THE NEW INTERPRETER'S® BIBLE
IN TWELVE VOLUMES

Volume Two

EDITORIAL BOARD

THE NEW INTERPRETER'S BIBLE

GENERAL ARTICLES
&
INTRODUCTION, COMMENTARY, & REFLECTIONS
FOR EACH BOOK OF THE BIBLE
INCLUDING
THE APOCRYPHAL / DEUTEROCANONICAL BOOKS
IN
TWELVE VOLUMES

VOLUME
II

ABINGDON PRESS
Nashville

THE NEW INTERPRETER'S® BIBLE
VOLUME II

Copyright © 1998 by Abingdon Press

All rights reserved.

This book is printed on recycled, acid-free paper.

Library of Congress Cataloging-in-Publication Data

The New Interpreter's Bible: general articles & introduction,
    commentary, & reflections for each book of the Bible, including the
Apocryphal/Deuterocanonical books.
        p. cm.
    Full texts and critical notes of the New International Version and
the New Revised Standard Version of the Bible in parallel columns.
        Includes bibliographical references.
        ISBN 0-687-27815-5 (v. 2: alk. paper)
        1. Bible—Commentaries. 2. Abingdon Press. I. Bible. English.
New International. 1994. II. Bible. English. New Revised
Standard. 1994.
BS491.2.N484   1994
220.7'7—dc20   94-21092
                                                                                CIP

The Hebraica® and Graeca® fonts used to print this work are available from Linguist's Software, Inc., PO Box 580, Edmonds, WA 98020-0580 tel (206) 775-1130.

PUBLICATION STAFF
President and Publisher: Neil M. Alexander
Editorial Director: Harriett Jane Olson
Project Director: Jack A. Keller, Jr.
Production Editor: Linda S. Allen
Hebrew and Greek Editor: Deborah A. Appler
Production and Design Manager: Walter E. Wynne
Designer: J. S. Laughbaum
Copy Processing Manager: Sylvia S. Street
Composition Specialist: Kathy M. Harding
Publishing Systems Analyst: Glenn R. Hinton
Prepress Manager: Billy W. Murphy
Prepress Systems Technicians: Thomas E. Mullins
                                                    J. Calvin Buckner
                                                    Phillip D. Elliott
Director of Production Processes: James E. Leath
Scheduling: Laurene M. Brazzell
                    Tracey D. Evans
Print Procurement Coordinator: Teresa S. Alspaugh

98 99 00 01 02 03 04 05 06 07—10 9 8 7 6 5 4 3 2 1

MANUFACTURED IN THE UNITED STATES OF AMERICA

CONSULTANTS

NEIL M. ALEXANDER
  President and Publisher
  The United Methodist Publishing House
  Nashville, Tennessee

OWEN F. CAMPION
  Associate Publisher
  Our Sunday Visitor
  Huntington, Indiana

MINERVA G. CARCAÑO
  Director
  Mexican American Program
  Perkins School of Theology
  Southern Methodist University
  Dallas, Texas

V. L. DAUGHTERY, JR.
  Pastor
  Park Avenue United Methodist Church
  Valdosta, Georgia

SHARON NEUFER EMSWILER
  Pastor
  First United Methodist Church
  Rock Island, Illinois

JUAN G. FELICIANO VALERA
  Pastor
  Iglesia Metodista "Juan Wesley"
  Arecibo, Puerto Rico

CELIA BREWER MARSHALL
  Lecturer
  University of North Carolina at Charlotte
  Charlotte, North Carolina

NANCY C. MILLER-HERRON
  Attorney and clergy member of the
    Tennessee Conference
  The United Methodist Church
  Dresden, Tennessee

ROBERT C. SCHNASE
  Pastor
  First United Methodist Church
  McAllen, Texas

BILL SHERMAN
  Pastor Emeritus
  Woodmont Baptist Church
  Nashville, Tennessee

RODNEY T. SMOTHERS
  Pastor
  Central United Methodist Church
  Atlanta, Georgia

WILLIAM D. WATLEY
  Pastor
  St. James African Methodist Episcopal Church
  Newark, New Jersey

TALLULAH FISHER WILLIAMS
  Superintendent
  Chicago Northwestern District
  The United Methodist Church
  Chicago, Illinois

SUK-CHONG YU
  Pastor
  San Francisco Korean United Methodist Church
  San Francisco, California

CONTRIBUTORS

ELIZABETH ACHTEMEIER
Adjunct Professor of Bible and Homiletics
Union Theological Seminary in Virginia
Richmond, Virginia
(Presbyterian Church [U.S.A.])
Joel

LESLIE C. ALLEN
Professor of Old Testament
Fuller Theological Seminary
Pasadena, California
(Baptist)
1 & 2 Chronicles

GARY A. ANDERSON
Associate Professor of Religious Studies
University of Virginia
Charlottesville, Virginia
(The Roman Catholic Church)
Introduction to Israelite Religion

DAVID L. BARTLETT
Lantz Professor of Preaching and
Communication
The Divinity School
Yale University
New Haven, Connecticut
(American Baptist Churches in the U.S.A.)
1 Peter

ROBERT A. BENNETT, PH.D.
Cambridge, Massachusetts
(The Episcopal Church)
Zephaniah

ADELE BERLIN
Robert H. Smith Professor of Hebrew Bible
Associate Provost for Faculty Affairs
University of Maryland
College Park, Maryland
Introduction to Hebrew Poetry

BRUCE C. BIRCH
Professor of Old Testament
Wesley Theological Seminary
Washington, DC
(The United Methodist Church)
1 & 2 Samuel

PHYLLIS A. BIRD
Associate Professor of Old Testament
Interpretation
Garrett-Evangelical Theological Seminary
Evanston, Illinois
(The United Methodist Church)
The Authority of the Bible

C. CLIFTON BLACK
Professor of New Testament
Perkins School of Theology
Southern Methodist University
Dallas, Texas
(The United Methodist Church)
1, 2, & 3 John

JOSEPH BLENKINSOPP
John A. O'Brien Professor of Biblical Studies
Department of Theology
University of Notre Dame
Notre Dame, Indiana
(The Roman Catholic Church)
Introduction to the Pentateuch

M. EUGENE BORING
I. Wylie and Elizabeth M. Briscoe Professor of
New Testament
Brite Divinity School
Texas Christian University
Fort Worth, Texas
(Christian Church [Disciples of Christ])
Matthew

WALTER BRUEGGEMANN
William Marcellus McPheeters Professor of Old
Testament
Columbia Theological Seminary
Decatur, Georgia
(United Church of Christ)
Exodus

DAVID G. BUTTRICK
Professor of Homiletics and Liturgics
The Divinity School
Vanderbilt University
Nashville, Tennessee
(United Church of Christ)
The Use of the Bible in Preaching

RONALD E. CLEMENTS
Samuel Davidson Professor of Old Testament
King's College
University of London
London, England
(Baptist Union of Great Britain and Ireland)
Deuteronomy

RICHARD J. CLIFFORD, S.J.
Professor of Old Testament
Weston Jesuit School of Theology
Cambridge, Massachusetts
(The Roman Catholic Church)
Introduction to Wisdom Literature

JOHN J. COLLINS
Professor of Hebrew Bible
The Divinity School
University of Chicago
Chicago, Illinois
(The Roman Catholic Church)
Introduction to Early Jewish Religion

ROBERT B. COOTE
Professor of Old Testament
San Francisco Theological Seminary
San Anselmo, California
(Presbyterian Church [U.S.A.])
Joshua

FRED B. CRADDOCK
Bandy Distinguished Professor of Preaching
and New Testament, Emeritus
Candler School of Theology
Emory University
Atlanta, Georgia
(Christian Church [Disciples of Christ])
Hebrews

SIDNIE WHITE CRAWFORD
Associate Professor of Hebrew Bible
and Chair of the Department of Classics
University of Nebraska—Lincoln
Lincoln, Nebraska
(The Episcopal Church)
Esther; Additions to Esther

JAMES L. CRENSHAW
Robert L. Flowers Professor of Old Testament
The Divinity School
Duke University
Durham, North Carolina
(Baptist)
Sirach

KEITH R. CRIM
Pastor
New Concord Presbyterian Church
Concord, Virginia
(Presbyterian Church [U.S.A.])
Modern English Versions of the Bible

R. ALAN CULPEPPER
Dean
The School of Theology
Mercer University
Atlanta, Georgia
(Southern Baptist Convention)
Luke

KATHERYN PFISTERER DARR
Associate Professor of Hebrew Bible
The School of Theology
Boston University
Boston, Massachusetts
(The United Methodist Church)
Ezekiel

ROBERT DORAN
Professor of Religion
Amherst College
Amherst, Massachusetts
1 & 2 Maccabees

THOMAS B. DOZEMAN
Professor of Old Testament
United Theological Seminary
Dayton, Ohio
(Presbyterian Church [U.S.A.])
Numbers

JAMES D. G. DUNN
Lightfoot Professor of Divinity
Department of Theology
University of Durham
Durham, England
(The Methodist Church [Great Britain])
  1 & 2 Timothy; Titus

ELDON JAY EPP
Harkness Professor of Biblical Literature
  and Chairman of the Department of Religion
Case Western Reserve University
Cleveland, Ohio
(The Episcopal Church)
  *Ancient Texts and Versions of the New
  Testament*

KATHLEEN A. ROBERTSON FARMER
Professor of Old Testament
United Theological Seminary
Dayton, Ohio
(The United Methodist Church)
  Ruth

CAIN HOPE FELDER
Professor of New Testament Language
  and Literature
The School of Divinity
Howard University
Washington, DC
(The United Methodist Church)
  Philemon

TERENCE E. FRETHEIM
Professor of Old Testament
Luther Seminary
Saint Paul, Minnesota
(Evangelical Lutheran Church in America)
  Genesis

FRANCISCO O. GARCÍA-TRETO
Professor of Religion and Chair of the
  Department of Religion
Trinity University
San Antonio, Texas
(Presbyterian Church [U.S.A.])
  Nahum

CATHERINE GUNSALUS GONZÁLEZ
Professor of Church History
Columbia Theological Seminary
Decatur, Georgia
(Presbyterian Church [U.S.A.])
  *The Use of the Bible in Hymns, Liturgy,
  and Education*

JUSTO L. GONZÁLEZ
Adjunct Professor of Church History
Columbia Theological Seminary
Decatur, Georgia
(The United Methodist Church)
  *How the Bible Has Been Interpreted in
  Christian Tradition*

DONALD E. GOWAN
Robert Cleveland Holland Professor of Old
  Testament
Pittsburgh Theological Seminary
Pittsburgh, Pennsylvania
(Presbyterian Church [U.S.A.])
  Amos

JUDITH MARIE GUNDRY-VOLF
Assistant Professor of New Testament
Fuller Theological Seminary
Pasadena, California
(Presbyterian Church [U.S.A.])
  Ephesians

DANIEL J. HARRINGTON
Professor of New Testament
Weston School of Theology
Cambridge, Massachusetts
(The Roman Catholic Church)
  Introduction to the Canon

RICHARD B. HAYS
Associate Professor of New Testament
The Divinity School
Duke University
Durham, North Carolina
(The United Methodist Church)
  Galatians

THEODORE HIEBERT
Professor of Old Testament
McCormick Theological
  Seminary
Chicago, Illinois
(Mennonite Church)
  Habakkuk

CARL R. HOLLADAY
Professor of New Testament
Candler School of Theology
Emory University
Atlanta, Georgia
  *Contemporary Methods of Reading the
  Bible*

MORNA D. HOOKER
  Lady Margaret's Professor of Divinity
  The Divinity School
  University of Cambridge
  Cambridge, England
  (The Methodist Church [Great Britain])
    Philippians

DAVID C. HOPKINS
  Professor of Old Testament
  Wesley Theological Seminary
  Washington, DC
  (United Church of Christ)
    Life in Ancient Palestine

DENISE DOMBKOWSKI HOPKINS
  Professor of Old Testament
  Wesley Theological Seminary
  Washington, DC
  (United Church of Christ)
    Judith

LUKE T. JOHNSON
  Robert W. Woodruff Professor of New
    Testament and Christian Origins
  Candler School of Theology
  Emory University
  Atlanta, Georgia
  (The Roman Catholic Church)
    James

WALTER C. KAISER, JR.
  President and Colman M. Mockler
    Distinguished Professor of Old Testament
  Gordon-Conwell Theological Seminary
  South Hamilton, Massachusetts
  (The Evangelical Free Church of America)
    Leviticus

LEANDER E. KECK
  Winkley Professor of Biblical Theology, Emeritus
  The Divinity School
  Yale University
  New Haven, Connecticut
  (Christian Church [Disciples of Christ])
    Introduction to The New Interpreter's Bible

CHAN-HIE KIM
  Professor of New Testament and Director of
    Korean Studies
  The School of Theology at Claremont
  Claremont, California
  (The United Methodist Church)
    Reading the Bible as Asian Americans

RALPH W. KLEIN
  Dean and Christ Seminary-Seminex Professor of
    Old Testament
  Lutheran School of Theology at Chicago
  Chicago, Illinois
  (Evangelical Lutheran Church in America)
    Ezra; Nehemiah

MICHAEL KOLARCIK, S.J.
  Assistant Professor
  Regis College
  Toronto, Ontario
  Canada
  (The Roman Catholic Church)
    Book of Wisdom

WILLIAM L. LANE
  Paul T. Walls Professor of Wesleyan
    and Biblical Studies
  Department of Religion
  Seattle Pacific University
  Seattle, Washington
  (Free Methodist Church of North America)
    2 Corinthians

ANDREW T. LINCOLN
  Professor of New Testament
  Wycliffe College
  University of Toronto
  Toronto, Ontario
  Canada
  (The Church of England)
    Colossians

J. CLINTON McCANN, JR.
  Evangelical Associate Professor of
    Biblical Interpretation
  Eden Theological Seminary
  St. Louis, Missouri
  (Presbyterian Church [U.S.A.])
    Psalms

ABRAHAM J. MALHERBE
  Buckingham Professor of New Testament
    Criticism and Interpretation, Emeritus
  The Divinity School
  Yale University
  New Haven, Connecticut
  (Church of Christ)
    *The Cultural Context of the New Testament:
    The Greco-Roman World*

W. EUGENE MARCH
Dean and Arnold Black Rhodes Professor
of Old Testament
Louisville Presbyterian Theological Seminary
Louisville, Kentucky
(Presbyterian Church [U.S.A.])
Haggai

JAMES EARL MASSEY
Dean Emeritus and
Distinguished Professor-at-Large
The School of Theology
Anderson University
(Church of God [Anderson, Ind.])
*Reading the Bible from Particular Social
Locations: An Introduction;
Reading the Bible as African Americans*

J. MAXWELL MILLER
Professor of Old Testament
Candler School of Theology
Emory University
Atlanta, Georgia
(The United Methodist Church)
Introduction to the History of Ancient Israel

PATRICK D. MILLER
Charles T. Haley Professor of Old Testament
Theology
Princeton Theological Seminary
Princeton, New Jersey
(Presbyterian Church [U.S.A.])
Jeremiah

PETER D. MISCALL
Adjunct Faculty
The Iliff School of Theology
Denver, Colorado
(Episcopalian)
Introduction to Narrative Literature

FREDERICK J. MURPHY
Professor
Department of Religious Studies
College of the Holy Cross
Worcester, Massachusetts
(The Roman Catholic Church)
Introduction to Apocalyptic Literature

CAROL A. NEWSOM
Associate Professor of Old Testament
Candler School of Theology
Emory University
Atlanta, Georgia
(The Episcopal Church)
Job

GEORGE W. E. NICKELSBURG
Professor of Christian Origins and Early Judaism
School of Religion
University of Iowa
Iowa City, Iowa
(Evangelical Lutheran Church in America)
*The Jewish Context of the New
Testament*

IRENE NOWELL
Associate Professor of Religious Studies
Benedictine College
Atchison, Kansas
(The Roman Catholic Church)
Tobit

KATHLEEN M. O'CONNOR
Professor of Old Testament Language,
Literature, and Exegesis
Columbia Theological Seminary
Decatur, Georgia
(The Roman Catholic Church)
Lamentations

GAIL R. O'DAY
Almar H. Shatford Associate Professor of Homiletics
Candler School of Theology
Emory University
Atlanta, Georgia
(United Church of Christ)
John

BEN C. OLLENBURGER
Professor of Biblical Theology
Associated Mennonite Biblical Seminary
Elkhart, Indiana
(Mennonite Church)
Zechariah

DENNIS T. OLSON
Associate Professor of Old Testament
Princeton Theological Seminary
Princeton, New Jersey
(Evangelical Lutheran Church in America)
Judges

CAROLYN OSIEK
Professor of New Testament
Department of Biblical Languages
and Literature
Catholic Theological Union
Chicago, Illinois
(The Roman Catholic Church)
Reading the Bible as Women

SAMUEL PAGÁN
President
Evangelical Seminary of Puerto Rico
San Juan, Puerto Rico
(Christian Church [Disciples of Christ])
Obadiah

SIMON B. PARKER
Associate Professor of Hebrew Bible and
Harrell F. Beck Scholar in Hebrew Scripture
The School of Theology
Boston University
Boston, Massachusetts
(The United Methodist Church)
*The Ancient Near Eastern Literary
Background of the Old Testament*

PHEME PERKINS
Professor of New Testament
Boston College
Chestnut Hill, Massachusetts
(The Roman Catholic Church)
Mark

DAVID L. PETERSEN
Professor of Old Testament
The Iliff School of Theology
Denver, Colorado
(Presbyterian Church [U.S.A.])
Introduction to Prophetic Literature

CHRISTOPHER C. ROWLAND
Dean Ireland's Professor of the Exegesis
of Holy Scripture
The Queen's College
Oxford, England
(The Church of England)
Revelation

ANTHONY J. SALDARINI
Professor of Biblical Studies
Boston College
Chestnut Hill, Massachusetts
(The Roman Catholic Church)
Baruch; Letter of Jeremiah

J. PAUL SAMPLEY
Professor of New Testament and
Christian Origins
The School of Theology and The Graduate Division
Boston University
Boston, Massachusetts
(The United Methodist Church)
1 Corinthians

JUDITH E. SANDERSON
Assistant Professor of Hebrew Bible
Department of Theology and Religious Studies
Seattle University
Seattle, Washington
*Ancient Texts and Versions of the Old
Testament*

EILEEN M. SCHULLER, O.S.U.
Professor
Department of Religious Studies
McMaster University
Hamilton, Ontario
Canada
(The Roman Catholic Church)
Malachi

FERNANDO F. SEGOVIA
Associate Professor of New Testament
and Early Christianity
The Divinity School
Vanderbilt University
Nashville, Tennessee
(The Roman Catholic Church)
Reading the Bible as Hispanic Americans

CHRISTOPHER R. SEITZ
Associate Professor of Old Testament
The Divinity School
Yale University
New Haven, Connecticut
(The Episcopal Church)
Isaiah 40–66

CHOON-LEONG SEOW
Henry Snyder Gehman Professor of Old Testa-
ment Language and Literature
Princeton Theological Seminary
Princeton, New Jersey
(Presbyterian Church [U.S.A.])
1 & 2 Kings

MICHAEL A. SIGNER
Abrams Professor of Jewish Thought and
Culture
Department of Theology
University of Notre Dame
Notre Dame, Indiana
*How the Bible Has Been Interpreted in
Jewish Tradition*

MOISÉS SILVA
Professor of New Testament
Westminster Theological Seminary
Philadelphia, Pennsylvania
(The Orthodox Presbyterian Church)
*Contemporary Theories of Biblical
Interpretation*

DANIEL J. SIMUNDSON
Professor of Old Testament
Luther Seminary
Saint Paul, Minnesota
(Evangelical Lutheran Church in America)
Micah

ABRAHAM SMITH
Associate Professor of New Testament
Andover Newton Theological School
Newton Centre, Massachusetts
(The National Baptist Convention, USA, Inc.)
1 & 2 Thessalonians

DANIEL L. SMITH-CHRISTOPHER
Associate Professor of Theological Studies
Department of Theology
Loyola Marymount University
Los Angeles, California
(The Society of Friends [Quaker])
*Daniel; Bel and the Dragon; Prayer of
Azariah; Susannah*

MARION L. SOARDS
Professor of New Testament Studies
Louisville Presbyterian Theological Seminary
Louisville, Kentucky
(Presbyterian Church [U.S.A.])
Acts

ROBERT C. TANNEHILL
Academic Dean and Harold B. Williams
Professor of Biblical Studies
Methodist Theological School in Ohio
Delaware, Ohio
(The United Methodist Church)
The Gospels and Narrative Literature

GEORGE E. TINKER
Associate Professor of Cross-Cultural Ministries
The Iliff School of Theology
Denver, Colorado
(Evangelical Lutheran Church in America)
Reading the Bible as Native Americans

W. SIBLEY TOWNER
The Reverend Archibald McFadyen Professor of
Biblical Interpretation
Union Theological Seminary in Virginia
Richmond, Virginia
(Presbyterian Church [U.S.A.])
Ecclesiastes

PHYLLIS TRIBLE
Baldwin Professor of Sacred Literature
Union Theological Seminary
New York, New York
Jonah

GENE M. TUCKER
Professor of Old Testament, Emeritus
Candler School of Theology
Emory University
Atlanta, Georgia
(The United Methodist Church)
Isaiah 1–39

CHRISTOPHER M. TUCKETT
Rylands Professor of Biblical Criticism
and Exegesis
Faculty of Theology
University of Manchester
Manchester, England
(The Church of England)
Jesus and the Gospels

RAYMOND C. VAN LEEUWEN
Professor of Religion and Theology
Eastern College
Saint Davids, Pennsylvania
(Christian Reformed Church in North America)
Proverbs

ROBERT W. WALL
Professor of Biblical Studies
Department of Religion
Seattle Pacific University
Seattle, Washington
(Free Methodist Church of North America)
Introduction to Epistolary Literature

DUANE F. WATSON
Associate Professor of New Testament Studies
Department of Religion and Philosophy
Malone College
Canton, Ohio
(The United Methodist Church)
2 Peter; Jude

RENITA J. WEEMS
  Associate Professor of Hebrew Bible
  The Divinity School
  Vanderbilt University
  Nashville, Tennessee
  (African Methodist Episcopal Church)
    Song of Songs

VINCENT L. WIMBUSH
  Professor of New Testament and
    Christian Origins
  Union Theological Seminary
  New York, New York
  (Progressive National Baptist Convention, Inc.)
    *The Ecclesiastical Context of the New
    Testament*

N. THOMAS WRIGHT
  Dean of Lichfield
  Lichfield Cathedral
  Staffordshire, England
  (The Church of England)
    Romans

GALE A. YEE
  Associate Professor of Old Testament
  Department of Theology
  University of Saint Thomas
  Saint Paul, Minnesota
  (The Roman Catholic Church)
    Hosea

FEATURES OF
THE NEW INTERPRETER'S BIBLE

The general aim of *The New Interpreter's Bible* is to bring the best in contemporary biblical scholarship into the service of the church to enhance preaching, teaching, and study of the Scriptures. To accomplish that general aim, the design of *The New Interpreter's Bible* has been shaped by two controlling principles: (1) form serves function, and (2) maximize ease of use.

General articles provide the reader with concise, up-to-date, balanced introductions and assessments of selected topics. In most cases, a brief bibliography points the way to further exploration of a topic. Many of the general articles are placed in volumes 1 and 8, at the beginning of the coverage of the Old and New Testaments, respectively. Others have been inserted in those volumes where the reader will encounter the corresponding type of literature (e.g., "Introduction to Prophetic Literature" appears in Volume 6 alongside several of the prophetic books).

Coverage of each biblical book begins with an "Introduction" that acquaints the reader with the essential historical, sociocultural, literary, and theological issues necessary to understand the biblical book. A short bibliography and an outline of the biblical book are found at the end of each Introduction. The introductory sections are the only material in *The New Interpreter's Bible* printed in a single wide-column format.

The biblical text is divided into coherent and manageable primary units, which are located within larger sections of Scripture. At the opening discussion of any large section of Scripture, readers will often find material identified as "Overview," which includes remarks applicable to the large section of text. The primary unit of text may be as short as a few verses or as long as a chapter or more. This is the point at which the biblical text itself is reprinted in *The New Interpreter's Bible*. Dealing with Scripture in terms of these primary units allows discussion of important issues that are overlooked in a verse-by-verse treatment. Each scriptural unit is identified by text citation and a short title.

The full texts and critical notes of the New International Version and the New Revised Standard Version of the Bible are presented in parallel columns for quick reference. (For the Apocryphal/Deuterocanonical works, the NIV is replaced by The New American Bible.) Since every translation is to some extent an interpretation as well, the inclusion of these widely known and influential modern translations provides an easy comparison that in many cases will lead to a better understanding of a passage. Biblical passages are set in a two-column format and placed in green tint-blocks to make it easy to recognize them at a glance. The NAB, NIV, and NRSV material is clearly identified on each page on which the text appears.

Immediately following each biblical text is a section marked "Commentary," which provides an exegetical analysis informed by linguistic, text-critical, historical-critical, literary, social-scientific, and theological methods. The Commentary serves as a reliable, judicious guide through the text, pointing out the critical problems as well as key interpretive issues.

The exegetical approach is "text-centered." That is, the commentators focus primarily on the text in its final form rather than on (a) a meticulous rehearsal of problems of scholarship associated with a text, (b) a thorough reconstruction of the pre-history of the text, or (c) an exhaustive rehearsal of the text's interpretive history. Of course, some attention to scholarly problems, to the pre-history of a text, and to historic interpretations that have shaped streams of tradition is important in particular cases precisely in order to illumine the several levels of meaning in the final form of the text. But the *primary* focus is on the canonical text itself. Moreover, the Commentary not only describes pertinent aspects of the text, but also teaches the reader what to look for in the text so as to develop the reader's own capacity to analyze and interpret the text.

Commentary material runs serially for a few paragraphs or a few pages, depending on what is required by the biblical passage under discussion.

Commentary material is set in a two-column format. Occasional subheads appear in a bold green font. The next level of subdivisions appears as bold black fonts and a third level as black italic fonts. Footnotes are placed at the bottom of the column in which the superscripts appear.

Key words in Hebrew, Aramaic, or Greek are printed in the original-language font, accompanied by a transliteration and a translation or explanation.

Immediately following the Commentary, in most cases, is the section called "Reflections." A detailed exposition growing directly out of the discussion and issues dealt with in the Commentary, the Reflections are geared specifically toward helping those who interpret Scripture in the life of the church by providing "handles" for grasping the significance of Scripture for faith and life today. Recognizing that the text has the capacity to shape the life of the Christian community, this section presents multiple possibilities for preaching and teaching in light of each biblical text. That is, instead of providing the preacher or teacher full illustrations, poems, outlines, and the like, the Reflections offer *several* trajectories of possible interpretation that connect with the situation of the contemporary listeners. Recognizing the power of Scripture to speak anew to diverse situations, not all of the suggested trajectories could be appropriated on any one occasion. Preachers and teachers want some specificity about the implications of the text, but not so much specificity that the work is done for them. The ideas in the Reflections are meant to stimulate the thought of preachers and teachers, not to replace it.

Three-quarter width columns distinguish Reflections materials from biblical text and Commentary.

Occasional excursuses have been inserted in some volumes to address topics of special importance that are best treated apart from the flow of Commentary and Reflections on specific passages. Set in three-quarter width columns, excursuses are identified graphically by a green color bar that runs down the outside margin of the page.

Occasional maps, charts, and illustrations appear throughout the volumes at points where they are most likely to be immediately useful to the reader.

CONTENTS

VOLUME XII

THE BOOK OF NUMBERS

INTRODUCTION, COMMENTARY, AND REFLECTIONS
BY
THOMAS B. DOZEMAN

THE BOOK OF
NUMBERS

INTRODUCTION

TITLE, STRUCTURE, AND CONTENT

T wo titles are associated with the fourth book of Moses. The title "Numbers" comes from the Vulgate (Vg, *Numeri*) and the Septuagint (LXX, *Arithmoi*). The talmudic name חומש הפקודים (*ḥômeš happĕqûddîm*, "the fifth of the census totals")[1] would also correlate most closely with the title "Numbers." A second title, "In the Wilderness," comes from the Masoretic Text (MT), where pentateuchal books are named either by their opening word or by a significant word in the first sentence. The two titles provide different points of view concerning the central themes and structure of Numbers.

Numbers. The title "Numbers" focuses on the characters in the book. It underscores the census of Israel, which takes place twice over a forty-year period. The first (or exodus) generation is counted in chap. 1 on Year 2, Month 2, Day 1 after the exodus (Num 1:1). A second generation is numbered in chap. 26, most likely in the fortieth year after the exodus. No date is given for this census, but it takes place after the death of Aaron in Num 20:22-29, which is dated as Year 40, Month 5, Day 1 in Num 33:38. Dennis T. Olson has argued that the numbering of Israel is the clue to the structure and thematic development of the book.[2] The two-part division results in the following structure: chapters 1–25, The Old Generation of Rebellion; chapters 26–36, The New Generation of Hope.

Comparison between the two halves of the book reveals thematic development. Numbers

---

1. See *m. Yoma* 7:1; *m. Menahot* 4:3.
2. Dennis T. Olson, *The Death of the Old and the Birth of the New: The Framework of the Book of Numbers and the Pentateuch,* BJS 71 (Chico, Calif.: Scholars Press, 1985) 83-124.

1–25 contains stories of rebellion. The establishment of the wilderness camp in Numbers 1–10 provides background for conflict. The people complain about the lack of meat in Numbers 11. They refuse to risk their lives to conquer Canaan in Numbers 13–14. And they continue to rebel against God and Moses in Numbers 16–17; 20–21; and 25. Rebellion leads to the death of the first generation. Numbers 26–36 focuses on the second generation. It is a story of hope. Rebellion gives way to negotiated solutions (Num 27:1-11; 31:14-15; 32:1-42), and the promise of land once again takes center stage (Numbers 27; 34–36).

In the Wilderness. The title "In the Wilderness" accentuates the setting of the book. The goal of Numbers is for Israel to leave the wilderness and enter the promised land of Canaan. The interrelationship of characters continues to be important to the book when the focus is on the setting. But it is their journey through the wilderness that provides the key to the plot structure. Numbers separates into three parts when the wilderness setting is emphasized: 1:1–10:10, Forming Community Around a Holy God; 10:11–21:35, The Wilderness Journey; 22:1–36:13, Preparing for Canaan on the Plains of Moab.

Numbers 1:1–10:10 contains revelation concerning the camp and the tabernacle. It takes place in the wilderness of Sinai. The purpose of instruction is to ready the people for Yahweh to dwell in the tabernacle at the center of the Israelite camp. The central theme is the holiness of God and its effects on Israel. Israel is counted in Numbers 1. The twelve tribes, priests, and Levites are arranged within the camp in Numbers 2. The Levites become the center of focus in Numbers 3–4. They guard the tabernacle at the center of the camp. Numbers 5–6 contain camp laws, which illustrate ways in which the holiness of God could be defiled. Numbers 7:1–10:10 narrows the subject matter from the social organization of the camp to the dedication of the tabernacle. This section includes sacrifices by each tribe, the observance of Passover, and preparation for the wilderness march.

Numbers 10:11–21:35 tells of the tragic wilderness journey of the first generation. The literature is organized around conflicts in which Israel rebels against God and the leadership of Moses. The people complain about food in Numbers 11–12 and question the ability of Moses to lead them through the wilderness. Israel doubts that God can bring them safely into the promised land in Numbers 13–15. The refusal of the first generation to enter Canaan leads to their death in the wilderness. Numbers 16–17 contains a series of conflict stories in which the priestly leadership of Moses and Aaron is challenged. Numbers 18–19 provide guidelines for approaching God. And Numbers 20–21 chronicles the deaths of Miriam and Aaron to provide the transition from the first to the second generation.

Numbers 22:1–36:13 describes the second generation of Israelites on the plains of Moab. The topics in this section anticipate an imminent possession of Canaan. Numbers 26 is a new census of the second generation. Numbers 28–29 provides instruction for worship in the land. Numbers 35 lists cities of asylum in Canaan. And Numbers 27; 32; 34; and 36 contain laws of inheritance. There is also a change of focus. Numbers 10:11–21:35 has an internal focus, exploring how rebellion by Israel threatens the holiness of God. Numbers 22:1–36:13 examines external threats to Israel in the story of Balak and Balaam in chapters 22–24 and the sin at Baal Peor in Numbers 25.

LITERARY FORM AND CONTEXT

Critical Study. Modern interpretation has focused on the literary formation of Numbers and its relation to the other books of the Pentateuch (Genesis, Exodus, Leviticus, and Deuteronomy). George Buchanan Gray outlined the literary formation of Numbers at the turn of the century using the documentary hypothesis.[3] According to this theory, the Pentateuch is composed of four literary sources (JEDP) written independently of each other. The Yahwist (J) was a tenth- or ninth-century BCE history. It was composed either during the united monarchy of David and Solomon (1000–922 BCE) or in the southern kingdom of Judah shortly after the split of the kingdoms (922 BCE). The Elohist (E) was an eighth-century BCE history, written for the northern kingdom of Israel (922–722 BCE). The book of Deuteronomy (D) is a seventh-century BCE document associated with the reform of Josiah in 621 BCE. And the Priestly (P) history was written in the sixth century BCE in the wake of the Babylonian exile (587–539 BCE).[4]

Gray concluded that Numbers was composed of J, E, and P. Examples of J include Israel's departure from Sinai (Num 10:29-32), request for meat (Num 11:4-15, 18-24*a*, 31-35), and a portion of the Balaam narrative (Num 22:22-35). The story of the seventy elders (Num 11:16, 17*a*, 24*b*-30), the vindication of Moses (Num 12:1-15), the embassies to Edom and to the Amorites (Num 20:14-21; 21:21-24*a*), and most of the Balaam narrative (Numbers 22–24) derive from E. J and E were separate histories that spanned the books of Genesis, Exodus, Numbers, and possibly also Joshua. They were combined in the seventh century BCE. The sign JE represents their combination.[5]

Gray also identified the work of a priestly school (P) in Numbers and concluded that most of the literature in Numbers belongs to this school. The symbol P represents a body of literature that includes both law and narrative. The distinctive literature within P is designated by the symbols Pg, Ps, and Px. Pg is a priestly history of sacred institutions, written after the Babylonian exile. It is composed independently of JE. Examples include the organization of the camp and dedication of the tabernacle in Num 1:1–10:10 and most of the laws dealing with life in the land of Canaan in Numbers 26–36. Gray also concluded that the priestly history (Pg) was expanded with additional stories (Ps) and legal material (Px). Thus the literature of the priestly school was not unified. He judged the war against Midian in Numbers 31 to be a narrative addition (Ps) and the directions concerning unintentional sin in Numbers 15:22-31 to be a legal addition (Px). The present form of Numbers results from the combination of the distinct literary sources (JE plus P).[6]

3. George Buchanan Gray, *Numbers,* ICC (Edinburgh, T. & T. Clark, 1903) xxix-xxxix.

4. Joseph Blenkinsopp, "Introduction to the Pentateuch," in *The New Interpreter's Bible,* vol. 1 (Nashville: Abingdon, 1994) 310-12.

5. Gray, *Numbers,* xxxi-xxxii.

6. Ibid., xxxiii-xxxix.

There are a number of lasting results from Gray's work. We know that Numbers was not written by one author, but contains literature spanning the history of Israel. This literature is preserved in two general histories, with different theological perspectives. There is a pre-priestly stratum of literature (JE), which makes up a small portion of the book. It consists of stories about Israel's wilderness wandering, beginning with their leaving Sinai in Numbers 10:29-36, and it continues through the account of Balaam in Numbers 22–24. Gray used the symbol JE to underscore that this literature was not unified. There is also a priestly stratum of literature (P). Most of Numbers derives from the priestly tradition. Priestly literature opens (Num 1:1–10:10) and closes (Numbers 26–36) the book. Priestly narrative and law are also woven throughout the middle portion of the book (e. g., Num 15:17-21, 22-31; 16:8-11; 17:1-5; 19). Two guidelines for interpretation emerge from the work of Gray. First, priestly theology dominates in the book of Numbers; the commentary will focus on priestly theology. Second, Numbers also contains a history of composition. Thus many stories will yield more than one meaning, since they include priestly and pre-priestly versions.

Two developments in pentateuchal studies influence the present commentary. Both are departures from the documentary hypothesis evident in Gray's commentary. The first is the character and date of pre-priestly literature in Numbers. Gray dated J in the ninth century and E in the eighth century BCE. A consequence of his early dating was the distinction of the J and E histories from Deuteronomy (D), written in the seventh century BCE. Thus, for Gray, there was no D literature in Numbers. Martin Noth sharpened this distinction by arguing that J and E in the Tetrateuch (Genesis, Exodus, Leviticus, and Numbers) were clearly separated from Deuteronomy (D).[7]

More recent research indicates a closer relationship between JE and D. The theme of covenant, for example, with Abraham (Genesis 15) and Israel (Exodus 19-34) carries through to Deuteronomy 1–11.[8] The same is true with other themes, such as the promise of land (e.g., Genesis 12; 24; Exodus 13; 30–33; Numbers 14; Deuteronomy 1–11; and Joshua 1).[9] The points of continuity between the Tetrateuch and Deuteronomy have prompted a reevaluation of the pre-priestly history.[10] John Van Seters maintains the name "Yahwist" to describe this history, but he redates the material from the early monarchical period to the exile. He also detects influence between J and Deuteronomy. But, according to Van Seters, J was written after Deuteronomy and the Deuteronomistic History (Joshua, Judges, Samuel, and Kings). Thus it represents a later perspective and not an earlier one.[11]

7. Martin Noth, *Numbers,* trans. James D. Martin, OTL (Philadelphia: Westminster, 1968) 4-11. Noth extended the argument to include later deuteronomistic (Dtr) additions, which tied Deuteronomy to the Deuteronomistic History (Joshua, Judges, Samuel, and Kings).

8. See Lothar Perlitt, *Bundestheologie im Alten Testament,* WMANT 36 (Neukirchen-Vluyn: Neukirchener Verlag, 1969); and Thomas B. Dozeman, *God on the Mountain,* SBLMS 37 (Atlanta: Scholars Press, 1988) 37-86.

9. Susan Boorer, *The Promise of Land as Oath: A Key to the Formation of the Pentateuch,* BZAW 205 (Berlin: de Gruyter, 1992); and Thomas B. Dozeman, *God at War: Power in the Exodus Tradition* (Oxford: Oxford University Press, 1996) 42-100.

10. Blenkinsopp, "Introduction to the Pentateuch," 312-13.

11. John Van Seters, *In Search of History: Historiography in the Ancient World and the Origins of Biblical History* (New Haven: Yale University Press, 1983); and *The Life of Moses: The Yahwist as Historian in Exodus-Numbers* (Louisville: Westminster/John Knox, 1994).

Other names for the pre-priestly history include Erhard Blum's designation of it as "D-Composition." This term designates literature in the Tetrateuch, Deuteronomy and the Deuteronomistic History.[12] Thus, for Blum also, there is a literary relationship between the Tetrateuch and Deuteronomy. In previous studies I have employed the term "deuteronomistic" to indicate the same close relationship between the pre-priestly Tetrateuch and Deuteronomy.[13]

The brief overview indicates how terminology is open to debate at the present time. In this commentary, I will simply use the term "pre-priestly" to indicate a history that is earlier than priestly tradition. It is composed in the late monarchical or the exilic period. It contains material from earlier periods in Israel's history as well, and it extends from Genesis through Kings.[14] Thus there is literary interdependence between the pre-priestly history in Numbers and Deuteronomy. Commentary will often include comparison between similar stories in these two books.

The second departure from the documentary hypothesis is the literary character of priestly tradition. Gray interpreted P as a history that was written independently of JE. The relationship between priestly and pre-priestly literature took place only when the distinct histories were combined to form the canonical Pentateuch. Thus the interweaving of the two histories was not important for interpretation. Martin Noth expressed doubts about this conclusion. He noticed more interaction between the two histories in the composition of P, concluding that P played a formative role in determining the literary shape of Numbers. This was true not only for the introduction (Numbers 1–10) and conclusion (Numbers 26–36), but also for the middle section, where Gray identified the JE narrative. Priestly writers provided the basic literary design of this section, according to Noth, by the way in which they had gathered the literature together in Numbers 11–12; 13–15; and 16–19.[15]

More recent scholars have continued to question whether the documentary hypothesis provides the best model for interpreting priestly tradition in Numbers. Wenham noted in passing that the composition of Numbers may be more the result of editors who interrelated older material with commentary.[16] Budd also questioned whether priestly tradition might better be interpreted as "midrashic commentary" on older literature, rather than an independent literary source. He took a middle position in his commentary. Priestly tradition is more than commentary, but not an independent document. P incorporates older material, according to Budd, along with interpretative comments, while also providing its own distinctive structure.[17] I, too, will interpret priestly tradition as a redaction of pre-priestly literature, rather than an independent history. This change in perspective assumes a dialogue between traditions in the formation of Numbers. As a result, interpretation must pay attention to the

---

12. Erhard Blum, *Studien zur Komposition des Pentateuch, BZAW* 189 (Berlin: de Gruyter, 1990).

13. Dozeman, *God on the Mountain* and *God at War.*

14. See Dozeman, *God at War,* 42-100, 171-83, for discussion of the pre-priestly history as including Genesis through Kings. For further discussion of terminology, see D. Carr, *Reading the Fractures of Genesis: Historical and Literary Approaches* (Louisville: Westminster John Knox, 1996) 143-293, who uses "Non-P" to designate pre-priestly tradition.

15. Noth, *Numbers,* 4-12.

16. Gordon J. Wenham, *Numbers: An Introduction and Commentary,* Tyndale Old Testament Commentaries (Leicester: Inter-Varsity, 1981) 20-21.

17. Philip J. Budd, *Numbers,* WBC 5 (Waco, Tex.: Word, 1984) xxii.

themes that arise in priestly literature and to the ways in which additions by priestly writers reinterpret and restructure the pre-priestly history.

Literary Form. According to Jacob Milgrom, Numbers contains the greatest variety of literature of any book in the Bible. He lists fourteen distinct genres: narrative (Num 4:1-3), poetry (Num 21:17-18), prophecy (Num 24:3-9), victory song (Num 21:27-30), prayer (Num 12:13), blessing (Num 6:24-26), lampoon (Num 22:22-35), diplomatic letter (Num 21:14-19), civil law (Num 27:1-11), cultic law (Num 15:17-21), oracular decision (Num 15:32-36), census list (Num 26:1-51), temple archive (Num 7:10-88), and itinerary (Num 33:1-49).[18] The literature, moreover, spans the history of Israel. The distinct literature within Numbers can be summarized in four stages of composition: (1) individual poetry, stories, records, and law; (2) the pre-priestly history; (3) the priestly history; and (4) the canonical book of Numbers.

Individual Poetry, Stories, Records, and Law. *Poetry.* Ancient poetry is concentrated in the story of Balaam in Numbers 22–24, but it is also woven throughout Numbers. The poems are very diverse in content. They include songs of war, water, blessing, prophecy, and even a foreign song:

6:24-26, priestly blessing;
10:35-36, Song of the Ark;
21:14-15, an excerpt from the Book of the Wars of Yahweh;
21:17-18, Song of the Well;
21:27-30, ballad over Heshbon;
23:7-10, 18-24; 24:3-9, 15-24, oracles of Balaam.

Stories, Inheritance Records, and Itineraries. Individual stories and other records were also in circulation prior to their incorporation into the pre-priestly and priestly histories. Topics include land inheritance, temple practice, and life experiences from the desert. Numbers also contains travels lists, known as itineraries. These lists are most likely from royal archives, perhaps associated with military campaigns:[19]

20–21,*[20] conquest in the Transjordan;
21:4-9, cult of Nehushtan;
21:10-20, itinerary list;
25:1-5, sin at Baal Peor;
32,* inheritance;
33,* itinerary list.

Law. There is debate surrounding the origin of priestly law. The majority view in the modern era was that priestly law is exilic or post-exilic in origin.[21] This conclusion has been countered by more recent arguments in favor of locating early forms of priestly law

18. Jacob Milgrom, *Numbers,* JPS Torah Commentary (Philadelphia: JPS, 1990) xiii.
19. See G. I. Davies, "The Wilderness Itineraries and the Composition of the Pentateuch," *VT* 33 (1983) 1-13.
20. The asterisk (*) indicates that a section of literature contains writing from more than one author.
21. See Julius Wellhausen, *Prolegomena to the History of Ancient Israel,* trans. J. S. Menzies and A. Black (Gloucester: Peter Smith, 1983; first published in 1883).

in the monarchical period.[22] The debate is difficult to resolve because all priestly law has been edited well into the post-exilic period. Possible examples of pre-exilic priestly law include the following:

5:5-10, restitution
5:11-28, the wife suspected of adultery
6:1-22, Nazirite vow
15:1-31,* law of sacrifice
19, red heifer
28–29,* aspects of the cultic calendar
30,* law of vows
34,* inheritance
35,* levitical cities.

The Pre-priestly History. Pre-priestly literature is concentrated in the middle portion of Numbers. It begins with Israel's departure from Mt. Yahweh in Num 10:29-36 and ends with a summary of the wilderness travel in Numbers 33. The pre-priestly history separates into two parts. It begins by outlining the complaints of Israel over food, water, and leadership (Numbers 11–12; 16) and the loss of the land by the first generation (Numbers 13–14). Numbers 20–21 provides transition from wilderness wandering to conquest of the Transjordan by the second generation. Numbers 22–24 and 25:1-5 explore threats to Israel by other nations. The story concludes with an account of Israel's inheritance of the Transjordan (Numbers 32) and a summary of the wilderness journey (Numbers 33). Pre-priestly literature includes the following:

10:29-36,* departure from Mt. Yahweh;
11:1-3, murmuring;
11:4-35, complaint about food and the selection of the seventy elders;
12,* conflict between Moses, Miriam, and perhaps Aaron;
13–14,* loss of the land;
16,* conflict between Moses and Dathan and Abiram;
20:14-21, conflict with Edom;
21:1-3, defeat of the king of Arad;
21:4-9, fiery serpents;
21:10-20, leaving the wilderness;
21:21-35, defeat of the Amorite kings Sihon and Og;
22–24,* the threat of Balak and the blessing of Balaam;
25:1-5, sin at Baal Peor;
32, inheritance of the Transjordan;
33,* summary of itinerary stops.

22. See Y. Kaufmann, *The Religion of Israel,* trans M. Greenberg (Chicago: University of Chicago Press, 1961).

Pre-priestly literature in Numbers is part of a history that includes the promise of land and nationhood to the ancestors in Genesis, as well as liberation from Egypt and the establishment of covenant at the mountain of God in Exodus. The departure of Israel from Mt. Yahweh in Numbers 10:29-36 indicates that the pre-priestly history once followed immediately after the establishment of covenant in Exodus 19–34. The role of the tent of meeting in Exodus 33 and Numbers 11–12 provides further support for this conclusion. In both Exodus 33 and Numbers 11–12, the tent of meeting is located outside the Israelite camp. This is unusual in the Pentateuch, because priestly writers place the tabernacle at the center of the camp in Exodus 35–40, Leviticus, and Numbers 1–10. As a result, Exodus 33 and Numbers 11–12 stand out in their present narrative context. But, in the pre-priestly history, Exodus 33 and Numbers 11–12 would have followed in rapid succession. The return of the tent of meeting in Deut 31:14-23 as the setting for the commissioning of Joshua to replace Moses suggests that the pre-priestly history also incorporated the book of Deuteronomy. The commissioning of Joshua leads into the conquest stories of the book of Joshua. Central themes of the pre-priestly history include the unfulfilled promise of land to the ancestors and the necessity of conquest to acquire it, salvation from Egypt as an event of liberation that provides an initial stage toward conquest, faith as fear of God that is able to withstand tests in the wilderness, the revelation of law, the establishment of covenant, and the idealization of Moses as a prophetic leader and teacher of law.

The Priestly History. Most literature in Numbers belongs to the priestly history. The priestly writers frame the pre-priestly history with law. Camp legislation is introduced in Numbers 1–10, while inheritance law and cultic legislation now conclude the book in Numbers 26–36. The priestly writers also add their interpretation to the conflict stories in Numbers 11–25 and interweave law with the narratives in Numbers 15; 18–19. The story of the loss of land in Numbers 13–14 includes a priestly interpretation, and it concludes with laws concerning life in the land in Numbers 15. A priestly leader, Korah, is added to the conflict with Dathan and Abiram in Numbers 16–17. This conflict, too, is followed by legislation in Numbers 18–19. Numbers 20–21 is less of a transition to the second generation for the priestly writers. They emphasize instead the death of Miriam and Aaron, as well as the sin of Moses. Israel's arrival on the plains of Moab in Numbers 22 signals transition from wilderness wandering to preparation for Canaan in the priestly history, although the death of the first generation is not complete until the second census in chap. 26. Priestly literature includes the following:

1:1–10:10, legislation concerning the camp and the tabernacle;
10:11-28, departure from Sinai;
12,* conflict between Moses, Miriam, and Aaron;
13–14,* loss of the land;
15,* law concerning life in the land;
16–17,* conflict between Moses and Korah;
18–19, law concerning the priesthood and death;
20:1, death of Miriam;

20:2-13, sin of Moses and Aaron;

20:22-29, death of Aaron;

25:6-18, sin at Baal Peor;

26, second census;

27:1-11, inheritance of the daughters of Zelophehad;

27:12-23, death of Moses;

28–29,* offerings and cultic calendar;

30,* law of vows;

31, law of booty;

33,* summary of Israel's itinerary stops;

34,* inheritance;

35,* levitical cities;

36, inheritance of the daughters of Zelophehad.

Priestly literature in Numbers is part of a history that begins with the story of creation in Genesis 1. It also includes the promise of land and nationhood to the ancestors in Genesis, the liberation from Egypt, and the establishment of the nation at the mountain of God in Exodus. The central event at Mt. Sinai is the revelation of the tabernacle cult. Its plans are revealed to Moses in Exodus 25–31, when the כבוד יהוה (*kĕbôd YHWH*, "the glory of Yahweh") descends on Mt. Sinai in Exod 24:15-18. Exodus 35–40 describes the construction of the tabernacle. It concludes with a theophany in Exod 40:16-38, when the *kĕbôd YHWH* leaves Mt. Sinai to enter the tabernacle. The book of Leviticus recounts the revelation of the sacrificial cult and the sanctification of the priesthood. These events also conclude with a theophany in Lev 9:23-24, when the *kĕbôd YHWH* appears at the altar in front of the tabernacle. The formation of the camp in Numbers 1–10 completes the revelation at Mt. Sinai in the priestly history. This episode, too, is marked by a theophany in Nums 7:89, when Moses enters the tabernacle to speak with God before the mercy seat.

The conclusion to the priestly history is not clear. There is evidence of editing by priestly writers in Deuteronomy. In particular, they enclose the book of Deuteronomy with the death of Moses. It is announced in Num 27:12-23 and 31:1-2, but not fulfilled until Deut 32:48-32 and 34:1-8. The framing may indicate that their history ends with the death of Moses.

The priestly history addresses the tragedy of the exile (587 BCE), when Israel lost their land to the Babylonians. One of its aims is to explore how Israel can once again be the people of God in the land of Canaan in the post-exilic period (539 BCE). Central themes of the priestly history include creation as the primary context for interpreting salvation, the relationship of creation and covenant, the unfulfilled promise of land, the holiness of God and the demand that it places on Israel to be holy like God, the importance of the sanctuary, the revelation of law, the atoning power of cultic ritual, the need for a sanctified priesthood, the danger of impurity, and the idealization of Moses as a priestly mediator.

The Canonical Book of Numbers. Numbers undergoes a final literary transformation. It is indicated by the way in which the book is presently framed. Numbers 1:1 opens with the statement, "The LORD spoke to Moses in the wilderness of Sinai, in the tent of meeting." The book closes in Num 36:13 with the similar theme: "These are the commandments and the ordinances that the LORD commanded through Moses to the Israelites." The effect of these verses is to separate the literature in Numbers to some degree from the other books in the Pentateuch. The opening and closing verses emphasize the authoritative nature of the literature. The framing also suggests a transformation of genre from history to law. The literature is not so much an episode in a larger history, when it is confined to Numbers. Instead, it resembles more a book of divine law revealed by God to Moses.

METHOD OF STUDY AND PRIESTLY RELIGION

Method of Study. The prominence of priestly ritual law in Numbers has made interpretation difficult. The rituals are not explained; their meaning is assumed. The layout of the camp (Numbers 2); distinctions between priests, Levites, and laity (Numbers 3–4); the dedication of the tabernacle with sacrifices (Numbers 7–9); and laws of inheritance (Numbers 27; 34–36) are outlined in detail without explanation. Gordon Wenham notes that the "sheer bulk of ritual law in the Pentateuch indicates its importance to biblical writers." Yet few of these texts have worked their way into the lectionary cycles of the church. Readings from Numbers in the *Revised Common Lectionary* are limited to three: the priestly blessing in Num 6:22-27, the selection of the seventy elders in Numbers 11, and the healing power of the copper snake in Num 21:4-9. The reason for the absence of Numbers in Christian teaching and preaching, according to Wenham, is that priestly ritual has been judged "dull to read, hard to understand, and apparently quite irrelevant to the church in the twentieth century." [23]

Social anthropologists have opened a window of interpretation into ritual law within the Bible. Anthropologists are trained to interpret living societies. Their research ranges from the most important events in a society to the everyday exchange between members. In most instances, the rules of interaction are known by all and thus usually unexplained. These rules reflect the deepest values of a people, and adhering to them gives rise to ritual behavior. They include important events like birth, marriage, worship practices, and burial of the dead. Yet other rules are mundane, like how and what people eat or acceptable forms of greeting each other on the street. [24] It is usually the outsider or foreigner who becomes aware of such rituals by unintentionally breaking them. All travelers know how easy it is to break the rules of another society.

Priestly laws are the unexplained rituals of ancient Israel. They take up most of the Pentateuch because they reveal their deepest values. Anthropologist Mary Douglas brought insight into the interpretation of priestly law with her study of Leviticus 11. [25] This text

---

23. Gordon J. Wenham, *Numbers: An Introduction and Commentary,* Tyndale Old Testament Commentaries (Leicester: Inter-Varsity, 1981) 25-29.

24. See, e.g., Thomas W. Overholt, *Cultural Anthropology and the Old Testament,* Guides to Biblical Scholarship, Old Testament (Minneapolis: Augsburg Fortress, 1996); and Robert R. Wilson, *Sociological Approaches to the Old Testament* (Philadelphia: Fortress, 1984).

25. Mary Douglas, *Purity and Danger: An Analysis of the Concepts of Pollution and Taboo* (London: Routledge and Kegan Paul, 1966), 41-57.

outlines the laws for clean and unclean food, known as "kashrut" (כשרות *kašrût*), kosher food law. The chapter consists of a long list of animals, fish, birds, and insects that are edible (clean) and inedible (unclean). Yet the underlying reason why only some split-hoofed animals were edible or why certain fish and birds were clean while others were not elude modern interpreters. Priestly writers gave no explanation, and the study of individual laws provides no insight.

Douglas assumed that the meaning of the text was in the interrelationship of all the laws and not in any one law. She concluded that what made something unclean was that it did not move as other land, air, or water creatures. Unclean animals, therefore, did not clearly conform to their species. The same was true for fish, birds, and insects. They broke the order (or natural law) of creation and thus were not fit for human consumption (at least by godly people). Priestly writers never state this principle. It only emerges when all the laws in Leviticus 11 are read together. The study of food laws in Leviticus 11 provides three important guidelines for interpreting priestly law in Numbers.

(1) Priestly law is concerned with the order of creation. Order, purity, and even holiness are interrelated in priestly law. The source of life is the holiness of God, which fashions order in the world. Life flourishes in a well-ordered creation. Disorder creates a condition that is threatening to holiness and all life in creation. It allows for impurity, which is not simply disorder, but, in its most extreme form, death.[26] Impurity is like a virus to the holiness of God. It can spread through contact, creating chaos and death in its wake. Priestly law is meant to safeguard the holiness of God from contagious impurity by reinforcing the order of creation. Eating habits are part of the system of safeguards for the holiness of God. So are the camp regulations in Numbers.

(2) The meaning of priestly ritual is not in any one law, but in the interrelationship of all the laws. Only by examining all the laws in Leviticus 11 was Douglas able to show that the principle of locomotion was the decisive factor for biblical writers in judging animals clean or unclean. The same is true for priestly law in Numbers. Theological insight requires that all the laws be interrelated. As a result, individual stories or laws in Numbers must be interpreted within the larger complex of literature.

(3) Priestly ritual has symbolic meaning. It creates a comprehensive worldview in which God, humans, and the created order are interrelated. Douglas concluded that in Leviticus 11 laws about animals were carried over into the human world. Thus just as animals separated into unclean (inedible), clean (edible), and sacrificial, so also humans separated into Gentile (unclean), Israelite (clean), and priest (sacrificial). Clean people eat clean food, and only priests sacrifice. The laws concerning the layout of the Israelite camp in Numbers will also have symbolic significance about God, about humans, and about creation.

Priestly Religion. Interpretation of Numbers requires an understanding of priestly religion. This is not an easy task for a modern Christian. We envision God as an intimate friend who

---

26. See Jacob Milgrom, *Numbers,* JPS Torah Commentary (Philadelphia: JPS, 1990) 344-46; and Kathrine Doob Sakenfeld, *Numbers: Journeying with God,* ITC (Grand Rapids: Eerdmans, 1995) 17-20.

dwells within us. We sing about "what a friend we have in Jesus." The focus of our piety is not on the vast gulf between God and ourselves, but on our own close, personal, and individual relationship with God. We may fear God, but it is the respect due a powerful companion. Our friendship with God leads to spontaneous prayer. These conversations take place at any time and in any location. They are not restricted to organized worship. They do not require special rituals. There is no need for a priest to mediate our prayer. And prayer certainly is not confined to church buildings. In fact, we envision our own bodies as the temple of God. The temple, sacrificial rituals, and God's relationship to humans are different in priestly religion.

Temple. The center of priestly religion is God dwelling in the Temple. When Solomon completed the Jerusalem Temple, he stated to Yahweh, "I have built you an exalted house, a place for you to dwell in forever." The same is true for the tabernacle in priestly religion. It is where God dwells on earth. Yahweh states to Moses, "Have [Israel] make me a sanctuary, so that I may dwell among them." The plans for the tabernacle in Exodus 25–31 are a pattern of God's heavenly home. Construction of the tabernacle allows God to descend to earth. Thus it connects heaven and earth. It is the *axis mundi*—the central point of creation where heaven and earth link.[27] All communication with God is channeled through cultic rituals in the tabernacle.

Temples are located on symbolic mountains. Solomon's Temple is on Mt. Zion (Psalm 48). Pre-priestly writers associate the tent of meeting in Exodus 33 with Mt. Horeb, which is also the mountain of theophany in Deuteronomy 4–5. Numbers 10:33-34 identifies the desert sanctuary of God as Mt. Yahweh. Priestly writers locate the tabernacle on Mt. Sinai (Exod 24:15-18). Yahweh has many mountain homes. Mountains symbolize the presence of God in the Temple and the role of the Temple in connecting heaven and earth. Different mountains indicate distinct forms of worship. Contemporary church architecture provides a partial analogy. Denominations favor distinct styles for church buildings because of different forms of worship. Churches are built with and without altars, with center aisles or in the round. But nearly all churches have steeples. Steeples convey the same message as mountains: They reach up to heaven and indicate communication between heaven and earth. The difference is that for ancient Israel temples are the only place where God can be approached.[28]

Sacrificial Ritual. Sacrifice and liturgical rituals result from the indwelling of God in the Temple. Worship rituals in the tabernacle, therefore, do not conjure up the presence of God. They are a response to Yahweh, who is already there. The word for worship is "work" or "service" (עבדה *ăbōdâ*). It states that sacrifice and worship rituals are acts of service to God, who has chosen to dwell with Israel.[29] Two-way communication results from the work of worship. Humans serve God through sacrifice. They also express their hopes and fears and seek blessing from God. In the process, God reveals law and makes promises.[30] Thus the act of worship manifests the presence of God in the sanctuary in a more concrete way through ritual drama.

---

27. Gary A. Anderson, "Introduction to Israelite Religion," *NIB* 1:277-79.
28. Thomas B. Dozeman, *God on the Mountain,* SBLMS 37 (Atlanta: Scholars Press, 1988).
29. Anderson, "Introduction to Israelite Religion," 279-80.
30. Wenham, *Numbers,* 29-30.

Sacrificial ritual in priestly religion continues in Christian sacraments. Baptism and eucharist result from prior actions of Jesus. Thus their observance by Christians is a response to God, who has chosen to dwell with us. Observance in worship is an act of service to God, in which Christ is made manifest through two-way communication. In baptism, for example, God forgives sins and defeats death. The congregation makes confession of faith to live a sin-free life and celebrates new life in Christ. Sacraments also provide partial analogy to the central role of the tabernacle in priestly religion. In most cases, they require ordained clergy for their administration. And they are usually performed publically at a sanctuary with established rituals.

God and Humans. Priestly religion does not envision God as an intimate friend of individuals. The starting point for priestly writers in Numbers is the gulf between God and humans. They achieve this by emphasizing the holiness of God. The word "holy" (קדשׁ *qōdeš*) means "to be separate." God is separate from humans in two different ways.

First, holiness distinguishes God from all things common. This is the separation between the sacred and the profane. God is sacred (holy), and humans are profane (common). This contrast makes God dangerous to humans.[31] Priestly writers convey this message by symbolizing the holiness of God as fire. Fire destroys life, but when applied carefully it can also purify. Priestly writers introduce the *kĕbôd YHWH* in Exod 24:17 as a devouring fire. Wholeness is another metaphor to contrast the sacred and the profane. Holiness is complete, and the profane world is not. The contrast between the sacred and the profane is prominent in the arrangement of the camp in Numbers 1–4.

Second, holiness also creates a contrast between health (purity) and disease (impurity). The contrast between purity and impurity intensifies the danger of God to humans. God embodies health, purity, and life. Death is the source of disease and all impurity. Thus corpses become a source of impurity for the priestly writers. Evil actions are also disease that pollutes and eventually kills a society. God is repelled by all forms of impurity. The contrast between purity and impurity is a central topic in the laws of defilement in Numbers 5–6.

The goal of priestly religion is to bring a holy God and a profane people together through the tabernacle cult. The arrangement of the camp and selection of Levites provides an ordered way for the sacred and the profane to dwell together. The *kĕbôd YHWH* also seeks to purify the tabernacle and the priesthood (Exodus 29; 40; Leviticus 9), allowing God to dwell with Israel. Ritual observance at the tabernacle monitors the health of Israel and transforms them into a holy people. But this transformation is not a story of intimate friendship. It is more an epic drama. Communication with God is not spontaneous and individual. It is ritualized and communal, requiring priestly intercessors. The reason for the heroic or grand scale to the drama is the holiness of God: Israel needs the *kĕbôd YHWH* for life, but the source of their life can be a consuming fire.

---

31. David P. Wright, "Holiness: Old Testament," in *Anchor Bible Dictionary,* 6 vols. (New York: Doubleday, 1992) 3:237-49.

THEOLOGICAL THEMES

The book of Numbers is a rich resource of theological reflection on community. Israel's formation at Sinai and the journey with God through the wilderness are intended to be a continuing model of how the people of God live out their faith in this world. The central theological themes in Numbers are embedded in the interplay of the wilderness setting, the journey toward the promised land, and the interaction of characters along the way.

Wilderness Setting. The wilderness is the primary setting for the book of Numbers. Israel is encamped in the wilderness of Sinai (Num 1:1) at the outset of the book, and the wilderness continues to be the setting for their journey toward the promised land of Canaan through Numbers 21. It is replaced by "the plains of Moab" in the Transjordan in Num 22:1. The following map provides the geographical boundaries of the wilderness.

The wilderness provides more than geographical background in Numbers. Biblical writers also use it to reflect theologically on salvation history. Gerhard von Rad characterized salvation history as a "canonical history."[32] It is a mixture of historical experience and cultic legend, recounting divine acts of salvation that formed the nation of Israel. The central topics of salvation history include the promise of land to the ancestors, the exodus, the wilderness wandering, the revelation at Sinai, and future life in the land of Canaan. The wilderness setting takes on a wide range of theological meanings in Numbers.

Place of Birth. The wilderness can represent Israel's birth as a nation. It is the setting for stories of Israel's youth and innocence, when they were courted by God (see Hos 2:16-17; 9:10). The formation of the camp in Numbers 1–10 is part of these positive stories. The wilderness is the place where Israel is organized, when structures of leadership are defined, when their relationship to God is revealed, and when systems of worship and government are developed.

Place of Testing. The wilderness also symbolizes a time of transition between slavery in Egypt and life in the land. A time of transition is not the same as a time of origin. This is a more complex meaning, in which an age of innocence is replaced by a time of testing. The test is whether Israel is able to live the life of faith outside the promised land. Testing gives rise to the possibility of failure, in which case the wilderness may be a negative time of rebellion, rather than a positive time of innocence and courtship (see Ezek 20:10-17). The failed journey of the first generation in Num 10:11–21:35 contains many negative stories of testing and rebellion.

Homeless Place. The destruction of a city or an entire land is often symbolized by the wilderness. The prophet Isaiah, for example, writes, "The fortified city is solitary, a habitation deserted and forsaken, like the wilderness" (Isa 27:10). Desolation imagery underscores that biblical writers do not view the wilderness as a natural home or an inviting setting.[33] It lies outside the security of civilized structures and is a dangerous place. Stories of complaint about

32. Gerhard von Rad, *Old Testament Theology I,* trans. D. M. G. Stalker (New York: Harper and Bros., 1962) 126, 129. See also Thomas L. Thompson, "Historiography [Israelite]," *ABD* 3:209-10.

33. Shemaryahu Talmon, "The 'Desert Motif' in the Bible and in Qumran Literature," in *Biblical Motifs in Origins and Transformations,* ed. A. Altmann, Philip W. Lown Institute of Advanced Judaic Studies, Brandeis University Studies and Texts 3 (Cambridge, Mass.: Harvard University Press, 1966) 39-44.

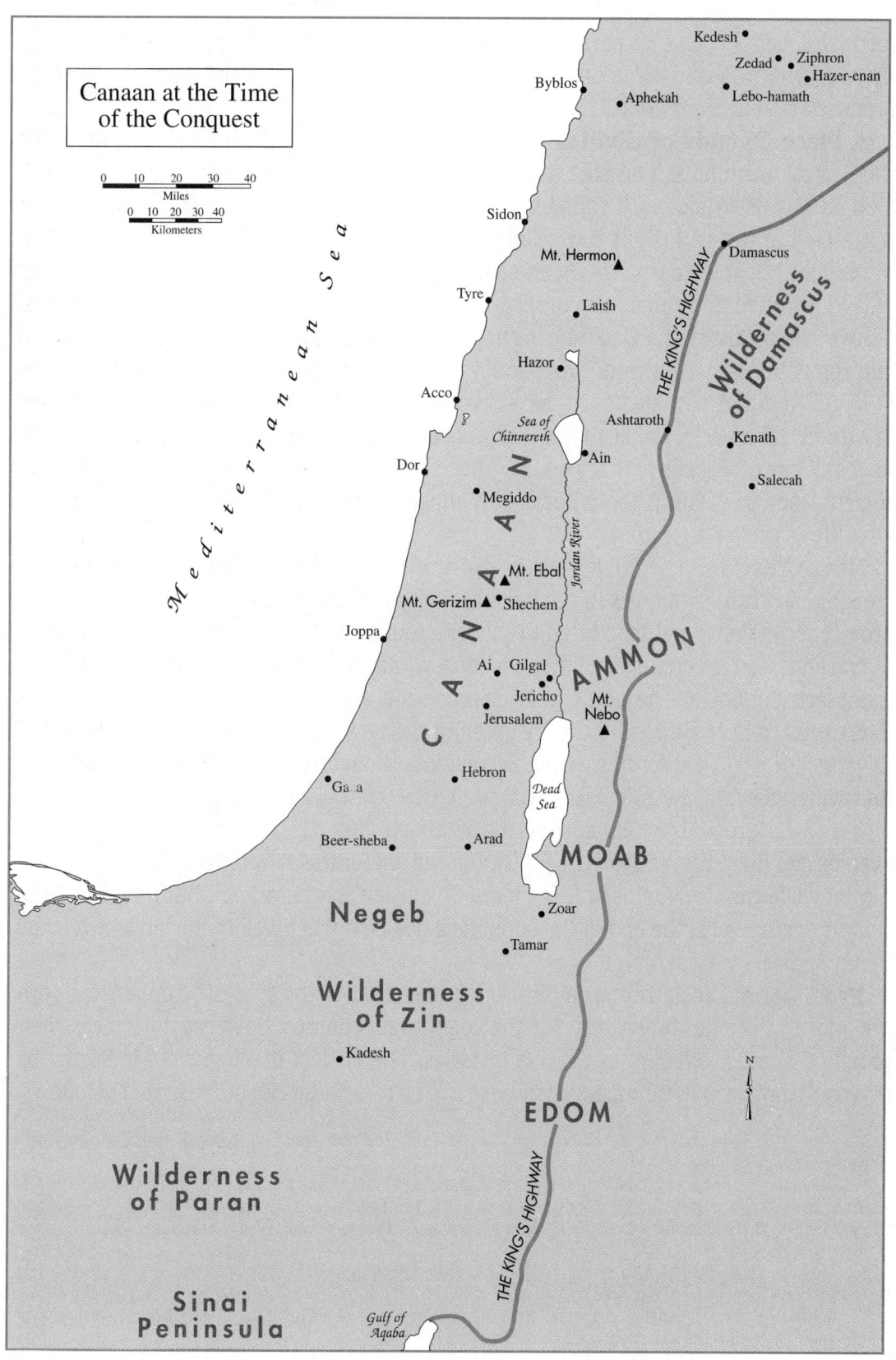

Canaan at the Time
of the Conquest

Miles
0 10 20 30 40

Kilometers
0 10 20 30 40

Kedesh

Zedad • Ziphron
Byblos • Hazer-enan
Aphekah Lebo-hamath

Mediterranean Sea

Sidon

Mt. Hermon ▲ Damascus

THE KING'S HIGHWAY

Tyre Laish

Wilderness
of Damascus

Hazor

Acco Sea of
Chinnereth Ashtaroth
Kenath

Ain

Dor Salecah

Megiddo

Jordan River

Mt. Ebal ▲
Mt. Gerizim ▲ • Shechem

C A N A A N

AMMON

Joppa

Ai • Gilgal
Jericho Mt.
Jerusalem Nebo ▲

Hebron

Gaza Dead
Sea

Beer-sheba Arad MOAB

Negeb Zoar

Tamar

Wilderness
of Zin

• Kadesh

N

EDOM

Wilderness
of Paran

THE KING'S HIGHWAY

Sinai
Peninsula Gulf of
Aqaba

food (Numbers 11) and water (Num 20:2-13) accentuate the danger of traveling through the wilderness. Divine judgment on the "rabble" in Numbers 11 and Moses' loss of the promised land in Num 20:2-13 underscore the need for faithful action in the desert.

A Place Outside of Civilization. The wilderness can take on a more subversive theological meaning as a symbol that criticizes civilization and encourages one to seek God outside its structures.[34] Yahweh is a God of the desert in Israel's oldest poetry, and not a God of the city (Deut 33:2; Judg 5:5; Ps 68:9, 18; Hab 3:3-4).[35] Often biblical heroes like Hagar (Genesis 16–18) and Moses (Exodus 3) must flee oppressive structures of civilization to find some form of salvation or relief in the wilderness. In these stories, Yahweh is presented as a God who is encountered outside of the confines of civilization and the nation-state. Encountering God in the desert puts one in tension with culture at large. Numbers participates in this subversive imagery. That Yahweh chooses to live in a desert tabernacle, rather than the temple of a king, is a criticism of civilization, with its many forms of security that seek to subvert faith in God. Failure to see the threats of society leads to death in the wilderness, while critical insight provides a path toward new life in the land.

New Creation. The wilderness is also the location for God's continuing work in creation. Sabbath re-emerges in the wilderness for the first time after Genesis 1. Signs of providence in water and food bring to the foreground the implications of salvation for all of creation. God is certainly active in creation within the wilderness, but the wilderness is not sacred or holy.[36] The land of Canaan represents a different quality of divine presence in creation, where God will actually dwell in the land. It represents the fulfillment of salvation for Israel and for this world. Second Isaiah underscores the distinction between the wilderness and the promised land, which he symbolizes as a garden in Zion. The wilderness is a road (Isa 40:3) and a place of miracles (Isa 41:18-19) that signals and may even lead to the return of Zion (Isa 53:3). But the wilderness is not Zion. The same is true for the wilderness in Numbers. It is a place of journey and miracles.[37] But the goal of the story is envisioned at the end of the book. One day God will dwell in the land with Israel (Num 35:34).

Promise of Land. The promise of land is central to the plot of Numbers for both pre-priestly and priestly writers. But theological reflection on how Israel achieves their promised home is different in the two histories. The distinct theologies are indicated by divergent travel routes through the wilderness. The two routes can be illustrated as follows.

34. Herbert N. Schneidau, *Sacred Discontent: The Bible and Western Tradition* (Baton Rouge: Louisiana State University Press, 1976) esp. 104-57.

35. The poems are characterized as the "March in the South" theophany tradition. A common feature of this poetry is that Yahweh dwells in the desert, not in the city. See Dozeman, *God on the Mountain,* 121-26; and Richard J. Clifford, *The Cosmic Mountain in Canaan and the Old Testament,* HSM 4 (Cambridge, Mass.: Harvard University Press, 1972).

36. Max Oelschlaeger, *The Idea of the Wilderness: From Prehistory to the Age of Ecology* (New Haven: Yale University Press, 1991) 41-53, esp. 50-51.

37. Robert L. Cohn, "Liminality in the Wilderness," in *The Shape of Sacred Space: Four Biblical Studies,* AAR Studies in Religion 23 (Missoula, Mont.: Scholars Press, 1981) 7-20.

Pre-priestly Kadesh Sequence of Travel

[1] from Mt. Yahweh (10:33)
    (Three days journey)
[2] Kibrothhattaqvah to Hazeroth (11:35)

KADESH/ZIN—Spy Story (13:21, 26)
—Spy Story (13:21, 26)
—Dathan and Abiram (chap. 16)
—Edom (20:14-21)

[3] Kadesh to Mount Hor (20:22)

Priestly Paran Sequence of Travel
[a] Sinai to Paran (10:12)

[b] Hazeroth to Paran (12:16)
PARAN
—Spy Story (Num 13:3, 26)
—Korah (Num 16–19)

[c] to Kadesh/Zin (20:1)

The sequence of travel in the pre-priestly history begins with Israel's departure from Mt. Yahweh on a three-day journey (10:33) to Hazeroth (11:35). The wilderness of Zin, or Kadesh, is an important setting in the pre-priestly history, even though it lacks a clear itinerary notice in the present form of Numbers. Israel arrives at Kadesh in the second year of their exodus from Egypt. It is the setting for the loss of the land in Numbers 13–14 (13:21, 26). The challenge to the leadership of Moses by Dathan and Abiram (chap. 16) and an unsuccessful negotiation with the Edomite king to cross his land (20:14-21) also take place at Kadesh. Israel leaves Kadesh when they journey to Mt. Hor (20:22).

Priestly writers change the sequence of travel. Israel departs from Sinai rather than Mt. Yahweh. Their next significant stopping point is the wilderness of Paran. This is stated both at the outset of their journey from Sinai (Num 10:12) and immediately preceding the spy story (Num 12:16). As a result, Paran is firmly established as the location of the spy story, which creates confusion in the present form of Numbers 13–14. The insertion of Paran results in Israel's arriving at Kadesh at the end of their wilderness trek in the fortieth year after they left Egypt (Num 20:1).

The two versions of travel represent different theologies of the promised land. Pre-priestly writers view the promised land from the wilderness location of Kadesh. Priestly writers achieve a different vantage point from Paran.[38] The two perspectives are expressed most clearly in the story of Israel's loss of the promised land in Numbers 13–14.

Kadesh and Holy War. Pre-priestly writers emphasize that Israel must acquire the courage to undertake holy war to leave the wilderness and to enter the promised land. Possession of the promised land requires a conquest of indigenous peoples no matter how dangerous such a war may appear. Holy war is an act of faith in the promises of God. The failure of the first generation to leave the wilderness in Numbers 13–14 is because they lack the courage of conquest. Joshua sends out spies from Kadesh to reconnoiter the southern border regions of the land. Upon their return, they report the goodness of the land and how fearsome the people appear to be, like the giant Anakim (Num 13:22-24, 26-30), which prompts rebellion (Num 14:2-4). Rebellion in this account is fear of the

38. See the detailed study of the different travel routes by Baruch A. Levine, *Numbers 1–20,* AB 4A (New York: Doubleday, 1993) 48-72.

giants to the point where the people lose faith in God to lead them to conquest. Divine judgment and the subsequent failure of the first generation to leave the wilderness is because the people lack the courage of conquest.

Paran and the Goodness of Creation. Priestly writers change the setting of Numbers 13–14 to Paran, and they introduce a new theology of the promised land. These writers eliminate the central role of conquest as the means for leaving the wilderness. Instead, they emphasize Israel's need to see the goodness of God in creation. In this account, Moses no longer sends out spies, but "explorers" from each tribe to evaluate the entire land of Canaan. Their goal is not espionage on the fortifications at the southern border of Canaan, but assessment of the quality of the whole land that Yahweh has promised. Thus the spies travel to the northernmost border of the land of Canaan (Num 13:21 *b*). Rebellion is not the fear of conquest, but the failure of the people to judge the land "good" (Num 13:31-33). The first generation still dies, but the plot no longer pushes ahead to an account of holy war. Priestly writers interpret the wilderness more in relationship to creation than to an exodus and conquest. Entering the promised land, in their version of the story, requires proper perception of its goodness, rather than a conquest of indigenous peoples.

Characters. The development of characters in Numbers evolves around the problem of how to build a theocratic society in the wilderness. The central character is Yahweh, and all other characters are defined in relation to God. The goal is to devise a way in which a holy God can be brought into relationship with humans who do not share this quality, and, hence, are at risk in the presence of God. Characters separate into three general groups: God, who embodies holiness; Israel, who lives in the sphere of holiness; and the nations, who live outside of the sphere of holiness.

God. There is unresolved tension in God that is central to the book of Numbers. It is the tension between holiness and covenant. Divine holiness results in separation from humans and creation. Holiness means that God is unlike creation and even repulsed by the pollution of sin. Covenant describes God's commitment to humans and creation in spite of sin.[39] God enters into a covenant with all of creation at the end of the flood in Gen 9:1-17. God makes a covenant with Abraham in Genesis 17, and God forms a covenant treaty with Israel in Exodus 19–34. Covenant is not easily harmonized with holiness, because it describes the relationship between God and humans, rather than separation. The result is a tension between divine holiness and Yahweh's commitment to creation and relationship with humans. The formation of a theocratic society around the wilderness tabernacle is the attempt to fulfill the divine obligations of covenant while safeguarding holiness.

The tension between holiness and covenant is never really resolved in the book of Numbers. Divine obligation to creation and to Israel fuels the plot of the story. Covenant prompts the exodus (Exod 6:2-8). It is also the driving force in the establishment of the wilderness sanctuary, when God descends from Mt. Sinai into the tabernacle (Exod

---

39. See Dozeman, *God on the Mountain,* 57-65.

40:35-36). Covenantal concern is manifested in divine communication with Moses (Num 1:1), in leading and guiding through the wilderness (Num 9:15-23), in the providential care of food and water (Numbers 11; 20), in healing (Num 21:1-9), in the quality of loving kindness (Num 14:18, 20), and in blessing (Num 6:21-27). The holiness of God emphasizes that divine leading is never casual and that divine grace is anything but cheap. Yahweh's repulsion to sin is underscored by the holy war imagery of the ark of the covenant (Num 10:33-36), by the precise details of the camp and priesthood (Num 1:1–10:10), and by the destructive power of divine wrath conceived in the wilderness (Num 11:1-3; 25).

The tension between holiness and covenant makes God dynamic and open to change. Obedience reinforces divine obligation (Caleb and Joshua in Numbers 13–14). Resistance to divine leading (Num 11:1-3), lack of faith in divine providence (Numbers 11), rejection of God's new creation (Numbers 13–14), and the worship of other gods (Numbers 25) prompt judgment and separation between God and Israel. Yet, even at these times, zealous action on behalf of God (Numbers 25), healing icons (Num 20:4-9), cultic rituals (Numbers 15), and intercession (Numbers 14) can persuade God to relent from acts of judgment.

Israel. Israel is the direct object of God's saving activity. They are formed out of divine covenantal obligation. Israelites are singled out for divine favor with the promise of land (Numbers 15). They experience special providence (Numbers 11) and divine guidance (Num 9:15-23). They are the ones who gather around the sanctuary and live in close proximity to God (Num 1:1–10:10). And, because of their special status, they are required to embody the qualities of divine holiness through cultic observances (Num 1:1–10:10; chaps. 28-29), in their march through the wilderness (Numbers 11–21; 25), and in their future life in the land of Canaan (Numbers 15; 35). Failure to do so results in death (Numbers 13–14; 25).

Numbers also explores forms of leadership for Israel. Leaders provide different ways for Israel to approach God, who dwells at the center of the camp. Divine holiness in the tabernacle is protected through the hierarchy of priests and Levites camped around it. Priestly leaders also provide a safe means for Israel to approach God through worship (Numbers 3–4; 8; 16–18). The seventy elders provide prophetic leadership in governing the people (Numbers 11). Numbers also outlines the role of lay tribal leaders (Numbers 1) and Nazirites (Numbers 6). The role of Moses throughout Numbers also provides theological reflection on both prophetic and priestly leadership. He models prophetic, charismatic leadership (Numbers 11–12); priestly, non-charismatic leadership (Numbers 16–18); and other intercessory roles (Numbers 13–14; 25).

The Nations. The nations are defined more in relationship to divine holiness than to covenant. They are separate from God and live outside of the wilderness camp. Some are associated with Canaan. They may be mythologized as giants, such as Anak, or the descendants of the Nephilim (Num 13:25-33). Others are simply described as ethnic groups, like the Amalekites, the Hittites, the Jebusites, and the Amorites (Num 13:27-29). In general, the nations are opponents of God who must be defeated by Israel in holy war, like Sihon, the Amorite king (Num 21:21-32), and Og of Bashan (Num 21:33-35). Divine concern for the nations is also evident in Numbers. The intercession of Moses in Num 14:13-19 is successful in part because of God's concern for the nations.

Other people and groups blur the line between "Israel" and "the nations." Resident aliens are one example of non-Israelites included in the camp (Num 9:1-14) and in Israel's future life in the land (Numbers 15; 35). "The rabble" in Num 11:4, on the other hand, represent members of the camp who belong outside the sphere of holiness. Balaam is a non-Israelite seer who knows Yahweh (Numbers 22–24), and the Midianites represent an entire ethnic group whose relationship with Israel is ambiguous. Jethro, or Hobab, the father-in-law of Moses, is a Midianite, whose guidance Moses requests (Num 10:29-32). Yet a Midianite woman threatens the purity of the Israelite camp in Numbers 25.

The following study will explore in more detail the theological themes of Numbers in two parts. A commentary section will interpret the meaning of the literature in the context of ancient priestly religion. Important words, the literary structure of chapters, distinct authorship, and divergent theological perspectives will be described. Reflections sections will include summaries of the central theological themes of pre-priestly and priestly writers. The reinterpretation of Numbers in New Testament literature will also be explored where applicable. And more concrete application for contemporary preaching and teaching will also be offered.

BIBLIOGRAPHY

Ashley, Timothy R. *Numbers.* NICOT. Grand Rapids: Eerdmans, 1993. A new translation and careful philological study from an evangelical perspective.

Budd, Phillip J. *Numbers.* WBC 5. Waco, Tex.: Word, 1984. A commentary with extensive review of the history of interpretation. Special attention is given to the history of composition of Numbers.

Gray, George Buchanan. *Numbers.* ICC. Edinburgh: T. & T. Clark, 1903. A classic commentary in the modern period. Full discussion of the history of composition is combined with detailed study of ancient Israelite religion.

Davies, Eryl W. *Numbers.* NCB. Grand Rapids: Eerdmans, 1995. A thorough and recent philological study based on the Revised Standard Version

Levine, Baruch A. *Numbers 1–20.* AB 4A. New York: Doubleday, 1993. A new translation of the text. Commentary is the most up-to-date comparative study of priestly terms in their larger ancient Near Eastern setting.

Milgrom, Jacob. *Numbers.* JPS Torah Commentary. Philadelphia: JPS, 1990. Commentary focuses on the meaning of priestly terms and is based on the New JPS translation. Seventy-seven essays at the end of the commentary summarize a lifetime of research by one of the foremost interpreters of priestly tradition.

Noth, Martin. *Numbers.* OTL. Philadelphia: Westminster, 1968. A classic historical-critical commentary.

Olson, Dennis T. *Numbers.* Interpretation. Louisville: Westminster John Knox, 1996. An insightful commentary comparing the fate of the first and second generation of Israelites to leave Egypt.

Sakenfeld, Katharine Doob. *Journeying with God: A Commentary on the Book of Numbers.* ITC. Grand Rapids: Eerdmans, 1995. A theological summary of Numbers paying particular attention to issues of purity and impurity in priestly religion.

Wenham, Gordon J. *Numbers: An Introduction and Commentary.* Tyndale Old Testament Commentaries. Leicester: Inter-Varsity, 1981. Commentary focuses on the structure of Numbers. Careful attention is given to the contribution of anthropology for interpreting priestly ritual.

OUTLINE OF NUMBERS

I. Numbers 1:1–10:10, Forming Community Around a Holy God at Sinai

   A. 1:1–6:27, Holiness and the Camp
   > 1:1–2:34, The First Census and the Arrangement of the Camp
   > 3:1–4:49, The Role of the Levites in the Cult, in the Camp, and on the March
   > 5:1–6:27, Camp Legislation to Prevent Defilement

   B. 7:1–10:10, Holiness and the Tabernacle
   > 7:1–8:26, The Dedication of the Tabernacle and the Levites
   > 9:1–10:10, The Celebration of Passover and Preparation for the Wilderness March

II. Numbers 10:11–21:35, The Wilderness Journey of the First Generation

   A. 10:11-36, Leaving Sinai

   B. 11:1–19:22, Murmuring and Death in the Wilderness
   > 11:1–12:16, Conflict Over Prophetic Leadership
   > 13:1–15:41, Conflict Over the Land
   > 16:1–17:13, Conflict Over Priestly Leadership
   > 18:1–19:22, Guidelines for Approaching God

   C. 20:1–21:35, Leaving the Wilderness

III. Numbers 22:1–36:13, Preparing for Canaan on the Plains of Moab

   A. 22:1–25:18, Threats to Israel on the Plains of Moab
   > 22:1–24:25, The Blessing of Balaam
   > 25:1-19, The Sin of Israel at Baal Peor

   B. 26:1–36:13, Instructions for Inheritance
   > 26:1-65, The Census of the Second Generation
   > 27:1-23, Inheritance, Death, and Succession
   > 28:1–30:16, Priestly Offerings, the Cultic Calendar, and Lay Vows
   > 31:1–33:56, Holy War
   > 34:1–36:13, Life in the Land

NUMBERS 1:1–10:10

FORMING COMMUNITY AROUND A HOLY GOD AT SINAI

OVERVIEW

Priestly authors compiled Num 1:1–10:10. The central theme underlying this section is holiness. Detailed instructions about the arrangement of the camp (Numbers 1–2), the different roles of priests and Levites (Numbers 3–4), the measures necessary to prevent contamination of the camp site (Numbers 5–6), and the elaborate process of dedicating the tabernacle (Num 7:1–10:10) are necessary responses to God's holiness.

Two points of tension provide insight into divine holiness: God is the source of all holiness; holiness is not inherent to creation or to humans. By its very nature, therefore, holiness divides. Its sacred character is set apart from our everyday, profane world.[40] As a result, the entrance of Yahweh into the Israelite camp is carefully orchestrated by priestly writers. The process extends for fifty-six chapters from Exodus 19 through Numbers 10. The camp legislation in Num 1:1–10:10 concludes a large section of literature about the revelation of Yahweh at Mt. Sinai in Exodus 19–40 and the formation of the sacrificial cult in Leviticus.

All movement in Exod 19:1–Num 10:10 is about Yahweh's descent from heaven to the tabernacle at the base of the mountain, where Israel is camped. Several attempts are necessary. The original descent of God (Exod 19:16-19) is aborted (Exod 19:20-25). The reason is that there were not enough safeguards to receive the holy presence of God. Yahweh states to Moses that more secure boundaries are necessary. These include stronger fences to keep the people back and a purified priesthood to mediate for Israel. A partial analogy might be nuclear energy. Its power is awesome, but dangerous, requiring complex structures to safeguard its radiation from humans and from our environment.

A second attempt at divine descent succeeds (Exod 24:15-18), when the יהוה כבוד (kĕbôd YHWH), "glory of the Lord," settles at the crest of Mt. Sinai to meet alone with Moses. This meeting results in blueprints for the tabernacle cult. The architectural plans of Exodus 25–31 guide the construction of the tabernacle in Exodus 35–40. The tabernacle allows God to descend from Mt. Sinai and enter into the sanctuary. But no one can get into the tabernacle, not even Moses (Exod 40:34-35).

The book of Leviticus opens with Moses outside of the tent of meeting, or tabernacle, as he is addressed by God (Lev 1:1). The divine instructions outline cultic procedures for approaching God, allowing Moses and Aaron to enter the tabernacle in Lev 9:23. Their entrance unleashes a theophany of the kĕbôd YHWH in the altar and blessing on the people (Lev 9:24). But even this situation ends in the death of Aaron's two eldest sons, Nadab and Abihu; fire from the altar burns them (Lev 10:1-3). The remainder of Leviticus explores other rituals that will allow the priesthood to approach God safely as representatives of the people.

Numbers 1:1 begins with Moses in the tent of meeting itself, rather than standing outside, as was the case in Lev 1:1. The opening verse indicates progress in the construction of safe procedures to approach God. The subject matter of Num 1:1–10:10 builds upon Leviticus by turning attention from ritual and sacrifice to the more external issues of forming community and creating society around a holy God. The layout of the camp in relation to the tabernacle at its center introduces degrees of holiness, depending on how close a person or place is situated to the tabernacle.[41]

---

40. David P. Wright, "Holiness: Old Testament," *ABD* 237-49.

41. J. Milgrom, *Cult and Conscience: The Asham and the Priestly Doctrine of Repentance,* SJLA 18 (Leiden: E. J. Brill, 1970).

There are degrees of holiness among priests, Levites, and people as well as among the tabernacle, the camp, and the wilderness area outside the camp. The closer to God, the holier. Gradations of holiness are a form of sacramental theology. Priestly writers describe how holiness emanating from the tabernacle creates a new social, political, and environmental order for Israel. The arrangement of the camp, the order for marching through the wilderness, and the role of priests and Levites describe the ethics of holiness.

NUMBERS 1:1–6:27, HOLINESS AND THE CAMP

OVERVIEW

These chapters outline the effects of divine holiness on Israel's social organization. The central question is how Israel should organize itself around Yahweh, who dwells in the sanctuary. The answer requires a detailed description of the interrelationships of characters in the wilderness camp. Such mundane matters as the organization of the tribes and their position within the camp take on a sacramental quality because of the nearness of the tabernacle.

Chapters 1–2 sketch the priestly ideal of religious community. Chapter 1 describes the social organization of Israel as twelve tribes with twelve lay leaders representing each tribe. Priestly writers employ a variety of social terminology to explore the nature of the community. The singling out of the Levites at the close brings into focus how the numbering and organization of Israel is being undertaken with an eye on the tabernacle. Chapter 2 describes the arrangement of the camp. Tribes are clustered in groups of three, surrounding the tabernacle from four directions. Throughout this chapter, placement within the camp carries theological significance. Campsites designate different relationships to the tabernacle.

Chapters 3–4 change the focus from the congregation of Israel at large to the Levites. The genealogy of Moses and Aaron is followed by a description of the function of the Levites. They are substitutes for the firstborn. The chapters close with a description of their ancestral houses, their number, their duties, and, finally, their placement in the camp in relationship to the tabernacle.

Chapters 5–6 describe camp legislation aimed at preventing defilement. Selective legislation from community to marriage relationships is presented to illustrate conditions or actions that might threaten holiness in the camp. Examples include leprosy, the relationship of neighbors, and jealousy within marriage. The law of the Nazirite follows, and the section closes with the priestly blessing on the people in the camp.

Numbers 1:1–6:27 is an idealistic picture of community to which the people of God must strive. The ideal character of the literature is reflected in its structure. Divine command (Num 1:1-3) to organize the people and the camp concludes with a priestly blessing (Num 6:21-27). Proper organization allows for the safe access to holiness, unleashing blessing on the camp.

Numbers 1:1–2:34, The First Census and the Arrangement of the Camp

NIV	NRSV
1 The Lord spoke to Moses in the Tent of Meeting in the Desert of Sinai on the first day of the second month of the second year after the Israelites came out of Egypt. He said: ²"Take	**1** The Lord spoke to Moses in the wilderness of Sinai, in the tent of meeting, on the first day of the second month, in the second year after they had come out of the land of Egypt, saying:

a census of the whole Israelite community by their clans and families, listing every man by name, one by one. ³You and Aaron are to number by their divisions all the men in Israel twenty years old or more who are able to serve in the army. ⁴One man from each tribe, each the head of his family, is to help you. ⁵These are the names of the men who are to assist you:

from Reuben, Elizur son of Shedeur;
⁶from Simeon, Shelumiel son of Zurishaddai;
⁷from Judah, Nahshon son of Amminadab;
⁸from Issachar, Nethanel son of Zuar;
⁹from Zebulun, Eliab son of Helon;
¹⁰from the sons of Joseph:
    from Ephraim, Elishama son of Ammihud;
    from Manasseh, Gamaliel son of Pedahzur;
¹¹from Benjamin, Abidan son of Gideoni;
¹²from Dan, Ahiezer son of Ammishaddai;
¹³from Asher, Pagiel son of Ocran;
¹⁴from Gad, Eliasaph son of Deuel;
¹⁵from Naphtali, Ahira son of Enan."

¹⁶These were the men appointed from the community, the leaders of their ancestral tribes. They were the heads of the clans of Israel.

¹⁷Moses and Aaron took these men whose names had been given, ¹⁸and they called the whole community together on the first day of the second month. The people indicated their ancestry by their clans and families, and the men twenty years old or more were listed by name, one by one, ¹⁹as the LORD commanded Moses. And so he counted them in the Desert of Sinai:

²⁰From the descendants of Reuben the firstborn son of Israel:

All the men twenty years old or more who were able to serve in the army were listed by name, one by one, according to the records of their clans and families. ²¹The number from the tribe of Reuben was 46,500.

²²From the descendants of Simeon:

All the men twenty years old or more who were able to serve in the army were counted and listed by name, one by one, according to the records of their clans and

²Take a census of the whole congregation of Israelites, in their clans, by ancestral houses, according to the number of names, every male individually; ³from twenty years old and upward, everyone in Israel able to go to war. You and Aaron shall enroll them, company by company. ⁴A man from each tribe shall be with you, each man the head of his ancestral house. ⁵These are the names of the men who shall assist you:

From Reuben, Elizur son of Shedeur.
⁶ From Simeon, Shelumiel son of Zurishaddai.
⁷ From Judah, Nahshon son of Amminadab.
⁸ From Issachar, Nethanel son of Zuar.
⁹ From Zebulun, Eliab son of Helon.
¹⁰ From the sons of Joseph:
    from Ephraim, Elishama son of Ammihud;
    from Manasseh, Gamaliel son of Pedahzur.
¹¹ From Benjamin, Abidan son of Gideoni.
¹² From Dan, Ahiezer son of Ammishaddai.
¹³ From Asher, Pagiel son of Ochran.
¹⁴ From Gad, Eliasaph son of Deuel.
¹⁵ From Naphtali, Ahira son of Enan.

¹⁶These were the ones chosen from the congregation, the leaders of their ancestral tribes, the heads of the divisions of Israel.

17Moses and Aaron took these men who had been designated by name, ¹⁸and on the first day of the second month they assembled the whole congregation together. They registered themselves in their clans, by their ancestral houses, according to the number of names from twenty years old and upward, individually, ¹⁹as the LORD commanded Moses. So he enrolled them in the wilderness of Sinai.

20The descendants of Reuben, Israel's firstborn, their lineage, in their clans, by their ancestral houses, according to the number of names, individually, every male from twenty years old and upward, everyone able to go to war: ²¹those enrolled of the tribe of Reuben were forty-six thousand five hundred.

22The descendants of Simeon, their lineage, in their clans, by their ancestral houses, those of them that were numbered, according to the number of names, individually, every male from twenty years old and upward, everyone able to go to war: ²³those enrolled of the tribe of Simeon were fifty-nine thousand three hundred.

NIV

families. ²³The number from the tribe of Simeon was 59,300.

²⁴From the descendants of Gad:

All the men twenty years old or more who were able to serve in the army were listed by name, according to the records of their clans and families. ²⁵The number from the tribe of Gad was 45,650.

²⁶From the descendants of Judah:

All the men twenty years old or more who were able to serve in the army were listed by name, according to the records of their clans and families. ²⁷The number from the tribe of Judah was 74,600.

²⁸From the descendants of Issachar:

All the men twenty years old or more who were able to serve in the army were listed by name, according to the records of their clans and families. ²⁹The number from the tribe of Issachar was 54,400.

³⁰From the descendants of Zebulun:

All the men twenty years old or more who were able to serve in the army were listed by name, according to the records of their clans and families. ³¹The number from the tribe of Zebulun was 57,400.

³²From the sons of Joseph:

From the descendants of Ephraim:

All the men twenty years old or more who were able to serve in the army were listed by name, according to the records of their clans and families. ³³The number from the tribe of Ephraim was 40,500.

³⁴From the descendants of Manasseh:

All the men twenty years old or more who were able to serve in the army were listed by name, according to the records of their clans and families. ³⁵The number from the tribe of Manasseh was 32,200.

³⁶From the descendants of Benjamin:

All the men twenty years old or more who were able to serve in the army were listed by name, according to the records of their clans and families. ³⁷The number from the tribe of Benjamin was 35,400.

³⁸From the descendants of Dan:

NRSV

²⁴The descendants of Gad, their lineage, in their clans, by their ancestral houses, according to the number of the names, from twenty years old and upward, everyone able to go to war: ²⁵those enrolled of the tribe of Gad were forty-five thousand six hundred fifty.

²⁶The descendants of Judah, their lineage, in their clans, by their ancestral houses, according to the number of names, from twenty years old and upward, everyone able to go to war: ²⁷those enrolled of the tribe of Judah were seventy-four thousand six hundred.

²⁸The descendants of Issachar, their lineage, in their clans, by their ancestral houses, according to the number of names, from twenty years old and upward, everyone able to go to war: ²⁹those enrolled of the tribe of Issachar were fifty-four thousand four hundred.

³⁰The descendants of Zebulun, their lineage, in their clans, by their ancestral houses, according to the number of names, from twenty years old and upward, everyone able to go to war: ³¹those enrolled of the tribe of Zebulun were fifty-seven thousand four hundred.

³²The descendants of Joseph, namely, the descendants of Ephraim, their lineage, in their clans, by their ancestral houses, according to the number of names, from twenty years old and upward, everyone able to go to war: ³³those enrolled of the tribe of Ephraim were forty thousand five hundred.

³⁴The descendants of Manasseh, their lineage, in their clans, by their ancestral houses, according to the number of names, from twenty years old and upward, everyone able to go to war: ³⁵those enrolled of the tribe of Manasseh were thirty-two thousand two hundred.

³⁶The descendants of Benjamin, their lineage, in their clans, by their ancestral houses, according to the number of names, from twenty years old and upward, everyone able to go to war: ³⁷those enrolled of the tribe of Benjamin were thirty-five thousand four hundred.

³⁸The descendants of Dan, their lineage, in their clans, by their ancestral houses, according to the number of names, from twenty years old and upward, everyone able to go to war: ³⁹those

NIV

All the men twenty years old or more who were able to serve in the army were listed by name, according to the records of their clans and families. ³⁹The number from the tribe of Dan was 62,700.

⁴⁰From the descendants of Asher:

All the men twenty years old or more who were able to serve in the army were listed by name, according to the records of their clans and families. ⁴¹The number from the tribe of Asher was 41,500.

⁴²From the descendants of Naphtali:

All the men twenty years old or more who were able to serve in the army were listed by name, according to the records of their clans and families. ⁴³The number from the tribe of Naphtali was 53,400.

⁴⁴These were the men counted by Moses and Aaron and the twelve leaders of Israel, each one representing his family. ⁴⁵All the Israelites twenty years old or more who were able to serve in Israel's army were counted according to their families. ⁴⁶The total number was 603,550.

⁴⁷The families of the tribe of Levi, however, were not counted along with the others. ⁴⁸The Lord had said to Moses: ⁴⁹"You must not count the tribe of Levi or include them in the census of the other Israelites. ⁵⁰Instead, appoint the Levites to be in charge of the tabernacle of the Testimony—over all its furnishings and everything belonging to it. They are to carry the tabernacle and all its furnishings; they are to take care of it and encamp around it. ⁵¹Whenever the tabernacle is to move, the Levites are to take it down, and whenever the tabernacle is to be set up, the Levites shall do it. Anyone else who goes near it shall be put to death. ⁵²The Israelites are to set up their tents by divisions, each man in his own camp under his own standard. ⁵³The Levites, however, are to set up their tents around the tabernacle of the Testimony so that wrath will not fall on the Israelite community. The Levites are to be responsible for the care of the tabernacle of the Testimony."

⁵⁴The Israelites did all this just as the Lord commanded Moses.

2 The Lord said to Moses and Aaron: ²"The Israelites are to camp around the Tent of

NRSV

enrolled of the tribe of Dan were sixty-two thousand seven hundred.

40The descendants of Asher, their lineage, in their clans, by their ancestral houses, according to the number of names, from twenty years old and upward, everyone able to go to war: ⁴¹those enrolled of the tribe of Asher were forty-one thousand five hundred.

42The descendants of Naphtali, their lineage, in their clans, by their ancestral houses, according to the number of names, from twenty years old and upward, everyone able to go to war: ⁴³those enrolled of the tribe of Naphtali were fifty-three thousand four hundred.

44These are those who were enrolled, whom Moses and Aaron enrolled with the help of the leaders of Israel, twelve men, each representing his ancestral house. ⁴⁵So the whole number of the Israelites, by their ancestral houses, from twenty years old and upward, everyone able to go to war in Israel— ⁴⁶their whole number was six hundred three thousand five hundred fifty. ⁴⁷The Levites, however, were not numbered by their ancestral tribe along with them.

48The Lord had said to Moses: ⁴⁹Only the tribe of Levi you shall not enroll, and you shall not take a census of them with the other Israelites. ⁵⁰Rather you shall appoint the Levites over the tabernacle of the covenant,ᵃ and over all its equipment, and over all that belongs to it; they are to carry the tabernacle and all its equipment, and they shall tend it, and shall camp around the tabernacle. ⁵¹When the tabernacle is to set out, the Levites shall take it down; and when the tabernacle is to be pitched, the Levites shall set it up. And any outsider who comes near shall be put to death. ⁵²The other Israelites shall camp in their respective regimental camps, by companies; ⁵³but the Levites shall camp around the tabernacle of the covenant,ᵃ that there may be no wrath on the congregation of the Israelites; and the Levites shall perform the guard duty of the tabernacle of the covenant.ᵃ ⁵⁴The Israelites did so; they did just as the Lord commanded Moses.

2 The Lord spoke to Moses and Aaron, saying: ²The Israelites shall camp each in their respective regiments, under ensigns by their an-

---

ᵃ Or treaty, or testimony; Heb eduth

NIV

Meeting some distance from it, each man under his standard with the banners of his family."

3On the east, toward the sunrise, the divisions of the camp of Judah are to encamp under their standard. The leader of the people of Judah is Nahshon son of Amminadab. 4His division numbers 74,600.

5The tribe of Issachar will camp next to them. The leader of the people of Issachar is Nethanel son of Zuar. 6His division numbers 54,400.

7The tribe of Zebulun will be next. The leader of the people of Zebulun is Eliab son of Helon. 8His division numbers 57,400.

9All the men assigned to the camp of Judah, according to their divisions, number 186,400. They will set out first.

10On the south will be the divisions of the camp of Reuben under their standard. The leader of the people of Reuben is Elizur son of Shedeur. 11His division numbers 46,500.

12The tribe of Simeon will camp next to them. The leader of the people of Simeon is Shelumiel son of Zurishaddai. 13His division numbers 59,300.

14The tribe of Gad will be next. The leader of the people of Gad is Eliasaph son of Deuel.ᵃ 15His division numbers 45,650.

16All the men assigned to the camp of Reuben, according to their divisions, number 151,450. They will set out second.

17Then the Tent of Meeting and the camp of the Levites will set out in the middle of the camps. They will set out in the same order as they encamp, each in his own place under his standard.

18On the west will be the divisions of the camp of Ephraim under their standard. The leader of the people of Ephraim is Elishama son of Ammihud. 19His division numbers 40,500.

20The tribe of Manasseh will be next to them. The leader of the people of Manasseh is Gamaliel son of Pedahzur. 21His division numbers 32,200.

a14 Many manuscripts of the Masoretic Text, Samaritan Pentateuch and Vulgate (see also Num. 1:14); most manuscripts of the Masoretic Text Reuel

NRSV

cestral houses; they shall camp facing the tent of meeting on every side. 3Those to camp on the east side toward the sunrise shall be of the regimental encampment of Judah by companies. The leader of the people of Judah shall be Nahshon son of Amminadab, 4with a company as enrolled of seventy-four thousand six hundred. 5Those to camp next to him shall be the tribe of Issachar. The leader of the Issacharites shall be Nethanel son of Zuar, 6with a company as enrolled of fifty-four thousand four hundred. 7Then the tribe of Zebulun: The leader of the Zebulunites shall be Eliab son of Helon, 8with a company as enrolled of fifty-seven thousand four hundred. 9The total enrollment of the camp of Judah, by companies, is one hundred eighty-six thousand four hundred. They shall set out first on the march.

10On the south side shall be the regimental encampment of Reuben by companies. The leader of the Reubenites shall be Elizur son of Shedeur, 11with a company as enrolled of forty-six thousand five hundred. 12And those to camp next to him shall be the tribe of Simeon. The leader of the Simeonites shall be Shelumiel son of Zurishaddai, 13with a company as enrolled of fifty-nine thousand three hundred. 14Then the tribe of Gad: The leader of the Gadites shall be Eliasaph son of Reuel, 15with a company as enrolled of forty-five thousand six hundred fifty. 16The total enrollment of the camp of Reuben, by companies, is one hundred fifty-one thousand four hundred fifty. They shall set out second.

17The tent of meeting, with the camp of the Levites, shall set out in the center of the camps; they shall set out just as they camp, each in position, by their regiments.

18On the west side shall be the regimental encampment of Ephraim by companies. The leader of the people of Ephraim shall be Elishama son of Ammihud, 19with a company as enrolled of forty thousand five hundred. 20Next to him shall be the tribe of Manasseh. The leader of the people of Manasseh shall be Gamaliel son of Pedahzur, 21with a company as enrolled of thirty-two thousand two hundred. 22Then the tribe of Benjamin: The leader of the Benjaminites shall be Abidan son of Gideoni, 23with a company as enrolled of thirty-five thousand four hundred.

NIV

²²The tribe of Benjamin will be next. The leader of the people of Benjamin is Abidan son of Gideoni. ²³His division numbers 35,400.

²⁴All the men assigned to the camp of Ephraim, according to their divisions, number 108,100. They will set out third.

²⁵On the north will be the divisions of the camp of Dan, under their standard. The leader of the people of Dan is Ahiezer son of Ammishaddai. ²⁶His division numbers 62,700.

²⁷The tribe of Asher will camp next to them. The leader of the people of Asher is Pagiel son of Ocran. ²⁸His division numbers 41,500.

²⁹The tribe of Naphtali will be next. The leader of the people of Naphtali is Ahira son of Enan. ³⁰His division numbers 53,400.

³¹All the men assigned to the camp of Dan number 157,600. They will set out last, under their standards.

³²These are the Israelites, counted according to their families. All those in the camps, by their divisions, number 603,550. ³³The Levites, however, were not counted along with the other Israelites, as the LORD commanded Moses.

³⁴So the Israelites did everything the LORD commanded Moses; that is the way they encamped under their standards, and that is the way they set out, each with his clan and family.

NRSV

²⁴The total enrollment of the camp of Ephraim, by companies, is one hundred eight thousand one hundred. They shall set out third on the march.

²⁵On the north side shall be the regimental encampment of Dan by companies. The leader of the Danites shall be Ahiezer son of Ammishaddai, ²⁶with a company as enrolled of sixty-two thousand seven hundred. ²⁷Those to camp next to him shall be the tribe of Asher. The leader of the Asherites shall be Pagiel son of Ochran, ²⁸with a company as enrolled of forty-one thousand five hundred. ²⁹Then the tribe of Naphtali: The leader of the Naphtalites shall be Ahira son of Enan, ³⁰with a company as enrolled of fifty-three thousand four hundred. ³¹The total enrollment of the camp of Dan is one hundred fifty-seven thousand six hundred. They shall set out last, by companies.ᵃ

32This was the enrollment of the Israelites by their ancestral houses; the total enrollment in the camps by their companies was six hundred three thousand five hundred fifty. ³³Just as the LORD had commanded Moses, the Levites were not enrolled among the other Israelites.

34The Israelites did just as the LORD had commanded Moses: They camped by regiments, and they set out the same way, everyone by clans, according to ancestral houses.

ᵃ Compare verses 9, 16, 24: Heb *by their regiments*

COMMENTARY

Numbers 1–2 recounts the census of the first generation of Israelites and the organization of the campsite. The two chapters are closely interrelated in subject matter and in literary design. Read together, they provide the overall organization of the congregation of Israel and their lay leadership, as compared to Numbers 3–4, where attention will turn to the non-lay leadership in the camp, consisting of priests and Levites.

Numbers 1–2 is organized loosely around divine command and fulfillment. The structure is

especially clear in Numbers 1, which opens with a stereotypical introduction, "The LORD spoke to Moses . . . " (see, e.g., 2:1; 3:5, 14, 40, 44; 4:1, 17, 21), indicating that all the following instructions are divine speech to Moses. The chapter concludes in v. 54 with the notice that the divine instructions were fulfilled "as the LORD had commanded Moses" (variations occur in 2:34; 3:51; 4:37, 41, 45, 49; 5:4; 8:4, 22; 9:20-23). Numbers 2:1-2 introduces a second divine command: "The LORD spoke to Moses and Aaron. . . . " Its fulfillment is indicated in 2:32-34: "The Israelites did just as the Lord had commanded Moses."

1:1. The place of divine instruction is the tent of meeting. (See Exodus 25–31 for a detailed description.) The Hebrew noun translated "meeting" (מוֹעֵד *mô'ēd*) in the phrase "tent of meeting" (אֹהֶל מוֹעֵד *'ōhel mô'ēd*) comes from the verb יעד (*yā'ad*), whose root meaning is "to appoint," "to meet," or "to gather by appointment." The noun *mô'ēd* can take on religious connotations by signifying appointed times and places when God and humans meet.

Appointed times are sacred festivals. The purposes of stars in Gen 1:14, for example, is to mark the liturgical year with its religious festivals. Here the noun *mô'ēd* is translated "seasons," thus signifying sacred time as compared to ordinary or profane time. The distinction between sacred and profane time is illustrated in Numbers in the description of Passover as having to be kept "at its appointed time" (במועדו *bĕmô'ădô*, 9:2), or when God states to Moses that the trumpet must be blown "at your appointed festivals" (מועדיכם *mô'ădêkem*, 10:10).

The tent of meeting in v. 1 signifies a sacred place. In this instance, the noun *mô'ēd* is the location where God and humans meet and where heaven and earth touch (see the section "Priestly Religion" in the Introduction, 13-14). In biblical tradition, sacred places like sanctuaries are often described using mountain imagery. The divine descent from Mt. Sinai to the sanctuary results in the tent of meeting becoming Israel's sacred place. It is the location where God now dwells and where the ark is lodged.

The indwelling of Yahweh in the tent of meeting is reinforced by the word "tabernacle" (מִשְׁכָּן *miškān*), which is frequently used by priestly authors to describe the wilderness sanctuary (over 40 times in Numbers; see 1:51). The noun "tabernacle" comes from the verb שכן (*šākan*), meaning "to dwell." This verb most likely refers to an impermanent dwelling of the divine. Thus God is able to leave this sanctuary home, if Israel does not maintain proper standards of holiness and justice.[42]

The two terms "tent of meeting" and "tabernacle" are not synonymous. The tent of meeting may represent an ancient tradition in which God was encountered in a tent for the purpose of receiving oracles (see Exod 33:7-11 and the Commentary on Numbers 11:1–12:16). Regardless of their earliest meaning, the tent of meeting and the tabernacle are brought together by priestly authors to designate the one wilderness sanctuary. The account of the divine descent into the sanctuary in Exod 40:34-35 illustrates how the terms are interchanged by the priestly writers.

The setting and time of the divine instruction in v. 1 intertwine the book of Numbers with other books in the Pentateuch. Reference to the wilderness of Sinai interrelates Num 1:1–10:10 with Exodus 19–40 and the book of Leviticus (see the Overview). The dating of events reinforces this interrelationship. The book of Numbers begins on Month 2, Day 1, Year 2 from the exodus. The following outline illustrates the important dates from the exodus in the priestly history.

I. The Exodus from Egypt (Exod 12:1),
   Month 1, Day 14, Year 1, The First Passover
II. Encampment at Sinai (Exod 19:1),
   Month 3, Year 1
   A. The Tabernacle (Exod 40:2), Month 1,
      Day 1, Year 2
   B. Census (Num 1:1), Month 2, Day 1,
      Year 2
   C. Late Observance of Passover (Num 9:1),
      Month 2, Day 14, Year 2
III. Departure from Sinai (Num 10:11), Month
   2, Day 20, Year 2

The system of dating is a priestly invention aimed at interpreting the liturgical calendar. It is not a historical chronology in any modern sense of the term.[43] Careful attention to dating and chronology provides insight into priestly theology, and not history. The exodus is a watershed event for the priestly authors. It ushers in a new age of salvation that is signified as Year 1. This is similar to the later distinction between B.C. and A.D. in classical Christian chronology, where the birth of Christ becomes the watershed event in time.

The events in the book of Numbers occur in

---

42. See Frank M. Cross, *Canaanite Myth and Hebrew Epic: Essays in the History of the Religion of Israel* (Cambridge, Mass.: Harvard University Press, 1963) 298-99; Tryggve N. D. Mettinger, *The Dethronement of Sabaoth: Studies in the Shem and Kadob Theologies,* ConBOT 18 (Lund: CWK Gleerup, 1982) 80-97.

43. See J. Hughes, *Secrets of the Times: Myth and History in Biblical Chronology,* JSOTSup 66 (Sheffield: Sheffield Academic, 1990).

the second year after the exodus. The entire period of Israel's encampment in the wilderness of Sinai, however, bridges the first and second years from Month 3, Year 1 (Exod 19:1), to Month 2, Day 20, Year 2 (Num 10:11). Thus Israel's stay at Sinai encompasses roughly one liturgical year. The significant event marking the transition from the first to the second year is the construction of the tent of meeting/tabernacle. It is completed on New Year's day of Year 2 (Month 1, Day 1, Year 2). The book of Numbers begins in the following month (Month 2, Day 1, Year 2) with the census of the people. The events in Num 1:1–10:10 last nineteen days.

1:2-3. God commands Moses in v. 2 to take a census of the "whole congregation of Israelites." The phrase combines distinct terms for designating the people. "Israelites" is from the Hebrew בני־ישׂראל (běnê-yiśrāʾēl), which is translated more literally "sons of Israel." It emphasizes kinship. In his study of social terminology, Norman Gottwald notes that the strictly biological meaning "sons" could become "an extended metaphor for describing clusters of persons according to certain common functions or traits." A contemporary example of this process would be the phrase "sons of liberty" in colonial North American history.[44]

Kinship language is reinforced in v. 2 by the terms "clans" and "ancestral houses" as descriptions of smaller groups within the Israelite community. The Hebrew משׁפחות (mišpāḥôt) is translated more naturally as "families" rather than "clans." It is avoided in English because the word most certainly refers to more than a nuclear family. It may be used to refer to a whole tribe (Judg 17:7) or more likely to an association of families within a tribe (Josh 7:14). The "ancestral houses" would appear to designate a group that is smaller than a "clan" or "family" (see Josh 7:14). The Hebrew ביה־אב (bêt-ʾāb, "father's house") is a patriarchal term that most likely signifies an extended family, including parents, children—married sons with their wives and unmarried daughters—as well as resident aliens. There is fluidity in the use of these terms throughout the book of Numbers. "Ancestral house," for example, may be equated with a "tribe" already

in v. 4, while the meaning of "clan" varies widely in the second census of chap. 26. The terminology reinforces a vision of the wilderness community as being related by genealogy.

The term "congregation" does not signify family ties. The Hebrew noun עדה (ʿēdâ), derives from the verb יעד (yāʿad), meaning "to appoint," "to meet," or "to gather by appointment." This same verb was discussed earlier in association with the tent of meeting. In some instances, "congregation" may designate a smaller group within Israel (27:3). The use of the terms "clans" and "ancestral houses" in v. 2 to describe smaller social units illustrates the preference of priestly writers to designate the entire community as the congregation. The priestly writers use the term "congregation" more than eighty times to designate the people in the wilderness. The congregation is that group of people who gather around the tent of meeting. Thus the act of gathering around the sanctuary as a community becomes the defining characteristic. In this case, proximity to holiness supersedes kinship. The LXX translation of ʿēdâ as "synagogue" underscores the liturgical background of the term "congregation."

Other uses of "congregation" in the book of Numbers elaborate on the term's social significance. In addition to gathering around the sanctuary, the congregation deliberates on the report of spies (14:5, 7) and has the power to reject the promise of land (14:27, 35, 36). The congregation is responsible for the purity of worship (15:24-26) and the people (31:16). The congregation also consults on legal matters (35:12, 24-25).

The purpose of the census is stated in v. 3. It fulfills the divine command from Exod 30:11-16, in which the census is a prerequisite for the people to live in proximity to the sanctuary. God tells Moses that a sanctuary tax is required of each adult male as an atonement for the people and that the money is to be used in service to the tabernacle. The collection of this tax is confirmed in Exod 38:26, where the number of registered males is given as 603,550. There are many parallels between the census of Numbers 1 and the sanctuary census in Exodus. Both number males twenty years of age and older (Exod 30:14; 38:26; Num 1:3); both use the verb "to consider" or "to muster" to describe the registration of the males (the verb פקד pāqad, Exod 30:12; Num 1:3; and

44. N. K. Gottwald, *The Tribes of Yahweh: A Sociology of the Religion of Liberated Israel, 1250–1050 BCE* (Maryknoll, N.Y.: Orbis, 1979) 239-44.

the noun פְּקֻדִים *pĕquddîm*, Num 1:21, 22, 44, etc.). Moreover, the number given for the census is the same (Exod 38:26; Num 1:43). The parallels to Exod 30:11-16 underscore the religious dimension of the census in Numbers 1. Numbering and organizing the people are a necessary safeguard for the community to live in the presence of God.

The census is also intended to prepare the community for war and to organize them into a regimented militia. The description of those being numbered in v. 3 includes military terminology. The combination of the verb יצא (*yāṣāʾ*, "to go out") and the noun צבא (*ṣābāʾ*, "war," "warfare," "service") indicates military action ("to go to war"), even though the noun *ṣābāʾ* can also describe religious service to the sanctuary (4:1, 23, 30). The priestly writers describe Israel's marching out of Egypt during the night of Passover with the same words (Exod 12:41), and the military meaning of the phrase is also clear in the war against Midian (Num 31:14, 36). War terminology encourages an interpretation of those being registered (*pĕquddîm*; 1:21, 22, 44, etc.) as forming regiments or army units. The military emphasis of the census underscores how God's presence with Israel not only transforms them as a people, but also puts them in conflict with other nations and cultures. As the congregation assembled around God, Israel becomes a militia representing holiness in a profane world. The march through the wilderness becomes a military campaign for God.

1:4-16. Leaders are chosen from each tribe. Verses 4 and 16 frame the actual listing of leaders in vv. 5-15. The tribe of Reuben begins the list of twelve tribes. Reuben also launches tribal lists in the choosing of the spies (chap. 13) and in the second census (chap. 26). The tribe of Judah begins lists that describe the order of the camp (chap. 2), the offerings presented to the tabernacle (chap. 7), the order of marching (chap. 10) through the wilderness, and the inheritance of the land (chap. 34). There may be an idealization of Judah in the distribution of the different tribal lists. Reuben is prominent in the numbering of the people and, more important, in the loss of the land. Judah heads tribal lists in more positive stories, including worshiping at the tabernacle and marching through the wilderness toward the promised land (see Commentary on 2:3-31).

The list of tribal leaders in vv. 5-15 proceeds in a stereotypical form: The tribe is named, followed by the name of the chosen leader and his father's name. The first entry provides illustration: from Reuben, Elizur son of Shedeur. The tribes of Reuben, Simeon, Judah, Issachar, and Zebulun are listed in this way (vv. 5-9) before the pattern is interrupted in v. 10, where Ephraim and Manasseh are listed as sons of Joseph. The original pattern returns for the remaining five tribes of Benjamin, Dan, Asher, Gad, and Naphtali (vv. 11-15).

The names in vv. 5-15 are, for the most part, confined to chaps. 1–10, where they appear four times (in chaps. 1; 2; 7; and 10). Scholars have sought with limited success to place these leaders in a particular historical setting of ancient Israel. George Buchanan Gray concluded that the list of names was not historical and that its composition was late,[45] while Martin Noth thought that the list was old and that it contained historical information about tribal Israel.[46] The debate is unresolvable. Yet, even if the list is ancient, the place and function of the leaders in a particular historical setting have been lost. Without a precise social context, what stands out is the distinctly theological composition of the names. Divine titles are often incorporated into a person's name to form a sentence. A number of names incorporating elements of names for the divine appear in the list, including Elizur ("El is my rock"), Shedeur ("Shaddai is light"), and Pedahzur ("the Rock has redeemed me"). A notable exception is the absence of the divine name Yahweh in any of the leaders' names.

The listing of tribal leaders (vv. 5-15) is framed in vv. 4 and 16 with a variety of terms that are meant to describe their social functions. The tribal leaders are designated as "the heads of ancestral houses" (v. 4), the "chosen ones from the congregation" (v. 16), the "leaders of ancestral tribes" (v. 16), and the "heads of the divisions of Israel" (v. 16). The language is difficult to sort out. "Leader" (נשׂיא *nāśîʾ*), "head" (ראשׁ *rōʾš*), and "division" (אלף *ʾelep*) may be descriptions of leadership roles from as early as Israel's pre-monarchical period. Yet, their usage and combination with other terms (like "congregation" and "ancestral

45. George Buchanan Gray, *Numbers*, ICC (Edinburgh: T. & T. Clark, 1903) 7-8.
46. Martin Noth, *Numbers*, OTL (Philadelphia: Westminster, 1968) 18-19.

tribe") point to a later time, suggesting that priestly authors are combining a rich history of social terminology. Theology would appear to take precedence over sociological precision in the portraits of lay leadership.

The language in vv. 4 and 16 provides insight into the idealization of lay leadership in priestly tradition. The notion of being "chosen" in v. 16 has political (Ezek 23:22) and cultic (1 Sam 9:13) meaning. The further description of these persons as "heads of the divisions of Israel" points to their responsibility as military leaders. These varied terms are carried over into the different roles the leaders perform in chaps. 1–10. They assist Moses in assembling the people for census (chap. 1), present offerings at the tabernacle (chap. 7), and lead the people in their military march through the wilderness (chaps. 2; 10).

1:17-47. The census of the first generation of Israelites is recorded in these verses. The setting and time of this census are stated in vv. 17-19, a repetition of v. 1. It takes place on Month 1, Day 1 in the wilderness of Sinai. Verses 20-43 list the registration of twenty-year-old males by tribe, beginning with Reuben, the firstborn. Verses 44-47 provide a summary conclusion. The procedure for counting in vv. 20-43 is stereotypical: Tribal identification is followed by the number. The summary of Reuben in vv. 20-21 provides an example of the two-part form: (1) the descendants of Reuben: their lineage in their clans, by their ancestral houses according to the number of names, individually, every male from twenty years old and upward, everyone able to go to war; (2) those enrolled of the tribe of Reuben were 46,500.

The first part of the census repeats many of the sociological terms introduced in v. 2. Males twenty years of age and older are numbered according to tribe, clan, and ancestral house. The additional word "lineage" (תולדות *tôlēdôt*, also translated as "generations") is added to the opening line. This is the same word used by the priestly authors to organize the book of Genesis ("These are the generations of . . ." [Gen 2:4; 5:1; 6:9; etc.]). Its appearance in the census accentuates the familial character of the wilderness group.

The number of males for each tribe is extremely large. The total of the census in Numbers 1 is 603,550 males over twenty years of age. George Buchanan Gray provides a detailed summary of the problems that arise when one attempts to interpret the census numbers literally as representing the number of people migrating from Egypt to Canaan. This number of males would require a total population of over 2,000,000 people in the Sinai peninsula.[47] So many people would overwhelm the environment of the Sinai. Moreover, the large total conflicts with other traditions in which the number of fighting males during Israel's tribal period is significantly less (see the reference to 40,000 males in Judg 5:8).

The numbers most likely have symbolic and theological value for the priestly writers. But deciphering what exactly they intended has proven elusive to modern interpreters. Two possibilities arise from the larger storyline of the Pentateuch. First, the enormous size of the wilderness group may signal the fulfillment of the divine blessing of fertility first promised to Abram in Gen 12:1-3. The census of Numbers 1 indicates that the Israelites have indeed become "a great nation." Second, the number of fighting males underscores Israel's potential power as God's "fighting host or militia." This military emphasis is reinforced by a phrase that repeats throughout the census: The males are all "able to go to war."

More precise interpretations of the numbers have also been offered. Philip J. Budd has suggested that the number of males represents theological reflection on the description of the tabernacle in Exodus 25–31. Exodus 38:26 uses the same figure of 603,550 for males over twenty, who were required to pay a half-shekel tax for the tabernacle. This figure may be derived from the cost of bases and hooks in the construction of the tabernacle. Exodus 38:27-28 states that the bases and hooks for the tabernacle required 100 talents (1 talent = 1,000 shekels) and 1,775 shekels of silver. The total shekels were 301,775 shekels. A half-shekel tax for this amount totals 603,550, the number of the census in Exod 38:26 and in Numbers 1.[48] Others suggest that the numbers are an instance of gematria—a process of valuation in which letters from the alphabet have a certain numerical worth. Georg Fohrer has noted that the numerical value of the Hebrew "sons of Israel" is 603, which when multiplied by

47. Gray, *Numbers*, 9-15.
48. Phillip J. Budd, *Numbers*, WBC 5 (Waco, Tex.: Word, 1984) 8-9.

1,000 nears the figure in Numbers 1. The figure 603,551 is achieved when the numerical value of the Hebrew "all the heads" (כל-ראש *kol-rō'š*) is included.[49] M. Barnouin regards Babylonian astronomy as the key to the numbering system by priestly writers. He argues that the tribal figures correspond to celestial movements that form the Babylonian calendar. In this case, the priestly writers' aim is to place the wilderness community in the widest social and cosmological context possible.[50] As a result, the numbering of the people has universal significance. The different hypotheses are tentative. Each illustrates, however, that the priestly authors are producing a highly stylized and theological history of Israel.

1:48-53. In these verses, the Levites are separated out from the other tribes. The text divides into two parts. Verses 48-50*a* define the special role of the Levites. They are not to be numbered with the other Israelites, because they are assigned special duties in caring for the tabernacle. Three special functions are spelled out in vv. 50*b*-53. The Levites perform service in the tabernacle (vv. 50, 53); they carry the tabernacle and its vessels on Israel's wilderness march (vv. 50, 51); and they must pitch their tents around the sanctuary, thus providing a buffer zone between the sanctuary and the congregation of Israel (v. 53).

The language in vv. 48-53 has given rise to different interpretations concerning the tasks of the Levites. The point of debate concerns the meaning of the concluding phrase in v. 53. The NRSV translation reads, "the Levites shall perform the guard duty of the tabernacle." The Hebrew is more ambiguous: "the Levites shall keep [שמר *šāmar*] the service [משמרת *mišmeret*] of the tabernacle." Interpretation hinges on what the "service of the tabernacle" means.

One reading emphasizes the cultic and religious work required of the Levites. Baruch Levine follows this line of interpretation and concludes that the "service" of the Levites must be defined in the context of their religious duties to God. In performing these duties, they contain the rage (קצף *qeṣep*) of God, mentioned in v. 53. Levitical service stops the divine wrath, which might other-

wise destroy the camp like a fire burning out of control. Thus they encircle the tabernacle in the camp, they carry the holy artifacts, and they care for both.[51]

Another reading emphasizes the relationship of the Levites to the congregation of Israel, rather than their service to God. This interpretation emphasizes more the role of Levites as protectors of the sanctuary. Jacob Milgrom follows this line of interpretation when he concludes that the phrase "to watch" or "to keep" (*šāmar*) a "service" (*mišmeret*) means "guard duty." The NRSV translation also reflects this interpretation. In this case, the service of the Levites is to keep Israel from coming too near to the divine. Divine rage results from encroachment by humans into the sacred space of God, which would be certain death.[52] The levitical encampment represents a border, and their service is both border guard and customs duty. The reason for guard duty is that all non-Levites are "outsiders" to the sacredness of the tabernacle (v. 51).

1:54. Chapter 1 concludes by underscoring that all divine commands have been completed.

2:1-2. These verses introduce a second divine command, this time directed to Moses and Aaron. The subject changes from the numbering of Israel to their arrangement in the campsite. The motivation behind the careful arrangement of the camp is the tent of meeting, which is situated at the center of the camp. The tribes are to be arranged around the tent of meeting (e.g., on its four sides), and they are to camp at some distance from it. The space between the tent of meeting and the tribes is not stated; Josh 3:4 may provide some help, since it states that the Israelites were required to leave a space of 2,000 cubits (1,000 yards) between themselves and the ark.

2:3-31. The arrangement of the tribes is delineated here. The language is stereotypical: Tribes are listed in groups of three, the names of lay leaders (chap. 1) are repeated, and the total number for every tribe is given. The literary structure of this section is determined by the geography of the campsite.

---

49. Georg Fohrer, *Introduction to the Old Testament,* trans. David E. Green (Nashville: Abingdon, 1968) 184.

50. M. Barnouin, "Les Recensements du Livre des Nombres et l'Astronomie Babylonienne," *VT* 27 (1977) 280-303.

51. Baruch A. Levine, *Numbers 1–20,* AB 4A (New York: Doubleday, 1993) 1-20, 141-42.

52. Jacob Milgrom, *Numbers,* JPS Torah Commentary (Philadelphia: JPS, 1990) 9-10, 342-44.

East of the Tent of Meeting (vv. 3-9)
Judah
Issachar
Zebulun

South of the Tent of Meeting (vv. 10-16)
Reuben
Simeon
Gad

The Tent of Meeting in the Center of the Camp (v. 17)
Levites

West of the Tent of Meeting (vv. 18-24)
Ephraim
Manasseh
Benjamin

North of the Tent of Meeting (vv. 25-31)
Dan
Asher
Naphtali

This outline illustrates how three tribes camp on each side of the tent of meeting, resulting in four groups of three tribes each. Moreover, there is a hierarchy in the relationship of the three tribes on each side. Judah, Reuben, Ephraim, and Dan are singled out as lead tribes. They are described as the "regimental encampment" (דגל מחנה *degel maḥănēh*, vv. 3, 10, 18, 25), in contrast to the others, who are designated simply as "tribes" (מטה *maṭṭeh*, "tribe"). Baruch Levine has demonstrated that the word דגל (*degel*) designates "a unit of the Persian military . . . where soldiers lived with their families."[53] His research underscores how priestly authors have incorporated military terminology from the exilic period and later to describe their ideal vision of Israel's early wilderness camp.

There is an additional distinction made in the placement of each regimental encampment around the sanctuary. Judah has first position (vv. 3-9). Its regiment is located on the east side of the tent of meeting; thus it guards the opening to the tent of meeting. Judah camps in the center of its regiment, with the tribes of Issachar and Zebulun on each side. Second comes Reuben to the

south (vv. 10-16), with the tribes of Simeon and Gad camped on each side. West of the tent of meeting is the regiment of Ephraim (vv. 18-24), accompanied by Manasseh and Benjamin. Finally, to the north lies Dan (vv. 25-31), flanked by Asher and Naphtali. Each ancestral house most likely had its own insignia or banner that marked their campsite (see vv. 1-2).

The arrangement of the regimental encampments on the four sides of the tent of meeting is also meant to provide the order for marching. This is indicated in the closing line of each section (vv. 9, 16, 24, 31). Thus the insignia or banner leads each ancestral house on its processional march through the wilderness.

The outline of vv. 3-31 illustrates how the order of the tribes changes from the census in chap. 1 to the arrangement of the camp in chap. 2. The change of order provides insight into the theological perspective of the priestly writers. The tribe of Reuben is the firstborn of the eponymous ancestors (see Genesis 29–30; 35). Thus it would be expected that Reuben would begin any listing of the tribes, as is the case in the first census in chap. 1, the second census in chap. 26, and the list of spies in chap. 13. But Reuben gives way to the tribe of Judah in the arrangement of the camp (chap. 2), in offerings for the tabernacle (chap. 7), in the order of marching toward the land (chap. 10), and in land distribution (chap. 34). As noted in the Commentary on 1:4-16, comparison suggests that the tribe of Reuben is associated with the numbering of Israel and with the loss of the land, while the tribe of Judah is associated with marching toward Canaan and acquiring the land. The contrast between the two lists is less a polemic against Reuben than an emphasis on the favored status of Judah, the representative tribe of the southern kingdom. The priestly writers see Israel's future with Judah, and the favored status of this tribe is reflected in their ideal vision of the camp. Judah camps in the central position on the east side of the tent of meeting so as to protect the door of the sanctuary.

Verse 17 underscores that the tent of meeting and the camp of the Levites are at the center of the four regimental encampments and the order of their marching. The camping arrangement of the priests and the Levites around the tent of meeting is described in more detail in chap. 3. Again, a heirar-

53. Levine, *Numbers 1–20,* 148.

chy emerges in which the Aaronid priests camp to the east of the tabernacle (3:38), the Kohathites to the south (3:35), the Gershonites to the west (3:23), and the Merarites to the north (3:35).

2:32-34. Three summary conclusions end the chapter. First, v. 32 gives the total number of Israelites as 603,550, a repetition from 1:46. Sec-ond, v. 33 underscores that the Levites were not included in the total number of Israelites, a repe-tition of 1:47 (vv. 32-33 do not include the military imagery from 1:46-47). Third, v. 34 notes the successful completion of the divine instruc-tions in vv. 1-2 and closes by anticipating Israel's march through the wilderness.

REFLECTIONS

1. The priestly writers view the entire world from the perspective of the camp, with the tabernacle representing the center point. This is not a common way of writing theology in contemporary culture. But location does influence each of us as we view the larger world. Consider a poster that came out several years ago by Steinberg entitled "A New Yorker's View of the World." The Hudson River is pictured as the outer reaches of the globe, because of the centrality of New York City for those who live in it. The poster illustrates how important even secular locations can become in structuring a vision of the world. The tabernacle plays an even stronger role in the priestly writer's view of the world. It was not simply a familiar or comfortable place to live. It is where Yahweh dwells.

Comparison of the priestly camp to other theological uses of geography, maps, and city plans in the Bible may assist further in understanding this genre of writing. The prophet Isaiah employs geographical descriptions of a new creation or a new Zion to describe the character of salvation (see Isa 65:17-25). The prophet Ezekiel provides a closer parallel to the priestly writers in Numbers 1–2. He, too, describes salvation geographically. It includes a new temple (Ezekiel 40–45), which produces life-giving water (Ezek 47:1-12). The prophet goes on to locate the Temple (Ezek 47:13-23) and the tribes in the land (Ezekiel 48). The book of Revelation provides an inner-biblical interpretation of the wilderness camp of the priestly writers. The camp becomes the new Jerusalem, which descends from heaven filled with divine glory. It is square, with three gates on each side to represent the twelve tribes of Israel (Rev 21:9-15).

Biblical writers employ geography to envision the salvation of God on earth. It is meant to be read symbolically. Yet, geographical imagery does remind us that salvation in the Bible is not an escape from this world to heaven. Rather, it is a transformation of it into the kingdom of God. Priestly writers provide a model for any church to envision its role in community. Write a map of the life of your church. Where is it located in your neighborhood, village, or city? What are its outer reaches? Where has it transformed the social character of its environment?

2. The priestly vision of religious community incorporates two perspectives, identity and mission, which continue to provide a paradigm for Christian community. Identity results from an inward focus on the relationship of Israel to God in the camp. It characterizes the Israelites as a holy people. It is the starting point for community. Mission results from an outward focus on the relationship of Israel to the world. Priestly writers employ military language to describe Israel's mission.

Identity is formed in worship. It is the first act in becoming a Christian community. When the focus of priestly writers is turned inward, toward the indwelling of God in the tabernacle, the Israelite camp is like a worshiping community. The presence of God forms their identity as a holy people. The arrangement of the camp is an outgrowth of the indwelling of God in the tabernacle at its center. Life in the camp, moreover, separates Israel from the profane world. The same is true in contemporary worship. Worship separates; it is where we acquire our identity as the people of God. We die to the world in baptism and feast with Christ in the eucharist. We also acquire a new ethical vision for life through preaching.

The inward focus of the camp is never an end in itself for priestly writers. Identity leads to mission. Thus the congregation encamped around the tabernacle can be transformed into an army that marches out through the wilderness. The military march is an outward focus. It explores Israel's relationship with the larger world. The militaristic language is symbolic and theological. Priestly writers do not glorify war (see the Commentary and Reflections on Numbers 31:1–33:56). War imagery accentuates the conflict between the holiness of God and the profane world, but with an eye on the people of God. Israel is caught up in this conflict. Life with God in the camp puts Israel in opposition to any form of security that would subvert faith in God. Thus their relationship to the world outside the camp is described with images of war. It accentuates the conflict between faith and culture. This tension is no less true for the church today. Worship gives rise to mission, and mission requires the church to continue the same wilderness march. We, too, appropriate war imagery to describe mission. This is not a glorification of war, but a theological statement about the many tensions that exist between the life of faith and our surrounding culture.

The priestly writers provide a continuing paradigm for Christian community. Identity without mission is self-indulgent religion. Mission without identity is not religion at all. Healthy Christian community requires a constant interrelationship of the two.

3. Numbers 1 provides guidelines for reflecting on the theological significance of administration. The chapter illustrates the priestly concern for order. It is important that the people are numbered precisely. Each group requires lay leaders. Levites are separated from other groups to encircle the tabernacle. Even the writing style of the chapter reflects this concern for balance. The divine commands (1:1) are fulfilled (1:54). The choosing of lay leaders (1:5-15) and the counting of the people (1:17-47) repeat the same phrases. All things are done decently and in good order. The aim of priestly writers, however, is not administration for its own sake. The ordering of the camp is a dynamic response to the presence of God in the community. Administration is intended to foster a new community in the wilderness.

Numbers 1 is not meant to be read in isolation. The larger literary context of the priestly history provides insight into the dynamic role of administration. In the creation story of Genesis 1, order subdues chaos, allowing for a rich diversity in creation. Yet, one need not scratch the surface very deeply to realize that the order of creation is a thin membrane, vulnerable to puncture and to the chaotic forces that swirl beneath its skin.[54] Tending to the structure of creation, therefore, has cosmological significance for priestly writers. The return to chaos (the flood) illustrates the consequences of ignoring the details.

The exodus from Egypt inaugurates a new creation for priestly writers. It is Year 1 of a new era, when Israel has passed through the chaotic waters of the Red Sea. Administrating the camp in Numbers 1 is part of this larger drama. Every detail of life in the wilderness matters, because the proper ordering of life and worship secures the presence of God.

Numbers 1 provides a continuing resource for evaluating administration. Power is easily abused for self-interest. Law, ritual, and hierarchy cannot be ends in themselves. Administration is always a dynamic response to the presence of God in community. It requires clear theological grounding. The goal of administration continues to be the creation of community in God's new creation. From the perspective of the priestly writers, serving on the board of trustees, chairing church committees, and participating in newsletters all strengthen the presence of God in community.

4. Numbers 1 contains a vision of community in which organization allows for innovation and difference. Priestly writers never state this explicitly. Instead, the message is embedded in the terminology used to describe Israel. The priestly vision of community in the wilderness

---

54. See Jon D. Levenson, *Creation and the Persistence of Evil: The Jewish Drama of Divine Omnipotence* (San Francisco: Harper & Row, 1985) 14-50, 66-127.

holds together myriad social terms that, when interpreted historically, appear contradictory. The most prominent contrast is membership in the group through kinship ("the sons of Israel") and through participation in worship ("the congregation"). These terms form different communities; yet, they exist side by side in Numbers 1. The bringing together of potentially conflicting terms indicates that priestly authors envision something new in the wilderness that defies past social models. Their vision can be summarized in the following manner: Social innovation takes place within the careful ordering of the community, and not in its destruction. And community does not require uniformity. Competing visions of community are allowed to exist together rather than in competition.

5. Numbers are important to the priestly writers. They seem preoccupied with the size of Israel. The commentary indicated that it may signify power and blessing. We, too, focus on numbers as a sign of power and of blessing. Bigger is often judged to be better. The emergence of megachurches is an example. The priestly writers provide two guidelines for reflecting on the size of our churches. The first is in the census. The significant message in numbering Israel is not the size of the group, but that each tribe and every member is accounted for and organized in the camp. The point of counting members is not to stress how large each tribe may be, but to ensure that no one is lost in the wilderness. The second point of emphasis is the large numbers. They are difficult to interpret. They do underscore the size of the group as a fulfillment of divine blessing, but they also emphasize that Israel is prepared to fulfill its mission. This is why the census is limited to males twenty years of age and older. The message of the priestly writers for our contemporary setting is that size must determine mission, not prestige. Larger churches may have the resources to undertake mission projects that are out of the reach of smaller congregations. Numbering members is one way to gauge mission.

6. The need to appease the wrath of God in the selection of Levites requires comment about priestly religion. God is not an intimate friend in priestly religion. The priestly writers stress, instead, the gulf between God and humans (see Introduction). God is holy and thus separate from humans. The indwelling of God bridges the gulf, but the combination of the sacred and the profane is a volatile mix. The priestly writer's concern for order is aimed at avoiding harmful consequences of living with God. Divine wrath results from any casual approach to God.

Divine wrath is not divine anger. The Israelites are not sinners in the hands of an angry God. They are redeemed humans who now live in the presence of the divine. They have access to power beyond their imagination. Such power is dangerous, because it will always effect change. Thus it must be approached carefully. The starting point of the priestly writers is the power of God to transform and make new. The wrath of God is a necessary by-product of such power. Electricity provides a partial analogy. The flow of generated electricity is constant. When properly wired, it can light and heat our homes. But when an exposed cord is touched with the bare hand, electricity has the power to kill.

The message of the priestly writers translates directly to contemporary Christians. Christians have access to the same power of God through sacraments. Baptism and participating in the eucharist will always effect change in us. Thus casual participation is dangerous, since we are held accountable once we lay claim to the power of God.

Numbers 3:1–4:49, The Role of the Levites in the Cult, in the Camp, and on the March

NIV	NRSV

NIV

3 This is the account of the family of Aaron and Moses at the time the LORD talked with Moses on Mount Sinai.

²The names of the sons of Aaron were Nadab the firstborn and Abihu, Eleazar and Ithamar. ³Those were the names of Aaron's sons, the anointed priests, who were ordained to serve as priests. ⁴Nadab and Abihu, however, fell dead before the LORD when they made an offering with unauthorized fire before him in the Desert of Sinai. They had no sons; so only Eleazar and Ithamar served as priests during the lifetime of their father Aaron.

⁵The LORD said to Moses, ⁶"Bring the tribe of Levi and present them to Aaron the priest to assist him. ⁷They are to perform duties for him and for the whole community at the Tent of Meeting by doing the work of the tabernacle. ⁸They are to take care of all the furnishings of the Tent of Meeting, fulfilling the obligations of the Israelites by doing the work of the tabernacle. ⁹Give the Levites to Aaron and his sons; they are the Israelites who are to be given wholly to him.ᵃ ¹⁰Appoint Aaron and his sons to serve as priests; anyone else who approaches the sanctuary must be put to death."

¹¹The LORD also said to Moses, ¹²"I have taken the Levites from among the Israelites in place of the first male offspring of every Israelite woman. The Levites are mine, ¹³for all the firstborn are mine. When I struck down all the firstborn in Egypt, I set apart for myself every firstborn in Israel, whether man or animal. They are to be mine. I am the LORD."

¹⁴The LORD said to Moses in the Desert of Sinai, ¹⁵"Count the Levites by their families and clans. Count every male a month old or more." ¹⁶So Moses counted them, as he was commanded by the word of the LORD.

¹⁷These were the names of the sons of Levi:
Gershon, Kohath and Merari.
¹⁸These were the names of the Gershonite clans:
Libni and Shimei.

ᵃ9 Most manuscripts of the Masoretic Text; some manuscripts of the Masoretic Text, Samaritan Pentateuch and Septuagint (see also Num. 8:16) to me

NRSV

3 This is the lineage of Aaron and Moses at the time when the LORD spoke with Moses on Mount Sinai. ²These are the names of the sons of Aaron: Nadab the firstborn, and Abihu, Eleazar, and Ithamar; ³these are the names of the sons of Aaron, the anointed priests, whom he ordained to minister as priests. ⁴Nadab and Abihu died before the LORD when they offered unholy fire before the LORD in the wilderness of Sinai, and they had no children. Eleazar and Ithamar served as priests in the lifetime of their father Aaron.

⁵Then the LORD spoke to Moses, saying: ⁶Bring the tribe of Levi near, and set them before Aaron the priest, so that they may assist him. ⁷They shall perform duties for him and for the whole congregation in front of the tent of meeting, doing service at the tabernacle; ⁸they shall be in charge of all the furnishings of the tent of meeting, and attend to the duties for the Israelites as they do service at the tabernacle. ⁹You shall give the Levites to Aaron and his descendants; they are unreservedly given to him from among the Israelites. ¹⁰But you shall make a register of Aaron and his descendants; it is they who shall attend to the priesthood, and any outsider who comes near shall be put to death.

¹¹Then the LORD spoke to Moses, saying: ¹²I hereby accept the Levites from among the Israelites as substitutes for all the firstborn that open the womb among the Israelites. The Levites shall be mine, ¹³for all the firstborn are mine; when I killed all the firstborn in the land of Egypt, I consecrated for my own all the firstborn in Israel, both human and animal; they shall be mine. I am the LORD.

¹⁴Then the LORD spoke to Moses in the wilderness of Sinai, saying: ¹⁵Enroll the Levites by ancestral houses and by clans. You shall enroll every male from a month old and upward. ¹⁶So Moses enrolled them according to the word of the LORD, as he was commanded. ¹⁷The following were the sons of Levi, by their names: Gershon, Kohath, and Merari. ¹⁸These are the names of the sons of Gershon by their clans: Libni and Shimei. ¹⁹The sons of Kohath by their clans: Amram,

NIV

¹⁹The Kohathite clans:

Amram, Izhar, Hebron and Uzziel.

²⁰The Merarite clans:

Mahli and Mushi.

These were the Levite clans, according to their families.

²¹To Gershon belonged the clans of the Libnites and Shimeites; these were the Gershonite clans. ²²The number of all the males a month old or more who were counted was 7,500. ²³The Gershonite clans were to camp on the west, behind the tabernacle. ²⁴The leader of the families of the Gershonites was Eliasaph son of Lael. ²⁵At the Tent of Meeting the Gershonites were responsible for the care of the tabernacle and tent, its coverings, the curtain at the entrance to the Tent of Meeting, ²⁶the curtains of the courtyard, the curtain at the entrance to the courtyard surrounding the tabernacle and altar, and the ropes—and everything related to their use.

²⁷To Kohath belonged the clans of the Amramites, Izharites, Hebronites and Uzzielites; these were the Kohathite clans. ²⁸The number of all the males a month old or more was 8,600.ᵃ TheKohathites were responsible for the care of the sanctuary. ²⁹The Kohathite clans were to camp on the south side of the tabernacle. ³⁰The leader of the families of the Kohathite clans was Elizaphan son of Uzziel. ³¹They were responsible for the care of the ark, the table, the lampstand, the altars, the articles of the sanctuary used in ministering, the curtain, and everything related to their use. ³²The chief leader of the Levites was Eleazar son of Aaron, the priest. He was appointed over those who were responsible for the care of the sanctuary.

³³To Merari belonged the clans of the Mahlites and the Mushites; these were the Merarite clans. ³⁴The number of all the males a month old or more who were counted was 6,200. ³⁵The leader of the families of the Merarite clans was Zuriel son of Abihail; they were to camp on the north side of the tabernacle. ³⁶The Merarites were appointed to take care of the frames of the taberna-

ᵃ28 Hebrew; some Septuagint manuscripts 8,300

NRSV

Izhar, Hebron, and Uzziel. ²⁰The sons of Merari by their clans: Mahli and Mushi. These are the clans of the Levites, by their ancestral houses.

21To Gershon belonged the clan of the Libnites and the clan of the Shimeites; these were the clans of the Gershonites. ²²Their enrollment, counting all the males from a month old and upward, was seven thousand five hundred. ²³The clans of the Gershonites were to camp behind the tabernacle on the west, ²⁴with Eliasaph son of Lael as head of the ancestral house of the Gershonites. ²⁵The responsibility of the sons of Gershon in the tent of meeting was to be the tabernacle, the tent with its covering, the screen for the entrance of the tent of meeting, ²⁶the hangings of the court, the screen for the entrance of the court that is around the tabernacle and the altar, and its cords—all the service pertaining to these.

27To Kohath belonged the clan of the Amramites, the clan of the Izharites, the clan of the Hebronites, and the clan of the Uzzielites; these are the clans of the Kohathites. ²⁸Counting all the males, from a month old and upward, there were eight thousand six hundred, attending to the duties of the sanctuary. ²⁹The clans of the Kohathites were to camp on the south side of the tabernacle, ³⁰with Elizaphan son of Uzziel as head of the ancestral house of the clans of the Kohathites. ³¹Their responsibility was to be the ark, the table, the lampstand, the altars, the vessels of the sanctuary with which the priests minister, and the screen—all the service pertaining to these. ³²Eleazar son of Aaron the priest was to be chief over the leaders of the Levites, and to have oversight of those who had charge of the sanctuary.

33To Merari belonged the clan of the Mahlites and the clan of the Mushites: these are the clans of Merari. ³⁴Their enrollment, counting all the males from a month old and upward, was six thousand two hundred. ³⁵The head of the ancestral house of the clans of Merari was Zuriel son of Abihail; they were to camp on the north side of the tabernacle. ³⁶The responsibility assigned to the sons of Merari was to be the frames of the tabernacle, the bars, the pillars, the bases, and all their accessories—all the service pertaining to

NIV

cle, its crossbars, posts, bases, all its equipment, and everything related to their use, 37as well as the posts of the surrounding courtyard with their bases, tent pegs and ropes.

38Moses and Aaron and his sons were to camp to the east of the tabernacle, toward the sunrise, in front of the Tent of Meeting. They were responsible for the care of the sanctuary on behalf of the Israelites. Anyone else who approached the sanctuary was to be put to death.

39The total number of Levites counted at the LORD's command by Moses and Aaron according to their clans, including every male a month old or more, was 22,000.

40The LORD said to Moses, "Count all the first-born Israelite males who are a month old or more and make a list of their names. 41Take the Levites for me in place of all the firstborn of the Israelites, and the livestock of the Levites in place of all the firstborn of the livestock of the Israelites. I am the LORD."

42So Moses counted all the firstborn of the Israelites, as the LORD commanded him. 43The total number of firstborn males a month old or more, listed by name, was 22,273.

44The LORD also said to Moses, 45"Take the Levites in place of all the firstborn of Israel, and the livestock of the Levites in place of their livestock. The Levites are to be mine. I am the LORD. 46To redeem the 273 firstborn Israelites who exceed the number of the Levites, 47collect five shekels[a] for each one, according to the sanctuary shekel, which weighs twenty gerahs. 48Give the money for the redemption of the additional Israelites to Aaron and his sons."

49So Moses collected the redemption money from those who exceeded the number redeemed by the Levites. 50From the firstborn of the Israelites he collected silver weighing 1,365 shekels,[b] according to the sanctuary shekel. 51Moses gave the redemption money to Aaron and his sons, as he was commanded by the word of the LORD.

4 The LORD said to Moses and Aaron: 2"Take a census of the Kohathite branch of the

a47 That is, about 2 ounces (about 55 grams)   b50 That is, about 35 pounds (about 15.5 kilograms)

NRSV

these; 37also the pillars of the court all around, with their bases and pegs and cords.

38Those who were to camp in front of the tabernacle on the east—in front of the tent of meeting toward the east—were Moses and Aaron and Aaron's sons, having charge of the rites within the sanctuary, whatever had to be done for the Israelites; and any outsider who came near was to be put to death. 39The total enrollment of the Levites whom Moses and Aaron enrolled at the commandment of the LORD, by their clans, all the males from a month old and upward, was twenty-two thousand.

40Then the LORD said to Moses: Enroll all the firstborn males of the Israelites, from a month old and upward, and count their names. 41But you shall accept the Levites for me—I am the LORD—as substitutes for all the firstborn among the Israelites, and the livestock of the Levites as substitutes for all the firstborn among the livestock of the Israelites. 42So Moses enrolled all the first-born among the Israelites, as the LORD commanded him. 43The total enrollment, all the firstborn males from a month old and upward, counting the number of names, was twenty-two thousand two hundred seventy-three.

44Then the LORD spoke to Moses, saying: 45Accept the Levites as substitutes for all the firstborn among the Israelites, and the livestock of the Levites as substitutes for their livestock; and the Levites shall be mine. I am the LORD. 46As the price of redemption of the two hundred seventy-three of the firstborn of the Israelites, over and above the number of the Levites, 47you shall accept five shekels apiece, reckoning by the shekel of the sanctuary, a shekel of twenty gerahs. 48Give to Aaron and his sons the money by which the excess number of them is redeemed. 49So Moses took the redemption money from those who were over and above those redeemed by the Levites; 50from the firstborn of the Israelites he took the money, one thousand three hundred sixty-five shekels, reckoned by the shekel of the sanctuary; 51and Moses gave the redemption money to Aaron and his sons, according to the word of the LORD, as the LORD had commanded Moses.

4 The LORD spoke to Moses and Aaron, saying: 2Take a census of the Kohathites sepa-

NIV

Levites by their clans and families. ³Count all the men from thirty to fifty years of age who come to serve in the work in the Tent of Meeting.

⁴"This is the work of the Kohathites in the Tent of Meeting: the care of the most holy things. ⁵When the camp is to move, Aaron and his sons are to go in and take down the shielding curtain and cover the ark of the Testimony with it. ⁶Then they are to cover this with hides of sea cows,ª spread a cloth of solid blue over that and put the poles in place.

⁷"Over the table of the Presence they are to spread a blue cloth and put on it the plates, dishes and bowls, and the jars for drink offerings; the bread that is continually there is to remain on it. ⁸Over these they are to spread a scarlet cloth, cover that with hides of sea cows and put its poles in place.

⁹"They are to take a blue cloth and cover the lampstand that is for light, together with its lamps, its wick trimmers and trays, and all its jars for the oil used to supply it. ¹⁰Then they are to wrap it and all its accessories in a covering of hides of sea cows and put it on a carrying frame.

¹¹"Over the gold altar they are to spread a blue cloth and cover that with hides of sea cows and put its poles in place.

¹²"They are to take all the articles used for ministering in the sanctuary, wrap them in a blue cloth, cover that with hides of sea cows and put them on a carrying frame.

¹³"They are to remove the ashes from the bronze altar and spread a purple cloth over it. ¹⁴Then they are to place on it all the utensils used for ministering at the altar, including the firepans, meat forks, shovels and sprinkling bowls. Over it they are to spread a covering of hides of sea cows and put its poles in place.

¹⁵"After Aaron and his sons have finished covering the holy furnishings and all the holy articles, and when the camp is ready to move, the Kohathites are to come to do the carrying. But they must not touch the holy things or they will die. The Kohathites are to carry those things that are in the Tent of Meeting.

¹⁶"Eleazar son of Aaron, the priest, is to have charge of the oil for the light, the fragrant incense,

NRSV

rate from the other Levites, by their clans and their ancestral houses, ³from thirty years old up to fifty years old, all who qualify to do work relating to the tent of meeting. ⁴The service of the Kohathites relating to the tent of meeting concerns the most holy things.

5When the camp is to set out, Aaron and his sons shall go in and take down the screening curtain, and cover the ark of the covenantª with it; ⁶then they shall put on it a covering of fine leather,ᵇ and spread over that a cloth all of blue, and shall put its poles in place. ⁷Over the table of the bread of the Presence they shall spread a blue cloth, and put on it the plates, the dishes for incense, the bowls, and the flagons for the drink offering; the regular bread also shall be on it; ⁸then they shall spread over them a crimson cloth, and cover it with a covering of fine leather,ᵇ and shall put its poles in place. ⁹They shall take a blue cloth, and cover the lampstand for the light, with its lamps, its snuffers, its trays, and all the vessels for oil with which it is supplied; ¹⁰and they shall put it with all its utensils in a covering of fine leather,ᵇ and put it on the carrying frame. ¹¹Over the golden altar they shall spread a blue cloth, and cover it with a covering of fine leather,ᵇ and shall put its poles in place; ¹²and they shall take all the utensils of the service that are used in the sanctuary, and put them in a blue cloth, and cover them with a covering of fine leather,ª and put them on the carrying frame. ¹³They shall take away the ashes from the altar, and spread a purple cloth over it; ¹⁴and they shall put on it all the utensils of the altar, which are used for the service there, the firepans, the forks, the shovels, and the basins, all the utensils of the altar; and they shall spread on it a covering of fine leather,ᵇ and shall put its poles in place. ¹⁵When Aaron and his sons have finished covering the sanctuary and all the furnishings of the sanctuary, as the camp sets out, after that the Kohathites shall come to carry these, but they must not touch the holy things, or they will die. These are the things of the tent of meeting that the Kohathites are to carry.

16Eleazar son of Aaron the priest shall have charge of the oil for the light, the fragrant incense, the regular grain offering, and the

---

ª6 That is, dugongs; also in verses 8, 10, 11, 12, 14 and 25

ª Or *treaty*, or *testimony;* Heb *eduth*   ᵇ Meaning of Heb uncertain

the regular grain offering and the anointing oil. He is to be in charge of the entire tabernacle and everything in it, including its holy furnishings and articles."

¹⁷The LORD said to Moses and Aaron, ¹⁸"See that the Kohathite tribal clans are not cut off from the Levites. ¹⁹So that they may live and not die when they come near the most holy things, do this for them: Aaron and his sons are to go into the sanctuary and assign to each man his work and what he is to carry. ²⁰But the Kohathites must not go in to look at the holy things, even for a moment, or they will die."

²¹The LORD said to Moses, ²²"Take a census also of the Gershonites by their families and clans. ²³Count all the men from thirty to fifty years of age who come to serve in the work at the Tent of Meeting.

²⁴"This is the service of the Gershonite clans as they work and carry burdens: ²⁵They are to carry the curtains of the tabernacle, the Tent of Meeting, its covering and the outer covering of hides of sea cows, the curtains for the entrance to the Tent of Meeting, ²⁶the curtains of the courtyard surrounding the tabernacle and altar, the curtain for the entrance, the ropes and all the equipment used in its service. The Gershonites are to do all that needs to be done with these things. ²⁷All their service, whether carrying or doing other work, is to be done under the direction of Aaron and his sons. You shall assign to them as their responsibility all they are to carry. ²⁸This is the service of the Gershonite clans at the Tent of Meeting. Their duties are to be under the direction of Ithamar son of Aaron, the priest.

²⁹"Count the Merarites by their clans and families. ³⁰Count all the men from thirty to fifty years of age who come to serve in the work at the Tent of Meeting. ³¹This is their duty as they perform service at the Tent of Meeting: to carry the frames of the tabernacle, its crossbars, posts and bases, ³²as well as the posts of the surrounding courtyard with their bases, tent pegs, ropes, all their equipment and everything related to their use. Assign to each man the specific things he is to carry. ³³This is the service of the Merarite clans as they work at the Tent of Meeting under the direction of Ithamar son of Aaron, the priest."

anointing oil, the oversight of all the tabernacle and all that is in it, in the sanctuary and in its utensils.

17Then the LORD spoke to Moses and Aaron, saying: 18You must not let the tribe of the clans of the Kohathites be destroyed from among the Levites. 19This is how you must deal with them in order that they may live and not die when they come near to the most holy things: Aaron and his sons shall go in and assign each to a particular task or burden. 20But the Kohathites[b] must not go in to look on the holy things even for a moment; otherwise they will die.

21Then the LORD spoke to Moses, saying: 22Take a census of the Gershonites also, by their ancestral houses and by their clans; 23from thirty years old up to fifty years old you shall enroll them, all who qualify to do work in the tent of meeting. 24This is the service of the clans of the Gershonites, in serving and bearing burdens: 25They shall carry the curtains of the tabernacle, and the tent of meeting with its covering, and the outer covering of fine leather[b] that is on top of it, and the screen for the entrance of the tent of meeting, 26and the hangings of the court, and the screen for the entrance of the gate of the court that is around the tabernacle and the altar, and their cords, and all the equipment for their service; and they shall do all that needs to be done with regard to them. 27All the service of the Gershonites shall be at the command of Aaron and his sons, in all that they are to carry, and in all that they have to do; and you shall assign to their charge all that they are to carry. 28This is the service of the clans of the Gershonites relating to the tent of meeting, and their responsibilities are to be under the oversight of Ithamar son of Aaron the priest.

29As for the Merarites, you shall enroll them by their clans and their ancestral houses; 30from thirty years old up to fifty years old you shall enroll them, everyone who qualifies to do the work of the tent of meeting. 31This is what they are charged to carry, as the whole of their service in the tent of meeting: the frames of the tabernacle, with its bars, pillars, and bases, 32and the pillars of the court all around with their bases,

---

ᵃ Heb *they*   ᵇ Meaning of Heb uncertain

34Moses, Aaron and the leaders of the community counted the Kohathites by their clans and families. 35All the men from thirty to fifty years of age who came to serve in the work in the Tent of Meeting, 36counted by clans, were 2,750. 37This was the total of all those in the Kohathite clans who served in the Tent of Meeting. Moses and Aaron counted them according to the LORD's command through Moses.

38The Gershonites were counted by their clans and families. 39All the men from thirty to fifty years of age who came to serve in the work at the Tent of Meeting, 40counted by their clans and families, were 2,630. 41This was the total of those in the Gershonite clans who served at the Tent of Meeting. Moses and Aaron counted them according to the LORD's command.

42The Merarites were counted by their clans and families. 43All the men from thirty to fifty years of age who came to serve in the work at the Tent of Meeting, 44counted by their clans, were 3,200. 45This was the total of those in the Merarite clans. Moses and Aaron counted them according to the LORD's command through Moses.

46So Moses, Aaron and the leaders of Israel counted all the Levites by their clans and families. 47All the men from thirty to fifty years of age who came to do the work of serving and carrying the Tent of Meeting 48numbered 8,580. 49At the LORD's command through Moses, each was assigned his work and told what to carry.

Thus they were counted, as the LORD commanded Moses.

pegs, and cords, with all their equipment and all their related service; and you shall assign by name the objects that they are required to carry. 33This is the service of the clans of the Merarites, the whole of their service relating to the tent of meeting, under the hand of Ithamar son of Aaron the priest.

34So Moses and Aaron and the leaders of the congregation enrolled the Kohathites, by their clans and their ancestral houses, 35from thirty years old up to fifty years old, everyone who qualified for work relating to the tent of meeting; 36and their enrollment by clans was two thousand seven hundred fifty. 37This was the enrollment of the clans of the Kohathites, all who served at the tent of meeting, whom Moses and Aaron enrolled according to the commandment of the LORD by Moses.

38The enrollment of the Gershonites, by their clans and their ancestral houses, 39from thirty years old up to fifty years old, everyone who qualified for work relating to the tent of meeting— 40their enrollment by their clans and their ancestral houses was two thousand six hundred thirty. 41This was the enrollment of the clans of the Gershonites, all who served at the tent of meeting, whom Moses and Aaron enrolled according to the commandment of the LORD.

42The enrollment of the clans of the Merarites, by their clans and their ancestral houses, 43from thirty years old up to fifty years old, everyone who qualified for work relating to the tent of meeting— 44their enrollment by their clans was three thousand two hundred. 45This is the enrollment of the clans of the Merarites, whom Moses and Aaron enrolled according to the commandment of the LORD by Moses.

46All those who were enrolled of the Levites, whom Moses and Aaron and the leaders of Israel enrolled, by their clans and their ancestral houses, 47from thirty years old up to fifty years old, everyone who qualified to do the work of service and the work of bearing burdens relating to the tent of meeting, 48their enrollment was eight thousand five hundred eighty. 49According to the commandment of the LORD through Moses they were appointed to their several tasks of serving or carrying; thus they were enrolled by him, as the LORD commanded Moses.

COMMENTARY

Numbers 3–4 turn from the Israelite congregation in general to focus on the specific role of the Levites in the cult, in the camp, and on the march. In priestly tradition, all cultic personnel—including Moses, Aaron, and Miriam—are descended from their ancestor Levi. Priestly writers outline the genealogy of Levi in Exod 6:16-25 into three clans of Gershon, Kohath, and Merari. This three-part division is reflected in Numbers 3–4, and it repeats in the levitical genealogy of 26:57-62. Figure 2 presents a partial genealogy of Levi.

All priests evolve from the eponymous ancestor Levi, the third son of Jacob's first wife, Leah (Gen 29:31-35). The folklore surrounding Levi and the Levites is that they are violent in service to Yahweh. Levi and Simeon destroy the family of Shechem to avenge the defilement of their sister, Dinah (Gen 34:25-31). This action is cursed in the last words of Jacob (Genesis 49). The patriarch characterizes it as uncontrolled and denies the Levites land in Canaan because of their violence (Gen 49:5-7). The Levites also slaughter 3,000 of their own family and friends to purge Israel from the sin of worshiping the golden calf (Exod 32:25-29). This action is praised in the song of Moses (Deuteronomy 33). Deuteronomy 33:8-11 attributes their priestly status (as the ones who consult the Thummin and the Urim) to their loyalty to Yahweh, even at the cost of family and children. Read together, these traditions account for the special status of the Levites as priests (Deuteronomy 33) who are without land in Canaan (Genesis 49). The special role is rooted in violence, motivated by allegiance to God. The violence is both praised (Deut 33:8-11) and cursed (Gen 49:25-29).

The priestly writers provide their own interpretation of the Levites in Numbers 3–4. Many historical problems surround the priestly presentation of the Levites. The genealogy of Levi in Num 26:57-62 indicates that the division of three clans in Numbers 3–4 is not original. Numbers 26:58 divides the house of Levi into five clans: Libnites, Hebronites, Mahlites, Mushites, and Korahites. This structure most likely reflects an earlier genealogy of Levi. Numbers 26:57 replaces the five-clan structure with the three-clan structure of Exod 6:16-25 and Numbers 3–4, thus bringing the older genealogy into conformity with

other priestly genealogies of Levi. Such modification suggests that the priesthood underwent change during the exilic period. Conflict between priestly families during the exile is evident in Ezek 44:11-13. The genealogy of Levi as three clans in Numbers 3–4 may represent the structure of the priesthood during the post-exilic period.

The division between Aaronide priests and Levites in the book of Numbers may also be an innovation by priestly writers during the period of the exile.[55] There does not appear to be a distinction between priests and Levites in the book of Deuteronomy, written toward the end of the monarchical period. In Deuteronomy, the term "levitical priests" (הכהנים הלוים hakkōhǎnîm halwiyyim) is a general reference for all priests (Deut 17:9, 18; 24:8; see also Deut 18:1; 21:5).[56] Yet, Numbers 3–4 assumes a clear distinction between Aaronide priests and all other Levites, even though they share the same family tree.

The difference between Aaronide priests and Levites in priestly tradition is indicated by their rites of ordination. Priests are consecrated to achieve their status of holiness. Levites undergo purification to assume their role in guarding the tabernacle. Levites achieve a position of holiness between that of Aaronide priests and the congregation of Israel in general. The consecration of the Aaronide priesthood was a central topic in the book of Leviticus, where the sacrificial system was described. The purification of the Levites becomes the focus in Numbers. Their role in the setting of the tabernacle and the camp is described in Numbers 1; 3–4; 8.

The literary structure of Numbers 3–4 follows the pattern of divine command and fulfillment. The stereotypical introduction, "The LORD spoke to Moses . . ." occurs seven times. Yahweh commands the Levites to be separated from the congregation of Israel (1:5), to be substitutes for all Israelite firstborn (3:11), and to be counted from one month of age and older (3:14). The command

---

55. For a brief overview of the problems surrounding the history of the Levites, see Baruch A. Levine, *Numbers 1–20*, AB 4A (New York: Doubleday, 1993) 171-78, 279-90; and M. D. Rehm, "Levites and Priests," *ABD* 4:297-310.

56. For a listing of references to Levites in Deuteronomy, see Rehm, "Levites and Priests," *ABD* 4:303-5.

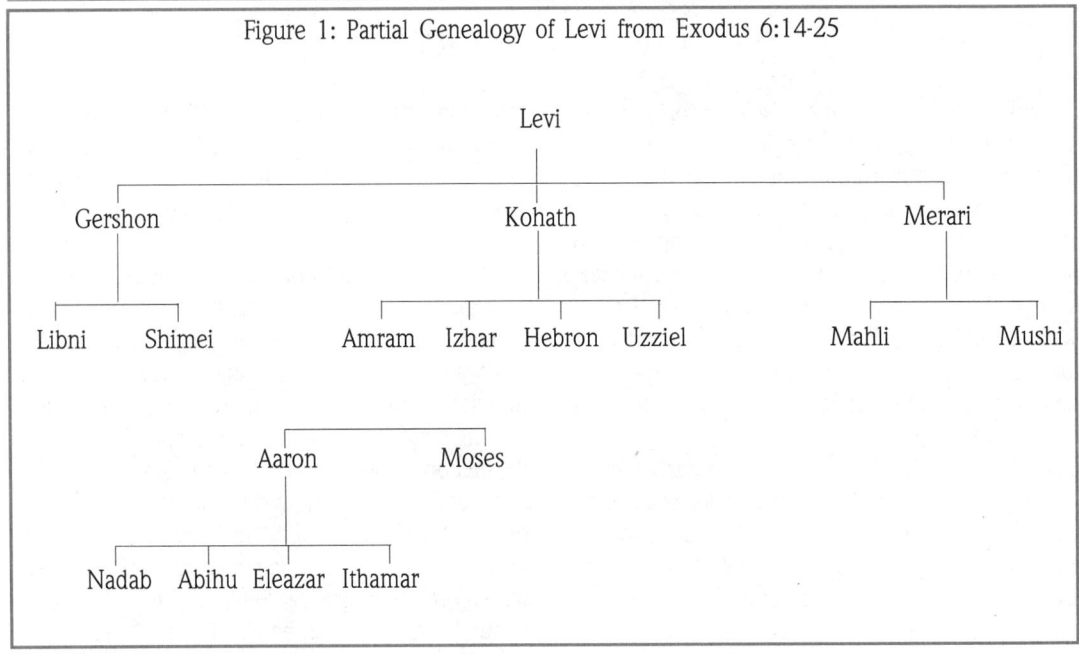

Figure 1: Partial Genealogy of Levi from Exodus 6:14-25

to be substitutes for all Israelite firstborn repeats in 3:44. Then God commands that the Kohathites from thirty to fifty years of age be counted and assigned duties for transporting the most holy objects of the tent of meeting (4:1) and that they not look at the holy objects in the tabernacle (4:17). The Gershonites and the Merarites from thirty to fifty years of age must also be counted and assigned duties for moving the remainder of the tent of meeting (4:21). The number of commands (seven) may be intentional, since it signifies completeness in priestly tradition. An additional command to number all Israelite firstborn appears in 3:40, where the verb "to say" (אמר 'āmar) replaces the verb "to speak" (דבר dābar), bringing the total number of introductory commands to eight.

The introductions divide loosely between a first census, in which the Levites are numbered to determine their role as substitutes for all Israelite firstborn, and a second census, in which each levitical ancestral house is assigned duties. Statements indicating fulfillment of the divine commands reinforce this two-part structure. Moses fulfills the requirements of the first census in 3:42, and he collects the redemption money in 3:51 "as the LORD had commanded." The fulfillment of the second census is recorded in 4:34-49.

3:1-10. The Levites are separated from the congregation. Verses 1-4 provide a genealogy of the Aaronide priesthood, and vv. 5-10 describe the Levites' relationship to the Aaronide priests.

3:1-4. Two introductory formulas are combined in these verses, both of which link chaps. 3–4 with a larger genealogical structure that runs throughout the Pentateuch. The two phrases are the *Toledot* (from תולדות *Tôlēdôt*, "Generations") formula ("This is the lineage of Moses and Aaron") in v. 1 and a naming formula ("These are the names of the sons of Aaron") in v. 2.

Most instances of the *Toledot* occur in Genesis. Yet the appearance of the phrase in Num 3:1 indicates that the priestly writers use the formula to emphasize the important role of Moses and Aaron in history. Its overall structure can be summarized in the following manner.

Several features of the *Toledot* provide insight into the priestly history. The story of creation in Genesis 1 is outside the structure of the *Toledot*. The special position of Genesis 1, outside of all genealogical development, allows for the story of creation to be both the beginning and the end of the priestly account of salvation history. The circular design to the priestly history encourages a reading of the *Toledot* structure both forward (from Genesis 2 to Numbers 3) and backward (from Numbers 3 to Genesis 2). The circular design of the *Toledot* structure reinforces the emphasis of priestly writers both to establish Israel's identity and to describe their mission as the people of God.

When the *Toledot* is read forward (from Genesis 2 to Numbers 3), it is a story of identity. The priestly history provides a genealogical account of salvation history as a process of divine election from the earliest humans to the wilderness generation. The first *Toledot* describes "the generations of the heavens and the earth" (Gen 2:4*a*). The scope of the *Toledot* narrows from all the families of the earth (Adam, Noah) to the Israelite ancestors (Abraham, Isaac, and Jacob) and, finally, to the genealogy of the Israelite priesthood in Num 3:1. This process of separation identifies Israel as the people of God.

When the *Toledot* is read backward, it provides a blueprint for mission. It is an outline of how the people of God must transform this world into the ideal of Genesis 1. Israel's mission in the priestly history is not simply to transform Israel (Jacob, Isaac, Abraham) or even all humans (Noah, Adam), but the very heavens and the earth themselves.

The circular design of the priestly history underscores how the genealogy of Moses and Aaron is the apex of salvation history. It is the turning point, where history moves back toward its ideal origin. Social and cosmological transformation must begin with the Aaronide priesthood and the Levites. They encircle the tabernacle and provide the starting point for guiding divine holiness into the world.

A naming formula in Num 3:2, "These are the names of the sons of Aaron . . . ," has been added to the *Toledot*. This formula is used more randomly throughout the Pentateuch to identify descendants of Ishmael (Gen 25:13), Esau (Gen 36:10, 40), Jacob (Gen 46:8; Exod 1:1), Levi (Exod 6:16), lay leaders (Num 1:5), spies (Num 13:16), the daughters of Zelophehad (Num 27:1), and tribal leaders in the land (Num 34:17, 19). The formula in Num 3:2 introduces Aaron's four sons, Nadab, Abihu, Eleazar, and Ithamar.

Numbers 3:3-4 recounts the death of Aaron's elder two sons, Nadab and Abihu. The reason for their death is that "they offered illicit [or strange] fire before Yahweh" (author's trans.). This is a reference to Leviticus 10, when Nadab and Abihu were killed by God immediately after the theophany of the כבוד יהוה (*kĕbôd YHWH*, "glory of God") in the altar of the tabernacle. Scholars debate just what is meant by the phrase "strange fire" (אש זרה *ʾēš zārâ*). The larger context of Leviticus 10 suggests that Nadab and Abihu sought to hoard holiness, rather than to use their special position as Aaronide priests as a means for channeling holiness to the entire congregation. Thus Moses warns Aaron immediately after the death of Nadab and Abihu that divine holiness is meant for "all the people" (Lev 10:3). The role of the priests and, more specifically, the Levites is certainly meant to provide boundaries between the sacred and the profane. Such boundaries, however, are not for the purpose of hoarding

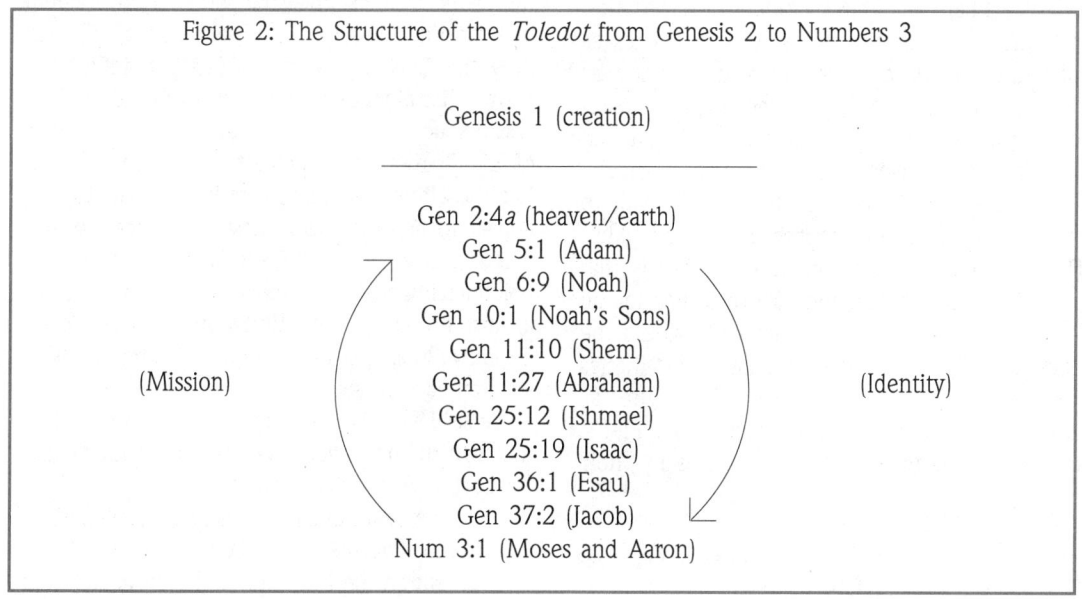

Figure 2: The Structure of the *Toledot* from Genesis 2 to Numbers 3

Genesis 1 (creation)

Gen 2:4*a* (heaven/earth)
Gen 5:1 (Adam)
Gen 6:9 (Noah)
Gen 10:1 (Noah's Sons)
Gen 11:10 (Shem)
Gen 11:27 (Abraham)
Gen 25:12 (Ishmael)
Gen 25:19 (Isaac)
Gen 36:1 (Esau)
Gen 37:2 (Jacob)
Num 3:1 (Moses and Aaron)

(Mission)

(Identity)

holiness for a few, but for holiness to influence as many as possible.

3:5-10. This section describes the relationship of the Levites to the Aaronide priesthood and to the congregation. The Levites are positioned between the priesthood and the congregation for the purpose of serving both groups in front of the tabernacle (vv. 6-7). George Buchanan Gray describes the Levites as a caste of servants for the priests.[57] This paragraph is filled with technical language that is not immediately apparent in translation. The command in v. 5 for Moses "to set them [the Levites] before Aaron the priest" indicates subordination, which is reaffirmed in v. 9 with the divine command to Moses: "you give the Levites to Aaron and his descendants." The verb "to give" (נתתה *nātattâ*) in this context is a technical term for dedication that signifies subordination.

The tasks of the Levites are twofold. They are "to perform duties" (שמרו את-משמרת *šāmĕrû ʾet-mišmeret*) for the priests and congregation in front of the tent of meeting and "to do the service" (לעבד את-עבדת *laʿăbōd ʾet-ʿăbōdat*) of the tabernacle. Jacob Milgrom has argued that the phrase "to perform duties" indicates guard duty.[58] Thus one of the tasks of the Levites is to guard the outer court of the tabernacle from encroachers. The second task is the hard labor of maintaining and transporting the tabernacle, which is described later in the chapter. The language used to indicate hard labor has overtones of slavery that will influence the special role of the Levites as substitutes for the firstborn. They are claimed by God as slaves for the divine. The threat of death to encroachers in v. 10 underscores the sacredness of the tabernacle and its danger to outsiders.

3:11-51. The purpose of the first census is to number all Levites one month of age and older. The reason for determining this number is that the Levites are to function as substitutes for all Israelite firstborn, who otherwise would be claimed by God. The theme of substitution frames this section. The divine claim on the Levites as substitutes for the firstborn is stated in vv. 11-13. The command to number the Levites by their

ancestral houses occupies the central section in vv. 14-39. And the issue of substitution for the firstborn returns in vv. 40-51.

3:11-13. These verses separate into three parts. Verse 11 begins the unit with the introduction, "Then the LORD spoke to Moses." Verse 12 states the divine claim on the Levites as acceptable substitutes for the firstborn. Although it is not stated in v. 12, the claim is on firstborn males. This is made clear in v. 40, where God requires Moses to count all firstborn males in the camp to determine how many persons are required for substitution. Verse 13 provides a historical reason for the divine claim on the firstborn by anchoring it in the exodus.

The text states that all firstborn are claimed by God and, thus, are considered holy in Israelite religion. Legal texts such as Exod 22:29-30 and 34:19-20 confirm the sacred status of the firstborn. Exodus 22:29 bluntly states that "the firstborn of your sons you shall give to me." The divine claim on the firstborn may have risen from the creative power of God as the giver of life. Perhaps there was a relationship with the Festival of First Fruits, also known as Weeks. This was a one-day festival in the spring, occurring fifty days after the Festival of Unleavened Bread, *Massot* (Exod 23:14-17). The few passages that mention the firstborn are not clear on this point, however. Another reason for the divine claim may have been that the firstborn assumed responsibility for burial and even worship of deceased parents. Remnants of such ancestral worship are evident in texts like Deut 26:1-14 (see esp. v. 14). Just how the holy status of the firstborn influenced early cultic practice is also unclear. Whether there was a special ritual, redemption, or even sacrifice of the firstborn is difficult to determine. Stories like the attempted sacrifice of Isaac in Genesis 22 appear to be polemics against child sacrifice. But it is not clear whether Genesis 22 is a late story polemicizing against an earlier Israelite practice or against non-Israelite cultic practice. In any case, Exod 34:20 speaks of redemption for the firstborn son rather than sacrifice.

Verse 13 roots the holy status of the Israelite firstborn in the exodus. The divine claim on the firstborn is historicized through the climactic final plague. The death of all firstborn Egyptian children and livestock at midnight (Exod 11:4-8; 12:29-32) is judgment on the Egyptians and their gods (Exod

57. George Buchanan Gray, *Numbers,* ICC (Edinburgh: T. & T. Clark, 1903) 21.

58. Jacob Milgrom, *Numbers,* JPS Torah Commentary (Philadelphia: JPS, 1990) 16

12:12). God spares the Israelite firstborn in the priestly history through the substitution of a one-year-old male lamb. This becomes the Feast of Passover (Exod 12:1-13; see also the non-priestly account in Exod 12:21-27). In this ritual, the blood of the lamb on the doorpost was a sign for God not to kill the Israelite firstborn at midnight.

The divine claim on the Israelite firstborn is a direct result of their being spared on Passover. Exodus 13:11-16 states that the sparing of the Israelite firstborn during the midnight plague in Egypt results in their becoming a special divine possession. Thus all firstborn were to be given over to God through sacrifice or redeemed in some way through substitution. The special status of the firstborn would begin once Israel entered the land of Canaan (Exod 13:15).

Numbers 3:13 follows the same line of interpretation as does Exod 13:11-16. It, too, states that the sacred status of the firstborn is a direct result of their being spared during the first Passover. Priestly writers, however, make three changes in Numbers. First, they describe the firstborn explicitly as having a holy status ("I consecrated for my own all the firstborn in Israel"). Second, they require redemption of the firstborn already in the wilderness, rather than commencing the requirement with Israel's future life in the land. As a result, the holy status of the firstborn is a present reality for priestly writers. Third, the priestly writers also provide a one-time means of substitution through the levitical priestly caste, who are dedicated to God.

3:14-39. The role of the Levites as substitutes for the firstborn requires that they be counted. Verses 14-20 provide an introduction to the section with the divine command to number the Levites. All levitical males from one month of age and older are to be numbered according to their ancestral houses. The reason for beginning at one month is unclear. The census of the congregation in chap. 1 began at the age of twenty, which appeared to correspond with the age of military service. The Levites, by contrast, are being numbered for the purpose of redemption of the firstborn and not for military service. Thus it appears that all levitical males of any age could function as a substitute. In his commentary on Numbers, W. Gunther Plaut notes that in Jewish tradition "a child must live a month before being consid-

ered fully viable" and that a child who dies earlier than one month of age is considered a stillborn.[59] Whether a similar tradition is at work already in the priestly writing cannot be determined, but remains a possibility.

The census of the Levites is introduced in v. 14 with the expected divine command, "Then the LORD spoke to Moses." The fulfillment of the divine command follows immediately in v. 16, even though the census continues to v. 51. Verse 16 reads, "So Moses enrolled them according to the word of the LORD [על-פי יהוה *'al-pî YHWH*], as he was commanded." The phrase "as he was commanded" is the expected language for indicating fulfillment of a divine command (see 1:54; 2:34). The additional phrase "according to the word of the LORD" is new, and it appears to create an unnecessary repetition. The purpose of this repetition may be to call attention to the levitical census and to underscore that their census is distinct from the general census of the people. Jacob Milgrom has gone so far as to argue that the phrase should be translated "oracle," thus signifying that the census of the Levites was actually taken by God rather than by Moses.[60] In this case, the role of Moses in the process is to record the divine count, rather than to undertake it himself. Milgrom's interpretation may account for the place of the fulfillment of the divine command already in the introduction, since the remainder of the section would consist of the recording of the divine count and not the count itself.

The census is separated into the three levitical ancestral houses of Gershon (vv. 21-26), Kohath (vv. 27-32), and Merari (vv. 33-37). Each paragraph follows the same structure: (1) a list of the clans of each ancestral house; (2) the number of males one month of age and older; (3) their placement in the camp; (4) the head of the ancestral house; and (5) a list of their responsibilities with regard to caring for the tabernacle (see *Fig.* 3, "The Levitical Ancestral Houses," 52; see also Commentary on 4:1-33).

Verses 38-39 turn attention from the levitical ancestral houses to the Aaronide priesthood, not for the purpose of numbering them, but to finish out the arrangement of the camp. The encampment of Moses and the Aaronide priesthood on

59. W. Gunther Plaut, *Numbers, The Torah: A Modern Commentary* 4 (New York: Union of American Hebrew Congregations, 1979) 26.
60. Milgrom, *Numbers,* 19.

the east side of the tabernacle is noted in v. 38, along with a description of the Aaronide priests' tasks within the tabernacle (as opposed to the other levitical houses, who labored outside). The total number of levitical males one month of age and older is given in v. 39 as 22,000.

3:40-51. The purpose of the census to substitute Levites for Israelite firstborn is restated. Verses 40-43 provide the number of firstborn Israelite males one month of age and older as 22,273. This census conflicts with the census of twenty-year-old males in chap. 1, where the total given was 603,550 (1:46). Harmonizing the two counts would require that each Israelite family have at least 14 children. The focus of the priestly writers, however, does not appear to be the census total from chap. 1, but the 22,000 Levites who were numbered in 3:14-39. Comparison indicates 273 more firstborn Israelites than Levites. The excess of 273 firstborn is important, because it creates a situation in which the priestly writers can provide a paradigm for redemption beyond the number of Levites. Each firstborn Israelite beyond the number of Levites must be redeemed at the price of five shekels, payable to the Aaronide priesthood. Substitution is also extended to cattle in v. 41. Levitical cattle substitute for firstborn cattle of the people of Israel. There is conflict between this law and 18:17, which states that all firstborn cattle must be sacrificed to Yahweh, rather than being redeemed. Moses fulfills the divine command in vv. 49-51.

4:1-49. Numbers 4 describes a second census. Its purpose is to define and distribute the workload of the Levites. The age of those counted changes from one month of age and higher to males between the ages of thirty and fifty (vv. 3, 23, 30). Divine command (vv. 1, 17, 21) indicates a hierarchy among the Kohathites (vv. 1-20), the Gershonites (vv. 21-28), and the Merarites (vv. 29-33). Moses undertakes the count in vv. 34-49.

All the Levites are placed under the direction of the Aaronide priests, but even here there is a difference in hierarchy. The Kohathites are supervised by Eleazar (v. 16), while the Gershonites and the Merarites are under the oversight of Ithamar (vv. 28, 33). The distinction in supervision arises from the separate jobs assigned to the ancestral houses. The Kohathites transport the most holy objects, while the Gershonites and the Merarites transport the remainder of the tabernacle and its court.

The tasks of the Kohathites are outlined in vv. 5-15. Once the Aaronide priests have packed the most holy objects, they must carry them on the march. These objects include the ark in the holy of holies (vv. 5-6), the table of showbread (vv. 7-8), the lampstand (vv. 9-10), the golden altar (v. 11), and all the utensils in the sanctuary (v. 12) as well as the altar of burnt offering in the courtyard (vv. 13-14).

Degrees of holiness are indicated by the position of the objects in the tabernacle and its courtyard. The most holy location is the holy of holies. The intensity of holiness lessens as one moves further from this location. Categories of holiness

Figure 3: The Levitical Ancestral Houses			
	Gershon	Kohath	Merari
1. Clans	Libnites	Amramites	Mahlites
	Shimeites	Izharites	Mushites
		Hebronites	
		Uzzielites	
2. Numbers	7,500	8,600	6,200
3. Placement in the Camp	West	South	North
4. Head of Ancestral House	Eliasaph son of Lael	Elizaphan son of Uzziel	Zuriel son of Abihail
5. Task	Tabernacle	Utensils	Frames

are maintained by the colors of the wrappings and by the process of packaging the objects for the march through the wilderness.

The most holy status of the ark is signified by the use of a veil in its storage for travel (v. 6). During periods of encampment, this veil separates the ark in the holy of holies from other objects in the tabernacle. There are two other wrappings for the ark in addition to the veil. Fine leather (perhaps from dolphin skin) surrounds the veil, which is itself covered with a blue cloth.

The table of showbread, the lampstand, the golden altar, and the utensils from the sanctuary are wrapped in blue cloth and then placed in fine leather. The altar of burnt offering in the courtyard is wrapped in purple and then placed in a fine leather covering.

Thus the packaging changes from the holy of holies (ark) to the sanctuary of the tabernacle (table of showbread, lampstand, golden altar, and utensils) to the courtyard (altar). This distinction is carried through to the colors. Note that on the march the ark would be the only blue object. All other objects have fine leather as their outer wrapping, although they are distinguished beneath by blue and purple cloth. The transportation of the holy objects is by far the most dangerous task of the Levites, and it elevates the status of the Kohathites. But even with their elevated position, they are warned never to touch the objects directly (v. 15). Only Aaronide priests are properly safeguarded for this task (vv. 17-20).

The task of the Gershonites is outlined in vv. 21-28. They are to carry the curtains of the tabernacle, its top, and all hangings from the court. The task of the Merarites is described in vv. 29-33. They are to carry the frames, bars, and pillars of the tabernacle and its court.

Moses fulfills the divine command in vv. 34-49. The section separates into four repetitive paragraphs: vv. 34-37, vv. 38-41, vv. 42-45, and vv. 46-49. In the first three sections, Moses and Aaron are described as counting the Kohathites (vv. 34-37), the Gershonites (vv. 38-41), and the Merarites (vv. 42-45) between the ages of thirty and fifty before their totals are given (Kohathites, 2,700; Gershonites, 2,630; Merarites, 3,200). A summary statement indicates the successful completion of the census. The final paragraph in vv. 46-49 follows the same structure in providing the total number of Levites, which is 8,580.

REFLECTIONS

1. The idealization of hierarchy in the priestly writer's vision of the camp requires careful theological reflection by modern interpreters, especially since priestly writing is often judged in the modern context as advocating elitism. Hierarchy in priestly theology is not for the purpose of limiting power to the few, but to distribute holiness to as many as possible. Thus, in teaching and preaching Numbers 3–4, it is important to remember that the focus of priestly writers is on the whole camp and not on individual members. This is true even when the topic narrows to the Levites or the Aaronide priesthood.

The starting point of priestly writers is the separation between God and humans (see Introduction). The incompatibility of holiness to our everyday world requires that a select few acquire a special status to serve the sacred for the many. Selection is not for privilege, but for service. Language of slavery is used to describe the role of the Levites (Num 3:5-10). The task of the Levites to carry the sacred objects of the tabernacle illustrates how holiness is not meant to be hoarded, but shared. These actions enable God to live in the camp and to move through the wilderness with Israel.

The Pauline vision of the body in 1 Corinthians 12 provides a New Testament analogy to the priestly vision of the camp. Paul, too, underscores that there are varieties of gifts in the church. But his focus, like that of the priestly writers, is on the whole body and not on the individual parts. All gifts, according to Paul, derive from the power of God (1 Cor 12:6). Gifts are evaluated, moreover, by whether they contribute to the common good (1 Cor 12:7) and not by the social position of a person with a particular gift. A camp of only Levites or Aaronide priests would be like a human body with only eyes and no ears (see 1 Cor 12:14-26). The diversity of the entire community is always stronger than any one person or group for both the priestly writers and Paul.

The priestly vision of the camp and the Pauline vision of the body challenge contemporary individualism in two ways. First, they remind us that the indwelling of God is not for individual persons to have a private relationship with God or to acquire prestige over others. It is intended to strengthen the community. The death of Nadab and Abihu (Num 3:2) indicates the rejection of such spiritual elitism by the priestly writers. Second, the distribution of leadership roles is always in service to the larger group. The Levites substitute for the firstborn, thus providing life to the community. The apostle Paul makes the same point when he concludes that honor and rank do not go together in the body of the church (1 Cor 12:24-25). Rank is always for the purpose of service to the weaker members. Weaker members hold the position of honor in the community.

2. The distinction among priests, Levites, and lay Israelites allows for theological reflection on different types of calling and ordination in the contemporary church. Degrees of holiness in the geography of the camp determine distinct ordinations. Three degrees of holiness emerge from the architecture of the tabernacle and its court. There is the holy of holies, where the ark is housed and God dwells (Num 4:5-6); the sanctuary of the tabernacle, where the holy objects, consisting of the table of showbread, the lampstand, the golden altar, and the utensils are housed (Num 4:7-12); and the outer court, where the altar of burnt offering is located (Num 4:13-14). The degrees of holiness give rise to the separation of priests and laity as well as to distinctions within the priesthood itself. Aaronide priests labor within the sanctuary. They are protected from death in viewing the sacred objects. Kohathite Levites rank higher than Gershonite and Merarite clans, because they carry the most sacred objects. The link between priests and laity is forged when all Levites substitute for the firstborn, thus providing a way for all Israelites to live in the camp.

We still evaluate ordination in much the same way within the contemporary church. We often think of preaching as separating ordained clergy from laity. This may be true in some churches, but it is the administration of the sacraments that provides the clearest line between clergy and laity. Baptism and the eucharist are the most holy rituals of the church. They are priestly functions of ministry that take place in the front or altar area of the church. The ordination required to discharge the sacraments is usually the most restricted of all offices in the church. But there are also many other ministries and offices in the church that broaden the role of leadership. Bishops, elders, deacons, and commissioned teachers are just a few examples of offices that emerge from the indwelling of Christ in the church. Gradations of holiness continue in the church for the same reason as in Numbers 3–4: God calls people to different tasks in order to disburse holiness through the community.

3. The divine claim on Israelite firstborn and their redemption by the Levites introduces language of service, salvation, and identity that lives on in Christian tradition. Numbers 3:11-13 states that God made the Israelite firstborn holy by not killing them during the night of Passover, when the Egyptian firstborn were destroyed. Firstborn, therefore, are a divine possession: "They are mine," says Yahweh. The divine claim of possession means that they should be given over to God, whether through sacrifice or through some other symbolic action. Levites redeem the firstborn by releasing them from their legal obligation through substitution. The Hebrew word "to redeem" (פדה *pādâ*) means "to buy back," implying that something is lost to the original owner. The thought behind Numbers 3 is that God, the Savior of Israel in Egypt, is compensated by the Levites. They are given over to God, they take on a special service in the camp, and they even lose their rights to the land. The identity of the Levites is formed in this act of substitution.

Redemption through substitution becomes a model for interpreting the ministry of Jesus and the life of all Christians. Jesus substitutes divine form for human and in this action acquires identity, according to the apostle Paul (Phil 2:6-11). The pattern continues in his own life, when Paul writes of himself, "It is no longer I who live, but it is Christ who lives in me. And the life I now live in the flesh I live by faith in the son of God, who lived in me and gave himself for me" (Gal 2:20 NRSV). In both of these instances, substitution leads to service and identity.

4. Numbers 3–4 illustrates the concern of the priestly writers to transform the entire environment of Israel. The smallest details take on importance. Holiness permeates objects like the ark, the table, the lampstand, the altar, and the utensils. It is even reflected in the different colors associated with the tabernacle: violet, purple, and crimson. We continue this practice in Christian tradition. The Christian year is made up of sacred seasons or times, like Advent, Epiphany, Lent, Easter, and Pentecost, which contrast to regular or ordinary time. Our seasons of worship are also distinguished by colors. For example, Advent and Lent are purple, Easter is white, and Pentecost is red. Ordinary time is green. Colors reflect different degrees of holiness just as in priestly tradition. Every church also has sacred objects. Some are objects common to all churches, like communion utensils or baptismal basins. Others are unique to local churches. Windows, paintings, artwork, or a special cross may each enrich our religious life. Paying attention to sacred objects in our church and the changing colors of the Christian year makes us conscious of the many concrete ways God changes the details of our lives.

5. The contemporary church is rediscovering how important the earth is for human health. The priestly history provides an important resource for reflecting on environmental theology. The *Toledot* formula in Num 3:1 indicates that Israel's life in the camp is part of a larger history that extends back to the origins of creation itself. Humans are defined as part of the earth. Salvation apart from the "heavens and the earth" would make no sense to the priestly writers (see the *Toledot* in Gen 2:4*a*). The quest of Israel within salvation history, according to priestly writers, is to rediscover the lost world of Genesis 1.

Numbers 5:1–6:27, Camp Legislation to Prevent Defilement

NIV

5 The LORD said to Moses, [2]"Command the Israelites to send away from the camp anyone who has an infectious skin disease[a] or a discharge of any kind, or who is ceremonially unclean because of a dead body. [3]Send away male and female alike; send them outside the camp so they will not defile their camp, where I dwell among them." [4]The Israelites did this; they sent them outside the camp. They did just as the LORD had instructed Moses.

[5]The LORD said to Moses, [6]"Say to the Israelites: 'When a man or woman wrongs another in any way[b] and so is unfaithful to the LORD, that person is guilty [7]and must confess the sin he has committed. He must make full restitution for his wrong, add one fifth to it and give it all to the

a2 Traditionally leprosy; *the Hebrew word was used for various diseases affecting the skin—not necessarily leprosy.* *b6 Or* woman commits any wrong common to mankind

NRSV

5 The LORD spoke to Moses, saying: [2]Command the Israelites to put out of the camp everyone who is leprous,[a] or has a discharge, and everyone who is unclean through contact with a corpse; [3]you shall put out both male and female, putting them outside the camp; they must not defile their camp, where I dwell among them. [4]The Israelites did so, putting them outside the camp; as the LORD had spoken to Moses, so the Israelites did.

5The LORD spoke to Moses, saying: [6]Speak to the Israelites: When a man or a woman wrongs another, breaking faith with the LORD, that person incurs guilt [7]and shall confess the sin that has been committed. The person shall make full restitution for the wrong, adding one-fifth to it, and giving it to the one who was wronged. [8]If the

a A term for several skin diseases; precise meaning uncertain

person he has wronged. ⁸But if that person has no close relative to whom restitution can be made for the wrong, the restitution belongs to the Lord and must be given to the priest, along with the ram with which atonement is made for him. ⁹All the sacred contributions the Israelites bring to a priest will belong to him. ¹⁰Each man's sacred gifts are his own, but what he gives to the priest will belong to the priest.' "

¹¹Then the Lord said to Moses, ¹²"Speak to the Israelites and say to them: 'If a man's wife goes astray and is unfaithful to him ¹³by sleeping with another man, and this is hidden from her husband and her impurity is undetected (since there is no witness against her and she has not been caught in the act), ¹⁴and if feelings of jealousy come over her husband and he suspects his wife and she is impure—or if he is jealous and suspects her even though she is not impure— ¹⁵then he is to take his wife to the priest. He must also take an offering of a tenth of an ephah[a] of barley flour on her behalf. He must not pour oil on it or put incense on it, because it is a grain offering for jealousy, a reminder offering to draw attention to guilt.

¹⁶" 'The priest shall bring her and have her stand before the Lord. ¹⁷Then he shall take some holy water in a clay jar and put some dust from the tabernacle floor into the water. ¹⁸After the priest has had the woman stand before the Lord, he shall loosen her hair and place in her hands the reminder offering, the grain offering for jealousy, while he himself holds the bitter water that brings a curse. ¹⁹Then the priest shall put the woman under oath and say to her, "If no other man has slept with you and you have not gone astray and become impure while married to your husband, may this bitter water that brings a curse not harm you. ²⁰But if you have gone astray while married to your husband and you have defiled yourself by sleeping with a man other than your husband"— ²¹here the priest is to put the woman under this curse of the oath—"may the Lord cause your people to curse and denounce you when he causes your thigh to waste away and your abdomen to swell.[b] ²²May this water that brings a curse

a15 That is, probably about 2 quarts (about 2 liters)   b21 Or causes you to have a miscarrying womb and barrenness

injured party has no next of kin to whom restitution may be made for the wrong, the restitution for wrong shall go to the Lord for the priest, in addition to the ram of atonement with which atonement is made for the guilty party. ⁹Among all the sacred donations of the Israelites, every gift that they bring to the priest shall be his. ¹⁰The sacred donations of all are their own; whatever anyone gives to the priest shall be his.

11The Lord spoke to Moses, saying: ¹²Speak to the Israelites and say to them: If any man's wife goes astray and is unfaithful to him, ¹³if a man has had intercourse with her but it is hidden from her husband, so that she is undetected though she has defiled herself, and there is no witness against her since she was not caught in the act; ¹⁴if a spirit of jealousy comes on him, and he is jealous of his wife who has defiled herself; or if a spirit of jealousy comes on him, and he is jealous of his wife, though she has not defiled herself; ¹⁵then the man shall bring his wife to the priest. And he shall bring the offering required for her, one-tenth of an ephah of barley flour. He shall pour no oil on it and put no frankincense on it, for it is a grain offering of jealousy, a grain offering of remembrance, bringing iniquity to remembrance.

16Then the priest shall bring her near, and set her before the Lord; ¹⁷the priest shall take holy water in an earthen vessel, and take some of the dust that is on the floor of the tabernacle and put it into the water. ¹⁸The priest shall set the woman before the Lord, dishevel the woman's hair, and place in her hands the grain offering of remembrance, which is the grain offering of jealousy. In his own hand the priest shall have the water of bitterness that brings the curse. ¹⁹Then the priest shall make her take an oath, saying, "If no man has lain with you, if you have not turned aside to uncleanness while under your husband's authority, be immune to this water of bitterness that brings the curse. ²⁰But if you have gone astray while under your husband's authority, if you have defiled yourself and some man other than your husband has had intercourse with you," ²¹—let the priest make the woman take the oath of the curse and say to the woman—"the Lord make you an execration and an oath among your peo-

NIV

enter your body so that your abdomen swells and your thigh wastes away.[a]"

"'Then the woman is to say, "Amen. So be it."

23"'The priest is to write these curses on a scroll and then wash them off into the bitter water. 24He shall have the woman drink the bitter water that brings a curse, and this water will enter her and cause bitter suffering. 25The priest is to take from her hands the grain offering for jealousy, wave it before the LORD and bring it to the altar. 26The priest is then to take a handful of the grain offering as a memorial offering and burn it on the altar; after that, he is to have the woman drink the water. 27If she has defiled herself and been unfaithful to her husband, then when she is made to drink the water that brings a curse, it will go into her and cause bitter suffering; her abdomen will swell and her thigh waste away,[b] and she will become accursed among her people. 28If, however, the woman has not defiled herself and is free from impurity, she will be cleared of guilt and will be able to have children.

29"'This, then, is the law of jealousy when a woman goes astray and defiles herself while married to her husband, 30or when feelings of jealousy come over a man because he suspects his wife. The priest is to have her stand before the LORD and is to apply this entire law to her. 31The husband will be innocent of any wrongdoing, but the woman will bear the consequences of her sin.'"

6 The LORD said to Moses, 2"Speak to the Israelites and say to them: 'If a man or woman wants to make a special vow, a vow of separation to the LORD as a Nazirite, 3he must abstain from wine and other fermented drink and must not drink vinegar made from wine or from other fermented drink. He must not drink grape juice or eat grapes or raisins. 4As long as he is a Nazirite, he must not eat anything that comes from the grapevine, not even the seeds or skins.

5"'During the entire period of his vow of separation no razor may be used on his head. He must be holy until the period of his separation to the LORD is over; he must let the hair of his head grow long. 6Throughout the period of his separation to the LORD he must not go near a dead body. 7Even if his own father or mother or brother or

a22 Or body and cause you to be barren and have a miscarrying womb
b27 Or suffering; she will have barrenness and a miscarrying womb

NRSV

ple, when the LORD makes your uterus drop, your womb discharge; 22now may this water that brings the curse enter your bowels and make your womb discharge, your uterus drop!" And the woman shall say, "Amen. Amen."

23Then the priest shall put these curses in writing, and wash them off into the water of bitterness. 24He shall make the woman drink the water of bitterness that brings the curse, and the water that brings the curse shall enter her and cause bitter pain. 25The priest shall take the grain offering of jealousy out of the woman's hand, and shall elevate the grain offering before the LORD and bring it to the altar; 26and the priest shall take a handful of the grain offering, as its memorial portion, and turn it into smoke on the altar, and afterward shall make the woman drink the water. 27When he has made her drink the water, then, if she has defiled herself and has been unfaithful to her husband, the water that brings the curse shall enter into her and cause bitter pain, and her womb shall discharge, her uterus drop, and the woman shall become an execration among her people. 28But if the woman has not defiled herself and is clean, then she shall be immune and be able to conceive children.

29This is the law in cases of jealousy, when a wife, while under her husband's authority, goes astray and defiles herself, 30or when a spirit of jealousy comes on a man and he is jealous of his wife; then he shall set the woman before the LORD, and the priest shall apply this entire law to her. 31The man shall be free from iniquity, but the woman shall bear her iniquity.

6 The LORD spoke to Moses, saying: 2Speak to the Israelites and say to them: When either men or women make a special vow, the vow of a nazirite,[a] to separate themselves to the LORD, 3they shall separate themselves from wine and strong drink; they shall drink no wine vinegar or other vinegar, and shall not drink any grape juice or eat grapes, fresh or dried. 4All their days as nazirites[b] they shall eat nothing that is produced by the grapevine, not even the seeds or the skins.

5All the days of their nazirite vow no razor shall come upon the head; until the time is

a That is one separated or one consecrated

57

NIV

sister dies, he must not make himself ceremonially unclean on account of them, because the symbol of his separation to God is on his head. ⁸Throughout the period of his separation he is consecrated to the LORD.

⁹"'If someone dies suddenly in his presence, thus defiling the hair he has dedicated, he must shave his head on the day of his cleansing—the seventh day. ¹⁰Then on the eighth day he must bring two doves or two young pigeons to the priest at the entrance to the Tent of Meeting. ¹¹The priest is to offer one as a sin offering and the other as a burnt offering to make atonement for him because he sinned by being in the presence of the dead body. That same day he is to consecrate his head. ¹²He must dedicate himself to the LORD for the period of his separation and must bring a year-old male lamb as a guilt offering. The previous days do not count, because he became defiled during his separation.

¹³"'Now this is the law for the Nazirite when the period of his separation is over. He is to be brought to the entrance to the Tent of Meeting. ¹⁴There he is to present his offerings to the LORD: a year-old male lamb without defect for a burnt offering, a year-old ewe lamb without defect for a sin offering, a ram without defect for a fellowship offering,ᵃ ¹⁵together with their grain offerings and drink offerings, and a basket of bread made without yeast—cakes made of fine flour mixed with oil, and wafers spread with oil.

¹⁶"'The priest is to present them before the LORD and make the sin offering and the burnt offering. ¹⁷He is to present the basket of unleavened bread and is to sacrifice the ram as a fellowship offering to the LORD, together with its grain offering and drink offering.

¹⁸"'Then at the entrance to the Tent of Meeting, the Nazirite must shave off the hair that he dedicated. He is to take the hair and put it in the fire that is under the sacrifice of the fellowship offering.

¹⁹"'After the Nazirite has shaved off the hair of his dedication, the priest is to place in his hands a boiled shoulder of the ram, and a cake and a wafer from the basket, both made without yeast. ²⁰The priest shall then wave them before the LORD as a wave offering; they are holy and belong to

ᵃ14 Traditionally *peace offering*; also in verses 17 and 18

NRSV

completed for which they separate themselves to the LORD, they shall be holy; they shall let the locks of the head grow long.

6All the days that they separate themselves to the LORD they shall not go near a corpse. ⁷Even if their father or mother, brother or sister, should die, they may not defile themselves; because their consecration to God is upon the head. ⁸All their days as naziritesᵇ they are holy to the LORD.

9If someone dies very suddenly nearby, defiling the consecrated head, then they shall shave the head on the day of their cleansing; on the seventh day they shall shave it. ¹⁰On the eighth day they shall bring two turtledoves or two young pigeons to the priest at the entrance of the tent of meeting, ¹¹and the priest shall offer one as a sin offering and the other as a burnt offering, and make atonement for them, because they incurred guilt by reason of the corpse. They shall sanctify the head that same day, ¹²and separate themselves to the LORD for their days as nazirites,ᵇ and bring a male lamb a year old as a guilt offering. The former time shall be void, because the consecrated head was defiled.

13This is the law for the naziritesᵃ when the time of their consecration has been completed: they shall be brought to the entrance of the tent of meeting, ¹⁴and they shall offer their gift to the LORD, one male lamb a year old without blemish as a burnt offering, one ewe lamb a year old without blemish as a sin offering, one ram without blemish as an offering of well-being, ¹⁵and a basket of unleavened bread, cakes of choice flour mixed with oil and unleavened wafers spread with oil, with their grain offering and their drink offerings. ¹⁶The priest shall present them before the LORD and offer their sin offering and burnt offering, ¹⁷and shall offer the ram as a sacrifice of well-being to the LORD, with the basket of unleavened bread; the priest also shall make the accompanying grain offering and drink offering. ¹⁸Then the naziritesᵃ shall shave the consecrated head at the entrance of the tent of meeting, and shall take the hair from the consecrated head and put it on the fire under the sacrifice of well-being. ¹⁹The priest shall take the shoulder of the ram, when it is boiled, and one unleavened cake out of the basket, and

ᵃ That is *those separated* or *those consecrated*

NIV

the priest, together with the breast that was waved and the thigh that was presented. After that, the Nazirite may drink wine.

²¹ "'This is the law of the Nazirite who vows his offering to the LORD in accordance with his separation, in addition to whatever else he can afford. He must fulfill the vow he has made, according to the law of the Nazirite.'"

²²The LORD said to Moses, ²³"Tell Aaron and his sons, 'This is how you are to bless the Israelites. Say to them:

²⁴ "'"The LORD bless you
  and keep you;
²⁵the LORD make his face shine upon you
  and be gracious to you;
²⁶the LORD turn his face toward you
  and give you peace."'

²⁷"So they will put my name on the Israelites, and I will bless them."

NRSV

one unleavened wafer, and shall put them in the palms of the nazirites,ᵃ after they have shaved the consecrated head. ²⁰Then the priest shall elevate them as an elevation offering before the LORD; they are a holy portion for the priest, together with the breast that is elevated and the thigh that is offered. After that the naziritesᵃ may drink wine.

21This is the law for the naziritesᵃ who take a vow. Their offering to the LORD must be in accordance with the naziriteᵇ vow, apart from what else they can afford. In accordance with whatever vow they take, so they shall do, following the law for their consecration.

22The LORD spoke to Moses, saying: ²³Speak to Aaron and his sons, saying, Thus you shall bless the Israelites: You shall say to them,

²⁴ The LORD bless you and keep you;
²⁵ the LORD make his face to shine upon you,
    and be gracious to you;
²⁶ the LORD lift up his countenance upon you,
    and give you peace.

27So they shall put my name on the Israelites, and I will bless them.

ᵃ That is *those separated* or *those consecrated*   ᵇ That is *one separated* or *one consecrated*

COMMENTARY

The legislation in Numbers 5–6 builds on the arrangement of the camp and the census in chaps. 1–4. The sections are tied together around the common problem of how Israel is to live in the presence of divine holiness. In chaps. 1–4, the holiness of God in the tabernacle gave rise to the social organization of Israel, the arrangement of the camp around the tent of meeting, and the role of the Levites. Chapters 5–6 present legislation to protect the holiness of the camp from impurity.

Biblical impurity and its relation to holiness requires definition. The holiness of God creates two different contrasts: sacred versus profane and pure versus impure.[61] The contrast of sacred versus profane is the contrast between the holy and the common. It has dominated Numbers 1–4.

Holiness separates by its very nature. God is holy; humans are not. They are common or profane. Thus care must be taken in bringing the two together. Humans must conform to divine holiness, symbolized as completeness. The quest for holiness requires taking on the order of holiness. The priestly writer's concern for order in the camp (chaps. 1–4) represents the desire to conform to holiness.

The dangers of physical and social impurity to the camp are central in chaps. 5–6. God's holiness remains the central theme. But the contrast is not between the sacred and the profane. It is between health and disease. The quest for completeness is replaced with medical images. Holiness is health. It must be protected from infection, contamination, pollution, and impurity. Contact with a corpse or the acquiring of a skin disease defiles. The medical language also describes the ethical life of Israel. Evil actions are contagious disease

61. Jacob Milgrom, *Numbers,* JPS Torah Commentary (Philadelphia: JPS, 1990) 334-46.

that pollutes and eventually kills the social body like cancer in a human body. The most basic contrast between holiness and impurity is life and death. The holiness of God is life. All forms of impurity, whether physical disease or immoral behavior, are death. The two are incompatible.

The laws of impurity in chaps. 5–6 are arranged in relationship to the tabernacle. They move from the outside of the camp (5:1-4) to the inside of the camp (5:5–6:21). The laws that focus on life within the camp (5:5–6:21) move in closer orbits toward the tabernacle at the center. Numbers 5:5-10 represents the broadest circle in the camp. It explores social relationships that defile. Numbers 5:11-31 narrows the circle. It turns attention to defilement within marriage relationships. Numbers 6:1-21 represents the smallest circle. It addresses the special human-divine relationship resulting from the Nazirite vow. This vow is the only way a non-priestly Israelite could attain a holy status. The section closes in 6:22-27 with the priestly blessing on the congregation. It is God's response to the purity of the camp. Comparison to Lev 9:22 indicates that the priestly blessing emanates from the door of the tabernacle, thus completing the movement toward the center of the camp.

Divine command and fulfillment reinforce the overall design of chaps. 5–6. The list of impurities in 5:1-4 requiring a person to be placed outside the camp is introduced by divine command in v. 1 ("The LORD spoke to Moses") and concludes with the notice of fulfillment in v. 4 ("The Israelites did so . . . as the LORD had spoken to Moses"). The different laws concerning relationships in the camp are introduced with divine command ("The LORD spoke to Moses," 5:5, 11; 6:1). They lack the formula of completion, however. The reason may be that they constitute ongoing legislation for the camp, rather than specific requirements to be implemented at the time of command. The priestly blessing on the congregation and the camp in 6:22-27 replaces the formula of completion.

5:1-4. This section is structured into four parts. It begins with the divine command in v. 1. The content of the command is stated in vv. 2-3*a*. Three forms of impurity threatening the purity of the camp are listed: (1) a skin disease described in Hebrew as צרעת (*ṣāra'at*); (2) abnormal bodily

discharges from the genitals; and (3) contact with a corpse. Any male or female with these conditions threatens the purity of the camp and must be expelled. Verse 3*b* states that the purpose of the legislation is not to protect people from disease, but to protect God's holiness from these threatening conditions. Verse 4 closes the unit by underscoring the completion of the command by the congregation.

The laws in vv. 1-4 stress that the life-giving power of holiness must be protected. But what exactly is being protected, and where is the conflict? Mary Douglas has argued that laws of impurity are symbolic of larger cosmological realities.[62] From her perspective, the point of conflict in Num 5:1-4 is not the specific diseases, but what they symbolize. The holiness of God at the center of the camp gives life that is whole and complete. The order of the camp is an outgrowth of divine holiness; as such, it reflects this abundant life. The camp symbolizes a whole new age of salvation. Following the interpretation of Douglas, we might conclude that the diseases and other impurities listed in v. 2 represent the disruption of the unblemished order of holiness symbolized by the camp. In other words, they represent different forms of "dirt" that must be removed to protect the order (or cleanliness) of the camp.

Jacob Milgrom takes the work of Douglas a step further. He concludes that each of the three forms of impurity listed in v. 2 represents the power of death in somewhat different ways.[63] Thus, according to Milgrom, the conflict addressed in vv. 1-4 is not simply order versus disorder, but the life-giving power of holiness versus death. The contamination to camp members by contact with a corpse clearly illustrates the conflict between holiness and death.

Defilement from skin disease addresses the same conflict. Although this condition is translated "leprosy" (צרעת *ṣāra'at*), the term most likely encompasses a variety of skin disorders described in more detail in Leviticus 13–14. Once again, it is not the health consequences of the disease that force a person from the camp, but its association with death, which is incompatible with holiness. The story of Miriam in Numbers 12 provides illustration. When she acquires *ṣāra'at* as punish-

---

62. Mary Douglas, *Purity and Danger* (London: Routledge and Kegan Paul, 1966).
63. Milgrom, *Numbers,* 344-46.

ment for opposing Moses, Aaron exclaims that her condition makes her like one of the dead (12:12).

The contrast between holiness and death is also the rationale for the impurity of discharge. The Hebrew word for "discharge" (זוב *zôb*) simply means "one flowing." Comparison to Leviticus 15, however, makes it clear that the context concerns abnormal discharge from the genitals of either males or females. Abnormal flowing of blood and semen, the sources of life, also symbolizes death.

In summary, vv. 1-4 outline two forms of power and their spheres of influence: life-giving holiness and death. Holiness emanates from God and is located in the tabernacle. Its sphere of power is the camp. The incompatibility of holiness and death demands that all signs of the latter be banished from the camp.

5:5–6:21. The perspective shifts in Num 5:5–6:21 from signs of death that must be banished from the camp to relationships within the camp that are incompatible with holiness. The topic changes from ritual impurity to moral offenses. The goal of the laws also appears to change. Their aim is no longer to remove threatening persons (or conditions) from the sphere of the holy, but to keep offenders within the camp. Thus restoration for violations of camp holiness is an important aspect of the legislation in this section.

5:5-10. These verses deal with the breakdown of community relationships. The first part of v. 5 underscores the broadly based social dimension of this law. It is addressed to all men and women in the camp. The violation described in v. 6 with the Hebrew phrase כי יעשו מכל־חטאת האדם (*kî ya ʿăśû mikkol-ḥaṭṭōʾt hāʾ ādām*) occurs only in this verse. It could be translated as "wrongs committed against another human" or as "wrongs committed by any human." The difference is whether the last word in the phrase, "the human" (האדם *hāʾ ādām*) is interpreted as a subjective genitive ("wrongs committed by any human") or as an objective genitive ("wrongs committed against another human"). Similar language occurs in Lev 6:1-7 (Lev 5:20-26 MT), where the former interpretation is intended. But the phrase in v. 6 is not exactly the same. The details of restitution in vv. 6-10 suggest that the sin being addressed is one of defrauding a neighbor, which favors the translation "wrongs committed against another human."

The issue in these verses is not secular crime,

however, but the violation of the sacred. The closing phrase of v. 6 makes this clear. It states that cheating and stealing "break faith with Yahweh." The Hebrew word "to break faith" (מעל *māʿal*) in conjunction with the preposition "with/against" (ב *bĕ*) is precise in indicating some form of sacrilege. God tends to be the offended party when this syntactical construction is used. Thus, for example, Moses is told by Yahweh in Deut 32:51 that he must die on Mt. Nebo and not enter the promised land, because Moses "broke faith [*māʿal*] with [*bĕ*] God" when he angrily struck the rock, instead of sanctifying God in the people's midst (see Numbers 20). The reason for the sacred dimension to community relationships in Num 5:5-10 is that the camp is the sphere of holiness. Holiness permeates all action.

The sacred character of the law is reinforced at the close of v. 6 when the offender is described as "incurring guilt." The Hebrew word for "guilt" (אשם *ʾāšām*) is a central term in the priestly description of Israel's cultic system. Guilt is a legal condition. It describes a situation resulting from illegal action. The removal of the condition of guilt requires ritual purification and restitution. The word is used no fewer than four times in vv. 6-8. A verbal form of the Hebrew word *ʾāšām* is used in vv. 6 and 8, while a noun form occurs in vv. 7 and 8. The noun has at least two meanings in priestly writing. It can designate a particular kind of sacrifice that is meant to alleviate guilt (as it does in 6:12); more specifically, it can indicate the actual content that is required for restitution. Verse 7 illustrates this latter meaning when it states that the one who has stolen must make full repayment "for what he has stolen" (the Hebrew translates literally, "his *ʾāšām*").[64]

The Hebrew verb meaning "to be guilty" is stative. Such verbs do not describe action, but the state or condition of something resulting from action (e.g., you cannot "cold" someone, but you can "be cold"). The stative aspect of the Hebrew verb is rendered in English as "is guilty" or, as in the case of the NRSV translation of v. 6, "incurs guilt." What the NRSV translation suggests is that defrauding in the camp becomes sacrilege that gives rise to a condition of guilt, which is incom-

64. Ibid., 35.

patible with holiness.[65] The imagery is medical. Such a person infects the camp with pollution, and a contaminated camp is incompatible with a holy God. The infected person must be cured. The offender must make confession, pay back the principal amount of what he or she stole, and add 20 percent (v. 7). These actions alleviate the condition of guilt created by the theft. Health is achieved. The offender is allowed to remain in the camp and continue living within the sphere of God's holiness.

A slightly different interpretation of vv. 6-7 has been offered by Jacob Milgrom, who argues that the Hebrew verb "to be guilty" can take on a psychological dimension when used without an object (as is the case in v. 6). In such instances, Milgrom suggests, the more accurate translation is "feel guilt."[66] Verses 6-7 state, according to Milgrom, that the offender must first feel guilt (become aware of his or her sin). Only then is confession meaningful and the reparation of guilt efficacious.

Verse 8 clarifies that restitution of theft remains a requirement even after the death of the injured party. The reason given for this requirement is that ultimately God is the offended party. Verse 8 closes by adding that God allocates the guilt offering to the priests. Verses 9-10 comment on the legislation of v. 8 by clarifying which priests receive the donation. The donation belongs to the priest who collects it.

5:11-31. These verses narrow the focus from relationships between all persons in the camp (vv. 5-10) to marriage. The danger of defilement is no longer defrauding in general, but adultery. The law is stated at the beginning (vv. 12-14) and the end (vv. 29-30) of the legislation.[67] It is aimed at a wife, who is suspected of "going astray." The verb "to go astray" (שׂטה *śāṭâ*) in vv. 12 and 29 can mean wickedness in general (Prov 4:15), but v. 13 makes it clear that sexual infidelity is intended. If the charge is true, such a wife is described as being unfaithful to her husband (v. 12) and thus defiled (v. 29).

The phrase in v. 12 indicating unfaithfulness (מעל *māʿal*) to (ב *bĕ*) a husband is unique, since

(as noted in the Commentary on 5:6) this expression tends to be used to indicate sacrilege, with God as the object. The repetition is certainly meant to relate the two laws. The unique usage in v. 12 may also be intended to indicate that adultery is a violation against God and, hence, a threat to the holiness of the camp. Such a broad interpretation of v. 12 is supported by v. 29, where the act of "going astray" is explicitly said to result in defilement (טמא *ṭāmēʾ*), thereby associating adultery with sacrilege. Genesis 20:6 provides an additional instance of adultery as sacrilege. Abimelech's potential sleeping with Sarah is described as sin against God. The religious dimension of the law is indicated by its frequent use throughout this section (vv. 12, 13, 14 [twice], 19, 20, 27, 28, 29).

Verses 15-31 outline a judicial ritual for determining the guilt or innocence of a suspected adulteress. The rationale for the ritual is that adultery is sacrilege. A woman guilty of such an action threatens the camp with contamination, not because she is ritually unclean from sexual intercourse, but because she is ethically unclean from violating her marriage relationship. The aim of the detailed ritual, therefore, is not to assuage a husband's jealousy (an infraction of civil law), but to avoid defilement of the camp (an infraction of sacred law). The magical character of the ordeal (vv. 15-28) for determining the guilt or innocence of the woman underscores the sacred dimension in which the law is meant to function.

Verse 15 states the condition for the ritual ordeal. A husband who suspects his wife of sexual infidelity must bring her to the priest along with a special offering, described as a "grain offering of jealousy" and a "grain offering of remembrance."

Verses 16-18 outline cultic instructions for the ritual ordeal. The priest places the woman before God (v. 16). He takes "holy water" and mixes it with dust from the floor of the tabernacle in an earthen vessel (v. 17). He also loosens the woman's hair and puts the special offering of jealousy and remembrance in her hands (v. 18).

Verses 19-26 prescribe an oath and accompanying sacrifices. The priest recites an oath while holding the mixture of water and dust in his own hands. The oath functions as a curse if the woman is guilty. Her "womb will discharge" and her "uterus will drop." The woman accepts the oath

---

65. Baruch A. Levine, *Numbers 1–20,* AB 4A (New York: Doubleday, 1993) 188-89.

66. J. Milgrom, *Cult and Conscience: The Asham and the Priestly Doctrine of Repentance,* SJLA 18 (Leiden: Press, 1970) 3-12.

67. See M. Fishbane, "Accusations of Adultery: A Study of Law and Scribal Practice in Numbers 5:11-31," *HUCA* 45 (1974) 35-36.

on herself by stating, "Amen, Amen" (vv. 19-22). The priest then writes down the words of the oath, washes the parchment in the mixture of water and dust, and makes the woman drink the potion while he sacrifices the grain offering of jealousy and remembrance (vv. 23-26).

Verses 27-28 indicate that the woman's reaction to the potion will determine her guilt or innocence. If she is guilty, the curse of the oath will take effect. If innocent, she will be immune to the curse and continue to conceive children.

The ritual contains technical language that is no longer clear to modern readers. The various descriptions of the offering in v. 15 ("offering of jealousy," "offering of remembrance," and "bringing iniquity to remembrance") lack precise parallels. Reference to "holy water" (מים קדשם *mayim qĕdōšîm*) in v. 17 is not explained and occurs nowhere else in the Old Testament. Perhaps the combination of water and dust symbolizes life and death. The symbolic significance of loosening the woman's hair in v. 18 may indicate mourning (Lev 10:6), a state of defilement as in leprosy (Lev 13:45), or shame.

Even more problematic is "the water of bitterness that brings a curse" (v. 19). The description of this potion is important for interpreting the entire ordeal, since it is the centerpiece of the ritual. Yet no clear consensus has emerged concerning the meaning of the word המרים (*hammārîm*). It is translated as "bitterness" in the NRSV and "bitter" in the NIV, from the root consonants מרר (*mrr*), "to be bitter." Other Hebrew roots have been suggested, which result in very different interpretations, including "water of rebellion" from the root מרי (*mry*, "to rebel")[68] and "water of instruction or revelation," from the root ירה (*yrh*, "to teach").[69]

The effect of the potion on the woman raises further questions. If the woman is innocent, she will be immune to the negative effects of the potion and will "be able to conceive children" (v. 29). If she is guilty, the potion will make her womb discharge and her uterus drop (vv. 21, 27). Interpreters are divided on the matter of whether the woman is pregnant. If pregnant and guilty of adultery, the phrase would mean that the potion induces an abortion. Innocence would result in a full-term delivery. If the woman is not pregnant and guilty, the phrase would indicate that the potion renders her physically unable to have children.

The process of the ritual has also prompted conflicting interpretations. Some scholars question whether the text is describing one ritual or a combination of distinct rituals and offerings. Martin Noth separated the text into a meal offering and a drink offering. He also identified three different forms of divine judgment. Holy water held secret power of judgment. The oath, in the form of a curse, could also trigger divine judgment. And the writing of words in a book was yet a third form of judgment.[70] More recent interpreters tend to view the text as describing one complex ritual.[71] But even here there is debate about whether the ritual should be characterized as an ordeal.

Such a magical ritual ordeal is unusual in the OT. There are other rituals from the ancient Near East in which guilt or innocence of a person is determined by a water ordeal. In the Code of Hammurabi, for example, a person accused of sorcery must go through a river ordeal to determine guilt or innocence,[72] as must a wife accused of adultery by a third party.[73] The closest parallel in the OT is Exod 32:20, where a similar ordeal may be implied when Moses makes the Israelites drink water mixed with powder from the destroyed golden calf. Perhaps the drinking of this mixture determined who would be killed by the Levites (Exod 32:25-29).

Tikva Frymer-Kensky questions whether Num 5:11-31 should be categorized as a trial by ordeal. She notes that the trial by ordeal includes two important features: The god's decision is manifested immediately, and the result of the ordeal is not the penalty for offense, requiring that the society execute judgment. Numbers 5:11-31 departs from both of these features. The divine decision is not immediately known at the end of the ritual, and the execution of judgment is reserved for God alone.[74] The second point is made explicit in v. 31, which states that the "woman shall bear

68. *BDB,* 598a; and G. R. Driver, "Two Problems in the Old Testament Examined in the Light of Assyriology," *Syria* 33 (1956) 73-77.

69. H. B. Brichto, "The Case of the SOTA and a Reconsideration of Biblical 'Law,'" *HUCA* 46 (1975) 66-67.

70. Martin Noth, *Numbers,* OTL (Philadelphia: Westminster, 1968) 48-49.

71. Jacob Milgrom, *Numbers,* JPS Torah Commentary (Philadelphia: JPS, 1990) 350-54.

72. James H. Charlesworth, ed. *Ancient Near Eastern Texts* (New York: Doubleday, 1985) 2:166.

73. Ibid., par. 130-31, 171.

74. T. Frymer-Kensky, "The Strange Case of the Suspected Sotah (Numbers V 11-31)," *VT* 34 (1984) 24.

her iniquity." The Hebrew of "to bear iniquity" (נשׂא את-עונה *nāśā’ ’et-‘ăwōnāh*) means that any punishment must come from God and not from the husband or the larger society, thus protecting the woman, to a certain degree, from her husband's jealousy.

The drinking of a magical potion certainly provides a strong parallel to the trial by ordeal. The differences highlighted by Frymer-Kensky, however, are significant. At the very least, they accentuate the theological aim of the priestly writers to address the danger of defilement to the camp, which in the end must be determined by God alone, and not by the people.

6:1-21. These verses describe the Nazirite. The name "Nazirite" comes from the Hebrew verb נזר (*nāzar*), meaning "to separate." Verse 3 states that a Nazirite is potentially any woman or man from the congregation who makes a vow to be separate or dedicated to God for a period of time. The act of vowing is described with the Hebrew פלא (*pālā’*). When used in conjunction with the word "vow" (נדר *neder*), it means simply "to fulfill a vow." The verb may indicate the need for an explicit statement by the person making the vow. Martin Noth thought that the verb also expressed an extraordinary pledge to God, since the verb can also mean something marvelous.[75] The consequence of such a vow was certainly special ordination. It resulted in lay Israelites' achieving a holy status. This special relationship between God and humans is the last to be explored in Numbers 5–6.

The holy status of Nazirites means that such persons are divine property during the period of their vow. They are separated out for God. The holy state of Nazirites may exceed that of regular priests. Nazirites occasion a third type of relationship that, if broken, would defile the camp. The purpose of priestly writers in these verses is to address potential problems of defilement that might arise in conjunction with the Nazirite vow. The particular details of the vow and the circumstances under which someone becomes a permanent Nazirite (e.g., Samson or Samuel) are not mentioned. Instead, vv. 1-8 provide enough conditions for addressing two potential situations of defilement. The first concerns accidental contamination from a corpse (vv. 9-12). Exposure to a dead family member, for example, contaminates a Nazirite, rendering such a person unable to fulfill the vow. The second (vv. 13-20) is guidelines for ending the vow and thus leaving the holy state of a Nazirite. The unit closes with a summary in v. 21.

Verses 1-8 describe the requirements for temporary Nazirite vows. Three restrictions characterize Nazirites during the period of their vow.

First, Nazirites cannot consume wine or any grape products, including raisins (vv. 3-4). The rationale for this prohibition is not given. George Buchanan Gray has suggested that abstinence from grape products represents a rejection of the settled agricultural life represented by Canaanite culture.[76] The story of the drunkenness of Noah (Gen 9:18-29) reflects a similar suspicion of Canaanite civilization. A rejection of agrarian culture in the Nazirite vow may be intended to symbolize intensified dependence on God.

Second, Nazirites cannot cut their hair during the period of the vow (v. 5). The story of the Nazirite Samson (Judges 13–16) illustrates how hair symbolizes strength. Refraining from cutting the hair during the period of the vow and offering it in sacrifice during the closing ritual (Num 6:18) most likely symbolizes the Nazirites' total dedication to God during their vow.

Third, the Nazirite cannot touch a corpse (v. 6), because the Nazirite is holy during the period of the vow. Holiness and death are incompatible. Nazirites would lose their state of holiness through contact with a corpse. The Nazirite vow takes precedence over all other relationships, including family. The Nazirite, therefore, is forbidden even to attend the funeral of a parent or sibling (vv. 7-8).

Once the requirements of the Nazirite vow are spelled out in vv. 1-8, the remainder of the text explores the dangers of defilement to those who undertake the vow. Verses 9-12 focus on cleansing from accidental defilement. Verses 13-20 outline proper procedures for ending the vow.

The cultic instructions in vv. 9-12 address the problem of corpse contamination to a Nazirite. Exposure to a corpse defiles a Nazirite, making him or her unable to fulfill the vow. The obligation of the vow remains in place, requiring the Nazirite to repeat the period of consecration.

---

75. Noth, *Numbers,* 55.

76. George Buchanan Gray, *Numbers,* ICC (Edinburgh: T. & T. Clark, 1903) 61-63.

Verses 9-12 are aimed at decontaminating both the sanctuary and the Nazirite, so that the person could begin the vow anew and thus fulfill the obligation to God. The text states that a contaminated Nazirite must undergo a seven-day period of purification, at the end of which his or her hair must be shaved (v. 9). On the eighth day, two turtle doves or pigeons are presented to the priest for sacrifice at the door of the tent of meeting (vv. 10-11). The first sacrifice is a sin offering, which purges the sanctuary from pollution. The second is a burnt offering, which may invoke divine presence. After rededication, the Nazirite presents a guilt offering of a one-year-old male lamb for expiation for the broken vow. Then the vow begins anew (v. 12).

A second situation in which Nazirites are vulnerable to defilement is the ending of their vow. Verses 13-20 outline the proper ritual for avoiding contamination when leaving the holy state of the Nazirite. The location of the rite is the door of the tent of meeting (v. 13). A complex series of sacrifices is required, including a burnt offering, a sin offering, an offering of well-being, and grain and drink offerings (vv. 14-15). The question arises as to why such a complex ritual is required and, more precisely, why a sin offering is necessary at the close of the period of the vow. Jacob Milgrom, who cites the medieval commentator Ramban (1194–1270 CE), is most likely correct that "self-removal from the sacred to the profane realm requires sacrificial expiation."[77] During the sacrifice, the consecrated hair of the Nazirite was shaved and destroyed in the fire to ensure that it not become the cause of some future defilement (v. 18). The priestly portion of the sacrifice is described in vv. 19-20; the unit ends by stating that after the ritual, the Nazirite can again drink wine.

6:22-27. A priestly blessing on the congregation closes the section on camp defilement in Numbers 5–6. The blessing in vv. 24-26 has been woven into its present framework (vv. 22-23, 27).

The act of blessing is deeply rooted in Israelite culture. It bears a wide range of meaning. On the one hand, Jacob's stealing of Esau's blessing and the latter's inability to acquire another from his father, Isaac (Gen 27:30-38), provides a glimpse into the near magical power of blessing. In that story, to bless is to bestow power for fertility and well-being, which, once spoken, takes on a life of its own. On the other hand, the expression of divine blessing appears to be no more than a stereotypical exchange for "Hello." The book of Ruth provides an example of how the invocation of divine blessing was part of the everyday language of greeting, for example, when the harvesters welcome Boaz with the words, "The LORD bless you" (Ruth 2:4).

The cultic use of divine blessing, as in vv. 24-26, functions someplace between the two examples noted above. The cultic use of the priestly blessing was widespread by the late monarchical period. Similar cultic language is richly attested in other liturgical literature. Psalm 129:8, for example, concludes with a priestly blessing on the worshipers, "The blessing of the LORD be upon you. We bless you in the name of the LORD" (see also Pss 128:5; 133:3; 134:3). The Hebrew inscription "the LORD bless you and keep you and be with you" was found on a jar at Kuntillet 'Ajrud in the upper Sinai, dating from the eighth-century BCE. This inscription indicates the use of a blessing very similar to Num 5:24-26 already in the middle of the monarchical period. The discovery of the priestly blessing in a burial cave in the area of Jerusalem known as the Valley of Hinnom (contemporary Keteph Hinnom) is even more striking. The blessing is written on two silver amulets that date from the late seventh century BCE. An amulet is an object believed to give magical powers of protection against evil to the one who wears it. The discovery of such an amulet in a grave raises further questions of whether the priestly blessing was meant to function in association with the dead. Baruch Levine suggests that the priestly blessing may have protected the dead on their way to Sheol.[78]

The priestly blessing has a simple structure, consisting of three lines, each of which contains two verbs: bless-keep (protect), shine-grace, lift-peace. The name "Yahweh" appears once in each line, in association with the first of the paired verbs.

Yahweh bless you and keep you;
Yahweh make his face to shine upon you
    and be gracious to you;
Yahweh lift up his countenance upon you—
    and give you peace

---

77. Milgrom, *Numbers,* 48.

78. Levine, *Numbers,* 236-44, esp. 242-43.

Two readings are possible from this structure. The six verbs could be interpreted to describe distinct actions of God. They can also be interpreted in pairs. The first verb in each line summarizes an activity of God upon the worshiper, and the second describes the results of God's actions. The use of the name "Yahweh" as the subject for only the first verb in each sentence favors the interpretation in which the verbs are paired.[79] The result is a threefold blessing. The first emphasizes concrete gifts—blessing and security (guarding). The second stresses the hope that God will be well disposed toward the person (to lighten or shine upon the worshiper) and thus temper judgment with mercy (to be gracious). The third asserts that God will pay attention (lift his face), thus providing fullness of life (peace). David Noel Freedman notes a variety of subtle stylistic devices in the Hebrew that aid in carrying out the meaning of the priestly blessing. These include a progression in the numbers of words (3, 5, 7) and consonants (15, 20, 25) in each line. The progression is framed by an opening ("The LORD bless you") and a closing ("and give you peace") cola of the same length (7 syllables in Hebrew).[80]

Numbers 6:22-23, 27 frames the priestly blessing within the context of Numbers 5–6. These verses take the form of divine instruction for the Aaronide priesthood. Numbers 6:22-23 indicate that the blessing is meant to function as a concluding benediction (vv. 22-23) to the instruction for camp purity in chaps. 5–6. Numbers 6:27 clarifies that it is God (rather than the priests) who blesses Israel.

The literary setting has puzzled scholars,[81] prompting some even to suggest that the text has been displaced from Lev 9:22, where Aaron is also described as blessing the people from the door of the tent of meeting.[82] But the function of the blessing as a concluding benediction on the camp and the congregation does correspond to other cultic uses of the priestly blessing in the Psalms (e.g., Psalm 129), suggesting that its present context is less arbitrary than many have suspected.

The overall design of Numbers 5–6 provides additional guidelines for interpreting the priestly blessing in its present context. The placement of the priestly benediction at the door of the tent of meeting follows naturally upon the inward movement of the laws of defilement. These laws began with contamination requiring expulsion from the camp (5:1-4), followed by three types of relationships within the camp with the power to defile. These relationships moved in an ever-closer orbit to the tabernacle at the center of the camp—from defrauding in general (5:5-10), to adultery (5:11-31), and through to the Nazirite vow (6:1-21). The location for expiatory rituals has tended to follow the same movement. The laws of defrauding and adultery require that the offender be presented "to the priest" (5:9, 15), while the defiled Nazirite must go "to the door of the tent of meeting" (6:10, 13). The door of the tent of meeting is also the location for the priestly blessing on the congregation (see Lev 9:22).

The priestly blessing has at least two functions in its present literary context. It provides yet another safeguard against defilement by blanketing the camp with the power of divine blessing. It also concludes Numbers 5–6 with a description of the ideal camp. The ideal is where God pays particular attention to persons, where blessing and security drive out the power of death, and where the achievement of wholeness and peace is possible.

79. P. D. Miller, Jr., "The Blessing of God," *Int.* 29 (1975) 240-51.
80. D. N. Freedman, "The Aaronic Benedictions," in *No Famine in the Land,* ed. J. W. Flanagan (Missoula, Mont.: Scholars Press, 1975) 411-42.
81. See, e.g., Milgrom, *Numbers,* 51.

82. Gray, *Numbers,* 71.

REFLECTIONS

1. The priestly writers encourage us to reflect theologically on the role of the church in health care. Medical care in modern society is increasingly separated from the life of faith. Doctors operate and prescribe medicine to combat disease. Ministers support the emotional needs of the family and the patient. We acknowledge the importance of both for human health, but the vocations are clearly separated between the physical and the spiritual. The priestly writers would have a difficult time understanding our clear separation of roles. Religion and health are more closely interwoven in their worldview. Their starting point in Numbers 5–6 is God as the source of both physical and moral health. Thus religious laws of defilement embrace both bodily and social diseases. Both are signs of death equally opposed by God.

What would it mean to translate the priestly worldview into our life? Their teaching on social defilement is not all that different from our own. We understand the power of social disease in the contemporary church. We employ the power of God to combat violence, greed, racism, the breakdown of the family, and many other illnesses that plague our society. And we expect God to bring about social change. Our expectations for God are less concrete when we shift from social to physical disease. The priestly teaching on physical defilement and the role of God in healing is more of a challenge. Yet their view of holiness requires that the church be actively involved in health care.

Employing the power of God to combat physical disease does not put the church in opposition to any other form of medical care. Cancer treatment requires operations and chemotherapy. But priestly writers would say that the church also has its own medicine to combat illness. And the New Testament witness to Jesus supports them. Jesus was a healer. It is one of the few things that both his followers and his opponents could agree about (Mark 4:20-27). This power is passed on to his followers. The sacraments of the church are a repository of Jesus' healing power. The water of baptism makes us new. The blood and body of Jesus flow in our veins through communion. These sacraments are resources for health to be dispensed freely by the church. Many churches have additional rituals of healing, some involving oil. The priestly writers infuse all dimensions of life with holiness. They encourage us to combat social and physical disease with the same expectation of change. Racism and cancer are both signs of death equally opposed by God.

2. The priestly laws of defilement are aimed at creating a healthy community. The details of their laws do not apply to the modern world. Skin diseases, semen, menstrual discharges, and contact with the dead are not the significant points to communicate when teaching Numbers 5–6. Two principles are important for healthy community. First, laws of defilement are universal to the human condition. They are not aimed at certain classes of people or races. All persons are liable for defilement. Second, the laws of defilement are inclusive in their intent. They are aimed at keeping people in the camp within the sphere of holiness, and not driving them away. Disease is identified so that it can be cured. It is not used to exclude anyone. This is especially evident with the laws of defilement within the camp (Num 5:5–6:21). They are aimed at restoration, not expulsion. It is also true with the laws requiring a person to leave the camp (Num 5:1-4). The larger body of priestly law includes rituals for reentry into the camp for those who have suffered skin disease (Leviticus 13–14), those who have had bodily discharges (Leviticus 15), and those who have been contaminated from contact with a corpse (Numbers 19). A healthy community has God at its center, cares equally for each member, and is socially inclusive.

3. The ritual ordeal of the suspected adulteress (Num 5:11-31) confronts the contemporary reader with a host of obstacles for interpretation. Much of the language of the text is no longer clear even to experts. The role of magic in the trial by ordeal is foreign to contemporary religious practice, and the unequal treatment of a husband and a wife regarding fidelity in marriage is viewed as unjust in contemporary society. Thus Numbers 5–6 forces the reader to think clearly about principles of interpretation. The central task is to determine how Scripture that is historically specific can function authoritatively for a contemporary reader, to whom the text may not only be unclear in its details, but even immoral in its prescribed practice as well.

The starting point for teaching this text is the association of adultery with sacrilege in Num 5:12. As noted in the commentary, the phrase "to break faith with" indicates that God is the offended party. Thus, even though the husband brings the woman to the priest in a "spirit of jealousy" (Num

5:13-15), the ordeal focuses on God and the woman, not the husband. Jealousy on the part of a wife is not mentioned. The limited focus on the husband's jealousy reflects the patriarchal society of ancient Israel. The priestly writers most likely shared the belief that sexual activity of a woman is an offense against the man, whether it be the woman's father or her husband (Deut 22:13-29).

Tikva Frymer-Kensky may be correct that the shift in focus from husband to God as judge is meant to protect the woman from her husband's jealousy in a patriarchal society. The principle underlying the ritual is that the accused is innocent until proven otherwise by God, in spite of jealousy. The aim of the ritual is to maintain the marriage relationship in a society where men are in sole control. Our ideal of marriage departs from the priestly writers. We seek an even distribution of power between the husband and the wife. But the aim of the priestly writers—to maintain a marriage even at the moment of jealousy—remains an important principle. But their limited application to men is too narrow for us. A contemporary interpretation would expand the principle to include a "spirit of jealousy" in both the husband and the wife. The destructive power of jealousy can infect both men and women in our society in ways that priestly writers could never have imagined.

4. Drinking "the water of bitterness" presents another obstacle in the interpretation of the trial by ordeal. The ability of the priest to make a potion that releases supernatural powers borders on magic, and "magic" is a bad word in the Judeo-Christian tradition. The God of the exodus cannot be manipulated through incantations or through sorcery (Deut 18:9-14). The power of Jesus cannot be induced through divination or bought with money (Acts 8:9-25). These confessions appear to conflict with the drinking of a magical potion. Why the aura of magic in warding off defilement? What is it about holiness and defilement that forced priestly theologians to incorporate rituals that did not easily fit into their own central beliefs?

Interpretation must focus on the power of God in the ritual. The point of emphasis is not on the ability of the priest to manipulate God with the use of a potion. It is, rather, on the tangible way in which holiness infiltrates the body of the woman. The setting of the ritual as self-curse focuses only on negative consequences. The requirement that a wife invoke God to destroy her uterus because of a husband's jealousy is so offensive that we are inclined to stop the process of interpretation. The underlying rationale, however, is worthy of reflection: The ingestion of holy water has health consequences (v. 16). It is the attempt of the priestly writers to communicate the physical effects of holiness that has pushed them to the limit of their theological discourse. Christians continue to share in their uneasy quest. We, too, confess that holiness is physical and that it infiltrates our bodies through tangible sacraments of water, wine, and bread.

5. The Nazirite vow provides a model for temporary leadership that is grounded in community. The Nazirite vow is a special calling of laypersons for a designated period of time. The content of the Nazirite vow does not appear to be the central point, and the priestly writers provide no reason for undertaking the Nazirite vow. What is emphasized is that laypersons take on a special calling for a limited period of time. It is done in public, and not in private. It is official, requiring rituals of commencement and conclusion, and it has communal and life-style consequences. The Nazirite is required to separate from everyday routine. Separation is not retreat from the world; Nazirites are not hermits. They remain part of the congregation, but their holy status brings them in a closer orbit of the tabernacle at the center of the camp. The Nazirite vow is a suggestive model for laypersons in the contemporary church to commit themselves to a special ministry for a limited period of time.

6. The priestly blessing (Num 6:22-24) is the most familiar passage in Numbers 5–6. The central message of the blessing is stated in the closing Hebrew word, שלום (šālôm), translated "peace." In English, "peace" connotes the absence of war. It can also describe a state of tranquility. These meanings are also in the Hebrew. But the peace of God in the priestly blessing embraces even more aspects of life, including good health, security, inner harmony, wellness, material prosperity, and a long life. The broad and rich meaning of "peace" in the priestly blessing reinforces the role of holiness in the life of Israel to bring about both social and physical health.

It was noted in the Commentary that the priestly blessing provides an ideal vision of the camp and that it functions as a conclusion to the laws of defilement in Numbers 5–6. The ideal of the priestly blessing continues in contemporary Jewish and Christian worship. It is included in most lectionary cycles as a topic for preaching. The blessing of God also continues to be the last word in many of our Sunday liturgies as a closing benediction.

The central task in preaching this text is to explore what blessing means. Is the bestowal of a blessing sacramental, or is it no more than a socially polite activity? What is it that we recieve at the close of a worship service? Is real divine power transmitted in blessing, or is the preacher simply telling us that the worship service is nearly over? The latter point creates a problem for interpreting the priestly benediction. Notice how the introduction to the priestly blessing (Num 6:22-23) stresses that only priests can bless. It is not a casual activity. The conclusion (Num 6:27) indicates how close the text is to the world of magic. The author must clarify that the priest does not possess the power to bless independently of God. The need for such clarification underscores that divine blessing has independent power that can be let loose in the congregation.

NUMBERS 7:1–10:10, HOLINESS AND THE TABERNACLE

OVERVIEW

The scope of the literature narrows in 7:1–10:10 from the effects of holiness on the camp to the tabernacle at its center. The subject matter also changes from the social organization of Israel to cultic rituals associated with the care and dedication of the sanctuary. Numbers 7–8 details the dedication of the tabernacle and the Levites. Numbers 9:1–10:10 describes the celebration of Passover and an account of theophany in the tabernacle, which prepares Israel for the wilderness march.

Numbers 7–8 progresses from rituals of dedication outside of the tabernacle (7:2-88) to divine instruction inside (7:89–8:26). In the first scene, leaders from each tribe present gifts at the altar in front of the tabernacle. The second scene takes place inside the tabernacle. It includes instruction for the lighting of the menorah and the duties of the Levites. The two parts are linked by the account of Moses entering the sanctuary to receive revelation from God (7:89).

Numbers 9:1–10:10 addresses cultic matters that prepare Israel for its wilderness march. The section opens with Passover instruction in 9:1-14.

The instructions include special provisions to postpone the feast for those unable to celebrate it at the appointed time. Numbers 9:15-23 is an account of theophany in the tabernacle. The section also includes a description of how the cloud will lead Israel on its wilderness journey. Numbers 10:1-10 concludes the section by describing the trumpets associated with the tabernacle and their use. They organize Israel for marching in the wilderness and for waging holy war in the land of Canaan.

The tabernacle is the center of focus throughout Numbers 7:1–10:10. Its significance is described in two ways: by its location in the camp and by its function in Israel's wilderness journey. The placement of the tabernacle at the center of the camp symbolizes its important role in Israel's cultic and communal life. The theophany to Moses indicates that the tabernacle is the location where God dwells. Rituals associated with the tabernacle explore its significance in Israel's history of salvation. The Passover provides a point of continuity with the past by underscoring how the God in the tabernacle is the Savior of the exodus. The cloud probes the significance of the sanctuary in Israel's present life as a guide in the wilderness. The trumpets also probe the present significance of the tabernacle when they are used to organize Israel for journeying in the wilderness. They also point to the future in their role of calling Israel to holy war in the promised land.

Numbers 7:1–8:26, The Dedication of the Tabernacle and the Levites

NIV

7 When Moses finished setting up the tabernacle, he anointed it and consecrated it and all its furnishings. He also anointed and consecrated the altar and all its utensils. [2]Then the leaders of Israel, the heads of families who were the tribal leaders in charge of those who were counted, made offerings. [3]They brought as their gifts before the LORD six covered carts and twelve oxen—an ox from each leader and a cart from every two. These they presented before the tabernacle.

[4]The LORD said to Moses, [5]"Accept these from them, that they may be used in the work at the Tent of Meeting. Give them to the Levites as each man's work requires."

[6]So Moses took the carts and oxen and gave them to the Levites. [7]He gave two carts and four oxen to the Gershonites, as their work required, [8]and he gave four carts and eight oxen to the Merarites, as their work required. They were all under the direction of Ithamar son of Aaron, the priest. [9]But Moses did not give any to the Kohathites, because they were to carry on their shoulders the holy things, for which they were responsible.

[10]When the altar was anointed, the leaders brought their offerings for its dedication and presented them before the altar. [11]For the LORD had said to Moses, "Each day one leader is to bring his offering for the dedication of the altar."

[12]The one who brought his offering on the first day was Nahshon son of Amminadab of the tribe of Judah.

[13]His offering was one silver plate weighing a hundred and thirty shekels,[a] and one silver sprinkling bowl weighing seventy shekels,[b]

[a]13 That is, about 3 1/4 pounds (about 1.5 kilograms); also elsewhere in this chapter   [b]13 That is, about 1 3/4 pounds (about 0.8 kilogram); also elsewhere in this chapter

NRSV

7 On the day when Moses had finished setting up the tabernacle, and had anointed and consecrated it with all its furnishings, and had anointed and consecrated the altar with all its utensils, [2]the leaders of Israel, heads of their ancestral houses, the leaders of the tribes, who were over those who were enrolled, made offerings. [3]They brought their offerings before the LORD, six covered wagons and twelve oxen, a wagon for every two of the leaders, and for each one an ox; they presented them before the tabernacle. [4]Then the LORD said to Moses: [5]Accept these from them, that they may be used in doing the service of the tent of meeting, and give them to the Levites, to each according to his service. [6]So Moses took the wagons and the oxen, and gave them to the Levites. [7]Two wagons and four oxen he gave to the Gershonites, according to their service; [8]and four wagons and eight oxen he gave to the Merarites, according to their service, under the direction of Ithamar son of Aaron the priest. [9]But to the Kohathites he gave none, because they were charged with the care of the holy things that had to be carried on the shoulders.

[10]The leaders also presented offerings for the dedication of the altar at the time when it was anointed; the leaders presented their offering before the altar. [11]The LORD said to Moses: They shall present their offerings, one leader each day, for the dedication of the altar.

[12]The one who presented his offering the first day was Nahshon son of Amminadab, of the tribe of Judah; [13]his offering was one silver plate weighing one hundred thirty shekels, one silver basin weighing seventy shekels, according to the shekel of the sanctuary, both of them full of choice flour mixed with oil for a grain offering; [14]one golden dish weighing ten shekels, full of incense; [15]one young bull, one ram, one male lamb a year old,

both according to the sanctuary shekel, each filled with fine flour mixed with oil as a grain offering; [14]one gold dish weighing ten shekels,[a] filled with incense; [15]one young bull, one ram and one male lamb a year old, for a burnt offering; [16]one male goat for a sin offering; [17]and two oxen, five rams, five male goats and five male lambs a year old, to be sacrificed as a fellowship offering.[b] This was the offering of Nahshon son of Amminadab.

[18]On the second day Nethanel son of Zuar, the leader of Issachar, brought his offering.

[19]The offering he brought was one silver plate weighing a hundred and thirty shekels, and one silver sprinkling bowl weighing seventy shekels, both according to the sanctuary shekel, each filled with fine flour mixed with oil as a grain offering; [20]one gold dish weighing ten shekels, filled with incense; [21]one young bull, one ram and one male lamb a year old, for a burnt offering; [22]one male goat for a sin offering; [23]and two oxen, five rams, five male goats and five male lambs a year old, to be sacrificed as a fellowship offering. This was the offering of Nethanel son of Zuar.

[24]On the third day, Eliab son of Helon, the leader of the people of Zebulun, brought his offering.

[25]His offering was one silver plate weighing a hundred and thirty shekels, and one silver sprinkling bowl weighing seventy shekels, both according to the sanctuary shekel, each filled with fine flour mixed with oil as a grain offering; [26]one gold dish weighing ten shekels, filled with incense; [27]one young bull, one ram and one male lamb a year old, for a burnt offering; [28]one male goat for a sin offering; [29]and two oxen, five rams, five male goats and five male lambs a year old, to be sacrificed as a fellowship offering. This was the offering of Eliab son of Helon.

[30]On the fourth day Elizur son of Shedeur, the leader of the people of Reuben, brought his offering.

[31]His offering was one silver plate weighing a hundred and thirty shekels, and one silver

a14 That is, about 4 ounces (about 110 grams); also elsewhere in this chapter   b17 Traditionally *peace offering;* also elsewhere in this chapter

for a burnt offering; [16]one male goat for a sin offering; [17]and for the sacrifice of well-being, two oxen, five rams, five male goats, and five male lambs a year old. This was the offering of Nahshon son of Amminadab.

[18]On the second day Nethanel son of Zuar, the leader of Issachar, presented an offering; [19]he presented for his offering one silver plate weighing one hundred thirty shekels, one silver basin weighing seventy shekels, according to the shekel of the sanctuary, both of them full of choice flour mixed with oil for a grain offering; [20]one golden dish weighing ten shekels, full of incense; [21]one young bull, one ram, one male lamb a year old, as a burnt offering; [22]one male goat as a sin offering; [23]and for the sacrifice of well-being, two oxen, five rams, five male goats, and five male lambs a year old. This was the offering of Nethanel son of Zuar.

[24]On the third day Eliab son of Helon, the leader of the Zebulunites: [25]his offering was one silver plate weighing one hundred thirty shekels, one silver basin weighing seventy shekels, according to the shekel of the sanctuary, both of them full of choice flour mixed with oil for a grain offering; [26]one golden dish weighing ten shekels, full of incense; [27]one young bull, one ram, one male lamb a year old, for a burnt offering; [28]one male goat for a sin offering; [29]and for the sacrifice of well-being, two oxen, five rams, five male goats, and five male lambs a year old. This was the offering of Eliab son of Helon.

[30]On the fourth day Elizur son of Shedeur, the leader of the Reubenites: [31]his offering was one silver plate weighing one hundred thirty shekels, one silver basin weighing seventy shekels, according to the shekel of the sanctuary, both of them full of choice flour mixed with oil for a grain offering; [32]one golden dish weighing ten shekels, full of incense; [33]one young bull, one ram, one male lamb a year old, for a burnt offering; [34]one male goat for a sin offering; [35]and for the sacrifice of well-being, two oxen, five rams, five male goats, and five male lambs a year old. This was the offering of Elizur son of Shedeur.

[36]On the fifth day Shelumiel son of Zurishaddai, the leader of the Simeonites: [37]his offering was one silver plate weighing one hundred thirty

NIV

sprinkling bowl weighing seventy shekels, both according to the sanctuary shekel, each filled with fine flour mixed with oil as a grain offering; ³²one gold dish weighing ten shekels, filled with incense; ³³one young bull, one ram and one male lamb a year old, for a burnt offering; ³⁴one male goat for a sin offering; ³⁵and two oxen, five rams, five male goats and five male lambs a year old, to be sacrificed as a fellowship offering. This was the offering of Elizur son of Shedeur.

³⁶On the fifth day Shelumiel son of Zurishaddai, the leader of the people of Simeon, brought his offering.

³⁷His offering was one silver plate weighing a hundred and thirty shekels, and one silver sprinkling bowl weighing seventy shekels, both according to the sanctuary shekel, each filled with fine flour mixed with oil as a grain offering; ³⁸one gold dish weighing ten shekels, filled with incense; ³⁹one young bull, one ram and one male lamb a year old, for a burnt offering; ⁴⁰one male goat for a sin offering; ⁴¹and two oxen, five rams, five male goats and five male lambs a year old, to be sacrificed as a fellowship offering. This was the offering of Shelumiel son of Zurishaddai.

⁴²On the sixth day Eliasaph son of Deuel, the leader of the people of Gad, brought his offering.

⁴³His offering was one silver plate weighing a hundred and thirty shekels, and one silver sprinkling bowl weighing seventy shekels, both according to the sanctuary shekel, each filled with fine flour mixed with oil as a grain offering; ⁴⁴one gold dish weighing ten shekels, filled with incense; ⁴⁵one young bull, one ram and one male lamb a year old, for a burnt offering; ⁴⁶one male goat for a sin offering; ⁴⁷and two oxen, five rams, five male goats and five male lambs a year old, to be sacrificed as a fellowship offering. This was the offering of Eliasaph son of Deuel.

⁴⁸On the seventh day Elishama son of Ammihud, the leader of the people of Ephraim, brought his offering.

⁴⁹His offering was one silver plate weighing a hundred and thirty shekels, and one silver sprinkling bowl weighing seventy shekels,

NRSV

shekels, one silver basin weighing seventy shekels, according to the shekel of the sanctuary, both of them full of choice flour mixed with oil for a grain offering; ³⁸one golden dish weighing ten shekels, full of incense; ³⁹one young bull, one ram, one male lamb a year old, for a burnt offering; ⁴⁰one male goat for a sin offering; ⁴¹and for the sacrifice of well-being, two oxen, five rams, five male goats, and five male lambs a year old. This was the offering of Shelumiel son of Zurishaddai.

⁴²On the sixth day Eliasaph son of Deuel, the leader of the Gadites: ⁴³his offering was one silver plate weighing one hundred thirty shekels, one silver basin weighing seventy shekels, according to the shekel of the sanctuary, both of them full of choice flour mixed with oil for a grain offering; ⁴⁴one golden dish weighing ten shekels, full of incense; ⁴⁵one young bull, one ram, one male lamb a year old, for a burnt offering; ⁴⁶one male goat for a sin offering; ⁴⁷and for the sacrifice of well-being, two oxen, five rams, five male goats, and five male lambs a year old. This was the offering of Eliasaph son of Deuel.

⁴⁸On the seventh day Elishama son of Ammihud, the leader of the Ephraimites: ⁴⁹his offering was one silver plate weighing one hundred thirty shekels, one silver basin weighing seventy shekels, according to the shekel of the sanctuary, both of them full of choice flour mixed with oil for a grain offering; ⁵⁰one golden dish weighing ten shekels, full of incense; ⁵¹one young bull, one ram, one male lamb a year old, for a burnt offering; ⁵²one male goat for a sin offering; ⁵³and for the sacrifice of well-being, two oxen, five rams, five male goats, and five male lambs a year old. This was the offering of Elishama son of Ammihud.

⁵⁴On the eighth day Gamaliel son of Pedahzur, the leader of the Manassites: ⁵⁵his offering was one silver plate weighing one hundred thirty shekels, one silver basin weighing seventy shekels, according to the shekel of the sanctuary, both of them full of choice flour mixed with oil for a grain offering; ⁵⁶one golden dish weighing ten shekels, full of incense; ⁵⁷one young bull, one ram, one male lamb a year old, for a burnt offering; ⁵⁸one male goat for a sin offering; ⁵⁹and for the sacrifice of well-being, two oxen, five rams, five male

both according to the sanctuary shekel, each filled with fine flour mixed with oil as a grain offering; [50]one gold dish weighing ten shekels, filled with incense; [51]one young bull, one ram and one male lamb a year old, for a burnt offering; [52]one male goat for a sin offering; [53]and two oxen, five rams, five male goats and five male lambs a year old, to be sacrificed as a fellowship offering. This was the offering of Elishama son of Ammihud.

[54]On the eighth day Gamaliel son of Pedahzur, the leader of the people of Manasseh, brought his offering.

[55]His offering was one silver plate weighing a hundred and thirty shekels, and one silver sprinkling bowl weighing seventy shekels, both according to the sanctuary shekel, each filled with fine flour mixed with oil as a grain offering; [56]one gold dish weighing ten shekels, filled with incense; [57]one young bull, one ram and one male lamb a year old, for a burnt offering; [58]one male goat for a sin offering; [59]and two oxen, five rams, five male goats and five male lambs a year old, to be sacrificed as a fellowship offering. This was the offering of Gamaliel son of Pedahzur.

[60]On the ninth day Abidan son of Gideoni, the leader of the people of Benjamin, brought his offering.

[61]His offering was one silver plate weighing a hundred and thirty shekels, and one silver sprinkling bowl weighing seventy shekels, both according to the sanctuary shekel, each filled with fine flour mixed with oil as a grain offering; [62]one gold dish weighing ten shekels, filled with incense; [63]one young bull, one ram and one male lamb a year old, for a burnt offering; [64]one male goat for a sin offering; [65]and two oxen, five rams, five male goats and five male lambs a year old, to be sacrificed as a fellowship offering. This was the offering of Abidan son of Gideoni.

[66]On the tenth day Ahiezer son of Ammishaddai, the leader of the people of Dan, brought his offering.

[67]His offering was one silver plate weighing a hundred and thirty shekels, and one silver sprinkling bowl weighing seventy shekels,

goats, and five male lambs a year old. This was the offering of Gamaliel son of Pedahzur.

[60]On the ninth day Abidan son of Gideoni, the leader of the Benjaminites: [61]his offering was one silver plate weighing one hundred thirty shekels, one silver basin weighing seventy shekels, according to the shekel of the sanctuary, both of them full of choice flour mixed with oil for a grain offering; [62]one golden dish weighing ten shekels, full of incense; [63]one young bull, one ram, one male lamb a year old, for a burnt offering; [64]one male goat for a sin offering; [65]and for the sacrifice of well-being, two oxen, five rams, five male goats, and five male lambs a year old. This was the offering of Abidan son of Gideoni.

[66]On the tenth day Ahiezer son of Ammishaddai, the leader of the Danites: [67]his offering was one silver plate weighing one hundred thirty shekels, one silver basin weighing seventy shekels, according to the shekel of the sanctuary, both of them full of choice flour mixed with oil for a grain offering; [68]one golden dish weighing ten shekels, full of incense; [69]one young bull, one ram, one male lamb a year old, for a burnt offering; [70]one male goat for a sin offering; [71]and for the sacrifice of well-being, two oxen, five rams, five male goats, and five male lambs a year old. This was the offering of Ahiezer son of Ammishaddai.

[72]On the eleventh day Pagiel son of Ochran, the leader of the Asherites: [73]his offering was one silver plate weighing one hundred thirty shekels, one silver basin weighing seventy shekels, according to the shekel of the sanctuary, both of them full of choice flour mixed with oil for a grain offering; [74]one golden dish weighing ten shekels, full of incense; [75]one young bull, one ram, one male lamb a year old, for a burnt offering; [76]one male goat for a sin offering; [77]and for the sacrifice of well-being, two oxen, five rams, five male goats, and five male lambs a year old. This was the offering of Pagiel son of Ochran.

[78]On the twelfth day Ahira son of Enan, the leader of the Naphtalites: [79]his offering was one silver plate weighing one hundred thirty shekels, one silver basin weighing seventy shekels, according to the shekel of the sanctuary, both of them full of choice flour mixed with oil for a grain offering; [80]one golden dish weighing ten shekels,

NIV

both according to the sanctuary shekel, each filled with fine flour mixed with oil as a grain offering; ⁶⁸one gold dish weighing ten shekels, filled with incense; ⁶⁹one young bull, one ram and one male lamb a year old, for a burnt offering; ⁷⁰one male goat for a sin offering; ⁷¹and two oxen, five rams, five male goats and five male lambs a year old, to be sacrificed as a fellowship offering. This was the offering of Ahiezer son of Ammishaddai.

⁷²On the eleventh day Pagiel son of Ocran, the leader of the people of Asher, brought his offering. ⁷³His offering was one silver plate weighing a hundred and thirty shekels, and one silver sprinkling bowl weighing seventy shekels, both according to the sanctuary shekel, each filled with fine flour mixed with oil as a grain offering; ⁷⁴one gold dish weighing ten shekels, filled with incense; ⁷⁵one young bull, one ram and one male lamb a year old, for a burnt offering; ⁷⁶one male goat for a sin offering; ⁷⁷and two oxen, five rams, five male goats and five male lambs a year old, to be sacrificed as a fellowship offering. This was the offering of Pagiel son of Ocran.

⁷⁸On the twelfth day Ahira son of Enan, the leader of the people of Naphtali, brought his offering. ⁷⁹His offering was one silver plate weighing a hundred and thirty shekels, and one silver sprinkling bowl weighing seventy shekels, both according to the sanctuary shekel, each filled with fine flour mixed with oil as a grain offering; ⁸⁰one gold dish weighing ten shekels, filled with incense; ⁸¹one young bull, one ram and one male lamb a year old, for a burnt offering; ⁸²one male goat for a sin offering; ⁸³and two oxen, five rams, five male goats and five male lambs a year old, to be sacrificed as a fellowship offering. This was the offering of Ahira son of Enan.

⁸⁴These were the offerings of the Israelite leaders for the dedication of the altar when it was anointed: twelve silver plates, twelve silver sprinkling bowls and twelve gold dishes. ⁸⁵Each silver plate weighed a hundred and thirty shekels, and each sprinkling bowl seventy shekels. Altogether, the silver dishes weighed two thousand four hun-

NRSV

full of incense; ⁸¹one young bull, one ram, one male lamb a year old, for a burnt offering; ⁸²one male goat for a sin offering; ⁸³and for the sacrifice of well-being, two oxen, five rams, five male goats, and five male lambs a year old. This was the offering of Ahira son of Enan.

84This was the dedication offering for the altar, at the time when it was anointed, from the leaders of Israel: twelve silver plates, twelve silver basins, twelve golden dishes, ⁸⁵each silver plate weighing one hundred thirty shekels and each basin seventy, all the silver of the vessels two thousand four hundred shekels according to the shekel of the sanctuary, ⁸⁶the twelve golden dishes, full of incense, weighing ten shekels apiece according to the shekel of the sanctuary, all the gold of the dishes being one hundred twenty shekels; ⁸⁷all the livestock for the burnt offering twelve bulls, twelve rams, twelve male lambs a year old, with their grain offering; and twelve male goats for a sin offering; ⁸⁸and all the livestock for the sacrifice of well-being twenty-four bulls, the rams sixty, the male goats sixty, the male lambs a year old sixty. This was the dedication offering for the altar, after it was anointed.

89When Moses went into the tent of meeting to speak with the LORD,ᵃ he would hear the voice speaking to him from above the mercy seatᵇ that was on the ark of the covenantᶜ from between the two cherubim; thus it spoke to him.

8 The LORD spoke to Moses, saying: ²Speak to Aaron and say to him: When you set up the lamps, the seven lamps shall give light in front of the lampstand. ³Aaron did so; he set up its lamps to give light in front of the lampstand, as the LORD had commanded Moses. ⁴Now this was how the lampstand was made, out of hammered work of gold. From its base to its flowers, it was hammered work; according to the pattern that the LORD had shown Moses, so he made the lampstand.

5The LORD spoke to Moses, saying: ⁶Take the Levites from among the Israelites and cleanse them. ⁷Thus you shall do to them, to cleanse them: sprinkle the water of purification on them, have them shave their whole body with a razor and wash their clothes, and so cleanse themselves.

ᵃ Heb *him*   ᵇ Or *the cover*   ᶜ Or *treaty*, or *testimony*; Heb *eduth*

NIV

dred shekels,^a according to the sanctuary shekel. ⁸⁶The twelve gold dishes filled with incense weighed ten shekels each, according to the sanctuary shekel. Altogether, the gold dishes weighed a hundred and twenty shekels.^b ⁸⁷The total number of animals for the burnt offering came to twelve young bulls, twelve rams and twelve male lambs a year old, together with their grain offering. Twelve male goats were used for the sin offering. ⁸⁸The total number of animals for the sacrifice of the fellowship offering came to twenty-four oxen, sixty rams, sixty male goats and sixty male lambs a year old. These were the offerings for the dedication of the altar after it was anointed.

⁸⁹When Moses entered the Tent of Meeting to speak with the LORD, he heard the voice speaking to him from between the two cherubim above the atonement cover on the ark of the Testimony. And he spoke with him.

8 The LORD said to Moses, ²"Speak to Aaron and say to him, 'When you set up the seven lamps, they are to light the area in front of the lampstand.'"

³Aaron did so; he set up the lamps so that they faced forward on the lampstand, just as the LORD commanded Moses. ⁴This is how the lampstand was made: It was made of hammered gold—from its base to its blossoms. The lampstand was made exactly like the pattern the LORD had shown Moses.

⁵The LORD said to Moses: ⁶"Take the Levites from among the other Israelites and make them ceremonially clean. ⁷To purify them, do this: Sprinkle the water of cleansing on them; then have them shave their whole bodies and wash their clothes, and so purify themselves. ⁸Have them take a young bull with its grain offering of fine flour mixed with oil; then you are to take a second young bull for a sin offering. ⁹Bring the Levites to the front of the Tent of Meeting and assemble the whole Israelite community. ¹⁰You are to bring the Levites before the LORD, and the Israelites are to lay their hands on them. ¹¹Aaron is to present the Levites before the LORD as a wave

NRSV

⁸Then let them take a young bull and its grain offering of choice flour mixed with oil, and you shall take another young bull for a sin offering. ⁹You shall bring the Levites before the tent of meeting, and assemble the whole congregation of the Israelites. ¹⁰When you bring the Levites before the LORD, the Israelites shall lay their hands on the Levites, ¹¹and Aaron shall present the Levites before the LORD as an elevation offering from the Israelites, that they may do the service of the LORD. ¹²The Levites shall lay their hands on the heads of the bulls, and he shall offer the one for a sin offering and the other for a burnt offering to the LORD, to make atonement for the Levites. ¹³Then you shall have the Levites stand before Aaron and his sons, and you shall present them as an elevation offering to the LORD.

¹⁴Thus you shall separate the Levites from among the other Israelites, and the Levites shall be mine. ¹⁵Thereafter the Levites may go in to do service at the tent of meeting, once you have cleansed them and presented them as an elevation offering. ¹⁶For they are unreservedly given to me from among the Israelites; I have taken them for myself, in place of all that open the womb, the firstborn of all the Israelites. ¹⁷For all the firstborn among the Israelites are mine, both human and animal. On the day that I struck down all the firstborn in the land of Egypt I consecrated them for myself, ¹⁸but I have taken the Levites in place of all the firstborn among the Israelites. ¹⁹Moreover, I have given the Levites as a gift to Aaron and his sons from among the Israelites, to do the service for the Israelites at the tent of meeting, and to make atonement for the Israelites, in order that there may be no plague among the Israelites for coming too close to the sanctuary.

²⁰Moses and Aaron and the whole congregation of the Israelites did with the Levites accordingly; the Israelites did with the Levites just as the LORD had commanded Moses concerning them. ²¹The Levites purified themselves from sin and washed their clothes; then Aaron presented them as an elevation offering before the LORD, and Aaron made atonement for them to cleanse them. ²²Thereafter the Levites went in to do their service in the tent of meeting in attendance on Aaron

NIV

offering from the Israelites, so that they may be ready to do the work of the LORD.

¹²"After the Levites lay their hands on the heads of the bulls, use the one for a sin offering to the LORD and the other for a burnt offering, to make atonement for the Levites. ¹³Have the Levites stand in front of Aaron and his sons and then present them as a wave offering to the LORD. ¹⁴In this way you are to set the Levites apart from the other Israelites, and the Levites will be mine.

¹⁵"After you have purified the Levites and presented them as a wave offering, they are to come to do their work at the Tent of Meeting. ¹⁶They are the Israelites who are to be given wholly to me. I have taken them as my own in place of the firstborn, the first male offspring from every Israelite woman. ¹⁷Every firstborn male in Israel, whether man or animal, is mine. When I struck down all the firstborn in Egypt, I set them apart for myself. ¹⁸And I have taken the Levites in place of all the firstborn sons in Israel. ¹⁹Of all the Israelites, I have given the Levites as gifts to Aaron and his sons to do the work at the Tent of Meeting on behalf of the Israelites and to make atonement for them so that no plague will strike the Israelites when they go near the sanctuary."

²⁰Moses, Aaron and the whole Israelite community did with the Levites just as the LORD commanded Moses. ²¹The Levites purified themselves and washed their clothes. Then Aaron presented them as a wave offering before the LORD and made atonement for them to purify them. ²²After that, the Levites came to do their work at the Tent of Meeting under the supervision of Aaron and his sons. They did with the Levites just as the LORD commanded Moses.

²³The LORD said to Moses, ²⁴"This applies to the Levites: Men twenty-five years old or more shall come to take part in the work at the Tent of Meeting, ²⁵but at the age of fifty, they must retire from their regular service and work no longer. ²⁶They may assist their brothers in performing their duties at the Tent of Meeting, but they themselves must not do the work. This, then, is how you are to assign the responsibilities of the Levites."

NRSV

and his sons. As the LORD had commanded Moses concerning the Levites, so they did with them.

23The LORD spoke to Moses, saying: 24This applies to the Levites: from twenty-five years old and upward they shall begin to do duty in the service of the tent of meeting; 25and from the age of fifty years they shall retire from the duty of the service and serve no more. 26They may assist their brothers in the tent of meeting in carrying out their duties, but they shall perform no service. Thus you shall do with the Levites in assigning their duties.

COMMENTARY

Numbers 7–8 explore the role of the tabernacle. The dedication of offerings by the twelve tribes in chap. 7 highlights the tabernacle's central role among the tribes. The chapter describes the presentation of sacrificial gifts at the altar by each tribe. The interior of the tabernacle becomes the setting for the dedication of the Levites in chap. 8.

7:1. This verse provides transition from the campsite in chaps. 1–6 to the dedication of the tabernacle in 7:1–10:10. The tabernacle is dedicated twice while Israel is encamped at Mt. Sinai (Exodus 19–Numbers 10), after its initial construction (Exodus 40) and again after the organization of the camp (Numbers 7). The chronology of Exodus 19–Numbers 10 suggests that the two dedications take place at the same time. The initial dedication takes place on Month 1, Day 1 of Year 2 after the exodus (Exod 40:1, 16). It is the day that Moses "set up the tabernacle." The second dedication appears to be on the same day. Numbers 7:1 reads: "On the day when Moses had finished setting up the tabernacle. . . ."

If the two dedications are interpreted as having taken place on the same day, then chronological time is suspended during the formation of the priesthood and cult in Leviticus and the organization of the congregation and camp in Numbers 1–6. It resumes in Num 7:1 (Month 1, Day 1, Year 2), when events once again follow a clear sequence of action, with twelve days of dedication offerings (Num 7:2-88); the dedication of Levites on the thirteenth day (Num 8:5-26); Passover on the fourteenth day (Num 9:1); a special observance of Passover one month later on Month 2, Day 14, Year 2 (Num 9:11); and the departure from Mt. Sinai on Month 2, Day 20, Year 2 (Num 10:11). The framing of events in Leviticus and Numbers 1–6 with the dedication of the tabernacle may be intended to accentuate its central role in the formation of the priesthood and the camp.

The disregard of chronology from Exodus 40 through Numbers 7 has bothered both ancient and modern interpreters. The rabbis note violations of sacrifice that occur in Num 7:1-88 because of the chronological problems, including the offering by a private individual that overrides the requirements of sabbath.[83] Jacob Milgrom has offered a modern resolution to the problem by translating the phrase "on the day" (ביום *běyôm*) in Num 7:1 indefinitely as "when," so that it need not designate the same day as Exod 40:2, 16.[84]

7:2-88. Sacrifice is important throughout Numbers 7. The priestly theology of sacrifice occurs primarily in the book of Leviticus, where it becomes clear that sacrifice can mean many things in ancient Israelite religion, including a means of expiation as well as a process of gaining union with God.[85] A basic meaning of sacrifice, however, is gift, and it is this meaning of sacrifice that stands out in these verses.

Dedication offerings are central to this section. Events take place in the courtyard of the tabernacle. The offerings are spontaneous gifts from the laity, not prompted by divine command. Initial gifts concern transportation of the tabernacle (vv. 2-9). The leaders of the tribes (see Commentary on 1:1–2:34) present a general offering of six wagons and twelve oxen for transporting it. Their gifts are distributed to the Gershonite and the Merarite Levites, since they are responsible for transporting the tabernacle. Two wagons and four oxen are given to the Gershonites to carry the curtains and coverings of the tabernacle (see 4:21-28), while four wagons and eight oxen are presented to the Merarites to carry the frames and other supporting material (see 4:29-33).

Verses 10-88 are an extensive account of gifts presented by each tribal leader over a twelve-day period. The order of gift-giving follows the sequence of tribes, in which Judah is first, rather than Reuben (see Commentary on 1:1–2:34). Each tribe brings identical gifts:

Grain Offering (מנחה *minḥâ*)
1 silver plate (130 shekels in weight =
    approx. 65 ozs.)
1 silver basin (70 shekels in weight =
    approx. 35 ozs.)
(both containing choice flour and oil)

83. *Sifre Num.* 51.
84. Jacob Milgrom, *Numbers,* JPS Torah Commentary (Philadelphia: JPS, 1990) 362-64.
85. See G. A. Anderson, "Sacrifice and Sacrificial Offerings," *ABD* 5:870-86, esp. 871-73.

Incense (קטרת *qĕṭōret*)

1 gold dish (10 shekels in weight = approx 5 ozs.)

Burnt Offering (עלה *'ōlâ*)

1 bull

1 ram

1 male lamb (one year old)

Sin Offering (חטאת *ḥaṭṭā't*)

1 male goat

Well-Being Offering (שלמים *šĕlāmîm*)

2 oxen

5 rams

5 male goats

5 male lambs (one year old)

The gifts presented by each tribal leader include all the central sacrifices in priestly tradition except the guilt offering (אשם *'āšām*).

The grain offering is prescribed in Leviticus 2, and its ritual is outlined in Lev 6:14-18. Grain offerings include choice floor, with oil, frankincense, and salt of the covenant, but never leaven. A portion is offered to God as smoke on the altar, while the remainder becomes the property of the priesthood.

Incense is associated with a number of sacrifices. An altar of incense stands inside the tabernacle (Exod 30:1-10).

The burnt offering (lit., "offering of ascent") could be from the herd, the flock, or even fowl. It is described in Leviticus 1 as an offering of atonement, but such a description is never repeated in priestly literature. Levine argues that the purpose of this offering was to attract God's attention by giving a gift that is totally consumed on the altar.[86] The ritual is described in Lev 6:8-13, where it is clear that the burnt offering was a continuous offering to God.

The sin offering alleviated the guilt of specific wrongful acts by cleansing or purging a person. For this reason, Milgrom has argued that the sacrifice is better translated as the purification offering.[87] It is described in Leviticus 4, and its ritual is outlined in Lev 6:24-29.

The offering of well-being, or peace offering, emphasizes fellowship and allegiance between the worshiper and God. Humans consume the sacrifice in an atmosphere of joy and celebration.

It is described in Leviticus 3, and its rituals are outlined in Lev 7:11-36 in association with thanksgiving, votive, and freewill offerings.

The presentation of the gifts by each tribe is described with the hiphil form of the Hebrew verb קרב (*qārab*), translated "to present" or "to bring near." The verb does not clarify whether the gifts are actually sacrificed or given as resources for future sacrifice. The order of the sacrifices suggests that actual sacrifice is not taking place. Within the cult, the sin offering was usually first, since it purified the sanctuary and the worshiper for worship itself. It would then be followed by a burnt offering, in which God's readiness to respond would be tested, giving way to the sacrifice of well-being. In contrast to this expected order of sacrifices, the sin offering comes after the burnt offering in the listing of gifts by the tribal leaders. The importance of the proper ordering of the offerings is still reflected in many Christian liturgies in which the confession of sin and divine pardon leads into the proclamation of a divine word and the eucharistic banquet.

The order of sacrifices suggests that the gifts are presented to the priesthood as resources for the cult. Levine has strengthened this interpretation. He notes that the tabular format of the records in 7:2-88 conforms to the manner in which temples kept track of their holdings.[88] These verses may be an example of bookkeeping from the archives of the Temple. The content of the gifts, however, is likely intended to convey the theological point that each tribe donates equally to the maintenance of the tabernacle, regardless of the tribe's size. The section also stresses that donations are spontaneous gifts to the Temple.

7:89. The opening phrase in this verse presents a problem. The Hebrew translates, "When Moses went into the tent of meeting to speak with him. . . ." The puzzle is the pronoun "him" (אתו *'ittô*). There is no mention of the divine name to provide an antecedent for the pronoun. As a consequence, scholars have argued that the verse is a late redactional insertion.[89] Note how the NRSV has resolved this problem by changing the pronoun "him" to the proper name "the LORD."

86. B. Levine, *In the Presence of the Lord,* (Leiden: E. J. Brill, 1974) 20-27, esp. 22-27.

87. J. Milgrom, *Studies in Cultic Theology and Terminology,* ed. J. Neusner, Studies in Judaism in Late Antiquity 36 (Leiden: E. J. Brill, 1983) 67-69.

88. Baruch A. Levine, *Numbers 1–20,* AB 4A (New York: Doubleday, 1993) 264.

89. George Buchanan Gray, *Numbers,* ICC (Edinburgh: T. & T. Clark, 1903) 77.

Regardless of the transmission history of this verse, it is clear that this verse signals transition from the sacrificial gifts outside of the tabernacle (vv. 2-88) to the divine instruction to Moses inside the shrine (chap. 8). The iconography within the tabernacle and the actions of Moses communicate the priestly writer's theology of divine cultic presence. Three aspects of v. 89 require commentary: the function of the verse within Numbers 7–8; the significance of the iconography in the description of the ark; and the role of this verse in the progression of events at Mt. Sinai (Exodus 19–Numbers 10).

First, 7:89 is pivotal for interpreting the overall structure of Numbers 7–8. Once this verse is in place, the divine speeches to Moses (8:1, 8, 23) concerning the menorah and the Levites acquire a more specific location within the tabernacle/tent of meeting. Change of location signals a new topic: from the tribal gifts (7:2-88) to rituals within the tabernacle and the divine claim on Levites as substitutes for Israelite firstborn (chap. 8). This claim separates Levites from the congregation, allowing them to approach the tabernacle as guardians of the shrine.

Second, the description of how God spoke with Moses in v. 89 is rich in priestly iconography. The priestly writers use visual imagery to communicate the presence of God. The fire of the כבוד יהוה (kĕbôd YHWH) is a central symbol for the presence of God throughout the revelation at Mt. Sinai (Exod 24:15-18; 40:34-35; Lev 9:23-24). But there are no representations or statues of God in the priestly tabernacle. Explicit statues of Yahweh would constitute idolatry for the priestly writers. Thus there is only a divine voice in the tabernacle.

The voice of God is located between the two cherubim that frame the mercy seat, which forms the top of the ark of the congregation. "Cover" is a more accurate translation than "mercy seat" for the Hebrew כפרת (kappōret). The translation "mercy seat" may derive from the rite of atonement that takes place at the ark (Leviticus 16). The name for the ark as "ark of the congregation" is distinctive to the priestly writers, who also identify the people of Israel as the "congregation" (4:5; Exod 25:22; 26:33, 34). The Hebrew העדת (hā'ēdut) signifies that Israel is a people in covenant with God. Thus the NRSV translates the Hebrew phrase ארן העדת ('ărōn hā'ēdut) as "ark

of the covenant," instead of "ark of the congregation" (NIV, "ark of the Testimony").

The iconography in the tabernacle is not an invention of the priestly writers. These objects were important in Israel's worship throughout the monarchical period. The priestly writers have reinterpreted the cherubim and the ark from the Jerusalem Temple of the monarchical period in order to describe how God was present with Israel even during the exile. The wilderness tabernacle represents this new period in Israel's worship life. It represents change within tradition. In the Jerusalem Temple, God was described as being enthroned upon two cherubim (Ps 99:1-5), massive winged statues ten cubits in height (one cubit = 18-22 inches), each with a single wing span of five cubits (1 Kgs 6:23-28; 8:7). Their wings stretched the width of the inner chamber of the Temple, touching in the middle to form a throne for God. The ark was placed in front of the wings of the cherubim as a footstool for God (Ps 99:1-5). Such iconography gave religious expression to Israel's belief that God dwelled or was enthroned in the Temple and ruled the land of Israel through the Davidic king.

The wilderness shrine is a theological response to the fall of the nation, the destruction of the Temple, and the loss of the monarchy in 587 BCE. The cherubim remain in the tabernacle, but they have been diminished in size and function. They are reduced from 10 cubits in height to figurines that sit on the cover of the ark, which has the dimensions of 2½ x 1½ cubits. No mention is made of divine enthronement, and the ark assumes a more central place of significance. It may yet be a footstool, if the Hebrew word for its covering (כפרת kappōret) is related to the Egyptian word meaning "sole of foot."[90] But its significance derives from the fact that it contains God's revelatory words from Mt. Sinai ("testimony"), and not that it provides a footrest for the enthroned God. The reinterpretation of the ark influences the function of the cherubim, who now appear as guardian angels of divine law in the wilderness, rather than as supports for divine enthronement in the land.[91]

Third, v. 89 plays an important role in the

---

90. M. Gürg, "Eine neue Deutung für kapporet," *ZAW* 89 (1977) 115-18.

91. For brief discussion, see T. N. D. Mettinger, *The Dethronement of Sabaoth: Studies in the Shem and Kabod Theologies,* ConBOT 18 (Lund: CWK Gleerup, 1982) 87-88.

progression of events at Mt. Sinai (Exodus 19–Numbers 10). Speech between God and Moses in the innermost part of the tabernacle concludes a process of revelation that began with the theophany of Yahweh on Mt. Sinai in Exodus 19. The original description of the ark, with its cover and two cherubim, appears in Exod 25:10-22. There Moses receives the blueprints for the tabernacle on the summit of Mt. Sinai. God also promises to meet with Moses in the tabernacle at the base of the mountain and to speak with him from above the cover of the ark. Numbers 7:89 fulfills that divine promise. It also emphasizes that the tabernacle is a location of divine speech for priestly writers, preserved as law. The emphasis on the cultic presence of God as speech is also evident in Exod 33:7-11, where Moses is described as entering the tent of meeting outside the camp to receive divine oracles. Priestly writers have combined this tradition of the tent of meeting with their description of the tabernacle, now at the center of the Israelite camp.

8:1-26. Moses is instructed in two matters regarding cultic personnel while inside the tabernacle. The first concerns Aaron and the menorah (vv. 1-4), and the second shifts to the role of the Levites (vv. 5-26). The format of divine command and fulfillment returns, providing structure for the two sections. Each separates into three parts: (1) divine instruction (vv. 1-2 and 5-19), (2) the execution of the instruction (vv. 3 and 20-22), and (3) further clarification of the topic (vv. 4 and 23-26).

8:1-4. The setting up of the lampstand, or menorah (מנורה *měnôrâ*), by Aaron is part of the dedication of the tabernacle. His action brings to conclusion a series of references to the menorah. The first command focused on its construction (Exod 25:31-40), which was fulfilled in Exod 37:17-24. A second divine command (Exod 30:8; Lev 24:1-4) indicated that lay Israelites were responsible to supply oil for the lamp and that Aaron and his sons were required to tend to its regular evening burning. Numbers 8:1-4 fulfills this command.

The divine instruction in vv. 1-2 is not so much about Aaron's responsibility to burn the menorah as it is on how the lights should be burned, especially their direction toward the altar. The details accentuate the divine presence in the tabernacle. The fifth vision of the prophet in Zechariah 4 may provide insight into the function

of the menorah, for he equates the seven lights with the eyes of God.

The menorah has additional symbolism. It is described with botanical imagery in Exod 25:31-40. Its shaft is called a stem (קנה *qāneh*), and its receptacles for lamps are branches (קנים *qānîm*). In her study of the menorah, Carol Meyers concludes that it is a stylized tree of life, symbolizing fertility in nature and the life-giving power of God. Such symbolism is common throughout the ancient Near East. Yet the construction of the tabernacle menorah points in particular to influence of Egyptian craft techniques.[92] When focus is limited to the OT, the image of the menorah as a stylized tree invites comparison to the tree of life in the garden of Eden (Gen 3:22-24). It relates the divine presence in the tabernacle to creation and holds out hope that Yahweh is able to restore fertility even in the wilderness.

8:5-26. This section focuses on the purification and dedication of the Levites. The Levites have been separated out for special attention throughout chaps. 1–8. They were separated from the other clans during the census (1:48-53). Chapters 3–4 detailed their separate census, service to the tabernacle, and special role as substitutes for Israelite firstborn. These verses now describe the process of dedication and status of the Levites in the camp. Divine command (vv. 5-19) and fulfillment (vv. 20-22) structure the section. A supplement specifying the age span for levitical service in the tabernacle ends the section (vv. 23-26). Commentary will focus on three topics: the purification and dedication of the Levites (vv. 5-14); the role of the Levites in ransoming the Israelite firstborn (vv. 15-18); and the ability of the Levites to atone for Israel (v. 19).

Verses 5-14 describe the dedication of the Levites for service and the ritual they must undergo in order to be purified. The process moves from purification (vv. 6-7) to sacrificial rites in the larger setting of the congregation (vv. 9-14).

Levites are not Aaronide priests. The distinction is significant. Aaronide priests must be consecrated (קדש *qādaš*) before assuming their office (Exodus 29; Leviticus 8). Consecration makes priests holy, allowing them to handle sacred objects in the tab-

---

92. Carol Meyers, "Lampstand," *ABD* 4:141-43; and her more extended study, *The Tabernacle Menorah*, AASOR Dissertation Series 2 (Missoula, Mont.: Scholars Press, 1976).

ernacle and to officiate at the altar. Levites are not consecrated. They are purified (טהר *ṭāhēr*) and presented to God as a divine possession. Purification separates Levites from the congregation, but purification does not result in Levites' achieving the holy status of priests. Levites do not handle sacred objects, they do not officiate at the altar, and they do not actually enter the tabernacle for their service. They guard it, and they carry it.

Verses 5-7 describe the purification of Levites through three actions. They are sprinkled with water of purification; they shave their entire bodies; and they wash their clothes. The practice of shaving for purification was mentioned in relation to the Nazirite vow in 6:9 and is prescribed in the purification of lepers in Lev 14:8. The washing of clothes also occurs in the purification of lepers (Lev 14:8), and was part of Israel's ritual of consecration in preparing for the initial theophany on Mt. Sinai (Exod 19:10).

The sprinkling of water is more difficult to interpret. The Hebrew translates literally "water of sin" or "sin offering" (מי חטאת *mê ḥaṭṭāʾt*). The term occurs nowhere else in the OT, hindering translation and interpretation. The absence of water in the sin offering makes the literal translation unlikely. Gray has suggested that the phrase "water of cleansing" (מי נדה *mê niddâ*), which is made from the ashes of the red cow (19:9), may also be the water in the levitical purification.[93] The aim of the ritual process is similar, to purify the Levites. The goal of purification has influenced the NRSV translation "water of purification" and the NIV's "water of cleansing." Completion of the three-step purification of the Levites leads to public rituals of sacrifice before the tabernacle.

Verses 9-13 describe the sacrifice of two bulls on the altar before the tent of meeting. The ritual begins with the entire congregation of Israel (perhaps represented by its elders) laying hands on the Levites (v. 10). The Levites in turn lay their hands on the bulls (v. 12), thereby linking the congregation, the Levites, and the sacrificial bulls in the ritual. These actions are punctuated with two elevation offerings by Aaron (vv. 11, 13).

The elevation offering is most likely a dedication to God. Its use in this ritual signifies that the Levites are being given to God as an offering. The elevation offering itself is a two-part ritual surrounding the sacrifice of the bulls. The Levites are given over to God for service by the congregation of Israel in the first elevation offering (v. 11). It emphasizes the separation between the Levites and the congregation of Israel that takes place in the laying on of hands. The sacrifice of the two bulls, on whom the Levites have laid hands, completes their transfer as a sacrifice from the congregation to God (v. 12). One bull is a sin offering and the other a burnt offering. The Levites are atoned by the bulls, allowing the Levites, in turn, to atone for Israel (v. 19). The second wave offering associates the Levites with the Aaronide priests as a result of their dedication to God (v. 13). They now "stand before Aaron and his sons."

The process by which Levites substitute for the Israelite firstborn is clarified in vv. 14-18. First, as a result of the ritual, Levites become a divine possession (v. 14). God states to Moses in v. 16: "They are unreservedly given to me from among the Israelites." Second, as a divine possession, Levites substitute for Israelite firstborn (vv. 16-18). The divine claim on the firstborn is rooted in the exodus, when God spared the Israelite firstborn, while killing all Egyptian firstborn (see the story in Exod 11:5-8; 12:29-30; and the priestly interpretation in Exod 12:12-13; see also the Commentary on Num 3:11-13). Third, once the Levites have substituted for the Israelite firsborn, God gives them to the Aaronide priesthood for service. God states in v. 19: "I have given the Levites as a gift to Aaron and his sons from among the Israelites."

Verse 19 states further that the Levites atone for Israel. This is not the same as their role of substitution for the Israelite firstborn. Nor is levitical atonement the blood-rite priests perform to purge the sanctuary of impurities that would otherwise drive God from the tabernacle (see, e.g., the ritual of the Day of Atonement in Leviticus 16). In fact, the Levites do not actually perform atonement themselves. Only priests can undertake this action. Instead, atonement is performed with the Levites through their position in the camp. Their role of atonement presupposes the dangerous presence of God in the sanctuary. They protect the Israelites who live in close proximity to God.[94]

The atonement performed by Levites is more

---

93. George Buchanan Gray, *Numbers,* ICC (Edinburgh: T. & T. Clark, 1903) 79.

94. See Jacob Milgrom, *Numbers,* JPS Torah Commentary (Philadelphia: JPS, 1990) 369-71.

along the lines of a ransom payment to God for protection. Exodus 30:11-16 provides an analogous understanding of atonement with regard to money. In this text, a temple tax on each Israelite is described as a ransom (atonement) payment for their lives, which protects them from any plague that might break out from the temple. The ransom is not an attempt to change divine motive, as if God required an extortion from humans in exchange for their lives. Nor is the ransom intended to be an indicator of human motive. The problem is not motive at all. Rather, the need for ransom arises when a holy God and the profane world are brought together. They are incompatible. Purification allows Levites to approach closer to the sanctuary than ordinary Israelites and even to carry it when journeying through the wilderness. Their guard duty provides a buffer zone between God in the tabernacle and the Israelite camp.

Verses 20-22 narrate the fulfillment of the divine commands concerning the Levites. Verses 23-26 are an addendum to the chapter, stating the age requirements for levitical service—from twenty-five years of age to fifty.

REFLECTIONS

1. The tribal offerings in Num 7:2-88 provide a model for church giving. God does not compel gifts from the tribes. The tribes spontaneously give gifts to God. There is no immediate benefit for the tribes as a reward for their giving. And all gifts are of equal value; no gift is better than another. Gift-giving by the tribes, moreover, is one of their last actions at Mt. Sinai. It signals their readiness to journey with God through the wilderness.

G. Van der Leeuw states that giving is essentially three things: It is personal, because the gift is part of oneself; it creates communion, because the personal nature of the gift creates a bond between the giver and the recipient; and it is reciprocal, because gifts prompt gifts. Van der Leeuw continues that the exchange of gifts creates a bond between God and the people of God: "The principal feature [of giving] is not that someone or other should receive something, but that the stream of life should continue to flow."[95]

The priestly writer's vision of gift giving fits Van der Leeuw's definition. Yahweh rescued Israel in the exodus. Israel receives providential care in the wilderness, and their camp is flooded with the life-giving power of holiness. These actions alone, however, do not conform to Van der Leeuw's definition of gift giving, because they have not yet generated an equal response in Israel. The saving power of God becomes a transforming gift for Israel when they participate in the same power of giving. It is the dynamic interaction of gift giving between God and Israel that transforms the camp and readies Israel for their journey. The apostle Paul also understood the power of giving. The death of Christ is God's gift to him. In return, Paul gives his life back to God. Gift prompts gift, and in the process new life is created (Gal 2:19-20).

We live in a materialistic culture that threatens the priestly vision of giving from many directions. Too many church budgets are raised through guilt, coercion, or the promise of rewards. We tend to emphasize the gift over the spontaneous act of giving. Pledge cards have levels of giving. Large donors acquire disproportionate privilege in the community. These are signs of weakness in the church. Nowhere is wealth a category for evaluating persons in the priestly camp. And our tendency to emphasize the gift actually hinders God's holiness from becoming a gift to us. This is not the principle of the priestly writers. We give in order to give, not to receive. In the process, the stream of life—holiness itself—becomes stronger. This is not a message for pledge Sunday. It is a message for every Sunday.

2. Contemporary worship revolves around preaching. The priestly writers remind us in Numbers 7–8 that worship rests on liturgical drama and sacrifice. The work of worship has its own rhythm of transformation, indicated by the order of sacrifices. Baruch Levine summa-

---

95. G. Van der Leeuw, *Religion in Essence and Manifestation,* trans. J. E. Turner (Princeton: Princeton University Press, 1986) 350-60.

rizes the liturgy of sacrifices in three steps: The sin offering purified, making the sanctuary ready for worship. The burnt offering followed as an invocation to God, signaling God's readiness to respond to worshipers. The offering of well-being culminated the process; it was a sacred meal shared by priest and worshipers in the presence of God.[96]

Sacrifice is also foundational for Christian worship, even though the slaughter of cattle is replaced by the blood of Jesus. The ordering of sacrifices structures our own worship. We approach God every Sunday with confession of sin, seeking divine pardon to purify us for worship. We offer prayers of invocation, the Word of God is proclaimed, and we share a sacred meal.

Preaching is essential to Christian worship. It provides vision, motivation, and inspiration for living. But preaching is not a sacrament, and it loses its power to transform when it is detached from the larger sacramental drama of worship. Preaching clarifies the power of God in our lives, but it is our participation in sacraments that brings us into communion with God. Worship is one of our gifts to God that strengthens holiness in our community.

3. The priestly writers understood the important role of symbols and icons in the worship of God. The Protestant church rests on the power of the Word. Jesus is the incarnate Word. Scripture is the written Word. And preaching is the spoken Word. But the emphasis on the Word often leads to the neglect of visual symbols for worship or even to rejection of religious icons as forms of idolatry. This is unfortunate, because God communicates through visual symbols. Numbers 7–8 is filled with sacred objects. The sacrificial altar, the cherubim, the ark, and the menorah all play a role in worship. These objects are not idols. They communicate the power and presence of God visually rather than through words. The interrelationship of iconography and divine speech in the revelation to Moses (Num 7:89) indicates the commitment of priestly writers to both words and sacramental icons in their theology of divine presence within the sanctuary.

The priestly writers provide us with a model to identify our own religious icons and to develop new ones. Many of the sacred objects in our local churches are universal symbols. They may be baptismal fonts and communion utensils. Each church will also have its own sacred objects. These may be windows, tapestries, paintings, statues, and furnishings. It is important to identify and use these objects for worship and teaching. They define community.

Priestly writers also provide a model for creating new religious symbols. We saw in the commentary that the cherubim and the ark represent new designs of traditional objects that reflect the changing circumstances of Israel. The contemporary church faces the same challenge that faced the priestly writers: Traditional symbols require constant reinterpretation as our culture changes. Television, computers, and other forms of communication require new designs for our traditional sacred objects. It is the priestly writers who provide biblical guidelines to meet this challenge.

4. There is no analogy for Levites in the contemporary church, which makes their role in the priestly camp difficult to understand. We have clergy in the church, whether priest or minister, and we have laity. But a Levite is neither. They represent a third category between priests and laity. Their dedication ceremony in Num 8:5-22 indicates that they are living sacrifices in the camp. Levites substitute for the divine claim on firstborn, serve the priesthood, and allow the camp to function by atoning for all Israelites.

Every church has Levites, whether we acknowledge it in the organizational structure of our church. Every church has members who substitute for others by taking on extra responsibility. They serve on committees beyond their appointed time. They teach Sunday school or vacation Bible school for an extra term. They clean the church on Saturday, paint a room, or set up coffee on Sunday. They are the first ones called in an emergency. Such persons relieve someone

---

96. Baruch A. Levine, *Numbers 1–20,* AB 4A (Yew York: Doubleday, 1993) 263-64.

else of responsibility every time they take on an extra task. They ransom other members from God's claim on their time. They are living sacrifices of great value.

The apostle Paul understood the important role of Levites when he wrote in Rom 12:1: "Present your bodies as a living sacrifice, holy and acceptable to God, which is your spiritual worship" (NRSV). God claims all Christians as a living sacrifice. There are always members in our churches who fulfill this claim for others.

Name your Levites. Honor them publicly in special ceremonies. The priestly writers provide a model with their dedication ceremony in Num 8:5-22. Lay hands on them to signify their role as substitutes who ransom other members. Indicate in some concrete way the value of their service. The modern equivalent of two bulls for the public dedication of Levites would challenge the annual budget of many churches today.

Numbers 9:1–10:10, The Celebration of Passover and Preparation for the Wilderness March

NIV

9 The LORD spoke to Moses in the Desert of Sinai in the first month of the second year after they came out of Egypt. He said, ²"Have the Israelites celebrate the Passover at the appointed time. ³Celebrate it at the appointed time, at twilight on the fourteenth day of this month, in accordance with all its rules and regulations."

⁴So Moses told the Israelites to celebrate the Passover, ⁵and they did so in the Desert of Sinai at twilight on the fourteenth day of the first month. The Israelites did everything just as the LORD commanded Moses.

⁶But some of them could not celebrate the Passover on that day because they were ceremonially unclean on account of a dead body. So they came to Moses and Aaron that same day ⁷and said to Moses, "We have become unclean because of a dead body, but why should we be kept from presenting the LORD's offering with the other Israelites at the appointed time?"

⁸Moses answered them, "Wait until I find out what the LORD commands concerning you."

⁹Then the LORD said to Moses, ¹⁰"Tell the Israelites: 'When any of you or your descendants are unclean because of a dead body or are away on a journey, they may still celebrate the LORD's Passover. ¹¹They are to celebrate it on the fourteenth day of the second month at twilight. They are to eat the lamb, together with unleavened bread and bitter herbs. ¹²They must not leave any of it till morning or break any of its bones. When they celebrate the Passover, they must follow all

NRSV

9 The LORD spoke to Moses in the wilderness of Sinai, in the first month of the second year after they had come out of the land of Egypt, saying: ²Let the Israelites keep the passover at its appointed time. ³On the fourteenth day of this month, at twilight,ᵃ you shall keep it at its appointed time; according to all its statutes and all its regulations you shall keep it. ⁴So Moses told the Israelites that they should keep the passover. ⁵They kept the passover in the first month, on the fourteenth day of the month, at twilight,ᵃ in the wilderness of Sinai. Just as the LORD had commanded Moses, so the Israelites did. ⁶Now there were certain people who were unclean through touching a corpse, so that they could not keep the passover on that day. They came before Moses and Aaron on that day, ⁷and said to him, "Although we are unclean through touching a corpse, why must we be kept from presenting the LORD's offering at its appointed time among the Israelites?" ⁸Moses spoke to them, "Wait, so that I may hear what the LORD will command concerning you."

⁹The LORD spoke to Moses, saying: ¹⁰Speak to the Israelites, saying: Anyone of you or your descendants who is unclean through touching a corpse, or is away on a journey, shall still keep the passover to the LORD. ¹¹In the second month on the fourteenth day, at twilight,ᵃ they shall keep it; they shall eat it with unleavened bread and bitter herbs. ¹²They shall leave none of it until

ᵃ Heb *between the two evenings*

the regulations. ¹³But if a man who is ceremonially clean and not on a journey fails to celebrate the Passover, that person must be cut off from his people because he did not present the LORD's offering at the appointed time. That man will bear the consequences of his sin.

¹⁴"'An alien living among you who wants to celebrate the LORD's Passover must do so in accordance with its rules and regulations. You must have the same regulations for the alien and the native-born.'"

¹⁵On the day the tabernacle, the Tent of the Testimony, was set up, the cloud covered it. From evening till morning the cloud above the tabernacle looked like fire. ¹⁶That is how it continued to be; the cloud covered it, and at night it looked like fire. ¹⁷Whenever the cloud lifted from above the Tent, the Israelites set out; wherever the cloud settled, the Israelites encamped. ¹⁸At the LORD's command the Israelites set out, and at his command they encamped. As long as the cloud stayed over the tabernacle, they remained in camp. ¹⁹When the cloud remained over the tabernacle a long time, the Israelites obeyed the LORD's order and did not set out. ²⁰Sometimes the cloud was over the tabernacle only a few days; at the LORD's command they would encamp, and then at his command they would set out. ²¹Sometimes the cloud stayed only from evening till morning, and when it lifted in the morning, they set out. Whether by day or by night, whenever the cloud lifted, they set out. ²²Whether the cloud stayed over the tabernacle for two days or a month or a year, the Israelites would remain in camp and not set out; but when it lifted, they would set out. ²³At the LORD's command they encamped, and at the LORD's command they set out. They obeyed the LORD's order, in accordance with his command through Moses.

10 The LORD said to Moses: ²"Make two trumpets of hammered silver, and use them for calling the community together and for having the camps set out. ³When both are sounded, the whole community is to assemble before you at the entrance to the Tent of Meeting. ⁴If only one is sounded, the leaders—the heads of the clans of Israel—are to assemble before you. ⁵When a trumpet blast is sounded, the tribes camping on

morning, nor break a bone of it; according to all the statute for the passover they shall keep it. ¹³But anyone who is clean and is not on a journey, and yet refrains from keeping the passover, shall be cut off from the people for not presenting the LORD's offering at its appointed time; such a one shall bear the consequences for the sin. ¹⁴Any alien residing among you who wishes to keep the passover to the LORD shall do so according to the statute of the passover and according to its regulation; you shall have one statute for both the resident alien and the native.

15On the day the tabernacle was set up, the cloud covered the tabernacle, the tent of the covenant;ᵃ and from evening until morning it was over the tabernacle, having the appearance of fire. ¹⁶It was always so: the cloud covered it by dayᵇ and the appearance of fire by night. ¹⁷Whenever the cloud lifted from over the tent, then the Israelites would set out; and in the place where the cloud settled down, there the Israelites would camp. ¹⁸At the command of the LORD the Israelites would set out, and at the command of the LORD they would camp. As long as the cloud rested over the tabernacle, they would remain in camp. ¹⁹Even when the cloud continued over the tabernacle many days, the Israelites would keep the charge of the LORD, and would not set out. ²⁰Sometimes the cloud would remain a few days over the tabernacle, and according to the command of the LORD they would remain in camp; then according to the command of the LORD they would set out. ²¹Sometimes the cloud would remain from evening until morning; and when the cloud lifted in the morning, they would set out, or if it continued for a day and a night, when the cloud lifted they would set out. ²²Whether it was two days, or a month, or a longer time, that the cloud continued over the tabernacle, resting upon it, the Israelites would remain in camp and would not set out; but when it lifted they would set out. ²³At the command of the LORD they would camp, and at the command of the LORD they would set out. They kept the charge of the LORD, at the command of the LORD by Moses.

10 The LORD spoke to Moses, saying: ²Make two silver trumpets; you shall make them

ᵃ Or *treaty*, or *testimony*; Heb *eduth*   ᵇ Gk Syr Vg: Heb lacks *by day*

NIV

the east are to set out. ⁶At the sounding of a second blast, the camps on the south are to set out. The blast will be the signal for setting out. ⁷To gather the assembly, blow the trumpets, but not with the same signal.

⁸"The sons of Aaron, the priests, are to blow the trumpets. This is to be a lasting ordinance for you and the generations to come. ⁹When you go into battle in your own land against an enemy who is oppressing you, sound a blast on the trumpets. Then you will be remembered by the LORD your God and rescued from your enemies. ¹⁰Also at your times of rejoicing—your appointed feasts and New Moon festivals—you are to sound the trumpets over your burnt offerings and fellowship offerings,ᵃ and they will be a memorial for you before your God. I am the LORD your God."

ᵃ10 Traditionally *peace offerings*

NRSV

of hammered work; and you shall use them for summoning the congregation, and for breaking camp. ³When both are blown, the whole congregation shall assemble before you at the entrance of the tent of meeting. ⁴But if only one is blown, then the leaders, the heads of the tribes of Israel, shall assemble before you. ⁵When you blow an alarm, the camps on the east side shall set out; ⁶when you blow a second alarm, the camps on the south side shall set out. An alarm is to be blown whenever they are to set out. ⁷But when the assembly is to be gathered, you shall blow, but you shall not sound an alarm. ⁸The sons of Aaron, the priests, shall blow the trumpets; this shall be a perpetual institution for you throughout your generations. ⁹When you go to war in your land against the adversary who oppresses you, you shall sound an alarm with the trumpets, so that you may be remembered before the LORD your God and be saved from your enemies. ¹⁰Also on your days of rejoicing, at your appointed festivals, and at the beginnings of your months, you shall blow the trumpets over your burnt offerings and over your sacrifices of well-being; they shall serve as a reminder on your behalf before the LORD your God: I am the LORD your God.

COMMENTARY

Numbers 9:1–10:10 is transitional between the organization of the camp and the tabernacle cult and Israel's march through the wilderness. As a result, the literature can be interpreted in two different ways: as a conclusion to the revelation of law and the cult at Mt. Sinai (Exodus 19–Numbers 10) and as an overview of the priestly interpretation of the wilderness journey (Numbers 11). Each vantage provides a somewhat different interpretation. As a concluding section, the repetition of theophany functions as the final snapshot of how Yahweh is present in the tabernacle. The final word of priestly writers is that God is available both day and night, but is not to be taken for granted. As an introduction to the following material in Numbers, the commentary on the cloud and the trumpets provides guidelines of how Israel must follow God in the wilderness. Three sections of commentary follow:

9:1-14, the celebration of Passover; 9:15-23, the role of the cloud on the wilderness march; 10:1-10, the function of the trumpets.

9:1-14. Passover concludes the organization of the camp and prepares Israel for the wilderness march. The literary setting of the Passover instruction is important for its interpretation in priestly tradition. It is introduced during the exodus (Exodus 12), and it concludes the revelation at Mt. Sinai (Num 9:1-14). Passover originally saved the firstborn sons of Israel from death in Egypt (Exodus 12), and Passover defines Israel as the congregation of God after the revelation, construction, and dedication of the tabernacle at Sinai. Thus Passover is Israel's constitutional feast. Participation in it solidifies the congregation as the people of God, whether native Israelite or resident alien. It prepares them to journey with God in the wilderness.

These verses do not contain the ritual for the observance of Passover; its statutes are mentioned only briefly in vv. 3, 11-12. The text presupposes the instruction from Exod 12:1-20, where Passover (Exod 12:1-14) is combined with unleavened bread (Exod 12:15-20). Passover is celebrated in households (Exod 12:3-4). The Passover lamb was a one-year-old male, selected on the tenth day of the month and slaughtered at twilight on the fourteenth day (Exod 12:6). Its blood was placed on the doorframe (Exod 12:7). The meat with the intestines was roasted over a fire and eaten with unleavened bread and bitter herbs. Any remaining meat was to be burned the next morning (Exod 12:8-10).

Verses 1-14 separate into three parts: the observance of Passover (vv. 1-5); the problem of observance posed by those who are unclean (vv. 6-8); and the solution to the problem by the creation of a second observance one month later (vv. 9-14).

Verses 1-5 recount both the divine command to observe Passover and its fulfillment. It takes place on the fourteenth day of the first month, most likely in the spring, probably the month Nisan, which corresponds roughly to April. This date is one month earlier than the beginning of the book (1:1), where God addresses Moses on the first day of the second month. The point of emphasis, however, is on the observance of a second Passover one month later. The emphasis on the second month places 9:1-14 within the chronology of Numbers 1–10 (see the Commentary on 7:1).

Verses 6-8 confirm the focus on a second observance of Passover one month later. The text presents a situation in which some Israelites were unable to observe Passover because of having been contaminated by contact with a corpse. They complain to Moses and Aaron about their dilemma, prompting Moses to seek a solution from God.

Verses 9-14 give the divine solution. A second Passover is sanctioned one month later. The solution is narrated in 2 Chronicles 30 in relation to Hezekiah's reformation. The divine decree to Moses, however, goes well beyond the problem of corpse contamination. God states three additional stipulations: Those who are on a trip and thus unable to observe Passover may also participate in the feast during the second month; resident aliens who choose to meet the requirements may also participate in Passover; and lack of participation by any Israelite will result in his or her being cut off from the congregation. Each of these declarations provides insight into the meaning of Passover for the priestly writers.

First, the problem posed by travel suggests the centralization of Israel's cult, which occurred in the seventh century BCE under the influence of the deuteronomic movement. Cult centralization with regard to Passover is narrated in the story of Josiah's reform (2 Kings 23, which required that all Israelites journey to Jerusalem to celebrate Passover as a national feast. This same practice is evident in Deut 16:5-7 and may also lie behind Num 9:1-14. The celebration of Passover as a family feast in Exod 12:1-20, however, raises questions about the exact details of Passover observance by the priestly writers.

Second, the stipulation regarding the resident alien is a signal that the wilderness setting of the priestly history is not to be taken literally. Resident aliens presuppose Israel's life in the land of Canaan. There could be no resident aliens in the wilderness, since all Israel would fall under this category. The emphasis on the resident alien signifies that membership in the congregation is open to outsiders. The priestly writer's vision of the camp is not limited to the twelve tribes of Israel. The inclusive character of the congregation is also reflected in the priestly writer's description of Passover at the exodus (Exod 12:43-49).

Third, Passover is the only feast in which all Israelites are required to participate (v. 13). Participation in Passover defines membership in the congregation. Conversely, avoidance of this constitutional feast results in being "cut off" from the group—most likely excommunication, but possibly even death. The unique status of Passover clarifies the importance of its celebration at the close of Israel's time at Sinai, where the community has been defined and organized for the first time.

9:15-23. This section describes the cloud associated with the tabernacle. The cloud symbolizes the presence of God. It is a common symbol throughout the ancient Near East to indicate the presence of the divine. The Akkadian word *melammu* designates a halo or bright disk that would surround a god or any other person or object that shared in divine power. The root of the imagery is most likely associated with the sun, especially viewed through mist or at the time of an eclipse, when there is a diffuse radiance around it. The encircling radiance, rather than the sun itself, is the *melammu* that in ancient Israelite religion becomes the cloud.

Psalm 97:1-2 provides illustration. This psalm celebrates the presence of God in the Temple with the imagery of enthronement:

The LORD is king! Let the earth rejoice;
  let the many coastlands be glad!
Clouds and thick darkness are all around him;
  righteousness and justice are
    the foundation of his throne. (Ps 97:1-2 NRSV)

God is not literally seen in this psalm—Yahweh dwells in thick darkness. Yet the psalmist is confident of the divine presence because the radiance of God appears in the form of the cloud. The cloud both symbolizes divine presence in the cult and also hides God from the direct view of worshipers. Sometimes this dual function of the cloud—to reveal and to hide God—is represented by a cultic mask. The long tradition in Christian art of portraits of Jesus and the saints with halos surrounding their heads is a continuation of the symbolism of the *melammu,* or cloud.[97]

Priestly writers interrelate two aspects of divine presence: God's presence in the tabernacle (vv. 15-16) and the cloud as a guide in Israel's wilderness march (vv. 17-22). Verse 23 provides a concluding summary by clarifying the divine authority behind the cloud.

Verses 15-16 state that when Moses set up the tabernacle, a cloud covered it continually, day and night. During the night, the cloud appeared as fire. The larger literary setting of this description is important for interpretation, since the cloud provides the framework for the priestly legislation at Mt. Sinai in Exodus 19–Numbers 10.

A "thick cloud" was first mentioned in the pre-priestly account of theophany in Exod 19:16. It was accompanied by thunder, lightning, and a blast of a trumpet to indicate the presence of God on the mountain. The image of the cloud is developed further by the priestly writers in their account of theophany on Mt. Sinai (Exod 24:15-18) and when God enters the tabernacle (Exod 40:34-38).

The priestly writers refine the imagery of the "thick cloud" (Exod 19:16) on Mt. Sinai in three ways in their description of theophany on the mountain (Exod 24:15-18). First, they state that the "glory of the LORD [כבוד יהוה *kĕbôd YHWH*]" resides within the cloud. When Moses ascends Sinai to receive plans for the tabernacle the cloud surrounds the *kĕbôd YHWH* (Exod 24:16). Second, the *kĕbôd YHWH* is a divine fire. The appearance of the glory of Yahweh was like a consuming fire on the top of Mount Sinai (Exod 24:17). And third, the cloud and the *kĕbôd YHWH* are not the same thing. The cloud first covers Mount Sinai (Exod 24:15), before the *kĕbôd YHWH* settles on it (Exod 24:16).

The cloud and the *kĕbôd YHWH* reappear in the tabernacle upon its completion (Exod 40:34-38). This theophany allows the priestly writers to transfer the presence of God from Sinai to the tabernacle. The *kĕbôd YHWH* now fills the tabernacle (Exod 40:35). The cloud and the *kĕbôd YHWH* remain separate. The cloud once again covers the *kĕbôd YHWH* (Exod 40:34). Yet the cloud also takes on a new role at the conclusion of this theophany. The "cloud of Yahweh" is able to lead Israel in the wilderness journey, appearing as fire at night (Exod 40:36-38).

The priestly writers return to the topic of the cloud in v. 15. They date this theophany to the same day as its first appearance on the tabernacle (Exod 40:34-38). Verse 15 begins, "On the day [וביום *ûbĕyôm*] the tabernacle was set up, the cloud covered the tabernacle" (see Exod 40:2, 16). The similar dating suggests that priestly writers are providing further commentary on the presence of God in the tabernacle at the close of Israel's stay at Mt. Sinai. Comparison with Exod 40:34-38 suggests three points of emphasis in Num 9:15-16. First, the priestly writers state explicitly that the cloud continually covered the tabernacle (v. 16). God is always available to Israel in their wilderness march. Second, there is no mention of the *kĕbôd YHWH* in Num 9:15-16, as there was in Exod 40:34-35. They have been separated throughout the previous theophanies. The absence of the *kĕbôd YHWH* may be cautionary warning at the end of Israel's time at Mt. Sinai that Yahweh is elusiveness in the wilderness. The presence of the cloud over the tabernacle does not guarantee the glory of Yahweh within the sanctuary. Third, the role of the cloud as a wilderness guide is greatly expanded from Exod 40:34-38. The brief

97. For examples of iconography and a detailed examination of the cloud imagery in its ancient Near Eastern context see G. E. Mendenhall, "The Mask of Yahweh," in *The Tenth Generation: The Origins of the Biblical Tradition* (Baltimore: The Johns Hopkins University Press, 1973) 32-66.

concluding description (Exod 40:36-38) becomes the central topic (Num 9:17-22).

Verses 17-22 provide a detailed summary of how the cloud guides Israel in the wilderness march. Verses 17-18 make clear that when the cloud arose from the sanctuary, Israel marched, and when it descended, they camped. Verses 19-22 reinforce the message through a variation in Israel's routine of travel and rest. Rest periods might include one night (v. 21), days, a month, or even longer periods of time (v. 22).

In following the cloud, Israel is "keeping the charge of the LORD" (vv. 19, 22). This expression may connote guard duty, as it does when used to describe the Levites (1:53). So precise a meaning in reference to the entire congregation of Israel seems unlikely. Here it appears that the charge of the congregation is the more general requirement that they follow the cloud in its rhythm of leading them through the wilderness. The imagery of travel with periods of unequal rest may refer to the priestly cultic calendar (see Numbers 28–29), where distinct feasts require different periods of rest. Observing these festivals throughout the liturgical year is how Israel "keeps the charge of the LORD" as they journey through the wilderness.

10:1-10. God commands Moses to make two silver trumpets (חצצרת *ḥăṣōṣĕrōt*). Josephus describes trumpets as narrow tubes, roughly eighteen inches in length, with a bell-shaped end.[98] Such instruments are common in Egyptian iconography. Reference to these particular trumpets is most common in priestly texts. They contrast to the שופר (*šôpār*; Exod 19:16, 19; 20:18) and the יבל (*yōbēl*; Exod 19:13), also mentioned during theophany at Mt. Sinai. Both of these terms refer to a smaller instrument in the shape of a ram's horn. The silver trumpets are mentioned only one other time in Numbers, during Israel's holy war against Midian (31:6). They occur frequently in Chronicles (1 Chr 13:8; 15:24, 28; 16:6, 42; 2 Chr 5:12; 13:12; 15:14; 20:28; 29:27).

Verses 1-2 describe the construction and purpose of the trumpets. They are made of hammered silver and are used both to summon the congregation and to prepare the camp for travel.

Verses 3-7 are a series of different signals for which the trumpets were used during Israel's wilderness march. When both trumpets are blown, the Israelites are to gather at the door of the tent of meeting (v. 3); one trumpet blast calls only the leaders (v. 4); one long blast signals that the east side of the camp is to set out (v. 5); a second long blast starts the south side of the camp (v. 6).

Verse 8 assigns responsibility for the blowing of trumpets to the Aaronide priests. According to 2 Chr 5:12, the total Aaronide priests who blow the trumpet are numbered at 120.

Verses 9-10 turn from the wilderness setting to the land, describing two more functions of the trumpets once Israel is in Canaan: They will summon the people to holy war (v. 9), and they will call Israel to the observance of feast days (v. 10). The books of Chronicles illustrate the role of the trumpets in holy war. They are associated most frequently with the ark (1 Chr 13:8; 15:24, 28; 16:6, 42) and are blown during battles (2 Chr 13:12; 20:28). The trumpets summon the people for assembly during the dedication of the Jerusalem wall (Neh 12:35, 41) and when the foundation of the post-exilic Temple is completed (Ezra 3:10).

Verse 10 concludes with a divine promise: Blowing the trumpets will prompt God to remember Israel, punctuated by the statement, "I am Yahweh [אני יהוה *'ănî YHWH*], your God." The final phrase is a revelation of the divine name, Yahweh, known as the self-introduction of God.[99] It is part of Israel's cultic life at least as early as the eighth century BCE. The prophet Hosea used it to express Yahweh's exclusive claim on Israel (Hos 12:10; 13:4, and the exilic prophets Ezekiel (e.g., Ezek 37:6) and Second Isaiah (e.g., Isa 42:8) used it frequently. When the phrase "your God" is added to the self-introduction, the relationship between Yahweh and Israel is emphasized.

The priestly writers use the self-introduction of Yahweh throughout the events of the exodus and revelation at Mt. Sinai. The commission to Moses (Exod 6:2, 7); the plagues (e.g., Exod 7:17; 10:2); and salvation at the sea (Exod 14:4, 18) are actions that reveal the name Yahweh. The establishment of the tabernacle cult (Exod 29:46), with its laws (e.g., Lev 19:11, 13, 16; 18:2, 5; 25:17, 38), also reveal the name Yah-

---

98. Josephus *Antiquities of the Jews* 3.291. See the discussion of musical instruments by Ivor H. Jones, "Musical Instruments," *ABD* 4:934-39, esp. 936.

99. Walter Zimmerli, *I Am Yahweh,* ed. Walter Brueggemann, trans. D. W. Stott (Atlanta: John Knox, 1982).

weh. Israel acquires power to communicate with God through the gift of the divine name, Yahweh. In the book of Numbers, the divine claim on the Israelite firstborn (3:13) was a revelation of the name Yahweh. Numbers 10:10 now closes the entire revelation at Mt. Sinai with a similar theophany of the name.

REFLECTIONS

1. Passover continues to be a constitutional feast for Christians. The Lord's supper is rooted in a Passover meal between Jesus and his disciples (Matthew 26; Mark 14; Luke 22). Jesus is the paschal lamb (John 1:29; 1 Cor 5:7). Even his bones are not broken in crucifixion, fulfilling priestly law (John 19:36; cf. Num 9:12). Participation in the Lord's supper defines the community. It is life-giving and dangerous, requiring preparation and self-examination. And it is inclusive (1 Cor 11:17-34). The Lord's supper is also expanded beyond the Passover rite of the priestly writers to include the death and resurrection of Jesus. The observance of Passover on Maundy Thursday of holy week demonstrates both its central role in Christian tradition and its reinterpretation. Churches gather to observe the seder meal (Passover) on Thursday evening. But it is followed by the three-day passion of Jesus, Good Friday through Easter Sunday, rather than the seven days of unleavened bread.

2. The imagery of the cloud over the tabernacle emphasizes the presence of God with Israel. It is not a symbol of God in heaven, separated from this world. The cloud over the tabernacle empowers Israel to "keep the charge of Yahweh" concretely in their march through the wilderness. The tradition of the cloud reappears in the transfiguration of Jesus (Matt 17:1-8; Mark 9:2-8; Luke 9:28-36). Too often this tradition is interpreted apart from its background in priestly tradition. Jesus' journey up the mountain is misinterpreted to indicate his separation from this world. The message of the transfiguration is just the reverse. It attests to the descent of God into our world in the person of Jesus, like the cloud over the tabernacle.

The tradition of the cloud in Luke-Acts provides illustration. The transfiguration of Jesus (Luke 9:28-37) employs the imagery of the cloud to highlight the presence of God, not separation. Jesus is on the mountaintop praying (Luke 9:29; see Exod 24:15-18). Moses and Elijah join him (Luke 9:30). Divine glory appears to the disciples (Luke 9:32; see Exod 24:17; 40:34-35) and is covered by the cloud (Luke 9:35; see Exod 24:15, 18; 40:34-38). The visual imagery of theophany culminates in a divine voice (Luke 9:35; see Exod 24:16; Num 7:89). The cloud returns during the ascension of Jesus (Acts 1:6-11) to cover him while he rises to heaven (Acts 1:9). The disciples are drawn away from this world by the event. They stand "gazing up toward heaven" (Acts 1:10). Two angels bring them back to earth with the question, "Men of Galilee, why do you stand looking up toward heaven?" (Acts 1:11). Once they turn their focus to Jerusalem rather than to heaven, they too are transfigured with the fire of the Holy Spirit (Acts 2:1-3). The message of the ascension is the same as that of the transfiguration. Both accentuate the immanence of God in this world, not the separation. The message of the cloud in biblical literature is that God is not encountered gazing into heaven. Following the cloud anchors us firmly in this world.

3. Priestly writers envision the life of faith as a wilderness journey in which God is the guide (Num 9:15-23). Success on this journey is moving in rhythm with God. Two features are noteworthy in preaching and teaching this material. First, the journey is long. The impression of the literary style in Num 9:15-23, with its complex syntax and many repetitions, is that Israel is about to embark on a long journey. The journey will include repeated stops of days, weeks, and even longer periods. Second, the journey has no clear ending. The emphasis is more on the rhythm of the cloud than on its destination. Israel keeps the charge of Yahweh by staying in harmony with the cloud's movement. The absence of a clear ending suggests that the life of faith rests more on the process of journey through the wilderness than on its conclusion. Yet, the final instruction on the trumpets forces a qualification of this conclusion. Journey for its own sake cannot be the final word of salvation in the priestly history. There is the divine promise of land, and it is introduced in conjunction with the trumpets. They bridge the wilderness march (Num 10:1-7) and life in the land (Num 10:9-10). The different signals of the trumpets even provide directions for finding the gift of the land in the wilderness. Moving and resting with God, following the signals of the trumpets for assemblies, marching, engaging in holy war, and observing feast days bring the promise of land near at hand.

4. Trumpets are important throughout the revelation at Mt. Sinai. They signal the presence of God and direct the people of God. The ram horns are blown during the theophany on the mountain (Exod 19:13, 16; 20:18). The priestly description of the silver trumpets adds further details for how God directs the people of God through the sound of the horn.

Trumpets continue the same role in the New Testament. They signal the end of history in Matt 24:30-31. This apocalyptic vision of the end also embraces the imagery of the cloud and the *kĕbôd YHWH*. Jesus is the Son of Man, who descends from heaven in glory on a cloud. Accompanying angels take over the priestly role of blowing the trumpets to assemble the elect from around the world. The apostle Paul takes up the imagery of the trumpet to signal the raising of the dead at the end of history (1 Cor 15:52). The book of Revelation provides the most extended account of trumpets at the end of history. Six angels blow trumpets in Revelation 8–9, prompting disruptions of nature and judgment on the wicked. A seventh angel sounds a trumpet in Rev 11:14-19 to announce the coming of the kingdom of God.

5. The legislation concerning the camp and the tabernacle concludes with a revelation of the divine name, Yahweh (Num 10:10). The phrase "I am Yahweh" is described as a self-introduction in the Commentary. Revelation of the divine name is a gift from God. God grants power to those who possess the name. Jacob's wrestling with God at the Jabbok River (Gen 32:22-32) illustrates the power of knowing names. Jacob wrestles all night with an unnamed divine being. Jacob overpowers his opponent and requests a name. He is never told the name, but in the process Jacob reveals his own name. As a consequence the opponent overpowers Jacob and renames him "Israel." Jacob concludes that next morning that his opponent was God, but the name "Yahweh" was never revealed to him. He names the location of his struggle simply "Peniel" ("The Face of God"). God reveals the special name, "Yahweh," to Moses at the outset of the exodus (Exod 3:13-15). The plagues reveal the power of the name "Yahweh" throughout the events of the exodus. The legislation at Mt. Sinai also reveals the name. Possession of the name "Yahweh" empowers Israel. They become God's people.

New Testament writers also employ the self-introduction to reveal the name "Jesus." The power of name is revealed to the disciples when Jesus approaches them walking on water (Mark 6:50). The disciples fear, thinking Jesus is a ghost. Jesus responds, "I am do not fear." The statement "I am" is a self-introduction like "I am Yahweh." When the high priest later asks Jesus whether he is the Messiah (Mark 14:62), Jesus responds, "I am." The use of "I am" as a divine name is developed most extensively in the Gospel of John.[100] Jesus is the "I am" (John 7:24, 28, 58; 13:19). Revelation of the name "Jesus" empowers believers to make requests to God (John 14:13; 17:23). Christian prayer arises from the power of the name. It is God's gift to us. When we punctuate our prayer "in the name of Jesus," we claim the power of God. We are empowered, like Israel at Sinai, to be the people of God. Jesus promises that whatever we ask in his name, God will do (John 15:16). Prayer offered in the name of Jesus and answered by God brings glory to God (John 14:13). Priestly writers would say that it strengthens holiness in our community and in our churches.

---

100. See Raymond E. Brown, *The Gospel According to John (I–XII)*, ed. D. N. Freedman (New York: Doubleday, 1966) 533-38.

THE WILDERNESS JOURNEY OF THE FIRST GENERATION

OVERVIEW

The holiness of God was the central theme of Num 1:1–10:10. The construction of the tabernacle (Exodus 25–40), the implementation of the sacrificial system, and the consecration of priests (Leviticus), as well as the organization of the camp and dedication of Levites (Numbers 1–10) allowed for the *kĕbôd YHWH* to descend from the summit of Sinai and dwell in the midst of Israel. Throughout this section, the people have remained in their encampment at the base of the mountain.

Israel departs from Mt. Sinai in Num 10:11–21:35. This section depicts the journey of the first generation of Israelites as a tragic story leading to death. The section is dominated by conflicts among God, Israel, and Moses that arise on the wilderness journey. Such conflicts were not possible as long as Israel was encamped at Mt. Sinai. Three of these conflicts are prominent: Challenges concerning leadership appear in chaps. 11–12 and 16–17. They frame a more central conflict (chaps.

13–14) over how Israel is to acquire the promised land of Canaan. Signs of hope are interspersed in legislation that points ahead to Israel's life in the land (chaps. 15; 18–19).

Conflicts over leadership center on Moses, whose authority is challenged twice. The charismatic and prophetic leadership of Moses is central to Numbers 11–12. Chapters 16–17 focus on his non-charismatic, priestly leadership. Resolution of conflicts through divine judgment serves to define more clearly these distinct leadership roles within the wilderness community. Chapters 13–14 describe the failure of the first generation of Israelites to secure the promised land of Canaan. Their failure, however, provides guidelines for success by a future generation (chaps. 15; 18–19). Chapters 20–21 provide transition from the failed journey of the first generation of Israelites to the second generation, who successfully undertake holy war.

NUMBERS 10:11-36, LEAVING SINAI

NIV	NRSV
[11]On the twentieth day of the second month of the second year, the cloud lifted from above the tabernacle of the Testimony. [12]Then the Israelites set out from the Desert of Sinai and traveled from place to place until the cloud came to rest in the Desert of Paran. [13]They set out, this first time, at the LORD's command through Moses. [14]The divisions of the camp of Judah went first, under their standard. Nahshon son of Amminadab was in command. [15]Nethanel son of Zuar was over the division of the tribe of Issachar, [16]and Eliab	[11]In the second year, in the second month, on the twentieth day of the month, the cloud lifted from over the tabernacle of the covenant.[a] [12]Then the Israelites set out by stages from the wilderness of Sinai, and the cloud settled down in the wilderness of Paran. [13]They set out for the first time at the command of the LORD by Moses. [14]The standard of the camp of Judah set out first, company by company, and over the whole company *a Or treaty, or testimony; Heb eduth*

NIV

son of Helon was over the division of the tribe of Zebulun. ¹⁷Then the tabernacle was taken down, and the Gershonites and Merarites, who carried it, set out.

¹⁸The divisions of the camp of Reuben went next, under their standard. Elizur son of Shedeur was in command. ¹⁹Shelumiel son of Zurishaddai was over the division of the tribe of Simeon, ²⁰and Eliasaph son of Deuel was over the division of the tribe of Gad. ²¹Then the Kohathites set out, carrying the holy things. The tabernacle was to be set up before they arrived.

²²The divisions of the camp of Ephraim went next, under their standard. Elishama son of Ammihud was in command. ²³Gamaliel son of Pedahzur was over the division of the tribe of Manasseh, ²⁴and Abidan son of Gideoni was over the division of the tribe of Benjamin.

²⁵Finally, as the rear guard for all the units, the divisions of the camp of Dan set out, under their standard. Ahiezer son of Ammishaddai was in command. ²⁶Pagiel son of Ocran was over the division of the tribe of Asher, ²⁷and Ahira son of Enan was over the division of the tribe of Naphtali. ²⁸This was the order of march for the Israelite divisions as they set out.

²⁹Now Moses said to Hobab son of Reuel the Midianite, Moses' father-in-law, "We are setting out for the place about which the LORD said, 'I will give it to you.' Come with us and we will treat you well, for the LORD has promised good things to Israel."

³⁰He answered, "No, I will not go; I am going back to my own land and my own people."

³¹But Moses said, "Please do not leave us. You know where we should camp in the desert, and you can be our eyes. ³²If you come with us, we will share with you whatever good things the LORD gives us."

³³So they set out from the mountain of the LORD and traveled for three days. The ark of the covenant of the LORD went before them during those three days to find them a place to rest. ³⁴The cloud of the LORD was over them by day when they set out from the camp.

³⁵Whenever the ark set out, Moses said,

"Rise up, O LORD!

May your enemies be scattered;

NRSV

was Nahshon son of Amminadab. ¹⁵Over the company of the tribe of Issachar was Nethanel son of Zuar; ¹⁶and over the company of the tribe of Zebulun was Eliab son of Helon.

17Then the tabernacle was taken down, and the Gershonites and the Merarites, who carried the tabernacle, set out. ¹⁸Next the standard of the camp of Reuben set out, company by company; and over the whole company was Elizur son of Shedeur. ¹⁹Over the company of the tribe of Simeon was Shelumiel son of Zurishaddai, ²⁰and over the company of the tribe of Gad was Eliasaph son of Deuel.

21Then the Kohathites, who carried the holy things, set out; and the tabernacle was set up before their arrival. ²²Next the standard of the Ephraimite camp set out, company by company, and over the whole company was Elishama son of Ammihud. ²³Over the company of the tribe of Manasseh was Gamaliel son of Pedahzur, ²⁴and over the company of the tribe of Benjamin was Abidan son of Gideoni.

25Then the standard of the camp of Dan, acting as the rear guard of all the camps, set out, company by company, and over the whole company was Ahiezer son of Ammishaddai. ²⁶Over the company of the tribe of Asher was Pagiel son of Ochran, ²⁷and over the company of the tribe of Naphtali was Ahira son of Enan. ²⁸This was the order of march of the Israelites, company by company, when they set out.

29Moses said to Hobab son of Reuel the Midianite, Moses' father-in-law, "We are setting out for the place of which the LORD said, 'I will give it to you'; come with us, and we will treat you well; for the LORD has promised good to Israel." ³⁰But he said to him, "I will not go, but I will go back to my own land and to my kindred." ³¹He said, "Do not leave us, for you know where we should camp in the wilderness, and you will serve as eyes for us. ³²Moreover, if you go with us, whatever good the LORD does for us, the same we will do for you."

33So they set out from the mount of the LORD three days' journey with the ark of the covenant of the LORD going before them three days' journey, to seek out a resting place for them, ³⁴the cloud

NIV	NRSV
may your foes flee before you." ³⁶Whenever it came to rest, he said, "Return, O Lᴏʀᴅ, to the countless thousands of Israel."	of the Lᴏʀᴅ being over them by day when they set out from the camp. 35Whenever the ark set out, Moses would say, "Arise, O Lᴏʀᴅ, let your enemies be scattered, and your foes flee before you." ³⁶And whenever it came to rest, he would say, "Return, O Lᴏʀᴅ of the ten thousand thousands of Israel."ᵃ

ᵃ Meaning of Heb uncertain

COMMENTARY

There are two accounts of Israel's departure from Mt. Sinai. Numbers 10:11-28 is the priestly account. It incorporates language, characters, and tribal organizations from 1:1–10:10. The priestly writers recount Israel's march from Sinai to Paran as a carefully orchestrated military maneuver with the tabernacle and the ark at the center of their march. They focus on the congregation of Israel as a whole and locate every tribe in the processional march, with God at the center. The repetition of language from Numbers 1–10 gives their version of departure a retrospective focus, as though the priestly writers wished to conclude the organization of the camp by showing how the Israelites moved through the wilderness.

Numbers 10:29-36 is the first occurrence of the pre-priestly history. It describes Israel's departure from Mt. Yahweh, with the ark of the covenant leading them three days in advance. The pre-priestly account has incorporated an even older hymn (10:35-36) about the role of the ark in holy war. No mention is made of the Israelites on the march. The focus, instead, is on the guidance of God. Divine leadership gives this account a forward focus, anticipating the conflicts over leadership that will take center stage in the following chapters.

10:11-12. The priestly account of leaving Sinai is tied to the closing celebrations surrounding the tabernacle in 9:1–10:10. The date of departure is on Month 2, Day 20 of the second year after the exodus, allowing for the completion of the second Passover prescribed in 9:1-14. The cloud guides Israel, as was described in 9:15-23.

Verse 12 indicates Israel's travel route through the wilderness. The priestly writers state that the people set out by stages from the wilderness of Sinai and that the cloud settled next in the wilderness of Paran. The priestly writers repeat this information in 12:16: "The people set out from Hazeroth, and camped in the wilderness of Paran." The wilderness of Paran thereby frames the pre-priestly version of Israel's departure from Mt. Yahweh (v. 33) and the events at Kibrothhattaveh and Hazeroth in chaps. 11–12 (these locations are stated in 11:35.) The priestly writers also change the setting of the spy story (chaps. 13–14; see 13:3, 26) and the rebellion of Korah (chaps. 16–19) from Kadesh to Paran. Israel leaves the wilderness of Paran in 20:1, when they arrive at Kadesh/Zin.

The priestly writers indicate important events by the rest stops in the wilderness journey. The summary of travel indicates that Paran is the most important setting for the priestly writers in the wilderness travel of the first generation (10:11–21:35). Although the priestly writers provide some commentary to the events in chaps. 11–12, they point ahead to the loss of the promised land (chaps. 13–15) and the rebellion of Korah against the Aaronide priesthood (chaps. 16–19) in the wilderness of Paran.

The exact location of the wilderness of Paran is unclear. It is described as a desert site between Midian and Egypt in 1 Kgs 11:18. This corresponds with similar references to Paran in Abram's war with the five kings (Gen 14:6) and to Ishmael and Hagar's home (Gen 21:21). The priestly writers' insertion of Paran in the spy story (Numbers 13–14) indicates some association with Kadesh, suggesting a larger area in the northern Sinai peninsula, rather than a specific station in the wilderness.

The wilderness of Paran also has theological significance. In ancient poetry, Paran is Yahweh's desert mountain. God is described as "the Holy One from Mount Paran" (Hab 3:3). In another poem (Deut 33:2), Yahweh wages holy war from Mt. Paran to rescue Israel. The priestly writers may be influenced by this tradition of theophany in emphasizing the wilderness of Paran. It was noted in the Introduction that the travel route has theological meaning for both the pre-priestly and the priestly writers. But the priestly writers have also reinterpreted the theological significance of Paran from the ancient poetry. It is neither a mountain home of God nor a setting for salvation. Instead, Paran has become the wilderness region where the first generation rebelled against God. As a result, God does not rescue Israel from Mt. Paran, but instead wages holy war against them in the wilderness of Paran.

10:13-28. This section describes the organization of Israel on the march. The image of the congregation as a regimented militia ties this account of its departure to the census in chap. 1 and to the organization of the camp in chap. 2. Numbers 10:14 contains the military phrase "the standard of the camp" (דגל מחנה *degel maḥănēh*) from Numbers 2:3, 10, 18, 25 to describe the four tribes that lead each regiment (Judah, Reuben, Ephraim, and Dan). The phrase "whole company" (צבא *ṣābā'*), designating those under the lead tribes, also repeats military language from Numbers 2. Thus the wilderness march bears overtones of holy war for the priestly writers.

Israel's organization on the march includes a description of the four standards, the leaders of each tribe (see Commentary on 1:1–2:34), and the transportation of the tabernacle with its holy objects by the three levitical families (see Commentary on 3:1–4:49). The priestly vision of Israel on the march in the wilderness can be illustrated in the following manner:

Standard 1 (Front)
Judah (Nahshon ben Amminadab)
Issachar (Nethanel ben Zuar)
Zebulun (Eliab ben Helon)
The Tabernacle
Gershonites
Merarites

Standard 2
Reuben (Elizur ben Shedeur)
Simeon (Shelumiel ben Zurishaddai)
Gad (Elisaph ben Deuel)
The Holy Objects
Kohathites

Standard 3
Ephraim (Elishama ben Ammihud)
Manasseh (Gamaliel ben Pedahzur)
Benjamin (Abidan ben Gideoni)
Standard 4 (Rear Guard)
Dan (Ahiezer ben Ammishaddai)
Asher (Pagiel ben Ochran)
Naphtali (Ahira ben Enan)

10:29-32. Verses 29-36 constitute a second account of Israel's departure, this time from Mt. Yahweh rather than from Mt. Sinai. Verses 29-32 report an exchange between Moses and his father-in-law, Hobab the son of Reuel. Moses requests his guidance and promises him a share in the goodness that Yahweh promises Israel. Hobab refuses and states his intention to return to Midian (v. 30). Moses repeats the request (vv. 31-32), adding that Hobab knows the terrain and can serve as the eyes for Israel in their wilderness journey. Moses again promises him a share in God's goodness, but receives no response from Hobab. The guiding role of the ark immediately following this exchange (vv. 33-36) suggests that God replaces Hobab in leading Israel on their wilderness journey.

There are several pentateuchal traditions about Moses' father-in-law. He is introduced as Reuel, the Midianite priest (Exod 2:15-22). His name changes to Jethro, the Midianite priest in the revelation to Moses on the mountain of God (Exod 3:1; 4:18) and in his visit to Moses after the exodus (Exod 18:1). Thus the name "Hobab, the son of Reuel, the Midianite" (Num 10:29-32) is unexpected and constitutes a third name. This name also occurs in Judg 4:11 to describe the father-in-law of Moses, where Hobab is a Kenite rather than a Midianite.

All pentateuchal stories about the father-in-law of Moses belong to the pre-priestly history. Thus the retention of three different names has puzzled interpreters. One suspects a rich tradition of folklore on how Israelites and Midianites are related. Midianites play a prominent and positive role in

Israel's earliest accounts of their origins. They appear three times in the pre-priestly history: (1) prior to the exodus, when Moses receives his initial command to free Israel (Exod 2:15-22; 3:1–4:20); (2) before the revelation at Sinai (Exodus 18); and (3) at the conclusion of the revelation at Sinai (Num 10:29-32). The Midianites provided safe haven for Moses (Exodus 2–3). Moses marries the Midianite Zipporah, and they have two sons, Gershom and Eliezar. Zipporah rescues Moses from an attack by God (Exod 4:24-26).

Stories about Moses' father-in-law frame the account of revelation at the sacred mountain. Jethro provides guidance in matters of worship and government (Exodus 18) prior to covenant ceremony between God and Israel (Exodus 19–24; 32–34). And the refusal of Hobab to lead Moses (Num 10:29-32) at the end appears less an abandonment than a transfer of leadership from himself to God, symbolized by the ark. These stories would have followed in rapid succession in the pre-priestly history without the extended description by the priestly writers of the tabernacle cult (Exodus 25–31; 35–40; Leviticus; Numbers 1–10). The Midianites receive a negative interpretation by the priestly writers. They plot with Balak to destroy Israel in the story of Balaam (Numbers 22–24), and Israel wages holy war against them (Numbers 25).

10:33-36. The departure of Israel (vv. 33-34) is followed by a poem about the ark (vv. 35-36). The poem is highlighted in the Hebrew Text (MT) by a pair of "inverted nuns" (*nun* is the letter *n* in the Hebrew alphabet). Such bracketing is rare in the Hebrew Bible; it may be a way by which scribes indicated the insertion of older poems into their present literary context.[101]

Israel's travel route through the wilderness is described in vv. 33-34. Israel departs from Mt. Yahweh on a three-day journey, with the ark leading them an additional three days. The cloud also hovers over Israel during the day (v. 33). The "three-day" journey most likely has religious and, perhaps, liturgical significance, since the exodus from Egypt was also a three-day journey (Exod 5:3; 15:22). No destination is provided (Num 10:12). The aim of the ark, "to seek out" (תור *tûr*) a resting place may be an addition by the priestly

writers. They use this verb repeatedly to describe the activity of the spies in chaps. 13–15.

The pre-priestly interpretation of the ark is central in this story. It leads Israel in their wilderness march, in contrast to the priestly version, where the ark travels in the middle of the tribal procession (3:27-32; 11:11-28). The poem (vv. 35-36) indicates the role of the ark in war. It represents God's power as a holy warrior who scatters enemies before returning to Israel. The poem is a couplet and may have served as a battle cry. The first line describes Yahweh's ability to attack the enemy. The NRSV translation "Arise" (NIV, "Rise up") does not convey the military imagery of the Hebrew קומה (*qûmâ*). It signifies advancing for the purpose of attacking. Psalm 68:1 employs the same language to describe the power of God in holy war. The second line envisions the successful return of Yahweh from battle along with the Israelite army. The verb "return" (שוב *šûb*) indicates that Yahweh rests on the ark. It is the divine throne, which symbolizes God's presence with Israel.

The ark is one of the most significant cult objects in Israel's history. The poem in vv. 35-36 may be an ancient liturgy, indicating the ark's original role in holy war. Such an interpretation corresponds with the stories in 1 Samuel 4–7, where the ark also represents the presence of God in war. The monarchy reinterpreted the ark by incorporating it into the iconography of the Temple as the footstool of the enthroned God (Ps 99:1-5). Previous commentary on Num 7:89 took note of how priestly writers renamed the ark as "the ark of the congregation" and how they gave it a more central place in the tabernacle as the location where God would speak with Moses and as the source of divine mercy.

The pre-priestly writers provide yet another interpretation of the ark in v. 33 by naming it "the ark of the covenant [ארון ברית *'ărôn běrît*]" This name is common in Deuteronomy (e.g., Deut 10:8, 31:9, 25) and in the Deuteronomistic History (e.g., Josh 3:3; 4:7; Judg 20:27; 1 Sam 4:3; 1 Kgs 3:15; 6:19; 8:1). The emphasis is on the Ten Commandments, which are contained within the ark on two stone tablets. The ark is holy because it contains the stipulations between God and Israel. The use of the term "ark of the covenant" in the pre-priestly history suggests that

---

101. See Baruch A. Levine, *Numbers 1–20*, AB 4A (New York: Doubleday, 1993) 318-19, for examples of this same scribal practice in Greek texts.

its authors share the theological perspective contained in Deuteronomy and in the Deuteronomistic History. God is present with the people of God through divine words codified as law. The law of God leads Israel in the wilderness march to the promised land.

REFLECTIONS

1. Israel's departure from Sinai envisions the life of faith as a journey with God. The imagery of journeying with God remains central to the Christian life. The life of Jesus is portrayed in the Gospels as a journey through the wilderness to Jerusalem. The disciples encounter Jesus as they journey on the road from Emmaus to Jerusalem (Luke 24). Numbers 10:11-36 contains specific insights for exploring the contemporary significance of this theme.

First, the larger literary context clarifies that journeying is not the first action for Israel in following God. The first action is worship. Numbers 1–10 is foundational for Israel's journey. The cultic icons of the tabernacle, the cloud, and the ark lead Israel. Without worship, the life of faith has no fuel or direction.

Second, Israel's journey with God is in the wilderness. It is not in the land. The theological significance of the wilderness (see Introduction) is important for interpretation. Yahweh is a desert God. Journeying with Yahweh takes one away from the security of home, land, and country. It destablizes Israel and transforms them. The same is true for the contemporary church. Baptism makes us citizens of Christ's church. Residency in the church creates new allegiances. The old passes away. We are propelled on a journey with God that may lead us away from the security of home and country.

Third, the positive role of Hobab, Moses' father-in-law, indicates the inclusive nature of community in the wilderness journey. Leadership may arise from unexpected persons, like Hobab the Midianite. Twice Moses offers Hobab a share in the goodness of God. The second offer is left open-ended. It is not Moses and Israel who decide to include Hobab in the wilderness camp, but the Midianite himself.

Fourth, God is three days ahead of Israel. The ark advances to protect Israel from enemies and to search for a resting place. It was noted in the commentary that this image has theological significance in the pre-priestly history. It continues in the New Testament. Jesus leads the church from the other side of Easter. The passion of Jesus from Good Friday through Easter also places him three days ahead of us. According to the writer of Hebrews, this makes Jesus a pioneer who lives on the frontier of a new salvation (Heb 2:10). He destroys death and seeks out a resting place for the church. Following Jesus, according to the writer of Hebrews, is like journeying with God through the wilderness (Hebrews 3–4).

2. The prominence of war imagery to depict the life of faith is an obstacle for teaching and preaching. Israel is a militia (Num 10:11-28), and the leading of God is glorified as victory over an enemy (Num 10:29-36). This imagery continues to be prominent in the church. The passion of Jesus is envisioned as a war against death, and Christians are soldiers of Christ. Teaching about holy war requires careful reflection on both its violent imagery and its social implications. Holy war is a theological metaphor to describe the conflict between God and death. The violent imagery indicates the power of death. Its grip on the world is strong; it is able to wage war against God and influence human society. God battles death in its many forms.

There are always social implications to holy war. Specific actions vary widely in the Bible. In Num 10:11-36, Israel must join in God's battle against death. Israel is Yahweh's militia. The demands are concrete and influence their way of life. But holy war does not describe political and military actions in support of the nation and its land. The Israelites have no land in Num 10:11-36. They are Yahweh's militia in the wilderness. They wage holy war by maintaining God's holiness, which may put them in conflict with others. The wars against the king of Arad (Num 21:1-3), King Sihon (Num 21:21-32), and the Midianites (Numbers 31) are instances of holy war.

The life and passion of Jesus are another model for waging holy war. Conflict is also central to the story of Jesus. He wages holy war by suffering for others, and in his suffering he defeats the power of death. In the case of Jesus, holy war theology becomes the basis for pacifism. Some Christian communities continue to wage holy war against death by turning the other cheek in social situations of violence. The two examples indicate broad social implications of holy war in the Bible from activism to pacifism. What they have in common is that conflicts of holy war are not determined by national policy. They are made clear through revelation in the church.

3. The symbolism of the ark is important for preaching, teaching, and worship. The commentary for Numbers 7:89 and 10:29-36 has outlined its significance throughout Israel's history of worship. It continues to inform Christian worship in two different ways. First, the holy war imagery of the ark is incorporated into the cross of Jesus. The cross symbolizes God's defeat of death. Its central place in our worship indicates the victory of God and the cost to God in winning this war. Thus there is victory in this symbol, but always at the price of suffering. The cross also becomes the standard or banner for the Christian church in our faith journey, in much the same way as the ark led Israel. The message is not one of triumphalism, but of challenge. The ark led Israel on a risky wilderness journey, filled with testing. The same is true when the cross becomes the emblem of the church. Jesus tells his disciples to pick up their cross and follow him. Second, the ark also indicated the central place of God's law in leading Israel. The title "ark of the covenant" pointed to the Ten Commandments contained in the chest. This symbolism of the ark continues in the central role of Scripture within Christian tradition. It is revelation that provides a road map for the Christian journey through the wilderness.

4. Biblical writers embrace both history and mythology to describe the power of God in the life of Israel. They describe historical periods and specific locations and infuse them with theological meaning. Thus their stories combine historical realism with supernatural actions of God. The use of Paran by the priestly writers is an example. It is both a location in the wilderness and the home of God. The same is true for many other locations in Israel's journey through the wilderness. There is a reason for this method of writing. Biblical writers always look for God in history, but they refuse to reduce the power of God to the events of history. This method of writing theology has become unfamiliar in the modern period of the church. We separate history and mythology, and often we force a choice between the two. The fundamentalist and modernist debate provides illustration. One perspective stresses solely the historical reliability of the wilderness stories. The other reduces historical tradition to ideas. Both interpretations are dissatisfactory because they are at odds with biblical literature. Preaching the wilderness stories requires the same easy movement between myth and history evidenced by the biblical writers.

NUMBERS 11:1–19:22, MURMURING AND DEATH IN THE WILDERNESS

OVERVIEW

These chapters outline the tragic wilderness journey of the first generation. The literature is organized around three conflicts, in which Israel rebels against God and the leadership of Moses.

Chapters 11–12 explore the prophetic leadership of Moses through a series of complaints. Numbers 11:1-3 introduces the section with a general story of complaint by the rabble in the camp, who are destroyed by fire. Israel murmurs about the lack of food in 11:4-35, prompting Moses to complain about his leadership role. Transfer of his prophetic spirit to the seventy elders becomes the central topic. Numbers 12 emphasizes the unique status of Moses as a prophetic leader when Miriam and Aaron challenge his privileged role to speak with God.

Chapters 13–15 tell how the first generation of Israelites lost the gift of the land. Chapters 13–14 recount the spying out of the land, the fear of Israel to wage holy war, and their inability to see the goodness of the land. Chapter 15 concludes the episode with legislation about sacrifices that Israel must perform when they eventually enter the land.

Chapters 16–17 explore priestly leadership in the wilderness camp. Chapter 16 tells of a rebellion against Moses by Dathan and Abiram, two leaders from the tribe of Reuben. Their story is combined with another rebellion by the Levite Korah, who challenges the priestly leadership of Moses and Aaron. Chapter 17 is the story of Aaron's budding staff, which confirms his leadership role as priest.

Chapters 18–19 are laws providing guidelines for approaching God in the tabernacle. Chapter 18 outlines the requirements for tithing, and chap. 19 contains the ritual for purification from corpse contamination. Guidelines for purification from the dead conclude the episode on a note of hope. Contamination from death can be purged from the community with the ashes of the red heifer. Murmuring and death in the wilderness are not God's last word for Israel.

Two themes are developed in 11:1–19:22. The first is death in the wilderness. Complaints by the first generation about Mosaic leadership and their rejection of the promised land create a tragic story. The people's rebellion results in their aimless wandering and eventual death. The second theme is the leadership of Moses. Rebellion is often against his leadership.

The Murmuring Stories. Numbers 11:1–19:22 is organized around episodes of complaint, known as the murmuring stories.[102] Threatening situations in the wilderness cause Israel to protest their present condition. Their complaint is accompanied by a longing to return to slavery in Egypt.

The murmuring stories begin at the exodus when the Israelites complain to Moses at the Red Sea during the attack by Pharaoh. They prefer their life of slavery in Egypt over the risky journey with God through the wilderness (Exod 14:11-12). Two rounds of murmuring stories follow their initial complaint at the Red Sea. The first sequence occurs in the march from Egypt to Sinai (Exodus 15–17). The second takes place during Israel's journey from Sinai to the plains of Moab (Num 11:1–19:22). The two sequences are separated by the revelation at Mt. Sinai (Exodus 19–Numbers 10). The formation of covenant and the creation of the tabernacle cult change God's response to the murmuring stories from assistance to judgment.

The Israelites raise three complaints in their initial journey from Egypt to Sinai (Exodus 15–17). The first concerns bitter or diseased water (Exod 15:22-26).[103] The second is about the lack of food in the wilderness (Exodus 16), and the third complaint is over the absence of water (Exod 17:1-7). The initial murmuring stories address the major environmental problems that arise in following God through the wilderness. Each problem is an appropriate concern about divine providence, prompting assistance from God. In the first story, Yahweh provides a way for Moses to purify the water. The crisis of food is solved by the miracle of manna, and in response to the third complaint, Moses draws water out of a rock. Israel's complaints do not indicate their lack of faith in God's leading. Instead, they occur during a period of courtship between God and Israel. God tests Israel in the incident of bitter water (Exod 15:22-26), and Israel tests God in their request for water from the rock (Exod 17:1-7). Complaint does not lead to divine judgment, but to rescue. The first sequence of murmuring stories corresponds to the prophet Hosea's interpretation of the wilderness as a period of innocence, when God courted Israel (Hos 2:14-15).

Numbers 11:1–19:22 repeats the murmuring stories about food (11:4-35) and water (20:2-13). The problem of health also returns in 21:4-9. Other murmuring stories include a general complaint about the wilderness (11:1-3), a protest about the threatening inhabitants in the land of

---

102. George W. Coats, *Rebellion in the Wilderness: The Murmuring Motif in the Wilderness Traditions of the Old Testament* (Nashville: Abingdon, 1968).

103. Norbert Lohfink, " 'I am Yahweh, your Physician' (Exodus 15:26): God, Society and Human Health in a Postexilic Revision of the Pentateuch (Exod. 15:2b, 26)," in *Theology of the Pentateuch: Themes of the Priestly Narrative and Deuteronomy,* trans. Linda M. Maloney (Minneapolis: Fortress, 1994) 35-95.

Canaan (chap. 14), and further criticism of the leadership of Moses and Aaron (chaps. 16–17). Murmuring after the events of Sinai changes God's response from assistance to judgment. The murmuring stories in 11:1–19:22 illustrate the loss of faith of the first generation and their eventual death in the wilderness.

The murmuring stories also provide a loose structure to the death of the first generation. Two stories of complaint frame the second wilderness period. The complaint of the rabble occurs as Israel leaves Sinai (11:1-3). There is also a complaint about food as the people leave the wilderness (21:4-9). Both stories are general complaints about the conditions of life in the wilderness. Each prompts immediate divine judgment. The first murmuring brings divine fire on the camp, while the second brings forth deadly fiery serpents. The immediacy of divine judgment indicates how the mood has changed from the period of courtship in Exodus 15–17. Murmuring is no longer appro-

priate testing of God's providence after the revelation of law, construction of the cult, and establishment of covenant at Mt. Sinai. It is rebellion against God and the leadership of Moses.

The Leadership of Moses. Divine judgment on the first generation allows for development in the leadership role of Moses as an intercessor. His prayer often stops divine judgment. The enhanced role of Moses as intercessor alerts the reader to issues of leadership that run throughout the murmuring stories in 11:1–19:22. The complaint about meat (chaps. 11–12) explores Moses' prophetic leadership. He models intercession by averting divine anger when Israel rejects the promised land and God wishes to destroy them immediately (chaps. 13–15). The priestly leadership of Moses and Aaron is central to the rebellion by Korah (chaps. 16–17). Thus models of leadership emerge from the conflicts between the first generation and Moses.

Numbers 11:1–12:16, Conflict Over Prophetic Leadership

NIV	NRSV

NIV

11 Now the people complained about their hardships in the hearing of the LORD, and when he heard them his anger was aroused. Then fire from the LORD burned among them and consumed some of the outskirts of the camp. ²When the people cried out to Moses, he prayed to the LORD and the fire died down. ³So that place was called Taberah,ᵃ because fire from the LORD had burned among them.

⁴The rabble with them began to crave other food, and again the Israelites started wailing and said, "If only we had meat to eat! ⁵We remember the fish we ate in Egypt at no cost—also the cucumbers, melons, leeks, onions and garlic. ⁶But now we have lost our appetite; we never see anything but this manna!"

⁷The manna was like coriander seed and looked like resin. ⁸The people went around gathering it, and then ground it in a handmill or crushed it in a mortar. They cooked it in a pot or made it into cakes. And it tasted like something made with olive oil. ⁹When the dew settled on the camp at night, the manna also came down.

a3 Taberah means burning.

NRSV

11 Now when the people complained in the hearing of the LORD about their misfortunes, the LORD heard it and his anger was kindled. Then the fire of the LORD burned against them, and consumed some outlying parts of the camp. ²But the people cried out to Moses; and Moses prayed to the LORD, and the fire abated. ³So that place was called Taberah,ᵃ because the fire of the LORD burned against them.

4The rabble among them had a strong craving; and the Israelites also wept again, and said, "If only we had meatˈ to eat! ⁵We remember the fish we used to eat in Egypt for nothing, the cucumbers, the melons, the leeks, the onions, and the garlic; ⁶but now our strength is dried up, and there is nothing at all but this manna to look at."

7Now the manna was like coriander seed, and its color was like the color of gum resin. ⁸The people went around and gathered it, ground it in mills or beat it in mortars, then boiled it in pots and made cakes of it; and the taste of it was like the taste of cakes baked with oil. ⁹When the

a That is Burning

NIV

[10]Moses heard the people of every family wailing, each at the entrance to his tent. The LORD became exceedingly angry, and Moses was troubled. [11]He asked the LORD, "Why have you brought this trouble on your servant? What have I done to displease you that you put the burden of all these people on me? [12]Did I conceive all these people? Did I give them birth? Why do you tell me to carry them in my arms, as a nurse carries an infant, to the land you promised on oath to their forefathers? [13]Where can I get meat for all these people? They keep wailing to me, 'Give us meat to eat!' [14]I cannot carry all these people by myself; the burden is too heavy for me. [15]If this is how you are going to treat me, put me to death right now—if I have found favor in your eyes—and do not let me face my own ruin."

[16]The LORD said to Moses: "Bring me seventy of Israel's elders who are known to you as leaders and officials among the people. Have them come to the Tent of Meeting, that they may stand there with you. [17]I will come down and speak with you there, and I will take of the Spirit that is on you and put the Spirit on them. They will help you carry the burden of the people so that you will not have to carry it alone.

[18]"Tell the people: 'Consecrate yourselves in preparation for tomorrow, when you will eat meat. The LORD heard you when you wailed, "If only we had meat to eat! We were better off in Egypt!" Now the LORD will give you meat, and you will eat it. [19]You will not eat it for just one day, or two days, or five, ten or twenty days, [20]but for a whole month—until it comes out of your nostrils and you loathe it—because you have rejected the LORD, who is among you, and have wailed before him, saying, "Why did we ever leave Egypt?"'"

[21]But Moses said, "Here I am among six hundred thousand men on foot, and you say, 'I will give them meat to eat for a whole month!' [22]Would they have enough if flocks and herds were slaughtered for them? Would they have enough if all the fish in the sea were caught for them?"

[23]The LORD answered Moses, "Is the LORD's arm too short? You will now see whether or not what I say will come true for you."

NRSV

dew fell on the camp in the night, the manna would fall with it.

[10]Moses heard the people weeping throughout their families, all at the entrances of their tents. Then the LORD became very angry, and Moses was displeased. [11]So Moses said to the LORD, "Why have you treated your servant so badly? Why have I not found favor in your sight, that you lay the burden of all this people on me? [12]Did I conceive all this people? Did I give birth to them, that you should say to me, 'Carry them in your bosom, as a nurse carries a sucking child,' to the land that you promised on oath to their ancestors? [13]Where am I to get meat to give to all this people? For they come weeping to me and say, 'Give us meat to eat!' [14]I am not able to carry all this people alone, for they are too heavy for me. [15]If this is the way you are going to treat me, put me to death at once—if I have found favor in your sight—and do not let me see my misery."

[16]So the LORD said to Moses, "Gather for me seventy of the elders of Israel, whom you know to be the elders of the people and officers over them; bring them to the tent of meeting, and have them take their place there with you. [17]I will come down and talk with you there; and I will take some of the spirit that is on you and put it on them; and they shall bear the burden of the people along with you so that you will not bear it all by yourself. [18]And say to the people: Consecrate yourselves for tomorrow, and you shall eat meat; for you have wailed in the hearing of the LORD, saying, 'If only we had meat to eat! Surely it was better for us in Egypt.' Therefore the LORD will give you meat, and you shall eat. [19]You shall eat not only one day, or two days, or five days, or ten days, or twenty days, [20]but for a whole month—until it comes out of your nostrils and becomes loathsome to you—because you have rejected the LORD who is among you, and have wailed before him, saying, 'Why did we ever leave Egypt?'" [21]But Moses said, "The people I am with number six hundred thousand on foot; and you say, 'I will give them meat, that they may eat for a whole month'! [22]Are there enough flocks and herds to slaughter for them? Are there enough fish in the sea to catch for them?" [23]The LORD

NIV

²⁴So Moses went out and told the people what the LORD had said. He brought together seventy of their elders and had them stand around the Tent. ²⁵Then the LORD came down in the cloud and spoke with him, and he took of the Spirit that was on him and put the Spirit on the seventy elders. When the Spirit rested on them, they prophesied, but they did not do so again.ᵃ

²⁶However, two men, whose names were Eldad and Medad, had remained in the camp. They were listed among the elders, but did not go out to the Tent. Yet the Spirit also rested on them, and they prophesied in the camp. ²⁷A young man ran and told Moses, "Eldad and Medad are prophesying in the camp."

²⁸Joshua son of Nun, who had been Moses' aide since youth, spoke up and said, "Moses, my lord, stop them!"

²⁹But Moses replied, "Are you jealous for my sake? I wish that all the LORD's people were prophets and that the LORD would put his Spirit on them!" ³⁰Then Moses and the elders of Israel returned to the camp.

³¹Now a wind went out from the LORD and drove quail in from the sea. It brought themᵇ down all around the camp to about three feetᶜ above the ground, as far as a day's walk in any direction. ³²All that day and night and all the next day the people went out and gathered quail. No one gathered less than ten homers.ᵈ Then they spread them out all around the camp. ³³But while the meat was still between their teeth and before it could be consumed, the anger of the LORD burned against the people, and he struck them with a severe plague. ³⁴Therefore the place was named Kibroth Hattaavah,ᵉ because there they buried the people who had craved other food.

³⁵From Kibroth Hattaavah the people traveled to Hazeroth and stayed there.

12 Miriam and Aaron began to talk against Moses because of his Cushite wife, for he had married a Cushite. ²"Has the LORD spoken only through Moses?" they asked. "Hasn't he also spoken through us?" And the LORD heard this.

ᵃ25 Or prophesied and continued to do so   ᵇ31 Or They flew
ᶜ31 Hebrew two cubits (about 1 meter)   ᵈ32 That is, probably about 60 bushels (about 2.2 kiloliters)   ᵉ34 Kibroth Hattaavah means graves of craving.

NRSV

said to Moses, "Is the LORD's power limited?ᵃ Now you shall see whether my word will come true for you or not."

24So Moses went out and told the people the words of the LORD; and he gathered seventy elders of the people, and placed them all around the tent. ²⁵Then the LORD came down in the cloud and spoke to him, and took some of the spirit that was on him and put it on the seventy elders; and when the spirit rested upon them, they prophesied. But they did not do so again.

26Two men remained in the camp, one named Eldad, and the other named Medad, and the spirit rested on them; they were among those registered, but they had not gone out to the tent, and so they prophesied in the camp. ²⁷And a young man ran and told Moses, "Eldad and Medad are prophesying in the camp." ²⁸And Joshua son of Nun, the assistant of Moses, one of his chosen men,ᵇ said, "My lord Moses, stop them!" ²⁹But Moses said to him, "Are you jealous for my sake? Would that all the LORD's people were prophets, and that the LORD would put his spirit on them!" ³⁰And Moses and the elders of Israel returned to the camp.

31Then a wind went out from the LORD, and it brought quails from the sea and let them fall beside the camp, about a day's journey on this side and a day's journey on the other side, all around the camp, about two cubits deep on the ground. ³²So the people worked all that day and night and all the next day, gathering the quails; the least anyone gathered was ten homers; and they spread them out for themselves all around the camp. ³³But while the meat was still between their teeth, before it was consumed, the anger of the LORD was kindled against the people, and the LORD struck the people with a very great plague. ³⁴So that place was called Kibroth-hattaavah,ᶜ because there they buried the people who had the craving. ³⁵From Kibroth-hattaavah the people journeyed to Hazeroth.

12 While they were at Hazeroth, Miriam and Aaron spoke against Moses because of the Cushite woman whom he had married (for he had indeed married a Cushite woman); ²and they

ᵃ Heb LORD's hand too short?   ᵇ Or of Moses from his youth
ᶜ That is Graves of craving

³(Now Moses was a very humble man, more humble than anyone else on the face of the earth.)

⁴At once the LORD said to Moses, Aaron and Miriam, "Come out to the Tent of Meeting, all three of you." So the three of them came out. ⁵Then the LORD came down in a pillar of cloud; he stood at the entrance to the Tent and summoned Aaron and Miriam. When both of them stepped forward, ⁶he said, "Listen to my words:

"When a prophet of the LORD is among you,
 I reveal myself to him in visions,
 I speak to him in dreams.
⁷But this is not true of my servant Moses;
 he is faithful in all my house.
⁸With him I speak face to face,
 clearly and not in riddles;
 he sees the form of the LORD.
Why then were you not afraid
 to speak against my servant Moses?"

⁹The anger of the LORD burned against them, and he left them.

¹⁰When the cloud lifted from above the Tent, there stood Miriam—leprous,ᵃ like snow. Aaron turned toward her and saw that she had leprosy; ¹¹and he said to Moses, "Please, my lord, do not hold against us the sin we have so foolishly committed. ¹²Do not let her be like a stillborn infant coming from its mother's womb with its flesh half eaten away."

¹³So Moses cried out to the LORD, "O God, please heal her!"

¹⁴The LORD replied to Moses, "If her father had spit in her face, would she not have been in disgrace for seven days? Confine her outside the camp for seven days; after that she can be brought back." ¹⁵So Miriam was confined outside the camp for seven days, and the people did not move on till she was brought back.

¹⁶After that, the people left Hazeroth and encamped in the Desert of Paran.

ᵃ10 The Hebrew word was used for various diseases affecting the skin—not necessarily leprosy.

said, "Has the LORD spoken only through Moses? Has he not spoken through us also?" And the LORD heard it. ³Now the man Moses was very humble,ᵃ more so than anyone else on the face of the earth. ⁴Suddenly the LORD said to Moses, Aaron, and Miriam, "Come out, you three, to the tent of meeting." So the three of them came out. ⁵Then the LORD came down in a pillar of cloud, and stood at the entrance of the tent, and called Aaron and Miriam; and they both came forward. ⁶And he said, "Hear my words:

When there are prophets among you,
 I the LORD make myself known to them
  in visions;
 I speak to them in dreams.
⁷ Not so with my servant Moses;
 he is entrusted with all my house.
⁸ With him I speak face to face—clearly, not
  in riddles;
 and he beholds the form of the LORD.
Why then were you not afraid to speak against my servant Moses?" ⁹And the anger of the LORD was kindled against them, and he departed.

10When the cloud went away from over the tent, Miriam had become leprous,ᵇ as white as snow. And Aaron turned towards Miriam and saw that she was leprous. ¹¹Then Aaron said to Moses, "Oh, my lord, do not punish usᶜ for a sin that we have so foolishly committed. ¹²Do not let her be like one stillborn, whose flesh is half consumed when it comes out of its mother's womb." ¹³And Moses cried to the LORD, "O God, please heal her." ¹⁴But the LORD said to Moses, "If her father had but spit in her face, would she not bear her shame for seven days? Let her be shut out of the camp for seven days, and after that she may be brought in again." ¹⁵So Miriam was shut out of the camp for seven days; and the people did not set out on the march until Miriam had been brought in again. ¹⁶After that the people set out from Hazeroth, and camped in the wilderness of Paran.

ᵃ Or devout ᵇA term for several skin diseases; precise meaning uncertain ᶜHeb do not lay sin upon us

COMMENTARY

Numbers 11–12 is a collection of stories compiled to explore the prophetic leadership of Moses.

Prophetic leadership is charismatic. The word *charisma* means "gift" in Greek. Moses is a gifted person. His power arises from his personality, and not from an inherited office of leadership. He is set apart from others, filled with the divine Spirit. He speaks with God face to face; he speaks for God to the community; and he intercedes on behalf of the people.

Chapters 11–12 describe the nature of Moses' charismatic leadership from different perspectives. Numbers 11:1-3 functions as an introduction, defining the mood and interaction of characters. Numbers 11:4-35 juxtaposes two different complaints—one by the people about the lack of meat and another by Moses about the burden of leadership. The complaint of Moses dominates the story. It provides the occasion to explore how his charismatic spirit can be transferred to others. The conflict between Miriam, Aaron, and Moses in Numbers 12 emphasizes the unique quality of Moses' prophetic spirit. Taken together, these stories explore the nature of charismatic leadership in the wilderness community.

11:1-3. This is an odd story, striking both in its context and in its content. It is a negative story about complaint, for which the reader is unprepared, especially after the account of Israel's leaving Sinai in 10:11-36. Its unexpected appearance at the outset of Israel's journey signals a change of mood in the book of Numbers from the formation of community at Sinai (chaps. 1–10) to conflict in the wilderness journey (chaps. 11–19). Conflict will provide opportunity for biblical writers to define more clearly the character of community and the leadership role of Moses.

Verses 1-3 lack specific details. They begin abruptly with an unexpected complaint by the people. Just as abruptly, God sends down fire to destroy rebels in the camp. The story moves quickly to a resolution and a concluding etiology. The location of this event is named Taberah (תבערה *tab'ērâ*; from בערה [*bě'ērâ*, "burning"]), because God uses fire to punish the people. The sequence includes the five basic elements in the murmuring stories: (1) complaint by the people; (2) divine punishment; (3) the cry of the people; (4) intercession by Moses; and (5) the end of divine judgment. This structure is somewhat different from the initial murmuring stories in Exodus 15–17, where complaint was not followed by divine punishment.

The language of vv. 1-3 introduces themes that the biblical writers will be addressing in chaps.

11–19. The Hebrew word translated "to complain" (אנן *'ānan*) in v. 1 appears only twice in the Hebrew Bible. The other occurrence is in Lam 3:39, where the negative character of complaint in Num 11:1-3 is reinforced. The author of Lam 3:37-39 states: "Who can command and have it done,/ if the LORD has not ordained it?/ Is it not from the mouth of the Most High/ that good and bad come?/ Why should any who draw breath complain/ about the punishment of their sins?" (NRSV). The writer of Lamentations leaves no room for the type of complaint signified by the Hebrew word *'ānan*. Numbers 11:1-3 shows how such complaint can actually prompt divine punishment.

Verse 2 states that divine fire destroyed all persons at the "outlying parts of the camp." Placement within the camp indicates moral action. The commentary on chaps. 1–10 provides illustration. God dwells at the center of the camp. The holiness of God radiates from the tabernacle and enhances life throughout the camp. The area outside the camp is of a different quality. Thus someone suffering from skin disease must be put outside the camp to avoid contaminating the community within the campsite (chap. 5). It is doubtful that priestly writers composed 11:1-3, but the pre-priestly authors are working with a similar understanding of holiness and community. Complaint does not characterize the people of God. Those who complain are not transformed members of the community. Their action places them at the edge of the camp. Divine fire at the edge of the camp defines the boundaries of community. Such borderline persons are pruned from the camp by fire. Yet Moses has the ability to intercede on behalf of those who are God's people. Thus conflict defines community and the leadership role of Moses. Both themes will continue throughout Numbers 11–19.

11:4-35. This is a distinct murmuring story. It is separated from vv. 1-3 by a new complaint, this time about the lack of meat in the wilderness. The story also occurs at a different location. The concluding etiology in v. 34 locates the story at Kibroth-hattaaveh ("graves of craving") as compared to Taberah ("burning") in v. 3. Verses 4-35 are also separated from chap. 12 by the itinerary notice in v. 35. The people journey from Kibroth-hattaaveh to Hazeroth for the next complaint story.

The juxtaposition of the themes of the people's desire for meat (vv. 4-9, 13, 18-23, 31-34) and Moses' complaint about the burden of leadership (vv. 10-12, 14-17, 24-30) raises questions concerning the authorship of these verses.[104] It is possible that the leadership theme was added to a complaint story about meat. The problem of leadership is embedded in that story and cannot be read independently of it, while the complaint about meat can be read as an independent story. Yet, it is not possible to distinguish the authors of the different themes. A careful study of the motifs favors a unified reading of the story. I read the entire account in vv. 4-35 as a pre-priestly complaint story, in which the subordinate theme of leadership is the central problem. Thus complaint about meat provides the setting for exploring how the charismatic spirit of Moses is distributed to others, first to the seventy elders and then to Eldad and Medad.

11:4-15. The opening section provides the setting and circumstances for the story. The complaint about meat is introduced in vv. 4-9. Verse 4 is important. It states that certain members of the camp, described as the "rabble" (אספסף ʾăsāpsup) had a strong "craving" (התאוה taʾăwâ). Because the term translated "rabble" occurs only once in the OT, it is difficult to know exactly what the biblical writers meant by using it. The rabble does not represent all the people, since the writers explicitly state that the activity of this group eventually affects all the Israelites.

The distinction in groups raises the question of identity. That the rabble is a sub-group of persons who have been gathered into the camp is basic to the Hebrew word, which includes the verbal form "to gather" (אסף ʾāsap). This may be a reference to the "mixed crowd" that left Egypt with Israel (Exod 12:38), but the language is not the same. It is more likely that the term indicates a fringe group that is defined by its action. The latter interpretation provides insight into the Hebrew word האספסף (hāʾsapsup), whose ending (סוף sôp) could mean "end," thus designating those gathered at the outer circumference of the camp: Their act of craving defines them as fringe members of the camp.

The craving for meat sets the story in motion.

It affects all Israelites who join in the complaint, and it continues to the end of the story, where the Hebrew word "craving" (taʾăwâ) becomes part of the place name, Kibroth-hattaavah. The craving for meat is a rejection of manna, the wilderness food first given to Israel in Exodus 16. This is indicated by an extended description in vv. 7-9 of the different ways that manna was served and eaten in the wilderness. The reference to manna indicates that the rabble has rejected divine providence in the wilderness through their desire for meat.

The story takes an unexpected turn from the complaint about the lack of meat to the problem of leadership. Verse 10 describes the circumstances in the camp. The people are crying at the openings of their tents. God is angry over their complaint for meat, and Moses also hears the crying of Israel and judges the situation to be very evil. The five elements of the murmuring story outlined in vv. 1-3 indicate intercession by Moses as the next action. Instead of seeking a remedy through intercession, however, Moses complains about the burden of leadership (vv. 11-15).

The exchange between Moses and God provides commentary on two previous stories. The first is Exodus 18, where Jethro advised Moses on the organization of the camp and recommended more leaders to govern the people. This story provided a prelude to the revelation of law at Sinai. The second story is Exodus 33, where Moses negotiated with God to continue leading Israel after the incident of the golden calf (Exodus 32). God desired to destroy Israel as punishment for the idolatry of the calf (Exod 32:9-10). Moses interceded for Israel and persuaded God not to destroy them (Exod 32:11-14). Exodus 33 contains a second intercession by Moses, in which he persuades God to accompany Israel in the wilderness. He states to Yahweh:

"See, you have said to me, 'Bring up this people'; but you have not let me know whom you will send with me. Yet you have said, 'I know you by name, and you have also found favor in my sight.' Now if I have found favor in your sight, show me our ways, so that I may know you and find favor in your sight." . . . He [Yahweh] said, "My presence will go with you, and I will give you rest." (Exod 33:12-14 NRSV)

Exodus 33 provides the background for interpreting the problems of leadership in Num 11:10-15. The description of the Israelites crying at the

---

104. See Martin Noth, *Numbers,* OTL (Philadelphia: Westminster, 1968) 83-85.

openings of their tents (v. 10) repeats the setting of Exod 33:7-11, where the Israelites are sitting at the entrances of their tents. The points of contact between Exodus 33 and the leadership story in Num 11:10-15 continue in Moses' speech. In his opening complaint, Moses poses the question, "Why have I not found favor in your sight?" This question presupposes Exod 33:12-23, where the phrase was at the center of the successful attempt to persuade God to lead Israel through the wilderness. Moses' complaint about leadership (vv. 12-15) is rooted in a theological problem about divine guidance and presence that was first addressed in Exodus 33.

The problem of leadership in vv. 12-15 is the conflicting expectations of Moses by God and the Israelites. Food is the central metaphor for addressing the problem. Moses' complaint juxtaposes God's (v. 12*b*) and the Israelite's (v. 13) views of appropriate food for the wilderness journey, each indicating different leadership models. Moses first states God's expectations for leadership. He raises a rhetorical question, meant as a complaint: "Did I conceive all this people? Did I give birth to them?" The implied answer to his question is that Moses did not give birth to Israel but that God has, which provides the force for the quotation about food in v. 12*b*: "Then why are you telling me, 'Carry them in your bosom as a nurse carries a suckling child?' " The imagery is feminine, involving conception and breast feeding. The expectation of God is that Moses will nurture Israel to maturity in the wilderness, eventually bringing them to the promised land. Manna in the wilderness symbolizes this stage in the Israelites' religious development. The view of the Israelites is contrasted to God's in v. 13. They do not want to mature through the wilderness journey. They want meat now. Moses quotes their demand in his complaint to God, "Give us meat to eat!" The impossibility of providing the two diets at the same time illustrates the burden of leadership. Two views of leadership collide in these quotations. God advocates breast feeding as a natural outgrowth of conception and birth over against the people, who want meat, and Moses is caught in the middle.

Moses concludes his complaint by appealing to the divine favor bestowed upon him in Exodus 33. As far as Moses is concerned, divine favor in the present contradictory situation is death, which

he requests. Death is better than the burden of leadership (v. 15). Two other prophets request death from God. Jonah wishes for death when a worm destroys a bush that has been giving him shade (Jonah 4:8). The prophet Elijah also requests death while fleeing from Jezebel in the wilderness (1 Kgs 19:4). His story provides a closer parallel to Moses, since Elijah is also a charismatic leader who believes that he is alone in following God.

11:16-23. God responds to both the problems of leadership and the Israelites' demand for meat in this section. The complaint by Moses about leadership is countered with instruction in vv. 16-17 on how to select seventy elders who will share in his spirit. The inner-biblical connections between Num 11:16-17 and Exodus 33 are again present. As was the case in Exodus 33, the tent of meeting is situated outside the camp, where it signifies a more prophetic encounter with God. Both Exodus 33 and Numbers 11 contrast the priestly writers' view that the tent of meeting is at the center of the camp and is equated with the priestly cult of the tabernacle.

The placement of the tent of meeting outside the camp signals that the complaint over leadership is meant to address problems of charismatic or prophetic leadership, rather than priestly leadership. This focus becomes even clearer from the details of the divine instruction. The seventy elders are scribes who, when stationed in front of the tent of meeting outside the camp, will received a portion of the spirit (רוח *rûaḥ*) of Moses, which will enable them to govern the people. The spirit of Moses refers to the spirit of prophecy (see Amos 9:7). The spirit is also central in the charismatic leadership of judges (Judg 3:10; 11:29). The word "scribe" (שטר *šōṭēr*) describes those who write documents, although their role in Numbers 11 is broader and includes administration. Reference to seventy may be symbolic. This number occurs frequently in the Old Testament. For example, there are seventy sons of Jacob (Exod 1:5); seventy elders accompany Moses upon the mountain (Exod 24:9-11); seventy princes are killed by Jehu (2 Kgs 10:6). The number seventy also is institutionalized in the Sanhedrin, the judicial body in Palestine during the Roman period.

God responds to the request for meat in vv. 18-23. The people are to consecrate themselves, an action they have not undertaken since the initial revelation of God on Mt. Sinai (Exod

19:10). God repeats the complaint of the people in v. 18, quoting their earlier words now as an indictment: "You have wailed in the hearing of the LORD, saying, 'If only we had meat to eat! Surely it was better for us in Egypt.'" Yahweh concludes that they will eat meat for no less than an entire month, until it comes out of their noses and becomes repulsive to them (vv. 19-20a). The reason for the negative tone is that the people's request for meat is really their rejection of the nurturing presence and providence of God in their midst (v. 20b).

The section ends with an aside in vv. 21-23, in which Moses reminds God of the 600,000 Israelites and the great quantities of cattle and fish needed to feed them. This number is a repetition of Exod 12:37, where this same number of people were described as having left Egypt. God responds to Moses with a rhetorical question: "Is the LORD's power limited?" The implied answer, no, moves the story to its completion in vv. 24-35.

11:24-35. The divine instructions are accomplished in this section. The selection of seventy elders is narrated in vv. 24-30. They are placed around the tent located outside the camp (v. 24). God descends in a cloud, takes some of the spirit of Moses, and places it on the seventy, causing them to prophesy momentarily (v. 25). The language in v. 25 is precise. It indicates that the seventy elders became ecstatic prophets when they received the spirit of Moses. The form of the verb "to prophesy" is hithpael, a form used to describe Saul when he was possessed by God and fell into a prophetic frenzy (1 Sam 10:10-11). But, just as the text is precise about the mantic behavior of the seventy elders, it is also equally explicit in stating that their behavior ceases.

The message of the story is paradoxical. The pre-priestly writers emphasize the importance of charismatic and prophetic leadership in the wilderness community. They state that elders from the people are able to participate in the power of the spirit of Moses, and thus they become charismatic leaders of the people. On the other hand, the pre-priestly writers do not want charismatic leadership to be uncontrolled. Thus the prophetic frenzy that overtakes the seventy elders and authenticates them is momentary and is not repeated. The story suggests that the pre-priestly writers idealize the power of prophecy, while they also wish for its traditional role to cease. Perhaps

this is why the seventy elders were described earlier as "scribes"—that is, inspired writers and interpreters of tradition, rather than classical prophets who spoke new words from God.

A similar development is evident in Deut 17:15-22. A prophet like Moses, who speaks oracles from Yahweh, is idealized (Deut 17:15-19). The Israelites are encouraged to look for another prophet like Moses. They will know that such a prophet has arisen when his spoken oracles are fulfilled (Deut 17:20-22). This criterion for judging the truth claims of a prophet, however, eliminates the power of prophetic oracles. The word of a prophet must be obeyed when it is spoken, not when it is fulfilled. The message of Deuteronomy 17 contains the same paradoxical message as Numbers 11. The prophetic spirit of Moses is idealized, while the traditional role of prophets is eliminated.

But charismatic power by definition cannot be completely controlled. The story of Eldad and Medad (vv. 26-30) emphasizes this point. It is a minority report to the previous story of the seventy elders. Verse 26 states that Eldad and Medad "were registered." Critics debate whether this means that they were numbered among the seventy elders, or simply were members of the community. In any case, the text clearly states that they were not at the tent of meeting outside the camp but within the camp. The Spirit of God spilled out upon them, causing the two to go into ecstatic frenzy like the seventy elders. Eldad and Medad represent the unpredictable side of charismatic leadership and hence a challenge to the orderly control of the spirit of Moses in vv. 24-25.

Joshua assumes a central role in the story of Eldad and Medad. He embodies the prophetic spirit of Moses more than does any other character in the Pentateuch. Joshua is introduced as the Israelites' gifted leader in holy war (Exod 17:8-13). He accompanies Moses onto Mt. Sinai to receive the tablets of the law (Exod 24:12-15; 32:17-19). His role in Num 11:26-30 links to Exodus 33, which states that Joshua remained in the tent of meeting alone when Moses left it. Joshua is a charismatic leader with a special role in the tent of meeting. He is concerned about the unpredictable presence of God's Spirit outside the tent of meeting in the camp. Wishing to control the spirit, he urges Moses to make Eldad and Medad stop prophesying: "My lord Moses, stop them!" (v. 28). This demand evokes a response from Moses: "Are you jealous for my sake? Would that all the LORD's people were prophets, and that the LORD would put his spirit on them!" Thus Moses rejects the desire of Joshua to control the transmission of his spirit to the seventy elders. He states that he does not hoard his own charismatic power; indeed, he wishes that all the people were prophets.

The exchange between Joshua and Moses ends in v. 30 with Moses gathering the seventy elders back into the camp. The use of the verb "to gather" (ʾāsap) repeats language from the opening section of the story (vv. 4-11). The incorporation of the seventy elders into the camp will be a contrast to those who leave the camp for meat in the following section.

The episode concludes by returning to the request of the Israelites for meat (vv. 31-35). Yahweh sends a wind from the sea that brings quails. The word "spirit" (rûaḥ), now meaning "wind" (v. 31), interrelates the selection of the seventy elders and the theme of meat. The story is miraculous and fantastic. Quails drop from heaven all around the camp (but not in it) until they are piled up two cubits deep (approx. 36-44 inches). The people who run out of the camp to catch these birds collect quail for two days, until the least that any one person possesses is ten homers of quail (approx. 89 bushels). But the feast no sooner begins than God kills the people with the meat still between their teeth. Thus all persons who chose to leave the camp for meat also choose death in the wilderness. The result is another pruning of the wilderness community. The miracle of quail answers the divine rhetorical question from v. 23, "Is the LORD's power limited?" Indeed, nothing is too difficult for God, but in this case the miracle comes with a price. Hence, the name of the place is "Graves of Craving" (Kibroth-hattaavah).

12:1-16. Chapter 12 is part of the pre-priestly history. The placement of the tent of meeting outside the camp ties chaps. 11 and 12 together. The broader literary connection to Exodus 33 continues, with the appearance of the pillar of cloud (v. 5; Exod 33:10). The literary relationships indicate that the pre-priestly history progressed from covenant renewal (Exodus 32–34) to the conflicts over prophetic leadership (Numbers 11–12). There are also signs of additional priestly

authorship: the characters of Miriam and Aaron, the seven-day period of purification from leprosy for Miriam (vv. 14-15; prescribed in Leviticus 13–14), and the reference to Paran in the closing itinerary notice (v. 16).

The charismatic leadership of Moses remains the central theme in the controversy between Miriam, Aaron, and Moses in this chapter, in which Miriam and Aaron claim the same prophetic authority as Moses. The central point of tension throughout the chapter is the need to maintain a hierarchy of authority among characters. Thus chap. 12 moves in the opposite direction of chap. 11, where the central problem was how the charismatic spirit of Moses could be passed on to the seventy elders, and even influence all members of the camp (11:29). The challenge from Miriam and Aaron sets in motion a story of divine revelation and punishment with a four-part structure.

12:1-3. These verses do not follow smoothly from chap. 11. Moses has no sooner told Joshua of his wish that all the people were prophets (11:29) than Miriam and Aaron challenge his own exclusive role of speaking for God. These opening verses present two problems for interpretation: determining why these particular characters are involved in the story and discerning the content of the challenge from Miriam and Aaron.

Why are the priest Aaron and his sister, Miriam, the ones who challenge Moses' special status as a charismatic leader? One would expect such a challenge from a more charismatic figure like Joshua or even the seventy elders, who now possess the spirit of Moses. Some scholars argue that Aaron is a late addition to the story and that Miriam alone originally challenged Moses.[105] Implied in this interpretation is the view that in early Israelite culture women played a more central and charismatic role, which was played down in later tradition.[106] The strength of this argument is that women assume charismatic leadership roles in the OT. In Exod 15:20, Miriam is presented as a charismatic prophet like Deborah (Judges 5) when she sings her victory song after the defeat of the

---

105. Martin Noth, *A History of Pentateuchal Traditions,* trans. Bernhard W. Anderson (Chico, Calif.: Scholars Press, 1981) 180-81.

106. For the role of Miriam in tradition, see P. Trible, "Subversive Justice: Tracing the Miriamic Traditions," in *Justice and the Holy: Essays in Honor of Walter Harrelson,* ed. D. A. Knight and P. J. Paris (Atlanta: Scholars Press, 1989) 102; and R. J. Burns, *Has the Lord Indeed Spoken Only Through Moses? A Study of the Biblical Portrait of Miriam,* SBLDS 84 (Atlanta: Scholars Press, 1987) 119-20.

Egyptian army at the sea. From this perspective, the anomaly of having a priest claim the charismatic spirit of Moses is resolved by interpreting the story at an earlier level of tradition. The challenge in Numbers 12 is between the two charismatic leaders of the exodus, Moses and Miriam.

The weakness of that interpretation is that it is difficult to edit out the character of Aaron. Often the verbal tenses presuppose two opponents against Moses, while the structure of the story, with its levels of intercession, implies all three characters. Even if one reconstructs a fairly coherent story with only Moses and Miriam, it still does not address Aaron's role in the present form of the story. Thus the problem of how many characters are involved is not easily resolved. It becomes even more problematic if we assume that Numbers 12 was written, or at least edited, by priestly authors, since this story is critical of Aaron, who ordinarily functions as their hero.

The reason for the central role of Miriam and Aaron in challenging Moses' charismatic authority may be their role in the exodus. They are the only other characters called prophets. Aaron is described as the prophet of Moses in Exod 7:1, while Miriam is called a prophet in Exod 15:20. In fact, outside of Miriam and Aaron, the only other character described as a prophet in the entire Pentateuch is Abraham (Gen 20:7), whose intercession for Abimelech provides background for interpreting Moses' mediation for Miriam in Num 12:11-15. The familial relationship of Miriam, Aaron, and Moses in priestly tradition may be another reason for their having this central role (Num 28:59). The family setting implied in the central characters of Numbers 12 also provides some context for the dispute over marriage that initiates the conflict.

Aaron and Miriam present two distinct complaints to Moses in vv. 1-2 that are not easily related. In v. 1, they complain about Moses' intermarriage to a Cushite woman. The topic changes in v. 2, when they question Moses' status as the only person to speak for God. The second challenge concerning Moses' special role as spokesperson for God conforms to the larger topic of charismatic authority. But the complaint concerning his wife appears to be isolated from the larger themes of the chapter.

Intermarriage between Israelites and foreigners

was forbidden in the post-exilic period. The emergence of this law may have provided the background of this story for both the pre-priestly and the priestly writers. Deuteronomy 7:3 states that Israel is to make no covenants with the people of the land, including intermarriage. Numbers 25 illustrates the corrupting influence of intermarriage with the Moabites (the pre-priestly version) and the Midianites (the priestly account). Ezra 9–10 recounts the policy in the post-exilic period whereby all foreign wives were sent away to their homes of origin. The complaint of Miriam and Aaron thus represents the policy on intermarriage in that Moses' marriage to a Cushite woman conflicts with this teaching.

Reference to Moses' marriage to a Cushite appears only in Num 12:1. The more developed tradition is that he married the Midianite woman Zipporah (Exodus 2–4, 18). The land of Cush refers to ancient Nubia (the kingdom south of Egypt), which is modern-day Ethiopia. Sporadic references to Cush in the OT suggest that it symbolized the outermost southern boundaries of the world for ancient Israel (Gen 2:13; Esth 1:1; 8:9). In this role it takes on exotic associations as a place of wealth (Job 28:19; Isa 45:14) and as a land populated by near mythic warriors, like Nimrod (Genesis 10).

The marriage of Moses to a Cushite woman stands in uneasy tension with authoritative teaching on intermarriage. It challenges the prescribed boundaries of the camp, and it is this quality that interrelates the two complaints of Miriam and Aaron in vv. 1-2. Their challenge concerning the special status of Moses as the authorative voice for God (v. 2) cannot be separated from their complaint concerning his marriage to the Cushite (v. 1). The two reinforce each other. By arguing that God also speaks through them, Miriam and Aaron are adding authority to their criticism of Moses' intermarriage. Their claim, furthermore, is supported by law. They represent the power of tradition; Moses has violated tradition.

Yet God supports Moses over against traditional law. Verse 3 sets the stage for refuting the challenge to Moses' authority, stressing his special quality as a devout person: "Moses was very humble, more so than anyone else on the face of the earth." The description of Moses as being humble (עָנָו 'ānāw) is not a psychological assessment. It describes his status before God. The "humble" are those who seek God (Pss 22:27; 69:33), hear God (Ps 34:3), rejoice in God (Ps 63:33), and do justice and righteousness (Isa 11:4). As a consequence, God hears the humble (Ps 10:17), saves them (Pss 76:10; 149:4), instructs them (Ps 25:9), and does not forget them (Pss 9:13; 10:12, 17). His humble nature makes Moses' status before God qualitatively different from that of any other person, including the other heroes of the exodus—Aaron and Miriam. His authority is not in any office, but in his personal qualities. Thus his actions are models of faithfulness to be repeated, not criticized.

Moses' marriage to a Cushite stands in uneasy tension with emerging teaching on intermarriage. It is an instance of inner-biblical interpretation, in which a story qualifies a broader teaching. The violation of marriage law is justified by Moses' personal quality of humility, and not by his having a special office of leadership. In this respect, Numbers 12 continues to explore the charismatic authority of Moses. The breaking of expected boundaries through marriage provides a point of contact with the unexpected spilling over of Moses' spirit onto Eldad and Medad in the previous story. Both stories challenge the structures of tradition. Each illustrates how charismatic power breaks boundaries. Joshua complained about this quality of uncontrolled ecstatic prophecy within the wilderness community by Eldad and Medad. Aaron and Miriam, the siblings of Moses, now complain about this quality in Moses' marriage, because it blurs the boundaries of the wilderness community.

12:4-10. This section describes God's response to the challenge of Aaron and Miriam. God suddenly calls Moses, Miriam, and Aaron to the tent of meeting outside the camp (v. 4). The presence of God is indicated by the pillar of cloud at the entrance of the tent (v. 5).

A divine oracle is given to Miriam and Aaron (vv. 6-8). The divine speech makes explicit the message implied in the narrator's comment in v. 3—namely, that Moses is incomparable, more humble than any person on earth. His charismatic authority is beyond that of the prophetic office. To prophets, Miriam and Aaron are told, God reveals messages through dreams and riddles (v. 6). To Moses, God speaks "mouth to mouth" (פֶּה אֶל־פֶּה peh 'el-peh). The phrase "mouth to mouth" occurs only in Num 12:8. The NIV and

the NRSV use the translation "face to face" to indicate the relationship between this oracle and Exodus 33, where the special status of Moses is established: "Yahweh used to speak to Moses face to face, as one speaks to a friend" (Exod 33:11). In 12:7, Moses is described as Yahweh's servant, entrusted with God's house. Thus Moses is trustworthy. He has even been allowed to see the form of God. The description of Moses links to the earlier account of his descent from Mt. Sinai with a shining face as a result of his nearness to God on the mountain (Exod 34:29-35).

The point of the divine oracle is that such direct communication with God is beyond that of prophets and places Moses in a special category. His charismatic authority transcends traditional categories. Consequently, prophets like Aaron and Miriam should fear Moses and certainly not challenge his special charismatic authority (v. 8) or his actions, including his intermarriage with the Cushite woman. Because Miriam and Aaron have not feared Moses, God strikes Miriam with severe leprosy so that her skin is white as snow (cf. Exod 4:6; 2 Kgs 5:27).

12:11-15. Miriam's leprosy provides the opportunity for Moses to demonstrate his special status as a charismatic leader. Aaron addresses Moses deferentially as "my lord" in acknowledging his and Miriam's sin. He requests intercession by Moses for Miriam, whose situation threatens to become like that of a stillborn baby (v. 12). Moses intercedes, requesting that God heal Miriam. Healing was God's first promise to Israel in the wilderness (Exod 15:26), and now Moses calls forth that power (Num 12:13).

The response of God to Moses' intercession is puzzling. Yahweh states, "If her father had but spit in her face, would she not bear her shame for seven days?" (v. 14). Spitting in the face may be a sign of contempt (Deut 25:9), an insult (Isa 50:6), or a source of impurity (Lev 15:8). The phrase may also be playing with sounds in the larger story. Rhetorically the verbal phrase "had but spit" (ירק ירק yārōq yāraq) repeats the sound (the literary device called paranomasia) of the opening challenge of Miriam and Aaron in v. 2: "Only [הרק hăraq] through Moses does the LORD speak?" The intention of such a sound play is reinforced by the similar rhetorical device in the exchange between Aaron and Moses in the previous verses, where Aaron pleads to Moses for help through negative requests ("Do not let [אל־נא 'al-nā']" in vv. 11-12), are translated into a positive petition to God by Moses in v. 13, "O God, please [אל נא 'ēl nā']."

12:16. The special status of Moses is illustrated by his successful intercession. Miriam is healed, but not without first being banished from the camp for seven days (see the instructions for leprosy in Leviticus 13). At the end of seven days, she is brought back into the camp, and Israel departs from Hazeroth to Paran (v. 16), the setting for the spy story in priestly tradition.

REFLECTIONS

Numbers 11–12 is a rich resource for theological reflection on the nature of community, the importance of prophetic leadership, and the uneasy relationship between tradition and social change.

1. The introductory story in Num 11:1-3 is a strong reminder that our identity as the people of God is determined by what we do, not by what we say or by our social location. We often prefer to identify ourselves on the basis of other criteria. But God recognizes us by our actions. When members of the wilderness community judge their journey as misfortune, God prunes them from the camp by fire. The rabble who complain about meat reinforce the same conclusion. They are not named individually. Anyone who craves meat more than the nourishment of God belongs to this group. The act of leaving the camp for meat determines identity. The stories illustrate how fluid our identity is as the people of God; it can change over time. Pruning takes place on the basis of life-style. A central goal in preaching and teaching these stories is to determine what we crave in the contemporary church that puts us in conflict with God's leading. The object of our craving changes. The meat desired by the rabble may be money, employment, or social prestige. The message of the story remains the same, however: God recognizes us by what we do. If we leave the camp in pursuit of the thing we crave, then we forfeit our identity as God's people. We die with the meat still in our teeth.

The conflict over food also contains a message about providence and the Christian life. The Christian life is goal oriented. It is like a wilderness journey. We make goals in life. We seek to discern the will of God in our planning; yet we often want God to conform to our timetable. The fast pace of modern life intensifies this desire. When we force God to accommodate to our life-style, we may turn providence into a commodity that serves our self-interest. The complaint over meat explores this temptation. Israel is at the outset of their wilderness journey, living on manna provided daily by God. Yet they desire meat. Spiritual growth in God's time is in conflict with the rabble, who desire divine grace on their own terms. Their desire for providence on their own terms creates ambiguity in determining who makes up the people of God in the camp.

Numbers 11 contains an important message for the contemporary church. Spiritual growth is not fast food. God often works on a different clock from that of our short-sighted, fast-paced culture. The rabble could not conform to God's timetable and were purged from the community. Those who remained in the camp and ate manna continued to journey with God. Sometimes God tests us by making us slow down.

2. A biblical understanding of charismatic leadership is crucial for the contemporary church. Contemporary culture is fixated on individual personalities. Celebrities attract our attention on television and in newsprint. They determine many trends in our society through advertising. Our tendency to worship fame has infiltrated the church, where we all too often are attracted by the superficial personality of individual preachers. But celebrity status in contemporary society and in the church is not the same as charismatic leadership. At the outset of the commentary, it was noted that prophetic leadership is charismatic and that the word *charisma* in Greek means "gift." Charismatic power is the quality of an individual's personality. It describes a gifted person whose personal strength makes him or her stand out from others. But charismatic persons are not necessarily famous. Max Weber adds a sociological dimension to charismatic leadership, concluding that such leaders are often agents of change during times of social crisis.[107] Numbers 11–12 provides a rich resource for evaluating the strengths and weaknesses of this form of leadership.

Too often charisma is used for self-promotion in our individualistic society. One reason for this is that charisma highlights individuals, hence the danger to confuse it with fame. Yet charismatic leadership is never about self-promotion. It is aimed at building community. The role of Moses in Numbers 11–12 provides illustration: He rejects self-promotion. He complains to God that his leading the people alone is inadequate. Thus it is Moses the charismatic leader who forces God to devise a way to pass on Moses' spirit to the seventy elders. His goal is not fame, but the distribution of his spirit to all members of the community, even when it threatens other leaders, like Joshua. Numbers 12:3 states the ideal: The most charismatic leader is the most humble person on earth. Humility is selflessness before God and others. Such persons do not hoard power jealously; they give it away. In preaching and teaching this story, it is important to clarify that Moses is not a celebrity. He is a charismatic leader.

The ability to intercede for others through prayer is a form of charismatic leadership. Intercession is certainly not limited to prophets. Priests intercede for the community through sacraments, a role that also has the power to influence God. But intercession through prayer in Numbers 11–12 is associated with Moses' prophetic leadership. The introductory story of murmuring in Num 11:1-3 accentuates Moses' power to stop divine judgment through prayer. The story of the quail in Num 11:4-35 develops Moses' role to intercede. His prayer provides a model for lamenting. He has expectations that arise from his past relationship with God. Thus he is able to complain to God about the burden of leadership. God hears his lament and responds to it. The conflict between Moses, Miriam, and Aaron in Numbers 12 demonstrates Moses' power to prompt divine healing through prayer. Intercession in each of these instances is more prophetic than priestly. In each case, God's actions are influenced through persuasion rather than by set rituals, and Moses changes divine action by interceding as a prophet.[108] Prophetic intercession is an important part of corporate worship. But it is not limited to public occasions. The discipline of private prayer is a form of charismatic leadership. Not all persons have this gift; yet all communities need such leaders.

Preaching is a form of charismatic leadership. But it is the role of the seventy elders in Numbers 11 that provides the model for Christian preaching, not Moses. The seventy elders receive a portion of Moses' spirit; thus they are charismatic leaders—but not of the quality of Moses. The seventy elders do not receive revelations, as was the case with classical prophets and Moses. When the spirit of Moses enters them, they prophesy only momentarily. Their charismatic leadership, then, is like that of a scribe. In Numbers 11, this means that they have responsibility to govern the community. The seventy elders govern by interpreting and applying the revelation received by Moses to Israel's life in the camp. In doing so, they model preaching in Christian tradition. Preaching is not classical prophecy. Preachers do not speak with God face to face, nor do they receive new oracles from God. Preaching is inspired interpretation. The truth claims of any sermon must be authenticated by Scripture. Thus ministers of the Word are a continuation of the office of the seventy elders. This analogy also provides insight into the goal of preaching. The role of the seventy elders was to apply the law of Moses to Israel's life; thereby they governed the people. The same is true in Christian preaching. The proclamation of the Word in worship is heard when it is applied to the life of the community.

107. Max Weber, *Essays in Sociology,* ed. and trans. H. H. Gerth and C. Wright Mills (Oxford: Oxford University Press, 1946).
108. P. D. Miller, Jr., *They Cried to the Lord: The Form and Theology of Biblical Prayer* (Minneapolis: Fortress, 1994) 262-80.

3. The Spirit of God cannot be controlled by human structures. It is a force for change that blows where it will. Thus there is always a subversive quality to communities that are attuned to charismatic leadership. Numbers 11–12 conveys this message in the story of Eldad and Medad. They illustrate how the charisma of God can appear in members who were not supposed to have such power. Their prophesying illustrates that the boundaries of even minimal forms of hierarchy can be broken immediately by the uncontrollable Spirit of God. The role of Moses in this episode illustrates how an ideal charismatic leader will promote and recognize such power in unexpected places, rather than view it as a challenge to his own authority, as did Joshua. The subversive character of charisma continues into the next story, where Miriam and Aaron challenge Moses because of his Cushite wife. Their complaint illustrates the way in which the charisma of God can break external boundaries as well as internal ones. The marriage of Moses to the Cushite is no less subversive to the structure of the community than was the unexpected prophesying of Eldad and Medad. When Numbers 11–12 are read together, they illustrate how charisma breaks established boundaries both within and outside of communities. Charismatic leadership forces communities to be self-critical, because the power of God can appear in unexpected forms, places, and persons.

Numbers 13:1–15:41, Conflict Over the Land

NIV

13 The LORD said to Moses, [2]"Send some men to explore the land of Canaan, which I am giving to the Israelites. From each ancestral tribe send one of its leaders."

[3]So at the LORD's command Moses sent them out from the Desert of Paran. All of them were leaders of the Israelites. [4]These are their names:

from the tribe of Reuben, Shammua son of Zaccur;

[5]from the tribe of Simeon, Shaphat son of Hori;

[6]from the tribe of Judah, Caleb son of Jephunneh;

[7]from the tribe of Issachar, Igal son of Joseph;

[8]from the tribe of Ephraim, Hoshea son of Nun;

[9]from the tribe of Benjamin, Palti son of Raphu;

[10]from the tribe of Zebulun, Gaddiel son of Sodi;

[11]from the tribe of Manasseh (a tribe of Joseph), Gaddi son of Susi;

[12]from the tribe of Dan, Ammiel son of Gemalli;

[13]from the tribe of Asher, Sethur son of Michael;

[14]from the tribe of Naphtali, Nahbi son of Vophsi;

[15]from the tribe of Gad, Geuel son of Maki.

NRSV

13 The LORD said to Moses, [2]"Send men to spy out the land of Canaan, which I am giving to the Israelites; from each of their ancestral tribes you shall send a man, every one a leader among them." [3]So Moses sent them from the wilderness of Paran, according to the command of the LORD, all of them leading men among the Israelites. [4]These were their names: From the tribe of Reuben, Shammua son of Zaccur; [5]from the tribe of Simeon, Shaphat son of Hori; [6]from the tribe of Judah, Caleb son of Jephunneh; [7]from the tribe of Issachar, Igal son of Joseph; [8]from the tribe of Ephraim, Hoshea son of Nun; [9]from the tribe of Benjamin, Palti son of Raphu; [10]from the tribe of Zebulun, Gaddiel son of Sodi; [11]from the tribe of Joseph (that is, from the tribe of Manasseh), Gaddi son of Susi; [12]from the tribe of Dan, Ammiel son of Gemalli; [13]from the tribe of Asher, Sethur son of Michael; [14]from the tribe of Naphtali, Nahbi son of Vophsi; [15]from the tribe of Gad, Geuel son of Machi. [16]These were the names of the men whom Moses sent to spy out the land. And Moses changed the name of Hoshea son of Nun to Joshua.

[17]Moses sent them to spy out the land of Canaan, and said to them, "Go up there into the Negeb, and go up into the hill country, [18]and see what the land is like, and whether the people who live in it are strong or weak, whether they

NIV

¹⁶These are the names of the men Moses sent to explore the land. (Moses gave Hoshea son of Nun the name Joshua.)

¹⁷When Moses sent them to explore Canaan, he said, "Go up through the Negev and on into the hill country. ¹⁸See what the land is like and whether the people who live there are strong or weak, few or many. ¹⁹What kind of land do they live in? Is it good or bad? What kind of towns do they live in? Are they unwalled or fortified? ²⁰How is the soil? Is it fertile or poor? Are there trees on it or not? Do your best to bring back some of the fruit of the land." (It was the season for the first ripe grapes.)

²¹So they went up and explored the land from the Desert of Zin as far as Rehob, toward Lebo^a Hamath. ²²They went up through the Negev and came to Hebron, where Ahiman, Sheshai and Talmai, the descendants of Anak, lived. (Hebron had been built seven years before Zoan in Egypt.) ²³When they reached the Valley of Eshcol,^b they cut off a branch bearing a single cluster of grapes. Two of them carried it on a pole between them, along with some pomegranates and figs. ²⁴That place was called the Valley of Eshcol because of the cluster of grapes the Israelites cut off there. ²⁵At the end of forty days they returned from exploring the land.

²⁶They came back to Moses and Aaron and the whole Israelite community at Kadesh in the Desert of Paran. There they reported to them and to the whole assembly and showed them the fruit of the land. ²⁷They gave Moses this account: "We went into the land to which you sent us, and it does flow with milk and honey! Here is its fruit. ²⁸But the people who live there are powerful, and the cities are fortified and very large. We even saw descendants of Anak there. ²⁹The Amalekites live in the Negev; the Hittites, Jebusites and Amorites live in the hill country; and the Canaanites live near the sea and along the Jordan."

³⁰Then Caleb silenced the people before Moses and said, "We should go up and take possession of the land, for we can certainly do it."

³¹But the men who had gone up with him said, "We can't attack those people; they are stronger

*21 Or *toward the entrance to* *23 Eshcol* means *cluster;* also in verse 24.

NRSV

are few or many, ¹⁹and whether the land they live in is good or bad, and whether the towns that they live in are unwalled or fortified, ²⁰and whether the land is rich or poor, and whether there are trees in it or not. Be bold, and bring some of the fruit of the land." Now it was the season of the first ripe grapes.

21So they went up and spied out the land from the wilderness of Zin to Rehob, near Lebo-hamath. ²²They went up into the Negeb, and came to Hebron; and Ahiman, Sheshai, and Talmai, the Anakites, were there. (Hebron was built seven years before Zoan in Egypt.) ²³And they came to the Wadi Eshcol, and cut down from there a branch with a single cluster of grapes, and they carried it on a pole between two of them. They also brought some pomegranates and figs. ²⁴That place was called the Wadi Eshcol,^a because of the cluster that the Israelites cut down from there.

25At the end of forty days they returned from spying out the land. ²⁶And they came to Moses and Aaron and to all the congregation of the Israelites in the wilderness of Paran, at Kadesh; they brought back word to them and to all the congregation, and showed them the fruit of the land. ²⁷And they told him, "We came to the land to which you sent us; it flows with milk and honey, and this is its fruit. ²⁸Yet the people who live in the land are strong, and the towns are fortified and very large; and besides, we saw the descendants of Anak there. ²⁹The Amalekites live in the land of the Negeb; the Hittites, the Jebusites, and the Amorites live in the hill country; and the Canaanites live by the sea, and along the Jordan."

30But Caleb quieted the people before Moses, and said, "Let us go up at once and occupy it, for we are well able to overcome it." ³¹Then the men who had gone up with him said, "We are not able to go up against this people, for they are stronger than we." ³²So they brought to the Israelites an unfavorable report of the land that they had spied out, saying, "The land that we have gone through as spies is a land that devours its inhabitants; and all the people that we saw in it are of great size. ³³There we saw the Nephilim (the Anakites come from the Nephilim); and to

a That is *Cluster*

NIV

than we are." ³²And they spread among the Israelites a bad report about the land they had explored. They said, "The land we explored devours those living in it. All the people we saw there are of great size. ³³We saw the Nephilim there (the descendants of Anak come from the Nephilim). We seemed like grasshoppers in our own eyes, and we looked the same to them."

14 That night all the people of the community raised their voices and wept aloud. ²All the Israelites grumbled against Moses and Aaron, and the whole assembly said to them, "If only we had died in Egypt! Or in this desert! ³Why is the Lord bringing us to this land only to let us fall by the sword? Our wives and children will be taken as plunder. Wouldn't it be better for us to go back to Egypt?" ⁴And they said to each other, "We should choose a leader and go back to Egypt."

⁵Then Moses and Aaron fell facedown in front of the whole Israelite assembly gathered there. ⁶Joshua son of Nun and Caleb son of Jephunneh, who were among those who had explored the land, tore their clothes ⁷and said to the entire Israelite assembly, "The land we passed through and explored is exceedingly good. ⁸If the Lord is pleased with us, he will lead us into that land, a land flowing with milk and honey, and will give it to us. ⁹Only do not rebel against the Lord. And do not be afraid of the people of the land, because we will swallow them up. Their protection is gone, but the Lord is with us. Do not be afraid of them."

¹⁰But the whole assembly talked about stoning them. Then the glory of the Lord appeared at the Tent of Meeting to all the Israelites. ¹¹The Lord said to Moses, "How long will these people treat me with contempt? How long will they refuse to believe in me, in spite of all the miraculous signs I have performed among them? ¹²I will strike them down with a plague and destroy them, but I will make you into a nation greater and stronger than they."

¹³Moses said to the Lord, "Then the Egyptians will hear about it! By your power you brought these people up from among them. ¹⁴And they will tell the inhabitants of this land about it. They have already heard that you, O Lord, are with these people and that you, O Lord, have been

NRSV

ourselves we seemed like grasshoppers, and so we seemed to them."

14 Then all the congregation raised a loud cry, and the people wept that night. ²And all the Israelites complained against Moses and Aaron; the whole congregation said to them, "Would that we had died in the land of Egypt! Or would that we had died in this wilderness! ³Why is the Lord bringing us into this land to fall by the sword? Our wives and our little ones will become booty; would it not be better for us to go back to Egypt?" ⁴So they said to one another, "Let us choose a captain, and go back to Egypt."

⁵Then Moses and Aaron fell on their faces before all the assembly of the congregation of the Israelites. ⁶And Joshua son of Nun and Caleb son of Jephunneh, who were among those who had spied out the land, tore their clothes ⁷and said to all the congregation of the Israelites, "The land that we went through as spies is an exceedingly good land. ⁸If the Lord is pleased with us, he will bring us into this land and give it to us, a land that flows with milk and honey. ⁹Only, do not rebel against the Lord; and do not fear the people of the land, for they are no more than bread for us; their protection is removed from them, and the Lord is with us; do not fear them." ¹⁰But the whole congregation threatened to stone them.

Then the glory of the Lord appeared at the tent of meeting to all the Israelites. ¹¹And the Lord said to Moses, "How long will this people despise me? And how long will they refuse to believe in me, in spite of all the signs that I have done among them? ¹²I will strike them with pestilence and disinherit them, and I will make of you a nation greater and mightier than they."

¹³But Moses said to the Lord, "Then the Egyptians will hear of it, for in your might you brought up this people from among them, ¹⁴and they will tell the inhabitants of this land. They have heard that you, O Lord, are in the midst of this people; for you, O Lord, are seen face to face, and your cloud stands over them and you go in front of them, in a pillar of cloud by day and in a pillar of fire by night. ¹⁵Now if you kill this people all at one time, then the nations who have heard about you will say, ¹⁶'It is because the Lord was not able to bring this people into the land he

NIV

seen face to face, that your cloud stays over them, and that you go before them in a pillar of cloud by day and a pillar of fire by night. ¹⁵If you put these people to death all at one time, the nations who have heard this report about you will say, ¹⁶'The LORD was not able to bring these people into the land he promised them on oath; so he slaughtered them in the desert.'

¹⁷"Now may the Lord's strength be displayed, just as you have declared: ¹⁸'The LORD is slow to anger, abounding in love and forgiving sin and rebellion. Yet he does not leave the guilty unpunished; he punishes the children for the sin of the fathers to the third and fourth generation.' ¹⁹In accordance with your great love, forgive the sin of these people, just as you have pardoned them from the time they left Egypt until now."

²⁰The LORD replied, "I have forgiven them, as you asked. ²¹Nevertheless, as surely as I live and as surely as the glory of the LORD fills the whole earth, ²²not one of the men who saw my glory and the miraculous signs I performed in Egypt and in the desert but who disobeyed me and tested me ten times— ²³not one of them will ever see the land I promised on oath to their forefathers. No one who has treated me with contempt will ever see it. ²⁴But because my servant Caleb has a different spirit and follows me wholeheartedly, I will bring him into the land he went to, and his descendants will inherit it. ²⁵Since the Amalekites and Canaanites are living in the valleys, turn back tomorrow and set out toward the desert along the route to the Red Sea.ᵃ"

²⁶The LORD said to Moses and Aaron: ²⁷"How long will this wicked community grumble against me? I have heard the complaints of these grumbling Israelites. ²⁸So tell them, 'As surely as I live, declares the LORD, I will do to you the very things I heard you say: ²⁹In this desert your bodies will fall—every one of you twenty years old or more who was counted in the census and who has grumbled against me. ³⁰Not one of you will enter the land I swore with uplifted hand to make your home, except Caleb son of Jephunneh and Joshua son of Nun. ³¹As for your children that you said would be taken as plunder, I will bring them in to enjoy the land you have rejected. ³²But you—

ᵃ25 Hebrew *Yam Suph;* that is, Sea of Reeds

NRSV

swore to give them that he has slaughtered them in the wilderness.' ¹⁷And now, therefore, let the power of the LORD be great in the way that you promised when you spoke, saying,
¹⁸ 'The LORD is slow to anger,
  and abounding in steadfast love,
  forgiving iniquity and transgression,
  but by no means clearing the guilty,
  visiting the iniquity of the parents
  upon the children
  to the third and the fourth generation.'
¹⁹Forgive the iniquity of this people according to the greatness of your steadfast love, just as you have pardoned this people, from Egypt even until now."

20Then the LORD said, "I do forgive, just as you have asked; ²¹nevertheless—as I live, and as all the earth shall be filled with the glory of the LORD— ²²none of the people who have seen my glory and the signs that I did in Egypt and in the wilderness, and yet have tested me these ten times and have not obeyed my voice, ²³shall see the land that I swore to give to their ancestors; none of those who despised me shall see it. ²⁴But my servant Caleb, because he has a different spirit and has followed me wholeheartedly, I will bring into the land into which he went, and his descendants shall possess it. ²⁵Now, since the Amalekites and the Canaanites live in the valleys, turn tomorrow and set out for the wilderness by the way to the Red Sea."ᵃ

26And the LORD spoke to Moses and to Aaron, saying: ²⁷How long shall this wicked congregation complain against me? I have heard the complaints of the Israelites, which they complain against me. ²⁸Say to them, "As I live," says the LORD, "I will do to you the very things I heard you say: ²⁹your dead bodies shall fall in this very wilderness; and of all your number, included in the census, from twenty years old and upward, who have complained against me, ³⁰not one of you shall come into the land in which I swore to settle you, except Caleb son of Jephunneh and Joshua son of Nun. ³¹But your little ones, who you said would become booty, I will bring in, and they shall know the land that you have despised. ³²But as for you, your dead bodies shall fall in this wilderness.

ᵃOr *Sea of Reeds*

NIV

your bodies will fall in this desert. ³³Your children will be shepherds here for forty years, suffering for your unfaithfulness, until the last of your bodies lies in the desert. ³⁴For forty years—one year for each of the forty days you explored the land—you will suffer for your sins and know what it is like to have me against you.' ³⁵I, the LORD, have spoken, and I will surely do these things to this whole wicked community, which has banded together against me. They will meet their end in this desert; here they will die."

³⁶So the men Moses had sent to explore the land, who returned and made the whole community grumble against him by spreading a bad report about it— ³⁷these men responsible for spreading the bad report about the land were struck down and died of a plague before the LORD. ³⁸Of the men who went to explore the land, only Joshua son of Nun and Caleb son of Jephunneh survived.

³⁹When Moses reported this to all the Israelites, they mourned bitterly. ⁴⁰Early the next morning they went up toward the high hill country. "We have sinned," they said. "We will go up to the place the LORD promised."

⁴¹But Moses said, "Why are you disobeying the LORD's command? This will not succeed! ⁴²Do not go up, because the LORD is not with you. You will be defeated by your enemies, ⁴³for the Amalekites and Canaanites will face you there. Because you have turned away from the LORD, he will not be with you and you will fall by the sword."

⁴⁴Nevertheless, in their presumption they went up toward the high hill country, though neither Moses nor the ark of the LORD's covenant moved from the camp. ⁴⁵Then the Amalekites and Canaanites who lived in that hill country came down and attacked them and beat them down all the way to Hormah.

15 The LORD said to Moses, ²"Speak to the Israelites and say to them: 'After you enter the land I am giving you as a home ³and you present to the LORD offerings made by fire, from the herd or the flock, as an aroma pleasing to the LORD—whether burnt offerings or sacrifices, for special vows or freewill offerings or festival offerings— ⁴then the one who brings his offering shall present to the LORD a grain offering of a tenth of

NRSV

³³And your children shall be shepherds in the wilderness for forty years, and shall suffer for your faithlessness, until the last of your dead bodies lies in the wilderness. ³⁴According to the number of the days in which you spied out the land, forty days, for every day a year, you shall bear your iniquity, forty years, and you shall know my displeasure." ³⁵I the LORD have spoken; surely I will do thus to all this wicked congregation gathered together against me: in this wilderness they shall come to a full end, and there they shall die.

36And the men whom Moses sent to spy out the land, who returned and made all the congregation complain against him by bringing a bad report about the land— ³⁷the men who brought an unfavorable report about the land died by a plague before the LORD. ³⁸But Joshua son of Nun and Caleb son of Jephunneh alone remained alive, of those men who went to spy out the land.

39When Moses told these words to all the Israelites, the people mourned greatly. ⁴⁰They rose early in the morning and went up to the heights of the hill country, saying, "Here we are. We will go up to the place that the LORD has promised, for we have sinned." ⁴¹But Moses said, "Why do you continue to transgress the command of the LORD? That will not succeed. ⁴²Do not go up, for the LORD is not with you; do not let yourselves be struck down before your enemies. ⁴³For the Amalekites and the Canaanites will confront you there, and you shall fall by the sword; because you have turned back from following the LORD, the LORD will not be with you." ⁴⁴But they presumed to go up to the heights of the hill country, even though the ark of the covenant of the LORD, and Moses, had not left the camp. ⁴⁵Then the Amalekites and the Canaanites who lived in that hill country came down and defeated them, pursuing them as far as Hormah.

15 The LORD spoke to Moses, saying: ²Speak to the Israelites and say to them: When you come into the land you are to inhabit, which I am giving you, ³and you make an offering by fire to the LORD from the herd or from the flock—whether a burnt offering or a sacrifice, to fulfill a vow or as a freewill offering or at your appointed festivals—to make a pleasing odor for the LORD, ⁴then whoever presents such an offering

NIV

an ephah[a] of fine flour mixed with a quarter of a hin[b] of oil. [5]With each lamb for the burnt offering or the sacrifice, prepare a quarter of a hin of wine as a drink offering.

[6]" 'With a ram prepare a grain offering of two-tenths of an ephah[c] of fine flour mixed with a third of a hin[d] of oil, [7]and a third of a hin of wine as a drink offering. Offer it as an aroma pleasing to the LORD.

[8]" 'When you prepare a young bull as a burnt offering or sacrifice, for a special vow or a fellowship offering[e] to the LORD, [9]bring with the bull a grain offering of three-tenths of an ephah[f] of fine flour mixed with half a hin[g] of oil. [10]Also bring half a hin of wine as a drink offering. It will be an offering made by fire, an aroma pleasing to the LORD. [11]Each bull or ram, each lamb or young goat, is to be prepared in this manner. [12]Do this for each one, for as many as you prepare.

[13]" 'Everyone who is native-born must do these things in this way when he brings an offering made by fire as an aroma pleasing to the LORD. [14]For the generations to come, whenever an alien or anyone else living among you presents an offering made by fire as an aroma pleasing to the LORD, he must do exactly as you do. [15]The community is to have the same rules for you and for the alien living among you; this is a lasting ordinance for the generations to come. You and the alien shall be the same before the LORD: [16]The same laws and regulations will apply both to you and to the alien living among you.' "

[17]The LORD said to Moses, [18]"Speak to the Israelites and say to them: 'When you enter the land to which I am taking you [19]and you eat the food of the land, present a portion as an offering to the LORD. [20]Present a cake from the first of your ground meal and present it as an offering from the threshing floor. [21]Throughout the generations to come you are to give this offering to the LORD from the first of your ground meal.

[22]" 'Now if you unintentionally fail to keep any of these commands the LORD gave Moses— [23]any of the LORD's commands to you through him, from

a4 That is, probably about 2 quarts (about 2 liters)   b4 That is, probably about 1 quart (about 1 liter); also in verse 5   c6 That is, probably about 4 quarts (about 4.5 liters)   d6 That is, probably about 1 1/4 quarts (about 1.2 liters); also in verse 7   e8 Traditionally *peace offering*   f9 That is, probably about 6 quarts (about 6.5 liters)   g9 That is, probably about 2 quarts (about 2 liters); also in verse 10

NRSV

to the LORD shall present also a grain offering, one-tenth of an ephah of choice flour, mixed with one-fourth of a hin of oil. [5]Moreover, you shall offer one-fourth of a hin of wine as a drink offering with the burnt offering or the sacrifice, for each lamb. [6]For a ram, you shall offer a grain offering, two-tenths of an ephah of choice flour mixed with one-third of a hin of oil; [7]and as a drink offering you shall offer one-third of a hin of wine, a pleasing odor to the LORD. [8]When you offer a bull as a burnt offering or a sacrifice, to fulfill a vow or as an offering of well-being to the LORD, [9]then you shall present with the bull a grain offering, three-tenths of an ephah of choice flour, mixed with half a hin of oil, [10]and you shall present as a drink offering half a hin of wine, as an offering by fire, a pleasing odor to the LORD.

[11]Thus it shall be done for each ox or ram, or for each of the male lambs or the kids. [12]According to the number that you offer, so you shall do with each and every one. [13]Every native Israelite shall do these things in this way, in presenting an offering by fire, a pleasing odor to the LORD. [14]An alien who lives with you, or who takes up permanent residence among you, and wishes to offer an offering by fire, a pleasing odor to the LORD, shall do as you do. [15]As for the assembly, there shall be for both you and the resident alien a single statute, a perpetual statute throughout your generations; you and the alien shall be alike before the LORD. [16]You and the alien who resides with you shall have the same law and the same ordinance.

[17]The LORD spoke to Moses, saying: [18]Speak to the Israelites and say to them: After you come into the land to which I am bringing you, [19]whenever you eat of the bread of the land, you shall present a donation to the LORD. [20]From your first batch of dough you shall present a loaf as a donation; you shall present it just as you present a donation from the threshing floor. [21]Throughout your generations you shall give to the LORD a donation from the first of your batch of dough.

[22]But if you unintentionally fail to observe all these commandments that the LORD has spoken to Moses— [23]everything that the LORD has commanded you by Moses, from the day the LORD gave commandment and thereafter, throughout

NIV

the day the LORD gave them and continuing through the generations to come— [24]and if this is done unintentionally without the community being aware of it, then the whole community is to offer a young bull for a burnt offering as an aroma pleasing to the LORD, along with its prescribed grain offering and drink offering, and a male goat for a sin offering. [25]The priest is to make atonement for the whole Israelite community, and they will be forgiven, for it was not intentional and they have brought to the LORD for their wrong an offering made by fire and a sin offering. [26]The whole Israelite community and the aliens living among them will be forgiven, because all the people were involved in the unintentional wrong.

[27]" 'But if just one person sins unintentionally, he must bring a year-old female goat for a sin offering. [28]The priest is to make atonement before the LORD for the one who erred by sinning unintentionally, and when atonement has been made for him, he will be forgiven. [29]One and the same law applies to everyone who sins unintentionally, whether he is a native-born Israelite or an alien.

[30]" 'But anyone who sins defiantly, whether native-born or alien, blasphemes the LORD, and that person must be cut off from his people. [31]Because he has despised the LORD's word and broken his commands, that person must surely be cut off; his guilt remains on him.' "

[32]While the Israelites were in the desert, a man was found gathering wood on the Sabbath day. [33]Those who found him gathering wood brought him to Moses and Aaron and the whole assembly, [34]and they kept him in custody, because it was not clear what should be done to him. [35]Then the LORD said to Moses, "The man must die. The whole assembly must stone him outside the camp." [36]So the assembly took him outside the camp and stoned him to death, as the LORD commanded Moses.

[37]The LORD said to Moses, [38]"Speak to the Israelites and say to them: 'Throughout the generations to come you are to make tassels on the corners of your garments, with a blue cord on each tassel. [39]You will have these tassels to look at and so you will remember all the commands of the LORD, that you may obey them and not prostitute yourselves by going after the lusts of

NRSV

your generations— [24]then if it was done unintentionally without the knowledge of the congregation, the whole congregation shall offer one young bull for a burnt offering, a pleasing odor to the LORD, together with its grain offering and its drink offering, according to the ordinance, and one male goat for a sin offering. [25]The priest shall make atonement for all the congregation of the Israelites, and they shall be forgiven; it was unintentional, and they have brought their offering, an offering by fire to the LORD, and their sin offering before the LORD, for their error. [26]All the congregation of the Israelites shall be forgiven, as well as the aliens residing among them, because the whole people was involved in the error.

[27]An individual who sins unintentionally shall present a female goat a year old for a sin offering. [28]And the priest shall make atonement before the LORD for the one who commits an error, when it is unintentional, to make atonement for the person, who then shall be forgiven. [29]For both the native among the Israelites and the alien residing among them—you shall have the same law for anyone who acts in error. [30]But whoever acts high-handedly, whether a native or an alien, affronts the LORD, and shall be cut off from among the people. [31]Because of having despised the word of the LORD and broken his commandment, such a person shall be utterly cut off and bear the guilt.

[32]When the Israelites were in the wilderness, they found a man gathering sticks on the sabbath day. [33]Those who found him gathering sticks brought him to Moses, Aaron, and to the whole congregation. [34]They put him in custody, because it was not clear what should be done to him. [35]Then the LORD said to Moses, "The man shall be put to death; all the congregation shall stone him outside the camp." [36]The whole congregation brought him outside the camp and stoned him to death, just as the LORD had commanded Moses.

[37]The LORD said to Moses: [38]Speak to the Israelites, and tell them to make fringes on the corners of their garments throughout their generations and to put a blue cord on the fringe at each corner. [39]You have the fringe so that, when you see it, you will remember all the commandments of the LORD and do them, and not follow the lust of your own heart and your own eyes. [40]So you

NIV	NRSV
your own hearts and eyes. ⁴⁰Then you will remember to obey all my commands and will be consecrated to your God. ⁴¹I am the LORD your God, who brought you out of Egypt to be your God. I am the LORD your God.'"	shall remember and do all my commandments, and you shall be holy to your God. ⁴¹I am the LORD your God, who brought you out of the land of Egypt, to be your God: I am the LORD your God.

COMMENTARY

Chapters 13–15 are pivotal in the book of Numbers. They tell the story of why the first generation of Israelites to leave Egypt lost the gift of the promised land (chaps. 13–14). The story concludes with legislation concerning sacrifices that Israel must observe when the next generation eventually enters the land (chap. 15). The episode introduces a distinctive method of composition, in which one account of a story is supplemented with an additional interpretation.[109] This method of composition allowed the biblical writers to present more than one interpretation in telling a single story. It occurs in the most important stories in the Pentateuch, including the flood story (Genesis 6–9), the exodus account (Exodus 1–15), and the revelation of God and forging of the covenant at Mt. Sinai and Mt. Horeb (Exodus 19–34; Deuteronomy 4–5). Given the importance of the loss of the promised land, it is not surprising that multiple interpretations of this story have been preserved in the Pentateuch. Deuteronomy 1:19-46 contains one such interpretation, while two additional versions are woven into Numbers 13–15. These interpretations present different perspectives on the nature of salvation, conceived as the divine gift of land, and, more particularly, how the people of God are to live in this world in order to realize the promise of salvation. A brief synopsis of Deut 1:19-45 provides a point of departure for commentary on Numbers 13–15.

The loss of the land by the first generation of Israelites is an important story in Deuteronomy. In Deut 1:19-46, Moses recounts the tragedy to the second generation who are preparing for conquest, thus setting the stage for the whole book.

The story separates into four parts: First, preparation for conquest (Deut 1:19-23) takes place at Kadesh-barnea, where the people request spies to scout out proper routes for invasion. Second, the act of spying out the land (Deut 1:24-25) is associated with the Wadi Eschol. The reconnaissance of the spies is for the purpose of war; yet they also bring back fruit, which provides the basis for a good report of the land itself. Third, the main section of the story consists of reactions to the spies' report by the people, by Moses, and by God (Deut 1:26-40). The people are unwilling to invade the land because they fear its inhabitants. The indigenous people are greater than they, the cities are fortified, and the giant race of the Anakim are present (Deut 1:26-28). Moses calls the people to faithfulness and holy war by reminding them of the power of God, which they witnessed in Egypt and in the wilderness (Deut 1:29-33). With the exception of Caleb and Joshua, God denies the first generation life in the land, promising instead to give it to their children (whom they feared would become booty if they invaded the land; Deut 1:34-40). Moses also is not allowed to enter the land because of the rebellion of the people. In his place, Joshua is appointed to lead the second generation in their invasion, while the first generation is directed to travel back into the wilderness. Fourth, the story ends with an account of a frantic and failed conquest because of the absence of God (Deut 1:41-46).

Deuteronomy 1:19-46 is not an independent story. Several important questions arise that cannot be answered simply by reading these verses. How did the people know about the fierce population, the fortified cities, and the Anakim? The spies' report does not contain this information. How did God know that Caleb had a different spirit from the other spies and that, as a consequence, he should receive land immediately?

---

109. This method of writing by supplementation is also called "redaction" and "conflation" in biblical studies, depending on one's overall view of the formation of the OT. See J. Trebolle, "Conflate Readings in the OT," *ABD* 1:1125-28; J. Blenkinsopp, "Introduction to the Pentateuch," *NIB* 1:305-18.

There is no mention of Caleb in the entire story. Then, too, when did Israel ever say that their children would be booty if they invaded the land? The literary genre of Deut 1:19-46 is a speech by Moses in which past events are recounted. The logical gaps in his speech suggest that it be read in conjunction with a pre-priestly version of Numbers 13–15. Thus Deut 1:19-46 provides a starting point for interpreting Numbers 13–15.

Two very different interpretations of why Israel lost the promised land are woven into the four-part story in Numbers. A pre-priestly version of the story shares many features with Deut 1:19-46, and it has been supplemented with a priestly interpretation of events. A brief summary of both points of view provides an overview for more detailed commentary of Numbers 13–15.

The pre-priestly version of Numbers 13–14 includes 13:17*b*-20, 22-24, part of 26, 27-30; 14:1*b*, 3-4, part of 5, 8-10*a*, 11-25, 39-45. This version locates Israel at Kadesh (13:26) and describes the spies' mission as reconnaissance for a conquest of the southern part of the land (13:17*b*-20). The spies go as far north as Hebron, take grapes from the Wadi Eschol, and bring back a report concerning the richness of the land and the fierceness of its people (13:22-24, 26-30). The Israelites murmur in response to the spies' report (14:1*b*, 3-4). The central portion of this story is dominated by God's desire to destroy Israel and the intercession of Moses to save them (most of 14:11-25), before it closes with an account of a failed attempt at conquest (14:39-45). The pre-priestly account of Numbers 13–14 contains many similarities to Deut 1:19-46 and, in most cases, fills in the gaps that exist in the latter version.

The priestly interpretation of Numbers 13–15 includes 13:1-3, 17*a*, 21, 25, part of 26, 32-33; 14:1*a*, 2, 5, part of 6, 17, 10*b*, 26-38; 15:1-41. This version changes the location of Israel's encampment to Paran (see the travel notice in 12:16 as well as references in 13:3, 26). The mission of the spies is reinterpreted from reconnaissance for invasion to an assessment of the land itself (13:17*a*). As a consequence, the spies go all the way to the northern boundary of Canaan in order to explore the entire land (13:21, 25). Failure is not a result of their fear to invade, but the negative assessment of the land as terrain that eats its inhabitants (13:31-33). The bad report of the land angers God (14:26-38). The priestly writers also extend the

story beyond the failed conquest of the pre-priestly version with the revelation of new law that points ahead to Israel's future life in the land (chap. 15).

13:1-20. This section describes Israel's preparation for conquest. It divides into a divine command to Moses (vv. 1-3), a list of tribal leaders (vv. 4-16), and Moses' instructions to the spies (vv. 17-20). The pre-priestly version of the spy story does not begin with a divine command. Instead, it commences with Moses' instructions that the spies proceed into the Negeb hills for reconnaissance (vv. 17*b*-20). An evaluation of the land is important to their mission. Moses instructs them to evaluate the land and its environment (vv. 18*a*, 20). Is the soil rich or poor? Are there trees? In addition they must gather fruit. The central portion of the instruction, however, focuses on the inhabitants and their fortifications (vv. 18*b*-19). Are the people strong or weak, many or few? Are their cities fortified? The focus is on gathering information for conquest. The notification that instruction took place in "the season of the first ripe grapes" (v. 20) may be pre-priestly or a later addition by priestly writers. It establishes the time of year in which grapes could be gathered in the Wadi Eschol.

The priestly writers change the dynamics of the story by adding the divine command in vv. 1-3 and by reinterpreting the mission of the spies in v. 17*a*. Verses 1-3 turn the spy story into a structure of divine command and fulfillment that predominates throughout chaps. 1–10. It even includes the introduction, "And the LORD spoke to Moses" (see 1:1; 2:1; 3:5, 14, 40, 44; 4:1). The priestly writers also change the mission of the leaders with the command in v. 17*a*, which the NRSV translates as, "Moses sent them to spy out the land of Canaan" (NIV, "Moses sent them to explore Canaan"). The Hebrew word translated "to spy out" is תור (*tûr*). The precise translation of the Hebrew is important for interpretation, especially since the NRSV translation is misleading. The primary meaning of the word is not the act of spying for the purpose of conquest. It is used in wisdom literature to describe how one searches for wisdom (Eccl 1:13; 2:3; 7:25) and how the righteous give advice to friends (Prov 12:26). Persons who embody this action during the reign of Solomon are described as "traders" (1 Kgs 10:15/ 2 Chr 9:14). In fact, only once is this verb used to describe the activity of spying with an aim toward invasion (Judg 1:23), and there the object of the activity is clearly a city. Neither people nor cities are ever the object of the verb in Numbers 13–15. Instead, the mission of the leaders is always directed to the land itself (13:16, 21, 25, 32 [twice]; 14:6-7, 36, 38), or more specifically the "land of Canaan" (13:1, 17)—a designation for the promised land that is characteristic of priestly authors (e.g., Gen 11:31; 12:5; 13:12; 16:33; 17:8).[110]

The meaning of the Hebrew word *tûr* is central to the priestly interpretation of Numbers 13–15. Of its twenty-three occurrences in the OT, twelve are in priestly additions to Numbers 13–15. Two additional occurrences also appear to be priestly commentary on the leading of the cloud in the wilderness march (at the end of Num 10:33-34 and in the account of the spy story in Deut 1:33, where the imagery of God's leading with the cloud also appears to be a priestly insertion).

Some commentators translate the verb in Numbers 13–15 as "to scout out" and underscore that such activity need not be of a military nature,[111] but the translation "to explore" may be even closer to the intended meaning (so NIV). Sean McEvenue concludes that the priestly writer's interpretation of the mission of the leaders is that "they are to know with their own eyes the good thing which Yahweh is about to give them, and they are to evaluate it, giving a favorable evaluation of it to the people."[112] The priestly writers' focus in the story is on the land, not the inhabitants. Theirs is not a story of conquest, but a theological assessment of the gift of salvation, conceived of as land.

Verses 4-16 provide a list of leaders from each tribe who are sent into the land. Most names on the list are unique to this passage. Whether this list was always part of the story or a later addition is difficult to confirm. Priestly writers are certainly fond of providing lists of tribal leaders (e.g., chaps. 1; 2; 7; 10; 26; 34). The list in these verses begins with the tribe of Reuben, as do the two census accounts by the priestly writers in Numbers 1 and 26. But the names are different from those of the first census. One argument for including the list of leaders in the pre-priestly version of the story

is that Caleb and Hoshea (= Joshua) are central characters in the story, and both are included in the list. Moreover, it is doubtful that the pre-priestly story actually begins with v. 17*b*, since the syntax presupposes a specific list of characters like the list of leaders in vv. 4-16. In its present context, however, the list is framed by priestly material (vv. 1-3, 17*a*), where emphasis falls on the mission of the leaders "to explore" the land.

13:21-33. The mission of the spies and their report is described in this section. Verses 21 and 22 each begin with the same word, "they went up" (ויעלו *wayya'ălû*). The repetition indicates two interpretations of the same event.

13:21. This verse constitutes the priestly description of the journey of the explorers. The command couples the verb "to go up" with the verb "to explore" (תור *tûr*) in order to describe the purpose of their mission as a theological evaluation of the land. In view of this, the priestly writers indicate that the parameters of their mission included the entire land of Canaan, extending from the wilderness of Zin in the south to Rehob, near Lebo-hamath, a city located in the extreme north of the land (1 Kgs 8:65).

13:22-24. This section is the pre-priestly account of the mission. It is limited to the southern boundary of the land, from the Negeb north to the city of Hebron, which is south of Jerusalem and adjacent to the Dead Sea. Here the mission is one of reconnaissance along the southern border for the purpose of conquest. Two points are stressed in the pre-priestly account of the mission. The first concerns the richness of the land in the Wadi Eschol (12:23-24), where the spies cut down a cluster of grapes so heavy that two men are required to carry it on a pole. This story closes in v. 24 by giving a name to this region: The valley is named "grape-cluster" (אשכול *'eškôl*) because of this event.

The second point of emphasis concerns the inhabitants (v. 22). The spies encounter Ahiman, Sheshai, and Talmai—a race of giants descended from Anak. This clan of giants acquires a near mythological status in stories about the conquest. They are mentioned in the account of the spy story in Deut 1:19-46 and in the story of Caleb's conquest of Hebron in Josh 14:12, 15; 15:13-19. Joshua is also described as killing indigenous Anakim in the hill country, leaving the remnants of this race of giants to live in Gaza, Gath, and

---

110. Sean E. McEvenue, *The Narrative Style of the Priestly Writer,* AnBib 50 (Rome: Pontifical Biblical Institute, 1971) 118-20.

111. See, e.g., Jacob Milgrom, *Numbers,* JPS Torah Commentary (Philadelphia: JPS, 1990) 100.

112. McEvenue, *The Narrative Style of the Priestly Writer,* 121.

Ashdod (Josh 11:21-22). They eventually give birth to Goliath, the giant killed by David (1 Samuel 17). The Anakim giants are mythologized even further in Deuteronomy 2, when they are also identified with the Rephaim, another superhuman race of giants (1 Chr 20:4-8) of whom Og of Bashan is one of the last descendants (Deut 2:11, 20). He required a sixteen-foot iron bed (Deut 3:11).

13:25-33. The report of the spies is recounted in this section. Again there are two versions. The pre-priestly spy story includes part of v. 26 ("And they came to Moses . . . at Kadesh, brought back word to them . . . and showed them the fruit of the land") and all of vv. 27-31. The spies declare the land rich in resources, stating that "it flows with milk and honey" (v. 27). But their report is dominated by an evaluation of the inhabitants and their fortifications. The people are strong, the cities are fortified, and the giant Anakim dwell there (v. 28). In addition to superhuman foes, they also report more a traditional list of opposing nations: Amalekites in the Negeb; Hittites, Jebusites, and Amorites in the hills; and Canaanites flanking the land by the sea and the Jordan River (v. 29). Variations of this list of enemy nations occur both in the Pentateuch (e.g., Gen 15:21; Exod 3:5, 8, 17; 32:3; Deut 1:7; 7:1; 20:17) and in the book of Joshua (Josh 3:10; 5:1; 11:1), always in stories about the promise of land and the conquest. In the pre-priestly story, Caleb is singled out from the other spies (v. 30). He acts on behalf of Moses by quieting the people, and he encourages them to undertake the conquest. But the group of spies counter his report with a negative one: The people will not be able to conquer the land because the inhabitants are stronger than they (v. 31). The loss of the land in the pre-priestly story arises from the fear of conquest.

The priestly writers' report of the spies includes part of v, 26 (reference to Aaron, the congregation, and the wilderness of Paran) and vv. 32-33. It also contains an assessment of the land and the population. But both are different. The report of the land takes place at Paran (v. 26), and it contradicts the pre-priestly version. The spies do not report that the land is good or that it "flows with milk and honey." Instead, they give a bad report of the land. The Hebrew phrase "bad report of the land" (דבת הארץ *dibbat hāʾāreṣ*) is limited to the priestly version of the story (v. 32; 14:36, 37), and it includes a sense of defamation or

slander. They state that the land eats its inhabitants (v. 32).

The report of the population in the land does not contradict the other version, although it does reinterpret it. The inhabitants are, indeed, great in size (v. 32). Descendants of Anak (v. 33), these giants are also identified with the Nephilim. The Nephilim are only mentioned twice in the OT, here and at the outset of the flood story (Gen 6:4). Both instances fit in well with priestly views concerning the need for proper boundaries in the world and how the violation of such boundaries creates defilement. Genesis 6:1-3 describes how divine beings took human wives. God, fearing their offspring, limited the human lifespan to 120 years. This story, with its focus on the mortality of humans, may very well be a pre-priestly introduction to the flood. Genesis 6:4 goes beyond Gen 6:1-3 by providing additional commentary, identifying the divine-human offspring as Nephilim ("fallen ones"). This interpretation fits in well with priestly theology in the Pentateuch.

Nephilim are not just heroic human giants. They are freaks of nature, because they blur the boundary between divine and human, originally established in creation. Nephilim are not intended for this earth, and their presence triggers the flood. The identification of the Nephilim in the land of Canaan (v. 33) accentuates its unnaturalness by recalling the monstrous conditions of the pre-flood world. Only the freakish Nephilim could live in a land that ate its inhabitants. Certainly nothing good could come from such land. The loss of the land in the priestly interpretation arises from slandering Canaan, rather than reporting on its goodness.

14:1-38. This section recounts various reactions to the spies' report by the people (vv. 1-4), by Moses and Aaron (v. 5), by Joshua and Caleb (vv. 6-10*a*), and by God. Moses assumes the role of intercessor (vv. 10*b*-38).

14:1-4. The reaction of the people is the same in both the pre-priestly and the priestly stories. They murmur, wishing they had died in Egypt or in the wilderness. They complain about divine leading, which, in their view, has brought them to the point of being slaughtered, and they fear that their children will become booty in a foolhardy invasion doomed to fail.

14:5. The response of Moses and Aaron to the report of the spies and to the murmuring of the people is stated in this verse: "[They] fell on their faces before all the assembly of the congregation of the Israelites." This posture usually signifies reverence. It could be an act of homage to a person, as when the brothers of Joseph fall on their faces before him (Gen 44:14; 50:18). More commonly, however, it is an act of reverence to God during a theophany. Thus the Israelites fall on their faces during the first revelation of God at the altar (Lev 9:24; see also Josh 5:14). But it can also signify anger, as in the case of Cain, when his offering was not accepted by God (Gen 4:5). Moses and Aaron are described as falling on their faces five times in Numbers. Two times they fall on their faces before the congregation (14:5; 16:4), two times before God (16:22, 45), and once the two actions are combined (20:6). When this ritual action takes place before the congregation, it signifies anger as a response to murmuring. During theophany, it is an act of homage that leads to intercession on behalf of the people. The response of Moses and Aaron in this verse, therefore, should be interpreted as anger against the people. Although the phrase is wide-ranging in biblical literature, this ritual act before the congregation appears to be commentary by the priestly writers.

14:6-10a. Joshua and Caleb respond to the people in this section. It is for the most part pre-priestly material, although there is some priestly commentary. The pre-priestly version includes the reference to "Joshua ben Nun and Caleb ben Jephunneh" (v. 6), the verb "to say" (אמר *'āmar*, v. 7), and all of vv. 8-9. They reaffirm God's power to fulfill the promise of land (v. 8), and they call the people to holy war with the command that they "not fear" (v. 9). The priestly writers reinterpret the mission of Joshua and Caleb as exploration (תור *tûr*) of the land (vv. 6-7). They insert the ritual act of tearing their clothes as a sign of mourning (v. 6), and they include a positive assessment of the land as a minority report that counters the previous negative report of the land. Thus Joshua and Caleb state in v. 7: "The land that we went through [as explorers] is an exceedingly good land." The priestly writers also portray the congregation's attempt to stone Joshua and Caleb (v. 10*a*).

14:10b-38. The glory of Yahweh (כבוד יהוה *kĕbôd YHWH*) appears at the entrance of the tent of meeting in v. 10*b*. God's reaction to the spies' report and the murmuring of the people appears

in vv. 11-38. This section can be separated into pre-priestly (vv. 11-25) and priestly (vv. 10*b*, 26-38) interpretations (although there is some priestly editing throughout vv. 11-25). The two sections are demarcated by repetition of divine questions to Moses, each of which employs different terminology. The pre-priestly version begins in v. 11: "How long [עד-אנה *'ad-'ānâ*] will this people [עם *'ām*] . . . ?" as compared to the priestly interpretation in v. 27: "How long [עד-מתי *'ad-mātay*] shall this wicked congregation [עדה *'ēdâ*]. . . ?" Each version moves to a point where God makes an oath, "as I live [חי-אני *ḥay-'ānî*]" (vv. 21, 28), that the murmuring generation of Israelites will not inherit the land. But the specific interpretations of the pre-priestly and the priestly writers are very different.

14:11-25. God complains that the people have rejected divine leading and do not believe in divine power, even though they have seen signs of it both in Egypt and in the wilderness (vv. 11, 21-22). As a result, the promised land is denied to all adults in the group except Caleb, who has a different spirit from the rest (vv. 23-24). The Israelites are then commanded to journey south along the Red Sea road (v. 25).

The central portion of the pre-priestly account (vv. 12-20) explores Moses' intercessory role, which, as noted, was first introduced in 11:1-3 and expanded upon in chaps. 11–12 (esp. 11:11-15). Some scholars argue that the intercessory role of Moses is a late addition to chaps. 13–15. Their reasons are that the section could be removed from 14:11, 21-25 without influencing the outcome of the story—more important, that Moses is not presented as interceding for Israel in Deut 1:19-46, which presupposes the pre-priestly account of the spy story in Numbers 13–14.[113]

The following commentary includes the intercession of Moses as part of the original account. This feature is not easily removed from the story. His actions are central for the delay of the promise of land to the next generation. Also, the role of Moses as intercessor is an important feature throughout the wilderness stories in Numbers 11–21. It reaches back to earlier wilderness stories

113. See George Buchanan Gray, *Numbers*, ICC (Edinburgh: T. & T. Clark, 1903) 155-59; McEvenue, *The Narrative Style of the Priestly Writer*, 94n. 4, 97-99; and N. Lohfink, "Darstellungskunst und Theologie in Dtn 1,6-3,29," *Bib* 41 (1960) 117-18.

(Exod 15:22-26) as well as to Moses' actions at Sinai (Exodus 32–34), making its removal from Numbers 14 even more difficult. Finally, gaps in Deut 1:19-45 have already illustrated how selectively this story has been constructed from Numbers 13–14. The absence of Moses' intercession for Israel in Deut 1:19-45 may be because it serves no purpose in an address to the second generation, who must now prepare for holy war. Instead, what matters (and what is stressed in Deut 1:19-45) is the need for the second generation to be courageous and not fear their impending invasion, as did the first generation.

The need for intercession in the pre-priestly story arises when God decides to destroy Israel and to form a new nation (v. 12). Moses intercedes for the people with a two-part argument about God's character. The first argument concerns holy war. He reminds God that killing off Israel at this point would lead the indigenous nations of the land to conclude that Yahweh is unreliable, incapable of fulfilling the promise of land.

The second argument turns on Yahweh's ability to change and thus forgive. This argument is presented as Moses selectively quotes the revelation of God's attributes from Exod 34:6-7. The literary context of Exod 34:6-7 aids in its interpretation. This revelation follows the intercession by Moses in Exodus 33 for the continuing presence of God with Israel. Despite Israel's sin in the golden calf episode (Exodus 32), Yahweh announces the decision to continue to lead Israel by revealing aspects of the divine character to Moses: (1) mercy and grace; (2) slow to anger; (3) rich in loving kindness and willing to dispense it to thousands; (4) bearer of iniquity; (5) yet not willing to cancel all guilt (6) so that punishment for iniquity might be extended to offspring to the fourth generation.

Exodus 34:6-7 is a liturgical confession about divine forgiveness in a culture that stressed collective responsibility and guilt. In this cultural setting, deferment of punishment was interpreted as the forgiving character of God. On the basis of these attributes, Moses asks God to forgive Israel (Exod 34:8-9). In Exodus 32–34, God's ability to defer punishment to a later generation allows Israel's story to continue after the incident of the golden calf. But such action gives rise to the proverb "The parents have eaten sour grapes, and the children's teeth are set on edge" (Ezek 18:2).

The intercession of Moses in Num 14:12-19 is an inner-biblical interpretation of Exod 34:6-7. In Num 14:17, Moses recalls God's earlier revelation and recites it in v. 18. Although the motifs of mercy, grace, and the dispensing of loving kindness are absent, the quotation by Moses does not appear to change the overall meaning of Exod 34:6-7. The people are still viewed collectively over several generations. The call for forgiveness in v. 19, therefore, is a request for deferment of punishment, like Exod 34:6-7.

The divine response to Moses in vv. 20-24 goes beyond his request; in doing so, it reinterprets Exod 34:6-7. God agrees to forgive in v. 20 as Moses requested. As a result, the entire nation is not destroyed instantly. In fact, no one is killed immediately in the pre-priestly story. But delayed execution does not lead to the gift of the land. Instead, the people are instructed to travel back into the wilderness on the Red Sea road (v. 25). The collective understanding of the people means that all members of the exodus generation—even Moses—must forfeit the land (with the exception of Caleb). This view is expressed in Deut 1:19-46, where Moses states that he cannot enter the land because of the people's murmuring.

What is new is that God redefines deferment of punishment by limiting its execution to the generation responsible for the sin. They may not die instantly as God had wished, but they will die in the wilderness without ever having reached the promised land. Thus God rejects deferment of punishment to later generations and, with it, the notion of accumulated guilt. The result of this new limitation on the traditional understanding of forgiveness is that the promise of salvation becomes intergenerational. This gives rise to a reversal of the traditional understanding. Divine forgiveness in the pre-priestly story means that the promise of land to Israel is deferred to a later generation, and not the punishment due their faithless ancestors.

14:26-38. Priestly writers provide their own interpretation of God's response in this section. They also reframe the dialogue between God and Moses in vv. 11-25 by describing more precisely how God was present in the tabernacle and how God leads Israel in the wilderness. In v. 10b, the priestly writers state that "the glory of Yahweh appeared on the tent of meeting," and they return to the topic of Yahweh's "glory" two more times

(vv. 21-22). These insertions bring the appearance of God into conformity with the central role that the glory of Yahweh assumes in priestly descriptions of theophany (Exod 24:12-18; 40:34-38; Lev 9:23). In v. 14, the priestly writers also emphasize how God leads Israel day and night with the pillar of cloud and the pillar of fire, respectively, which is how they described the wilderness march in 9:15-23. But their theological evaluation of the loss of the land is contained in 14:26-38.

The priestly version of God's response to the murmuring of the people begins with their typical introduction, "And the LORD spoke to Moses and Aaron" (v. 26). The priestly writers move even further from the traditional way of viewing the people collectively over several generations. In fact, it is not clear whether the priestly writers view even a single generation collectively. Instead, they focus on detailed retribution for distinct groups, measured out in proportion to the offense. Thus God punishes the people according to what they have actually said (v. 28). Those who murmured will die in the wilderness rather than live in the land with God (v. 30). These persons include those who were numbered in the census (chap. 1) as being over twenty years of age (v. 29); Joshua and Caleb are the only exceptions. The children will inherit the land instead of their parents (v. 31). Furthermore, the length of the punishment is determined by the offense. The forty days of exploring the land will be translated into forty years of wilderness wandering (vv. 34-35). The leaders, who actually defamed the land with their evil report, die instantly before God (vv. 36-37). Because the priestly writers appear to stress individual responsibility, it is not surprising that a second story is necessary to explain why Moses was not allowed to enter the land (see 20:1-13).

14:39–15:41. The episode concludes with an account of Israel's failed attempt at conquest (14:39-45), which is supplemented by the priestly writers with divine law about Israel's future life in the land (chap. 15).

14:39-45. The pre-priestly story ends with an account of profane war. Moses tells the people of the divine decision to defer the gift of land, which prompts confession of sin and the decision to invade (v. 40). Moses condemns this decision as yet another transgression against God. It can only lead to the slaughter of the people, because God will not fight for them (vv. 41-43). The closing scene of the story has the people ascending into the hills for battle, while the ark of Yahweh remains in the camp (v. 44). The inevitable consequence is narrated in v. 45: The people are pummeled all the way to the city of Hormah, a location south of Hebron.

15:1-41. The priestly writers provide a more positive ending to the loss of the land in chaps. 13–14 by ending the story with legislation (chap. 15), which emphasizes Israel's future life in the land and, hence, God's commitment to fulfill the promise of salvation. Thus the law in this chapter is meant to provide commentary on the actions in chaps. 13–14. The chapter separates into three parts. An initial division between vv. 1-16 and 17-31 is indicated by the repetition of vv. 1-2 in vv. 17-18. This repetition includes the stereotypical introduction, "The LORD spoke to Moses, saying: Speak to the Israelites and say to them" (vv. 1-2*a*, 17-18*a*), and a reference to life in the land, which gives the law a future orientation, "When you come into the land . . ." (vv. 2*b*, 18*b*). A third section, vv. 32-41, contains legislation intended for the wilderness setting.

15:1-16. This section contains detailed prescriptions of what ingredients should accompany different sacrifices. Verses 3-16 state that every offering by fire, whether a whole burnt offering or a sacrifice in which only part of the animal is burnt, must be accompanied by both a grain offering and a drink offering. Similar requirements with slightly different measurements also appear in Leviticus 2 and Ezek 46:5-7, 11, 14. The following guidelines are given in vv. 4-10 (a hin is approx. 3.6 liters and an ephah is approx. 22 liters):

Animal	Grain Offering (and oil)	Drink Offering (wine)
Lamb	¹⁄₁₀ ephah + (¼ hin)	¼ hin
Ram	²⁄₁₀ ephah + (⅓ hin)	⅓ hin
Bull	³⁄₁₀ ephah + (⅕ hin)	⅕ hin

A refrain throughout these verses is that the sacrifices are a "pleasing odor for the LORD" (vv. 3, 7, 10, 13, 14). The conception of God as being attracted to sacrifice by its aroma is rooted in the mythology of the ancient Near East. In the *Epic of Gilgamesh,* for example, Utnapishtim, the survivor of the flood, describes his sacrifice to the gods after the flood:

"The gods smelled the savor,
The gods smelled the sweet savor,
The gods crowded like flies about the sacrificer."[114]

The OT parallel to Utnapishtim occurs when Noah sacrifices to God after the flood with the result that "the LORD smelled the pleasing odor" (Gen 8:21). Priestly writers use this phrase both in Leviticus 1–3 and in Numbers 15 to indicate that an offering is accepted by God and, hence, will effect power from God. Verses 11-16 underscore that the basis of the requirements for sacrifice are rooted in the gift of the land. Verse 13 states that all native Israelites (אזרח 'ezrāḥ, sing.) are required to perform the sacrifices listed in vv. 4-10. A native Israelite is one who owns land.

Priestly writers also extend the law to the resident alien (גר gēr; also the "stranger" or "sojourner"), if they choose to participate. The priestly writers incorporate resident aliens into civil law and cultic practice in a number of different ways. For example, the resident alien must avoid leaven during the observance of unleavened bread (Exod 12:19), must not work on the Day of Atonement (Lev 16:29-31), must refrain from eating blood (Lev 17:10-12), must abide by Israelite sexual practices (Lev 18:26), must not sacrifice to Molech (Lev 20:2), and must undergo purification if defiled by a corpse (Num 19:10). They must have access to cities of refuge (Num 35:15). Furthermore, resident aliens may observe cultic rites like Passover if they undergo circumcision (Exod 12:48-49; Num 9:14) and other sacrificial rituals (Lev 17:8; 22:18-20; Num 15:26). The laws concerning the resident alien provide a social and theological window into Israel's self-identity, because the Israelites viewed themselves as resident aliens in a land that God owned (Lev 25:23).

Two points stand out in these verses. First, the promise of land is not negated by the disobedience of the congregation, nor is it even in question. The detailed legislation on sacrifice underscores that Israel will, indeed, live in the land. Second, specific details of the sacrifices emphasize the productivity of the land. When Israel lives in the promised land, there will be cattle, grain, oil, and wine for repeated sacrifices to God. This picture

114. *The Epic of Gilgamesh*, ll. 159-61 in *ANET*, 95.

of fertility counters the bad report of the leaders (13:32-33). A land that eats its inhabitants does not produce the abundance of meat, meal, oil, and wine listed in vv. 1-16.

15:17-31. This second section of legislation is also directed to Israel's future life in the land. Verses 17-21 anchor the legislation firmly in the future context of the land when God states that a donation from the first batch of dough is required whenever anyone eats "bread of the land" (vv. 19-20). The Hebrew word translated "dough" (עריסה 'ărîsâ) is not clear. The translation "dough" is from the Septuagint, but it may also refer to barley food, or even more likely a baking vessel. Similar legislation is repeated in Ezek 44:30 and Neh 10:38. The point of the legislation in Num 15:17-21 is that the donation is required from generation to generation. This law sets the stage for the priestly writers to return to the topic of corporate and individual responsibility that is central to Numbers 13–14.

Verses 22-31 explore three types of transgression in order to illustrate the limitations of forgiveness and the different ways in which forgiveness operates: unintentional corporate sin (vv. 22-26); unintentional individual sin (vv. 27-29); and intentional sin (vv. 30-31). Verses 22-26 explore unintentional corporate sin. If an act of transgression is committed without the people's knowing it, corporate forgiveness of both native Israelites and resident aliens is possible. Forgiveness, in this case, requires that the priest sacrifice a bull for a burnt offering and a male goat for a sin offering. This ritual atones for the entire congregation. (It is also outlined in Lev 4:13-21.)

Verses 27-29 describe how unintentional individual transgression can be forgiven. The sacrifice of a female goat by the priest atones for either a native Israelite or a resident alien. (This ritual is also described in Lev 4:27-31.)

Verses 30-31 are the point of emphasis in the section. They describe high-handed transgression. The Hebrew phrase "high-handed" (ביד רמה bĕyād rāmâ) also was used to characterize Israel as it left Egypt (Exod 14:8), where it is translated "boldly." In the legal context of Num 15:30-31, "high-handed" transgressions are best interpreted as intentional or premeditated sin. There is no forgiveness for premeditated transgression. Such persons must bear their guilt, which means that they are "cut off" (כרת kārat) from the people.

The exact meaning of this phrase in priestly tradition is not clear. It may have a collective sense, meaning a family line is discontinued. This meaning would qualify the more individual focus of 14:26-38. But it may also be more individual in its meaning, in which case it would signify a loss of status, excommunication, death, or even a judgment by God after death. The bad report of the land by the leaders of Israel (who die instantly) and the murmuring of the people (who are condemned to die in the wilderness) are instances of premeditated transgression that fall under the final category.

15:32-41. The third section of law in this chapter switches from the setting of the land to the wilderness. Verses 32-36 describe the case of a person collecting sticks on the sabbath who is taken into custody and brought to Moses for judgment. The infraction is without precedent, requiring special revelation for a resolution. Other instances where an ambiguous situation demanded new law in the form of an oracle from God include the blasphemer (Lev 24:10-23), the second Passover (9:6-13), and the rights of the daughters of Zelophehad (27:1-11; 36:1-12). In none of these situations is there clear precedent in priestly law—even though the non-priestly Book of the Covenant does prescribe legislation against blasphemy (Exod 22:28[27]).

But the incident in vv. 32-36 is perplexing, because the priestly writers do indeed address sabbath law in a number of different places. The priestly theologians prescribe sabbath law in the Decalogue (Exod 20:10-11), where work is forbidden because of the structure of creation (Gen 2:1-3). They return to the topic during the revelation of the tabernacle (Exod 31:12-17; 35:1-3), reiterating the prohibition against work and including an additional prohibition against home fires on the sabbath. Again their argument is based on an analogy with creation. Thus, when Israel is at a loss of what to do with the person gathering sticks on the sabbath, the reader is also at a loss, because there is, in fact, clear precedent for action from other texts. The rabbis saw the problem and suggested that the new thing requiring an oracle from God is not sabbath law, but the nature of the punishment. More modern commentators speculate that the ambiguity of the situation involves gathering wood and whether that is work.[115]

The wilderness setting for the story offers yet another perspective for interpretation. From this point of view, vv. 32-36 address the question of whether sabbath observance is tied only to the land or is in effect in all places. The emphasis on the wilderness as the setting for the legislation (v. 32) suggests that the point of clarity in the divine oracle is that sabbath law is always in effect, whether Israel is in its land or not. The basis for the universal requirement of sabbath law in priestly tradition arises from the structure of creation (Gen 2:1-3). It is simply part of the intended fabric of this world. Thus, in the priestly history, sabbath reemerges immediately in the wilderness in conjunction with the providential gift of manna (Exod 16:22-31). And because sabbath observance is universal in scope, picking up sticks on this day—even in the wilderness outside of the land—is a capital offense against God, requiring the death penalty.

The priestly writers close the unit in vv. 37-41 by calling Israel to remember God's legislation through the act of sewing blue tassels to the corners of their garments (see the parallel in Deut 22:12). Blue tassels are intended to be an aid to faithful living in that such symbols will remind the Israelites of Yahweh's promise of land; the priestly writers state the principle in v. 39. Looking at the blue cords will prevent the Israelites from exploring (13:1, 17, 21, 25, 32 [twice]; 14:6, 7, 36, 38) according to their own hearts' desire, which led to adultery (14:33) and loss of the land. Thus tassels are a sign of hope about a future life in the land. Finally, the authority for the divine commands is rooted in Yahweh's power as demonstrated in the event of the exodus (v. 41).

115. See, e.g., Milgrom, *Numbers*, 126, 408-10.

REFLECTIONS

1. The central role of creation in the priestly writers' account of the Israelites' loss of the land is timely for the contemporary church. The Israelites fail to see the value of the land.

Even worse, their leaders give a bad report that defames it. They conclude that the land of Canaan eats its inhabitants and that only unnatural Nephilim are able to live in its environment.

The priestly writers' version of Israel's pivotal sin in the wilderness reads like a parable of the contemporary church. God's good gift of creation is nearly absent in our worship life. We focus on our personal relationship with Jesus and our social responsibility to other humans. Both are essential to the Christian life. But each rests on a more foundational divine gift: the earth itself. We have failed to identify ourselves as creatures of God within the ecosystem of the earth, and our blindness has given rise to "bad reports" of the land, which defame the earth.

A central goal in preaching and teaching this story is to explore ways in which we have defamed the earth by being blind to its goodness. Environmental pollution, overdevelopment, and irresponsible use of resources are ways in which we slander the earth through blindness. We no longer need to mythologize the results of such pollution as did the priestly writers. We have abundant evidence of Nephilim created by our toxic environment. And the result of our blindness is the same as that of the wilderness generation of Israelites: We lose God's gift of the land.

Preaching on the environment must move beyond a message of doom and judgment. The priestly writers are not pessimists. The power of God's promise means that pollution is not the last word on the land. Atonement for moral blindness is possible. The priestly writers also point ahead to a future vision of a rich and productive earth. When God's promise is fulfilled, Israel will recognize their produce as a gift from God and return it through sacrifice. Priestly writers not only envision a bright future based on God's promise, but they also provide guidelines for Israel's present life in the wilderness. The future vision of the land begins by organizing the wilderness journey within the rhythm and cycles of creation. Sabbath rest is the first act in living in harmony with creation.

Sabbath law is about worship. The first step in addressing our abuse of the earth is to celebrate its gift in worship; otherwise, we remain blind. We are only beginning to awaken to the central role of creation in Jesus' proclamation of the kingdom of God. Identifying the earth as God's gift of salvation and ourselves as creatures within it brings God's kingdom into view. We must return to the insight of the ancient Israelites that they were resident aliens on God's land. We continue to sojourn on God's property, and our worship must include recognition of this gift. Leadership in environmental ethics will then flow from our worship life.

2. There is a growing conflict in the church between social justice and environmental theology. The argument is that the church has limited resources and cannot undertake two distinct missions. The message of Numbers 13–15 is that the two cannot be separated. The pre-priestly writers interpret the loss of the land as a failure of holy war. Holy war often symbolizes struggles for social justice in the Bible. The exodus is Yahweh's holy war against the oppressive empire of Egypt. It is an event of liberation for Israel. The message of the pre-priestly writers is that the Israelites fear to risk their lives for social justice, and as a consequence they lose the gift of salvation. The priestly writers emphasize the important role of seeing the goodness of the land in order to possess it. They stress a theology of creation. Both interpretations are interwoven in Numbers 13–15; neither is given precedence. The message arising from the composition of Numbers 13–15 is that social justice and environmental justice are inseparable.

3. The message in the loss of the land is salvation, not judgment, when interpretation focuses on God. Three insights into the character of God are important for preaching. First, God is able to change. This is the central message of the story. The Israelites' rejection of the land should have stopped the story of salvation. They broke the conditions of their covenant by refusing to follow God, sealing their fate. God continues the story by changing the conditions of their relationship. Yahweh's forgiveness of Israel indicates a transformation by God, not by Israel. There is no such thing as fate in the Bible. The future is open, because God is in a personal relationship with the Israelites. The result is that Yahweh is steadfast, constant, and enduring, according to biblical writers. Second, God's grace is most clear during times of judgment. It is the crisis of the loss of land that brings forth new insight into Yahweh's mercy. Third, the mercy of God goes beyond our expectations. Moses presented his best argument to God, requesting that God defer punishment at the present time, so that the Israelites might endure the wilderness march. God shatters Moses' meager request by eliminating deferred punishment altogether and replacing it with the promise of land as the point of continuity between the generations. The result is that the transforming power of salvation (not guilt) passes from generation to generation.

4. Moses models intercession in Numbers 13–14. He approaches Yahweh on the basis of tradition. He quotes the best liturgy at his disposal (Exod 34:6-7). He presents additional arguments to dissuade God from judgment, including past promises by Yahweh to the Israelites and the perception of God by other nations. Moses is idealized, moreover, both as a prophet (Num 14:11-25) and as a priest (Num 14:26-38) as he mediates for the people. The power to intercede is not limited to any one office. Central to Moses' intercession is the knowledge that Yahweh is able to change judgment into forgiveness. But what is most striking in this story is that even Moses, the greatest intercessor, underestimates Yahweh's ability to transform disaster into hope. The message that arises from this story is that there is no limit to the power of intercession. Moses demonstrates that it is not possible to undervalue the persuasive power of intercession with God. Yahweh is full of surprises. Jesus models the same boldness in his intercession with God, and he encourages his disciples to do the same (see John 14–17).

5. The message of the loss of the land is judgment when interpretation focuses on the Israelites. A sermon on the Israelites is a meditation on the destructive power of fear. Fear blinds the first generation to God's leading. Fear turns salvation into a foolhardy enterprise that will ensure the death of children. Fear changes the good gift of the land into a place of death. Fear transforms other humans into monsters (Anakim) and freaks of nature (Nephilim). And an immature response to fear leads to a suicidal war. Fear in each case is a form of death. God has the power to defeat it, but not independent of the Israelites. Thus the first generation dies in the wilderness because they refuse to let go of their fear and give it to God.

The task of preaching is to discern the destructive power of fear in contemporary life. What keeps your congregation from following God's leading? Is it fear of losing money or the risk of changing a life-style? Do members of your church mask their fear by belittling or slandering the salvation of God? Have any concluded that the land is not worth the risk and, therefore, is a foolhardy endeavor? Do members in your church turn other humans into monsters and thus feed racism? Is God's gift of creation respected or abused? The destructive power of fear can push the promised land further into our future, as it did for the Israelites in the wilderness.

Numbers 16:1–17:13, Conflict Over Priestly Leadership

NIV	NRSV
16Korah son of Izhar, the son of Kohath, the son of Levi, and certain Reubenites—Dathan and Abiram, sons of Eliab, and On son of Peleth—became insolent[a] 2and rose up against Moses. With them were 250 Israelite men, well-known community leaders who had been appointed members of the council. 3They came as	**16**Now Korah son of Izhar son of Kohath son of Levi, along with Dathan and Abiram sons of Eliab, and On son of Peleth—descendants of Reuben—took 2two hundred fifty Israelite men, leaders of the congregation, chosen from the assembly, well-known men,[a] and they confronted Moses. 3They assembled against Moses and against
a1 Or Peleth—took ⌊men⌋	*a Cn: Heb and they confronted Moses, and two hundred fifty men . . . well-known men*

a group to oppose Moses and Aaron and said to them, "You have gone too far! The whole community is holy, every one of them, and the LORD is with them. Why then do you set yourselves above the LORD's assembly?"

[4]When Moses heard this, he fell facedown. [5]Then he said to Korah and all his followers: "In the morning the LORD will show who belongs to him and who is holy, and he will have that person come near him. The man he chooses he will cause to come near him. [6]You, Korah, and all your followers are to do this: Take censers [7]and tomorrow put fire and incense in them before the LORD. The man the LORD chooses will be the one who is holy. You Levites have gone too far!"

[8]Moses also said to Korah, "Now listen, you Levites! [9]Isn't it enough for you that the God of Israel has separated you from the rest of the Israelite community and brought you near himself to do the work at the LORD's tabernacle and to stand before the community and minister to them? [10]He has brought you and all your fellow Levites near himself, but now you are trying to get the priesthood too. [11]It is against the LORD that you and all your followers have banded together. Who is Aaron that you should grumble against him?"

[12]Then Moses summoned Dathan and Abiram, the sons of Eliab. But they said, "We will not come! [13]Isn't it enough that you have brought us up out of a land flowing with milk and honey to kill us in the desert? And now you also want to lord it over us? [14]Moreover, you haven't brought us into a land flowing with milk and honey or given us an inheritance of fields and vineyards. Will you gouge out the eyes of[a] these men? No, we will not come!"

[15]Then Moses became very angry and said to the LORD, "Do not accept their offering. I have not taken so much as a donkey from them, nor have I wronged any of them."

[16]Moses said to Korah, "You and all your followers are to appear before the LORD tomorrow—you and they and Aaron. [17]Each man is to take his censer and put incense in it—250 censers in all—and present it before the LORD. You and Aaron are to present your censers also." [18]So each

[a]14 Or you make slaves of; or you deceive

Aaron, and said to them, "You have gone too far! All the congregation are holy, every one of them, and the LORD is among them. So why then do you exalt yourselves above the assembly of the LORD?" [4]When Moses heard it, he fell on his face. [5]Then he said to Korah and all his company, "In the morning the LORD will make known who is his, and who is holy, and who will be allowed to approach him; the one whom he will choose he will allow to approach him. [6]Do this: take censers, Korah and all your[a] company, [7]and tomorrow put fire in them, and lay incense on them before the LORD; and the man whom the LORD chooses shall be the holy one. You Levites have gone too far!" [8]Then Moses said to Korah, "Hear now, you Levites! [9]Is it too little for you that the God of Israel has separated you from the congregation of Israel, to allow you to approach him in order to perform the duties of the LORD's tabernacle, and to stand before the congregation and serve them? [10]He has allowed you to approach him, and all your brother Levites with you; yet you seek the priesthood as well! [11]Therefore you and all your company have gathered together against the LORD. What is Aaron that you rail against him?"

[12]Moses sent for Dathan and Abiram sons of Eliab; but they said, "We will not come! [13]Is it too little that you have brought us up out of a land flowing with milk and honey to kill us in the wilderness, that you must also lord it over us? [14]It is clear you have not brought us into a land flowing with milk and honey, or given us an inheritance of fields and vineyards. Would you put out the eyes of these men? We will not come!"

[15]Moses was very angry and said to the LORD, "Pay no attention to their offering. I have not taken one donkey from them, and I have not harmed any one of them." [16]And Moses said to Korah, "As for you and all your company, be present tomorrow before the LORD, you and they and Aaron; [17]and let each one of you take his censer, and put incense on it, and each one of you present his censer before the LORD, two hundred fifty censers; you also, and Aaron, each his censer." [18]So each man took his censer, and they put fire in the censers and laid incense on them, and they stood at the entrance of the tent of

[a] Heb his

NIV

man took his censer, put fire and incense in it, and stood with Moses and Aaron at the entrance to the Tent of Meeting. [19]When Korah had gathered all his followers in opposition to them at the entrance to the Tent of Meeting, the glory of the LORD appeared to the entire assembly. [20]The LORD said to Moses and Aaron, [21]"Separate yourselves from this assembly so I can put an end to them at once."

[22]But Moses and Aaron fell facedown and cried out, "O God, God of the spirits of all mankind, will you be angry with the entire assembly when only one man sins?"

[23]Then the LORD said to Moses, [24]"Say to the assembly, 'Move away from the tents of Korah, Dathan and Abiram.'"

[25]Moses got up and went to Dathan and Abiram, and the elders of Israel followed him. [26]He warned the assembly, "Move back from the tents of these wicked men! Do not touch anything belonging to them, or you will be swept away because of all their sins." [27]So they moved away from the tents of Korah, Dathan and Abiram. Dathan and Abiram had come out and were standing with their wives, children and little ones at the entrances to their tents.

[28]Then Moses said, "This is how you will know that the LORD has sent me to do all these things and that it was not my idea: [29]If these men die a natural death and experience only what usually happens to men, then the LORD has not sent me. [30]But if the LORD brings about something totally new, and the earth opens its mouth and swallows them, with everything that belongs to them, and they go down alive into the grave,[a] then you will know that these men have treated the LORD with contempt."

[31]As soon as he finished saying all this, the ground under them split apart [32]and the earth opened its mouth and swallowed them, with their households and all Korah's men and all their possessions. [33]They went down alive into the grave, with everything they owned; the earth closed over them, and they perished and were gone from the community. [34]At their cries, all the Israelites around them fled, shouting, "The earth is going to swallow us too!"

[a]30 Hebrew *Sheol*; also in verse 33

NRSV

meeting with Moses and Aaron. [19]Then Korah assembled the whole congregation against them at the entrance of the tent of meeting. And the glory of the LORD appeared to the whole congregation.

[20]Then the LORD spoke to Moses and to Aaron, saying: [21]Separate yourselves from this congregation, so that I may consume them in a moment. [22]They fell on their faces, and said, "O God, the God of the spirits of all flesh, shall one person sin and you become angry with the whole congregation?"

[23]And the LORD spoke to Moses, saying: [24]Say to the congregation: Get away from the dwellings of Korah, Dathan, and Abiram. [25]So Moses got up and went to Dathan and Abiram; the elders of Israel followed him. [26]He said to the congregation, "Turn away from the tents of these wicked men, and touch nothing of theirs, or you will be swept away for all their sins." [27]So they got away from the dwellings of Korah, Dathan, and Abiram; and Dathan and Abiram came out and stood at the entrance of their tents, together with their wives, their children, and their little ones. [28]And Moses said, "This is how you shall know that the LORD has sent me to do all these works; it has not been of my own accord: [29]If these people die a natural death, or if a natural fate comes on them, then the LORD has not sent me. [30]But if the LORD creates something new, and the ground opens its mouth and swallows them up, with all that belongs to them, and they go down alive into Sheol, then you shall know that these men have despised the LORD."

[31]As soon as he finished speaking all these words, the ground under them was split apart. [32]The earth opened its mouth and swallowed them up, along with their households—everyone who belonged to Korah and all their goods. [33]So they with all that belonged to them went down alive into Sheol; the earth closed over them, and they perished from the midst of the assembly. [34]All Israel around them fled at their outcry, for they said, "The earth will swallow us too!" [35]And fire came out from the LORD and consumed the two hundred fifty men offering the incense.

[36][a]Then the LORD spoke to Moses, saying: [37]Tell Eleazar son of Aaron the priest to take

[a]Ch 17.1 in Heb

NIV

[35]And fire came out from the LORD and consumed the 250 men who were offering the incense.

[36]The LORD said to Moses, [37]"Tell Eleazar son of Aaron, the priest, to take the censers out of the smoldering remains and scatter the coals some distance away, for the censers are holy— [38]the censers of the men who sinned at the cost of their lives. Hammer the censers into sheets to overlay the altar, for they were presented before the LORD and have become holy. Let them be a sign to the Israelites."

[39]So Eleazar the priest collected the bronze censers brought by those who had been burned up, and he had them hammered out to overlay the altar, [40]as the LORD directed him through Moses. This was to remind the Israelites that no one except a descendant of Aaron should come to burn incense before the LORD, or he would become like Korah and his followers.

[41]The next day the whole Israelite community grumbled against Moses and Aaron. "You have killed the LORD's people," they said.

[42]But when the assembly gathered in opposition to Moses and Aaron and turned toward the Tent of Meeting, suddenly the cloud covered it and the glory of the LORD appeared. [43]Then Moses and Aaron went to the front of the Tent of Meeting, [44]and the LORD said to Moses, [45]"Get away from this assembly so I can put an end to them at once." And they fell facedown.

[46]Then Moses said to Aaron, "Take your censer and put incense in it, along with fire from the altar, and hurry to the assembly to make atonement for them. Wrath has come out from the LORD; the plague has started." [47]So Aaron did as Moses said, and ran into the midst of the assembly. The plague had already started among the people, but Aaron offered the incense and made atonement for them. [48]He stood between the living and the dead, and the plague stopped. [49]But 14,700 people died from the plague, in addition to those who had died because of Korah. [50]Then Aaron returned to Moses at the entrance to the Tent of Meeting, for the plague had stopped.

17 The LORD said to Moses, [2]"Speak to the Israelites and get twelve staffs from them, one from the leader of each of their ancestral

NRSV

the censers out of the blaze; then scatter the fire far and wide. [38]For the censers of these sinners have become holy at the cost of their lives. Make them into hammered plates as a covering for the altar, for they presented them before the LORD and they became holy. Thus they shall be a sign to the Israelites. [39]So Eleazar the priest took the bronze censers that had been presented by those who were burned; and they were hammered out as a covering for the altar— [40]a reminder to the Israelites that no outsider, who is not of the descendants of Aaron, shall approach to offer incense before the LORD, so as not to become like Korah and his company—just as the LORD had said to him through Moses.

[41]On the next day, however, the whole congregation of the Israelites rebelled against Moses and against Aaron, saying, "You have killed the people of the LORD." [42]And when the congregation had assembled against them, Moses and Aaron turned toward the tent of meeting; the cloud had covered it and the glory of the LORD appeared. [43]Then Moses and Aaron came to the front of the tent of meeting, [44]and the LORD spoke to Moses, saying, [45]"Get away from this congregation, so that I may consume them in a moment." And they fell on their faces. [46]Moses said to Aaron, "Take your censer, put fire on it from the altar and lay incense on it, and carry it quickly to the congregation and make atonement for them. For wrath has gone out from the LORD; the plague has begun." [47]So Aaron took it as Moses had ordered, and ran into the middle of the assembly, where the plague had already begun among the people. He put on the incense, and made atonement for the people. [48]He stood between the dead and the living; and the plague was stopped. [49]Those who died by the plague were fourteen thousand seven hundred, besides those who died in the affair of Korah. [50]When the plague was stopped, Aaron returned to Moses at the entrance of the tent of meeting.

17 [a]The LORD spoke to Moses, saying: [2]Speak to the Israelites, and get twelve staffs from them, one for each ancestral house, from all the leaders of their ancestral houses. Write each man's

a Ch 17.16 in Heb

NIV

tribes. Write the name of each man on his staff. ³On the staff of Levi write Aaron's name, for there must be one staff for the head of each ancestral tribe. ⁴Place them in the Tent of Meeting in front of the Testimony, where I meet with you. ⁵The staff belonging to the man I choose will sprout, and I will rid myself of this constant grumbling against you by the Israelites."

⁶So Moses spoke to the Israelites, and their leaders gave him twelve staffs, one for the leader of each of their ancestral tribes, and Aaron's staff was among them. ⁷Moses placed the staffs before the LORD in the Tent of the Testimony.

⁸The next day Moses entered the Tent of the Testimony and saw that Aaron's staff, which represented the house of Levi, had not only sprouted but had budded, blossomed and produced almonds. ⁹Then Moses brought out all the staffs from the LORD's presence to all the Israelites. They looked at them, and each man took his own staff.

¹⁰The LORD said to Moses, "Put back Aaron's staff in front of the Testimony, to be kept as a sign to the rebellious. This will put an end to their grumbling against me, so that they will not die." ¹¹Moses did just as the LORD commanded him.

¹²The Israelites said to Moses, "We will die! We are lost, we are all lost! ¹³Anyone who even comes near the tabernacle of the LORD will die. Are we all going to die?"

NRSV

name on his staff, ³and write Aaron's name on the staff of Levi. For there shall be one staff for the head of each ancestral house. ⁴Place them in the tent of meeting before the covenant,ᵃ where I meet with you. ⁵And the staff of the man whom I choose shall sprout; thus I will put a stop to the complaints of the Israelites that they continually make against you. ⁶Moses spoke to the Israelites; and all their leaders gave him staffs, one for each leader, according to their ancestral houses, twelve staffs; and the staff of Aaron was among theirs. ⁷So Moses placed the staffs before the LORD in the tent of the covenant.ᵃ

8When Moses went into the tent of the covenantᵃ on the next day, the staff of Aaron for the house of Levi had sprouted. It put forth buds, produced blossoms, and bore ripe almonds. ⁹Then Moses brought out all the staffs from before the LORD to all the Israelites; and they looked, and each man took his staff. ¹⁰And the LORD said to Moses, "Put back the staff of Aaron before the covenant,ᵃ to be kept as a warning to rebels, so that you may make an end of their complaints against me, or else they will die." ¹¹Moses did so; just as the LORD commanded him, so he did.

12The Israelites said to Moses, "We are perishing; we are lost, all of us are lost! ¹³Everyone who approaches the tabernacle of the LORD will die. Are we all to perish?"

ᵃ Or *treaty,* or *testimony;* Heb *eduth*

COMMENTARY

Numbers 16–17 explores priestly leadership in the wilderness community through a series of challenges to the authority of Moses and Aaron. This section provides a counterpart to Numbers 11–12, where charismatic, prophetic leadership was examined. Priestly leadership is not charismatic. It does not arise spontaneously through the power of personality, as was the case in Numbers 11–12. Rather, it emerges in response to holiness. The formal structures of the priestly office are meant to protect people from the danger of divine holiness, while also providing a safe means to worship God. The Aaronide priests are noncharis-

matic leaders. They are born into their leadership role, not called like the seventy elders. They lack the visible signs of charismatic authority evident in the seventy elders, whose ecstatic behavior confirmed their divine call. Numbers 16–17 examine the proper exercise of priestly power.

Numbers 16:1-2 lists the many characters who come into conflict with Moses. They include a Levite from the family of Kohath named Korah, two Reubenites named Dathan and Abiram, perhaps a third character named On, also a Reubenite, and 250 unnamed leaders of Israel. Scholars have long noted that the cast of characters in

16:1-2 do not appear to be original. On plays no role in the story, and reference to him may actually be the result of textual corruption. Even with the absence of On, Reubenites and Levites do not form a natural coalition, which has raised the question of whether the characters come from different authors. This suspicion is strengthened by the tradition in Deut 11:6, where Dathan and Abiram appear independently of Korah. Their complaints also appear to be separated in Numbers 16–17.

Deuteronomy 11:6 provides a window into the pre-priestly version of the story. It states that Dathan and Abiram, both Reubenites, were swallowed up by the earth in the wilderness, along with their entire households. All the Israelites witnessed this event. The narrative account to which Deut 11:6 refers is contained in Num 16:25-34, suggesting that much of this material was present before priestly writers reworked the story. Dathan and Abiram also play a central role in Num 16:12-15, which provides the conflict leading to their destruction in 16:25-34. In this section, they complain about Moses' leadership using language similar to other murmuring stories. Moses has made himself prince, they charge, even though he has led Israel from fertile Egypt to die in the wilderness. The exact contours of the Dathan and Abiram story are difficult to determine, because these men play such a subordinate role in the present form of the story, in which they are referred to only five times (16:1, 12, 24, 27 [twice]).

The priestly writers have thoroughly reworked the story of Dathan and Abiram, adding a new conflict between Korah, Moses, and Aaron over priestly leadership. In fact, they have supplemented and edited the material to such an extent that the present form of the story is, for all practical purposes, their interpretation. Korah now dominates the conflict. He is referred to eleven times (16:1, 5, 6, 8, 16, 19, 24, 27, 32; 17:5, 14) as a Levite who is supported by a congregation of 250 leaders. Together Korah and his supporters challenge the special priestly status of Moses and Aaron. The issue in the priestly version of the story is no longer Moses' ability to lead in the wilderness, but holiness and, more precisely, who has the power and privilege to approach God at the altar.

The priestly editing of the Dathan and Abiram story results in a new drama with three parts: an opening conflict with Korah (Dathan and Abiram) over priestly leadership (16:1-17); theophany and judgment at the tent of meeting to resolve the conflict (16:18-35); and a cultic etiology concerning hammered plates on the altar as a memorial of the conflict (16:36-40[17:1-5]). The priestly writers also extend the story with an additional episode. Numbers 16:41–17:13[17:6-28] is a conflict between all the Israelites and Moses and Aaron. It arises from the deaths of Korah, Dathan, and Abiram, and it follows the same three-part structure of that story: opening conflict, theophany as judgment, and etiological conclusion. The opening conflict is a complaint by the congregation of Israel over the deaths of Korah, Dathan, and Abiram (16:41). The glory of Yahweh (כבוד יהוה *kĕbôd YHWH*) appears at the tent of meeting to judge the Israelites (16:42-50). The episode concludes with an etiology concerning Aaron's budding staff as a memorial of the conflict and as a sign of priestly authority (chap. 17).

The priestly interpretation of chaps. 16–17 will provide the framework for more detailed commentary. Their reading yields a story line of two episodes: 16:1-40, the challenge to priestly leadership by other leaders; 16:41–17:13, the challenge to priestly leadership by the people.

16:1-40. The challenge to Moses and Aaron by other leaders is the central conflict in chaps. 16–17. It establishes the main themes surrounding non-charismatic leadership, and it sets the stage for the second episode in 16:41–17:12.

16:1-17. The setting and themes for the conflict over non-charismatic leadership are established in this section. The introduction of the challengers in vv. 1-2 is stylized. Three groups are each identified in three ways. A linear genealogy of three generations is given for Korah (Izhar-Kohath-Levi) and for Dathan and Abiram (Eliab-Peleth [= Pellu]-Reuben), while the 250 leaders are described as (1) leaders of the congregation who were (2) chosen from the assembly and (3) are well-known men. The genealogy of Dathan and Abiram presents the most problems for interpretation. The ancestry list assumes that On, the son of Peleth, appears as the result of textual corruption, perhaps repetition of the closing letters of the preceding word. He certainly plays no role in the story, nor does he occur in any other references to this event (27:1-4, Korah; Deut 11:6, Dathan and Abiram; Ps 106:16-18, Dathan and

Abiram). The reference to Pellu in place of Peleth is based on the second census of Israel in 26:5-11 (see also Exod 6:14), where Dathan and Abiram are listed in the genealogy of Reuben and are identified with Korah and the 250 leaders. No mention of On appears in this text. The family line of Korah is repeated in the levitical genealogies of Exod 6:16-24 and 1 Chr 6:16-30.

The complaint of the challengers in v. 3 concerns priestly leadership. They oppose the social structure in which priests alone are able to approach God. They counter with an egalitarian vision of the camp, stating that all the congregation is holy, because God dwells in its midst. Indeed, their claim is supported throughout the priestly literature as an ideal for Israel. Repeatedly in priestly tradition, Yahweh promises to dwell in Israel's midst (Exod 29:45), and the people are called to be holy. The opening divine speech at Mt. Sinai envisioned Israel as a "priestly kingdom and a holy nation" (Exod 19:6); this ideal returns throughout the priestly corpus, appearing as recently as the closing verses of the previous story, where Israel is once again called to be holy (15:40). The thrust of the challengers' complaint is that this future ideal is, in fact, a present reality, rendering the structural hierarchy of the priesthood both unnecessary and oppressive.

The egalitarian ideal of holiness leads to the accusation that Moses and Aaron "have gone too far!" (רב-לכם *rab-lākem*) in "exalting themselves above [על *'al*] the assembly of the LORD." The form of the verb translated "to exalt yourselves" (תתנשאו *titnaśśě'û*) is used to describe non-charismatic forms of hierarchy and power. Such power is good when it describes Yahweh as the LORD who is exalted over all (1 Chr 29:11), including Israelite kings who reign as God's representatives (2 Chr 32:23) and even the kingdom of Israel (Num 23:24; 24:7). But such power is evil when it is grasped for selfish reasons. Such persons are foolish (Prov 30:31-32), as illustrated by Adonijah, who rashly grasped for the power of kingship (1 Kgs 1:5). The challengers use the term negatively against Moses and Aaron. The expression "to exalt oneself above" signifies oppression. The only other occurrence of this phrase is in Ezek 29:15, where the prophet condemns past Egyptian oppression by describing how the future nation will be lowly,

so much so that Egypt "will never again exalt itself above nations."

Moses responds to the challengers in vv. 4-17. His initial response (v. 4) is anger against the congregation: He falls on his face. As was the case in the spy story (14:5), this action signals dissatisfaction and anger. It differs from the same action performed before God, where it signifies reverence (v. 22; 17:10). After the ritual act of falling on his face before the congregation, Moses addresses the challengers in three parts. Two addresses to Korah and his group (vv. 5-7, 16-17) frame a separate confrontation with Dathan and Abiram (vv. 12-15). Thus one detects editing, in which the priestly interpretation of events in vv. 5-7 and vv. 16-17 has come to dominate the pre-priestly story about Dathan and Abiram.

The confrontation with Dathan and Abiram in vv. 12-15 takes place at their tents. Moses sends for them, but they respond, "We will not go up [לא-נעלה *lō' na'ăleh*]!" This expression frames the confrontation in vv. 12 and 14, and it contains a broader complaint against Moses, since it is also used to describe Yahweh's choice of Moses to lead the Israelites into the land of Canaan. Yahweh's commissioning of Moses in Exod 3:8 includes rescue from Egypt ("I have come down to deliver them [Israel] from the Egyptians") and leadership into the promised land ("and to bring them up [ולהעלתו *ûlěha'ălōtô*] out of that land to a good and broad land, a land flowing with milk and honey").[116] By refusing to appear before Moses, Dathan and Abiram are also rejecting his leadership.

Their complaint to Moses is filled with irony. They state, "Is it too little that you have brought us up [עלה *'ālâ*] out of a land flowing with milk and honey to kill us in the wilderness?" (v. 13). They employ language of salvation from Egypt, but reverse its meaning. Dathan and Abiram use the word "to go up" (*'ālâ*) in order to describe their exodus from Egypt, rather than the more traditional word for leaving Egypt, "to go out" (יצא *yāṣā'*), as in the phrase, "Yahweh brought Israel out of Egypt" (Exod 13:3, 9, 14, 16).[117]

---

116. J. N. M. Wijngaards, "הוציא and העלה: A Twofold Approach to the Exodus," *VT* 15 (1965) 91-102.

117. H. D. Preuss, "יצא," in *TDOT,* ed. G. J. Botterweck and H. Ringgren (Grand Rapids: Eerdmans, 1990) 6:225-50; Thomas B. Dozeman, *God at War: Power in the Exodus Tradition* (Oxford: Oxford University Press, 1996) 51-53.

They also use metaphorical language of Canaan ("a land flowing with milk and honey") to describe the land of Egypt. As a result, Moses is accused of leading the people from an Egyptian paradise to die in the wilderness. This accusation echoes the other murmuring stories, where hardships in the wilderness prompt complaint. (See the commentary on the murmuring stories in the Overview to Num 11:1–19:22.)

The complaint of Dathan and Abiram also exceeds the other murmuring stories, because it is not limited to a failure of leadership by Moses. Their complaint includes the accusation that Moses has abused his power. They accuse Moses of having proclaimed himself leader and, in the process, "lording it over" (v. 13, שׂרר *śārar*). The same accusation was lodged earlier against Moses in Exod 2:14, where, in the midst of a dispute between two Hebrews, one asks him sarcastically, "Who made you a ruler [שׂר *śar*] and judge over us?" The verb indicates that the conflict concerns non-charismatic, civil leadership, especially how it is evaluated and justified. This focus ties the pre-priestly Dathan and Abiram story with the priestly writers' story of Korah. The difference between the two is that the former focuses on civil leadership, as opposed to the sacral interests of the priestly writers.

Moses' response in v. 15 provides the model for non-charismatic, civil leadership. His actions come into clearer light when they are compared to the earlier story in Exod 2:11-15, where he was accused of the same abuse. In that account, Moses executed justice on his own. Seeing an Egyptian abuse an Israelite, Moses killed the Egyptian (Exod 2:12). Confronted by an Israelite about the source of his authority, Moses fled Egypt (Exod 2:13-15). He repeats neither of these actions in Num 16:12-15. Confronted by the same charge from Dathan and Abiram, Moses neither executes judgment on his own nor flees. Instead, he turns the matter over to God and provides evidence that he has not abused his leadership power (v. 15): He has not taken a single donkey from any of his accusers, nor has he harmed them in any way. Moses also requests that God vindicate him by not accepting his accusers' sacrifice. Thus the matter is adjudicated in a larger context than Moses' sphere of power.

Priestly writers frame the conflict over civil leadership (vv. 12-15) with the conflict between Moses, Aaron, and Korah over priestly leadership (vv. 5-11, 16-17). The technique of repeating material before (vv. 5-11) and after (vv. 16-17) another episode (vv. 12-15) is called resumptive repetition. The introductory and concluding sections become the points of emphasis as the result of this type of editing.[118] The effect of the repetition is that Korah's confrontation now dominates the narrative. With these additions, the issue is no longer the ability of Moses to lead Israel into Canaan, but who is allowed to approach God in the sanctuary. The social background for such an inter-priestly conflict about access to the cult is most likely the post-exilic period. H. Gese has suggested that the priestly version of Numbers 16 is intended to clarify the subordinate role of Korahite cultic singers to Aaronide priests in the rituals of the post-exilic Temple.[119]

Although Moses' role changes from civil to priestly leadership, his response to Korah is similar to the incident with Dathan and Abiram. Moses does not adjudicate the conflict himself, but turns the matter over to God (vv. 5-7a), before stating his own criticism of Korah and his company (vv. 7b-11). A ritual is devised (vv. 5-7a) to determine who will achieve holy status and thus be able to draw near to God. The ritual involves censers (מחתות *maḥtôt*), flat bronze pans used to draw ashes from the fire at the altar. In this ritual, however, the censers are used with קטרת (*qĕṭōret*), "incense," according to the NIV and NRSV translations. The participants are to draw fire from the altar with their censers and place incense on them before God. But the meaning of *qĕṭōret* is difficult to determine. It may refer to either an incense offering or a sacrificial burning.[120] In any case, Moses states that through this action Yahweh will reveal who within the tribe of Levi is allowed to represent the people in God's presence.

The ritual with "censers" and "incense" provides many parallels to Lev 10:1-3, where Aaron's two sons, Nadab and Abihu, also take censers, put fire on them, burn incense before God, and die. The Nadab and Abihu story also defines the

---

118. C. Kuhl, "Wiederaufnahme. Ein Literar Prinzip?" *ZAW* 64 (1952) 1-10.

119. H. Gese, "Zur Geschichte der Kältsänger am zweiten Tempel," in *Abraham unser Vater: Juden und Christen im Gespräch über die Bibel* (Leiden: Brill, 1963) 232-33. See also the work of D. L. Peterson, *Late Israelite Prophecy: Studies in Deutero-Prophetic Literature and in Chronicles,* SBLMS 23 (Missoula, Mont.: Scholars Press, 1977).

120. See M. Haran, "The Uses of Incense in the Ancient Israelite Ritual," *VT* 10 (1960) 116-28, esp. 116-17.

leadership role of priests by criticizing a potential abuse of their power. Moses' statement to Aaron in Lev 10:3 provides the point of the criticism in the form of an oracle from Yahweh:

Through those who are near me
  I will show myself holy,
and before all the people
  I will be glorified. (Lev 10:3 NRSV)

The oracle indicates that priestly offerings at the altar are not for private access to God or for personal benefit or prestige, but for the sake of all the people. From this statement it appears that Nadab and Abihu were killed by God for having performed a private ritual for their own benefit. The literary parallels may signal a continuation of the same theme in the challenge by Korah.

In contrast to Lev 10:1-3, the point of the ritual in Num 16:5-7 is not to criticize the power of priests, but to defend it. Thus the conflict with Korah moves in the opposite direction from the story of Nadab and Abihu. The defense of priestly power is made clear in the speech of Moses (vv. 7*b*-11): It is not Moses and Aaron who have "gone too far" (רב-לכם *rab-lākem*), but Korah and his company of Levites (v. 7*b*). The evidence is their dissatisfaction in serving the tabernacle as Levites and their desire for the power of Aaronide priests. Moses states that by questioning the leadership of the priesthood, they are actually rebelling against God. The outcome of the ritual test at the close of the scene (v. 35), where fire destroys those of Korah's company who had burned incense, is already foreshadowed in the speech of Moses.

16:18-35. This section describes the divine execution of judgment on Dathan, Abiram, Korah, and the 250 leaders. Its literary structure is organized by the technique of resumptive repetition, as was also evident in vv. 4-17. The execution of judgment against Dathan and Abiram in the pre-priestly story (vv. 24-34) is framed by priestly material in vv. 18-23 and 35. Interpretation will begin with the judgment against Dathan and Abiram in vv. 24-34, then turn to the reinterpretation of this event by the priestly writers with their new introduction (vv. 18-23) and conclusion (v. 35).

The beginning of the pre-priestly story of Dathan and Abiram is not clear. It most likely included divine instruction to Moses similar to that of vv. 23-24, if not those precise words. The refusal of Dathan and Abiram to meet with Moses prompts Moses to go to their tents, along with the elders of Israel (v. 25). The setting of the story, therefore, is not at the tent of meeting, but at the tents of Dathan and Abiram (v. 28).

God's judgment (vv. 31-34) is preceded by a two-part speech by Moses to Israel (vv. 26-30). First, Moses warns the people to separate themselves from the tents of Dathan and Abiram in order to avoid the judgment that is about to fall on these men and their entire households (vv. 26-27). Second, Moses outlines the test by which Israel will be able to evaluate the complaint by Dathan and Abiram that Moses has abused his power of leadership (vv. 28-30). If nothing happens to Dathan and Abiram and they die natural deaths, then the people will know that Moses was not sent by God (v. 29). But if the ground swallows the households of Dathan and Abiram, sending them down to Sheol alive, then Israel will know that in challenging Mosaic leadership they have rejected God (v. 30). The judgment is executed swiftly in vv. 31-34. The ground swallows the households of Dathan and Abiram, and they descend alive and screaming into Sheol for all Israel to witness.

The priestly writers edit the confrontation with Dathan and Abiram by adding Korah to the story (vv. 24, 27, 32) and by describing Israel as a congregation (v. 24). Perhaps they also insert the emphasis on Israel's coming to a knowledge of God (v. 28), since this is a common motif in the priestly interpretation of the exodus (e.g., Exod 6:7) and in priestly law (e.g., Exod 29:45). Most important, however, the priestly writers frame the story of Dathan and Abiram with a new introduction (vv. 18-23) and conclusion (v. 35). The introduction superimposes the command and fulfillment structure characteristic of priestly literature onto Numbers 16. The instruction of Moses that Korah and his company perform the ritual with censers (vv. 6-7, 17) is carried out in v. 18, before the tent of meeting. Verse 35 brings this ritual to a close by describing how the participants are destroyed by fire.

The centerpiece of the priestly story is the theophany in vv. 18-21 and the intercession by Moses and Aaron in v. 22. The performance of the ritual act with censers (v. 18) prompts the appearance of the glory of Yahweh before the entire congregation of Israel (v. 19) for the purpose of judgment. God commands Moses and

Aaron to separate themselves from the congregation, so that all the people can be destroyed with fire (vv. 20-21). The threat of destruction to all Israel is a new element in the story, allowing the priestly writers to idealize Moses and Aaron in the role of priestly intercessors on behalf of the people (v. 22). Their intercession begins with the ritual act of falling on their faces, this time as an act of reverence intended to divert the divine wrath that is about to consume Israel. Moses and Aaron ask God why all the congregation should perish as a consequence of the sin of one person.

The intercession of Moses and Aaron builds on the revelation of individual responsibility, which the priestly writers introduced in the story concerning the loss of the land (14:26-38). There, also, the glory of Yahweh appeared for the purpose of judging the people (14:10). What is different, however, is the view that God supports priestly intercession. As priests, Moses and Aaron appeal to the universal power of God as Creator, rather than to the more particular power of God as Israel's Savior and covenant partner. In his previous roles of intercession (chaps. 11–12; 14), Moses functioned as a prophet who enjoyed special favor in the eyes of God (11:11). His charisma gave him the power to intercede through prayer, and successful intercession grew out of his persuasive rhetorical arguments (14:13-17), reminding God of past covenantal commitments to Israel (14:18) as a basis for forgiveness (14:19).

The priestly intercession of Moses and Aaron in v. 22 lacks rhetorical persuasion and makes no reference to Israel's unique salvation history. Instead, it presents the facts of creation. God is addressed with the more general name *El* ("God"), rather than with the covenantal name, *Yahweh* ("LORD"), in order to emphasize that God is the creative source of all life. The implication of the epitaph "God of the spirits of all flesh" is that such a deity cannot be the source of indiscriminate death. This argument requires no request that God forgive—only that punishment be limited to the guilty. The call for the Israelites to separate themselves from the rebellious group (v. 24) indicates the successful intercession by Moses and Aaron to save the nation of Israel. The deaths of Dathan and Abiram (vv. 24-34), rather than of the entire nation, become one stage of a more selective punishment aimed only at the guilty. The

destruction by fire of the 250 participants in the ritual at the close of the scene completes the punishment of the guilty in the priestly interpretation of the story (v. 35).

16:36-40. The story ends with a cultic etiology concerning the origin of hammered plates on the altar. These plates are made from the censers of the 250 participants in Korah's company who challenged the special status of the Aaronide priesthood and were killed by God. The censers are hammered into plates for the altar because they become holy in the ritual—the cause of death for the participants. By handling holy censers, the 250 participants commit sin worthy of capital punishment. As a consequence, Eleazar, the priest and son of Aaron, now handles the censers and fashions them into a new cultic object that symbolizes priestly authority, with a warning about encroachment: Any person outside of the clan of Aaron who approaches the altar will suffer the same consequences as did Korah and his company. The hammered plates on the altar serve as God's answer to the challenge of v. 3 that Moses and Aaron "have gone too far! All the congregation are holy, every one of them, and the LORD is among them." All the congregation of the wilderness community are not equally holy, and the separation of a special priesthood to approach God is not in itself oppressive.

16:41–17:13. The priestly writers add an entire story to the conflict over priestly leadership in these verses (= 17:6-28 MT) that focuses on all of the people, rather than select leaders. This section repeats the three-part structure of the preceding conflict: complaint, theophany and judgment, and concluding cultic etiology.

16:41. The challenge to priestly leadership by the people occurs on the day following the death of Korah and his company. It begins when the congregation murmurs against Moses and Aaron, accusing them of murdering the "people of Yahweh" (עם יהוה 'am YHWH). The phrase "people of Yahweh" is not one of the priestly writers' regular designations for Israel. They prefer the word "congregation" (עדה 'ēdâ), which is, indeed, how Israel is described by the narrator in the opening of this verse. The phrase "people of Yahweh" may indicate a special covenantal relationship between God and Israel in which governance is less hierarchical than the careful stratifications of holiness being advocated by the priestly writers. Note that Moses used this very term in 11:29 in presenting to Joshua the charismatic ideal that "all people of Yahweh [*am YHWH*] were prophets and that Yahweh would put his spirit on them." The repetition of the phrase in the people's complaint indicates that the priestly writers intend to address the relationship of charismatic and non-charismatic forms of leadership in this story by using Moses' own words from a past story as a challenge to his role as a priest.

16:42-50. Theophany and intercession by Moses and Aaron once again constitute the centerpiece of the story. The description of theophany in vv. 42-45 even repeats the details from vv. 19-21. It, too, begins by establishing a setting at the tent of meeting, where the congregation (rather than Korah) assembles against Moses, prompting the appearance of the glory of Yahweh (v. 19; see v. 42). Yahweh commands Moses and Aaron to separate themselves from their challengers, so their opponents can be consumed instantly with fire (vv. 20-21; see vv. 44-45).

Moses and Aaron again intercede for the people (vv. 46-50). They fall on their faces (v. 45), and Moses directs Aaron to perform a ritual of atonement for the people against divine wrath that has taken the form of a plague. The plague indicates the anger of God that brings death. Exodus 12:13 provides an analogy to this story, where an independent "destroyer" also executed divine judgment on the Egyptians by killing all unprotected firstborn. The ritual of atonement is an antidote that stops the plague.

Moses' instructions underscore the holy status of Aaron, for he is commanded to perform the very ritual that led to the deaths of Korah and his company (v. 46). Aaron takes his censer, puts fire from the altar on it along with incense, and uses the holy fire to appease the avenging wrath, now moving through the camp. The intercessory role of Aaron is emphasized when he leaves the confines of the altar and stands in the midst of the people in order to atone for them (v. 47). Atonement in this context is a rite of expiation that makes appeasement for the people and, in the process, wards off the divine wrath. Such a ritual of atonement, with a censer rather than blood, is unique to this passage.[121]

Aaron's intercession stops the divine wrath, but not before 14,700 Israelites are killed (vv. 48-49).

His actions challenge the opening complaint of the people: "You have killed the people of Yahweh" (v. 41). When the crisis is over, he returns to Moses at the entrance of the tent of meeting (v. 50).

17:1-13. This section contains a cultic etiology about the budding staff of Aaron, which rests in front of the ark of the covenant in the tent of meeting. The story begins with a divine command to Moses (vv. 1-5) that he collect a staff from the leader of each tribe. Many of the social terms used to describe Israel from Numbers 1–4 recur here, such as Israelites, ancestral house, leader; but the focus is on the Hebrew word for "staff" (מטה *maṭṭeh*), which can mean both "staff" and "tribe." Moses is to write the name of each tribal leader on his staff. Aaron represents the Levites. He is to place the staffs before the ark of the covenant, described with the priestly term עדות (*ʿēdût*, "testimony"). The one whose staff buds is God's chosen priestly leader. This sign of divine election is intended to stop any further murmuring by the people.

Moses executes the divine command (vv. 6-7) and returns the next day for the results. Aaron's staff is the only one that has budded. It is filled with ripe almonds, visible to all the Israelites (vv. 8-9). Aaron's budding staff is to be placed before the ark. Its symbolic meaning is stated in v. 10: The budding staff of Aaron is a warning to rebels to cease complaining about the role of the priesthood lest they die. Although Aaron's staff functions as a warning to rebellious Israelites in the present construction of the story, the meaning of Aaron's budding staff is actually positive. The choice of almonds may signify watchfulness, as in Jer 1:11. The whiteness of the budding almond may symbolize purity and holiness, as it does in Isa 1:18.[122] In more general terms, the budding staff symbolizes the ability of the Aaronide priesthood to approach God and live.[123] Thus the two cultic etiologies in chaps. 16–17 complement each other in confirming the necessity of priestly intercessors. The hammered plates on the altar are a warning against encroachment by non-priests, while the budding staff is a sign of the divine choice of the Aaronide priesthood to represent the people before God.

---

121. Haran, "The Uses of Incense in the Ancient Israelite Ritual," 122.

122. Gordon J. Wenham, *Numbers: An Introduction and Commentary*, Tyndale Old Testament Commentaries (Leicester: Inter-Varsity, 1981) 139-40.

123. For comparisons to the budding staff of Aaron in other ancient folklore, see George Buchanan Gray, *Numbers*, ICC (Edinburgh: T. & T. Clark, 1903) 216-17.

The story ends in vv. 12-13 on a more negative note about the danger of encroachment. Israel expresses its fear to approach God with the question, "Are we all to perish?"

REFLECTIONS

1. The office of priest is often misinterpreted and ignored in the contemporary church. The most prominent current image is the phrase "the priesthood of all believers" (1 Pet 2:5, 9). It has come to mean that all Christians are priests, thereby making a special office of priesthood irrelevant. The roots of this interpretation reflect important conflicts over hierarchy and the abuse of clerical power during the Reformation period. But the lasting effects of these controversies can be harmful to Christian community. Our contemporary interpretation of "the priesthood of all believers" resembles the position of Korah, when he stated that "all the congregation are holy, every one of them." Both judge the special office of priest unnecessary and oppressive. Numbers 16–17 is a strong criticism of Korah, and it presents two challenges to many contemporary churches.

First, when we disperse the office of priest to the entire congregation, clergy fail to claim the full resources of God available through ordination. Ordination to Word (prophetic office) and sacraments (priestly office) continue in most denominations, but the emphasis is on preaching the Word, not administering sacraments. Yet every ordained clergy is both a prophet and a priest. Clergy who preach the Word and interpret Scripture empower churches to live Spirit-filled lives. But God offers additional power to transform humans through baptism and the eucharist, requiring priestly mediation. The ideal of the priestly writers is the claim of Korah that Israel become a kingdom of priests (Exod 19:6). The message of Numbers 16–17 is that the ideal is not yet a present reality. Priestly mediators represent an important step in reaching this goal. They stand between the dead and the living and transmit God's holiness and health to the community (Num 16:48).

Second, congregations fail to realize the dangerous power of Christian sacraments when the office of priest is ignored or casually dispersed to all members. The death of Korah and his followers (Num 16:31-35) indicates that the holiness of God is strong medicine, never to be taken for granted. The same message undergirds 1 Peter. The call for Christians to become a "priesthood of all believers" is embedded in a baptismal sermon (1 Pet 1:3–4:11), the force of which presupposes the essential role of the priestly office in creating Christian community. The audience of 1 Peter consists of new Christians. Baptism has transformed them, creating tension between their former life and their new identity in Christ (1 Pet 1:13-16). They are now exiles in this world on a journey with God (1 Pet 1:17-21; 2:11-12), but they have not yet reached their goal. These new Christians are vulnerable, like newborn infants. The water of baptism is spiritual milk that will make them grow (1 Pet 2:1-3).

The message of 1 Peter is similar to that of Numbers 16–17. The call to be a royal priesthood is the goal for these new Christians (1 Pet 2:4-10) as it is for the priestly writers (Exod 19:6). But the goal has not yet been attained. The Christians in 1 Peter are aliens and exiles like the Israelites in the wilderness, where the life of faith is also a journey between Egypt and the promised land. The mediation of sacraments is the spiritual source for waging war against evil and achieving the goal of salvation (1 Pet 2:11-12). First Peter does not eliminate the office of priest. On the contrary, it presents an argument for the central role of this office in the life of Christians.

2. Numbers 16 provides a model of intercession based on priestly ritual, rather than prophetic words. Aaron stands between the dead and the living to stop the plague from sweeping through the camp. He does not halt the plague through persuasive prayer, but by burning incense and thereby atoning for the people (Num 16:46-48). The healing role of priestly intercession is a distinctive form of ministry. It extends the power of sacraments into the community through rituals. The power of the priest to intercede by action is a reminder that effective ministry is not necessarily saying the right words. Aaron models a ministry of presence. His ritual action calls forth the healing power of God. Sharing the eucharist with homebound members of your church, performing rituals of healing with oil, or simply sitting at the bedside of a sick person is similar to the priestly intercession of Aaron. These are ritual forms of intercession, bringing the power of the sacraments into the lives of Christians. The goal of priestly intercession is to maintain the health of the community by providing safe access to the healing power of holiness.

3. Clergy misconduct through the abuse of power is no less dangerous to Christian community today than it was to the wilderness community of Israel. The complaint of Dathan and Abiram that Moses "lords it over them" (Num 16:13) and Korah's accusation that Moses and Aaron "exalt themselves" (Num 16:3) reflect a long tradition of exploitation by civil and ecclesiastical leaders. The prophets repeatedly condemn the self-interest of princes, kings, and priests. Amos condemned both Jeroboam, the king, and his priest, Amaziah, for turning justice into poison (Amos 7). He is followed by Hosea (chaps. 4–5) and Jeremiah (chaps. 7; 26). Prophetic judgment warns us that power is a dangerous gift, easily exploited. Numbers 16–17 are a manual on conflict resolution for people in positions of power. The response of Moses to the challenges of Korah, Dathan, and Abiram provides two criteria for evaluating authentic leadership during times of conflict.

First, leaders do not themselves adjudicate conflicts over their own leadership. In neither the challenge to his civil leadership by Dathan and Abiram, nor that to his priestly leadership by Korah does Moses adjudicate the matter himself. In both instances, he places the challenge to his authority in a larger context than his own sphere of power, so that the outcome is open to public evaluation. In the case of Dathan and Abiram, God was called upon to evaluate the truth of their accusation through a public display of judgment. Due process is followed. The same is true with the challenge to the priestly leadership of Moses by Korah. In both instances, all Israel sees the outcome of the tests. Resolution is always public, not a private agreement among a few.

Second, leadership is authentic when power is used for the good of the whole community, rather than for a select few. Priests and Levites hold office for the sake of the community. They protect people from the danger of holiness, while also mediating its life-giving power to them through rituals. Priests and Levites bear the responsibility for encroachment themselves through substitution. Their office increases their responsibilities, not their privileges.

Numbers 18:1–19:22, Guidelines for Approaching God

NIV	NRSV
18 The LORD said to Aaron, "You, your sons and your father's family are to bear the responsibility for offenses against the sanctuary, and you and your sons alone are to bear the responsibility for offenses against the priesthood. ²Bring your fellow Levites from your ancestral tribe to join you and assist you when you and your sons minister before the Tent of the Testimony. ³They are to be responsible to you and are to perform all the duties of the Tent, but they must not go near the furnishings of the sanctuary or the altar, or both they and you will die. ⁴They	**18** The LORD said to Aaron: You and your sons and your ancestral house with you shall bear responsibility for offenses connected with the sanctuary, while you and your sons alone shall bear responsibility for offenses connected with the priesthood. ²So bring with you also your brothers of the tribe of Levi, your ancestral tribe, in order that they may be joined to you, and serve you while you and your sons with you are in front of the tent of the covenant.ᵃ ³They shall perform duties for you and for the whole tent. But they

ᵃ Or *treaty,* or *testimony;* Heb *eduth*

are to join you and be responsible for the care of the Tent of Meeting—all the work at the Tent—and no one else may come near where you are.

⁵"You are to be responsible for the care of the sanctuary and the altar, so that wrath will not fall on the Israelites again. ⁶I myself have selected your fellow Levites from among the Israelites as a gift to you, dedicated to the LORD to do the work at the Tent of Meeting. ⁷But only you and your sons may serve as priests in connection with everything at the altar and inside the curtain. I am giving you the service of the priesthood as a gift. Anyone else who comes near the sanctuary must be put to death."

⁸Then the LORD said to Aaron, "I myself have put you in charge of the offerings presented to me; all the holy offerings the Israelites give me I give to you and your sons as your portion and regular share. ⁹You are to have the part of the most holy offerings that is kept from the fire. From all the gifts they bring me as most holy offerings, whether grain or sin or guilt offerings, that part belongs to you and your sons. ¹⁰Eat it as something most holy; every male shall eat it. You must regard it as holy.

¹¹"This also is yours: whatever is set aside from the gifts of all the wave offerings of the Israelites. I give this to you and your sons and daughters as your regular share. Everyone in your household who is ceremonially clean may eat it.

¹²"I give you all the finest olive oil and all the finest new wine and grain they give the LORD as the firstfruits of their harvest. ¹³All the land's firstfruits that they bring to the LORD will be yours. Everyone in your household who is ceremonially clean may eat it.

¹⁴"Everything in Israel that is devoted[a] to the LORD is yours. ¹⁵The first offspring of every womb, both man and animal, that is offered to the LORD is yours. But you must redeem every firstborn son and every firstborn male of unclean animals. ¹⁶When they are a month old, you must redeem them at the redemption price set at five shekels[b] of silver, according to the sanctuary shekel, which weighs twenty gerahs.

¹⁷"But you must not redeem the firstborn of an

a14 The Hebrew term refers to the irrevocable giving over of things or persons to the LORD.   b16 That is, about 2 ounces (about 55 grams)

must not approach either the utensils of the sanctuary or the altar, otherwise both they and you will die. ⁴They are attached to you in order to perform the duties of the tent of meeting, for all the service of the tent; no outsider shall approach you. ⁵You yourselves shall perform the duties of the sanctuary and the duties of the altar, so that wrath may never again come upon the Israelites. ⁶It is I who now take your brother Levites from among the Israelites; they are now yours as a gift, dedicated to the LORD, to perform the service of the tent of meeting. ⁷But you and your sons with you shall diligently perform your priestly duties in all that concerns the altar and the area behind the curtain. I give your priesthood as a gift;[a] any outsider who approaches shall be put to death.

8The LORD spoke to Aaron: I have given you charge of the offerings made to me, all the holy gifts of the Israelites; I have given them to you and your sons as a priestly portion due you in perpetuity. ⁹This shall be yours from the most holy things, reserved from the fire: every offering of theirs that they render to me as a most holy thing, whether grain offering, sin offering, or guilt offering, shall belong to you and your sons. ¹⁰As a most holy thing you shall eat it; every male may eat it; it shall be holy to you. ¹¹This also is yours: I have given to you, together with your sons and daughters, as a perpetual due, whatever is set aside from the gifts of all the elevation offerings of the Israelites; everyone who is clean in your house may eat them. ¹²All the best of the oil and all the best of the wine and of the grain, the choice produce that they give to the LORD, I have given to you. ¹³The first fruits of all that is in their land, which they bring to the LORD, shall be yours; everyone who is clean in your house may eat of it. ¹⁴Every devoted thing in Israel shall be yours. ¹⁵The first issue of the womb of all creatures, human and animal, which is offered to the LORD, shall be yours; but the firstborn of human beings you shall redeem, and the firstborn of unclean animals you shall redeem. ¹⁶Their redemption price, reckoned from one month of age, you shall fix at five shekels of silver, according to the shekel of the sanctuary (that is, twenty gerahs). ¹⁷But the

a Heb as a service of gift

NIV

ox, a sheep or a goat; they are holy. Sprinkle their blood on the altar and burn their fat as an offering made by fire, an aroma pleasing to the Lord. [18]Their meat is to be yours, just as the breast of the wave offering and the right thigh are yours. [19]Whatever is set aside from the holy offerings the Israelites present to the Lord I give to you and your sons and daughters as your regular share. It is an everlasting covenant of salt before the Lord for both you and your offspring."

[20]The Lord said to Aaron, "You will have no inheritance in their land, nor will you have any share among them; I am your share and your inheritance among the Israelites.

[21]"I give to the Levites all the tithes in Israel as their inheritance in return for the work they do while serving at the Tent of Meeting. [22]From now on the Israelites must not go near the Tent of Meeting, or they will bear the consequences of their sin and will die. [23]It is the Levites who are to do the work at the Tent of Meeting and bear the responsibility for offenses against it. This is a lasting ordinance for the generations to come. They will receive no inheritance among the Israelites. [24]Instead, I give to the Levites as their inheritance the tithes that the Israelites present as an offering to the Lord. That is why I said concerning them: 'They will have no inheritance among the Israelites.'"

[25]The Lord said to Moses, [26]"Speak to the Levites and say to them: 'When you receive from the Israelites the tithe I give you as your inheritance, you must present a tenth of that tithe as the Lord's offering. [27]Your offering will be reckoned to you as grain from the threshing floor or juice from the winepress. [28]In this way you also will present an offering to the Lord from all the tithes you receive from the Israelites. From these tithes you must give the Lord's portion to Aaron the priest. [29]You must present as the Lord's portion the best and holiest part of everything given to you.'

[30]"Say to the Levites: 'When you present the best part, it will be reckoned to you as the product of the threshing floor or the winepress. [31]You and your households may eat the rest of it anywhere, for it is your wages for your work at the Tent of Meeting. [32]By presenting the best part of it you

NRSV

firstborn of a cow, or the firstborn of a sheep, or the firstborn of a goat, you shall not redeem; they are holy. You shall dash their blood on the altar, and shall turn their fat into smoke as an offering by fire for a pleasing odor to the Lord; [18]but their flesh shall be yours, just as the breast that is elevated and as the right thigh are yours. [19]All the holy offerings that the Israelites present to the Lord I have given to you, together with your sons and daughters, as a perpetual due; it is a covenant of salt forever before the Lord for you and your descendants as well. [20]Then the Lord said to Aaron: You shall have no allotment in their land, nor shall you have any share among them; I am your share and your possession among the Israelites.

[21]To the Levites I have given every tithe in Israel for a possession in return for the service that they perform, the service in the tent of meeting. [22]From now on the Israelites shall no longer approach the tent of meeting, or else they will incur guilt and die. [23]But the Levites shall perform the service of the tent of meeting, and they shall bear responsibility for their own offenses; it shall be a perpetual statute throughout your generations. But among the Israelites they shall have no allotment, [24]because I have given to the Levites as their portion the tithe of the Israelites, which they set apart as an offering to the Lord. Therefore I have said of them that they shall have no allotment among the Israelites.

[25]Then the Lord spoke to Moses, saying: [26]You shall speak to the Levites, saying: When you receive from the Israelites the tithe that I have given you from them for your portion, you shall set apart an offering from it to the Lord, a tithe of the tithe. [27]It shall be reckoned to you as your gift, the same as the grain of the threshing floor and the fullness of the wine press. [28]Thus you also shall set apart an offering to the Lord from all the tithes that you receive from the Israelites; and from them you shall give the Lord's offering to the priest Aaron. [29]Out of all the gifts to you, you shall set apart every offering due to the Lord; the best of all of them is the part to be consecrated. [30]Say also to them: When you have set apart the best of it, then the rest shall be reckoned to the Levites as produce of the threshing floor, and as

will not be guilty in this matter; then you will not defile the holy offerings of the Israelites, and you will not die.'"

19 The LORD said to Moses and Aaron: [2]"This is a requirement of the law that the LORD has commanded: Tell the Israelites to bring you a red heifer without defect or blemish and that has never been under a yoke. [3]Give it to Eleazar the priest; it is to be taken outside the camp and slaughtered in his presence. [4]Then Eleazar the priest is to take some of its blood on his finger and sprinkle it seven times toward the front of the Tent of Meeting. [5]While he watches, the heifer is to be burned—its hide, flesh, blood and offal. [6]The priest is to take some cedar wood, hyssop and scarlet wool and throw them onto the burning heifer. [7]After that, the priest must wash his clothes and bathe himself with water. He may then come into the camp, but he will be ceremonially unclean till evening. [8]The man who burns it must also wash his clothes and bathe with water, and he too will be unclean till evening.

[9]"A man who is clean shall gather up the ashes of the heifer and put them in a ceremonially clean place outside the camp. They shall be kept by the Israelite community for use in the water of cleansing; it is for purification from sin. [10]The man who gathers up the ashes of the heifer must also wash his clothes, and he too will be unclean till evening. This will be a lasting ordinance both for the Israelites and for the aliens living among them.

[11]"Whoever touches the dead body of anyone will be unclean for seven days. [12]He must purify himself with the water on the third day and on the seventh day; then he will be clean. But if he does not purify himself on the third and seventh days, he will not be clean. [13]Whoever touches the dead body of anyone and fails to purify himself defiles the LORD's tabernacle. That person must be cut off from Israel. Because the water of cleansing has not been sprinkled on him, he is unclean; his uncleanness remains on him.

[14]"This is the law that applies when a person dies in a tent: Anyone who enters the tent and anyone who is in it will be unclean for seven days, [15]and every open container without a lid fastened on it will be unclean.

[16]"Anyone out in the open who touches some-

produce of the wine press. [31]You may eat it in any place, you and your households; for it is your payment for your service in the tent of meeting. [32]You shall incur no guilt by reason of it, when you have offered the best of it. But you shall not profane the holy gifts of the Israelites, on pain of death.

19 The LORD spoke to Moses and Aaron, saying: [2]This is a statute of the law that the LORD has commanded: Tell the Israelites to bring you a red heifer without defect, in which there is no blemish and on which no yoke has been laid. [3]You shall give it to the priest Eleazar, and it shall be taken outside the camp and slaughtered in his presence. [4]The priest Eleazar shall take some of its blood with his finger and sprinkle it seven times towards the front of the tent of meeting. [5]Then the heifer shall be burned in his sight; its skin, its flesh, and its blood, with its dung, shall be burned. [6]The priest shall take cedarwood, hyssop, and crimson material, and throw them into the fire in which the heifer is burning. [7]Then the priest shall wash his clothes and bathe his body in water, and afterwards he may come into the camp; but the priest shall remain unclean until evening. [8]The one who burns the heifer[a] shall wash his clothes in water and bathe his body in water; he shall remain unclean until evening. [9]Then someone who is clean shall gather up the ashes of the heifer, and deposit them outside the camp in a clean place; and they shall be kept for the congregation of the Israelites for the water for cleansing. It is a purification offering. [10]The one who gathers the ashes of the heifer shall wash his clothes and be unclean until evening.

This shall be a perpetual statute for the Israelites and for the alien residing among them. [11]Those who touch the dead body of any human being shall be unclean seven days. [12]They shall purify themselves with the water on the third day and on the seventh day, and so be clean; but if they do not purify themselves on the third day and on the seventh day, they will not become clean. [13]All who touch a corpse, the body of a human being who has died, and do not purify themselves, defile the tabernacle of the LORD; such

[a] Heb *it*

NIV

one who has been killed with a sword or someone who has died a natural death, or anyone who touches a human bone or a grave, will be unclean for seven days.

¹⁷"For the unclean person, put some ashes from the burned purification offering into a jar and pour fresh water over them. ¹⁸Then a man who is ceremonially clean is to take some hyssop, dip it in the water and sprinkle the tent and all the furnishings and the people who were there. He must also sprinkle anyone who has touched a human bone or a grave or someone who has been killed or someone who has died a natural death. ¹⁹The man who is clean is to sprinkle the unclean person on the third and seventh days, and on the seventh day he is to purify him. The person being cleansed must wash his clothes and bathe with water, and that evening he will be clean. ²⁰But if a person who is unclean does not purify himself, he must be cut off from the community, because he has defiled the sanctuary of the LORD. The water of cleansing has not been sprinkled on him, and he is unclean. ²¹This is a lasting ordinance for them.

"The man who sprinkles the water of cleansing must also wash his clothes, and anyone who touches the water of cleansing will be unclean till evening. ²²Anything that an unclean person touches becomes unclean, and anyone who touches it becomes unclean till evening."

NRSV

persons shall be cut off from Israel. Since water for cleansing was not dashed on them, they remain unclean; their uncleanness is still on them.

14This is the law when someone dies in a tent: everyone who comes into the tent, and everyone who is in the tent, shall be unclean seven days. ¹⁵And every open vessel with no cover fastened on it is unclean. ¹⁶Whoever in the open field touches one who has been killed by a sword, or who has died naturally,ᵃ or a human bone, or a grave, shall be unclean seven days. ¹⁷For the unclean they shall take some ashes of the burnt purification offering, and running water shall be added in a vessel; ¹⁸then a clean person shall take hyssop, dip it in the water, and sprinkle it on the tent, on all the furnishings, on the persons who were there, and on whoever touched the bone, the slain, the corpse, or the grave. ¹⁹The clean person shall sprinkle the unclean ones on the third day and on the seventh day, thus purifying them on the seventh day. Then they shall wash their clothes and bathe themselves in water, and at evening they shall be clean. ²⁰Any who are unclean but do not purify themselves, those persons shall be cut off from the assembly, for they have defiled the sanctuary of the LORD. Since the water for cleansing has not been dashed on them, they are unclean.

21It shall be a perpetual statute for them. The one who sprinkles the water for cleansing shall wash his clothes, and whoever touches the water for cleansing shall be unclean until evening. ²²Whatever the unclean person touches shall be unclean, and anyone who touches it shall be unclean until evening.

ᵃ Heb lacks *naturally*

COMMENTARY

The priestly writers present detailed guidelines for approaching God in Numbers 18–19. These chapters constitute the third episode to the conflicts surrounding priestly leadership. The first episode contained complaints by Korah, Dathan, and Abiram about the leadership of Moses and Aaron (16:1-40). The people challenged priestly leadership in the second episode (16:41–17:13).

It closed with the people expressing their fear to approach God, "Are we all to perish?" The guidelines for approaching God in chaps. 18–19 are the response to the Israelites' fear of perishing in the presence of Yahweh.

18:1-32. 18:1-7. This section provides a response to the fear of Israel expressed in 17:12-13. The section consists of a divine speech directed to Aaron, rather than to Moses (v. 1)—unusual in priestly literature, where nearly all divine speech is directed to Moses. Aaron is addressed directly by God only three other times. Two of them also occur in chap. 18 (vv. 8 and 20), while the one other time appears in Lev 10:8. There Aaron is commanded to maintain purity in a situation of lethal divine wrath (Lev 10:1-2). Thus the direct address to Aaron appears in situations of danger, while also accentuating the authority of the priesthood.

The danger of divine wrath is addressed in 17:5. God tells Aaron that if the priests perform their duties at the sanctuary and at the altar, divine wrath will not strike Israel. Thus the priesthood is a divine gift aimed at protecting Israel from the danger of divine holiness (v. 7). The nature of the gift is spelled out in more detail, as the responsibilities of the priests and the Levites are described. Israel is protected from divine wrath at one level by the Aaronide priests, who perform the duties of the sanctuary and the altar (vv. 1, 3*b*, 5*a*). Any encroachment on the sanctuary becomes their responsibility. Israel is further protected by the Levites, who serve the Aaronide priests. Their subordinate role is indicated (v. 2) through a play on words. The verb stating that the Levites "will be joined" (לוה *lāwâ*) to the Aaronite priests derives from the same root in Hebrew as does the noun "Levi" (לוי *lēwî*). The Levites serve the priests by performing service for the tent of meeting (vv. 2-4), but they are restricted from handling holy utensils or from serving at the altar.

18:8-20. This section is framed by two divine speeches to Aaron (vv. 8, 20). The first speech consists of vv. 8-19. In this section, God outlines the compensation that priests will receive for performing their sacred duties. Such compensation is called emolument, and it consists of either a portion of a sacrifice or a redemption payment. The second speech actually includes vv. 20-24, although vv. 21-24 have been separated from v. 20 in the Commentary because the focus changes from the Aaronide priesthood to the Levites. Verse 20 appears to be a later addition to a section of priestly law (vv. 8-19, 21-24) in which the compensation for priests (vv. 8-19) and Levites (vv. 21-24) was outlined. In v. 20, God informs Aaron that priests forfeit land ownership as a conse-

quence of their office, because God is their special possession among the people of Israel.

Two kinds of priestly emoluments are described in vv. 8-19. The first is compensation that comes "from the most holy" (מקדש הקדשים *miqqōdeš haqqŏdāšîm*) offerings. These are described in vv. 8-10 as three sacrifices: grain, sin, and guilt offerings (see the Commentary on 7:1-89 for a description of these sacrifices). The sacrifices are described as being reserved for priests "from the fire" (מן-האש *min-hāʾēš*). This phrase most likely refers to offering by fire (see also 15:2). The burnt offering is not mentioned because it is a holocaust, meaning that no portion remains for the priests to eat. Compensation from most holy sacrifices is limited to priests who are ritually clean—that is, they have not been contaminated by skin disease, bodily discharge, or contact with the dead. Furthermore, such compensation can only be eaten within the sacred precinct of the tent of meeting.

The second compensation is from "holy" (הקדשים *haqqŏdāšîm*) offerings and contributions. Unlike the most holy offerings, compensation from holy offerings can be eaten outside of the precinct of the tent of meeting by anyone in a priest's family who is ritually clean. Contributions within this lesser category are described in vv. 11-19. They include all dedicated offerings (v. 11); the first fruits of grain, wine, and oil (vv. 12-13); any devoted thing (v. 14); and the firstborn of clean animals (vv. 15-18). Verse 19, a concluding summary, states that the compensation of priests is a "covenant of salt," which probably connotes permanence. The phrase is used in v. 19 in conjunction with other language that indicates permanence (the compensation is a "perpetual due"). The two other uses of the phrase (Lev 2:13; 2 Chr 13:15) also support such an interpretation. In Lev 2:13, the salting of sacrifices appears to be a binding requirement, while in 2 Chr 13:15 the divine covenant with David is also described as a "covenant of salt," meaning that it is eternal. The phrase may also indicate obligations, since salt was regularly included in sacrifices (Lev 2:13).

The reference to "devoted things" in v. 14 requires comment. It is a translation of the Hebrew word חרם (*ḥērem*), which means "to separate" or "to set aside." Thus it is one of the words used to designate holiness. Yet the semantics of *ḥērem* are often negative. It can designate property that is taken away from individual owners and seized by the temple (Lev 27:16-25, esp. v. 21). People, too, can become *ḥērem* because of worshiping other gods (Exod 22:20) or as booty from holy war (Joshua 1–7). Verse 14 states that priests are allowed to possess devoted property as part of their compensation.

God owns the firstborn, and vv. 15-18 state that the firstborn belong to the priesthood as part of their payment. God's claim on firstborn humans has been addressed twice before in Numbers (3:11-13; 8:14-19; the Levites substitute for them). The divine claim on the firstborn returns in 18:15-18 in the context of compensation for priests. Firstborn of humans and of unclean animals one month of age must be redeemed at the cost of five shekels, which is paid to the priests (vv. 15-16). Clean animals, such as cows, sheep, and goats cannot be redeemed. They are holy, and God does not relinquish claim on them. Their blood must be dashed against the altar, and the fat must be burned, while their flesh becomes compensation for the priests (vv. 17-18).

18:21-24. The divine command to Aaron in v. 20 that priests cannot possess land continues into vv. 21-24, even though the topic changes to levitical compensation. Thus vv. 20-24 constitute a single unit of literature in the present form of the text. Levites are to receive a tithe (or one-tenth of Israel's produce) in return for their service of maintaining the tent of meeting and performing guard duty. The point of emphasis in this section is the role of guarding, which the Levites fulfill in protecting tent of meeting from encroachment. This role means that the Israelites will not be able to approach the sanctuary. If any layperson does so, the Levites bear the responsibility for the violation of the sacred space. Thus the responsibility of the Levites as guards becomes another way of alleviating Israel's fear, stated in 17:12-13, that God's presence in their midst is lethal. God's instructions to Aaron indicate that in the future only Levites would perish for any offense of encroachment.

The Levites receive a general tithe from all Israelites for the dangerous task of guarding the sanctuary (v. 21). This compensation substitutes for ownership of land in Canaan (v. 24). In these verses, the priestly writers provide few details on the nature of the tithe. What is clear is that the tithe is not a voluntary donation. It is more like a tax required of all Israelites. Such taxes, which

are not unique to Israel, appear to have been a general policy of governments in the ancient Near East. Thus, for example, when Samuel lists the oppressive actions that a king will impose on Israel, he includes a royal tithe levied against all Israelites (1 Sam 8:15, 17).

Royal taxes, moreover, are closely associated with a temple tithe in the ancient Near East because of the intertwining of king and cult. The same close interrelationship also appears to have arisen during Israel's monarchical period. The book of Genesis contains etiologic stories in which the patriarchs legitimate tithing as a royal temple tax to the cultic sites of the kings. Abram tithes to Melchizedek, the king-priest of Salem (= Jerusalem) in Gen 14:20, while Jacob does the same at Bethel in Gen 28:22 (see also Amos 4:4).

The royal tithe becomes more exclusively a temple tax for the priestly writers, who envision a theocracy rather than a monarchy. References to the tithe in Deuteronomy provide some background for this transition. Tithing is addressed in the call for cult centralization in Deut 12:6, 11, 17, where it is required of all Israelites living in the land. The tithe must be brought to the cultic center by each Israelite family unit, who are then required to have a feast at the temple. The act of tithing, therefore, would appear to require a yearly religious pilgrimage to the central sanctuary (although there were exceptions). Individuals could redeem their tithe of produce if the trip from the village to the central cult site was too far.

The emphasis on cult centralization throughout Deuteronomy 12 suggests that this tithing practice was an innovation. The normal practice of tithing during the monarchical period must have occurred in local settings. Thus cult centralization presented new hardships for local levitical priests, whose incomes from tithing would have been cut off. The inclusion of the local Levite, along with all household slaves, in the family feast at the central sanctuary reinforces this conclusion. The more detailed law of the tithe in Deut 14:22-29 provides a solution to the financial problem imposed on local levitical priests through the centralization of the tithe. It prescribes two different tithes. The yearly tithe, described in vv. 22-27, consists of produce (grain, wine, oil) and firstlings of flocks that are given at the central sanctuary, thus conforming to the requirement of cult centralization in Deuteronomy 12. Deuteronomy 14:28-29 states that every third year the tithe is given locally for the Levite, for orphans, and for widows; Deut 26:12 calls this the Year of the Tithe. (Deuteronomy makes no clear distinction between Aaronide priests and Levites.)

The priestly law of the tithe in Num 19:21-24 addresses more specifically the emerging hierarchy of priests that arises from cult centralization, with the distinction between Aaronide and levitical priests. Tithes are clearly compensation to Levites (18:21-24). Thus one of the implications of serving the tent of meeting is that the Levites become responsible for collecting the temple tax. Nehemiah 10:38-39 provides a window into this responsibility when it describes the Levites as traveling from village to village to collect tithes for the post-exilic Temple. This scenario suggests that the priestly writers eliminate the yearly requirement of a pilgrimage by each Israelite family. In the process, they fashion a new office for local levitical priests: tax collection. Perhaps local collection of the tithe was one way in which Levites guarded against the encroachment outlined in Num 18:21-24. In any case, Lev 27:30-33 indicates that tithes consisted of produce and animals. Produce could be redeemed at a 20 percent surcharge, while animals could not be redeemed. The tithe was stored in the central temple (2 Chr 31:5, 6, 12; Neh 12:44; Mal 3:10).

18:25-32. Another implication of the distinction between Aaronide and levitical priests is that Levites themselves must tithe. Their tithe is described in Num 18:25-32. The requirement that Levites tithe is introduced in a divine speech to Moses, not Aaron (v. 25). The divine command is clear: The Levites also must give one-tenth of their wages to the temple. The best portion of the general tithe they receive from Israel must be given to the priest (v. 29). The penalty for withholding the tithe is death (v. 32). The remaining nine-tenths of Israel's tithe consists of levitical wages, which are no longer tied to the sanctuary in any way. This is the meaning of v. 30, where the remaining tithe is reckoned as "produce of the threshing floor, and as produce of the wine press."

19:1-22. Numbers 19 changes the focus from Aaronide priests and Levites (Numbers 18) to ordinary Israelites. The topic of the chapter is corpse contamination and the threat of defilement that it poses to the sanctuary.

Baruch Levine has argued that "the hidden agenda of Numbers 19 is the cult of the dead."[124] It is the belief that the dead lived on as ghosts. Dead ancestors were memorialized in the ancient Near East through burial rituals and continual care through offerings of food and drink. Observance ensured protection from evil.[125] Israelites observed the cult of the dead at least with regard to kings. The burial of Asa in 2 Chr 16:13-14 may refer to such a practice. The prophet Ezekiel lists the burial of kings within the Temple as one of the practices in the monarchical period that defiled the sanctuary, forcing God to abandon it (Ezek 43:6-9).[126] Prohibitions against sacrificing to the dead are stated in the law of first fruits (Deut 26:13-15), again suggesting an ongoing practice. Scholars speculate whether the responsibility of caring for the dead originally fell on the firstborn, giving them sacred status (see the Commentary on 3:11-13).[127] In the cult of the dead, the ancestral ghosts remained part of the community, and authority within society remained focused on the past.[128]

The priestly writers oppose worshiping the dead or giving them any authority in the community of the living. Death becomes the most extreme form of defilement for priestly writers. Far from providing power to the living, it pollutes those whom it touches and drives God away. Thus the priestly writers forbid priests to officiate at funerals, removing the mediatorial power of the priesthood from burial ceremonies (Lev 21:1-15). They also remove all burial rituals from the sanctuary. Those contaminated from contact with the dead are expelled from the camp (Num 5:1-4). Rejection of the cult of the dead indicates the priestly writers' future orientation in understanding the power of salvation. They deny past actions of ancestors as determining the fate of Israelites.

124. Baruch A. Levine, *Numbers 1–20*, AB 4A (New York: Doubleday, 1993) 472.

125. Jerold S. Cooper, "The Fate of Mankind: Death and Afterlife in Ancient Mesopotamia," in *Death and Afterlife: Perspectives of World Religions*, ed. Hiroshi Obayashi, Contributions to the Study of Religion 13 (New York: Greenwood, 1992) 19-33, esp. 27-30.

126. One of the innovations of the Josianic reform at the close of the monarchical period was the elimination of ancestral worship, at least as the official practice of the state (2 Kings 23:15-16).

127. Jacob Milgrom, *Numbers,* JPS Torah Commentary (Philadelphia: JPS, 1990) 432.

128. George E. Mendenhall, "From Witchcraft to Justice: Death and Afterlife in the Old Testament," in Obayashi, *Death and Afterlife,* 71-72.

Authority rests in Yahweh's promise about the future gift of the land. Worship of the ancestors could only lead to death.[129]

Numbers 19 outlines procedures for Israelites to be purified from corpse contamination and thus reenter the camp. Contamination occurs through touching or simply from being in the proximity of the dead. Any person contaminated by death becomes a threat to God's life-giving holiness in the sanctuary. This is the only time that this topic is addressed in the OT. Its placement at this particular juncture in Numbers answers the Israelites' question from 17:12-13: How are they to live in the sphere of divine holiness and not perish? Thus, contrary to many interpreters,[130] chap. 19 is an integral part of the conflicts over priestly leadership in chaps. 16–19. Thomas Mann has gone so far as to argue that holiness and death are the central themes throughout these chapters for the priestly writers and that these themes extend through 20:2-13, where Moses and Aaron are also condemned to death because of their violation of holiness.[131]

The central ingredient in the ritual in this chapter is the "water of cleansing" (מי נדה *mê niddâ*). Water bears cleansing properties throughout priestly law. It is used, for example, to cleanse lepers (Leviticus 14). But the water of cleansing is a special potion, derived mainly from the ashes of a red heifer, that has the power to purify those who have been contaminated through contact with the dead. The water of cleansing also appears in 31:23, where it is used as a detergent to purify warriors after holy war.

The four references to the water of cleansing in chap. 19 (vv. 9, 13, 20-21) span three sections. Verses 1-10*a* describe how the potion is made from the ashes of a red heifer, as well as other ingredients. Verses 10*b*-13 and 14-22 describe conditions for using the potion: vv. 10*b*-13 state that the water must be used for both Israelites and resident aliens; vv. 14-22 outline the different conditions that make someone impure.

Scholars debate whether Numbers 19 consists of two sections (vv. 1-13, 14-22) or three (vv. 1-10*a*, 10*b*-13, and 14-22).[132] They also question whether the chapter constitutes an original unit of law or is the final result of an ongoing process of supplementation. Verses 10*b*-13 may, indeed, be a later addition to vv. 1-10*a* and 14-22, since these verses clarify that contamination from the dead affects both Israelites and resident aliens. The commentary will follow the three-part structure of vv. 1-10*a*, vv. 10*b*-13, and vv. 14-22. But even here questions arise concerning the headings to the different sections. Verses 1-10*a* and vv. 14-22 are introduced with clear headings: "This is the [statute of the] law." Verses 10*b*-13 begin with the words "a perpetual statute," perhaps a summary conclusion to vv. 1-10*a*, in which case the middle section consists of vv. 11-13.

19:1-10a. This section consists of legislation aimed at Israelites, not at their priests (v. 2). It describes a ritual of riddance or exorcism, which decontaminates persons from defilement through contact with the dead. Verses 1-2 describes the animal to be used, vv. 3-6 the details of the ritual, and vv. 7-10*a* its effects on all the participants. Israel is to present a cow for sacrifice. The Hebrew is unclear, but it would appear that the priestly writers intend that the cow be full grown, and not a calf. Four conditions are stated concerning the cow. It must be red, perhaps to symbolize blood. It must be physically perfect (NIV, "without defect or blemish"; NRSV, "without defect, in which there is no blemish"). The Hebrew word used in this instance, תמימה (*tĕmîmâ*), means "complete" or "whole." The cow must be without blemish, and it must never have been yoked. Gray is probably correct to conclude that the prohibition against a yoke precludes that the animal has been used for profane work, such as plowing.[133] The two cows used by the Philistines to return the ark to Israel (1 Sam 6:7) also meet this requirement, suggesting that they were being presented to Israel for sacrifice.

The ritual is described in vv. 3-6. It required priestly supervision by Eleazar: the cow must be slaughtered in his presence and then burned in fire. The blood of the cow must be sprinkled seven times in the direction of the entrance of the

129. See ibid., 67-81, for discussion of the historical character of ancient Israelite religion and how this perspective conflicted with worship of the ancestors.

130. See, e.g., Martin Noth, *Numbers*, OTL (Philadelphia: Westminster, 1968) 139.

131. T. W. Mann, "Holiness and Death in the Redaction of Numbers 16:1–20:13," in *Love and Death in the Ancient Near East: Essays in Honor of Marvin H. Pope*, ed. J. H. Marks and R. M. Good (Guilford: Four Quarters, 1987) 181-90.

132. For a summary of positions see Phillip J. Budd, *Numbers*, WBC 5 (Waco, Tex.: Word, 1984) 209-10.

133. George Buchanan Gray, *Numbers*, ICC (Edinburgh: T. & T. Clark, 1903) 249.

tent of meeting. All of these actions resemble a sacrifice (e.g., Lev 4:6; 14:7; see also the ritual of atonement in Leviticus 16). But the ritual of the red cow takes place outside the camp, away from the altar. Thus it is not technically a sacrifice, even though it is specifically described as a purification (sacrifice) in v. 9. The unique function of the ashes of the red cow to eliminate impurity from corpse contamination partially explains this irregularity, since persons so defiled were banished from the camp (5:1-4). It also provides background for another exceptional feature of the ritual: The blood is burned in the fire along with the skin, flesh, and dung of the cow (v. 5). Blood in the ashes of the red cow is the ritual detergent that purifies,[134] along with three additional ingredients: cedar wood, hyssop, and crimson (v. 6). These ingredients are also used in the purification of the leper (Leviticus 14), but the precise reasons for their combination are not clear. Cedar is aromatic, as is hyssop, which is associated with a ritual of purification in Ps 51:7: "Purge me with hyssop, and I shall be clean." Crimson, or red, may have symbolic significance in association with blood.

Verses 7-10*a* describe the effects of the ritual on all the participants. The water of cleansing (מי נדה *mê niddâ*) purifies. The Hebrew word translated "cleansing" (נדה *niddâ*) probably comes from a verb meaning "to cast off" (נדה *nādâ*).[135] Gray states that this word tends to describe ritual impurity, such as menstrual blood (Lev 12:2; Ezek 18:6).[136] In the reference to menstruation, Levine notes the ambiguity of whether the casting off describes the flow of blood or the social isolation of women during menstruation.[137] In v. 9, the act of casting off with water removes impurity, hence the translation "water of cleansing." A ritual of washing with water to purify Levites was described in 8:7 as the "water of purification" (מי חטאת *mê ḥaṭṭā't*). This term returns in 19:9, where the water of cleansing is described as a purification offering (חטאת *ḥaṭṭā't*) for ordinary Israelites. The water of cleansing provides a way for Israelites to reenter the camp safely after expulsion on account of corpse contamination (5:1-4), and thus to continue to live in the sphere of divine holiness.

Paradoxically, all three individuals involved in performing the ritual become impure and thus must undergo separate acts of purification, involving the washing of clothes (see also 8:7; Exod 19:10) and bathing before reentering the camp. The priest who supervises the ritual and the layperson who burns the red cow must wash their clothes and bathe before entering the camp at evening. The ritually clean person who gathers the ashes of the red cow is required to wash his clothes before reentering the camp at evening.

19:10b-13. The central point in this section is that both Israelites and resident aliens (see Commentary on 9:1-14 and 15:1-16) are susceptible to defilement from the dead. Purification lasts seven days and requires washing with the water of cleansing on the third and seventh days. Failure to perform the purification ritual results in being cut off from the congregation, meaning excommunication or perhaps even execution.

19:14-22. This section provides more detailed commentary concerning the circumstances under which someone becomes defiled from contact with the dead (vv. 14-16) and the ritual processes for using the water of cleansing (vv. 17-22). If someone dies inside a tent, all persons and all open vessels in that tent will be contaminated for seven days (v. 14). Here contamination is thought to permeate an entire space irrespective of actual contact with the dead. Defilement from a corpse in an open field, however, requires contact. This form of contamination also lingers for seven days (v. 15). Contamination in the open field is defined more precisely as contact with a human who has been killed or someone who has died of natural causes or even contact with human bones. Thus, according to priestly writers, the impurity of the dead is permanent.[138]

The procedures for purification are outlined in vv. 17-22. Ashes from the red cow must be mixed with running water. The Hebrew in v. 17 differs slightly from the NRSV's "running water" and the NIV's "fresh water." The ashes of the red cow are described as "dust" in Hebrew, while running water is literally "living water" (מים חיים *mayim ḥayyîm*). Living water is water that is not stagnant, but spring fed. A ritually clean person is required to dip hyssop into the potion and sprinkle it on

---

134. Milgrom, *Numbers,* 159, 438-43.
135. Levine, *Numbers,* 463.
136. Gray, *Numbers,* 252.
137. Levine, *Numbers,* 463-64.

138. Ibid., 467.

contaminated persons and objects on the third and seventh days (v. 18). As was the case for those preparing the ingredients, the person performing the ritual is also rendered unclean until evening, requiring the washing of clothes and a bath. Verses 21-22 add two further clarifications about ritual impurity: The water of cleansing contaminates through touch, making a person unclean until evening, and contamination from the dead can be spread by touching something that an unclean person has touched. Verse 20 underscores the necessity of purification for any person contaminated by the dead, since they pose a threat to the sanctuary. Failure to follow proper procedures leads to being cut off from the assembly.

REFLECTIONS

1. The ritual of cleansing with the ashes of the red heifer is the most detailed treatment of death in the Old Testament. Upon first reading, the priestly theology of death appears to be far removed from the New Testament, where resurrection from the dead is central. The priestly writers do not share a belief in resurrection, but their theology of death informs New Testament teaching in a number of ways.

First, death is defined over against holiness by priestly writers and in New Testament literature. Death is a power that is incompatible with the holiness of God, and thus it defiles. Those infected with corpse contamination are expelled from the camp (Num 5:1-4). In the same way, life in Christ and death are incompatible for Christians (Rom 5:12-21; 7–8).

Second, the power of death is combated through sacraments of atonement. Those contaminated from contact with the dead must be purified with the water of cleansing from the red heifer in order to reenter the camp. Christians, too, are purged from the power of death through sacraments. Baptism defeats death (1 Pet 3:19-21), while the eucharist is a messianic feast in the kingdom of God.

Third, the mediation between holiness and death is a priestly form of leadership. A priest is required to oversee the making of the ashes from the red heifer. In Christian tradition, Jesus becomes the ashes of the red heifer in his role as high priest (Heb 9:11-14). The administration of Jesus' cleansing power through sacraments remains a priestly function of ministry. Power in this situation is rooted not in personality, but in formal structures of healing that emerge from the holiness of Jesus. The defeat of death is central to the priestly writers and to the Christian faith. The points of continuity indicate how influential the priestly theology of death is to the formation of Christian theology and liturgy.

2. There is a future orientation in the priestly writers' view of community that is foundational to Christian teaching. It emerges from their emphasis on individual responsibilty and divine forgiveness, first articulated in Numbers 13–15. The identity of Israel rests on Yahweh's promise of the land, according to the priestly writers, and not on the past actions of the ancestors. This future orientation is carried over into the teaching on death. Dead ancestors are not allowed to influence the living. Death itself is banished from the camp. The identity of the community is formed, instead, by marching ahead to the promised land.

The church extends the future orientation of the priestly writers in its teaching on death. Death is not only banished from the camp, but it is also defeated in the resurrection of Jesus and in the promise of his future return. But the foundation for this teaching rests in priestly tradition. The future orientation of the priestly writers is the building block of Christian sacraments. Baptism creates an eschatological community, in which the past loses authority for Christians because death has been defeated. Christians continue to reflect on past tradition, but only to understand the present and the future, not to worship the past of the ancestors. Christians feast with the saints in the eucharist, but this is not a cult of the dead in which the past holds authority over the present. It is an eschatological banquet in which the present and the future merge in Christ.

3. The laws regarding priestly and levitical tithes provide guidelines for reflecting on the special position of clergy within the church. Two aspects of the priestly office stand out in Numbers 18.

First, priests are paid by the congregation through tithing. Tithing, moreover, is not a gift; it is an obligation of the laity. It is one way in which the congregation of Israel is able to appoach God. Supporting priests and Levites financially allows them to fulfill their office and thus protect Israel from the danger of holiness. The command to support clergy continues into the New Testament. Paul refers to the obligation of Christians to tithe (1 Cor 9:13-14). The author of 1 Timothy is even more direct in demanding pay for preachers and teachers (1 Tim 5:17-18).

Second, priests forfeit land ownership because of their special calling. They are set apart in this respect from other members of the congregation. Numbers 18:20 states that the priests' special status with Yahweh replaces their right to inherit land. Celibacy among Roman Catholic priests provides a partial analogy to the special status of priests in Numbers 18. They give up marriage and family in exchange for their special status with God. Finding an analogy for Protestant clergy is more difficult. Yet the question is important for any clergyperson. What are clergy called to forfeit because of their special status with God?

NUMBERS 20:1–21:35, LEAVING THE WILDERNESS

NIV

20 In the first month the whole Israelite community arrived at the Desert of Zin, and they stayed at Kadesh. There Miriam died and was buried.

²Now there was no water for the community, and the people gathered in opposition to Moses and Aaron. ³They quarreled with Moses and said, "If only we had died when our brothers fell dead before the LORD! ⁴Why did you bring the LORD's community into this desert, that we and our livestock should die here? ⁵Why did you bring us up out of Egypt to this terrible place? It has no grain or figs, grapevines or pomegranates. And there is no water to drink!"

⁶Moses and Aaron went from the assembly to the entrance to the Tent of Meeting and fell facedown, and the glory of the LORD appeared to them. ⁷The LORD said to Moses, ⁸"Take the staff, and you and your brother Aaron gather the assembly together. Speak to that rock before their eyes and it will pour out its water. You will bring water out of the rock for the community so they and their livestock can drink."

NRSV

20 The Israelites, the whole congregation, came into the wilderness of Zin in the first month, and the people stayed in Kadesh. Miriam died there, and was buried there.

2Now there was no water for the congregation; so they gathered together against Moses and against Aaron. ³The people quarreled with Moses and said, "Would that we had died when our kindred died before the LORD! ⁴Why have you brought the assembly of the LORD into this wilderness for us and our livestock to die here? ⁵Why have you brought us up out of Egypt, to bring us to this wretched place? It is no place for grain, or figs, or vines, or pomegranates; and there is no water to drink." ⁶Then Moses and Aaron went away from the assembly to the entrance of the tent of meeting; they fell on their faces, and the glory of the LORD appeared to them. ⁷The LORD spoke to Moses, saying: ⁸Take the staff, and assemble the congregation, you and your brother Aaron, and command the rock before their eyes to yield its water. Thus you shall bring water out

NIV

⁹So Moses took the staff from the LORD's presence, just as he commanded him. ¹⁰He and Aaron gathered the assembly together in front of the rock and Moses said to them, "Listen, you rebels, must we bring you water out of this rock?" ¹¹Then Moses raised his arm and struck the rock twice with his staff. Water gushed out, and the community and their livestock drank.

¹²But the LORD said to Moses and Aaron, "Because you did not trust in me enough to honor me as holy in the sight of the Israelites, you will not bring this community into the land I give them."

¹³These were the waters of Meribah,ᵃ where the Israelites quarreled with the LORD and where he showed himself holy among them.

¹⁴Moses sent messengers from Kadesh to the king of Edom, saying:

"This is what your brother Israel says: You know about all the hardships that have come upon us. ¹⁵Our forefathers went down into Egypt, and we lived there many years. The Egyptians mistreated us and our fathers, ¹⁶but when we cried out to the LORD, he heard our cry and sent an angel and brought us out of Egypt.

"Now we are here at Kadesh, a town on the edge of your territory. ¹⁷Please let us pass through your country. We will not go through any field or vineyard, or drink water from any well. We will travel along the king's highway and not turn to the right or to the left until we have passed through your territory."

¹⁸But Edom answered:

"You may not pass through here; if you try, we will march out and attack you with the sword."

¹⁹The Israelites replied:

"We will go along the main road, and if we or our livestock drink any of your water, we will pay for it. We only want to pass through on foot—nothing else."

²⁰Again they answered:

"You may not pass through."

Then Edom came out against them with a large and powerful army. ²¹Since Edom refused to let

ᵃ13 Meribah means quarreling.

NRSV

of the rock for them; thus you shall provide drink for the congregation and their livestock.

9So Moses took the staff from before the LORD, as he had commanded him. ¹⁰Moses and Aaron gathered the assembly together before the rock, and he said to them, "Listen, you rebels, shall we bring water for you out of this rock?" ¹¹Then Moses lifted up his hand and struck the rock twice with his staff; water came out abundantly, and the congregation and their livestock drank. ¹²But the LORD said to Moses and Aaron, "Because you did not trust in me, to show my holiness before the eyes of the Israelites, therefore you shall not bring this assembly into the land that I have given them." ¹³These are the waters of Meribah,ᵃ where the people of Israel quarreled with the LORD, and by which he showed his holiness.

14Moses sent messengers from Kadesh to the king of Edom, "Thus says your brother Israel: You know all the adversity that has befallen us: ¹⁵how our ancestors went down to Egypt, and we lived in Egypt a long time; and the Egyptians oppressed us and our ancestors; ¹⁶and when we cried to the LORD, he heard our voice, and sent an angel and brought us out of Egypt; and here we are in Kadesh, a town on the edge of your territory. ¹⁷Now let us pass through your land. We will not pass through field or vineyard, or drink water from any well; we will go along the King's Highway, not turning aside to the right hand or to the left until we have passed through your territory."

18But Edom said to him, "You shall not pass through, or we will come out with the sword against you." ¹⁹The Israelites said to him, "We will stay on the highway; and if we drink of your water, we and our livestock, then we will pay for it. It is only a small matter; just let us pass through on foot." ²⁰But he said, "You shall not pass through." And Edom came out against them with a large force, heavily armed. ²¹Thus Edom refused to give Israel passage through their territory; so Israel turned away from them.

22They set out from Kadesh, and the Israelites, the whole congregation, came to Mount Hor. ²³Then the LORD said to Moses and Aaron at Mount Hor, on the border of the land of Edom, ²⁴"Let Aaron be gathered to his people. For he

ᵃ That is Quarrel

154

NIV

them go through their territory, Israel turned away from them.

²²The whole Israelite community set out from Kadesh and came to Mount Hor. ²³At Mount Hor, near the border of Edom, the LORD said to Moses and Aaron, ²⁴"Aaron will be gathered to his people. He will not enter the land I give the Israelites, because both of you rebelled against my command at the waters of Meribah. ²⁵Get Aaron and his son Eleazar and take them up Mount Hor. ²⁶Remove Aaron's garments and put them on his son Eleazar, for Aaron will be gathered to his people; he will die there."

²⁷Moses did as the LORD commanded: They went up Mount Hor in the sight of the whole community. ²⁸Moses removed Aaron's garments and put them on his son Eleazar. And Aaron died there on top of the mountain. Then Moses and Eleazar came down from the mountain, ²⁹and when the whole community learned that Aaron had died, the entire house of Israel mourned for him thirty days.

21 When the Canaanite king of Arad, who lived in the Negev, heard that Israel was coming along the road to Atharim, he attacked the Israelites and captured some of them. ²Then Israel made this vow to the LORD: "If you will deliver these people into our hands, we will totally destroy[a] their cities." ³The LORD listened to Israel's plea and gave the Canaanites over to them. They completely destroyed them and their towns; so the place was named Hormah.[b]

⁴They traveled from Mount Hor along the route to the Red Sea,[c] to go around Edom. But the people grew impatient on the way; ⁵they spoke against God and against Moses, and said, "Why have you brought us up out of Egypt to die in the desert? There is no bread! There is no water! And we detest this miserable food!"

⁶Then the LORD sent venomous snakes among them; they bit the people and many Israelites died. ⁷The people came to Moses and said, "We sinned when we spoke against the LORD and against you. Pray that the LORD will take the snakes away from us." So Moses prayed for the people.

a2 The Hebrew term refers to the irrevocable giving over of things or persons to the LORD, often by totally destroying them; also in verse 3. b3 Hormah means destruction. c4 Hebrew Yam Suph; that is, Sea of Reeds

NRSV

shall not enter the land that I have given to the Israelites, because you rebelled against my command at the waters of Meribah. ²⁵Take Aaron and his son Eleazar, and bring them up Mount Hor; ²⁶strip Aaron of his vestments, and put them on his son Eleazar. But Aaron shall be gathered to his people,[a] and shall die there." ²⁷Moses did as the LORD had commanded; they went up Mount Hor in the sight of the whole congregation. ²⁸Moses stripped Aaron of his vestments, and put them on his son Eleazar; and Aaron died there on the top of the mountain. Moses and Eleazar came down from the mountain. ²⁹When all the congregation saw that Aaron had died, all the house of Israel mourned for Aaron thirty days.

21 When the Canaanite, the king of Arad, who lived in the Negeb, heard that Israel was coming by the way of Atharim, he fought against Israel and took some of them captive. ²Then Israel made a vow to the LORD and said, "If you will indeed give this people into our hands, then we will utterly destroy their towns." ³The LORD listened to the voice of Israel, and handed over the Canaanites; and they utterly destroyed them and their towns; so the place was called Hormah.[b]

4From Mount Hor they set out by the way to the Red Sea,[c] to go around the land of Edom; but the people became impatient on the way. ⁵The people spoke against God and against Moses, "Why have you brought us up out of Egypt to die in the wilderness? For there is no food and no water, and we detest this miserable food." ⁶Then the LORD sent poisonous[d] serpents among the people, and they bit the people, so that many Israelites died. ⁷The people came to Moses and said, "We have sinned by speaking against the LORD and against you; pray to the LORD to take away the serpents from us." So Moses prayed for the people. ⁸And the LORD said to Moses, "Make a poisonous[e] serpent, and set it on a pole; and everyone who is bitten shall look at it and live." ⁹So Moses made a serpent of bronze, and put it upon a pole; and whenever a serpent bit someone, that person would look at the serpent of bronze and live.

a Heb lacks to his people   b Heb Destruction   c Or Sea of Reeds
d Or fiery; Heb seraphim   e Or fiery; Heb seraph

NIV

⁸The LORD said to Moses, "Make a snake and put it up on a pole; anyone who is bitten can look at it and live." ⁹So Moses made a bronze snake and put it up on a pole. Then when anyone was bitten by a snake and looked at the bronze snake, he lived.

¹⁰The Israelites moved on and camped at Oboth. ¹¹Then they set out from Oboth and camped in Iye Abarim, in the desert that faces Moab toward the sunrise. ¹²From there they moved on and camped in the Zered Valley. ¹³They set out from there and camped alongside the Arnon, which is in the desert extending into Amorite territory. The Arnon is the border of Moab, between Moab and the Amorites. ¹⁴That is why the Book of the Wars of the LORD says:

". . . Waheb in Suphah[a] and the ravines,
    the Arnon¹⁵and[b] the slopes of the ravines
that lead to the site of Ar
    and lie along the border of Moab."

¹⁶From there they continued on to Beer, the well where the LORD said to Moses, "Gather the people together and I will give them water."

¹⁷Then Israel sang this song:
"Spring up, O well!
    Sing about it,
¹⁸about the well that the princes dug,
    that the nobles of the people sank—
    the nobles with scepters and staffs."

Then they went from the desert to Mattanah, ¹⁹from Mattanah to Nahaliel, from Nahaliel to Bamoth, ²⁰and from Bamoth to the valley in Moab where the top of Pisgah overlooks the wasteland.

²¹Israel sent messengers to say to Sihon king of the Amorites:

²²"Let us pass through your country. We will not turn aside into any field or vineyard, or drink water from any well. We will travel along the king's highway until we have passed through your territory."

²³But Sihon would not let Israel pass through his territory. He mustered his entire army and marched out into the desert against Israel. When he reached Jahaz, he fought with Israel. ²⁴Israel, however, put him to the sword and took over his

a14 The meaning of the Hebrew for this phrase is uncertain.   b14,15 Or "I have been given from Suphah and the ravines / of the Arnon 15to

NRSV

10The Israelites set out, and camped in Oboth. 11They set out from Oboth, and camped at Iye-abarim, in the wilderness bordering Moab toward the sunrise. 12From there they set out, and camped in the Wadi Zered. 13From there they set out, and camped on the other side of the Arnon, in[g] the wilderness that extends from the boundary of the Amorites; for the Arnon is the boundary of Moab, between Moab and the Amorites. 14Wherefore it is said in the Book of the Wars of the LORD,

"Waheb in Suphah and the wadis.
The Arnon¹⁵and the slopes of the wadis
    that extend to the seat of Ar,
    and lie along the border of Moab."[a,b]

16From there they continued to Beer;[c] that is the well of which the LORD said to Moses, "Gather the people together, and I will give them water." 17Then Israel sang this song:

"Spring up, O well!—Sing to it!—
¹⁸ the well that the leaders sank,
    that the nobles of the people dug,
    with the scepter, with the staff."

From the wilderness to Mattanah, 19from Mattanah to Nahaliel, from Nahaliel to Bamoth, 20and from Bamoth to the valley lying in the region of Moab by the top of Pisgah that overlooks the wasteland.[d]

21Then Israel sent messengers to King Sihon of the Amorites, saying, 22"Let me pass through your land; we will not turn aside into field or vineyard; we will not drink the water of any well; we will go by the King's Highway until we have passed through your territory." 23But Sihon would not allow Israel to pass through his territory. Sihon gathered all his people together, and went out against Israel to the wilderness; he came to Jahaz, and fought against Israel. 24Israel put him to the sword, and took possession of his land from the Arnon to the Jabbok, as far as to the Ammonites; for the boundary of the Ammonites was strong. 25Israel took all these towns, and Israel settled in all the towns of the Amorites, in Heshbon, and in all its villages. 26For Heshbon was the city of King Sihon of the Amorites, who had fought against the former king of Moab and captured all

a Gk: Heb which is in   b Meaning of Heb uncertain   c That is Well   d Or Jeshimon land from the Arnon to the Jabbok, but only as far as the Ammonites, because their border was fortified. ²⁵Israel captured all the cities of the Amorites and occupied them, including Heshbon and all its surrounding settlements. ²⁶Heshbon was the city of Sihon king of the Amorites, who had fought against the former king of Moab and had taken from him all his land as far as the Arnon.

²⁷That is why the poets say:
"Come to Heshbon and let it be rebuilt;
    let Sihon's city be restored.

²⁸"Fire went out from Heshbon,
    a blaze from the city of Sihon.
It consumed Ar of Moab,
    the citizens of Arnon's heights.

²⁹Woe to you, O Moab!
    You are destroyed, O people of Chemosh!
He has given up his sons as fugitives
    and his daughters as captives
    to Sihon king of the Amorites.

³⁰"But we have overthrown them;
    Heshbon is destroyed all the way to Dibon.
We have demolished them as far as Nophah,
    which extends to Medeba."

³¹So Israel settled in the land of the Amorites.

³²After Moses had sent spies to Jazer, the Israelites captured its surrounding settlements and drove out the Amorites who were there. ³³Then they turned and went up along the road toward Bashan, and Og king of Bashan and his whole army marched out to meet them in battle at Edrei.

³⁴The LORD said to Moses, "Do not be afraid of him, for I have handed him over to you, with his whole army and his land. Do to him what you did to Sihon king of the Amorites, who reigned in Heshbon."

³⁵So they struck him down, together with his sons and his whole army, leaving them no survivors. And they took possession of his land.

his land as far as the Arnon. ²⁷Therefore the ballad singers say,

"Come to Heshbon, let it be built;
    let the city of Sihon be established.
²⁸ For fire came out from Heshbon,
    flame from the city of Sihon.
It devoured Ar of Moab,
    and swallowed upᵃ the heights of the
        Arnon.
²⁹ Woe to you, O Moab!
    You are undone, O people of Chemosh!
He has made his sons fugitives,
    and his daughters captives,
    to an Amorite king, Sihon.
³⁰ So their posterity perished
    from Heshbonᵇ to Dibon,
    and we laid waste until fire spread to
        Medeba."ᶜ

³¹Thus Israel settled in the land of the Amorites. ³²Moses sent to spy out Jazer; and they captured its villages, and dispossessed the Amorites who were there.

³³Then they turned and went up the road to Bashan; and King Og of Bashan came out against them, he and all his people, to battle at Edrei. ³⁴But the LORD said to Moses, "Do not be afraid of him; for I have given him into your hand, with all his people, and all his land. You shall do to him as you did to King Sihon of the Amorites, who ruled in Heshbon." ³⁵So they killed him, his sons, and all his people, until there was no survivor left; and they took possession of his land.

ᵃ Gk: Heb *and the lords of*   ᵇ Gk: Heb *we have shot at them; Heshbon has perished*   ᶜ Compare Sam Gk: Meaning of MT uncertain

COMMENTARY

Numbers 20–21 is a loose collection of stories clustered around three general locations: Kadesh, Mt. Hor, and the Transjordan. Kadesh is the location for Miriam's death (20:1), the failure of leadership by Moses and Aaron (20:2-13), and a conflict with the Edomites concerning passage through their land (20:14-21). Mount Hor is the location for Aaron's death (20:22-29), the defeat of the Canaanite king of Arad at Hormah (21:1-3), and the attack by fiery serpents as Israel journeys around Edom on the Red Sea road (21:4-9). A series of Transjordanian locations concludes the section, providing the setting for Israel's defeat of the Amorite kings Sihon and Og (21:10-35).

This synopsis illustrates how chaps. 20–21 provide a transition in the book of Numbers from wandering and death in the wilderness to successful holy war in the Transjordan. The transitional character of this section creates ambiguity about its central themes. It can be read both as a story about the death of the first generation in the wilderness and as a story about the successful inauguration of holy war by the second generation. Its different points of focus have spawned debate among interpreters concerning the place of chaps. 20–21 in the larger structure of the book. This debate may be unresolvable, since the ambiguity has been built into the literature itself by the pre-priestly and priestly authors.

The pre-priestly stories include the following sequence: The conflict with Edom (20:14-21) follows the spy story (chaps. 13–14) and the rebellion of Dathan and Abiram (chap. 16). These stories take place at Kadesh. The defeat of the Canaanite king of Arad (21:1-3) and the attack by fiery serpents (21:4-9) occur in the vicinity of Mt. Hor. And the defeat of the Amorite kings, Sihon and Og (21:10-35), takes place in the Transjordan.

The pre-priestly writers emphasize positive themes in chaps. 20–21, focusing on the second generation's leaving the wilderness and beginning their initial conquest of Transjordan. This conclusion is based on comparison to Deut 1:46–3:17. The death of the first generation is never stated in chaps. 20–21, nor anywhere else in the pre-priestly version of Numbers, but it appears in Deuteronomy. There are differences between Numbers 20–21 and Deut 1:46–3:17, especially with regard to geography. Deuteronomy 2:3-13 notes that Israel went through Edom and Moab, while Num 20:14-21 makes no mention of Moab and enlarges the confrontation with Edom before concluding that Israel did not go through this land. Yet the accounts are similar enough to suggest some form of relationship between the two, at least concerning the first and second generations.

Reference to the Wadi Zered in Deuteronomy and in Numbers provides an anchor point for discerning the transition from the first to the second generations. In Deuteronomy, the first generation of Israelites dies during the wilderness journey between Kadesh-barnea and the Wadi Zered. Deuteronomy 1:46–2:2 locates the wilderness wandering of the first generation in the region of Mt. Seir. Deuteronomy 2:7 states that the duration of this wandering is forty years. Deuteronomy 2:13-15 adds that travel from Kadesh-barnea to the Wadi Zered took thirty-eight years and that, during this time, the entire first generation of Israelites died. Their deaths provide transition in Deut 2:16-17 to holy war against Sihon and Og by the second generation of Israelites.

The Wadi Zered is also embedded in Num 20:10-20, where it signifies transition from the wilderness to the border of the Amorite kingdom at Arnon (vv. 12-13). This point of transition marks the beginning of holy war in the book of Numbers, just as it does in Deuteronomy. The parallel to Deuteronomy suggests that the second generation is the focal point at this juncture in Numbers. But the exact point of transition between generations is not clear. According to Numbers 20–21, the first generation may have died off already at Kadesh. The story of holy war at Mt. Hor against the King of Arad (21:1-3) may point to action by the second generation, in which case it provides a contrast to the defeat of the first generation at the same location immediately after the loss of the land (14:39-45). Such an interpretation would correspond to the perspective of Deuteronomy, where the first generation never engages in a successful holy war after the spy story. Even without locating the precise point of transition from the first to the second generation in Numbers 20–21, it is clear that the pre-priestly version of events is oriented toward the future conquest of the Transjordan by the second generation.

The priestly writers add three stories. They include Miriam's death at Kadesh, along with an itinerary notice indicating Israel's arrival there (20:1). The failure of leadership by Moses and Aaron is also included at Kadesh (20:2-13). The priestly writers locate the death of Aaron at Mt. Hor (20:22-29).

The priestly writers focus on the theme of

death in the wilderness for the first generation by highlighting both the failure of the leadership and the deaths of the heroes of the exodus—Miriam, Aaron, and Moses. Thus their reading of chaps. 20–21 is not oriented toward a future conquest. In fact, the second generation of Israelites does not become a clear focus of the priestly writers until the second census in chap. 26 (see 26:63-65). For them, the deaths of the first generation are not complete until chap. 25, when Phinehas the priest slaughters all those who worshiped the baal of Peor (chap. 25).

This overview illustrates that interpretation must deal with two points of view in Numbers 20–21. The pre-priestly writers turn their focus toward the land, emphasizing that the second generation of Israelites will leave the wilderness and begin the conquest of the Transjordan. The priestly writers focus on the wilderness in order to explore the theme of the deaths of the leaders of the exodus.

20:1. The section begins with a travel notice that Israel has entered the wilderness of Zin and is encamped at Kadesh. Two terms are used to describe the people: "Israelites" and "the whole congregation." The combination of these terms occurs only in this itinerary notice and in the itinerary notice in v. 22. Some scholars suggest that reference to Kadesh was already present in the pre-priestly story—not as an itinerary notice but to remind the reader that Israel is still encamped there. "The whole congregation" (כל־העדה *kol-hā'ēdâ*) is one of the central phrases used by the priestly writers. This phrase, along with reference to the wilderness of Zin (see 13:21; 27:14; 33:36; 34:3-4, all P) suggest that the itinerary notice is the work of the priestly writers. The date for Israel's arrival at Kadesh in the priestly itinerary lacks reference to year and day. It simply states the "first month." Comparison to 33:38-39, however, indicates that it is the fortieth year of wilderness wandering. The itinerary notice is significant to the priestly history. It places Israel at Kadesh only at the end of the wilderness journey, as compared to the pre-priestly version, in which Israel arrives at Kadesh in the second year of the wilderness journey (chaps. 13–14).

In spite of their different chronologies, both histories portray Kadesh as the setting for negative stories. In the pre-priestly history, Kadesh was the general location for a series of negative accounts about the first generation of Israelites to leave Egypt. The events take place over an extended period of time and include the loss of the land (chaps. 13–14), the defeat at Hormah (14:39-45), and the challenge to Moses' leadership by Dathan and Abiram (chap. 16). The priestly writers also view events at Kadesh negatively, but their focus is narrowed to a shorter period of time and to the leadership of the first generation of Israelites to leave Egypt. Paran is the place where Israel loses the land. Kadesh, on the other hand, is the place where Miriam dies and is buried (Num 20:1). It is also the place where Moses and Aaron disobey God and lose the gift of the land (20:2-13).

Miriam's death is noted almost in passing. No reason for her death is given, nor is any mention made of mourning rites (cf. the deaths of Aaron in 20:29 and Moses in Deut 34:8). Yet her death is significant because of her role in the exodus, both as the savior of Moses (Exod 2:1-10) and as the one who sang a victory song of salvation at the Red Sea (Exod 15:20-21). Along with Moses and Aaron, she is one of the three leaders of the exodus. Whether her death in the wilderness at Kadesh is meant to be a result of her earlier challenge to Moses' leadership (chap. 12) is unclear; no direct connection is drawn. But her death at Kadesh foreshadows the deaths of Moses and Aaron, the other two heroes of the exodus.

20:2-13. The priestly writers follow Miriam's death notice with a story about the disobedience of Moses and Aaron, which results in their not being able to enter the promised land of Canaan. This story is a continuation of the idealization of Moses as a leader, which has been a central theme throughout chap. 11–21. In this case, however, Moses models the failure of leadership. This section is an outgrowth of the priestly emphasis on individual responsibility, introduced in the story of the loss of the land (14:26-35). Individual responsibility before God means that Moses and Aaron could no longer be denied entrance into the promised land simply because of the collective sin of the people, as was the case in Deuteronomy. Thus the central purpose of this story is clear: The priestly writers recount the sin of Moses and Aaron that denies them entrance into the promised land. In the process, they illustrate failure of leadership in the wilderness community.

Yet the interpretation of the sin of Moses has puzzled interpreters. Scholars debate whether his sin lies in striking the rock, in his character, in his speech to the people, or perhaps in some feature no longer recorded in the text.[139]

Verses 2-13 recount a four-part murmuring story about lack of water. It begins with a complaint against Moses and Aaron by the congregation (vv. 2-6) includes motifs found also in other murmuring stories. The people question why Moses has brought them up from Egypt to die of thirst in the desert. The second scene (vv. 7-8) consists of a theophany of the glory of Yahweh at the entrance of the tent of meeting, where Moses and Aaron receive instruction about procuring water. They must (1) take the rod from its position before Yahweh; (2) assemble the people; and (3) speak to the rock in order to bring forth from it water for the Israelites and their cattle. Commentators debate whether the rod in this story belongs to Moses or to Aaron. The location of the rod before Yahweh in the tent of meeting suggests that it is the budding rod of Aaron, since this is where Moses was commanded to place it (17:10).

In the third scene (vv. 8-11), Moses only partially executes the divine order. He takes the rod from before Yahweh and assembles the people. Instead of speaking to the rock, however, he addresses the people and strikes the rock twice with the rod. Thus one aspect of Moses' sin is his failure to follow the divine command, especially the last requirement of speaking to the rock. The final scene (vv. 12-13) consists of a divine speech in which the sin of Moses is described as not having trusted in Yahweh and not sanctifying God before Israel. The word "to sanctify" in Hebrew (הקדיש *hiqdîš,* hiphil from קדש *qādaš*) is a pun on the place name "Kadesh." The two words include the same consonants in Hebrew (ק *q;* ד *d;* ש *š*). The episode concludes with an etiology on the "waters of Meribah" (מי מריבה *mê měrîbâ*). The place name "Meribah" includes the root consonants from the verb "to quarrel" (ריב *rîb*). The etiology combines the quarrelling of Israel with the sanctifying presence of Yahweh: "These are the waters of Meribah, where the people of Israel quarreled [*rîb*] with Yahweh, and by which he showed his holiness [*qādaš,* niphal]."

The etiology indicates that vv. 2-13 are meant to be read as a positive story of divine provision in the wilderness. It is the only murmuring story in the entire book of Numbers that does not prompt divine anger and judgment against Israel. By contrast, the general complaint in 11:1-3; the desire for meat in 11:4-35 (esp. v. 10); the complaint of Miriam and Aaron in 12:9; the spy story in 14:11-12, 26-35; and the Korah, Dathan, and Abiram rebellion in 16:21, 45 all result in divine anger and judgment on the people.

The positive orientation of the need for water in 20:2-13 is reinforced by its many parallels to Exod 17:1-7, where Israel also complains about lack of water without prompting divine punishment. Furthermore, both stories use the verb "to quarrel" (*rîb*) in the complaint of the people, giving both accounts legal overtones (20:3; Exod 17:2). The Hebrew verb translated "to quarrel" (*rîb*) frequently means "to conduct a legal case," while the noun often refers to a lawsuit.[140] The legal dimension of both stories is reflected in their similar etiology of Meribah (20:13; Exod 17:7). The positive character of Israel's legal complaint in these verses is very important for interpreting the sin of Moses. It suggests that Israel's desire for water has been voiced in the proper way and that God intends to respond appropriately by supplying water to them.

Moses' sin includes both his actions and his words to Israel. His sin of action is clear from the synopsis of the story. He does not follow divine instructions in responding to the people's dispute. Striking the rock conveys divine anger in response to Israel's legal claim, when, in fact, there is none. In this action, Moses demonstrates his own lack of faith in the very structures he should uphold. Thus God accuses him of not trusting and, hence, of not being able to mediate divine holiness in the midst of the people. Moses fails as a leader by not following the appropriate means of communication and accountability between God and Israel.

This sin is compounded by Moses' angry address to Israel before he strikes the rock with this rod: "You rebels!" (המרים *hammōrîm*). The sinful nature of Moses' words comes into full view when they are interpreted against the backdrop of the rebellion of Korah in chaps. 16–17. Israel's

---

139. Jacob Milgrom, *Numbers,* JPS Torah Commentary (Philadelphia: JPS, 1990) 448-56.

140. *BDB,* 936; and *KB,* 888b-89a.

complaint in 20:3 first established a connection between these two stories: "Would that we had died [גוענו *gāwaʿnû*] when our kindred died [בגוע *bigwaʿ*] before the LORD!" The word translated "to die" (גוע *gāwaʿ*) repeats the exclamation of the people at the conclusion of the Korah rebellion (17:12-13): "Are we all to perish [*gāwaʿ*] [in approaching God]?" The repetition suggests that their legal complaint in 20:2-13 for water may be one way in which Israel is able to approach God without perishing. Yet Moses does not discern the appropriateness of their action. He misinterprets their legal complaint as rebellion against God. In doing so, he fails as a leader by not discerning proper ways for Israel to approach God in the wilderness.

Moses' failure of leadership and his self-indictment are conveyed ironically through Aaron's rod, which he was required to remove from the tent of meeting. It provides yet another connection to the rebellion of Korah. In fact, the budding of Aaron's rod prompted Israel's exclamation of fear in 17:12-13. They were afraid because this rod became a sign to rebels not to complain against God. The structure of 20:2-13, suggests, however, that Israel's legal complaint about water is not an instance of rebellion through murmuring. Indeed, the peculiar divine command to Moses that he take the rod with him when he draws water from the rock, but not wield it against the rock, reinforces the positive context of the people's legal complaint. Thus, when Moses uses the rod to strike the rock, he is doing more than simply disobeying divine instructions. He is also judging the situation as an act of rebellion by the people against God. This action is consistent with his message that the people are rebels. Instead, he becomes the rebel through his misuse of the rod, which prompts his own death sentence, rather than Israel's.

20:14-21. The final story associated with Kadesh concerns Israel's request to pass through the land of Edom. Moses sends messengers from Kadesh to the king of Edom. The account takes the form of diplomatic correspondence, which includes naming the recipient, a messenger formula, identification of the sender and his rank, the present predicament and motive for the message, and finally the request itself.[141]

In v. 14, the recipient of the message is identified as "the King of Edom." This is followed by a messenger formula, "Thus says your brother Israel," including the name of the sender, "Israel," and his rank, "brother." The latter refers to the ancestral story of the brothers Jacob and Esau (Gen 25:19–33:20). Israel's approach of Edom is reminiscent of Jacob's approach to Esau in Genesis 32–33.

Verses 16-17, a description of Israel's present situation, includes a synopsis of the exodus. The ancestors of the Israelites went down to Egypt and lived there many years. But they were oppressed by the Egyptians, prompting their cry to God for help. The Lord heard their cry and sent an angel, who brought them out of Egypt. This summary of the exodus is similar to accounts in Deut 26:5-9 and Judg 11:16-18, though not in all details. The reference to the angel, or more precisely in Hebrew, "divine messenger" (מלאך *malʾāk*) is unique to this version of the exodus. The same word is used to describe the human messengers whom Moses sends to the king of Edom. The most prominent characteristic of the divine messenger is leading Israel in holy war. The divine messenger was present at the confrontation with Egypt at the Red Sea (Exod 14:19), and God promises that the divine messenger will lead Israel in conquest of the land (Exod 23:20-33; 33:2). Thus holy war overtones are present in the message to the King of Edom, but not when the exodus is recounted from the setting of the promised land in Deut 26:5-9 and Judg 11:16-18.

Moses requests permission for the Israelites to pass through the land of Edom on the King's Highway (v. 17), a trade route running north and south from southern Arabia to Syria. He promises that they will stay on this route, harming no field and drinking no water. The central motif in this request is that the people be allowed to "cross over" (עבר *ʿābar*) the land, a word that occurs three times in this single verse. The literal meaning of the request "to cross over" is "to travel"—Israel wishes to pass through the land. But the word also bears overtones of conquest. The final refrain in the Song of the Sea (Exod 15:16), for example, describes Israel's conquest as "crossing over" the nations, which in this hymn includes Edom. The language suggests that the central theme of the book of Numbers is changing from

---

141. Gordon J. Wenham, *Numbers: An Introduction and Commentary*, Tyndale Old Testament Commentaries (Leicester: Inter-Varsity Press, 1981) 152.

wilderness wandering to conquest, even though no holy war against Edom occurs.

Verses 18-21 recount the exchange between Israel and Edom. Both nations are represented by individuals, recalling the ancestral stories of Jacob and Esau, in which the nations of Israel and Edom are represented by persons. Edom refuses Israel's request for passage in v. 18 and even threatens war. Israel responds in v. 19 by repeating the request and offering to pay for water. The story ends in vv. 20-21 with the king of Edom refusing to allow the Israelites to cross over and even meeting them with an army, thus forcing "Israel to turn away from him."

The closing line, "So Israel turned away from Edom," is suggestive. On one level it is a geographical statement. Israel looked for another route to the promised land around Edom. But one wanders if it also reflects Israel's experience during the exile. The title "King of Edom" is certainly anachronistic for the setting of the story, since Edom was an independent state only from the eighth to the sixth centuries BCE, the end of Israel's monarchical period.[142] The treachery of the Edomites in the immediate aftermath of Jerusalem's destruction is specifically mentioned in Israel's anguished lament of the exile (Ps 137:7), and it is also the topic of the exilic prophet Obadiah. Read from the perspective of the exile, the pre-priestly story of Num 20:14-21 functions as an etiology that describes how Israel's brother nation, the Edomites, refused to assist in a time of need, thus causing Israel to turn away from them.

20:22-29. An itinerary notice in v. 22 indicates that Israel leaves Kadesh and arrives at Mt. Hor. Two events are addressed in these verses: the death of Aaron and the passing on of the office of high priest. The story is closely linked with the preceding stories in this chapter. Mount Hor stands in the proximity of Edom, the location of vv. 14-21, and Aaron's death is a result of his earlier disobedience at Kadesh (vv. 2-13). The account of Aaron's death follows the pattern of divine command to Moses (vv. 23-26) and its fulfillment (vv. 27-28). It concludes with mourning rituals (v. 29).

The death of Aaron is a significant event in the book of Numbers and, indeed, in the entire Pen-

tateuch. His death, along with the deaths of Miriam and Moses, will mark the end of the generation of Israelites who were liberated from Egypt. One indication of Aaron's significance is that his death is remembered in two different traditions within the Pentateuch. Deuteronomy 10:6 locates his death at Moserah; Num 20:2-13 places it at Mt. Hor. The complete itinerary list of the wilderness march in Numbers 33 makes it clear that these locations were not regarded as the same. In 33:31-37, Moserah is seven stops removed from Mt. Hor. Both traditions contain a notice of Eleazar's succeeding Aaron as high priest.

The details surrounding the death of Aaron further attest to his importance in tradition. Like Moses (Deut 34:1-8), he dies on a mountaintop and is gathered to his ancestors, prompting mourning for thirty days. The usual period of mourning was seven days (Gen 50:10; Job 2:13). Thus the month-long period of mourning indicates the prominence of Aaron. Moses is the only other person whose death prompted a thirty-day period of mourning (Deut 34:1-8). Numbers 33:38-39 dates Aaron's death to Year 40, Month 5, Day 1 after the exodus from Egypt, making him 123 years old. According to the priestly writers, he undertook the exodus at 83 years of age (Exod 7:7). The phrase "was gathered to his people" is applied to many of the male heroes in the Pentateuch: e.g., Abraham (Gen 25:8); Ishmael (Gen 25:17); Isaac (Gen 35:29); Jacob (Gen 49:33); and Moses (Num 27:13; 31:2; Deut 32:50). It provides a glimpse into Israel's view of Sheol as a place where one is united with ancestors. Whether this was Israel's only view of the afterlife or whether Sheol was limited to men is unclear.

Aaron's death also provides occasion for the priestly writers to model succession of leadership in the office of high priest. The office is inherited; thus it is a non-charismatic form of leadership. There is no transfer of a prophetic spirit or laying on of hands. Instead, Eleazar is invested with the signs of the office. Aaron is stripped of his priestly vestments, and they are placed on Eleazar. The Israelites know that Aaron has died, because they see the priestly vestments on Eleazar. The vestments of the high priest are described in Lev 8:7-9. They include a tunic with sash and robe, the decorated band of the ephod, a breastpiece containing the Urim and Thummin, and a turban

142. J. R. Bartlett, "The Rise and Fall of the Kingdom of Edom," *PEQ* 104 (1972) 26-37.

with a golden ornament and a holy crown. The procedure for transferring these sacred garments from one high priest to another is described in Exod 29:29-30. The ritual of investiture includes anointing and ordination over a seven-day period within the tent of meeting. These details are not specifically recounted in Num 20:22-29.

21:1-3. These verses tell a story of divine deliverance and a successful holy war against the Canaanite king of Arad in the Negeb at Hormah. The episode is clearly out of place in its present literary context, for it is inserted between the death of Aaron at Mt. Hor (20:22) and Israel's departure from Mt. Hor to travel south around Edom (21:4). Thus it momentarily transports Israel to a military campaign in the north, while the itinerary has them traveling south on the Red Sea road. A tradition of victory against Arad in the Negeb is preserved in Judg 1:16, but Num 21:1-3 does not appear to be the same story. Furthermore, the geographical references suggest that no such kingdom of Arad existed during the Late Bronze Age. Interpretation will focus on the literary purpose of 21:1-3 at this juncture in the book of Numbers.

Numbers 21:1-3 is structured as a story of divine deliverance in a threatening situation. The king of Arad attacks Israel and takes captives (v. 1). Israel asks God for help, vowing to place all the cities of Arad under the חרם (ḥērem) ban (v. 2). Under the ḥērem ban, all property would be given over to God through destruction, rather than becoming booty for the warriors. God hears the Israelites' request and gives the Canaanites to them in battle (v. 3a). As Israel had vowed, they turn all the cities over to God by destroying them. Hence the etiological name "Hormah," from the Hebrew word חרם (ḥērem). Milgrom has suggested that the story is meant to underscore the sin of Moses by presenting his failed attempt at holy war in Canaan after being denied entry into the land.[143] But Moses is conspicuously absent from this story. Furthermore, this is a positive story about Israel, and not about specific leaders.

The setting of the story at Hormah provides a connection to Israel's failed attempt at holy war

at the close of the spy story in 14:39-45, which also took place at Hormah. The meaning of the story most likely lies in this repetition. Both stories focus on Israel, rather than on specific leaders, and both are paradigmatic for holy war. The first story provides a negative example of holy war, illustrating what not to do. Divine direction is rejected, war is waged out of desperation, and Israel is defeated. In 21:1-3, holy war is waged as a response to oppression, divine direction is sought before the battle, ḥērem vows are made to ensure that war is not motivated by self-interest, and Israel is successful. Levine's suggestion that the repetition marks a transition from the first to the second generation may also be correct, although there are no clear statements to this effect in the story.[144] What is clear is that the insertion of holy war at Hormah is one more instance of the transition from wilderness wandering to conquest of the promised land in Numbers 20–21.

21:4-9. The final murmuring story occurs when Israel leaves Mt. Hor and journeys south around Edom on the Red Sea road (v. 4). The story moves briskly without providing many details; in this respect, it resembles the first murmuring story after Israel's departure from Sinai (11:1-3). In both instances, general complaint leads immediately to divine punishment, prompting confession by the people and the request for intercession by Moses, whose prayer persuades God to eliminate the punishment. These parallels in structure underscore that the stories of Israel's wilderness journey from Sinai to the plains of Moab are framed by instances of murmuring and successful intercession by Moses.

Israel's final complaint is directed against both Moses and God (vv. 4-5). It includes the idealization of Egypt, characteristic of most of the murmuring stories. The specific complaint by Israel about the wilderness is presented as incoherent ranting. They have neither bread nor water, yet they do not like the miserable food in their possession!

God responds in v. 6 by sending poisonous serpents to bite and kill many of the people. The translation "poisonous" serpents is from the Hebrew word שרפים (śĕrāpîm), which comes from the verb meaning "to burn" (שרף śārap). These

---

143. Milgrom, *Numbers*, 458. For fuller discussion of *ḥērem*, see P. Stern, *The Biblical Herem: A Window on Israel's Relgious Experience*, BJS 211 (Atlanta: Scholars Press, 1991); N. Lohfink, "haram," *TDOT* 5:180-99.

144. Baruch A. Levine, *Numbers 1–20*, AB 4A (New York: Doubleday, 1993) 60.

snakes are not simply a natural disaster. They are divine agents of punishment and potential healing. The seraph is mentioned in Isa 14:29 and 30:6-7 as a flying serpent. The seraphim are also active in the call of the prophet Isaiah (Isaiah 6). They are part of the iconography of the Temple, stationed above Yahweh's throne. They are winged creatures, associated with the fire of divine holiness. Their fire is life-threatening; yet, they also are able to purify the prophet. Bronze serpents have been found throughout the ancient Near East, providing ample parallels for interpreting vv. 4-9.[145] Yet the association of the seraphim with Yahweh's throne most likely derives from Egyptian religion, where the raised and swollen head of the cobra is often depicted on the pharaoh's headdress as a protective goddess, Wadjyt. Her function was to spit fiery venom onto the enemies of the king.[146] Thus in Egypt the cobra's function was twofold: to protect and to destroy.

Verses 4-9 illustrate the twofold character of the seraph serpents as well. God sends them to punish Israel for murmuring, but the point of the story is to explore the healing property of the snake. As a consequence, once the people have confessed their sin and requested intercession by Moses (v. 7), God instructs Moses to make a seraph and to place it on a pole or banner as an antidote to the snake bites (v. 8). The story ends with an account of Moses making a bronze replica of the seraph, called נחש נחשת (*něḥaš něḥōšet*, "the serpent of bronze"). This serpent has the power to heal anyone who looks at it. The cultic roots of story in vv. 4-9 may derive from religious practice in the Jerusalem Temple. It contained a bronze serpent named Nehushtan, which was destroyed by King Hezekiah (2 Kgs 18:4).

21:10-20. This section consists of travel notices (vv. 10-13, 16*a*, 18*b*-20) and two songs (vv. 14-15, 17-18*a*). It separates into two parts: vv. 10-18*a* recount the final stages of Israel's wilderness march to the Arnon River; vv. 18*b*-20 note Israel's exit from the wilderness and then briefly summarize the journey from Mattanah to Mt. Pisgah.

The travel notices give specific stopping sites with detailed geographical locations, extending

from Oboth in the wilderness (v. 10) to a valley in the fields of Moab near Mt. Pisgah (v. 20). The specific locations include Oboth, Iye-abarim, the Wadi Zered, the Arnon River, Beer, Mattanah, Nahaliel, Bamoth, and Pisgah. The location of Oboth (v. 10) is unknown, but it must be south of the Dead Sea. The next stopping point, Iye-abarim (v. 11), is also unknown and may simply be a reference to "the ruins on the other side." The Wadi Zered (v. 12), however, is likely the modern Wadi el-Hesa, which flows into the southern portion of the Dead Sea from the east. The Arnon River (v. 13) is also a firmly fixed point. It flows from the east into the Dead Sea at its midpoint. These two sites indicate that the writers of these verses envision Israel as moving north into the Transjordan on the east side of the Dead Sea. Yet Beer (v. 16), as well as Mattanah, Nahaliel, Bamoth, and Pisgah (vv. 19-20), are all unknown.

The journey of the Israelites into the Transjordan is also recounted in Deuteronomy 2 and in Numbers 33, with different routes and other locations. In Deuteronomy 2, Israel journeys from Kadesh (Deut 2:19, 46) through Edom and Moab (Deut 2:1-13) to the Wadi Zered (Deut 2:13-15), before crossing into Moab at Ar (Deut 2:18). Then they cross the Arnon to battle Sihon (Deut 2:24) from their camp in the wilderness at Kedemoth (Deut 2:26). Comparison with Num 21:10-20 reveals several differences: Israel journeys through Edom rather than around it; nearly all of the sites mentioned in Num 21:10-20 are absent from Deuteronomy, with the exception of the Wadi Zered and the Arnon River; and the reference to Kedemoth in Deuteronomy is absent from Num 21:10-20.

The itinerary in Numbers 33 records Israel's journey to Oboth, Iye-abarim, Dibon-gad, Almon-diblathaim, the mountains of Abarim before Nebo, and, finally, the plains of Moab by the Jordan, opposite Jericho (33:41-48). This list includes neither the Wadi Zered nor the Arnon River, while it locates Iye-abarim in the land of Moab, placing it significantly further north than envisioned by the writers of 21:10-20, where Iye-abarim is south of the Wadi Zered.

The differences between Num 21:10-20, Numbers 33, and Deuteronomy 2, along with the lack of historical detail, suggest that geography is being employed for theological purposes in all of the travel lists. The geographical descriptions that accompany the different sites in Num 21:10-20

---

145. See K. R. Joines, "The Bronze Serpent in the Israelite Cult, *JBL* 87 (1968) 245-56.

146. Stephen Quirke, *Ancient Egyptian Religion* (London: British Museum, 1992) 31-32.

provide a window into the theological aims of the authors. The most important description is that of the wilderness. It is mentioned three times in the short section (vv. 10, 13, 18*b*). The first two references (vv. 10, 13) place Israel in the wilderness. Iye-abarim is in the wilderness at the border of Moab (v. 10). The Arnon River (v. 13) is also described as being in the wilderness, this time at the border of the Amorites. The third reference marks the Israelites' departure from the wilderness as they journey to Mattanah (v. 18*b*). The three references to the wilderness indicate that one purpose of Num 21:10-20 is to mark the transition from Israel's wilderness wandering to its conquest of fertile land.

This transition is underscored by the inclusion of two songs. The first is about holy war at the River Arnon (vv. 14-15). The second is about the gift of water at Beer (vv. 17-18). Holy war and flowing, spring-fed water mark an end to the wilderness wanderings.

The first song (vv. 14-15) is a fragment of poetry from an anthology of war poems, entitled The Book of the Wars of Yahweh. It is the only example of poetry from this collection. The fragmentary character of the poem is indicated by the first line, "Waheb in Suphah" (את־והב בסופה *'et-wāhēb běsûpâ*). The initial word, את (*'et*), is a direct object marker. It has no translation value by itself. Instead, it indicates that the following phrase is meant to be the direct object of a verb; yet, no verb (or subject) is present. The NRSV and the NIV interpret the Hebrew as a place name, Waheb in Suphah. This reading emphasizes geography through a series of place names: Waheb in Suphah, the Arnon, Ar, and the border of Moab. With this reading, the poetic insertion reinforces the place names of the itinerary in vv. 10-20.

But the title the Book of the Wars of Yahweh also signals that the poem is about holy war. Christensen has proposed a reconstruction of the song that emphasizes the holy war theme of the fragment by reading the direct object marker as a verb, "he came" (אתה *' ātâ*), and the place name, Weheb, as the divine name *YHW* (without the final H). Also, rather than regarding the Hebrew סופה (*Sûpâ*) as a place name, he interprets the word to mean "whirlwind," as it does in all other instances of its use in the OT. This reading turns

the opening phrase into a complete sentence, "Yahweh came in a whirlwind."[147] The use of natural imagery like the whirlwind to describe the approach of Yahweh to aid Israel in holy war is characteristic of ancient poetry (e.g., Judg 5:4; Ps 68:6). As a holy war poem, the song foreshadows the subsequent war with the Amorite kings Sihon and Og in vv. 21-35. In fact, the story of war against Sihon and Og likely occurred at this place in Numbers in the pre-priestly history, making it presently out of sequence.

A second song in vv. 17-18*a* concerns water. The location for the song is Beer ("well"). Scholars have classified the poem as a work song.[148] Yet, its function in the present text is celebrative. Verse 16 indicates that the water at Beer is a divine gift to the people. The song in vv. 17-18 is Israel's response to God's providence. The people sing, "Spring up, O well!—Sing to it!" The Song of the Well provides yet another point of transition in the book of Numbers from wilderness wandering to fertile land, where water wells simply spring up from the ground. Indeed, Israel officially leaves the wilderness at this point in its journey (v. 18*b*), moving quickly to the valley in Moab and looking back upon the wasteland of the wilderness from the top of Pisgah (v. 20).

21:21-35. The defeat of the Amorite kings Sihon and Og is reported three times in the OT. The story in these verses is presented as the original narrative of the victory. Moses recounts the event to the second generation of Israelites in Deut 2:26-3:7, and Jephthah, the judge, tells it to the Ammonite king who claims the territory as his own (Judg 11:19-26). Each of these stories, independent of the others, includes a request by Israel to pass through the kingdom of Sihon, his refusal and attack, Israel's victory at Jahaz, and the conquest of the Amorite kingdom from the Arnon to the Jabbok rivers. But there are differences as well. Numbers 21:27-30 includes a poem that is absent from the other accounts. Numbers 21:33-34 and Deut 3:1-7 extend the story to include the defeat of Og of Bashan. These differences have occassioned debate over the precise interrelationship between the three stories, which

---

147. D. L. Christensen, "Num 21:14-15 and the Book of the Wars of Yahweh," *CBQ* 36 (1974) 359-60.
148. Eissfeldt, *The Old Testament: An Introduction,* trans. P. Ackroyd (New York: Harper & Row, 1965) 88.

has bearing on the composition of the Tetrateuch (Genesis–Numbers), Deuteronomy, and the Deuteronomistic History (Joshua, Judges, Samuel, and Kings).[149] For the purposes of this commentary, it is important to note that there are no indications that Num 21:21-35 is part of the priestly history. All debate concerns the literary character of the pre-priestly history. Thus the conquest of the Transjordan will be interpreted as part of the pre-priestly history.

The request to pass through the kingdom of Sihon (vv. 21-22) is very similar to the story about Edom (20:14-21). Messengers are sent to the king, requesting permission to pass through the land. Promises are made: Travel will be restricted to the King's Highway, and Israel will drink no water, eat no food, or tred on any field or vineyard. There are also differences between the two stories. In 20:14-21, Moses sent messengers to Edom; they recounted the exodus and underscored the kinship ties between the two peoples. In 21:21-22, Israel sends the messengers to Sihon, the exodus is not recounted, and no kinship ties are claimed.

The war is narrated in vv. 23-32. Verse 23 describes Sihon's attack, which takes place in the wilderness at Jahaz. The exact location of this city is unknown, although Jeremiah also mentions it (Jer 48:21, where it is referred to as Jahzah), and it appears in the Mesha Inscription as a location next to Dibon.[150] The war itself provides a transition from the wilderness to the Transjordan. The wilderness setting for the attack by Sihon signals that the battle is out of place in the book of Numbers, since Israel already left the wilderness on the way to Pisgah (20:18b-20). The battle fits better with the preceding events in 20:10-20, where Israel traveled to the Arnon (20:10-13) and celebrated their holy war victory (20:14-15).

Verses 24-25 and 31-32 outline the extent of Israel's conquest. The central location is Heshbon, the city of King Sihon (v. 25). The Israelites also take all the towns and villages of the Amorites, from the Arnon to the Jabbok as far as the Ammonite border (vv. 24-25). Verses 31-32 confirm the successful conquest and include the capture of Jazer, most likely a location further north (see 32:1). This northern location provides transition to the defeat of Og of Bashan in vv. 33-35.

The accounts of conquest in vv. 24-25 and 31-32 frame a poem about Heshbon (vv. 26-30). Scholars have sought to interpret the Song of Heshbon as an Israelite taunt of Sihon.[151] But v. 26 makes is clear that it is an Amorite ballad, celebrating Sihon's defeat of the Moabites.[152] The song reaffirms this conclusion. Verses 27-29 recount the defeat of the Moabites. Heshbon is identified as King Sihon's (v. 27b), as a result of his conquering the Moabites up to the Arnon. The act of conquest is pictured as fire and flames (v. 28). The Moabites are addressed directly in v. 29 with a lament that their god, Chemosh, has given their sons and daughters over as captives. As a result, the final line of v. 29 states that the Moabites are captives "to an Amorite king, Sihon." But this line is most likely a later addition, since it breaks the poetic structure of parallel lines in vv. 27b-29.

Interpretation of the poem becomes much more difficult in v. 30. The opening line is unclear. The NRSV translation, "So their posterity perished from Heshbon to Dibon," follows the LXX, which has changed נִיר (nîr, "yoke"?) to נִין (nîn, "offspring"). Hanson has suggested restoring v. 30 so that it reads, "The dominion of Moab has perished."[153] The closing line in v. 30 is also difficult. The NRSV has changed the relative pronoun (אֲשֶׁר ʾăšer) to the noun "fire" (אֵשׁ ʾēš) to translate, "and we laid waste until fire spread to Medaba."

The purpose of the Ballad of Heshbon is difficult to determine. By attributing the song to Israelites, scholars have sought to interpret it as a taunt against the Amorites. But the context resists this interpretation. Perhaps the ballad addresses Israel's relationship with the Moabites, since the defeat of the Moabites by Sihon is the central point of the poem. Jeremiah 48:45-46, where portions of the Ballad of Heshbon reappear as

---

149. See J. Van Seters, "The Conquest of Sihon's Kingdom: A Literary Examination," *JBL* 91 (1972) 182-97; and "Once Again—the Conquest of Sihon's Kingdom," *JBL* 99 (1980) 117-19; J. R. Bartlett, "The Conquest of Sihon's Kingdom: A Literary Re-examination," *JBL* 97 (1978) 347-51. Van Seters argues that Num 21:21-35 is the latest of the three texts, meaning that the pre-priestly history would be later than Deuteronomy and the Deuteronomistic History. Bartlett, on the other hand, argues that Deuteronomy is a later development of the story in Numbers.

150. *ANET,* 320.

151. Martin Noth, *Numbers,* OTL (Philadelphia: Westminster, 1968) 163-66; George Buchanan Gray, *Numbers,* ICC (Edinburgh: T. & T. Clark, 1903) 300.

152. See Jacob Milgrom, *Numbers,* JPS Torah Commentary (Philadelphia: JPS, 1990) 462-63.

153. P. D. Hanson, "The Song of Heshbon and David's Nir," *HTR* 61 (1968) 297-320, esp. 304.

judgment oracles against Moab, provides some support for this interpretation. The message of the Ballad of Heshbon at this juncture in Numbers is that the Moabites have no claim on Israelite property in the Transjordan, since they had been defeated already by Sihon.

The conquest of the Amorites in the Transjordan ends in vv. 33-35 with an account of the defeat of Og, king of Bashan. Yahweh commands Moses to attack Og, and his defeat takes place at Edrei. The subsequent defeat of Og is repeated in Deut 3:1-7. Deuteronomy 3:11 provides further lore on Og of Bashan as one of the last of the Rephaim. His bed measures nine cubits long (approx. 16 feet) and is preserved at the Ammonite city Rabbah.

REFLECTIONS

1. The power of leadership is dangerous. It can breed arrogance, making people intolerant of conflict and blind to due process. The fall of Moses is a paradigm of such abuse. He is impatient. Moses first demonstrated impatience when he killed the Egyptian taskmaster (Exod 2:11-15), forcing him to flee for his life. In Num 20:2-13, Moses' impatience cost him entry into the promised land. Anger forces him to exploit his power by not following the legal channels of accountability between God and Israel. In the process, he places himself above the law and plays God. The tragedy of the story resides in his blindness and confused motivation. He accuses the Israelites of being rebels in their legal complaint against God, when all the time he is the rebel himself. The continuing message of this tragedy is clear: No one is above the law, not even Moses the law-giver.

2. The paradoxical role of the snakes in the story of the bronze serpent invites theological reflection on their twofold role: Their bite kills; yet, the bronze serpent heals. What makes the snakes kill or heal? The Commentary indicated that the Israelites' complaint in this story is more an impatient tirade than a response to any life-threatening crisis. The people are sick of eating manna, and they desire something more interesting. God's response is to send fiery snakes to torment them. They are divine agents of death in response to Israel's trivial complaints about life in the wilderness. But the bronze snake has the power to heal. It is the medical antidote to the bite of the seraphim. Healing, however, does not just happen independently of the Israelites. The people are required to gaze at the snake in order to access its healing power.

Two themes for preaching emerge from the paradoxical role of the snakes. First, actions by Israel determine whether the seraphim are agents of death or life. Trivial and self-indulgent complaints lead to death. Faith in the power of the bronze serpent heals. This is also the message of Jesus to Nicodemus, when he refers to the story of the bronze snake: "And just as Moses lifted up the serpent in the wilderness, so must the Son of Man be lifted up, that whoever believes in him may have eternal life" (John 3:14-15). Belief in the Son of Man is a requirement for eternal life.

Second, even in their most trivial moment of pointless haranguing, God devises medicine to heal Israel. The message is that Israel cannot become so terminally ill that Yahweh is unable to heal them. Yahweh made this promise in the first wilderness story (Exod 15:22-26). The last story (Num 21:4-9) illustrates its truth. The same message returns in the discourse of Jesus to Nicodemus. The love of God has no boundaries, "for God so loved the world that he gave his only son" (John 3:16).

3. The bronze snake raises questions concerning the role of the church in health care. Does the snake really heal? The relationship between God, the church, and health care is an uneasy topic for contemporary Christians. It can be avoided by reading the story of the bronze serpent metaphorically, as an illustration about trusting in God and avoiding self-indulgent trivia. A more literal interpretation of the healing power of the bronze snake and its application to Jesus

(John 3:14-15) requires reflection on Christian sacraments. The healing power of God begins in baptism, when Christians are re-created. It is when God opens the medicine chest, infuses humans with divine serum, and defeats death. Communion contains divine vitamins that give strength. The church claims the promises of God to heal in these two sacraments. They are not metaphors about social formation; they are divine medicine. The healing power of God flows from one's having been re-created in baptism. The teaching of Jesus to Nicodemus reinforces the point when Jesus offers Nicodemus eternal life, telling him that he must be born anew. The reference is not to his funeral, but to his baptism. It is the moment of his new birth.

4. The two battles of Israel at Hormah (Num 14:39-45; 21:1-3) provide some guidelines for reflecting on just war. Warfare that is a response to oppression and includes no aspect of self-gain is possible for the people of God, according to the writers of Num 21:1-3. Here Israel responds to a threat, seeks divine guidance, and bans all personal profit from war. In contrast, war initiated by the people of God and undertaken out of fear for personal gain is condemned in Num 14:39-45. It is war that leads to death in the wilderness. (See the Reflections on 31:1–33:56 for further discussion of the *ḥērem* ban as sacrifice to God.)

NUMBERS 22:1–36:13

PREPARING FOR CANAAN ON THE PLAINS OF MOAB

OVERVIEW

Numbers 22:1–36:13 is the third and final section of the book of Numbers. The central theme of preparation for Canaan builds upon the two previous sections. The holiness of God was the central theme in 1:1–10:10. Holiness provided the backdrop for the priestly writers to explore the organization of the camp around the tabernacle. The wilderness journey of the first generation was the central theme of 10:11–21:35. In this section, both pre-priestly and priestly writers explored the life of faith as a journey with God through the threatening wilderness. Lack of faith expressed in the form of murmuring led to death, while faithfulness required that Israel follow God regardless of the threat. The first generation failed and died, leaving the divine promise of land to the second generation.

The third and final section in Numbers, 22:1–36:13, is signaled by a change of setting from the wilderness to the plains of Moab. This change of setting indicates a transition in theme from the wilderness wandering of the first generation to final preparations for Canaan by the second generation. The setting looks ahead to Jericho across the Jordan River and away from the desert that lies behind. The topics in 22:1–36:13 reinforce the anticipation of imminent possession of the land of Canaan. They include a new census of the people (chap. 26), instructions regarding the cultic calendar of Israel once the people enter the land (chaps. 28–29), cities of asylum in Canaan (chap. 35), and detailed laws concerning inheritance (chaps. 27; 32; 34; 36).

There are two accounts of Israel's final preparation for entering Canaan. The pre-priestly history moves briskly in four stages: the blessing of Balaam, when Israel is threatened by Balak's desire to have them cursed (chaps. 22–24); the sin

at Baal Peor (25:1-5); the inheritance of land in the Transjordan (chap. 32); and a summary of Israel's wilderness travels (chap. 33).

The priestly history greatly enlarges Moses' instructions to Israel in 22:1–36:13. Yet it follows in general the outline of the pre-priestly history. The threats to Israel on the plains of Moab are expanded with the addition of the Midianites. The priestly writers include the Midianites with Balak, king of Moab, as those who wish that Israel be cursed (22:4, 7). They also include the Midianites in Israel's sin at Baal Peor (25:6-18), and they add an account of holy war against the Midianites (chap. 31). Thus the Midianites become the central threat to Israel on the plains of Moab.

The priestly writers also expand the second part of the pre-priestly history concerning laws of inheritance. They begin this section with a second census (chap. 26), which signals a new beginning for the second generation of Israelites. Then, inheritance laws for daughters frame an extended section of law governing Israel's possession of the land. The inheritance of the daughters of Zelophehad appears in 27:1-11 and chap. 36. Within this framework, the priestly writers address a range of issues surrounding the inheritance of the land, including the announcement of the death of Moses and guidelines for succession of leadership (27:12-23), a cultic calendar and legislation regarding vows (chaps. 28–30), and holy war (chap. 31). Most noteworthy, they extend the rights of inheritance to include all of the promised land of Canaan (chaps. 34–36). The pre-priestly history is limited in scope to the inheritance of the Transjordan area (chap. 32).

The priestly expansion of 22:1–36:13 was undertaken with an eye on Deuteronomy, since the divine announcement to Moses of his impending death in 27:12-14 is not fulfilled until the closing chapters of Deuteronomy (Deut 32:48-52; 34:1-7). Thus the pattern of divine announcement and fulfillment, so characteristic of priestly writers, is employed at the close of the book of Numbers to incorporate the entire book of Deuteronomy into the final section of their history under the theme of "Instructions for Inheritance."

The preceding summary indicates that most of the literature in Numbers 22:1–36:13 is part of the priestly history, even though the pre-priestly literature provides the general structure for the section. Commentary will proceed in two parts. Chapters 22–25 will explore threats to Israel on the plains of Moab by other nations. Chapters 26–36 conclude the book by looking ahead to Israel's future life in the land.

NUMBERS 22:1–25:18, THREATS TO ISRAEL ON THE PLAINS OF MOAB

OVERVIEW

Points of tension change throughout the book of Numbers. Numbers 1:1–10:10 focused on the internal life of Israel within the camp. The danger of holiness within the tabernacle gave rise to the layout of the camp as a means to protect Israel as they lived in proximity to God. The transition from the stationary camp at Sinai to the wilderness march in 10:11–21:25 continued to focus on Israel's relationship with God. Central themes in this section included lack of faith in the divine promise of land, conflicts over leadership, and various forms of defilement. All of these threats were self-imposed, internal conflicts over land and leadership, and they led to the death of the first generation.

In 22:1–25:18, the point of tension changes from internal to external threats to the wilderness community. This change in focus is signaled by a new setting, the plains of Moab, and by a new cast of characters, the second generation. Two somewhat different external threats are explored. The first is the danger of being cursed by another nation. The story of Balak and Balaam in chaps. 22–24 probes the protective role of God outside the boundaries of the Israelite community. Israel plays no active role in this story. The second external threat is the danger of seduction of worshiping the gods of another nation. In contrast to the threat from Balak and Balaam, Israel is a central character in 25:1-5, where their sin at Baal Peor illustrates how other nations can defile Israel through intermarriage and syncretistic worship, and thus bring death into the camp. The priestly writers intensify this external danger by inserting a series of stories about the Midianites (22:4, 7; 25:6-18).

Numbers 22:1–24:25, The Blessing of Balaam

NIV

22 Then the Israelites traveled to the plains of Moab and camped along the Jordan across from Jericho.[a]

[2] Now Balak son of Zippor saw all that Israel had done to the Amorites, [3] and Moab was terrified because there were so many people. Indeed,

[a] 1 Hebrew *Jordan of Jericho;* possibly an ancient name for the Jordan River

NRSV

22 The Israelites set out, and camped in the plains of Moab across the Jordan from Jericho. [2] Now Balak son of Zippor saw all that Israel had done to the Amorites. [3] Moab was in great dread of the people, because they were so numerous; Moab was overcome with fear of the people of Israel. [4] And Moab said to the elders of Midian, "This horde will now lick up all that is

Moab was filled with dread because of the Israelites.

⁴The Moabites said to the elders of Midian, "This horde is going to lick up everything around us, as an ox licks up the grass of the field."

So Balak son of Zippor, who was king of Moab at that time, ⁵sent messengers to summon Balaam son of Beor, who was at Pethor, near the River,ᵃ in his native land. Balak said:

"A people has come out of Egypt; they cover the face of the land and have settled next to me. ⁶Now come and put a curse on these people, because they are too powerful for me. Perhaps then I will be able to defeat them and drive them out of the country. For I know that those you bless are blessed, and those you curse are cursed."

⁷The elders of Moab and Midian left, taking with them the fee for divination. When they came to Balaam, they told him what Balak had said.

⁸"Spend the night here," Balaam said to them, "and I will bring you back the answer the LORD gives me." So the Moabite princes stayed with him.

⁹God came to Balaam and asked, "Who are these men with you?"

¹⁰Balaam said to God, "Balak son of Zippor, king of Moab, sent me this message: ¹¹'A people that has come out of Egypt covers the face of the land. Now come and put a curse on them for me. Perhaps then I will be able to fight them and drive them away.'"

¹²But God said to Balaam, "Do not go with them. You must not put a curse on those people, because they are blessed."

¹³The next morning Balaam got up and said to Balak's princes, "Go back to your own country, for the LORD has refused to let me go with you."

¹⁴So the Moabite princes returned to Balak and said, "Balaam refused to come with us."

¹⁵Then Balak sent other princes, more numerous and more distinguished than the first. ¹⁶They came to Balaam and said:

"This is what Balak son of Zippor says: Do not let anything keep you from coming to me, ¹⁷because I will reward you handsomely and

ᵃ5 That is, the Euphrates

around us, as an ox licks up the grass of the field." Now Balak son of Zippor was king of Moab at that time. ⁵He sent messengers to Balaam son of Beor at Pethor, which is on the Euphrates, in the land of Amaw,ᵃ to summon him, saying, "A people has come out of Egypt; they have spread over the face of the earth, and they have settled next to me. ⁶Come now, curse this people for me, since they are stronger than I; perhaps I shall be able to defeat them and drive them from the land; for I know that whomever you bless is blessed, and whomever you curse is cursed."

⁷So the elders of Moab and the elders of Midian departed with the fees for divination in their hand; and they came to Balaam, and gave him Balak's message. ⁸He said to them, "Stay here tonight, and I will bring back word to you, just as the LORD speaks to me"; so the officials of Moab stayed with Balaam. ⁹God came to Balaam and said, "Who are these men with you?" ¹⁰Balaam said to God, "King Balak son of Zippor of Moab, has sent me this message: ¹¹'A people has come out of Egypt and has spread over the face of the earth; now come, curse them for me; perhaps I shall be able to fight against them and drive them out.'" ¹²God said to Balaam, "You shall not go with them; you shall not curse the people, for they are blessed." ¹³So Balaam rose in the morning, and said to the officials of Balak, "Go to your own land, for the LORD has refused to let me go with you." ¹⁴So the officials of Moab rose and went to Balak, and said, "Balaam refuses to come with us."

¹⁵Once again Balak sent officials, more numerous and more distinguished than these. ¹⁶They came to Balaam and said to him, "Thus says Balak son of Zippor: 'Do not let anything hinder you from coming to me; ¹⁷for I will surely do you great honor, and whatever you say to me I will do; come, curse this people for me.'" ¹⁸But Balaam replied to the servants of Balak, "Although Balak were to give me his house full of silver and gold, I could not go beyond the command of the LORD my God, to do less or more. ¹⁹You remain here, as the others did, so that I may learn what more the LORD may say to me." ²⁰That night God came to Balaam and said to him, "If the men have

ᵃ Or land of his kinsfolk

NIV

do whatever you say. Come and put a curse on these people for me."

[18] But Balaam answered them, "Even if Balak gave me his palace filled with silver and gold, I could not do anything great or small to go beyond the command of the LORD my God. [19] Now stay here tonight as the others did, and I will find out what else the LORD will tell me."

[20] That night God came to Balaam and said, "Since these men have come to summon you, go with them, but do only what I tell you."

[21] Balaam got up in the morning, saddled his donkey and went with the princes of Moab. [22] But God was very angry when he went, and the angel of the LORD stood in the road to oppose him. Balaam was riding on his donkey, and his two servants were with him. [23] When the donkey saw the angel of the LORD standing in the road with a drawn sword in his hand, she turned off the road into a field. Balaam beat her to get her back on the road.

[24] Then the angel of the LORD stood in a narrow path between two vineyards, with walls on both sides. [25] When the donkey saw the angel of the LORD, she pressed close to the wall, crushing Balaam's foot against it. So he beat her again.

[26] Then the angel of the LORD moved on ahead and stood in a narrow place where there was no room to turn, either to the right or to the left. [27] When the donkey saw the angel of the LORD, she lay down under Balaam, and he was angry and beat her with his staff. [28] Then the LORD opened the donkey's mouth, and she said to Balaam, "What have I done to you to make you beat me these three times?"

[29] Balaam answered the donkey, "You have made a fool of me! If I had a sword in my hand, I would kill you right now."

[30] The donkey said to Balaam, "Am I not your own donkey, which you have always ridden, to this day? Have I been in the habit of doing this to you?"

"No," he said.

[31] Then the LORD opened Balaam's eyes, and he saw the angel of the LORD standing in the road with his sword drawn. So he bowed low and fell facedown.

[32] The angel of the LORD asked him, "Why have

NRSV

come to summon you, get up and go with them; but do only what I tell you to do." [21] So Balaam got up in the morning, saddled his donkey, and went with the officials of Moab.

[22] God's anger was kindled because he was going, and the angel of the LORD took his stand in the road as his adversary. Now he was riding on the donkey, and his two servants were with him. [23] The donkey saw the angel of the LORD standing in the road, with a drawn sword in his hand; so the donkey turned off the road, and went into the field; and Balaam struck the donkey, to turn it back onto the road. [24] Then the angel of the LORD stood in a narrow path between the vineyards, with a wall on either side. [25] When the donkey saw the angel of the LORD, it scraped against the wall, and scraped Balaam's foot against the wall; so he struck it again. [26] Then the angel of the LORD went ahead, and stood in a narrow place, where there was no way to turn either to the right or to the left. [27] When the donkey saw the angel of the LORD, it lay down under Balaam; and Balaam's anger was kindled, and he struck the donkey with his staff. [28] Then the LORD opened the mouth of the donkey, and it said to Balaam, "What have I done to you, that you have struck me these three times?" [29] Balaam said to the donkey, "Because you have made a fool of me! I wish I had a sword in my hand! I would kill you right now!" [30] But the donkey said to Balaam, "Am I not your donkey, which you have ridden all your life to this day? Have I been in the habit of treating you this way?" And he said, "No."

[31] Then the LORD opened the eyes of Balaam, and he saw the angel of the LORD standing in the road, with his drawn sword in his hand; and he bowed down, falling on his face. [32] The angel of the LORD said to him, "Why have you struck your donkey these three times? I have come out as an adversary, because your way is perverse[a] before me. [33] The donkey saw me, and turned away from me these three times. If it had not turned away from me, surely just now I would have killed you and let it live." [34] Then Balaam said to the angel of the LORD, "I have sinned, for I did not know that you were standing in the road to oppose me. Now therefore, if it is displeasing to you, I will

[a] Meaning of Heb uncertain

you beaten your donkey these three times? I have come here to oppose you because your path is a reckless one before me.[a] [33]The donkey saw me and turned away from me these three times. If she had not turned away, I would certainly have killed you by now, but I would have spared her."

[34]Balaam said to the angel of the LORD, "I have sinned. I did not realize you were standing in the road to oppose me. Now if you are displeased, I will go back."

[35]The angel of the LORD said to Balaam, "Go with the men, but speak only what I tell you." So Balaam went with the princes of Balak.

[36]When Balak heard that Balaam was coming, he went out to meet him at the Moabite town on the Arnon border, at the edge of his territory. [37]Balak said to Balaam, "Did I not send you an urgent summons? Why didn't you come to me? Am I really not able to reward you?"

[38]"Well, I have come to you now," Balaam replied. "But can I say just anything? I must speak only what God puts in my mouth."

[39]Then Balaam went with Balak to Kiriath Huzoth. [40]Balak sacrificed cattle and sheep, and gave some to Balaam and the princes who were with him. [41]The next morning Balak took Balaam up to Bamoth Baal, and from there he saw part of the people.

23 Balaam said, "Build me seven altars here, and prepare seven bulls and seven rams for me." [2]Balak did as Balaam said, and the two of them offered a bull and a ram on each altar.

[3]Then Balaam said to Balak, "Stay here beside your offering while I go aside. Perhaps the LORD will come to meet with me. Whatever he reveals to me I will tell you." Then he went off to a barren height.

[4]God met with him, and Balaam said, "I have prepared seven altars, and on each altar I have offered a bull and a ram."

[5]The LORD put a message in Balaam's mouth and said, "Go back to Balak and give him this message."

[6]So he went back to him and found him standing beside his offering, with all the princes of Moab. [7]Then Balaam uttered his oracle:

[a]32 The meaning of the Hebrew for this clause is uncertain.

return home." [35]The angel of the LORD said to Balaam, "Go with the men; but speak only what I tell you to speak." So Balaam went on with the officials of Balak.

[36]When Balak heard that Balaam had come, he went out to meet him at Ir-moab, on the boundary formed by the Arnon, at the farthest point of the boundary. [37]Balak said to Balaam, "Did I not send to summon you? Why did you not come to me? Am I not able to honor you?" [38]Balaam said to Balak, "I have come to you now, but do I have power to say just anything? The word God puts in my mouth, that is what I must say." [39]Then Balaam went with Balak, and they came to Kiriath-huzoth. [40]Balak sacrificed oxen and sheep, and sent them to Balaam and to the officials who were with him.

[41]On the next day Balak took Balaam and brought him up to Bamoth-baal; and from there he could see part of the people of Israel.[a]

23 [1]Then Balaam said to Balak, "Build me seven altars here, and prepare seven bulls and seven rams for me." [2]Balak did as Balaam had said; and Balak and Balaam offered a bull and a ram on each altar. [3]Then Balaam said to Balak, "Stay here beside your burnt offerings while I go aside. Perhaps the LORD will come to meet me. Whatever he shows me I will tell you." And he went to a bare height.

[4]Then God met Balaam; and Balaam said to him, "I have arranged the seven altars, and have offered a bull and a ram on each altar." [5]The LORD put a word in Balaam's mouth, and said, "Return to Balak, and this is what you must say." [6]So he returned to Balak,[b] who was standing beside his burnt offerings with all the officials of Moab. [7]Then Balaam[c] uttered his oracle, saying:

"Balak has brought me from Aram,
　the king of Moab from the eastern
　　mountains:
'Come, curse Jacob for me;
　Come, denounce Israel!'
[8] How can I curse whom God has not cursed?
　How can I denounce those whom the
　　LORD has not denounced?
[9] For from the top of the crags I see him,
　from the hills I behold him;

[a] Heb lacks *of Israel*　[b] Heb *him*　[c] Heb *he*

NIV

"Balak brought me from Aram,
  the king of Moab from the eastern
    mountains.
'Come,' he said, 'curse Jacob for me;
  come, denounce Israel.'
⁸How can I curse
  those whom God has not cursed?
How can I denounce
  those whom the Lᴏʀᴅ has not denounced?
⁹From the rocky peaks I see them,
  from the heights I view them.
I see a people who live apart
  and do not consider themselves one of the
    nations.
¹⁰Who can count the dust of Jacob
  or number the fourth part of Israel?
Let me die the death of the righteous,
  and may my end be like theirs!"

¹¹Balak said to Balaam, "What have you done
to me? I brought you to curse my enemies, but
you have done nothing but bless them!"

¹²He answered, "Must I not speak what the
Lᴏʀᴅ puts in my mouth?"

¹³Then Balak said to him, "Come with me to
another place where you can see them; you will
see only a part but not all of them. And from
there, curse them for me." ¹⁴So he took him to
the field of Zophim on the top of Pisgah, and
there he built seven altars and offered a bull and
a ram on each altar.

¹⁵Balaam said to Balak, "Stay here beside your
offering while I meet with him over there."

¹⁶The Lᴏʀᴅ met with Balaam and put a message
in his mouth and said, "Go back to Balak and
give him this message."

¹⁷So he went to him and found him standing
beside his offering, with the princes of Moab.
Balak asked him, "What did the Lᴏʀᴅ say?"

¹⁸Then he uttered his oracle:
"Arise, Balak, and listen;
  hear me, son of Zippor.
¹⁹God is not a man, that he should lie,
  nor a son of man, that he should change
    his mind.
Does he speak and then not act?
  Does he promise and not fulfill?
²⁰I have received a command to bless;
  he has blessed, and I cannot change it.

NRSV

Here is a people living alone,
  and not reckoning itself among the
    nations!
¹⁰ Who can count the dust of Jacob,
  or number the dust-cloudᵃ of Israel?
Let me die the death of the upright,
  and let my end be like his!"

11Then Balak said to Balaam, "What have you
done to me? I brought you to curse my enemies,
but now you have done nothing but bless them."
¹²He answered, "Must I not take care to say what
the Lᴏʀᴅ puts into my mouth?"

13So Balak said to him, "Come with me to
another place from which you may see them; you
shall see only part of them, and shall not see them
all; then curse them for me from there." ¹⁴So he
took him to the field of Zophim, to the top of
Pisgah. He built seven altars, and offered a bull
and a ram on each altar. ¹⁵Balaam said to Balak,
"Stand here beside your burnt offerings, while I
meet the Lᴏʀᴅ over there." ¹⁶The Lᴏʀᴅ met
Balaam, put a word into his mouth, and said,
"Return to Balak, and this is what you shall say."
¹⁷When he came to him, he was standing beside
his burnt offerings with the officials of Moab.
Balak said to him, "What has the Lᴏʀᴅ said?"
¹⁸Then Balaam uttered his oracle, saying:
"Rise, Balak, and hear;
  listen to me, O son of Zippor:
¹⁹ God is not a human being, that he should
    lie,
  or a mortal, that he should change his
    mind.
Has he promised, and will he not do it?
  Has he spoken, and will he not fulfill it?
²⁰ See, I received a command to bless;
  he has blessed, and I cannot revoke it.
²¹ He has not beheld misfortune in Jacob;
  nor has he seen trouble in Israel.
The Lᴏʀᴅ their God is with them,
  acclaimed as a king among them.
²² God, who brings them out of Egypt,
  is like the horns of a wild ox for them.
²³ Surely there is no enchantment against
    Jacob,
  no divination against Israel;
now it shall be said of Jacob and Israel,

ᵃ Or fourth part

174

NIV

21"No misfortune is seen in Jacob,
　no misery observed in Israel.*d*
The LORD their God is with them;
　the shout of the King is among them.
22God brought them out of Egypt;
　they have the strength of a wild ox.
23There is no sorcery against Jacob,
　no divination against Israel.
It will now be said of Jacob
　and of Israel, 'See what God has done!'
24The people rise like a lioness;
　they rouse themselves like a lion
that does not rest till he devours his prey
　and drinks the blood of his victims."

25Then Balak said to Balaam, "Neither curse them at all nor bless them at all!"

26Balaam answered, "Did I not tell you I must do whatever the LORD says?"

27Then Balak said to Balaam, "Come, let me take you to another place. Perhaps it will please God to let you curse them for me from there." 28And Balak took Balaam to the top of Peor, overlooking the wasteland.

29Balaam said, "Build me seven altars here, and prepare seven bulls and seven rams for me." 30Balak did as Balaam had said, and offered a bull and a ram on each altar.

24 Now when Balaam saw that it pleased the LORD to bless Israel, he did not resort to sorcery as at other times, but turned his face toward the desert. 2When Balaam looked out and saw Israel encamped tribe by tribe, the Spirit of God came upon him 3and he uttered his oracle:

"The oracle of Balaam son of Beor,
　the oracle of one whose eye sees clearly,
4the oracle of one who hears the words of
　　God,
　who sees a vision from the Almighty,*e*
　who falls prostrate, and whose eyes are
　　opened:

5"How beautiful are your tents, O Jacob,
　your dwelling places, O Israel!

6"Like valleys they spread out,
　like gardens beside a river,
like aloes planted by the LORD,
　like cedars beside the waters.

NRSV

'See what God has done!'
24 Look, a people rising up like a lioness,
　and rousing itself like a lion!
It does not lie down until it has eaten the
　　prey
　and drunk the blood of the slain."

25Then Balak said to Balaam, "Do not curse them at all, and do not bless them at all." 26But Balaam answered Balak, "Did I not tell you, 'Whatever the LORD says, that is what I must do'?"

27So Balak said to Balaam, "Come now, I will take you to another place; perhaps it will please God that you may curse them for me from there." 28So Balak took Balaam to the top of Peor, which overlooks the wasteland.*a* 29Balaam said to Balak, "Build me seven altars here, and prepare seven bulls and seven rams for me." 30So Balak did as Balaam had said, and offered a bull and a ram on each altar.

24 Now Balaam saw that it pleased the LORD to bless Israel, so he did not go, as at other times, to look for omens, but set his face toward the wilderness. 2Balaam looked up and saw Israel camping tribe by tribe. Then the spirit of God came upon him, 3and he uttered his oracle, saying:

"The oracle of Balaam son of Beor,
　the oracle of the man whose eye is clear,*b*
4 the oracle of one who hears the words of
　　God,
　who sees the vision of the Almighty,*c*
　who falls down, but with eyes uncovered:
5 how fair are your tents, O Jacob,
　your encampments, O Israel!
6 Like palm groves that stretch far away,
　like gardens beside a river,
　like aloes that the LORD has planted,
　like cedar trees beside the waters.
7 Water shall flow from his buckets,
　and his seed shall have abundant water,
his king shall be higher than Agag,
　and his kingdom shall be exalted.
8 God who brings him out of Egypt,
　is like the horns of a wild ox for him;
he shall devour the nations that are his foes
　and break their bones.
　He shall strike with his arrows.*d*

NIV

7Water will flow from their buckets;
  their seed will have abundant water.

"Their king will be greater than Agag;
  their kingdom will be exalted.

8"God brought them out of Egypt;
  they have the strength of a wild ox.
They devour hostile nations
  and break their bones in pieces;
  with their arrows they pierce them.
9Like a lion they crouch and lie down,
  like a lioness—who dares to rouse them?

"May those who bless you be blessed
  and those who curse you be cursed!"

10Then Balak's anger burned against Balaam. He struck his hands together and said to him, "I summoned you to curse my enemies, but you have blessed them these three times. 11Now leave at once and go home! I said I would reward you handsomely, but the LORD has kept you from being rewarded."

12Balaam answered Balak, "Did I not tell the messengers you sent me, 13'Even if Balak gave me his palace filled with silver and gold, I could not do anything of my own accord, good or bad, to go beyond the command of the LORD—and I must say only what the LORD says'? 14Now I am going back to my people, but come, let me warn you of what this people will do to your people in days to come."

15Then he uttered his oracle:

"The oracle of Balaam son of Beor,
  the oracle of one whose eye sees clearly,
16the oracle of one who hears the words of
      God,
  who has knowledge from the Most High,
  who sees a vision from the Almighty,
  who falls prostrate, and whose eyes are
      opened:

17"I see him, but not now;
  I behold him, but not near.
A star will come out of Jacob;
  a scepter will rise out of Israel.
He will crush the foreheads of Moab,
  the skulls[a] of[b] all the sons of Sheth.[c]
18Edom will be conquered;

a17 Samaritan Pentateuch (see also Jer. 48:45); the meaning of the word in the Masoretic Text is uncertain.   b17 Or possibly Moab, / batter   c17 Or all the noisy boasters

NRSV

9 He crouched, he lay down like a lion,
  and like a lioness; who will rouse him up?
Blessed is everyone who blesses you,
  and cursed is everyone who curses you."

10Then Balak's anger was kindled against Balaam, and he struck his hands together. Balak said to Balaam, "I summoned you to curse my enemies, but instead you have blessed them these three times. 11Now be off with you! Go home! I said, 'I will reward you richly,' but the LORD has denied you any reward." 12And Balaam said to Balak, "Did I not tell your messengers whom you sent to me, 13'If Balak should give me his house full of silver and gold, I would not be able to go beyond the word of the LORD, to do either good or bad of my own will; what the LORD says, that is what I will say'? 14So now, I am going to my people; let me advise you what this people will do to your people in days to come."

15So he uttered his oracle, saying:
"The oracle of Balaam son of Beor,
  the oracle of the man whose eye is clear,[a]
16 the oracle of one who hears the words of
      God,
  and knows the knowledge of the Most
      High,[b]
who sees the vision of the Almighty,[c]
  who falls down, but with his eyes
      uncovered:
17 I see him, but not now;
  I behold him, but not near—
a star shall come out of Jacob,
  and a scepter shall rise out of Israel;
it shall crush the borderlands[d] of Moab,
  and the territory[e] of all the Shethites.
18 Edom will become a possession,
  Seir a possession of its enemies,[f]
  while Israel does valiantly.
19 One out of Jacob shall rule,
  and destroy the survivors of Ir."

20Then he looked on Amalek, and uttered his oracle, saying:
"First among the nations was Amalek,
  but its end is to perish forever."

21Then he looked on the Kenite, and uttered his oracle, saying:

a Or closed or open   b Or of Elyon   c Traditional rendering of Heb Shaddai   d Or forehead   e Some Mss read skull   f Heb Seir, its enemies, a possession

NIV

Seir, his enemy, will be conquered,
but Israel will grow strong.
[19]A ruler will come out of Jacob
and destroy the survivors of the city."
[20]Then Balaam saw Amalek and uttered his
oracle:

"Amalek was first among the nations,
but he will come to ruin at last."
[21]Then he saw the Kenites and uttered his
oracle:

"Your dwelling place is secure,
your nest is set in a rock;
[22]yet you Kenites will be destroyed
when Asshur takes you captive."
[23]Then he uttered his oracle:

"Ah, who can live when God does this?[a]
[24]   Ships will come from the shores of Kittim;
they will subdue Asshur and Eber,
but they too will come to ruin."
[25]Then Balaam got up and returned home and
Balak went his own way.

[a]23 Masoretic Text; with a different word division of the Hebrew A
people will gather from the north.

NRSV

"Enduring is your dwelling place,
and your nest is set in the rock;
[22] yet Kain is destined for burning.
How long shall Asshur take you away
captive?"
[23]Again he uttered his oracle, saying:
"Alas, who shall live when God does this?
[24]   But ships shall come from Kittim
and shall afflict Asshur and Eber;
and he also shall perish forever."
[25]Then Balaam got up and went back to his
place, and Balak also went his way.

COMMENTARY

Numbers 22–24 opens with Israel encamped on the plains of Moab beside the Jordan River, across from Jericho. The change in setting marks a transition from the first generation in the wilderness to the second generation. Israel has grown into a great nation, fulfilling the divine blessing of fertility to the ancestors (Gen 12:1-4). The second generation is so numerous, in fact, that it threatens Balak, the king of Moab, in much the same way that the previous generation had threatened Pharaoh in Egypt (Exodus 1–2). Numbers 22–24 tell how Balak sought to weaken Israel's ability to reproduce by hiring a Mesopotamian diviner named Balaam to curse them.

The Central Theme of Numbers 22–24. The central problem in these chapters is the external threat that Balak poses to Israel through his request to have Balaam curse them. Israel is unaware of this threat. Thus the people play no active role in the story. Yahweh, however, is an active character. Through a series of revelations to Balaam, God protects Israel from the threat of a curse by commanding only blessings from the seer. The whole story ends with Israel remaining unaware of either the threat or God's salvation.

Divine revelation to a non-Israelite diviner is unusual in the Old Testament, and it creates tension for the storytellers. One message of the story is comforting: God's protective care for the people of God is universal in scope, influencing actions well beyond Israel's immediate horizon. Another message of the story is more problematic: The revelation of Yahweh, and even acts of salvation, are not limited to the Israelites or their cultic practices. Balaam, the Mesopotamian, is a Yahwistic diviner, even though he is neither an Israelite nor part of the wilderness community; nor does he participate in the cult of the tabernacle. This tension provides insight into the history of tradition that surrounds Balaam in general and the composition of Numbers 22–24 in particular.

The Legend of Balaam Outside of the

Old Testament. The discovery in 1967 at Tell Deir 'Alla of a text about a diviner named Balaam son of Beor has provided unexpected information concerning the legendary significance of Balaam as a diviner who lived in the Transjordan. Tell Deir 'Alla is located near the Jabbok and Jordan rivers. The text was written on lime-plaster, which appears to have covered either a pillar or a wall of an eighth-century BCE temple. One hundred and nineteen fragments of the lime-plaster were recovered, but only twelve pieces fit together.[154] These twelve pieces tell of the night vision of a seer, Balaam son of Beor, who sees a coming disaster, causing him to fast and to weep. Balaam describes his vision of a divine counsel, in which the goddess Shagar (most likely a fertility goddess) and the Shaddai-gods decide to cause a drought on earth. The drought is accompanied by reversals in nature and in society. Balaam warns that darkness will eclipse light, weak birds will overpower stronger ones, the wise will be laughed at by their pupils, and the poor will take the place of the rich.[155] The Deir 'Alla text provides two starting points for interpreting Numbers 22–24. First, the role of Balaam in Numbers 22–24 arises from Israel's larger cultural context, where the character had achieved legendary significance as a diviner by the eighth century BCE. Second, Balaam appears to be a positive character in the Deir 'Alla text, rather than a negative or sinister diviner.

The Poems in Numbers 22–24. These chapters were composed around four poems, or oracles, of Balaam. Israel is the subject of the first three oracles, while the final poem predicts disaster on nations that surround Israel. In the oracles directed to Israel, Balaam addresses the central themes of the Pentateuch. These themes are the divine promises to the ancestors that they would be fertile (e.g., Gen 12:1-4) and that they would possess a land (e.g., Gen 17:1-8). In the first poem (23:7-10), Balaam affirms that the fertility of Israel is a result of God's blessing and that, for this reason, he cannot curse them. In the second (23:18-24), Balaam underscores the reliability of

God's promises to Israel against any attempt at divination. And in the third (24:3-9), Balaam predicts that Israel will possess land, become a kingdom, and be successful in warfare. The fourth poem (24:15-24) changes in focus from Israel to other nations. It is a series of smaller oracles about imminent tragedy awaiting a number of nations, including Moab, Edom, Amalek, the Kenites, and Asshur.

The age of the poems is debated. W. F. Albright argued that the poems originated very early in Israel's history, perhaps as early as the thirteenth century BCE, because of similarities in grammar, language, and writing style to other northwest Semitic texts of this period.[156] Others, like George Buchanan Gray and Sigmund Mowinckel, argued that the nationalistic perspective of the poems and their optimistic outlook suggested, instead, the early monarchical period.[157] There is further debate concerning the literary context of the poems. If composed in the thirteenth century BCE, they were meant to be read independently from their present narrative context. Gray writes that "the poems were obviously written to fit into a story of Balaam: see 23:7ff., 18, 20; 24:3, 15; though it is only in the first two that a close structural connection with a story of Balaam is found."[158] Jacob Milgrom extended this argument to suggest that all the poems were composed for the sake of the narrative.[159] If the poems are early and independent, then they constitute the oldest level of tradition in Numbers about a non-Israelite diviner name Balaam. But they may also simply reflect a more archaic writing style that was fashioned for literary effect in Numbers 22–24. Regardless of their date of composition, it is clear that throughout the oracles Balaam is presented in a positive light as a diviner who speaks only what Yahweh reveals to him.

The Narrative in Numbers 22–24. The narrative portions of these chapters contain a history of commentary, which has made the flow of the story uneven (especially in chap. 22). Clarifications within the text about central char-

---

154. See Klaas A. D. Smelik, *Writings from Ancient Israel: A Handbook of Historical and Religious Documents,* trans. G. I. Davies (Louisville: Westminster/John Knox, 1991) 79-92.

155. For translation and exegesis of the Deir 'Alla text, see Jo Ann Hackett, *The Balaam Text from Deir 'Alla, HSM* 31 (Chico, Calif.: Scholars Press, 1984). For interpretation of the role of Balaam in the Deir 'Alla text as a diviner and seer, see Michael S. Moore, *The Balaam Traditions: Their Character and Development,* SBLDS 113 (Atlanta: Scholars Press, 1990) 66-96.

156. W. F. Albright, "The Oracles of Balaam," *JBL* 63 (1944) 207-33. See the review of Albright's work by D. A. Robertson, *The Linguistic Evidence in Dating Early Hebrew Poetry,* SBLDS 3 (Missoula, Mont.: Scholars Press, 1972) 145.

157. George Buchanan Gray, *Numbers,* ICC (Edinburgh: T. & T. Clark, 1903) 313-14; Sigmund Mowinckel, "Die Ursprung der Bil'amsage," *ZAW* 7 (1930) 233-71, esp. 268-69.

158. Gray, *Numbers,* 313.

159. Jacob Milgrom, *Numbers,* JPS Torah Commentary (Philadelphia: JPS, 1990) 467-68.

acters and locations are one indication of additions to the narrative. For example, later writers felt it necessary to identify Balak as the king of Moab (22:4*b*), even though this information was already assumed at the outset of the story (22:2). There is also a more precise identification of Balak's advisers as "elders of Moab" (זִקְנֵי מוֹאָב *ziqnê-mô'āb*, 22:7), in addition to their role as "princes of Moab" (שָׂרֵי-מוֹאָב *śārê-mô'ab*, 22:8, 15, 21). The additional notice that Balaam's home at Pethor on the Euphrates was "in the land of Amaw" (22:5) may also be later commentary.[160]

Later writers also added new motifs and episodes to the story, of which two stand out. The first is the inclusion of the "elders of Midian" (זִקְנֵי מִדְיָן *ziqnê midyān*, 22:4, 7) as co-conspirators with Balak against Israel. The priestly writers are most likely responsible for the addition of this motif to the story, since it provides the basis for their story of holy war against Midian in chap. 31. The second addition is the story of Balaam's journey to Balak (22:22-35). This episode disrupts the larger narrative in a number of ways. It creates a literary tension between the divine command that Balaam go to Balak (22:20) and the divine anger against Balaam for disobeying God by journeying to Balak (22:22). This episode also introduces a negative interpretation of Balaam in what would otherwise be a positive story of a non-Israelite seer. The authors of 22:22-35 may have been priestly writers, but such an identification is by no means clear.

The literary overview of the narrative in Numbers 22–24 indicates a history of composition. The earliest version is a positive story of a non-Israelite seer, Balaam, who serves Yahweh and is unable to curse Israel as Balak requests. Both the poems and the narrative (excluding 22:22-35) idealize Balaam as a seer. He is frequently presented as using the divine name "Yahweh" ("LORD") in Numbers 22–24, which reinforces the positive portrait of him. In the opening narrative (22:1-21), Balaam refers to Yahweh four times (22:8, 13, 18, 19); in one instance, he even confesses that Yahweh is his God (22:18). In the sequence of oracles (22:36–24:25), Balaam continues to use the name "Yahweh," both in the narrative (23:5, 12, 23; 24:13) and in the poetry (23:8, 21; 24:6). Scholars debate whether the positive story of

Balaam existed independently or whether it was composed by pre-priestly writers to fit in at this point in their history.[161] A clear resolution to this debate is not possible from a literary study of these chapters.

The addition of 22:22-35 introduces a new interpretation of Balaam as an anti-hero. In this episode, he is presented as a disobedient seer who is more blind to divine leading than is his donkey. The authors of this episode are difficult to identify. They may have been priestly writers, since it is clear that the priestly writers interpret Balaam negatively, associating him with the Midianites in Numbers 31. Thus it is possible that the positive portrayal of Balaam reflects the pre-priestly version of Numbers 22–24 and that the negative reinterpretation of this story is by the priestly writers. In this case, the latter would have included the insertion of the Midianites as co-conspirators with Balak (22:4, 7), along with a negative episode about Balaam's disobedience and blindness (22:22-35). The death of both the Midianites and Balaam in the priestly account of holy war in chap. 31 lends support to this hypothesis.

But the language of Num 22:22-35 does not show clear signs of priestly authorship. In fact, the frequent use of the "messenger of Yahweh" (מַלְאַךְ יְהוָה *mal'ak YHWH*, 22:22-27, 31-32, 34-35) is a strong argument against priestly authorship, since this designation of God is not part of their theological vocabulary. In this case, the history of composition does not follow the pattern of pre-priestly and priestly authorship. Thus the literary study of the poetry and the narrative points to several possible histories of composition that may account for the present form of the story of Balaam in Numbers 22–24.

What remains clear is that the story of a non-Israelite Yahwistic seer has prompted a complex history of commentary. The reason for the ongoing commentary is the theological problem that is posed when a non-Israelite seer claims to be a Yahwist, even though he functions outside of Israel's cultic institutions. One suspects that the history of commentary is a compilation of different answers to this theological problem.

The Divine Names. Scholars have used the two divine names, *Elohim* ("God") and *Yahweh* ("LORD") to gain insight into the compositional

---

160. See Gray, *Numbers*, 307-22.

161. See Martin Noth, *Numbers*, OTL (Philadelphia: Westminster, 1968) 166-94.

history of Numbers 22–24.[162] Noth, for example, concluded that two versions of the narrative, Yahwistic (J) and Elohistic (E), are discernible in these chapters. The Elohistic version, according to Noth, includes most parts of 22:2-21 and 22:41–23:27, while the Yahwistic encompasses most of 22:22-40 and 23:28–24:19.[163] The distribution of the divine names in these chapters is, indeed, striking. But an overview indicates that their use is for literary and theological reasons, and not the result of a history of composition.

The many names used for God in Numbers 22–24 can be summarized as follows: The personal name of God, *Yahweh* ("Lord") appears seventeen times, nine times in speeches by Balaam (22:8, 13, 18-19; 23:3, 8, 12, 26; 24:6, 13), twice by Balak (23:17; 24:11), and five times by the narrator of the story (22:28, 31; 23:5, 16; 24:1). *Elohim* ("God") occurs nine times, once by Balaam (22:38), once by Balak (23:27), and seven times by the narrator of the story (22:9, 10, 12, 20, 22; 23:4; 24:2). The combination *Yahweh-Elohim* ("Lord God") is used twice in speeches by Balaam (22:18; 23:21). Other names for God also appear in speeches by Balaam: *El* ("God"), seven times (23:19, 22, 23; 24:8, 16, 23); *Elyon* ("Most High"), once (24:16); and *Shaddai* ("Almighty"), twice (24:4, 16). The ten references to the "messenger of Yahweh" are confined to the episode of Balaam and his donkey (22:22-25).

The range of divine names employed in Numbers 22–24 indicates that the biblical writers are exploring the different ways in which the God of Israel is known to other people. Thus the variety of divine names serves literary and theological purposes. For example, in the opening scene (22:1-21), Balaam only refers to God as *Yahweh* ("Lord"; 22:8, 13, 18-19), while the narrator of the story uses only the name *Elohim* ("God"; 22:9-10, 12, 20). This technique presents a contrast between the narrator, who speaks in more general language about the God of Israel in relationship to the non-Israelite seer Balaam, and Balaam, who claims knowledge of Yahweh. Such a carefully constructed contrast is not the result of combining two narrative accounts. A stronger hypothesis asserts that the variety of divine names is the work of a single author. Indeed, the result

of this technique is a portrayal of Balaam as someone who knows the God of Israel and most of the important names for God. How he chooses to use such knowledge is one of the central tensions of the story. The reticence on the part of the narrator to name Balaam's God as Yahweh simply highlights this tension.

22:1-21. This section tells of the fear of Balak, king of Moab. He hears of Israel's defeat of the Amorite kings, Og and Sihon, and he seeks to weaken them by hiring a diviner named Balaam to curse the people. Verses 1-20 provide the setting for the entire story of Balaam (v. 1), outline the nature of the Israelite threat to Balak (vv. 2-4), and describe two missions of Balak to Balaam to hire him to curse Israel (the first mission appears in vv. 5-14, the second in vv. 15-20).

22:1. The setting of the story takes the form of an itinerary notice, but it lacks the location of Israel's departure. It simply states that they journeyed and camped "in the plains of Moab," located more precisely as "across the Jordan from Jericho." The broken form of the itinerary emphasizes the new setting, rather than the point of departure.

The change of setting to the plains of Moab indicates that Israel has left the wilderness. Leaving the wilderness does not fulfill the divine promise of land in the Pentateuch, however, because the plains of Moab are not Canaan. Instead, it signals the fulfillment of the promise of fertility; the second generation has become a great nation once again. The central focus on fertility is underscored by the fear of the Moabites (vv. 2-4); the number of the Israelites terrifies them.

The location "in the plains of Moab across the Jordan from Jericho" is a favorite expression of the priestly writers. It is the location for the second census of Israel (26:3, 63); the waging of holy war against Midian (31:12); the appointing of levitical cities (35:1); the final legislation of Moses in the book of Numbers (36:13); and for the death of Moses (Deut 34:1, 8). The priestly writers' use of this location throughout chaps. 22–36 provides strong evidence for attributing the travel notice in 22:1 to them.[164]

But this itinerary notice may be part of the pre-priestly history along with a similar reference in 33:50—the conclusion to the full list of wil-

162. Gray, *Numbers,* 309-14.
163. Noth, *Numbers,* 171-75.

164. Gray, *Numbers,* 306-7.

derness travel stops. Verse 1 introduces "the plains of Moab" as the location for two external threats to Israel: the first by Balak (chaps. 22–24) and the second the incident at Baal Peor (25:1-5). The plains of Moab in 33:50 is the setting for the divine command that Israel cross the Jordan and conquer the Canaanites. Crossing the Jordan for conquest is not a theme in the priestly history.[165] Read together, 22:1 and 33:50 frame the final section of Numbers in the pre-priestly history and point the reader ahead to additional instruction by Moses in Deuteronomy, also in the "land of Moab" (Deut 29:1).

22:2-4. This section describes the nature of the Israelite threat to Balak and the Moabite nation. Verse 3 states that Moab fears Israel. Two words are used to describe their fear, and both are important for interpretation. The first word, "dread" (גור *gûr*) characterizes persons who are confronted by power, either divine (Deut 9:19) or human (1 Sam 18:15), and who are unsure of how such power will be used. The second word, "to be overcome with fear" (קוץ *qûṣ*) bears connotations of abhorrence. Again, the context of the word indicates a confrontation of power amid the threat of war. The word is used to describe the fear that Ahaz, the Judahite king, had for Damascus and the northern kingdom of Israel during war (Isa 7:16). A more important parallel for Num 22:3 is Exod 1:12, where the fear of the Egyptians over the unchecked population growth of the Israelites is described with the same word.

The reason for the Moabite fear is twofold. Israel's power to wage war is evident from its defeat of the Amorites (v. 1). The more explicit reason, however, is the size of Israel (v. 3). Balak's speech to the Midianites in v. 4 underscores this fact. He fears the impact that so many Israelites will have on the environment of his country: "The horde will now lick up [resources] as an ox licks up the grass of the field." The fertility of Israel fulfills one of two divine promises to the ancestors: population (Gen 12:1-4) and land (Gen 17:1-8). At the outset of chap. 22, the second generation has once again become numerous, just as the first generation had become in Egypt (Exodus 1).

The parallel between Numbers 22 and Exodus 1 is important for interpretation. It signals that the

165. Ibid., 449-52.

change in setting from the wilderness to the "plains of Moab" is more than a transition from the first to the second generation in the pre-priestly history. It also marks for a second time the fulfillment of the divine promise of fertility that was made to the ancestors. The connection to the first generation in Egypt goes beyond mere numbers of persons to include a threatening dimension. Israelite fertility in the second generation creates the same dread in the Moabites that it did in the Egyptians (Exod 1:12). The parallels to Egypt will continue with Balak's message to Balaam (vv. 5-6).

The renaming of Balak in v. 4 as the son of Zippor, and the description of him as "king of Moab at that time," provide transition from the opening description of Moabite fear to their plan of action. The meaning of "Zippor" is not clear, although the name appears in a feminine form, "Zipporah" (the wife of Moses).

The closing temporal phrase in v. 4, "at that time" (בעת ההוא *bā'ēt hahî'*), to indicate when Balak was king of Moab gives the story a didactic quality. It is a favorite device for narrating historical stories in Deuteronomy (Deut 1:9, 16, 18; 2:34; 3:4, 8, 12, 18, 21, 23; 4:14; 5:5; 9:20 10:1), where past events are recalled for the purpose of teaching. The phrase has a similar didactic function in Num 22:4. As a result, the story is less an unfolding drama than a lesson from the past: how God foiled Balak's plan to hire Balaam to curse Israel.

22:5-14. This section describes the first mission to Balaam, who is introduced in v. 5 by lineage and location. He is the son of Beor. His home is Pethor ("on the river"). "The river" almost always means the Euphrates, accounting for the NRSV translation. Pethor may be Pitru, a location in Syria, south of Carchemish. The additional identification "in the land of Amaw" is unclear; the Hebrew translates "in the land of his people."

Balak's request to Balaam (vv. 5-6) takes the form of a speech to his messengers. His words recount many themes from the exodus. The expression "a people has come out of Egypt" consists of a form of the Hebrew verb "to go forth" or "to go out" (יצא *yāṣā'*), with the prepositional phrase "from Egypt" (ממצרים *mimmiṣrayim*). It is used in Exodus to describe the mission of Moses (Exod 3:10-12) and the exodus itself (e.g., Exod 13:3, 8-9; 14:11). As noted, the primary fear of

Balak concerns the fertility of Israel. This fear, too, is expressed in language from the exodus. Balak's description of the number of Israelites encamped on his land as "having spread over the face of the earth" recalls the plague of locusts (Exod 10:5). His statement that the number of Israelites implies that "they are stronger than [he]" echoes Pharaoh's fear at the outset of the exodus (Exod 1:9).

The fertility of Israel is a direct result of God's blessing; God states this to Balaam explicitly in v. 12. Balak requests that Balaam curse the Israelites, because cursing, the opposite of blessing, disrupts fertility. The cursed earth in Gen 3:17-19, for example, is transformed from a fertile garden into ground that brings forth thorns and thistles. Thus the objective power of cursing and blessing is central to the story. Balak hopes that having Israel cursed will weaken it, allowing him to drive the Israelites from his land. "Driving out" (שׁרג *gāraš*) Israel from the land is language of conquest. It occurs in a Moabite inscription (The Moabite Stone or Mesha Stele), in which the king Mesha boasts of conquest over Israel.[166] It also appears elsewhere in the OT, for example, when God promised that the divine messenger would "drive out" the inhabitants of Canaan (Exod 23:20-33).

Balaam possesses the power to curse and to bless. Balak affirms this power in v. 6 with language reminiscent of the divine promise to Abraham (Gen 12:3). Whomever Balaam blesses is blessed, and whomever he curses is cursed. Attributing such power to Balaam indicates that such power is not unique to Israel, but may also be possessed by a non-Israelite. The primeval hero of the flood, Noah, also possessed the power to bless and to curse. He cursed Canaan (Gen 9:25) and blessed Shem (Gen 9:26). The description of Balaam also conveys the objective quality of blessing and cursing, in which the words set into motion powers that cannot be reversed. Isaac's blessing of Jacob by mistake (Gen 27:27-29), and his inability to reverse it upon learning of his error, is similar.

Balaam's power to bless and to curse is described in v. 7 as "divination" (קסם *qesem*). Divination is the science of predicting the future through interpretation of natural phenomena. It took many forms in the ancient Near East, including the casting of lots (1 Sam 14:42-43) and the

166. *ANET,* 320-21.

reading of animal entrails. It was most certainly common in ancient Israel, but it came to be condemned as a practice that conflicted with Yahwistic faith. The clearest statement on this point is Deut 18:9-14, but such teaching is also found in other places; 2 Kings 17:7-23, supports the teaching of Deuteronomy by listing divination as one of the reasons for the destruction of the northern kingdom. Ezekiel, too, condemns the practice (Ezek 13:9). Thus the reference to divination in association with Balaam raises the question of whether the term is meant to be a negative commentary on the seer. It appears not to be. "Diviner" is not a title Balaam claims for himself, and his subsequent actions do not conform to such practice. In fact, the characterization of Balaam as a diviner is made indirectly through the description of the payment of Balak's messengers as "the fees for divination."

Verses 8-14 describe Balaam's intercession with God to discern whether or not to curse Israel. Throughout the passage, Balaam is presented in a positive light. In v. 8 he explicitly states that he is unable to make a decision without instruction from Yahweh. As a result, the episode is structured around Balaam's seeking instruction from God during the night (vv. 8-11) and returning with an answer at dawn (v. 13). Balaam refuses Balak's request to curse Israel.

Several features of vv. 8-14 are important for interpretation. Perhaps the most noteworthy is that Balaam refers to God with the personal name "Yahweh" ("LORD," v. 8). "Yahweh" is the name for God given to Moses in Exodus 3 with the specific instruction that he share this name with Israel. Thus it is not a general epithet for God; rather, it requires knowledge of Israel's unique history of salvation. Balaam's use of the name "Yahweh," then, is astonishing, because he has no knowledge of Israel. Note that in the nighttime exchange between Balaam and God, Balaam has no firsthand knowledge of Israel. Describing the request of Balak (v. 11), Balaam refers generically to "a people" that has come out of Egypt and now covers the land of Moab. His description is merely a repetition of the message conveyed to him (see vv. 5-6). The biblical writers present Balaam as a diviner who has come to possess the special divine name "Yahweh" through independent revelation.

The portrait of God is also noteworthy. God is presented as having a special relationship with a non-Israelite formed outside of the structure of Israel's history of salvation. Nowhere in God's reply to Balaam is Israel referred to by name, nor are they called God's people (v. 12). Instead, God tells Balaam that he cannot curse "the people" because they are blessed. In this brief exchange, the biblical writers succeed in presenting a glimpse into God's relationship with a diviner. The Israelites are peripheral to the scene. In fact, they are unaware of the threat posed by Balak and the intercession of Balaam (v. 13).

22:15-21. This section describes the second mission to Balaam. The language intensifies. Balak sends many more distinquished officials (v. 15). Their message to Balaam is prefaced with the messenger formula, "Thus says Balak son of Zippor. . . . " The message itself is filled with pleas, exclamations, and even demands (vv. 16-17). Nothing should hinder Balaam from traveling to Moab. Balak assures Balaam through his messengers that no price is too high, if only he will come and curse this people. Balaam's response is equally strong (v. 18). No amount of money could make him act contrary to the command of Yahweh, his God. The portrait of Balaam is even more positive as a result of this second mission. Once again, Balaam inquires of God during the night for an answer to Balak's request (vv. 19-20). This time God instructs Balaam to return with the officials of Balak, but to speak only the words that God commands him.

22:22-35. The account of Balaam's journey to Balak is a separate story. Originally the two previous missions of Balak's officials (vv. 1-21) probably continued uninterrupted into v. 36, where Balaam arrives at Moab and informs Balak that he can only speak what God tells him (the command from v. 20).

Several literary features indicate that vv. 22-35 were inserted into the Balaam cycle of stories. Yahweh's anger at Balaam's decision to travel to Moab (v. 22) directly contradicts the divine command that he undertake the trip (v. 20). The portrayal of Balaam changes significantly from a diviner who carefully discerns the direction of God's leading to a blind and impatient seer whose donkey has more sense and clairvoyance than he. The appearance of the messenger of Yahweh is confined to this section; and the internal structure of vv. 22-35, with their three-part repetition of action, also suggests a self-contained story. All of

these factors lead to the conclusion that these verses were a later addition to the Balaam cycle of stories, intended to introduce a negative interpretation of the non-Israelite diviner.

Numbers 22:22-35 is folklore—a burlesque, even slapstick story about a clairvoyant animal who speaks a word of common sense to a blind seer. The story divines between a confrontation with the messenger of Yahweh (vv. 22-27) and the interpretation of the message (vv. 28-35).

22:22-27. Verse 22 sets the stage for the story, describing how the messenger of Yahweh blocks the road and functions as Balaam's adversary on his journey to Moab. The word "adversary" (שטן *śāṭān*) is also used to describe God's opponent in Job 1. Here God or the messenger of Yahweh opposes Balaam. There is no clear distinction between the messenger of Yahweh and God in this particular folk tale. Other references to Yahweh's messenger indicate that this manifestation of God is able to wage holy war for Israel (Exod 23:20-33) and to lead Israel through the wilderness (Exod 14:19). Numbers 22:22-35 bears overtones of war, since the messenger states that he seeks to kill Balaam (v. 33).

There are three encounters with the messenger of Yahweh, all seen by the donkey (vv. 23, 25, 27), but not by Balaam or his servants (who disappear from the story after v. 22). The encounters are increasingly intense. First, the messenger of Yahweh forces the donkey from the road (v. 23). Then he forces the donkey against the wall (vv. 24-25). Finally, he blocks the donkey's path altogether, causing it to lie down (vv. 26-27). In each of these instances, the donkey saves Balaam's life, but the diviner is blind to his rescue and responds with increasingly violent acts against the donkey.

22:28-35. The donkey and the messenger of Yahweh address Balaam. The donkey interprets events for Balaam in vv. 28-30, followed by a more detailed interpretation from the messenger of Yahweh in vv. 31-35. Speaking animals are a common feature of folk literature, but they are unusual in biblical stories. The only other talking animal in the OT is the serpent in the garden of Eden (Genesis 2). In both instances, a talking animal appears not to be unusual to the human character. Balaam does not show surprise that his donkey is able to engage him in conversation;

instead, he responds immediately as if they conversed regularly.

The donkey's interpretation of events (vv. 28-30) is based on common sense. It questions why Balaam has beaten it three times. The question casts Balaam in the role of the fool. He has misinterpreted the donkey's actions as ruthless, rather than salvific. If he had a sword, Balaam swears, he would kill the donkey. Yet the nearest sword is in the hand of the messenger of Yahweh, and it is aimed at Balaam! The donkey does not share its clairvoyance with Balaam. Rather, it reflects on experience, reminding Balaam of past service. The donkey questions whether its behavior has ever been ruthless. Balaam responds that no, it has not. The implication of their conversation is that Balaam has no business attributing sinister motive to his donkey, even though he does not understand the animal's unexpected behavior. His accumulated experience with the donkey should suffice to warrant his trust.

Yahweh's messenger provides the second interpretation of the events in vv. 31-35. Finally, Balaam's eyes are opened to the presence of his swordbearing divine adversary, prompting an act of worship. The messenger of Yahweh repeats the donkey's question—why the beatings? The new information supplied by God in vv. 32-33 builds on the commonsense conclusion offered by the donkey. The animal was not acting ruthlessly. On the contrary, it saved Balaam from a divine attack, for God would surely have killed him and left the animal alive. Had the animal acted in response to Balaam's sinister assumption, the diviner would now be dead. His eyes now opened, Balaam confesses his sin, while also claiming ignorance. He then offers to return to his home. The episode ends in v. 35 with the messenger repeating the divine instruction from v. 20 that Balaam continue on in his journey, but speak only what God instructs him to say.

22:36–24:13. Balaam's oracles concerning Israel comprise the heart of the Balaam cycle. The section evolves around three episodes. Numbers 22:36-40 provides both a conclusion to the opening story about Balak's envoys to Balaam (22:1-21) and an introduction to Balaam's three oracles about Israel (22:41–24:13). The three oracles separate into episodes consisting of 22:41–23:12; 23:13-26; and 23:27–24:13. Similar in form, each begins with Balak taking Balaam to a specific location to curse Israel. In each scene, Balaam sacrifices on seven altars, prompting a word from God that leads to a poetic oracle. Balaam's oracles are blessings rather than curses. This unexpected reversal leads in each case to an exchange between Balaam and Balak, in which Balak appears dumbfounded that the diviner has blessed Israel rather than cursed it. Balaam responds that he can only say what God commands him to say. The portrait of Balaam throughout this section is positive. Further commentary will demonstrate that development of character occurs within the repetitive structure of the oracles.

22:36-40. The geographical locations are important to the story. Balak travels to the border of Moab to meet Balaam, who enters the country from the north. The setting is Ir-moab, a site on the Arnon River. Ir-moab should, perhaps, be translated "City of Moab." The location does not correspond to any known contemporary site, but it does relate to a city mentioned in 21:15, 28 called Ar of Moab, the setting for the Moabites' destruction in the Book of the Wars of Yahweh (21:15) and in the Ballad of Heshbon (21:28). These inner-biblical references lend a somber tone to the account of Balaam's arrival in Moab, foreshadowing the downfall of the Moabites.

Ir-moab serves as the setting for an exchange between Balak and Balaam (vv. 37-38). Balak questions why Balaam has been delayed: Did Balaam not think that he, Balak, had the power to honor him? Balaam dismisses this question by introducing divine direction, as opposed to reward from Balak. Balaam states that he is only able to speak the words that God puts in his mouth, a repetition of the divine instruction in vv. 20, 35. Thus this encounter of Balaam and Balak can be read as a continuation either of vv. 1-21 or of vv. 22-35. In either case, Balaam is presented as a positive character. The scene closes with Balak taking Balaam to Kiriath-huzoth ("City of Streets") for sacrifices.

22:41–23:12. The events surrounding the first oracle progress in three stages. The setting and procedures for divination are described in 22:41–23:6. Balaam's oracle follows in 23:7-10. The concluding exchange between Balaam and Balak is described in 23:11-12. This three-part structure continues throughout the sequence of oracles, along with repetition in actions and dialogue between Balaam and Balak. Variations within the stereotypical actions convey development in the plot.

Numbers 22:41 states both the time (dawn) and the location (Bamoth-baal) of the first oracle. It also describes what Balaam saw from this location, but the Hebrew is ambiguous. The text states literally that Balaam saw "the extremity or outer edge of the people" (קצה העם *qĕṣēh hā'ām*). But it does not indicate which outer edge of the people the writer intends. If it is the furthermost edge, then Balaam is viewing the entire people of Israel encamped below Bamoth-baal. If it is the closest edge, then he is viewing only a small section of the people. The NRSV adopts the latter reading: "from there he [Balaam] saw part of the people of Israel."[167] The NEB follows the former reading so that Balaam saw "the full extent of the Israelite host."[168] The two readings provide distinctive plot structures to the story. In each, however, the name "Israel" is an unwarranted addition, since it is absent from the text. The Commentary on 22:1-21 indicated that the absence of a proper name for Israel was important to the perspective of the narrative.

Divination is central to the Balaam oracles, and sight is central to divination. Milgrom writes that in a story about divination "the object must be within sight for a curse to be effective." He quotes Democritus to illustrate the power of the evil eye:

From the eyes issue images which are neither without sensation nor without volition, and are filled with the wickedness and malice of those from whom they proceed: imprinting themselves firmly upon the person to be enchanted, they become part of him, and disturb and injure both his body and mind.[169]

The importance of sight for cursing can be interpreted in two ways in the story of Balaam. The NRSV translation of 22:41 yields a three-part plot that increases in scope. Balaam sees only the outer edge of the people for the first oracle (at Bamoth-baal, 22:41–23:12). He sees a greater portion of the people for the second oracle (on Pisgah, 23:13-26). Finally, Balaam views all of Israel for the third oracle (on Peor, 23:27–24:13).

The NEB interpretation (Balaam saw all of Israel from Bamoth-baal) creates a satirical story of reversal, rather than a story that increases in scope and drama. This reading suggests that the first episode (22:41–23:12) is the most threatening, because Balaam is able to fix his eye on the entire people. Balak's inability to induce a curse on Israel, even when Balaam has them firmly fixed in his eye, gives rise to satire: Balak then tries to conjure up a curse by limiting Balaam's view of Israel. In 22:13, Balak takes Balaam to Pisgah, where he can see only part of the people, in the hope that a more limited viewing might induce a curse from Balaam. When this attempt fails (23:13-26), Balak takes Balaam to Peor, where the seer "overlooks the wasteland" (23:27-28). The people are not mentioned in the introduction to the third oracle, nor does Balak refer to the need for Balaam to view Israel. One way to interpret the absence of these motifs is that Balaam has turned away from Israel altogether. Numbers 20:10-20 indicates that Israel has left the desert. Balak provides commentary on this unorthodox action when he states that perhaps he may induce enough divine favor to prompt Balaam into cursing the people (23:27). But this action backfires (24:1-2): Balaam departs from Balak, discontinues his process of divination, and looks upon all of Israel, tribe by tribe, for a final oracle of blessing.

The divination procedure is described in 23:1-6. Balaam requires the construction of no less than seven altars—a sacred number of completeness—each to be used for sacrificing a bull and a ram. These are extravagant sacrifices, the most valued sacrifices in the book of Leviticus (chap. 4). According to Num 23:2, the sacrifices are performed by both Balak and Balaam. But the inclusion of Balaam may be a latter addition, since the verbs describing the act of sacrificing are third-person singular, referring to Balak alone. The larger context also supports this reading. In 22:36-40, only Balak sacrificed, and in 23:3, when Balaam instructs Balak to remain beside his sacrifice, he uses the second-person singular pronoun, "your sacrifice." The sacrifices are part of a ritual of divination, perhaps intended to prompt God's appearance. The encounter between Balaam and God is separated from Balak and his sacrifices, for Balaam is described as going to a bare height. His aim in 23:3 is to meet Yahweh ("the LORD"; the narrator describes the encounter between Balaam

---

167. See George Buchanan Gray, *Numbers,* ICC (Edinburgh: T. & T. Clark, 1903) 342.

168. See Eryl W. Davies, *Numbers,* NCB (Grand Rapids: Eerdmans, 1995) 253-54.

169. Jacob Milgrom, *Numbers,* JPS Torah Commentary (Philadelphia: JPS, 1990) 193-94. The quotation is from Plutarch *Symposium* 5.7.6.

and God by using both the general divine name "God" [v. 4] and the personal name "Yahweh" [v. 5].

The oracle in 23:7-10 constitutes the divine word to Balaam. The Hebrew word for "oracle" is מָשָׁל (*māšāl*, v. 7). This word is unusual in the present context, because it is not used to describe the sayings of OT prophets. Yet all of Balaam's speeches are described with this word. *Māšāl* has a range of meanings, including "parable" or "allegory" (Ezek 17:2), "proverb" (Prov 1:1), and "taunt" (Isa 14:4). It appears that the biblical writers have introduced an element of ambiguity regarding the genre of Balaam's speeches. Read in isolation from their narrative context, Balaam's speeches resemble prophetic oracles. But when the narrative context is emphasized, the oracles provide commentary on surrounding events, in which case they are more like parables or wisdom sayings about Israel's journey with God. The final oracle against the nations (24:15-24) bears characteristics of a taunt.

Balaam's initial oracle consists of three stanzas: 23:7-8 presents the central theme of the poem—namely, the inability of Balaam to curse if it is not God's will; 23:9 describes the distinctive character of Israel; and 23:10 makes allusion to the fertility of Israel. It is composed in synonymous parallelism, a poetic device in which two lines provide variation on a similar theme, of which 23:7 provides an illustration:

"*Balak* has brought me *from Aram*,
　the *king of Moab* from the eastern mountains:
'Come, *curse* Jacob for me;
　Come, *denounce* Israel!'"

The first pair and the last pair of lines are parallel and synonymous, because they state essentially the same thing. Lines one and two state that Balak commissioned Balaam. The repetition between the lines adds information. Balak is the king of Moab, and Balaam came from Aram by the eastern mountains. Lines three and four state that the content of the commission is a curse. Repetition clarifies the nature of cursing as denouncing and the object of the curse as Jacob/Israel. Synonymous parallelism continues throughout: v. 8 contains two lines that are synonymous, while vv. 9-10 contain four lines consisting of two pairs of synonymous parallelism, like v. 7.

The speech of Balaam takes on different mean-ing, depending on whether it is read in isolation as a prophetic oracle or in its present narrative context as commentary on the story. When the poem is read in isolation, Balaam's speech resembles prophetic discourse, and the message takes precedence over the messenger. The central theme of the oracle as prophetic discourse is Balaam's inability to curse if it is contrary to God's will. The limited focus on the northern kingdom (e.g., Jacob/Israel) may indicate the original setting of the Balaam oracles prior to their incorporation within the pre-priestly history.

Balaam's speech can also be read as commentary on the larger story. That the biblical writers intend for such a reading is clear from the careful way in which the oracle has been interwoven into its narrative context. The reference to Aram (22:7) harks back to 22:5, where Balaam's homeland was identified as Pethor, a location most likely near the Euphrates. The recounting of Balak's commission that Balaam curse Israel, then, ties the oracle into the opening episode in 22:1-21. Balaam's view of Israel "from the top of the crags" links the oracle to the narrative introduction (22:41). Finally, Balaam's reference to the number of Israelites reinforces the population motif, which prompted Balak to act in the first place (22:5).

The oracle in 23:7-10 loses its prophetic quality when read as commentary on the larger narrative context. What stands out, instead, is the autobiographical nature of Balaam's speech. "I" statements by Balaam come into focus throughout the sequence of the three stanzas. The first two stanzas begin with "I" statements by Balaam that recount past events in the narrative—his commissioning by Balak to curse Israel (v. 7) and his present location "at the top of the crags" (v. 9*a*). Statements about Israel's present condition conclude each of these stanzas—he cannot curse a people whom God has not cursed (v. 8), and Israel is distinct from the nations (v. 9*b*). The third stanza reverses this structure. It begins with a statement about Israel's present condition (their great number [v. 10*a*]), and concludes with yet another self-reference by Balaam. This time Balaam's "I" statement is a wish that he might be like Israel (v. 10*b*).

Read in the larger context of the narrative, the first episode emphasizes Balaam's coming to knowledge of the nation of Israel, not his inability to curse when doing so is against the divine will.

In this regard, it is noteworthy that Israel is named by Balaam, since he did not know the name of the people in his earlier exchange with God (22:11-12). The first oracle indicates development in Balaam. God has revealed to Balaam the name of this people and their special status with regard to God (v. 8) and the nations (v. 9). As a consequence, Balaam wishes to join Israel rather than curse them (v. 10).

Numbers 23:11-12 concludes the first oracle with an exchange between Balak and Balaam that provides insight into these two characters. Balak is angry with Balaam for having blessed Israel rather than cursing them, even though Balaam has not actually blessed Israel in the first oracle. The language of Balak indicates his expectation that Balaam would functioned as a sorcerer. A sorcerer is someone who attempts to alter the future; thus Balak wishes to alter the Israelites' destiny by having Balaam curse them. Balaam responds by repeating a motif that has already occurred in 22:38 and 23:3: He can only speak what God tells him. This response indicates that Balaam sees himself as a diviner, and not as a sorcerer.[170] Diviners predict the future, but they do not seek to alter it. The two perceptions of Balaam's role signal a tension that runs throughout the narrative: Is Balaam's power positive or negative? Balak wishes to use the power of Balaam negatively. But Balaam appears in a positive light as a diviner who conveys the divine will, but does not seek to manipulate it through sorcerery.

23:13-26. The setting for the second oracle is established in vv. 13-17. Balak takes Balaam to a new location at the top of Mt. Pisgah in the field of Zophim. Pisgah appears as one of Israel's traveling stops in 21:20. The location of the field of Zophim, however, is uncertain. The name may be a pun on the meaning of the word "watchers" (צֹפִים *ṣōpîm*). The new setting of the second oracle means that Balaam can only see a part of Israel. As in the first oracle, seven altars are built, and a bull and a ram are sacrificed on each. Balaam departs from Balak to receive a word of divination from God and then returns to him with a message. Note that in this case, however, Balak asks Balaam, "What has Yahweh said?" The question indicates a new understanding in Balak that

Yahweh (the Lord) is the deity who empowers Balaam.

Verses 18-24 contain the second oracle of Balaam. It, too, is structured in eleven parallel lines (vv. 18, 19*a*, 19*b*, 20, 21*a*, 22, 23*a*, 23*b*, 24*a*, 24*b*), and it separates into three stanzas. Verses 18-19 contrast Balak and God; vv. 20-22 describe God's power in the history of Israel; and vv. 23-24 turn the focus from God to Israel in order to describe the power of Israel and the futility of seeking enchantments against it. When the oracle is read within the larger narrative context, the direct address to Balak (v. 18) stands out. In contrast to the autobiographical nature of the first oracle, the second oracle is intended to teach Balak about God and Israel.

Verses 18-19 are composed of three parallel lines:

"Rise, Balak, and hear;
    listen to me, O son of Zippor:
God is not a human being, that he should lie,
    or a mortal, that he should change his mind.
Has he promised, and will he not do it?
    Has he spoken, and will he not fulfill it?"

The oracle is addressed to Balak, described in the second line as "son of Zippor." The point of the oracle is to teach Balak something about God and Israel. The teaching will take place by contrasting Balak and God. Verse 19*a* provides two contrasts: Unlike Balak, God is neither a man (אִישׁ *'îš*) nor the "son of a human" (בֶּן־אָדָם *ben-'ādām*). As a result, God neither "lies" (כּוּב *kāzab*) nor "changes his mind" (נִחַם *niḥam*).

The contrast between the divine and the human is used in biblical literature to emphasize that God is not bound to human expectations or desires. The meaning of such contrasts must be determined by the specific context of the text under study. For example, a similar contrast occurs in Hos 11:9, where the incomparability of God to humans is stated in order to emphasize that God is not bound to predictable results of legal justice and thus can change. The contrast between God and humans is meant to emphasize transformation in God's character. Unlike humans, God can forgive, even though the situation requires judgment.

The context of the Balaam oracle is just the opposite of Hosea, since the threatening situation is that Balak wishes to change the future through sorcery. Balaam's response is that such human

<hr />

170. See Michael S. Moore, *The Balaam Traditions: Their Character and Development,* ed. J. J. M. Roberts and Charles Talbert, SBLDS 113 (Atlanta: Scholars Press, 1990) 113-18; and Milgrom, *Numbers,* 469-71.

manipulation is useless in relationship to God. Thus the emphasis in this literary setting is the reliability and constancy of divine promises and blessings, rather than God's ability to change. The background for Balaam's proclamation about divine nature over against human nature might be the words of the psalmist, "Everyone is a liar" (Ps 116:11)—meaning all humans. Balaam's point to Balak would be that God is not "everyone." "Lying" (כזב *kāzab*) in v. 19 refers to more than telling a falsehood. It has to do with failing to fulfill an oracle or a promise (see Hab 2:3). Balaam's revelation to Balak is that God does not fail to fulfill promises.

God does not "change his mind." Again it is important to emphasize the context of the Balaam oracle. The point of this oracle is that God cannot be manipulated through sorcery. No act of magical divination can influence God. When God promises salvation, God is reliable and will not change, even under the threat of outside sorcery (v. 19*b*). There are other stories in which the ability of God to "change his mind" is a central theme, especially where the power of intercession through prayer is at issue. Examples include the intercession of Moses for Israel during the sin of the golden calf (Exod 32:9-14), and the spy story (Numbers 14). The ability of God to change is also an important theme in Jonah 3 and Joel 2. In these texts, the biblical writers encourage intercessory prayer as a way of influencing divine action.

The second stanza (vv. 20-22) consists of four paired lines. The poetic structure of this stanza is less clear than the synonymous parallelism of the opening stanza, although there is repetition between the lines, as is evident in vv. 20-21.

See, I received a command to bless;
    he has blessed, and I cannot revoke it.
He has not beheld misfortune in Jacob;
    nor has he seen trouble in Israel.
The LORD their God is with them,
    acclaimed as a king among them.

But in many cases, as in v. 22, the second line adds new material with little or no repetition:

God, who brings them out of Egypt,
    is like the horns of a wild ox for them.

Verses 20-22 describe the power of God in more detail by recounting Israel's history of salvation as an outgrowth of divine blessing. Verse 20 affirms

God's intention to bless Israel, and vv. 21-22 state that God is the king of Israel and has rescued Israel through the exodus. Again this information is intended for Balak; he is being called to understand Israel's unique history of salvation.

The third stanza (vv. 23-24) changes from past events of salvation history to the present; note the transitional word "now" in v. 23*b*. Each verse consists of four paired lines, beginning with a direct address to Balak about his desire for sorcery:

Surely there is no enchantment against Jacob,
    no divination against Israel;

The oracle ends by comparing Israel to a lion:

Look, a people rising up like a lioness,
    and rousing itself like a lion!

Comparison of Israel to a lion is unusual (but see Gen 49:9; Deut 33:20; Mic 5:8). In ancient Near Eastern iconography, kings are often pictured as lions on the hunt. The symbolism most likely is meant to underscore the power of the state to protect against the wild forces of nature. Such symbolism ties in well with Balak's concern about the Israelite threat. Balaam's message, then, is that Balak and the Moabite state cannot protect themselves against Israel (v. 24*b*):

It [Israel the lion] does not lie down until it has
    eaten the prey
    and drunk the blood of the slain.

When the imagery of Israel as a lion is viewed within the larger context of ancient Near Eastern iconography, a degree of irony emerges in the story. In the opening scene of the story, Balak expressed his fear of Israel with the imagery of domestic cattle: "This horde will now lick up all that is around us, as an ox licks up the grass of the field" (22:4). The concluding point of Balaam's second oracle is that Balak has underestimated the threat of Israel. They are a lion and not an ox. They will lick up not only the grass of the fields of Moab, but also its people.

The conclusion to the second oracle (vv. 25-26) follows the pattern of the first oracle by presenting an exchange between Balaam and Balak. Balak is angry and prefers that Balaam say nothing at all. Balaam's response is to reaffirm his position: He can only say what God tells him to speak.

23:27–24:13. The third oracle of Balaam follows the general pattern of the previous two. The episode consists of an introduction (23:27–24:2), the presentation of an oracle (24:3-9), and a conclusion (24:10-13). The three sections also include details from the other two. In the introduction, Balak takes Balaam to a new location, Peor, where seven altars are constructed and a bull and a ram are sacrificed on each. The episode concludes with an exchange between Balak and Balaam, in which Balak again expresses anger over the content of the oracle.

The third episode departs from the other two in significant ways. The introduction in 23:27–24:2 contains a series of new motifs. The episode begins with speech by Balak, as before, but his reference to God marks a development in the story. He opines that "perhaps it will please God" that Balaam curse Israel from this new location (23:27). Peor is expected, since each oracle has taken place at a different place. But the notice that Peor overlooked the wasteland departs from the previous episodes, where Balaam's view of Israel was always described. Israel is not mentioned at the outset of the third oracle. Thus the text is ambiguous about what Balaam sees on Peor. Is he looking at Israel or toward the desert from whence they emerged?

Numbers 24:1-2 provides three further points of contrast to the previous episodes. First, Balaam's perception of events is stated: He saw that "it pleased the LORD to bless Israel." Balaam's insight contradicts Balak's opening statement (23:27) that "perhaps it will please God" to curse Israel. Second, Balaam departs from the procedure of seeking omens. The change of practice must be inferred, since the word for seeking omens was not actually used in the earlier episodes. Yet the statement that Balaam did not look for omens "as at other times" clarifies that the writers wish to contrast this episode with the previous ones. Third, Balaam is filled with the "spirit of God" as he gazes over the entire population of Israel, tribe by tribe. The reference to the Spirit is certainly a positive feature, drawing Balaam into the orbit of charismatic leadership, which was explored in chaps. 11–12 in relationship to the seventy elders (see 11:17, 25).

The introduction of the "spirit of God" (24:2) suggests that Balaam achieves a new level of clairvoyance in the third oracle (24:3-9). The content of the oracle supports this interpretation, with its repetition of the technical word for "or-

acle" (נְאֻם *nĕʾum*) in 24:3-4. This word frequently appears in the oracles of Israelite prophets. Hosea 2:13 provides an example:

I will punish her for the festival days of the Baals,
    when she offered incense to them
and decked herself with her ring and jewelry,
    and went after her lovers,
and forgot me, says the LORD. (NRSV)

This example illustrates that the word "oracle" tends to end prophetic discourses, rather than begin them (as in the saying of Balaam), and that oracles are attributed to God rather than to a human speaker. In spite of these departures in form, it appears that the biblical writers intend to present a positive portrayal of Balaam, whose three oracles about Israel progress in insight and clairvoyance until the third closely resembles the form of Israelite prophecy. The first oracle (23:7-10) was autobiographical, describing Balaam's coming to knowledge of Israel. The second (23:18-24) was directed at Balak; it taught Balak about God and Israel. The third (24:3-9) is prophetic discourse about Israel's fate. It is not intended to be instruction for either Balaam or Balak, but is addressed to Israel (in the opening [v. 3] and closing [v. 9] verses). These are the first occurrences in which Balaam addresses Israel directly in any of his oracles.

The third oracle is structured primarily in parallel lines, separating loosely into three stanzas. The poetic structure of the third oracle departs from the strict parallelism of the previous two. Parallel lines still dominate, occurring nine times (vv. 3, 5, 6*a*, 6*b*, 7*a*, 7*b*, 8*a*, 9*a*, 9*b*). Unlike the previous oracles, tricolons also appear in vv. 4 and 8*b*. Verses 3-4 provide an introduction, vv. 5-7 describe the Israelite camp with fertility imagery, and vv. 8-9 describe the power of Israel as an extension of God's power.

Balaam introduces himself as a diviner in 24:3-4. The opening lines are not clear. The NRSV reads:

"The oracle of Balaam son of Beor,
    the oracle of the man whose eye is clear."

The translation suggests clairvoyance, even though the meaning of the Hebrew is uncertain. It assumes that the Hebrew word שְׁתֻם (*šātam*) means "to be open." But a somewhat similar word, שָׂתַם (*śātam*), means "to be closed" in Lam 3:8. Thus the question arises whether Balaam's eye is open or closed. In either case, the intent of the verse is to state that his inner eye is receptive to the revelation of God. Verse 4 reinforces this interpretation:

the oracle of one who hears the words of God [El],
    who sees the vision of the Almighty [Shaddai],
    who falls down, but with eyes uncovered.

Falling down may refer to an ecstatic trance for the purpose of achieving clairvoyance. Balaam identifies the God of his revelation with two names. The first is a general name for God, "El," and the second is a more specific name for God, "Shaddai." The exact meaning of "Shaddai" is uncertain. It may derive from the word "mountain" or "steppe." This name for God appears in other poetry (Gen 49:25), and it is used by the priestly writers as a name for God during Israel's ancestral period (Gen 17:1; Exod 6:3). Most occurrences of "Shaddai" in the OT appear in the book of Job. It is noteworthy that the Dier 'Allah text (the non-Israelite account of Balaam) also employs "Shaddai" to describe a group of deities.

Numbers 24:5-7 describes the Israelite camp using fertility imagery. Four agricultural metaphors in 24:6 point to Israel's possession of land, as compared to the emphasis on population in the opening episodes of the story. The comparisons between camp and land are in the second person in reference to Israel—"your tents" and "your encampments." The camp is fertile like palm groves, a garden beside the river, the aloe tree, and cedars. The imagery is of a rich and fertile land.

Verse 7 appears to continue the imagery of a fertile land, although it does not follow clearly from vv. 5-6. There is a shift in v. 7 to the third person to describe Israel—"his buckets," "his seed," "his king," and "his kingdom." The water flowing from Israel's buckets in v. 7*a* signifies prosperity, while the reference to the seed of Israel may refer to posterity or allude to deep roots as a sign of health. Verse 7*b* concludes the stanza with explicit statements about the future kingdom of Israel. The strength of their king is compared to Agag, the Amalekite king who was defeated by Saul (1 Sam 15:8). The reference to Agag, with its allusions to Saul, points to the possibility that the Balaam oracles may have functioned independently in the northern kingdom. The LXX reinterprets this line in a more eschatological vein

by changing Agag to Gog, the legendary enemy of Israel described in Ezekiel 38–39.

Numbers 24:8-9 concludes the oracle, introducing the exodus in order to describe Israel's power. Verse 8 repeats 23:22, where God was also described as Israel's Savior through the exodus. The verse extends the imagery of holy war even further: Israel has the power to devour nations, break their bones, and strike with arrows. Verse 9 concludes by returning to the metaphor of a lion, which also ended the previous oracle (23:24). The former reference indicated Israel's ability to attack without relenting. The present metaphor shifts to the power of a lion at rest, secure in its rule. The concluding couplet (v. 9*b*) returns to the theme of blessing and cursing. Those who bless Israel are themselves blessed, and those who curse Israel are cursed. This two-sided outcome to anyone who interacts with Israel relates the Balaam oracles to the original divine promise to Abram (Gen 12:3).

Numbers 24:10-13 recounts the exchange between Balak and Balaam. Balak is even more angry with Balaam. He claps his hands, restates his original intention that Balaam curse Israel, and reminds Balaam of the reward that he had promised. But Balak also adds new insight to the situation by recognizing that it was Yahweh who hindered Balaam from cursing Israel and receiving reward. Balaam's response in 24:12-13 is stereotypical. He repeats his inability to say anything contrary to Yahweh's direction, regardless of reward.

24:14-25. The final section of the Balaam story contains an oracle against Moab (vv. 15-17) and Edom (vv. 18-19), as well as an additional series of oracles against the nations that will surround Israel (vv. 20-24). The transition to this oracle takes place quickly in v. 14. Balaam tells Balak that he is leaving Moab to return to his own people, but before leaving, he offers Balak advice. The verb יעץ (yā'aṣ) can take on the meaning "to advise," as in the counsel that Jethro gives Moses in Exod 18:19, or it can mean "to plan," as in the recounting of the Balak story in Mic 6:5. The reference to the future indicates that Balaam's advice to Balak is prophetic. Thus the following oracle is divine revelation about Moab's future in relation to Israel.

The oracle against Moab (vv. 15-17) includes an introduction (vv. 15-16) and a prediction of their fate (v. 17). The introduction repeats language from the third oracle about Israel (24:3-9):

"The oracle of Balaam son of Beor,
    the oracle of the man whose eye is clear [v. 15 =
      Num 24:4]
the oracle of one who hears the words of God [El],
    and knows the knowledge of the Most High [Elyon],
who sees the vision of the Almighty [Shaddai],
    who falls down, but with his eyes uncovered."
    (v. 16 = Num 24:5)

The first couplet in v. 15 names Balaam and states his clairvoyance with the couplet from v. 3. Verse 16 departs from v. 4, however, with the addition of the line "and knows the knowledge of the Most High [*Elyon*]." The introduction includes a series of important names for God, including *El, Elyon,* and *Shaddai.* The divine name *Elyon,* a non-Israelite title for God, first occurs in Gen 14:18-20, 22, where Melchizedech, the high priest of Salem, blesses Abram in the name of Elyon. It is also employed in the Song of Moses, where the "Most High" is described as the creator God, who "apportioned the nations" and "divided humankind" (Deut 32:8).

Verse 17 predicts the fate of Moab. The future orientation of the saying is indicated by its opening couplet. The vision of Moab is "not now," nor is it "near." The content of the eschatological vision contains royal imagery for Jacob/Israel. The reference to a star coming from Jacob is unusual in OT literature; yet, such imagery tends to have royal connotations, as in Isa 14:12, where the king of Babylonian is called "Day Star." The reference to a scepter is more explicitly a reference to royalty, for the scepter is the insignia of kings (Amos 1:5, 8). Balaam's prediction is that a royal figure will rise out of Israel to destroy Moab. This may be a reference to David, who defeats the Moabites (2 Sam 8:2, 13-14). But it need not be anchored in any particular historical period. The oracle may be intended as eschatological discourse, in which case the poem reflects messianic speculation in Second Temple Judaism and even later. Evidence of the messianic interpretation in Second Temple Judaism is reflected in later rabbinic (*Targum Onkelos*) and Christian (Rev 22:16) tradition. The leader of the Jewish revolt against Rome in the second century CE, Bar-Kochba ("son of the star") illustrates the continuing influence of the messianic reading of Balaam's oracle.

The closing line of v. 17 is not clear. It states that the future royal figure will crush Moab as well as the Sethites. Seth was the third son of Adam and Eve (Gen 4:26; 5:1-8). The inclusion of the Sethites suggests that the author is predicting the defeat of all humanity descended from Seth, which would include the Israelites. Such speculation about the end time is possible, but the rationale for including Israel in this judgment is not immediately apparent. In view of this problem, scholars have also sought a more regional meaning to the Sethites, since it is in parallel with Moab. Egyptian execration texts from the second millennium BCE provide one solution, since they mention a nomadic tribe named Shutu that lived in Canaan.[171]

Verses 18-19 predict the fate of Edom. Both the poetry and the change of subject present problems for interpretation. The identification of Edom with Seir in the first couplet is expected (see Judg 5:4), but the placement of the word "his enemy" (איביו *'ōyĕbāyw*) in the second line of v. 18 disrupts the rhythm of the poetry and does not make sense. The Hebrew translates literally, "Edom will be a possession, Seir will be a possession of his enemies." Some interpreters judge "his enemies" to be a gloss, while others suggest that it be transferred to v. 19*a* to read: "Jacob will rule over his enemies."

The change in subject in vv. 18-19 is also surprising, since Edom has not been part of the Balaam cycle of stories. It may indicate that vv. 18-19 are an addition to an oracle that originally ended with the prediction of Moab's destruction. Yet the language of the poetry ties in to the larger context of Numbers. Israel was not allowed to attack the Edomites in 20:14-21, even though they failed to show Israel hospitality during their journey toward Canaan. The future destruction of Edom could be read as a response to this earlier incident. This interpretation also raises problems, however, since the reference to Ir in v. 19*b* ties back to Moab rather than to Edom. It is the city mentioned in the Ballad of Heshbon (21:27-30) and the location where Balak first met Balaam (22:36).

Verses 20-24 are not related to vv. 16-19. It begins with a new introduction, which broadens the scope of Balaam's final oracle to include judgments on Amalek (v. 20), the Kenites (vv.

---

171. W. F. Albright, "The Oracles of Balaam," *JBL* 63 (1944) 220n. 89.

21-22), and an unnamed nation (vv. 23-24). Unlike vv. 15-19, Israel is not mentioned in these final three oracles. Verses 20-24 may consist of three separate oracles, since the judgment against each nation has a separate introduction. The first two are introduced by the words "Then he [Balaam] looked on . . . and uttered his oracle," while the last oracle only includes the words "he uttered his oracle." Thus vv. 20-24 are best characterized as prophetic oracles against foreign nations, a genre developed extensively in the classical prophets (e.g., Isaiah 13–23; Jeremiah 46–51).

The future destruction of the Amalekites is predicted in vv. 20-21. The reason for their inclusion at this juncture in the story is not clear. They are remembered as a nomadic tribe that opposed Israel early in its history, but presented no great threat during the monarchical period (Judges 6–7; 2 Sam 12:2-26). The description of them as "first among the nations" is open to several interpretations. It may be historical, but the OT provides very little evidence to evaluate such an interpretation. Another possibility arises from the literary structure of the poetic unit, in which "first among the nations" is an antonym of "end" in the second line.[172] A third interpretation arises from the larger story of the Pentateuch, where the Amalekites are the first nation to attack Israel during its wilderness journey (Exod 17:8-16).

The oracle against the Kenites in vv. 21-22 may arise from an association between Amalekites and Kenites in Israel's national experience (1 Sam 15:6). But Israel's memory of the Kenites is not that they are enemies. According to Judg 4:11, Moses' father-in-law was a Kenite, while in 1 Sam 15:4-9 Saul spares the Kenites in his conquest of the Amalekites because they "showed kindness to all the people of Israel when they came up out of Egypt."

The judgment against the Kenites may have to do more with their occupation as metalworkers, since the name "Kenite" means "smithy." The manipulation of metals is a form of alchemy that took on magical characteristics in the ancient world. It allowed nations to forge new materials for war, for work, and for construction that made a civilized, urban life possible. Verse 22 identifies the Kenites as descendants of Cain, who is the

eponymous ancestor of all "smiths" and, indeed, of all forms of civilization, including city building, commerce, and art (Gen 4:17-24). The negative evaluation of Cain in the Pentateuch is partially a judgment against civilization in general. The judgment of the biblical writers is that, in spite of all of its splendor, civilization is built on blood and violence. It began with the murder of Abel by Cain, and it increased to the point where Lamech, a descendent of Cain, kills a youth for merely striking him and boasts about it to his wives (Gen 4:23-24). Thus the judgment against the Kenites may be rooted in a broadly based critique of their manipulation of metal as a central component in the development of civilization and its empires. Balaam states that the destiny of Kain is to burn and to be taken captive by Asshur. In the OT, Asshur nearly always means the Assyrian Empire (Gen 10:22; Isa 10:5), which points to the eighth century BCE as one possible date for the composition of the poem.

The poem ends in Num vv. 23-24 with an additional oracle whose introduction lacks a specific nation as the object of the speech. The poem is nearly impossible to interpret in its present form. It begins as a woe oracle, "Alas!" The NRSV translation ("who shall live when God does this?") follows the MT text, where מִשֻּׂמוֹ (*miśśumô*) is derived from the verb "to determine" (שׂוּם *śûm*). The problem with that translation is that "this" is ambiguous. If "this" is taken to be a person, then it may refer to Asshur from the preceding verse (v. 22). The oracle then traces the downfall of Asshur and an unknown nation named Eber. In the LXX, Eber is taken to be a reference to the Hebrews. Others have conjectured a possible reference to a nomadic tribe or to a descendent of Midian (Gen 25:4). Still other problems of interpretation remain. The downfall of Asshur and Eber is brought about by ships from Kittim. Kittim was a city on Crete (Isa 23:1), but it can also designate Greeks (1 Macc 1:1) and the Romans (Dan 11:30). Such late historical references raise the possibility that subsequent world events affecting the history of Second Temple Judaism have prompted the additions in vv. 20-24. The story of Balaam ends in v. 25 with the diviner returning home.

---

172. See Jacob Milgrom, *Numbers,* JPS Torah Commentary (Philadelphia: JPS, 1990) 209.

REFLECTIONS

1. Every church has persons who see the power of God at work outside the community of faith. Their focus of ministry is often beyond the walls of the church. They identify the Spirit of God at work in unexpected places. They form coalitions with non-church groups. They build bridges with other faith communities. Such persons often make other members of their own church uncomfortable, because they are willing to push the boundaries for discerning the Spirit of God in the world. These persons are diviners. They are like Balaam.

Balaam models a third office of leadership in the book of Numbers: the seer. Prophetic and priestly leaders originate from within the worship life of Israel. Their forms of leadership and their responsibilities are distinct; the Commentary on Numbers 11–12 and 16–17 outlines these differences. Yet their sources of authority are similar. Revelation at the tent of meeting is central in the selection of Aaronide priests and the seventy elders. Both require divine confirmation to the entire community, through established forms of revelation. They represent tradition. Prophets channel the Spirit of God within the Israelite camp, and priests mediate the "glory of the Lord" through the tabernacle cult. Their focus of leadership remains within the community of faith.

The seer is a distinct form of religious leadership. Balaam's commission is never provided; he is simply introduced as a diviner. His religious authority is not confirmed through the tent of meeting, like that of prophets and priests. He is an outsider who knows God. The positive role of Balaam models the leadership of the seer. He is an outsider who divines the Spirit of God in Israel. The message of the story is that the reader also discern the Spirit of God in Balaam.

Two insights into the leadership role of the seer emerge from the story. First, a seer does not fear the unknown, as Balak does, whose first reaction to a new people is to destroy them. Instead, a seer seeks insight from God in order to evaluate the unfamiliar. The Israelites are unknown to Balaam; yet, he does not act out of fear. He divines in order to gain insight, not to destroy. Second, a seer builds bridges between people. Balak sought to destroy what was foreign to him. Balaam was able to discern the Spirit of God at work in a new situation, gain insight into others who are different, and make new alliances. He identified with Israel, and his oracles model this process. Balaam acquired self-understanding as he learned more about Israel. In the end, he blesses the people, rather than cursing them.

Every church needs seers in addition to priests and prophets. It is a form of mission. Christians also need to recognize seers in other faith communities. Our contemporary setting requires two additional comments on the seer that are implicit in the story of Balaam, but not articulated. First, the leadership role of a seer is not for the purpose of conversion. Balaam is not an Israelite, nor is the point of his story that he becomes an Israelite. Instead, he is idealized as one who is able to see God's Spirit at work in another community. At the conclusion of the story, he returns to his own home. Second, the clairvoyance of the seer is a gift from God. It does not occur outside of revelation or religious tradition. Balaam is grounded in his own relationship with God. The power of a seer is the ability to identify God's Spirit in others while embracing one's own faith tradition. Recognizing this special gift of leadership strengthens the church, both within its community of faith and in its larger role in the world.

2. Evaluating the authenticity of a seer is a problem. The role of a seer is meant to push us beyond what is familiar and orthodox. Thus, by its very nature, the leadership of the seer often takes away our ability to evaluate. How do we live with seers? How do we know when their divination is the voice of God, encouraging us to move into new and unfamiliar frontiers of faith, or whether it is destructive? The story of Balaam, his donkey, and the messenger of

Yahweh answers these questions. Balaam is once again the model, but this time through satire. He represents limited vision in this story, and his donkey takes on the leadership role of the seer.

The central theme of the episode is common sense in community, arising through shared experience. The donkey provides the teaching. Balaam fell prey to the fear of Balak by attributing sinister intentions to the animal when he was unable to understand its motives in veering off the road. The leadership role of the seer is modeled in this action. The seer is often required to lead us off the straight and narrow path to avoid dangers from God that most of us never see. The message of the story is that we evaluate what we cannot see by judging the morality of the seer. The donkey reminds Balaam of past service. Their shared experience warrants trust, even when one of the party is blind to the situation. The messenger of Yahweh confirms the commonsense insight of the donkey. Veering from the path saved Balaam from an attack by God. Recognizing the leadership role of seers is urgent, but evaluating it is even more important. The message of the foolish Balaam and his donkey is that without trust the leadership of a seer will always appear sinister.

3. The role of the church in interfaith dialogue raises many uncertain questions about religious pluralism in contemporary society. Balaam provides a model for evaluating religious persons outside of Judeo-Christian tradition. There is a long tradition in Jewish and Christian theology that knowledge of God is not limited to special revelation, but also includes a more general revelation. Special revelation includes unique events of salvation history and the acts of worship that grow out of those events. The Day of Atonement, for Jews, and Easter, for Christians, are festivals of special revelation. General revelation is the confession that God is also known more broadly through creation. Psalm 19:1 gives voice to general revelation when the psalmist declares, "The heavens are telling the glory of God;/ and the firmament proclaims God's handiwork" (NRSV). General revelation is potentially universal in scope, since any person living in this world has the potential of seeing the power of God in creation.

The story of Balaam fits neither category of special or general revelation. Balaam does not have some vague sense of divinity that emerges from the creation itself. He knows Yahweh through divination; yet, he did not acquire this knowledge from Israel. In fact, he has no knowledge of Israel or of their past history with God. Thus he has not acquired his knowledge of God through Israel's special revelation. But Balaam's knowledge of God is not simply the result of a general revelation, arising through the speech of creation. He is a diviner who performs specific cultic acts at night to prompt revelation. His acts of divination represent another religion, in which, surprisingly, not only El, Elyon, or Shaddai, but also even Yahweh is worshiped. One result of this surprising turn of events is that the story of Balaam confronts readers of the Bible with the revelation that God maintains active and personal relationships with human beings through other religious structures. The challenge for the church is to fashion an understanding of God that is firmly grounded in Christ, while not limiting God's power of salvation to Christian sacraments.

4. The Israelites are not active in the story of Balaam. Their absence allows biblical writers to explore the power of God's providence through blessing. The commentary on the priestly benediction (Num 6:22-27) outlined a variety of meanings that are conveyed in the act of blessing in ancient Israel. Three additional aspects of blessing provide the basis for theological reflection on Numbers 22–24.

First, blessing is evident through population and fertility. God blesses humanity in Gen 1:26-28 to be fertile. God blesses Abram in Gen 12:1-3 with the promise that his family will be fertile and develop into a great nation. This meaning is also evident in Numbers 22, where it is emphasized that Israel is once again a great population. The divine blessing is evident in the growth of Israel's second generation. This theme presents a special challenge to the contemporary church. We continue to confess that every human life and the ability to have children are gifts from God. But a large population is no longer a sign of blessing. It is even becoming a curse on the earth as we continue to strain natural resources to accommodate an ever-increasing number of people. Overpopulation and a limited view of the earth's resources were not topics of reflection for biblical writers.

Second, blessing means well-being, health, and peace. Numbers 22–24 explores the protective power of divine blessing. Israel assumes a passive and defenseless role throughout the drama. The interaction between God, Balaam, and Balak illustrates how God's blessing encircles Israel, protecting them in ways they do not even know. The message of the story is that God's blessing is reliable. The second oracle of Balaam provides commentary (Num 23:18-24). God's promises reach their goal. They cannot be revoked.

Third, blessing is dynamic. It is an active force that pulsates with life and, in doing so, confronts people with the power of God. The opening verses of Numbers 22 underscore the dynamic quality of blessing by emphasizing how Israel threatened Balak and the Moabites. The second generation of Israelites creates the same dread in the Moabites as in the Egyptians who were confronted by the first generation (Exodus 1). Thus Balak's desire to curse them is a response to the active power of blessing that emanates through Israel. Balaam, too, underscores the dynamic quality of blessing in his third oracle when he describes the interactive nature of blessing. Blessing will flow out to those who bless Israel, and it will bring a curse on those who curse Israel. Balaam and Balak represent the two ways in which the divine blessing on Israel can influence other nations. Both are confronted by the power of divine blessing, and each comes to a knowledge of Yahweh. Their separate reactions, however, determine whether divine blessing on Israel leads to their own blessing or to a curse. Balaam recognizes the power of divine blessing on Israel and claims it for himself. Balak, on the other hand, is threatened by Israel and seeks an antidote to their blessing through a curse. In the process, he becomes cursed. The central message in preaching about the dynamic quality of blessing is not the fate of Balaam and Balak, however. It is the reliability of God's blessing for the Israelites. God is active in dynamic ways, even when they are unaware.

5. Balaam is reinterpreted as a negative character in other Old Testament passages, in rabbinical tradition, and in the New Testament. In Numbers 31, Balaam, along with the Midianite kings, is killed by Israel for having induced them to sin at Baal Peor. In Deut 23:1-6, Balaam is accused of seeking to curse Israel. New Testament writers continue the negative interpretation of Balaam. In Rev 2:14, the story of Balaam and Balak is actually reversed, so that it is Balaam who is teaching Balak how he might make Israel stumble, while in Jude 11 and 2 Pet 2:15 Balaam is presented as divining for financial gain. The negative portrayal of Balaam is also in rabbinical literature. Three non-Israelites are singled out as advising Pharaoh on how to treat Israelites in Egypt. Job and Jethro are righteous Gentiles, but Balaam is characterized as being a wicked and blasphemous diviner.[173] He is accused of using his power of divination for greedy purposes.[174]

The negative interpretations of Balaam tend to emphasize his greed. This theme grows out of a more fundamental judgment about Balaam as being an idolater and a magician. Idolatry is the belief that there is a power distinct from God that does not transcend the systems of this world. Magic is the desire to utilize this power for personal gain; thus it represents greed in humans.

The history of interpretation illustrates the fluidity of Scripture over time. A positive character in Numbers 22–24 is used negatively in other texts. The teaching on idolatry as greed in the New Testament and in rabbinical literature contains a strong message for our materialistic

---

173. *B. Sota* 11a; *B. Sanh.* 106a; *Exod. Rab.* 1:9.
174. *M. Abot* 5:18. See Judith R. Baskin, *Pharaoh's Counsellors: Job, Jethro, and Balaam in Rabbinic and Patristic Tradition,* ed. J. Neusner et al., BJS 47 (Chico, Calif.: Scholars Press, 1983). For additional studies on the Balaam traditions see Michael S. Moore, *The Balaam Traditions: Their Character and Development,* and John T. Greene, *Balaam and His Interpreters: A Hermeneutical History of the Balaam Traditions,* ed. Shaye J. D. Cohen et al., BJS 244 (Atlanta: Scholars Press, 1992).

culture. It warns against reducing God to systems of social power to be used for personal gain. But the negative interpretations of Balaam must not silence his positive portrayal. Reclaiming his positive role in Numbers 22–24 is urgent in our ever-increasingly pluralistic world. The contemporary church requires the leadership of seers who are able to discern the Spirit of God in inter-religious dialogue and to guide us in new forms of social ethics.

Numbers 25:1-19, The Sin of Israel at Baal Peor

NIV

25 While Israel was staying in Shittim, the men began to indulge in sexual immorality with Moabite women, [2]who invited them to the sacrifices to their gods. The people ate and bowed down before these gods. [3]So Israel joined in worshiping the Baal of Peor. And the LORD's anger burned against them.

[4]The LORD said to Moses, "Take all the leaders of these people, kill them and expose them in broad daylight before the LORD, so that the LORD's fierce anger may turn away from Israel."

[5]So Moses said to Israel's judges, "Each of you must put to death those of your men who have joined in worshiping the Baal of Peor."

[6]Then an Israelite man brought to his family a Midianite woman right before the eyes of Moses and the whole assembly of Israel while they were weeping at the entrance to the Tent of Meeting. [7]When Phinehas son of Eleazar, the son of Aaron, the priest, saw this, he left the assembly, took a spear in his hand [8]and followed the Israelite into the tent. He drove the spear through both of them—through the Israelite and into the woman's body. Then the plague against the Israelites was stopped; [9]but those who died in the plague numbered 24,000.

[10]The LORD said to Moses, [11]"Phinehas son of Eleazar, the son of Aaron, the priest, has turned my anger away from the Israelites; for he was as zealous as I am for my honor among them, so that in my zeal I did not put an end to them. [12]Therefore tell him I am making my covenant of peace with him. [13]He and his descendants will have a covenant of a lasting priesthood, because he was zealous for the honor of his God and made atonement for the Israelites."

[14]The name of the Israelite who was killed with the Midianite woman was Zimri son of Salu, the leader of a Simeonite family. [15]And the name of the Midianite woman who was put to death was

NRSV

25 While Israel was staying at Shittim, the people began to have sexual relations with the women of Moab. [2]These invited the people to the sacrifices of their gods, and the people ate and bowed down to their gods. [3]Thus Israel yoked itself to the Baal of Peor, and the LORD's anger was kindled against Israel. [4]The LORD said to Moses, "Take all the chiefs of the people, and impale them in the sun before the LORD, in order that the fierce anger of the LORD may turn away from Israel." [5]And Moses said to the judges of Israel, "Each of you shall kill any of your people who have yoked themselves to the Baal of Peor."

6Just then one of the Israelites came and brought a Midianite woman into his family, in the sight of Moses and in the sight of the whole congregation of the Israelites, while they were weeping at the entrance of the tent of meeting. [7]When Phinehas son of Eleazar, son of Aaron the priest, saw it, he got up and left the congregation. Taking a spear in his hand, [8]he went after the Israelite man into the tent, and pierced the two of them, the Israelite and the woman, through the belly. So the plague was stopped among the people of Israel. [9]Nevertheless those that died by the plague were twenty-four thousand.

10The LORD spoke to Moses, saying: [11]"Phinehas son of Eleazar, son of Aaron the priest, has turned back my wrath from the Israelites by manifesting such zeal among them on my behalf that in my jealousy I did not consume the Israelites. [12]Therefore say, 'I hereby grant him my covenant of peace. [13]It shall be for him and for his descendants after him a covenant of perpetual priesthood, because he was zealous for his God, and made atonement for the Israelites.'"

14The name of the slain Israelite man, who was killed with the Midianite woman, was Zimri son of Salu, head of an ancestral house belonging to the Simeonites. [15]The name of the Midianite

NIV

Cozbi daughter of Zur, a tribal chief of a Midianite family.

¹⁶The LORD said to Moses, ¹⁷"Treat the Midianites as enemies and kill them, ¹⁸because they treated you as enemies when they deceived you in the affair of Peor and their sister Cozbi, the daughter of a Midianite leader, the woman who was killed when the plague came as a result of Peor."

NRSV

woman who was killed was Cozbi daughter of Zur, who was the head of a clan, an ancestral house in Midian.

16The LORD said to Moses, 17"Harass the Midianites, and defeat them; 18for they have harassed you by the trickery with which they deceived you in the affair of Peor, and in the affair of Cozbi, the daughter of a leader of Midian, their sister; she was killed on the day of the plague that resulted from Peor."

COMMENTARY

Numbers 22–25 describes two external threats to Israel. The first (chaps. 22–24) is Balak's desire to conjure up a curse on Israel. The Balaam cycle of stories illustrates God's protective power even at those times when Israel is unaware of it. The second external threat to Israel (chap. 25) involves its active participation in worshiping other gods and in mixed marriages. As a result, the worship of the golden calf at Mt. Sinai (Exodus 32) is repeated on the plains of Moab, with the same consequences for the Israelites.

Numbers 25 contains two stories about how Israel's complicity in external threats to their purity can lead to death. The pre-priestly story (vv. 1-5) treats the threat of worshiping the gods of surrounding nations. The Moabites are the central characters. Israel is described as "the people" (העם *hā ʿām*). The daughters of Moab entice the Israelites to worship their gods. The foreign god worshiped by Israel is a local deity named Baal of Peor. Yahweh responds in anger, commanding Moses to punish the leaders of the tribes by impaling them. Judges assist Moses in carrying out the divine decree. Parallels to the story of the golden calf (Exodus 32) include the worship of a foreign god with sacrifice (v. 2; Exod 32:6), divine rage (v. 4; Exod 32:10), and slaughter of the offenders (v. 5; Exod 32:28).

The priestly writers add a second story in vv. 6-18. In this account, an Israelite man publicly brings a Midianite woman into his family. Israel is described with the priestly term "the congregation of the children of Israel" (עדת בני-ישראל *ʿǎdat běnê-yiśrāʾēl*). Sexual imagery indicates the cen-

tral theme as intermarriage between an Israelite and a Midianite. In response, Phinehas, the priest, spears the couple through their stomachs as they lie in their tent. Divine anger in the form of a plague ceases with this action. Additional parallels to the golden calf appear, including plague as divine punishment (v. 9; Exod 32:35); slaughter of the guilty, resulting in atonement (vv. 8-10; Exod 32:28-30); and the establishment of a special office (Levites to serve Yahweh [Exod 32:28-29] and Phinehas to the perpetual priesthood [Num 25:12-13]).

The differences between the two stories in Numbers 25 are clear: The pre-priestly story warns against worshiping Moabite gods. Moses and the tribal judges assume responsibility for purity of worship. The priestly story moves beyond worship to intermarriage with Midianites, and the priesthood assumes responsibility for Israel's purity. More detailed commentary will bring to light further differences. In spite of their differences, however, both stories share underlying similarities that provide an important starting point for commentary: (1) Other nations present an external threat to Israel; (2) the external threat requires Israel's active participation; (3) resisting the threat implies clear boundaries between Israel and other nations; and (4) both stories qualify the universal focus on revelation of the Balaam cycle of stories.

25:1-5. The account of Israel's idolatry consists of three parts. The event and its location are described in vv. 1-3*a*, the divine response appears in vv. 3*b*-4, and the action of Moses (v. 5) concludes the episode.

The setting of the story is Shittim (v. 1). It is

not one of the itinerary notices, but simply states that Israel "was staying" or "dwelt" at Shittim. Similar notices occur in 20:1 and 21:25, 31. Israel dwells at Kadesh (20:1), in the city of the Amorites (21:25), and in the land of the Amorites (21:35). Shittim has no clear modern counterpart. The word translates as the thorny tree "acacias." Shittim wood is used in the construction of the ark and the tabernacle (e.g., Exod 25:5, 10, 13; 26:32, 37). Shittim reappears in the itinerary travel list of Numbers 33 as Abel-Shittim (33:49), and it is associated with the crossing of the Jordan (Josh 2:1; 3:1; 4:18). The literary function of the new setting is that it separates the events in Numbers 25 from the Balaam cycle of stories in Numbers 22–24, which took place while Israel was encamped on the plains of Moab (see 22:1).

Events move quickly in vv. 1-3a. The NRSV translation emphasizes a sexual relationship between Israelite men and Moabite women. The Hebrew, however, is ambiguous. The central verb of the sentence is חלל (ḥālal), meaning "to pollute," and it is combined with the verb זנה (zānâ), meaning "to fornicate" or "to engage in illicit extramarital relations." Thus sexual nuances are undoubtedly part of the story. Leviticus 21:9 uses the latter verb to describe sexual practice, but the language may be intended to describe the worship of other gods, since the verb "to fornicate" can also be used metaphorically to described false worship (e.g., Jer 2:20). The book of Hosea illustrates how both meanings may be combined (Hos 2:7; 4:13-14), and this may also be the case in v. 1b.

The larger context of vv. 1-3a indicates that the pre-priestly writers are concerned primarily with the worship of other gods. Israel's act of fornication entails sacrificing to the Moabite deities, eating the food of the sacrifices, and, finally, worshiping Moabite gods. The result (v. 3) is that Israel becomes attached to Baal of Peor. The Hebrew word describing Israel's attachment is translated "yoked" (צמד ṣāmad) in the NRSV and "joined" in the NIV. The idea is not oppression or servitude, but bonding, hence the imagery of fornication to describe Israel's action in relationship to Yahweh. The particular deity is odd, given that Chemosh was the Moabite god. Baal is the Canaanite storm god of fertility who appears in a variety of local manifestations in the OT; in addition to Baal Peor (vv. 1-5), other manifestations

include Baal-hermon (Judg 3:3) and Baal-hazor (2 Sam 13:23).

The divine response in vv. 3b-4 is anger. Other occurrences of such anger include the golden calf incident (Exod 32:10-11), the divine responses to Israel's murmuring (Num 11:1-3; 11:10, 33), the challenge of Aaron and Miriam (Num 12:9), and Balaam (Num 22:22). Many of these instances are accompanied by a plague, which has prompted commentators to assume a similar situation in Numbers 25. But no mention is made of a plague in the pre-priestly story (vv. 1-5). It is first introduced in the priestly addition (vv. 6-18).

Although God's anger is directed to Israel in general, the chiefs of the people are singled out for judgment in v. 4. The term "chiefs" (ראשים rāʾšîm) has appeared two other times in Numbers. In 10:4, they are described as heads of the tribes who represent the people at special meetings announced by a single trumpet blast. The chiefs reappear as spies in 13:3. The use of the term in 25:4 suggests that divine judgment is not limited to the guilty but falls indiscriminately on all leaders. They are to be hanged in the sun. Reference to the sun suggests a public execution. The manner of death is most likely impalement. Similar language describes the death of Saul's seven sons (2 Sam 21:6, 9), who were impaled by Gibeonites. Wenham has suggested that the act of impalement in the sun indicates that the corpses were not buried.[175] Such impalement without burial signifies divine curse (Deut 21:22-23) and is actually forbidden in the promised land of Canaan because of its power to defile the land. The text is not clear about the burial of the corpses, but it is clear that the impalement is not meant primarily as a warning to Israel. Rather, it functions to appease God by expiating Israel from apostasy.

Moses executes the divine command in v. 5. But instead of impaling the leaders in general, he commands judges to kill only the guilty individuals. Thus there is no correspondence between the divine command of v. 4 and Moses' actions in v. 5. The reference to judges relates this text with Exodus 18, where, upon the advice of Jethro, Moses elected judges to command companies of ten, fifty, one hundred, and one thousand. The

---

175. Gordon J. Wenham, *Numbers: An Introduction and Commentary*, Tyndale Old Testament Commentaries (Leicester: Inter-Varsity, 1981) 186-87.

relationship between these judges and the chiefs mentioned in v. 4 is not clear. In addition, there is no indication that impalement is used to kill the offenders.

The lack of correspondence has puzzled commentators. Some have suggested that 25:1-5 consists of two different stories, now only partially woven together. But this is unlikely. What is striking about the story is that even though God demands indiscriminate death to appease divine anger, Moses follows the principle of punishing only the guilty. In so doing, Moses is following and extending God's own instructions from the story of the spies, where punishment was reserved for the guilty generation, while grace was extended indiscriminately to the next generation (14:11-25). The action of Moses in v. 5 is an extension of the spy story, in that he is distinguishing between the innocent and the guilty within the same generation. The lack of comment on the striking difference between the divine command and the action of Moses suggests that his method is the proper extension of law and grace from the story of the spies.

25:6-19. The priestly writers add their own interpretation of Israel's sin at Baal Peor. It is a story of intermarriage between an Israelite man and a Midianite woman, who are executed by Phinehas the priest. The story is structured in four parts that modulate between a description of events and divine speeches evaluating the events. Verses 6-9 provide the central narrative, with divine discourse in vv. 10-13 affirming the action of Phinehas. Verses 14-15 return to the story line by providing the names of the executed couple, while vv. 16-18 conclude the episode with a divine judgment on the Midianites.

The priestly version of the sin at Baal Peor is narrated in vv. 6-9. The wording of v. 6 indicates that the priestly writers intend for their story to be read in conjunction with the previous story, even though the connection is at best loose. For the priestly writers, the crisis with Moabites evolves into a crisis with Midianites. The setting for the story is cultic. The congregation is weeping at the door of the tent of meeting. The offense is that an Israelite man brings a Midianite woman into the Israelite camp for the purpose of marriage. The action is described as taking place in the sight of Moses and the congregation, suggesting a public act of intermarriage. The couple is described

in v. 8 as being in the tent. The Hebrew word translated "tent" is קבה (*qubbâ*); it occurs only in this story. Scholars debate what the priestly writers intend by using this word. The setting of the story suggests that it may refer to a chamber of the tent of meeting, since Moses and the congregation were weeping at the door of the tent of meeting. Another possible interpretation is that it is a marriage canopy. In either case, it is clear that the imagery of the priestly story is meant to be explicitly sexual. The couple is having intercourse either in the tent of meeting or in a separate marriage tent.

Phinehas is introduced in this story for the first time in the book of Numbers. He is mentioned one previous time in the Pentateuch, in the priestly genealogy of Exod 6:16-25, where he is identified as a grandson of Aaron through the line of Eleazar. His name is Egyptian and means "dark-skinned one." In the genealogy of 1 Chronicles 9, Phinehas is described as chief over all the levitical gatekeepers (see 1 Chr 9:17-20). Phinehas functions as guard of the camp in this story. He is singled out as acting to protect the camp from the pollution of an intermarriage between an Israelite man and a Midianite woman. Phinehas will return in the same role against Midianites in chap. 31, when he leads Israel in a holy war. Thus, in the priestly version of the sin at Baal Peor, Phinehas saves Israel from divine wrath in his role as guard.

Verses 7-9 describe how Phinehas takes a spear, enters the tent where the couple is lying, and stabs either the woman or both of them through the stomach. At this point in the story, a plague is mentioned for the first time. The reader is told that the execution stops the plague, but not before 24,000 Israelites are killed. The action of Phinehas in killing the couple, and its effects in appeasing divine wrath in the form of a plague, parallels the story of Aaron in 16:41-50[17:6-15]. In both stories, priestly acts of ritual intercession provide antidotes to disease that stems from divine wrath.

The central theme in the divine speech of vv. 10-13 is jealousy. God demands an exclusive relationship with Israel. The word "jealousy" (קנא *qānā´*) conveys qualities of vigilance, intolerance, and absolute devotion. God states in v. 11 that Phinehas has absorbed God's jealousy ("he was jealous with my jealousy in their midst"). Phinehas's act has a fanatical quality to it, which is idealized in later tradition by Zealots (4 Macc 18:12). In absorbing God's jealousy and acting it out precisely on those who are guilty, Phinehas has saved Israel from God's more indiscriminate punishment of a general plague on all Israelites. Here the action of Phinehas parallels that of Moses from the preceding story (v. 5), in that each hero focuses divine anger on the guilty, rather than on all the people.

The divine speech in vv. 10-13 affirms the action of Phinehas, interprets its significance theologically, and bestows special status upon him and his clan. Phinehas is given a covenant of peace from God. The language may indicate wholeness and health as the Hebrew word "peace" (שלום šālôm) often does (see 6:22-27; Isa 54:10). But, as Milgrom has suggested, it may have a more precise meaning in this case—namely, that Phinehas is protected from revenge by Zimri's clan.[176] In this case, the text would be stating that those who protect the sanctuary from encroachment do not incur blood guilt. Indeed, such action saves Israel. God makes a second covenant concerning the status of Phinehas's clan: They will be priests forever. The enduring quality of the promise is similar to the covenant made with King David (Ps 89:29-37). Both are unconditional and permanent.

Verses 14-15 return to the narrative by naming the couple. The Israelite male was Zimri, whose father was Salu, a chief in the tribe of Simeon. The Midianite woman was Cozbi, whose father was Zur, a tribal head. Including the names of the couple gives the incident concreteness. Perhaps their status indicates that the prohibition against intermarriage could not be circumvented

by those with power. More certainly, it is clear that the mention of the Midianites serves a larger purpose for priestly writers—eliminating their influence on Israelite religion. The concluding speech by God (vv. 16-18) provides a bridge to chap. 31, where Israel will declare holy war on Midian.

God commands Moses (vv. 16-18) to show hostility (צרור ṣārôr) against Midian, because Midian showed hostility (צררים ṣōrĕrîm) against it. Midian's hostility toward Israel takes the form of trickery or deceit, according to the priestly writers. The Hebrew word used to describe their deceit is נכל (nēkel). It occurs in only two other passages in the OT: It characterizes the action of Joseph's brothers in deciding to kill him (Gen 37:18), and Pharaoh is described as acting in a deceitful manner when he oppressed Israel in Egypt (Ps 105:25). These passages suggest that trickery leads to either death or oppression. For the priestly writers, intermarriage between an Israelite and a Midianite is also trickery, leading to the same outcome. God calls the Israelites to holy war against the Midianites.

Verse 19 is an incomplete sentence. It includes only the phrase "after the plague." The NRSV and the NIV have merged the verse with the second census in Numbers 26. This may be the original intention of the priestly writers. The temporal clause may also have been intended to connect chaps. 25 and 31, "After the plague the LORD spoke to Moses, saying," (31:1). The strength of this interpretation is that Numbers 31 fulfills the divine command to wage holy war against Midian (25:17-18).

176. Milgrom, *Numbers,* 216.

REFLECTIONS

1. The Christian life has an irresolvable tension within it. The incarnation of Jesus and his proclamation of the kingdom of God root salvation in this world. Christians are called to embrace life here and now, and all people. The gospel is inclusive. Jesus provides the model by accepting outsiders, like the Samaritan woman (John 4). The pattern continues in Acts as disciples venture out to the ends of the earth. At the same time, discipleship requires radical and even fanatical denial. Everything must be renounced by disciples, according to Jesus (Luke 14:25-33). He even states, "Whoever comes to me and does not hate father and mother, wife and children, brothers and sisters, yes, and even life itself, cannot be my disciple" (Luke 14:26 NRSV). The truth of the gospel cannot be understood by focusing on one pole of the tension or in seeking a resolution between embracing the world and denying it altogether. The tension generates a vision of the Christian life, encapsulated in the saying, "Christians must be in the world, but not of it."

The threats to Israel on the plains of Moab (Numbers 22–25) create the same tension. Balaam, the Mesopotamian seer, breaks all boundaries in demonstrating the universal power of Yahweh in the world (Numbers 22–24). The pre-priestly writers barely make this point before they qualify it with a message of radical exclusion in following Yahweh (Num 25:1-5). The Mesopotamian seer may be a Yahwist, but Israel had better maintain clear boundaries with their more immediate Moabite neighbors. The two stories stand side by side. Neither negates the other, nor is a resolution between them offered. The priestly writers intensify the tension by making it personal. They move from the social domain of the pre-priestly writers to the family and marriage (Num 25:6-19). Their conclusion is that following Yahweh may require renouncing family. Preaching Numbers 22–25 is no different from preaching the Gospels. No single story carries the entire message. The central message in Numbers 22–25 emerges from the tension between the stories. It is that Israel must be in the world (Numbers 22–24), but not of it (Numbers 25).

2. The jealousy of God is an important topic for theological reflection. It is a central theme throughout Numbers 25, both in the story of the Moabites (Num 25:1-5) and in intermarriage between an Israelite and a Midianite (Num 25:6-19). Jealousy is about divine passion. It stresses that Yahweh is not indifferent to Israel or to their relationships in this world. It conveys strong imagery of intolerance for any allegiance outside of the relationship to God. Commentators tend to water down the violent and suspicious characteristics that accompany a description of God as being jealous. But the content of the stories in Numbers 25 suggest just the opposite. God is fanatical in demanding exclusive allegiance—so fanatical, in fact, that punishment is enacted indiscriminately. The jealousy of God is an important message to preach. God is not casual about our commitments. God is jealous about how we worship (Num 25:1-5) and how we live (Num 25:6-18).

Seduction in Numbers 25 aids in interpreting jealousy. It describes the process by which Israel is pulled away from Yahweh, prompting God's jealous reaction. The threats to Israel are external. The pollution represented by Moabites and Midianites, therefore, requires Israel's active participation in order for it to enter the camp. The sexual imagery throughout Numbers 25 indicates the Israelites' active role in seeking partners other than Yahweh, prompting the jealous response.

There is every reason to believe that priestly writers were literal in their message against intermarriage. Laws against intermarriage during the Second Temple period are stated in Ezra 9–10 (see Commentary on 11:1–12:16). One need not continue to read the story literally, however, to preach and to teach its central message. Entering into a relationship with God is filled with passion, and God demands exclusive devotion, requiring that we create boundaries in our lives. In the contemporary church, these boundaries are ethical. The constant factor in reinterpreting this story in the modern world is divine jealousy. God continues to be an enraged spouse whenever we are seduced by other allegiances.

3. There is yet another example of leadership in Numbers 25, which also provides insight into God. Both Moses and Phinehas act on principles that arise from the story of the spies in Numbers 13–15. The principle is that God limits punishment to the guilty. The striking feature of Moses' leadership is that he applies this principle even when it goes against the command of God. God is enraged in Num 25:1-5 and wishes to destroy indiscriminately. Moses departs from the direct command of Yahweh and kills only the guilty. The action of Moses is not determined by the passion of the moment, nor does he resort to direct intercession with God as he has tended to do in the past. Instead, his action is based on God's own instructions from the spy story that punishment be reserved for the guilty.

The lack of intercession to justify Moses' action has prompted scholars to judge the story incomplete. But his action requires no intercession, since the divine principle of punishing only the guilty has already been established. Moses even advances the teaching from the spy story, since he now distinguishes between the guilty and the innocent of the same generation. Phinehas models the same principle in a priestly leadership role. By executing the guilty and halting the plague on all the people, he also qualifies indiscriminate divine wrath so that the innocent are not punished.

The role of Scripture emerges as central in preaching this story. Moses models leadership based on principles of past revelation, not on the passion of the moment. A central message of the story is that God is also bound by the principles of Scripture. Moses does not execute the divine command to kill all of the Israelites. Yet, there is no indication that he is disobeying God. Mosaic leadership in Num 25:1-5 provides a model of searching Scripture to resolve conflict. The rabbis give image to the central role of Scripture by envisioning God as also studying Torah.[177]

177. *m.'Abod. Zar* 3.b.

NUMBERS 26:1–36:13, INSTRUCTIONS FOR INHERITANCE

OVERVIEW

Priestly literature frames the book of Numbers. Chapters 1–10 describe the first generation at Mt. Sinai, fashioning the wilderness camp around the tabernacle. They perish because of rebellion against God. Chapters 26–36 are also priestly tradition, with the exception of chaps. 32–33, which focuses on the second generation preparing for life in the land. The central theme, inheritance, provides a new beginning to the Israelites' quest for the promised land, signaled through repetition in the structure of Numbers. The census of the second generation (chap. 26) repeats the first (chap. 1). There is also a change of leadership. Eleazar replaces Aaron as high priest (26:1), and Joshua succeeds Moses to lead Israel into the promised land (27:12-23). The theme of inheritance loosely organizes chaps. 27–36. Inheritance law of daughters frames the section (27:1-11; 36:1-13), while possession of the Transjordan (chap. 32) and Canaan (chap. 34), along with the distribution of levitical cities (chap. 35) are woven throughout the section.

The census (chap. 26) signals transition from the first to the second generation. The tribes and the Levites are recounted on the plains of Moab.

In chap. 27, the central theme of land inheritance is established with the request by the daughters of Zelophehad to take possession of their father's property, since they lack male siblings. The chapter also includes the announcement of Moses' death and Joshua's succession of him to lead Israel into the land of Canaan.

Divine command to Moses in chaps. 28–30 outlines the sacrificial responsibilities for each day, week, month, and year. The commands include priestly duties for cultic sacrifices, the Israelite cultic calendar for worship festivals, and the obligations of vows by laypersons—especially women.

Holy war is the central theme of chaps. 31–33, and chap. 31 returns to the threat of Midian introduced in the Balaam cycle of stories (chaps. 22–24) and in the priestly version of Israel's sin at Baal Peor (chap. 25). God declares holy war against Midian in chap. 31, providing the occasion to describe the laws pertaining to booty. Chapter 32 outlines the inheritance of the Transjordan as the outcome of war. Chapter 33 reviews the wilderness journey to prepare the Israelites for continued war in Canaan.

The land of Canaan takes center stage in the

final section (chaps. 34–36). Chapter 34 describes its boundaries; chap. 35 outlines the Levites' role in the land and their cities of refuge; and chap. 36 closes the book by returning to the topic of inheritance by daughters. The request of the daughters of Zelophehad is modified to ensure that land stays within the possession of the original tribe, regardless of marriage.

Numbers 26:1-65, The Census of the Second Generation

NIV

26After the plague the LORD said to Moses and Eleazar son of Aaron, the priest, [2]"Take a census of the whole Israelite community by families—all those twenty years old or more who are able to serve in the army of Israel." [3]So on the plains of Moab by the Jordan across from Jericho,[a] Moses and Eleazar the priest spoke with them and said, [4]"Take a census of the men twenty years old or more, as the LORD commanded Moses."

These were the Israelites who came out of Egypt:

[5]The descendants of Reuben, the firstborn son of Israel, were:

    through Hanoch, the Hanochite clan;
    through Pallu, the Palluite clan;
    [6]through Hezron, the Hezronite clan;
    through Carmi, the Carmite clan.

[7]These were the clans of Reuben; those numbered were 43,730.

[8]The son of Pallu was Eliab, [9]and the sons of Eliab were Nemuel, Dathan and Abiram. The same Dathan and Abiram were the community officials who rebelled against Moses and Aaron and were among Korah's followers when they rebelled against the LORD. [10]The earth opened its mouth and swallowed them along with Korah, whose followers died when the fire devoured the 250 men. And they served as a warning sign. [11]The line of Korah, however, did not die out.

[12]The descendants of Simeon by their clans were:

    through Nemuel, the Nemuelite clan;
    through Jamin, the Jaminite clan;
    through Jakin, the Jakinite clan;
    [13]through Zerah, the Zerahite clan;
    through Shaul, the Shaulite clan.

[14]These were the clans of Simeon; there were 22,200 men.

NRSV

26After the plague the LORD said to Moses and to Eleazar son of Aaron the priest, [2]"Take a census of the whole congregation of the Israelites, from twenty years old and upward, by their ancestral houses, everyone in Israel able to go to war." [3]Moses and Eleazar the priest spoke with them in the plains of Moab by the Jordan opposite Jericho, saying, [4]"Take a census of the people,[a] from twenty years old and upward," as the LORD commanded Moses.

The Israelites, who came out of the land of Egypt, were:

5Reuben, the firstborn of Israel. The descendants of Reuben: of Hanoch, the clan of the Hanochites; of Pallu, the clan of the Palluites; [6]of Hezron, the clan of the Hezronites; of Carmi, the clan of the Carmites. [7]These are the clans of the Reubenites; the number of those enrolled was forty-three thousand seven hundred thirty. [8]And the descendants of Pallu: Eliab. [9]The descendants of Eliab: Nemuel, Dathan, and Abiram. These are the same Dathan and Abiram, chosen from the congregation, who rebelled against Moses and Aaron in the company of Korah, when they rebelled against the LORD, [10]and the earth opened its mouth and swallowed them up along with Korah, when that company died, when the fire devoured two hundred fifty men; and they became a warning. [11]Notwithstanding, the sons of Korah did not die.

12The descendants of Simeon by their clans: of Nemuel, the clan of the Nemuelites; of Jamin, the clan of the Jaminites; of Jachin, the clan of the Jachinites; [13]of Zerah, the clan of the Zerahites; of Shaul, the clan of the Shaulites.[b] [14]These are the clans of the Simeonites, twenty-two thousand two hundred.

15The children of Gad by their clans: of Zephon, the clan of the Zephonites; of Haggi, the

---

[a]3 Hebrew *Jordan of Jericho;* possibly an ancient name for the Jordan River; also in verse 63

[a] Heb lacks *take a census of the people:* Compare verse 2   [b] Or *Saul . . . Saulites*

NIV

¹⁵The descendants of Gad by their clans were:

through Zephon, the Zephonite clan;

through Haggi, the Haggite clan;

through Shuni, the Shunite clan;

¹⁶through Ozni, the Oznite clan;

through Eri, the Erite clan;

¹⁷through Arodi,[a] the Arodite clan;

through Areli, the Arelite clan.

¹⁸These were the clans of Gad; those numbered were 40,500.

¹⁹Er and Onan were sons of Judah, but they died in Canaan.

²⁰The descendants of Judah by their clans were:

through Shelah, the Shelanite clan;

through Perez, the Perezite clan;

through Zerah, the Zerahite clan.

²¹The descendants of Perez were:

through Hezron, the Hezronite clan;

through Hamul, the Hamulite clan.

²²These were the clans of Judah; those numbered were 76,500.

²³The descendants of Issachar by their clans were:

through Tola, the Tolaite clan;

through Puah, the Puite[b] clan;

²⁴through Jashub, the Jashubite clan;

through Shimron, the Shimronite clan.

²⁵These were the clans of Issachar; those numbered were 64,300.

²⁶The descendants of Zebulun by their clans were:

through Sered, the Seredite clan;

through Elon, the Elonite clan;

through Jahleel, the Jahleelite clan.

²⁷These were the clans of Zebulun; those numbered were 60,500.

²⁸The descendants of Joseph by their clans through Manasseh and Ephraim were:

²⁹The descendants of Manasseh:

through Makir, the Makirite clan (Makir was the father of Gilead);

through Gilead, the Gileadite clan.

³⁰These were the descendants of Gilead:

through Iezer, the Iezerite clan;

through Helek, the Helekite clan;

³¹through Asriel, the Asrielite clan;

[a17] Samaritan Pentateuch and Syriac (see also Gen. 46:16); Masoretic Text *Arod*   [b23] Samaritan Pentateuch, Septuagint, Vulgate and Syriac (see also 1 Chron. 7:1); Masoretic Text *through Puvah, the Punite*

NRSV

clan of the Haggites; of Shuni, the clan of the Shunites; ¹⁶of Ozni, the clan of the Oznites; of Eri, the clan of the Erites; ¹⁷of Arod, the clan of the Arodites; of Areli, the clan of the Arelites. ¹⁸These are the clans of the Gadites: the number of those enrolled was forty thousand five hundred.

19The sons of Judah: Er and Onan; Er and Onan died in the land of Canaan. ²⁰The descendants of Judah by their clans were: of Shelah, the clan of the Shelanites; of Perez, the clan of the Perezites; of Zerah, the clan of the Zerahites. ²¹The descendants of Perez were: of Hezron, the clan of the Hezronites; of Hamul, the clan of the Hamulites. ²²These are the clans of Judah: the number of those enrolled was seventy-six thousand five hundred.

23The descendants of Issachar by their clans: of Tola, the clan of the Tolaites; of Puvah, the clan of the Punites; ²⁴of Jashub, the clan of the Jashubites; of Shimron, the clan of the Shimronites. ²⁵These are the clans of Issachar: sixty-four thousand three hundred enrolled.

26The descendants of Zebulun by their clans: of Sered, the clan of the Seredites; of Elon, the clan of the Elonites; of Jahleel, the clan of the Jahleelites. ²⁷These are the clans of the Zebulunites; the number of those enrolled was sixty thousand five hundred.

28The sons of Joseph by their clans: Manasseh and Ephraim. ²⁹The descendants of Manasseh: of Machir, the clan of the Machirites; and Machir was the father of Gilead; of Gilead, the clan of the Gileadites. ³⁰These are the descendants of Gilead: of Iezer, the clan of the Iezerites; of Helek, the clan of the Helekites; ³¹and of Asriel, the clan of the Asrielites; and of Shechem, the clan of the Shechemites; ³²and of Shemida, the clan of the Shemidaites; and of Hepher, the clan of the Hepherites. ³³Now Zelophehad son of Hepher had no sons, but daughters: and the names of the daughters of Zelophehad were Mahlah, Noah, Hoglah, Milcah, and Tirzah. ³⁴These are the clans of Manasseh; the number of those enrolled was fifty-two thousand seven hundred.

35These are the descendants of Ephraim according to their clans: of Shuthelah, the clan of the Shuthelahites; of Becher, the clan of the Becherites; of Tahan, the clan of the Tahanites.

NIV

through Shechem, the Shechemite clan;
[32]through Shemida, the Shemidaite clan;
through Hepher, the Hepherite clan.
[33](Zelophehad son of Hepher had no sons; he had only daughters, whose names were Mahlah, Noah, Hoglah, Milcah and Tirzah.)
[34]These were the clans of Manasseh; those numbered were 52,700.

[35]These were the descendants of Ephraim by their clans:
through Shuthelah, the Shuthelahite clan;
through Beker, the Bekerite clan;
through Tahan, the Tahanite clan.
[36]These were the descendants of Shuthelah:
through Eran, the Eranite clan.
[37]These were the clans of Ephraim; those numbered were 32,500.

These were the descendants of Joseph by their clans.

[38]The descendants of Benjamin by their clans were:
through Bela, the Belaite clan;
through Ashbel, the Ashbelite clan;
through Ahiram, the Ahiramite clan;
[39]through Shupham,[a] the Shuphamite clan;
through Hupham, the Huphamite clan.
[40]The descendants of Bela through Ard and Naaman were:
through Ard,[b] the Ardite clan;
through Naaman, the Naamite clan.
[41]These were the clans of Benjamin; those numbered were 45,600.

[42]These were the descendants of Dan by their clans:
through Shuham, the Shuhamite clan.
These were the clans of Dan: [43]All of them were Shuhamite clans; and those numbered were 64,400.

[44]The descendants of Asher by their clans were:
through Imnah, the Imnite clan;
through Ishvi, the Ishvite clan;
through Beriah, the Beriite clan;
[45]and through the descendants of Beriah:

a39 A few manuscripts of the Masoretic Text, Samaritan Pentateuch, Vulgate and Syriac (see also Septuagint); most manuscripts of the Masoretic Text *Shephupham*   b40 Samaritan Pentateuch and Vulgate (see also Septuagint); Masoretic Text does not have *through Ard*

NRSV

[36]And these are the descendants of Shuthelah: of Eran, the clan of the Eranites. [37]These are the clans of the Ephraimites: the number of those enrolled was thirty-two thousand five hundred. These are the descendants of Joseph by their clans.

[38]The descendants of Benjamin by their clans: of Bela, the clan of the Belaites; of Ashbel, the clan of the Ashbelites; of Ahiram, the clan of the Ahiramites; [39]of Shephupham, the clan of the Shuphamites; of Hupham, the clan of the Huphamites. [40]And the sons of Bela were Ard and Naaman: of Ard, the clan of the Ardites; of Naaman, the clan of the Naamites. [41]These are the descendants of Benjamin by their clans; the number of those enrolled was forty-five thousand six hundred.

[42]These are the descendants of Dan by their clans: of Shuham, the clan of the Shuhamites. These are the clans of Dan by their clans. [43]All the clans of the Shuhamites: sixty-four thousand four hundred enrolled.

[44]The descendants of Asher by their families: of Imnah, the clan of the Imnites; of Ishvi, the clan of the Ishvites; of Beriah, the clan of the Beriites. [45]Of the descendants of Beriah: of Heber, the clan of the Heberites; of Malchiel, the clan of the Malchielites. [46]And the name of the daughter of Asher was Serah. [47]These are the clans of the Asherites: the number of those enrolled was fifty-three thousand four hundred.

[48]The descendants of Naphtali by their clans: of Jahzeel, the clan of the Jahzeelites; of Guni, the clan of the Gunites; [49]of Jezer, the clan of the Jezerites; of Shillem, the clan of the Shillemites. [50]These are the Naphtalites[a] by their clans: the number of those enrolled was forty-five thousand four hundred.

[51]This was the number of the Israelites enrolled: six hundred and one thousand seven hundred thirty.

[52]The LORD spoke to Moses, saying: [53]To these the land shall be apportioned for inheritance according to the number of names. [54]To a large tribe you shall give a large inheritance, and to a small tribe you shall give a small inheritance; every tribe shall be given its inheritance according to its

a Heb *clans of Naphtali*

through Heber, the Heberite clan;

through Malkiel, the Malkielite clan.

⁴⁶(Asher had a daughter named Serah.)

⁴⁷These were the clans of Asher; those numbered were 53,400.

⁴⁸The descendants of Naphtali by their clans were:

through Jahzeel, the Jahzeelite clan;

through Guni, the Gunite clan;

⁴⁹through Jezer, the Jezerite clan;

through Shillem, the Shillemite clan.

⁵⁰These were the clans of Naphtali; those numbered were 45,400.

⁵¹The total number of the men of Israel was 601,730.

⁵²The LORD said to Moses, ⁵³"The land is to be allotted to them as an inheritance based on the number of names. ⁵⁴To a larger group give a larger inheritance, and to a smaller group a smaller one; each is to receive its inheritance according to the number of those listed. ⁵⁵Be sure that the land is distributed by lot. What each group inherits will be according to the names for its ancestral tribe. ⁵⁶Each inheritance is to be distributed by lot among the larger and smaller groups."

⁵⁷These were the Levites who were counted by their clans:

through Gershon, the Gershonite clan;

through Kohath, the Kohathite clan;

through Merari, the Merarite clan.

⁵⁸These also were Levite clans:

the Libnite clan,

the Hebronite clan,

the Mahlite clan,

the Mushite clan,

the Korahite clan.

(Kohath was the forefather of Amram; ⁵⁹the name of Amram's wife was Jochebed, a descendant of Levi, who was born to the Levites[a] in Egypt. To Amram she bore Aaron, Moses and their sister Miriam. ⁶⁰Aaron was the father of Nadab and Abihu, Eleazar and Ithamar. ⁶¹But Nadab and Abihu died when they made an offering before the LORD with unauthorized fire.)

[a]59 Or *Jochebed, a daughter of Levi, who was born to Levi*

enrollment. ⁵⁵But the land shall be apportioned by lot; according to the names of their ancestral tribes they shall inherit. ⁵⁶Their inheritance shall be apportioned according to lot between the larger and the smaller.

57This is the enrollment of the Levites by their clans: of Gershon, the clan of the Gershonites; of Kohath, the clan of the Kohathites; of Merari, the clan of the Merarites. ⁵⁸These are the clans of Levi: the clan of the Libnites, the clan of the Hebronites, the clan of the Mahlites, the clan of the Mushites, the clan of the Korahites. Now Kohath was the father of Amram. ⁵⁹The name of Amram's wife was Jochebed daughter of Levi, who was born to Levi in Egypt; and she bore to Amram: Aaron, Moses, and their sister Miriam. ⁶⁰To Aaron were born Nadab, Abihu, Eleazar, and Ithamar. ⁶¹But Nadab and Abihu died when they offered unholy fire before the LORD. ⁶²The number of those enrolled was twenty-three thousand, every male one month old and upward; for they were not enrolled among the Israelites because there was no allotment given to them among the Israelites.

63These were those enrolled by Moses and Eleazar the priest, who enrolled the Israelites in the plains of Moab by the Jordan opposite Jericho. ⁶⁴Among these there was not one of those enrolled by Moses and Aaron the priest, who had enrolled the Israelites in the wilderness of Sinai. ⁶⁵For the LORD had said of them, "They shall die in the wilderness." Not one of them was left, except Caleb son of Jephunneh and Joshua son of Nun.

NIV

⁶²All the male Levites a month old or more numbered 23,000. They were not counted along with the other Israelites because they received no inheritance among them.

⁶³These are the ones counted by Moses and Eleazar the priest when they counted the Israelites on the plains of Moab by the Jordan across from Jericho. ⁶⁴Not one of them was among those counted by Moses and Aaron the priest when they counted the Israelites in the Desert of Sinai. ⁶⁵For the LORD had told those Israelites they would surely die in the desert, and not one of them was left except Caleb son of Jephunneh and Joshua son of Nun.

COMMENTARY

Numbers 26 recounts the census of the second generation of Israelites. The chapter consists of divine command to Moses and to Eleazar, the son of Aaron. As in the first census, the Levites are separated out, resulting in the following outline: vv. 1-4, the setting for the census; vv. 5-56, the numbering of the tribes; vv. 57-62, the numbering of the Levites; vv. 63-65, conclusion.

26:1-4. The reference to the plague in 25:19 ties the introduction of the census in Numbers 26 to the story of the sin at Baal Peor. Only after the plague does God command Moses and Eleazar to undertake a new census of the second generation. This sequence suggests that for priestly writers the first generation does not die off completely until the Baal Peor episode. This interpretation of the transition from the first to the second generation departs from the pre-priestly history, where the second generation appeared already to be active in the conquest of Og and Sihon in the Transjordan (see Commentary on 20:1–21:35).

These verses loosely parallel the divine command for a census in 1:1-4. In each case, the census is presented as a divine command; the command focuses on males, twenty years of age and older, who are able to go to war. There are also differences, which indicate how the story line in the book of Numbers has progressed. The second command is directed to Moses and Eleazar, as compared to Moses and Aaron. The transition in priestly leadership parallels the change in generations signaled by

the new census. The setting also indicates progression from the wilderness of Sinai in chap. 1 to the plains of Moab in chap. 26.

The text of vv. 1-4 presents some difficulties, suggesting that parts of the introduction may have been lost in transmission. First, the wording of the divine command for a census in v. 2 is an abbreviated form of 1:2. The former lacks the division of the Israelites into clans and ancestral houses. Second, and more problematic, is an apparent gap in logic between v. 3 and v. 4. Verse 3 ends with the word "saying," which indicates that v. 4 is a direct quotation of Moses and Eleazar. Yet v. 4 is clearly missing the first part of the quotation. The NRSV translation has supplied the words, "Take a census of the people" in v. 4*a* (NIV, "Take a census of the men"), even though these words are absent in the MT. A third and final problem in v. 4 concerns the ending of the verse. Some scholars have argued that the reference to "Israelites, who came out of the land of Egypt" is the second object of the statement, "The LORD commanded." In this case, the second census fulfills a divine command both to Moses and to the first generation of Israelites (i.e., those who came out of Egypt). The NRSV translation interprets v. 4*b* as supplying the heading for the next section concerning the numbering of the second generation. This would appear to be the stronger reading. Yet it, too, creates a problem, since the second generation of Israelites are not those who came out of Egypt.

26:5-56. A literary relationship exists between the

list of tribes in Numbers 26 and that in Genesis 46. The difference is that the list in Genesis 46 is about individuals, while Numbers 26 is about clans. The census in Numbers 26 follows a two-part pattern in which each tribe is identified by clan, followed by the total number of able-bodied fighting men over the age of twenty years. Commentary and departures in format are interspersed throughout this pattern with regard to the tribes of Reuben, Judah, Manasseh, and Asher. Careful attention to the commentary and to the departures in format will provide insight into the aims of the priestly writers concerning the second census and its introductory function for the remainder of the book of Numbers (see *Fig.* 4, "The Structure and Number of the Clans").

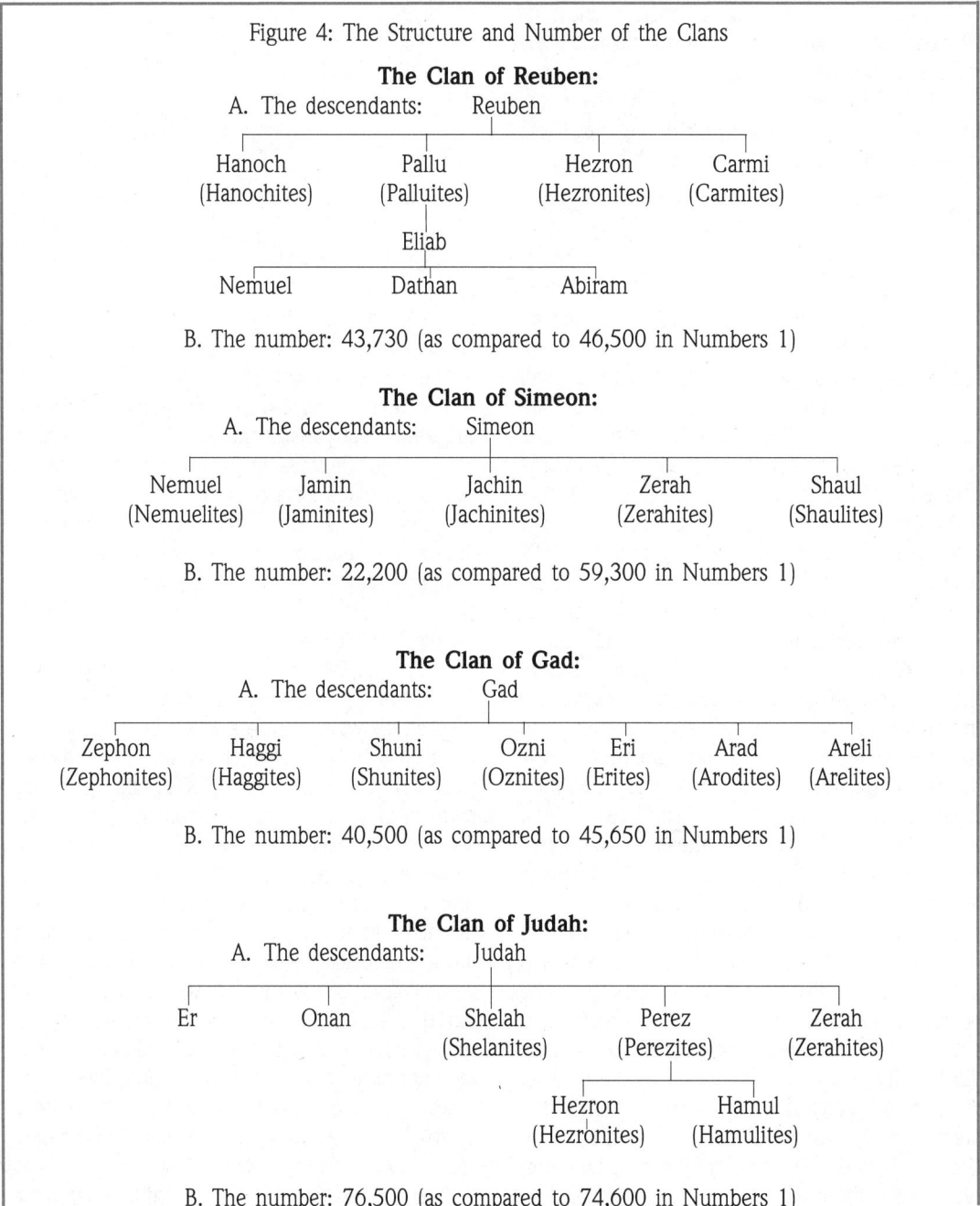

Figure 4: The Structure and Number of the Clans

The Clan of Reuben:

A. The descendants: Reuben

Hanoch (Hanochites)   Pallu (Palluites)   Hezron (Hezronites)   Carmi (Carmites)

Eliab

Nemuel   Dathan   Abiram

B. The number: 43,730 (as compared to 46,500 in Numbers 1)

The Clan of Simeon:

A. The descendants: Simeon

Nemuel (Nemuelites)   Jamin (Jaminites)   Jachin (Jachinites)   Zerah (Zerahites)   Shaul (Shaulites)

B. The number: 22,200 (as compared to 59,300 in Numbers 1)

The Clan of Gad:

A. The descendants: Gad

Zephon (Zephonites)   Haggi (Haggites)   Shuni (Shunites)   Ozni (Oznites)   Eri (Erites)   Arad (Arodites)   Areli (Arelites)

B. The number: 40,500 (as compared to 45,650 in Numbers 1)

The Clan of Judah:

A. The descendants: Judah

Er   Onan   Shelah (Shelanites)   Perez (Perezites)   Zerah (Zerahites)

Hezron (Hezronites)   Hamul (Hamulites)

B. The number: 76,500 (as compared to 74,600 in Numbers 1)

The Clan of Issachar:

A. The descendants: Issachar

Tola	Puvah	Jashub	Shimron
(Tolaites)	(Punites)	(Jashubites)	(Shimronites)

B. The number: 64,300 (as compared to 54,400 in Numbers 1)

The Clan of Zebulun:

A. The descendants: Zebulun

Sered	Elon	Jahleel
(Seredites)	(Elonites)	(Jahleelites)

B. The number: 60,500 (as compared to 57,400 in Numbers 1)

The Clan of Joseph:

A. Manasseh (vv. 29-34)

1. The descendants: Manasseh

Machir
(Machirites)

Gilead
(Gileadites)

Iezer	Helek	Asriel	Shechem	Shemida	Hepher
(Iezerites)	(Helekites)	(Asrielites)	(Shechemites)	(Shemidaites)	(Hepherites)

Zelophehad

(daughters)   Mahlah Noah Hoglah Milcah Tirzah

2. The number: 52,700 (as compared to 32,200 in Numbers 1)

B. Ephraim (vv. 35-37)

1. The descendants: Ephraim

Shuthelah	Becher	Tahan
(Shuthelahites)	(Becherites)	(Tahanites)

Eran
(Eranites)

2. The number: 32,500 (as compared to 40,500 in Numbers 1)

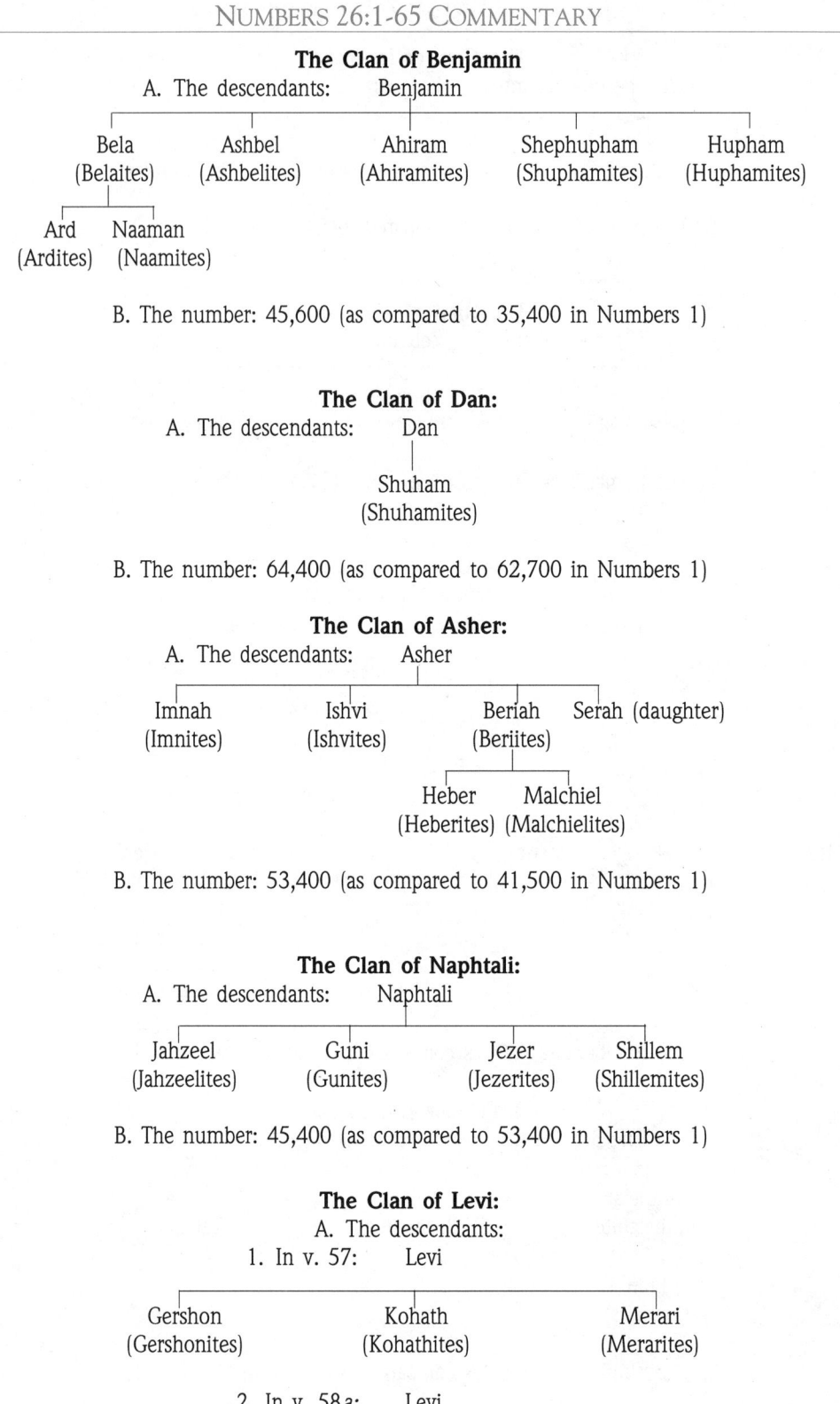

The Clan of Benjamin

A. The descendants: Benjamin

Bela	Ashbel	Ahiram	Shephupham	Hupham
(Belaites)	(Ashbelites)	(Ahiramites)	(Shuphamites)	(Huphamites)

Ard   Naaman
(Ardites)   (Naamites)

B. The number: 45,600 (as compared to 35,400 in Numbers 1)

The Clan of Dan:

A. The descendants: Dan

Shuham
(Shuhamites)

B. The number: 64,400 (as compared to 62,700 in Numbers 1)

The Clan of Asher:

A. The descendants: Asher

Imnah	Ishvi	Beriah	Serah (daughter)
(Imnites)	(Ishvites)	(Beriites)	

Heber   Malchiel
(Heberites) (Malchielites)

B. The number: 53,400 (as compared to 41,500 in Numbers 1)

The Clan of Naphtali:

A. The descendants: Naphtali

Jahzeel	Guni	Jezer	Shillem
(Jahzeelites)	(Gunites)	(Jezerites)	(Shillemites)

B. The number: 45,400 (as compared to 53,400 in Numbers 1)

The Clan of Levi:

A. The descendants:

1. In v. 57: Levi

Gershon	Kohath	Merari
(Gershonites)	(Kohathites)	(Merarites)

2. In v. 58a: Levi

Libnites	Hebronites	Mahlites	Mushites	Korahites

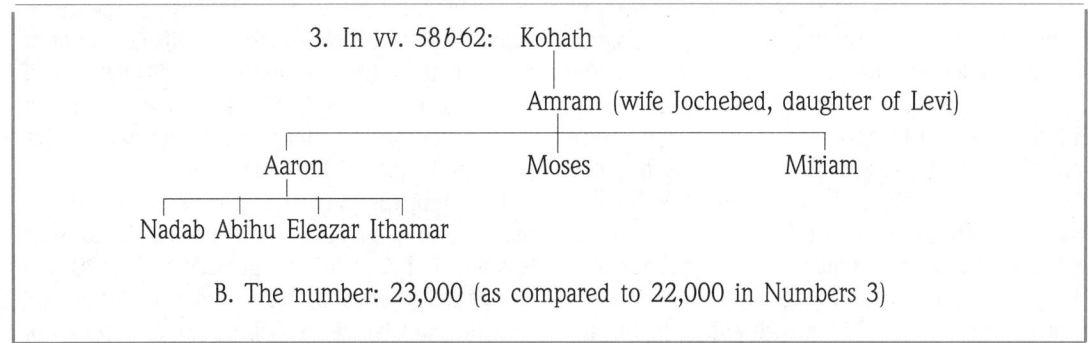

3. In vv. 58*b*-62: Kohath

Amram (wife Jochebed, daughter of Levi)

Aaron   Moses   Miriam

Nadab Abihu Eleazar Ithamar

B. The number: 23,000 (as compared to 22,000 in Numbers 3)

26:5-18. The clans of Reuben in vv. 5-7 have been expanded three generations to include Dathan and Abiram from the conflict with Moses over leadership in chap. 16. In vv. 8-11, the priestly writers associate the rebellion of Dathan and Abiram with the levitical leader Korah. Yet in the census all three leaders appear to have died together by being swallowed up by the earth, as compared to chap. 16, where Korah and his company die separately by fire.

The point of focus is not the manner of the deaths of these characters. Rather, it would appear to lie with the closing line that punishment of the guilty persons does not extend throughout their clan. The continuation of Korah's descendants in v. 11 makes this point explicit. In biblical tradition, the clan of Korah is remembered as temple singers. Psalms like 42, 44–49, 84–85, and 87 are attributed to this clan of Levites. In 1 Chr 9:19, the clan of Korah is described as temple guards. The emphasis on the continuation of the Korah clan beyond the sin of their eponymous ancestor conforms to the priestly emphasis on individual responsibility for sin that has been developed throughout the book of Numbers.

26:19-27. The numbering of Judah departs from the expected format in two ways. First, it records the deaths of two sons, Er and Onan, who "died in the land of Canaan." Second, the clan structure of Judah is extended with an additional generation through the line of Perez. Both of these departures provide commentary on inheritance laws in the land of Canaan through reference to the story of Judah and Tamar in Genesis 38.

The reference to the deaths of Er and Onan harks back to the opening of Genesis 38. Er was the husband of Tamar, killed by Yahweh because of unspecified wicked behavior before having produced any heirs. Onan also is killed by God for not performing the levirate law with Tamar, the widow of Er. The levirate law required that, in instances where a husband died without leaving offspring, the dead man's brother must produce children with his sister-in-law in order to carry on the clan of the lost brother. The levirate law, therefore, has to do with inheritance rights (see Deut 25:5-10; Ruth 4:1-12). In Genesis 38, Onan let his sperm fall to the ground rather than impregnate Tamar, knowing that the offspring would not be his (meaning that these offspring would not enhance his inheritance). Reference to his death in Num 26:19 may be intended to underscore that such behavior continues to be worthy of death in the land of Canaan.

The second departure in the account of the census of Judah is the additional information that his line continued through Perez to include Hezron and Hamul. The significance of naming Hezron and Hamul requires interpretation of the three remaining sons of Judah: Shelah, Perez, and Zerah. All three play a role in Genesis 38. Shelah was the last of Judah's three sons, whom he kept from performing the levirate law with Tamar after the death of Onan. Perez and Zerah are not part of Judah's original offspring in Genesis 38. Instead, they are introduced at the close of the story as twins born to Tamar by Judah, who unwittingly fulfilled the levirate law by impregnating Tamar, whom he thought to be a prostitute. Through a reversal in birth, Perez becomes the firstborn of these twins. The grandchildren of Judah through the line of Perez balance the two lost sons of Judah, and, in so doing, may be intended to affirm the continuing relevance of the levirate inheritance law for the second generation of Israelites, who are about to reenter the land of Canaan.

26:28-43. The clan structure of Joseph departs significantly in form from the other sections of this chapter. The splitting of Manasseh and Ephraim under Joseph is unique among the tribes; it goes back to Genesis 48, where Manasseh and Ephraim are introduced as sons of Joseph. The central event in Genesis 48 is that Jacob blesses the younger Ephraim over the firstborn, Manasseh. The blessing of Ephraim is reflected in the first census in Numbers 1, where Ephraim (1:32-33) is listed before Manasseh (1:34-35). The reversal of the order of Manasseh and Ephraim in chap. 26 is thus noteworthy, given the story of blessing in Genesis 48 and the more prominent place of Ephraim in Numbers 1.

The reversal of order between Manasseh and Ephraim here places Manasseh in the special seventh position within the census. The number seven plays a significant role in the priestly history from the outset, from God's resting on the seventh day (Gen 2:1-3), through the importance of seven in the construction of the tabernacle (Exod 24:12-18), and on into the laws of Jubilee (Leviticus 25). In each of these instances, the number seven marks a transition in the priestly history and the incorporation of something new. The same is true with Manasseh, the seventh clan in the census of the second generation.

The clan structure of Manasseh is also unique in Numbers 26 because of the linear depth of the genealogy. It is structured into seven generations: (1) Joseph, (2) Manasseh, (3) Machir, (4) Gilead, (5) the six offspring of Gilead, (6) Zelophehad, and (7) the daughters of Zelophehad. The intention of the priestly writers emerges at this point. Manasseh is the seventh tribe, and the daughters of Zelophehad are the seventh generation of Manasseh. One begins to suspect that the daughters of Zelophehad will represent a new transition in the priestly history. Indeed, they become central characters in the concluding structure of Numbers, since they frame the remainder of the material in the book (27:1-11; 36:1-13). The new thing that the daughters of Zelophehad represent is the right of daughters to inherit apart from levirate law.

Comparison to other accounts of the genealogy of Manasseh underscores that vv. 25-32 have been constructed for social, literary, and theological purposes, instead of for purely historical reasons. Other descriptions of the genealogy of Manasseh appear in Josh 17:1-3, where Gilead is a son of Manasseh, rather than a grandson (as in

Num 26:29). In Num 32:39, Gilead is not a descendant of either Manasseh or Machir, but a city that is conquered by Manasseh and thus given over to the tribe by Moses. Still other genealogies occur in 1 Chr 2:21-23 and 7:14-19.

The comparison illustrates how cities and territories are personified and related in ancient Israelite tradition through genealogy. The daughters of Zelophehad may also have originally represented smaller regions within the territory of Manasseh. Tirzah, the name of one of the five daughters of Zelophehad, appears as a Canaanite city-state on one of the Samaria ostraca.[178] The incorporation of geographical relationships into clan systems, as well as the variety of genealogies, underscores the social and theological function of this genre of literature in the Bible over against a strictly historical purpose. Whatever the origin of the daughters of Zelophehad may have been, in priestly tradition they have come to represent a transition in inheritance law with regard to daughters. The central point of the genealogy is that daughters who are unable to carry on their clan lines through the levirate law are able to inherit independently. The details of this change in practice will be explained in 27:1-11 and 36:1-13.

26:44-50. The genealogy of Asher is the last to depart from the standard format of the census. The new feature in this genealogy is the listing of Serah as the daughter of Asher. She is the only recorded daughter of an eponymous ancestor; her place in the genealogy of Asher is also noted in Gen 46:17 and 1 Chr 7:30. The purpose for her status in the genealogy is not immediately apparent. One suspects that she is meant to be interpreted in relation to the daughters of Zelophehad, since they are the only women mentioned in the census of non-levitical tribes. If this is the case, her preservation in the clan structure of Asher may illustrate the rights of daughters to inherit independent of the levirate law.[179]

---

178. Jacob Milgrom, *Numbers,* JPS Torah Commentary (Philadelphia: JPS, 1990) 224-25; Timothy R. Ashley, *Numbers,* NICOT (Grand Rapids: Eerdmans, 1993) 535-37; and J. Sasson, "A Genealogical 'Convention' in Biblical Chronography," *ZAW* 90 (1978) 171-85.

179. Milgrom (*Numbers,* 226) cites the work of Moses ben Nahman (Ramban), a medieval Jewish commentator (1194–1270) whose reference to the Targum on Serah has "the name of the daughter of the wife of Asher." This reference does not exist in any extant Targum texts. It suggests, however, an interpretation that would relate Serah and the daughters of Zelophehad.

26:51-56. The total number of the second census is given in v. 51 as 601,730, which is slightly smaller than the first census total of 603,550. It is difficult to discern any pattern or overall message in the numbers for each tribe or in the different totals between the first and second census. The tribes that decreased in number include Reuben (-2,770), Simeon (-37,100), Gad (-5,150), Ephraim (-8,000), and Naphtali (-8,000). The tribes that increased in number include Judah (+1,900), Issachar (+9,900), Zebulun (+3,100), Manasseh (+20,500), Benjamin (+10,200), Dan (+1,700), and Asher (+11,900).

Verses 52-56 make it clear that the purpose of the census is to determine the proportion of inheritance for each tribe. These verses most likely reflect a history of interpretation, since two contradictory methods for determining inheritance are proposed side by side. In vv. 52-54, God instructs Moses that inheritance of land will be determined by the size of each tribe. This conclusion fits well with the overall intent of the chapter to determine the size of each tribe. But the divine instruction moves in a completely different direction in v. 55, where God states that inheritance will be determined by lot. The practice of casting lots to determine divine will is common in biblical literature. The choice of Saul as Israel's leader in 1 Samuel 10 provides some insight into the religious character of casting lots. In that story, Samuel casts lots at the cultic site at Mizpah. The lot eventually falls to Saul, thus indicating to Samuel God's choice of leader.

The revision of the method of inheritance in Num 26:52-56 from the size of each tribe (vv. 52-54) to the casting of lots (v. 55) brings this chapter into conformity with the account of inheritance in the book of Joshua (14:2; 15:1; 16:1; 17:1), even as it creates internal contradiction within Numbers 26. Verse 56 would appear to be still later commentary that seeks to relate the two methods of inheritance. It states that inheritance will be both by lot and by size.

26:57-62. The clan structure of Levi separates into three parts. Verse 57 presents the traditional division of the levitical clans into the three houses of Gershon, Kohath, and Merari; v. 58a departs from the traditional division by listing five houses of Libnites, Hebronites, Mahlites, Mushites, and

Horahites; and vv. 58b-62 provide commentary on the opening genealogy in v. 57.

The first genealogy of the levitical clans (v. 57) begins with the introduction: "This is the enrollment of the Levites by their clans." Following this introduction is the three-part division of the Levites into the houses of Gershonites, Kohathites, and Merarites. This structure is the most prominent tradition of the Levites in the OT. It is first stated in the family genealogy of Gen 46:11. It reappears in the levitical genealogy of Exod 6:16-25 and is reflected in the first census of the Levites in Numbers 3; it also occurs in 1 Chr 5:27–6:34. Within this structure, the three levitical houses split further in the following manner: Gershon (Libnites and Shimeites); Kohath (Amramites, Izharites, Hebronites, and Uzzielites); and Merari (Mahlites and Mushites).

Verse 58a begins with a separate introduction: "These are the clans of Levi." This introduction suggests that this verse is not a continuation of v. 57. The content confirms this conclusion, since v. 58a presents a distinctive genealogy of Levi, consisting of five sons or clans: Libnites, Hebronites, Mahlites, Mushites, and Korahites. These clans have been subordinated under the three-clan structure of the genealogy in v. 57. Scholars speculate that v. 58a may represent an older tradition concerning the clan structure of the Levites that was eventually replaced by the more prominent three-part division.[180]

The explanation and additional genealogy in vv. 58b-62 are a continuation of the opening genealogy in v. 57. The concern here is with the clan of Kohath, which is not mentioned in the second genealogy of v. 58a. When v. 57 and vv. 58b-62 are read together, they parallel closely the levitical genealogy in Exod 6:16-25. Both texts trace the family line of Aaron and Moses back to Levi through the ancestors of Amram and Kohath. Both texts also identify the mother of Aaron and Moses, and hence the wife of Amram, as Jochebed. Comparison of these genealogies also brings to light differences, which may indicate the intention of the priestly writers in Numbers 26.

Verses 57 and 58b-62 weave together information from four previous stories or genealogies. Verse 59 states that Jochebed, the wife of Amram,

180. K. Mühlenbrink, "Die levitischen Überlieferung des Alten Testaments," *ZAW* 12 (1934) 184-231.

is the daughter of Levi. This is a reinterpretation of Exod 6:20, where Jochebed is the sister of Kohath rather than of Levi. The identification of Miriam as a sister of Aaron and Moses refers to Exod 15:21, where Miriam was identified as Aaron's sister when she took on the prophetic role of singing a victory hymn after Israel's salvation at the sea. These identifications certainly provide for a more precise interpretation of the birth of Moses in Exod 2:1-10, since the unnamed mother in this episode can be identified with Jochebed and the sister with Miriam. But one suspects that the intentions of the priestly writers go beyond a desire to provide inner-biblical interpretation on the birth of Moses. The changing status of Miriam in the priestly genealogy may be tied to social developments within the post-exilic priesthood. The nature of these developments, however, is not immediately clear from the text.

Her prophetic role of singing in Exod 15:21 may relate to the priestly reinterpretation of prophecy during the post-exilic period, when the levitical temple choir of Korahites takes over the role of prophets (see the prophetic role of the Korahite Levites' singing during holy war in 2 Chronicles 20). Finally, the statement that Nadab and Abihu, Aaron's eldest sons, were killed by God for offering "illicit fire" ties back to Lev 10:1-2 and Num 3:4.

26:63-65. The conclusion to the census refers to the spy story of Numbers 13–14, where God condemned the first generation to death in the wilderness. These verses stress that all of the first generation, who were counted in the wilderness of Sinai, are dead, with the exception of Joshua and Caleb. The point of the conclusion is not so much the death of the first generation as it is the new beginning for the second generation.

REFLECTIONS

1. All churches have a genealogy. The history of every congregation includes important persons, families, and clergy who have shaped the character of community. Genealogies are not simply recorded history. They live on in churches. The persons listed in a genealogy represent the continuing values of a congregation. Leadership is often determined through conformity to the ideals memorialized in the genealogy. Genealogies represent the continuing social power of past tradition. One of the first responsibilities for any minister upon arrival at a new church is to uncover its genealogy. To ignore this central task almost guarantees failure.

The ancient Near East is a far more tradition-based society than is modern Western culture. As a result, at the time of the priestly writers, genealogies exerted even more power over community. This insight provides a window into the radical character of the priestly genealogy in Numbers 26. It is certainly rooted in tradition, with the historic division of the tribes. But its central feature throughout is the inclusion of new heroes into the Israelites' founding genealogy. The daughters of Zelophehad, Serah, and Miriam are memorialized as founding members of the community. The Commentary has illustrated that the incorporation of new characters into the genealogy indicates change in social practice during the post-exilic period with regard to inheritance and leadership.

The genealogy of the second generation provides a model for social change. The starting point for engaging the priestly writers' use of genealogy is to raise the question, Who is in our genealogy and who is left out? Does our idealized past adequately empower our present community? Genealogy is a mirror of our ideals. Thus the way we shape our founding genealogy is one way of introducing change while embracing the power of tradition. The priestly writers provide illustration. They reaffirm the value of levirate law in the genealogy of Judah. At the same time, they introduce inheritance of daughters independent of levirate law in the genealogy of Manasseh. Tradition and change stand side by side. The point of the priestly writers is that the second generation is not simply an extension of the first. They represent both continuity and change in following the leading of Yahweh into the promised land.

2. The genealogy of the second generation probes the character of God and what is required in following God. Numbers 26 provides commentary on the divine promises of nationhood and land first given to Abram (Genesis 12). The central message of the priestly writers is that God is reliable in fulfilling promises and that their fulfillment requires human participation.

One of the central themes of the Pentateuch is the divine promise to the ancestors that they would become a great nation (Gen 12:1-4). The literary structure of the book of Numbers, with its division into a census of the first (chap. 1) and the second (chap. 26) generations, develops this theme in three ways. First, the death of the first generation in the wilderness indicates that disobedience can disqualify an entire generation from God's promise of nationhood. The message is that divine promise requires our participation for its fulfillment. Second, the birth of a new generation in the wilderness emphasizes that hope lies with God, who is faithful to promises. Olson illustrates this point: "Numbers presents a radical and decisive distinction between the old rebellious generation of death and the new generation of hope. . . . The focus is not on a gradual spiritual improvement on the part of the people. Rather, the focus is on the activity of God, who, though intolerant of rebellion, remains faithful to his promise."[181] God's commitment to the promise of salvation lays the basis for individual responsibility in the book of Numbers. Promise of salvation, not human guilt, becomes intergenerational. As a result, the second generation is given the opportunity to participate anew with God in realizing salvation. Third, the census of the second generation illustrates the subtle ways in which God is reliable to promises. The number of Israelites in Numbers 26 illustrates that the divine promise of nationhood was in effect even when Israel was disobedient in the wilderness.

A second theme running throughout the Pentateuch is the promise of land to the ancestors (Gen 12:7). The census of the second generation also develops this theme. The story line of the book of Numbers progresses from the wilderness of Sinai in Numbers 1 to the plains of Moab in Numbers 26, where the city of Jericho in the land of Canaan is already in view. The purpose of taking a census changes along with the new setting. The census of the first generation was for the purpose of war. Preparation for war continues in the census of the second generation, but it is the theme of inheritance that takes center stage. Unlike the first generation, the second is on the threshold of taking possession of the promised land. The second generation not only embodies the fulfillment of the divine promise of nationhood through their numbers, but they are also in a position to receive the divine promise of land.

The interaction of the two divine promises, nationhood and land, provides a springboard for teaching and preaching. The contrast between the first and the second generations provides models of failure and success. God is faithful to promises. Some promises, like the promise of nationhood to Israel in the wilderness, are being fulfilled in the present time. The first generation failed to recognize the power of God in their midst and died in the wilderness. The second census is a recognition of God's faithfulness to promise. The Israelites are once again a great nation. Recognition provides the basis for journeying ahead and realizing the future promise of land just over the horizon.

181. Dennis T. Olson, *The Death of the Old and the Birth of the New: The Framework of the Book of Numbers and the Pentateuch,* BJS 71 (Chico, Calif.: Scholars Press, 1985) 180.

Numbers 27:1-23, Inheritance, Death, and Succession

27 The daughters of Zelophehad son of Hepher, the son of Gilead, the son of Makir, the son of Manasseh, belonged to the clans of

27 Then the daughters of Zelophehad came forward. Zelophehad was son of Hepher son of Gilead son of Machir son of Manasseh son

Manasseh son of Joseph. The names of the daughters were Mahlah, Noah, Hoglah, Milcah and Tirzah. They approached ²the entrance to the Tent of Meeting and stood before Moses, Eleazar the priest, the leaders and the whole assembly, and said, ³"Our father died in the desert. He was not among Korah's followers, who banded together against the LORD, but he died for his own sin and left no sons. ⁴Why should our father's name disappear from his clan because he had no son? Give us property among our father's relatives."

⁵So Moses brought their case before the LORD ⁶and the LORD said to him, ⁷"What Zelophehad's daughters are saying is right. You must certainly give them property as an inheritance among their father's relatives and turn their father's inheritance over to them.

⁸"Say to the Israelites, 'If a man dies and leaves no son, turn his inheritance over to his daughter. ⁹If he has no daughter, give his inheritance to his brothers. ¹⁰If he has no brothers, give his inheritance to his father's brothers. ¹¹If his father had no brothers, give his inheritance to the nearest relative in his clan, that he may possess it. This is to be a legal requirement for the Israelites, as the LORD commanded Moses.'"

¹²Then the LORD said to Moses, "Go up this mountain in the Abarim range and see the land I have given the Israelites. ¹³After you have seen it, you too will be gathered to your people, as your brother Aaron was, ¹⁴for when the community rebelled at the waters in the Desert of Zin, both of you disobeyed my command to honor me as holy before their eyes." (These were the waters of Meribah Kadesh, in the Desert of Zin.)

¹⁵Moses said to the LORD, ¹⁶"May the LORD, the God of the spirits of all mankind, appoint a man over this community ¹⁷to go out and come in before them, one who will lead them out and bring them in, so the LORD's people will not be like sheep without a shepherd."

¹⁸So the LORD said to Moses, "Take Joshua son of Nun, a man in whom is the spirit,ᵃ and lay your hand on him. ¹⁹Have him stand before Eleazar the priest and the entire assembly and commission him in their presence. ²⁰Give him some of your authority so the whole Israelite

ᵃ18 Or Spirit

of Joseph, a member of the Manassite clans. The names of his daughters were: Mahlah, Noah, Hoglah, Milcah, and Tirzah. ²They stood before Moses, Eleazar the priest, the leaders, and all the congregation, at the entrance of the tent of meeting, and they said, ³"Our father died in the wilderness; he was not among the company of those who gathered themselves together against the LORD in the company of Korah, but died for his own sin; and he had no sons. ⁴Why should the name of our father be taken away from his clan because he had no son? Give to us a possession among our father's brothers."

5Moses brought their case before the LORD. ⁶And the LORD spoke to Moses, saying: ⁷The daughters of Zelophehad are right in what they are saying; you shall indeed let them possess an inheritance among their father's brothers and pass the inheritance of their father on to them. ⁸You shall also say to the Israelites, "If a man dies, and has no son, then you shall pass his inheritance on to his daughter. ⁹If he has no daughter, then you shall give his inheritance to his brothers. ¹⁰If he has no brothers, then you shall give his inheritance to his father's brothers. ¹¹And if his father has no brothers, then you shall give his inheritance to the nearest kinsman of his clan, and he shall possess it. It shall be for the Israelites a statute and ordinance, as the LORD commanded Moses."

12The LORD said to Moses, "Go up this mountain of the Abarim range, and see the land that I have given to the Israelites. ¹³When you have seen it, you also shall be gathered to your people, as your brother Aaron was, ¹⁴because you rebelled against my word in the wilderness of Zin when the congregation quarreled with me.ᵃ You did not show my holiness before their eyes at the waters." (These are the waters of Meribath-kadesh in the wilderness of Zin.) ¹⁵Moses spoke to the LORD, saying, ¹⁶"Let the LORD, the God of the spirits of all flesh, appoint someone over the congregation ¹⁷who shall go out before them and come in before them, who shall lead them out and bring them in, so that the congregation of the LORD may not be like sheep without a shepherd." ¹⁸So the LORD said to Moses, "Take Joshua son of Nun, a

ᵃ Heb lacks with me

NIV

community will obey him. ²¹He is to stand before Eleazar the priest, who will obtain decisions for him by inquiring of the Urim before the LORD. At his command he and the entire community of the Israelites will go out, and at his command they will come in."

²²Moses did as the LORD commanded him. He took Joshua and had him stand before Eleazar the priest and the whole assembly. ²³Then he laid his hands on him and commissioned him, as the LORD instructed through Moses.

NRSV

man in whom is the spirit, and lay your hand upon him; ¹⁹have him stand before Eleazar the priest and all the congregation, and commission him in their sight. ²⁰You shall give him some of your authority, so that all the congregation of the Israelites may obey. ²¹But he shall stand before Eleazar the priest, who shall inquire for him by the decision of the Urim before the LORD; at his word they shall go out, and at his word they shall come in, both he and all the Israelites with him, the whole congregation." ²²So Moses did as the LORD commanded him. He took Joshua and had him stand before Eleazar the priest and the whole congregation; ²³he laid his hands on him and commissioned him—as the LORD had directed through Moses.

COMMENTARY

Three events are interwoven in Numbers 27. The chapter begins with a legal claim by the daughters of Zelophehad (vv. 1-11) concerning their right to inherit land in the absence of male offspring. The topic changes from inheritance to death in vv. 12-14. Moses is told by God that he is about to die because of his rebellion in the wilderness of Zin. The divine announcement occasions a transition to the account of Joshua's succession of Moses (vv. 15-23).

27:1-11. This section presents a legal case about inheritance. The daughters of Zelophehad claim the right of inheritance, requiring a special revelation from God. These verses contain the initial ruling, while chap. 36 will return to the topic in order to clarify restrictions on the inheritance of daughters.

The setting for the legal case is stated in v. 2: It takes place at the door of the tent of meeting before Moses, Eleazar the priest, the leaders, and the entire congregation. The genealogy of the daughters of Zelophehad is outlined in v. 1, a repetition of the clan structure of Manasseh from 26:28-35. The problem of inheritance, which the daughters present, is not covered in any of the existing law codes in Torah. This is one of only four stories in which an ambiguous legal situation requires special revelation for its solution; the others are the case of the blasphemer (Lev 24:10-

23); the second Passover (Num 9:6-14); and sabbath law (Num 15:32-36).

The daughters present their legal problem in vv. 3-4. Their father has died in the wilderness, leaving no sons to inherit. In view of this situation, they request the right to inherit. The circumstances of the death of Zelophehad are spelled out in detail: He "died for his own sins." By stating that their father "died for his own sins," his daughters appeal to the principle of individual responsibility for guilt. This statement is contrasted with an alternative possibility—namely, that he might have been a participant in Korah's rebellion. The implication of the contrast is that participation in a sin like the rebellion of Korah could result in loss of land or inheritance rights,[182] even though 26:11 indicates that such sin does not lead to the death of an entire family. Thus it appears that Zelophehad is being described as having died for the general sin of unfaithfulness, which characterized the entire first generation, and not for any particular offense. As a result, no circumstances exist to justify the loss of inheritance to his family. On the basis of this situation, his daughters claim the right to inherit in order to perpetuate the clan name of their father.

182. J. Weingreen, "The Case of the Daughters of Zelophehad," *VT* 16 (1966) 518-21.

Their request is without precedent, and Moses refers the matter to God (vv. 5-11). God concurs with the legal claim of the daughters and provides judgment on the case in v. 7. Moses is to transfer the inheritance of Zelophehad to his daughters, so that they are able to take possession of the land. Three theological foundations undergird the divine ruling. The first is that God owns the land. This principle is stated most clearly in the context of the Jubilee law of Leviticus 25, where God declares divine ownership: "For the land is mine" (Lev 25:23). Second, divine ownership means that the status of Israel is that of a tenant of the land; again see Lev 25:23: "With me you are but aliens and tenants." No humans have an inherent right to any portion of the land, because all receive land as a divine gift. Third, the social implication of this divine gift is that each Israelite's right to a portion of land is inalienable. No parcel of land can be permanently sold or taken away from its clan of origin. Once again, see Lev 25:24: "You will provide for the redemption of the land." Joshua 17:3-6 narrates the fulfillment of the divine ruling in Num 27:5-7: The daughters of Zelophehad each receive a portion of the promised land.

Verses 8-11 extend the claim of the daughters of Zelophehad into four general case laws. The first codifies their situation: (1) If a man dies without sons, then the inheritance is passed on to his daughters (v. 8). The next three case laws go beyond the story of vv. 1-7. These laws emphasize that inheritance in Israel was patrilineal, meaning that inheritance is passed to males through the father's side. Thus, (2) if a man died without sons or daughters, then his inheritance would pass on to his brother or brothers (v. 9); (3) if there were no brothers, then the father's brothers would inherit (v. 10); and (4) if there were no uncles, then the nearest kinsmen of his clan would inherit (v. 11a). The divine ruling is judged to be "a statute and ordinance" (לחקת משפט *lĕḥuqqat mišpāṭ*). This designation of divine law occurs only one other time (35:29), as a conclusion to the laws concerning the cities of refuge.

27:12-14. The impending death of Moses is announced by God in this section. God commands Moses to ascend the Abarim mountain range, located on the northern end of the Dead Sea. From there he will be able to see the promised land before he dies. The reason for his sentence

is his sin at Meribath-kadesh (20:2-13). In this story, the priestly writers advocate the principle of individual responsibility for guilt. Moses cannot enter the promised land of Canaan because of his failure of leadership in not following the legal structures of communication and authority concerning Israel's complaint about water. Instead of following God's instructions, Moses condemns Israel as rebels. The point of the story is that in accusing the Israelites of being rebels, Moses himself becomes guilty of the charge. Thus Moses does not enter Canaan as a result of his own actions, as compared to Deut 1:37; 3:23-29, where he must share vicariously in the collective guilt of the first generation.

The announcement concerning the death of Moses in vv. 12-14 is repeated in Deut 32:48-52 before it is finally fulfilled in Deut 34:1-8. This structure of divine announcement and fulfillment is yet another illustration of how the book of Numbers is meant to be read within the larger context of the Pentateuch. The present structure of the Pentateuch encourages a reading of Numbers 27–Deuteronomy 34 as representing the final series of addresses by Moses to Israel. The remainder of Numbers focuses primarily on inheritance law, while in Deuteronomy Moses recounts the exodus and wilderness periods (Deuteronomy 1–11) to the second generation, as well as the private revelation of God that he received at Mt. Horeb (Deuteronomy 12–26). It is only when the education of the second generation is completed that Moses finally ascends Mt. Nebo in the Abarim range to view the promised land before dying (Deut 34:1-8), thus fulfilling the original divine commandment (Num 27:12-14).

No specific dates are given for the divine announcement to Moses in vv. 12-14. In fact, no specific dates for speeches or narrative events appear again in the book of Numbers. As a result, the timeframe between the announcement (vv. 12-14; Deut 32:48-52) and his death (Deut 34:1-8) is not immediately clear. The introduction to Deuteronomy, however, dates the speeches of Moses in this book to Year 40, Month 11, Day 1 after the exodus. This date was most likely supplied by the priestly writers. The death of Moses in Deut 34:1-8 also shows signs of priestly influence, including the statement that Israel mourned Moses for thirty days after his death (v.

8). Note that the death of Aaron was mourned for the same period of time (Num 20:29).

The manner in which the priestly writers have framed the book of Deuteronomy with dates suggests that Moses' address in Deuteronomy took place on one day and that at the close of the speeches, "on that very day" (Deut 32:48), God commanded Moses to ascend the mountain. In that case, the speeches of Moses and the thirty days of mourning for his death complete the fortieth year of Israel's journey from Egypt. The absence of dates in Numbers 27–36 raises the question of whether the priestly writers intended for the entire section of Num 27:12–Deut 34:8 to take place on one day. The only story in Numbers 27–36 that presents a problem is the war with Midian in chap. 31. Although that war is not dated, the action of this story and the seven-day requirement for purification (31:24) require a somewhat looser timeframe than the single day in which Moses ostensibly promulgated the book of Deuteronomy.

The dating by priestly writers bears theological significance, underscoring how important the fortieth year is in the priestly history. It is a time of both death and new hope. It is the year when the second generation of Israelites are numbered (Numbers 26) in preparation for the gift of the land. Yet it is also the year in which the leaders of the exodus die: Miriam, Aaron, and Moses. The deaths of the leaders of the exodus began with Miriam (20:1). Her demise at Kadesh in the wilderness of Zin is dated to Month 1 with no year given. Comparison of her death with the deaths of Aaron and Moses indicates, however, that the complete date is most likely Year 40, Month 1. The death of Aaron at Mt. Hor is recounted immediately thereafter in 20:22-29. No date is given in this story, but in 33:38-39 Aaron's death is dated as Year 40, Month 5, Day 1; and 20:29 indicates that his death is followed by thirty days of mourning. Finally, the announcement and death of Moses on Year 40, Month 11, Day 1, along with the thirty days of mourning after his death, complete the forty-year death cycle of the leaders of the exodus. The overview of dates shows that Miriam and Aaron died in the first half of Year 40 in the priestly history, while the death of Moses concludes the second half of the year. Death and life are thus intermingled in Year 40, leading to the final topic of succession of leadership.

27:15-23. The transfer of the Mosaic spirit to Joshua provides occasion for the priestly writers to explore how charismatic non-priestly power is transferred. This story provides a counterpart to the succession of Aaron by Eleazar in 20:22-29, where the transfer of non-charismatic priestly power was modeled. The succession of Eleazar was signaled by the transfer of vestments representing the office of high priest. Once the people saw Aaron's vestments on Eleazar, the succession of priestly leadership was complete. The transfer of Moses' charismatic spirit is not tied to vestments of an office. Furthermore, succession of Moses' charismatic spirit is initiated by his own request in vv. 15-17.

In v. 16, Moses addresses Yahweh as the "God of the spirits of all flesh." This is the same language of intercession that the priestly writers used in 16:20-22, when Moses and Aaron interceded for Israel during the rebellion of Korah. In Numbers 16, reference to the divine Spirit in creation was used to underscore that the creator God could not be the source of indiscriminate death. In chap. 27, the language is employed to argue that Israel will always need a non-priestly leader.

Two images in vv. 15-17 demonstrate that the request of Moses for a leader is about civil or lay leadership. First, the image of a leader who "goes out" (יצא *yāṣā'*) and "comes in" (בוא *bô'*) before the people has military overtones. David is described in 1 Sam 18:13 as "going out" and "coming in" while leading his army. The language can also refer more generally to Israel's salvation history. The exodus is an experience of "going out." Yahweh is described as the God "who brought Israel out from Egypt" (Exod 20:1). The gift of the land is historicized in salvation history as Israel's "coming in" or "entering" the land (Exod 12:25; 13:3). Yahweh is described as the God "who will bring Israel into the land of Canaan" (Exod 13:5). Second, the image of a shepherd is also royal rather than priestly. Kings are described as shepherds of the sheep (1 Kgs 22:17; Ezek 34:6).

The divine response appears in vv. 18-21. Joshua is chosen to succeed Moses in his charismatic role as Israel's military leader. He fulfills the charismatic ideal of leadership in that he already possesses the spirit. The reference to the spirit of Joshua most likely ties this story to Numbers 11, where a portion of the spirit of Moses was placed on the seventy elders. Joshua is not specifically mentioned as being one of the seventy elders, but he is identified in 11:28 as "the assistant of Moses and one of his chosen men." Joshua certainly fulfills the requirements for a lay, charismatic, military leader. He is an Ephraimite (13:8) who plays a role in waging holy war already in Exod 17:9. He accompanies Moses up the mountain in Exod 24:13 and returns with Moses in Exod 32:17 to discover the golden calf. Joshua is associated with the early tradition of the tent of meeting in Exod 33:11, where it functions more as an oracular tent than as a cultic shrine. He is a hero of the spy story (14:6, 30, 38) and eventually the hero of the conquest (the book of Joshua). The succession of Joshua is also noted in Deut 34:9.

The priestly point of view of charismatic lay leaders is evident in the divine instructions for the transfer ritual. As was the case in the selection of the seventy elders, only a portion of the "author- ity" of Moses will actually be transferred to Joshua. In v. 20 the word "authority" (הוד *hôd*) replaces the language of "spirit" from 11:17, but the point is most likely the same: After Moses, non-charismatic leaders will not have his status, which was a position of authority even above that of priests. Instead, charismatic lay leaders will possess only part of his spirit or authority. Joshua, therefore, will be subordinate to the high priest, Eleazar. Joshua's ritual of ordination makes this point clear. The transfer of charismatic power is accomplished through the laying on of hands, but confirmation of the authority of Joshua must take place through Eleazar, who will discern the char- acter of the charisma through the Urim.

The Urim and Thummim are most likely divin- ing stones used by priests to inquire judgments from God. They are mentioned in Deut 33:8 as belonging to the Levites in general. In this text, the Levites' possession of the Urim and Thummim arises from their zealous devotion to God above family. As a consequence, the Levites acquire three functions: They transmit divine law to Israel, they burn incense, and they sacrifice on the altar. The function of conveying divine judgments

through teaching may be associated with the Urim and Thummim.

Priestly writers limit the use of the Urim and Thummim to the high priest. In Exod 28:30, the Urim and Thummim are part of the special garments of the high priest, which include an underrobe made of wool and an ephod, or outer garment, of gold, wool, and linen placed over the underrobe. Over the ephod garment is a breastplate, also made of gold, wool, and linen containing two onyx stones with the names of the twelve tribes of Israel and an additional set of twelve stones. The high priest represented the people before God when wearing the breastplate. The Urim and Thummim could also be attached to the breastplate in a pouch. The high priest would wear the Urim and Thummim in the inner sanctuary when seeking a divine judgment on behalf of the people. The details of the inquiry are not provided. If the Urim and Thummim were stones, however, then the ritual may have resembled the casting of lots, in which questions were posed to God requiring a yes or no answer. The brief statement by Saul in 1 Sam 14:41 provides a glimpse into how the Urim and Thummim functioned as a casting of lots. In this story, Saul requests Urim to designate guilt in himself and Jonathan and Thummim to designate guilt in the people of Israel. The Urim and Thummim are also mentioned in Ezra 2:63 and Neh 7:65 without ex- planation or comment.

The choice of Joshua to succeed Moses may also provide an illustration of how the Urim and Thummim functioned in ancient Israel in relation- ship to the high priest. For Joshua's selection to be official, Eleazar, the high priest, "inquired for him [Joshua] by the judgment of the Urim before the Yahweh" (v. 21). The important point in v. 21 is that charismatic leaders must be authenti- cated by the priest. Their authority was not trans- ferred independently of the high priest.

Verses 22-23 mark the fulfillment of the divine command. Moses takes Joshua to Eleazar and commissions Joshua before the priest and all the congregation of Israel.

REFLECTIONS

1. The priestly writers characterize human life on earth as renting space, not owning land. Their insight provides the starting point for theological reflection on the role of humans in creation and its implications for social ethics.

The central word used to designate family inheritance of land in Num 27:6-11 is נחלה (*naḥălâ*). In his study of this term, J. Herrmann concluded that it tends to focus on a portion of a tribal possession rather than the land of Canaan as a whole. Thus the term for "inheritance" has a concrete dimension. The land designated as "inheritance" is allotted to someone. The apportionment is by divine ordination, with the result that it is a lasting possession of the family.[183] Thus the laws of inheritance in Num 27:6-11 emphasize the inalienable right of family possession of property.

The story of Naboth's vineyard in 1 Kings 21 illustrates the inalienable right of family inheritance. In this story, Naboth refuses to sell his property to the king because it is his ancestral inheritance. When Ahab offers to pay Naboth full price for the land, Naboth responds, "God forbid that I should give you my ancestral inheritance." The story of Naboth's vineyard brings to light the theological background of inheritance law in ancient Israel. The land is a divine gift to Israel. Possession of a particular allotment of land by an ancestral family transforms the status of that clan into land-tenants of God, who is the owner of the property. Being a tenant of God actually guarantees one rights in God's land as an heir of the gift. Ahab the king, in the story of Naboth's vineyard, understood the theological foundations of land possession. When Naboth refused to sell his land, Ahab's immediate response was to honor the claim. His downfall was in forcing possession of the land for himself.

The present form of the Pentateuch is structured around the theological affirmation that the land of Canaan belongs to God, not to the Israelites. The ancestral stories in Genesis and the salvation of Israel from Egypt are built around the divine promise of land. The laws of inheritance in Num 27:6-11 are part of the same theme. The second generation of Israelites represents the fulfillment of the first promise of God to the ancestors that Israel would one day be a great nation (Gen 12:1-4). They are on the threshold of fulfilling the second promise of God, in becoming tenants of God in the land of Canaan. The promise of land, however, is not fulfilled in the Pentateuch as is the promise of descendants. It remains a goal for Israel to be realized in the near future.

Throughout the Old and New Testaments the imagery of being a tenant on God's land is both an image of salvation and the basis for ethical accountability of the people of God. The image of Israel as a tenant of God in Canaan is a central metaphor for salvation in prophetic literature. The prophet Micah describes the land of Israel as "the portion of the people" (Mic 2:4). Jeremiah describes Canaan as Israel's inheritance from God (Jer 3:19). Judgment in the book of Amos is pictured as the Israelites' losing status as God's tenants in the land because of their unethical behavior (Amos 2:6-16; 7). The parable of the vineyard by the prophet Isaiah (Isa 5:1-7) also presupposes the theological basis of inheritance law, when the prophet declares that Israel will lose the vineyard because they are unworthy tenants.

The same theology of inheritance is taken up in the New Testament. The proclamation of the kingdom of God by Jesus is a continuation of the promise of land to the ancestors (Mark 1:15). God, the Creator, owns the earth and is reestablishing divine rule. Humans are called to recognize God's ownership and become renters in God's land. The apostle Paul often refers to inheritance law to describe salvation in Christ (Rom 8:17; Gal 4:7).[184] The ethical responsibility of inheritance is explored in the parable of the wicked tenants in the vineyard (Matt 21:33-46; Mark 12:1-12; Luke 20:9-19), which represents a Christian reinterpretation of Isa 5:1-7. Christian identity is formed in the understanding that we live as guests and renters in God's creation.

The divine promise of land throughout the Pentateuch, the prophetic call for ethical behavior in God's land, and the central place of the kingdom of God in the ministry of Jesus (Mark 1:15) all remind us that salvation is not simply about people. These related themes affirm that

---

183. J. Herrmann, "נחלה:" *TDNT,* ed. G. Kittel (Grand Rapids: Eerdmans, 1965) 3:769-76. See also Christopher J. H. Wright, *God's People in God's Land: Family, Land, and Property in the Old Testament* (Grand Rapids: Eerdmans, 1990) 3-23.

184. Paul L. Hammer, "Inheritance (NT)," *ABD* 3:415-17.

God's salvation is rooted in creation itself. The challenge for the contemporary church is to reaffirm the central role of the earth as part of God's kingdom. Salvation is not restricted to people and population (the promise of fertility and nationhood); it also requires the proper environment for humans (the promise of land). All humans rent space on earth as tenants of God. The church is called to be a model tenant, strengthening the earth, not weakening it. An understanding of salvation that highlights individuals or social systems at the expense of creation misses the central message of inheritance, which runs throughout Scripture.

2. The request of the daughters of Zelophehad for the right to inherit presupposes a situation in which daughters have no legal rights of inheritance. In ancient Israel, sons inherited property in a patrilineal system, while daughters received a dowry to take into marriage (Judg 1:13-15). Given this situation, the request of the daughters of Zelophehad to inherit is certainly meant to provide a model of change within tradition. The structure of the text, with its emphasis on obtaining a special revelation from God, makes this point clear. But the exact nature of the change in inheritance law is unclear.

Two interpretations of the request of the daughters of Zelophehad are possible. First, if the request for inheritance by daughters is meant to be a rejection of the levirate law, then the change in tradition is significant. It would mean that daughters have a right to inherit independent of any male. George Buchanan Gray interpreted these women's request of the daughters of Zelophehad as such a rejection, because no mention of levirate law is made to resolve the problem of the lack of males to inherit.[185] He further reasoned that a rejection of levirate law would also conform to priestly legislation against incest (Lev 18:16; 20:21). Second, if the request for inheritance by daughters is an extension of levirate law, then less change in traditional practice is intended. The marriage restrictions in Numbers 36 concerning daughters who inherit favors this second reading. It suggests that daughters who held land would turn it over to their husbands after marriage, thus maintaining the patrilineal system of inheritance.

The request of the daughters of Zelophehad for the right to inherit has caught the attention of modern readers because of the issues of gender rights implied in their legal request. A careful reading of Num 27:1-11; 36 certainly emphasizes that change is indeed built into biblical tradition. As such, it provides a basis for evaluating change in gender roles in our own culture. But these texts also underscore how the social background of biblical literature is often far removed from contemporary life and unable to provide concrete models for contemporary social concerns. The power of the text for teaching and preaching is not in its specific teaching on inheritance of daughters, but in its modeling of social change. Priestly writers affirm change in inheritance law as special revelation from God.

3. The book of Numbers has modeled many forms of leadership. Charismatic leadership was outlined in Numbers 11–12. Non-charismatic, priestly leadership came into focus in Numbers 16–19. All leadership in the book of Numbers is derived from Moses; yet, no subsequent leader equals his status. God said as much to Miriam and Aaron in Num 12:6-8. The passing on of only a portion of Moses' spirit to Joshua in Num 27:20 underscores the same point, and Moses himself states the same in Deut 18:15. As the leader of the exodus and the one to receive the special revelation of God from the mountain, Moses is a hero of unparalleled stature. It is this unique quality of Moses that prompts New Testament writers to make comparisons to Jesus—not in the sense that Jesus is Moses, but that, like Moses, Jesus is an incomparable hero who represents something new from God (John 1:17; Rom 5:14).

185. George Buchanan Gray, *Numbers,* ICC (Edinburgh: T. & T. Clark, 1903) 398.

Numbers 28:1–30:16, Priestly Offerings, the Cultic Calendar, and Lay Vows

NIV

28 The LORD said to Moses, [2]"Give this command to the Israelites and say to them: 'See that you present to me at the appointed time the food for my offerings made by fire, as an aroma pleasing to me.' [3]Say to them: 'This is the offering made by fire that you are to present to the LORD: two lambs a year old without defect, as a regular burnt offering each day. [4]Prepare one lamb in the morning and the other at twilight, [5]together with a grain offering of a tenth of an ephah[a] of fine flour mixed with a quarter of a hin[b] of oil from pressed olives. [6]This is the regular burnt offering instituted at Mount Sinai as a pleasing aroma, an offering made to the LORD by fire. [7]The accompanying drink offering is to be a quarter of a hin of fermented drink with each lamb. Pour out the drink offering to the LORD at the sanctuary. [8]Prepare the second lamb at twilight, along with the same kind of grain offering and drink offering that you prepare in the morning. This is an offering made by fire, an aroma pleasing to the LORD.

[9]" 'On the Sabbath day, make an offering of two lambs a year old without defect, together with its drink offering and a grain offering of two-tenths of an ephah[c] of fine flour mixed with oil. [10]This is the burnt offering for every Sabbath, in addition to the regular burnt offering and its drink offering.

[11]" 'On the first of every month, present to the LORD a burnt offering of two young bulls, one ram and seven male lambs a year old, all without defect. [12]With each bull there is to be a grain offering of three-tenths of an ephah[d] of fine flour mixed with oil; with the ram, a grain offering of two-tenths of an ephah of fine flour mixed with oil; [13]and with each lamb, a grain offering of a tenth of an ephah of fine flour mixed with oil. This is for a burnt offering, a pleasing aroma, an offering made to the LORD by fire. [14]With each bull there is to be a drink offering of half a hin[e] of wine; with the ram, a third of a hin[f]; and with

NRSV

28 The LORD spoke to Moses, saying: [2]Command the Israelites, and say to them: My offering, the food for my offerings by fire, my pleasing odor, you shall take care to offer to me at its appointed time. [3]And you shall say to them, This is the offering by fire that you shall offer to the LORD: two male lambs a year old without blemish, daily, as a regular offering. [4]One lamb you shall offer in the morning, and the other lamb you shall offer at twilight;[a] [5]also one-tenth of an ephah of choice flour for a grain offering, mixed with one-fourth of a hin of beaten oil. [6]It is a regular burnt offering, ordained at Mount Sinai for a pleasing odor, an offering by fire to the LORD. [7]Its drink offering shall be one-fourth of a hin for each lamb; in the sanctuary you shall pour out a drink offering of strong drink to the LORD. [8]The other lamb you shall offer at twilight[a] with a grain offering and a drink offering like the one in the morning; you shall offer it as an offering by fire, a pleasing odor to the LORD.

[9]On the sabbath day: two male lambs a year old without blemish, and two-tenths of an ephah of choice flour for a grain offering, mixed with oil, and its drink offering— [10]this is the burnt offering for every sabbath, in addition to the regular burnt offering and its drink offering.

[11]At the beginnings of your months you shall offer a burnt offering to the LORD: two young bulls, one ram, seven male lambs a year old without blemish; [12]also three-tenths of an ephah of choice flour for a grain offering, mixed with oil, for each bull; and two-tenths of choice flour for a grain offering, mixed with oil, for the one ram; [13]and one-tenth of choice flour mixed with oil as a grain offering for every lamb—a burnt offering of pleasing odor, an offering by fire to the LORD. [14]Their drink offerings shall be half a hin of wine for a bull, one-third of a hin for a ram, and one-fourth of a hin for a lamb. This is the burnt offering of every month throughout the months of the year. [15]And there shall be one male goat for a sin offering to the LORD; it shall be offered in addition to the regular burnt offering and its drink offering.

---

a5 That is, probably about 2 quarts (about 2 liters); also in verses 13, 21 and 29   b5 That is, probably about 1 quart (about 1 liter); also in verses 7 and 14   c9 That is, probably about 4 quarts (about 4.5 liters); also in verses 12, 20 and 28   d12 That is, probably about 6 quarts (about 6.5 liters); also in verses 20 and 28   e14 That is, probably about 2 quarts (about 2 liters)   f14 That is, probably about 1 1/4 quarts (about 1.2 liters)

a Heb *between the two evenings*

NIV

each lamb, a quarter of a hin. This is the monthly burnt offering to be made at each new moon during the year. [15]Besides the regular burnt offering with its drink offering, one male goat is to be presented to the LORD as a sin offering.

[16]"'On the fourteenth day of the first month the LORD's Passover is to be held. [17]On the fifteenth day of this month there is to be a festival; for seven days eat bread made without yeast. [18]On the first day hold a sacred assembly and do no regular work. [19]Present to the LORD an offering made by fire, a burnt offering of two young bulls, one ram and seven male lambs a year old, all without defect. [20]With each bull prepare a grain offering of three-tenths of an ephah of fine flour mixed with oil; with the ram, two-tenths; [21]and with each of the seven lambs, one-tenth. [22]Include one male goat as a sin offering to make atonement for you. [23]Prepare these in addition to the regular morning burnt offering. [24]In this way prepare the food for the offering made by fire every day for seven days as an aroma pleasing to the LORD; it is to be prepared in addition to the regular burnt offering and its drink offering. [25]On the seventh day hold a sacred assembly and do no regular work.

[26]"'On the day of firstfruits, when you present to the LORD an offering of new grain during the Feast of Weeks, hold a sacred assembly and do no regular work. [27]Present a burnt offering of two young bulls, one ram and seven male lambs a year old as an aroma pleasing to the LORD. [28]With each bull there is to be a grain offering of three-tenths of an ephah of fine flour mixed with oil; with the ram, two-tenths; [29]and with each of the seven lambs, one-tenth. [30]Include one male goat to make atonement for you. [31]Prepare these together with their drink offerings, in addition to the regular burnt offering and its grain offering. Be sure the animals are without defect.

29 "'On the first day of the seventh month hold a sacred assembly and do no regular work. It is a day for you to sound the trumpets. [2]As an aroma pleasing to the LORD, prepare a burnt offering of one young bull, one ram and seven male lambs a year old, all without defect. [3]With the bull prepare a grain offering of three-tenths of an ephah[a] of fine flour mixed with oil; with the

a3 That is, probably about 6 quarts (about 6.5 liters); also in verses 9 and 14

NRSV

[16]On the fourteenth day of the first month there shall be a passover offering to the LORD. [17]And on the fifteenth day of this month is a festival; seven days shall unleavened bread be eaten. [18]On the first day there shall be a holy convocation. You shall not work at your occupations. [19]You shall offer an offering by fire, a burnt offering to the LORD: two young bulls, one ram, and seven male lambs a year old; see that they are without blemish. [20]Their grain offering shall be of choice flour mixed with oil: three-tenths of an ephah shall you offer for a bull, and two-tenths for a ram; [21]one-tenth shall you offer for each of the seven lambs; [22]also one male goat for a sin offering, to make atonement for you. [23]You shall offer these in addition to the burnt offering of the morning, which belongs to the regular burnt offering. [24]In the same way you shall offer daily, for seven days, the food of an offering by fire, a pleasing odor to the LORD; it shall be offered in addition to the regular burnt offering and its drink offering. [25]And on the seventh day you shall have a holy convocation; you shall not work at your occupations.

[26]On the day of the first fruits, when you offer a grain offering of new grain to the LORD at your festival of weeks, you shall have a holy convocation; you shall not work at your occupations. [27]You shall offer a burnt offering, a pleasing odor to the LORD: two young bulls, one ram, seven male lambs a year old. [28]Their grain offering shall be of choice flour mixed with oil, three-tenths of an ephah for each bull, two-tenths for one ram, [29]one-tenth for each of the seven lambs; [30]with one male goat, to make atonement for you. [31]In addition to the regular burnt offering with its grain offering, you shall offer them and their drink offering. They shall be without blemish.

29 On the first day of the seventh month you shall have a holy convocation; you shall not work at your occupations. It is a day for you to blow the trumpets, [2]and you shall offer a burnt offering, a pleasing odor to the LORD: one young bull, one ram, seven male lambs a year old without blemish. [3]Their grain offering shall be of choice flour mixed with oil, three-tenths of one ephah for the bull, two-tenths for the ram, [4]and one-tenth for each of the seven lambs; [5]with one

NIV

ram, two-tenths*a*; *4*and with each of the seven lambs, one-tenth.*b* *5*Include one male goat as a sin offering to make atonement for you. *6*These are in addition to the monthly and daily burnt offerings with their grain offerings and drink offerings as specified. They are offerings made to the LORD by fire—a pleasing aroma.

7" 'On the tenth day of this seventh month hold a sacred assembly. You must deny yourselves*c* and do no work. *8*Present as an aroma pleasing to the LORD a burnt offering of one young bull, one ram and seven male lambs a year old, all without defect. *9*With the bull prepare a grain offering of three-tenths of an ephah of fine flour mixed with oil; with the ram, two-tenths; *10*and with each of the seven lambs, one-tenth. *11*Include one male goat as a sin offering, in addition to the sin offering for atonement and the regular burnt offering with its grain offering, and their drink offerings.

12" 'On the fifteenth day of the seventh month, hold a sacred assembly and do no regular work. Celebrate a festival to the LORD for seven days. *13*Present an offering made by fire as an aroma pleasing to the LORD, a burnt offering of thirteen young bulls, two rams and fourteen male lambs a year old, all without defect. *14*With each of the thirteen bulls prepare a grain offering of three-tenths of an ephah of fine flour mixed with oil; with each of the two rams, two-tenths; *15*and with each of the fourteen lambs, one-tenth. *16*Include one male goat as a sin offering, in addition to the regular burnt offering with its grain offering and drink offering.

17" 'On the second day prepare twelve young bulls, two rams and fourteen male lambs a year old, all without defect. *18*With the bulls, rams and lambs, prepare their grain offerings and drink offerings according to the number specified. *19*Include one male goat as a sin offering, in addition to the regular burnt offering with its grain offering, and their drink offerings.

20" 'On the third day prepare eleven bulls, two rams and fourteen male lambs a year old, all without defect. *21*With the bulls, rams and lambs, prepare their grain offerings and drink offerings according to the number specified. *22*Include one

a3 That is, probably about 4 quarts (about 4.5 liters); also in verses 9 and 14   *b4* That is, probably about 2 quarts (about 2 liters); also in verses 10 and 15   *c7* Or *must fast*

NRSV

male goat for a sin offering, to make atonement for you. *6*These are in addition to the burnt offering of the new moon and its grain offering, and the regular burnt offering and its grain offering, and their drink offerings, according to the ordinance for them, a pleasing odor, an offering by fire to the LORD.

*7*On the tenth day of this seventh month you shall have a holy convocation, and deny yourselves;*a* you shall do no work. *8*You shall offer a burnt offering to the LORD, a pleasing odor: one young bull, one ram, seven male lambs a year old. They shall be without blemish. *9*Their grain offering shall be of choice flour mixed with oil, three-tenths of an ephah for the bull, two-tenths for the one ram, *10*one-tenth for each of the seven lambs; *11*with one male goat for a sin offering, in addition to the sin offering of atonement, and the regular burnt offering and its grain offering, and their drink offerings.

*12*On the fifteenth day of the seventh month you shall have a holy convocation; you shall not work at your occupations. You shall celebrate a festival to the LORD seven days. *13*You shall offer a burnt offering, an offering by fire, a pleasing odor to the LORD: thirteen young bulls, two rams, fourteen male lambs a year old. They shall be without blemish. *14*Their grain offering shall be of choice flour mixed with oil, three-tenths of an ephah for each of the thirteen bulls, two-tenths for each of the two rams, *15*and one-tenth for each of the fourteen lambs; *16*also one male goat for a sin offering, in addition to the regular burnt offering, its grain offering and its drink offering.

*17*On the second day: twelve young bulls, two rams, fourteen male lambs a year old without blemish, *18*with the grain offering and the drink offerings for the bulls, for the rams, and for the lambs, as prescribed in accordance with their number; *19*also one male goat for a sin offering, in addition to the regular burnt offering and its grain offering, and their drink offerings.

*20*On the third day: eleven bulls, two rams, fourteen male lambs a year old without blemish, *21*with the grain offering and the drink offerings for the bulls, for the rams, and for the lambs, as prescribed in accordance with their number; *22*also

a Or *and fast*

male goat as a sin offering, in addition to the regular burnt offering with its grain offering and drink offering.

23"'On the fourth day prepare ten bulls, two rams and fourteen male lambs a year old, all without defect. 24With the bulls, rams and lambs, prepare their grain offerings and drink offerings according to the number specified. 25Include one male goat as a sin offering, in addition to the regular burnt offering with its grain offering and drink offering.

26"'On the fifth day prepare nine bulls, two rams and fourteen male lambs a year old, all without defect. 27With the bulls, rams and lambs, prepare their grain offerings and drink offerings according to the number specified. 28Include one male goat as a sin offering, in addition to the regular burnt offering with its grain offering and drink offering.

29"'On the sixth day prepare eight bulls, two rams and fourteen male lambs a year old, all without defect. 30With the bulls, rams and lambs, prepare their grain offerings and drink offerings according to the number specified. 31Include one male goat as a sin offering, in addition to the regular burnt offering with its grain offering and drink offering.

32"'On the seventh day prepare seven bulls, two rams and fourteen male lambs a year old, all without defect. 33With the bulls, rams and lambs, prepare their grain offerings and drink offerings according to the number specified. 34Include one male goat as a sin offering, in addition to the regular burnt offering with its grain offering and drink offering.

35"'On the eighth day hold an assembly and do no regular work. 36Present an offering made by fire as an aroma pleasing to the LORD, a burnt offering of one bull, one ram and seven male lambs a year old, all without defect. 37With the bull, the ram and the lambs, prepare their grain offerings and drink offerings according to the number specified. 38Include one male goat as a sin offering, in addition to the regular burnt offering with its grain offering and drink offering.

39"'In addition to what you vow and your freewill offerings, prepare these for the LORD at your ap-

one male goat for a sin offering, in addition to the regular burnt offering and its grain offering and its drink offering.

23On the fourth day: ten bulls, two rams, fourteen male lambs a year old without blemish, 24with the grain offering and the drink offerings for the bulls, for the rams, and for the lambs, as prescribed in accordance with their number; 25also one male goat for a sin offering, in addition to the regular burnt offering, its grain offering and its drink offering.

26On the fifth day: nine bulls, two rams, fourteen male lambs a year old without blemish, 27with the grain offering and the drink offerings for the bulls, for the rams, and for the lambs, as prescribed in accordance with their number; 28also one male goat for a sin offering, in addition to the regular burnt offering and its grain offering and its drink offering.

29On the sixth day: eight bulls, two rams, fourteen male lambs a year old without blemish, 30with the grain offering and the drink offerings for the bulls, for the rams, and for the lambs, as prescribed in accordance with their number; 31also one male goat for a sin offering, in addition to the regular burnt offering, its grain offering, and its drink offerings.

32On the seventh day: seven bulls, two rams, fourteen male lambs a year old without blemish, 33with the grain offering and the drink offerings for the bulls, for the rams, and for the lambs, as prescribed in accordance with their number; 34also one male goat for a sin offering, besides the regular burnt offering, its grain offering, and its drink offering.

35On the eighth day you shall have a solemn assembly; you shall not work at your occupations. 36You shall offer a burnt offering, an offering by fire, a pleasing odor to the LORD: one bull, one ram, seven male lambs a year old without blemish, 37and the grain offering and the drink offerings for the bull, for the ram, and for the lambs, as prescribed in accordance with their number; 38also one male goat for a sin offering, in addition to the regular burnt offering and its grain offering and its drink offering.

39These you shall offer to the LORD at your appointed festivals, in addition to your votive pointed feasts: your burnt offerings, grain offerings, drink offerings and fellowship offerings.ᵃ' "

⁴⁰Moses told the Israelites all that the LORD commanded him.

30 Moses said to the heads of the tribes of Israel: "This is what the LORD commands: ²When a man makes a vow to the LORD or takes an oath to obligate himself by a pledge, he must not break his word but must do everything he said.

³"When a young woman still living in her father's house makes a vow to the LORD or obligates herself by a pledge ⁴and her father hears about her vow or pledge but says nothing to her, then all her vows and every pledge by which she obligated herself will stand. ⁵But if her father forbids her when he hears about it, none of her vows or the pledges by which she obligated herself will stand; the LORD will release her because her father has forbidden her.

⁶"If she marries after she makes a vow or after her lips utter a rash promise by which she obligates herself ⁷and her husband hears about it but says nothing to her, then her vows or the pledges by which she obligated herself will stand. ⁸But if her husband forbids her when he hears about it, he nullifies the vow that obligates her or the rash promise by which she obligates herself, and the LORD will release her.

⁹"Any vow or obligation taken by a widow or divorced woman will be binding on her.

¹⁰"If a woman living with her husband makes a vow or obligates herself by a pledge under oath ¹¹and her husband hears about it but says nothing to her and does not forbid her, then all her vows or the pledges by which she obligated herself will stand. ¹²But if her husband nullifies them when he hears about them, then none of the vows or pledges that came from her lips will stand. Her husband has nullified them, and the LORD will release her. ¹³Her husband may confirm or nullify any vow she makes or any sworn pledge to deny herself. ¹⁴But if her husband says nothing to her about it from day to day, then he confirms all her vows or the pledges binding on her. He confirms them by saying nothing to her when he hears about them. ¹⁵If, however, he nullifies them some

offerings and your freewill offerings, as your burnt offerings, your grain offerings, your drink offerings, and your offerings of well-being.

40ᵃ So Moses told the Israelites everything just as the LORD had commanded Moses.

30 Then Moses said to the heads of the tribes of the Israelites: This is what the LORD has commanded. ²When a man makes a vow to the LORD, or swears an oath to bind himself by a pledge, he shall not break his word; he shall do according to all that proceeds out of his mouth.

3When a woman makes a vow to the LORD, or binds herself by a pledge, while within her father's house, in her youth, ⁴and her father hears of her vow or her pledge by which she has bound herself, and says nothing to her; then all her vows shall stand, and any pledge by which she has bound herself shall stand. ⁵But if her father expresses disapproval to her at the time that he hears of it, no vow of hers, and no pledge by which she has bound herself, shall stand; and the LORD will forgive her, because her father had expressed to her his disapproval.

6If she marries, while obligated by her vows or any thoughtless utterance of her lips by which she has bound herself, ⁷and her husband hears of it and says nothing to her at the time that he hears, then her vows shall stand, and her pledges by which she has bound herself shall stand. ⁸But if, at the time that her husband hears of it, he expresses disapproval to her, then he shall nullify the vow by which she was obligated, or the thoughtless utterance of her lips, by which she bound herself; and the LORD will forgive her. ⁹(But every vow of a widow or of a divorced woman, by which she has bound herself, shall be binding upon her.) ¹⁰And if she made a vow in her husband's house, or bound herself by a pledge with an oath, ¹¹and her husband heard it and said nothing to her, and did not express disapproval to her, then all her vows shall stand, and any pledge by which she bound herself shall stand. ¹²But if her husband nullifies them at the time that he hears them, then whatever proceeds out of her lips concerning her vows, or concerning her pledge of herself, shall not stand. Her husband has nullified them, and the LORD will forgive her.

ᵃ39 Traditionally *peace offerings*

ᵃ Ch 30.1 in Heb

NIV

time after he hears about them, then he is responsible for her guilt."

[16]These are the regulations the LORD gave Moses concerning relationships between a man and his wife, and between a father and his young daughter still living in his house.

NRSV

[13]Any vow or any binding oath to deny herself,[a] her husband may allow to stand, or her husband may nullify. [14]But if her husband says nothing to her from day to day,[b] then he validates all her vows, or all her pledges, by which she is obligated; he has validated them, because he said nothing to her at the time that he heard of them. [15]But if he nullifies them some time after he has heard of them, then he shall bear her guilt.

16These are the statutes that the LORD commanded Moses concerning a husband and his wife, and a father and his daughter while she is still young and in her father's house.

[a] Or to fast   [b] Or from that day to the next

COMMENTARY

The priestly duties for cultic sacrifices are outlined in chaps. 28–29, while chap. 30 adds material on lay vowing, especially by women. Chapters 28–29 are clearly unified. The chapters are structured as divine command (28:1) and fulfillment by Moses (29:40[30:1]), a common feature of the priestly writers throughout Numbers. The content of these chapters also encourages that they be read as a single unit, since together they describe Israel's worship through one annual cycle.

Numbers 30 is less clear in its relationship to chaps. 28–29; yet, it appears that the priestly writers intend to interrelate chaps. 28–30. No new divine command to Moses at the outset of chap. 30 separates the instruction on vows from the legislation regarding priestly sacrifices in chaps. 28–29. Instead, the instruction concerning vows follows immediately after 29:40[30:1 MT], where it states that Moses conveyed to Israel all of the divine commands. The reference to votive, freewill, burnt, grain, drink, and well-being offerings in 29:39 may have provided the transition from priestly sacrifices in chaps. 28–29 to the topic of lay vows in chap. 30, since vowing often included sacrifices at the cult site. Thus it appears that legislation regarding vows in general, but especially vows by women (chap. 30), has been loosely attached to the information on priestly sacrifices in chaps. 28–29. The result is that chaps. 28–30 present a contrast between lay (chap. 30) and priestly (chaps. 28–29) responsibilities for sacrifices. The emphasis on priestly

responsibilities also contrasts with chap. 15, where other lay responsibilities for cultic sacrifice were outlined.

The commentary on Numbers 28–30 will follow the pattern of the priestly writers, in which instructions for priestly sacrifice are arranged by frequency. These sacrifices are followed by the legislation on vowing.

28:1-2. These verses provide a general introduction to chaps. 28–29. Verse 1 indicates that chaps. 28–29 are divine instruction to Moses. The introduction is vague, making it difficult to integrate this section into the larger design of the book. Two problems stand out. First, no specific location is given for the divine instruction to Moses. The present context of Numbers 28 would suggest that the divine commands follow the commissioning of Joshua by Eleazar at the door of the tent of meeting (27:12-23). Yet, the relationship between these two chapters is not clearly defined. Second, the intended audience indicates that the commands are directed to the Israelites in general, even though the content of the instruction deals primarily with priestly responsibilities for sacrifices. Perhaps the leadership role of Eleazar in the preceding commissioning of Joshua has prompted the priestly writers to outline at this point the comprehensive cultic responsibilities of priests for conducting sacrifices on behalf of Israel. Also, there has been a tendency in priestly tradition to place priestly requirements within the context of all Israel, which may explain why the commands are directed to all Israelites rather than to the priests alone. The focus on all Israel for communicating priestly responsibilities holds the priesthood accountable in their office of mediation. Their power is not intended to be held privately. The deaths of Nadab and Abihu for offering private sacrifices provide a strong warning against separating priestly mediation from the entire Israelite congregation (Lev 10:1-2).

Verse 2 indicates that the focus of chaps. 28–29 is sacred time or, more precisely, "appointed time" (מועד *môʿēd*). God tells Moses that each offering by fire must be made "at its appointed time." The appointed time refers to sacred seasons that structure Israel's cultic life. Proper observance of sacred time through sacrifice will create a "pleasing odor" to God. (See the Commentary on 1:1–2:34 for further discussion of "appointed time," where the Hebrew word is used in the phrase "tent of meeting" to indicate a sacred place as opposed to its temporal meaning here. See the Commentary on 13:1–15:41 for interpretation of the phrase "pleasing odor.")

The emphasis on God's claim over time is new to the book of Numbers. References to "appointed times" have occurred in relationship to Passover (9:2) and to trumpets (10:10). For the most part, however, the focus of chaps. 1–10 was place, including the legislation concerning the holiness of the camp (chaps. 1–6) and the tabernacle (chaps. 7–10). The central role of setting in the wilderness and the quest for land also gave the travel stories in chaps. 11–25 a geographical focus.

But the divine claim on time is deeply rooted in the priestly history, appearing already in Genesis 1. In this account of creation, the planets and the stars, as well as the sun and the moon, function to direct Israel's worship life. All heavenly bodies exist to indicate sacred or "appointed times" (Gen 1:14-19). The priestly writers state in Gen 1:14 that the stars are "for signs and for seasons and for days and years." The NRSV translation "for seasons" is the same Hebrew word translated as "appointed time" in Num 28:2. Numbers 28–29 provides detailed commentary on Gen 1:14 by outlining the priestly responsibilities for sacrificing on days, months, and seasons of the year. The temporal rhythms of sacrifice outlined in these chapters are meant to put Israel in harmony with God's ideal vision for creation.

28:3-8. The first sacrifice prescribed is "the regular burnt offering" (v. 6). This is the daily offering by the priests, also known as the *Tamid* (תמיד *tāmîd*), from the Hebrew word translated "regular." The regular burnt offering consists of:

Animal	Grain Offering (and oil)	Drink Offering
lamb	⅒ ephah (¼ hin)	¼ hin

The daily offering was performed twice each day, once in the morning and again at twilight. Thus two lambs with the accompanying grain and drink offerings were required. Each lamb was to be one year of age and without blemish. This requirement of age and quality continues throughout all festival sacrifices of lambs. The accompanying grain offering (מנחה *minḥâ*) consisted of choice flour and beaten oil. The drink offering was most likely wine, although v. 7 describes it simply as "strong drink." The proportions of the daily offering are the same as those given in chap. 15 (see the Commentary on 15:1-16 for an explanation of the quantities ephah and hin). The priestly writers anchor the requirement of a daily offering in the revelation at Sinai, described in Exod 29:38-42.

The practice of a daily offering is already evident in the monarchical period. A morning burnt offering and an evening cereal offering are described in 2 Kgs 16:15. The prophet Ezekiel describes only a morning offering, indicating the practice of *Tamid* during the exilic period (Ezek 46:13-15). The practice of a daily offering was so important to Israel that its cessation during the time of Antiochus IV (167 BCE) was interpreted as marking the end of an epoch in Jewish history (see Dan 8:11; 11:31; 12:11). The Christian practice of morning and evening vespers is an outgrowth of the divine requirement for daily offering in priestly tradition.

28:9-10. Sabbath required special sacrifice by the priests. The day was already set apart from others by the priestly writers in their account of creation, when God rested on this day (Gen 2:1-3). The amount of the offering on sabbath was equal to the daily offering, and it was accumulative, meaning that it was offered in addition to the daily offering. Thus sabbath required a double offering. The burnt offering includes:

Animal	Grain Offering (and oil)	Drink Offering
2 lambs	⅒ ephah/lamb	¼ hin/lamb

These verses do not explicitly state the amount of oil and wine used in this offering, but only that the grain offering was to be accompanied by oil and the drink offering. The proportions listed above follow the quantities of the daily burnt offering. The only other mention of a requirement for sabbath sacrifice appears in the book of Ezekiel, where the prophet states that the prince (or king) must offer six lambs, one ram, one ephah of grain with the ram, and as much grain with the lambs as he wishes.

28:11-15. The monthly offering by priests was to take place on the first day of the month. Once again, these verses do not explicitly state the amount of oil to be used, but only that the grain offering was to be accompanied by oil. The burnt offering includes:

Animal	Grain Offering (and oil)	Drink Offering (wine)
2 bulls	3/10 ephah/bull	1/2 hin/bull
1 ram	2/10 ephah	1/3 hin
7 lambs	1/10 ephah/lamb	1/4 hin/lamb

+

1 goat as a sin offering

The quantity of the sacrifice on New Moon indicates its importance in the priestly calendar. It equals the number of offerings for Passover and First Fruits. Other references to New Moon in the OT suggest that lunar observance was an old custom in Israel. An observance of New Moon is mentioned in the story of Jonathan and David (1 Sam 20:5, a family meal) and again in the story of the prophet Elisha (2 Kgs 4:23), where it appears that the Israelites visited holy persons on this day. The festival is also mentioned in Amos 8:5 and Hos 2:11. A form of lunar observance occurs in Protestant churches that celebrate the eucharist on the first Sunday of each month.

28:16–29:38. The yearly sacrifices focus on months 1 and 7, with the Festival of Weeks, or First Fruits, occurring between these months. (Its observance, according to Lev 23:15-16, was fifty days after an initial presentation of a sheaf of grain to the priest.) The underlying structure of the yearly festivals of the priestly cultic calendar follows in general an old pattern of worship in Israel, in which the cultic year was organized around three agricultural festivals: a seven-day Feast of Unleavened Bread in spring, followed by First Fruits when they were ready, and concluded by the Feast of Ingathering in autumn. This tri-partite cultic calendar is preserved in Exod 23:14-17 (see also Exod 34:22-23).[186]

But the priestly calendar also indicates change in worship. The Feast of Unleavened Bread in the spring (Month 1) in Exod 23:15 had become attached to Passover by the time of the priestly writers, while the Feast of Ingathering in autumn (Month 7) in Exod 23:16 was renamed the Feast of Booths, or Succoth (see Lev 23:33-36). The feast days of Blowing the Horn on the first day, as well as Atonement, had also been added to Month 7. The addition of two feasts in Month 7 suggests that for the priestly writers the fall was the high point of worship in the liturgical year.

The purpose of Num 28:16–29:37 is to catalogue the required sacrifices by priests during the yearly festivals. The yearly rituals repeat the cultic calendar outlined in Leviticus 23. This repetition may be intended to contrast lay and priestly responsibilities, as the following outline illustrates:

Comparison of Leviticus 23 and Numbers 28–29 demonstrates that the two cultic calendars complement each other with different emphases. Both are focused on Israel's future life in the land of Canaan. Yet Leviticus 23 outlines the role of lay Israelites during the yearly festivals, while Numbers 28–29 focus on the role of priests. Note, for example, that Leviticus 23 makes no mention of daily or monthly sacrifices, since these activities are performed by priests at the central cultic location independently of lay Israelites. Sabbath is mentioned in both texts, but the emphasis is different in each: Leviticus 23 describes the duties of lay Israelites, while Numbers 28 outlines the priestly responsibilities for sacrifices.

The yearly festivals in Leviticus 23 are also aimed at lay Israelites, as compared to Numbers 28–29, where, once again, the focus is on priestly sacrifices. The festivals in Month 1 provide illustration: In Leviticus 23, Passover is specified as taking place at twilight, thus locating the time of family observance. Unleavened Bread requires two convocations for all Israelites. The ritual associated with First Fruits, or Weeks, is described in detail, and the time of the festival is determined precisely by its focus on lay Israelite participation.

---

186. See "Agricultural and Civil Calendar," in *The New Interpreter's Bible,* vol. 1 (Nashville: Abingdon, 1994) 275.

Figure 5: Cultic Calendars in Leviticus 23 and Numbers 28–29

Leviticus 23
I. Daily Sacrifice (Not Included)

2. Sabbath (Lev 23:3)
   Emphasis: No Work by Israelites
3. Monthly Sacrifice (Not Included)

4. Yearly Festivals (Lev 23:5-43)
   A. Month 1
      (1) Day 14
      Passover (23:5)
      Emphasis: Time (Twilight)
      (2) Days 15-21
         Unleavened Bread (23:6-8)
         Emphasis: Days 15 and 21
         Convocation by Israel
   B. First Fruits (23:9-22)
      Emphasis: Role of Lay Israelites
      (1) First Fruits to Priest
      (2) Sacrifice by Israelites
      (3) Determining Date
   C. Month 7
      (1) Day 1
         Blowing the Horn (23:23-25)
         Emphasis: Convocation by Israel
            No Work
      (2) Day 10
         Day of Atonement (23:26-32)
         Emphasis: Convocation by Israel
            No Work
      (3) Days 15-21
         Feast of Booths (23:33-43)
         Emphasis: Role of Lay Israelites
            (a) Construction of Booths
            (b) Interpretation

Numbers 28–29
1. Daily Sacrifice (Num 28:2-6)
   Emphasis: Sacrifices by Priests
2. Sabbath (28:9-10)
   Emphasis: Sacrifices by Priests
3. Monthly Sacrifice (Num 28:11-15)
   Emphasis: Sacrifices by Priests
4. Yearly Festivals (Num 28:16–29:39)
   A. Month 1
      (1) Day 14
      Passover (28:16)

      (2) Days 15-21
         Unleavened Bread (28:17-24)
         Emphasis: Daily Offerings
         by Priests
   B. First Fruits (28:26-31)
      Emphasis: Sacrifices by Priests

   C. Month 7
      (1) Day 1
         Blowing the Horn (29:1-6)
         Emphasis: Sacrifices by Priests

      (2) Day 10
         Not Named (29:7-11)
         Emphasis: Sacrifice by Priests

      (3) Days 15-21
         Not Named (29:12-38)
         Emphasis: Sacrifice by Priests

In chaps. 28–29, the emphasis is sacrifice by the priests. The same contrast holds true for the festivals in Month 7: The Blowing of the Horn, Atonement, and the Feast of Booths describe the role of lay Israelites in Leviticus 23, as compared to the focus on priestly sacrifices in Numbers 28–29.

Scholars debate the literary relationship between Leviticus 23 and Numbers 28–29. The latter appears to presuppose Leviticus 23 at several points.[187] The

outline illustrates that neither the Day of Atonement on Month 7, Day 10, nor the Feast of Booths on Month 7, Days 15-21, is specifically named in Numbers 28–29, suggesting a dependent relationship to Leviticus 23. Some scholars interpret the formality of the language and the precise details of Numbers 28–29 as signs of late composition.[188] In general, scholars have assumed

187. George Buchanan Gray, *Numbers,* ICC (Edinburgh: T. & T. Clark, 1903), 402-7; Phillip J. Budd, *Numbers,* WBC 5 (Waco, Tex.: Word, 1984) 312-15.

188. Martin Noth, *Numbers,* OTL (Philadelphia: Westminster, 1968) 219-20. Cf., however, L. R. Fisher, "A New Ritual Calendar from Ugarit," HTR 63 (1970) 485-501; and see the criticism of Timothy R. Ashley, *Numbers,* NICOT (Grand Rapids: Eerdmans, 1993) 561.

that Numbers 28–29 is a later composition than Leviticus 23. But the complementary nature of the two texts, with their different points of emphasis, may provide sufficient reason for their distinct locations in the priestly history. Even the consensus concerning the later composition of Numbers 28–29 has been challenged recently by Israel Knohl, who argues that the present form of Leviticus 23 represents the latest view of the priestly writers.[189]

The important point for this commentary is the more general conclusion that Numbers 28–29 and Leviticus 23 are part of the priestly history, rather than the pre-priestly history. The cultic calendar in Deuteronomy 16 most likely reflects more closely the point of view of the writers of the pre-priestly history. Still, other cultic calendars that contrast both the deuteronomic and the priestly interpretation of festivals include the older calendars contained in Exod 23:14-17; 34:18-26, mentioned above, and most notably Ezek 45:18-25, where a distinctive list of priestly sacrifices is proposed.

28:16. The Passover offering is observed on Month 1, Day 14. No further description is given of Passover, because there are no sacrifices by priests at the central cult on this day. Passover in priestly tradition is a family observance. The priestly interpretation of Passover appears in Exod 12:1-13, 43-49, which states that the Passover offering required one male lamb, one year of age and without blemish. It was to be slaughtered at twilight (see also Lev 23:5) and eaten during the night by families. Numbers 9:1-14 contains legislation granting observance on Month 2, Day 14 for those unable to participate in Passover at its designated time.

28:17-25. The Feast of Unleavened Bread was observed on Month 1, Days 15-21. A convocation of all Israelites was required on the first and last days of the feast. In addition, priestly sacrifice was required on all seven days. The sacrifices are the same as for New Moon, although no drink offering is specifically mentioned. Like the New Moon and sabbath sacrifices, these offerings are in addition to other prescribed sacrifices, like the daily offerings. The burnt offering includes:

189. I. Knohl, "The Priestly Torah Versus the Holiness School: Sabbath and the Festivals," *HUCA* 58 (1987) 65-117; and *The Sanctuary of Silence: The Priestly Torah and the Holiness School* (Minneapolis: Fortress, 1995).

Animal	Grain Offering (and oil)
2 bulls	$^3/_{10}$ ephah/bull
1 ram	$^2/_{10}$ ephah
7 lambs	$^1/_{10}$ ephah/lamb
+	
1 goat as a sin offering	

28:26-31. The Feast of Weeks is an agricultural festival that is not fixed in the priestly calendar. Calculations for determining its date are not even given here; more precise directions for its observance are provided in Lev 23:9-22. It was determined by counting fifty days, seven sabbaths from the day on which the sheaf of first fruit was presented to the priests. In Exod 23:16, this feast is called the "festival of harvest," because it celebrated the harvest of barley. Its name in priestly tradition underscores the timing of its celebration: seven weeks after Unleavened Bread. The Feast of Weeks required a convocation of all Israelites and the cessation of all work. (This festival corresponds with Pentecost in the Christian calendar.) The amount of the burnt offering required by priests follows the expected formula of major feasts:

Animal	Grain Offering (and oil)
2 bulls	$^3/_{10}$ ephah/bull
1 ram	$^2/_{10}$ ephah
7 lambs	$^1/_{10}$ ephah/lamb
+	
1 goat as a sin offering	

29:1-6. A horn was blown on Month 7, Day 1. The blowing of a similar horn was used to direct Israel on its march (10:5-6), and later the blowing of a horn will be used for waging war against Midian (31:6). Here the blowing of the horn distinguishes the seventh month from other months, in much the same way that sabbath is distinguished from other days. Thus the New Moon on Month 7 is separated out as a special day of convocation without work. The priestly sacrifices on this day are in addition to the already prescribed New Moon offerings. The amount of burnt offerings required by the priest are:

Animal	Grain Offering (and oil)
1 bull	$^3/_{10}$ ephah
1 ram	$^2/_{10}$ ephah
7 lambs	$^1/_{10}$ ephah/lamb
+	
1 goat as a sin offering	

29:7-11. The Day of Atonement is observed on Month 7, Day 10. Its name does not appear in these verses, but is derived from Lev 23:27; the complex ritual is outlined in Leviticus 16. The purpose of the Day of Atonement is to purge the sanctuary of the defilement accumulated through human use. The contamination from human sin is transferred to a goat, which is then sent out into the wilderness (Lev 16:20-22). Here it is stipulated that this day is a time of self-denial, which most likely is the practice of fasting. In addition, Israelites were to perform no work and to hold a convocation. The central point of these verses is to outline the requirements for priestly offerings. They include:

Animal	Grain Offering (and oil)
1 bull	$\frac{3}{10}$ ephah
1 ram	$\frac{2}{10}$ ephah
7 lambs	$\frac{1}{10}$ ephah/lamb
+	
1 goat as a sin offering	

29:12-38. The Feast of Booths was celebrated on Month 7, Days 15-21, with an extra day of sacrifice on Day 22. The extra eighth day may be a later addition to the festival. The name of the festival is absent in these verses. Other designations for the fall festival include the Feast of Ingathering (Exod 23:16); during the monarchical period, it is simply referred to as "the Feast" (1 Kgs 8:22), suggesting its predominant role in the liturgical year. The name Feast of Booths derives from Lev 23:34, where it is described with the Hebrew word סכות (sukkôt), meaning "booths" or "tabernacles." This word refers to the temporary dwellings of farmers during harvest. These were interpreted by the priestly writers as reminders of Israel's wilderness travels (Lev 23:43). During the festival, all Israel was required to refrain from work and to hold a convocation.

Verses 12-38 are primarily concerned with outlining the extensive sacrifices required by priests during the eight days of the festival. Unique to this festival is the descending number of bull sacrifices from thirteen on Day 15 to seven on Day 21. This pattern accentuates the importance of the number seven. On the seventh day of the festival in the seventh month and on the twenty-first day of the month (3 x 7) seven bulls are sacrificed. The number seven is central throughout the calendar. There are seven feasts, and seven days of observance for Unleavened Bread and Booths. In addition, the seventh day of the week and the seventh month are holy times. Thus the sacrifice of seven bulls on the seventh day of the seventh

month is most certainly a significant moment in the liturgical year for the priestly writers. The daily sacrifices on Days 15-21 include:

Animal	Grain Offering (and oil)
1-7 bulls	$\frac{3}{10}$ ephah/bull
2 rams	$\frac{2}{10}$ ephah/ram
7 lambs	$\frac{1}{10}$ ephah/lamb
+	
1 goat as a sin offering	

On Day 22, a day of transition from the Feast of Booths to ordinary time, the sacrifices include:

Animal	Grain Offering (and oil)
1 bull	$\frac{3}{10}$ ephah
1 ram	$\frac{2}{10}$ ephah
7 lambs	$\frac{1}{10}$ ephah/lamb
+	
1 goat as a sin offering	

The total number of sacrifices for the Feast of Booths require no less than 71 bulls, 15 rams, 105 lambs, and 8 goats. These sacrifices are in addition to the daily offerings.

29:39-40. The conclusion to the cultic calendar stresses that the preceding list of sacrifices is intended to be public offerings. Private offerings, like those described in chap. 15, are in addition to the public cycle of sacrifice. The section closes by indicating that Moses fulfilled the divine instructions by relaying the information concerning public offerings to Israel.

30:1-16. This chapter contains instruction by Moses concerning vowing. Vows were most likely accompanied by private offerings, since they include dedication to God at a sanctuary. Hannah, for example, makes a vow at the central cult site of Shiloh. The content of her vow is that if God gives her a male child, she will dedicate that child to God as a Nazirite (1 Sam 1:11). Her son, Samuel, is the dedication of this vow. When Hannah fulfills her vow and brings Samuel to Eli at the temple of Shiloh, however, she also brings a private sacrifice consisting of one "three-year old bull, an ephah of flour, and a skin of wine" (1 Sam 1:24). It may be this link between vowing and lay sacrifice that accounts for the linkage of Numbers 30 with chaps. 28–29.

The story of Hannah illustrates that vows are promises in which a person invokes God's name. These vows are binding in much the same way as covenants. In this chapter, two types of vows are addressed. They are distinguished in translation by the words "vow" (נדר *neder*) and "pledge" (אסר *'issār*), which occur in tandem in nearly every verse of the chapter. Although both words require the fulfillment of promises made to God, each designates a different action. The word "vow" indicates a situation in which a person promises to do something for God in exchange for divine help. Jacob illustrates such a vow (Gen 28:20-22) when he promises to construct a sanctuary for God at Bethel, if God protects him on his journey. A "pledge" is a promise that involves an action of self-denial. The Nazirites illustrate this type of vow, since their pledge involved giving up wine. The distinction between "vow" and "pledge" does not continue outside of Numbers 30; the Hebrew word *neder* is used to describe both types of promises. Thus, for example, the abstinence by Nazirites in Numbers 6 is described as a "vow" rather than a "pledge."

This chapter focuses primarily on vows by women. It is the second chapter in the section of chaps. 27–36 to focus on the role of women in ancient Israelite society. Chapter 27 outlined the rights of daughters to inherit, and chap. 30 sketches out situations in which women can make and fulfill vows. Both chapters illustrate that ancient Israelite society was patriarchal, since the intended audience in both appears to be men. Inheritance of daughters takes place only in exceptional situations where there is no male heir. The underlying concern in this chapter is the financial obligations that accompany vows. The legislation regarding vowing by women is primarily concerned to outline the conditions under which either fathers or husbands are able to annul them.

Gordon Wenham has illustrated that the laws on vowing divide into two groups, consisting of vv. 2-8 and vv. 9-15.[190] Each half, in turn, separates into three categories. The first category concerns unbreakable vows. Verse 2 states that any vow made by a man is binding. The complement to this is v. 9, which states that any vow by a widow or divorced woman is also unbreakable.

The second category concerns vows by women that can be annulled by men without penalty. Verses 3-5 state that a father can annul a vow by his daughter, if he immediately expresses disapproval. Such an action by the father will prompt divine forgiveness of the daughter. The complement to this is vv. 10-12, which states that a husband can nullify the vow of his wife, if he expresses disapproval immediately at the time of hearing.

The third category addresses situations in which a husband desires to nullify the vow of his wife after a period of time. Verses 6-8 address the situation in which a husband wishes to annul a vow that was made by his wife and approved by her father prior to their marriage. The law states that husbands may annul the previous vows of their brides without penalty. The complement to this law is vv. 13-15, which state that if a husband does not act immediately to nullify a vow of his wife, then he must bear the guilt for any future action on his part to annul the vow.

190. Gordon J. Wenham, *Numbers: An Introduction and Commentary,* Tyndale Old Testament Commentaries (Leicester: Inter-Varsity, 1981) 206.

REFLECTIONS

1. Our contemporary world is obsessed with time. It is an obstacle to be overcome in reaching goals faster. Manufacturing technology is aimed at a never-ending quest to accomplish more in less time. Computers and the World Wide Web accelerate our communication in order to save time. Family life includes more and more activity in the same twenty-four-hour period. Food is now even evaluated by time—fast food is a growth industry in Western culture. Progress in each of these different areas of modern life is measured by overcoming the limits of time. The priestly writers view time differently in Numbers 28–29. They provide an excellent resource for reflecting theologically on the significance of time in contemporary life and especially sacred time in our worship life.

Time is holy for the priestly writers. The importance of time is not its speed in reaching a goal, but its rhythm in relationship with objects in creation. Thus time highlights interrelationships in creation. Genesis 1 lays the foundation for this insight. Creation is an evolution of opposites, from dark to light, from water to air, from sea to dry land, and from profane time to sacred time. Time, according to the priestly writers, is part of the pattern of contrasts that imposes order on chaos. But priestly writers value time even beyond its role in containing chaos. It holds the key to holiness. The ideal rhythm of time is woven into the pattern of creation, including day and night (Gen 1:3-5), sabbath (Gen 2:1-3), and months and years (Gen 1:14-19). These rhythms are not obstacles to be overcome by humans. On the contrary, human life is enriched when it corresponds to the temporal patterns of creation. Conforming to the rhythm of creation is the only way to achieve holiness.

Sabbath is central to the priestly vision of sacred time. Genesis 1 once again is the source of their teaching. God sanctifies sabbath (Gen 2:3) by resting on this day. Sanctification of sabbath imposes yet another temporal order on creation—sacred and profane time—providing a paradigm for the worship week of humans. This message is clear from the story of manna (Exodus 16), the Decalogue (Exodus 20), the instructions for the tabernacle (Exodus 31 and 35), and the case of the man picking up sticks on the sabbath (Numbers 15). Humans rest on sabbath because God rested on sabbath (Gen 2:1-3). This moment in creation is sanctified.

Only sabbath time is holy, according to the priestly writers. No other part of creation is given holy status in Genesis 1. The earth is not holy. The stars, sun, and moon are not holy. Animals, birds, and humans are not holy. All of these parts of creation are good, but none is sacred. God cannot be identified with objects or creatures in creation. Only time is holy in Genesis 1. God sanctifies the sabbath, because it marks the moment of completion. On sabbath, the finished creation interacts as an organism, alive and in balance. This is what allows for divine rest. The organism is not holy, but the moment of sabbath rest is holy. Any additional work would disrupt the balance of the whole. Thus when humans rest on sabbath, it takes on eschatological significance for the priestly writers. It is a window into this original sacred moment, when the organism of creation conformed to God's intentions.

Priestly writers lay the foundation for their view of sacred time in Genesis 1, but God's claim on time continues into the book of Numbers. The presence of God in the tabernacle influences not only the way Israel is organized in the camp, but also how their days, weeks, months, and years are structured. Thus time itself divides between sacred and profane. Transitional moments in the day (at dawn and twilight), in the week (on sabbath), in the month (on the first day), and in the year (at major festivals) are infused with holiness, creating a contrast with ordinary time. Work is replaced by worship, and sacrificial rites are performed. Participation in the cultic rhythms of Numbers 28–29 is eschatological. It transports Israel to the sacred moment when creation was balanced and God rested.

The change in the observance of sabbath from Saturday to Sunday in early Christian worship accentuates the eschatological nature of sabbath rest established by priestly writers. The resurrection of Jesus prompted Christians to move sabbath from Saturday to Sunday in order to memorialize the resurrection on a weekly basis. Sabbath as Sunday becomes the first day of the new creation in the kingdom of God, ushered in through the passion of Jesus. The message in Christian worship is the same as that of the priestly writers: Time is never an obstacle to be overcome. Just the opposite; we participate in holiness by conforming to the rhythm of God's time in creation.

2. The priestly cultic calendar also provides an occasion to reflect more generally on sacred time in the Christian liturgical year. Christians share the confession of the priestly writers that God claims time, creating a contrast between sacred and profane time. Christians also profess that sacred time provides a rhythm suggestive of God's vision for time. Furthermore, the Christian calendar has evolved from the priestly calendar in Numbers 28–29 in much the same way as the priestly calendar evolved from the older cultic calendar in Exod 23:14-17. Comparison between the priestly and the Christian calendars underscores how the fall festivals in the priestly calendar—those that occur in Month 7—do not continue in Christian tradition.

Advent and Christmas are not a continuation of the priestly fall festivals. Instead, they represent a late innovation in Christian tradition that departs from Jewish tradition.

The center of the Christian year is Holy Week in the spring. Holy Week in Christian tradition builds off of the spring festival of Passover in Month 1, Day 14. Passover is embedded in a week-long festival for Christians that now includes the three-day passion of Jesus from Good Friday to Easter Sunday morning, where much of the priestly rituals from the Day of Atonement are relocated. Pentecost is the Christian reinterpretation of the Feast of Weeks in the priestly calendar. Thus the Festival of First Fruits for Christians becomes the gift of the Holy Spirit to the apostles. In this way, the church becomes the first fruits of the kingdom of God. The comparisons underscore how Christians, like the priestly writers, profess that time is holy and that the life of faith must be organized according to the rhythm of God's time.

3. Numbers 28–29 model the power of public intercession through sacrifice. This is true for all the public offerings by the priests, but such power is reflected especially in the *Tamid,* the daily regular burnt offerings, because it occurs independently of a convocation by Israel. The *Tamid* is a form of priestly intercession that takes place every morning and every evening. It is aimed at maintaining the health and well-being of the community as a whole and the entire creation as well. What is noteworthy for contemporary teaching and preaching is that the *Tamid* takes place without the personal involvement of those whom it is intended to benefit. The ritual itself creates an environment of health.

The ever-growing emphasis on individualized and personal religion in modern culture has tended to minimize the power of public intercession like the *Tamid.* As a result, the power of God in contemporary culture is often limited in scope to individual persons, while the action of God to save tends to be conditioned on personal, human involvement. The focus on lay Israelite involvement, emphasized in Leviticus 23, indicates that priestly writers certainly support individual participation in worship. The message of priestly writers in Numbers 28–29, however, is that daily ritual sacrifice by priests also influences God and that such influence is independent of direct lay participation. The *Tamid* is rooted in the belief that the Temple (for Christians, the church) has the power to influence the outcome of world events through ritual intercession. Such intercession actually aids in keeping the world in balance. The message of the priestly writers is that we are more powerful collectively than we are individually. The writer of Matthew states the same insight somewhat differently with the proclamation that the church holds the keys to the kingdom of God (Matt 16:13-20).

4. The patriarchal structure of Numbers 30, in which women play a subordinate role to men, renders the passage socially irrelevant to modern culture, for which the goal is for men and women to have equal status under the law. But the social structure of Numbers 30 should not obscure its essential point: the power of making vows with God. The challenge of Numbers 30 for modern readers is not a literal reading of ancient Israelite social structure, but a literal reading of the power of making vows. Too often, modern interpreters reverse this order and look to ancient texts for irrelevant social models, while ignoring the underlying religious dimension of the text.

Vows imply the active presence of God in the life of people. Vows were often made at times of crisis. Hannah's request for a son (1 Samuel 1) and Israel's request for divine help in war (Num 21:2) illustrate typical situations in which vows were made. The legal background of Numbers 30 underscores how seriously both Israel and God evaluated promises. Vows were not interpreted metaphorically in ancient Israel as expressions of wishful thinking on the part of Israelites. They were legally binding for both God and humans. Thus vows imply that God is a concrete and active force in human affairs. Ancient Israel expected God to be faithful to the contract. They also held themselves accountable. Thus once spoken a vow took on a life of its own. The NRSV translation in Num 30:2, "he shall not break his word," literally means "to desecrate." Failure to fulfill a vow threatened to profane the sanctuary, influencing the health of the entire community.

Vowing implies an awareness of God in the outcome of concrete human events. This, and not the social structure of the text, is the central message and challenge for contemporary preaching and teaching on Numbers 30. Vows hold God and the person making the vow accountable. They also are public contracts, whose fulfillment strengthens the community of faith. We make vows constantly in the church. There are vows for positions of leadership (ordination vows), marriage, baptism, tithing, and so forth. Numbers 30 reminds us that both God and we have legal obligations when we make vows. The chapter also invites reflection on more individual vows for specific occasions or periods of time. These are less common in the life of the church, but are no less important to the health of a community.

Numbers 31:1–33:56, Holy War

NIV

31 The LORD said to Moses, [2]"Take vengeance on the Midianites for the Israelites. After that, you will be gathered to your people."

[3]So Moses said to the people, "Arm some of your men to go to war against the Midianites and to carry out the LORD's vengeance on them. [4]Send into battle a thousand men from each of the tribes of Israel." [5]So twelve thousand men armed for battle, a thousand from each tribe, were supplied from the clans of Israel. [6]Moses sent them into battle, a thousand from each tribe, along with Phinehas son of Eleazar, the priest, who took with him articles from the sanctuary and the trumpets for signaling.

[7]They fought against Midian, as the LORD commanded Moses, and killed every man. [8]Among their victims were Evi, Rekem, Zur, Hur and Reba—the five kings of Midian. They also killed Balaam son of Beor with the sword. [9]The Israelites captured the Midianite women and children and took all the Midianite herds, flocks and goods as plunder. [10]They burned all the towns where the Midianites had settled, as well as all their camps. [11]They took all the plunder and spoils, including the people and animals, [12]and brought the captives, spoils and plunder to Moses and Eleazar the priest and the Israelite assembly at their camp on the plains of Moab, by the Jordan across from Jericho.[a]

[13]Moses, Eleazar the priest and all the leaders of the community went to meet them outside the camp. [14]Moses was angry with the officers of the army—the commanders of thousands and commanders of hundreds—who returned from the battle.

[15]"Have you allowed all the women to live?" he asked them. [16]"They were the ones who followed

a12 Hebrew *Jordan of Jericho;* possibly an ancient name for the Jordan River

NRSV

31 The LORD spoke to Moses, saying, [2]"Avenge the Israelites on the Midianites; afterward you shall be gathered to your people." [3]So Moses said to the people, "Arm some of your number for the war, so that they may go against Midian, to execute the LORD's vengeance on Midian. [4]You shall send a thousand from each of the tribes of Israel to the war." [5]So out of the thousands of Israel, a thousand from each tribe were conscripted, twelve thousand armed for battle. [6]Moses sent them to the war, a thousand from each tribe, along with Phinehas son of Eleazar the priest,[a] with the vessels of the sanctuary and the trumpets for sounding the alarm in his hand. [7]They did battle against Midian, as the LORD had commanded Moses, and killed every male. [8]They killed the kings of Midian: Evi, Rekem, Zur, Hur, and Reba, the five kings of Midian, in addition to others who were slain by them; and they also killed Balaam son of Beor with the sword. [9]The Israelites took the women of Midian and their little ones captive; and they took all their cattle, their flocks, and all their goods as booty. [10]All their towns where they had settled, and all their encampments, they burned, [11]but they took all the spoil and all the booty, both people and animals. [12]Then they brought the captives and the booty and the spoil to Moses, to Eleazar the priest, and to the congregation of the Israelites, at the camp on the plains of Moab by the Jordan at Jericho.

13Moses, Eleazar the priest, and all the leaders of the congregation went to meet them outside the camp. [14]Moses became angry with the officers of the army, the commanders of thousands and

a Gk: Heb adds *to the war*

Balaam's advice and were the means of turning the Israelites away from the LORD in what happened at Peor, so that a plague struck the LORD's people. [17]Now kill all the boys. And kill every woman who has slept with a man, [18]but save for yourselves every girl who has never slept with a man.

[19]"All of you who have killed anyone or touched anyone who was killed must stay outside the camp seven days. On the third and seventh days you must purify yourselves and your captives. [20]Purify every garment as well as everything made of leather, goat hair or wood."

[21]Then Eleazar the priest said to the soldiers who had gone into battle, "This is the requirement of the law that the LORD gave Moses: [22]Gold, silver, bronze, iron, tin, lead [23]and anything else that can withstand fire must be put through the fire, and then it will be clean. But it must also be purified with the water of cleansing. And whatever cannot withstand fire must be put through that water. [24]On the seventh day wash your clothes and you will be clean. Then you may come into the camp."

[25]The LORD said to Moses, [26]"You and Eleazar the priest and the family heads of the community are to count all the people and animals that were captured. [27]Divide the spoils between the soldiers who took part in the battle and the rest of the community. [28]From the soldiers who fought in the battle, set apart as tribute for the LORD one out of every five hundred, whether persons, cattle, donkeys, sheep or goats. [29]Take this tribute from their half share and give it to Eleazar the priest as the LORD's part. [30]From the Israelites' half, select one out of every fifty, whether persons, cattle, donkeys, sheep, goats or other animals. Give them to the Levites, who are responsible for the care of the LORD's tabernacle." [31]So Moses and Eleazar the priest did as the LORD commanded Moses.

[32]The plunder remaining from the spoils that the soldiers took was 675,000 sheep, [33]72,000 cattle, [34]61,000 donkeys [35]and 32,000 women who had never slept with a man.

[36]The half share of those who fought in the battle was:

337,500 sheep, [37]of which the tribute for the LORD was 675;

the commanders of hundreds, who had come from service in the war. [15]Moses said to them, "Have you allowed all the women to live? [16]These women here, on Balaam's advice, made the Israelites act treacherously against the LORD in the affair of Peor, so that the plague came among the congregation of the LORD. [17]Now therefore, kill every male among the little ones, and kill every woman who has known a man by sleeping with him. [18]But all the young girls who have not known a man by sleeping with him, keep alive for yourselves. [19]Camp outside the camp seven days; whoever of you has killed any person or touched a corpse, purify yourselves and your captives on the third and on the seventh day. [20]You shall purify every garment, every article of skin, everything made of goats' hair, and every article of wood."

[21]Eleazar the priest said to the troops who had gone to battle: "This is the statute of the law that the LORD has commanded Moses: [22]gold, silver, bronze, iron, tin, and lead— [23]everything that can withstand fire, shall be passed through fire, and it shall be clean. Nevertheless it shall also be purified with the water for purification; and whatever cannot withstand fire, shall be passed through the water. [24]You must wash your clothes on the seventh day, and you shall be clean; afterward you may come into the camp."

[25]The LORD spoke to Moses, saying, [26]"You and Eleazar the priest and the heads of the ancestral houses of the congregation make an inventory of the booty captured, both human and animal. [27]Divide the booty into two parts, between the warriors who went out to battle and all the congregation. [28]From the share of the warriors who went out to battle, set aside as tribute for the LORD, one item out of every five hundred, whether persons, oxen, donkeys, sheep, or goats. [29]Take it from their half and give it to Eleazar the priest as an offering to the LORD. [30]But from the Israelites' half you shall take one out of every fifty, whether persons, oxen, donkeys, sheep, or goats—all the animals—and give them to the Levites who have charge of the tabernacle of the LORD."

[31]Then Moses and Eleazar the priest did as the LORD had commanded Moses:

³⁸36,000 cattle, of which the tribute for the LORD was 72;

³⁹30,500 donkeys, of which the tribute for the LORD was 61;

⁴⁰16,000 people, of which the tribute for the LORD was 32.

⁴¹Moses gave the tribute to Eleazar the priest as the LORD's part, as the LORD commanded Moses.

⁴²The half belonging to the Israelites, which Moses set apart from that of the fighting men— ⁴³the community's half—was 337,500 sheep, ⁴⁴36,000 cattle, ⁴⁵30,500 donkeys ⁴⁶and 16,000 people. ⁴⁷From the Israelites' half, Moses selected one out of every fifty persons and animals, as the LORD commanded him, and gave them to the Levites, who were responsible for the care of the LORD's tabernacle.

⁴⁸Then the officers who were over the units of the army—the commanders of thousands and commanders of hundreds—went to Moses ⁴⁹and said to him, "Your servants have counted the soldiers under our command, and not one is missing. ⁵⁰So we have brought as an offering to the LORD the gold articles each of us acquired— armlets, bracelets, signet rings, earrings and necklaces—to make atonement for ourselves before the LORD."

⁵¹Moses and Eleazar the priest accepted from them the gold—all the crafted articles. ⁵²All the gold from the commanders of thousands and commanders of hundreds that Moses and Eleazar presented as a gift to the LORD weighed 16,750 shekels.ᵃ ⁵³Each soldier had taken plunder for himself. ⁵⁴Moses and Eleazar the priest accepted the gold from the commanders of thousands and commanders of hundreds and brought it into the Tent of Meeting as a memorial for the Israelites before the LORD.

32 The Reubenites and Gadites, who had very large herds and flocks, saw that the lands of Jazer and Gilead were suitable for livestock. ²So they came to Moses and Eleazar the priest and to the leaders of the community, and said, ³"Ataroth, Dibon, Jazer, Nimrah, Heshbon, Elealeh, Sebam, Nebo and Beon— ⁴the land the LORD subdued before the people of Israel—are suitable for livestock, and your servants have livestock. ⁵If we have found favor in your eyes,"

ᵃ52 That is, about 420 pounds (about 190 kilograms)

32The booty remaining from the spoil that the troops had taken totaled six hundred seventy-five thousand sheep, ³³seventy-two thousand oxen, ³⁴sixty-one thousand donkeys, ³⁵and thirty-two thousand persons in all, women who had not known a man by sleeping with him.

36The half-share, the portion of those who had gone out to war, was in number three hundred thirty-seven thousand five hundred sheep and goats, ³⁷and the LORD's tribute of sheep and goats was six hundred seventy-five. ³⁸The oxen were thirty-six thousand, of which the LORD's tribute was seventy-two. ³⁹The donkeys were thirty thousand five hundred, of which the LORD's tribute was sixty-one. ⁴⁰The persons were sixteen thousand, of which the LORD's tribute was thirty-two persons. ⁴¹Moses gave the tribute, the offering for the LORD, to Eleazar the priest, as the LORD had commanded Moses.

42As for the Israelites' half, which Moses separated from that of the troops, ⁴³the congregation's half was three hundred thirty-seven thousand five hundred sheep and goats, ⁴⁴thirty-six thousand oxen, ⁴⁵thirty thousand five hundred donkeys, ⁴⁶and sixteen thousand persons. ⁴⁷From the Israelites' half Moses took one of every fifty, both of persons and of animals, and gave them to the Levites who had charge of the tabernacle of the LORD; as the LORD had commanded Moses.

48Then the officers who were over the thousands of the army, the commanders of thousands and the commanders of hundreds, approached Moses, ⁴⁹and said to Moses, "Your servants have counted the warriors who are under our command, and not one of us is missing. ⁵⁰And we have brought the LORD's offering, what each of us found, articles of gold, armlets and bracelets, signet rings, earrings, and pendants, to make atonement for ourselves before the LORD." ⁵¹Moses and Eleazar the priest received the gold from them, all in the form of crafted articles. ⁵²And all the gold of the offering that they offered to the LORD, from the commanders of thousands and the commanders of hundreds, was sixteen thousand seven hundred fifty shekels. ⁵³(The troops had all taken plunder for themselves.) ⁵⁴So Moses and Eleazar the priest received the gold from the commanders of thousands and of hundreds, and

they said, "let this land be given to your servants as our possession. Do not make us cross the Jordan."

[6]Moses said to the Gadites and Reubenites, "Shall your countrymen go to war while you sit here? [7]Why do you discourage the Israelites from going over into the land the LORD has given them? [8]This is what your fathers did when I sent them from Kadesh Barnea to look over the land. [9]After they went up to the Valley of Eshcol and viewed the land, they discouraged the Israelites from entering the land the LORD had given them. [10]The LORD's anger was aroused that day and he swore this oath: [11]'Because they have not followed me wholeheartedly, not one of the men twenty years old or more who came up out of Egypt will see the land I promised on oath to Abraham, Isaac and Jacob— [12]not one except Caleb son of Jephunneh the Kenizzite and Joshua son of Nun, for they followed the LORD wholeheartedly.' [13]The LORD's anger burned against Israel and he made them wander in the desert forty years, until the whole generation of those who had done evil in his sight was gone.

[14]"And here you are, a brood of sinners, standing in the place of your fathers and making the LORD even more angry with Israel. [15]If you turn away from following him, he will again leave all this people in the desert, and you will be the cause of their destruction."

[16]Then they came up to him and said, "We would like to build pens here for our livestock and cities for our women and children. [17]But we are ready to arm ourselves and go ahead of the Israelites until we have brought them to their place. Meanwhile our women and children will live in fortified cities, for protection from the inhabitants of the land. [18]We will not return to our homes until every Israelite has received his inheritance. [19]We will not receive any inheritance with them on the other side of the Jordan, because our inheritance has come to us on the east side of the Jordan."

[20]Then Moses said to them, "If you will do this—if you will arm yourselves before the LORD for battle, [21]and if all of you will go armed over the Jordan before the LORD until he has driven his enemies out before him— [22]then when the land is subdued before the LORD, you may return and

brought it into the tent of meeting as a memorial for the Israelites before the LORD.

32 Now the Reubenites and the Gadites owned a very great number of cattle. When they saw that the land of Jazer and the land of Gilead was a good place for cattle, [2]the Gadites and the Reubenites came and spoke to Moses, to Eleazar the priest, and to the leaders of the congregation, saying, [3]"Ataroth, Dibon, Jazer, Nimrah, Heshbon, Elealeh, Sebam, Nebo, and Beon— [4]the land that the LORD subdued before the congregation of Israel—is a land for cattle; and your servants have cattle." [5]They continued, "If we have found favor in your sight, let this land be given to your servants for a possession; do not make us cross the Jordan."

[6]But Moses said to the Gadites and to the Reubenites, "Shall your brothers go to war while you sit here? [7]Why will you discourage the hearts of the Israelites from going over into the land that the LORD has given them? [8]Your fathers did this, when I sent them from Kadesh-barnea to see the land. [9]When they went up to the Wadi Eshcol and saw the land, they discouraged the hearts of the Israelites from going into the land that the LORD had given them. [10]The LORD's anger was kindled on that day and he swore, saying, [11]'Surely none of the people who came up out of Egypt, from twenty years old and upward, shall see the land that I swore to give to Abraham, to Isaac, and to Jacob, because they have not unreservedly followed me— [12]none except Caleb son of Jephunneh the Kenizzite and Joshua son of Nun, for they have unreservedly followed the LORD.' [13]And the LORD's anger was kindled against Israel, and he made them wander in the wilderness for forty years, until all the generation that had done evil in the sight of the LORD had disappeared. [14]And now you, a brood of sinners, have risen in place of your fathers, to increase the LORD's fierce anger against Israel! [15]If you turn away from following him, he will again abandon them in the wilderness; and you will destroy all this people."

[16]Then they came up to him and said, "We will build sheepfolds here for our flocks, and towns for our little ones, [17]but we will take up arms as a vanguard[a] before the Israelites, until we

[a] Cn: Heb *hurrying*

be free from your obligation to the Lord and to Israel. And this land will be your possession before the Lord.

²³"But if you fail to do this, you will be sinning against the Lord; and you may be sure that your sin will find you out. ²⁴Build cities for your women and children, and pens for your flocks, but do what you have promised."

²⁵The Gadites and Reubenites said to Moses, "We your servants will do as our lord commands. ²⁶Our children and wives, our flocks and herds will remain here in the cities of Gilead. ²⁷But your servants, every man armed for battle, will cross over to fight before the Lord, just as our lord says."

²⁸Then Moses gave orders about them to Eleazar the priest and Joshua son of Nun and to the family heads of the Israelite tribes. ²⁹He said to them, "If the Gadites and Reubenites, every man armed for battle, cross over the Jordan with you before the Lord, then when the land is subdued before you, give them the land of Gilead as their possession. ³⁰But if they do not cross over with you armed, they must accept their possession with you in Canaan."

³¹The Gadites and Reubenites answered, "Your servants will do what the Lord has said. ³²We will cross over before the Lord into Canaan armed, but the property we inherit will be on this side of the Jordan."

³³Then Moses gave to the Gadites, the Reubenites and the half-tribe of Manasseh son of Joseph the kingdom of Sihon king of the Amorites and the kingdom of Og king of Bashan—the whole land with its cities and the territory around them.

³⁴The Gadites built up Dibon, Ataroth, Aroer, ³⁵Atroth Shophan, Jazer, Jogbehah, ³⁶Beth Nimrah and Beth Haran as fortified cities, and built pens for their flocks. ³⁷And the Reubenites rebuilt Heshbon, Elealeh and Kiriathaim, ³⁸as well as Nebo and Baal Meon (these names were changed) and Sibmah. They gave names to the cities they rebuilt.

³⁹The descendants of Makir son of Manasseh went to Gilead, captured it and drove out the Amorites who were there. ⁴⁰So Moses gave Gilead to the Makirites, the descendants of Manasseh, and they settled there. ⁴¹Jair, a descendant of Manasseh, captured their settlements and called

have brought them to their place. Meanwhile our little ones will stay in the fortified towns because of the inhabitants of the land. ¹⁸We will not return to our homes until all the Israelites have obtained their inheritance. ¹⁹We will not inherit with them on the other side of the Jordan and beyond, because our inheritance has come to us on this side of the Jordan to the east."

20So Moses said to them, "If you do this—if you take up arms to go before the Lord for the war, ²¹and all those of you who bear arms cross the Jordan before the Lord, until he has driven out his enemies from before him ²²and the land is subdued before the Lord—then after that you may return and be free of obligation to the Lord and to Israel, and this land shall be your possession before the Lord. ²³But if you do not do this, you have sinned against the Lord; and be sure your sin will find you out. ²⁴Build towns for your little ones, and folds for your flocks; but do what you have promised."

25Then the Gadites and the Reubenites said to Moses, "Your servants will do as my lord commands. ²⁶Our little ones, our wives, our flocks, and all our livestock shall remain there in the towns of Gilead; ²⁷but your servants will cross over, everyone armed for war, to do battle for the Lord, just as my lord orders."

28So Moses gave command concerning them to Eleazar the priest, to Joshua son of Nun, and to the heads of the ancestral houses of the Israelite tribes. ²⁹And Moses said to them, "If the Gadites and the Reubenites, everyone armed for battle before the Lord, will cross over the Jordan with you and the land shall be subdued before you, then you shall give them the land of Gilead for a possession; ³⁰but if they will not cross over with you armed, they shall have possessions among you in the land of Canaan." ³¹The Gadites and the Reubenites answered, "As the Lord has spoken to your servants, so we will do. ³²We will cross over armed before the Lord into the land of Canaan, but the possession of our inheritance shall remain with us on this side of*ᵃ the Jordan."

33Moses gave to them—to the Gadites and to the Reubenites and to the half-tribe of Manasseh son of Joseph—the kingdom of King Sihon of the

ᵃ Heb *beyond*

them Havvoth Jair.*a* *42*And Nobah captured Kenath and its surrounding settlements and called it Nobah after himself.

33 Here are the stages in the journey of the Israelites when they came out of Egypt by divisions under the leadership of Moses and Aaron. *2*At the LORD's command Moses recorded the stages in their journey. This is their journey by stages:

*3*The Israelites set out from Rameses on the fifteenth day of the first month, the day after the Passover. They marched out boldly in full view of all the Egyptians, *4*who were burying all their firstborn, whom the LORD had struck down among them; for the LORD had brought judgment on their gods.

*5*The Israelites left Rameses and camped at Succoth.

*6*They left Succoth and camped at Etham, on the edge of the desert.

*7*They left Etham, turned back to Pi Hahiroth, to the east of Baal Zephon, and camped near Migdol.

*8*They left Pi Hahiroth*b* and passed through the sea into the desert, and when they had traveled for three days in the Desert of Etham, they camped at Marah.

*9*They left Marah and went to Elim, where there were twelve springs and seventy palm trees, and they camped there.

*10*They left Elim and camped by the Red Sea.*c*

*11*They left the Red Sea and camped in the Desert of Sin.

*12*They left the Desert of Sin and camped at Dophkah.

*13*They left Dophkah and camped at Alush.

*14*They left Alush and camped at Rephidim, where there was no water for the people to drink.

*15*They left Rephidim and camped in the Desert of Sinai.

*16*They left the Desert of Sinai and camped at Kibroth Hattaavah.

a*41* Or *them the settlements of Jair*   b*8* Many manuscripts of the Masoretic Text, Samaritan Pentateuch and Vulgate; most manuscripts of the Masoretic Text *left from before Hahiroth*   c*10* Hebrew *Yam Suph;* that is, Sea of Reeds; also in verse 11

Amorites and the kingdom of King Og of Bashan, the land and its towns, with the territories of the surrounding towns. *34*And the Gadites rebuilt Dibon, Ataroth, Aroer, *35*Atroth-shophan, Jazer, Jogbehah, *36*Beth-nimrah, and Beth-haran, fortified cities, and folds for sheep. *37*And the Reubenites rebuilt Heshbon, Elealeh, Kiriathaim, *38*Nebo, and Baal-meon (some names being changed), and Sibmah; and they gave names to the towns that they rebuilt. *39*The descendants of Machir son of Manasseh went to Gilead, captured it, and dispossessed the Amorites who were there; *40*so Moses gave Gilead to Machir son of Manasseh, and he settled there. *41*Jair son of Manasseh went and captured their villages, and renamed them Havvoth-jair.*a* *42*And Nobah went and captured Kenath and its villages, and renamed it Nobah after himself.

33 These are the stages by which the Israelites went out of the land of Egypt in military formation under the leadership of Moses and Aaron. *2*Moses wrote down their starting points, stage by stage, by command of the LORD; and these are their stages according to their starting places. *3*They set out from Rameses in the first month, on the fifteenth day of the first month; on the day after the passover the Israelites went out boldly in the sight of all the Egyptians, *4*while the Egyptians were burying all their firstborn, whom the LORD had struck down among them. The LORD executed judgments even against their gods.

5So the Israelites set out from Rameses, and camped at Succoth. *6*They set out from Succoth, and camped at Etham, which is on the edge of the wilderness. *7*They set out from Etham, and turned back to Pi-hahiroth, which faces Baal-zephon; and they camped before Migdol. *8*They set out from Pi-hahiroth, passed through the sea into the wilderness, went a three days' journey in the wilderness of Etham, and camped at Marah. *9*They set out from Marah and came to Elim; at Elim there were twelve springs of water and seventy palm trees, and they camped there. *10*They set out from Elim and camped by the Red Sea.*b* *11*They set out from the Red Sea*b* and camped in the wilderness of Sin. *12*They set out from the wilderness of Sin and camped at Doph-

a That is *the villages of Jair*   a Or *Sea of Reeds*

¹⁷They left Kibroth Hattaavah and camped at Hazeroth.

¹⁸They left Hazeroth and camped at Rithmah.

¹⁹They left Rithmah and camped at Rimmon Perez.

²⁰They left Rimmon Perez and camped at Libnah.

²¹They left Libnah and camped at Rissah.

²²They left Rissah and camped at Kehelathah.

²³They left Kehelathah and camped at Mount Shepher.

²⁴They left Mount Shepher and camped at Haradah.

²⁵They left Haradah and camped at Makheloth.

²⁶They left Makheloth and camped at Tahath.

²⁷They left Tahath and camped at Terah.

²⁸They left Terah and camped at Mithcah.

²⁹They left Mithcah and camped at Hashmonah.

³⁰They left Hashmonah and camped at Moseroth.

³¹They left Moseroth and camped at Bene Jaakan.

³²They left Bene Jaakan and camped at Hor Haggidgad.

³³They left Hor Haggidgad and camped at Jotbathah.

³⁴They left Jotbathah and camped at Abronah.

³⁵They left Abronah and camped at Ezion Geber.

³⁶They left Ezion Geber and camped at Kadesh, in the Desert of Zin.

³⁷They left Kadesh and camped at Mount Hor, on the border of Edom. ³⁸At the LORD's command Aaron the priest went up Mount Hor, where he died on the first day of the fifth month of the fortieth year after the Israelites came out of Egypt. ³⁹Aaron was a hundred and twenty-three years old when he died on Mount Hor.

⁴⁰The Canaanite king of Arad, who lived in the Negev of Canaan, heard that the Israelites were coming.

kah. ¹³They set out from Dophkah and camped at Alush. ¹⁴They set out from Alush and camped at Rephidim, where there was no water for the people to drink. ¹⁵They set out from Rephidim and camped in the wilderness of Sinai. ¹⁶They set out from the wilderness of Sinai and camped at Kibroth-hattaavah. ¹⁷They set out from Kibroth-hattaavah and camped at Hazeroth. ¹⁸They set out from Hazeroth and camped at Rithmah. ¹⁹They set out from Rithmah and camped at Rimmon-perez. ²⁰They set out from Rimmon-perez and camped at Libnah. ²¹They set out from Libnah and camped at Rissah. ²²They set out from Rissah and camped at Kehelathah. ²³They set out from Kehelathah and camped at Mount Shepher. ²⁴They set out from Mount Shepher and camped at Haradah. ²⁵They set out from Haradah and camped at Makheloth. ²⁶They set out from Makheloth and camped at Tahath. ²⁷They set out from Tahath and camped at Terah. ²⁸They set out from Terah and camped at Mithkah. ²⁹They set out from Mithkah and camped at Hashmonah. ³⁰They set out from Hashmonah and camped at Moseroth. ³¹They set out from Moseroth and camped at Bene-jaakan. ³²They set out from Bene-jaakan and camped at Hor-haggidgad. ³³They set out from Hor-haggidgad and camped at Jotbathah. ³⁴They set out from Jotbathah and camped at Abronah. ³⁵They set out from Abronah and camped at Ezion-geber. ³⁶They set out from Ezion-geber and camped in the wilderness of Zin (that is, Kadesh). ³⁷They set out from Kadesh and camped at Mount Hor, on the edge of the land of Edom.

38Aaron the priest went up Mount Hor at the command of the LORD and died there in the fortieth year after the Israelites had come out of the land of Egypt, on the first day of the fifth month. ³⁹Aaron was one hundred twenty-three years old when he died on Mount Hor.

40The Canaanite, the king of Arad, who lived in the Negeb in the land of Canaan, heard of the coming of the Israelites.

41They set out from Mount Hor and camped at Zalmonah. ⁴²They set out from Zalmonah and camped at Punon. ⁴³They set out from Punon and camped at Oboth. ⁴⁴They set out from Oboth and camped at Iye-abarim, in the territory of Moab. ⁴⁵They set out from Iyim and camped at Dibon-

NIV

⁴¹They left Mount Hor and camped at Zalmonah.

⁴²They left Zalmonah and camped at Punon.

⁴³They left Punon and camped at Oboth.

⁴⁴They left Oboth and camped at Iye Abarim, on the border of Moab.

⁴⁵They left Iyim*ᵃ* and camped at Dibon Gad.

⁴⁶They left Dibon Gad and camped at Almon Diblathaim.

⁴⁷They left Almon Diblathaim and camped in the mountains of Abarim, near Nebo.

⁴⁸They left the mountains of Abarim and camped on the plains of Moab by the Jordan across from Jericho.*ᵇ* ⁴⁹There on the plains of Moab they camped along the Jordan from Beth Jeshimoth to Abel Shittim.

⁵⁰On the plains of Moab by the Jordan across from Jericho the LORD said to Moses, ⁵¹"Speak to the Israelites and say to them: 'When you cross the Jordan into Canaan, ⁵²drive out all the inhabitants of the land before you. Destroy all their carved images and their cast idols, and demolish all their high places. ⁵³Take possession of the land and settle in it, for I have given you the land to possess. ⁵⁴Distribute the land by lot, according to your clans. To a larger group give a larger inheritance, and to a smaller group a smaller one. Whatever falls to them by lot will be theirs. Distribute it according to your ancestral tribes.

⁵⁵"'But if you do not drive out the inhabitants of the land, those you allow to remain will become barbs in your eyes and thorns in your sides. They will give you trouble in the land where you will live. ⁵⁶And then I will do to you what I plan to do to them.'"

ᵃ45 That is, Iye Abarim   ᵇ48 Hebrew *Jordan of Jericho;* possibly an ancient name for the Jordan River; also in verse 50

NRSV

gad. ⁴⁶They set out from Dibon-gad and camped at Almon-diblathaim. ⁴⁷They set out from Almon-diblathaim and camped in the mountains of Abarim, before Nebo. ⁴⁸They set out from the mountains of Abarim and camped in the plains of Moab by the Jordan at Jericho; ⁴⁹they camped by the Jordan from Beth-jeshimoth as far as Abel-shittim in the plains of Moab.

50In the plains of Moab by the Jordan at Jericho, the LORD spoke to Moses, saying: ⁵¹Speak to the Israelites, and say to them: When you cross over the Jordan into the land of Canaan, ⁵²you shall drive out all the inhabitants of the land from before you, destroy all their figured stones, destroy all their cast images, and demolish all their high places. ⁵³You shall take possession of the land and settle in it, for I have given you the land to possess. ⁵⁴You shall apportion the land by lot according to your clans; to a large one you shall give a large inheritance, and to a small one you shall give a small inheritance; the inheritance shall belong to the person on whom the lot falls; according to your ancestral tribes you shall inherit. ⁵⁵But if you do not drive out the inhabitants of the land from before you, then those whom you let remain shall be as barbs in your eyes and thorns in your sides; they shall trouble you in the land where you are settling. ⁵⁶And I will do to you as I thought to do to them.

COMMENTARY

Numbers 31–33 are bound together by the theme of war. The section opens with the divine command that Israel destroy the Midianites for their seduction of the people at Baal Peor. Chapter 32 outlines the rules for participation in holy war by the tribes of Reuben, Gad, and Manasseh;

these are the tribes who chose to settle in the Transjordan. Chapter 33 recounts Israel's entire wilderness journey as a military march, concluding with the warning that Israel must drive out all of the indigenous people of Canaan if they expect God to lead them in the land.

Both the pre-priestly and the priestly histories emphasize the theme of holy war. The pre-priestly history includes the rules for participation in holy war (chap. 32), along with the review of the wilderness march and the call for holy war (chap. 33). The priestly writers preface the pre-priestly history with the account of holy war against Midian (chap. 31), while adding additional commentary throughout the section.

31:1-54. This chapter tells of holy war against the Midianites. Scholars debate whether this war is historical or fictional.[191] The complete destruction of all Midianite males without one Israelite fatality suggests that the story is a literary construction by the priestly writers, intended to provide the framework for their interpretation of holy war legislation. The role of the central characters throughout the story is important for discerning the teaching of the priestly writers on war. Joshua does not lead this holy war. Moses and the priests oversee the war. Eleazar the high priest determines what constitutes acceptable booty from holy war, while Phinehas, the son of Eleazar, actually leads the troops.

Holy war against Midian provides the literary setting for the priestly writers to return to the topic of external threats to Israel—the central theme of chaps. 22–25. The story of Balaam (chaps. 22–24) explored the external threat presented by Balak of Moab in seeking to curse Israel, while the sin of Israel at Baal Peor (25:1-5) illustrated the danger of intermingling with surrounding people. The priestly writers weave Midianites into both of these stories. Midianites assist in hiring Balaam to curse Israel (22:4, 7), and they intermarry with Israelites at Baal Peor (25:6-18). Holy war against Midian concludes the topic of external threats to Israel. It represents the most extreme measures for maintaining purity. The divine command that Israel "harass" the Midianites because of the incident at Baal Peor (25:16-18) foreshadows the holy war in chap. 31.

Booty is the central concern underlying the rules and procedures for holy war in Numbers 31.

Other topics also addressed include the selection and participation of warriors from the tribes, leadership, the role of priests in sanctioning holy war, purification of warriors from contact with the dead, and the price of ransom to the temple. Central topics concerning the booty acquired during holy war include foreign objects and persons that can be taken into the Israelite camp without polluting the community; the division of booty among warriors and other Israelites; and the amount of booty given to priests and Levites. The quantity of booty acquired in the holy war against Midian exceeds 800,000 animals and 16,750 shekels of gold. The unrealistic quantity indicates that plunder from war is the central concern of the priestly writers.

Even more specific is the priestly writers' concern for the role of women as booty. No fewer than 32,000 virgins are taken as booty. This chapter is the fourth time in Numbers 22–36 that the priestly writers turn their attention to women. Chapter 25 addressed the threat of Midianite women to the purity of the Israelite camp; chap. 27 outlined the inheritance rights of Israelite daughters in the absence of a male heir; and chap. 30 described the legal rights of Israelite daughters and wives to make vows. Now, chap. 31 returns to the topic of Midianite women entering the Israelite camp, this time as the spoils of holy war.

Chapters 25 and 31 are meant to be read together. Numbers 25 introduces the threat of intermarriage between Midianites and Israelites, and chap. 31 outlines conditions by which foreign women can become part of the Israelite community. In 25:6-18, intermarriage with Midianites was unacceptable to the priestly writers, since it threatened the purity of the Israelite camp. Holy war, however, eliminates the threat of cultural intermingling, since it envisions the extermination of entire cultures and religions. Under such conditions, chap. 31 suggests that Israelite males are able to assimilate foreign virgins into their families.

· Deuteronomy 20 and 21:10-14 provide the background for the priestly legislation regarding booty from holy war. Two features, in particular, provide a starting point for interpreting women as booty. The first is the general law regarding spoils of war in Deuteronomy 20: (1) From cities within the promised land, no booty is allowed; everything must be destroyed (Deut 20:16-18); (2) from all peoples outside the promised land, holy war

---

191. For arguments favoring its historicity, see Jacob Milgrom, *Numbers,* JPS Torah Commentary (Philadelphia: JPS, 1990) 490-91; and Gordon J. Wenham, *Numbers: An Introduction and Commentary,* Tyndale Old Testament Commentaries (Leicester: Inter-Varsity, 1981) 209. For arguments in support of the fictive character of the chapter, see George Buchanan Gray, *Numbers,* ICC (Edinburgh: T. & T. Clark, 1903) 417-20; and Eryl W. Davies, *Numbers,* NCB (Grand Rapids: Eerdmans, 1995) 320.

requires only that all adult males be killed. Acceptable plunder in these instances includes women, children, livestock, and everything else (Deut 20:10-15). The priestly story of holy war against Midian falls under the second category regarding holy war booty, and it even appears to follow the guidelines of Deuteronomy 20. The booty taken by Phinehas and the Israelite warriors in Num 31:9 includes women, children, cattle, flocks, and all other goods.

Deuteronomy 21:10-14 also provides background for interpreting Numbers 31, which states that Israelite males are allowed to marry any woman acquired as booty in holy war. Read in conjunction with the general laws of holy war in Deuteronomy 20, this law implies that Israelites could wed non-virgin foreign women. The larger context of Deuteronomy 21 indicates that such marriages influence inheritance laws. Marriage law is not directly addressed in Numbers 31; yet it, too, would be affected by the story of the war with Midian. The priestly story of holy war against Midian departs from the guidelines of Deut 21:10-14. Moses voices the concern of the priestly writers in Num 31:14-18. His anger over taking male children and non-virgin women as booty indicates priestly opposition to the breadth of the laws in Deuteronomy 20 and 21:10-14. The new law voiced by Moses narrows the scope of acceptable booty to female virgins.

31:1-18. Holy war against Midian is undertaken at divine command (vv. 1-2). God instructs Moses to take vengeance on the Midianites—a response to 25:6-18, where Midianites are blamed by the priestly writers for Israel's sin at Baal Peor. The divine instruction also indicates that this is one of the last commands Moses will receive. After this incident, he will die. The instruction of Moses to Israel is recorded in vv. 3-4, where he states that war with Midian is an execution of divine vengeance. In addition, he indicates the number and distribution of warriors. Israel's army is to include 1,000 male warriors from each of the twelve tribes; thus all tribes participate in holy war equally.

Verses 5-12 are a brief account of the battle, anchoring the institution of holy war in the cult. The troops are led by the priest Phinehas, who already assumed the position of holy warrior when he killed the Midianite woman Cozbi and the Israelite man Zimri for the sin of intermarriage (25:6-18). Now, he leads the Israelite army in executing God's vengeance on the entire nation of Midian for this sin. Not only is Israel led by a priest, but also it takes "vessels of the sanctuary" into battle. The text is not clear about the exact nature of these objects. Scholars suggest three possibilities: holy war clothing for the priest (Deut 22:5), the ark (Num 10:35; 14:44; 1 Sam 4:4), or the trumpets (cited in Num 31:6).[192] The phrase "vessels of the sanctuary" is used earlier in Numbers (3:31; 4:15; 18:3) to indicate furniture, thus favoring a reference to the ark or trumpets over the priestly clothing.

A description of the actual battle against Midian is absent. Instead, vv. 7-12 list the results of the war. Those killed in the battle are listed in vv. 7-8. The Midianite dead include all the males (v. 7), the five kings of Midian (Evi, Rekem, Zur, Hur, and Reba; v. 8/ Josh 13:21), and Balaam son of Beor (v. 8). The booty is listed in v. 9. It includes all Midianite women and children, all cattle and flocks, and all goods. With towns and settlements burned, the army returns to Moses, Eleazar, and Israel on the plains of Moab. (Other wars with Midian in biblical literature include Gideon's war with them in Judges 6–9 and the obscure reference to the Day of Midian in Ps 83:10; Isa 9:3.)

The response of Moses in vv. 13-18 indicates that the priestly writers' focus is on the booty. As noted earlier, the booty taken from the Midianites follows the instructions for holy war in Deuteronomy 20 and 21:10-14. Yet Moses is angry. The cause of his anger is the Midianite women taken as booty (vv. 15-16). He accuses them of seduction in the incident at Baal Peor. The priestly writers also reinterpret the Balaam stories more negatively by accusing the diviner, rather than the Moabite king Balak, of threatening Israel. Balaam's sin is not having cursed Israel through divination, as King Balak desired in the story of Numbers 22–24, however. Rather, it is the seduction of Israel by Midianite women. The priestly writers are much less generous about granting Balaam an authentic relationship with God outside of the Israelite cult than were the pre-priestly writers. Balaam the diviner, who knows God independently of the cultic rituals of the tabernacle, represents for the priestly writers a type of religious pimp, while the Midianite women are his prostitutes. They must all be killed according to new and more rigorous rules for booty.

192. See Davies, *Numbers,* 323; Gray, *Numbers,* 420.

Verses 17-18 state the priestly law of booty in both a negative and a positive form. The negative statement is that all male children and non-virgin women must be killed. The positive form of the law is that virgins are acceptable booty. Israelites may keep them "alive for themselves." The meaning of this phrase is not clear. Comparison to Deut 21:10-14 and Judges 21 suggests that it refers to marriage. Deuteronomy 21:10-14 indicates that Israelite men are allowed to marry any women taken as plunder in holy war, without stipulating that the women must be virgins. Judges 21 provides a closer parallel to Num 31:18. In this story, an army of 12,000 soldiers (1,000 soldiers from each tribe, as Moses required in Num 31:4-6) defeats Jabesh-gilead in a holy war. They spare only the virgins, who are then given to the Benjaminites as wives.

31:19-24. The procedures for purifying humans and objects after holy war is outlined in this section. Purification is necessary, because death defiles all participants in war; and contact with the dead threatens the holiness of the camp. Numbers 5:1-4 stated the initial rule that any person defiled by contact with a corpse must be expelled from the camp. Numbers 19 outlined the general procedures for purification from contamination by corpses. Central to the process of purification was the "water of cleansing" made from the ashes of the red heifer. The priestly writers intend that these verses be read in relation to chap. 19, which not only refers to the rituals associated with the water of cleansing, but also describes the legislation with the same language: Both are "the statute of the law that the LORD has commanded" (19:2; 31:21).

These verses also add new information to chap. 19 by applying the purification ritual to war. Soldiers must go through the seven-day ritual outside the camp, with cleansing taking place on the third and seventh days. Verse 19 makes it clear that such purification applies both to Israelite warriors and to their human booty. Finally, 31:21-24 provides the guidelines for purifying objects taken as booty. Eleazar, rather than Moses, outlines these procedures. Metals must pass through fire and be purified with the water of cleansing. Objects that cannot withstand fire are purified only with the water of cleansing. At the end of the process, all clothes must be washed before an Israelite warrior can reenter the camp.

The teaching of the priestly writers is that war pollutes. This is a significant departure from other stories in which participation in war makes soldiers holy. David and his soldiers, for example, are in a holy state in 1 Sam 21:4-5 and thus are able to eat holy bread. In 2 Samuel 11, Uriah the Hittite refuses to have sex with his wife, Bath-sheba, because he has been consecrated for war. These stories suggest that participation in war is a sacred act, making its participants holy. For the priestly writers, participation in war requires the most rigorous form of purification. Killing in war does not sanctify its participants but defiles them even when the war has been commanded by God, raising the question of whether there is such a thing as "holy war" in priestly teaching.

31:25-47. The inventory and distribution of booty are outlined in this section. Verses 25-30 provide the formula for distribution. The booty is divided equally among warriors and all other Israelites. The principle of equal distribution of the spoils among warrior and citizen is illustrated in David's defeat of the Amalekites in 1 Samuel 30. Each group is then taxed by the temple at a different rate. Warriors pay 1/500th of their booty to the priesthood, while civilians pay 1/50th of their booty to the Levites. (See Numbers 7; 18; and 28 for other discussion of taxation for the temple and priesthood.)

Verses 31-47 apply the formula of distribution to the Midianite booty. The total booty from the war with Midian is exceptionally large:

	Total	Warriors/ Citizens	Priests	Levites
Sheep	675,000	337,500	675	6,750
Oxen	72,000	36,000	72	720
Donkeys	61,000	30,500	61	610
Virgins	32,000	16,000	32	320

31:48-54. The chapter closes with the officers' taking a census of the warriors and reporting to Moses that not a single soldier has died in the battle with Midian. They bring a gift of gold and jewelry, weighing 16,750 shekels, to Moses and Eleazar, which, they state, is intended to make atonement for themselves to God. Atonement does not indicate an offering of thanksgiving. Rather, it is a form of ransom to God in order to avoid divine wrath, perhaps associated with the census. Second Samuel 24 tells of a plague that occurred as a result of David's census. Exodus 30:12 states that whenever a census is taken, it must be accompanied by a ransom in order to avoid a plague. Given the priestly teaching on war as an act of defilement, it may be that ransom is required from soldiers because of their participation in war, even though it was sanctioned by God.

32:1-42. The themes of holy war and inheritance are interwoven in this chapter. The opening (vv. 1-5) and closing (vv. 33-42) sections of the chapter focus on the inheritance of the Transjordan by the tribes of Reuben, Gad, and Manasseh. The dialogue between Moses and the tribes of Reuben and Gad in the central section of the chapter (vv. 6-32) concerns participation in holy war as a condition for inheritance. These two themes were likely always related in the chapter. Yet a history of composition lies behind Numbers 32, suggesting that the emphasis has changed from inheritance in the pre-priestly history to holy war in the priestly history.[193]

The stories of inheritance in vv. 1-5 and 33-42 are part of the pre-priestly history. They outline the territory and the cities that Israel took over after conquering King Sihon of the Amorites and King Og of Bashan. The request for land and the account of settlement provide continuity with the story of the Transjordanian conquest in chap. 21, where the central theme was holy war. The focus of the pre-priestly narrative in chap. 32 is less on holy war than on the city-building activities of the Transjordanian tribes after the conquest. In the pre-priestly history, chap. 32 is about inheriting land east of the Jordan. The accounts of inheritance are not unified, since the opening section (vv. 1-5) focuses only on the Reubenites and the Gadites, while the closing section (vv. 33-42) suddenly adds Manasseh. The list of cities in chap. 32 contrasts to others found in Deut 3:8-17 and Josh 13:8-13. Some form of the stipulation that participation in holy war is a condition for inheritance (vv. 6-32) is also most likely present in the pre-priestly history, since Deuteronomy and Joshua stress that the conquest of Canaan was a unified invasion by all Israel.

The influence of the priestly writers is also evident throughout Numbers 32. Eleazar the priest plays a prominent role in negotiating with the tribes of Reuben and Gad. Israel is described as the congregation (Exod 32:2), a favorite term of the priestly writers. Details from the priestly account of the loss

of the land by the first generation (Numbers 13–14) appear in the speech of Moses (vv. 6-15), and the instruction of Moses to Eleazar about holy war and inheritance (vv. 28-32) conforms to the priestly account of the commissioning of Joshua in 27:12-23. Additions by the priestly writers change the emphasis in chap. 32 from inheritance to holy war, continuing the theme from chap. 31. The war with Midian in chap. 31 outlined the requirements for participation, purification, offerings, and booty in holy war. Chapter 32 returns to the topic of participation in holy war as a prerequisite for inheritance.

The interweaving of holy war and inheritance provides transition in the book of Numbers. When the theme of holy war is emphasized, the chapter provides a contrast to the failure of the first generation (chaps. 13–14) to undertake such a war. The second generation successfully carries out holy war in chap. 21, where Israel wages war against Sihon and Og, and again in chap. 31, where Israel wages war against Midian. Chapter 32 extends the commentary on holy war by outlining the requirements of participation. The theme of inheritance looks toward the conclusion of the story, indicating that the second generation has left the wilderness, already achieved part of its inheritance, and is about to complete the story of salvation by realizing the divine promise of land though conquest.

32:1-5. The order in which the tribes are listed in the opening verse has caught the attention of commentators, because it changes after v. 1. Gad takes precedence over Reuben in vv. 2, 6, 25, 29, 31, and 33. Gad is also the tribe identified most strongly with the Transjordan. The census of David in 2 Sam 24:5, for example, mentions only Gad; the Mesha stone also mentions only Gad.[194]

The tribes of Reuben and Gad are described as owning a great number of cattle, and the land east of the Jordan is rich for grazing. The area of the Transjordan that was of interest to the Reubenites and the Gadites is the land of Jazer and Gilead (v. 2). Jazer was mentioned as a location in the account of the conquest of Sihon (21:32). Gilead may refer to all of the area east of the Jordan, but here it designates a smaller section in the southern region, between the Arnon and Yarmuk rivers (vv. 3, 34-37). The nine towns listed in v. 3 cluster in the southern region of

193. The history of composition in Numbers 32 is especially complicated. For an overview of past interpretations, see Phillip J. Budd, *Numbers,* WBC 5 (Waco, Tex.: Word, 1984) 337-42.

194. See "Mesha Stele," *ABD* 4:708-9.

Gilead. These cities are also mentioned in vv. 34-38, where they are distributed between Gad and Reuben. The only variation from the southern location for Gilead appears in v. 39, where Gilead may designate a region further north.

Reuben and Gad make their request to Moses, Eleazar, and the entire congregation of Israel (vv. 3-5). They note that the land of Jazer and Gilead is good for grazing and ask that it be given to them, that Moses "not make [them] cross the Jordan." The Hebrew verb "to cross" (עבר *ʿābar*) is more than a description of travel, especially when used in conjunction with the Jordan. In such instances, it signifies conquest. The verb is used repeatedly in Joshua 3–5, where Israel's crossing of the Jordan for conquest is described. Thus the request of Reuben and Gad is ambiguous. It may mean that they wish the Transjordan for their inheritance, but it may also mean that they wish to avoid participating in the conquest of the promised land west of the Jordan.[195]

32:6-27. Moses interprets the request of the Reubenites and the Gadites as a desire to inherit land without participating fully in holy war. This leads to two rounds of negotiations (vv. 6-19 and 20-27). The first round (vv. 6-19) includes a warning by Moses that holy war requires the participation of all Israelites (vv. 6-15). In response, the tribes of Gad and Reuben propose a solution (vv. 16-19). In the second round of negotiations, Moses formalizes the proposed solution into law (vv. 20-24), to which the Reubenites and the Gadites agree (vv. 25-27).

Moses' initial response in vv. 6-15 is anger. He recounts the story of the spies, when the first generation lost the land because they feared holy war. This analogy is made in vv. 6-9 along with two accusations. First, the Reubenites and the Gadites are accused of discouraging the entire group from waging holy war (v. 7). This was the sin of their fathers at Kadesh-barnea (vv. 8-9). Second, they are accused of instigating disunity within the entire group (v. 6). Here is one of the central points of the chapter: Moses asks, "Shall your brothers go to war while you sit here?"

The need for all Israel to participate in holy war is stressed by the way the sin at Kadesh-barnea is recounted in vv. 10-15. Twice the anger of the Lord

is cited (vv. 10, 13) as a response to the lack of faith of the first generation. Verses 10-12 state how divine anger resulted in the loss of the land for the first generation of Israelites, with the exception of Caleb and Joshua. Verse 13 describes how divine anger led to forty years of wandering in the wilderness. The point of recounting the original loss of the land is stated in vv. 14-15, where the speech of Moses switches from the past to the present tense. The demand placed on the second generation is that they assume collective responsibility for participation in holy war, at least within the same generation. By not participating in holy war with the other tribes, Reuben and Gad endanger the gift of the land for their entire generation. They threaten to "destroy all this people" (v. 15).

The response by the tribes of Reuben and Gad in vv. 16-19 forges a solution to the requirement that all Israelites participate in holy war. A two-part procedure is outlined in vv. 16-18. First, the tribes of Reuben and Gad will fortify cities for their families and build corrals for their flock (composed of stone walls). Second, a fighting force will join the other tribes in holy war. The language in v. 17 suggests that they even offer to be the shock troops, who will lead Israel in battle. The warriors from the tribes of Reuben and Gad, moreover, will not return to the Transjordan until all fighting is completed. The concluding statement in v. 19, that neither Reuben nor Gad will inherit land as a result of their participation, indicates that their solution to the Moses' accusation is meant to provide a paradigm for participation in holy war by settled tribes, whose involvement is out of obligation to the group, rather than for their own self-interest.

The proposed solution is reformulated by Moses as law (vv. 20-24), to which the Reubenites and the Gadites formally agree (vv. 25-27). Moses formulates the proposal as an oath. Repeatedly in vv. 20-24 he states that the agreement for participation in war is being made "before the LORD." The consequences of the oath are stated in both a positive and a negative form. If the Reubenites and the Gadites fulfill their obligations for holy war, then they will be free of their oath agreement and thus able to inherit land in the Transjordan; the legal background for the fulfillment of such oaths is stated in Deut 24:5. If they renege on their oath, their "sin will find them out." Sin is an active force in this

---

195. Milgrom (*Numbers,* 268) underscores the central role of עבר (*ʿābar*) by noting that it is used seven times: Num 32:5, 7, 21, 27, 29, 30, 32.

statement. (See the story of Cain and Abel in Gen 4:7, where the same view of sin is expressed.) The phrase implies a curse in an oath situation. But no specific punishments are outlined. Moses ends the statement by implying the positive form of the law. He sends the Reubenites and the Gadites off to build their cities. These tribes agree (vv. 25-27) and promise to join in the holy war on the west side of the Jordan.

32:28-32. The public ratification of the negotiations in vv. 6-27 is stated in this section through repetition of the oaths from vv. 20-24. Those present include Eleazar the priest, Joshua son of Nun, and the heads of the tribes. The leadership structure is reminiscent of 27:15-23, where Joshua was also commissioned before Eleazar. The ratification of holy war legislation before Eleazar anchors holy war firmly in the orbit of the cult. If the tribes are faithful in their participation, they will be allowed to possess the land of Gilead. The negative form in v. 30 is unclear. Lack of fulfillment will result in Reuben and Gad inheriting land west of the Jordan with the other tribes. The confusion is that the consequences of not participating in holy war appear to be positive. Perhaps what is meant is that they will forfeit possession of the Transjordan. The same ambiguity is evident in the earlier negative form of the oath (v. 23). The tribes of Gad and Reuben, however, agree to the oath in vv. 31-32.

32:33-42. The theme of participation in holy war gives way to inheritance in the final section of the chapter. In v. 33, Moses charges the tribes east of the Jordan with securing the towns taken from Sihon and Og. Surprisingly, the tribe of Manasseh is mentioned for the first time in this chapter, along with the tribes of Reuben and Gad. Although Manasseh is absent from the negotiations in this chapter, the presence of this tribe at the conclusion of the chapter conforms to other accounts of land distribution east of the Jordan in Deut 3:13; 4:43; 29:8 and in Josh 12:6; 13:29-31. Verses 34-38 repeat the list of nine towns mentioned at the outset of the chapter, along with five others, which are now distributed between the tribes of Gad (Dibon, Ataroth, Aroer, Atroth-shophan, Jazer, Jogbehah, Beth-nimrah and Beth-haran) and Reuben (Heshbon, Elealeh, Kiriathaim, Nebo, Baal-meon and Sibmah).

Numbers 32 concludes with an independent account of conquest by the tribe of Manasseh (vv. 39-42). Machir conquers the Amorites in Gilead, here a more northern region than the previous references to Gilead at the opening of the chapter. Jair, another ancestor in the tribe of Manasseh, is described as renaming Amorite villages after himself. Independent action by one tribe contradicts the emphasis on holy war as requiring participation by all Israelites. The picture of singular tribes waging war independently conforms to the account of Judges 1.

33:1-56. This chapter provides a transition in the book of Numbers. It looks back to review Yahweh's leading in the wilderness by listing Israel's stopping points in the wilderness march (vv. 1-49), and it looks ahead to the conquest of the promised land with a warning that Israel continue to engage in holy war after crossing the Jordan (vv. 50-56). In the pre-priestly history, this chapter ends the book of Numbers. The review of the wilderness march and the concluding call for holy war probably led to the book of Deuteronomy, where Moses once again reviews the wilderness period and calls the second generation to holy war. In the priestly history, by contrast, Numbers 33 provides a transition to the final section on inheritance in Numbers 34–36.

The list of stopping points in vv. 1-49 has received a great deal of attention. Scholars debate whether the list of forty-two locations is ancient (and the source of the stopping points that run throughout Exodus and Numbers) or a late literary construction. There is clear evidence of priestly additions to the list. The priestly writers add commentary to bring the wilderness march into conformity with their history. They weave their interpretation of the exodus into vv. 1-4 by providing a date, a description of Israel leaving Egypt with a "high hand," and an interpretation of the exodus as a judgment on the Egyptian gods. All of these motifs are part of the priestly account of the exodus (see Exod 7:5; 14:8). The priestly writers also include Pi-harhiroth (v. 7) as the location of the confrontation at the sea in Exod 14:1-4. Finally, priestly writers also include the notice of Aaron's death at the close of the itinerary list; this information derives from the account of Aaron's death in 20:22-29.

Evidence of priestly additions, however, does not solve the problem of the origin or purpose of the list, nor does it clarify the relationship of Numbers 33 to the list of stopping points running throughout Exodus and Numbers. A comparison illustrates the similarities and differences between these accounts of Israel's wilderness travel:

Figure 6: Israel's Wilderness Travel in Exodus–Numbers and in Numbers 33

Numbers 33	Exodus–Numbers Itinerary Stops and Other Locations	
	Similarities	*Differences*
Ramses	Ramses (Exod 12:37)	
Succoth	Succoth (12:37)	
Etham	Etham (13:20)	
Pi-harhiroth	Pi-harhiroth (14:2)	
		Red Sea–Shur (15:22)
Marah	Marah (15:23)	
Elim	Elim (15:27)	
Red Sea		
Wilderness of Sin	Wilderness of Sin (16:1)	
Dophkah		
Alush		
Rephidim	Rephidim (17:1)	
Wilderness of Sinai	Wilderness of Sinai (19:1)	
		Sinai–Paran (Num 10:12)
		Three days from Mt. Yahweh (10:33)
Kibroth-hattaavah	Kibroth-hattaavah (11:35)	
Hazeroth	Hazeroth (11:35)	
		Hazeroth—Paran (12:16)
Rithmah		
Rimmon-perez		
Libnah		
Rissah		
Kehelathah		
Mt. Shepher		
Haradah		
Makheloth		
Tahath		
Terah		
Mithkah		
Hashmonah		
Moseroth		
Bene-jaakan		
Hor-haggidgad		
Jotbathah		
Abronah		
Ezion-geber		
Wilderness of Zin (Kadesh)	Wilderness of Zin (Kadesh) (13:26; 20:1)	
Kadesh—Mt. Hor	Kadesh—Mt. Hor (20:22)	
Zalmonah		
Punon		
Oboth	Oboth (21:10)	
Iye-abarim	Iye-abarim (21:11)	
		Zered—Mattanah—Nahaliel—Bamoth —Pisgah (region of Moab) (21:12-20)
Dibon-gad		
Almon-diblathaim		
Mountains of Abarim (Nebo)		
Plains of Moab	Plains of Moab (22:1)	

Comparison of the stopping points in Exodus–Numbers and in Numbers 33 indicates that the latter contains many more locations than appear in the travel accounts of Exodus–Numbers. Further comparison throughout Scripture reveals that sixteen of the places mentioned in Numbers 33 occur nowhere else. The obscurity of the locations may indicate that the document, or at least parts of it, is old and that it provides the source for the more abbreviated version in Exodus–Numbers. But such a conclusion is difficult to confirm.[196]

The purpose for preserving Numbers 33 is no more clear than its age. It may indicate pilgrimage sites, as Noth suggested.[197] More promising, however, is the conclusion by Davis.[198] Comparing Numbers 33 with other ancient Near Eastern texts of a similar nature, Davis concluded that it shares characteristics of records associated with military campaigns. The style in which military campaigns were recorded in the ancient Near East progressed in the same manner as do the travel notices: They set out at A and encamped at B; they set out from B and encamped at C. This genre indicates that, regardless of whether Numbers 33 is an ancient source or a late literary creation, in its present journey as a military march. This is certainly how the list functions in the chapter. The successful completion of Israel's military march, indicated by the summary in 33:1-49, provides the background for the command and warning in 33:50-56 that Israel continue its holy war across the Jordan.

The emphasis on holy war is reinforced by commentary in Numbers 33. Narrative commentary is interspersed especially at the beginning and end of the list of stopping points. Commentary at the beginning of the list includes the exodus (vv. 1-4), the location of Etham at the edge of the wilderness (v. 6b), the confrontation at the sea (vv. 7b-8a), and the lushness of the oasis at Elim (v. 9b). Commentary at the end of the list identifies the Wilderness of Zin as Kadesh (v. 36b) and includes Israel's approach to Edom (v. 37b), the death of Aaron (vv. 38-40), the detection of Israel's approach by the

Canaanite king of Arad (v. 40), and Israel's entry into the land of Moab (v. 44b). The distribution of commentary indicates that it is not so much the wilderness journey that concerns the biblical writers, but a reading of salvation history as a holy war within the structure of an exodus and a conquest. There is no commentary on the wilderness journey from the Red Sea to Kadesh (vv. 10-36). The structure of salvation history in this chapter as an exodus and conquest certainly conforms to its literary setting, where the recounting of Israel's history (vv. 1-49) is intended to provide background for the command by God in vv. 50-56 that Israel complete the holy war by conquering Canaan.

Numbers 33 is composed of different kinds of locations. Most of the list consists of precise locations of cities (e.g., Rameses) or of oases (e.g., Elim). But there are also three more general designations of wilderness areas (Wilderness of Sin, Wilderness of Sinai, Wilderness of Zin), as well as the more general reference to the Plains of Moab. (These are indicated in the list above by the use of italics.)

33:1-11. Verse 1 establishes the military nature of the entire chapter. Israel is envisioned as an army or military host under the command of Moses and Aaron (see the Commentary on 1:3). Verse 2 is unusual in describing Moses as writing down the stopping points in Israel's journey. The last occasion on which Moses was described as writing down information was Exod 24:4, where he was described as writing down divine commandments at Mt. Sinai. Thus Moses authors both law and history in the book of Numbers.

The events of the exodus are described in vv. 3-8 and of Israel's journey into the wilderness in vv. 9-11. The description of the exodus separates into the death of the Egyptian firstborn (vv. 3-4) and the confrontation at the sea (vv. 5-8). The recounting of these events tends to follow the priestly interpretation: The exodus is dated to Month 1, Day 15 (v. 3), the day after the Passover. Israel's departure from Egypt repeats the priestly description of the event in Exod 14:8, in which Israel does not sneak away during the night (see Exod 12:29-39), but marches boldly out of Egypt. The additional comment in v. 4 that the exodus took place in full sight of all the Egyptians, who are still burying their firstborn dead, has no parallel in the story of the exodus. But the interpretation of the death of the firstborn as a judg-

196. See Martin Noth, *Numbers,* OTL (Philadelphia: Westminster, 1968) 242-46; F. M. Cross, *Canaanite Myth and Hebrew Epic* (Cambridge, Mass.: Harvard University Press, 1972) 309-21; G. I. Davies, "The Wilderness Itineraries: A Comparative Study," *TynBul* 25 (1974) 46-81; and *The Way of the Wilderness: A Geographical Study of the Wilderness Itineraries in the Old Testament,* SOTSMS 5 (Cambridge: Cambridge University Press, 1979); and Jacob Milgrom, *Numbers,* JPS Torah Commentary (Philadelphia: JPS, 1990) 497-99.

197. Noth, *Numbers,* 242-44.

198. Davies, "The Wilderness Itineraries," 46-81.

ment against the Egyptian gods repeats the priestly account of events in Exod 7:5.

The confrontation at the sea (vv. 5-8) also follows in general the priestly interpretation from Exod 14:1-4. In the pre-priestly story of the exodus, Israel is said to journey from Rameses to Succoth (Exod 12:37) and from Succoth to Etham, located at the "edge of the wilderness" (Exod 13:20). In the pre-priestly version of the exodus, the confrontation at the Red Sea takes place in the vicinity of Etham, which may indicate a location in the wilderness, rather than in Egypt. The priestly writers change the location in Exod 14:1-4 by having Israel turn around and travel back into Egypt to Pi-hahiroth, a site they place between Migdol and the sea, in front of Baal-zephon. The confrontation at the sea in vv. 5-8 shows the same reinterpretation of location as does Exod 14:1-4. Israel travels from Rameses through Succoth to Etham, before turning back to Pi-hahiroth. The comparison of accounts indicates that the pre-priestly writers favor a wilderness location for the confrontation at the Red Sea, while priestly writers place the confrontation in Egypt.

The account of Israel's entry into the wilderness (vv. 9-11) departs from both the pre-priestly and the priestly versions of the exodus. In the pre-priestly version, Israel crossed the Red Sea (Exod 13:18; 15:22) in its journey from Etham (Exod 13:20) to the Wilderness of Shur (Exod 15:22), the location for the story of bitter water at Marah. The oasis of Elim then follows (Exod 15:27). The priestly account follows this sequence but interjects Pi-hahiroth between Etham and the Wilderness of Shur as the location for the confrontation at the sea. The sequence of locations in v. 9 no longer associates the Red Sea with the crossing of water. It is instead a wilderness campsite that Israel reaches only after several days of travel from Elim. The different accounts can be illustrated in the following manner:

Pre-priestly Exodus	Priestly Exodus	Numbers 33
Rameses	Rameses	Rameses
Succoth	Succoth	Succoth
Etham	Etham	Etham
(Edge of Wilderness)	(Edge of Wilderness)	(Edge of Wilderness)
Red Sea (Sea of Confrontation)		
Pi-hahiroth	Pi-hahiroth	
Wilderness Shur/Marah (Three Days Journey)	Wilderness Shur/Marah (Three Days Journey)	Wilderness Etham/Marah (Three Days Journey)
Elim	Elim	Elim
		Red Sea (Wilderness Location)

Etham is interpreted in this chapter both as a particular place and as a more general wilderness region, which replaces the Wilderness of Shur. More significantly, however, the lists indicate two interpretations of the Red Sea—both as the sea of confrontation with the Egyptians and as a wilderness location. These two interpretations run throughout OT literature. In the Song of the Sea in Exodus 15, the Red Sea is the sea of confrontation, where Pharaoh and his army are destroyed (Exod 15:4). This interpretation is reflected in the book of Joshua, where the Red Sea is dried up by God (Josh 2:10), is crossed over by Israel (Josh 4:23), and is the location of Pharaoh's destruction (Josh 24:6). This interpretation is also implied in Exod 13:18 and 15:22, where references to the Red Sea frame the confrontation at the sea. But Exod 13:18 also indicates that the Red Sea can be envisioned as a road through the wilderness. Numbers 21:4 reflects this interpretation, as do Deut 1:40; 2:1. The Red Sea is the setting for God's central act of salvation. Its two interpretations provide commentary on the meaning of divine salvation. It is a single event in time, when Yahweh destroyed the Egyptians, but salvation at the Red Sea also implies journeying with God through the wilderness. The designation of the Red Sea as a place of destruction and a wilderness road carries both of these meanings.

33:12-37. The march of Israel from the Wilderness of Sin (v. 12) to the Wilderness of Zin (v. 37) contains twenty-four stopping points. Fourteen of the stopping points occur only in this chapter, six correspond to travel notices in Exodus–Numbers, and four correspond to an account of Israel's travels in Deut 10:6-9. The locations that occur only in this chapter include Dophkah and Alush (vv. 12b-14a), as well as the twelve locations between Rithman and Hashmonah (vv. 18b-30a).

The five locations that occur in Exodus–Numbers are as follows: The Wilderness of Sin is the location for the story of manna (Exodus 16). The four stopping points after Alush in vv. 14b-18a follow loosely the account of Israel's travel in Exodus 17–Numbers 12. Rephidim is the location of the war with the Amalekites (Exodus 17); the Wilderness of Sinai is the location for the revelation of law (Exodus 19–Num 10:10), and Kibroth-hattaavah is the location of Israel's murmuring for meat and of the selection of the seventy elders (11:4-35). Hazeroth is the location of the confrontation between Aaron, Miriam, and Moses (11:35; 12:16).

Four locations in vv. 20b-34a correspond loosely to a travel sequence in Deut 10:6-9, which describes Israel's journey after receiving the second copy of the tablets of law. In this account, Israel journeys in the following sequence: Meeroth-bene-jaaken, Moserah, Gudgodah-Jotbathah. Moserah is described in Deut 10:6 as the place of Aaron's death (Mt. Hor in Num 20:22-29; 33:38), while Jotbathah is the location where the Levites were first set apart from the other tribes to guard the ark, in place of receiving an inheritance of land.

This section concludes by tracing Israel's travels from Abronah to Ezion-geber and finally to the Wilderness of Zin, identified as Kadesh. Ezion-geber is most likely located at the head of the Gulf of Akaba (1 Kgs 9:26; 22:48), making the travel distance to Kadesh exceptionally long.

33:38-49. More extended commentary returns in the account of Israel's travels from Kadesh to the Plains of Moab. The purpose of the commentary is to accentuate the theme of holy war. The death of Aaron at Mt. Hor begins the section. His death notice in vv. 38-39 includes information that is lacking in 20:22-29. The date is given as Year 40, Month 5, Day 1 from the exodus, and his age is 123 years. This corresponds to Exod 7:7, where priestly writers date his age as 83 years at the time of the exodus. The death of Aaron

indicates a transition in chap. 33 from wilderness travel to holy war.

Aaron's death is followed immediately by commentary (v. 40) concerning the Canaanite king of Arad. Accentuating the theme of holy war, the writer refers to the story in 21:1-3, where Arad attacked Israel and took captives. Israel's response was to enter into a vow of holy war with God, which was successful. Reference to this event sets the stage for the instruction in vv. 50-56 about Israel's need to wage holy war in Canaan. The additional place sites in vv. 41-49 reinforce the theme of holy war by referring to locations in Israel's war against King Sihon, the Amorite. Oboth (v. 43) is mentioned in 21:10; Iye-Abarim (v. 34) in 21:11; and Dibon-gad (v. 35) in 21:30. The section concludes by noting Israel's present location on the Plains of Moab.

33:50-56. Holy war in Canaan is the central theme of this section. It is signaled by the reference to Israel's crossing over the Jordan (v. 51), which was also central to the negotiations between Moses and the tribes of Reuben and Gad (chap. 32). The holy war material corresponds to similar instruction in the pre-priestly history during the giving of law at Sinai (Exod 23:20-23), in Deuteronomy as teaching by Moses (Deut 7:1-6), and in the Deuteronomistic History as teaching by Joshua (Josh 23:1-13). Israel is to expel the land's inhabitants (v. 52), destroy their idols (v. 52), and take possession of their land (v. 53). The final warning in v. 55, that the inhabitants of Canaan will become a "snare" to Israel if they fail to execute holy war, also repeats language from the same group of texts (Exod 23:33; Deut 7:16; Josh 23:13). The influence of the priestly writers is also evident. The reference to "figured stones" in v. 52 elsewhere occurs only in Lev 26:1, while the allotment of the land in v. 54 repeats the instructions from 26:52-56.

REFLECTIONS

The teaching on war is central in Numbers 31–33, but it also permeates the entire book. The book of Numbers is violent. The opening verses characterize the numbering of Israel at Mt. Sinai as a registration for the draft, focusing on males who are eligible for war (Num 1:3). The march through the wilderness is a military expedition, with each tribe representing a division (Num 11:13-28) led by the ark (Num 10:34-36). The loss of the land is a military failure (Numbers 13–14), culminating in the slaughter of Israelites (Num 14:39-45). The faithfulness of the second generation is charted by military victories over the king of Arad (Num 21:1-3), over Og, and over Sihon (Num 21:10-35). The prominence of war in Numbers requires careful theological reflection. How do we interpret these stories? Is war being glorified in the book of Numbers? Are the Israelite wars models for contemporary ethics of war, so that conquest stories in the Bible call for continuing conquest today? Or is war metaphorical commentary on the life of faith and the need for worshiping communities to maintain purity as the people of God? Whether metaphorical or literal, is violent imagery necessary at all? The following reflections will summarize the teaching on war in the book of Numbers and explore its significance for contemporary Christian teaching.

1. The first important insight is that no unified teaching on war is presented in the book of Numbers. Rather, war is a topic of debate among the different writers of Numbers. Even a brief summary indicates conflict over the significance of killing other human beings in battle.

The battle against the king of Arad (Num 21:1-3) teaches that killing in war is an act of sacrifice to God, requiring the extermination of the entire population. Extermination is described as חרם *ḥērem*, meaning that the enemy is devoted to God as an offering in exchange for divine assistance in battle. Susan Niditch notes the "terrifying completeness" in the *ḥērem* ban as sacrifice. The ethics of such violence, however, are paradoxically rooted in respect for the value of human life. "The ban validates the enemy as human and valuable and does not turn him into a monster worthy of destruction." As a result, the death of each enemy "is a mirror of the self, that which God desires for himself."[199] Sacrificing the enemy to God is an attempt to address the guilt in killing fellow human beings in war. Participation in war, according to this teaching, may be holy, but it is certainly not something to be glorified.

The pre-priestly writers envision war as divine judgment against nations that worship false gods (see the list of nations in Num 13:25-29 and their false worship in Exod 23:20-33). The symbolism of the ark as marching before Israel in the wilderness toward the promised land, scattering enemies before it, and returning to protect the camp (Num 10:34-36) locates God within war (see also Deut 20:1, which encourages Israel not to fear in war because "the LORD your God is with you"). The first generation's fear of invading the indigenous nations of Canaan (Numbers 13–14) is a rejection of God and indicates lack of faith in the divine promise of salvation. The second generation, in contrast, illustrates faith in defeating Og and Sihon in the Transjordan (Num 21:10-35). War in the pre-priestly history is rightful conquest of opponents deserving of death as divine judgment on idolatry. They are defined impersonally as the "other." The indigenous populations of Canaan become the giant Anakim. Such mythologizing dehumanizes them, making their slaughter a just act of divine judgment. The killing of Sihon and Og provides illustration; Og is even identified later as one of the Anakim (Deut 3:11).

The priestly writers interpret war as a necessary evil. War maintains purity in a polluted world. Military imagery characterizes the people of God as a community (Num 1:3) in their journey throughout the wilderness (Num 11:13-28). War itself is sanctioned by God (Num 25:16-18; 31:1). Priests participate in war and even take cultic objects into battle (Num 31:6). But there is no clear indication that Yahweh is actually present in battle, making it holy. To the contrary, participation in war defiles all participants. Killing in war is dissociated from God. Warriors and all objects of war require the most severe processes of purification before reentry into the camp is allowed. War, according to the priestly writers, exacts an enormous price. Killing separates participants from God, even when the cause is deemed just (i.e., sanctioned by God).

The brief summary indicates that war is a debated topic among the writers of Numbers. No single view is presented as the authoritative teaching. The three positions summarized do not exhaust the teaching; war songs (Num 21:14-14, 26-30), the refusal to go to war against Edom

---

199. Susan Niditch, *War in the Hebrew Bible: A Study in the Ethics of Violence* (Oxford: Oxford University Press, 1993) 50. Niditch summarizes a range of teachings on war that provide an excellent resource for a more broadly based study of war in the OT.

(Num 20:14-21), war oracles against the nations by Balaam (Num 24:15-24), and the passive role of Israel during the threat from Balak (Numbers 22–24) add still other voices to the debate on war. Other Old Testament books expand the discussion of how the people of God respond to acts of violence (see, for example, the holy war of Joshua, the pacifism of Isaiah, and the cultic interpretation of war in Chronicles). Too often the pre-priestly teaching of war as justified conquest is allowed to dominate Old Testament teaching on war. Any use of Numbers as a resource for contemporary reflection on war must begin with the understanding that it provides a resource for contemporary debate on war, rather than a single authoritative teaching.

2. Interpretation of war stories in Numbers is complicated by their metaphorical use to address theological themes of faithfulness to God and of the need for Israelites to be separate from the nations. Thus holy war takes on broad theological significance in Numbers. It provides the underlying structure of salvation history as a liberation from Egypt and conquest of the promised land. The wilderness journey in Numbers 33 reflects this theology. It symbolizes Israel's march as one of unconditional faith in the power of God to lead. Compromise with surrounding nations signifies lack of faith that can lead only to doom, causing God to turn against Israel and to use the nations as a "snare" to take the land away from Israel.

More explicit stories of war may also be theological in their intent. The execution of the *ḥērem* ban against the king of Arad at Hormah (Num 21:1-3) may be a theological story about faithfulness to God in a time of crisis, as compared to the faithlessness of the first generation in their earlier battle at Hormah (Num 14:39-45). There is no evidence that the *ḥērem* ban as sacrifice to God was ever practiced. The priestly writers also use war imagery to write theology. The Midianites represent an external threat of pollution. They are a borderline people in the priestly history, with close ties to Israel through Moses. In this position, they are dangerous characters who have the power to seduce Israel, requiring their extermination. The description of the war as the extermination of all Midianites without the loss of one single Israelite indicates that holy war is used metaphorically to address problems of cultural intermingling, hence the focus on booty and especially virgins as potential wives.

War as a metaphor for theology does not eliminate its violent imagery as a model for living a faithful life. Conflict permeates the themes of faithfulness and purity throughout the book of Numbers. Holy war imagery encourages contemporary teachers and preachers to accentuate that the life of faith includes struggle, requiring discipline to fulfill its mission. In the end, however, the metaphorical use of war in Numbers brings one full circle to concrete problems of war and violence—including the role of the church in times of war.

3. Roland Bainton summarizes three historic Christian positions toward war: pacifism, the crusade, and the just war.[200] In the book *War: A Primer for Christians,* Joseph Allen briefly summarizes each position.[201] Pacifism is rooted in the principles that God forbids killing (Exod 20:13), warns against relying on force against enemies (Hos 7:11), and ideally envisions the world at peace (Isa 2:4). These principles are most clearly stated in Jesus' command not to resist evil (Matt 5:39).[202] The crusade includes these features: Justifiable war is a religious conflict between good and evil (Judges 4–5), the goals in war are absolute and unlimited (Deut 7:1-2), and the means of war are unrestrained (Josh 6:21; 8:24).[203] Just-war theory emerged in the fourth and fifth centuries CE, when Christian theologians like Ambrose and Augustine began to evaluate the Roman Empire's use of power. Augustine, for example, argued that the state had a moral obligation to protect people, avenge injuries, and restore justice and peace

---

200. Roland H. Bainton, *Christian Attitudes Toward War and Peace: A Historical Survey and Critical Re-evaluation* (Nashville: Abingdon, 1960) 14.
201. Joseph L. Allen, *War: A Primer for Christians* (Nashville: Abingdon, 1991).
202. Ibid., 16-30.
203. Ibid., 7-15.

in society. Two principles informed his theology: War should not be waged for selfish reasons, and it should be directed toward helping other people.[204]

The book of Numbers does not separate into the three categories of Christian teaching on war. The crusade model is the clearest of the three, occurring in the conquest stories. There is no clear teaching on pacifism. The inactive role of Israel during the threat by Balak may touch on the topic, since evil is not resisted. But inactivity by Israel is not the central point. The avoidance of war with Edom might also support features of pacifism (Num 20:14-21). Individual principles stated in pacifism and in the crusade model do occur in Numbers. Peace, not war, is the ideal for creation (Num 6:22-27). Killing defiles (Numbers 31). Reliance on one's own power in war is condemned, as is warring for self-interest (Num 14:39-45). And God must declare all war through the cult.

The need for God to declare war leads to the conclusion that there is no teaching on just war in Numbers. Israel is a theocracy in the wilderness throughout the book. All war in Numbers is waged through the sanctuary. No state has the power to declare war in Numbers. Those that do are destroyed (Balak, the king of Arad, Sihon, and Og). The central role of just-war theory in contemporary Christian teaching underscores how theological reflection on war is an ongoing responsibility for the people of God throughout history. The church now evaluates the actions of nation-states in Western history. Such a practice was not envisioned by the writers of Numbers. The absence of just-war theory in Numbers, however, is also a caution for contemporary Christians. We often concede too much power to the state, and thus fail to take full moral authority for the role of the church at times of war. The book of Numbers does not present a single teaching on war, but all of its different writers agree that evaluation of and participation in war are responsibilities of the sanctuary, not of the state.

204. Ibid., 31-52.

Numbers 34:1–36:13, Life in the Land

NIV

34 The LORD said to Moses, [2]"Command the Israelites and say to them: 'When you enter Canaan, the land that will be allotted to you as an inheritance will have these boundaries:

[3]" 'Your southern side will include some of the Desert of Zin along the border of Edom. On the east, your southern boundary will start from the end of the Salt Sea,[a] [4]cross south of Scorpion[b] Pass, continue on to Zin and go south of Kadesh Barnea. Then it will go to Hazar Addar and over to Azmon, [5]where it will turn, join the Wadi of Egypt and end at the Sea.[c]

[6]" 'Your western boundary will be the coast of the Great Sea. This will be your boundary on the west.

[7]" 'For your northern boundary, run a line from the Great Sea to Mount Hor [8]and from Mount Hor to Lebo[d] Hamath. Then the boundary will go

a3 That is, the Dead Sea; also in verse 12   b4 Hebrew Akrabbim
c5 That is, the Mediterranean; also in verses 6 and 7   d8 Or to the entrance to

NRSV

34 The LORD spoke to Moses, saying: [2]Command the Israelites, and say to them: When you enter the land of Canaan (this is the land that shall fall to you for an inheritance, the land of Canaan, defined by its boundaries), [3]your south sector shall extend from the wilderness of Zin along the side of Edom. Your southern boundary shall begin from the end of the Dead Sea[a] on the east; [4]your boundary shall turn south of the ascent of Akrabbim, and cross to Zin, and its outer limit shall be south of Kadesh-barnea; then it shall go on to Hazar-addar, and cross to Azmon; [5]the boundary shall turn from Azmon to the Wadi of Egypt, and its termination shall be at the Sea.

6For the western[b] boundary, you shall have the Great Sea and its[b] coast; this shall be your western boundary.

7This shall be your northern boundary: from the Great Sea you shall mark out your line to Mount Hor; [8]from Mount Hor you shall mark it

a Heb Salt Sea   b Syr: Heb lacks its

NIV

to Zedad, ⁹continue to Ziphron and end at Hazar Enan. This will be your boundary on the north.

¹⁰"'For your eastern boundary, run a line from Hazar Enan to Shepham. ¹¹The boundary will go down from Shepham to Riblah on the east side of Ain and continue along the slopes east of the Sea of Kinnereth.^a ¹²Then the boundary will go down along the Jordan and end at the Salt Sea.

"'This will be your land, with its boundaries on every side.'"

¹³Moses commanded the Israelites: "Assign this land by lot as an inheritance. The LORD has ordered that it be given to the nine and a half tribes, ¹⁴because the families of the tribe of Reuben, the tribe of Gad and the half-tribe of Manasseh have received their inheritance. ¹⁵These two and a half tribes have received their inheritance on the east side of the Jordan of Jericho,^b toward the sunrise."

¹⁶The LORD said to Moses, ¹⁷"These are the names of the men who are to assign the land for you as an inheritance: Eleazar the priest and Joshua son of Nun. ¹⁸And appoint one leader from each tribe to help assign the land. ¹⁹These are their names:

Caleb son of Jephunneh,
    from the tribe of Judah;
²⁰Shemuel son of Ammihud,
    from the tribe of Simeon;
²¹Elidad son of Kislon,
    from the tribe of Benjamin;
²²Bukki son of Jogli,
    the leader from the tribe of Dan;
²³Hanniel son of Ephod,
    the leader from the tribe of Manasseh son
    of Joseph;
²⁴Kemuel son of Shiphtan,
    the leader from the tribe of Ephraim son
    of Joseph;
²⁵Elizaphan son of Parnach,
    the leader from the tribe of Zebulun;
²⁶Paltiel son of Azzan,
    the leader from the tribe of Issachar;
²⁷Ahihud son of Shelomi,
    the leader from the tribe of Asher;
²⁸Pedahel son of Ammihud,

^a11 That is, Galilee   ^b15 Jordan of Jericho was possibly an ancient name for the Jordan River.

NRSV

out to Lebo-hamath, and the outer limit of the boundary shall be at Zedad; ⁹then the boundary shall extend to Ziphron, and its end shall be at Hazar-enan; this shall be your northern boundary.

10You shall mark out your eastern boundary from Hazar-enan to Shepham; ¹¹and the boundary shall continue down from Shepham to Riblah on the east side of Ain; and the boundary shall go down, and reach the eastern slope of the sea of Chinnereth; ¹²and the boundary shall go down to the Jordan, and its end shall be at the Dead Sea.^a This shall be your land with its boundaries all around.

13Moses commanded the Israelites, saying: This is the land that you shall inherit by lot, which the LORD has commanded to give to the nine tribes and to the half-tribe; ¹⁴for the tribe of the Reubenites by their ancestral houses and the tribe of the Gadites by their ancestral houses have taken their inheritance, and also the half-tribe of Manasseh; ¹⁵the two tribes and the half-tribe have taken their inheritance beyond the Jordan at Jericho eastward, toward the sunrise.

16The LORD spoke to Moses, saying: ¹⁷These are the names of the men who shall apportion the land to you for inheritance: the priest Eleazar and Joshua son of Nun. ¹⁸You shall take one leader of every tribe to apportion the land for inheritance. ¹⁹These are the names of the men: Of the tribe of Judah, Caleb son of Jephunneh. ²⁰Of the tribe of the Simeonites, Shemuel son of Ammihud. ²¹Of the tribe of Benjamin, Elidad son of Chislon. ²²Of the tribe of the Danites a leader, Bukki son of Jogli. ²³Of the Josephites: of the tribe of the Manassites a leader, Hanniel son of Ephod, ²⁴and of the tribe of the Ephraimites a leader, Kemuel son of Shiphtan. ²⁵Of the tribe of the Zebulunites a leader, Eli-zaphan son of Parnach. ²⁶Of the tribe of the Issacharites a leader, Paltiel son of Azzan. ²⁷And of the tribe of the Asherites a leader, Ahihud son of Shelomi. ²⁸Of the tribe of the Naphtalites a leader, Pedahel son of Ammihud. ²⁹These were the ones whom the LORD commanded to apportion the inheritance for the Israelites in the land of Canaan.

35 In the plains of Moab by the Jordan at Jericho, the LORD spoke to Moses, saying: ²Command the Israelites to give, from the inheritance that they possess, towns for the Levites to live in; you shall also give to the Levites pasture

NIV

the leader from the tribe of Naphtali."

²⁹These are the men the LORD commanded to assign the inheritance to the Israelites in the land of Canaan.

35 On the plains of Moab by the Jordan across from Jericho,ᵃ the LORD said to Moses, ²"Command the Israelites to give the Levites towns to live in from the inheritance the Israelites will possess. And give them pasturelands around the towns. ³Then they will have towns to live in and pasturelands for their cattle, flocks and all their other livestock.

⁴"The pasturelands around the towns that you give the Levites will extend out fifteen hundred feetᵇ from the town wall. ⁵Outside the town, measure three thousand feetᶜ on the east side, three thousand on the south side, three thousand on the west and three thousand on the north, with the town in the center. They will have this area as pastureland for the towns.

⁶"Six of the towns you give the Levites will be cities of refuge, to which a person who has killed someone may flee. In addition, give them forty-two other towns. ⁷In all you must give the Levites forty-eight towns, together with their pasturelands. ⁸The towns you give the Levites from the land the Israelites possess are to be given in proportion to the inheritance of each tribe: Take many towns from a tribe that has many, but few from one that has few."

⁹Then the LORD said to Moses: ¹⁰"Speak to the Israelites and say to them: 'When you cross the Jordan into Canaan, ¹¹select some towns to be your cities of refuge, to which a person who has killed someone accidentally may flee. ¹²They will be places of refuge from the avenger, so that a person accused of murder may not die before he stands trial before the assembly. ¹³These six towns you give will be your cities of refuge. ¹⁴Give three on this side of the Jordan and three in Canaan as cities of refuge. ¹⁵These six towns will be a place of refuge for Israelites, aliens and any other people living among them, so that anyone who has killed another accidentally can flee there.

¹⁶"'If a man strikes someone with an iron object so that he dies, he is a murderer; the murderer shall be put to death. ¹⁷Or if anyone has a stone in his hand that could kill, and he strikes

---

ᵃ1 Hebrew *Jordan of Jericho;* possibly an ancient name for the Jordan River   ᵇ4 Hebrew *a thousand cubits* (about 450 meters)   ᶜ5 Hebrew *two thousand cubits* (about 900 meters)

NRSV

lands surrounding the towns. ³The towns shall be theirs to live in, and their pasture lands shall be for their cattle, for their livestock, and for all their animals. ⁴The pasture lands of the towns, which you shall give to the Levites, shall reach from the wall of the town outward a thousand cubits all around. ⁵You shall measure, outside the town, for the east side two thousand cubits, for the south side two thousand cubits, for the west side two thousand cubits, and for the north side two thousand cubits, with the town in the middle; this shall belong to them as pasture land for their towns.

6The towns that you give to the Levites shall include the six cities of refuge, where you shall permit a slayer to flee, and in addition to them you shall give forty-two towns. ⁷The towns that you give to the Levites shall total forty-eight, with their pasture lands. ⁸And as for the towns that you shall give from the possession of the Israelites, from the larger tribes you shall take many, and from the smaller tribes you shall take few; each, in proportion to the inheritance that it obtains, shall give of its towns to the Levites.

9The LORD spoke to Moses, saying: ¹⁰Speak to the Israelites, and say to them: When you cross the Jordan into the land of Canaan, ¹¹then you shall select cities to be cities of refuge for you, so that a slayer who kills a person without intent may flee there. ¹²The cities shall be for you a refuge from the avenger, so that the slayer may not die until there is a trial before the congregation.

13The cities that you designate shall be six cities of refuge for you: ¹⁴you shall designate three cities beyond the Jordan, and three cities in the land of Canaan, to be cities of refuge. ¹⁵These six cities shall serve as refuge for the Israelites, for the resident or transient alien among them, so that anyone who kills a person without intent may flee there.

16But anyone who strikes another with an iron object, and death ensues, is a murderer; the murderer shall be put to death. ¹⁷Or anyone who strikes another with a stone in hand that could cause death, and death ensues, is a murderer; the murderer shall be put to death. ¹⁸Or anyone who strikes another with a weapon of wood in hand that could cause death, and death ensues, is a murderer; the murderer shall be put to death. ¹⁹The avenger of blood is the one who shall put

NIV

someone so that he dies, he is a murderer; the murderer shall be put to death. [18]Or if anyone has a wooden object in his hand that could kill, and he hits someone so that he dies, he is a murderer; the murderer shall be put to death. [19]The avenger of blood shall put the murderer to death; when he meets him, he shall put him to death. [20]If anyone with malice aforethought shoves another or throws something at him intentionally so that he dies [21]or if in hostility he hits him with his fist so that he dies, that person shall be put to death; he is a murderer. The avenger of blood shall put the murderer to death when he meets him.

[22]" 'But if without hostility someone suddenly shoves another or throws something at him unintentionally [23]or, without seeing him, drops a stone on him that could kill him, and he dies, then since he was not his enemy and he did not intend to harm him, [24]the assembly must judge between him and the avenger of blood according to these regulations. [25]The assembly must protect the one accused of murder from the avenger of blood and send him back to the city of refuge to which he fled. He must stay there until the death of the high priest, who was anointed with the holy oil.

[26]" 'But if the accused ever goes outside the limits of the city of refuge to which he has fled [27]and the avenger of blood finds him outside the city, the avenger of blood may kill the accused without being guilty of murder. [28]The accused must stay in his city of refuge until the death of the high priest; only after the death of the high priest may he return to his own property.

[29]" 'These are to be legal requirements for you throughout the generations to come, wherever you live.

[30]" 'Anyone who kills a person is to be put to death as a murderer only on the testimony of witnesses. But no one is to be put to death on the testimony of only one witness.

[31]" 'Do not accept a ransom for the life of a murderer, who deserves to die. He must surely be put to death.

[32]" 'Do not accept a ransom for anyone who has fled to a city of refuge and so allow him to go back and live on his own land before the death of the high priest.

[33]" 'Do not pollute the land where you are. Blood-

NRSV

the murderer to death; when they meet, the avenger of blood shall execute the sentence. [20]Likewise, if someone pushes another from hatred, or hurls something at another, lying in wait, and death ensues, [21]or in enmity strikes another with the hand, and death ensues, then the one who struck the blow shall be put to death; that person is a murderer; the avenger of blood shall put the murderer to death, when they meet.

[22]But if someone pushes another suddenly without enmity, or hurls any object without lying in wait, [23]or, while handling any stone that could cause death, unintentionally[a] drops it on another and death ensues, though they were not enemies, and no harm was intended, [24]then the congregation shall judge between the slayer and the avenger of blood, in accordance with these ordinances; [25]and the congregation shall rescue the slayer from the avenger of blood. Then the congregation shall send the slayer back to the original city of refuge. The slayer shall live in it until the death of the high priest who was anointed with the holy oil. [26]But if the slayer shall at any time go outside the bounds of the original city of refuge, [27]and is found by the avenger of blood outside the bounds of the city of refuge, and is killed by the avenger, no bloodguilt shall be incurred. [28]For the slayer must remain in the city of refuge until the death of the high priest; but after the death of the high priest the slayer may return home.

[29]These things shall be a statute and ordinance for you throughout your generations wherever you live.

[30]If anyone kills another, the murderer shall be put to death on the evidence of witnesses; but no one shall be put to death on the testimony of a single witness. [31]Moreover you shall accept no ransom for the life of a murderer who is subject to the death penalty; a murderer must be put to death. [32]Nor shall you accept ransom for one who has fled to a city of refuge, enabling the fugitive to return to live in the land before the death of the high priest. [33]You shall not pollute the land in which you live; for blood pollutes the land, and no expiation can be made for the land, for the blood that is shed in it, except by the blood of the one who shed it. [34]You shall not defile the land in which you live, in which I also dwell; for I the LORD dwell among the Israelites.

[a] Heb *without seeing*

shed pollutes the land, and atonement cannot be made for the land on which blood has been shed, except by the blood of the one who shed it. ³⁴Do not defile the land where you live and where I dwell, for I, the LORD, dwell among the Israelites.'"

36 The family heads of the clan of Gilead son of Makir, the son of Manasseh, who were from the clans of the descendants of Joseph, came and spoke before Moses and the leaders, the heads of the Israelite families. ²They said, "When the LORD commanded my lord to give the land as an inheritance to the Israelites by lot, he ordered you to give the inheritance of our brother Zelophehad to his daughters. ³Now suppose they marry men from other Israelite tribes; then their inheritance will be taken from our ancestral inheritance and added to that of the tribe they marry into. And so part of the inheritance allotted to us will be taken away. ⁴When the Year of Jubilee for the Israelites comes, their inheritance will be added to that of the tribe into which they marry, and their property will be taken from the tribal inheritance of our forefathers."

⁵Then at the LORD's command Moses gave this order to the Israelites: "What the tribe of the descendants of Joseph is saying is right. ⁶This is what the LORD commands for Zelophehad's daughters: They may marry anyone they please as long as they marry within the tribal clan of their father. ⁷No inheritance in Israel is to pass from tribe to tribe, for every Israelite shall keep the tribal land inherited from his forefathers. ⁸Every daughter who inherits land in any Israelite tribe must marry someone in her father's tribal clan, so that every Israelite will possess the inheritance of his fathers. ⁹No inheritance may pass from tribe to tribe, for each Israelite tribe is to keep the land it inherits."

¹⁰So Zelophehad's daughters did as the LORD commanded Moses. ¹¹Zelophehad's daughters—Mahlah, Tirzah, Hoglah, Milcah and Noah—married their cousins on their father's side. ¹²They married within the clans of the descendants of Manasseh son of Joseph, and their inheritance remained in their father's clan and tribe.

¹³These are the commands and regulations the LORD gave through Moses to the Israelites on the plains of Moab by the Jordan across from Jericho.ᵃ

ᵃ13 Hebrew *Jordan of Jericho;* possibly an ancient name for the Jordan River

36 The heads of the ancestral houses of the clans of the descendants of Gilead son of Machir son of Manasseh, of the Josephite clans, came forward and spoke in the presence of Moses and the leaders, the heads of the ancestral houses of the Israelites; ²they said, "The LORD commanded my lord to give the land for inheritance by lot to the Israelites; and my lord was commanded by the LORD to give the inheritance of our brother Zelophehad to his daughters. ³But if they are married into another Israelite tribe, then their inheritance will be taken from the inheritance of our ancestors and added to the inheritance of the tribe into which they marry; so it will be taken away from the allotted portion of our inheritance. ⁴And when the jubilee of the Israelites comes, then their inheritance will be added to the inheritance of the tribe into which they have married; and their inheritance will be taken from the inheritance of our ancestral tribe."

5Then Moses commanded the Israelites according to the word of the LORD, saying, "The descendants of the tribe of Joseph are right in what they are saying. ⁶This is what the LORD commands concerning the daughters of Zelophehad, 'Let them marry whom they think best; only it must be into a clan of their father's tribe that they are married, ⁷so that no inheritance of the Israelites shall be transferred from one tribe to another; for all Israelites shall retain the inheritance of their ancestral tribes. ⁸Every daughter who possesses an inheritance in any tribe of the Israelites shall marry one from the clan of her father's tribe, so that all Israelites may continue to possess their ancestral inheritance. ⁹No inheritance shall be transferred from one tribe to another; for each of the tribes of the Israelites shall retain its own inheritance.'"

10The daughters of Zelophehad did as the LORD had commanded Moses. ¹¹Mahlah, Tirzah, Hoglah, Milcah, and Noah, the daughters of Zelophehad, married sons of their father's brothers. ¹²They were married into the clans of the descendants of Manasseh son of Joseph, and their inheritance remained in the tribe of their father's clan.

13These are the commandments and the ordinances that the LORD commanded through Moses to the Israelites in the plains of Moab by the Jordan at Jericho.

COMMENTARY

The priestly writers are the authors of the closing section of the book of Numbers. They are also responsible for the overall design of Numbers 26–36. The commentary on chap. 26 indicated that the priestly writers used the second census to show that the divine promise of descendants was fulfilled at this point in Israel's salvation history. The divine promise of descendants (Gen 12:2) is one of two promises of salvation to the ancestors that runs throughout the Pentateuch.

The second promise of salvation to the ancestors is that of land (Gen 12:7). The priestly writers set their focus squarely on this second theme in Numbers 34–36. Chapter 34 outlines the boundaries of the promised land of Canaan and lists the leaders from each tribe who will assist in land distribution. Chapter 35 provides a list of the levitical cities in the land and the laws regarding cities of refuge. Chapter 36 returns one final time to inheritance by the daughters of Zelophehad.

The subject matter of Numbers 34–36 provides two initial insights that aid in interpretation. First, the concluding section of Numbers is about Israel's future life in the land. Second, chaps. 34–36 follow a division between the people of Israel and the Levites that was also important to the priestly writers in the opening section of Numbers 1–10, where Israel's life in the camp was described. Thus the social structure surrounding the holiness of God in the camp is extended to the land.

34:1-29. 34:1-15. The spies travel from the Wilderness of Zin in the south to Rehob, near Lebo-hamath in the north, in the priestly version of their mission (13:21). The geographical locations from the spy story return in these verses, where the priestly writers fill in the boundaries of the promised land of Canaan. Two details are noteworthy. The first is that the priestly vision of Canaan in vv. 1-12 is of a large geographical area. The second is that in spite of their expansionist view of the land, the Transjordan is not specifically included in vv. 13-15.

The priestly vision of the promised land in vv. 1-12 does not correspond to its boundaries in any known time in Israel's political history. It is an ideal vision of the land as a divine gift. The description of its borders progresses in a circle that moves in a clockwise direction from south (vv.

1-5), to west (v. 6), to north (vv. 7-9), and to east (vv. 10-12). The circle begins and ends with the Dead Sea. The list of locations includes:

(1) The southern boundary (Num 34:1-5)
    Wilderness of Zin
      along Edom
    Dead Sea
    Akrabbim
    Zin
    Kadesh-barnea
      (outer limit south)
    Hazar-addar
    Azmon Wadi Egypt
    The (Great) Sea
(2) The western boundary (Num 34:6)
    The Great Sea
(3) The northern boundary (Num 34:7-9)
    The Great Sea
    Mount Hor
    Lebo-hamath
    Zedad (outer limit north)
    Ziphron
    Hazar-enan
(4) The eastern boundary (Num 34:10-12)
    Hazar-enan
    Shepham
    Riblah on the East Side
      of Ain
    Sea of Chinnereth
    Jordan
    Dead Sea

Many of the locations cited in vv. 1-12 are difficult to place. Nevertheless, the listing of exact boundaries for Canaan underscores that, for priestly writers, the promise of land must be interpreted concretely. The fulfillment of promises is not to be sought in another world. God's quest for renewal is aimed at this world.

There appear to be two descriptions of the southern boundary of the land in vv. 1-5, a general description ("the wilderness of Zin along the side of Edom," v. 3a) and a more detailed account of specific locations (vv. 3b-5). Kadesh-barnea marks the southernmost boundary for the priestly writers. The Great Sea, or Mediterranean, links the southern, western, and northern borders, although the particular location where the northern border meets the Mediterranean is unknown. The furthermost boundary on the north is Zedad. This location is in the vacinity of Lebo-hamath, thus providing a link with the priestly interpretation of the spy story, which mentions "Rehob, near Lebo-hamath" as the northernmost destination of the spies (13:21). But Rehob is not mentioned in chap. 34. The location of Hazar-enan, which provides the corner point for the northern and eastern borders, is also unknown. The eastern border, however, is clearly marked by the Jordan River.

Two related descriptions of the boundaries of Canaan occur in Josh 15:1-12 and Ezek 47:15-20. The description in Joshua begins with the southern boundary, but progresses counterclockwise: south, east, north, west. The eastern boundary is the Dead Sea, while the northern boundary is the northern point of the Dead Sea and includes many more locations than does Numbers 34. Ezekiel 47:15-20 begins with the northern boundary rather than the southern, as in Joshua 15 and in Numbers 34. Like Numbers 34, it also progresses clockwise: north, east, south, west and follows closely the boundaries of Numbers 34.

Surprisingly, the boundaries of the promised land appear to exclude the Transjordan. The eastern boundary of the land mentioned in vv. 10-12 indicates as much, since it runs along the Jordan River. The concluding commentary by Moses in vv. 13-15 reinforces this point. The promised land includes only what is apportioned to the nine tribes west of the Jordan. The land east of the Jordan, taken by the tribes of Reuben, Gad, and half of Manasseh, is regarded by Moses as their inheritance, but he does not include it in the boundaries of Canaan. Cities of refuge, however, are designated for the Transjordan in chap. 35. Perhaps the limitation of the promised land to territory west of the Jordan accounts for Reuben's loss of firstborn status to the tribe of Judah in the priestly list of the tribes in vv. 16-29.

34:16-29. Ten tribal leaders are named to assist Eleazar and Joshua in distributing the land. The number is ten, rather than twelve, because the tribes of Reuben and Gad chose to inherit in the Transjordan. The names of the tribal leaders are new with the exception of Caleb, who, along with Joshua (see Numbers 13–14), is allowed to inherit land.

The order of the tribes follows the direction of the boundaries from vv. 1-15, moving from south to north. The tribes who will settle in the south include Judah, Simeon, Benjamin, and Dan. The Joseph tribes, Manasseh and Ephraim, will settle in the central portion of Canaan. The northern tribes include Zebulun, Issachar, Asher, and Naphtali. The result of listing the tribes from south to north is that Judah heads the list. This, too, may be by design, since the tribe of Judah has headed the list of tribes in situations that point toward the inheritance of the land, including the order of the camp (chap. 2), the presentation of offerings (chap. 7), the order of marching (chap. 10), and now inheritance (chap. 34). These lists contrast other situations in which Reuben heads the lists: the first census (chap. 1), the spy story (chap. 13), and the second census (chap. 26).

35:1-34. The Levites are separated from the other tribes in the promised land, just as they were in the wilderness camp. The divine command to Moses in vv. 1 and 9 indicates the two general topics of the chapter. In vv. 1-8, God states that, unlike other tribes, the Levites will receive no land, because they are a divine possession. Instead, they receive special cities located throughout the land. The levitical cities now complement the tithe that the Levites receive, which was described (18:21-24) as a substitute for inheriting land.

Verses 9-34 return to the topic of the special role of Levites as a divine possession and their ability to protect Israel from the danger of divine wrath. The protective role of the Levites in the camp is now extended to the entire land. God states to Moses that a small number of levitical cities will take on the power of protection that characterized the Levites in the camp. These cities will be havens of refuge for persons who are guilty of certain kinds of homicide. Much of chap. 35 outlines the conditions under which individuals might seek asylum in a city of refuge.

35:1-8. The priestly description of sacrifices for the priests and Levites (18:21-25) contained the divine commandment that the Levites not inherit land. The priestly writers provide further details of this divine command by stating that the Levites will own cities rather than land. This section is introduced as divine instruction to Moses (v. 1) and includes information about the boundaries of a levitical city along with its pastureland (vv. 2-5) as well as the number of such cities and the process by which they will be selected from each tribe's territory (vv. 6-8).

The inheritance of cities instead of land by Levites carries forward a theological design that the priestly writers first developed in their description of the wilderness camp. Four times the Levites were singled out in chaps. 1–10 to indicate their special status as a divine possession and to outline how that status influenced their role in the camp. They were counted separately from the other tribes in 1:48-53, where their role of maintaining a buffer zone between God and Israel was noted. Numbers 2:17 provided a visual illustration of this role by noting how the Levites camped around the tabernacle, creating a protective space between God and the people. Chapters 3–4 described in detail the work of the Levites in caring for the tabernacle and their special status as substitutes for Israel's firstborn. Finally, chap. 8 added further background on the Levites' ability to atone for Israel's firstborn as substitutes. Atonement was understood as a ransom for protection of the firstborn. Such ransom was possible because the Levites were a divine possession. Here, the priestly writers describe how the special status of Levites as a divine possession affects their life in the land.

How the Levites actually lived in the land of Canaan is no clearer from biblical literature than is the history of their development (see the Commentary on 3:1–4:49). The prophet Ezekiel contradicts 35:1-8 by stating that the Levites do inherit land (Ezek 48:3-22). Deuteronomy 18:1-8 provides some agreement with Num 35:1-8 in stating that the Levites do not inherit land. Yet, there is no mention of levitical cities in Deut 18:1-8. In fact, Deut 18:6 suggests that the Levites are scattered throughout all of Israel's cities, and not in specially designated cities. Given the contradictory information in Scripture and the clear signs of theological design by the priestly writers regarding the role of the Levites, scholars debate whether there is any historical value to Num 35:1-8. The debate over the history of levitical cities is complicated, however, by Judges 21, which may contain older tradition concerning such cities. There are clear signs that priestly editing in Judges 21 seeks to make the chapter function as the fulfillment of Num 35:1-8. Chapter 35

may also contain older information on levitical cities from Israel's monarchical period.[205]

Several literary questions arise in vv. 1-8. In an attempt to harmonize the priestly material on levitical cities with Deuteronomy, some commentators have questioned whether the command that Levites "live in" cities (v. 2) indicates possession or some form of leasing. But Lev 25:32-34 makes it clear that the priestly writers intend for Levites to own their cities. The designated pastureland of the cities in vv. 4-5 presents a more puzzling problem. Verse 4 states that pastureland shall extend for 1,000 cubits, while v. 5 expands the dimension to 2,000 cubits. Verses 6-8 change the focus from the dimensions of levitical cities to their number and location. Levitical cities will number forty-eight in all, while six will have special status as "cities of refuge." Selection of levitical cities is to be determined by size, with larger tribes contributing more.

35:9-15. The more narrow topic of levitical cities of refuge is indicated with a new introduction in v. 9. Verse 11 states that cities of refuge function as places of asylum. There are indications that early in Israel's history the altars of sanctuaries, rather than selected cities, functioned as locations of asylum. Two examples appear in the opening chapters of 1 Kings, where Adonijah competes with Solomon for succession to the throne of David. Upon hearing of the selection of Solomon, both Adonijah (1 Kgs 1:49-53) and Joab, David's general who supported Adonijah for the throne (1 Kgs 2:28-35), flee to the sanctuary and "grasp the horns of the altar" for protection from Solomon. The priestly designation of levitical cities of refuge thus indicates a rejection of the sanctuary altar as the place for asylum. Indeed, contact with the altar kills humans, according to the priestly writers (4:15). The rejection of the altar as the place of refuge is evident in Deuteronomy (Deut 4:41-43) and in the Deuteronomistic History (Joshua 21); thus it is not an innovation by the priestly writers. Scholars debate when the transfer of asylum from altar to designated cities occurred. It may have been early in the monarchical period. Perhaps the prophet Hosea refers to Gilead and Shechem as places of refuge (Hos

205. See W. F. Albright, "The List of Levitical Cities," in L. Ginzberg, *Jubilee Volume* (New York: American Academy for Jewish Research, 1945) 49-73.

6:7-10). Another possible time would be during the reign of Josiah in the late seventh century BCE, when he centralized the cult in Jerusalem.

The specific crime for which the cities of refuge are intended to provide asylum is homicide. Verse 12 indicates that asylum is granted from the avenger (גֹּאֵל *gō'ēl*). The avenger, or next of kin, performed many duties. Boaz functions as the *gō'ēl* in fulfilling the levirate vow with Ruth (Ruth 3:13). The *gō'ēl* may be called upon to redeem family property or a relative from slavery (Leviticus 25). In these cases, the word *gō'ēl* is often translated "redeemer." The shedding of blood is a debt that pollutes the land. In this situation, the *gō'ēl* is responsible for "redeeming" the debt of blood that occurs with homicide. The traditional role of the avenger of blood indicates that justice surrounding murder was a matter of the clan or family. The priestly law in v. 12 does not eliminate the avenger's role. On the contrary, it affirms the role of the avenger and anchors it even more broadly in the theology of the land (vv. 33-34). But the priestly writers do transfer the execution of justice surrounding homicide from the family to the state. The city of refuge functions as an asylum until the guilt or innocence of the one who killed could be determined by a trial before the congregation.

Verses 13-15 indicate the number and location of the cities of refuge and the range of persons having access to their protection. The six cities are distributed evenly on both sides of the Jordan, with three in Canaan and three in the Transjordan. They are not named in this chapter, but they are listed in Deut 4:41-43 and Joshua 21 as Bezer, Ramoth, and Golan in the Transjordan (Deut 4:41-43), and Shechem (Josh 21:21), Golan (Josh 21:27), and Kedesh (Josh 21:32) in Canaan. Cities of asylum functioned for all Israelites, as well as for resident aliens in the land (see the Commentary on 15:1-16).

35:16-28. The priestly writers introduced the distinction between intentional and unintentional sins with regard to sacrifices in chap. 15. Unintentional sins (15:22-29) could be forgiven, while intentional or "high-handed" sins (15:30-31) could not. The priestly writers extend the distinction based on intention to homicide in this section. Verses 16-21 provide criteria for determining intention and the procedure to be followed in

executing punishment, while vv. 22-28 outline the procedures that must be followed if someone kills another unintentionally.

Verses 16-21 describe instances of intentional homicide. Guilt can be determined in two ways. First, the object used to kill indicates motive. An iron object (v. 16), a stone (v. 17), or a piece of wood (v. 18) is considered a weapon. The use of such instruments indicates motive to kill. Thus anyone who kills another person with one of these objects is guilty of intentional homicide. Second, motive must be examined independently of weapons. Thus, if someone kills another simply with the fist and it is determined that it was done out of hatred or enmity, then that person is guilty of murder (vv. 20-21). The procedure to be followed in cases of murder is stated in v. 19: The guilty person must be executed by the avenger of blood.

Verses 22-28 describe instances of unintentional homicide. Accidental death through pushing or while working with stone (v. 22) requires a trial by the congregation. Even when the congregation determines that blood was shed unintentionally, there is no such thing as innocence. Absence of motive does not absolve someone from blood guilt. The procedure for unintentional homicide involves the cities of refuge, which function in two ways. First, they shelter persons guilty of shedding blood. Thus they become a type of prison, keeping those who have slain other humans from moving freely about the land. Second, they are places of refuge. Thus the slayer is rescued from the avenger of blood. But, if at any time the slayer leaves the city of refuge, he or she may be killed by the avenger of blood without penalty. The guilt of shedding blood unintentionally can be atoned for only by the high priest, upon whose death all persons guilty of unintentional homicide are atoned for. At that time, they are allowed to leave the city of refuge and return home.

35:29-34. The chapter concludes by stating that the rules surrounding homicide are confirmed civil law. The same designation of law is used with regard to the inheritance rights of the daughters of Zelophehad (27:11).

Three additions to the laws of homicide (vv. 30-32) and a theological grounding for all the laws in the chapter (vv. 33-35) are given. The first addition concerns witnesses. Verse 30 states that no one can be convicted of murder on the basis of only one witness; there must be two or more witnesses. The second concerns convicted murderers. Verse 31 states that no ransom is possible for convicted murderers under any circumstance; they must be executed. The third addition concerns those guilty of unintentional homicide. Verse 32 states that no person guilty of manslaughter is able to ransom an early release from a city of refuge before the death of the high priest. For priestly writers, money cannot atone for the shedding of human blood.

The rationale for the strict laws regarding homicide is provided in vv. 33-34: Blood pollutes the land. The story of Cain's murder of Abel illustrates vividly the polluting power of human blood on the land (Gen 4:10). God knows of Cain's act of murder because the ground screams when Abel's blood soaks into it. Thus murder is a violent act of cosmic proportions that cannot be reduced to mere finances. No monetary expiation is possible for any form of homicide. The debt of blood once shed requires the blood of the perpetrator. Finally, the laws of homicide are placed in the largest context possible: Murder is not simply an act of cosmic consequences, it also influences God, who has chosen to dwell in the land. Human blood that has been shed in the land and not accounted for through proper expiation can drive even God away.

36:1-13. The final chapter of the book of Numbers returns to a problem surrounding the inheritance of the daughters of Zelophehad, first addressed in 27:1-11. As a result, chaps. 27–36 are framed by the theme of the inheritance of daughters in the land. Inheritance in general has also been a central theme throughout the final section of the book. The theme of holy war in chaps. 31–33 emphasized Israel's claim on the land of Canaan, with the concluding paragraph (33:50-56) focusing clearly on the conquest of the land. Chap. 34 outlined the boundaries of land to be inherited, while chap. 35 underscored the danger of defiling the land through the shedding of blood. Chapter 36 returns to the topic of inheritance in order to emphasize the inalienable right of each tribe to dwell in the land.

36:1-4. The original claim of the daughters of Zelophehad in 27:1-11 was that their father had died without sons, thus threatening the family's right to inherit land. On the basis of this situation, they claimed the right to inherit in order to preserve the basic principle that possession of land was inalienable. Their claim is supported by God and extended by Moses (27:8-11) into case law. In the Commentary on 27:8-11, three principles were noted as undergirding the law that extends inheritance rights to daughters: (1) God owns the land; (2) divine ownership means that the land is a divine gift to Israel, whose status in the land is that of a tenant; and (3) each person's right to land is inalienable. As noted earlier, these principles are stated most clearly in the Jubilee law of Leviticus 25.

The daughters of Zelophehad are from the tribe of Manasseh. The leaders of that tribe now address Moses (vv. 1-4) to bring to light a problem in the case law of 27:8-11. The problem concerns intertribal marriage, particularly with daughters like those of Zelophehad, who have inherited land. Under the present law, their possession of land would be transferred to their husbands, in which case the tribe of Manasseh would lose part of its inheritance. In other words, by solving a problem of inheritance at the level of the family, Moses has created a new problem of inheritance at the level of the tribe. Reference to the law of Jubilee in v. 4 is used to confirm that the principle of inalienable rights is being contradicted. The tribal leaders state that at the time of Jubilee the land will permanently transfer to the husband's tribe. This reference to the Jubilee has puzzled commentators, because it applies to debts and not to inheritance (see Leviticus 25). Furthermore, one would expect that a strict application of the Jubilee law would return the land to the tribe of Manasseh. In any case, in Numbers 36 it is used to underscore that the land will leave the possession of the tribe of Manasseh, thus violating their right to inalienable possession.

36:5-12. Moses agrees and adds an addendum to his previous ruling from 27:8-11. The ruling is that daughters who inherit land must marry within their own tribe. Thus the principle of the inalienable right of possession of land by tribes is maintained: "No inheritance shall be transferred from one tribe to another." The section concludes by naming again the daughters of Zelophehad and by stating that they have fulfilled the new law; each has married within the clan of Manasseh.

36:13. The book of Numbers ends with a subscription, stating that the book contains divine commandments delivered to Moses on the plains of Moab. The subscription certainly provides a conclusion to the legislation on homicide in chap. 35 and on inheritance in chap. 36. But upon further analysis, it appears that the subscription is also intended to provide a conclusion to the book of Numbers. A similar subscription occurs at the end of Leviticus, in which Lev 27:34 states that it contains divine commandments presented by Moses at Mt. Sinai. Numbers uses the same conclusion, but changes the location to "the plains of Moab by the Jordan at Jericho." The book of Numbers ends with the promised land of Canaan in clear view of all the Israelites.

REFLECTIONS

1. The central message of Jesus is the good news of a new creation. The Gospel of Mark provides illustration: Jesus begins his ministry with the proclamation that the kingdom of God is near (Mark 1:15). Too often we interpret Jesus' mission as being directed solely at humans. Nothing could be further from the truth. The good news of salvation for humans, according to Jesus, arises in recognizing God's claim on creation and entering into the domain of God's rule. The kingdom of God does not exist solely in the human heart, nor is it limited to human relationships. It embraces the earth and all life within it. The substitution of kinship language for the kingdom of God in contemporary liturgy is well intended in its attempt to avoid overly sexist imagery, but it is an anthropocentric misreading of the gospel. The promise of salvation is much larger than God's relationship with us.

Jesus' proclamation of the kingdom of God is rooted in the message of the priestly writers at the close of the book of Numbers, where the focus rests on God's promise of the land. The priestly writers trace Israel's journey with God through the wilderness and follow its growth from one generation to the next. The promise of descendants explores the importance of Israel's relationship with God. But the goal of salvation in the book of Numbers is the promise of land. The story does not end with the census of the second generation in chapter 26. The promise of descendants alone does not complete the story of salvation history. The second generation still requires land.

The promise of land in the priestly history gives concreteness to salvation history. Numbers 34 even provides specific boundaries. Yet the overall structure of the priestly history suggests that the promise of land reaches out to include all creation. God's commitment to creation in priestly tradition is evident in Genesis 1, when all aspects of the world are judged to be good. The importance of creation for human salvation is made clear by priestly writers in their conclusion to the flood story, where God makes a covenant (Gen 9:1-17) never again to abandon the world through a flood because of the sin of humans. God's commitment to the creation provides the broader context and mission for interpreting Israel's journey with God. Jesus' proclamation of the kingdom of God is an extension of the priestly writers' vision of salvation.

2. The priestly writers' laws of homicide arise from their vision of a new creation. Life has sanctity, and blood defiles the earth. Life in God's land is intended to transform human relationships. All shedding of blood pollutes the land. No amount of money can atone for such bloodshed. Murder is far more than an act against society. It is a violation against creation, inducing a debt to the land. Even accidental death defiles the land. Not a single life is expendable in God's land, according to the priestly writers. Every death must be accounted for in the land economy of the priestly writers. We all understand debt in our contemporary capitalistic society. Our news media spend hours reporting on national debt, interest paid on inter-fund borrowing, trade deficits, and the like. Few of us are free from family or personal debt on property. Imagine our present debt to the earth in the priestly writers' economy of value. There are so many deaths daily in our cities that news organizations cannot report on all of them. With every violent death, we take another loan from the kingdom of God, according to the priestly writers, reducing our equity in God's salvation.

3. The Commentary indicated that asylum in ancient Israel was originally associated with the sanctuary altar. The basic premise of asylum, according to Jacob Milgrom, is "that those who touch the altar absorb its sanctity and are removed from and immune to the jurisdiction of the profane world."[206] The priestly writers remove asylum from the altar to designated cities, and they focus more particularly on sanctuary from blood vengeance. But the basic principle remains the same: Asylum suspended the normal practice of justice, allowing for evaluation by the congregation. Cities of refuge are difficult to translate into modern society, requiring theological reflection on the role of the church as a place of asylum in modern culture. Certainly redemption takes place in the church. but the social implications of redemption concerning asylum from national law are less clear. The sanctuary movement in North America, for example, provided asylum for migrants from the U.S. Immigration and Naturalization Service, prompting debate among church people whether the action was ethical. Regardless of one's position on this particular issue, the possibility of asylum is a reminder that the church can never be subsumed under the law of any nation-state.

4. The priestly description of levitical cities and of the entire land of Canaan is a vision between utopia and historical reality. Menahan Haran notes how the measurement of each city as an exact square of 2,000 cubits, the Jubilee legislation of release, and even the distinction between Aaronide priests and Levites conforms to an idealized theological program. But realism is mixed throughout. Levitical cities are dispersed away from the temple and even outside of the boundaries of Canaan, not what one might expect from a purely fictional story.[207] The result is that neither utopian fiction nor historical reality is allowed to outweigh the other. They are intertwined in the priestly writers' vision of the land, giving rise to two conclusions at the close of the book of Numbers. First, utopian imagery denotes that the story of Numbers is incomplete. Life in the land with God represents a new quality of life. It is an ideal to be reached at the end of the wilderness journey. Second, the realism of the priestly writers indicates that the ideal vision is obtainable in this world. Biblical writers offer the content of the book of Numbers as a manual for achieving life in the promised land.

206. Jacob Milgrom, *Numbers,* JPS Torah Commentary (Philadelphia: JPS, 1990) 504.
207. Menahem Haran, *Temples and Temple Service in Ancient Israel: An Inquiry into the Biblical Cult Phenomena and the Historical Setting of the Priestly School* (Winona Lake: Eisenbrauns, 1985) 122-29.

THE BOOK OF DEUTERONOMY

INTRODUCTION, COMMENTARY, AND REFLECTIONS
BY
RONALD E. CLEMENTS

THE BOOK OF
DEUTERONOMY

INTRODUCTION

THE BOOK AND ITS LITERARY SETTING

The Contents of the Book. Deuteronomy is the fifth book of the Hebrew Bible and is ascribed to Moses, making it the concluding book, or scroll, of the Pentateuch. Its title, which derives from the Greek (Septuagint, or LXX) text of Deut 17:18, indicates that it is a "second law." The title is wholly appropriate, since it describes the law given by Moses in the plains of Moab immediately prior to the crossing of the river Jordan and Israel's entry into the land promised to its ancestors, Abraham, Isaac, and Jacob. It is, therefore, a "second law," or more precisely a second giving of the law that had first been given as the terms of the covenant concluded through the mediation of Moses on Mt. Sinai between the Lord as God and the people of Israel, immediately after their deliverance from slavery in Egypt.

Although it contains two main collections of legal, or quasi-legal, material, the book of Deuteronomy is much more than a book of law. The first of these collections is set out in Deut 5:6-21, where the Ten Commandments are repeated from their first disclosure in Exod 20:2-17. The second collection is to be found in chapters 12–26 and contains an extensive collection of laws and legislative prescriptions (concerning, for example, how law is to be administered). The relationship between the Ten Commandments and the laws of chapter 26 has remained a very important issue for the understanding of the book and its background.

In addition to these collections of commandments and laws there is a narrative beginning in chapters 1–3 that summarizes the story of Israel's life in the wilderness from the first revelation on Mt. Sinai (which Deuteronomy consistently refers to as Mt. Horeb) to the time when the people were ready to launch their assault upon the promised land under Joshua. The narrative conclusion (chap. 34) tells of the death of Moses in the plains of Moab, before the crossing of the Jordan. In addition to this narrative framework there is a significant series of exhortations and warnings in chapters 6–11 and similar admonitory speeches, presented as blessings and curses, in chapters 27–28. Further hortatory addresses and poems in chapters 29–33 complete the framework of the law code. Scholars, therefore, have found it useful to distinguish between the "law code" of chapters 12–26 and the "framework" of chapters 1–11 and 27–34.

Sermon-like speeches and laws may at first appear as unlikely companions in a single literary work, but throughout there is a high level of consistency and homogeneity of style in Deuteronomy that makes it in general the most easily recognized of the entire OT. This closeness of stylistic presentation does not point to one single author, but to a particular group of writers, preachers, and reformers who shared a consistency of purpose that has created a work of coherence, clarity, and intense passion. The writers very evidently set out to compose a comprehensive guidebook for Israel to live as the people of the LORD God.

The Form and Forms of the Book. When we inquire as to the overall form and character of the book, the overall title of "law" proves to be inadequate. Deuteronomy describes its own chief contents as being composed of "law" (תורה *tôrâ*, "instruction," "directive," "guidance") and further defines this as being made up of "decrees, statutes, and ordinances" (Deut 4:44). Certainly there are laws, such as would appear in a statute book for the handling of criminal cases, which are present in the book, but there is much else besides. Moreover, many of the so-called laws are in the nature of religious regulations; some are ethical directives concerning good behavior in the home and in society in general, and some are institutional directives for setting up governmental organizations. Besides all these there are regulations controlling family law and custom. If we seek a comprehensive term to describe what is to be found in the book, then "polity" is almost certainly the most helpful term.

From a formal perspective, there is a surprising shift between the high prominence given to Moses in the framework, particularly in chapters 1–11, and in the lack of reference to Moses in the law code of chapters 12–26, apart from being referred to by inference in the regulation concerning prophecy in Deut 18:18. This accords with the very marked rhetorical style of the exhortations of the framework and the more crisp style of the law code. Obviously the authors of the finished book have drawn material from different sources over an extended period of time. Although they have imposed a general level of stylistic and theological consistency on the work, this variety in the different types of material and its varied origins still shows through.

If the subject matter of the book can best be described as declaring a national "polity" for Israel,[1] extending from constitutional permission for a monarchy (Deut 17:14-20) to rules of personal hygiene in a military encampment (Deut 23:12-14), then its form can

---

1. S. Dean McBride, "Polity of the Covenant People: The Book of Deuteronomy," *Int* 41 (1987) 229-44.

best be described as "preached law."[2] It is law only in a modified sense, however, since it is addressed to an entire nation, even demanding that its most important requirements be taught to children (Deut 6:7) and making use of a high degree of exhortation and rhetorical persuasion. Even specific laws that call for precise and careful definition are sometimes supplemented by exhortations to observe them for religious reasons (e.g., in showing generosity to former slaves, Deut 15:12-18).

The formal legal parts of the book can be usefully compared with earlier formulations of laws covering similar cases, most particularly in the law code of Exod 20:22–23:19, which has come to be described as "the book of the covenant" (cf. Exod 24:7). This older law code can clearly be seen to have been available to the authors of the laws of Deuteronomy, who can be shown to have based many of their own rulings on it.[3]

The form of the Ten Commandments has a distinctiveness all its own and requires to be considered separately for its importance in regard to the origins both of these commandments and of the book of Deuteronomy.

The law code proper of chapters 12–26 necessarily invites comparison with the form and structure of comparable law codes of the ancient Near East. The similarities and the contrasts are both worthy of close attention and can be considered in connection with the introduction to that code.

The speeches of warning and exhortation ascribed to Moses are distinctive in their style and represent the most marked and characteristically "deuteronomic" feature of the book. Whoever the authors were, it is evident that they were accomplished speakers and preachers. A further aspect of the form of the book as a whole relates to the possibility that ancient Near Eastern treaty forms, themselves originally secular in character, may have been employed by its authors to shape the work.[4] While not in itself implausible, at most the extent of this influence would appear to be limited to the introduction of the blessing and curse formulas of chapters 27–29 and will be considered in that connection. Beyond this, support for the assumption of the influence of ancient Near Eastern treaty forms is chiefly in the awareness that the book of Deuteronomy displays many affinities in its forms and vocabulary with the bureaucratic language and conventions of a state administrative circle.

Deuteronomy in the Old Testament. Deuteronomy now appears as the fifth and final book of the five books of Moses that make up the Pentateuch (Genesis–Deuteronomy). In Jewish tradition, all of them are ascribed to the authorship of Moses, and they form the first, and most foundational, part of the canon of the Hebrew Bible. Taken as a whole, they provide the basis for the heirs of Abraham, who are also viewed as persons bound in covenant to the LORD God through the revelation given through Moses on Mt. Sinai (Horeb), to govern their lives as the people of God.

2. G. von Rad, *Studies in Deuteronomy,* trans. D. Stalker, SBT 9 (London: SCM, 1953) 11-24

3. Cf. E. Otto, *Theologische Ethik des Alten Testaments* (Stuttgart: W. Kohlhammer, 1994) 18-31.

4. See J. G. McConville, *Law and Theology in Deuteronomy,* JSOTSup 33 (Sheffield: JSOT, 1984). A more cautious and critical position is presented by Dennis J. McCarthy, *Treaty and Covenant,* AnBib 21A (Rome: Pontifical Biblical Institute, 1978) 157-205.

However, so extensive a work as the Pentateuch was certainly not written at one period of history and by one writer alone. It has been brought together from a variety of source documents and traditions in order to present the fullest and most basic constitution of Israel. Within this great anthology, which shows many features of being a "collection of collections," Deuteronomy is neither the earliest nor the latest to have been composed, even though it now forms the last of the five books. Rather, it stands very much as a midpoint, and even a balance point, for the Pentateuch as a whole.

Because Deuteronomy has such a distinctive style and lays down such precise and specific requirements over a number of major issues relating to worship, it has proved helpful in enabling scholars to identify (within certain limits) what is "pre-deuteronomic" from what is "post-deuteronomic." It is not surprising, therefore, that in the course of critical biblical scholarship, which has sought to trace, as far as possible, the main lines of the literary growth of the Pentateuch, the attention to Deuteronomy has been very pronounced. It represents a kind of center, both for the literary composition of the Pentateuch and for the development of Israel's religious life.

Seen in such a light, the book of Deuteronomy, or at least some major part of it, can be said to have once formed an independent work that was later joined to other writings, before finally being given its present position. Whereas we might have expected that these other writings would have been the other books of the Pentateuch, the majority opinion among present-day scholars is that this was certainly not the case. It was instead first joined with the six historical books of Joshua–2 Kings, which in the Hebrew canon make up the Former Prophets (Joshua, Judges, 1–2 Samuel, 1–2 Kings). As a consequence, it has become a widespread scholarly practice to refer to these six books as "the deuteronomic (or deuteronomistic) history" because they explicitly presuppose a tradition of divinely given law by which events and persons are judged. This law, which is sometimes explicitly referred to as a law book, is clearly a body of the laws contained in Deuteronomy. There is also a consensus to accept that the first three chapters of Deuteronomy were composed in order to provide an introduction to this large work, comprising both law book and historical narrative. At most, some parts of Deuteronomy 1–3 may have provided a much more brief introduction to the original deuteronomic law book before it was combined with the history.

During the post-exilic period, the deuteronomic writings were supplemented by a large body of additional material, consisting partly of narrative and partly of additional rulings of a priestly and ritual character. This additional material has usually been described as belonging to a priestly (or P) documentary source, although much of it may actually have been incorporated piecemeal into a combined work. Essentially the Pentateuch can be seen to have been composed of the combined deuteronomic and priestly material, together with such earlier (pre-deuteronomic) traditions as had been preserved in conjunction with Deuteronomy.

At this stage, the book of Deuteronomy was separated from the history of the Former

Prophets, of which it had at one time been a part, to constitute a separate work that is our present Pentateuch. This contains all the essential traditions and rulings governing the existence and life of Israel as the people of the LORD God, given before Israel entered the promised land. Within this immensely formative document, Deuteronomy can readily be seen to have a most important place. In terms of religious ideas and practice, it marks the first great comprehensive stage in the collecting, harmonizing, and unifying of regulations governing Israelite belief and practice. It represents, therefore, a primary stage in the formation of the Hebrew canon, or "rule," of faith, even though the term as such is not used. Nevertheless, all the main features of defining, controlling, and focusing faith and practice, which later the provision of a scriptural canon sought to supply, are evident in Deuteronomy. It can justifiably be regarded, therefore, as providing a center for the Pentateuch and for the Hebrew Bible as a whole.

In addition to the links between Deuteronomy and the historical books of the Former Prophets, it is also important to note that there are significant contacts between Deuteronomy and the prophecies of Jeremiah. At one time these were explained in terms of an influence, either from the prophet Jeremiah upon the authors of the law book, or vice versa. If the deuteronomic law book, with its distinctive preaching style, were part of a contemporary tradition that the prophet Jeremiah was familiar with, then it could be argued that Jeremiah sometimes made use of this high-flown rhetorical style.

However, all such explanations must now be set aside in favor of a more literary, but potentially more complex, explanation for such noteworthy contacts between a prophet and the authors of a law book. Certainly the evidence that these contacts provide is important for determining the date of Deuteronomy, but their origin can be explained in a rather different fashion from supposing that a direct influence of a prophet upon lawmakers took place. The use of the so-called deuteronomic style in the book of Jeremiah, which is in reality more a matter of a distinctive vocabulary and a distinctive set of theological ideas than a matter of style in the technical sense, is not uniformly present throughout the book. It appears particularly in the narrative sections and in a series of homilies on specific themes and topics. The reason for the presence of these homilies and for the use of this narrative style is to be found in the fact that the extant book of Jeremiah has come down to us in a deuteronomic dress. It has, in fact, been edited in circles that stood close to the authors of Deuteronomy.

Taken overall, therefore, we can identify a situation in which, besides the book of Deuteronomy, the scribes who produced the final form of the history of Joshua–2 Kings and the extant written version of the prophecies of Jeremiah were all deeply influenced by the belief in a Mosaic law given by Moses in the plains of Moab. The law book of Deuteronomy can then be seen to provide an excellent viewpoint for understanding one of the most formative periods in the development of Israel's faith and of the formation of a central part of the biblical literature.

THE CHARACTER OF DEUTERONOMY

Having drawn attention to what has been described as the style of the deuteronomic authors, it is now possible to consider what precisely this style consisted of.[5] In a broad sense, the features that mark a particular author, or group of authors, have to do with the way in which ideas are presented so that the literary purpose is achieved. We can infer the purpose of the authors of Deuteronomy with considerable confidence. It was first and foremost to define a pattern of conduct, especially religious conduct, which was regarded as conforming to the terms of the covenant the LORD God had made with Israel. Such conduct required especially single-minded and exclusive allegiance to worship the LORD God alone. No other God was to be set alongside this one deity, nor was any form of image or physical representation of any god, even of the LORD, to be tolerated. In accordance with this purpose, sacrificial worship was to be restricted to one location only, which the LORD God would signify. Sanctuaries, cult objects, and religious practices pertaining to other gods and goddesses were all banned and condemned to be actively destroyed. A particular program of festivals was further defined as appropriate to the worship of the LORD God.

Alongside this very stringent code of religious practice was placed a related, and interwoven, code of moral and social behavior, which was partly defined in terms of dealing with criminal behavior through an established, although rather mixed, legal administration. Much further than this, however, were many rules governing family life, military commitments, and commercial dealings that were all intended to bear the stamp of the covenant made between the LORD and Israel.

If defining what God's covenant implied was the primary purpose of the book of Deuteronomy, in parallel with it went the goal of persuading the readers of the book of the rightness and necessity of this. To this end a highly developed rhetorical style of speech is employed, marked by long parentheses, many repetitions, and a strong probing into questions of motive and attitude that search the hearts of the reader. The psychology of faith is richly explored, more so than anywhere else in the entire Bible, with constant appeals to remember, not to forget, to avoid self-satisfied complacency, and to bear constantly in mind the deceitfulness of the human heart. The overall evaluation that the deuteronomic authors place upon the goodwill and good intentions of their readers is not high! They are assumed to be prone to disloyalty, as the deuteronomic authors insist their ancestors had been.

In line with this rich and often intensely passionate appeal to religious loyalty and steadfastness is a deep feeling that Israel is one single people throughout all its generations. The chosen setting in which the laws and exhortations of the book are given is that of Israel, standing poised in the plains of Moab and waiting to cross the river Jordan to take possession of the land. Yet, the author is fully aware that this was a generation that lay in

5. See the comprehensive survey in M. Weinfeld, *Deuteronomy and the Deuteronomic School* (Oxford: Oxford University Press, 1972) 320-65.

the very distant past, so that the fiction of such a time and place is only thinly maintained. The reality that Israel has long been in the land and that its experience there has often been painful and distressing is frequently evident in the book. Yet, the author uses extensively the phrase "all Israel" and views the passing of the generations as a fact that changes nothing concerning the way in which Israel stands face to face before God. The "here and now" of the authors is both the situation recognized for the readers and that which is selected for the setting of the speeches and laws given through Moses. Moreover, even this collapsing of the interval of time between the generation that first awaited entry into the land and that of the readers is stretched further to embrace the generation that stood at the foot of Mt. Horeb to whom Moses first brought the tablets of law. Israel is one people, and this oneness stretches laterally across all twelve of its member tribes and vertically through its generations.

It is in the rhetorical flourishes and insights into human psychology that the distinctiveness of the deuteronomic vocabulary shows itself most markedly. This is what we should expect, since the defining of behavior requisite to the careful formulation of laws was necessarily governed by the subject matter dealt with. However, alongside the distinctive vocabulary of this preaching style there is also a very evident theological vocabulary relating to the way in which Israel is regarded as being bound to the LORD God and, therefore, must repudiate the forms of illicit religion through which the people have been tempted. These religious traditions, which are ascribed to the former occupants of the land, are regarded as particularly alluring and contrary to the attitude of mind that is appropriate to true worship. So we find that the concept of covenant, the dangers of idolatry, the persistence of the worship of the Baals and Asherah, and the importance of gratitude as an essential component of serving God all stand prominently in view within the deuteronomic horizon.

Whether we consider the topic from a theological, a historical, a political, or a sociological perspective, the subject of the land that had been promised to the ancestors of Israel—Abraham, Isaac, and Jacob—is of paramount significance.[6] The primary gift of God to Israel under the terms of the covenant is this land. Consequently, the most serious consequence of disobeying the terms of the covenant is threatened as the loss of this land and the possibility of being expelled from it.

However, besides these broad theological and literary features that characterize Deuteronomy, there are other features that are of great interest to the careful reader. Not least among these is the contribution that Deuteronomy makes to the knowledge and evaluation of the development of a system of law in ancient Israel. The fact that it is possible to compare closely the text of the deuteronomic laws with those made earlier in the Book of the Covenant makes it possible to see how new questions had arisen in legal administration and how this had been progressively improved and elaborated. Conversely,

---

6. L. Perlitt, "Motive und Schichten der Landtheologie im Deuteronomium," *Deuteronomium-Studien* (Tübingen: J. C. B. Mohr, 1994) 97-108.

several features of the deuteronomic law code reveal that this administration had displayed shortcomings and serious limitations. Furthermore, the fact that, in some cases, later versions of rulings dealing with essentially the same problem are also preserved in the latest parts of the Pentateuch enable us to construct a valuable chronology of legal and ethical development.

THE DATE OF DEUTERONOMY

A question that has loomed prominently in the modern study of the book of Deuteronomy concerns the question of the date at which it was written. In 2 Kings 22–23, the biblical historian recounts how a "book of the law," which was subsequently identified as "the law of the covenant between God and Israel" (2 Kgs 22:11–23:3), was found in the Temple during renovations in the reign of King Josiah (639–609 BCE). This led to an extensive cultic reform in which a complete destruction of the ancient sanctuary of Bethel took place and many of the old Canaanite rural shrines were destroyed in order to centralize sacrificial worship exclusively in Jerusalem. Since the work of the great nineteenth-century biblical scholar W. M. L. de Wette, this law book has been identified with some part, if not the whole, of the book of Deuteronomy. For a time, there was something of a scholarly consensus that the law book thus rediscovered was probably only the law code of Deuteronomy 12–26. Such conclusions must now certainly be substantially modified.

In the present reconsideration of the issues, the value of this piece of historical criticism has been heavily undermined by the recognition that the account of how the law book was discovered is clearly an attempt by the biblical historian to introduce to the reader the law book of Deuteronomy. The story is itself, therefore, a part of the deuteronomic character of the presentation of history in 1–2 Kings and by itself neither confirms nor denies that the book of Deuteronomy was composed somewhere close to that time.[7]

The report of the discovery of the law book in Josiah's time, then, is relevant to an understanding of the date of origin of the book of Deuteronomy, but does not settle the issue. In reality it never could have done, since it leaves unclear how much older the law book was at the time when it was rediscovered. Nor does it explain what part or form of the book of Deuteronomy was given a new life at this time.

Some parts of Deuteronomy cannot have been written as early as King Josiah's reign, since they make allusion to the disasters that befell Jerusalem in the sixth century BCE (e.g., Deut 29:21-28). Other parts could be, and have frequently been held to be, considerably older. Much depends, then, on which part of Deuteronomy is being discussed when the question of time of composition is under consideration. Too much has been built on the assumption that the law code of chapters 12–26 was significantly older in its complete form than the framework of chapters 1–11 and 27–34. The position adopted in

7. See E. Würthwein, "Die Josianische Reform und das Deuteronomium" *ZTK* 73 (1976) 395-423.

the present commentary is that the original law code on which the present code was based almost certainly did originate in Josiah's reign, but that this has been extensively revised and added to in the wake of the disasters that overtook Judah in the sixth century BCE.

Overall the question of the date at which the book was composed must be regarded as dependent in part on a careful analysis of the various component sections and layers that are evident within the book. Neither the law code of chapters 12–26, nor the book as a whole was composed at a stroke and at one time.

Of great significance is the question of how much of the book was composed after the disastrous events that overtook the kingdom of Judah at the hands of the Babylonian forces at the beginning of the sixth century. Some reflections of these events are evident in the book, although they have frequently been held to be present only in the concluding parts of the framework. The view adopted here is that these events are far more strongly reflected than this and have deeply influenced several major features of Deuteronomy. Most prominent are the demand for cult centralization, the greatly weakened role ascribed to the king, the desacralizing of several aspects of the cultus, and most probably the overall awareness that, in the future, the true Israelite who is loyal to the covenant will be dependent on a written law for guidance. If this is the case, then a great deal of the spiritual character and strategy that have contributed to making the book of Deuteronomy what it is are a consequence of what happened to Judah at the beginning of the sixth century BCE.

However, this does not properly settle the issue of the date of Deuteronomy as a written document. Those scholars are undoubtedly correct who have recognized that some form of connection exists between the book and the steps taken by King Josiah in the late seventh century to reform worship around Jerusalem. The relationship is more oblique, however, than has often been assumed, and in signficant measure the book of Deuteronomy in its final form must be regarded as a long-term product of the reforms initiated by Josiah, rather than simply the prompting cause of those reforms.

After the breakup of the united Israelite kingdom at Solomon's death, the divided kingdoms of Israel and Judah pursued separate paths and eventually the northern kingdom fell prey to Assyrian intervention by the end of the eighth century. Judah survived, though at the cost of painful and humiliating submission to Assyrian demands that only slackened when, by the middle of the seventh century, the Mesopotamian influence weakened. Josiah's measures were essentially an attempt to rebuild a united kingdom of Israel, with its capital in Jerusalem and under a Davidic king, along the lines that tradition credited to David and Solomon.

Josiah was only partially successful in achieving his goal, and his death in battle in 609 BCE set a limit to further restoration of the ideal kingdom of "all Israel." In these reforms, clearly the role of the Davidic monarchy had of necessity been significantly curtailed, since it was the excessive impositions of the monarchy under Solomon that had brought about the earlier breakup (1 Kgs 12:4). However, the relief from Assyrian control in Judah proved to be only short-lived, and Babylonian power swiftly replaced it, thereby putting an end to the belief that God had spared and preserved Jerusalem during the preceding centuries for the sake of Jerusalem and the Davidic kingship.

The disastrous events that brought a fearful siege and eventual surrender of Jerusalem to the Babylonians in 598 and again in 587 BCE ended with the destruction of the Temple in Jerusalem and the removal of the last of the Davidic kings from his Jerusalem throne. All of these events form part of the background to the composition of the book of Deuteronomy and are, in varied ways, reflected in its pronouncements and exhortations. What was left of the old kingdom of Israel, which Josiah had sought to restore and revive, now found itself in ruins. The people were once again in a situation closely akin to that chosen by the author of Deuteronomy for the setting of the book. They stood at the borders of the land, sorely stricken by military defeats that seemed to defy explanation and in danger of losing altogether their sense of nationhood, of commitment to the LORD as God, and of any direction as to how to prepare for a difficult future. More than at any other period in its history the threat of a return to the "old gods" of the land presented Israel with a temptation and appeal that were almost irresistible.

The book of Deuteronomy, together with its supporting historical and prophetic writings, is a magnificent response to this situation of political and religious crisis. It is a serious review of Israel's past and a challenge to renew commitment and loyalty to God and to look for the time when a new Israel would take shape and the land would once again belong to those who had kept faith with the God who gave it.

THE AUTHORS OF THE BOOK

The Authors and Their Interests. To some extent the answers that we have sought to provide to the date of the book go some way toward also answering the question concerning who the authors were. If they were persons who were active over a period of more than a century, then clearly they represented not simply a small interest group that emerged at one moment of crisis, but a movement that retained momentum for a significant length of time. We can best seek to track down more fully who they were from the particular interests they reveal in the book they have left.

Among such interests we can certainly place the high premium they set on the commitment to an exclusive worship of the LORD God alone. No image was to be tolerated of any kind, and no other God was to be set alongside this one deity. That this falls short of an absolute monotheism in which the very existence of any other God is altogether denied may be admitted, but nevertheless the portrayal that is made of such deities is so negative and derisive in its tone as to present them as powerless nonentities that deserve little more than contempt. Certainly the deuteronomic doctrine of God contributed greatly to the emergence of a more fully explicit monotheism in subsequent biblical writings.[8]

It is unlikely that this movement, which aimed at worshiping "the LORD alone,"

8. Cf. N. Lohfink, "Gott im Buch Deuteronomium," *Studien zum Deuteronomium und zur deuteronomistischen Literatur* II, SBA 12 (Stuttgart: Katholisches Bibelwerk, 1991) 25-53.

originated among these deuteronomic authors. It certainly found support among several of the eighth-century prophets, and it seems likely that this prophetic influence was an important factor. But so, too, were the political crises that had beset Israel during the eighth century, when the incursions from Mesopotamia effectively broke up the temporary stability that had left the Levant to sort out its own affairs, looking chiefly to Egypt as the major external power to be reckoned with.

The very concept of a law book, the markedly literate social world the book presumes, and the polished rhetorical style, which shares many features in common with the Israelite tradition of wisdom,[9] point us also to recognize that the authors of Deuteronomy had close links with the royal administration, where education flourished. Certainly this must have been the Jerusalem court, even though the general tenor of the deuteronomic attitude to kingship is certainly not that of an ardent pro-Davidic court circle. Many of its most marked features represent a strong expression of antipathy to the high-flown and exaggerated court style of the royal psalms, with their mythological coloring for the place of the king in the world of lesser mortals.

Strongly supportive of the conclusion that the deuteronomic authors themselves stood close to the circles of power that hovered around the king is the fact that the authors of this law book display every confidence in their ability to control the administration of the nation. King Josiah had assumed the throne in Jerusalem as a mere boy, placed there by those described as "the people of the land" (2 Kgs 21:23-24). In particular the control of legal affairs, the expectation of enforcing new legal rulings, combined with the assumption of a right to speak for "all Israel," points to a circle of patrician and skilled administrators.

A further feature of the deuteronomic legislation is to be found in its interest in the cultus and in the levitical priesthood. This has led several scholars to look to a circle of levitical priests, or ex-priests, as the authors of Deuteronomy, perhaps drawn from among those who had been forced from their duties and service in sanctuaries during the eighth-century incursions of Assyria. Yet, overall the intellectual outlook and concern of the book are not priestly. It is, on the contrary, very distinctively non-mystical and unsympathetic to the ideas of priestly cultic power, redolent of a holiness that could kill, which echoes in several of the priestly (P) sections of the Pentateuch.[10] It seems certain that the authors of Deuteronomy were not traditional priests, even though they recognized the value and authority of the services that Israel's priests performed.

Taken together, all of these considerations point to the recognition that the authors of Deuteronomy are unlikely to have belonged to any one professional class. If this were the case, then they have contrived to show a considerable knowledge, not only of governmental administration, but also of ideas that were current among both the prophetic and the priestly circles current in Judah during the seventh and sixth centuries BCE. This is by no means impossible. Nevertheless, if we think in terms of a deuteronomic movement,

9. M. Weinfeld, *Deuteronomy and the Deuteronomic School* (Oxford: Oxford University Press, 1972) 244-81.
10. Ibid., 282-97.

encouraged and inspired by the strong nationalistic and Yahwistic faith that arose in the wake of the humiliations and sufferings inflicted by Assyria, then we shall certainly be close to the truth. Since, in any case, we know and understand the aims and thinking of the deuteronomic authors from the literature that they have given to us, it is perhaps of only limited value to endeavor to define more precisely who they were. For the most part they remain anonymous, although it is tempting to speculate from the names of men linked with King Josiah, and later the prophet Jeremiah, who may have been among their number.

Deuteronomy and the Northern Kingdom. One of the features of the book of Deuteronomy that has repeatedly attracted the attention of biblical scholars is the extent to which it shows familiarity with, and even a strong empathy with, traditions that appear to have originated within the old northern, or Ephraimite, kingdom of Israel. This region had broken from any allegiance to the Davidic monarchy when Rehoboam became king, and it was effectively dismembered as a political entity at the end of the eighth century BCE by Assyrian intrusion and territorial realignments, including mass deportations of sections of the population.

Scholars as distinct as A. C. Welch,[11] Albrecht Alt,[12] and G. von Rad[13] have drawn attention to different features of the book that show a stong link to territorial, political, and religious aspects of the dismembered northern kingdom. But they have not agreed as to what these northern interests are. More recently, the commentary by E. Nielsen[14] has added further support for such a conclusion. Josiah clearly had political ambitions to regain as much of this lost territory as it was possible to achieve and to restore it to a reborn kingdom of a united Israel. That he was only partially successful in doing so does not weaken the insight that this had been a prime goal he sought to achieve.

The insights gained from this can all too readily be overpressed. In particular, we must conclude that many aspects of the book are to be traced to the devastating effect that Babylonian interventions in Judah at the beginning of the sixth century had upon the veneration for the Davidic dynasty of kings and the Jerusalem Temple. Josiah's reform had encouraged hope that a new era of prosperity for Israel was about to dawn. Now the discrediting of an overconfident and complacent faith in both the Temple and the kingship demanded a major reappraisal of them. It is this reappraisal, and not the resurgence of old northern Israelite traditions, that is most prominent in the deuteronomic legislation.

Nevertheless, set in a guarded perspective, it seems evident that the deuteronomic ambition to present a legislative program that was designed for, and acceptable to, "all Israel" was genuine enough. It could not hope to achieve this by simply retaining the excessive Judahite claims that had first broken the kingdoms apart in the tenth century. It would appear, then, that the deuteronomic movement did not ultimately prevail to

11. A. C. Welch, *The Code of Deuteronomy: A New Theory of Its Origin* (London: Nisbet, 1924).

12. A. Alt, "Die Heimat des Deuteronomiums," *Kleine Schriften zur Geschichte des Volkes Israel II* (Munich: C. H. Beck, 1953) 250-75.

13. G. von Rad, *Deuteronomy,* OTL (Philadelphia: Westminster, 1966).

14. E. Nielsen, *Deuteronomium,* HAT I/6 (Tübingen: J. C. B. Mohr, 1995).

establish the final form of the Mosaic Torah. More cult-oriented traditions, almost certainly originating in a central circle of the Jerusalem priestly aristocracy, acquired new impetus and dominance in the post-exilic period. Fundamental, therefore, as the deuteronomic movement was in establishing the central lines of the post-exilic Jewish faith, the final definition of this called for a noticeably different tradition from that of Deuteronomy to be added to it, and in substantial measure to overlay it.

Moses in the Book of Deuteronomy. It is a feature of the book that cannot easily be overlooked that it is prominently presented as the product and teaching of Moses. In chapters 1–11 and again in 31–34, this great leader of Israel's formative beginnings dominates the scene. Not only is much of the book presented under the form of a speech of Moses, but also his figure is set in the forefront of faith. To a remarkable extent he is presented as a man who stands over against the great majority of his people. He is a leader, and they need to be led. His faith contrasts with their mean-spiritedness. He is a person of prayer, but they are faithless and full of complaints. He is for going on, when they are for going back. It is not simply that Moses stands between the people and God, as a chosen mediator would inevitably do, but that he is of a different temper and insight from all of them. In heeding the words of Moses, the people of Israel are assured that they will be drawing inspiration from the most worthy of sources.

Certainly the earlier traditions of Israel's origins had given a significant role to Moses as the one who had led the people out of slavery in Egypt, but none of this material had placed so high a valuation upon his person. He is a figure of faith in a way that shows a remarkable new sensitivity concerning what is needed in such a person. He appears as the most worthy of national leaders.

There is no easy, simple explanation of why the deuteronomic authors display so great an interest in Moses. In part it can be seen as a consequence of the feeling of leaderless malaise that the deuteronomic authors diagnosed as part of their nation's ills. They needed a new Moses! Yet this is not sufficient to explain such a prominent new interest in this historic figure. Certainly it cannot be traced to the belief that the authors of the book held any specific professional attachment to Moses, either as a prophet or a priest, for they do not place any significant emphasis on either task, even though Moses is more prophet than priest. Rather, it must lie chiefly in the feeling of disillusionment with the institution of kingship, and in particular with the kings who were of the dynasty of David. They had promised much and had, in the person of Josiah, given cause for hope that the LORD God would once again hold all nations in derision before the power vested in the chosen scion of the house of David (see Ps 2:4-11). This had proved to be a tragically misguided faith, as even those who had placed great confidence in the ambitions of Josiah and his less honorable successors found out so tragically (see 2 Kgs 23:29-30).

We must also recognize that there is present in all the deuteronomic literature a refreshing, if sometimes startling, consciousness that all human institutions are no more than human. Claims to divinity or to possess unlimited access to divine power, when vested in any human being become a serious threat to fundamental features of human society. So the deuteronomic authors put more trust in law than in lawmakers, and more in God than in human beings.

They also shared a remarkably insightful and commendable awareness of the way in which human beings are easily led. The markedly dismissive portrait they present of the contemporaries of Moses, with very few exceptions, reveals much of this social awareness that all human leaders seem readily capable of commanding a following, even when leading their people astray. Accordingly, by presenting the true ideal of human leadership in a figure of the past, who is forthrightly declared to have been more cognizant of the divine ways than any other (Deut 34:10-12), the deuteronomists establish a firm role model through whom all other expressions of human leadership are to be judged. In painting such a picture of the great leader of the nation, they reinforce their claims that the Mosaic law deserves the most urgent and undeviating attention.

DEUTERONOMY IN JEWISH AND CHRISTIAN TRADITION

Deuteronomy in the Hebrew Bible and in Jewish Tradition. To a quite remarkable degree the book of Deuteronomy establishes a standard for the interpretation of the entire Hebrew Bible. This is not surprising, since it is in Deuteronomy that we first hear defined the content of the Mosaic teaching as *torah*. Subsequently, such a title has been employed to characterize the entire contents of the Pentateuch and to establish its essential purpose. Its English translation as "law," by means of its ancient Greek and Latin counterparts, has meant that from a Jewish perspective the entire biblical tradition is understood to consist of law. That it could equally well have been translated as "instruction" or "guidance" is undoubtedly true, although had this been the case the note of authority that has so characterized its reception in Judaism (and Christianity) would certainly have been much reduced.

Moreover, as has already been noted, the fact that the deuteronomic law expresses a development of an earlier code of laws and was itself subsequently used as the basis for yet further elaboration and clarification has meant that it provides a pattern for all subsequent Jewish biblical interpretation. The eventual formulation and publication of a code of Mishnah stands very much in a straight line with the idea that Deuteronomy itself represents a "second giving" of the law of God's covenant. If we are at all to understand the Jewish perspective on the interpretation of the biblical tradition, then we shall undoubtedly need to pay full attention to the fact that Deuteronomy presents its contents as *torah*, and what it implies by doing so.

Deuteronomy in New Testament Perspective. From a New Testament viewpoint, the book of Deuteronomy was clearly a work of immense importance as a central formative work that had shaped contemporary Jewish practice. Allusions to and citations from the book in the New Testament writings are to be found more frequently than is the case with any other Old Testament book. Moreover, it cannot be overlooked that the teaching of Jesus concerning the first, and most important, of all the commandments takes the form of a quotation from Deut 6:4-5 (see Luke 10:25-28). In a similar fashion, the story of the temptation of Jesus in the wilderness uses citations from Deuteronomy as the primary means for countering the suggestions made by Satan (Matt 4:1-11).

However, it is not simply in these specific key moments that the teaching of Deuteronomy has exercised a major influence on the New Testament tradition. More pervasively, it can be recognized that the inward psychologizing and spiritualizing of religious commitment, which is so marked a feature of the deuteronomic teaching, pervades the early Christian tradition. It is the inwardness of faith, the emphasis on attitude beside action, and the focus on love, obedience, and gratitude that have made the deuteronomic teaching so fundamental to New Testament faith.

Moreover, one of the significant aspects of the deuteronomic interpretation of a divine *torah* lies in the way it brings together religious, ethical, and social concerns under a single umbrella. It may be held to have desacralized religion, removing much of the mystical and quasi-magical notions of cultic power. As such it promotes a rather "secularized" interpretation of religious commitment. In another direction, however, it can be held to have spiritualized a wide range of everyday activities, spiritualizing their significance. It can be seen to have moralized and personalized ideas of religious loyalty to a remarkable degree. Not only is the individual called upon to respond to God in obedience, but also such obedience is made the subject of deep heart searching and self-examination. Without the teaching of Deuteronomy, it is hard to see how the religious and ethical arguments that characterize the conflicts between Jesus and his Jewish contemporaries could have arisen. From the perspective of grasping the nature of the New Testament and its reflection of Christian controversies with the contemporary Jewish tradition, a close study of the teaching of Deuteronomy becomes essential.

Deuteronomy in Historical and Ethical Perspective. What has been noted in regard to the place of Deuteronomy in Old and New Testament tradition has viewed it in a predominantly positive and constructive light. On any reckoning its influence in shaping the main lines of biblical tradition has been very strong. Yet, once it is viewed in a wider historical and ethical perspective, a number of serious questions arise that can only be answered negatively.[15] Most prominent in this regard is the uncompromising vehemence with which Deuteronomy demands the wholesale extermination of all ethnic and religious communities that had occupied the land prior to the Israelite conquest. Moreover the very assumption that Israel could be the beneficiary of a divinely given entitlement to conquer, repress, and exterminate an entire population in order to gain possession of their land undermines the many richer ethical and spiritual insights the book contains.[16] It reflects deeply upon not only the concept of Israel as a people of God, but also on the understanding of God that it exemplifies.

15. See F. E. Deist, "The Dangers of Deuteronomy: A Page from the Reception History of the Book," in *Studies in Deuteronomy in Honour of C. J. Labuschagne,* ed. F. Garcia Martinez et al. (Leiden: E. J. Brill, 1994) 13-30.
16. Cf. Susan Niditch, *Warfare in the Hebrew Bible* (New York: Oxford University Press, 1994).

From a historical perspective, therefore, the influence of Deuteronomy has been far from uniform and not at all consistently helpful. That there are inherent dangers and defects in its teaching must be frankly reckoned with. Certainly we can moderate this ethical criticism of the book with the help of two important provisos, neither of which adequately resolves the problems raised.

The first of these provisos concerns the fact that the book is an uneven composition; it has many strands. The stratum of legislative demand that calls for the extermination of all the previous occupants of the land and the death penalty for any Israelite who tolerates or encourages the perpetuation of their religion stands alongside much more tolerant and humane considerations for the weak and the oppressed. Even informing on one's neighbor is encouraged if religious loyalty is at stake (Deut 13:6-11). To this extent, the punishment demanded for those who presume to practice the religions of Baal and Asherah and the other traditions of the land's previous occupants stands in contrast with a more considered awareness of the need to show consideration and compassion to the oppressed and to distinguish between distinct categories of foreign aliens (Deut 23:3-8). How and why the frenetic and cruel demand for a rigid exclusivism in promoting the worship of the LORD alone was to be applied in the light of the parallel concern for love and compassion is never adequately made clear from the book's contents. Presumably it was an attitude the authors felt to be necessary when the very survival of their religious tradition was under threat.

The second proviso concerns the fact that, in calling for the extermination of the previous inhabitants of the land, the book was undoubtedly propagating a historical anachronism. These peoples had long since ceased to retain any clear and separate ethnic identity, having undoubtedly largely been absorbed into the Israelite kingdom that flourished under David and Solomon. Yet this does not properly resolve the difficulty, since almost certainly the deuteronomic authors did have in mind a real contemporary community and its leaders, whom they regarded as enemies and who were believed to pose a danger to the program that they themselves were seeking to propagate. Thus we are left with the difficulty that, in seeking to promote a richly ethical and responsible interpretation of Israel's religious faith, the authors of Deuteronomy were prepared to recommend the most uncompromising and repressive measures. Sadly, the long history of humankind's subsequent religious conflicts has shown how many have been willing to follow that lead and have failed to set it under a necessary critical scrutiny.

A further critical perspective on the teaching of Deuteronomy is also a necessary part of the introduction to the book. From within the biblical tradition, one of its most innovative features has been its emphasis on the ideas of Israel's divine election, of its privileged covenant status in relationship to God, and of the many claims to advantage and power that this covenant relationship confers. In itself such teaching can be seen as an important step in seeking to theologize and rationalize the inherited ideas that flourished in the ancient world of competing national powers with national deities, each seeking advantage over others. In many respects the history of international conflict that characterized the ancient Near East during the half millennium from the days of David to the end of the Davidic monarchy witnessed the absurdity of such notions. The impetus toward monotheism and to a concept of one world rendered the belief in many competing gods totally obsolete.

So Deuteronomy stands apart from the confused and confusing picture of a world in which many gods fought for the allegiance of human beings. It moves strongly in the direction of a true monotheism. Yet in order to accommodate its national, as well as its more universal, concepts appropriate to belief in a deity who wielded supreme authority over the universe, it makes use of ideas that have themselves become fraught with danger. In spite of the high place given to the notion of a covenant between the supreme deity and human beings in Deuteronomy and the biblical tradition that drew from it, it remains a limiting and imperfect concept for the expression of religious ideas. All too readily conferred privileges, rather than the call to a spiritual obedience, have assumed the most prominent place, sometimes with disastrous consequences.

BIBLIOGRAPHY

Commentaries:

Craigie, P. C. *The Book of Deuteronomy.* NICOT. Grand Rapids: Eerdmans, 1976. Although rather strongly conservative in its literary and historical perspectives, this remains a useful and clearly written exposition.

Driver, S. R. *Deuteronomy.* 3rd ed. ICC. Edinburgh: T. & T. Clark, 1902. Very dated now in its critical assessments, but a classical work by an outstanding scholar; it is still indispensable for its comments on the Hebrew text and vocabulary of the book.

Mayes, A. D. H. *Deuteronomy.* NCB. London: Marshall, Morgan & Scott, 1979. An exposition from a modern critical perspective that gives an excellent account of the theological and literary developments in which Deuteronomy arose.

Miller, P. D. *Deuteronomy.* Interpretation. Louisville: Westminster John Knox, 1990. Written in nontechnical language and aimed at the preacher and general reader; places high emphasis on the ethical and religious issues raised by Deuteronomy.

von Rad, G. *Deuteronomy.* OTL. Philadelphia: Westminster, 1966. A strikingly fresh theological understanding of Deuteronomy that has remained central to subsequent research; although brief in compass, it is valuable for its insights into central issues of biblical theology.

Thompson, J. A. *Deuteronomy.* Tyndale Old Testament Commentaries. London: IVF, 1974. Conservative in outlook and rather too dependent on analogies between Deuteronomy and ancient Near Eastern treaty documents, this is nevertheless a clear and positive exposition.

Weinfeld, M. *Deuteronomy 1–11.* AB 5. New York: Doubleday, 1991. Although so far incomplete, this commentary is indispensable for the serious student because of its summaries and accounts of early and medieval Jewish interpretation. When used in conjunction with Weinfeld's study of the religious and ethical background to the book, it provides a well-balanced account of the central place of Deuteronomy in the growth of the OT and the development of ancient Israelite religion.

Special Studies:

Braulik, G. *The Theology of Deuteronomy. Collected Essays of Georg Braulik OSB.* Bibal Collected Essays 2. Translated by Ulrika Lindblad. N. Richland Hills, Tex.: Bibal, 1994. Along with N. Lohfink, the author has played a central role in research into the legal structure and ethical background of Deuteronomy.

Christensen, D. L., ed. *A Song of Power and the Power of Song: Essays on the Book of Deuteronomy.* Sources for Biblical and Theological Study 3. Winona Lake: Eisenbrauns, 1993. An excellent resource for the serious student; it brings together a wide range of the most significant critical essays reflecting contemporary research into the background and interpretation of Deuteronomy.

Haran, M. *Temples and Temple Service in Ancient Israel.* Oxford: Oxford University Press, 1978. An essential resource for understanding the priestly and ritual background reflected in the legislative prescriptions of Deuteronomy.

Harrelson, W. *The Ten Commandments and Human Rights.* OBT. Philadelphia: Fortress, 1980.

N. Lohfink, ed. *Das Deuteronomium: Entstehung, Gestalt und Botschaft.* BETL 68. Leuven: J. P. Peeters, 1985.

———. *Studien zum Deuteronomium und zur deuteronomistischen Literatur I.* SBA 8. Stuttgart: Katholisches Bibelwerk, 1990.

———. *Studien zum Deuteronomium und zur deuteronomistischen Literatur II.* SBA 12. Stuttgart: Katholisches Bibelwerk, 1991.

———. *Studien zum Deuteronomium und zur deuteronomistischen Literatur III.* SBA 20. Stuttgart: Katholisches Bibelwerk, 1995.

———. *Theology of the Pentateuch: Themes of the Priestly Narrative and Deuteronomy.* Translated by L. M. Maloney. Minneapolis: Augsburg Fortress, 1994. A sample of the work of an author who has become an outstanding world authority on the book of Deuteronomy.

Olson, D. T. *Deuteronomy and the Death of Moses.* OBT. Minneapolis: Augsburg Fortress, 1994.

von Rad, G. *Studies in Deuteronomy.* Translated by D. Stalker. SBT 9. London: SCM, 1953.

Weinfeld, M. *Deuteronomy and the Deuteronomic School.* Oxford: Oxford University Press, 1972.

OUTLINE OF DEUTERONOMY

DEUTERONOMY 1:1–3:29

INTRODUCTION TO ISRAEL'S STORY

OVERVIEW

Like many introductions to a major piece of literature, the introduction to the book of Deuteronomy hides much behind its simplicity and brevity. It presents a central guide to the significance and authority of the words that follow and establishes for them a unique place within the social and religious history of Israel, as well as within the literary structure of the Hebrew Bible.

In order to appreciate its character, it is essential to bear in mind certain central critical observations regarding chapters 1–3 and their significance for the book of Deuteronomy and for the writings that follow it. In a major, pathfinding work on the history of the books of Joshua, Judges, 1–2 Samuel, and 1–2 Kings, Martin Noth argued that Deuteronomy 1–3 must be regarded as the introduction, not simply to the law book of Deuteronomy, but to the entire narrative history that follows in these six books.[17] Following the order of the Hebrew canon, these books belong together as "the Former Prophets" (the book of Ruth appears separately among the five scrolls). So the book of Deuteronomy provides the beginning for the history of Israel under the monarchy that follows it, a history that Noth believed could be appropriately described as "the Deuteronomistic History." Seen as a whole, since it comprises a work of substantial length, the Deuteronomistic History offers a record of God's polity for Israel in the law book and an account of how the nation had subsequently fared under this code of laws. Israel did well when it displayed obedience, but experienced disaster when the people turned back from it.

Against such a background, we can see that Deuteronomy 1–3 contains a short historical résumé describing the adventures of Israel from the time of God's revelation at Mt. Horeb to the eve of the people's crossing of the river Jordan and their entry into the land promised to their ancestors. In order to provide such a historical setting for the giving of the law that forms the heart of the book, the writers employed information drawn from narrative sources that are still preserved in parts of Genesis–Numbers. So it partially summarizes a story that has already been told.

The law of Deuteronomy is presented as a speech of Moses given on the eve of this crossing and the subsequent conquest, recapitulating with elaborations and variations the law already given through Moses at Mt. Horeb. So the book's title as "a second law" is quite fitting. The introductory narrative's historical continuation is to be found in the account of Moses' death (chaps. 31 and 34) and the preparations for crossing the river Jordan under Joshua (Joshua 1–11).

Noth's case for recognizing this larger literary setting and purpose for the introduction to Deuteronomy has been widely accepted and must be upheld as valid, with two major cautionary provisos. The first of these is that many scholars have rightly sought to give recognition to the intricate, and rather piecemeal, composition of Deuteronomy 1–3. A basic text appears to have been progressively enlarged and expanded in several stages. A second significant point has been argued by S. Mittmann[18] in claiming that a part of this ground text was aimed at providing an introduction to the Decalogue of Deut 5:6-21. On any reckoning,

---

17. M. Noth, *The Deuteronomistic History,* JSOTSup 15 (Sheffield: JSOT, 1981). The original German text was published in 1943.

18. S. Mittmann, *Deuteronomium 1,1-6,3 literarkriotisch und traditionsgeschichtlich untersucht,* BZAW 139 (Berlin: de Gruyter, 1975). A review of the problems is presented in L. Perlitt, "Deuteronomium 1-3 im Streit der exegetischen Methoden," *Das Deuteronomium. Entstehung, Gestalt und Botschaft,* ed. N. Lohfink, BETL 68 (Leuven: Peeters, 1985) 149-63; L. Perliit, *Deuteronomum-Studien* (Tübingen: J. C. B. Mohr, 1994) 32-49.

this "Commandment Code" must be regarded as the central "law" of Deuteronomy and as a key to understanding the aims and assumptions of the deuteronomic movement. The more detailed code of Deuteronomy 12–26 can then be seen as an elaboration and outworking of this central, and relatively brief, list of commandments.

In this light, the introduction of Deuteronomy 1–3 serves a twofold goal: It prepares for the declaration of the basic commandments by Moses, unwaveringly placing him as the central figure in affirming the divine origin and authority of Israel's law, and it shows that Israel's history had a beginning *before* it entered the land promised to its ancestors. Law and narrative history, therefore, are the central means used by the deuteronomists to present their message explaining what it meant for Israel to be the people of the LORD God.

We should not be surprised, then, that there is some unevenness of form and content in chaps. 1–3, which is to be explained by recognizing that more than one editorial hand has been at work. Yet, the precise analysis and ordering of this compositional process remain uncertain, and little is to be gained by pressing the various scholarly conjectures to the point of assurance.[19] More significant is the recognition that the many rough edges in the literary flow of these introductory chapters are themselves a result of the need to bind the book of Deuteronomy closely to the four

books that precede it (i.e., Genesis–Numbers). It is not difficult to recognize that the authors of Deuteronomy have drawn upon narratives, still preserved in these preceding books, that tell of the revelation of the LORD God to the patriarchs and to Moses. So Deuteronomy has a special place in the Hebrew Bible and represents a uniquely important literary bond. It forms the final section of the five books of the Pentateuch—the books of Moses—but also joins directly and closely to the story that follows in those books that the Hebrew Bible describes as the Former Prophets. The introductory chapters thus fulfill a key role in establishing this literary bond.[20]

Since the wide acceptance of Noth's study has led to a strong emphasis on the connections between Deuteronomy and the Former Prophets, it is salutary to bear in mind the importance of the fact that its present canonical form and shape also tie it inseparably to Genesis–Numbers. It forms the final book of Moses, declaring repeatedly and unequivocally that Israel's origins began with Moses and not with the kingship that occupies so large a place in the story that follows. The nation had its start before the land was entered and conquered, and not after this had been achieved. It began with a covenant made on Mt. Horeb and with a law embodied in this, not with laws made and administered by kings and a royal court.

19. A valuable survey of positions is to be found in N. Lohfink, "Dtn 1,6–3,29," in *Studien zum Deuteronomium und zur deuteronomistischen Literatur I*, SBA 8 (Stuttgart: Katholisches Biblewerk, 1990) 15-44.

20. A review of the issues is to be found in N. Lohfink, "Deuteronomum und Pentateuch. Zum Stand der Forschung," in *Studien zum Deuteronomum und zur deuteronomistischen Literatur III*, SBA 20 (Stuttgart: Katholisches Bibelwerk, 1995) 13-38.

DEUTERONOMY 1:1-5, EDITORIAL PREFACE

NIV	NRSV
1 These are the words Moses spoke to all Israel in the desert east of the Jordan—that is, in the Arabah—opposite Suph, between Paran and Tophel, Laban, Hazeroth and Dizahab. ²(It takes eleven days to go from Horeb to Kadesh Barnea by the Mount Seir road.) ³In the fortieth year, on the first day of the eleventh month, Moses proclaimed to the Israelites all that the LORD had commanded him con-	**1** These are the words that Moses spoke to all Israel beyond the Jordan—in the wilderness, on the plain opposite Suph, between Paran and Tophel, Laban, Hazeroth, and Di-zahab. ²(By the way of Mount Seir it takes eleven days to reach Kadesh-barnea from Horeb.) ³In the fortieth year, on the first day of the eleventh month, Moses spoke to the Israelites just as the LORD had commanded him to speak to them. ⁴This was after

NIV

cerning them. [4]This was after he had defeated Sihon king of the Amorites, who reigned in Heshbon, and at Edrei had defeated Og king of Bashan, who reigned in Ashtaroth.

[5]East of the Jordan in the territory of Moab, Moses began to expound this law, saying:

NRSV

he had defeated King Sihon of the Amorites, who reigned in Heshbon, and King Og of Bashan, who reigned in Ashtaroth and[a] in Edrei. [5]Beyond the Jordan in the land of Moab, Moses undertook to expound this law as follows:

[a] Gk Syr Vg Compare Josh 12.4: Heb lacks *and*

COMMENTARY

Bearing these preliminary remarks in mind, we can note the points that the introduction to the book establishes in 1:1-5: (1) The words that follow are the work, and carry the unique authority, of Moses, the great founding father of Israel (note especially the threefold references to Moses in vv. 1, 3, 5). (2) They were given to Israel in the wilderness, before the crossing of the river Jordan and the entry into the land (v. 3). The author's perspective as one living within this land is made clear in v. 5 with the reference to "beyond the Jordan." (3) By defeating King Sihon of the Amorites and King Og of Bashan, Israel has a claim to certain territories east of the Jordan; this point has been drawn from Num 21:21-35 and is taken up again later. What history proved about Israel's claims to the land is a feature that was clearly of great importance to the author. Past events carried a strong contemporary relevance. (4) What Moses sets out in this second act of lawgiving is not a new or different law from that which had already been given, but rather represents an exposition and reaffirmation of that law. The Hebrew verb באר (*bēʾēr*, piel) used in v. 5

for "to expound" is unusual (cf. 27:8; Hab 2:2) and suggests both amplification and emphasis as well as "making plain," all of which are features that well characterize the book of Deuteronomy.

Taken as an introduction both to the book of Deuteronomy and to the larger history that follows it, some significant features are brought out in these verses. Israel's law is neither a "law of the land" nor a "law of the king" (one may compare King Hammurabi's famous law code). Israel's law is truly a divine law and stands above both land and kingship. Moreover, this law is addressed to the entire nation—"all Israel" (v. 1). Even children are to be taught the law and are expected to respond to it in a manner appropriate to their age (6:20).

The victories over Sihon and Og (v. 4) in the region to the east of Jordan take on something of an exemplary role. They show that, when obedient to the law, Israel can win great victories. Throughout the deuteronomic literature the questions of military organization and effectiveness appear prominently as major issues. So stories of defeat and victory achieved in the past constantly assume exemplary status.

REFLECTIONS

The most striking and fundamental feature of the introduction to Deuteronomy is its emphasis on Moses and the revelation of God given at Mt. Horeb. This man and this event provide the point of origin of the religion and faith of Israel, through which God had disclosed the special divine calling and destiny of Israel. Israel's very existence was bound up irrevocably to faith. This faith gave assurance of the reality of God and of the divine engagement with the world and its peoples. It was also, and inevitably, a fragile and vulnerable faith, since the demands of God's revelation and the divine covenant could be refused. Deuteronomy is very, almost excessively, conscious of this vulnerability. Faith is a question of human responsiveness, and such responsiveness may not be forthcoming. Deuteronomy has much to say about the shadowy side of Israel's beginnings, the acts of failure, the timid refusals to rise to the challenge that

God's calling had made possible, and the denial of the great vision of the promise that Moses had made possible from the beginning.

It is wholly in line with this biblical consciousness of the vulnerability of faith that the early rabbinic commentators were struck by the contrast between the eleven-day journey from Mt. Horeb to Kadesh-barnea and the thirty-eight-year interval before Israel finally set out to cross the Wadi Zered (2:14). Time had passed, and a generation had died out, all because the majority of Israelites lacked the courage and faith to act according to God's promise. So there had been, from the very beginning, a faithless generation.

The entire deuteronomic literature is imbued with this sensitivity to the psychology of faith. It records a noble story of the past and sets out an insightful constitution for the moral life of the nation. Yet, above both these informational literary tasks it makes an urgent appeal for faith and courage. This document was evidently intended to be read in public worship, and seems constantly aware that its readers and hearers were facing a challenge similar to that which confronted the first generation traveling with Moses to the borders of the promised land. That entire generation had failed, with the result that it—along with Moses—died before entering the land. Only their children, rearmed spiritually under the leadership of Joshua, had ventured to believe that God's promise would be fulfilled and that they would enjoy the fruits of freedom the exodus had given to their forebears.

It is on account of this intense faith consciousness that the book of Deuteronomy has retained its appeal and been able to continue to speak to succeeding generations. The generation lost in the wilderness was a perpetual reminder that the summons to faith is inescapable and essential for every subsequent generation.

DEUTERONOMY 1:6-45, FAITH AFFIRMED, TESTED, AND JUDGED

NIV	NRSV
[6]The LORD our God said to us at Horeb, "You have stayed long enough at this mountain. [7]Break camp and advance into the hill country of the Amorites; go to all the neighboring peoples in the Arabah, in the mountains, in the western foothills, in the Negev and along the coast, to the land of the Canaanites and to Lebanon, as far as the great river, the Euphrates. [8]See, I have given you this land. Go in and take possession of the land that the LORD swore he would give to your fathers—to Abraham, Isaac and Jacob—and to their descendants after them."	[6]The LORD our God spoke to us at Horeb, saying, "You have stayed long enough at this mountain. [7]Resume your journey, and go into the hill country of the Amorites as well as into the neighboring regions—the Arabah, the hill country, the Shephelah, the Negeb, and the seacoast—the land of the Canaanites and the Lebanon, as far as the great river, the river Euphrates. [8]See, I have set the land before you; go in and take possession of the land that I[a] swore to your ancestors, to Abraham, to Isaac, and to Jacob, to give to them and to their descendants after them."
[9]At that time I said to you, "You are too heavy a burden for me to carry alone. [10]The LORD your God has increased your numbers so that today you are as many as the stars in the sky. [11]May the LORD, the God of your fathers, increase you a thousand times and bless you as he has promised! [12]But how can I bear your problems and your	[9]At that time I said to you, "I am unable by myself to bear you. [10]The LORD your God has multiplied you, so that today you are as numerous as the stars of heaven. [11]May the LORD, the God of your ancestors, increase you a thousand times more and bless you, as he has promised you! [12]But
	[a] Sam Gk: MT *the LORD*

burdens and your disputes all by myself? ¹³Choose some wise, understanding and respected men from each of your tribes, and I will set them over you."

¹⁴You answered me, "What you propose to do is good."

¹⁵So I took the leading men of your tribes, wise and respected men, and appointed them to have authority over you—as commanders of thousands, of hundreds, of fifties and of tens and as tribal officials. ¹⁶And I charged your judges at that time: Hear the disputes between your brothers and judge fairly, whether the case is between brother Israelites or between one of them and an alien. ¹⁷Do not show partiality in judging; hear both small and great alike. Do not be afraid of any man, for judgment belongs to God. Bring me any case too hard for you, and I will hear it. ¹⁸And at that time I told you everything you were to do.

¹⁹Then, as the LORD our God commanded us, we set out from Horeb and went toward the hill country of the Amorites through all that vast and dreadful desert that you have seen, and so we reached Kadesh Barnea. ²⁰Then I said to you, "You have reached the hill country of the Amorites, which the LORD our God is giving us. ²¹See, the LORD your God has given you the land. Go up and take possession of it as the LORD, the God of your fathers, told you. Do not be afraid; do not be discouraged."

²²Then all of you came to me and said, "Let us send men ahead to spy out the land for us and bring back a report about the route we are to take and the towns we will come to."

²³The idea seemed good to me; so I selected twelve of you, one man from each tribe. ²⁴They left and went up into the hill country, and came to the Valley of Eshcol and explored it. ²⁵Taking with them some of the fruit of the land, they brought it down to us and reported, "It is a good land that the LORD our God is giving us."

²⁶But you were unwilling to go up; you rebelled against the command of the LORD your God. ²⁷You grumbled in your tents and said, "The LORD hates us; so he brought us out of Egypt to deliver us into the hands of the Amorites to destroy us. ²⁸Where can we go? Our brothers have made us lose heart. They say, 'The people are stronger and taller than we are; the cities are large, with walls up to the sky. We even saw the Anakites there.'"

how can I bear the heavy burden of your disputes all by myself? ¹³Choose for each of your tribes individuals who are wise, discerning, and reputable to be your leaders." ¹⁴You answered me, "The plan you have proposed is a good one." ¹⁵So I took the leaders of your tribes, wise and reputable individuals, and installed them as leaders over you, commanders of thousands, commanders of hundreds, commanders of fifties, commanders of tens, and officials, throughout your tribes. ¹⁶I charged your judges at that time: "Give the members of your community a fair hearing, and judge rightly between one person and another, whether citizen or resident alien. ¹⁷You must not be partial in judging: hear out the small and the great alike; you shall not be intimidated by anyone, for the judgment is God's. Any case that is too hard for you, bring to me, and I will hear it." ¹⁸So I charged you at that time with all the things that you should do.

¹⁹Then, just as the LORD our God had ordered us, we set out from Horeb and went through all that great and terrible wilderness that you saw, on the way to the hill country of the Amorites, until we reached Kadesh-barnea. ²⁰I said to you, "You have reached the hill country of the Amorites, which the LORD our God is giving us. ²¹See, the LORD your God has given the land to you; go up, take possession, as the LORD, the God of your ancestors, has promised you; do not fear or be dismayed."

²²All of you came to me and said, "Let us send men ahead of us to explore the land for us and bring back a report to us regarding the route by which we should go up and the cities we will come to." ²³The plan seemed good to me, and I selected twelve of you, one from each tribe. ²⁴They set out and went up into the hill country, and when they reached the Valley of Eshcol they spied it out ²⁵and gathered some of the land's produce, which they brought down to us. They brought back a report to us, and said, "It is a good land that the LORD our God is giving us."

²⁶But you were unwilling to go up. You rebelled against the command of the LORD your God; ²⁷you grumbled in your tents and said, "It is because the LORD hates us that he has brought us out of the land of Egypt, to hand us over to the Amorites to destroy us. ²⁸Where are we headed? Our kindred have made our hearts melt by re-

NIV

²⁹Then I said to you, "Do not be terrified; do not be afraid of them. ³⁰The Lord your God, who is going before you, will fight for you, as he did for you in Egypt, before your very eyes, ³¹and in the desert. There you saw how the Lord your God carried you, as a father carries his son, all the way you went until you reached this place."

³²In spite of this, you did not trust in the Lord your God, ³³who went ahead of you on your journey, in fire by night and in a cloud by day, to search out places for you to camp and to show you the way you should go.

³⁴When the Lord heard what you said, he was angry and solemnly swore: ³⁵"Not a man of this evil generation shall see the good land I swore to give your forefathers, ³⁶except Caleb son of Jephunneh. He will see it, and I will give him and his descendants the land he set his feet on, because he followed the Lord wholeheartedly."

³⁷Because of you the Lord became angry with me also and said, "You shall not enter it, either. ³⁸But your assistant, Joshua son of Nun, will enter it. Encourage him, because he will lead Israel to inherit it. ³⁹And the little ones that you said would be taken captive, your children who do not yet know good from bad—they will enter the land. I will give it to them and they will take possession of it. ⁴⁰But as for you, turn around and set out toward the desert along the route to the Red Sea.ᵃ"

⁴¹Then you replied, "We have sinned against the Lord. We will go up and fight, as the Lord our God commanded us." So every one of you put on his weapons, thinking it easy to go up into the hill country.

⁴²But the Lord said to me, "Tell them, 'Do not go up and fight, because I will not be with you. You will be defeated by your enemies.'"

⁴³So I told you, but you would not listen. You rebelled against the Lord's command and in your arrogance you marched up into the hill country. ⁴⁴The Amorites who lived in those hills came out against you; they chased you like a swarm of bees and beat you down from Seir all the way to Hormah. ⁴⁵You came back and wept before the Lord, but he paid no attention to your weeping and turned a deaf ear to you.

ᵃ40 Hebrew *Yam Suph;* that is, Sea of Reeds

NRSV

porting, 'The people are stronger and taller than we; the cities are large and fortified up to heaven! We actually saw there the offspring of the Anakim!'" ²⁹I said to you, "Have no dread or fear of them. ³⁰The Lord your God, who goes before you, is the one who will fight for you, just as he did for you in Egypt before your very eyes, ³¹and in the wilderness, where you saw how the Lord your God carried you, just as one carries a child, all the way that you traveled until you reached this place. ³²But in spite of this, you have no trust in the Lord your God, ³³who goes before you on the way to seek out a place for you to camp, in fire by night, and in the cloud by day, to show you the route you should take."

34When the Lord heard your words, he was wrathful and swore: ³⁵"Not one of these—not one of this evil generation—shall see the good land that I swore to give to your ancestors, ³⁶except Caleb son of Jephunneh. He shall see it, and to him and to his descendants I will give the land on which he set foot, because of his complete fidelity to the Lord." ³⁷Even with me the Lord was angry on your account, saying, "You also shall not enter there. ³⁸Joshua son of Nun, your assistant, shall enter there; encourage him, for he is the one who will secure Israel's possession of it. ³⁹And as for your little ones, who you thought would become booty, your children, who today do not yet know right from wrong, they shall enter there; to them I will give it, and they shall take possession of it. ⁴⁰But as for you, journey back into the wilderness, in the direction of the Red Sea."ᵃ

41You answered me, "We have sinned against the Lord! We are ready to go up and fight, just as the Lord our God commanded us." So all of you strapped on your battle gear, and thought it easy to go up into the hill country. ⁴²The Lord said to me, "Say to them, 'Do not go up and do not fight, for I am not in the midst of you; otherwise you will be defeated by your enemies.'" ⁴³Although I told you, you would not listen. You rebelled against the command of the Lord and presumptuously went up into the hill country. ⁴⁴The Amorites who lived in that hill country then came out against you and chased you as bees do. They beat you down in Seir as far as Hormah.

ᵃ Or *Sea of Reeds*

NRSV

45When you returned and wept before the LORD, the LORD would neither heed your voice nor pay you any attention.

COMMENTARY

The story of Israel's beginnings up to the eve of entry into the land is now sketched out more fully by means of certain incidents, selected because they bring to the surface key constitutional and theological motifs.

1:6-8. The first of these key motifs is that of the promise of the land given to Israel's first ancestors (Gen 12:7; 15:18).[21] This theme is the *leitmotif* that now binds the entire Genesis story to that of the exodus and the revelation at Mt. Horeb. It gives coherence to the wide variety of local and tribal traditions that constitute the story of the patriarchal period of Israel's existence (Genesis 12–50). In its developed literary form, it appears as one of the ways in which local and individual narrative memories, which naturally focused on specific regions and clans, were woven together into a larger whole. Tribal tradition became national tradition, since each tribe had its own particular story to tell to make its own contribution to the larger picture.

This summary history was consequently able to bring together a wide compass of ancestral traditions belonging to each of Israel's member clans and tribes. It set them under one overarching heading: God's promise of the land. This, then, provides a central theological motif, because the land is presented as belonging to Israel as the outworking of a divine purpose and the product of divine action. So the theology of God as Land-giver functions as a unifying principle, bringing diverse stories and memories about settlement of the land into one connected story.

The phrase "the LORD our God" (v. 6) is typically deuteronomic, occurring no less than twenty-three times in the book. Even more common is the expression "the LORD your/our God," which is to be found no less than 276 times. The title "Amorite" is widely attested in Mesopotamian

documents from the second and third centuries BCE to designate "west land" or "westerner." In biblical usage, it is found alongside the related title "Canaanite" to describe the pre-Israelite inhabitants of the territory Israel had settled. Predominantly Amorite peoples occupied the hill country, whereas the Canaanites were settled mainly along the coastal areas (see Josh 13:3-4). The extent of the land Israel was destined to occupy is regarded from a perspective of its maximum coverage; yet even this appears to be heavily idealized (see 11:24; Josh 1:4). That the land itself was the subject of an older covenant made between the LORD God and Abraham is described in Gen 15:18-21, but significantly the covenant there lacks any element of a binding set of obligations that dominate the deuteronomic presentation of the covenant at Horeb.

1:9-18. The deuteronomist has clearly drawn his information regarding the institution of an order of lay judges from the literary sources now preserved in Exodus 18 and Numbers 11. Noticeably, the complaint by Moses concerning the heavy burden imposed by having to adjudicate the disputes that arose between members of the community, which in Numbers 11 is directed toward God, is here directed toward the people. The deuteronomic author has evidently felt a need to heighten the image and role of Moses. The placing of this action at this point highlights the importance to Israel of a fair and acceptable system of juridical authority vested in reputable leaders chosen from among the tribes (v. 13). Throughout the legal section of the book (chaps. 12–26), the question of the administration of law receives considerable attention and reflects a variety of institutional responsibilities, embracing priests, elders, and appointed judges.[22]

Comparison with other peoples of the ancient Near East reveals the prominent role of kingship

21. W. Brueggemann, *The Land: Place as Gift, Promise and Challenge in Biblical Faith,* OBT (Philadelphia: Fortress, 1977).

22. J. C. Gertz, *Die Gerichtsorgainisation Israels im deuteromistischen Gesetz,* FRLANT 165 (Göttingen: Vandenhoeck & Ruprecht, 1994).

in establishing and promoting systems of law administration.[23] This was evidently true to a significant extent for ancient Israel, as various narrative reports show. It was, inevitably, open to abuse so that a highly critiqued aspect of the institution of monarchy was that it failed to institute and maintain a responsible judicial system over which the king personally presided, at least in a nominal fashion (see Jer 22:15-17). It is apparent that the deuteronomic concern to place the issue of law and legal administration at the head of its requirements, as is achieved by setting this summary report here, reflects the prominence given to the matter. Fundamental to the entire deuteronomic outlook is a concern with public justice, and underlying this ambition is a scarcely disguised awareness of the complexity of the many issues raised and the vulnerability of existing systems to abuse and corruption. The high profile accorded to Moses as the supreme lawgiver has in part been shaped by the consciousness that Israel's kings had often fallen short in this regard.

Verse 15 occasions some difficulty concerning the manner of choice of the judges. Since v. 13 has shown that the power to choose the appropriate individuals was to rest with the people, it is surprising to find here that those chosen are simply approved by Moses and are already designated as "leaders of your tribes." This might point to a mere twelve such judges, whereas Numbers 11 specifies seventy elders. Furthermore, although the title "commanders" (שׂרים *śārîm*) could be construed widely to describe various types of officials, the division of the people into thousands, hundreds, fifties, and tens suggests patterns of military organization and obligation. Probably the inclusion of the verse was intended to allow this wider jurisdiction of the judges for military activity. It provides one of a larger number of indications that, at the time of the composition of this introduction, Israel was aware that it was itself deeply threatened militarily. Arrangements for local community defense were necessary and involved the raising of a civil militia.

1:19-33. Once again this historical survey by the deuteronomic author makes direct use of older written sources that are now preserved in Numbers 13–14. The literary dependence on the part of Deuteronomy is evident, but there are some significant variations. These would appear to have been introduced in order to highlight the central theme that failure to occupy the land immediately was a result of misguided fear on the part of the people and faithlessness toward God.

Mayes points out that the deuteronomist not only summarizes the story contained in his source, but also presupposes that the reader is familiar with it.[24] The reiteration of the divine promise of the land and its accompanying injunction to show no fear or alarm at the danger and immensity of the task are characteristic deuteronomic themes (vv. 21, 29). The gift of the land is both a promise and a divine command to act. The proposal to send out spies to evaluate and report on the nature of the territory to be conquered is presented as originating from the people themselves: "All of you came to me and said. . . ." There is a collective responsibility for the mission and a shared culpability for the consequences of it.

1:34-45. The earliest version of the story clearly possessed much local flavor and focused in detail on the contrast between the attitude of Caleb, with his consequent position of privilege, shared with Joshua (Num 14:6, 24, 30, 38), and that of the people more generally. This motif is retained, but serves now to contrast Caleb's faithfulness with the lack of it from the wider community. He is said to have displayed "complete fidelity to the LORD." The popular response to the spies' report, advocating caution and promoting fear, is presented as a fundamental reason for disobeying the divine command to proceed immediately to prepare for entry into the land. The reprehensible and unbelieving attitude of the community as a whole, with the exceptions of Joshua and Caleb, is made the subject of particular emphasis (v. 27). The people even go so far as to accuse God of perpetrating a vindictive deceit upon them by leading them on to disaster. Throughout the reader is directly drawn into the story by being shown contrasting attitudes in which his or her own loyalties and sympathies would be bound to agree with those of the narrator. Those who choose the path of disobedience through fear pay a heavy price for their timidity!

23. K. W. Whitelam, *The Just King: Monarchical Judicial Authority in Ancient Israel* (Sheffield: JSOT, 1979).

24. A. D. H. Mayes, *Deuteronomy,* NCB (London: Marshall, Morgan & Scott, 1979) 127.

Taken as a carefully selected incident, the report of which is drawn from older sources relating to the conquest and settlement of the land, the narrative seeks to demonstrate that success in the occupation and enjoyment of the land was entirely a matter of obedience to God's clearly given commands and to an unwavering trust in the reliability of the divine promises. These had been given first to the patriarchal ancestors of Israel and subsequently reaffirmed through Moses. Such a call for undeviating faith in God, no matter how daunting the danger or massive the task, is wholly in line with the later narrative of Joshua 1–9. This is itself undoubtedly a late narrative compilation on the part of the deuteronomic school. It recounts how the occupation of the land was finally achieved in a swift coordinated campaign in which obedience or disobedience toward the divine law was the deciding factor. In both Deuteronomy and the book of Joshua the historical recollections and reconstructions of the past are made to elucidate from them lessons of faith. These lessons relate consistently to questions of faith in the promises of God and the neccessity for obedience to a clearly known divine law.

The report of the popular dismay at God's anger over the people's response and their subsequent regret for their lack of faith (vv. 41-45) is employed as a means of further reinforcing the central message. It is a message that holds together both the deuteronomic understanding of warfare and the conviction that Israel's occupation of the land and its obedience to God's law are inseparably linked. The LORD's presence must remain in the midst of the people if they are to secure victory (v. 42). Without this presence, no victory can be won and defeat becomes inevitable. It is in line with this that the eventual conquest of Jericho is presented, not as a battle but as a ritual

procession led by priests (Josh 6:1-21). Faith and obedience to the law, not military expertise and force of arms, are the needful elements of security and assurance for the retention of God's gifts. For Deuteronomy, the most central of those gifts was the gift of the land.

In Num 14:43, 45 the enemy is identified as "the Amalekites and Canaanites" so that their designation here as "Amorites" (v. 44) is a mark of the general leveling shown by the deuteronomic author in using this term for the pre-Israelite occupants of all the land. The concluding affirmation in v. 45 that God refused to listen to the remorse expressed by the people for their lack of faith reveals the strength of the deuteronomic doctrine of divine retribution. Some offenses against God's commands are such that human entreaties, no matter how passionately felt and expressed, cannot bring about a withdrawal of the divine anger.

The theme that prayerful entreaty and intercession may sometimes prove to be unavailing is an important feature of the deuteronomic understanding of Israel's history. This appears to have become even more marked in those parts of the deuteronomic literature that derive from the latest period of the composition of the book. The theme is explored extensively in the lengthy account of Moses' intercession in Deuteronomy 9. Although a clear chronology is unobtainable for the various stages of theological development of the deuteronomic movement, such evidence as we have points to a deepening sense of foreboding and a consciousness of the depth of the divine anger. If this is true, it would also serve to relate to, and perhaps in part explain, the level of frenetic intensity, combined with merciless severity, with which the demand for enforcing obedience to the law is presented in certain parts of the books of Deuteronomy and Joshua.

REFLECTIONS

Two issues immediately call for attention in surveying this summary report of Israel's generation-long sojourn in the wilderness after the revelation on Mt. Horeb. The occupation of the land is understood as an unquestioned consequence of God's purpose and gracious will toward Israel. No thought is given to the needs, feelings, or survival of the existing occupants of that land. They appear only as shadowy, half-identifiable people whose misfortune it was to have been in the way of a more favored people. The deuteronomic literature is uncompromising on the issue. Such a partisan attitude accords badly with either modern Jewish or

Christian awareness of the universal sovereignty and grace of God. This view may be mitigated to some extent by recognizing its historical inadequacy as a way to understand and interpret the many extensive, and usually violent, population movements that shaped several millennia of human settlement in the ancient Near East. Such movements and extensive migrations occurred, invariably with triumphant consequences for the victors and no pity or redress for the vanquished.

The rise of Israel as a nation toward the end of the second millennium BCE was one particular instance of a complex pattern of similar actions that took place over the region. The deuteronomic literature is the biblical record of one such instance among many similar major social and political movements, and that record survives with a distinctive theological interpretation stamped upon it.

Of special importance to us is the fact that it is the deuteronomic movement and its literary achievements that established the best-known paradigm for such developments by creating a canonical biblical interpretation for Israel's version. In spite of intense historical research and the use of comparative data to show how it comes about that nations and a national consciousness emerge, the full details of how Israel stepped onto the historical stage of national history can be traced only imperfectly. The early history of many of its constituent tribes and of the regions where they settled is far from clear. What we are left with is a single coordinated theological interpretation of a series of past events that saw within them unfolding images of divine grace, beneficence, and a summons to courage and a high moral vision.

Alongside these images were set also some negative metaphors of divine anger, retribution, and discriminatory punishment and rejection. It then becomes no easy task to isolate the more positive imagery, ideas, and symbols from the less helpful negative concepts and themes.

One way in which this can be attempted is by recognizing that the deuteronomic construct of how Israel came to birth as a nation was itself the product of men and women facing a major crisis.[25] The book itself suggests at many places that it was composed at a time when the continuance of Israel's existence as a state, with a land and kingship of its own, was all but at an end. The deuteronomic literature is essentially a twilight literature, written in the shadow of catastrophe when much of Israel's territory had already been lost, when defeat had faced the nation many times, and when the great expectations associated with the days of David and Solomon were a richly colored memory.

In a very powerful way the authors felt that their own contemporaries, the hearers and readers of the book, were facing the same threats and dangers that had faced their forebears who had first entered the land. A new generation of Anakim (giants) had come upon the scene and had threatened to take and keep possession of the land. Nor can the authors of the book hide their conviction that many of their contemporaries were displaying the same fear and defeatist thinking that had kept the generation that had first sent spies to reconnoiter the land imprisoned in the wilderness. The call to faith and obedience was urgent; the belief that, however great the opposition, the LORD God was greater still fired their imagination. The fervor of their appeal is unmistakable. It is in large measure this sense of urgency and its accompanying call to firmer loyalty to God that have made the book of Deuteronomy a rich source of spiritual resources for both Jews and Christians. That this call to loyalty should have fallen short of recognizing that the Canaanites, too, were human beings and also children of God should not hide from us the fact that there is a better, as well as an insidiously dangerous, aspect to the deuteronomic theology.

25. See W. Brueggemann, *The Land,* 46: "It is as though Israel's traditionists had intuitively known that this is the hour of destiny; as though Israel knows that hard, disciplined reflection is never more needed than at this moment, when the new situation of land requires a new Israel with a new faith."

DEUTERONOMY 1:46–3:29,
THE FIRST CAMPAIGNS—PEACEFUL AND MILITARY

NIV

⁴⁶And so you stayed in Kadesh many days—all the time you spent there.

2 Then we turned back and set out toward the desert along the route to the Red Sea,ᵃ as the LORD had directed me. For a long time we made our way around the hill country of Seir.

²Then the LORD said to me, ³"You have made your way around this hill country long enough; now turn north. ⁴Give the people these orders: 'You are about to pass through the territory of your brothers the descendants of Esau, who live in Seir. They will be afraid of you, but be very careful. ⁵Do not provoke them to war, for I will not give you any of their land, not even enough to put your foot on. I have given Esau the hill country of Seir as his own. ⁶You are to pay them in silver for the food you eat and the water you drink.'"

⁷The LORD your God has blessed you in all the work of your hands. He has watched over your journey through this vast desert. These forty years the LORD your God has been with you, and you have not lacked anything.

⁸So we went on past our brothers the descendants of Esau, who live in Seir. We turned from the Arabah road, which comes up from Elath and Ezion Geber, and traveled along the desert road of Moab.

⁹Then the LORD said to me, "Do not harass the Moabites or provoke them to war, for I will not give you any part of their land. I have given Ar to the descendants of Lot as a possession."

¹⁰(The Emites used to live there—a people strong and numerous, and as tall as the Anakites. ¹¹Like the Anakites, they too were considered Rephaites, but the Moabites called them Emites. ¹²Horites used to live in Seir, but the descendants of Esau drove them out. They destroyed the Horites from before them and settled in their place, just as Israel did in the land the LORD gave them as their possession.)

¹³And the LORD said, "Now get up and cross the Zered Valley." So we crossed the valley.

ᵃ1 Hebrew *Yam Suph*; that is, Sea of Reeds

NRSV

46After you had stayed at Kadesh as many days as you did,

2 ¹we journeyed back into the wilderness, in the direction of the Red Sea,ᵃ as the LORD had told me and skirted Mount Seir for many days. ²Then the LORD said to me: ³"You have been skirting this hill country long enough. Head north, ⁴and charge the people as follows: You are about to pass through the territory of your kindred, the descendants of Esau, who live in Seir. They will be afraid of you, so, be very careful ⁵not to engage in battle with them, for I will not give you even so much as a foot's length of their land, since I have given Mount Seir to Esau as a possession. ⁶You shall purchase food from them for money, so that you may eat; and you shall also buy water from them for money, so that you may drink. ⁷Surely the LORD your God has blessed you in all your undertakings; he knows your going through this great wilderness. These forty years the LORD your God has been with you; you have lacked nothing." ⁸So we passed by our kin, the descendants of Esau who live in Seir, leaving behind the route of the Arabah, and leaving behind Elath and Ezion-geber.

When we had headed out along the route of the wilderness of Moab, ⁹the LORD said to me: "Do not harass Moab or engage them in battle, for I will not give you any of its land as a possession, since I have given Ar as a possession to the descendants of Lot." ¹⁰(The Emim—a large and numerous people, as tall as the Anakim—had formerly inhabited it. ¹¹Like the Anakim, they are usually reckoned as Rephaim, though the Moabites call them Emim. ¹²Moreover, the Horim had formerly inhabited Seir, but the descendants of Esau dispossessed them, destroying them and settling in their place, as Israel has done in the land that the LORD gave them as a possession.) ¹³"Now then, proceed to cross over the Wadi Zered."

So we crossed over the Wadi Zered. ¹⁴And the length of time we had traveled from Kadesh-barnea until we crossed the Wadi Zered was

ᵃ Or *Sea of Reeds*

[14]Thirty-eight years passed from the time we left Kadesh Barnea until we crossed the Zered Valley. By then, that entire generation of fighting men had perished from the camp, as the LORD had sworn to them. [15]The LORD's hand was against them until he had completely eliminated them from the camp.

[16]Now when the last of these fighting men among the people had died, [17]the LORD said to me, [18]"Today you are to pass by the region of Moab at Ar. [19]When you come to the Ammonites, do not harass them or provoke them to war, for I will not give you possession of any land belonging to the Ammonites. I have given it as a possession to the descendants of Lot."

[20](That too was considered a land of the Rephaites, who used to live there; but the Ammonites called them Zamzummites. [21]They were a people strong and numerous, and as tall as the Anakites. The LORD destroyed them from before the Ammonites, who drove them out and settled in their place. [22]The LORD had done the same for the descendants of Esau, who lived in Seir, when he destroyed the Horites from before them. They drove them out and have lived in their place to this day. [23]And as for the Avvites who lived in villages as far as Gaza, the Caphtorites coming out from Caphtor[a] destroyed them and settled in their place.)

[24]"Set out now and cross the Arnon Gorge. See, I have given into your hand Sihon the Amorite, king of Heshbon, and his country. Begin to take possession of it and engage him in battle. [25]This very day I will begin to put the terror and fear of you on all the nations under heaven. They will hear reports of you and will tremble and be in anguish because of you."

[26]From the desert of Kedemoth I sent messengers to Sihon king of Heshbon offering peace and saying, [27]"Let us pass through your country. We will stay on the main road; we will not turn aside to the right or to the left. [28]Sell us food to eat and water to drink for their price in silver. Only let us pass through on foot— [29]as the descendants of Esau, who live in Seir, and the Moabites, who live in Ar, did for us—until we cross the Jordan into the land the LORD our God is giving us." [30]But

[a]23 That is, Crete

thirty-eight years, until the entire generation of warriors had perished from the camp, as the LORD had sworn concerning them. [15]Indeed, the LORD's own hand was against them, to root them out from the camp, until all had perished.

16Just as soon as all the warriors had died off from among the people, [17]the LORD spoke to me, saying, [18]"Today you are going to cross the boundary of Moab at Ar. [19]When you approach the frontier of the Ammonites, do not harass them or engage them in battle, for I will not give the land of the Ammonites to you as a possession, because I have given it to the descendants of Lot." [20](It also is usually reckoned as a land of Rephaim. Rephaim formerly inhabited it, though the Ammonites call them Zamzummim, [21]a strong and numerous people, as tall as the Anakim. But the LORD destroyed them from before the Ammonites so that they could dispossess them and settle in their place. [22]He did the same for the descendants of Esau, who live in Seir, by destroying the Horim before them so that they could dispossess them and settle in their place even to this day. [23]As for the Avvim, who had lived in settlements in the vicinity of Gaza, the Caphtorim, who came from Caphtor, destroyed them and settled in their place.) [24]"Proceed on your journey and cross the Wadi Arnon. See, I have handed over to you King Sihon the Amorite of Heshbon, and his land. Begin to take possession by engaging him in battle. [25]This day I will begin to put the dread and fear of you upon the peoples everywhere under heaven; when they hear report of you, they will tremble and be in anguish because of you."

26So I sent messengers from the wilderness of Kedemoth to King Sihon of Heshbon with the following terms of peace: [27]"If you let me pass through your land, I will travel only along the road; I will turn aside neither to the right nor to the left. [28]You shall sell me food for money, so that I may eat, and supply me water for money, so that I may drink. Only allow me to pass through on foot— [29]just as the descendants of Esau who live in Seir have done for me and likewise the Moabites who live in Ar—until I cross the Jordan into the land that the LORD our God is giving us." [30]But King Sihon of Heshbon was not willing to let us pass through, for the

NIV

Sihon king of Heshbon refused to let us pass through. For the LORD your God had made his spirit stubborn and his heart obstinate in order to give him into your hands, as he has now done.

³¹The LORD said to me, "See, I have begun to deliver Sihon and his country over to you. Now begin to conquer and possess his land."

³²When Sihon and all his army came out to meet us in battle at Jahaz, ³³the LORD our God delivered him over to us and we struck him down, together with his sons and his whole army. ³⁴At that time we took all his towns and completely destroyed[a] them—men, women and children. We left no survivors. ³⁵But the livestock and the plunder from the towns we had captured we carried off for ourselves. ³⁶From Aroer on the rim of the Arnon Gorge, and from the town in the gorge, even as far as Gilead, not one town was too strong for us. The LORD our God gave us all of them. ³⁷But in accordance with the command of the LORD our God, you did not encroach on any of the land of the Ammonites, neither the land along the course of the Jabbok nor that around the towns in the hills.

3 Next we turned and went up along the road toward Bashan, and Og king of Bashan with his whole army marched out to meet us in battle at Edrei. ²The LORD said to me, "Do not be afraid of him, for I have handed him over to you with his whole army and his land. Do to him what you did to Sihon king of the Amorites, who reigned in Heshbon."

³So the LORD our God also gave into our hands Og king of Bashan and all his army. We struck them down, leaving no survivors. ⁴At that time we took all his cities. There was not one of the sixty cities that we did not take from them—the whole region of Argob, Og's kingdom in Bashan. ⁵All these cities were fortified with high walls and with gates and bars, and there were also a great many unwalled villages. ⁶We completely destroyed[a] them, as we had done with Sihon king of Heshbon, destroying[a] every city—men, women and children. ⁷But all the livestock and the plunder from their cities we carried off for ourselves.

⁸So at that time we took from these two kings

a34 The Hebrew term refers to the irrevocable giving over of things or persons to the LORD, often by totally destroying them.

NRSV

LORD your God had hardened his spirit and made his heart defiant in order to hand him over to you, as he has now done.

31The LORD said to me, "See, I have begun to give Sihon and his land over to you. Begin now to take possession of his land." ³²So when Sihon came out against us, he and all his people for battle at Jahaz, ³³the LORD our God gave him over to us; and we struck him down, along with his offspring and all his people. ³⁴At that time we captured all his towns, and in each town we utterly destroyed men, women, and children. We left not a single survivor. ³⁵Only the livestock we kept as spoil for ourselves, as well as the plunder of the towns that we had captured. ³⁶From Aroer on the edge of the Wadi Arnon (including the town that is in the wadi itself) as far as Gilead, there was no citadel too high for us. The LORD our God gave everything to us. ³⁷You did not encroach, however, on the land of the Ammonites, avoiding the whole upper region of the Wadi Jabbok as well as the towns of the hill country, just as[a] the LORD our God had charged.

3 When we headed up the road to Bashan, King Og of Bashan came out against us, he and all his people, for battle at Edrei. ²The LORD said to me, "Do not fear him, for I have handed him over to you, along with his people and his land. Do to him as you did to King Sihon of the Amorites, who reigned in Heshbon." ³So the LORD our God also handed over to us King Og of Bashan and all his people. We struck him down until not a single survivor was left. ⁴At that time we captured all his towns; there was no citadel that we did not take from them—sixty towns, the whole region of Argob, the kingdom of Og in Bashan. ⁵All these were fortress towns with high walls, double gates, and bars, besides a great many villages. ⁶And we utterly destroyed them, as we had done to King Sihon of Heshbon, in each city utterly destroying men, women, and children. ⁷But all the livestock and the plunder of the towns we kept as spoil for ourselves.

8So at that time we took from the two kings of the Amorites the land beyond the Jordan, from the Wadi Arnon to Mount Hermon ⁹(the Sidonians call Hermon Sirion, while the Amorites call

a GkTg: Heb and all

NIV

of the Amorites the territory east of the Jordan, from the Arnon Gorge as far as Mount Hermon. ⁹(Hermon is called Sirion by the Sidonians; the Amorites call it Senir.) ¹⁰We took all the towns on the plateau, and all Gilead, and all Bashan as far as Salecah and Edrei, towns of Og's kingdom in Bashan. ¹¹(Only Og king of Bashan was left of the remnant of the Rephaites. His bed*a* was made of iron and was more than thirteen feet long and six feet wide.*b* It is still in Rabbah of the Ammonites.)

¹²Of the land that we took over at that time, I gave the Reubenites and the Gadites the territory north of Aroer by the Arnon Gorge, including half the hill country of Gilead, together with its towns. ¹³The rest of Gilead and also all of Bashan, the kingdom of Og, I gave to the half tribe of Manasseh. (The whole region of Argob in Bashan used to be known as a land of the Rephaites. ¹⁴Jair, a descendant of Manasseh, took the whole region of Argob as far as the border of the Geshurites and the Maacathites; it was named after him, so that to this day Bashan is called Havvoth Jair.*c*) ¹⁵And I gave Gilead to Makir. ¹⁶But to the Reubenites and the Gadites I gave the territory extending from Gilead down to the Arnon Gorge (the middle of the gorge being the border) and out to the Jabbok River, which is the border of the Ammonites. ¹⁷Its western border was the Jordan in the Arabah, from Kinnereth to the Sea of the Arabah (the Salt Sea*d*), below the slopes of Pisgah.

¹⁸I commanded you at that time: "The Lord your God has given you this land to take possession of it. But all your able-bodied men, armed for battle, must cross over ahead of your brother Israelites. ¹⁹However, your wives, your children and your livestock (I know you have much livestock) may stay in the towns I have given you, ²⁰until the Lord gives rest to your brothers as he has to you, and they too have taken over the land that the Lord your God is giving them, across the Jordan. After that, each of you may go back to the possession I have given you."

²¹At that time I commanded Joshua: "You have seen with your own eyes all that the Lord your God has done to these two kings. The Lord will

---

a11 Or *sarcophagus*   *b11* Hebrew *nine cubits long and four cubits wide* (about 4 meters long and 1.8 meters wide)   *c14* Or *called the settlements of Jair*   *d17* That is, the Dead Sea

NRSV

it Senir), ¹⁰all the towns of the tableland, the whole of Gilead, and all of Bashan, as far as Salecah and Edrei, towns of Og's kingdom in Bashan. ¹¹(Now only King Og of Bashan was left of the remnant of the Rephaim. In fact his bed, an iron bed, can still be seen in Rabbah of the Ammonites. By the common cubit it is nine cubits long and four cubits wide.) ¹²As for the land that we took possession of at that time, I gave to the Reubenites and Gadites the territory north of Aroer,*a* that is on the edge of the Wadi Arnon, as well as half the hill country of Gilead with its towns, ¹³and I gave to the half-tribe of Manasseh the rest of Gilead and all of Bashan, Og's kingdom. (The whole region of Argob: all that portion of Bashan used to be called a land of Rephaim; ¹⁴Jair the Manassite acquired the whole region of Argob as far as the border of the Geshurites and the Maacathites, and he named them—that is, Bashan—after himself, Havvoth-jair,*b* as it is to this day.) ¹⁵To Machir I gave Gilead. ¹⁶And to the Reubenites and the Gadites I gave the territory from Gilead as far as the Wadi Arnon, with the middle of the wadi as a boundary, and up to the Jabbok, the wadi being boundary of the Ammonites; ¹⁷the Arabah also, with the Jordan and its banks, from Chinnereth down to the sea of the Arabah, the Dead Sea,*c* with the lower slopes of Pisgah on the east.

18At that time, I charged you as follows: "Although the Lord your God has given you this land to occupy, all your troops shall cross over armed as the vanguard of your Israelite kin. ¹⁹Only your wives, your children, and your livestock—I know that you have much livestock—shall stay behind in the towns that I have given to you. ²⁰When the Lord gives rest to your kindred, as to you, and they too have occupied the land that the Lord your God is giving them beyond the Jordan, then each of you may return to the property that I have given to you." ²¹And I charged Joshua as well at that time, saying: "Your own eyes have seen everything that the Lord your God has done to these two kings; so the Lord will do to all the kingdoms into which you are about to cross. ²²Do

---

a Heb *territory from Aroer*   *b* That is *Settlement of Jair*   *c* Heb *Salt Sea*

NIV

do the same to all the kingdoms over there where you are going. ²²Do not be afraid of them; the LORD your God himself will fight for you."

²³At that time I pleaded with the LORD: ²⁴"O Sovereign LORD, you have begun to show to your servant your greatness and your strong hand. For what god is there in heaven or on earth who can do the deeds and mighty works you do? ²⁵Let me go over and see the good land beyond the Jordan—that fine hill country and Lebanon."

²⁶But because of you the LORD was angry with me and would not listen to me. "That is enough," the LORD said. "Do not speak to me anymore about this matter. ²⁷Go up to the top of Pisgah and look west and north and south and east. Look at the land with your own eyes, since you are not going to cross this Jordan. ²⁸But commission Joshua, and encourage and strengthen him, for he will lead this people across and will cause them to inherit the land that you will see." ²⁹So we stayed in the valley near Beth Peor.

NRSV

not fear them, for it is the LORD your God who fights for you."

23At that time, too, I entreated the LORD, saying: 24"O Lord GOD, you have only begun to show your servant your greatness and your might; what god in heaven or on earth can perform deeds and mighty acts like yours! 25Let me cross over to see the good land beyond the Jordan, that good hill country and the Lebanon." 26But the LORD was angry with me on your account and would not heed me. The LORD said to me, "Enough from you! Never speak to me of this matter again! 27Go up to the top of Pisgah and look around you to the west, to the north, to the south, and to the east. Look well, for you shall not cross over this Jordan. 28But charge Joshua, and encourage and strengthen him, because it is he who shall cross over at the head of this people and who shall secure their possession of the land that you will see." 29So we remained in the valley opposite Beth-peor.

COMMENTARY

1:46–2:8a. The author continues his story by reporting a journey that has already been recounted in Num 20:14 concerning the Israelites' passage through the territory of Edom. By the time the author wrote, Edom and Esau had evidently come to be effectively identified as one. This had taken place as a result of the westward spread of Edom into Seir, a territory that had been occupied by the descendants of Esau. The awareness of a blood relationship between Jacob and Esau (Gen 27:1-45) accounts for the insistence on a peaceful passage through the territory of Esau's descendants. Their land had been assigned to them by the LORD God (v. 5), and any provisions acquired from them by the Israelites had to be paid for (v. 6). The mention of this need to buy provisions gave rise to the slightly jarring note that God provided for Israel all necessary sustenance during the forty-year wilderness period (v. 7). This was believed not to exclude the purchase of goods, although no indication is made of whence the purchase money would come.

Altogether the narrative down to 3:11 recounts five encounters with nations settled east of Jordan that follow a closely similar pattern.[26] In three of them, Edom, Moab, and Ammon, peaceful negotiations avoid any conflict. However, in the last two, involving Sihon and Og, hostilities arise that enable and entitle Israel to take possession of their respective territories. Undoubtedly this motif of using historical traditions to maintain a claim on territory was an important feature of deuteronomic writing. From a purely historical perspective, most of the land east of the Jordan appears to have been lost to Israel subsequent to the death of Solomon. Nevertheless, we must take it as highly probable that changing allegiances and feuding among local clans led to many fluctuations of political and religious affiliation. We cannot, therefore, assume that there was a fixed and settled border in Transjordan, or across much of

26. For these nations, see J. R. Bartlett, "The Moabites and Edomites," in *Peoples of Old Testament Times,* ed. D. J. Wiseman (Oxford: Oxford University Press, 1973) 229-58; M. Noth, *Aufsätze zur biblischen Landes und Altertumskunde I,* ed. H. W. Wolff (Neukirchen-Vluyn: Neukirchener Verlag, 1971) 391-433.

the land occupied at some stage by the Israelites. Certainly also the Mesopotamian incursions into the region from the ninth century BCE on led to further shifts and realignments. The deuteronomic author here was clearly endeavoring to maintain a political horizon that retained a contemporary relevance for his time. A relatively conciliatory attitude toward the Edomites is commanded in 23:7-8.

2:8b-23. The next ethnic community settled east of the Jordan whose territory had to be crossed was that of Moab. How Israel did so in order to reach its own promised land is recounted in vv. 8*b*-18. This is followed by a brief warning concerning the necessity for avoiding conflict with the people of Ammon (v. 9); further elaboration of this particular caution is then given in v. 37. Apparently the route envisaged by the author for Israel's journey did not require incursion into Ammonite territory, which lay still farther to the east.

The injunction not to harass Moab follows the pattern of the preceding report of avoiding conflict with Edom. It has no precise counterpart in the earlier source used by the author, but was introduced to complete the picture of the long journey from Kadesh to the land. The tolerant and peace-seeking attitude toward both Moab and Ammon contrasts sharply with the more hostile and un-compromising sentiment expressed in the law of 23:3-6. Obviously, allegiances changed at different periods during the time covered by the composition of the deuteronomic literature. We must assume that changing political events had led to quite fundamental changes of attitude on the part of the Israelites. We may particularly bear in mind that the story of the Ammonite involvement in the protection of the murderers of the Judahite governor Gedaliah after the disaster of 587 BCE (Jer 41:15) provides evidence of friction. For al-most two centuries, in fact, it appears that the military pressures imposed on the region from Mesopotamia inevitably led to fluctuating, and often treacherous, shifts of allegiance.

The brief note in v. 14 concerning the period of thirty-eight years spent in the wilderness ac-cords with the author's affirmation that the entire generation that had spurned God's promise and been fearful of attempting to enter the land had to die out. This was to be their punishment for their lack of courage and disobedience. The inter-val of thirty-eight years shows that the author has

deducted two years to account for the time in reaching Mt. Horeb and the period spent there and at Kadesh. The punishment is here restricted (cf. 1:35) to those who were of age for military service ("warriors," NRSV). It is in accord with this convic-tion that no military action could be undertaken before these adults had passed from the scene, since the LORD was no longer in Israel's midst (1:42).

The point that the generation who died in the wilderness was experiencing God's punishment for their fearfulness is hardly consistent with the em-phasis that has been put on God's special provision for the people during these years (2:7); but in reality two separate theological points are being made. On one side, God's faithfulness and care are exemplified, while on the other the divine punishment of dis-obedience is also revealed.

The explanatory notes in vv. 10-12 and 20-23 concerning the identities and character of the pre-Israelite inhabitants of the land are of special interest and display an antiquarian flavor.[27] Al-ready the report of the spies had brought infor-mation concerning the height of the inhabitants. Now various names are ascribed to them: Emim, Anakim, Rephaim, Zamzummim, and Avvim. The name "Rephaim" is not an ethnic term, and appears in Ps 88:10 and Isa 14:9 as a title for the spirits of the dead. It seems to convey the mean-ing "healer" or "restorer." What is apparently the same name is found in Ugaritic as an honorific title for the god Baal. Emim are mentioned in Gen 14:5, Anakim in Num 13:33 and Judg 1:20; and Avvim in Josh 13:3. These latter are undoubtedly understood to have been the original occupants of southwest Palestine, but it is in any event probable that frequent population shifts took place in the region. Both the difficult climate and the vulnerable political situation vis-à-vis Egypt brought frequent changes. From the perspective of tracing historically some of the major ethnic movements of the region, the mention of the displacement of the Avvim by the Caphtorim from Caphtor (Crete) indicates their likely links with the Philistines, whose origin from Caphtor is else-where referred to (Jer 47:4; Amos 9:7).

2:24–3:11. The fact that the disobedient and fainthearted generation that had refused to under-

27. See L. Perlitt, "Riesen im Alten Testament. Ein literarisches Motiv im Wirkungsfeld des Deuteronomismus," in *Deuteronomium-Studien* (Tübingen: J. C. B. Mohr, 1994) 205-46.

take an immediate march to occupy the land had died out is now fully recognized by the author. A worthier and more faith-engendered enterprise could now begin. Forceful dispossession of the previous inhabitants of the land would now have to commence, and two instances from Israel's historical tradition are adduced to bear this out.

From the author's point of view, these stories serve a double purpose, on the one hand establishing the claim that the land promised to Israel included territory to the east of Jordan. Throughout the report the writer's own location west of the Jordan is presupposed. On the other hand, these accounts of victories gained east of the Jordan provided exemplary instances of how success in conquering the land was to be achieved. Victory would be a gift of God so that great emphasis is placed on the elements of panic and confusion the enemy were to experience, reducing their defense to the point of being ineffective.[28] King Sihon of Heshbon and King Og of Bashan are the example cases that show that victory comes from the LORD and brings with it the right to take possession of conquered territory.[29]

The narrative at this point draws upon material from Num 20:17, 19 and 21:21-23, which has been adapted to bring out the deuteronomist's particular religious interests. It especially concerns the art of warfare, beginning with a characteristic emphasis on the psychological factors—the generating of fear and foreboding in the hearts of the enemy (v. 25) and the demand for unflinching courage and faith on the part of Israel's warriors. It is noteworthy that the possibility of avoiding conflict altogether is raised in vv. 27-29, with the offer of a peaceful passage through Sihon's territory. We may compare the instructions for the conduct of war set out in 20:1-20. The discrepancies and unevenness further bear out that the deuteronomic law book was produced from varied materials over a period of time and is far from being homogeneous and unified.

The refusal to accept Israel's offer of peace then provides a reason for the beginning of conflict, which in turn entitles Israel to take possession of Sihon's territory, which is now considered to have become forfeit.[30] The point is of interest since it

further reflects the deuteronomic sensitivity to questions of human responsibility and the unresolved tensions that lie hidden in the phrase "God had hardened his spirit" (v. 30).

The narrative brings to light the fact that Heshbon was Sihon's chief city so that the region over which he ruled was not extensive. Kingship did not necessarily imply leadership either of a large territory or of a large national community. He appears more to have been an urban chieftain than the ruler of a nation. His control was mainly a regional one, and the point is important for understanding the rise of monarchy as an institution in which territorial, rather than kinship, factors played a large role.

The narrative concerning the defeat and dispossession of the two kings from Transjordan enables us for the first time to perceive details of the distinctive and prominent deuteronomic theology of warfare.[31] It has become customary to describe this deuteronomic doctrine as that of "holy war," although serious caveats and objections need to be considered in regard to such a title. Most especially it must be regarded as extremely doubtful that the deuteronomic authors were simply reflecting a far older and widely practiced set of conventions regarding the conduct of war. Certainly both contemporary experience and past customs and conventions are to be traced in the deuteronomic presentation, but ultimately its distinctive, and effectively unique, character must be recognized. So, too, is it necessary to draw attention to several highly stylized and theoretical features that are introduced into it.

It is important to the deuteronomic interpretation of warfare that it is chiefly considered from the point of view of the conquest and retention of the land. So it was seen as a religious duty, and those who participated in it were consecrated to their task. In turn this consecration imposed restraints and set limits on what could be gained from the victorious outcome of such battles. It is certainly not the case that such a deuteronomic understanding of a form of consecration to warfare was intended only in the case of defensive battles. On the contrary, almost all that is presented on

---

28. See M. C. Lind, *Yahweh Is a Warrior: The Theology of Warfare in Ancient Israel* (Scottdale, Pa.: Herald, 1980) 147-48, "Reliance upon Yahweh's Miracle."

29. For the historical background, see J. R. Bartlett, "Sihon and Og, Kings of the Amorites," *VT* 20 (1970) 257-77.

30. S. Niditch, *Warfare in the Hebrew Bible. A Study in the Ethics of Violence* (New York: Oxford University Press, 1993) 127-28.

31. G. von Rad, *Studies in Deuteronomy,* trans. David Stalker, SBT 9 (London: SCM, 1953) 45-59, and *Holy War in Ancient Israel,* trans. Marva J. Dawn (Grand Rapids: Eerdmans, 1991) 115-27; M. C. Lind, *Yahweh Is a Warrior,* 146-68.

the subject is subordinated to the claim that the gift of the land that Israel occupied was a direct gift from God.[32] It had been promised to Israel's ancestors and so belonged to Israel as a consequence of its election by the LORD God. It is this promise and the related claim to a special election that rendered the commitment to take the land in warfare a religious task.

The most striking aspect of the deuteronomic doctrine of warfare is the claim that the primary qualifications demanded of Israel were faith and courage. The victory would come as a gift of God, a situation exemplified in the story of the conquest of Jericho. Little real fighting would be necessary, and the elements of religious ritual were every bit as important as the task of actual fighting. Through and through the conduct of war is viewed as a supernatural activity in which Israel's warriors would face little risk to themselves, if only they exemplified the right kind of courage and obedience.

Considering the period at which this deuteronomic doctrine of warfare emerged, we can feel certain that it represents a heavily theologized and theoretical response to Israel's deep consciousness of military weakness. In the two centuries from the middle of the eighth century BCE to the middle of the sixth, Israel and Judah had suffered fearsome defeats in the face of the imperial spread of Mesopotamian power. Neither Israel's own military strength nor that which could be called upon by the formation of alliances with Egypt and other neighboring powers proved adequate to face such a threat. The deuteronomic doctrine, therefore, must be viewed as an attempt to piece together a new understanding of warfare and a new explanation for the seeming failures of national policy. It has undoubtedly drawn upon beliefs, customs, and a military awareness that made its novelties and strong claims for acts of divine intervention a further cause for total obedience to the LORD as God. As a practical formula for military reorganization and renewal, it appears strained and unconvincing. Yet as a basis for appeal for a new sense of national reawakening and a renewal of national pride, it merits close attention for its spiritual intensity.

The emphasis on the sovereignty of the divine power is well brought out in v. 33 with its insistence that "the LORD gave him

over to us." Even so, the unevenness of the deuteronomic ideology reappears once it is recognized that the actions of the people in these battles do not properly conform to those laid down later in the regulations of 20:10-18.

3:12-17. Bashan was an area in Transjordan, to the north of Gilead, highly regarded for its rich, fertile land, which is the meaning its very name conveys (Amos 4:1; Mic 7:14). No older pre-deuteronomic account has been preserved of the defeat of King Og, although Josh 12:4 reports the ruler's name and tells of his control over this rich territory. Verse 2, which appears as a paranthetical addition, reiterates the primary injunction to show no fear in the face of a powerful enemy.

The story of Israel's journeyings and experiences under the leadership of Moses is now brought to a conclusion with a summary account of the allocation of land east of the Jordan to the tribes of Reuben, Gad, and Manasseh. The region on the east of the river Jordan that is here claimed for Israel was very extensive, stretching from Mt. Hermon in the north to the boundary of Moab at the river Arnon in the south. The central region of Gilead was divided by the Jabbok. All told, the deuteronomic historical narratives appear to show a special anxiety to reaffirm Israel's claim to this desirable region, noted for its agricultural lushness and contrasting with the more rugged hill country to the west of Jordan and the semi-desert region to the south. Not least was this Transjordanian territory felt to be of great significance for the security of the Jordan valley and the protection of its trade routes.

The vulnerability of the region to incursions from the east, from which aggressive marauding tribespeople came repeatedly, accounts for much of its violent history. During the period of Israel's monarchy, it appears that this area of the Transjordan was subjected to a whole series of conflicts, bringing constant realignments of allegiance. Little clear historical recollection has been preserved of Reuben's checkered and unfortunate history. At a very early period in the emergence of Israel as a nation it appears to have suffered as a consequence of its exposed position. That the tribal territory of Manasseh straddled the Jordan was important to its survival within Israel. Those tribes who had settled in the attractive lands to the east of Jordan were too exposed to a variety of threats

32. W. Brueggemann, *The Land: Place as Gift, Promise and Challenge in Biblical Faith,* OBT (Philadelphia: Fortress, 1977) 45-53.

to be able to maintain themselves with any confidence. It is also noteworthy that the settlement of Israelite tribes to the east of the Jordan posed something of a problem for the deuteronomist's concern with the centralizing of worship in Jerusalem; as a result, the issue receives separate attention in Josh 22:1-34. Overall it seems clear that the deuteronomist was aware of the weak position of the tribes settled east of the Jordan, but that his convictions concerning the oneness of Israel, understood in a very wide compass, has encouraged attention to their territory.

Joshua 12:4 records that King Og of Bashan belonged among the Rephaim (cf. Deut 3:13). The writer here clearly regarded this as evidence of Og's great stature and strength, leading to the intriguing antiquarian notice in v. 11 regarding his iron bed. The REB follows a scholarly suggestion that this can best be understood as a reference to a "sarcophagus of basalt." That it should have been thirteen feet long and six feet wide (NRSV, "nine cubits by four") would then not be so surprising. It would, in fact, be factually quite feasible and would indicate little regarding the king's actual physical stature.

Much of the information set out here regarding the tribal settlements of Israel has been drawn from Num 32:9. Nevertheless it has been added to, and tailored into, a carefully structured unity. A measure of difficulty appears in that v. 12 reports that the half tribe of Manasseh was allocated the territory of Bashan and the northern half of Gilead. This has then been amplified in v. 15 to record that Gilead was ascribed to Machir, who was one son of Manasseh, whereas Bashan was given to another son, Jair. A judge named Jair is mentioned in Judg 10:3-5 as having originated from Gilead and is said to have judged Israel for twenty-two years. This would be in accord with 1 Chr 2:21-22, which makes Jair the great-grandson of Manasseh's son Machir. It may be that the author here was seeking to systematize such evidence as he had, but it is also necessary to bear in mind that the same name could frequently recur across several generations.

The overall purpose of this narrative unit is clear: It is concerned to trace the story of Israel's beginnings from the time of the revelation of God on Mt. Horeb to the eve of the people's entry into the land. Some supplementation of the original narrative appears to have taken place with a view to adding interesting additional detail and clarifying information mentioned only briefly in the basic account.

3:18-29. Essentially the original account of the first campaign to occupy the land, which dealt with the region of Transjordan, appears to have been drawn by the author from material preserved in the book of Numbers. Nevertheless, it has been carefully systematized and filled out. The historical details have been set in the background in order to illuminate more fully certain basic theological themes that the deuteronomists regarded as matters of great importance.

Prominent among these themes is the uniqueness of the leadership afforded by Moses, who now dominates the scene.[33] It is a remarkable feature of chaps. 1–11 that the name and achievements of Moses are given immense emphasis that contrasts with the absence of his name from chaps. 12–26.

In this first campaign, where his presence is evident, Moses' personal conduct contrasts with the lamentably poor response shown by the Israelites more generally to the privileges and opportunities that had been granted to them. Where he shows obedience and faith, the people display distrust and fear. So Moses himself is exonerated from all blame, and it is the people who must carry the guilt of this. We may note nevertheless that, according to v. 26, Moses was forced to suffer on the people's account; so he had to share the privations and punishment of the people whose leader he had become. It is more a shared punishment than a vicarious punishment, but it is not difficult to see that it could later be understood in this fashion (see 32:51; Num 20:12).

The leadership of Moses is clearly intended to be exemplary, and his success is only vitiated because the people as a whole fail to heed his commands, or do so only reluctantly. So the people enjoy success in their military campaigns while the leadership of Moses remains available to them. They are able without difficulty to conquer the territories of Sihon and Og and to deal effectively with Edom and Moab. When we seek to find some explanation for this exceptional emphasis on one man, which the deuteronomic authors have obviously taken some pains to stress

33. See G. W. Coats, *Moses: Heroic Man, Man of God,* JSOTSup 57 (Sheffield: JSOT, 1988).

beyond what their sources declared, two points emerge. The first of these is provided by the portrayal of the confused, defeatist, and timid spirit displayed by the majority in Israel. This was evidently an attitude of mind that the writer clearly believed reflected the mood of his own readers. They were tempted to relapse into the same mood of defeatist despair, lacking worthy leadership. Yet they themselves could no longer enjoy the direct leadership of Moses, who had himself not entered the land.

So this gave rise to the second of the points regarding this unusual emphasis. If the people could no longer enjoy the leadership of Moses, they could bask in the benefit of the great gift Moses had brought to them. This was the gift of the law of the LORD, and this is the message the book of Deuteronomy was concerned to present. It was, indeed, the great legacy Moses had given to Israel.

It might have been assumed that the leadership of Moses was simply handed on to his successor in the person of Joshua (vv. 21, 28). Yet, there is a subtle delicacy and distinctiveness in the manner in which the deuteronomists present the succession of Joshua. He is not another Moses, since there could never be such a figure, but Joshua is most emphatically the successor to the

great leader. So his role is significantly different, and his task is to ensure that the commands and instructions of Moses are faithfully carried out. He is the administrator of a new order, and this new order is that of living in accordance with the law that Moses had revealed to the people. In a sense, Joshua is the first deuteronomist, since he is the leader of the generation that was called upon to shape its life and actions in accordance with what had been laid down by the founding father of the nation. To this extent, the very uniqueness of Moses makes the succession of Joshua indispensable. The lawgiver must give way to the first administrator of the law. This issue is so important that it is dealt with further in chaps. 31 and 34.

The concluding geographical note leaves Israel poised at the border of the promised land and being brought face to face with a new temptation. Halted in the valley opposite Beth-peor, the Israelites face the dangerous possibility of accepting and worshiping the gods of the land they are about to occupy. The reference to the location must intend the same place referred to as Baal-peor, which is clearly presumed in 4:3 to be the case. In Josh 13:20, the location is connected with Mt. Pisgah (cf. Hos 9:10). As often occurred, the name of the deity and his sanctuary has served to provide a name for the entire town.

REFLECTIONS

The entire deuteronomic theology of war is composed of the various exhortations, regulations, and narratives that deal with the military aspects of Israel's national life. Precisely because this theology of war enters so strongly and extensively into the larger biblical narrative tradition, it has given rise to some of the sharpest and most keenly felt objections to the morality of the biblical revelation. A number of considerations need to be borne in mind that may offer some reasoned understanding of this feature of Deuteronomy.

A number of political and religious concerns, closely bound up with the deuteronomic authors' contemporary anxieties, may be discerned. From a political and legal standpoint, it mattered greatly to affirm that the whole land promised to Abraham's descendants had been occupied and settled by Israel. The previous inhabitants had simply been wiped out. Not only was this a gross exaggeration, but it fits badly with the deuteronomic writers' insistence, given in the narrative history that follows, that Israel was persistently and deeply led into disloyalty to God by the temptation to emulate the religion of those who survived in the land. The theory of a wholesale extermination of the previous inhabitants of the land was intended to give assurance that Israel's forebears had at first enjoyed a good and unrestricted start to life in the land. Furthermore, it was necessary to reassert the claim that the entire land had at one time belonged to Israel by right of conquest.

However, even the felt need to provide a clean sheet for the record of Israel's origins in the land, with its highly selective and stylized character, cannot account for the insensitivity and cruelty with which the demand for a religiously motivated genocide is expressed. This fact alone forces us to recognize that the deuteronomic authors were keenly aware of Israel's weakness when faced with the contemporary threat from the military might of Babylon. Behind that more than a century of humiliating subjugation to the Assyrians had effectively led to the loss of a large part of the territory occupied by the northern tribes and had left a legacy of almost abject helplessness on the part of those who remained. Faced with forces that had developed effective techniques of siege breaking and whose cohorts were manned by well-trained and unpitying soldiers, Israel's weakness was all too evident. So we can understand, even if we cannot justify, that Deuteronomy responded to such a threat by a new harshness and severity of its own and by reasserting with a passionate zeal the conviction that the LORD God was greater than all the powers ranged against them. So this book idealized the past in order to compensate for the inadequacies of the present. Most striking of all, the deuteronomic authors sought to rearm faith as a means for combating the sense of helplessness they so readily associate with their readers. All was not lost, and a new commitment of faith could bring a new age in which even the great achievements of Joshua would no longer appear strange and out of place.

Yet, we dare not overlook the impassioned commitment to military force and expectations that the deuteronomists express. Even allowing its presence in other parts of the biblical literature, there exists within it a great consciousness of the cruelty and barbarity of war and of the irreplaceable gift of peace and security. At best, all that the modern reader can hope to salvage from the shadowed and dangerous encouragement the deuteronomists give to warfare as a means of achieving the divine will are some elements of its psychological and spiritual relevance. The appeal to courage and faith, and even to an unremitting resistance to evil, has provided a rich imagery for a portrayal of human life as a "spiritual warfare." We may compare especially John Bunyan's extensive use of both the language and the ideas drawn from the deuteronomists in his work *The Holy War Made by Shaddai upon Diabolus for the Regaining of the Metropolis of the World* (1682).

DEUTERONOMY 4:1–11:32

THE COMMANDMENTS OF GOD

DEUTERONOMY 4:1-43, THE GREAT SUMMONS TO OBEDIENCE

OVERVIEW

The deuteronomic literature is through and through colored by its use of speeches, prayers, and occasional historical reflections that have a strong impact on the reader. In the case of speeches, which are made by the leading figures within the narrative, the distance between the original hearers of the speech and the readers of the book is swallowed up. The message takes on a degree of timelessness. Such speeches and prayers are characterized by some of the most searching theological reflections to be found anywhere in the OT. This amply confirms the widely recognized feature that the deuteronomic movement was heavily innovative in its theological grasp and intentions.

The speech that is here ascribed to Moses has been introduced into the narrative of the lawbook at a relatively late stage.[34] Almost certainly it can be recognized as one of the very latest units to have been composed and incorporated into the book. This is borne out by the reference in v. 3 linking the speech to Israel's encampment at Baal-peor, waiting to cross the Jordan and to enter the land. This event, with all its tensions and temptations, is seen as a decisive moment for Israel's past, calling for special caution and heart searching. Yet the speech is wholly deuteronomic in its character and clearly recognizes that many of the former citizens of Israel had, by this time, been dispersed into exile among the nations (vv. 27-31). This fact adds to the awareness that acute temptations and difficulties were facing many Israelites in a perilous and uncertain future. In a quite special way, therefore, it addresses these people (v. 29), recognizing their yearning at a distance for the land and conscious that it was, for the present at least, lost to them (cf. Jer 29:12-13). It urges them not to abandon their loyalty to the LORD God, reassuring them that they, in turn, will not be abandoned by God.

The difficult situation of such people, separated from the Temple and its ministry, is reflected in v. 9, which introduces an injunction to make the commandments the subject of teaching within the home, particularly emphasizing the necessity of instructing children in them. This consciousness that the law was not simply a matter for elders and recognized officials, but a textbook to be used for instruction in the home, becomes a highly distinctive characteristic of Deuteronomy. It is a book for a whole community and for everyone who cares about the LORD God, not simply a charter for leaders and officials.

---

34. N. Lohfink, "Verkündigung des Hauptgebots in der jüngsten Schicht des Deuteronomiums (Dt 4,1-40)," in *Studien zum Deuteronomium und deuteronomistischen Literatur I*, SBA 8 (Stuttgart: Katholisches Bibelwerk, 1995) 167-92.

Deuteronomy 4:1-20, A Warning Against Idolatry

NIV

4 Hear now, O Israel, the decrees and laws I am about to teach you. Follow them so that you may live and may go in and take possession of the land that the LORD, the God of your fathers, is giving you. ²Do not add to what I command you and do not subtract from it, but keep the commands of the LORD your God that I give you.

³You saw with your own eyes what the LORD did at Baal Peor. The LORD your God destroyed from among you everyone who followed the Baal of Peor, ⁴but all of you who held fast to the LORD your God are still alive today.

⁵See, I have taught you decrees and laws as the LORD my God commanded me, so that you may follow them in the land you are entering to take possession of it. ⁶Observe them carefully, for this will show your wisdom and understanding to the nations, who will hear about all these decrees and say, "Surely this great nation is a wise and understanding people." ⁷What other nation is so great as to have their gods near them the way the LORD our God is near us whenever we pray to him? ⁸And what other nation is so great as to have such righteous decrees and laws as this body of laws I am setting before you today?

⁹Only be careful, and watch yourselves closely so that you do not forget the things your eyes have seen or let them slip from your heart as long as you live. Teach them to your children and to their children after them. ¹⁰Remember the day you stood before the LORD your God at Horeb, when he said to me, "Assemble the people before me to hear my words so that they may learn to revere me as long as they live in the land and may teach them to their children." ¹¹You came near and stood at the foot of the mountain while it blazed with fire to the very heavens, with black clouds and deep darkness. ¹²Then the LORD spoke to you out of the fire. You heard the sound of words but saw no form; there was only a voice. ¹³He declared to you his covenant, the Ten Commandments, which he commanded you to follow and then wrote them on two stone tablets. ¹⁴And the LORD directed me at that time to teach you the

NRSV

4 So now, Israel, give heed to the statutes and ordinances that I am teaching you to observe, so that you may live to enter and occupy the land that the LORD, the God of your ancestors, is giving you. ²You must neither add anything to what I command you nor take away anything from it, but keep the commandments of the LORD your God with which I am charging you. ³You have seen for yourselves what the LORD did with regard to the Baal of Peor—how the LORD your God destroyed from among you everyone who followed the Baal of Peor, ⁴while those of you who held fast to the LORD your God are all alive today.

⁵See, just as the LORD my God has charged me, I now teach you statutes and ordinances for you to observe in the land that you are about to enter and occupy. ⁶You must observe them diligently, for this will show your wisdom and discernment to the peoples, who, when they hear all these statutes, will say, "Surely this great nation is a wise and discerning people!" ⁷For what other great nation has a god so near to it as the LORD our God is whenever we call to him? ⁸And what other great nation has statutes and ordinances as just as this entire law that I am setting before you today?

⁹But take care and watch yourselves closely, so as neither to forget the things that your eyes have seen nor to let them slip from your mind all the days of your life; make them known to your children and your children's children— ¹⁰how you once stood before the LORD your God at Horeb, when the LORD said to me, "Assemble the people for me, and I will let them hear my words, so that they may learn to fear me as long as they live on the earth, and may teach their children so"; ¹¹you approached and stood at the foot of the mountain while the mountain was blazing up to the very heavens, shrouded in dark clouds. ¹²Then the LORD spoke to you out of the fire. You heard the sound of words but saw no form; there was only a voice. ¹³He declared to you his covenant, which he charged you to observe, that is, the ten commandments;ᵃ and he

ᵃ Heb *the ten words*

NIV

decrees and laws you are to follow in the land that you are crossing the Jordan to possess.

¹⁵You saw no form of any kind the day the LORD spoke to you at Horeb out of the fire. Therefore watch yourselves very carefully, ¹⁶so that you do not become corrupt and make for yourselves an idol, an image of any shape, whether formed like a man or a woman, ¹⁷or like any animal on earth or any bird that flies in the air, ¹⁸or like any creature that moves along the ground or any fish in the waters below. ¹⁹And when you look up to the sky and see the sun, the moon and the stars—all the heavenly array— do not be enticed into bowing down to them and worshiping things the LORD your God has apportioned to all the nations under heaven. ²⁰But as for you, the LORD took you and brought you out of the iron-smelting furnace, out of Egypt, to be the people of his inheritance, as you now are.

NRSV

wrote them on two stone tablets. ¹⁴And the LORD charged me at that time to teach you statutes and ordinances for you to observe in the land that you are about to cross into and occupy.

15Since you saw no form when the LORD spoke to you at Horeb out of the fire, take care and watch yourselves closely, ¹⁶so that you do not act corruptly by making an idol for yourselves, in the form of any figure—the likeness of male or female, ¹⁷the likeness of any animal that is on the earth, the likeness of any winged bird that flies in the air, ¹⁸the likeness of anything that creeps on the ground, the likeness of any fish that is in the water under the earth. ¹⁹And when you look up to the heavens and see the sun, the moon, and the stars, all the host of heaven, do not be led astray and bow down to them and serve them, things that the LORD your God has allotted to all the peoples everywhere under heaven. ²⁰But the LORD has taken you and brought you out of the iron-smelter, out of Egypt, to become a people of his very own possession, as you are now.

COMMENTARY

In its content, this great hortatory speech falls into two parts (vv. 1-20 and 21-40) that nevertheless remain closely interlinked. The first part declares unequivocally that on Mt. Horeb the LORD made a covenant with Israel that had as its central feature a series of ten commandments, written on two stone tablets (v. 13). This is the first point at which the deuteronomic author has explicitly described the events that took place on Mt. Horeb as constituting a covenant agreement. It becomes one of the key themes, encapsulated in the key term "covenant" (ברית *bĕrît*), by which the bilateral commitments between the LORD as God and Israel as a people are described.[35] Its usage is spread rather unevenly throughout the book of Deuteronomy and the literature influ-

enced by it, strongly pointing to the conclusion that it was not an original part of the deuteronomic theological vocabulary, but was introduced into it at a particular stage. A major consequence of its use was to indicate both a conditional element in Israel's special relationship to the LORD God and a heightened sense of the exclusiveness of the moral and spiritual demands imposed on Israel. This provides the basis for the second part of the speech in v. 21.

A transition to this second section is provided by vv. 15-20, which focus attention on the demands of the second commandment, with its complete rejection of the use of any image or idol in the worship of God. It is a complete rebuttal of the validity of any such image, uncompromising and far-reaching in its firmness. Only in the prophetic passage in Isa 44:9-20 do we find any comparable treatment of the theological objections to idolatry. The speech here clearly recognizes that idolatry had remained a persistent and powerful temptation to Israel, by its very vigor clearly

35. For the deuteronomic background of covenant terminology, see L. Perlitt, *Bundestheologie im Alten Testament,* WMANT 36 (Neukirchen-Vluyn: Neukirchener Verlag, 1969); D. J. McCarthy, *Old Testament Covenant: A Survey of Current Opinions* (Oxford: Blackwell, 1972); D. R. Hillers, *Covenant: The History of a Biblical Idea* (Baltimore: Johns Hopkins University Press, 1969); E. W. Nicholson, *God and His People: Covenant and Theology in the Old Testament* (Oxford: Oxford University Press, 1986).

indicating that this was a temptation Israel had not often resisted.

The origins and primary reasons for the rejection of the use of images for God in Israel remain obscure and have been heavily discussed.[36] The very associations of images with alien forms of religion in which the LORD had either no place at all or only a very subordinate one within a larger pantheon would clearly have strengthened the call to reject their use. It is likely also that iconographic imagery was closely linked to aspects of cultus involving fertility rituals, which the more carefully guarded features of the Israelite religious inheritance strongly opposed. Idols, therefore, had many unwelcome associations. To what extent an unapproved tradition in the use of idols, involving images among which even the LORD God could be represented, was present in ancient Israel has never become wholly clear from archaeological research. It seems likely that such representations existed, but that they may have been subjected to much official opposition and condemnation.

Certainly in the deuteronomic movement the prohibition of the use of images was one of the most keenly felt, and strongly argued, features pertaining to the Israelite tradition. It is also a feature in which the passionate condemnations of the deuteronomists have left the strongest imprint on the biblical literature. Accordingly, a special interest attaches to the explanations and theological justification for this rejection, set out here. Valuable as it is, it nonetheless falls short of providing a wholly convincing rationale for so major a feature of religion.

As to the speech itself we may confidently regard its balanced literary structure as indicative that it has been constructed as a unity. Throughout it displays the strong rhetorical style that is so characteristic of the deuteronomists. This, in itself, provides evidence that behind the book of Deuteronomy stands a well-established and effective preaching style that must have become part of an intense preaching and didactic activity within the community.

4:1-8. The opening part of the address declares that what Moses presented to the people consisted of "statutes and ordinances." These key terms used in legal administration are further defined in v. 8 as

constituting תורה (tôrâ).[37] This term, which has familiarly entered into the English-language biblical tradition, more widely denotes "instruction" or "direction." Clearly it includes laws, but much else besides. It was an appropriate term by which to describe cultic instruction, but it could also be used to describe moral direction. It cannot have been a distinctive neologism on the part of the deuteronomists, but their use of it, particularly to describe the varied contents of Moses' teaching, undoubtedly raised its importance for the development of Israel's religious life. Taken as a description of the material set out in the book of Deuteronomy, it can helpfully be described as "polity,"[38] since what is set out covers a great deal of direction for the constitutional structure of Israel as a national community.

The importance of this comprehensive designation of the divine revelation as Torah cannot easily be overestimated. No other requirement, whether passed as a royal edict, imposed as a local priestly convention, or revealed through a prophet could displace it or override it. It offered a categorical rule of life. At the same time, this comprehensiveness, expressed through its being linked with other, more diverse titles of a predominantly legal character, asserted that it carried an all-sufficient authority. It was a rule of life, controlling public behavior as well as religious practice and political affairs. Taken as a whole it offered a guidebook for education and contained a wisdom that established life goals and guidelines for all human living. To some extent, its all-encompassing role as a direction for human life is modified and limited by its being presented as the conditions of a covenant between Israel and God, but it nevertheless remains both a human document and a national one.[39]

Here, as repeatedly in the book, we encounter a strong emphasis on the various psychological aspects relating to religious loyalty and spiritual

36. W. Zimmerli, "Das Zweite Gebot," *Gottes Offenbarung. Gesammelte Aufsätze,* Theologische Bücherei 19 (Munich: Kaiser Verlag, 1963) 234-48.

37. See B. Lindars, "Torah in Deuteronomy," in *Words and Meanings: Essays Presented to David Winton Thomas,* ed. P. R. Ackroyd and B. Lindars (Cambridge: Cambridge University Presss, 1968) 117-36; G. Braulik, "Die Ausdrücke für 'Gesetz' im Buch Deuteronomium," *Studien zur Theologie des Deuteronomiums,* Stuttgarter Biblische Aufsatzbände 2 (Stuttgart: Katholisches Bibelwerk, 1988) 11-38.

38. S. Dean McBride, "Polity of the Covenant People: The Book of Deuteronomy," *Int* 41 (1987) 229-44.

39. G. Braulik, "Deuteronomy and Human Rights," in *The Theology of Deuteronomy: Collected Essays of Georg Braulik, O.S.B.,* trans. Ulrika Lindblad, Bibal Collected Essays 2 (N. Richland Hills, Tex.: Bibal, 1994) 131-50.

sincerity. So there are repeated exhortations concerning the commandments to "watch . . . do not forget . . . nor let them slip from your mind." This is combined with a strong emphasis on the inner psychological dimension of obedience. The people must not "become complacent" or "act corruptly" (i.e., be guilty of self-delusion, v. 25).

4:9-14. In these verses, the author presupposes that the reader is fully familiar with the events that took place on Mt. Horeb and are recorded in Exodus 19–20. He expects the reader to know this story well and to have reflected upon it, taking full cognizance of the impressive awesomeness of the events that occurred.

Through skillful literary artistry, the author brings into unity three distinct generations of Israelites: "You once stood before the LORD your God at Horeb." However, the adults of the first generation had died in the wilderness, and a new generation now stood poised to enter the land. Yet this community, too, is the author's backward projection into the past, since he is wholly mindful of the readers and hearers whom he now addresses. All three generations are nevertheless one people who constitute "all Israel," united through their generations. From within this unity, Moses still speaks to the present generation.

The nature of the "fire" (vv. 11-12) on Mt. Horeb has provided few useful clues to the original location of the mountain or its geological character. It is only since early Christian times that its identification with Jebel Musa, the highest mountain of the Sinai peninsula, has been firmly claimed. Other possibilities for a location closer to the oasis of Kadesh, and even more distant ones, have been canvassed in an effort to defend the interpretation of the "fire" on the mountain as a manifestation of volcanic activity. Yet this latter claim would carry the entire episode much too far to the east to be a convincing alternative. The theophany tradition that was so central to the Israelite recollection of the significance of the mountain has undoubtedly woven together various images.[40] Some of these appear to be natural phenomena such as storms and volcanic activity, but features of a sanctuary, with its altar fire

burning, have been woven into the tradition as well. So, by itself, the fire imagery, which was in any case a widely established feature of a divine presence, enables us to determine little at all about the original location of the holy mountain.

4:15-20. The strong polemic against idolatry in these verses proceeds to deal with the central theme of the speech as a whole. The temptation posed by the sanctuary at Baal-peor has rendered it necessary. It concerns the vital necessity of maintaining the second commandment, prohibiting any Israelite from using an image as a focus for worship. From within the context of the Ten Commandments, this second commandment (5:8-10) presumes that such an image would be some form of the representation of the LORD God, since to worship any other deity alongside the LORD was already precluded. In reality, however, it seems probable that the subjects covered by the first two commandments could readily become intertwined.

The reference in v. 17 to the likeness of any human or animal form greatly extends the prohibition to cover creatures that could be understood as consorts, or servants, of the LORD God. In general, in the ancient Near East deities were conceived of as being grouped into pantheons in which a number of deities were placed in a certain order and were themselves pictured as being surrounded by a number of lesser deities and heavenly servants, some with human form and some with part-human or animal form. The world of the gods was portrayed as comparable to the earthly world, but populated by a mixture of beings.

Alongside the representations of human-like and animal-like beings existed many stylized symbols that were also thought to possess divine power, or at least to make such power accessible. Prominent among these were portrayals of the sun and the moon and other heavenly bodies (v. 19). So an "image" could take many forms, and even the biblical narrative tradition contained recollections of the use of symbolic artifacts, used in the Jerusalem Temple as symbols of special potency (1 Kgs 6:23-36). The prophet Ezekiel's descriptions of bizarre imagery in the very heart of the Jerusalem Temple reveal how complex such symbolism could become (Ezek 8:5, 10). More important, the repeated condemnations of it in prophecy make plain that the use of such symbolism, what each symbol was thought to mean or

40. The development of such a tradition from a variety of traditional features is proposed by Jörg Jeremias, *Theophanie, Die Geschichte einer alttestamentlichen Gattung*, WMANT 10 (Neukirchen-Vluyn: Neukirchener Verlag, 1965).

convey, and whether it was acceptable within the Israelite tradition of worship were all highly contested issues. It would certainly appear that the deuteronomic authors, and the exilic age more generally, marked a period when a much more stringent interpretation of the second commandment became strenuously advocated.

The polemic set out here, that Israel heard a voice but saw no form of deity when the LORD God was revealed as being present at Mt. Horeb (v. 15), does little to clarify the reasons why such a prohibition arose in Israel and why it was felt to carry such immense importance. From a practical perspective, however, it is not difficult to see why, with the deuteronomists and the period of the exilic age, the issue had become a major one.

If Israel were to retain any clear uniformity and identity within its religious tradition, then the use of unrestrained and uncontrolled iconography of any form of deity whatsoever existed as a major threat. Images could mean almost anything and could readily be associated with more than one deity, with such bewildering lack of positive control or integrity that their use could not be tolerated at all. Indeed, it seems highly probable that it was the recognition that this was already the situation for many Israelites that made the intensity of the deuteronomic polemic so necessary. Without the rejection of the plethora of images and symbols that had become commonplace, the deuteronomists saw that Israel's religious tradition would simply disintegrate. (See Reflections at 4:21-43.)

Deuteronomy 4:21-43, A Warning Against Complacency

NIV

21The LORD was angry with me because of you, and he solemnly swore that I would not cross the Jordan and enter the good land the LORD your God is giving you as your inheritance. 22I will die in this land; I will not cross the Jordan; but you are about to cross over and take possession of that good land. 23Be careful not to forget the covenant of the LORD your God that he made with you; do not make for yourselves an idol in the form of anything the LORD your God has forbidden. 24For the LORD your God is a consuming fire, a jealous God.

25After you have had children and grandchildren and have lived in the land a long time—if you then become corrupt and make any kind of idol, doing evil in the eyes of the LORD your God and provoking him to anger, 26I call heaven and earth as witnesses against you this day that you will quickly perish from the land that you are crossing the Jordan to possess. You will not live there long but will certainly be destroyed. 27The LORD will scatter you among the peoples, and only a few of you will survive among the nations to which the LORD will drive you. 28There you will worship man-made gods of wood and stone, which cannot see or hear or eat or smell. 29But if from there you seek the LORD your God, you will find him if you look for him with all your

NRSV

21The LORD was angry with me because of you, and he vowed that I should not cross the Jordan and that I should not enter the good land that the LORD your God is giving for your possession. 22For I am going to die in this land without crossing over the Jordan, but you are going to cross over to take possession of that good land. 23So be careful not to forget the covenant that the LORD your God made with you, and not to make for yourselves an idol in the form of anything that the LORD your God has forbidden you. 24For the LORD your God is a devouring fire, a jealous God.

25When you have had children and children's children, and become complacent in the land, if you act corruptly by making an idol in the form of anything, thus doing what is evil in the sight of the LORD your God, and provoking him to anger, 26I call heaven and earth to witness against you today that you will soon utterly perish from the land that you are crossing the Jordan to occupy; you will not live long on it, but will be utterly destroyed. 27The LORD will scatter you among the peoples; only a few of you will be left among the nations where the LORD will lead you. 28There you will serve other gods made by human hands, objects of wood and stone that neither see, nor hear, nor eat, nor smell. 29From there you will seek the LORD your God, and you will find

NIV

heart and with all your soul. ³⁰When you are in distress and all these things have happened to you, then in later days you will return to the LORD your God and obey him. ³¹For the LORD your God is a merciful God; he will not abandon or destroy you or forget the covenant with your forefathers, which he confirmed to them by oath.

³²Ask now about the former days, long before your time, from the day God created man on the earth; ask from one end of the heavens to the other. Has anything so great as this ever happened, or has anything like it ever been heard of? ³³Has any other people heard the voice of God*ᵃ* speaking out of fire, as you have, and lived? ³⁴Has any god ever tried to take for himself one nation out of another nation, by testings, by miraculous signs and wonders, by war, by a mighty hand and an outstretched arm, or by great and awesome deeds, like all the things the LORD your God did for you in Egypt before your very eyes?

³⁵You were shown these things so that you might know that the LORD is God; besides him there is no other. ³⁶From heaven he made you hear his voice to discipline you. On earth he showed you his great fire, and you heard his words from out of the fire. ³⁷Because he loved your forefathers and chose their descendants after them, he brought you out of Egypt by his Presence and his great strength, ³⁸to drive out before you nations greater and stronger than you and to bring you into their land to give it to you for your inheritance, as it is today.

³⁹Acknowledge and take to heart this day that the LORD is God in heaven above and on the earth below. There is no other. ⁴⁰Keep his decrees and commands, which I am giving you today, so that it may go well with you and your children after you and that you may live long in the land the LORD your God gives you for all time.

⁴¹Then Moses set aside three cities east of the Jordan, ⁴²to which anyone who had killed a person could flee if he had unintentionally killed his neighbor without malice aforethought. He could flee into one of these cities and save his life. ⁴³The cities were these: Bezer in the desert plateau, for the Reubenites; Ramoth in Gilead, for the Gadites; and Golan in Bashan, for the Manassites.

ᵃ33 Or of a god

NRSV

him if you search after him with all your heart and soul. ³⁰In your distress, when all these things have happened to you in time to come, you will return to the LORD your God and heed him. ³¹Because the LORD your God is a merciful God, he will neither abandon you nor destroy you; he will not forget the covenant with your ancestors that he swore to them.

32For ask now about former ages, long before your own, ever since the day that God created human beings on the earth; ask from one end of heaven to the other: has anything so great as this ever happened or has its like ever been heard of? ³³Has any people ever heard the voice of a god speaking out of a fire, as you have heard, and lived? ³⁴Or has any god ever attempted to go and take a nation for himself from the midst of another nation, by trials, by signs and wonders, by war, by a mighty hand and an outstretched arm, and by terrifying displays of power, as the LORD your God did for you in Egypt before your very eyes? ³⁵To you it was shown so that you would acknowledge that the LORD is God; there is no other besides him. ³⁶From heaven he made you hear his voice to discipline you. On earth he showed you his great fire, while you heard his words coming out of the fire. ³⁷And because he loved your ancestors, he chose their descendants after them. He brought you out of Egypt with his own presence, by his great power, ³⁸driving out before you nations greater and mightier than yourselves, to bring you in, giving you their land for a possession, as it is still today. ³⁹So acknowledge today and take to heart that the LORD is God in heaven above and on the earth beneath; there is no other. ⁴⁰Keep his statutes and his commandments, which I am commanding you today for your own well-being and that of your descendants after you, so that you may long remain in the land that the LORD your God is giving you for all time.

41Then Moses set apart on the east side of the Jordan three cities ⁴²to which a homicide could flee, someone who unintentionally kills another person, the two not having been at enmity before; the homicide could flee to one of these cities and live: ⁴³Bezer in the wilderness on the tableland belonging to the Reubenites, Ramoth in Gilead belonging to the Gadites, and Golan in Bashan belonging to the Manassites.

COMMENTARY

4:21-31. The second part of Moses' speech begins in these verses and provides a passage that both develops the theme of the divine fire and combines it with a further warning concerning the threat posed by idolatry. It strengthens the notion of God's consistent and implacable hostility to any form of disobedience against the commandments. The LORD is a devouring fire and a deity whose will cannot be flouted or thwarted. Proof of this fact is found in the tradition that even Moses could fall victim to the divine anger, not on his own account but on account of the faithlessness of the disobedient generation who had perished in the wilderness. They represented a perpetual example, whose misfortune and punishment existed as a warning for all the later generations of Israelites.

Verse 26 adopts the legal formula of summoning heaven and earth as witnesses, since God has no peer among human beings to act as witnesses to the veracity of the divine revelation. Since the summoning of witnesses was a prominent feature of the form of ancient Near Eastern vassal treaties, it could well be that it is on the analogy of such a political-legal formulation that this deuteronomic usage has been based. Yet even this is not a necessary conclusion, since the role of witnesses in lawsuits was familiar enough to the deuteronomists; more important, it was very familiar to every Israelite, so that the employment of such a mode of address would have been readily understood.

The threat voiced in v. 27 that God's punishment for disobedience would take the form of the people's being dispersed among the nations points strongly in the direction of a late origin for this speech, almost certainly after the disasters of 598 and 587 BCE had taken place. As a specific threat, however, it is in line with the deuteronomic concern with the land.

Disobedience to God's covenant and its commandments would result in failure to enjoy life in the promised land. Moses himself is made the prime example of this, although in his case it was not as a consequence of his personal disobedience, but that of his contemporaries. He was debarred from enjoying entry in the land, with all its fruits, on account of the disobedience and unbelief of others. Now the message is spelled out very clearly that failure to respond fully to God's basic demands by showing unswerving loyalty and rejecting any form of idolatry would result in punishment and expulsion from the land. This was clearly the fate that had already befallen some in Israel, whose loss was already known to the readers of Deuteronomy (v. 27).

In this context, it is important to recognize that the concept of "exile among the nations" is already, in this deuteronomic address, beginning to take on a more comprehensive and rounded form as a doctrine of a scattering that could become a long-term condition. Dispersal among the nations was assuming the status of becoming the major threat to the entire nation.

The large-scale deportations to Babylon in 598 and 587 BCE, which already followed even larger mass deportations perpetrated by the Assyrians after the fall of Samaria in 722 BCE, had generated a picture of all Israel effectively returning to the "wilderness." There is, however, an important message of hope set out in vv. 29-31, with its assurance that, even there, God would not abandon them (cf. 1 Kgs 8:45).

4:32-43. The final section of this address in vv. 32-40 returns to the theme of the covenant between God and Israel. It is couched in the heavily rhetorical form that characterizes much of the deuteronomic writing, effectively demonstrating that much of the material in the introduction to the law code was spoken before it came to be written down. The use of rhetorical questions ("For ask now about former ages," v. 32), the emphasis on all the manifestations of God's presence and power ("by trials, by signs, by wonders," v. 34), and the identification of the contemporary hearers of the deuteronomic address with the first generation that had witnessed God's action ("Before your very eyes") all bear the marks of skilled preachers and persuaders.

The reference in v. 37 to the claim that God "loved your ancestors" reveals the interesting manner in which the deuteronomic authors treat the earlier patriarchal period. So far as its historical details are concerned, these writers offer little by way of specific references to either the persons or the events recounted in the book of Genesis. It is not, however, a period that had little meaning for Israel, since it is presented as one in which a continued and purposeful providence was manifested.

The concluding section raises more strikingly than anywhere else in the deuteronomic literature the question of the full extent of the conditional element in Israel's covenant relationship with God. All the rhetoric and warnings are based on the dangers Israel faced and the possibility that disobedience would bring a terrible outburst of the divine wrath and a permanent scattering among the nations. Yet the reflection on this possibility in vv. 37-40 shrinks from this ultimate conclusion without giving a final verdict. All the passion and rhetoric the deuteronomists can call to their aid is directed toward warding off such a terrible threat.

Could the covenant ultimately be broken off permanently and forever on God's side because of the people's disobedience? No answer is given, and in any case it was wholly in line with the deuteronomic theology that it would be events themselves, not theological theorizing, that decided the issue. So far as the present was concerned, all was not yet lost. The land could be held, the exiles could return to their former homeland, and a new nation could arise from the ashes of the old.

A brief note is inserted in vv. 41-43 concerning the establishing of cities of refuge east of the river Jordan. This prepares the way for the next major section, which introduces the primary commandments of the covenant between God and Israel. It has been placed here to complete the details of the arrangements made by Israel for life under the law and in order to maintain the claim to territory east of the Jordan. The establishing of cities of refuge to which a person accused of murder could flee to avoid peremptory vengeance is dealt with in 19:1-10, where the manner of their functioning is more fully explained; but it is not made clear that three of the cities of refuge were to be located east of the Jordan, nor is the precise identification of these sites clarified.

It was obviously important to maintain the jurisdiction of Israelite law across its entire territory, in much the same manner that it was important to provide suitable opportunity for Israelite worship throughout its entire land. For that reason, as a kind of preparation for the further declaration of the divine law (which is made in v. 44), the narrator has recognized that, in upholding Israel's claim to possess territory across the Jordan, the necessary facilities for the proper administration of this claim had to be provided. So this list has been introduced at this point. The names of the cities concerned are in agreement with those mentioned in Josh 20:8, which almost certainly provides the source of the author's information.

To the uninitiated reader, the inclusion of the list makes an awkward interruption of the text, but the reasoning that underlies it is a carefully considered one. The sign and "proof" of Israel's claim to territory was that the divine law was upheld and authoritative there. In similar fashion, Mesopotamian rulers set up tablets of law in order to demonstrate the system of justice that applied as "the law of the land." For Israel's law to be applicable required that the authority for its administration was fully in place. Accordingly, the narrator explains that this had been done as soon as Israel had opportunity to act.

REFLECTIONS

The theological perceptiveness and depth of this great speech ascribed to Moses undoubtedly represent a classical exposition of the deuteronomists' skill and artistry. Their tools are the tools of rhetoric, and their aim is to persuade the reader that faith in God and the scrupulous avoidance of all idolatry are wholly desirable and beneficial goals in life. So they set about imparting to their readers a renewed sense of who they really are and what dangers are currently facing them. Yet this is achieved by identifying the present readership with a generation that had long since passed away. They can even appeal to present readers to believe that they actually witnessed some of the events they can only have known as stories and names from a distant past.

Even more startling, they are shown to be waiting to cross over the Jordan and to begin life as a nation—an event that even their most distantly and carefully remembered forebears would not have experienced directly. Yet, in some sense, through the power of the spoken and written word, the past lives again for them, since they can find in it the key to their own situation. The richness of the land encourages them to believe the word of God and take possession of the land; yet, the sanctuary of Baal-peor and the temptations of idolatry raise a sinister threat to the enjoyment of the land.

The weapon by which the folly of idolatry is countered is an appeal to historical events and to the absurdity of idolatry. Since God's glory and power had been revealed on Mt. Horeb, then an image made of stone or wood could convey nothing of the true majesty of God. It was more appropriate and meaningful to recall the unimaginable glory of fire and smoke filling the heavens than to suppose that a man-made artifact could conjure up divine power.

For the modern reader, the question of idolatry appears to pose no threat at all, if it is viewed simply in terms of using visual aids to conjure up images and memories of God and the divine power. Even Paul in the Epistle to the Colossians interprets idolatry in terms closer to the tenth, rather than the second, commandment when he describes its error as that of covetousness (Col 3:5). For the biblical tradition, the intensity of opposition to idolatry appears to lie in its pretentiousness of claiming that God can be manipulated and used to serve some desirable human goal. It turns God into an object and makes human beings the subject who can conjure up divine power to suit themselves. Over against this the biblical presentation, mediated through storytelling and metaphor, presents God as the subject who always finds us and calls us out of a darkness that we cannot penetrate. The very domain of God is that of impenetrable fire that we cannot enter and explore. The most terrible blasphemy is to believe that God can be kept "in one's pocket." To suppose that we can describe God or present a portrait of divinity is to lose the biblical sense that only the verbal images of fire and light convey insight of the truth about God. When we think that we can see something more than this, we begin to deceive ourselves.

For the modern world, the effective opposite to a religious interpretation of life would appear to be a secular one. An image of one god is no more and no less meaningful than an image of any other. Some may simply appear more beautiful and elegant than others. There is, nonetheless, a salutary warning in the biblical shrinking away from idolatry that demands serious consideration. Religious faith has immense power, and when such faith is misdirected or misrepresented, then quite fearful consequences can ensue. So often the effective opposite of real faith in a real God appears to be a distorted and defective search for images of a false deity. Bogus religions are with us still in abundance, flourishing in the very tolerance the deuteronomic authors would have rejected. By losing awareness of the dimension of transcendence and mystery that must clothe any language we employ to describe the Creator and Sovereign of the universe, the very universe itself becomes trivialized and the majesty of life is brought into contempt.

DEUTERONOMY 4:44–5:5, INTRODUCTION TO THE COVENANT LAW

NIV

⁴⁴This is the law Moses set before the Israelites. ⁴⁵These are the stipulations, decrees and laws Moses gave them when they came out of Egypt ⁴⁶and were in the valley near Beth Peor east of the Jordan, in the land of Sihon king of the Amorites, who reigned in Heshbon and was de-

NRSV

44This is the law that Moses set before the Israelites. ⁴⁵These are the decrees and the statutes and ordinances that Moses spoke to the Israelites when they had come out of Egypt, ⁴⁶beyond the Jordan in the valley opposite Beth-peor, in the land of King Sihon of the Amorites, who reigned

NIV

feated by Moses and the Israelites as they came out of Egypt. [47]They took possession of his land and the land of Og king of Bashan, the two Amorite kings east of the Jordan. [48]This land extended from Aroer on the rim of the Arnon Gorge to Mount Siyon[a] (that is, Hermon), [49]and included all the Arabah east of the Jordan, as far as the Sea of the Arabah,[b] below the slopes of Pisgah.

5 Moses summoned all Israel and said:

Hear, O Israel, the decrees and laws I declare in your hearing today. Learn them and be sure to follow them. [2]The LORD our God made a covenant with us at Horeb. [3]It was not with our fathers that the LORD made this covenant, but with us, with all of us who are alive here today. [4]The LORD spoke to you face to face out of the fire on the mountain. [5](At that time I stood between the LORD and you to declare to you the word of the LORD, because you were afraid of the fire and did not go up the mountain.) And he said:

a48 Hebrew; Syriac (see also Deut. 3:9) *Sirion*   *b49* That is, the Dead Sea

NRSV

at Heshbon, whom Moses and the Israelites defeated when they came out of Egypt. [47]They occupied his land and the land of King Og of Bashan, the two kings of the Amorites on the eastern side of the Jordan: [48]from Aroer, which is on the edge of the Wadi Arnon, as far as Mount Sirion[a] (that is, Hermon), [49]together with all the Arabah on the east side of the Jordan as far as the Sea of the Arabah, under the slopes of Pisgah.

5 Moses convened all Israel, and said to them:

Hear, O Israel, the statutes and ordinances that I am addressing to you today; you shall learn them and observe them diligently. [2]The LORD our God made a covenant with us at Horeb. [3]Not with our ancestors did the LORD make this covenant, but with us, who are all of us here alive today. [4]The LORD spoke with you face to face at the mountain, out of the fire. [5](At that time I was standing between the LORD and you to declare to you the words[b] of the LORD; for you were afraid because of the fire and did not go up the mountain.) And he said:

a Syr: Heb *Sion*   *b* Q Mss Sam Gk Syr Vg Tg: MT *word*

COMMENTARY

The narrative introduction in 4:44-49 prepares for the disclosure of the divine law that is to be the hallmark of the covenant relationship between God and Israel. The law proper is then prepared for by a speech of Moses couched in the first person in 5:1-5. This speech adds the personal authority of Moses to the law and explains the time and circumstances of its revelation to the people. The law itself, in the form of the Ten Commandments, then follows in 5:6-21. These commandments are formulated as the direct speech of God, adding a yet higher level of authority to them as the unmistakable demand placed upon Israel as the people of the LORD God.

The addresses from Moses that follow the disclosure of these commandments in 5:22–11:32 serve as a means of emphasizing their importance, warning of the dangers and temptations of neglecting or disregarding them, and adding further exhortations to observe them. The law code that follows in 12:1–26:19 then serves as a fuller elaboration and

explication of these basic Ten Commandments. So the book of Deuteronomy itself is presented as an ellipse with its focus on two collections of law. The first of these is brief, sharply declaratory in form, and repeats, with minor variations, the list of commandments the reader of the books of Genesis–Numbers will already be familiar with from Exod 20:2-17. Moses himself refers to such an earlier disclosure in 5:4-5.

However, this sense of an elliptical structure with two separate law collections is more apparent than real, and it is evident that the deuteronomic authors did not intend to imply that there were two separate "covenant" law codes; nor did they in any way recognize or assume this to be the case. God's covenant law was one law. The fundamental and primary declaration of that was the Decalogue of Deut 5:6-21. The law code of chaps. 12–26, even though it is formulated very differently, is viewed as an explication and commentary of the essential commandments of 5:6-21.

It is regrettable that, in attempting to unravel the literary sequence by which the component elements of Deuteronomy were composed and brought together, many scholars assumed that the "original" law of Deuteronomy was that of chaps. 12–26 and that the introduction of the Ten Commandments into chap. 5 was a secondary development from a literary point of view. This was claimed even when it was recognized that the Ten Commandments were written earlier than the laws of chaps. 12–26 and were initially formed as an independent collection.

However, it remains clear from the Mosaic exhortations of 5:22–11:32 that the Ten Commandments stand at the head of all that the deuteronomic authors understood by the concept of God's covenant law. The more detailed collections of regulations and case law collected into the code of chaps. 12–26 appear as an elaboration of this primary law, and actually bear significant indications that they owe much of their own structure and order to the desire to maintain this. (The connection between the Ten Commandments and the order of the law code of chaps. 12–26 is dealt with more fully in the Commentary on 12:1-28.)

4:44-49. In the light of these considerations, the transitional introduction to the Ten Commandments, which begins in v. 44, serves to bind the whole series together. It is, then, not simply the preamble to the Ten Commandments, but to the whole collection of 4:44–26:32. While it would be overly hasty to assume that this large literary unit ever existed in precisely its present form and textual content, nevertheless it is reasonable to infer that it provides us with the best guide to what the "original" shape of Deuteronomy was. Even when we accept that many expansions have been introduced into this, it offers a reasonable guide to the core issues that shaped the deuteronomic movement.

The opening declaration in vv. 44-45 offers us the fullest description of how the deuteronomic authors themselves understood their literary work. It is especially noteworthy in view of the fact that much of the deuteronomic literature consists of narrative, as we have already encountered, and, in chaps. 6–11, of hortatory speeches. Yet here the heart of the deuteronomic writing is described as "instruction" (תורה *tôrâ*), which consists of "decrees" (עדה *'ēdōt*), "statutes" (משפטים

mišpāṭîm), and "ordinances" (חקים *ḥuqqîm*). These are all predominantly legal terms, although it is difficult to defend the claim that they had previously pertained only to very precisely defined areas of legal and administrative affairs. In any case, we must ultimately be guided by the actual content of the deuteronomic writing, which contains many laws, but also much in the way of religious directives for worship, besides some fundamental constitutional matters covering kingship, military service, and even family customs relating to marriage settlements. Overall the material is comprehensive in scope and was obviously intended to be so.

Furthermore, since the Ten Commandments form a primary formulation of demands that are not in the strictest sense laws at all, we sense that they were aimed at achieving a maximal level of coverage. All life is to be brought under the umbrella of God's authority and to conform to a call for righteous living. God's covenant touches every area of life and reaches into every home and every corner of daily activity. So it was appropriate that the opening declaration concerning God's law should make it abundantly clear that no other law stood above that which God has given. So there is a transcendent, otherworldly dimension to God's law, even though it is wholly directed toward very practical, this-worldly affairs. It sanctifies everyday life by showing that every activity engages human life with responsibilities and demands that fall under the designation of "holy." This is what it means for Israel to be a holy people.

Verses 46-49 then simply recapitulate the outline story of the situation in which Israel found itself when Moses declared to them, for a second time, the demands of the covenant law first given on Mt. Horeb. At first appearance, such a summary may appear repetitive, as also does the strong affirmation that it was a law mediated through the person of Moses. Both the situation and the name of the great leader, however, were vital for the entire deuteronomic claim that this was a binding law for all Israel. The miscellany and variety of traditions that had at one time characterized the different tribal and regional communities of Israel were now emphatically combined into one.

Indeed, the claim to unity—one God, one land, one people, one law—was a vital and indispensable feature of what the authors of Deuteronomy were striving for. The opposite threat was not simply disunity, although this was obvious, but the realization that disunity would inevitably lead to diversity, disintegration, and death—the death of Israel among the nations once its belief in its own nationhood had been eroded to the point of emptiness. Memories of Israel's past were not a luxury to be savored in quiet contemplation but a reality to be seized and held on to as the very lifeblood through which Israel could survive as a people. So the deuteronomic rhetoric is not a piece of cosmetic artistry, but a determined effort to hold on to the very core of what it meant to be Israel.

5:1-5. The declaration concerning the covenant made on Mt. Horeb makes plain that the commandments that constitute the heart of God's law belong inseparably to that covenant. So it is especially affirmed that this was not simply a reassertion of an ancient covenant made with Israel's ancestors (v. 2), but that it is central to the birthplace of the nation on Mt. Horeb. The covenant, therefore, was binding upon the entire nation and was inseparable from its religious commitment to the Lord as God. There could be no effective retention of a faith commitment to the LORD as God that did not, in the very nature of that commitment, include as a central feature the recognition of the Ten Commandments and the necessity of their observance. So faith and morality belonged together, as did deliverance (from Egyptian slavery) and law (embodied in the commandments). Freedom without law would be no freedom at all.

REFLECTIONS

The situation the deuteronomists saw themselves addressing highlights the special relevance of their work. They were calling upon their readers to think back to first principles in order to deal adequately with a new and threatening era, one in which disaster had succeeded disaster and the surviving remnant of Israel was facing the dissolution of the very institutions that had held it together. Because of the threat to the Davidic monarchy and the prospect that even the Temple and its priesthood would not be forever available to give shape and structure to life, Israel was facing a new, and more perilous, Jordan crossing in which dispersion among the nations was a serious threat. Only by reclaiming the central truths concerning the LORD as God, the covenant of Horeb, and the fundamental commandments that it presented could the nation's life be held together.

The political and historical consequences of this had become terrifyingly evident by the time the deuteronomic movement took hold. That movement had striven to recover the unity and "soul" of the nation by looking back to its beginnings. Unity was now to be sought, not in the institutions of kings and priests, but in the fundamentals of law, justice, and family life. So what is now unfolded in this remarkable presentation of the law of the covenant given to Israel by Moses on Mt. Horeb is a carefully considered judgment concerning everything that was deemed essential for Israel to be, and to remain, Israel.

The picture given of Moses "standing between the LORD and you" (5:5) once again bridges the gap of the generations. By this powerful rhetorical device, the figure of Moses once again confronts a new generation with his disclosure of the voice of God. Such an assertion does not correspond to any one specific incident recorded in the earlier narratives in which Moses acted as mediator between the people and God. In the earlier reports, the leader had ascended the mountain, and only seventy elders had been permitted to accompany him as representatives of the people (Exodus 24). However, it is the overall portrayal of Moses as the indispensable mediator who could interpret the will of God that forms the essential basis of the claim that Moses stood between them and God. So it is not simply in the narrow historical sense that Moses acted as go-between for every man, woman, and child within Israel. In a wider, theological and figurative sense, Moses was the mediator without whom the nation could not have come to birth and without whose words it could not survive. Once again the ordinary mass of human beings who constituted the community of Israel are portrayed in a less than flattering manner. They are "afraid because of the fire" (5:5); yet Moses dare not be afraid, since his negotiating between the LORD and the people is vital for their existence.

The role of Moses as mediator between God and human beings may suggest to Christian readers a similar role of Jesus. For instance, the Gospel of Matthew, with the five major discourses of Jesus, may reflect the Evangelist's view of Jesus as a new Moses offering a new Torah that fulfills the old.

DEUTERONOMY 5:6-21, THE TEN COMMANDMENTS: THE COVENANT RULE

OVERVIEW

In a quite fundamental way, the Ten Commandments dominate the book of Deuteronomy, as they have tended to dominate popular perceptions of the entire Hebrew Bible.[41] They represent law in a very basic sense, even though they are not laws in a technical and formal manner. Moreover, their very dominance has generally been found to lie in the fact that they represent a form of "higher law" that stands behind and above all human systems of law.

However, from a strictly literary perspective they constitute simply one series, or collection, of laws presented as having been given at Mt. Horeb (Mt. Sinai in the Exod 20:2-17 account). Since a large part of the Pentateuch from Exod 19:1 to Deut 34:12 consists of a wide variety of collections of laws and regulations, one might have expected that the Ten Commandments would simply be submerged within this larger framework. Yet, this is not so. By their presentation in the foremost experience of revelation on the mountain (Exodus 20) and their repetition on the eve of the entry into the land (Deuteronomy 5), they are placed in positions of pre-eminence. These commandments possess an importance above and beyond that of other laws contained within the narrative. It is a recognition of this importance in Jewish and Christian tradition that has set them apart as deserving special attention and as being representative not simply of laws, but of principles, and even human rights, that still matter greatly to human society.

Certainly, from both a historical and a literary point of view, this series of Ten Commandments has raised many searching and complex questions.[42] The very fact of their being set out twice calls attention to them. All the more does this occasion surprise from a narrative structural perspective, in that their first expression in Exodus 20 fits awkwardly in a larger narrative setting in which the tablets upon which they were inscribed were destroyed. The second set of tablets (Exod 34:10-26) then contains a rather different series of laws, which are no longer ten in number.

However, it is the relationship between the list of commandments in Exod 20:2-17 and those in Deut 5:6-21 that calls for the closest examination. Essentially the commandments are the same, although the wording of some of them is rather different, and, in particular, the sabbath commandment in Exod 20:8-11 is noticeably longer and more elaborate. This commandment also shows a connection with, and a dependence on, the creation narrative of Gen 1:1–2:4a, which is of post-exilic date and is ascribed to the priestly

---

41. The literature on the Ten Commandments is now very extensive. Among recent studies the following are particularly accessible and significant: E. Nielsen, *The Ten Commandments in New Perspective,* trans. D. J. Bourke, SBT second series 7 (London: SCM, 1968); J. J. Stamm and M. E. Andrew, *The Ten Commandments in Recent Research,* SBT second series 2 (London: SCM, 1967); Anthony Phillips, *Ancient Israel's Criminal Law: A New Approach to the Decalogue* (Oxford: Blackwell, 1970); Walter Harrelson, *The Ten Commandments and Human Rights,* OBT (Philadelphia: Fortress, 1980).

42. For the special importance of the Deuteronomy 5 version of the Decalogue, see N. Lohfink, "The Decalogue in Deuteronomy 5," in *Theology of the Pentateuch: Themes of the Priestly Narrative and Deuteronomy,* trans. Linda M. Maloney (Edinburgh: T. & T. Clark, 1994) 248-64.

(P) source. In seeking to defend the historical and literary priority of the Exodus 20 version of the commandments, therefore, scholars have found themselves compelled to accept that a number of later additions and elaborations have been made to it. In fact, to make such a defense at all has consistently called for recognition of an older, more basic form of the Ten Commandments, sometimes described as a Primary Decalogue.[43] All such concern to unravel the complex literary history of the Ten Commandments, and to defend a very early literary origin for them, probably in a rather different form, raises a host of questions that require separate consideration. Certainly, even from a purely literary perspective, the conclusion seems assured that the list of the commandments was inserted in the narrative of Exodus 20 at a late stage. The case for claiming that this version was the more original, therefore, must be regarded as very dubious.

We must proceed on the basic premise that the formulation of the Ten Commandments in Deut 5:6-21 remains their earliest literary presentation. Because of their importance, a further listing of them was brought forward to introduce them into Exodus 20 at a relatively late stage in the final formation of the Pentateuch. Certainly, these Ten Commandments are thoroughly in keeping with the aims, the tenor, and the literary techniques of the deuteronomists. Moreover, they represent for the deuteronomists the expression of the most basic demands imposed on Israel by God's covenant made on Mt. Horeb. They represent Torah in a manner that no other brief summary account can possibly rival. The remainder of the Torah is, in effect, simply an elaboration and enlargement of these basic commands.

All of these considerations do not of themselves tell us about the actual date of origin of the Ten Commandments, nor do they imply that they are not fundamentally the work of Moses. Yet they are the work of Moses in essentially the same sense and with the same literary and historical provisos that pertain to the book of Deuteronomy

as a whole. We can then more directly address the question of the literary origin of this vitally significant ethical masterpiece.

The Date of Origin of the Ten Commandments. To a number of scholars, it has appeared that the literary formulation of the Ten Commandments can be of no earlier date than the remainder of Deuteronomy and should almost certainly be ascribed to a relatively late period in the history of Israel under the monarchy. It may even be later still. To others it has appeared a highly probable, if not virtually certain, conclusion that these commandments represent the most clearly attested legacy of the work of Moses. If they are not to be credited to so great a figure, then who else could lay claim to a work of such eminent ethical value and significance?

Yet, when focused in sharper detail, two such contrasting conclusions are merely reflections of larger questions that can be answered with more clarity and confidence. They show that the original question is really rather inadequately formulated and that we are called upon to answer broader issues in order to recognize this.

On one side, we can define the question simply in terms of asking at what stage the verbal written list of Ten Commandments, as we now possess them in Deut 5:6-21, was made. The answer to this would seem to be that it was made either contemporaneously with, or perhaps somewhat earlier than, the remainder of Deut 4:44–26:19. It certainly appears likely that such a list of Ten Commandments was composed earlier as an independent document, and some such list may have existed from a very early period of Israel's history. To make such a deduction, however, is inevitably a speculative proceeding, and it has usually carried with it the belief that the original form was briefer and probably consisted simply of ten prohibitions, all with a similar formal structure.

There seems little point in rigorously pursuing such historical speculations, however, since they effectively form a subject area of their own and lead to no certain results. It is sufficient to note that we have no firm support outside the present text for claiming a very early date for the written Ten Commandments.

On the other side exists the more directly ethical, and not purely literary, question concerning the stage at which the demands now con-

---

43. Lohfink (ibid., 248), while setting aside the case for a more primitive list of ten prohibitions, suggests that the present series may have arisen as an expansion of the sabbath commandment, thereby effectively reversing the usual order of literary growth. Since it is certain that the formulation of the Ten Commandments has made use of earlier material, it would appear of limited value to speculate of what form such a list may have taken and what it may, or may not, have included.

tained in these individual commandments became binding upon Israel. This is to ask at what period these basic commandments, and the conduct they seek to regulate, became formative features of Israel's faith, fundamental to its recognition of the LORD as the God who had made a covenant with Israel as a people.

The answer to this would certainly carry us much further back and bring us closer to the person and work of Moses. What the formulation of these Ten Commandments has endeavored to achieve is a focusing and clarifying of the most basic demands that belong to the worship of the LORD as God. They are not, therefore, a novel creation of the deuteronomists, introducing fresh moral ideas and demands. Rather, they are a bold and effective attempt to focus emphatically on certain fundamental features of faith in the LORD as God that had a long history.

When we ask about an era in which human beings first recognized the folly of wanton killing, unchecked theft, or carefree adultery, we look in vain for clear dates, for certain fundamental ethical demands belong inescapably to all human society. The ancient Near East amply attests the deep concern on the part of human communities to control, suppress, and punish violent and socially disruptive behavior. For millennia, in fact, it belonged to the protective role of the kin group to deal with such matters. The problems and issues the commandments deal with can then be seen to be of varying periods in their origin, many of them as old as human civilization. It is in their concern to deal with these problems in a fundamental and practical way that the commandments display their great originality. So we must face the fact that it is essentially the deuteronomists who have formulated this literary list of Ten Commandments in this unique fashion.

The Ten Commandments as Fundamental Teaching. The creative innovation brought by the Ten Commandments lies in bringing together a basic series of ten primary demands, in formulating them in a readily memorable fashion, and in highlighting their significance as basic to all human life, when it is to be lived "before God." Their originality lies not in their "discovery" of new ethical demands, but in their stress on the importance of these basic demands for

human living.[44] They combine this emphasis with a simple listing technique devised for teaching purposes by using the number ten. So their importance lies not in the novelty of discovering new areas of life that needed to be controlled and regulated, since these belong to the human situation as such, but to a special emphasis that is focused on them.

Second, it is clearly of the utmost importance to the Ten Commandments as a comprehensive list that they combine duties to God and duties to fellow human beings. In a significant measure, it is this combination, making the recognition of a transcendent God the foundation for a respectful and truly moral concern for other human beings, that marks their distinctiveness. In effect, they recognize that the question of what duties exist toward other persons is also a question concerning who these other persons are. It recognizes that the answer lies in the fact that they, too, are children of God, deserving of the regard that derives from the createdness of all things and all people. So morality and moral obligation have a divine origin and meaning.

It has often been customary to draw attention to the negative aspects of the formulation of the commandments in that eight of the ten are set out as prohibitions: "You shall not. . . ." However, this is less significant than may at first glance appear. There is no real basis for the attempts that have sometimes been advocated for recasting all ten as original prohibitions. This is simply to rewrite the commandments—a hazardous proceeding! In any event, the subject areas covered were clearly of far greater importance than the tidiness of maintaining a consistent form. Furthermore, once the manner in which the extended law code of Deuteronomy 12–26 is recognized as being structured as an amplification of the Ten Commandments, then such a criticism becomes even more markedly misplaced. It depends on the conduct being dealt with whether a prohibition or an injunction is the most appropriate form for the commandment.

Form of the Commandments. The question of the form of the commandments has been much discussed, and only certain main features can be

44. E. Otto, *Theologische Ethik des Alten Testaments* (Stuttgart: W. Kohlhammer, 1994) 215-19, describes the Ten Commandments as presenting the sum of the divinely authorized and ordained ethic of the Hebrew Bible.

examined in detail. It is, as a foremost consideration, of great significance that they are presented as direct speech of God. It is otherwise almost always only prophets who adopt so bold a formula for their utterances. Yet, in the case of the commandments, this direct-speech formula accords fully with the religious dimension that pervades them all and gives to them their unique authority. Even to reduce them to the level of the speech of Moses would deprive them of some element of their remarkable authority. They belong unequivocally to the spiritual understanding and meaning of life. To recognize that these commandments are the voice of God is a paramount consideration.

The distinctive commandment form of address (usually called "apodeictic" from the pioneering study by A. Alt)[45] in which active prohibition, or demand, is expressed adds rhetorical vigor to this sense of authority and separates them from more familiar legal formulations—i.e., case laws (Alt, casuistic laws). That it represents a direct adaptation and shift from a form of clan (or family) instruction in which the familial head controlled the conduct of the kin group appears an unnecessary conclusion. Nonetheless, the point is important in showing that the direct apodeictic form was not a uniquely legal device, nor was it exclusive to a narrow pattern of teaching and authority. We must reaffirm that, essentially, form follows content, rather than dictates it.

In similar fashion, the much explored attempt to bring fresh illumination to the form of the commandments by comparing them with ancient Near Eastern treaty formulations must be set aside as having little bearing on the understanding of the Decalogue. This is not to deny that such treaties may, more broadly, have exercised some literary influence on the deuteronomists. The commandments, in the form they now possess, make eminent sense in and for themselves as a major feature of the deuteronomic measures to ensure Israel's survival. Two centuries of painful history have served to shape and direct those measures.

A further issue relates to the number ten and to its function within the overall purpose of the list. Basically this may be held as a useful didactic device, almost certainly drawn from reference to

the ten fingers of a person's hands. That such commandments were incised on tablets of stone and retained inside the sacred ark as a covenant document (31:9-13, 24-26) can at most be seen as a secondary concern to heighten their significance for Israel's faith, rather than as a feature that dictated their formulation. Their relative brevity can owe nothing to such lapidary preservation, since other Near Eastern law codes, inscribed on stone tablets, could be of considerable length and discursiveness.

We may conclude, in consequence, that studies of the distinctive form of the Ten Commandments, illuminating and extensive as they have been, should not lead us to attempt to regard the form as uniquely meaningful. Certainly it should not encourage us to attempt to redraft any of the commandments in an attempt to re-create a more original Primary Decalogue. Such attempts are too speculative to offer a serious basis for research. Since the issues covered by the commandments were of primary importance to society, it is evident that other attempts to deal with them would have been made.

Contents of the Ten Commandments. It is surprising, in view of the relative brevity of a list of a mere ten commandments, that uncertainty has existed on precisely how the division into ten separate commandments should be counted. Furthermore, in view of their exceptional significance, it is surprising that certain of them remain a little obscure as to their precise meaning and intent, notably in relation to the misuse of the divine name and the range of conduct covered by the prohibition against unlawful killing (murder, v. 17).

It has also been a matter of considerable concern that, precisely on account of their formulation as commandments, they lack any specific indication of what punishment is to be meted out to offenders. Since they are tied closely to the sense of a covenant relationship that exists between the LORD God and Israel, it could be assumed that exclusion from the covenant community would be the inevitable and appropriate punishment. Yet this is not spelled out, and the seriousness of the offenses dealt with must be held not to be of equal importance. In the case of the tenth commandment, which warns against covetousness, it is difficult to envisage any effective form of punishment. The attempt to elevate all ten of the commandments to cover capital crimes

---

45. A. Alt, "The Origins of Israelite Law," in *Essays on Old Testament History and Religion,* trans. R. A. Wilson (Oxford: Blackwell, 1966) 79-132.

involving the death penalty must be set aside as highly implausible. We are left, then, with a list of commandments that deal with fundamental religious and social issues, some of which overlap with offenses for which specific legal action is called for.

The opening declaration of v. 6 unswervingly ties the commandments to the LORD God, who has delivered Israel out of the slavery of Egypt. Certainly the awareness of a commitment to God as a primary assumption permeates all the commandments. It is Israel's faith that must shape its conduct. From a historical perspective, this has frequently been seen as a limitation of the commandments, since they appear as eliciting a special demand from Israelites and Jews, and in a strictly formal sense are not necessarily applicable to all humankind. Yet, in historical retrospect and with minor adjustments (notably in connection with the sabbath), the commandments have readily been recognized as a universal human document. Their concern is for the welfare of human beings as such and for the harmony and good order of all human society. This does not claim for them a level of absolute authority, since too many issues are either left unclear or left out, for this to be possible. Nevertheless, they have been expounded and understood within both Judaism and Christianity as an essentially universal ethical document of immense value.

Deuteronomy 5:6-7, The First Commandment

NIV	NRSV
[6]"I am the LORD your God, who brought you out of Egypt, out of the land of slavery. [7]"You shall have no other gods before[a] me." [a]7 Or *besides*	6I am the LORD your God, who brought you out of the land of Egypt, out of the house of slavery; [7]you shall have no other gods before[a] me. [a] Or *besides*

COMMENTARY

The demand "You shall have no other gods before me" (the marginal note in the NRSV, suggesting "besides" instead of "before," is relevant) must be intended to preclude the acceptance of other gods alongside, and in addition to, the LORD. However, it could also imply "in preference to," which was undoubtedly important to the deuteronomic emphasis on the uniqueness and sovereignty of the LORD as God. It falls short of a strict monotheism, since it does not deny the existence of other deities. Since also it is addressed to Israelites ("you"), it leaves untouched the legitimacy of the worship of other gods by other peoples (cf. 4:28). Obviously this was an unclear area of polemic, and the commandment was directly aimed at achieving a pragmatic rejection of acceptance of other deities alongside the LORD in Israel, rather than attempting a more theoretical monotheism. In other features of the deuteronomic apologetic there is a more positive assertiveness in denying that other deities have any power to obstruct, or frustrate, the sovereign will of the LORD as God. (See Reflections at 5:21.)

Deuteronomy 5:8-10, The Second Commandment

NIV	NRSV
[8]"You shall not make for yourself an idol in the form of anything in heaven above	8You shall not make for yourself an idol, whether in the form of anything that is in heaven

NIV	NRSV
or on the earth beneath or in the waters below. ⁹You shall not bow down to them or worship them; for I, the LORD your God, am a jealous God, punishing the children for the sin of the fathers to the third and fourth generation of those who hate me, ¹⁰but showing love to a thousand ⌐generations⌐ of those who love me and keep my commandments."	above, or that is on the earth beneath, or that is in the water under the earth. ⁹You shall not bow down to them or worship them; for I the LORD your God am a jealous God, punishing children for the iniquity of parents, to the third and fourth generation of those who reject me, ¹⁰but showing steadfast love to the thousandth generation[a] of those who love me and keep my commandments. [a] Or to thousands

COMMENTARY

The prohibition on the use of images returns to a subject that has already been dealt with polemically in the speech ascribed to Moses in 4:15-20. The assumption certainly appears to be that such images would be images of the LORD God, although elsewhere the rejection of all symbolic imagery as representative of divine powers is maintained. Iconographic symbolism of various kinds was effectively the norm in ancient Near Eastern religions so that the absolute rejection of

them for the worship of the LORD in Israel is striking. All the more is this the case when we recognize that certain forms of iconography, especially the cherubim (cf. 1 Kgs 6:23-30), existed within the Jerusalem Temple itself. Clearly the dividing line between symbols was not easily drawn, and this becomes even more marked when we consider the use of various forms of geometric symbolism within worship. (See Reflections at 5:21.)

Deuteronomy 5:11, The Third Commandment

NIV	NRSV
¹¹"You shall not misuse the name of the LORD your God, for the LORD will not hold anyone guiltless who misuses his name."	11You shall not make wrongful use of the name of the LORD your God, for the LORD will not acquit anyone who misuses his name.

COMMENTARY

The reference to "the third and fourth generation of those who reject me" points to a deep sense of the solidarity of the extended family living within a single household. Four generations within one household was the maximum that was likely to be encountered.

The precise aim of the third commandment is more obscure in the precise range of activities that it sought to prohibit than might at first appear. The Hebrew specifically prohibits the invoking of God's name to what is "empty," "void," "false" (שָׁוְא šāwʾ). It could be construed as referring to false and deceitful

oaths, or even a false image or idol. Most probably, however, it refers to the use of the divine name to back up a wide range of harmful or false utterances. These would have included magical utterances as well as deceitful oaths. Modern English versions have endeavored to show the wide range of harmful activities covered by offering a slight paraphrase of the Hebrew; e.g., GNB, "for evil purposes." While the Bible generally shows a deep concern with the threat of perjury in legal affairs, it is also conscious that the line between magic and religion was often difficult to define.

It should also be noted that the reference to "the name of the LORD your God" refers to God in the third person, although the commandments as a whole are the direct speech of God (hence, "my name" might have been expected). This feature, however, simply reflects that instructional material from teaching in the cultus, as well as in legal matters, has been secondarily incorporated into the commandment form. It is, in any case,

not at all surprising that in a prohibition of this nature, it was advantageous to identify precisely the divine name that was not to be subjected to misuse. The name expressed the very reality and being of God, so that to misuse it or to trivialize its use was a serious affront to the very foundations on which the commandment form rested. (See Reflections at 5:21.)

Deuteronomy 5:12-15, The Fourth Commandment

12"Observe the Sabbath day by keeping it holy, as the LORD your God has commanded you. 13Six days you shall labor and do all your work, 14but the seventh day is a Sabbath to the LORD your God. On it you shall not do any work, neither you, nor your son or daughter, nor your manservant or maidservant, nor your ox, your donkey or any of your animals, nor the alien within your gates, so that your manservant and maidservant may rest, as you do. 15Remember that you were slaves in Egypt and that the LORD your God brought you out of there with a mighty hand and an outstretched arm. Therefore the LORD your God has commanded you to observe the Sabbath day."

12Observe the sabbath day and keep it holy, as the LORD your God commanded you. 13Six days you shall labor and do all your work. 14But the seventh day is a sabbath to the LORD your God; you shall not do any work—you, or your son or your daughter, or your male or female slave, or your ox or your donkey, or any of your livestock, or the resident alien in your towns, so that your male and female slave may rest as well as you. 15Remember that you were a slave in the land of Egypt, and the LORD your God brought you out from there with a mighty hand and an outstretched arm; therefore the LORD your God commanded you to keep the sabbath day.

COMMENTARY

In v. 12, the fourth commandment is the first of the two that abandon the prohibition form. It has been suggested, therefore, that it may have existed earlier in a form such as "You shall do no work on the sabbath day." Yet this would represent a far more fundamental change than might at first appear, since to keep the day "holy" (קדש qādaš) involved positive obligations of prayer and worship, rather than simple abstention from work. The parallel clause in Exod 20:8 reads "Remember [זכר zākar] the sabbath day to keep it holy," which occasions some surprise in view of the considerable emphasis the deuteronomic exhortations and admonitions place on "remembering" as a religious obligation.

The sabbath combines two features, making it likely that its observance was itself a combination of two elements of religious tradition. The first of these was the importance of reckoning time within a sacred calendar, so that the division of time into weeks, months, and years was seen as part of the sacred order of life (see Gen 1:14). The sabbath, therefore, was an especially "holy" day because it marked a basic temporal division of life and its holiness served to regulate the entire week. At the same time, the importance of rest and relaxation, especially in periods when work was a particularly heavy burden (cf. Exod 23:12; 34:21) served an important purpose for human well-being. So the necessity of granting rest to all creatures, even slaves and domestic animals, was important. Time and space both formed elements within the structure of life that had to be observed by confessing their holiness. Human beings did not create the order of time, but experienced it as something given and, therefore, to be accepted and consecrated.

It seems likely that the sabbath title was itself originally closely linked to the lunar cycle of the calendar, probably as the day of the full moon ("new moons and sabbaths"). Since this was linked to a seven-day periodic cycle, the use of the term has been extended to cover every seventh day, rather than only one within the lunar cycle.

The enlargement of the sabbath commandment in vv. 13-15 is noteworthy and indicative of the kind of expansion that has suggested that at least in this case the original wording was shorter. If this is true, it would serve to confirm a perspective corroborated elsewhere in the OT that this particular commandment was especially vulnerable to indifference and neglect. We may note that trading on the sabbath appears commonplace in the time of the prophet Amos (Amos 8:5) and that even the rigor of Nehemiah could not achieve the willing observance of sabbath, but that he had to be content with rendering it impossible for traders to enter Jerusalem on the sabbath (Neh 13:15-22). The aim of the expansion here is clearly to apply persuasion in order to encourage its effective observance, especially in granting sabbath rest as a concession to slaves (vv. 14-15). That it was ever customary to enforce it by imposing capital punishment (cf. Num 15:32-36) appears very unlikely. Once again, we can note the great importance the deuteronomists attached to rhetoric and the art of persuasion. (See Reflections at 5:21.)

Deuteronomy 5:16, The Fifth Commandment

NIV

16"Honor your father and your mother, as the LORD your God has commanded you, so that you may live long and that it may go well with you in the land the LORD your God is giving you."

NRSV

16Honor your father and your mother, as the LORD your God commanded you, so that your days may be long and that it may go well with you in the land that the LORD your God is giving you.

COMMENTARY

The commandment to honor father and mother, like the preceding one, is couched in a positive form. Older legislation (cf Exod 21:15, 17) shows that the striking or cursing of a parent was treated with the utmost seriousness so that, if this commandment were to be recast into the negative prohibition form, it would greatly narrow the activities it sought to preclude. As it stands, the positive formulation was clearly of great significance in seeking to secure respect for parents in terms of obedience and seeking the overall welfare of the family unit over which the parents presided. Such a demand also possessed strong economic overtones, since the problems of old age and failing health could undoubtedly impose severe economic strains.

That this commandment, like the preceding one, has also been given a supplemental promissory extension ("that your days may be long") is a further instance of the recognition made by the commandments that it was impossible to legislate for a right attitude. The hope instead is to encourage that attitude through persuasion. Such an assurance concerning the attainment of a secure old age shows that the problems of aging were especially in view in the framing of the commandment.

The high profile given to the question of old age, and the strains and temptations that this could bring within a family unit, is marked out by its inclusion in the list of ten primary obligations. Expectations and calculations show that average life expectancy cannot have been very high in ancient Israel—certainly not in comparison with modern developed societies.[46] Yet a high infant mortality rate was a major feature of life for all ancient societies, and those who reached adulthood

46. The problems in calculating life expectancy in ancient Israel are dealt with in H. W. Wolff, *Anthropology of the Old Testament,* trans. Margaret Kohl (London: SCM, 1973) 119-20.

could clearly hope to reach a full span of years (see Psalm 90). That many such adults passed the point where they could usefully work may have provided a serious temptation for poverty-stricken households to exclude them from active participation in the household routine or even to expel them altogether. (See Reflections at 5:21.)

Deuteronomy 5:17, The Sixth Commandment

NIV	NRSV
[17]"You shall not murder."	17You shall not murder.[a]
	[a] Or *kill*

COMMENTARY

The prohibition "You shall not kill [murder]" was clearly not intended to preclude necessary killing in time of war or capital punishment. Still less can it have had in mind questions relating to the slaughter of animals, although this was not a matter of complete indifference (cf. Gen 9:5-6). The Hebrew verb translated "murder" (רצח *rāṣaḥ*) is not the simple expression for any sort of killing, but relates to various forms of violent illegitimate acts of slaughter. Since there were clear laws dealing with homicide and the difficulties that could arise in regard to distinguishing it from accidental killing (cf. 17:8; Exod 21:12-14), it is evident that the translation "murder" must be rather inadequate in connection with this particular commandment. It was evidently designed to exclude various forms of wanton killing, but

would appear particularly to envisage actions in which the normal legislative processes would be unlikely, or even powerless, to act.

This prohibition would relate directly to vengeance killing, for which a person accused of a serious crime was peremptorily punished without resort to investigation and a fair trial. It is evident that a custom of clan-based "blood revenge" was widely current in biblical times and proved difficult to eradicate. It is also noteworthy that the unjustified killing of a thief is made the subject of special legislative provision (see Exod 22:2-3). Clearly there were ways of indulging in wanton killing that slipped through the laws against homicide, and it is all such actions that are prohibited by this commandment. (See Reflections at 5:21.)

Deuteronomy 5:18, The Seventh Commandment

NIV	NRSV
[18]"You shall not commit adultery."	18Neither shall you commit adultery.

COMMENTARY

The prohibition against adultery raises once again the concern of the commandments to protect the family as a unit and to ensure the right of the paternal head of the household to the

paternity of his children. This leaves open the question of whether the charge of adultery was limited to women, so that sexual promiscuity of adult males was tolerated (see the story of Judah's visit to a supposed prostitute in Genesis 38). Obviously the commandment, by itself, is not entirely clear on this point, making the supplementary laws dealing with such sexual matters in chaps. 22–23 of great importance. It is noteworthy that such sayings as Prov 30:20 recognize the difficulties of proving a woman's adulterous con-

duct and the danger posed by an unreasonably suspicious husband is dealt with in 22:13-21. Similarly, it is a feature of the biblical tradition that it retains the archaic provision for trial by testing in respect of a wife accused of infidelity (Num 5:11-31). (See Reflections at 5:21.)

Deuteronomy 5:19, The Eighth Commandment

NIV	NRSV
19"You shall not steal."	19Neither shall you steal.

COMMENTARY

The prohibition against theft occasions surprise on account of its inclusion in a series of commandments that, for the most part, relate to matters either beyond the regular competence of the law to deal with or to such matters that stood on the border between clear-cut offenses that the law could handle and those that were unclear or could easily be flouted. Obviously simple theft by itself could not have been considered a capital crime, and there is no reason for limiting the commandment to the kidnapping of persons, which would have been a capital offense (cf. Exod 21:16).

Undoubtedly the growth of prosperity in ancient Israel and the building of large and opulent households in a society in which many persons were

gravely impoverished created major inequalities between the wealthy and the near destitute. The protection of property, therefore, became a matter of increasing prominence for the law to deal with, especially when matters of proof of ownership were difficult to establish. Clearly theft was often an occasion for unresolvable disputes and dissensions, which the intervention of third parties could not always be relied upon to settle (cf. Exod 22:9). Accordingly we find that such matters as the use of false weights (25:13-15) and the removal of territorial boundary markers (19:14) were forms of cheating and theft that ancient courts often found difficult to deal with for lack of satisfactory evidence. (See Reflections at 5:21.)

Deuteronomy 5:20, The Ninth Commandment

NIV	NRSV
20"You shall not give false testimony against your neighbor."	20Neither shall you bear false witness against your neighbor.

COMMENTARY

The offense of bearing false witness against another person primarily concerns perjury in a legal proceeding (Exod 23:1). The ease with which false acusations might be brought against an innocent person is well illustrated by the story

of Naboth's vineyard (2 Kgs 21:16, esp. vv. 8-10). That such cases could include the leveling of capital charges against an enemy was clearly a major problem for ancient society. In many psalms, the complaint of the psalmist is that he or she is suffering as a result of malicious accusations and that only God can truly bring a verdict of innocence.

Not only could malevolent accusations of a very serious kind lead to the punishment, and even death, of the accused person, but it is also clear that a related problem existed in regard to the laws of evidence. Since major accusations required a minimum of two witnesses if they were to be upheld, it was clearly a great temptation for a plaintiff to secure the support of a person to act as a second witness and, in so doing, commit perjury (cf. the provision of 19:15-21). The person may have acted with some misguided feeling of

trust, but would thereby undermine completely the protective procedures of the law.

Certainly the inclusion of this particular commandment further strengthens the broad recognition that the entire series of commandments was specially designed to support and back up the resources of the law, rather than to exist as an independent series of laws as such. They do not circumvent the normal juridical processes, and they were clearly not intended to do so. They were, however, fully conscious that the law was a fragile and limited instrument for the good order of society and that, for its effectiveness, it required a positive and law-respecting attitude on the part of the entire community. (See Reflections at 5:21.)

Deuteronomy 5:21, The Tenth Commandment

NIV	NRSV
21"You shall not covet your neighbor's wife. You shall not set your desire on your neighbor's house or land, his manservant or maidservant, his ox or donkey, or anything that belongs to your neighbor."	21Neither shall you covet your neighbor's wife. Neither shall you desire your neighbor's house, or field, or male or female slave, or ox, or donkey, or anything that belongs to your neighbor.

COMMENTARY

The injunction "Neither shall you covet" would appear to overlap with the eighth commandment, prohibiting theft, since the "vigorous desiring" that is denoted by coveting would undoubtedly include the nurturing of desires and the plotting of schemes whereby the property of a neighbor might become one's own. The weakness of the case for seeing a particularly strong and active intention behind the verb and the concern to recognize a more serious offense than mere desiring has led Anthony Phillips to suggest that this commandment entailed plotting to deprive an elder of his status.[47] Yet the argument for such an interpretation rests largely on a concern to defend the overall claim for the commandments that they relate to serious forms of criminal behavior. Once such an assumption is left aside,

there is no difficulty in taking the command at its plain surface meaning. It is a prohibition against the harboring of a dangerous and selfish attitude of mind in which a wide variety of potential criminal actions could be nurtured. As such it is indicative of the deep attention given in the series of commandments as a whole to those broad issues of morality that extended beyond the law, but that the legal system was designed to serve.

There is much in Deuteronomy to indicate that it was addressed to a community for whom the implementation of the demands of the law was often weak and uncertain. The community, therefore, needed to ensure that it was not "lawless" in the larger sense that there was no regard for basic human rights and for protection from violence. The extension of the list to include property belonging to a neighbor that might arouse covetous desires is quite possibly an expansion of what

47. Anthony Phillips, *Ancient Israel's Criminal Law: A New Approach to the Decalogue* (Oxford: Blackwell, 1970) 149-52.

was originally a much briefer formulation. It is, nevertheless, surprising that it should include a wife among the property of another, even though the commandments already include a prohibition against adultery.

This commandment fulfills a valuable role in contributing to a wider understanding of the purpose of the series of Ten Commandments, which were to be learned as a part of basic education, rather than set out in a court of law. It shows that they cannot have been laws in the formal juridical sense. However much coveting could be recognized as a dangerous and undesirable attitude of mind, it was scarcely the kind of offense that could be made subject to legal action or redress. Moreover, the claim that has sometimes been raised that the commandment ethic repre-

sents a rather negative ideal by failing to recognize the inwardness of true morality clearly cannot be sustained in this particular case. It is of special interest for the fuller understanding of the social development of ancient Israel that those commandments that deal with property appear to recognize most fully the weaknesses endemic to the legal processes available to the community. Ownership of goods and property, the protection of honest trading practices, and the restraint of exploitative commercial deals were all well recognized as immensely important benefits for the health and good order of the community. They were, at the same time, notoriously difficult areas to guard from abuse by the limited and haphazard legal processes available to ancient Israel.

REFLECTIONS

The Ten Commandments must be recognized as one of the great contributions the Hebrew Scriptures have made to humankind, certainly to the development of Western civilization. The Ten Commandments came into existence as a teaching aid, concerned with the moral education of a whole community. It is appropriate, therefore, that they be recognized as deliberately limiting their compass to a mere ten fundamental issues. The remarkable feature is that, in doing so, they nevertheless maintain an extraordinary comprehensiveness. The range of conduct they cover is extensive, and their breadth becomes all the more evident once the needless criticism that they are merely negative is set aside. If later generations developed a form of casuistry, seeking to keep the letter of the law but to deny its spirit and intention, then this was certainly never within the purview of those who compiled such a list.

Those who preserved the commandments were only too conscious that the law and its processes were vulnerable to abuse and could be treated as rather blunt instruments for attaining effective redress for wrongs suffered. Already by the time of Deuteronomy it was evident that many Israelites would be compelled to live under the jurisdiction of foreign powers, with all the limitations that this imposed and the unlikelihood of obtaining justice from well-established juridical systems. For much of their history, in fact, Jews have had to become self-regulating so far as many areas of conduct are concerned. Recognition of this necessity for all human beings is, to a significant degree, present in the Ten Commandments. "Morality is too important simply to be left to the law and its officers." Such at least would appear to be a major assumption undergirding the concern of the Ten Commandments.

It is regrettable that a misinformed apologetic has led to a misguided tendency to contrast the supposed externalism and supposed negativity of the Ten Commandments with the more emphatically inward and positive love orientation of the New Testament tradition. Clearly the Ten Commandments were not concerned to cover every possible area of social and ethical concern. Nor could they have done so. Their primary aim was to restrain abuses and to prevent the deficiencies of the authorized legislative system from destroying community life. This aim the commandments have clearly served very effectively to maintain.

It is a paramount feature of the Ten Commandments that they combine religious duties with those toward the family and the community more generally. In a secular, modern social context, it is not difficult to see that this appeal to an ultimate transcendent authority can cause problems. The commandments do not formally purport to be for all humankind but for Israel, and they might seem to lose a certain degree of their claim upon us when they are regarded simply as a series of demands imposed by an ancient God upon an ancient people. Yet to think in such terms is to misread the commandments.

The great value and historical importance of the Ten Commandments lie in their focus on certain fundamental issues that belong to the human condition. They recognize that the right ordering and protection of humans from abuse and exploitation are of the utmost importance to human survival and human happiness. Still today it becomes necessary to appeal to such fictive concepts as "natural law" and "natural justice" in order to protect the awareness that there is a measure of ultimate concern that belongs to the welfare of human beings. So even though the mode of appeal employed by the commandments seems to require modification and adaptation, the centrality of the issues with which they deal is unaffected. Whether we express such a feeling of ultimate demand in terms of "God says . . ." or "human dignity requires . . ." the issues remain quite fundamentally the same. Seen in the context of ancient Israel's life, the Ten Commandments can still be reflected upon profitably and seriously as one of the great ethical documents of humankind. They have proved to be a primary contribution made by the biblical tradition to the shaping of civilization.

DEUTERONOMY 5:22–11:32, MOSAIC EXHORTATIONS

Deuteronomy 5:22-33, The Request for a Mediator and the Authority of the Commandments

NIV

22These are the commandments the LORD proclaimed in a loud voice to your whole assembly there on the mountain from out of the fire, the cloud and the deep darkness; and he added nothing more. Then he wrote them on two stone tablets and gave them to me.

23When you heard the voice out of the darkness, while the mountain was ablaze with fire, all the leading men of your tribes and your elders came to me. 24And you said, "The LORD our God has shown us his glory and his majesty, and we have heard his voice from the fire. Today we have seen that a man can live even if God speaks with him. 25But now, why should we die? This great fire will consume us, and we will die if we hear the voice of the LORD our God any longer. 26For what mortal man has ever heard the voice of the living God speaking out of fire, as we have, and survived? 27Go near and listen to all that the LORD

NRSV

22These words the LORD spoke with a loud voice to your whole assembly at the mountain, out of the fire, the cloud, and the thick darkness, and he added no more. He wrote them on two stone tablets, and gave them to me. 23When you heard the voice out of the darkness, while the mountain was burning with fire, you approached me, all the heads of your tribes and your elders; 24and you said, "Look, the LORD our God has shown us his glory and greatness, and we have heard his voice out of the fire. Today we have seen that God may speak to someone and the person may still live. 25So now why should we die? For this great fire will consume us; if we hear the voice of the LORD our God any longer, we shall die. 26For who is there of all flesh that has heard the voice of the living God speaking out of fire, as we have, and remained alive? 27Go near, you yourself, and hear all that the LORD our God

NIV

our God says. Then tell us whatever the LORD our God tells you. We will listen and obey."

28The LORD heard you when you spoke to me and the LORD said to me, "I have heard what this people said to you. Everything they said was good. 29Oh, that their hearts would be inclined to fear me and keep all my commands always, so that it might go well with them and their children forever!

30"Go, tell them to return to their tents. 31But you stay here with me so that I may give you all the commands, decrees and laws you are to teach them to follow in the land I am giving them to possess."

32So be careful to do what the LORD your God has commanded you; do not turn aside to the right or to the left. 33Walk in all the way that the LORD your God has commanded you, so that you may live and prosper and prolong your days in the land that you will possess.

NRSV

will say. Then tell us everything that the LORD our God tells you, and we will listen and do it."

28The LORD heard your words when you spoke to me, and the LORD said to me: "I have heard the words of this people, which they have spoken to you; they are right in all that they have spoken. 29If only they had such a mind as this, to fear me and to keep all my commandments always, so that it might go well with them and with their children forever! 30Go say to them, 'Return to your tents.' 31But you, stand here by me, and I will tell you all the commandments, the statutes and the ordinances, that you shall teach them, so that they may do them in the land that I am giving them to possess." 32You must therefore be careful to do as the LORD your God has commanded you; you shall not turn to the right or to the left. 33You must follow exactly the path that the LORD your God has commanded you, so that you may live, and that it may go well with you, and that you may live long in the land that you are to possess.

COMMENTARY

This section rounds off the preceding declaration of the Ten Commandments by reporting the manner of their reception by Israel. It then paves the way for the long series of exhortations and admonitions that form the main content of chaps. 6–9. There is a certain measure of ambivalence in the fact that vv. 22-27 reaffirm the fearful and awesome nature of the LORD as God. The fear-inspiring majesty that had been revealed on Mt. Horeb is now experienced afresh, once the commandments have been repeated. It is as though the commandments themselves are in some measure a manifestation of the presence of God. As the people hear once again the demands that are presented, by that very experience, they encounter God afresh. All the traditional elements that constitute a theophany are again manifested here—fire, cloud, impenetrable darkness, and an awesome sound (thunder).

Taken as a whole, these features marvelously combine the sense of a genuine revelation with the inevitable hiddenness of God. The people have heard the divine voice again as the com-

mandments have been repeated to them. They cannot doubt that God is present with them still through the divine law and that, even though they are now poised on the banks of the Jordan ready to enter the land, all the majesty and awe of the presence manifested on Mt. Horeb will accompany them. Where the law is read and heard, there God is truly present. God reveals both the majesty and the otherness that belong to the very essence of deity, and yet remains essentially hidden. God cannot be seen, touched, or defined, yet through the commandments given on Mt. Horeb the majesty of a divine otherness is felt and known.

A note of ambivalence colors the account of Israel's response to the giving of the commandments in vv. 22-27. The people are terrified at what they have felt and heard, so they turn again to Moses, asking that he act as mediator for them. Alongside this is the contrasting motif that it had been a unique and remarkable privilege for them to see God and still remain alive (vv. 24, 26). The two themes run in parallel and are not easily reconciled. It is in consequence of this that many interpreters have seen here the work of an editor who has expanded upon the original narrative in the same vein that runs through chap. 4. However the text has been brought to its present shape, there is a necessary complementarity about the two themes. God is the holy One who inspires fear and dread, manifesting a reality that cannot be grasped. Yet such fear and dread are themselves uplifting and irresistibly fascinating. Israel had enjoyed a unique privilege in encountering God. The enduring legacy of that encounter was that the Israelites could live life at a new level through their reception of, and obedience to, the divine commandments.

The importance of the role of Moses as mediator continues to dominate chaps. 6–9. There are, however, certain related themes needing to be dealt with. Since the commandments are presented as having been inscribed on two stone tablets (v. 22), written by the very hand of God and received by Moses, their divine origin could not be stated more forcibly. They are of God, and it becomes fundamental to their role and effectiveness that this divine origin should be permanently recognized.

On account of this divine origin, they required no list of specific punishments for disobedience, since it is fundamental to the deuteronomic perspective that Israel's very relationship to God would be placed in jeopardy were Israel to disobey these commandments. Only in the list of blessings and curses set out in the epilogue to the book as a whole in chaps. 27–30 is there an attempt to focus on the question of what would happen to Israel were it to fail to live up to its high calling. Through and through Israel's relationship to God is seen as conditional. Yet, only when the terms of blessing and cursing are spelled out in detail do the full consequences and risks of this conditional status become explicit.

Throughout the structure of the book, therefore, there is a certain momentum that gathers strength, in which the possibility of disaster becomes ever more openly recognized. But this does not extinguish the element of hope. Rather, it serves to reinforce it. Hope is not a predestined future from which Israel cannot escape. Rather, it is an opportunity to be seized and striven for in much the same manner as the nation's forebears had seized their opportunity when they crossed the Jordan and set foot on the new territory. When faced with the vital question of how this rich and hopeful future could be grasped, the deuteronomists give one clear and unequivocal answer—by paying heed to the commandments God had given and following their guidance faithfully.

The reception of the Ten Commandments by the people is then further reflected upon in vv. 28-33. Their ultimate purpose is well expressed in v. 33. It is to promote a way of life that would be prosperous and beneficial to the social and political well-being of Israel: "and that you may live long in the land." The theme of the temptations of life in the land, combined with the potential threat of being expelled from it, now begins to hover like the shadow of a bird of prey over the remainder of the book. It is a theme that is more broadly enlarged upon in the great work of history that follows the law book from the deuteronomic authors. The theme generates a somber mood, and at times it gives rise to a frenetic intensity of aggressive demand and intolerance, which characterizes the entire theological outlook of the deuteronomists.

So Moses, and the first generation of the nation who enjoyed the prospect of entry into the land, were looking to a future that the readers of the book knew only too well still eluded them. They could empathize with that earlier band of nation seekers, since they shared their expectations, and yet were equally fearful of its consequences. If there were an advantage that the original readers of Deuteronomy enjoyed—but was not appreciated by their national ancestors about whom the book was written—it was a realization attained through hindsight of the importance of the commandments God had given. If only that earlier generation had heeded God's law, then the people would not now be faced with the prospect of beginning again.

So there is an unmistakable sense of tension that permeates Deuteronomy and that now unfolds with remarkable intensity in a series of exhortations and warnings, ascribed to Moses, that set out clearly the choices facing Israel. There is, woven into them, a certain wistfulness in which the authors of the book read back some of their own emotional stresses and anxieties: "If only they had such a mind as this" (v. 29); "You must be careful to do . . ." (v. 32). Repeatedly the warning note is sounded in Deuteronomy. There is a consciousness that Israel is wavering in its loyalty and is as uncertain of the outcome of its own painful choices as that first generation had been. Quite clearly the "if only" is meant with utmost seriousness. All kinds of unknown threats and dangers lay awaiting the people, just as that earlier generation had experienced them when they first set foot on the bed of the river Jordan. The only guidance they possessed by which to negotiate the perils they faced was in the commandments by which they could be assured of divine protection and support.

REFLECTIONS

It is appropriate that the giving of the Ten Commandments should be followed by a formal sequel that summarizes their central importance for the life and future of Israel. This short episode binds together two very distinct and differing interpretations of the divine transcendence. On one side is a physical awesomeness that is unbearably terrifying and potentially destructive—storm clouds, fire, unbearable light. But the disclosure of the commandments calls forth a life-enhancing moral seriousness. God is the author of life and the source of love. The divine law is itself a body of truths concerning the high dignity of human beings and the immense seriousness of the moral responsibility they bear. Only those who pay no heed to the ethical dimension of the divine nature and who pay no regard to this moral priority have need to fear God. So, for all their seeming brevity and simple directness, the Ten Commandments are awesome in their significance. They hold the key to human welfare and the possibility of building a truly God-willed order of life on earth.

The deuteronomic modes of address continually fluctuate between the singular and the plural. Sometimes it appears that the authors of the work are addressing one solitary person, as though the future of God's law and the future life of the nation hung wholly upon the response of that one person. At other times, the plural form of address is employed, creating a more profound sense of the social nature of the community and of the collective responsibility shared among all its members.

A key toward understanding the relationship between these two dimensions of human identity—the individual and the collective—is found in the deuteronomic portrait of Moses. More than any other person, he is presented as distinctive and unique. When others are afraid, he is fearless. When others are in despair, he is fired with courage. When others would turn back, he is for going on. He stands alone, and yet he is never alone. On him rests the survival of the nation, and without him they cannot go forward. In the conclusion to Deuteronomy's narrative, Moses himself dies in the wilderness, being debarred from the future that he has made possible for others. Yet even this failure to enjoy the fruits of his own vision is not on his own account. He must forfeit his future, so that the nation might have theirs! With such perceptive awareness of the complex intertwining of collective and individual elements of human responses, the deuteronomic literature sees a profoundly spiritual and theological dimension in the concept of community.

A whole plethora of phrases ("Be careful. Do not forget. If only . . .") indicate how firmly and confidently the deuteronomists point to the simplicity of the way to the future. If Israel willed, it could readily and immediately enjoy the fruits of the land, with the prospect of unclouded days ahead. Yet the very repetitions and passionate pleading indicate that the deuteronomists were all too conscious that it had not been that simple and could not be so. The Israelites so easily could have achieved everything that was promised, yet they singularly failed to do so. The deuteronomic authors do not disguise this feeling from their readers, who were already looking back on a ruined nation. So even within this insistence on the simplicity of God's directive, with a mere ten brief commandments being all that was necessary to unlock the gate to an almost paradisaical future, there is a consciousness of the faulty humans with whom God had to work. Deep within the human psyche lie forces and leanings that are not so easily governed, so that even Moses had to be denied the future that he strove so unselfishly to bring to others.

Deuteronomy 6:1-25, The Call to Diligent Observance

6 These are the commands, decrees and laws the LORD your God directed me to teach you to observe in the land that you are crossing the Jordan to possess, ²so that you, your children and their children after them may fear the LORD your God as long as you live by keeping all his decrees and commands that I give you, and so that you may enjoy long life. ³Hear, O Israel, and be careful to obey so that it may go well with you and that you may increase greatly in a land flowing with milk and honey, just as the LORD, the God of your fathers, promised you.

⁴Hear, O Israel: The LORD our God, the LORD is one.ª ⁵Love the LORD your God with all your heart and with all your soul and with all your strength. ⁶These commandments that I give you today are to be upon your hearts. ⁷Impress them on your children. Talk about them when you sit at home and when you walk along the road, when you lie down and when you get up. ⁸Tie them as symbols on your hands and bind them on your foreheads. ⁹Write them on the doorframes of your houses and on your gates.

¹⁰When the LORD your God brings you into the land he swore to your fathers, to Abraham, Isaac and Jacob, to give you—a land with large, flourishing cities you did not build, ¹¹houses filled with all kinds of good things you did not provide, wells you did not dig, and vineyards and olive groves you did not plant—then when you eat and are satisfied, ¹²be careful that you do not forget the LORD, who brought you out of Egypt, out of the land of slavery.

¹³Fear the LORD your God, serve him only and take your oaths in his name. ¹⁴Do not follow other gods, the gods of the peoples around you; ¹⁵for the LORD your God, who is among you, is a jealous God and his anger will burn against you, and he will destroy you from the face of the land. ¹⁶Do not test the LORD your God as you did at Massah.

6 Now this is the commandment—the statutes and the ordinances—that the LORD your God charged me to teach you to observe in the land that you are about to cross into and occupy, ²so that you and your children and your children's children may fear the LORD your God all the days of your life, and keep all his decrees and his commandments that I am commanding you, so that your days may be long. ³Hear therefore, O Israel, and observe them diligently, so that it may go well with you, and so that you may multiply greatly in a land flowing with milk and honey, as the LORD, the God of your ancestors, has promised you.

4Hear, O Israel: The LORD is our God, the LORD alone.ª ⁵You shall love the LORD your God with all your heart, and with all your soul, and with all your might. ⁶Keep these words that I am commanding you today in your heart. ⁷Recite them to your children and talk about them when you are at home and when you are away, when you lie down and when you rise. ⁸Bind them as a sign on your hand, fix them as an emblemᵇ on your forehead, ⁹and write them on the doorposts of your house and on your gates.

10When the LORD your God has brought you into the land that he swore to your ancestors, to Abraham, to Isaac, and to Jacob, to give you—a land with fine, large cities that you did not build, ¹¹houses filled with all sorts of goods that you did not fill, hewn cisterns that you did not hew, vineyards and olive groves that you did not plant—and when you have eaten your fill, ¹²take care that you do not forget the LORD, who brought you out of the land of Egypt, out of the house of slavery. ¹³The LORD your God you shall fear; him you shall serve, and by his name alone you shall swear. ¹⁴Do not follow other gods, any of the gods of the peoples who are all around you, ¹⁵because the LORD your God, who is present with you, is

ª4 Or *The LORD our God is one LORD;* or *The LORD is our God, the LORD is one;* or *The LORD is our God, the LORD alone*

ª Or *The LORD our God is one LORD,* or *The LORD our God, the LORD is one,* or *The LORD is our God, the LORD is one*   ᵇ Or *as a frontlet*

NIV

17Be sure to keep the commands of the LORD your God and the stipulations and decrees he has given you. 18Do what is right and good in the LORD's sight, so that it may go well with you and you may go in and take over the good land that the LORD promised on oath to your forefathers, 19thrusting out all your enemies before you, as the LORD said.

20In the future, when your son asks you, "What is the meaning of the stipulations, decrees and laws the LORD our God has commanded you?" 21tell him: "We were slaves of Pharaoh in Egypt, but the LORD brought us out of Egypt with a mighty hand. 22Before our eyes the LORD sent miraculous signs and wonders—great and terrible—upon Egypt and Pharaoh and his whole household. 23But he brought us out from there to bring us in and give us the land that he promised on oath to our forefathers. 24The LORD commanded us to obey all these decrees and to fear the LORD our God, so that we might always prosper and be kept alive, as is the case today. 25And if we are careful to obey all this law before the LORD our God, as he has commanded us, that will be our righteousness."

NRSV

a jealous God. The anger of the LORD your God would be kindled against you and he would destroy you from the face of the earth.

16Do not put the LORD your God to the test, as you tested him at Massah. 17You must diligently keep the commandments of the LORD your God, and his decrees, and his statutes that he has commanded you. 18Do what is right and good in the sight of the LORD, so that it may go well with you, and so that you may go in and occupy the good land that the LORD swore to your ancestors to give you, 19thrusting out all your enemies from before you, as the LORD has promised.

20When your children ask you in time to come, "What is the meaning of the decrees and the statutes and the ordinances that the LORD our God has commanded you?" 21then you shall say to your children, "We were Pharaoh's slaves in Egypt, but the LORD brought us out of Egypt with a mighty hand. 22The LORD displayed before our eyes great and awesome signs and wonders against Egypt, against Pharaoh and all his household. 23He brought us out from there in order to bring us in, to give us the land that he promised on oath to our ancestors. 24Then the LORD commanded us to observe all these statutes, to fear the LORD our God, for our lasting good, so as to keep us alive, as is now the case. 25If we diligently observe this entire commandment before the LORD our God, as he has commanded us, we will be in the right."

COMMENTARY

The giving of the Ten Commandments provides a fitting climax to the entire story of God's action with, and toward, Israel, which has occupied the books of Genesis through Numbers. It has three central themes: the promise to the ancestors of the nation that Israel would enter and occupy a land "flowing with milk and honey"; the exodus from Egypt, which rescued the people from slavery; and the giving of the law, now enshrined in the Ten Commandments.

A summary of these events now provides the basis for a renewed appeal to make ready for the crossing of the Jordan to take possession of the land (v. 1). The immediate threat posed by the present inhabitants of the land and the task of defeating them is taken as a relatively minor difficulty. More serious and prolonged is the threat posed by the temptation to forget the law that Moses had just reaffirmed. So before all other dangers are faced, there must be a carefully nurtured preparation—spiritual, psychological, and practical—to ensure that this law would never be forgotten. It must remain imprinted on the mind of every single Israelite, both young and old. Chapter 6, then, was carefully constructed, and its component themes are easily identified.

6:1-3. The opening section focuses afresh on the centrality of the law as the climactic gift of God. Israel's story, from the days of the patriarchs to the eve of the conquest, has now reached its climax, and the time has come to set in motion the plans and forces to bring Israel to its triumphant achievement. Israel can now contemplate the prospect of life in the land, where the people will enjoy an untroubled and undiminished future.

6:4-9. These verses set out the requisite attitude of mind needed to maintain the centrality of the commandments' authority. They must be taught to children from their earliest days, worn as a sign on the body, and fixed permanently upon the doorways of every house (vv. 8-9). The response to be aroused by explaining the meaning of this sign is later set out in vv. 20-25 (cf. Exod 12:24-27; 13:11-16). In between, there is a parenthesis (vv. 10-19) that breaks up the straightforward formula of the sign, followed by its explanation. This parenthesis contains a series of admonitions reinforcing the demand of the first commandment. The LORD alone is to be feared as God, and all temptation to act otherwise must be rigidly and firmly rejected. This parenthesis appears to have been inserted later into the original unit and serves to add yet more emphasis to a feature that was already heavily stressed.

Many of the most basic of the deuteronomic characteristic features come to the surface in this chapter, so that it has quite appropriately become one of the most often repeated, and readily memorable, parts of the book. Of prominent interest is the command to love God (v. 5), which, from this point onward, becomes a central aspect of the entire biblical tradition, shaping much of the Jewish and Christian spirituality that has been built upon it. For Deuteronomy, this demand for a loving attitude toward God is closely related to the concept of moral obedience. It reflects an attitude of giving priority to the demands of God. Commentators have regarded it as being closely linked to the teaching of the prophet Hosea (esp. Hos 11:1), in which God's exceptional love for Israel is stressed. There is to be a strong reciprocal bond of affection and commitment between Israel and the LORD as God.

Attempts to explore the similarities and parallels between the deuteronomic teaching and the form and characteristics of international treaties have noted that a demand for love is to be found in both of them.[48] If the deuteronomic authors were familiar with this treaty form, then it could be argued that they have consciously adapted this important demand for a loving attitude on the part of an Israelite worshiper toward God on the analogy of the treaty between a vassal partner and an overlord.

Yet such an argument appears strained and implausible in view of the importance of the issue and the widespread feature in Deuteronomy of pointing out the necessity for the nurturing of a right attitude toward God. Since love is vitally important in family life, and since there is widespread use throughout the biblical tradition of employing kinship metaphors to describe divine-human relationships, the employment of the love concept by the deuteronomists can hardly occasion surprise. It is simply one further example of the introduction of human metaphors and analogies to describe the fundamental features of the spiritual life.

A further important aspect of the deuteronomic teaching is evident in the injunction to teach "these words" (הדברים האלה *haddĕbārîm hā'ēlleh*), which must refer to the Ten Commandments, to children. The inference is clear that those who are addressed are regarded as lay citizens of Israel who will carry out such instruction in their homes. Such a practice reflects an important similarity between the teaching of Deuteronomy and the biblical wisdom tradition (see, e.g., 4:9; Prov 2:1).

The confessional affirmation of the Shema (v. 4) is very terse, so that ascertaining the precise meaning is fraught with uncertainties. "The LORD is our God, the LORD alone" (cf. NIV; REB). The Hebrew affirmation falls short of expressing a clear-cut denial of the existence of other deities, but is adamant that there is only one LORD God who is to be worshiped by Israel. This, then, amounts to a denial that the LORD can have more than one manifestation (i.e., a denial that the deity could be known in different forms, or manifestations, in different sanctuaries), and it is a firm rejection of the notion that there could be any consort or retinue of lesser gods surrounding the

48. W. L. Moran, "The Ancient Near Eastern Background of the Love of God in Deuteronomy," *CBQ* 25 (1963) 77-87. For a review of the issue, see D. J. McCarthy, "Notes on the Love of God in Deuteronomy and the Father-Son Relationship Between Yahweh and Israel," in *Institution and Narrative: Collected Essays,* AnBib 108 (Rome: Pontifical Biblical Institute, 1985) 301-4.

LORD.[49] This latter feature was clearly virtually the norm in traditional forms of Canaanite religion, where one deity was supreme but other gods and goddesses served as helpers and servants. There would also appear to be substantial evidence that unofficial practice in Israel frequently countenanced the acceptance of other gods alongside the LORD. That this was the case, even though not officially approved, lends weight to the conviction that it was a concern to repudiate such practice that has motivated the form of the confessional recital of faith here.

It is possible to construe either literally or metaphorically the instructions in vv. 8-9 to bind this confessional affirmation "as a sign on your hand" and to fix them to the doorposts of the house. If taken metaphorically, the implication would be that the commandments are to be remembered at all times. The force of the construction can then be understood as "when you are at home and when you are away."

The injunction has consistently been understood literally within Jewish tradition, giving rise to the use of phylacteries, small leather containers to hold the texts of Exod 13:1-10, 11-16; and Deut 6:4-9; 11:13-21 inscribed on scrolls (cf. Matt 23:5). It seems probable that a literal understanding was intended from the outset, making the use of such important confessional texts affirming religious loyalty and identity a counterpart to the widespread use of semi-magical amulets and religious jewelry among non-Israelite peoples. Such amulets were thought to provide divine healing power (cf. Ezek 13:18) and would certainly have been familiar objects to the deuteronomic authors. It would have been a positive form of religious apologetic, therefore, to provide continued reminders of the commandments and of the need for total loyalty to the LORD as God—a requirement that could easily be infringed by resorting to popular semi-magical practices.

6:10-19. This parenthetical section reiterates commands that have already been given and marks a further aspect of the extent to which the deuteronomic writers were conscious of human weakness. Security, prosperity, and the general feeling that God's promises had been fulfilled could readily lead to a sense of complacency (v. 11; cf. 8:11-20). In such a circumstance a belief could arise that the requirements of the divine law were no longer important and could safely be set aside. So there could emerge an attitude of indifference to the divine law and a feeling that God's gifts, having once been received, would not subsequently be taken away. Once given, they would forever be the spiritual possession of Israel. Against all such complacency, the authors of these exhortations offer a sharp rebuke.

It is likely that we should recognize that behind such forms of spiritual psychologizing the deuteronomic authors were seeking not simply to forestall future eventualities, but were also very mindful of attitudes and events that had already overtaken Israel. We are entitled to assume, therefore, that in this rather pessimistic exploration of the psychology of apostasy these authors were assessing the mood and attitude of some of their readers. Clearly they had encountered such a spirit and were here concerned to oppose it by uncovering its element of self-delusion. It belonged to their belief, and the entire strategy of their work, to set the Mosaic *torah* in the forefront of the life of Israel, out of a conviction that this had never really been the case in the past. So the disasters that had already overtaken the nation were, to the knowledge of these authors, entirely explainable. The right attitude toward the law of God on the part of Israel had been seriously lacking from the earliest times since the nation had taken possession of the land.

The central understanding of what constituted the sum of Israel's religious duties is then set out clearly in v. 13: Israel must fear the LORD, serve God unswervingly, and invoke no other divine name in affirming its oaths. The contrast between this and the simple formula of Israel's visible commitment to God set out in Exod 23:17 is quite noteworthy. Formal outward duties toward the LORD are certainly required (and are specified in 16:1-17), but alongside this, and undergirding them, lies a prior commitment of attitude that would affect every part of the year and every aspect of life. It is this concern to match outward observance with inward attitude and reflection that forms so large a feature of what is new and striking in Deuteronomy. The entire understanding of religious commitment has taken on a

49. G. Braulik, "Das Deuteronomium und die Geburt des Monotheismus," *Studien zur Theologie des Deuteronomiums,* SBA 2 (Stuttgart: Katholisches Bibelwerk, 1988) 257-300.

more inward, and more recognizably spiritual, stance. It is on this account that the book has acquired a central place in the formation of a reasoned theological explication of what constitutes the service of God.

Once again the element of conditionality in Israel's relationship with the LORD is given renewed emphasis. The author does not shun from declaring what failure to adhere to God's demands will entail: "he would destroy you from the face of the earth" (v. 15).

The warning against putting the LORD God "to the test" (נסה *nāsâ*, v. 16) can most readily be understood in the present context as a reference to the temptation to see whether God would, indeed, punish Israel if it failed to adhere to the law—i.e., the test would be a bold flouting of God's law to see if punishment would ensue. This fits closely the general theme of the unit, and it would be out of place to see here a reference to seeking a "sign" from God as indicative that a prophetic word was to be fulfilled (as in Isa 7:10, 14).

6:20-25. The unit that brings the section to a conclusion is important for the manner in which it formulates a short credo-like summary of Israel's history as an answer to the question put by children concerning the "sign" of God's law, which was binding upon Israel. The use of short historical summaries of the past as a demonstrative affirmation of the love of God toward Israel and the reason why this people were bound to respond to this love by obedience is a major feature of the deuteronomic rhetoric. It comes to its fullest expression in the more elaborate summary set out in 26:5*b*-10*a* and can more fully be examined there. Its importance lies in the manner in which it reflects the consistent deuteronomic assertion that God's law is a further manifestation of the divine grace that belongs with, and is related to, God's deliverance of the people from Egypt. Deliverance and response are both seen to be expressions of the same divine love without which Israel could not exist. So the law itself is viewed as an instrument of grace.

REFLECTIONS

The most striking and memorable feature of this entire hortatory address concerning the importance of God's commandments and the steps Israel must take to ensure that it never forgets them lies in its command to love God. All the familiar vocabulary of worship concerning the necessity to fear God, to revere God's name, and to offer service and gifts at a sanctuary at the appropriate times of the year is fully present in Deuteronomy. Yet now there comes a fresh, and less obviously expected, demand that seeks to provide motivation and reason for all the rest: Israel is to *love* God. Clearly elements of tension and near contradiction can readily arise, since it is a far from straightforward undertaking to show love toward a power that may hurl one swiftly to destruction and may take away everything that one possesses. Yet, with this intrusion of the concept of love into the framework of the deuteronomic understanding of faith and spirituality a breakthrough of immense importance has been made. In fact, the strong emphasis placed on all the gifts and benefits God has showered upon Israel represents a move in the direction of recognizing the *loveliness* of God. God becomes the supreme expression of love, motivating, inspiring, and making possible a deeper understanding of the nature of love in the lives of human beings.

Were it not for the placing of such a demand in a position of great prominence here, it could be claimed that the assertions concerning the requirement to love God and to confess the divine love in the Old Testament are often muted. Sometimes assertions of God's love are severely modified by the limits placed on them. The LORD God has many enemies, and the focus placed on the concept of divine wrath frequently reduces worship to a cringing submissiveness. Features of a more violent portrayal of the divine being then come to the fore. Yet it must be recognized that the understanding that love lies at the heart of worship is a leaven that must ultimately affect the entire understanding of faith. There is, therefore, a direct path from the command in Deuteronomy to love God to the New Testament assertion in 1 John 4:8: "Whoever does not love does not know God, for God is love."

A second aspect of the deuteronomic teaching emerges very forcibly in Deuteronomy 6. This concerns the heavy psychologizing of faith and all its concerns. Commitment to God cannot simply be presented as the performance of certain outward duties that will be publicly observed and recognized. Rather, all knowledge of God becomes a matter of heart searching and looking inward. The authors seem to display an almost Freudian awareness that self-delusion is always a possibility in religion. So there may arise a sense of complacency that calculates in a mean-spirited fashion that sufficient regard for God and the divine demands has been made and that no outward signs of divine wrath are likely to overwhelm the formally correct worshiper.

For Deuteronomy, however, such can never be the obedience that God seeks, which must ultimately flow out from a sense of love toward God. Again there is a note of duality and ambivalence in the overall perspectives set out in Deuteronomy. At times the most violent and cruel responses are demanded by way of punishment upon those who refuse the message of God's love. Yet alongside these harsh demands, tempering them and ultimately outlasting them, is an awareness that true faith and a true spirit of obedience can only be attained from within the human spirit. So the key words for understanding the kind of obedience that is sought after lie in the injunctions: "Observe diligently"; "Remember . . ."; "Love!"

The short unit (6:20-25) that brings this hortatory address to a close is also of great significance for the overall grasp of the message of the Pentateuch in its full compass. This concerns the combining of a message of deliverance and liberation with a call for obedience and a high regard for God's command. The Pentateuch is a story of freedom and promise. But it is also a call to obedience and righteousness. There can be no liberation without law and no freedom without justice.

All too easily there can arise within religious reflection an imbalance precisely because one feature is emphasized to the detriment of another. So the threat of legalism and the pursuit of righteousness as a path to salvation can become stultifying and self-destructive. But Deuteronomy is in no sense a legalistic book, affirming only the awesome demands of the law with threats and warnings lest it be disobeyed. Such elements are certainly present, but they are combined with an assertion of divine love and grace, which calls for a similar attitude of love by way of response. It recognizes that, for the divine love and grace to become real and effective in human society, it must be reciprocated in human actions. So the path is left open for the recognition that to love God is loving to obey the divine commandments.

Deuteronomy 7:1-26, When You Live in the Land

NIV	NRSV
7 When the LORD your God brings you into the land you are entering to possess and drives out before you many nations—the Hittites, Girgashites, Amorites, Canaanites, Perizzites, Hivites and Jebusites, seven nations larger and stronger than you— [2]and when the LORD your God has delivered them over to you and you have defeated them, then you must destroy them totally.[a] Make no treaty with them, and show them	7 When the LORD your God brings you into the land that you are about to enter and occupy, and he clears away many nations before you—the Hittites, the Girgashites, the Amorites, the Canaanites, the Perizzites, the Hivites, and the Jebusites, seven nations mightier and more numerous than you— [2]and when the LORD your God gives them over to you and you defeat them, then you must utterly destroy them. Make no covenant with them and show them no mercy. [3]Do not intermarry with them, giving your daugh-

[a]2 The Hebrew term refers to the irrevocable giving over of things or persons to the LORD, often by totally destroying them; also in verse 26.

NIV

no mercy. ³Do not intermarry with them. Do not give your daughters to their sons or take their daughters for your sons, ⁴for they will turn your sons away from following me to serve other gods, and the LORD's anger will burn against you and will quickly destroy you. ⁵This is what you are to do to them: Break down their altars, smash their sacred stones, cut down their Asherah poles* and burn their idols in the fire. ⁶For you are a people holy to the LORD your God. The LORD your God has chosen you out of all the peoples on the face of the earth to be his people, his treasured possession.

⁷The LORD did not set his affection on you and choose you because you were more numerous than other peoples, for you were the fewest of all peoples. ⁸But it was because the LORD loved you and kept the oath he swore to your forefathers that he brought you out with a mighty hand and redeemed you from the land of slavery, from the power of Pharaoh king of Egypt. ⁹Know therefore that the LORD your God is God; he is the faithful God, keeping his covenant of love to a thousand generations of those who love him and keep his commands. ¹⁰But

those who hate him he will repay to their
    face by destruction;
he will not be slow to repay to their face
    those who hate him.

¹¹Therefore, take care to follow the commands, decrees and laws I give you today.

¹²If you pay attention to these laws and are careful to follow them, then the LORD your God will keep his covenant of love with you, as he swore to your forefathers. ¹³He will love you and bless you and increase your numbers. He will bless the fruit of your womb, the crops of your land—your grain, new wine and oil—the calves of your herds and the lambs of your flocks in the land that he swore to your forefathers to give you. ¹⁴You will be blessed more than any other people; none of your men or women will be childless, nor any of your livestock without young. ¹⁵The LORD will keep you free from every disease. He will not inflict on you the horrible diseases you knew in Egypt, but he will inflict them on all who

*5 That is, symbols of the goddess Asherah; here and elsewhere in Deuteronomy

NRSV

ters to their sons or taking their daughters for your sons, ⁴for that would turn away your children from following me, to serve other gods. Then the anger of the LORD would be kindled against you, and he would destroy you quickly. ⁵But this is how you must deal with them: break down their altars, smash their pillars, hew down their sacred poles,* and burn their idols with fire. ⁶For you are a people holy to the LORD your God; the LORD your God has chosen you out of all the peoples on earth to be his people, his treasured possession.

7It was not because you were more numerous than any other people that the LORD set his heart on you and chose you—for you were the fewest of all peoples. ⁸It was because the LORD loved you and kept the oath that he swore to your ancestors, that the LORD has brought you out with a mighty hand, and redeemed you from the house of slavery, from the hand of Pharaoh king of Egypt. ⁹Know therefore that the LORD your God is God, the faithful God who maintains covenant loyalty with those who love him and keep his commandments, to a thousand generations, ¹⁰and who repays in their own person those who reject him. He does not delay but repays in their own person those who reject him. ¹¹Therefore, observe diligently the commandment—the statutes and the ordinances—that I am commanding you today.

12If you heed these ordinances, by diligently observing them, the LORD your God will maintain with you the covenant loyalty that he swore to your ancestors; ¹³he will love you, bless you, and multiply you; he will bless the fruit of your womb and the fruit of your ground, your grain and your wine and your oil, the increase of your cattle and the issue of your flock, in the land that he swore to your ancestors to give you. ¹⁴You shall be the most blessed of peoples, with neither sterility nor barrenness among you or your livestock. ¹⁵The LORD will turn away from you every illness; all the dread diseases of Egypt that you experienced, he will not inflict on you, but he will lay them on all who hate you. ¹⁶You shall devour all the peoples that the LORD your God is giving over to you, showing them no pity; you shall not serve their gods, for that would be a snare to you.

*Heb *Asherim*

hate you. [16]You must destroy all the peoples the LORD your God gives over to you. Do not look on them with pity and do not serve their gods, for that will be a snare to you.

[17]You may say to yourselves, "These nations are stronger than we are. How can we drive them out?" [18]But do not be afraid of them; remember well what the LORD your God did to Pharaoh and to all Egypt. [19]You saw with your own eyes the great trials, the miraculous signs and wonders, the mighty hand and outstretched arm, with which the LORD your God brought you out. The LORD your God will do the same to all the peoples you now fear. [20]Moreover, the LORD your God will send the hornet among them until even the survivors who hide from you have perished. [21]Do not be terrified by them, for the LORD your God, who is among you, is a great and awesome God. [22]The LORD your God will drive out those nations before you, little by little. You will not be allowed to eliminate them all at once, or the wild animals will multiply around you. [23]But the LORD your God will deliver them over to you, throwing them into great confusion until they are destroyed. [24]He will give their kings into your hand, and you will wipe out their names from under heaven. No one will be able to stand up against you; you will destroy them. [25]The images of their gods you are to burn in the fire. Do not covet the silver and gold on them, and do not take it for yourselves, or you will be ensnared by it, for it is detestable to the LORD your God. [26]Do not bring a detestable thing into your house or you, like it, will be set apart for destruction. Utterly abhor and detest it, for it is set apart for destruction.

[17]If you say to yourself, "These nations are more numerous than I; how can I dispossess them?" [18]do not be afraid of them. Just remember what the LORD your God did to Pharaoh and to all Egypt, [19]the great trials that your eyes saw, the signs and wonders, the mighty hand and the outstretched arm by which the LORD your God brought you out. The LORD your God will do the same to all the peoples of whom you are afraid. [20]Moreover, the LORD your God will send the pestilence[a] against them, until even the survivors and the fugitives are destroyed. [21]Have no dread of them, for the LORD your God, who is present with you, is a great and awesome God. [22]The LORD your God will clear away these nations before you little by little; you will not be able to make a quick end of them, otherwise the wild animals would become too numerous for you. [23]But the LORD your God will give them over to you, and throw them into great panic, until they are destroyed. [24]He will hand their kings over to you and you shall blot out their name from under heaven; no one will be able to stand against you, until you have destroyed them. [25]The images of their gods you shall burn with fire. Do not covet the silver or the gold that is on them and take it for yourself, because you could be ensnared by it; for it is abhorrent to the LORD your God. [26]Do not bring an abhorrent thing into your house, or you will be set apart for destruction like it. You must utterly detest and abhor it, for it is set apart for destruction.

[a] Or hornets: Meaning of Heb uncertain

COMMENTARY

The look ahead to a future life in the land that Israel was shortly to occupy affirmed that it was to be lived in the light of the commandments of God (6:1-2). Careful safeguards were to be implemented to ensure that Israel forgot neither these commandments nor their inescapable link to the promise of God through which the land had been occupied. Forgetfulness and complacency were clearly inner spiritual temptations to which the nation could all too easily fall prey (6:10-13). Yet a more visible and persistent hazard needed also to be considered in the form of the presence of sanctuaries to alien deities, like that at Baal-peor, and especially the deeply rooted traditional religious practices of the people already occupying the land.

7:1-6. Three fundamental rules are laid down with uncompromising sternness to obviate the dangers to Israel posed by these alluring temptations. First the former occupants of the land themselves were to be exterminated: "You must utterly destroy them" (v. 2). No treaties or covenants that might qualify this demand were to be entertained (v. 3). It is the most uncompromising demand for genocide, based on religious principles, that could possibly be expressed. In historical and theological perspective, we are bound to seek some degree of qualification, and hermeneutical distance, to place between the modern world and such a horrifying demand.[50] Nevertheless, it is appalling in the fearfulness of what it demands and contrasts strangely with the preceding affirmation concerning the loving aspects of God and of obedience. Deuteronomy presents us with several strange anomalies and paradoxes!

As a second step, no intermarriage was to be tolerated between the young people of Israel and those of the groups already inhabiting the land who are, somewhat inconsistently, assumed to have survived the calls for their removal. In this demand we can recognize a deep-seated and long-established feature of societies in which kinship played a prominent role. This was the practice of endogamy (marriage within the larger kin group; cf. Gen 24:1-9), although such marriage was necessarily restricted within kinship affinities to preclude the most immediate family kin.

In view of the concern to preclude intermarriage of Israelites with former inhabitants of the land, it is surprising to find that the important ruling presented in the law code of Deuteronomy (21:10-14) takes it for granted that an Israelite man might take as a wife a woman taken as a prisoner of war. In this case, it would undoubtedly have involved the crossing of a wide ethnic gap. Almost certainly such a ruling stands closer to actual practice in Israel, whereas the hortatory injunction of v. 4 represents a stylized concern to remove every temptation from Israel whereby God's law might be neglected.

The third instruction, designed to remove the danger of Israel's becoming enmeshed in practices and beliefs of the former religion of the land, demands that all the physical symbols of that religion be destroyed (v. 5). The justification for this action is that Israel is a people holy to the LORD God (v. 6).

The use of the term "holy" (קדוש qādôš) in such a context is itself full of distinctive meaning. It represents one of the most basic and lastingly significant aspects of the deuteronomic teaching.[51] In origin, the concept of holiness related directly to the sphere of cultic activity and connoted a quality of separateness and of being imbued with a special divine power. So holiness is not only a quality of persons and things, but also a power possessed by them. It was applicable primarily to holy places and objects, but it naturally extended, in a quasi-physical fashion, to cover those persons whose activities required that they work in close proximity to, and relationship with, such objects (cf. the experience of Moses in Exod 3:5).

In itself, therefore, the direct application to persons was not the remarkable feature of the deuteronomic teaching on holiness, but rather the extension of it to cover an entire nation. Israel as a whole was regarded as a holy nation. The formulation of v. 6, therefore, combines cultic and legal vocabulary in a way that has had lasting consequences for Jewish and Christian thinking.

A further important part of the deuteronomic understanding of the term "holy" lies in the assertion that the covenant relationship between Israel and the LORD God was itself the consequence of a unique act of divine choice. So the vocabulary of divine election is introduced as a vital part of Israel's thinking about the nature and meaning of its unique relationship to the LORD as God. Once again we find an extended application of a basic traditional concept, a feature that repeatedly characterizes the deuteronomic movement. Old ideas are given new clothes, and this process is consistently in the direction of adding the colors of ritual and worship to fundamental political and ethical terminology. It is not surprising, then, that scholars have found it difficult to determine whether Deuteronomy can best be understood as the work of priests or that of lawyers. So many features of both areas of social life are brought together and skillfully combined. On one hand, religion is partially secularized, but on the

---

50. The subject of the deuteronomic repudiation of any acceptance of peace with the inhabitants of the land is covered by G. Schmitt, *Du sollst keinen Frieden Schliessen mit den Bewohnen des Landes,* BWANT V:11 (Stuttgart: W. Kohlhammer, 1970) 13-24, 131-44.

51. J. G. Gammie, *Holiness in Israel,* OBT (Minneapolis: Fortress, 1989) 106-16; M. Weinfeld, *Deuteronomy and the Deuteronomic School* (Oxford: Oxford University Press, 1972) 225-32.

other hand, secular life is sacralized in a new way. This then is part of what it means for Israel to be a holy nation.

The very existence of Israel as a nation-state, together with the life within it that is to be regulated and shaped by the observance of the Ten Commandments, is recognized as the goal of a prior act of God's choice.[52] Close study of the background to this deuteronomic teaching brings to light a clear and discernible shift of thought. The concept of divine choice in early Israel was directly related to two institutions: God's choice of Mt. Zion as the location for the divine abode (cf. Psalm 78) and God's choice of the Davidic dynasty to provide a line of kings under whom Israel might live and be governed (cf. Psalms 89; 132).

Now the foreground of the divine purpose is taken up with Israel itself as a nation. The whole people is chosen; the whole nation is holy! So an important shift takes place, almost certainly anticipating, if not directly reflecting, the already accomplished fact that both the Davidic kingship and the Temple that stood on Mt. Zion might be lost to Israel. Would Israel's chosen status be forfeited because of such disasters? Clearly the deuteronomic authors give a clear and resounding no to such a possibility. Israel itself as a people is the object of God's choice. King and Temple might serve them and symbolize the reality of this election, but they do not themselves embody it or empower it.

7:7-11. This section forms a short parenthesis, almost certainly brought into the text at a late stage, that digresses more fully on the question of the mystery of divine election. Taken at a merely surface level, the belief that Israel had been selected to exist in a unique relationship to God could relapse into a doctrine of self-justification and self-congratulation. It is a risk endemic to all concepts of being especially chosen and favored. It could, in fact, become an article of faith that would encourage the very complacency 6:10-13 had warned Israel to resist. Accordingly, this parenthesis both warns against this, arguing that it would be a complete misreading of the situation, and reasserts the inscrutable and unqualified nature of divine love (v. 8).

52. A valuable study of the whole concept of election in relation to Israel is to be found in H. Wildberger, *Jahwes Eigentumsvolk,* ATANT 37 (Zurich: Zwingli Verlag, 1959). See also Paul D. Hanson, *The People Called: The Growth of Community in the Bible* (San Fransisco: Harper & Row, 1987) 167-76.

The author then proceeds to reaffirm, if any such reaffirmation were still needed, that Israel has been chosen by God and must therefore maintain its obligations toward the divine covenant that was the consequence of this choice (v. 9). Very clearly, all the references in this section to the divine law presuppose them to be the commandments given at Mt. Horeb—i.e., the Ten Commandments.

This unit is particularly important on two counts. First, it brings into sharp focus an awareness of the existence and potential destiny of other nations. The command that the nations that had previously occupied Israel's land should be exterminated was recognized as inadequate, although we here encounter a distinction between those nations who were rival claimants to the land and more distant nations, with whom Israel must deal. Already the journey through the wilderness had highlighted the possibility of such a distinction.

A second issue, also of considerable importance, now emerges into the light of day and concerns the question of the permanence of the covenant relationship between the LORD God and Israel. Could this covenant be annulled? Could Israel forfeit its unique and privileged position before God? The assertion in v. 10, which declares that God "repays in their own person those who reject him," would appear to indicate that this conditional uncertainty was indeed the case. Yet, it is noteworthy that the warning is couched in the singular form, indicating that it envisaged that it would be individuals who might turn away from their privileged status, without the entire nation's falling away and being destroyed as a result. The question of the conditional element within the deuteronomic covenant theology was to become one fraught with serious consequences for later generations of Jews, and also to become one that intruded itself into Christian apologetic toward Jews (cf. Romans 9–11); it raises too large a set of questions to be considered here. Clearly the deuteronomic authors did not believe that such a falling away had happened, and they clearly hope to forestall its ever happening.

7:12-16. This section resumes the assurance that obedience to the law will bring great success and prosperity to Israel so that the nation as a whole will have no need to remain in fear of its former inhabitants. Essentially it centers upon an affirmation of divine blessing (vv. 13-16) that closely follows the traditional formulas of blessing proclaimed in the rituals of Israel's worship. What is promised covers the full range of traditional benefits to be desired: fertility in flocks and herds and in the soil, healthy children, and protection from illness and disease. All those people who stood in the way of Israel's possession of the land would be quickly removed. We can well summarize all these benefits as comprising "life," a concept that lies at the heart of the deuteronomic understanding of the meaning of salvation.

What is especially significant for an understanding of the deuteronomic theology is that this "life" is set within the context of the covenant and is made conditional upon obedience to the commands that stand at the center of this covenant. Effectively it asserts that without obedience to the commandments there can be no blessing. The consequences of this for the overall understanding of worship, as seen by the deuteronomists, is far reaching. Ritual and prayer, with all their many forms and requirements, are not effective, save within this larger context of covenant life. The commandments hold the key to the path of blessing—a feature that is taken up afresh in the latter part of the book.

7:17-26. The problem of the nations who were already settled in the land then occupies the final section of the chapter. From the point of view of the deuteronomists, seeing the threat posed by these nations at a considerable distance in time from the direct encounter with them when Israel settled in the land, their existence provided opportunity for fundamental theological reflection. The same fundamental outlook on the question of the threat and the perils of warfare with these people is then set out. God will give victory as a reward for loyalty. The reassuring promise of v. 22 that the nations of the land could only be destroyed piecemeal and over time stands in obvious tension with the admonition that Israel is to make a quick end of them (v. 2). It is possible that it has been introduced out of a positive historical knowledge that there had not, in reality, been any wholesale slaughter of the previous inhabitants of the land.[53] More plausibly, however, the reassurance has been introduced into the text at a late stage in order to offer some clear explanation as to why the presence of these people and their religious establishments would remain a serious temptation for later generations of Israel. Overall, there is considerable incongruity in the reasoning that the previous inhabitants would have to remain for some time until the number of Israelites was sufficient to prevent the land's being overrun by wild animals.

The final warning against the temptation of seizing possession of the images of gods or any other cult objects that had belonged to the former inhabitants serves as a further reinforcement of the deuteronomic polemic against religious images. It is basically this sin of which Achan and his household are accused in Josh 7:20-21, when they are charged with having taken "a beautiful mantle from Shinar" from among the spoils of the city of Ai, an offense for which they pay the ultimate price. The infringement is against the rules of holy war, which are assumed to be a necessary part of Torah, and the offense is given vaguely cultic overtones. The terminology used in Deuteronomy to describe the unacceptibility of such religious objects is that they are "an abhorrent thing" (v. 26). The concept of "abhorrence"/"abomination" (תועבה *tô'ēbâ*) is important for the deuteronomists (cf. 18:10; 22:5) and is used to justify the rejection of a number of objects and practices as hostile to the essential meaning of God's law.[54] Elsewhere it is widely used by the sages in the book of Proverbs to describe unacceptability within the moral sphere, although older usage links it closely to cultic objects and actions. Objects used within one religious tradition are regarded as abhorrent to the god of another.

---

53. G. Schmitt, *Du sollst keinen Frieden schliessen mit den Bewohnen des Landes,* 134, cites the observation of P. Kleinert, published in 1870, that in historical reality there had been no such wholesale slaughter of the previous inhabitants so that the deuteronomic demand represents an idealized and fictionalized perspective on the past.

54. See Weinfeld, *Deuteronomy and the Deuteronomic School,* 226, 265-70.

REFLECTIONS

Taken as a whole, Deuteronomy 7 reflects theologically on the problem posed by the previous inhabitants of the land. It is noteworthy that, in the basic form of the promise of the land given to the patriarchs of Israel, the question of the existence of these peoples is not properly taken into consideration. Yet it was clear to the ancient writers that rich, arable farmland, which is the warm and glowing picture given of the land of Israel, would not be left unoccupied. A "return to the wild" is a condition of curse that is sometimes used in prophetic threats of future defeat and destruction, both for Israel and for other nations.

Accordingly, the realization that the land Israel occupied had had previous inhabitants becomes an increasingly prominent feature of the deuteronomic picture of the course of Israel's early history—a conquest of the land—and of its subsequent problems—a mixture of non-Israelite religious traditions with many sanctuaries and cult objects. The theological response made to this realization is twofold in nature. First, there is a dramatic theology of warfare, with the belief that victory in war is entirely a gift of God, and the deuteronomic authors have already provided the reader with outline summaries of how such campaigns involve supernatural, divine intervention, sending the enemy into a panic and depriving them of the power to resist.

The second feature of the deuteronomic concern with the existence and religious activities of the previous inhabitants—the Canaanites—is one of religious apologetic. It is primarily the relics of the religion of these peoples that are claimed to have brought disunity and idolatry to Israel in the past. The continued existence of such relics and practices is a threat in the present as well. So the portrayal of the danger posed by the previous occupants is viewed as a present religious one, since the integrity and purity of Israel's faith are held to have been established at the beginning, but progressively lost thereafter.

It is reasonable to conclude that the deuteronomic authors were fully aware that among their readers were many who still held fast to the wide variety of amulets, cult objects, and general religious bric-a-brac with which daily life was surrounded. Almost certainly many of these readers did not regard the retention of these pious artifacts as hostile to God or a flagrant infringement of the commandments. For many readers, these were no more than ancient features of community life and household religion with which they were understandably reluctant to part. The vigor with which the fear is expressed that Israel will continue to venerate the "old gods" of the land and will perpetuate practices that originated before Israel occupied it reveals something of the situation in which the deuteronomic authors found their readers.

By far the most adequate explanation for this fear, and for the ruthless punishments demanded for breaking the rule of maintaining an exclusive purity in the worship of the LORD God, is that it emerged after the Jerusalem Temple had been destroyed in 587 BCE. This single event had dealt a massive blow to the prestige and credibility of the traditional worship of the LORD God. With the destruction of Jerusalem went the destruction of much that had been popularly believed about the power of God to protect the people of Judah. In such a time of crisis, it is fully understandable that there was a widespread popular return to the simple, long-established forms of religion associated with households, local communities, and local shrines that had a strong domestic flavor and enjoyed a seemingly ineradicable following. The deuteronomic polemic represents a major fighting back for the maintenance of an "official" expression of Israel's faith. The fuller outworking of this is then to be seen in the greatly reinterpreted expression of cultic life that the deuteronomic lawmakers set out in Deuteronomy 12–13.

It was important for the deuteronomic polemic—if it was to achieve its goal of retraining, unifying, harmonizing, and strengthening faith in and commitment to the LORD as God—that veneration of the "old gods" be eradicated. Since their antiquity could not be denied, it was important that their orthodoxy and acceptability to the LORD be challenged. A major feature of the deuteronomic theology is that it identifies those features of Israel's religious tradition that it repudiates as belonging to the former inhabitants of the land.

As a feature of religious apologetic, this aggressive repudiation and rejection of popular and quasi-magical forms of religion is recognizable as a survival technique that has left a powerful legacy within both Judaism and Christianity. Exclusivism in religion, combined with a sharp intolerance of any alien religious tradition, can readily become regressive and destructive. Strong and forceful moves to promote a fuller and firmer hold on the positive aspects of faith seem almost invariably destined to align themselves with harsh, and often cruel, reactions against all that threatens them. In order to establish what is new and positive, the hostility to what is old and familiar becomes aggressive and destructive.

Within the biblical tradition this awareness of bold affirmation and repressive defensiveness becomes very pronounced in Deuteronomy and the writings it has influenced, pointing strongly to the situation of crisis out of which it emerged. Since situations of crisis can be reconstructed only in part, we can only partially understand the justification of radical exclusivism. However, this fact in itself does little to soften the dangerous and destructive tendencies of such exclusivism. That it represents a violent and iconoclastic repudiation of well-established religious traditions in order to retain faith in Israel's God in the wake of unexpected catastrophe can readily be recognized. Nevertheless, in seeking to embrace for faith in the LORD God of Israel a painful experience of disaster, it has left a dangerous legacy of intolerance that has in turn set in motion further tragedies.

Deuteronomy 8:1-20, Take Care to Remember God's Commandment

NIV

8 Be careful to follow every command I am giving you today, so that you may live and increase and may enter and possess the land that the LORD promised on oath to your forefathers. ²Remember how the LORD your God led you all the way in the desert these forty years, to humble you and to test you in order to know what was in your heart, whether or not you would keep his commands. ³He humbled you, causing you to hunger and then feeding you with manna, which neither you nor your fathers had known, to teach you that man does not live on bread alone but on every word that comes from the mouth of the LORD. ⁴Your clothes did not wear out and your feet did not swell during these forty years. ⁵Know then in your heart that as a man disciplines his son, so the LORD your God disciplines you.

⁶Observe the commands of the LORD your God, walking in his ways and revering him. ⁷For the LORD your God is bringing you into a good land—a land with streams and pools of water, with springs flowing in the valleys and hills; ⁸a land with wheat and barley, vines and fig trees, pomegranates,

NRSV

8 This entire commandment that I command you today you must diligently observe, so that you may live and increase, and go in and occupy the land that the LORD promised on oath to your ancestors. ²Remember the long way that the LORD your God has led you these forty years in the wilderness, in order to humble you, testing you to know what was in your heart, whether or not you would keep his commandments. ³He humbled you by letting you hunger, then by feeding you with manna, with which neither you nor your ancestors were acquainted, in order to make you understand that one does not live by bread alone, but by every word that comes from the mouth of the LORD.ª ⁴The clothes on your back did not wear out and your feet did not swell these forty years. ⁵Know then in your heart that as a parent disciplines a child so the LORD your God disciplines you. ⁶Therefore keep the commandments of the LORD your God, by walking in his ways and by fearing him. ⁷For the LORD your God is bringing you into a good land, a land with

ª Or by anything that the LORD decrees

NIV

olive oil and honey; ⁹a land where bread will not be scarce and you will lack nothing; a land where the rocks are iron and you can dig copper out of the hills.

¹⁰When you have eaten and are satisfied, praise the LORD your God for the good land he has given you. ¹¹Be careful that you do not forget the LORD your God, failing to observe his commands, his laws and his decrees that I am giving you this day. ¹²Otherwise, when you eat and are satisfied, when you build fine houses and settle down, ¹³and when your herds and flocks grow large and your silver and gold increase and all you have is multiplied, ¹⁴then your heart will become proud and you will forget the LORD your God, who brought you out of Egypt, out of the land of slavery. ¹⁵He led you through the vast and dreadful desert, that thirsty and waterless land, with its venomous snakes and scorpions. He brought you water out of hard rock. ¹⁶He gave you manna to eat in the desert, something your fathers had never known, to humble and to test you so that in the end it might go well with you. ¹⁷You may say to yourself, "My power and the strength of my hands have produced this wealth for me." ¹⁸But remember the LORD your God, for it is he who gives you the ability to produce wealth, and so confirms his covenant, which he swore to your forefathers, as it is today.

¹⁹If you ever forget the LORD your God and follow other gods and worship and bow down to them, I testify against you today that you will surely be destroyed. ²⁰Like the nations the LORD destroyed before you, so you will be destroyed for not obeying the LORD your God.

NRSV

flowing streams, with springs and underground waters welling up in valleys and hills, ⁸a land of wheat and barley, of vines and fig trees and pomegranates, a land of olive trees and honey, ⁹a land where you may eat bread without scarcity, where you will lack nothing, a land whose stones are iron and from whose hills you may mine copper. ¹⁰You shall eat your fill and bless the LORD your God for the good land that he has given you.

11Take care that you do not forget the LORD your God, by failing to keep his commandments, his ordinances, and his statutes, which I am commanding you today. ¹²When you have eaten your fill and have built fine houses and live in them, ¹³and when your herds and flocks have multiplied, and your silver and gold is multiplied, and all that you have is multiplied, ¹⁴then do not exalt yourself, forgetting the LORD your God, who brought you out of the land of Egypt, out of the house of slavery, ¹⁵who led you through the great and terrible wilderness, an arid wasteland with poisonousª snakes and scorpions. He made water flow for you from flint rock, ¹⁶and fed you in the wilderness with manna that your ancestors did not know, to humble you and to test you, and in the end to do you good. ¹⁷Do not say to yourself, "My power and the might of my own hand have gotten me this wealth." ¹⁸But remember the LORD your God, for it is he who gives you power to get wealth, so that he may confirm his covenant that he swore to your ancestors, as he is doing today. ¹⁹If you do forget the LORD your God and follow other gods to serve and worship them, I solemnly warn you today that you shall surely perish. ²⁰Like the nations that the LORD is destroying before you, so shall you perish, because you would not obey the voice of the LORD your God.

ª Or fiery; Heb seraph

COMMENTARY

The warnings concerning the threat that will be posed by the presence, and more particularly the religious artifacts and practices, of the former occupants of the land is now followed by a sermon addressed directly to the heart of every Israelite. Its message is passionate and consistent:

"Take care to remember that the LORD God who gave you the land, also gave you the commandments to observe."

8:1-10. The address opens with its fundamental theme: "This entire commandment that I command you today you must diligently observe" (v.

1). What follows is essentially a sermon on this text, amplifying its importance and pointing out the likely personal temptations that will be encountered and that might lead to failure to fulfill such a demand. The conclusion is sharp and decisive: "If you do forget . . . you shall surely perish" (v. 19).[55] The sermon raises yet again the question of the extent to which the deuteronomic theology of covenant contains a radical conditional element that could contemplate the annihilation of Israel as a nation. Here the warning seems clear enough that the possibility exists that Israel, as a nation, could perish from the land. At the same time, this was evidently what the deuteronomists believed was now inevitable. Theirs is a kind of "last appeal," contemplating the possibility of disaster, but hoping to avert it.

By appealing to "this entire commandment," the author was clearly referring to the Ten Commandments, rather than to any wider range of laws. There are sufficient signs of variation in the chapter to suggest that an earlier unit (vv. 7-11*a*) has subsequently been amplified in close conformity with the message of 4:1-40. Yet overall the signs of a resultant unity are strong, with evidence of a chiastic structure.

The danger of forgetting the LORD God focuses on two issues that are closely inter-related and that envisage different contents for what has been forgotten. The first is that Israel may forget the providential care of God during the years in the wilderness (vv. 2-5), a period of trial and testing in which a parental discipline had been imposed on the people. This represents an interesting and important development of the theme concerning what the wilderness period of Israel's existence signified. For the prophets Hosea and Jeremiah, it had been a honeymoon time in Israel's life (Jer 2:2-8; Hos 2:14; 9:10). Ezekiel, however, placed a more radically negative interpretation on this phase of Israel's history (Ezek 20:10-26). He regarded it as having been as fully a time of religious unfaithfulness as was all of Israel's subsequent history. For this prophet, no part of Israel's past had been untainted by a deep inner obsession with idolatry, thereby sharply implying that the

roots of such idolatry lay in Israel's inner consciousness, and not in historical circumstances.

The deuteronomic position marks a kind of neutral middle ground. The wilderness period was neither wholly good nor wholly bad, but an occasion when the challenges and temptations of disobedience had first been fully felt. The outcome of Israel's wilderness period had then proved to be that Israel had been taught a lesson and had been humbled by it. The meaning must clearly be that Israel had experienced sufficient adversity at that time and had learned the inner deceitfulness of the human heart, so that such punishment as had been inflicted amounted to a severe lesson. So it was a time of trial during which the seriousness of Israel's intent to maintain loyalty to God's covenant had been tested and the consequences of disobedience had begun to be felt. Throughout there is the assumption that the experience of deprivation had forced upon Israel the necessity of depending on God's provision—even right up to the point when severe hunger and thirst threatened personal disaster.

This interesting spiritual interpretation of the harshness and vulnerability of life in the semi-desert of the Sinai region has given rise to some of the most theologically perceptive and memorable features of the entire book. The manna that was to be found on some of the scrub vegetation of the region, and is the product of insect secretion that is edible and possesses a sweet taste, is interpreted as a supernaturally provided food from God. Its meaning, however, is found not simply in its nutritional value for desert travelers, but in its role as a sign of God's providential care. More than this, it becomes a sign that the acknowledgment of such direct dependence upon God is its ultimate purpose. So we are brought to a justly famous and meaningful pronouncement: "One does not live by bread alone, but by every word that comes from the mouth of the LORD" (v. 3).

A third feature of the experience of Israel's wilderness generation is then added and places further emphasis on the overall interpretation that it was a time of testing and of demonstration of divine providence: "The clothes on your back did not wear out and your feet did not swell these forty years" (v. 4). The comment is repeated in 29:5 and is made into a meaningful symbol of

55. The necessity of remembering as a primary religious duty is a fundamental aspect of the deuteronomic theology. See B. S. Childs, *Memory and Tradition in Israel,* SBT 37 (London: SCM, 1962) 45-56.

divine providence in Nehemiah's great prayer reviewing Israel's history (Neh 9:21).

The saying reflects the richly varied manner in which the deuteronomists combine practical and spiritual features in using inherited historical traditions to generate a doctrine of divine providence. In this case, the central point made is that God's care is sufficient for all human need. To ask for more than this becomes a mark of human arrogance and greed, with a consequent loss of the essential perception that the most fundamental of all human needs are spiritual. Accordingly, the Word of God is the most precious gift, and it alone makes possible life within the divine order.

8:11-20. By contrast, the abundant provisions of life within the boundaries of the promised land rendered possible a life of richness and prosperity (vv. 7-10). Wheat, barley, vines, figs, pomegranates, olives, and honey all amount to an abundance and variety of diet that contrast dramatically with the sparse rations of the wilderness years. It is precisely this richness and abundance that is seen as a temptation to forget God and the divine commandments (vv. 11-14). It then becomes a striking reflection of the way in which the physical terrain and climate in the biblical lands have been shaped into a series of spiritual lessons about the human condition and the inter-relationship between bodily and spiritual needs. The one becomes the guidebook to the other.

For such a small region, Palestine reveals a great variety of ecological features. These vary from the semi-desert of the south and east to the sub-tropical vegetation in the upper Jordan valley. In consequence, the mixed possibilities of agriculture, the major variations of climate, and the harshness of the more mountainous and desert regions all create problems and uncertainties for the maintenance of a settled population. For many areas, drought and consequent famine remain regular threats, whereas violent storms manifest the violence, as well as the beneficence, of the rainfall. The author here brilliantly interprets these uncertainties and variations as a combination of privileges, tests, and temptations to which each inhabitant is called upon to make an appropriate spiritual response. This response is unerringly seen as a need to remember the LORD God. Abundance and prosperity are signs of God's grace and beneficence, but such welcome beneficence can quickly turn to manifestations of divine anger when the God-ordained pattern of life is flouted (vv. 15-16).

The concluding section in vv. 19-20 presents a solemn adjuration that to forget that the LORD is God and to tolerate and pursue the worship of other gods would plunge Israel into the pit of destruction: "I solemnly warn you today that you shall surely perish" (v. 19). The covenant itself makes known the conditions of security, prosperity, and survival in the land. So the possibility of ultimate failure to heed the simple lessons of the wilderness years could lead to an even more drastic failure to remain secure and prosperous in the land that God had given. If Israel could not take note of the message inherent in the basic traditions about its own past, it would have to learn more fearful and destructive lessons within its own history in the present. It was not as if there was not ample evidence in all that Israel knew of its own past to take the solemn warning to heart: "Like the nations that the LORD is destroying before you, so shall you perish" (v. 20). Evidently, this was not yet a catastrophe that had actually come to pass. Yet it was an imminent possibility that the deuteronomic author recognized and strove with great rhetorical artistry to impress upon the reader.

REFLECTIONS

Coming immediately after the alarming and ruthless injunctions of chapter 7, with their insistence that Israel spare no effort to root out every one of the previous occupants of the land and the relics of their detested religions, the artistry and spiritual perceptiveness of chapter 8 provide a splendid and welcome relief. It is unquestionably one of the most memorable and instructive passages in the entire book. It is small wonder, then, that this chapter has provided the basis on which the meaning and message of the temptations of Jesus in the wilderness are constructed (Matt 4:1-11). Human life can have no higher wealth and no more necessary sustenance than that provided by the Word of God. Whereas most people spend their lives seeking to secure themselves from famine by ensuring a plentiful food supply and from cold and destitution by surrounding themselves with fine and warm clothing, they fail to see that the most basic of all essentials for life is to be found in the Word of God. Real poverty is poverty of the spirit, and even those who feel secure because they have no fear of hunger and destitution may fail to see this. Indeed, the opposite result may obtain and the very plentiful supplies of food and clothing may lead to a complacency that encourages the thought that "God is no longer necessary for my life."

So the deuteronomic authors draw out from a vague and historically little-known phase of Israel's earlier existence some remarkable lessons. In the forefront is the perceptive observation that it is in the memory of years of famine and want that the value of an abundance of food and clothing is most fully appreciated. The privilege of possession becomes the richer and the more genuinely appreciated when it can be accepted in the shadow of want. So far as precise details are concerned, it seems evident that a good deal of historical and literary license has been taken with the facts and conditions of Israel's life in the wilderness. Neither the unexpected discovery and sweetness of manna nor the food offered by exhausted quail or other wild creatures found in the wilderness could possibly supply food for an entire nation for thirty-eight years. Yet it is sufficient for the authors to realize that there are unexpected manifestations of God's providential care that even the hard pressed and the near destitute may find. So this unexpected provision and the conviction that even worn-out clothes could last a little longer to protect a nation on the march provide the basis for important spiritual lessons.

However much we may be inclined to dismiss the poetic exaggeration and special pleading of the author, we can only marvel at his insight into truths that have continued to have a profound influence on the spiritual tradition of both Jews and Christians. There may be more to be learned in times of trial and deprivation than can possibly be learned in times of wealth and plenty. Moreover, spiritual truths may become more apparent and more readily accepted in such times as well. Consistently, the Bible and the spiritual tradition built upon it have viewed with suspicion and criticism the dangers of wealth and plenty. It is not that these desirable attainments are wrong in themselves, but that they become an occasion for neglect of a more profound spiritual truth: Without an inward peace and an awareness of God, the most lavish of possessions can appear tawdry. So the New Testament parable can present the hearing and responding to the gospel message as a discovery comparable to the finding of a treasure of incalculable price that makes the surrender of all other treasures an easy option (Matt 13:45-46).

A further feature characterizes the remarkable artistry and insight of this chapter in its ability to deduce searching lessons from the basic facts of geology, climate, and ecology. The wilderness, with all its hazards, provides the basis for important tests of character and personal resilience (8:15). By contrast, the richer agricultural land of Israel offers the opportunity for rich farming and the building of fine homes. In such a land trade can bring yet greater wealth (8:12-13). Here, however, more subtle temptations may arise in that complacency and a sense of self-achievement may displace the due recognition that there is nothing that was not ultimately a gift of God. Even the power to achieve anything is itself God's gift (8:17-18). Success and prosperity, too, therefore, are tests of character, in their own way more subtle and more dangerous than the wilderness. Whereas the wilderness poses an open and readily recognized challenge, the settled land offers instead a hidden allure that may, in the end, prove more effectively destructive of the knowledge of God and of the divine covenant. So the message is clear: "Remember the LORD your God, for it is he who gives you power to get wealth" (8:18 NRSV).

Deuteronomy 9:1-7, Be Prepared and Be Humble

NIV

9 Hear, O Israel. You are now about to cross the Jordan to go in and dispossess nations greater and stronger than you, with large cities that have walls up to the sky. ²The people are strong and tall—Anakites! You know about them and have heard it said: "Who can stand up against the Anakites?" ³But be assured today that the LORD your God is the one who goes across ahead of you like a devouring fire. He will destroy them; he will subdue them before you. And you will drive them out and annihilate them quickly, as the LORD has promised you.

⁴After the LORD your God has driven them out before you, do not say to yourself, "The LORD has brought me here to take possession of this land because of my righteousness." No, it is on account of the wickedness of these nations that the LORD is going to drive them out before you. ⁵It is not because of your righteousness or your integrity that you are going in to take possession of their land; but on account of the wickedness of these nations, the LORD your God will drive them out before you, to accomplish what he swore to your fathers, to Abraham, Isaac and Jacob. ⁶Understand, then, that it is not because of your righteousness that the LORD your God is giving you this good land to possess, for you are a stiff-necked people.

⁷Remember this and never forget how you provoked the LORD your God to anger in the desert. From the day you left Egypt until you arrived here, you have been rebellious against the LORD.

NRSV

9 Hear, O Israel! You are about to cross the Jordan today, to go in and dispossess nations larger and mightier than you, great cities, fortified to the heavens, ²a strong and tall people, the offspring of the Anakim, whom you know. You have heard it said of them, "Who can stand up to the Anakim?" ³Know then today that the LORD your God is the one who crosses over before you as a devouring fire; he will defeat them and subdue them before you, so that you may dispossess and destroy them quickly, as the LORD has promised you.

4When the LORD your God thrusts them out before you, do not say to yourself, "It is because of my righteousness that the LORD has brought me in to occupy this land"; it is rather because of the wickedness of these nations that the LORD is dispossessing them before you. ⁵It is not because of your righteousness or the uprightness of your heart that you are going in to occupy their land; but because of the wickedness of these nations the LORD your God is dispossessing them before you, in order to fulfill the promise that the LORD made on oath to your ancestors, to Abraham, to Isaac, and to Jacob.

6Know, then, that the LORD your God is not giving you this good land to occupy because of your righteousness; for you are a stubborn people. ⁷Remember and do not forget how you provoked the LORD your God to wrath in the wilderness; you have been rebellious against the LORD from the day you came out of the land of Egypt until you came to this place.

COMMENTARY

This brief sermon urging Israel yet again to prepare themselves for the crossing of the Jordan and the entry into the land serves as a transition piece. It summarizes and reinforces the call to courage, loyalty, and obedience as the three prerequisites for entry into the land. At the same time it introduces a further admonitory note. The entire corpus of traditions concerning Israel's status as a people in covenant with the LORD God could have a damaging and misleading effect. The

promise of the ancestors, the making of the covenant on Mt. Horeb, and the giving of the law could all have the consequence of encouraging Israel to believe that it was a very remarkable and special people. Had not the LORD God chosen them from among all peoples to be a chosen and privileged nation, pre-eminent above all others on this account?

The preparation for crossing the Jordan and occupying the land could reinforce this conviction still further. God was about to drive out and destroy peoples who were already settled there—and these people included the Anakim, a race of powerful giants! Surely such a people must be very special indeed to merit so many privileges and to have received so many advantages from God.

This short sermon faces the issue squarely and knocks away completely any such complacent belief. The nations who were about to be expelled and destroyed from the land were deeply tainted with the spirit and deeds of wickedness (vv. 4-5). It was not, therefore, because of Israel's righteousness that such privileges and opportunities were being accorded to them. Rather, it was as a necessary punishment visited on the erstwhile occupants of the land, whose evil deeds called for judgment. The terms employed to describe the conduct that is respectively described as either bad or good, wicked or righteous, has a directly legal background. Yet their reference here appears extended to cover a wide range of activities, of which the major offense is to be found in their false religious beliefs and practices. So legal terminology is employed to condemn what are fundamentally false religious pursuits. From the author's perspective, these pursuits could then be seen readily to flout the requirements of the Ten Commandments.

The message concerning God's gracious election of Israel has a double-edged significance. It represents a marvelous privilege and opportunity, but it is also not without its element of warning and danger. If the previous occupants of the land had been dispossessed and destroyed because of their wickedness, should not Israel be fully warned of the possibility of the same fate awaiting them should they, in turn, prove to be disobedient?

Two contrasting comments then add further force to this note of warning. First, God had given this privileged opportunity to Israel because of the promise given on oath to the national ancestors: Abraham, Isaac, and Jacob (v. 5). Second, and more ominous, Israel must look into its own heart to see what sentiments resided there. The historical traditions the nation had so jealously preserved would reveal a darker side to the nation's conduct in the past and the dangerous inner propensities of spirit that had all too often been displayed. They were a stubborn people and had been rebellious against God since the day they had come out of Egypt (vv. 6-7).

REFLECTIONS

Short as it is, this further exhortation to courage and boldness in facing the challenge of taking possession of the land, even from the grip of such feared opponents as the Anakim, touches a very salutary note. God's election does not mean groundless and unmerited favoritism. Were that the case, God would have been shown to flout the very righteousness the covenant declared and upheld. That God must be fair and just, and therefore no supporter of undeserved favoritism, is strongly argued by Peter in Acts 10:34-35. God does not, and cannot, have favorites, since it is the divine purpose to uphold justice and righteousness. Even to entertain the idea that this could be the case is an affront to the very character of divinity.

A deeper aspect of this deuteronomic teaching is its probing of human thought and attitudes. It searches the inner recesses of the human heart. Pride was one of the medieval church's seven deadly sins. It becomes even more deadly when it takes the form of spiritual pride, which may occur even though it is established on the most worthy spiritual premises of God's gifts and assurances. Hidden feelings of stubborn rebelliousness may remain cloaked behind an outward display of good behavior. Yet, however well masked they are, the sentiment of pride will eventually show up. So the deuteronomic author here probes into the inner motives and attitudes of every person, demanding an introspective soul-searching that is remarkable in a document that has sometimes mistakenly been held to be legalistic in its tendencies. God's acts of election call for an inner response, summoning feelings of gratitude and love and resisting any temptation to human self-congratulation: "Let the one who boasts, boast in the LORD" (1 Cor 1:31 NRSV).

Deuteronomy 9:8–10:11, The Great Intercessor

NIV

[8]At Horeb you aroused the LORD's wrath so that he was angry enough to destroy you. [9]When I went up on the mountain to receive the tablets of stone, the tablets of the covenant that the LORD had made with you, I stayed on the mountain forty days and forty nights; I ate no bread and drank no water. [10]The LORD gave me two stone tablets inscribed by the finger of God. On them were all the commandments the LORD proclaimed to you on the mountain out of the fire, on the day of the assembly.

[11]At the end of the forty days and forty nights, the LORD gave me the two stone tablets, the tablets of the covenant. [12]Then the LORD told me, "Go down from here at once, because your people whom you brought out of Egypt have become corrupt. They have turned away quickly from what I commanded them and have made a cast idol for themselves."

[13]And the LORD said to me, "I have seen this people, and they are a stiff-necked people indeed! [14]Let me alone, so that I may destroy them and blot out their name from under heaven. And I will make you into a nation stronger and more numerous than they."

[15]So I turned and went down from the mountain while it was ablaze with fire. And the two tablets of the covenant were in my hands.[a] [16]When I looked, I saw that you had sinned against the LORD your God; you had made for yourselves an idol cast in the shape of a calf. You had turned aside quickly from the way that the LORD had commanded you. [17]So I took the two tablets and threw them out of my hands, breaking them to pieces before your eyes.

[18]Then once again I fell prostrate before the LORD for forty days and forty nights; I ate no bread and drank no water, because of all the sin you had committed, doing what was evil in the LORD's sight and so provoking him to anger. [19]I feared the anger and wrath of the LORD, for he was angry enough with you to destroy you. But again the LORD listened to me. [20]And the LORD was angry enough with Aaron to destroy him, but at that

[a]15 Or And I had the two tablets of the covenant with me, one in each hand

NRSV

8Even at Horeb you provoked the LORD to wrath, and the LORD was so angry with you that he was ready to destroy you. [9]When I went up the mountain to receive the stone tablets, the tablets of the covenant that the LORD made with you, I remained on the mountain forty days and forty nights; I neither ate bread nor drank water. [10]And the LORD gave me the two stone tablets written with the finger of God; on them were all the words that the LORD had spoken to you at the mountain out of the fire on the day of the assembly. [11]At the end of forty days and forty nights the LORD gave me the two stone tablets, the tablets of the covenant. [12]Then the LORD said to me, "Get up, go down quickly from here, for your people whom you have brought from Egypt have acted corruptly. They have been quick to turn from the way that I commanded them; they have cast an image for themselves." [13]Furthermore the LORD said to me, "I have seen that this people is indeed a stubborn people. [14]Let me alone that I may destroy them and blot out their name from under heaven; and I will make of you a nation mightier and more numerous than they."

15So I turned and went down from the mountain, while the mountain was ablaze; the two tablets of the covenant were in my two hands. [16]Then I saw that you had indeed sinned against the LORD your God, by casting for yourselves an image of a calf; you had been quick to turn from the way that the LORD had commanded you. [17]So I took hold of the two tablets and flung them from my two hands, smashing them before your eyes. [18]Then I lay prostrate before the LORD as before, forty days and forty nights; I neither ate bread nor drank water, because of all the sin you had committed, provoking the LORD by doing what was evil in his sight. [19]For I was afraid that the anger that the LORD bore against you was so fierce that he would destroy you. But the LORD listened to me that time also. [20]The LORD was so angry with Aaron that he was ready to destroy him, but I interceded also on behalf of Aaron at that same time. [21]Then I took the sinful thing you had made, the calf, and burned it with fire and crushed it, grinding it thoroughly, until it was

NIV

time I prayed for Aaron too. [21]Also I took that sinful thing of yours, the calf you had made, and burned it in the fire. Then I crushed it and ground it to powder as fine as dust and threw the dust into a stream that flowed down the mountain.

[22]You also made the LORD angry at Taberah, at Massah and at Kibroth Hattaavah.

[23]And when the LORD sent you out from Kadesh Barnea, he said, "Go up and take possession of the land I have given you." But you rebelled against the command of the LORD your God. You did not trust him or obey him. [24]You have been rebellious against the LORD ever since I have known you.

[25]I lay prostrate before the LORD those forty days and forty nights because the LORD had said he would destroy you. [26]I prayed to the LORD and said, "O Sovereign LORD, do not destroy your people, your own inheritance that you redeemed by your great power and brought out of Egypt with a mighty hand. [27]Remember your servants Abraham, Isaac and Jacob. Overlook the stubbornness of this people, their wickedness and their sin. [28]Otherwise, the country from which you brought us will say, 'Because the LORD was not able to take them into the land he had promised them, and because he hated them, he brought them out to put them to death in the desert.' [29]But they are your people, your inheritance that you brought out by your great power and your outstretched arm."

10 At that time the LORD said to me, "Chisel out two stone tablets like the first ones and come up to me on the mountain. Also make a wooden chest.[a] [2]I will write on the tablets the words that were on the first tablets, which you broke. Then you are to put them in the chest."

[3]So I made the ark out of acacia wood and chiseled out two stone tablets like the first ones, and I went up on the mountain with the two tablets in my hands. [4]The LORD wrote on these tablets what he had written before, the Ten Commandments he had proclaimed to you on the mountain, out of the fire, on the day of the assembly. And the LORD gave them to me. [5]Then I came back down the mountain and put the tablets in the ark I had made, as the LORD commanded me, and they are there now.

[a]1 That is, an ark

NRSV

reduced to dust; and I threw the dust of it into the stream that runs down the mountain.

[22]At Taberah also, and at Massah, and at Kibroth-hattaavah, you provoked the LORD to wrath. [23]And when the LORD sent you from Kadesh-barnea, saying, "Go up and occupy the land that I have given you," you rebelled against the command of the LORD your God, neither trusting him nor obeying him. [24]You have been rebellious against the LORD as long as he has[a] known you.

[25]Throughout the forty days and forty nights that I lay prostrate before the LORD when the LORD intended to destroy you, [26]I prayed to the LORD and said, "Lord GOD, do not destroy the people who are your very own possession, whom you redeemed in your greatness, whom you brought out of Egypt with a mighty hand. [27]Remember your servants, Abraham, Isaac, and Jacob; pay no attention to the stubbornness of this people, their wickedness and their sin, [28]otherwise the land from which you have brought us might say, 'Because the LORD was not able to bring them into the land that he promised them, and because he hated them, he has brought them out to let them die in the wilderness.' [29]For they are the people of your very own possession, whom you brought out by your great power and by your outstretched arm."

10 At that time the LORD said to me, "Carve out two tablets of stone like the former ones, and come up to me on the mountain, and make an ark of wood. [2]I will write on the tablets the words that were on the former tablets, which you smashed, and you shall put them in the ark." [3]So I made an ark of acacia wood, cut two tablets of stone like the former ones, and went up the mountain with the two tablets in my hand. [4]Then he wrote on the tablets the same words as before, the ten commandments[b] that the LORD had spoken to you on the mountain out of the fire on the day of the assembly; and the LORD gave them to me. [5]So I turned and came down from the mountain, and put the tablets in the ark that I had made; and there they are, as the LORD commanded me.

[6](The Israelites journeyed from Beeroth-benejaakan[c] to Moserah. There Aaron died, and there

[a] Sam Gk: MT *I have*   [b] Heb *the ten words*   [c] Or *the wells of the Bene-jaakan*

NIV

⁶(The Israelites traveled from the wells of the Jaakanites to Moserah. There Aaron died and was buried, and Eleazar his son succeeded him as priest. ⁷From there they traveled to Gudgodah and on to Jotbathah, a land with streams of water. ⁸At that time the LORD set apart the tribe of Levi to carry the ark of the covenant of the LORD, to stand before the LORD to minister and to pronounce blessings in his name, as they still do today. ⁹That is why the Levites have no share or inheritance among their brothers; the LORD is their inheritance, as the LORD your God told them.)

¹⁰Now I had stayed on the mountain forty days and nights, as I did the first time, and the LORD listened to me at this time also. It was not his will to destroy you. ¹¹"Go," the LORD said to me, "and lead the people on their way, so that they may enter and possess the land that I swore to their fathers to give them."

NRSV

he was buried; his son Eleazar succeeded him as priest. ⁷From there they journeyed to Gudgodah, and from Gudgodah to Jotbathah, a land with flowing streams. ⁸At that time the LORD set apart the tribe of Levi to carry the ark of the covenant of the LORD, to stand before the LORD to minister to him, and to bless in his name, to this day. ⁹Therefore Levi has no allotment or inheritance with his kindred; the LORD is his inheritance, as the LORD your God promised him.)

10I stayed on the mountain forty days and forty nights, as I had done the first time. And once again the LORD listened to me. The LORD was unwilling to destroy you. ¹¹The LORD said to me, "Get up, go on your journey at the head of the people, that they may go in and occupy the land that I swore to their ancestors to give them."

COMMENTARY

The warning to Israel that, as a nation, it was a people prone to rebelliousness against God (9:7) is now backed up by a long sermon demonstrating more fully this very point. Israel should not, on its past record, trust in itself. It could only trust in Moses and the power of intercessory prayer.[56] The text for this sermon is provided by the historical report, now preserved in Exod 32:1-35, that told how the Israelites, even while Moses was on Mt. Horeb in conversation with God, had manufactured an image of a golden calf. So the very historical tradition Israel had retained demonstrated that from the very beginning of Israel's spiritual journey, which began at Mt. Horeb, deep sin had been committed against the second commandment. Even while the covenant was in the process of being made, Israel was in the process of flouting one of its most solemn requirements.

Before even the writing on the tablets, written by the finger of God, had been seen by human eyes, and before they had been handed over to the people, these people were enmeshed in idolatry. The message is taken as decisively clear that, when left to their own devices, the people invariably go deeply astray. At the time when they were waiting at the foot of the mountain, the effrontery of such an act is taken to have been so serious that it would have brought an end to Israel's hopes of fulfilling God's promise to them. Had it not been for the intercession of Moses, they would have perished there and then. He had placed his own person between God and the people and had been willing to die with them, rather than see everything that had been promised come to nothing.

The narrative is complex from a literary point of view. It has been given its present literary location because it serves to illustrate and reinforce the warning of 9:7: "You have been rebellious against the LORD from the day you came out of the land of Egypt" (NRSV). Yet from a narrative viewpoint it appears out of historical sequence, particularly when set beside similar historical narratives in Deuteronomy 1–3. It deals with an event that had occurred at Mt. Horeb at the time when negotiations for the covenant were still

56. The fullest recent study by E. Aurelius, *Der Fürbitte Israels. Eine Studie zum Mosebild im Alten Testament,* ConBOT 27 (Lund: Almqvist & Wiksell International, 1988) 8-56, is most valuable. See also S. E. Balentine, *Prayer in the Hebrew Bible,* OBT (Minneapolis: Fortress, 1993) 19, 21; H. Graf Reventlow, *Gebet im Alten Testament* (Stuttgart: W. Kohlhammer, 1986) 229-35.

being completed and before Israel had ventured farther into the wilderness.

The story is told here by Moses in the first person, and it interprets this act of spiritual betrayal from his point of view. In contrast, the report of the event in Exodus 32 saw the action from the people's, and Aaron's, perspective.

The narrative in its final form is certainly not from one single literary mold. The report of the final outcome of the events that occurred and of the reprieve that was granted to Israel is given in 10:10-11. This is linked directly to a great prayer of intercession ascribed to Moses in 9:25-29. The intervening instructions concerning the need for the making of a sacred ark (10:1-5) and for the placing of this in the custody of the Levites (10:6-9) have been introduced at this particular point to show where the law of God was to be found and from whom it could be heard. To some degree it implies, without explicitly declaring, that the ark and the law of God replaced any need in Israel for the kind of symbolic image of deity that had been sought after in the manufacture of the golden calf.

The account of the actual intercession of Moses appears to be given twice. It is first reported in 9:18-19, where no actual prayer is recounted, and then again in 9:25-29, where the vital text of the prayer is given. It certainly appears, therefore, that a shorter report of Moses' action has undergone a measure of subsequent expansion. The central core of the original report, which focuses on the issues of the necessity for complete obedience to God's commandments and the efficacious power of prayer, can be seen to be based directly on the account given in Exodus 32. In its enlarged form, with the subsequent expansions, the major emphasis is placed on the rebellious tendency Israel had persistently displayed, which is viewed with an almost fatalistic and despairing inevitability. Left to itself, Israel is almost beyond the hope of redemption. Without a spiritual giant of the stature of Moses, Israel would have perished at the very beginning of its existence as the chosen people of the LORD God. The warning from this presentation is clear: When no comparable figure to that of Moses exists, then Israel must take even greater care to remain obedient to God's commandments. The mediatorial role of Moses carries over to affirm the mediation provided by God's law.

We can note some of the most prominent features that make this account of Moses' intercessory prayer a central basis for the expression of the deuteronomic theology. It reveals how human beings are related to God through prayer and the vital role that spiritual leadership plays in building this relationship. The covenant between God and Israel is presented as synonymous with the Ten Commandments, which were inscribed on the two tablets. These are then described as "the tablets of the covenant" (9:9, 11, 15; cf. 4:13). The dramatic action of Moses in smashing the tablets (9:17) is both a mark of the leader's anger, which itself reflects the anger of God, and also a deliberate sign-action. It aimed at demonstrating in visible fashion the fact that the people had broken the covenant on their side so that it would now be regarded as no longer valid and in force. Only the prayer of Moses alters the situation to rescue the covenant from this act of annulment. In making such a gesture of breaking the tablets it seems highly probable that Moses is enacting a dramatic gesture comparable to that employed in negotiating and revoking major international treaties.

The formal expression of the people's disobedience is given outward and visible form in the manufacture of an image of a calf, cast from gold. Similar images of bull calves, made either from clay or wood overlaid with metal, have been found at a number of sites in the Holy Land. The bull-calf form, symbolizing strength and fertility, was a popular image so that the portrayal of such an image at this vital moment in Israel's history was undoubtedly intended as a typical example of the way in which Israel had flouted the demands of the second commandment throughout a long history. The bull-calf images set up by Jeroboam I at Bethel and Dan (1 Kgs 12:28-29) were probably especially in the author's mind, in which case a degree of political feeling has intruded into the account, since such images were proof of the indifference to the demand for one single sanctuary at the place the LORD would choose.

We are clearly left with the question of what precisely the rationale was for such images and how it came about that they were so widely popular for so long throughout Israel's history. Undoubtedly such an image expressed both male power and fertility, making it a suitable symbol of the life-giving power of God. Since the Jerusalem Temple possessed images of cherubim (winged lion-like creatures; cf. Ezek 10:14), it may be asked why the cherubim images were acceptable, while the bull-calf images were not. No clear answer can be given to show precisely how the image was believed to relate to, and embody the power of, that which it symbolized.

Undoubtedly the bull-calf image was thought to be more than a pedestal for the invisible deity. Yet the manner of identity between the deity and its image is never clearly or directly stated. To some extent the two were never wholly identified, although the sense of the power of deity in a suitable image that represented divine presence (the Hebrew uses the word פנים [pānîm] for "face, presence") was all-important. Not only does the deuteronomic theology reject the sexual associations of the bull-calf image, but it also strongly opposes the sense of immediacy in the identity between deity and image that was fundamental to the religious symbolism of the entire ancient Near East. It has been noted, and is relevant to the deuteronomic theology, that in the ancient Near Eastern texts from Ugarit the god El is frequently described as having the form of a bull. Yet so is the deity Baal, indicating that there was no restriction of the most popular power and fertility symbolism to one single deity. That bull imagery had been popularly linked with the LORD God of Israel, therefore, is wholly understandable.

Many sections of the population of ancient Israel had simply adopted the imagery of a bull calf as a suitable symbol for deity, basing the practice on the older tradition that had existed in the land. This almost certainly went back to the time of the very beginning of the domestication of cattle for agricultural use and for food. Many of the most widely used forms of such an image would appear to have been retained in the homes of individual families, so that their presence at the major shrines was not the only manifestation of their presence. Even centralized control over the practice at Israel's sanctuaries would not eradicate the popularity of such symbols. The deuteronomists now seek to repudiate all further use of such iconography from the homes and rural shrines of Israel. It had become, in their skillful reworking of the ancient tradition, a tangible expression of all that was most tempting, and yet seemingly most ineradicable, in the inherited legacy of the religious life in the land. This deuteronomic narrative polemic then appears as the expression of a major effort to remove these popular religious bull-calf images and their associated customs from the homes and thought world of Israel.

So the account of the great intercessory prayer of Moses serves a dual pupose. On the one hand, it reveals the deceitfulness of sin by showing how seemingly natural and inevitable it was that Israel should fall into idolatry if it failed to give the most strenuous heed to the Ten Commandments. On the other hand, it also exalted the memory and image of the person of Moses. Without him Israel would have perished at its very beginning. He was the spiritual giant who towered above all others, since not even the patriarchs had carried the destiny of the nation on their shoulders in quite the fashion that Moses had done. Israel had been spared, not for its own sake, but for the sake of God's honor and for the sake of the self-denying intervention of Moses.

Before the final outcome of Moses' great work of intercession is reported in 10:10-11, two short narrative reports are inserted in the story. The first of these (10:1-5) tells of the making of an ark, and the second (10:6-9) of the resumption of the journey and the setting apart of the Levites to carry and keep custody of the ark. The reason for their inclusion here, which introduces a rather disconnected flow to the story of Moses' prayer and its successful outcome, must lie in their relevance to the custody and proclamation of the law. Since these commandments were vital to Israel's obedience, it was essential to know where the law was kept and who its custodians were. The answers to these questions were that the tablets containing the commandments had been entrusted to the Levites, who were commissioned by God to retain custody of the ark and to convey God's blessing to the people. In this way, the ark and the Levites between them maintained much of the unique ministry of Moses on behalf of the people. In turn, this perspective tells something of considerable importance about the authors of Deuteronomy and about their major theological reassessment of one of the leading features of Israel's worship.

The early history of the ark in ancient Israel is shrouded in obscurity. It is introduced to us as a mobile sanctuary in Num 10:34-35, where the accompanying invocation and prayers indicate that it had a close link to the concept of the LORD God as Israel's Leader in battle. The fact that it could be addressed directly as though it were God reveals how closely the divine presence was believed to be linked to it. This fact has given rise to the belief that, in spite of its name and box-like form, it was regarded as the throne of the invisible deity seated upon it. However, doubts remain as to its original significance and role since its name clearly implies that it was a container of some description. Its connection with warfare and the belief in God's leadership and power in battle appear as the most certain of its associations.

Not until the time of King David was the ark brought to Jerusalem and established permanently in a tent there (2 Sam 6:12-19). From this time onward, at least, it was evidently regarded as the most important of Israel's sacred artifacts and as a feature that made the shrine of Jerusalem more important than others, even before the Temple was built there. So the presence of the ark in Jerusalem played an important part in making the city the political capital of all Israel and in relating the traditions of it to one of the oldest features of Israel's religious inheritance.

For the deuteronomists, this older interpretation of the ark called for considerable modification, and it is this deuteronomic reinterpretation that is now set out in 10:1-5. It has been widely recognized as among the latest literary units to have been introduced into the book. It is also quite likely that an older account of the making of the ark once stood after Exod 33:6, where it would have followed the account of the making of the golden calf. With the literary reshaping of the Pentateuch in its later stages, this account was regarded as no longer relevant and so was lost, being replaced by the deuteronomic revised viewpoint.

It is a striking feature of the deuteronomic theology that the direct identification of the ark with the presence of God is effectively set aside and its role as a container contrastingly emphasized. It is regarded as the focal shrine memorializing and expressing the covenant between Israel and the LORD as God. So it could even be described as "the ark of the covenant," although this cannot have been its earliest designation, and its original relationship to any covenant ideology appears doubtful. Later Jewish tradition was of the

belief that several of the most important relics of Israel's national history had been kept in it (cf. Heb 9:4).

It is, however, not difficult to see that when the Judean state collapsed in 587 BCE and the Temple of Jerusalem was destroyed, the significance of the ark effectively perished with it. It is possible that the ark had not even survived that long and had been removed earlier, but this appears unlikely. In any case, as a symbol of the divine power to bring victory in battle, the ark now became totally discredited. For its deuteronomic reinterpretation, however, its significance now lay not in what it was in itself, but solely in what it contained: the sacred book of Torah. Since that law of God's covenant had not perished, then the loss of the ark no longer mattered greatly. An allusion to its loss and to the unimportance of this for Jerusalem's future is to be found in Jer 3:15-16, and this note must undoubtedly be credited to a deuteronomic editor of Jeremiah's prophecies.

The short narrative in 10:6-9 carries us back to the period of Israel's wilderness journeyings. Its inclusion here must be a consequence of the desire to show both that the ark had accompanied the Israelites in the wilderness and that it was in the custody, and under the protection of, the Levites. The brief note in 10:9 explaining that the Levites had no permanent inheritance of land, but were maintained by the gifts of the people for their role of ministry before the LORD, introduces us to them and to their significance for the deuteronomists, showing that they, too, were agents of the covenant relationship.

The role of the Levites, as set out in the book of Deuteronomy, has aroused considerable discussion and deserves close attention, since it undoubtedly served to magnify their importance to Israel's life.[57] It presents a seemingly ambivalent attitude toward them. As in the brief note here, the Levites are recognized as guardians, and by implication interpreters, of the law of the covenant. So they are revered as faithful teachers who were authorized as the law's interpreters and also as those who could be expected to promote

---

57. M. Haran, *Temples and Temple Service in Ancient Israel* (Oxford: Oxford University Press, 1978) 58-83; Aelred Cody, *A History of Old Testament Priesthood*, AnBib 35 (Rome: Pontifical Biblical Institute, 1969) 125-45; A. H. J. Gunneweg, *Leviten und Priester*, FRLANT 89 (Göttingen, 1965); J. A. Emerton, "Priests and Levites in Deuteronomy," *VT* 12 (1962) 128-38.

allegiance to it with the utmost zeal. At the same time, there are several passages in the book, especially in the law code section (chaps. 12–26), which align them so directly with the poor as to suggest that they were a relatively impoverished group whose claim on the people for support was in need of strong encouragement. G. von Rad in particular has seen the close association of the Levites with the authors of Deuteronomy to be one of identity.[58] The powerful rhetorical preaching style that colors chaps. 6–9 could then reflect the work of teaching Levites, who were the strongest and most respected of those whose loyalty to the LORD God was above question. That such loyalty to God was their prime duty (cf. the story of the ruthlessness in displaying loyalty to the LORD in Exod 32:25-29) could then serve to explain, if not to justify, those parts of the book that advocate complete ruthlessness in demanding adherence to the LORD.

Attractive as some aspects of this attempt to identify the Levites as Deuteronomy's authors is, it appears, by itself, to be too incomplete an understanding of the latter. Other aspects of the

work point strongly to other interests and traditions. More significant for an understanding of the deuteronomic interpretation of the distinctive position of the Levites is the question of their priestly status. While Deuteronomy assumes that all priests are Levites, it clearly recognizes that many Levites are teachers, rather than priests, and are not formally carrying out priestly duties. In seeking to relate the situation of the law book to Josiah's reform, this was understood by von Rad to point to those Levites who had been displaced as a result of the Assyrian incursions into northern Israel during the eighth century BCE.

However, the deuteronomic awareness that the Levites were in special need of consideration for support from Israel's tithes and charitable gifts, and that they were not all fulfilling priestly duties, can be far better explained as a consequence of what had happened in 587 BCE, when the Temple was destroyed. The Levites had been effectively left without an altar to serve. As custodians of Israel's sacral traditions they were, nevertheless, able to fulfill a primary role as teachers and guides for prayer. It is in such a capacity that the deuteronomic legislation seeks to retain for them a primary function as guardians of Israel's faith.

---

58. G. von Rad, *Studies in Deuteronomy*, trans. D. Stalker, SBT 9 (London: SCM, 1953) 60-69.

REFLECTIONS

The story of Moses' great act of intercession, and the role of intercessory prayer generally in the biblical portrait of religious life, marks a high point of deuteronomic theology. We have consistently noted the turning to an inner spiritual dimension of faith that characterizes so much of this book. It is wholly consonant with this that the history of Joshua–2 Kings, which carries so many of the trademarks of deuteronomic thinking, should also present many of the great turning points of the national history being negotiated through sermons or prayers.

Whereas the inherited patterns of religion in the ancient Near East had consistently been physical, external, and visual in form, that of Deuteronomy is contrastingly inward, rational, and reflective. In general the human endeavor to make the divine world accessible through ritual and the veneration of artifacts is regarded by the deuteronomists at best with suspicion and at worst with deep hostility. Without an inner probing and searching of the heart, there could be no true access to the world of divine power and a divine presence. Almost all other forms of religious activity are viewed as largely adjuncts to prayer. Only by acts of remembering, heart searching, and loving can the human mind seize the key to the heavenly realities. Even the most august and respected of Israel's shrines could be no more than a place where the divine name could be found, through which prayer could be offered. In fact, even prayer offered from a distant land toward this place would be heard and honored (1 Kgs 8:44).

Yet prayer could easily lapse into the most isolated and individualistic expression of religious faith. Instead of promoting a sense of community and shared faith within a larger congregation, it could become isolationist and solipsistic, with each individual Israelite praying on a spiritual island of his or her own making. Yet, according to the deuteronomic perspective, prayer was never to be isolationist, and so intercessory prayer was one of its most basic and fundamental expressions. Individuals were bound up with one another in the community of faith, enabling the strong to carry the weak and the stumbling and fainthearted to be carried along by those of courage and insight. In all Israel's history there was no one whose courage and insight could match those of the figure of Moses.

The interjection of the two narratives in 10:1-9 regarding the ark and the Levites brings us face to face with an important aspect of the deuteronomic thinking. We have already noted the striking manner in which the forms of address used in the sermonic exhortations to the reader introduce a note of contemporaneity in regard to events of the past. The generations of Israel who stood at the foot of Mt. Horeb or who waited anxiously to set foot across the river Jordan to enter the promised land or who now constituted the surviving readership to whom Deuteronomy was addressed, all made up one Israel. A timeless unity bound the generations of the nation together to make them one so that decisions and choices of the past remained real options for the present. Israel was facing the same challenges and possibilities that its earlier generations had faced.

This is an important rhetorical device employed in Deuteronomy to create a sense of urgency and immediacy. The past lived on in that it had left open future choices and decisions that each Israelite man and woman still faced. It is, however, more than a skillfull literary technique, since the authors clearly believed that God's choice of Israel and the covenant that had been made with the people were lasting covenants. The consequences remained real and valid for the generations who had passed since the Jordan was first crossed.

For this ongoing reality of the covenant to be accepted and realized within Israel there needed to be a continued ministry of teaching, prayer, and responsiveness to keep alive the blessing that the covenant had brought. Israel would remain on its land, its fields and flocks would prosper and be fertile, and the power that had defeated all Israel's enemies so victoriously at the beginning would still give victory in later years (cf. the role of the ark and the Levites in achieving the model victory at Jericho, Josh 6:12-21). So the ministry of the Levites, the making and care of the sacred ark, the reading and hearing of the law, and all the rites and customs that gave vitality and visible expression to religion had to be maintained. Israel would then continue to be a blessed people.

This awareness that salvation could be a *present* condition, and not merely an event that had happened in the past, was a vital aspect of the deuteronomic theology. For all the careful historical focus on events of the past, and not least the lessons of the failures and rebelliousness of the past, the present mattered greatly to the deuteronomic authors.

Deuteronomy 10:12–11:7, The Law Carries Both Curse and Blessing

NIV	NRSV
¹²And now, O Israel, what does the LORD your God ask of you but to fear the LORD your God, to walk in all his ways, to love him, to serve the LORD your God with all your heart and with all your soul, ¹³and to observe the LORD's commands and decrees that I am giving you today for your own good?	12So now, O Israel, what does the LORD your God require of you? Only to fear the LORD your God, to walk in all his ways, to love him, to serve the LORD your God with all your heart and with all your soul, ¹³and to keep the commandments of the LORD your God*a* and his decrees that I am commanding you today, for your own well-being.
¹⁴To the LORD your God belong the heavens,	*a* Q Ms Gk Syr: MT lacks *your God*

NIV

even the highest heavens, the earth and everything in it. ¹⁵Yet the LORD set his affection on your forefathers and loved them, and he chose you, their descendants, above all the nations, as it is today. ¹⁶Circumcise your hearts, therefore, and do not be stiff-necked any longer. ¹⁷For the LORD your God is God of gods and Lord of lords, the great God, mighty and awesome, who shows no partiality and accepts no bribes. ¹⁸He defends the cause of the fatherless and the widow, and loves the alien, giving him food and clothing. ¹⁹And you are to love those who are aliens, for you yourselves were aliens in Egypt. ²⁰Fear the LORD your God and serve him. Hold fast to him and take your oaths in his name. ²¹He is your praise; he is your God, who performed for you those great and awesome wonders you saw with your own eyes. ²²Your forefathers who went down into Egypt were seventy in all, and now the LORD your God has made you as numerous as the stars in the sky.

11 Love the LORD your God and keep his requirements, his decrees, his laws and his commands always. ²Remember today that your children were not the ones who saw and experienced the discipline of the LORD your God: his majesty, his mighty hand, his outstretched arm; ³the signs he performed and the things he did in the heart of Egypt, both to Pharaoh king of Egypt and to his whole country; ⁴what he did to the Egyptian army, to its horses and chariots, how he overwhelmed them with the waters of the Red Sea*a* as they were pursuing you, and how the LORD brought lasting ruin on them. ⁵It was not your children who saw what he did for you in the desert until you arrived at this place, ⁶and what he did to Dathan and Abiram, sons of Eliab the Reubenite, when the earth opened its mouth right in the middle of all Israel and swallowed them up with their households, their tents and every living thing that belonged to them. ⁷But it was your own eyes that saw all these great things the LORD has done.

*a4 Hebrew *Yam Suph;* that is, Sea of Reeds

NRSV

¹⁴Although heaven and the heaven of heavens belong to the LORD your God, the earth with all that is in it, ¹⁵yet the LORD set his heart in love on your ancestors alone and chose you, their descendants after them, out of all the peoples, as it is today. ¹⁶Circumcise, then, the foreskin of your heart, and do not be stubborn any longer. ¹⁷For the LORD your God is God of gods and Lord of lords, the great God, mighty and awesome, who is not partial and takes no bribe, ¹⁸who executes justice for the orphan and the widow, and who loves the strangers, providing them food and clothing. ¹⁹You shall also love the stranger, for you were strangers in the land of Egypt. ²⁰You shall fear the LORD your God; him alone you shall worship; to him you shall hold fast, and by his name you shall swear. ²¹He is your praise; he is your God, who has done for you these great and awesome things that your own eyes have seen. ²²Your ancestors went down to Egypt seventy persons; and now the LORD your God has made you as numerous as the stars in heaven.

11 You shall love the LORD your God, therefore, and keep his charge, his decrees, his ordinances, and his commandments always. ²Remember today that it was not your children (who have not known or seen the discipline of the LORD your God), but it is you who must acknowledge his greatness, his mighty hand and his outstretched arm, ³his signs and his deeds that he did in Egypt to Pharaoh, the king of Egypt, and to all his land; ⁴what he did to the Egyptian army, to their horses and chariots, how he made the water of the Red Sea*a* flow over them as they pursued you, so that the LORD has destroyed them to this day; ⁵what he did to you in the wilderness, until you came to this place; ⁶and what he did to Dathan and Abiram, sons of Eliab son of Reuben, how in the midst of all Israel the earth opened its mouth and swallowed them up, along with their households, their tents, and every living being in their company; ⁷for it is your own eyes that have seen every great deed that the LORD did.

*a Or Sea of Reeds

COMMENTARY

The sermons that have advocated and reinforced the covenant commandments by a process of exhortation and reflection on past events are now brought to a climax by further admonitions. These recapitulate points that have already been made, but lend a further note of urgency to the consciousness of the covenant and its law. The demands of the covenant are both simple and yet inexhaustible. They can easily be remembered, and yet the nature of the human mind and the inevitable temptations of alien religious traditions make constant vigilance a necessity. One thing that is constantly needed is to fear God, to pursue the path marked out by the divine laws and to hold to them by maintaining an unbroken attitude of love toward God. "Only to fear the LORD your God" (v. 12) remained a perpetual admonition and command. Yet this one thing posed a demand that knew no limit, since it was a demand that could only be responded to with the whole of one's being—heart, soul, and mind.

10:12-22. Once again the unique privilege and opportunity that have been conferred on Israel as a consequence of the mysterious act of God's choice of them are reasserted (v. 15). Israel could neither evade nor deny the opportunity that lay ahead. Nevertheless, it was not an opportunity to be faced lightly. It was no easy thing to be the recipient of God's choice and call. The LORD was to be celebrated as God of gods, Lord of lords, and One who could not be swayed or bribed by human plans or devious practices. Accordingly, vv. 18-19 digress to assert that Israel's conduct must show the same pattern of right dealing as that displayed by the divine nature. It is noteworthy that the interpretation of what such right acting entailed for the orphan, the widow, and the stranger (or resident alien) was to provide each with food and clothing. The point is subsequently taken up more fully in the law code of chaps. 12–26.

The appeal to the historical tradition regarding Israel's origins as slaves in the land of Egypt (vv. 19, 22) is used by the deuteronomists on several occasions to sustain a basic ethical injunction of care and empathy toward the weaker and more destitute members of society. In this way, the very "national" tradition of Israel was one in which a sensitivity to those who were deprived and abused

held a prominent place. For the deuteronomists, the very understanding of righteousness included a strong bias toward the weak and the poor.

The point is a significant one and serves to explain the distinctive nature of the commandments and the remarkable deuteronomic concern to combine a strong demand for an inward disposition of love with a sharply defined formal system of legislation. Clearly love and law were in no way regarded as concepts that stood in contrast. It is precisely this combination of law and an ethic of love that makes it impossible to interpret the Ten Commandments as representing a system of law in an exclusively juridical sense. They were to be the guideposts of a social order built on an ethic of unity and of a responsive concern to a knowledge of divine love.

The theological nature of the deuteronomic ethic is reinforced by a return once again to the insistence that reverence for the LORD as God, and unswerving loyalty to the divine commandments, demanded an exclusive use of the name of the LORD alone when sacred oaths and vows were needed (v. 20). This single-minded emphasis reveals the theological underpinning of the deuteronomic ethic. Without a prior exclusive reverence for the LORD as God, the fundamental grounds for accepting the demands of righteous action would be undermined.

11:1-7. These verses provide further insight into the deuteronomic theology of worship and the manner in which this is combined with a strong moral demand. Israel was called upon to obey the commandments of God—a point that has already been established as the controlling theme of chaps. 5–11. Yet it should never appear difficult or unwelcome to Israel to yield this obedience, since the people had themselves witnessed the saving power of the LORD as God. Once again the sense of contemporaneity and the rhetorical bridge that bound together Israel's many generations create a sense of unity and reassert the claim of God on every generation of Israel. The truths of the past became the springboard of action for the present.

At a first reading, the insistence that the readers of the book "must acknowledge his greatness" (v. 2) would appear to be unremarkable. Yet it glosses over the point already made earlier regarding the period of thirty-eight years spent wandering aimlessly in the wilderness until the generation that had shown complete distrust of God's Word had died out. Those whom the author so emphatically insists have most reason to trust and acknowledge the power of God from the evidence of what their own eyes had witnessed are assumed to be most at risk to disobey the commandments of God.

The point made in v. 2 that "it was not your children" becomes all the more remarkable when it is recognized that the text of Deuteronomy was quite evidently and consciously being addressed to a much later generation still. The great power of God had been demonstrated to the full to those Hebrew slaves who had experienced the marvelous deliverance from Egypt and who had witnessed the overthrow of the pursuing Egyptian army (v. 4). That generation had been given firsthand knowledge of who the LORD God was and of the divine majesty. Yet all this had taken place with the most immense consequences for the present, which the author brings out with a kind of double entendre in the key phrase "to this day" (עד היום הזה 'ad hayyôm hazzeh, v. 4). It is both the day when Moses addressed Israel as the people faced the prospect of entering the land and it is the day of the reader who stands trembling with anxiety and concern as to whether there can be any future at all for the remnant of Israel. The former glory now appeared to be sadly tarnished. Israel's spiritual armor had rusted, and its moral courage in believing the Word of God had been gradually ebbing away. The reawakening call of Deuteronomy is that "this day" is still "God's today." Salvation is viewed as a reality that has consequences for all succeeding generations of Israelites. Past events prove the possibility of present salvation.

At this point, the narrative takes up a more unexpected point. Not only had there existed an external threat from the Egyptian forces that had pursued Israel, but there was also a more insidious threat from within in the figures of Dathan and Abiram, who had rebelled against the authority of Moses. A point of special interest regarding the method of the deuteronomic writer appears in that it is evident that the source of the information presented here is the report of the rebellion given in Numbers 16. There, where the present priestly text is now preserved, "all the men of Korah," along with Dathan and Abiram, are the rebels who suffer dire punishment for their folly. The deuteronomic author, however, must have followed an earlier version of the pentateuchal source (JE?) that mentioned only Dathan and Abiram and not Korah.

The reference to this internal threat comes unexpectedly at this particular point. Nevertheless, it fits in well with the broader deuteronomic perspective that Israel not only faced external enemies, spearheaded by powerful foreign peoples with massive armies, but also internal ones, led by rebels from within the nation. More threatening and dangerous still in the eyes of the deuteronomists was the threat that every man, woman, and child within the nation would forget the greatness of God's achievements in the past. The lessons of the past needed to be learned all over again, and the courage of the few, which had given birth to the nation and had dared to believe the Word of God, had to be learned all over again.

REFLECTIONS

Few subjects can appear more confusing and difficult for the untutored mind than the uses of history. What is it that history teaches? For some it may appear to have no lessons or meaning at all, while for others it may, as in Marxist dogma, operate as if on rails, to "prove" that one consequence necessarily follows another and that society is moving in unstoppable necessity toward a classless utopia. To some people, one period of history appears much like any other, illustrating the same features and uncovering the same mix of human vision and human weakness. To others all episodes of human history are utterly unique and unrepeatable and, therefore, incapable of teaching anything at all that might be relevant to another period.

In fact, history sometimes teaches us easily discernible truths, and sometimes history teaches us nothing at all. Certainly much seems so startlingly to repeat itself that one generation finds itself having to fight again the battles and learn again the lessons that earlier generations had fought and learned. As the biblical Ecclesiastes could repeat as a proverbial maxim, "There is nothing new under the sun" (Eccl 1:9). Yet there is an element of uniqueness about the past that makes the course of history unforeseeable and the study of it so fascinating. To a noticeable extent, each generation of the human race has had to work out its own salvation.

The brief period that Israel's ancestors spent marching from the oasis of Kadesh to the banks of the river Jordan, after they had wasted a fruitless lifetime of a generation meandering aimlessly in a wasteland, provided the deuteronomic authors with object lessons for their own generation. These lessons learned about the past and already recorded in Israel's national history were also lessons for the present, when read and interpreted discerningly. And such is what the deuteronomists have done in using these stories. They are, in effect, sermons, and the "texts" for these sermons are provided by extracted records from episodes reported in earlier material, for the most part still preserved for us in the Pentateuch.

The method of the deuteronomic authors is relatively easy to follow, and the rhetorical skill with which the reader is invited to heed the message of the past is unmistakable and highly praiseworthy. When we examine closely the theological undergirding that has shaped the way the stories are retold and the lessons that are deduced from them, we see that these writers have resorted to simple paradigms with a rather simplistic presentation, suggesting that the same features are repeated from one generation to the next. Nowhere is this deuteronomistic style of making history fit into a formula more evident than in the framework to the book of Judges.

It would be a mistake, however, to regard the deuteronomic interpretation of history as a fixed and stylized sequence of repetitions, in which only the names of persons and locations change but the essential outcome appears predetermined. Hidden within these anecdotal paradigms is a very powerful and existential view of the past. While the past is seen to conform to certain patterns, what these patterns bring to the fore is the sense of challenge and uniqueness that belongs to each situation, a sense that a time has come that is full of opportunity and danger, and that it will not come again. By such a theological reflection the past events of Israel's beginning period become the text for showing the reader the challenge of the present. The sense that repeatedly faces the reader is one of wistful reflection: "If only they had. . . ." Some people behaved well in the past, but some behaved badly and foolishly. So the opportunity passed them by, and a time of spiritual richness was lost. Yet no serious reader can fail to see how he or she is still being faced with the same challenge: "Today, if you will hear his voice. . . ." So the message of the past becomes a call to action in the present. The very fact that there existed an open gateway in the past reveals that there are still gates that may be opened in the present.

Deuteronomy 11:8-32, Be Diligent to Keep the Commandments

NIV

8Observe therefore all the commands I am giving you today, so that you may have the strength to go in and take over the land that you are crossing the Jordan to possess, 9and so that you may live long in the land that the LORD swore to your forefathers to give to them and their descendants, a land flowing with milk and honey. 10The land you are entering to take over is not like the land of Egypt, from which you have come, where you planted your seed and irrigated it by foot as in a vegetable garden. 11But the land you

NRSV

8Keep, then, this entire commandment that I am commanding you today, so that you may have strength to go in and occupy the land that you are crossing over to occupy, 9and so that you may live long in the land that the LORD swore to your ancestors to give them and to their descendants, a land flowing with milk and honey. 10For the land that you are about to enter to occupy is not like the land of Egypt, from which you have come, where you sow your seed and irrigate by foot like a vegetable garden. 11But the land that you are

NIV

are crossing the Jordan to take possession of is a land of mountains and valleys that drinks rain from heaven. ¹²It is a land the LORD your God cares for; the eyes of the LORD your God are continually on it from the beginning of the year to its end.

¹³So if you faithfully obey the commands I am giving you today—to love the LORD your God and to serve him with all your heart and with all your soul— ¹⁴then I will send rain on your land in its season, both autumn and spring rains, so that you may gather in your grain, new wine and oil. ¹⁵I will provide grass in the fields for your cattle, and you will eat and be satisfied.

¹⁶Be careful, or you will be enticed to turn away and worship other gods and bow down to them. ¹⁷Then the LORD's anger will burn against you, and he will shut the heavens so that it will not rain and the ground will yield no produce, and you will soon perish from the good land the LORD is giving you. ¹⁸Fix these words of mine in your hearts and minds; tie them as symbols on your hands and bind them on your foreheads. ¹⁹Teach them to your children, talking about them when you sit at home and when you walk along the road, when you lie down and when you get up. ²⁰Write them on the doorframes of your houses and on your gates, ²¹so that your days and the days of your children may be many in the land that the LORD swore to give your forefathers, as many as the days that the heavens are above the earth.

²²If you carefully observe all these commands I am giving you to follow—to love the LORD your God, to walk in all his ways and to hold fast to him— ²³then the LORD will drive out all these nations before you, and you will dispossess nations larger and stronger than you. ²⁴Every place where you set your foot will be yours: Your territory will extend from the desert to Lebanon, and from the Euphrates River to the western sea.ᵃ ²⁵No man will be able to stand against you. The LORD your God, as he promised you, will put the terror and fear of you on the whole land, wherever you go.

²⁶See, I am setting before you today a blessing and a curse— ²⁷the blessing if you obey the commands of the LORD your God that I am giving

ᵃ24 That is, the Mediterranean

NRSV

crossing over to occupy is a land of hills and valleys, watered by rain from the sky, ¹²a land that the LORD your God looks after. The eyes of the LORD your God are always on it, from the beginning of the year to the end of the year.

13If you will only heed his every command-mentᵃ that I am commanding you today—loving the LORD your God, and serving him with all your heart and with all your soul— ¹⁴then heᵇ will give the rain for your land in its season, the early rain and the later rain, and you will gather in your grain, your wine, and your oil; ¹⁵and heᵇ will give grass in your fields for your livestock, and you will eat your fill. ¹⁶Take care, or you will be seduced into turning away, serving other gods and worshiping them, ¹⁷for then the anger of the LORD will be kindled against you and he will shut up the heavens, so that there will be no rain and the land will yield no fruit; then you will perish quickly off the good land that the LORD is giving you.

18You shall put these words of mine in your heart and soul, and you shall bind them as a sign on your hand, and fix them as an emblemᶜ on your forehead. ¹⁹Teach them to your children, talking about them when you are at home and when you are away, when you lie down and when you rise. ²⁰Write them on the doorposts of your house and on your gates, ²¹so that your days and the days of your children may be multiplied in the land that the LORD swore to your ancestors to give them, as long as the heavens are above the earth.

22If you will diligently observe this entire com-mandment that I am commanding you, loving the LORD your God, walking in all his ways, and holding fast to him, ²³then the LORD will drive out all these nations before you, and you will dispos-sess nations larger and mightier than yourselves. ²⁴Every place on which you set foot shall be yours; your territory shall extend from the wilderness to the Lebanon and from the River, the river Euphrates, to the Western Sea. ²⁵No one will be able to stand against you; the LORD your God will put the fear and dread of you on all the land on which you set foot, as he promised you.

ᵃ Compare Gk: Heb *my commandments*   ᵇ Sam Gk Vg: MT *I*
ᶜ Or *as a frontlet*

NIV

you today; 28the curse if you disobey the commands of the LORD your God and turn from the way that I command you today by following other gods, which you have not known. 29When the LORD your God has brought you into the land you are entering to possess, you are to proclaim on Mount Gerizim the blessings, and on Mount Ebal the curses. 30As you know, these mountains are across the Jordan, west of the road,ᵃ toward the setting sun, near the great trees of Moreh, in the territory of those Canaanites living in the Arabah in the vicinity of Gilgal. 31You are about to cross the Jordan to enter and take possession of the land the LORD your God is giving you. When you have taken it over and are living there, 32be sure that you obey all the decrees and laws I am setting before you today.

ᵃ30 Or *Jordan, westward*

NRSV

26See, I am setting before you today a blessing and a curse: 27the blessing, if you obey the commandments of the LORD your God that I am commanding you today; 28and the curse, if you do not obey the commandments of the LORD your God, but turn from the way that I am commanding you today, to follow other gods that you have not known.

29When the LORD your God has brought you into the land that you are entering to occupy, you shall set the blessing on Mount Gerizim and the curse on Mount Ebal. 30As you know, they are beyond the Jordan, some distance to the west, in the land of the Canaanites who live in the Arabah, opposite Gilgal, beside the oakᵃ of Moreh.

31When you cross the Jordan to go in to occupy the land that the LORD your God is giving you, and when you occupy it and live in it, 32you must diligently observe all the statutes and ordinances that I am setting before you today.

ᵃ Gk Syr: Compare Gen 12.6; Heb *oaks* or *terebinths*

COMMENTARY

A final sermon brings the introduction to the deuteronomic law code to a close and summarizes the message of what has been declared in the previous addresses of chaps. 5–11. The message remains unequivocal: The Ten Commandments are vitally important and must never be forgotten. So the opening words, "Keep then this entire commandment" (v. 8), are effectively complemented by the concluding injunction: "You must diligently observe all the statutes and ordinances that I am setting before you today" (v. 32). In the center of this section (vv. 18-21), we are presented with a further summary recapitulation of the various injunctions as to how Israel may learn to keep these important commandments. Here we find repeated directives that have already been made earlier. Israel must learn to keep the words of the commandments consistently in mind—to bind them as a sign to the hand, to teach them to children, and to think upon them wherever and whenever it is practically possible. All of this further insistence upon the central position of the commandments is necessary for one overriding

reason: Continued settlement in the land and retention of its ownership are conditional upon doing so.

A number of features in the section carry us deeply into the theological world of the deuteronomists. Taken in their entirety, the series of commandments can be summed up by the singular term "the commandment" (המצוה *hammiṣwâ*, v. 8; cf. 5:31). Virtually every blessing of life that made it sustainable are presented as being dependent upon obedience to these basic demands.

What is striking in contrast to the appeal to history as a motivating reason for such observance in 10:12–11:7 is that here an appeal is made to the beauty, the fertility, and the general desirability of Israel's land, shortly to be won and occupied, that provides such a motive. Since scholars have frequently contrasted the biblical appeals to history and historical recollection with an appeal to the natural world and the natural order of things, the section here deserves the closest attention. In a poetic and somewhat exaggerated fashion, the very geology and climate of the biblical landscape is made into an assertion concerning the directness of God's concern with it: "The eyes of the LORD your God are always on it, from the beginning of the year to the end of the year" (v. 12).

Such attention to the fertility and desirability of the biblical territory is highly meaningful when read in the context of the religious tradition of the ancient Near East. It is wholly typical of the deuteronomistic theology to contrast the Israelites' land favorably with the seemingly hostile territory of Egypt (v. 10). Yet more immediately relevant for an appreciation of the significance of the deuteronomic theology is its consciousness of the popular appeal of Canaanite religion on account of its claim to uphold the vitality and seasonal efficacy of the natural order of life. Baal and his consort Anat were presented as givers of "life," so that it can be misleading to focus exclusively on their appeal as givers of "fertility" in abstraction from this. The fertility of fields and flocks, the productivity of the soil, and the seasonal regularity of the rainfall were all regarded as aspects of life. Such life could then be regarded as the gift of the Cannanite deities, whose rituals were designed to promote its preservation and continuance.

Baal was lord of storms and thunder, master of the rainfall, and on this account he was revered as the giver of life. Anat, his heavenly consort, was both his defender and his helper and the bearer of new life. By controlling the seasonal order, these deities brought life to the soil and security to the people whose very existence depended on its productivity and on the health of flocks and herds. Because drought and consequent famine were ever-present threats, neither god nor goddess could easily be ignored.

Keeping in mind an awareness of this intense Canaanite preoccupation with rainfall and the fertility of the soil, one can see the special significance of the description of Israel's land as one "flowing with milk and honey" (v. 9). Whereas the land of the Israelites was irrigated by the seasonal rainfall, Egypt was dependent upon irrigation "by foot" (v. 10), an allusion to the need for human effort to power the mechanical systems in use in ancient Egypt. The fact that the human-designed systems of irrigation made the Nile and its surrounding land into "the granary of Egypt" and that Israel's ancestor Jacob had fled to Egypt in order to find food in a time of famine is tactfully

passed over. The author has made use of an understandable degree of poetic license to express his own overpowering delight in the land of Israel and the horror with which he contemplates the possibility of its loss.

Awareness of the variations of climate and the marginal levels of rainfall in the semi-desert regions of Israel's land are here employed to promote a sense of the immediacy of its dependence upon God. The coming of the rains in the spring and fall of the year becomes a vital mark of a beneficent providence and so makes the question, "Who is it who gives the rain?" a primary one for religion (v. 14). In a very real sense, it was the same awareness and the raising of the same question that were a prominent feature of Canaanite religion and that made Baal, lord of storms and thunder, so forceful a factor in the Canaanite mythology and pantheon. What is then particularly striking in this homily is the interposing of obedience to the Ten Commandments as a vital requirement for the life-sustaining climate of the region to be maintained. Not Baal, but the LORD God of Israel is the giver of life. The LORD God alone is the life-ensuring One without whose cooperation and power the fertility of the land would wither away. So this important combining of ethical demand with natural promise results in a powerful moralizing and spiritualizing of the interpretation of nature.

We can well appreciate the note of urgency in the warning: "Take care, or you will be seduced into turning away, serving other gods and worshiping them" (v. 16). Precisely because the gods and goddesses of Canaan were venerated as "deities of the land," who were its sustainers and protectors, it was an inevitable temptation for those who lived on it, and who were dependent upon its produce, to feel under obligation to them. All the more must this have been the case when the LORD God of Israel was regarded as merely the God of Mt. Horeb who had intervened to rescue the nation's ancestors in Egypt. The sense of geographical and temporal distance made the appeal of "the gods of the land" appear more immediate and relevant to the people of Israel once they had settled in it.

The concluding section of this sermonic address in vv. 26-31, which brings to a close the whole series of homilies advocating careful observance of the commandments beginning in chap. 6, proclaims both the promise of blessing and the threat of curse. This theme then returns far more extensively in chaps. 27–29.

The simple contrasting of the consequences of blessing and curse in vv. 26-30 serves to set the commandments once more in the very forefront of all life and activity. Whether the one or the other is to be the experience of Israel will be wholly determined by whether Israel, taken as a single entity, displays obedience to the commandments. This highlights the pre-eminence attached to religious commitment, combined with a concern for morality, which is embodied in the commandments. Both here and even more fully in the larger exposition of the hope of blessing and the threat of curse in chaps. 27–29, there are important elements of the harmonization and integration of a wide variety of human experiences into a consolidated pattern. For many people, concepts of blessing and, even more particularly, of curse were treated in a quasi-magical fashion. They were believed to possess a vitality of their own. Persons, families, and places could all be thought of as being the subjects of curse or of blessing. Certain individuals were regarded as being capable of uttering words of either blessing or curse that could not thereafter be canceled. Some persons could be thought of as having been "born under a curse," while others were thought of as "children of blessing." It was no insignificant matter for the deuteronomic authors, therefore, to seek to discern a coherence and wholeness in the entire arena of life by insisting that both blessing and curse lay in the hands of the One God, who had spoken to Israel through the commandments.

Behind concepts of blessing and curse there lay a deep consciousness throughout the entire ancient Near East of the power of the spoken word. Words uttered in the name of a deity, whether threatening or reassuring, were words fraught with power. It is the consciousness of this fact that makes inclusion of the misuse of the name of the LORD an important prohibition among the commandments (5:11). To link the powerful name of God with words spoken in deliberately contrived malice, or in order to secure undeserved protection, was to abuse the divine name.

Since words declaring curse or blessing from any god were words of special significance, especially was this so when such words were spoken with appeal to the name of Israel's God. All too easily the fear of such words plunged innocent people into a sea of fear and anxiety that would become destructive. Conversely, the misguided belief that words promising security and prosperity would be unstoppable in their effect could breed a dangerous complacency. A considerable importance, therefore, attaches to what Deuteronomy has to teach on this subject. It presents a feature that permeates the book as a whole and marks the whole deuteronomic outlook in insisting that all faith and spiritual understanding are subject to God's ethical demands.

Religion must inevitably be related to the language and concepts of power and authority. But both power and authority may be abused when they become separated from the wider ethical needs and demands of the human community. Since blessing and curse may be seen as the outworking of human power and authority, then it matters greatly that there should be a tight integration of spiritual, ethical, and political authority. It is just such integration that Deuteronomy seeks to promote and to bring about.

How successful the writers of Deuteronomy were in achieving this in practice we do not adequately know. But we can see in its prescriptive assertions concerning the subordination of all spiritual and political agencies to the ultimate authority of one God that it recognized the central significance of the issue: It declared an unequivocal no to the belief that religious power, even when designed to bring about blessing, could be bestowed without regard for the most fundamental notions of right and wrong. God offers "blessing, if you obey the commandments of the LORD your God . . . and the curse, if you do not" (vv. 27-28).

REFLECTIONS

The careful reader may at first be taken aback by the repetitiveness and seeming overstatement of the deuteronomic emphasis on the commandments of God. So exaggerated is the concern that its repetitiveness sounds rather obsessive. Everywhere, every day, and without exception, the commandments are to be remembered and reflected upon. Moreover, the author of the homilies urging obedience to these commandments probes into the human psyche to uncover the temptations and self-justifying reasonings that might lead any Israelite, once settled safely in the land, to neglect to obey them. The passage of time and the comfort and complacency induced by success are seen to present inevitable temptations. Why should the biblical writers be so insistent, and why should they be so negative in their assessment of how future generations of Israelites would behave? Could it not be assumed that, having once seen and known what was good and right, obedience to God's commandments would commend itself so obviously to everyone as to elicit a natural and unforced obedience? Clearly the deuteronomists did not think so.

The reasons for such negative assessments immediately reveal themselves. First, behind the deuteronomic homilies lies a deep and long experience of human life and attitudes that have given rise to these warnings. The writers were well aware of what had happened in the later years of Israel's life under a monarchy. All Israel's systems of law, of government, of education, and of religious practice and instruction had been severely tested and found wanting since the time when Israel's ancestors had crossed the Jordan and settled in the land. Those very institutions that had claimed so much for themselves—the kingship, the priesthood, the civil judges, and the wealthy heads of families—had all claimed more than they had delivered in promising the success of a healthy, moral, and prosperous nation.

It is for this reason that so much of the Hebrew Bible that deals with the period from the conquest of the land to the collapse of the first Jewish state is a literature of protest. The stories point to weaknesses, betrayals, and failures, and only seldom to a few outstanding leaders and reformers who summoned the nation back to higher goals and worthier ideals than they had achieved. The prophets, with their decisive invective and threats, are more characteristic of the voices from this past than are the words of epic storytellers and poets of triumphant success. By the time of the deuteronomists, Israel felt itself to be lingering under judgment and in need of a new beginning and a return to more fundamental values than it currently embraced. It looked for the recapturing of such values and ideals in the figure and teaching of Moses.

The warnings and admonitions set out here by the deuteronomists were not speculative probings in the darkness, but were themselves the result of serious reflection and deep, heart-searching questions concerning the mysterious nature of evil and the possibilities of self-deception that every human being must feel. There is a mystery of iniquity that means that it is one thing to promulgate good laws and another to ensure that they are obeyed. It is relatively easy to teach high ideals, but another story altogether when it comes to winning acceptance for them. Kings may celebrate righteousness and justice as the very foundations on which their thrones rest, but that celebration does not prevent them from following in the footsteps of Ahab. Loyalty to one LORD God could quickly become confused and undermined by fear of magical powers and age-old respect for local traditions and conventions. The deuteronomic portrait of the actions of Jeroboam I, whatever its precise historical basis, is profoundly insightful (1 Kings 12). The capacity for pandering to human weakness and naïveté may cloud the vision of better things for any community. Nations may be born in moments of splendid insight and glorious endeavor, only to perish in a wasteland of disillusionment and self-deception. The modern social historian and shrewd observer of behavior will find similar enough pictures of the human scene in our time.

In the shaping of these deuteronomic sermons, the repetition of the emphatic conditional warning is meant with the most intense seriousness: "Take heed . . . do not forget . . . days will come when you will indeed be tempted to forget the LORD God and to set aside the divine commandments." So there is a powerful and meaningful catalog of explanations and admonitions, uttered in a highly charged rhetorical style to which every generation of Israelites was urged to pay attention. Even when all the outward signs of obedience would appear to be intact and secure, there could nevertheless arise a deceptive inner aversion to them. Those who felt most assured of their rectitude had reason to be most watchful lest they be the ones to lead Israel astray.

It is important that the spiritual depth of the deuteronomic concern to teach love for God, and to go so far as to demand that it be given with a whole heart and mind and effort, should have its counterpart in a recognition of the inwardness and deceptiveness of evil. Even circumcision itself—the physical proof of submission to the covenant of God—must be matched with a circumcision of the heart (Deut 10:16). Consciousness of the covenant and all that it stood for had to motivate the inner springs of thought and action. This was true because it is in the heart also that forgetfulness, complacency, and indifference to the love of God arise. Evil can no longer be regarded simply as the fault of society, of other people, or even of one's own past mistakes. It has to be traced deep down into the inner workings of the human heart. Wherever the deuteronomists had been nurtured in their understanding of the nature of evil, it was clearly no simple doctrine of ritual error or social oppression. It demanded a degree of personal self-examination. It is this aspect of the deuteronomic teaching that has made it such a powerful instrument in the shaping of both Jewish and Christian piety. To suppose that the Hebrew Bible thinks of sin only in formal and external categories is to fail to heed the very warnings that Deuteronomy declares so loudly.

The second feature of these homilies is their intense moralizing of faith, which they express through repeated calls to obey the commandments. To the modern reader, it may appear self-evident that true religion is about love, honesty, truthfulness, and integrity in all aspects of conduct. Without such virtues faith and worship lose their meaning and become lifeless formalities. Yet such convictions were not normal, or widespread, in the ancient world. Even in the modern world they are less commonplace than might be supposed. Religion that promises power, but evades the insistent demands of right speaking and right dealing, possesses an ever-current appeal.

All such belief is an illusion, and the deuteronomic authors of these memorable homilies assert the point with all the passion and vigor that their rhetoric could express. Without the commandments, all faith would become empty and all devotion would be robbed of its real connection with God. The love of God can never be an excuse for evading the demands of the commandments. On the contrary, it is just such love that opened the range of possibilities for human living that the commandments disclosed.

DEUTERONOMY 12:1–26:19

THE DEUTERONOMIC LAW CODE

OVERVIEW

That a new beginning is to be found at 12:1 is evident from the clear introductory formula: "These are the statutes and ordinances. . . ." It marks the commencement of a law corpus that extends as far as 26:15. The issues dealt with by these laws can be outlined as follows: 12:1–14:21, laws dealing with unity and purity of worship; 14:22–16:17, regulations concerning the sacred divisions of time; 16:18–18:22, order within the community and the officials of the state; 19:1–21:9, matters of life and death; 22:1-30, boundaries of life and society; 23:1–25:19, matters of general conduct; and 26:1-15, first fruits and tithes.

It will be seen from this summary that a wide range of religious, personal, and social matters are dealt with. In contrast, a number of concerns that one might have anticipated to be present in a law code that aimed at being fully comprehensive are not covered. Many issues relating to property, marriage, and health do not appear, whereas some of the issues that are covered appear to be relatively peripheral. Nevertheless, a comparison of the material in the deuteronomic law code with the forms and content of other ancient Near Eastern legal collections has proved highly instructive.

The Date of the Code of Deuteronomy 12–26. With the rise of a historical-critical approach to the study of the book of Deuteronomy in the nineteenth and early twentieth centuries it became a widely accepted opinion among scholars, to the point of becoming almost a consensus conclusion, that the law code of chaps. 12–26 represented the oldest part of the book of Deuteronomy. It was widely regarded as the "original" Deuteronomy. The introduction of chaps. 5–11 and the epilogue of chaps. 27–32 were then regarded as later expansions of this original text. The historical "preamble" of chaps. 1–3 could

then be taken as a still later addition, with 4:1-40 being brought in as one of the very latest expansions to the book. Such a comprehensive set of conclusions regarding the literary growth of the book, however, cannot now be sustained quite in this form, even though no firm consensus has been able to replace it.

Many of the observations that gave rise to this reconstruction of a straightforward process of aggregation of the material remain valid, even though the conclusions based on them must now be viewed with circumspection. Undoubtedly there is material of varying dates set both in the introductory chaps. of 5–11 and in the laws of chaps. 12–26. Reconstructing a precise literary chronology of this development, however, is fraught with uncertainty. Moreover, the belief that much of the material in Deuteronomy, including some of the most influential theological developments to be found in chaps. 12–26, is to be dated after the debacle of 587 BCE had occurred must now be seriously considered. Whereas the earlier critical views of the growth of Deuteronomy fully allowed for the presence of post–587 material in the framework of the book, it must now be regarded as certain that this observation applies to the code as well.

This is the case not only in respect of the prominent issue of the law of centralization of the cultus (12:1-28), but also in regard to the constitutional regulation for the monarchy (17:14-20). We cannot then simply draw the conclusion that the laws of chaps. 12–26 were in their present form before the introduction and epilogue were added to them.

The Diversity of Laws in Deuteronomy 12–26. The reader of the law code of chaps. 12–26 will be struck by the sharp contrasts that are evidenced within it. The extreme severity of the punishments prescribed for those who fail to maintain the purity of worship demanded in 12:1–14:21 contrasts starkly with the emphasis on love and charity that emerges in other sections of the legislation (e.g., 15:7-11). Moreover, the relatively humane and practical attitude toward non-Israelites, whether resident aliens or members of a foreign nation (e.g., 23:3-6), contrasts with the barbarism that demands the extermination of the previous inhabitants of the land (12:30-32; 13:12-60). Overall, too, the intermingling of rules concerning the conduct of worship and the observance of prescribed festivals mixes awkwardly with detailed instructions for the administration of law in a precise juridical sense.

When examined more closely still, it is striking that the formal administration of law does not lie securely in the hands of one single set of officials. Instead there is a threefold division between the authority of established officials appointed to administer law, elders of the community, and levitical priests, since a number of legal responsibilities are assigned to them as a court of last resort. Clearly at varying stages each of these groups could become involved in examining and adjudicating both civil disputes and criminal offenses.[59]

We must also consider the question of the precise literary and social character of the law code of chaps. 12–26. In what sense is it a law code, and for whom, precisely, was it written? It has already been noted that its overall character can be described as one of prescribing a "polity" for a nation-state.[60] It is clearly not simply a handbook for legal officials, since it is addressed to responsible adult members of the Israelite community more widely. It deals with several matters that would broadly have come under the purview of the levitical priests concerning the timing of the major religious festivals and the activities to be undertaken at them. Included also, however, are matters relating to family law, including marriage obligations and questions involving inheritance. Domestic arrangements too, therefore, fall within its scope. It is wide ranging, if not properly comprehensive, and shows every sign of having been built up from more than one source over an extended period of time.

A further feature of the code is that it includes some rulings of a highly theoretical character that still carry the appearance of being unworkable. This concerns such matters as the laws of debt release (15:1-11). There is good reason to question whether the brutal laws aimed at the extermination of apostate members of the community could ever seriously have been implemented on a wide scale under the safeguards laid down for capital crimes, such as murder and rape. They appear more to be intended as a deterrent than as a workable set of laws. Their threatened penalties are more in line with the intense passion and rhetoric of the sermons in the introduction than with the cautionary safeguards of the laws dealing with crimes of violence.

The Deuteronomic Law Code and the Book of the Covenant of Exod 20:22–23:19.

In many of its judicial rulings, the deuteronomic law code shows connections and affinities with the similar collection of laws in Exod 20:22–23:19, which has come to be known as "the Book of the Covenant."[61] This was clearly the earliest Israelite law collection that was given a formal statutory position in Israel's legal administration. It shows many points of contact with similar law collections of the ancient Near East, making it evident that a long history of keeping written records of legal decisions existed and was familiar to the ancient Israelites. That this code of laws could have been composed and used in the period when Israel was still a tribal society, as argued by M. Noth,[62] is doubtful. Rather it must itself have arisen under a period of monarchic rule, probably in northern Israelite territory, among a governmental circle familiar with Near Eastern practice.

For an understanding of the deuteronomic laws it is important to recognize that the evidence points uniformly to the conclusion that the deuteronomic material is later than that of the Book of the Covenant and that, in part, the deuteronomic laws were designed to expand, clarify, and, where necessary, modify the rulings of the Book

---

59. See J. C. Gertz, *Die Gerichtsorganisation Israels im deuteronomistischen Gesetz*, FRLANT 165 (Göttingen: Vandenhoeck & Ruprecht, 1994).

60. L. Perlitt, "Der Staatsgedanke im Deuteronomium," in *Language and Theology in the Bible: Essays in Honour of James Barr*, ed. S. E. Balentine and J. Barton (Oxford: Oxford University Press, 1994) 182-98.

61. E. Otto, "Vom Bundesbuch zum Deuteronomium. Die deuteronomische Redaktion in Dtn 12-26," in *Biblische Theologie und gesellschaftliche Wandel.Festschrift für N. Lohfink, S.J.*, ed. G. Braulik, W. Gross, and S. McEvenue (Freiburg: Herder Verlag, 1993) 260-78.

62. M. Noth, "The Laws in the Pentateuch: Their Assumptions and Meaning," in *The Laws of the Pentateuch and Other Essays,* trans. D. R. Ap-Thomas (Edinburgh: Oliver & Boyd, 1966) 1-107.

of the Covenant. It is certain, therefore, that the deuteronomic lawmakers were able to draw upon the older law collection.[63]

The Deuteronomic Law Code and the Ten Commandments. Significant for present understanding of the nature of the code of chaps. 12–26 are the indications that the ordering of its legal material, with minor modifications and adaptations, is structured on the basis of the Ten Commandments. This has been argued by Braulik[64] and is set out in the work of Olson,[65] who lists the links with the commandments as follows:

1. First Commandment—Deut 12:1–13:18, No Other gods to Be Worshiped.

2. Second Commandment—14:1-21, God's Name to Be Honored.

3. Third Commandment—14:22–16:17, The Sabbath to Be Remembered.

4. Fourth Commandment—16:18–18:22, Parents and Civil Authority to Be Respected.

5. Fifth Commandment—19:1–22:8, Issues of Life and Death.

6. Sixth Commandment—22:9–23:18, Prohibition of Adultery.

7. Seventh Commandment—23:19–24:7, Prohibition of Theft.

8. Eighth Commandment—24:8–25:4, Prohibition of False Testimony.

9. Ninth Commandment—25:5-12, Prohibition of Coveting a Neighbor's Wife.

10. Tenth Commandment—25:13–26:15, Prohibition of Inordinate Desiring.

The possibility of such a recognition simply confirms what we can in any case readily deduce from the theological emphases of the book of Deuteronomy: that the deuteronomic "law, Torah" par excellence is embodied in the Ten Commandments. The broader spectrum of laws and religious regulations set out in the law code, and that in many cases correlate directly with legislative material in ancient Near Eastern law codes, are to be interpreted as an amplification of these commandments.

Of great significance for understanding the structure of Deuteronomy 12–26 is the fact that the particular issues that fall under a particular commandment heading are not always transparently clear. Moreover, there are certainly some rulings that fall outside any such watertight listing, either because they have been inserted secondarily or because they form "link" passages, assisting in forming a bridge between separate groups of rulings. It would then appear to be the case that the major legal "source" for the deuteronomic legislation has been provided by the older Book of the Covenant, but this required substantial revision and amplification in order to render it a more suitable guidebook for the post–587 restoration of Israel. In such a light, the ordering of chaps. 12–26 to conform to the pattern of the Ten Commandments can only have represented a stage of final redaction.

The Deuteronomic Law Code and Ancient Near Eastern Laws. There are close affinities between the form of many of the legislative pronouncements contained in Deuteronomy 12–26 and that of ancient Near Eastern law codes. Predominantly these are a type of "case law" (or casuistic law, to use A. Alt's terminology)[66] in which a particular offense is described as a hypothetical event, and the appropriate action to be taken by way of imposing punishment is laid down. It would certainly appear that the source for the determining of such considered judgments lies in records of actual cases dealt with. In any case, the connection with the legal tradition of the ancient Near East was already initiated in the Book of the Covenant and so is simply carried further in the deuteronomic revisions of this.

Interspersed with properly legal pronouncements in Deuteronomy is a wide variety of religious instructions concerned with requirements for worship as well as exhortations and provisions for matters of state concerning the institution of kingship and the role of prophets. It comes as a surprise that Moses' name is absent from the laws, although the framework implies that he is the

---

63. See E. Otto, *Theologische Ethik des Alten Testaments,* 175-208; and "Aspects of Legal Reforms and Reformulations in Ancient Cuneiform and Israelite Law," in *Theory and Method in Biblical and Cuneiform Law,* ed. B. M. Levinson, JSOTSup 181 (Sheffield: Sheffield Academic, 1994) 160-96.

64. G. Braulik, "The Sequence of Laws in Deuteronomy 12–26 and in the Decalogue," in *A Song of Power and the Power of Song: Essays on the Book of Deuteronomy,* ed. D. L. Christensen, Sources for Biblical and Theological Study 3 (Winona Lake: Eisenbrauns, 1993) 313-35; and "Zur Abfolge der Gesetze in Deuteronomium 16,18–21,23. Weitere Beobachtungen," *Biblica* 69 (1988) 63-91.

65. Dennis T. Olson, *Deuteronomy and the Death of Moses,* OBT (Minneapolis: Fortress, 1994).

66. A. Alt, "The Origins of Israelite Law," in *Essays on Old Testament History and Religion,* trans. R. A. Wilson (Oxford: Blackwell, 1966) 88-103.

spokesman of them. This is then reinforced in the law dealing with false prophecy in 18:15-22, which presumes the direct speech of Moses as being himself a true prophet. In other respects, the laws are anonymous, although they are throughout expressed with an absolute level of authority commensurate with their origin as divinely given and ordained.[67]

It is predominantly the presence of provisions of a cultic nature that betrays unmistakably their origin in a situation after the catastrophe of 587 BCE, which effectively put an end to the old Israelite state and with it an established temple cultus. All the indications are that what we are presented with in the law code of Deuteronomy 12–26 is a programmatic legislative document designed for the administration of a restored state of Israel after the debacle that had brought an end to the old kingdom. Its basis, however, lies in an earlier

document of a predominantly juridical nature, showing close affinities with Mesopotamian legal practice and originating in the first half of the seventh century BCE. That this original "proto-Deuteronomy" was already in existence to enable it to form the basis for Josiah's reform in the latter half of that century would appear highly probable. However, it underwent considerable expansion during the latter half of the sixth century to form the present code of chaps. 12–26. Certainly the religious and nationalistic circle behind Josiah's reform also stand behind the book of Deuteronomy.

In this law code, as in the case of the book as a whole, a central core of material that bears a direct relationship to the long-standing tradition of written law in the ancient Near East has been adapted and expanded by its incorporation into a distinctively Israelite framework and structure. What was initially a system of legal administrative rulings compiled at a time of fundamental national and legal reform has been developed into a program for the renewal of Israel after a period of national disaster.

67. N. Lohfink, "Das Deuteronomium; Jahwegesetz oder Mosegesetz? Die Subjektzuordnung bei Woitern für 'Gesetz' in Dtn und in der dtr Literatur," *Studien zum Deuteronomium und zur deuteronomistischen Literatur III*, SBA 20 (Stuttgart: Katholisches Bibelwerk, 1991) 157-66.

DEUTERONOMY 12:1–14:21, LAWS DEALING WITH THE UNITY AND PURITY OF WORSHIP

Deuteronomy 12:1-28, The Law of the Central Sanctuary

NIV	NRSV
12 These are the decrees and laws you must be careful to follow in the land that the LORD, the God of your fathers, has given you to possess—as long as you live in the land. ²Destroy completely all the places on the high mountains and on the hills and under every spreading tree where the nations you are dispossessing worship their gods. ³Break down their altars, smash their sacred stones and burn their Asherah poles in the fire; cut down the idols of their gods and wipe out their names from those places.	**12** These are the statutes and ordinances that you must diligently observe in the land that the LORD, the God of your ancestors, has given you to occupy all the days that you live on the earth.
⁴You must not worship the LORD your God in their way. ⁵But you are to seek the place the LORD your God will choose from among all your tribes to put his Name there for his dwelling. To that	2You must demolish completely all the places where the nations whom you are about to dispossess served their gods, on the mountain heights, on the hills, and under every leafy tree. ³Break down their altars, smash their pillars, burn their sacred poles[a] with fire, and hew down the idols of their gods, and thus blot out their name from their places. ⁴You shall not worship the LORD your

a Heb *Asherim*

NIV

place you must go; ⁶there bring your burnt offerings and sacrifices, your tithes and special gifts, what you have vowed to give and your freewill offerings, and the firstborn of your herds and flocks. ⁷There, in the presence of the LORD your God, you and your families shall eat and shall rejoice in everything you have put your hand to, because the LORD your God has blessed you.

⁸You are not to do as we do here today, everyone as he sees fit, ⁹since you have not yet reached the resting place and the inheritance the LORD your God is giving you. ¹⁰But you will cross the Jordan and settle in the land the LORD your God is giving you as an inheritance, and he will give you rest from all your enemies around you so that you will live in safety. ¹¹Then to the place the LORD your God will choose as a dwelling for his Name—there you are to bring everything I command you: your burnt offerings and sacrifices, your tithes and special gifts, and all the choice possessions you have vowed to the LORD. ¹²And there rejoice before the LORD your God, you, your sons and daughters, your menservants and maidservants, and the Levites from your towns, who have no allotment or inheritance of their own. ¹³Be careful not to sacrifice your burnt offerings anywhere you please. ¹⁴Offer them only at the place the LORD will choose in one of your tribes, and there observe everything I command you.

¹⁵Nevertheless, you may slaughter your animals in any of your towns and eat as much of the meat as you want, as if it were gazelle or deer, according to the blessing the LORD your God gives you. Both the ceremonially unclean and the clean may eat it. ¹⁶But you must not eat the blood; pour it out on the ground like water. ¹⁷You must not eat in your own towns the tithe of your grain and new wine and oil, or the firstborn of your herds and flocks, or whatever you have vowed to give, or your freewill offerings or special gifts. ¹⁸Instead, you are to eat them in the presence of the LORD your God at the place the LORD your God will choose—you, your sons and daughters, your menservants and maidservants, and the Levites from your towns—and you are to rejoice before the LORD your God in everything you put your hand to. ¹⁹Be careful not to neglect the Levites as long as you live in your land.

NRSV

God in such ways. ⁵But you shall seek the place that the LORD your God will choose out of all your tribes as his habitation to put his name there. You shall go there, ⁶bringing there your burnt offerings and your sacrifices, your tithes and your donations, your votive gifts, your freewill offerings, and the firstlings of your herds and flocks. ⁷And you shall eat there in the presence of the LORD your God, you and your households together, rejoicing in all the undertakings in which the LORD your God has blessed you.

8You shall not act as we are acting here today, all of us according to our own desires, ⁹for you have not yet come into the rest and the possession that the LORD your God is giving you. ¹⁰When you cross over the Jordan and live in the land that the LORD your God is allotting to you, and when he gives you rest from your enemies all around so that you live in safety, ¹¹then you shall bring everything that I command you to the place that the LORD your God will choose as a dwelling for his name: your burnt offerings and your sacrifices, your tithes and your donations, and all your choice votive gifts that you vow to the LORD. ¹²And you shall rejoice before the LORD your God, you together with your sons and your daughters, your male and female slaves, and the Levites who reside in your towns (since they have no allotment or inheritance with you).

13Take care that you do not offer your burnt offerings at any place you happen to see. ¹⁴But only at the place that the LORD will choose in one of your tribes—there you shall offer your burnt offerings and there you shall do everything I command you.

15Yet whenever you desire you may slaughter and eat meat within any of your towns, according to the blessing that the LORD your God has given you; the unclean and the clean may eat of it, as they would of gazelle or deer. ¹⁶The blood, however, you must not eat; you shall pour it out on the ground like water. ¹⁷Nor may you eat within your towns the tithe of your grain, your wine, and your oil, the firstlings of your herds and your flocks, any of your votive gifts that you vow, your freewill offerings, or your donations; ¹⁸these you shall eat in the presence of the LORD your God at the place that the LORD your God will choose, you

NIV

20When the LORD your God has enlarged your territory as he promised you, and you crave meat and say, "I would like some meat," then you may eat as much of it as you want. 21If the place where the LORD your God chooses to put his Name is too far away from you, you may slaughter animals from the herds and flocks the LORD has given you, as I have commanded you, and in your own towns you may eat as much of them as you want. 22Eat them as you would gazelle or deer. Both the ceremonially unclean and the clean may eat. 23But be sure you do not eat the blood, because the blood is the life, and you must not eat the life with the meat. 24You must not eat the blood; pour it out on the ground like water. 25Do not eat it, so that it may go well with you and your children after you, because you will be doing what is right in the eyes of the LORD.

26But take your consecrated things and whatever you have vowed to give, and go to the place the LORD will choose. 27Present your burnt offerings on the altar of the LORD your God, both the meat and the blood. The blood of your sacrifices must be poured beside the altar of the LORD your God, but you may eat the meat. 28Be careful to obey all these regulations I am giving you, so that it may always go well with you and your children after you, because you will be doing what is good and right in the eyes of the LORD your God.

NRSV

together with your son and your daughter, your male and female slaves, and the Levites resident in your towns, rejoicing in the presence of the LORD your God in all your undertakings. 19Take care that you do not neglect the Levite as long as you live in your land.

20When the LORD your God enlarges your territory, as he has promised you, and you say, "I am going to eat some meat," because you wish to eat meat, you may eat meat whenever you have the desire. 21If the place where the LORD your God will choose to put his name is too far from you, and you slaughter as I have commanded you any of your herd or flock that the LORD has given you, then you may eat within your towns whenever you desire. 22Indeed, just as gazelle or deer is eaten, so you may eat it; the unclean and the clean alike may eat it. 23Only be sure that you do not eat the blood; for the blood is the life, and you shall not eat the life with the meat. 24Do not eat it; you shall pour it out on the ground like water. 25Do not eat it, so that all may go well with you and your children after you, because you do what is right in the sight of the LORD. 26But the sacred donations that are due from you, and your votive gifts, you shall bring to the place that the LORD will choose. 27You shall present your burnt offerings, both the meat and the blood, on the altar of the LORD your God; the blood of your other sacrifices shall be poured out beside[a] the altar of the LORD your God, but the meat you may eat.

28Be careful to obey all these words that I command you today,[b] so that it may go well with you and with your children after you forever, because you will be doing what is good and right in the sight of the LORD your God.

[a] Or on   [b] Gk Sam Syr: MT lacks today

COMMENTARY

The most prominent and widely discussed feature of chaps. 12–26 is to be found in its prescription for one single sanctuary where alone an altar was to be set up and where officially approved sacrifices and burnt offerings were to be made to the LORD God of Israel. In conjunction with this there is to be a corresponding freeing of the usual festive slaughter of domestic animals from cultic restraints so that their killing and eating are made into a purely secular, or profane, act (12:20-28). We have no reason to doubt that at least by the end of the seventh century BCE the identity of this central sanctuary was taken to be Jerusalem, since the reforming activities of Josiah's reign openly presuppose this.[68] Behind this, however, from the time of Solomon's building of a Temple in Jerusalem, the centralization formula is openly associated with that city in the narratives of 1 Kings (1 Kgs 11:32, 36; 14:21; 2 Kgs 21:7; 23:7).

In a formal sense it is evident that the claim to a centralized cultus is carried back by the deuteronomic legislation to the time of Moses through the prescription for the building of an ark and the setting of it in a tent of meeting. Wherever these cult objects are carried is then taken as fulfilling the requirements of a centralized cult until the time when the ark is carried into Jerusalem (2 Sam 5:6-10) and a tent was set up for it there. From that point, Jerusalem became the designated shrine, and a Temple was built there in Solomon's reign. In historical, rather than theological, perspective, it was evidently the building of the celebrated Temple in Jerusalem that provided the effective moment of cult centralization in Israel. Even this action established a pre-eminent national sanctuary, rather than an exclusive one. Not until Josiah's time were active steps taken to restore the central role of the Jerusalem sanctuary to the position of unrivaled pre-eminence it had lost. Since the Jerusalem Temple enjoyed a close association with the Davidic royal dynasty, whose power and privileges it was intended to convey, it represented a political, as much as a religious, institution. In celebrating the deity who was believed to dwell there, it necessarily also celebrated the royal house whom God was believed to have chosen to rule over Israel.

12:1-4. Verse 1 provides a fresh description of the contents of the law code of chaps. 12–26, describing it as being made up of "statutes and ordinances." This compares closely with 4:45, but lacks the designation "decrees" (NRSV), which is set alongside the other two there. The term "ordinances" (מִשְׁפָּטִים *mišpāṭîm*) must certainly identify the juridical rulings that constitute the oldest part of the law code. "Statutes" (חֻקִּים *ḥuqqîm*) would then aptly fit as a description of the regulations contained in chaps. 12–26 concerning what is specifically due to the LORD God. Horst has defined them as the "charter rights of YHWH," comparing them to a form of "Privilege Law" in which tenants of a medieval lord were given protection and rights of land use, in return for which they were required to render certain dues back to the lord.[69]

Overall the broad scope of the issues dealt with in the law code indicates that in its present form it was intended to serve as a comprehensive policy document for the religious, social, and moral life of Israel in its entirety. It addresses the reader as "you," allowing a very open transition from the narrative setting of Moses addressing the gathered community of Israel in the plains of Moab to a timeless inclusiveness in which all Israelites of all generations are included. The contents of the code, however, leave it in no doubt that Israel is assumed to constitute a nation like other nations, to possess a territory of its own, and to have the authority to administer all its civil and religious affairs, including those of the highest levels of government. From a literary and historical perspective, it is evident that this represents something of an ideal situation, since several aspects of Deuteronomy show it to be a program for reform and restoration that was shaped after the collapse of the surviving kingdom of Judah in 587 BCE. What level of freedom was allowed under the Judean puppet administration during the period of Babylonian control is unclear, as also is the extent to which the deuteronomic authors were justified in their expectations of exercising political control.

Many of the same observations apply in respect of the authority of the assumed speaker of the laws, which remains that of the person of Moses. He addresses the reader directly and refers consistently to the LORD God in third-person speech forms, but nevertheless assumes an absolute and unquestioned right to obedience on all matters—religious, civil, and personal.

After the introduction in v. 1, the preparation for establishing right and appropriate worship in the land is spelled out. Verses 2-4 affirm the bold demand that characterizes one of the more uncompromisingly assertive aspects of the deuteronomic legislation. Israel is to identify and destroy all the sanctuaries, altars, religious artifacts, and symbols that had previously existed in the land. There was to be a new beginning, achieved by

68. See R. E. Clements, "Deuteronomy and the Jerusalem Cult Tradition," *VT* 15 (1965) 300-312. The extensive discussion concerning the law of cult centralization is fully reviewed in E. Reuter, *Kultzentralisation. Entstehung und Theologie von Dtn 12,* BBB 87 (Frankfürt: Herder Verlag, 1993).

69. F. Horst, "Das Privilegrecht Jahwes," originally published in 1930 and reprinted in *Gottes Recht. Studien zum Recht im Alten Testament,* Th B12 (Munich: Kaiser Verlag, 1961) 150-54. On the two terms, see N. Lohfink, "Die huqqim umispatim und ihre Neubegrenzung durch Dtn 12,1," *Studien zum Deuteronomium und zur deuteronomistischen,* 229-56.

the rooting out of every vestige of the previous religious life that existed within it. Since there was to be no continuance of veneration for the former gods and goddesses worshiped in the land, all that pertained to them was to be sytematically destroyed. The location and character of these older sanctuaries are described in such a way as to make their identity easily recognized and so as to explain their dangerous nature.

The description of these worship sites as being "on the mountain heights" (v. 2) shows that they were predominantly of a rural character. They could apparently be found "under every leafy tree," because such vegetation revealed the life-giving fertilizing power of the deities who were believed to make available and to release their divine life-sustaining energy there. On hills and mountain heights they could be regarded as being situated near the divine realm above the clouds.

At such sanctuaries were to be found a few simple, but nevertheless essential, religious symbols: an altar where offerings could be slaughtered and burned, alongside a sacred pole and a stone pillar. These appear to denote respectively the male and female aspects of the life-producing and sustaining power of God. It seems probable that many of these sacred columnar symbols bore explicit sexual symbolism (cf. Ezek 16:17).

Side by side with these larger fixed symbols would have been images, usually set up in small sheltered structures, to which prayers could be addressed. The relative simplicity of such furnishings and their location in open-air sites outside the major cities appear to have been characteristic of them.

The rural character of these pre-Israelite sanctuaries described in the deuteronomic law is significant. Certainly before the Israelite occupation of the land all the major cities had at one time been centers of celebrated and important sanctuaries. This fact becomes evident from the stories of Israel's ancestors preserved in Genesis. Many of the city names were acquired on the basis of the sanctuaries that lay within their boundaries.

The rural character of this pattern of religion, of which the deuteronomic authors disapprove so strongly, is noteworthy since the portrait of Israelite life the deuteronomic legislation presupposes is quite markedly urban in character. This accords also with the fact that the general tradition of legal development in the ancient Near East also displays

a major role for the great cities that served as centers of administration and culture. It is not difficult to discern, therefore, that, hidden within the opposition between the Israelite Yahwistic tradition of religion promoted by Deuteronomy and that which is rejected as belonging to the former inhabitants, lie broader social and cultural differences. Deuteronomy represents a strongly centralized pattern of administration, operated through city life, whereas the amorphous, varied, but persistently popular forms of rural unofficial religion appeared to hinder and be a threat to this.

These wider considerations concerning the context in which the deuteronomic law of centralization appears indicate that it represents a strong concern to uphold and protect a form of official Israelite religion over against a more mixed and varied conglomerate of traditions and customs that possessed a more domestic and unofficial character. At the same time, this observation needs to be modified by the recognition that the strong concern of the deuteronomists that the fundamental principles of the knowledge and worship of the Lord God of Israel should be taught to children in every home and should become an inseparable feature of everyday life brought about a new form of domesticated religion. In the deuteronomic legislation, in spite of the importance attached to the centralization of the cultus, this cultus itself impinges less forcibly and directly upon the life of the people as a whole. There is a marked element of de-sacralizing and de-mythologizing the older forms and customs of Israelite religion, especially when we compare the deuteronomic theological ideas with many features still retained in the Jerusalemite psalmody.

12:5-12. The second of the features contained in this distinctive deuteronomic formula for the chosen sanctuary is that it was to be the location where the Lord God's name would be placed.[70] Much discussion has focused on this definition of the chosen sanctuary, which has clearly been designed to avoid the implication that God's actual presence could be found in the Temple. We have noted that this appears as a consequence of what had happened with the Temple's destruction

---

70. See G. von Rad, *Studies in Deuteronomy,* trans. M. Kohl, SBT 9 (London: SCM, 1953); T. N. D. Mettinger, *The Dethronement of Sabaoth: Studies in the Shem and Kabod Theologies,* ConBOT 18 (Lund: C. W. K. Gleerup, 1982) esp. 59-62.

in 587 BCE. God dwells in heaven, not on earth, but can make the divine power available to Israel through the placing of God's name. In some sense the divine name then appears as a kind of surrogate or mediating power through which God remains accessible without actually being present. An emphatic deuteronomic emphasis on God's dwelling in heaven is placed in the mouth of Solomon for the prayer at the dedication of the Temple in 1 Kgs 8:27-30. In the later priestly theology that dominates the final form of the pentateuchal accounts of the Mosaic tabernacle, the presence of God is designated as a manifestation of the divine "glory" (Exod 40:34-38).

Since the deuteronomic authors do not themselves define precisely what role the name fulfills, it is unhelpful to seek to establish a doctrine of the name as a manifestation of divine eminence that is then to be contrasted with the aspect of transcendence implicit in the idea that God dwells in heaven. The term "name" (שׁם *šēm*) is essentially no more than the deuteronomic explanation for the significance of the Temple as a place for prayer and as the designated location to which tithes and burnt offerings were to be brought. The distinctive form of "name theology" appears fundamentally to have originated as a reformulation and reinterpretation of the older formula for the setting up of an altar to the LORD in the Book of the Covenant (Exod 20:24).

In this way the directness of the identity between the earthly and the heavenly divine dwelling places is relaxed, without altogether losing the sense of the uniqueness of the earthly sanctuary and the reality of the divine power manifested there. The result was undoubtedly a strong reinforcement of the sense of otherness and transcendence belonging to the LORD as God, without forfeiting the belief in the importance of a special sanctuary with all its traditional symbolism. Clearly this deuteronomic development was conscious of the damaging effect on Israel's theology that had been brought about by the threat to, and eventual destruction of, the Jerusalem Temple at the hands of foreign armies.

The primary function for the sanctuary chosen by the LORD as God (vv. 6-7) is that it should be the location to which all Israel's offerings are brought. The list of these is comprehensive and was clearly intended to be all-inclusive in order to preclude the presentation of unorthodox offerings elsewhere. The emphasis on eating together and rejoicing in the presence of God is characteristic of the deuteronomic interpretation of worship as a celebratory occasion. That certain of the offerings would be made in acts of contrition and self-abasement is not discounted, but the more festive tone is presented as the more typical.

Verses 8-12 reiterate the basic demand set out in the preceding section, but offer a further explanation for the evident fact that Israel had not always restricted holy offerings to the one designated sanctuary chosen by the LORD God. Clearly Israelites could not have been expected to do so until they had entered and occupied the land as a nation. Only then would they enjoy the "rest" (i.e., the permanent security and peace) that God had promised to them.

12:13-19. These verses appear to be the oldest section of the pronouncements dealing with the rules for cult centralization. It reasserts the vital importance of the ruling contained in the Book of the Covenant that Israel's burnt offerings were to be presented only at the altar specifically designated for that purpose by the LORD God. More significant is its freeing of most forms of slaughter of domestic animals for food, placing them on a level with animals caught and killed in the hunt (v. 15). This action must undoubtedly be a departure from previous practice in which all forms of the slaughter of domestic animals had been bound by the tightly knit rules of the cultus. It would appear that this concession had been rendered necessary by the requirement that burnt offerings and tithes should be presented only at the designated central sanctuary.

It was necessary, in amplifying this concession for the slaughter of domestic animals for food, to make plain that it did not represent an abrogation of the tithe offering (vv. 17-19). This was still required, since its origins indicate that it was a deeply embedded feature of the concept of a natural cycle of life. As the new life of the crops appeared each season, so it was necessary that the appropriate portion should be set apart for God as a gift for the deity, the giver of life. It served also as a means of support for the levitical priesthood, and this requirement is especially reaffirmed (v. 19). What is a new and startling innovation in the deuteronomic reformulation of the demand for the tithe is the concession spelled out in 14:24-27, decreeing that, if the distance to the central sanctuary should prove too far away to carry the tithe offering there, then it was to be sold and fresh produce bought so that it would remain possible to hold a festive meal in the presence of God.

The designation of the appointed sanctuary leaves no doubt that one single sanctuary was intended (vv. 14, 18), and the context in which this demand is set shows that it was closely connected with, if not originally intended to uphold, the concern to preclude an uncontrolled, haphazard range of cultic activities. Older non-Israelite forms of ritual activity, linked almost certainly with other deities besides the LORD God of Israel, would continue if there were not a tightly monitored central priestly oversight. It is this that the deuteronomic authors were concerned to establish.

The injunction to be careful to show special favor to the Levites (vv. 18-19) was evidently inserted at this point because they had at one time resided close to the sanctuaries where they would assist in the presentation of the festal offerings. They would then naturally expect to be invited to share in the meal in return for this help. The freeing of some animal slaughter from the strict religious requirements pertaining to offerings created a situation in which the needs of the Levites could easily be overlooked. Their mention here introduces one of several instances where Deuteronomy points to the activities of Levites that were not exclusively priestly in character. Although the Levites were to serve as priests, the service of the sanctuary was evidently not their only duty within Israel.

Overall the purpose of the demand for cult centralization would appear to be clearly evident. It was to maintain a pure cultus. Nor can we doubt that the sanctuary where this demand was implemented was Jerusalem. But was it always intended to be so? The recognition that many aspects of the deuteronomic legislation show a northern Israelite background has suggested that possibly some major sanctuary in the north was originally the chosen location. Yet it would seem extremely unlikely that this should have been the case, not least because Josiah's reforming activities specially targeted the chief rival sanctuary to Jerusalem for destruction and desecration (2 Kgs 23:15-20). If some other location than Jerusalem were the intended location, then no adequate evidence now remains to defend such a claim. On the contrary, not only was Jerusalem assumed to be the chosen location, but also there is a wealth of evidence to support the belief that the claims to the unique pre-eminence of Jerusalem-Zion as the sanctuary uniquely chosen and blessed by the LORD God had a very long history in Israel. It had only been subjected to question when the two kingdoms were divided (1 Kgs 12:25-33).

How far King Josiah's reign witnessed an effective centralizing of worship in Jerusalem remains historically unclear. That some major attempt was made to refurbish and reinvigorate the unique claims of the Jerusalem Temple in his day appears certain. Yet it was in the wake of the Temple's destruction in 587 BCE that the demand for centralization in Jerusalem acquired a fresh importance. This event also gave renewed impetus to such a demand, precisely because it had put a serious question mark against this sanctuary. The very trust that had been placed in it and the high-flown celebration of its power to secure Israel's defense against all enemies had proved misdirected. Moreover, its links with the monarchy and with Davidic dynastic rights to kingly status over Israel had also proved ill founded. After 587 BCE there were many reasons why the Temple site in Jerusalem should be abandoned along with the ruined building. The deuteronomic demand for the retention of the practice of bringing tithes to Jerusalem and prohibiting ritual slaughter at any other sanctuary secured a place for Jerusalem in Israel's future.

Certainly the interpretation of Jerusalem's role as a sanctuary was much changed and its function within the religious life of the community was much revised with it. Nevertheless the deuteronomic law of cult centralization effectively defended Jerusalem's unique place within Israel's cultic history, exalting it as the sole legitimate place to which tithes and sacrificial offerings could be brought.

12:20-28. Taken together the twofold concessions toward a secularizing and demythologizing of two fundamental cultic activities—the presentation of the tithes and the slaughter of domestic animals for food—represent a major shift in cultic legislation introduced by Deuteronomy. The concessions have, in the first instance, been rendered necessary for the reason that the law code itself describes: "If the place where the LORD your God will choose to put his name is too far from you" (v. 21; cf. 14:24). That there were other important considerations after the Temple had been destroyed cannot be doubted. It also appears likely that for whoever had formulated the deuteronomic legislation, the older cultic notions of holiness held little attraction. For all their attention to matters of ritual and cultic life, their intellectual world had closer affinities with that of lay administrators than with that of a class of priests. So there is throughout many aspects of their work a remarkable atmosphere of demythologization and de-sacralization of life. It cannot then have been too difficult a step for them to take to value most cultic actions as expressions of gratitude and affection for God, rather than of obligatory encroachment into the mysterious sphere of a mystic life force that permeated the natural world.[71]

There was, however, an inevitable danger in granting permission for a regular pattern of non-

71. See M. Weinfeld, *Deuteronomy and the Deuteronomic School* (Oxford: Oxford University Press, 1972) 191-224.

cultic slaughter of animals. The very roots of all such ritual actions that involved the taking of life and the shedding of blood, even that of domestic animals, was that blood was regarded as sacred. No blood could be shed in total innocence, since it required interference with the very life force of the natural order of the world. Was it not likely, then, that if such slaughter was not undertaken with the blessing of the LORD God of Israel it would be performed in the name of some other deity? Such would appear to be the fear behind the special provisions and distinctions laid down in vv. 20-28. A careful distinction was to be made between the profane slaughter of animals that was now permitted and the sacred donations and burnt offerings that were to be brought to the central sanctuary (vv. 26-27). The latter were sacred and required a cloak of ritual protection. The former were not and needed no such cultic situation or assistance. The one proviso remained that, since the blood was sacred, it was to be poured out on the ground (v. 24). It was not to be consumed.

REFLECTIONS

The law of the central sanctuary in Deuteronomy 12 marks the most obvious and readily recognizable platform of the deuteronomic legislation in the entire book. The claim for cultic centralization at one single sanctuary highlights a major attempt to regularize and control forms of ritual activity and cultic expression at the foremost of Israel's shrines. The theme of centralization, used as a means of establishing uniformity and of eliminating deviations and a plurality of religious expressions, represents a combination of ideological and pragmatic considerations.

As a testimony to the inner spiritual development of Israel's faith, the forthright demand for the centralization of all cultic activity at one single sanctuary represents something of an extreme development. Coming as it undoubtedly did at the very close of a period when the Temple of Jerusalem had dominated the religious life of Judah, it represented a triumph for the unique claims of this historical sanctuary. It might have been expected, therefore, that the deuteronomic theology of the sanctuary and its cultus would have been characterized by the themes of Mt. Zion, its unique claims to divine pre-eminence, and its assurance of a unique measure of divine protection. In fact, we should certainly have expected it to express in full measure the Zion theology that is still preserved for us in the celebratory psalms of Zion (especially Psalms 46, 48, 84). Yet it does not do this, and these particular Zion themes are wholly absent from the deuteronomic formulations of faith. At most the notion that one particular sanctuary had been especially "chosen" by the LORD God of Israel retains the outer shell of such a Zion theology.

Even more startling, the very concept of a divine "presence" at the sanctuary and the assurance that this one sanctuary could offer a blessing found at no other place have been abandoned. They have been replaced by a theology of the divine "name," linking the sanctuary to a relationship with the LORD God in which prayer and moral obedience held pride of place. Even though the chosen sanctuary represents something external to the worshiper, it nevertheless demands a relationship with God in which an inner spiritual seeking and remembering are as important as the outward location. It could then be boldly asserted that the significance of the chosen sanctuary is as valid for those who remained at a distance from it as for those who daily lived their lives in its shadow. Even the concept of dwelling in the house of God took on a broader spiritual meaning.

It is here, more profoundly than in any other of its assertions, that the remarkable tensions and paradoxes of the deuteronomic theology and spirituality appear. Because it was to stand alone as the sole valid place to which offerings could be brought and where the name of God would be established on earth, the central sanctuary is exalted in importance in Deuteronomy above anything that had previously pertained to Israelite worship. At the same time, the role played by this one solitary house of prayer and ritual service was balanced against the opening out and domestication of religious activity, so that every home, and even every child's nursery, would be a place where the name of God would be remembered and the commandments taught. As the cultus became more tightly controlled and monitored, much of its purpose and usefulness was replaced by a far simpler work of teaching, nurturing, and honoring the name and demands of God in everyday life. In a real sense the doors of the inner sanctuary of the Temple, which the high priest alone was permitted to enter, were opened and the presence of God, which was revered and honored there, was made available across the length and breadth of Israel.

Such a religious development became all the more important because the next generation of Israelites, instead of crossing the River Jordan to enter the land as Joshua and the first generation after Moses had done, found themselves crossing in the other direction into exile. It was understandable that they could be dismissed and even ridiculed by some as those who "had gone far from the LORD" (Ezekiel 11). It was the deuteronomic theology that assured them that they had not gone beyond the range of the divine care and love. They could, indeed, "sing the songs of Zion in a foreign land" (Psalm 137). God would maintain their cause.

Deuteronomy 12:29–13:18, The Perpetual Temptation: Apostasy

NIV

[29]The LORD your God will cut off before you the nations you are about to invade and dispossess. But when you have driven them out and settled in their land, [30]and after they have been destroyed before you, be careful not to be ensnared by inquiring about their gods, saying, "How do these nations serve their gods? We will do the same." [31]You must not worship the LORD your God in their way, because in worshiping their gods, they do all kinds of detestable things the LORD hates. They even burn their sons and daughters in the fire as sacrifices to their gods.

[32]See that you do all I command you; do not add to it or take away from it.

13 [1]If a prophet, or one who foretells by dreams, appears among you and announces to you a miraculous sign or wonder, [2]and if the sign or wonder of which he has spoken takes place, and he says, "Let us follow other gods"

NRSV

[29]When the LORD your God has cut off before you the nations whom you are about to enter to dispossess them, when you have dispossessed them and live in their land, [30]take care that you are not snared into imitating them, after they have been destroyed before you: do not inquire concerning their gods, saying, "How did these nations worship their gods? I also want to do the same." [31]You must not do the same for the LORD your God, because every abhorrent thing that the LORD hates they have done for their gods. They would even burn their sons and their daughters in the fire to their gods. [32a]You must diligently observe everything that I command you; do not add to it or take anything from it.

13 [b]If prophets or those who divine by dreams appear among you and promise you omens or portents, [2]and the omens or the portents de-

a Ch 13.1 in Heb   *b* Ch 13.2 in Heb

NIV

(gods you have not known) "and let us worship them," [3]you must not listen to the words of that prophet or dreamer. The LORD your God is testing you to find out whether you love him with all your heart and with all your soul. [4]It is the LORD your God you must follow, and him you must revere. Keep his commands and obey him; serve him and hold fast to him. [5]That prophet or dreamer must be put to death, because he preached rebellion against the LORD your God, who brought you out of Egypt and redeemed you from the land of slavery; he has tried to turn you from the way the LORD your God commanded you to follow. You must purge the evil from among you.

[6]If your very own brother, or your son or daughter, or the wife you love, or your closest friend secretly entices you, saying, "Let us go and worship other gods" (gods that neither you nor your fathers have known, [7]gods of the peoples around you, whether near or far, from one end of the land to the other), [8]do not yield to him or listen to him. Show him no pity. Do not spare him or shield him. [9]You must certainly put him to death. Your hand must be the first in putting him to death, and then the hands of all the people. [10]Stone him to death, because he tried to turn you away from the LORD your God, who brought you out of Egypt, out of the land of slavery. [11]Then all Israel will hear and be afraid, and no one among you will do such an evil thing again.

[12]If you hear it said about one of the towns the LORD your God is giving you to live in [13]that wicked men have arisen among you and have led the people of their town astray, saying, "Let us go and worship other gods" (gods you have not known), [14]then you must inquire, probe and investigate it thoroughly. And if it is true and it has been proved that this detestable thing has been done among you, [15]you must certainly put to the sword all who live in that town. Destroy it completely,[a] both its people and its livestock. [16]Gather all the plunder of the town into the middle of the public square and completely burn the town and all its plunder as a whole burnt offering to the LORD your God. It is to remain a ruin forever, never to be rebuilt. [17]None of those condemned

[a]15 The Hebrew term refers to the irrevocable giving over of things or persons to the LORD, often by totally destroying them.

NRSV

clared by them take place, and they say, "Let us follow other gods" (whom you have not known) "and let us serve them," [3]you must not heed the words of those prophets or those who divine by dreams; for the LORD your God is testing you, to know whether you indeed love the LORD your God with all your heart and soul. [4]The LORD your God you shall follow, him alone you shall fear, his commandments you shall keep, his voice you shall obey, him you shall serve, and to him you shall hold fast. [5]But those prophets or those who divine by dreams shall be put to death for having spoken treason against the LORD your God—who brought you out of the land of Egypt and redeemed you from the house of slavery—to turn you from the way in which the LORD your God commanded you to walk. So you shall purge the evil from your midst.

[6]If anyone secretly entices you—even if it is your brother, your father's son or[a] your mother's son, or your own son or daughter, or the wife you embrace, or your most intimate friend—saying, "Let us go worship other gods," whom neither you nor your ancestors have known, [7]any of the gods of the peoples that are around you, whether near you or far away from you, from one end of the earth to the other, [8]you must not yield to or heed any such persons. Show them no pity or compassion and do not shield them. [9]But you shall surely kill them; your own hand shall be first against them to execute them, and afterwards the hand of all the people. [10]Stone them to death for trying to turn you away from the LORD your God, who brought you out of the land of Egypt, out of the house of slavery. [11]Then all Israel shall hear and be afraid, and never again do any such wickedness.

[12]If you hear it said about one of the towns that the LORD your God is giving you to live in, [13]that scoundrels from among you have gone out and led the inhabitants of the town astray, saying, "Let us go and worship other gods," whom you have not known, [14]then you shall inquire and make a thorough investigation. If the charge is established that such an abhorrent thing has been done among you, [15]you shall put the inhabitants of that town to the sword, utterly destroying it

[a] Sam Gk Compare Tg: MT lacks your father's son or

NIV

things[a] shall be found in your hands, so that the LORD will turn from his fierce anger; he will show you mercy, have compassion on you, and increase your numbers, as he promised on oath to your forefathers, [18]because you obey the LORD your God, keeping all his commands that I am giving you today and doing what is right in his eyes.

[a]17 The Hebrew term refers to the irrevocable giving over of things or persons to the LORD, often by totally destroying them.

NRSV

and everything in it—even putting its livestock to the sword. [16]All of its spoil you shall gather into its public square; then burn the town and all its spoil with fire, as a whole burnt offering to the LORD your God. It shall remain a perpetual ruin, never to be rebuilt. [17]Do not let anything devoted to destruction stick to your hand, so that the LORD may turn from his fierce anger and show you compassion, and in his compassion multiply you, as he swore to your ancestors, [18]if you obey the voice of the LORD your God by keeping all his commandments that I am commanding you today, doing what is right in the sight of the LORD your God.

COMMENTARY

The admonitory address in 12:29–13:18 represents the reverse side of the concern for purity of religious practice and integrity that motivates the law of the central sanctuary. It reinforces this with a style loosely based on typical case-law legislation: "If prophets arise . . . if anyone . . . if you hear. . . ."

12:29-32. This introductory unit to the regulations dealing with persons who seek to lead Israel into apostasy explains why such fierce regulations were necessary. The barbarism of the practices that were associated with the gods worshiped by the previous inhabitants included horrifying forms of child sacrifice.

This repugnant practice, the precise details of which remain obscure, even though they are clearly credible, constitutes an important aspect of the deuteronomic polemic against the older religious life of the land.[72] It was clearly based on firm knowledge and recognizable traditions. At several points the deuteronomic polemic concerning certain of Judah's rulers mentions that the kings were guilty of such practices (Ahaz, 2 Kgs 16:3; 17:31; Manasseh, 2 Kgs 21:6). That the practice was more widespread is attested by the prophet Jeremiah (Jer 7:31), in whose time the high place of Tophet, in the valley of Ben-Hinnom in Jerusalem, is identified as the location where such actions were carried out. In several OT

passages such actions are linked with Moloch (or Molk). Later Judaism, as testified by the translation of this word in the Greek and Latin versions, took this to be the name of a deity to whom such child offerings were dedicated. More probably it designates the type of offering intended, or even its purpose in fulfillment of a vow.

The prophet Ezekiel (Ezek 20:25-26; cf. Ezek 16:20) refers to the currency in Israel of an evil law (= religious custom) that was assumed to require the sacrifice of a firstborn child. This would appear to be a reference to the "giving" to God of the firstborn child in Exod 22:28-29 (cf. Exod 13:1-2). That the firstborn of animals were sacrificed to God is certain (Exod 13:11-15; 34:19-20) However, it is clear that in historical times such actions concerning the sacrifice of human infants were discounted by the claim that the firstborn could be redeemed. Overall the evidence concerning any widespread prevalence of the sacrifice of human infants, either to some non-Israelite deity or even in the name of the LORD was not widespread. Yet certainly such actions did take place (see 1 Kgs 16:34; 2 Kgs 3:27), although the instances that provide circumstantial detail show it to have been a relatively rare occurrence. That child sacrifice was practiced seems certain nevertheless, and the deuteronomic author here has undoubtedly made use of this knowledge to justify the severity of the actions called for in eliminating all

72. See R. de Vaux, *Ancient Israel: Its Life and Institutions,* trans. John McHugh (London: Darton, Longman & Todd, 1961) 441-46.

traces of the worship of the former inhabitants of the land.

13:1-5. It is evident that the activities of prophets could not easily be regulated. Their voices could be raised in support of novelties and innovations in religion as powerfully as in support of a return to fundamental loyalties. The mechanism of appeal employed by prophets was that displayed in their own preaching and rhetorical skills. There could therefore be false prophets as well as true ones. Such truth and falseness lay not only in whether they were able to foresee the outcome of events, but also in their claims to disclose a valid understanding of God's will for human society. So prophets might appear who would turn the minds of people back to the veneration of discarded gods and goddesses or to the practices, now cloaked in the name of the LORD God of Israel, that had marked the worship of these ancient deities.

With its interest in establishing firm lines of control over the entire range of Israel's religious life, it is no surprise that Deuteronomy is alone among Israel's law books in including restrictions and regulations that sought to distinguish the work of true prophets from false. The confrontation between the prophets Jeremiah and Hananiah recounted in Jeremiah 28 shows how two contrasting messages, each purporting to derive from the LORD God of Israel, could cause confusion. The legislation in Deut 13:1-5, however, is concerned more directly with the activities of prophets who urged the worship of other deities besides the LORD. That this should have happened is wholly intelligible, but becomes especially so if we recognize that this ruling has arisen in the wake of the destruction of the Jerusalem Temple by the Babylonian armies. Such an action would inevitably have been popularly interpreted as a sign of the powerlessness of Israel's God to protect even the Temple upon which the divine name was set.

In the wake of such an event there must have been many prophetic voices loudly declaring that such a disaster had happened because the "old gods" of the land had been offended at having been abandoned. The very zeal for the exclusive worship of the LORD would have been turned into an argument for its own mistakenness. In the deuteronomic ruling, such false prophets are condemned and repudiated. Their falseness is seen to lie in their attempts to seduce Israelites away from

an exclusive worship of the LORD as God. Whatever their apparent credibility as prophets and dream interpreters, if they incited Israelites to acknowledge any other god than the LORD God of Israel they were automatically to be identified as false and punished accordingly. This was to take the form of public execution by stoning (v. 5).

In the description of the false prophets, it is striking that they are regarded as being closely allied to interpreters of dreams (v. 1), which would appear to be a rather limited form of semi-religious activity. It is otherwise only in popular wisdom tales that dream interpretation receives wide attention in the biblical tradition, despite its similarity to prophecy in its claim to be able to foresee future events. It is primarily the mantic wisdom portrait of the figure of Daniel that otherwise links prophecy and dream interpretation closely together. In making such an association between dreams and prophetic speech, the deuteronomic authors would certainly appear to establish a significant gap between their own work as lawmakers and prophetic oracle giving. This evidence would certainly indicate that the links between these zealous reforming writings and the actual prophets was a rather tenuous one. Such a description jars considerably with the recognition that Moses was a prophet (cf. 18:15; 34:10).

Although the deuteronomists appear to have favored such vigorous and forthright prophets as Jeremiah, their own estimate of prophecy, at least in chap. 13, appears seriously compromised. While favoring those who proclaimed an uncompromising loyalty to the LORD as God, they recognized the dangers of unregulated prophecy and saw its role within the life of the nation as a relatively marginal one.

The formula used to justify the execution of false prophets ("So you shall purge the evil from your midst," v. 5) represents a particular purpose for imposing punishment that is several times used by the deuteronomic authors. It is evidently a purely religious categorization of evil and retains many of the features of the taboo-like concept of "guilt" (עָוֹן *āwōn*), which viewed it as a form of infection that could bring harmful consequences upon an entire community. By punishing the false prophets so severely, the Israelite community was thought to be protecting itself.

13:6-11. There can be no question but that

the deuteronomic authors felt the threat of apostasy to be very real and urgent, regarding it as the major challenge to the survival of Israel as a people and a massive threat to Israel's hope of retaining occupancy of the land promised to their ancestors. Much of the sense of a crisis situation and of the feeling that few people could be wholly trusted to carry out the deuteronomic demands is revealed in this further elaboration of the insistence that any person who was found to be guilty of encouraging the worship of other gods than the LORD God of Israel was to be put to death. There is a threefold pattern in what is demanded in this unit. Most striking of all is the recognition that such disloyalty to the LORD God could arise within members of one's own household. The most immediate kin—brother, sister, son, daughter, or even a person's own spouse—could be responsible for abandoning faith in the LORD and turning to other gods. So an Israelite who wished to be loyal to the nation's ancestral faith was commanded to inform upon his or her most immediate relatives, eyeing them with suspicion and reporting on even their most private conversations. Also, and in stark contrast to the more consistent deuteronomic demands for love and compassion to those who are the weaker members of society, there was to be no pity or compassion shown. Religious loyalty was to be set above every other form of kinship and community bond, and all natural feelings were to be set aside.

Another feature is also of importance. This is to be found in v. 11 and relates to the intention that the brutal punishment meted out to an offender was intended to serve as a warning to others. The victims of such a cruel repression of apostasy were to be used as examples to ensure that others were suitably impressed to take heed of the warning.

It is a point of significant legal interest to note that no provisions are laid out in line with those required for similar cases in 17:6 that a minimum of two witnesses were required for the charge to be upheld. Since informing on members from within one's closest kin group would usually require the disclosure of private information, it is evident that such supporting testimony would usually have been difficult to obtain. It must also be regarded as certain that the overall intention of this harsh legislation was to deter, and it can hardly have anticipated that

a large number of cases would ensue. Nor, in fact, are we made aware in respect of the deuteronomic law code generally what degree of effective authority the lawmakers possessed to implement their policies. There are clearly several indications that suggest that this was not high and that the exilic revision of the original deuteronomic law code was an attempt to establish guidelines and policies for a future that remained politically very uncertain. It is worthy of note that, at a later time, even so influential a figure as Nehemiah was unable to take direct action against those who flagrantly broke the sabbath rules. He had to be content simply with making their trading activities unworkable (Neh 13:15-22).

13:12-18. The last of the three cases concerning apostasy from commitment to the LORD as Israel's God envisages a situation in which entire towns are guilty of such defection. A significantly new point arises in that, in addition to the total destruction of all the inhabitants of the town, their livestock and all their possessions are to be destroyed along with them. They are regarded as having been infected with the non-Israelite religious practices, and among the spoil taken from them would certainly have been some objects of an expressly religious nature. The degree of hostility that is expressed is startling, as is the belief that a quasi-physical threat would arise from the retention of any of these objects.

The case that most immediately relates to the injunction of v. 17, "Do not let anything devoted to destruction stick to your hand," is that reported of Achan at the time of the Israelite conquest. His appropriation of a "mantle from Shinar" and a large quantity of silver and gold were held responsible for Israel's failure to capture Ai at the first attempt (Josh 7:1-26). It is only in a very extended sense that the original requirement of the so-called holy war devotion of all captured persons and objects to the "ban" (חרם *ḥērem*) can be said to cover the character and purpose of what is described here. The purpose is wholly religious in intent, regarding any object that has been associated with an alien religious tradition as dangerously unacceptable. It is fit only to be destroyed, whatever its value.

In several respects this further demand for the elimination of all objects, persons, and practices associated with the mixed religious traditions that existed in the land before the Israelites established in it their unique worship of the LORD God is surprising. It would appear, superficially at least, to be of a highly theoretical nature. Especially is this the case when the demand for the elimination of religious rivals is viewed in the actual historical context the deuteronomic authors were facing in Judah in the mid-sixth century BCE. It must, nevertheless, reveal to us something of that situation. Evidently the representatives of the pure Israelite faith that the deuteronomists strove for were not that powerful and evidently could not count on widespread support within the land. Whole towns were regarded as likely to defect from their ancestral faith. Throughout Deuteronomy we are made constantly aware that, in demanding so stringent an interpretation of what loyalty to God demanded, its authors were not only introducing a new rigidity and intolerance of defectors, but also desperately trying to secure a faith that they believed to be in danger of being lost.

In view of the appalling consequences that such cruelly harsh judgment of religious apostasy has had in the history of the interpretation of Deuteronomy,[73] it is open to question whether the authors of Deuteronomy were in any position to carry it into effect. This must certainly remain a matter of uncertainty, even though this fact does little to lessen its bitter message. Many aspects of the deuteronomic legal requirements appear to display a markedly theoretical character, setting a program for the future that it was hoped to enforce, rather than recording one that had actually shaped the life of a community. To this extent, the severity of what is demanded must certainly reflect the deep anxieties of the deuteronomic authors to impose their will upon an unwilling community.

73. See F. E. Deist, "The Dangers of Deuteronomy: A Page from the Reception History of the Book," in *Studies in Deuteronomy in Honour of C. J. Labuschagne on the Occasion of His 65th Birthday,* ed. F. Garcia Martinez et al. (Leiden: E. J. Brill, 1994) 13-30.

REFLECTIONS

The modern reader, influenced by two and a half thousand years of religious history, will perhaps experience anxiety and shock at the uncompromising intolerance and harshness with which these cruel demands are set out. One is shocked not only by the bland resort to capital punishment for purely religious offenses, but also by the lack of protection against their being abused and misapplied and the insistence that there be no feelings of compassion and pity for those so treated. The urgent necessity for religious tolerance in modern secular societies, coupled with the historical knowledge of trials and executions carried out upon many hapless victims, requires that these laws be viewed in their more limited historical context, rather than as a broad spiritual demand. Yet even in such a limited setting the reasons why they arose in ancient Israel, by whom they were invented, and how far they were actually carried into effect all remain obscure.

It is certainly important to recognize inherent dangers of such legislation. We need to read it critically, in the light of later Jewish and Christian moral ideals. It can in no way be elevated to provide a pattern for modern religious goals, and modern attempts to appeal to it, even in a modified fashion, are fraught with the gravest dangers.

The first requirement, therefore, is certainly that we should set these harsh regulations in their historical context and recognize the significance of their considerable limitations. It is almost impossible to know whether they were ever carried into effect in more than a few instances. Clearly, even the story of Achan's punishment is intended to support the legislation, rather than provide a certain historical reflection of its implementation. By the time the laws were incorporated into the deuteronomic law code, it was certainly the case that only very limited power and authority remained in the hands of the religious authorities. These laws, in their character, represent something of a middle stage between the age-old holiness restriction, exemplified in the book of Numbers, that believed God would intervene directly to punish infringements of the laws of holiness, and the rather more political assumptions of the state legislative authorities, who believed that it was their duty to protect the community from religious apostasy. After the collapse of the Judean state in 587 BCE (the most plausible period when these laws were composed), it is far from clear that the continuing political authority in Judah possessed either the will or the authority to implement such rules as are advocated by the deuteronomists.

When we ask, then, who was responsible for having composed and advocated such a harsh policy of religious uniformity and repression, it would appear that it arose among a group of reforming zealots who sought to restore Israel's national pride and religious integrity in the face of the threat of its imminent dissolution. They undoubtedly found inspiration and traditional examples for their policy in the circles of Yahwistic Levites; they may well have included some Levites among their numbers. The reforming zeal of certain prophets also gave them traditional encouragement.

These historical observations, however, do little to soften the stern rigor that is demanded as a way of countering the undoubtedly real threat of religious apostasy and national defection from faith in the LORD as Israel's God. At most we can understand such measures by reflecting that the crisis situation both in politics and in religion that the deuteronomists must certainly have faced has spawned a reaction of extreme severity. The terrible consequences of witch-hunts and religious persecutions in the much later experience of seventeenth-century Europe and North America highlight the dangers of this deuteronomic teaching.

A twofold anxiety reverberates through Deuteronomy 13. On one side lies the question of how the disasters Israel had experienced could have been avoided. On the other side is the question concerning how a repetition of such disasters in the future might be prevented. Israel's prevalent resort to idolatry and the popularity of a mixture of religious customs and activities that involved recognition of minor deities besides the LORD God appeared primarily to blame. It is the determination to eradicate such practices at whatever cost to individual lives and freedom that is expressed in this chapter.

There have been attempts to rescue some spiritual meaning and integrity for these deuteronomic demands by a form of spiritualizing interpretation. The threats and dangers the legislation seeks to counter are viewed, not as physical enemies and opponents, but as hidden spiritual enemies who are to be defeated solely by faith and continued allegiance to the one LORD God.

Nevertheless, the stratum of religious intolerance in the deuteronomic legislation is abundantly evident. The modern reader is forced to remember the terrible history of religious intolerance and the social disasters to which it has given rise, and to remember as well the critique from later New Testament and rabbinical perspectives upon what is demanded in Deuteronomy 13.

Deuteronomy 14:1-21, Maintaining the Holiness of God's Name

NIV

14 You are the children of the LORD your God. Do not cut yourselves or shave the front of your heads for the dead, [2]for you are a people holy to the LORD your God. Out of all the peoples on the face of the earth, the LORD has chosen you to be his treasured possession.

[3]Do not eat any detestable thing. [4]These are the animals you may eat: the ox, the sheep, the goat, [5]the deer, the gazelle, the roe deer, the wild goat, the ibex, the antelope and the mountain sheep.[a] [6]You may eat any animal that has a split hoof

[a]5 The precise identification of some of the birds and animals in this chapter is uncertain.

NRSV

14 You are children of the LORD your God. You must not lacerate yourselves or shave your forelocks for the dead. [2]For you are a people holy to the LORD your God; it is you the LORD has chosen out of all the peoples on earth to be his people, his treasured possession.

[3]You shall not eat any abhorrent thing. [4]These are the animals you may eat: the ox, the sheep, the goat, [5]the deer, the gazelle, the roebuck, the wild goat, the ibex, the antelope, and the mountain-sheep. [6]Any animal that divides the hoof and has the hoof cleft in two, and chews the cud, among the animals, you may eat. [7]Yet of those

NIV

divided in two and that chews the cud. [7]However, of those that chew the cud or that have a split hoof completely divided you may not eat the camel, the rabbit or the coney.[a] Although they chew the cud, they do not have a split hoof; they are ceremonially unclean for you. [8]The pig is also unclean; although it has a split hoof, it does not chew the cud. You are not to eat their meat or touch their carcasses.

[9]Of all the creatures living in the water, you may eat any that has fins and scales. [10]But anything that does not have fins and scales you may not eat; for you it is unclean.

[11]You may eat any clean bird. [12]But these you may not eat: the eagle, the vulture, the black vulture, [13]the red kite, the black kite, any kind of falcon, [14]any kind of raven, [15]the horned owl, the screech owl, the gull, any kind of hawk, [16]the little owl, the great owl, the white owl, [17]the desert owl, the osprey, the cormorant, [18]the stork, any kind of heron, the hoopoe and the bat.

[19]All flying insects that swarm are unclean to you; do not eat them. [20]But any winged creature that is clean you may eat.

[21]Do not eat anything you find already dead. You may give it to an alien living in any of your towns, and he may eat it, or you may sell it to a foreigner. But you are a people holy to the LORD your God.

Do not cook a young goat in its mother's milk.

a[7] That is, the hyrax or rock badger

NRSV

that chew the cud or have the hoof cleft you shall not eat these: the camel, the hare, and the rock badger, because they chew the cud but do not divide the hoof; they are unclean for you. [8]And the pig, because it divides the hoof but does not chew the cud, is unclean for you. You shall not eat their meat, and you shall not touch their carcasses.

[9]Of all that live in water you may eat these: whatever has fins and scales you may eat. [10]And whatever does not have fins and scales you shall not eat; it is unclean for you.

[11]You may eat any clean birds. [12]But these are the ones that you shall not eat: the eagle, the vulture, the osprey, [13]the buzzard, the kite of any kind; [14]every raven of any kind; [15]the ostrich, the nighthawk, the sea gull, the hawk of any kind; [16]the little owl and the great owl, the water hen [17]and the desert owl,[a] the carrion vulture and the cormorant, [18]the stork, the heron of any kind; the hoopoe and the bat.[b] [19]And all winged insects are unclean for you; they shall not be eaten. [20]You may eat any clean winged creature.

[21]You shall not eat anything that dies of itself; you may give it to aliens residing in your towns for them to eat, or you may sell it to a foreigner. For you are a people holy to the LORD your God.

You shall not boil a kid in its mother's milk.

a Or pelican   b Identification of several of the birds in verses 12-18 is uncertain

COMMENTARY

The fundamental requirement that Israel should worship the LORD God alone and that it should devote all offerings and tithes to this one deity at the place set apart as the sole legitimate place of worship demanded further amplification. A more detailed set of rules was needed to explain and demonstrate those varied aspects of life and activity where the holy regard for the LORD as God could be imperiled. Accordingly the distinctions between "holy" and "profane" needed to be fully defined. Entering the world where such distinctions prevailed meant entering a complex domain of categories, ideas, and demarcations that do not readily translate into comparable categories of modern life.

Verse 1 affirms, rather unexpectedly, the conviction, clearly both ancient and deeply felt, that the Israelites comprised a nation who were all "children of the LORD your God." Clearly in the deuteronomic context this affirmation was to be interpreted metaphorically, thereby asserting the close and unbreakable relationship that bound Israel to God.[74] A more carefully worded deuteronomic pronouncement of what was implicit in

74. The importance of Deuteronomy 14 as a reflection of the deuteronomic worldview is well set out by A. D. H. Mayes, "Deuteronomy 14 and the Deuteronomic World View," in Martinez, *Studies in Deuteronomy in Honour of C. J. Labuschagne on the Occasion of His 65th Birthday*, 165-82.

Israel's special relationship to God is then given in terms of Israel's having been chosen by God; thus it had become God's uniquely treasured possession. All of this meant that Israel was holy to the LORD God (v. 2).

Thus it is possible to see this entire section as an elaboration of the second commandment, defining what it meant for Israel to uphold the correct use of the divine name.[75] Since the name of God was required to be set apart as holy, the proper observance of all that was implicit in holiness formed an indispensable guideline for daily life. The consequence of this demand was that a wide range of everyday concerns, especially those involving food, had to be carefully monitored and the rules of holiness maintained. It was as if the whole of Israel's life were set under a great umbrella of the sacred and this protecting shelter kept in proper repair because God's name was attached to it.

We must then proceed to ask what this notion of holiness entailed. Of all the major religious concepts of antiquity, the concept of holiness has proved to be one of the most difficult to reinterpret into a modern setting.[76] It is evident that, even by the time of the NT writings, the varied meanings attached to holiness were sufficiently mixed and indistinct to make it a problematic term for use in a Christian context. Similarly with Judaism, the partial overlap with notions of purity and cleanliness, as well as of acceptability to God, called for a complex and prolonged series of reinterpretations.

This complexity is due, in part at least, to the fact that in ancient times the idea of holiness was given a physical, or quasi-physical, connotation. Holiness was a quality attached to places, persons, or things. At the same time, this quasi-physical property of holiness was fundamentally linked to ideas of separation and distinctness. Consequently it involved the careful marking of boundaries. The holiness associated with God demanded, by this very affinity, a careful separation from all that was unclean and that could threaten this holiness. Holiness and uncleanness, if allowed to come together, were a dangerous mixture. Just as idola-

try and the worship of gods other than the LORD God of Israel broke into and threatened the purity of worship, so also uncleanness threatened the boundaries of Israel's holiness.

It is in the light of this that Deut 14:1-21 reaffirms the understanding that Israel was a people holy to the LORD God, and then proceeds to show how this called for a careful screening of actions and creatures that might bring uncleanness, thereby threatening Israel's holiness. This could occur either in a purely individual fashion or more broadly in regard to the nation as a whole. So there could be no self-laceration or symbolic disfiguring for the dead (v. 1), nor could the people eat anything that was abhorrent to God and so constituted an abomination (תועבה *tôʿēbâ*). We see here that an original body of relatively basic and concise legislation has been expanded by the inclusion of more extensive details relating to which animals were to be regarded as clean and which as unclean (vv. 4-20). The listing of the clean and unclean creatures relates closely to the comparable list in Leviticus 11. An original catalog of ten clean animals (Deut 14:4*b*-5), followed by a list of ten unclean birds, has later been amplified by the inclusion of a further list of birds taken from Lev 11:18, which brings the total to twenty.

For the modern reader, this defining of the distinction between clean and unclean animals has led to substantial problems of understanding. The context clearly shows that these dietary rules originally belonged within the larger context of a distinction between what was holy and what was profane. To eat anything that was classed as "unclean," which described the fundamental category to which the creature belonged and not its temporary condition, is here regarded as an infringement of the demand that Israel should be a holy people. All the people's activities were required to conform to the rules governing the distinctions between holiness and uncleanness.

While Israel remained a national community, it is evident that a broad social consensus established an easily enforced pattern of activities that reduced the risk of casual or unintentional breaking of the rules concerning holiness. However, once the Jewish communities found themselves increasingly living a scattered existence, intermixed with non-Jewish communities, these dietary rules became more difficult to enforce and, therefore, subject to closer attention and care. Once this situation had occurred,

75. D. T. Olson, *Deuteronomy and the Death of Moses,* OBT (Minneapolis: Augsburg Fortress, 1994) 70-73.

76. See J. G. Gammie, *Holiness in Israel,* OBT (Minneapolis: Fortress, 1989) 102-24.

such rules themselves became important badges of religious commitment and identity, as they have remained for certain sections of the Jewish community to the present day.

It is evident that these dietary rules functioned as rules of hygiene, and it is largely in such terms that they have subsequently been understood in Jewish tradition. For example, the consumption of carrion-eating birds, such as the vulture, carried an evident health risk. It seems unlikely, however, that such hygienic considerations formed more than one possible feature for the rationale of such a list.[77] In seeking to establish a safe and secure order of life, ancient societies established a complex system of symbols in which an order of creation was perceived. It was a matter of primary importance to uphold this social symbol system that rejected "disorderly," or "mixed," forms of life. Boundaries of cleanness and wholeness had to be recognized and maintained. So, for example, the eating of fish that lacked both fins and scales was prohibited.

What is surprising in the biblical account of creation in Genesis 1 is that it fails to incorporate any mention of the existence of such unclean forms of animal life, which only become apparent to the reader in the account of the great flood (cf. Gen 7:2). The fact that all creation could be defined as "good" (e.g., Gen 1:4, 10) can only be understood in a relative sense that does not include the clean/unclean distinction. Even the story of the great flood only partially resolves the question of the non-edibility of unclean creatures.

By the time the list in Deut 14:1-21 was compiled, Israel had become well aware of the differing dietary habits pertaining to neighboring communities, so that their association with the worship of idols and alien deities would have added an intensified feeling of rejection to those creatures defined as unclean. Already such a distinction may have influenced Deuteronomy, even though it cannot have been an association with non-Israelite religion that gave rise to the compilation in the first instance.

Undoubtedly the boundary that was feared most of all, and that consequently needed to be observed with the greatest possible care, was that relating to life and death. So Israel had to keep itself well clear of participating in forms of self-mutilation for the dead, no matter how symbolic and restrained such behavioral patterns were (v. 1). It was also essential for Israel to avoid eating the carcass of a clean animal that had died of apparent natural causes (v. 21). It is against such a background also that we must understand the prohibition against boiling a kid in its mother's milk (v. 21). Life and death could not be mixed in such a fashion. The action thus referred to is prohibited elsewhere in earlier legal formulations (Exod 23:19; 34:26). These older prohibitions strongly point to such a practice as having once formed part of a ritual action, possibly itself intended to assist in ensuring safe childbirth or some related concern.

The fact that matters relating to death form the beginning and end of the series (vv. 1, 21) seems clearly to point to a deliberate pattern of inclusio to show that death marked a kind of ultimate boundary. In Israel in particular the ultimate nature of death is strongly recognized, thereby precluding forms of ritual and mythology that laid claim to a consistent crossing and recrossing of the boundary between life and death.

77. Most influential in recent study has been the work of anthropologist Mary Douglas, *Purity and Danger: An Analysis of Concepts of Pollution and Taboo* (London: Routledge and Kegan Paul, 1966) 53.

REFLECTIONS

There is a certain historical irony in the fact that the biblical dietary laws became so pronounced a feature of Jewish life. Clearly this had already taken place by the close of the formation of the Hebrew Bible, even though it is in the New Testament and the Mishnah that the wider consequences of this become apparent. Even the prohibition against boiling a kid in its mother's milk, the original significance of which has remained relatively obscure, has become a major identifying feature of Jewish food hygiene through the ages. At the same time, these rules, which were aimed at achieving a measure of careful conformity to the perceived order of the natural world, have in the passage of time become archaic and have instead functioned largely as distinguishing features of traditional faith and religious commitment.

At a very early stage of the parting of the ways between Judaism and Christianity, the Jewish dietary laws concerning clean and unclean food became a primary cause for the separation of the two communities (see Mark 7:17-23; Acts 10:9-16). At the same time, it is firmly recognizable that the Jewish rules relating food to the concept of a divine Torah contributed strongly to maintaining a close relationship between the concept of holiness and everyday patterns of life. From being a concept concerning the mysterious power, and inherent dangers, of the divine order of life, holiness came to be largely related to practical hygiene and healthy living.

A further consideration involves another primary issue of contemporary concern. That human beings should exercise control, or dominion, over the animal and natural world (Gen 1:28) can be easily, and dangerously, misinterpreted to imply complete human freedom to exploit natural resources and the natural environment without restraint. The destructive consequences of doing so, leading at times to the extinction of valued forms of animal and plant life and the devastation of large areas of the earth, reducing once fruitful areas to wastelands, have all been visible effects of such uncontrolled exploitation.

It is important that the modern reader recognize that the biblical concept of holiness included a wide recognition of the divine createdness and orderliness of all things, viewing all creation as part of a grand design that had to be respected and upheld. While it would be too much to claim that the concept of holiness as set out in Deut 14:1-21 consciously presented a clear-cut awareness of an ecological balance in the natural world, it is undoubtedly significant in its recognition that the human species belongs within a larger whole.

The biblical perspective is clearly one of concern to accept the wholeness of the natural world, to recognize and learn its innate orderliness and patterns, and to act so as to maintain and respect the various features of this order, so far as it touched upon human life. The very biblical notion of creation is itself a declaration of belief in one world. Human beings are seen to be part of this natural order of life, which even extends to inanimate objects. Although it is not difficult for the modern reader to note that the biblical distinctions between clean and unclean creatures include much that is primitive and unscientific, the fact that such distinctions were made points to fundamentally important principles. There exists a pattern and inter-relatedness between all creatures, in which even unclean creatures have a positive place and role to play. Life is believed to involve a complex intermeshing of different forms and expressions that all contribute distinctive features to make up the whole.

A further feature of the listing of animals in Deut 14:1-21 relates to teaching about the fixed and unalterable boundary between life and death. The passages of birth and death are of the most extreme significance and demand the greatest care. Accordingly, the passage into life itself, which takes place at birth for human beings and for flocks and herds, was surrounded with special prayers and rites. This mysterious cycle of life is also seen in the pattern of the seasons and of vegetational growth. But most of all it was seen in the passage from life into death, even the death of an animal. Such an event brought into play processes of decay and dissolution, which are mysterious and frightening. For human beings this is especially true, since death marks a departure and the crossing of a frontier that can never thereafter be recrossed.

Death marks the end of an individual existence and the transition to a new, and less welcome, form of being that could not be fully understood. It was impossible for persons of antiquity to confront death as a "natural" event, for all the circumstances that related to it pointed to its unnaturalness and, therefore, its dangerous character. The reflective disquisition on the fact of death in Ecclesiastes 8 reflects the immense problems in coming to terms with death as a part of the natural order and, therefore, as part of a divine design. It is not surprising, then, to find that Canaanite religion conceived of death in wholly unnatural and hostile terms as personified in the figure of Mot, the archenemy of Baal, the giver of life.

It is evident that, when confronted with the reality of death in the presence of a corpse or in the solemn duty of taking leave of a dead person at a funeral, a wide range of customs and rituals existed, some of which blatantly challenged the belief in the sovereignty of the LORD as God. It is also evident that such customs and rituals could pose serious problems for the loyal Israelite, since death was itself understood to be a form of uncleanness, the effects of which had to be countered.

Even in the modern world it is recognizable that, when faced with the presence of death, it becomes all too easy to relapse into an anxious evasiveness and pretense, rather than to accept that God is the one and only deliverer who enables us to contemplate the existence of another world beyond the boundary of death. So the biblical prohibitions warning against engaging in customs and rituals that evade the reality of death as itself a feature of the God-given order still carry a relevant message concerning the sacredness of life and the fact that God alone, as Lord of life, is also Lord of death.

DEUTERONOMY 14:22–16:17, REGULATIONS CONCERNING THE SACRED DIVISIONS OF TIME

Deuteronomy 14:22–15:23, The Worship of God in the Sacred Order of Time

NIV

22Be sure to set aside a tenth of all that your fields produce each year. 23Eat the tithe of your grain, new wine and oil, and the firstborn of your herds and flocks in the presence of the LORD your God at the place he will choose as a dwelling for his Name, so that you may learn to revere the LORD your God always. 24But if that place is too distant and you have been blessed by the LORD your God and cannot carry your tithe (because the place where the LORD will choose to put his Name is so far away), 25then exchange your tithe for silver, and take the silver with you and go to the place the LORD your God will choose. 26Use the silver to buy whatever you like: cattle, sheep, wine or other fermented drink, or anything you wish. Then you and your household shall eat there in the presence of the LORD your God and rejoice. 27And do not neglect the Levites living in your towns, for they have no allotment or inheritance of their own.

28At the end of every three years, bring all the tithes of that year's produce and store it in your towns, 29so that the Levites (who have no allotment or inheritance of their own) and the aliens, the fatherless and the widows who live in your towns may come and eat and be satisfied, and so

NRSV

22Set apart a tithe of all the yield of your seed that is brought in yearly from the field. 23In the presence of the LORD your God, in the place that he will choose as a dwelling for his name, you shall eat the tithe of your grain, your wine, and your oil, as well as the firstlings of your herd and flock, so that you may learn to fear the LORD your God always. 24But if, when the LORD your God has blessed you, the distance is so great that you are unable to transport it, because the place where the LORD your God will choose to set his name is too far away from you, 25then you may turn it into money. With the money secure in hand, go to the place that the LORD your God will choose; 26spend the money for whatever you wish—oxen, sheep, wine, strong drink, or whatever you desire. And you shall eat there in the presence of the LORD your God, you and your household rejoicing together. 27As for the Levites resident in your towns, do not neglect them, because they have no allotment or inheritance with you.

28Every third year you shall bring out the full tithe of your produce for that year, and store it within your towns; 29the Levites, because they have no allotment or inheritance with you, as well as the resident aliens, the orphans, and the widows in your towns, may come and eat their fill

NIV

that the LORD your God may bless you in all the work of your hands.

15 At the end of every seven years you must cancel debts. [2]This is how it is to be done: Every creditor shall cancel the loan he has made to his fellow Israelite. He shall not require payment from his fellow Israelite or brother, because the LORD's time for canceling debts has been proclaimed. [3]You may require payment from a foreigner, but you must cancel any debt your brother owes you. [4]However, there should be no poor among you, for in the land the LORD your God is giving you to possess as your inheritance, he will richly bless you, [5]if only you fully obey the LORD your God and are careful to follow all these commands I am giving you today. [6]For the LORD your God will bless you as he has promised, and you will lend to many nations but will borrow from none. You will rule over many nations but none will rule over you.

[7]If there is a poor man among your brothers in any of the towns of the land that the LORD your God is giving you, do not be hardhearted or tightfisted toward your poor brother. [8]Rather be openhanded and freely lend him whatever he needs. [9]Be careful not to harbor this wicked thought: "The seventh year, the year for canceling debts, is near," so that you do not show ill will toward your needy brother and give him nothing. He may then appeal to the LORD against you, and you will be found guilty of sin. [10]Give generously to him and do so without a grudging heart; then because of this the LORD your God will bless you in all your work and in everything you put your hand to. [11]There will always be poor people in the land. Therefore I command you to be open-handed toward your brothers and toward the poor and needy in your land.

[12]If a fellow Hebrew, a man or a woman, sells himself to you and serves you six years, in the seventh year you must let him go free. [13]And when you release him, do not send him away empty-handed. [14]Supply him liberally from your flock, your threshing floor and your winepress. Give to him as the LORD your God has blessed you. [15]Remember that you were slaves in Egypt and the LORD your God redeemed you. That is why I give you this command today.

NRSV

so that the LORD your God may bless you in all the work that you undertake.

15 Every seventh year you shall grant a remission of debts. [2]And this is the manner of the remission: every creditor shall remit the claim that is held against a neighbor, not exacting it of a neighbor who is a member of the community, because the LORD's remission has been proclaimed. [3]Of a foreigner you may exact it, but you must remit your claim on whatever any member of your community owes you. [4]There will, however, be no one in need among you, because the LORD is sure to bless you in the land that the LORD your God is giving you as a possession to occupy, [5]if only you will obey the LORD your God by diligently observing this entire commandment that I command you today. [6]When the LORD your God has blessed you, as he promised you, you will lend to many nations, but you will not borrow; you will rule over many nations, but they will not rule over you.

[7]If there is among you anyone in need, a member of your community in any of your towns within the land that the LORD your God is giving you, do not be hard-hearted or tight-fisted toward your needy neighbor. [8]You should rather open your hand, willingly lending enough to meet the need, whatever it may be. [9]Be careful that you do not entertain a mean thought, thinking, "The seventh year, the year of remission, is near," and therefore view your needy neighbor with hostility and give nothing; your neighbor might cry to the LORD against you, and you would incur guilt. [10]Give liberally and be ungrudging when you do so, for on this account the LORD your God will bless you in all your work and in all that you undertake. [11]Since there will never cease to be some in need on the earth, I therefore command you, "Open your hand to the poor and needy neighbor in your land."

[12]If a member of your community, whether a Hebrew man or a Hebrew woman, is sold[a] to you and works for you six years, in the seventh year you shall set that person free. [13]And when you send a male slave[b] out from you a free person, you shall not send him out empty-handed. [14]Provide liberally out of your flock, your threshing

---

[a] Or *sells himself or herself*   [b] Heb *him*

NIV

¹⁶But if your servant says to you, "I do not want to leave you," because he loves you and your family and is well off with you, ¹⁷then take an awl and push it through his ear lobe into the door, and he will become your servant for life. Do the same for your maidservant.

¹⁸Do not consider it a hardship to set your servant free, because his service to you these six years has been worth twice as much as that of a hired hand. And the LORD your God will bless you in everything you do.

¹⁹Set apart for the LORD your God every first-born male of your herds and flocks. Do not put the firstborn of your oxen to work, and do not shear the firstborn of your sheep. ²⁰Each year you and your family are to eat them in the presence of the LORD your God at the place he will choose. ²¹If an animal has a defect, is lame or blind, or has any serious flaw, you must not sacrifice it to the LORD your God. ²²You are to eat it in your own towns. Both the ceremonially unclean and the clean may eat it, as if it were gazelle or deer. ²³But you must not eat the blood; pour it out on the ground like water.

NRSV

floor, and your wine press, thus giving to him some of the bounty with which the LORD your God has blessed you. ¹⁵Remember that you were a slave in the land of Egypt, and the LORD your God redeemed you; for this reason I lay this command upon you today. ¹⁶But if he says to you, "I will not go out from you," because he loves you and your household, since he is well off with you, ¹⁷then you shall take an awl and thrust it through his earlobe into the door, and he shall be your slave[a] forever.

You shall do the same with regard to your female slave.[b]

18Do not consider it a hardship when you send them out from you free persons, because for six years they have given you services worth the wages of hired laborers; and the LORD your God will bless you in all that you do.

19Every firstling male born of your herd and flock you shall consecrate to the LORD your God; you shall not do work with your firstling ox nor shear the firstling of your flock. ²⁰You shall eat it, you together with your household, in the presence of the LORD your God year by year at the place that the LORD will choose. ²¹But if it has any defect—any serious defect, such as lameness or blindness—you shall not sacrifice it to the LORD your God; ²²within your towns you may eat it, the unclean and the clean alike, as you would a gazelle or deer. ²³Its blood, however, you must not eat; you shall pour it out on the ground like water.

[a] Or bondman   [b] Or bondwoman

COMMENTARY

14:22-29. The section that now follows concerns the temporal order in that the passage of time, like the dimension of terrestrial space, was viewed as part of the sacred order of things; 14:22 marks the transition to those dues required to be given to God in return for the privilege of divine protection. Both in the annual seasons and in the larger context of the progression through the years, time was regarded as the gift of God and as a carefully designed and ordered dimension of the natural world. The fact that the heavenly bodies could be interpreted as visible signs of the

passage of time (Genesis 1) enables us to see that the Israelites saw the world as a created whole, so that space and time were interlocking arenas subject to certain sacred rules. In just the same way that it was necessary in the terrestrial and animal realms to observe the fixed distinctions between locations and species, so also it was essential to maintain and acknowledge the sacred nature of the temporal realm.

To "observe the sabbath day to keep it holy" (5:12), therefore, was not simply a convenient way of enjoying a break within a busy routine. It was, rather, the acknowledgment of the immense mystery and inescapability of the passage of time. It was, in its link to the story of creation (cf. Gen 2:2-3), a recognition of the createdness of time and of the distinction between the "now" of present human experience and the "then" and "hereafter" that can only be thought about, but never actually experienced. So the marking and observance of the sabbath by prayer and rest from work formed the simplest and most basic of the distinctions that shaped and ordered the temporal realm.

The first of the rules concerning time is set out in 14:22-29 and concerns the offering of the tithe of the produce of the fields. All the harvest—grain, wine, and oil—was to be divided and marked off in this fashion, as were also the firstlings of flocks and herds. At first glance, the rules appear more in the nature of a tax rather than an act of recognition of the movement of time. Yet it was precisely the life-giving effect of the progress of the seasons that made the yielding of the tithe and the offering of firstlings actions that acknowledged the divine power present in the progress of time.

The tithe undoubtedly had very ancient origins, serving both as a gift and, more important, as an act of consecration. It maintained the orderliness and integrity of the cycle of life. And it expressed the return to God of some part of what the worshiper had received from God, since, just as some of the crop had to be retained for seed, so also some further part had to be handed back for the use of the divine giver. So the tithe came to fulfill many significant purposes. It reminded the worshiper that, in harvesting the crops or counting the offspring of flocks and herds, there had occurred an act of receiving, and not simply of producing. The worshiper had participated in a life-sustaining cycle in which he or she had co-operated, but over which only God had ultimate control.

It was also of great importance to the deuteronomic authors that the tithe fulfilled a second role in providing a supply of food for the support of the levitical priesthood and the poor of the community. They, too, held a place within the larger community, and it was essential that they, too, be provided for and that their basic needs be met.

At a third level, one of the key ways by which the deuteronomists understood the power and value of worship was that of remembering. The Israelite citizen was repeatedly urged to remember that all the major benefits of life—land, freedom, fertility, and a welcoming climate—were gifts from God. By such acts of remembering it was intended to engender a feeling of gratitude and an awareness of dependence that renewed the desire to remain loyal to God and to display a proper obedience to the divine commandments. So the calculation and yielding up of tithes was a formal temporal requirement that gave outward expression to the inward act of remembering.

Against such a background of allied purposes being served by the offering of tithes, we can understand the unusually bold pronouncement of the deuteronomistic legislation that permitted the sale of the actual tithe offering and the use of the money gained in this fashion to buy other goods at the location of the central sanctuary. The offering could be eaten there "in the presence of the LORD your God" (vv. 23-24). This is clearly a concession to the recognition that the demand for the restriction of formal offerings to one single centralized sanctuary could result in some worshipers' residing at too great a distance from this sanctuary for it to be practical to carry the offerings there. It represents one of the relatively few major elements in the deuteronomic legislation outside the actual formulation of the law of the sanctuary that seeks to compensate and allow for its consequences. It has been noted by several scholars that a large element of unreality pertains to such a law at a time when the social and political unity of Judah and Israel were progressively being broken apart.

The unique significance of such a concession is that it amounts to a desacralizing of the actual tithe itself, which is thereby no longer regarded as holy in itself. Offerings attain this holiness only through their relationship to the loyalty and religious intention of the worshiper, who uses such a gift to acknowledge the sovereignty of God over the cycle of the natural world.

The ruling that the tithe of every third year was to be wholly given for the benefit of the Levites marks a further element of the deuteronomic legislation that recognized that the Levites were in special need of support—a feature already remarked upon in connection with the social and political affinities of the deuteronomists. It is, at the same time, startling in its assumption that such a system of triennial additional support for the Levites, who are assumed in any case to benefit from the usual tithe offering, would be sufficient to enhance their situation within the community.

15:1-11. A further feature in the deuteronomic concern for the sacred observance of the order of time is presented with the legislation demanding the acceptance of a year for the remission of debts at the end of a forty-nine-year cycle. The Hebrew word for "remission" (שמטה *šĕmiṭṭâ*) means literally "letting fall"; it occurs in Exod 23:11 in relation to the cultivation of land. In that context, it undoubtedly meant "to leave uncultivated" and referred to the practice of allowing land to remain fallow every seventh year. Thereby the natural life cycle of the land, as God's gift, could be honored and its vitality renewed. Through such a practice we can recognize the importance of the acceptance of a cyclical pattern operating in the temporal order. Just as the seasons of the year evidence a pattern of use, decay, and renewal, so also a similar pattern can be observed through a sequence of years.

Here the law has been transferred across to the larger realm of commerce and property transactions, and is primarily applied to the making of loans for commercial purposes. By the time this deuteronomic legislation was formulated Israel had moved deeply into a capital-acquiring, land-owning economy in which wealth and poverty were prominent features. It is taken for granted that debts would be incurred for the purchase of land and other property and that there would be further, risk-laden business ventures. For the successful, these could lead to the amassing of considerable wealth and the acquisition of influence and power. For the less fortunate, such ventures could lead to ruin and destitution. So the more egalitarian patterns of life that had operated reasonably well in the social structure of extended families and clans, where property was largely held in trust throughout a large group, were eroding and being replaced by more individualistic patterns of economic life. Some people were doing considerably less well than others, and the legislation proposed by the deuteronomists was evidently designed to alleviate the consequences and effects of this and to make possible a recurring pattern of renewals and restarts, based on the analogy of agricultural routines.

It is assumed that debts will have been incurred for commercial ventures. Where these ventures have prospered it is then further taken for granted that the debt will have been repaid; if not, the debtor is not to be saddled with the burden of it beyond the set period of six years.

This legislation concerning the year of "release" has proved something of a puzzle for commentators. How could such a law have been upheld without the imposition of a form of negative interest, in which the value of the capital sum would have steadily depreciated over a period of six years? The "mean thinking" outlined in v. 9 appears to be a perfectly sensible response to the situation and to have implied that a fixed cycle of seven years was envisioned. This would have meant a cycle in which all loans were made and incurred within an already established timetable. Undoubtedly the proximity of the time of remission would have brought an effective standstill to a wide range of financial and property loans. The legislation, therefore, appears to be unduly theoretical, so much so as to render it unworkable except as a form of social charity.

The most positive estimate of it would appear to be a recognition that without some form of larger social restraint the unchecked operation of commercial pressures and risks brought business activity to the level of uncontrollability, leaving the successful virtual monopolistic rulers and locking the less fortunate into debt and poverty from which they could not escape. The proposed legislation set out here can then be viewed as an attempt to break into this situation by limiting the extent to which the commercial and financial pressures of the economy could be allowed to shape and control society more generally.

From a purely literary perspective, the original brief formulation of the legislation appears to have been expanded in the manner in which it defines the neighbor, referred to in v. 2 as a "member of the community" (אח *ʾāḥ*; lit., " brother").[78] Similarly the warning against mean thinking in vv. 7-11 appears to be a later addition to the original ruling. It recognizes quite openly the difficulty

---

78. L. Perlitt, "Ein einzig Volk von Brüdern. Zur deuteronomischen Herkunft der biblischen Bezeichnung Bruder," *Deuteronomium-studien,* FAT 8 (Tübingen: J. C. B. Mohr, 1994) 50-73.

that would arise in persuading free citizens, who would themselves have faced quite regularly major financial risks in farming, to maintain in spite of these risks an exceedingly generous spirit. Such observations serve only to strengthen the awareness that this was an area of legislation that sought to build on a long-standing history of cyclical renewal in agriculture and that assumed a strong sense of obligation concerning the wider moral and social problems of wealth and poverty.

Behind all such laws we can discern the shifting social and economic patterns of Israelite life in which some measure of accommodation to the commercial practices of the ancient Near East was sought. It perceives the need for sophisticated commercial development, but at the same time tempers this with traditions and rules that reflect older patterns of a kinship-based society concerned with protecting the weaker and less fortunate members of society. The deuteronomic legislation, which is incorporated into a deep awareness of the divine ordering of the temporal realm, reflects much of the "in-between" character of Israelite life at the close of the monarchic period. Much adaptation in the forms of economic activity and social urbanized community life had brought great changes. Yet these could bring, and probably to some degree already had brought, disruptive and disturbing transformations in society. The consequences had been far from ethically helpful, or even commercially successful, so that this deuteronomic ruling proposes important ameliorating restrictions to restrain commercial activity.

In spite of its idealistic character, this particular deuteronomic law gives voice to some of the most passionately expressed pleas on behalf of the poor that are to be found in the Bible. The tersely worded command, "Open your hand to the poor" (v. 11), spells out a great depth of feeling concerning social justice that permeates the legislation of Deuteronomy. It marks an attempt, as does the book of Deuteronomy more largely, to marry conscience to legislative action. It frankly recognizes that laws, especially those regulating commercial activity, cannot function effectively unless there is a willingness to implement them with a genuine compassion and integrity of respect for the entire community. Even the fact that there is any legislation at all reveals the recognition that mere appeals to goodwill are an insufficient basis for any society to implement justice

and compassion in its activities. Law requires love, but love also demands law!

15:12-18. The third of the commitments enjoined in this section dealing with the temporal realm concerns the acquisition, retention, and release of slaves. In line with the general tenor of the entire section, the emphasis is on generosity and the showing of compassion toward a fellow Israelite. In this case, the slave, whether a man or a woman, is understood to be a member of the community, a "brother." Clearly this is how the term 'āḥ is intended to be understood in this passage, indicating an ethnic affiliation rather than membership in a particular social class. It is closely equivalent to the concept of an "Israelite," a term the deuteronomists do not employ, even though the legislation implies such a concept.

The use of the term עברי ('ibrî) is to be explained from the fact that it has been taken and adapted, like the deuteronomic law itself, from the older law concerning slavery in Exod 21:2-6. In this case, the term 'ibrî certainly carried the connotation of social status, indicating the legal situation of a person who had fallen into slavery. The law in Deuteronomy was intended to provide an amendment to the older law and to modify its effect and purpose in a number of ways. Male and female slaves are placed on an equal footing (v. 17b), and provision is to be made to enable a released slave to maintain a viable position in the community (vv. 13-15).

Most striking of all, however, the law requiring the release of slaves after six years of service sets the whole question of such release within the larger context of the remission of debts. This release is assumed to take place within the fixed seven-year cycle requiring the remission of debts, rather than to represent the usual period of service into which a person would be sold to work as a slave. The law presupposes throughout that the situation of slavery has been occasioned through debt. In dire circumstances, a person might sell either himself or members of his or her family (see Amos 2:6) into slavery as a means of paying off a debt. But there were other ways in which people might be enslaved in ancient Israel, as in the ancient Near East generally. Some prisoners of war were kept as slaves, some slaves were victims of kidnapping (see the law of Exodus 21), and some persons may have been sold into slavery. The restriction of the present law to deal only with Hebrew slaves—i.e., those who were ethnically from the community—does not take into account those other slaves who were of alien origin and whose servitude was assumed in most cases to be permanent. The implication, therefore, is that this ruling was concerned primarily with ameliorating the consequences of debt slavery.

The fact that the legislation in Exodus deals only with the case of male slaves, whereas that in Deuteronomy is extended to cover females as well, reveals something of the changing social status of women by the time the deuteronomic legislation was written. Since the slave was clearly expected to be accorded certain minimal rights, in regard to both length of servitude and protection against abuse (Exodus 22, which deals with cases of physical injury resulting in a slave's death), their social position was evidently only a little lower than that of the hired laborer, whose employment is referred to in v. 18.

Verse 15 is an appeal to the tradition of the experience of Israel's ancestors as slaves in Egypt (cf. 5:15; 16:12; 24:18, 22), according to which the Egyptians furnished the departing Israelites with gifts before sending them away (Exod 3:21-22; 11:2; 12:35-36). Quite certainly the legislative requirement of providing adequate means for a released slave to function as an independent citizen has served to shape this unexpected feature of the narrative tradition.

The law dealing with the release of slaves reveals much of the same ambivalence and complexity that are found more broadly in this section covering temporal matters affecting social and commercial activity. On one side we find a deep compassion and studied realism concerning the humiliation and deprivation of status and protection to which fellow Israelites were subjected when sold into slavery. Over against this is a well-intended appeal to a spirit of generosity and goodwill designed to alleviate the worst consequences of slavery. The tightening up of the law in order to prevent exploitation and cruelty is evident, although the difficulty in doing much in this direction is everywhere evident. The appeal to the goodwill of the slave-owning citizen is then made in order to improve the lot of the slave.

A striking and alarming instance of the operation of this appeal for generosity and compassion

concerning the release of slaves is provided by the report in Jer 34:8-22. When Jerusalem was under siege by the army of Babylon, those citizens who owned slaves released them. The reasoning behind this action was almost certainly largely selfish and cynical: It relieved the owners of the responsibility of providing food for these unfortunates. When the siege was temporarily lifted, the former slaveowners repossessed them, assuming, prematurely as it turned out, that the threat of defeat and starvation had passed. The prophet Jeremiah's unrestrained condemnation of such a cruel and cynical act is ample evidence that he shared wholly the spirit of compassion and concern that underlies these deuteronomic regulations.

15:19-23. The law concerning the dedication of the firstborn males in the herds and flocks belonging to Israelites upholds an ancient ritual tradition. The birth of these animals was the manifestation of new life, and so they were to be returned to God, as the giver of life, in the form of a sacrifice. Together with the offering of firstfruits in the harvest as a means of promoting and upholding the cyclical order of the natural world, such offerings acknowledged the sovereignty of God over the temporal realm. New life implied the regenerative power of God in the world and, accordingly, had to be acknowledged with gratitude and honor. Behind the practice we can discern deep convictions regarding the belief that all life is a consequence of divine energy and power, which must be channeled and protected to ensure its continuance.

Throughout the many regulations for the ordering, upholding, and proper understanding of worship and the temporal order that are to be found in Deuteronomy, we can sense a deep spirit of respect for its given nature. Time is a gift of God, as much a feature of the shaping and structuring order of things as is space itself. It possesses measurements and symbols that can be noted and acknowledged. At the same time, it imposes limits on human activities. Just as human work potential was not to be exploited to the point of exhaustion, but was to be restrained by the renewing and life-restoring gift of the sabbath, so also the land was not to be exploited to the point of denuding it of its productiveness. Similarly, all commercial and social life was to be placed within boundaries that gave place for the renewing and regenerating life of God. Even capital acquisition, debt, and slavery were not conditions that could be allowed to run in perpetuity. They belong within the human scheme of things and require limits and boundaries, giving room for the renewing miracle of God's grace and power.

REFLECTIONS

The section that began in 14:22 and extends as far as 15:23 represents an amplification of the law of the sabbath, a law that reflects a consciousness of the divine order of time. Time is as much a gift of God as is the territorial domain of space. In the modern world, astrophysics has reawakened our own awareness that there exists a space-time continuum, so that all that exists does so within a framework of created time. We should not feel surprise, then, that in much the same way that we feel a compunction to devote some space to God by the establishing of a sanctuary, or holy place, that expresses to others and reminds us of the divine relatedness of space, so also time calls for the same degree of sacred setting apart.

The most elementary and foundational setting apart of time is that which occurs with the sabbath, a brief interval of one day in a sequence of seven, marking this divine givenness of time. It is important, therefore, that the biblical record traces the origin of the sabbath back to creation itself, thereby fitting it into a foundational level of the world's existence. It is also significant that the worshiper is called upon both to observe (i.e., "keep and acknowledge") the sabbath day and to remember to sanctify it through prayer and thanksgiving. It is a time set apart for celebration and rejoicing; it is altogether regrettable that, in the course of an overzealous interpretation in both Judaism and Christianity, the sabbath should at times become a day fraught with anxiety and boredom. Its primary function is to establish a pattern of renewal, enabling the exhaustion and stress of a work-laden week to be relieved by a revitalizing opportunity and freedom for renewal. Even the slave was to enjoy the freedom the sabbath provided, since no other human being was empowered to demand the wholeness of a person's time, which belonged to God the Creator.

The legislation within the present section, however, is not focused on the sabbath directly, but with other intervals and consequences in the passage of time. These focused on three particular issues. The first of these is the passage of the seasons in the agricultural year and the process of birth, maturity, and rebirth within the flocks and herds. The passing of the old into decay and inaction, followed by subsequent renewal with new growth and new births is evident. Time formed a part of the enabling stream of life, since it made visible and effective the experience of decay and renewal. It was vitally important, therefore, that this cycle of the seasons should be sanctified by marking its progress with appropriate offerings to God.

The second of the patterns of decay and renewal that is dealt with concerns commercial transactions in which debts were incurred. Some debt escape provision was called for lest a state of permanent indebtedness, with a consequent permanent crippling of a person's ability to participate in normal business life and activity, should be brought about. The legislation has consistently appeared strange and unworkable, even though the charitable and compassionate reasons for its introduction are laudable enough and clearly possess much ethical value. It marked an attempt to prevent a situation in which citizens could be permanently tied down with a burden of unrepayable debt. The deuteronomic legislation strived to avoid this situation with rulings that established an outer limit to the time scale of debt and sought, by doing so, to avert the consequences that would place an impossible burden on an individual household.

The pattern of such legislation, like the title "a year of release" (lit., "letting fall," "leaving alone"), has evidently been carried over from an agricultural setting with its institution of a fallow year. So economic and commercial activities were not to be allowed to determine and destroy an individual's life in such a way that ignored the God-ordained pattern of decay and renewal.

However unworkable such a legislative rule appears to be in purely commercial terms, it nevertheless reflects certain profound truths concerning the nature of human life and of the world order. The book of Deuteronomy clearly reveals a picture in which Israel's social and economic transformation, which characterizes the nation's development during the period of the monarchy, had brought major social inequalities and injustices. The prophets, particularly Amos, Micah, and Isaiah, cried out forcefully against the effect of these changes. Yet their only response appears to have been to appeal for the growth of a national conscience over the issue. The deuteronomic legislation, however, seeks to achieve more than this, by making law follow the dictates of the prophetic conscience. It seems unlikely that such laws proved practically workable or could easily have been put into effect. The issues they deal with, however, have remained powerful and significant, not least during the nineteenth and twentieth centuries. The consequences of uncontrolled capitalistic activity have repeatedly incurred world-shattering consequences to the detriment of other aspects of human social development.

The law attempts to translate into legislative regulation the biblical concern to subordinate commercial activity to a larger range of moral and social factors that shape human life and social development. Just as the sabbath provided a breathing space within the working week, so also the year of release was designed to provide a kind of commercial breathing space within the temporal realm.

The third of the issues dealt with relates to slavery, and in particular to the practice of debt slavery, in which a person sold oneself or members of one's family into slavery in order to pay off debts that had otherwise become unrepayable. The analogy with the sabbath, and with the regulation for the year of release, becomes evident. Even the misfortune of being sold into slavery was not to become a life sentence for an individual. For that to occur, human dignity and human freedom would be so deeply undermined that it would contradict the belief that all human beings had been fashioned in the image of God. So a limit was set, based on the cycle of six plus one. Thus an Israelite's slavery would be brought to an end with the arrival of the year of release and the possibility of a new beginning.

It is in this regard that a particular level of human interest is introduced into the legislation, since it openly recognized that, after six years of slavery, the unfortunate citizen in such a situation would not have remained in the same condition he or she had been in before misfortune struck. Life is never as simple as that! In order to be a truly free citizen it would be necessary to have capital to buy property and to begin again. Moreover it was quite likely that, if the slave was a young person, he or she would have reached puberty and probably would have contracted a marriage while enslaved. All these eventualities had to be taken into account. So the deuteronomic legislation is frank and realistic, even when it falls back upon rather idealistic appeals. Freedom would not be freedom if the capital to work and farm as a free citizen were lacking. Marriage commitments had to be balanced against the rights and expectations of the former lord and owner of the slaves, whose outlay also needed to be protected.

The rulings that are ultimately set out resort to a fundamental deuteronomic appeal to the slaveowner to be generous and compassionate in dealing with a former slave. A slaveowner had to remember that Israel's own ancestry could be traced back to men and women who had themselves been slaves in Egypt. It was essential, therefore, to treat slaves with understanding and compassion, realizing that it was only by the grace of the LORD God that one's own family was no longer in such a position.

How effective such appeals were to careful land- and slaveowners, on whose goodwill there were evidently many demands, remains wholly unknown. But the fact that such appeals are present and mark an important feature of the deuteronomic laws is itself significant. Laws cannot embrace every possible eventuality or deal with every aspect of a situation. They can be abused, misinterpreted, or applied so callously and unthinkingly as to undermine the very justice they were intended to maintain. So it was vital that the hearer or reader of the law should regard every fellow citizen as a human being, feeling the same pains and loyalties as well as facing the same dangers and challenges. It was essential to remember, when surveying one's misfortunes and mistakes, that these were risks that might subsequently befall oneself. So it was necessary that law should be administered and tempered by love, a demand that shapes the memorable saying of Lev 19:15: "You shall love your neighbor as yourself."

Deuteronomy 16:1-17, The Festival Calendar

NIV

16Observe the month of Abib and celebrate the Passover of the LORD your God, because in the month of Abib he brought you out of Egypt by night. [2]Sacrifice as the Passover to the LORD your God an animal from your flock or herd at the place the LORD will choose as a dwelling for his Name. [3]Do not eat it with bread made with yeast, but for seven days eat unleavened bread, the bread of affliction, because you left Egypt in haste—so that all the days of your life you may remember the time of your departure from Egypt. [4]Let no yeast be found in your possession in all your land for seven days. Do not let any of the meat you sacrifice on the evening of the first day remain until morning.

[5]You must not sacrifice the Passover in any town the LORD your God gives you [6]except in the place he will choose as a dwelling for his Name. There you must sacrifice the Passover in the evening, when the sun goes down, on the anniversary[a] of your departure from Egypt. [7]Roast it and eat it at the place the LORD your God will choose. Then in the morning return to your tents. [8]For six days eat unleavened bread and on the seventh day hold an assembly to the LORD your God and do no work.

[9]Count off seven weeks from the time you begin to put the sickle to the standing grain. [10]Then celebrate the Feast of Weeks to the LORD your God by giving a freewill offering in proportion to the blessings the LORD your God has given you. [11]And rejoice before the LORD your God at the place he will choose as a dwelling for his Name—you, your sons and daughters, your menservants and maidservants, the Levites in your towns, and the aliens, the fatherless and the widows living among you. [12]Remember that you were slaves in Egypt, and follow carefully these decrees.

a6 Or down, at the time of day

NRSV

16Observe the month[a] of Abib by keeping the passover to the LORD your God, for in the month of Abib the LORD your God brought you out of Egypt by night. [2]You shall offer the passover sacrifice to the LORD your God, from the flock and the herd, at the place that the LORD will choose as a dwelling for his name. [3]You must not eat with it anything leavened. For seven days you shall eat unleavened bread with it—the bread of affliction—because you came out of the land of Egypt in great haste, so that all the days of your life you may remember the day of your departure from the land of Egypt. [4]No leaven shall be seen with you in all your territory for seven days; and none of the meat of what you slaughter on the evening of the first day shall remain until morning. [5]You are not permitted to offer the passover sacrifice within any of your towns that the LORD your God is giving you. [6]But at the place that the LORD your God will choose as a dwelling for his name, only there shall you offer the passover sacrifice, in the evening at sunset, the time of day when you departed from Egypt. [7]You shall cook it and eat it at the place that the LORD your God will choose; the next morning you may go back to your tents. [8]For six days you shall continue to eat unleavened bread, and on the seventh day there shall be a solemn assembly for the LORD your God, when you shall do no work.

9You shall count seven weeks; begin to count the seven weeks from the time the sickle is first put to the standing grain. [10]Then you shall keep the festival of weeks to the LORD your God, contributing a freewill offering in proportion to the blessing that you have received from the LORD your God. [11]Rejoice before the LORD your God—you and your sons and your daughters, your male and female slaves, the Levites resident in your towns, as well as the strangers, the orphans, and

a Or new moon

NIV

¹³Celebrate the Feast of Tabernacles for seven days after you have gathered the produce of your threshing floor and your winepress. ¹⁴Be joyful at your Feast—you, your sons and daughters, your menservants and maidservants, and the Levites, the aliens, the fatherless and the widows who live in your towns. ¹⁵For seven days celebrate the Feast to the LORD your God at the place the LORD will choose. For the LORD your God will bless you in all your harvest and in all the work of your hands, and your joy will be complete.

¹⁶Three times a year all your men must appear before the LORD your God at the place he will choose: at the Feast of Unleavened Bread, the Feast of Weeks and the Feast of Tabernacles. No man should appear before the LORD empty-handed: ¹⁷Each of you must bring a gift in proportion to the way the LORD your God has blessed you.

NRSV

the widows who are among you—at the place that the LORD your God will choose as a dwelling for his name. ¹²Remember that you were a slave in Egypt, and diligently observe these statutes.

13You shall keep the festival of booths^a for seven days, when you have gathered in the produce from your threshing floor and your wine press. ¹⁴Rejoice during your festival, you and your sons and your daughters, your male and female slaves, as well as the Levites, the strangers, the orphans, and the widows resident in your towns. ¹⁵Seven days you shall keep the festival to the LORD your God at the place that the LORD will choose; for the LORD your God will bless you in all your produce and in all your undertakings, and you shall surely celebrate.

16Three times a year all your males shall appear before the LORD your God at the place that he will choose: at the festival of unleavened bread, at the festival of weeks, and at the festival of booths.^a They shall not appear before the LORD empty-handed; ¹⁷all shall give as they are able, according to the blessing of the LORD your God that he has given you.

^a Or *tabernacles*; Heb *succoth*

COMMENTARY

For the community of ancient Israel, the passage of time was characterized most dramatically by the routines and processes of agriculture. There was a time for sowing and a time for harvesting, a time for plowing and readying the soil for the coming season of growth and a time for reaping, threshing, and storing the crops. Each of these seasons of the agricultural year was accompanied by an appropriate religious festival, and this festival was inevitably closely bound up with memories and recollections of the divine power and beneficence that had made agricultural growth possible.

In the life of the Canaanite peoples from whom Israel had taken over the land, these festivals were also present and were inevitably closely patterned on the seasonal activities that marked the winning of crops from the soil. Such had certainly been the case for several thousands of years, probably with little variation in the rituals of seasonal

activity. The major festivals were interpreted, and in a measure sanctified, by the telling of myths and stories of the work and exploits of the gods who watched over the activities of the human beings who strove to gain from the soil the food to sustain life. With a kind of impertinent boldness, such mythology could even view the gods as enjoying their leisure, while their human slaves worked for the life-sustaining food, some of which they also would enjoy. So farming and religion went hand in hand.

It is in taking full account of this intimate bond between religion, mythology, and the agricultural year, as it was experienced by the previous inhabitants of the land, that we can see the reasoning behind the deuteronomistic fervor to promote a fresh understanding of seasonal time. The sanctuaries, holy places, rituals, and stories of the gods and goddesses of the land, which the deuteronomists sought strenuously to remove from the memorials and sacred sites of the land, were deeply ingrained in daily life. There was an understandable reluctance on the part of ordinary people, bordering closely on a kind of incomprehension, to abandon beliefs and practices upon which the very productivity of the land seemed to depend. So the most vital and inescapable requirement for the provision of an interpretation of time that fully honored the Lord as God was one in which the festivals of the agricultural year were celebrated wholly in honor of this one divine name.

The festival calendar[79] presented in 16:1-17 marks the final section of the collection of laws dealing with the sanctification of time. It provides us with one of the most forthright indications of the manner in which the aims of the deuteronomists have led to revisions of earlier customs. Older formulations of Israel's list of annual religious celebrations are to be found in Exod 23:14-19 and 34:18-26. We must assume that these formulations, already in written form, were available to the deuteronomistic authors.

By comparing the different calendars of events and their carefully prescribed wording, we can trace a number of changes that have been introduced over time. Even though we cannot always know when these changes were actually introduced, they nevertheless reveal the directional trend of religious development in Israel. These festivals undoubtedly marked a high point in the year and established the most evident public face of religious life. All families everywhere were bound to participate, since the life of the entire community depended on the success of the farming year. Moreover, such festivals provided the most powerful activities that generated a form of social bonding. They were joyous celebratory occasions, so that to have absented oneself or one's family from them would have been to turn one's back on the community as a whole. To do so would have been unthinkable, so that even the slaves and resident aliens, to whom much of what was done may have appeared strange, were required to participate.

In large measure, the aims of the deuteronomists can be seen quite clearly to have been to consolidate, to unify, and to "Israelitize" the festivals, which already had a long history behind them. They were to be performed in honor of the Lord God alone, to be divested of any of the sexual connotations and implications that the idea of new life invariably suggested to an ancient society, and to recall the slavery and humble, landless origins from which Israel had sprung.

16:1-8. From a literary perspective, the most remarkable new feature of the regulations set out in 16:1-17, when compared with the earlier formulations of the book of Exodus, is to be found in the close conjunction of the celebration of Passover with that of Unleavened Bread in the springtime of the year. Although there may have been some older connection between the two simply because they both took place in the same season, the Passover was essentially a festival for sheep farmers, whereas that of Unleavened Bread was related to a cereal harvest from the sown land. In such distinctions lay deep differences of economy, life-style, and necessarily of religious concern. So it is certainly the deuteronomistic sacred calendar that has formally striven to connect the two together and to provide for each a single coherent relationship to Israel's tradition of the exodus.

The Passover celebration took on a close association with the tradition of Israel's deliverance from slavery in Egypt. By doing so, it elevated the sense of salvation and protection afforded by the sacrificial and blood-smearing rituals of the passover event into a memorializing of that event, which marked the nation's birth. It represents a striking example of the manner in which a far older religious celebration, linked originally to a change of pasturage in the spring and to a warding off of dangerous powers, could become thoroughly "Israelitized." The combination of act and word could be transformed by adding new words to outdated forms. More than any other single seasonal religious event, Passover expressed and proclaimed the manner and circumstances of Israel's beginnings and the unique indebtedness to the Lord as God.

The title "Passover" is applied both to the sacrificial lamb, which provided the central ritual material for the celebration, and to the act of celebration itself. The oldest narrative account of its introduction into Israel is given in Exod 12:29-39 (usually ascribed to the pre-deuteronomic source J). However, this narrative record was enlarged in the post-exilic

---

79. See "Agricultural and Civil Calendar," in *The New Interpreter's Bible,* vol. 1 (Nashville: Abingdon, 1994) 275.

age, with evident post-deuteronomic features. It seems certain that in the process of this literary development much of the tradition available to the deuteronomistic authors has been discarded.

The term "Passover" (פֶּסַח *pesaḥ*, from פָּסַח *pāsaḥ*, "to hop," "to leap") refers to the divine grace in "passing over" Israel when "the angel of the LORD" threatened the firstborn of Egypt with death (Exod 11:5). Yet this is a very strained and implausible explanation for the origin of the name, and it remains a strong possibility that we should regard the actual verb here as a homonym meaning "to protect," since protection was clearly the primary purpose of the ritual.

The celebration was to take place during the first month of the year, Abib (March-April; cf. Exod 13:4; 23:15). The later post-exilic festival calendar established this date more precisely as the fourteenth or fifteenth day of Abib.

It is reported in 2 Kgs 23:21-22 that the Passover had not been celebrated by Israel from the time of the judges until the reign of King Josiah (cf. Josh 5:10-12). However, it is improbable that it was an entirely fresh restoration in Josiah's reign of a custom from so far back. Passover must have remained a significant celebration among some elements of the community throughout the monarchic era, possibly among the more marginal, sheep-farming segment. All the indications are that it was the purpose of the deuteronomistic legislation to regularize, standardize, and reinterpret religious celebrations that had previously been observed in a more haphazard fashion. It would then certainly appear that this was true of the spring celebration, which the deuteronomists now sought to establish as a unified festival of Passover-Mazzot, effectively combining the two celebrations into a single event.

The original Festival of Mazzot (Unleavened Bread) is related to the agricultural year, designed to establish an interval between the us...ig up of the leavened meal from one year and the introduction of new leaven from the new year's first crop. In the narrowest sense, it was not a religious celebration performed at a sanctuary, but a domestic provision related to the grain harvest and the food supply. It even possessed certain hygienic considerations.

Yet the original farming connotations are left aside in the acquisition of a new significance in terms of eating the bread of affliction as an act of remembering the season of affliction Israel's ancestors had experienced in Egypt. Old festival celebrations were filled with new content, and, in the process, ritual actions that can be traced to an agricultural context were invested with new meaning that related them overtly to Israel's historical commitment to the LORD as God.

16:9-17. The other two festivals specified in the deuteronomistic legislation, the Feast of Weeks (vv. 9-12) and the Feast of Booths (vv. 13-17), complete the religious observances of the year. They, too, possess an obviously agricultural character. The celebration of Weeks was to take place seven weeks after the first cutting of the early harvest. The post-exilic, amplified regulations for the celebration of this festival, set out in Lev 13:15-16, require that it be held on the fiftieth day after the sabbath following the offering of the first sheaf. This gave to it the title "Pentecost" (πεντηκοστή *pentēkostē*, "fiftieth"). It marked the complete harvesting of the grain crop and required that an appropriate offering, related to the size of the yield, be made.

Unlike the events of Passover and Mazzot, which recalled painful episodes from the nation's past, the Feast of Weeks was through and through a joyful celebration. It provided opportunity for thanksgiving for the food supply for the coming year. Such a reassuring provision contrasted with the scarcity of food that had pertained in Egypt (v. 12). Firm insistence is made that the entire household, including slaves, should join in the celebration, along with the disadvantaged, non-landowning members of the community, which included resident aliens, orphans, and widows.

The third of the annual festival celebrations is defined as the Festival of Booths, which, like Mazzot, lasted seven days (v. 13). This festival was celebrated when the last of the produce of the agricultural year—the vintage and olive harvests—was acknowledged with gratitude. Since this celebration took place in the late summer, its outdoor nature was characterized by the making of simple shelters from branches and scrub foliage, forming the booths, or tabernacles, in which the celebrants protected themselves from the cool night air. In turn, these rough shelters were later reinterpreted as imitations of the temporary shelters made by the Israelites when they fled from Egypt and set out into the wilderness.

It is in this fashion that the deuteronomistic interpretation, or more strictly reinterpretation, of Israel's agricultural festivals has drawn all of them into a relatively coherent and consistent pattern of worship. They mark the passage of the seasons, originally being locally related to the harvest, but later fixed at specific days within particular months. Their original agricultural character was not abandoned, but was overlaid with a distinctive theological set of images and ideas.

It would be easy to overstate the primary agricultural significance of these celebrations. They were primarily signposts and markers of the passage of time throughout the year. This could be recognized to possess a pattern of rise and fall, of new birth, followed by decay and death until the new season heralded a resurgence of new life. Naturally the harvesting of the crops provided the materials with which this process of decay and revitalization could be recognized and expressed. Yet they were far more than simple token gifts of gratitude for an adequate food supply. They enabled the entire community to become part of this seasonal rise and fall of the passage of time. Men and women grew accustomed to the passing of the weeks and months in which their own life cycle was mirrored in a simpler, more basic form. God was "the living God," and in worshiping this life-bestowing power people are looked to be renewed with new life.

It is clear that, in giving new meaning to these festivals and in emphasizing their significance as memorials of events from the national past, the deuteronomists were concerned to break with aspects that were no longer regarded as helpful. At the same time, it is evident from the demand for compulsory participation in these celebrations that they were also seen to be vitally important moments of social bonding and renewal. Being present on such occasions was the most obvious and deeply felt way an individual family knew that they were part of the community of the LORD God.

For the deuteronomists it is wholly in line with the concern to coordinate and regularize the celebration of these festivities that they were required to be performed at the one central sanctuary (vv. 6, 11, 15). Obviously this imposed considerable difficulties and restrictions on their actual performance, since it is unthinkable that whole communities would vacate their towns and homesteads to journey to Jerusalem for seven days or more. Such a restriction became increasingly difficult because of the ever-enlarging dispersion of the Judean population into scattered and loosely connected settlements. The breakup of the former nation and the progressive migration into more distant lands turned the original population of a single nation into a miscellany of aliens resident in many lands. Except in the context of a pilgrimage, the celebration at a central sanctuary became progressively more difficult. Nevertheless, the importance of the deuteronomistic legislation cannot be overstated, and the religious foundations of the dispersion were laid firmly on the memorializing and celebration of a national past, with a strong forward look to its re-creation at a future time. It is among these foundations that the sacred festival calendar of ancient Israel held a place of exceptional significance. The deuteronomistic legislation provided a pattern of ritual that was readily adaptable and required only basic domestic materials for performance.

It seems certain that the primary aim of the deuteronomists had been to create a closer uniformity of practice and to promote a healthy sense of national unity in honor of the one LORD God. In historical reality, it appears most probable that it was less the creation of a new unity than the prevention of further disunity of religious practice that was its greatest achievement. It is noteworthy that, in the fifth century BCE, the Jewish community established at Yeb (Elephantine) in Egypt celebrated the Passover, even though it is evident that much of their practice and religious outlook were highly heterodox from the standards set by the deuteronomists. Nevertheless, the sacred festival calendar marked the passage of time through the year in very much the same way that the observance of the sabbath marked the passage of days into weeks. Time itself was sanctified and made holy by being filled with religious content and meaning.

REFLECTIONS

Religion implies a strong measure of continuity, so it is not surprising to find in Deuteronomy a series of regulations promoting the observance of three major religious festivals throughout the year. Nor should we be surprised that these festivals bear all the indications of close connections with the practice of agriculture. Quite certainly these celebrations had belonged inseparably to the skills and techniques of raising crops from the land and husbanding flocks and herds with only limited subsistence and rainfall. They were, in many of their details, ancient by the time of Moses. Their origins must go back to the very earliest stages of organized agriculture in the ancient Near East.

The deuteronomistic festival calendar is not, however, simply a calendar of the agricultural year. Rather, it has been transformed by associating each of the main seasonal celebrations with events from Israel's national past. The renewing of the farming year has been transformed into a celebration of human freedom—Passover freedom from the slavery of Egypt, the wickedness of human oppression and obstinacy in Pharaoh's refusal to let Israel go free, and the entitlement to own land, to plant crops, and to own flocks. Passover had been turned into a festival of human freedom, not only in the narrowly political sense, but also in its recognition that to live meant to be free to enjoy the fruits of life in food, well-being, and pride of possession. So Israel's gifts of the land are seen first and foremost as the fruits of the larger gift of historic acts of deliverance. The rituals were recast in the form of mini-dramas that reenacted significant moments from the past so that entire families could feel themselves caught up once again in the great turning points by which the nation of Israel had been given birth.

The modern reader is inevitably surprised at the way these ancient festival celebrations combine the physical with totally spiritual connotations. There is no sharp dichotomy between the benefits and the blessings of the material world and the inner meaning and "message" the worshiper is bidden to draw from the celebration. Most striking to our modern perspective is the total absence of any sense of distinction between wealth and poverty in the manner in which the celebration takes place. The entire community is not simply invited to take part, but is duty bound to do so. Even those who stood most at the margins of society were required to participate. These celebrations relate to the community in its entirety and wholeness, so that all can be seen to benefit from the food that sustains them. The festival celebrations exemplify a belief in the essential unity and oneness of the community before God.

By the time the written deuteronomistic legislation regarding the calendar of sacred festivals was composed, Israel was on the verge of national collapse. In fact, by this period much of the nation had already succumbed to the destructive impact of Mesopotamian imperialism upon the region. One of the remarkable features of this reworking and revitalizing of an ancient festival calendar, therefore, lies in the way it provided a simple pattern of ritual and celebration that could take place even far away from the central sanctuary for which it had originally been designed. Even Israelites living in the lands of their dispersion could continue sanctifying and "nationalizing" the passage of the seasons, even in environments in which the original agricultural connections became less and less evident.

The world of commerce was also incorporated into a seasonal calendar of time that had wholly different origins and significance from the historical events it commemorated. Acts of national thanksgiving survived as reminders that Israel had once been a nation and could become so again. Recollections of events that freed them from slavery continued to provide for Jews a self-image of people who were free, responsible, and law-abiding in their commitment to the larger social environment. This was true because such concepts were woven into the very meaning of time and history.

Few features of the biblical worldview contrast more directly with a modern secular worldview than in the understanding of time. For the secularist, time represents no more than an undifferentiated stream of possibility in which no one aspect is qualitatively distinguished from any other. Modern cosmology, by the unimaginable eons of time over which it has traced the processes of creation, has served to remove the sense of the creativity of time from the realms of everyday living. Similarly, time has been given a predominantly oppressive and negative quality—it is always "running out," like the sand from an hourglass.

In contrast, the biblical perception of time calls attention to its rhythmic, cyclical patterns. It is regrettable that, in a desire to magnify the historical sequential nature of time as a process, beginning at creation and proceeding to an as yet unknown end point, an earlier generation of biblical scholarship sought to denigrate the significance of the rhythmic, cyclical aspects of the Hebraic portrayal of time. Beginning with the visible symbols of the heavenly bodies and their observable and predictable movements, the biblical portrayal of time regarded it as a rhythmic, cyclical order. The cycle of seven days in which the regular occurrence of the sabbath presented both a period of rest and renewal and a recapturing of the potential of the primal sabbath of creation (Gen 2:2-3) provided the model of a larger pattern.

Days, weeks, and years were brought together in a pattern in which work and leisure, followed by times of release and recommencement, formed part of a divine plan. For the ancient Israelites who participated in and formulated this sacred calendar, time did not conform to the pattern of an undifferentiated stream. It had its moments of rise and fall, death and rebirth. In regarding time as "holy" and in accepting its given place in the divine scheme of things, the Israelites accepted a balance that conformed to the natural rhythm of life.

It is helpful to reflect on whether the modern secular perception of time has destroyed this balance and, by denying its natural rhythms, generated a far more stressful, uncontrolled, and uncontrollable environment. Because time is no longer perceived as holy, and not, therefore, subject to religious imagery and obligations, it has instead become a bewildering maze that can only be negotiated with patience and care. Rest and leisure no longer possess a "natural" and given place within the scheme of things, with the strange consequence that for some it is difficult to find room for it at all, while others look for ways to fill its boredom.

So we moderns have had to learn techniques of "time management" as a means of dealing with the unregulated and unmanageable pressures of a pattern of time that has no formal order. The abandonment of any attempt to understand time in relation to the natural rhythms and patterns of life and the seasonal order has meant that life in the modern world has become a markedly stress-inducing and destabilizing affair.

It is also important to reflect that the abandonment of religious connotations and associations for many of the major turning points of the seasonal calendar has resulted in a greatly weakened sense of its social connotation. Whereas the ancient festival days recalled the essential, if largely ideal, belief in the unity and united origins of the community, the modern secular marking of time retains few indications of such an ideal unity. As a consequence, a sense of otherness and alienation emphasizes the distinctions and differences within community life, rather than a calling back to a primary feeling of a common heritage.

DEUTERONOMY 16:18–18:22, PUBLIC AUTHORITY AND LEADERSHIP

OVERVIEW

The section 16:18–18:22 moves into a new area of legislation and concerns questions of public authority and leadership.[80] In the broad context of the Ten Commandments it appears as an elaboration of the commandment concerning the honoring of parents, since this marked the primary and most basic form of acknowledgment of a concept of social order. Parenthood, with all the responsibilities and commitments of the family as the primary kin group, established the groundwork for a wider spectrum of authority and leadership that provided a structural backbone for society as a whole. So the natural authority that arose within the family is taken as indicative of a necessary and given order that enables economic, moral, and household discipline to be managed and controlled.

Ultimately these forms of public authority can be seen to cover four specific areas of activity. In turn, these conferred authority upon and required submission to four professional, or semi-professional, social classes: the judiciary, which depended primarily on a body of publicly appointed judges; the levitical priesthood, which emerged from a particular family lineage; the monarchy, which traced its origin to an act of divine choice and appointment, but that in practice was dependent upon a unique family dynasty; the charismatic prophets, who represented a divinely selected and appointed class of leadership.

All of these groups of public leaders are viewed as necessary for the proper maintenance of social order, although how their relative levels of authority were to be balanced against one another is not spelled out. Each is necessary and to some extent exists within a kind of social oligarchy. It is not made clear how an operating balance between the various competing interests was to be achieved. There is an underlying assumption that each of these classes of leader administers the higher authority of God and that some kind of divine ordering and balance would manifest itself.

We should not be surprised, then, that no predetermined method of resolving conflicts of authority within Israelite society is laid down. The significance of what is set out in the deuteronomic legislation lies in its acceptance of a specific place for each of four main forms of authority, allowing each to serve as a check and balance over the other three areas. In this way, there would be no monopoly of public authority that could lead to abuses of power. In this regard, the most striking feature, when viewed against the larger context of the ancient Near East, is the limited authority accorded to the kingship as a public institution. Its existence appears to be conceded, rather than warmly demanded, and it is set under a positive code of restraints.

It is also noteworthy that even the basic form of authority in which parents exercised control over their children is placed under certain limits. This indicates a clear recognition that no one form of authority, however basic, was allowed to exercise a dominant position over the others.

From the perspective of the time of origin of the legislation set out here, a measure of openness has to be accepted. The provision for the institution of monarchy clearly points to the expectation of the continuance of this institution, but even this appears as one of the latest insertions into the section as a whole. It is provided for in such a manner as to suggest that its continuance was uncertain and that the institution of a monarchy was not essential to Israel's existence as a nation.

The time scale within which this legislative section concerning public leadership and authority

80. J. C. Gertz, *Die Gerichtsorganisation Israels im deuteronomistischen Gesetz*, FRLANT 165 (Göttingen: Vandenhoeck & Ruprecht, 1994) 28-97; U. Rütersworden, *Von der politischen Gemeinschaft zur Gemeinde. Studien zum Dt 16,18–18,22*, BBB 65 (Frankfurt: Herder Verlag, 1987); N. Lohfink, "Distribution of the Functions of Power: The Laws Concerning Public Offices in Deuteronomy 16:18–18:22," in *A Song of Power and the Power of Song: Essays on the Book of Deuteronomy*, ed. D. L. Christensen, Sources for Biblical and Theological Study 3 (Winona Lake: Eisenbrauns, 1993) 336-52; E. Otto, "Von der Gerichtsordnung zum Verfassungsentwurf. Deuteronomische Gestaltung und Deuteronomistische Interpretation im Ämtergesetz. Dtn 16,18–18,22," *Wer ist wie du, HERR, unter den Göttern? Studien zur Theologie und Religionsgeschichte Israels für Otto Kaiser zum 70. Geburtstag*, ed. Ingo Kottsieper et al. (Göttingen: Vandenhoeck & Ruprecht, 1994) 142-55.

was composed cannot be determined with any certainty, and such a question need not be thought of as an issue of great significance. The provisions set out in this section endorse a situation concerning the institutional life of ancient Israel, which emerged over a very long period. They point to a fundamental trend in the organizational structure and life of the society, rather than to a sudden reformation. Certainly we should regard them as being related to the major changes in Israel's political existence that occurred during the reign of King Josiah (639–609 BCE). Yet many of these changes likely were consequential upon the changes introduced during this king's reign, rather than serving as the immediate cause of them. If we may single out one feature that is wholly remarkable, it is that the monarchy is provided for; instead of being the foundational basis on which all other features of the state are based, however, it is itself presented as simply one part of a higher divine order for society.

Broader policy shifts can be discerned within the area of the major reduction in the power of the monarchy. The kingship is given little overt instruction as to its function, either militarily or judicially. The primary concern is that this institution should endorse and uphold the Mosaic (deuteronomic) constitution, and not act outside its scope. Also evident is a broad recognition that society functions primarily as a collection of townships with little power ascribed to the heads of larger family groups of clans and tribes. The elders of towns are presented as more directly active as a resource of authority, rather than family or clan chiefs, although presumably these elders came from powerful families. Nevertheless, it is the strong focus on cities and towns as the seats of local administration that betrays the strong development of urbanized communities.

Another feature of this deuteronomic concern with public leadership and authority is that it points to a situation in which the more formal structure of a nation-state is no longer regarded as the sole ultimate authority. Claims to the righteousness and justice that uphold the royal throne are no longer made. Instead legal disputes are handled under a variety of lesser powers, including those of the levitical priesthood and the elders of local townships. It would certainly appear to be the case that the final form of the picture set out in these regulations

envisages a community in which a strong and effectively administered central government could no longer be relied upon. This would point to the conclusion that the final draft of this legislation was made after the debacles of 598 and 587 BCE, when the central Jerusalem administration collapsed. Although the framework of a national monarchic state is retained, the historical figure of Moses and the concept of a written Torah provide the constitutional foundations upon which the whole polity is established.

Few factors impinge more heavily upon the harmony and well-being of society than its forms and structures of public authority. This is especially true in those areas that control legal powers, social and family policy, and commercial protection and promotion. Ultimately the justification for all such exercise of public leadership is traced back to the supreme authority of God, from whom all forms of human authority are derived. This is most emphatically expressed in the Pauline assertion that "the powers which exist are ordained of God," but it underlies all the Hebraic biblical presentation of the nature of a divine social order. It also becomes evident in a far wider spectrum of political and social order of the ancient Near East.

So far as claims to a religious basis for political order are concerned, two patterns appear prominent: the monarchy and a priestly theocracy. The monarchy, in which the royal power is itself presented as absolute, is derived directly from God, making it a theocracy. Ironically, it is typically portrayed in the biblical reports of the Pharaonic administration of Egypt with its unlimited powers carried to the lengths of absurdity.

A second form of divine rule through human agency may also lay claim to unlimited power when a priestly theocracy is allowed to dominate. In practice it appears that both in Egypt and in Babylon an administration established on a balance between kingly and priestly rule prevailed. Yet even in these forms of state development the necessity for careful protection of both royal and priestly power remained essential, and the need for constant vigilance was paramount.

From the biblical perspective it would appear that a considerable level of residual authority remained with the heads of major family and tribal groups. Furthermore, repeated challenges to kingly authority by individual prophets is a marked feature of the historical tradition. Clearly such prophets could not have been unsupported and unconnected with popular feeling and the local interests of the community, whose interests they voiced. Overall, therefore, the biblical tradition is strongly critical of kingship as an institution and relatively unsympathetic toward the claims to public authority of the most celebrated priestly families. Thus a special interest attaches to the deuteronomic presentation of the forms and duties vested in these different expressions of public leadership and authority.

Deuteronomy 16:18–17:13, Judicial Authority

NIV	NRSV

NIV

[18]Appoint judges and officials for each of your tribes in every town the LORD your God is giving you, and they shall judge the people fairly. [19]Do not pervert justice or show partiality. Do not accept a bribe, for a bribe blinds the eyes of the wise and twists the words of the righteous. [20]Follow justice and justice alone, so that you may live and possess the land the LORD your God is giving you.

[21]Do not set up any wooden Asherah pole[a] beside the altar you build to the LORD your God, [22]and do not erect a sacred stone, for these the LORD your God hates.

17 Do not sacrifice to the LORD your God an ox or a sheep that has any defect or flaw in it, for that would be detestable to him.

[2]If a man or woman living among you in one of the towns the LORD gives you is found doing evil in the eyes of the LORD your God in violation of his covenant, [3]and contrary to my command has worshiped other gods, bowing down to them or to the sun or the moon or the stars of the sky, [4]and this has been brought to your attention, then you must investigate it thoroughly. If it is true and it has been proved that this detestable thing has been done in Israel, [5]take the man or woman who has done this evil deed to your city gate and stone that person to death. [6]On the testimony of two or three witnesses a man shall be put to death, but no one shall be put to death on the testimony of only one witness. [7]The hands of the witnesses must be the first in putting him to death, and then the hands of all the people. You must purge the evil from among you.

[8]If cases come before your courts that are too difficult for you to judge—whether bloodshed, lawsuits or assaults—take them to the place the

NRSV

18You shall appoint judges and officials throughout your tribes, in all your towns that the LORD your God is giving you, and they shall render just decisions for the people. [19]You must not distort justice; you must not show partiality; and you must not accept bribes, for a bribe blinds the eyes of the wise and subverts the cause of those who are in the right. [20]Justice, and only justice, you shall pursue, so that you may live and occupy the land that the LORD your God is giving you.

21You shall not plant any tree as a sacred pole[a] beside the altar that you make for the LORD your God; [22]nor shall you set up a stone pillar—things that the LORD your God hates.

17 You must not sacrifice to the LORD your God an ox or a sheep that has a defect, anything seriously wrong; for that is abhorrent to the LORD your God.

2If there is found among you, in one of your towns that the LORD your God is giving you, a man or woman who does what is evil in the sight of the LORD your God, and transgresses his covenant [3]by going to serve other gods and worshiping them—whether the sun or the moon or any of the host of heaven, which I have forbidden— [4]and if it is reported to you or you hear of it, and you make a thorough inquiry, and the charge is proved true that such an abhorrent thing has occurred in Israel, [5]then you shall bring out to your gates that man or that woman who has committed this crime and you shall stone the man or woman to death. [6]On the evidence of two or three witnesses the death sentence shall be executed; a person must not be put to death on the evidence of only one witness. [7]The hands of the witnesses shall be the first raised against the person to execute the death penalty, and after-

a21 Or *Do not plant any tree dedicated to Asherah*

a Heb *Asherah*

NIV

LORD your God will choose. [9]Go to the priests, who are Levites, and to the judge who is in office at that time. Inquire of them and they will give you the verdict. [10]You must act according to the decisions they give you at the place the LORD will choose. Be careful to do everything they direct you to do. [11]Act according to the law they teach you and the decisions they give you. Do not turn aside from what they tell you, to the right or to the left. [12]The man who shows contempt for the judge or for the priest who stands ministering there to the LORD your God must be put to death. You must purge the evil from Israel. [13]All the people will hear and be afraid, and will not be contemptuous again.

NRSV

ward the hands of all the people. So you shall purge the evil from your midst.

[8]If a judicial decision is too difficult for you to make between one kind of bloodshed and another, one kind of legal right and another, or one kind of assault and another—any such matters of dispute in your towns—then you shall immediately go up to the place that the LORD your God will choose, [9]where you shall consult with the levitical priests and the judge who is in office in those days; they shall announce to you the decision in the case. [10]Carry out exactly the decision that they announce to you from the place that the LORD will choose, diligently observing everything they instruct you. [11]You must carry out fully the law that they interpret for you or the ruling that they announce to you; do not turn aside from the decision that they announce to you, either to the right or to the left. [12]As for anyone who presumes to disobey the priest appointed to minister there to the LORD your God, or the judge, that person shall die. So you shall purge the evil from Israel. [13]All the people will hear and be afraid, and will not act presumptuously again.

COMMENTARY

The major series of deuteronomic regulations authorizing the setting up of such public leaders is set out in 16:18–17:13. It concerns the setting up of an order of juridical officials to oversee the administration of law. Who exactly was to be given the duty of selecting and installing such legal officials is not made explicit, but it would appear to be the community itself. Traditionally such selection would have rested in the hands of the royal administration, and it cannot be ruled out that this was originally intended here. The royal court claimed complete authority over the administration of justice, making this a major feature of the beneficent claims of kingship for the community. Failure to uphold such a juridical system is made a primary prophetic accusation against King Jehoiakim (Jer 22:13-17). If those who were appointed under the deuteronomic legislation were to be given office through the centralized royal administration, then it is also to

be borne in mind that this opened the way to conflicts of loyalty between such officials and the heads of local townships and clans.

The very existence of the deuteronomic law code, with its many important contacts with legal procedures and formulations, which are well evidenced from the wider world of the ancient Near East, indicates the high level of skill and sophistication that was required. Such persons were not simply judges in the modern sense, but were held responsible for careful record-keeping of cases dealt with and for obtaining familiarity with the rulings and principles of legislation that had developed over a long period in the ancient Near East. Clearly such a legal official would be held responsible for controlling the conduct of cases and for ensuring the fairness of the proceedings. There is an abundance of testimony from the speech forms used by prophets, as well as from reports of cases, that a well-established protocol for the hearing of cases was observed.

16:18-20. The remarkably forthright declaration of the principles of impartiality and evenhandedness in the administration of cases set out in vv. 19-20 undoubtedly reflects long experience of actual situations. The custom of presenting gifts as a token of friendship and esteem readily developed into the corruption of giving bribes to secure a favorable verdict. Probably just as difficult to eradicate was the practice of honoring powerful and wealthy families in such a manner that their influence could easily be secured to subvert justice. In a society where kinship loyalties had traditionally provided a powerful bonding factor in upholding social harmony and cohesion, it could often prove difficult to override such loyalties in the interest of justice. The very concepts of loyalty and integrity (to one's family) could actually serve to undermine, rather than foster, a true spirit of justice.

That the task of a judge in ancient Israel could be a difficult one to fulfill honorably, and was persistently susceptible to abuse, becomes evident from the repeated sharp strictures of both prophets and the authors of proverbial instruction concerning the administration of justice. By reading between the lines of what is demanded, it is not difficult to recognize the prevalence of familiar forms of distortion and abuse. Clearly major problems arose for the administration of justice over the difficulty in assessing the truthfulness of witnesses and the rudimentary nature of the laws of evidence. In consequence, a high premium was placed on the insight, experience, and resolute determination of legal officials to ensure fair trials. These requirements for the selection of suitable officials for the task, as set out in 16:20, point us to recognize that the administration of justice formed a high priority for the general harmony and well-being of ancient Israelite society.

Issues concerning the administration of justice are further dealt with in 17:8-13, which provides for a way of dealing with cases of a serious nature in which the local judicial process, presided over by a judge, was unable to come to a satisfactory verdict, providing the basis for what we might describe as a system of appeals. The intervening regulations that are set out in 16:21–17:7 deal with fundamental questions of religious disloyalty

and apostasy. Three specific cases are considered: (1) setting up a sacred pole as an Asherah or a stone pillar as a related non-Israelite cult symbol; (2) presenting a defective animal as a sacred offering to God; and (3) open blasphemy.

16:21-22. Clearly the practice of establishing simple, and basically primitive, shrines to a local deity had a long history in the land occupied by Israel. Such simple sanctuaries were local features that could often claim to have existed from times of great antiquity and were not, therefore, to be ignored or set aside. The sharp deuteronomic polemic against them indicates that they enjoyed a good deal of popular support. For the authors of Deuteronomy, these shrines are now viewed as a serious threat to the purity and integrity of the worship of the LORD as God. It seems highly probable that in many instances the local communities that venerated such symbols regarded them as acceptable adjuncts to the worship of the LORD as Israel's God. They could also readily provide explanations for why the one great God of Israel should have appeared in many forms.

Throughout the Deuteronomic History we find a consistent zeal and fervor to maintain a rigid religious purity, with every indication that forms of religious practice that had at one time appeared acceptable, and even normal, within Israel were now outlawed and classed as objectionable and dangerous. Moreover, the deuteronomists, who were themselves clearly not priests, had no restraint in expecting to use the full force of the law to implement their stringent demands.

It is not at all clear why these prohibitions against long-established, and now rejected, cultic features should have been introduced into a series of instructions for the administration of justice. We may consider that they were felt to be necessary at this point because the simple resolution of difficult legal cases by the Levites at a local sanctuary, as laid down in the older Book of the Covenant, were in need of revision when only one central sanctuary was permitted. Resort to any traditional, but non-Yahwistic, sanctuary as a place where difficult legal matters could be settled, therefore, was firmly outlawed. It had become necessary to preclude that the concern to deal with local juristic problems should have led to any recognition of small sanctuaries that were repudiated on religious grounds. In other words, it was not to be permitted that non-Yahwistic sanctuaries should be tolerated simply because they were needed for settling legal disputes.

17:1. The use of blemished animals as sacrificial offerings is prohibited by the ruling laid down in this verse, which defines such an offering as an "abomination" (תועבה *tōʿēbâ*) to God. This was undoubtedly a significant term in the vocabulary of evil and wrongdoing for the deuteronomists, since it expressed a strong note of divine repugnance, without entering further into discussion of how it conflicted with the divine order of life. Neither this nor the preceding prohibition gives any ruling on the punishment to be imposed on offenders, should they be guilty of contravening the deuteronomic ruling.

17:2-7. This is not the case, however, with the third of the condemnatory prohibitions, which concerns a blatant infringement of the first commandment. It brings us face to face once again with the extremely harsh treatment demanded by the deuteronomic legislators for any citizens who defected from a total commitment to the worship and devotion to the LORD as God. This was brought out earlier in the rulings of chap. 13 concerning incitement by prophets to turn away from exclusive loyalty to the LORD. The situation envisaged in the present law concerns acts of outright apostasy. It would seem most probable that it has been introduced at this point as a further elaboration of the prohibition against the retention of non-Israelite cult symbols that was raised in 16:21–17:1. The penalty for blatant acts of apostasy is unequivocal and final: Any person found guilty of such an offense was to be put to death.

It is clear that such cases represented extremely dangerous instances where the legal system could be abused and where unscrupulous persons could concoct a charge of apostasy in order to avenge themselves upon people against whom they held a grudge. Thus the rules governing witnesses and their evidence are reaffirmed in 17:6-7 to ensure that those who made such accusations were directly implicated in their consequences. The presence of this ruling may reflect on the fact that such cases called for the most careful judicial handling. More probable, however, it seems that the whole stratum of harsh anti-apostasy legislation in Deuteronomy, imposing capital punishment for such offenses and calling for the

extermination of non-Israelite residents in the land, marks a consistent, coherent, but relatively late, stratum in the growth of the deuteronomic corpus. After the political disasters that witnessed the collapse of the Judean state in 587 BCE, a harsh and bitter attempt was made to effect a religious "cleansing" of the land from those elements of the population who had abandoned their exclusive loyalty to the LORD as God, or who had never observed such a commitment.

17:8-13. The ruling set out concerning legal cases that could not be resolved through the usual judicial processes maintains the ancient custom of settling such disputes by resorting to the services of a priest at a sanctuary. In most cases, this would have called for the use of the sacred lot, rather than depending on any kind of special priestly legal expertise. It is of interest that the type of dispute envisaged as needing such priestly resolution is primarily one that involved physical violence (v. 8). The various kinds of bloodshed mentioned refer to distinctions between intentional and accidental assaults leading to the death of the victim. A similar understanding must apply to the phrase "one kind of assault and another." In such cases, the intention of the assailant was of critical importance, but was obviously frequently difficult to determine. Similarly, even accidental injury could be brought about through culpable negligence on the part of a person's ill-judged actions. The issues relating to "one kind of legal right and another" must refer to claims over property in which proof of ownership could often be difficult to establish.

The recognition of the difficulties inherent in such cases, where the expertise and experience of a judge could be most heavily tested, reflects two prominent features of ancient Israelite law. The first concerns the relatively undeveloped laws of evidence, for which a verdict depended on assessing the accused person's intention at the time of the offense. The second concerns the reluctance in such cases in which insufficient and inconclusive evidence was available to allow the case to be dropped altogether. Belief that a divine decision could be obtained in spite of the difficulties of the case by resorting to the help of a levitical priest at a sanctuary enabled the determination of disputes lacking adequate proof by a different route altogether. The results may often have been arbitrary, but were simply imposed on the persons concerned.

The conclusion set out in vv. 12-13 specifying the death penalty for anyone who refused to accept the verdict of the priest in such instances can be taken to indicate that the arbitrary nature of the verdicts arrived at in such cases could often give rise to further bitterness and recrimination. Quite evidently, even the inclusion of provisions to involve the priestly authorities in settling diffi-cult legal cases was only a partial, and apparently contested, means of assistance. Overall the picture we obtain from the regulations providing for a wide-ranging legal system in ancient Israel reflects the importance of a system of criminal justice in maintaining peaceful and non-violent relationships in society. At the same time, the provisions that are made highlight the difficulties that all such systems experience and the need for protecting the innocent as well as punishing the guilty.

REFLECTIONS

The provision of publicly appointed judges, combined with a strong insistence on the necessity for their impartiality and integrity in the performance of their duties, reflects the high importance the development of law encounters in any society. We find ample evidence of such developments throughout the ancient Near East, and they are well represented in the legal sections of the Old Testament. The belief in a foundation of law that undergirds and protects all human societies was one of the major products of the rise of civilization in the ancient Near East. The achievements of (even partial) justice have provided a legacy from which all of Western civilization has benefited.

From as far back as clear historical evidence can take us it was initially the members of a person's own clan or tribe who sought to protect individuals and to impose punishment on wrongdoers. Family heads and tribal chiefs used their wisdom and experience to sort out disputes and to settle quarrels. When members of other clans and tribes were involved, a system of blood revenge operated as far as could be attained. Quite often such a primitive system of justice based on avenging wrongdoing must have been cruel and have caught up many innocent persons in its actions. To establish a system of redress and punishment based on individual responsibility and guilt, therefore, stood in the forefront of building a fairer and more peaceful society. Yet to achieve this called for considerable care and experience of human behavior. Questions of responsibility and guilt consistently called for ways of determining the relative degrees of guilt when two persons were caught up in a violent quarrel. Fairness demanded insight into matters of intentions and self-control. So inevitably forms of law that set out the principles and guidelines by which men and women should be judged became carefully worded and carefully balanced statements. Time and again the verdicts that were to be reached depended on the good sense, integrity, and fair-mindedness of the persons who judged the case. Perhaps more precisely it was the people themselves, including both the victim and the accused, who were to "judge" the case, and it was the responsibility of the judge to show how this was to be done and to ensure, so far as was possible, that it was done.

Yet even with the best of intentions all forms of public authority could be abused and manipulated to serve more selfish and partisan ends. Even kings could abuse their authority, as is amply shown by the biblical portrait of the Egyptian pharaoh in the story of how Israel suffered oppression in Egypt. So in any township or city, judges were fallible human beings who could behave in unsatisfactory ways.

It is in the light of this that much of the biblical tradition, even when it boldly upholds a public judicial system and supports the necessity for its operation in a civilized society, is constantly aware of its vulnerability and limitations. Whether we look at biblical stories of how royal figures such as Ahab could distort justice to support their selfish aims (1 Kings 21), how prophets complained of major abuses perpetrated by high public figures (Jeremiah 22), or even how psalmists and sages warned of corruption and injustice in judicial affairs, we are brought face to face with an awareness of the problems that the cry for justice entailed.

It is important in the light of this to note how persistently the biblical tradition of justice focuses not simply on the insistent demand "justice and only justice shall you pursue," but that it recognizes the many hindrances to this. All judicial systems are subject to limitations and weaknesses and can rise no higher than the honesty and conscientiousness of the persons who administer them. It is a major feature of the Ten Commandments that they frankly recognize these difficulties and endeavor to counter them. The prohibition against wrong use of the divine name, the sharp repudiation of giving false evidence ("bearing false witness," KJV), and not least the prohibition against coveting a neighbor's property indicate that possessing good laws is not sufficient in itself to create a just and worthy society. Personal honor and integrity also have a role to play, as does a willingness to seek out and deal with public wrongs. Laws can be no more "lawful" than the willingness and determination of those who administer them.

We sense once again the importance that Deuteronomy, and the biblical tradition more generally, attaches to the claim that justice and righteousness are fundamental features of the divine order of life. They are not simply human constructions for the convenience of men and women living in society, but are gifts of God by which a truly holy and righteous world order can be achieved. In many respects, we can see how basic, and sometimes inadequate, the laws set out in the Bible appear to be when compared with the more sophisticated legal formulations with which we work in the modern world. Nevertheless, the insights, principles, and especially the sense of the divine basis for law that the Bible presents remain valid for our acceptance and recognition. We, too, are called upon to pursue justice and righteousness with impartiality and fervor, since the lives, freedom, and well-being of all human beings depend on this. If we are sometimes tempted to feel superior to persons in antiquity, we may nonetheless profit from the clarity and directness with which they set out the goals of righteous living.

Deuteronomy 17:14–18:22, Kings, Priests, and Prophets

NIV

[14] When you enter the land the LORD your God is giving you and have taken possession of it and settled in it, and you say, "Let us set a king over us like all the nations around us," [15] be sure to appoint over you the king the LORD your God chooses. He must be from among your own brothers. Do not place a foreigner over you, one who is not a brother Israelite. [16] The king, moreover, must not acquire great numbers of horses for himself or make the people return to Egypt to get more of them, for the LORD has told you, "You are not to go back that way again." [17] He must not take many wives, or his heart will be led astray. He must not accumulate large amounts of silver and gold.

[18] When he takes the throne of his kingdom, he is to write for himself on a scroll a copy of this law, taken from that of the priests, who are Levites. [19] It is to be with him, and he is to read

NRSV

[14] When you have come into the land that the LORD your God is giving you, and have taken possession of it and settled in it, and you say, "I will set a king over me, like all the nations that are around me," [15] you may indeed set over you a king whom the LORD your God will choose. One of your own community you may set as king over you; you are not permitted to put a foreigner over you, who is not of your own community. [16] Even so, he must not acquire many horses for himself, or return the people to Egypt in order to acquire more horses, since the LORD has said to you, "You must never return that way again." [17] And he must not acquire many wives for himself, or else his heart will turn away; also silver and gold he must not acquire in great quantity for himself. [18] When he has taken the throne of his kingdom, he shall have a copy of this law written for him in the presence of the levitical priests. [19] It shall remain

NIV

it all the days of his life so that he may learn to revere the LORD his God and follow carefully all the words of this law and these decrees ²⁰and not consider himself better than his brothers and turn from the law to the right or to the left. Then he and his descendants will reign a long time over his kingdom in Israel.

18 The priests, who are Levites—indeed the whole tribe of Levi—are to have no allotment or inheritance with Israel. They shall live on the offerings made to the LORD by fire, for that is their inheritance. ²They shall have no inheritance among their brothers; the LORD is their inheritance, as he promised them.

³This is the share due the priests from the people who sacrifice a bull or a sheep: the shoulder, the jowls and the inner parts. ⁴You are to give them the firstfruits of your grain, new wine and oil, and the first wool from the shearing of your sheep, ⁵for the LORD your God has chosen them and their descendants out of all your tribes to stand and minister in the LORD's name always.

⁶If a Levite moves from one of your towns anywhere in Israel where he is living, and comes in all earnestness to the place the LORD will choose, ⁷he may minister in the name of the LORD his God like all his fellow Levites who serve there in the presence of the LORD. ⁸He is to share equally in their benefits, even though he has received money from the sale of family possessions.

⁹When you enter the land the LORD your God is giving you, do not learn to imitate the detestable ways of the nations there. ¹⁰Let no one be found among you who sacrifices his son or daughter inᵃ the fire, who practices divination or sorcery, interprets omens, engages in witchcraft, ¹¹or casts spells, or who is a medium or spiritist or who consults the dead. ¹²Anyone who does these things is detestable to the LORD, and because of these detestable practices the LORD your God will drive out those nations before you. ¹³You must be blameless before the LORD your God.

¹⁴The nations you will dispossess listen to those who practice sorcery or divination. But as for you, the LORD your God has not permitted you to do so. ¹⁵The LORD your God will raise up for you a prophet like me from among your own brothers.

ᵃ10 Or *who makes his son or daughter pass through*

NRSV

with him and he shall read in it all the days of his life, so that he may learn to fear the LORD his God, diligently observing all the words of this law and these statutes, ²⁰neither exalting himself above other members of the community nor turning aside from the commandment, either to the right or to the left, so that he and his descendants may reign long over his kingdom in Israel.

18 The levitical priests, the whole tribe of Levi, shall have no allotment or inheritance within Israel. They may eat the sacrifices that are the LORD's portionᵃ ²but they shall have no inheritance among the other members of the community; the LORD is their inheritance, as he promised them.

3This shall be the priests' due from the people, from those offering a sacrifice, whether an ox or a sheep: they shall give to the priest the shoulder, the two jowls, and the stomach. ⁴The first fruits of your grain, your wine, and your oil, as well as the first of the fleece of your sheep, you shall give him. ⁵For the LORD your God has chosen Leviᵇ out of all your tribes, to stand and minister in the name of the LORD, him and his sons for all time.

6If a Levite leaves any of your towns, from wherever he has been residing in Israel, and comes to the place that the LORD will choose (and he may come whenever he wishes), ⁷then he may minister in the name of the LORD his God, like all his fellow-Levites who stand to minister there before the LORD. ⁸They shall have equal portions to eat, even though they have income from the sale of family possessions.ᵃ

9When you come into the land that the LORD your God is giving you, you must not learn to imitate the abhorrent practices of those nations. ¹⁰No one shall be found among you who makes a son or daughter pass through fire, or who practices divination, or is a soothsayer, or an augur, or a sorcerer, ¹¹or one who casts spells, or who consults ghosts or spirits, or who seeks oracles from the dead. ¹²For whoever does these things is abhorrent to the LORD; it is because of such abhorrent practices that the LORD your God is driving them out before you. ¹³You must remain completely loyal to the LORD your God. ¹⁴Although these nations that you are about to dispossess do

ᵃ Meaning of Heb uncertain   ᵇ Heb *him*

NIV

You must listen to him. [16]For this is what you asked of the LORD your God at Horeb on the day of the assembly when you said, "Let us not hear the voice of the LORD our God nor see this great fire anymore, or we will die."

[17]The LORD said to me: "What they say is good. [18]I will raise up for them a prophet like you from among their brothers; I will put my words in his mouth, and he will tell them everything I command him. [19]If anyone does not listen to my words that the prophet speaks in my name, I myself will call him to account. [20]But a prophet who presumes to speak in my name anything I have not commanded him to say, or a prophet who speaks in the name of other gods, must be put to death."

[21]You may say to yourselves, "How can we know when a message has not been spoken by the LORD?" [22]If what a prophet proclaims in the name of the LORD does not take place or come true, that is a message the LORD has not spoken. That prophet has spoken presumptuously. Do not be afraid of him.

NRSV

give heed to soothsayers and diviners, as for you, the LORD your God does not permit you to do so.

[15]The LORD your God will raise up for you a prophet[a] like me from among your own people; you shall heed such a prophet.[b] [16]This is what you requested of the LORD your God at Horeb on the day of the assembly when you said: "If I hear the voice of the LORD my God any more, or ever again see this great fire, I will die." [17]Then the LORD replied to me: "They are right in what they have said. [18]I will raise up for them a prophet[a] like you from among their own people; I will put my words in the mouth of the prophet,[c] who shall speak to them everything that I command. [19]Anyone who does not heed the words that the prophet[d] shall speak in my name, I myself will hold accountable. [20]But any prophet who speaks in the name of other gods, or who presumes to speak in my name a word that I have not commanded the prophet to speak—that prophet shall die." [21]You may say to yourself, "How can we recognize a word that the LORD has not spoken?" [22]If a prophet speaks in the name of the LORD but the thing does not take place or prove true, it is a word that the LORD has not spoken. The prophet has spoken it presumptuously; do not be frightened by it.

[a] Or prophets   [b] Or such prophets   [c] Or mouths of the prophets
[d] Heb he

COMMENTARY

17:14-20. Central to the understanding of public authority in ancient Israel was acceptance of the king as supreme earthly ruler. So we are now given instructions for the setting up of a monarchy as the first of three primary institutions for the administration and life of the community. The other two are those of priests and prophets. Already the regulations concerning the appointment of law officials have presupposed acceptance of an order of levitical priests. Now we are presented with an explicit instruction concerning the place, character, and function of the king in ancient Israel. It is unique within the Pentateuch as a formulation declaring the constitutional position of the king and the basic duties that are entrusted

to him. We can, however, note that the hymnic celebrations of the Davidic king in a significant number of psalms forthrightly express an absolute claim for the divine choice and support for the kingly office. What is surprising about the deuteronomic ruling is that it regards the monarchy as a permitted concession, rather than a necessary foundation of national existence. We may contrast the very different perspective given in Lam 4:20, where the kingship is regarded as indispensable.

So the regulations governing the kingship that are set out in these verses are distinctive for the quite modest claims made for the king and for the restrictions placed on the role and prestige of the public office. It cuts the monarchy down to size, clearly showing it to be a human institution, subject to normal human temptations. Undoubtedly this guarded attitude must reflect the uncertainty with which the deuteronomists viewed it.[81] It is also a noteworthy feature that the particular limitations imposed on the king in vv. 16-17 are aimed at preventing another ruler of the character of Solomon, whose excesses had effectively caused the breakup of the old united kingdom that David had built. There can be no doubt at all that the reason for this cutting down to human dimensions of the office of king was a consequence of Israel's experience and an awareness of the dangers of the oppressiveness kings could bring. The prophet Samuel's warning concerning kings and their excessive claims and demands (1 Sam 8:11-18) was a message the deuteronomists had taken to heart.

In order to appreciate the special character of what the deuteronomists declare concerning Israel's kings, we must see it against the background of the ancient Near Eastern world.[82] Fundamental to this context was the claim that kings were appointed by God, chosen and supported by an act of divine will, enabling kings to exercise a form of "divine" rule on earth. Human kings were presented as acting on behalf of, and in the place of, God. So kingship purported to be a form of theocracy in which the human agent, whether claimed as "son of God" or simply as the "anointed of God," exercised a divine rule. So whatever kings did was claimed to be by divine authority and to possess an absolute, unquestionable right. Human societies simply "received" their kings as emissaries of God, rather than choosing and appointing them. It is on account of such excessive claims that kingship could consistently appear as a powerful, but inherently oppressive, form of government.

Yet kingship was not all bad, and it is impossible to consider the rise and success of the progress of civilization in the ancient world without it. Kings were powerful, relatively efficient, and militarily successful. They claimed to administer justice, to deter brigands and robbers, and to

put down all forms of wrongdoing. They presented themselves as the friends of widows and the weak. In order to fulfill all these duties, they produced great codes of law, amassed powerful armies, promoted trade, built great temples and palaces, and founded schools and colleges of scribes. So they achieved much, but frequently did so at a terrible human cost.

Looking at kingship in such a light, we can understand the carefully moderated acceptance of kingship that the deuteronomists advocate. Kingship, even that of the revered house and dynasty of David, was an institution that had a tarnished history.

Nevertheless, the assertion that the ruler was to be "a king whom the LORD your God will choose" (v. 15) maintains the long-standing tradition that kings were not humanly appointed but were the subject of divine election. Such had certainly been declared with regard to the dynasty of David (Pss 89:3-4; 132:11-12), and the restriction of succession to members of this dynasty must certainly have been intended by the deuteronomists.

The rule of the king, further, expressly spells out that the king was to be "one of your own community" (מקרב אחיך miqqereb 'aheyka; lit., "one from among your brothers"). This has a twofold significance, consciously emphasizing the human status of the king and eliminating the mythological language of the king's origins from a divine birth, making him "Son of God," as in Egypt. Also, it ensured that the king was a native Israelite, thereby precluding that a foreigner could usurp the throne of Israel. In all of this the deuteronomic legislation very plainly sets limits to the titles, religious claims, and supernatural status of the king, such as had surrounded the varied portraits of kingship current in antiquity. The king is very clearly a human figure with a particular task to perform within the life of Israel as a nation.

Historically we can place the origins of this deuteronomic view of kingship in the situation of Josiah's reign. This was a period in which a major attempt was made, in the disastrous aftermath of a century of Assyrian interference, to reestablish a single united people of Israel under a native ruler of the house of David. The price that such a ruler had to pay was that he should not repeat the excesses of Solomon.[83] So the roots of this deuter-

81. F. Crüsemann, *Der Widerstand gegen das Königtum. Die antikönigliche Texte des Alten Testaments und der kampf um den frühe israelitischen Staat,* WMANT 49 (Neukirchen-Vluyn: Neukirchener Verlag, 1978); G. E. Gerbrandt, *Kingship According to the Deuteronomistic History,* SBLDS 87 (Atlanta: Scholars Press, 1986) esp. 89-115.

82. This background is excellently described in H. Frankfort, *Kingship and the Gods: A Study of Ancient Near Eastern Religion as the Integration of Society and Nature* (Chicago: University of Chicago Press, 1948).

83. This historical background to the changed perception of kingship in Josiah's time is described in R. Albertz, *A History of Israelite Religion in the Old Testament Period,* trans. J. Bowden (London: SCM, 1994) 1:198-206.

onomic reformed view of a limited monarchy are to be traced back to the political situation of Josiah's reign. However, more than this would appear to underlie the surprising degree of uncertainty concerning whether there needed to be a continuing Davidic monarchy in Israel at all. Certainly for Josiah's reform the supporting role of the king was vital to the whole success of the program. We must conclude, therefore, that this level of doubt expressed in vv. 14-20 regarding the future of the institution has entered in the wake of the disastrous blow to the Jerusalem monarchy in 587 BCE. After that, its future was far from clearly evident, and the noncommittal historical note in 2 Kgs 25:27-30 corroborates this to be the later deuteronomic viewpoint.

The requirement that the king should have prepared a copy of the written law of Moses (vv. 18-19), which is a reference to the deuteronomists' own law code, and that he should read from it "all the days of his life" accords with the report of David's instructions to Solomon (1 Kgs 2:1-4). It has all the marks of being a rather idealistic demand that affirmed the priority of Moses and the Mosaic law over the institution of kingship. It would support the overall deuteronomic demand that the historical figure of Moses and the Mosaic written law should provide the basis for limiting the absolute freedom of the king to control religious, military, and legal affairs.

18:1-14. The next major institution to be subjected to the legislative purview of the deuteronomists is that of the priesthood. Here the deuteronomic instructions make provision for all Levites to serve as priests, whether they were already resident in the city of the central shrine or whether they had earlier been resident in other towns, but now wished to continue their ministry at the central sanctuary (vv. 6-7). The ruling explicitly specifies that they are then to enjoy equal privileges and rewards for their services as those of other priests working in the city. (That this privilege was not conceded is reported in 2 Kgs 23:9.)

The origin of the Levites as a class of religious ministrants is shrouded in historical uncertainty and cannot be brought into a wholly clear light. It is claimed both here and elsewhere in the Bible that they at one time constituted a separate tribe, but became scattered as a consequence of a major upheaval that befell them (cf. Genesis 34). Yet

this claim is not easily substantiated, and such a portrayal of the origins of what was essentially a varied range of religious devotees bears traces of a highly stylized and theoretical account of persons who had no specific territorial holding of their own. Their primary characteristic was an unswerving and uncompromising loyalty to the LORD as sole deity and a concomitant expertise in the knowledge of divine service that qualified them to be priests.

Certainly at an earlier time in Israel not all priests were Levites (even David's sons could become priests; 2 Sam 8:18), but this simply reflects that early Israel lacked any narrowly defined summary of the duties exclusive to priests. It was undoubtedly held from an early period of Israel's development that it was advantageous for a priest to be a Levite (cf. Judg 17:12-13). It would appear, therefore, that the deuteronomic legislation moves strongly in the direction of imposing some uniformity by permitting all Levites to serve as priests. However, such a situation was more than a little theoretical if by the time this legislation was set out the Jerusalem Temple had been destroyed and the levitical communities scattered.

That they did not all do so becomes clear from subsequent definitions of priestly duties and restrictions contained in the book of Ezekiel and the later priestly (P) parts of the Pentateuch. In fact, in the post-exilic age, the Levites became a class of second-rank sanctuary ministers. Their duties especially concerned the more verbal aspects of public worship with the offering of public prayer, the singing of psalms, and the delivery of sermon-like exhortations.

The deuteronomic concern to set out a program for the worship of Israel at only one central sanctuary involved a number of competing, and often conflicting, claims relating to the history of the priesthood. The events of the sixth century BCE had undoubtedly brought not only disruption to the activities of the Jerusalem priesthood, but also serious divisions within it. These conflicts were not easily resolved, and when the time came for the rebuilding and refurbishing of the destroyed Temple fresh compromises became necessary. In fact, the entire period is shrouded in obscurity so far as the history of the priesthood is concerned.[84] The deu-

---

84. M. Haran, *Temples and Temple Service in Ancient Israel* (Oxford: Oxford University Press, 1978); A. Cody, *A History of Old Testament Priesthood,* AnBib 35 (Rome: Pontifical Biblical Institute, 1969).

teronomic ruling concerning the role of the Levites and their potential status as priests marks an important step in defining their position within the nation. From the evidence of the existence of levitical cities, it would appear that not all Levites were involved with the service of a sanctuary. Thus the deuteronomic ruling points to a firm encouragement for the Levites to become more fully involved in Israel's cultic affairs.

Two particular points concerning the levitical priesthood are well reflected in the deuteronomic legislation. The first is its recognition that the Levites were wholly dependent upon the gifts and tithe offerings of the people. Since they possessed no substantial tribal territory of their own, the Levites' adherence to the traditional allegiance to the LORD as God was their title-deed to a role in Israel's life.

If the overall perspective adopted by this commentary—that Deuteronomy 12–26 reflects a concern to legislate for religious renewal in the wake of the disasters of 587 BCE—is valid, then this degree of concern for the welfare of the Levites is particularly fitting. Without a fully functioning Temple and temple cultus to administer, the position of the levitical priesthood had become precarious. So it was especially significant that the deuteronomists were deeply committed to securing the survival of the levitical priesthood.

It is certainly also a matter of significance for the development of Israel's priesthood that the deuteronomic instructions and provisions brought a variety of priestly duties and activities under a single, uniform set of regulations. In the wider concern to eradicate deviations of practice and to expunge the risk of continuing resort to non-Yahwistic deities and rituals, the priestly function itself has here become more closely defined.

Since priestly duties involved the service of the altar, the careful and ritually acceptable slaughter and presentation of sacrifices were among the more obvious of priestly functions. Yet, alongside these duties were many others involving instruction in prayer, the obtaining of oracles, and the handling of a range of issues covering matters of hygiene and ritual purity. Although many areas relating to the latter either do not appear at all or do so only marginally in the deuteronomic law book, it can be concluded that the deuteronomic provisions for the priesthood generated a strong

unifying impulse. This was not an accidental offshoot of the reformers' work, but rather represented a positive tendency designed to uphold an integrated and unified tradition. So far as the deuteronomists were concerned, all worship was a matter of wider concern to society and to the possibility of maintaining an Israelite state. Therefore, it needed to be carefully regulated and supervised. The deuteronomic tendency to treat matters of religious allegiance and worship as matters involving the state and its legislative powers is a striking aspect of its assumptions and interests. It is wholly in line with this deuteronomic tendency that precise instructions are given concerning which parts of the sacrificial offering and what proportion of the first fruits were to be given to the Levites as their due (vv. 3-4).

The inclusion of a series of prohibitions concerning cultic and quasi-cultic activities set out in vv. 9-14 can be seen as a practical consequence of the endorsement given to the approved levitical priesthood. With a faithful and loyal order of priestly servants, Israel would have no need to resort to the mixed range of rituals and divinatory practices that are outlawed here. It would appear that many of them had been popular and widely used responses to a variety of social needs, especially those concerned with health and hygiene.

The reference to making a son or daughter "pass through fire" (v. 10) marks a particularly repugnant form of religious commitment attested in the OT (cf. 2 Kgs 21:6). It relates to human sacrifice, as condemned in 12:31. The remaining categories of cultic activity that are outlawed in vv. 10-14 relate to forms of oracle giving, divination, and the manipulation of magic powers through the uttering of spells or counterspells. In this we encounter a particularly influential aspect of the deuteronomic theology, which strove to eliminate any form of acceptance of or deference to arbitrary spiritual powers, whether they were believed to be beneficial or harmful. All spiritual powers and controls, whether public or private, are made subject to the overriding sense of the unique, personal, and gracious nature of the LORD as God. Belief in the sovereignty of one divine controlling power and its superiority to all human powers and to all forms of spiritual power to which human beings might claim access was of paramount importance. No compulsive manipulation of divine forces, secret invocation of divine names and titles, or even appeal to the spirits of departed ancestors was to be permitted in Israel. All worship is personalized and subjected to recognized categories of reasoned personal communication. Personal prayer, not magical formulas, is the basis for humans' communication with God and with the divine world. Public worship was to be saturated with awareness that symbols, words, and ritual actions could only be adjuncts to support this personal communion of human beings with God. Neither ritual nor the spoken word could be depersonalized so as to provide a mechanistic interpretation of spiritual realities.

18:15-22. So far we have been introduced to the roles of three classes of public institutional authority: royal, juridical, and priestly. In the course of time, each was liable to acquire a degree of rigidity and permanence in the wielding of power. For both kings and priests authority was based on an inherited status, conferred upon them as a birthright. In consequence, the public power structures based on these roles easily became inflexible. They tended to become detached from actual personal needs, and so became unresponsive to the changing religious and social circumstances of the community. To counter this inflexibility, prophets offered a measure of corrective challenge and the possibility of innovation.

We are now introduced to a fourth, and more controversial, class of public leaders. These were the prophets who would arise from time to time to bring a new word from God that could affect both the national and the private lives of persons in Israel.

Taken in its broad compass, the picture of ancient Israelite religion given to us by the biblical writings is of a spiritual and religious life in which prophets figured very prominently. This accords with the realities of the situation as they were actually experienced. Prophets consistently and regularly appeared as charismatically endowed, and often richly eloquent, speakers and preachers. Their authority was claimed to be, and was usually accepted as, direct, God-given, and unconfined to any one family, locality, or tribal group. To outsiders and opponents, prophets appeared to be self-appointed speakers, but to their followers they were God-appointed revealers of truth that came through no other avenue of spiritual knowledge.

Prophets gave expression to a fundamentally different kind of authority from that of priests and kings precisely because it appeared as a spontaneous breaking-in of knowledge and truth from God alone. The speech forms used by such prophets conformed to this claim to a divine origin, in which they presented themselves as the very mouth of God to speak to Israel. It is this spontaneous, uncontrolled—and uncontrollable—feature of prophetic activity that made it both a powerful instrument for change and renewal and a danger to all attempts at religious conformity and orthodoxy. In the light of their concern to create and impose a uniform Mosaic Torah, it is understandable that the deuteronomists should have viewed prophets and their activities with some misgivings. Already we have encountered the sharp ruling and ferocious penalties that endeavored to deal with any prophet who presumed to speak a message in the name of a deity other than that of the LORD God of Israel (13:1-5). Yet prophecy could not be altogether denied, and it appears that the rigorous contention, which the deuteronomists so eagerly endorsed, that Israel should worship the LORD alone as God was itself a product of prophetic tradition. Besides which, prophets must often have received a strong popular following in ancient Israel, making any attempt to limit or nullify their activities quite impossible. So the deuteronomic legislative ruling concerning prophets bears a twofold requirement: Prophets should be "from among your own people" (i.e., native Israelites), and they should be "like Moses."

Although it has been argued that there may have existed in Israel a specific order of official prophets who would fulfill an inter-tribal role for the whole community and would thereby have a national significance "like Moses," no firm evidence for this is available. Rather, the formulation must be not the reconstruction of an ancient office within the nation, but a major attempt by the deuteronomists to see prophecy in perspective. The importance of prophecy could not be denied, but its haphazard and random appearance meant that it had to be treated with great care. It is for this reason that this legislation allows prophecy a place in the religious and public life of Israel, but hedges it about with restrictions. Prophets must be "like Moses," by which it is intended to affirm that their teaching must accord with the words and spirit of Moses as Israel's unique leader.

The second test for the acknowledgment of a true prophet is that the prophet's messages should be proved true by the actual outcome of events (v. 22). This must be judged a reasonable, but in practice rather unhelpful, test to apply. Since prophecies often took the form of warnings and threats in times of crisis, it may have been of little assistance to find that such warnings were true when it was too late to heed their message. Similarly the reverse situation would be equally valid. Yet in truth the ruling, for all its theoretical nature, provides an important guide to the way in which prophecy was understood by the deuteronomists.

Already there existed a substantial body of written tradition of the words and messages of earlier prophets that are now preserved for us. These messages, emanating from as early as the eighth century BCE from such figures as Amos and Isaiah, had foretold the terrible disasters Israel had subsequently suffered. So this deuteronomic ruling serves as a form of endorsement and approval for these figures, recognizing that they had formed a genuine succession in the spirit of Moses. In substantial measure, their words had already shown themselves to be true prophecies by the time that deuteronomic legislation was composed, and it is the need to draw attention to this that has occasioned its composition. We may compare the rough and ready guide to the differences between true and false prophecy that is set out in Jer 28:8-9, where the influence of the deuteronomists is certainly evident.

In large measure it agreed well with the overall sense of crisis they felt and with their urgent appeals for obedience to the law Moses had given for the deuteronomic authors to point to the way in which prophecies of doom had already proved true to events. The distinctive word of prophecy could not be ignored as a valid and authoritative word from God. Yet this did not open the door for every prophet to be heard and listened to with confidence. Many prophets came with deceitful messages of false hope, just as Hananiah had endeavored to beguile the hearers of Jeremiah (Jer 28:1-4; 29:8-9). Not every prophetic message was from God, and only that which was in agreement with the terms and spirit of Moses and the law was to be accepted.

Overall the presence of prophets within the national life of Israel, both in a larger historical perspective and in the contemporary scene, provided the deuteronomists with an unsettling and complex agency of religious leadership. It claimed an immediate and unquestioned authority and could thereby easily endanger the zeal for conformity and unswerving loyalty the deuteronomists demanded. Yet it had held a rich and influential place in Israel's history and was, in any case, widely respected. The prophets' place could not be denied and had contributed much to the deuteronomic sense that Israel's present crisis had been foretold by divine warnings. So the formula that is put forward is that all true prophets must be "like Moses," thereby drawing a line around the range of their teaching and at the same time indicating that Moses was a more than ordinary prophet.

REFLECTIONS

The fourfold listing of public leadership authorized by the deuteronomic legislators represents a uniquely balanced assessment of the power structures of human societies in general. A striking mixture of leadership based on inherited status and popular acclamation jostles alongside religious and social factors in shaping public life. Kings are brought down from their high thrones, but prophets, too, who could sometimes appear as kingmakers, are commissioned for their work within strict limits. Law officers are heralded as the custodians of justice and fairness, but their task is seen to be almost impossible to fulfill without the added input of priestly agents who could pronounce a verdict from God.

In an avowedly religious writing like the book of Deuteronomy, we might have expected to find evidence of claims for a priestly hierarchy, such as existed in many ancient societies and have occasionally reappeared in Christian history. Throughout the ancient Near East also we find that all writing of a political nature has emerged from within powerful monarchies in which the role of the king is presented as supreme and beyond all question. Such portrayals of the kingly office as absolute and as the only divinely approved form of human government find some limited expression in the Old Testament (see Psalm 2). Yet much of the biblical literature offers a more truthful and circumscribed portrait of kings, revealing their weaknesses and corruptibility. The deuteronomic ruling, therefore, places their power within necessary restraints and openly insists that they are themselves simply servants of a higher power and a more perfect justice.

Perhaps most of all we might have expected to find in the deuteronomic rulings an endorsement of prophecy as the sure and certain word from God to guide the people of Israel along a difficult and uncharted course. Yet here, too, we find major limitations, even if their expression is so brief and simplistic as to be difficult to apply to individual cases. Prophets, like kings, were to be administrators and leaders in a social order that had been laid down by Moses and ultimately looked to God as its author and founder.

So we find in Deuteronomy a sensitive balance in which judges, kings, priests, and prophets are each accorded an appropriate, if rather loosely defined, range of authority. Very markedly the royal power is sharply curtailed and set under a higher power based on the tradition of Moses. Priestly authority and the right of priests to claim the economic support of the community are firmly endorsed, but are placed within boundaries that exclude a range of mantic activities that are now viewed as dangerous and subversive. All priestly claims to be able to negotiate with the spirits of departed ancestors or to pierce the hidden mysteries of the future are eliminated. Israelite priests could not be shamans wielding magical power, nor could prophets and soothsayers ply their trade, preying on popular griefs and fears.

No indication is given as to how the judges and law officers were to be appointed, and this may well have been left open for local communities to decide. To what extent the royal administration exercised influence on this matter is left unclear.

The picture generated by this deuteronomic legislation concerning public authority left significant areas of overlap between the separate lines of interest and control. Township elders appear still to have exercised considerable power in local affairs, but no sharp line defining each respective sphere of influence is drawn. Nor is it evident how disputes were to be settled when conflicts of interest arose. However, the legislation provides an interesting recognition that a variety of insights and interests was appropriate to the good ordering of a society. In particular, legal disputes were not left under the exclusive control of any one professional group or section of the community. Some degree of interactive checks and restraints is envisaged that conceived of Israelite society as functioning as an organic unit. For the health of the whole, each part was required to be vitally active and consciously alert.

Undergirding the whole picture of society that is presupposed by these rules governing public authority is an affirmed divine foundation. Israel is conceived of as existing by an act of divine election, and so its social order is to be shaped by a polity given by Moses in the name of God. The concept of divine revelation colors and illuminates everything; yet, it is not a traditional theocracy in which kings or priests assume the role of deity. In place of an autocratic, and easily corruptible, imperial bureaucracy there is an awareness of a need for flexibility and the embracing of change. In spite of its form and reputation as a law book, Deuteronomy is strongly committed to granting the freedom of responsible officers to deal with a wide range of basic matters on an ad hoc basis. Unlike the later developments of Jewish life in which a vast number of rules and instructions were formulated to cover everyday activities, Deuteronomy leaves much to the good sense and integrity of responsible citizens.

Particular importance attaches to the deuteronomic concern to allow that a variety of channels of public jurisdiction were to be recognized and given the freedom to act in concert, and even to react upon each other. Nor is any undue emphasis placed here on the strictly religious, over against the more openly secular, structures of the community.

It is not by mere chance that the deuteronomic movement as a whole has been viewed as providing a kind of center or balance point for the entire development of the Old Testament. It quite evidently marked a point of transition, consciously aware that, with the decline and eventual collapse of the kingdoms of Israel and Judah between the eighth and sixth centuries BCE, an experiment had come to an end. Israel had entered the world of nations, had striven to express a divine ideal within this national reality, and had fallen apart in the face of unstoppable pressures from Mesopotamian imperialism. From within this declining national ethos the deuteronomists sought to retrieve many of the fundamental values and achievements it had brought to birth. A commitment to law, justice, brotherly love, and national solidarity had established ideals that were worth preserving for the future.

Such ideals, however, remain weak and powerless unless they are incorporated into the operating structures of social and political life. It is never sufficient to have just laws. It is essential that such laws be administered justly. Similarly, the righteous authority of judges and rulers to put down wrongdoing and punish the lawless can only work when these officers of the state act justly. More subtly still, both priests and prophets can uphold a vision and awareness of the spiritual dimension of life. Yet these persons, too, can distort their offices to pander to the fears and sufferings of a community by preying on those fears. Even religion can be abused and traded for spurious claims to know what cannot be known and to deal in unholy fire!

DEUTERONOMY 19:1–21:23, MATTERS OF LIFE AND DEATH

OVERVIEW

The series of laws that now follow deals with issues of life and death. They can helpfully be regarded as having been brought together to provide an elaboration and explication of the sixth commandment ("You shall not murder," 5:17). This commandment applied to more than simply the overt criminal acts that can be covered by the modern criminal category of murder. Even the ancient laws covering this crime encountered difficulties with the necessity for distinguishing between a deliberate act of killing, the causing of death by accident, and the varying degrees of culpability that could emerge between the two extremes. At the very least, the commandment against unjustified killing raised a host of questions concerning the intention of the offender, the possibility of provocation, and the extent to which social conventions of revenge may have played a role.

When we add to these variable factors the indirect responsibility for a person's premature death, a vast number of further issues arise. Injury might lead to dangerous infections, resulting in prolonged suffering and death, and carelessness and indifference can lead to an innocent person's suffering a fatal accident. Who, then, was to blame? Homicide was seldom a simple matter, and further complexities arose when the circumstances of death were suspicious, but no obvious culprit could be found. The stories in 2 Samuel present excellent examples of the problem of apportioning blame for homicide, as in the case of David's responsibility for Uriah's death (2 Sam 12:9) and Joab's responsibility for the killing of Abner (2 Sam 3:26-30).

Overall the problem of distinguishing between intentional and accidental killing occasioned difficulties for the lawmakers of antiquity, as it still does today. When we add to these problems the accountability for accidental death or for the death of a slave, we can see that the direct commandment "You shall not murder" opened up a range of further issues. Issues of life and death stretched into areas that, at first reckoning, appeared to be only peripherally related to the question of murder.

Deuteronomy 19:1-21, Issues of Life and Death: Murder

19 When the LORD your God has destroyed the nations whose land he is giving you, and when you have driven them out and settled in their towns and houses, ²then set aside for yourselves three cities centrally located in the land the LORD your God is giving you to possess. ³Build roads to them and divide into three parts the land the LORD your God is giving you as an inheritance, so that anyone who kills a man may flee there.

⁴This is the rule concerning the man who kills another and flees there to save his life—one who kills his neighbor unintentionally, without malice aforethought. ⁵For instance, a man may go into the forest with his neighbor to cut wood, and as he swings his ax to fell a tree, the head may fly off and hit his neighbor and kill him. That man may flee to one of these cities and save his life. ⁶Otherwise, the avenger of blood might pursue him in a rage, overtake him if the distance is too great, and kill him even though he is not deserving of death, since he did it to his neighbor without malice aforethought. ⁷This is why I command you to set aside for yourselves three cities.

⁸If the LORD your God enlarges your territory, as he promised on oath to your forefathers, and gives you the whole land he promised them, ⁹because you carefully follow all these laws I command you today—to love the LORD your God and to walk always in his ways—then you are to set aside three more cities. ¹⁰Do this so that innocent blood will not be shed in your land, which the LORD your God is giving you as your inheritance, and so that you will not be guilty of bloodshed.

¹¹But if a man hates his neighbor and lies in wait for him, assaults and kills him, and then flees to one of these cities, ¹²the elders of his town shall send for him, bring him back from the city, and hand him over to the avenger of blood to die. ¹³Show him no pity. You must purge from Israel the guilt of shedding innocent blood, so that it may go well with you.

¹⁴Do not move your neighbor's boundary stone set up by your predecessors in the inheritance you receive in the land the LORD your God is giving you to possess.

19 When the LORD your God has cut off the nations whose land the LORD your God is giving you, and you have dispossessed them and settled in their towns and in their houses, ²you shall set apart three cities in the land that the LORD your God is giving you to possess. ³You shall calculate the distances[a] and divide into three regions the land that the LORD your God gives you as a possession, so that any homicide can flee to one of them.

4 Now this is the case of a homicide who might flee there and live, that is, someone who has killed another person unintentionally when the two had not been at enmity before: ⁵Suppose someone goes into the forest with another to cut wood, and when one of them swings the ax to cut down a tree, the head slips from the handle and strikes the other person who then dies; the killer may flee to one of these cities and live. ⁶But if the distance is too great, the avenger of blood in hot anger might pursue and overtake and put the killer to death, although a death sentence was not deserved, since the two had not been at enmity before. ⁷Therefore I command you: You shall set apart three cities.

8 If the LORD your God enlarges your territory, as he swore to your ancestors—and he will give you all the land that he promised your ancestors to give you, ⁹provided you diligently observe this entire commandment that I command you today, by loving the LORD your God and walking always in his ways—then you shall add three more cities to these three, ¹⁰so that the blood of an innocent person may not be shed in the land that the LORD your God is giving you as an inheritance, thereby bringing bloodguilt upon you.

11 But if someone at enmity with another lies in wait and attacks and takes the life of that person, and flees into one of these cities, ¹²then the elders of the killer's city shall send to have the culprit taken from there and handed over to the avenger of blood to be put to death. ¹³Show no pity; you shall purge the guilt of innocent blood from Israel, so that it may go well with you.

a Or prepare roads to them

NIV

¹⁵One witness is not enough to convict a man accused of any crime or offense he may have committed. A matter must be established by the testimony of two or three witnesses.

¹⁶If a malicious witness takes the stand to accuse a man of a crime, ¹⁷the two men involved in the dispute must stand in the presence of the LORD before the priests and the judges who are in office at the time. ¹⁸The judges must make a thorough investigation, and if the witness proves to be a liar, giving false testimony against his brother, ¹⁹then do to him as he intended to do to his brother. You must purge the evil from among you. ²⁰The rest of the people will hear of this and be afraid, and never again will such an evil thing be done among you. ²¹Show no pity: life for life, eye for eye, tooth for tooth, hand for hand, foot for foot.

NRSV

14You must not move your neighbor's boundary marker, set up by former generations, on the property that will be allotted to you in the land that the LORD your God is giving you to possess.

15A single witness shall not suffice to convict a person of any crime or wrongdoing in connection with any offense that may be committed. Only on the evidence of two or three witnesses shall a charge be sustained. ¹⁶If a malicious witness comes forward to accuse someone of wrongdoing, ¹⁷then both parties to the dispute shall appear before the LORD, before the priests and the judges who are in office in those days, ¹⁸and the judges shall make a thorough inquiry. If the witness is a false witness, having testified falsely against another, ¹⁹then you shall do to the false witness just as the false witness had meant to do to the other. So you shall purge the evil from your midst. ²⁰The rest shall hear and be afraid, and a crime such as this shall never again be committed among you. ²¹Show no pity: life for life, eye for eye, tooth for tooth, hand for hand, foot for foot.

COMMENTARY

The three issues that come first under the purview of this section of the deuteronomic legislation deal with the provision of three cities of refuge west of the river Jordan (vv. 1-13), the removal of a neighbor's boundary marker (v. 14), and the question of what kind of evidence was admissible to substantiate a criminal charge, especially if it carried the death penalty (vv. 15-21).

19:14. It certainly appears out of place that the shifting of a boundary marker should have been included among rules dealing with offenses that carried the possibility of capital punishment. It may be that such a criminal act had come to be regarded as so serious a problem that it had to be deterred by the most serious punishment. It cannot, in any case, altogether be ruled out that such actions had given rise to violent quarrels in which deaths had occurred.

We must also keep in mind that the problem attendant upon the illegal shifting of boundary markers may have been introduced at this point precisely because it illustrated the major problems attendant upon the laws of evidence admissible in legal cases. Without any form of mapping procedure it is likely that it was virtually impossible to attain proof that a marker had been moved. The particular problem would then have been brought into the series of cases concerning issues of life and death, since it highlighted the importance of securing admissible evidence. Beyond this we can note that the primacy of land as the most basic form of wealth made any attempt to deprive a citizen of it a serious matter. To be cheated out of land eroded the very ability of a farmer to maintain himself and his family.

19:1-13. The regulations set out concerning the provision of three cities of refuge west of the river Jordan was an important matter for the administration of law. Their existence greatly affected the possibility of giving a fair trial to an accused person. Any person who was suspected of or accused of involvement in the death of another could flee to a designated city in order to secure a fair trial. By presenting oneself at such a location, the accused person was to be protected from any of the victim's family members who were seeking immediate vengeance. In Num 35:6, 11, these cities are described as "cities of refuge," although that precise title is not employed here. The setting apart of three similarly functioning cities east of the Jordan is dealt with in Deut 4:41-43 as well, drawing special attention to the importance attached to such provision in Israel's legal administration. It would certainly appear that the passage in 4:41-43 is of later origin than the law of 19:1-13. It elaborates on the clause of 19:8-10 that allows for the designation of additional cities "in the event of Israel's territory being enlarged." In the final shaping of the book of Deuteronomy, adequate account had to be taken, not only of the ideal borders of the territory of Israel, but also of the fact that many loyal citizens had by this time been scattered outside the traditional territory of Israel.

We can take it for granted that the designation of specific cities as places of refuge was a feature of considerable antiquity in Israel and was not simply a deuteronomic measure aimed at compensating the loss of protection afforded by the many sanctuaries extant in the earliest period. Such cities were of vital significance if a credible and uniform system of law were to operate within the nation. This is not to suppose that, prior to their introduction, Israel was essentially a lawless society, but rather that the power to administer justice and to punish criminal acts was almost exclusively the prerogative of the heads of the large extended families. Their impartiality could not be relied upon, and, in any event, when dealing with offenses perpetrated by those outside of their immediate kin group a straightforward practice of vengeance taking was the norm. True justice meant fairness for all, and this involved preventing the taking of innocent life in cases where the guilty could not be reached or identified and ensuring that any accused person was given an opportunity to present whatever defense he or she could offer. The process of law was deeply committed to protecting the innocent by ensuring that punishment was never arbitrary or untried.

So the purpose of designating cities of refuge was not to provide a means whereby offenders could protect themselves from the due course of justice, but to provide places where a proper examination of the charges could be made and a verdict arrived at by a more impartial court than would be presented by the victim's family or local townspeople. For the system to work effectively, it was necessary that experienced and trained officials be available in the cities to which the criminal had fled in order for proper legal procedures to be followed. The situation once again draws special attention to the point that, when we consider the difficulties encountered in biblical times for the administration of justice, and when we listen to the persistent cries preserved in the literature of the period of those who felt denied this, it is clear that it was primarily in matters of procedure that the greatest difficulties arose. It was usually possible to discern what distinguished right from wrongful actions, but problems arose with the need for a procedure to ensure that the innocent were not punished with the guilty, or even instead of them.

Where serious crimes were concerned, especially those in which the death of a person was involved, the custom of exacting punitive revenge by a near relative of the victim existed as a long-standing and publicly acknowledged tradition. It represented a rough and ready means of protecting against crime and was chiefly operated from within a social setting in which kin groups and kinship obligations were paramount.

The term used here to identify the pursuer of the accused as "the avenger of blood" (גאל הדם gōʾēl haddām) indicates a person who was expected to be acting "in hot anger" (יחם לבבו yēḥam lēbābô, v. 6). It strongly suggests that such a pursuer would be a near relative of the victim who would be seeking revenge. However, it is possible that the townspeople of the victim may have acted to appoint such an avenging deputy. In any case, it is the elders of the victim's city (v. 12) who are charged with seeking out and punishing the accused. The Hebrew is sufficiently open to allow that such elders may have been those from the designated city to which the fugitive had fled. In this case, it is possible that they would have been regarded as especially experienced in handling such matters and fully conversant with the law. In any case, it was an issue of importance for the avenging person to obtain some degree of public recognition of the elder's intentions and purpose lest he should later be accused of the fugitive's death.

Behind these procedures and the provision of designated cities for the sorting out of serious legal offenses it appears that a primary concern was to enable the community more broadly to implement a proper distinction between accidental and intentional killing. Such a need involved careful examination of witnesses and the assurance that punitive action was not taken simply on the word of a single witness. Overall, we can see why more than one community could become caught up in such procedures and why it was necessary to allow time for the investigation of the charges to be conducted fully.

19:15-21. The need to distinguish manslaughter from murder raised serious problems concerning the admissibility of evidence and the broader background of the relationship between the accused person and the victim. The formula in v. 11 makes plain that a primary factor in determining guilt was whether a previous history of enmity between the two persons was known. It is in this regard that the laws of evidence set out in this section are significant. The important issues dealt with concern the requirement that at least two witnesses be available to substantiate the guilt of the accused person. This must often have proved a major obstacle to the prosecution of a satisfactory case. Many murders would have taken place where no reliable witnesses could be found. The danger posed by a malicious witness, which is dealt with in v. 16, would then sometimes have referred not simply to a totally false accusation (as in the instance of the charges against Naboth, 2 Kings) but to a person who could be persuaded to come forward with corroborative evidence that had no real basis of truth. The harsh punishment of bearing false witness testifies to the serious problem for justice posed by the danger of perjury. In general, in the biblical period the laws of evidence were relatively undeveloped and unsophisticated. This fact alone must undoubtedly have been a strong factor in keeping alive the older tradition of justice by revenge when the legal system was unable to deal with a case satisfactorily.

Another significant way the instructions set out here reflect the development of the ancient Israelite legal system concerns the variety of legal, or quasi-legal, authorities who could become involved in the handling of a particular case. The rules governing proceedings in the cities of refuge for a person accused of homicide refer to the authority of city elders (v. 12). In the rules of procedure against a witness accused of perjury, reference is made to both priests and judges. It would have been unusual, but not impossible, for all three classes of judicial authority—elders, priests, and judges—would all have been involved at the same time. It seems likely, therefore, that a substantial measure of openness was left so that, in changing social circumstances, any of the three sources of legal expertise could become involved in a particular case. In general it seems that an appeal to the priests to settle a dispute was not so much a question of their independent legal knowledge, but rather of their access to the sacred lot, which could be called upon to reach a verdict when other means failed.

The sternness of the rule of making the punishment equal to that which might have been inflicted on the accused person—"life for life, eye for eye, tooth for tooth," the *lex talionis* (v. 21)—is a reflection on the problem posed by perjury. It is not a deliberate relapse into expressly physical forms of punishment involving maiming, which the biblical law codes largely shun, but a deep realization that harsh dissuasive measures were needed to deal with offenses that could undermine the entire legal system. The same general observation may well account for the unexpected inclusion of a warning against the removal of a neighbor's landmark (v. 14). Where the legal system showed itself to be vulnerable, it inevitably countered by calling for very severe punishments. Carried to an extreme, this approach to the problems of law appears in the gross demands for capital punishment for those who repudiated the Mosaic legal system altogether by blatant apostasy.

REFLECTIONS

The three laws set out in Deuteronomy 19 are centered especially on cases of homicide and the varying circumstances by which a person could be held responsible for another's death.

The foremost distinction lay between determining whether it had been done intentionally or accidentally. The guideline concerning proof of earlier enmity between the parties concerned could only serve as a very rough and provisional guide. Obviously even two friends could fall out, and one might become violent in a dangerous, and perhaps uncharacteristic, fit of rage. Similarly in the course of daily work, it might be possible to misuse a tool or weapon so recklessly as to endanger another person's life.

In such circumstances, it was wholly understandable that the immediate relatives and dependents of the victim should seek revenge for what had happened. This is a state of affairs that can be traced far back into the kinship structures of tribal groups. Wanton violence and killing were not tolerated within any normal community of human beings. Yet conflicts and quarrels between families and tribes might often go unpunished when there was no effective means of imposing punishment across family and tribal boundaries. The growth of systems of law that operated on a territorial, and ultimately a nationwide, level was of the utmost importance. It became compellingly necessary once large townships and cities embraced a wide mixture of tribal and ethnic groups. Therefore, it became the goal of a satisfactory legal system to deal with all human beings on an equal footing—a feature that is partially affirmed in the deuteronomic concept of membership in the community (lit., of "brothers"). Although this fell short of treating all human beings as standing on an equal footing, it nevertheless marked a major step forward and cut directly across the family and clan boundaries that must still have molded the feelings controlling moral attitudes within the nation.

So acts involving bodily violence, sometimes resulting in death, needed the greatest care to determine whether they should be treated as criminal acts. The law needed to protect innocent persons as well as to punish the guilty. Such cases largely turned on assessment of intention, and so raised the question as to how such intentions could be discovered, and when discovered, how they could be proved. The problems were clearly many, and the modern reader is well aware that they remain fundamental aspects of our own legal system.

For Christian readers, the presumption in the Sermon on the Mount of personal responsibility for nurturing good attitudes (Matt 5:21-26) intensifies the debate about the issue. Moreover, the dangers of too easily and hastily giving way to feelings of anger are strongly emphasized. When pressed even further, the modern reader is made aware of the fact that issues of provocation may also be summoned in defense of a person who commits a violent crime (Matt 5:38-42). Once we begin to judge our actions, and the actions of others, we are forced to recognize that the motives and restraints that determine them are many and complex.

Each of us has limits beyond which, if we are pushed, we may experience an emotional explosion. So even when we are compelled to judge others for the sake of public well-being and justice, we know that we are never wholly and completely innocent of the desires for revenge and for hurting those who have hurt and wounded us. It is in such a context that the very personal admonition of Jesus is to be heard and reflected on. It is not too subtle and illusory to suggest that sometimes the very strength and fervor of our anxiety to see punishment brought upon wrongdoers lies not in an altruistic desire to protect others around us, but in a half-conscious guilty fear that we, too, given the right circumstances, can become dangerous and violent persons. All too easily we can overlook the fact that the stark simplicity and terse formulations of the Old Testament laws hide from us the deep and considered judgments that undergird them.

It is important to give room to the sophisticated concern of the biblical teachers of proverbial wisdom that whether we are peaceable or violent persons may lie far back, before we ever commit either peaceful or angry actions. The person who consorts with violent persons is likely to become as violent as those companions (Prov 1:10-19). Similarly, by yielding to impulses of ill temper or outbursts of violence, a person will smooth the path to more ill-tempered and violent outbursts at a later time. Every day of our lives we are becoming new persons as a consequence of the emotions we yield to or learn to contain. Ultimately when we ask ourselves what kind of person we have become, we may look back on actions of which we are ashamed. We may not have realized at the time what our actions would lead to, and we shall probably have dismissed them as "uncharacteristic." Nevertheless, what was uncharacteristic yesterday can quickly develop into what is all too characteristic today.

Deuteronomy 20:1-20, Issues of Life and Death: Warfare

NIV

20 When you go to war against your enemies and see horses and chariots and an army greater than yours, do not be afraid of them, because the LORD your God, who brought you up out of Egypt, will be with you. ²When you are about to go into battle, the priest shall come forward and address the army. ³He shall say: "Hear, O Israel, today you are going into battle against your enemies. Do not be fainthearted or afraid; do not be terrified or give way to panic before them. ⁴For the LORD your God is the one who goes with you to fight for you against your enemies to give you victory."

⁵The officers shall say to the army: "Has anyone built a new house and not dedicated it? Let him go home, or he may die in battle and someone else may dedicate it. ⁶Has anyone planted a vineyard and not begun to enjoy it? Let him go home, or he may die in battle and someone else enjoy it. ⁷Has anyone become pledged to a woman and not married her? Let him go home, or he may die in battle and someone else marry her." ⁸Then the officers shall add, "Is any man afraid or fainthearted? Let him go home so that his brothers will not become disheartened too." ⁹When the officers have finished speaking to the army, they shall appoint commanders over it.

¹⁰When you march up to attack a city, make its people an offer of peace. ¹¹If they accept and open their gates, all the people in it shall be subject to forced labor and shall work for you. ¹²If they refuse to make peace and they engage you in battle, lay siege to that city. ¹³When the LORD your God delivers it into your hand, put to the sword all the men in it. ¹⁴As for the women, the children, the livestock and everything else in the city, you may take these as plunder for yourselves. And you may use the plunder the LORD your God gives you from your enemies. ¹⁵This is how you are to treat all the cities that are at a distance from you and do not belong to the nations nearby.

NRSV

20 When you go out to war against your enemies, and see horses and chariots, an army larger than your own, you shall not be afraid of them; for the LORD your God is with you, who brought you up from the land of Egypt. ²Before you engage in battle, the priest shall come forward and speak to the troops, ³and shall say to them: "Hear, O Israel! Today you are drawing near to do battle against your enemies. Do not lose heart, or be afraid, or panic, or be in dread of them; ⁴for it is the LORD your God who goes with you, to fight for you against your enemies, to give you victory." ⁵Then the officials shall address the troops, saying, "Has anyone built a new house but not dedicated it? He should go back to his house, or he might die in the battle and another dedicate it. ⁶Has anyone planted a vineyard but not yet enjoyed its fruit? He should go back to his house, or he might die in the battle and another be first to enjoy its fruit. ⁷Has anyone become engaged to a woman but not yet married her? He should go back to his house, or he might die in the battle and another marry her." ⁸The officials shall continue to address the troops, saying, "Is anyone afraid or disheartened? He should go back to his house, or he might cause the heart of his comrades to melt like his own." ⁹When the officials have finished addressing the troops, then the commanders shall take charge of them.

10When you draw near to a town to fight against it, offer it terms of peace. ¹¹If it accepts your terms of peace and surrenders to you, then all the people in it shall serve you at forced labor. ¹²If it does not submit to you peacefully, but makes war against you, then you shall besiege it; ¹³and when the LORD your God gives it into your hand, you shall put all its males to the sword. ¹⁴You may, however, take as your booty the women, the children, livestock, and everything else in the town, all its spoil. You may enjoy the spoil of your enemies, which the LORD your God

NIV

¹⁶However, in the cities of the nations the LORD your God is giving you as an inheritance, do not leave alive anything that breathes. ¹⁷Completely destroy[a] them—the Hittites, Amorites, Canaanites, Perizzites, Hivites and Jebusites—as the LORD your God has commanded you. ¹⁸Otherwise, they will teach you to follow all the detestable things they do in worshiping their gods, and you will sin against the LORD your God.

¹⁹When you lay siege to a city for a long time, fighting against it to capture it, do not destroy its trees by putting an ax to them, because you can eat their fruit. Do not cut them down. Are the trees of the field people, that you should besiege them?[b] ²⁰However, you may cut down trees that you know are not fruit trees and use them to build siege works until the city at war with you falls.

[a]17 The Hebrew term refers to the irrevocable giving over of things or persons to the LORD, often by totally destroying them.   [b]19 Or down to use in the siege, for the fruit trees are for the benefit of man.

NRSV

has given you. ¹⁵Thus you shall treat all the towns that are very far from you, which are not towns of the nations here. ¹⁶But as for the towns of these peoples that the LORD your God is giving you as an inheritance, you must not let anything that breathes remain alive. ¹⁷You shall annihilate them—the Hittites and the Amorites, the Canaanites and the Perizzites, the Hivites and the Jebusites—just as the LORD your God has commanded, ¹⁸so that they may not teach you to do all the abhorrent things that they do for their gods, and you thus sin against the LORD your God.

19If you besiege a town for a long time, making war against it in order to take it, you must not destroy its trees by wielding an ax against them. Although you may take food from them, you must not cut them down. Are trees in the field human beings that they should come under siege from you? ²⁰You may destroy only the trees that you know do not produce food; you may cut them down for use in building siegeworks against the town that makes war with you, until it falls.

COMMENTARY

We are now presented with two sections concerned with Israel's conduct in time of war. Already we have noted the strong and forthright manner in which the deuteronomic legislation deals with issues involving the aims and conduct of war, and the subject has left an indelible stamp on the entire deuteronomic theology and ethic. Here we are brought face to face with two speeches, the first of which was to be delivered by a priest to the assembled soldiers before a battle (vv. 2-4). This is followed by another that was to be delivered by undefined officials at a similar time (vv. 5-8). Only after these formal speeches had been made were the mustered military forces to be returned to the charge of their commanders (v. 9).

The first speech, which was to be given by a priest, sets out the religious nature of the battle that was to come and gives assurance that it would be God who would accompany the forces to fight against Israel's enemy and give the victory. The address by the officials allows a modest number of exemptions from military service on what could be regarded as compassionate grounds. These include the building of a new house, the planting of a new vineyard, or engagement to be married.

However, when we look at the implications more closely we see that the reasons for exemption have less to do with compassion for persons with overriding personal commitments than with larger issues concerning morale in battle. The central issue is that of courage and wholehearted commitment in battle. Those who were preoccupied with personal concerns and undue anxieties about their personal survival could be the cause of undermining the morale of the entire army (v. 8). Throughout there appears a realization that morale was a subtle and complex factor in battle and that even a few defaulters could sap the determination of the army.

A central issue that permeates both speeches is the claim that warfare was a religious duty in which victory could only come directly from God. For such victories to be obtained the primary requirements were not military technology but unbroken moral courage and unwavering faith in the power of God to give success. This is exactly the formula that is singled out as bringing success in defeating kings Sihon and Og (2:24–3:13) and that is claimed to have brought about the overthrow of Jericho at the outset of the campaign to claim possession of the land (Josh 6:1-27).

The entire ideology relating to warfare in Deuteronomy has been labeled that of "holy war," and it has been held to represent an ancient Israelite concept of obligation for military action that the deuteronomists resuscitated from an earlier period. Certainly a number of ancient ideas and customs relating to warfare have been called upon by the deuteronomists to create their particular presentation regarding Israel's military potential. Overall the book of Deuteronomy is a startlingly and dangerously militaristic work, reflecting the situation its authors saw to be facing Israel. Nevertheless, it appears doubtful in the extreme that what the deuteronomists propose as a way for Israel to achieve great success in its military campaigns represents a viable and ancient practice that was being revived at the close of the monarchic period. Such an assumption would not explain the highly theological and theoretical tone of what is demanded and the extraordinary claim that warfare could largely be left in the hands of the priests.

The ideology of warfare that is set out in Deuteronomy must be held as largely a creation of the deuteronomists themselves, although undoubtedly drawing upon various elements of custom and tradition.[85] These elements served the deuteronomists' purpose in stressing the religious over against the strictly military and technological features of ancient warfare. Overall the view of warfare in Deuteronomy must be regarded as a response to the calamities and disasters that had befallen the twilight years of the kingdom of Judah in the late seventh and early sixth centuries BCE. It represents the deuteronomists' answer to the catastrophe of 587 BCE and to the military prowess of Assyria and Babylon. It evidences much the same tone and manner as the prophet Isaiah in repudiating the boastful claims of the Assyrian Rabshakeh when calling upon the citizens of Judah to surrender.

It is highly dubious whether the deuteronomic program for battle can be regarded as significantly more than a theoretical set of rules for the conduct of war; therefore, it is one that was never properly put to the test. It is more concerned with theology and the belief in the divine control of history than with what happened on the battlefield. As with many features of the law code of Deuteronomy 12–26, a core of established rules and customs has been incorporated into a larger framework of religious ideology aimed at renewing and reestablishing the central role of faith in the LORD God as the key to Israel's future. It is true that it reflects experience of war, but this would appear largely to have been the tragic battles Israel and Judah fought in defense of their land once the grip of Mesopotamian rule on the Levant had tightened. In recognizing Israel's weakness and helplessness in the face of Mesopotamian military strength, Deuteronomy looks to a renewed faith in God as a basis for defense.

Once this background is taken fully into account and full cognizance is taken of the religious, rather than the military, features of what is demanded, we can better understand the distinctive character of Deuteronomy's perspective on warfare. It looks for divinely wrought miracles, rather than effective campaign strategies. It portrays as the exemplary guide to success in warfare the qualities shown in the defeat of Goliath by the boy David, in whom the virtues of faith and courage were the primary qualifications for victory (1 Sam 17:45-47). It is in line with this religious and theological interpretation of warfare that the deuteronomists saw warfare primarily as a means for the taking and retaining of possession of the land. The demand for the annihilation of the previous inhabitants is wholly in line with this aim (vv. 17-18). For the deuteronomists, war was a God-ordained means of land acquisition and religious purification.[86]

An unfortunate consequence of the assumption that the deuteronomic theology of warfare represents a viewpoint that was typical and widely adopted in ancient Israel is that its demands have

---

85. This point is particularly well presented in A. Rofé, "The Laws of Warfare in the Book of Deuteronomy: Their Origins, Intent and Positivity," *JSOT* 32 (1985) 23-44. See also G. von Rad, *Studies in Deuteronomy,* trans. D. Stalker, SBT 9 (London: SCM, 1953) 45-59, and *Holy War in Ancient Israel,* trans. Marva J. Dawn (Grand Rapids: Eerdmans, 1991) 115-27; Millard C. Lind, *The Theology of Warfare in Ancient Israel* (Scottdale, Pa.: Herald, 1980) 146-68.

86. Susan Niditch, *War in the Hebrew Bible* (New York: Oxford University Press, 1993) 28-55.

frequently been regarded as characteristic of ancient Israel as a whole. This is not the case, as its religious purpose and highly theoretical nature bear out. There is much in the literature that points to Israel's warfare as having been more restrained and less theologically charged than either the book of Deuteronomy or the historical writings it has influenced would suggest.

Certainly the late reflections on the reasons for Israel's defeat at the hands of the Babylonian ruler Nebuchadnezzar (Jer 27:5-7) would point to the eventual abandonment of the exaggerated hopes of God-ordained victory that the deuteronomic doctrine led some to expect. At most we must conclude that the biblical writings contain a variety of viewpoints concerning warfare and its demands. Accordingly the emphatic deuteronomic doctrine on the subject must be set in a larger context that shows it to have been an unusually one-sided portrayal of the aims, methods, and possibilities warfare proffered to ancient Israel. It is certainly not the only viewpoint regarding war the Bible contains.

Some awareness that different situations called for different responses and that the harsh demand for the extermination of all the previous occupants of the land on religious grounds was an extreme position is shown by the qualification set out in vv. 10-14. In this case, it is urged that, before a town was besieged, terms of surrender should be offered to its inhabitants, with forced slave labor being the price such surrender incurred (v. 11). After the capture of a town that had been besieged and defeated, only the men were to be put to death,

with the women, children, and property falling to the victors as spoil (v. 13). However, the addition of vv. 15-18 limits these concessions to towns outside the land of Israel proper. The concession is important for two reasons. The first lies in its recognition that Israel's aims and practices in the conduct of war were unusual and abnormal for warfare in the ancient world. More significant, it also recognizes that the reasons for this harsh and unyielding demand were wholly religious in nature, once again revealing how the deuteronomic concern with the first commandment has ultimately colored its entire legislative program.

When examined from a historical-critical perspective, both in regard to other literary developments within the deuteronomic movement and in the light of a knowledge of the practice of warfare in antiquity, the distinctively deuteronomic character of what is demanded in the conduct of war can be clearly and readily seen. It represents far more than the revival of an ancient practice of the so-called holy war, even though some elements of ancient custom have been incorporated into it. Nor is it at all likely that it represents a serious attempt during the reign of King Josiah to restore some military credibility after the disastrous consequences of more than a century of Assyrian control. In sum, it marks a particular stratum of deuteronomic thought that viewed warfare in precisely the same manner as it viewed the administration of criminal law, as a means whereby the purity of Israel's religion, as expressed in the deuteronomic law code, could be enforced.

REFLECTIONS

The aims and methods of warfare as set out in this deuteronomic passage are among the most disturbing and dangerous of all the teaching that is to be found within the book. The realization that this ideology of warfare has an exclusive religious basis and motivation, and that it has frequently been said to constitute a doctrine of "holy war," has heightened, rather than softened, the intense moral objections to it. It is nothing less than a demand for a policy of religious and ethnic genocide. Clearly its total contradiction to the Christian demand for the love of one's enemy (Matt 5:43-45) stands out starkly. The deuteronomic viewpoint has created a popular image of the militaristic aggressiveness of Old Testament literature generally, by the very drama and abnormality of the story of how Jericho was captured as the first of the campaigns within the land, when the deuteronomic formula was held to have been adopted.

Various lines of Christian and Jewish apologetic have repeatedly been adopted with a view to rescuing the demands for such genocidal belligerence from its obvious, and directly literal, consequences. The first is essentially a hermeneutical ploy and endeavors to isolate the demand for faith, courage, and unconditional loyalty to the LORD God from its genocidal expression. So it is argued that the demand for the slaughter of those who practice idolatry and who repudiate their loyalty to the LORD God may be set aside, to be replaced by a more tolerant and reasoned policy of persuading such persons to see the error of their ways. Loyalty to God is applauded and endorsed, but the method demanded for dealing with God's enemies is repudiated. Whatever merit lies in such a stance, it cannot be said to deal effectively with the heart of the problem without facing more directly the dangerous nature of any such demand for violence against religious opponents. Too much of Jewish and Christian history has been stained with blood by those who did not realize that the deuteronomic demands should not be taken literally. In this regard, the firm repudiation of such a doctrine of genocide in the New Testament needs to be given its full weight.

Possibly a more fruitful path has been pursued by those who, like John Bunyan in *The Holy War,* have sought to regard the concept of a biblically justified holy warfare typologically as an allegory of the conflict between good and evil for control of the human soul. It is not a doctrine of how Israelites should deal with Canaanites, but a doctrine outlining the demands, difficulties, and dangers of the spiritual warfare that every serious believer in a righteous God must face. Not only does Bunyan allegorize the broad concept of warfare into a spiritual struggle, but also, in his marginal notes, he connects individual acts of heroism and violence to particular virtues or temptations. It must undoubtedly be recognized that an imaginative, spiritually uplifting, and purposeful set of guidelines for the pursuit of the spiritual life can be wrung from even the most unlikely sources. Provided the imaginative reader is fully aware of the literary technique that is being adopted, and of the inherent dangers of the literal interpretation of the material, then quite positive and constructive ideas and guidelines can be adduced.

Yet neither of these two hermeneutical approaches has engaged seriously enough with the moral dangers and threats posed by the literal interpretation of the text. They have arisen primarily out of a deep consciousness that the literal demands of the text are totally unacceptable and have usually failed to face this issue seriously enough. Clearly the intention of the original authors of the text, insofar as we can understand it, was that their demands should be taken seriously. Moreover the very seriousness of their intent was a vital reason for the harsh and uncompromising measures they proposed to adopt. We are compelled, therefore, to face up to this serious demand for genocide as a product of a community that undoubtedly believed that it should have been attempted, even if history suggests that it was not actually undertaken.

It is the more historical perspective, relating both to the circumstances and to the background of the deuteronomists and of what we can discover historically concerning the manner in which Israel took possession of the land and waged warfare in defense of it, that has drawn most attention from modern critics. Undoubtedly the previous Canaanite inhabitants of the land Israel occupied were not exterminated. There is a deep illogicality inherent in the deuteronomic doctrine that they had been. Had this been the case, the fervor to remove all relics of the religion of these people and all knowledge of their customs would not have been needed.

Yet whatever amelioration of anxiety and conscience such modern historical knowledge may give to the critical reader of the text, it nevertheless fails to deal adequately with the moral and historical problems it raises for us. The very existence of the deuteronomic doctrine of religious warfare and its methods demands that we acknowledge that it clearly came into existence as a serious ideology of a segment within ancient Israel. That this community felt itself to be threatened and its survival to be in doubt if such measures were not adopted may also be granted. That the historical Canaanites and their immediate ethnic descendants were no longer easily to be found may be granted. Nevertheless, there clearly were in existence people whom the deuteronomic authors identified as Canaanites and whom they feared so greatly, and detested so fervently, that the deuteronomists called for their total extermination. Who exactly these people were and why such a sharp and fearful conflict with them had arisen remains totally obscure. Yet certainly it appears that such a community existed and that, under the guise of fighting an ancient ideological battle concerning the uniqueness of Israel's God, the deuteronomists pieced together a harsh religious doctrine concerning the purpose, methods, and possibilities of warfare (the fruits of which they expected to be miraculous).

The Commentary has sought to interpret the manner and content of the deuteronomic legislation against the background of the twilight days of Judah's history. The movement certainly continued its activity after the final collapse of Judah and the destruction of its Temple in 587 BCE. Yet it appears not to have survived this catastrophe for very long, so that new movements carried the future spiritual and intellectual movements of the new Judaism in very different directions. Most prominent among these new directions were a more tolerant spirit, the hope of an ultimate spread of the knowledge of the LORD God to all nations and peoples, and a willingness to live, work, and learn alongside non-Jewish neighbors. So a broader intellectual outlook accompanied a more tolerant spirit, and the excesses of the deuteronomic calls for genocide were left aside. The attempts that have arisen from time to time to reactivate the deuteronomic demand for a renewed religious warfare in the face of some new spiritual crisis have only served to reinforce the moral objections to it. In interpreting it, therefore, it is valuable that its literal meaning should be frankly recognized, its dire consequences properly appraised, and its moral limitations reasserted.

Deuteronomy 21:1-23, Issues of Life and Death: Murder, Capital Offenses, and Inheritance

NIV	NRSV
21 If a man is found slain, lying in a field in the land the LORD your God is giving you to possess, and it is not known who killed him, [2]your elders and judges shall go out and measure the distance from the body to the neighboring towns. [3]Then the elders of the town nearest the body shall take a heifer that has never been worked and has never worn a yoke [4]and lead her down to a valley that has not been plowed or planted and where there is a flowing stream. There in the valley they are to break the heifer's neck. [5]The priests, the sons of Levi, shall step forward, for the LORD your God has chosen them to minister and to pronounce blessings in the name of the LORD and to decide all cases of dispute and assault. [6]Then all the elders of the town nearest the body shall wash their hands over the heifer whose neck was broken in the valley, [7]and they shall declare: "Our hands did not shed this blood, nor did our eyes see it done. [8]Accept this atonement for your people Israel, whom you have redeemed, O LORD, and do not hold your people guilty of the blood of an innocent man." And the bloodshed will be atoned for. [9]So you will purge from yourselves the guilt of shedding innocent	**21** If, in the land that the LORD your God is giving you to possess, a body is found lying in open country, and it is not known who struck the person down, [2]then your elders and your judges shall come out to measure the distances to the towns that are near the body. [3]The elders of the town nearest the body shall take a heifer that has never been worked, one that has not pulled in the yoke; [4]the elders of that town shall bring the heifer down to a wadi with running water, which is neither plowed nor sown, and shall break the heifer's neck there in the wadi. [5]Then the priests, the sons of Levi, shall come forward, for the LORD your God has chosen them to minister to him and to pronounce blessings in the name of the LORD, and by their decision all cases of dispute and assault shall be settled. [6]All the elders of that town nearest the body shall wash their hands over the heifer whose neck was broken in the wadi, [7]and they shall declare: "Our hands did not shed this blood, nor were we witnesses to it. [8]Absolve, O LORD, your people Israel, whom you redeemed; do not let the guilt of innocent blood remain in the midst of your people Israel." Then they will be absolved of bloodguilt. [9]So you shall

NIV

blood, since you have done what is right in the eyes of the LORD.

¹⁰When you go to war against your enemies and the LORD your God delivers them into your hands and you take captives, ¹¹if you notice among the captives a beautiful woman and are attracted to her, you may take her as your wife. ¹²Bring her into your home and have her shave her head, trim her nails ¹³and put aside the clothes she was wearing when captured. After she has lived in your house and mourned her father and mother for a full month, then you may go to her and be her husband and she shall be your wife. ¹⁴If you are not pleased with her, let her go wherever she wishes. You must not sell her or treat her as a slave, since you have dishonored her.

¹⁵If a man has two wives, and he loves one but not the other, and both bear him sons but the firstborn is the son of the wife he does not love, ¹⁶when he wills his property to his sons, he must not give the rights of the firstborn to the son of the wife he loves in preference to his actual firstborn, the son of the wife he does not love. ¹⁷He must acknowledge the son of his unloved wife as the firstborn by giving him a double share of all he has. That son is the first sign of his father's strength. The right of the firstborn belongs to him.

¹⁸If a man has a stubborn and rebellious son who does not obey his father and mother and will not listen to them when they discipline him, ¹⁹his father and mother shall take hold of him and bring him to the elders at the gate of his town. ²⁰They shall say to the elders, "This son of ours is stubborn and rebellious. He will not obey us. He is a profligate and a drunkard." ²¹Then all the men of his town shall stone him to death. You must purge the evil from among you. All Israel will hear of it and be afraid.

²²If a man guilty of a capital offense is put to death and his body is hung on a tree, ²³you must not leave his body on the tree overnight. Be sure to bury him that same day, because anyone who is hung on a tree is under God's curse. You must not desecrate the land the LORD your God is giving you as an inheritance.

NRSV

purge the guilt of innocent blood from your midst, because you must do what is right in the sight of the LORD.

¹⁰When you go out to war against your enemies, and the LORD your God hands them over to you and you take them captive, ¹¹suppose you see among the captives a beautiful woman whom you desire and want to marry, ¹²and so you bring her home to your house: she shall shave her head, pare her nails, ¹³discard her captive's garb, and shall remain in your house a full month, mourning for her father and mother; after that you may go in to her and be her husband, and she shall be your wife. ¹⁴But if you are not satisfied with her, you shall let her go free and not sell her for money. You must not treat her as a slave, since you have dishonored her.

¹⁵If a man has two wives, one of them loved and the other disliked, and if both the loved and the disliked have borne him sons, the firstborn being the son of the one who is disliked, ¹⁶then on the day when he wills his possessions to his sons, he is not permitted to treat the son of the loved as the firstborn in preference to the son of the disliked, who is the firstborn. ¹⁷He must acknowledge as firstborn the son of the one who is disliked, giving him a double portion[a] of all that he has; since he is the first issue of his virility, the right of the firstborn is his.

¹⁸If someone has a stubborn and rebellious son who will not obey his father and mother, who does not heed them when they discipline him, ¹⁹then his father and his mother shall take hold of him and bring him out to the elders of his town at the gate of that place. ²⁰They shall say to the elders of his town, "This son of ours is stubborn and rebellious. He will not obey us. He is a glutton and a drunkard." ²¹Then all the men of the town shall stone him to death. So you shall purge the evil from your midst; and all Israel will hear, and be afraid.

²²When someone is convicted of a crime punishable by death and is executed, and you hang him on a tree, ²³his corpse must not remain all night upon the tree; you shall bury him that same day, for anyone hung on a tree is under God's curse. You must not defile the land that the LORD your God is giving you for possession.

a Heb two-thirds

COMMENTARY

A total of six separate rulings are presented in chap. 21, dealing broadly with matters relating to the boundary between life and death. Included among them are questions of inheritance, and hence of the protection and preservation of the family name and household. It is possible to see in the structure of the units a chiastic pattern (ABCC'B'A'), a literary device used to connect the rulings. Overall the concern is to counter the disruptive consequences of death in the life of a family and of the community more generally. There is evident a desire to discern a coherent boundary between life and death and a drawing together of anxieties and beliefs relating to religion with those that relate more directly to basic legal and ethical concerns.

21:1-9. The first of the rulings deals with the matter of the discovery of a dead body in the open countryside. Two factors immediately become evident: the likelihood that a murder has been committed, with the perpetrator of the crime remaining unknown, and a religious conviction that any unburied corpse would defile the land and thereby destroy its holy, life-upholding character.

The response to this situation is twofold. First, the elders of the town nearest to the place where the body was discovered must take responsibility for its safe burial in a location where the land has not been used for farming. They are to take the body to a wadi where there is running water to perform a ritual that will remove the defilement associated with a corpse. The land will then be protected against the defiling effect of the presence of death upon it. The ritual involves breaking the neck of a heifer that has never been worked. Then the elders are required to wash their hands over the carcass of the dead heifer. At the same time, a formal declaration of their innocence of the crime and a prayer that the guilt it has incurred may be forgiven are made.

The reasoning behind these carefully specified actions is not openly expressed. Clearly, from a practical viewpoint, it was an acknowledgment that the crime was taken seriously, but that nothing further could be done to identify the circumstances of the death or to apprehend the person, or persons, responsible for it. However, behind this avowal of innocence we discern that the killing of the unworked heifer at a place not used for agriculture indicates that the action was intended to remove the consequences of the probable crime from the sphere where it might bring harm. The ritual reenacted the original killing by substituting the heifer for the victim and carrying its attendant blood guilt away from the life-supporting productive land of the nearby township. The land's holiness was preserved and its legal system affirmed, even though no actual proceedings were undertaken.

21:10-13. The second of the regulations presented concerns the treatment of a woman taken as a captive in war and subsequently married by her captor, or purchaser.[87] She was to be allowed a full month's mourning for the loss of her former home and parents, after which she could become the wife of an Israelite citizen. The ruling demands that she then be fully integrated into the community and family, being given the full status of an Israelite woman. This newly acquired status guaranteed her a full measure of freedom commensurate with other Israelite women. She was to be regarded as a full member of the household and not demeaned as a slave-wife. The implication is clearly that life in Israel was characterized by a particular status as a mother and wife and that this status was to be granted to all the wives of the household, irrespective of their origin. They were assumed to be responsible for bearing children who would then bring new life into the community, so it was vital that they, too, should acquire a normal position in the household commensurate with their age. The ruling is concerned with the life and growth of the household within society more generally, and the aim is to protect this new life by noting the boundaries that were to be upheld and those that were not. The circumstances of a woman's origin were not to form a permanent barrier once her marriage had taken place.

21:14. The ruling that follows is essentially a rider to the primary declaration.[88] It asserts that the status acquired by becoming a wife and po-

---

87. C. J. H. Wright, *God's People in God's Land: Family, Land, and Property in the Old Testament* (Ann Arbor: Books on Demand, 1990) 213-16.
88. Ibid., 193.

tential mother in Israel was unalterable and could not thereafter be withdrawn. Such a woman could not be returned to the level of a slave after her marriage to an Israelite citizen, since this circumstance had brought to her full recognition as an Israelite woman.

21:15-17. A further ruling is in the same vein, but covers a wider range of possible cases than that of the children of a woman who had been elevated from slave status of a prisoner of war to become a wife and potential mother. The firstborn son of an Israelite household enjoyed a unique status as the primary heir of the family and was accordingly entitled to a significantly increased share in the family inheritance. More than this, it was the privilege and duty of the firstborn son to become the head of the family estate. In the course of time, when the father had to surrender his control over family affairs through physical weakness or death, then the eldest son would assume his mantle.

The ruling set out here simply asserts that, in a household in which there is more than one wife, the status of the firstborn son was unalterable. It is a matter of particular interest that the reason why a father might attempt to remove this status is assumed to lie, not in the ill favor of the son or his lack of business ability, but in the unloved status of the mother. Not only might a paternal head of a household seek to take revenge on an unloved wife by depriving her son of the inheritance to which he was entitled, but also the potential influence of a more favored, or more probably a younger, wife was not to be allowed to disrupt the established structure of the household or the status of its individual members. Clearly such a ruling had in its favor the need to preserve the customary rights and good order of a household as well as the necessity for eliminating the possibility of continuous intrigue and squabbling within a polygamous family.

It is noteworthy that David's reported action in supporting the claim of Solomon to succeed to the throne of Israel (1 Kgs 1:15-31) appears to contravene this ruling. In general, such a firm imposition of the rights of inheritance within a family was concerned to maintain a secure social order. It carries special interest in regard to the royal household of Judah and Israel, where an extensive practice of polygamy prevailed and

where the process by which an heir apparent was chosen is not fully known. Obviously primogeniture was important, but it seems unlikely to have been an exclusive factor. Unfortunately, insufficient information is provided to clarify the procedure, although the practice of naming the mother of the royal successor indicates the special status she acquired through her son's position. This is wholly in line with the present ruling, which closely connects the mother's position with that of the inheritance of the family estate. The need to preserve and promote the economic strength and integrity of the household was a primary feature, with far-reaching consequences for the health and stability of society more generally.

21:18-21. The ruling that follows allows for the death penalty to be inflicted on a rebellious and wanton son.[89] It continues on the same general principle as the preceding regulation. Maintaining the vitality and good order of the household was fundamental to the interests of the larger community. It marked one of the boundaries of life, since once the economic strength of a household had been undermined, the viability of that household more broadly was placed in jeopardy. All its members could be threatened, even though the trouble had arisen on account of a single one of them.

It is in the light of the importance of the household in general as the primary economic unit of society that the relatively severe and uncompromising discipline enjoined here is to be understood. As well as permitting, in certain circumstances, the complete removal of a troublesome son, it also takes full account of the fact that this was a practice that could easily be abused. In such cases, this action would frustrate the intention of the ruling that precedes it. The possibility that a troublesome son might even be put to death by his parents is in line with the generally stern approach advocated by Israel's sages and educators in endorsing the need for strong parental discipline.

In the case envisaged, the procedure for examining the culprit and enforcing the harsh penalty is noteworthy. All that the parents were permitted to do was to report the matter to the elders of the town, who would then initiate their own investigation. Only after they had been satisfied

89. Ibid., 77-78, 230-31.

that the accusation was justified could the death penalty be inflicted. The cruel method of execution by stoning was preferred in cases where a wide measure of shared responsibility for the verdict and its consequences was to be upheld. Those who had made and approved the charges had to carry the risk of blood guilt for their actions. When this was a whole township, then the whole community was to be involved.

D. Olson points out that in the Mishnah, where this particular ruling is evaluated, so many qualifications were introduced to determine the nature of the rebellious son's guilt that it is unlikely that the punishment was ever carried out.[90] Clearly we can discern beneath the surface of the ruling a deep consciousness that polygamous households could often be torn apart by fierce feuds. The broader context of the ruling given is that relating to the cycle of life, death, and new birth, which inevitably shaped and characterized the life of an extended family. There is accordingly a strong concern to protect the strength and hope inherent in every new life within a household. This was especially important where that new life was the formal heir to the family's estate. All too easily the jealousies and feuds of one generation could

be carried forward into the next with disastrous consequences. Family survival and stability were important, but all too easily the tensions that arose within it could destroy the very entity that should have been protected.

21:22-23. The last of the rulings contained in the chapter deals with the necessity for the removal of the corpse of an executed criminal on the day of the execution. There was obviously a temptation for the community to display the victim's body for exemplary purposes. The motive for the requirement set out in the present rule is firmly spelled out: The decaying corpse in the open countryside would defile the land (v. 23). Death is treated as a living force with its own power to replicate itself and to endanger the lives of others. It is no surprise to find that in Canaanite mythology a deity named Mot ("Death") appears in various legendary guises as a kind of anti-God.

All the more would the defiling effect of a corpse left in the open be felt to constitute a danger when the dead person had been executed as a criminal. Execution by hanging from a tree marked out the victim as a person under God's curse. It is this observation that is taken up and commented upon by Paul in Gal 3:3 in reference to the atoning work of the death of Jesus by crucifixion, itself taken as a form of hanging from a tree.

90. D. T. Olson, *Deuteronomy and the Death of Moses*, OBT (Minneapolis: Augsburg Fortress, 1994) 98.

REFLECTIONS

The series of rulings set out in this chapter deals with the mysterious cycle of life and death and with the need for noting the boundary between the two. In general, it might have been supposed that a clear-cut dividing line existed between life and death that everyone would recognize. However, the problem of noting and observing the boundary was brought about because all kinds of circumstances can arise in which actions in life fail to take account of the seriousness of this dividing line and, in consequence, fail to allow its ultimacy to be recognized. We can see this most clearly in respect to the concern to protect the progeny within a family from the effects of actions that were not of their own making. In particular, the right of the firstborn was to remain inalienable. The mother who had been born a slave and had borne children to the man who had taken and married her could not afterward be returned to the status of a slave. New life was a God-ordained reality that was not to be interfered with or manipulated to accommodate the whims and preferences of a capricious head of a household.

The underlying assumptions that govern these rulings represent a mixture of traditional religious concern about death, viewing it in a quasi-physical fashion as a power of supernatural dimensions that had to be feared and that could have ongoing consequences, as the spread of disease from a rotting corpse so obviously exemplified. Woven into this mixture of concerns, sometimes rather taboo-ridden in nature, lie a wider concern for justice, a righteous order of family life, and the promotion of health and well-being in society. So religious and legal considerations become intertwined. Boundaries have to be noted and their reality upheld. Life must be separated from death so that just as death itself marked a final shutdown on a human life, so also did birth bring about the opening of a new scene, with new potential and new opportunities.

Throughout the chapter there is the deep conviction that all life is sacred and a gift from God. Hence the taking of innocent life, even when its cause cannot be explained, must be atoned for. Those associated with the taking of a life must be absolved from guilt, both to declare their innocence and to explain their inability to bring the culprit to justice. Only so could the natural cycle of justice be fulfilled. When the established law required the taking of the culprit's life in punishment for a capital crime, even then the seriousness of such an act needed to be publicly recognized so that the corpse of the executed person had to be removed on the same day as the execution for proper burial. All taking of life represented acts of intrusion into the sphere of the sacred, whether this was justified in the punishment of a criminal or unexplained in the finding of a corpse in the country.

It is the awareness of the sacredness of life that marks out marriage as a step in life's journey with immense, potentially immeasurable, consequences. Even when the marriage was to a woman who had been taken as a captive and turned into a slave, that marriage could never be reduced simply to a master/slave relationship. Marriage, with its expectation of bringing new life into being, could not thereafter be regarded as a matter of no consequence.

By a similar reasoning, the firstborn son of such a marriage would retain unalterably the rights and privileges that came to him from that union. Even the contention that a son was unworthy of his position and privilege within a household and that his status brought shame and the risk of disaster to a household had to be treated with the greatest circumspection. If the accusation was proved to the satisfaction of the town elders, then he was potentially subject to the death penalty. If it was not proved, then he retained his position within the family.

All these rulings represent the outworking of a belief in the sanctity of life, its unique quality as a divine gift, and the necessity of guarding and upholding its power within the family and the community at large. Legal matters relating to life and death were never merely legal matters, since they marked the encounter of humankind with the most demanding and uncrossable of all barriers—that which separated the living from the dead. To take life, whether by a criminal act or in judicial punishment, was to enter into the religious domain. To give birth to new life as a wife and mother was similarly to participate in a process in which God was also involved.

All of this has much to instruct the modern reader regarding the strong feelings, scruples, and sensitivities that colored life in the biblical world. Life had an incommensurate value that could not be matched by mere monetary compensation, any more than a newly discovered corpse could be quietly buried as though nothing untoward had happened. All life had to be accounted for, to the community at large so far as this was possible, but to God always, since the Author and Giver of life could be reckoned to watch over every creature.

Few aspects of the impact of a secular worldview on modern life highlight more directly our different attitude from the people of antiquity than in this question of the sanctity of life. Abortion, invitro fertilization, and euthanasia pose deep moral concerns and uncertainties. Yet the issues do not end here, since it is possible, even while adopting a guarded and responsible attitude to these issues, to lose sight of lesser questions.

Life for every individual is a unique, unrepeatable experiment and adventure. It happens to each of us only once. Consequently its opportunities, possibilities, and dangers have to be faced anew by each person individually. With each new birth there is a new divine act of creation. So the boundaries between life and death, as this ancient legislative compilation reminds us, are not simply the moments of birth and death. These we can mark by essential religious services, reminding ourselves and the community that something remarkable and unique has taken place. Yet the boundary between life and death is more widely felt than is to be comprehended in these dramatic experiences. There are many moments when the resurgence of life over death may be established by our choices and actions. Conversely some experiences can so diminish life and its quality that we may sense that death itself has made inroads upon us.

A further reflection is important in view of the fact that it has sometimes been argued that the fundamental commandment "Thou shalt not kill" ("do no murder") is too negative to provide an adequate guideline for normal conduct. This was capriciously and cynically put by the Victorian poet A. H. Clough in his satirical poem "A Decalogue for Today":

> Thou shalt not kill, but need not strive
> officiously to keep alive.

Such a viewpoint is contrary to the message and purpose of the commandment, as the present chapter of legislation fully bears out. Acknowledging the boundary between life and death, and acting accordingly, is a vital requirement for living. To act negligently so that another's life is lost or so that serious injury results (cf. Deut 22:8) is as much a failure to heed the commandment as is a willful act of murder. It is the sanctity of life itself that needs to be protected and upheld.

The question of the boundary between life and death was of great concern in ancient Israel, since it formed a significant border between morality, religious feeling, and social responsibility. So questions of primal anxieties as to what lies beyond the grave mingled with the practical affairs of inheritance and family structure, as well as determining whether someone could be held responsible when a death occurred accidentally or indirectly. In our secular world, we have sought, by using a host of euphemisms and verbal screens, to hide from ourselves the natural fear of death. In trying to remove the demons of fear, we have often only driven them underground. It is a great merit of the deuteronomic legislation that, however much it may appear to simplify the mysteries of life and death, it frankly recognizes that they cannot be ignored.

DEUTERONOMY 22:1-30, MAINTAINING THE DIVINE ORDER OF LIFE

NIV

22 If you see your brother's ox or sheep straying, do not ignore it but be sure to take it back to him. ²If the brother does not live near you or if you do not know who he is, take it home with you and keep it until he comes looking for it. Then give it back to him. ³Do the same if you find your brother's donkey or his cloak or anything he loses. Do not ignore it.

⁴If you see your brother's donkey or his ox fallen on the road, do not ignore it. Help him get it to its feet.

⁵A woman must not wear men's clothing, nor a man wear women's clothing, for the LORD your God detests anyone who does this.

⁶If you come across a bird's nest beside the road, either in a tree or on the ground, and the mother is sitting on the young or on the eggs, do not take the mother with the young. ⁷You may

NRSV

22 You shall not watch your neighbor's ox or sheep straying away and ignore them; you shall take them back to their owner. ²If the owner does not reside near you or you do not know who the owner is, you shall bring it to your own house, and it shall remain with you until the owner claims it; then you shall return it. ³You shall do the same with a neighbor's donkey; you shall do the same with a neighbor's garment; and you shall do the same with anything else that your neighbor loses and you find. You may not withhold your help.

4You shall not see your neighbor's donkey or ox fallen on the road and ignore it; you shall help to lift it up.

5A woman shall not wear a man's apparel, nor shall a man put on a woman's garment; for

NIV

take the young, but be sure to let the mother go, so that it may go well with you and you may have a long life.

⁸When you build a new house, make a parapet around your roof so that you may not bring the guilt of bloodshed on your house if someone falls from the roof.

⁹Do not plant two kinds of seed in your vineyard; if you do, not only the crops you plant but also the fruit of the vineyard will be defiled.ᵃ

¹⁰Do not plow with an ox and a donkey yoked together.

¹¹Do not wear clothes of wool and linen woven together.

¹²Make tassels on the four corners of the cloak you wear.

¹³If a man takes a wife and, after lying with her, dislikes her ¹⁴and slanders her and gives her a bad name, saying, "I married this woman, but when I approached her, I did not find proof of her virginity," ¹⁵then the girl's father and mother shall bring proof that she was a virgin to the town elders at the gate. ¹⁶The girl's father will say to the elders, "I gave my daughter in marriage to this man, but he dislikes her. ¹⁷Now he has slandered her and said, 'I did not find your daughter to be a virgin.' But here is the proof of my daughter's virginity." Then her parents shall display the cloth before the elders of the town, ¹⁸and the elders shall take the man and punish him. ¹⁹They shall fine him a hundred shekels of silverᵇ and give them to the girl's father, because this man has given an Israelite virgin a bad name. She shall continue to be his wife; he must not divorce her as long as he lives.

²⁰If, however, the charge is true and no proof of the girl's virginity can be found, ²¹she shall be brought to the door of her father's house and there the men of her town shall stone her to death. She has done a disgraceful thing in Israel by being promiscuous while still in her father's house. You must purge the evil from among you.

²²If a man is found sleeping with another man's wife, both the man who slept with her and the woman must die. You must purge the evil from Israel.

ᵃ9 Or *be forfeited to the sanctuary*   ᵇ19 That is, about 2 1/2 pounds (about 1 kilogram)

NRSV

whoever does such things is abhorrent to the LORD your God.

6If you come on a bird's nest, in any tree or on the ground, with fledglings or eggs, with the mother sitting on the fledglings or on the eggs, you shall not take the mother with the young. 7Let the mother go, taking only the young for yourself, in order that it may go well with you and you may live long.

8When you build a new house, you shall make a parapet for your roof; otherwise you might have bloodguilt on your house, if anyone should fall from it.

9You shall not sow your vineyard with a second kind of seed, or the whole yield will have to be forfeited, both the crop that you have sown and the yield of the vineyard itself.

10You shall not plow with an ox and a donkey yoked together.

11You shall not wear clothes made of wool and linen woven together.

12You shall make tassels on the four corners of the cloak with which you cover yourself.

13Suppose a man marries a woman, but after going in to her, he dislikes her 14and makes up charges against her, slandering her by saying, "I married this woman; but when I lay with her, I did not find evidence of her virginity." 15The father of the young woman and her mother shall then submit the evidence of the young woman's virginity to the elders of the city at the gate. 16The father of the young woman shall say to the elders: "I gave my daughter in marriage to this man but he dislikes her; 17now he has made up charges against her, saying, 'I did not find evidence of your daughter's virginity.' But here is the evidence of my daughter's virginity." Then they shall spread out the cloth before the elders of the town. 18The elders of that town shall take the man and punish him; 19they shall fine him one hundred shekels of silver (which they shall give to the young woman's father) because he has slandered a virgin of Israel. She shall remain his wife; he shall not be permitted to divorce her as long as he lives.

20If, however, this charge is true, that evidence of the young woman's virginity was not found, 21then they shall bring the young woman out to the entrance of her father's house and the men

NIV

²³If a man happens to meet in a town a virgin pledged to be married and he sleeps with her, ²⁴you shall take both of them to the gate of that town and stone them to death—the girl because she was in a town and did not scream for help, and the man because he violated another man's wife. You must purge the evil from among you.

²⁵But if out in the country a man happens to meet a girl pledged to be married and rapes her, only the man who has done this shall die. ²⁶Do nothing to the girl; she has committed no sin deserving death. This case is like that of someone who attacks and murders his neighbor, ²⁷for the man found the girl out in the country, and though the betrothed girl screamed, there was no one to rescue her.

²⁸If a man happens to meet a virgin who is not pledged to be married and rapes her and they are discovered, ²⁹he shall pay the girl's father fifty shekels of silver.^a He must marry the girl, for he has violated her. He can never divorce her as long as he lives.

³⁰A man is not to marry his father's wife; he must not dishonor his father's bed.

^a29 That is, about 1 1/4 pounds (about 0.6 kilogram)

NRSV

of her town shall stone her to death, because she committed a disgraceful act in Israel by prostituting herself in her father's house. So you shall purge the evil from your midst.

22If a man is caught lying with the wife of another man, both of them shall die, the man who lay with the woman as well as the woman. So you shall purge the evil from Israel.

23If there is a young woman, a virgin already engaged to be married, and a man meets her in the town and lies with her, ²⁴you shall bring both of them to the gate of that town and stone them to death, the young woman because she did not cry for help in the town and the man because he violated his neighbor's wife. So you shall purge the evil from your midst.

25But if the man meets the engaged woman in the open country, and the man seizes her and lies with her, then only the man who lay with her shall die. ²⁶You shall do nothing to the young woman; the young woman has not committed an offense punishable by death, because this case is like that of someone who attacks and murders a neighbor. ²⁷Since he found her in the open country, the engaged woman may have cried for help, but there was no one to rescue her.

28If a man meets a virgin who is not engaged, and seizes her and lies with her, and they are caught in the act, ²⁹the man who lay with her shall give fifty shekels of silver to the young woman's father, and she shall become his wife. Because he violated her he shall not be permitted to divorce her as long as he lives.

30^aA man shall not marry his father's wife, thereby violating his father's rights.^b

^a Ch 23.1 in Heb   ^b Heb *uncovering his father's skirt*

COMMENTARY

The group of laws that now commence relate to a wide range of issues governing both social responsibility and personal conduct. They have, as a common connecting principle, a concern to maintain the proper boundaries of life and to uphold the realm that we should describe as "the natural order." In some of them, the anxiety to respect what are considered to be the boundaries of a given created scheme of things is very prominent, whereas in others it is less clearly apparent. Braulik sees this unit as marking a transition from the topic of "preserving life" to that of "sexuality."[91] These laws are concerned with marriage,

91. G. Braulik, "The Sequence of Laws in Deuteronomy 12-26 and in the Decalogue," 322, 332.

the raising of a family, and the protection of the household, and they represent a pattern of order that could only be satisfactorily maintained provided that its structural boundaries were protected and upheld. Certainly the upholding of the sexual order represents a central concern, since the gender distinction between male and female is perceived to be one of the foremost of the structural boundaries of the created world.

However, within the central concern to clarify and define the boundaries of sexual conduct and to protect against sexual abuses, there are several other foundational lines that are perceived as lending support and stability to society. Regulations protecting these boundaries act like fences to keep everything in its place and to prevent the falling apart of society as a result of a breach in the invisible boundaries that contain it.

22:1-4. As well as protecting the integrity of the family, the first of the regulations (vv. 1-3) can be interpreted as an elaboration of the commandment concerning the avoidance of coveting a neighbor's wife or property. The matter of finding oxen or sheep straying across the known limits of a neighbor's property, or more simply of discovering a stray animal, the ownership of which was not known, on one's own land imposed an obligation. This obligation consisted simply of returning the stray beast to its rightful owner. The need to respect a neighbor as a fellow citizen of Israel who enjoyed the same right to respect and protection as one sought for oneself extended also to property. This necessity even extended as far as the obligation to return any object belonging to a neighbor that might be found by chance. As the legislation is set out, it appears as a fuller elaboration of the earlier law contained in Exod 23:4-5.

The ruling that lost property must be returned to its rightful owner may at first appear as a transparently obvious duty. However, it was clearly a matter of considerable importance in regard to the question of respecting established boundaries. The head of a family could expect to be master of the property that belonged to his household. There were, however, necessary limits to this right, so that what is decreed here sets out certain limits as a matter of principle. When a neighbor's animal strayed onto another person's property, then it was the duty of that person to

return it. Location did not determine ownership, even when the rightful owner of lost property was not immediately known.

A further extension of this principle is then affirmed in v. 4 by its imposition of an obligation to come to the help of a neighbor's beast, even when the misfortune that had befallen it occurred on public land. The obligation to assist an injured animal extended across the boundaries defined by ownership.

22:5. A more subtle and psychologically more complicated ruling is put forward here by the introduction of a number of regulations governing the protection of sexual boundaries. These rules prohibit the practice of transvestism as a forbidden crossing of one of the foremost distinctions established at creation (Gen 1:27). The boundary defined by gender was regarded as all-pervasive. It is possible that some forms of transvestism were practiced in cultic ceremonies of which the deuteronomists disapproved, so that they are here outlawed as idolatrous and non-Israelite. However, the overall context of the ruling shows that it was concerned to uphold what were perceived to be given boundaries of the natural order, rather than being a further ruling to outlaw acts of apostasy from the LORD God.

We can reasonably assume that some persons in ancient Israel experienced problems and difficulties in establishing their gender orientation, as has been the case in human society generally. However, the ruling set out here must certainly be interpreted as based on the fundamental awareness that formal gender distinctions marked one of the formative structural boundaries of life. Such boundaries were not to be blurred or willfully crossed. To do so would amount to a negation of the divine order.

It is significant that the prohibition against transvestism is not sanctioned by any specific punitive measure to be taken against those who contravene its demands. It is not difficult to recognize that any such punitive action would have been difficult to enforce, but it is also clear that the social sanction of shame and repudiation by the community at large would have carried a considerable force. The formula that expresses this awareness of social stigma and repudiation is that certain actions are described as "abhorrent to the LORD your God." The use of such a formula draws attention to the fact that, quite apart from setting out a legal code for action against civil and criminal misdemeanors, the book of Deuteronomy contains much that reflects the less overtly enforced ethos of the community. It was taken as natural that such an ethos should have been regarded as an expression of the mind and will of God.

22:6-7. The prohibition contained in v. 6 regarding the rather limited protection that was to be afforded to wild birds displays a concern to maintain the boundary between life and death by a refusal to take the mother with the fledgling birds and eggs. Since the mother provided the womb from which life came, then, when the eggs and fledglings were taken, presumably for food, life and death were not to be mixed together. In this fashion the respect for life and the need to avoid entanglement with death were maintained by not permitting death to overrule life completely.

22:8. The regulation demanding that an adequate protective parapet be built on the roof of a house to reduce the risk of accidents follows a similar concern to protect life. The rooftop of a house, whether it was built of mudbrick or stone, was a part of the living space of an ancient Israelite's home. It could be expected that it would be in use throughout much of the year. Failure to ensure that it incorporated reasonable protection against injury and death through accidental falls was adjudged to incur blood guilt. That such a term is used at all for injury caused in this fashion is noteworthy since it is otherwise almost exclusively applied to cases of homicide or the willful inflicting of serious bodily injury.

It would appear from these rulings that the ancient Israelite legislators were uncomfortable with the notion of an accident for which no responsibility could be apportioned. Accordingly even the earlier legislation regarding an unpremeditated act that resulted in a person's death is described as having been brought about by "an act of God" (Exod 21:13). We have already noted a deep concern in the legislation in 21:1-9, dealing with the discovery of a corpse in open country, to ensure that no blood guilt was incurred simply because the real culprit was not known and could not be apprehended. The local community was required to demonstrate that it was innocent of the crime.

It is noteworthy that the Jewish sage referred to as Qohelet, writing in the third century BCE (Eccl 9:11-12) seems to have been the first to have left a written recognition of the concept of pure chance that could bring about personal accident or misfortune for which no one, not even God, was directly to be blamed.

22:9-11. Three rulings set out in these verses quite directly reflect the importance of maintaining the given boundaries of the natural order and of avoiding any willful crossing of them. A vineyard was not to be planted with the seed of another crop, since this would mix the two and contravene a given order of life. The very force of life would be confused if the established boundaries of its many varied manifestations were not respected. It is rather surprising that the mixing of crops that is contemplated was to have occurred in a vineyard. A parallel ruling in Lev 19:19 specifies that it was not to be undertaken in a field. This would appear to have provided a broader, and more plausible, context, since it is the principle of mixing different crops in a single field that is prohibited. However, the deuteronomic formulation appears to have been content simply to specify a typical and reasonably likely case of infringement, whereas the ruling in Leviticus is more tersely formulated and is focused on the general principle. It is in line with this that the deuteronomic ruling specifies a penalty, in that both crops would become forfeit to the local sanctuary, whereas in Leviticus this is not specified.

The prohibition against plowing with both an ox and a donkey (v. 10) was not the result of a compassionate concern to avoid using together two beasts of unequal strength. It is possible that the verb translated "plow" (חרש *ḥāraš*) should be taken to imply "mate together," thereby occasioning the miscegenation of species. However, none of the standard English versions follow such a suggestion, which appears instead to have arisen out of a desire to find a rational explanation for a procedure that otherwise might have appeared insignificant. It would comply with the larger context, which is concerned with avoiding any mixture of species. However, it is possible to understand the verb in its literal sense and to interpret it as a prohibition against bringing animals together in any fashion that might lead to miscegenation.

A similar concern to maintain the observed order of things, and of avoiding any unwarranted mixture, appears further in the regulation of v. 11, which prohibits the making of garments of a combination of wool and linen; this ruling is also repeated in Lev 19:19. The Hebrew uses a noun "mixed stuff" (שעטנז *ša'aṭnēz*), which is clearly a loan word, to describe the mixed cloth. It may indicate that such clothing was intended to have special, semi-magical power, either for the cure of illnesses or for the warding off of evil spirits. It has then simply been brought into line with a general concern to avoid crossing the given boundaries of life, save in certain specified exceptional cases.

22:12. The ruling concerned with the making of tassels on the four corners of a cloak is related to a practice of unknown origin. In Num 15:38-39, it is explained in terms of symbols to remind members of the community of Israel that they possessed obligations to uphold the divine commandments. The very general nature of this obligation strongly suggests that the original purpose of such tassels was either unknown or had come to be regarded as inappropriate, so that it required to be replaced by a more general reason.

22:13-30. The remaining six rulings in the section are all concerned with marriage and sexual relationships. This undoubtedly provided one of the most central and important areas of the given boundaries of life, which called for especially careful handling. At a basic level it represented a particularly difficult feature of life to grasp conceptually, just as it also marked an area of potentially disruptive, and even destructive, social force if its boundaries were not respected.

Gender differences were quite evidently perceived to be fundamental to life, reaching across from the human sphere to embrace also the animal world and even the sphere of vegetation. Male and female principles were widely perceived to pervade all creation, and it is a striking exception that the OT does not carry this through into the divine sphere, which the rest of the ancient Near East so clearly did. The boundaries of gender and sexuality, therefore, had to be respected, as we have already seen in regard to human dress codes.

More than this was entailed, however, since at times these boundaries had to be crossed in order to permit sexual relationships to lead to the establishment of wholly new households (cf. Gen 2:24). Moreover the making of such relationships and marriages required the crossing of the boundaries of the most close-knit family kinship structures, since incestuous sexual connections were precluded and

a wide degree of openness in permitting marriages to take place outside the immediate kin group was permitted. Already the ruling of 21:10-14, which allowed marriage to a woman who had been taken as a prisoner of war illustrates this fact. Some boundaries might have been, and even had been, crossed in normal sexual activities, but these trespasses in turn established new boundaries that could not thereafter be broken.

Accordingly sexual relationships called for very careful handling, and a considerable number of subordinate protective rulings were required in order to set appropriate limits. These guaranteed protection and stability so that proper order could be upheld within the sphere of sexual activity. Throughout the regulations there is a pervasive awareness that a sexual relationship implied the crossing of a boundary that could not thereafter be uncrossed. Accordingly the loss of a woman's virginity and the setting up of a sexual partnership in marriage could never thereafter be ignored either by the individuals concerned or by the kin groups to which each of them belonged. Nor was this solely a matter that concerned the procreation of children, since major financial implications were also tied up with marriage.

The first of the cases that the deuteronomic legislation deals with (vv. 13-19) concerns precisely the recognition that marriage and the commencement of a sexual relationship brought into being a wholly new situation that had not before existed. Such a relationship could not thereafter be denied or revoked simply by an accusation on the part of the husband that the wife was not a virgin at the time of the marriage. The parents of the woman are then given the responsibility of providing to the town elders evidence of the woman's virginity at the time of the marriage. If this evidence is taken to be sufficient and satisfactory, then a heavy fine, amounting to one hundred shekels of silver (v. 19), was to be imposed on the husband and paid over to the wife's father. Such a sum must have represented a very substantial amount of capital. Thereafter the husband is refused any right to divorce the woman, who, together with her family who had been responsible for her, was regarded as having been subjected to a considerable level of social shame as a result of the false accusation regarding her virginity.

Very little indication is given to indicate why

the husband might have been tempted to behave in such a fashion. He is said simply to have accused his bride of wanton or capricious conduct. However, it is more evident from the response that the woman's parents make in repudiation of such accusations that a primary concern lay in the charge that the bride was not a virgin at the time of her marriage. There is an imputation that the woman's family may have known this and acted deceitfully in marrying her off, when her value as a bride would have been reduced. The paternity of her children would then be put in doubt. There is also the very real possibility that the husband might have been acting out of unreasoned jealousy. Having taken a bride in good faith, he could not simply afterward revoke his responsibilities.

The "proofs of virginity" the parents are to bring to the elders are usually taken to be the bloodstains resulting from the first sexual union. However, it has very plausibly been argued that the reference is to proofs of menstruation, showing that the woman was not pregnant at the time of her marriage.

Verses 20-21 deal with the situation when no proofs of the woman's virginity could be produced. In this event, the accusations are assumed to be justified, and the woman was to be returned to the entrance of her father's house. She was then to be publicly executed by stoning. The location is significant, since it is throughout assumed that she was in the custody of her father until the time of her marriage. He is then held to have been responsible for ensuring that she remained a virgin until the time of her marriage. Throughout the male domination of women is heavily marked, since the woman passes from the custody of her father to that of her husband.

The whole situation is noteworthy and was clearly aimed at ensuring the man's right to certain knowledge of the paternity of his children. The harsh punishment for the woman's failure to fit in with these demands is striking, especially as there is a strong measure of responsibility leveled at her father. The severity of the assumed offense is measured by its being categorized as an act of "outrage" (נבלה *nĕbālâ*; cf. the purging formula used in 5:18). In view of the penalty to be inflicted, the KJV's translation "folly" appears remarkably weak. In the prophetic literature, Hos 2:2 and Jer 3:8 point to a situation in which the woman's punishment for such

action is only that she should be divorced. In the light of this, the deuteronomic legislation demands a stricter enforcement of the moral code regarding charges of sexual misconduct.

Verses 22-29 deal with cases of rape and adultery. The fundamental ruling is set out directly in v. 22. If a man is found having sexual intercourse with the wife of another man, then both are to be put to death. The method of execution is not specified, but the formula for purging evil from Israel is expressed, which most plausibly indicates death by stoning. The primary concern must certainly be to protect the husband's rights to the paternity of his children. At the same time, the close interconnection between a social kinship structure and the complex boundaries posed by human sexuality points to a fervent anxiety to protect the formal lines of these distinctions.

A number of subordinate considerations are then introduced that have a direct bearing on the broader concern to preclude irregular sexual relationships. The first of these appears in vv. 23-27 and relates to a situation in which the woman is a virgin and is engaged to be married, but the formal marriage has not yet taken place. If, in this circumstance, the woman is found in an illicit sexual union, then both she and the man concerned are held to be equally guilty and are to suffer the same penalty as if the woman were already married. The ruling is important in establishing the contractual importance of the engagement arrangement, since this is taken as tantamount to marriage itself. The formal financial arrangements that were a part of the marriage contract are assumed to have been completed so that the husband-to-be has already acquired certain basic rights over his future bride.

The severity of the punishment, which is one of a number of instances in which capital punishment is laid down for a sexual offense, was obviously designed to have a strong deterrent effect. This is further borne out by the employment of the purging formula, indicating the strong concern to influence the conduct of Israel as a whole. It may well indicate that, in spite of the concern to ensure that young women remained under the supervision and custody of responsible males, there was a deep awareness that such offenses as are dealt with were often difficult to prove and disturbing in their social effect.

However, the situation raises a further important consideration, since it was necessary to allow that the woman may have been seized, overpowered, and raped against her will. Thus a qualification is introduced calling for the fullest and most severe punishment to be inflicted on the woman only in cases where the offense took place within the township boundaries. Outside of these it is assumed that the woman would have been unable to cry out and summon help to protect her. The hypothetical situation in which she is portrayed as doing so is then described extensively in vv. 25-27. The conclusion is drawn that, in such a case, only the man is deserving of death, while the woman is presumed to be innocent of any intention to violate the terms of her engagement.

At first reflection the case appears to express a perfectly reasonable and straightforward situation. Its ruling, however, is of considerable interest and importance for the insights it provides into the social implications of human sexuality. Attention has been drawn to the range of boundaries that controlled the structure of human society, in which those concerning sexual relationships were of paramount importance. In the case of the rape of an unmarried woman, a major social boundary had been transgressed. This is shown by the situation envisaged in the ruling in vv. 28-29, concerning the case of a young unmarried woman who is seized and raped by a man who may or may not be married. The culprit is then obliged to compensate the unmarried woman's father with fifty shekels of silver. He is also required to marry the woman with no subsequent entitlement to divorce her. Clearly, by his having established a sexual relationship with her it is assumed that a boundary had been crossed. The consequences of this had then to be fully accepted both by the man and by the victim, together with her family.

The ruling highlights the special significance of the case covered by vv. 25-27 in which the woman is presumed to be innocent of having committed an offense since it took place in open country. Although declared to be innocent, no indication is given as to what her future status would be, although she was engaged to be married at the time she was taken by another man. The discerning critic will note throughout that the rulings display a rather hypothetical nature since, although the concessionary caveat of v. 24 applies when no help to prevent an offense was available, the case defined in v. 28 requires that the offending couple be caught in the act.

From a legal perspective it becomes apparent in these regulations, as in many of the provisions contained in the deuteronomic law code, that a particularly weak feature of the legislative processes of ancient Israel concerned rules governing the admissibility of evidence. The sense of fairness and the general desire on the part of the elders who are made responsible for administering the laws to maintain order with compassion were obviously of paramount importance. It would appear that the rulings arrived at were intended to provide guidelines and to be related to particular cases as the situation demanded.

A concluding ruling in v. 30 prohibiting the marriage of a son to his father's wife serves as a connecting link between the rules of sexual conduct that have preceded it and those that follow. Together they cover fundamental issues regarding the structural boundaries of the community. It may be presumed here that the designated father's wife was a stepmother of the son and that the father was presumed to be dead by the time of the marriage. The background concerns that are envisaged, therefore, are those relating to questions of inheritance. The biblical laws provide evidence of a widespread and long-held assumption that a son could inherit his father's wives and concubines (Gen 35:22; 49:4; 2 Sam 3:7; 16:22; 1 Kgs 2:22). These latter figure as part of the household capital.

REFLECTIONS

Two considerations will appear uppermost to the modern reader of these deuteronomic laws. The first is to note the firm and unmodified patriarchal structure of ancient Israelite society. This male-oriented world assumed throughout that, from birth to death, the place of every female member of the community was determined by her relationship to men. Initially this relationship was to her father, who remained her effective guardian and owner until the time of her marriage to an agreed suitor. This patriarchal dominance is startlingly shown by the fact that the young woman's father was required to be compensated if she was seized and raped in open country before formal arrangements for her betrothal and marriage had been negotiated (22:29). The culprit was then compelled to marry his victim with no right for a subsequent divorce. The young woman's wishes were not even considered. To the modern reader, such heavy restrictions placed on the ability of a woman to initiate and control her position in society must appear deeply disturbing and demeaning.

The second consideration that must strike the modern reader very forcefully is the pervasive awareness that sexual relationships could not be regarded, and treated in law, simply as a private matter between two consenting adults. A much wider social context was recognized as being affected by all such relationships. Behind all of the rules governing sexual behavior we are made deeply aware that human sexuality was never simply an individual matter, since it concerned the families from which the individuals came and the children they were likely to produce and for whom they had to accept responsibility. Sexual relationships could not be treated simply as the concern only of the two central parties.

So far as the male domination of social and sexual relationships is concerned within this patriarchal structure, some degree of protection of women's rights and participation in family and social life was afforded. She was protected against malicious accusations and slanders regarding her virginity on the part of a husband who became jealous or who wished for some reason to be rid of a wife he had taken (22:13-19). If the charge could reasonably be disproved to the satisfaction of impartial judges, then no divorce was possible. On the other hand, if no such proof were forthcoming, the woman could be put to death as an adulteress (v. 27) on the basis of her husband's accusations against her.

A woman was also afforded some protection in the case of rape when it could be assumed that she had been overpowered and had been unable to cry out for help. A further limiting consideration to the male domination of women's position in society is the ruling in 22:30 that a woman who had been widowed could not thereafter be passed on like other family property to the son and heir.

Behind all of these rules governing sexual behavior, we are made deeply conscious that sexual relationships introduced a distinctive boundary in society that gave rise to many complications. That this boundary was set up to protect male interests, both personal and economic, is markedly evident and must appear deeply disturbing in a modern setting. Perhaps also it should be noted that the entire legal structure of the community appears to have been heavily affected by questions of property, inheritance, and the protection of capital within a family context generally. Sexuality and sexual desire are little reflected upon as issues in themselves. Rather, on account of the importance of the preservation and extension of a family, sexuality is safeguarded within this larger setting.

Throughout these rulings is an assumption that it was the male members of society who had the power to initiate relationships between the sexes, even though the woman who was guilty of adultery or who was the unwilling but unprotected victim of certain forms of rape paid a terrible price for her vulnerability. This background highlights the important changes introduced in Israel by the new and liberating teachings of Jesus about equality before God.

DEUTERONOMY 23:1–25:19, MATTERS OF GENERAL CONDUCT

Deuteronomy 23:1-18, The Boundaries of the Community

23No one who has been emasculated by crushing or cutting may enter the assembly of the LORD.

²No one born of a forbidden marriage[a] nor any of his descendants may enter the assembly of the LORD, even down to the tenth generation.

³No Ammonite or Moabite or any of his descendants may enter the assembly of the LORD, even down to the tenth generation. ⁴For they did not come to meet you with bread and water on your way when you came out of Egypt, and they hired Balaam son of Beor from Pethor in Aram Naharaim[b] to pronounce a curse on you. ⁵However, the LORD your God would not listen to Balaam but turned the curse into a blessing for you, because the LORD your God loves you. ⁶Do not seek a treaty of friendship with them as long as you live.

⁷Do not abhor an Edomite, for he is your brother. Do not abhor an Egyptian, because you lived as an alien in his country. ⁸The third generation of children born to them may enter the assembly of the LORD.

⁹When you are encamped against your enemies, keep away from everything impure. ¹⁰If one of your men is unclean because of a nocturnal emission, he is to go outside the camp and stay there. ¹¹But as evening approaches he is to wash himself, and at sunset he may return to the camp.

¹²Designate a place outside the camp where you can go to relieve yourself. ¹³As part of your equipment have something to dig with, and when you relieve yourself, dig a hole and cover up your excrement. ¹⁴For the LORD your God moves about in your camp to protect you and to deliver your enemies to you. Your camp must be holy, so that he will not see among you anything indecent and turn away from you.

¹⁵If a slave has taken refuge with you, do not hand him over to his master. ¹⁶Let him live among

23No one whose testicles are crushed or whose penis is cut off shall be admitted to the assembly of the LORD.

2Those born of an illicit union shall not be admitted to the assembly of the LORD. Even to the tenth generation, none of their descendants shall be admitted to the assembly of the LORD.

3No Ammonite or Moabite shall be admitted to the assembly of the LORD. Even to the tenth generation, none of their descendants shall be admitted to the assembly of the LORD, ⁴because they did not meet you with food and water on your journey out of Egypt, and because they hired against you Balaam son of Beor, from Pethor of Mesopotamia, to curse you. ⁵(Yet the LORD your God refused to heed Balaam; the LORD your God turned the curse into a blessing for you, because the LORD your God loved you.) ⁶You shall never promote their welfare or their prosperity as long as you live.

7You shall not abhor any of the Edomites, for they are your kin. You shall not abhor any of the Egyptians, because you were an alien residing in their land. ⁸The children of the third generation that are born to them may be admitted to the assembly of the LORD.

9When you are encamped against your enemies you shall guard against any impropriety.

10If one of you becomes unclean because of a nocturnal emission, then he shall go outside the camp; he must not come within the camp. ¹¹When evening comes, he shall wash himself with water, and when the sun has set, he may come back into the camp.

12You shall have a designated area outside the camp to which you shall go. ¹³With your utensils you shall have a trowel; when you relieve yourself outside, you shall dig a hole with it and then cover up your excrement. ¹⁴Because the LORD your God travels along with your camp, to save you and to hand over your enemies to you, therefore your camp must be holy, so that he may not see

a2 Or *one of illegitimate birth*   b4 That is, Northwest Mesopotamia

NIV

you wherever he likes and in whatever town he chooses. Do not oppress him.

[17]No Israelite man or woman is to become a shrine prostitute. [18]You must not bring the earnings of a female prostitute or of a male prostitute[a] into the house of the LORD your God to pay any vow, because the LORD your God detests them both.

[a]18 Hebrew *of a dog*

NRSV

anything indecent among you and turn away from you.

[15]Slaves who have escaped to you from their owners shall not be given back to them. [16]They shall reside with you, in your midst, in any place they choose in any one of your towns, wherever they please; you shall not oppress them.

[17]None of the daughters of Israel shall be a temple prostitute; none of the sons of Israel shall be a temple prostitute. [18]You shall not bring the fee of a prostitute or the wages of a male prostitute[a] into the house of the LORD your God in payment for any vow, for both of these are abhorrent to the LORD your God.

[a] Heb *a dog*

COMMENTARY

The legislation we have been considering until now has presumed that a clear distinction can be drawn between the Israelite proper, the resident alien who had settled within Israel, and the foreigner whose place within the Israelite community was purely temporary. The weak and exposed position of such a person then needed to be protected by certain conventions of hospitality and did not assume any permanent adoption within the community of Israel (cf. 14:21). Such persons may have been caravan traders and emissaries from foreign lands. Obviously individuals and their families could move from one status to another, but only within certain well-established limits and conventions.

The deuteronomic literature makes membership in the Israelite community a matter of paramount importance and effectively addresses its own demands and standards to men and women who were assumed to belong within this community of privilege. In fact, by its historical recollections and direct modes of address, Deuteronomy functions as literature that actively promotes a sense of belonging within this community.

Yet who did belong within this people, and where were its boundaries to be drawn? In the traditional portrayal of its own national origins, Israel was made up of a group of twelve tribes that comprised large extended families. Accordingly a sense of kinship and family structure

belonged indispensably to a person's sense of identity. Birth and family origin were evidently of paramount importance. Each person also existed, however, within a series of networks that centered first on the immediate family circle of parents, children, and their close relatives. Around this circle were larger circles to be drawn of a wider extended family who might all exercise varying degrees of influence and authority over an individual. Such families could draw other members into their embrace through marriage, the acquisition of slaves, and negotiations in which persons from other regions were adopted into the extended family on a client basis. As a result, only as a kind of notional outer limit did the idea of being an Israelite figure significantly. For the most part the more immediate circle defined the necessary pattern of relationships that governed social and religious life.

It is strongly arguable that the book of Deuteronomy contributed a great deal to strengthen and reinforce the awareness that a marked boundary separated those who were within Israel from those who stood outside the privileges of the covenant community.[92] The deuteronomic legislation both

92. See G. Braulik, "Deuteronomy and Human Rights," in *The Theology of Deuteronomy: Collected Essays of Georg Braulik OSB,* Bibal Collected Essays 2, trans. Ulrika Lindblad (N. Richland Hills, Tex.: Bibal, 1994) 131-50.

idealizes the boundaries of Israel by its concepts of membership (lit., "brotherhood") and at the same time seeks in practical terms to regularize and define the status of those who belonged within the community. To a very meaningful degree such membership carried far-reaching consequences, since the person who betrayed his or her primary allegiance to the LORD as God could pay a terrible price for doing so (cf. 13:12-18).

Much of the explanation for this heavy deuteronomic attention to the boundaries of the community must lie within the particular historical and social context in which the law book was composed. A strong sense that the people of Israel were threatened with breakup and dissolution and that the ready-made givenness of clan and tribal affiliations no longer played a decisive role pervades Deuteronomy. We cannot evade the conclusion that it was precisely the fact of this social breakup and disorientation that provided the major background concern the deuteronomists were anxious to address.

23:1-8. What we find as a set of rules defining the limits of the Israelite community is a list of exclusions. The first two categories arise directly out of concern with the sexual boundaries that were dealt with in the preceding section. By appearing here, they serve as a useful transition element in the overall structure of the laws. The other exclusions arose from historical, ethnic, and less obviously defined considerations. A major point of concern relating to these factors must have been connected with the particular social and historical context in which Deuteronomy was composed. It is probable that these rules of exclusion had a very early origin, possibly from as far back as the pre-monarchic period. They may have emerged at a major border city, such as Gilgal in the Jordan valley, where trade and communication routes met. Joshua 2:9-11 and 9:9-10 reflect situations in which the acceptance of outsiders into the Israelite cultic community required to be dealt with. It seems unlikely, however, that before the deuteronomic legislation sought to regularize the situation there was any uniform Israelite policy on such matters. Individual clan and tribal groups pursued their own preferences according to local circumstances. It would then have been a consequence of the disruption arising from Assyrian interventions in the late eighth century BCE that a more considered policy was called for.

Obviously the question of membership in the Israelite community, with its consequent privileges, was a point of importance for individual families and even whole clusters of families at every stage throughout the nation's history. The necessity for regularizing and standardizing conventions of community allegiance in the age of Josiah, with the desire to reestablish a united Israel, made this a major social issue. It became all the more urgent after the disaster of 587 BCE, when large-scale movements of population took place and normal administrative practices collapsed altogether.

So it appears as an issue of unique importance in the context of the deuteronomic concern to integrate a code of practice applicable to all members of the community. All who claimed that they were full members of the Israelite covenant community and loyal worshipers of the LORD God had to establish their claims for acceptance by the recognized authority. As a result, what had no doubt earlier been varied and uncoordinated conventions needed to be fixed within a single set of rules. Whereas the separate individual rulings were almost certainly of considerable antiquity and here given a somewhat rationalized explanation, we are here presented with a set of rules to establish the cultic and social boundaries applicable to all Israelites. For the deuteronomic authors, the question of who was within and who was outside the recognized boundaries of the covenant people was of the utmost importance. It could ultimately prove to be a matter of life or death if the strict terms of the demands of religious loyalty were implemented.

After the collapse of the old Judahite state, membership in the cultic community, even without a continuing sacrificial cultus in the Temple, became a vital and irreplaceable badge of acceptance within society. The final composition of this list of community membership would therefore appear to have taken place sometime during the middle of the sixth century BCE.

The ruling in v. 1, which excludes any male whose sexual organs had been severely damaged or removed, represents an ancient sensitivity to the belief that sexual potency was a mark of divine blessing and wholeness. In consequence, any serious impairment of sexual health, which was a humiliation frequently inflicted on males defeated in battle, represented a separation from the life-giving power of the living God.

Similarly, the ruling in v. 2, which excludes the progeny of illicit sexual unions from the cultic community, must refer to those children who were born to women whose relationships conflicted with the regulations previously laid down for married status. The permanent exclusion of the Ammonites and the Moabites from entry into Israel, even to the tenth generation (vv. 3-6), reflects the long-standing antipathy and conflict between Israel and these peoples. The term "tenth generation" should probably not be taken literally, but simply implies no limit to the exclusion.

It seems highly probable that both Ammon and Moab had callously exploited Israel's weakness after the Babylonian campaign of 588–587 BCE, thereby adding further support to a date for the list at this time (for Ammonite involvement in Israel's misfortunes, see Jer 41:15). By plundering Israelite villages and harrying refugees from the Babylonian forces, these people had added further wounds to a long history of bitter suspicion and conflict.

The adducing of historical motives in v. 4 in the form of a tradition relating back to the beginning period of Israel's journeyings in the wilderness contains some unexpected features. Deuteronomy 2:29 relates that the Moabites gave food and drink to Israel at this time, although nothing is said in respect of the Ammonites on this matter. In order to provide a suitable reason, however, the deuteronomic author makes reference to the anti-Israelite stance of Balaam, the Moabite prophet (Numbers 22–24).

The prophetic oracles against Moab preserved in the prophetic literature of the OT (Isa 15:1–16:14; Amos 2:1-3) show how intense was the bitterness felt toward the Moabites. It is the awareness of the strength of this hostility that forms a significant feature of the context of the story of Ruth.

It comes as something of a surprise that a relatively open and more relaxed attitude is adopted toward both the Edomites and the Egyptians. In spite of the vigorously unsympathetic, even hostile portrayal of the Egyptian pharaoh in the story of the exodus, it is evident that close political and commercial relationships existed between Israel and Egypt. For two centuries both Israel and Judah had relied, rather unwisely, on promises of Egyptian military support against the Assyrians and the Babylonians.

In the case of the Edomites, it is noteworthy that 2:1-8 identifies Edom with Esau, the brother of Jacob/Israel. This identification had its origins in the Edomite occupation of the region of Seir, a territory where Esau's descendants established their settlements. Overall it is apparent that membership in the cultic community of Israel had, by the time these rulings were formally promulgated as law, taken on a range of major social, economic, and political consequences.

23:9-14. The rulings set out in these verses concern the hygienic conditions that were to prevail in the Israelite military camp. Two features come prominently to the fore. The first is that warfare was perceived to be an activity when extra precautions were necessary because of its hazardous nature. It was also regarded as a partially sacred activity that has drawn to it rather misleadingly the idea of "holy war." Warfare entailed the shedding of blood so that warriors were required to be protected from any blood guilt that might be incurred by acts of killing. It was also important that a military camp should be so arranged that the divine presence would be secured, since it was this presence that ensured victory according to the deuteronomic theology of warfare.

In a practical perspective, it is also to be borne in mind that, with large numbers of men living in hastily prepared and ill-protected conditions, disease became a serious threat and proper handling of food was easily neglected. The basic, if seemingly mundane, requirements for personal hygiene set out in vv. 12-13 made practical good sense. It is a consistently developed feature of Deuteronomy that warfare and military service were mandatory obligations for all able-bodied male members of the community. What is envisaged in the deuteronomic literature is a citizen army, rather than a professional fighting elite.

23:15-16. The law regarding the right of slaves to receive protection and the right to permanent domicile in the community occasions some degree of surprise. The Babylonian law code of Hammurabi required that fugitive slaves be returned to their former masters. The ruling here reflects a more humanitarian concern that recurs in the deuteronomic legislation, especially in regard to the protection of slaves. It found explicit justification in the traditional memory of the period of slavery suffered by Israel's ancestors in Egypt. God alone was the ultimate judge of all human conduct, so the commercial and social interests that it was the business of the state legislation to protect had to be subordinated to this belief in an ultimate divine order of right.

The choice granted to a slave to take up residence in any of Israel's cities exhibits a considerable degree of personal freedom. The formula that is used ("in any place they choose in any one of your towns") links this freedom of choice with the freedom of God in establishing the location of the nation's central sanctuary (cf. 12:5). It also recognizes frankly that full social freedom was not simply a matter of status but also one of opportunity to express and fulfill a normal pattern of life. A comparable concern is reflected in the admonition to ensure that a freed slave had sufficient capital to set up a viable homestead (cf. 15:12-18).

This protection and right of domicile for a runaway slave can be considered a development of the earlier law of Exod 22:21 prohibiting the oppression or exploitation of an alien.[93] In a similar fashion, this adduces as a motive the experience of Israel's ancestors in Egypt: "you were aliens in the land of Egypt." Certainly there are close similarities, but it is improbable that Israel simply equated the status of a slave with that of a resident alien, although clearly a runaway slave would seek recognition as an alien in a foreign region. Both categories of persons represented disadvantaged, and consequently vulnerable, members of the community, so that the attitude of the deuteronomists appears as the outcome of a conscious broadening of concern for classes of weak and oppressed persons.

23:17-18. In these verses, the practice of cultic prostitution appears as an acknowledged

---

93. C. van Houten, *The Alien in Israelite Law,* JSOTSup 107 (Sheffield: Sheffield Academic, 1991) 45, 87-88.

fact in ancient Israel during the period of the monarchy and to have required the employment of both male and female practitioners. The deuteronomic literature displays a sharp hostility to the practice; this hostility must certainly have represented a long-held antipathy to the practice in the official Israelite cultus (cf. Gen 38:21-2; 1 Kgs 14:24; 15:12). In its origin in the ancient Near East, the custom appears widely attested and to have been related to rituals in which sexual union was performed as a type of sympathetic magic designed at reactivating the natural forces of life. The prohibition of such activity to the daughters and sons of Israel points firmly in the direction of recognizing that those employed in such services were usually of foreign, non-Israelite origin. The ruling here is surprising in that, while prohibiting such ritual service to Israelites, the law nevertheless frankly recognizes the freedom of such activities to continue. A further discouragement of such activity is maintained by prohibiting that any fee paid for such practice should be contributed to the temple treasury. It would appear that this had at one time been an established custom.

The name given to a male prostitute in v. 18 is "dog" (כלב *keleb*), which appears to have strong pejorative tones. Less plausibly, it could be understood in the sense of "faithful follower." The use of such a name needs to be considered in conjunction with the general hostility to all forms of cult prostitution. The deuteronomic attitude is clearly hostility and repudiation, but not to the point where it possessed the assurance and authority to bar the practice altogether. Although the deuteronomic authors usually assume with great confidence that they have, or can expect to have, the authority to implement their legislative proposals, this is one of a number of instances in the book where their ability to do so faced some inevitable limitations. In this regard, there are significant similarities between the authors of Deuteronomy and the sages of Proverbs in condemning and repudiating popular forms of prostitution, while at the same time acknowledging its prevalence.

REFLECTIONS

The laws set out in Deut 23:1-18 deal with defining the boundaries of the community, ethnically, socially and, to a lesser extent, morally. The legislation about community membership was a matter of primary concern and was to be exemplified by participation in the formal worship of the sanctuary at the major festivals. Membership established privileges and brought assurances concerning welfare and opportunities for prosperity within the national life. Ideally the covenant instituted on Mt. Horeb and expressed through the Ten Commandments determined the nature of this covenant community. However, human communities are living entities that necessarily create their own boundaries. The orderliness and well-being of the entire group could be threatened from within by disruptive sexual behavior, so rules were set forth to regulate behavior and to contain consequences within proper limits. At the edges also, a community's general stability and vitality could be threatened by the intrusion of unwelcome outsiders.

At the same time, the need to show vigor and firmness in maintaining the internal purity and integrity of the community had to be tempered with the need to display compassion and openness. So Israel had to accept the right of entry of aliens and foreigners on a regulated basis and especially to show a humanitarian protection and right of residence to fugitive slaves, since to have denied this would have made a mockery of Israel's own central tradition concerning its origin in an act of divine deliverance from slavery in Egypt.[94]

All such concerns are real and pressing issues in the modern world. The enthusiasm to maintain high standards and firm boundaries all too readily becomes harsh and unrealistic. Yet openness and laxity can equally easily tear away the very heart of the commitment to a sense of high calling established through God's election and covenant promises.

What we are faced with in these laws are ancient perceptions showing where boundaries were to be drawn. Attention is fixed on the manner in which historical and kinship obligations had to be modified in the light of the need to maintain the health and compassionate outreach of a caring society.

94. Braulik, "Deuteronomy and Human Rights," 145.

Deuteronomy 23:19–25:4, Justice and Compassion in the Community

NIV	NRSV
[19]Do not charge your brother interest, whether on money or food or anything else that may earn interest. [20]You may charge a foreigner interest, but not a brother Israelite, so that the LORD your God may bless you in everything you put your hand to in the land you are entering to possess.	19You shall not charge interest on loans to another Israelite, interest on money, interest on provisions, interest on anything that is lent. [20]On loans to a foreigner you may charge interest, but on loans to another Israelite you may not charge interest, so that the LORD your God may bless you in all your undertakings in the land that you are about to enter and possess.
[21]If you make a vow to the LORD your God, do not be slow to pay it, for the LORD your God will certainly demand it of you and you will be guilty of sin. [22]But if you refrain from making a vow, you will not be guilty. [23]Whatever your lips utter you must be sure to do, because you made your	21If you make a vow to the LORD your God, do not postpone fulfilling it; for the LORD your God will surely require it of you, and you would incur guilt. [22]But if you refrain from vowing, you will not incur guilt. [23]Whatever your lips utter

vow freely to the LORD your God with your own mouth.

²⁴If you enter your neighbor's vineyard, you may eat all the grapes you want, but do not put any in your basket. ²⁵If you enter your neighbor's grainfield, you may pick kernels with your hands, but you must not put a sickle to his standing grain.

24 If a man marries a woman who becomes displeasing to him because he finds something indecent about her, and he writes her a certificate of divorce, gives it to her and sends her from his house, ²and if after she leaves his house she becomes the wife of another man, ³and her second husband dislikes her and writes her a certificate of divorce, gives it to her and sends her from his house, or if he dies, ⁴then her first husband, who divorced her, is not allowed to marry her again after she has been defiled. That would be detestable in the eyes of the LORD. Do not bring sin upon the land the LORD your God is giving you as an inheritance.

⁵If a man has recently married, he must not be sent to war or have any other duty laid on him. For one year he is to be free to stay at home and bring happiness to the wife he has married.

⁶Do not take a pair of millstones—not even the upper one—as security for a debt, because that would be taking a man's livelihood as security.

⁷If a man is caught kidnapping one of his brother Israelites and treats him as a slave or sells him, the kidnapper must die. You must purge the evil from among you.

⁸In cases of leprous*ᵃ* diseases be very careful to do exactly as the priests, who are Levites, instruct you. You must follow carefully what I have commanded them. ⁹Remember what the LORD your God did to Miriam along the way after you came out of Egypt.

¹⁰When you make a loan of any kind to your neighbor, do not go into his house to get what he is offering as a pledge. ¹¹Stay outside and let the man to whom you are making the loan bring the pledge out to you. ¹²If the man is poor, do not go to sleep with his pledge in your possession. ¹³Return his cloak to him by sunset so that he may sleep in it. Then he will thank you, and it

---

ᵃ8 The Hebrew word was used for various diseases affecting the skin—not necessarily leprosy.

you must diligently perform, just as you have freely vowed to the LORD your God with your own mouth.

24If you go into your neighbor's vineyard, you may eat your fill of grapes, as many as you wish, but you shall not put any in a container.

25If you go into your neighbor's standing grain, you may pluck the ears with your hand, but you shall not put a sickle to your neighbor's standing grain.

24 Suppose a man enters into marriage with a woman, but she does not please him because he finds something objectionable about her, and so he writes her a certificate of divorce, puts it in her hand, and sends her out of his house; she then leaves his house ²and goes off to become another man's wife. ³Then suppose the second man dislikes her, writes her a bill of divorce, puts it in her hand, and sends her out of his house (or the second man who married her dies); ⁴her first husband, who sent her away, is not permitted to take her again to be his wife after she has been defiled; for that would be abhorrent to the LORD, and you shall not bring guilt on the land that the LORD your God is giving you as a possession.

5When a man is newly married, he shall not go out with the army or be charged with any related duty. He shall be free at home one year, to be happy with the wife whom he has married.

6No one shall take a mill or an upper millstone in pledge, for that would be taking a life in pledge.

7If someone is caught kidnaping another Israelite, enslaving or selling the Israelite, then that kidnaper shall die. So you shall purge the evil from your midst.

8Guard against an outbreak of a leprous*ᵃ* skin disease by being very careful; you shall carefully observe whatever the levitical priests instruct you, just as I have commanded them. 9Remember what the LORD your God did to Miriam on your journey out of Egypt.

10When you make your neighbor a loan of any kind, you shall not go into the house to take the pledge. 11You shall wait outside, while the person to whom you are making the loan brings the pledge out to you. 12If the person is poor, you shall not sleep in the garment given you as*ᵇ* the

---

ᵃ A term for several skin diseases; precise meaning uncertain   *ᵇ* Heb lacks *the garment given you as*

NIV

will be regarded as a righteous act in the sight of the LORD your God.

14Do not take advantage of a hired man who is poor and needy, whether he is a brother Israelite or an alien living in one of your towns. 15Pay him his wages each day before sunset, because he is poor and is counting on it. Otherwise he may cry to the LORD against you, and you will be guilty of sin.

16Fathers shall not be put to death for their children, nor children put to death for their fathers; each is to die for his own sin.

17Do not deprive the alien or the fatherless of justice, or take the cloak of the widow as a pledge. 18Remember that you were slaves in Egypt and the LORD your God redeemed you from there. That is why I command you to do this.

19When you are harvesting in your field and you overlook a sheaf, do not go back to get it. Leave it for the alien, the fatherless and the widow, so that the LORD your God may bless you in all the work of your hands. 20When you beat the olives from your trees, do not go over the branches a second time. Leave what remains for the alien, the fatherless and the widow. 21When you harvest the grapes in your vineyard, do not go over the vines again. Leave what remains for the alien, the fatherless and the widow. 22Remember that you were slaves in Egypt. That is why I command you to do this.

25 When men have a dispute, they are to take it to court and the judges will decide the case, acquitting the innocent and condemning the guilty. 2If the guilty man deserves to be beaten, the judge shall make him lie down and have him flogged in his presence with the number of lashes his crime deserves, 3but he must not give him more than forty lashes. If he is flogged more than that, your brother will be degraded in your eyes.

4Do not muzzle an ox while it is treading out the grain.

NRSV

pledge. 13You shall give the pledge back by sunset, so that your neighbor may sleep in the cloak and bless you; and it will be to your credit before the LORD your God.

14You shall not withhold the wages of poor and needy laborers, whether other Israelites or aliens who reside in your land in one of your towns. 15You shall pay them their wages daily before sunset, because they are poor and their livelihood depends on them; otherwise they might cry to the LORD against you, and you would incur guilt.

16Parents shall not be put to death for their children, nor shall children be put to death for their parents; only for their own crimes may persons be put to death.

17You shall not deprive a resident alien or an orphan of justice; you shall not take a widow's garment in pledge. 18Remember that you were a slave in Egypt and the LORD your God redeemed you from there; therefore I command you to do this.

19When you reap your harvest in your field and forget a sheaf in the field, you shall not go back to get it; it shall be left for the alien, the orphan, and the widow, so that the LORD your God may bless you in all your undertakings. 20When you beat your olive trees, do not strip what is left; it shall be for the alien, the orphan, and the widow.

21When you gather the grapes of your vineyard, do not glean what is left; it shall be for the alien, the orphan, and the widow. 22Remember that you were a slave in the land of Egypt; therefore I am commanding you to do this.

25 Suppose two persons have a dispute and enter into litigation, and the judges decide between them, declaring one to be in the right and the other to be in the wrong. 2If the one in the wrong deserves to be flogged, the judge shall make that person lie down and be beaten in his presence with the number of lashes proportionate to the offense. 3Forty lashes may be given but not more; if more lashes than these are given, your neighbor will be degraded in your sight.

4You shall not muzzle an ox while it is treading out the grain.

COMMENTARY

The makeup of a community is a complex reality, bearing all the characteristics of growth, like a living body, rather than of a fixed structure, like a building. This sensitivity to the vitality of a community in terms of growth and decay is well reflected in the earliest narratives of the Hebrew patriarchs shown in the book of Genesis. It places a marked emphasis on the extended family and on ties of kinship as providing a set of values and associations that require to be acknowledged in all aspects of life. The consciousness of clan and tribal affiliation continues to be reflected strongly in the stories relating to the earliest phase of Israel's settlement in the land and in the accounts of the origins of the Israelite monarchy. For Deuteronomy, the concept of Israel's divine election and of a covenant bond between the nation and the LORD God embraced these kinship ties, vesting them with a powerful religious significance and creating the idea that the entire nation was a people of one kin. So they could be portrayed pictorially as one large family, which the Hebrew expressed in its patriarchal fashion as "a nation of brothers."

Quite clearly various factors contributed to the breakdown of this feeling of social solidarity, which appears to have been strongest in the earliest period of Israel's life. It may well be that it was never more than a projected ideal that was only partially felt by the various member clans and tribes. For the most part, it becomes consistently evident that in the earliest times a sense of identity and belonging was generated most firmly through the immediate affiliation of the extended family and clan, rather than of the nation in its broad extent. We can see that, over time, other factors, especially those of regional associations and status within a city or community, became important.

In this process of development from tribal groups to cities inevitable changes occurred in patterns of religious loyalty. Greater prosperity emerged, but the increased acquisition and influence of wealth created new social boundaries, which gave rise to fresh problems. Accordingly it became the business of the law to monitor and control these.

Far too little is known regarding the development of the Israelite economy, although it would appear from the legislation in the book of Deuteronomy that ownership of land, the protection of rights of inheritance, and general expectations of prosperity and well-being were all matters that were accorded high priority in the attention of Israel's lawmakers. The position of families within the community could not be viewed in isolation from matters of property and wealth. These contributed to defining the status of a family. It is evident from the deuteronomic laws that silver had become a means of exchange and a highly prized form of capital. Mercantile enterprise was common, and contacts with other nations for purposes of trade were generally experienced. For all the consciousness of military threats and political uncertainties that surround the final form of the book, the broad outlook of the book of Deuteronomy can be described as one of general economic stability. Israel, as it is portrayed within the laws, is a community of opportunity and of social and commercial sophistication.

It is against this background that the laws set out in 23:19-25 are to be interpreted. To an extent, they reflect a guarded acceptance of the principle that it was the duty of the law to protect capital, to promote commercial enterprise, and to secure respect and encouragement for personal industry and effort. Over against this, however, there appears a deep consciousness that, if left unregulated, economic enterprise and protectiveness could undermine the very basis of the community with its kinship values and commitments. A nation of landowners and mercantilists could not easily also be a nation of brothers and sisters.

The laws set out in 23:19–25:4 are predominantly aimed at achieving a balance between accepting the necessity for commercial enterprise and the protection of family capital, while at the same time setting limits to both. They may broadly be seen as an elaboration of the aims and intentions that undergird the commandment "You shall not steal" (5:19). They establish guidelines to show what constituted misappropriation of another's property and what was required to uphold the traditional compassion of the extended family to protect the weaker and more vulnerable members of the community.

23:19-23. The law here protects against the prevalent practice of usury, in which excessive rates of interest were charged on loans of capital and on goods purchased. As a result, the borrower, assumed to be already in economic constraints, was mercilessly exploited. The response exhibited by this legislation is to prohibit the taking of any interest at all from a fellow Israelite, but to allow it, with no specified restrictions, from foreigners. The custom of such selective business dealings was probably not wholly an innovation at this point of time, since it is probable that local, kinship-based trading practices of this kind were quite common. What is new is the extension of this pattern to cover an entire national, covenant-based community. The status as a citizen of Israel could, from this time, carry quite major economic consequences.

The law concerning the fulfillment of vows must similarly reflect the uncertainties of the economic order. Vows to present goods and produce to the sanctuary at the end of the harvest or of some commercial enterprise could readily prove to be inconvenient, or even hopelessly optimistic, in their calculation. Behind all such actions often lay the unexpressed belief that such vows might serve as a form of inducement to God so that the enterprise would be blessed. Any delay in paying what had been vowed is here prohibited out of the theological conviction that words spoken to God, even in secret, were binding promises in which the integrity and good faith of the giver were at stake. Undoubtedly we find throughout biblical history evidence of the belief that vows were a sign of the trustworthiness and good faith of the true worshiper. Gifts to God were an evident proof of the reality of faith in the divine governance of the world (cf. Eccl 5:4-6).

23:24-25. The reality of the economic order, tempered by the necessity to display compassion and charity to a needy neighbor, are reflected in these two laws. The background assumption to them is undoubtedly that of a long-standing custom that allowed a local person or a traveler to pluck grapes from a neighbor's vineyard when passing through. A similar convention existed with regard to the standing grain in a neighbor's field at harvesttime. To allow a modest plucking of the crop was a mark of hospitality and goodwill, but was quite evidently

never intended to provide an impoverished neighbor with a continued means of charitable support. So a charitable concession could easily be abused when it was exploited by deliberate scroungers. Both laws then provide illuminating expressions of the deuteronomic spirit and of the general social context in which its legislative program was developed. Old customs, nurtured in a world of neighborly trust and the conventions appropriate to a close-knit community with strong kinship ties, were overtaken by a harsher economic environment in which those customs were susceptible to exploitation.

Where vines were grown and fields planted with crops for commercial purposes rather than home use, new protective measures were called for. Even neighbors could become greedy and exploitative in using old customs to get something for themselves at another's expense. This ruling, therefore, is aimed at protecting the rights of the landowner while at the same time seeking to preserve what was valuable of the neighborly attitudes of ancient customs.

From the perspective of legislative development, these laws also serve to highlight the inevitable reflections and ramifications consequent upon the broad sweep of the commandment prohibiting stealing. It sought to determine what constituted theft in specific circumstances and endeavored to show that this was not incompatible with ancient customs of a charitable nature. We may presume that these rulings still left open a rather indeterminate area of judgment for local elders to define when a reasonable right had been abused.

24:1-4. The law that prohibits the remarriage to her former husband of a woman who had subsequently been divorced by him and married to another is of special interest.[95] There are no close parallels to it in other ancient Near Eastern law codes, and the reasoning that underlies it is not wholly clear. It appears also to be awkwardly placed, since it might have been expected to appear alongside the other laws concerning sexual behavior in 22:13-30. It can best be regarded as

---

95. The issue is discussed in G. Wenham, "The Restoration of Marriage Reconsidered," *JJS* 30 (1979) 36-40; R. Westbrook, "The Prohibition of Marriage in Deuteronomy 24:1-4," *Studies in Bible*, ed S. Japhet, Scripta Hierosolumitana 31 (Jerusalem: Magnes, 1986) 385-405; E. Otto, "Das Verbot der Wiederherstellung einer geschiedenen Ehe. Deuteronomium 24,1-4 im Kontext des israelitischen und jüdäischen Eherechts" *UF* 24 (1992) 301-9.

a transition piece that concerns property rights and inheritance as well as sexual behavior.

The ruling itself is clear enough and is further reflected in the prophetic report of Hosea 1–3 and the saying recorded in Jer 3:1-2. It reveals an underlying awareness that such action could only promote social confusion and would make nonsense of the proper boundaries of sexual conduct. The circumstances that are said to have brought about the divorce in the first instance ("because he finds something objectionable about her," v. 1) are vague and ill-defined. Similarly, the situation envisaged is one in which the woman is then divorced again by her second husband on the grounds that "he dislikes her." The second husband is then assumed to be still living at the time when the proposed remarriage to the first husband occurs. Overall the background conviction expressed by the law recognizes the seriousness of marriage, permits rather arbitrary grounds for divorce, but takes full account of the fact that divorce introduces considerable complications in the preservation of acceptable social boundaries. While some degree of arbitrariness in permitting divorce in the first place is allowed, any relapse into a fickle marital exchange is prohibited. The concern is to exclude the possibility altogether of remarriage to a former spouse after a divorce. Such action would represent a serious breach of respect for acknowledged social structures.

24:5. The law grants the unusual concession that a newly married man was to be freed from military or other public service for one year after his marriage. The underlying assumption appears to be that marriage is a solemn undertaking that establishes a new household unit within society. Therefore, it both carries obligations and fulfills certain promises in regard to the upholding and extension of the extended family unit. It is assumed that children would result from the marriage and thereby secure the future of the new household unit, preserving the name of the husband should he fall victim in his military service. Such concern for the protection of a new family unit was important for society, and by granting this concession to a newly married man his adulthood and manhood would be confirmed. Widows with children, especially sons, were more favorably placed than widows without offspring, as the book of Ruth illustrates (cf. Ruth 1:11-13).

The law serves as a noteworthy attempt to define the boundary between private right, closely linked to the values of the extended family, and public duty. To yield complete priority to one consideration over the other would ultimately have jeopardized the future health and well-being of society as a whole. It also has relevance in displaying an awareness that, even in times of military emergency, it was not appropriate that one generation should be sacrificed in the expectation that a future generation would thereby benefit from what they had forgone. Each generation is seen as a whole in and for itself, with its own expectation of establishing families and households in which an individual adult male would ensure that his name was preserved.

24:6. This law is a sharp reminder of the level of poverty that could be experienced in ancient Israel. The two millstones with which grain would be ground into flour are regarded as forming a basic minimum of household utensils. Without them, a family would be reduced to begging and would lose all ability to remain self-supporting. It is prohibited, therefore, that such vital domestic utensils be taken as a pledge against a loan of provisions or money of any kind. Such a ruling reflects on the way in which the protection of property and the authority of the law to enforce commercial, or loan, transactions was subjected to specific limits. When the enforcement of such transactions would reduce a fellow Israelite to the point of complete destitution, then to do so was prohibited. Similar limits to the enforcement of business transactions are set out in vv. 10-13.

24:7. The law that prohibits kidnapping follows the differently worded, but essentially equivalent, law of Exod 21:16. The subject of kidnapping is also covered in the law code of Hammurabi, which deals with the kidnapping of an infant son of a free citizen. This would certainly suggest that the crime, intended for the acquisition of slaves, was a serious one in antiquity. In a tribally structured community, members of an alien tribe could readily have been regarded as reasonable targets for such hostile acts, with marauding bands capturing and enslaving their unfortunate victims, many of whom would have been children. It appears as a prevalent and deeply disruptive aspect of ancient banditry, which the centrally based authority of the urban communities strove hard to control and eliminate.

The directive that such a prohibition applied only to "another Israelite" is a surprising, and rather disturbing, weakening of the basic principle of the law. It is occasionally a feature of the deuteronomic legislation that it is made to apply only to Israelites, allowing a lower standard of conduct to operate toward outsiders (cf. 14:21; 15:3; 23:20). This reflects the strong background of election and covenant ideology that permeates the legislation, extending privileges and status to all Israelites, but at the same time heightening in a negative fashion a sense of exclusion for those outside the privileged circle.

24:8-9. Concern for neighborly conduct toward a fellow Israelite also motivates the law regarding the prevention of the spread of infectious skin diseases. A considerable debate has taken place regarding the precise medical identification of the skin disease, or diseases, covered by the Hebrew word צרעת (*ṣāraʿat*).[96] No satisfactory evidence has arisen to indicate that the disease was leprosy, which became a scourge in medieval times, but was not known in the ancient Near East. The complex rulings set out in Leviticus indicate a recognition that some skin afflictions were more contagious, and therefore more dangerous, than others; but precise identification was difficult. All the indications are that various types of skin afflictions were covered by the term *ṣāraʿat* and that it was left to the experience and traditional knowledge of the levitical priest to pronounce the level of risk posed by the condition. The purpose of the law here was clearly to protect the community at large from heedless and uncaring persons who might have been tempted to ignore whatever warnings had been given regarding their condition. By remaining in active social circulation, they risked infecting other people. The law, in effect, sought to give a measure of authority and control to the priests over such matters. Nevertheless, it leaves open the question of what further active steps could be taken to restrict the movements of a person who was unwilling to comply with the priestly restraints.

96. The varied range of diseases and manifestations (since the term is also used of buildings) covered by the Hebrew term is examined in the light of modern medical and scientific understanding in David P. Wright and R. N. Jones, "Leprosy," ABD 4:277-82.

The adducing of the example of Moses' sister Miriam (Num 12:14-15) is an instructive instance of the awareness that the law lacked any specific penalty and that difficulties could arise in seeking to enforce restrictions on an uncooperative member of the community. The biblical tradition recounts that Miriam had been afflicted with a severe skin disease as punishment for her critical attitude toward Moses. The author clearly intends to warn that a similar misfortune could befall any Israelite who flouted the restrictions demanded by the law of v. 8. Throughout there is a fundamental assumption that affliction with disease, and any consequent recovery from it, were matters that lay entirely in the hands of God to control. Hidden within this also lies the belief that disease could be a punishment for sin, an assumption that is challenged in the book of Job.

24:10-13. The rulings set out in these verses return to deal with issues arising from the economic order. Once again they concern the treatment of a neighbor who has fallen upon hard times and who has been compelled to seek a loan of goods or silver. Even the most necessary items of personal clothing could be offered and taken in pledge against a loan. When proceeding to take possession of the pledge, the creditor was not permitted to enter the house of the debtor. Nor, if the pledge took the form of the debtor's only cloak, could this last piece of property be withheld overnight. Throughout there is a deep consciousness of the disruptive consequence that the legally backed enforcement of commercial transactions could have on the social life and stability of a community. The caring and neighborly concern that would almost certainly have been strongly felt within communities in which the values of the extended family were still strongly maintained could easily be broken and undermined in the harsher context of the economic life of large urban communities.

The deuteronomic law is at pains to protect and uphold the personal rights of possession of property and aims to protect—and where necessary enforce—the honoring of commercial and monetary dealings. Yet there were limits, and these limits established new restrictions that were to be respected. Fundamental among these was the boundary established between Israelites and non-Israelites, which had come to acquire a paramount significance in the deuteronomic horizon.

There was also a boundary set by an individual's household, which became an expression of his or her individual citizenship and a sanctuary of privacy. Thus it could not be invaded arbitrarily, even in the legitimate act of taking possession of something given in pledge to secure a loan.

If the item pledged was the cloak that was vital to the well-being and personal identity of a citizen, then, under the same principle, this was to be returned at nightfall. The duty of the law to protect commercial dealings was thereby set within certain limits that could not be crossed. At all stages of Israelite/Jewish history in the biblical period, it appears that debt slavery represented a real, and potentially deeply disturbing, threat. In upholding the economic order, wider issues of a humanitarian kind could be set aside. Children could be sold off in order to pay debts (Amos 2:6), and starvation and ruination faced an impoverished family.

24:14-15. Problems of poverty and the economic order also surface in the law regarding the prompt payment of wages. The ruling presupposes that labor was normally paid for on a daily basis and that those who were available for work on these terms were wholly dependent upon what they earned. It is significant that, as in the case of the previous laws dealing with the limits imposed on the enforcement of monetary dealings, these are addressed to those who are assumed to be members of the free landowning section of the community. The appeal is essentially one that sought to maintain a sensitive and fair attitude toward the poorer members of society, as well as to those who could suddenly find themselves thrown into unexpected poverty. The motive for such a charitable disposition is held to lie with God, who is the protector of the poor, so that the ungenerous person, even when legally in the right, might nevertheless incur guilt from God (v. 15).

24:16-18. The same line of argument to support a compassionate and caring interpretation of justice reverberates through the three laws that follow. Of great importance is the ruling in v. 16, which precludes the infliction of the death penalty on the children of the actual culprit. The rule is cited in 2 Kgs 14:6 in connection with Amaziah's execution of his father's murderers, but the sparing of their children.

The law is concerned with the administration of human justice, rather than with the effect of divine punishment on a family or community, and so, in this respect at least, it stands apart from the warning given in the Decalogue (5:9). We may also note the cruel punishment inflicted upon Achan's entire household in Josh 7:24 and the severe punishment urged for those who transgress the first commandment (Deut 13:15).

The principle behind the law was clearly felt to be important and reflects directly on the way in which the development of a centralized system of law, administered through law officers and elders, was able to check and restrain the custom of vengeful mutilations and killings that characterized the strong vengeance orientation of family solidarity in early Israel. Repeatedly we find that the deuteronomic legislators were concerned to secure fairness and parity of treatment across the whole community. How effective such a legal code was in the manner of its operation is impossible to determine and clearly depended much on the good sense of those who administered it.

The awareness of an "all Israel" consciousness that strongly pervades the book of Deuteronomy, setting a sharp distinction between those who were within the community and those who were outside it, is reflected in the law of v. 17. The resident alien and the orphan belonged within the basic community, yet lacked the full support that would ordinarily have been afforded by a surrounding kinship circle. As a result, they became more than usually vulnerable to exploitation and abuse. They enjoyed only a dependent, client status in society,[97] so they had to rely on the protection and representative mediation of others if they were to secure legal or financial redress in contentious matters. They were, therefore, especially vulnerable and virtually powerless if they were unable to obtain the support of a patron. The admonition here, which once again falls back on the historical recollection of Israel's ancestral origins in the slavery of Egypt, warns categorically against any exploitation of this weakness. We can once again perceive the real degree of sensitivity the deuteronomic legislators display toward recognizing that a system of law could be no more just and fair than the level of integrity and goodwill shown by those who administered it. Even laws carved on tablets of

97. The deuteronomic legislation on the subject of the resident alien, and its social background, is well covered in C. van Houten, *The Alien in Israelite Law,* JSOTSup 107 (Sheffield: Sheffield Academic, 1991) 68-108.

stone were powerless if those who were responsible for applying those laws were indifferent to the claims of society's weakest members. An added touch of authority is thus imposed on the administration by the concluding comment: "therefore I command you to do this" (v. 18).

24:19-22. These admonitions concerning the requirement to leave a forgotten sheaf of grain or the gleanings of the olive trees and vines for the poorer members of society to harvest must certainly reflect an ancient custom. It was a way of providing some assistance for the poor that enabled them to share both in the workload of harvest and in its rejoicing and fruits. Obviously such charitable provision made available a necessary means of subsistence for the landless and provided an important means of social bonding and collective sharing. The community was ultimately seen as a single entity that could prosper as a whole, but in which even the least fortunate were to participate.

25:1-3. The legislation concerning the manner and circumstances in which a punishment of flogging was to be administered provides a valuable insight into the way Deuteronomy envisaged the application of its legal rulings. A dispute between two persons, evidently over a serious matter in view of the potential punishment, was to be brought before judges who would decide on the guilt or innocence of the accused person. If the guilty verdict were upheld, then the punishment of flogging was to be carried out in the presence of the judge. He was also to ensure that the punishment was administered exactly as had been determined and that it was neither lessened nor exceeded. A maximum number of lashes, forty, is then prescribed in v. 3 on the grounds that to exceed this number would lead to the neighbor's being "degraded in your sight." It was the custom in later Jewish practice for this to be limited to thirty-nine in order to avoid any accidental overstepping of the number (cf. 2 Cor 11:24).

25:4. The ruling in this verse gives a measure of protection for animals by affirming that an ox was not to be muzzled while treading out the grain. The ruling has consistently been understood literally in rabbinic interpretations, which must certainly be regarded as correct. In 1 Cor 9:9, Paul understands the ruling allegorically as indicating that workers deserve their reward. Clearly the issue had become a matter of discussion in learned Jewish circles, and the fact that it displays a concern for the welfare of animals is significant. Creation was looked upon as a coherent reality, the order of which needed to be respected in all its parts.

REFLECTIONS

The series of laws that commenced in 23:19 ranges over a number of issues that appear, at first glance, to have little in common. Yet this seeming randomness in the subject matter is more apparent than real, since the prevailing concern is to mark out exceptions in the rigorous application of certain laws. In consequence, there is a relatively broad basis of attention to situations in which human welfare and dignity, or even that of animals, are protected against overly zealous administration of justice.

The upholding of the right of a citizen to pick grapes or pluck grain from a neighbor's vineyard or field maintains a customary freedom, while aiming to prevent deliberate theft or exploitation of another's property. Similarly the refusal to allow a neighbor to enter the house of another in order to take possession of property that had been offered in pledge guaranteed the neighbor's independence and right of privacy in his or her own home.

This series of rulings reveals a sensitive and practical attitude toward the administration of law and justice. To press one facet or ruling of the law to the detriment of other matters of moral and social concern would have been to make a mockery of the law. There is displayed here a genuine recognition that laws protecting property and possessions could easily enforce the rights of the property owner at the expense of the dignity and social standing of another. Property could become a cause of division and dissension in an unwelcome and unforeseen way. As a broad principle, it appears that it was felt to be the business of the legal system to uphold the binding nature of legal transactions, to enforce payment of debts, and to defend the enterprise of landowners in farming and developing their land commercially without interference and exploitation by envious neighbors. Yet all such developments could trespass heavily on ancient customs aimed at providing some protection and support for the poorer members of society. The law, if pressed too zealously, could lead to sharper social and economic divisions, with the poor becoming poorer and the rich getting richer. To prevent the breakup of a community and the consequent loss of human dignity if the poor became utterly destitute, some restraining guidelines were necessary, thus the guidelines illustrated by these laws. Ultimately even working animals represented an important resource that deserved to be respected and protected.

These laws make us aware that it is the business of the law to protect the community as a whole, and not just the more successful members of it. The earlier structure of Israelite society had leaned heavily upon the commitment of the extended family to protect its weaker members and to provide the conditions for sharing property and its benefits widely throughout the group. But fundamental shifts in Israel's economy, a series of moves toward more sophisticated and diverse forms of urban living, and increased openness to the larger world of the ancient Near East had all made heavy inroads into these older structures with their strong sense of kinship values. Progress was welcome, but it often came at a price that the smaller rural communities of Israel could ill afford. Wealth and the promotion of trade threatened to undermine many of the older values and supportive customs. Accordingly a major interest in the legislation set out here indicates a concern to retain what could be preserved of these older values and customs by setting limits to the rights of the landowning section of the community.

The attitude that it displayed regarding personal property is of particular interest, since there is a bold recognition of its importance to individual persons. Considerations of health, of human dignity, and of the need for a person to retain a minimum of resources to be self-supporting all came under the purview of the lawmakers. As a result, such unlikely sounding possessions as a millstone, a cloak, or other items of personal property that might be used as a token pledge to secure a loan are all made the subject of specific rulings. There emerges a sensitivity to the recognition that what a person is as a member of the community cannot properly be separated from that person's basic possessions. Food, warmth, work, and the right to privacy in one's own house are all viewed as central features of an individual's dignity. Therefore, it becomes the duty of the law to consider property in its relationship to a person's overall position in society. What was a minor item for the wealthy could represent a priceless treasure to the poor.

Deuteronomy 25:5-19, Protecting the Family

NIV	NRSV
⁵If brothers are living together and one of them dies without a son, his widow must not marry outside the family. Her husband's brother shall take her and marry her and fulfill the duty of a brother-in-law to her. ⁶The first son she bears shall carry on the name of the dead brother so that his name will not be blotted out from Israel.	5When brothers reside together, and one of them dies and has no son, the wife of the deceased shall not be married outside the family to a stranger. Her husband's brother shall go in to her, taking her in marriage, and performing the duty of a husband's brother to her, ⁶and the firstborn whom she bears shall succeed to the name of the deceased brother, so that his name may not be blotted out of Israel. ⁷But if the man
⁷However, if a man does not want to marry his brother's wife, she shall go to the elders at the town gate and say, "My husband's brother refuses to carry on his brother's name in Israel. He will not fulfill the duty of a brother-in-law to me." ⁸Then the elders of his town shall summon him	has no desire to marry his brother's widow, then his brother's widow shall go up to the elders at the gate and say, "My husband's brother refuses to perpetuate his brother's name in Israel; he will

NIV

and talk to him. If he persists in saying, "I do not want to marry her," [9]his brother's widow shall go up to him in the presence of the elders, take off one of his sandals, spit in his face and say, "This is what is done to the man who will not build up his brother's family line." [10]That man's line shall be known in Israel as The Family of the Unsandaled.

[11]If two men are fighting and the wife of one of them comes to rescue her husband from his assailant, and she reaches out and seizes him by his private parts, [12]you shall cut off her hand. Show her no pity.

[13]Do not have two differing weights in your bag—one heavy, one light. [14]Do not have two differing measures in your house—one large, one small. [15]You must have accurate and honest weights and measures, so that you may live long in the land the LORD your God is giving you. [16]For the LORD your God detests anyone who does these things, anyone who deals dishonestly.

[17]Remember what the Amalekites did to you along the way when you came out of Egypt. [18]When you were weary and worn out, they met you on your journey and cut off all who were lagging behind; they had no fear of God. [19]When the LORD your God gives you rest from all the enemies around you in the land he is giving you to possess as an inheritance, you shall blot out the memory of Amalek from under heaven. Do not forget!

NRSV

not perform the duty of a husband's brother to me." [8]Then the elders of his town shall summon him and speak to him. If he persists, saying, "I have no desire to marry her," [9]then his brother's wife shall go up to him in the presence of the elders, pull his sandal off his foot, spit in his face, and declare, "This is what is done to the man who does not build up his brother's house." [10]Throughout Israel his family shall be known as "the house of him whose sandal was pulled off."

[11]If men get into a fight with one another, and the wife of one intervenes to rescue her husband from the grip of his opponent by reaching out and seizing his genitals, [12]you shall cut off her hand; show no pity.

[13]You shall not have in your bag two kinds of weights, large and small. [14]You shall not have in your house two kinds of measures, large and small. [15]You shall have only a full and honest weight; you shall have only a full and honest measure, so that your days may be long in the land that the LORD your God is giving you. [16]For all who do such things, all who act dishonestly, are abhorrent to the LORD your God.

[17]Remember what Amalek did to you on your journey out of Egypt, [18]how he attacked you on the way, when you were faint and weary, and struck down all who lagged behind you; he did not fear God. [19]Therefore when the LORD your God has given you rest from all your enemies on every hand, in the land that the LORD your God is giving you as an inheritance to possess, you shall blot out the remembrance of Amalek from under heaven; do not forget.

COMMENTARY

The laws that now bring the present section to a close appear to have only a slight connection with those that have preceded them. Yet this lack of connection is more apparent than real, since the overall concern of the laws set out in vv. 5-12 is with the need to protect the family. More precisely, they are concerned to protect the economic interests of the family by safeguarding its capital and its importance as an inheritance. We have already noted in Deuteronomy that the family unit is focused

in a relatively narrow way on an individual household and its property rather than the much larger extended kin group. We have seen how this could be threatened by irresponsible sexual behavior on the part of the head of the family and, more directly, by misconduct on the part of the women of the household, whether wives or daughters, for whom the family head was responsible.

Yet the household was not simply a kin group built around a sense of belonging. A prime concern of the law prohibiting adultery was a need to ensure the family head of his right to the paternity of the children his wives were expected to bear him. He was entitled to be assured, in accordance with the commandment prohibiting adultery (5:18), that his children were truly his. They would become part of the economic unit of the household and would eventually become its heirs. So the viability and success of the household as a primary unit of society depended on the extent to which there were legitimate heirs to its wealth and a willingness on their part to concern themselves with its welfare. The security of a household and its property were very much a matter entrusted to its male head and the eldest son, who could expect to take his father's place in due course. It then became a matter of honor that this heir apparent should pay proper respect to his parents, once they passed an effective working age. The law permitted harsh measures to be taken against a wastrel son, while at the same time it strove to ensure that the inheritance rights of each son were fully protected in accordance with birth order. The boundary lines of such matters were of the utmost significance. Where it might well have seemed practical to allow the head of the household to act as he saw fit in planning for future eventualities, the law fully recognized the dangers of doing so. In a polygamous household, bitter tensions could arise to bring the family to the point of destruction. Accordingly there was a deep interest on the part of society more generally to concern itself with the rights and expectations of wives and their children.

25:5-10. The law regarding levirate marriage (the title is taken from the Latin *levir,* "husband's brother") gives formal approval to measures aimed at coping with a situation in which a woman was widowed without having a son to assume the male role within the household.[98] The custom appears to rest on a well-established practice that most probably operated on an ad hoc basis. It seems unlikely that it was either a common practice or that it was legally enforceable. Had it been the normal convention in the circumstance of early widowhood, it is hard to understand why in the OT the misfortunes and near destitution of widows and orphans appear to be a persistent, and acutely felt, social problem.

The requirement that a widow could not be

98. R. Westbrook, *Family and Property in Biblical Law,* JSOTSup 113 (Sheffield: Sheffield Academic, 1991) 69-89.

married outside the family was evidently intended to ensure that the property of the deceased husband remained within his family's control. It also marks a situation in which the patriarchal structure of Israelite society was itself closely guarded, since, had women been entitled to inherit ancestral property in accordance with the prescription given in Num 27:8, the problem would not have arisen. As it is, the concern of the law is to provide the possibility of the birth of a male heir to the deceased, who would eventually take responsibility for the family estate. Accordingly, the explanation for the marriage to the deceased husband's brother set out in vv. 5-6 is that it should lead to the birth of a male heir who would then be counted as the original husband's firstborn for the purposes of inheritance.

The narrative episode of Gen 38:12-30 goes further even than this in recognizing all the offspring of such a relationship as constituting the family of the deceased brother. However, the point is not of major importance, since the intention of the arrangement was achieved once a firstborn son to the deceased had been born. The overall concern is with the economic preservation of the original household, rather than with the regulation of sexual relationships or the provision of a home for an unfortunate widow. The contrary law contained in the holiness code (Lev 18:16; 20:21), which forbids the contracting of such levirate marriages, is probably later in origin but must also reflect the fact that such a practice had never been widely adopted.

It is the shadow of this unease concerning the practice that has given rise to the further regulations in vv. 7-10, which provide for the possibility of the husband's brother opting out of any such commitment. The reasons why this might be desirable followed two main paths. A primary factor would certainly be that the husband's brother might himself be in a position to acquire his brother's property, adding it to property of his own. This could readily have arisen when the brother was in line to take over a family estate that would have gone to his deceased brother. By marrying his widowed sister-in-law, he would be reducing his own household's prospects. It could also have been the case that the value of his own property might be diminished and his status in the community lessened if a major entitlement remained in the name of his dead brother.

The law frankly recognizes the possibility of such a refusal to implement the requirement of marriage to a widow. Accordingly, the right to make such a refusal is upheld, but it is countered to some extent by imposing a ceremony of public shaming and humiliation. This took the form of a ritualized action of removing the sandal from the non-compliant brother's foot and spitting in his face. Clearly the offense, such as it is, is regarded as failure to uphold the integrity of a family and its estate. The sandal was the token of "walking over" a piece of land as a sign of ownership. Its removal signified that the owner of the sandal had not shown proper regard for his (extended) family's property.

The demand that such a ceremonial act of shaming be carried out is interesting, since shame was clearly a matter that exercised a powerful influence on patterns of social behavior. It was, however, primarily a social matter and is clearly one that the deuteronomic lawmakers do not otherwise consider a major means of enforcing right conduct.

Overall the problem that the custom of levirate marriage sought to deal with was one occasioned by the growth of wealthy property-owning households. It can then be seen in the context, and against the background, of the older strong sense of kinship ties and the heavily protective desire to keep property and wealth within the immediate extended family. Formal codes of social legislation like that of Deuteronomy came strongly to the fore as society became more urbanized and more affluent. It is understandable, therefore, that the book of Deuteronomy should have felt it a prime duty to give the full backing of the law to commercial loans and transactions and to the right of owning and developing private property. At the same time, it clearly remained fully sensitive to the moral value latent in kinship ties. Therefore, it could resort to the language of family membership (brotherhood and sisterhood) as a means of evoking a strong sense of mutual responsibility. In the case of the legislation for levirate marriage, which was obviously not a common practice, it tries to retain something of the older commitment to the extended family in a more commercially minded age.

25:11-12. The law that follows provides the only example among the OT laws in which physi-

cal mutilation is prescribed as a legal punishment, apart from the broad reference to the practice in the *lex talionis* (cf. 19:21). The quarrel outlined in v. 11 is described as one between "brothers" (אחים *'āḥîm*); it may have been intended in a narrow literal sense (as in the NRSV) or be understood to cover any male member of the community. The context could favor the narrower and more literal interpretation, since the concern was evidently not simply with immodest or unseemly behavior, but with an action that could result in preventing a male member of a household from producing offspring. The harshness of the punishment prescribed would then become more readily intelligible in a situation that would not simply have been humiliating to a man, but would have had major consequences for him.

25:13-16. The concluding law covers the problem of a trader working with different kinds of weights, all carrying the same nominal value. The general problem of maintaining a fair system of standard weights and measures was quite evidently a persistent problem for ancient society once the practice of barter as well as of direct sales with monetary values was in widespread use. By using a heavier weight for buying than for selling, it was easy to cheat the unwary. It must certainly have been one of the most widespread forms of cheating simply because it was difficult for the purchaser to detect or for the authorities to stamp out (cf. Ps 12:2; Prov 20:23; Amos 8:5). Even standard weights employed in antiquity suffered considerable variation through wear and tear, besides which there may also have existed regional variations, since new weights were balanced from older, worn ones. One of the most desirable benefits of official royal oversight of trading practices was a concern to enforce standard weights. Nevertheless, even with these efforts, it seems probable that the honesty of the officials was little superior to the dishonesty of the traders. Against such a background, the deep disgust at such cheating is expressed by the idea of such practices as constituting an "abomination" (תועבה *tô'ēbâ*).

25:17-19. The remarks concerning Amalek and the necessity for maintaining a continued hostility and watchfulness toward this people bring an unexpected note to the conclusion. The verses would appear to have been added at a late stage in order to round off the series of regulations and laws, probably at a time when Amalekite brigands became a renewed threat to the Israelite community. The historical reference to Amalekite treachery is to Exod 17:8-17, although the accusation made here goes beyond the details recorded there. In any event, this historical memory can scarcely have provided a sufficient basis for the unrelenting animosity and distrust that are expressed. Israel's experience had clearly shown the Amalekites to be unsatisfactory people with whom to have any dealings whatsoever and persons with whom it was impossible to make real peace, in spite of attempts to do so.

REFLECTIONS

The laws contained in 25:5-19 appear to be a miscellany, but, as with the preceding group, a number of underlying basic concerns draw them together. The major interest lies in preserving the family household as an integrated unit and in upholding its viability. The death of any prominent male member of a household posed a potential threat to its economic strength since there had then to take place either a handing over of the deceased person's estate to his male heirs or a fundamental realignment of expectation within the surviving male family members. Without any males to administer a household's capital stock, its future was placed in jeopardy or collapsed altogether (as envisaged by Qoheleth in Eccl 4:7-8; 5:13-17). Obviously it was impractical to apportion the estate in equal shares to all, even to only the male children, since this would have broken up its consolidated value. We may assume that its capital value was often not great, with many persons being dependent upon it. To have divided an estate into equal shares, however attractive this may have appeared in simple fairness, would have destroyed its viability, since this was largely in terms of arable land.

In the light of this need, the eldest son, ordinarily the firstborn (and assumed to have reached adulthood by the time such a major responsibility fell to him) had the lion's share. Yet this privilege also carried immense responsibility since it meant that all the other members of the family, especially the women, were almost entirely dependent upon him. In a polygamous household in which there may be many sons, it is obvious that rivalries within the family could become bitter and sometimes violent. Much was at stake, then, and the structure of the household unit, with its roots in the extended family, was closely tied to the economic viability of the whole community. Strong households made for strong townships, provided a reasonable harmony, and common interest was established between them. In the case of the premature death of the head of a household, the problems became greatly exacerbated, especially if the inheriting son were still a minor. Personal interests had to be subordinated to the need to hold together the value of the household's capital assets and to the concern to keep this under efficient male control.

From the perspective of hindsight, and with a less narrowly structured pattern of social groupings in which male domination can no longer be conceded, the limitations of the Israelite situation become apparent. We can at best seek to understand it and to understand the motives and concerns that gave rise to it. We should also recognize that such legislation as is presented here was itself a reflection of social attitudes and assumptions that had grown up over many centuries, and even millennia.

Of special interest to us is the recognition of the importance of building strong and positive relationships within a household. Throughout the book of Proverbs, the sages who were its authors offer strong warnings against disruptive behavior within a household. Quarrelsome speech, nagging complaints, undisciplined children, as well as violent and uncontrolled anger are all made the targets of their admonitions. At first it may appear a rather trivial concern with matters that are a part of ordinary human experience. However, the sages clearly regarded such matters important, because any conduct that could bring dissension and conflict within a household might eventually bring the entire household to ruin.

The strong biblical emphasis on the family as the foundational unit of society is important and relevant to the modern world. It represents a major line of defense against dehumanization and economic weakness, since the household unit is crucial for coping with varied human demands. At the same time, it is important, in seeking to defend and protect family life, to recognize those factors that can make it vulnerable or that can lead to its becoming an oppressive, rather than a liberating and supportive, institution. One aspect of the legislation in Deuteronomy is the manner in which it seeks to achieve a shift of focus from a social context in which dependence on the family was all-important to one in which a wider range of conventions and attitudes retained its strengths, while at the same time seeking to curtail its weaknesses.

Clearly the strongest and most successful families in ancient Israel had the resources with which to protect themselves from the economic misfortunes of life. There were, however, weaker members of the community who lacked an effective basis of family support, such as resident aliens and freed slaves, or who had been unfortunate enough to fall victim to misfortune, such as those widowed early in life and no longer within range of their families. The story of Ruth skillfully captures a scenario in which two women, Ruth and her mother-in-law, Naomi, find themselves in such a situation.

One of the measures adopted by the deuteronomic legislators with a view to retaining the benefits of the family values of Israelite society, as it had existed in its earliest phase, is to classify every member of the community as a "brother" or "sister." To learn to think of other members of society as part of one great national family was clearly aimed at enhancing respect for them and protecting their interests. Yet more than a purely verbal basis of support is needed if family life is to be protected in Israel and if the weaker members of the community are to be kept from starvation and destitution. So there are important legislative steps to be taken, aimed in part at guaranteeing that families behave responsibly by ensuring consistency and fairness in matters of inheritance and by seeking to assist them to retain their economic viability. A cornerstone in this policy is undoubtedly that of seeking to ensure that deaths, particularly that of the patriarchal head of a successful family, did not become a destructive event for the family's future.

DEUTERONOMY 26:1-19, LITURGY AND THANKFULNESS

NIV

26 When you have entered the land the LORD your God is giving you as an inheritance and have taken possession of it and settled in it, ²take some of the firstfruits of all that you produce from the soil of the land the LORD your God is giving you and put them in a basket. Then go to the place the LORD your God will choose as a dwelling for his Name ³and say to the priest in office at the time, "I declare today to the LORD your God that I have come to the land the LORD swore to our forefathers to give us." ⁴The priest shall take the basket from your hands and set it down in front of the altar of the LORD your God.

NRSV

26 When you have come into the land that the LORD your God is giving you as an inheritance to possess, and you possess it, and settle in it, ²you shall take some of the first of all the fruit of the ground, which you harvest from the land that the LORD your God is giving you, and you shall put it in a basket and go to the place that the LORD your God will choose as a dwelling for his name. ³You shall go to the priest who is in office at that time, and say to him, "Today I declare to the LORD your God that I have come into the land that the LORD swore to our ancestors to give us." ⁴When the priest takes the

NIV

[5]Then you shall declare before the LORD your God: "My father was a wandering Aramean, and he went down into Egypt with a few people and lived there and became a great nation, powerful and numerous. [6]But the Egyptians mistreated us and made us suffer, putting us to hard labor. [7]Then we cried out to the LORD, the God of our fathers, and the LORD heard our voice and saw our misery, toil and oppression. [8]So the LORD brought us out of Egypt with a mighty hand and an outstretched arm, with great terror and with miraculous signs and wonders. [9]He brought us to this place and gave us this land, a land flowing with milk and honey; [10]and now I bring the firstfruits of the soil that you, O LORD, have given me." Place the basket before the LORD your God and bow down before him. [11]And you and the Levites and the aliens among you shall rejoice in all the good things the LORD your God has given to you and your household.

[12]When you have finished setting aside a tenth of all your produce in the third year, the year of the tithe, you shall give it to the Levite, the alien, the fatherless and the widow, so that they may eat in your towns and be satisfied. [13]Then say to the LORD your God: "I have removed from my house the sacred portion and have given it to the Levite, the alien, the fatherless and the widow, according to all you commanded. I have not turned aside from your commands nor have I forgotten any of them. [14]I have not eaten any of the sacred portion while I was in mourning, nor have I removed any of it while I was unclean, nor have I offered any of it to the dead. I have obeyed the LORD my God; I have done everything you commanded me. [15]Look down from heaven, your holy dwelling place, and bless your people Israel and the land you have given us as you promised on oath to our forefathers, a land flowing with milk and honey."

[16]The LORD your God commands you this day to follow these decrees and laws; carefully observe them with all your heart and with all your soul. [17]You have declared this day that the LORD is your God and that you will walk in his ways, that you will keep his decrees, commands and laws, and that you will obey him. [18]And the LORD has declared this day that you are his people, his

NRSV

basket from your hand and sets it down before the altar of the LORD your God, [5]you shall make this response before the LORD your God: "A wandering Aramean was my ancestor; he went down into Egypt and lived there as an alien, few in number, and there he became a great nation, mighty and populous. [6]When the Egyptians treated us harshly and afflicted us, by imposing hard labor on us, [7]we cried to the LORD, the God of our ancestors; the LORD heard our voice and saw our affliction, our toil, and our oppression. [8]The LORD brought us out of Egypt with a mighty hand and an outstretched arm, with a terrifying display of power, and with signs and wonders; [9]and he brought us into this place and gave us this land, a land flowing with milk and honey. [10]So now I bring the first of the fruit of the ground that you, O LORD, have given me." You shall set it down before the LORD your God and bow down before the LORD your God. [11]Then you, together with the Levites and the aliens who reside among you, shall celebrate with all the bounty that the LORD your God has given to you and to your house.

12When you have finished paying all the tithe of your produce in the third year (which is the year of the tithe), giving it to the Levites, the aliens, the orphans, and the widows, so that they may eat their fill within your towns, [13]then you shall say before the LORD your God: "I have removed the sacred portion from the house, and I have given it to the Levites, the resident aliens, the orphans, and the widows, in accordance with your entire commandment that you commanded me; I have neither transgressed nor forgotten any of your commandments: [14]I have not eaten of it while in mourning; I have not removed any of it while I was unclean; and I have not offered any of it to the dead. I have obeyed the LORD my God, doing just as you commanded me. [15]Look down from your holy habitation, from heaven, and bless your people Israel and the ground that you have given us, as you swore to our ancestors—a land flowing with milk and honey."

16This very day the LORD your God is commanding you to observe these statutes and ordinances; so observe them diligently with all your heart and with all your soul. [17]Today you have

NIV

treasured possession as he promised, and that you are to keep all his commands. [19]He has declared that he will set you in praise, fame and honor high above all the nations he has made and that you will be a people holy to the LORD your God, as he promised.

NRSV

obtained the LORD's agreement: to be your God; and for you to walk in his ways, to keep his statutes, his commandments, and his ordinances, and to obey him. [18]Today the LORD has obtained your agreement: to be his treasured people, as he promised you, and to keep his commandments; [19]for him to set you high above all nations that he has made, in praise and in fame and in honor; and for you to be a people holy to the LORD your God, as he promised.

COMMENTARY

The significance and attractiveness of the two liturgical confessions that bring to a close the main legal section of Deuteronomy can scarcely be overrated. Each provides an illuminating glimpse into the minds of the deuteronomists and reveals why this law book has been so influential in the development of both Jewish and Christian thought.

It should be noted that Deuteronomy 26 provides a carefully structured inclusio to balance the opening of the more directly worded instructions for the establishment of a central place of worship in chap. 12. There the primary importance of the sanctuary is declared, with its controlling position in shaping the life of the community in all its aspects. It is described with relative simplicity as a place at which prayers could be made and to which offerings could be brought. It was to be a sanctuary where God would become accessible to the people by the presence there of the divine name. In chap. 26 we have a concluding resumption of the theme concerning the central place worship was to have in the life of every member of the Israelite nation. Whereas chap. 12 provides the means and institutional structure for the religious dimension of Israel's life, chap. 26 fills this structure with content and ideas. And whereas chap. 12 determines the outward pattern and location of worship, chap. 26 determines the shape of the liturgical prayers, confessions, and theological meaning of worship.

Most of all this content is set out as an expression of the thankfulness with which Israel was to celebrate before God the immensity of the gift that the divine choosing, calling, and preservation of the nation had made possible. From a literary and historical perspective, it should be noted that, contrary to the widely canvassed view of Gerhard von Rad[99] that this confessional recital of God's gracious dealings with Israel had an early origin, its relatively late deuteronomic composition must be fully recognized.[100] It marks a late, and revisionist, view of the meaning of worship for Israel, rather than a very early one. It is pervasively and characteristically an expression of the deuteronomic understanding of worship and of the embedding of all social relationships and moral seriousness in this.

To be an Israelite was to be a beneficiary of a long history of God's gracious providence and care, which had made slaves into free and prosperous citizens. This is the message that echoes through the confessional recital of the past in 25:5-10a. This summary account has been constructed and worded on the basis of the outline history of Israel's origins, now contained in Genesis–Numbers. Clearly only a part of the present tradition was available to the deuteronomists, although the main structural outlines had been established in the form with which we are familiar.

26:1-4. The introductory rubric explains the

99. G. von Rad, "The Form-critical Problem of the Hexateuch," in *The Problem of the Hexateuch and Other Essays,* trans. E. W. T. Dicken (Edinburgh: Oliver & Boyd, 1965) 3.

100. See L. Rost, "Das kleine geschichtliche credo," *Das kleine Credo und andere Studien zum Alten Testament* (Heidelberg: Quelle & Meyer, 1965) 11-25; N. Lohfink, "Zum 'kleinen geschichtlichen Credo' Dtn 26,5-9," and "Dt,6-9: Ein Beispiel altisraelitischer Geschichtstheologie," in *Studien zum Deuteronomium und zur deuteronomistichen Literatur I,* SBA 8 (Stuttgart: Katholisches Bibelwerk, 1990) 263-304.

circumstances in which this confessional recital was to be made. A token gift of the firstfruits of the harvest was to be placed in a basket and handed to the priest at the central sanctuary (v. 2). The priest was then to place this basket of gifts before the altar as a gesture acknowledging that the produce belonged to God. It represents a part of what God had given to the worshiper. The occasion for this action was evidently intended to be the Festival of Ingathering, which took place in the late summer (14:22-29). The whole procedure, which is carefully specified, is an open acknowledgment that the land itself is a gift from God. It has acquired this religious significance because it was the land that had been promised on oath by God to the nation's ancestors (v. 3).

The handing over of the basket of fruit and produce is only one part of the prescribed act of worship. Probably rituals that were not all that dissimilar had been performed in honor of the local Baals by non-Israelites. As important as the presentation of the gift was the confessional declaration showing how the land had been given to Israel's ancestors when they were landless and impoverished.

26:5-10a. These verses contain what can best be described as Israel's confession of faith. It was a kind of creed, declaring the story of God's actions that had shaped the nation's faith. It anchored Israel's possession of the land to its knowledge of God and tied both to events from the nation's past. In this fashion, Israel's faith was inseparably linked to the territory on which the produce had been grown and elicited from the story of the past a message concerning the nature and purpose of God. It was this message that gave assurance, faith, and hope for the future.

Such a confession defines the Being of God in an oblique manner by affirming and recalling those actions through which God had become known and accessible to Israel. It transforms a simple act of giving into an assertion of the gracious and generous nature of God and avers yet again the dependence of the worshiper on God for the sustenance that makes life possible. It renounces, by implication, any claim upon God other than that of God's own gracious and outgoing nature. Israel had been brought into existence by divine grace and continued to be saved

by grace alone. In this simple thanksgiving ceremony, the declaration of that grace was reaffirmed as Israel's continually renewed confession of faith.

The detailed elements of the historical summary that constitutes this creed are brief and are drawn from the outline part of the story that binds together the narrative of the present books of Genesis to Joshua. The "wandering Aramaean" (the phrase ארמי אבד [ărammî ʾōbēd] conveys the sense of "vulnerable" or "destitute," since a landless person was without security of food and protection) was Jacob, who had sought refuge from famine in the land of Egypt. It was while he was in Egypt that his descendants had grown to such numbers that they were reckoned to constitute a "nation." (For the deuteronomic authors of this creedal confession, the sheer growth in number of the Israelites is regarded as the primary factor that had elevated them to nationhood.

This affirmation draws attention to the unexpected omission in the recited account of Israel's beginnings of any mention of the covenant made on Mt. Horeb (Sinai). In the exodus story, it is especially the revelation of God on the sacred mountain and the making of the covenant between the LORD God and Israel that elevated Israel to the status of nation (Exod 19:5-6). Yet here this status is seen as having already been conferred by the growth in number of Jacob's descendants. Surprisingly the report of the making of the covenant on Mt. Horeb is passed over in silence.

For von Rad and Noth, this failure to make reference to the Horeb event was seen as a significant guide to the manner in which Israel's tradition concerning its past had been built up, with the tradition of the revelation on Mt. Horeb being grafted in at a relatively late stage.[101] It is questionable, however, whether this omission is particularly significant and whether it represents a valid conclusion that can be drawn. In any case, once the fact that this creedal recital of the story of Israel's origins is seen to be a deuteronomic composition, then the basis for drawing such conclusions is largely removed.

The reason for the absence of any reference to the events of God's revelation on Mt. Horeb must

---

101. A critical survey of the problem arising from this is presented in E. W. Nicholson, *Exodus and Sinai in History and Tradition* (Oxford: Blackwell, 1973) 1-32.

lie in the theological motives that led to the formulation of this historical summary as a concentration on God's reaching out to Israel. The Horeb revelation, with its code of commandments, together with the entire deuteronomic legislation, which gave sharper definition to the demands of the covenant, belonged to the sphere of Israel's response. In this regard, the entire law code of Deuteronomy 12–26 is viewed as a spelling out of the content and purpose of the revelation made on Horeb. The covenant at Horeb and the covenant made in the plains of Moab (29:1) are not two different covenants, but two occasions for affirming what is viewed essentially as one covenant relationship, brought about by God's election of Israel. Seen in such a light, the purpose of recalling how God had stretched out a mighty hand to bring Israel out of Egypt "with a terrifying display of power and with signs and wonders" (v. 8) was aimed at showing that all Israel possessed had been given to it. Israel's duty to obey these laws was a necessary way of responding to all the privileges to which its continued existence on the land bore testimony. God was Israel's inescapable benefactor to whom it both had been and forever would be totally indebted. Without God, Israel was nothing.

We cannot leave aside consideration of the centrality of the importance of land for the larger perspective of the theology of the deuteronomists. Throughout the years in which the deuteronomic movement came into being and through which it had flourished and gained maturity, the threat of the loss of the land had grown in scale to be a major threat. For much of the nation, it had already become a reality by the time this confessional recital was composed. The roots of this aspect of deuteronomic theology are traceable to the shock and alarm that had arisen when the first Assyrian depredations of Israel's territory had occurred during the latter half of the eight century BCE. By the beginning of the sixth century, when the deuteronomic movement reached maturity, very little of the original territory that had constituted the Davidic-Solomonic empire remained under the control of Jerusalem. In reciting the tradition of how the land had originally been given to Israel, each surviving member of this once great nation was recalling what had been his or her ancestral inheritance.

This fact lends added force to the emphasis on the manner in which Israel had been brought out

of Egypt, "with signs and wonders." This distinctive deuteronomic formulation (cf. 4:34; 6:22; 7:19; 11:2-3; 29:2; 34:11)[102] reflects directly the central theme of the plague narrative (Exodus 6–12) and of the providential wonders by which Israel had been sustained in the wilderness. Such actions on God's part served to provide evidence that the LORD was indeed God and that the exercise of divine power was the reason for Israel's escape from Egypt, survival in the wilderness, and conquest of the land. It had not been in Israel's power to achieve these victories, since they were gifts conferred by the power of God.

Such a theological message clearly had taken on a special relevance at a time when Israel was contemplating the greatness of the past and was staring a more ruinous present in the face. By recalling the gracious divine purpose that had brought Israel into being in the first place, a firm basis for hope for the future was established.

26:10b-15. The second of the confessional recitals by which Israel was to affirm the giving of firstfruits of the land to God and the tithe of the produce for the upkeep of the Levites and the care of the destitute is more functional. The requirement that Israel should tithe the increase of all its produce annually was established in 14:22, whereas here the tithe is reckoned only at the end of a three-year period. The annual levy is then counted as the firstfruits. No specific reference is made to the requirement that this offering be presented at the central sanctuary, as laid down in 14:23 and 15:20, although this should probably be taken for granted.

Throughout the chapter the emphasis is firmly placed in demonstrating that the giving of this triennial tithe for the upkeep of the sanctuary servants and the destitute (for the three categories of the needy: resident aliens, orphans, and widows; cf. 1:16; 14:29) was to be fulfilled "in accordance with your entire commandment that you commanded me" (v. 13) and was not a voluntary act of charity. To this extent the confessional recital represents a stringent declaration of the importance of the tithe as a visible expression of Israel's observance of the law. This con-

---

102. For the significance of this formula in the deuteronomic presentation of the exodus from Egypt, see B. S. Childs, "Deuteronomic Formulae of the Exodus Traditions, *Hebräische Wortforschung. Festschrift zum 80. Geburtstag von Walter Baumgartner,* SVTP 16 (Leiden: E. J. Brill, 1967) 30-39.

forms also with the requirement that a full declaration be made that the commandments had been kept in their entirety. The offerings had not been spoiled by having been eaten, or set apart, while the worshiper was in an unclean (cultically unacceptable) condition.

In this fashion the offering of the triennial tithe became an act of wider significance than simply providing support for the ministers of Israel's worship and giving charitable assistance to the poor. It was a public expression of the religious good standing and the law-abiding faithfulness of the worshiper. To have been negligent in this offering would have had serious consequences for membership within the community as a whole. The effect was clearly twofold: It both reinforced the importance of the tithe as a sign of the willingness to keep the commandments in their full range, and it ensured that the tithe was not reduced to a mere optional extra that could be treated with indifference.

There is a measure of dignity and open-ended expectation in the prayer with which this second confessional recollection of the past is made: "Look down from your holy habitation, from heaven . . . and bless your people Israel" (v. 15). The past could be remembered with gratitude; the present could be viewed only with anxiety and alarm; the future could now be striven for and secured by renewing obedience to God's commandments.

26:16-19. The concluding section affirms that the covenant between God and Israel, the laws for which have been set out in the preceding chapters and give to this covenant a human dimension, has been agreed upon, sealed, and ratified.[103] Both parties to the covenant are fully aware of the terms and consequences relating to it and have willingly agreed to abide by them. Israel is therefore already bound to the commandments and has been so since its entry into the land.

From a literary perspective, this section completes the framework to the laws that began in 12:1, and it links directly to the exhortation by Moses (11:1-32) for Israel to keep the commandments. The preparatory period in the wilderness has come to an end, and now the promises and expectations for the future need to be fulfilled. There is, therefore, a note of dramatic finality

about the time reference: "this very day." The time of preparation is over. The period of fulfillment has begun when obedience must prevail.

From a formal perspective, there can be little reason to doubt that the pattern of covenant making portrayed here, together with much of the terminology employed, has been drawn and adapted from international treaty making between nations and cities. To such treaties, God, or the respective deities named by the signatory parties, could be invoked to act as witness and guardian. The fundamental difference here is that the LORD God is one party to the covenant and Israel is the other. There is no invoking of third parties to act as witnesses or patron overseers, because the LORD God acts throughout as initiator, guardian, and witness to it.

At the same time, there is a solemn and serious intent behind the securing of agreement from all the people of Israel. This is further reinforced in the following section (27:1-10) by affirming that Moses was accompanied by the elders of Israel (27:1) and the Levites (27:9), who act as the people's representatives. All Israel has been drawn into the covenant with the LORD as God since its entry into the land.

We should not overlook the point that the strongly worded formula insisting that "this very day" saw the covenant bond between Israel and God inaugurated is repeated in each and every day in which Israel continues to exist. A renewed immediacy of the commandments is brought into being every time they are read and remembered. By them Israel must live, and no letup in their importance is contemplated. So the repetition of the today formula in vv. 17-18 carries forward to each new day Israel's obligation, which forms its response to God's covenant making.

It is significant that not only has Israel been bound to God by the covenant and has thereby become committed to keeping the commandments, but also God is bound by what is promised from the divine side. Israel will be set high above all nations (v. 19). The formula that follows is ambiguous whether the reference to "fame, praise, and honor" refers to Israel (NRSV and NIV) or to God (NEB and REB).

Clearly the text displays a certain level of reticence in suggesting that Israel has a claim on God by which the LORD is bound to bless them

---

103. See N. Lohfink, "Dt 26,17-19 und die Bundesformel," *Studien zum Deuteronomium und zur deuteronomistischen Literatur I,* SBA 8 (Stuttgart: Katholisches Bibelwerk, 1990) 211-61.

and to keep them secure in their land. The divine initiative and sovereignty are carefully protected. Nevertheless, the covenant implies that the bond between Israel and God carries obligations for God as well as for Israel. It is God who has taken the initiative to deliver, uphold, and render holy the people of Israel.

REFLECTIONS

Few passages in the book of Deuteronomy have attracted quite so much attention as the short confessional recital of Deut 16:5-10a. The reason for this lies in its history-centered emphasis. It portrays God as "the God who acts" by constructing a brief review of particular past events relating to Israel's origins, which paints a picture of the love, purpose, and power of God. Without defining the attributes of God in the conventional language of classical theology, it nevertheless infers and implies many of those attributes. So the worshiper can sense that he or she knows God because of events that bear directly on the worshiper's own experience and perceptions of the world.

Moreover, because these events are related directly to the situation of the worshiper, making reference to the land on which the crops offered to God had been grown, a bridge is built between the past and the present and between God and human beings. The realization that it was my ancestor who was landless and destitute and that it was my forebears who were slaves and my predecessors who first entered and took possession of this land made faith personal and real.

Seen in this light, the importance of well-planned worship and a well-structured liturgy becomes obvious. Such worship forms a continuous bridge between the generations and between the unseen world of God and the known earthly realm of home and work. Worship becomes a process of bonding in much the same way that an infant becomes bonded to its mother—through care and contact. Far from such worship's being an optional extra, it fulfills a vital role in life. It establishes an indispensable sense of identity, relating the individual to the larger community in which life has to be lived and generating a sense of orientation and hope to the environment and its future. All this in a mere half dozen verses!

To contrast this emphasis on the action of God in directing events with other, especially Canaanite, religious traditions—suggesting that whereas they represented gods of nature, Israel worshiped a God of history—has undoubtedly been a serious misinterpretation of the situation. Undoubtedly it was a widespread feature of much ancient Near Eastern religion, as indeed of religions generally, to claim that a god, known by whatever name, had the power to initiate and control events. It is hard to see how it could have been otherwise if the deity concerned were not regarded as impossibly remote and inaccessible. It belongs to the most basic notion of divinity that gods possess power over events, persons, and processes in this world. At most the contrast suggested has relevance in relation to a degree of emphasis on historical processes or the natural order. In a very real way, most of the world's great religious traditions have focused attention on the power of God, or the gods, to intervene directly in human activities and affairs, either at a national or a personal level. We can understand that a deity who did nothing at all for human beings would attract few worshipers, since it is the consciousness of divine power that lies at the heart of faith.

It is scarcely adequate as an interpretation of the specific setting in Deuteronomy 26 to contrast the idea of a God of history with a God of nature, since the chapter is directly related to the offering of the fruits of the soil. The very fact that the Israelite worshiper was commanded to recite this short summary of Israel's early history as an accompaniment to the presentation of a harvest thank offering relates the gifts of nature very directly to the land and to the historical events through which Israel had come to possess it. It is very much a scholarly abstraction to separate too sharply God's power in nature from God's power in history, since these are simply modern abstractions by which we grasp our experience of the world in its totality.

Absolute contrasts between history and nature and between the God of history and the gods of nature, therefore, are mistaken. We can discern a remarkable wholeness and balance in the Israelite confession of faith. God is related personally and directly to each Israelite's actual situation. Faith is tied indissolubly to the demands, tasks, and necessities of daily life. The world of faith and the world of food, clothing, and territory are one world.

A similar significance attaches to the omission in this confession of any reference to the giving of the law on Mt. Sinai. In view of all that has been noted concerning the importance of the concept of covenant law to Deuteronomy and the fact that this chapter is clearly intended to serve as a kind of summarizing conclusion to the specific legal parts of the book of Deuteronomy, it becomes unthinkable to suppose that the author quite intentionally bypassed any reference to the giving of the law. Only by taking the confession out of its present context altogether could this assumption be made. To some degree, it is probably this fact that has led the author to give added emphasis to the law in the shorter second confession (26:12-15). This was to be recited in accompaniment to the offering of the triennial tithe, where the bringing of the tithe is a public act of avowing that the worshiper intends to keep the commandments in their entirety.

Overall the recital of God's providential care, which has given Israel the land, and the acknowledgment that there are laws that belong to the covenant by which Israel must respond to God belong together. Law and grace are two parallel manifestations of God's commitment to Israel. Obedience to God is not a way of gaining God's favor, but a proper way of responding to it. It is because all of life's most precious assets can be seen as having derived from God that an obedient path of rightly using these assets is a proper human response.

In the theology of Deuteronomy, special importance attaches to this linking together of law and grace in that the book is deeply committed to emphasizing both concepts. It is because God is gracious that God gives the law. To emphasize one aspect to the detriment of the other or to take objection to Deuteronomy because it places the Ten Commandments so high in the divine scheme of things would be to distort the balance the book expresses. All the more does this become evident when we take full account of the way in which the central law code of the book (chaps. 12–26) is given a historical framework and an epilogue that looks to the future of Israel.

The very structure of the law code in chapter 12 begins with instructions for the building of a sanctuary and the setting up of an altar where God's presence would continue to be made available to Israel. This sanctuary would be the location of the divine name, making God accessible to the people, but at the same time providing a center of focus for the people and the place to which prayers could be offered. The same law code then concludes here with a resumption of the instruction to bring to God a thank offering. Law is set within a context of prayer and worship, which themselves form part of the armory of grace that has been given to Israel.

DEUTERONOMY 27:1–30:20

EPILOGUE

OVERVIEW

The section that begins in 27:1 and extends to 30:20 has all the appearance of being a rather randomly shaped miscellany, providing an epilogue to the giving of the law through Moses, which has now been completed in all its essentials. In this epilogue, the four chapters are broadly held together by the themes of blessing and curse, with a marked predominance of the latter. It appears that life under the law has more things that may go amiss and bring pain than it possesses of positive blessings. This appearance of one-sidedness may be partly due to the usefulness of curses as a didactic tool, exercising an admonitory role. It may also be due in part to a consciousness that historically Israel had failed to live up to its obligations to keep God's commandments. To this extent, the book of Deuteronomy carries something of a "last chance" appeal to restore the commandments to their rightful place in the daily agenda of Israel's existence.

Even granted such ameliorating comments regarding the heavy weight of curses that now unfold, it must be clearly stated that, in spite of the formulaic language, the major part of the curse section that colors the epilogue is not a true series of curses at all. In essence, a curse is the invoking of harm and evil upon a specified enemy, or wrongdoer, whether known or unknown. Curses are a form of negative prayer, aimed at inflicting hurt. We find here, however, that a substantial section of the material formulated under the heading of curse is not really a curse at all. It is, rather, a stylized confessional reflection on the historical experience of Israel. It contains much that is a shrill cry of pain for all that Israel has suffered and brings this cry to God in confession, since the commandments have been grievously neglected. It even goes so far as to pinpoint specific events and sufferings that can quite readily be related to known historical events.

DEUTERONOMY 27:1-10, THE LAW IS BOTH BLESSING AND CURSE

NIV

27 Moses and the elders of Israel commanded the people: "Keep all these commands that I give you today. ²When you have crossed the Jordan into the land the Lᴏʀᴅ your God is giving you, set up some large stones and coat them with plaster. ³Write on them all the words of this law when you have crossed over to enter the land the Lᴏʀᴅ your God is giving you, a land flowing with milk and honey, just as the Lᴏʀᴅ, the God of your fathers, promised you. ⁴And when you have crossed the Jordan, set up these stones on Mount

NRSV

27 Then Moses and the elders of Israel charged all the people as follows: Keep the entire commandment that I am commanding you today. ²On the day that you cross over the Jordan into the land that the Lᴏʀᴅ your God is giving you, you shall set up large stones and cover them with plaster. ³You shall write on them all the words of this law when you have crossed over, to enter the land that the Lᴏʀᴅ your God is giving you, a land flowing with milk and honey, as the Lᴏʀᴅ, the God of your ancestors, promised you.

NIV

Ebal, as I command you today, and coat them with plaster. ⁵Build there an altar to the Lord your God, an altar of stones. Do not use any iron tool upon them. ⁶Build the altar of the Lord your God with fieldstones and offer burnt offerings on it to the Lord your God. ⁷Sacrifice fellowship offerings*a* there, eating them and rejoicing in the presence of the Lord your God. ⁸And you shall write very clearly all the words of this law on these stones you have set up."

⁹Then Moses and the priests, who are Levites, said to all Israel, "Be silent, O Israel, and listen! You have now become the people of the Lord your God. ¹⁰Obey the Lord your God and follow his commands and decrees that I give you today."

a7 Traditionally peace offerings

NRSV

⁴So when you have crossed over the Jordan, you shall set up these stones, about which I am commanding you today, on Mount Ebal, and you shall cover them with plaster. ⁵And you shall build an altar there to the Lord your God, an altar of stones on which you have not used an iron tool. ⁶You must build the altar of the Lord your God of unhewn*a* stones. Then offer up burnt offerings on it to the Lord your God, ⁷make sacrifices of well-being, and eat them there, rejoicing before the Lord your God. ⁸You shall write on the stones all the words of this law very clearly.

9Then Moses and the levitical priests spoke to all Israel, saying: Keep silence and hear, O Israel! This very day you have become the people of the Lord your God. ¹⁰Therefore obey the Lord your God, observing his commandments and his statutes that I am commanding you today.

a Heb whole

COMMENTARY

As an opening presentation of this epilogue to the deuteronomic law code, renewed instructions are given for the setting up of a monument to the commandments at a suitable location west of the river Jordan. This monument is to be located on Mt. Ebal, in fulfillment of the instruction first given in 11:29-30.

Such monuments were not unusual in antiquity; the law tablet of King Hammurabi is undoubtedly the most famous. Special interest attaches here to the precise detail that it was to be constructed from a heap of large stones covered with plaster (vv. 2, 4) so that the words could more readily be inscribed upon it. Clearly the author was familiar with such a technique of rendering a stone surface more amenable to an ancient script.

The directive in v. 2, which insists upon the stone's being set up "on the day that you cross over the Jordan into the land that the Lord your God is giving you," certainly points to a location close to the western bank of the Jordan, which would appear to exclude the more distant location of Mt. Ebal. This was close to Shechem, a city that repeatedly appears as a central location of Israel's earliest covenant traditions. Verse 4 un-

derstands the law table set up on Mt. Ebal to be a second set of memorial symbols, in addition to the stones set up immediately after the Israelites' crossing of the Jordan. There would appear to be some confusion, then, with the stone monuments set up at Gilgal, on the west bank of the Jordan, which were directly associated with Israel's entry into the land (Josh 4:1-9). Either the time reference is to be understood very loosely as indicating no more than "the time when . . ." or more likely the report here represents a drawing together of the tradition concerning the ancient stone circle of Gilgal with the inscribing of the Ten Commandments on stone tablets (Deut 5:22) and the knowledge of a monumental pillar set up on the sacred Mt. Ebal.

The example of such law monuments as the law code of Hammurabi would indicate that they could serve not only as memorials to great rulers and their achievements, but also as important territorial boundary markers, signifying the rule of justice that prevailed in the land. They laid claim to the land as a region in which the rule of law was upheld and, when set out in the name of and bearing the image of the ruler of the land, they affirmed the justice of that ruler. In the case presented here, the fact of such a monument declared that justice in the land was inseparably linked to the name of the LORD God.

From the perspective of the history and development of law, it is noteworthy that this tradition reflects, even in a rather incomplete fashion, the long-established convention that related law to territory. The monument indicated that the law of God given through Moses represented the law of the land, modifying and extending the connection between law and established political authority.

Mount Ebal (v. 4) was traditionally associated with the curse, whereas Mt. Gerizim was the sacred mountain of the Samaritan community. It is then a matter of some importance that the text of the Samaritan Pentateuch records the name of Mt. Gerizim here. It may be that the Hebrew (MT) text is the original one and that this was subsequently altered in the Samaritan tradition to accord directly with Samaritan territorial claims. It is equally possible, however, that the Samaritan recording of the name "Gerizim" here is the older tradition and that the change was introduced after the break between Samaritans and Jews had occurred.

The building of an altar constructed from natural, uncut stones on which sacrifices of burnt offerings were to be made is prescribed in vv. 5-7. The instruction represents something of an enigma, since the deuteronomic law of cult centralization explicitly precluded the making and use of any such altar for formal cultic worship outside "the place which the LORD your God will choose." This was clearly a reference to Jerusalem, so that an altar on Mt. Ebal (or Gerizim) would have contradicted such a limitation. It certainly appears strange that the author here appears to be indifferent to the demand for the centralized control of the cultus at one place. Either he was well aware that an altar had once been in use on Mt. Ebal, or it may simply be the case that an altar on Mt. Ebal may have been regarded as permissible, and even necessary, until such time as the ark had been brought into Jerusalem. The historical narratives recounting Israel's actions immediately after the conquest are fully aware that an authorized cultus had been in use from the earliest crossing of the Jordan.

The story of the setting up of this monument to the law of the covenant reflects the intensity of the author's concern to relate the keeping of the commandments to the formal conduct of worship. The horizons of the deuteronomic author are firmly bounded by the political history of the Israelite people as a nation, together with all the institutional features of a national life. These included acceptance of a single, unified government that could administer law and a sanctuary through which the cultus could be regulated. At the same time, this law is presented as the product of a divine revelation that was made prior to the formation of the nation in all the range of its territorial and social expression. Accordingly, the law is seen to have existed before Israel's organized national life, since the formation of the nation was seen to be the consequence of the covenant between the LORD God and Israel. So, in the eyes of the deuteronomic authors of the book of the law, the entire territory west of the Jordan that Israel occupied was "the land of the law." It was wholly appropriate, therefore, that from the very outset of Israel's entry into the land, the claim of the law upon it should be affirmed and memorialized.

REFLECTIONS

Long before formal history ever came to be written, human beings marked their achievements and sent signals into the future by the raising of monuments. Some of these monuments, in the form of sacred stone pillars and circles of great stones arranged in a meaningful pattern, still exist. They stand as mute witnesses to human triumphs and values that can be recaptured only very inadequately. They speak of a sense of the divine power and purpose for humankind that could be visualized and expressed in no other way than through the setting up of a symbol that could not be ignored.

Ancient Israel was familiar with such stone circles and pillar monuments that had become familiar landmarks by the beginning of the biblical period and were already ancient by that time. The pillar that stood on Mt. Ebal was evidently among the most familiar of such historic landmarks, while the great circle of stones that stood beside the river Jordan at Gilgal was another. But what was it that these great monuments witnessed to? Even to think of them in terms of merely human achievements and triumphs of early engineering skill would be to distort and falsify the message they expressed. In truth, they were human achievements, setting forth as they did signs of the immense physical effort and engineering skills that made their erection possible. Yet the intention behind their creation lay elsewhere, since it was to point to the world behind and beyond that which can be seen. They sought to embody a transcendent meaning in a very earthly symbol.

For the deuteronomic authors, mindful of the long traditions that had made the prominent heights of Mt. Ebal and Mt. Gerizim into major national monuments, the question was what they signified. It seems likely that a great variety of popular interpretations existed, linked to the separate tribes and clans who visited these sites. This consciousness of mixed tribal and partisan traditions is still later reflected in the manner in which the later Jewish and Samaritan communities saw in these two distinct mountain heights an expression of their own jealously guarded traditions.

For the deuteronomic authors, however, the twin realities of these mountains testified to the twin realities for which Israel had come into existence. These were the law of Moses, which constituted Israel's national charter, and the blessing and curses that such a law activated into real life.

The introductory speeches ascribed to Moses have emphasized well enough the either/or nature of the challenges and decisions facing Israel. The very setting of the deuteronomic law book on the eve of Israel's entry into the land highlights this sense of a choice facing Israel and its future. There was a path leading to blessing and success and a path leading to failure and despair. The author of the epilogue to the book now seeks with considerable artistry and skill to focus attention on this existential dimension of the future. Just as every person must choose between two paths (cf. Psalm 1), so also now an entire nation found itself at a similar point in its history. The monument on the mountain of Ebal served as a kind of signpost from the past, continually pointing to that fork in the road where the momentous decision for or against God's covenant had to be made.

The concept of the law as a gift of divine grace, which makes possible a life lived in an aura of blessing, points to an understanding of human existence that recognizes that life has a potency. Whereas we have grown accustomed to thinking of infancy and childhood as an age of innocence from which we slowly fall away as experience and failures make us conscious of what we might have become, but failed to be, the biblical perspective is rather different. Infancy and childhood are ages of potency, and all our life is a stage of becoming.

Just as the deuteronomic author could look back on the beginning period of Israel's history as a time of challenge and choices, so also each human life is a continual process of meeting such challenges and making choices. It belongs to our human condition to "become what we are," which is a child of God, created in the divine image and destined to seek and find fellowship with the Creator. In order to achieve this, however, it is necessary to follow that pattern and way of life that accords with the divine image and purpose. So there is a need for God's law to serve as a map by which to trace a route through the complex paths of life.

It is in this context that the Old Testament perspective concerning the centrality of Torah, which means "guidance" or "instruction" as fully as it means "law," must be understood. Law becomes a directive for living, but it is a directive that speaks of curse as well as blessing. The contrast between the two serves as a warning that Torah is not simply about knowing what is right, but choosing the right path. To know what is right is the gift and grace of the law. Yet knowing is not the same as choosing and doing. Failure to respond in a positive fashion means that the very law that was designed to bring blessing becomes a monument of misery and despair by reminding us of all that we failed to achieve.

The tensions between law and grace, with which the apostle Paul wrestles so vehemently in Romans and Galatians, are not tensions that first emerged in the New Testament period. Already they have begun to come to the surface in a quite sharp and pointed fashion in the book of Deuteronomy. It is one of the advantages of turning back to Deuteronomy in the light of Paul's inner conflicts and turmoil to see why law is both a means of grace and a threat of curse.

For those setting out on the path of entry into the land promised to Israel's ancestors, the law appeared at first as the indispensable key to success and achievement. Yet for those, like the deuteronomic authors, looking back over what had happened since the death of Moses there was a consciousness of failure and disaster. The law had been the guidebook Israel had failed to follow. Accordingly the epilogue to the code of laws (chaps. 27–30) brings a consciousness of this fact very forcefully to the reader. The book of Deuteronomy is an optimistic document, setting out a story full of promise and hoped-for achievement. Yet hidden away in many of its warning speeches and poetry is a very gloomy and despairing note. It is a warning concerning the curse of the law and the pain of regret felt by authors surveying the prospect of a world that might have been. Only by coming to terms with this note of gloom and near despair does a fresh message of hope and renewal come to the surface.

DEUTERONOMY 27:11-26, BEHAVIOR NOT PERMITTED IN ISRAEL

NIV

¹¹On the same day Moses commanded the people:

¹²When you have crossed the Jordan, these tribes shall stand on Mount Gerizim to bless the people: Simeon, Levi, Judah, Issachar, Joseph and Benjamin. ¹³And these tribes shall stand on Mount Ebal to pronounce curses: Reuben, Gad, Asher, Zebulun, Dan and Naphtali.

¹⁴The Levites shall recite to all the people of Israel in a loud voice:

¹⁵"Cursed is the man who carves an image or casts an idol—a thing detestable to the LORD, the work of the craftsman's hands—and sets it up in secret."

Then all the people shall say, "Amen!"
¹⁶"Cursed is the man who dishonors his father or his mother."

Then all the people shall say, "Amen!"
¹⁷"Cursed is the man who moves his neighbor's boundary stone."

Then all the people shall say, "Amen!"
¹⁸"Cursed is the man who leads the blind astray on the road."

Then all the people shall say, "Amen!"
¹⁹"Cursed is the man who withholds justice from the alien, the fatherless or the widow."

NRSV

11The same day Moses charged the people as follows: ¹²When you have crossed over the Jordan, these shall stand on Mount Gerizim for the blessing of the people: Simeon, Levi, Judah, Issachar, Joseph, and Benjamin. ¹³And these shall stand on Mount Ebal for the curse: Reuben, Gad, Asher, Zebulun, Dan, and Naphtali. ¹⁴Then the Levites shall declare in a loud voice to all the Israelites:

15"Cursed be anyone who makes an idol or casts an image, anything abhorrent to the LORD, the work of an artisan, and sets it up in secret." All the people shall respond, saying, "Amen!"

16"Cursed be anyone who dishonors father or mother." All the people shall say, "Amen!"

17"Cursed be anyone who moves a neighbor's boundary marker." All the people shall say, "Amen!"

18"Cursed be anyone who misleads a blind person on the road." All the people shall say, "Amen!"

19"Cursed be anyone who deprives the alien, the orphan, and the widow of justice." All the people shall say, "Amen!"

20"Cursed be anyone who lies with his father's

NIV

Then all the people shall say, "Amen!"

20"Cursed is the man who sleeps with his father's wife, for he dishonors his father's bed."

Then all the people shall say, "Amen!"

21"Cursed is the man who has sexual relations with any animal."

Then all the people shall say, "Amen!"

22"Cursed is the man who sleeps with his sister, the daughter of his father or the daughter of his mother."

Then all the people shall say, "Amen!"

23"Cursed is the man who sleeps with his mother-in-law."

Then all the people shall say, "Amen!"

24"Cursed is the man who kills his neighbor secretly."

Then all the people shall say, "Amen!"

25"Cursed is the man who accepts a bribe to kill an innocent person."

Then all the people shall say, "Amen!"

26"Cursed is the man who does not uphold the words of this law by carrying them out."

Then all the people shall say, "Amen!"

NRSV

wife, because he has violated his father's rights."[a] All the people shall say, "Amen!"

21"Cursed be anyone who lies with any animal." All the people shall say, "Amen!"

22"Cursed be anyone who lies with his sister, whether the daughter of his father or the daughter of his mother." All the people shall say, "Amen!"

23"Cursed be anyone who lies with his mother-in-law." All the people shall say, "Amen!"

24"Cursed be anyone who strikes down a neighbor in secret." All the people shall say, "Amen!"

25"Cursed be anyone who takes a bribe to shed innocent blood." All the people shall say, "Amen!"

26"Cursed be anyone who does not uphold the words of this law by observing them." All the people shall say, "Amen!"

[a] Heb uncovered his father's skirt

COMMENTARY

The general assertion that disobedience to the law of God could place an individual Israelite under the curse now leads to a highly distinctive formal series of curses in which particular forms of conduct are outlawed. The careful formal structure and the particular deeds that are forbidden strongly suggest that the series was at one time an independent formulation. It would then have been introduced at this point because it provides an excellent illustration of the way in which disobedience to the law could result in a person's being placed under a curse.[104] It is also noteworthy for the manner in which it shows how the set forms of public worship could be used to reinforce and influence moral conduct, especially over conduct that might appear marginal and difficult to control by any other means.

Among modern scholars, Albrecht Alt,[105] in his pioneering study of the form of the Ten Commandments, drew special attention to this series of twelve curses since they illustrated how an appeal to divine authority and an implicit threat of direct punishment from God could be used to shape fundamental matters of social behavior. In arguing that the Ten Commandments were originally composed for instruction and declaration within a form of worship, a feature that had earlier been proposed by Mowinckel, Alt drew attention to this dodecalogue of curses. Although there is some overlap with the contents of the commandments, it is not specifically the particular actions condemned that provide the point of comparison.

104. For the relationship between these curses and the law, see E. Bellefontaine, "The Curses of Deuteronomy 27: Their Relationship to the Prohibitive," in *A Song of Power and the Power of Song: Essays on the Book of Deuteronomy,* ed. D. L. Christensen, SBT 3 (Winona Lake, Ind.: Eisenbrauns, 1993) 256-68.

105. A. Alt, "The Origins of Israelite Law," in *Essays on Old Testament History and Religion,* trans. R. A. Wilson (Oxford: Blackwell, 1966) 114-22.

A feature that is explicit in some of these curses is that they concern wrongful actions that would have been carried out in secret. Alt went further than to accept that this was true of those deeds where their private and secret nature was explicitly mentioned and proposed that it was actually true of all. There are substantive reasons for thinking that this was the case and that the actions outlawed in these curses, with the exception of the first and last, which are almost certainly additional to an original ten, were all deeds that would have been carried out privately and away from public knowledge. Such an understanding has a significant bearing on the interpretation of certain of them, which might otherwise be understood more broadly.

The reason why these particular actions are singled out and made the subject of publicly recited curses, to which the individual members of Israel are required to respond with a cry of "Amen," is that they dealt with matters that could not reasonably have been dealt with by the processes of law. This was not because the actions were not "illegal" in the sense that they were contrary to the commands and spirit of the law. Rather, it was precisely because these actions were carried out privately that it was highly improbable that any formal public action could have been taken against them.

It is noteworthy that no specific penalty is attached to these curses, since "living under a curse" must have been regarded as a dangerous and potentially serious condition. That it necessarily carried with it the implication that such persons would have been outlawed from the community, or even regarded as being under sentence of death, can by no means be taken for granted. It would have been left open as to what effect the curse would bring.

The form of the curse was not the only way in which the rituals and formal proceedings of the cultus were employed to influence individual conduct in a direct and publicly recognized fashion. We find that admission to the Temple could also carry with it strong admonitions regarding the forms of conduct that God hated and would render a person unfit to appear in the divine presence in the sanctuary (cf. Psalms 15; 27). There are good reasons, therefore, for accepting that, in a slightly modified form, this dodecalogue

of curses once existed as a separate composition and that, like the short listing of the Ten Commandments, it was intended as a means of reminding worshipers of the moral demands of God's holiness. God could be expected to take action against the person who knowingly flouted the divine order of life.

There is little reason to suppose that this list of curses for public recital was very much earlier in its origin than the time of the deuteronomic authors of the law book. It has then been incorporated into the epilogue to the law code as a formal example of the way in which the law made it essential to distinguish between following the path of blessing and following the way of the curse.

Almost certainly the present list of twelve curses has been enlarged from a more original list in which only ten such curses were included.[106] The first, which concerns the general prohibition against worshiping alien gods, and the last, which is little more than a repeated summary of all the preceding prohibitions, have then been added in order to bring the number up to twelve. The reason for this proceeding can only be that it was felt appropriate to make the number of curses equivalent to the number of the tribes of Israel, whose representatives are held to have been present for the public recital of the curses.

27:11-14. The introduction to the list in vv. 11-13 describes the twelve tribes of Israel as gathered together and divided into two groups of six. One group is then placed on Mt. Gerizim for the blessing, and the second group is located on Mt. Ebal for the curses. In this way, the author has made the declaration of the list of twelve curses fit directly into a narrative context relating to the Israelites' entry into the land, the designation of the two historic mountains as centers of blessing and curse, and the presence of all twelve tribes in the land after their crossing of the Jordan.

The tribal names have been taken from the list of the sons of Jacob, set out in the narrative of Genesis 29–30. The first group appears to be the more favored tribes, which is appropriate to their proximity to the mount of blessing. These comprise the sons born to Jacob's wives, Leah and Rachel. The second group is made up of the

---

106. H. Gese, "Der Dekalog als Ganzheit betrachtet," *Vom Sinai zum Zion. Alttestamentliche Beiträge zur biblischen Theologie* (Munich: Chr. Kaiser, 1974) 71-72.

descendants of Jacob's concubines, together with Reuben and Zebulon. The first group was the tribes who had settled in the central and southern territories, which corresponds with their favored associations of blessing. The latter group had settled the less favored territory of Galilee and the Transjordan.

Overall it appears that this assembling of representatives of the tribes, if not the whole nation of tribes, in such a massive convocation is a literary device of the deuteronomic author. It suits the broad theological affirmation that all Israel equally came under the law and so all were equally subject to the contingencies of blessing and curse. It was also a point at issue that the list of twelve activities subjected to the formula of curse were prohibited to all Israel.

27:15. There are strong reasons for concluding that the first and last of the twelve curses have been added to an original list of ten. The first of them relates to the setting up of an image "in secret," presenting a particular variation of the more familiar prohibition against the use of any image at all in worship. It could have been the case that, since the series of curses relates to actions and activities that were unlikely to be dealt with by the normal processes of public prosecution and punishment, a scribe felt it appropriate that this offense, which was taken by the deuteronomic authors with the utmost seriousness, also deserved to be included.

By establishing the nature of the first offense as one committed in secret, we can recognize that the formal use of ritual curses against potential offenders was intended to operate as an adjunct to the law. Actions that the law was unlikely to deal with are nonetheless reprehensible, and those who commit them deserve to be outlawed from the community.

The curses, therefore, serve as a form of public condemnation, inviting ostracism from the community and asking God to punish the offender, but without offering any clear indication of how this would come about. To a considerable extent, the instruction that those assembled are required to respond to the levitical declaration of the curse with a loud "Amen" shows that it was a matter of individual conscience and sense of guilt that made the curse effective. At the same time, the recital of such curses gave a powerful declaration of the will of the community, affirming that those

who committed certain actions were banished. There is, then, a degree of affinity with the use of the formula that declared certain objects or actions "abhorrent to the LORD," thereby showing that they were wholly contrary to the divine will. They caused offense and a sense of outrage.

27:16. The curse upon those guilty of dishonoring their parents relates directly to the offense covered by the laws of Exod 21:17 and Lev 20:9. It is obviously closely connected with the commandment of the Decalogue that enjoins the honoring of parents (5:16). The fact that essentially all of these rulings deal with substantially the same moral issue of showing respect for parents, making provision for them, and acting so as to maintain the strength and integrity of the household is significant. Clearly an outright act of cursing parents, or rejecting them when they became infirm, was a particularly detestable offense. At the same time, the different verbal formulations used indicate that whether a positive or negative construction was used was a relatively minor issue.

27:17. The prohibition against the removal of a neighbor's boundary marker concerns an issue that has already been dealt with, potentially very severely, in the legislative ruling of 19:14. Its reappearance here further demonstrates the sensitivity to the problem that was felt and further illustrates the point that it was one for which effective action through processes of law was difficult to obtain. Both this and the preceding curse relate to forms of conduct that would have been undertaken furtively and in private, where it would be difficult to produce satisfactory proof to enable action to be taken.

27:18-19. Much the same background of furtive, unprovable misconduct is illustrated by the deliberate misleading of a blind person, which is cursed in v. 18. It is closely paralleled by the admonition of Lev 19:14, which deals with abuse of both blind and deaf persons. It is linked here to a general injunction not to deprive handicapped or disadvantaged members of the community from access to the public processes of justice (v. 19), which belongs alongside the widely expressed deuteronomic concern to grant to such persons the same privileges that other members of the community enjoyed (14:29; 16:14).

27:20-23. The curses set out here deal with sexual relationships. The curse upon sexual contact between a man and his stepmother (v. 20) must be compared with the law of 22:30, which precludes a marriage between two such persons. This raises the issue of whether the conduct that is made the subject of the curse envisages a marriage or simply a casual sexual encounter. In view of the preceding curses, which relate to misconduct of a secretive and furtive nature, it would appear that it is the latter situation that is envisaged. Since a marriage with a stepmother, who is probably assumed to be widowed, was already precluded, the intention here may have been to prohibit the sexual abuse of a woman who is likely a member of the same household as the man upon whom the curse is laid. By taking advantage of a woman who was a dependent member of the household, the culprit could probably escape public detection.

A similar background of private, secretive activity would then be covered by the curse upon anyone who had had sexual contact with an animal (v. 21). An earlier legal prohibition against such acts is found in the laws of the Book of the Covenant in Exod 22:19. It seems highly likely that such bizarre sexual acts once formed part of rituals aimed at securing special power through the life force present in the animal. It would have displayed some of the same reasoning that made the visual portrayal of various forms of mixed human and animal creatures a prominent feature of the religious symbolism of ancient Egyptian religion. A more complete and wide-ranging list of forbidden sexual relationships is set out in Lev 20:13-21.

It seems highly probable that this list of curses against forbidden sexual behaviors was not intended to be a redrafting of marginal cases relating to family law. Israelite custom had at one time clearly not precluded marriage to a halfsister (Gen 20:12; 2 Sam 13:13), although a later prohibition is found in Lev 18:9; 20:17. Rather, the curses were aimed at prohibiting sexual abuse, especially of vulnerable female members of a household who would be unlikely to have effective means of redress against a senior male. Unmarried sisters, halfsisters, and widowed in-laws were all likely to have been part of a household and, therefore, susceptible to sexual abuse. It is certainly a prominent feature that the list of curses regarding such actions focuses directly on the issue of sexual relationships.

27:24. The extent of the harm inflicted on another person covered by this curse is not precisely defined. The RSV's "strikes" has been strengthened in the NRSV to "strikes down" (נכה *nākâ*). Clearly a violent blow leading to death or serious injury is primarily in mind, although it is not explicitly spelled out whether there was any intent to kill. That such an act is said to be carried out in secret points to a carefully planned attempt to inflict harm upon another.

27:25. Bribery was a persistent problem throughout the ancient world, and it appears only to have increased in its effectiveness with the introduction of more complex and sophisticated legal systems. The particular offense of receiving payment to shed innocent blood would have covered payments made for "contract killing," but more probably it refers to the committing of perjury in a capital lawsuit that could lead to the death penalty's being imposed upon an innocent person, thereby amounting to murder.

27:26. The concluding curse effectively summarizes all the preceding ones and serves to reinforce the level of authority that attaches to them. It adds nothing new and appears to have been introduced primarily with a view to increasing the number of such curses to twelve, thereby matching the number of tribes said to have been present to affirm them.

Overall this series of curses, in which the entire community bound itself to refrain from actions that might otherwise go unpunished, was clearly intended to augment the efficacy of the law, rather than to add to its demands in any specifically detailed fashion. Some of the conduct that is outlawed would have been undetected because of its secretive nature, but other actions may have lacked effective witnesses to make a reliable prosecution possible.

The formulation as a series of curses is essentially artificial and achieves little more than the simple declaration that certain types of conduct were "abhorrent to" God. A curse in the fullest sense was believed to possess a measure of dynamic efficacy, invoking divine action to harm a specified person or group. Here the curse form has been converted essentially into a didactic device to draw popular attention to conduct the community as a whole would not tolerate. The popular response whereby each member present acknowledged the wrongfulness of such prohibited actions is expressed by the utterance of the single word *Amen.* This in itself was used as a way of personalizing and directing the message of the curse to each person present. What we find here appears to have been a further didactic means introduced by the deuteronomists to fill some of the gaps brought on by a laxity in moral order and family discipline. The deuteronomists recognized quite openly that there were several important areas of conduct that could not appropriately be handled by the established legal arrangements.

REFLECTIONS

It is a significant and thought-provoking point of awareness that the Old Testament has frequently been characterized by Christians as a book of law. The book of Deuteronomy, possibly rather more directly than any other Old Testament writing, appears to exemplify this commitment to law. Yet we have already had much opportunity to note that the deuteronomic authors were primarily interested in presenting law as both a gift of the grace of God, which had brought Israel into existence in the first place, and a way through which Israel could enjoy a life of blessing. It would be a mistake, then, to interpret the book of Deuteronomy as a whole as presenting law as a kind of negative contrast to the concept of divine love and an ethic of grace.

So in a very profound sense, the book of Deuteronomy, like the Old Testament as a whole, is a book about law. Yet law itself has more than one sense, which becomes very complex when put in a theological context. In the first, and most obvious, manner, law refers to those statutes that represent pronouncements of a legal system through which human conduct in society is to be governed. It stretches across many areas of conduct in families and in business as well as between neighbors. It regulates all sorts of morally reprehensible behavior, from violence and wanton killing to cheating and taking advantage of disadvantaged and helpless members of the community.

For any citizen of the modern world, the administration and trust in a system of law are vital if a community is to live at peace with itself and if the full potential of human opportunities is to be realized. At the same time, we are all too conscious that law can be a very blunt and imperfect instrument by which human conduct and affairs are to be regulated. Laws have to be administered fairly, and, in much of modern life, it becomes impossible to devise a law to cover every situation that might arise. We have become all too conscious of these problems in connection with such painful issues as sexual abuse within a family and with problems of corruption among those who are called upon to uphold the law. Quite obviously the knowledge that "there is a law against it!" does not mean that particular forms of undesirable conduct never take place. It only means that the law cannot do everything.

It is against such a backdrop that we can see the considerable relevance of the series of curses in Deuteronomy 27. It would appear as a strange and objectionable proceeding were we to conduct such a public ritual of cursing in a modern setting. Yet we are forced to do many things that are surprisingly similar. We are called upon to educate people concerning undesirable forms of conduct; we are impelled to teach respect for the law and for the needs and rights of other human beings. Education for right conduct is as important as the legal system that is called upon to enforce it.

We can certainly go further than this, since it is also a prevalent modern concern that legal systems are often very clumsy and inadequate social institutions for handling many personal matters. To mislead a blind person on the road so that he or she stumbles into a wall or a ditch will appear to most people a very cruel form of a practical joke. Yet it would make little sense to formulate a law against such behavior, for the root of the problem lies in a lack of compassion and an inability of some persons to empathize with the needs and difficulties of others. Only by educating for compassion and for respect for each individual can we address some behaviors. Such concerns require instruction, example, and teaching, rather than laws.

In a more deeply philosophical vein, this list of public curses highlights the awareness that all systems of law must ultimately reckon with a fundamental understanding of human nature. The dignity of all human beings, and, therefore, their right to command respect and compassion, is in the final resort a question for theology and not simply a matter of what is educationally useful. The understanding that human beings are fashioned in "the image of God" (Gen 1:26) is a basic biblical assertion that seeks to encapsulate this sense of human dignity and human potential. It is in educating to declare the religious nature and destiny of humankind that both the importance and the limitations of human laws can best be understood.

DEUTERONOMY 28:1-68, GOD'S ORDER: BLESSING AND CURSE

NIV

28 If you fully obey the LORD your God and carefully follow all his commands I give you today, the LORD your God will set you high above all the nations on earth. [2]All these blessings will come upon you and accompany you if you obey the LORD your God:

[3]You will be blessed in the city and blessed in the country.

[4]The fruit of your womb will be blessed, and the crops of your land and the young of your livestock—the calves of your herds and the lambs of your flocks.

[5]Your basket and your kneading trough will be blessed.

[6]You will be blessed when you come in and blessed when you go out.

[7]The LORD will grant that the enemies who rise up against you will be defeated before you. They will come at you from one direction but flee from you in seven.

[8]The LORD will send a blessing on your barns and on everything you put your hand to. The LORD your God will bless you in the land he is giving you.

[9]The LORD will establish you as his holy people, as he promised you on oath, if you keep the commands of the LORD your God and walk in his ways. [10]Then all the peoples on earth will see that you are called by the name of the LORD, and they will fear you. [11]The LORD will grant you abundant

NRSV

28 If you will only obey the LORD your God, by diligently observing all his commandments that I am commanding you today, the LORD your God will set you high above all the nations of the earth; [2]all these blessings shall come upon you and overtake you, if you obey the LORD your God:

3Blessed shall you be in the city, and blessed shall you be in the field.

4Blessed shall be the fruit of your womb, the fruit of your ground, and the fruit of your livestock, both the increase of your cattle and the issue of your flock.

5Blessed shall be your basket and your kneading bowl.

6Blessed shall you be when you come in, and blessed shall you be when you go out.

7The LORD will cause your enemies who rise against you to be defeated before you; they shall come out against you one way, and flee before you seven ways. [8]The LORD will command the blessing upon you in your barns, and in all that you undertake; he will bless you in the land that the LORD your God is giving you. [9]The LORD will establish you as his holy people, as he has sworn to you, if you keep the commandments of the LORD your God and walk in his ways. [10]All the peoples of the earth shall see that you are called by the name of the LORD, and they shall be afraid of you. [11]The LORD will make you abound in prosperity, in the fruit of your womb, in the fruit

NIV

prosperity—in the fruit of your womb, the young of your livestock and the crops of your ground—in the land he swore to your forefathers to give you.

[12]The LORD will open the heavens, the storehouse of his bounty, to send rain on your land in season and to bless all the work of your hands. You will lend to many nations but will borrow from none. [13]The LORD will make you the head, not the tail. If you pay attention to the commands of the LORD your God that I give you this day and carefully follow them, you will always be at the top, never at the bottom. [14]Do not turn aside from any of the commands I give you today, to the right or to the left, following other gods and serving them.

[15]However, if you do not obey the LORD your God and do not carefully follow all his commands and decrees I am giving you today, all these curses will come upon you and overtake you:

[16]You will be cursed in the city and cursed in the country.

[17]Your basket and your kneading trough will be cursed.

[18]The fruit of your womb will be cursed, and the crops of your land, and the calves of your herds and the lambs of your flocks.

[19]You will be cursed when you come in and cursed when you go out.

[20]The LORD will send on you curses, confusion and rebuke in everything you put your hand to, until you are destroyed and come to sudden ruin because of the evil you have done in forsaking him.[a] [21]The LORD will plague you with diseases until he has destroyed you from the land you are entering to possess. [22]The LORD will strike you with wasting disease, with fever and inflammation, with scorching heat and drought, with blight and mildew, which will plague you until you perish. [23]The sky over your head will be bronze, the ground beneath you iron. [24]The LORD will turn the rain of your country into dust and powder; it will come down from the skies until you are destroyed.

[25]The LORD will cause you to be defeated before your enemies. You will come at them from one direction but flee from them in seven, and you will become a thing of horror to all the kingdoms

[a]20 Hebrew me

NRSV

of your livestock, and in the fruit of your ground in the land that the LORD swore to your ancestors to give you. [12]The LORD will open for you his rich storehouse, the heavens, to give the rain of your land in its season and to bless all your undertakings. You will lend to many nations, but you will not borrow. [13]The LORD will make you the head, and not the tail; you shall be only at the top, and not at the bottom—if you obey the commandments of the LORD your God, which I am commanding you today, by diligently observing them, [14]and if you do not turn aside from any of the words that I am commanding you today, either to the right or to the left, following other gods to serve them.

[15]But if you will not obey the LORD your God by diligently observing all his commandments and decrees, which I am commanding you today, then all these curses shall come upon you and overtake you:

[16]Cursed shall you be in the city, and cursed shall you be in the field.

[17]Cursed shall be your basket and your kneading bowl.

[18]Cursed shall be the fruit of your womb, the fruit of your ground, the increase of your cattle and the issue of your flock.

[19]Cursed shall you be when you come in, and cursed shall you be when you go out.

[20]The LORD will send upon you disaster, panic, and frustration in everything you attempt to do, until you are destroyed and perish quickly, on account of the evil of your deeds, because you have forsaken me. [21]The LORD will make the pestilence cling to you until it has consumed you off the land that you are entering to possess. [22]The LORD will afflict you with consumption, fever, inflammation, with fiery heat and drought, and with blight and mildew; they shall pursue you until you perish. [23]The sky over your head shall be bronze, and the earth under you iron. [24]The LORD will change the rain of your land into powder, and only dust shall come down upon you from the sky until you are destroyed.

[25]The LORD will cause you to be defeated before your enemies; you shall go out against them one way and flee before them seven ways. You shall become an object of horror to all the

NIV

on earth. ²⁶Your carcasses will be food for all the birds of the air and the beasts of the earth, and there will be no one to frighten them away. ²⁷The LORD will afflict you with the boils of Egypt and with tumors, festering sores and the itch, from which you cannot be cured. ²⁸The LORD will afflict you with madness, blindness and confusion of mind. ²⁹At midday you will grope about like a blind man in the dark. You will be unsuccessful in everything you do; day after day you will be oppressed and robbed, with no one to rescue you.

³⁰You will be pledged to be married to a woman, but another will take her and ravish her. You will build a house, but you will not live in it. You will plant a vineyard, but you will not even begin to enjoy its fruit. ³¹Your ox will be slaughtered before your eyes, but you will eat none of it. Your donkey will be forcibly taken from you and will not be returned. Your sheep will be given to your enemies, and no one will rescue them. ³²Your sons and daughters will be given to another nation, and you will wear out your eyes watching for them day after day, powerless to lift a hand. ³³A people that you do not know will eat what your land and labor produce, and you will have nothing but cruel oppression all your days. ³⁴The sights you see will drive you mad. ³⁵The LORD will afflict your knees and legs with painful boils that cannot be cured, spreading from the soles of your feet to the top of your head.

³⁶The LORD will drive you and the king you set over you to a nation unknown to you or your fathers. There you will worship other gods, gods of wood and stone. ³⁷You will become a thing of horror and an object of scorn and ridicule to all the nations where the LORD will drive you.

³⁸You will sow much seed in the field but you will harvest little, because locusts will devour it. ³⁹You will plant vineyards and cultivate them but you will not drink the wine or gather the grapes, because worms will eat them. ⁴⁰You will have olive trees throughout your country but you will not use the oil, because the olives will drop off. ⁴¹You will have sons and daughters but you will not keep them, because they will go into captivity. ⁴²Swarms of locusts will take over all your trees and the crops of your land.

NRSV

kingdoms of the earth. ²⁶Your corpses shall be food for every bird of the air and animal of the earth, and there shall be no one to frighten them away. ²⁷The LORD will afflict you with the boils of Egypt, with ulcers, scurvy, and itch, of which you cannot be healed. ²⁸The LORD will afflict you with madness, blindness, and confusion of mind; ²⁹you shall grope about at noon as blind people grope in darkness, but you shall be unable to find your way; and you shall be continually abused and robbed, without anyone to help. ³⁰You shall become engaged to a woman, but another man shall lie with her. You shall build a house, but not live in it. You shall plant a vineyard, but not enjoy its fruit. ³¹Your ox shall be butchered before your eyes, but you shall not eat of it. Your donkey shall be stolen in front of you, and shall not be restored to you. Your sheep shall be given to your enemies, without anyone to help you. ³²Your sons and daughters shall be given to another people, while you look on; you will strain your eyes looking for them all day but be powerless to do anything. ³³A people whom you do not know shall eat up the fruit of your ground and of all your labors; you shall be continually abused and crushed, ³⁴and driven mad by the sight that your eyes shall see. ³⁵The LORD will strike you on the knees and on the legs with grievous boils of which you cannot be healed, from the sole of your foot to the crown of your head. ³⁶The LORD will bring you, and the king whom you set over you, to a nation that neither you nor your ancestors have known, where you shall serve other gods, of wood and stone. ³⁷You shall become an object of horror, a proverb, and a byword among all the peoples where the LORD will lead you.

³⁸You shall carry much seed into the field but shall gather little in, for the locust shall consume it. ³⁹You shall plant vineyards and dress them, but you shall neither drink the wine nor gather the grapes, for the worm shall eat them. ⁴⁰You shall have olive trees throughout all your territory, but you shall not anoint yourself with the oil, for your olives shall drop off. ⁴¹You shall have sons and daughters, but they shall not remain yours, for they shall go into captivity. ⁴²All your trees and the fruit of your ground the cicada shall take over. ⁴³Aliens residing among you shall ascend above

NIV

⁴³The alien who lives among you will rise above you higher and higher, but you will sink lower and lower. ⁴⁴He will lend to you, but you will not lend to him. He will be the head, but you will be the tail.

⁴⁵All these curses will come upon you. They will pursue you and overtake you until you are destroyed, because you did not obey the LORD your God and observe the commands and decrees he gave you. ⁴⁶They will be a sign and a wonder to you and your descendants forever. ⁴⁷Because you did not serve the LORD your God joyfully and gladly in the time of prosperity, ⁴⁸therefore in hunger and thirst, in nakedness and dire poverty, you will serve the enemies the LORD sends against you. He will put an iron yoke on your neck until he has destroyed you.

⁴⁹The LORD will bring a nation against you from far away, from the ends of the earth, like an eagle swooping down, a nation whose language you will not understand, ⁵⁰a fierce-looking nation without respect for the old or pity for the young. ⁵¹They will devour the young of your livestock and the crops of your land until you are destroyed. They will leave you no grain, new wine or oil, nor any calves of your herds or lambs of your flocks until you are ruined. ⁵²They will lay siege to all the cities throughout your land until the high fortified walls in which you trust fall down. They will besiege all the cities throughout the land the LORD your God is giving you.

⁵³Because of the suffering that your enemy will inflict on you during the siege, you will eat the fruit of the womb, the flesh of the sons and daughters the LORD your God has given you. ⁵⁴Even the most gentle and sensitive man among you will have no compassion on his own brother or the wife he loves or his surviving children, ⁵⁵and he will not give to one of them any of the flesh of his children that he is eating. It will be all he has left because of the suffering your enemy will inflict on you during the siege of all your cities. ⁵⁶The most gentle and sensitive woman among you—so sensitive and gentle that she would not venture to touch the ground with the sole of her foot—will begrudge the husband she loves and her own son or daughter ⁵⁷the afterbirth from her womb and the children she bears. For

NRSV

you higher and higher, while you shall descend lower and lower. ⁴⁴They shall lend to you but you shall not lend to them; they shall be the head and you shall be the tail.

⁴⁵All these curses shall come upon you, pursuing and overtaking you until you are destroyed, because you did not obey the LORD your God, by observing the commandments and the decrees that he commanded you. ⁴⁶They shall be among you and your descendants as a sign and a portent forever.

⁴⁷Because you did not serve the LORD your God joyfully and with gladness of heart for the abundance of everything, ⁴⁸therefore you shall serve your enemies whom the LORD will send against you, in hunger and thirst, in nakedness and lack of everything. He will put an iron yoke on your neck until he has destroyed you. ⁴⁹The LORD will bring a nation from far away, from the end of the earth, to swoop down on you like an eagle, a nation whose language you do not understand, ⁵⁰a grim-faced nation showing no respect to the old or favor to the young. ⁵¹It shall consume the fruit of your livestock and the fruit of your ground until you are destroyed, leaving you neither grain, wine, and oil, nor the increase of your cattle and the issue of your flock, until it has made you perish. ⁵²It shall besiege you in all your towns until your high and fortified walls, in which you trusted, come down throughout your land; it shall besiege you in all your towns throughout the land that the LORD your God has given you. ⁵³In the desperate straits to which the enemy siege reduces you, you will eat the fruit of your womb, the flesh of your own sons and daughters whom the LORD your God has given you. ⁵⁴Even the most refined and gentle of men among you will begrudge food to his own brother, to the wife whom he embraces, and to the last of his remaining children, ⁵⁵giving to none of them any of the flesh of his children whom he is eating, because nothing else remains to him, in the desperate straits to which the enemy siege will reduce you in all your towns. ⁵⁶She who is the most refined and gentle among you, so gentle and refined that she does not venture to set the sole of her foot on the ground, will begrudge food to the husband whom she embraces, to her own son, and to her own daugh-

NIV

she intends to eat them secretly during the siege and in the distress that your enemy will inflict on you in your cities.

58If you do not carefully follow all the words of this law, which are written in this book, and do not revere this glorious and awesome name—the LORD your God— 59the LORD will send fearful plagues on you and your descendants, harsh and prolonged disasters, and severe and lingering illnesses. 60He will bring upon you all the diseases of Egypt that you dreaded, and they will cling to you. 61The LORD will also bring on you every kind of sickness and disaster not recorded in this Book of the Law, until you are destroyed. 62You who were as numerous as the stars in the sky will be left but few in number, because you did not obey the LORD your God. 63Just as it pleased the LORD to make you prosper and increase in number, so it will please him to ruin and destroy you. You will be uprooted from the land you are entering to possess.

64Then the LORD will scatter you among all nations, from one end of the earth to the other. There you will worship other gods—gods of wood and stone, which neither you nor your fathers have known. 65Among those nations you will find no repose, no resting place for the sole of your foot. There the LORD will give you an anxious mind, eyes weary with longing, and a despairing heart. 66You will live in constant suspense, filled with dread both night and day, never sure of your life. 67In the morning you will say, "If only it were evening!" and in the evening, "If only it were morning!"—because of the terror that will fill your hearts and the sights that your eyes will see. 68The LORD will send you back in ships to Egypt on a journey I said you should never make again. There you will offer yourselves for sale to your enemies as male and female slaves, but no one will buy you.

NRSV

ter, 57begrudging even the afterbirth that comes out from between her thighs, and the children that she bears, because she is eating them in secret for lack of anything else, in the desperate straits to which the enemy siege will reduce you in your towns.

58If you do not diligently observe all the words of this law that are written in this book, fearing this glorious and awesome name, the LORD your God, 59then the LORD will overwhelm both you and your offspring with severe and lasting afflictions and grievous and lasting maladies. 60He will bring back upon you all the diseases of Egypt, of which you were in dread, and they shall cling to you. 61Every other malady and affliction, even though not recorded in the book of this law, the LORD will inflict on you until you are destroyed. 62Although once you were as numerous as the stars in heaven, you shall be left few in number, because you did not obey the LORD your God. 63And just as the LORD took delight in making you prosperous and numerous, so the LORD will take delight in bringing you to ruin and destruction; you shall be plucked off the land that you are entering to possess. 64The LORD will scatter you among all peoples, from one end of the earth to the other; and there you shall serve other gods, of wood and stone, which neither you nor your ancestors have known. 65Among those nations you shall find no ease, no resting place for the sole of your foot. There the LORD will give you a trembling heart, failing eyes, and a languishing spirit. 66Your life shall hang in doubt before you; night and day you shall be in dread, with no assurance of your life. 67In the morning you shall say, "If only it were evening!" and at evening you shall say, "If only it were morning!"—because of the dread that your heart shall feel and the sights that your eyes shall see. 68The LORD will bring you back in ships to Egypt, by a route that I promised you would never see again; and there you shall offer yourselves for sale to your enemies as male and female slaves, but there will be no buyer.

COMMENTARY

The surprisingly long series of blessings and curses found in Deuteronomy 28 provokes discussion and comment on account of its somber and threatening tone. Curses outnumber blessings by a considerable margin and give the impression that the overall effect of the deuteronomic legislation was predominantly negative. There were more things that could go wrong than could go right! There is undoubtedly some justification for this impression, and a detailed examination of several of the features of the list of curses will show how and why it has arisen.

It is important, therefore, that we remember that this section forms part of the epilogue to the law code; and to a significant extent it reflects an awareness of how Israel has fared under the law. There is, in consequence, a sense of failure and non-achievement since Israel has not kept the law. This sensitivity to failure and to the belief that in retrospect the law of Moses had proved to be Israel's undoing can, however, only be regarded as a superficial and limited sense of what this long section of blessing and curses has to teach.

From a formal perspective two issues have dominated discussion of the chapter and have a very direct bearing on its interpretation. The first of these concerns the presence of comparable lists of threats and curses in ancient Near Eastern vassal treaties. Considerable discussion has taken place over the extent to which the overall shape of Deuteronomy, as well as several of its basic constituent parts, have been influenced by, and even directly adapted from, these vassal treaties. Certainly in the later Assyrian treaty documents, for example, the enumeration of a long and deliberately intimidating list of curses that will befall the vassal should the demands of the treaty not be complied with is very marked. These certainly bear comparison with the curses that appear in Deuteronomy 28, although there is no reason for supposing that specific wording was adapted to one from the other. From a literary perspective, therefore, it is undoubtedly conceivable that the authors of Deuteronomy were familiar with the employment of a series of threatening curses of warning and admonition to encourage the vassal to stick to the terms of the treaty.

However, to concede this point draws attention to a rather formal literary aspect of Deuteronomy, and it seems highly probable that the addition of the blessings and curses in this chapter was made at a relatively late stage in the composition of the book. They do not fit the nature and content of the laws that have occupied the central part of the book since these laws prescribe their own punishments and penalties where necessary and do not need additional reinforcement by a further series of punitive threats. It is primarily the setting of the law code within the larger context of a review of Israel's history and its experience as a nation that has occasioned the inclusion of these curses.

This perception is more fully confirmed when we look at the particular content of the curse lists. For the most part they cannot truly be regarded as curses in the formal sense at all but are more in the nature of a historical reflection on the history of Israel and its present situation. Even the actual verbal formulation as curses is abandoned throughout most of them so that we are presented with a broad declaration that failure to keep the terms of the covenant law will result in punishment. This is then followed by a detailed look at specific circumstances relevant to Israel in this light.

It becomes clear from close examination that the present chapter is not from a single hand. An initial section in vv. 1-46 represents the foundational basis of the whole. Even this primary unit bears all the hallmarks of having been built up around a relatively concise core text that has then undergone expansion. The concluding verses are then introduced as an editorial transition piece preparing for the historical perspective that follows. The intention throughout appears to be essentially didactic and reflective, rather than offering a real attempt to provide additional warnings to Israel concerning the dangers of any failure to keep the law. Although there are some overlaps with the kind of admonition contained in the secular vassal-treaty form, the situation in Deuteronomy is essentially of a different nature. Overall there is a broad desire to teach the seriousness of the law, closely comparable with the general message that is to be found in the prologue to the law book in the speeches of Moses in chapters 6–9.

A second section has subsequently been joined on in vv. 47-57 that gives a further and noticeably even more threatening tone to the curses. It spells out with added detail the horrors of life under the curse, although it refrains altogether from using the formal structure of cursing or the relevant vocabulary. Rather it points to events that have clearly already befallen Israel and seeks to understand these in the light of the situation threatened by the curse for those who disobey the law. In such a setting the notion of curse is little more than a very open and broad way of coming to terms with the mysterious nature of evil and the specific misfortunes that have overtaken Israel.

A further section has then been added even later in vv. 58-68, offering yet more detailed instances of the almost unbearable pain of life under God's curse. It quite directly relates this to the post–587 BCE circumstances when many former citizens of Judah had been forced to become refugees, fleeing into exile and slavery. A sense of inevitable retribution for disobedience to God's covenant law is provided by the fact that these very refugees sought asylum back in Egypt, willingly selling themselves as slaves and so reversing completely the story of how Israel's ancestors had been rescued by the hand of God from there. Because the present generation of Israel had failed to remember that its ancestors had been slaves in Egypt, they were compelled by the irony of divine justice to find out what that really meant!

We are certainly faced here with a progressive series of literary additions. The second of these (vv. 47-57) bears unmistakable indications that it was composed shortly after the siege and destruction of Jerusalem in 588–87 BCE. Its message illustrating the agony and suffering of the people of Judah shows significant connections of theme and purpose with the book of Lamentations.

Similarly the third section (vv. 58-68) bears all the marks of having been written later still, when the pain and wretchedness of those refugees who had fled from Judah could be readily envisaged. There is no doubt a deliberate element of poetic license in this in which the author has imaginatively reconstructed the plight of destitute people selling themselves into slavery rather than facing death by starvation. Nevertheless, the verses have been designed to fit the present context very skillfully, alerting the reader to interpret the text, not in a documentary and historical fashion as a testimony of the last days of Moses, but as a contemporary warning of the plight into which fellow-Israelites had fallen in recent days. Once again the author collapses the long historical distance between the men and women who followed Moses through the wilderness and were awaiting the moment to enter the land and those who were experiencing the present time of distress. Israel is one Israel, both laterally through the twelve tribes and also vertically through its many generations.

Both of these later sections can be seen to be rhetorically molded literary compositions aimed at offering contemporary relevance for the reader concerning the reality of the curses that have been listed. By drawing on memories and events from the reader's recent past, they serve to intensify the message that disobedience to God's law would bring the most terrifying consequences. For the author these events served to confirm the urgency of the warnings. Only the first of the sections retains the formal blessing-curse structure, and even this exhibits substantial modifications from the true curse form.

From a historical and theological viewpoint this series of three rhetorical "curses" is a forward-looking epilogue that abandons the narrative perspective of the situation in the Plains of Moab and establishes the setting for the second giving of the law. Already the admonitory addresses in chapters 6–9 have made clear that Israel faced a decisive either/or challenge. To obey the law that Moses had given would bring success and lasting security and peace; to flout its demands would conversely lead to appalling suffering and catastrophe. The epilogue now draws on recent memory to confirm this very point.

It is arguable that a first intimation of this more somber note of warning for Israel is to be found in the first address concerning blessing and curse in vv. 1-46. Here for the first time is a marked indication that curse will, in the end, prove to be a more powerful feature of Israel's history than blessing. As soon as we move on to examine the addresses of vv. 47-57 and 58-68, we are made yet more conscious of the predominance of curse. Moreover, it becomes incontrovertibly clear that we are no longer contemplating possible events of an uncertain future but instead are looking back on certain events of a grievously painful past. Not only is there a wealth of circumstantial detail that carries us beyond the generalizations of hard choices, but we are also given terrifying pictures of recent events. This is especially the case in the last discourse. No longer is the question: "Will curse rather than blessing be the fate of Israel?" Instead, there is a deeper theological anxiety that asks whether God can have any future purpose for Israel at all, if it must lead to such terrible personal suffering. Has not the law itself become a curse, and has it not acted as a millstone around Israel's neck to plunge it into a whirlpool of disaster?

28:1-46. The primary address in 28:1-44 begins in vv. 1-14 with a restatement of the meaning and possibility of blessing that would accrue to those who obeyed the commandments. The theme throughout is transparently clear and thoroughly deuteronomic in its character: "If you will obey the LORD your God by diligently observing all his commandments" (vv. 1, 13b-15). The commandments hold the key to understanding life, prosperity, and security. All aspects of human need are claimed to be covered by the comprehensive sweep of God's law since they relate to family life, agriculture (v. 4), and military success (v. 7). The message is twofold in its thrust: The righteousness of the law is the key to human happiness; therefore, the opposite truth must also be entertained, that where such success and prosperity are lacking there must have been a neglect of obedience to the commandments.

The somber note of this necessary deduction is then spelled out explicitly by the curse formulations of vv. 16-44. The concluding summary in vv. 45-46 then serves as a transition piece reiterating a conclusion that has become obvious: Disobedience will bring terrible consequences. The verses prepare the reader for the harsher message to come in the sections that follow.

So far as the basic unit of vv. 1-44 is concerned, we are clearly still very much in the theological thought world of the deuteronomists. Retribution for good to those who obey and for ill to those who disobey is the key feature. We hear the confident deuteronomic doctrine that God is wholly just and fair in all dealings with the people of Israel. The covenant has made the terms clear so that there can be no impugning of the idea of the divine justice. Israel can remain assured that it receives from God only what it deserves.

The date of composition of this section is best indicated by the reference in v. 36 to the removal of the king of Judah to a foreign land. This is most probably a reference to the imprisonment and removal into exile of King Jehoiachin in 598 BCE (cf. 2 Kings 20), rather than to the events of 587 BCE when King Zedekiah was removed from his royal throne in Jerusalem altogether and taken to Babylon and to his death there. Had these latter

disastrous and final consequences for the Davidic kingship already taken place, it seems unlikely that the lesser misfortune that befell Jehoiachin would alone have been referred to. If this is the case, then the original unit must have been composed during the period of political upheaval consequent upon Judah's first disastrous encounter with the might of Babylon in 598 BCE and the even worse disasters of 587 BCE.

The language employed in this lengthy disquisition on the possibilities of either blessing or curse, especially that used in the much shorter blessing section, is strongly reminiscent of the celebratory language of worship. Conversely, the language of the curse section gives explicit expression to the kinds of misfortune that could readily have been invoked at almost any time upon Israel's enemies. All that has changed is that these curses envisage Israel itself becoming the LORD's enemy. To a significant extent it is arguable that the whole section represents a particular adaptation of the kind of prophetic threat/curse that a cultic prophet would have been expected to deliver against the enemies of Israel.

Such "national" curses were simply developments of the more personal style of curse in which an individual invoked evil upon another in the name of a particular deity. The belief that words had power in themselves, especially when reinforced by the power of a god, meant that they were believed to be capable of bringing harm upon those who were named as the targets of the curse.

There is in this deuteronomic setting a considerable shift from this primitive stage of word-magic since the belief in the power of words to bring harm is wholly subsumed under the larger notion that it is the law of God alone that has the power to bring blessing or to inflict harm. There can then be no other, unforeseen power that would occasion harm; still less could the belief be upheld that random curses brought with them power to inflict injury and hurt.

In spite of the overweight of curses over blessings in vv. 1-44, there is nonetheless a profoundly rational and systematizing theology undergirding it. It shares much in common with the view of the authors of proverbial wisdom, who entertained a strong confidence in the justice that pervaded all things and in the effective outworking of a pattern of retribution in daily life.

The transitional unit in vv. 45-46 introduces into the message of blessing and curse a more deeply disturbing warning regarding the power of God's commandments. When things go wrong because Israel has disobeyed the law, there will be no avenue of escape from the terrible and inevitable retribution that will come. Justice will be done, and it will be seen to have been done when Israel remembers the commandments of God and surveys its own history in their light. The commandments themselves will be the "sign and portent" of disaster for future generations. The wording is very significant since it carries a deliberate echo of the triumphant assurance with which Deuteronomy had recorded the story of how the LORD God had brought up Israel from Egypt "with signs and wonders."

Respecting the epilogue to the law code, the message of 28:1-46 is of a different theological character from the admonitions of chapters 6–9. The latter are prospective in viewpoint and educative in intention. The former, however, is retrospective of Israel's actual history and serves as a theodicy, justifying God's ways with Israel. What has happened is what could have been expected to happen in view of Israel's behavior since it entered the land.

The predominance of curses over blessings in chapter 28 can then find its explanation in the conviction that this is in fact how Israel's history has proved to be. Disaster had come, and what was needed at this juncture was an explanation for it. Where many had simply drawn the conclusion that the LORD God of Israel was impotent when faced with the conflicting power of the gods of surrounding nations, the deuteronomic author endeavors to reassert the truth of the LORD's sovereignty. Israel had been called by God to fulfill the demands of the law. Now it must be content to be judged by it.

In the light of this distinctive use of a series of curses to present a theodicy of the final collapse of the first Israelite kingdom, we can discern some significant undercurrents in the theological message that is set forth. Most striking is the insistence on the sovereign power of the LORD God. The theological stance is very close to that of the prophecies ascribed to Isaiah in Isaiah 37:22-29. It is the LORD God of Israel who controls the power processes of historical events and not the supposedly superior gods of Mesopotamia.

So we find in vv. 20-37 no fewer than ten assertions that what has happened has been determined by the LORD God:

v. 20, "The LORD will send upon you . . .
v. 21, "The LORD will make the pestilence cling to you . . .
v. 22, "The LORD will afflict you . . .
v. 24, "The LORD will change . . .
v. 25, "The LORD will cause you . . .
v. 27, "The LORD will afflict you . . .
v. 28, "The LORD will afflict you . . .
v. 35, "The LORD will strike you . . .
v. 36, "The LORD will bring you . . .
v. 37, " . . . among all the peoples where the LORD will lead you."

Behind these assertions lies a firm intention to reaffirm one of the central tenets of a true monotheism: The LORD God of Israel is a sovereign deity over all other claims to godhood. Though the existence of other gods is not denied (cf. v. 36), their powerlessness before the LORD God of Israel is heavily emphasized and their uselessness shown in that they are not real gods at all but merely objects of wood and stone.

A striking feature of this basic series of blessings and curses lies in the incompleteness of the picture it offers concerning what the future will hold for Israel under the curse. Verse 20 envisages the possibility that Israel may be destroyed, and this threat of complete annihilation is repeated further in vv. 21-24. The transitional summary in v. 45 reaffirms the warning yet again. Some slight concession appears to be introduced in v. 36, giving a glimpse of Judah's king and his people being taken into exile, where they will be forced to serve alien gods. No more substantial expression of hope for the future than this is provided.

28:47-57. When we turn to the addition in vv. 47-57, there is a significant shift both in formal structure and theological viewpoint. The literary form of the curse is abandoned altogether and instead graphic illustrative detail is given of Israel's sufferings at the hands of an unnamed enemy. The agent of God's punishment is specified as "a nation from far away" (v. 49). No fuller identification is made, but Babylon must certainly be intended. The most striking feature is the detailed description of a prolonged and horrifying siege that will bring unendurable famine and will lead to gruesome acts of cannibalism (vv. 53-57), even involving parents and their children. These are undoubtedly no longer generalized sketches of human suffering but rather are specific recollections of horrors that took place in Jerusalem during the Babylonian siege of Jerusalem between the years of 588–587 BCE. There is, therefore, a close similarity of date and theological intention between this rhetorical address and the book of Lamentations.

Overall the purpose of the address appears to have been to provide a full confession on Israel's part, insisting that it has been guilty of disobedience to God's laws. The element of theodicy is strongly present in the implied insistence that it is not the powerlessness of Israel's God that has brought about the nation's misfortunes but rather the terrible indifference shown to the divine commandments given through Moses.

28:58-68. The final addition in vv. 58-68 is important, not for any fuller theological development of the theodicy, but for the clear and extensive message concerning Israel's exile. Of great interest is the last great shift in deuteronomic theology and the embracing of the notion of a painful and lasting flight from the land of Israel and a prolonged period of exile. Still no hint at all is made of an eventual end to this exile and to a return to the land once conquered by Israel under Joshua. For a nation for which the land had occupied so prominent and central a position, the awareness of expulsion from it takes on a singularly threatening character. One of the closest parallels to the passage is in Jer 25:10-14, with its realization that a long and painful time of exile is the fate that awaits Israel.

A particular feature of this passage lies in the attention given to those who would flee to Egypt (vv. 60, 68) and offer themselves for sale as slaves (v. 68). Egypt appears to be the preferred destination of the Judean survivors who fled there after the murder of Gedaliah (cf. Jer 43:1–44:30), and the return there is seen as a tragic reversal of the original deliverance. The exodus had given birth to Israel as a nation, and the return to seek refuge in that land takes on the character of a loss of nationhood. Noteworthy, too, is the complete absence of any further reference to the group of exiles from Judah who had been taken to Babylon in 598 BCE, together with the Davidic ruler Jehoiachin. At this point the expectation that the renewal of Israel as a nation would come about when those who had been taken to Babylon returned to their native land has not been defined clearly enough to show how the rebirth of Israel would come about.

Obviously, the fate of those who had either been taken as exiles to Babylon or who had fled to neighboring lands such as Egypt had come to preoccupy the deuteronomic authors. Yet even up to this point hope for the continuance of some form of government and stability in the land had not been altogether abandoned, and expectations of the exiles' eventual return has no firm place in Israel's hope.

By the time the prophecies of Isaiah 40–55 and the major prophetic collections of Jeremiah and Ezekiel had been given a literary shape, all hope for Israel's future had become focused on a return from Babylon of those who had been forcibly taken there. This was clearly the situation that emerged by the beginning of the sixth century BCE. In the meantime all confidence in the surviving administration in the ruined land of Judah had been abandoned, and with this one of the central planks of the deuteronomic theology had perished.

REFLECTIONS

There is a surprising appropriateness in the manner in which the deuteronomic law code is followed by an epilogue that declares the role of the law in human experience. Why should a person be obedient to the law, and what are the benefits to be obtained by doing so? The first part of Deuteronomy 28 responds to these unfocused questions in the most straightforward and predictable way: Those who obey the law will be blessed and will achieve happiness and prosperity (Deut 28:2-14); conversely, those who disobey the law will be cursed and will suffer misfortune and ruin (vv. 16-44). Such is the deuteronomic doctrine of retribution that governs both the law book and the written story of Israel's history shaped by its doctrines. God is a God of justice, and divine retribution is inevitable.

However, it is not only the deuteronomic writings and much of the biblical literature but also the experience of life that encourage such a belief. Were it not so, we should have neither need nor respect for law and good behavior since it is a fundamental conviction that they point us to recognize the order and moral structure of our world and of the place of human beings within it.

Yet if a doctrine of retribution is true, it is certainly not the whole truth about life and cannot therefore be made into a universal truth that is always valid. Evildoers often do not get their deserts, and correspondingly very good people may suffer horrendous misfortunes. The book of Job is the richest biblical exploration of the doctrine of retribution. So theologians conclude that the shadow of the cross stretches not only across the whole of the biblical literature but in a very real sense across the whole of life. The problem of unmerited pain and undeserved misfortune becomes a major part of the human story.

The fact that the simplest enumeration of blessings and curses in an either/or choice begins the epilogue of Deut 28:1-44 (the blessings of vv. 3-6 contrast directly with the curses of vv. 16-19 and may well have been adapted from a simple formula used in worship) draws attention to the shifts and differences of thought that emerge in the additions that have subsequently been joined to it.

Verses 47-57 were undoubtedly added in the wake of the setbacks and disasters that befell Judah once the kingdom came under Babylonian control and King Jehoiakim was foolhardy enough to rebel. The nightmare consequences of the sieges of Jerusalem in 599–598 BCE and again in 588–587 are then brought more directly into the picture. Although the simple doctrine of retribution is still held on to, it is already evident from the horrifying instance of cannibalism that the doctrine had worn extremely thin! A simple doctrine that men and women only suffer what they deserve surely did not account for this. At the least it forcibly raised the point that those who were responsible for bringing about a situation (the king and the royal administration) were not the only ones to suffer its consequences. Many innocent persons were brought down in the judgment.

It seems clear that these additions, which are in a formal sense merely illustrations of what it means to live under God's curse, actually do far more than this. They raise the question whether a simple teaching that evil and misfortune are a consequence of disobedience to God's law is really enough to explain the facts of the real world! Clearly the author has drawn upon known instances of barbarism, and the miseries that befell the inhabitants of a city under siege cannot properly be fitted into any such doctrine. The mystery of evil goes deeper than this, and it is pointless to give inadequate answers to such major questions.

Very much the same problem, arising out of the same circumstances, appears in the laments brought together in the book of Lamentations. The author is confessing guilt and unburdening his grief and shock but is also trying to focus a question that remains blurred and only half defined. Can such appalling actions as are attested in Deut 28:33-57 (cf. Lam 2:20), in which every vestige of normal human feeling and compassion is overthrown, really have been intended by God as a punishment?

At a single stroke the very framing of such a question forces us to recognize that "theology after the holocaust" can never be the same as it was before. New depths of human misery have been plumbed; new horrors have been inscribed on the walls of human history; new nightmares have been experienced that can never afterward be erased from human consciousness. The unknown author of Deut 28:47-57 has not given us an answer but has set a question before us that would have been very much easier to ignore.

The second of the additions made to the simplistic assertions of the blessing-curse formulation is also profoundly interesting. This is given in vv. 58-68 and represents a straightforward updating of Israel's story in the wake of what happened to a large section of the population of Judah after the events of 587 BCE. Thousands were compelled to flee from their homes, to confront a burned and ravaged countryside, and to come to terms with the unwelcome truth that homes, households, and freedom had all been lost.

With bitter irony the picture given in these verses is of a tragic reversal of the triumphalist story of Israel's beginnings portrayed in Deuteronomy 1–3. The plight of slavery in Egypt, the sound of the taskmaster's lash, and the humiliation of being sold as a slave in the market-place—all these miseries had been part of the traditional story of everything that God had rescued Israel from. Now Israel was once again to experience these cruel sufferings. The wheel of fate seemed to have turned full circle!

However, the message the author of these verses draws from this ironic contrast between Israel's beginnings and endings is not a fatalistic doctrine of despair. As Jesus was later to appeal to the citizens of Jerusalem in the name of God, "If you, even you, had only recognized on this day the things that make for peace! But now they are hidden from your eyes" (Luke 19:42), so there is here a poignant awareness that God's possibilities are never exhausted. God had given Israel a lifeline of hope through the revelation of the commandments, but Israel had refused to grasp it. For those readers who were still indifferent to the claim of these commandments, the message had now become very plain. The pain of the past, however, did not eliminate the reality of hope for the future.

DEUTERONOMY 29:1–30:20, THE GREAT FAREWELL ADDRESS OF MOSES

NIV

29 These are the terms of the covenant the LORD commanded Moses to make with the Israelites in Moab, in addition to the covenant he had made with them at Horeb.

2 Moses summoned all the Israelites and said to them:

Your eyes have seen all that the LORD did in Egypt to Pharaoh, to all his officials and to all his land. 3 With your own eyes you saw those great trials, those miraculous signs and great wonders. 4 But to this day the LORD has not given you a mind that understands or eyes that see or ears that hear. 5 During the forty years that I led you through the desert, your clothes did not wear out, nor did the sandals on your feet. 6 You ate no bread and drank no wine or other fermented drink. I did this so that you might know that I am the LORD your God.

7 When you reached this place, Sihon king of Heshbon and Og king of Bashan came out to fight against us, but we defeated them. 8 We took their land and gave it as an inheritance to the Reubenites, the Gadites and the half-tribe of Manasseh.

9 Carefully follow the terms of this covenant, so

NRSV

29 a These are the words of the covenant that the LORD commanded Moses to make with the Israelites in the land of Moab, in addition to the covenant that he had made with them at Horeb.

2 b Moses summoned all Israel and said to them: You have seen all that the LORD did before your eyes in the land of Egypt, to Pharaoh and to all his servants and to all his land, 3 the great trials that your eyes saw, the signs, and those great wonders. 4 But to this day the LORD has not given you a mind to understand, or eyes to see, or ears to hear. 5 I have led you forty years in the wilderness. The clothes on your back have not worn out, and the sandals on your feet have not worn out; 6 you have not eaten bread, and you have not drunk wine or strong drink—so that you may know that I am the LORD your God. 7 When you came to this place, King Sihon of Heshbon and King Og of Bashan came out against us for battle, but we defeated them. 8 We took their land and gave it as an inheritance to the Reubenites, the Gadites, and the half-tribe of Manasseh. 9 There-

a Ch 28.69 in Heb   b Ch 29.1 in Heb

NIV

that you may prosper in everything you do. [10]All of you are standing today in the presence of the LORD your God—your leaders and chief men, your elders and officials, and all the other men of Israel, [11]together with your children and your wives, and the aliens living in your camps who chop your wood and carry your water. [12]You are standing here in order to enter into a covenant with the LORD your God, a covenant the LORD is making with you this day and sealing with an oath, [13]to confirm you this day as his people, that he may be your God as he promised you and as he swore to your fathers, Abraham, Isaac and Jacob. [14]I am making this covenant, with its oath, not only with you [15]who are standing here with us today in the presence of the LORD our God but also with those who are not here today.

[16]You yourselves know how we lived in Egypt and how we passed through the countries on the way here. [17]You saw among them their detestable images and idols of wood and stone, of silver and gold. [18]Make sure there is no man or woman, clan or tribe among you today whose heart turns away from the LORD our God to go and worship the gods of those nations; make sure there is no root among you that produces such bitter poison.

[19]When such a person hears the words of this oath, he invokes a blessing on himself and therefore thinks, "I will be safe, even though I persist in going my own way." This will bring disaster on the watered land as well as the dry.[a] [20]The LORD will never be willing to forgive him; his wrath and zeal will burn against that man. All the curses written in this book will fall upon him, and the LORD will blot out his name from under heaven. [21]The LORD will single him out from all the tribes of Israel for disaster, according to all the curses of the covenant written in this Book of the Law.

[22]Your children who follow you in later generations and foreigners who come from distant lands will see the calamities that have fallen on the land and the diseases with which the LORD has afflicted it. [23]The whole land will be a burning waste of salt and sulfur—nothing planted, nothing sprouting, no vegetation growing on it. It will be like the destruction of Sodom and Gomorrah, Admah

[a]19 Or way, in order to add drunkenness to thirst."

NRSV

fore diligently observe the words of this covenant, in order that you may succeed[a] in everything that you do.

10You stand assembled today, all of you, before the LORD your God—the leaders of your tribes,[b] your elders, and your officials, all the men of Israel, [11]your children, your women, and the aliens who are in your camp, both those who cut your wood and those who draw your water— [12]to enter into the covenant of the LORD your God, sworn by an oath, which the LORD your God is making with you today; [13]in order that he may establish you today as his people, and that he may be your God, as he promised you and as he swore to your ancestors, to Abraham, to Isaac, and to Jacob. [14]I am making this covenant, sworn by an oath, not only with you who stand here with us today before the LORD our God, [15]but also with those who are not here with us today. [16]You know how we lived in the land of Egypt, and how we came through the midst of the nations through which you passed. [17]You have seen their detestable things, the filthy idols of wood and stone, of silver and gold, that were among them. [18]It may be that there is among you a man or woman, or a family or tribe, whose heart is already turning away from the LORD our God to serve the gods of those nations. It may be that there is among you a root sprouting poisonous and bitter growth. [19]All who hear the words of this oath and bless themselves, thinking in their hearts, "We are safe even though we go our own stubborn ways" (thus bringing disaster on moist and dry alike)[c]— [20]the LORD will be unwilling to pardon them, for the LORD's anger and passion will smoke against them. All the curses written in this book will descend on them, and the LORD will blot out their names from under heaven. [21]The LORD will single them out from all the tribes of Israel for calamity, in accordance with all the curses of the covenant written in this book of the law. [22]The next generation, your children who rise up after you, as well as the foreigner who comes from a distant country, will see the devastation of that land and the afflictions with which the LORD has afflicted it— [23]all its soil burned out by sulfur and salt,

[a] Or deal wisely   [b] Gk Syr: Heb your leaders, your tribes   [c] Meaning of Heb uncertain

NIV

and Zeboiim, which the LORD overthrew in fierce anger. ²⁴All the nations will ask: "Why has the LORD done this to this land? Why this fierce, burning anger?"

²⁵And the answer will be: "It is because this people abandoned the covenant of the LORD, the God of their fathers, the covenant he made with them when he brought them out of Egypt. ²⁶They went off and worshiped other gods and bowed down to them, gods they did not know, gods he had not given them. ²⁷Therefore the LORD's anger burned against this land, so that he brought on it all the curses written in this book. ²⁸In furious anger and in great wrath the LORD uprooted them from their land and thrust them into another land, as it is now."

²⁹The secret things belong to the LORD our God, but the things revealed belong to us and to our children forever, that we may follow all the words of this law.

30 When all these blessings and curses I have set before you come upon you and you take them to heart wherever the LORD your God disperses you among the nations, ²and when you and your children return to the LORD your God and obey him with all your heart and with all your soul according to everything I command you today, ³then the LORD your God will restore your fortunes^a and have compassion on you and gather you again from all the nations where he scattered you. ⁴Even if you have been banished to the most distant land under the heavens, from there the LORD your God will gather you and bring you back. ⁵He will bring you to the land that belonged to your fathers, and you will take possession of it. He will make you more prosperous and numerous than your fathers. ⁶The LORD your God will circumcise your hearts and the hearts of your descendants, so that you may love him with all your heart and with all your soul, and live. ⁷The LORD your God will put all these curses on your enemies who hate and persecute you. ⁸You will again obey the LORD and follow all his commands I am giving you today. ⁹Then the LORD your God will make you most prosperous in all the work of your hands and in the fruit of your womb, the young of your livestock and the crops of your

^a3 Or *will bring you back from captivity*

NRSV

nothing planted, nothing sprouting, unable to support any vegetation, like the destruction of Sodom and Gomorrah, Admah and Zeboiim, which the LORD destroyed in his fierce anger— ²⁴they and indeed all the nations will wonder, "Why has the LORD done thus to this land? What caused this great display of anger?" ²⁵They will conclude, "It is because they abandoned the covenant of the LORD, the God of their ancestors, which he made with them when he brought them out of the land of Egypt. ²⁶They turned and served other gods, worshiping them, gods whom they had not known and whom he had not allotted to them; ²⁷so the anger of the LORD was kindled against that land, bringing on it every curse written in this book. ²⁸The LORD uprooted them from their land in anger, fury, and great wrath, and cast them into another land, as is now the case." ²⁹The secret things belong to the LORD our God, but the revealed things belong to us and to our children forever, to observe all the words of this law.

30 When all these things have happened to you, the blessings and the curses that I have set before you, if you call them to mind among all the nations where the LORD your God has driven you, ²and return to the LORD your God, and you and your children obey him with all your heart and with all your soul, just as I am commanding you today, ³then the LORD your God will restore your fortunes and have compassion on you, gathering you again from all the peoples among whom the LORD your God has scattered you. ⁴Even if you are exiled to the ends of the world,^a from there the LORD your God will gather you, and from there he will bring you back. ⁵The LORD your God will bring you into the land that your ancestors possessed, and you will possess it; he will make you more prosperous and numerous than your ancestors.

6Moreover, the LORD your God will circumcise your heart and the heart of your descendants, so that you will love the LORD your God with all your heart and with all your soul, in order that you may live. ⁷The LORD your God will put all these curses on your enemies and on the adversaries who took advantage of you. ⁸Then you shall again obey the LORD, observing all his command-

^a Heb *of heaven*

NIV

land. The LORD will again delight in you and make you prosperous, just as he delighted in your fathers, [10]if you obey the LORD your God and keep his commands and decrees that are written in this Book of the Law and turn to the LORD your God with all your heart and with all your soul.

[11]Now what I am commanding you today is not too difficult for you or beyond your reach. [12]It is not up in heaven, so that you have to ask, "Who will ascend into heaven to get it and proclaim it to us so we may obey it?" [13]Nor is it beyond the sea, so that you have to ask, "Who will cross the sea to get it and proclaim it to us so we may obey it?" [14]No, the word is very near you; it is in your mouth and in your heart so you may obey it.

[15]See, I set before you today life and prosperity, death and destruction. [16]For I command you today to love the LORD your God, to walk in his ways, and to keep his commands, decrees and laws; then you will live and increase, and the LORD your God will bless you in the land you are entering to possess.

[17]But if your heart turns away and you are not obedient, and if you are drawn away to bow down to other gods and worship them, [18]I declare to you this day that you will certainly be destroyed. You will not live long in the land you are crossing the Jordan to enter and possess.

[19]This day I call heaven and earth as witnesses against you that I have set before you life and death, blessings and curses. Now choose life, so that you and your children may live [20]and that you may love the LORD your God, listen to his voice, and hold fast to him. For the LORD is your life, and he will give you many years in the land he swore to give to your fathers, Abraham, Isaac and Jacob.

NRSV

ments that I am commanding you today, [9]and the LORD your God will make you abundantly prosperous in all your undertakings, in the fruit of your body, in the fruit of your livestock, and in the fruit of your soil. For the LORD will again take delight in prospering you, just as he delighted in prospering your ancestors, [10]when you obey the LORD your God by observing his commandments and decrees that are written in this book of the law, because you turn to the LORD your God with all your heart and with all your soul.

[11]Surely, this commandment that I am commanding you today is not too hard for you, nor is it too far away. [12]It is not in heaven, that you should say, "Who will go up to heaven for us, and get it for us so that we may hear it and observe it?" [13]Neither is it beyond the sea, that you should say, "Who will cross to the other side of the sea for us, and get it for us so that we may hear it and observe it?" [14]No, the word is very near to you; it is in your mouth and in your heart for you to observe.

[15]See, I have set before you today life and prosperity, death and adversity. [16]If you obey the commandments of the LORD your God[g] that I am commanding you today, by loving the LORD your God, walking in his ways, and observing his commandments, decrees, and ordinances, then you shall live and become numerous, and the LORD your God will bless you in the land that you are entering to possess. [17]But if your heart turns away and you do not hear, but are led astray to bow down to other gods and serve them, [18]I declare to you today that you shall perish; you shall not live long in the land that you are crossing the Jordan to enter and possess. [19]I call heaven and earth to witness against you today that I have set before you life and death, blessings and curses. Choose life so that you and your descendants may live, [20]loving the LORD your God, obeying him, and holding fast to him; for that means life to you and length of days, so that you may live in the land that the LORD swore to give to your ancestors, to Abraham, to Isaac, and to Jacob.

a Gk: Heb lacks *If you obey the commandments of the LORD your God*

COMMENTARY

The art of rhetoric and speech making was highly prized and highly developed by both the ancient Greeks and Romans. Moving the minds of fellow human beings by artistry with words—appealing, informing, cajoling, and persuading—has been among the most influential of human artistic achievements. Because it is an art that has been exploited by demagogues and abused in the pursuit of dangerous and selfish ends, it is one that many responsible and educated people view with suspicion. It is an art that can easily be misused and that can unleash feelings and ambitions that eventually lead to great suffering and destruction.

Yet, rightly used and directed, a skillfully prepared and delivered speech can take on a life-transforming importance. Few persons, in fact, can claim that they have never been so deeply moved by a powerful speech or sermon that they have changed the direction of their lives. Certainly the speech that is presented in Deut 29:1–30:20 as the farewell address of Moses to the people of Israel is a brilliant example of the rhetorician's art. It appears as the third of the great addresses of Moses that make up the book of Deuteronomy.[107] Studied from the perspective of its rhetorical techniques and stylistic devices it stands out as among the most brilliant dramatic compositions that the Old Testament contains.

Clearly an addition to the original law book of Deut 4:44–16:19, the speech is also of considerable historical and theological significance in that it is addressed specifically and openly to a community of Israel who found themselves at a wholly new juncture in their national history. They had by this time been driven out from the land promised to their ancestors, Abraham, Isaac, and Jacob. This land, which represented God's central material gift to Israel and by which they had been embodied a nation, had by this time been lost. Through its possession they had been able, however imperfectly, to express their nationhood and to fulfill the promise of freedom that had been assured by their deliverance from Egypt. From it all that sustains life could be obtained in such abundance that they had become the envy of less fortunate neighbors. Thereby the promises implicit in the covenant God had made on Mt. Horeb had found a measure of fulfillment. Yet by the time this address was composed the land had been ravaged and its productivity ruined. Even more disturbing, it no longer remained under the political control of those whose religious loyalty meant that it could safely be entrusted to their care. For the deuteronomic authors Israel had been driven into exile—a picture that is graphically and effectively drawn in 28:58-68.

This new situation exhibited with considerable realism the human vulnerability of Israel. In the eyes of the deuteronomists it was also a fearful confirmation of the importance of obedience to the law of Moses. Yet, even beyond these two glaring physical facts, it was a fundamental theological problem. Without possession of the land how could there be an Israel at all? A restored nation could only come into being by a new journey through the wilderness and a new act of taking possession of the land. In a remarkable way, therefore, the situation that the deuteronomic authors used to reaffirm the central importance of the law of Moses—Israel waiting in the plains of Moab and poised to cross the Jordan into the promised land—had to be repeated. Israel was once again exiled in the wilderness; as a nation it was once again wrestling to break free from bondage to alien nations; it had once again to recross the Jordan and repossess the land.

In the form of a farewell speech by Moses to the assembled people of Israel, this splendid address is delivered to an Israel that had been driven into exile. It was a people landless, demoralized, and confused—a people seeking to find a path of hope in a situation that seemed hopeless. So a wide array of rhetorical skills is used as a means of appeal to reawaken and rearm Israel morally and spiritually. The very faith in the power of the LORD God that seemed to have been discredited and largely disowned by the people is now summoned back into being. The address is therefore a supreme appeal to faith, courage, and hope. If ever the art of rhetoric was needed, it was needed now!

Seen against such a background the speech emerges as a strong appeal to faith, urging Israel

---

107. An excellent critique and exposition of the speech, with an analysis of its rhetorical techniques, is presented in Timothy A Lenchak, *"Choose Life!" A Rhetorical-Critical Investigation of Deuteronomy 28, 69-30, 20,* AnBib 129 (Rome: Pontifical Biblical Institute, 1993).

to accept its past failures, to recognize its hopeless position without faith in God, and to return to a renewed loyalty to the covenant and its commandments. A new beginning was possible, and a new day would dawn when the failures of the past and the wretchedness of the present would be set behind Israel. A new life would open up for the people once they had resettled in their ancient homeland.

The speech of 29:1–30:20 must be regarded as a unity, although it divides into separate sections. Throughout it displays a coherence and consistency of theme, style, and purpose. It undoubtedly belongs to the latest among the strata of material that has been incorporated into the book and displays several important theological and literary links with the viewpoint of Jer 24:1-24; 25:1-10; 30:18-22; 31:1-34. Its central message is the insistence on the possibility of repentance and the return of Israel to nationhood as part of a great purpose that God would bring about. The situation of those addressed is clearly described in 30:1. Israel's disobedience after the first settlement in the land and its being scattered among the nations in punishment for turning to other gods is presupposed as having taken place. Now a new choice faced the people: They could either abandon God and the covenant altogether, as the fainthearted among them had already begun to do, or they could return in sincerity and truth to keep God's covenant and to remain unwaveringly loyal to the LORD as God.

The appeal of the address is clear and decisive, and the situation in which the original hearers/readers were placed is allowed to show through very clearly. The address has a threefold purpose: It makes clear that, by the grace of the LORD God, Israel's renewal is a genuine possibility; it thrusts aside the objections that could be raised against trusting in this possibility; and it uncovers and refutes the unspoken thoughts of despair and disillusionment the people secretly nursed. The whole message is set out with great psychological insight and outstanding rhetorical skill.

(1) The opening declaration of 29:1 sets the scene by establishing the genuineness of Israel's opportunity to repent and in pointing to the new situation this would bring about. Israel is once again poised on the edge of the land, exactly as its ancestors were when they stood across the Jordan in the plains of Moab. Just as Moses'

address to their ancestors had amounted to a new covenant "in addition to the covenant made with them at Horeb" (v. 1), so also this "new covenant" was a fresh possibility once again. In effect, what is envisaged is not so much a totally new covenant, but rather a renewed covenant.

This is the first point at which the deuteronomic legislation has been explicitly presented as being a new covenant in addition to that made on Horeb. This does not contain a new additional set of commandments but is rather a restatement of the Horeb covenant. Its secondary and supplementary character had become necessary because Israel had failed to observe its terms and to grasp the importance of its commandments. Verse 4 declares categorically that throughout its generations Israel had consistently not grasped the greatness of God's power. The immediate reference in its historical guise is to the tradition of Israel's rebellion in the wilderness, now understood symbolically as a repeated obstinacy and willful disobedience that lay hidden in the hearts of the people. It is the "blindness and deafness" of which the prophet Isaiah had accused them (Isa 6:10), and it is the "stiff-necked obstinacy" that the prophet Jeremiah had found among his contemporaries.

The accusation serves to highlight the truth that the thirty-eight years spent wandering in the wilderness were symbolic of the whole failed history of Israel in the land from the time of the conquest under Joshua to the removal of Zedekiah from the throne in 587 BCE. From the author's point of view the accusation was still true that "but to this day the LORD has not given you a mind to understand, or eyes to see, or ears to hear" (v. 4). The phrase "but to this day" establishes again the sense of contemporaneity between Moses addressing Israel in the plains of Moab and the author addressing Israel as it now found itself scattered among the nations. Accordingly, the idea of a second covenant made on the plains of Moab established the grounds for confidence that Israel could reenter and repossess the land as Joshua had done. By seeing its situation in this light Israel could experience a renewing of its commitment to the covenant at Horeb as Moses had urged the people to do centuries before. There are significant connections of historical context and theological ideas with the promise of the new covenant of Jer 31:31-34.

The essential content of the message is then made incontrovertibly plain in the words of 30:1-

5, which leaves no uncertainty as to what Israel, scattered and demoralized as it was, must now do: "Return to the LORD your God" (v. 2); "The LORD will restore your fortunes and have compassion on you" (v. 3). This will then lead to God's further initiative in renewal: "gathering you again from all the peoples" (v. 3); "The LORD will bring you into the land that your ancestors possessed, and you will possess it" (v. 5).

The possibilities that faced Israel as it reflected on the renewal of the Horeb covenant made on the far side of the river Jordan is thereby clearly stated. Yet the message made a demand on the present generation, the same demand that had been made on every Israelite since the original Horeb covenant had been established: They must choose between following the way of God or abandoning it. They could either remain totally loyal to the covenant, obeying its commandments (vv. 15-20), or they could turn away; but in doing so they would also abandon the promise of hope altogether. In this case they would be throwing away the only lifeline that was within their grasp.

With magnificent evangelical passion the author makes a final appeal: "Choose life so that you and your descendants may live" (v. 19). One thing alone remained for Israel to do; the remainder lay in the power of God. Nevertheless, this one act was the essential key that would enable them to pass through the doorway of hope. Choose life!

(2) The second of the aims of this address is to thrust aside the objections that the survivors of Israel nursed in their hearts, that made such a message of hope appear impossible. Foremost among these was the belief that God's actions and power were not sufficient for such a restoration. The influence the LORD God of Israel possessed over the course of human affairs was not enough to ensure Israel's eventual success. So ran the unexpressed objections to returning at this point of history to a deep and exclusive commitment to the LORD as God. Had not the entire course of events in the years of Judah's final demise given proof of God's powerlessness before the gods of the nations?

The response to this objection is to look back once again to the story of Israel's beginnings when the nation journeyed through the wilderness. There God had shown extraordinary providential care for Israel (vv. 5-6), and there great victories had been won over King Sihon of Heshbon and

King Og of Bashan (v. 7; cf. Deut 2:26–3:17). The territory on the far side of the Jordan occupied by Reuben, Gad, and part of Manasseh had been swiftly claimed. When faith and loyalty had been strong and Moses' leadership still a reality, then Israel had been assured of success.

The second of the objections that were aroused concerned the uncertainty and confusion surrounding the requirement that Israel should obey the commands of the covenant. How could the people know that they had fulfilled what was required? Here the author of the address presents a very central feature of God's covenant with Israel. It did not involve mysterious, unknown, or unfulfillable demands on the part of God. The commandments were clear, plain, and fully knowable by every citizen in Israel, both young and old: "The secret things belong to the LORD our God, but the revealed things belong to us and to our children forever, to observe all the words of this law" (v. 29).

It could not be denied that there was a mysterious side to God's Being that humans did not, and could not, know. What mattered was that the truths that concerned humankind had been fully disclosed in the covenant. Essentially the same truth is reaffirmed in 30:11-14 in words that leave no doubt as to the central position the deuteronomists saw the law of God to hold. These words are vitally and centrally related to the biblical concept of divine revelation and of a moral order of life that is indissolubly linked to it.

A third objection that must have been openly spoken and not merely privately reflected on is found in vv. 22-26. The key element is the ruined state of the land, forcefully described in v. 23: "all its soil burned out by sulfur and salt, nothing planted, nothing sprouting, unable to support any vegetation, like the destruction of Sodom and Gomorrah, Admah and Zeboiim." The picture must have been unforgettably etched on the minds of many of the hearers and readers of this remarkable sermon.

However, in a masterful twist of rhetorical artistry, the words of this objection are not placed on the lips of the hearers and readers. Instead, they are put into the mouths of the children of future generations of Israelites and of foreigners who will comment on such devastation—and they will know precisely the reason why such devastation had come! It is "because they abandoned the covenant of the

LORD, the God of their ancestors" (v. 25). Children as yet unborn and foreigners who survey the scene from outside will know the truth that the Israelites want to hide from themselves. It is not the powerlessness of the LORD God that is responsible for the ruin of the land but the disobedience and faithlessness of the people of Israel. They blame God, but they should look into their own hearts where they will see that they can only blame themselves. Such is the writer's rhetorical skill that even a seemingly unanswerable objection does have an answer when men and women "have a mind to understand" (v. 4).

(3) The third aim of this long address is to uncover and remove the fears and disillusionment that had reduced the author's readers to near despair. Why did the situation and the future outlook appear so different to the author from the way it appeared to the readers? To answer this question the author probes deeply into the psychology of faith. Faith is a perspective on life and the world that requires a proper understanding. Just as the first generation of Israelites in the wilderness had failed miserably to understand the call and challenge of God (v. 4), so also, the author implies, many of his contemporaries still do not understand. The human mind is deceptively liable to seek easy answers to complex questions. As a consequence, there are those who are ready to turn aside from trusting God at the first sign that the situation has become difficult: "It may be that there is among you a man or woman, or a family or tribe, whose heart is already turning away from the LORD our God" (v. 18). The deuteronomic account of their ancestors wandering in the wilderness provided many examples of such a cowardly lack of faith (Deut 8:1-10).

Alongside such mean-spirited faithlessness there was also the temptation to indulge in a selfish complacency. People were saying to themselves: "We are safe even though we go our own stubborn ways" (v. 19). By self-indulgently contemplating their own remarkable good fortune in at least surviving, they were willing to abandon altogether any concern with larger issues of faith and national destiny in order to look after themselves, thus paying no attention to the larger fate of the nation.

All such want of faith the author describes as "a root sprouting poisonous and bitter growth" (v. 18). Clearly these were thoughts that the author was hearing daily, or, if they were not openly spoken, they certainly represented widely felt but unspoken reflections of despondency and despair. By drawing them out into the open and putting them in plain speech, such thoughts could be shown up for the self-centered, unworthy, and faithless realities that they were. Those who were too timid to speak such words would thereby be shamed into admitting to themselves that they had entertained them.

Another objection also came to the author's attention and must certainly have cut deeply into the message of hope. Its essential thought line ran: Even granting that all that is said about the covenant, its law, and its promise for the future, does not the covenant itself, backed up by the entire past history of Israel, show that the same disasters would overtake the nation again? If disobedience to the law carried such terrible consequences, and if the nature of Israel in the future remained what it had been in the past, would not the same consequences inevitably befall Israel yet again? One way or another the nation was doomed!

This serious objection is countered by the words of 30:6: "God will circumcise your heart and the heart of your descendants so that you will love the LORD your God with all your heart and with all your soul, in order that you may live." God would transform the inner mind and spirit of Israel by "circumcising" the hearts of the people in order to implant the will to obey the commandments. The theology is virtually identical to that expressed in Jer 31:33-34 and Ezek 36:25-27. By a spiritual transformation the power of God would create a new spirit of obedience within every Israelite. God would give the power and the willingness to obey.

To some extent a certain level of ambivalence and inconsistency in the author's presentation is discernible here. After such a strong emphasis on the need to obey the commandments and on the terrible consequences of failure to do so, it is remarkable that God's love and compassion are so great that in the future God will give Israel the power to obey. The sharpness of earlier warnings is to this extent compromised. However, in spite of this inconsistency, it is very significant that this same issue was to recur more than once in both Jewish and Christian attempts to combine the concepts of law and grace. That law should be an instrument of grace and that grace should bring us to fulfill God's law have remained important emphases in Christian exegesis through such different figures as Paul, Augustine, and Martin Luther.

With this threefold armory of rhetoric—stating a

clear and decisive message, showing its conformity to all that its readers truly believed, and exposing the shamefulness and emptiness of those who were inclined to reject it—the author concludes with a renewed challenge: "Choose life so that you and your descendants may live!" (30:19).

The address clearly belongs to the middle of the sixth century BCE, closely contemporaneous with the book of Lamentations and displaying many connections with the edited collection of Jeremiah's prophecies, which bears a deuteronomic stamp.

Taken in the context of its origin, the deuteronomic movement had striven desperately to avert the disasters that had befallen the surviving king-

dom of Judah at the hands of the Babylonians. In its aftermath they found a land that was economically ruined, politically divided, and spiritually demoralized.

In this splendid speech ascribed to Moses, this late deuteronomic author makes a decisive appeal for a renewal of faith and loyalty. Rightly discerning that spiritual confusion was the foremost issue to be dealt with, in this address he introduces into the deuteronomic theology a new dimension of hope. No longer could the future be hoped for in terms of averting catastrophe. It needed to be seen in terms of renewal and recovery after the worst had taken place.

REFLECTIONS

In many ways this outstanding example of the ancient preacher's art needs little by way of further reflection. It contains so many timeless truths, and its allusions and references to events are reasonably self-explanatory within the overall perspective of the deuteronomic movement. Nevertheless, it has a powerful contemporary relevance in its strong emphasis on issues of personal faith. In a modern secular world where religion appears so frequently as a matter of choice, embraced and held on to by relatively few persons in a society that has largely grown indifferent to religion, its central importance for human development is easily overlooked. The author of this address recognizes that faith and loyalty to God are central antidotes to despair. Hope in God becomes a larger, surer, and more comprehensive basis of hope than is to be found anywhere else.

Despair of the future is a kind of social disease. Whether that social sickness is a consequence of the turmoil and ruination caused by warfare, as this ancient author witnessed, or whether it is caused by deprivation, unemployment, and social alienation, the effects are very similar. Hopelessness generates despondency. It deenergizes and dehumanizes persons so that they no longer reach to grasp the possibilities that life brings. It generates impulses of self-pity and self-condemnation. It begins to regard death as a welcome release instead of the closure of the period of opportunity.

So the appeal to faith and hope is not merely a religious appeal to generate support for religious enterprise but an appeal to enter into a full humanity. It is an appeal to seek out the deep wellsprings of human ambition and to expect the future to be open and desirable. It is an appeal to discover afresh what it truly means to be a human being.

Seen in this light the appeal to faith set out here gains greatly from the recognition that it originates in the worst of times. It is a call to hope that emerged out of a situation of deep gloom and emptiness. Not simply a challenge to embrace particular articles of faith or partisan leanings, it is, rather, an appeal to heart searching and self-examination, a remarkably personal and direct challenge that highlights the way in which, in the final analysis, faith is a necessity for every human being.

As a rhetorical composition made with great skill and based on a tradition of preaching eloquence, it makes an appropriate "last sermon" from the person and genius of Moses. It bears close comparison with the roughly contemporary and similarly directed speech ascribed to Joshua in Josh 24:1-28. In view of popular familiarity with the latter speech, it is surprising that this address of Moses has not been more fully explored. It brings out many of the same points made in the address of Joshua; it counters similar popular objections and expresses the same fundamental challenge to make firm decisions of faith. It is, then, a fitting testimony to the figure of Moses as a giant of faith, leaving a clear call to face the future with courage and with hope.

APPENDIX

OVERVIEW

Although the figure of Moses and the acclamation of his leadership as the unique mediator between God and Israel dominate the book of Deuteronomy, nevertheless, the book prepares Israel for life without the presence of this unique leader. Because the written law is the legacy and testament of Moses to Israel, Deuteronomy gives details of the preparations for the leader's inevitable death. It contains instructions that are designed to show how the contents of this book of law are to be preserved, protected, and administered.

What we now encounter in the final chapters of the book is an appendix that provides details concerning where the law book was to be kept, who were to be its trusted custodians, and what arrangements were to be made to ensure that Israel remained familiar with its contents. In addition to these essential preparations, there is a practical note on the fact and circumstances of Moses' death, together with two beautiful hymnic poems, the Song of Moses and the Blessing of Moses, that provide a kind of summary of what Moses means to all the future generations of Israel. In spite of their ascription to Moses, these cannot have been composed directly by him since they refer to events that happened long after his death. Nevertheless, they brilliantly convey the sense of a person whose gift to humankind was the gift of faith and for whom the greatest blessing that can be afforded is the discovery of this faith.

In addition to the arrangements for the preservation and custody of the law book, instructions are given for the installation of Moses' successor, Joshua, and an address entrusting him with his high task.

From a literary perspective this appendix to the law book displays considerable unevenness. Both of the major poems have clearly been added to the text at a late stage, but even allowing for this the flow of events is ragged. The basic themes concerning arrangements for the law book, the succession of Joshua, and the fact of Moses' death before the crossing of the Jordan are referred to at more than one point and intersect each other. It can only be concluded that these materials were added as a supplement to the law book and that this literary process of revision resulted in repetitions.

DEUTERONOMY 31:1-29, PREPARATIONS FOR LIFE UNDER THE LAW OF MOSES

NIV	NRSV
31 Then Moses went out and spoke these words to all Israel: [2]"I am now a hundred and twenty years old and I am no longer able to lead you. The LORD has said to me, 'You shall not cross the Jordan.' [3]The LORD your God himself will cross over ahead of you. He will destroy these nations before you, and you will take possession of their land. Joshua also will cross over ahead of	**31** When Moses had finished speaking all[a] these words to all Israel, [2]he said to them: "I am now one hundred twenty years old. I am no longer able to get about, and the LORD has told me, 'You shall not cross over this Jordan.' [3]The LORD your God himself will cross over before you. He will destroy these nations before you, and you

a Q Ms Gk: MT *Moses went and spoke*

NIV

you, as the LORD said. ⁴And the LORD will do to them what he did to Sihon and Og, the kings of the Amorites, whom he destroyed along with their land. ⁵The LORD will deliver them to you, and you must do to them all that I have commanded you. ⁶Be strong and courageous. Do not be afraid or terrified because of them, for the LORD your God goes with you; he will never leave you nor forsake you."

⁷Then Moses summoned Joshua and said to him in the presence of all Israel, "Be strong and courageous, for you must go with this people into the land that the LORD swore to their forefathers to give them, and you must divide it among them as their inheritance. ⁸The LORD himself goes before you and will be with you; he will never leave you nor forsake you. Do not be afraid; do not be discouraged."

⁹So Moses wrote down this law and gave it to the priests, the sons of Levi, who carried the ark of the covenant of the LORD, and to all the elders of Israel. ¹⁰Then Moses commanded them: "At the end of every seven years, in the year for canceling debts, during the Feast of Tabernacles, ¹¹when all Israel comes to appear before the LORD your God at the place he will choose, you shall read this law before them in their hearing. ¹²Assemble the people—men, women and children, and the aliens living in your towns—so they can listen and learn to fear the LORD your God and follow carefully all the words of this law. ¹³Their children, who do not know this law, must hear it and learn to fear the LORD your God as long as you live in the land you are crossing the Jordan to possess."

¹⁴The LORD said to Moses, "Now the day of your death is near. Call Joshua and present yourselves at the Tent of Meeting, where I will commission him." So Moses and Joshua came and presented themselves at the Tent of Meeting.

¹⁵Then the LORD appeared at the Tent in a pillar of cloud, and the cloud stood over the entrance to the Tent. ¹⁶And the LORD said to Moses: "You are going to rest with your fathers, and these people will soon prostitute themselves to the foreign gods of the land they are entering. They will forsake me and break the covenant I made with them. ¹⁷On that day I will become angry

NRSV

shall dispossess them. Joshua also will cross over before you, as the LORD promised. ⁴The LORD will do to them as he did to Sihon and Og, the kings of the Amorites, and to their land, when he destroyed them. ⁵The LORD will give them over to you and you shall deal with them in full accord with the command that I have given to you. ⁶Be strong and bold; have no fear or dread of them, because it is the LORD your God who goes with you; he will not fail you or forsake you."

⁷Then Moses summoned Joshua and said to him in the sight of all Israel: "Be strong and bold, for you are the one who will go with this people into the land that the LORD has sworn to their ancestors to give them; and you will put them in possession of it. ⁸It is the LORD who goes before you. He will be with you; he will not fail you or forsake you. Do not fear or be dismayed."

⁹Then Moses wrote down this law, and gave it to the priests, the sons of Levi, who carried the ark of the covenant of the LORD, and to all the elders of Israel. ¹⁰Moses commanded them: "Every seventh year, in the scheduled year of remission, during the festival of booths,ᵃ ¹¹when all Israel comes to appear before the LORD your God at the place that he will choose, you shall read this law before all Israel in their hearing. ¹²Assemble the people—men, women, and children, as well as the aliens residing in your towns—so that they may hear and learn to fear the LORD your God and to observe diligently all the words of this law, ¹³and so that their children, who have not known it, may hear and learn to fear the LORD your God, as long as you live in the land that you are crossing over the Jordan to possess."

¹⁴The LORD said to Moses, "Your time to die is near; call Joshua and present yourselves in the tent of meeting, so that I may commission him." So Moses and Joshua went and presented themselves in the tent of meeting, ¹⁵and the LORD appeared at the tent in a pillar of cloud; the pillar of cloud stood at the entrance to the tent.

¹⁶The LORD said to Moses, "Soon you will lie down with your ancestors. Then this people will begin to prostitute themselves to the foreign gods in their midst, the gods of the land into which

ᵃ Or tabernacles; Heb succoth

NIV

with them and forsake them; I will hide my face from them, and they will be destroyed. Many disasters and difficulties will come upon them, and on that day they will ask, 'Have not these disasters come upon us because our God is not with us?' 18And I will certainly hide my face on that day because of all their wickedness in turning to other gods.

19"Now write down for yourselves this song and teach it to the Israelites and have them sing it, so that it may be a witness for me against them. 20When I have brought them into the land flowing with milk and honey, the land I promised on oath to their forefathers, and when they eat their fill and thrive, they will turn to other gods and worship them, rejecting me and breaking my covenant. 21And when many disasters and difficulties come upon them, this song will testify against them, because it will not be forgotten by their descendants. I know what they are disposed to do, even before I bring them into the land I promised them on oath." 22So Moses wrote down this song that day and taught it to the Israelites.

23The LORD gave this command to Joshua son of Nun: "Be strong and courageous, for you will bring the Israelites into the land I promised them on oath, and I myself will be with you."

24After Moses finished writing in a book the words of this law from beginning to end, 25he gave this command to the Levites who carried the ark of the covenant of the LORD: 26"Take this Book of the Law and place it beside the ark of the covenant of the LORD your God. There it will remain as a witness against you. 27For I know how rebellious and stiff-necked you are. If you have been rebellious against the LORD while I am still alive and with you, how much more will you rebel after I die! 28Assemble before me all the elders of your tribes and all your officials, so that I can speak these words in their hearing and call heaven and earth to testify against them. 29For I know that after my death you are sure to become utterly corrupt and to turn from the way I have commanded you. In days to come, disaster will fall upon you because you will do evil in the sight of the LORD and provoke him to anger by what your hands have made."

NRSV

they are going; they will forsake me, breaking my covenant that I have made with them. 17My anger will be kindled against them in that day. I will forsake them and hide my face from them; they will become easy prey, and many terrible troubles will come upon them. In that day they will say, 'Have not these troubles come upon us because our God is not in our midst?' 18On that day I will surely hide my face on account of all the evil they have done by turning to other gods. 19Now therefore write this song, and teach it to the Israelites; put it in their mouths, in order that this song may be a witness for me against the Israelites. 20For when I have brought them into the land flowing with milk and honey, which I promised on oath to their ancestors, and they have eaten their fill and grown fat, they will turn to other gods and serve them, despising me and breaking my covenant. 21And when many terrible troubles come upon them, this song will confront them as a witness, because it will not be lost from the mouths of their descendants. For I know what they are inclined to do even now, before I have brought them into the land that I promised them on oath." 22That very day Moses wrote this song and taught it to the Israelites.

23Then the LORD commissioned Joshua son of Nun and said, "Be strong and bold, for you shall bring the Israelites into the land that I promised them; I will be with you."

24When Moses had finished writing down in a book the words of this law to the very end, 25Moses commanded the Levites who carried the ark of the covenant of the LORD, saying, 26"Take this book of the law and put it beside the ark of the covenant of the LORD your God; let it remain there as a witness against you. 27For I know well how rebellious and stubborn you are. If you already have been so rebellious toward the LORD while I am still alive among you, how much more after my death! 28Assemble to me all the elders of your tribes and your officials, so that I may recite these words in their hearing and call heaven and earth to witness against them. 29For I know that after my death you will surely act corruptly, turning aside from the way that I have commanded you. In time to come trouble will befall you, because you will do what is evil in the sight of the LORD, provoking him to anger through the work of your hands."

COMMENTARY

The primary text (31:1-13) covers two basic issues: First, Moses acknowledges to Israel that he is old and will soon die (v. 1). Accordingly, he commissions Joshua as his successor (vv. 1-8).[108] Second, he writes down the law hitherto spoken to Israel (v. 9). This is placed in the custody of the levitical priests (vv. 9-13) with instructions for it to be read every seventh year (v. 10). The two essential concerns are then outlined. The injunction to Israel in 31:13 reads like a suitable final admonition for the book.

However, 31:14–32:44 resumes and repeats both issues concerning the law book and the leadership succession and also a third theme and theological viewpoint relating to the disobedience of Israel. This is then used as a basis for introducing the Song of Moses. The theme of this song is the sovereign greatness of Israel's God, the national disobedience, and Israel's eventual vindication by God. The introduction is in 31:16-22, and the matter of Joshua's succession to leadership is taken up afresh in 31:23, followed by arrangements for the law's preservation. The precise literary and compositional sequence that has led to this unevenness is not wholly clear, although it would certainly appear that the insertion of the Song of Moses at a late stage has disrupted a smooth narrative sequence.

A number of broad literary observations must also be made. It is evident that in its original form the law book of Deuteronomy must have been composed as an independent and self-contained work. At a significant second stage of development, it was adapted to provide the opening section of the history that now stretches across six books from Joshua to 2 Kings. Within this larger literary setting the Mosaic handing over of the leadership of the nation to Joshua became an important issue. Joshua became a link figure who brought together the story of the giving of the law with the story of how the land was conquered.

As a third phase of literary growth, Deuteronomy was once more separated from the historical work and reformulated as the final book of the Pentateuch. It then rounded off the story of Moses' achievements; more important, it made the Pentateuch a kind of constitutional charter for the nation of Israel, given through Moses and completed before Israel entered the land. It thereby applied to everyone included in the covenant, not merely to those living within the land. This point held considerable significance for later generations of Jewish readers.

From a historical and theological perspective the material contained in Deuteronomy 29–34 reflects a number of major issues regarding the nature of religious leadership and of the importance of sacred Scripture as a witness to, and product of, God's revelation to Israel. Moses was the supreme revealer and spokesman of God throughout his lifetime. Yet his inevitable death would remove from Israel this source of guidance and judgment (31:1).

With Moses no longer present in their midst, how would Israel face the future? Who, or what, would replace this divine guidance? Clearly no single person, not even one as obedient and courageous as Joshua, could do so. The primary response to this need is found in the provision of the book of the law that is placed in the custody of the levitical priests. From this time on Israel would be "the people of the book."

One of the implications of this action is that the levitical priests would now take responsibility for teaching and administering the law. However, as we have already seen, the urgent need to teach the commandments of God is made a responsibility of every household (cf. Deut 6:7). All Israel was to be caught up in learning, obeying, and teaching God's commandments. Life after Moses would necessarily, therefore, be of a significantly different order from what it had been while Moses was still alive.

In many respects the more surprising feature of the arrangements made for Israel after the death of Moses is that Joshua is entrusted with national leadership. It might have appeared that the pro-

---

108. G. W. Coats, "Legendary Motifs in the Moses Death Reports," in *A Song of Power and the Power of Song: Essays on the Book of Deuteronomy,* ed. D. L. Christensen, SBT 3 (Winona Lake, Ind.: Eisenbrauns, 1993) 181-91; N. Lohfink, "Die deuteronomistische Darstellung des Übergangs der Führung Israels von Moses auf Josue. Ein Beitrag zur alttestamentlichen Theologie des Amtes," *Studien zum Deuteronomium und zur deuteronomistischen Literatur I,* SBA 8 (Stuttgart: Katholisches Bibelwerk, 1990) 83-97; G. W. Coats, *The Moses Tradition,* JSOTSup 161 (Sheffield: Sheffield Academic, 1993) 76-81; and *Moses: Heroic Man, Man of God,* JSOTSup 57 (Sheffield: Sheffield Academic, 1988) 145-54.

vision of the law book would have made this unnecessary. We can, then, best understand the role of Joshua and the according to him of a leadership role as preparation for the ultimate introduction of a monarchy. The deuteronomic historian then shows how a leadership succession emerged from Moses to Joshua, from Joshua to the judges, and then ultimately to the kingship that finally results in the dynasty of David. This picture accords with the law of the king in Deut 17:14-20, which permits such an institution but views its primary responsibility as one of knowing and administering the Mosaic law.

The provision for the reading of the law every seventh year at the Festival of Booths (31:10) is significant. The interval between readings would appear to be unusually long if such an act were intended as an effective instrument of education. At most it would symbolically demonstrate that the law was a fundamental feature of Israel's faith and worship. Nevertheless, it would seem very probable that the reading of sections of the law in a service of worship, and in particular at the Feast of Booths (Tabernacles) held in the fall of the year, was a feature of the Israelite cultus. Certainly in later Jewish worship the giving of the law on Mt. Sinai (Horeb) came to be the foremost focus for thanksgiving at the fall celebration. Just as worship was an occasion to recall the providential care of God in the past, so also the reading of the law was a way of ensuring that Israel remained mindful of its proper response in the present.

The second of the major provisions in installing Joshua as leader concerned the transition from life in the wilderness (preparation) to life in the land (fulfillment). From a literary perspective we have already noted that this established a narrative continuity between the period of revelation at Horeb and in the plains of Moab and the period of active response in Joshua and all that followed.

A more restrained and hidden motif, however, would also appear to be found in the background to such an action. This concerned the eventual introduction of the monarchy, which the law book permits but does not absolutely require (Deut 17:14-20). There is abundant evidence from the way 1 and 2 Samuel and 1 and 2 Kings deal with the monarchy that the deuteronomic authors viewed the institution very critically. Yet they certainly did not preclude it, provided that it acted

within the confines set by the divine commandments in the law book (Deuteronomy 17: cf. also 1 Kings 2). So Joshua's installation is shown to be a necessity in order to provide Israel with military leadership, a task that is eventually seen as the primary one fulfilled by a king.

The report of the manner of Joshua's installation in 31:7-8, 23 employs a well-established formula, strongly suggesting that it was drawn from a cultic, or possibly a civil, ceremony for such appointments. Certainly behind the rather heavy emphasis placed by the deuteronomic authors on warfare and on Israel's military commitments lies an awareness of the nation's vulnerability to Mesopotamian power during the eighth and seventh centuries. Consistently the unspoken question arises as to how Israel can compensate for this weakness, and the answer given is that God must fight on their behalf. Only with such divine support can Israel match and overpower the strength of its enemies. So Joshua is bidden to be a man of courage and faith, ensuring that both he and all his soldiers are wholly devoted to the LORD God.

The section dealing with the tent of meeting in 31:14-15, 23 shows close parallels to Exod 33:7-11, presenting the tent as a simple sanctuary that the later priestly pentateuchal author has elaborated into the tabernacle. This is a temple in all but name and clearly prefigures the building of the Temple that Israelite tradition recognized as the work of Solomon.

The deuteronomic author here does not go so far as the later priestly writer in elaborating the details of the sanctuary but nevertheless uses the tradition concerning such a tent of meeting to show how the cultus instituted by Moses had been performed before the Temple was built. The emphasis in v. 3 on the assurance that the presence of the LORD will go with Israel has not been fully harmonized with the deuteronomic doctrine that the name of God will make God's presence available. The concern for God's presence with the people was especially relevant in connection with the installation of Joshua as leader since he would have to lead them into battle.

The issue of Moses' succession is further resumed in 34:9 and Josh 1:1-9, where the installation formula is repeated. This repetition has become necessary, as well as that concerning the manner and time of Moses' death, in order to allow for the inclusion of the two major poems, the Song of Moses and the Blessing of Moses, which round off Moses' literary legacy to Israel. The era of Moses is complete before the age of conquest and life in the land can begin. This accords with the literary division between the Pentateuch and the narrative history of the former prophets (Joshua–2 Kings) that follows. The division may appear to be primarily a literary feature, but it had considerable significance for contemporary readers, many of whom, like Moses, now found themselves excluded from the land, either by exile to Babylon and elsewhere or by being forced to flee to other lands for refuge. For such people the land promised to the nation's patriarchal ancestors had once again become a hope for the future rather than a present reality.

The placement of the book of the law in the custody of the levitical priests (31:9, 25-26) placed a responsibility on them to become both its guardians and its administrators. It would certainly appear likely that prominent Levites were among the leading figures of the deuteronomic movement. It would also seem likely that, with such a trust given into their hands, the levitical priests also now assumed a new role as interpreters of the law.

The ruling that the book, or scroll, of the law should be kept beside the ark accords with its functional role, which is how the deuteronomic law book interpreted its significance. God's relationship to Israel was mediated through the covenant rather than through the symbolism of "presence" in a temple and its furnishings. As a visible token that God was "with" Israel the ark

had served in the pre-Temple period as a reminder of the LORD's leadership in battle (cf. Num 10:45-46). By interpreting the central sanctuary as the location of the divine name, the ark had almost become irrelevant save as a container for the scroll of the covenant law. The belief that Israel had neglected such a central role for the law draws forth yet another reminder that the nation could again in the future fail to fulfill the possibilities implicit in its elect covenant status. Future generations "will surely act corruptly, turning aside from the way that I have commanded you" (v. 29).

Such an adverse warning of future apostasy on the part of Israel serves to provide a suitable scene-setting introduction to the Song of Moses (32:1-43). The requirement that the Israel of the future must learn to become "the people of the book" allows the possibility that yet again the people may choose to disobey the covenant commandments. What then? The response to such a question is given in vv. 16-22: Because God will then no longer be able to speak to the people through the law, which they have rejected; instead, they will have to learn through the punishments and disasters that will befall them. This advance warning of Israel's future apostasy then serves to prepare the reader for the message of the Song of Moses. In it, the strongest warnings are given against faithlessness and religious disloyalty. At the same time, and with consummate skill, the poem declares the message of hope that, in spite of future disloyalty, God will ultimately ensure that the people of Israel are vindicated and that they will triumph over their enemies.

REFLECTIONS

Life after Moses would never be the same again! That Moses was about to die becomes an important feature of the book of Deuteronomy. Once Moses was dead and had become a figure of past history, buried in the wilderness before Israel had even crossed the Jordan, a new order would prevail. In a very real sense, it is not only the book of Deuteronomy but also the entire Old Testament that owes its existence to the death of Moses. It was the need for guiding, shaping, and advancing an order of life without Moses that made the writing of the book of the law essential. Had Moses lived forever, then every generation of Israel would have been able to enjoy the benefits of his inspiration and leadership in the same way as had those who had followed him in the wilderness.

The impression left by the biblical accounts of Israel's time spent in the wilderness is that the entire story of the nation would have been very different had Moses been immortal. Later generations would not have been so easily led astray or so willing to abandon their faith and high destiny, had Moses been able to rebuke and chide them as he had done to the faithless generation in the wilderness.

Yet such was not possible, for even the most outstanding of human leaders must die, and the task they have worked at must be carried on by others. So it becomes important that there be a successor to Moses, chosen while Moses was still alive so that he could be introduced to and accepted by the people during Moses' lifetime. Almost certainly this is what took place in later years with Israel's kingship, since the time of transition to a new ruler was fraught with unrest and dangers. A crown prince had to be appointed while the existing ruler was still living in order to secure a smooth transition in the threat of rival claimants.

Yet the situation was different with Moses! A successor, even a man of the stature and skill of Joshua, could not be another Moses. Something irreplaceable would have disappeared from the nation's life. Accordingly it was necessary that special and unique provisions be made so that the teaching and spiritual leadership Moses had given should be preserved in a new way for future generations. This could come about through the writing down of the book of the law, which Moses had personally given in the name of God. Through the preservation and reading of this book of law, Moses would live on. His guidance would be permanently enshrined in a book, which would eventually grow to comprise the five books of Moses, the Pentateuch (Genesis–Deuteronomy). Through them the unique gift of Moses would contribute to each new generation of Israelites. Moses would, in a sense, be contemporary with them all.

Seen in such a light, all biblical religion is built on Torah, "instruction." It is founded on a collection of writings that make possible defiance of death and its destructiveness. It requires scribes, interpreters, and custodians, because it is a faith that requires both literacy and literature. It demands scholars and scholarship, since otherwise the truth once committed to these ancient scrolls would be lost. Both Jews and Christians then become "people of the book" and are able to share in the benefits of the revelation given to Moses.

At many, and probably all, periods of their respective histories, both Jews and Christians have encountered problems from those who have believed that this book-orientation of their religion is irksome and tiresome. Should not religion be free and completely open to wherever the Spirit may lead? Such has been the reasoning of those who have felt constrained by the need for biblical instruction. Yet such freedom has all too often become a byway to disaster, akin to exploring a land without a map.

This is not to decry the need for openness and fresh spiritual leadership, but to recognize the importance of a firm basis of truth enshrined in the belief in God's past revelation to Moses and the prophets and, above all, in Jesus of Nazareth. There is certainly also a danger that the very scrolls and books that make up the Bible have been turned into an unreasoned fetish—symbols of divine action that no longer speak or contain any message by which we can chart life's journey.

In a remarkable manner, the picture set out in Deuteronomy 31 dealing with the arrangements that would become necessary once Moses had died expresses a constantly repeated pattern of faith and understanding. The work of Moses would be enshrined in a book, but there was still a need for continued leadership by new generations of persons like Joshua. The combination of God's order for Israel's future was that the given truth of the law should inspire fresh leadership as represented by Joshua. The book of the law alone would not be sufficient, yet neither would leadership without the law prevail. It would quickly go astray, just as the book of Judges portrays Israel doing once Joshua had passed from the scene.

The balance between the two kinds of authority—the authority of the book and the authority of the charismatic leader—must be firmly kept, even though it cannot be rigidly defined. At times, biblical religion has become "bookish" and textbound, knowing the words of the law but denying its spirit (cf. 2 Cor 3:6). At other times, new prophets of "the Spirit" have arisen, claiming the power and appearance of spiritual leadership, but all too readily going astray by departing from the foundation laid within the biblical text. In a very real way, all subsequent Jewish and Christian experience, both in its high points and in its failures, has been a coming to terms with the fact that Moses is dead.

DEUTERONOMY 31:30–32:52, THE SONG OF MOSES

<table>
<tr><td>NIV</td><td>NRSV</td></tr>
<tr><td>

30And Moses recited the words of this song from beginning to end in the hearing of the whole assembly of Israel:

32 Listen, O heavens, and I will speak; hear, O earth, the words of my mouth.
2Let my teaching fall like rain
    and my words descend like dew,
like showers on new grass,
    like abundant rain on tender plants.

3I will proclaim the name of the LORD.
    Oh, praise the greatness of our God!
4He is the Rock, his works are perfect,
    and all his ways are just.
A faithful God who does no wrong,
    upright and just is he.

5They have acted corruptly toward him;
    to their shame they are no longer his
        children,
    but a warped and crooked generation.*a*
6Is this the way you repay the LORD,
    O foolish and unwise people?
Is he not your Father, your Creator,*b*
    who made you and formed you?

7Remember the days of old;
    consider the generations long past.
Ask your father and he will tell you,
    your elders, and they will explain to you.
8When the Most High gave the nations their
        inheritance,
    when he divided all mankind,
he set up boundaries for the peoples
    according to the number of the sons of
        Israel.*c*
9For the LORD's portion is his people,
    Jacob his allotted inheritance.

</td><td>

30Then Moses recited the words of this song, to the very end, in the hearing of the whole assembly of Israel:

32 Give ear, O heavens, and I will speak; let the earth hear the words of my mouth.
2 May my teaching drop like the rain,
    my speech condense like the dew;
like gentle rain on grass,
    like showers on new growth.
3 For I will proclaim the name of the LORD;
    ascribe greatness to our God!

4 The Rock, his work is perfect,
    and all his ways are just.
A faithful God, without deceit,
    just and upright is he;
5 yet his degenerate children have dealt
        falsely with him,*a*
    a perverse and crooked generation.
6 Do you thus repay the LORD,
    O foolish and senseless people?
Is not he your father, who created you,
    who made you and established you?
7 Remember the days of old,
    consider the years long past;
ask your father, and he will inform you;
    your elders, and they will tell you.
8 When the Most High*b* apportioned the
        nations,
    when he divided humankind,
he fixed the boundaries of the peoples
    according to the number of the gods;*c*
9 the LORD's own portion was his people,
    Jacob his allotted share.

10 He sustained*d* him in a desert land,

</td></tr>
</table>

a5 Or Corrupt are they and not his children, / a generation warped and twisted to their shame *b6 Or Father, who bought you* *c8 Masoretic Text; Dead Sea Scrolls (see also Septuagint) sons of God*

a Meaning of Heb uncertain *b Traditional rendering of Heb Elyon* *c Q Ms Compare Gk Tg: MT the Israelites* *d Sam Gk Compare Tg: MT found*

NIV

¹⁰In a desert land he found him,
 in a barren and howling waste.
He shielded him and cared for him;
 he guarded him as the apple of his eye,
¹¹like an eagle that stirs up its nest
 and hovers over its young,
that spreads its wings to catch them
 and carries them on its pinions.
¹²The LORD alone led him;
 no foreign god was with him.

¹³He made him ride on the heights of the land
 and fed him with the fruit of the fields.
He nourished him with honey from the rock,
 and with oil from the flinty crag,
¹⁴with curds and milk from herd and flock
 and with fattened lambs and goats,
with choice rams of Bashan
 and the finest kernels of wheat.
You drank the foaming blood of the grape.

¹⁵Jeshurunᵃ grew fat and kicked;
 filled with food, he became heavy and
  sleek.
He abandoned the God who made him
 and rejected the Rock his Savior.
¹⁶They made him jealous with their foreign gods
 and angered him with their detestable idols.
¹⁷They sacrificed to demons, which are not
  God—
 gods they had not known,
 gods that recently appeared,
 gods your fathers did not fear.
¹⁸You deserted the Rock, who fathered you;
 you forgot the God who gave you birth.

¹⁹The LORD saw this and rejected them
 because he was angered by his sons and
  daughters.
²⁰"I will hide my face from them," he said,
 "and see what their end will be;
for they are a perverse generation,
 children who are unfaithful.
²¹They made me jealous by what is no god
 and angered me with their worthless idols.
I will make them envious by those who are
  not a people;
I will make them angry by a nation that
  has no understanding.

ᵃ15 *Jeshurun* means *the upright one*, that is, Israel.

NRSV

 in a howling wilderness waste;
he shielded him, cared for him,
 guarded him as the apple of his eye.
¹¹ As an eagle stirs up its nest,
 and hovers over its young;
as it spreads its wings, takes them up,
 and bears them aloft on its pinions,
¹² the LORD alone guided him;
 no foreign god was with him.
¹³ He set him atop the heights of the land,
 and fed him withᵃ produce of the field;
he nursed him with honey from the crags,
 with oil from flinty rock;
¹⁴ curds from the herd, and milk from the flock,
 with fat of lambs and rams;
Bashan bulls and goats,
 together with the choicest wheat—
 you drank fine wine from the blood of
  grapes.
¹⁵ Jacob ate his fill;ᵇ
 Jeshurun grew fat, and kicked.
 You grew fat, bloated, and gorged!
He abandoned God who made him,
 and scoffed at the Rock of his salvation.
¹⁶ They made him jealous with strange gods,
 with abhorrent things they provoked him.
¹⁷ They sacrificed to demons, not God,
 to deities they had never known,
to new ones recently arrived,
 whom your ancestors had not feared.
¹⁸ You were unmindful of the Rock that bore
  you;ᶜ
 you forgot the God who gave you birth.

¹⁹ The LORD saw it, and was jealous;ᵈ
 he spurnedᵉ his sons and daughters.
²⁰ He said: I will hide my face from them,
 I will see what their end will be;
for they are a perverse generation,
 children in whom there is no faithfulness.
²¹ They made me jealous with what is no god,
 provoked me with their idols.
So I will make them jealous with what is
  no people,
 provoke them with a foolish nation.
²² For a fire is kindled by my anger,

ᵃ Sam Gk Syr Tg: MT *he ate*   ᵇ Q Mss Sam Gk: MT lacks *Jacob ate his fill*   ᶜ Or *that begot you*   ᵈ Q Mss Gk: MT lacks *was jealous*   ᵉ Cn: Heb *he spurned because of provocation*

NIV

²²For a fire has been kindled by my wrath,
  one that burns to the realm of death[a]
    below.
It will devour the earth and its harvests
  and set afire the foundations of the
    mountains.

²³"I will heap calamities upon them
  and spend my arrows against them.
²⁴I will send wasting famine against them,
  consuming pestilence and deadly plague;
I will send against them the fangs of wild beasts,
  the venom of vipers that glide in the dust.
²⁵In the street the sword will make them
    childless;
  in their homes terror will reign.
Young men and young women will perish,
  infants and gray-haired men.
²⁶I said I would scatter them
  and blot out their memory from mankind,
²⁷but I dreaded the taunt of the enemy,
  lest the adversary misunderstand
and say, 'Our hand has triumphed;
  the LORD has not done all this.'"

²⁸They are a nation without sense,
  there is no discernment in them.
²⁹If only they were wise and would understand
    this
  and discern what their end will be!
³⁰How could one man chase a thousand,
  or two put ten thousand to flight,
unless their Rock had sold them,
  unless the LORD had given them up?
³¹For their rock is not like our Rock,
  as even our enemies concede.
³²Their vine comes from the vine of Sodom
  and from the fields of Gomorrah.
Their grapes are filled with poison,
  and their clusters with bitterness.
³³Their wine is the venom of serpents,
  the deadly poison of cobras.

³⁴"Have I not kept this in reserve
  and sealed it in my vaults?
³⁵It is mine to avenge; I will repay.
  In due time their foot will slip;
their day of disaster is near
  and their doom rushes upon them."

^a22 Hebrew *to Sheol*

NRSV

  and burns to the depths of Sheol;
it devours the earth and its increase,
  and sets on fire the foundations of the
    mountains.
²³ I will heap disasters upon them,
  spend my arrows against them:
²⁴ wasting hunger,
    burning consumption,
    bitter pestilence.
The teeth of beasts I will send against them,
  with venom of things crawling in the
    dust.
²⁵ In the street the sword shall bereave,
  and in the chambers terror,
for young man and woman alike,
  nursing child and old gray head.
²⁶ I thought to scatter them[a]
  and blot out the memory of them from
    humankind;
²⁷ but I feared provocation by the enemy,
  for their adversaries might misunderstand
and say, "Our hand is triumphant;
  it was not the LORD who did all this."

²⁸ They are a nation void of sense;
  there is no understanding in them.
²⁹ If they were wise, they would understand
    this;
  they would discern what the end would
    be.
³⁰ How could one have routed a thousand,
  and two put a myriad to flight,
unless their Rock had sold them,
  the LORD had given them up?
³¹ Indeed their rock is not like our Rock;
  our enemies are fools.[a]
³² Their vine comes from the vinestock of Sodom,
  from the vineyards of Gomorrah;
their grapes are grapes of poison,
  their clusters are bitter;
³³ their wine is the poison of serpents,
  the cruel venom of asps.

³⁴ Is not this laid up in store with me,
  sealed up in my treasuries?
³⁵ Vengeance is mine, and recompense,
  for the time when their foot shall slip;

^a Gk: Meaning of Heb uncertain

NIV

36The LORD will judge his people
    and have compassion on his servants
when he sees their strength is gone
    and no one is left, slave or free.
37He will say: "Now where are their gods,
    the rock they took refuge in,
38the gods who ate the fat of their sacrifices
    and drank the wine of their drink offerings?
Let them rise up to help you!
Let them give you shelter!

39"See now that I myself am He!
    There is no god besides me.
I put to death and I bring to life,
    I have wounded and I will heal,
    and no one can deliver out of my hand.
40I lift my hand to heaven and declare:
    As surely as I live forever,
41when I sharpen my flashing sword
    and my hand grasps it in judgment,
I will take vengeance on my adversaries
    and repay those who hate me.
42I will make my arrows drunk with blood,
    while my sword devours flesh:
    the blood of the slain and the captives,
    the heads of the enemy leaders."

43Rejoice, O nations, with his people,*a, b*
    for he will avenge the blood of his servants;
he will take vengeance on his enemies
    and make atonement for his land and
        people.

44Moses came with Joshua*c* son of Nun and spoke all the words of this song in the hearing of the people. 45When Moses finished reciting all these words to all Israel, 46he said to them, "Take to heart all the words I have solemnly declared to you this day, so that you may command your children to obey carefully all the words of this law. 47They are not just idle words for you—they are your life. By them you will live long in the land you are crossing the Jordan to possess."

48On that same day the LORD told Moses, 49"Go up into the Abarim Range to Mount Nebo in Moab, across from Jericho, and view Canaan, the land I am giving the Israelites as their own possession. 50There on the mountain that you have

NRSV

because the day of their calamity is at hand,
    their doom comes swiftly.

36 Indeed the LORD will vindicate his people,
    have compassion on his servants,
when he sees that their power is gone,
    neither bond nor free remaining.
37 Then he will say: Where are their gods,
    the rock in which they took refuge,
38 who ate the fat of their sacrifices,
    and drank the wine of their libations?
Let them rise up and help you,
    let them be your protection!

39 See now that I, even I, am he;
    there is no god besides me.
I kill and I make alive;
    I wound and I heal;
    and no one can deliver from my hand.
40 For I lift up my hand to heaven,
    and swear: As I live forever,
41 when I whet my flashing sword,
    and my hand takes hold on judgment;
I will take vengeance on my adversaries,
    and will repay those who hate me.
42 I will make my arrows drunk with blood,
    and my sword shall devour flesh—
with the blood of the slain and the captives,
    from the long-haired enemy.

43 Praise, O heavens,*a* his people,
    worship him, all you gods!*b*
For he will avenge the blood of his
        children,*c*
    and take vengeance on his adversaries;
he will repay those who hate him,*b*
    and cleanse the land for his people.*d*

44Moses came and recited all the words of this song in the hearing of the people, he and Joshua*e* son of Nun. 45When Moses had finished reciting all these words to all Israel, 46he said to them: "Take to heart all the words that I am giving in witness against you today; give them as a command to your children, so that they may diligently observe all the words of this law. 47This is no trifling matter for you, but rather your very life;

---

a43 Or *Make his people rejoice, O nations*   b43 Masoretic Text; Dead Sea Scrolls (see also Septuagint) *people, / and let all the angels worship him /*   c44 Hebrew *Hoshea,* a variant of *Joshua*

a Q Ms Gk: MT *nations*   b Q Ms Gk: MT lacks this line   c Q Ms Gk: MT *his servants*   d Q Ms Sam Gk Vg: MT *his land his people*   e Sam Gk Syr Vg: MT *Hoshea*

NIV

climbed you will die and be gathered to your people, just as your brother Aaron died on Mount Hor and was gathered to his people. [51]This is because both of you broke faith with me in the presence of the Israelites at the waters of Meribah Kadesh in the Desert of Zin and because you did not uphold my holiness among the Israelites. [52]Therefore, you will see the land only from a distance; you will not enter the land I am giving to the people of Israel."

NRSV

through it you may live long in the land that you are crossing over the Jordan to possess."

48On that very day the LORD addressed Moses as follows: [49]"Ascend this mountain of the Abarim, Mount Nebo, which is in the land of Moab, across from Jericho, and view the land of Canaan, which I am giving to the Israelites for a possession; [50]you shall die there on the mountain that you ascend and shall be gathered to your kin, as your brother Aaron died on Mount Hor and was gathered to his kin; [51]because both of you broke faith with me among the Israelites at the waters of Meribath-kadesh in the wilderness of Zin, by failing to maintain my holiness among the Israelites. [52]Although you may view the land from a distance, you shall not enter it—the land that I am giving to the Israelites."

COMMENTARY

The poem of 32:1-43, which forms the Song of Moses, has already been introduced in 31:16-22, so that 31:30 links back to 31:22. The narrative continuation in 32:44-52 then resumes the report of the arrangements for Moses' death and tells of how the great leader was refused permission by God to enter the land, but was instead allowed to ascend Mt. Nebo in order to see it.

The song must certainly have been composed as an independent unit and, as its literary setting shows, has been incorporated into the book at a late stage. In vocabulary and style, it is a composition of a very different type from the legal and hortatory addresses of Deuteronomy, being highly poetic in its imagery. Nevertheless its inclusion rests on its suitability as a further warning to Israel against continued disobedience and apostasy. Its concluding message of hope that Israel, in spite of its unfaithfulness, will ultimately be vindicated by God conveys an important additional perspective to the deuteronomic viewpoint. The impact of the repeated warnings and curses could have left an expectation of the future that was ultimately negative and threatening. Instead, the song brings an assurance of Israel's ultimate triumph among the nations.

Literary Form. The basic imagery and form

of the song are that of the presentation of a lawsuit, modeled closely on features that would have characterized the presentation of a case in a court of law. Both the chosen vocabulary and the speech forms adhere to this purported setting in bringing an indictment against Israel. This is then abandoned at 32:28 when the narrator, who assumes divine authority, turns to accuse the nations of misunderstanding. Finally, in 32:39-42 a verdict is declared against these unnamed nations who have been guilty of foolishness and wanton violence. A concluding summons to the gods of the nations to praise the LORD in 32:43 then reaffirms the divine plan to cleanse the land.

The fact that it is initially the nation of Israel that is indicted invites comparison with the use of a similar lawsuit form by certain prophets (e.g., Isaiah 1). In turn, this prophetic usage invites comparison with the form of international vassal treaties, which set out in a formal legal manner the requirements imposed on a vassal by his sovereign overlord. It displays a distinctively set form. However, all the indications are that the song here is a distinctive artistic composition that has simply used the basic lawsuit form, with which most readers would have been familiar, for rhetorical purposes. It presumes that God is both judge and plaintiff, and it accuses both Israel and foreign nations. The use of the lawsuit form provides the basis for an effectively reasoned challenge against Israel, but then turns to make it a reason for hope by its assurance of vindication over the nations. Overall there are some similarities with the didactic style of the wisdom literature as well as with the use of legal language by Israel's prophets in justifying threats against Israel.

Time of Origin. So far as the time of composition of the song is concerned, it is evident from the references to Israel's misfortunes and defeats in battle (vv. 22-33) that a long and painful history has confirmed the seriousness of the warnings against apostasy that have already been given. Israel has proved itself disobedient, and defeats and sufferings have already come (vv. 23-24). But precise details of how Israel has been defeated, or by whom, are lacking, and the impression is created that it is a situation that has existed for some time.

A primary purpose of the song is to provide assurance that punishment will eventually come to Israel's enemies, who have tormented and ravaged the land. The time for this punishment is held to be not far off. It seems likely that the poem was originally composed independently, almost certainly in the post-exilic age, and very possibly at a time when Deuteronomy had come to form the final part of the Pentateuch. If this is the case, then the ascription to Moses (31:22) can only be understood as a literary device that has used the figure of the great leader to stress the authority and relevance of the message the song contains. Its appropriateness lies in its message of Israel's vindication.

Formal Structure. The highly poetic form of the song means that it poses many problems for the translator as a consequence of textual uncertainties. It makes full use of the prophetic device in which God speaks directly in the first person, declaring what the present situation is and what is about to happen. At other points, it adopts a distinctly wisdom didactic manner. All told, this mixing of formal rhetorical speech forms with an incomplete adoption of a trial scene points to an author well versed in literary poetic skills.

Content. The song divides into separate units, with a major turning point between v. 27 and v. 28, where the speaker turns to rebuke Israel's enemies. They are accused of failing to understand

what has really happened when they have inflicted torment and misfortune upon Israel. God then declares that the time for action against these enemies will soon come, which will lead to Israel's vindication. A concluding appeal to the gods of the defeated nations to praise the LORD is made in v. 43, rounding off the note of assurance that, in spite of present appearances, God will vindicate the people.

32:1-9. God is Israel's Creator and Sustainer. Yet the people are accused of having forgotten this fact and have dealt treacherously against their divine benefactor. They have abused the divine care. All the more is this a punishable offense because Israel was the most favored of all nations from the time of its creation (vv. 8-9). The title used for God in v. 8, "Most High" (עליון, 'elyôn), refers to the LORD God, but was an ancient title that could be used to celebrate any divine power who sat at the head of a pantheon of gods. It has been chosen here to give poetic expression to the mythical idea of many deities, of which the LORD was head, with Israel being uniquely the LORD's people and the lesser deities acting as guardians of other nations. The NRSV follows the text of a Qumran fragment and of the Septuagint. It reflects a belief that there were many gods for other nations, with the LORD being only the chief among them. Later scribal objections to this use of a polytheistic idea, even for poetic purposes, has occasioned the variant readings of v. 8 (see the NRSV's marginal note).

32:10-18. The affirmation of the LORD's unique providential care of Israel moves on to the theme of the years spent wandering through the wilderness and the miraculous manner in which the survival of Israel was ensured. The author views the entire wilderness experience as one demonstrating the total sufficiency of God's care for the people. The traditional stories of how the people were fed with manna and quail from the skies and water from the rock have been made the subject of poetic hyperbole in v. 13. They are then linked in v. 14 to the richness of Israel's land. The rare name "Jeshurun" for Israel (v. 15; cf. 33:5, 26; Isa 44:2) makes an apparent verbal play on the concept of uprightness. Yet Israel has turned its back on God through complacency, taking for granted the richness and sufficiency of the land and provoking God to anger by turning to worship false gods and demons (vv. 16-17).

32:19-27. Having seen how the people have responded to the care lavished upon them, God determines that they must be punished in order to bring them to their senses. The form this punishment will take is then determined as attacks by unnamed enemies, who are described as "no people" and "a foolish nation" (v. 21). We can only assume that a succession of foreign invaders is intended here (Assyria, Babylon, Persia) and that the titles are deliberately derogatory. That it is the work of God is explicitly shown by being spoken throughout by the poet in the first person, assuming the role of both creator and judge. In a subtle change of theme, God pauses to reflect that the punishment of Israel may be misunderstood as a mark of divine weakness, thereby demanding that further action be taken to dispel such a mistaken view (v. 27).

32:28-32. The theme that Israel's enemies are "a foolish people" is further explored in vv. 28-31 by showing that the exaggerated and arrogant nature of their claims cannot possibly be true (v. 30). Imagery of God as Israel's "Rock" (צור *sûr*) and the poetic assurances that God will give stunning victories to those who put their trust in divine aid are all turned around. Because this has not happened, then it can only be that God has been angry with Israel, not because the divine power is inadequate to meet such demands.

32:33-38. These verses then turn sharply against the enemies for their cruel and wanton behavior. At this point the poem indulges in a degree of moral inconsistency. God has had to use these cruel enemies to punish Israel, but will now turn to exact vengeance on them for their own false religion (v. 37). The gods who guide these nations, like guardian angels, will appear to be greater than the LORD! Then it will be Israel's turn to be the object of divine compassion (v. 36). Great play is now made of the emptiness and powerlessness of the gods of the nations, who can do nothing to protect them from the vengeance of the LORD God. At this point, the claims of "the gods of the nations," which were alluded to in v. 8, are shown to be worthless, demonstrating that in reality these are no gods at all.

32:39-43. The final unit of the Song of Moses (vv. 39-42) makes a forthright declaration that the

LORD has complete power over all peoples so that when the time comes for vengeance upon Israel's enemies, this power will prove to be unstoppable. An unexplained feature arises in the description of the enemy as "the long-haired enemy." The reference may be not to a particular physical characteristic, but to the fact that warriors wore their hair long as a mark of consecration or as a sign of leadership. The final summons to praise in v. 43 is startling in calling upon the heavens to praise God's people and in summoning all the lesser gods to worship the LORD.

32:44-52. This short unit summarizes the challenging and admonitory element contained in the Song of Moses (vv. 44-47). It warns that the threat of apostasy on the part of Israel is real ("no trifling matter") and that failure to take the warning to heart could jeopardize Israel's continued settlement of the land. From the writer's viewpoint, these were eventualities that had already become real and serious threats. The narrative of vv. 48-52 then picks up the announcement from 31:21 that Moses had brought the people to the very border of the promised land.

The story of how Moses ascended Mt. Nebo to view the promised land, now being fully aware that he would not be allowed to enter it, contains a number of instructive features. Most prominent is the warning that Moses was not to be allowed to enter the land because he had broken faith with God. In 3:26, the author firmly stated that Moses was innocent of doubting God and that it was the people who had sinned. However, the priestly writer of Num 20:1-13 has developed the notion that Moses, too, had been led to question whether God could bring water from the rock. Therefore, he had been led to sin against God. The accusation that Moses had failed to maintain the divine holiness among the Israelites appears to have called for a deliberate play upon the name of Meribath-kadesh (cf. Num 20:13, 24; 27:14). This form of the name for the oasis of Kadesh appears as a priestly coining, probably because it was the location where conflict and contention (מריבה *měrîbâ*) had arisen. Historically the name almost certainly owes its origin to the fact that disputes were brought there for judgment. In this unexpected charge against Moses, it is taken to imply that he had been contentious over the matter of holiness.

The author here has undoubtedly been influenced by the priestly tradition, using the brief note here to record Moses' offense, which serves to reinforce the connection between sinning against the LORD and taking possession of the land. The close literary link with the priestly (P) tradition of the Pentateuch indicates the late stage at which the note has been brought in here, almost certainly when the book of Deuteronomy had been combined with Genesis–Numbers to form the closing chapter of the story of Israel's beginnings.

From the reader's perspective, Moses' exclusion from the land had undoubtedly become a major issue in view of the seeming hopelessness of the situation for those who had been exiled from their homeland. The recollection of the tradition that Moses himself had been denied entry into the land gave a dimension of hope and encouragement for its repossession.

❖ ❖ ❖ ❖

EXCURSUS: MONOTHEISM AND THE SONG OF MOSES

The theme that permeates the theological message of the Song of Moses (Deut 32:1-43) is that of monotheism. God is one, and there is no other who is comparable in power or purpose. In a strictly formal sense, the poem does not declare a monotheistic faith, for it repeatedly refers to the existence of other deities besides the LORD God of Israel. They first appear in 32:8 as the guardians of the non-Israelite nations, with each one being allocated a particular nation and territory to watch over. They reemerge in 32:16 as "strange gods" and in the following verse as "deities they had never known" and "new ones recently arrived." In the context of the deuteronomic religious polemic, such a dismissive charge fits rather awkwardly, since the primary accusation concerning the deities Israel was repeatedly tempted to worship is that they were the gods of the former occupants of the land. The primary point is that all such gods are weak and powerless beside the God of Israel, and they must submit to the will and purpose of the LORD. All of this is already conveyed in the opening section, where an early form of a creation myth is alluded to in which the Most High God (the LORD) is the primary creator figure, using the lesser gods as servants.

The gods worshiped by other peoples are referred to again in 32:37 and in the final summons to praise in 32:43. Such references appear to conflict with the declaration of a more absolute monotheistic faith in 32:39, which denies any power at all to other gods. We may regard the tension that arises between faith in one absolute deity and the belief that other gods have a relative degree of authority apportioned them by the Most High God as partly poetic hyperbole and partly a desire to show how weak other gods really are. It can be argued that if other nations believe their gods exist, then in some sense they do exist for them. The poet does not finally resolve the issue, but uses the idea of non-Israelite gods in order to emphasize to the fullest possible extent the absolute power of the LORD (cf. Ps 96:4-5).

It may at first glance appear to be a somewhat unexpected development that the Song of Moses, the great architect of Israel's faith, should be equivocal over the question of monotheism and whether other gods besides the LORD have real existence. Yet such an inference is more apparent than real, because the direction of this poem is to show the sovereign power of the LORD in all the history of Israel. When things went well for Israel, it was because God was showing mercy to the people. When things went badly, it was because it was necessary that they be punished.

Yet these other nations rashly assumed that their gods were greater and more powerful than the LORD God of Israel (32:27). Such was certainly not the case, but merely a foolish misunderstanding, for, in fact, no god is greater than the LORD God of Israel. Because this is true, then ultimately the power of this God will prevail on earth, bringing judgment over Israel's enemies and providing vindication for Israel.

A subordinate theme of the poem is the relationship between many gods and many nations. The conventional mythical perspective in which each nation has its own deity is assumed in 32:8, so that the various competing claims among them for precedence are assumed to have a measure of validity.[109] Yet this can only on the surface seem to be the case, but cannot be so in reality. Once it is admitted that one God is superior to all other gods, then these others cannot be gods at all. They must be mere idols, since the very essence of divinity is the concept of creative power. Once that creative power is made subordinate and relative to a superior power, then these so-called deities are reduced to mere appearances. So, by a rather historical form of polemic, the poet insists that there can only be one true God.

The debate over one God or many, which reverberates through the Old Testament, can be reduced to a rather arid and abstract debate about theories and speculations. More relevant is the question of a single all-powerful and all-encompassing divine will that controls the universe. That there should be lesser powers (sons of gods, demons, idols, no gods) then becomes irrelevant. It is the issue of the sovereignty of the LORD God of Israel that is so majestically argued for in this song.

---

109. The importance of such a belief for the rise of nation-states in the ancient Near East is shown by Daniel I. Block, *The Gods of the Nations: Studies in Near Eastern National Theology* (Winona Lake, Ind.: Eisenbrauns, 1988).

❖   ❖   ❖   ❖

REFLECTIONS

There is a consistent undercurrent of practicality about the faith expressed in this poem. Although it employs the formal language concerning God and the divine power as Creator, it focuses all such faith on more immediately knowable and practical issues. These concern the way in which Israel saw itself and its situation. That the latter was a time of frustration, tension, and suffering is readily apparent. In highly poetic language, Israel's present time of crisis is echoed in 32:24-25. Bitter pestilence and "the teeth of beasts" have been sent against the people. There is no respect of person, either on the grounds of age or gender (32:25). The hidden question in such experiences is, Why has God allowed this to happen? The poem's answer is to argue that it had become necessary for a time, but that the time would soon pass. Rather than abandon faith in God's control over events, the author believes that it is possible to explain them in terms of the complex character of God. The divine will for the loyalty and uprightness of Israel had to be combined with the belief that Israel's enemies were God's enemies, too, and must eventually be punished. So the issue of monotheism, which can easily slip back into becoming sterile and theoretical, must be rescued from this by focusing on the way in which it helps to explain the mixed and complex nature of the way we experience life. It is far better that we retain a sense of the oneness and wholeness of human history and human experience, than that we seek to explain away its varied faces by supposing that rivalries and conflicts between a multitude of gods are their cause.

DEUTERONOMY 33:1-29, THE BLESSING OF MOSES

33 This is the blessing that Moses the man of God pronounced on the Israelites before his death. [2]He said:

"The LORD came from Sinai
　and dawned over them from Seir;
　he shone forth from Mount Paran.
He came with[a] myriads of holy ones
　from the south, from his mountain slopes.[b]
[3]Surely it is you who love the people;
　all the holy ones are in your hand.
At your feet they all bow down,
　and from you receive instruction,
[4]the law that Moses gave us,
　the possession of the assembly of Jacob.
[5]He was king over Jeshurun[c]
　when the leaders of the people assembled,
　along with the tribes of Israel.

[6]"Let Reuben live and not die,
　nor[d] his men be few."

[7]And this he said about Judah:

"Hear, O LORD, the cry of Judah;
　bring him to his people.
With his own hands he defends his cause.
　Oh, be his help against his foes!"
[8]About Levi he said:

"Your Thummim and Urim belong
　to the man you favored.
You tested him at Massah;
　you contended with him at the waters of
　　Meribah.
[9]He said of his father and mother,
　'I have no regard for them.'
He did not recognize his brothers
　or acknowledge his own children,
but he watched over your word
　and guarded your covenant.
[10]He teaches your precepts to Jacob
　and your law to Israel.
He offers incense before you
　and whole burnt offerings on your altar.
[11]Bless all his skills, O LORD,

---

a2 Or from   b2 The meaning of the Hebrew for this phrase is uncertain.   c5 Jeshurun means the upright one, that is, Israel; also in verse 26.   d6 Or but let

33 This is the blessing with which Moses, the man of God, blessed the Israelites before his death. [2]He said:

The LORD came from Sinai,
　and dawned from Seir upon us;[a]
　he shone forth from Mount Paran.
With him were myriads of holy ones;[b]
　at his right, a host of his own.[c]
[3] Indeed, O favorite among[d] peoples,
　all his holy ones were in your charge;
they marched at your heels,
　accepted direction from you.
[4] Moses charged us with the law,
　as a possession for the assembly of Jacob.
[5] There arose a king in Jeshurun,
　when the leaders of the people
　　assembled—
　the united tribes of Israel.

[6] May Reuben live, and not die out,
　even though his numbers are few.

[7]And this he said of Judah:

O LORD, give heed to Judah,
　and bring him to his people;
strengthen his hands for him,[e]
　and be a help against his adversaries.

[8]And of Levi he said:

Give to Levi[f] your Thummim,
　and your Urim to your loyal one,
whom you tested at Massah,
　with whom you contended at the waters
　　of Meribah;
[9] who said of his father and mother,
　"I regard them not";
he ignored his kin,
　and did not acknowledge his children.
For they observed your word,
　and kept your covenant.
[10] They teach Jacob your ordinances,

---

a Gk Syr Vg Compare Tg: Heb upon them   b Cn Compare Gk Sam Syr Vg: MT He came from Ribeboth-kodesh,   c Cn Compare Gk: meaning of Heb uncertain   d Or O lover of the   e Cn: Heb with his hands he contended   f Q Ms Gk: MT lacks Give to Levi

NIV

and be pleased with the work of his hands.
Smite the loins of those who rise up against
  him;
  strike his foes till they rise no more."

¹²About Benjamin he said:

"Let the beloved of the LORD rest secure in
  him,
  for he shields him all day long,
  and the one the LORD loves rests between
    his shoulders."

¹³About Joseph he said:

"May the LORD bless his land
  with the precious dew from heaven above
  and with the deep waters that lie below;
¹⁴with the best the sun brings forth
  and the finest the moon can yield;
¹⁵with the choicest gifts of the ancient
    mountains
  and the fruitfulness of the everlasting hills;
¹⁶with the best gifts of the earth and its fullness
  and the favor of him who dwelt in the
    burning bush.
Let all these rest on the head of Joseph,
  on the brow of the prince among*a* his
    brothers.

¹⁷In majesty he is like a firstborn bull;
  his horns are the horns of a wild ox.
With them he will gore the nations,
  even those at the ends of the earth.
Such are the ten thousands of Ephraim;
  such are the thousands of Manasseh."

¹⁸About Zebulun he said:

"Rejoice, Zebulun, in your going out,
  and you, Issachar, in your tents.
¹⁹They will summon peoples to the mountain
  and there offer sacrifices of righteousness;
they will feast on the abundance of the seas,
  on the treasures hidden in the sand."

²⁰About Gad he said:

"Blessed is he who enlarges Gad's domain!
  Gad lives there like a lion,
  tearing at arm or head.
²¹He chose the best land for himself;
  the leader's portion was kept for him.
When the heads of the people assembled,
  he carried out the LORD's righteous will,
  and his judgments concerning Israel."

a16 Or of the one separated from

NRSV

and Israel your law;
  they place incense before you,
  and whole burnt offerings on your altar.
¹¹ Bless, O LORD, his substance,
  and accept the work of his hands;
crush the loins of his adversaries,
  of those that hate him, so that they do
    not rise again.

¹²Of Benjamin he said:

The beloved of the LORD rests in safety—
  the High God*a* surrounds him all day long—
  the beloved*b* rests between his shoulders.

¹³And of Joseph he said:

Blessed by the LORD be his land,
  with the choice gifts of heaven above,
  and of the deep that lies beneath;
¹⁴ with the choice fruits of the sun,
  and the rich yield of the months;
¹⁵ with the finest produce of the ancient
    mountains,
  and the abundance of the everlasting hills;
¹⁶ with the choice gifts of the earth and its
    fullness,
  and the favor of the one who dwells on
    Sinai.*c*
Let these come on the head of Joseph,
  on the brow of the prince among his
    brothers.

¹⁷ A firstborn*d* bull—majesty is his!
  His horns are the horns of a wild ox;
with them he gores the peoples,
  driving them to*e* the ends of the earth;
such are the myriads of Ephraim,
  such the thousands of Manasseh.

¹⁸And of Zebulun he said:

Rejoice, Zebulun, in your going out;
  and Issachar, in your tents.
¹⁹ They call peoples to the mountain;
  there they offer the right sacrifices;
for they suck the affluence of the seas
  and the hidden treasures of the sand.

²⁰And of Gad he said:

Blessed be the enlargement of Gad!

*a Heb above him   b Heb he   c Cn: Heb in the bush   d Q Ms
Gk Syr Vg: MT His firstborn   e Cn: Heb the peoples, together*

NIV

²²About Dan he said:

"Dan is a lion's cub,
    springing out of Bashan."
²³About Naphtali he said:
"Naphtali is abounding with the favor of the
    LORD
and is full of his blessing;
    he will inherit southward to the lake."
²⁴About Asher he said:
"Most blessed of sons is Asher;
    let him be favored by his brothers,
    and let him bathe his feet in oil.
²⁵The bolts of your gates will be iron and
        bronze,
    and your strength will equal your days.

²⁶"There is no one like the God of Jeshurun,
    who rides on the heavens to help you
    and on the clouds in his majesty.
²⁷The eternal God is your refuge,
    and underneath are the everlasting arms.
He will drive out your enemy before you,
    saying, 'Destroy him!'
²⁸So Israel will live in safety alone;
    Jacob's spring is secure
in a land of grain and new wine,
    where the heavens drop dew.
²⁹Blessed are you, O Israel!
    Who is like you,
    a people saved by the LORD?
He is your shield and helper
    and your glorious sword.
Your enemies will cower before you,
    and you will trample down their high
        places.^a"

^a29 Or *will tread upon their bodies*

NRSV

Gad lives like a lion;
    he tears at arm and scalp.
²¹ He chose the best for himself,
    for there a commander's allotment was
        reserved;
he came at the head of the people,
    he executed the justice of the LORD,
    and his ordinances for Israel.

²²And of Dan he said:
    Dan is a lion's whelp
        that leaps forth from Bashan.

²³And of Naphtali he said:
    O Naphtali, sated with favor,
        full of the blessing of the LORD,
        possess the west and the south.

²⁴And of Asher he said:
    Most blessed of sons be Asher;
        may he be the favorite of his brothers,
        and may he dip his foot in oil.
²⁵ Your bars are iron and bronze;
        and as your days, so is your strength.

²⁶ There is none like God, O Jeshurun,
        who rides through the heavens to your
            help,
        majestic through the skies.
²⁷ He subdues the ancient gods,^a
        shatters^b the forces of old;^c
he drove out the enemy before you,
        and said, "Destroy!"
²⁸ So Israel lives in safety,
        untroubled is Jacob's abode^d
in a land of grain and wine,
        where the heavens drop down dew.
²⁹ Happy are you, O Israel! Who is like you,
        a people saved by the LORD,
    the shield of your help,
        and the sword of your triumph!
Your enemies shall come fawning to you,
        and you shall tread on their backs.

^a Or *The eternal God is a dwelling place*   ^b Cn: Heb *from underneath*   ^c Or *the everlasting arms*   ^d Or *fountain*

COMMENTARY

Another poem is brought in as the final utterance of Moses, through which he is able to survey and to "bless" all the future generations of Israelites. It bears close comparison with the similar blessing of Jacob in Gen 49:1-28 and, less directly, with the list of the Israelite tribes in Num 1:5-15. Behind both this poetic prayer and the one ascribed to Jacob we are confronted with the intense belief that so great a figure could both foresee the destiny of each tribe and pronounce blessing upon each.

The poem is essentially split into two parts with a hymnic praise of God in vv. 2-5 and 26-29. This then serves as a framework for the blessing formula for each tribe, which captures for each a divine message concerning their individual destiny. Moses thereby gives to each tribe his own gift of divine understanding and power, and at the same time the diverse gifts and characteristics of each tribe are recognized and affirmed to be gifts of God.

33:2-5, 26-29. Almost certainly we must conclude that the two elements of the poem were originally separate, the framework being taken from a psalm celebrating the kingship and triumphant power of the LORD God. It shares many features and a common vocabulary with the "enthronement psalms," which celebrate the power of God over creation and over all Israel's potential enemies. It must certainly be of early pre-exilic origin, but it is unlikely to have been written earlier than the building of the Jerusalem Temple.

A particularly memorable feature of the poem is the description of a divine theophany in vv. 2-3, in which God is seen as coming in triumph to Israel from Mt. Sinai and the southern hill country to appear before Israel in their land. Similar theophanic descriptions appear in Ps 68:7-10, 17-23 and Hab 3:3-15.[110] The divine passage from the southern mountains conveys many of the features of a powerful electrical storm in which dark clouds and brilliant flashes of lightning display both the power and the wrath of God. Such storm-theophany imagery appears in Ps 29:3-9,

and there are many indications that the Canaanite Baal tradition drew heavily upon the conception of Baal as a god of storms and thunder who rode upon the clouds (cf. 33:26). It is noteworthy, however, that the LORD comes from Sinai, pointing to an amalgamation of the historical tradition concerning God's unique act of self-disclosure on Mt. Sinai (Exodus 19–24) with the more stereotypical imagery of a divine theophany in a thunderstorm. The reference to Mt. Sinai is unique in the book of Deuteronomy; elsewhere the mountain of revelation is consistently referred to as Mt. Horeb (see the Commentary on 1:2). The linking of the divine appearance with the giving of the law is possibly an editorial attempt to combine traditional cultic language with the central importance attached to the law.

In a similar fashion, the note that "there arose a king in Jeshurun" (v. 5) could refer either to Moses as king or, more probably, to the celebration of the LORD as divine King over Israel. While Israel lived under a human monarchy, the conception prevailed that the earthly ruler was the servant and representative of God, who was the heavenly King. So human kingship mirrored the divine. Nevertheless, the idea of divine kingship was flexible, which subsequently gave rise to ideas of a theocracy in which no earthly king was needed.

The second part of the framework (vv. 26-29) proclaims many of the established features of the psalms that express the theme of God's kingship (esp. Psalms 95–100). These verses focus especially on God's triumph over all other deities and the destruction of Israel's enemies (vv. 27, 29), so that Israel can live in peace. These enemies, who are essentially regarded as constituting a potential, rather than an immediate and known threat to Israel's security, are not identified. The psalm itself is an affirmation of divine triumph and victory that was designed to promote and achieve such peace and safety.

The use of this hymnic declaration of the LORD's victories at this point has considerable theological significance for its reflection of a subtle change of context in its future hope. There can be no doubt that in its original cultic context it was a stereo-

---

110. J. Jeremias, *Theophanie, Die Geschichte einer alttestamentlichen Gattung,* WMANT 10 (Neukirchen-Vluyn: Neukirchener Verlag, 1965).

typical formula aimed at declaring that any potential aggressor against Israel would be swiftly dealt with (cf. Ps 2:10-11). However, here the overall context at the close of the book of Deuteronomy reflects a situation in which Israel's vulnerable position among the nations of the world was prominently in mind. How will Israel ultimately fare in the world of nations, and how will the God of Israel prove victorious in a world that venerates many strange gods? No longer is the situation abstract and undefined. Through Israel's experience, it proves to be vitally significant. As a consequence, the dimension of hope was pressed further into the future in the expectation of a more distant, but ultimately more glorious, triumph over the nations in which Israel would be vindicated in their land. This hope is clearly set out in the shaping of the canonical books of prophecy, but is less clearly evident in the pentateuchal collection. Here the psalm has effectively been read as prophecy.

33:6-25. The central part of the blessing of Moses consists of sayings directed to the traditional twelve tribes, each of which was descended from Jacob, the nation's ancestor. The listing of the twelve tribes is variously arrived at between the tribal genealogies of Num 1:5-15 and 26:5-62 and the "blessing" compositions. Here the name of Simeon is missing, but is compensated for by the fact that Joseph is divided into two, with Ephraim and Manasseh each constituting a complete tribe. The precise history of each of these tribes is impossible to trace, and it is questionable whether such a list of short, and sometimes cryptic, sayings such as are preserved in the blessing-poems provide sufficient information to reconstruct the earliest stages of the tribal history.[111] Even the significance of the well-preserved tradition concerning the existence and inter-relationship of the twelve tribes before the formation of the Israelite state under Saul and David remains shrouded in uncertainty.

Two major historical questions make it difficult to arrive at a date for the composition of this list of sayings. The first question relates to the sense of tribal awareness that prevailed in Israel. Quite certainly during the period of the monarchy, the territorial upheavals, especially those brought on

by Mesopotamian interference in the region, led to a disintegration of the older sense of tribal unity that had held Israel together. Increasingly, the effective solidarity of the twelve-tribe group, based on a feeling of kin-based "belonging," waned. It was the purpose of such "blessing" sayings, then, to promote and preserve such feelings.

Second, it is not clear whether these sayings were originally independent or were an expression of the concern to keep alive the memory of an original "family" of twelve tribes who shared a common ancestor. The fact that the names of these twelve were not uniformly preserved argues against this, but evidently the number twelve remained significant. All we can conclude is that these tribal sayings seek to encapsulate the destiny of each of the member tribes and that it was important for the author of the blessing of Moses to keep alive the consciousness of this. It is plausible that the inclusion of the blessing in Deuteronomy 33, on the eve of the move into the promised land, was made at the time when the book of Deuteronomy became the final chapter of the written Torah, the five books of Moses.

33:6, Reuben. The first saying is addressed appropriately to Reuben, the firstborn of Jacob. It recognizes the fact that, within the biblical period, Reuben had become a very small tribe, so much so that its actual history is no longer reported in the extant tradition. It remained little more than a name and a memory.

33:7, Judah. This saying takes full account of the separateness of this tribe and its problem with unnamed adversaries. Who these might have been, and why this tribe had become separate from the remainder of Israel ("his people") is not explained. It may be that the saying originated in the period of the divided monarchy. Judah's enemies are likely to have been Edom and Moab, the other national groups settled in the south and to the east of the Jordan valley. When compared with the Judah saying in the blessing of Jacob (Gen 49:10), it is significant that the rise of Israel's kingship from within Judah is now passed over.

33:8-11, Levi. The saying addressed to Levi is the longest of those preserved in the blessing. It appears to be composite in origin, having been expanded by the addition of vv. 9b-10. Verse 11, then, would have been the original conclusion to the Judah saying. The original Levi saying allocates

111. H.-J. Zobel, *Stammesspruch und Geschichte*, BZAW 95 (Berlin: Alfred Töpelmann, 1965).

to them a role in dispensing priestly oracular judgment through the Urim and Thummim (cf. 1 Sam 14:18-19). The Massah and Meribah incident is recounted in Exod 17:1-7, where the link with Levi can only be through the testing of Moses. The unflinching and cruel loyalty of Levi refers to the incident in Exod 32:25-29, but must also, more generally, have been related to their historic commitment to total loyalty to the LORD God of Israel, to whose service they were dedicated. Their role as teachers of the law fits closely with the task envisaged for them by the deuteronomists and became increasingly their responsibility in the early post-exilic age.

33:12, Benjamin. This saying alludes to Benjamin's favored status as the youngest, and especially loved, son of Jacob (Gen 44:20); it probably also contains a hidden political message. Many features of the Israelite tradition, as reflected in Deuteronomy, reveal a deep suspicion of the Judahite claims to superiority among the tribes, to which the tribe of Benjamin fell victim. The conflict over the beginnings of the kingship between Saul (a Benjaminite) and David (a Judahite) were evidently a long-felt source of tension.

33:13-17, Ephraim and Manasseh. The Joseph saying is particularly long and is full of nature imagery regarding the fertility of the land occupied by the tribes of Ephraim and Manasseh. It rejoices in the fertility of the soil and its productivity ("choice fruits of the sun"; "rich yield of the months"; v. 14) and presupposes that the Joseph tribes are the most favored of Israel. The explicit mention of both Ephraim and Manasseh in v. 17 must have originated with the author's desire to ensure that all twelve tribal names received a mention in the blessing. The fact that the saying is so forthright in favoring the Joseph tribes, coupled with the omission of any mention of Judah's kingly status, would fit the broad deuteronomic reflection of an "all Israel" perspective. It is a further reflection of the broad Ephraimite (northern) traditions preserved in the book.

33:18-19, Zebulun and Issachar. These two northern tribes had settled on the hinterland of the Phoenician seaports of Tyre and Sidon and were evidently able to benefit from the maritime trade that developed in the first millennium BCE. Hence, they could be said to "suck the affluence of the seas." The OT preserves relatively sparse information concerning them.

33:20-21, Gad. The strongest of the tribes settled to the east of the Jordan, Gad is reputed for its belligerent and aggressive character (cf. Gen 49:19). This tribe appears to have absorbed much of the territory of its neighbor, Reuben, and was undoubtedly settled in the rich cultivated region in the upper Jordan valley. No obvious explanation appears as to why Gad was especially praised for having "executed the justice of the LORD."

33:22, Dan. The metaphor of Dan as "a lion's whelp that leaps forth from Bashan" is probably best explained as referring to the fact that this tribe had settled in the forested region of the upper Jordan, where, in antiquity, wildlife abounded. The region, with its ready access to the trading routes to Syria and Mesopotamia, made it an important security frontier for Israel, but also left the tribe vulnerable. Accordingly, its toughness was both needed and celebrated as its great virtue.

33:23, Naphtali. This tribe was settled to the north and west of the Sea of Galilee and is another of the twelve tribes about which little historical information is preserved in the biblical tradition. The rich territory that was their traditional land holding has drawn for them a very favored picture in this blessing, but little concrete detail can be gleaned from it.

33:24-25, Asher. The desirable settlement area of this tribe is reflected in the high level of blessing ascribed to it, but once again the reference to their military prowess ("Your bars are iron and bronze," v. 25) indicates the threats that were constantly endangering their ability to hold on to this might. The concluding saying, "and as your days, so is your strength," gives assurance that this tribe will prove strong enough to withstand these attacks.

REFLECTIONS

The blessing of Moses is appropriately set as the final hymnic assurance to bring both the book of Deuteronomy and the entire collection of the Mosaic Torah to a close. It has been a law addressed to Israel, full of warnings, threats, and exhortations to heed the Word of God and to be obedient to the law that has been given to Israel through the covenant. Now Moses is to bid final farewell to the nation he has led and nurtured for a full generation. Like a youth leaving home to go to a distant city to learn or work, Israel is being released to face an uncertain future. The message of the blessing is one of the most prayerful desires for the nation's success and well-being. Moses has bequeathed to the tribes all that he has to give them. The tribes, in return, have revealed the responsive, as well as dangerous, aspects of who they are. Now all that remains is to commit them all to God.

The author undoubtedly felt a great significance attached to the sense of wholeness and inclusiveness of Israel at this point. Certainly by the time Deuteronomy came to be written the fortunes of several of the tribes had long been clouded and almost totally lost. More relevant than the breakup and dispersion of the tribal groupings that had characterized the earliest form of Israel was the exiled and fugitive status that had befallen much of the nation. This fate is well reflected in the formulas of curse that characterize chapters 28–30.

But curse cannot be the ultimate fate of Israel as a nation, and the grounds for believing this are set out here in the context of the hymnic celebration of God's power. So this final formulaic blessing with which Moses parts from the tribes and their representatives is a final pointer to trust in the power of God as the only source and assurance of ultimate success. It is, in the most literal sense, a poem that bids, "Fare well!"

DEUTERONOMY 34:1-12, THE DEATH OF MOSES

NIV

34 Then Moses climbed Mount Nebo from the plains of Moab to the top of Pisgah, across from Jericho. There the LORD showed him the whole land—from Gilead to Dan, [2]all of Naphtali, the territory of Ephraim and Manasseh, all the land of Judah as far as the western sea,[a] [3]the Negev and the whole region from the Valley of Jericho, the City of Palms, as far as Zoar. [4]Then the LORD said to him, "This is the land I promised on oath to Abraham, Isaac and Jacob when I said, 'I will give it to your descendants.' I have let you see it with your eyes, but you will not cross over into it."

[5]And Moses the servant of the LORD died there in Moab, as the LORD had said. [6]He buried him[b] in Moab, in the valley opposite Beth Peor, but to this day no one knows where his grave is. [7]Moses was a hundred and twenty years old when he died, yet his eyes were not weak nor his strength gone. [8]The Israelites grieved for Moses in the plains of Moab thirty days, until the time of weeping and mourning was over.

[a]2 That is, the Mediterranean   [b]6 Or He was buried

NRSV

34 Then Moses went up from the plains of Moab to Mount Nebo, to the top of Pisgah, which is opposite Jericho, and the LORD showed him the whole land: Gilead as far as Dan, [2]all Naphtali, the land of Ephraim and Manasseh, all the land of Judah as far as the Western Sea, [3]the Negeb, and the Plain—that is, the valley of Jericho, the city of palm trees—as far as Zoar. [4]The LORD said to him, "This is the land of which I swore to Abraham, to Isaac, and to Jacob, saying, 'I will give it to your descendants'; I have let you see it with your eyes, but you shall not cross over there." [5]Then Moses, the servant of the LORD, died there in the land of Moab, at the LORD's command. [6]He was buried in a valley in the land of Moab, opposite Beth-peor, but no one knows his burial place to this day. [7]Moses was one hundred twenty years old when he died; his sight was unimpaired and his vigor had not abated. [8]The Israelites wept for Moses in the plains of Moab thirty days; then the period of mourning for Moses was ended.

9Joshua son of Nun was full of the spirit of

NIV

⁹Now Joshua son of Nun was filled with the spirit[a] of wisdom because Moses had laid his hands on him. So the Israelites listened to him and did what the LORD had commanded Moses.

¹⁰Since then, no prophet has risen in Israel like Moses, whom the LORD knew face to face, ¹¹who did all those miraculous signs and wonders the LORD sent him to do in Egypt—to Pharaoh and to all his officials and to his whole land. ¹²For no one has ever shown the mighty power or performed the awesome deeds that Moses did in the sight of all Israel.

a9 Or Spirit

NRSV

wisdom, because Moses had laid his hands on him; and the Israelites obeyed him, doing as the LORD had commanded Moses.

10Never since has there arisen a prophet in Israel like Moses, whom the LORD knew face to face. ¹¹He was unequaled for all the signs and wonders that the LORD sent him to perform in the land of Egypt, against Pharaoh and all his servants and his entire land, ¹²and for all the mighty deeds and all the terrifying displays of power that Moses performed in the sight of all Israel.

COMMENTARY

The final chapter of Deuteronomy has undoubtedly been given its present shape by the editor who made it the final chapter of the Pentateuch. It reports the death of the great leader Moses, with further emphasis that he did not set foot in the land (v. 4) and with a renewed declaration that Joshua was fully empowered as the successor to Moses (v. 9). The final word is a eulogy in praise of Moses as the unequaled leader of the nation. His physical strength was unimpaired (v. 7), but more pertinent, he was able to wield a miraculous divine power against Pharaoh and all his servants, more than any other leader or prophet in Israel (vv. 10-12).

This ascription of Moses' unique miracle-working power is significant as a reflection of the conception of charismatic leadership with which he was believed to have been endowed, and as a mark of a distinct shift of emphasis from that which prevails more extensively in the book of Deuteronomy. Until now, the emphasis has been on Moses' ability to prevail with God in prayer (9:25-29), his unflinching courage and commitment at a time when the majority of the nation had been discouraged and cowardly in the face

of the report of the spies (1:26-45), and his mediation with God on Israel's behalf in bringing the tablets of the law by which they can live as a nation. The transition to a more priestly, power-conscious sense of virtue is quite striking.

In the final form of the biblical books of law, the emphasis on righteousness and justice, rather than priestly power and authority, is uppermost. It is noteworthy that in v. 10 Moses is described as a prophet, in whom the prophetic skills were more fully developed than in any other. This accords with the law relating to true and false prophets in 18:18, where Moses is introduced as a superior prophet. Overall if one title more than any other is sought to describe the role Moses has played in Israel, it is "prophet." In the end, however, Moses' very uniqueness makes it impossible to describe his role as that of prophet, priest, military commander, or king. At different times, he fulfills tasks appropriate to each one of these roles. Yet he surpasses them all and thereby ties Israel to a person and a past history from which it can never afterward be separated. He is the one "whom the LORD knew face to face."

INTRODUCTION TO NARRATIVE LITERATURE

PETER D. MISCALL

In the late 1960s increasing numbers of scholars suggested that the methods of historical criticism, particularly source and form analysis, had reached an impasse and new approaches were needed. In subsequent years, literary criticism, in its many contemporary forms, has become the area most consistently explored for new ways of studying biblical literature, particularly narrative. Muilenburg's influential essay "Form Criticism and Beyond" built the foundation for rhetorical criticism, one of the first of the new ways to read biblical narratives as they appear in the canonical text.[1] Rhetorical criticism is defined as "the isolation of a discrete literary unity, the analysis of its structure and balance, and the attention to key words and motifs."[2] Its early results are enshrined in the 1974 Muilenberg festschrift, *Rhetorical Criticism*. This approach can contribute much to the close reading of a text, but because of its limited focus, it has not developed into a major approach to biblical narrative.

Rhetorical criticism competed with the influx of French structuralism and of other traditional brands of literary criticism that were influenced by the American New Criticism of the 1930s through the 1960s. A 1971 collection of French essays appeared in translation in 1974 as *Structural Analysis and Biblical Exegesis*.[3] *Semeia*, a journal devoted to new trends in biblical studies, issued its first volume in 1974, "A Structuralist Approach to the Parables." "Classical Hebrew Narrative," its third volume, appeared the following year. The issue included both structuralist and traditional literary approaches. *Semeia: An Experimental Journal for Biblical Criticism* continues to be a major sounding board for new approaches to biblical studies. In its issues, one can track most of the developments in biblical studies over the past two and a half decades, whether these developments flowered and lasted or withered on the vine.

Structuralism is noted for its attention to structure, both manifest and deep. Rhetorical criticism shares its concern for the obvious textual marks of structure, such as repeated terms and phrases, plot elements, and characters. Deep structure, however, is a theoretical category referring to the arrangement of a story—e.g., in terms of plot elements or of the relationships of the characters—that is abstracted from the actual text through the application of modes of structural analysis. Structuralism is characterized by this abstract concern, by its fascination with specialist terminology—"synchronic," "diachronic," "actant" (instead of character)—and by its use of diagrams and quasi-mathematical formulas,

---

1. James Muilenberg, "Form Criticism and Beyond," *JBL* 88 (1969) 1-18.
2. Bernhard W. Anderson, "Introduction," *Rhetorical Criticism: Essays in Honor of James Muilenberg*, ed. Jared J. Jackson and Martin Kessler (Pittsburgh: Pickwick, 1974) xi.
3. R. Barthes, F. Bovon, et al., eds., *Structural Analysis and Biblical Exegesis* (Pittsburgh: Pickwick, 1974).

such as the semiotic square and cube. Structuralism and rhetorical criticism remain valuable to biblical studies for the detailed textual focus they demand and for the original insights they produce.

Structuralism in particular, with its technical terminology and quasi-scientific claims, contrasts with "standard" literary approaches—those that employ the more familiar terminology of plot, setting, character, and theme and focus on these issues. They are no less probing or fruitful in their analyses. A collection of essays entitled *Literary Interpretations of Biblical Narratives* was published in 1974.[4] Intended for literature teachers in secondary schools and colleges, the collection had an impact on biblical studies and was one of the earliest of a long series of works devoted to the study of biblical narrative. The entire methodological shift that was occurring in the 1970s affected all areas of biblical studies— Old and New Testaments—including narrative, prophetic, wisdom, and epistolary literature. Our concern, however, lies with the Hebrew narrative in the OT; comments on other areas will be indirect.

The Sheffield periodical, *Journal for the Study of the Old Testament,* began appearing in 1976. It continues to be a major forum for diverse studies of biblical narrative. As with *Semeia,* one can track in its pages many of the changes and developments over the past twenty years of biblical studies.

Robert Alter's "A Literary Approach to the Bible" appeared in December 1975; it was devoted to Hebrew narrative and was followed in ensuing years by a series of articles on biblical narrative.[5] These articles, rewritten to various degrees, were gathered into Alter's influential *The Art of Biblical Narrative,* published in 1981.[6] Without arguing for a strict dividing line, I use this book and date to mark the beginning of a new stage in work on Hebrew narrative.

To simplify the work of a decade, we can say that in the 1970s those biblical scholars who were disenchanted, for a variety of reasons, with the methods and results of historical criticism were in search of new approaches to biblical study. This was a time of experimentation and often of heated debate between historical critics and the practitioners of various types of literary study of narrative. In particular, those debates addressed the central issue of whether one should focus on the biblical text in its canonical form or attempt to reconstruct earlier forms of the text. "The text-as-it-stands" and "the final form of the text" were two catchphrases of the period. The debate continues to the present day, although it is less heated and less prevalent.

The 1980s and 1990s witnessed the multiplication of methods and of in-depth interpretations of biblical narrative. Alongside the traditional historical-critical approaches were others: narratology, literary criticism, feminism, post-structuralism, and ideology critique. Scholars who employed the newer approaches could be as, if not more, acrimonious in their disputes among themselves as in those with historical critics. The recent *The Postmodern Bible* is an excellent overview of this diversity as it has developed over the last few decades and as it stands today.[7] I turn now from these controversies to a presentation of the literary study of biblical narrative as it has developed in the last generation. The presentation is general, but with pointers to some of the twists that individual critics give to both method and interpretation.

NARRATIVE AND NARRATOLOGY

A *narrative* is the telling, by a *narrator* to an audience, of a connected series or sequence of events. The series of events involve *characters* and their interrelationships, and the events occur in a place or places, the *setting.* The *plot* is the events selected and the particular order in which they are presented. A *theme* is an idea, an abstract concept, that emerges from the narrative's presentation and treatment of its material.

"Narrative" can refer to a short piece, to an episode (e.g., Rebekah and Jacob's deception of Isaac in Genesis 27), or to a larger work, such as Genesis itself or even the whole of Genesis through 2 Kings. Although others may make a distinction, I use "story" as a synonym for narrative—e.g., the story of Sarah and Hagar in Genesis 16 and Israel's primary story in Genesis–2 Kings.

Twentieth-century study of narrative, ancient and modern, from the epic to the novel, has developed into the specialized area of *narratology,* which endeavors to define narrative and its categories (e.g., narrator and character) on a theoretical and abstract level. Narratology is a subdivision of the larger field

4. K. R. R. Gros Louis, J. S. Ackerman, and T. S. Warshaw, eds., *Literary Interpretations of Biblical Narratives* (Nashville: Abingdon, 1974).

5. Robert Alter, "A Literary Approach to the Bible," *Commentary* 60 (1975), 70-77.

6. Robert Alter, *The Art of Biblical Narrative* (New York: Basic, 1981).

7. The Bible and Culture Collective, *The Postmodern Bible* (New York: Yale University Press, 1995).

of *poetics* (not to be equated with the study of poetry only), which strives for a science of literature, a study of the basic elements and rules of any type of literature. Poetics is to literature what the study of grammar and syntax is to language. In such theoretical studies, actual narratives provide examples and illustrations. Narratology and poetics describe specific categories, with various subdivisions, that can be applied in the analysis of any narrative (or other type of literature); they offer tools to the literary critic, but do not engage in the in-depth reading and interpretation of texts for their own sake. These are the fields that have both refined and expanded our understanding of the mechanics and intricacies of, for example, characterization and point of view.

The works of Berlin,[8] Bar-Efrat,[9] and Gunn-Fewell[10] are fine examples of the genre that focuses on Hebrew narrative. They all employ extended examples of analysis, and Gunn-Fewell intersperse their theoretical presentations with extended readings of given narratives, including the fiery furnace episode in Daniel 3. Both Alter's *The Art of Biblical Narrative*[11] and Sternberg's *The Poetics of Biblical Narrative*[12] are inextricable mixes of theoretical comments and involved readings of chosen stories, mainly from Genesis–2 Kings.

One of the more important changes in this methodological shift is the explicit concern to describe and to appreciate biblical narrative in its own right as a literary category. Scholars engaged in this work describe the narratives as they appear in the Bible, rather than judging them according to norms and expectations developed from other Western literature, especially those of the modern realistic novel. In the works just listed, the authors take pains to explicate the narratological terms and concepts they employ and, at the same time, to show in detail how they apply to actual biblical narratives. Narrative study is a contemporary response to the original, critical insight and demand of Spinoza and others that the Bible be read like other literature. At relevant points, I will note the impact of this shift in focus for the specific categories I am presenting.

8. Adele Berlin, *Poetics and Interpretation of Biblical Narrative* (Sheffield: Almond, 1983).

9. Shimon Bar-Efrat, *Narrative Art in the Bible* (Sheffield: Almond, 1989; Hebrew ed., 1979).

10. David M. Gunn and Danna N. Fewell, *Narrative in the Hebrew Bible* (New York: Oxford, 1993).

11. Alter, *The Art of Biblical Narrative.*

12. Meir Sternberg, *The Poetics of Biblical Narrative: Ideological Literature and the Drama of Reading* (Bloomington: Indiana University Press, 1985).

Narrative and History. Before proceeding to biblical narrative itself, I address one final methodological issue: the relation of narrative study to the study of the history of Israel, on the one hand, and the history of biblical writing, on the other hand. Although it can have significant impact on both, expecially the latter, narrative study can proceed on its own by bracketing historical questions that are presently characterized by wide-ranging diversity of opinion and heated controversy. That is, we can discuss the narrative of Samuel, Saul, and David in 1 Samuel and beyond without having to answer, or even ask, the question of what "really happened" in those ancient times. This does not deny the relevance of issues of historicity. It neither affirms nor denies the historicity of specific characters and events, whether Joshua and the conquest, Samson and his exploits, David's relationship with Bathsheba, or the courtship of Ruth and Boaz. It asserts that these stories can be fruitfully read for what they tell us about people and how they relate to others, including God, and for what they tell us about the workings of biblical narrative, general and specific.

Moreover, it allows us to bracket questions of the historical development of narrative style—not to deny the relevance of the issues, but to be able to proceed with narrative analysis without becoming embroiled in all the debates about the history of the writing and editing of the biblical text. Narrative and literary analyses have enough debates and diversity of opinion of their own!

The Narrative and the Author. This topic takes us immediately to a central distinction developed in twentieth-century criticism that is relevant to all narrative, ancient and modern. The author is the actual historical person (or persons) who wrote the work in question. (In reference to the Bible, I am not taking a stand on the issue of oral or written composition.) For example, Herman Melville wrote *Moby Dick* in the mid-nineteenth century. The narrator, on the other hand, is a literary and abstract personage. Within the text, he tells us the story that we are reading and must be distinguished from the actual author. *Moby Dick* is narrated by Ishmael ("Call me Ishmael"), not by Melville.

This distinction allows biblical readers to discuss the narratives in depth, and in the detail of their presentation, without having to identify an actual author by name or impersonal title, by place, and by date. There is, in addition, the category of the "implied author," the hypothetical person inferred as the author from the text's style and content. This person might or might not be similar to the actual author. However, this category is too abstract and debated to be explored in this article.

STYLE

Style refers to form, to how a narrative is told. Style can be used across the spectrum to describe a single story (e.g., Genesis 27), a traditional section (e.g., the Pentateuch), or an entire corpus (e.g., Genesis–2 Kings). At this point I shall describe three primary, and often noted, characteristics of biblical narrative—indeed, of the whole OT. Then I shall discuss how these and other stylistic features affect the respective narrative categories. These three traits are the *episodic nature* of the material; the great *diversity* in terms of both form and content; and the prevalence of *repetition* of many different aspects of narrative.

The *episodic nature* is my phrase for the quality that allows us to read stories individually and separate from their context without feeling that we have lost the heart of the tale. This quality creates the impression that large segments of narrative are composed of stories strung together in a loose chronological frame, without further significant connection or relation. Examples are the Abraham cycle in Genesis 12–25, the wilderness wanderings episodes in Numbers 11–36, the judges stories in Judges 3–16, and the accounts of the last years of Israel and Judah in 2 Kings. These share a *paratactic style*—that is, scenes or stories are juxtaposed without connecting or transitional phrases.

The paratactic style is present at the level of individual sentences in the narrator's preference for "and" over subordinating conjunctions such as "so," "then," or "because." This characteristic is often obscured in modern translations, including the NIV and the NRSV, that use subordinating conjunctions in order to avoid too many repetitions of "and." The story of the war of the kings and of Abram's rescue of Lot in Genesis 14 closes with Abram's declaration that he will accept nothing from the king of Sodom. The following episode of promise and covenant is introduced by the indefinite phrase "after these things" (NRSV) or "after this" (NIV). The narrator gives us no hint of how much time, if any, has elapsed or whether we should think of a change of place. And he relates the story in chapter 15 with sentences connected by "and"; both the NIV and

the NRSV use "but," "then," and "also" in place of some of the simple connectives. The story closes with the Lord's far-reaching promise to Abram and his descendants. Genesis 16, like chapter 15, opens abruptly with no indication of any time lapse or change in locale: "And Sarai, the wife of Abram, bore him no children." Both the NIV and the NRSV attempt to lessen the abruptness by using "now" as an introduction. Others, such as the NJB and the REB, mirror the terseness with a plain "Abram's wife Sarai. . . . " (Note, however, the shift in the order of the characters such that Abram is named first; the NIV and the NRSV keep Sarai first.)

Another well-known and diversely interpreted juxtaposition of two stories occurs in the two creation stories in Gen 1:1–2:4*a* and 2:4*b*-25. To cite this example does not mean that we must accept the hypothesis that two different sources or authors are in evidence here, nor does it mean that we must attempt to harmonize the two stories and explain away all contrasts. Rather, we should accept the juxtaposition, even if it produces sharp contrasts or even contradictions, as part of the narrative style and then work at describing its effects upon readers and intepreters. Episodic and paratactic are descriptive, and not judgmental or evaluative, terms.

The narrator frequently proceeds by presenting contrasting or opposing views, stories, character portrayals, and such, whether placed side-by-side or at some remove. One example of the latter is the Moses who displays weaknesses in Exodus 17–18 and the Moses of Exod 33:7-11 and 34:29-35, who speaks with God face to face. Another is the near-silent Bathsheba of 2 Samuel 11–12 and the politically effective speaker of 1 Kings 1–2. This episodic style leaves room for readers to infer and to conjecture possible transitions and connections, but it never provides enough textual evidence to cinch any one interpretation. The myriad ways that have been proposed for relating or not relating the two creation stories is ample evidence for the process of unending inference triggered by this stylistic trait.

Diversity is a second catchword frequently used to describe biblical narrative. Not only do the two creation stories differ in their depictions of God, of creation, and of humanity, but also they differ in how the narrator presents the material. The first story is so highly and tightly structured that some question whether narrative or story adequately describes the text; perhaps a theological treatise or an ancient "scientific" document is a better descriptor. The second tale is a looser narrative with characters in potential conflict, and with the segment on the rivers in 2:10-14 in the center but without explicit relevance to the rest of the story. It is a fine example of the paratactic style.

This diversity in both content and form, along with the episodic aspect, confronts the reader constantly from the opening pages of Genesis through the close of 2 Kings and beyond. Genesis comprises narratives ranging from the terseness of the depiction of Lamech in 4:18-24 and of the tale of divine beings and human women in 6:1-4 to the lengthy and tightly woven story of Joseph and his brothers. The sagas of Abraham and his family, and of Jacob and his family or families, lie between these two poles, with the Abraham story the more episodic. Indeed, the latter has been referred to as the "Abraham Cycle," but never as a tightly woven tale. The strictly narrative portions of Genesis are broken at points by genealogies (e.g., chaps 5 and 36) and a poem, Jacob's blessing (49:1-27).

Once readers move beyond Genesis to the rest of the Pentateuch, however, they are confronted with an even greater range of diversity. The strictly narrative portions are mixed with genealogies; a wide variety of ritual, legal, and technical descriptions and prescriptions; and the lengthy rehearsal of all of this in the sermons in Deuteronomy. "Strictly narrative portions" refers to separate stories such as the call of Moses in Exodus 3–4, the manna in Exodus 16, spying out the land in Numbers 13–14, and Moses' final moments in Deuteronomy 34, as opposed to other materials. But all of this material, including stories, "laws," the description of the tabernacle, poems, and sermons, is still part of the overall narrative of Genesis–2 Kings. The flow of the narrative, the forward movement in time and events, may slow or even stop for the presentation of these other materials, but the latter are still part of the narrative. Much of Exodus through Deuteronomy consists of lengthy speeches by characters, mainly God and Moses. We must keep all of this together in order to describe accurately the narrative corpus of Genesis–2 Kings. Awareness of diversity in form and content is also necessary for reading other narrative portions of the OT, such as Chronicles, Ezra-Nehemiah, and Ruth. Diversity may appear in different aspects and ways in these works than in Genesis–2 Kings, but it is present nonetheless.

Joshua–2 Kings continues the mixing. In these books, the narrator relates the history of Israel in the land from conquest to exile. He does so with the same variation in style—from the comparatively tightly woven story of Samuel, Saul, and then David in 1–2 Samuel to the much looser episodes of Judges and 2 Kings. (I use the traditional term "books" without regarding them—e.g., Genesis and Joshua—as separate works by separate authors; for Genesis–2 Kings, I take the "books" to be more like chapters in a contemporary work.) At points the material is punctuated with poems, such as those in Judges 5, 1 Samuel 2, and 2 Samuel 22, and by the speeches of characters, e.g., of Jotham in Judges 9, of Samuel in 1 Samuel 12, and of Ahijah in 1 Kings 11. The speeches, including overviews by the narrator, such as in 2 Kings 17, place the particular narratives in the larger setting of the story of Israel from its creation to the disaster of the exile.

Repetition is the third and final trait I shall discuss. It, like the other traits, appears in the opening pages of the OT. Genesis 1 is divided into six days by the formula "And there was evening and there was morning, the X day." Genesis 2 "repeats" the first chapter. There are two genealogies for Lamech (Gen 4:17-24; 5:1-31), and three stories of a patriarch (Abraham, Isaac) claiming that his wife (Sarah, Rebekah) is his sister (Gen 12:10-20; and 26:6-11). Ten plagues ravage Egypt, and God produces two copies of the stone tablets. In Exodus 25–31 the Lord, in great detail, commands Moses and the Israelites to build a tabernacle; in Exodus 35–40, with much the same detail, the narrator describes the actual construction of the tabernacle. This is the longest and most detailed repetition in the OT.

One of the most, if not the most, repeated stories is that of Israel from Genesis through 2 Kings and beyond, which is recited by the narrator, by God, or by another character at many different stages in the larger narrative. The story is anticipated in the Lord's declarations to Abraham in Gen 15:13-16 and to Moses in Exod 23:20-33 and Deut 31:16-21. Moses refers to it often in his speeches in Deuteronomy (e.g., Deut 26:1-11; 31:26-29; Joshua summarizes it in Josh 24:1-15, as does the narrator in 2 Kgs 17:7-20).

The story is repeated in a wide variety of ways from the brief declaration of the first commandment, "I am the Lord your God, who brought you out of the land of Egypt, out of the house of slavery" (Exod 20:2), to the lengthy versions in

Deuteronomy 31 and Joshua 24. The repetition of Israel's story exemplifies both diversity and *diversity amid regularity*, since the same story is repeated. Diversity in biblical narrative is not endless or unlimited, but variation within set boundaries and a set number of narrative elements. A notable example is the Decalogue. It appears first as the Lord's direct speech in Exodus 20 and then is cited by Moses, in slightly different form, in Deuteronomy 5.

The versions of the story of God and Israel vary not only in terms of their length, but also in terms of their content. The sentence cited from Exod 20:2 refers only to the exodus from Egypt, while Joshua traces the story from the days of Abraham to the entrance into the land in his own day. In Deut 31:16-21, the Lord begins the tale with Moses and then looks off into Israel's future of sin and misery. Moses himself speaks of this distant future in Deut 4:25-31 with a more optimistic view of the outcome. An unnamed prophet tells of the exodus and entrance into the land with no mention of patriarchs or the wandering in the wilderness (Judg 6:8-10). Ezra's recital in Neh 9:6-37 is a full, detailed version that includes all the stages down to Ezra's own day, a time of suffering for past sins.

THE NARRATOR

In accepted literary terms, the biblical narrator is *omniscient* in the sense of possessing potential knowledge of all the characters and events presented, even the thoughts of God (see Gen 6:5-7; 18:17-21). The narrator is *reliable* to the extent that we can trust what we are told. Gunn and Fewell define this characteristic:

> A reliable narrator always gives us accurate information; or put another way, does not make mistakes, give false or unintentionally misleading information, or deliberately deceive us.[13]

They recognize, however, that the many factual contrasts and contradictions in Genesis–2 Kings, the focus of many source and traditio-historical studies, and the presence of ironic statements require us to modify our understanding of what is reliable. Their general rule is the one followed in this article: "In practice, some such scale of reliability is a helpful rule of thumb in reading biblical narrative."[14]

Finally, this is a *third-person* narrator who is not identified by name or title and who does not use "I."

In most ancient literature, narrators are voices, disembodied presences who narrate what we are reading and who seldom explicitly identify themselves or mark their presence. Genesis opens, "In the beginning God created the heavens and the earth," with no textual comment as to who is telling us this. The same narratorial style is employed throughout Genesis–2 Kings. For contrast, we can turn to Nehemiah ("In the month of Chislev, in the twentieth year, while I was in Susa" [1:1]) or to Ecclesiastes/Qoheleth ("I, the Teacher [Qoheleth], when king over Israel in Jerusalem, applied my mind" [1:12]). These are the exceptions and not the rule in biblical narrative.

The narrator's *point of view* is generally from outside or above the characters and the actions of the narrative, but material can be presented through the eyes of a character. For example, part of the formula that closes each day of creation is the repeated "and God saw that it was good"—a report of God's reaction and evaluation, not of the narrator's. Genesis 18 opens with the narrator's report, followed by what Abraham himself saw: "The LORD appeared to Abraham. . . . He looked up and saw three men standing near him" (NRSV). A similar contrast is drawn between the report and a character's perception in Exod 3:2. "There the angel of the LORD appeared to him in a flame of fire out of a bush: he looked, and the bush was blazing, yet it was not consumed" (NRSV).

In narratology, both within and beyond biblical studies, critics have proposed a wide range of distinctions and subdivisions to deal with all the complexities and nuances of the narrator and the point of view in narrative, ancient and modern. These can be valuable in the close reading and analysis of a narrative, but they are beyond the scope of this article. I refer the reader to the works of Berlin,[15] Bar-Efrat,[16] and Bal[17] for both the complexities and the varieties. There is little critical consensus in this matter of further distinctions.

These characteristics are only the general framework within which the very capable and resourceful narrator works. This storyteller may be able to know all about the characters and events but is very selective

13. Gunn and Fewell, *Narrative in the Hebrew Bible,* 53.
14. Ibid., 54.

15. Berlin, *Poetics and Interpretation of Biblical Narrative.*
16. Bar-Efrat, *Narrative Art in the Bible.*
17. Mieke Bal, *Narratology: An Introduction to the Theory of Narrative* (Toronto: University of Toronto Press, 1985).

and deliberate in exactly what is told us about them and how and when we are told. Such sparseness of narrative detail, whether in terms of characters, events, or setting, has long been noted in biblical narrative. What has changed in the contemporary scene is the judgment and evaluation of this stylistic trait; this change applies to many of the other stylistic traits discussed above, particularly the episodic and repetitive nature of the narrative. These traits have been variously observed in the past, but have almost always been judged as marks of the primitive and simplistic nature of biblical narrative. Critics took them as signs of a lack of literary ability and sophistication and not as essential keys to reading and analyzing the narrative. Contemporary literary critics speak, on the other hand, of the art of biblical narrative and of the artistic sophistication of the narrator, who can accomplish so much with apparently so little.

I turn now to discuss each of the other aspects of narrative: theme, setting, plot, and character. I deal with the initial three first because they can be presented more briefly. This is not to turn our backs completely on the narrator, since all that we know about these other four comes through the narration. We will have opportunity to comment further on the narrator's style—diversity, repetition, selectivity, etc.—and to relate it to the particulars of the narrative.

THEME, SETTING, AND PLOT

Theme is a rich, overarching category containing all of the ideas, concepts, and issues that a narrative treats, explicitly or implicitly, in what it says and how it says it. Thematic content can derive from both narrative form and content, and it is developed from the study of all other aspects of a narrative. Themes are generally spoken of in abstract terms: e.g., covenant, divine and human responsibilities, justice and injustice, mercy, prophetic (charismatic) and monarchic (dynastic) leadership, war, wisdom, law, love, the strengths and the failings of families, friendship, loyalty, and betrayal. This short list illustrates the wide range of issues that biblical narrative addresses. In addition, themes can be grouped into comprehensive classifications, such as political, theological, sociological, and historical, and then studied in relation to other topics within those classifications. The relation of one classification to another can be developed—e.g., what does the depiction of the monarchy

in Samuel–Kings tell us about the narrator's (or author's) theology of state and of history?

Plot comprises the events that occur in the course of a narrative and can be looked at from two different perspectives. First, plot reflects a *pattern,* since the events, the actions, occur in a certain order and arrangement; they form a series. Second, one central binding element in the series is a *temporal framework.* The events form a sequence, a continuum that is bound in large part by chronology, by the flow of time. Genesis–2 Kings presents the story of humanity, especially Israel, from the creation of the world to the fall of Judah and Jerusalem c. 600–580 BCE. But there is great variety in the presentation of the plot—e.g., the amount of space and detail accorded a given event or period of time and the clarity, or lack thereof, in noting the passage of time.

Focus on plot raises the issues of causality and resolution. They, especially the former, are complicated by the episodic nature and brevity of biblical narrative, whether on the level of individual scenes and even sentences of one story, or on the level of the grouping of narratives into larger works, such as Exodus or all of Genesis–2 Kings. Specific events, stories, and even whole books frequently follow one upon another in time with little or no indication of any other connection between them. I included one example of this in the discussion of Genesis 15–16. The final statement in the clash between Michal and David (2 Samuel 6) is another good example of paratactic style characterized by the use of "and." The mutual anger and resentment between Michal and her husband are revealed in their heated exchange. The story closes: "And Michal the daughter of Saul had no child to the day of her death" (2 Sam 6:23 NRSV). The narrator thereby reports "the objective fact of Michal's barrenness . . . but carefully avoids any subordinate conjunction or syntactical signal that would indicate a clear causal connection between the fact stated and the dialogue that precedes it."[18] Is the childlessness divine punishment, one spouse refusing conjugal relations with the other, or "a bitter coincidence, the last painful twist of a wronged woman's fate"?[19]

The transition from Joshua to Judges provides another example of a reading difficulty caused by the juxtaposition of stories without an explicit statement of chronology and the flow of events. The book of

18. Alter, *Art of Biblical Narrative,* 125.
19. Ibid., p. 125.

Joshua closes with Israel in firm possession of much of the land and unified in its worship of the Lord; Josh 24:31 speaks of Israel in the singular: "Israel served the Lord." In the final verses, the narrator reports the passing of Joshua and his generation. The book of Judges opens with "after the death of Joshua" without, however, specifying the amount of elapsed time. Further, we immediately encounter "the children of Israel," who see themselves as a group of tribes without a leader, not as the united people, the singular "Israel" of Josh 24:31 led by Joshua and his comrades.

The division and isolation of the tribes narrated in Judges 1 is mirrored in the narrator's jagged style, which recounts each event, however brief, separately. Narrative form reflects content. A brief speech from a divine messenger (Judg 2:1-5) in part accounts for this sorry state of affairs. In Judg 2:6–3:6, the narrator provides a lengthy explanation both for what has happened and for what will continue to happen. The narrator's exposition breaks the chronology by backing up and telling us, after the reports in chap. 1, what happened after the death of Joshua and his generation, and then by looking ahead to the pattern of the future, the careers of the judges (Judges 3–16). The narrative of Judges 17–21 is not explicitly anticipated in this overview.

Both the stories of the judges and those about the characters and tribes in Judges 17–21 are presented in an episodic manner. They are apparently bound by chronology, with one judge and crisis following upon the other in time; they are also connected by themes of violence and war, both foreign and civil, and by themes of ignorance, confusion, and anonymity. As with chap. 1, the confusions and divisions narrated continue to be mirrored in the broken, paratactic form of the narration. The narrator forces readers to experience some of the bewilderment and bafflement of the characters of the narrative.

The chronological ties are only apparent. The narrator punctuates the text with explicit statements of elapsed time—e.g., "the Israelites served Cushan-rishathaim eight years" (Judg 3:8 NRSV); "the land had rest forty years" (Judg 3:11; 5:31 NRSV); and "he [Samson] had judged Israel twenty years" (Judg 16:31 NRSV). Depending on how one adds up or overlaps the figures, a two- to three-century period is covered in the stories of the judges. However, the narrator, in an aside, jolts us with the information that Israel has moved only one generation from the close of Joshua. The last verse of the book of Joshua reports the passing

of Eleazar, son of Aaron; and Judg 20:27-28 notes that "Phinehas son of Eleazar, son of Aaron, ministered before [the ark] in those days." This genealogical notice forces us to rethink the previous material in Judges as simultaneous events or as events narrated after or before they have occurred, and not as events narrated in a straightforward plot line.

In historical-critical analyses, Judges has served as a prime target for different types of source and traditio-historical methods that divide the book into separate stories, groups of stories, or redactional levels. Critics employing these methods regard the narrative traits as pointing to the lack of a consistent narrative and conclude that the book cannot be read as a whole.[20] A contemporary literary critic, such as Josipovici, recognizes the literary problems and then, reflecting the shift in how such literary characteristics are evaluated, accepts them as part of the book: "The book of Judges is indeed oddly fragmented and jagged, even by the standards of the Bible, but that is part of what it is about, not something to be condemned."[21]

Plot, finally, leads us to question whether a narrative leaves its reader with a sense of resolution, a feeling that all the loose ends have been tied up. This applies to a single episode such as the Tamar and Shechem story in Genesis 34, the entire Abraham cycle in Gen 11:10–25:18, the book of Genesis, or the whole of Genesis–2 Kings. The endings of both the Abraham story and the entire book of Genesis leave the reader with a sense of completion. Abraham "died in a good old age, an old man and full of years, and was gathered to his people" (Gen 25:8); he was blessed by the Lord in all things (Gen 24:1). He had seen to the proper marriage of his son Isaac; and the matter of his other wives and sons, including Ishmael, is summarized in the genealogies in Gen 25:1-6 and chaps. 12–18. Genesis ends with the proper burial of Jacob in the family plot at Machpelah, and with all his remaining family in Egypt having finally reached a high degree of trust and reconciliation. The story continues in Exodus but centuries later, and with an almost entirely new cast of characters, except for God and Jacob's "sons," who have now become the people Israel.

On the other hand, Genesis 34 ends with the city of Shechem plundered and Jacob terrified that the

20. See Robert G. Boling, *Judges*, AB 6A (Garden City, N.Y.: Doubleday, 1975).

21. Gabriel Josipovici, *The Book of God: A Response to the Bible* (New Haven: Yale University Press, 1988) 110.

violent acts of his sons will result in his and his house's destruction by the Canaanites. The story ends with a question: "Should our sister be treated like a whore?" Thus the story is left open-ended, in regard both to Jacob's fears and to the query itself. All of Genesis–2 Kings ends, perhaps "stops" is a better term, with the description of King Jehoiachin residing in Babylon and being maintained in fine style by the king of Babylon. The ambiguity of the scene is evident, in the divided opinion of many commentators. Is it a positive sign that the Judean king yet lives on with ample support, or is it a negative sign of pathetic subjection and a fast-fading, last glimmer of hope? Is eating at another king's table a mark of honor or of humiliation? Note the similar ambiguity surrounding Mephibosheth's presence at David's table (2 Samuel 9). Is this only the fulfillment of a pledge to Jonathan, or is it an effective way of keeping an eye on a survivor of the house of Saul?[22]

Setting is the locale, the place where events happen, where characters reside. It refers to the cosmic, the heavens and earth of Genesis 1; to the large scale of countries and areas such as Canaan, Egypt, and the wilderness; to the smaller scale of cities, towns, and designated sites such as Shechem, Zoar, and the field of Machpelah, and to particular places within these sites. When the Lord appears to Abraham, it is "by the oaks of Mamre, as he sat at the entrance of his tent in the heat of the day" (Gen 18:1). Such details, including the notice of the time of day, add specificity to the narrative and, in this case, can lead us to wonder if Abraham first thinks he is seeing a heat mirage. The absence of any explicit indication of setting can serve to keep our attention on other aspects of the narrative. Genesis 15 and 17, both covenant stories, are appropriate examples.

In Genesis–2 Kings one broad concern is whether the setting is in Canaan/Israel, in a foreign country such as Egypt or Babylon, or in the intermediate zone of the wilderness. The setting may be actual or potential—i.e., promised or threatened—and is closely related to the actions of the people Israel, of God, and of the other nations and people involved in the ongoing narrative. This relation of setting with plot and character is a major part of the entire thematics and pattern

of covenant and promise, possession or loss of the land, and both exodus and exile.

On a smaller scale, setting, especially as it fits or does not fit with the characters and actions placed there, can be significant in a story. Abram, in Egypt, expects the Egyptians to be amoral and to resort to murder to avoid adultery (Gen 12:10-20). Pharaoh and the Egyptians do nothing of the sort, and Pharaoh is shocked at Abram's behavior when he learns the truth. In the future, an Israelite king in the holy city of Jerusalem will act in just this way as he arranges for Uriah's death to cover his adultery with Bathsheba (2 Samuel 11). Awareness of similarities and contrasts in plot and setting heightens our appreciation of the characterization of the main players, particularly Abram and David.

A contrasting example of the significance of Jerusalem occurs in Judges 19. Late in the day a servant suggests to his Levite master that they spend the night in "Jebus" (i.e., Jerusalem), but the Levite wants to press on to Gibeah of Benjamin, since Jebus is "a city of foreigners, who do not belong to the people of Israel" (Judg 19:10-12). It soon turns out that the men of Gibeah are more like the men of Sodom than like those whom the Levite and most readers would expect to encounter in an Israelite city.

Sisera, the commander of Jabin's army and a man of cities and broad battlefields, dies at the hand of a woman, Jael, in the confines of her tent (Judges 4). The male space of cities and the great outdoors contrasts with the female space of indoors and tents to the detriment of males. Sisera dies in a tent, and Barak discovers his enemy's corpse there and not on a battlefield. The same contrast is found between Michal's looking "out of the window" at David dancing in the street (2 Sam 6:16) and Jezebel's looking "out of the window" at Jehu (2 Kgs 9:30). The contrast of male and female space at the beginning of the David and Bathsheba episode in 2 Samuel 11 anticipates the dark portrayal of David—one already foreshadowed by the story of Pharaoh in Gen 12:10-20. David is in Jerusalem in the king's house, while Joab and the army are away at war with the Ammonites; from the roof of his house, he sees Bathsheba, and this sets the sordid tale in motion.

Genesis ends and Exodus begins in Egypt. The same setting allows us to focus on the passage of time and on the change in characters and situation. The narrator passes over the intervening centuries in silence, but the arrival of a new king "who did not know Joseph"

22. Leo G. Perdue, " 'Is There Anyone Left of the House of Saul . . .?' Ambiguity and the Characterization of David in the Succession Narrative," *JSOT* 30 (1984) 67-84.

(Exod 1:8) expresses, in as brief a manner as possible, the potentially threatening new conditions. The gap in time does not pose a problem for the plot, since the narrator's concern is with how Israel first came to Egypt and then with why and how they left. Judges ends, in accord with its episodic style, with the grotesque story of the rape of the young women of Shiloh at the annual festival. In terms of plot resolution the book ends or stops with the noncommittal statement about Israel's having no king and the people's doing whatever they want.

In the Hebrew Bible, but not in the Septuagint arrangement that underlies most English Bibles, 1 Samuel follows immediately with the story of Hannah, Elkanah, and Samuel. It is set in Shiloh and revolves about events at the annual festival in that city. But this common setting with the close of Judges is not accompanied by common elements of plot or character. We have no idea of elapsed time, if there is any; perhaps we are to read 1 Samuel 1 as saying that Hannah and her family were at Shiloh during the mass rape. Only after reading further into 1 Samuel do we realize that the narrative is finally moving on beyond the repetitive cycles of Judges. The narrator does not signal this shift at the start.

CHARACTER AND CHARACTERIZATION

I discuss this topic last because many, if not most, contemporary narrative studies focus on it and, directly or indirectly, relate the treatment of other narrative aspects to the development of characters. This includes works such as Moyers's *Genesis* television series and Miles's *God: A Biography*,[23] both of which are outside the mainstream of biblical studies. Many of my previous examples point to the significance of plot, setting, and style for our appreciation of characters. *Character* refers to the personages depicted in the narrative—e.g., Abraham and Rebekah—while *characterization* refers to all of the means that the narrator employs to portray them.

Characterization was not dealt with in any depth by either rhetorical criticism or structuralism because of their central concern with the text's structure, apparent or deep, and because of the latter's strong tendency to regard characters as actants. An actant is described in terms of relationships to others and by the use of adjectives attached to the actant. This technical terminology reflects structuralism's desire to align itself with science.

Before the advent of contemporary literary approaches, biblical studies regarded characterization in biblical narrative as minimal because of its lack of many of the devices for character development (e.g., detailed physical descriptions and in-depth psychological portraits) employed in other literature, especially the modern novel. The inability to describe the portrayal of characters in biblical narrative left mainline biblical studies unable to explain or engage the testimony of so many artists, teachers, and other expositors—Jewish and Christian—to the existence of such powerful individual characters as Abraham, Sarah, Moses, Ruth, and David.

The change in the evaluation of the biblical style of characterization is signaled in the title of one of Alter's chapters, "Characterization and the Art of Reticence."[24] He, and many others, now celebrate the Bible's sparseness and laconic style, seeking to describe how the biblical narrator can depict such powerful and memorable individuals without employing all of the familiar narrative modes.

Alter describes an ascending scale of reliability in the ways that the narrator presents a character. Although his is not the final word on the subject, it is a solid and accessible starting point. The lowest level of the scale includes a character's actions or appearance; these facts reveal little or nothing about motivations for actions or about the significance of the physical trait. Next is direct speech, by a character or by other characters concerning him or her. This moves us into the realm of claims and assertions about motives, feelings, intentions, etc., but here too we have to evaluate the assertions, weighing them against what others, including the narrator, tell us about the situation. The Amalekite's claim to have killed Saul (2 Samuel 1) is a lie that contradicts the narrator's reliable report that Saul killed himself in battle (1 Samuel 31).

Next comes inward speech, a character's interior monologue, which gives us some certainty regarding what she or he feels and thinks. In Gen 18:17-19, we learn precisely why the Lord's plans for Sodom and Gomorrah will be revealed to Abraham; in contrast, we know *what* Abraham argues for regarding the city, but we do not know *why*. Because the

23. See Bill Moyers, *Genesis: A Living Conversation* (New York: Doubleday, 1996); Jack Miles, *God: A Biography* (New York: Random House, 1995).

24. Alter, *The Art of Biblical Narrative,* 114-30.

men with the Lord are going toward Sodom (Gen 18:16, 22), we assume that Abraham means Sodom when he says "the city." Perhaps Lot and his family are at the front of his mind, and not just the righteous in general. Such assumptions and conjectures are typical of the process a reader goes through in evaluating and developing a portrait of a character.

Finally there is the reliable narrator's report of what the characters feel, think, and plan. Even here, however, the narrator may only state the feeling or intention without offering any explanation or motive for it. At the center of the story of Absalom's revolt, the narrator informs us that "the LORD had ordained to defeat the good counsel of Ahithophel, so that the LORD might bring ruin on Absalom" (2 Sam 17:14 NRSV). This announces the intention but not the motives of the Lord, especially whether this ruin of Absalom is meant for the benefit of David. In Genesis 37, Joseph's reports of his dreams result in his brother's hatred and jealousy, "but his father kept the matter in mind" (37:11 NRSV).

Since brevity and selectivity play major roles in the depiction of character, reliability needs qualification in the sense that we cannot rely on the narrator to tell us all the facts, motives, intentions, etc., that we need. The modes that grant certainty are employed sparingly and usually report minimal amounts of information. This reticence can clothe characters in varying ways and degrees in ambiguity, mystery, and depth. Abner's death at Joab's hands is the convenient removal of a potential rival of David, and readers have wondered whether David had some role in this murder, as he will in the subsequent death of Uriah (2 Samuel 11). The narrator could resolve this question for us, but instead only asserts the king's popularity with the people and their conviction of his innocence: "All the people and all Israel understood that day that the king had no part in the killing of Abner son of Ner" (2 Sam 3:37). We learn that Isaac and Rebekah favor Esau and Jacob respectively; a motive is provided for Isaac's love but not for Rebekah's: "Isaac loved Esau, because he was fond of game; but Rebekah loved Jacob" (Gen 25:28 NRSV).

The narrator employs repetition to great effect in the depiction of characters. Repetition extends from specific details to whole stories and is one of the most, if not the most, employed devices in the narrator's literary tool kit. A character's own statement can be repeated at a different time or in a different place. We gain insight into God's frustration with and eventual toleration of human sin in that God first sends the flood and then promises never to send another because the human heart is always inclined to evil (Gen 6:5; 8:21). The narrator can tell us one thing and the character another. The character may be lying outright or simply tailoring the facts to fit an agenda. Both David and Solomon speak of the Lord's presence and establishment of Solomon's reign (1 Kgs 2:45 NRSV). Solomon proclaims to Shimei that "King Solomon shall be blessed, and the throne of David shall be established before the LORD forever" (1 Kgs 2:44-45). But the narrator makes no mention of the Lord in the closing report: "The kingdom was established in the hand of Solomon" (1 Kgs 2:46 NRSV; see 2:12).

Similar are the many instances when a character repeats what another character has said but alters it. Determining what the alterations are and how they reflect on the characters and the situation is a central process in our development and appreciation of biblical characterization. In Isaac's proposal to bless Esau, he emphasizes the hunt and food and does not mention the Lord. When Rebekah repeats this to Jacob, she shortens the description of the hunt and adds that the blessing is to be "before the LORD" (Gen 27:1-7). She tailors the repetition to impress Jacob more strongly. When Elisha first hears of Naaman's request for healing, he asks that Naaman be sent to Elisha "that he may learn that there is a prophet in Israel" (2 Kgs 5:8 NRSV). Once Naaman, an Aramean, is healed, he asserts, "Now I know that there is no God in all the earth except in Israel" (5:15). The contrast redounds to the honor of the foreigner and to the disgrace of the self-centered prophet.

Issues of change and complexity are central to appreciating biblical characterization. Characters can change for the better or for the worse. Judah develops from the self-centered brother and father-in-law of Genesis 37–38 into the responsible and knowledgeable son and brother of Genesis 43–44. In 1 Samuel, Saul gradually degenerates from the capable, although wary, king and soldier of his early career into the crazed and jealous ruler who spends his time and resources in the pursuit of David. David, at the same time, learns a lesson about the political and personal value of restraint in his chance encounter with Saul in the cave and through Abigail's argument that killing Nabal would haunt him in the future (1 Samuel 24–25). David then applies this lesson in deliberate fashion by hunting down Saul and demonstrating that he will not kill him, even though he has the ability to do so whenever he wants (1 Samuel 26).

On the other hand, lack of change or the persistence of personality, particularly in new situations, adds to characterization. Esau's impetuous nature leads him to sell his birthright in Gen 25:29-34, but results in his emotional welcome of Jacob in Genesis 33. In both instances Esau is a man of the moment who does not consider matters of the future or of the past. Samuel, even in death, remains the harsh prophet and Saul's implacable foe (1 Samuel 13–15; 28). Jacob, unlike David, does not learn from his own experience that parental favoritism can tear a family apart; he plays favorites with Joseph, who, like Jacob, ends up spending twenty years in a foreign land before seeing his brothers again.

Complexity points to the multifaceted aspect of many character portrayals, including both the change and the persistence of personality traits. Seldom do characters fit into simple moral categories, and seldom can they be described using only one or two adjectives. They are portrayed with personal and moral strengths and weaknesses, and they demonstrate these in a variety of settings. Complexity combines with the capability of change to produce the rich and full individuals we meet in the pages of the OT. Even characters who appear once are seldom mere stereotypes, present only to advance the plot or to serve as a foil to other people, as evidenced by Abraham's servant (Genesis 24), by Rahab (Joshua 2), by Samson's parents (Judges 13), and by Abigail (1 Samuel 25).

Characters. Discussion of the portraits of a few individuals furthers the presentation and underlines differences in how specific biblical people have been perceived. The 1970s produced a growing number of studies of major personalities such as Joseph, Moses, and David that developed some of the aspects of complexity and change. In the 1980s, the rate of growth accelerated, and the tenor of many of these studies shifted. Again, Alter's work is a helpful benchmark.

Besides complexity and change, Alter discussed the role of ambiguity in the depiction of a character such as David. I use David as a major illustration because a large number of works treat him directly or indirectly and because of the distinct shift in the evaluation of his character. Ambiguity of character arises when we are given some information that leads us to speculate about a particular trait, motive, or such, but we are not given enough information finally to resolve the question. In the example from Genesis 25, we know that Rebekah loves Jacob. Because we are given a motive for Isaac's love of Esau, we can wonder what Rebekah's reasons might be.

At various points in his discussion, Alter draws attention to this mainly in the portrayal of David. We are at times told how others view and react to David, whether in fear or in love. Saul, Jonathan, Michal, and all the people love David (1 Sam 16:21, 18:1-3, 16, 20), and Saul comes to fear him (1 Sam 18:12, 29). But we are never told what David feels toward any of these people. David is "very much afraid of King Achish" (1 Sam 21:12 NRSV), so it is not that the narrator never tells us what David feels or thinks. When Saul proposes that David marry one of his daughters, Merab and then Michal, the narrator uses inner monologue to reveal Saul's ulterior motive (that David would die in battle with the Philistines, 1 Sam 18:17, 21, 25). Of David, he tells us that he "was well pleased to be the king's son-in-law" (1 Sam 18:26 NRSV) but not why he was pleased or whether he has any inkling of Saul's intentions. David kills two hundred Philistines to collect double the required number of foreskins, but the narrator provides no light on David's reasons.

In evaluating David's—indeed, any character's—assertions and claims about self, about others, and about the general situation, we must take account of the setting for the statements. It is striking how many of David's pronouncements are made publicly so that, in evaluating them for their sincerity and truth, we have to ask whether David speaks honestly, only for public effect, or for a mix of the two. When David confronts Goliath in view of both the Israelite and Philistine armies, he proclaims the Lord's power (1 Sam 18:45-47). Once Goliath is dead, however, no one—including David and the narrator—makes any mention of the Lord or of the assembled people coming to acknowledge his feat. At a crucial point in his flight from Saul, David speaks "in his heart" or "to himself" of the necessity of fleeing to the Philistines to escape Saul; in this very private moment David says nothing of the Lord.

Ambiguity means that we are presented a choice of ways of understanding David, or any character depicted in this mode. Is David only the pious shepherd and chosen king of Jewish and Christian tradition? Is he a violent, grasping man who will stop at almost nothing to achieve his goals? Or is he a complex mix of both of these, a true "political animal" to use a contemporary phrase? He ends his life displaying the same mixture of piety and power. He speaks to Solomon of fidelity to the Lord and then gives him a "hit list" of potential enemies (2 Kgs 2:1-9). The various studies and commentaries of the last twenty or so years have developed, in their own ways, each of these views with a variety of nuances and perspectives.

Character studies of David are prime examples of changes in the study of biblical narrative in both method and content. The brevity, selectivity, and repetitive nature of the narrator are now celebrated as integral parts of the depiction of characters. In addition, the characters themselves are regarded as complex, multifaceted, and capable of change, and not as cardboard stereotypes of righteousness or sin, faith or disobedience, success or failure. This includes a willingness to recognize that the biblical narrators are deliberately portraying both positive and negative sides of people and institutions. Biblical narrative is not a one-sided story of saints versus sinners, evil kings versus good prophets, and so forth.

Instead of dividing 1 Samuel into pro-monarchical and anti-monarchical sources, for example, we can read the book as a sophisticated and multifaceted evaluation of monarchy. The presentation includes kingship and the related systems of priests, judges, and prophets. This mode of reading works with both the abstract (prophecy) and the concrete (Samuel) without trying fully to separate them. That is, we cannot talk of the narrator's view(s) of monarchy separate from the personalities of Samuel, Saul, David, and the others associated with them. The many, and often contradictory, critical and historical stands that scholars have taken concerning 1 Samuel reflect, in part, the very complexity of the multiple viewpoints and beliefs expressed in the text.

Samuel is another example of rich characterization. He is a leader with aspects of priest, judge, and prophet; and he is a leader who is asked by the people and commanded by God to appoint his own successor. In 1 Samuel 8, Samuel threatens the people with the reality of kingship, but both the people and the Lord repeat their request and command. Samuel responds ambiguously, and not with immediate obedience: "Samuel then said to the people of Israel, 'Each of you return home' " (1 Sam 8:22 NRSV). Chapters 10–11, then, depict a prophet dragging his feet in carrying out his commission. Since

Samuel is unwilling to appoint a king immediately, God sends him a candidate, Saul. Samuel has a love/hate relationship with Saul that carries both personal and political implications. Saul, for his part, is a capable military leader in his campaign against the Ammonites, but he can never envision himself totally separate from Samuel. Because of this latter trait, Samuel, perhaps, thinks of Saul as a leader whom he can influence or even control. Hence Samuel's angry reaction to the Lord's regret at ever making Saul king is a complex mix of emotions (1 Sam 15:10-11).

The Role of Women. Concern with characters has heightened our awareness of the roles women play in biblical narrative. This awareness has been accompanied by a focus on the issue of gender in both biblical narrative and commentary. Phyllis Trible, in her rhetorical and feminist readings, was one of the first to focus on questions of gender in the creation stories and other biblical narratives.[25] She challenges traditional views that assert God's strict maleness in Genesis 1 and that see a straightforward story of disobedience in Genesis 3. Starting with her work, critics have produced more readings of the opening chapters of Genesis that explore in detail the ways the narrator develops the plot, setting, and characters of the story.[26] In these readings, the garden story becomes a fuller and richer narrative, not the simple story of sin committed by the one-dimensional figures Adam and Eve.

This leads into the large and growing number of feminist studies of biblical narrative. Many focus on the women in the narratives, whether they are major or minor characters, and portray them in depth and with independence. Sarah, Rebekah, Miriam, Deborah, Michal, Bathsheba—all take on a life of their own and no longer exist solely as the mothers, daughters, or wives of men. This holds even if the women are not given proper names of their own—e.g., the wife of Manoach, Samson's mother, and the daughter of Jephthah.

In addition, and just as significant, feminist studies draw our attention to the patriarchal and male society that forms a narrative's setting. These studies do not have to deal only or mainly with women in the text. Setting here refers to the entire range of social, religious, and political beliefs, perspectives,

25. Phyllis Trible, *God and the Rhetoric of Sexuality* (Philadelphia: Fortress, 1978), and *Texts of Terror: Literary-Feminist Readings of Biblical Narratives* (Philadelphia: Fortress, 1984).
26. Gunn and Fewell, *Narrative in the Hebrew Bible,* 194-205.

and assumptions that form the often unspoken background for the stories. Setting in this sense is usually evident only after close study of the text. The fact that most studies refer to the biblical narrator as "he" reflects the dominant male perspective of the narrative. Feminist studies, however, show us that it is a dominant, but not a totally commanding, perspective. Finally, reflecting the contemporary willingness to look at the darker parts and aspects of the Bible, feminist studies can confront us with troubling issues such as the role and treatment of women in the world of biblical narrative.[27]

The Character of God. The LORD (*YHWH*), God (*Elohim*), has seldom been treated as a character, mainly because of the powerful influence of Christianity and Judaism. However, as with the shift to full character portrayal with humans, God as a character with strengths and weaknesses is often a major part of the study of biblical narrative. God is not viewed as above or outside of the story, but as an integral part of it: "We can read the character of God in Hebrew narrative more elusively, positing of God the enigmatic ambiguities found in complex human characters."[28] A character portrayal of God takes into account all divine actions and statements, as well as whatever is said of or to God by another, including the narrator. This data is then evaluated as with any human character.

The divine presence varies from the implicit to the explicit. As an explicit presence, the Lord speaks and acts as in Genesis 1–11 and 12–25 (the primeval and the Abraham stories, respectively) while as an implicit presence, the Lord is referred to by others, as in the Joseph story, but seldom appears directly. (The book of Esther is an extreme example of the latter.) The Lord appears only once in the Joseph story, when in a vision of God, Jacob is assured of divine presence and support during his upcoming stay in Egypt. True to the narrator's selective style, the Lord says, "Joseph's own hand will close your eyes," and neither confirms nor negates Joseph's claims that his rise to power in Egypt was part of a divine plan to preserve the family (Gen 45:4-9; 50:19-20). This relates to the variation between clarity and ambiguity of the portrait in terms of whether the Lord is actually determining and involved in events and of any possible motives for such activity. Previously I noted the limited extent of the narrator's ascription of Absalom's fall to the divine intention (2 Sam 17:14).

Narrative critics are willing to look at the dark side of human characters like Abraham and David, and of human society in general. The latter is evidenced in the mistreatment of women and in the prevalence of violence as the chief way to deal with problems. The focus on the human side is matched by a concern with understanding and evaluating God, who is not only involved with this human scene but is often also the initiator, the one who sets violent events in motion. The flood, the conquest, the seemingly unending wars of Samuel–Kings, and the destruction of Judah and Jerusalem are prime examples. Humans, whether individuals or the whole people, are flawed or far worse; and God is the One who chooses them to play a role in the divine plan. Critics have begun raising the question of how all of this reflects on God.

Biblical studies are presently enmeshed in assessing and debating the impact and relevance of all these changes, particularly the emphasis on the dark side, both human and divine, of the story. The task is to read the Bible as it is and to hold together its glory and its dread, and not to deny one to maintain only the other.

BIBLIOGRAPHY

Alter, Robert. *The Art of Biblical Narrative.* New York: Basic, 1981.

Bal, Mieke. *Narratology: An Introduction to the Theory of Narrative.* Toronto: University of Toronto Press, 1985. An excellent introduction to general narratology.

Bar-Efrat, Shimon. *Narrative Art in the Bible.* Sheffield: Almond, 1989 (Hebrew ed., 1979). A solid introduction that covers more topics than Berlin's work.

Berlin, Adele. *Poetics and Interpretation of Biblical Narrative.* Sheffield: Almond, 1983. A solid introduction that focuses on character and point of view.

The Bible and Culture Collective. *The Postmodern Bible.* New York: Yale University Press, 1995. By a group of scholars; an overview of the variety of contemporary ways of interpreting the Bible.

Gunn, David M., and Danna N. Fewell. *Narrative in the Hebrew Bible.* New York: Oxford, 1993. A solid introduction that combines theoretical discussion with in-depth readings of a variety of narratives.

Josipovici, Gabriel. *The Book of God: A Response to the Bible.* New Haven: Yale University Press, 1988. An insightful, general reading of both the OT and the NT by a comparative literature scholar.

Miles, Jack. *God: A Biography.* New York: Random House, 1995. The depiction or biography of God in the OT from Genesis through Chronicles; a fine and non-technical introduction to the issues involved in regarding God as a character in the Bible.

Moyers, Bill, *Genesis: A Living Conversation.* New York: Doubleday, 1996. The companion to the PBS series, which is available in video and audio form; a powerful expression of the tensions between traditional views of Genesis and contemporary readings that raise moral issues from the narrative.

Sternberg, Meir. *The Poetics of Biblical Narrative: Ideological Literature and the Drama of Reading.* Bloomington: Indiana University Press, 1985. An often-cited and debated work noted for its insights, its detail, and its controversial claims.

---

27. For example, see Danna N. Fewell and David M. Gunn, *Gender, Power, and Promise: The Subject of the Bible's First Story* (Nashville: Abingdon, 1993); J. Cheryl Exum, *Fragmented Women: Feminist (Sub)Versions of Biblical Narratives* (Valley Forge, Pa.: Trinity, 1993).
28. Gunn and Fewell, *Narrative in the Hebrew Bible,* 85.

THE BOOK OF JOSHUA

INTRODUCTION, COMMENTARY, AND REFLECTIONS
BY
ROBERT B. COOTE

THE BOOK OF
JOSHUA

INTRODUCTION

The book of Joshua tells of Israel's conquest of Canaan, which appears to climax the long opening story of the Bible. In Genesis, God promises to give the land of Canaan to the descendants of Abraham, Isaac, and Israel. After delivering the descendants of Israel from Egypt and forcing them to remain in the desert long enough for an entire generation to die out and a new generation to take their place, God fulfills this promise. Near the end of the book of Numbers, with Moses still in command, the Israelites conquer the promised land east of the Jordan River and finally arrive at the Jordan. Deuteronomy consists of a long speech by Moses to Israel, including the last major installment of the law Moses passes on to Israel. At the end of Deuteronomy, Moses dies.

The book of Joshua continues the story from this point. First God commissions Joshua. Then, in an orgy of terror, violence, and mayhem, God takes the land of Canaan west of the Jordan away from its inhabitants and gives it to Israel under Joshua's command. Joshua, with the help of the priest Eleazar, distributes the conquered land to the tribes of Israel. Having aged, like Moses he bids his people farewell, dies, and is buried. Thus the book of Joshua explains how under Joshua's command Canaan was conquered, the Canaanites were slaughtered, and their lands were expropriated and redistributed to the tribes of Israel. It forms a triumphant finale to the Bible's foundational epic of liberation, the savage goal toward which God's creation of Israel and delivery of Israel from slavery in Egypt appears to point from the start.

COMPOSITION DURING THE MONARCHICAL PERIOD

It is possible, but unlikely, that this story was recorded as it happened in history. The story is composed of diverse ingredients. These include set speeches, folk narratives (some with auxiliary additions), echoes of rituals, excerpts from supposed ancient sources, lists, territorial descriptions of differing kinds, material repeated elsewhere in the Bible but in different form, and a double ending. The story purports to be about tribal warfare, but several features point to a monarchical as much as a tribal viewpoint. These include the precise delineation of territory covering a sweeping area, the notion of a unified conquest involving mass murder, and the portrayal of strict military loyalty and absolute obedience to a single commander. While Joshua plays a singular role in the story, however, he appears only sporadically, mostly in frameworks, large and small, as though he might not have belonged originally to all the parts—or to any of them. It is surprising that a hero from the tribe of Ephraim, whose territory lay at the heart of early Israel, should be the protagonist of a conquest narrative that focuses almost entirely on the territory of Benjamin, with scarcely anything at all to say about Ephraim. Similarly, Joshua rarely, if ever, acts on his own initiative, but moves only on Yahweh's orders. This contrasts, for example, with the account of David, who acts for himself, albeit in response to God's election; but it comports, as will become clear, with the scheme behind the later composition of the book of Joshua. This scheme held that for centuries Joshua, together with Israel under his command, was unique in his obedience to Yahweh. The first five books of the Bible are composed of at least five distinctive layers and strands, and the book of Joshua appears to be in line with at least two of these, long known as D and P, the first in a major way and the second in a minor way. Many towns are destroyed in Joshua, and these often do not agree with the archaeological evidence of the period before the Israelite monarchy, when the story is supposed to have taken place. In sum, these features of the book of Joshua indicate that it was not composed all at once as an accurate account of an episode in the history of pre-monarchic Israel. Instead, they point to a gradual composition, which took place mainly during the period of the monarchy, from two hundred to six hundred years after the supposed events occurred. Other features make clear that the monarchic perspective of Joshua derives specifically from the house of David.

The book of Joshua is not a simple account of historical events. It is a complex narrative shaped by writers belonging to several different contexts. Most of these contexts can be identified with at least some probability. The clearest is what most scholars regard as the basic context of the D strand, or Deuteronomistic History—namely, the reform of Josiah (c. 640–609 BCE) in the late seventh century. A significant part of Josiah's reform was the reconquest of what had been Israel, and Joshua's conquest of Canaan was taken as a precursor of Josiah's reconquest of Israel. Another earlier context was the reign of Hezekiah (c. 714–687 BCE). Hezekiah was the first Davidic king to begin his reign after the fall of Samaria in 722 BCE, when the non-Davidic kingdom of Israel came to an end. Analysis has shown that much of the books of Kings was composed under Hezekiah, and it is possible that much in the books of Joshua and Judges comes from his reign as well. He, too, wanted to reconquer Israel. The likelihood is that it was Hezekiah who adopted Joshua as a Davidic hero. Before Hezekiah, Joshua was an Israelite hero, probably introduced into wider popularity by Jeroboam I, the usurper of what had been Davidic Israel, whose home was not far from the tomb of Joshua. While it is not always possible to assign particular parts of Joshua to an exact source, these are the main events that helped to shape the book prior to the Babylonian exile of the house of David. During the exile, a few minor changes may have been made in line with the exilic revision of the entire Deuteronomistic History. After the exile, the parts of Joshua that seem related to the priestly strand in the Pentateuch were written, during the Persian period. The source and context of a few parts of Joshua remain a mystery.

That the book of Joshua was written mainly during the period of the Davidic monarchy no longer occasions surprise. In the last twenty years, much research has been devoted to the study of early Israel, particularly with regard to the tide of village settlements that arose in the hill country of Palestine during the Early Iron Age.[1] The Early Iron Age lasted during the twelfth and eleventh centuries BCE, after the supposed time of Joshua and before the time of David. While an exact identification between these new settlements and early Israel cannot be proved, historians and archaeologists believe that the inhabitants of most of these villages were related in some way to Israel as described in the Bible.

Settlement shifts are not uncommon in the history of Palestine. They have been going on for at least five thousand years, and many are comparable to the Early Iron Age shift. While the interpretation of these shifts will remain under investigation for the foreseeable future, so far one thing is clear: Century-long settlement shifts in Palestine are not typically caused by blitzkriegs; therefore, it is improbable that the Early Iron Age settlement shift was prompted by an onslaught of tribal outsiders of the sort described by the book of Joshua. Most scholars now think that the people of Israel were indigenous to Palestine, and were not outsiders. There is nothing in the archaeological record to suggest that the Early Iron Age population of highland Palestine had a mainly pastoral-nomadic background, as suggested by the Bible, or that any sizable segment of the population of Palestine at that time originated outside of Palestine, again as suggested by the Bible, except the Aegean "Sea Peoples," represented by the Philistines. (Hittites are named in Joshua, where they are seen as indigenous; it is conceivable that they settled in Palestine during the Late Bronze Age, but more likely the term has its Neo-Assyrian meaning of the inhabitants of greater Syria.)

Several passages in Joshua itself, as well as in Judges, contradict the picture of a single triumphant assault. Moreover, the picture in Joshua leaves an important question unanswered: What was the nature of early Israel? One of the biggest mistakes readers of the Bible can make is to project modern notions of nationalism onto the ancient world or to

---

1. The standard work is Israel Finkelstein, *The Archaeology of the Israelite Settlement* (Jerusalem: Israel Exploration Society, 1988).

assume, with the eighteenth-century thinker Johann Gottfried Herder and his Romantic and modern followers, that a given people whose existence as such is mistakenly taken for granted naturally expresses its singularity through a homogeneous folk spirit. In the commentary, "nation" is used to refer to what historians call the "political nation," rulers over a changing body of subjects. Early Israel represented not a nation, but a shifting confederation of tribes.

A tribe was a political network of families united by external threat and claiming a common putative ancestor. Tribal loyalty competed with other political and social loyalties and tended to be stronger among the stronger members of the alliance. Thus "tribe," like "nation," referred mainly to the political identity and function of an elite. Anthropological study of tribal societies, combined with historical evidence, shows that notions of defined patriarchal descent and kinship like those described in the Bible tend to be putative and fictional, reflecting not historical kinship but political relations, both among tribes and tribal alliances and between tribes and a central government. The biblical descriptions of the tribes of Israel, like those in J and P, reflect the interests of a state or governing elite with the ability or desire to centralize. The description of the "tribes" in Joshua is no different: It reflects, not the disorderly tribal relations that must have characterized early Israel, as illustrated in the early "Song of Deborah" in Judges 5, but the politics of radical reform and centralization. Thus in Joshua the tribes of Israel are presented in a rationalized manner, united in harmonious kinship.

The sources used by the writers of the book of Joshua may contain sparse material going back in some way to early Israel, but the book of Joshua in its present form was written long after the time of early Israel. The emergence of Israel and its settlement of the central highlands of Palestine are now understood mainly through archaeology and comparative history rather than the Bible.[2] To inquire about the historical contexts of the book of Joshua means to look at the house of David, and not early Israel. In this regard, Joshua resembles the Pentateuch, which precedes it. Virtually all of the Pentateuch, while purporting to describe early Israel, was written during the period of the Israelite and Davidic monarchies or later and reflects chiefly their circumstances and concerns.

CONTEXT OF DEUTERONOMISTIC HISTORY

To understand the book of Joshua, it is important to recognize that it is part, and how it is part, of a much larger work: the Deuteronomistic History. This is a conglomerate of monarchic historical sources, some of them probably tracing back to the court of David

2. For early Israel, see Robert B. Coote, *Early Israel: A New Horizon* (Minneapolis: Fortress, 1990); Coote, "Early Israel," *Scandinavian Journal of the Old Testament* 5 (1991) 35-46; Coote, "Conquest," in *Eerdmans Dictionary of the Bible,* ed. David Noel Freedman, Astrid B. Beck, and Allen C. Myers (Grand Rapids: Eerdmans, forthcoming); Michael G. Hasel, "Israel in the Merneptah Stela," *BASOR* 296 (1994) 45-61; Israel Finkelstein and Nadav Na'aman, eds., *From Nomadism to Monarchy: Archaeological and Historical Aspects of Early Israel* (Jerusalem: Israel Exploration Society, 1994); Israel Finkelstein, "The Great Transformation: The 'Conquest' of the Highlands Frontiers and the Rise of the Territorial States," in *The Archaeology of Society in the Holy Land,* ed. Thomas E. Levy (New York: Facts on File, 1995) 349-65.

himself, that have been edited according to a single overarching conception. That conception is the house of David's claim to the sovereignty of Israel. The Deuteronomistic History was composed out of these sources mainly during the reigns of Hezekiah and later Josiah to support their programs of centralization. Joshua cannot be understood apart from the Deuteronomistic History. But what about the story of the Tetrateuch, the first four books of the Bible, which precedes the Deuteronomistic History? Should Joshua also be read in the light of the Tetrateuch, especially the parts that pre-date the great priestly revision of it in the late sixth century BCE? Joshua presumes aspects of the Tetrateuch's story, but there is little of importance in Joshua that must be understood mainly in terms of the pre-priestly Tetrateuch. (Joshua also contains priestly passages. These are considered briefly at the end of this Introduction.) For example, Joshua assumes the Tetrateuch's representation of Davidic sovereignty, even though the Tetrateuch contains hardly a hint of a forthcoming conquest.

If we ask what gave God the right to dispossess the Canaanites of their land, the scriptural answer is to be found near the beginning of the Tetrateuch, in Noah's curse of Canaan in Gen 9:25-26: "Cursed be Canaan;/ lowest of slaves shall he be to his brothers. . . . Blessed by [Yahweh] my God be Shem [an ancestor of Israel];/ and let Canaan be his slave" (NRSV; cf. Josh 16:10; 17:13; Judg 1:28; 1 Kgs 9:20-21). The reason why Noah cursed Canaan was that Canaan's father, Ham, had seen Noah naked when Noah lay drunk in his tent (Gen 9:21-22). This curse laid the basis for God's promise to Abram made "between Bethel and Ai" (Gen 13:3): "All the land that you see I will give to you and to your offspring forever" (Gen 13:15 NRSV; Bethel and Ai lie about a mile and a half apart; cf. Josh 12:19).

The source of this myth was the court of the house of David, which early on produced the "history" of the world and of Israel that forms the basis of the Tetrateuch. The myth of God's promise of land to Israel, essential to the story of Joshua, together with the related myths of a unified nation descended from a single family arriving from outside, originated in its present form to help the house of David explain its sovereignty over greater Israel. However, the house of David exercised such sovereignty for only a short period in its five-hundred-year history, during the reigns of its founder David and his son Solomon in the tenth century BCE. Thereafter the house of David ruled little more than the highland territory of Judah, while the rest of Israel had its own kings and foreign rulers. For centuries the house of David looked back on the reigns of David and Solomon as the Golden Age and never gave up the hope of reconquering Israel and restoring Davidic rule to its original glory.

Such claims are not uncommon in dynastic histories. For instance, in the Mayflower Compact of 1621, the Pilgrims acknowledged the sovereignty of their king, James I (of the King James Bible), whom they called "king of Great Britain, *France,* and Ireland." The kings of England had not ruled in France for a long time, but they maintained the title in theory up through the eighteenth century. James I inherited this proprietary title from his great-grandmother on both sides, Margaret Tudor, daughter of Henry VII, and she from distant forebears. In the same way, the house of David maintained its title to Israel, inherited from David, in theory for hundreds of years. The ambition to reconquer Israel and make that title real again became pronounced in the late Assyrian period, after the fall of Samaria, Israel's capital, in 722 BCE, when there were no more opposing kings of Israel. Two Davidic kings in particular are known to have pursued policies leading to a projected reconquest of Israel: Hezekiah in the late eighth century BCE and Josiah in the late seventh century.

To the extent that the promise of the land plays an important role in the Tetrateuch, the book of Joshua appears to bring the Tetrateuch's story to its expected conclusion. However, originally the book of Joshua was *not* the ending of this story. When this story was first composed, the book of Joshua had not even been thought of. As already indicated, the Romantic idea that a single popular folk narrative lies behind the various strands of the biblical story from Genesis to Joshua has no basis. Even within the Pentateuch, Deuteronomy does not belong to the original story, but begins a new story, the Deuteronomistic History, which apparently was meant to be a sequel to the original pre-priestly Tetrateuch story.[3]

Two strands of narrative made up the bulk of the pre-priestly Tetrateuch story. These were the early house of David's history of Israel, called J, and a slightly later northern Israelite supplement, called E. The J and E strands give little indication of how God's promise of land is to be fulfilled. They seem to take it for granted that David (in the case of J) and the kings of Israel (in the case of E) possess sovereignty over the land of Israel, as sanctioned by God, and devote most of their attention to other concerns. These strands cannot be traced into Deuteronomy and Joshua. They end, not with a conquest, as in Joshua, but with the culmination of their own distinctive themes, in Exodus (for E) and in Numbers (for J).[4]

Not only do the earliest strands of the Pentateuch conclude before Deuteronomy and Joshua, fail to appear in Deuteronomy and Joshua, and fail to refer to a conquest, but they also give no indication that the promise of the land is to be fulfilled in a blitzkrieg and attempted ethnic cleansing. Nor is there a hint of God's command to exterminate the Canaanites, to say nothing of the particular contours and emphases of the book of Joshua. The curse of slavery on Canaan is not the same as extermination, as recognized in the book of Joshua (Josh 16:10; 17:13). The figure of Joshua himself appears in the Tetrateuch, but he has little if anything to do with the main themes of J and E, and was probably introduced there by scribes in the court of Hezekiah or Josiah. In Exod 17:8-16, a text that belongs to neither J nor E, Joshua appears out of nowhere to help defeat the Amalekites. He appears again in Numbers 13–14, also in connection with the Amalekites. This is a J

---

3. Deuteronomy became a part of a five-book Pentateuch, or Torah, late in the OT period, when the notion of an "Age of Moses" became a primary basis for partitioning Scripture. At that time the rest of the Deuteronomistic History, beginning with Joshua, became a part of the section of the Scriptures later called the Prophets.

4. Hans Walter Wolff, "The Kerygma of the Yahwist," in *The Vitality of Old Testament Traditions,* eds. Walter Brueggemann and Hans Walter Wolff, 2nd ed. (Atlanta: John Knox, 1982) 41-66; Robert B. Coote and David Robert Ord, *The Bible's First History* (Philadelphia: Fortress, 1989); Robert B. Coote, *In Defense of Revolution: The Elohist History* (Minneapolis: Fortress, 1991).

story about the Judahite town of Hebron, later David's first capital, and its eventual Judahite conqueror, Caleb. Here Joshua, an Ephraimite, is introduced rather artificially as a new character (Num 13:8, 16) to play a supplementary and presumably secondary role to Caleb, who is of primary interest in the J strand. It is even implied in Josh 14:12 that Joshua was not one of the spies.

The Amalekites play a major role in the Deuteronomistic History (Deut 25:17, 19; Judg 3:13; 5:14; 6:3, 33; 7:12; 10:12; 12:15; 1 Sam 14:48; 15:2-3, 5-7, 18, 20, 32; 28:18; 30:1, 13, 18; 2 Sam 1:1, 8, 13; 8:12; most of these passages have a connection with the founding of the house of David), but only a minor part in the Tetrateuch, except for these two passages involving Joshua (Gen 14:7; 36:12, 16; Num 24:20).[5] As for the notion of mass extermination, it figures in the Tetrateuch in only two stories, Joshua's attack on the Amalekites in Exodus 17 and Israel's attack on Hormah in Numbers 21, a duplicate of the attack on the Amalekites in Num 14:39-45.[6] It may be no coincidence that the Amalekites were later said to have been finally exterminated under Hezekiah (1 Chr 4:41-43).[7] It was probably in the court of Hezekiah, where the overall plot of the Deuteronomistic History was first conceived and Joshua was first given a significant role in the Davidic history of Israel, that the association of Joshua with the Amalekites was apparently introduced into the Tetrateuch.

NARRATIVE STRUCTURE

The story of Joshua has two parts. Israel's land east of the Jordan has already been conquered under Moses. The story of Joshua concerns mainly the west side of the Jordan.[8] First, Joshua leads the tribes of Israel in the conquest of the west side of the Jordan. What begins in Josh 1:1-6 concludes in 12:7-24. Second, Joshua oversees the distribution to the twelve tribes of all the land conquered (Joshua 13–31). The distribution includes the designation of refuges for manslayers and the assignment of towns and pasture to the Levites. After giving permission to the tribes from east of the Jordan to build an altar beside the Jordan to witness to their desire not to be separated from the west-bank tribes, and after giving a double farewell—a speech followed by a covenanting ceremony, ending with the erection of a stone as a witness that all Israel has committed to Joshua's Yahweh—Joshua dies and is buried (Joshua 22–24).

5. The first and last of these passages probably belong to the J strand. The middle two belong to a separate text regarding the Edomites that may have been incorporated into the J strand.

6. The verb החרים (heḥĕrîm, "dedicate" in the sense of "exterminate") occurs in the Tetrateuch only in Num 21:2-3, as a folk explanation of the name "Hormah," "Extermination" (cf. Josh 12:14). The name probably derives from the notion of a sacred or prohibited precinct.

7. Outside of Exodus 17 and Numbers 13–14, Joshua appears parenthetically in Exod 24:13; 32:17 (texts that belong to neither J nor E); 33:11 (Joshua is introduced as an aside, with no close tie to the story); Num 11:28 (Joshua is a superfluous double to the "young man" in v. 27); and Num 27:18, 22; 32:12, 28; 34:17, all texts, basically priestly, that come after the end of J and E. See George W. Ramsey, "Joshua," ABD, 3:999.

8. In the long history of Palestine, the Jordan has rarely formed a prominent natural boundary as it does in the Deuteronomistic History. The tribe of Manasseh traditionally occupied both sides of the Jordan precisely because it was not a boundary. In the biblical period, the Jordan as boundary appears to be attested for the first time in the eighth and seventh centuries BCE, as an administrative expedient instituted by the Assyrians, who, not surprisingly, were outsiders.

The plot of conquest and distribution represents only the bare bones of the narrative. By the time most of the account of the conquest is completed (Joshua 1–9), only two towns have been captured and destroyed, Jericho and Ai, and the inhabitants of another town, Gibeon, accommodated. The three towns that dominate the narrative of conquest lie in the small territory of Benjamin, nearly within sight of one another. They represent a tiny part of the land to be conquered. Why is this the case? The story uses conquest not only to foreshadow the house of David's reconquest, but also to confirm its sovereignty and elaborate on its policy of centralization.

Most of the narrative of conquest is taken up with three localities of great significance for the house of David's claim to sovereignty: Gilgal, Bethel, and Gibeon. (This assumes that the story of Ai bears on its neighbor Bethel.) At Gilgal, Samuel determined to depose Saul in favor of David, thereby establishing the house of David (see Commentary on 4:19–5:12). Bethel plays a critical role in the entire Deuteronomistic History. Its altar symbolized the "sin of Jeroboam." By usurping the sovereignty of the house of David in Israel, Jeroboam violated the first law of Moses, which stipulates that the service of Yahweh has to be performed at one shrine only. The sin of Jeroboam was then committed by all the subsequent kings of Israel, who thus stood in the way of the house of David's reconquest of Israel. Gibeon played a decisive role in the conflict between the house of Saul and the house of David, which led to David's usurping the throne and becoming king of Israel. It was at Gibeon that David's men defeated Abner's men and launched David's war of usurpation (2 Sam 2:12–3:1). David later consolidated his sovereignty by complying with the Gibeonites' demand for the execution of seven remaining sons and grandsons of Saul on the grounds that Saul had "put the Gibeonites to death." Although the incident referred to is not mentioned elsewhere, it makes direct reference to Josh 9:3-27 (2 Sam 21:1-14).

The story signals radical Davidic centralization by highlighting Joshua's fulfillment of Yahweh's command. Following the quasi-royal commissioning of Joshua, in which he begins his career as not only a second Moses but also the prototype of the ideal king in the Deuteronomistic History, the main narrative focuses on three examples (involving the three localities Gilgal, Ai, and Gibeon) of how the law of חרם (ḥērem; Deut 7:1; 20:16-18), which requires that all opponents be killed and no booty be taken, applies in order to sharpen the definition of how people are to relate to Yahweh's command, as enforced by Joshua, and to God's service, or cult, in its extraordinary deuteronomistic form. The first example involves Rahab and her family. They are Canaanites, but because Rahab shows loyalty to Yahweh by saving the Israelite spies and making possible the conquest of Jericho, at Joshua's direction she and her family are not slaughtered with the rest of the people of Jericho. In contrast, in the second example the Judahite Achan violates the law of ḥērem by withholding booty from Jericho. Achan and his family are Israelites, but this does not protect them from the consequences of their disloyalty. As a result of Achan's violation, at Joshua's direction, Achan and his family are stoned to death by "all Israel." The stoning of Achan makes possible the conquest of Ai.[9] The third example involves the Hivites of Gibeon. They trick Joshua into thinking they live far away, and in line with Deut 20:10-15 Joshua exempts them from *ḥērem* annihilation. When he finds that he has been deceived, he keeps his oath to them and does not destroy them, but makes them slaves of Yahweh's cult, laying the foundation for David's later annihilation of the house of Saul.

The concluding section concerning the conquest in Joshua relates two short campaigns of extermination. The first was prompted by Joshua's compact with the Gibeonites and instigated by the Amorite king of Jerusalem, the future city of David. In the second, Joshua overthrows a horde of Canaanite and alien kings led by the king of Hazor. The section ends with a list of thirty-one kings defeated and killed, largely in the order in which they were killed in the narrative, starting with the kings of Jericho, Ai, and Jerusalem.

The second half of Joshua's story concerns the distribution of the conquered land. Following an age-old pattern, victory in war ensues in the division of the spoils. The spoils other than land have mostly been "dedicated" to Yahweh through *ḥērem*, leaving only the land to distribute. The distribution of land places the greatest weight on Judah (Joshua 14–15) and Benjamin (Josh 18:11-28). As followers of David, Judahites ended up in Jerusalem (15:63), but the town itself was located within the territory of Benjamin (18:28). The distribution of land is by lot at Gilgal for Judah, Ephraim, and Manasseh, then at Shiloh for the remaining tribes. The land goes to tribes defined in terms of specified territories, an artificial conception that reflects the point of view of a central state concerned to regulate a population that threatens to regard itself as opposed to the state and, therefore, ready to make its own use of tribal designations and tribal rhetoric.

Centralizing monarchs strove to curtail not only tribal independence, but also acts of revenge that subverted the rule of the king through royally sanctioned law. Hence, once the tribal allotments are defined, Joshua assigns the cities of refuge from the avenger of blood, required in Deut 19:1-13 (cf. Num 35:9-34). According to deuteronomistic law, Levites are to control the document of the law laid down by Moses and thus oversee the house of David's jurisdiction. Members of the tribe of Levi do not receive a tribal territory, but are assigned towns and pasturage throughout the other territories (Joshua 21). Then a lengthy account in Joshua 22 details how Joshua helps to settle a dispute over an altar that threatens to duplicate the altar destined to be located at the Davidic Temple in Jerusalem. This ostensible exception to the deuteronomistic law of centralization must be meticulously justified.

Finally, Joshua pronounces two farewells. In the first he stresses absolute obedience to the command of Yahweh, the same emphasis with which the entire narrative began. In the second farewell, he performs a covenanting ceremony at Shechem, deep in the heartland of Israel, where little else has happened to this point. Here the gathered people in formation are encouraged to vow their loyalty to Joshua's, or the deuteronomist's,

---

9. This episode also sets up a contrast with the Judahite Caleb, whose clan figures in the rise of David (Joshua 14). Because once Caleb, unlike Achan, alone obeyed Yahweh's command in battle, he later became the first member of the first tribe to receive a land grant on the west side of the Jordan.

Yahweh. This ceremony has points of contact with Deuteronomy 27 and Josh 8:30-35, though it does not appear to belong to the monarchic Deuteronomistic History.

The narrative concludes with the death and burial of Joshua. Joshua's burial is important, because Joshua was likely to have been revered as a local hero, or saint, after his death, in a saint's cult centered at his tomb. Especially after death, such saints (Elijah and Elisha are probably examples) could become the focal point of political movements among villagers in the countryside, and it was important for central authorities to suppress them or to co-opt them. This is probably why few instances of such movements are found in the Bible before early Christianity. The tomb of Moses was potentially so important that the deuteronomistic historian asserts that its location is unknown, presumably in a bid to prevent anyone from starting a resistance movement around it. The figure of Joshua, an Ephraimite hero, has been thoroughly pre-empted in the house of David's history of the conquest so that he will be of little use to Israelites who might want to continue to resist the house of David.

MAIN FEATURES OF THE DEUTERONOMISTIC HISTORY

Since Joshua must be understood as part of the Deuteronomistic History, it is essential to recall the main features of that work. It is a lengthy and multifarious work, a corpus of manifold overlapping sources in successive editions that probably span almost four hundred years. However, its basic story is straightforward. Like most basic stories in the Bible, it treats of sovereignty expressed in terms of jurisdiction exercised through a religious shrine and cult. In the world of the Bible, government, politics, and religion are inseparable. Translations using "religious" language, like "worship" in place of "fear," which occurs several times in Joshua, often do not adequately express the political significance of shrines and cults in the Bible. The reason is that such translations do not have a juridical and jurisdictional connotation in modern English, as terms referring to the services in and of cults invariably have in the Bible.[10] The deuteronomistic story is the story of a set of laws that must be obeyed and eventually established through a particular shrine and its cult if the promised land is to be kept. If this story is thought to be mainly "religious," despite the essential role of this law, then it may be seriously misunderstood.

The deuteronomistic story begins when this law is delivered to the "nation" by Moses. Keeping the law, Joshua conquers Canaan. After Joshua dies, the nation fails to keep the law. Enemies afflict the nation, as one "judge" after another succeeds only in temporarily saving some of them. The first law of Moses delivered at the Jordan calls for centering the

10. The NRSV translates forms of חרם (ḥāram, "devote," "consecrate," "sanctify") with "destroy" or "annihilate," thereby misleadingly excluding the "religious" sense of the term, presumably because the practice was perceived by the translators as highly negative and hence not religious, and limiting its meaning to a "secular" sense; this is the reverse of the translators' approach to "fear," where they chose to exclude its secular sense, which takes in the entire sphere of jurisdiction, and limit its meaning to the religious sense of "worship," a term that, perhaps, was felt to make "fear," which here was unmistakably religious, sound more positive. The traditional translation of ḥērem is "ban," emphasizing the prohibition.

cult of Yahweh at one shrine only (Deut 12:1-14). David captures Jerusalem, and there his son Solomon builds the Temple, and this turns out to be the one shrine. Solomon, however, tolerates other shrines. Therefore, Yahweh takes the sovereignty of Israel away from the house of David and gives it to Jeroboam, who is no better. He immediately reactivates the cult of Bethel, violating Moses' cardinal law. As a result, the sovereignty of Israel must ultimately revert to the house of David. The story leaves no doubt how: At the precise moment Jeroboam is to inaugurate the secessionist cult of Bethel at its forbidden altar, a "man of God" from Judah, still held by the house of David, suddenly appears. He proclaims that a future scion of the house of David, whose name, here revealed three hundred years in advance, will be Josiah, is destined to destroy that very altar (1 Kgs 13:1-6). Two hundred years later, the story reaches a preliminary climax. The kingdom of Israel, whose kings have persisted in the "sin of Jeroboam," is obliterated, and the sovereignty of what had been Israel is taken over by the king of Assyria. The cult at Bethel, however, remains intact. Within three more generations, the long-awaited Josiah is born. During refurbishment of the Temple, ordered by Josiah, the law of Moses, which seems to have dropped out of sight, is rediscovered. Like Joshua, Josiah obeys it. He embarks on a triumphant rampage, destroying every shrine in sight other than the Temple—and most notably Bethel—throughout Judah and what had been Israel, which now may be reconstituted and brought once again under the sovereignty and direct jurisdiction of the house of David.

In sum, the Deuteronomistic History tells of how Israel under Joshua acquired its land in the first place, then how the house of David took it over, lost it, and under Josiah looked to recover it. It is a story of revanchism: The land once lost is to be reconquered. At the end of the story, the reconquest is not told in detail. In fact, it seems scarcely to be mentioned (cf. 2 Kgs 23:19-20). It is not clear whether the writer of this stage of the Deuteronomistic History meant to end his work by referring to the reconquest in this highly abbreviated form or simply to present the basis for a policy of reconquest. Whether Josiah's reconquest ever actually took place, the structure of the overall deuteronomistic story shows clearly how that reconquest was conceived. The story begins with the proclamation and recording of the law of Moses and the conquest of the land. It ends with the rediscovery of the law of Moses and the reconquest of the land. Thus the earlier conquest pre-figures the later reconquest. Joshua, as will become evident, pre-figures Josiah and may be said to be modeled on Josiah. In essence, the book of Joshua is a representation, incorporating sources of various kinds, of either the plan for or the course of the house of David's reconquest of Israel under Josiah.

The main deuteronomistic account ended with Josiah. The debacle of the Babylonian exile of the house of David necessitated updating the history. Minor additions appear in several places, and a coda brings the story to about 560 BCE. This updating had little effect on Joshua. Joshua 23:15-16 is the best candidate for an exilic addition.

Josiah's reform is the goal of the Deuteronomistic History and the event that more than any other provides the context for the book of Joshua. Josiah's reform is an example of a practice known throughout ancient history, including numerous times in the Bible, in which a ruler refurbished the state shrine or temple and, in the name of the state god(s), promulgated a roster of reform laws that headlined the easement of debts. Such appeals to commoners were a standard feature of the reigns of the protodemocratic rulers called "tyrants" (an impartial term) in Greece during the seventh century BCE. The famous reforms of Draco (624 BCE) and Solon (594 BCE) in Athens were nearly contemporary with Josiah's reform. The centerpiece of such reform laws was usually debt remission. Other forms of debt easement included the manumission of debt slaves (indentured servants trapped in interminable indebtedness), the prohibition or limiting of interest, and regulations governing the holding of securities for loans. All these are found in Josiah's deuteronomistic reform law (Deut 15:1-18; 23:19-20; 24:6, 10-13, 17-18).

The purposes of such ruler reforms are well known. They are summarized by Chaney, who studied the many ancient parallels to the abundant biblical texts related to such reforms.[11] In the ancient world, the lower classes were usually heavily in debt. Periodically their accumulated indebtedness threatened economic, social, and political order. One purpose of debt reform was to "ameliorate economic abuses severe enough to threaten the viability of the state." By the time of Josiah's reform in 622 BCE, economy and society under the house of David had been extensively commercialized in the context of the Assyrian "peace." Such commercialization typically had the effect of concentrating agricultural land in the hands of the wealthy through a combination of high rents and taxation and manipulation of the debt mechanism. It is not difficult to imagine that Josiah's reform answered to a clamor for debt relief.

A second purpose was to restore the reputation of the ruler, to allow him to "project a public image as a just statesman who took good care of his subjects, especially the weak and disadvantaged." Josiah's reform came after eighty years of Assyrian domination of the house of David. The dynasty's tradition of strength, longevity, and autonomy only served to point up its current weakness, since it had been suffered to govern for the last three generations only by the indulgence of and at the behest of its imperial master. It is almost certain that the house of David encouraged the commercialization that swelled indebtedness in its realm, and at the same time was poorly positioned to prevent disregard for and abuse of debt easement provisions sanctioned by age-old custom or spelled out in existing law rosters. Thus the house of David was in need of a policy that would counteract charges of callousness and injustice from the impoverished.

The third purpose of such reforms was to undermine opponents by implementing debt remission laws in a selective, partial manner, in order to "weaken elite factions that threatened the ruler's hold on power." The dominant political relations and political conflicts concerned the ruling class, who were also the creditor class. This class typically

---

11. Marvin L. Chaney, "Debt Easement in Israelite History and Tradition," in *The Bible and the Politics of Exegesis,* ed. David Jobling, Peggy L. Day, and Gerald T. Sheppard (Cleveland: Pilgrim, 1991) 131. The quotations on this subject that follow are from this article.

divided into contending factions. The reform of Josiah appears to have been partly the work of a faction only recently come to power. Josiah himself, who became king at the age of eight, would have reached his majority only a few years before the reform. Upon coming of age, he had either to break out of the clutches of his regents altogether or to gain control of them and join forces with them to enhance their combined power. It is likely that Josiah followed the second course. It seems that with the backing of the court newcomers who had held the regency, he promulgated a policy of debt remission designed to weaken eminent households long in power in the court and its Temple in Jerusalem, some perhaps going as far back as the early years of the house of David.

The modern reader may react very differently to two of the most important aspects of Josiah's reform: debt easement, on the one hand, and, on the other hand, a revanchist reconquest patterned after the destructive devotion of Canaan's indigenous populace—men, women, and children—which amounts to ethnic cleansing if not genocide. Group-based debt easement may be regarded by most people today as a laudable policy, even an acceptable foundation for an entire ethical program, though in practice usually only so long as, unlike the ideal in Deuteronomy, creditors can control the process. The same people today, however, would probably regard ethnic cleansing as wholly outside the bounds of ethics, categorically indefensible under any circumstances. Yet God, through Moses, commands both, and both as part of the *same* policy and program, within the space of five chapters in Deuteronomy. Clearly the world of Joshua is not the same as our world, and this ambiguity, like many other features of the book of Joshua, requires careful attention to the ancient context.

The deuteronomistic account of Josiah's reform is based largely on typical elements of ancient royal reforms (2 Kgs 22:3–23:24). These include the repair of the dynastic Temple, the announcement of a reform law featuring debt remission, radical centralization of cult and jurisdiction, and territorial expansion. These elements are integral to one another and together enhance the reforming monarch's sovereignty and jurisdiction. Such acts were performed by Josiah with one end in view: the greater power of the house of David embodied in Josiah.

In the deuteronomist's account, the reform begins when Josiah orders his high priest Hilkiah to supervise the refurbishing of the Davidic Temple. In the ancient Near East, repairing a temple was tantamount to rebuilding it, or even building it in the first place. It represented the reassertion of strong rule through the reconfirmation of the dynasty. According to the deuteronomist, only one previous Davidic king had ordered the Temple repaired, and that was Jehoash (2 Kgs 11:1–12:16). Jehoash and Josiah had much in common. Jehoash's father, Ahaziah, had been assassinated, just as Josiah's father, Amon, was. Like Josiah, Jehoash needed to overcome the detriment of a lengthy minority, begun when he was seven years old, much like Josiah at eight. Jehoash's minority, like Josiah's, began with the aggressive restoration of the house of David by a forceful priest. The restoration of the dynasty was carried out in spite of alien overlords controlling Jerusalem, in Jehoash's case the Omrids, in Josiah's the Assyrians. In both cases the overlords promoted exceptional commercial development, producing the need for a temple-centered debt reform.

In the course of the repair ordered by Josiah, Hilkiah discovers the law of Moses, ostensibly long lost or long in desuetude. This is the law laid out in Deuteronomy 12–26, which was immediately written down and then heeded, or nearly so, under Joshua (Josh 1:7-8). As noted, although it is possible that this document, the "document of the law" within the Deuteronomistic History, contains archaic elements predating the monarchy, it is not likely, and the whole clearly reflects a radical monarchic reform. The writing of supposedly ancient, hidden books of vision, law, and wisdom for discovery is a commonplace of history.[12] The writer of Deuteronomy may well have consulted ancient sources, but by and large those parts of the law in Deuteronomy not already composed for Hezekiah's reform were probably composed under Josiah, in preparation for Josiah's centralizing reform, the aim of the history as a whole. Moses had introduced his law by insisting over and over that it was essential if the Israelites were to keep the land they were about to conquer. No law of Moses, no land of Israel. Having transgressed this law, the political nation of Israel lost its land with the fall of Samaria. The only hope for recovering the land of Israel, to say nothing of keeping the land of Judah, is to recover the law. And here it is, in the hands of Josiah's priest Hilkiah, ready to launch the house of David on its long-anticipated reconquest of Israel.

The two primary accents of this law have been mentioned: centralization, both cultic and judicial, and the periodic remission of debt. These policies are effected by radical rulings indeed, in all likelihood previously unheard of among Israelites in the form in which they occur in Deuteronomy. The Temple of the house of David, the shrine that Yahweh is to choose to place his name there, makes all other shrines, including other shrines dedicated to Yahweh, illegitimate (Deut 12:2-12; 12:29–13:18). Throughout the Deuteronomistic History, the presence of Yahweh is signified by the presence of Yahweh's name. In the deuteronomistic conception, the name of Yahweh encapsulates the political character of the central cult, which, like all cults, combines the religious and judicial aspects of the cult. The name of Yahweh is invoked not only in worship and supplication, but also, equally important and sometimes simultaneously, in judicial oaths that sanction true witness and just judgment in the adjudication of cases and disputes. To judge from the account in Deuteronomy of Moses' appointment of the judiciary (which may borrow from the E-strand account in the Tetrateuch, Exod 18:13-27). Josiah proposed to extend and rationalize central Davidic jurisdiction and to this end planned, for judicial purposes, to organize the entire subject people into surveillance cells of ten households each (Deut 1:9-18; cf. Deut 16:18-20).

Shrines and their jurisdictions outlawed by Moses' first law include those devoted to

---

12. See Jonathan Z. Smith, "The Temple and the Magician," in *Map Is Not Territory: Studies in the History of Religions* (Leiden: Brill, 1978) 176, esp. note 19.

other Palestinian deities like Baal, Astarte, and Asherah, as well as the sun, the moon, and the host of heaven (stars, constellations). The status of the cults of the foreign peoples deported to Palestine by the Assyrians (identified in 2 Kgs 17:29-31) is ambiguous, since Josiah is not said to destroy them. The outlawed shrines include those devoted to departed heroes similar to Joshua and Moses. Josiah preempts the shrine of Joshua rather than outlawing it. Preempting the shrine or shrines of Moses, which must have existed, was apparently thought to be beyond even the militant, insurgent power of Josiah. Accordingly, it was officially declared not only that Moses died on the far side of the Jordan (probably an accepted tradition, although neither J nor E had addressed the matter), but also that "no one knows the burial place of Moses to this day" (Deut 34:6). It is not likely that this was a popular or widely accepted view. In the face of popular piety and practice to the contrary, it probably is one of the pronouncements and rulings put forward in their account of Moses that Josiah and his faction were unable to maintain.

The main rite of the central shrine, like nearly all ancient shrines, is sacrifice, which often entails the eating of meat; so the deuteronomistic historian goes into where and how meat may be eaten (Deut 12:13-27; 14:3-29). This subject resumes in Deut 15:19-23 and continues by implication through the rulings regarding keeping the three main feasts at the central shrine (Deut 16:1-17). In addition, this opening section of laws regarding centralization deals with the disposition of the Judahite levitical priests, who seemed to preside at now outlawed non-Jerusalemite shrines. They are made wards of the central shrine, but are expected to reside throughout the kingdom (Joshua 21).

In Deuteronomy 15, the historian reaches the second primary accent of the law: debt remission. This was a radical law: "At the end of seven years you shall remit all debts" held by fellow Israelites, that is, subjects of the house of David who have covenanted to keep the laws of Moses. Foreigners may be dunned indefinitely; as Frick points out, the Deuteronomistic History, like the Tetrateuch, presents "national" identity, not class, as the primary social category and takes little interest in the amelioration of poverty in the rest of the history outside Deuteronomy.[13] Like all land-reform and debt-reform laws, this one was short-lived, even though similar laws occur, like ruler's reforms, throughout biblical history (cf. Exod 22:25-27; Lev 25:8-55; Neh 5:1-13; and numerous prophetic oracles that assume such laws, like Isa 3:13-15 and Amos 2:6-8; Jer 34:8-22 is reminiscent of Deut 15:1-18 but seems not to represent a full-scale royal reform). The lender is not permitted to deny the needy person's request for a loan, no matter how close the seventh year, the year of remission, may be. The condition described in Deut 15:11 is frequently misunderstood because of the use of this verse in the New Testament (Matt 26:11; Mark 14:7; John 12:8); the Hebrew text in Deuteronomy does not say that the poor will never cease, an outcome that would be quite unlikely given this law as formulated and given the abundant produce of the land (Deut 15:4). Instead, it says that when you enter the

13. Frank S. Frick, *"Cui Bono?*—History in the Service of Political Nationalism: The Deuteronomistic History as Political Propaganda," *Semeia* 66 (1994) 79-92.

land, "since the poor shall not yet have ceased," open your hand to them. An exceptional feature of this legislation is the optimism and goodwill it expresses: The Israelite is not only to forgive debts owed, but to do so readily and joyously. This attitude is expressed particularly in regard to the release of the debt slave, another form of debt remission, which in the deuteronomistic conception recapitulates the deliverance from Egypt (see Commentary on 2:1–6:27).

Josiah's reform continues when he orders all the elders of Judah—those town and village heads who are referred to throughout the law—to gather in Jerusalem, together with all the nobles, priests, cult emissaries, courtiers, and plebs already there. "In the ears" of this great assembled gathering, the entire nation under the house of David, Josiah himself reads the complete law of Moses, discovered in the Temple. Josiah then makes a covenant to keep the law in all its parts, and the assembled nation joins him with one accord (2 Kgs 23:1-3).

This pristine accord, reminiscent of Joshua's fighting nation, ignites Josiah's campaign of cult purification, beginning with Judah. In obedience to the first law, Josiah purges and purifies the cult of the Temple and suppresses or purges all other cults as rivals to the one shrine and one cult serving the one Yahweh (2 Kgs 23:4-14). He dislodges and demolishes or incinerates the apparatus and artifacts of the cults of Baal, Asherah, and the sun, the moon, and the stars, presumably with Astarte and Ashtar at their head. These are the Canaanite deities that helped to advance the house of David's long-standing trade relations and are associated particularly with Solomon and, for the Assyrian period, with Ahaz and Manasseh. Like most populist reforms, Josiah's reform touts its aversion to commerce, a root cause of the creation of debt slaves out of villagers forced to mortgage their labor and of the amassing of landholdings mortgaged by debt slaves into cash-crop estates. Altars and high places in and about Jerusalem he destroys, as well as all altars in Judah, "from Geba to Beer-sheba." These include the "high places" at the gate of the governor of the city, whose name happens to be Joshua; these high places at the gate probably sanction the jurisdiction assumed by this strong man, until Josiah puts an end to his insubordination (2 Kgs 23:8). The priests of all these abolished cults are left in their localities, but now they are dependent on the central cult, to which are owed all the contributions previously made to the demolished shrines (2 Kgs 23:9). This has been taken as a signal expression of the economic exploitation entailed in cult centralization, as the priests called Levites in Deuteronomy are forced to become wards of the Davidic Temple.[14] Many scholars theorize that these priests were installed by the house of David early in its history as partisans for Davidic rule in the hinterland. Apparently Josiah feels this settlement calls for reorganization (cf. Josh 21:1-42). Josiah puts a stop to child sacrifice in Jerusalem, thus confirming his right to supplant household patriarchs in determining the fate of their sons and daughters. The culmination of Josiah's purge of Judah comes with the wrecking of the shrines installed by Solomon (23:13-14). These were the shrines that, in the reformers'

14. W. Eugene Claburn, "The Fiscal Basis of Josiah's Reforms," *JBL* 92 (1973) 11-22.

view, brought about the house of David's loss of Israel in the first place. With their destruction, the way is cleared for the reconquest of Israel.

Having thus purged Judah, Josiah turns to Israel. The revanchism of the house of David, dormant for more than three hundred years but festering for the preceding one hundred years, has come to a head. The ancient prophecy of the man from Judah at the altar of Jeroboam in Bethel—the altar by which generations of kings of Israel presumed to sanction the hated non-Davidic jurisdictions of Israel, jurisdictions condemned from the very start by Moses as recorded in the document found in the Davidic Temple—is to be fulfilled. Josiah begins with the altar at Bethel (23:15-18). He destroys the altar and its shrine. He removes the bones from saints' tombs nearby and incinerates them on the remains of the altar, as the man from Judah foretold. The remains of that same man lie in his own tomb; his bones Josiah leaves in peace, a relic of three centuries of impudence and its epochal requital.

Josiah continues on from Bethel, ravaging the remaining shrines of Israel founded under the kings of Israel, treating them all as he had the shrine at Bethel. Apparently, Josiah spares the priests of the outlawed shrines in Judah, but slaughters the priests in Israel. Finally he returns to Jerusalem (23:19-20). The brevity of this account has been noted. The historian may leave the details of the reconquest of Israel to be worked out, having previewed its salient highlights in the conquest of Canaan by Joshua. The key detail of Josiah's rampage through Israel is what is not said; as noted, Josiah does not attack the cults of the Assyrian populace planted by imperial force within the territory of what had been Israel (2 Kgs 17:34), but only "the shrines of the high places . . . which kings of Israel had made" (2 Kgs 23:19 NRSV).

Josiah's historian thus makes a clear distinction between indigenous cults and alien cults. The significance of this distinction goes beyond the possibility that the writer wished to avoid arousing Assyrian ire or resistance over the extent of Josiah's reconquest. Josiah accepts Assyrian settlement policy in this territory, just as he defines the territory in terms of Assyrian bounds, and he respects the separate jurisdictions sanctioned by these recently established cults. These were presumably limited jurisdictions for each imperial local group represented, like the Babylonians, Cuthites, and Hamathites. In the absence of any indication to the contrary, Josiah apparently lets these groups be, along with the judicial and property relations, including landholdings, under their aegis.

Josiah's concern lies not only with the pre-Assyrian populace and their leaders and cults, represented both by the so-called Canaanite people and by the contemporary inhabitants who correspond to the other distinct groups peopling the land Joshua fought to possess. These were the Canaanite "nations," called in varying order and combinations Canaanites, Hittites, Hivites, Perizzites, Girgashites, Amorites, and Jebusites (Josh 3:10; 9:1; 11:3; 12:8; 24:11; later they were idealistically regarded as seven in number). These Canaanite entities are also thought of in general as either Canaanites or Amorites. The latter distinction appears to represent the notion that the Amorites are native to the uplands of Palestine and the Canaanites to the lowlands (Num 13:29; Josh 11:3; 13:2-5). The cultures of the uplands and lowlands were distinct from each other during both the Late Bronze and Iron ages in Palestine.[15]

Most of the leaders of this native populace, especially of those who were subject to the kings of Israel, had been dispersed and deported a hundred years earlier than Josiah. The populace came under the new leaders planted by the Assyrians. These, the deuteronomistic historian explains, had been forced by Yahweh to acknowledge the cult of Bethel and hence its laws and jurisdiction, as part of their duty for taking over landholding rights and privileges in territory disposed of by Yahweh (2 Kgs 17:24-28).[16] The primary landholding relations of the newcomers, in other words, were those regulated from Bethel, and these were abolished when Josiah ransacked Bethel. Their private cults, which they had set up after the arrangement with Bethel and continued to practice following Josiah's reconquest, had little or no bearing on the loyalty of landholders, including themselves, to Jerusalem. As the historian explains at length in 2 Kgs 17:24-41, the descendants of these people do not now adhere to the law of Yahweh (Bethel having been destroyed) and, falling for the most part outside the scope of rural landholding in Israel, do not come under the jurisdiction of the house of David. From the Josianic deuteronomist's perspective, their overlord remains the king of Assyria.

Some may find it surprising that the presence of Assyria, rather than its absence, figures in the background of Josiah's reform. It used to be thought that the main event that made Josiah's reform possible was the collapse of Assyria at the end of the seventh century BCF leaving a temporary power vacuum into which Josiah could step. The great Assurbanipal died in 627, Nineveh fell in 612, and by 609 virtually nothing was left of the once great empire. Assyria was fast being replaced by Babylon. Here was a window of opportunity, it seemed, that induced Josiah to reform.

However, in recent years views have changed. It is true that Josiah's reform advanced a nationalist and populist revival in which all things foreign were open to ridicule. This meant that any natives of Palestine who as the result of a hundred years of Assyrian cultural domination continued to imitate Assyrian style or custom or tout Assyrian ties were fair game for disparagement. But such disparagement leaves no trace in the deuteronomistic account of Josiah's reform, or anywhere in the Deuteronomistic History. It is now clear that the Assyrians did not require conquered peoples to worship Assyrian gods and that Josiah's purging of the Temple and the cults of Judah was not an anti-Assyrian act.[17] Apparently the deuteronomist makes a distinction between regional and indigenous people,

15. Rivka Gonen, *Burial Patterns and Cultural Diversity in Late Bronze Age Canaan* (Winona Lake, Ind.: Eisenbrauns, 1992), esp. 38-39; Elizabeth M. Bloch-Smith, "The Cult of the Dead in Judah: Interpreting the Material Remains," *JBL* 111 (1992) 213-24, esp. 214-19.

16. The lions sent by God to ravage the Assyrian plantations for not acknowledging the judicial authority of Bethel (2 Kgs 17:26) are ironically akin to the lion sent by God to kill the man of God from Judah for dining with the anonymous old prophet in Bethel (1 Kgs 13:11-32).

17. Mordechai Cogan, "Judah Under Assyrian Hegemony: A Reexamination of *Imperialism and Religion,*" *JBL* 112 (1993) 403-14.

on the one hand, and the newcomers planted by the Assyrians, the people of Babylon, Cuth, Hamath, and Sepharvaim, and the Assyrians themselves, who were still in place in 622 BCE, on the other hand. Josiah attacks the cults of the indigenous, but not of the Assyrian newcomers.[18]

Astonishingly, Josiah's historian says nothing about Assyria or Assyrians at either the beginning or the end of his history. Moses says nothing about them, nor, most remarkably, do they appear at all after Hezekiah's reign. The Assyrians are treated with an understandably negative slant in the account of Hezekiah's reign, since Hezekiah was known to have rebelled against Assyria. That account may incorporate a source from Hezekiah's time, as indicated by the ample role played by the prophet Isaiah. The deuteronomistic writers themselves do not give the named prophets so much attention, except when distinct sources are incorporated in their history, as with Samuel, Elijah, and Elisha. Thus it is not surprising that the Assyrians appear in a somewhat unsympathetic light in relation to Hezekiah. The deuteronomistic view is better seen in the treatment of the fall of Samaria, which immediately precedes the account of Hezekiah's reign. Here the king of Assyria is presented as simply carrying out God's judgment (2 Kgs 17:1-34).

In his attack against rivals in Israel, Josiah seems to defer to long-standing Assyrian administrative boundaries. Josiah probably remained a nominal Assyrian vassal to the end of his reign and never had a reason to be anti-Assyrian. If the main impulse of Josiah's reform was anti-Assyrian, there is no sign of it in the Deuteronomistic History.

Thus for understanding Joshua as much as Josiah, the account of Josiah's campaign against the cults of the north is significant as much for what it does not say as for what it does say. By not having to attack the Assyrian newcomers, Josiah's historian makes it all the easier to develop the era of Joshua as the prototype for Josiah's reconquest, in which the long-resident peoples, "Amorite" and "Canaanite" agriculturists and commercialists, are the primary target.

When Josiah arrives back in Jerusalem, two final acts bring his reform to a close. The first is the keeping of the feast of Passover "as prescribed in this document of the covenant" (2 Kgs 23:21-23). The deuteronomistic law of Moses requires that the feast be kept at the central shrine. Like most of the reform legislation, this is a radical innovation. As described in the Tetrateuch, the Passover is an intrinsically local, household rite, centered on the extended family as the patriarch's household. By now it comes as no surprise that Josiah wishes to suppress such extended family rites, as is implied clearly in Deut 16:1-17. In the deuteronomistic conception, as seen above, the Passover celebrates the archetypal release from debt. The history of the nation as the Davidic "nation" in the land of Canaan, therefore, begins and ends with a Passover. The first Passover is represented by the national crossing of the Jordan, followed by the celebration of Passover (Josh 3:1–5:10). On apparently the second day of that first Passover in the land, the manna ceases and the

18. This distinction may have been disregarded or found unacceptable by the later writer who added 2 Kgs 17:34b-40 to the history written under Josiah. See *The New Oxford Annotated Bible,* ed. Bruce M. Metzger and Roland E. Murphy (New York: Oxford University Press, 1991) 489.

nation eats for the first time of the produce of the land (Josh 5:11-12). The second Passover comes under Josiah, at the conclusion of his reform, and is the first in history to be in full compliance with the final law of Moses. For this alone, Josiah would have ranked supreme among the kings of Israel in deuteronomistic terms.

The second of Josiah's final acts is to remove from Judah "the mediums, wizards, teraphim, idols, and all the abominations . . . in Judah and Jerusalem" (2 Kgs 23:24 NRSV). To the extent that these are not redundant, they refer to local saints and their devices and representations, of the kind prohibited in Deut 18:9-14. The burden of this act is clear from the juxtaposition of the prohibition in Deuteronomy 18 with the text in which Moses says that "Yahweh will raise up a prophet like myself, whom you shall heed" (18:15). To obey Moses is to refuse to consult an oracle or saint who does not represent Moses. Elijah, and to a lesser extent Elisha, came close to looking something like Moses, but no one in the Deuteronomistic History actually both looks and sounds like Moses. The only way Moses does reappear is in the document containing his words, found in the Temple at Josiah's instigation. The authenticity of this document is confirmed by the prophet Huldah, so no further search for judgment, wisdom, or truth is required.

THE POLITICAL CONTEXT OF JOSIAH'S REFORM

The political context of Josiah's reform forms the primary backdrop for the story of Joshua. Josiah's support came not from the political middle, but instead from the two political extremes. One was the empires in control of Palestine: Egypt and its ally Assyria.[19] The other was a particular rural family and its allies and clients, a non-Jerusalemite family with deep Israelite roots, whose most famous member was Jeremiah, from Anathoth in Benjamin, just north of Jerusalem. This family traced its putative lineage back to Shiloh and was eager to promote a populist correction. From Shiloh's once venerable shrine came the prophet Samuel, who anointed David and sanctioned his usurpation of Saul, and the prophet Ahijah, who sanctioned Jeroboam's usurpation of the house of David (1 Kgs 11:29-39; 12:15) and then turned to a third dynast (14:1-18). Jeroboam bypassed Shiloh when he restored the cult of Israel at his borders, a common strategy, in Bethel and Dan. The importance of traditions from Benjamin in the book of Joshua and its failure to mention Egypt or Assyria are among the direct reflexes of this twofold source of support for Josiah.

---

19. In this regard, Josiah followed in the footsteps of his grandfather Manasseh. See Anson F. Rainey, "Manasseh, King of Judah, in the Whirlpool of the Seventh Century B.C.E.," in *Kinattūtu ša dārâti: Raphael Kutscher Memorial Volume*, ed. Anson F. Rainey (Tel Aviv: Institute of Archaeology, 1993) 147-64; J. P. J. Olivier, "Money Matters: Some Remarks on the Economic Situation in the Kingdom of Judah During the Seventh Century B.C.," *Biblische Notizen* 73 (1994) 90-100; Israel Finkelstein, "The Archaeology of the Days of Manasseh," in *Scripture and Other Artifacts: Essays on the Bible and Archaeology in Honor of Philip J. King*, ed. Michael D. Coogan, J. Cheryl Exum, and Lawrence E. Stager (Louisville: Westminster John Knox, 1994) 169-87; Richard Nelson, "*Realpolitik* in Judah (687–609 B.C.E.)," in *Scripture in Context II: More Essays on the Comparative Method*, ed. William W. Hallo, James C. Moyer, and Leo G. Perdue (Winona Lake, Ind.: Eisenbrauns, 1983) 177-89; J. Maxwell Miller and John H. Hayes, *A History of Ancient Israel and Judah* (Philadelphia: Westminster, 1986) 365-401; Duane L. Christensen, "Zephaniah 2:4-15: A Theological Basis for Josiah's Program of Political Expansion," *CBQ* 46 (1984) 669-82, esp. 678-81; Robert Althann, "Josiah," *ABD* 3:1015-18.

Not everyone, conceivably even the partisans' original backers, was enthusiastic about Josiah's pretensions. The Deuteronomistic History deals extensively with opponents of and foils to centralization. Indeed, its treatment of opponents, whether actual or metaphorical, comprises the great bulk of the history, and an understanding of these opponents as the deuteronomist presents them is of great importance for interpreting the book of Joshua. First there are the "Canaanites" of various kinds, who play an essential role in the preview of Josiah's reconquest and reassignment of land titles played out under Joshua. Then there are the local heroes of the type represented by the "saviors" and "judges" of the book of Judges, climaxing with Saul, in all of whose days the Israelites, in the absence of a rightful king, do "each what is right in his own eyes," contrary to the deuteronomistic law of centralization. Then come the opponents of David from among the house of Saul and its supporters and from David's own sons, possibly not unlike bypassed sons of Manasseh. Then follow the several dynasties of the kings of Israel (especially Jeroboam I and Ahab) who reject the pretensions of the house of David and its cult in Jerusalem, even when allied with it. All of these represent in Josiah's own day the kinds of opponents he must vanquish if his plan of conquest and political dominance is to succeed: men who, like Hiel of Bethel, fortify strategic sites like Jericho to their own advantage (Josh 6:26; 1 Kgs 16:34); indigenous landholders and traders in the Assyrian provinces who may identify themselves as Israelites following the norms of Bethel but not of Jerusalem; popular regional warlords, strongmen, and outlaws; prophets other than those who directly support the house of David; opposing claimants to the sovereignty of Israel from rival elite households or from the house of David itself. None can rival Josiah, the Deuteronomistic History proclaims, for the cogency and legitimacy of his claim of sovereignty.[20]

Josiah and his supporters promote a policy of "ethnic" cleansing based on the idea that "Canaanites"—that is, opponents in both Judah and the north headed by landowners and urban elite with commercial affiliations and their families, a large group under the Assyrian and Egyptian empires in Palestine—deserved to be murdered and all their property destroyed by the monarchy. As a "nationality," the category "Canaanite," like that of "Israelite," was a social construction, not an unchangeable historical reality. In the world of the Bible, there were no such nations as we understand the term.[21] Like virtually all distinctions of race, ethnic identity, and nationality, as well as the very definitions of such concepts, categories like "Canaan" and "Israel" were not natural but cultural.

The several kinds of opponents to Josiah treated throughout the Deuteronomistic History appear in the book of Joshua in the character of the seven "great and strong nations" named in Josh 3:10 (cf. Deut 7:1; Josh 11:3; Acts 13:19). In the deuteronomistic conception, these are the original inhabitants of the land of Canaan, of whom the

---

20. Richard D. Nelson, *The Double Redaction of the Deuteronomistic History* (Sheffield: JSOT, 1981) 122.

21. Benedict Anderson, *Imagined Communities: Reflections on the Origin and Spread of Nationalism* (New York: Verso, 1983); Ernest Gellner, *Nations and Nationalism* (Ithaca: Cornell University Press, 1983); Eric J. Hobsbawm, *Nations and Nationalism Since 1780* (New York: Cambridge University Press, 1990); Mario Liverani, "Nationality and Political Identity," *ABD* 4:1031-37; John Hutchinson and Anthony D. Smith, eds., *Nationalism* (New York: Oxford University Press, 1994).

"Canaanites" in particular are only one group. "Canaan" was a general term of uncertain origin for the southeastern Mediterranean coast and its hinterland, for which the terms "Palestine" and "the land of Israel" are often used in modern academic literature. Use of the term "Canaan" goes back to the Egyptian New Kingdom period, when Egypt held imperial sovereignty in Palestine, and even earlier. The term occurs in the phrases "the inhabitants [i.e., landholding elite] of Canaan" (Exod 15:15) and "the kings of Canaan" (Judg 5:19) already in early Israelite women's battle songs. It refers to the territory destined to come under David's sovereignty in the J strand, which adapts early Israelite tribal traditions so as implicitly to pit David against the king of Egypt in the post–New Kingdom struggle for Canaan. In J, the land of Canaan is mythically pictured as a "land oozing milk and honey"—that is, a largely uncultivated land (cf. Isa 7:18-25), peopled almost exclusively by city dwellers, the "Canaanite" elite descended from Ham (Gen 10:15-18). In a few texts in the Bible, "Canaanite" appears to mean "merchant," functionaries of the "kings of Canaan." The most interesting of these texts is Zeph 1:11, in which the "people of Canaan" are condemned. In this text, probably written in the time of Josiah, and perhaps in his court, "the people of Canaan" parallel "all who weigh out silver"—i.e., traders from "Canaan" resident in Jerusalem—precisely the people Josiah was most determined to suppress. The deuteronomistic historian, therefore, appears to have taken over the term "Canaan" from the house of David's history of early Israel and added to it the nuance of "trader," if that nuance was not already present.

Then, still using traditional sources and with no independent knowledge of his own (note, for example, that six of the "nations" are listed in Exod 3:8, probably an original J text), the deuteronomistic historian peoples the land of Canaan with a multifarious ancient elite of seven or so "nations" (Canaanites, Amorites, Hittites, Hivites, Girgashites, Perizzites, Jebusites; in the MT, the group numbers seven only in Deut 7:1; Josh 3:10; 24:11). Some of their names occur in the historical record outside the Bible. This is particularly the case with "Hittite" and "Amorite," a Semitic term (meaning "Westerner") used by the Egyptians like "Canaan" as a general geographic designation, this time for the Mediterranean coast and its hinterland north of Canaan. All may have existed at some time in ancient Canaan. It is important to realize that although modern historians can show that among these "nations" at least so-called Amorites, Hittites, and possibly Hivites lived long before the time of Josiah, mainly outside of Canaan, Josiah's historian, like scribes of the house of David probably going back to its beginning, believed that all these "nations" were, unlike "Israel," indigenous to Canaan. Thus they were all "Canaanites" in the sense of the original elites of the land of "Canaan," and all, in terms of J's genealogy of the "nations," sons of Ham as distinct from the sons of Shem, from whom Israel was descended.

In sum, for his understanding of "Canaan" and "Canaanite," which in his history figure almost exclusively prior to Saul and David, the deuteronomist had to look no further than the scrolls available to him in Josiah's scriptorium. He simply followed the written tradition of the house of David, to which he belonged. In line with this tradition, the ancient "land of

Canaan" was the territory destined to be held by the united tribes of Israel ruled by the house of David. The original "inhabitants" or "kings" of Canaan would have to be dispossessed. The list of thirty-one kings (petty city lords) of Canaan in Josh 12:9-24, however fictional, fits exactly the Davidic concept of pre-Davidic Canaan as the land of the "kings of Canaan." Such a concept of Canaan apparently existed among tribal Israelites who formed their ostensible political identity partly over against the petty states of Canaan long before David. But this pre-existence makes little difference for understanding the book of Joshua, since it has little to do with early Israel. In the context of Davidic sovereignty in "Canaan," "Canaanite" meant "not Israelite," and as a fictive representation of contemporary political identity it meant "not submitting to the sovereignty of the house of David."

As an expression of Josiah's reform, the story of Joshua's conquest, patterned on Josiah's reconquest, "functions as an instrument of coercion" and intimidation, encouraging the submission of all subjects.[22] The historian wants to terrorize the populace, particularly its recalcitrant political leaders, into submission to Josiah by showing what happens to a class of people ("Canaanites") whose interests are opposed to the interests of Josiah's monarchy and of the peasantry under him. The writer also shows that obedience to Josiah can take precedence over supposed ethnic affiliation: Canaanites can submit and be saved (Rahab, the Gibeonites), and if a Judahite belonging to the Israelite in-group disobeys the commander-in-chief, he can be repudiated and killed (Achan). "The primary purpose of the conquest narrative is to send a message to internal rivals, potential Achans, that they can make themselves into outsiders very easily."[23] Josiah's historian "uses the rhetoric of warfare and nationalism as an encouragement and a threat to its own population to submit voluntarily to the central authority of a government struggling to organize itself and to [re]create its own ideological framework of inclusion. In order to justify violent action [to that end], the dynamics of the literature of warfare usually consist of a division [often outrageously overstated] between self and other," us and them.[24]

22. Lori L. Rowlett, "Inclusion, Exclusion and Marginality in the Book of Joshua," *JSOT* 55 (1992) 15-23; Rowlett, *Joshua and the Rhetoric of Violence: A "New Historicist" Analysis* (Sheffield: Sheffield Academic, 1996).

23. Rowlett, "Inclusion, Exclusion and Marginality in the Book of Joshua," 23.

24. Ibid., 23. See also Danna Nolan Fewell, "Joshua," in *The Women's Bible Commentary,* ed. Carol A. Newsom and Sharon H. Ringe (Louisville: Westminster/John Knox, 1992) 63-66; Peter Machinist, "Outsiders or Insiders: The Biblical View of Emergent Israel and Its Contexts," in *The Other in Jewish Thought and History: Constructions of Jewish Culture and Identity,* ed. L. J. Silverstein and R. I. Cohn (New York: New York University Press, 1994) 35-60; E. Theodore Mullen, *Narrative History and Ethnic Boundaries: The Deuteronomistic History and the Creation of Israelite National Identity* (Atlanta: Scholars Press, 1992), which holds that the Deuteronomistic History is mainly an exilic composition. For more on Josiah's reform and the Deuteronomistic History, see Steven L. McKenzie, "Deuteronomistic History," *ABD* 2:160-68; Jeffries M. Hamilton, *Social Justice and Deuteronomy: The Case of Deuteronomy 15* (Atlanta: Scholars Press, 1992); Shigeyuki Nakanose, *Josiah's Passover: Sociology and the Liberating Bible* (Maryknoll, N.Y.: Orbis, 1993); Gary N. Knoppers, *Two Nations Under God: The Deuteronomistic History of Solomon and the Dual Monarchies,* vol. 1: *The Reign of Solomon and the Rise of Jeroboam* (Atlanta: Scholars Press, 1993), vol. 2: *The Reign of Jeroboam, the Fall of Israel, and the Reign of Josiah* (Atlanta: Scholars Press, 1994); William G. Dever, "The Silence of the Text: An Archaeological Commentary on 2 Kings 23," in *Scripture and Other Artifacts: Essays on the Bible and Archaeology in Honor of Philip J. Kings,* ed. Michael D. Coogan, J. Cheryl Exum, and Lawrence E. Stager (Louisville: Westminster John Knox, 1994) 143-68; Erik Eynikel, *The Reform of King Josiah and the Composition of the Deuteronomistic History* (Leiden: E. J. Brill, 1995); Hieronymus Cruz, "Centralization of Cult by Josiah: A Biblical Perspective in Relation to Globalization," *Jeevadhara* 25 (1995) 65-71; William Schniedewind, "The Problem with Kings: Recent Study of the Deuteronomistic History," *Religious Studies Review* 22 (1996) 22-27.

VALUES IN THE BOOK OF JOSHUA

Much about the book of Joshua is repulsive, starting with ethnic cleansing, the savage dispossession and genocide of native peoples, and the massacre of women and children—all not simply condoned but ordered by God. These features are worse than abhorrent; they are far beyond the pale. Excoriable deeds and many others of at least questionable justifiability have been committed with the sanction of the book of Joshua, such as the decimation of the Native American peoples. People who regard themselves as peaceable Christians tend to shun the book of Joshua as not simply unedifying but irreconcilable with their faith, or to justify a tacit Marcionism by equating the worst parts of the book of Joshua with the entire OT. The book of Joshua scarcely appears in the ecumenical lectionary for preaching used in many denominations; not only are its most repugnant passages ignored, but most of the rest of the book is too. The current lectionary prescribes only three passages from Joshua, all innocuous: the crossing of the Jordan (3:7-17), the keeping of Passover at Gilgal (5:9-12), and the covenant at Shechem (24:1-3, 14-25). That the last pericope, with its lofty if paternalistic avowal "as for me and my household, we will serve the LORD," is assigned twice while most of the book is assigned not at all only corroborates the aversion and bowdlerizing selectivity with which people attuned to "family values" tend to hold Joshua at arm's length.

It is possible to abstract the narrative of Joshua so as to extract from it pure qualities or values that are positive and affirmable. The stories can be taken to illustrate reliance on the power of God, whose provision, both short-term and long-run, does not fail. They illustrate the importance of grace, allegiance, obedience to authority, community solidarity, the family, and deterring hasty revenge. This is one way to rescue the text of Joshua from peremptory dismissal. However, with such a sidestepping approach study is not necessary, and commentaries need play no role.

The purpose of a careful study of the book of Joshua is not in the first place to redeem it but to understand it better, and through it to understand ourselves better. In order to understand the book of Joshua better, along with other helps we need to use the imperfect knowledge of it that is available—with all its mere likelihoods and probabilities, its uncertainties, puzzles, gaps, and voids. When looked at in terms of its historical context, the values represented in the book of Joshua, whether ostensibly bad or good, are not pure, like offhand abstractions, but multifaceted, mixed, and ambiguous. Even within the limited and relatively well understood context of Josiah's reform, significant interpretive issues arise that are difficult to address. Josiah marshaled the harsh forces of centralization for the sake of his poor subjects, promulgating a program of debt remission, which, if carried out, would have eliminated poverty among his subjects within his lifetime—an unheard-of boon. Or did he marshal the sympathies of the poor for the sake of his program of centralization? Where does the balance lie? Such ambiguities cannot finally be resolved but must be grappled with if the Word of God is to be discovered in the book of Joshua.

What does the book of Joshua show us about ourselves? If we attend to it carefully, it may suggest to us our own affinities with the atrocities, violence, coercion, and prejudicial categorizing as means to social betterment that are its main events. The point of such insight through God's Word is not to exaggerate our sins or grovel in them, but to encounter a greater reality in which we may not be as innocent as we suppose when averting our gaze from this book or disavowing it out of hand. The book of Joshua can help us to overcome consciousnesses mystified through the ignorance, fear, and conflict that to one degree or another affect all human beings.

PRIESTLY ADDITIONS TO JOSHUA

The main priestly strand (P) as a unified composition is confined to the Tetrateuch. But at least one passage of priestly character is found in Deut 32:48-52. Some historians have argued that the priestly strand predates and hence provides a source for at least the beginning parts of the Deuteronomistic History. Most, however, continue to believe that, while preserving earlier tradition from the time of their service as the priesthood of the house of David in Jerusalem, P was composed in its present form during or just after the Babylonian exile of the house of David. This sequence suggests what is probably the simplest explanation for the quasi-priestly additions to the Deuteronomistic History as well, which are most evident in the book of Joshua.

The Deuteronomistic History reflects a levitical control of tradition against the established priesthood. In contrast, in the post-exilic period the reestablished priesthood, who identified with the figure of Aaron, again found themselves in power and thus in a position to modify the Deuteronomistic History to make it conform more with the priestly Tetrateuch and express their special interests, and this they seem to have done in a modest way. For example, while the list of levitical cities in Joshua 21 may date originally from the late eighth or seventh century BCE, in its present form it is a priestly composition that was probably composed in the post-exilic period. Thus its assignment of Anathoth to the Aaronid priests (Josh 21:18) may represent, not long-standing tradition, but a form of Aaronid revenge against the deuteronomistic cabal of more than a century earlier. The similar bias can be seen in the account of Josiah's reform in 2 Chronicles 34–35, which, like the rest of Chronicles, reflects the influence of both the Aaronid rulers of the post-exilic period and the Levite underlings. Ignoring a foundational theme of the Deuteronomistic History, the account in Chronicles makes no mention at all of Josiah's attack against Bethel, the erstwhile Aaronid shrine.

A less likely explanation of the priestly additions to Joshua is to suppose that an exilic deuteronomist used priestly sources. Either way, the priestly tradition met in Joshua should be understood primarily in relation to the priestly strand in the Tetrateuch rather than in relation to the Deuteronomistic History, even though it is doubtful that a continuation of the P strand or any other unified priestly substratum underlies the present book of Joshua.

A notable instance of a priestly addition is the insertion of Eleazar in Josh 14:1; 17:4;

and 21:1. Eleazar was the third son of Aaron and his designated heir. In later genealogies, he is the link between Aaron and the Zadokite Aaronids displaced by Josiah but restored to power following the Babylonian exile, at least putatively (1 Chr 6:3-15, 50-53; Ezra 7:1-5). In the deuteronomistic view, Joshua is the direct successor of Moses and is obedient to Moses' charge and commands, both without intermediary. In Josh 14:1; 17:4; 19:51; and 21:1, however, Eleazar appears to come between Moses and Joshua, as in Num 32:28 and 34:17. This contrasts with the deuteronomistic emphasis. (Eleazar is mentioned in Deut 10:6, but this is likely to be a priestly addition.) In the priestly strand, Eleazar joins Moses to hear Yahweh's order to enumerate the clans of the tribes of Israel in preparation for the apportionment of the conquered land (Numbers 26). This order is given before Joshua is commissioned (Num 27:12-23). Then, at Joshua's commissioning, Yahweh makes it explicit to Moses that Joshua is subordinate to Eleazar (Num 27:20-21).

In Joshua 13–21, the word מטה (*maṭṭeh*) rather than שבט (*šēbeṭ*) is used for "tribe," and scholars have sometimes taken this, together with other supposed differences, to indicate a comprehensive priestly source for the account of the allotment of territories to the tribes. This remains doubtful. Clearly Joshua 13–21 as currently phrased fulfills priestly directions given in the book of Numbers, tying together the themes of promise and fulfillment in the Tetrateuch and Joshua. This is true even when there are differences between the two books on the same subject. Thus priestly writers had a hand in composing the agreements between Numbers and Joshua, and it is not necessary to look further to explain the priestly characteristics found in these chapters.

Others have noted similarities between the book of Joshua and Chronicles. Such may be particularly significant in the account of the crossing of the Jordan (Joshua 3–4). The liturgical character of this account, which apparently originated in a ritual reenactment, is enhanced by the ceremonial role of the priests, much in the style of Chronicles. Because circumcision appears nowhere else in the Deuteronomistic History but plays a cardinal role in the priestly strand, the account of circumcision in Josh 5:2-8, which appears to interrupt the narrative, represents a priestly addition.

BIBLIOGRAPHY

Boling, Robert G., and G. Ernest Wright. *Joshua.* AB 6 Garden City, N.Y.: Doubleday, 1982. A thorough treatment of textual, literary, archaeological, historical, and interpretive issues; the introduction was written by G. Ernest Wright before his death in 1974.

Chaney, Marvin L. "Debt Easement in Israelite History and Tradition." In *The Bible and the Politics of Exegesis.* Edited by David Jobling, Peggy L. Day, and Gerald T. Sheppard. Cleveland: Pilgrim, 1991. 127-39.

———. "Joshua." In *The Books of the Bible.* Edited by Bernhard W. Anderson. New York: Charles Scribner's Sons, 1989). A concise but nuanced analysis of the book of Joshua as a deuteronomistic composition.

Coogan, Michael D. "Joshua." In *The New Jerome Biblical Commentary.* Edited by Raymond E. Brown, Joseph A. Fitzmyer, and Roland E. Murphy. Englewood Cliffs, N.J.: Prentice Hall, 1990. 110-31. Pays particular attention to literary and archaeological issues, acutely sensitive to the problems of placing the book of Joshua in its historical context.

Curtis, Andrian H. *Joshua.* Sheffield: Sheffield Academic, 1994. A succinct and balanced introduction to the basic issues of Joshua interpretation, with a partly annotated bibliography for each issue.

Doorly, William J. *Obsession with Justice: The Story of the Deuteronomists.* New York: Paulist, 1994. An introduction written for laypeople by a retired minister; usable with congregations.

Hamlin, E. John. *Inheriting the Land: A Commentary on the Book of Joshua.* Grand Rapids: Eerdmans, 1983. A fluent commentary attuned to historical, social, and interpretive issues; the author, who taught for many years in Singapore and Thailand, uses his experience in Asia to draw out the implications of Joshua from an international perspective.

Hess, Richard S. *Joshua: An Introduction and Commentary.* Downer's Grove, Ill.: Inter-Varsity, 1996. A knowledgeable interpretation of Joshua as reflecting Late Bronze Age conditions, particularly attentive to historical and archaeological data and interpretation.

McCarter, P. Kyle. *Joshua.* Hermeneia. Minneapolis: Fortress, forthcoming.

Na'aman, Nadav. "The 'Conquest of Canaan' in the Book of Joshua and in History." In *From Nomadism to Monarchy: Archaeological and Historical Aspects of Early Israel.* Edited by Israel Finkelstein and Nadav Na'aman. Jerusalem: Israel Exploration Society (1994) 218-81.

Nelson, Richard D. *Joshua.* OTL. Louisville: Westminster/John Knox, 1997. Particularly useful for preaching and teaching in the church, by one of the foremost scholarly interpreters of the Deuteronomistic History.

Niditch, Susan N. *War in the Hebrew Bible: A Study in the Ethics of Violence.* New York: Oxford University Press, 1993. A lively and insightful contemplation of the many facets of this contentious issue.

Soggin, J. Alberto. *Joshua: A Commentary.* Philadelphia: Westminster, 1972. An older work still valuable for its concise articulation of basic exegetical matters.

Woudstra, Marten H. *The Book of Joshua.* Grand Rapids: Eerdmans, 1981. An intelligent and informed discussion by a scholar who believes "the picture drawn by the book of Joshua to be true and reliable," with a particular interest in theological considerations.

OUTLINE OF JOSHUA

I. Joshua 1:1-18, Joshua Receives His Commission

II. Joshua 2:1–12:24, Joshua Conquers Canaan and Destroys Its People

    A. 2:1–6:27, The Destruction of Jericho at Passover
        2:1-24, Rahab's Help
        3:1–4:18, Crossing the Jordan
        4:19–5:12, Camped at Gilgal
        5:13–6:21, Destruction of Jericho
        6:22-27, Saving Rahab and Her Family

    B. 7:1–8:29, The Destruction of Achan and Ai

    C. 8:30-35, An Altar on Mt. Ebal

    D. 9:1–10:43, Destruction to the South

JOSHUA RECEIVES HIS COMMISSION

NIV

1 After the death of Moses the servant of the Lord, the Lord said to Joshua son of Nun, Moses' aide: ²"Moses my servant is dead. Now then, you and all these people, get ready to cross the Jordan River into the land I am about to give to them—to the Israelites. ³I will give you every place where you set your foot, as I promised Moses. ⁴Your territory will extend from the desert to Lebanon, and from the great river, the Euphrates—all the Hittite country—to the Great Sea*a* on the west. ⁵No one will be able to stand up against you all the days of your life. As I was with Moses, so I will be with you; I will never leave you nor forsake you.

⁶"Be strong and courageous, because you will lead these people to inherit the land I swore to their forefathers to give them. ⁷Be strong and very courageous. Be careful to obey all the law my servant Moses gave you; do not turn from it to the right or to the left, that you may be successful wherever you go. ⁸Do not let this Book of the Law depart from your mouth; meditate on it day and night, so that you may be careful to do everything written in it. Then you will be prosperous and successful. ⁹Have I not commanded you? Be strong and courageous. Do not be terrified; do not be discouraged, for the Lord your God will be with you wherever you go."

¹⁰So Joshua ordered the officers of the people: ¹¹"Go through the camp and tell the people, 'Get your supplies ready. Three days from now you will cross the Jordan here to go in and take possession of the land the Lord your God is giving you for your own.'"

¹²But to the Reubenites, the Gadites and the half-tribe of Manasseh, Joshua said, ¹³"Remember the command that Moses the servant of the Lord gave you: 'The Lord your God is giving you rest and has granted you this land.' ¹⁴Your wives, your children and your livestock may stay in the land that Moses gave you east of the Jordan, but all

a4 That is, the Mediterranean

NRSV

1 After the death of Moses the servant of the Lord, the Lord spoke to Joshua son of Nun, Moses' assistant, saying, ²"My servant Moses is dead. Now proceed to cross the Jordan, you and all this people, into the land that I am giving to them, to the Israelites. ³Every place that the sole of your foot will tread upon I have given to you, as I promised to Moses. ⁴From the wilderness and the Lebanon as far as the great river, the river Euphrates, all the land of the Hittites, to the Great Sea in the west shall be your territory. ⁵No one shall be able to stand against you all the days of your life. As I was with Moses, so I will be with you; I will not fail you or forsake you. ⁶Be strong and courageous; for you shall put this people in possession of the land that I swore to their ancestors to give them. ⁷Only be strong and very courageous, being careful to act in accordance with all the law that my servant Moses commanded you; do not turn from it to the right hand or to the left, so that you may be successful wherever you go. ⁸This book of the law shall not depart out of your mouth; you shall meditate on it day and night, so that you may be careful to act in accordance with all that is written in it. For then you shall make your way prosperous, and then you shall be successful. ⁹I hereby command you: Be strong and courageous; do not be frightened or dismayed, for the Lord your God is with you wherever you go."

10Then Joshua commanded the officers of the people, ¹¹"Pass through the camp, and command the people: 'Prepare your provisions; for in three days you are to cross over the Jordan, to go in to take possession of the land that the Lord your God gives you to possess.'"

12To the Reubenites, the Gadites, and the half-tribe of Manasseh Joshua said, ¹³"Remember the word that Moses the servant of the Lord commanded you, saying, 'The Lord your God is providing you a place of rest, and will give you this land.' ¹⁴Your wives, your little ones, and your

NIV

your fighting men, fully armed, must cross over ahead of your brothers. You are to help your brothers [15]until the LORD gives them rest, as he has done for you, and until they too have taken possession of the land that the LORD your God is giving them. After that, you may go back and occupy your own land, which Moses the servant of the LORD gave you east of the Jordan toward the sunrise."

[16]Then they answered Joshua, "Whatever you have commanded us we will do, and wherever you send us we will go. [17]Just as we fully obeyed Moses, so we will obey you. Only may the LORD your God be with you as he was with Moses. [18]Whoever rebels against your word and does not obey your words, whatever you may command them, will be put to death. Only be strong and courageous!"

NRSV

livestock shall remain in the land that Moses gave you beyond the Jordan. But all the warriors among you shall cross over armed before your kindred and shall help them, [15]until the LORD gives rest to your kindred as well as to you, and they too take possession of the land that the LORD your God is giving them. Then you shall return to your own land and take possession of it, the land that Moses the servant of the LORD gave you beyond the Jordan to the east."

16They answered Joshua: "All that you have commanded us we will do, and wherever you send us we will go. [17]Just as we obeyed Moses in all things, so we will obey you. Only may the LORD your God be with you, as he was with Moses! [18]Whoever rebels against your orders and disobeys your words, whatever you command, shall be put to death. Only be strong and courageous."

COMMENTARY

The Josianic book of Joshua begins and ends with characteristically deuteronomistic speeches and narratives (Joshua 1; 22–23; 24:29-31). The deuteronomistic opening consists of three speeches. In the first speech, Yahweh recommissions Joshua (1:1-9); in the second Joshua gives his first order to his army officers (1:10-11); and in the third, the two and a half Transjordanian, or east-bank, tribes declare their willingness to obey Joshua's orders and to guarantee obedience from others on pain of death (1:12-18). The opening thus establishes Joshua's authority. The whole is framed by the formulaic phrases "I/he will be with you . . . be strong and courageous" (1:5-7, 17-18).

The narrative opens with the phrase "after the death of Moses." This is the deuteronomistic writer's way of demarcating the end of the period of Moses, when the law was laid down, and the commencement of the period of Joshua. The period of Joshua ends, and the period of the judges begins "after the death of Joshua" (Judg 1:1). The period of the judges ends, and the period of the kings proper, starting with the rule of David and

his establishment of what his distant successors insisted was the single shrine laid down by Moses, begins "after the death of Saul" (2 Sam 1:1).

The period of Joshua features the conquest and distribution of the land under the law of Moses, so it is not surprising that these are the main themes of Yahweh's opening speech to Joshua. Here Yahweh recommissions Joshua to succeed Moses and command Israel in the conquest of the land west of the Jordan. The deuteronomistic character of the first speech is particularly evident, as it repeats several phrases from the account of Yahweh's commissioning of Joshua in Deut 31:7-23. It also pictures Joshua reading the document of the law day and night, as is decreed for the king in Deut 17:18-20.

The words that frame the entire opening section also frame the first speech, in chiastic order. Yahweh commands Joshua to cross the Jordan and conquer the land, since "as I was with Moses I will be with you . . . be strong and courageous. . . . Be strong and courageous, for [I] Yahweh your God am with you" (1:5-6, 9; cf. 1:7). From the first commissioning of Joshua in Deut 3:28, it is clear that these repeated words reiterate the operative clauses of the commission: "Be strong and courageous. . . . I will be with you." Moreover, Yahweh's encouragement of Joshua to "be strong and courageous" is reminiscent of the encouragement Moses offered to Joshua (Deut 3:23; 31:7). Unfortunately, this correspondence is not evident in the NRSV, since the same Hebrew words are translated differently each time. The words also echo what Moses said to the entire nation as they prepared for conquest (Deut 31:6), and they are repeated by Joshua to encourage his fighters to debase their Canaanite captives before he executes them (Josh 10:25).

In Deuteronomy, the commissioning of Joshua (Deut 31:14, 23) is nested within the larger account of the disposition of the law of Moses (Deut 31:9-29). Both accounts of Joshua's commissioning (Deuteronomy 31; Joshua 1) thus stress the importance of the law of Moses. It is this law that justifies the house of David's claim to the land and thus justifies the conquest as reconquest, and it is this law through which the house of David will exercise its jurisdiction over the conquered land. This is one of many indications that Joshua is cast in the role of the monarch, a role he plays throughout this story. As Nelson explains, these indications suggested to listeners in Josiah's court the identification of Joshua with Josiah.[25] Like a king, Joshua is to study the law of Moses every day. As in the installation of a king, Joshua is commissioned with a form used for office holders in general, but with the addition of obedience to the law, which makes the installation specifically royal (cf. 1 Kgs 2:2-4).

Similarly, the opening section emphasizes that Joshua is the successor to Moses. Just as Yahweh was with Moses, so also Yahweh is with Joshua; what Yahweh commanded Moses, Joshua is commanded to do also; as the tribes obeyed Moses, they will obey Joshua; only may Yahweh be with Joshua as with Moses. Joshua's immediate succession upon the death of Moses does not follow the consensual or charismatic pattern of tribal leadership, but the royal pattern of smooth dynastic succession, like Solomon's succession (cf. 1 Kgs 2:2). This succession is stressed throughout the book. As Joshua is about to lead Israel across the

Jordan, just as Moses led Israel through the sea, Yahweh tells Joshua that he will be exalted, so that "they may know that I will be with you as I was with Moses" (3:7). When the crossing is finished, the writer notes that "all Israel feared him as they had feared Moses." Here "fear" (ירא yārē') connotes obedience to Joshua's command as to Moses' law. Joshua meets the commander of Yahweh's army in a scene reminiscent of Moses' meeting with the angel of Yahweh at the burning bush (Exod 3:2-6).

There are still other indications that Joshua is portrayed royally. Like a king, Joshua is assigned to lead a united family of "tribes," a family that, contrary to a genuinely early tradition like the Song of Deborah in Judges 5, suffers no internal conflict or dissension. As Chaney observes, in phrases like "all the Israelites," "all Israel," and "all the men of Israel," the notion of national unity "punctuates the book of Joshua like a drumbeat."[26] Like a king, Joshua is to exercise the royal power to partition land taken in conquest. As though upon a king who individually embodies his subjects, Yahweh concentrates the promise of victory and land upon the single individual Joshua (Josh 1:5). In contrast, the same promise in Deut 11:24-25 had been expressed to the entire nation. In the third of the opening speeches, the people pledge their absolute obedience to Joshua in place of Moses, as to a king; this motif is a commonplace in ancient Near Eastern vassal treaties, which demand that loyalty owed to a sovereign must be transferred to that sovereign's successor.

The commissioning of Joshua involves more than the pattern of royal appointment and succession. It also involves what Assyrian kings in Josiah's time and for centuries before referred to as the "trust-inspiring oracle" of the king's god. The first speech of the book of Joshua is just such a war oracle. In it, Yahweh encourages his lieutenant Joshua by declaring that since Yahweh will be fighting in the same battle and "will not fail you or forsake you" (1:5), Joshua should "be not frightened or dismayed" (1:9). This is a routine battle motif in the ancient Near East.[27] Assyrian kings, for example, went to battle "at the com-

25. Richard D. Nelson, "Josiah in the Book of Joshua," *JBL* 100 (1981) 531-40.

26. Marvin L. Chaney, "Joshua," in *The Books of the Bible,* ed. Bernhard W. Anderson (New York: Charles Scribner's Sons, 1989) 1:108.
27. Jeffrey J. Niehaus, "Joshua and Ancient Near Eastern Warfare," *JETS* 31 (1988) 37-50.

mand of my lord Ashur." In the Ugaritic texts, the god El visits King Keret in a dream and commands him to make war against Pabil, king of Udum. Thus the diction of Yahweh's speech parallels that of Deut 20:1, 8 in the law for making war, which, next to the slaughter of the Canaanite peoples, deals primarily with the need for dedication and fearlessness in the troops. Moreover, the comparison of Josh 1:9 and 10:25 should remove the modern temptation to treat Yahweh's "trust-inspiring" words as anything other than a prelude to rout and mayhem.

The priestly account of Moses' commissioning of Joshua (Num 27:12-23) is distinct from, but probably dependent upon, the deuteronomistic treatment of the same theme.

The land is the land Yahweh has given to the nation of Israel. Note the repetition of "give," "gave," and "given" (נתן *nātan*) throughout this opening section. The nation in this narrative consists of the idealized subjects of the house of David, and the land is the land claimed by those who held the Davidic title in the period after the fall of Samaria in 722 BCE. The narrator refers almost exclusively to the "land" rather than to its present inhabitants. The inhabitants are referred to only in 1:5, where it is evident that the trust Yahweh must inspire is trust that the inhabitants who are to be attacked will not destroy their Israelite attackers. Without this reference to the land's present inhabitants, it might be easy to forget that the land is not just to be claimed but expropriated, and that even as myth the story is not about giving a land without a people to a people without a land.

The scope of the claimed territory is described in two ways. One way reflects the ideal that the territory of Israel should match what was conceived to be the greatest extent of Davidic suzerainty under David and Solomon. The description in 1:4 is similar to several such descriptions, which differ from one another, usually in minor ways (Deut 1:7; 11:24; Josh 9:1; 10:40; 11:16; 12:7-8).[28]

---

28. The phrase "all the land of the Hittites" does not occur in the LXX and is probably an example of the kind of expansion that recurs often in the Hebrew text of Joshua. See P. Kyle McCarter, *Textual Criticism: Recovering the Text of the Hebrew Bible* (Philadelphia: Fortress, 1986), 27-29; Emanuel Tov, *Textual Criticism of the Hebrew Bible* (Minneapolis: Fortress, 1992), 283-84, 327-29. However, there is nothing surprising in this designation for the late Assyrian period.

The other way concerns the boundary of the Jordan River. The Jordan is often thought of as a natural boundary, a concept greatly reinforced by the eastern boundary of the modern state of Israel. The modern boundary was determined at the Conference of Versailles following World War I as part of the British Mandate in Palestine. The conference mapmakers based their work on the deuteronomistic conception. This boundary was based on the system of Assyrian provinces in Palestine. It is not surprising that the two known instances of treating the Jordan as a political boundary should represent state-level determinations and have nothing to do with the people in the area themselves, who rarely if ever have treated the Jordan as a boundary. Typically, those who held or inhabited one side of the Jordan at any point held the other side as well. The fact that during most of a history of six hundred years or more, including the time of Josiah, "Israel" held land on both sides of the Jordan is quite in line with regional custom. That the tribe of Manasseh was conceived as having been divided by the deuteronomistic boundary makes the point even clearer.

Just as the first speech in the opening of Joshua refers immediately to the crossing of the Jordan as the archetypal boundary crossing, the second speech refers directly to the crossing. Joshua gives orders through his "officers." The Hebrew term שטרים (*šōṭĕrîm*) means "scribes" and is a clear indication of the organized, if not bureaucratic, character of their office and the monarchic character of the narrative's context. The order is for the people to use the following three days to prepare provisions for crossing the Jordan and campaigning on the other side. The three days represent the time Israelite spies were concealed in Jericho, as part of the narrative framing and contextualizing of the crossing of the Jordan during Passover.

The third exchange, which equals the first in length, addresses head-on the closest thing to an internal division that the book of Joshua admits: the two and a half tribes who hold land to the east rather than to the west of the Jordan. The theme of this exchange is the obedience of the two and a half tribes. The ones whose loyalty might most be in question, since they already possess their lands and are separated by the Jordan, show themselves to be model followers of Joshua, to the point of avowing the death penalty for disobedience. There is an ironic element to their protestation, since it looks forward to the deuteronomistic close of the book of Joshua. There the same two and a half tribes appear to commit a dire transgression of the first law of Moses, prohibiting more than one altar by building an altar in the territory of Manasseh on the west bank of the Jordan, before the site of the single shrine prescribed by Moses had been settled upon. This apparent transgression leaves the two and a half tribes open to the charge of disloyalty, and the rest of the tribes prepare to make war against them, until the misunderstanding is cleared up. Thus the deuteronomistic composer of the book of Joshua frames the whole with a narrative defusing of the issue of potential "tribal" disloyalty.

REFLECTIONS

1. Most modern societies have a strong democratic and republican ethos, and the embodiment of a cause in a single individual can become complex and subtle. The constant turnover in officeholders and in leaders of political parties at all levels reflects this ethos. Moreover, the causes that are important to most Americans do not look like agrarian guerrilla causes. In our diverse and pluralistic society, causes are often deliberately designed more or less to overarch significant differences among people. The broad evangelical movement in American Protestantism provides an excellent example of a typical American pattern. For a hundred and fifty years or more, it has encompassed a great diversity of denominations and produced a multiplicity of leaders, at the same time standing for an identifiable alternative form of spirituality. Leaders recognized as embodiments of causes with national scope might include Susan B. Anthony, Mary Baker Eddy, Martin Luther King, Jr., Barry Goldwater, Gloria Steinem, Ralph Nader, and Billy Graham. Innumerable parallels exist for regional and local causes. Leaders have the ability to sharpen one set of distinctions in order to neutralize and incorporate all the other many distinctions that mark our lives. This realization invites us to reflect on the diversity of forces and interests represented by Joshua, even though his biblical portrait is inevitably one dimensional. It also bears on the role of the minister, who as leader frequently is challenged to embody both the congregation's diversity and its sense of common purpose.

2. In the Gospel of Mark, the story of Jesus begins, like the story of Joshua, with a commissioning. God commissions Jesus, like Joshua, to embody his "nation" as the monarch. This notion did not originate with Mark. It represents the subjects' usual sense of their monarch, not just in ancient Israel, but in agrarian societies in general. It also represents part of the meaning of such notions as being "in Christ" or "the body of Christ," which occur frequently, especially in the letters of Paul, the earliest-known Christian writings. Although the meaning of such notions is not exhausted by their sociopolitical origin, it is worth remembering that they do not begin with a vague or mystical experience, but parallel concrete experience, in this instance the experience of a collective or social identity "in" the monarch. This dimension of being "in" Christ suggests a collective experience that can be added to the necessary individualistic feeling or understanding of the phrase.

JOSHUA 2:1–12:24

JOSHUA CONQUERS CANAAN AND DESTROYS ITS PEOPLE

JOSHUA 2:1–6:27, THE DESTRUCTION OF JERICHO AT PASSOVER

OVERVIEW

Nearly the entire first half of the conquest narrative deals directly or indirectly with the fall of Jericho. The battle of Jericho is the most famous incident in the book of Joshua and one of the most famous incidents in the Bible. Often people who know little else about the Bible are aware that Joshua fought the battle of Jericho and the walls came tumbling down. The picture of the mighty walls of Jericho collapsing at the mere blast of seven horns and the shouts of the Israelite host encircling the town has captured the imagination for centuries. The attention given Jericho in the book of Joshua is a measure of its importance as a paradigm for God's leading the campaign to conquer Canaan. The great fighting force of Israelites need do no more than march around the outside of the town, blow seven horns, shout at the appointed moment—and above all obediently follow these unusual commands. God does the rest, until the Israelites rush in to ravage the now defenseless town and annihilate its inhabitants.

Of course, the battle of Jericho was not always so singularly prominent. It is scarcely mentioned outside of Joshua (2 Macc 12:15; Heb 11:30; and indirectly 1 Kgs 16:34, referring to the curse of Joshua in Josh 6:26). Apparently it held less fascination for the biblical writers than it does for us. Moreover, the battle of Jericho is only one among many interrelated themes in this section of Joshua; the others, while perhaps less famous, are just as important, if not more so. The account of the fall of Jericho is plaited out of numerous thematic strands and interconnected plots, which

intertwine like the multiple plots of an effective television drama. They all relate to one another, and the battle itself takes its place within the assemblage. In interpreting any one theme or plot from this section, it is essential to keep in mind how it is related to the others.

If there is a master plot that draws all together, it is not the battle per se, but the recapitulation of the first Passover, from the saving of the Israelite firstborn to the crossing of the sea. This is represented especially by the crossing of the Jordan, which is the centerpiece of the account. Among other links to the Passover, two stand out. Rahab is to hang out a red cord and keep her family inside to avoid slaughter by the forces of Yahweh, just as the Israelites marked their homes with streaks of blood on the first Passover night. The seven days of the battle of Jericho apparently fall on the seven days of Passover. For the writers of the Deuteronomistic History, this is the last authentic Passover before the one decreed by Josiah in his eighteenth year, which practically brings the Josianic stage of the Deuteronomistic History to its grand climax (2 Kgs 23:21-23).

All the other themes and plots in this section relate to one another through the Passover, although, like the elements of many passages in the Bible, they are intensely multivalent. There are many such themes and plots. We can scan them here briefly. Joshua replays the role of Moses in the deliverance from slavery in Egypt. Yahweh is with Joshua as he was with Moses, as proved by Yahweh's miraculous support of Joshua in the crossing and the battle in tandem. The role of the levitical priests in the crossing stresses their deuteronomistic importance as trustees of the law of Moses in the ark (they are called "the priests, the Levites" in Josh 3:3, typically the deuteronomistic designation). Their feet play the same role in the crossing that the hand of Moses does in the original, by signaling the parting of the water for the passing of the law of Moses. The Jordan serves as the great boundary, where the desert trek (and with it manna) ends and the promised land (and with it the produce of the land) begins. The fall of Jericho and destruction of everyone in it serve as paradigms for the guerrilla tactics favored by Joshua's "weak" band in the face of local power and for the projected success of Joshua's rampage, especially as regards obedience to God's command. When Jericho is destroyed, Rahab and her father's household are saved. Rahab's family is the subject of the frame to this entire section. She and her family represent two significant themes. One theme is the inclusion of Canaanites on the side of Yahweh in contrast to the exclusion of the Israelite Achan and his family in the episode that follows. The other theme, assuming that Rahab's prostitution indicates her family's poverty, is the rescue of Rahab's family from indebtedness, just as in the Deuteronomistic History Passover validates Josiah's septennial debt remission by commemorating the saving of Israelite debt slaves from Egypt. This second theme concerning Rahab is the only reason her family is mentioned at all. Rahab and her family are saved from the ban. The ban exemplified in the destruction of Jericho epitomizes the unconditionality of Josiah's reform and reconquest, in theory at least, and it ties this account of Jericho and Rahab to the ensuing account of Achan and Ai, which illustrates the consequences of violating the law of the ban. The two cairns of twelve stones memorialize "tribal" Israel, which might resist royal encroachment but which Josiah aims to incorporate. The second cairn also stands specifically for Gilgal, here established as a sacred shrine like that at Horeb, where Moses was confronted by the fire of Yahweh in the bush. Except for allusions to the present scene, Gilgal plays a role elsewhere in the Deuteronomistic History only as the shrine where Samuel both appointed and determined to depose Saul in favor of David, for violating the law of the

ban. Although based on the "cairn" of stones, the name "Gilgal" is taken by the narrator to refer to the "rolling away" of the "shame of Egypt," which from the deuteronomistic perspective at least, signifies debt slavery. By highlighting Gilgal, and hence the later rejection of King Saul in favor of David, the narrative reinforces the point that the entire Jericho episode, but especially the crossing of the Jordan (2:9-10; 4:23-24), is meant, as was the first Passover, to inspire fear in "all the inhabitants of the land" and "all the people of the earth," who are specified as "the kings of the Amorites" and "the kings of the Canaanites" (5:1). Finally, having completed the desert trek, the new generation of Israelite men are straightaway circumcised, a condition for keeping the Passover (Exod 12:48).

It may be difficult for a reader or preacher to hold together all at once the many interrelated motifs, themes, and plots contained in this major section of the book of Joshua. We can review them once again, one by one: Joshua's authority; the Passover allusions and their significance; Rahab and debt remission; the priestly curators of the law of Moses; the Jordan as a boundary; obedience to God's command; the unconditionality of Josiah's reform, but the inclusion of indebted "Canaanites"; and the support represented in Gilgal for the house of David against opposing "tribes" and kings. The best way to relate one theme to another is to ask regarding any particular element or incident what theme or themes it contributes to, and then how it is related to Passover, recalling that Passover in the Deuteronomistic History signifies the saving of a nation of debt slaves, the populist base for Josiah's reform.

The deuteronomist follows an interpretation of debt slavery that is extremely important for the book of Joshua. When debt slaves are set free in the seventh year, Josiah's law prescribes, they are to be liberally provided with sheep, goats, grain, and wine (Deut 15:12-14). The reason is given: "You yourselves were once slaves in Egypt and Yahweh freed you from slavery and provided you with plenty—so now you are to do the same" (Deut 15:15). This reason contains something of a surprise. In the Tetrateuch's version of the exodus, what Israel suffered in Egypt was continuous corvée, or a state-imposed statute tax on labor in the form of slavery. The deuteronomistic conception, which the writers of Deuteronomy and Joshua were probably not alone in holding, is different. For them the exodus from Egypt represented liberation from debt slavery, not corvée slavery.

The deuteronomistic historian certainly knew the important difference between corvée slavery and debt slavery, but in principle the historian had little problem with corvée slavery. No deuteronomistic law deals with corvée. Samuel may refer to it in 1 Sam 8:17, a text incorporated by the historian, but there no deuteronomistic elaboration is given. David himself instituted corvée (2 Sam 20:24), and Solomon's Temple, Yahweh's exclusive shrine, was built by Israelite corvée slaves (1 Kgs 5:13, 12:4; seemingly contradicted by 1 Kgs 9:22).

Just as debt remission was a great theme of temple reform in the ancient Near East, so also debt slavery becomes an overriding concern of the deuteronomist. As a commemoration of the exodus, therefore, the feast of Passover in the Deuteronomistic History marks liberation from debt slavery. That is why Passover is the next major subject addressed in the laws after the remission of debt (15:19–16:8).[29] The deuteronomistic interpretation of the slavery in Egypt as debt slavery is also clear from the frequent deuteronomistic

use of the verb "redeem" (פדה *pādâ*) as though from debt (cf. e.g., Exod 21:8; Lev 19:20), to refer to Yahweh's deliverance of Israel from the "house of slavery" in Egypt (examples include Deut 7:8; 9:26; 13:6; 15:15; 24:18; 2 Sam 7:23; Mic 6:4 (part of a deuteronomistic passage).

The importance of this deuteronomistic understanding of the Passover becomes clear in the interpretation of the crossing of the Jordan (as Israel crossed the sea in the exodus), the keeping of Passover, and the conquest of Jericho in Joshua 2–6. All these episodes are framed by the story of the deliverance of Rahab and her family. Rahab is a prostitute. That is, she is a woman who is forced by poverty—and by her poor father or brothers—to seek income that would either help to keep her family from falling disastrously into debt or to pay off the debt they have already incurred. The story of the deliverance of Rahab and her family expresses more than the safeguarding of one Canaanite family from death by *ḥērem,* the ritual slaying of enemies "devoted" to Yahweh for the sake of central rule. It also epitomizes, in combination with the epitome of the reconquest that the crossing of the Jordan and the fall of Jericho represent, the selective deliverance from debt servitude that stands at the center of Josiah's reform in the form of the law of debt remission.

---

29. The deuteronomistic treatment of Passover begins appropriately with rules concerning the eating of the firstborn of herd and flock. This is the subject that also forms an envelope around the law of Passover in Exod 13:1-16.

Joshua 2:1-24, Rahab's Help

NIV

2 Then Joshua son of Nun secretly sent two spies from Shittim. "Go, look over the land," he said, "especially Jericho." So they went and entered the house of a prostitute[a] named Rahab and stayed there.

[2]The king of Jericho was told, "Look! Some of the Israelites have come here tonight to spy out the land." [3]So the king of Jericho sent this message to Rahab: "Bring out the men who came to you and entered your house, because they have come to spy out the whole land."

[4]But the woman had taken the two men and hidden them. She said, "Yes, the men came to me, but I did not know where they had come

a1 Or possibly *an innkeeper*

NRSV

2 Then Joshua son of Nun sent two men secretly from Shittim as spies, saying, "Go, view the land, especially Jericho." So they went, and entered the house of a prostitute whose name was Rahab, and spent the night there. [2]The king of Jericho was told, "Some Israelites have come here tonight to search out the land." [3]Then the king of Jericho sent orders to Rahab, "Bring out the men who have come to you, who entered your house, for they have come only to search out the whole land." [4]But the woman took the two men and hid them. Then she said, "True, the men came to me, but I did not know where they came from. [5]And when it was time to close the gate at dark, the men went out. Where the men went I do not know. Pursue them quickly,

NIV

from. ⁵At dusk, when it was time to close the city gate, the men left. I don't know which way they went. Go after them quickly. You may catch up with them." ⁶(But she had taken them up to the roof and hidden them under the stalks of flax she had laid out on the roof.) ⁷So the men set out in pursuit of the spies on the road that leads to the fords of the Jordan, and as soon as the pursuers had gone out, the gate was shut.

⁸Before the spies lay down for the night, she went up on the roof ⁹and said to them, "I know that the Lord has given this land to you and that a great fear of you has fallen on us, so that all who live in this country are melting in fear because of you. ¹⁰We have heard how the Lord dried up the water of the Red Sea*ᵃ* for you when you came out of Egypt, and what you did to Sihon and Og, the two kings of the Amorites east of the Jordan, whom you completely destroyed.*ᵇ* ¹¹When we heard of it, our hearts melted and everyone's courage failed because of you, for the Lord your God is God in heaven above and on the earth below. ¹²Now then, please swear to me by the Lord that you will show kindness to my family, because I have shown kindness to you. Give me a sure sign ¹³that you will spare the lives of my father and mother, my brothers and sisters, and all who belong to them, and that you will save us from death."

¹⁴"Our lives for your lives!" the men assured her. "If you don't tell what we are doing, we will treat you kindly and faithfully when the Lord gives us the land."

¹⁵So she let them down by a rope through the window, for the house she lived in was part of the city wall. ¹⁶Now she had said to them, "Go to the hills so the pursuers will not find you. Hide yourselves there three days until they return, and then go on your way."

¹⁷The men said to her, "This oath you made us swear will not be binding on us ¹⁸unless, when we enter the land, you have tied this scarlet cord in the window through which you let us down, and unless you have brought your father and mother, your brothers and all your family into your house. ¹⁹If anyone goes outside your house

---

ᵃ10 Hebrew *Yam Suph*; that is, Sea of Reeds   *ᵇ10* The Hebrew term refers to the irrevocable giving over of things or persons to the Lord, often by totally destroying them.

NRSV

for you can overtake them." ⁶She had, however, brought them up to the roof and hidden them with the stalks of flax that she had laid out on the roof. ⁷So the men pursued them on the way to the Jordan as far as the fords. As soon as the pursuers had gone out, the gate was shut.

8Before they went to sleep, she came up to them on the roof ⁹and said to the men: "I know that the Lord has given you the land, and that dread of you has fallen on us, and that all the inhabitants of the land melt in fear before you. ¹⁰For we have heard how the Lord dried up the water of the Red Sea*ᵃ* before you when you came out of Egypt, and what you did to the two kings of the Amorites that were beyond the Jordan, to Sihon and Og, whom you utterly destroyed. ¹¹As soon as we heard it, our hearts melted, and there was no courage left in any of us because of you. The Lord your God is indeed God in heaven above and on earth below. ¹²Now then, since I have dealt kindly with you, swear to me by the Lord that you in turn will deal kindly with my family. Give me a sign of good faith ¹³that you will spare my father and mother, my brothers and sisters, and all who belong to them, and deliver our lives from death." ¹⁴The men said to her, "Our life for yours! If you do not tell this business of ours, then we will deal kindly and faithfully with you when the Lord gives us the land."

15Then she let them down by a rope through the window, for her house was on the outer side of the city wall and she resided within the wall itself. ¹⁶She said to them, "Go toward the hill country, so that the pursuers may not come upon you. Hide yourselves there three days, until the pursuers have returned; then afterward you may go your way." ¹⁷The men said to her, "We will be released from this oath that you have made us swear to you ¹⁸if we invade the land and you do not tie this crimson cord in the window through which you let us down, and you do not gather into your house your father and mother, your brothers, and all your family. ¹⁹If any of you go out of the doors of your house into the street, they shall be responsible for their own death, and we shall be innocent; but if a hand is laid upon any who are with you in the house, we shall bear

---

ᵃ Or *Sea of Reeds*

NIV

into the street, his blood will be on his own head; we will not be responsible. As for anyone who is in the house with you, his blood will be on our head if a hand is laid on him. ²⁰But if you tell what we are doing, we will be released from the oath you made us swear."

²¹"Agreed," she replied. "Let it be as you say." So she sent them away and they departed. And she tied the scarlet cord in the window.

²²When they left, they went into the hills and stayed there three days, until the pursuers had searched all along the road and returned without finding them. ²³Then the two men started back. They went down out of the hills, forded the river and came to Joshua son of Nun and told him everything that had happened to them. ²⁴They said to Joshua, "The LORD has surely given the whole land into our hands; all the people are melting in fear because of us."

NRSV

the responsibility for their death. ²⁰But if you tell this business of ours, then we shall be released from this oath that you made us swear to you." ²¹She said, "According to your words, so be it." She sent them away and they departed. Then she tied the crimson cord in the window.

22They departed and went into the hill country and stayed there three days, until the pursuers returned. The pursuers had searched all along the way and found nothing. ²³Then the two men came down again from the hill country. They crossed over, came to Joshua son of Nun, and told him all that had happened to them. ²⁴They said to Joshua, "Truly the LORD has given all the land into our hands; moreover all the inhabitants of the land melt in fear before us."

COMMENTARY

The story of Rahab is the story of her father's house, as she repeats (2:12, 18; cf. 6:25): father, mother, brothers, sisters, and all who belong to them (2:13, 18; 6:23)—indeed, her entire extended family (6:23; the NRSV translates the phrase "father's house" [בית אב *bêt 'āb*] as "family"). The mention of Rahab's mother next to her father reflects the subverting of patriarchal households in Josiah's reform. Rahab's family's fate is tied to her own, not because as the wealthiest member of the family she provides for the rest of them, as some have suggested,[30] but for just the opposite reason: It has fallen to her as a mere daughter to help supply her family's dire need through the unwanted and demeaning necessity of prostitution, for it is the poverty of her extended household that has forced her into prostitution in the first place.

There are several reasons besides the deuteronomistic Passover basis of this narrative for assuming that Rahab is a prostitute because her family is in debt. Poverty was by far the most common cause of prostitution in the ancient world, as it is in our world as well. Most of the story works like

many of the folkloristic narratives of the Bible, by dealing in stereotypical extremes. Rahab takes the side of the "outside agitators," on the extreme margins of society, against the king, at the extreme pinnacle of society. She advises the spies to escape to the hills, the traditional refuge of outlaws against royal authority. Her story is basically a folk narrative about poor people against kingly power, not about a well-off, if socially marginal, sexual escort. The narrative's characters represent stock figures rather than nuanced individuals: a typical prostitute and her family, a typical king, typical outlaw spies. Moreover, the only reason why the prostitute's family is brought into the story is that her story is their story—her prostitution reflects their poverty, and their poverty in all likelihood means their indebtedness. The story is adopted to appeal to debtor families who, far from condemning Rahab because of her prostitution or her act of deception, would sympathize with her and her family as fellow indigents and cheer her on as she dares to make fools out of the king and his men, to whom her family would have owed their debts.

There is no indication that Rahab owns the

30. See, e.g., Athalya Brenner, *The Israelite Woman: Social Role and Literary Type in Biblical Narrative* (Sheffield: JSOT, 1985) 79-81.

house she resides in, as is often assumed. It is probably her father's house, since the rest of her family are assumed to be living in Jericho. The house would have been kept in the family in part through Rahab's prostitution. The phrase "the house of a prostitute" in v. 1 does not require that the prostitute own the house; the phrase "your house" in v. 18 does not occur in the Hebrew text, which has only "inside the house" (אליך הביתה *ʾēlayik habbaytâ*). There is no reason to regard Rahab as a "madame," as some do, or an innkeeper, as later tradition sometimes attempted to suggest (see the note to 2:1 and 6:17 in the NIV). Rahab's prostitution is the narrator's way of addressing the issue of indebtedness, for in most instances in the ancient world prostitution alternated with debt slavery. Often, if a poor family did not submit to one alternative, it was forced to submit to the other, if not to both. Rahab represents the indebted, as we might expect in a deuteronomistic text highlighting Passover, and her deliverance and the deliverance of her father's entire house in conjunction with the slaughter of their creditors are tantamount to the remission of their debts.

The basic story of the prostitute against the king has been co-opted by the deuteronomistic writers for its populist appeal.[31] Most of the narrative assumes that Rahab and her family are on the side of the spies and opposed to the king and his henchmen. In this aspect, the story pits the poor against the rich, the marginal against the dominant, and Rahab belongs on the side of the poor Israelites. The deuteronomist is opposed to all local warlords and minor rulers, like those featured throughout the narrative of conquest and enumerated in 12:9-24, a list headed by the king of Jericho. These represent the likes of Josiah's adversaries, the potent oppressors of Josiah's poor subjects and the target of his law of debt remission. In origin, the story tells about collusion between disaffected insurgents and a disaffected prostitute who have an interest in joining forces but who need to give guarantees that can be trusted. For this reason, the bulk of the narrative

details the dialogue between spies (called messengers in 6:17, 25) and a prostitute as they negotiate the risky business of agreeing to terms and taking the requisite oaths (2:9*a*, 12-21).

In contrast to such a theme, however, in a few lines Rahab refers to herself as one with the king (2:9*b*-11). These lines have been added to the basic story by the deuteronomistic historian, in line with the conceptual polarization of Israelite and Canaanite. They interrupt the thread of Rahab's opening to her parley with the spies: "I know Yahweh has given you the land . . . so, since I have dealt kindly with you, swear. . . ." The first of the interjected phrases, "that dread of you has fallen on us" (v. 9*b*), and the rest of vv. 10-11 have numerous deuteronomistic parallels, especially in Deuteronomy and Joshua.[32] Yahweh, the God of heaven and earth, promotes the interests of the "nation" of the chosen grantees against the other nations of the earth. In this aspect, the story pits the supposed Israelite nation against the Canaanite nations, and Rahab belongs on the side of the Canaanites rather than the Israelites (her "us," "we," and "our" include the king and his men). The flax drying on the roof of Rahab's house is the first direct indication that events are occurring during the time of Passover. Flax was harvested and laid out to dry just before the barley harvest, and, as reckoned by the agricultural calendar, it was the barley harvest that marked the time of Passover.

Rahab refers to two causes of her people's fear: the drying up of the sea at Passover and the slaughter of the Amorite kings, Sihon and Og. It is partly ironic that in this speech she mentions the Passover—and mentions it first—since it is in the context of Passover and the debt remission it validates that the rest of her story puts her on the side of the Israelite poor. Looked at another way, however, it is appropriate. Having completed the new trek through the Jordan on dry land, Joshua constructs the cairn of stones at Gilgal to commemorate the crossing on dry land ("dry" [יבש *yābēš*] is repeated three times) so that all the

---

31. For the social analysis of the Rahab story presented here, see Marvin L. Chaney, "Ancient Palestinian Peasant Movements and the Formation of Premonarchic Israel," in *Palestine in Transition: The Emergence of Ancient Israel,* ed. David Noel Freedman and David F. Graf (Sheffield: Almond, 1983) 67-69. Cf. Norman K. Gottwald, *The Tribes of Yahweh: A Sociology of the Religion of Liberated Israel 1250–1050 B.C.E.* (Maryknoll, N.Y.: Orbis, 1979) 885-86.

32. In addition to numerous deuteronomistic phrases, note that Rahab says the Israelites carried out the ban of extermination against Sihon and Og (2:10; NIV, "completely destroyed"; NRSV, "utterly destroyed"). Her statement agrees in this respect with the deuteronomistic account of the battles against Sihon and Og in Deut 2:31–3:7 ("ban" in Deut 2:34; 3:6). The account in the Tetrateuch, in contrast, mentions no such ban (Num 21:21-35). This part of Rahab's deuteronomistic speech thus points up in retrospect the rescue of her father's house, which sets up the marked contrast between Josh 6:17-21, where the ban involves "Canaanite" exceptions, and Deut 2:31–3:6, where there are no "Amorite" exceptions.

peoples of the earth may know that Yahweh is mighty and so that they may learn, like the Israelites, to fear Yahweh (4:22-24). In the deuteronomistic view, for both Rahab and Joshua the purpose of crossing on dry land is to put fear in the hearts of the nations so that they will collapse in the face of Joshua—that is, so that they are forced to acknowledge the justice of Israel's liberation from Egypt. This is what Joshua comments on when the spies report to him (vv. 23-24), even though they have spent three days scouting out the hill country as well.

The phrase "inhabitants of the land" can be and was construed in two ways, only one of which applied in the folk narrative. The Hebrew translated "inhabitants" (יושבים *yôšĕbîm*) means, literally, "the ones who sit." In many passages, it can refer either to rulers who sit on thrones (e.g., Amos 1:5: "I will cut off the enthroned one [NRSV, inhabitants] from Emeq-aven, and the one who holds the scepter from Beth-eden") or to the strong who "sit" on their estates as the wealthy landowning class (e.g., the "lords" of Philistia and Canaan in Exod 15:14-15; note the parallels, "chiefs" and "leaders"). This is the meaning of the phrase in the folk narrative, which stresses the gulf between the rich (not "inhabitants," but "landowners") and the poor. The second phrase in v. 9*b*, "all the landowners of the country melt in fear before you," is likely original to the folk narrative, since it is not deuteronomistic but is identical to the popular poetic line in Exod 15:15 (NRSV, "all the inhabitants of Canaan melted away"). From the perspective of Rahab's deuteronomistic avowals, however, for which the distinction between Israelite and Canaanite is primary, the phrase probably was taken to mean "inhabitants," as though "Canaanite" were a national category embracing all people regardless of social class, including women and children. From this perspective, king and prostitute, the richest and the poorest in the town, belonged to the same category of people.

As in the rest of Joshua, the LXX often represents a different Hebrew original from the MT. In several places in Joshua 2, the LXX seems more in tune with the folk narrative, in which the spies come to the town to make contacts there, than the deuteronomistic use of it. In the LXX of v. 2, the king is told that some spies have come to search out the *town*, not the land. In v. 13, the LXX has "the house of my father," again the social unit responsible for covering family debts, instead of the MT's "my father" at the head of the list of individuals. In v. 18, the LXX has "if we come to the edge of the town" rather than "come to the land" (NIV, "enter the land"; NRSV, "invade the land"). The idea that in origin the story applied only to some town fits with 6:17, 25, where the spies are called "messengers," as though they had had business with someone in the town. Finally, the long phrase in v. 15*b*, "for her house was on the outer side of the town wall and she resided within the wall itself," does not occur in the LXX and seems to be a late explanatory addition that accords poorly with the fall of Jericho's walls and survival of Rahab's house (6:20, 22). It is sometimes suggested that Rahab's house stood miraculously while the rest of the wall fell down. This is unlikely, since it finds no association or resonance elsewhere in the text.

As already indicated, the red cord hung out by Rahab to protect her family from the impending slaughter is intentionally reminiscent of the blood of the pascal lamb, which protected the Israelite debt slaves at Passover (Exod 12:7, 13). Even this quasi-liturgical motif could have played a role in the original folk narrative, if conceived in terms of the Passover feast as a family rite rather than the state rite it becomes in deuteronomistic legislation.

Thus the historian conceives a role for both Rahabs: the Rahab who represents the impoverished in social terms and the Rahab who represents the Canaanites in national terms. The one is meant to appeal to the poor debtors among Josiah's subjects, the other to "Canaanite" clients of Josiah's landed elite opponents who might be enticed to submit to Josiah's sovereign command.

REFLECTIONS

1. Probably most readers of Joshua who reside in the so-called developed world, or First World, when presented with the story of a prostitute are apt to appropriate it primarily in moral terms. Prostitution is bad, and a prostitute is a morally reprehensible individual; so Rahab must be a questionable character. Thus it is not surprising, such an interpretation might conclude, that she is a Canaanite, and in the end never really better than the rest of her fellow Canaanites. Such an interpretive approach must be abandoned, however, because it fails to take account of the pre-industrial contexts and meaning of prostitution.[33] Furthermore, it lacks any realistic analysis of modern prostitution and its causes, lumping poor and dominated prostitutes together with wealthy and independent prostitutes, even though the former far outnumber the latter, and assuming that prostitutes may simply exercise freedom of choice to engage in "immoral" behavior.

As in the book of Joshua, debt, slavery, and extermination played an important role in the development of American identity and racial and ethnic classifications. In the colonial period of United States history, indentured servitude, a form of debt slavery, played a significant role in helping thousands of needy people, almost entirely young men, emigrate from Britain and begin a new life in America. These debt contracts provided a socially accepted and constructive way for landowners and householders to capitalize on the labor pool available for work in the colonies and for the sons of the poor to find a new dignity in the independence they soon achieved. At the same time, in using the debt contract to bootstrap themselves to prosperity, they became part of the advancing tide of deception, mayhem, and dispossession that confronted the Native American populace.

In the highlands of Central and South America, European colonists put Native Americans to work in mines and on vast latifundia as serfs and slaves. Descendants of these groups exist today in large numbers, though often they are poor and discriminated against. In the tropical lowlands, the colonists exterminated or expelled the natives and imported chattel slaves from Africa, mainly for sugar and later cotton production. This labor development led directly to the definition of "whites" versus "blacks" that still prevails in the United States. In the temperate climes, colonists drove back the native population and brought in British and northern European indentured servants, whose story eventually contributed to the myth of North American resourcefulness and self-reliance.

Debt slavery and debt prostitution still exist around the world. Debt slavery was outlawed in Pakistan in 1992, but is still common there, for example, on sugar plantations. Recently the president of Brazil was forced to admit that slavery, outlawed in Brazil in 1888, is common on the orange, coffee, and other plantations of the Amazon region. Most Brazilian slaves indenture themselves to estate owners to pay for the long journey from the northeast of Brazil. Once on location, they are forced to buy all their needs from the estate owner and soon find it impossible to repay their debt, which only continues to grow. In a similar way, prostitutes are frequently enslaved in East Asia and other parts of the world.[34]

It may come as more of a surprise that slaves are still found in the United States. Recently state officials in Los Angeles raided a sweatshop housing seventy-four immigrant Thai workers, mostly women, being paid slave wages for seventeen hours of work a day, supposedly toward paying off their fares to America. The state figured they were owed $3.5 million in back-pay, but instead laid plans to deport them, against the desire of many locals that all seventy-four be given green cards—in other words, be treated the way Rahab was treated by Joshua. As with many such attempts to enforce the law, this incident was regarded as a sign of the much wider practice of peonage and prostitution among poor Asian immigrants in southern California.

In comparable ways, such practices could be verified in many other parts of the country. The picture is complicated by a recent case in Chicago in which a woman was charged with selling her child to pay off a drug debt. With the reformist values represented in Joshua 2, God would

33. See, e.g., Gideon Sjoberg, *The Preindustrial City: Past and Present* (New York: Free Press, 1960).
34. For prostitution in the contemporary world, see Rita Nakashima Brock and Susan Brooks Thistlethwaite, *Casting Stones: Prostitution and Liberation in Asia and the United States* (Minneapolis: Fortress, 1996).

attack the creditor, pay the woman's debt, and redeem the child. In Chicago, the public faulted all three parties in the case—dealer, woman, and child—but focused most attention on the mother's wrongdoing, as though Rahab were most at fault because she is a prostitute.

When interpreting biblical texts, it is often worthwhile to identify the protagonists not with most of the people in the church, but with others whose lives are more like those in the text. The examples of forced indebtedness mentioned here represent a burden that has weighed on the poor for at least four millennia, and one that will, it seems, continue in more or less the same guise for the foreseeable future. Those who interpret Scripture in churches that are not poor need to recognize how this text (and many others) resonates with the experience of the poor.

By the same token, even within the church there are many, especially women, who, while not slaves, are oppressed by coercion of one kind or another. Thus in satisfying the needs of others they are unable to maintain their own importance and well-being.

2. Rahab is mentioned twice in the New Testament. In Heb 11:31, Rahab becomes one in the train of forebears who survived or prospered by faith, and in James she is a model of those who are "justified by works and not by faith alone" (Jas 2:24). The partial contrast between these two texts (Hebrews expounds on faith, while James advocates works) points up inevitable partiality of interpretation, even for New Testament writers dealing with the Scriptures. Nevertheless, these texts also complement each other. Brief though they are, both attribute to Rahab the same faith marked by the same work: safeguarding the Israelite spies. Thus in concert they articulate the familiar biblical theme that "faith without works is dead" (Jas 2:17, 26). From this biblical perspective, the figure of Rahab reminds the interpreter that faith may be expounded in terms not only of doctrine, but also of lives lived. Moreover, the lives of the faithful include not only deeds performed, but also perseverance and patience maintained in the face of adversity. To be faithful is both to do and to endure, and the vector of a person's faith manifests itself through both.

Joshua 3:1–4:18, Crossing the Jordan

NIV

3 Early in the morning Joshua and all the Israelites set out from Shittim and went to the Jordan, where they camped before crossing over. ²After three days the officers went throughout the camp, ³giving orders to the people: "When you see the ark of the covenant of the LORD your God, and the priests, who are Levites, carrying it, you are to move out from your positions and follow it. ⁴Then you will know which way to go, since you have never been this way before. But keep a distance of about a thousand yards[a] between you and the ark; do not go near it."

⁵Joshua told the people, "Consecrate yourselves, for tomorrow the LORD will do amazing things among you."

⁶Joshua said to the priests, "Take up the ark of the covenant and pass on ahead of the people." So they took it up and went ahead of them.

a4 Hebrew *about two thousand cubits* (about 900 meters)

NRSV

3 Early in the morning Joshua rose and set out from Shittim with all the Israelites, and they came to the Jordan. They camped there before crossing over. ²At the end of three days the officers went through the camp ³and commanded the people, "When you see the ark of the covenant of the LORD your God being carried by the levitical priests, then you shall set out from your place. Follow it, ⁴so that you may know the way you should go, for you have not passed this way before. Yet there shall be a space between you and it, a distance of about two thousand cubits; do not come any nearer to it." ⁵Then Joshua said to the people, "Sanctify yourselves; for tomorrow the LORD will do wonders among you." ⁶To the priests Joshua said, "Take up the ark of the covenant, and pass on in front of the people." So they took up the ark of the covenant and went in front of the people.

NIV

[7]And the LORD said to Joshua, "Today I will begin to exalt you in the eyes of all Israel, so they may know that I am with you as I was with Moses. [8]Tell the priests who carry the ark of the covenant: 'When you reach the edge of the Jordan's waters, go and stand in the river.'"

[9]Joshua said to the Israelites, "Come here and listen to the words of the LORD your God. [10]This is how you will know that the living God is among you and that he will certainly drive out before you the Canaanites, Hittites, Hivites, Perizzites, Girgashites, Amorites and Jebusites. [11]See, the ark of the covenant of the Lord of all the earth will go into the Jordan ahead of you. [12]Now then, choose twelve men from the tribes of Israel, one from each tribe. [13]And as soon as the priests who carry the ark of the LORD—the Lord of all the earth—set foot in the Jordan, its waters flowing downstream will be cut off and stand up in a heap."

[14]So when the people broke camp to cross the Jordan, the priests carrying the ark of the covenant went ahead of them. [15]Now the Jordan is at flood stage all during harvest. Yet as soon as the priests who carried the ark reached the Jordan and their feet touched the water's edge, [16]the water from upstream stopped flowing. It piled up in a heap a great distance away, at a town called Adam in the vicinity of Zarethan, while the water flowing down to the Sea of the Arabah (the Salt Sea [a]) was completely cut off. So the people crossed over opposite Jericho. [17]The priests who carried the ark of the covenant of the LORD stood firm on dry ground in the middle of the Jordan, while all Israel passed by until the whole nation had completed the crossing on dry ground.

4 When the whole nation had finished crossing the Jordan, the LORD said to Joshua, [2]"Choose twelve men from among the people, one from each tribe, [3]and tell them to take up twelve stones from the middle of the Jordan from right where the priests stood and to carry them over with you and put them down at the place where you stay tonight."

[4]So Joshua called together the twelve men he had appointed from the Israelites, one from each tribe, [5]and said to them, "Go over before the ark

a16 That is, the Dead Sea

NRSV

7The LORD said to Joshua, "This day I will begin to exalt you in the sight of all Israel, so that they may know that I will be with you as I was with Moses. [8]You are the one who shall command the priests who bear the ark of the covenant, 'When you come to the edge of the waters of the Jordan, you shall stand still in the Jordan.'" [9]Joshua then said to the Israelites, "Draw near and hear the words of the LORD your God." [10]Joshua said, "By this you shall know that among you is the living God who without fail will drive out from before you the Canaanites, Hittites, Hivites, Perizzites, Girgashites, Amorites, and Jebusites: [11]the ark of the covenant of the Lord of all the earth is going to pass before you into the Jordan. [12]So now select twelve men from the tribes of Israel, one from each tribe. [13]When the soles of the feet of the priests who bear the ark of the LORD, the Lord of all the earth, rest in the waters of the Jordan, the waters of the Jordan flowing from above shall be cut off; they shall stand in a single heap."

14When the people set out from their tents to cross over the Jordan, the priests bearing the ark of the covenant were in front of the people. [15]Now the Jordan overflows all its banks throughout the time of harvest. So when those who bore the ark had come to the Jordan, and the feet of the priests bearing the ark were dipped in the edge of the water, [16]the waters flowing from above stood still, rising up in a single heap far off at Adam, the city that is beside Zarethan while those flowing toward the sea of the Araban, the Dead Sea,[a] were wholly cut off. Then the people crossed over opposite Jericho. [17]While all Israel were crossing over on dry ground, the priests who bore the ark of the covenant of the LORD stood on dry ground in the middle of the Jordan, until the entire nation finished crossing over the Jordan.

4 When the entire nation had finished crossing over the Jordan, the LORD said to Joshua: [2]"Select twelve men from the people, one from each tribe, [3]and command them, 'Take twelve stones from here out of the middle of the Jordan, from the place where the priests' feet stood, carry them over with you, and lay them down in the place where you camp tonight.'" [4]Then Joshua summoned the twelve men from

a Heb Salt Sea

NIV

of the LORD your God into the middle of the Jordan. Each of you is to take up a stone on his shoulder, according to the number of the tribes of the Israelites, ⁶to serve as a sign among you. In the future, when your children ask you, 'What do these stones mean?' ⁷tell them that the flow of the Jordan was cut off before the ark of the covenant of the LORD. When it crossed the Jordan, the waters of the Jordan were cut off. These stones are to be a memorial to the people of Israel forever."

⁸So the Israelites did as Joshua commanded them. They took twelve stones from the middle of the Jordan, according to the number of the tribes of the Israelites, as the LORD had told Joshua; and they carried them over with them to their camp, where they put them down. ⁹Joshua set up the twelve stones that had been*c* in the middle of the Jordan at the spot where the priests who carried the ark of the covenant had stood. And they are there to this day.

¹⁰Now the priests who carried the ark remained standing in the middle of the Jordan until everything the LORD had commanded Joshua was done by the people, just as Moses had directed Joshua. The people hurried over, ¹¹and as soon as all of them had crossed, the ark of the LORD and the priests came to the other side while the people watched. ¹²The men of Reuben, Gad and the half-tribe of Manasseh crossed over, armed, in front of the Israelites, as Moses had directed them. ¹³About forty thousand armed for battle crossed over before the LORD to the plains of Jericho for war.

¹⁴That day the LORD exalted Joshua in the sight of all Israel; and they revered him all the days of his life, just as they had revered Moses.

¹⁵Then the LORD said to Joshua, ¹⁶"Command the priests carrying the ark of the Testimony to come up out of the Jordan."

¹⁷So Joshua commanded the priests, "Come up out of the Jordan."

¹⁸And the priests came up out of the river carrying the ark of the covenant of the LORD. No sooner had they set their feet on the dry ground than the waters of the Jordan returned to their place and ran at flood stage as before.

c9 Or Joshua also set up twelve stones

NRSV

the Israelites, whom he had appointed, one from each tribe. ⁵Joshua said to them, "Pass on before the ark of the LORD your God into the middle of the Jordan, and each of you take up a stone on his shoulder, one for each of the tribes of the Israelites, ⁶so that this may be a sign among you. When your children ask in time to come, 'What do those stones mean to you?' ⁷then you shall tell them that the waters of the Jordan were cut off in front of the ark of the covenant of the LORD. When it crossed over the Jordan, the waters of the Jordan were cut off. So these stones shall be to the Israelites a memorial forever."

8The Israelites did as Joshua commanded. They took up twelve stones out of the middle of the Jordan, according to the number of the tribes of the Israelites, as the LORD told Joshua, carried them over with them to the place where they camped, and laid them down there. ⁹(Joshua set up twelve stones in the middle of the Jordan, in the place where the feet of the priests bearing the ark of the covenant had stood; and they are there to this day.)

10The priests who bore the ark remained standing in the middle of the Jordan, until everything was finished that the LORD commanded Joshua to tell the people, according to all that Moses had commanded Joshua. The people crossed over in haste. ¹¹As soon as all the people had finished crossing over, the ark of the LORD, and the priests, crossed over in front of the people. ¹²The Reubenites, the Gadites, and the half-tribe of Manasseh crossed over armed before the Israelites, as Moses had ordered them. ¹³About forty thousand armed for war crossed over before the LORD to the plains of Jericho for battle.

14On that day the LORD exalted Joshua in the sight of all Israel; and they stood in awe of him, as they had stood in awe of Moses, all the days of his life.

15The LORD said to Joshua, ¹⁶"Command the priests who bear the ark of the covenant,*a* to come up out of the Jordan." ¹⁷Joshua therefore commanded the priests, "Come up out of the Jordan." ¹⁸When the priests bearing the ark of the covenant of the LORD came up from the middle of the Jordan, and the soles of the priests' feet touched dry ground, the waters of the Jordan returned to their place and overflowed all its banks, as before.

a Or treaty, or testimony; Heb eduth

COMMENTARY

The battle of Jericho may not be much celebrated in the rest of the Bible, but the main event that precedes it, Israel's march through the Jordan River on dry land, is referred to or alluded to in several important passages in the OT and plays an extremely significant role in the NT Gospels. One of the most famous references occurs in Mic 6:4-5. There God explains briefly what God has done for Israel, redeeming them from slavery in Egypt by leading them out behind Moses, Aaron, and Miriam; protecting them from Balak and Balaam; and having them pass over (a commonly accepted emendation) "from Shittim to Gilgal." This is one of those places in the Bible where the failure to mention Joshua along with the other prominent characters in the story occasions surprise, particularly since Miriam is mentioned only here outside the Tetrateuch and since the entire passage, Mic 6:1-5, has a marked deuteronomistic tone.[35] As with other references to it, the event itself holds more significance than does the leadership of Joshua, who probably was joined to this event no earlier than the time of Hezekiah. Many commentators have noticed what they consider to be repetitions and inconsistencies in the narrative that suggest a composite text and a complicated history of composition; the text is multivalent, but genuine inconsistencies are probably only apparent.

Perhaps the lack of reference to Joshua in Mic 6:5 is even more surprising, given that one of the main themes in Joshua 3–4 is the magnification (NIV, NRSV, "exalted") of Joshua to the stature of Moses. The section is partially framed by the commencement and fulfillment of this theme in 3:7 and 4:14, with the result that all Israel "feared [Joshua] as they had feared Moses." Joshua's command, however, goes little further than giving orders. For drama, the main role is played by the priests bearing the ark containing the law of Moses, which more than anything else represents the presence of the "living God." (The phrase "the

ark of the covenant of Yahweh your God" occurs only here and in Deut 31:26, where Moses commands the Levites to put the new document of law on the ark.) It is the priests who, by stepping into the river, accomplish what Moses did by extending his hand toward the sea to part the waters and who, by stepping out again, cue the waters to return, as again Moses did with his hand. It is they who station themselves in the midst of the watercourse as the massed assembly of Israelites, including forty thousand men armed for war, trek safely across at a distance of no less than two thousand cubits, or about two-thirds of a mile. It is their position in the watercourse that is marked by a cairn of twelve stones, gathered and placed by Joshua. Moreover, Joshua's commemoration of the event stresses Yahweh's power in dividing and drying up the waters, not his own (4:6-7, 21-24). In a surprisingly democratic gesture, Joshua orders the Israelites to appoint twelve of their number, one from each tribe, to gather the stones that will form the cairn at Gilgal. Nevertheless, the significance of the ark's crossing for Joshua is clear: The living God, whose law of dispossession and centralization rests in the ark and who gives orders through Joshua, will drive out the seven Canaanite nations before the Israelite host (3:9-11). In a word, this crossing of the Jordan spells reconquest under Joshua. This is the emphasis that Josiah's historian wants the story to have.

It was not always so. The crossing of the Jordan played various roles in the thinking and writing found in the Bible and engendered several different interpretations. The deuteronomistic portrayal of the crossing of the Jordan has a ritual character and may have been based on a rite that was periodically carried out more or less as described.[36] The ritual involved a re-enactment of the crossing of the sea at Passover. The re-enactment entailed a division of the water in the river into two walls or heaps on either side and the crossing of Israel on dry land, exactly the points Joshua takes to be the significance of the stones. Scholars have noted that neither of these familiar

35. James L. Mays, *Micah,* OTL (Philadelphia: Westminster, 1976) 127-36. For example, the last phrase in Mic 6:5, "in order to know the judgments of Yahweh," is similar to Josh 4:24, "in order for all the peoples of the earth to know the hand of Yahweh." The NRSV translation of Mic 6:5 assumes that the unspecified subject of the infinitive "to know" is "you," but it is at least as likely to be the rest of the world, and more likely to be both, as in Joshua. The phrase "in order to know" occurs three times in the Deuteronomistic History and once in Ezek 38:16.

36. See Frank M. Cross, *Canaanite Myth and Hebrew Epic* (Cambridge, Mass.: Harvard University Press, 1973) 77-144; Bernard F. Batto, *Slaying the Dragon: Mythmaking in the Biblical Tradition* (Louisville: Westminster/John Knox, 1992) 128-52.

features of the event is mentioned in the earliest accounts of the exodus victory at the sea—namely, the ancient victory song in Exod 15:1-18 and the J and E accounts in Exodus 14. These features were apparently introduced into the Exodus account on the basis of the ritual at the Jordan. The earliest allusion to the splitting of the waters at the Jordan is in 2 Kings 2, which concerns the Jordan, and not the sea. This account dates to the latter part of the ninth century BCE, but its use of the tradition of crossing implies that the ritual re-enactment is already a well-established practice. It is not known exactly what form the re-enactment took or how the splitting of the waters was accomplished, as through damming or rechanneling at Adam, about fifteen miles north of the crossing at Jericho, or otherwise represented. The stopping of the waters of the Jordan at Passover, however, or even just the idea of stopping them, would have been particularly dramatic at that time of the year, which saw the Jordan in flood following the winter rainy season and with snow beginning to melt on Mt. Hermon at its source (3:15).

The most explicit equation of the sea and the Jordan appears in Psalm 114: The sea fled, the Jordan turned back as Israel left Egypt for Judah, God's sanctuary, and Israel, God's sovereign possession. The original passage through the sea not only consists of dry land but it also leads into the desert; the passage through the Jordan, which is modeled after it, does so as well. In fact, nearly the entire way from the Jordan to either Ai or Jerusalem goes through the Benjaminite or Judean desert, including some of the most barren landscape in the world. This way may have served as the ritual way reflected, for example, in the grand elaboration that is the subject of most of Isaiah 40–55, written less than a hundred years after the Deuteronomistic History. An ancient wayfarer in the new exodus proclaimed by Isaiah would have journeyed not directly west across the Syrian desert, a route that never would have entered the poet's mind under any circumstances, but via the fertile crescent all the way from Babylon to the Jordan at Jericho without passing through any desert at all. Thus the way of the new exodus in Isaiah's conception passes through the desert only metaphorically until its last stage, from the Jordan to Jerusalem. This ritual way may be reflected

already in Exod 15:13-18, which, like Psalm 114, truncates the journey from the sea to Yahweh's sanctuary and abode in Palestine, presumably Jerusalem. Little is lost by reading the entire song in Exod 15:1-18 as though it referred to the Jordan in place of the "sea" named in Exod 15:4.

The equation of the sea and the Jordan River was ultimately based on the same myth that the Exodus narrative itself makes use of: the divine warrior's defeat of the forces of chaos and infertility, personified by the cosmic sea. The role of the sea is played by Tiamat in the famous Babylonian creation narrative called *Enuma elish*. The same role in the Ugaritic myth of Baal, culturally closer to Israelite tradition, is played by a character called Sea, but given the twofold epithet of "Prince Sea" and "Judge River."[37] This mythic motif is adopted many times in the Bible to describe the establishment of Yahweh's cult as the source of fertility. Among the oldest of these is Hab 3:1-19, in which Yahweh does battle against both River and Sea (3:8-10, 15). Elsewhere, "Sea" and "River" appear in the Bible in their mythic form as dragons (e.g., Job 26:12-13; Pss 74:11-15; 77:16-20; Isa 27:1; 51:9-11).[38]

What is perhaps most striking about all of these references to the tradition in its archetypal form is that not only do they make no mention of Joshua, but also they imply nothing about conquest or reconquest. Joshua and conquest are developments of the tradition of the crossing of the sea or the river that must be attributed to the deuteronomistic writers, whether under Hezekiah or Josiah.

Having left Shittim headed west, Israel camps next to the Jordan for three days. After this time of ritual preparation, Joshua's officers tell the people to watch for the ark carried by the levitical priests. When they see it moving, they are to follow it, "because you have not passed over on [this] way previously" (3:4). This caution looks very much like an alert to participants in the ritual who might think they were quite well acquainted with the way they were to follow, either because

37. The Ugaritic terms translated "prince" and "judge" both signify "ruler" with little distinction between them.

38. The dragon is sometimes called Leviathan. In Job 9:13; 26:12; Ps 89:11; and Isa 51:9, it is called "Rahab." The dragon is sometimes said to be split, like the waters in Joshua 3–4 and Exodus 14. Although the two names "Rahab," one of the sea dragon (רהב *rahab*) and the other of the woman in Joshua 2 (רחב *rāḥāb*), look alike in English, they are spelled differently in Hebrew and are not related, despite the proximity of the motif of splitting or cutting off the river in Joshua 3–4.

they lived nearby and were used to using the designated route or one close by or because they had participated in the ritual before. Thinking they knew the route, people massed for the day for the crossing might, if not otherwise cautioned, be inclined to follow their whim and cross whenever they pleased, perhaps at one of the fords mentioned in 2:7, rather than in order and at a place requiring or reflecting the stopping of the waters. Furthermore, they move quickly (4:10), as the Israelites did on the first Passover night (Deut 16:3; cf. Exod 12:11; Isa 52:12). This is probably an allusion to the first Passover, although the Hebrew expression is different. The NRSV leaves no doubt about the allusion by translating מהר (*māhar*) as "in haste," as though the Hebrew were the same as in Deut 16:3; the NIV more accurately translates "hurried."

No wonder that Micah said "from Shittim to Gilgal," since next to the command of Joshua, a deuteronomistic accent, and the role of the levitical priests, a deuteronomistic or priestly accent, the main point of the narrative is the gathering of the stones for the two memorial cairns that give Gilgal its name. The association of the crossing with Gilgal goes back well before the Deuteronomistic History. That is the subject of the next section.

REFLECTIONS

1. Israel crosses the Jordan to reach the land granted to it by Yahweh at the very beginning of its history, beginning with Israel's grandfather Abraham. This grant was alluded to even earlier in human history, through Noah's curse of Canaan. In the Old Testament world, land was the fundamental good, the irreducible basis of life, joy, and fulfillment, the entity whose disposition most other forms of social existence were shaped to serve. Modern interpreters may tend to think of land as a material good, without quite the status or value of spiritual goods. To be religious today is to emphasize spirituality over materiality. Such a distinction was foreign to the Old Testament world. There was then no clearer knowledge of God than that God was the one who gave to Israelites their land and that to keep their land they must heed the law laid down by God, including stipulations governing material goods. Land, law, people—these are the components of historical existence in ancient Canaan or Palestine that pointed to the one known as Yahweh, the Lord of all. Moreover, materiality depends on particularity, and both are ultimate, not penultimate, essentials of faith in ancient Israel.

This understanding of God and God's people as particular sits awkwardly with the Christian propensity to universalize God and the related Protestant propensity to individualize and spiritualize the life of faith. Thus Christians rightly marvel at God's creation in general and give thanks for individual blessings, especially those involving personal relationships. The focus on the land in Joshua might suggest, in addition, special attention to some particularity of the created order, such as the ecological soundness of the local environment or the ecological impact of economic policy. Or it might suggest special attention to particular material blessings, those received as well as those not received, as they appear to depend on group affiliations like family, nation, race, or class. Both the universal and the particular are essential. Working out how they are related to each other is like working out how a nation or a church or a congregation can be unified and diverse, one and many, at the same time, affirming what is distinctive about individuals and groups and what all people have in common. It is especially important to be aware of how wealth as such sometimes encourages the tendency to spiritualize and individualize. The classical liberal heritage essential to most denominations and to our national well-being now must be tempered with a clear recognition that particular identities—troublesome, upsetting, and morally ambiguous though they may appear, especially when they are somebody else's—are as significant as universal identities.

2. The crossing of the sea and the river to the land serves as a great symbol in the traditions of Israel and the house of David. It is repeated, recalled, and recast as the nucleus of what it means to become the redeemed people of God. Thus this part of Joshua can often be interpreted with integrity in the light of latter narratives of redemption.

Perhaps the best example of such recapitulation in the Old Testament is found in the elaborate vision of the return from Babylon to Jerusalem laid out in Second Isaiah (Isaiah 40–55; cf. Isaiah 35). This is probably the longest and most elaborate example of sustained metaphorical and rhetorical brilliance in the Old Testament. The poet polemicizes against the complacency of the second and third generations of the court in exile, who have little interest in leaving the place they experienced as the capital of their world and returning to the provincial backwater of Zion. To fire them up, the poet puts before them an image of Israel departing from Egypt in order to make known God's redeeming justice. The central component of this image is crossing through the water on dry land. Over and over this figure is elaborated, ramified, and developed.

The people of Israel, those addressed by Second Isaiah, are again Yahweh's servant, as they were of old. They are the servant of Yahweh in three distinct senses: (1) as a slave redeemed by Yahweh, as in the original exodus; (2) as a suppliant to Yahweh, drawn to worship Yahweh, also as in the first exodus (in Second Isaiah, the servant in this sense has to be encouraged to ask for help); and (3), the most important, as an officer in Yahweh's court. As such, Israel is called and appointed to serve in the court of the greatest lord of all, the Creator of the world and of Israel at the sea, and his anointed one, Cyrus, instead of the false gods of Babylon, whose service looks attractive to the Judahites. The servant (in all three senses) once was afflicted: The generation of the court of the house of David who came before suffered the punishment of exile. But now the servant is to be requited, by being raised high once again (one of several metaphors for return to Jerusalem), so that the nations can once again see and fear.

The resonant strain of intense transitions and new beginnings, the fresh confidence of initiations and the liberating encouragement derived from evidences of God's renewed attentions—these features of the story of Israel crossing the Jordan are replayed in the significant places where Scripture recalls this story. The interpreter and preacher may develop these positive themes at length to reflect their intensity in Joshua and Second Isaiah. At the same time, the question of who might suffer under the onslaught of such exuberant assurance and determination can never be overlooked.

3. The figure of the suffering and raised servant in Second Isaiah, who re-embodies Israel's crossing the Jordan, subsequently plays a momentous role in the early church's conception of Jesus. This is especially the case with the earliest of the canonical Gospels, Mark. The Isaian background to Mark's portrayal of Jesus is clearly indicated by, for example, the quote from Isaiah regarding the coming of the Lord's servant in Mark 1:2-3. Just as myth and rite are combined in the Old Testament text, so also they are combined in the New Testament, especially in the rite of baptism, which recapitulates the crossing of the sea. The baptism of Jesus at the Jordan, repeating the experience of Elisha in 2 Kings 2, serves as paradigm. Since the names "Joshua" and "Jesus" are the same, it would have come as no surprise for early Christians to hear the story of their Lord, Jesus, begin, as it does in Mark, with a scene reminiscent of Joshua's leading Israel across the Jordan River (Mark 1:1-13), as though Jesus were repeating that great episode in the story of his namesake, itself recapitulating Israel's escape from slavery across the parted waters of the sea on dry land (Exod 14:5–15:21).

To the modern reader, the reminiscence may not be obvious at first. The passage may seem to be nothing more than a description of the baptism of Jesus. But to the hearer conversant with Scripture, numerous allusions would be unmistakable, of which a few can be considered here. The writer of Mark even declares that he is going to make the allusions by citing a scriptural amalgam from Exodus, Isaiah, and Malachi, which together refer to the return of Elijah as a voice of one crying in the desert, heralding the "great and terrible day of the Lord" (Mal 3:1; 4:5). This reference to Elijah immediately draws the hearer back to the moment when Elijah was last seen on earth. That moment is described in 2 Kgs 2:1-14, in a scene intentionally modeled on Joshua's crossing the Jordan in imitation of Israel crossing the sea during Passover, and that in turn provides one of the models for Mark's description of Jesus' baptism. Elijah leads Elisha through the parted waters of the Jordan from west to east. As Elijah is swept alive into the heavens in a swirl of war chariots, his prophetic spirit passes to Elisha, who takes up Elijah's mantle, strikes the Jordan, and, like Moses at the sea and Joshua at the Jordan, passes through the parted waters from east to west.

This, in adapted form, is what happens to Jesus. Mark, having alluded to all of this and more, opens his Gospel with the appearance of John, who looks like Elijah on the same day he summarily destroyed troops of the state's hostile armed men by summoning fire from heaven (2 Kgs 1:8-12; Mark 1:6). Indeed, it seems that John the Baptist is Elijah (Mark 9:11-13). Elijah has returned to announce the coming of the Lord and the preparation of the way to the Temple, leading to the restoration of God's kingdom on earth on a "great and terrible day." The anointing of Jesus with the Spirit as he re-enacts the climactic event of Passover, the crossing of the sea (here the Jordan), makes him all at once the new Moses, the new Joshua, as well as the new David, ready to draw together a new fighting host, storm Jerusalem, recapture and restore the Temple of the house of David, and re-establish God's rule on earth.[39] In the light of the deuteronomistic paralleling of Moses, Joshua, and Josiah, Jesus as the Davidic Messiah might almost be thought of at this point (Mark 1:11) as Josiah redivivus. As the Gospel of Mark develops, however, it becomes clear that Jesus is the antitype of such a messiah and that those who mistake him for another Josiah are deeply mistaken and disloyal.

Prior to the writing of Mark, there had developed a great debate in the early church regarding just how and to what extent Jesus embodied the material hopes of the house of David. It is sometimes easy to forget that the earliest Christians did not always see eye to eye on even the most basic issues.[40] Most, if not all, of the writings in the New Testament take similar positions on subjects about which early Christians vehemently disagreed; so it is often necessary to look behind the New Testament texts to see what subjects the early Christians were debating. One such subject was political: the substantive relationship between the "kingdom of God" and the historical kingdom of the house of David. Would Jesus, having risen from the grave and thus foiled those of the Temple and imperial states who had tried to stop him, return at the head of the heavenly host that once swept away Elijah and then brought him back as John? Would Jesus as the new Joshua/Josiah complete the recovery and repurification of the Temple, the reconquest of Israel, the reassertion of the law of God through Moses as the basis of Israel's righteousness, and the installation of the church's members, starting with its "pillars," as Jesus' vice-regents to rule the world? Many believed this was what Jesus meant to do. Others tended to focus attention on the church less as the new political nation in the usual sense and more as a new commonality with its own distinctive destiny.

There were several reasons for this debate, but it became particularly acute as more and more Gentiles were baptized as Christians. Many, if not most, Gentiles regarded the specifically Davidic political aspirations of the early church as the new Israel as of little moment. That was not what Jesus meant to them. Paul, who at first was probably something of a maverick in the church, became the spokesperson for many such Gentiles. The Jewish monarchy, the Temple (newly restored by the non-Davidic Herodians), and the law of Moses have their own validity, which even Gentiles may affirm, but Jesus as Messiah has introduced a new basis for righteousness quite apart from these fundamental Davidic institutions, for Gentiles and Jews alike. The dispute often came down to the question of whether circumcision, the sign of the covenant of Abraham that laid the basis for the covenant of Moses, would be required of Gentile male converts, as it had been of an entire generation of uncircumcised Israelite adult

---

39. The Greek εἰς (eis) in Mark 1:9 appears to mean "into and through," as in Mark 7:31.
40. See Michael Goulder, *St. Peter versus St. Paul: A Tale of Two Missions* (Louisville: Westminster John Knox, 1995).

male followers of Moses and Joshua as soon as they had crossed the Jordan (Josh 5:2-8) and before keeping Passover (Josh 5:10; cf. Exod 12:48). That is, was the church, in essence, a new form of the old Davidic nation, bound to the law of Moses, or was it something else?

Mark was written in the midst of this debate. Much was at stake. The early Christian sect was a Jewish sect and struggled with the same basic issues other Jews struggled with: What, in line with God's will, was the basis of the ethnic and judicial integrity of the Jews, and how were Jews to relate to the Gentiles, with whom they shared life in the cities of the Roman and Persian empires, where most Jews lived? The Jewish position, ultimately abandoned by the "orthodox" church on the basis of divergent interpretations, nevertheless involved affirmations we can still understand and value, such as ethnic integrity and the refusal to compromise with the will of God as revealed in Scripture.

By making the rite of baptism and the baptism of Jesus a primary basis of his version of the gospel, and by showing how baptism recapitulates the basic themes of the exodus and the crossing of the Jordan under Joshua, Mark lays a basis for understanding the inclusion of the Gentiles in terms of just those scriptural texts that most clearly formed the basis for distinguishing between Israel and the Gentiles. In this sense, the Gospel of Mark represents a radical reinterpretation of the old Joshua in terms of the new Joshua, or Jesus. The preacher may wish to reflect on the importance of not simply rejecting or repudiating what appears to be non-Christian in Joshua, but of interpreting the New Testament transformation of the themes of Joshua in their first-century context, where the integrity of the ethnic and judicial identity of the Jews and their relationships with Gentiles were at stake.

Joshua 4:19–5:12, Camped at Gilgal

NIV

[19]On the tenth day of the first month the people went up from the Jordan and camped at Gilgal on the eastern border of Jericho. [20]And Joshua set up at Gilgal the twelve stones they had taken out of the Jordan. [21]He said to the Israelites, "In the future when your descendants ask their fathers, 'What do these stones mean?' [22]tell them, 'Israel crossed the Jordan on dry ground.' [23]For the LORD your God dried up the Jordan before you until you had crossed over. The LORD your God did to the Jordan just what he had done to the Red Sea[a] when he dried it up before us until we had crossed over. [24]He did this so that all the peoples of the earth might know that the hand of the LORD is powerful and so that you might always fear the LORD your God."

5 Now when all the Amorite kings west of the Jordan and all the Canaanite kings along the coast heard how the LORD had dried up the Jordan before the Israelites until we had crossed over, their hearts melted and they no longer had the courage to face the Israelites.

[a]23 Hebrew *Yam Suph*; that is, Sea of Reeds

NRSV

19The people came up out of the Jordan on the tenth day of the first month, and they camped in Gilgal on the east border of Jericho. [20]Those twelve stones, which they had taken out of the Jordan, Joshua set up in Gilgal, [21]saying to the Israelites, "When your children ask their parents in time to come, 'What do these stones mean?' [22]then you shall let your children know, 'Israel crossed over the Jordan here on dry ground.' [23]For the LORD your God dried up the waters of the Jordan for you until you crossed over, as the LORD your God did to the Red Sea,[a] which he dried up for us until we crossed over, [24]so that all the peoples of the earth may know that the hand of the LORD is mighty, and so that you may fear the LORD your God forever."

5 When all the kings of the Amorites beyond the Jordan to the west, and all the kings of the Canaanites by the sea, heard that the LORD had dried up the waters of the Jordan for the Israelites until they had crossed over, their hearts melted, and there was no longer any spirit in them, because of the Israelites.

[a]Or *Sea of Reeds*

NIV

²At that time the LORD said to Joshua, "Make flint knives and circumcise the Israelites again." ³So Joshua made flint knives and circumcised the Israelites at Gibeath Haaraloth.*ᵃ*

⁴Now this is why he did so: All those who came out of Egypt—all the men of military age—died in the desert on the way after leaving Egypt. ⁵All the people that came out had been circumcised, but all the people born in the desert during the journey from Egypt had not. ⁶The Israelites had moved about in the desert forty years until all the men who were of military age when they left Egypt had died, since they had not obeyed the LORD. For the LORD had sworn to them that they would not see the land that he had solemnly promised their fathers to give us, a land flowing with milk and honey. ⁷So he raised up their sons in their place, and these were the ones Joshua circumcised. They were still uncircumcised because they had not been circumcised on the way. ⁸And after the whole nation had been circumcised, they remained where they were in camp until they were healed.

⁹Then the LORD said to Joshua, "Today I have rolled away the reproach of Egypt from you." So the place has been called Gilgal*ᵇ* to this day.

¹⁰On the evening of the fourteenth day of the month, while camped at Gilgal on the plains of Jericho, the Israelites celebrated the Passover. ¹¹The day after the Passover, that very day, they ate some of the produce of the land: unleavened bread and roasted grain. ¹²The manna stopped the day after*ᶜ* they ate this food from the land; there was no longer any manna for the Israelites, but that year they ate of the produce of Canaan.

a3 Gibeath Haaraloth means hill of foreskins.   b9 Gilgal sounds like the Hebrew for roll.   c12 Or the day

NRSV

2At that time the LORD said to Joshua, "Make flint knives and circumcise the Israelites a second time." 3So Joshua made flint knives, and circumcised the Israelites at Gibeath-haaraloth.*ᵃ* 4This is the reason why Joshua circumcised them: all the males of the people who came out of Egypt, all the warriors, had died during the journey through the wilderness after they had come out of Egypt. 5Although all the people who came out had been circumcised, yet all the people born on the journey through the wilderness after they had come out of Egypt had not been circumcised. 6For the Israelites traveled forty years in the wilderness, until all the nation, the warriors who came out of Egypt, perished, not having listened to the voice of the LORD. To them the LORD swore that he would not let them see the land that he had sworn to their ancestors to give us, a land flowing with milk and honey. 7So it was their children, whom he raised up in their place, that Joshua circumcised; for they were uncircumcised, because they had not been circumcised on the way.

8When the circumcising of all the nation was done, they remained in their places in the camp until they were healed. 9The LORD said to Joshua, "Today I have rolled away from you the disgrace of Egypt." And so that place is called Gilgal*ᵇ* to this day.

10While the Israelites were camped in Gilgal they kept the passover in the evening on the fourteenth day of the month in the plains of Jericho. 11On the day after the passover, on that very day, they ate the produce of the land, unleavened cakes and parched grain. 12The manna ceased on the day they ate the produce of the land, and the Israelites no longer had manna; they ate the crops of the land of Canaan that year.

a That is the Hill of the Foreskins   b Related to Heb galal to roll

COMMENTARY

This entire section concerns Gilgal: the setting up of the twelve-stone cairn for which Gilgal is named (the cairn has its independent significance), the giving of the meaning of the name "Gilgal" for this narrative, and the keeping of the feast of Passover as the blessed nation at Gilgal. Israel no

longer is to eat manna, as they did in the desert, but the newly harvested produce of the land. The keeping of Passover looks ahead to Josiah's Passover, on the deuteronomistic assumption that the rite had not been kept the way it should have been for the entire time between Joshua and

Josiah (2 Kgs 23:21-22). In the midst of this section, a later priestly writer has inserted an account of the circumcision of the new generation in the promised land.

The Benjaminite shrine at Gilgal plays a significant role as early as the prophetic sources for the history of David. Gilgal was where Samuel anointed Saul king of Israel (1 Sam 11:14-15) and then later determined to depose him, because Saul had violated a battle command of Yahweh (the same חרם [ḥērem][41] command violated by Achan at Gilgal [Josh 7:1–8:29]). Gilgal was where Samuel anointed David king in Saul's place (1 Sam 13:8-14). In the deuteronomistic conception, the beginning of Saul's reign leads directly to its fruitless end, both tied to Gilgal.

Samuel anoints Saul king and tells Saul to wait for him at Gilgal for seven days, until Samuel comes and offers sacrifices (1 Sam 10:1-8). Saul arrives at Gilgal and waits seven days, but Samuel does not come. To prevent his forces from further slipping away from inaction, Saul offers the sacrifices himself. Instantly Samuel appears, with no explanation for his delay, and denounces Saul for his disobedience. The price for Saul's error will be the loss of his kingdom to a rival. This first hint of the coming greatness of the house of David is announced at Gilgal.

The turning point between Saul and David occurs in 1 Samuel 15, again at Gilgal, in the midst of Saul's ongoing conflict with the Philistines. Here the issue is ḥērem, the primary issue in the stories of Rahab (Joshua 2; 6), Achan (Joshua 7–8), and the Gibeonites (Joshua 9) that make up most of the narrative of conquest in the book of Joshua. Moreover, here the issue of ḥērem all of a sudden has to do not with the Philistines, but with the Amalekites, just as in the stories that introduce Joshua in the Tetrateuch. Samuel has ordered Saul to slaughter the Amalekites, man, woman, and child, together with all their livestock. Saul destroys the Amalekites, but spares their king, Agag, along with choice cattle and sheep, in order to sacrifice them, as he later claims, in Gilgal. When the book of Joshua was composed, this violation of ḥērem

apparently became the example for Achan in Joshua 7, whose violation of ḥērem also occurs at Gilgal. At Gilgal, where once again Samuel meets up with Saul, Samuel is again unimpressed with Saul's sacrifice. Again he accuses Saul of disobedience: "Since you have rejected the word of Yahweh, Yahweh has rejected you from being king over Israel." Saul repents, but to no avail. Samuel himself "hews Agag in pieces" and departs from Gilgal, never to see Saul again until the day Saul is to die in battle, when, again disobeying the deuteronomistic law, Saul summons the ghost of Samuel from the dead to consult him one last, futile time. Leaving Saul in Gilgal, Samuel proceeds immediately to anoint David as Saul's eventual successor (1 Sam 16:1-13), thereby initiating all that the deuteronomist holds dear: the sovereignty of the house of David over all Israel, exercised through the deuteronomistic law of Moses and centered in the Temple in Jerusalem.

Apart from these two extremely significant episodes—Joshua's crossing the Jordan and setting up a base camp at Gilgal and Samuel's rejection of Saul in favor of David—and allusions to them, Gilgal plays practically no role in the Bible. It is, however, also associated with the crossing of the Jordan in 2 Kgs 2:1-18, and as a camp for Elisha and an impoverished following in 2 Kgs 4:38. These last two texts were probably written in the late ninth or early eighth century, some hundred years before Hezekiah and two hundred years before Josiah. Gilgal is mentioned several times as an Israelite shrine in the eighth- or seventh-century BCE texts of both Hosea and Amos (Hos 4:15; 9:15; 12:11; Amos 4:4; 5:5), in addition to the passage in Mic 6:5, already noted. In four of these prophetic passages, Gilgal is paired with Bethel, as in 2 Kgs 2:1-2. The geography suggested by this combination has led many scholars to posit two different Gilgals (in addition to at least two others), one near the Jordan and the other in the hill country, but the matter is uncertain.[42] In this commentary, they are taken to be the same.

Elijah and Elisha journey from Gilgal to Bethel to Jericho to the Jordan, and then across the Jordan, heading east. Apart from Bethel, this is the journey of the Israelites in Joshua in reverse, and nearly such if Bethel should substitute for Ai, from which the

---

41. When someone or something falls into the classification ḥērem, he, she, or it is a possession of Yahweh and, therefore, not for general use. When the spoils of war (whether people, animals, or property) were declared ḥērem, they were to be destroyed. See P. Stern, *The Biblical Ḥērem: A Window on Israel's Religious Experience* (Atlanta: Scholars Press, 1991); N. Lohfink, "*ḥaram*," *TDOT* 5:180-99.

42. Wade R. Kotter, "Gilgal," in *The Anchor Bible Dictionary,* ed. David Noel Freedman, 6 vols. (New York: Doubleday, 1992) 2:1022-24.

Israelites returned to Gilgal (Josh 8:23; 9:6; the detour to the vicinity of Shechem in Josh 8:30-35 is a secondary addition). Gilgal is clearly an important Israelite shrine, with an early association with the ritual recapitulation of the crossing of the sea. The exodus allusions in 2 Kings 2 include not just the many ways in which Elijah and Elisha imitate Moses, which are easy to recognize, but the following story in which Elisha, having recrossed the Jordan westward, like Joshua, and ended up at Jericho, purifies a spring of water at Jericho. This purification follows the river crossing immediately just as the purification of the waters of Marah follows the crossing of the sea in Exodus 14–15 (Exod 15:22-25; cf. Exod 15:27). This sequence matches the most common sequence of themes in the mythic accounts of the defeat or splitting of sea and river, which is frequently followed by a production of fresh water or allusion to such an event (e.g., Job 9:9; 38:22-38; Pss 46:4; 65:9-13; 74:15; 77:20; 89:11-12; 114:6). The tie between Gilgal and the myth of the sea splitting was ancient and distinct.

Passover allusions continue in the entire Jericho account, right up to its end. These include the seven days of the siege of Jericho, which represent the seven days of the Passover begun in 5:10. The possibility that the seven days may have been added after the main composition of the Deuteronomistic History will be considered in the next section. Given that the siege occurs during Passover, the crossing of the Jordan, while symbolically representing the Passover, is said to occur four days before Passover (4:19). Since the crossing does not coincide with Passover, Joshua's interpretation of the stones that will form the cairn of Gilgal makes the comparison of the crossing at the Jordan with the crossing at the sea explicit, which is done only here. For twelve stones representing the twelve tribes of Israel, see Exod 24:4 and 1 Kgs 18:31.

The Amorite kings hear about the drying up of the Jordan and are utterly dispirited. The phrasing of this line recalls Rahab's deuteronomistic speech (2:10-11; a similar transitional phrase is used also in 9:1; 10:1; 11:1). The Amorites are specified as being "to the west" because "beyond the Jordan" usually means the east bank. The sequel to this disheartening follows directly in 5:9, since the mass circumcision is an insertion. The local kings have heard about Israel's miraculous crossing to the land, and the shame of slavery in Egypt is

removed. The conjunction of these two themes goes all the way back to Exod 15:13-17, ostensibly one of the earliest texts in the Bible. It is repeated numerous times, not least in Numbers 22–24 in the story of Balaam's refusal to curse the passing escaped slaves. This is the meaning the narrator hears in the name "Gilgal," a name that in fact more likely derives from the cairns. All three meanings given to the cairns and to Gilgal—"Yahweh cut off the waters for the ark" (4:7), "Yahweh dried up the waters for crossing so the nations might hear about it" (4:22-24), and "Yahweh removed the shame of Egypt" (5:9)—are related, and the second flows directly into the preface to the third: "so that all the nations may know . . . the Amorite kings heard."

On the fourteenth day of the month, Passover begins. The manna that fed the Israelites for forty years in the desert ceases, and the invaders eat of the produce of the land of Canaan (there is a pun between "produce" [עבור ʾābûr] in 5:11, 12 and "pass on" or "cross over" [עבר ʾābar] in 3:4, 6 and 4:5).[43] How do they get the grain, having just arrived? As invaders, they take it, just as they take the land itself.

A priestly writer has inserted an account of the circumcision of the new generation of Israelites who replaced those who died out during the forty-year desert trek. Priestly tradition makes circumcision a prerequisite for participation in Passover (Exod 12:43-49). Thus the writer inserted his account here because he wanted to make sure everyone was circumcised before Passover began. Except as a metaphor (Deut 10:16; 30:6), circumcision plays no role in the Deuteronomistic History outside of this text. Except for the phrase "not having listened to the voice of Yahweh," this insertion has no significant resonances with the text in the Deuteronomistic History that serves as its basis, the foundational account of the rebellion against Yahweh's command to conquer the land in Deut 1:19-40, which set the scene for Joshua's succession and conquest.

For the P strand, however, circumcision is an extremely important rite. There is little doubt that Israelites, like nearly all people in the ancient Near East, practiced circumcision during the entire biblical

---

43. The Hebrew word for "produce" in 5:11-12 is rare in the Bible, occurring only here for certain and possibly one or two other places. There are indications that it is a loanword from Assyrian.

period as a surveillance ritual designed to test the loyalty that men with sons owed to their fraternal interest group.[44] But circumcision became a significant article of Israelite or Davidic covenantal understanding only for the Davidic priestly tradition represented in the P strand. There circumcision represents nothing less than the sign of the second of the three "eternal" covenants of P: the covenant of Abraham, required of all sons of Abraham. While circumcision later came to represent a supposed distinctive feature of Jews among the "nations," this was not its significance for the P strand. The rite was too common for that, and in any case P itself presents Abraham as the father of a "multitude of nations" (Gen 17:5). Davidic priests probably stressed the importance of circumcision because of their special concern for reproduction ("be fruitful and multiply," Gen 1:28 and repeated many times in P) and interest in male privilege in the sacrificial cult.[45]

The phrase "a second time" (5:2) is potentially confusing. It does not mean that these Israelites have already been circumcised once. The phrase may be secondary, having arisen due to an am-

---

44. On circumcision in P, see Robert B. Coote and David Robert Ord, *In the Beginning: Creation and the Priestly History* (Minneapolis: Fortress, 1991) 67-75, a discussion based in part on Karen Ericksen Paige and Jeffrey M. Paige, *The Politics of Reproductive Ritual* (Berkeley: University of California Press, 1981) 122-66.

45. Nancy B. Jay, *Throughout Your Generations Forever: Sacrifice, Religion, and Paternity* (Chicago: University of Chicago Press, 1992).

biguity created by a word in Yahweh's command that occurs in the Hebrew text but is not directly translated in either the NRSV or the NIV: "sit" (καθίζω *kathizō* LXX) or "do again" (שנית *šēnît* MT): "make flint knives and sit/again circumcise the Israelites." The LXX may represent the original meaning of this Hebrew word; if so, when it took on the MT meaning "do again," it may have been reinforced by "a second time." Perhaps more likely the MT meaning was original, in the sense of "resume" a practice that has been suspended. The practice would then have been started, if not resumed, a second time: "Start again to circumcise the Israelites. . . ."

The phrase "a land flowing [better: oozing] with milk and honey" was present already in the ancient Davidic history of the nation, the J strand. There it described the land of Canaan as untilled and largely uncultivated (cf. Isa 7:14-25), as though the Canaanites were nearly all just town-dwelling rulers or merchants. The deuteronomistic concept of the land of Canaan is the opposite (Deut 8:7-8), and hence this phrase acquires the connotation of extreme abundance in the Deuteronomistic History, as though milk and honey could provide a square meal that a hardworking peasant man or woman would choose instead of a satisfying batch of bread and olives. It is the deuteronomistic concept rather than the J concept that came to dominate the biblical and modern use of the phrase.

REFLECTIONS

1. Gilgal is named for a memorial cairn, which is seen to signify the removal of the shame of poverty, indebtedness, and peonage ("the shame of Egypt"). It is thus a memorial both to the war that was, the war against slavery in Egypt (cf. Deut 6:21; 26:6; 28:68), which resulted in crossing the sea, and the war that will be, the war against the Canaanites, whose land must be forfeited to the former slaves, while the Canaanites themselves, in line with the curse of Canaan, become Israel's slaves. It may be useful to think of our own war memorials, especially to the two great wars that took place on our own soil, the War of Independence and the Civil War. Both wars were fought against slavery, and hence monuments from those wars could be regarded, like Gilgal, as monuments against slavery. The first war was fought against "slavery" to a government in which the colonists felt they had no representation. During the American Revolution, the word *slavery* was used often to describe England's treatment of the colonists. The second war was fought to assert the right of the United States over the right of constituent states to decide issues of slavery. This war resulted in the emancipation of slaves and the outlawing of slavery in the United States.

The analogy with Gilgal holds if slavery is defined very broadly. It is also important, however, to recognize how the analogy does not fit, because if slavery is only broadly defined, then the full meaning of Joshua will not become apparent. Obviously nothing in Joshua or the deuteronomistic reform suggests the value of representation in government. The reform is authoritarian and largely totalitarian. The law is said to come from Moses not Josiah, but that does not mean that it is based on representation. The slavery eliminated by the Civil War was chattel slavery. The Deuteronomistic History takes no stand on chattel slavery, which figures prominently in the house of David's JE history without censure, and the history condones the imposition of corvée, or statute enslavement, on the Canaanites. Later parts of the Old Testament may take sides against chattel slavery, but the New Testament as a body ends up indifferent to it, and in some cases supportive of it, despite important texts like Gal 3:28. Using Scripture to help invalidate and eradicate slavery is a relatively recent development in the church's history, as in our nation's history.

Is it possible that by focusing on political slavery and chattel slavery, the two forms abolished by our great wars against slavery, Americans have given themselves permission to divert their attention from the ongoing jeopardy of poverty, which continues to lead to different forms of impoverished labor and debt slavery, which the Bible always opposes or sharply limits? Looking more closely at the relationship between poverty and work, even in an age when the world of jobs is drastically changing, leads to the realization that missing from our land are public monuments to a war against coercive, extortionate labor in all its forms. The gap between rich and poor is now greater in the United States than in any other so-called developed country. America's twentieth-century "war on poverty" has failed for a variety of reasons, and it has been replaced by a new form of what some are calling a "war against the poor."[46] The United States is not alone. The monument at Gilgal provides the opportunity to reflect on the chronic war against the poor that all rich people and nations have been accused of waging.

2. Circumcision is in some ways the most important subject in the New Testament. The basis for including uncircumcised Gentiles was a point of contention from the start. When the view represented by Paul eventually came to prevail, baptism in effect became a substitute for circumcision. The issue is basic to Paul's Letter to the Romans, 1 Corinthians, and most explicitly Galatians, and thus underlies a substantial portion of the Pauline corpus. In Mark, the Gospel that leads the way in integrating the Pauline perspective with the church's gospel, the paradigmatic scene of Jesus's baptism makes clear allusion to the extensive symbolization of the circumcision of the firstborn in order, like Paul, to set aside the significance of the rite in favor of baptism, whose imagery in turn is pervasive and fundamental.[47] There were many different views of baptism in the early church, but these all tend to merge inconsistently from the perspective of the New Testament canon, which is dominated by the writings and views of Paul and in which the primary concern is to invalidate the necessity of circumcision rather than give a single coherent explanation of baptism.

3. The keeping of Passover by eating the produce of the land recalls Deut 8:3. There, in the desert, bread is contrasted to the command of Yahweh. Here, in the land, bread and Yahweh's command, found in the law of Moses, come together: The abundance of prosperity made possible by possession of the land depends on obedience to Moses, to Joshua, and to Josiah. It is not clear whether the Israelites stole the grain or bartered for it, a gap that confirms that it functions mainly as a symbol here. The availability of grain rather than the lack of it is now to remind the Israelites of their dependence on Yahweh and the law. The weight of exhortation to this effect in Deuteronomy and Joshua is perhaps an indication of how easy it is for the opposite to occur: God's blessing often leads us to forget its ultimate source instead of remembering it.

---

46. Herbert J. Gans, *The War Against the Poor: The Underclass and Antipoverty Policy* (New York: Basic, 1996).
47. See Jon D. Levenson, *The Death and Resurrection of the Beloved Son: The Transformation of Child Sacrifice in Judaism and Christianity* (New Haven: Yale University Press, 1993) 173-232.

13Now when Joshua was near Jericho, he looked up and saw a man standing in front of him with a drawn sword in his hand. Joshua went up to him and asked, "Are you for us or for our enemies?"

14"Neither," he replied, "but as commander of the army of the LORD I have now come." Then Joshua fell facedown to the ground in reverence, and asked him, "What message does my Lord[a] have for his servant?"

15The commander of the LORD's army replied, "Take off your sandals, for the place where you are standing is holy." And Joshua did so.

6 Now Jericho was tightly shut up because of the Israelites. No one went out and no one came in.

2Then the LORD said to Joshua, "See, I have delivered Jericho into your hands, along with its king and its fighting men. 3March around the city once with all the armed men. Do this for six days. 4Have seven priests carry trumpets of rams' horns in front of the ark. On the seventh day, march around the city seven times, with the priests blowing the trumpets. 5When you hear them sound a long blast on the trumpets, have all the people give a loud shout; then the wall of the city will collapse and the people will go up, every man straight in."

6So Joshua son of Nun called the priests and said to them, "Take up the ark of the covenant of the LORD and have seven priests carry trumpets in front of it." 7And he ordered the people, "Advance! March around the city, with the armed guard going ahead of the ark of the LORD."

8When Joshua had spoken to the people, the seven priests carrying the seven trumpets before the LORD went forward, blowing their trumpets, and the ark of the LORD's covenant followed them. 9The armed guard marched ahead of the priests who blew the trumpets, and the rear guard followed the ark. All this time the trumpets were sounding. 10But Joshua had commanded the people, "Do not give a war cry, do not raise your voices, do not say a word until the day I tell you

a14 Or lord

13Once when Joshua was by Jericho, he looked up and saw a man standing before him with a drawn sword in his hand. Joshua went to him and said to him, "Are you one of us, or one of our adversaries?" 14He replied, "Neither; but as commander of the army of the LORD I have now come." And Joshua fell on his face to the earth and worshiped, and he said to him, "What do you command your servant, my lord?" 15The commander of the army of the LORD said to Joshua, "Remove the sandals from your feet, for the place where you stand is holy." And Joshua did so.

6 Now Jericho was shut up inside and out because of the Israelites; no one came out and no one went in. 2The LORD said to Joshua, "See, I have handed Jericho over to you, along with its king and soldiers. 3You shall march around the city, all the warriors circling the city once. Thus you shall do for six days, 4with seven priests bearing seven trumpets of rams' horns before the ark. On the seventh day you shall march around the city seven times, the priests blowing the trumpets. 5When they make a long blast with the ram's horn, as soon as you hear the sound of the trumpet, then all the people shall shout with a great shout; and the wall of the city will fall down flat, and all the people shall charge straight ahead." 6So Joshua son of Nun summoned the priests and said to them, "Take up the ark of the covenant, and have seven priests carry seven trumpets of rams' horns in front of the ark of the LORD." 7To the people he said, "Go forward and march around the city; have the armed men pass on before the ark of the LORD."

8As Joshua had commanded the people, the seven priests carrying the seven trumpets of rams' horns before the LORD went forward, blowing the trumpets, with the ark of the covenant of the LORD following them. 9And the armed men went before the priests who blew the trumpets; the rear guard came after the ark, while the trumpets blew continually. 10To the people Joshua gave this command: "You shall not shout or let your voice be heard, nor shall you utter a word, until the day I tell you to shout. Then you shall shout." 11So

NIV

to shout. Then shout!" [11]So he had the ark of the LORD carried around the city, circling it once. Then the people returned to camp and spent the night there.

[12]Joshua got up early the next morning and the priests took up the ark of the LORD. [13]The seven priests carrying the seven trumpets went forward, marching before the ark of the LORD and blowing the trumpets. The armed men went ahead of them and the rear guard followed the ark of the LORD, while the trumpets kept sounding. [14]So on the second day they marched around the city once and returned to the camp. They did this for six days.

[15]On the seventh day, they got up at daybreak and marched around the city seven times in the same manner, except that on that day they circled the city seven times. [16]The seventh time around, when the priests sounded the trumpet blast, Joshua commanded the people, "Shout! For the LORD has given you the city! [17]The city and all that is in it are to be devoted[a] to the LORD. Only Rahab the prostitute[b] and all who are with her in her house shall be spared, because she hid the spies we sent. [18]But keep away from the devoted things, so that you will not bring about your own destruction by taking any of them. Otherwise you will make the camp of Israel liable to destruction and bring trouble on it. [19]All the silver and gold and the articles of bronze and iron are sacred to the LORD and must go into his treasury."

[20]When the trumpets sounded, the people shouted, and at the sound of the trumpet, when the people gave a loud shout, the wall collapsed; so every man charged straight in, and they took the city. [21]They devoted the city to the LORD and destroyed with the sword every living thing in it—men and women, young and old, cattle, sheep and donkeys.

[a]17 The Hebrew term refers to the irrevocable giving over of things or persons to the LORD, often by totally destroying them; also in verses 18 and 21.   [b]17 Or possibly *innkeeper*; also in verses 22 and 25

NRSV

the ark of the LORD went around the city, circling it once; and they came into the camp, and spent the night in the camp.

[12]Then Joshua rose early in the morning, and the priests took up the ark of the LORD. [13]The seven priests carrying the seven trumpets of rams' horns before the ark of the LORD passed on, blowing the trumpets continually. The armed men went before them, and the rear guard came after the ark of the LORD, while the trumpets blew continually. [14]On the second day they marched around the city once and then returned to the camp. They did this for six days.

[15]On the seventh day they rose early, at dawn, and marched around the city in the same manner seven times. It was only on that day that they marched around the city seven times. [16]And at the seventh time, when the priests had blown the trumpets, Joshua said to the people, "Shout! For the LORD has given you the city. [17]The city and all that is in it shall be devoted to the LORD for destruction. Only Rahab the prostitute and all who are with her in her house shall live because she hid the messengers we sent. [18]As for you, keep away from the things devoted to destruction, so as not to covet[a] and take any of the devoted things and make the camp of Israel an object for destruction, bringing trouble upon it. [19]But all silver and gold, and vessels of bronze and iron, are sacred to the LORD; they shall go into the treasury of the LORD." [20]So the people shouted, and the trumpets were blown. As soon as the people heard the sound of the trumpets, they raised a great shout, and the wall fell down flat; so the people charged straight ahead into the city and captured it. [21]Then they devoted to destruction by the edge of the sword all in the city, both men and women, young and old, oxen, sheep, and donkeys.

[a] Gk: Heb *devote to destruction* Compare 7.21

COMMENTARY

The focus now shifts again to Jericho, destined for siege and destruction. Recall why Jericho plays the role it does as emblem for the entire conquest. With its spring-fed oasis, Jericho dominated the lower Jordan plain, as it had for six thousand years or more. During Josiah's reign, and not during the pre-Davidic period of Israel's history, Jericho, which lay about four miles west of the Jordan, was the prime urban settlement beside the Jordan where it flows closest to Jerusalem in the highland. Thus Jericho helps to mark the boundary of the land to be conquered under Joshua. Jericho also dominated the route south to the rest of the western side of the Dead Sea basin. Here was concentrated the increased production of incense in Palestine, in which the house of David under Manasseh and Josiah took great interest.

Moreover, Jericho may have been a center of resistance to Josiah's rule. In defiance of Joshua's curse (Josh 6:26) Jericho was rebuilt, according to the Deuteronomistic History, during the reign of Ahab, more than two centuries before Josiah, by a certain Hiel of Bethel (1 Kgs 16:34).[48] The deuteronomistic historian probably takes this Hiel to be an example of the kind of semi-independent warlord whom Josiah must suppress. Thus Coogan suggests that Hiel's rebuilding of Jericho, which to judge by the poetic character of the reference in 1 Kings had a historical basis, "was a kind of rebellious secession, disapproved of by the deuteronomistic historians."[49] Indeed, it is quite conceivable that Hiel had a self-governing successor in Jericho in Josiah's day who would then have been the real "king of Jericho" targeted by the story in Joshua. During the Late Bronze and Iron ages, which began in the sixteenth century BCE and lasted for nine hundred years, until the fall of Jerusalem, Jericho was most extensively settled during the seventh and early sixth centuries; before then, settlement was sparse at best, though the site was well known, since it was always strategically important due to its location and springs, regardless of whether it was settled.

In the prelude to the battle against Jericho, the commander of Yahweh's army appears before Joshua with drawn sword. There is no indefinite "once" as in the NRSV; this scene belongs with what follows, including Yahweh's battle instructions and Israel's first march around Jericho. The

entire episode takes place without a break on the first day of Passover (5:13–6:11). Angels often appear as men, even when they speak as Yahweh, so Joshua at first does not recognize the commander for what he is. Joshua challenges him: Is he an Israelite or an enemy? The commander reveals his remarkable identity. That such appearances, concomitant with the routine war oracle, are typical in traditional battle accounts is indicated by a remarkable Homeric parallel in which Athena, goddess of war and Odysseus' protector, appears to Odysseus prior to his battle with the suitors to assure him of victory.[50] In this scene, even in Athena's presence Odysseus wonders out loud how he is going to succeed; he seems no more aware than Joshua of the might that is standing before him.

Confronted by Yahweh's commander, Joshua instantly collapses in obeisance and asks what word the angel has for him. This represents an extremely critical moment, since Joshua now knows that, as when he was commissioned by Yahweh, he is to learn in advance the outcome of the battle through the equivalent of a divine war oracle delivered directly from the source rather than through an intervening messenger or prophet. Joshua is not looking for a command (contrary to the NRSV), but that is the first thing he receives. The commander's instruction recalls Moses standing before the burning bush at Horeb (Exod 3:1-12). His instruction makes Gilgal equivalent to Horeb, the site where Moses was told at length, despite numerous protestations, that God would be with him (Exod 3:12–4:17), and where, after delivering Israel from slavery in Egypt, God formed a covenant with Israel, conveyed the first ten laws, and anticipated the entire rest of the law (Deuteronomy 5). At Horeb, God also referred to the land oozing milk and honey and to the seven nations inhabiting the land, who are to be dispossessed (Exod 3:8)—starting here at Jericho. The commander's instruction confirms that the shrine at Gilgal is to be a sacred shrine like Horeb.

What, then, is to be the outcome of the battle? The comparison implies that Yahweh will fight on the side of Israel to fulfill the salvation of the former slaves. This scene thus resumes the insistence that Yahweh is with Joshua as with Moses

48. The LXX of 1 Kgs 16:34 shows the full form of Hiel's name, Ahiel.
49. Michael D. Coogan, "Archaeology and Biblical Studies: The Book of Joshua," in *The Hebrew Bible and Its Interpreters,* ed. William Propp, Baruch Halpern, and David Noel Freedman (Winona Lake, Ind.: Eisenbrauns, 1990) 22; "Joshua," in *The Jerome Biblical Commentary,* 116.

50. Homer *Odyssey* 20:30-55.

612

(3:7; 4:14) and forms a framework with the concluding line of the Jericho episode to the same effect (6:27). Thus the entire first quarter of the book of Joshua may be said to be dedicated to verifying that Joshua and his royal successor Josiah represent the authority of Yahweh.

The chapter division should be ignored. After a narrator's comment on the state of Jericho (6:1), Yahweh delivers the expected war oracle, including an assigned battle plan (6:2). The fluid alternation of the figure of man, angel, and Yahweh should occasion no surprise; such alternation occurs several times in Genesis (e.g., Gen 18:1–19:28). Yahweh's battle plan, while surprising, is not so preposterous as it may at first seem. It can be interpreted in terms of guerrilla tactics, where feint, deception, display, discipline, and surprise can go a long way toward compensating for a weak position, like that of a tribal force facing a well-armed and sealed fortress town. In addition, the narrative has a clear theological point: Israel cannot fight without Yahweh's help, though Yahweh is able to do a great deal without Israel's help. The narrative highlights how Yahweh's might almost effortlessly makes up for Israel's weakness (6:16: "Yahweh has given you the town").

The battle plan consists mostly of normal military procedures: blowing horns (see, e.g., 1 Sam 13:3; Amos 2:2; Hos 5:8; Zeph 1:16), marching in formation, rallying behind the palladium, shouting, charging. Comparison can be made with Joshua's battle against Ai (Joshua 8) and with Gideon's battle against the Midianites, which conveys much the same theological point (Judg 7:2-23). The number seven—seven priests, horns, and days—is known in military contexts. For example, in the Ugaritic texts, King Keret sets out with a mighty force to besiege King Pabil in his town, and the journey takes seven days.[51] The seven plagues that Yahweh inflicts on Pharaoh and his household in the original J account of the exodus (the E and P strands add three more plagues) probably stem from such a tradition (see Deut 7:18-20). At the same time, all the military elements except charging are characteristic of liturgical acts as well. The LXX does not include a reference to these groups of seven in the instructions to Joshua, possibly pointing to an earlier stage of the story, before its liturgical elaboration,

if not by the deuteronomists then perhaps by priestly writers in the exilic or post-exilic period. In any case, the "Day of Yahweh," the day on which Yahweh arrives to vindicate a just judgment (typically in battle), the language of war, and the language of liturgy merge into a common diction, based on the common symbolism of God's fearsome advent as divine warrior and magistrate. Such a merging can be seen in such passages as Hos 5:8–6:6; Joel 2; and Zephaniah 1. This characteristic merging makes it possible for a narrator to describe the fall of Jericho as virtually a liturgical continuation of the crossing of the Jordan, whether or not there was a later liturgical recasting of the narrative.

At the climactic moment when Joshua gives the command to shout, all must hold their breath while he expands on the dedication of the goods, livestock, and people to Yahweh—that is, their disposal to the temple or their annihilation (6:15-19). This dedication is the pivotal motif underlying both the exemption of Rahab and her family, because Rahab in effect has loyally championed the dedication of Jericho, and, in the sequel, the execution of Achan and his family for Achan's violation of the same dedication. The phrase "bringing trouble upon it/bring disaster on it" (6:18) links this narrative directly to the crime and punishment of Achan (7:25). References to dedications of various kinds using the term חרם (ḥērem) occur throughout the OT. The deuteronomistic law for the dedication, or ban, of enemy spoil is laid down in Deut 20:10-18 (cf. Deut 7:1-3) as part of the procedure for warring against the natives of Canaan, and in Deut 13:12-18 as part of the procedure for punishing Israelite localities that practice idolatry. Every living thing is to be slaughtered as the means of dedicating them to Yahweh, and indestructible (chiefly metallic; note the anachronistic mention of iron) property of any worth is to be dedicated to the treasury of Yahweh (6:19). The NIV translation of 6:18a accurately renders the MT; the NRSV follows a widely accepted emendation based on the LXX. The LXX reading provides a further direct link with the story of Achan in 7:21. The ambiguity of choosing between such variants, however, which occur often in biblical study, is illustrated by the ties that both variants have to Deut 7:25-26, which make them not only valid but apropos. The Aramaic version of 6:19 refers to the "treas-

51. Michael D. Coogan, *Stories from Ancient Canaan* (Philadelphia: Westminster, 1978) 60-64.

ury *of the temple* of Yahweh," as does the MT, though not the LXX, in 6:24 (NRSV and NIV, "house"). There is nothing startling about this variant, since the term "treasury" by itself implies the existence of a substantial and commanding central shrine. The mention of a temple, whether by a deuteronomistic writer or later scribes, makes an anachronistic reference to the shrine of the house of David in Jerusalem and an allusion to Josiah's program of centralization.

This anachronism is telling in more ways than one. The narrator may have been aware that the complete and unconditional dedication of enemy spoil is not a tribal but a state institution, and that it would not make sense in the narrative in the absence of a state temple. To see why this is true, it is necessary to look more closely at the institution of dedication.

The Hebrew root used to mean "dedication" (חרם *ḥrm*) occurs in all the Semitic languages as a synonym of the root קדש (*qdš*), which in Hebrew is the more common root, usually translated by the English idea of "holy." Both roots mean "to set apart," "treat as sacred," "dedicate," or "forfeit." Concepts like holy, holiness, sanctuary, and sanctified that in Hebrew are usually formed from the root *qdš* are frequently formed in other Semitic languages from the root *ḥrm.* In Arabic, for example, a sanctuary precinct is called *ḥaram* and the sanctuary *ḥarîm.* The latter word has come into English as "harem," the section of the patriarchal household "set apart" for women and, like "banned" items in Hebrew, "prohibited." The two roots occur together in Hebrew in Lev 27:28: "every dedicated thing [*ḥērem*] is most holy [קדש-קדשׁים *qōdeš-qādāšîm*] to Yahweh," so that every person so dedicated must be put to death. A less barbaric use of the two terms occurs in Lev 27:16-25, concerning a field dedicated (*qdš*) to Yahweh, which under specified conditions "shall be holy [*qdš*] to Yahweh as a dedicated [*ḥrm*] field" (Lev 27:21). It must be realized that there is some redundancy in such phrases: Something "set apart" is something "set apart." The prohibitive use of *qdš* in Hebrew is illustrated in Deut 22:9: If a person sows a vineyard with seed, "the whole yield will be forfeit [תקדש *tiqdaš*—that is, will be holy, or prohibited]."[52]

Not surprisingly, the ritual dedication of rivals and

enemies, an excellent excuse for exterminating them, was practiced elsewhere in the ancient Near East, but how extensively is not known. The closest parallel comes from the so-called Mesha Stela, a Moabite inscription from the mid-ninth century BCE. In it the king of Moab, Mesha (probably the king referred to in 2 Kgs 1:1; 3:5), vaunts his reconquest of territory earlier lost to Omri and Ahab, kings of Israel (making Mesha a sort of non-Davidic precursor of Josiah). Mesha's state god was an avatar of Ashtar named Kemosh. In the midst of the account of his reconquest, Mesha declares that "Kemosh said to me, 'Go, take Nebo from Israel!' So I went by night and fought against it from the break of dawn until noon, taking it and slaying all, seven thousand men, boys, women, girls, and maid-servants, for I had dedicated [*ḥrm*] them to Ashtar-Kemosh. From there I took the vessels(?) of Yahweh and hauled them before Kemosh."[53]

Another parallel often pointed out comes from the Mari letters, clay tablets from Mari, located on the middle Euphrates River near the present border between Syria and Iraq, which were written a thousand years before Josiah.[54] These letters concern many subjects, including the struggles of the kings of Mari to curb, pre-empt, or accommodate the tribes inhabiting territory under their sovereignty. In these struggles, the king of Mari claimed propriety over the spoils of warfare or intimidation on behalf of his god, much like Joshua. The king termed the violation of his prerogative "eating the *asakku* of the king or god." Eventually this expression became generalized to cover any breach of contract. The Akkadian word *asakku* originated as a loanword from Sumerian, where it referred to a particular demon that could be relied on to avenge a violation of propriety, and hence to something prohibited or taboo. The Akkadian term, therefore, was functionally, though not semantically, equivalent to Hebrew *ḥērem.*

In a recent response to the comparison of "eating the *asakku* of the king or god" with the violation of *ḥērem,* it has been suggested that the *asakku* taboo at Mari was an administrative device for

52. See Marvin H. Pope, "Devoted," in *Interpreter's Dictionary of the Bible,* ed. George A. Buttrick (Nashville: Abingdon, 1962) 1:838-39; Norbert Lohfink, "*ḥrm*," in *Theological Dictionary of the Old Testament,* ed. G. J. Botterweck and H. Ringgren (Grand Rapids: Eerdmans, 1982) vol. 3.

53. James B. Pritchard, *Ancient Near Eastern Texts* (Princeton: Princeton University Press, 1955) 320-21; Klass A. D. Smelik, *Writings from Ancient Israel: A Handbook of Historical and Religious Documents* (Louisville: Westminster/John Knox, 1991) 33-34.

54. Abraham Malamat, *Mari and the Early Israelite Experience* (New York: Oxford University Press, 1989) 70-79.

regulating the distribution of booty, whereas the biblical concept of *ḥērem* was religious, entailing a self-denying vow of abstinence from the normal fruits of victory in order to arouse God's sympathy with Israel's cause.[55] The latter point helps to broaden the function of *ḥērem* in war. However, the perceived contrast between the two institutions depends on the unlikely distinction between the realms of religion and taboo and may not take seriously enough that in war *ḥērem* was imposed by decree rather than voluntarily adopted.

The last point forms an important part of another major response to the original proposal.[56] Gottwald agrees with the comparison of "eating the *asakku*" with the violation of *ḥērem*, but rejects the assumption that the Mari institution was comparable with Israelite tribal practice in the pre-monarchic period. As Gottwald points out, it was not the tribes of Mari who imposed proprietary taboo, but the king, representing the central government and dominant cult. The same applies, according to Gottwald, to the great majority of other parallels that have been adduced.[57] By the same token, therefore, the description of *ḥērem* in Joshua must be regarded as a reflection of the reform of Josiah and possibly Hezekiah, and not a description of pre-Davidic tribal warfare.[58]

Ironically the fall and capture of Jericho and the dedication of every living thing in it, the sum of what most people know about Joshua, only two verses (6:20-21; see Overview to 9:1–10:43). Much has been made of Jericho not only because it is the first of the cities Joshua destroys, and not only because of the particularly dramatic fashion in which it is destroyed, but because its destruction appears to lend itself to archaeological confirmation. The archaeological evidence from Palestine, however, fails to agree with a Late Bronze Age destruction of Jericho and with few, if any, of the other episodes of destruction described in Joshua. Most archaeologists now believe that Jericho, Ai, and Gibeon had no significant occupation during the Late Bronze Age, when the incidents in Joshua would have occurred. Some of the cities supposedly destroyed in Joshua's campaign show evidence of destruction more or less in the requisite period, but their dates of destruction can vary significantly; Hazor was destroyed as early as a century before Lachish.

It does not do, however, to deal with the sites selectively in order to focus on the few apparent consistencies between archaeology and the book of Joshua. For the aggregate of evidence, William Dever, the dean of American biblical archaeologists, summarizes as follows:

First, of a total of sixteen sites clearly said by the Bible to have been destroyed, only three have produced archaeological evidence for a destruction ca. 1200 B.C.: Bethel, Lachish, and Hazor. This is virtually the same evidence adduced by Albright and Wright a generation ago; we can add only the newer data from Lachish for changing Albright's 1230 B.C. date to ca. 1175–50 B.C. Of the remaining thirteen sites, seven claimed by the Bible as Israelite destructions either were not even occupied in the period, or show no trace of a destruction. Finally, for six of these sixteen Biblical sites, archaeology is simply silent: they have not been positively located, or they have not yet been excavated sufficiently to yield evidence.

Second, if we look at the picture the other way around, of the twelve sites said by the Bible *not* to have been destroyed by the Israelites (mostly in Judges 1), five have been excavated and indeed show no destruction ca. 1200 B.C. The other six either have not been dug or have produced evidence that is inconclusive.

Finally, there are at least twelve other Late Bronze-Iron I sites of this horizon, either unidentified or not mentioned by name in the Bible. Of these, six were destroyed in all likelihood by the Philistines or "Sea Peoples," and one by the Egyptian Pharaoh Merneptah. The other six were destroyed by unknown agents—perhaps one or two of them by the Israelites, although there is no Biblical tradition to that effect and no way of ascertaining archaeologically the identity of the destroyers.

In conclusion, it may be stated confidently that the archaeological evidence today is overwhelmingly against the classic conquest model of Israelite origins, as envisioned in the book of Joshua and in much Biblical scholarship until recently.[59]

---

55. Moshe Greenberg, "Is There a Mari Parallel to the Israelite Enemy-*ḥērem*?" *Eretz-Israel* 24 (1993) 49-53, Hebrew with English summary p. 233*.

56. Norman K. Gottwald, *The Tribes of Yahweh* (Maryknoll, N.Y.: Orbis, 1979) 543-46.

57. See further Moshe Weinfeld, *The Promise of the Land: The Inheritance of the Land of Canaan by the Israelites* (Berkeley: University of California Press, 1993) 76-98; Phillip D. Stern, *The Biblical ḥērem: A Window on Israel's Religious Experience* (Atlanta: Scholars Press, 1991).

58. See Paul D. Hanson, "War and Peace in the Hebrew Bible," *Int.* 38 (1984) 241-61; T. Raymond Hobbs, *A Time for War: A Study of Warfare in the Old Testament* (Wilmington, Del.: Michael Glazier, 1989); Sa-Moon Kang, *Divine War in the Old Testament and the Ancient Near East* (Berlin: De Gruyter, 1989); Stern, *The Biblical Ḥērem*; Susan Niditch, *War in the Hebrew Bible: A Study in the Ethics of Violence* (New York: Oxford University Press, 1993); J. P. U. Lilley, "Understanding the *ḥērem*," *TynBul* 44 (1993) 169-77.

59. William G. Dever, "The Israelite Settlement in Canaan: New Archaeological Models," in *Recent Archaeological Discoveries and Biblical Research* (Seattle: University of Washington Press, 1990) 61; see also 37-84. See also Dever, "Archaeology and the Israelite 'Conquest,'" in *ABD* 3:545-58; Coogan, "Archaeology and Biblical Studies," 19-32.

In a more recent summary of the discrepancies between archaeology and Joshua, Israeli archaeologist Nadav Na'aman confirms Dever's conclusion. Many sites, Na'aman points out, supposedly conquered or otherwise mentioned were not occupied in the Late Bronze Age. These include Heshbon, Arad, Ai, Jarmuth, Hebron, and Gibeon. The first four were not occupied for the entire second millennium BCE. The destruction of Late Bronze Age urban culture was gradual, not sudden, over a period of more than a hundred years. Joshua 10–11 makes it appear that Lachish and Hazor were destroyed at practically the same time. The evidence shows that Hazor was destroyed about mid-thirteenth century, and Lachish in the second half of the twelfth century. During the thirteenth and most of the twelfth centuries, Egyptian forces were in Canaan and left a marked Egyptian influence on the material culture of Palestine, especially in the eleventh century, but there is no mention of Egypt in the account of Joshua's conquest. Many cities were destroyed as Egypt pulled out of Palestine in the 1130s, including Bethshean, Megiddo, Ashdod, Tel Sera, and Tell el-Fer'ah. These sites, however, were destroyed much later than the supposed conquest, and they were all in the lowland, not the highland settled by the Israelites.[60] Moreover, John Peterson's archaeological analysis of levitical settlements in Joshua 21, showing that on the basis of the history of occupation at each site, the list could not have been compiled before the eighth century BCE, has been widely accepted.[61] As pointed out by many, the same is probably true of the most complete of the site lists, that of Judah in Joshua 15.

60. Nadav Na'aman, "The 'Conquest of Canaan' in the Book of Joshua and in History," in *From Nomadism to Monarchy: Archaeological and Historical Aspects of Early Israel,* ed. Israel Finkelstein and Nadav Na'aman (Jerusalem: Israel Exploration Society, 1994) 218-81, esp. 223.

61. John L. Peterson, "A Topographical Survey of the Levitical 'Cities' of Joshua 21 and 1 Chronicles 6: Studies on the Levites in Israelite Life and Religion" (Th.D. diss., Seabury-Western Theological Seminary, Evanston, 1977).

REFLECTIONS

1. There is probably nothing in the Bible more offensive to modern sensibilities than God's sanction of genocide against the Canaanites. In a discerning discussion of biblical theology in relation to natural theology, James Barr notes that proponents of a pure biblical theology have unfortunately been left either excusing this offense on false grounds—the Canaanites were wicked and deserved God's judgment; or the practice was common, and thus the Israelites were no worse than their neighbors; or the practice negated an ethic of plunder and exploitation—or ignoring it in the hope that most people would regard it as a minor matter or forget that it was in the Bible. It is probably not possible, concludes Barr, to accept the divine sanction of the practice and remain moral at the same time.[62]

An alternative apologetic looks at first more promising. This is to take a quasi-Marcionite approach. Genocide was commanded by the God of the Old Testament, whereas the God of the New Testament takes the opposite approach by incorporating the Gentiles, symbolized by the same seven "nations" of Canaanites anathematized in the Davidic scriptures, in the new covenant in Jesus Christ. This approach can emphasize changes in God or in history, analogous to progressive revelation, in which the old is replaced by the new. Or from a historical perspective, it can point out an apparent major difference between the Old Testament and the New Testament. The Old Testament presumes the integrity of a functioning nation or subset of humanity constituted under monarchic sovereignty by a distinctive law for life in a given territory, and thus of the wars that such integrity requires. In contrast, the New Testament repudiates that concept of Israel in favor of the notion of a community of faith, or trust, constituted not by a law but by mutual deference and love, ruled not by an earthly monarch schooled in the martial arts and existing to be served, but by an ecclesiastical collective

62. James Barr, *Biblical Faith and Natural Theology* (Oxford: Clarendon, 1993) 207-21.

representing the heavenly prince of peace, schooled in the arts of concord and goodwill and existing to serve.

Such an approach is no sooner stated than its flaws become apparent. While there is significant truth to the contrast, at the same time there is a great deal in the Old Testament that accords with what has just been said about the New Testament, as the New Testament writers themselves endlessly aver. By the same token, it would be a selective reading of the New Testament, indeed, to deny that one of its central concepts is the victory of the church through a great war sustained by God in fulfillment of the church's earliest Scriptures, the Old Testament. In that war, some are to die and others live, according to the inscrutable will of God. Moreover, the history of the church, for at least the last seventeen hundred years, shows that its concept of power and authority owes more to supposed Old Testament notions of privilege, sovereignty, and rule, than to the New Testament ideal of universal peace. Until quite recently all the major churches have been extremely powerful institutions, often with the force of states at their disposal, and in some cases they were states or virtual states in their own right. Even today, to state the obvious, much military havoc continues to be wrought in the name of the Prince of peace.

2. God's war against the Canaanites gives the interpreter more than the occasion for disavowing genocide. It prompts us to reflect on at least two major issues: the function of violence and the dynamics of genocide in our own world. Recognizing that social order takes on the character of the sacred, even within modern secular societies, René Girard observes in his broad comparative treatment of the subject that violence in the name of the sacred usually represents a reaction to a threat to social order, whether actual or perceived.[63] Since communities that define the sacred deal in symbolic realities, they typically project the threat onto collective scapegoats who, whether more or less justifiably, symbolize the threat. Scapegoat victims can be enemies, ritual victims, or surrogate victims from the community itself. All ultimately represent the threat and must be destroyed. In the end, the tendency is to see all disorder as external rather than internal to the community. The common enemy must be sacrificed so the community can survive. The political opportunism made possible by sacred violence is evident. Without reference to the Bible, Girard lists four essentials to scapegoating: a crisis, the involvement of the divine in the selection of victims, a perceived difference between scapegoat and scapegoaters, and the sacrality of the king or other figurehead of sacred social order. All these apply to the narrative of Joshua, and they can be illustrated in our own world.

As for the dynamics of genocide, the role of the state or a comparable governing entity is essential. Ethnic cleansing is not a process that emerges in the "natural" interaction of people with one another. People are not angels, but left on their own they will not form grandiose concepts of false identity with which to divide the world into types whose moral characters form such opposites that one type must be destroyed by the other. This is a feat, to judge from known instances, to which people must be induced. The treatment of Jews pursued by the Nazi government in Central Europe is only the most notorious example of this rule; obviously many average people participated willingly in the persecution of Jews, but without the Nazi government there would have been no genocide. The same is true of the treatment of Tamils in Sri Lanka; of Serbs, Croats, and Bosnians in the former Yugoslavia; of Tutsis and in turn Hutus in Rwanda, and so on. These modern instances of ethnic cleansing represent not the inevitable struggle of one essential kind of humanity against another, as many of the participants themselves have been led to believe, but the result of government manipulation of popular insecurity, residual resentments, and latent or perceptible distinctions in the populace.

Without historical analysis, of course, this feature of the book of Joshua has been, and is,

---

63. See René Girard, *Violence and the Sacred* (Baltimore: Johns Hopkins University Press, 1977). See also James G. Williams, *The Bible, Violence, and the Sacred: Liberation from the Myth of Sanctioned Violence* (San Francisco: HarperCollins, 1996).

quite invisible. Even today it is possible for most readers of the Bible to believe that Canaanites and Israelites were actually completely different from each other.

3. The interpreter may prefer to bracket the political assumptions of the text and focus on the *esprit de corps* demonstrated by the guerrilla tactics of Israel's band of fighters. Their faith in the God who fought with them and for them, and their fear of what God might do if they were disobedient (see Joshua 7), led them to extraordinary commitment and feats of bravery. This is the spirit needed by any group set on facing daunting challenges and achieving difficult goals.

Joshua 6:22-27, Saving Rahab and Her Family

NIV

²²Joshua said to the two men who had spied out the land, "Go into the prostitute's house and bring her out and all who belong to her, in accordance with your oath to her." ²³So the young men who had done the spying went in and brought out Rahab, her father and mother and brothers and all who belonged to her. They brought out her entire family and put them in a place outside the camp of Israel.

²⁴Then they burned the whole city and everything in it, but they put the silver and gold and the articles of bronze and iron into the treasury of the LORD's house. ²⁵But Joshua spared Rahab the prostitute, with her family and all who belonged to her, because she hid the men Joshua had sent as spies to Jericho—and she lives among the Israelites to this day.

²⁶At that time Joshua pronounced this solemn oath: "Cursed before the LORD is the man who undertakes to rebuild this city, Jericho:

"At the cost of his firstborn son
  will he lay its foundations;
at the cost of his youngest
  will he set up its gates."

²⁷So the LORD was with Joshua, and his fame spread throughout the land.

NRSV

22Joshua said to the two men who had spied out the land, "Go into the prostitute's house, and bring the woman out of it and all who belong to her, as you swore to her." ²³So the young men who had been spies went in and brought Rahab out, along with her father, her mother, her brothers, and all who belonged to her—they brought all her kindred out—and set them outside the camp of Israel. ²⁴They burned down the city, and everything in it; only the silver and gold, and the vessels of bronze and iron, they put into the treasury of the house of the LORD. ²⁵But Rahab the prostitute, with her family and all who belonged to her, Joshua spared. Her family*a* has lived in Israel ever since. For she hid the messengers whom Joshua sent to spy out Jericho.

26Joshua then pronounced this oath, saying,
  "Cursed before the LORD be anyone who
    tries
      to build this city—this Jericho!
  At the cost of his firstborn he shall lay its
      foundation,
  and at the cost of his youngest he shall
      set up its gates!"

27So the LORD was with Joshua; and his fame was in all the land.

a Heb *She*

COMMENTARY

In a typical narrative frame, the end of the story of Jericho returns to its beginning. Joshua sends the same two men whom he sent in 2:1 into Jericho, to the house of Rahab. In what amounts to a compound conclusion (a small frame at the end of the large frame) the narrator refers in v. 25 yet again to the sending of the two men. The entire extended family is safely removed and given quarters outside the Israelite camp. This act brings the narrative as such to a close. The rest is summary and result, as is clear from the Hebrew syntax. In contrast to the rest of Jericho, which is put to the torch, Rahab and all her family with all their property are saved, to endure as aliens in the midst of Israel, a living testimony to the value of loyalty to Yahweh's and Israel's cause. Rahab and her family do not become Israelites, but still she contrasts with Achan as a model of loyalty in contrast to Achan's disloyalty. It may be assumed that in the narrative world of this text Rahab, whether a historical or legendary character, was able to discontinue her prostitution; even if not Israelite and not in line to receive a land grant, a household playing the role that hers does can expect relief from poverty and its degradations.

The NRSV translation "her family" in v. 25 is preferable to the NIV's "she"; Rahab's family rather than she alone may, in fact, be the subject of the verb "live," but in any case the sense pertains to Rahab's entire family, and not just to Rahab herself. However, the NRSV's "lived in Israel" is a seriously misleading anachronism. The NIV gets this right: Rahab's family "lives among the Israelites." This is the meaning of the Hebrew expression "in the midst of" (בקרב *bĕqereb*) here, which occurs also in 13:13 and 16:10 with reference to Canaanites. As shown by its translation of the latter two passages, the NRSV takes "Israel" to be a territory, equivalent to the expression "land of Israel"; neither that expression nor its sense occurs in Joshua. "Israel" here means the populace under tribal heads subjected to the house of David.

The entire narrative concerning Jericho concludes with the best clue to its significance in the first place. Joshua puts a curse on anyone who dares to rebuild Jericho (v. 26)—and someone does. Rebuilding Jericho does not mean just residing there, as some apparently do in the interim (18:21; Judg 3:13; 2 Sam 10:5), but refortifying it as a center of power. In the days of Ahab, long before Josiah, Hiel rebuilt Jericho, and in fulfillment of Joshua's curse it cost him two sons (1 Kgs 16:34; reported in the LXX of Josh 6:26). Whether the sons died as intentional sacrifices to the rebuilding or in some other way is disputed. The text is ambiguous in this regard. The main

reason for believing that sacrifice was the cause of their deaths is the convention of guaranteeing such an undertaking by child sacrifice. The poetic character of Joshua's curse may suggest the use of a ritual formula. Whether or not a rite of child sacrifice was involved, the death of Hiel's two sons answers to the saving of Rahab and her family; more important, it provides a final allusion to Passover in this section. The prescription for the Passover meal in Exod 13:1-16 is framed by references to the sacrifice of all firstborn males, with children to be redeemed (13:1-2, 11-16), and the Passover law in Deuteronomy 16 is immediately preceded by the deuteronomistic equivalent of the same law of sacrifice (Deut 15:19-23). The sacrifice of the firstborn, of course, duplicates the devastating slaughter of the firstborn of Pharaoh and the rest of the Egyptians on Passover night. It can be no accident that the deuteronomistic historian brings his grand account of the first Passover in the promised land to a conclusion by referring to the fitting death of the firstborn sons of the rebuilder of Jericho. Like all the onetime kings of Canaan, he is no better than Pharaoh and deserves the same fate (see Deut 7:17-24), as does anyone who might be tempted to follow his example by trying to establish an independent center of power.

The final line of this section summarizes the entire story, beginning with the commissioning of Joshua (1:5). Joshua's success in the miraculous crossing of the Jordan and capture of Jericho demonstrates that Yahweh stands behind him—or before him. Joshua's fame reaches the entire land. The Hebrew for "fame" (שמע *šōma*ʿ) means literally "what was heard" about him. The phrase recalls one of the main themes of the exodus: When Yahweh brought Israel out of Egypt with miraculous shows of power, kings trembled in fear and prepared to resist. The implications of Yahweh's power on Joshua's behalf are the same. Having heard about Joshua, the fearful kings combine forces to attempt to repulse the arrogant expropriator and his pretentious God (9:1). Of course, failure and weakness can produce a comparable fame and embolden opponents (see 7:8-9).

REFLECTIONS

Joshua's unconditional good fortune and victory suggest that Yahweh was "with him," as the narrator categorically states (6:27). This continues the emphasis of Josh 1:5, 9, "I will be with you . . . Yahweh is with you." Here the statement looks forward more than backward. However, without the benefit of lengthy hindsight, to equate blessing with righteousness and success with God's favor constitutes an arrogant audacity. A common prophetic theme in the Bible is how often the confidence of those who attribute their success to God's favor turns out to be premature. As history unfolds, sooner or later apparent blessing turns into wretched curse, as God turns the tables on the wealthy, the self-confident, and the self-assured, whose prosperity and accomplishments prove to be delusions. The deuteronomist, a notoriously unequivocal champion of God's justice, knows that this is true as long as God's justice prevails and is manifest.

From a prophetic perspective, the deuteronomistic writer realizes that despite Joshua's success there is no way to indicate with certainty without the passage of narrative time that God was, indeed, with Joshua. Thus the writer juxtaposed this claim with a curse, or forecast, by Joshua that later—much later—comes true. Together, curse and fulfillment supply the necessary proof, once the hearer of this part of the story hears what happens to Hiel in the time of Ahab. Of course, it is likely that the writer included this prophetic curse precisely because hearers were already familiar with the fate of Hiel. The writer was not content to allow the conquest of Jericho, betokening the conquest of Canaan, the very foundation of the house of David's later distinction, to satisfy the need for the prophetic perspective of time, because the later reconquest of the land is just what was at issue. Joshua captured the land, and David ruled it, but whether God really was with Joshua and David and, therefore, was to be with the writer's contemporary, Josiah, and give to him the rule of the land is not yet proven, because at the time the writer wrote, Josiah had not yet completed the reconquest.

Thus the brief notice that "the LORD was with Joshua" (6:27 NRSV), placed as it is immediately following Joshua's foretelling of the future, evidences the deuteronomist's awareness that making theological pronouncements based on ostensible success but without the benefit of the history God still has in store is not only a risk, but vain presumption. Of course, the deuteronomist himself nevertheless ends up being presumptuous: He crafts a narrative proof, but the narrative goes on and on. There is history yet to follow, not just the fulfillment of Joshua's curse, and not just the reign of Josiah himself. From the prophetic perspective, history was not over, and it is still not over. God continues to reign and to shape history to accomplish God's just will; hence theological presumption grounded in success and prosperity remains as perilous as ever.

JOSHUA 7:1–8:29, THE DESTRUCTION OF ACHAN AND AI

NIV

7 But the Israelites acted unfaithfully in regard to the devoted things[a]; Achan son of Carmi, the son of Zimri,[b] the son of Zerah, of the

[a]1 The Hebrew term refers to the irrevocable giving over of things or persons to the LORD, often by totally destroying them; also in verses 11, 12, 13 and 15.   [b]1 See Septuagint and 1 Chron. 2:6; Hebrew *Zabdi*; also in verses 17 and 18.

NRSV

7 But the Israelites broke faith in regard to the devoted things: Achan son of Carmi son of Zabdi son of Zerah, of the tribe of Judah, took some of the devoted things; and the anger of the LORD burned against the Israelites.

2Joshua sent men from Jericho to Ai, which is

NIV

tribe of Judah, took some of them. So the LORD's anger burned against Israel.

²Now Joshua sent men from Jericho to Ai, which is near Beth Aven to the east of Bethel, and told them, "Go up and spy out the region." So the men went up and spied out Ai.

³When they returned to Joshua, they said, "Not all the people will have to go up against Ai. Send two or three thousand men to take it and do not weary all the people, for only a few men are there." ⁴So about three thousand men went up; but they were routed by the men of Ai, ⁵who killed about thirty-six of them. They chased the Israelites from the city gate as far as the stone quarries[a] and struck them down on the slopes. At this the hearts of the people melted and became like water.

⁶Then Joshua tore his clothes and fell facedown to the ground before the ark of the LORD, remaining there till evening. The elders of Israel did the same, and sprinkled dust on their heads. ⁷And Joshua said, "Ah, Sovereign LORD, why did you ever bring this people across the Jordan to deliver us into the hands of the Amorites to destroy us? If only we had been content to stay on the other side of the Jordan! ⁸O Lord, what can I say, now that Israel has been routed by its enemies? ⁹The Canaanites and the other people of the country will hear about this and they will surround us and wipe out our name from the earth. What then will you do for your own great name?"

¹⁰The LORD said to Joshua, "Stand up! What are you doing down on your face? ¹¹Israel has sinned; they have violated my covenant, which I commanded them to keep. They have taken some of the devoted things; they have stolen, they have lied, they have put them with their own possessions. ¹²That is why the Israelites cannot stand against their enemies; they turn their backs and run because they have been made liable to destruction. I will not be with you anymore unless you destroy whatever among you is devoted to destruction.

¹³"Go, consecrate the people. Tell them, 'Consecrate yourselves in preparation for tomorrow; for this is what the LORD, the God of Israel, says: That which is devoted is among you, O Israel.

[a]5 Or as far as Shebarim

NRSV

near Beth-aven, east of Bethel, and said to them, "Go up and spy out the land." And the men went up and spied out Ai. ³Then they returned to Joshua and said to him, "Not all the people need go up; about two or three thousand men should go up and attack Ai. Since they are so few, do not make the whole people toil up there." ⁴So about three thousand of the people went up there; and they fled before the men of Ai. ⁵The men of Ai killed about thirty-six of them, chasing them from outside the gate as far as Shebarim and killing them on the slope. The hearts of the people melted and turned to water.

6Then Joshua tore his clothes, and fell to the ground on his face before the ark of the LORD until the evening, he and the elders of Israel; and they put dust on their heads. ⁷Joshua said, "Ah, Lord GOD! Why have you brought this people across the Jordan at all, to hand us over to the Amorites so as to destroy us? Would that we had been content to settle beyond the Jordan! ⁸O Lord, what can I say, now that Israel has turned their backs to their enemies! ⁹The Canaanites and all the inhabitants of the land will hear of it, and surround us, and cut off our name from the earth. Then what will you do for your great name?"

10The LORD said to Joshua, "Stand up! Why have you fallen upon your face? ¹¹Israel has sinned; they have transgressed my covenant that I imposed on them. They have taken some of the devoted things; they have stolen, they have acted deceitfully, and they have put them among their own belongings. ¹²Therefore the Israelites are unable to stand before their enemies; they turn their backs to their enemies, because they have become a thing devoted for destruction themselves. I will be with you no more, unless you destroy the devoted things from among you. ¹³Proceed to sanctify the people, and say, 'Sanctify yourselves for tomorrow; for thus says the LORD, the God of Israel, "There are devoted things among you, O Israel; you will be unable to stand before your enemies until you take away the devoted things from among you." ¹⁴In the morning therefore you shall come forward tribe by tribe. The tribe that the LORD takes shall come near by clans, the clan that the LORD takes shall come near by households, and the household that the LORD takes shall

NIV

You cannot stand against your enemies until you remove it.

14" 'In the morning, present yourselves tribe by tribe. The tribe that the LORD takes shall come forward clan by clan; the clan that the LORD takes shall come forward family by family; and the family that the LORD takes shall come forward man by man. 15He who is caught with the devoted things shall be destroyed by fire, along with all that belongs to him. He has violated the covenant of the LORD and has done a disgraceful thing in Israel!' "

16Early the next morning Joshua had Israel come forward by tribes, and Judah was taken. 17The clans of Judah came forward, and he took the Zerahites. He had the clan of the Zerahites come forward by families, and Zimri was taken. 18Joshua had his family come forward man by man, and Achan son of Carmi, the son of Zimri, the son of Zerah, of the tribe of Judah, was taken.

19Then Joshua said to Achan, "My son, give glory to the LORD,[a] the God of Israel, and give him the praise.[b] Tell me what you have done; do not hide it from me."

20Achan replied, "It is true! I have sinned against the LORD, the God of Israel. This is what I have done: 21When I saw in the plunder a beautiful robe from Babylonia,[c] two hundred shekels[d] of silver and a wedge of gold weighing fifty shekels,[e] I coveted them and took them. They are hidden in the ground inside my tent, with the silver underneath."

22So Joshua sent messengers, and they ran to the tent, and there it was, hidden in his tent, with the silver underneath. 23They took the things from the tent, brought them to Joshua and all the Israelites and spread them out before the LORD.

24Then Joshua, together with all Israel, took Achan son of Zerah, the silver, the robe, the gold wedge, his sons and daughters, his cattle, donkeys and sheep, his tent and all that he had, to the Valley of Achor. 25Joshua said, "Why have you brought this trouble on us? The LORD will bring trouble on you today."

Then all Israel stoned him, and after they had stoned the rest, they burned them. 26Over Achan

a19 A solemn charge to tell the truth   b19 Or and confess to him
c21 Hebrew Shinar   d21 That is, about 5 pounds (about 2.3 kilograms)   e21 That is, about 1 1/4 pounds (about 0.6 kilogram)

NRSV

come near one by one. 15And the one who is taken as having the devoted things shall be burned with fire, together with all that he has, for having transgressed the covenant of the LORD, and for having done an outrageous thing in Israel.' "

16So Joshua rose early in the morning, and brought Israel near tribe by tribe, and the tribe of Judah was taken. 17He brought near the clans of Judah, and the clan of the Zerahites was taken; and he brought near the clan of the Zerahites, family by family,[a] and Zabdi was taken. 18And he brought near his household one by one, and Achan son of Carmi son of Zabdi son of Zerah, of the tribe of Judah, was taken. 19Then Joshua said to Achan, "My son, give glory to the LORD God of Israel and make confession to him. Tell me now what you have done; do not hide it from me." 20And Achan answered Joshua, "It is true; I am the one who sinned against the LORD God of Israel. This is what I did: 21when I saw among the spoil a beautiful mantle from Shinar, and two hundred shekels of silver, and a bar of gold weighing fifty shekels, then I coveted them and took them. They now lie hidden in the ground inside my tent, with the silver underneath."

22So Joshua sent messengers, and they ran to the tent; and there it was, hidden in his tent with the silver underneath. 23They took them out of the tent and brought them to Joshua and all the Israelites; and they spread them out before the LORD. 24Then Joshua and all Israel with him took Achan son of Zerah, with the silver, the mantle, and the bar of gold, with his sons and daughters, with his oxen, donkeys, and sheep, and his tent and all that he had; and they brought them up to the Valley of Achor. 25Joshua said, "Why did you bring trouble on us? The LORD is bringing trouble on you today." And all Israel stoned him to death; they burned them with fire, cast stones on them, 26and raised over him a great heap of stones that remains to this day. Then the LORD turned from his burning anger. Therefore that place to this day is called the Valley of Achor.[b]

8 Then the LORD said to Joshua, "Do not fear or be dismayed; take all the fighting men with you, and go up now to Ai. See, I have handed over to you the king of Ai with his people,

a Mss Syr: MT man by man   b That is Trouble

NIV

they heaped up a large pile of rocks, which remains to this day. Then the LORD turned from his fierce anger. Therefore that place has been called the Valley of Achor[a] ever since.

8 Then the LORD said to Joshua, "Do not be afraid; do not be discouraged. Take the whole army with you, and go up and attack Ai. For I have delivered into your hands the king of Ai, his people, his city and his land. ²You shall do to Ai and its king as you did to Jericho and its king, except that you may carry off their plunder and livestock for yourselves. Set an ambush behind the city."

³So Joshua and the whole army moved out to attack Ai. He chose thirty thousand of his best fighting men and sent them out at night ⁴with these orders: "Listen carefully. You are to set an ambush behind the city. Don't go very far from it. All of you be on the alert. ⁵I and all those with me will advance on the city, and when the men come out against us, as they did before, we will flee from them. ⁶They will pursue us until we have lured them away from the city, for they will say, 'They are running away from us as they did before.' So when we flee from them, ⁷you are to rise up from ambush and take the city. The LORD your God will give it into your hand. ⁸When you have taken the city, set it on fire. Do what the LORD has commanded. See to it; you have my orders."

⁹Then Joshua sent them off, and they went to the place of ambush and lay in wait between Bethel and Ai, to the west of Ai—but Joshua spent that night with the people.

¹⁰Early the next morning Joshua mustered his men, and he and the leaders of Israel marched before them to Ai. ¹¹The entire force that was with him marched up and approached the city and arrived in front of it. They set up camp north of Ai, with the valley between them and the city. ¹²Joshua had taken about five thousand men and set them in ambush between Bethel and Ai, to the west of the city. ¹³They had the soldiers take up their positions—all those in the camp to the north of the city and the ambush to the west of it. That night Joshua went into the valley.

¹⁴When the king of Ai saw this, he and all the men of the city hurried out early in the morning

a26 Achor means trouble.

NRSV

his city, and his land. ²You shall do to Ai and its king as you did to Jericho and its king; only its spoil and its livestock you may take as booty for yourselves. Set an ambush against the city, behind it."

3So Joshua and all the fighting men set out to go up against Ai. Joshua chose thirty thousand warriors and sent them out by night ⁴with the command, "You shall lie in ambush against the city, behind it; do not go very far from the city, but all of you stay alert. ⁵I and all the people who are with me will approach the city. When they come out against us, as before, we shall flee from them. ⁶They will come out after us until we have drawn them away from the city; for they will say, 'They are fleeing from us, as before.' While we flee from them, ⁷you shall rise up from the ambush and seize the city; for the LORD your God will give it into your hand. ⁸And when you have taken the city, you shall set the city on fire, doing as the LORD has ordered; see, I have commanded you." ⁹So Joshua sent them out; and they went to the place of ambush, and lay between Bethel and Ai, to the west of Ai; but Joshua spent that night in the camp.[a]

10In the morning Joshua rose early and mustered the people, and went up, with the elders of Israel, before the people to Ai. ¹¹All the fighting men who were with him went up, and drew near before the city, and camped on the north side of Ai, with a ravine between them and Ai. ¹²Taking about five thousand men, he set them in ambush between Bethel and Ai, to the west of the city. ¹³So they stationed the forces, the main encampment that was north of the city and its rear guard west of the city. But Joshua spent that night in the valley. ¹⁴When the king of Ai saw this, he and all his people, the inhabitants of the city, hurried out early in the morning to the meeting place facing the Arabah to meet Israel in battle; but he did not know that there was an ambush against him behind the city. ¹⁵And Joshua and all Israel made a pretense of being beaten before them, and fled in the direction of the wilderness. ¹⁶So all the people who were in the city were called together to pursue them, and as they pursued Joshua they were drawn away from the city.

a Heb among the people

NIV

to meet Israel in battle at a certain place overlooking the Arabah. But he did not know that an ambush had been set against him behind the city. ¹⁵Joshua and all Israel let themselves be driven back before them, and they fled toward the desert. ¹⁶All the men of Ai were called to pursue them, and they pursued Joshua and were lured away from the city. ¹⁷Not a man remained in Ai or Bethel who did not go after Israel. They left the city open and went in pursuit of Israel.

¹⁸Then the LORD said to Joshua, "Hold out toward Ai the javelin that is in your hand, for into your hand I will deliver the city." So Joshua held out his javelin toward Ai. ¹⁹As soon as he did this, the men in the ambush rose quickly from their position and rushed forward. They entered the city and captured it and quickly set it on fire.

²⁰The men of Ai looked back and saw the smoke of the city rising against the sky, but they had no chance to escape in any direction, for the Israelites who had been fleeing toward the desert had turned back against their pursuers. ²¹For when Joshua and all Israel saw that the ambush had taken the city and that smoke was going up from the city, they turned around and attacked the men of Ai. ²²The men of the ambush also came out of the city against them, so that they were caught in the middle, with Israelites on both sides. Israel cut them down, leaving them neither survivors nor fugitives. ²³But they took the king of Ai alive and brought him to Joshua.

²⁴When Israel had finished killing all the men of Ai in the fields and in the desert where they had chased them, and when every one of them had been put to the sword, all the Israelites returned to Ai and killed those who were in it. ²⁵Twelve thousand men and women fell that day—all the people of Ai. ²⁶For Joshua did not draw back the hand that held out his javelin until he had destroyed[a] all who lived in Ai. ²⁷But Israel did carry off for themselves the livestock and plunder of this city, as the LORD had instructed Joshua.

²⁸So Joshua burned Ai and made it a permanent heap of ruins, a desolate place to this day. ²⁹He hung the king of Ai on a tree and left him there until evening. At sunset, Joshua ordered them to

^a26 The Hebrew term refers to the irrevocable giving over of things or persons to the LORD, often by totally destroying them.

NRSV

¹⁷There was not a man left in Ai or Bethel who did not go out after Israel; they left the city open, and pursued Israel.

18Then the LORD said to Joshua, "Stretch out the sword that is in your hand toward Ai; for I will give it into your hand." And Joshua stretched out the sword that was in his hand toward the city. ¹⁹As soon as he stretched out his hand, the troops in ambush rose quickly out of their place and rushed forward. They entered the city, took it, and at once set the city on fire. ²⁰So when the men of Ai looked back, the smoke of the city was rising to the sky. They had no power to flee this way or that, for the people who fled to the wilderness turned back against the pursuers. ²¹When Joshua and all Israel saw that the ambush had taken the city and that the smoke of the city was rising, then they turned back and struck down the men of Ai. ²²And the others came out from the city against them; so they were surrounded by Israelites, some on one side, and some on the other; and Israel struck them down until no one was left who survived or escaped. ²³But the king of Ai was taken alive and brought to Joshua.

24When Israel had finished slaughtering all the inhabitants of Ai in the open wilderness where they pursued them, and when all of them to the very last had fallen by the edge of the sword, all Israel returned to Ai, and attacked it with the edge of the sword. ²⁵The total of those who fell that day, both men and women, was twelve thousand—all the people of Ai. ²⁶For Joshua did not draw back his hand, with which he stretched out the sword, until he had utterly destroyed all the inhabitants of Ai. ²⁷Only the livestock and the spoil of that city Israel took as their booty, according to the word of the LORD that he had issued to Joshua. ²⁸So Joshua burned Ai, and made it forever a heap of ruins, as it is to this day. ²⁹And he hanged the king of Ai on a tree until evening; and at sunset Joshua commanded, and they took his body down from the tree, threw it down at the entrance of the gate of the city, and raised over it a great heap of stones, which stands there to this day.

NIV

take his body from the tree and throw it down at the entrance of the city gate. And they raised a large pile of rocks over it, which remains to this day.

COMMENTARY

The story of the capture and destruction of Ai is immediately related to the preceding story of the capture and destruction of Jericho by means of a similar beginning, in which Joshua sends men to spy out the land (2:1; 7:2), and a similar ending, in which a primary site is given an etymology related to a heap of stones (Gilgal in 4:7, 20; 5:9; Jericho is not a heap of stones because it was rebuilt by Hiel). Jericho and Gilgal play a central role in each story: Achan hides spoil from Jericho in the camp in Gilgal. More important, the story of Ai mirrors the story of Jericho in that both highlight an individual, in one case, Rahab, in the other, Achan. The two individuals are contrasted. Rahab is loyal to the Israelite cause; Achan is disloyal to the same cause. Moreover, the two stories are linked through the *ḥērem* at Jericho, the dedication of every living thing and all material goods to Yahweh. Rahab is spared from the application of that dedication, and Achan is snared for violating it. In other words, the loyal Canaanite is included and the disloyal Israelite is excluded. This correspondence alone is the basis for the integration of over half the narrative of conquest in the book of Joshua (chaps. 2–8).

Indeed, the correspondence extends to the following major episode as well, in chaps. 9–10 (8:30-35 is to be bracketed as a later addition). The following episode must be brought into the discussion of the present section. Joshua's campaign to the south in chap. 9 begins with the attempt of the Canaanite kings to band together to defend themselves. The men of Gibeon decide not to join their coalition and instead, at the risk of getting themselves dedicated to Yahweh, trek to Gilgal and trick Joshua into making a compact with them. Having escaped dedication to Yahweh, the Gibeonites submit to Joshua as servants of the central altar of Yahweh, "in the place that he should choose" (9:27; cf. Deut 12:2-5). The story of the Gibeonites, like the stories of Rahab and

Achan, lays the groundwork for the related battle account. Joshua comes to the rescue of the Gibeonites when they are attacked by five Amorite kings in the Canaanite alliance, led by the king of Jerusalem. Joshua kills the five kings and captures and dedicates most of their towns and others (except Jerusalem, left for David to capture).

The Gibeonites are Canaanites (Hivites). The inclusion of the Gibeonites parallels the inclusion of Rahab and her family, forming a frame around the story of the exclusion of Achan (note the tie between 6:27 and 9:1, immediately surrounding the story of Achan and Ai). Together these three stories comprise over three-quarters of the narrative of conquest (chaps. 2–10). As a set they make this one point: Those who submit may be saved and included, while those who rebel will be excluded and exterminated. It is now widely recognized that this point provides a counterpoint to the ostensible premise of the conquest according to the law of dedication, which posits that for the sake of all Israelites, all Canaanites are to be exterminated. Thus the conquest narrative makes two conflicting points at once. The first point is that as "nations" the Canaanites and the Israelites are implacable and irreconcilable opponents without exception, the Canaanites to be eradicated and the Israelites to be delivered. The second point, or counterpoint, is that exceptions are possible: Canaanites may find a placable reception, and Israelites can be eradicated.

Point and counterpoint may not seem consistent with each other, but both are consistent with Josiah's goal of reconquering and ruling Israel as efficiently as possible. The first point applies mainly to the "kings" of Canaan and their forces, claimants to autonomous sovereignty in their own spheres. The narrative allows for no exception to these and at the end drives home the point by listing by locality, or jurisdiction, all thirty-one kings eradicated (12:7-24). The counterpoint applies to the indebted and intimidated commoners among the Canaanites, the erstwhile subjects and clients of these kings. For these, loyalty and submission may sometimes forestall eradication, providing a basis for the corvée, or statute servitude (NRSV and NIV, "forced labor"), of Canaanites remaining in Israelite territory at the conclusion of Joshua's campaigns of conquest (see 16:10; 17:13; Deut 20:11; Judg 1:28, 30, 33, 35; 1 Kgs 9:20-21; cf. Deut 20:16). Thus the Deuteronomistic History, like the Prophets in general, makes use of two distinctions at once, without either taking precedence, a quasi-ethnic, or "national," distinction and a quasi-socioeconomic, or "class," distinction.

The intersection of the two distinctions may be best represented by the conflicting treatments of Canaanites in Joshua. Most Canaanites are slaughtered, the narrative implies. Many others are subjected to corvée slavery; the Israelites treat them as slaves in the same manner as the Israelites were treated as slaves in Egypt. The latter correspondence seems not to mean much to the deuteronomist, even though he must have known that the slavery described in Exod 1:11-14 was corvée servitude. As previously shown, the deuteronomist thought of Israel's slavery in Egypt as debt slavery rather than corvée (see Commentary on 2:1–6:27). Israel's enslavement of Canaanites represents mainly the fulfillment of Noah's curse of Canaan in the foundational Davidic history of Israel, the J strand. The Gibeonites have a privileged form of corvée duty imposed on them when they submit to becoming slaves of the central shrine of Yahweh. A few Canaanites may be delivered outright, and these are represented by Rahab, whose family has palpably been, or is liable to be, reduced to debt slavery. The narrative, therefore, focuses particular attention on those Canaanites who, in terms of fundamental deuteronomistic ideals, look like Israelites—slaves serving Yahweh—and are, therefore, treated as such and are saved. The message seems to be that "Canaanites" looking for mercy had better have a demonstrable grasp of Josiah's program of debt remission, promulgated from Yahweh's altar in Jerusalem. Thus the pattern in which the two main points of Joshua intersect suggests not contradiction, but rather no more tension than is inherent in the policies of Josiah they are meant to reflect.

It is now possible to see that the story of the fall of Ai represents more than a temporary setback followed by one more step forward in Joshua's unstoppable conquest, or the deserved punishment of a man who disobeyed the word of the Lord—or, in terms of classical American liberalism, the much less condonable punishment of his innocent family. While it is important to look at the story of Achan and Ai in further detail, it is equally important to realize that it does not, and as such never did, stand in isolation. Nevertheless, like the stories of Rahab, the crossing of the Jordan, and probably the fall of Jericho, the story of Ai seems to be based in part on a separate folk narrative, reflecting outlaw or guerrilla tactics of just the kind that Josiah must have had to neutralize or co-opt in order to prevent their being used against him.

The name "Ai" means "ruin" (תל *tēl*), and a ruin it was, whether in the Late Bronze Age of the exodus or the Late Iron Age of Josiah. Two thousand years before Josiah, in the Early Bronze Age, Ai had been a significant highland town. Between then and the time of Josiah, however, the site had been settled as an unwalled village for only about a century and a half, during the Early Iron Age. By the time of Saul and David, it had fallen into desuetude. Ai lies not far from Bethel, with which it is clearly associated in the mind of the narrator (7:2; 8:17). It is likely that Ai symbolically stood in part for Bethel and its cult, loathed by the deuteronomists.[64] The present story explains how Ai came to be a ruin, as Bethel would in the time of Josiah. It is thus one of the many etiologies in Joshua—i.e., stories that explain some notable feature of the landscape.

In the case of Ai, there are two such features, described in 8:28-29. The first is the ruin of the supposed town, which Joshua reduces to a "perpetual devastated ruin" that exists "to this day" (8:28). Here the Hebrew word for "ruin" is *tēl.* Even today the word "tel" is used to describe mounds artificially built up through centuries of human settlement at a site. Such tells dot the

---

64. This suggestion has nothing to do with the very unlikely theory still proposed by some scholars that the destruction of Ai, described in Joshua 8 as Late Bronze Age history, actually applied to Bethel instead, which, unlike Ai, was destroyed at the end of the Bronze Age, according to excavators. In this view, the account of the fall of Bethel became secondarily attached to the ruin at Ai, as over time Bethel was rebuilt and Ai abandoned. For the problems surrounding the interpretation of the supposed Late Bronze destruction of Bethel, see William G. Dever, "Beitin, Tell," *ABD* 1:651-52.

landscape throughout the Near East. Indeed, the present-day Aramaic name for Ai is et-Tell, "the tell." The second etiology is the one that ties this story to the story of Jericho. This etiology actually occurs twice. The first time is when the Israelites raise over Achan's corpse "a great heap of stones to this day" (7:26). The second time is when the king of Ai is captured alive and executed and his corpse exposed until it is deposited at the entrance to what is left of Ai and covered with "a great heap of stones to this day" (8:29). The word for "heap" (גל gal) is the same as in "Gilgal," associated with its two heaps of stones. (The name "Gilgal" results from a regular transformation of the reduplicated form גלגל [galgal], "stone heap" or "heaps.") Achan's crime occurs in the camp in Gilgal. Thus the same etiology applies to Achan and the king of Ai; its significance cannot be missed. The two etiologies for Ai at the end of the story are themselves linked by a pun on the word tēl, since the word for "hanging" the king's corpse on a tree in order to expose it is תלא (tālāʾ; see 10:26; Deut 21:22-23).

Like the story of Jericho, the story of Ai is a story within a story. The two attacks on Ai, the first a failure and the second a success, enclose the story of the discovery and execution of Achan, which turns failure into success. However, since Achan is fully identified at the outset (7:1), the failed attack is itself framed by the Achan story, which thereby is shown to be equal in significance to the fall of Ai, just as Rahab's story is as significant as the fall of Jericho.

There are two important parallels to the story of the fall of Ai. One is the battle between the Benjaminites and Israelites at Gibeah in Judges 20. There the Benjaminites play the role of the men of Ai. The Israelites attack the Benjaminites twice and are put to rout, as in the story of Ai. The Israelites appeal to Yahweh, and when Yahweh indicates support, they prepare the same ruse as at Ai. One division lies in ambush. The other draws the Benjaminites out of the town, allowing the first to put the town to the torch. Seeing the town on fire, the Benjaminites retreat and are cut down in flight by the recombined Israelite forces. The two stories have nearly identical plots. One may be based on the other, but it is more likely that they are two exemplars of a common folk narrative of tribal or brigand warfare.

The first parallel does not include an Achan. The men of Gibeah have committed a great wrong, but their story does not mesh with the story of the battle, as Achan's does. For the combined plots, it is necessary to look at a second parallel. This is the story in Deut 1:9-45, which summarizes events in Numbers 13–14. This is an important story, because it lays the basis for the conquest under Joshua rather than Moses (Deut 1:37-40). Moses orders the Israelites to take the land, starting with the Amorites in the highland. They hesitate and appeal for a reconnoitering. The spies bring a favorable report, but out of fear they still refuse to attack. Yahweh punishes their disobedience: They shall die in the desert without ever entering the land, and Joshua will lead the next generation in taking the land. When they hear this, they change their minds and are ready to attack. Yahweh orders them not to, but they disobey once again and attack anyway. They are routed "as far as Hormah," the very town named for the ḥērem the Israelites are supposed to inflict (Num 21:2-3).

This story parallels the first half of the Ai story. The great wrong committed by Achan is paralleled by the disobedience of all the Israelites. As a result, the attack, when finally made, is a failure. The attack will succeed only when the crime is punished: An entire generation must die in the desert, and only then will Joshua's attack succeed. With respect to this story at the beginning of the Deuteronomistic History, which is followed by the several examples of successful Yahweh-ordered dispossessions (Deut 2:1–3:17), the parallel to the second half of the Ai story is nothing other than the whole of the conquest under Joshua. The story of Ai has immense resonances, indeed.

It is not surprising that Achan plays the same role as all the Israelites in the foundational story in Deuteronomy 1, for a striking aspect of the Ai story is the assumption of collective punishment. One person's sin arouses God's wrath against the entire nation (7:11, 20). Put in terms of Josiah's program, a single violation of the reform law is tantamount to their wholesale violation. The term used in 7:1 for Achan's transgression, translated "broke faith" (מעל māʿal), is used elsewhere in the book of Joshua only in chap. 22, where it refers to the alleged violation of the fundamental law of cult centralization (22:16, 20, 22, 31). The narrative thus reflects not only the collective perspective of social solidarity and community responsibility, but also the theoretical extremism of Joshua's program of centralization and reconquest, enforced through the terror of collective guilt investigated by means of a judicial lottery.

Joshua's reform calls for a highly regimented society, what we might term today a police state. Josiah's plan, probably based on earlier tradition, is to organize the state magistry down to supervised units of ten (Deut 1:9-18), in which one member could easily spy on another. Such small and rationally demarcated surveillance cells could not always correspond to households or clans, and probably were intentionally designed not to. Within households, family members were required to inform on each other (Deut 13:6-11), in a militant undermining of the patriarchal household consonant with other components of Josiah's law, which tended to isolate individuals from their lineal networks of aid and support in the process of undermining patriarchal households in order to strengthen the power of the monarchy.

It is important to grasp this feature of Josiah's reform, which is evident in the laws in Deuteronomy (Deuteronomy 12–26) and has received considerable scholarly attention. The most impor-

tant households under Josiah's power would have functioned as the magistrates of the realm, judging cases coming before them as they deemed appropriate. The mere publication of a law like Josiah's served to curtail the power of this class of patriarchs, regardless of what was in that law. When the law prescribes that every tenth person is to be a magistrate (Deut 1:15), then clearly the power of any one of them is circumscribed. The basic political conflict in most pre-industrial societies pitted the central power against peripheral powers. Peripheral powers came in many forms. The most common included rival claimants to the throne: landed aristocrats or great nobles, paramilitary commanders, regional warlords or outlaws (anyone beyond the law of the realm), and local saints, alive or dead, who claimed a separate power and authority. Beyond such prominent potential opponents, in a more general way every head of household in the realm represented an alternative power and authority, and Josiah was not the first monarch bent on centralizing authority and power in such a way as to curb the authority and power of every male head of household subject to his jurisdiction.

❖   ❖   ❖   ❖

EXCURSUS: DEUTERONOMISTIC REPRESSION OF PATRIARCHAL AUTHORITY

Like the laws centralizing the cult and remitting debts after seven years, those designed to curb the authority and prerogatives of patriarchal heads represented a fundamental departure from customary practice if not customary ideals. These laws appear mostly in the latter part of the collection of Moses' laws, mostly in Deuteronomy 19–25, but in some instances the same thrust is evident in earlier laws. A good example of how radical such legislation can be appears as a corollary of the law of the sole cult: "If your brother, son, daughter, wife, or kin entices you in secret with the words, 'Let us go and serve others gods' . . . you shall not yield to him or listen to him, nor shall your eye pity him, nor shall you spare him, nor shall you conceal him; but you shall kill him" (Deut 13:6-9 author's trans.). The patriarchal head of household, in other words, has lost the right to protect his kin from the state's ruling.

In an analysis of family transgressions in Deuteronomy carrying the death penalty, Stulman has shown that deuteronomistic legislation tends to limit the power of fathers and husbands and consolidate those powers in local tribunals under state authority, all under the jurisdiction of the central shrine (Deut 17:8-13).[65] The state—that is, the Davidic Temple and court—restricts the power of the male head of household by obligating the state to act against family wrongs, by involving town elders in the legal process, and by requiring punishment to be

---

65. Louis Stulman, "Sex and Familial Crimes in the D Code: A Witness to Mores in Transition," *JSOT* 53 (1992) 47-63.

executed in public at the town gate. The household patriarch is no longer the final authority in his own household. As with many parallel examples, this centralizing state attempts to regulate sexual matters, like virginity, adultery, and incest, in the interests of controlling the families and their heads. The laws may seem to confirm the prerogatives of town elders, but this is unlikely to be the case; at the very beginning of the history, the basis of a nationalized and regimented judiciary exercised through local authorities is laid down (Deut 1:9-18; 16:18-20), and in many cases described in Deuteronomy, the scope of the elders' rulings is significantly reduced.

These findings confirm a similar study by Steinberg, who concluded that the laws in Deuteronomy 19–25 posit increased centralized control over family matters.[66] By supporting the nuclear family at the expense of the extended family, these laws tend to subvert the venerable kinship-based social system in favor of government oversight through councils of regulated town and village elders. It is often noticed that these laws help to preserve the nuclear family by limiting the power of men and creating rights for women. The deuteronomist, however, is not interested in the rights of women for their own sake, but for the sake of the nuclear family, which is more important than the individual. In order to safeguard these new rights, legal decisions affecting the nuclear family are taken out of the hands of the father or husband and given to the town elders, who are often beholden to set orders. This departure from custom can be seen by comparing Exod 22:16-17 with Deut 22:28-29. Both texts deal with the case of a man who has intercourse with a virgin who is not engaged. In Exodus, a bride-price is negotiated between the man and the woman's father, and her father decides whether she is to marry the man. In Deuteronomy, the bride-price is fixed at fifty shekels of silver, marriage is required, and no divorce is allowed; the woman's father is not even mentioned. Nowadays, such legislation might be called an invasion of privacy, and that is certainly the way it would have been experienced by householding men under Josiah's rule.

There are many such laws in Deuteronomy. Some involve routine attempts at state imposition, such as regulating blood revenge instead of allowing it to run rampant as an excuse for falling into factions and gathering private forces among families and clans (Deut 19:1-13) or preventing a man's preference for one wife over another from overriding the rights of primogeniture for both the firstborn son and his mother (Deut 21:15-17). Other laws are much less expected. An alien woman captured in battle and then married may not later be sold as a slave (Deut 21:10-14). A father and mother may discipline a defiant son, but neither may kill him, as was the accepted custom (Exod 21:15, 17). They must turn him over to the town elders, or magistrates, at the gate and together make public proclamation of their complaint; the elders then would arrange for the public execution of the son by the men of the town, presumably after satisfying themselves that the case is valid. A man who charges that his bride was not a virgin must present his case, together with evidence collected by the father and the mother of the bride, to the town elders rather than settling the matter in private. If the case goes against the accuser, he is to be fined a hundred shekels of silver and may never divorce the woman. If his case is sustained, she is to be stoned to death at the door of her father's house by the men of the town rather than by her father (Deut 22:13-21). If a man has intercourse with a married woman, both are stoned to death; neither the woman's husband nor her father or brothers may save her (Deut 22:22). The law of levirate marriage may seem to be an exception (Deut 25:5-10), but it, too, is designed primarily to shift the emphasis from the extended family to the nuclear family by keeping the property of the dead man within the immediate family and by ensuring that later offspring born to his wife and brother bear the dead man's name and provide support to the widow in her old age. If a brother refuses, the widow initiates legal action against him before the elders, who supervise a rite of spitting

---

66. Naomi Steinberg, "The Deuteronomic Law Code and the Politics of State Centralization," in *The Bible and the Politics of Exegesis*, ed. David Jobling, Peggy L. Day, and Gerald T. Sheppard (Cleveland: Pilgrim, 1991) 161-70.

and humiliation, so that the brother's shame is sure to be public "throughout Israel" (see Commentary on Josh 17:1-13).[67]

67. Tikva Frymer-Kensky, "Deuteronomy," in *The Women's Bible Commentary*, ed. Carol A. Newsom and Sharon H. Ringe (Louisville: Westminster/John Knox, 1992) 52-62.

❖   ❖   ❖   ❖

As with the law of debt remission, it is important to understand the deuteronomistic repression of patriarchal authority for the sake of the monarch, because it is a part of the portrayal of Joshua. This connection with Joshua goes well beyond the provision of cities of refuge, for example (Joshua 20; cf. Deut 19:1-13). Joshua represents the single ruler at the head of a united Israel. One individual leads the conquest. In the account of the conquest and distribution of land, all references to managing the competing and conflicting interests of particular "tribes" and their heads are dispensed with (cf. Judges 4–5). Assuming that references to Eleazar the priest are not deuteronomistic, all mention of other collaborating or competing chiefs, of dependable or jealous chiefs, or of lieutenants or aids is suppressed. All these, it might be expected, would be essential to an account of a campaign like Joshua's, but they are missing. Just as Rahab and her indebted family are integral to the first major narrative in Joshua, so also it is no accident that Achan and his family are integral to the second narrative, the conquest of Ai. Just as Rahab's story illustrates the deliverance of the debt slave, so also Achan's story illustrates the authority and power of the monarch over local patriarchs, even if the patriarch, like Achan, belongs to the same "tribe" as the monarch. As Joshua narrows his probe by lot through tribes, clans, households, and individuals in search of the man who violated the law of ḥērem, the detailing of Achan's social location points up his social isolation. No one steps forward to take Achan's side, to protect him or save him, or to help him hide or escape. The entire "nation" unanimously joins the monarch in the pitiless eradication of lawlessness in the person of this patriarch—and his nuclear family (strangely, his wife is not mentioned). This is more than an expression of corps solidarity. It is an epitome of the potency and command projected in Josiah's reform.

Besides the guilt of the isolated and vulnerable Achan, Israel's collective guilt is the narrative version of the categorical rhetoric of the laws themselves. As in the case of the two seemingly contradictory principles explained above, the assumption of an absolute law must be weighed against exceptions. This narrative immediately declares an exception: No sooner is Achan executed than Yahweh gives the Israelites permission to keep the spoil of Ai (8:2, 27), just as they spared Rahab.

Achan also plays a significant role in the emergence of the house of David. Achan's violation of ḥērem finds its later echo in Saul's violation of ḥērem, especially since both take place in Gilgal (1 Sam 15:10-33). Saul's kingship was revoked for his disobedience at Gilgal (1 Sam 13:7-14) for having made a sacrifice against orders from Samuel while the Philistines were camped "east of Beth-aven," thus not far from Ai (Josh 7:2; 1 Sam 13:5).[68] Saul was not executed right away for his crimes, but his death and the death of his son and heir Jonathan in battle against the Philistines are regarded as due punishment for failing to kill the king of the Amalekites as Joshua had killed the king of Ai (1 Sam 28:15-19).

A few further details require comment. The initial proposal that only a small force would be needed to take Ai is ironic (7:3). The proposal makes clear that the spies trust Yahweh and are ready to rely on Yahweh's strength. However, they are unaware that Yahweh is angry, as the narrator has openly stated. The attack on Ai is doomed from the start, trust or not. The term "thousand" in military contexts like this probably does not mean "a thousand," but a much smaller number. What number it does mean is uncertain and was presumably variable. One suggestion is that the "thousand" (אלף *'elep*) is the fighting unit of the "clan" (משפחה *mišpāḥâ*), the putative social unit above the extended household. A likely parallel has been found in the Mari letters (see

68. For these and further parallels between Achan and Saul, see Michael D. Coogan, "Joshua," in *The New Jerome Biblical Commentary*, ed. Raymond E. Brown, Joseph A. Fitzmyer, and Roland E. Murphy (Englewood Cliffs, N.J.: Prentice Hall, 1990) 117.

Commentary on 5:13–6:21), in which the word for "thousand" also is used for a clan unit.[69]

Joshua's lament (7:7-9) concludes with an argument popular in prayers of complaint, the most common form of prayer in the Bible (e.g., Pss 74:10, 18; 79:9; 83:4, 16, 18; 106:8; 109:21; 143:11). "When the Canaanites have cut off our name," he asks, "what are you going to do to restore your name?" Petitioners frequently remind God of the risk of God's being mocked as powerless if those ready to acknowledge God's help suffer great harm. Joshua tears his clothes as he does in Num 14:6, but there the appeal is to the people rather than to God. Here Joshua's appeal to God is closer to that of Moses, his precursor in Deut 9:25-29.

Yahweh responds vehemently. Achan's sin is everyone's sin. The repetitive counts of the charge are driven home in a series of clauses joined with "also" (גם *gam*), repeated five times like a bass drum beat. This pounding accent has been left out of both the NRSV and the NIV translations (7:11). The measure-for-measure character of God's justice is evident: Because Israel has violated the *ḥērem*, they have become a *ḥērem*, until they purge the *ḥērem*, both the perpetrator and the goods stolen (7:12; cf. 7:25).

Joshua goes through the hierarchy of social units, from tribe to clan to household to the men of the household (גברים *gĕbārîm*, "men," 7:14, 18; the NRSV's "one" is gratuitous), apparently by lot. The closest parallel is 1 Sam 10:20-21, in which Saul, having been chosen by Yahweh to be king, is publicly selected by lot. The narrative makes the result of the process of selecting Achan known in advance. Therefore, the point of tracing the process step-by-step twice (7:14, 16-18) is not the suspense of discovering who did it, or even the sharpened resemblance between Achan and David's unruly adversary Saul, but the intense judicial urgency to get to the culprit, to zero in on him and deal with him. There is no trial, even by ordeal. Yahweh knows who did it (cf. 22:20-22), and the process allows what Yahweh knows to be dramatically re-

vealed, a practice common to sacred violence. There is a thin line between doing God's will and engaging in a witch hunt. As part of the history behind Josiah's reform, the narrative resolves this ambiguity by demonstrating that the process leads to the truth. This makes the Achan story a judicial exemplar of the same magnitude as David's self-condemnation for adultery and murder (2 Sam 12:1-15) or Solomon's solution to the case of the prostitute's son by using the discerning mind given to him by Yahweh (1 Kgs 3:3-28). When the lot falls on Achan, he is forced to confess. The parallel between "give glory to God" in 7:19 and the same phrase in John 9:24 is indicative: The man is known to be a sinner; the issue is getting him to admit it. The public process excludes the possibility that Achan's family may have informed on him, so they are guilty by association and accordingly suffer the same punishment of stoning, a form of both communal judicial responsibility and controlled mob violence.

Achan's name is taken as a pun on the word "trouble," for which the valley where Achan is executed is named, "Achor" (עכור *ʿākôr*). His name occurs as "Achar" in 1 Chr 2:7. The valley takes on a positive valence in Hos 2:17 and Isa 65:10.

Joshua's use of his lance (8:18, 26; NRSV, "sword"; NIV, "javelin") to signal the defeat of the town (not to launch the ambush) recalls Moses' holding high of his staff while Joshua, at his first appearance, defeated the Amalekites (Exod 17:8-13). Again a parallel from the Mari letters suggests an age-old practice or convention.[70] In the different textual traditions of 8:11-13, there is confusion over details, but the general picture is clear. The mention of Bethel in 8:17 is surprising; since it does not appear in the LXX, most take it to be secondary. Despite the proximity of Bethel to Ai, there is no reason for its mention other than the importance of Bethel to the deuteronomists. Hence it is impossible to tell whether it was one of the original historians who mentioned it or a late copyist.

69. Abraham Malamat, "A Recently Discovered Word for 'Clan' in Mari and Its Hebrew Cognate," in *Solving Riddles and Untying Knots: Biblical, Epigraphic, and Semitic Studies in Honor of Jonas C. Greenfield,* ed. Ziony Zevit et al. (Winona Lake, Ind.: Eisenbrauns, 1995) 177-79.

70. Moshe Anbar, "La critique biblique à la lumière des Archives royales de Mari: Jos 8," *Bib* 75 (1994) 70-74.

Reflections

1. This lengthy passage plays collective responsibility off against individual responsibility. The killing of Achan's family does not take away from this point: Their fate is tied to his individual act, discovery, and punishment. The point is easy to see. As Joshua proceeds to make a conspicuous example of Achan, the culprit's fellow Israelites can breathe a sigh of relief that with his death the basic problem has been taken care of and things will now go well. Life turns out to be orderly and manageable, so long as people realize that the authority of the central power is absolute and, as indicated by success at the lottery, infallible. This is the nature of collective discipline under fire. Under such circumstances, in the face of perceived pressure, threat, and danger, it is more difficult than usual to assess the nature of the central power's authority. Where does it come from? How does it work? What does it want? How does it expect to get it? Sometimes it may be necessary not to question authority. However, people in authority almost always would prefer that their authority not be questioned. When disorder under their command can be reduced to a single person's wrongdoing, so much the better. If it takes blaming a particular group or class of people, that can be done, too, as long as a problem can be identified in such a way as to be eliminated when the guilty party is eliminated. This is why there is such a narrow gap between analyzing social problems as a matter of policy, on the one hand, and scapegoating, on the other hand.

2. Joshua's "lament" follows the form of a prayer of complaint, of which there are many biblical examples. One important feature of such complaints is that they were typically performed in public, as here, even when they concern primarily an individual. Job's complaint is another familiar example: Job cries out to God in the presence of his friends. Recently, the purposes of such performances have been analyzed.[71] The enemies are not always simply the well-to-do and powerful who make the psalmist suffer. They can be friends, neighbors, and even family members as well. Often plaintiffs can expect that their loud public prayer will be heard by their enemies. The plaintiff may thereby expose the enemies and gain protection from further harassment or may voice indictments or threats against the enemies without having to confront them directly or may issue harsh commands or advice to the enemies, in the hope of deterring or converting them. Such a practice makes the collective nature of biblical prayer evident and contrasts strongly with the modern sense that prayer is mainly private, especially if it is a complaint.

Like any ancient plaintiff, Joshua can expect to arouse the sympathy of the elders and through them of the entire "nation," for whom he prays in any case, and draw the community together into a tighter unit than before. Joshua's prayer is immediately answered, a somewhat rare occurrence with complaints in the Bible. Indeed, the rhetoric of complaint, which is probably much more familiar to church people in their private lives than in their worship lives, is mostly self-contained. The plea to Yahweh for a response tends to be simple, whereas the elaboration of the difficulties, charges, and instructions is voiced mainly to the overhearing community, where the cry may gradually work its effect. Yahweh's response begins in typical fashion: When the complaint concerns the nation, the fault usually lies with a collective enemy, even when the guilty party has been the nation itself. Having accused the nation of wrongdoing, however, Yahweh then orders a procedure for conspicuous public discovery and punishment.

Nowadays if a person in prayer dares to complain to God at all, the complaint is routinely voiced in solitary devotions as a personal matter between the individual and God. The rarity of individual public complaint in church is a measure not only of the commendable dignity and discretion that characterize modern well-to-do congregations, but also of the extent to which congregations have difficulty dealing with conflict openly. Modern congregants can be grateful if their lives are relatively

---

71. Gerald T. Sheppard, " 'Enemies' and the Politics of Prayer in the Book of Psalms," in *The Bible and the Politics of Exegesis,* ed. David Jobling, Peggy L. Day, and Gerald T. Sheppard (Cleveland: Pilgrim, 1991) 61-82.

free of the powerlessness, oppression, deceit, rancor, and anguish that afflicted the ancient suppliant and found expression in the open court, as it were, of public complaint. At the same time, disagreements, tensions, and conflict are a fact of modern congregational life, and little good comes from pretending otherwise. Congregants may want to consider regaining some of the communal integrity and mutual care in loving expressions of anger and frustration that seem to have existed in some biblical communities, while striving to avoid the hostility, backbiting, and self-righteousness that frequently seemed also to be included. Such care might be nurtured if prayerful complaints could be heard and respected in church.

There is no simple solution to the spiritual dilemma that openness and dignity can be difficult to reconcile. It is important to remember that the ancient cultic setting of judicial prayer is significantly different from the modern worship service. It may be that, following a discussion of needs and expectations and the formulation of a common understanding, a weekly prayer meeting would best serve for introducing prayerful complaints. It must also be remembered that while dignity is important, at the cost of communion among the faithful it is not a significant biblical value. The tendency of the Bible is for corporate reliance on the grace of God to make possible the openness that builds trust and to obviate individuals' struggle for dignity as crucial to self-worth.

JOSHUA 8:30-35, AN ALTAR ON MT. EBAL

NIV

30Then Joshua built on Mount Ebal an altar to the LORD, the God of Israel, 31as Moses the servant of the LORD had commanded the Israelites. He built it according to what is written in the Book of the Law of Moses—an altar of uncut stones, on which no iron tool had been used. On it they offered to the LORD burnt offerings and sacrificed fellowship offerings.[a] 32There, in the presence of the Israelites, Joshua copied on stones the law of Moses, which he had written. 33All Israel, aliens and citizens alike, with their elders, officials and judges, were standing on both sides of the ark of the covenant of the LORD, facing those who carried it—the priests, who were Levites. Half of the people stood in front of Mount Gerizim and half of them in front of Mount Ebal, as Moses the servant of the LORD had formerly commanded when he gave instructions to bless the people of Israel.

34Afterward, Joshua read all the words of the law—the blessings and the curses—just as it is written in the Book of the Law. 35There was not a word of all that Moses had commanded that Joshua did not read to the whole assembly of Israel, including the women and children, and the aliens who lived among them.

a31 Traditionally *peace offerings*

NRSV

30Then Joshua built on Mount Ebal an altar to the LORD, the God of Israel, 31just as Moses the servant of the LORD had commanded the Israelites, as it is written in the book of the law of Moses, "an altar of unhewn[a] stones, on which no iron tool has been used"; and they offered on it burnt offerings to the LORD, and sacrificed offerings of well-being. 32And there, in the presence of the Israelites, Joshua[b] wrote on the stones a copy of the law of Moses, which he had written. 33All Israel, alien as well as citizen, with their elders and officers and their judges, stood on opposite sides of the ark in front of the levitical priests who carried the ark of the covenant of the LORD, half of them in front of Mount Gerizim and half of them in front of Mount Ebal, as Moses the servant of the LORD had commanded at the first, that they should bless the people of Israel. 34And afterward he read all the words of the law, blessings and curses, according to all that is written in the book of the law. 35There was not a word of all that Moses commanded that Joshua did not read before all the assembly of Israel, and the women, and the little ones, and the aliens who resided among them.

a Heb *whole*   b Heb *he*

COMMENTARY

Joshua makes an unexpected jump to and from Mt. Ebal, which lies just north of Shechem in the center of the northern highland, a long day's march each way, of which there is no mention. There he publishes the law of Moses by writing it on stones and reading it aloud, in its entirety, to the whole nation of Israel—men, women, children, and resident aliens—assembled on Mt. Ebal and Mt. Gerizim astride one of the most strategic passes in highland Canaan (in what by Josiah's time was the heart of Israel). This unopposed theatrical production supposedly takes place before the conquest of Canaan has scarcely begun; the book of Joshua posits no military campaign here at all (there is no king of Shechem listed in 12:9-24, and the only nearby town in that list is the last, Tirzah). Joshua does not reappear at Shechem until chap. 24, the last chapter, after his deuteronomistic farewell in chap. 23. This section thus comes as a sudden surprise and does not fit well with the surrounding narrative. The end of the Ai story flows smoothly into the beginning of the story of the alliance of the Canaanite kings and the covenant with the Gibeonites (8:29; 9:1-2; 10:1). This section is evidently not part of the main deuteronomistic narrative.

This widely held perception is based on more than intuition. The present section does not have a fixed place in the textual record. In the LXX, it appears after 9:1-2. In the fragments of the oldest known text of Joshua, 4QJosh[a] from the Hasmonean period (approximately 150–50 BCE), it is followed by the report of circumcision now found in 5:2-8 and evidently preceded by the crossing of the Jordan in Joshua 3–4, which might help to explain the similarities between 5:1 and 9:1-2. Whichever of the three attested placements of this section is the original one—if, indeed, there was an original placement—such textual differences in sequence, of which there are many in the Bible, often arise with sections whose positions are not fixed because of their secondary nature.[72] Moreover, this section is directly related to Deuteronomy 27 (with Deut 11:29-30) and Joshua 24,

both of which also concern Shechem and themselves appear to be secondary to their contexts.

The affinities of this movable section are thus clear. Its significance is less so, but must depend in part on the role of Shechem. Shechem occurs seldom in the Deuteronomistic History. Besides the passage just mentioned and two incidental references in the town list of Manasseh (17:2, 7), Shechem figures in just six other places in the history, of which all except two are brief. However, together these show that Shechem laid claim to being one of the most important localities in highland Israel. Shechem is named as one of the towns of the Levites (21:21) and, much more important, the only town of refuge in the Israelite heartland (20:7). Another brief mention (Judg 21:19) describes the main road north from Jerusalem and Bethel as the road to Shechem. The fourth mention (Judg 8:31; 9:1-57) is the lengthiest. It concerns the story of Abimelech of Shechem, said to have killed seventy of his brothers, induced the lords of Shechem to make him king, and ruled as a tyrant for three years, when, after he has foiled an attempted coup, a woman crushes his skull with a millstone while he is attacking the town of Thebez. For the Deuteronomistic History, next to the kings of Israel themselves and even more than Hiel of Jericho (Josh 6:26; 1 Kgs 16:24), Abimelech of Shechem serves as the plainest example of the dangers of letting an Israelite other than a Davidic king set himself up as an independent power.

This political significance of Shechem is confirmed by the final two references. Both occur in 1 Kings 12 and figure directly in the house of David's loss of Israel to a rival king. First, Solomon's heir, Rehoboam, goes to Shechem in order to get "all Israel" to make him king; all except the tribe of Judah spurn him and make Jeroboam their king instead (12:1-24; this treatment of Shechem has obvious similarities with the story of how Abimelech is made king). Then Jeroboam, now king of Israel, immediately rebuilds Shechem (cf. Hiel of Jericho) and resides there, making it the first capital of anti-Davidic Israel (1 Kgs 12:25). For the deuteronomist, there is no question that Jeroboam's rebuilding of Shechem both

72. Emanuel Tov, *Textual Criticism of the Hebrew Bible* (Minneapolis: Fortress, 1992) 339. Similarly, another suggested explanation for the sequence in 4QJosh[a] is that Josh 5:2-8, which also is a secondary addition, may have been placed after 8:30-35 following the battle of Ai.

prefigures Hiel and echoes Abimelech, who is nothing but a useless bramble, as Jothan vividly proclaims (Judg 9:7-15) from the same Mt. Gerizim upon which half the Israelites are standing to hear the law of Moses in Josh 8:33-35, commencing with the law of Davidic centralization.

Shechem thus stands for the archrival power in Israel to the house of David. Shechem was destroyed by the Assyrians in the eighth century BCE, probably around the time of the fall of Samaria. It was shoddily reconstructed during the seventh century. Assyrian pottery styles suggest the domination of outsiders at that time. The irony is that, though secondary, this section of Joshua may fit the circumstances of Josiah's reform at least as well as the main narrative of Joshua. For Josiah, however, Shechem's importance would have been not its concentration of power, but its symbolic role as a historic political center in Israel.

Moreover, it is no accident that the two main texts dealing with Shechem and kingship describe something akin to an election of the king (Judg 9:6, 16; 1 Kgs 12:1, 20) and that Deuteronomy 27 and Joshua 24 both involve elements of a public covenanting ceremony. According to Judg 9:4, the god of Shechem was Baal-berith, "Lord of the covenant," perhaps known as El-berith, "God of the covenant."[73] Shechem was regarded as a covenant-making center. While this tradition clearly pre-dates Josiah—indeed, may go back as early as the Late Bronze Age—there is no reason to believe that the two additions to Joshua involving Shechem reflect the early history of Israel as such, any more than the folkloric elements on which the accounts of Joshua's battles in the main deuteronomistic narrative are partly based reflect the history of early Israel. While covenant-making forms were already ancient by the time of Josiah, the emphasis on covenant associated with Shechem in the OT is found exclusively in deuteronomistic texts, and for covenantal forms in the Deuteronomistic History one need look no further than common practice in the Neo-Assyrian period and later.

Deuteronomy 27 prescribes a ceremonial ratification of some facet of the deuteronomistic covenant under Moses, at a strategic location glaringly symbolic of both rebellion against Davidic rule and covenantal accord with it. Joshua 8:30-35 sees that

ratification carried out, with Joshua in the role of Moses. Joshua 24:1-28, of a slightly different character, reiterates the ratification with a stress on the reincorporation of the putative tribes of Israel. The establishment of the shrine for Joseph's bones in Josh 24:32 may belong to the same set of additions. Recent study suggests that the particular form to which the covenantal elements in Deuteronomy 27 and Joshua 8 contribute is the sacred enactment of a land grant, akin to the Babylonian *kudurru*.[74] The typical land-grant ceremony included the setting up of a boundary stone, here represented by the stones on which the law is written; a description of the plot of land and the circumstances of its transfer (Deut 27:1-10); the witnesses present; and curses on violators of the grant (cf. Josh 8:17). If this comparison is correct, these two texts were inserted in order to supply a missing piece in the account of God's granting to the Israelites the land of the Canaanites. That missing piece is the public formalization of the grant, tied to Yahweh's basic judicial covenant with Israel (the deuteronomistic covenant).

If the first two texts (with Deut 11:29-30) relate in any way to Josiah's reform, they may reflect either an alternative, less dictatorial approach to the highland heartland of Israel, an approach not articulated in the main narrative, or a later stage in the reform, when forces of resistance aroused by the reform and organized around Shechem had to be simultaneously mastered and accommodated. It is striking that 8:30 describes the building of an altar, presumably a temporary central shrine that later was to be replaced by the Temple in Jerusalem. This represents a different concept of the central shrine from that of the main deuteronomistic narrative, which displays a vehement reaction to the building of an altar in Joshua 22 and makes no reference to an existing altar at Shechem. It is also noteworthy that resident aliens are mentioned in Joshua only in 8:33, 35 (cf. Deut 27:19) and 20:9. These were apparently socially and politically isolated and vulnerable non-natives who were not required to keep all the laws of Moses (see Deut 14:21), but who were expected to become clients of the house of David and its cult of Yahweh for the protection of their interests rather than of one of the organized alien groups

---

73. G. Ernest Wright, *Shechem: The Biography of a Biblical City* (New York: McGraw-Hill, 1965) 133-37.

74. Andrew E. Hill, "The Ebal Ceremony as Hebrew Land Grant?" *JETS* 31 (1988) 399-406.

planted by the Assyrians and coming partly under the jurisdiction of Bethel after the fall of Samaria (see Deut 1:16). The phrase that contrasts with "alien" in 8:33, "indigenous" (אזרח *'ezrāḥ*; NRSV and NIV, "citizen"), is a predominantly priestly term that occurs only here in the Deuteronomistic History.

The altar that Joshua builds harks back to the Tetrateuch. It is built, ostensibly in obedience to Deut 27:5-6, of rough stones, not hewn with tools of iron. This anachronistic reference to iron follows the rule in Exod 20:25, reflecting traditional tribal rather than state practice. It represents a concern of little interest to the main deuteronomistic narrative, which describes the abundant use of dressed stones for building the Temple (1 Kgs 5:17; 7:9-12; cf. 6:7, which implies that there is a rule not against the use of iron tools but against hearing them being used at the building site). Most altars known from excavations at Israelite sites are made of hewn stones. The publication of law on plastered stones erected in a public place (Deut 27:2-4, 8) is also an activity of state and not a tribal custom. Joshua appears here as much in the guise of a monarch as he does in any other passage. Moreover, in having a "copy" of the law written, he fulfills the duty laid on the king in Deut 17:18. Joshua's copy is for public display rather than his private use, one more indication that this set of texts related to Shechem is secondary to the main Deuteronomistic History. After

the blessings and curses are pronounced from the two mountains (cf. Deut 27:12-13), Joshua reads all the written blessings and curses, a standard part of ancient Near Eastern covenants, presumably here the same as those in Deut 28:1-68 (the curses in Deut 27:15-26 are not matched by blessings). The final confirmation that Joshua here plays the role of the king comes with the phrase "before all the assembly of Israel," which in the Deuteronomistic History occurs only in 1 Kgs 8:22, when Solomon, having just blessed "all the assembly of Israel" (1 Kgs 8:14), makes his prayer of dedication for the Temple (cf. Deut 31:30).

Joshua's altar received a great deal of renewed attention when an Iron I site that apparently included an altar and was used for cultic purposes was discovered on the slopes of Mt. Ebal in 1980. The excavator identified the site as probably Joshua's altar.[75] To others, such an identification made little sense. "Since the division of the land in Joshua is an ideal picture . . . the mere presence of premonarchic remains within the ideal tribal boundaries does not require their construction or use by the members of that tribe."[76]

75. Adam Zertal, "Has Joshua's Altar Been Found on Mount Ebal?" *BAR* 11 (1985) 26-43; "An Early Iron Age Cultic Site on Mount Ebal," *Tel Aviv* 13-14 (1986–87) 105-65.

76. Michael D. Coogan, "Archaeology and Biblical Studies: The Book of Joshua," in *The Hebrew Bible and Its Interpreters,* ed. William Propp, Baruch Halpern, and David Noel Freedman (Winona Lake: Eisenbrauns, 1990) 27. For further, see Adam Zertal, "Ebal, Mount," *ABD* 2:255-58.

JOSHUA 9:1–10:43, DESTRUCTION TO THE SOUTH

OVERVIEW

With the destruction of Ai, the way lies open for the Israelites' wider assault in Canaan. So far the Deuteronomistic History has presented the conquest, which to this point has covered only a tiny part of the land, in terms of two attacks, one against Jericho and the other against Ai, construed as offensive actions on Joshua's initiative (2:1; 7:2), under Yahweh's orders (6:2-5; 8:1-2).[77] The

conquest of the rest of the land is presented in terms of two wider campaigns, against kings to the south and kings to the north. Although still the populace is slaughtered, the focus shifts even more than before to the kings, whose role is also cast into profile by the Gibeonites, who are said to have no king.

These two campaigns are parallel in several ways. In both, Yahweh delivers a war oracle to Joshua ordering him to attack and assuring victory

77. The MT and the LXX of Josh 9:3 show a variation between "what Joshua had done" and "what Yahweh had done."

(10:8; 11:6); Joshua attacks the hostile kings and their armies by surprise (10:9; 11:7); Yahweh does battle on Israel's side (10:10-14; 11:8); and the Israelite force routs its foes (10:10, 14; 11:8). Then Joshua kills the salient kings and destroys their towns (10:16-39; 11:10-15). In each case, the narration concludes with an acclamatory summary of death and destruction (10:40-43; 11:16-20). These two narratives are construed as struggles first against highland opponents ("Amorites") in the south and then lowland opponents in the north, who use chariots and are joined by allies from all over Canaan. The difference between highland and lowland warfare was a reality, and Josiah had to succeed at both if he was to reconquer Israel. But the many parallels between the two accounts, and between them and stereotypical ancient Near Eastern campaign accounts, show that they are literary compositions rather than historical reports.[78]

In addition, both of these campaigns are construed as defensive actions against offensive alliances. The initiative for battle comes not from Joshua, but from the kings. Nevertheless, the kings are the pawns of Yahweh. Yahweh makes the kings too stubborn ("hardens their hearts") to yield submissively to Israel's takeover, in order to make sure that they can be dedicated and exterminated without mercy (11:20). Yahweh's act of provocation shifts the onus for the conquest onto the dispossessed rather than the usurper, while the ultimate justification for usurpation remains with the sovereign Yahweh, who, having granted the land of the supposedly powerful Canaanites to the supposedly weak Israelites, guarantees that the land is taken.

Yahweh thus grants the land, provokes its holders into aggression, contributes the main force in response, and orders that the opposing populace be annihilated. The decisive role played by Yahweh is one reason why the narratives of the battles per se in Joshua are as brief as they are, as was also the case with the paradigmatic battle against Jericho. The book of Joshua tells nothing like the elaborate detail and embellishments that characterize heroic descriptions of intrepid fighting and dying in the Homeric epics and comparable traditions. Not even particulars such as are

found in more succinct women's songs, like those of Miriam (Exod 15:1-18; cf. Exod 15:20-21) or of Deborah (Judg 5:1-31), seem to figure much in these accounts. Instead, the campaign accounts are marked by the spare formulaic prose of scribal war diaries, royal campaign annals, and monarchic Egyptian "day books," which frequently put forth grandiose claims of victories achieved by the kings of the ancient Near East with the help of their gods, accounts rich only in stereotyped hyperbole.[79] This part of Joshua is interrupted by varied detail only infrequently, as in the brief excerpt from the "Yashar" document, apparently an ancient collection of poems of diverse types (10:12-13; cf. 2 Sam 1:17-27; 1 Kgs 8:12-13).

The numerous great and petty kings who appear in the book of Joshua have suggested to many a picture of Canaanite society splintered by conflict and feud into myriad tiny city-states, with no overarching political organization and identity. This is the way Late Bronze Age Canaan is usually thought of, giving the book of Joshua the appearance of historical reliability. This picture has seemed to find confirmation in the Amarna letters, written by numerous rival rulers and governors to the Egyptian court at Thebes and Akhetaten during the fourteenth century BCE.

What sense does such a picture make for the time of Josiah, when supposedly political fragmentation was a thing of the past and the house of David and the kings of Israel had brought swaths of territory under their sovereignty for centuries? Of course, the kings of Israel were no longer in the picture, and in any case the success of these rulers in controlling territory varied greatly over the centuries. The maps of OT times showing homogeneous sovereignty are frequently deceptive in this regard, especially when a single map covers centuries rather than decades. The picture of society in the book of Joshua offers a poor match for the Amarna era. It has already been pointed out that the locales named in Joshua differ markedly from what is known of settlement at that time and that references to iron are a serious anachronism. Within roughly the bounds covered by the book of Joshua, the Amarna letters suggest

78. K. Lawson Younger, *Ancient Conquest Accounts: A Study in Ancient Near Eastern and Biblical History Writing* (Sheffield: JSOT, 1990).

79. James K. Hoffmeier, "The Structure of Joshua 1–11 and the Annals of Thutmose III," in *Faith, Tradition, and History: Old Testament Historiography in Its Near Eastern Context,* ed. A. R. Millard, James Hoffmeier, and David W. Baker (Winona Lake, Ind.: Eisenbrauns, 1994) 165-79.

altogether only a handful of kings or warlords at any one time, some controlling quite extensive areas, and not the thirty-three, including Sihon and Og, listed in Joshua 12 (Judg 1:7 refers to no less than seventy).

Moreover, the term "king" can refer to many levels and degrees of sovereignty, from the imperial monarch to the lord of a large town. The picture in Joshua is one of a peculiar uniformity, where each town has its own king. Such a picture would be a figment of imagination for any age, whatever the extent of its political fragmentation. It resembles the Homeric picture of the age of "kings," which, like the book of Joshua, is an eighth- or seventh-century projection back to the Bronze Age. In Homer, "kings" are local lords and heads of households up against powerful but feuding local aristocracies striving to keep kingly prerogatives to a minimum. These kings must maintain their status "by might," like Odysseus's having to fight against the suitors. The picture of "kings" in Joshua is a negative idealization corresponding to the positive idealization of the twelve tribes of Israel as a uniformity.

There is little reason to look further than Josiah's reform for the source of these opposed idealizations. The opposition of "tribe" and "state" was a widespread and popular notion that by itself says nothing about time, place, and circumstance. The book of Joshua, however, as part of the Deuteronomistic History, gives this opposition a specific setting. In the context of Josiah's reform, the two "nations" represent antitheses. The "Israelite" populace under Josiah's rule are granted their traditional "tribal" identities in theory, opposed to "state" impositions and exactions by the likes of Canaanite "kings" or local and regional strongmen; in fact, these tribal identities are severely curtailed by the royal court's typical rationalizing of tribal policy and by the severe curtailment of patriarchal prerogatives represented by the deuteronomistic law of Moses.

In contrast, Josiah's opposition is embodied in the "kings" of the "Canaanite" peoples. These kings are nowhere described with qualities or actions, other than their plain opposition, which would justify their destruction. None is even named until Josh 10:3, and thereafter only the kings of Gezer, Hazor, and Madon are named; all the rest are nameless. They are given no family or extended household ties; as beneficiaries of commerce in the deuteronomistic conception, they are assumed to place money ahead of family ties, unlike "tribes." The destruction of the kings of Canaan is justified in the narrative, not by who they are or what they do, but simply by the claim of the divine territorial grant together with the categorical distinction of "tribe" versus "king" that permeates the narrative. The one person in the narrative who acts in any detail like a king— namely, Joshua—is, of course, never called a king. The "kings" as a lot are clones of the king of Jericho as the successor of Hiel. Like Hiel, they are strongmen who set up rival sovereignties and carve out rival jurisdictions, presumably once condoned by Assyria and Egypt, who must be suppressed and when possible eliminated if Josiah's reform and reconquest are to succeed. It is no accident that, according to the story, the Gibeonites, the foil to the kings of the south, live in a great town (10:2) but have no king (cf. 9:11).

Nowhere was this more the case than in the region of the Shephelah, or Judahite foothills to the west and southwest of Joshua's camp, and of the northern great valley under control of "kings" of the north. These two areas were of great strategic and economic importance in the late seventh century. Bringing them under the aegis of the house of David would represent a major step toward assuring the submission of the highland enclosed by them. Such a strategy was similar to the one David used to consolidate his power to the extent that he did. This strategy is probably the main reason why the deuteronomist can reduce the account of Joshua's extensive conquest to the two campaigns in chaps. 10 and 11.

Joshua 9:1-27, Saving the Gibeonites

NIV

9 Now when all the kings west of the Jordan heard about these things—those in the hill country, in the western foothills, and along the entire coast of the Great Sea[a] as far as Lebanon (the kings of the Hittites, Amorites, Canaanites, Perizzites, Hivites and Jebusites)— ²they came together to make war against Joshua and Israel.

³However, when the people of Gibeon heard what Joshua had done to Jericho and Ai, ⁴they resorted to a ruse: They went as a delegation whose donkeys were loaded[b] with worn-out sacks and old wineskins, cracked and mended. ⁵The men put worn and patched sandals on their feet and wore old clothes. All the bread of their food supply was dry and moldy. ⁶Then they went to Joshua in the camp at Gilgal and said to him and the men of Israel, "We have come from a distant country; make a treaty with us."

⁷The men of Israel said to the Hivites, "But perhaps you live near us. How then can we make a treaty with you?"

⁸"We are your servants," they said to Joshua.

But Joshua asked, "Who are you and where do you come from?"

⁹They answered: "Your servants have come from a very distant country because of the fame of the LORD your God. For we have heard reports of him: all that he did in Egypt, ¹⁰and all that he did to the two kings of the Amorites east of the Jordan—Sihon king of Heshbon, and Og king of Bashan, who reigned in Ashtaroth. ¹¹And our elders and all those living in our country said to us, 'Take provisions for your journey; go and meet them and say to them, "We are your servants; make a treaty with us."' ¹²This bread of ours was warm when we packed it at home on the day we left to come to you. But now see how dry and moldy it is. ¹³And these wineskins that we filled were new, but see how cracked they are. And our clothes and sandals are worn out by the very long journey."

¹⁴The men of Israel sampled their provisions but did not inquire of the LORD. ¹⁵Then Joshua

a1 That is, the Mediterranean   *b4* Most Hebrew manuscripts; some Hebrew manuscripts, Vulgate and Syriac (see also Septuagint) *They prepared provisions and loaded their donkeys*

NRSV

9 Now when all the kings who were beyond the Jordan in the hill country and in the lowland all along the coast of the Great Sea toward Lebanon—the Hittites, the Amorites, the Canaanites, the Perizzites, the Hivites, and the Jebusites—heard of this, ²they gathered together with one accord to fight Joshua and Israel.

3But when the inhabitants of Gibeon heard what Joshua had done to Jericho and to Ai, ⁴they on their part acted with cunning: they went and prepared provisions,[a] and took worn-out sacks for their donkeys, and wineskins, worn-out and torn and mended, ⁵with worn-out, patched sandals on their feet, and worn-out clothes; and all their provisions were dry and moldy. ⁶They went to Joshua in the camp at Gilgal, and said to him and to the Israelites, "We have come from a far country; so now make a treaty with us." ⁷But the Israelites said to the Hivites, "Perhaps you live among us; then how can we make a treaty with you?" ⁸They said to Joshua, "We are your servants." And Joshua said to them, "Who are you? And where do you come from?" ⁹They said to him, "Your servants have come from a very far country, because of the name of the LORD your God; for we have heard a report of him, of all that he did in Egypt, ¹⁰and of all that he did to the two kings of the Amorites who were beyond the Jordan, King Sihon of Heshbon, and King Og of Bashan who lived in Ashtaroth. ¹¹So our elders and all the inhabitants of our country said to us, 'Take provisions in your hand for the journey; go to meet them, and say to them, "We are your servants; come now, make a treaty with us."' ¹²Here is our bread; it was still warm when we took it from our houses as our food for the journey, on the day we set out to come to you, but now, see, it is dry and moldy; ¹³these wineskins were new when we filled them, and see, they are burst; and these garments and sandals of ours are worn out from the very long journey." ¹⁴So the leaders[b] partook of their provisions, and did not ask direction from the LORD. ¹⁵And Joshua made peace with them, guaranteeing their lives by a treaty; and the leaders of the congregation swore an oath to them.

a Cn: Meaning of Heb uncertain   *b* Gk: Heb *men*

NIV

made a treaty of peace with them to let them live, and the leaders of the assembly ratified it by oath.

[16]Three days after they made the treaty with the Gibeonites, the Israelites heard that they were neighbors, living near them. [17]So the Israelites set out and on the third day came to their cities: Gibeon, Kephirah, Beeroth and Kiriath Jearim. [18]But the Israelites did not attack them, because the leaders of the assembly had sworn an oath to them by the LORD, the God of Israel.

The whole assembly grumbled against the leaders, [19]but all the leaders answered, "We have given them our oath by the LORD, the God of Israel, and we cannot touch them now. [20]This is what we will do to them: We will let them live, so that wrath will not fall on us for breaking the oath we swore to them." [21]They continued, "Let them live, but let them be woodcutters and water carriers for the entire community." So the leaders' promise to them was kept.

[22]Then Joshua summoned the Gibeonites and said, "Why did you deceive us by saying, 'We live a long way from you,' while actually you live near us? [23]You are now under a curse: You will never cease to serve as woodcutters and water carriers for the house of my God."

[24]They answered Joshua, "Your servants were clearly told how the LORD your God had commanded his servant Moses to give you the whole land and to wipe out all its inhabitants from before you. So we feared for our lives because of you, and that is why we did this. [25]We are now in your hands. Do to us whatever seems good and right to you."

[26]So Joshua saved them from the Israelites, and they did not kill them. [27]That day he made the Gibeonites woodcutters and water carriers for the community and for the altar of the LORD at the place the LORD would choose. And that is what they are to this day.

NRSV

[16]But when three days had passed after they had made a treaty with them, they heard that they were their neighbors and were living among them. [17]So the Israelites set out and reached their cities on the third day. Now their cities were Gibeon, Chephirah, Beeroth, and Kiriath-jearim. [18]But the Israelites did not attack them, because the leaders of the congregation had sworn to them by the LORD, the God of Israel. Then all the congregation murmured against the leaders. [19]But all the leaders said to all the congregation, "We have sworn to them by the LORD, the God of Israel, and now we must not touch them. [20]This is what we will do to them: We will let them live, so that wrath may not come upon us, because of the oath that we swore to them." [21]The leaders said to them, "Let them live." So they became hewers of wood and drawers of water for all the congregation, as the leaders had decided concerning them.

[22]Joshua summoned them, and said to them, "Why did you deceive us, saying, 'We are very far from you,' while in fact you are living among us? [23]Now therefore you are cursed, and some of you shall always be slaves, hewers of wood and drawers of water for the house of my God." [24]They answered Joshua, "Because it was told to your servants for a certainty that the LORD your God had commanded his servant Moses to give you all the land, and to destroy all the inhabitants of the land before you; so we were in great fear for our lives because of you, and did this thing. [25]And now we are in your hand: do as it seems good and right in your sight to do to us." [26]This is what he did for them: he saved them from the Israelites; and they did not kill them. [27]But on that day Joshua made them hewers of wood and drawers of water for the congregation and for the altar of the LORD, to continue to this day, in the place that he should choose.

COMMENTARY

The construing of the conquest as defensive is brought to the fore through the story of the Gibeonites, which begins with this episode, nested within the story of hostilities with the

Canaanite kings. For the main deuteronomistic narrative, the reaction of the kings in 9:1-2 must be to the destruction of Ai and its king. As the text stands, however, they could just as well be reacting to the threat to their sovereignties represented by Joshua's exhibition of Moses' law in Shechem in 8:30-35. But that passage is secondary, as explained above, and it would seem untidy first to focus attention on the hill country around Shechem and then to describe reactions far to the south or to the north of Shechem without mentioning reactions in or around Shechem itself. Joshua attacks the five Amorite kings when they attack Gibeon; both attacks stem from the treaty between the Gibeonites and the Israelites.

Gibeon, which lay seven miles southwest of Ai and six miles northwest of Jerusalem, was not inhabited in the Late Bronze Age but in the time of David. It plays the role it does in Joshua for three reasons. First, it figured in the events surrounding David's rise to power against the house of Saul (2 Sam 2:12–3:1). Second, the house of David patronized the Gibeonites, who apparently already served as slaves of the cult of Yahweh, which David co-opted. Thus this story, for the deuteronomists at least, serves as the etiology of the Gibeonites' cult duty (9:24, 27; cf. 6:19; "the place that he should choose" is the central shrine in Jerusalem). Third, David used an attack by the rival house of Saul against the Gibeonites as his excuse to put to death the heirs of the erstwhile Israelite king (2 Sam 21:1-14; see Introduction). Thus David's avenging the Gibeonites echoes Joshua's defense of the Gibeonites against the Amorite kings (cf. Josh 9:18 with 2 Sam 21:2). Some have supposed that the later story served as the basis of the present story.[80]

The Gibeonites' story emphasizes their submission. They know, somehow, the law of *ḥērem*, which continues as a primary theme in the nar-

80. The tradition was that Gibeonites served in the Temple until at least the time of Josiah, if not in the Persian period as well. In 1 Chr 9:35-44, a Gibeonite genealogy follows immediately after the catalog of Temple servants. See Joseph Blenkinsopp, *Ezra–Nehemiah,* OTL (Philadelphia: Westminster, 1988) 90.

rative, and its distinction between near and distant towns (Deut 20:10-18), and they decide to try to avoid being wiped out through an acquiescent ruse rather than resistance. Their ruse recalls Yahweh's care of the Israelites during their lengthy trek in Deut 8:4 and 29:5. Their deuteronomistic lines in 9:9-10 make them like Rahab, intimidated by the exodus and the killing of Sihon and Og (2:10), and they are saved by an oath, as was Rahab. The role of the "leaders of the congregation" or "assembly" marks a priestly addition to the story, as evident from priestly vocabulary in 9:15*b,* 17-21, from the way 9:22 follows on 9:16, and from the apparent duplication between 9:17-21 and 9:22-27. Exactly what comes from the priestly writer is not entirely certain, but the reason for the addition seems clear. As far as the deuteronomist is concerned, the Gibeonites' ruse works because they pull it off, and they submit; Joshua is tricked, and once the covenant is sealed and corvée duty (Deut 20:11; cf. 29:11) is imposed on the Gibeonites, the matter is closed. The priestly writer, however, seems troubled by Joshua's responsibility and the possibility that Joshua himself failed to obey the law of Moses. The wrongdoing involved, therefore, is shifted to the "leaders of the congregation," whose oath, rather than Joshua's covenant, prevents the Israelites from dedicating the Gibeonites to death after discovering the ruse. It is probably the priestly writer who blames the "men" for not consulting Yahweh to avoid being tricked (9:14).

The NRSV's "live among us" (9:7, 16, 22) makes for a possible anachronism, as though Israelites live all around Gibeon. Like many features of the book of Joshua, this would fit the context of Josiah, but this time the translation is faulty. The NIV's translation, "live near us," is to be preferred.

REFLECTIONS

The Gibeonites are representatives of one of the indigenous "nations" in Joshua. These are the Gentiles, as they are later called on the basis of the Latin word for "nation." The book of Joshua is based in part on the sharp contrast between Israelite and Canaanite. In the New Testament, a similar contrast between Jew and Gentile plays an extremely significant role. The letters of Paul and the four Gospels make much of incorporating the Gentiles into the people of God. Although the history of how this came about is complex, one of the most important themes of the New Testament is this inclusion of outsiders within the new covenant in Jesus. Considering the book of Joshua, this is a striking development. It is possible to point to many clues in the Old Testament that this was God's intent all along, and Paul and the Gospels are quick to adduce the relevant passages from Scripture. The book of Joshua largely contradicts this point of view. Nevertheless, it is brought into service of it by pointing out the faith of Rahab and of the Israelites, since faith instead of circumcision became the new basis of belonging to the people of God.

The Gentile "nations" were traditionally said to be seven in number; this number refers to the lists of Canaanite nations that occur frequently in Joshua, even though only a few of these lists contain exactly seven nations. One of the great ironies of the Bible is that the Gentiles are conceived of in this way as belonging originally to the land of Canaan before the Israelites ever arrived. God first takes away the land of the "Gentiles," and then later incorporates them into the new "Israel." This stunning reversal imbues the New Testament, providing the core conviction behind some of its keenest polemic and most serene assurance.

No sooner did the church of both Jew and Gentile form, however, than it began drawing lines of demarcation and boundaries of its own for purposes of exclusion. Taking for granted our inclusion as "Gentiles," we perhaps assume too quickly that the problem of inclusion was resolved during the first centuries and is no longer relevant.

The basis on which Joshua accepted the Gibeonites clearly does not have to do with a principle of inclusion. But in relation to the New Testament it does raise the issue of the inclusion of the Gentiles (Hivites included) and points us toward an aspect of the New Testament that is too easily neglected: The New Testament favors the inclusion of those who have been excluded, and it does so to the remarkable extent of dispensing with the core institutions and values—the Temple and the law of Moses—that were important not only to the book of Joshua, but in the time of the early church played the primary role in defining what it meant to be Jewish as well. In the beginning, this issue represented a radical and threatening innovation (see Reflections at 3:1–4:18).

How might the church today express a similar commitment to inclusion? Some possible challenges that some churches have already taken on are dissolving denominational boundaries, dissolving national church boundaries, publicizing and instituting a commitment to diversity in the congregation to counteract the tendency toward congregational homogeneity, and welcoming the homeless into the church. In these and other ways, Christians can be challenged to renew the church's commitment to inclusion.

Joshua 10:1-43, Destruction of the Jerusalem Coalition

NIV

10 Now Adoni-Zedek king of Jerusalem heard that Joshua had taken Ai and totally destroyed[a] it, doing to Ai and its king as he had done to Jericho and its king, and that the people of Gibeon had made a treaty of peace with Israel and were living near them. [2]He and his people were very much alarmed at this, because Gibeon was an important city, like one of the royal cities; it was larger than Ai, and all its men were good

[a]1 The Hebrew term refers to the irrevocable giving over of things or persons to the LORD, often by totally destroying them; also in verses 28, 35, 37, 39 and 40.

NRSV

10 When King Adoni-zedek of Jerusalem heard how Joshua had taken Ai, and had utterly destroyed it, doing to Ai and its king as he had done to Jericho and its king, and how the inhabitants of Gibeon had made peace with Israel and were among them, [2]he[a] became greatly frightened, because Gibeon was a large city, like one of the royal cities, and was larger than Ai, and all its men were warriors. [3]So King Adoni-zedek of Jerusalem sent a message to King Hoham of

[a] Heb they

NIV

fighters. [3]So Adoni-Zedek king of Jerusalem appealed to Hoham king of Hebron, Piram king of Jarmuth, Japhia king of Lachish and Debir king of Eglon. [4]"Come up and help me attack Gibeon," he said, "because it has made peace with Joshua and the Israelites."

[5]Then the five kings of the Amorites—the kings of Jerusalem, Hebron, Jarmuth, Lachish and Eglon—joined forces. They moved up with all their troops and took up positions against Gibeon and attacked it.

[6]The Gibeonites then sent word to Joshua in the camp at Gilgal: "Do not abandon your servants. Come up to us quickly and save us! Help us, because all the Amorite kings from the hill country have joined forces against us."

[7]So Joshua marched up from Gilgal with his entire army, including all the best fighting men. [8]The LORD said to Joshua, "Do not be afraid of them; I have given them into your hand. Not one of them will be able to withstand you."

[9]After an all-night march from Gilgal, Joshua took them by surprise. [10]The LORD threw them into confusion before Israel, who defeated them in a great victory at Gibeon. Israel pursued them along the road going up to Beth Horon and cut them down all the way to Azekah and Makkedah. [11]As they fled before Israel on the road down from Beth Horon to Azekah, the LORD hurled large hailstones down on them from the sky, and more of them died from the hailstones than were killed by the swords of the Israelites.

[12]On the day the LORD gave the Amorites over to Israel, Joshua said to the LORD in the presence of Israel:

"O sun, stand still over Gibeon,
     O moon, over the Valley of Aijalon."
[13]So the sun stood still,
     and the moon stopped,
     till the nation avenged itself on[a] its enemies,
as it is written in the Book of Jashar.

The sun stopped in the middle of the sky and delayed going down about a full day. [14]There has never been a day like it before or since, a day when the LORD listened to a man. Surely the LORD was fighting for Israel!

[a]13 Or nation triumphed over

NRSV

Hebron, to King Piram of Jarmuth, to King Japhia of Lachish, and to King Debir of Eglon, saying, [4]"Come up and help me, and let us attack Gibeon; for it has made peace with Joshua and with the Israelites." [5]Then the five kings of the Amorites—the king of Jerusalem, the king of Hebron, the king of Jarmuth, the king of Lachish, and the king of Eglon—gathered their forces, and went up with all their armies and camped against Gibeon, and made war against it.

6And the Gibeonites sent to Joshua at the camp in Gilgal, saying, "Do not abandon your servants; come up to us quickly, and save us, and help us; for all the kings of the Amorites who live in the hill country are gathered against us." [7]So Joshua went up from Gilgal, he and all the fighting force with him, all the mighty warriors. [8]The LORD said to Joshua, "Do not fear them, for I have handed them over to you; not one of them shall stand before you." [9]So Joshua came upon them suddenly, having marched up all night from Gilgal. [10]And the LORD threw them into a panic before Israel, who inflicted a great slaughter on them at Gibeon, chased them by the way of the ascent of Beth-horon, and struck them down as far as Azekah and Makkedah. [11]As they fled before Israel, while they were going down the slope of Beth-horon, the LORD threw down huge stones from heaven on them as far as Azekah, and they died; there were more who died because of the hailstones than the Israelites killed with the sword.

12On the day when the LORD gave the Amorites over to the Israelites, Joshua spoke to the LORD; and he said in the sight of Israel,

"Sun, stand still at Gibeon,
     and Moon, in the valley of Aijalon."
[13] And the sun stood still, and the moon
          stopped,
     until the nation took vengeance on their
          enemies.

Is this not written in the Book of Jashar? The sun stopped in midheaven, and did not hurry to set for about a whole day. [14]There has been no day like it before or since, when the LORD heeded a human voice; for the LORD fought for Israel.

15Then Joshua returned, and all Israel with him, to the camp at Gilgal.

NIV

¹⁵Then Joshua returned with all Israel to the camp at Gilgal.

¹⁶Now the five kings had fled and hidden in the cave at Makkedah. ¹⁷When Joshua was told that the five kings had been found hiding in the cave at Makkedah, ¹⁸he said, "Roll large rocks up to the mouth of the cave, and post some men there to guard it. ¹⁹But don't stop! Pursue your enemies, attack them from the rear and don't let them reach their cities, for the LORD your God has given them into your hand."

²⁰So Joshua and the Israelites destroyed them completely—almost to a man—but the few who were left reached their fortified cities. ²¹The whole army then returned safely to Joshua in the camp at Makkedah, and no one uttered a word against the Israelites.

²²Joshua said, "Open the mouth of the cave and bring those five kings out to me." ²³So they brought the five kings out of the cave—the kings of Jerusalem, Hebron, Jarmuth, Lachish and Eglon. ²⁴When they had brought these kings to Joshua, he summoned all the men of Israel and said to the army commanders who had come with him, "Come here and put your feet on the necks of these kings." So they came forward and placed their feet on their necks.

²⁵Joshua said to them, "Do not be afraid; do not be discouraged. Be strong and courageous. This is what the LORD will do to all the enemies you are going to fight." ²⁶Then Joshua struck and killed the kings and hung them on five trees, and they were left hanging on the trees until evening.

²⁷At sunset Joshua gave the order and they took them down from the trees and threw them into the cave where they had been hiding. At the mouth of the cave they placed large rocks, which are there to this day.

²⁸That day Joshua took Makkedah. He put the city and its king to the sword and totally destroyed everyone in it. He left no survivors. And he did to the king of Makkedah as he had done to the king of Jericho.

²⁹Then Joshua and all Israel with him moved on from Makkedah to Libnah and attacked it. ³⁰The LORD also gave that city and its king into Israel's hand. The city and everyone in it Joshua put to the sword. He left no survivors there. And

NRSV

¹⁶Meanwhile, these five kings fled and hid themselves in the cave at Makkedah. ¹⁷And it was told Joshua, "The five kings have been found, hidden in the cave at Makkedah." ¹⁸Joshua said, "Roll large stones against the mouth of the cave, and set men by it to guard them; ¹⁹but do not stay there yourselves; pursue your enemies, and attack them from the rear. Do not let them enter their towns, for the LORD your God has given them into your hand." ²⁰When Joshua and the Israelites had finished inflicting a very great slaughter on them, until they were wiped out, and when the survivors had entered into the fortified towns, ²¹all the people returned safe to Joshua in the camp at Makkedah; no one dared to speak^a against any of the Israelites.

²²Then Joshua said, "Open the mouth of the cave, and bring those five kings out to me from the cave." ²³They did so, and brought the five kings out to him from the cave, the king of Jerusalem, the king of Hebron, the king of Jarmuth, the king of Lachish, and the king of Eglon. ²⁴When they brought the kings out to Joshua, Joshua summoned all the Israelites, and said to the chiefs of the warriors who had gone with him, "Come near, put your feet on the necks of these kings." Then they came near and put their feet on their necks. ²⁵And Joshua said to them, "Do not be afraid or dismayed; be strong and courageous; for thus the LORD will do to all the enemies against whom you fight." ²⁶Afterward Joshua struck them down and put them to death, and he hung them on five trees. And they hung on the trees until evening. ²⁷At sunset Joshua commanded, and they took them down from the trees and threw them into the cave where they had hidden themselves; they set large stones against the mouth of the cave, which remain to this very day.

²⁸Joshua took Makkedah on that day, and struck it and its king with the edge of the sword; he utterly destroyed every person in it; he left no one remaining. And he did to the king of Makkedah as he had done to the king of Jericho.

²⁹Then Joshua passed on from Makkedah, and all Israel with him, to Libnah, and fought against Libnah. ³⁰The LORD gave it also and its king into

^a Heb *moved his tongue*

he did to its king as he had done to the king of Jericho.

³¹Then Joshua and all Israel with him moved on from Libnah to Lachish; he took up positions against it and attacked it. ³²The LORD handed Lachish over to Israel, and Joshua took it on the second day. The city and everyone in it he put to the sword, just as he had done to Libnah. ³³Meanwhile, Horam king of Gezer had come up to help Lachish, but Joshua defeated him and his army—until no survivors were left.

³⁴Then Joshua and all Israel with him moved on from Lachish to Eglon; they took up positions against it and attacked it. ³⁵They captured it that same day and put it to the sword and totally destroyed everyone in it, just as they had done to Lachish.

³⁶Then Joshua and all Israel with him went up from Eglon to Hebron and attacked it. ³⁷They took the city and put it to the sword, together with its king, its villages and everyone in it. They left no survivors. Just as at Eglon, they totally destroyed it and everyone in it.

³⁸Then Joshua and all Israel with him turned around and attacked Debir. ³⁹They took the city, its king and its villages, and put them to the sword. Everyone in it they totally destroyed. They left no survivors. They did to Debir and its king as they had done to Libnah and its king and to Hebron.

⁴⁰So Joshua subdued the whole region, including the hill country, the Negev, the western foothills and the mountain slopes, together with all their kings. He left no survivors. He totally destroyed all who breathed, just as the LORD, the God of Israel, had commanded. ⁴¹Joshua subdued them from Kadesh Barnea to Gaza and from the whole region of Goshen to Gibeon. ⁴²All these kings and their lands Joshua conquered in one campaign, because the LORD, the God of Israel, fought for Israel.

⁴³Then Joshua returned with all Israel to the camp at Gilgal.

the hand of Israel; and he struck it with the edge of the sword, and every person in it; he left no one remaining in it; and he did to its king as he had done to the king of Jericho.

31Next Joshua passed on from Libnah, and all Israel with him, to Lachish, and laid siege to it, and assaulted it. ³²The LORD gave Lachish into the hand of Israel, and he took it on the second day, and struck it with the edge of the sword, and every person in it, as he had done to Libnah.

33Then King Horam of Gezer came up to help Lachish; and Joshua struck him and his people, leaving him no survivors.

34From Lachish Joshua passed on with all Israel to Eglon; and they laid siege to it, and assaulted it; ³⁵and they took it that day, and struck it with the edge of the sword; and every person in it he utterly destroyed that day, as he had done to Lachish.

36Then Joshua went up with all Israel from Eglon to Hebron; they assaulted it, ³⁷and took it, and struck it with the edge of the sword, and its king and its towns, and every person in it; he left no one remaining, just as he had done to Eglon, and utterly destroyed it with every person in it.

38Then Joshua, with all Israel, turned back to Debir and assaulted it, ³⁹and he took it with its king and all its towns; they struck them with the edge of the sword, and utterly destroyed every person in it; he left no one remaining; just as he had done to Hebron, and, as he had done to Libnah and its king, so he did to Debir and its king.

40So Joshua defeated the whole land, the hill country and the Negeb and the lowland and the slopes, and all their kings; he left no one remaining, but utterly destroyed all that breathed, as the LORD God of Israel commanded. ⁴¹And Joshua defeated them from Kadesh-barnea to Gaza, and all the country of Goshen, as far as Gibeon. ⁴²Joshua took all these kings and their land at one time, because the LORD God of Israel fought for Israel. ⁴³Then Joshua returned, and all Israel with him, to the camp at Gilgal.

COMMENTARY

The campaign to the south sparked by Joshua's defense of Gibeon occurs in three stages. The first stage involves the attack against the five allied kings. This attack continues to feature Gibeon; in separate incidents, at Gibeon the Israelites slaughter the allied army, from Gibeon to Azekah Yahweh pommels the retreating enemy with giant hailstones, and at Gibeon the sun stands still, helping Israel against its enemies. But the spotlight of the campaign as such is first on a group of kings led by the king of Jerusalem, and then on a group of towns whose territories blanket the Shephelah and Judahite highland. In the second stage, Joshua pursues and executes the five kings. In the third stage, the towns of most of these kings, along with other towns, are dedicated and destroyed. The narrative structure of this third stage highlights the destruction of Gezer (10:33), which dominates the primary gateway to the Aijalon Valley and the road between the Philistine coast and the Benjaminite and northern Judahite hills around Jerusalem.

The five Amorite kings are organized by the king of Jerusalem. The relationship between Adoni-zedek and another king, Adoni-bezek, probably also of Jerusalem, in Judg 1:4-7 is unclear. Their names are less similar than they look in English, but the LXX of Josh 10:1, 3 takes Adoni-zedek to be Adoni-bezek. This is one of a group of related puzzles and inconsistencies. There appears to be a duplication between Joshua and Judges of the accounts concerning several of these towns. The account in Joshua 15 concerning Jerusalem (which, according to 2 Sam 5:6-9, was not captured until David did so) and Hebron and Debir, all in the Judahite highland, seems to have an approximate duplicate in Judges 1. According to Judg 1:4-13, the Judahites, who take the lead in Judges 1 unlike in the wars of Joshua, capture these three towns in the era after the death of Joshua. Judges 1:8 describes the capture and destruction of Jerusalem, contrary to Josh 15:63 (with which Judg 1:21 agrees, except that in Joshua it is the Judahites who live in Jerusalem and in Judges it is the Benjaminites). Judges 1:10 describes the capture of Hebron, but with no mention of Caleb, as in Josh 15:13-14. Judges

1:11-15 describes the capture of Debir in a nearly verbatim doublet of Josh 15:15-19. Joshua 11:21 raises fresh questions about the destruction of Hebron and Debir. The parallels between Judges 1 and Joshua 15 must be placed next to the account concerning the same towns in Joshua 10: here Jerusalem under Adoni-zedek or Adoni-bezek is not captured, but Hebron and Debir are (10:36-39). To top things off, Debir, the king of Eglon (10:3), is the only person supposedly with this name; all other Debirs are names of places, of which there are at least two. Is the writer confused about Debir?

There is no simple solution to these discrepancies, which are not the only matters on which Joshua and the beginning of Judges disagree. It is not likely that these differences arose in conflicting traditions about whether the conquest of Canaan was quick or gradual, an explanation that was popular not long ago. More likely, they arose beginning with the differing deuteronomistic concepts of the two eras, one of Joshua, the other of the judges and saviors. In Joshua the conquest was in theory complete, or virtually so; exceptions were just that, as the Israelites took effective control of the land. In the era of the judges and saviors, from the start Israel's control was much less than complete, and the accent is on the troubling presence everywhere of Israel's opponents.

Judges 1 is a deuteronomistic composition based on the contrast between Jerusalem, on the one hand (Judg 1:4-8, 21), and Bethel and Dan, where Jeroboam established his anti-Jerusalem shrines, on the other hand (Judg 1:22-26, 34). The references to Jerusalem enclose an account of Judah's successes in conquest, and the references to Bethel and Dan enclose an account of the failure in conquest of the rest of the northern Israelite tribes that, under Jeroboam, broke away from the house of David. The capture of Bethel (Judg 1:22-26) forms an unmistakable parallel to the capture of Jericho under Joshua, but without explicit sanction for sparing the Canaanite helper and his family from dedication. The account of the northern tribes forms an antithesis to the book of Joshua: Each tribe fails to drive out the Canaanites (Judg 1:27-34), though some are able to subject them to corvee slavery (forced labor). In the case of Manasseh and Ephraim, this is true in the book of Joshua as well (Josh 16:10; 17:12-13).

The structural contrast between Jerusalem and Bethel and Dan in Judges 1 is confirmed in the scene at Bochim ("Weepers"), which the LXX correctly takes to be Bethel, where in violation of the deuteronomistic law of centralization "they sacrificed to Yahweh" (Judg 2:1-5). Following a duplication of the death and burial of Joshua, which re-marks the boundary between Joshua's generation and the next (Judg 2:6-10), the deuteronomistic lesson of the era of the judges is laid out in full (Judg 2:11–3:6): Without a monarch devoted to the law of Moses and surrounded by leftover Canaanite peoples, generation after generation of Israelites prove unable to resist, oppose, or do battle against Canaanite power and Canaanite gods. This lesson is illustrated many times over in the main narrative of Judges, leading off with the stereotypical case of the Judahite deliverer Othniel (Judg 3:7-11).[81]

Given these two different concepts underlying the era of Joshua in contrast to the era of Judges— the rapid and successful conquest of Canaan in contrast to the cyclical failure to control the land conquered—it is not surprising that similar names and traditions are given different treatment in them and that, as typical in textual transmission, further confusion has arisen through subsequent attempts to reconcile or harmonize accounts. The supposed gradual conquest in Judges 1 probably reflects no more actual history, to say nothing of better history, than the book of Joshua's sudden conquest, and there is no reason to continue to contrast the two accounts as history at all. From a historical perspective, the two books are both best interpreted as reflecting monarchical politics in the late eighth and seventh centuries BCE.

As the Amorites flee from the Israelites toward the southwest, Yahweh attacks them with hail.

Yahweh controls the heavens; this use of meteorological elements in battle is a commonplace in biblical war (see, e.g., Judg 5:20-21, where the stars represent windows opened to let in the cosmic flood [cf. Gen 7:11]; Hab 3:8-12; Job 38:22-23).

The same conception lies behind the episode encapsulated in the poetic excerpt in 10:12-13, which is too fragmentary to give a clear picture (the LXX's "God" for "the nation" is probably a later interpretation, consistent with v. 14b). The prose interpretation in v. 13b takes it to refer to an extension of daylight, presumably in order to allow Israel to complete its slaughter of the enemy. This oldest interpretation is found also in Sir 46:4. However, the prayer puts the sun over Gibeon and the moon over Aijalon (hence it cannot refer to a solar eclipse), and thus must have been pronounced at daybreak, not late in the day. Moreover, the day is not unique because the sun stopped, but because God "heeded a human voice." This cannot mean that God has never answered a prayer; it probably means that God has never taken orders from anyone in battle. Several recent interpretations make a comparison between Joshua's prayer and ancient Near Eastern omens. Certain sets of omens use "wait" and "stand" to refer to the sun and moon in their normal motions, not their miraculous deviation from their usual course or pace. This is probably the case with Joshua's prayer. According to some omens, if the sun and the moon appear together on the fourteenth day after new moon, there will be peace in the land; if the sun and the moon do not appear together until the fifteenth day, there will be catastrophic war. One interpretation along these lines supposes that Joshua seeks a favorable omen.[82] Another suggests that Joshua does not believe in omens himself but wants the Amorites to receive a discouraging omen.[83]

Neither v. 15 nor v. 43 appears in the LXX, but the narrative cusps that these verses mark are obvious nevertheless. In typical framework style, the second stage of the battle is enclosed by references to the cave where the kings hide (vv.

---

81. A somewhat lengthy addition to the end of Joshua in the LXX describes the life and burial of the priest Phinehas, the apostasy of the Israelites, and Yahweh's delivering them "into the hands of Eglon king of Moab and he ruled over them eighteen years." The mention of Eglon's rule connects this variant of the end of the book of Joshua to Judg 3:12, suggesting to some that at least in one edition of Joshua and Judges the entire Jerusalem-dominated or deuteronomistic section in Judg 1:1–3:11 may have been missing, to be added secondarily. See Alexander Rofé, "The End of the Book of Joshua According to the Septuagint," *Henoch* 4 (1982) 17-36; Emanuel Tov, *Textual Criticism of the Hebrew Bible* (Minneapolis: Fortress, 1992) 330-32.

82. John R. Holladay, "The Day(s) the Moon Stood Still," *JBL* 87 (1968) 166-78.
83. John H. Walton, "Joshua 10:12-15 and Mesopotamian Celestial Omen Texts," in *Faith, Tradition, and History: Old Testament Histiography in Its Near Eastern Context,* ed. A. R. Millard, James K. Hoffmeier, and David W. Baker (Winona Lake: Eisenbrauns, 1994) 181-90.

16, 27). The cave is sealed with stones until the rout and slaughter of the enemy are complete. Joshua has the Israelites bring the kings out of the cave and symbolically vanquish them; then he executes them, hangs each corpse on a tree until sunset, removes them, throws them back into the cave, and seals the entrance with the same stones.

The final stage of the battle of the south entails the fulfillment of *ḥērem* against three of the kings' towns and several others: Makkedah, Libnah, and Lachish, then Eglon, Hebron, and Debir. In each town, every person is put to death. In between these two sets of three towns, Joshua does battle against the kings of Gezer and his force ("people" in such a context usually refers to the group under arms). The structure of the narrative gives Gezer a particular prominence.[84] Gezer is not destroyed, nor are the inhabitants of the town itself slaughtered (16:10; Judg 1:19). Gezer's location gave it great strategic importance, and it continued to be occupied following its destruction during Sennacherib's campaign. Assyrian tablets have been found in this stratum of occupation, and the likelihood is that it was for some time an imperial administrative center, under Assyrian or Egyptian control, whose destruction Josiah had no reason to portray (though what were probably similar circumstances did not discourage him from having the destruction of Hazor portrayed—indeed, singling it out for burning, possibly because it was in fact beyond his reach; 11:10-11).

The summary of the southern campaign is given by region (v. 40), boundaries (v. 41), and length of time (v. 42).[85] From Gibeon south, not one human survivor remained and nothing was left alive. This obvious exaggeration was not even intended to be consistent with other parts of Joshua and Judges. Its purpose is to contribute to the deuteronomistic idealization of the era of Joshua. The "slopes" are probably the eastern escarpment of the Judahite and Benjaminite hills, dropping down to the Jordan and the Dead Sea basin. Goshen is distinct from the region of the same name in Egypt.

84. K. Lawson Younger, Jr., "The 'Conquest' of the South (Jos 10, 28-39)," *BZ* 39 (1995) 255-64.

85. Ibid., 258-59, 264.

REFLECTIONS

1. The contradiction between a complete destruction and an incomplete destruction in the south points up what Daniel Hawk calls the "contesting plots" in Joshua.[86] Tensions tend to arise in Joshua either because the narrator juxtaposes contrary events or because the narrator gives an interpretation that is inconsistent with the events being narrated. This happens in two main areas. One is the complete (Josh 10:28-42; 11:12-23; 12:7-24; 21:43-45; 23:9-10; 24:11-13) versus the incomplete (Josh 9:14-27; 11:19, 22; 15:63; 16:10; 17:11-12; 19:47) conquest. The other is the contrast between a quick and total obedience to Yahweh (Josh 1:16-18; 4:10; 8:30-35; 24:16-18, 21) and a slow reluctance or inability to obey (Josh 2:1-21; 7:1; 9:1-27; 18:1-10; 24:19-20).[87] Hawk looks at the narrative all at once and sees these not as irreconcilable differences resulting from a complex process of composition, but as narrative facets integral to a plot that seeks to "exemplify the tension between the structuring operations of dogma and the circumstances of experience."[88] The narrator's struggle with ambiguity mirrors the reader's perception that while structuring life according to a plan is essential, "reality resists and provokes our concords with dissonances and uncertainties. Israel laid claim to fulfillment, but continued to tell its story under the impulse of a promise yet to be realized."[89] The ambiguities and inconsistencies of Joshua reflect a narrator grappling with a reality less plastic than desired and throwing up challenges to his tenets and assertions. In this view, reading the book of Joshua becomes an exercise in adjusting hopes and expectations to the way things are

86. L. Daniel Hawk, *Every Promise Fulfilled: Contesting Plots in Joshua* (Louisville: Westminster/John Knox, 1991).
87. Ibid., 15-16.
88. Ibid., 20.
89. Ibid., 145.

without abandoning basic principles, a continually startling metaphor for adult learning. For readers of the Bible in the church, this can be a worthwhile lesson in looking or listening carefully to what the Bible is saying despite the expectations inevitably brought to it.

2. The forced repulsion, expulsion, or eradication of peoples is an age-old story of domination and despair, of which the decimation of Native Americans is, for present-day Americans, the most trenchant and consequential instance.[90] The story does not abate, and the twentieth century has produced some of the worst examples in history. For many, the Jewish Holocaust in Nazi Europe marks the nadir of the human capacity for the heinous atrocity of genocide.[91]

The tragic sequel to the suffering of the Jewish people in Europe is the suffering of the Palestinian people in what became the state of Israel and, in 1967, the occupied territories of the West Bank. The history of twentieth-century Palestine is a vexed and contentious subject, but one thing is indisputable: The outcome for hundreds of thousands of natives of Palestine has been an unending disaster. In 1948 the conquest of Joshua was replayed, with Palestinians in the role of the Canaanites. Assisted by Arab armies, the Palestinians were able to hold on to much of the highlands of Palestine until 1967, when Israeli forces captured the rest of biblical Canaan west of the Jordan. The history of this period is complex, but the result for most Palestinians was oppression, expulsion, and destruction, and in many cases death. The 1948 war produced 750,000 Palestinian refugees, families and communities whose children fifty years later often still live in the same camps to which their parents fled.[92]

The story of expulsion and ethnic cleansing has been repeated innumerable times and in many places since. Notable recent examples include East Timor (where since 1975 one-third of the population has been killed by its own government), Cambodia (one-fifth of the population), Sri Lanka, the former Yugoslavia, and Rwanda. The historian does no service to the memory of the victims of these horrendous events by making facile comparisons between them; however, one common feature important for comprehending the book of Joshua stands out: Ethnic cleansing does not occur today, and probably never did occur, except as devised, promoted, organized, and carried out under the direction of a state or dominant government seeking to centralize and expand. As one recent commentator put it regarding recent wars in Africa, "Ethnic differences do not in themselves cause wars. But when they are exploited by politicians, in countries where one man or one party has taken over the state, the results can be disastrous."[93] Such generalizations confirm that the cleansing portrayed in the book of Joshua did not originate among the populace of ancient Palestine, including the highland tribal people identified as Israel. One key feature of modern ethnic cleansing is the use of the media to foster hatred. Although probably publicized little further than Josiah's wider court, the book of Joshua, together with the rest of the Deuteronomistic History, helped to serve this function in Josiah's reform.[94]

90. Robert Allen Warrior, "A Native American Perspective: Canaanites, Cowboys, and Indians," *Christianity and Crisis,* September 11, 1989, 261-65; reprinted in *Voices from the Margin: Interpreting the Bible in the Third World,* ed. R. S. Sugirtharajah (Maryknoll, N.Y.: Orbis, 1995) 277-85.

91. Douglas K. Huneke, *The Stones Will Cry Out: Pastoral Reflections on the Shoah* (Westport, Conn.: Greenwood, 1995).

92. Walid Khalidi, ed., *All That Remains: The Palestinian Villages Occupied and Depopulated by Israel in 1948* (Washington: Institute for Palestine Studies, 1992); Nur Masalha, *Expulsion of the Palestinians: The Concept of "Transfer" in Zionist Political Thought, 1882–1948* (Washington: Institute for Palestine Studies, 1992); Naim S. Ateek, "A Palestinian Perspective: Biblical Perspectives on the Land," in *Faith and the Intifada: Palestinian Christian Voices* (Maryknoll, N.Y.: Orbis, 1992): 108-16, reprinted in Sugirtharajah, *Voices from the Margin,* 267-76; W. Eugene March, *Israel and the Politics of Land: A Theological Case Study* (Louisville: Westminster/John Knox, 1994).

93. See *The Economist,* July 1, 1995, 17.

94. To understand ethnic cleansing in the book of Joshua, interpreters should familiarize themselves with at least one well-studied modern example. For Cambodia: Ben Kiernan, *The Pol Pot Regime: Race, Power, and Genocide in Cambodia Under the Khmer Rouge, 1957–79* (New Haven: Yale University Press, 1996). For Sri Lanka: Anthony Spaeth, "Inventing an Ethnic Rivalry," *Harper's* (November 1991) 67-78; David Little, *Sri Lanka: The Invention of Enmity* (Washington: United States Institute of Peace, 1994). For Yugoslavia: Misha Glenny, *The Fall of Yugoslavia: The Third Balkan War* (New York: Penguin, 1992); Laura Silber and Allan Little, *The Death of Yugoslavia* (New York: Penguin, 1995); Norman Cigar, *Genocide in Bosnia: The Policy of "Ethnic Cleansing"* (College Station: Texas A. & M. University Press, 1995). For Rwanda: Alex de Waal, "The Genocidal State: Hutu Extremism and the Origins of the 'Final Solution' in Rwanda," *The Times Literary Supplement,* July 1, 1994, 3-4; Robert Block, "The Tragedy of Rwanda," *The New York Review of Books,* October 20, 1994, 3-8; Gérard Prunier, *The Rwanda Crisis: History of a Genocide* (New York: Columbia University Press, 1995); *Genocide in Rwanda: The Planning and Execution of Mass Murder* (New York: Human Rights Watch, 1996). In general: *Slaughter Among Neighbors: The Political Origins of Ethnic, Racial, and Religious Violence* (New Haven: Yale University Press, 1995).

JOSHUA 11:1-15, DESTRUCTION TO THE NORTH

NIV

11 When Jabin king of Hazor heard of this, he sent word to Jobab king of Madon, to the kings of Shimron and Acshaph, ²and to the northern kings who were in the mountains, in the Arabah south of Kinnereth, in the western foothills and in Naphoth Dor*ᵃ* on the west; ³to the Canaanites in the east and west; to the Amorites, Hittites, Perizzites and Jebusites in the hill country; and to the Hivites below Hermon in the region of Mizpah. ⁴They came out with all their troops and a large number of horses and chariots—a huge army, as numerous as the sand on the seashore. ⁵All these kings joined forces and made camp together at the Waters of Merom, to fight against Israel.

⁶The LORD said to Joshua, "Do not be afraid of them, because by this time tomorrow I will hand all of them over to Israel, slain. You are to hamstring their horses and burn their chariots."

⁷So Joshua and his whole army came against them suddenly at the Waters of Merom and attacked them, ⁸and the LORD gave them into the hand of Israel. They defeated them and pursued them all the way to Greater Sidon, to Misrephoth Maim, and to the Valley of Mizpah on the east, until no survivors were left. ⁹Joshua did to them as the LORD had directed: He hamstrung their horses and burned their chariots.

¹⁰At that time Joshua turned back and captured Hazor and put its king to the sword. (Hazor had been the head of all these kingdoms.) ¹¹Everyone in it they put to the sword. They totally destroyed*ᵇ* them, not sparing anything that breathed, and he burned up Hazor itself.

¹²Joshua took all these royal cities and their kings and put them to the sword. He totally destroyed them, as Moses the servant of the LORD had commanded. ¹³Yet Israel did not burn any of the cities built on their mounds—except Hazor, which Joshua burned. ¹⁴The Israelites carried off for themselves all the plunder and livestock of these cities, but all the people they put to the sword until they completely destroyed them, not

ᵃ2 Or in the heights of Dor   ᵇ11 The Hebrew term refers to the irrevocable giving over of things or persons to the LORD, often by totally destroying them; also in verses 12, 20 and 21.

NRSV

11 When King Jabin of Hazor heard of this, he sent to King Jobab of Madon, to the king of Shimron, to the king of Achshaph, ²and to the kings who were in the northern hill country, and in the Arabah south of Chinneroth, and in the lowland, and in Naphoth-dor on the west, ³to the Canaanites in the east and the west, the Amorites, the Hittites, the Perizzites, and the Jebusites in the hill country, and the Hivites under Hermon in the land of Mizpah. ⁴They came out, with all their troops, a great army, in number like the sand on the seashore, with very many horses and chariots. ⁵All these kings joined their forces, and came and camped together at the waters of Merom, to fight with Israel.

6And the LORD said to Joshua, "Do not be afraid of them, for tomorrow at this time I will hand over all of them, slain, to Israel; you shall hamstring their horses, and burn their chariots with fire." ⁷So Joshua came suddenly upon them with all his fighting force, by the waters of Merom, and fell upon them. ⁸And the LORD handed them over to Israel, who attacked them and chased them as far as Great Sidon and Misrephoth-maim, and eastward as far as the valley of Mizpeh. They struck them down, until they had left no one remaining. ⁹And Joshua did to them as the LORD commanded him; he hamstrung their horses, and burned their chariots with fire.

10Joshua turned back at that time, and took Hazor, and struck its king down with the sword. Before that time Hazor was the head of all those kingdoms. ¹¹And they put to the sword all who were in it, utterly destroying them; there was no one left who breathed, and he burned Hazor with fire. ¹²And all the towns of those kings, and all their kings, Joshua took, and struck them with the edge of the sword, utterly destroying them, as Moses the servant of the LORD had commanded. ¹³But Israel burned none of the towns that stood on mounds except Hazor, which Joshua did burn. ¹⁴All the spoil of these towns, and the livestock, the Israelites took for their booty; but all the people they struck down with the edge of the sword, until they had destroyed them, and they did not leave any who breathed. ¹⁵As the LORD

NIV	NRSV
sparing anyone that breathed. [15]As the LORD commanded his servant Moses, so Moses commanded Joshua, and Joshua did it; he left nothing undone of all that the LORD commanded Moses.	had commanded his servant Moses, so Moses commanded Joshua, and so Joshua did; he left nothing undone of all that the LORD had commanded Moses.

COMMENTARY

Consistent with the standard narrative transition in Joshua (see 5:1; 9:1; 10:1), the king of the greatest of the far northern towns, Hazor, hears about what has just happened in the south, and he tries to turn the tables on the Israelites. He organizes a northern alliance similar to the southern alliance just defeated. The southern alliance involved a few Amorite kings; this alliance includes all the Canaanite groups, who together produce a multitude under arms, with a multitude of chariots, the ancient equivalent of tanks pitted against Israel's infantry. Joshua's counterpart is Jabin, the king of Hazor, and it is hard to separate him from the Jabin who is the "king of Canaan" ruling in Hazor in the time of Deborah, several generations after Joshua (Judg 4:2, 7, 23-24). Many scholars rightly believe that the two accounts in Josh 11:1-15 and Judges 4–5 are variants of each other, or that one is based on the other. Both involve a battle against a Canaanite coalition in the Jezreel Valley. The "waters of Merom" (11:5)

compare with the "waters of Megiddo" (Judg 5:19) and may be involved in a pun in the phrase "heights of the field" (5:18). The nature of the woman's song, probably ancient, in Judges 5 and some of its contents suggest that some pre-Davidic battle involving tribal "Israel" might lie far in the background of these accounts.

The Israelites burn the chariots and hamstring the horses, making them unusable in warfare (Gen 49:6; 2 Sam 8:4). Surprisingly the Israelites leave the towns they attack "on their tells" (cf. 8:28), excepting Hazor, and as with Ai dedicate to God only the inhabitants of the towns, taking the livestock and other spoil as booty. How the precedent of Ai justifies this exception to the law of ḥērem is unclear. Regardless, the conclusion that follows immediately explains that this was not a violation of the law, since Joshua has from the beginning and without exception obeyed all that Yahweh ordered Moses to tell the Israelites to do.

REFLECTIONS

Christians have always looked to God for support in their battles with superior forces, both material and spiritual. Virtually every church and denomination has a tradition of overcoming adversity against great odds with the help of the Lord. Expressions of God's help are readily found in church liturgies and hymns. In the comparatively peaceful world of middle-class America, where such adversity is more likely to be experienced in a spiritual rather than a material mode, it is easy to forget the struggles our forebears in the faith had to endure. It might be useful to go through the church's hymnal and discuss some of these struggles. An example is the great Reformed hymn based on Psalm 68, "Let God Arise and Show His Face." Its lines, in their sixteenth-century context of religious wars, were not sung metaphorically:

And all that hate him shall give place,
and all his foes shall scatter.
Just as the smoke away doth blow,
so shall his arm disperse the foe,
and all opponents banish.
But let the righteous all rejoice.[95]

95. This hymn was translated by Margaret House in 1949 for the World Student Christian Federation hymnal, published in 1951.

This "Battle Hymn of the Huguenots" was used by, among others, the Pilgrims at Plymouth. The mortal foes referred to in this hymn are fellow Christians, although Protestants did not always regard Catholics as such for the first two hundred years or so of the Reformation. The nature of the struggle in the Reformation use of this hymn—in France, Britain, the Lowlands, or elsewhere—tended to be a civil war, not a war against "external" enemies. In this respect, it may not be so different from the struggle represented in the book of Joshua.

It is too facile simply to dismiss such hymns as barbaric and hence irrelevant. How do we take sides with a God who battles cancer, oppression, and death without raising the flag for the "God of our side"? To be faithful is to be partisan, and there is no more poignant expression of partisanship than the church's heritage of militaristic hymns, even if today we choose to reject or muffle their martial blare and spiked animosity. In any case, except in churches that are explicitly and unreservedly pacifist, the muting of the church's legacy of bellicosity tends to be selective. Christians may intend no longer to kill like Joshua, but happily they can "choose their fight" within the often shifting and ambiguous constraints of love and justice. Then the great battle hymns may have a great positive effect. Models may include the writer of Eph 6:10-17, who does not stint in rhetorically arming the Christian warrior to the hilt, and the Reformer Martin Luther, who, in "A Mighty Fortress Is Our God," composed, in part with martial metaphor, one of the enduring monuments to the calling of Christian faith.

JOSHUA 11:16–12:24, SUMMARY OF DESTRUCTION

NIV

16So Joshua took this entire land: the hill country, all the Negev, the whole region of Goshen, the western foothills, the Arabah and the mountains of Israel with their foothills, 17from Mount Halak, which rises toward Seir, to Baal Gad in the Valley of Lebanon below Mount Hermon. He captured all their kings and struck them down, putting them to death. 18Joshua waged war against all these kings for a long time. 19Except for the Hivites living in Gibeon, not one city made a treaty of peace with the Israelites, who took them all in battle. 20For it was the LORD himself who hardened their hearts to wage war against Israel, so that he might destroy them totally, exterminating them without mercy, as the LORD had commanded Moses.

21At that time Joshua went and destroyed the Anakites from the hill country: from Hebron, Debir and Anab, from all the hill country of Judah, and from all the hill country of Israel. Joshua totally destroyed them and their towns. 22No

NRSV

16So Joshua took all that land: the hill country and all the Negeb and all the land of Goshen and the lowland and the Arabah and the hill country of Israel and its lowland, 17from Mount Halak, which rises toward Seir, as far as Baal-gad in the valley of Lebanon below Mount Hermon. He took all their kings, struck them down, and put them to death. 18Joshua made war a long time with all those kings. 19There was not a town that made peace with the Israelites, except the Hivites, the inhabitants of Gibeon; all were taken in battle. 20For it was the LORD's doing to harden their hearts so that they would come against Israel in battle, in order that they might be utterly destroyed, and might receive no mercy, but be exterminated, just as the LORD had commanded Moses.

21At that time Joshua came and wiped out the Anakim from the hill country, from Hebron, from Debir, from Anab, and from all the hill country of Judah, and from all the hill country of Israel;

NIV

Anakites were left in Israelite territory; only in Gaza, Gath and Ashdod did any survive. [23]So Joshua took the entire land, just as the LORD had directed Moses, and he gave it as an inheritance to Israel according to their tribal divisions.

Then the land had rest from war.

12 These are the kings of the land whom the Israelites had defeated and whose territory they took over east of the Jordan, from the Arnon Gorge to Mount Hermon, including all the eastern side of the Arabah:

[2]Sihon king of the Amorites,
who reigned in Heshbon. He ruled from Aroer on the rim of the Arnon Gorge—from the middle of the gorge—to the Jabbok River, which is the border of the Ammonites. This included half of Gilead. [3]He also ruled over the eastern Arabah from the Sea of Kinnereth[a] to the Sea of the Arabah (the Salt Sea[b]), to Beth Jeshimoth, and then southward below the slopes of Pisgah.

[4]And the territory of Og king of Bashan,
one of the last of the Rephaites, who reigned in Ashtaroth and Edrei. [5]He ruled over Mount Hermon, Salecah, all of Bashan to the border of the people of Geshur and Maacah, and half of Gilead to the border of Sihon king of Heshbon.

[6]Moses, the servant of the LORD, and the Israelites conquered them. And Moses the servant of the LORD gave their land to the Reubenites, the Gadites and the half-tribe of Manasseh to be their possession.

[7]These are the kings of the land that Joshua and the Israelites conquered on the west side of the Jordan, from Baal Gad in the Valley of Lebanon to Mount Halak, which rises toward Seir (their lands Joshua gave as an inheritance to the tribes of Israel according to their tribal divisions— [8]the hill country, the western foothills, the Arabah, the mountain slopes, the desert and the Negev—the lands of the Hittites, Amorites, Canaanites, Perizzites, Hivites and Jebusites):

[9]the king of Jericho	one
the king of Ai (near Bethel)	one
[10]the king of Jerusalem	one

a3 That is, Galilee   b3 That is, the Dead Sea

NRSV

Joshua utterly destroyed them with their towns. [22]None of the Anakim was left in the land of the Israelites; some remained only in Gaza, in Gath, and in Ashdod. [23]So Joshua took the whole land, according to all that the LORD had spoken to Moses; and Joshua gave it for an inheritance to Israel according to their tribal allotments. And the land had rest from war.

12 Now these are the kings of the land, whom the Israelites defeated, whose land they occupied beyond the Jordan toward the east, from the Wadi Arnon to Mount Hermon, with all the Arabah eastward: [2]King Sihon of the Amorites who lived at Heshbon, and ruled from Aroer, which is on the edge of the Wadi Arnon, and from the middle of the valley as far as the river Jabbok, the boundary of the Ammonites, that is, half of Gilead, [3]and the Arabah to the Sea of Chinneroth eastward, and in the direction of Beth-jeshimoth, to the sea of the Arabah, the Dead Sea,[a] southward to the foot of the slopes of Pisgah; [4]and King Og[b] of Bashan, one of the last of the Rephaim, who lived at Ashtaroth and at Edrei [5]and ruled over Mount Hermon and Salecah and all Bashan to the boundary of the Geshurites and the Maacathites, and over half of Gilead to the boundary of King Sihon of Heshbon. [6]Moses, the servant of the LORD, and the Israelites defeated them; and Moses the servant of the LORD gave their land for a possession to the Reubenites and the Gadites and the half-tribe of Manasseh.

[7]The following are the kings of the land whom Joshua and the Israelites defeated on the west side of the Jordan, from Baal-gad in the valley of Lebanon to Mount Halak, that rises toward Seir (and Joshua gave their land to the tribes of Israel as a possession according to their allotments, [8]in the hill country, in the lowland, in the Arabah, in the slopes, in the wilderness, and in the Negeb, the land of the Hittites, Amorites, Canaanites, Perizzites, Hivites, and Jebusites):

[9] the king of Jericho	one
the king of Ai, which is next to Bethel	one
[10] the king of Jerusalem	one
the king of Hebron	one
[11] the king of Jarmuth	one
the king of Lachish	one

a Heb Salt Sea   b Gk: Heb the boundary of King Og

NIV		NRSV	
the king of Hebron	one	12 the king of Eglon	one
11the king of Jarmuth	one	the king of Gezer	one
the king of Lachish	one	13 the king of Debir	one
12the king of Eglon	one	the king of Geder	one
the king of Gezer	one	14 the king of Hormah	one
13the king of Debir	one	the king of Arad	one
the king of Geder	one	15 the king of Libnah	one
14the king of Hormah	one	the king of Adullam	one
the king of Arad	one	16 the king of Makkedah	one
15the king of Libnah	one	the king of Bethel	one
the king of Adullam	one	17 the king of Tappuah	one
16the king of Makkedah	one	the king of Hepher	one
the king of Bethel	one	18 the king of Aphek	one
17the king of Tappuah	one	the king of Lasharon	one
the king of Hepher	one	19 the king of Madon	one
18the king of Aphek	one	the king of Hazor	one
the king of Lasharon	one	20 the king of Shimron-meron	one
19the king of Madon	one	the king of Achshaph	one
the king of Hazor	one	21 the king of Taanach	one
20the king of Shimron Meron	one	the king of Megiddo	one
the king of Acshaph	one	22 the king of Kedesh	one
21the king of Taanach	one	the king of Jokneam in Carmel	one
the king of Megiddo	one	23 the king of Dor in Naphath-dor	one
22the king of Kedesh	one	the king of Goiim in Galilee,*a*	one
the king of Jokneam in Carmel	one	24 the king of Tirzah	one
23the king of Dor (in Naphoth Dor*a*)	one	thirty-one kings in all.	
the king of Goyim in Gilgal	one		
24the king of Tirzah	one		
thirty-one kings in all.			

*a*23 Or *in the heights of Dor*

a Gk: Heb *Gilgal*

COMMENTARY

The summary of the northern campaign (11:16-20) serves as the beginning of the summary of the entire war of conquest (11:23–12:24). The emphasis on kings and the significance of Yahweh's provocation have been discussed already. The first summary concludes with a seemingly unrelated note that Joshua defeated the Anakim from Hebron, Debir, and Anab (11:21), major towns in the heart of Judah, and from the rest of Judah and Israel (note the geographical anachronism). The Anakim were strong giants (Deut 9:2), and they are said to remain in the Philistine towns that in the late seventh century BCE lay in Egyptian-

controlled territory well beyond Josiah's control. The Anakim were Judah's own indigenous giants, analogous to the Rephaim, Emim, and Zamzummim who were dispossessed by Yahweh in the accounts of Deuteronomy 2. If Joshua 12–14, containing further summary and introduction, were bracketed, the reference to Joshua's giving Israel its inheritances, mentioned here for the first time in the book of Joshua, could flow cleanly into 15:1. It is thus not a coincidence that the story that immediately precedes 15:1 concerns Caleb's inheritance of Hebron, whose earlier name was the "town of Arba," the greatest of the

Anakim. The repetition of the concluding formula in both 11:23 and 14:15, "the land had rest from war" (a deuteronomistic formula; see 14:15; Judg 3:11, 30; 5:31; 8:28), confirms that the account of the whole, in which the grant to Judah is both the first and the most extensive land grant on the west side of the Jordan, lays great stress on the conquest and disposition of the first of David's towns, Hebron. This is probably also why Joshua plays his most extensive role in the Tetrateuch as a secondary addition to the narrative of spying out Hebron with Caleb in Numbers 13–14 (note the Anakim in Num 13:22, 28, 33; see Introduction and discussion of 14:6-15).

The grand summary of the war of conquest begins with a cover statement (11:23), then gives two lists of kings, those defeated on the east side of the Jordan (12:1-6) and those on the west side (12:7-24). The first list includes just Sihon and Og, who have already been referred to several times. Og is said to be one of the last of the Rephaim, another race of giants who once inhabited the lands of Israel (Deut 3:11). Traditionally the Rephaim were the "hale" ones, mostly upper-class ancestors sufficiently robust and vital to survive death and live in the underworld (Job 26:5; Isa 14:9; 26:14). Living warriors borrowed the title to suggest that they would be able to survive death. The territory of the kingdoms of Sihon and Og is delineated, and it is made clear that the two and a half eastern tribes have their title to that land from Moses. This brief description previews the more detailed account in 13:8-33.

The second list is thought by many to be an independent source. Josiah may have drawn up a list of towns to be brought under his jurisdiction to the west of the Jordan, including some abandoned settlements; recall that a "king" represents the embodiment of a jurisdiction. The inclusion of lists and catalogs was popular with ancient narrators. The list contains thirty-one kings in the MT, twenty-nine in the LXX. The meaning of the word "one" (אחד 'eḥād), which follows each place name, is an intriguing mystery; it is missing from the most important LXX MSS. The overall description of the territory that introduces the list moves from north to south, possibly because the immediately preceding section ended with the territory of Og in the northern Transjordan. This list of kings begins by following more or less the order of appearance in Joshua until it reaches Geder, Hormah, and Arad, which lie in the south but are not mentioned in Joshua 1–11. The narrative order resumes with Libnah and Makkedah, to which Adullam is added. The rest of the list shows little order, except that certain places are roughly adjacent to each other, like Adullam, near Libnah and Makkedah; Tappuah, near Bethel; Hepher, near Aphek and possibly Lasharon (if it is in fact a place name); Taanach, near Megiddo; and Jokneam, near Dor. The "king of Goiim in Galilee" is of dubious identity. The MT has "Gilgal" for the LXX's "Galilee" (cf. NRSV and NIV), and "Goiim" (גוים gôyim) means simply "nations" (cf. Isa 9:1).

The inclusion of Gezer, where Canaanites are said to remain (16:10; Judg 1:29), shows that the list is indeed a list of kings who embody sovereignties or jurisdictions, and not a list of localities. As such, it represents not destroyed towns or even simply eliminated kings, but one by one the separate jurisdictions that Josiah means to appropriate, establishing in place of their multiplicity a single sovereignty based on a single law sanctioned by a single cult under one single God (cf. Deut 6:4).

REFLECTIONS

The final summary of the conquest comes as a list of kings. Given the appalling incidence of mass slaughter in the narrative of conquest, this focus comes as a bit of a surprise. It invites us to engage in an exercise that is almost always instructive when we are confronted with a binary opposition of any kind. That exercise is to look for the "hidden third." What is missing, the interpreter may ask, in the choice between two alternatives? What in the case of Joshua might be missing in the distinction between Canaanite and Israelite as categories? If "Canaanite" means the kings of the Canaanites, as it does in this passage, then we may spot an opening that suggests that subjects, in contrast to kings, may fall into a different category from that of kings, despite the earlier narrative. If so, the king's subjects of the one category and those of the other might fall into a single class, one opposed to kings. In such a new binary opposition, the missing third might be discovered to be the debt enslaved, possessing the characteristic that earlier grouped Rahab with the escaped slaves of Israel (see Commentary on 2:1–6:27). In this case, the narrator has already invited us to inquire about the "hidden third."

In our church life as much as elsewhere, we are frequently confronted with seemingly all-encompassing alternatives, from trivial matters to the sublime. There are people who dress up for church and those who do not. There are those who claim to have a personal saving relationship with Jesus and those who do not. There is social justice and personal piety. There are those who baptize infants and those who do not. There are those who go to church and those who do not. There are the married and the unmarried, those with children and those without, those who own their own home and those who do not, those with a college degree and those without.

Whenever we realize that the world has been dichotomized, it is worth asking whether the assumptions behind the dichotomy are as true as they at first seem. While there is, given the "descent rule" in the history of American racism, an important social reality to the simple distinction between "black" and "white" in American culture, it is also a profoundly false distinction. One person confessed that when she was quite young and heard the words *black* and *white,* she was confused. She looked around at her classmates and saw people of Chinese, Filipino, Japanese, African, and Nordic descent, and she looked at the color of their skin: ivory, biscuit, buff, brick, sandalwood, clay, tobacco, hazelnut, and so forth. We may become irritated with the "rowdy, assertive babble about definitions and categories" that other people use, but how often do we examine our own cherished assumptions about how the world divides up?[96]

Looking for the hidden third also has the propensity to lead to compromise. For instance, a reviewer of essays by the Israeli writer Amos Oz points out his "political conviction . . . that the struggle between Israel and the Palestinians is a struggle of 'right against right,' that it is futile to insist on pure justice. Compromise, however inconsistent and unsatisfying, is the only solution. 'I was not born to blow rams' horns and liberate the land from the 'foreign yoke,' Mr. Oz writes."[97]

96. The phrase is from Frank Kermode, in *The New York Times Book Review,* July 9, 1995, 7.
97. Tova Reich in *The New York Times Book Review,* June 25, 1995, 18.

JOSHUA 13:1–21:45

JOSHUA REDISTRIBUTES THE LAND

OVERVIEW

Joshua and his men have conquered the land by dispossessing its holders and barbarously putting them to death. Now, in the pattern of the war leader, Joshua undertakes to distribute the confiscated land to his men and their families. Until now the Israelites have obediently forborne the taking of booty, a routine means of compensation, but it is high time for them to receive grants of land. The distribution is told as a story in which each tribe is granted a portion of land defined by lists of towns or regions or descriptions of boundaries. Modern readers are liable to find this part of the book of Joshua of less interest than the earlier part. The pace of the story slows so as hardly to seem like a story at all. Precisely where a given tribe's territory lies can be of little interest to anyone other than those directly involved at the time. Twenty-six centuries later, the interpreter may know little about the presumptions, stresses, contentions, and surprises contained in the account of allocation that no doubt gripped the interest of its first hearers.

Indeed, unlike the modern reader, the ancient hearer would have found this part of the story of great interest, including many details that are now lost to us, since it dealt with the most important factor in the life of practically every person in the ancient world: access to land. In North America and many other parts of the world today, what most tends to attract attention is violence and sex. In Joshua's world, it was violence and land.

This story is a fictionalized account of an existing administrative arrangement. Such fictionalizations are not uncommon in pre-modern literature, and in talking about them historians will sometimes say that a scheme or organization has been "narrativized." This story, however, would have been of limited, and now unknown, administrative usefulness. There is reason to believe that the tribal lists existed at least in part before Hezekiah's or Josiah's historian made use of them. The descriptions of the tribal allotments are quite uneven, as though they might have been incorporated as available from haphazard sources: Some are detailed, some spare; some consist mainly of town lists or of regional descriptions, others of boundary descriptions, and no tribe is given a full description using both types of material. They appear to be at best only partly adjusted to fit Josiah's particular administrative purposes. Comparable ancient Near Eastern lists often appear in administrative texts, including those dealing with landholdings, which are usually already in the hands of their holders, as they are for the most part in Joshua 13–19.[98]

The possible dates of the supposed constituent lists are much debated. Whatever the dates of the incorporated lists, the story of the allotment comes from the deuteronomist, though it may be based on an earlier version from the court of Hezekiah. Given the variety of the descriptions of the different allotments and the schematized nature of the whole, the primary point of the allotment cannot be administrative, but must involve the story as such. Moreover, the story seems designed to illustrate not just the range of the assertive lord's reconquest, which is immediately said to fall significantly short of its goal, but more important the magnitude of his momentous capacity to make land grants at will in the territories he does control.

A later priestly hand has introduced Eleazar into the picture next to Joshua, but only in the

---

98. Richard S. Hess, "Asking Historical Questions of Joshua 13–19: Recent Discussion Concerning the Date of the Boundary Lists," in *Faith, Tradition, and History: Old Testament Historiography in Its Near Eastern Context*, ed. A. R. Millard, James K. Hoffmeier, and David W. Baker (Winona Lake, Ind.: Eisenbrauns, 1994) 191-205.

frame of the allotments, and spuriously named ahead of Joshua (14:1; 18:1; 19:51; 21:1-2; in 13:7 and 14:6, Joshua functions on his own or with the tribal heads, the deuteronomistic concept). The same hand may also be responsible for mentions of the tent of meeting and the use of the characteristic priestly word for "tribe" (מטה *maṭṭeh*) throughout the allotments. Overall there are many differences between the MT and the LXX in the text of this whole section, suggesting that what often happens in the transmission of MSS has happened here: Attempts to make clearer a somewhat irregular text, which furthermore was susceptible to scribal adjustment as soon as political and administrative circumstances began to change, have only made the text muddier.

The story emphasizes the role of Joshua as the supervisor of allocation. Three distinct notions of land redistribution are combined in the story, based on three different model contexts. Joshua plays the dominant role in each. The three contexts are the warlord's council or monarch's court, the village, and the tribe. In real life it was unusual for these three forms of redistribution to overlap. In the story of Joshua, they do overlap, so that none appears complete in itself, but only as part of a political metaphor with three discernible dimensions. Each dimension makes an essential contribution to what the deuteronomist wants to convey through the story of allotment.

The monarchic dimension emerges directly from the narrative plot of the book of Joshua, as one more of its numerous monarchic features. The military chief distributes captured land to his loyal retainers and supporters and their families. The monarch as conqueror represents a sovereign or arbitrary power. Joshua acts on his own sovereign's behalf, directing the lottery through which Yahweh makes the otherwise inscrutable allocation known. The imperiousness of Joshua's allocation becomes evident when it is remembered that from a tribal viewpoint tribal territories are not assigned by the state but are negotiated among the tribes. The monarch's arbitrariness emerges most conspicuously in 18:2-7. There Joshua first orders a survey for setting up the divisions of the land. Once the divisions are demarcated, the lottery takes place to determine which tribe gets which division. The premise of the narrative is that the tribes do not already inhabit a particular

territory, as though Joshua were like the king of Assyria, able to transfer whole populations, urban or tribal, from one location to another by divinely sanctioned fiat. There is little doubt that Josiah accommodated the "tribes" under his sovereignty in their usual territories, at least for the most part, but such is not the message of this story. This story's message is that the monarch, in obedience to God, claims the power to put people where he wants—if he wants. The modern reader might regard God's command to slaughter innocent people as the most outrageous atrocity in the book of Joshua. Ancient tribalists probably would not have agreed, but were likely to have regarded Joshua's arrogation of the right to assign tribal territories as the greatest offense, if they grasped the implication of this story.

This dimension is probably the main one behind the use of the term נחלה (*naḥălâ*), translated "inheritance," although the term has an important part to play in the other dimensions as well. The basic meaning of this term is "land grant" and of its verb "to receive or make a land grant."[99] Such a grant frequently becomes heritable, so it is not surprising that the term can take on the meaning of inheritance. But inheritance is not its primary meaning in Joshua, even though the tribal territories are taken as permanent. The story of Joshua does not emphasize the land as it is to be inherited by later generations, but rather land that is to be granted and received as a grant now, when both strong men and commoners are forced to respond to the pretensions of this belligerent upstart. The grant originates with Yahweh, the leading conqueror, who here carries out the sovereign decision to give to the "Israelites" the land that belongs to the "Canaanites."

In the Deuteronomistic History, the grant, a basis of the covenant, is made on condition; hence it is limited as to heritability from the start. Typically such conditions lie within the prerogative of the sovereign making the grant. Even when grants are made "in perpetuity," they can be reassigned with little or no difficulty, since even such grants remain in effect only at the pleasure of the grantor. Many examples of such reassignment are known from ancient texts. In this di-

99. P. Kyle McCarter and Robert B. Coote, "The Spatula Inscription from Byblos," *BASOR* 212 (December 1973) 20-21 (with correction, *BASOR* 214, 41).

mension, the grants may be represented as heritable to the extent that Josiah wishes to be seen empowering the "Israelite" debtors against the depredations of "Canaanite" large landholders and creditors engaged in agricultural trade. This dimension, however, addresses more than the peasants of tribal Israel. It also addresses the powerful among Josiah's followers or among those he wants to coax into following him, to whom the portrayal of allocation promises a grant not so much of land, but of the rights to the produce of lands farmed by the peasants of the towns and villages named in the form of taxes, rents, or tribute.

The second dimension concerns the village. Villagers in ancient Palestine typically practiced a form of periodic repartitioning of arable land by lot. The participants in the lottery were those who headed households who did not hold parts of the land itself, but cultivation rights to the whole of the arable land. This practice, which was widespread in agrarian societies and can still be found in many parts of the world today, had a number of purposes. In Palestine it made it easier to leave fallow a large proportion of the arable land belonging to the farmers of a given village as a single block of land. The village animals could then graze in and manure this fallow block without wandering into the patchwork of adjacent cultivated plots that would exist if the fallow land were not so blocked. Thus each year a different section of the village's arable land was available for cultivation. As year by year cultivation rotated from section to section, the land to be cultivated was repartitioned by lot among the farming families. Redistribution spread the advantage of farming the better lands among the families at random. It also allowed the village to pay its taxes on arable land as a commonality, affording leverage against the tax collector.[100] The repartitional lottery forms the background to a number of biblical texts, including Pss 16:5-6; 125:3; and Mic 2:5.

In this dimension, the land of Canaan is like a village's total arable land, Joshua is the foremost elder in the village, and the tribal heads, where they figure, are the heads of households holding cultivation rights in the village. The Israelite tribes represent villagers who find their cultivation rights newly authorized, like peasants whose debts have

been remitted, rather than relentlessly jeopardized or already lost through unpaid arrears. Periodic redistribution stood for values that villagers held dear, such as security, stability, cooperation, solidarity, productivity, and equal opportunity. It is necessary not to romanticize these values, but to recognize that when the deuteronomist "narrativizes" the tribal territories as he does, among other things he confirms an entire set of popular ideals consonant with Josiah's radical program of debt reform.

The third dimension is tribal. As already seen, tribes tended to define themselves from the top down according to putative genealogies, often through tribal heads in negotiation with state authorities. The dynamics of internal tribal politics, and of relations between tribes and rival powers, were extremely fluid and variable.[101] Tribal states like the one projected by the Deuteronomistic History are by no means rare in the history of the Middle East, but their notions of tribal constituencies were subject to erratic alteration. Nevertheless tribal ideals typically expressed egalitarianism, opposition to the state, a seamless solidarity to which all contributed voluntarily, pride of superiority over the mere peasant, and the honor of both self-reliance and mutual aid. These are the ideals that the deuteronomist can affirm through his story of the allocation of the land of Canaan among the tribes of Israel.

More often than not tribes are a bother to strong rulers, who prefer to keep them under control on the periphery of their realm. Why would a centralizing monarch like Josiah agree to have his nation portrayed as a great tribal family? Josiah might instead be expected to follow in the footsteps of Solomon and attempt to neutralize tribal loyalty and influence in his realm. This is what many scholars believe Solomon did, on the basis of the list of districts in 1 Kgs 4:7-19. One reason why Josiah went along with the ancient Davidic concept of tribal Israel is that, although it is impossible to know for certain, it is doubtful that Israelite tribal sentiments played a significant role in his time independent of central policy, except possibly in Judah and Benjamin. Josiah had little to lose and much to gain from this portrayal,

---

100. Robert B. Coote, *Early Israel: A New Horizon* (Minneapolis: Fortress, 1990) 20.

101. Philip S. Khoury and Joseph Kostiner, *Tribes and State Formation in the Middle East* (Berkeley: University of California Press, 1990) 38-44, 109-26, 252-75; Coote, *Early Israel*, 75-83.

since he meant to control both it and the politics it represented. In its treatment of the tribes of Israel, the Deuteronomistic History clearly announced that among putative Israelites no tribal politics would be licensed that did not fall within the definitions laid down by the court in Jerusalem. The recognition of the tribes of Israel had been an important facet of central reform under Hezekiah and probably Manasseh, and when Josiah inherited this strategy he saw no reason to repudiate it.

In the Deuteronomistic History, the tribes of Israel play an important role before David. After David, they play practically no role at all, being scarcely mentioned in the book of Kings. Presumably like Hezekiah's scribe before him, the deuteronomist got his concept of the tribes from JE, the Davidic history of early Israel, with its Israelite supplement as reappropriated by Hezekiah's court. The tribes are in J because in the Late Bronze and Early Iron ages early Israel was a powerful, but shifting and variable, tribal entity, and in the tenth century BCE, when J was written, the tribal concept of Israel remained a lively and potent force. The portrayal of the tribes in J, however, is already highly idealized and stylized from the order of their birth, to their numbering exactly twelve over a period of several hundred years, to their stories, which are mainly two: the tension between Judah and Joseph, resolved in the crisis over Benjamin and in tearful reconciliation among all the tribal brothers, and their nearly problem-free solidarity in the exodus and desert trek, during which individual names scarcely appear, the same as under Joshua.[102] The fixed number of twelve tribes represents David's tribal policy, which, unlike Josiah, he was probably forced to adopt, because the tribes were strong and the monarchy weak. There is some indication of traditional relations and territories in J, especially in the etymologies of the tribes in Genesis 29–30 and the archaic blessings in Genesis 49. The overriding tribal issue in J, however, is the relationship between Judah and Joseph, the two core highland areas south and north, with Benjamin between them and the key to their reconciliation. This is practically a geographical constant in the history of Palestine, and thus it occurs also in Joshua 14–18 (see 18:11).

There is an evident element of reality in Joshua's portrayal of the tribes. As indicated, the lists of towns and borders probably come from existing documents of some kind. In several cases the territories represent natural regions, though the bearing of this point can be questioned; historically, tribes in Palestine claim not natural regions over an extended period of time, but changeable territories determined by a complex combination of geographical, demographic, economic, and especially political factors. Again it is essential to remember that while some tribal names may persist for some time in the history of Syria and Palestine, the usual pattern is for at least some names and relationships to change in little more than decades, making the persistence of twelve names in exactly the same genealogical relationship over several centuries of extreme social change implausible. Seven years after the fall of Samaria, in about 715 BCE, Sargon II resettled four named Arab tribes within the bounds of former Israel.[103] The deuteronomist makes no mention of these tribes, even though they must have quickly related with whatever may have been left of old Israelite tribal identities at the time. In any case, the tribal territories in Joshua are based on a maximalist, hardly practical notion, that has, for example, highland Judah incorporating Ashdod and Gaza (15:47) and coastal Asher incorporating Tyre (19:29), bounds that are politically quite improbable.

The tribal dimension does more than affirm a set of supposed tribal ideals. It also expresses specific political relationships, as the tribal metaphor always does. In Joshua's account, as in Judges 1, Judah comes first and is given the most complete treatment of all the tribes (Joshua 15). This reflects the Davidic origin of the book of Joshua, despite Joshua's Ephraimite origin. Next, the boundaries of Ephraim and the western half of Manasseh are given. Their town lists are missing. The statement is made, however, that Manasseh includes major towns within the bounds of Issachar and Asher (17:11-13). Clearly the concept includes more than a given territory. Manasseh is the heartland of political Israel during nearly its entire history, from pre-monarchic times to Josiah. Its dominance is expressed in its inclu-

---

102. Robert B. Coote and David Robert Ord, *The Bible's First History* (Philadelphia: Fortress, 1989) 167-206, 257-97.

103. D. D. Luckenbill, *Ancient Records of Assyria and Babylonia,* vol. 2 (Chicago: University of Chicago Press, 1927) par. 17; available also in James B. Pritchard, ed., *The Ancient Near East: An Anthology of Texts and Pictures* (Princeton: Princeton University Press, 1958) 196, and Pritchard, *Ancient Near Eastern Texts Relating to the Old Testament,* 3rd ed. (Princeton: Princeton University Press, 1969) 286.

sion of the likes of Megiddo, one of the great towns of Palestine in many ages, not least the age of Josiah. By now five tribes have received their allotments. Once the two tribes of Joseph, Ephraim and Manasseh, have received their allotments, the scene shifts to Shiloh in Ephraim, where the seven remaining tribes are dealt with,

starting with Benjamin (Joshua 18–19). Following a list of towns of refuge for manslayers (Joshua 20), a list of the towns and pasturage assigned to the Levites brings the distribution to a close.[104]

104. See Kurt Elliger, "Tribes, Territories of," in *IDB*, 4:701-10; Zecharia Kallai, "Tribes, Territories of," *IDBSup*, 920-23.

JOSHUA 13:1-7, "REDISTRIBUTE THIS LAND"

NIV

13 When Joshua was old and well advanced in years, the LORD said to him, "You are very old, and there are still very large areas of land to be taken over.

²"This is the land that remains: all the regions of the Philistines and Geshurites: ³from the Shihor River on the east of Egypt to the territory of Ekron on the north, all of it counted as Canaanite (the territory of the five Philistine rulers in Gaza, Ashdod, Ashkelon, Gath and Ekron—that of the Avvites); ⁴from the south, all the land of the Canaanites, from Arah of the Sidonians as far as Aphek, the region of the Amorites, ⁵the area of the Gebalites*; and all Lebanon to the east, from Baal Gad below Mount Hermon to Lebo* Hamath.

⁶"As for all the inhabitants of the mountain regions from Lebanon to Misrephoth Maim, that is, all the Sidonians, I myself will drive them out before the Israelites. Be sure to allocate this land to Israel for an inheritance, as I have instructed you, ⁷and divide it as an inheritance among the nine tribes and half of the tribe of Manasseh."

a5 That is, the area of Byblos   b5 Or to the entrance to

NRSV

13 Now Joshua was old and advanced in years; and the LORD said to him, "You are old and advanced in years, and very much of the land still remains to be possessed. ²This is the land that still remains: all the regions of the Philistines, and all those of the Geshurites ³(from the Shihor, which is east of Egypt, northward to the boundary of Ekron, it is reckoned as Canaanite; there are five rulers of the Philistines, those of Gaza, Ashdod, Ashkelon, Gath, and Ekron), and those of the Avvim ⁴in the south; all the land of the Canaanites, and Mearah that belongs to the Sidonians, to Aphek, to the boundary of the Amorites, ⁵and the land of the Gebalites, and all Lebanon, toward the east, from Baal-gad below Mount Hermon to Lebo-hamath, ⁶all the inhabitants of the hill country from Lebanon to Misrephoth-maim, even all the Sidonians. I will myself drive them out from before the Israelite only allot the land to Israel for an inheritance, as I have commanded you. ⁷Now therefore divide this land for an inheritance to the nine tribes and the half-tribe of Manasseh."

COMMENTARY

Joshua is now all of a sudden old (14:10 suggests that five to seven years have passed since the beginning of the conquest), though not so old that "many years" cannot pass before his final address to Israel (23:1). This represents the deuteronomistic conception in which Joshua's career has three stages: He conquers, distributes the

land, and bids farewell. Joshua conquers what he can between his maturity and his old age. Much land within the ideal borders is left to conquer, but Joshua has come to the end of his fighting years and must go ahead and distribute what he has captured before he dies. When the distribution is complete, he dies, but before doing so he makes a final deuteronomistic speech, again in the pattern of Moses.

Much land remains to be possessed. This phrase at first seems to anticipate the frequent references to the incomplete conquest that follow (13:13; 14:12; 15:63; 16:10; 17:12-13, 15-18; Judg 1:21-35; 3:1-6). However, these later passages refer almost entirely to Canaanites remaining within or near the bounds of conquest described in Joshua 2–12. The notable exception is Judg 3:1-6, which refers for the most part to the same coastal territory described in the present passage but then defines its inhabitants according to the standard list of seven "nations," minus the Girgashites. The land described in the present passage falls into three sections, covering the entire Mediterranean coastland from south to north, with most of interior Lebanon as the hinterland of the third section.

The first section of land covers the territory of the Philistines. This includes the Geshur in the south (cf. 1 Sam 27:8), different from the Geshur in the north, mentioned in 12:5. Of course, for the Late Bronze Age the confederated pentapolis under five Philistine rulers is an anachronism; the Philistines did not come to Palestine before the twelfth century BCE, and the pentapolis is unlikely to have formed long before its earliest historical attestation, which probably occurs in 1 Samuel 4–6 in the Davidic era, two hundred years later. The Avvim or Avvites are the pre-Philistine giants of the region of the kind that Yahweh regularly dispossesses in favor of new inhabitants (Deut 2:23; cf. the Rephaim in Josh 13:12) as paradigms for dispossession of the Canaanites. The second section of land covers the "Canaanite" coast between the first and third sections, Philistia and Phoenicia, which were culturally distinct. This section is probably designated "from Arah to Aphek," as in the NIV, even though Arah is said to be under the rule of the Sidonians, the contemporary term for "Phoenicians." The third section comprises the Phoenician towns and their hinterland as far as the Anti-Lebanon mountains. The dominant rulers are those of Byblos (Gebal) and Sidon.

In the long history of Palestine, the stretch of coastal lowland from next to the Sinai Peninsula to what is now Lebanon has often been part of a different cultural or political matrix from that of the highland, or hill country. Nowhere in the Bible is this difference better illustrated than in the story of Samson, who as the rough-and-ready highlander smashes, bumps, jostles, pushes, and shoves his blunt way through adventures, but never slices or cuts, sharp actions that are left to the supposedly refined and civilized lowlanders.[105] Material cultural differences between lowland and highland similar to those that contributed to the ethnic distinction between "Israelite" and "Canaanite"—a distinction that was always at least as much political and social as cultural—are attested in other regions of the Near East possessing a comparable topography.[106] During the roughly five hundred years of Israelite monarchies, the kings of Israel and Judah rarely controlled the great towns along the coast. Towns in this region thrived on sea trade and great swaths of arable land, which enabled them to withstand highlander sieges and to field chariots in battle, which highlanders on their own could not do. Lowland towns tended to remain under the power of local rulers or oligarchies, who themselves were frequently overpowered by imperial forces and brought directly under the sway of Egypt or Mesopotamia. Highland monarchs and chieftains frequently allied with lowland powers, local or imperial. During the reign of Josiah, who was probably allied with the rulers of Assyria or Egypt who were in virtual full control of the Palestine coastal area, highland rule along the coast could be nothing more than an ambition, part of a scheme presented for political effect. Even Josiah's supposed Davidic model fails him on this score, since particularly along the northern coast David could do no more than make agreements with existing rulers.

The NRSV is probably correct to suppose that Yahweh's promise in v. 6 refers to all the sections and peoples named, not just the highland Sidonians, as in the NIV. With the conquest of this territory in the offing, Yahweh instructs Joshua to distribute what territory he has.

105. David E. Bynum, "Samson as a Biblical *phēr oreskōos* [Wild Man of the Mountains]," in *Text and Tradition: The Hebrew Bible and Folklore*, ed. Susan Niditch (Atlanta: Scholars Press, 1990) 57-73.

106. Gloria A. London, "A Comparison of Two Contemporaneous Lifestyles of the Late Second Millennium B.C.E.," *BASOR* 273 (1989) 37-55.

REFLECTIONS

Much of the literature available for Bible study tends to be somewhat more tranquil and aseptic than the Bible itself. This is particularly true when it comes to dealing with matters of land and property. Land was the most important material resource for the people of the Bible, and yet it is rarely discussed, either for what it meant in the biblical period or for how it might shed light on our attitudes to the nearest modern equivalent: capital. One of the benefits of the book of Joshua is that it brings us quickly and unavoidably into the turmoil, tribulation, anxiety, and violence of land relations in ancient Palestine, and the sharing of resources in our own world, where often the same turmoil prevails.

JOSHUA 13:8-33, LAND FOR THE TRIBES BEYOND THE JORDAN

NIV

⁸The other half of Manasseh,ᵃ the Reubenites and the Gadites had received the inheritance that Moses had given them east of the Jordan, as he, the servant of the LORD, had assigned it to them.

⁹It extended from Aroer on the rim of the Arnon Gorge, and from the town in the middle of the gorge, and included the whole plateau of Medeba as far as Dibon, ¹⁰and all the towns of Sihon king of the Amorites, who ruled in Heshbon, out to the border of the Ammonites. ¹¹It also included Gilead, the territory of the people of Geshur and Maacah, all of Mount Hermon and all Bashan as far as Salecah— ¹²that is, the whole kingdom of Og in Bashan, who had reigned in Ashtaroth and Edrei and had survived as one of the last of the Rephaites. Moses had defeated them and taken over their land. ¹³But the Israelites did not drive out the people of Geshur and Maacah, so they continue to live among the Israelites to this day.

¹⁴But to the tribe of Levi he gave no inheritance, since the offerings made by fire to the LORD, the God of Israel, are their inheritance, as he promised them.

¹⁵This is what Moses had given to the tribe of Reuben, clan by clan:

¹⁶The territory from Aroer on the rim of the

NRSV

8With the other half-tribe of Manassehᵃ the Reubenites and the Gadites received their inheritance, which Moses gave them, beyond the Jordan eastward, as Moses the servant of the LORD gave them: ⁹from Aroer, which is on the edge of the Wadi Arnon, and the town that is in the middle of the valley, and all the tableland fromᵇ Medeba as far as Dibon; ¹⁰and all the cities of King Sihon of the Amorites, who reigned in Heshbon, as far as the boundary of the Ammonites; ¹¹and Gilead, and the region of the Geshurites and Maacathites, and all Mount Hermon, and all Bashan to Salecah; ¹²all the kingdom of Og in Bashan, who reigned in Ashtaroth and in Edrei (he alone was left of the survivors of the Rephaim); these Moses had defeated and driven out. ¹³Yet the Israelites did not drive out the Geshurites or the Maacathites; but Geshur and Maacath live within Israel to this day.

14To the tribe of Levi alone Moses gave no inheritance; the offerings by fire to the LORD God of Israel are their inheritance, as he said to them.

15Moses gave an inheritance to the tribe of the Reubenites according to their clans. ¹⁶Their territory was from Aroer, which is on the edge of the Wadi Arnon, and the town that is in the middle of the valley, and all the tableland by Medeba; ¹⁷with Heshbon, and all its towns that are in the tableland; Dibon, and Bamoth-baal, and Beth-baal-meon, ¹⁸and

ᵃ8 Hebrew *With it* (that is, with the other half of Manasseh)

ᵃ Cn: Heb *With it*   ᵇ Compare Gk: Heb lacks *from*

NIV

Arnon Gorge, and from the town in the middle of the gorge, and the whole plateau past Medeba ¹⁷to Heshbon and all its towns on the plateau, including Dibon, Bamoth Baal, Beth Baal Meon, ¹⁸Jahaz, Kedemoth, Mephaath, ¹⁹Kiriathaim, Sibmah, Zereth Shahar on the hill in the valley, ²⁰Beth Peor, the slopes of Pisgah, and Beth Jeshimoth ²¹—all the towns on the plateau and the entire realm of Sihon king of the Amorites, who ruled at Heshbon. Moses had defeated him and the Midianite chiefs, Evi, Rekem, Zur, Hur and Reba—princes allied with Sihon—who lived in that country. ²²In addition to those slain in battle, the Israelites had put to the sword Balaam son of Beor, who practiced divination. ²³The boundary of the Reubenites was the bank of the Jordan. These towns and their villages were the inheritance of the Reubenites, clan by clan.

²⁴This is what Moses had given to the tribe of Gad, clan by clan:

²⁵The territory of Jazer, all the towns of Gilead and half the Ammonite country as far as Aroer, near Rabbah; ²⁶and from Heshbon to Ramath Mizpah and Betonim, and from Mahanaim to the territory of Debir; ²⁷and in the valley, Beth Haram, Beth Nimrah, Succoth and Zaphon with the rest of the realm of Sihon king of Heshbon (the east side of the Jordan, the territory up to the end of the Sea of Kinnereth^a). ²⁸These towns and their villages were the inheritance of the Gadites, clan by clan.

²⁹This is what Moses had given to the half-tribe of Manasseh, that is, to half the family of the descendants of Manasseh, clan by clan:

³⁰The territory extending from Mahanaim and including all of Bashan, the entire realm of Og king of Bashan—all the settlements of Jair in Bashan, sixty towns, ³¹half of Gilead, and Ashtaroth and Edrei (the royal cities of Og in Bashan). This was for the descendants of Makir son of Manasseh—for half of the sons of Makir, clan by clan.

³²This is the inheritance Moses had given when

NRSV

Jahaz, and Kedemoth, and Mephaath, ¹⁹and Kiriathaim, and Sibmah, and Zereth-shahar on the hill of the valley, ²⁰and Beth-peor, and the slopes of Pisgah, and Beth-jeshimoth, ²¹that is, all the towns of the tableland, and all the kingdom of King Sihon of the Amorites, who reigned in Heshbon, whom Moses defeated with the leaders of Midian, Evi and Rekem and Zur and Hur and Reba, as princes of Sihon, who lived in the land. ²²Along with the rest of those they put to death, the Israelites also put to the sword Balaam son of Beor, who practiced divination. ²³And the border of the Reubenites was the Jordan and its banks. This was the inheritance of the Reubenites according to their families with their towns and villages.

24Moses gave an inheritance also to the tribe of the Gadites, according to their families. ²⁵Their territory was Jazer, and all the towns of Gilead, and half the land of the Ammonites, to Aroer, which is east of Rabbah, ²⁶and from Heshbon to Ramath-mizpeh and Betonim, and from Mahanaim to the territory of Debir,^a ²⁷and in the valley Beth-haram, Beth-nimrah, Succoth, and Zaphon, the rest of the kingdom of King Sihon of Heshbon, the Jordan and its banks, as far as the lower end of the Sea of Chinnereth, eastward beyond the Jordan. ²⁸This is the inheritance of the Gadites according to their clans, with their towns and villages.

29Moses gave an inheritance to the half-tribe of Manasseh; it was allotted to the half-tribe of the Manassites according to their families. ³⁰Their territory extended from Mahanaim, through all Bashan, the whole kingdom of King Og of Bashan, and all the settlements of Jair, which are in Bashan, sixty towns, ³¹and half of Gilead, and Ashtaroth, and Edrei, the towns of the kingdom of Og in Bashan; these were allotted to the people of Machir son of Manasseh according to their clans—for half the Machirites.

32These are the inheritances that Moses distributed in the plains of Moab, beyond the Jordan east of Jericho. ³³But to the tribe of Levi Moses gave no inheritance; the LORD God of Israel is their inheritance, as he said to them.

NIV

he was in the plains of Moab across the Jordan east of Jericho. [33]But to the tribe of Levi, Moses had given no inheritance; the LORD, the God of Israel, is their inheritance, as he promised them.

COMMENTARY

Before narrating the distribution of the land conquered west of the Jordan (chaps. 14–19), the narrator defines the land conquered by Moses east of the Jordan (13:8-13), just as he had earlier reviewed its conquest (1:12-15; Deut 2:24–3:22). He then defines the division of that land among the tribes of Reuben and Gad and half the tribe of Manasseh (13:15-32). Also included are two references to the tribe of Levi, who receives no land grant (13:14, 33).

Moses' triumph over the kings Sihon and Og serves as the great exemplar for dispossession by Israel, and the deuteronomist misses no opportunity to refer to it. As in chaps. 1–12, the capture of the territory of Sihon and Og is assumed to be complete. Sweeping conquest is one thing, total ethnic cleansing and the imposition of coercive jurisdiction another. Now for the first time it appears that the dispossession is incomplete; Geshurites and Maacathites survive, under the control of Moses' law. The possible implication of shifting the focus to kings rather than to the entire populace begins to be borne out. This is the first of five references in Joshua to incomplete dispossession (see 14:12; 15:63; 16:10; 17:12-13, 15-18). The inescapable and terrible force of Moses' law is exemplified: The Israelites kill Balaam (cf. Num 31:8) for practicing "divination" (Numbers 22–24) in violation of deuteronomistic law (Deut 18:10; 2 Kgs 17:17). This law is not alone in the OT in condemning "divination," which can include consulting the dead (1 Sam 28:8); the prophets condemn it, too, but nearly always for what the "diviner" says, in contexts where divining seems simply to parallel other mantic forms (see Isa 3:2; Jer 27:9; 29:8; Ezek 13:9; Mic 3:6, 8). In Gen 30:27, Jacob divines with no apparent stigma attached at all. Balaam is a particularly unfortunate victim of Moses' pogrom, since (according to his story in J) he obeyed Yahweh at

considerable personal risk and pronounced four blessings upon Israel, despite being hired by the king of Moab to curse them. But even Balaam admitted that Yahweh left him no choice in the matter, and the deuteronomist remembers him as a prophet whose vocation would have condemned him regardless and who would have cursed Israel for the king's pay if Yahweh had not stopped him (Deut 23:4-5; cf. Josh 24:9-10).

The names "Geshur" and "Maacah" can stand for the people of Geshur and Maacah, as often is the case with the term "Israel" (13:13). Thus the NIV translates "in the midst of Israel" in this verse as "among the Israelites." This seemingly minor point is actually quite important. The NRSV may be potentially misleading: "Israel" here does not mean a territory, whether state or tribal, a modern anachronism. In four of the five references to incomplete dispossession, a similar description occurs, but three different expressions are used. The same expression as in 13:13, "in the midst of" (בקרב *běqereb*) occurs in 16:10. That the text is referring to "the Ephraimites" (NIV) rather than to the territory of Ephraim is clear from 15:63. The third reference (in 17:12) is to a territory rather than to a people, and so it makes that distinction explicit: "in that land."

Long before Josiah, the Levites are seen to possess no arable land. In his ancient "blessing" of Levi, Jacob curses their notorious ire and promises to "apportion" them out—instead of giving them a portion—in Jacob and so disperse them in Israel (Gen 49:7). It is tempting to suppose that Jacob's curse gets it backward, since it is easier to imagine that the Levites' ire may result from their landlessness rather than the other way around. Instead of land, they are assigned towns to live in with pasturage for grazing livestock (chap. 21; Num 35:1-8). In the present section, the Levites are mentioned twice, first after the summary introduction (13:14) and then after the details of the allotments and the conclusion (13:33). Several of the Levites' towns with pasturage (chap. 21) lie east of the Jordan, so the narrator includes a reminder that while Levites are to be found east of the Jordan, they are not included in the apportionment of land there. Their "grant" is Yahweh, meaning the cult of Yahweh, supplied with the produce of the land by others (Deut 10:9; 14:22-29; 18:1-

8).[107] The Levites do not provide their own staples, but are wards of the monarchy, whether in their towns or at the central shrine. The phrase "the offerings by fire to" is missing from the LXX of 13:14; the two variants are juxtaposed in Deut 18:1-2. The Levites are discussed further in the Commentary on 21:1-45.

107. This idiom is the source of the word "clergy," which derives ultimately from the notion of service for God as κλῆρος (*klēros*), Greek for "lot" or "inheritance."

REFLECTIONS

The monarchic role is projected onto Moses, as it has been on Joshua, and not for the first time in Scripture, since Moses played a role akin to that of David in the house of David's early history, represented by the J strand in the Tetrateuch. The interpreter is reminded that the continual process of interpretation and reinterpretation of people, events, and passages as the Bible is produced over many hundreds of years often includes viewing the old in terms of the new, the unfamiliar in terms of the familiar, and the ostensibly unuseful in terms of the useful. This process of interpretation continues without a break to the present. Updating—making the text present today—entails the hermeneutical dilemma, with the inevitable benefits and perils, of loosening the grip of historical rootedness that defines the subject merely on its own terms.

The killing of Balaam reminds us once again of the dispensability of human beings to those in power who feel the need to put principle ahead of lives. Again the reader is faced with the profound clash of values between Josiah's publicized intent to end poverty in Israel and his unyielding determination to eliminate all sources of authority other than his own. The one requires the other, the revolutionary argument runs, and the lives of individuals cannot stand in the way of the greater good. Even people who do not stand to lose their lives immediately might find room for skepticism. Equivalents of this dilemma, with less at stake, frequently confront us: When can we be sure that some greater good really does justify the suffering or wrong along the way?

In some instances the answer is easy. No recognizable good can justify the deaths of millions in famine and of thousands in military purges. In other cases, the answer appears easy, but can become more complicated depending on perspective. Today so-called terrorism is frequently perpetrated in the name of the supposed greater good of national liberation. The outrage against this notion is nearly universal, even among those presumed to be its beneficiaries. Yet it is possible at least to begin to grasp the frustration of terrorists, without justifying their acts. In the land of Joshua, present-day Israel and the occupied territories of Palestine, for example, those able to countenance terrorism can point to the vast imbalance of Palestinian suffering resulting from the Israelis' struggle to secure the good of a Jewish state in Palestine. The justification of war itself is a grand and recurrent instance of the same problem. The extremities of war present genuine dilemmas in their own right. Toward the end of what many have called the last "Good War," for instance, the United States killed over a hundred thousand civilians of Hiroshima and Nagasaki in a successful attempt to avert the deaths of as many or more Americans and Japanese in the planned Allied invasion of Japan.

Comparable uncertainty attends many instances closer to home of suffering or potential wrong caused for supposed short-term or long-term gains. Civil disobedience involving coercion or harm, doctor-assisted suicide, abortion on demand, and capital punishment all pose social dilemmas of great public import. Moreover, in the workplace as well as among friends and family, most people at some time wonder whether to qualify the imperatives of telling the truth and honoring private property in order to achieve what they regard as a greater good.

In this way, the killing of Balaam along with the rest of the onetime inhabitants of Reuben's territory, to say nothing of the general slaughter described by Joshua or its apparent foundation in Josiah's revanchist reform, raises an issue that, in one form or another, no one escapes.

JOSHUA 14:1-5, INHERITANCE BY LOT

NIV

14 Now these are the areas the Israelites received as an inheritance in the land of Canaan, which Eleazar the priest, Joshua son of Nun and the heads of the tribal clans of Israel allotted to them. ²Their inheritances were assigned by lot to the nine-and-a-half tribes, as the LORD had commanded through Moses. ³Moses had granted the two-and-a-half tribes their inheritance east of the Jordan but had not granted the Levites an inheritance among the rest, ⁴for the sons of Joseph had become two tribes—Manasseh and Ephraim. The Levites received no share of the land but only towns to live in, with pasturelands for their flocks and herds. ⁵So the Israelites divided the land, just as the LORD had commanded Moses.

NRSV

14 These are the inheritances that the Israelites received in the land of Canaan, which the priest Eleazar, and Joshua son of Nun, and the heads of the families of the tribes of the Israelites distributed to them. ²Their inheritance was by lot, as the LORD had commanded Moses for the nine and one-half tribes. ³For Moses had given an inheritance to the two and one-half tribes beyond the Jordan; but to the Levites he gave no inheritance among them. ⁴For the people of Joseph were two tribes, Manasseh and Ephraim; and no portion was given to the Levites in the land, but only towns to live in, with their pasture lands for their flocks and herds. ⁵The Israelites did as the LORD commanded Moses; they allotted the land.

COMMENTARY

The tribal allotments east of the Jordan having been defined, the story turns to the tribes west of the Jordan in the land of Canaan. Here the scene is set for the entire main allotment. In this scene, the remaining tribes are treated as though they were farming households in a great village. The village elders—here the patriarchal heads of the tribes—have gathered along with all the heads of cultivating households for the periodic redistributive lottery, as described above. The main item of business before the lottery itself is to decide exactly how many parties or households, here tribes, are participating. Thus v. 2 is the key to this section: The grants are to be apportioned by lot, and nine and a half parties will be participating. The number is explained. The whole group comprises the twelve sons of Israel. Two and a half have already received their grants, and

Levi is not to receive a grant of land. The number is now down to eight and a half. However, Joseph is represented by his two sons, to make up for Levi's receiving only towns and pasturage. The result is nine and a half lottery participants.

The Levites are similarly mentioned in 18:7 in the midst of a new setting up for apportionment, this time at Shiloh. Again the crucial question is how many cultivating units the land is to be divided among, and the answer (seven) is again painstakingly explained (18:5-7).

Throughout agrarian history the world over, periodic reallocations of land within cultivating communities have nearly always been carried out by lot. The lottery ensures fairness and allows a community to express its solidarity. As in Palestine, periodic reallocation has been practiced not because people in close communities love to share wealth with one another, but in order to meet a particular need. Although such needs may take different forms, they typically arise from the advantage to the community as a whole of not fixing land as permanent properties. As explained above, in Palestine the community of dry farmers, who must put their land in fallow every second or third year to maintain its productivity, benefits from being able to enclose all of a given year's fallow land in a single block rather than in scattered fields, thereby greatly reducing the fencing, hedging, or surveillance required and making it easier to graze flocks and other livestock safely. The main disadvantage of reallocation is that it takes away the incentive for individuals or households to improve the land they work. Since over time the advantage accrues to and the disadvantage diminishes the community as a whole, it is important for the community not only to share the benefits and drawbacks as equally as possible, by preventing individuals or households from taking particular advantage of the system, but also to make a public display of this intent to sustain the level of cooperation required for such a system to work. This the lottery does.

Redistribution applied only to arable land, which was used for raising grain. Arable land was cultivated anew each year it was not in fallow, and so it did not necessitate long-term investment. Redistribution was not used with land planted in perennial crops, on the other hand, chiefly vineyards and olive orchards. These did require an investment by individuals or households, which they would be reluctant to hazard in a common land pool. During periods of the commercialization of agriculture, such as the eighth and seventh centuries BCE in Palestine, land tended to concentrate in the hands of big landholders, including the deuteronomistic "Canaanites," who could pressure growers into raising grain, grapes, or olives as cash crops rather than diversifying production for subsistence and risk management. Such commercialization is what Josiah's reform was professed to have been designed to counteract.

There were other popular non-village uses of the lottery in land distribution. One took place when groups of tribal or village farmers agreed to cultivate a big landholder's tract of land under a collective sharecropping agreement. Yet another use sometimes compared with Joshua was the lottery imposed by the powerful planters of Greek colonies for the

distribution of land, as prescribed, for example, in highly rational detail by Plato in his *Laws*.[108] By this analogy, the conquest constitutes a colonization, and colonizations often were conquests. The Greek concepts of lottery and inherited land were closely related, in the same way that a grant in Hebrew tended to become an inheritance. Indeed, the evidence for the use of the lot in the distribution of land is more common in the Greek sources than in the OT, especially since over 150 Greek colonies were founded around the Mediterranean and the Black Sea within roughly a hundred years, and most within fifty years, of Josiah's reform and the main writing of the book of Joshua.

The idea of this common Greek practice, which like Joshua's distribution was part of a complex mix of political and religious procedures centered in conquest and with a popular—or populist—tinge, may have been based on communal repartitioning like that just described, which it must be assumed was practiced. But what is most noteworthy is that virtually all of the attested instances involve a powerful leader or ruler whose lottery stands for an intrusion of supremacy, and that most of the instances may have been more idealistic than practical. The earliest is the famous example of Nausithoos, legendary king of the Phaiakians.[109] Described as "godlike," Nausithoos led his people to a faraway land where, after building a walled town and temples to the gods, he distributed land to his people by lot. Another example comes from Herodotus's description of the legendary Egyptian king Sesostris.[110] He was the legendary greatest of all Egyptian conquerors and the builder of all of Egypt's myriad canals. Herodotus reports that "it was this king who divided the land among all the Egyptians, giving to each man as an allotment a square, equal in size. . . . If the river should carry off a portion of the allotment, the man would come to the king himself and signify what had happened, whereupon the king sent men to inspect and remeasure by how much the allotment had grown less, so that for the future it should pay proportionally less

108. Plato *Laws* 745 b-3. See Moshe Weinfeld, "The Pattern of the Israelite Settlement in Canaan," in *Congress Volume: Jerusalem 1986*, ed. J. A. Emerton, VTSup 40 (Leiden: Brill, 1988) 270-83, esp. 271, 279-80. In Plato's theory, after capturing land, the lawgiver founds and builds the city and its temples and divides the city, the land, and the people into twelve equal divisions ("tribes"), to whom the land is then allotted.
109. Homer *Odyssey* 6.6-10.
110. Herodotus *History* 2.102-110.

of the assigned tax. I think it was from this that geometry was discovered."[111] Sesostris was no ordinary individual. Although in his *Laws* Plato describes a government less autocratic than his earlier utopias, its rationalized regimentation, provisions for surveillance, and communal conformity under a powerful "lawgiver" who imposes the death penalty on anyone encouraging deviance provide illuminating parallels to Josiah's deuteronomistic Israel.

In the ancient world, distribution of land by lot was ubiquitous. It is also likely, however, that it was farming collectives who practiced it in fact, while rulers practiced it mainly in theory. What the Greek parallels suggest is not that Joshua engages in a procedure with historical veracity, but that his is the role of the powerful despot whose image of fairness and equality shows his determination to be an autocrat for the people—autonomous, self-reliant, and unconstrained by the powerful men and households of his realm. It has been pointed out that land division was the most important part of colonization and equality of division the most important issue (cf. Num 26:52-56; Ezek 47:13–48:35); at the same time, it is probable that "the highly oligarchic societies of Greece cannot conceivably have founded colonies in which the citizens were equal."[112] While evidence points to an insistence on equality in theory in the classical period, from which all literary references come, "archaeological evidence and strong arguments from probability make it doubtful if such principles were observed in the colonization of at least the early Archaic period."[113]

There is no reason to believe that Josiah's domain was any less oligarchic than Greece was at the same time. Plato's lawgiver must deal with intractable strong men and anyone else who might be reluctant to submit to an autocrat in return for a parsimonious parcel of land:

All the arrangements now described will never be likely to meet with such favorable conditions that the whole program can be carried out according to plan. This requires that the citizens will raise no objection to such a mode of living together, and will tolerate being restricted for life to fixed and limited amounts of property and to families such as we have stated, and being deprived of gold and of the other things which the lawgiver is clearly obliged by our regulations to forbid, and will submit also to the arrangements he has defined . . . almost as if he were telling nothing but dreams, or molding a city and citizen out of wax.[114]

The deuteronomistic historian uses the narrative device of the redistributive lottery metaphorically, not unlike the Greek examples just given. Whether Josiah made grants of land to retainers and followers by lot, or planned to do so, does not much matter. The metaphor of the lottery allows the narrator of Joshua to make several points about Josiah at once. One point is the implied power of the monarchic distributor. In effect, the lottery makes Joshua's allocations arbitrary rather than either rational or, ironically, according to custom. This is the prerogative every centralizing monarch covets and the Greek examples illustrate: the latitude to ignore logic or convention and to neutralize individuals and families of long-standing influence. The result is analogous as well to that achieved in Athens by the introduction, possibly as early as Cleisthenes (late sixth century BCE) or even Solon (early sixth century BCE) of election of magistrates by lottery, making it more difficult for the long-standing elite to gain powerful positions by virtue of family connections or wealth.[115] A second point palliates the first. It is not Joshua who decides who goes where and who gets what, but Yahweh, whose will the lottery reveals. Ostensibly Joshua's role in the protracted narrative of distribution is quite restricted. This is one of the items in the book of Joshua that scholars sometimes take as an indication that Joshua has been secondarily made the hero of existing stories. This time, however, Joshua's detachment is integral to the story: The village headman stands by to guarantee—as far as his credibility extends—the fairness of the lottery not by producing particular results in his

111. Ibid., 2.109. See *Herodotus: The History,* trans. David Greene (Chicago: University of Chicago Press, 1987) 175.

112. A. J. Graham, "The Colonial Expansion of Greece," in *The Cambridge Ancient History,* 2nd ed. (Cambridge: Cambridge University Press, 1982) 3:151. The tribal allotments in Ezekiel illustrate the extreme theoretical pitch possible when equal distribution is seen by the ruling class: Israel falls exclusively on the west side of the Jordan, and the envisioned allotments, adjoining one another along absolutely straight-line borders, are equal in their north-south dimension only, regardless of topography or east-west breadth.

113. Ibid., 152. The Archaic period covers the eighth, seventh, and sixth centuries BCE in Greece and the Aegean.

114. Plato *Laws,* 745e, LCL.

115. Josiah Ober, *Mass and Elite in Democratic Athens: Rhetoric, Ideology, and the Power of the People* (Princeton: Princeton University Press, 1989) 76-79.

own interest, but by ensuring that chance is random, or up to God. A third point is made bypicturing Joshua as distributing all the conquered land in a manner that reminds hearers of the way villagers redistribute their arable land in contrast to their vineyards and orchards. This picture might suggest that the amount of village arable land is to increase and the land devoted to cash crops decrease, so that villagers are less likely to be forced into the market, especially during the winter, to purchase staple grain at inflated prices.[116] A fourth point is to affirm the villagers' values expressed through the lottery. As mentioned above, these include security, mutual aid, and equal opportunity, all confirming the fundamental value of the debt remission that forms the heart of Josiah's reform legislation.

116. See Marvin L. Chaney, "Bitter Bounty: The Dynamics of Political Economy Critiqued by the Eighth-Century Prophets," in *Reformed Faith and Economics,* ed. Robert L. Stivers (Lanham: University Press of America, 1989) 15-30.

REFLECTIONS

The lottery outwardly manifests the sovereignty of God, since people receive by lottery whatever God chooses to grant. The sovereignty of God is an essential biblical doctrine, but a doctrine always in potential tension with reason. Christian theologians have struggled with this dilemma since the beginning of the church. The tension is seen clearly in the grant of Canaan to God's chosen people. Neither the grant nor the choice of Israel has a reason. Of course, for both a reason is given: to justify the grant, Ham saw his father naked; to justify the choice of Israel, having been blessed, Abraham obediently threw himself on the grace of God. But even if by these acts Ham and Abraham set themselves apart from all other human beings, the interpreter can still ask whether these acts reasonably lead to and warrant Israel's barbarous dispossession of the "Canaanites." To ask such a question is not to question God's sovereignty, but to pose the problem of theodicy, or God's responsibility for evil, in terms of the biblical text historically rather than abstractly understood—even though in the biblical writer's eyes the conquest of Canaan was a great good. Conversely, the fictional distribution by lot of holdings that fall more or less where they already have in the past verges on making the lottery have no reason: What is the point of a lottery when the outcome is known in advance, from the perspective of writer and hearer? As previously noted, at best it points up the sovereignty of God, which in this instance is at least fair (for the Israelite tribes), if arbitrary. But divine sovereignty in this sense is little more than an abstraction. In reality, the doctrine of God's sovereignty has always served both to thwart power and to support power. The interpreter, therefore, must take the unavoidable next step and ask how the abstraction of God's sovereignty is applied in reality, whether by powers reflected in the text, like Josiah, or by modern claimants to the power of the text.

The Christian doctrines of God's sovereignty and election are based in the Bible on the metaphor of the caprice of the autonomous, all-powerful ruler. Yahweh, the God of both the Old Testament and the New Testament, is a gracious despot. Theologically these doctrines are indispensable, but they have posed an intellectual challenge to the church in all ages; and they produce especially troubling implications in the modern context. In the pre-industrial, agrarian era of the Bible, authority was hierarchical. Arbitrary authority was thus expected and in the end usually accepted, and often glorified. This biblical notion of authority did not drop from the sky. It derived from and was sustained by a clear and definable social and political context. The modern context is different, and hence the modern concept of authority is different. In the modern context, authority is experienced as fundamentally democratic, and hence arbitrary authority is fundamentally unacceptable. The ancient concept of authority found in the Bible cannot trump the modern concept, because the ancient concept had a social and political basis no less than the modern concept. The great watershed occurred in North Atlantic culture during the seventeenth and eighteenth centuries. The distinction now prevails over most of the world.

In theory, God is treated as an exception to this development: God's authority is categorically other than democratic authority. In this way, the biblical concept is saved. However, theory becomes fact when in the name of God power is exercised by some individual, group, church, or nation. God may be absolutely sovereign and arbitrary, but humans using power in the name of God are not. They must be reasonable.

The tendency is to ignore these implications rather than grapple with them. A recent survey found that most Americans no longer thought of God as king, lord, or father, but as friend. Without denying the truth of the popular conviction that God is our friend, insofar as it sidesteps most questions of power it leaves most of the Bible out of the picture—and potentially allows the religious justification of the abuse of power in through the back door. When some people exercise power over or against others in the name of God without having to give a reasonable answer to the question, "What gives God the right. . . ?" then injustice is likely to occur.

As the basis for the use of power in the name of God, the sovereignty of God is a two-edged sword. The classical liberal approach to God's sovereignty is rooted in the Age of Reason and is now accepted, explicitly or implicitly, by most Western or Westernized Christians. This approach follows in the natural law tradition. It holds that justice can be discerned by reason and that God must be reasonable. This seems in theory to limit God's freedom, but the alternative may be worse. If God is not limited by reason, then anything is possible; and if anything is possible, then injustice can be justified. By what right does Josiah reconquer the jurisdictions of Davidic Israel? By right of inheritance and the rationale of social justice. What would Josiah's opponents argue against him? To begin with, they might point out that David himself usurped those jurisdictions from Saul. But what about David's purported divine right to usurp, a major theme of the Bible?

There is no ending point to this progression or to the dilemmas evoked in the doctrine of God's sovereignty, essential though it is. Today some Christians would think it presumptuous and arrogant to reason about God's sovereignty, authority, and justice. God is just, so their assumption goes, but God answers to no one. This doctrine leads directly to the problem of Job. In the face of God's overwhelming sovereignty, Job surrenders the right to question God's justice. In the world of the Bible, where the vast majority had no claim to a share in power, and in theory, it may be tolerable to look no further than Job. In our world and in the real world of power, the responsible interpreter and trusting believer, even while affirming the categorical otherness of God, does look further, and like the psalmist refuses to abandon the right to question God.

JOSHUA 14:6–15:63, LAND FOR JUDAH

OVERVIEW

The tribes gather at Gilgal for the distribution of their allotments of land. If the redistributive lottery implies that all the tribes are equal, the descriptions of their territories quickly dispel this impression. Among the tribes, Judah, the tribe of the house of David, takes precedence, both by being first to receive its land grant in Canaan and by having its grant be the one most thoroughly delineated. Judah takes precedence among the tribes because it is the homeland of David, and for Josiah it is the one best known, most important, and largely already held.

The description of Judah's holding falls into four sections. The first and third are narrative; they focus on Caleb and the taking of Hebron and Debir, towns in central Judah (14:6-15; 15:13-19). The second and fourth are lists; they detail the allotment of Judah, first according to its boundaries, then according to its towns, which are grouped in twelve districts (15:1-12, 20-63).

As they appear, the two lists cannot pre-date the seventh century, and probably Josiah, since they include towns not settled before then. Earlier dates for the lists are often proposed, but there is little agreement about their pre-Josianic form. The interpretation of these and subsequent tribal lists is made difficult by numerous variations in the texts and versions, which indicate a complex history of revision and adjustment, probably both before and after Josiah, and by doubt or complete ignorance about the location of many of the places. Judah's boundaries are not always consistent with the boundaries described for adjacent tribes; the most obvious disagreement may involve Jerusalem, which is mentioned apropos of Judah in 15:63 but assigned to Benjamin in 18:28.

Joshua 14:6-15, Hebron for Caleb

NIV

[6]Now the men of Judah approached Joshua at Gilgal, and Caleb son of Jephunneh the Kenizzite said to him, "You know what the LORD said to Moses the man of God at Kadesh Barnea about you and me. [7]I was forty years old when Moses the servant of the LORD sent me from Kadesh Barnea to explore the land. And I brought him back a report according to my convictions, [8]but my brothers who went up with me made the hearts of the people melt with fear. I, however, followed the LORD my God wholeheartedly. [9]So on that day Moses swore to me, 'The land on which your feet have walked will be your inheritance and that of your children forever, because you have followed the LORD my God wholeheartedly.'[a]

[10]"Now then, just as the LORD promised, he has kept me alive for forty-five years since the time he said this to Moses, while Israel moved about in the desert. So here I am today, eighty-five years old! [11]I am still as strong today as the day Moses sent me out; I'm just as vigorous to go out to battle now as I was then. [12]Now give me this hill country that the LORD promised me that day. You yourself heard then that the Anakites were there and their cities were large and fortified, but, the LORD helping me, I will drive them out just as he said."

[13]Then Joshua blessed Caleb son of Jephunneh and gave him Hebron as his inheritance. [14]So Hebron has belonged to Caleb son of Jephunneh the Kenizzite ever since, because he followed the LORD, the God of Israel, wholeheartedly. [15](Hebron used to be called Kiriath Arba after Arba, who was the greatest man among the Anakites.)

Then the land had rest from war.

[a]9 Deut. 1:36

NRSV

[6]Then the people of Judah came to Joshua at Gilgal; and Caleb son of Jephunneh the Kenizzite said to him, "You know what the LORD said to Moses the man of God in Kadesh-barnea concerning you and me. [7]I was forty years old when Moses the servant of the LORD sent me from Kadesh-barnea to spy out the land; and I brought him an honest report. [8]But my companions who went up with me made the heart of the people melt; yet I wholeheartedly followed the LORD my God. [9]And Moses swore on that day, saying, 'Surely the land on which your foot has trodden shall be an inheritance for you and your children forever, because you have wholeheartedly followed the LORD my God.' [10]And now, as you see, the LORD has kept me alive, as he said, these forty-five years since the time that the LORD spoke this word to Moses, while Israel was journeying through the wilderness; and here I am today, eighty-five years old. [11]I am still as strong today as I was on the day that Moses sent me; my strength now is as my strength was then, for war, and for going and coming. [12]So now give me this hill country of which the LORD spoke on that day; for you heard on that day how the Anakim were there, with great fortified cities; it may be that the LORD will be with me, and I shall drive them out, as the LORD said."

[13]Then Joshua blessed him, and gave Hebron to Caleb son of Jephunneh for an inheritance. [14]So Hebron became the inheritance of Caleb son of Jephunneh the Kenizzite to this day, because he wholeheartedly followed the LORD, the God of Israel. [15]Now the name of Hebron formerly was Kiriath-arba;[a] this Arba was[b] the greatest man among the Anakim. And the land had rest from war.

[a]That is the city of Arba   [b]Heb lacks this Arba was

COMMENTARY

This is the first of two stories that feature Caleb as a champion in the allotment of Judah—and a parade example of just the kind of individual who was likely to raise an objection to the lottery on the grounds that he constitutes an exception. Caleb wants his grant before the lottery gets started. Caleb has good grounds, and Joshua recognizes them. Caleb is a living legend, a hero of a different order, not one more foot soldier.

These stories should not be mistaken for chance footnotes to the main theme. Caleb is not an incidental figure for the book of Joshua. At some stage the figure of Joshua was joined to the story of Caleb, which told how Caleb was the only faithful Israelite in a reconnoitering of the land. Once he had turned into the only faithful Israelite in the generation of the exodus and the only Israelite of that generation—including Moses— deserving to inherit land in Canaan (Numbers 13–14; cf. Num 32:12), the question of who will lead Israel into the land arises. Will it be Moses himself, or will someone else be required? And if someone else, why not Caleb? Maybe the house of David before Hezekiah told stories about Caleb's leading a conquest of Israel.

Caleb's name means "dog" (כלב *keleb*). Dogs were usually thought of as fierce curs in the ancient world, and the name carried mostly negative connotations, not much better than "rat" or "skunk" today. By itself it is the tag of a mean man, not simply "Yahweh's best friend." But the name, which was actually quite common in the ancient world, could also be used affirmatively to mean a faithful and submissive servant. Caleb and Joshua are the deuteronomists' models of faithful servants. Joshua got into Caleb's story to help connect the earlier Davidic history of Israel, the JE parts of the Tetrateuch, to the history of the house of David's right to reconquer Israel. Caleb's story is repeated at length by Moses at the beginning of the Deuteronomistic History as an object lesson in obedience to the command to conquer the land without fear (Deut 1:19-45). It has already formed part of the groundwork of Joshua's succession to Moses, since, unlike Caleb, even Moses is indeed prevented from crossing the Jordan (cf. Deut 3:23-28). Then two further related

stories about Caleb are told here in Joshua 14–15, and the second is repeated in Judg 1:11-15. Finally, Caleb's nephew Othniel, who figures in the latter story, becomes the Judahite "judge" (Judg 3:7-11), the first to fill that role, serving as a paradigm for all the judges who follow.

Caleb plays an important role in the allotment of Judah for the same reason he was singled out in J. As the eponymous ancestor of a—possibly the—major clan of Hebron, he represents the center of Judah and the town that David made his first capital. For the modern historian, the Calebites' role in the rise of David remains indistinct, but enough evidence is preserved to indicate that it must have been significant.[117] Caleb is said to have descended from the Kenizzites, one of the "pre-Israelite" peoples of Canaan (Gen 15:19; cf. Gen 36:11). Apparently the Calebites came to prominence among the Israelites (cf. the example of Uriah "the Hittite," 2 Sam 11:3–12:10; 23:39) and were worked into the genealogy of Judah, a process of which the genealogies in 1 Chronicles 2 and 4:15 are somewhat confusing vestiges. The first husband of David's wife Abigail was a Calebite nicknamed Nabal, "fool," whom David may have had killed in a move to supplant him (1 Samuel 25).[118] The narrator in Joshua 14–15 has a grasp of this and much more of Caleb's part in the Davidic heritage (and possibly more that is unknown to us), and by telling two stories about Caleb's land holdings he pays homage to it.

The two stories imply that Hebron and Debir have not yet been captured and so contradict the earlier conquest of Hebron and Debir (10:36-39; 12:10, 13). This inconsistency, intensified by 11:21-22, where Joshua is given all the credit for defeating the Anakim and Caleb none, cannot be resolved—though clearly Joshua, the likely newcomer to the house of David's story, had to prove himself equal to the Judahite hero, who is not modest about his abilities (14:11). Along with the story of Caleb's faithfulness, these two stories derive from a pre-deuteronomistic tradition of Caleb's exploits, of much the same character as

---

117. Mark J. Fretz and Raphael I. Panetz, "Caleb," *ABD* 1:808-10.
118. Jon D. Levenson, "1 Samuel 25 as Literature and as History," *CBQ* 40 (1978) 11-28; Jon D. Levenson and Baruch Halpern, "The Political Import of David's Marriages," *JBL* 99 (1980) 507-18.

the saga accounts found, for example, in Joshua 2 and 7–8. The final phrase of the first story, "the land had rest from war" (14:15), is surprising, since there is no battle account, and it seems to contradict the summary phrase in 11:23. It is apparently used to cap the allusion to dispossession in the mention of the Anakim (14:12, 15), just as the elliptical version of the phrase caps

comparable episodes in Judges (Judg 3:11, 30; 5:31; 8:28). Nonetheless it would seem to go better at the end of 15:19, after Hebron and Debir are again fully captured. A sure sign of the independence of the tradition of Caleb's faithfulness is 14:12, which implies that Joshua was not one of the spies in Numbers 13–14 (even in Deut 1:36-38, Joshua is almost an afterthought).

REFLECTIONS

Caleb gets his personal grant of land at the beginning of a distribution that finds Joshua getting his personal grant of land at the end (19:49-50). These two individual grants bracket the grants to the west-bank tribes. The two great heroes of obedience—the old-timer and the newcomer—are given equivalent recognition. This is a stately variation on the projection of Josiah's exploits into Israel's venerable past, in which attention is diverted from the big man of the present, Josiah, to his illustrious predecessors, and in deference to the traditional Judahite hero, Caleb receives his grant first. The careful balance between Caleb and Joshua is maintained only up to a point. Joshua defeats the Anakim of Hebron before Caleb offers to do the same. Joshua grants Caleb his land, not the other way around. It is always an act of graciousness to defer to predecessors and others of the past, to honor those who have gone before, who have spent their lives and thus may manifest more clearly than ourselves what God can do through a given individual. Leaders especially would do well to remember that it does not cost the living to honor the dead, or the young to honor the old, or the incumbent to honor previous holders of their office. Such respect gives the chance to show gratefulness for the gifts of life, youth, or responsibility by sharing the advantages they confer.

Joshua 15:1-63, Land for Judah

NIV

15 The allotment for the tribe of Judah, clan by clan, extended down to the territory of Edom, to the Desert of Zin in the extreme south.

²Their southern boundary started from the bay at the southern end of the Salt Sea,ᵃ ³crossed south of Scorpionᵇ Pass, continued on to Zin and went over to the south of Kadesh Barnea. Then it ran past Hezron up to Addar and curved around to Karka. ⁴It then passed along to Azmon and joined the Wadi of Egypt, ending at the sea. This is theirᶜ southern boundary.

⁵The eastern boundary is the Salt Sea as far as the mouth of the Jordan.

The northern boundary started from the bay of the sea at the mouth of the Jordan,

ᵃ2 That is, the Dead Sea; also in verse 5   ᵇ3 Hebrew *Akrabbim*
ᶜ4 Hebrew *your*

NRSV

15 The lot for the tribe of the people of Judah according to their families reached southward to the boundary of Edom, to the wilderness of Zin at the farthest south. ²And their south boundary ran from the end of the Dead Sea,ᵃ from the bay that faces southward; ³it goes out southward of the ascent of Akrabbim, passes along to Zin, and goes up south of Kadesh-barnea, along by Hezron, up to Addar, makes a turn to Karka, ⁴passes along to Azmon, goes out by the Wadi of Egypt, and comes to its end at the sea. This shall be your south boundary. ⁵And the east boundary is the Dead Sea,ᵃ to the mouth of the Jordan. And the boundary on the north side runs from the bay of the sea at the mouth of the Jordan; ⁶and the boundary goes up to Beth-hoglah, and passes along north of Beth-arabah; and the boundary goes

ᵃ Heb *Salt Sea*

NIV

NRSV

⁶went up to Beth Hoglah and continued north of Beth Arabah to the Stone of Bohan son of Reuben. ⁷The boundary then went up to Debir from the Valley of Achor and turned north to Gilgal, which faces the Pass of Adummim south of the gorge. It continued along to the waters of En Shemesh and came out at En Rogel. ⁸Then it ran up the Valley of Ben Hinnom along the southern slope of the Jebusite city (that is, Jerusalem). From there it climbed to the top of the hill west of the Hinnom Valley at the northern end of the Valley of Rephaim. ⁹From the hilltop the boundary headed toward the spring of the waters of Nephtoah, came out at the towns of Mount Ephron and went down toward Baalah (that is, Kiriath Jearim). ¹⁰Then it curved westward from Baalah to Mount Seir, ran along the northern slope of Mount Jearim (that is, Kesalon), continued down to Beth Shemesh and crossed to Timnah. ¹¹It went to the northern slope of Ekron, turned toward Shikkeron, passed along to Mount Baalah and reached Jabneel. The boundary ended at the sea.

¹²The western boundary is the coastline of the Great Sea.ᵃ

These are the boundaries around the people of Judah by their clans.

¹³In accordance with the Lord's command to him, Joshua gave to Caleb son of Jephunneh a portion in Judah—Kiriath Arba, that is, Hebron. (Arba was the forefather of Anak.) ¹⁴From Hebron Caleb drove out the three Anakites—Sheshai, Ahiman and Talmai—descendants of Anak. ¹⁵From there he marched against the people living in Debir (formerly called Kiriath Sepher). ¹⁶And Caleb said, "I will give my daughter Acsah in marriage to the man who attacks and captures Kiriath Sepher." ¹⁷Othniel son of Kenaz, Caleb's brother, took it; so Caleb gave his daughter Acsah to him in marriage.

¹⁸One day when she came to Othniel, she urged himᵇ to ask her father for a field. When she got off her donkey, Caleb asked her, "What can I do for you?"

up to the Stone of Bohan, Reuben's son; ⁷and the boundary goes up to Debir from the Valley of Achor, and so northward, turning toward Gilgal, which is opposite the ascent of Adummim, which is on the south side of the valley; and the boundary passes along to the waters of En-shemesh, and ends at En-rogel; ⁸then the boundary goes up by the valley of the son of Hinnom at the southern slope of the Jebusites (that is, Jerusalem); and the boundary goes up to the top of the mountain that lies over against the valley of Hinnom, on the west, at the northern end of the valley of Rephaim; ⁹then the boundary extends from the top of the mountain to the spring of the Waters of Nephtoah, and from there to the towns of Mount Ephron; then the boundary bends around to Baalah (that is, Kiriath-jearim); ¹⁰and the boundary circles west of Baalah to Mount Seir, passes along to the northern slope of Mount Jearim (that is, Chesalon), and goes down to Beth-shemesh, and passes along by Timnah; ¹¹the boundary goes out to the slope of the hill north of Ekron, then the boundary bends around to Shikkeron, and passes along to Mount Baalah, and goes out to Jabneel; then the boundary comes to an end at the sea. ¹²And the west boundary was the Mediterranean with its coast. This is the boundary surrounding the people of Judah according to their families.

13According to the commandment of the Lord to Joshua, he gave to Caleb son of Jephunneh a portion among the people of Judah, Kiriath-arba,ᵃ that is, Hebron (Arba was the father of Anak). ¹⁴And Caleb drove out from there the three sons of Anak: Sheshai, Ahiman, and Talmai, the descendants of Anak. ¹⁵From there he went up against the inhabitants of Debir; now the name of Debir formerly was Kiriath-sepher. ¹⁶And Caleb said, "Whoever attacks Kiriath-sepher and takes it, to him I will give my daughter Achsah as wife." ¹⁷Othniel son of Kenaz, the brother of Caleb, took it; and he gave him his daughter Achsah as wife. ¹⁸When she came to him, she urged him to ask her father for a field. As she dismounted from her donkey, Caleb said to her, "What do you wish?" ¹⁹She said to him, "Give me a present; since you have set me in the land of the Negeb, give me

ᵃ12 That is, the Mediterranean; also in verse 47   ᵇ18 Hebrew and some Septuagint manuscripts; other Septuagint manuscripts (see also note at Judges 1:14) Othniel, he urged her

ᵃ That is the city of Arba

675

NIV

¹⁹She replied, "Do me a special favor. Since you have given me land in the Negev, give me also springs of water." So Caleb gave her the upper and lower springs.

²⁰This is the inheritance of the tribe of Judah, clan by clan:

²¹The southernmost towns of the tribe of Judah in the Negev toward the boundary of Edom were:

Kabzeel, Eder, Jagur, ²²Kinah, Dimonah, Adadah, ²³Kedesh, Hazor, Ithnan, ²⁴Ziph, Telem, Bealoth, ²⁵Hazor Hadattah, Kerioth Hezron (that is, Hazor), ²⁶Amam, Shema, Moladah, ²⁷Hazar Gaddah, Heshmon, Beth Pelet, ²⁸Hazar Shual, Beersheba, Biziothiah, ²⁹Baalah, Iim, Ezem, ³⁰Eltolad, Kesil, Hormah, ³¹Ziklag, Madmannah, Sansannah, ³²Lebaoth, Shilhim, Ain and Rimmon—a total of twenty-nine towns and their villages.

³³In the western foothills:

Eshtaol, Zorah, Ashnah, ³⁴Zanoah, En Gannim, Tappuah, Enam, ³⁵Jarmuth, Adullam, Socoh, Azekah, ³⁶Shaaraim, Adithaim and Gederah (or Gederothaim)ª—fourteen towns and their villages.

³⁷Zenan, Hadashah, Migdal Gad, ³⁸Dilean, Mizpah, Joktheel, ³⁹Lachish, Bozkath, Eglon, ⁴⁰Cabbon, Lahmas, Kitlish, ⁴¹Gederoth, Beth Dagon, Naamah and Makkedah—sixteen towns and their villages.

⁴²Libnah, Ether, Ashan, ⁴³Iphtah, Ashnah, Nezib, ⁴⁴Keilah, Aczib and Mareshah—nine towns and their villages.

⁴⁵Ekron, with its surrounding settlements and villages; ⁴⁶west of Ekron, all that were in the vicinity of Ashdod, together with their villages; ⁴⁷Ashdod, its surrounding settlements and villages; and Gaza, its settlements and villages, as far as the Wadi of Egypt and the coastline of the Great Sea.

⁴⁸In the hill country:

Shamir, Jattir, Socoh, ⁴⁹Dannah, Kiriath Sannah (that is, Debir), ⁵⁰Anab, Eshtemoh, Anim, ⁵¹Goshen, Holon and Giloh—eleven towns and their villages.

⁵²Arab, Dumah, Eshan, ⁵³Janim, Beth Tappuah, Aphekah, ⁵⁴Humtah, Kiriath Arba (that

ª36 Or Gederah and Gederothaim

NRSV

springs of water as well." So Caleb gave her the upper springs and the lower springs.

20This is the inheritance of the tribe of the people of Judah according to their families. ²¹The towns belonging to the tribe of the people of Judah in the extreme south, toward the boundary of Edom, were Kabzeel, Eder, Jagur, ²²Kinah, Dimonah, Adadah, ²³Kedesh, Hazor, Ithnan, ²⁴Ziph, Telem, Bealoth, ²⁵Hazor-hadattah, Kerioth-hezron (that is, Hazor), ²⁶Amam, Shema, Moladah, ²⁷Hazar-gaddah, Heshmon, Beth-pelet, ²⁸Hazar-shual, Beer-sheba, Biziothiah, ²⁹Baalah, Iim, Ezem, ³⁰Eltolad, Chesil, Hormah, ³¹Ziklag, Madmannah, Sansannah, ³²Lebaoth, Shilhim, Ain, and Rimmon: in all, twenty-nine towns, with their villages.

33And in the lowland, Eshtaol, Zorah, Ashnah, ³⁴Zanoah, En-gannim, Tappuah, Enam, ³⁵Jarmuth, Adullam, Socoh, Azekah, ³⁶Shaaraim, Adithaim, Gederah, Gederothaim: fourteen towns with their villages.

37Zenan, Hadashah, Migdal-gad, ³⁸Dilan, Mizpeh, Jokthe-el, ³⁹Lachish, Bozkath, Eglon, ⁴⁰Cabbon, Lahmam, Chitlish, ⁴¹Gederoth, Beth-dagon, Naamah, and Makkedah: sixteen towns with their villages.

42Libnah, Ether, Ashan, ⁴³Iphtah, Ashnah, Nezib, ⁴⁴Keilah, Achzib, and Mareshah: nine towns with their villages.

45Ekron, with its dependencies and its villages; ⁴⁶from Ekron to the sea, all that were near Ashdod, with their villages.

47Ashdod, its towns and its villages; Gaza, its towns and its villages; to the Wadi of Egypt, and the Great Sea with its coast.

48And in the hill country, Shamir, Jattir, Socoh, ⁴⁹Dannah, Kiriath-sannah (that is, Debir), ⁵⁰Anab, Eshtemoh, Anim, ⁵¹Goshen, Holon, and Giloh: eleven towns with their villages.

52Arab, Dumah, Eshan, ⁵³Janim, Beth-tappuah, Aphekah, ⁵⁴Humtah, Kiriath-arba (that is, Hebron), and Zior: nine towns with their villages.

55Maon, Carmel, Ziph, Juttah, ⁵⁶Jezreel, Jokdeam, Zanoah, ⁵⁷Kain, Gibeah, and Timnah: ten towns with their villages.

58Halhul, Beth-zur, Gedor, ⁵⁹Maarath, Beth-anoth, and Eltekon: six towns with their villages.

NIV

is, Hebron) and Zior—nine towns and their villages.

⁵⁵Maon, Carmel, Ziph, Juttah, ⁵⁶Jezreel, Jokdeam, Zanoah, ⁵⁷Kain, Gibeah and Timnah—ten towns and their villages.

⁵⁸Halhul, Beth Zur, Gedor, ⁵⁹Maarath, Beth Anoth and Eltekon—six towns and their villages.

⁶⁰Kiriath Baal (that is, Kiriath Jearim) and Rabbah—two towns and their villages.

⁶¹In the desert:

Beth Arabah, Middin, Secacah, ⁶²Nibshan, the City of Salt and En Gedi—six towns and their villages.

⁶³Judah could not dislodge the Jebusites, who were living in Jerusalem; to this day the Jebusites live there with the people of Judah.

NRSV

60Kiriath-baal (that is, Kiriath-jearim) and Rabbah: two towns with their villages.

61In the wilderness, Beth-arabah, Middin, Secacah, ⁶²Nibshan, the City of Salt, and En-gedi: six towns with their villages.

63But the people of Judah could not drive out the Jebusites, the inhabitants of Jerusalem; so the Jebusites live with the people of Judah in Jerusalem to this day.

COMMENTARY

The territory of Judah is described in two sections, by boundaries (15:1-12) and by towns (15:20-63); only the descriptions of Benjamin (18:11-28) and Naphtali (19:32-39), and fragmentarily Zebulun (19:10-16), Issachar (19:17-23), and Asher (19:24-31) match this pattern. These two Judahite lists are separated by the second story of Caleb (15:13-19; cf. Judg 1:11-15).

Four boundaries of Judah are described in the order of south, east, north, and west. Judah is bounded on three sides by natural features—sink, desert, and sea—and consists of the southern portion of ancient Canaan. The southern boundary runs from the border with Edom in the Arabah below the Dead Sea west to the Mediterranean at Wadi el-Arish, on the edge of the Sinai desert southwest of Gaza (15:1-4), although a few localities named later may fall below this line. The eastern boundary is the Dead Sea (15:5a). The northern boundary runs from the mouth of the Jordan at the northern end of the Dead Sea west to the Mediterranean at Jabneel, modern Yavne south of Tel Aviv (15:5b-11). This boundary, which in the highland Judah shares with Benjamin and in the foothills and lowland with Dan, separates Judah from the rest of Israel. Hence it is not surprising that it is described in more detail than

any other and that it agrees almost entirely with Benjamin's southern boundary (18:15-19, described west to east). The brief description of Dan includes no boundary list (19:41-46). Judah's western boundary is the Mediterranean Sea (15:12a).

The town list (15:20-63) almost certainly represents an administrative division of Judah into twelve districts. Because the districts are partly ideals, if not utopian, the list would seem to come from either Hezekiah's or Josiah's reform program. In Sennacherib's account of the siege of Jerusalem, Hezekiah is said to be allied with several of the Philistine towns named. Several of the towns were settled only in the seventh century BCE. Hezekiah, therefore, is the less likely candidate. The list's relatively high degree of clarity suggests a recently composed document.

Scholars do not agree on how exactly the list represents the assumed twelve districts. The best solution would seem to be that represented by the NIV paragraphs, which differ from the NRSV only in combining vv. 45-47. This division produces eleven districts: one in the Negeb; four in the Shephelah (the western foothills or lowland); five in the highland; and one in the desert. The missing district, the tenth in sequence, is supplied by the LXX of the end of v. 59. It was lost by a classic case of homoioteleuton (an occurrence in writing of the same or similar endings near together), in which a scribe accidently skipped from "villages" at the end of v. 59 to "villages" at the end of the lost text and continued to copy from there. The lost text, representing a sixth highland district, reads "Tekoa, Ephrathah (that is, Bethlehem), Peor, Etam, Koloun, Tatam, Sores, Kerem, Gallim, Bether, Manahath—eleven towns and their villages." This correction is worth noting because it restores a large district in the northeast corner of Judah. This district centers on Bethlehem and borders Jerusalem and thus is of utmost importance to the house of David. It represents a surprising gap in the MT and an unfortunate omission from the marginal notes of both the NRSV and the NIV.

The town lists' sums do not always match the number of towns named; there are more than 29 towns in the first district (15:21-32), as apparently the list has grown without the sum's being recalculated. The new eleventh district, consisting of only two towns (15:60), seems too small. Many believe that the list for this district may have been transferred to the list for Benjamin (18:21-28), since Kiriath-jearim occurs in both lists (however, cf. 18:14) and Beth-arabah from the last district (15:61) is included as well (18:22). Three great Philistine towns make up an extremely broad and rich fifth district (15:45-47) whose towns and villages are neither listed nor tallied. This region, which no king of Judah, including probably even David, ever controlled, shows that the entire town list for Judah resembles a wish list as much as an administrative list (cf. 11:22; 13:2-3). The section concludes by noting that the Judahites cannot expel the Jebusites from Jerusalem, a failure later laid on the Benjaminites and contrasted to Caleb's success in capturing Hebron (Judg 1:20-21). The capture of Jerusalem, the deuteronomistic center, awaits the arrival of David (2 Sam 5:6).

Between the two Judahite lists, the Calebite capture of Hebron and Debir is narrated (15:13-19; cf. Judg 1:11-15, 20). The deuteronomist gets the names of the individual Anakim from Num 13:22. The main episode explains how the Calebite Othniel came to rule Debir, but its principal theme is more specific than that. The purpose of the story is to answer the question, How did the ruler of Debir acquire the rights to the two springs that bubble into the brown soil a mile and a half north of the town, its closest fresh water supply?[119] Unfortunately, the answer, and thus the point of the story, is something of a mystery. The point hinges on the connection between what Achsah does while sitting on her donkey—or "from" her donkey—and the gift she receives. No one knows for certain what either of these is. The meaning of the verb translated "dismount" (צנח ṣānaḥ, which occurs only here, in the parallel in Judg 1:14, and in Judg 4:21) and the noun translated "springs" (גלה gullōt) is uncertain. Neither the verb nor the noun represents the usual expression for its respective translation, and both translations are probably incorrect. An Akkadian cognate to the verb means "have diarrhea" (leading the great philologist G. R. Driver mistakenly to translate it "make a noise"—that is, break wind—in the NEB); and the noun גלה (gullâ), which can mean "bowl," comes from a Hebrew root also found in several words for excrement (גל gel, גלל gālāl, גלול gillûl). One plain meaning of Caleb's question to Achsah is, "What's the matter?" If the visual and verbal pun is not the obvious but lamentably scatological one, in which Achsah's diarrhea leaves pools beneath her donkey, evoking both the likeness of and a term for muddy spring basins (גלה מים gullōt māyim, "watery excrement," "watery basins"), then it remains beyond our ken.[120]

119. Robert G. Boling and G. Ernest Wright, *Joshua*, AB 6 (Garden City, N.Y.: Doubleday, 1982) 376.

120. For an alternative view, see the comments of Danna Nolan Fewell in "Textual Incites: Achsah and the (E)razed City of Writing," in *Judges and Method: New Approaches in Biblical Studies*, ed. Gale A. Yee (Minneapolis: Fortress, 1995) 129-41.

REFLECTIONS

Judah is home to the deuteronomist, so Judah's allocation gets the most careful and complete description. The small land is subdivided into twelve districts, and the settlements in each are detailed in turn. Organized administration looks good to us, and so it did to the government in Jerusalem that gave us this list. To the people in the towns, villages, and tents of the land, it looked different. People in Palestine tended not to care for administration, just as they did not like the census, which was useful mainly for taxation, conscription, or surveillance (cf. 2 Sam 24:1-17). There is always a tension between the governing and the governed that goes quite beyond the civil realm. What are the purposes of administration? How are its purposes to be achieved? The governing and the governed must find a common answer to these questions if rule is to succeed. In the ancient era, self-justifying government tended toward an autocratic tyranny. In the modern era, it tends toward a bureaucratic tyranny, though autocracy is always a danger as well. The idealistic scheme of the allocation to Judah raises the issue of the ends of government policy, or of any policy imposed by one on another. Whose interests are served? Does Josiah know best? The question arises even when it is acknowledged that it is God's plan and that God knows best, since even God's plan may serve one side's interests more than another's. The interpreter is again catapulted into the hermeneutical circle.

For the community of faith today, these questions arise whenever individual believers undertake to assess the roles and policies of governments and administrations in the light of their Christian beliefs. The biblical pattern for connecting administrative policy with strategic commitments becomes visible in this and most texts in Joshua when one recognizes its relationship to the centralizing and reforming laws of Deuteronomy. In this case, the ideal of relief for the majority poor, encapsulated in Deut 15:1-18, is affirmed in a "national" covenant with God. In the modern world, the establishment of tolerance and pluralism in the United States Constitution, which by the intention of its authors, but to the frustration of many, makes no mention of God, means that commitments based on faith are expressed through individuals and groups, including those holding public office, attempting to influence government rather than through government as such. The ideal is for as many as possible of those who are under a particular government, including Christian believers, to participate in the process of influencing that government, from voting to lobbying to acting responsibly in office. This is the case not only in the United States, but in most constitutional democracies.

A closer parallel to the biblical pattern of policy and faith can be expressed in the church itself. Although in the modern era neither nation nor theocracy, the church is the institution wherein the policies of administration and the interests and requirements of members can be brought together in a common undertaking in obedience to God. Most modern churches are representative to some degree. Representation usually helps to reduce the gap between the interests of administrators and those of members. Ambiguities continue to arise, however, concerning who is to be represented and how, and concerning the potential tension between the authority of the Bible and the authority of the majority. As overall conserving institutions, churches also struggle with whether the inertia of bureaucracies and entrenched leadership works for or against God. The preacher might want to reflect on the attitudes appropriate to those who hold church office, including the office of preacher. Given the ambiguities of church governance, the classical disciplines of Christian discipleship take on all the more importance: prayer, ongoing Bible study, unassuming consultation, an eagerness to be guided by the Holy Spirit, and a generous respect for and estimation of fellow members.

JOSHUA 16:1–17:18, LAND FOR THE SONS OF JOSEPH

COMMENTARY

The allotments for Ephraim and Manasseh follow immediately without a transition. The two tribes representing the sons of Joseph rank with Joseph's brothers their uncles; long after the event, the priestly strand in Genesis explained that Jacob simply declared it so (Gen 48:5-6). Historical geography tells us more. Since before David the highlands of Ephraim and Manasseh had formed much of the heartland of Israel, the mountains whose productivity the tribes of Israel significantly enhanced, in which they found refuge, and from which they launched their offensives against lowland rivals. As mentioned above, the reconciliation of Joseph and Judah formed the core of the story of the sons of Israel in J, the early Davidic history of Israel, and the three towns that became capitals of Israel once the Israelites had thrown off the yoke of the house of David—Shechem, Tirzah, and Samaria—lay in Manasseh.

The younger son, Ephraim, precedes Manasseh (cf. 17:1) because Jacob crossed his hands when he blessed them, declaring that Ephraim would become the greater (Gen 48:8-20). This tale is from J and was known to the deuteronomists. The stress on both brothers' greatness in Gen 48:19 is recalled by the tribes' complaint that they are numerous and Joshua's response at the end of this section (Josh 17:14-18), even though the Hebrew terms differ. The importance of Manasseh is nowhere clearer than in the naming of Hezekiah's son and heir, likely part of his bid for Israelite support.

This section has four parts. The southern boundary is drawn (16:1-3), followed by the allotments of the two sons (16:4-10; 17:1-13). The section concludes with the tribes' appeal for more land and Joshua's response confining them to the highland (17:14-18).

Joshua 16:1-10, Land for Ephraim

<table>
<tr><td>

NIV

16 The allotment for Joseph began at the Jordan of Jericho,[a] east of the waters of Jericho, and went up from there through the desert into the hill country of Bethel. [2]It went on from Bethel (that is, Luz),[b] crossed over to the territory of the Arkites in Ataroth, [3]descended westward to the territory of the Japhletites as far as the region of Lower Beth Horon and on to Gezer, ending at the sea.

[4]So Manasseh and Ephraim, the descendants of Joseph, received their inheritance.

[5]This was the territory of Ephraim, clan by clan:

The boundary of their inheritance went from Ataroth Addar in the east to Upper Beth Horon [6]and continued to the sea. From Micmethath on the north it curved eastward

</td><td>

NRSV

16 The allotment of the Josephites went from the Jordan by Jericho, east of the waters of Jericho, into the wilderness, going up from Jericho into the hill country to Bethel; [2]then going from Bethel to Luz, it passes along to Ataroth, the territory of the Archites; [3]then it goes down westward to the territory of the Japhletites, as far as the territory of Lower Beth-horon, then to Gezer, and it ends at the sea.

4The Josephites—Manasseh and Ephraim—received their inheritance.

5The territory of the Ephraimites by their families was as follows: the boundary of their inheritance on the east was Ataroth-addar as far as Upper Beth-horon, [6]and the boundary goes from there to the sea; on the north is Michmethath; then on the east the boundary makes a turn toward Taanath-shiloh, and passes along beyond

</td></tr>
</table>

[a]1 *Jordan of Jericho* was possibly an ancient name for the Jordan River.
[b]2 Septuagint; Hebrew *Bethel to Luz*

NIV

to Taanath Shiloh, passing by it to Janoah on the east. ⁷Then it went down from Janoah to Ataroth and Naarah, touched Jericho and came out at the Jordan. ⁸From Tappuah the border went west to the Kanah Ravine and ended at the sea. This was the inheritance of the tribe of the Ephraimites, clan by clan. ⁹It also included all the towns and their villages that were set aside for the Ephraimites within the inheritance of the Manassites.

¹⁰They did not dislodge the Canaanites living in Gezer; to this day the Canaanites live among the people of Ephraim but are required to do forced labor.

NRSV

it on the east to Janoah, ⁷then it goes down from Janoah to Ataroth and to Naarah, and touches Jericho, ending at the Jordan. ⁸From Tappuah the boundary goes westward to the Wadi Kanah, and ends at the sea. Such is the inheritance of the tribe of the Ephraimites by their families, ⁹together with the towns that were set apart for the Ephraimites within the inheritance of the Manassites, all those towns with their villages. ¹⁰They did not, however, drive out the Canaanites who lived in Gezer: so the Canaanites have lived within Ephraim to this day but have been made to do forced labor.

COMMENTARY

The narrator launches right in by delineating the boundary between the tribes of Joseph and Benjamin, from Jericho to Gezer by way of Bethel. Jericho and Bethel themselves lie in Benjamin (18:21-22). In the hills north of this line are found the holdings of the sons of Joseph.

The heading (v. 4) marks the descriptions of the two allotments as parallel (vv. 5-10; 17:1-13). Both contain boundary lists, but no proper town lists. Both pay heed to towns under one tribe's jurisdiction but lying within the bounds of another tribe (v. 9; 17:8-9, 11), an indication that traditional jurisdictions had to be honored notwithstanding the partly artificial tribal bounds postulated by the central government. Both descriptions mention that Ephraim and Manasseh are unable to expel all the Canaanites from large towns under their control, but are able to impose corvée duty on them (v. 10; 17:12-13; cf. Judg 1:27-29), at last fulfilling the curse of Canaan, which justified the conquest in the first place (Gen 9:25).

REFLECTIONS

The fulfillment of the curse of Canaan expresses at best a backhanded compliment. The Davidic historian gives these two tribes of Joseph—always troublesome to Judah—the credit for fulfilling the curse, but as little credit as possible. Each of the likely rulers behind the composition of this section, Josiah and Hezekiah, knows that he must compromise with these powerful folk of the old Israelite hills, so the writer acknowledges their power ("put to forced labor"), but at the same time recalls their weaknesses ("did not drive them out").

Sometimes it is necessary to limit the esteem bestowed on worthy rivals with whom compromise is unavoidable. Prudence suggests that those given charge should pay the necessary compliments to those who could stand in their way, but without exaggerating to disguise reluctance. Acknowledge the opponent's strength, but with moderation. This the text subtly but tactfully does. The text is in keeping with scriptural advice to speak moderately and treat enemies with kindness. A good example of such advice is found in Prov 25:11-28, which Paul cites in Rom 12:14-21 and which the Gospel of Matthew follows in Matt 5:43-48.

All three of these texts (Prov 25:22; Matt 5:45; Rom 12:19) place the treatment of rivals in the context of God's judgment (cf. Matt 13:24-30). Undergirded by the judgment of God, the prescribed ideal for rulers in both the Old Testament and the New Testament is meekness. Probably Hezekiah and Josiah each saw himself, on the model of their ancestor David, as appropriately meek in the face of God's judgment. The ambiguity in the text arises from the fact that such prescriptions for meekness were almost always made from a position of actual strength; the Bible's proverbial wisdom tends to be court wisdom. Whether the advice that the strong be meek is appropriate for those who are already weak and poor, or the best way to bring the judgment of God to bear on the plight of the weak and poor is a question worth careful consideration by anyone who is not.

Joshua 17:1-13, Land for Manasseh

NIV

17 This was the allotment for the tribe of Manasseh as Joseph's firstborn, that is, for Makir, Manasseh's firstborn. Makir was the ancestor of the Gileadites, who had received Gilead and Bashan because the Makirites were great soldiers. [2]So this allotment was for the rest of the people of Manasseh—the clans of Abiezer, Helek, Asriel, Shechem, Hepher and Shemida. These are the other male descendants of Manasseh son of Joseph by their clans.

[3]Now Zelophehad son of Hepher, the son of Gilead, the son of Makir, the son of Manasseh, had no sons but only daughters, whose names were Mahlah, Noah, Hoglah, Milcah and Tirzah. [4]They went to Eleazar the priest, Joshua son of Nun, and the leaders and said, "The LORD commanded Moses to give us an inheritance among our brothers." So Joshua gave them an inheritance along with the brothers of their father, according to the LORD's command. [5]Manasseh's share consisted of ten tracts of land besides Gilead and Bashan east of the Jordan, [6]because the daughters of the tribe of Manasseh received an inheritance among the sons. The land of Gilead belonged to the rest of the descendants of Manasseh.

[7]The territory of Manasseh extended from Asher to Micmethath east of Shechem. The boundary ran southward from there to include the people living at En Tappuah. [8](Manasseh had the land of Tappuah, but Tappuah itself, on the boundary of Manasseh, belonged to the Ephraimites.) [9]Then the boundary continued south to the Kanah Ravine. There were towns belonging to Ephraim lying among the towns of Manasseh, but the boundary of Manasseh was the northern side of the ravine

NRSV

17 Then allotment was made to the tribe of Manasseh, for he was the firstborn of Joseph. To Machir the firstborn of Manasseh, the father of Gilead, were allotted Gilead and Bashan, because he was a warrior. [2]And allotments were made to the rest of the tribe of Manasseh, by their families, Abiezer, Helek, Asriel, Shechem, Hepher, and Shemida; these were the male descendants of Manasseh son of Joseph, by their families.

3Now Zelophehad son of Hepher son of Gilead son of Machir son of Manasseh had no sons, but only daughters; and these are the names of his daughters: Mahlah, Noah, Hoglah, Milcah, and Tirzah. [4]They came before the priest Eleazar and Joshua son of Nun and the leaders, and said, "The LORD commanded Moses to give us an inheritance along with our male kin." So according to the commandment of the LORD he gave them an inheritance among the kinsmen of their father. [5]Thus there fell to Manasseh ten portions, besides the land of Gilead and Bashan, which is on the other side of the Jordan, [6]because the daughters of Manasseh received an inheritance along with his sons. The land of Gilead was allotted to the rest of the Manassites.

7The territory of Manasseh reached from Asher to Michmethath, which is east of Shechem; then the boundary goes along southward to the inhabitants of En-tappuah. [8]The land of Tappuah belonged to Manasseh, but the town of Tappuah on the boundary of Manasseh belonged to the Ephraimites. [9]Then the boundary went down to the Wadi Kanah. The towns here, to the south of the wadi, among the towns of Manasseh, belong to Ephraim. Then the boundary of Manasseh goes along the north side of the wadi and ends at the

NIV

and ended at the sea. ¹⁰On the south the land belonged to Ephraim, on the north to Manasseh. The territory of Manasseh reached the sea and bordered Asher on the north and Issachar on the east.

¹¹Within Issachar and Asher, Manasseh also had Beth Shan, Ibleam and the people of Dor, Endor, Taanach and Megiddo, together with their surrounding settlements (the third in the list is Naphoth*).

¹²Yet the Manassites were not able to occupy these towns, for the Canaanites were determined to live in that region. ¹³However, when the Israelites grew stronger, they subjected the Canaanites to forced labor but did not drive them out completely.

*11 That is, Naphoth Dor

NRSV

sea. ¹⁰The land to the south is Ephraim's and that to the north is Manasseh's, with the sea forming its boundary; on the north Asher is reached, and on the east Issachar. ¹¹Within Issachar and Asher, Manasseh had Beth-shean and its villages, Ibleam and its villages, the inhabitants of Dor and its villages, the inhabitants of En-dor and its villages, the inhabitants of Taanach and its villages, and the inhabitants of Megiddo and its villages (the third is Naphath).* ¹²Yet the Manassites could not take possession of those towns; but the Canaanites continued to live in that land. ¹³But when the Israelites grew strong, they put the Canaanites to forced labor, but did not utterly drive them out.

a Meaning of Heb uncertain

COMMENTARY

Manasseh, the firstborn of Joseph, has to give way to Ephraim, but his own firstborn he treats better. To Machir (NIV, "Makir") goes the first grant, east of the Jordan in the fertile Gilead and Bashan (vv. 1-2; cf. 13:29-31). West of the Jordan, Manasseh's grant goes to clans descended from six sons, including the five granddaughters from one of them, making a total of ten main divisions (vv. 5-6). Lesser claimants join Machir in the east (v. 6).

The six clan names represent regions or localities. The significance of Shechem is obvious. Three others—Helek, Asriel, and Shamida—occur in the Samaria ostraca from the eighth century BCE as notable sources of wine and oil. These all cluster within eight miles of Samaria. Hepher is Zelophehad's father. His name appears in the district list found in the account of Solomon's reign (1 Kgs 4:10). The area of Hepher is now known to have been in the Dothan Valley north of Samaria. As suggested by the name "Tirzah," Jeroboam I's second capital, northeast of Shechem, the groups tracing themselves to Hepher's granddaughters may cluster farther east.

The story of the daughters of Zelophehad (vv. 3-6) is taken directly from Num 27:1-11 so that Joshua can be said to fulfill another of Moses'

commands. Whatever the source of the passage in Numbers, it is introduced there as part of the priestly editing of the Tetrateuch, and it appears here in the book of Joshua as a priestly addition as well (cf. Eleazar, v. 4).

The issue raised by the daughters in Numbers 27 is the order of inheritance in case a married man has no sons. The deuteronomists have their own solution to that problem—namely, levirate (brother-in-law) marriage (Deut 25:5-10). Based on ancient and widespread custom, the levirate law requires that when a man who has had no sons dies, regardless of whether he has had daughters, his brother is to marry his widow, the vulnerable and marginalized daughter-in-law in the family, and bestow the inheritance of the deceased on the widow's firstborn in the name of the deceased and in his line. Thereafter the firstborn, beholden to his mother, may marry with his inheritance on his own account, since he is male, regardless of the wishes of his paternal uncles, including his biological father. Whether or not the widow had daughters, the uncles neither acquire the land nor dispose of it. The purpose of the levirate is to strengthen the wife-centered nuclear family at the expense of the patriarchal extended family (see the Commentary on 7:1–

8:29). Although widely attested in pre-industrial societies, the levirate was frequently unpopular (cf. Gen 38:1-11). The continuance of the deceased brother's inheritance diminished the size of the inheritances of the surviving brothers, especially if the deceased was the firstborn. By trying to enforce the levirate, Josiah hoped to reduce the concentration of wealth in a given patriarchal household's hands.

The priestly rule laid down in response to the daughters of Zelophehad is different (Num 27:8-11). It allows the widow to be ignored by requiring that the property pass unencumbered to the daughters, if there are any. Even though they are then without father and brothers, they are beholden as usual, being female, to marry with their inheritance not on their own account, but according to the wishes of their paternal uncles, returning the advantage to the patriarchal family (cf. Num 36:1-12). If there are no daughters, the land passes directly to the paternal uncles of either the first or the second generation back. It is little wonder that the priestly writer of vv. 3-6 does not spell out the point of Moses' ruling regarding the daughters of Zelophehad, given its incongruence with the law of levirate marriage.[121]

The description of Manasseh's allotment is confined to vv. 7-9, even shorter than Ephraim's sketchy account. The dearth of information on the territory of these two tribes fits with the failure of the narrative of conquest to devote any attention at all to the conquest of this territory. The contrast with the full description of Judah (chap. 15) is meant to be noticed. However, people of Manasseh held the great towns of the Jezreel Valley even though they did not lie within the tribal bounds, a demonstration of their power (v. 11). Perhaps Josiah had to depend on the heads of Ephraim and Manasseh to organize their own administration. These Jezreel towns are on Joshua's list of conquest (12:21, 23), but the men of Manasseh are not powerful enough to carry out completely the ethnic cleansing of their territory (v. 12; Judg 1:27), unlike Judah.

121. For an analysis of feminist readings of Num 27:1-11, see Katharine Doob Sakenfeld, "In the Wilderness, Awaiting the Land: The Daughters of Zelophehad and Feminist Interpretation," *The Princeton Seminary Bulletin* 9 (1988) 179-96; also Sakenfeld, "Feminist Biblical Interpretation," *Theology Today* 46 (1989) 154-68.

REFLECTIONS

The inheritance of the daughters of Zelophehad represents an empowerment. The deuteronomist clearly regarded empowerment as a zero-sum game: Power given to nuclear households was power taken away from extended households. Such a notion of power is often a valid one, particularly in contexts where power is distributed unequally and a justifiable struggle for power ensues. In the Bible, God's judgment often takes just this form, taking power away from one and giving it to another. This understanding inheres in the pervasive biblical metaphor of justification and its rhetorical expression, which over and over hold that to declare one party innocent is to declare another guilty and that the justification of one requires the condemnation of another. If the wrongful use of power is at stake, as it usually is in the Bible, then the judgment of God against it is understandably construed as a dialectic. Moreover, it is often pointed out that in agrarian societies experience usually dictates a zero-sum notion of the common good, so that by analogy the redistribution of any quantity must entail mutual gain and loss.

An alternative view holds that to empower one person is to empower others. The amount of compassion, affirmation, capability, self-respect, and self-fulfillment available is limitless, more than enough for all to have all they need. This view, in keeping with the focus on self-actualization in our individualistic culture, likewise has validity. It works well in contexts in which the wrongful use of power is not at issue, and thus tends to neglect much of what is in the Bible. It is a view in tune not only with the individualizing tendencies in our society, but also with the classical liberal tenets of universal likeness of individuals, individual worth and the opportunity of choice, and general social amelioration and progress. These liberal assumptions are inherent in our national political, economic, and social institutions and in our sense of competition among competitors sharing equal opportunity. Thus they tend to prevail over the contending assumption of dissension and strife between inimical opponents. It is possible that the individualizing view is favored by those who are better off and do not have to struggle to make ends meet.

Joshua 17:14-18, The Hill Country for the Sons of Joseph

NIV

14The people of Joseph said to Joshua, "Why have you given us only one allotment and one portion for an inheritance? We are a numerous people and the LORD has blessed us abundantly."

15"If you are so numerous," Joshua answered, "and if the hill country of Ephraim is too small for you, go up into the forest and clear land for yourselves there in the land of the Perizzites and Rephaites."

16The people of Joseph replied, "The hill country is not enough for us, and all the Canaanites who live in the plain have iron chariots, both those in Beth Shan and its settlements and those in the Valley of Jezreel."

17But Joshua said to the house of Joseph—to Ephraim and Manasseh—"You are numerous and very powerful. You will have not only one allotment 18but the forested hill country as well. Clear it, and its farthest limits will be yours; though the Canaanites have iron chariots and though they are strong, you can drive them out."

NRSV

14The tribe of Joseph spoke to Joshua, saying, "Why have you given me but one lot and one portion as an inheritance, since we are a numerous people, whom all along the LORD has blessed?" 15And Joshua said to them, "If you are a numerous people, go up to the forest, and clear ground there for yourselves in the land of the Perizzites and the Rephaim, since the hill country of Ephraim is too narrow for you." 16The tribe of Joseph said, "The hill country is not enough for us; yet all the Canaanites who live in the plain have chariots of iron, both those in Beth-shean and its villages and those in the Valley of Jezreel." 17Then Joshua said to the house of Joseph, to Ephraim and Manasseh, "You are indeed a numerous people, and have great power; you shall not have one lot only, 18but the hill country shall be yours, for though it is a forest, you shall clear it and possess it to its farthest borders; for you shall drive out the Canaanites, though they have chariots of iron, and though they are strong."

COMMENTARY

In case those great sons of Joseph begin to think they have a right to take over in power in those strong lowland towns, the narrator tells a story in which Joshua orders them to be satisfied with the highland (vv. 14-18). The "portion" (vv. 5, 14) is the same in Hebrew as a "cord" (חבל ḥebel), since a cord was laid out when dividing up parcels of farming land by lot (cf. Amos 7:17; Mic 2:5); this is a direct reflex of the communal practice behind the metaphor of division by lot (see Commentary on 14:1-5; elsewhere in Joshua, "portion" translates various words). The references to forests and maquis do not imply a Bronze Age date, as sometimes suggested. The forests, which by NT times may have been nearly as sparse as they were into the twentieth century CE, were still widespread in the monarchic period, and it would have involved no strain of the imagination to picture the hills covered with them. (A number of reasons for the denuding of the Palestine hills have been suggested; goats may have been the main culprits.) The mention of iron, on the other hand, is an obvious anachronism, since iron did not come into common use in Palestine until the tenth century BCE or later (cf. 6:19, 24; 22:8). The sons of Joseph should have little difficulty in expelling Canaanites from the highland, since chariots of iron (weaponry, fixtures, plating) would not have been of much use to them in the hills (cf. Num 13:29).

JOSHUA 18:1-10, LAND SURVEY AND LOTS AT SHILOH

NIV

18 The whole assembly of the Israelites gathered at Shiloh and set up the Tent of Meeting there. The country was brought under their control, ²but there were still seven Israelite tribes who had not yet received their inheritance.

³So Joshua said to the Israelites: "How long will you wait before you begin to take possession of the land that the LORD, the God of your fathers, has given you? ⁴Appoint three men from each tribe. I will send them out to make a survey of the land and to write a description of it, according to the inheritance of each. Then they will return to me. ⁵You are to divide the land into seven parts. Judah is to remain in its territory on the south and the house of Joseph in its territory on the north. ⁶After you have written descriptions of the seven parts of the land, bring them here to me and I will cast lots for you in the presence of the LORD our God. ⁷The Levites, however, do not get a portion among you, because the priestly service of the LORD is their inheritance. And Gad, Reuben and the half-tribe of Manasseh have already received their inheritance on the east side of the Jordan. Moses the servant of the LORD gave it to them."

⁸As the men started on their way to map out the land, Joshua instructed them, "Go and make a survey of the land and write a description of it. Then return to me, and I will cast lots for you here at Shiloh in the presence of the LORD." ⁹So the men left and went through the land. They wrote its description on a scroll, town by town, in seven parts, and returned to Joshua in the camp at Shiloh. ¹⁰Joshua then cast lots for them in Shiloh in the presence of the LORD, and there he distributed the land to the Israelites according to their tribal divisions.

NRSV

18 Then the whole congregation of the Israelites assembled at Shiloh, and set up the tent of meeting there. The land lay subdued before them.

2There remained among the Israelites seven tribes whose inheritance had not yet been apportioned. ³So Joshua said to the Israelites, "How long will you be slack about going in and taking possession of the land that the LORD, the God of your ancestors, has given you? ⁴Provide three men from each tribe, and I will send them out that they may begin to go throughout the land, writing a description of it with a view to their inheritances. Then come back to me. ⁵They shall divide it into seven portions, Judah continuing in its territory on the south, and the house of Joseph in their territory on the north. ⁶You shall describe the land in seven divisions and bring the description here to me; and I will cast lots for you here before the LORD our God. ⁷The Levites have no portion among you, for the priesthood of the LORD is their heritage; and Gad and Reuben and the half-tribe of Manasseh have received their inheritance beyond the Jordan eastward, which Moses the servant of the LORD gave them."

8So the men started on their way; and Joshua charged those who went to write the description of the land, saying, "Go throughout the land and write a description of it, and come back to me; and I will cast lots for you here before the LORD in Shiloh." ⁹So the men went and traversed the land and set down in a book a description of it by towns in seven divisions; then they came back to Joshua in the camp at Shiloh, ¹⁰and Joshua cast lots for them in Shiloh before the LORD; and there Joshua apportioned the land to the Israelites, to each a portion.

COMMENTARY

The scene shifts from Gilgal to Shiloh, situated halfway between Ai and Shechem, for the allotment of land to the remaining seven tribes.

Eleazar is a priestly addition, as is probably the mention of the tent of meeting, which occurs only here and in the corresponding summary in 19:51

(cf. 1 Sam 2:22 MT). While sudden, the shift to Shiloh belongs to the deuteronomistic story. Together the Deuteronomistic History and the book of Jeremiah imply that the family of Hilkiah, the priest of Josiah's reform, traditionally came from Shiloh. Shiloh is the only location before Jerusalem to be described, in a deuteronomistic text, as "my place . . . where I made my name dwell at first" (Jer 7:12 NRSV; cf. Deut 12:5; Judg 18:31; 1 Samuel 1–3; Ps 78:60). This gives Shiloh a unique status in deuteronomistic eyes. Moreover, the significance of Hilkiah's name (חלקיהו *ḥilqiyyāhû*), which means "Yahweh is my portion," is made clear by v. 7 (cf. 13:14, 33; 14:3-4). The Levites have no "portion" of land (also 14:4), since "the priesthood of Yahweh is their grant" (also 13:33; as noted above, this phrase lies behind the origin of the English word "clergy," which ultimately derives from Greek κλῆρος [*klēros*, "lot," "inheritance"]). Hence Hilkiah's name: "[the priesthood of] Yahweh is my portion," in lieu of a portion of land. And hence in Hilkiah's ancestral home the majority of Israelite tribes, seven of twelve, receive their portions—and the Levites do too (21:2). (The assignment of Anathoth to the Aaronids in 21:18, which may be reflected in the epigonic prose of Jer 11:21-23, is probably a Persian period maneuver.)

The faction that most directly supported Josiah's partisan program appears to have been a Levite group originally from Shiloh in Ephraim and then from Anathoth in Benjamin. The nature of this faction goes far toward explaining the book of Joshua's enthusiasm for its Ephraimite hero and the special attention it gives to Benjaminite traditions in Joshua 1–9 and to Gilgal in Benjamin and Shiloh in Ephraim as the sites where the distribution of the land takes place (14:6; 18:1). As outsiders this faction represented the interests of a particular segmentary power rather than of the segmentary powers in general or of the ancestral priesthood in Jerusalem. The established priesthood had been made unpopular by their trade and debt practices, and they suffered discredit at court because of their inconsistent loyalties. It is also probable that the established priesthood, whose ancestry according to later texts went all the way back to Aaron, had deep ties with the early priests of Bethel. The priests of Bethel were also putatively descended from Aaron, as indicated by the similarity of

Jeroboam's golden calves with the golden calf fabricated by Aaron in Exodus 32. As pointed out by Friedman, when Josiah turns the "Asherah" of the Temple and the extraneous altars into "dust" (NRSV has also "rubble") and scatters the dust on graves and in the wadi, he performs an act described only one other time in the Deuteronomistic History, indeed, in the entire Bible—namely, what Moses said he did to Aaron's golden calves (Deut 9:21; 2 Kgs 23:6, 12; cf. Exod 32:20).[122]

From Jeremiah and the Deuteronomistic History, it is possible to know something about Josiah's upstart priestly supporters, though not nearly as much as desired. The reform faction centered on the priestly family of Hilkiah, who discovered the document of Moses' Torah in the Temple, and the scribal families of Shaphan, who brought the document to Josiah and read it to him, together with Neriah, the father of the prophet Jeremiah's amanuensis Baruch.[123] The "faithful priest" referred to in 1 Sam 2:35 is almost always taken to be Zadok, the eponym (supplied with an Aaronid genealogy) of the dominant priestly family in Jerusalem from Solomon onward. But despite Zadok's supposed importance, he is of practically no interest to the Deuteronomistic History except to be implicated in the failure of Solomon's reign. The "faithful priest" who is to perform what Yahweh "thinks and wills" is more likely, at least in the conception of Josiah's deuteronomist, to be the non-Zadokite Hilkiah than Zadok, the priest on whose watch the house of David polluted the cult of Yahweh and lost its sovereignty over Israel (cf. 1 Chr 5:29-31; 9:10-11).

Jeremiah belonged to this faction. Friedman gives a concise summary: "When Jeremiah sent a letter to the exiles in Babylon, it was delivered for him by Gemariah, son of *Hilkiah,* and by Elasah, son of *Shaphan.* When Jeremiah wrote a scroll of prophecies against Josiah's son Jehoiakim, it was read at the chamber of Gemariah, son of *Shaphan.* Gemariah, son of Shaphan, stood by Jeremiah at critical moments in his life, as did

122. Richard Elliott Friedman, *Who Wrote the Bible?* (New York: Summit, 1987) 113.
123. Ibid., 120-26; J. Andrew Dearman, "My Servants the Scribes: Composition and Context in Jeremiah 36," *JBL* 109 (1990) 403-21; Patricia Dutcher-Walls, "The Social Location of the Deuteronomists: A Sociological Study of Factional Politics in Late Pre-Exilic Judah," *JSOT* 52 (1992) 77-94.

Ahikam, son of Shaphan, who saved Jeremiah from being stoned. And Gedaliah, son of Ahikam, son of Shaphan, when he was appointed governor of Judah by Nebuchadnezzar, took Jeremiah under protection."[124] The book of Jeremiah is the only prophecy to refer to Shiloh, which is described with the deuteronomistic phrase "the place where Yahweh caused his name to dwell" (Jer 7:12). Jeremiah was the son of a priest from Anathoth, just north of Jerusalem (Jer 1:1; 11:21-23; 36:6-15), presumably descended from Abiathar, the priest of the house of Eli at Shiloh who served David and was banished by Solomon to Anathoth. Jeremiah's prophetic book was composed with language and ideas practically identical to those of the Deuteronomistic History, and his father's name was Hilkiah.[125] It is usually assumed that the priest of Josiah's reform and Jeremiah's father were two different men, but Friedman has pointed out that they could have been the same. In any case, like the deuteronomistic historian (who may have been Shaphan), Jeremiah identified as his prophetic forebears Samuel, the oracle behind the house of David, and Moses, the medium of the house of David's law (Jer 15:1).

How did such village-based families, minor segmentary powers in their own right but with little or no obvious strength in Jerusalem, come to power in the house of David, presumably during Josiah's youth? There is no way to know for certain (just as there is no way to know how Draco and Solon came to power in Greece), but it is worth speculating about from what is known about the house of David in the later Assyrian period and from what little is said, but is implied on a grand scale, in the Deuteronomistic History. In the history's account, members of the court of Amon, Manasseh's son and successor and Josiah's father, murdered Amon after a rule of only two years. (It is not known why Amon was murdered, but since he was not born until Manasseh was forty-five years old, he is likely to have had, like Solomon, older brothers with connections who thought the throne was rightfully theirs.) In the ensuing turmoil, segmentary powers (the meaning of עַם־הָאָרֶץ [*am-hā'āreṣ;* NRSV, "the people of the land"] in this context) of some ilk intervened to avenge the murder (2 Kgs 21:24). Momentarily in control, the avengers placed on the throne the eight-year-old Josiah and provided, it must be presumed, for a regency—today we might call them Josiah's handlers—to manage his responsibilities during his minority and to look after their own advantage. It is quite likely that their chosen partisans, Hilkiah and Shaphan and their families, were the regency.

These partisans developed a liking for power and, partly to further their own interests in local conflicts (cf. Jer 32:6-15), encouraged their ward, as he grew older, in renewing the house of David's offensive against opposing segmentary powers, who among other things may still have been attempting to gain their own hold on the house of David. The cabal's means was a partisan populist reform, designed to garner support from an oppressed populace. Depending on whether Josiah in his teens and twenties continued to be dependent on his segmentary patrons, he either turned the tables on them or, with his plan to reconquer Israel and reallocate its lands, set out to help them fulfill their greatest dream of regaining land in erstwhile Israel. (Again, Hilkiah's name means "Yahweh is my portion of land.") The partisans' work was made easier by Egypt and Assyria, who gave them permission, albeit ambivalent, to press the reform.

Shiloh is one of the few Early Iron Age sites potentially associated with early Israel that have been excavated. Scant remains were found at the Late Bronze Age level, but a major settlement existed in the Early Iron period, whose pottery was "strongly in the overall Late Bronze tradition with respect to all individual types," not distinctively "Israelite."[126] The same description applies, in Dever's view, to the possible shrine identified by the excavator.[127] Shiloh was resettled as a village during the period of the monarchy, as evidenced by scattered remains in Stratum IV at the site. Its significance for the deuteronomist may be more symbolic than substantive.

---

124. Friedman, *Who Wrote the Bible?* 125. Hundreds of personal names from around the time of Josiah are attested on ostraca, seals, and seal impressions, but only a few agree with figures mentioned in the Bible. Of those that do, most are mentioned in Jeremiah 36 and related texts, particularly Baruch, Seraiah, and Gemariah.
125. Baruch Halpern, "Shiloh," *ABD* 5:1215.

126. William G. Dever, *BAR* 21/6 (November-December 1995) 10, review of Israel Finkelstein, *Shiloh: The Archaeology of a Biblical Site* (Tel Aviv: Institute of Archaeology, 1993).
127. Ibid., 8.

REFLECTIONS

1. The scene of redistribution shifts to Shiloh as soon as the territory of the tribes of Joseph, where Shiloh lies, is alloted. From the standpoint of Josiah's age, as opposed to the putative age of Joshua, this privileging of Shiloh (under Josiah no more than a small town that for hundreds of years had had little or no import) is extraordinary. It is tied, of course, to the traditional background of the deuteronomistic cabal, who regarded themselves as small and insignificant, the truly powerless amid the struggles of the powerful, dependent on Yahweh alone for whatever success they achieve. Their history recalls how they were reduced to a thin line of survival that ended up in one lone individual, Abiathar, who lost out in contention with Zadok, priest of the Davidic temple, and was banished to Anathoth. Josiah's cabal thought of themselves as this thin line of succession come back, looking to restore the prerogatives of David's support of the tribal cult under Abiathar, possibly involving the Levites as well. This tribal cult originally functioned alongside of, but separate from, David's private household cult under Zadok. Since the latter had enjoyed all the benefits since Solomon, it was time for the descendants of Abiathar to have their turn. The desire to have their own privileges restored lies behind the role of Shiloh in the book of Joshua. Their sense of lone vulnerability is abundantly personified in Jeremiah as portrayed in the book of Jeremiah.

The concept of ethnic cleansing in Joshua does not pit the strong against the weak, as was the case with genocide against Jews in Europe and Native Americans in the United States. The deuteronomist pictures a weak Israel fighting against a strong Canaanite, whom they may nevertheless, with Yahweh's help, annihilate. The Canaanites are "great and strong nations" (23:9; Deut 7:1). "Israel" is weak and must fight using guerrilla tactics. The deuteronomistic examples of God removing one people in favor of another involve the dispossession of giants, as the Canaanites/Amorites are described in Numbers 14–15, and Israel in Joshua fights against kings and towns—that is, centers of power. The powerful in the deuteronomist's conception are the opponents: the indigenous commercial populace, opposing claimants to sovereignty, especially the erstwhile wicked kings of the north. Josiah thought of himself as the head of "a people humble and lowly who shall seek refuge in the name of Yahweh—the remnant of Israel" (Zeph 3:12-13). It is possible that Hezekiah (from whom Zephaniah may have been descended) thought the same before him. The basis of this attitude by Josiah is his experience: growing up a youth in court, dependent on his regents, heading up a cabal that, even if possessing some power, was only one power among many in the realm. In a populist vein, he aggressively took up the cause of the poor, and in this way was no different from many other kings, not least his ancestor David, who regarded himself as beset by enemies on all sides—as he may in fact, like Josiah, have been.

Feeling weak does not excuse genocide. This is always the claim of the perpetrators of ethnic cleansing or genocide, including the European settlers and Americans against Native Americans and the Nazis against the Jews. But in assessing any political violence, the relations of power must be examined carefully—even when it is difficult to see how they could justify certain forms of violence. This is particularly true of political terrorists, who in desperation lash out against civilians in their struggle for their nations in the face of state power.

2. The rehabilitation of Shiloh and its priesthood is not unlike affirmative action in our own time. In reflecting on the actions of Josiah's reform faction, we are led to think as well about the right that some people have for special consideration due to past wrongs. Affirmative action is a corrective policy based on the recognition that institutions tend to re-create themselves, unless acted on from outside. The deuteronomistic cabal were such outsiders, interfering with the age-old pattern of priestly privilege and service in Jerusalem. From the deuteronomists' perspective, some corrective to institutional inertia seemed justified.

What do we as present-day Christians do with affirmative action policies designed to correct institutional inertia that favors whites over people of color? The book of Joshua obviously does not speak directly to the complexity of our multiracial society. But it does suggest a biblical precedent for taking seriously the reality of institutional inertia and for seeking possible remedies for it. The Shiloh issue remains important for us: What can be done to counter the disadvantages and wrongs of the past that still bear on the present?

JOSHUA 18:11-28, LAND FOR BENJAMIN

NIV

¹¹The lot came up for the tribe of Benjamin, clan by clan. Their allotted territory lay between the tribes of Judah and Joseph:

¹²On the north side their boundary began at the Jordan, passed the northern slope of Jericho and headed west into the hill country, coming out at the desert of Beth Aven. ¹³From there it crossed to the south slope of Luz (that is, Bethel) and went down to Ataroth Addar on the hill south of Lower Beth Horon.

¹⁴From the hill facing Beth Horon on the south the boundary turned south along the western side and came out at Kiriath Baal (that is, Kiriath Jearim), a town of the people of Judah. This was the western side.

¹⁵The southern side began at the outskirts of Kiriath Jearim on the west, and the boundary came out at the spring of the waters of Nephtoah. ¹⁶The boundary went down to the foot of the hill facing the Valley of Ben Hinnom, north of the Valley of Rephaim. It continued down the Hinnom Valley along the southern slope of the Jebusite city and so to En Rogel. ¹⁷It then curved north, went to En Shemesh, continued to Geliloth, which faces the Pass of Adummim, and ran down to the Stone of Bohan son of Reuben. ¹⁸It continued to the northern slope of Beth Arabah[a] and on down into the Arabah. ¹⁹It then went to the northern slope of Beth Hoglah and came out at the northern bay of the Salt Sea,[b] at the mouth of the Jordan in the south. This was the southern boundary.

²⁰The Jordan formed the boundary on the eastern side.

a18 Septuagint; Hebrew slope facing the Arabah *b19 That is, the Dead Sea*

NRSV

11The lot of the tribe of Benjamin according to its families came up, and the territory allotted to it fell between the tribe of Judah and the tribe of Joseph. 12On the north side their boundary began at the Jordan; then the boundary goes up to the slope of Jericho on the north, then up through the hill country westward; and it ends at the wilderness of Beth-aven. 13From there the boundary passes along southward in the direction of Luz, to the slope of Luz (that is, Bethel), then the boundary goes down to Ataroth-addar, on the mountain that lies south of Lower Beth-horon. 14Then the boundary goes in another direction, turning on the western side southward from the mountain that lies to the south, opposite Beth-horon, and it ends at Kiriath-baal (that is, Kiriath-jearim), a town belonging to the tribe of Judah. This forms the western side. 15The southern side begins at the outskirts of Kiriath-jearim; and the boundary goes from there to Ephron,[a] to the spring of the Waters of Nephtoah; 16then the boundary goes down to the border of the mountain that overlooks the valley of the son of Hinnom, which is at the north end of the valley of Rephaim; and it then goes down the valley of Hinnom, south of the slope of the Jebusites, and downward to En-rogel; 17then it bends in a northerly direction going on to En-shemesh, and from there goes to Geliloth, which is opposite the ascent of Adummim; then it goes down to the Stone of Bohan, Reuben's son; 18and passing on to the north of the slope of Beth-arabah[b] it goes down to the Arabah; 19then the boundary passes on to the north of the slope of Beth-hoglah; and the boundary ends at the northern bay of the Dead Sea,[c] at the south end of the Jordan: this is the southern border. 20The Jordan forms its

a Cn See 15.9. Heb westward *b Gk: Heb to the slope over against the Arabah* *c Heb Salt Sea*

NIV

These were the boundaries that marked out the inheritance of the clans of Benjamin on all sides.

²¹The tribe of Benjamin, clan by clan, had the following cities:

Jericho, Beth Hoglah, Emek Keziz, ²²Beth Arabah, Zemaraim, Bethel, ²³Avvim, Parah, Ophrah, ²⁴Kephar Ammoni, Ophni and Geba—twelve towns and their villages.

²⁵Gibeon, Ramah, Beeroth, ²⁶Mizpah, Kephirah, Mozah, ²⁷Rekem, Irpeel, Taralah, ²⁸Zelah, Haeleph, the Jebusite city (that is, Jerusalem), Gibeah and Kiriath—fourteen towns and their villages.

This was the inheritance of Benjamin for its clans.

NRSV

boundary on the eastern side. This is the inheritance of the tribe of Benjamin, according to its families, boundary by boundary all around.

21Now the towns of the tribe of Benjamin according to their families were Jericho, Beth-hoglah, Emek-keziz, ²²Beth-arabah, Zemaraim, Bethel, ²³Avvim, Parah, Ophrah, ²⁴Chephar-ammoni, Ophni, and Geba—twelve towns with their villages: ²⁵Gibeon, Ramah, Beeroth, ²⁶Mizpeh, Chephirah, Mozah, ²⁷Rekem, Irpeel, Taralah, ²⁸Zela, Haeleph, Jebus*ᵃ* (that is, Jerusalem), Gibeah*ᵇ* and Kiriath-jearim*ᶜ*—fourteen towns with their villages. This is the inheritance of the tribe of Benjamin according to its families.

ᵃ Gk Syr Vg: Heb *the Jebusite*   *ᵇ* Heb *Gibeath*   *ᶜ* Gk: Heb *Kiriath*

COMMENTARY

Benjamin consists of a lozenge-shaped territory, its northern boundary with Ephraim extending from Jericho to Kiriath-jearim, and its southern boundary reaching east from Kiriath-jearim back to the Jordan at its entrance into the Dead Sea (vv. 11-20). Thus its eastern border consists of a few miles of the Jordan River. Most of this recapitulates what has previously been recorded (15:5-

9; 16:1-3). The two lists of towns (vv. 21-28) add up to twenty-six. Several of these have already been assigned to Judah. Jerusalem is on the border between Benjamin and Judah, but appears to be regarded as lying, like all the significant localities in the opening three-quarters of the conquest narrative, within the bounds of Benjamin.

JOSHUA 19:1-51, LAND FOR THE REMAINING SIX TRIBES

NIV

19 The second lot came out for the tribe of Simeon, clan by clan. Their inheritance lay within the territory of Judah. ²It included:

Beersheba (or Sheba),*ᵃ* Moladah, ³Hazar Shual, Balah, Ezem, ⁴Eltolad, Bethul, Hormah, ⁵Ziklag, Beth Marcaboth, Hazar Susah, ⁶Beth Lebaoth and Sharuhen—thirteen towns and their villages;

⁷Ain, Rimmon, Ether and Ashan—four towns and their villages— ⁸and all the villages

ᵃ2 Or Beersheba, Sheba; 1 Chron. 4:28 does not have Sheba.

NRSV

19 The second lot came out for Simeon, for the tribe of Simeon, according to its families; its inheritance lay within the inheritance of the tribe of Judah. ²It had for its inheritance Beer-sheba, Sheba, Moladah, ³Hazar-shual, Balah, Ezem, ⁴Eltolad, Bethul, Hormah, ⁵Ziklag, Beth-marcaboth, Hazar-susah, ⁶Beth-lebaoth, and Sharuhen—thirteen towns with their villages; ⁷Ain, Rimmon, Ether, and Ashan—four towns with their villages; ⁸together with all the villages all around these towns as far as Baalath-beer,

around these towns as far as Baalath Beer (Ramah in the Negev).

This was the inheritance of the tribe of the Simeonites, clan by clan. [9]The inheritance of the Simeonites was taken from the share of Judah, because Judah's portion was more than they needed. So the Simeonites received their inheritance within the territory of Judah.

[10]The third lot came up for Zebulun, clan by clan:

The boundary of their inheritance went as far as Sarid. [11]Going west it ran to Maralah, touched Dabbesheth, and extended to the ravine near Jokneam. [12]It turned east from Sarid toward the sunrise to the territory of Kisloth Tabor and went on to Daberath and up to Japhia. [13]Then it continued eastward to Gath Hepher and Eth Kazin; it came out at Rimmon and turned toward Neah. [14]There the boundary went around on the north to Hannathon and ended at the Valley of Iphtah El. [15]Included were Kattath, Nahalal, Shimron, Idalah and Bethlehem. There were twelve towns and their villages.

[16]These towns and their villages were the inheritance of Zebulun, clan by clan.

[17]The fourth lot came out for Issachar, clan by clan. [18]Their territory included:

Jezreel, Kesulloth, Shunem, [19]Hapharaim, Shion, Anaharath, [20]Rabbith, Kishion, Ebez, [21]Remeth, En Gannim, En Haddah and Beth Pazzez. [22]The boundary touched Tabor, Shahazumah and Beth Shemesh, and ended at the Jordan. There were sixteen towns and their villages.

[23]These towns and their villages were the inheritance of the tribe of Issachar, clan by clan.

[24]The fifth lot came out for the tribe of Asher, clan by clan. [25]Their territory included:

Helkath, Hali, Beten, Acshaph, [26]Allammelech, Amad and Mishal. On the west the boundary touched Carmel and Shihor Libnath. [27]It then turned east toward Beth Dagon, touched Zebulun and the Valley of Iphtah El, and went north to Beth Emek and Neiel, passing Cabul on the left. [28]It went to Abdon,[a]

[a]28 Some Hebrew manuscripts (see also Joshua 21:30); most Hebrew manuscripts *Ebron*

Ramah of the Negeb. This was the inheritance of the tribe of Simeon according to its families. [9]The inheritance of the tribe of Simeon formed part of the territory of Judah; because the portion of the tribe of Judah was too large for them, the tribe of Simeon obtained an inheritance within their inheritance.

10The third lot came up for the tribe of Zebulun, according to its families. The boundary of its inheritance reached as far as Sarid; [11]then its boundary goes up westward, and on to Maralah, and touches Dabbesheth, then the wadi that is east of Jokneam; [12]from Sarid it goes in the other direction eastward toward the sunrise to the boundary of Chisloth-tabor; from there it goes to Daberath, then up to Japhia; [13]from there it passes along on the east toward the sunrise to Gath-hepher, to Eth-kazin, and going on to Rimmon it bends toward Neah; [14]then on the north the boundary makes a turn to Hannathon, and it ends at the valley of Iphtah-el; [15]and Kattath, Nahalal, Shimron, Idalah, and Bethlehem—twelve towns with their villages. [16]This is the inheritance of the tribe of Zebulun, according to its families—these towns with their villages.

17The fourth lot came out for Issachar, for the tribe of Issachar, according to its families. [18]Its territory included Jezreel, Chesulloth, Shunem, [19]Hapharaim, Shion, Anaharath, [20]Rabbith, Kishion, Ebez, [21]Remeth, En-gannim, En-haddah, Beth-pazzez; [22]the boundary also touches Tabor, Shahazumah, and Beth-shemesh, and its boundary ends at the Jordan—sixteen towns with their villages. [23]This is the inheritance of the tribe of Issachar, according to its families—the towns with their villages.

24The fifth lot came out for the tribe of Asher according to its families. [25]Its boundary included Helkath, Hali, Beten, Achshaph, [26]Allammelech, Amad, and Mishal; on the west it touches Carmel and Shihor-libnath, [27]then it turns eastward, goes to Beth-dagon, and touches Zebulun and the valley of Iphtah-el northward to Beth-emek and Neiel; then it continues in the north to Cabul, [28]Ebron, Rehob, Hammon, Kanah, as far as Great Sidon; [29]then the boundary turns to Ramah, reaching to the fortified city of Tyre; then the boundary turns to Hosah, and it ends at the sea; Mahalab,[a]

[a] Cn Compare Gk: Heb *Mehebel*

Rehob, Hammon and Kanah, as far as Greater Sidon. 29The boundary then turned back toward Ramah and went to the fortified city of Tyre, turned toward Hosah and came out at the sea in the region of Aczib, 30Ummah, Aphek and Rehob. There were twenty-two towns and their villages.

31These towns and their villages were the inheritance of the tribe of Asher, clan by clan.

32The sixth lot came out for Naphtali, clan by clan:

33Their boundary went from Heleph and the large tree in Zaanannim, passing Adami Nekeb and Jabneel to Lakkum and ending at the Jordan. 34The boundary ran west through Aznoth Tabor and came out at Hukkok. It touched Zebulun on the south, Asher on the west and the Jordan*a* on the east. 35The fortified cities were Ziddim, Zer, Hammath, Rakkath, Kinnereth, 36Adamah, Ramah, Hazor, 37Kedesh, Edrei, En Hazor, 38Iron, Migdal El, Horem, Beth Anath and Beth Shemesh. There were nineteen towns and their villages.

39These towns and their villages were the inheritance of the tribe of Naphtali, clan by clan.

40The seventh lot came out for the tribe of Dan, clan by clan. 41The territory of their inheritance included:

Zorah, Eshtaol, Ir Shemesh, 42Shaalabbin, Aijalon, Ithlah, 43Elon, Timnah, Ekron, 44Eltekeh, Gibbethon, Baalath, 45Jehud, Bene Berak, Gath Rimmon, 46Me Jarkon and Rakkon, with the area facing Joppa.

47(But the Danites had difficulty taking possession of their territory, so they went up and attacked Leshem, took it, put it to the sword and occupied it. They settled in Leshem and named it Dan after their forefather.)

48These towns and their villages were the inheritance of the tribe of Dan, clan by clan.

49When they had finished dividing the land into its allotted portions, the Israelites gave Joshua son of Nun an inheritance among them, 50as the LORD had commanded. They gave him the town he asked for—Timnath Serah*b* in the hill country of Ephraim. And he built up the town and settled there.

a34 Septuagint; Hebrew west, and Judah, the Jordan, *b50 Also known as Timnath Heres (see Judges 2:9)*

Achzib, 30Ummah, Aphek, and Rehob—twenty-two towns with their villages. 31This is the inheritance of the tribe of Asher according to its families—these towns with their villages.

32The sixth lot came out for the tribe of Naphtali, for the tribe of Naphtali, according to its families. 33And its boundary ran from Heleph, from the oak in Zaanannim, and Adami-nekeb, and Jabneel, as far as Lakkum; and it ended at the Jordan; 34then the boundary turns westward to Aznoth-tabor, and goes from there to Hukkok, touching Zebulun at the south, and Asher on the west, and Judah on the east at the Jordan. 35The fortified towns are Ziddim, Zer, Hammath, Rakkath, Chinnereth, 36Adamah, Ramah, Hazor, 37Kedesh, Edrei, En-hazor, 38Iron, Migdal-el, Horem, Beth-anath, and Beth-shemesh—nineteen towns with their villages. 39This is the inheritance of the tribe of Naphtali according to its families— the towns with their villages.

40The seventh lot came out for the tribe of Dan, according to its families. 41The territory of its inheritance included Zorah, Eshtaol, Ir-shemesh, 42Shaalabbin, Aijalon, Ithlah, 43Elon, Timnah, Ekron, 44Eltekeh, Gibbethon, Baalath, 45Jehud, Bene-berak, Gath-rimmon, 46Me-jarkon, and Rakkon at the border opposite Joppa. 47When the territory of the Danites was lost to them, the Danites went up and fought against Leshem, and after capturing it and putting it to the sword, they took possession of it and settled in it, calling Leshem, Dan, after their ancestor Dan. 48This is the inheritance of the tribe of Dan, according to their families—these towns with their villages.

49When they had finished distributing the several territories of the land as inheritances, the Israelites gave an inheritance among them to Joshua son of Nun. 50By command of the LORD they gave him the town that he asked for, Timnath-serah in the hill country of Ephraim; he rebuilt the town, and settled in it.

51These are the inheritances that the priest Eleazar and Joshua son of Nun and the heads of the families of the tribes of the Israelites distributed by lot at Shiloh before the LORD, at the entrance of the tent of meeting. So they finished dividing the land.

NIV

⁵¹These are the territories that Eleazar the priest, Joshua son of Nun and the heads of the tribal clans of Israel assigned by lot at Shiloh in the presence of the LORD at the entrance to the Tent of Meeting. And so they finished dividing the land.

COMMENTARY

The remaining six tribes are given cursory treatment, as much because there is little related narrative material as because the lists are short. The allotments are numbered according to their order at Shiloh, beginning with Benjamin (18:11; 19:1). Having finished with Benjamin, Judah's neighbor to the north, the narrator turns to Simeon, Judah's close neighbor to the south, then to the remaining five tribes farther north, beyond Manasseh. Simeon lies wholly within Judah, and several of the towns listed occur in Judah's lists. Simeon seems to consist of two districts; the one centered on Beersheba contains fourteen towns, not thirteen as stated in v. 6. The ideal of fairness is touted again in v. 9. Asher includes great Phoenician towns within its bounds, another case of utopian dreaming (vv. 24-31). The towns listed for Naphtali are described as being fortified (vv. 35-38); for Palestine in the Late Bronze Age, only a handful of walled settlements are known from archaeology; most settlements were unwalled.

Dan (vv. 40-48) represents a case of a tribe that migrates. They move from their territory northwest of Judah (cf. Judg 5:17, 13-16) to the far north, around the sources of the Jordan River at the base of Mt. Hermon (v. 47). The story of Dan's migration is told more fully in Judges 18 (cf. Judg 1:34-35). Leshem probably is a variant of Laish (Judg 18:7, 14, 27, 29). Traditions of Dan relate to both locations, and it is possible that

the tribe was divided (cf. Judges 13–18). The town list for Dan (vv. 41-46) applies to the southern location, for which the writer has left room between the facing western boundaries of Judah (15:10-11) and Joseph (16:3). The list is apparently artificially constructed, mostly out of names for the Judah lists. The compiler begins with Zorah and Eshtaol, which are known from the story of Samson (Judg 13:2, 25) and are named in Judah's second district (15:33). He may then incorporate what was originally the fifth district before that became the Philistine region (15:45-47), heedless of the overlap with several towns mentioned in the Judahite boundary list (Beth-shemesh [Ir-shemesh], Timnah, Ekron).

When all the tribes have been assigned their grants, the Israelites obey God's command (presumably delivered via Joshua himself) to give Joshua the land grant of his choice (vv. 49-50). Joshua chooses Timnath-serah in Ephraim, with which thereafter he is traditionally associated and where his tomb and shrine rest. The name of his town appears as Timnath-heres in the LXX and Judg 2:9. The tomb, a saint's shrine in the time of Josiah that the resurgent monarch wishes to control rather than outlaw, is mentioned three times in the space of a few chapters (here; 24:29; and Judg 2:9; see the discussion at Josh 24:29). The conclusion at v. 51 brings to a close the process of allocation that began in 14:1.

JOSHUA 20:1-9, TOWNS FOR REFUGE

NIV

20 Then the LORD said to Joshua: [2]"Tell the Israelites to designate the cities of refuge, as I instructed you through Moses, [3]so that anyone who kills a person accidentally and unintentionally may flee there and find protection from the avenger of blood.

[4]"When he flees to one of these cities, he is to stand in the entrance of the city gate and state his case before the elders of that city. Then they are to admit him into their city and give him a place to live with them. [5]If the avenger of blood pursues him, they must not surrender the one accused, because he killed his neighbor unintentionally and without malice aforethought. [6]He is to stay in that city until he has stood trial before the assembly and until the death of the high priest who is serving at that time. Then he may go back to his own home in the town from which he fled."

[7]So they set apart Kedesh in Galilee in the hill country of Naphtali, Shechem in the hill country of Ephraim, and Kiriath Arba (that is, Hebron) in the hill country of Judah. [8]On the east side of the Jordan of Jericho[a] they designated Bezer in the desert on the plateau in the tribe of Reuben, Ramoth in Gilead in the tribe of Gad, and Golan in Bashan in the tribe of Manasseh. [9]Any of the Israelites or any alien living among them who killed someone accidentally could flee to these designated cities and not be killed by the avenger of blood prior to standing trial before the assembly.

[a]8 *Jordan of Jericho* was possibly an ancient name for the Jordan River.

NRSV

20 Then the LORD spoke to Joshua, saying, [2]"Say to the Israelites, 'Appoint the cities of refuge, of which I spoke to you through Moses, [3]so that anyone who kills a person without intent or by mistake may flee there; they shall be for you a refuge from the avenger of blood. [4]The slayer shall flee to one of these cities and shall stand at the entrance of the gate of the city, and explain the case to the elders of that city; then the fugitive shall be taken into the city, and given a place, and shall remain with them. [5]And if the avenger of blood is in pursuit, they shall not give up the slayer, because the neighbor was killed by mistake, there having been no enmity between them before. [6]The slayer shall remain in that city until there is a trial before the congregation, until the death of the one who is high priest at the time: then the slayer may return home, to the town in which the deed was done.'"

[7]So they set apart Kedesh in Galilee in the hill country of Naphtali, and Shechem in the hill country of Ephraim, and Kiriath-arba (that is, Hebron) in the hill country of Judah. [8]And beyond the Jordan east of Jericho, they appointed Bezer in the wilderness on the tableland, from the tribe of Reuben, and Ramoth in Gilead, from the tribe of Gad, and Golan in Bashan, from the tribe of Manasseh. [9]These were the cities designated for all the Israelites, and for the aliens residing among them, that anyone who killed a person without intent could flee there, so as not to die by the hand of the avenger of blood, until there was a trial before the congregation.

COMMENTARY

It may seem at first that chaps. 20–21, the related lists of towns for refuge and the levitical towns, form an addition to the deuteronomistic Joshua, since its conclusion (21:43-45) apparently duplicates the conclusion at 19:51. But 19:51 concludes the grants of land in Canaan, and 21:43-45 concludes the whole of the allocation that began in 13:1. Chapters 20–21 include set-tlements on both the east and the west sides of the Jordan; thus they mirror the description of the eastern tribal territories in chap. 13.

Moreover, both chap. 20 and chap. 21 have a deuteronomistic logic in that they fit the known purposes of Josiah's reform. The towns of refuge are designed to enhance the central power's control of cycles of violence. Clearly Josiah's reform was not meant to eliminate or even to reduce violence. But one of its purposes was to take as much as possible of the violence that did occur out of the hands of families and commonalities and put it in the hands of the state. In Athens, Draco's reform in 621 BCE, the year after Josiah's reform, had as its main purpose the melioration of the vendetta.

The levitical towns contribute to Josiah's control of and solicitude for the Levites. Conceivably the levitical towns are the vestige of a genuinely ancient institution, perhaps going back, as many have suggested, to the house of David's patronage of a scattered tribe of militant supporters (a hypothesis that is often overly romanticized). Barred from holding arable land (thus limited to pastureland) and, therefore, from turning into a landholding elite, as dependents of the centralizing monarch they could serve in the role of dispersed and intimidating trustees of the central shrine's law, well known for their militancy and readiness to use violence. However, whether these two chapters are primarily deuteronomistic or priestly in their present form is another question.

The tension between clan justice, especially as expressed in the blood feud or vendetta, and the prerogatives of central justice, with its interest in the supposed dispassionate weighing of evidence and circumstance, is an age-old theme. In industrialized societies, where large middle and influential upper classes have the benefit of well-developed systems of law, courts, and police, it is sometimes easy to forget how fragile and tenuous the maintenance of social order can be. In theory, people who are relatively poor or racially stigmatized enjoy the same benefits, but their lives often come closer than do those of well-off whites to the disorder, lawlessness, and capriciousness that characterized most societies before the modern era.

Under such circumstances, the blood feud functions as a form of primitive justice. According to the basic principle, in the absence of police and courts households undertake to avenge the murder of one of their own. The responsibility for revenge falls on kin in the same proportion as for redemption from debt, so that in Hebrew the "redeemer" (גאל *gōʾēl*) is also the "avenger." Justice is a private matter. In practice, blood guilt serves more often as the basis for a negotiated settlement with compensation than as a justification for answering one killing with an-

other. People usually—not always—prefer to work things out rather than pursue the potentially endless cycle of revenge and counterrevenge. This is important, because it relates directly to the purpose of the biblical towns of refuge, which represent a kind of compromise between private justice and monarchic justice, which in the deuteronomistic conception is overseen by a controlled magistracy.

While the institution of assigned urban asylums seems to make sense, it has the look of idealistic central planning often found in biblical law. The term used for "asylum" (מקלט *miqlāṭ*) occurs only in reference to these towns in priestly texts (Numbers 35; 1 Chronicles 6; and priestly parts of Joshua 20–21). There are no stories or historical accounts in the OT in which such towns appear. Elsewhere in the OT, asylum is provided by altars, as prescribed in the ancient law in Exod 21:13-14 (cf. 1 Kgs 1:50; 2:28). Outside of deuteronomistic or priestly legislation, such altars might be available practically anywhere. It is likely that the idea for asylum towns originated with the deuteronomists, forced on them as a repercussion of their radical law of centralization: The monarchy must support asylum; if altars outside Jerusalem are now illegal and, therefore, no longer available for asylum, something must take their place, and that something cannot depend on the availability of altars (cf. Deut 19:6, which recognizes distance to asylum as the problem).

Moses' order for asylum towns is given in two places, Deut 19:1-13 and Num 35:9-34. The deuteronomistic law calls for assigning three towns in the three main regions of highland Canaan, and another three towns if the east bank of the Jordan is conquered. The conquest of the east is described in Deut 2:26–3:17, so the three asylum towns there are designated already in Deut 4:41-43, one for each tribal territory. They are apparently major towns in the seventh century BCE, but none is mentioned in Joshua other than in chap. 21, where all the towns of refuge appear also in the list of levitical towns. The towns to the west are assigned by region rather than by tribe; Hebron and Shechem are the traditional centers of their regions ("Ephraim" [20:7] is used broadly, since Shechem belongs to Manasseh [17:2]), and Kedesh in Galilee serves for the deuteronomist the same northern urban and strategic functions as Dan did for the kings of Israel.[128] Killers who flee to one of these towns turn their case over to the magistracies of both the asylum town and the town of the person killed.

There is nothing in the priestly law that indicates the existence of asylum towns before Josiah's reform, even though there is no doubt that earlier monarchs wanted to control the vendetta. The protection of Cain at the beginning of the J strand (Gen 4:1-16) is an early reflection of this concern. However, several significant elements appear in the priestly law that are not in the deuteronomistic law. One is that the killer's justification for initial asylum is strictly defined rather than being left mostly to the town's magistrates. Second, the case is quickly brought to trial before the "congregation," the priestly concept of the collective of all Israel. Third, killers judged innocent of murder by the congregation may return to their asylum and must remain there "until the death of the high priest," when they can return home.

Both versions of the law of asylum are evident in Joshua 20, but an important textual variation affects the interpretation of these two versions and their origin. In the LXX, 20:4-6 is almost entirely missing; there the text of 20:1-3, 6 states simply that the towns required by Moses are to be designated so that the killer "without intent" (NIV, "accidentally") may flee there until there is a trial before the congregation. The phrase "by mistake" (NIV, "unintentionally") is missing from the LXX. Now "without intent" occurs in Numbers 35 and "by mistake" in Deuteronomy 19. It has also been noticed that the LXX text looks like it is based entirely on the priestly version of the law and that the longer MT version shows apparent deuteronomistic additions that have no part in the priestly law, not only "by mistake" (there

is no "or" in the Hebrew text), but also the negotiations between killer and town magistracy by which they must make a preliminary judgment in the case, before it goes before the "congregation" (20:4-5).

Some have regarded the magistrate's preliminary judgment as seriously inconsistent with the priestly law. Believing that the LXX version of Joshua 20 preserves a consistent understanding of the law, they reason that it represents, excepting one or two phrases, the earlier form of Joshua 20, and therefore that the earlier form follows the priestly rather than the deuteronomistic law.[129]

It is important to remember, however, that people have an interest in making an institution like the asylum towns work and in order to do so would have to be willing to give a killer the benefit of the doubt in a preliminary trial. With this in mind, the simpler explanation is that the MT of Joshua 20, the version familiar from the translations, represents the text's pre-LXX form (a deuteronomistic text with later priestly supplements) and that the shorter LXX text represents the alterations of a later scribe who had no particular need to see the system work. This scribe was disturbed by an apparent inconsistency between Deuteronomy 19 and Numbers 35 and, assuming that with the more determinate priestly law at the magistrates' disposal no preliminary trial would be needed, removed it, along with the vague "by mistake." In sum, the deuteronomistic version is more workable, the priestly version more defined, organized, and indeed centralized, but at the same time more theoretical; the MT represents the usual combination of the two on a deuteronomistic base, the LXX a revision in the direction of priestly strictness.[130]

128. John L. Peterson, "Kedesh, 3," *ABD* 4:11-12.

129. Alexander Rofé, "Joshua 20—Historico-Literary Criticism Illustrated," in *Empirical Models for Biblical Criticism*, ed. Jeffrey H. Tigay (Philadelphia: University of Pennsylvania Press, 1985) 131-47.
130. See A. Graeme Auld, "Cities of Refuge in Israelite Tradition," *JSOT* 10 (1978) 26-40.

REFLECTIONS

People who live in the so-called developed world, especially those who are not poor, may tend to take for granted the degree of basic law and order, or social peace, that they enjoy as the result of belonging to a comparatively democratic, wealthy, and well-policed society. There is vast room for improvement in the policing of society in developed countries, but compared with early agrarian and present-day poorer societies, the majority of their inhabitants are fortunate. Because we do not have to worry daily about ongoing vendettas, we may underestimate the boon that any attempt to control them, as with the town of refuge, represented. Such refuge may have been indispensable in the absence of effective alternatives.

JOSHUA 21:1-45, TOWNS WITH PASTURE LANDS FOR THE LEVITES

NIV

21 Now the family heads of the Levites approached Eleazar the priest, Joshua son of Nun, and the heads of the other tribal families of Israel ²at Shiloh in Canaan and said to them, "The LORD commanded through Moses that you give us towns to live in, with pasturelands for our livestock." ³So, as the LORD had commanded, the Israelites gave the Levites the following towns and pasturelands out of their own inheritance:

⁴The first lot came out for the Kohathites, clan by clan. The Levites who were descendants of Aaron the priest were allotted thirteen towns from the tribes of Judah, Simeon and Benjamin. ⁵The rest of Kohath's descendants were allotted ten towns from the clans of the tribes of Ephraim, Dan and half of Manasseh.

⁶The descendants of Gershon were allotted thirteen towns from the clans of the tribes of Issachar, Asher, Naphtali and the half-tribe of Manasseh in Bashan.

⁷The descendants of Merari, clan by clan, received twelve towns from the tribes of Reuben, Gad and Zebulun.

⁸So the Israelites allotted to the Levites these towns and their pasturelands, as the LORD had commanded through Moses.

⁹From the tribes of Judah and Simeon they allotted the following towns by name ¹⁰(these towns were assigned to the descendants of Aaron who were from the Kohathite clans of the Levites, because the first lot fell to them):

¹¹They gave them Kiriath Arba (that is, Hebron), with its surrounding pastureland, in the hill country of Judah. (Arba was the forefather of Anak.) ¹²But the fields and villages around the city they had given to Caleb son of Jephunneh as his possession.

¹³So to the descendants of Aaron the priest

NRSV

21 Then the heads of the families of the Levites came to the priest Eleazar and to Joshua son of Nun and to the heads of the families of the tribes of the Israelites; ²they said to them at Shiloh in the land of Canaan, "The LORD commanded through Moses that we be given towns to live in, along with their pasture lands for our livestock." ³So by command of the LORD the Israelites gave to the Levites the following towns and pasture lands out of their inheritance.

4The lot came out for the families of the Kohathites. So those Levites who were descendants of Aaron the priest received by lot thirteen towns from the tribes of Judah, Simeon, and Benjamin.

5The rest of the Kohathites received by lot ten towns from the families of the tribe of Ephraim, from the tribe of Dan, and the half-tribe of Manasseh.

6The Gershonites received by lot thirteen towns from the families of the tribe of Issachar, from the tribe of Asher, from the tribe of Naphtali, and from the half-tribe of Manasseh in Bashan.

7The Merarites according to their families received twelve towns from the tribe of Reuben, the tribe of Gad, and the tribe of Zebulun.

8These towns and their pasture lands the Israelites gave by lot to the Levites, as the LORD had commanded through Moses.

9Out of the tribe of Judah and the tribe of Simeon they gave the following towns mentioned by name, ¹⁰which went to the descendants of Aaron, one of the families of the Kohathites who belonged to the Levites, since the lot fell to them first. ¹¹They gave them Kiriath-arba (Arba being the father of Anak), that is Hebron, in the hill country of Judah, along with the pasture lands around it. ¹²But the fields of the town and its

NIV

they gave Hebron (a city of refuge for one accused of murder), Libnah, [14]Jattir, Eshtemoa, [15]Holon, Debir, [16]Ain, Juttah and Beth Shemesh, together with their pasturelands—nine towns from these two tribes.

[17]And from the tribe of Benjamin they gave them Gibeon, Geba, [18]Anathoth and Almon, together with their pasturelands—four towns. [19]All the towns for the priests, the descendants of Aaron, were thirteen, together with their pasturelands.

[20]The rest of the Kohathite clans of the Levites were allotted towns from the tribe of Ephraim:

[21]In the hill country of Ephraim they were given Shechem (a city of refuge for one accused of murder) and Gezer, [22]Kibzaim and Beth Horon, together with their pasturelands—four towns.

[23]Also from the tribe of Dan they received Eltekeh, Gibbethon, [24]Aijalon and Gath Rimmon, together with their pasturelands—four towns.

[25]From half the tribe of Manasseh they received Taanach and Gath Rimmon, together with their pasturelands—two towns. [26]All these ten towns and their pasturelands were given to the rest of the Kohathite clans.

[27]The Levite clans of the Gershonites were given:
from the half-tribe of Manasseh,
Golan in Bashan (a city of refuge for one accused of murder) and Be Eshtarah, together with their pasturelands—two towns;
[28]from the tribe of Issachar,
Kishion, Daberath, [29]Jarmuth and En Gannim, together with their pasturelands—four towns;
[30]from the tribe of Asher,
Mishal, Abdon, [31]Helkath and Rehob, together with their pasturelands—four towns;
[32]from the tribe of Naphtali,
Kedesh in Galilee (a city of refuge for one accused of murder), Hammoth Dor and Kartan, together with their pasturelands—three towns.
[33]All the towns of the Gershonite clans were thirteen, together with their pasturelands.

[34]The Merarite clans (the rest of the Levites) were given:

NRSV

villages had been given to Caleb son of Jephunneh as his holding.

13To the descendants of Aaron the priest they gave Hebron, the city of refuge for the slayer, with its pasture lands, Libnah with its pasture lands, [14]Jattir with its pasture lands, Eshtemoa with its pasture lands, [15]Holon with its pasture lands, Debir with its pasture lands, [16]Ain with its pasture lands, Juttah with its pasture lands, and Beth-shemesh with its pasture lands—nine towns out of these two tribes. [17]Out of the tribe of Benjamin: Gibeon with its pasture lands, Geba with its pasture lands, [18]Anathoth with its pasture lands, and Almon with its pasture lands—four towns. [19]The towns of the descendants of Aaron—the priests—were thirteen in all, with their pasture lands.

20As to the rest of the Kohathites belonging to the Kohathite families of the Levites, the towns allotted to them were out of the tribe of Ephraim. [21]To them were given Shechem, the city of refuge for the slayer, with its pasture lands in the hill country of Ephraim, Gezer with its pasture lands, [22]Kibzaim with its pasture lands, and Beth-horon with its pasture lands—four towns. [23]Out of the tribe of Dan: Elteke with its pasture lands, Gibbethon with its pasture lands, [24]Aijalon with its pasture lands, Gath-rimmon with its pasture lands—four towns. [25]Out of the half-tribe of Manasseh: Taanach with its pasture lands, and Gath-rimmon with its pasture lands—two towns. [26]The towns of the families of the rest of the Kohathites were ten in all, with their pasture lands.

27To the Gershonites, one of the families of the Levites, were given out of the half-tribe of Manasseh, Golan in Bashan with its pasture lands, the city of refuge for the slayer, and Beeshterah with its pasture lands—two towns. [28]Out of the tribe of Issachar: Kishion with its pasture lands, Daberath with its pasture lands, [29]Jarmuth with its pasture lands, En-gannim with its pasture lands—four towns. [30]Out of the tribe of Asher: Mishal with its pasture lands, Abdon with its pasture lands, [31]Helkath with its pasture lands, and Rehob with its pasture lands—four towns. [32]Out of the tribe of Naphtali: Kedesh in Galilee with its pasture lands, the city of refuge for the

NIV

from the tribe of Zebulun,

Jokneam, Kartah, [35]Dimnah and Nahalal, together with their pasturelands—four towns;
[36]from the tribe of Reuben,

Bezer, Jahaz, [37]Kedemoth and Mephaath, together with their pasturelands—four towns;
[38]from the tribe of Gad,

Ramoth in Gilead (a city of refuge for one accused of murder), Mahanaim, [39]Heshbon and Jazer, together with their pasturelands—four towns in all.

[40]All the towns allotted to the Merarite clans, who were the rest of the Levites, were twelve.

[41]The towns of the Levites in the territory held by the Israelites were forty-eight in all, together with their pasturelands. [42]Each of these towns had pasturelands surrounding it; this was true for all these towns.

[43]So the LORD gave Israel all the land he had sworn to give their forefathers, and they took possession of it and settled there. [44]The LORD gave them rest on every side, just as he had sworn to their forefathers. Not one of their enemies withstood them; the LORD handed all their enemies over to them. [45]Not one of all the LORD's good promises to the house of Israel failed; every one was fulfilled.

NRSV

slayer, Hammoth-dor with its pasture lands, and Kartan with its pasture lands—three towns. [33]The towns of the several families of the Gershonites were in all thirteen, with their pasture lands.

[34]To the rest of the Levites—the Merarite families—were given out of the tribe of Zebulun: Jokneam with its pasture lands, Kartah with its pasture lands, [35]Dimnah with its pasture lands, Nahalal with its pasture lands—four towns. [36]Out of the tribe of Reuben: Bezer with its pasture lands, Jahzah with its pasture lands, [37]Kedemoth with its pasture lands, and Mephaath with its pasture lands—four towns. [38]Out of the tribe of Gad: Ramoth in Gilead with its pasture lands, the city of refuge for the slayer, Mahanaim with its pasture lands, [39]Heshbon with its pasture lands, Jazer with its pasture lands—four towns in all. [40]As for the towns of the several Merarite families, that is, the remainder of the families of the Levites, those allotted to them were twelve in all.

[41]The towns of the Levites within the holdings of the Israelites were in all forty-eight towns with their pasture lands. [42]Each of these towns had its pasture lands around it; so it was with all these towns.

[43]Thus the LORD gave to Israel all the land that he swore to their ancestors that he would give them; and having taken possession of it, they settled there. [44]And the LORD gave them rest on every side just as he had sworn to their ancestors; not one of all their enemies had withstood them, for the LORD had given all their enemies into their hands. [45]Not one of all the good promises that the LORD had made to the house of Israel had failed; all came to pass.

COMMENTARY

The list of levitical towns, which includes all the towns of refuge in Joshua 20, fulfills the command of Moses described in the priestly text in Num 35:1-8, of which it is an elaboration. Like all the town lists in Joshua, this one has generated much discussion regarding date, and proposals have ranged from the earliest to the latest periods, from pre-monarchic to Persian times. After surveying the archaeological evidence for the sites listed, Peterson concluded that the list could not have

been composed before the eighth century BCE, and his results have been widely accepted.[131] The list is dependent on both the list of allotments in Joshua 13–19 and the list of towns of refuge in Joshua 21, and is duplicated with variations in the

131. John L. Peterson, "A Topographical Surface Survey of the Levitical 'Cities' of Joshua 21 and 1 Chronicles 6: Studies on the Levites in Israelite Life and Religion" (Th.D. diss., Seabury-Western Theological Seminary, Evanston, 1977). This work is cited often in the secondary literature; see esp. Robert G. Boling and G. Ernest Wright, *Joshua,* AB 6 (New York: Doubleday, 1982) 487-96.

Persian-period priestly version of the house of David's history, in 1 Chr 6:39-66. Nowhere else does the Deuteronomistic History show an interest in the levitical genealogy by which Joshua 21 is structured. Once more the distribution is headed by Eleazar before Joshua, a priestly earmark (21:1). The list displays a degree of formality not found in the deuteronomistic parts of Joshua. Four levitical groups (the usual three plus the Aaronids) receive four towns from each of the twelve tribes, except that Judah and Simeon together give up nine instead of eight and thus Naphtali gives up three. Since all the towns in a given tribe go to one of the Levite groups, the four groups receive respectively 13, 13, 12, and 11 towns, the least possible deviation from the ideal of 12 towns apiece.[132] The imbalance is created by the Aaronids' receiving an additional town in Judah and Simeon. By itself the imbalance does not indicate, as some have supposed, that the writer was forced to accommmodate a pre-existing list; there is nothing to stop a writer from changing a source to fit his scheme. The so-called imbalance makes its own point: the primacy of Aaron.

The present list's emphasis is on the family of Aaron, and the imbalance contributes to this emphasis. The Aaronids claim the levitical towns in Judah, including Hebron, which has already in Joshua been granted to Caleb (14:6-15; 15:13), and including Debir, which Caleb has granted to his nephew (15:15-19). Technically Caleb's rights are honored by means of a distinction, which is found only here in the book of Joshua, between the town and its pasturelands, on the one hand, and its villages and their arable land, on the other hand (21:11-12). It is as if each town, consistent with the glaringly unrealistic scheme of Num 35:5, possessed no adjacent arable land. The Aaronids here also lay claim to Anathoth, the traditional home of the rivals of the Aaronids, the Elide remnant behind the deuteronomistic reform (21:18). Indeed, the Aaronids receive more towns than do all the rest of their Kohathite branch, or than either of the other two levitical branches.[133] The Aaronids claim the levitical towns of Judah, Simeon, and Benjamin, the three territories closest to Jerusalem, presumably a reflection of their Persian-period dominance.

In Num 35:1-8, Moses prescribes a mythical rational allotment of levitical towns: The pasturage extends exactly two thousand cubits from the town wall (Num 35:5; all 48 towns are walled)—where usually the best garden and arable land would be expected—and more towns are to be taken from the larger tribes (Num 35:8). In Joshua 21, Eleazar and Joshua distribute the towns by lot (21:4-6, 8, 10). Many have supposed that the two passages contradict each other, but this is unlikely. The difference between mythical theory and fulfillment by lot characterizes most if not all of the connections between Numbers and Joshua.[134] That the Aaronids are first to come up by lot does not contradict their appointment as the main priestly family in the Tetrateuch. The mythic picture of towns surrounded with pastureland is apparently confirmed in 21:42. The allocation is said to be in direct fulfillment of Moses' command (21:2-3, 8).

In sum, in Joshua 22, the Aaronids are the focus of an artificial composition dependent on deuteronomistic parts of Joshua but devoid of deuteronomistic features, excepting perhaps the sparseness of levitical towns in Ephraim and Manasseh. The Aaronids dominate the Jerusalemite heartland, and the other Levites are pushed to the margins, from the perspective of Jerusalem. The Aaronid towns lie beyond the bounds of the Persian province of Yehud to the south, in the Edomite marches, and to the west, in the Philistine marches. This distribution may express the hope of the Persian-period Aaronids to expand their power. As Ben Zvi has concluded, this list "provides a glimpse into the world of claims, disappointments and hopes of the post-monarchic period" when the Aaronid priests ruled Jerusalem.[135]

The grand concluding statement in 21:43-45 is contradicted many times in the book of Joshua. This represents the era of Joshua, according to the deuteronomistic concept, at its most prominent, and the contradictions serve only to point up how strongly held the ideal was.

---

132. Ehud Ben Zvi, "The List of Levitical Cities," *JSOT* 54 (1992) 86-87.

133. Ibid., 77-106.

134. Ibid., 81n. 1.

135. Ibid., 105. See also Nadav Na'aman, *Borders and Districts in Biblical Historiography: Seven Studies in Biblical Geographical Lists* (Jerusalem: Simor, 1986) 203-36; John R. Spencer, "Levitical Cities," *ABD* 4:310-11.

REFLECTIONS

The traditional dominant priestly families of the house of David returned, under the putative headship of Aaron, to harass the Levites, whose reform was long since dead and whose protestations are most pronounced in Isaiah 56–66. This is one of the many turns of events in the history of God's people that make it difficult or impossible to state categorically what God is up to. Eventually the priestly offices behind this chapter fell into oblivion following the fall of the Temple in 70 CE, which radically changed the face not only of Judaism but of Christianity as well. Whether the early church looked for a priestly messiah in addition to their royal messiah is unclear, but following the fall of the Temple such an idea, if it was ever held, lost all appeal. The restoration of comparable offices—an established and endowed cult leadership allied with the state—awaited the establishment of Christianity in the fourth and fifth centuries CE. Even then, the established priesthood rarely became hereditary, as it was in the Bible.

The failure of the church's priesthood to become hereditary was a measure not of the church's weakness but of its strength, the ability to prevent the prorogative of appointing priests, and with them their endowments, from falling out of the hands of the church's central authorities. This principle came under greatest threat at the time of emerging modern states in the fifteenth and sixteenth centuries. Clearly the Reformation also represented a diminishing of the church's central power. In Protestant churches, typically whatever of their support wealthier ministers were able to preserve passed to their heirs rather than back to the church. More important, in many instances appointments to endowments ended up in the hands mostly of laymen, as in Scotland for over two hundred years.

The endowment of the church today and the relationship of that endowment to the ministry of the church raise significant issues regarding the future of churches. As churches become wealthier in endowment, frequently the ministers and priests of the church become poorer. This is particularly the case in Protestant old-line churches, where, for example, the educational indebtedness of the pastorate has reached unprecedented levels. Because the ministry and priesthood have become so thoroughly professionalized, and because a profession that pays poorly may fail to attract the most able and qualified persons to its ranks, churches run the risk of enhancing their financial stability at the cost of an effective ministry. Add to this potential development the shrinking of membership in old-line churches, and the picture of churches resting on secure endowments but unsure ministries and uncertain memberships begins to take shape. The threat of identities and ministries driven mainly by endowment rather than vision, not a new situation in the history of the church, must be taken seriously. The purpose of such reflection is not to presume to prophesy about the future of the church, but to prompt the interpreter to consider the church's endowment and its current disposition in the light of God's will for the church.

A SECOND ALTAR: LEGAL OR NOT?

NIV

22 Then Joshua summoned the Reubenites, the Gadites and the half-tribe of Manasseh ²and said to them, "You have done all that Moses the servant of the LORD commanded, and you have obeyed me in everything I commanded. ³For a long time now—to this very day—you have not deserted your brothers but have carried out the mission the LORD your God gave you. ⁴Now that the LORD your God has given your brothers rest as he promised, return to your homes in the land that Moses the servant of the LORD gave you on the other side of the Jordan. ⁵But be very careful to keep the commandment and the law that Moses the servant of the LORD gave you: to love the LORD your God, to walk in all his ways, to obey his commands, to hold fast to him and to serve him with all your heart and all your soul."

⁶Then Joshua blessed them and sent them away, and they went to their homes. ⁷(To the half-tribe of Manasseh Moses had given land in Bashan, and to the other half of the tribe Joshua gave land on the west side of the Jordan with their brothers.) When Joshua sent them home, he blessed them, ⁸saying, "Return to your homes with your great wealth—with large herds of livestock, with silver, gold, bronze and iron, and a great quantity of clothing—and divide with your brothers the plunder from your enemies."

⁹So the Reubenites, the Gadites and the half-tribe of Manasseh left the Israelites at Shiloh in Canaan to return to Gilead, their own land, which they had acquired in accordance with the command of the LORD through Moses.

¹⁰When they came to Geliloth near the Jordan in the land of Canaan, the Reubenites, the Gadites and the half-tribe of Manasseh built an imposing altar there by the Jordan. ¹¹And when the Israelites heard that they had built the altar on the border of Canaan at Geliloth near the Jordan on the Israelite side, ¹²the whole assembly of Israel gathered at Shiloh to go to war against them.

¹³So the Israelites sent Phinehas son of Eleazar,

NRSV

22 Then Joshua summoned the Reubenites, the Gadites, and the half-tribe of Manasseh, ²and said to them, "You have observed all that Moses the servant of the LORD commanded you, and have obeyed me in all that I have commanded you; ³you have not forsaken your kindred these many days, down to this day, but have been careful to keep the charge of the LORD your God. ⁴And now the LORD your God has given rest to your kindred, as he promised them; therefore turn and go to your tents in the land where your possession lies, which Moses the servant of the LORD gave you on the other side of the Jordan. ⁵Take good care to observe the commandment and instruction that Moses the servant of the LORD commanded you, to love the LORD your God, to walk in all his ways, to keep his commandments, and to hold fast to him, and to serve him with all your heart and with all your soul." ⁶So Joshua blessed them and sent them away, and they went to their tents.

7Now to the one half of the tribe of Manasseh Moses had given a possession in Bashan; but to the other half Joshua had given a possession beside their fellow Israelites in the land west of the Jordan. And when Joshua sent them away to their tents and blessed them, ⁸he said to them, "Go back to your tents with much wealth, and with very much livestock, with silver, gold, bronze, and iron, and with a great quantity of clothing; divide the spoil of your enemies with your kindred." ⁹So the Reubenites and the Gadites and the half-tribe of Manasseh returned home, parting from the Israelites at Shiloh, which is in the land of Canaan, to go to the land of Gilead, their own land of which they had taken possession by command of the LORD through Moses.

10When they came to the region[a] near the Jordan that lies in the land of Canaan, the Reubenites and the Gadites and the half-tribe of Manasseh built there an altar by the Jordan, an

ᵃ Or to Geliloth

the priest, to the land of Gilead—to Reuben, Gad and the half-tribe of Manasseh. [14]With him they sent ten of the chief men, one for each of the tribes of Israel, each the head of a family division among the Israelite clans.

[15]When they went to Gilead—to Reuben, Gad and the half-tribe of Manasseh—they said to them: [16]"The whole assembly of the LORD says: 'How could you break faith with the God of Israel like this? How could you turn away from the LORD and build yourselves an altar in rebellion against him now? [17]Was not the sin of Peor enough for us? Up to this very day we have not cleansed ourselves from that sin, even though a plague fell on the community of the LORD! [18]And are you now turning away from the LORD?

" 'If you rebel against the LORD today, tomorrow he will be angry with the whole community of Israel. [19]If the land you possess is defiled, come over to the LORD's land, where the LORD's tabernacle stands, and share the land with us. But do not rebel against the LORD or against us by building an altar for yourselves, other than the altar of the LORD our God. [20]When Achan son of Zerah acted unfaithfully regarding the devoted things,[a] did not wrath come upon the whole community of Israel? He was not the only one who died for his sin.' "

[21]Then Reuben, Gad and the half-tribe of Manasseh replied to the heads of the clans of Israel: [22]"The Mighty One, God, the LORD! The Mighty One, God, the LORD! He knows! And let Israel know! If this has been in rebellion or disobedience to the LORD, do not spare us this day. [23]If we have built our own altar to turn away from the LORD and to offer burnt offerings and grain offerings, or to sacrifice fellowship offerings[b] on it, may the LORD himself call us to account.

[24]"No! We did it for fear that some day your descendants might say to ours, 'What do you have to do with the LORD, the God of Israel? [25]The LORD has made the Jordan a boundary between us and you—you Reubenites and Gadites! You have no share in the LORD.' So your descendants might cause ours to stop fearing the LORD.

[26]"That is why we said, 'Let us get ready and build an altar—but not for burnt offerings or

altar of great size. [11]The Israelites heard that the Reubenites and the Gadites and the half-tribe of Manasseh had built an altar at the frontier of the land of Canaan, in the region[a] near the Jordan, on the side that belongs to the Israelites. [12]And when the people of Israel heard of it, the whole assembly of the Israelites gathered at Shiloh, to make war against them.

13Then the Israelites sent the priest Phinehas son of Eleazar to the Reubenites and the Gadites and the half-tribe of Manasseh, in the land of Gilead, [14]and with him ten chiefs, one from each of the tribal families of Israel, every one of them the head of a family among the clans of Israel. [15]They came to the Reubenites, the Gadites, and the half-tribe of Manasseh, in the land of Gilead, and they said to them, [16]"Thus says the whole congregation of the LORD, 'What is this treachery that you have committed against the God of Israel in turning away today from following the LORD, by building yourselves an altar today in rebellion against the LORD? [17]Have we not had enough of the sin at Peor from which even yet we have not cleansed ourselves, and for which a plague came upon the congregation of the LORD, [18]that you must turn away today from following the LORD! If you rebel against the LORD today, he will be angry with the whole congregation of Israel tomorrow. [19]But now, if your land is unclean, cross over into the LORD's land where the LORD's tabernacle now stands, and take for yourselves a possession among us; only do not rebel against the LORD, or rebel against us[b] by building yourselves an altar other than the altar of the LORD our God. [20]Did not Achan son of Zerah break faith in the matter of the devoted things, and wrath fell upon all the congregation of Israel? And he did not perish alone for his iniquity!' "

21Then the Reubenites, the Gadites, and the half-tribe of Manasseh said in answer to the heads of the families of Israel, [22]"The LORD, God of gods! The LORD, God of gods! He knows; and let Israel itself know! If it was in rebellion or in breach of faith toward the LORD, do not spare us today [23]for building an altar to turn away from following the LORD; or if we did so to offer burnt offerings or grain offerings or offerings of well-being on it, may

---

[a]20 The Hebrew term refers to the irrevocable giving over of things or persons to the LORD, often by totally destroying them.   [b]23 Traditionally *peace offerings*, also in verse 27

[a] Or *at Geliloth*   [b] Or *make rebels of us*

NIV

sacrifices.' [27]On the contrary, it is to be a witness between us and you and the generations that follow, that we will worship the LORD at his sanctuary with our burnt offerings, sacrifices and fellowship offerings. Then in the future your descendants will not be able to say to ours, 'You have no share in the LORD.'

[28]"And we said, 'If they ever say this to us, or to our descendants, we will answer: Look at the replica of the LORD's altar, which our fathers built, not for burnt offerings and sacrifices, but as a witness between us and you.'

[29]"Far be it from us to rebel against the LORD and turn away from him today by building an altar for burnt offerings, grain offerings and sacrifices, other than the altar of the LORD our God that stands before his tabernacle."

[30]When Phinehas the priest and the leaders of the community—the heads of the clans of the Israelites—heard what Reuben, Gad and Manasseh had to say, they were pleased. [31]And Phinehas son of Eleazar, the priest, said to Reuben, Gad and Manasseh, "Today we know that the LORD is with us, because you have not acted unfaithfully toward the LORD in this matter. Now you have rescued the Israelites from the LORD's hand."

[32]Then Phinehas son of Eleazar, the priest, and the leaders returned to Canaan from their meeting with the Reubenites and Gadites in Gilead and reported to the Israelites. [33]They were glad to hear the report and praised God. And they talked no more about going to war against them to devastate the country where the Reubenites and the Gadites lived.

[34]And the Reubenites and the Gadites gave the altar this name: A Witness Between Us that the LORD is God.

NRSV

the LORD himself take vengeance. [24]No! We did it from fear that in time to come your children might say to our children, 'What have you to do with the LORD, the God of Israel? [25]For the LORD has made the Jordan a boundary between us and you, you Reubenites and Gadites; you have no portion in the LORD.' So your children might make our children cease to worship the LORD. [26]Therefore we said, 'Let us now build an altar, not for burnt offering, nor for sacrifice, [27]but to be a witness between us and you, and between the generations after us, that we do perform the service of the LORD in his presence with our burnt offerings and sacrifices and offerings of well-being; so that your children may never say to our children in time to come, "You have no portion in the LORD." ' [28]And we thought, If this should be said to us or to our descendants in time to come, we could say, 'Look at this copy of the altar of the LORD, which our ancestors made, not for burnt offerings, nor for sacrifice, but to be a witness between us and you.' [29]Far be it from us that we should rebel against the LORD, and turn away this day from following the LORD by building an altar for burnt offering, grain offering, or sacrifice, other than the altar of the LORD our God that stands before his tabernacle!"

30When the priest Phinehas and the chiefs of the congregation, the heads of the families of Israel who were with him, heard the words that the Reubenites and the Gadites and the Manassites spoke, they were satisfied. [31]The priest Phinehas son of Eleazar said to the Reubenites and the Gadites and the Manassites, "Today we know that the LORD is among us, because you have not committed this treachery against the LORD; now you have saved the Israelites from the hand of the LORD."

32Then the priest Phinehas son of Eleazar and the chiefs returned from the Reubenites and the Gadites in the land of Gilead to the land of Canaan, to the Israelites, and brought back word to them. [33]The report pleased the Israelites; and the Israelites blessed God and spoke no more of making war against them, to destroy the land where the Reubenites and the Gadites were settled. [34]The Reubenites and the Gadites called the altar Witness;[d] "For," said they, "it is a witness between us that the LORD is God."

[d] Cn Compare Syr: Heb lacks *Witness*

COMMENTARY

At last, with conquest and land distribution concluded, Israel's fighting force has dispersed to new homelands, whose ethnic cleansing they have well begun if not ended. For the first time in over forty-five years of migration and fighting, the descendants of Jacob can look forward to a settled existence. Five generations after God had, within sight of the scene of the great battle of Ai (Joshua 7–8), promised the land to Jacob and his offspring (Gen 28:13-15; cf. Gen 13:3, 14-17), that promise now reaches its fulfillment as the households and clans of the children of Israel embark on the final stage of their long journey home—unaware that the troubled period of the "saviors" and "judges," when "there was no king in Israel," lies just ahead.

Not only have the loyal east Jordan tribes fought side by side with their kin in the west bank, but with their own land grants from Moses already in hand, they have also patiently attended the ceremony in which Joshua allots the remaining land and sends the happy recipients home. Now the men of the east Jordan tribes stand alone before Joshua at Shiloh, waiting to be dismissed. Joshua applauds their loyalty and, with a last admonition to love Yahweh and obey Moses, sends them on their way back to their families. Scarcely out of Joshua's sight, they come to the Jordan and, before crossing, build an altar, as though Moses' law of centralization had gone in one ear and out the other. Fearful that God would answer such an outrageous act of hostility with collective punishment, the west-bank tribes hurry back to Shiloh to make war against their own people (cf. Judges 20). They dispatch a delegation to reason with the rebels. Surely, the delegation complains, the rebels remember what happened when one man, Achan, broke the law—the whole nation was made to pay the price of defeat. At once the alleged culprits invoke Yahweh as the God of gods (22:22, 34), reaffirming Yahweh's oneness, and declare their innocence. They built the altar, they say, in Manasseh on the west side of the Jordan, not in order to break away from Israel's one cult and jurisdiction and establish their own on the east side—the sin of Jeroboam before its time—but to create a suitable monument to their right to belong to the jurisdiction of Israel and to hold their lands by that right. Separated from the heartland by the Jordan, they will not allow themselves to be disowned and thereby dispossessed by some future kin who, mistaking the Jordan for a national boundary, might shout across the river, "You have no portion [of land] in Yahweh"—that is, "Since we bar you from the central cult of Yahweh, your claim to land under its sovereignty is invalid" (note how this theme both begins and ends the expression of the tribes' concern in 22:25-27). The delegation from Shiloh is convinced by this protestation, since after all the east-bank tribes had shared the struggle to the end, and they return and mollify the rest of Israel.

As just told, these events continue the deuteronomistic story. This is the second time a second altar appears in the book of Joshua (see 8:30-35). Unlike the previous altar, this altar belongs to the original deuteronomistic narrative of Joshua and, ironically, plays a central role. Despite appearances, it is not the main subject. The main subject is the Jordan River, to whose significance the altar is a witness. The point of these events is that the Jordan may be a symbolic and administrative boundary, but it is not a national boundary. The Deuteronomists have to make this point clearly at the end of the entire story of Joshua, since at the beginning of the story they laid so much emphasis on the Jordan as a boundary (e.g., 1:2, 11, 14-15; 3:1–5:1; 7:7; 9:1; 12:1, 7; 15:5; 16:1; Deut 2:29; 3:17; 9:1; 11:31; 12:10; 30:18; 31:13).

Quite by plan, this episode forms part of a fourfold frame around the whole deuteronomistic narrative of conquest and allotment. At the beginning: (1) Joshua received his commission and mustered the Israelites; (2) Joshua called on the east-bank tribes to fight with their west-bank kin until the war was over, and they loyally consented; (3) Rahab was loyal; (4) all Israel crossed the Jordan from east to west in a heroic entrance into the promised land. The last deuteronomistic parts of the book of Joshua mirror the first, in reverse order: The east-bank tribes arrive at the Jordan prepared to cross from west to east (compare 4); they commit an act that looks like Achan's disloyalty (presaged when Joshua mentions spoil, 22:8), in contrast to Rahab's loyalty (3); they reaffirm their loyalty to their west-bank kin (2); and Joshua musters all the Israelites to bid them farewell (1). This narrative plan shows that the writer matched the story of Israel's crossing of the Jordan (chaps. 3–5) with the story of the building of the altar at the Jordan (chap. 22), confirming that the main issue is the status of the Jordan, an issue for which the attention-getting apparent act of disregard for the cardinal law of centralization provides a perfect vehicle.

In the light of this correspondence, it is no accident that the place where the east-bank tribes arrive at the Jordan and build their altar is called גלילות (gĕlîlôt, v. 10). Whether this is a descriptive term (NRSV, "region near the Jordan") or a place name (NIV, "Geliloth"), it plays on the name "Gilgal," the site of the first crossing and of Achan's crime. The word is uncommon and puzzled the LXX translators. They rendered the first occurrence "Gilgal" and the second "Gilead"; the first makes some symbolic sense, the second some geographical sense, since Gilead lies nearby to the east. Wordplay was already a feature of the tradition on which this episode is based. Like the story in Gen 31:44-54, it explains the meaning of Gilead, "the cairn of witness" (in vv. 9, 13, 15, 32, the name refers not just to Gilead proper, but to the east bank in general).

The discussion so far has ignored much of Joshua 22, because this chapter is filled with priestly language and motifs that have been added to make the original deuteronomistic story considerably longer than it once was.[136] Although it is not always certain what was added, most of the priestly phrases appear in the section of the story dealing with the delegation, of which Phinehas the son of Eleazar is made the leader, presumably in place of Joshua. Identifiable traces of priestly additions include the phrase involving "possession" (vv. 9, 19); the "sons of Reuben or Gad" in place of simply Reuben or Gad; the priestly word for "tribe" (v. 14 and elsewhere); "treachery"; the "whole congregation"; the ten "chiefs"; the sin of Peor, where Phinehas played the saving role (Num 25:1-13; cf. the absence of Phinehas in Deut 4:3-4); the "defiled land"; the phrase "where Yahweh's tabernacle now stands" (v. 19); the elaboration of altar offerings; probably "copy" (v. 28); possibly the phrase "that stands before his tabernacle" (v. 29); all of v. 31; and "destroying" the land (v. 33). The priestly additions seem designed to highlight Phinehas's concern for purity and the priestly succession from Eleazar to Phinehas, anticipating Eleazar's death and burial (24:33).

136. John S. Kloppenborg, "Joshua 22: The Priestly Editing of an Ancient Tradition," *Bib* 62 (1981) 347-71.

REFLECTIONS

The east-bank tribes are portrayed as so anxious not to be excluded from the "nation" under Joshua that they risk the appearance of violating what is arguably the chief of all the laws Moses laid down as they themselves first stood near the banks of the Jordan: the law of the central altar (Deut 12:1-14). How were the other tribes to know that their altar was meant as a memorial rather than as a bid either to build and control the central altar or to build a second altar to rival the future central altar? The grave danger of misunderstanding gives a poignant edge to the narrative's characterization of the fear of exclusion. The east-bank tribes' fear of exclusion went as deep as it did because the social boundaries of the "nation" were defined so unconditionally and so violently.

There lies here an acutely disquieting irony: The more exactly and emphatically the edge of the sword (overt, as in the world of Joshua, or covert, as often in ours) marks the dividing line between those who belong and those who do not, between those who are in and those who are out, the more those who are in may be troubled with the possibility of ending up with those who are out. Such is the nature of division and factioning, as prevalent with supposedly constructive as well as destructive acts of distinguishing. There is a lesson in this text worth reflecting on: Is it not often the case that the more definite the criteria distinguishing those who belong from those who do not, the more the purpose of such criteria becomes questionable and the criteria themselves self-defeating? Given the nature of human beings, the more precise and systematic the division of one group from another becomes, the more untidy it becomes. The probable reason is that division arises from fear, and fear engenders more fear.

In addition, the present narrative raises an important issue regarding how people in a group work out an understanding of themselves and their values and identity. The story is that the east-bank tribes felt they had to test an important point of possible future legal contention: Could the Jordan be construed as a national boundary? Nothing had been said or done that necessitated such a conclusion, but neither had it clearly been ruled out, and the great emphasis on the Jordan, despite the continued solicitude for the east-bank tribes, left the matter in potential limbo.

Perhaps the closest parallel to this episode today, when laws provide one of the best delineations of values, is the testing of laws in a constitutional or quasi-constitutional system of jurisprudence. If there is a question of the meaning of a law, let it be violated, either substantively or technically. Through the ensuing process, the exact limits of the law will be discovered.

Sometimes in order to determine one point of law, an ancillary or corollary point must be raised. The west-bank tribes ruled on the irregular altar, but what they were really addressing was the issue of the river, and the resulting "national" constituency.

In general, a group's values and identity can often best be measured by concrete actions or decisions rather than by statements of principle. What beliefs and commitments define a group, including a church or a congregation? The answer lies in what they do when particular uncertainties or dilemmas arise. It is often observed, moreover, that there is no better indicator of the values of a group or organization than its budget, which defines the investment of resources, time, and money. To what is a church or congregation committed? Read its budget.

JOSHUA BIDS FAREWELL

OVERVIEW

At the end of his life, Joshua gathers all the tribes together one last time to hear his farewell speech. In the original deuteronomistic narrative, this speech was followed directly by Joshua's death and burial and the deuteronomists' final characterization of the period of Joshua (24:29-31). Joshua 24:1-28 interrupts this sequence to describe a covenant at Shechem. Joshua 24 is not clearly deuteronomistic (see Commentary on 24:1-28). Its historical and literary affinities are uncertain. It summarizes the history from Abraham to Joshua from available scripture, uses stock motifs from covenant rites, and has possible connections with Josh 8:30-35.[137] In some ways it is redundant with chap. 23, from which it may borrow the list of heads gathered (23:2; 24:1; but cf. 8:33), so that Joshua ends up admonishing both the political nation and the popular nation twice.

137. For recent study of covenant, see Robert A. Oden, Jr., "The Place of Covenant in the Religion of Israel," in *Ancient Israelite Religion* (Philadelphia: Fortress, 1987) 429-47; Robert Davidson, "Covenant Ideology in Ancient Israel," in *The World of Ancient Israel: Sociological, Anthropological and Political Perspectives,* ed. Ronald E. Clements (Cambridge: Cambridge University Press, 1989) 323-47; George E. Mendenhall and Gary A. Herion, "Covenant," *ABD* 1:1179-1202.

JOSHUA 23:1-16, LOVE YAHWEH OR LOSE YOUR LAND

NIV

23 After a long time had passed and the LORD had given Israel rest from all their enemies around them, Joshua, by then old and well advanced in years, ²summoned all Israel—their elders, leaders, judges and officials—and said to them: "I am old and well advanced in years. ³You yourselves have seen everything the LORD your God has done to all these nations for your sake; it was the LORD your God who fought for you. ⁴Remember how I have allotted as an inheritance for your tribes all the land of the nations that remain—the nations I conquered—between the Jordan and the Great Sea*a* in the west. ⁵The LORD your God himself will drive them out of your way. He will push them out before you, and you will take possession of their land, as the LORD your God promised you.

a4 That is, the Mediterranean

NRSV

23 A long time afterward, when the LORD had given rest to Israel from all their enemies all around, and Joshua was old and well advanced in years, ²Joshua summoned all Israel, their elders and heads, their judges and officers, and said to them, "I am now old and well advanced in years; ³and you have seen all that the LORD your God has done to all these nations for your sake, for it is the LORD your God who has fought for you. ⁴I have allotted to you as an inheritance for your tribes those nations that remain, along with all the nations that I have already cut off, from the Jordan to the Great Sea in the west. ⁵The LORD your God will push them back before you, and drive them out of your sight; and you shall possess their land, as the LORD your God promised you. ⁶Therefore be very steadfast to observe and do all that is written in the book of the law of Moses,

NIV

6"Be very strong; be careful to obey all that is written in the Book of the Law of Moses, without turning aside to the right or to the left. 7Do not associate with these nations that remain among you; do not invoke the names of their gods or swear by them. You must not serve them or bow down to them. 8But you are to hold fast to the LORD your God, as you have until now.

9"The LORD has driven out before you great and powerful nations; to this day no one has been able to withstand you. 10One of you routs a thousand, because the LORD your God fights for you, just as he promised. 11So be very careful to love the LORD your God.

12"But if you turn away and ally yourselves with the survivors of these nations that remain among you and if you intermarry with them and associate with them, 13then you may be sure that the LORD your God will no longer drive out these nations before you. Instead, they will become snares and traps for you, whips on your backs and thorns in your eyes, until you perish from this good land, which the LORD your God has given you.

14"Now I am about to go the way of all the earth. You know with all your heart and soul that not one of all the good promises the LORD your God gave you has failed. Every promise has been fulfilled; not one has failed. 15But just as every good promise of the LORD your God has come true, so the LORD will bring on you all the evil he has threatened, until he has destroyed you from this good land he has given you. 16If you violate the covenant of the LORD your God, which he commanded you, and go and serve other gods and bow down to them, the LORD's anger will burn against you, and you will quickly perish from the good land he has given you."

NRSV

turning aside from it neither to the right nor to the left, 7so that you may not be mixed with these nations left here among you, or make mention of the names of their gods, or swear by them, or serve them, or bow yourselves down to them, 8but hold fast to the LORD your God, as you have done to this day. 9For the LORD has driven out before you great and strong nations; and as for you, no one has been able to withstand you to this day. 10One of you puts to flight a thousand, since it is the LORD your God who fights for you, as he promised you. 11Be very careful, therefore, to love the LORD your God. 12For if you turn back, and join the survivors of these nations left here among you, and intermarry with them, so that you marry their women and they yours, 13know assuredly that the LORD your God will not continue to drive out these nations before you; but they shall be a snare and a trap for you, a scourge on your sides, and thorns in your eyes, until you perish from this good land that the LORD your God has given you.

14"And now I am about to go the way of all the earth, and you know in your hearts and souls, all of you, that not one thing has failed of all the good things that the LORD your God promised concerning you; all have come to pass for you, not one of them has failed. 15But just as all the good things that the LORD your God promised concerning you have been fulfilled for you, so the LORD will bring upon you all the bad things, until he has destroyed you from this good land that the LORD your God has given you. 16If you transgress the covenant of the LORD your God, which he enjoined on you, and go and serve other gods and bow down to them, then the anger of the LORD will be kindled against you, and you shall perish quickly from the good land that he has given to you."

COMMENTARY

Joshua's farewell speech is replete with deuteronomistic phraseology. As a set piece of exhortation, it compares with Moses' lengthy prologue and epilogue to the law (Deuteronomy 6–11; 29–31). This is not surprising, since Moses' entire speech in Deuteronomy, including the law, is cast,

like Joshua's speech here, as a farewell. Joshua's last speech also compares with David's in 1 Kgs 2:1-9; moreover, Joshua and David are the only persons in the Deuteronomistic History who at death's door say they are "about to go the way of all the earth" (23:14; 1 Kgs 2:2). Joshua's last speech corresponds structurally to Yahweh's first (1:2-9), in which Joshua is commissioned like a monarch; thus Joshua takes his leave from the story the same way he entered it: looking like the Davidic dynast for whom he stands.

Joshua emphasizes that what made Israel's victories possible was Yahweh's fighting on their side. If their success is not to be reversed, the Israelites must remain subjects of Yahweh, obedient to the law of Moses. This is Moses' theme put in the diction of conquest: Obey the law and take the land; continue to obey the law or lose the land. When encountering this rhetoric, the reader must not lose sight of exactly what this law entails, beginning with chillingly brutal ethnic conflict, ruthless centralization, and benevolent debt remission. Joshua emphasizes the exclusive character of Israel, different in kind from the other "nations," so that association and intermarriage are excluded (vv. 7, 12). This exclusion has more than a polemical social or "ethnic" thrust. Marriages sealed alliances, and in Josiah's world the main purpose of alliances was to create political and economic networks for siphoning the produce of Palestine into the channels of trade. As conceived here, intermarriage is a facet of the commercialization that Josiah, through his reform, is seen to set himself against.

The interdiction of intermarriage does not correspond to any of the deuteronomistic laws of Moses and plays an explicit role elsewhere in the Deuteronomistic History only in Deut 7:3 and perhaps Judges 21, which it is sometimes thought to anticipate. It is perfectly consistent, however, with the reform plan to eliminate rival cults, stem the commodification of agriculture, and interpose the state in the affairs of patriarchal households. Intermarriage becomes an even greater concern in the Persian period, when, with the resurgence of Aegean traders in the eastern Mediterranean, commercialization remained a threat to the populace, and opposing it remained a useful basis for popular appeal. The interdiction of marriage is thus a possible indication that the end of Joshua 23 may include changes or additions from the hand of the exilic or later editor of the Deuteronomistic History (see Introduction). The "if" in v. 12 is not ambiguous; however, the clauses in v. 15-16 are ambiguous and can be read as factual or conditional. Thus v. 15 may be understood modally: "Yahweh may bring upon you all the bad worse [curse]." Verse 16 may begin with either a conditional "if" (both NRSV and NIV) or a factual "when." The Hebrew may favor "when," the exilic sense.

The "great and strong" nations in v. 9 recall the description of the tribes of Joseph in 17:17, even though the Hebrew terms are different. Power is always relative, and Yahweh helps to keep it that way.

REFLECTIONS

The prohibition of intermarriage in terms of ethnic affiliation brings up the issue of definitions of race and ethnicity in our own culture. Race and ethnicity are socially constructed categories. This does not mean that they are unreal, but that they have no inherent or essential reality apart from the political, social, and economic history that gives rise to them. Not only particular "races," but also the notion of race itself has a historical origin. The "white" race in North America represents an instructive example. The historical contingencies that led to the emergence of "whites" were complex, but its many facets have been well studied in recent years. These include the development of the so-called descent rule for eliminating intermediate identities (a single identifiable black ancestor made one black); the bureaucratic fondness for the classification "Caucasian," as though it represented a scientific category, even though it was invented by an eighteenth-century German naturalist who simply thought people from the Caucasus were the most beautiful; and the process by which in the United States during the nineteenth century the Irish, who in the British context played a role similar to that of Africans in the United States, came to be identified as "white."[138]

The prohibition of intermarriage in Joshua 23 targeted marriage alliances between major

138. See Ivan Hannaford, "The Idiocy of Race," *The Wilson* Quarterly 18:2 (Spring 1994) 8-44, and *Race: The History of an Idea in the West* (Baltimore: Johns Hopkins University Press, 1996); Marvin Harris, *Patterns of Race in the Americas* (New York: Norton, 1974); Stephen Jay Gould, "The Geometer of Race," *Discover* 15:11 (November 1994) 64-69; Noel Ignatiev, *How the Irish Became White* (New York: Routledge, 1995).

land owners under the supposed jurisdiction of the Temple, and hence "Judean," on the one hand, who were in a position to commercialize agriculture to the detriment of commoners and, on the other hand, traders with Mediterranean links. The prohibition is stated in "ethnic" terms, but its purpose, like marriage among the elite in the ancient world, was largely political and economic. In reflecting on parallels to the prohibition in modern times, the interpreter thus should focus on the undue or unjust advantage gained by the wealthy through questionable alliances.

JOSHUA 24:1-28, COVENANT AT SHECHEM

NIV

24 Then Joshua assembled all the tribes of Israel at Shechem. He summoned the elders, leaders, judges and officials of Israel, and they presented themselves before God.

²Joshua said to all the people, "This is what the LORD, the God of Israel, says: 'Long ago your forefathers, including Terah the father of Abraham and Nahor, lived beyond the River*a* and worshiped other gods. ³But I took your father Abraham from the land beyond the River and led him throughout Canaan and gave him many descendants. I gave him Isaac, ⁴and to Isaac I gave Jacob and Esau. I assigned the hill country of Seir to Esau, but Jacob and his sons went down to Egypt.

⁵" 'Then I sent Moses and Aaron, and I afflicted the Egyptians by what I did there, and I brought you out. ⁶When I brought your fathers out of Egypt, you came to the sea, and the Egyptians pursued them with chariots and horsemen*b* as far as the Red Sea.*c* ⁷But they cried to the LORD for help, and he put darkness between you and the Egyptians; he brought the sea over them and covered them. You saw with your own eyes what I did to the Egyptians. Then you lived in the desert for a long time.

⁸" 'I brought you to the land of the Amorites who lived east of the Jordan. They fought against you, but I gave them into your hands. I destroyed them from before you, and you took possession of their land. ⁹When Balak son of Zippor, the king of Moab, prepared to fight against Israel, he sent for Balaam son of Beor to put a curse on you. ¹⁰But I would not listen to Balaam, so he blessed you again and again, and I delivered you out of his hand.

*a2 That is, the Euphrates; also in verses 3, 14 and 15   *b6 Or charioteers   *c6 Hebrew* Yam Suph; *that is, Sea of Reeds*

NRSV

24 Then Joshua gathered all the tribes of Israel to Shechem, and summoned the elders, the heads, the judges, and the officers of Israel; and they presented themselves before God. ²And Joshua said to all the people, "Thus says the LORD, the God of Israel: Long ago your ancestors—Terah and his sons Abraham and Nahor—lived beyond the Euphrates and served other gods. ³Then I took your father Abraham from beyond the River and led him through all the land of Canaan and made his offspring many. I gave him Isaac; ⁴and to Isaac I gave Jacob and Esau. I gave Esau the hill country of Seir to possess, but Jacob and his children went down to Egypt. ⁵Then I sent Moses and Aaron, and I plagued Egypt with what I did in its midst; and afterwards I brought you out. ⁶When I brought your ancestors out of Egypt, you came to the sea; and the Egyptians pursued your ancestors with chariots and horsemen to the Red Sea.*a* ⁷When they cried out to the LORD, he put darkness between you and the Egyptians, and made the sea come upon them and cover them; and your eyes saw what I did to Egypt. Afterwards you lived in the wilderness a long time. ⁸Then I brought you to the land of the Amorites, who lived on the other side of the Jordan; they fought with you, and I handed them over to you, and you took possession of their land, and I destroyed them before you. ⁹Then King Balak son of Zippor of Moab, set out to fight against Israel. He sent and invited Balaam son of Beor to curse you, ¹⁰but I would not listen to Balaam; therefore he blessed you; so I rescued you out of his hand. ¹¹When you went over the Jordan and came to Jericho, the citizens of Jericho fought against you, and also the Amorites, the Perizzites,

a Or Sea of Reeds

NIV

[11]" 'Then you crossed the Jordan and came to Jericho. The citizens of Jericho fought against you, as did also the Amorites, Perizzites, Canaanites, Hittites, Girgashites, Hivites and Jebusites, but I gave them into your hands. [12]I sent the hornet ahead of you, which drove them out before you— also the two Amorite kings. You did not do it with your own sword and bow. [13]So I gave you a land on which you did not toil and cities you did not build; and you live in them and eat from vineyards and olive groves that you did not plant.'

[14]"Now fear the LORD and serve him with all faithfulness. Throw away the gods your forefathers worshiped beyond the River and in Egypt, and serve the LORD. [15]But if serving the LORD seems undesirable to you, then choose for yourselves this day whom you will serve, whether the gods your forefathers served beyond the River, or the gods of the Amorites, in whose land you are living. But as for me and my household, we will serve the LORD."

[16]Then the people answered, "Far be it from us to forsake the LORD to serve other gods! [17]It was the LORD our God himself who brought us and our fathers up out of Egypt, from that land of slavery, and performed those great signs before our eyes. He protected us on our entire journey and among all the nations through which we traveled. [18]And the LORD drove out before us all the nations, including the Amorites, who lived in the land. We too will serve the LORD, because he is our God."

[19]Joshua said to the people, "You are not able to serve the LORD. He is a holy God; he is a jealous God. He will not forgive your rebellion and your sins. [20]If you forsake the LORD and serve foreign gods, he will turn and bring disaster on you and make an end of you, after he has been good to you."

[21]But the people said to Joshua, "No! We will serve the LORD."

[22]Then Joshua said, "You are witnesses against yourselves that you have chosen to serve the LORD."

"Yes, we are witnesses," they replied.

[23]"Now then," said Joshua, "throw away the foreign gods that are among you and yield your hearts to the LORD, the God of Israel."

NRSV

the Canaanites, the Hittites, the Girgashites, the Hivites, and the Jebusites; and I handed them over to you. [12]I sent the hornet[a] ahead of you, which drove out before you the two kings of the Amorites; it was not by your sword or by your bow. [13]I gave you a land on which you had not labored, and towns that you had not built, and you live in them; you eat the fruit of vineyards and oliveyards that you did not plant.

[14]"Now therefore revere the LORD, and serve him in sincerity and in faithfulness; put away the gods that your ancestors served beyond the River and in Egypt, and serve the LORD. [15]Now if you are unwilling to serve the LORD, choose this day whom you will serve, whether the gods your ancestors served in the region beyond the River or the gods of the Amorites in whose land you are living; but as for me and my household, we will serve the LORD."

[16]Then the people answered, "Far be it from us that we should forsake the LORD to serve other gods; [17]for it is the LORD our God who brought us and our ancestors up from the land of Egypt, out of the house of slavery, and who did those great signs in our sight. He protected us along all the way that we went, and among all the peoples through whom we passed; [18]and the LORD drove out before us all the peoples, the Amorites who lived in the land. Therefore we also will serve the LORD, for he is our God."

[19]But Joshua said to the people, "You cannot serve the LORD, for he is a holy God. He is a jealous God; he will not forgive your transgressions or your sins. [20]If you forsake the LORD and serve foreign gods, then he will turn and do you harm, and consume you, after having done you good." [21]And the people said to Joshua, "No, we will serve the LORD!" [22]Then Joshua said to the people, "You are witnesses against yourselves that you have chosen the LORD, to serve him." And they said, "We are witnesses." [23]He said, "Then put away the foreign gods that are among you, and incline your hearts to the LORD, the God of Israel." [24]The people said to Joshua, "The LORD our God we will serve, and him we will obey." [25]So Joshua made a covenant with the people that day, and made statutes and ordinances for them

[a] Meaning of Heb uncertain

NIV

²⁴And the people said to Joshua, "We will serve the LORD our God and obey him."

²⁵On that day Joshua made a covenant for the people, and there at Shechem he drew up for them decrees and laws. ²⁶And Joshua recorded these things in the Book of the Law of God. Then he took a large stone and set it up there under the oak near the holy place of the LORD.

²⁷"See!" he said to all the people. "This stone will be a witness against us. It has heard all the words the LORD has said to us. It will be a witness against you if you are untrue to your God."

²⁸Then Joshua sent the people away, each to his own inheritance.

NRSV

at Shechem. ²⁶Joshua wrote these words in the book of the law of God; and he took a large stone, and set it up there under the oak in the sanctuary of the LORD. ²⁷Joshua said to all the people, "See, this stone shall be a witness against us; for it has heard all the words of the LORD that he spoke to us; therefore it shall be a witness against you, if you deal falsely with your God." ²⁸So Joshua sent the people away to their inheritances.

COMMENTARY

Joshua re-calls the tribes to Shechem, last seen in 8:30-35, here introduced with a similar jump in location (for Shechem, see the Commentary on 8:30-35). The most distinctive aspect of this secondary passage is at the same time its closest link to 8:30-35: Joshua's publication of statutes and ordinances, which are recorded with the rest of the ceremony in the "document of the law of God" (24:25-26; cf. 8:32, 34-35). Joshua's new role as lawgiver puts him unusually at odds with the exclusive authority of the commandments and laws of Moses elsewhere in the book of Joshua. The law document here is referred to in the same way that the whole law of Moses—not just the law in Deuteronomy—is referred to in Neh 8:18 (cf. Neh 8:8; 10:29-30), confirming the impression that this passage was written later than most of the Deuteronomistic History. In 24:5, Aaron joins Moses, just as he does in the priestly additions to the Tetrateuch. Part of the distinctiveness of this passage is the way Joshua stands alone over against the Israelites rather than as first among them (cf. Josiah in 2 Kgs 23:1-3) to challenge them to faithfulness (24:15). (Joshua's challenge, if not his stance, has often appealed to preachers, helping to gain this idiosyncratic pericope its place in lieu of nearly all of the rest of Joshua in the church's common lectionary.) In the preceding chapter, Joshua had admonished the Israelites, but in the same congratulatory vein in which he had

sent the east-bank tribes on their way (22:2-7). In contrast, now all of a sudden he challenges the Israelites' apostasy to Mesopotamian and other gods. Even if these gods are meant to be the same as those mentioned in 23:16, read as fact rather than condition (see the Commentary on 23:1-16), the responses from Yahweh and Joshua contrast sharply: in the first instance immediate expulsion; in the second, the opportunity to repent. Precisely this contrast is what most typically differentiates the Josianic deuteronomist from the exilic deuteronomist. Whether or not Joshua 24 was written by the latter, its author was evidently not the former.

The central concern of this passage is the apostasy and idolatry of the Israelites. They apparently assume naively that they can serve Yahweh and other gods at the same time; this seems to be the reason for Joshua's response to their assertion of loyalty to Yahweh (24:16-19). Joshua induces them to foreswear their allegiance to "foreign gods" who are either of the east, in Mesopotamia, where Abraham left to migrate to Canaan, stopping first at Shechem (Gen 12:6), or of the Amorites in the conquered land (24:14-15; cf. 24:2). The rehearsal of the ancestors' history and the concern for idolatry are both reminiscent of the exilic deuteronomist (cf. Deut 4:1-40, especially the concern for idolatry in Deut 4:15-20 and the importance of the "fathers" [NRSV, "ancestors"] in Deut 4:31, 37; 2 Kgs 21:10-15); the concern for Mesopotamian gods appears to imply exile or continued residence in Mesopotamia. But there are still too few identifiable deuteronomistic features of the narrative to say that it was written by the same hand that is behind the main exilic deuteronomistic passages, as well as otherwise surprising omissions. Why, for example, does the writer of Joshua 24 not emphasize Baal of Peor (as Deut 4:3-4 does) in the account of Israel's history in 24:2-10? Much like Joshua 22, the narrative ends with the setting up of a monumental stone as a witness to the people's commitment to testify against themselves should they forsake Yahweh for foreign gods.

Shechem is a medial locale in the original Israelite highlands, including the region assigned to the tribes of Joseph. Thus it might be expected to play a greater role in the main narrative of conquest than it does. (This discrepancy is addressed in the discussion of Josh 8:30-35.) The present passage does not make up for this lack of attention—or Davidic slight—to Shechem, nor to the whole of Manasseh and Ephraim, excepting Shiloh, even though Joshua comes from Ephraim. In reality, Shechem lay more or less beyond the sphere of the house of David in every period but its beginning.

Verse 13 brings out as well as any other text in Joshua the nature of the conquest as dispossession and ethnic cleansing. It refers not to the historical Iron I settlement of the hill country, which occurred largely on previously unoccupied terrain, but to the unmerciful displacement of the vanquished.

Yahweh's deliverance of the Israelites calls for a response, which Joshua puts to the people in vv. 14-15. The NRSV's "revere" in place of "fear" (ירא yārē'; cf. NIV) reflects the contemporary change in many liberal churches from patriarchal piety to the piety of familiarity and friendship with God; in the world of the Bible, the meaning was fear and its effects, especially fealty toward the lord and his commandments—obedience to Yahweh and the law. Both the NRSV ("in sincerity and in faithfulness") and the NIV ("with all faithfulness") may miss the meaning of the Hebrew phrase "with integrity and with faithfulness" (בתמים ובאמת bĕtāmîm ûbe'ĕmet). It is possible that the phrase expresses a single idea, as the NIV suggests: "with a true faithfulness." It is equally possible, though, that the first term retains a separate meaning—namely, the congruence of professed and actual obedience. "Sincerity" may be understood in this way, but in contemporary English it may have too strong a subjective valence to capture a congruence that can be measured point by point against the standard of specific stipulations. The patriarchal character of Joshua's charge, quite contrary to the individualism that is important to nearly all modern churches, comes through clearly: As head of his household (the ביה-אב [bêt-'āb], or "house of the father"), Joshua not only speaks for all the men, women, and children in his charge, but he has also decided for them what they will do. The "people" who respond are not the whole populace, each individual speaking for himself or herself, but the "elders, heads, judges, and officials" (v. 1, apparently adopted from 23:2)—the patriarchal heads, who agree on behalf of the households in their charge.

REFLECTIONS

Joshua's charge at Shechem highlights loyalty and professions of loyalty. The text suggests reflecting on the character of loyalty and the object of loyalty.

The nature of loyalty in this text is typical for the Bible. Loyalty tended to be objective, definable according to a known norm or expectation, explicitly affirmed, and in principle strictly judged, even if by no one but God. Loyalty also had a significant subjective component; however, loyalty, including to God, centered not on the warm experience of acceptance, trust, and support that characterizes interpersonal relationships at their best in our culture, but on the trepidation, deference, habitual caution, and hopeful dependence that characterized a person's relationship with social superiors, those who truly were lord and master. Thus the fear commanded by Joshua included, and at the same time had to answer to, an element of anxiety that a lord might act erratically or impulsively. Joshua spells out the saving acts of God not only to magnify the burden on the listening patriarchal heads—feared in turn by their own subordinates—to respond, but also to assure the heads, and through them their subordinates, of God's consistency, to allay their fear of capriciousness.

In patriarchal or authoritarian settings, which some have opted for in the church as elsewhere, such loyalty may seem unexceptional. But for many others in the church, those influenced by modern ideas of democracy, self-responsibility, self-worth, toleration of differences, overlooking the faults of others, and liberal love, such loyalty may seem peculiar and repugnant. There are probably benefits and liabilities to both kinds of loyalty, biblical and modern, which careful reflection will bring out. Not everyone will choose to reflect in this way, however, since to do so is to embrace the great dilemma of faithfulness to God in modern times, approaching God, whom the Bible reveals as the supreme patriarch, as modern classical liberal individuals.

This dilemma is all the more profound because it arises within and is reinforced by the prevailing political context of modern times, the constitutional society, with the United States as the example to the world. As modern believers, we do what biblical believers did; we express our faith in terms of our political culture. In the Bible, political culture—relations of power for achieving and maintaining social order—meant that orders were handed down from above in an altogether patriarchal mode. For us, political culture ideally means that we ourselves determine the laws we live by. This is now true in most parts of the world, which comes as a source of encouragement and joy to most Americans. Hence, culturally speaking, "the people" in Joshua 24 are vastly different from the people featured as "we the people" in the preamble to the Constitution of the United States. This difference is eclipsed by the apparent choice made by the people in Josh 24:16-24. But it must be remembered that "the people" in Joshua 24 are not choosing the system of government they would institute or which laws they would live by, but simply which lord and master they would subordinate themselves to. The object of their loyalty is both *God,* who has handed down the law, and the *law* that comes from God. The object of our comparable loyalty is the state, which, in theory, we, the people, have constituted.

Practically speaking, for modern believers the acute dilemma epitomized by this text is resolved in the modern notion of religion, which excludes the political by definition. Thus those who want to include a political dimension in their definition of religion have to say so explicitly. As modern people, we instinctively accept this truncated notion of religion, the very foundation of the modern multiconfessional nation. It is essential to realize, however, that this notion of religion does not apply to the Bible and that if we wish to reflect wisely on the meaning of loyalty in the Bible, we have no choice but to include the political dimension in our thinking.

JOSHUA IS BURIED

NIV

NIV

²⁹After these things, Joshua son of Nun, the servant of the LORD, died at the age of a hundred and ten. ³⁰And they buried him in the land of his inheritance, at Timnath Serah*ᵃ* in the hill country of Ephraim, north of Mount Gaash.

³¹Israel served the LORD throughout the lifetime of Joshua and of the elders who outlived him and who had experienced everything the LORD had done for Israel.

³²And Joseph's bones, which the Israelites had brought up from Egypt, were buried at Shechem in the tract of land that Jacob bought for a hundred pieces of silver*ᵇ* from the sons of Hamor, the father of Shechem. This became the inheritance of Joseph's descendants.

³³And Eleazar son of Aaron died and was buried at Gibeah, which had been allotted to his son Phinehas in the hill country of Ephraim.

ᵃ30 Also known as Timnath Heres (see Judges 2:9)   ᵇ32 Hebrew hundred kesitahs; a kesitah was a unit of money of unknown weight and value.

NRSV

29After these things Joshua son of Nun, the servant of the LORD, died, being one hundred ten years old. ³⁰They buried him in his own inheritance at Timnath-serah, which is in the hill country of Ephraim, north of Mount Gaash.

31Israel served the LORD all the days of Joshua, and all the days of the elders who outlived Joshua and had known all the work that the LORD did for Israel.

32The bones of Joseph, which the Israelites had brought up from Egypt, were buried at Shechem, in the portion of ground that Jacob had bought from the children of Hamor, the father of Shechem, for one hundred pieces of money;*ᵃ* it became an inheritance of the descendants of Joseph.

33Eleazar son of Aaron died; and they buried him at Gibeah, the town of his son Phinehas, which had been given him in the hill country of Ephraim.

ᵃ Heb one hundred qesitah

COMMENTARY

Joshua was an Ephraimite hero, a saint venerated at his tomb. This may be as close as we can get to the historical Joshua, who almost certainly existed, but whose celebrated deeds just as certainly lie hidden in the mists of time. There are many kinds of deeds for which legendary heroes were venerated. Having been an Israelite tribal paramilitary leader is more than consistent with such veneration, as would having played a role like that of a Greek colonizer, a comparison broached in the discussion of 18:1-7. However, the all-Israel concept of the book of Joshua is extremely unlikely, both politically and geographically, to derive from traditions about such an Ephraimite local hero. Timnath-serah was located in the western part of Ephraim, midway between the town of Bethel, high in the hills, and the town of Aphek, in the coastal plain (cf. 19:49; Judg

2:6-9).[139] It is nowhere near any of the locations that play a significant role in the account of conquest. As explained in the Introduction, Joshua's name was probably introduced into the wider political arena by Jeroboam, who was born and raised close by Joshua's tomb, and into the house of David's history in the time of Hezekiah.

In contrast to our sparse knowledge of the historical Joshua, often there is a good deal of historical evidence for the colonizers. Most of these were roughly contemporary with Josiah, about whom considerably more is known than about Joshua. The colonizers' power was great, as we have seen, but what happened to these powers after the colonizers' death is usually un-

139. According to various Jewish, Samaritan, Christian, and Muslim traditions, the tomb of Joshua is located in seven widely separated places in Palestine, Lebanon, and Syria.

clear. What is clear is something that can probably also be assumed about Joshua: After he died he "became a hero, who was worshipped with ritual and offerings in the belief that he was immortal and would, if propitiated, care for the welfare of his foundation."[140] While barring possible offerings to the saint, Josiah apparently acquiesed in the veneration of Joshua at his tomb, a concession to popular piety made possible by the co-opting of his prestige in the Deuteronomistic History. To judge from a parallel to Josiah's suppression of popular saints, this may have saved him at least some trouble. In the 1830s the governor of Palestine was Ibrahim Pasha, who ruled during a nine-year Egyptian occupation. Ibrahim expropriated many of the lands that held the shrines of saints in an attempt to reduce their power and influence. It is said that when his soldiers tried to capture a village containing the tomb of a saint, they were attacked and driven back by a swarm of bees, which the villagers said were the saint himself defending his shrine.[141]

140. A. J. Graham, "The Colonial Expansion of Greece," in *The Cambridge Ancient History,* 2nd ed. (Cambridge: Cambridge University Press, 1982) 3:152. The generic role of such heroes in the local and regional politics of Palestine is explored in Scott D. Hill, "The Local Hero in Palestine in Comparative Perspective," in *Elijah and Elisha in Socioliterary Perspective,* ed. Robert B. Coote (Atlanta: Scholars Press, 1992) 37-73.
141. Philip J. Baldensperger, "Order of Holy Men in Palestine," *PEFQ* 25 (1984) 35.

The LXX of 24:30 contains a significant addition. It says that placed with Joshua in his tomb were the flint knives used to circumcise Israelites at Gilgal as Yahweh had commanded them to do, and that the knives are there "to this day." This may belong to the original Deuteronomistic History or it may, like 5:2-7, be a priestly touch. Either way, the notion that artifacts associated with the hero rest in his tomb with him is an authentic one, no different from the innumerable examples from the veneration of saints worldwide. In addition, in Palestine it was believed that objects left at a saint's shrine—such as plows, jewelry, or other valuables—came under the care of the saint and would be protected from theft.

The deuteronomistic summary of the period of Joshua follows directly on Joshua's death and burial. In the LXX this summary is placed before Joshua's death and burial, probably a rationalizing correction. The final two notices regarding Joseph's bones and the death and burial of Eleazar are secondary, the latter related to priestly additions to Joshua, the former possibly related to the addition of 24:1-28. It is striking that all three of these final burial notices pertain to the territory of the tribes of Joseph (Manasseh in the case of Joseph's bones, Ephraim in the case of Joshua and Eleazar), and not to the territory of Judah.

REFLECTIONS

Given that his tomb became enshrined, Joshua continued as a living spirit in his own right, so that Josiah did not simply pose as Joshua returned. However, the line between being a particular saint and only looking like that saint was less rigid and probably less significant in the biblical period than we might expect. For example, as is well known, in the Gospel of Mark, John the Baptist first appears at exactly the place where Elijah had last appeared, on the east side of the Jordan, and wearing a leather belt that makes him look like Elijah (Mark 1:6; cf. 2 Kgs 1:8). Not surprisingly, in the story some believe that John was actually Elijah returned (Mark 6:15). Modern readers might assume that the writer of Mark meant to make fun of such an idea. This would be a hasty assumption, though, since Jesus himself identifies John as Elijah (Mark 9:9-13), and he does so even though Elijah has just reappeared with Moses in his presence in the transfiguration (the mountain is symbolic of Mt. Horeb, which both Moses and Elijah visited; see Mark 9:2-8). Later this identification plays an important role in Jesus' death (Mark 15:34-37). Was Elijah on the mountain actually John come back? For the last time? This important irony in Mark partakes of the inevitable ambiguity that arises when a living individual reminds many of a deceased individual: The living person embodies the spirit of the deceased, not just in appearance or manner but frequently in quite substantial terms.

This is the way Josiah is presented in the Deuteronomistic History—that is, as the embodiment of the first heroic Israelite conqueror of Canaan, Joshua. Joshua's own separate role as a living spirit was not necessarily thereby usurped, even if the active veneration of Joshua might have been discouraged under deuteronomistic law. Josiah was not Joshua, but he might as well have been, given the important similarities between the two men, as between Elijah and John. Furthermore, we may think of saints as peace-loving doers of good for all people; but throughout history saints, whether in the Middle East or worldwide, including Christian saints, could be militant and brutal, as was Elijah, who on at least one occasion single-handedly slaughtered 850 people in cold blood (1 Kgs 18:1-40). Controlling cults of saints was important not only to Josiah in the biblical period or to Ibrahim Pasha in the nineteenth century, but to many other rulers, including Christian rulers.[142]

The veneration of saints and of the dead has varied much in the history of Christianity. Regardless of diverse official views regarding the dead, however, there may be few believers—or non-believers, for that matter—who doubt that the dead live on in some sense, especially those who lived exemplary or heroic lives, or whose lives were simply bound particularly close to ours. We often find that their continued presence is particularly intense at, but by no means limited to, the place of their burial or the disposal of their ashes. It may be useful to reflect on the continuing presence of the spirit of the departed, which can always be affirmed pastorally even without an elaborate or developed view of how such spirits relate to the fate of the dead or to material reality.

Christians belonging to traditions with a less developed sense of the effect of departed spirits or the influence of saints may want at least to bring to mind the importance of such figures in other traditions more in keeping with the perceptions and experiences of the biblical world. There are probably hundreds of such figures in the contemporary Christian world, in addition to the existing canonized saints of the Roman Catholic Church. Jesus Malverde is one of them. Malverde's shrine is found in Culiacan, in the Pacific Coast state of Sinaloa in Mexico. Around the turn of the century, Malverde is believed to have roamed the Culiacan hills, robbing the rich and feeding the poor, until the government caught up with him and executed him in 1909. All year a continuous stream of devotees, drawn largely from the poor and highland inhabitants of Sinaloa, come to Malverde's shrine to ask for favors—for health, safety, job success, protection from the government—and to give him thanks for his continuous deeds of kindness and assistance. The stories about Malverde are legion. They differ greatly, however, even over critical details like the manner of the saint's death. Historians have found no clear evidence that Malverde ever existed. But to his followers, he not only existed but is more powerful than ever, and they can make contact with him at his shrine, not far from the site of his death. "Thanks to God and Malverde," one follower was quoted as having said, "there's something for everyone. Not much, but something."[143]

142. Peter Brown, *The Cult of the Saints: Its Rise and Function in Latin Christianity* (Chicago: University of Chicago Press, 1981).
143. *San Francisco Sunday Examiner,* March 2, 1997.

THE BOOK OF JUDGES

INTRODUCTION, COMMENTARY, AND REFLECTIONS
BY
DENNIS T. OLSON

THE BOOK OF
JUDGES

INTRODUCTION

The book of Judges is one of the most exciting, colorful, and disturbing books of the Bible. It combines stories of political intrigue and assassination, lies and deception, rape and murder, courage and fear, great faith and idolatry, power and greed, sex and suicide, love and death, military victories and civil war. The book portrays a major transition in the biblical story of Israel. Before the book of Judges, Israel was under the leadership of Moses in the wilderness (Exodus–Deuteronomy) and then Joshua in the initial conquest of the land of Canaan (Joshua). After the book of Judges, Israel was ruled by kings, beginning with Saul, David, and Solomon and concluding with Judah's defeat and exile to Babylon (1–2 Samuel; 1–2 Kings; see 2 Kings 24–25). The turbulent transition between Moses and Joshua, on one hand, and the kings of Israel, on the other hand, is portrayed in the book of Judges. The book presents the varied tales of twelve warrior rulers, called judges, who led ancient Israel for brief periods in times of military emergency.

The book's title, "Judges," may bring to mind images of wise people who arbitrate legal cases in courts. Indeed, one of the so-called judges, Deborah, appears to function in this way as a mediator of disputes (4:4-5). However, the term "judge" (שׁפט *šōpēṭ*) in Hebrew can also mean "rule" or "ruler," and it is this meaning of the term that applies to the major characters in the book.[1] They are primarily warrior rulers who led Israel in fighting oppressive enemies. The judges were also involved in maintaining Israel's religious life and institutions with varying degrees of success (2:17; 5:1-31; 6:25-27; 8:22-28).

1. Temba L. J. Mafico, "Judge, Judging," in *The Anchor Bible Dictionary,* 6 vols. (New York: Doubleday, 1992) 3:1104.

JUDGES AND HISTORY

Scholars have debated the value of the book of Judges in reconstructing the early history of ancient Israel after its settlement in the land of Canaan in the twelfth and eleventh centuries BCE. Some commentators assume that many of the events and people recounted in Judges do reflect actual historical situations in this early period, although the stories have been significantly reshaped and edited.[2] For example, scholars argue that the ongoing struggle of the Israelites with other nations in Canaan over a long period of time in Judges may provide a more accurate picture of the conquest of Canaan than does the quick and total conquest as depicted in some parts of Joshua (Josh 11:23). Scholars also point to the Song of Deborah and Barak in Judges 5 as one of the most ancient parts of the Bible, with its origin in the period of the judges or the early monarchy.

Yet, scholars are also cautious about using Judges to reconstruct early Israelite history.[3] For example, if one adds all of the years of enemy oppression and the length of the judges' rule throughout the book (e.g., 3:8, 11), the total comes to 480 years. But, that is far too long a period to fit the roughly 300 years between the exodus, dated sometime in the thirteenth century, and the rise of kingship in the tenth century BCE. Moreover, some of the judges' stories may have originally been tales of local heroes and chieftains of small clan or tribal groups. The tales were then later rewritten so that they became stories of leaders of larger Israelite coalitions as they were incorporated into the book of Judges. Still other scholars believe that we simply do not have adequate evidence from archaeological or other textual sources to evaluate the overall historicity of the events in Judges.

METHODS IN THE INTERPRETATION OF JUDGES

The lively characters, the moral difficulties, the turbulent social context, and the theological questions that animate the book of Judges have occasioned a wide spectrum of response in the history of biblical interpretation. The rabbinic debate over whether Jephthah's daughter was actually offered as a burnt sacrifice and the ancient Christian interpretation of the death of Samson as a typological prefigurement of the death of Jesus are only two of many intriguing examples of the ancient approportion of Judges. Modern historical-critical interpretation of Judges has paid the most attention to the history of the composition of the book in the light of proposals for the growth of the larger Deuteronomistic History (Deuteronomy and Joshua–2 Kings). Most scholars agree that Judges emerged through several stages of collecting, writing, and editing.[4] Originally separate stories of local clan or tribal heroes were assembled into a larger connected narrative.

2. Robert G. Boling, *Judges,* AB 6A (Garden City, N.Y.: Doubleday, 1975) 9-29.
3. J. Alberto Soggin, *Judges,* OTL (Philadelphia: Westminster, 1981) 6-12.
4. An insightful survey and proposal for the editorial shaping of Judges is offered by Lawson Stone, "From Tribal Confederation to Monarchic State: The Editorial Perspective of the Book of Judges" (Ph.D. diss., Yale University; Ann Arbor: University Microfilms, 1987). Much of my view of the overall structure and movement of Judges is indebted to Stone's work.

Editorial sections were added at key junctures in and around the stories. A definitive two-part introduction (1:1–2:5; 2:6–3:6) and a two-part conclusion (17:1–18:31; 19:1–21:25) were also added in two or more editorial stages. This process occurred over many generations, culminating in two or three definitive periods of editorial shaping, including the time of King Hezekiah (eighth century BCE), King Josiah (seventh century BCE), and sometime after the exile of Judah to Babylon (sixth–fifth century BCE). The audience for the final form of Judges probably included the people of Judah, who had experienced the exile to Babylon and the disintegration of their social, political, and religious life (2 Kings 24–25). Judges continued to be read and interpreted in new contexts and thus lived on as a biblical paradigm for future generations.

The book of Judges has been an exceptionally fertile ground for a wide variety of newer approaches to biblical interpretation.[5] Narrative analyses of plot, character, point of view, repetition, and theme have proved to be profitable avenues of study. Judges contains one of the Bible's largest concentrations of female characters, nineteen in all. The variety of women in Judges has offered a rich resource for feminist scholarship on the relationship of women, power, and violence. Social-scientific criticism has found grist for its mill in the questions of the formation of Israelite society in the judges period, the function of kinship association in a tribal society, and the role of the judges as chieftains in the rise of Israelite kingship. Structuralist, deconstructive, and ideological criticisms have also found Judges to be amenable to their various strategies and methods of reading. The approach of this commentary on Judges is somewhat eclectic, using insights from various methods as they seem most helpful with a given text or issue. However, this commentary has a general tilt toward redactional and narrative analysis of the final form of the text, along with an overriding theological interest in the questions, issues, and struggles raised by the text for understanding the relationships of God, humans, and the world. This study of Judges is also informed by the Russian literary theorist Mikhail Bakhtin and his notion of competing dialogical voices and themes that are held together but not absorbed into one another.[6]

THE SHIFT FROM REPETITIVE CYCLES TO GRADUAL DECLINE

The book of Judges is often associated with a repetitive pattern or cycle outlined in 2:11-19 and repeated throughout the narratives of individual judges: Israel does evil, God sends an enemy; Israel cries in distress, God sends a judge or deliverer; Israel again does evil, and the cycle repeats. The cyclical pattern probably defined an earlier editorial layer of Judges. However, editors of the final form made important changes and additions that

---

5. A survey of new methods as applied to Judges is Gale Yee, ed., *Judges and Method: New Approaches in Biblical Studies* (Minneapolis: Fortress, 1995).

6. Among other works, see Mikhail Bakhtin, *Problems of Dostoevsky's Poetics,* ed. and trans. Caryl Emerson (Minneapolis: University of Minnesota Press, 1984), and *The Dialogic Imagination: Four Essays by M. M. Bakhtin,* ed. Michael Holquist (Austin: University of Texas Press, 1981). An example of a biblical scholar's application of Bakhtin's insights to some aspects of Judges is Robert Polzin, *Moses and the Deuteronomist: A Literary Study of the Deuteronomic History* (New York: Seabury, 1980).

redefined the basic movement of the book's plot. These changes redefined the judges era from its characterization as a series of flat cycles in endless repetition to a downward slide and increasingly severe disintegration of Israel's social and religious life. These changes included altering the two-part introduction to Judges so that it described the gradual deterioration of the twelve tribes' conquest of Canaan (1:1–2:5) and the gradual decline of Israel's faithfulness to the covenant with God (2:6–3:6).

The stories of the individual judges (3:7–16:31) also have been edited to exhibit a similar gradual decline from initial success and faithfulness among the early judges (Othniel, Ehud, Deborah, and Barak) to eventual ineffectiveness and unfaithfulness among the later judges (Jephthah, Samson). In the final chapters of Judges, Israel is portrayed as having no king or ruler, and "all the people did what was right in their own eyes" (17:6; 21:25). Israel disintegrates into religious and social chaos in this final phase of the judges era (17:1–21:25). God allowed Israel to hit bottom as punishment for its increasing sinfulness and idolatry. Yet in the midst of Israel's unraveling and near-death experiences, glimpses of hope emerge. Samson's shaved hair began to grow back (16:22). A faithful house of God remained functioning in northern Israel at Shiloh in spite of the idolatrous cult at Dan (18:30). The tribe of Benjamin was pulled back from the brink of extinction and death (20:46–21:24). God remained present and active even in the midst of sinful and tragic circumstances (20:18, 21, 28, 35).

IMPORTANT THEMES IN DIALOGICAL TENSION

The book of Judges contains a wide array of dialogical perspectives on key themes. The book holds together seemingly opposed or disjunctive viewpoints on the same subject. Only a few examples are cited here; more detailed discussions of these dialogical tensions will occur throughout the commentary. This dialectical character of Judges was the basis for Martin Buber's proposal that Judges contains two "books," an anti-monarchical book that opposes dynastic kingship (chaps. 1–12) and a pro-monarchical book that supports dynastic kingship (chaps. 13–21).[7] The first anti-kingship section offers a critique of foreign kings, like Adoni-bezek (1:5-7), fat King Eglon (3:15-25), and King Jabin of Canaan (4:23-24). In this same section, Gideon rejects the offer to become a king over Israel (8:22-23), and Jotham ridicules Abimelech's disastrous attempt to become an Israelite king (9:7-15). In contrast, Buber argued that the second half of Judges, chapters 13–21, is pro-kingship in that it laments the chaos and disintegration of Israel in a time when "there was no king in Israel" and "all the people did what was right in their own eyes" (17:6; 18:1; 19:1; 21:25).

However, in my judgment the book's view of kingship is more consistent throughout the book than Buber suggests, but no less dialectical.[8] The book of Judges affirms the need

---

7. Martin Buber, "The Books of Judges and the Book of Judges," in *The Kingship of God* (New York: Harper & Row, 1967) 66-84.

8. Stone, "From Tribal Confederation to Monarchic State," 77-84, 373-89. Stone reaches similar but not identical conclusions on Buber and Judges' view of kingship.

for human kingship in Israel *at this particular time in Israel's history* at the end of the judges era. However, the editors and readers of the final form of Judges and the Deuteronomistic History also know that kingship, like the institution of judgeship, will be flawed, temporary, and eventually collapse. Kingship in Israel, like the judges, will in time be replaced by another form of human leadership, which will be necessary but also provisional and imperfect. The era of the judges thus becomes a paradigm of any human institution, mode of governance, or ideology—necessary but provisional, helpful for a time, but eventually replaced by another.

Examples of other themes held in dialogical tension throughout Judges include the interplay of religion and politics, the well-being of women and the health of society, the benefits and threats of relationships with people of other nations, human character as both noble and deeply flawed, the subtle interplay of divine and human agency and actions, and small signs of hope in the midst of horrendous chaos and social disintegration. One final and overriding tension throughout Judges is the interplay of God's justice or punishment and God's mercy or compassion. God repeatedly punishes Israel for its continual evil, and yet God cannot let Israel go. This increasingly intense dance between divine justice and mercy raises questions as the reader moves through the chapters of Judges: How far can God's patience and mercy be stretched until it reaches a breaking point? How far can Israel stray from the covenant before God gives up on Israel altogether? The angel's words in 2:1-5 pose the tension. On one hand, God affirms to Israel, "I will never break my covenant with you" (2:1). But on the other hand, God promises to punish Israel because "you have not obeyed my command" (2:2). In the end, God's mercy will sustain God's relationship with Israel, but Israel will go through a time of national chaos and death in order for a new generation to be born and a new way forward to emerge as Israel's experiment in kingship opens up into the narratives about the rise of kingship in 1–2 Samuel.

BIBLIOGRAPHY

Commentaries:

Boling, Robert G. *Judges,* AB 6A. Garden City, N.Y.: Doubleday, 1975. A fresh translation with a commentary focused on linguistic, historical, archaeological, and text-critical matters; assumes that Judges underwent several stages of editing, although many of its narratives reflect actual historical events and persons dating from the twelfth and eleventh centuries BCE.

Gray, John. *Joshua, Judges, Ruth.* NCBC. Grand Rapids: Eerdmans, 1986. A historical-critical commentary concerned with understanding the history of composition and redaction of Judges and the meaning of terms and phrases in their ancient Near Eastern context.

Hamlin, E. John. *Judges: At Risk in the Promised Land.* ITC. Grand Rapids: Eerdmans, 1990. A commentary of theological reflection on Judges in dialogue with other biblical texts, including the New Testament; having taught for many years in an Asian context, the author seeks to make connections between Judges and contemporary global issues related to gender, race, class, and ecology.

Soggin, J. Alberto. *Judges.* OTL. Philadelphia: Westminster, 1981. A historical-critical commentary that is more skeptical about judgments concerning the historicity of the events and persons in Judges; covers issues of text, form, archaeology, geography, and history of composition.

Other studies:

Bal, Mieke. *Death and Dissymmetry: The Politics of Coherence in the Book of Judges.* Chicago: University of Chicago Press, 1988. A provocative feminist and literary analysis of the relationship of gender and violence throughout Judges as a sign of cultural upheaval and transition; argues that the male violence against the three daughters in Judges (Jephthah's daughter, Samson's wife, and Levite's concubine) is answered by the violent retribution of three displaced mothers (Jael, the woman with the millstone, and Delilah).

Brenner, Athalya, ed. *A Feminist Companion to Judges.* Sheffield: JSOT, 1993. A stimulating collection of feminist and womanist studies of the book's many and varied female characters, including leaders, mothers, wives, and daughters.

Klein, Lillian R. *The Triumph of Irony in the Book of Judges.* Sheffield: Almond, 1989. Argues for the widespread use of irony as one of the major literary devices at work in the book of Judges; traces the differing perspectives and levels of knowledge among the narrator, the characters, God, and the reader and the effects of such differences on interpretation.

Marcus, David. *Jephthah and His Vow.* Lubbock, Tex.: Texas Tech Press, 1986. A fascinating study of the history of traditional Jewish, Christian, and modern critical interpretation of the story of Jephthah and his vow concerning the sacrifice of his daughter.

Polzin, Robert. *Moses and the Deuteronomist: A Literary Study of the Deuteronomic History.* New York: Seabury, 1980. An insightful literary study of Deuteronomy, Joshua, and Judges that traces the thematic tensions and dialogic interplay between various narrative voices; argues that the central conflict is the voice of dogmatic authoritarianism versus the voice of critical traditionalism.

Trible, Phyllis. *Texts of Terror: Literary-Feminist Readings of Biblical Narratives.* Philadelphia: Fortress, 1984. Contains chapters on Jephthah's daughter in Judges 11 and the Levite's concubine in Judges 19; a close reading of the biblical text that follows its rhetoric and traces the effects of male violence on the women who become its tragic victims.

Stone, Lawson. "From Tribal Confederation to Monarchic State: The Editorial Perspective of the Book of Judges." Ph.D. dissertation, Yale University. Ann Arbor: University Microfilms, 1987. A detailed and well-argued redaction-critical study that proposes that later editors constructed a coherent and artful structure for the whole book of Judges, culminating in a pattern of deterioration from faithfulness and triumph among the early judges to tragedy and internal conflict among the later judges and the end of the judges period.

Webb, Barry. *The Book of the Judges: An Integrated Reading.* Sheffield: JSOT, 1987. A thorough literary and narrative analysis of the whole book of Judges, highlighting its literary artfulness, its structural coherence, and the meaningful repetition of key motifs throughout the book.

Yee, Gale A., ed. *Judges and Method: New Approaches in Biblical Studies.* Minneapolis: Fortress, 1995. Helpful methodological essays that explain and apply a number of new literary and sociological methods in biblical interpretation using selected texts from the book of Judges; the various approaches include narrative, social-scientific, feminist, structuralist, deconstructive, and ideological criticisms.

OUTLINE OF JUDGES

I. Judges 1:1–3:6, Introduction: Judges as an Era of Decline

    A. 1:1–2:5, From Success to Failure: The Conquest of Canaan

JUDGES 1:1–3:6

INTRODUCTION: JUDGES AS AN ERA OF DECLINE

OVERVIEW

The first major section of Judg 1:1–3:6 establishes the definitive pattern or paradigm for understanding the movement and structure of the entire book. The pattern defines the era of the Israelite judges as a series of generations who slide downward from initial successes and faithfulness to increasing failures and apostasy. The pattern is presented twice from two different perspectives within this introductory section. Judges 1:1–2:5 focuses on Israel's increasing failure in the military *conquest* of Canaan, and 2:6–3:6 focuses on Israel's growing unfaithfulness to the *covenant* with God. Israel's military inability or unwillingness to eradicate the Canaanites from the promised land becomes a symptom of a deeper problem—namely, Israel's failure to keep the covenant and worship the Lord alone.

Many scholars believe that this introduction in two parts reflects at least two stages in the writing and editing of the book of Judges.[9] The earliest part of the introduction is embedded within 2:6–3:6 and may have once functioned on its own as a prelude to an earlier version of the book. This earlier introduction defined the era of the judges as a cyclical and repetitive pattern of Israel's apostasy, God's punishment, and God's deliverance through a judge. The elements of this cyclical pattern are evident in 2:11-19: (1) Israel worshiped other gods (2:11-13); (2) the Lord became angry and handed Israel over to an enemy, who oppressed them (2:14-16); (3) Israel cried out, and the Lord responded in mercy by sending a judge to deliver Israel from its enemy (2:18); and (4) Israel would relapse into disobedience and apostasy, and the cycle would begin again (2:19). This

cyclical pattern was then attached to a series of stories of heroic individuals called judges. These judges were temporary leaders who formed loose alliances of Israelite tribes, won military victories against enemies, resolved intertribal conflicts, and restored peace for a time, until Israel sinned again and the next enemy threatened Israel once more.

The theology implied in such a cyclical and repetitive pattern is more mechanical than relational, more static than dynamic, more predictable than surprising and unexpected. But generations of Israelites who heard and passed on these stories about God and the judges came to believe that more needed to be said about the ways of God with Israel. Israel's experience with God was not as cyclical or predictable as this early introduction suggested. Israel was constantly surprised by God's unexpected ways both in judgment and in deliverance. For example, the prophet Jeremiah stunned the complacent leaders of his day with a surprising word of judgment from God for ignoring the deep wound of unfaithfulness among God's people: "They have treated the wound of my people carelessly, saying 'Peace, peace,' when there is no peace" (Jer 6:14 NRSV). On the other hand, the prophet of Isaiah 40–55 delivered unexpected words of God's promise of hope and a return home to a beleaguered and despondent audience of exiles in Babylon: "For you shall go out in joy, and be led back in peace" (Isa 55:12 NRSV). God's interactions with God's people were often surprising and contrary to guaranteed or predictable cycles from a human perspective.

Thus a later editor and community made additions to the earlier introduction that changed its orientation from a flat-line cyclical pattern to a downward slide, a decline from faithfulness in early generations to a deepening sinfulness and

---

9. For various perspectives on the history of the composition of this introductory section of Judges, see Robert G. Boling, *Judges,* AB 6 (Garden City, N.Y.: Doubleday, 1975) 29-38.

apostasy in later generations. The book of Judges explores the surprising ways in which God acted and related to Israel through the judges in the midst of this deterioration of Israel's social and religious life. As we shall see, one key addition was the insertion of 2:17, which demoted the judges from entirely positive and heroic deliverers to leaders who gained temporary military success but ultimately failed as religious leaders. Another addition was 2:20–3:6, including God's climactic pronouncement of a change in strategy in 2:20-21. Later generations also added a second and entirely new introduction to the book in 1:1–2:5.[10] Much of this later introduction that now begins the book of Judges is reworked material drawn from the preceding book of Joshua. This later introduction presents the last stages of the conquest of Canaan after the death of the leader Joshua as a downward spiral that moves from moderate successes by the southern tribe of Judah (1:1-21) to increasingly negative failures by the northern tribes of "the house of Joseph" (1:22-36).

These later editorial changes and additions created an important shift in the book's theology from a cyclical and mechanistic view of God's ways with Israel. The expanded two-part introduction paints a much more relational, dynamic, and intense portrait of God's anger and mercy in response to the growing failure and faithlessness of Israel in the period of the judges. The book of Judges is no longer a predictable cycle of temporary military heroes in Israel's history. Under the careful shaping of later editors, Judges introduces the record of Israel's slow and bumpy decline into apostasy and disintegration, a decline that even the judges sent by the Lord could not finally prevent or impede. The actual narratives of the judges in 3:7–16:31 have been shaped in the final form of the book to reflect this gradual decline in Israel's life and faith as a community of God's people. By the time we reach the final chapters of the book, the reader will be shocked by, but not wholly unprepared for, the horrific disintegration of Israel's religious and social fabric that Judges 17–21 narrates in tragic detail. A major theological question remains hanging over the end of the book of Judges: Now that the conquest of Canaan has been only partial, and now that the era of the judges has ended in failure and tragedy, what new strategy will God adopt in relating to and leading God's people? By the time we reach the end of Judges, Israel's life as a community will be so dramatically flawed that God will need to find a whole new way of leading and relating to God's people.

One other element to note in this opening section is the different time sequence within the two parts of the introduction. The time period associated with the first introductory section in 1:1–2:5 begins only "*after* the death of Joshua" (1:1). The brief narratives or notices about the conquest of Canaan that follow are all set in a time when Joshua is gone and off the stage. However, the time associated with the second introductory section in 2:6–3:6 takes the reader back in time and opens with a flashback scene when Joshua is still alive: "When Joshua dismissed the people . . ." (2:6). This section then moves through a series of generational phases: the lifetime of Joshua (2:6-7), a faithful generation of Israelites who outlived Joshua (2:7), and a new generation who did not know the Lord (2:10). This latter generation marks the beginning of a series of generations to whom God sends the judges to rescue Israel.

10. For details and arguments for this later redactional shaping of the introduction to Judges, see E. Theodore Mullen, "Judges 1:1–3:6: The Deuteronomistic Reintroduction of the Book of Judges," *HTR* 77 (1984) 33-54; and Lawson Stone, "From Tribal Confederation to Monarchic State: The Editorial Perspective of the Book of Judges" (Ph.d. diss., Yale University; Ann Arbor: University Microfilms, 1987) 190-259.

JUDGES 1:1–2:5, FROM SUCCESS TO FAILURE: THE CONQUEST OF CANAAN

OVERVIEW

This first of two parts of the introduction to Judges begins "after the death of Joshua" (1:1). A later editor or writer carefully constructed this introductory piece by borrowing some source material from the book of Joshua, restructuring it, and then adding other material to form a three-part section. Each section is marked at the beginning by the verb "to go up" (עלה 'ālâ) with the meaning of "invade" or "attack": "Judah *shall go up*" (1:1-2); "The house of Joseph also *went up*" (1:22); and "Now the angel of the LORD *went up*" (2:1).[11] This tripartite series of military engagements moves from some moderate successes by the southern tribes led by Judah in 1:1-21 to a spiral of declining failures by the northern Israelite tribes of the "house of Joseph" (1:22, 35) in 1:22-36 to a final "going up" by the "angel of the LORD" in a climactic judgment speech against "all the Israelites" (2:4) in 2:1-5. This culminating divine speech marks a dramatic reversal of the conquest of Canaan; previously God had gone up and fought *for* Israel, but now God goes up and fights *against* Israel!

This portrait of a decline from Judah's initial triumphs to the failures of the northern "house of Joseph" to the divine indictment against all Israel has been constructed by an editor who borrowed and shaped material taken from the book of Joshua. Judges 1:1–2:5 quotes directly from several texts within the book of Joshua with some subtle, but important, changes:[12]

Josh 14:6, 13, 15;
    15:13-14 ⟶ Judg 1:10, 20

| (Caleb captures | (Judah captures |
| Hebron) | Hebron) |

Josh 15:13-19   Judg 1:11-15

(Othniel captures	(Othniel captures
Kiriath-Sepher	Kiriath-Sepher
during the lifetime	after the death
of Joshua)	of Joshua)

Josh 15:63 ⟶ Judg 1:21

| (Judah could not | (Benjaminites could |
| capture Jerusalem) | not capture Jerusalem) |

Josh 17:11-13 ⟶ Judg 1:27-28

(Manasseh's failure	(Manasseh's failure
is given less	is given more
prominence)	prominence)

Josh 16:10 ⟶ Judg 1:29

(Ephraim's failure is	(Ephraim's failure
given less	is given more
prominence)	prominence)

In addition to these direct quotations, Judges also draws a number of more indirect allusions from the book of Joshua:

Joshua 10 ⟶ Judg 1:5-7

(Joshua's victory	(Judah's victory over
over King	King Adonibezek;
Adonizedek;	Jerusalem captured)
Jerusalem not	
captured)	

Josh 17:16-18 ⟶ Judg 1:19

(Ephraim's failure	(Judah's failure in
excused by	north excused by
enemy's iron	enemy's iron chariots)
chariots)	

Joshua 13–19 ⟶ Judg 1:30-35

(tribal list moves	(tribal list moves from
from south to	south to north; added
north)	failure reports to some
	northern tribes)

Josh 5:13-15 ⟶ Judg 2:1-5

(angelic commander	(angel of the Lord
of the Lord's army	indicts Israel;
is neither friend	allows Canaanites to
nor enemy of	remain in land as
Israel)	enemies of Israel)

A writer composed Judg 1:1–2:5 by gathering and shaping these quotations and allusions, cementing them together with the writer's own additions. The specifics of the quotations and the allusions will be considered in the Commentary sections below. However, a general anachronism or problem in time sequences arises in these reappropriations of material from Joshua into Judg 1:1–2:5. The book of Joshua assumes that these events happened *during* the lifetime of Joshua. However, when the writer of Judg 1:1–2:5 incor-

---

11. A. G. Auld, "Judges 1 and History: A Reconsideration," *VT* 25 (1975) 276; G. F. Moore, *Judges,* ICC (New York: Scribners, 1901) 40. The same verb (עלה *ālâ,* "to go up") is used in the sense of entering into a battle in Judg 1:1-4, 16, 22; 2:1.

12. This list of quotations and allusions drawn from Joshua and their interpretation is adapted from Stone, "From Tribal Confederation to Monarchic State," 196-248; Mullen, "Judges 1:1–3:6," 33-54; and Marc Brettler, "The Book of Judges, Literature as Politics," *JBL* 108 (1989) 395-418.

porated them into the introduction to Judges, the writer altered the chronological frame to a time "*after* the death of Joshua" (Judg 1:1). But this anachronism was allowed to stand in service to the writer's larger goal of portraying a graduated decline from Judah's initial successes to the growing failure of the northern tribes to a general indictment of all Israel.

Judges 1:1-21, Judah First: Moderate Success

NIV

1 After the death of Joshua, the Israelites asked the LORD, "Who will be the first to go up and fight for us against the Canaanites?"

²The LORD answered, "Judah is to go; I have given the land into their hands."

³Then the men of Judah said to the Simeonites their brothers, "Come up with us into the territory allotted to us, to fight against the Canaanites. We in turn will go with you into yours." So the Simeonites went with them.

⁴When Judah attacked, the LORD gave the Canaanites and Perizzites into their hands and they struck down ten thousand men at Bezek. ⁵It was there that they found Adoni-Bezek and fought against him, putting to rout the Canaanites and Perizzites. ⁶Adoni-Bezek fled, but they chased him and caught him, and cut off his thumbs and big toes.

⁷Then Adoni-Bezek said, "Seventy kings with their thumbs and big toes cut off have picked up scraps under my table. Now God has paid me back for what I did to them." They brought him to Jerusalem, and he died there.

⁸The men of Judah attacked Jerusalem also and took it. They put the city to the sword and set it on fire.

⁹After that, the men of Judah went down to fight against the Canaanites living in the hill country, the Negev and the western foothills. ¹⁰They advanced against the Canaanites living in Hebron (formerly called Kiriath Arba) and defeated Sheshai, Ahiman and Talmai.

¹¹From there they advanced against the people living in Debir (formerly called Kiriath Sepher). ¹²And Caleb said, "I will give my daughter Acsah in marriage to the man who attacks and captures Kiriath Sepher." ¹³Othniel son of Kenaz, Caleb's younger brother, took it; so Caleb gave his daughter Acsah to him in marriage.

¹⁴One day when she came to Othniel, she

NRSV

1 After the death of Joshua, the Israelites inquired of the LORD, "Who shall go up first for us against the Canaanites, to fight against them?" ²The LORD said, "Judah shall go up. I hereby give the land into his hand." ³Judah said to his brother Simeon, "Come up with me into the territory allotted to me, that we may fight against the Canaanites; then I too will go with you into the territory allotted to you." So Simeon went with him. ⁴Then Judah went up and the LORD gave the Canaanites and the Perizzites into their hand; and they defeated ten thousand of them at Bezek. ⁵They came upon Adoni-bezek at Bezek, and fought against him, and defeated the Canaanites and the Perizzites. ⁶Adoni-bezek fled; but they pursued him, and caught him, and cut off his thumbs and big toes. ⁷Adoni-bezek said, "Seventy kings with their thumbs and big toes cut off used to pick up scraps under my table; as I have done, so God has paid me back." They brought him to Jerusalem, and he died there.

8Then the people of Judah fought against Jerusalem and took it. They put it to the sword and set the city on fire. ⁹Afterward the people of Judah went down to fight against the Canaanites who lived in the hill country, in the Negeb, and in the lowland. ¹⁰Judah went against the Canaanites who lived in Hebron (the name of Hebron was formerly Kiriath-arba); and they defeated Sheshai and Ahiman and Talmai.

11From there they went against the inhabitants of Debir (the name of Debir was formerly Kiriath-sepher). ¹²Then Caleb said, "Whoever attacks Kiriath-sepher and takes it, I will give him my daughter Achsah as wife." ¹³And Othniel son of Kenaz, Caleb's younger brother, took it; and he gave him his daughter Achsah as wife. ¹⁴When she came to him, she urged him to ask her father for a field. As she dismounted from her donkey, Caleb said to her, "What do you wish?" ¹⁵She

NIV

urged him[a] to ask her father for a field. When she got off her donkey, Caleb asked her, "What can I do for you?"

[15]She replied, "Do me a special favor. Since you have given me land in the Negev, give me also springs of water." Then Caleb gave her the upper and lower springs.

[16]The descendants of Moses' father-in-law, the Kenite, went up from the City of Palms[b] with the men of Judah to live among the people of the Desert of Judah in the Negev near Arad.

[17]Then the men of Judah went with the Simeonites their brothers and attacked the Canaanites living in Zephath, and they totally destroyed[c] the city. Therefore it was called Hormah.[d] [18]The men of Judah also took[e] Gaza, Ashkelon and Ekron—each city with its territory.

[19]The LORD was with the men of Judah. They took possession of the hill country, but they were unable to drive the people from the plains, because they had iron chariots. [20]As Moses had promised, Hebron was given to Caleb, who drove from it the three sons of Anak. [21]The Benjamites, however, failed to dislodge the Jebusites, who were living in Jerusalem; to this day the Jebusites live there with the Benjamites.

[a]14 Hebrew; Septuagint and Vulgate *Othniel, he urged her*   [b]16 That is, Jericho   [c]17 The Hebrew term refers to the irrevocable giving over of things or persons to the LORD, often by totally destroying them. [d]17 *Hormah* means *destruction.*   [e]18 Hebrew; Septuagint *Judah did not take*

NRSV

said to him, "Give me a present; since you have set me in the land of the Negeb, give me also Gulloth-mayim."[a] So Caleb gave her Upper Gulloth and Lower Gulloth.

16The descendants of Hobab[b] the Kenite, Moses' father-in-law, went up with the people of Judah from the city of palms into the wilderness of Judah, which lies in the Negeb near Arad. Then they went and settled with the Amalekites.[c] [17]Judah went with his brother Simeon, and they defeated the Canaanites who inhabited Zephath, and devoted it to destruction. So the city was called Hormah. [18]Judah took Gaza with its territory, Ashkelon with its territory, and Ekron with its territory. [19]The LORD was with Judah, and he took possession of the hill country, but could not drive out the inhabitants of the plain, because they had chariots of iron. [20]Hebron was given to Caleb, as Moses had said; and he drove out from it the three sons of Anak. [21]But the Benjaminites did not drive out the Jebusites who lived in Jerusalem; so the Jebusites have lived in Jerusalem among the Benjaminites to this day.

[a] That is *Basins of Water*   [b] Gk: Heb lacks *Hobab*   [c] See 1 Sam 15.6: Heb *people*

COMMENTARY

This opening section of Judges is an example of inner-biblical exegesis. The later editor who wrote this introductory material did so by selecting, rearranging, and reinterpreting selected earlier biblical accounts of the conquest of Canaan, drawn from Joshua 14–19. The interpretive rewriting has given the material a moderately pro-Judah slant. The southern tribe of Judah is highlighted as the first tribe chosen by God to lead the next phase of the conquest of Canaan "after the death of Joshua." Judah leads several other southern groups in military engagements, some Israelite and some non-Israelite. The Israelite tribe of Simeon (vv. 3-17) was associated with

Judah, since the tradition held that its allotted land lay within Judah's territory (Josh 19:1). Caleb and Othniel (vv. 11-15, 20) were apparently Kenizzites and not originally Israelites. Joshua 14:6, 14 narrates the adoption of Caleb the Kenizzite and his clan into the tribal allotment of Judah and celebrates Caleb's faithfulness as one of the Israelite spies of Numbers 13–14. The Kenites, another non-Israelite group whose ancestor was the father-in-law of Moses, joined Judah as well for a time (Judg 1:16).

The section divides into four subsections: vv. 1-7, Judah's defeat of King Adoni-bezek; vv. 8-10, Judah's conquest of the cities of Jerusalem and

Hebron; vv. 11-16, the conquests of foreigners who have been adopted into Judah's tribe: Othniel, his wife Achsah, and the Kenites; and vv. 17-21, further conquests by Judah and Simeon and some minor setbacks. The material borrowed from the book of Joshua to write much of this section has been given a moderately pro-Judah slant. But the seeds of some failure and signs of Judah's weakness remain and prepare for the angel's indictment against "all the Israelites" in 2:1-5.

1:1-7. These verses begin with a time designation, marking the beginning of an entirely new era: "After the death of Joshua." The preceding era, when Joshua led Israel in battle against the Canaanites, had been marked by a similar notice of the death of Moses in Josh 1:1. In the same way, a future new era under King David will commence in 2 Sam 1:1 and be marked by the same formula: "After the death of Saul." Thus v. 1 launches the reader into an important time of transition between the conquest of Canaan under Joshua and the unification of all Israel under King David. The book of Judges forms the first half of that time of transition, a time when God will experiment with judges as a way of leading Israel. In the second half of the transition to the Israelite kingship in 1 Samuel, God will experiment for the first time with human kingship under Saul. Both of these experiments, the judges and the kingship under Saul, will begin favorably but end in tragedy. Ultimately, the Davidic kingship itself will run aground at the end of the present form of 2 Kings as even southern Judah under a Davidic king will end up with the Jerusalem Temple destroyed, the city sacked, and much of Judah's population forcibly taken into exile in Babylon (2 Kgs 25:1-26). But the hope of a return of a Davidic king to Jerusalem continued even at the end of the book of 2 Kings (2 Kgs 25:27-30; see 2 Samuel 7) and in the prophetic promises of a Davidic messiah who would return to lead Israel in some distant future day (e.g., Isaiah 11).

However, in this time of transition after the death of Joshua and before the rise of the Davidic kingship, the Israelite tribes gather to initiate a second phase of the conquest of Canaan. The generation of Israelites under Joshua had not completely routed all the Canaanites from the land, and thus a second phase of military engagements

was required. The tribes inquire of the Lord through an oracle, using a question very much parallel to an oracular inquiry at the end of the book of Judges in 20:18:

"Who shall go up first for us against the Canaanites, to fight against them?" (1:1 NRSV)

"Which of us shall go up first to battle against the Benjaminites?" (20:18 NRSV)

In each case of the twin oracles, the answer will be "Judah shall go up first." However, in 1:1 the enemy is external, the Canaanites. In 20:18, Israel will have disintegrated into civil war among the tribes; the enemy will become internal, Israel fighting against itself. But for now, Judah is chosen to lead first. The pre-eminence of Judah has been affirmed previously in the biblical narrative as far back as the blessing of Jacob in Gen 49:8-10 and in Judah's leadership in the arrangement of the holy war camp in Num 10:14. Joshua 14 begins the allotment of lands among the tribes with the tribe of Judah. The southern tribe of Judah will eventually become the southern kingdom of Judah. Jerusalem will become its capital and the site of Solomon's Temple and the palace of the Davidic kings. Thus Judah's prominence among the twelve tribes of Israel is a recurring theme throughout the biblical narrative, and Judah's leadership in this phase of the conquest is in line with that theme.

Judah invites its fellow southern tribe of Simeon (see Josh 19:1) to join its forces (v. 3). The first of Judah's conquests involves the defeat of an army of ten thousand at Bezek. Scholars are unsure about the location of Bezek, although it may be identified with the one other occurrence of the name in the OT in 1 Sam 11:8, where it is a place name near Shechem. But the focus of the narrative is on the enemy king who is captured, King Adoni-bezek. The name invites comparison with the text of Joshua 10, where the great leader Joshua defeated a king with a similar name, Adoni-zedek of Jerusalem (Josh 10:1). Like the great leader Joshua, who defeated Adoni-zedek, Judah defeats a Canaanite king, Adoni-bezek. But Judah goes even a step further. Joshua defeated the king of Jerusalem but did not actually capture the city, as it remained in Jebusite hands (Josh 15:8). According to Judg 1:8, Judah was able to do what Joshua could not—namely, capture Jerusalem. In this way, the story elevates Judah's accomplishments to the same level as Joshua and pushes them even a notch higher. In capturing the city of Jerusalem, Judah does what Joshua could not.[13]

King Adoni-bezek is captured. His thumbs and big toes are cut off as a sign not just of disablement but also of humiliation and revenge, a practice known elsewhere among the cultures of the ancient Near East. What is striking is that this foreign king acknowledges God's victory and the moral judgment of God. The king is reaping what he has sown; he is receiving the same punishment he had arrogantly exacted against countless other rulers. The text affirms the ability of those outside the community of God's people to discern God's ways and moral order. King Abimelech had feared God and corrected his unintentional error of taking Sarah, the wife of Abraham, as a wife (Gen 20:1-18). Likewise, even the Egyptian pharaoh acknowledged to Moses in the midst of the ten plagues, "This time I have sinned; the LORD is in the right, and I and my people are in the wrong. Pray to the LORD!" (Exod 9:27-28 NRSV). The story reminds Israel that even foreign rulers can discern their own transgression against God's moral order. Even these kings know they cannot do "whatever is right in their own eyes" (see Judg 17:6).

Judah's army brings King Adoni-bezek to Jerusalem, where he dies (v. 7). There at the city of Jerusalem, where Israel's own kings will one day come to power in David and Solomon and all the Davidic kings who follow, we are reminded that the arrogance of power will come to ruin. Kingship itself lives under and is responsible to the rule of a larger and divine moral order. No political order or ideology, whether of Joshua or Judah or judges or kings, can escape responsibility or judgment under God's ultimate rule.

1:8-10. The narrative continues with Judah's temporary capture of the city of Jerusalem. The capture is temporary, because the city will apparently be entrusted by Judah to the tribe of Benjamin, since the city lay within the boundaries of Benjamin's allotment of land (Josh 18:16, 28). So although Judah is able to make the initial assault on the city, Benjamin will be unable to hold on to the city and will not be able to drive out the Jebusite inhabitants of Jerusalem (v. 21). This scenario is

somewhat at odds with the previous conquest reports in the book of Joshua, which states that it was Judah (not Benjamin) who was unable to drive out the Jebusites from Jerusalem (Josh 15:63). The writer of Judges 1 has clearly constructed a more favorable portrait of Judah's military success in line with the overall goal of portraying a movement of decline in Judges 1 from success to failure. But in the end, even Judah will be included in the indictment and failure of "all the Israelites" in 2:1-5.

After Jerusalem, Judah moves to the Negev and other areas of southern Canaan, including the city of Hebron (vv. 9-10). Again, the writer of chap. 1 revises the narrative of the book of Joshua in order to exalt Judah's accomplishment. In Josh 15:13-14, Caleb the Kenizzite is named as the one who captures Hebron, but in Judg 1:10 it is Judah. Caleb becomes subsumed under the tribe of Judah, although the wider biblical tradition knows the Kenizzites as being descended from Edom and not Israel (Gen 15:19; 36:11, 15, 42).

1:11-16. The next story in vv. 11-15 recounts Caleb's promise to give his daughter Achsah in marriage to whoever attacks and conquers the city of Debir, otherwise known as the city of Kiriath-sepher. The story is almost a repetition of the same story told in Josh 15:15-19. Othniel son of Kenaz accepts Caleb's challenge, conquers the city, and receives Achsah as his wife. It is grammatically ambiguous who the phrase "Caleb's younger brother" modifies in v. 13, either Othniel himself (making Othniel a brother or cousin to Caleb) or Othniel's father (making Othniel a nephew to Caleb). The latter is more likely in terms of the narrative, since Caleb was a contemporary of Joshua and at least one or two generations have come and gone since the death of Joshua (2:7-10; 3:7-11). However, the central character in this mini-narrative is not Othniel but Achsah, the wife of Othniel and daughter of Caleb. Achsah emerges as a shrewd and able negotiator with her father, Caleb. The Hebrew text of v. 14 makes her the primary subject of the action: "*She* urged him [her husband, Othniel] to ask" her father Caleb for a piece of land to go along with Achsah. The Greek and Latin versions of the verse reverse the order, "*he* [Othniel] urged her to ask," but the NRSV and the NIV have rightly followed the Hebrew text. Achsah is in

---

13. Stone, "From Tribal Confederation to Monarchic State," 214-16.

charge. She gets Othniel to ask for a piece of land. She herself then slides off her donkey, approaches her father, and asks him for yet another favor. Since she and Othniel are getting land in the dry region of the Negev, she also asks for Gulloth-mayim (גלת מים *gullōt māyim*), meaning in Hebrew "Springs/Basins of Water." Her father, Caleb, responds by giving her not one but two sources of water, Upper Gulloth ("Upper Springs") and Lower Gulloth ("Lower Springs").

While one commentator has dismissed this mini-narrative as "a charming personal tale," vv. 11-15 in fact play an important role in introducing key themes and characters that will emerge later in the book of Judges. Barry Webb summarizes the connections with later material in Judges:

All three characters in this vignette will assume greater significance in the larger narrative which is yet to unfold. Othniel will reappear as the first judge (3.7-11). In the light of 2.7, Caleb will appear as a representative of 'the elders who outlived Joshua' and in whose days Israel still served Yahweh. On the other hand, his promise to give Achsah to whoever would take Debir for him (12bc) will find a grotesque and tragic parallel in Jephthah's vow (11.30-31). Achsah's practical shrewdness and resourcefulness in seizing the initiative from both Othniel and Caleb—the two male heroes of the story—introduces a motif which will recur at crucial points in 3.6–16.31, particularly at 4.17-22 (Jael), 9.53-54 (the 'certain woman' of Thebez) and 16.14-21 (Delilah). Othniel's marriage to Achsah will also assume greater significance in the light of 3.6.[14]

The last sentence in Webb's summary alludes to the primary indictment against Israel in Judg 3:6. Later generations of Israelites have been marrying wives from the Canaanites and other non-Israelite people of the land and, as a result, have worshiped their gods and neglected the worship of Yahweh, the God of Israel. Othniel's marriage to Achsah is a model of remaining within the fold of Israel both in marriage and in faithfulness to God. Othniel will be portrayed as a model judge. But gradually even the judges, as well as the people, will deteriorate into intermarriage and unfaithfulness, culminating in Samson's liaisons with foreign women (chaps. 13–16). Judges repeatedly affirms the interconnectedness of the social and theological dimensions of Israel's life; the character of Israel's social and human relationships

reflects Israel's relationship to God. The two cannot be separated.

As if to underscore that Israel is still to remain open to some foreign nations while avoiding entanglement with other evil nations (e.g., the native Canaanites), v. 16 speaks well of the Kenites, descendants of Moses' father-in-law and adopted members of the Israelite community. The NRSV supplies the name of the Kenite ancestor, Hobab; the NIV reflects the Hebrew Masoretic Text, which lists no name, only "the Kenite." The difference in the translation reflects some confusion in the larger biblical tradition about the name of Moses' father-in-law. He is called Hobab the Midianite in Num 10:29, Reuel the Midianite in Exod 2:16-22, and Jethro the Midianite in Exod 18:1-27. Later in Judg 4:11, a note will appear about a man named Heber the Kenite, a descendant of "Hobab, the father-in-law of Moses." Thus one can infer that within the book of Judges, the father-in-law of Moses is assumed to be Hobab the Kenite. The word "Kenite" (קיני *qênî*) is related to the Hebrew word for "iron smith" (קין *qyn*) and may reflect the group's vocation as metal workers, tracing their ancestry back to Cain and those who "made all kinds of bronze and iron tools" (Gen 4:22). The Kenites went up with Judah from the "city of palms" (probably Jericho; Deut 34:3) to the Negeb. The NIV reflects the MT, which says that the Kenites settled with "the people," meaning presumably the Israelites. The NRSV, however, bases its change of the text from the Kenites settling among "the people" to the Kenites settling "with the Amalekites" on the narrative in 1 Sam 15:6. There King Saul instructs the Kenites to flee from the Amalekites because Saul is about to invade and kill off all the Amalekites. But because the Kenites have been kind to the Israelites throughout their history (see Num 10:29-32), Saul wishes to spare them and so urges them to separate themselves from the Amalekites. In any case, the Kenites are portrayed as foreigners who are welcomed and have a favorable relationship with Israel. The Kenites live as a liminal people, able to move among various nations and cross boundaries among cultures. This characteristic will play a role later in the story of Heber the Kenite and his wife, Jael, in the story of the death of the Canaanite general Sisera in chap. 4.

1:17-21. These verses continue with a number

14. Barry Webb, *The Book of the Judges: An Integrated Reading* (Sheffield: JSOT, 1987) 87.

of other victories by the tribes of Judah and Simeon against various Canaanite cities. Judah captured Zephath and "devoted it to destruction" in a holy war ban in obedience to the special laws of holy war in Deut 20:10-18; thus the city's name was changed to "Hormah," meaning "Destruction" (v. 17). Verse 18 names three out of five principal Philistine strongholds that Judah conquered according to the Hebrew text: Gaza, Ashkelon, and Ekron. The Septuagint version of v. 18 reads that "Judah did *not* take" these cities, which may reflect the following verse about Judah's inability to drive out the inhabitants of the plain (v. 19). The Septuagint may also have in mind the reports of the continuing existence of the lords of the five Philistine cities in 3:3; the continuing threat of the Philistines, including Gaza in the Samson cycle (16:1-3); and the note in Josh 13:3 that these three Philistine cities were not conquered by Israel (see also 1 Sam 5:6-12). On the other hand, the Hebrew text, which affirms Judah's capture of the three Philistine cities, corresponds to the note in Josh 15:45-47 that these cities were part of the inheritance of the tribe of Judah.

In any case, v. 19 affirms that "the LORD was with Judah" so that they could take the hill country; at the same time it concedes that Judah could not drive out the inhabitants of the plain. The reason given is the enemy's superior military technology: "they had chariots of iron." The writer of Judges 1 has taken over this apparently reasonable explanation or excuse from Josh 17:16-18; there it was used to explain *Ephraim's* failure, but now in v. 19 it excuses the failure of *Judah.* A possible theological conundrum enters here. If Judah is obedient and the Lord is with Judah, why is Judah unable to be successful against any enemy and any odds? "Is anything too hard for the LORD?" (Gen 18:14). The underlying lesson is that it may take time and other circumstances for God to accomplish God's will against certain powers and enemies. God will eventually lead Israel to victory against Sisera and his "iron chariots" in 4:13, 16. God will "begin" to conquer the Philistines with Samson the judge (13:5), but the Philistines and their iron chariots will remain a threat until the time of the kingships of Saul and David, when they will finally be overcome (1 Sam 13:19-22; 2 Sam 8:1). God may not always act immediately or in the way we would like, but God does remain true to God's

ultimate promises. Such apparent delays or alternate routes in God's work to overcome evil and oppression are not necessarily caused by the sinfulness of the person or community involved. Judah is obedient and faithful, and God is with Judah; nevertheless, Judah encounters some enemies that cannot be overcome in the present moment. The Aramaic Targum tries to take the blame from God and put it on Judah. The Targum paraphrases the text of v. 19 by adding, "Because they [Judah] sinned they were not able to drive out the inhabitants." But the Targum's explanatory addition commits the same error as did Job's friends, who tried to convince the righteous Job that some secret or unknown sin must have caused his suffering. In the end, God condemns the friends and exonerates Job, who maintained his innocence in his suffering throughout his ordeal. Some failures, oppressions, or suffering occur without some sin causing them.

Finally, vv. 20-21 conclude with one positive note and one negative note. Verse 20 affirms that Caleb received the city of Hebron as his inheritance (see 15:13-14). Earlier in the chapter (v. 10), Judah was named as the one who captured Hebron; once again we see that the editor has subsumed Caleb the Kenizzite under the tribe of Judah. Caleb successfully drove out the "sons of Anak," who were notorious fighters in Canaan. When the Israelite spies had first surveyed the land of Canaan in Numbers 13–14, their reports about the unusually tall and powerful "sons of Anak" had frightened the Israelite people into disobedience so that they refused to enter the promised land and, as a result, were condemned by God to wander in the wilderness forty more years. Caleb had been one of two faithful spies (the other being Joshua) who urged the Israelites to trust God and enter the land, but to no avail (Num 13:22, 28, 30-33). Now Caleb defeats the "sons of Anak" and proves his words of assurance and trust in God to be true.

The final negative note reports that "the Benjaminites" did not drive out the Jebusite people who lived in Jerusalem (v. 21). This is a virtual quotation from Josh 15:63 with one major change: The writer of Judges 1 has substituted Benjamin for Judah as the one responsible for the failure to drive out the Jebusites. As the narrative of Judges 1 now stands, Judah is seen as having successfully conquered Jerusalem (v. 8) and then entrusted the city to the tribe of Benjamin, since it was in their territory (Josh 18:28). But the Benjaminites were not able to hang on to Jerusalem or defeat its inhabitants (v. 21). This is all in line with the generally pro-Judah character of Judges 1, which we have noted at several points. The mention of Benjamin, a northern tribe, and its failure provides a transition into the next section of Judges 1, which relates the gradual deterioration and failure of the northern tribes to drive out the inhabitants of Canaan as God has commanded (Deut 20:16-18). The negative note about Benjamin here at the beginning of Judges is also a precursor to the grievous crime committed by the Benjaminites in Judges 19–21.

REFLECTIONS

1. This introductory section of Judges consists largely of rewritten material borrowed from the book of Joshua that has been given a decidedly pro-Judah and pro-David slant. The two cities, Jerusalem (1:7-8, 21) and Hebron (1:10, 20), form inclusios at the beginning and end of the unit. These two cities figure prominently in the narratives about King David as sites of his coronation and his capital city (2 Samuel 5). Although Benjamin was not able to drive out the Jebusites (Judg 1:21), King David did and claimed Jerusalem as "the city of David" (2 Sam 5:6-10). Just as God was with the tribe of Judah in its victories (Judg 1:19), so also God was "with David" in his victories (2 Sam 5:10). But these claims are not just political ideology or propaganda, although such motivations probably played some role in the formation of this material. The pro-Judah and pro-David perspectives affirm God's faithfulness in carrying out the blessing and promises of God over time, extending from Jacob's blessing of Judah in Gen 49:8-12 to the promise of an eternal dynasty to King David in 2 Sam 7:8-17.

This section was labeled Judah's "Moderate Success" for two reasons. First of all, Judah was not solely responsible for its victories. Judah received assistance from the tribe of Simeon, Caleb the Kenizzite and his clan, the Kenites, and most important God (Judg 1:19). Thus the narratives are not just about Judah's solo achievements. Ultimately, Judah owes whatever victories it achieves to God. Second, Judah is explicitly unsuccessful in ousting "the inhabitants of the plain," which acknowledges a partial failure on Judah's part (Judg 1:19). This concession as it stands is not found in the source material in the book of Joshua. The text is apparently a creation of the writer of Judges 1, conflating two traditions in Joshua: Judah's inability to drive out the Jebusites from Jerusalem (Josh 15:63) and Ephraim's inability to drive out the inhabitants of the plain because of their iron chariots (Josh 17:16-18). The writer has not obscured Judah's failure, and the enemy's iron chariots provide some reasonable excuse. Yet the text causes the reader to linger a moment over Judah's failure and wonder whether somehow all is not well even with this leading and favored tribe of Israel. Judah seems faithful and obedient, and yet Judah is not invincible and may be pulled into the greater failures of the northern tribes, who will occupy our attention in the next section of Judges 1.

2. The question of Israel's relationship to foreigners is raised in Judg 1:1-21 by juxtaposing Judah's true foreign enemies ("Canaanites and Perizzites, 1:5) and Judah's true foreign friends (Caleb and the Kenizzites and the Kenites, 1:11-16). This tension between foreigners who are helpful and welcome and foreigners who are oppressive and dangerous resonates with the theme of Israel's fluid relationship to foreigners throughout the book of Judges. Jael, a foreign woman and a Kenite, will be an agent of God's saving Israel (Judg 4:11, 17-24). On the other hand, foreign nations will constantly threaten and oppress Israel. Deep in the ethos of the community of God's people is a concern to welcome the stranger and the foreigner because Israel remembered its primal memory of what it was to be a stranger and a foreigner in the land of Egypt (Lev 19:33-34; Deut 24:17-18). Yet, Israel's memory was also littered with the temptations and oppressions of foreign nations and their gods, which often caused Israel to lose its way. Discernment and vigilance were constant requirements in Israel's interaction with foreigners, their values, their culture, and their gods. The same remains equally true of communities of God today. In the end, however, the book of Judges also reminds Israel that its own worst enemy could be itself; the threat to God's people is as much internal as external (Judges 17–21).

3. The two mini-narratives in this opening section grab the reader's interest and attention: the story of King Adoni-bezek with his thumbs and toes cut off (Judg 1:4-7) and the story of Achsah, who boldly asked for a spring of water from her father and received a double portion, two springs (Judg 1:11-15). The two narratives juxtapose at the beginning two ruling metaphors that will weave in and out of the book of Judges: the metaphor of law, retribution, and just punishment for sin and the metaphor of gracious and generous parental love. This dialectic of retributional law and generous love will interlace with a variety of relationships within Judges: the relationship of God and Israel and of Israel with other nations, intertribal relationships within Israel, relationships of parents and children, relationships of men and women. The necessary dialogical relationship between the two will sometimes be balanced and appropriate. At other times, the balance will be skewed and the subsequent relationships will become increasingly distorted, with disastrous results. Like the twins Jacob and Esau wrestling within their mother's womb (Gen 25:22-23), this delicate tug between lavish parental love and forgiveness and a more legal retribution wrestles within the deepest recesses of God's character:

> "a God merciful and gracious,
> slow to anger,
> and abounding in steadfast love and faithfulness,
> keeping steadfast love for the thousandth generation,
> forgiving iniquity and transgression and sin,
> yet by no means clearing the guilty,
> but visiting the iniquity of the parents
> upon the children . . .
> to the third and fourth generation." (Exod 34:6-7 NRSV)

The book of Judges will illustrate this dance between law and love as God struggles with an increasingly unfaithful and disobedient Israel. In the end, God's love will prevail in that God will remain faithful to the promises made to Israel. But it will be a tough love that allows Israel in various generations to experience the tragic consequences of its own increasing disobedience.

4. The book of Judges contains a greater number of interesting women characters than does any other book of the Bible. We are introduced to the first woman in Judges 1: Achsah, daughter of Caleb and wife of Othniel. Achsah is both a passive object, the prize offered by her father for a military victory, and an active subject, a bold petitioner who seeks to ensure her own well-being and the well-being of her family. Danna Nolan Fewell makes this observation about Achsah's role in Judges:

> Her status as a daughter sets the stage for all the other daughters of Judges whose fates will be decided by their fathers and husbands. Hence her story introduces the theme of female vulnerability, which will reach painful crescendos with the fates of Jephthah's daughter, Samson's bride, the Levite's wife, the women of Benjamin, Jabesh-Gilead, and Shiloh. And yet, Achsah's situation suggests that even in patriarchy women can sometimes have power, especially when they are treated with esteem by men in their family. Unfortunately, Achsah's endogamous marriage and her demand for a home on cultivable soil also serve to accentuate all the daughters who are sold to foreigners (Judg 3:6), who are, in fact, dispossessed from the landholdings of Israel. Consequently, as the story of a woman, Achsah's brief debut raises all sorts of unresolved issues about power, control, possession, personhood, and the social health of the Israelite nation.[15]

---

15. Danna Nolan Fewell, "Deconstructive Criticism: Achsah and the (E)razed City of Writing," in *Judges and Method: New Approaches to Biblical Studies,* ed. Gale Yee (Minneapolis: Fortress, 1995) 140.

The picture of Achsah dismounting from her donkey in boldness and self-assurance to ask her father for springs of water (Judg 1:14) at the beginning of Judges contrasts with another picture at the end of Judges. There the limp body of another woman, the Levite's concubine, who has been gang raped and abused and finally murdered, is placed lifeless on a donkey (Judg 19:25-28). Somewhere between this beginning and this end of Judges, things have gone terribly wrong. The next text, Judg 1:22-36, will begin to explore Israel's descent into failure, unfaithfulness, and disintegration.

Judges 1:22-36, The "House of Joseph": Failed Conquests

NIV

22Now the house of Joseph attacked Bethel, and the LORD was with them. 23When they sent men to spy out Bethel (formerly called Luz), 24the spies saw a man coming out of the city and they said to him, "Show us how to get into the city and we will see that you are treated well." 25So he showed them, and they put the city to the sword but spared the man and his whole family. 26He then went to the land of the Hittites, where he built a city and called it Luz, which is its name to this day.

27But Manasseh did not drive out the people of Beth Shan or Taanach or Dor or Ibleam or Megiddo and their surrounding settlements, for the Canaanites were determined to live in that land. 28When Israel became strong, they pressed the Canaanites into forced labor but never drove them out completely. 29Nor did Ephraim drive out the Canaanites living in Gezer, but the Canaanites continued to live there among them. 30Neither did Zebulun drive out the Canaanites living in Kitron or Nahalol, who remained among them; but they did subject them to forced labor. 31Nor did Asher drive out those living in Acco or Sidon or Ahlab or Aczib or Helbah or Aphek or Rehob, 32and because of this the people of Asher lived among the Canaanite inhabitants of the land. 33Neither did Naphtali drive out those living in Beth Shemesh or Beth Anath; but the Naphtalites too lived among the Canaanite inhabitants of the land, and those living in Beth Shemesh and Beth Anath became forced laborers for them. 34The Amorites confined the Danites to the hill country, not allowing them to come down into the plain. 35And the Amorites were determined also to hold out in Mount Heres, Aijalon and Shaalbim, but when the power of the house of Joseph increased, they

NRSV

22The house of Joseph also went up against Bethel; and the LORD was with them. 23The house of Joseph sent out spies to Bethel (the name of the city was formerly Luz). 24When the spies saw a man coming out of the city, they said to him, "Show us the way into the city, and we will deal kindly with you." 25So he showed them the way into the city; and they put the city to the sword, but they let the man and all his family go. 26So the man went to the land of the Hittites and built a city, and named it Luz; that is its name to this day.

27Manasseh did not drive out the inhabitants of Beth-shean and its villages, or Taanach and its villages, or the inhabitants of Dor and its villages, or the inhabitants of Ibleam and its villages, or the inhabitants of Megiddo and its villages; but the Canaanites continued to live in that land. 28When Israel grew strong, they put the Canaanites to forced labor, but did not in fact drive them out.

29And Ephraim did not drive out the Canaanites who lived in Gezer; but the Canaanites lived among them in Gezer.

30Zebulun did not drive out the inhabitants of Kitron, or the inhabitants of Nahalol; but the Canaanites lived among them, and became subject to forced labor.

31Asher did not drive out the inhabitants of Acco, or the inhabitants of Sidon, or of Ahlab, or of Achzib, or of Helbah, or of Aphik, or of Rehob; 32but the Asherites lived among the Canaanites, the inhabitants of the land; for they did not drive them out.

33Naphtali did not drive out the inhabitants of Beth-shemesh, or the inhabitants of Beth-anath, but lived among the Canaanites, the inhabitants of the land; nevertheless the inhabitants of Beth-shemesh and of Beth-anath became subject to forced labor for them.

NIV

too were pressed into forced labor. [36]The boundary of the Amorites was from Scorpion[a] Pass to Sela and beyond.

[a]36 Hebrew *Akrabbim*

NRSV

34The Amorites pressed the Danites back into the hill country; they did not allow them to come down to the plain. [35]The Amorites continued to live in Har-heres, in Aijalon, and in Shaalbim, but the hand of the house of Joseph rested heavily on them, and they became subject to forced labor. [36]The border of the Amorites ran from the ascent of Akrabbim, from Sela and upward.

COMMENTARY

The first introductory section of Judges now turns its attention from Judah's "going up" to fight the Canaanites in 1:1-2 to the "house of Joseph," who "went up" to fight against the city of Bethel in 1:22. The "house of Joseph" in the Joshua source material typically refers only to the two tribes of Manasseh and Ephraim, who traced their ancestry back to Joseph (Gen 48:1; Josh 16:4). But in chap. 1, the "house of Joseph" has a broader function and becomes the umbrella designation for all the northern tribes. The "house of Joseph" forms an inclusio from the beginning of the section in v. 22 to the end of the section in v. 35 with a number of specific northern tribes being named between the two occurrences. Just as Judah had represented the southern tribes, so also the house of Joseph represents the northern tribes of Israel.

Two narrative trajectories dominate vv. 22-36, one geographical and the other military. The geographical trajectory moves from south to north, from Bethel and the tribal territories of Ephraim and Manasseh (v. 22-29) northward through the territories of Zebulun, Asher, Naphtali (vv. 30-33), and on to the northernmost tribe of Dan (v. 34). The accompanying military trajectory involves a movement from initial victory (vv. 22-26) to growing military failures by the northern tribes, culminating in Dan's expulsion from its territory (v. 34). The correlation of these two trajectories suggests that the deeper one moves into northern territory in Israel, the more one moves into failure and deficiency. These two trajectories form part of the strategy of the pro-southern Judah and anti-northern perspective of the writer of Judges 1.[16]

1:22-26. The account of the military experiences begins with the northern tribes' successful campaign against Bethel, formerly known as Luz. Verse 22 affirms that "the LORD was with them," just as the Lord had been with Judah (v. 19). The small narrative of Bethel's capture involves an account of Israelite spies convincing a native of the city to show them the way into the city. God's presence and clever human ingenuity combine to bring a victory. But the price for the man's advice is that he and his family will be spared and let go when Israel invades the city. This story of Bethel echoes the story of Rahab, the Canaanite harlot, and Israel's defeat of the city of Jericho in Joshua 2 and 6. Like the man at Bethel, Rahab had helped the Israelite spies in Jericho in exchange for Israel's sparing of her and her family. In both cases, Israel had seemed to be obedient and victorious. But the careful reader will notice that something is missing in the attack against Bethel that was present in the account of Judah's victory against Zephath (v. 17). Judah devoted the whole city to destruction, every living being, in accord with the holy wars of Deut 20:16-18. Bethel's capture by the house of Joseph disobeyed the holy war laws, since the man and his family were allowed to live, disobeying the holy war provisions that everyone in the Canaanite city be killed and devoted to God. Indeed, the story of Israel's capture of Jericho when Rahab and her family were allowed to live may be read as an unintentional, but nevertheless real, violation of this same holy war law in Deuteronomy.[17] The same ambiguity and tension concerning Israel's disobedience of the holy war laws, which prescribe

16. Lawson Stone, "From Tribal Confederation to Monarchic State: The Editorial Perspective of the Book of Judges" (Ph.D. diss., Yale University; Ann Arbor: University Microfilms, 1987) 237-39; Theodore Mullen, "Judges 1:1–3:6: The Deuteronomistic Reintroduction of the Book of Judges," *HTR* 77 (1984) 50-52.

17. L. Daniel Hawk, *Every Promise Fulfilled: Contesting Plots in Joshua* (Louisville: Westminster/John Knox, 1991) 59-71, 92-93.

total destruction, by allowing Rahab to live (Joshua 2; 6) is also evident in the story of Bethel and the resident of Bethel who was spared (Judg 1:22-26). God does lead Israel to victory in both cases, but the reader senses that the seeds of disobedience and disintegration may already have been sown.

1:27-36. The sequence of events involving the northern tribes and their military engagements now proceeds into a gradual decline in stages from this initial victory at Bethel. The first stage involves the northern tribes of Manasseh, Ephraim, and Zebulun. They "did not drive out" all the Canaanite inhabitants of several of the cities within their territory. They allowed the Canaanites to continue to live in their land (vv. 27, 29-30). In two of the three cases, they also put the Canaanites to "forced labor" so that the Israelite tribes remained the most numerous and dominant population in their territory (vv. 28, 30). The second stage of decline involves the next two tribes of Asher and Naphtali. Neither of these tribes drive out all the Canaanites. Moreover, in the case of Manasseh, Ephraim, and Zebulun, the Canaanites live among the Israelites. The Canaanites remain a minority among the more numerous Israelite population. But in the case of Asher and Naphtali, we have a reversal. The Canaanites do not live among the people of Asher and Naphtali; instead, Asher and Naphtali "lived among the Canaanites" (vv. 32, 33). Asher and Naphtali are portrayed as the less numerous minority within a predominantly Canaanite population. They have lost even more ground than the preceding tribes. But in the case of Naphtali, even as a minority Israel did manage to subject the Canaanites to forced labor (v. 33).

Finally, the whole tribe of Dan is unable to continue to live in its own designated territory, for the Amorites (an alternate name for the Canaanites) have driven them completely out of the plain "back into the hill country" (v. 34). Dan becomes a refugee tribe in search of a home territory. Dan's tragic story will resume at the end of the book of Judges with the story of Dan's forcible theft of the idolatrous shrine of Micah and Dan's migration with the shrine to the far north of Israel (chaps. 17–18).

As in the section concerning Judah in vv. 1-21, the writer of vv. 22-36 has selected, revised, and added to source material from Joshua 14–19 in order to construct this account. The failure of Manasseh and Ephraim to drive out the Canaanites completely is reported in Josh 17:11-13 along with a number of other items about these tribes. However, the writer of Judg 1:27-29 has highlighted only the account of the failures of Ephraim and Manasseh. Moreover, Josh 17:12 says that these northern tribes *could not* drive out the Canaanites. However, the writer of Judg 1:27, 29 deleted the "could not" and changed it simply to "did not" drive them out. The change is subtle but telling. The Joshua account makes the failure to drive out the Canaanites a matter of power and ability; they wanted to but were not able. The failure is somewhat excusable. The Judges 1 account, however, suggests less excusable reasons for the failure: The failure of Manasseh and Ephraim to drive out the Canaanites may have involved less a lack of ability and more a lack of desire. Perhaps they *could* have driven the Canaanites out, but they did not *want* to do so. If Manasseh was able to subject the Canaanites to forced labor, they also should have been able to drive them out (v. 28). The northern tribes apparently desired to enter into covenants with the Canaanites and their gods rather than obey the covenant with the Lord and worship the Lord alone. This theological issue will indeed be the underlying motivation for Israel's future, which will be revealed in the angel's speech in 2:1-5.

Another change made by the writer of Judges 1 was the addition of failure reports for the three tribes of Zebulun, Asher, and Naphtali. Failure reports for these three tribes do not exist in the Joshua source material, and so the editor of Judges 1 has composed and added them, using the Ephraim and Manasseh material as a model. The writer of Judges 1 clearly wishes to underscore the thoroughgoing failure of the northern tribes. Finally, concerning the tribe of Dan, the writer has again selected only the failure report (v. 34) out of a larger section detailing both Dan's successes and failures in Josh 19:40-48.

The section ends with a general summary of the overall experience of the "house of Joseph" (vv. 35-36). The Amorites or Canaanites continue to live in various cities, but the northern tribes continue to hold the balance of power and thus subject the Amorites to forced labor (vv. 30,

32-33). However, this affirmation that the Canaanites were allowed to live and were subjected to forced labor only reminds the reader of the northern tribes' transgression of the holy war law in Deuteronomy, which mandates the total annihilation of all Canaanites from the land. The holy war provision that allows the enemy to live and be subject to forced labor applies only to "towns that are very far from you" that lie outside the borders of Canaan (Deut 20:11, 15-18 NRSV). Once again we are reminded of the growing failure of the northern tribes to carry out the commands of God. Verse 36 concludes with a southern boundary established for the Amorites, as if to suggest that the Amorites and the Canaanites will now remain a permanent fixture in the land of Canaan with their own established borders. The Canaanites are here to stay!

REFLECTIONS

1. We see again the perspective of the writer of Judges 1 generally to be more charitable to southern Judah and less charitable to the northern "house of Joseph" in this summation of the continuing conquest of Canaan after the death of Joshua. But at least two factors mitigate against any kind of absolute distinction of good or bad in assessing the two groups. First of all, the text affirms that the Lord was with both Judah (1:19) and the house of Joseph (1:22). God plays no favorites and remembers the covenant promises to all Israel. Second, the descriptions of both Judah and the house of Joseph include successes and failures; neither group is all perfect or all evil. Judah could not drive out the inhabitants of the plain (1:19), although its portrait emerges as largely positive. The house of Joseph successfully captured Bethel (1:22-26), although its overall portrait emerges as largely negative. The narrative avoids the creation of an absolute villain in the northern tribes or an absolute hero in southern Judah. The character of these communities remains human, realistic, and as morally complex as any human community or individual. Rarely can blame be assessed simply on one party or another in any dispute, conflict, or tragedy. And rarely are motives absolutely pure and complex actions totally unambiguous. Although a relative distinction is possible between the more successful Judah and the less successful northern tribes of Joseph, their fate and destiny remain bound together as brother tribes. The apostle Paul spoke of the body of Christ and the need for one group or member to refrain from claiming absolute superiority over another member in order that "there may be no dissension within the body, but the members may have the same care for one another. If one member suffers, all suffer together with it; if one member is honored, all rejoice together with it" (1 Cor 12:25-26 NRSV). Relative distinctions remain from a human perspective. But as the divine angel's speech will reveal in 2:1-5, those distinctions dissolve as God views people and events through divine eyes. The angel will speak to "all the Israelites" as a community or body without distinction of its parts (Judg 2:4).

2. The geographical trajectory from southern Judah to the various northern tribes of Israel roughly reflects the same south-to-north sequence of geographical affiliations of the individual major judges that will appear in the narratives of Judges 13–16. The first major judge is Othniel, from southern Judah (3:7-11), and the last judge is Samson, from what will become the far northern tribe of Dan (13:2). The geographical progression of the individual judges runs in the following sequence: Judah (Othniel), Benjamin (Ehud), Issachar/Naphtali (Deborah/Barak), Manasseh (Gideon), Gad (Jephthah), and Dan (Samson). Thus Judges 1 provides a kind of geographical guide to the main body of judge stories that will follow in Judges 3–16.

This geographical trajectory will also be matched by a similar theological trajectory from initial success to a downward slide of failure and unfaithfulness among the individual judges. The stories will move from the initial victorious judges in Judges 3–5 to the ambiguous figure of Gideon, who moves from victory to unfaithfulness in Judges 6–8. The era of the major judges will end with the tragic figures of Jephthah and Samson (Judges 10–16). The final chapters (Judges 17–21) will conclude the internal religious social disintegration of Israel as a community. Thus Judges 1 functions as a road map, both geographical and theological, for the rest of the book.

3. The failures of the Israelite conquest and the disobedience of the holy war laws of Deuteronomy in allowing some of the Canaanites to live (contrary to the law in Deut 20:16-18) do not represent rash or overt rebellions against the Lord. Judah is not able to defeat its enemies because of their iron chariots. The northern Joseph tribes defeat some of the Canaanites, but not all of them. Those Canaanites who remain are subjected to forced labor. The Canaanites are at least subdued, albeit by a means the law reserves for nations far away from Canaan (Deut 20:10-15). At least on the surface, the Israelites seem to be making some good-faith effort to continue the conquest.

Yet Judges 1 gives the sense of a growing deterioration in strength and resolve of the Israelite tribes. Israel does not seem to intend to be unfaithful, but gradually the seeds of disobedience that were sown begin to grow. Step by step, the web of transgression and failure begins to be spun. Like the serpent's gradual temptation of Adam and Eve with a few seemingly innocent questions (Gen 3:1-7) or King David's gradual entanglement with adultery and then murder in the case of Bathsheba and Uriah (2 Samuel 11), Israel is gradually drawn into deeper disobedience and entanglements with the Canaanites and their gods. Such is often the nature of temptation and the downward spiral into disobedience. Originally good people and communities and institutions can become corrupted from the inside, even if on the surface all seems, at least for the moment, to be well. That will happen to the people of Israel, both north and south, to the institutions of the judges, and to the institution of Israelite kingship, which will follow the era of the judges.

Judges 2:1-5, Judgment on All the Israelites

NIV

2 The angel of the Lord went up from Gilgal to Bokim and said, "I brought you up out of Egypt and led you into the land that I swore to give to your forefathers. I said, 'I will never break my covenant with you, ²and you shall not make a covenant with the people of this land, but you shall break down their altars.' Yet you have disobeyed me. Why have you done this? ³Now therefore I tell you that I will not drive them out before you; they will be ⌞thorns⌟ in your sides and their gods will be a snare to you."

⁴When the angel of the Lord had spoken these things to all the Israelites, the people wept aloud, ⁵and they called that place Bokim.ª There they offered sacrifices to the Lord.

ª5 Bokim means weepers.

NRSV

2 Now the angel of the Lord went up from Gilgal to Bochim, and said, "I brought you up from Egypt, and brought you into the land that I had promised to your ancestors. I said, 'I will never break my covenant with you. ²For your part, do not make a covenant with the inhabitants of this land; tear down their altars.' But you have not obeyed my command. See what you have done! ³So now I say, I will not drive them out before you; but they shall become adversariesª to you, and their gods shall be a snare to you." ⁴When the angel of the Lord spoke these words to all the Israelites, the people lifted up their voices and wept. ⁵So they named that place Bochim,ᵇ and there they sacrificed to the Lord.

ª OL Vg Compare Gk: Heb sides   ᵇ That is Weepers

COMMENTARY

The climactic conclusion to this first introductory section of Judges features the sudden appearance and judgment speech of "the angel of the LORD." Who is this angel or messenger of God who makes a dramatic intrusion into the narrative? The last appearance of the angel was back in Josh 5:13-15 near the cities of Jericho and Gilgal (Josh 5:10). There Joshua was about to lead the Israelite army in an attack against Jericho, when the angel suddenly appeared as a man with a drawn sword and confronted Joshua. Joshua asked this divine warrior, "Are you one of us, or one of our adversaries?" The angel replied, "Neither; but as commander of the army of the LORD I have now come" (Josh 5:13-14 NRSV). Joshua's response was to bow to the ground and worship, for he realized he was in the Lord's presence.

The Lord had promised Israel in the covenant at Mt. Sinai that the angelic divine warrior would lead Israel into the promised land (Exod 23:20-33; 33:2; Num 20:16). But on the eve of the conquest of the first Canaanite city of Jericho, the angel had reminded Joshua that God remains free to fight either for or against Israel. God is neither "one of us" nor "one of our adversaries." God ultimately transcends all humanly engineered divisions and remains sovereign to judge or deliver whomever God wills. The special name of God, Yahweh, from the Hebrew verb "to be" (היה *hāyâ*) conveys this divine freedom: "I AM WHO I AM" (Exod 3:13-14 NRSV) and "I will be gracious to whom I will be gracious, and will show mercy on whom I will show mercy" (Exod 33:19 NRSV). It is this same angelic agent of God's power and transcendent freedom who "went up from Gilgal [the site of the angel's last appearance] to Bochim" to encounter a new generation of Israelites "after the death of Joshua."

The verb "to go up" (עלה *'ālâ*) had been used to mark the beginning of the military engagements of southern Judah (1:1-2) and then the engagements of the northern house of Joseph (1:22) against the Canaanites. In 2:1, the same verb signals a third "going up" in battle, but this time it is the divine angel's "going up" in a holy war attack, not against the Canaanites, but against the Israelites! The reader recalls the angel's reminder to Joshua (Josh 5:13-14) that God is absolutely free to be for us or against us. Israel cannot smugly assume that God will always fight on its side. The form of this holy war attack on Israel is not military weaponry but a verbal indictment: The angel speaks words of judgment like a prosecuting attorney presenting an airtight case of evidence against the accused defendant Israel.

The angelic prosecutor begins the case, reminding Israel that God has met all the divine obligations under the covenant made at Mt. Sinai in Exodus 19–24 and reaffirmed in the book of Deuteronomy. God brought Israel up from Egypt and has now brought them into the promised land of Canaan. The angel reports God's absolute and irrevocable commitment: "I said, 'I will never break my covenant with you'" (v. 1). Israel was obligated for its part of the covenant to maintain an exclusive relationship with the Lord. Israel was not allowed to make any covenants with "the inhabitants of the land," and Israel was required to tear down the altars of the Canaanite gods (v. 2).

The angel then levels the charge that while God has kept God's side of the covenant, Israel has not. The covenant at Mt. Sinai clearly stated Israel's covenant obligations to drive out the inhabitants of the land of Canaan and not make covenants with them or their gods. The Canaanites "shall not live in your land, or they will make you sin against me; for if you worship their gods, it will surely be a snare to you" (Exod 23:31-33 NRSV; see also Deut 7:1-6). Israel has disobeyed God's command of exclusive loyalty by allowing many of the Canaanites and their gods and worship sites to remain in the land. The angel then points to the failures to oust the Canaanites from the land, which have just been narrated in Judges 1, and says, "See what you have done!" The evidence is plain enough: Israel has failed to carry out the conquest of Canaan as commanded.

The angelic prosecutor suddenly shifts roles and becomes a divine judge. The angel reports God's verdict, which involves a dramatic change in strategy in God's plans concerning Israel and the promised land. God's original plan and hope was that Israel would eliminate all the Canaanites from the promised land, leaving a secure paradise free from all temptations of other cultures and gods. The vision is not unlike the garden of Eden in Genesis 1–2, a perfect place of human habitation without enticements to disobey or follow other gods. But just as the plan for the humans in the garden of Eden collapsed and required a new strategy by God, so also the plan for Israel in Canaan has fallen apart. God resolves not to drive out the Canaanites but instead allows them to remain among the Israelites in Canaan. The Canaanites shall become ongoing "adversaries" (NRSV) or "thorns in your sides" (NIV); the difference in translation reflects a text-critical problem with the Hebrew text that requires some emending to make sense. But the issue is not just a social or political issue with the Canaanites. It is also theological. God resolves to allow the Canaanite gods to remain in the land as a continuing "snare" to test the faith and loyalty of Israel (v. 3).

The speech of the angel is concluded, but we as readers may wonder at whom this verbal onslaught is aimed. Judah seems to have been moderately successful in its conquest, and even the northern house of Joseph has made a determined attempt to oust or subdue at least some of the Canaanites. But the narrator quickly informs us that the angel's indictment targets "all the Israelites" (v. 4). No tribe is exempt from this blanket condemnation. All have sinned and fallen short. There is no room for one tribe to gloat over the misfortunes or denunciation of another.

In response to the angel's judgment speech and verdict, the people lift up their voices and "weep" with a loud and public wailing of lament and grief. They recognize that their relationship to God and the land in which they and their children will live has been dramatically altered. Canaan will not be a pure paradise of milk and honey without temptations or worries. Canaan will be for Israel a land like any other, with other nations, other cultures, other values, and other gods constantly gnawing at Israel's heart and allegiance. Like the garden of

Eden, the perfect land of promise has been forever lost. Because this was a place where the Israelites wept at the loss of their great promise, they name the place "Bochim," which in Hebrew means "Weepers" (בכים *bōkîm*). This place of wailing and weeping becomes a memorial to dashed hopes and forfeited futures because of the sinfulness of Israel. The Israelites acknowledge the place as a holy site of divine revelation by making sacrifices to the Lord on the spot (vv. 4-5).

This dramatic and tearful climax to this introductory section of Judges finds an important counterpart at the end of the book. Only two places in the entire book of Judges explicitly mention "all the Israelites": 2:4, at the beginning, and 20:26, at the end of the book. Moreover, these two contexts also share the portrait of all Israel weeping and lamenting before God. In v. 4, the Israelites weep once, but by the end of the book the weeping and the wailing have intensified into a triple chorus of Israel's crying and lamenting to God on three closely related occasions at Bethel (20:23, 26; 21:2). This series of weeping and lament brackets the book, and the intensification of the cry at the end provides further indication that we are headed for a downhill slide in terms of Israel's fortunes and faithfulness as we move through the book of Judges. These bookends of weeping in Judges enclose numerous other cries and laments throughout the book. Israel repeatedly cried out to God because of the oppression of its enemies (3:9, 15; 4:3; 6:7; 10:10). Like Israel, Jephthah's daughter wept over the loss of what her life could have been had it not been for her father's foolish vow, which cut short her life (11:37-38). Israelite women continued to weep in an annual ritual in remembrance of her loss and pain (11:40). Judges is a book that takes seriously the reality of human suffering and anguish, whether brought on by our own sinfulness or by external forces and enemies who oppress us.

REFLECTIONS

1. The severe indictment of the angel of the Lord breaks into the narrative somewhat abruptly. The last things we have heard about the Lord's activity are the positive notes that the Lord was with Judah and with the house of Joseph in their victories (1:19, 22). Suddenly God breaks in as an angelic messenger and summarily condemns all the Israelites for the failure of their conquest of Canaan. In fact, a reader who has worked through both the book of Joshua and the first chapter of Judges may have reason to wonder what God thinks about Israel's moderate, but partial, success in defeating and eradicating the Canaanites. Even within the book of Joshua, which portrays a fairly successful conquest, one may see two "contesting plots" throughout the book, one affirming the success and obedience of the Israelite conquest and the other hinting at the conquest's failures and Israel's disobedience.[18] But now in Judg 2:1-5, we have the definitive divine assessment over all of Joshua and Judges 1: Israel has failed in the conquest and disobeyed God's command. The period of the conquest is over, and Canaanites will remain scattered over the land as a constant threat, temptation, and thorn in Israel's side.

2. For modern readers, the notion of holy war, the act of killing—especially the killing of women and children—and the near annihilation of a native population of Canaanites will seem alien and reprehensible in the extreme. From a larger biblical and moral view, the notion of a holy war seems hard to justify. Other texts in the Old Testament promulgate a very different vision for God's people, a vision of peace rather than war among nations (e.g., Isa 2:2-4). But Judg 2:1-5 reminds us that the holy war concept is only a temporary measure, confined to this limited period in Israel's story. No later biblical texts ever counsel Israel to take up a holy war again. The holy war as an act of human violence against other humans does not function in the Bible as a continuing paradigm for the actions of God's people. The goal of the holy war against Canaan was not achieved. The goal had been to define a clear boundary that would protect Israel from contact with the "other" in its social, political, and religious life. Israel was forced throughout its history to struggle to discern when to welcome and when to resist the culture, values, and philosophies of other nations and peoples. The struggle between separateness and absorption, strict isolation and negotiated assimilation, remains a challenge for every community of God's people who strive to live in the world but not be of it.

Although the paradigm of holy war as human violence against other humans was seen as a dead end, that does not mean that the notion of holy war and God as divine warrior ceased. In fact, the image of the divine warrior remains a lively theological motif throughout the Old Testament and on into the New Testament.[19] Israel continued to wage battles against the enemies of God's will, but the battles became more and more for Israel a battle of words, persuasion, obedience, and education through devotion and study of God's Word of Scripture (Josh 1:7-9).[20]

3. The two mini-narratives in Judges 1—the story of King Adoni-bezek, who received his just legal punishment, and the story of Caleb's daughter Achsah, who graciously received more than she asked for from her father—illustrate the dialogical dance between law and lavish love, between a *quid pro quo* legalism and a more familial model of forgiveness and unconditional love. This interplay between a legal-political model and a more domestic-familial model gets at the inherent tension in God's covenant with Israel. God pledges undying commitment to Israel in words similar to a parental vow to a child: "I will never break my covenant with you" (2:1). At the same time, God brings Israel to court in a forensic indictment more akin to a courtroom. The scene ends with one resolution (the Canaanites will remain in the land), but the next step God will take in responding to Israel's weeping is not resolved. Has the covenant relationship between God and Israel ended because of Israel's unfaithfulness? Or will God continue to work with Israel in spite of its ongoing disobedience? And if so, how will God proceed with Israel into the future? The answers to these questions remain open, but the second half of the two-part introduction to Judges in 2:6–3:6 will begin to address the root causes and the next steps God will take to address these issues.

18. L. Daniel Hawk, *Every Promise Fulfilled: Contesting Plots in Joshua* (Louisville: Westminster/John Knox, 1991) 56-116.
19. Richard Nysse, "Yahweh Is a Warrior," *Word & World* (Spring 1987) 192-201.
20. Dennis T. Olson, *Deuteronomy and the Death of Moses: A Theological Reading* (Minneapolis: Fortress, 1994) 162-64.

JUDGES 2:6–3:6, FROM FAITHFULNESS TO SIN: THE COVENANT WITH GOD

OVERVIEW

Judges 2:6–3:6 presents the second half of the two-part introduction to the book of Judges. This two-part introduction provides the lens through which the reader will interpret the varied stories of individual judges that will follow in chaps. 3–16. The first half of this introductory interpretive lens, 1:1–2:5, focused largely on external events, reporting the successes and failures of Israel's military campaign in Canaan. Very little was said of God's reactions and feelings about the events until 2:1-5. Suddenly the angel appeared with a stinging rebuke of Israel's failure to oust the Canaanites totally from the land. The root causes of God's displeasure were only briefly touched on in the rebuke: "their gods shall be a snare to you" (2:3). This theological or religious dimension of Israel's failure will become the major theme to be explored in much more depth in the second half of the introduction, 2:6–3:6. The second introductory half will also reveal much more of God's inner emotions and feelings in relationship to Israel's constant rebellion and worship of other gods. Descriptions of the Lord's anger, sorrow, and compassion will swirl around the downward spiral of Israel's growing unfaithfulness like eddies in a wildly turbulent river. The river will have its moments of calm, but they will soon give way again to increasingly rocky rapids, heading inexorably toward the final waterfall that will dash Israel into a splintered social and religious heap (chaps. 17–21).

The reader will also notice a striking shift from specificity to generalization as we move from the first to the second half of the introduction to Judges. The first half, 1:1–2:5, was saturated with specific names of Israelite tribes, people, and places. Certain tribes were singled out in contrast to others. The second half, 2:6–3:6, speaks less of individual tribes or persons and much more about all the Israelites together. This pan-Israelite perspective ties in with the angel's speech, directed to "all the Israelites" at the end of the first introductory section (2:4). Only one person,

Joshua, is highlighted as a faithful leader of a past generation. The distinctions in this section focus less on individual tribes or people than on differences among generations of Israelites; the faithfulness of the generations of Joshua and the next generation of elders (2:7-10a) contrasts sharply with the growing unfaithfulness of the generations after them, for they "did not know the LORD or the work that he had done for Israel" (2:10).

One major interpretive challenge is the need to account for the disjunction in time as we move from events in the first unit of 1:1–2:5 to the second unit in 2:6–3:6. All the events in the first unit are set in a time "after the death of Joshua" (1:1). Suddenly, as we encounter the second unit beginning in 2:6, the clock winds back in time to a moment when Joshua is still alive: "when Joshua dismissed the people . . ." (2:6). Why do we have this abrupt flashback in time? We will see that it allows the writer to draw the necessary contrast between the faithful generation of Joshua and his contemporaries and the downward slide of subsequent generations of Israelites who worship other gods and rebel against the Lord. Just as the first half of the introduction had begun with a fairly positive portrait of Judah, to which the northern tribes' experience could be contrasted, so also the second half begins with a fairly positive portrait of Joshua and his generation, to which later generations can be contrasted. Thus the two introductions form a parallel portrait of Israel on a downward slope from initial victory and faithfulness to increasing defeat and apostasy. The parallels move along two axes, one tribal or geographical (south to north) and the other temporal or generational (from Joshua's generation to post–Joshua generations). Together, the two introductions invite the reader to understand the narratives that comprise the main body of the book in chaps. 3–16 as more than merely a revolving or cyclical circle of events that always returns to the same point. Rather, the stories of the judges trace a rough trajectory or line that moves toward deterioration, culminating in the tragedy of Samson and the religious crisis of chaps. 17–18 and the social and political crisis of chaps. 19–21.[21]

What can be known about the history of how this second part of the introduction to Judges was composed? Many scholars agree that 2:6–3:6 contains within it the remnants of an earlier preface to the stories of the judges. This earlier preface presented the era of the judges of Israel as a time of cyclical repetition in which God sent temporary deliverers, called judges, to save Israel from its enemies. This earlier preface accentuated the heroism and faithfulness of the judges as leaders of Israel; the judges were always able to bring

Israel back to God and back to a sense of political and social security. The core of this early form of the preface is likely 2:10-16, 18-19 and 3:1-4. However, a later editor added a number of crucial verses to this core: 2:6-9, 17, 20-23 and 3:5-6.[22] These editorial additions changed the orientation of the preface from a repetitive cycle celebrating heroic judges to a linear story of Israel's gradual deterioration, a deterioration in which even the judges participated. These editorial changes brought this earlier preface in line with other parts of the book of Judges as they came to be edited later: the later preface in 1:1–2:5, the judges stories themselves as later edited and shaped to show a decline (chaps. 3–16), and the concluding chapters portraying Israel at its moment of greatest failure and disintegration at the end of the judges era (chaps. 17–21).

21. Similar conclusions about the larger function of the dual introductions in the light of the whole book of Judges have been argued independently from both a redaction-critical perspective (Lawson Stone, "From Tribal Confederation to Monarchic State: The Editorial Perspective of the Book of Judges" [Ph.D. diss., Yale University; Ann Arbor: University Microfilms, 1987] 248-59, 460-77) and a formalistic literary perspective (Barry Webb, *The Book of the Judges: An Integrated Reading* [Sheffield: JSOT, 1987] 81-122). Both Stone and Webb build on a number of important earlier works on Judges, both literary and redaction-critical in scope.

22. Rudolph Smend, "Das Gesertz und die Völker: ein Beitrag zu deuteronomistichen Redaktionsgeschichte," *Probleme biblischer Theologie: Gerhard von Rad zum 70 Geburtstag,* ed. H. W. Wolff (Munich: Chr. Kaiser Verlag, 1971) 494-509.

Judges 2:6-10, A New Generation Is Born

NIV

[6]After Joshua had dismissed the Israelites, they went to take possession of the land, each to his own inheritance. [7]The people served the LORD throughout the lifetime of Joshua and of the elders who outlived him and who had seen all the great things the LORD had done for Israel.

[8]Joshua son of Nun, the servant of the LORD, died at the age of a hundred and ten. [9]And they buried him in the land of his inheritance, at Timnath Heres[a] in the hill country of Ephraim, north of Mount Gaash.

[10]After that whole generation had been gathered to their fathers, another generation grew up, who knew neither the LORD nor what he had done for Israel.

[a]9 Also known as *Timnath Serah* (see Joshua 19:50 and 24:30)

NRSV

[6]When Joshua dismissed the people, the Israelites all went to their own inheritances to take possession of the land. [7]The people worshiped the LORD all the days of Joshua, and all the days of the elders who outlived Joshua, who had seen all the great work that the LORD had done for Israel. [8]Joshua son of Nun, the servant of the LORD, died at the age of one hundred ten years. [9]So they buried him within the bounds of his inheritance in Timnath-heres, in the hill country of Ephraim, north of Mount Gaash. [10]Moreover, that whole generation was gathered to their ancestors, and another generation grew up after them, who did not know the LORD or the work that he had done for Israel.

COMMENTARY

2:6. The setting for the military campaigns in 1:1–2:5 was a time "*after* the death of Joshua."

Judges 2:6-9 marks a brief flashback to a time *before* the death of Joshua and is essentially a rearrangement of material drawn from the scene in Josh 24:28-31 just before Joshua's death. Joshua had assembled all Israel in a great assembly at Shechem (Josh 24:1). He reminded the people of God's faithfulness, which the Lord had shown to Israel through the first phase of the conquest, and he called on the people of Israel to renew their commitment to the covenant with the Lord. Then Joshua dismissed the Israelites (Josh 24:28), and that is where Judg 2:6 picks up the action. All the Israelites who have been fighting together as one army in Canaan during Joshua's lifetime have disbanded into individual tribes, each responsible for completing the conquest within its individual tribal allotments of territory.

2:7. This verse underscores the faithful worship of the Lord by the people during the period of the leadership of Joshua and then the elders who outlived him. They had known and trusted in the Lord because they were eyewitnesses to "all the great work that the LORD had done for Israel." God's great works during the leadership of Joshua and the elders included protection and guidance of the new generation at the end of the wilderness period in Numbers 26–36 and the first stage of the conquest of Canaan in the book of Joshua. Thus Joshua and the elders who ruled the generation after him effectively taught and led the people in the ways of the Lord. They had been direct witnesses and participants in the drama of God's great acts of power and deliverance in the wilderness and in Canaan.

2:8-9. Joshua died and was buried in his home territory of Ephraim (Num 13:8, 16) at the age of 110 years. He received the honored title of "the servant of the LORD" (v. 8), first used for Moses (Josh 1:1) and to be used again for certain faithful kings (David, Hezekiah, Zerubbabel) and prophets, culminating in the Suffering Servant figure in Isaiah 40–55 (see Isa 52:13–53:12). But no leader comparable to Moses or Joshua with the title of "servant of the LORD" arose in the generation immediately after the death of Joshua and the next generation of elders. Moses and Joshua represent unique and unrepeatable leaders in a special time of Israel's history.

2:10. This verse sets the stage for a definitive shift from the era of Moses, Joshua, and the elders to a new era defined by a generation "who did not know the LORD or the work that he had done for Israel." The phrase is reminiscent of the dra-

matic change in relationships that occurred at the beginning of the book of Exodus. Israel had enjoyed good fortune when Joseph had been favored by an earlier pharaoh. But then "a new king arose over Egypt, who did not know Joseph" (Exod 1:8). This lack of knowing caused a sudden shift in the nature of Israel's relationship to pharaoh and the Egyptians. They became slaves instead of a favored people. In 2:10, it is Israel who no longer knows the Lord, and as a result the nature of the relationship between God and Israel will dramatically change. The verb "to know" (ידע yāda') signifies here an intimate and personal knowledge and relationship with another. The verb can describe the intimacy of sexual intercourse between a man and a woman (Gen 4:1). Moses described the special bond between God and himself with the words, "I know you by name" (Exod 33:12). Knowing God involves loyalty in a covenant relationship, a sense of mutual trust, obedience to God's commands, and an acknowledgment of God's power and sovereignty (Exod 29:45-46). The generations of Joshua and the elders had such a knowledge of the Lord because of their direct and personal experience of God's mighty acts of deliverance. But a new generation arises without such a foundation and knowledge and relationship with God.

The narrative movement from one generation to another has formed an important structural framework for much of the OT narrative up to this point. Genealogical formulas that mark the end of one generation and the beginning of another form the major narrative backbone for the book of Genesis (e.g., Gen 2:4; 5:1; 10:1; 25:19). The beginning of the book of Exodus marks the rise of a new generation of Israelites along with the rise of a new king who did not know Joseph (Exod 1:1-8). Two census lists of the twelve tribes of Israel in Numbers 1 and 26 define the structure of Numbers as the story of two very different generations. The first generation counted in the census list in Numbers 1 was increasingly rebellious against God and Moses in the wilderness. Because of their rebellion, climaxed by the refusal to enter the promised land in the spy story of Numbers 13–14, God condemned this generation to die in the desert without entering the land of Canaan. The Lord would allow only the new generation of their "little ones" born in the wilderness to come into Canaan, along with the two faithful spies out of the old generation, Joshua and Caleb (Num 14:20-35). The rise of this new generation of hope and promise was marked by the second census list in Numbers 26. The census included no members of the old rebellious wilderness generation of Israelites except Joshua and Caleb (Num 26:63-65).[23]

The theme of a generational transition from an old rebellious generation to a new generation of hope and promise in the book of Numbers was taken up again in Moses' speech in the book of

23. Dennis T. Olson, *Numbers,* Interpretation (Louisville: John Knox, 1996) 3-6, 75-89.

Deuteronomy (Deut 1:26-40). This shift from an earlier unfaithful generation to a later faithful generation (led by Joshua) provides the necessary background to Judg 2:6-9, which is a mirror image of what happens in Numbers. In Judg 2:6-9, an earlier faithful generation (led by Joshua and then the elders who outlived Joshua) dies and a later unfaithful generation, who "did not know the LORD," rises up. Thus, while the book of Numbers had ended on a hopeful note about the rise of a new faithful generation of promise, the book of Judges begins on a pessimistic note about the rise of a new unfaithful generation of rebellion.

REFLECTIONS

1. The text raises the issue of the nature of faith and knowing God and the role of eyewitness testimony from those who have seen the works of God directly and firsthand. Being a firsthand witness to God's powerful acts of mercy and deliverance does not automatically create or guarantee faith. The old wilderness generation in the book of Numbers had been eyewitnesses to the dramatic Red Sea deliverance out of Egypt and God's thunderous revelation on the top of Mt. Sinai in the book of Exodus. But those direct experiences of God's awesome presence and power did not prevent the old generation from constantly rebelling against God. Faith in God is a fragile gift that must be continually nurtured and nourished through a community of faith, prayer, study, and practice. No faithful person can rely on any one dramatic event or conversion or miracle to sustain faith over the long haul. Many in Jesus' time saw firsthand the powerful signs of healing and forgiveness and teaching of Jesus' ministry, but even then many did not believe in him or understand his ministry (Mark 6:6). Even some of Jesus' own disciples had difficulty understanding the shape and purpose of his life and work (Mark 8:31-33; 9:32). His own disciple Judas betrayed him (Matt 26:14-16; 47-50). Even Peter "the rock" denied Jesus three times (Matt 26:69-75). When the apostle Paul preached at Athens about what he had seen and heard about Jesus, some listeners scoffed, some were mildly interested, and still others actually joined Paul and became believers (Acts 17:32-34).

2. If seeing God's work directly does not always lead to believing, then it is also true that believing and knowing God can happen without seeing in some direct, firsthand way. The fact that the new generation in Judg 2:10 did not see the great works of God firsthand, as had the previous generation of Joshua and the elders, did not excuse the new generation from the expectation that they too would come to know, love, and obey the Lord. Jesus' words in response to doubting Thomas's demand for tangible proof remind us that believing without seeing not only is possible but also promises a particular blessing: "Have you believed because you have seen me? Blessed are those who have not seen and yet have come to believe" (John 20:29 NRSV). A deep faith and knowledge of God can come through hearing, learning, and doing as well as through seeing.

3. This text raises the urgent question of how faith is or is not passed from one generation to the next. The text reminds us that the heritage of faith is not something automatically inherited by passive osmosis from one generation to the next. A faithful generation can have unfaithful children. Faith and the knowledge of God are always only one generation away from extinction. The question, Will our children have faith? remains a pressing and urgent issue in the community of God's people. The traditions of faith require constant attention, teaching, discussion, and living out day by day if they are to have a chance to be passed on to the next generation (Deut 6:1-9). Even when parents are diligent in teaching the faith to their children, it may be that faith will not sprout or will die down for some period in a child's life. Faith is not something even parents can program into their children; it is finally a matter between God and the individual or community in question. We may contribute to the process, but we have no ultimate control over whether someone has faith in God.

Judges 2:11-23, The Pattern: Apostasy, Punishment, and Mercy

NIV

[11]Then the Israelites did evil in the eyes of the LORD and served the Baals. [12]They forsook the LORD, the God of their fathers, who had brought them out of Egypt. They followed and worshiped various gods of the peoples around them. They provoked the LORD to anger [13]because they forsook him and served Baal and the Ashtoreths. [14]In his anger against Israel the LORD handed them over to raiders who plundered them. He sold them to their enemies all around, whom they were no longer able to resist. [15]Whenever Israel went out to fight, the hand of the LORD was against them to defeat them, just as he had sworn to them. They were in great distress.

[16]Then the LORD raised up judges,[a] who saved them out of the hands of these raiders. [17]Yet they would not listen to their judges but prostituted themselves to other gods and worshiped them. Unlike their fathers, they quickly turned from the way in which their fathers had walked, the way of obedience to the LORD's commands. [18]Whenever the LORD raised up a judge for them, he was with the judge and saved them out of the hands of their enemies as long as the judge lived; for the LORD had compassion on them as they groaned under those who oppressed and afflicted them. [19]But when the judge died, the people returned to ways even more corrupt than those of their fathers, following other gods and serving and worshiping them. They refused to give up their evil practices and stubborn ways.

[20]Therefore the LORD was very angry with Israel and said, "Because this nation has violated the covenant that I laid down for their forefathers and has not listened to me, [21]I will no longer drive

[a]16 Or leaders; similarly in verses 17-19

NRSV

11Then the Israelites did what was evil in the sight of the LORD and worshiped the Baals; [12]and they abandoned the LORD, the God of their ancestors, who had brought them out of the land of Egypt; they followed other gods, from among the gods of the peoples who were all around them, and bowed down to them; and they provoked the LORD to anger. [13]They abandoned the LORD, and worshiped Baal and the Astartes. [14]So the anger of the LORD was kindled against Israel, and he gave them over to plunderers who plundered them, and he sold them into the power of their enemies all around, so that they could no longer withstand their enemies. [15]Whenever they marched out, the hand of the LORD was against them to bring misfortune, as the LORD had warned them and sworn to them; and they were in great distress.

16Then the LORD raised up judges, who delivered them out of the power of those who plundered them. [17]Yet they did not listen even to their judges; for they lusted after other gods and bowed down to them. They soon turned aside from the way in which their ancestors had walked, who had obeyed the commandments of the LORD; they did not follow their example. [18]Whenever the LORD raised up judges for them, the LORD was with the judge, and he delivered them from the hand of their enemies all the days of the judge; for the LORD would be moved to pity by their groaning because of those who persecuted and oppressed them. [19]But whenever the judge died, they would relapse and behave worse than their ancestors, following other gods, worshiping them and bowing down to them. They would not drop any of their practices or their stubborn ways. [20]So the

NIV

out before them any of the nations Joshua left when he died. ²²I will use them to test Israel and see whether they will keep the way of the LORD and walk in it as their forefathers did." ²³The LORD had allowed those nations to remain; he did not drive them out at once by giving them into the hands of Joshua.

NRSV

anger of the LORD was kindled against Israel; and he said, "Because this people have transgressed my covenant that I commanded their ancestors, and have not obeyed my voice, ²¹I will no longer drive out before them any of the nations that Joshua left when he died." ²²In order to test Israel, whether or not they would take care to walk in the way of the LORD as their ancestors did, ²³the LORD had left those nations, not driving them out at once, and had not handed them over to Joshua.

COMMENTARY

With the announced death of Joshua in 2:8 and the rise of a new generation after him, we have arrived back again at the same time frame with which the book of Judges began, "after the death of Joshua" (1:1). What follows in 2:11-23 will describe God's unique angle of interpretation and reaction to the military campaigns reported earlier in 1:1-36. In a sense, God's judgment on the new generations and their unfaithfulness in 2:11-23 functions as an expanded commentary on the angel's brief indictment speech, which has already appeared in 2:1-5. This expansion of God's reaction will zero in on the underlying problem for which the partial military failures in Judges 1 are only symptoms. The root problem is not military strategy or ideological differences among tribes or the relative failure of one tribe or group in comparison to another. The core problem is *all* Israel's abandonment of the Lord and *all* Israel's increasing propensity to worship other gods. The real issue is a religious and theological problem that applies to "all the Israelites."

2:11-15. These verses provide the details of what Israel has done and God's reaction to it. The Israelites did "evil" and "worshiped the Baals." The plural "Baals" likely refers to numerous local cults in Canaan all directed in worship to the principal Canaanite god, Baal. This god is mentioned with some frequency in the OT, but the Bible provides few details of the Canaanite fertility cult with which Baal is associated. However, archaeologists have uncovered and deciphered cuneiform tablets from Ugarit that provide some of the background myths for the Baal cult. Baal is portrayed in the Ugaritic myths as a weather god, manifested in thunderstorms ("Rider of the Clouds"), who struggles with the sea god, named Yam, and the god of death, named Mot. The chaos of the sea and the threat of death threatened the annual cycles of rain and fertility, but Baal in the end overcomes the forces of death and ensures the annual springtime rains and seasons of agricultural planting and harvests. The worship of Baal probably involved annual rituals that dramatized and encouraged Baal's victory over death and infertility. The cult was no doubt popular in an agrarian setting like Canaan, and this new generation of Israelites has been drawn into Baal worship instead of observing their covenant obligation to worship and love the Lord alone (Deut 5:6-7; 6:4-15). Verse 13 mentions Baal again, along with a Canaanite fertility goddess named Astarte, who was a consort of Baal and part of the broader Canaanite pantheon.

The flip side of worshiping other gods is abandoning the Lord. Israel's abandonment is particularly egregious for two reasons: The Lord is "the God of their ancestors," and the Lord is the one "who had brought them out of the land of Egypt" (v. 12). The Lord has been Israel's faithful God reaching far back into Israel's history to the time of Abraham, Isaac, and Jacob. Moreover, the Lord is the one who gave Israel its future by rescuing it from slavery and bringing it to the land of Canaan. Now Israel has taken the gift of the land and rejected the gift-giver by worshiping other gods. These reminders of God's past faithfulness prepare the reader for God's heated response of anger, which appears in triplicate in this section (v. 12, 14, 20).

God's righteous anger gives way to action in judgment on Israel, described as "giving them over" to plunderers and "selling them into the power" of their enemies (v. 14). God drops all divine defenses from around the Israelites so that they become vulnerable to those who attack them. But God also takes a more active role as well. Whenever Israel's army marched into battle, the Lord's hand "was against them to bring misfortune" (v. 15). Here the motif of God as enemy mirrors the angel of the Lord, who "went up" in a reversal of the holy war to fight against Israel with a verbal indictment in vv. 1-5. God's reaction should have been no surprise, since God had clearly stated time and again that the worship of other gods would lead to God's anger and destructive fury. Deuteronomy 7:4 is an example where Moses speaks on behalf of God about the consequences of Israel's worshiping other gods: "Then the anger of the LORD would be kindled against you, and he would destroy you quickly." According to the covenant, God has the legal right to impose the death penalty on Israel as a people; such is the severity of the transgression of bowing down to other deities.

2:16. What seemed to be a screaming locomotive heading for Israel's destruction is suddenly derailed. God raised up "judges, who delivered them out of the power of those who plundered them." God is both enemy and friend, both wounder and healer. The judges provide temporary relief from the enemy's oppression. The earlier nucleus of this section probably presented this sequence of events in a revolving or cyclical pattern:

(a) Israel worshiped other gods.

(b) God became angry and allowed enemies to attack Israel.

(c) God raised up a judge who delivered Israel and returned Israel to worshiping the Lord.

(d) Israel reverted to its old ways of worshiping other gods after the judge died, and then the cycle started all over again (a-d).

2:17. This cyclical pattern appears if the reader moves from v. 16 immediately to vv. 18-19, skipping v. 17. Verse 17 is probably a later editorial addition to the old nucleus of this section. Once added, v. 17 transforms the earlier positive characterization of the judges as military

leaders and religious reformers into something else. According to v. 17, the judges do, indeed, remain effective military deliverers who rescue Israel from enemies. But they fail in the more important theological task of teaching the people about their sole loyalty to the Lord: The Israelites "did not listen even to their judges; for they lusted after other gods and bowed down to them."

2:18-19. These verses add two more pieces of important information, one about God and one about Israel. Concerning God, we are told the reason why God repeatedly sent judges generation after generation to deliver Israel from the very enemies God had allowed to plunder Israel. The Lord was "moved to pity by their groaning." The verb נחם (niḥam, niphal), translated "move to pity" (NRSV) or "had compassion" (NIV), signifies sorrow at the hurt or pain of another and a desire to come to the victim's aid. The word "groaning" (נאקה nĕʾāqâ) refers not to any repentant attitude on the part of the Israelites, but to cries of lament due to pain and oppression. God responds to deliver them not because Israel has promised to reform or is sorry for sin. God responds simply because God has compassion on this oppressed but still rebellious people. The same Hebrew word is used in Exod 2:23-24 for the groaning of the Israelite slaves in Egypt, which caused God to hear and to act to deliver them from oppression. The cries of oppressed people have a special avenue to God's heart and a unique claim on God's compassion, irrespective of whether the oppressed are themselves wholly virtuous.

Concerning Israel, v. 19 informs us that the Israelites during the era of the judges are on a downhill slide into apostasy and idolatry. Whenever the judges died, the Israelites who were not faithful even during the tenure of the judges (v. 17) behaved even worse than the previous generation of ancestors. God's hope was that the judges would not only save Israel from its enemies but also strengthen Israel's resolve to drive the Canaanites and their gods totally out of the promised land. But Israel under the judges refused to drop any of their sinful ways. They increasingly strayed from the Lord and continued more and more to worship other gods. In their final edited form, vv. 6-19 have portrayed a steady decline from the faithfulness of the early generations under Joshua and the elders to the increasing apostasy and rebellion of Israel throughout the era of the judges. We see, then, a parallel movement in the characterization of Israel from good to bad to worse in the two parts of the introduction to the book of Judges: 1:1-36, increasing military failure to oust the Canaanites, and 2:6-19, increasing theological failure to worship the Lord alone.

2:20-23. The first part of the introduction to Judges ended with a climactic speech by the angel of the Lord. The speech indicted Israel and reported God's change in plans. God would allow the Canaanites to stay in the land, and their gods would remain as a constant "snare" to Israel (vv. 1-5). This second half of the introduction also ends with a climactic speech by God, indicting Israel and reporting God's change in plans concerning the Canaanites (vv. 20-23). The third appearance of God's anger in this section occurs in v. 20. The previous two occurrences of the divine anger had been part of the repeated cycle of God's anger in the more global response of God's looking back over the whole sweep of the many generations of the judges era and their failures and disappointments. Thus God, in a culminating but understandable and righteous rage, gives up on the holy war plan to wipe out the Canaanites. Instead, the Canaanites will remain in the land "in order to test Israel, whether or not they would take care to walk in the way of the Lord" (v. 22). Israel will never be free from temptations and forces that will seek to lure its faith and allegiance away from the Lord. Israel's faith will be under constant scrutiny and testing. God's dream of bringing Israel into the promised land of milk and honey with no cares or temptations where Israel would have no choice but to worship the Lord alone has been forfeited and lost forever. Verses 6-23 have revealed God's inner struggle and process to arrive at that painful conclusion. The divine dream has been shattered. Yet God's compassion moves God to pick up the pieces and move on with a new reality and strategy for continuing in relationship with the inescapably unruly people of Israel.

REFLECTIONS

1. The book of Judges does not go into great detail in describing the particulars of the other religions and gods that Israel worshiped. The narrative mentions the names of Baal and Astarte, but little other information is provided. The lack of specificity and the repeated general charge of "worshiping other gods" invites later generations to fill in this story with the particular temptations and gods of their own age and setting. What gods in our own time and place lure us away from loyalty and devotion to the Lord? What temptations in our surrounding culture cause us to ignore the call to "love the Lord your God with all your heart, and with all your soul, and with all your might" (Deut 6:5 NRSV)? Such temptations are not limited to other organized religions or cults. All the many pressures, values, and enticements of our culture that demand our time, energy, resources, and loyalty can become false gods insofar as our devotion to them supersedes our devotion to the Lord. For example, Deuteronomy 7–11 explores the ways in which devotion to arrogant militarism, self-sufficient materialism, or self-righteous moralism can become substitutes for true worship of God (Deut 7:7, 17; 8:17; 9:4). The nature of the false gods we worship may be as varied as the human imagination that manufactures them.

2. We encounter again the theme of the dialogical struggle between God's anger and God's compassion, the battle between the requirements of the law and the compassion of gracious love. As was noted earlier, there is a juxtaposition of these two competing paradigms in the legalism of the judgment of King Adoni-bezek (Judg 1:4-7) and the compassion and generosity of parental love shown by Caleb to his daughter Achsah (Judg 1:11-15). The angel's speech in 2:1-5 displayed a similar tension between God's unconditional covenant faithfulness (2:1) and Israel's covenant disobedience and God's just punishment (2:2-3). This dialectical dance between God's heartfelt compassion and God's angry judgment becomes the dominating theme of 2:6-23. As Israel accelerates its downward slide into rebellion and apostasy, God allows enemies to plunder Israel in punishment for its sin. But at the same time, God interrupts the judgment for a time by sending judges who deliver Israel from their enemies. Israel experiences God as both enemy and friend. Just as the angelic divine warrior who confronted Joshua (Josh 5:13-15) was not solely an adversary or solely an ally, so also God both judges and delivers God's people. In the Song of Moses in Deuteronomy 32, God proclaims:

> See now that I, even I, am he;
>   there is no god beside me.
> I kill and I make alive;
>   I wound and I heal;
>   and no one can deliver from my hand. (Deut 32:39 NRSV)

Like Jacob in the wrestling match with God in Genesis 32, God wrestles and injures, but also blesses and cares for, God's people. This is the painful lesson the rebellious people of God must constantly learn: There is no other god or savior to heal our woes other than the same God who alone has the power both to judge and to deliver.

3. The power of the cry of the oppressed Israelites to move God, even though they remained mired in their idolatrous sin, reminds us of the hold that the poor and the oppressed have on God's heart. It was the cry of the Israelite slaves that caught God's attention and initiated the course of events that toppled an arrogant pharaoh from power (Exod 2:23-24). As a result, God later commanded the Israelites to treat those who were poor or oppressed in their own communities with generosity and compassion. Otherwise, "your neighbor might cry to the LORD against you, and you would incur guilt" (Deut 15:9 NRSV). The cry of the oppressed peoples of the earth has power to provoke God's action to judge the arrogant and the powerful and to raise up the poor and the downtrodden (1 Sam 2:1-10; Luke 1:46-55).

Judges 3:1-6, Nations Remain to Test Israel

NIV

3 These are the nations the LORD left to test all those Israelites who had not experienced any of the wars in Canaan ²(he did this only to teach warfare to the descendants of the Israelites who had not had previous battle experience): ³the five rulers of the Philistines, all the Canaanites, the Sidonians, and the Hivites living in the Lebanon mountains from Mount Baal Hermon to Lebo*ᵃ* Hamath. ⁴They were left to test the Israelites to see whether they would obey the LORD's commands, which he had given their forefathers through Moses.

⁵The Israelites lived among the Canaanites, Hittites, Amorites, Perizzites, Hivites and Jebusites. ⁶They took their daughters in marriage and gave their own daughters to their sons, and served their gods.

ᵃ3 Or to the entrance to

NRSV

3 Now these are the nations that the LORD left to test all those in Israel who had no experience of any war in Canaan ²(it was only that successive generations of Israelites might know war, to teach those who had no experience of it before): ³the five lords of the Philistines, and all the Canaanites, and the Sidonians, and the Hivites who lived on Mount Lebanon, from Mount Baal-hermon as far as Lebo-hamath. ⁴They were for the testing of Israel, to know whether Israel would obey the commandments of the LORD, which he commanded their ancestors by Moses. ⁵So the Israelites lived among the Canaanites, the Hittites, the Amorites, the Perizzites, the Hivites, and the Jebusites; ⁶and they took their daughters as wives for themselves, and their own daughters they gave to their sons; and they worshiped their gods.

COMMENTARY

The two-part introduction to Judges (1:1–2:5 and 2:6–3:6) concludes with a brief summary of the nations that God allowed to remain in the promised land. God had resolved in 2:21 not to drive out "any of the nations that Joshua left," and 3:1-6 tells the reader precisely who those nations are. The list of nations in v. 3—Philistines, Canaanites, Sidonians, and Hivites—was probably derived from Josh 13:2-6 and includes nations that were neighbors to the central part of Canaan on its northern and western boundaries. The king of Hazor in the far north of Canaan will be featured in the story of Deborah, Barak, and Jael (chaps. 4–5), and the Philistines will be the prime oppressors in the Samson story (chaps. 13–16). The additional list of nations in v. 5 is the more conventional summary of the inhabitants of Canaan that one finds scattered throughout the book of Joshua (Josh 3:10; 9:1; 11:3; 12:8; 24:11).

Why did the Lord allow these nations to remain in Canaan? Two seemingly contradictory reasons are given. Verses 1-2 argue that the other nations were left in Canaan to help succeeding generations of Israelites learn how to fight in a war and gain military experience. The text says this was the "only" reason. Verse 4 offers a second, different reason. God allowed the other nations to remain in Canaan to test Israel "to know whether Israel would obey the commandments of the LORD." This second reason has been the primary way in which the preceding verses explained why

God allowed the Canaanites to stay in the land (2:3, 22-23). Many scholars simply dismiss the first reason about pedagogy for military battle an insertion by a later naïve or inept editor. That may be the case, but the two reasons can be read as more complementary than contradictory. God's commandments do include rules on how to conduct holy war (cf. Deut 20:10-18, which has the same list of nations as in Judg 3:5). Thus a good part of knowing whether Israel would obey God's commandments (reason 2) includes testing how Israel will fight its battles against other peoples and other gods (reason 1). Also, following God's commandments inevitably draws the faithful person or community into some sort of conflict with other forces, powers, and communities who may resist God's will and God's way. The challenge to obey God in the face of countervailing forces entails learning how to do battle against such forces. Such battles need not be fought with weapons of violence, but with weapons of words, Scripture, study, persuasion, prayer, worship, community support, and acts of love, reconciliation, and forgiveness. Future visions of nations and their vocation in the world moved away from military violence to visions of peace, servanthood, and education in the ways of the Lord (Isa 2:1-4):

They shall beat their swords into plowshares,
  and their spears into pruning hooks;
nation shall not lift up sword against nation,
  neither shall they learn war any more. (Isa 2:4 NRSV)

REFLECTIONS

1. Some people may be troubled by the notion that God deliberately places tests and temptations before us to try our souls. After all, we pray in the Lord's prayer, "Lead us not into temptation" (Matt 6:13 NIV). However, the motif of God's testing the faith of God's people is a significant theme in the Old Testament. God tested Abraham when God ordered him to sacrifice Isaac (Gen 22:1). The psalmist invites such testing: "Prove me, O LORD, and try me; test my heart and mind" (Ps 26:2 NRSV; cf. Ps 66:10). The prophets likewise speak of God's testing of Israel (Jer 9:7; Zech 13:9). The entire book of Job involves God's test of Job's faith and devotion to God (Job 1). While some New Testament traditions likewise affirm God's testing of the faithful (Heb 11:17), other traditions deny that God tempts anyone (Jas 1:13). Satan, or the devil, is often portrayed as the chief source of temptation and testing (Matt 4:1-11; Luke 22:3; Rev 2:10).

How are we to understand these disparate traditions about God's testing and tempting of

God's people? It seems clear that God does at times test people and their faith. But God tests them not to tempt them into sin but to refine and strengthen their commitment to God. Using the analogy of the purification of precious metals, God will at times put the people of God "into the fire, refine them as one refines silver, and test them as gold is tested" (Zech 13:9 NRSV). But, of course, there are times when suffering or evil comes upon us from forces or powers other than God or ourselves. Then we join with God in battle against a common enemy. But each challenge and difficulty in life is an opportunity to ask the question, Is God testing me and my community? But even when we discern that God may be testing our faith, the apostle Paul reminds us that God is both the one who tests and the one who provides:

> No testing has overtaken you that is not common to everyone. God is faithful, and he will not let you be tested beyond your strength, but with the testing he will also provide the way out so that you may be able to endure it. (1 Cor 10:13 NRSV)

Again we see the portrait of God as both enemy and friend, judge and deliverer, tempter and rescuer. In the book of Judges, God resolves to leave the Canaanites in the land to tempt Israel as a test of faith (3:1, 4). But in the course of the generations of testing, God will provide judges who will deliver Israel for a time. God will not abandon Israel entirely to its own devices. God will ensure that somehow the story of God and of God's people will go on in spite of the testing, the failures, and the unfaithfulness of God's people.

2. The concluding verse in this unit, 3:6, provides a narrative transition that sets the stage for the series of individual judge stories that will typically begin with Israel doing evil in the sight of the Lord. Verse 6 describes the nature of Israel's evil as the intermarriage of Israelite men and women with the sons and daughters of the other nations. The consequence of such intermarriage was that the Israelites "worshiped their gods." This association of intermarriage and apostasy takes seriously the risks and challenges of close and intimate relationships with those who do not share our core values, beliefs, and faith. Marriages, close friendships, peer groups, gangs, and other tightly knit communities (such as cults) have enormous power to shape our loyalties and thinking. As was noted in the Commentary on 1:1-21, Israel often had to wrestle with the nature of its relationships to other peoples and nations. Sometimes Israel fought against and isolated itself from other nations (Judg 1:4; cf. Ezra and Nehemiah), and sometimes Israel embraced people of foreign nations (Judg 1:16; cf. Ruth and Jonah).

A curious double message exists in the biblical material concerning intermarriage. On the one hand, prominent ancestors and leaders of Israel intermarried in good faith with women of other nations and peoples (Joseph and his Egyptian wife, Gen 41:45; Moses and his Midianite wife, Exod 2:21; Moses and his Cushite wife, Num 12:1; Boaz and his Moabite wife, Ruth, Ruth 4:13). On the other hand, some biblical laws and narratives offer strict warnings against intermarriage because it may lead to abandoning the Lord and worshiping other gods (Exod 34:11-16; Num 25:1-18; Deut 7:1-6; 1 Kgs 11:1-13).

Two things need to be said. First of all, many of the warnings against intermarriage occurred only in regard to certain transitional times in Israel's history and in regard to certain evil nations, like the Canaanites, at the time of the settlement in the land. The settlement in Canaan was the moment of Israel's birth as a nation. Such times of transition in Israel's history were precarious. Israel's identity as the people of God was fragile, vulnerable, and easily swayed. Israel needed a time of separation to gain a sense of its boundaries and identity as a people among the other nations. The time of Ezra and Nehemiah and the rebuilding of a fragile community of returned exiles in Judah in the post-exilic period was also a time of delicate transition and community formation. In that context, the leaders decreed an end to intermarriage with foreign spouses, echoing the concerns of these earlier texts from Exodus, Deuteronomy, and Judges (Ezra 9–10).

Second, other traditions in the Old Testament are much more open to the notion of intermarriage and regular interaction with people of other nations. Books like Ruth and Jonah come to mind, along with the stories in Genesis in which the foreigners sometimes appear more noble and virtuous than do the Israelites (Gen 12:10-20; 20:1-18; 34:1-31). Some of these stories may have come from a time when Israel was more secure in its identity and thus better able to be open and inclusive of other peoples and nations. In any case, as we come to the end of this two-part introduction to the book of Judges, we know that we are about to embark upon a path that will lead from Israel's initial success and faithfulness downward into the growing disintegration and unfaithfulness of the fragile Israelite community.

THE INDIVIDUAL JUDGES: A DOWNWARD SPIRAL

OVERVIEW

The two-part introduction to the book of Judges in 1:1–3:6 provided the defining pattern for understanding the movement and structure of the book of Judges. This generalized pattern portrayed the time of Israel's judges as a series of Israelite generations who experienced a downward political and religious spiral in their leadership, in their faith in God, and in their social unity. The individual judge stories in the main body of 3:7–16:31 have been edited and shaped to conform to this same introductory paradigm of military, political, and religious decline. The tales of individual judges begin with the model judge Othniel (3:7-11), who stands apart from the rest and provides the standard of proper judgeship by which all the other judges may be evaluated. The individual judge narratives include a total of twelve judges, six "major judges," with extended narratives (Othniel, Ehud, Deborah, Gideon with his son Abimelech, Jephthah, and Samson), and six "minor judges," with brief notices interspersed among the major judge stories (Shamgar, Tola, Jair, Ibzan, Elon, and Abdon).

The Six Major Judges: From Victory to Tragedy. We may discern a downward progression in three phases or stages among the six major judge stories.[24] The first phase (3:7–5:31) includes judges who are largely victorious and faithful: Othniel, the model judge; Ehud, the left-handed Benjaminite ("son of the right hand"); and the story of Deborah, Barak, and Jael. This first phase culminates in the poetic Song of Deborah, which sings the praises of God and hu-

mans. The second phase (6:1–10:5) is transitional in character and begins the downward slide of the judges. Gideon is himself a transitional figure, moving from victory and faithfulness (albeit in a somewhat cowardly and tentative manner) to idolatry and hints of political power grabbing in the midst of a rhetoric of pious humility. The subtle negative shift in Gideon's character emerges full blown in his son Abimelech, whose arrogance and power grabbing are anything but subtle. Abimelech declares himself king and kills his own brothers in a familial and civil war. He dies in shame fighting a war started over a challenge to his personal honor. Gideon and Abimelech mark a turning point from positive to negative in the succession of individual judges. More and more the judges will fight for themselves and against Israel's interests rather than for God and for the interests of a united people of Israel.

The third group of judges after Gideon and Abimelech descend further into military failure, religious unfaithfulness, and personal tragedy (10:6–16:31). Jephthah the judge is victorious in battle but feels forced to kill his one and only child, a daughter, because of a foolish vow to God. Jephthah also fights and kills 42,000 members of a fellow Israelite tribe, an act as abhorrent as killing one's own family member. The other tragic figure in this third and last group of Israelite judges is Samson. Although great expectations are attached to his birth as a specially chosen Nazirite, Samson is a judge who leads no one but himself. He is a playboy who parties with foreigners, a hot-headed rogue who regularly violates his nazirite vows to God, and a love-struck fool who is humiliated by Israel's enemies. In the end, Samson kills himself along with a large number of

24. My understanding of the overall shape of the book of Judges, 3:7–6:31 in particular, is informed by the redaction-critical study of, among others, Lawson Stone, "From Tribal Confederation to Monarchic State: The Editorial Perspective in the Book of Judges" (Ph.D. diss., Yale University; Ann Arbor: University Microfilms, 1987) 260-391, and the literary work of Barry Webb, *The Book of the Judges: An Integrated Reading* (Sheffield: JSOT, 1987) 123-79.

Philistine leaders in one last desperate act of personal revenge.

This three-stage descent from victory and faithfulness to tragedy and religious distortion among the individual judges is the result of an intentional process of careful literary editing in two or more stages. Many of the judge stories probably originated as entertaining heroic tales about the military victories or exploits of a local tribal ancestor. These independent tales were retold and gradually came to be collected and edited into a coherent series of deliverers or judges. The resulting series of judge stories may have been formed on the model of a common genre of ancient Near Eastern literature called the royal annals or chronicles, in which a succession of rulers and their stories were brought together into a coherent whole.[25] The role of these originally local judges was expanded to a national level; they were portrayed as leading not only a local tribe or small coalition but "all Israel" for a given period of years. Much of the local color and detail of each of the stories remained. However, later editors also reworked the stories in crucial ways so that the reader was given a sense of a gradual and progressive deterioration in the quality of the judges and their rule.

Six important elements of the first judge story, that of Othniel (3:7-11), functioned as a definitive norm or standard of a faithful judge against which all the other judge stories could be implicitly assessed. These six elements include (1) the nature of the evil done by the Israelite people, (2) the description of the enemy's oppression, (3) the divine reaction to the Israelites' cry, (4) the judges' success in uniting and delivering Israel, (5) a focus on God's victory against the enemies of Israel versus a focus on the details of the judge's own personal life and desire for vengeance, and (6) the proportion of the number of years the judge ruled in peace versus the number of years the enemy oppressed Israel. As we move from the earlier to the later judges in chaps. 3–16, we will note the progressive deterioration in actualizing these six criteria of the model judge. As the discussion below will show, these six criteria have been used by the writers and editors of Judges to portray a dramatic religious and political decline during the era of the judges:

(1) The nature of Israel's evil moves from an unspecified evil in the early judge stories (3:12; 4:1a) to a more and more explicit charge of idolatry and worshiping foreign gods in the later judge stories (6:10; 8:24-27, 33-35; 10:6).

(2) The descriptions of the enemy's oppression in the early judge narratives are relatively short and generic (3:13; 4:2), but the descriptions of the oppression in the last two stages of the judge narratives become longer and more severe (6:1-6; 10:6-16).

(3) God's reaction to the Israelites' cry of distress is immediate and positive in the early judge tales (3:15; 4:3-7). In contrast, Israel's cry of distress in the later stories evokes a mediated rebuke from God (6:7-10) and then a direct divine rejection (10:10-14) because of Israel's increasing sinfulness and the judges' increasing failure to lead. This decline culminates in the final judge story of Samson, which contains no Israelite cry of distress at all; the traditional power of the oppressed human's cry to God has been lost (13:1).

(4) The judges' success in uniting and saving Israel from its oppressing enemy begins on a high note. The early judges are victorious (3:29-30; 4:23-24). They united Israel, including the northern Ephraimites, to their cause (3:27; 5:14). The degree to which the Israelite tribe of Ephraim is included or excluded becomes an indicator of Israel's health throughout these narratives. The later judges have some success against external enemies (8:28). However, Gideon becomes entangled in a brief internal conflict with his fellow Israelite tribe of Ephraim (8:1-3). Gideon's conflict with Ephraim is quickly resolved without bloodshed, but this intra-Israel conflict escalates with the later judges who slay fellow Israelites. Abimelech murders seventy of his own brothers (9:5), Jephthah kills his own daughter and fights and kills 42,000 people of the tribe of Ephraim (12:1-6). The last judge, Samson, is a one-man army who does not unite or lead any tribes of Israel in concerted action against their enemy. His success is limited, as he will only "begin to deliver Israel from the hand of the Philistines" (13:5).

(5) The focus of the early judge narratives is less on the human judge in terms of biographical detail and more on God and the praise of God (3:15, 28; 4:23; 5:1-11, 31). We know very little about the origins, divine call, or personal lives of the early judges, Othniel, Ehud, and Deborah. The

25. Barnabas Lindbars, *Judges 1–5: A New Translation and Commentary* (Edinburgh: T. & T. Clark, 1995) 125.

spotlight in their stories is on the military victory itself and on God's role in achieving it. However, the later judge stories gradually lessen the attention on God and increase the amount of biographical detail dedicated to the individual judges, beginning with Gideon. By the time we reach Jephthah and Samson, their personal stories and self-serving desire for personal vengeance simply crowd out the actual account of any military victory or of God's role in it. Like the later judges, Israel has become more and more concerned with looking at itself and less and less concerned with looking to God for guidance and help.

(6) The decreasing proportion of the number of years Israel had rest or peace under each judge to the number of years of enemy oppression is yet another marker of the decline of the judges period. The ideal standard is set in the Othniel account with a long forty years of peace (a round number for a generation), in contrast to only an eight-year period of oppression (3:8, 11). The early judges all meet or exceed this standard.

Judge	Years of Peace	Years of Oppression
Ehud (3:14, 30)	80	18
Deborah (4:3; 5:31)	40	20
Gideon (6:1; 8:28)	40	7
Jephthah (10:8; 12:7)	6	18
Samson (13:1; 16:31)	20	40

Gideon is a transitional figure in the decline of the judges. He meets the standard set by Othniel in chap. 3 of at least forty years of peace (8:28), but this notice is marred by an accompanying indictment that "all Israel prostituted themselves" to an idolatrous ephod made by Gideon (8:27). Gideon's son Abimelech solidifies the decline in that he kills members of his own Israelite family and then himself is killed in battle, so no years of peace are recorded for him; Abimelech falls entirely outside the paradigm. The notices for the last two judges, Jephthah and Samson, reveal that the decline has continued. The formula that the "land had rest" for a specified number of years is absent in the later stories of Jephthah and Samson, replaced simply with the number of years they were judges. In the case of the later judgeships, the years of oppression far exceed the number of

years the judge actually ruled. The progression in these chronological notices associated with the major judges throughout 3:7–16:31 clearly reveals a gradual decline in the fortunes of Israel and the judges' effectiveness as leaders.

The Six Minor Judges: From Victory to Trivial Pursuit. The same sense of gradual decline appears in the sequence of the six so-called minor judges. The brief notices of these judges intrude at three junctures among the major judge narratives: Shamgar in 3:31, Tola and Jair in 10:1-5, and Ibzan, Elon, and Abdon in 12:8-15. These three junctures correspond to the three phases or stages in the decline of the judges as a whole. The first minor judge, Shamgar, successfully kills six hundred of the dreaded enemy, the Philistines, and is said to have "delivered Israel" (3:31). The focus only on Shamgar's military success fits his present literary location among the early judges who were faithful and successful. The next two minor judges, Tola and Jair, who rule twenty-three and twenty-two years respectively, appear in the second transitional stage after Gideon and the disastrous rule of his son Abimelech. The narrator reports that Tola "rose to deliver Israel," but the narrator provides no indication that the second minor judge, Jair, accomplished anything for the well-being of Israel. All that is reported is the rather bizarre personal note that Jair had thirty sons who rode on thirty donkeys and had thirty towns. This mixed report of deliverance of Israel and no deliverance of Israel mirrors the transitional nature of this section of Judges, moving from success to failure in Gideon and Abimelech.

Finally, the third interpolation of minor judges (Ibzan, Elon, and Abdon) in 12:8-15 appears between the narratives of Jephthah and Samson. In line with the relative decline and failure of the last of the major judges, no mention of delivering Israel or any other beneficial effect is reported for these three minor judges. Moreover, the length of their successive judgeships is relatively short: seven years (Ibzan), ten years (Elon), and eight years (Abdon). The relative shortness of their tenures corresponds to the relative brevity of the judgeships of Jephthah and Samson, indicating again a sense of decreasing effectiveness as leaders. The focus of the brief reports concerning these later minor judges, like the later major judges, is on their personal lives and individual concerns rather than the national welfare (finding spouses for their sons and daughters, the number of their children and grandchildren riding on donkeys). The concern for Israel's national welfare among the early judges has been gradually diluted into personal agendas, individual familial concerns, and trivial pursuits among the last judges.

Geographical Sequence and the Decline of the Judges. It was noted in the discussion of the introductory section of Judges 1 that a trend from positive success to gradually increasing failure characterized the geographical movement from southern to northern Israel in the first chapter of the book of Judges. A similar geographical movement from southern Judah through middle and northern Israelite tribes and clans is evident in the sequence of individual judge stories in 3:6–16:31. The sequence begins with the positive model of Othniel, who is related to Caleb from the tribe of Judah. The sequence then continues from south to north through Israel's landscape as we move through the tribal designations provided for many, but not all, of the judges: Judah (Othniel, 1:10-15; 3:9), Benjamin (Ehud, 3:15), Ephraim (Deborah, 4:4), Issachar (Tola, 10:1), Zebulun (Elon, 12:12), and Dan (Samson, 13:2). These geographical progressions from southern Judah to the far northern Dan are accompanied by a deteriorating progression in the effectiveness and faithfulness of the judges and the Israelites. Both of these progressions—geographical and religious-political—mirror the structure and progression evident in the introduction to the book in chap. 1. Many of the other judges, particularly those in the latter stages of the judges era, are not listed by their affiliation with one of the twelve tribes of Israel. They are listed only by their minor clan or village designations: Abiezrite (Gideon, 6:11), Gilead (Jephthah, 11:1), Bethlehem (Ibzan, 12:8), and Pirathon (Abdon, 12:13). These increasingly minor clan affiliations, as opposed to full tribal attachments, contribute further to the sense of increasing disunity and disintegration within the nation of Israel toward the end of the period of the judges.

Thus the editing of the six major judge narratives, the three minor judge interpolations, and the overall geographical progression from the southern to the northern tribes all conspire to shape the reading of these judge stories. The once independent judge narratives have been brought together and formed into a sequence of gradual decline and disintegration. The judges' political leadership and Israel's religious faithfulness begin on a high note with the earliest judges, but end in tragedy and disunity with the last judges, Jephthah and Samson. Although the political and religious institution of the judges and their temporary mode of leadership was satisfactory for a time, it soon proved to be inadequate for the long haul. Israel and God would together need to find a new way to unify and lead Israel as its national life continued in the land of Canaan.

JUDGES 3:7-11, OTHNIEL, THE MODEL JUDGE

NIV

⁷The Israelites did evil in the eyes of the Lord; they forgot the Lord their God and served the Baals and the Asherahs. ⁸The anger of the Lord burned against Israel so that he sold them into the hands of Cushan-Rishathaim king of Aram Naharaim,ᵃ to whom the Israelites were subject for eight years. ⁹But when they cried out to the Lord, he raised up for them a deliverer, Othniel son of Kenaz, Caleb's younger brother, who saved them. ¹⁰The Spirit of the Lord came upon him,

ᵃ8 That is, Northwest Mesopotamia

NRSV

7The Israelites did what was evil in the sight of the Lord, forgetting the Lord their God, and worshiping the Baals and the Asherahs. ⁸Therefore the anger of the Lord was kindled against Israel, and he sold them into the hand of King Cushan-rishathaim of Aram-naharaim; and the Israelites served Cushan-rishathaim eight years. ⁹But when the Israelites cried out to the Lord, the Lord raised up a deliverer for the Israelites, who delivered them, Othniel son of Kenaz, Caleb's younger brother. ¹⁰The spirit of the Lord came upon him,

NIV

so that he became Israel's judge[a] and went to war. The LORD gave Cushan-Rishathaim king of Aram into the hands of Othniel, who overpowered him. [11]So the land had peace for forty years, until Othniel son of Kenaz died.

[a]10 Or *leader*

NRSV

and he judged Israel; he went out to war, and the LORD gave King Cushan-rishathaim of Aram into his hand; and his hand prevailed over Cushan-rishathaim. [11]So the land had rest forty years. Then Othniel son of Kenaz died.

COMMENTARY

The numerous episodes of individual judges or deliverers in 3:7–16:31 begin with a judge who is a relative of the honored ancestor Caleb and a member of the prestigious southern tribe of Judah. His name is Othniel. We have encountered Othniel already in the first chapter of Judges. Caleb, of the tribe of Judah, offered his daughter Achsah in marriage to the one warrior who would attack and defeat the Canaanite city of Kiriath-sepher. Caleb's nephew Othniel accepted the challenge, defeated the Canaanites, and married Achsah (1:11-15; see Josh 15:13-19). None of these details are carried forward into this brief narrative in 3:7-11. Instead, what we have is a collation of all the stock formulas and stereotypical phrases that occurred in the summary framework in 2:11-19 and will recur with important and meaningful variations over the course of the more expansive individual judge narratives that will follow in chaps. 3–16. Scholars have long recognized the stereotypical form of the Othniel episode as being composed of these formulaic phrases and motifs: Israel's doing evil, the Lord's anger, oppression from the enemy, the Lord's raising up of a judge, and so forth. Some scholars have concluded from its brevity and artificiality that the Othniel episode is of little value for interpreting Judges, perhaps functioning only to make up a judge for the tribe of Judah, since Judah did not have a representative among the other judge stories.

However, the Othniel episode in the present form of Judges has a central role as the standard against which all the other judge stories may be compared and evaluated.[26] As was discussed in the Overview to 3:7–16:31, the variations in key

motifs and phrases in the judge stories portray a sequence of gradual degradation in the political, military, and religious effectiveness of the Israelite judges. Othniel's story gathers together all the significant stereotypical phrases that are scattered among the other judge stories as if to say to the reader, "Now these are the phrases and elements to which you should pay attention as you evaluate the following stories of judges." The Overview to 3:7–16:31 also noted how six elements or criteria embedded within the Othniel story play a crucial role in the appraisal of the judges who will follow Othniel: (1) the nature of Israel's evil, (2) the description of the enemy's oppression, (3) God's reaction to the Israelites' cry of distress, (4) the judge's success in uniting and delivering Israel, (5) a focus on God's victory or the judge's personal life and desire for vengeance, and (6) the proportion of the number of years the judge ruled in peace ("the land had rest X years") and the number of years the enemy oppressed Israel. The Othniel episode contains largely positive dimensions of these six elements, while later judge stories will gradually exhibit more negative dimensions relative to the criteria implied in the model story of Othniel.

Othniel's story is the first specific example of the generalized pattern of what will occur in the era of the judges, laid out earlier in 2:11-19. The story begins with the Israelites doing evil, which is expressed as both "forgetting the LORD" and "worshiping the Baals and Asherahs." The time period presumably returns the reader to the time of 2:11, when Joshua and his generation have died. The new generation has forgotten all that Israel's God has done for them and instead has sought security and salvation in the gods of Canaan, the local cults of the male god Baal and the female consort Asherah. This apostasy provokes

26. Lawson Stone, "From Tribal Confederation to Monarchic State," 260-89.

God's anger so that God gives the Israelites over to an enemy king named Cushan-rishathaim from Aram-naharaim. The king's name in Hebrew means "Cusan of Double Wickedness," an obviously villainous and perhaps satirical royal name for which we have no historical record. The place name Aram-naharaim means "Aram of the Two Rivers" and refers to the area of northwest Mesopotamia where two rivers flow.

God and the Cry of the Oppressed. The enemy oppression of Israel lasted only eight years, one of the shortest periods of oppression among the judge stories (3:8). In the midst of their oppression, the Israelites "cried out to the LORD," and God responded by sending the judge-deliverer named Othniel to save them. Some interpreters have understood this cry to God as Israel's cry of repentance and remorseful acknowledgment of the sin of worshiping other gods. However, the Hebrew verb זעק (zāʿaq, "to cry out"), as it is used elsewhere in the OT, does not carry the connotation of repentance but simply someone in distress who is calling desperately to God for help. That the cry of the oppressed has a special power and leverage with the gods is a common ancient Near Eastern motif that the OT shares.[27] However, the story of Othniel adds an additional religious and moral dimension. In spite of Israel's worship of other gods, Israel's God graciously responds to their cry and saves them in spite of their sin (3:9). However, the time will come in the judges era when Israel's idolatrous transgression will increase to such an extent that God will respond with a rebuke when the Israelites cry out about oppression (6:7-10). Later, God will respond even more negatively to Israel's cry with a word of outright rejection, even though Israel adds words of confession and repentance to the cry for help (10:10-16). The growing depth of Israel's sin will eventually make even the powerful cry of the oppressed ineffectual in moving God to saving action. For now in the Othniel story, Israel's cry for aid receives an immediate and positive response: God quickly sends Othniel to save Israel.

The Spirit of the Lord and the Judges. God raises up Othniel as "the spirit of the LORD" comes upon him. The effect of the divine Spirit

on the judge is another important criterion by which to evaluate the judges. With Othniel, the effect is positive as he is empowered and immediately victorious (3:10). However, the divine Spirit in the book of Judges can have either positive or negative effects. For Othniel, God's Spirit is a positive gift that changes him and leads him into powerful, decisive, and faithful action. The result is similar to the effect of God's Spirit coming upon Saul in 1 Sam 10:6-7. For the other early judges, like Ehud and Deborah, the text does not say that they were given a divine Spirit at all but rather a divine word (3:20; 4:6). When God's Spirit does return to play a role in the judges narrative, it comes upon Gideon—but with little effect or change. Before the Spirit of the Lord comes upon him, Gideon is cowardly, hesitant, and secretive (6:11-33). After the Spirit of the Lord has come upon him (6:34), Gideon does not change. The cowardly Gideon continues to need repeated reassurance from God through signs and dreams (6:36–7:15). The effect of the divine Spirit's coming on Jephthah is even more negative. Before receiving the Spirit, Jephthah had been an able and cool-headed negotiator of conflicts (11:1-28). After "the spirit of the LORD" comes upon him (11:29), Jephthah begins to act in rash, careless, and impulsive ways by making a foolish vow that causes his daughter's death (11:30-40). The Spirit-filled Jephthah also erupts in a hot-headed killing spree, slaying 42,000 fellow Israelites over a petty disagreement (12:1-6).

The misuse of the divine Spirit's power comes to a climax in Samson, upon whom the divine Spirit comes several times (13:25; 14:6, 19; 15:14). Again, however, the Spirit of the Lord simply impels Samson to act powerfully but with unthinking impulse, violence, and faithlessness. The Spirit's untamed power leads Samson to slay a lion and later eat honey from its carcass. The spirit-driven Samson kills thirty and then a thousand Philistine warriors at close range with the jawbone of an ass. The problem is that Samson is a Nazirite from birth (Judges 13) and is prohibited from touching anything unclean, especially a dead body or corpse. His close contact with countless corpses, both animal and human, repeatedly breaks his nazirite vow to God. Therefore, Othniel embodies the ancient ideal of a faithful judge empowered in a special way by the Spirit of the

---

27. Richard Boyce, *The Cry to God in the Old Testament* (Atlanta: Scholars Press, 1988); Stone, "From Tribal Confederation to Monarchic State," 311-26.

Lord. But when the divine Spirit gradually reappears in later judges, the Spirit is no longer a positive force. In the hands of unfaithful leaders like Gideon, Jephthah, and Samson, the divine Spirit becomes ineffectual and ultimately dangerous and destructive in the extreme.[28]

The Lord's Rest. The brief episode of Othniel ends with the affirmation that it is "the LORD" who gave the enemy king into the hands of the judge Othniel (3:10). The ultimate agent of Israel's deliverance is not Othniel's personal skills or prowess but God's faithfulness and compassion.

Even though Israel forgets the Lord and worships other gods, God remains true to the covenant relationship and promises made to Israel's ancestors over many generations. Thus "the land had rest forty years," roughly the equivalent of one generation. The land at rest signifies peace, security, and the absence of conflict with enemies. The land at rest is the ultimate goal of the judge's leadership and deliverance according to the ideal set by Othniel, but it will be a goal that later judges (Jephthah and Samson) will not be able to achieve (12:7; 16:31).

28. Stone, "From Tribal Confederation to Monarchic State," 332-38.

REFLECTIONS

1. Othniel is the first ideal and faithful leader within a system of Israelite governance and polity depicted as the era of the judges. This system of temporary leaders who arose at certain crisis periods in Israel's early nationhood will eventually deteriorate and collapse by the end of the book of Judges. The judges were eventually replaced by kings who ruled as an ongoing dynasty in ancient Israel (1–2 Samuel; 1–2 Kings). But even within the flawed system and structure of the judges, Othniel emerges as an ideal ruler for this time and context. Good leaders can work faithfully and successfully within any number of secular political systems or religious polities. We are sometimes prone to label some governmental or economic systems as inherently "anti-Christian" or "evil," especially when they are different from our own. But God's success with Othniel as part of the ultimately flawed system of judges suggests that we need to be open to the possibility of God's faithful working in and through a wide variety of human political systems, social organizations, and economic structures. God is not permanently tied to any one human institution or structure or ideology.

2. The role of "the spirit of the LORD" with Othniel and the other judges suggests the need to accompany reliance on God's Spirit with leaders who have been shaped by faithful guidance from the tradition and memory of what God has done and proclaimed in the past. God's Spirit does, indeed, give special power to leaders, but that power may be abused by unfaithful or misguided leaders. Thus leadership that claims legitimacy through God's Spirit needs to be evaluated and checked by appeals to Scripture, by conformity to the church's tradition, and by other voices both within and outside the community.

3. The victory against the enemy king and the resulting rest or peace Israel enjoyed during Othniel's tenure as their temporary leader was ultimately the work of God. It was "the LORD" who gave the king into Othniel's hand. Human beings are the vehicles through which God works, but God is the one who in the end accomplishes God's purposes. In similar ways, the apostle Paul spoke of his work and the work of his colleague Apollos in proclaiming the gospel in the Christian community of Corinth. Growth in faith had been the result, but Paul knew it was ultimately not his doing: "What then is Apollos? What is Paul? Servants through whom you came to believe, as the Lord assigned to each. I planted, Apollos watered, but God gave the growth." Othniel may have planted and watered, but it was God who won the victory. Thus the first judge we meet recedes into the background with little detail about his personal life. As God is remembered as the One who finally is responsible for the victory, the final words of the story usher the first judge off the stage with the words, "Othniel the son of Kenaz died."

JUDGES 3:12-31, EHUD AND SHAMGAR

¹²Once again the Israelites did evil in the eyes of the LORD, and because they did this evil the LORD gave Eglon king of Moab power over Israel. ¹³Getting the Ammonites and Amalekites to join him, Eglon came and attacked Israel, and they took possession of the City of Palms.^a ¹⁴The Israelites were subject to Eglon king of Moab for eighteen years.

¹⁵Again the Israelites cried out to the LORD, and he gave them a deliverer—Ehud, a left-handed man, the son of Gera the Benjamite. The Israelites sent him with tribute to Eglon king of Moab. ¹⁶Now Ehud had made a double-edged sword about a foot and a half^b long, which he strapped to his right thigh under his clothing. ¹⁷He presented the tribute to Eglon king of Moab, who was a very fat man. ¹⁸After Ehud had presented the tribute, he sent on their way the men who had carried it. ¹⁹At the idols^c near Gilgal he himself turned back and said, "I have a secret message for you, O king."

The king said, "Quiet!" And all his attendants left him.

²⁰Ehud then approached him while he was sitting alone in the upper room of his summer palace^d and said, "I have a message from God for you." As the king rose from his seat, ²¹Ehud reached with his left hand, drew the sword from his right thigh and plunged it into the king's belly. ²²Even the handle sank in after the blade, which came out his back. Ehud did not pull the sword out, and the fat closed in over it. ²³Then Ehud went out to the porch^e; he shut the doors of the upper room behind him and locked them.

²⁴After he had gone, the servants came and found the doors of the upper room locked. They said, "He must be relieving himself in the inner room of the house." ²⁵They waited to the point of embarrassment, but when he did not open the doors of the room, they took a key and unlocked them. There they saw their lord fallen to the floor, dead.

^a13 That is, Jericho   ^b16 Hebrew a cubit (about 0.5 meter)   ^c19 Or the stone quarries; also in verse 26   ^d20 The meaning of the Hebrew for this phrase is uncertain.   ^e23 The meaning of the Hebrew for this word is uncertain.

¹²The Israelites again did what was evil in the sight of the LORD; and the LORD strengthened King Eglon of Moab against Israel, because they had done what was evil in the sight of the LORD. ¹³In alliance with the Ammonites and the Amalekites, he went and defeated Israel; and they took possession of the city of palms. ¹⁴So the Israelites served King Eglon of Moab eighteen years.

¹⁵But when the Israelites cried out to the LORD, the LORD raised up for them a deliverer, Ehud son of Gera, the Benjaminite, a left-handed man. The Israelites sent tribute by him to King Eglon of Moab. ¹⁶Ehud made for himself a sword with two edges, a cubit in length; and he fastened it on his right thigh under his clothes. ¹⁷Then he presented the tribute to King Eglon of Moab. Now Eglon was a very fat man. ¹⁸When Ehud had finished presenting the tribute, he sent the people who carried the tribute on their way. ¹⁹But he himself turned back at the sculptured stones near Gilgal, and said, "I have a secret message for you, O king." So the king said,^a "Silence!" and all his attendants went out from his presence. ²⁰Ehud came to him, while he was sitting alone in his cool roof chamber, and said, "I have a message from God for you." So he rose from his seat. ²¹Then Ehud reached with his left hand, took the sword from his right thigh, and thrust it into Eglon's^b belly; ²²the hilt also went in after the blade, and the fat closed over the blade, for he did not draw the sword out of his belly; and the dirt came out.^c ²³Then Ehud went out into the vestibule,^d and closed the doors of the roof chamber on him, and locked them.

²⁴After he had gone, the servants came. When they saw that the doors of the roof chamber were locked, they thought, "He must be relieving himself^e in the cool chamber." ²⁵So they waited until they were embarrassed. When he still did not open the doors of the roof chamber, they took the key and opened them. There was their lord lying dead on the floor.

²⁶Ehud escaped while they delayed, and passed beyond the sculptured stones, and escaped

^aHeb he said   ^bHeb his   ^cWith Tg Vg: Meaning of Heb uncertain   ^dMeaning of Heb uncertain   ^eHeb covering his feet

²⁶While they waited, Ehud got away. He passed by the idols and escaped to Seirah. ²⁷When he arrived there, he blew a trumpet in the hill country of Ephraim, and the Israelites went down with him from the hills, with him leading them.

²⁸"Follow me," he ordered, "for the LORD has given Moab, your enemy, into your hands." So they followed him down and, taking possession of the fords of the Jordan that led to Moab, they allowed no one to cross over. ²⁹At that time they struck down about ten thousand Moabites, all vigorous and strong; not a man escaped. ³⁰That day Moab was made subject to Israel, and the land had peace for eighty years.

³¹After Ehud came Shamgar son of Anath, who struck down six hundred Philistines with an oxgoad. He too saved Israel.

to Seirah. ²⁷When he arrived, he sounded the trumpet in the hill country of Ephraim; and the Israelites went down with him from the hill country, having him at their head. ²⁸He said to them, "Follow after me; for the LORD has given your enemies the Moabites into your hand." So they went down after him, and seized the fords of the Jordan against the Moabites, and allowed no one to cross over. ²⁹At that time they killed about ten thousand of the Moabites, all strong, able-bodied men; no one escaped. ³⁰So Moab was subdued that day under the hand of Israel. And the land had rest eighty years.

31After him came Shamgar son of Anath, who killed six hundred of the Philistines with an oxgoad. He too delivered Israel.

COMMENTARY

The first judge who appears after the model judge, Othniel, is a crafty and deceptive assassin named Ehud. The narrative of Ehud contains entertaining elements of satire, suspense, and humor that probably reflect a previous history of oral storytelling as the tale was passed from one generation to the next. The present literary form of the story retains these elements and adds to them a theological concern in line with the larger framework of the cycle of judge stories. Two of the central theological issues that emerge in this story are the interaction of human and divine agency or causality and the hidden and unexpected ways in which God acts to save God's people.

3:12-14. The story of the judge Ehud begins with the Israelites again doing "what was evil in the sight of the LORD." This refrain echoes the opening formula at the beginning of the recurring pattern, noted in the Introduction (2:11-19) and in the paradigm established by the judge Othniel (3:7-11). The nature of Israel's evil is not spelled out in any detail. In the later judges, such as Gideon and Jephthah, the evil will increasingly be described as the serious offense of worshiping other foreign gods (6:8-10; 10:6); here the evil is unspecified. The evil is sufficient to move God to punish the Israelites by "strengthening" King

Eglon of Moab against Israel. The other judge stories portray God as either "selling" or "giving over" Israel to its enemy, suggesting a more active and direct divine role in handing Israel over to its oppressors (4:2; 6:1; 10:7; 13:1). In the Ehud story, God simply strengthens the Moabite king in his own already established plans to conquer and oppress Israel. Moreover, the Moabite King Eglon engineers some strengthening of his own by forming a military alliance with the neighboring "Ammonites and Amalekites" (3:13). Thus the Moabite Eglon and his Ammonite and Amalekite allies unknowingly carry out God's purposes to defeat and punish Israel for a period of eighteen years. They capture in particular "the city of palms," usually identified as the town of Jericho, near the Jordan River and the border between Israel and Moab and Ammon.

3:15-30. After eighteen years under the tyranny of the Moabite King Eglon, Israel cries out to God, and God responds by raising up a "deliverer" named Ehud. Ehud is from the tribe of Benjamin, a tribe whose territory is just north of Judah and thus in line with the general south-to-north trajectory of the tribal affiliations of the individual judge stories, beginning with Othniel of southern Judah (vv. 7-11). The other significance of Ehud's being from the tribe of Benjamin is that the name "Benjamin" in Hebrew (בנימין *binyāmîn*) means "son of the right hand." The text notes that Ehud is "a left-handed man" (v. 15). In other words, Ehud is a "left-handed son of the right hand"! As a reader, we may expect something extraordinary, unusual, and unexpected from this character Ehud, and we will not be disappointed. His left-handedness will play an important role in a crafty assassination plot against the king of Moab. But what exactly does it mean that Ehud is left-handed? The phrase in Hebrew literally means "bound or restricted in his right hand." Some interpreters have suggested that Ehud was handicapped with a deformed or withered right hand. Others suggest he was simply left-handed. Still others link Ehud with an elite group of Benjaminite warriors who were specially trained to be left-handed or ambidextrous, which gave them an advantage in battle (20:15-16). For the purposes of the Ehud story, all that is required to make the story work is that he is left-handed, and thus we assume its straightforward meaning.

The Israelites choose Ehud to be their envoy to carry tribute to the Moabite King Eglon. The tribute is a burdensome tax of money or produce exacted as a reminder that the Israelites are under the rule of the Moabite king, who is free to take from them whatever he wishes for his royal coffers. In choosing Ehud as tribute bearer, the Israelites are apparently unaware that Ehud himself has a secret plan in mind to bring down the Moabite king. Ehud manufactures a "sword with two edges," which symbolizes the double-edged nature not only of the sword but also of the words Ehud will use with King Eglon at the opportune moment. Ehud fastens the sword on his right thigh so that he can cross over with his left hand and draw the sword. The plan seems to be that since most people are right-handed, the bodyguards to the king will assume that Ehud is right-handed and thus check only Ehud's left thigh for a weapon. If so, they will fail to notice the concealed weapon on his right side.

After these preparations, Ehud leads an entourage of Israelites to offer the tribute of produce and money to King Eglon (vv. 17-18). The vocabulary of "presenting the tribute" is related to religious rituals of offering sacrifices to the gods as an acknowledgment of their power and the people's allegiance. Such a ceremony may have been involved in Ehud's presenting the tribute. The ritual and sacrificial charater of the scene is further suggested by the narrator's interjection, "Now Eglon was a very fat man." Eglon's name in Hebrew (עגלון *'eglôn*) is related to the noun "young bull" or "fatted calf" (עגל *'ēgel*), which is an animal that may be killed or sacrificed on an altar in an offering to God (Lev 9:2-3, 8). What we have, then, is a very fat "young bull" king who himself is about to be killed and offered as a tribute and a sacrifice. Ehud leaves with his Israelite companions to go back home after presenting the tribute. However, Ehud turns back at the "sculptured stones" (NRSV) or "idols" (NIV) near Gilgal (v. 19). When he does his deed against the king and returns back home on his escape, he will again pass by the same "sculptured stones/idols" (v. 26). The reference to these carved stones or idols and Ehud's passing by or passing over them forms a meaningful inclusio to the scene about to be narrated: Ehud's killing of the fat Moabite king is his way of leading Israel to bypass and leave behind the Moabite powers and gods that have oppressed them for eighteen years. Politics and religion are here intimately tied together.

As Ehud returns to the king's palace, he is allowed to speak with the king since he has just presided over giving a lavish tribute or offering to Eglon. Ehud says to King Eglon, "I have a secret message for you, O king." The Hebrew word for "message" (דבר *dābār*) can mean a "word" or a "thing." Like his sword, Ehud's words are double-edged. The king expects to hear "a secret word," but Ehud really has "a secret thing," a sword. The Moabite king immediately orders "Silence!" All the king's attendants take the order as an invitation to exit the throne room, leaving the king and Ehud alone in the "roof chamber" of the palace. In double-edged irony, Ehud speaks a second time to the king and reveals the divine origin of this "message": "I have a message [word/thing] from God for you." The king anxiously rises from his throne to receive the secret and divine message, unseating himself from the seat of power. Ehud promptly reaches "with his left hand," takes the dagger "from his right thigh," and thrusts it into Eglon's very fat belly (v. 21).

The text pauses here with some grotesque detail: The king's mountain of fat swallows up the sword, handle and all, so that Ehud does not draw the weapon back out. The final phrase in v. 22 contains an unusual Hebrew word whose meaning is uncertain. Some translate it as does the NRSV: "the dirt came out," meaning the contents of the king's colon. This translation, derived from the Aramaic Targum and the Vulgate versions, would give some added reason why the king's attendants would later assume he was taking his time on the toilet. Another translation is represented by the NIV: "[the sword] which came out his back." Still others suggest the phrase refers to Ehud's escape route: "and he [Ehud] went out the hole [of the toilet?]." Ehud next goes out into the vestibule or porch and locks the outer doors to give himself time to escape (v. 23).[29]

The scene shifts to the king's servants who had exited and now come back to check on the king. They note that the doors of the roof chamber are locked from the inside. The locked doors and perhaps the smell of defecation cause them to assume the fat king must be "relieving himself" on his royal toilet. They wait until they are embarrassed and become concerned. Finally, they take a key and unlock the doors. As they fling open the doors, their eyes witness a horrifying sight: "there was their lord lying dead on the floor" (v. 25).

While the Moabite servants are left frozen and staring in horror, the scene shifts once again to Ehud as he escapes. He again passes by "the sculptured stones/idols," a sign of leaving behind the Moabite lords and their gods (v. 26). Ehud's crafty assassination of King Eglon earns him the loyalty of the Israelites as they make him their military leader. Ehud reveals the real force behind his success as he exhorts the Israelites, "Follow me, for the Lord has given your enemies into your hand" (v. 28). The Moabite "lord" was already dead, and Israel's Lord had already sealed the victory of Israel against its oppressors. The military

victory against the Moabites that follows again involves craft and deception. The Israelite warriors lie in wait at the fords of the Jordan River, which separates Moab from Canaan. They ambush about ten thousand Moabites who try to cross the river "and so Moab was subdued that day under the hand of Israel" (v. 30). The result was eighty years of rest in the land.

3:31. After the conclusion of the Ehud narrative, we encounter the first of the six so-called minor judges who appear at three junctures among the other major judge stories (3:31; 10:1-5; 12:8-15). The first minor judge is "Shamgar son of Anath." Most of the other judges have tribal or clan designations that indicate they are clearly of Israelite origin, but Shamgar does not. He is listed as the "son of Anath." "Shamgar" is not a typical Israelite name, and "Anath" is the name of a Canaanite goddess and consort to the god Baal. Thus some have argued that Shamgar may have been a foreign mercenary who joined and led Israel's federation of tribes for a time. All we are told of Shamgar is that he killed six hundred Philistines "with an oxgoad" (v. 31). Just as Ehud's exploits centered on the uniqueness of his method and the weapon used, so also the brief note about Shamgar focuses on his single-handed and heroic method and weapon, the oxgoad. Shamgar is not as subtle or secretive as Ehud; Shamgar uses brute strength and a blunt oxgoad to defeat the enemy, the Philistines. For all of his suspect lineage and his brutal tactics, however, Shamgar is affirmed as part of the line of judges. Shamgar comes "after him [Ehud]," and the narrator affirms that Shamgar "too delivered Israel" just as Ehud had done (vv. 15, 31). The Song of Deborah will later recall and celebrate "the days of Shamgar son of Anath" (5:6), and Israel will be reminded that God had previously defeated the Philistines (10:11). Using Shamgar, God saves Israel for a time but does so again through quite unexpected and unpredictable means and people.

29. For a detailed historical reconstruction of Eglon's assassination, see Baruch Halpern, *The First Historians: The Hebrew Bible and History* (New York: Harper & Row, 1988) 39-75.

REFLECTIONS

1. The story is first and foremost about the "left-handed" ways of God both to judge and to deliver Israel. God's ways are not our ways. The unexpected and often hidden means by which God works should make us cautious about being overly confident that we know exactly where, when, and how God will act in a given situation or context. God begins by choosing an unlikely fat Moabite king and his Ammonite and Amalekite allies who unknowingly carry out God's punishment upon a sinful Israel. In response to Israel's cry of distress, God reverses course and compassionately chooses another unlikely agent, a deliverer named Ehud whose odd left-handedness, hidden weapon, and deceptive words lead to the death of the Moabite oppressor and temporary rest for Israel. The hand of God works through the "left hand" of Ehud to subdue the Moabites "under the hand" of Israel and to give Moab "into the hand" of Israel (3:15, 21, 28, 30).

2. A related theme that emerges from this story is the intricate way in which God's agency is woven in and through the words, actions, and plans of human groups and individuals. God "strengthens" the Moabites in their already existent plan to conquer Israel. At the same time, the Moabites strengthen themselves by joining an alliance with Ammon and the Amalekites. Ehud devises on his own initiative an intricate plan to kill the Moabite king, but he (unlike the Moabites) acknowledges that it was "the LORD" working through him. Ehud's plan of assassination was in many ways ingenious. Yet the high number of fortuitous coincidences that were required to make Ehud's plan effective suggests a divine hand working behind the scenes to ensure success. Ehud just happened to be the one chosen to carry Israel's tribute to King Eglon. Ehud just happened to be allowed to have a second audience with the king. Ehud happened to be left-handed, and the bodyguards of the king just happened not to check Ehud's right side for a sword. The servants just happen to exit the throne room and leave Ehud alone with the king when the king had simply told the servants to be quiet and not necessarily to leave. Ehud somehow fortuitously found the time and the means to escape undetected. The large number of seeming coincidences suggests a divine hand behind it all.

As we look back over our own lives, Ehud's story may lead us to consider whether those seemingly chance encounters, fortuitous opportunities, and timely coincidences we have experienced may not have had a divine hand at work in them. It may be difficult to know at the time of the events themselves, but time and hindsight sometimes allow us to look back and trace a divine plan at work, sometimes faintly and sometimes quite clearly.

3. This story about the very fat King Eglon of Moab and his stupid Moabite servants may be seen as an example of antagonistic and even vicious ethnic humor. One can well imagine Israelites laughing heartily at the "toilet joke" about the obese king of Moab. Is this just an ethnic slur against Moabites that has inadvertently found its way into the Bible? Or does the satire of the Ehud story play a larger role within the increasing deterioration of Israel within the book of Judges? In terms of bawdy humor and bumbling characters who are constantly outwitted, the story of Ehud and Eglon at the beginning of the judge stories finds its closest counterpart at the end of the judge stories in the story of Samson (Judges 13–16). Like the story of Ehud and the Moabites, the tale of Samson and the Philistines is full of humor, riddles, bumbling mistakes, and deceptions. But the biting satire in the tale of Samson turns the tables on Israel: Samson, the hero and symbol of Israel, becomes the bumbling fool, the deceived playboy, and finally the one who brings death on himself. The laughter over Ehud's victory over the Moabites will become the weeping over Samson's tragic life and suicidal death. By the end of Judges, Israel will be no different from any other nation or group.[30] In fact, Israel will become its own worst enemy. God's people cannot claim greater numerical strength, material advantage, or moral superiority to the Moabites, the Philistines, or even the Canaanites (Deut 7:7; 8:17; 9:4-7). In the end, the only thing that makes Israel distinct from every other nation is that God's presence and activity stir among this chosen people of God, both to judge and to save (Exod 33:16).

30. Lowell Handy, "Uneasy Laughter: Ehud and Eglon as Ethnic Humor," *Scandinavian Journal of the Old Testament* 6 (1992) 233-46.

The same is true of God's people today. Writing to the Christians at Rome, the apostle Paul reminded them that they had no right to boast about their superiority over any other people: "Therefore you have no excuse, whoever you are, when you judge others; for in passing judgment on another you condemn yourself, because you, the judge, are doing the very same things" (Rom 2:1 NRSV).

JUDGES 4:1–5:31, DEBORAH, BARAK, AND JAEL

OVERVIEW

Judges 4–5 concludes the first of three phases in the story of the gradual decline of Israel and the decline in the effectiveness of the individual judges as leaders of Israel. The three phases move from (1) victorious and faithful judges (3:7–5:31) to (2) a transitional stage that begins a decline into idolatry and social disunity within Israel (6:1–10:5) to (3) an increasingly serious deterioration of Israel as a social and religious community led by increasingly tragic and misguided judges (10:6–16:31). Chapters 4–5 contain some seeds of Israel's future deterioration, but these chapters largely celebrate a positive victory over Israel's Canaanite enemies.

Judges 4–5 follow the general pattern of judge stories established in the paradigm in 2:11-19 and in the story of the model judge Othniel (3:7-11). The Israelites do evil, the Lord sells them into the hand of the enemy, Israel cries out to the Lord, and the Lord raises up a judge who delivers them for a period of time. One of the unique wrinkles in Judges 4–5 is that it is not altogether clear who the actual judge is in this account. Indeed, the task of the judge as exemplified in the previous judge stories (Othniel, Ehud, Shamgar) is shared among three major characters in the story: Deborah, who is a woman prophet and acts as a judge in the sense of arbitrating disputes rather than leading military attacks; Barak, who is Israel's military general but is never called a judge; and Jael, who is a non-Israelite woman who kills the enemy Canaanite general named Sisera when he comes to her tent for refuge. This ambivalence about the real judge or hero of this story will play an important role in the narrative's plot as well as in the theological interpretation of the account.

Another major distinguishing element of Judges 4–5 is that the same account of Deborah, Barak, and Jael is conveyed to the reader in two different versions: a prose narrative account (chap. 4) and a poetic song that combines elements of a hymn of victory and a ballad that retells a story in poetic form (chap. 5). The closest biblical analogy to this juxtaposition of narrative and song to recount the same event is the account of Moses leading the Israelites in the crossing of the Red Sea in Exodus 14 (prose) and Exodus 15 (song). The two versions, the narrative in Judges 4 and the song in Judges 5, display a number of similarities as well as key differences. The story and the song both contain the same list of main characters: the Lord, Deborah, Barak, Jael, and Sisera the Canaanite general. They both recount the battle and victory against the Canaanite Sisera and the roles played by Deborah and Barak as leaders of Israel. In both the song and the narrative, Jael the Kenite woman offers hospitality to Sisera and then kills him.

Significant differences also characterize the prose and poetic versions of the Deborah-Barak-Jael account. Although playing no direct role in the story itself, the name of the Canaanite King Jabin appears in the outer framework of the prose story at the beginning (4:2) and at the end (4:23-24). In contrast, Jabin is not mentioned at all in the song of Judges 5, although there is a reference to unnamed "kings of Canaan" (5:19). A number of themes are present in the poetic song that are absent from the prose narrative: a more extensive description of the conditions of Israel's oppression (5:6-8), the description of cosmic disturbances and effects with the appearance of the Lord as the divine warrior (5:4-5, 19-22), the contrast between some Israelite tribes who participated in the battle and those who refused to participate (5:13-18), and the final scene of Sisera's mother and her advisers waiting for the return of her son, who will never come back home (5:28-30).

Two other broader differences between the narrative and poetic versions of Judges 4–5 have been proposed and debated among interpreters of these texts. One debate revolves around the question of whether the narrative and the poem differ in their primary focus on human activity or divine activity. A second debate argues about whether either the poem or the narrative reflects a woman's perspective versus a man's perspective.

On the contrast between a focus on divine agency versus human agency, some interpreters have argued that the story in Judges 4 subsumes all human action under the providential and divine plan of God with the oracle that Sisera would be defeated by "the hand of a woman" (4:9). God is the focus of the narrative version. On the other hand, these same interpreters argue that the poem in Judges 5 places human motives, emotions, and actions in the foreground (the oppressed Israelites, 5:6-8; the enthusiasm and the hesitation of some Israelite tribes, 5:13-18; the emotional scene of Sisera's mother waiting for her son to return, 5:28-30). Other scholars argue just the opposite: The prose narrative in chap. 4 highlights the interactions among the humans, while the poem of chap. 5 places the spotlight on God and plays down the role of the humans (the song's opening praise of God, 5:1-5; the refrain "bless the LORD," 5:2, 9; the battle as "the triumphs of the LORD," 5:11; the concluding prayer concerning the enemies and the friends of the Lord, 5:31). Still others claim that both the narrative and the poem place God as the center, subsuming all human action to the divine purpose and plan.[31] In fact, the widely divergent views of human and divine agencies suggest a complex intertwining and subtle dialectic between the divine plan and human freedom that cannot be easily distinguished or separated in either the prose or the poetic account.

Another broad category of proposed differences between the narrative of Judges 4 and the poetry of Judges 5 involves whether one or the other version reflects a feminine versus a masculine perspective. Mieke Bal argues that cultural studies of oral cultures suggest that certain genres tend to be tied to women and other genres to men. Feminine genres tend more toward lyric poetry, contain few details, and highlight activities around the village and family. Bal finds these feminine characteristics more evident in the poem of Judges 5. The poem's images of Deborah as "a mother in Israel" (5:7), Jael as "most blessed of women" (5:24), and the pathos of the scene with Sisera's mother and her female advisers suggest a feminine orientation to the song of Judges 5. In contrast, masculine genres tend to favor epic narrative, the inclusion of many details, and adventures centered outside the village or family. Bal finds these elements more clearly in the narrative prose of Judges 4 and argues that the main plot line in the narrative of chap. 4 wrestles with the distinctly masculine issue of honor and shame in relation to a woman: The two males in the story, Barak and Sisera, lose honor and status because of a woman, Jael, who either kills or steals glory from the men.[32] Other interpreters have argued the opposite. The narrative in Judges 4, they suggest, displays more of a woman's perspective, celebrating the prowess of a woman and upsetting the expected conventions of a typical male heroic tale. On the other hand, they maintain that the poem in Judges 5 has a more masculine character, since the focus is on the battle with Sisera's army and God's fighting on behalf of the Israelites.

As with the false dichotomy of divine versus human agency, both the prose and the poetic accounts defy any simple attempts to separate them into discrete masculine and feminine perspectives. The prose account in Judges 4 does feature powerful women in Deborah and Jael. Some of Barak's glory as a male warrior does fall upon Jael when Barak discovers that she is the one who has killed the Canaanite general Sisera (4:9, 22). However, Barak remains the victorious leader of Israel's militia who defeated all of Sisera's army. That Barak received help from God (4:6-7, 15) and from Deborah (4:8-9, 14) as well as from Jael is not a matter of great shame. Rahab, the Canaanite harlot, helped the faithful Joshua and his army in conquering the city of Jericho with no shame or dishonor upon Joshua for hav-

31. See Julius Wellhausen, *Prolegomena to the History of Israel* (Gloucester, Mass.: P. Smith, 1973 [1878]) 240-42; Barry Webb, *The Book of the Judges: An Integrated Reading* (Sheffield: JSOT, 1987) 141-44; Mieke Bal, *Murder and Difference: Gender, Genre and Scholarship on Sisera's Death* (Bloomington: Indiana University Press, 1988) 38, 44-50; Yairah Amit, "Judges 4: Its Content and Form," *JSOT* 39 (1987) 89-111; James W. Watts, *Psalm and Story: Inset Hymns in Hebrew Narrative* (Sheffield: JSOT, 1992) 86-87.

32. Bal, *Murder and Difference*, 111-34; A Globe, "The Literary Structure and Unity of the Song of Deborah," *JBL* 93 (1974) 495.

ing received aid from a woman (Josh 2:1-24; 6:22-25). The death of Sisera at the hands of Jael is a different matter. A great warrior's being killed at the hands of a woman was an ignoble death (Judg 9:52-57). However, the Canaanite Sisera had already been dishonored by his retreat and abandonment of his army; Jael's killing of him simply caused him further dishonor.

In the present form of the text, with the song of chap. 5 following the prose account, the reader sees both Barak and Deborah together singing a song (5:1). Barak does not appear woefully shamed or dishonored but praised along with others. The song does not praise only men or only women but all those who participated in saving Israel: God (5:2-5, 20-21, 31), Deborah (5:7, 12), Jael (5:24-27), some of the Israelite tribes (5:13-18), and Barak (5:9, 12). The praise of God begins and ends the song as an affirmation that God integrates and works across the many boundaries of gender, tribe, nation, and creation within the poem (male/female, Israelite/non-Israelite, some tribes/not other tribes, human/non-human forces of nature). The only boundary that remains is the one between Israel and their Canaanite foes. But even that boundary may be crossed by God in the light of 5:31, which speaks of judgment upon the Lord's enemies and blessing upon the Lord's friends. The next verse tells us that "the Israelites did what was evil in the sight of the LORD" (6:1), suggesting that Israel will soon become again God's enemies, virtually indistinguishable from the Canaanite enemies of God (2:1-5). God will fight against Israel until it again cries in distress.

The existence of two versions of the same event, the narrative in Judges 4 and the poetic song in Judges 5, raises issues of relative dating and dependence of each text on the other. Which of the two accounts is earlier? Was one account written on the basis of the other? Or were the narrative and the poetic versions written independently from a common source and later combined? Most scholars agree that the poetic song in Judges 5 is the earlier of the two accounts because of its archaic Hebrew language and style. The prose narrative reflects standard classical Hebrew from a time later in Israel's history. The most plausible reconstruction of the composition of the two accounts may be that the poetic Song of Deborah and Barak was written first. The

narrative of Judges 4 was composed on the basis of the earlier poem in Judges 5 and perhaps also in the light of the Ehud story in 3:12-30. Notable echoes exist between the Deborah-Barak-Jael story and the preceding Ehud narrative. The prose version retold the story with important thematic differences and thus may have functioned independently for a time. But eventually an editor brought the prose (Judges 4) and poetic (Judges 5) versions together and placed them within the larger framework and collection of individual judge stories to make up the present book of Judges.

Two principal motifs intimated in Judges 4–5 will play an increasing role in portraying the gradual deterioration of Israel under the judges in chapters that follow. The first motif is the leader's desire for reassurance or a sign when called to fight against the enemy. In 4:6-10, the Israelite general Barak places a condition on accepting God's call to go and fight the Canaanite oppressors. Barak refuses to go into battle unless Deborah, the prophet of the Lord, goes along with him. As we move into the later stories in Judges, this motif of a leader's need for divine assurance or a sign will become more prominent in the stories of Gideon (6:36-40) and Jephthah (11:29-33). Increasingly, the leaders of Israel will be less trusting and require more divine guarantees to bolster their confidence. The second motif, which will become ever more significant in the deterioration of Israel's social and political fabric, is the disunity within the tribal confederation of Israel. The Song of Deborah and Barak in Judges 5 chastises several of Israel's tribes for their failure to join the other Israelite tribes in the battle against the Canaanites (Judg 5:13-18, 23). This theme of tribal disunity will recur in mild form in the Gideon episode (8:1-3), but it will begin to grow more grave in Abimelech's killing of his own brothers (9:5), in Jephthah's killing of 42,000 of his Ephraimite countrymen (12:1-6), in Samson's inability to lead any Israelite tribal coalitions at all and Judah's betrayal of Samson (15:9-17), and ultimately in the civil war among the Israelite tribes against the tribe of Benjamin in the concluding section of Judges (20:12-48). Thus Judges 4–5 begins to plant the seed for the gradual decline in Israel's fortunes and sense of unity as we move through the book of Judges. However, the story of Deborah, Barak, and Jael remains for the most part a positive portrait of a time in Israel when judges ruled effectively and faithfully as the Canaanites are defeated, the Lord is praised, and "the land had rest forty years" (5:31).

Judges 4:1-24, The Story of Sisera's Death

NIV

4 After Ehud died, the Israelites once again did evil in the eyes of the LORD. ²So the LORD sold them into the hands of Jabin, a king of Canaan, who reigned in Hazor. The commander of his army was Sisera, who lived in Harosheth Haggoyim. ³Because he had nine hundred iron chariots and had cruelly oppressed the Israelites for twenty years, they cried to the LORD for help.

⁴Deborah, a prophetess, the wife of Lappidoth, was leading^a Israel at that time. ⁵She held court under the Palm of Deborah between Ramah and Bethel in the hill country of Ephraim, and the Israelites came to her to have their disputes decided. ⁶She sent for Barak son of Abinoam from Kedesh in Naphtali and said to him, "The LORD, the God of Israel, commands you: 'Go, take with you ten thousand men of Naphtali and Zebulun and lead the way to Mount Tabor. ⁷I will lure Sisera, the commander of Jabin's army, with his chariots and his troops to the Kishon River and give him into your hands.'"

⁸Barak said to her, "If you go with me, I will go; but if you don't go with me, I won't go."

⁹"Very well," Deborah said, "I will go with you. But because of the way you are going about this,^{b} the honor will not be yours, for the LORD will hand Sisera over to a woman." So Deborah went with Barak to Kedesh, ¹⁰where he summoned Zebulun and Naphtali. Ten thousand men followed him, and Deborah also went with him.

¹¹Now Heber the Kenite had left the other Kenites, the descendants of Hobab, Moses' brother-in-law,^{c} and pitched his tent by the great tree in Zaanannim near Kedesh.

¹²When they told Sisera that Barak son of Abinoam had gone up to Mount Tabor, ¹³Sisera gathered together his nine hundred iron chariots and all the men with him, from Harosheth Haggoyim to the Kishon River.

NRSV

4 The Israelites again did what was evil in the sight of the LORD, after Ehud died. ²So the LORD sold them into the hand of King Jabin of Canaan, who reigned in Hazor; the commander of his army was Sisera, who lived in Harosheth-ha-goiim. ³Then the Israelites cried out to the LORD for help; for he had nine hundred chariots of iron, and had oppressed the Israelites cruelly twenty years.

4At that time Deborah, a prophetess, wife of Lappidoth, was judging Israel. ⁵She used to sit under the palm of Deborah between Ramah and Bethel in the hill country of Ephraim; and the Israelites came up to her for judgment. ⁶She sent and summoned Barak son of Abinoam from Kedesh in Naphtali, and said to him, "The LORD, the God of Israel, commands you, 'Go, take position at Mount Tabor, bringing ten thousand from the tribe of Naphtali and the tribe of Zebulun. ⁷I will draw out Sisera, the general of Jabin's army, to meet you by the Wadi Kishon with his chariots and his troops; and I will give him into your hand.'" ⁸Barak said to her, "If you will go with me, I will go; but if you will not go with me, I will not go." ⁹And she said, "I will surely go with you; nevertheless, the road on which you are going will not lead to your glory, for the LORD will sell Sisera into the hand of a woman." Then Deborah got up and went with Barak to Kedesh. ¹⁰Barak summoned Zebulun and Naphtali to Kedesh; and ten thousand warriors went up behind him; and Deborah went up with him.

11Now Heber the Kenite had separated from the other Kenites,^{a} that is, the descendants of Hobab the father-in-law of Moses, and had encamped as far away as Elon-bezaanannim, which is near Kedesh.

12When Sisera was told that Barak son of Abinoam had gone up to Mount Tabor, ¹³Sisera called out all his chariots, nine hundred chariots

---

^{a}4 Traditionally *judging* ^{b}9 Or *But on the expedition you are undertaking* ^{c}11 Or *father-in-law*

^{a} Heb *from the Kain*

NIV

¹⁴Then Deborah said to Barak, "Go! This is the day the LORD has given Sisera into your hands. Has not the LORD gone ahead of you?" So Barak went down Mount Tabor, followed by ten thousand men. ¹⁵At Barak's advance, the LORD routed Sisera and all his chariots and army by the sword, and Sisera abandoned his chariot and fled on foot. ¹⁶But Barak pursued the chariots and army as far as Harosheth Haggoyim. All the troops of Sisera fell by the sword; not a man was left.

¹⁷Sisera, however, fled on foot to the tent of Jael, the wife of Heber the Kenite, because there were friendly relations between Jabin king of Hazor and the clan of Heber the Kenite.

¹⁸Jael went out to meet Sisera and said to him, "Come, my lord, come right in. Don't be afraid." So he entered her tent, and she put a covering over him.

¹⁹"I'm thirsty," he said. "Please give me some water." She opened a skin of milk, gave him a drink, and covered him up.

²⁰"Stand in the doorway of the tent," he told her. "If someone comes by and asks you, 'Is anyone here?' say 'No.'"

²¹But Jael, Heber's wife, picked up a tent peg and a hammer and went quietly to him while he lay fast asleep, exhausted. She drove the peg through his temple into the ground, and he died.

²²Barak came by in pursuit of Sisera, and Jael went out to meet him. "Come," she said, "I will show you the man you're looking for." So he went in with her, and there lay Sisera with the tent peg through his temple—dead.

²³On that day God subdued Jabin, the Canaanite king, before the Israelites. ²⁴And the hand of the Israelites grew stronger and stronger against Jabin, the Canaanite king, until they destroyed him.

NRSV

of iron, and all the troops who were with him, from Harosheth-ha-goiim to the Wadi Kishon. ¹⁴Then Deborah said to Barak, "Up! For this is the day on which the LORD has given Sisera into your hand. The LORD is indeed going out before you." So Barak went down from Mount Tabor with ten thousand warriors following him. ¹⁵And the LORD threw Sisera and all his chariots and all his army into a panic^a before Barak; Sisera got down from his chariot and fled away on foot, ¹⁶while Barak pursued the chariots and the army to Harosheth-ha-goiim. All the army of Sisera fell by the sword; no one was left.

17Now Sisera had fled away on foot to the tent of Jael wife of Heber the Kenite; for there was peace between King Jabin of Hazor and the clan of Heber the Kenite. ¹⁸Jael came out to meet Sisera, and said to him, "Turn aside, my lord, turn aside to me; have no fear." So he turned aside to her into the tent, and she covered him with a rug. ¹⁹Then he said to her, "Please give me a little water to drink; for I am thirsty." So she opened a skin of milk and gave him a drink and covered him. ²⁰He said to her, "Stand at the entrance of the tent, and if anybody comes and asks you, 'Is anyone here?' say, 'No.'" ²¹But Jael wife of Heber took a tent peg, and took a hammer in her hand, and went softly to him and drove the peg into his temple, until it went down into the ground—he was lying fast asleep from weariness—and he died. ²²Then, as Barak came in pursuit of Sisera, Jael went out to meet him, and said to him, "Come, and I will show you the man whom you are seeking." So he went into her tent; and there was Sisera lying dead, with the tent peg in his temple.

23So on that day God subdued King Jabin of Canaan before the Israelites. ²⁴Then the hand of the Israelites bore harder and harder on King Jabin of Canaan, until they destroyed King Jabin of Canaan.

^a Heb adds *to the sword*; compare verse 16

COMMENTARY

Judges 4 is a narrative account of a coalition of three judge-like figures who save Israel only

through the combination of unique contributions that each person makes. Deborah is a prophet and a judge in the sense of arbitrator. She brings God's word to fight the Canaanites and accompanies the Israelite warriors into battle with words of encouragement and guidance. Barak is the general of Israel's army who leads the victory against the Canaanites but fails to kill his Canaanite counterpart, the general Sisera. Jael is not an Israelite but a Kenite who invites Sisera, the Canaanite general, into her tent and then proceeds to kill him. All three contribute to saving Israel, but none of them can lay sole claim to the title of "judge" in this period. This shifting and inconclusive identity of the major judge in this story will contribute to a sense of suspense within the narrative plot as well as the theological significance of the story.

4:1-3. The cycle of events in this chapter begins in the same way the earlier judge paradigm had established (2:11-19) and the previous model of Othniel had confirmed (3:7-11). "After Ehud died," Israel "again" begins to do evil in God's sight (v. 1). The death of the previous judge Ehud leaves a vacuum into which Israel slips in disobedience to God. The next step is also expected: God sells Israel into the hand of an enemy, King Jabin of Canaan. The Canaanites are the fourth set of enemies Israel has faced in this first phase of the judges period. With the judge Othniel, the enemy had come from some distance in the far north and east in Mesopotamia. With Ehud, the enemy had been a closer neighbor to the east, Moab. Shamgar fought against the Philistines, Israel's close neighbor to the west. Now for the first time Israel faces a more internal enemy, King Jabin of Canaan, who is said to reign in the far north of Canaan at Hazor (v. 2). Many interpreters believe this King Jabin may be related in some way to the "King Jabin of Hazor" who led a coalition of Canaanite kings against Joshua and Israel as reported in Joshua 11. Joshua successfully conquered the coalition, and Josh 11:10 notes that Joshua "took Hazor, and struck its king down with the sword." Is this the same Jabin, or is "Jabin" a common royal name among Canaanite rulers? Some scholars suggest that Judges 4–5 is a retelling of the same event as recorded in Joshua 11 with some changes. Others suggest that the name of Jabin has been imported into the present text of Judges 4, since Jabin plays no active role in the story itself and is never mentioned in the song in Judges 5. The mention of "the kings of Canaan" in 5:19 may have occasioned the link with the account in Joshua 11.

In any case, King Jabin remains a shadowy figure in the background to Judges 4; general Sisera is the one Canaanite who grabs the spotlight and generates any narrative interest in the story.

As we would expect, the next step in the cycle of events is Israel's cry to God for help (v. 3). However, a note is added that the Canaanite commander "had nine hundred chariots of iron." The mention of iron provides a glimpse into the major cultural shift in technology occurring in the ancient Near East at this time from the earlier Bronze Age to the early phase of the Iron Age (1200–1000 BCE). The Canaanites were the more established, powerful, and richer culture in comparison to the Israelites. Thus the Canaanites had access to the most recent military technology, which they used to maintain their power and "cruelly" oppress the Israelites. The Canaanite oppression lasted a total of twenty years, slightly longer than the eighteen years before Ehud and the eight years before Othniel (3:8, 14).

4:4-11. In the previous judge stories, Israel's cry of distress had immediately caused God to raise up a judge to save Israel (3:9, 15). Thus we expect the next person named to be the judge who will lead Israel's army against the enemy. That person is Deborah, a woman described as a prophet, the wife of Lappidoth (or alternatively "woman of torches"), and who was "judging" Israel. The Hebrew word "judge" (שׁפט šōpēṭ) can have the sense either of ruler and military commander (as in the preceding judge stories) or arbitrator of disputes (as in the story of Moses in Exod 18:13-16). Deborah fulfills the latter sense of judging as she sits "under the palm of Deborah" in the hill country of Ephraim and the Israelites come to her for judgment in disputes (v. 5).

As the reader wonders whether Deborah is, indeed, the expected judge or deliverer sent to lead Israel into battle against the Canaanites, the narrative introduces a second possible candidate. His name is Barak. Deborah delivers an oracle from the Lord to Barak, commanding him to take ten thousand warriors from the tribes of Naphtali and Zebulun to fight the Canaanites. God promises to "draw out" the Canaanite commander Sisera with his chariots and troops, "and I will give him into your hand" (v. 7). The vocabulary of God's giving the enemy "into your hand" echoes similar words used for the preceding judges (3:10, 28). We now expect Barak to step immediately into the shoes of previous judges, bravely leading Israel against Sisera and his troops. But Barak interrupts with unexpected words of caution and hesitation. Barak seeks the reassurance of Deborah's presence with him as he goes out into battle. If Deborah is willing to go with him, Barak will go. But if Deborah will not go with him, Barak will not go, in spite of God's direct command to him (v. 8).

Barak's request for Deborah's presence has been variously interpreted. Some see Barak here as cowardly, afraid, and distrusting of God. A real judge would not need the assistance of anyone, much less a woman, to lead Israel into battle. In this understanding, the request for Deborah's presence would be unusual and unnecessary. Other interpreters see Barak's request as a gracious and insistent invitation to Deborah as God's prophet to join him so that she might bless the military expedition and share in the glory of the Lord's victory over the Canaanites. In this understanding, it would not be unusual for the woman prophet Deborah to accompany a military expedition and offer divine oracles of encouragement and strategy. The narrator does not provide an explicit evaluation of Barak's statement, and so we are left to wonder about Barak's inner motivation.

Deborah's response to Barak is no less ambiguous. Her reply is emphatic: "I will *surely* go with you." But what is the tone of her speech? "Of course I will go with you, Barak; that's what I would expect to do, since I am a prophet of God and this is God's battle." Or is the tone more like this: "Well, all right, if you insist, I will surely go with you, but it really shows a lack of trust in God on your part"? The same ambiguity pertains to the second half of her response, and here the NRSV and the NIV translations differ significantly in the nuances they give to the Hebrew. In the NRSV, Deborah says she will surely go with Barak, but Barak should know that the road on which he is going will not lead to his glory, since the Lord will give his counterpart, the Canaanite commander Sisera, "into the hand of a woman" (v. 9). Although susceptible to either a negative or a positive reading, the NRSV translation could suggest that Deborah's words are merely a statement of fact that does *not* reflect negatively on Barak's request for her presence with him. Losing

some glory to a woman may well be a trade-off Barak is quite willing to make in exchange for Deborah's prophetic presence with his army. The NIV gives a more one-sided and negative interpretation to Deborah's response. She agrees to go with Barak, but she adds, "because of the way you are going about this, the honor will not be yours, for the LORD will hand Sisera over to a woman" (v. 9). Here the lack of honor for Barak is interpreted as a negative punishment for the unfaithful request to have Deborah accompany him. The way Barak is going about this is all wrong and a punishable offense against God.

In my judgment, the NIV interprets Deborah's statement too narrowly. As the NRSV rightly translates, Deborah's response is ambiguous and should be translated in a way that maintains the uncertainty. The narrative is intentionally drawing the reader in to ponder the ambiguous possibilities in the statements of these two characters. The ambiguity is part of a larger narrative strategy that builds suspense and leads the reader on to determine who the real judge might be. In the flow of the narrative, the reader initially would think that Deborah was the judge (v. 4), but then Barak takes over as a more likely candidate (vv. 6-7). However, Barak's ambiguous statement makes us think twice about his suitability (v. 8). Now Deborah's declaration that Sisera (the individual or Sisera and his whole army?) will be delivered into the hand of a woman causes us to wonder whether Deborah will after all emerge as the true judge and heroine in place of Barak (v. 9). But we are not sure at this point, and so we read on. Deborah does go up with Barak to the place of battle at Kedesh, and Barak does summon his ten thousand warriors, so the stage is now set for the battle to begin (v. 10).

One peculiar note suddenly drops into the story without any preparation. It is a piece of information provided by the narrator to the reader that will become important later in the story. A man named Heber from the non-Israelite nation of the Kenites had separated himself from the other Kenites and encamped "near Kedesh," the place where the battle is about to begin. The Kenites had a special relationship with Israel in that Moses' father-in-law, Hobab, had been a Kenite (v. 11; see 1:16). One interesting possibility concerning Heber the Kenite is the Kenites' traditional association with iron smithing and iron work (see Gen 4:22). Although Heber had a familial association with Israel, had Heber separated from the other Kenites in order to ply his trade as an iron smith with the 900 iron chariots of the Canaanites? Is Heber an ally of Israel or of Canaan? Later in this story, we will learn that "there was peace between King Jabin of Hazor and the clan of Heber the Kenite" (v. 17). That fact will play a role in the ongoing suspense and drama of the story. For now, the note about Heber the Kenite (v. 11) is simply inserted between Israel's preparing for battle (vv. 6-10) and Canaan's preparing for battle (vv. 12-13). Heber's placement between Israel and Canaan signifies his ambiguous position on the narrative boundary between them. With all the other ambiguities of this story, the reader wonders what the role of this liminal character and his clan will be.

4:12-16. The Canaanite commander Sisera hears of Israel's preparations for war and assembles "all his chariots, nine hundred chariots of iron, and all the troops" (vv. 12-13). As for Israel, Deborah speaks an oracle of divine encouragement to Barak: "Up! For this is the day on which the LORD has given Sisera into your hand" (v. 14). What does this oracle mean? Has the earlier oracle that Sisera would be given into the hand of a woman (v. 9) been rescinded? Or is this merely a way of saying that Barak and his forces will win a general victory against the Canaanites, even though Sisera himself will fall under the hand of a woman? Again, we as readers do not know. We do know that God is with the Israelites and fights for them as the divine warrior. Thus the Lord throws Sisera's army and chariots into confusion and panic, just as the Lord had done against Pharaoh and his chariots in the exodus from Egypt (Exod 14:24). Barak defeats the entire army of Sisera with the Lord's help, except for Sisera, who runs away on foot (vv. 15-16).

4:17-22. As in v. 11, the narrator interrupts the flow of the story with another note informing the reader that the fleeing Sisera has escaped to the tent of Jael, who is the wife of Heber the Kenite. Sisera had fled there, "for there was peace" between Heber's Kenite clan and the Canaanite king Jabin, whose army Sisera commanded (v. 17). Now we surmise that Heber had separated from the other Kenites (v. 11) in order to ally himself and his family with the Canaanites.

The narrative resumes with Jael welcoming Sisera warmly into her tent, addressing him as "my lord" and insisting that he need have no fear. He enters Jael's tent, and she covers him with a rug. He asks for "a little water to drink," and Jael gives him sleep-inducing milk instead (vv. 18-19). Jael here acts as a mother. The mighty warrior Sisera is turned into a little child, tucked into bed for the night and hiding from any monsters who might threaten him. Sisera instructs Jael to stand watch at the entrance to the tent. If anyone comes by and asks "Is anyone here?" Sisera tells Jael to say no (v. 20). The question in Hebrew (הֲיֵשׁ־פֹּה אִישׁ *hăyēš-pōh 'îš*) can mean literally, "Is *a man* here?" Ironically, Sisera's own words reveal that his masculinity has been reduced to that of an infant. On the surface, Sisera seems safe and secure in the womb-like tent of mother Jael, falling asleep from the weariness of battle and the heaviness of milk.

The story suddenly takes a dramatic and wholly unexpected turn. Jael takes a sharp tent peg and a hammer "in her hand" and drives the peg forcefully into the soft temple of Sisera's sleeping head so that he dies (v. 21). Commentators have long observed the sudden shift from material to sexual imagery here in a scene of reverse rape, the woman Jael forcibly thrusting and violently penetrating Sisera's body. The sexual imagery will become more explicit in the poetic version in 5:26-27.[33] The Israelite general Barak pursues Sisera but arrives after Jael has killed Sisera in his sleep. Jael welcomes Barak into her tent and shows him the body of Sisera, "lying dead, with the tent peg in his temple" (v. 22). Is Barak happy to share the glory with Jael? Is he despondent that he did not have the singular glory of killing his Canaanite counterpart? The narrative does not tell us.

Now the perplexity over whether Deborah or Barak is the true judge or hero is in some ways made even more complicated. Jael, a non-Israelite woman, is added to the list of those who helped save Israel from its Canaanite enemy. She replaces

---

33. See Robert Alter, *The Art of Biblical Poetry* (New York: Basic, 1985) 43-50; Meir Sternberg, *The Poetics of Biblical Narrative: Ideological Literature and the Drama of Reading* (Bloomington: Indiana University Press, 1981) 270-83; Mieke Bal, *Murder and Difference: Gender, Genre and Scholarship on Sisera's Death* (Bloomington: Indiana University Press, 1988) 111-34; and Danna Nolan Fewell and David Gunn, "Women, Men, and the Authority of Violence in Judges 4 and 5," *JAAR* 58 (1990) 389-411.

Deborah as the one who fulfills Deborah's oracle that Sisera would be given "into the hand of a woman" (vv. 9, 21). Neither Deborah, Barak, nor Jael emerges as the singular hero or judge in this story. Moreover, the puzzle continues with new questions. What motivated Jael to kill Sisera? Why did she defy the peace agreement between her husband and the Canaanites? Did she act out of a deep loyalty to Israel and Israel's God? Or did she realize the Israelites had won the battle and so defect to the Israelite cause for pragmatic reasons to save her own life? Her motives remain a mystery. All we know is that God used Jael for the purpose of defeating Israel's enemy, no matter what her motives were.

4:23-24. The artful indirection, suspense, and sharing of glory among Deborah, Barak, and Jael point ultimately to the overarching and integrating agency of God. In the final analysis, "*God* subdued King Jabin of Canaan" (v. 23). God and Jabin were the shadowy but ultimate power brokers in the battle between Israel and Canaan. In that ultimate struggle, it was God who prevailed. But God's purposes were achieved through a coalition of human actors, none of whom could take ultimate credit for the victory.[34] The final verse in the narrative suggests that Israel continued to wage war against other Canaanite forces of King

34. Yairah Amit, "Judges 4: Its Content and Form," *JSOT* 39 (1987) 89-111.

Jabin for a time, bearing harder and harder upon him until he was destroyed (v. 24).

The climactic point in chap. 4 is not the battle but the scene in Jael's tent and the assassination of Sisera. Several similarities between this central scene in chap. 4 and the stories of the preceding two judges, Ehud and Shamgar (3:12-31), stand out. Like Ehud, Jael kills the enemy alone in a private room through an act of deception. Like Ehud, who had brought tribute to King Eglon to seek his favor, Jael offers milk, refuge, and rest to Sisera. The same Hebrew verb (תקע *tāqaʿ*, "to drive," "to thrust") is used for Ehud's assassination of Eglon (3:21) and for Jael's assassination of Sisera (4:21). Just as Ehud's deed was unexpectedly done by his left hand, so also Jael's deed was unexpectedly done through a foreign woman's hand (4:9). Like Shamgar, who fashioned an unconventional weapon out of an oxgoad (3:31), Jael used a tent peg as her unusual weapon. Thus the three judge stories—Ehud, Shamgar, and Deborah-Barak-Jael—are tied together as examples of temporary victories that God leads on behalf of an oppressed Israel through the agency of unexpected human agents. This first phase of the judge stories in 3:7–5:31 portrays faithfulness and effectiveness on the part of Israel's leaders and judges. When the judge or judges are alive, Israel prospers. But when the judge dies, Israel reverts to its old evil ways.

REFLECTIONS

1. The most dramatic feature of this story is the image of two strong, independent, and courageous women: Deborah, the prophet and arbitrator of disputes, and Jael, the non-Israelite assassin. These are not the first strong women in Judges. Achsah, daughter of Caleb and Othniel's wife, had been a strong and independent negotiator with her father (1:11-15). Indeed, the book of Judges contains the largest number of women characters of any book of the Bible, nineteen in all. But the portraits and fate of the women of Judges follow a trajectory similar to that of the judges period as a whole. The judge stories and the portraits of women begin as healthy, strong, and faithful. The first women we encounter all have names (Achsah, Deborah, Jael). But increasingly, as Israel and the judges begin their decline, the fate of women will decline as well. The many women characters become nameless (except for Delilah in the Samson story). Women gradually lose their independent power and become objects and victims, first inadvertently and willingly (Jephthah's daughter and his foolish vow in chap. 11), but then more intentionally and unwillingly (Samson's women in chaps. 14–16, the Levite's concubine in chap. 19, the 400 young virgins of Jabesh-Gilead and the women dancers at Shiloh in chap. 21). The book of Judges offers a wide spectrum of the possible experiences of women, both positive and negative. In the ancient world as well as our own, the health and well-being of women provide an important barometer to measure the core health and values of a society or community.

2. Judges 4 depicts God's working in and through a nexus of human activities involving shared leadership, mutual responsibility, and glory that is distributed among several of the main characters (Deborah, Jael, and Barak). Although many interpreters argue that Judges promotes a strictly centralized and royal mode of leadership (see the refrain in 17:6 and 21:25), Judges 4 also appears to recognize the ability of God to work effectively through more complex systems where power may be decentralized, duties may be distributed, and no one leader need take all the credit or responsibility. As we reflect on various models or polities within our families, congregations, denominations, or other political entities, we may be assured that God is able to work through any variety of structures or systems. The question may be what is most appropriate and helpful in a given context, time, and tradition.

3. The Bible honors the common ancient Near Eastern custom of hospitality to strangers and sojourners. Abraham and Sarah welcomed three strangers who turned out to be the Lord present among them (Genesis 18). Hebrews 13:2 uses their story to commend its readers to show hospitality to strangers, "for by doing that some have entertained angels without knowing it" (NRSV). Many of Israel's laws urged hospitality to strangers and sojourners, since Israel had been a sojourner in Egypt (Exod 22:21; Lev 19:33-34; Deut 10:19). Jael breaks this hospitality code rather egregiously in first welcoming and then killing Sisera, the Canaanite general. Not only does she break the hospitality code, but she also breaks the peace pact between the Canaanites and her own Kenite clan. Yet the narrative never explicitly condemns or raises concerns about her act; indeed, her slaying of Sisera is praised in the next chapter in the song (Judg 5:24-27). But Jael's act inevitably raises difficult moral questions, and the narrative does not let the reader off the hook by providing much insight into Jael's motives or thoughts. On this issue, the story in Judges 4 draws the reader into moral reflection without providing an explicit evaluation. The situation is similar to the scene of Moses killing the Egyptian foreman in Exod 2:11-15; no overt moral assessment is made in the text of Moses' act of using violence for the sake of social justice. However, the story raises the questions and issues in a way that forces the reader to wrestle with them.

4. Two narrative strategies seem to be working at cross-purposes in Judges 4. On one hand, the cyclical framework (4:1-3, 23) commonly found in the other judge stories suggests a foreordained sequence of events with God clearly in control. The predictability of the sequence of events affirms the ultimate sovereignty of God. On the other hand, the intensity of misdirection and suspense throughout Judges 4 (will the real judge please stand up?) suggests unpredictability and the need for God to adjust the divine plan to make room for human freedom and decisions. God's oracle through Deborah promises Barak that the Lord will deliver Sisera into his hand (4:7). However, his request that Deborah accompany him seems to cause a change in God's oracle and plan: "the Lord will sell Sisera into the hand of a woman" (4:9). But later, Deborah reiterates that God has given Sisera into Barak's hand (4:14). In the end, God accomplishes the salvation promised, but we as human readers ponder the often untraceable combination of human and divine "hands" at work in a given situation. In the end, God's will for the world will prevail, but God also makes adjustment to human freedom and actions along the way. As the people of God, we can be confident that God is at work in and through our lives and communities to accomplish God's will, even when we may be unaware. Indeed, God may work through outsiders or those on the margin of our community in ways we would never expect. At the same time, we can be hopeful that the prayers, words, and actions of faithful individuals, leaders, and communities will be taken seriously and incorporated into the larger plans of God to bring about change and redemption in line with the purposes of God.

Judges 5:1-31, The Song of Deborah and Barak

5 On that day Deborah and Barak son of Abinoam sang this song:

²"When the princes in Israel take the lead,
    when the people willingly offer
        themselves—
    praise the LORD!

³"Hear this, you kings! Listen, you rulers!
    I will sing to*ᵃ* the LORD, I will sing;
    I will make music to*ᵇ* the LORD, the God of
        Israel.

⁴"O LORD, when you went out from Seir,
    when you marched from the land of Edom,
the earth shook, the heavens poured,
    the clouds poured down water.
⁵The mountains quaked before the LORD, the One
        of Sinai,
    before the LORD, the God of Israel.

⁶"In the days of Shamgar son of Anath,
    in the days of Jael, the roads were
        abandoned;
    travelers took to winding paths.
⁷Village life*ᶜ* in Israel ceased,
    ceased until I,*ᵈ* Deborah, arose,
    arose a mother in Israel.
⁸When they chose new gods,
    war came to the city gates,
and not a shield or spear was seen
    among forty thousand in Israel.
⁹My heart is with Israel's princes,
    with the willing volunteers among the
        people.
    Praise the LORD!

¹⁰"You who ride on white donkeys,
    sitting on your saddle blankets,
    and you who walk along the road,
consider ¹¹the voice of the singers*ᵉ* at the
        watering places.
    They recite the righteous acts of the LORD,
    the righteous acts of his warriors*ᶠ* in Israel.

"Then the people of the LORD
    went down to the city gates.

5 Then Deborah and Barak son of Abinoam sang on that day, saying:

² "When locks are long in Israel,
    when the people offer themselves
        willingly—
    bless*ᵃ* the LORD!

³ "Hear, O kings; give ear, O princes;
    to the LORD I will sing,
    I will make melody to the LORD, the God of
        Israel.

⁴ "LORD, when you went out from Seir,
    when you marched from the region of
        Edom,
the earth trembled,
    and the heavens poured,
    the clouds indeed poured water.
⁵ The mountains quaked before the LORD, the
        One of Sinai,
    before the LORD, the God of Israel.

⁶ "In the days of Shamgar son of Anath,
    in the days of Jael, caravans ceased
    and travelers kept to the byways.
⁷ The peasantry prospered in Israel,
    they grew fat on plunder,
because you arose, Deborah,
    arose as a mother in Israel.
⁸ When new gods were chosen,
    then war was in the gates.
Was shield or spear to be seen
    among forty thousand in Israel?
⁹ My heart goes out to the commanders of
        Israel
    who offered themselves willingly among the
        people.
    Bless the LORD.

¹⁰ "Tell of it, you who ride on white donkeys,
    you who sit on rich carpets*ᵇ*
    and you who walk by the way.
¹¹ To the sound of musicians*ᵇ* at the watering
        places,

---

*a3 Or of   b3 Or / with song I will praise   c7 Or Warriors   d7 Or
you   e11 Or archers*; the meaning of the Hebrew for this word is
uncertain.   *f11 Or villagers*

a Or You who offer yourselves willingly among the people, bless
b Meaning of Heb uncertain

NIV

¹²'Wake up, wake up, Deborah!
    Wake up, wake up, break out in song!
Arise, O Barak!
    Take captive your captives, O son of
        Abinoam.'

¹³"Then the men who were left
    came down to the nobles;
the people of the LORD
    came to me with the mighty.
¹⁴Some came from Ephraim, whose roots were in
        Amalek;
    Benjamin was with the people who followed
        you.
From Makir captains came down,
    from Zebulun those who bear a
        commander's staff.
¹⁵The princes of Issachar were with Deborah;
    yes, Issachar was with Barak,
    rushing after him into the valley.
In the districts of Reuben
    there was much searching of heart.
¹⁶Why did you stay among the campfires^a
    to hear the whistling for the flocks?
In the districts of Reuben
    there was much searching of heart.
¹⁷Gilead stayed beyond the Jordan.
    And Dan, why did he linger by the ships?
Asher remained on the coast
    and stayed in his coves.
¹⁸The people of Zebulun risked their very lives;
    so did Naphtali on the heights of the field.

¹⁹"Kings came, they fought;
    the kings of Canaan fought
at Taanach by the waters of Megiddo,
    but they carried off no silver, no plunder.
²⁰From the heavens the stars fought,
    from their courses they fought against Sisera.
²¹The river Kishon swept them away,
    the age-old river, the river Kishon.
    March on, my soul; be strong!
²²Then thundered the horses' hoofs—
    galloping, galloping go his mighty steeds.
²³'Curse Meroz,' said the angel of the LORD.
    'Curse its people bitterly,
because they did not come to help the LORD,
    to help the LORD against the mighty.'

^a16 Or saddlebags

NRSV

there they repeat the triumphs of the LORD,
    the triumphs of his peasantry in Israel.

"Then down to the gates marched the people
    of the LORD.

¹² "Awake, awake, Deborah!
    Awake, awake, utter a song!
Arise, Barak, lead away your captives,
    O son of Abinoam.
¹³ Then down marched the remnant of the
        noble;
    the people of the LORD marched down for
        him^a against the mighty.
¹⁴ From Ephraim they set out^b into the valley,^c
    following you, Benjamin, with your kin;
from Machir marched down the
        commanders,
    and from Zebulun those who bear the
        marshal's staff;
¹⁵ the chiefs of Issachar came with Deborah,
    and Issachar faithful to Barak;
    into the valley they rushed out at his
        heels.
Among the clans of Reuben
    there were great searchings of heart.
¹⁶ Why did you tarry among the sheepfolds,
    to hear the piping for the flocks?
Among the clans of Reuben
    there were great searchings of heart.
¹⁷ Gilead stayed beyond the Jordan;
    and Dan, why did he abide with the
        ships?
Asher sat still at the coast of the sea,
    settling down by his landings.
¹⁸ Zebulun is a people that scorned death;
    Naphtali too, on the heights of the field.

¹⁹ "The kings came, they fought;
    then fought the kings of Canaan,
at Taanach, by the waters of Megiddo;
    they got no spoils of silver.
²⁰ The stars fought from heaven,
    from their courses they fought against Sisera.
²¹ The torrent Kishon swept them away,
    the onrushing torrent, the torrent Kishon.
    March on, my soul, with might!

^a Gk: Heb me   ^b Cn: Heb From Ephraim their root   ^c Gk: Heb in
Amalek

²⁴"Most blessed of women be Jael,
 the wife of Heber the Kenite,
 most blessed of tent-dwelling women.
²⁵He asked for water, and she gave him milk;
 in a bowl fit for nobles she brought him
 curdled milk.
²⁶Her hand reached for the tent peg,
 her right hand for the workman's hammer.
She struck Sisera, she crushed his head,
 she shattered and pierced his temple.
²⁷At her feet he sank,
 he fell; there he lay.
At her feet he sank, he fell;
 where he sank, there he fell—dead.

²⁸"Through the window peered Sisera's mother;
 behind the lattice she cried out,
'Why is his chariot so long in coming?
 Why is the clatter of his chariots delayed?'
²⁹The wisest of her ladies answer her;
 indeed, she keeps saying to herself,
³⁰'Are they not finding and dividing the spoils:
 a girl or two for each man,
 colorful garments as plunder for Sisera,
 colorful garments embroidered,
 highly embroidered garments for my neck—
all this as plunder?'

³¹"So may all your enemies perish, O LORD!
 But may they who love you be like the sun
 when it rises in its strength."
Then the land had peace forty years.

²² "Then loud beat the horses' hoofs
 with the galloping, galloping of his steeds.

²³ "Curse Meroz, says the angel of the LORD,
 curse bitterly its inhabitants,
because they did not come to the help of the
 LORD,
 to the help of the LORD against the
 mighty.

²⁴ "Most blessed of women be Jael,
 the wife of Heber the Kenite,
 of tent-dwelling women most blessed.
²⁵ He asked water and she gave him milk,
 she brought him curds in a lordly bowl.
²⁶ She put her hand to the tent peg
 and her right hand to the workmen's
 mallet;
she struck Sisera a blow,
 she crushed his head,
 she shattered and pierced his temple.
²⁷ He sank, he fell,
 he lay still at her feet;
at her feet he sank, he fell;
 where he sank, there he fell dead.

²⁸ "Out of the window she peered,
 the mother of Sisera gazed^a through the
 lattice:
'Why is his chariot so long in coming?
 Why tarry the hoofbeats of his chariots?'
²⁹ Her wisest ladies make answer,
 indeed, she answers the question herself:
³⁰ 'Are they not finding and dividing the
 spoil?—
 A girl or two for every man;
spoil of dyed stuffs for Sisera,
 spoil of dyed stuffs embroidered,
 two pieces of dyed work embroidered for
 my neck as spoil?'

³¹ "So perish all your enemies, O LORD!
 But may your friends be like the sun as it
 rises in its might."

And the land had rest forty years.

^a Gk Compare Tg: Heb *exclaimed*

COMMENTARY

The Song of Deborah and Barak in this chapter is considered by most scholars to be one of the oldest pieces of literature in the Old Testament, perhaps dating to the twelfth century BCE. Its archaic Hebrew vocabulary and syntax have caused significant debates and disagreements about how best to translate certain lines of the poem. A comparison of the NRSV and the NIV translations reveals significant differences in 5:2*a*, 7*a*, 14*a*, and 16*a*, and these represent only the tip of the scholarly iceberg of studies devoted to this ancient poem.[35] The poetic song in Judges 5 provides an alternative version of the story of God's victory and the Canaanites' defeat, narrated in prose form in Judges 4. The song fills in some additional details, adds whole new scenes, lacks the narrative version's important theme of Barak's loss of glory, and adds other themes not present in Judges 4. The song seems to assume that the reader is familiar with the events as narrated in the story. For example, Sisera appears without prior explanation or introduction in the poem itself in 5:20. The poem combines elements of a hymn of praise and a ballad that recounts a story in poetic form.

5:1-11. The overriding theme of this section of the poem is the overwhelming power of God contrasted with the weakness of Israel in the face of the Canaanites' oppression. The song is sung by both Deborah and Barak "on that day," presumably immediately after the victory narrated in chap. 4, which concludes with the same phrase in 4:23, "on that day." This first section is framed by a related pair of themes at the beginning and the end: a note of joy and thanksgiving for those Israelites who volunteered to fight, followed by the refrain, "Bless the LORD!" (vv. 2, 9), and an imperative call for foreign kings to hear the song that Deborah and Barak are singing to the Lord (v. 3), matched by an imperative call to foreign

travelers to listen to musicians as "they repeat the triumphs of the LORD" and "of his peasantry in Israel" (vv. 10-11).

Between these two framing sections, the poem draws a striking contrast between the powerful appearance of God as a divine warrior and the oppression and weakness of Israel in the face of the Canaanite tyranny (vv. 4-8). The scene in vv. 4-5 depicts the awesome cosmic disturbances that accompany the appearance of the Lord, who is ready for battle against the enemies of God. As God the divine warrior marches from the east in Edom to Israel, nature erupts with explosive force: Mountains quake; the earth trembles; the skies unleash a powerful and pounding rainstorm.

In contrast, Israel in the days of Shamgar and Jael was weak and powerless. Travelers and caravans avoided the roads for fear of the Canaanites. Normal life and commerce were interrupted (vv. 6-7). The NIV may be closer than the NRSV to the meaning of v. 7*a*: The normal life of Israel's peasantry ceased. This negative situation continued "until" (NIV) Deborah arose "as a mother in Israel." The phrase is probably more than just an endearing title. "Mother in Israel" (אם בישראל *ʾēm bĕyiśrāʾēl*) may represent the place and office of a wise woman prophet who delivers divine oracles to resolve disputes (see 4:5; 2 Sam 20:16-19).[36] Verse 8*a* is difficult to understand, having to do either with Israel's apostasy in choosing new gods (NIV and NRSV) or, more probably, with Deborah's choosing new recruits for Israel's army. Unfortunately, these new recruits had no weapons: "not a shield or spear was seen" (v. 8). Thus a weak and weaponless Israel will face the mighty Canaanites in battle. But the determining factor will not be the relative weakness or strength of these human forces. In this holy war conflict, the one truly relevant factor will be that God, the powerful divine warrior, will be fighting for Israel and against Canaan. Thus the rag tag army of Israel marches down from its humble highland settlements to the lowland walled and gated cities of Canaan: "Then down to the gates marched the people of the LORD" (v. 11*b*).

5:12-18. The important contrast in this section

35. A few representative studies include Michael D. Coogan, "A Structural and Literary Analysis of the Song of Deborah," *CBQ* 40 (1978) 143-66; Frank M. Cross and David Noel Freedman, *Studies in Ancient Yahwistic Poetry* (Missoula, Mont.: Scholars Press, 1975); and A. Globe, "The Literary Structure and Unity of the Song of Deborah," *JBL* 93 (1974) 493-512. On the importance of contrasts in the structure of the poem, see G. Gerleman, "The Song of Deborah in Light of Stylistics," *VT* (1951) 168-79; and Frank Yamada, "The Rhetorical Use of Contrast in the Song of Deborah (Judges 5)," a paper presented at the Society of Biblical Literature Annual Meeting, San Francisco, November 22, 1997.

36. James W. Watts, *Psalm and Story: Inset Hymns in Hebrew Narrative* (Sheffield: JSOT, 1992) 90.

is between those Israelite tribes that valiantly joined the battle and those other tribes who were reluctant or refused to do so. The section begins with a call to Deborah to "utter a song" as a call to battle and a call to Israel's military leader, Barak, to lead away his captives. A "remnant" (שָׂרִיד *śārîd*) of all the Israelite tribes responds to their leaders' call to battle as they march down "against the mighty" Canaanites (v. 13). This faithful remnant includes the tribes of Ephraim, Benjamin, Zebulun, Issachar, Naphtali, and the half-tribe of Manasseh, known as Machir (vv. 14-15*a*, 18). However, other Israelite tribes were hesitant and stayed at home rather than help their fellow Israelites. The "clans of Reuben" experienced "great searchings of heart" in deciding whether to leave their flocks of sheep to go to war (vv. 15*b*-16). The east Jordan tribe of Gilead refused to cross the Jordan River and come to the aid of Israel's other tribes. The tribes of Dan and Asher preferred the relative security of their ships and the seacoast to the dangers of war (v. 17). The tribes' reluctance reveals a lack of trust in God and a lack of commitment to the unity of Israel as the people of God. Nevertheless, the war against Canaan begins with an already weak Israel at half strength but, more important, with God fighting on Israel's side.

5:19-22. This section of the poem narrates the battle scene between Israel's God and the Canaanite kings. The section begins with the confident Canaanite kings who come and fight beside the waters of Megiddo (v. 19). The section ends with the loud beating of Canaanite horses' hooves galloping in retreat (v. 22). On the surface, it seemed that Canaan's army was fighting only a weak and weaponless Israelite militia. But Israel's God was also fighting. God used the forces of nature, the stars and the rainstorm, to defeat the Canaanite general Sisera and his army of chariots (vv. 20-21; see 4:2). The torrential rains and flooding torrents of the wadi Kishon rendered Sisera's chariots useless in the lowland mud. God unleashed forces far beyond the control or power of Israel's small human army to win the victory over Israel's Canaanite oppressor.

5:23-30. The next poetic unit juxtaposes a vehement curse and a lavish blessing. The curse is aimed at a presumably Israelite clan, Meroz, for its unwillingness to "come to the help of the LORD . . .

against the mighty" (v. 23). The blessing is pronounced upon Jael, the non-Israelite wife of Heber the Kenite, who is remembered as "the most blessed of women" (v. 24). The rest of the unit retells in gory detail the way in which Jael assassinated the Canaanite general Sisera. The unit concludes with a poignant scene depicting Sisera's mother waiting in vain for her son to return home from battle.

Sisera had come to this "tent-dwelling woman" and asked her for water. But Jael gave him milky "curds in a lordly bowl," a mild sedative to set him up for her deadly deed (v. 25). The action slows down to a slow-motion crawl in the next two verses as Jael takes a tent peg in one hand and a mallet in the other. She then strikes Sisera with a crushing blow to the head, shattering and piercing his temple. Unlike the narrative version of this scene, where Sisera is lying asleep in the tent (4:18-21), here he appears to be standing or perhaps sitting in a chair. When Jael penetrated his body with the tent peg, "he sank, he fell, he lay still . . . he sank, he fell . . . he fell dead" (v. 27). Sisera falls dead literally in Hebrew "between her feet" or "between her legs" (בֵּין רַגְלֶיהָ *bên ragleyhā*, v. 27), a sexual euphemism found elsewhere in the Bible (Deut 28:57; Ezek 16:25). The sexual overtones of this death scene have been frequently noted, reaching as far back as the ancient Jewish rabbinical interpreters. This woman nurturer-turned-warrior symbolizes the close interplay of sexuality and death, of rape and war.[37] But the tables have been turned. Used to killing men and raping woman, general Sisera is himself killed and "raped" by a woman. The non-Israelite Jael here becomes a cipher for Israel and Sisera a cipher for Canaan's military might. The supposedly weaker Israel had been repeatedly oppressed and pillaged by the arrogant Canaanites in the past. But now with the help of Israel's divine warrior, mighty Canaan has fallen into defeat and death.

For the closing scene of this unit, the narrator turns our attention to a scene in a Canaanite city where the mother of general Sisera waits at her window for her son to return from battle. Sisera's mother wonders aloud and discusses with her women advisers why her son is taking such a long time to return (vv. 28-29). Their arrogant confi-

---

37. Susan Niditch, "Eroticism and Death in the Tale of Jael," in *Gender and Difference in Ancient Israel,* ed. Peggy Day (Minneapolis: Fortress, 1989) 43-57.

dence that Sisera has surely been victorious is matched only by their greedy anticipation of fine clothes and other spoil that Sisera will steal from those whom he has defeated (v. 30). But one line in this chatter of smug Canaanite women leaps out in the light of what has happened earlier in the poem. One of the reasons they imagine for the delay in his return is the time it takes to rape the women of those who have been defeated. The NRSV and the NIV translations read "a girl or two for every man" (v. 30). The Hebrew is even more crude: "A womb [רחם *raḥam*] or two for every man." But these Canaanite women (and their men) have not reckoned with the "one or two women" who are the heroes of this poem, Deborah and Jael. Nor have they reckoned with the God of Israel, against whom no human army can withstand. Thus Deborah, Barak, Jael, and God upended the prideful plans of Sisera and his Canaanite soldiers: the Canaanites "got no spoils of war" (v. 19), and Sisera "fell . . . between her feet . . . there he fell dead" (v. 27).

5:31. The poem comes to a close with a final prayer that contrasts the enemies and the friends of the Lord: "So perish all your enemies, O LORD!" The defeat and death of the Canaanites represent the fate of all God's enemies, those powers and principalities that resist the will of God for Israel and the world. But the poem requests of God a very different fate for those who are faithful and love God: "But may your friends be like the sun as it rises in its might." After the turbulent rainstorm and the clouds of battle and the stars fighting from heaven have concluded their work (vv. 4, 20-21), they now can step aside and allow a faithful Israel to assume its place of honor like the sun shining in full strength in the sky. Judges 5, so filled with the noise and tumult of war and earthquakes and thunderstorms, now ends quietly with the words, "And the land had rest forty years."

REFLECTIONS

1. The dominant feature of the Song of Deborah and Barak is its series of strong and dramatic contrasts: the powerful divine warrior and a weak Israel, the willing bravery of some Israelite tribes and the passive reluctance of others, the defeated human army of the Canaanites and God's victorious forces of nature and the stars of heaven, Jael as a woman killing and "raping" Sisera, and Sisera's mother under the illusion that her son would be the one killing and raping. Poetry is elevated speech that heightens contrasts, interprets reality, discerns truth, stretches imagination, and leads us deeper into mysteries in more playful, poignant, and powerful ways than ordinary prosaic discourse. Judges 4 provides us with the prose narrative version of the story, but the poetry of Judges 5 leads us to see more deeply the meanings and mysteries of God, who fights against God's enemies and for God's friends. One of the ministerial tasks of preaching, teaching, and counseling in a community of faith is to help people take up the prosaic and mundane realities of their lives and the events of our world and explore the deeper and divine realities, truths, and mysteries that lie embedded within them. The poetry of Judges 5 provides one of many models for thinking about ministry as poetic reflection on the seemingly mundane and ordinary parts of our lives. Just as poetry interprets prose, so also the pastor interprets the everyday life of his or her parishioners.

2. If the poem of Judges 5 is a series of contrasts, the primary contrast is between God's power and effective use of forces from outside Israel versus the weakness and the timidity of Israel's contribution to the major battle with the Canaanites. Israel was relatively poor, militarily weak, virtually weaponless, and not unified in its resolve. The source of Israel's salvation would have to come from outside itself—from God, from the forces of nature that God used against Canaan (the thunderstorm), and from Jael the Kenite. Similarly, as Christians we confess that our salvation against the enemy forces of sin and death is rooted, not in our own efforts or capacities to save ourselves, but in the work of God and the agents through whom God works to bring to us the words and deeds of God's sustaining love. Just as Israel was saved through

God's complex integration of forces of nature, Jael the Kenite, and the bravery of some of the Israelite tribes, so, too, God works to ensure that we are nurtured in our faith and life through a complex integration of people, communities, family, friends, gifts of nature, and the like. Life in its fullness is a true gift from God.

3. Although God and forces outside of Israel itself were largely responsible for the victory against the Canaanites, the poem also makes clear that it matters whether God's own people remain unified and work together toward the purposes of God. God has chosen in some way to be contingent on active human participation in the ongoing drama of God's saving ways with God's people and the world. God's people ought not to take lightly the obligation to help one another, particularly in times of crisis, threat, or danger. The body of Christ requires all its members to be united together under the one head, who is Christ: "If one member suffers, all suffer together with it; if one member is honored, all rejoice together with it" (1 Cor 12:26 NRSV). The poem in Judges 5 is an important model in this regard. The prose story of Judges 4 tells of how Barak lost glory when Jael killed the Canaanite commander Sisera before Barak had the opportunity (4:9, 22). But the poem of Judges 5 shows Barak immediately afterward joining Deborah in singing not only the praises of God but also the praises of Jael, the "most blessed of women" (5:24). Some commentators argue that the song in Judges 5 was originally only the Song of Deborah (5:7) and that Barak's name was added only later to the introduction in 5:1. If that is true, the present form of the text still affirms Barak's willingness to overcome his loss of glory and rejoice together with other members of the community.

4. Some features of this poem may be troubling to those people of God who cherish the hopes for peace (Isa 2:1-11), the resistance to violence (Matt 5:38-48), and the refusal to take vengeance (Rom 12:9) that are themes we find elsewhere in the Bible. What do we do with Judges 5 and its image of God as divine warrior; the ruthless violence of Jael against Sisera, which seems to be applauded; and the desire for vengeance against one's enemies (5:31)? These are not issues that can be easily resolved, because they require ongoing reflection over all of Scripture and its diverse witnesses. But we can offer a few brief guidelines.

First of all, the image of God as divine warrior is pervasive throughout many different traditions in the Old Testament and even into the New Testament. But typically, as in Judges 5, God as divine warrior fights on behalf of the weak and the powerless against arrogant forces of oppression, death, and rebellion against God. When Jesus sent out seventy of his followers to preach and to heal and they returned to him, Jesus proclaimed that underlying the apparently mundane character of their ministry was an ongoing cosmic battle against the power of evil: "I watched Satan fall from heaven like a flash of lightning" (Luke 10:18 NRSV).

Second, the violence of Jael against Sisera was done by a non-Israelite acting as an advocate for the sake of others, and not to save herself. The poem portrays the act as God's just punishment upon the arrogance and greed of an oppressor as exemplified in the scene with Sisera's mother (5:28-30). The narrator of the poem does not present the story of Jael as a model to be emulated by God's people when they are attacked so much as it is a portrait of the judgment God will bring upon those who live by violence and oppression. The Bible is fully aware of the ambiguity and danger in any use of violence even for reasons we may convince ourselves are just, but there are times when oppressors will bring God's judgment of violence on themselves. Sisera is one such example.

Finally, the prayer to God that all the Lord's enemies might perish (5:31) relinquishes this natural human desire for vengeance to God. The petitioner can let go of these negative feelings toward an enemy and entrust any just vengeance to God. The book of Psalms contains many so-called imprecatory psalms asking God for vengeance, and they serve this positive purpose, letting go of our sinful human inclinations to do vengeance and entrusting God to perform whatever justice needs to be done (see Psalms 7; 54; 143).

JUDGES 6:1–10:5, THE DOWNHILL SLIDE BEGINS: GIDEON AND ABIMELECH; TOLA AND JAIR

OVERVIEW

The accounts of the individual judges or deliverers in 3:7–16:31 divide into three major phases of gradual decline in military effectiveness and religious faithfulness. The first phase included Othniel, the model judge (3:7-11), and the two faithful and victorious judges, Ehud (3:12-30) and Deborah (4:1–5:31). As we move into the second phase of the judges period, two major characters stand out: Gideon (6:1–8:35) and his renegade son Abimelech (9:1-57). This second phase of the judges period is marked by a transition from victory and faithfulness to idolatry and the reckless and selfish use of military might and violence. Gideon's initial military victories against the Midianite enemies are impressive, but Gideon is also cowardly, hesitant, and often doubtful of God's ability to accomplish what God has promised. Moreover, Gideon himself shifts from being an idol breaker to an idol maker. Although Gideon secretly destroys an altar of the pagan god Baal early in his career, he later fashions a golden ephod, used in obtaining oracles from God. The ephod itself becomes an object of worship and thus an idol in place of the Lord.

The transition into decline in this second phase of the judges period becomes even more pronounced with Gideon's son Abimelech (9:1-57). Abimelech's mother, a Canaanite, was a concubine or a woman servant whom Gideon had taken as a wife. Abimelech declares himself king over Israel after Gideon's death. He kills Gideon's seventy other Israelite sons to solidify his power. He enlists the support of his mother's people, the residents of Shechem. However, Abimelech eventually falls out of favor even with the Shechemites and ends up destroying their town and killing all the inhabitants of Shechem. Finally, Abimelech himself is killed in an ignoble manner as God's repayment for the disgraceful way in which he ruled over Israel (9:56-57). Previous and effective judges like Ehud and Deborah had united Israel, defeated the enemy, and praised God for their victories. Abimelech does the opposite: He causes divisions within Israel, kills his own people, and fights for his own honor and glory. Abimelech is a sign that the strategy of leading Israel through the temporary leaders called judges is in serious danger of unraveling.

The two minor judges who conclude this second phase, Tola and Jair (10:1-5), provide a parallel to the pair of major judges in this section. The major judge Gideon had been somewhat successful. In a similar way, Tola, the first minor judge, likewise "rose to deliver Israel." But just as the second major judge, Abimelech, had been a failure and gained nothing for Israel, so, too, there is no notice that the second minor judge, Jair, accomplished any deliverance or victory for Israel. The period of the judges has clearly moved into a transition into decline in this second phase. The third phase of the individual judge accounts will slide even further into internal dissension, fragmentation, civil war, and tragedy with the stories of Jephthah (10:6–11:15) and Samson (13:1–16:31). But that downward slide has already begun in this second phase with Gideon, Abimelech, Jair, and Tola.

One recurring image that binds together the stories of Gideon and Abimelech is that of the rock or stone. The first rock is the one on which Gideon sets his offering or present to the angel of God. The angel miraculously causes fire to burn on the rock, consuming Gideon's offering (6:17-21). In this case, the rock is part of a sign of reassurance to Gideon that God is indeed powerfully present with him as he fights the enemy. The second rock or stone image is the "one stone" on which Abimelech kills the seventy sons of Gideon in order to protect his arrogant claim to power (9:5, 18). The third stone is the "millstone" that "one woman" throws from atop the city wall of Shechem onto Abimelech's head, crushing his skull. Lying half-dead next to the millstone, Abimelech orders his servant to kill him with a sword so that people will not say of Abimelech, "A woman killed him" (9:53-54). In these stories, the motif of the stone moves from a sign of divine assurance for Gideon to the stone as an executioner's block for the murder of seventy of Abimelech's half-brothers to a skull-crushing millstone that brings poetic justice onto Abimelech's own head. The stone image further illustrates the transition from faithfulness to disaster in the stories of Gideon and Abimelech.

Judges 6:1–8:35, Gideon: From Idol Breaker to Idol Maker

OVERVIEW

Two features of the story of Gideon the judge merit special attention by the reader. The first feature involves the important alterations or additions to the normal judge cycles of events, first given in 2:11-19. The elements of that recurring cycle include (1) Israel's doing evil, (2) the Lord's becoming angry and sending enemies against Israel, (3) Israel's crying in distress, and (4) the Lord's sending judges to save them. But when the judge died, Israel again did evil, and the cycle would repeat. The Gideon story modifies and expands some of these cyclical elements. First of all, the nature of Israel's evil is left unspecified in the early judge stories (3:12; 4:1). The Gideon account, however, charges the Israelites with the specific and serious evil of worshiping idols and other gods (6:10; 8:24-27, 33-35). Second, the severity of the oppression of the enemy (the Midianites, the Amalekites, and people of the east) is spelled out in much more detail than in the earliest judges accounts (6:2-6). Third, God had previously responded to Israel's cry of distress by immediately sending a judge to save them. In the Gideon story, however, God first rebukes the Israelites for their worship of other gods through the judgment speech of a prophet (6:7-10). Fourth, the Gideon story greatly expands the process of raising up or calling a judge. Gideon is hesitant and resistant to God's call (6:11-24). When Gideon does finally accept God's call to be a judge, he acts like a secretive and cowardly trickster in need of constant reassurance. He is not the bold, confident, and courageous military leader we have seen before in Ehud and Deborah (6:25-40; 7:9-15). Finally, Gideon's function as judge is to be not only a military leader but also a religious leader who unifies the people in the praise and worship of the Lord. The Song of Deborah and Barak in Judges 5, which precedes the Gideon story, illustrates this religious function of the judge. Gideon does well in this regard early on when he breaks down an idol and pulls down an altar to the pagan god Baal (6:25-32). However, by the end of his career, Gideon himself constructs an object that becomes an idol that the Israelites worship as a god (8:25-28). Unlike the Deborah story, which ends in the praise of the Lord, Gideon's story ends in the worship of the Canaanite god Baal-berith (8:33). All of these changes to the typical judges cycle suggest that we have entered into a new and more negative phase in the judges era.

A second feature of the Gideon story is the number of allusions to other important biblical figures and events that echo throughout the episodes. The exodus out of Egypt (Exodus 14–15), the call of Moses (Exodus 3), the idolatry of the golden calf at Mt. Sinai (Exodus 32), the golden calves of King Jeroboam (1 Kings 12), Micah's idolatrous ephod of silver (Judges 17–18), the angels' visit to Abraham and Sarah (Genesis 18), Jacob's combative encounter with God and his name change to "Israel" at Penuel (Genesis 32), Elijah's encounter with the Baal prophets and the burned sacrifice on the altar on Mt. Carmel (1 Kgs 18:20-40), and Joshua's victory at Jericho with the trumpets and the falling city walls all find echoes in this Gideon story. These reverberations suggest that an earlier version of the Gideon story has been significantly reshaped and edited in dialogue with a wide range of other biblical traditions.[38] The task in the commentary below will be to determine the function of these many echoes in the interpretation of the stories. In general, these parallels will reflect negatively on Gideon's career. Gideon is somewhat successful in his military victories, but in the end he loses the most important battle, which is trusting the Lord and keeping Israel faithful.

---

38. A. Graeme Auld, "Gideon: Hacking at the Heart of the Old Testament," *VT* 39 (1989) 257-67.

Judges 6:1-32, A Timid Gideon Pulls Down Baal's Altar

6 Again the Israelites did evil in the eyes of the LORD, and for seven years he gave them into the hands of the Midianites. ²Because the power of Midian was so oppressive, the Israelites prepared shelters for themselves in mountain clefts, caves and strongholds. ³Whenever the Israelites planted their crops, the Midianites, Amalekites and other eastern peoples invaded the country. ⁴They camped on the land and ruined the crops all the way to Gaza and did not spare a living thing for Israel, neither sheep nor cattle nor donkeys. ⁵They came up with their livestock and their tents like swarms of locusts. It was impossible to count the men and their camels; they invaded the land to ravage it. ⁶Midian so impoverished the Israelites that they cried out to the LORD for help.

⁷When the Israelites cried to the LORD because of Midian, ⁸he sent them a prophet, who said, "This is what the LORD, the God of Israel, says: I brought you up out of Egypt, out of the land of slavery. ⁹I snatched you from the power of Egypt and from the hand of all your oppressors. I drove them from before you and gave you their land. ¹⁰I said to you, 'I am the LORD your God; do not worship the gods of the Amorites, in whose land you live.' But you have not listened to me."

¹¹The angel of the LORD came and sat down under the oak in Ophrah that belonged to Joash the Abiezrite, where his son Gideon was threshing wheat in a winepress to keep it from the Midianites. ¹²When the angel of the LORD appeared to Gideon, he said, "The LORD is with you, mighty warrior."

¹³"But sir," Gideon replied, "if the LORD is with us, why has all this happened to us? Where are all his wonders that our fathers told us about when they said, 'Did not the LORD bring us up out of Egypt?' But now the LORD has abandoned us and put us into the hand of Midian."

¹⁴The LORD turned to him and said, "Go in the strength you have and save Israel out of Midian's hand. Am I not sending you?"

¹⁵"But Lord,ᵃ" Gideon asked, "how can I save Israel? My clan is the weakest in Manasseh, and I am the least in my family."

ᵃ15 Or sir

6 The Israelites did what was evil in the sight of the LORD, and the LORD gave them into the hand of Midian seven years. ²The hand of Midian prevailed over Israel; and because of Midian the Israelites provided for themselves hiding places in the mountains, caves and strongholds. ³For whenever the Israelites put in seed, the Midianites and the Amalekites and the people of the east would come up against them. ⁴They would encamp against them and destroy the produce of the land, as far as the neighborhood of Gaza, and leave no sustenance in Israel, and no sheep or ox or donkey. ⁵For they and their livestock would come up, and they would even bring their tents, as thick as locusts; neither they nor their camels could be counted; so they wasted the land as they came in. ⁶Thus Israel was greatly impoverished because of Midian; and the Israelites cried out to the LORD for help.

⁷When the Israelites cried to the LORD on account of the Midianites, ⁸the LORD sent a prophet to the Israelites; and he said to them, "Thus says the LORD, the God of Israel: I led you up from Egypt, and brought you out of the house of slavery; ⁹and I delivered you from the hand of the Egyptians, and from the hand of all who oppressed you, and drove them out before you, and gave you their land; ¹⁰and I said to you, 'I am the LORD your God; you shall not pay reverence to the gods of the Amorites, in whose land you live.' But you have not given heed to my voice."

¹¹Now the angel of the LORD came and sat under the oak at Ophrah, which belonged to Joash the Abiezrite, as his son Gideon was beating out wheat in the wine press, to hide it from the Midianites. ¹²The angel of the LORD appeared to him and said to him, "The LORD is with you, you mighty warrior." ¹³Gideon answered him, "But sir, if the LORD is with us, why then has all this happened to us? And where are all his wonderful deeds that our ancestors recounted to us, saying, 'Did not the LORD bring us up from Egypt?' But now the LORD has cast us off, and given us into the hand of Midian." ¹⁴Then the LORD turned to him and said, "Go in this might of yours and

NIV

¹⁶The Lord answered, "I will be with you, and you will strike down all the Midianites together."

¹⁷Gideon replied, "If now I have found favor in your eyes, give me a sign that it is really you talking to me. ¹⁸Please do not go away until I come back and bring my offering and set it before you."

And the Lord said, "I will wait until you return."

¹⁹Gideon went in, prepared a young goat, and from an ephah^a of flour he made bread without yeast. Putting the meat in a basket and its broth in a pot, he brought them out and offered them to him under the oak.

²⁰The angel of God said to him, "Take the meat and the unleavened bread, place them on this rock, and pour out the broth." And Gideon did so. ²¹With the tip of the staff that was in his hand, the angel of the Lord touched the meat and the unleavened bread. Fire flared from the rock, consuming the meat and the bread. And the angel of the Lord disappeared. ²²When Gideon realized that it was the angel of the Lord, he exclaimed, "Ah, Sovereign Lord! I have seen the angel of the Lord face to face!"

²³But the Lord said to him, "Peace! Do not be afraid. You are not going to die."

²⁴So Gideon built an altar to the Lord there and called it The Lord is Peace. To this day it stands in Ophrah of the Abiezrites.

²⁵That same night the Lord said to him, "Take the second bull from your father's herd, the one seven years old.^b Tear down your father's altar to Baal and cut down the Asherah pole^c beside it. ²⁶Then build a proper kind of^d altar to the Lord your God on the top of this height. Using the wood of the Asherah pole that you cut down, offer the second^e bull as a burnt offering."

²⁷So Gideon took ten of his servants and did as the Lord told him. But because he was afraid of his family and the men of the town, he did it at night rather than in the daytime.

²⁸In the morning when the men of the town got up, there was Baal's altar, demolished, with

^a19 That is, probably about 3/5 bushel (about 22 liters)   ^b25 Or Take a full-grown, mature bull from your father's herd   ^c25 That is, a symbol of the goddess Asherah; here and elsewhere in Judges   ^d26 Or build with layers of stone an   ^e26 Or full-grown; also in verse 28

NRSV

deliver Israel from the hand of Midian; I hereby commission you." ¹⁵He responded, "But sir, how can I deliver Israel? My clan is the weakest in Manasseh, and I am the least in my family." ¹⁶The Lord said to him, "But I will be with you, and you shall strike down the Midianites, every one of them." ¹⁷Then he said to him, "If now I have found favor with you, then show me a sign that it is you who speak with me. ¹⁸Do not depart from here until I come to you, and bring out my present, and set it before you." And he said, "I will stay until you return."

¹⁹So Gideon went into his house and prepared a kid, and unleavened cakes from an ephah of flour; the meat he put in a basket, and the broth he put in a pot, and brought them to him under the oak and presented them. ²⁰The angel of God said to him, "Take the meat and the unleavened cakes, and put them on this rock, and pour out the broth." And he did so. ²¹Then the angel of the Lord reached out the tip of the staff that was in his hand, and touched the meat and the unleavened cakes; and fire sprang up from the rock and consumed the meat and the unleavened cakes; and the angel of the Lord vanished from his sight. ²²Then Gideon perceived that it was the angel of the Lord; and Gideon said, "Help me, Lord God! For I have seen the angel of the Lord face to face." ²³But the Lord said to him, "Peace be to you; do not fear, you shall not die." ²⁴Then Gideon built an altar there to the Lord, and called it, The Lord is peace. To this day it still stands at Ophrah, which belongs to the Abiezrites.

²⁵That night the Lord said to him, "Take your father's bull, the second bull seven years old, and pull down the altar of Baal that belongs to your father, and cut down the sacred pole^a that is beside it; ²⁶and build an altar to the Lord your God on the top of the stronghold here, in proper order; then take the second bull, and offer it as a burnt offering with the wood of the sacred pole^a that you shall cut down." ²⁷So Gideon took ten of his servants, and did as the Lord had told him; but because he was too afraid of his family and the townspeople to do it by day, he did it by night.

²⁸When the townspeople rose early in the morning, the altar of Baal was broken down, and the sacred pole^a beside it was cut down, and the

^a Heb Asherah

NIV

the Asherah pole beside it cut down and the second bull sacrificed on the newly built altar!

²⁹They asked each other, "Who did this?"

When they carefully investigated, they were told, "Gideon son of Joash did it."

³⁰The men of the town demanded of Joash, "Bring out your son. He must die, because he has broken down Baal's altar and cut down the Asherah pole beside it."

³¹But Joash replied to the hostile crowd around him, "Are you going to plead Baal's cause? Are you trying to save him? Whoever fights for him shall be put to death by morning! If Baal really is a god, he can defend himself when someone breaks down his altar." ³²So that day they called Gideon "Jerub-Baal,ᵃ" saying, "Let Baal contend with him," because he broke down Baal's altar.

ᵃ32 Jerub-Baal means let Baal contend.

NRSV

second bull was offered on the altar that had been built. ²⁹So they said to one another, "Who has done this?" After searching and inquiring, they were told, "Gideon son of Joash did it." ³⁰Then the townspeople said to Joash, "Bring out your son, so that he may die, for he has pulled down the altar of Baal and cut down the sacred poleᵃ beside it." ³¹But Joash said to all who were arrayed against him, "Will you contend for Baal? Or will you defend his cause? Whoever contends for him shall be put to death by morning. If he is a god, let him contend for himself, because his altar has been pulled down." ³²Therefore on that day Gideonᵇ was called Jerubbaal, that is to say, "Let Baal contend against him," because he pulled down his altar.

ᵃ Heb *Asherah*   ᵇ Heb *he*

COMMENTARY

The story of Gideon is a tale of a leader who changes from a timid but faithful leader who relies on God to a bold but ultimately unfaithful leader who takes matters into his own hands. Militarily, Gideon ends up relying on his own skill and direction rather than God. Religiously, Gideon ends up crafting an idol with his own hands that leads Israel away from God. As we begin the Gideon story, however, we encounter a faithful Gideon who works in the mold of Moses when he was called to lead Israel out of the slavery of Egypt (Exodus 3).

6:1-10. The familiar refrain of v. 1 marks the start of another major episode in the judges stories: Israel again does evil in the sight of the Lord (see 2:11; 3:7, 12; 4:1). The quick return to evil on Israel's part is disappointing in the light of the exuberant song that praised God's faithfulness so strongly in Judges 5. In response to Israel's ingratitude, God predictably hands Israel over to an enemy. The previous enemy in chaps. 4–5 had been the native Canaanites. The defeat of the Canaanite army left a power vacuum in Canaan, which allowed marauding desert tribes from the east to invade the land. Thus the enemy God

sends against Israel is the desert peoples of the "Midianites," "Amalekites," and "the people of the east" (v. 3). These roving desert nations were traditional enemies of Israel dating back to the period of Moses and the wilderness (Exod 17:8-16; Num 31; Deut 25:17-19). The effects of their attacks against Israel are described in great detail. Their military incursions force Israel to hide and live in mountain caves like cowering animals (v. 2). The desert marauders destroy Israel's crops and steal all their livestock (vv. 3-4). The vast number of Midianites is like a locust plague swarming over the land, causing images of the plagues of Egypt to sweep across the mind's eye (Exodus 7–13). This time, however, it is Israel who suffers God's torments. Israel's economic devastation is immense (v. 6). Predictably, Israel "cried out to the Lᴏʀᴅ for help."

On the heels of this cry, the reader has come to expect God's swift appointment of a judge or deliverer (3:9, 15). In 4:3-4, God had worked through a woman prophet named Deborah to guide Israel's general Barak to victory. Now in 6:7-8, God again raises up a prophet. But this prophet has a mission different from that of Deborah, who immediately called up Israel's army to fight. This unnamed prophet rebukes Israel, reminding the people that their cry of distress is not to be taken as an automatic guarantee of God's gracious response. The prophet rehearses God's past faithfulness in liberating Israel from Egypt and bringing them to the land of Canaan (vv. 8-9). The single most important obligation Israel had in its relationship with this faithful God was exclusive loyalty to the Lord and the worship of no other gods (v. 10). But God concludes in the words of the anonymous prophet, "You have not given heed to my voice." There is something of a narrative pause here, and we wonder as readers whether God has reached the limits of divine patience. Will God decide at this point not to send a judge to deliver Israel as God had done in the past?

6:11-24. The answer to the question of whether God will respond to Israel's cry comes in the form of an "angel of the LORD." God's deliverance in chaps. 4–5 had begun with Deborah the judge, who "used to sit under the palm of Deborah" (4:5). Similarly, God's deliverance in chap. 6 begins with the "angel" who "sat under the oak at Ophrah" (v. 11). The oak tree belongs to an Israelite named Joash from the Abiezrite clan, which is part of the tribe of Manasseh (Josh 17:2). Joash has a son, Gideon, who has been secretly threshing grain in the unlikely locale of a winepress in order to avoid detection by the Midianites (v. 11). For the first time in Judges, an angel of the Lord speaks directly to one who will become a judge—that is, to Gideon. We have heard this angel speak before to all Israel in 2:1-5. In that speech, the angel had reaffirmed God's unconditional commitment to the covenant with Israel. Yet at the same time, the angel condemned Israel for not tearing down the altars of the Canaanite gods in their midst. This tension between God's faithfulness and Israel's continual failure to maintain exclusive loyalty to the Lord alone returns as a major theme here in the Gideon story.

The angel addresses young Gideon, hiding in the winepress, with words of affirmation: "The LORD is with you, you mighty warrior." The dissonance between this timid young man hiding in fear from the enemy and the angel's description of him as a "mighty warrior" introduces an ongoing theme in the early part of Gideon's career as a judge. But Gideon is interested in discussing another dissonance with the angel. If the angel's assurance that "the LORD is with us" is true, and if the prophet's earlier words about God saving Israel from Egypt are true, then why "has the LORD cast us off and given us into the hand of Midian" (v. 13)? The angel, to whom the question is addressed, suddenly becomes "the LORD." The Lord turns and points at Gideon and says, in effect, "You are the answer to your own question." God orders Gideon to use "this might of yours" to go and save Israel from the hand of Midian. The Lord concludes by answering Gideon's question with another question: "Am I not sending you?"

However, Gideon intends this encounter with God to remain in the realm of the theoretical and abstract. Gideon does not anticipate becoming an active part of the solution to the problem he posed to the angel. Thus Gideon strenuously objects to God's commission to save Israel from the Midianites. Gideon asks, "How can I deliver Israel?" He is the weakest member of the smallest clan of the tribe of Manasseh. Gideon does not have the qualifications or the resources for the job. But in the ways of the Lord, Gideon's weakness is a virtue. Gideon's inadequacy allows room for what is most important and determinative in this mission: God's presence and God's strength. What really matters in the end, says God, is that "I will be with you" (v. 16). Gideon is still not satisfied. He trades on God's favoring of him and asks for an additional "sign" to prove that "it is you who speak with me" (v. 17).

The angel promptly responds to Gideon's request and miraculously lights a fire on a rock with the tip of a staff. The fire burns Gideon's sacrifice of meat and unleavened bread. Then the angel disappears as soon as the sign or proof of the angel's divine identity is given (vv. 19-21). When Gideon sees this sign, he knows he has seen "the angel of the LORD face to face." A recurring tradition in the OT states that no human can see the dangerous holiness of God face to face and live (13:22; Gen 16:13; 32:30; Exod 20:19; 33:23). Although God's visible angelic form has disappeared, the Lord's invisible presence remains and soothes the terrified Gideon with the words, "Peace be to you. . . . You shall not die." Gideon gratefully responds to this promise by doing the same thing Jacob had done when the angel appeared to him with similar assurance that "I will be with you" (Gen 28:10-22). Like Jacob, Gideon builds an altar near the rock where the sacrifice had been burned. In the light of God's promise of peace, Gideon calls the place "The Lord is peace." At his hometown of Ophrah, Gideon sets up an altar to the Lord (v. 24).

This opening portrait of Gideon connects with three other biblical figures: Moses, Elijah, and Jacob. God's call to Gideon to save an oppressed Israel mirrors God's call to Moses to deliver an enslaved Israel from Egypt in Exodus 3. Like Gideon, Moses objected to God's call, but God promised Moses, "I will be with you" and then gave a "sign" of reassurance (Exod 3:11-12). God also infused Moses' staff with miraculous power to convince the people of God's presence with him (Exod 4:1-5), just as the angel used a staff to light a fire as proof for Gideon. The miraculous fire on the altar is also reminiscent of the prophet Elijah and his contest with the prophets of Baal on Mt. Carmel when the Lord caused a water-soaked altar built by Elijah to burst into flames (1 Kgs 18:20-40). And like Gideon, the ancestor Jacob built an altar at a special stone or rock where God appeared and gave the place a name (Gen 28:10-22). Like Gideon, Jacob also saw God face to face and lived when he wrestled with God at Penuel (Gen 32:30). This cluster of associations with some of the most important figures of the OT raises enormous expectations about Gideon's tenure as judge and deliverer of Israel. Will Gideon be the one to end Israel's oppression, like Moses, to defeat the Baal cults of Canaan, like Elijah, or even to wrestle a blessing from God, like Jacob?

6:25-32. God begins Gideon's career as judge by instructing him to use a bull to pull down his father's altar. This family altar was dedicated to the worship, not of the Lord, but of the Canaanite god Baal, and the accompanying sacred pole was for the worship of Asherah, a Canaanite goddess and consort to Baal. The bull was also a frequent image for the god Baal. Thus Gideon uses a bull to pull down the altar of Baal the bull. Then Gideon kills the bull and sacrifices it on the new altar dedicated to the worship of the Lord. The initial temptation to cheer enthusiastically for Gideon's brave act of religious reform is tempered by a note concerning his timidity; he does the deed at night and in secret for fear of his family (v. 27). Gideon has not yet fully lived up to the angel's description of him as a bold and "mighty warrior" (v. 12).

The townspeople are outraged when they discover the desecrated Baal altar the next morning. When they determine Gideon is responsible and seek to kill him, Gideon's father intervenes and urges the people to let the god Baal fight his own fight. "Will you contend for Baal?" he asks. "If he is a god, let him contend for himself" (v. 31). The Lord had earlier told Gideon that victory would come not because of Gideon's human strength or weakness but because of the Lord's presence and power. Gideon's father applies the same test to the god Baal. If Baal is truly a god, then Baal by his own power will exact revenge on Gideon for destroying his altar. The incident becomes the occasion for a second name given to Gideon: "Jerubbaal." The name is taken to mean "Let Baal contend [רִיב *rîb*] against him" (v. 32). Some scholars believe "Jerubbaal" may have referred to an earlier individual with whom the later and separate tradition of Gideon became secondarily identified. The story of Abimelech, son of Jerubbaal, in Judges 9 consistently uses only the name "Jerubbaal." Moreover, other OT references to the judges mention only Jerubbaal and not Gideon (1 Sam 12:11; 2 Sam 11:21). However, the present form of the text clearly attaches the two names to one person: "Jerubbaal (that is, Gideon)" (7:1; 8:35). Gideon's oscillation between two names will reflect his double-sided character. Early on, Gideon is a faithful but weak servant of the Lord, a destroyer of idols and entirely dependent on God's leading. Later, Gideon will become a bold military leader who relies not on God but on his own human skill. He will end up making God into his own humanly crafted idol (8:24-27). Such a complex character may well deserve at least two different names.

Reflections

1. Like Moses and Jeremiah and countless others whom God has called to service, Gideon felt inadequate to do the task God had given him. The Bible continually reminds us, however, that success in the vocations to which God summons people depends primarily on God's presence and God's power working in and through them. God will work in spite of and sometimes through their weaknesses. When the apostle Paul repeatedly complained to God about the "thorn in his flesh" that made him weak, the Lord replied, "My grace is sufficient for you, for power is made perfect in weakness" (2 Cor 12:9 NRSV). Elsewhere Paul describes the gospel of a crucified and broken Messiah as foolishness for unbelievers. But that portrait of suffering love on the cross is the power and wisdom of God, which exceeds all human wisdom and power. Paul reminds his hearers that they are in the same cruciform mold as their Lord: "Consider your own call, brothers and sisters: not many of you were wise by human standards, not many were powerful, not many were of noble birth." But God chose what was weak and despised in the world so that "no one might boast in the presence of God" (1 Cor 1:26-29 NRSV). The God of Gideon is the God of Jesus Christ, choosing the weakest of the weak to accomplish God's mission in the world.

2. In the course of being called by God, Gideon raises a recurring issue in the life of faith. God has been faithful in the past and has promised God's blessing into the present and the future. In the midst of his people's blessing, however, Gideon asks the hard question: "If the LORD is with us, why then has all this happened to us?" The Bible provides many different responses to that question of theodicy posed elsewhere in the psalms of lament, the confession of Jeremiah, or the complaints of the righteous sufferer Job. The answers to the "Why?" of suffering varies, depending on the circumstances. Sometimes the sin of the people has brought it upon them. Sometimes God uses evil to accomplish a greater good (Gen 50:20). Sometimes the reason for suffering remains a profound mystery without any rational resolution, as in the book of Job. In the case of Gideon's question and circumstance, the narrative gives two responses. One response is implied already in the beginning of the story: "The Israelites did what was evil in the sight of the LORD" (6:1). Their own sin brought their enemy upon them. But God's second and more direct response to Gideon's query about their suffering is this: "Go . . . and deliver Israel" (6:14). Get involved. Do something about it. But at the same time, remember that success depends on the faithfulness and promise of God: "I will be with you" (6:16).

3. Gideon is the first judge whose inner character and feelings are explored in depth. What emerges is a complex character who will develop and change over his lifetime. His two names, Gideon and Jerubbaal, suggest a split personality, two inner masters fighting to control the one person. Gideon begins in this early part of his story as faithful and dependent on God's guidance. At the same time, he is timid, weak, and afraid. Later, Gideon will become much bolder and stronger as a leader. But he will also rely less on God and more on his own power and wisdom. In the end, he will lead Israel into idolatry, even as he tries to be faithful to God and refuses the kingship offered to him by the Israelites.

The tug of war within Gideon reflects the tensions and divided loyalties within many of God's people who seek to be faithful to God and yet who feel constantly pulled to other commitments and loyalties. We struggle to pull down altars to other gods and allegiances in our lives and erect a true altar of worship and service to the Lord. But we remain divided and wrestle with God all through our lives. As a desperate father pleaded with Jesus to help his afflicted child, he knew his own divided self, "I believe; help my unbelief!" (Mark 9:24 NRSV). The apostle Paul also knew of this civil war within his own body: "For I do not do the good I want, but the evil I do not want is what I do" (Rom 7:19 NRSV). Gideon's own divided character testifies to these inner civil wars of allegiance that rage within many who struggle to be faithful servants of God.

Judges 6:33–8:3, Gideon's Victory

NIV	NRSV

NIV

³³Now all the Midianites, Amalekites and other eastern peoples joined forces and crossed over the Jordan and camped in the Valley of Jezreel. ³⁴Then the Spirit of the LORD came upon Gideon, and he blew a trumpet, summoning the Abiezrites to follow him. ³⁵He sent messengers throughout Manasseh, calling them to arms, and also into Asher, Zebulun and Naphtali, so that they too went up to meet them.

³⁶Gideon said to God, "If you will save Israel by my hand as you have promised— ³⁷look, I will place a wool fleece on the threshing floor. If there is dew only on the fleece and all the ground is dry, then I will know that you will save Israel by my hand, as you said." ³⁸And that is what happened. Gideon rose early the next day; he squeezed the fleece and wrung out the dew—a bowlful of water.

³⁹Then Gideon said to God, "Do not be angry with me. Let me make just one more request. Allow me one more test with the fleece. This time make the fleece dry and the ground covered with dew." ⁴⁰That night God did so. Only the fleece was dry; all the ground was covered with dew.

7 Early in the morning, Jerub-Baal (that is, Gideon) and all his men camped at the spring of Harod. The camp of Midian was north of them in the valley near the hill of Moreh. ²The LORD said to Gideon, "You have too many men for me to deliver Midian into their hands. In order that Israel may not boast against me that her own strength has saved her, ³announce now to the people, 'Anyone who trembles with fear may turn back and leave Mount Gilead.'" So twenty-two thousand men left, while ten thousand remained.

⁴But the LORD said to Gideon, "There are still too many men. Take them down to the water, and I will sift them for you there. If I say, 'This one shall go with you,' he shall go; but if I say, 'This one shall not go with you,' he shall not go."

⁵So Gideon took the men down to the water. There the LORD told him, "Separate those who lap the water with their tongues like a dog from those who kneel down to drink." ⁶Three hundred men lapped with their hands to their mouths. All the rest got down on their knees to drink.

NRSV

³³Then all the Midianites and the Amalekites and the people of the east came together, and crossing the Jordan they encamped in the Valley of Jezreel. ³⁴But the spirit of the LORD took possession of Gideon; and he sounded the trumpet, and the Abiezrites were called out to follow him. ³⁵He sent messengers throughout all Manasseh, and they too were called out to follow him. He also sent messengers to Asher, Zebulun, and Naphtali, and they went up to meet them.

³⁶Then Gideon said to God, "In order to see whether you will deliver Israel by my hand, as you have said, ³⁷I am going to lay a fleece of wool on the threshing floor; if there is dew on the fleece alone, and it is dry on all the ground, then I shall know that you will deliver Israel by my hand, as you have said." ³⁸And it was so. When he rose early next morning and squeezed the fleece, he wrung enough dew from the fleece to fill a bowl with water. ³⁹Then Gideon said to God, "Do not let your anger burn against me, let me speak one more time; let me, please, make trial with the fleece just once more; let it be dry only on the fleece, and on all the ground let there be dew." ⁴⁰And God did so that night. It was dry on the fleece only, and on all the ground there was dew.

7 Then Jerubbaal (that is, Gideon) and all the troops that were with him rose early and encamped beside the spring of Harod; and the camp of Midian was north of them, below^a the hill of Moreh, in the valley.

²The LORD said to Gideon, "The troops with you are too many for me to give the Midianites into their hand. Israel would only take the credit away from me, saying, 'My own hand has delivered me.' ³Now therefore proclaim this in the hearing of the troops, 'Whoever is fearful and trembling, let him return home.'" Thus Gideon sifted them out;^b twenty-two thousand returned, and ten thousand remained.

⁴Then the LORD said to Gideon, "The troops are still too many; take them down to the water and I will sift them out for you there. When I

^a Heb *from*   ^b Cn: Heb *home, and depart from Mount Gilead'"*

[NIV column]

7The LORD said to Gideon, "With the three hundred men that lapped I will save you and give the Midianites into your hands. Let all the other men go, each to his own place." 8So Gideon sent the rest of the Israelites to their tents but kept the three hundred, who took over the provisions and trumpets of the others.

Now the camp of Midian lay below him in the valley. 9During that night the LORD said to Gideon, "Get up, go down against the camp, because I am going to give it into your hands. 10If you are afraid to attack, go down to the camp with your servant Purah 11and listen to what they are saying. Afterward, you will be encouraged to attack the camp." So he and Purah his servant went down to the outposts of the camp. 12The Midianites, the Amalekites and all the other eastern peoples had settled in the valley, thick as locusts. Their camels could no more be counted than the sand on the seashore.

13Gideon arrived just as a man was telling a friend his dream. "I had a dream," he was saying. "A round loaf of barley bread came tumbling into the Midianite camp. It struck the tent with such force that the tent overturned and collapsed."

14His friend responded, "This can be nothing other than the sword of Gideon son of Joash, the Israelite. God has given the Midianites and the whole camp into his hands."

15When Gideon heard the dream and its interpretation, he worshiped God. He returned to the camp of Israel and called out, "Get up! The LORD has given the Midianite camp into your hands." 16Dividing the three hundred men into three companies, he placed trumpets and empty jars in the hands of all of them, with torches inside.

17"Watch me," he told them. "Follow my lead. When I get to the edge of the camp, do exactly as I do. 18When I and all who are with me blow our trumpets, then from all around the camp blow yours and shout, 'For the LORD and for Gideon.'"

19Gideon and the hundred men with him reached the edge of the camp at the beginning of the middle watch, just after they had changed the guard. They blew their trumpets and broke the jars that were in their hands. 20The three companies blew the trumpets and smashed the jars. Grasping the torches in their left hands and hold-

[NRSV column]

say, 'This one shall go with you,' he shall go with you; and when I say, 'This one shall not go with you,' he shall not go." 5So he brought the troops down to the water; and the LORD said to Gideon, "All those who lap the water with their tongues, as a dog laps, you shall put to one side; all those who kneel down to drink, putting their hands to their mouths,[a] you shall put to the other side." 6The number of those that lapped was three hundred; but all the rest of the troops knelt down to drink water. 7Then the LORD said to Gideon, "With the three hundred that lapped I will deliver you, and give the Midianites into your hand. Let all the others go to their homes." 8So he took the jars of the troops from their hands,[b] and their trumpets; and he sent all the rest of Israel back to their own tents, but retained the three hundred. The camp of Midian was below him in the valley.

9That same night the LORD said to him, "Get up, attack the camp; for I have given it into your hand. 10But if you fear to attack, go down to the camp with your servant Purah; 11and you shall hear what they say, and afterward your hands shall be strengthened to attack the camp." Then he went down with his servant Purah to the outposts of the armed men that were in the camp. 12The Midianites and the Amalekites and all the people of the east lay along the valley as thick as locusts; and their camels were without number, countless as the sand on the seashore. 13When Gideon arrived, there was a man telling a dream to his comrade; and he said, "I had a dream, and in it a cake of barley bread tumbled into the camp of Midian, and came to the tent, and struck it so that it fell; it turned upside down, and the tent collapsed." 14And his comrade answered, "This is no other than the sword of Gideon son of Joash, a man of Israel; into his hand God has given Midian and all the army."

15When Gideon heard the telling of the dream and its interpretation, he worshiped; and he returned to the camp of Israel, and said, "Get up; for the LORD has given the army of Midian into your hand." 16After he divided the three hundred men into three companies, and put trumpets into

---

[a] Heb places the words *putting their hands to their mouths* after the word *lapped* in verse 6   [b] Cn: Heb *So the people took provisions in their hands*

NIV

ing in their right hands the trumpets they were to blow, they shouted, "A sword for the LORD and for Gideon!" [21]While each man held his position around the camp, all the Midianites ran, crying out as they fled.

[22]When the three hundred trumpets sounded, the LORD caused the men throughout the camp to turn on each other with their swords. The army fled to Beth Shittah toward Zererah as far as the border of Abel Meholah near Tabbath. [23]Israelites from Naphtali, Asher and all Manasseh were called out, and they pursued the Midianites. [24]Gideon sent messengers throughout the hill country of Ephraim, saying, "Come down against the Midianites and seize the waters of the Jordan ahead of them as far as Beth Barah."

So all the men of Ephraim were called out and they took the waters of the Jordan as far as Beth Barah. [25]They also captured two of the Midianite leaders, Oreb and Zeeb. They killed Oreb at the rock of Oreb, and Zeeb at the winepress of Zeeb. They pursued the Midianites and brought the heads of Oreb and Zeeb to Gideon, who was by the Jordan.

8 Now the Ephraimites asked Gideon, "Why have you treated us like this? Why didn't you call us when you went to fight Midian?" And they criticized him sharply.

[2]But he answered them, "What have I accomplished compared to you? Aren't the gleanings of Ephraim's grapes better than the full grape harvest of Abiezer? [3]God gave Oreb and Zeeb, the Midianite leaders, into your hands. What was I able to do compared to you?" At this, their resentment against him subsided.

NRSV

the hands of all of them, and empty jars, with torches inside the jars, [17]he said to them, "Look at me, and do the same; when I come to the outskirts of the camp, do as I do. [18]When I blow the trumpet, I and all who are with me, then you also blow the trumpets around the whole camp, and shout, 'For the LORD and for Gideon!'"

19So Gideon and the hundred who were with him came to the outskirts of the camp at the beginning of the middle watch, when they had just set the watch; and they blew the trumpets and smashed the jars that were in their hands. [20]So the three companies blew the trumpets and broke the jars, holding in their left hands the torches, and in their right hands the trumpets to blow; and they cried, "A sword for the LORD and for Gideon!" [21]Every man stood in his place all around the camp, and all the men in camp ran; they cried out and fled. [22]When they blew the three hundred trumpets, the LORD set every man's sword against his fellow and against all the army; and the army fled as far as Beth-shittah toward Zererah,[a] as far as the border of Abel-meholah, by Tabbath. [23]And the men of Israel were called out from Naphtali and from Asher and from all Manasseh, and they pursued after the Midianites.

24Then Gideon sent messengers throughout all the hill country of Ephraim, saying, "Come down against the Midianites and seize the waters against them, as far as Beth-barah, and also the Jordan." So all the men of Ephraim were called out, and they seized the waters as far as Beth-barah, and also the Jordan. [25]They captured the two captains of Midian, Oreb and Zeeb; they killed Oreb at the rock of Oreb, and Zeeb they killed at the wine press of Zeeb, as they pursued the Midianites. They brought the heads of Oreb and Zeeb to Gideon beyond the Jordan.

8 Then the Ephraimites said to him, "What have you done to us, not to call us when you went to fight against the Midianites?" And they upbraided him violently. [2]So he said to them, "What have I done now in comparison with you? Is not the gleaning of the grapes of Ephraim better than the vintage of Abiezer? [3]God has given into your hands the captains of Midian, Oreb and Zeeb; what have I been able to do in comparison with you?" When he said this, their anger against him subsided.

[a] Another reading is *Zeredah*

COMMENTARY

After God's call to Gideon and his secretive destruction of the Baal altar, Gideon faces his next challenge. He must lead a military battle against the Midianite and Amalekite invaders. He is successful in his military endeavors only because of God's involvement. But Gideon remains fearful and in need of reassurance from God until the end of this section, when he begins to assert more of himself and his own diplomatic skill as a leader.

6:33-40. "The spirit of the LORD" comes upon Gideon in preparation for the battle against the Midianites, the Amalekites, and other desert peoples of the east (v. 34). God's Spirit had once earlier come upon a judge, the model deliverer named Othniel (3:10). Then the Spirit had given Othniel the power and courage to unite Israel and defeat the enemy. In the case of Gideon, however, the Spirit of the Lord seems to have little effect in changing Gideon in any significant way. *Before* receiving the divine Spirit, Gideon had been timid, fearful, and in need of signs of reassurance (vv. 15, 17, 27). Now *after* receiving the Spirit, Gideon still remains tentative, doubtful, and in need of signs of reassurance (vv. 36-40; 7:9-15). When the Spirit of the Lord returns and comes upon later judges, like Jephthah and Samson, the unbridled power of the Spirit will create more negative and even disastrous consequences. Already with Gideon, the era of the judges inspired by a temporary divine Spirit has taken a negative turn, a decline that will become more pronounced as the period of the judges continues.

As Gideon musters his armies from some of the middle and northern tribes of Israel (Manasseh, Asher, Zebulun, and Naphtali), he asks God for a sign that "you will deliver Israel by my hand" (v. 36). He lays out fleece or wool shorn from sheep on the threshing floor overnight. If there is moist dew on the fleece alone and the ground remains dry, then Gideon will take that as a sign that God will deliver Israel. However, that dew would condense on wool and evaporate from the warmer stone floor of a threshing floor in the coolness of night is a completely natural and expected result in everyday experience. This may be a sign of a natural sort, but it is no miracle. So using the words of old Abraham when he once bargained

with God over the fate of Sodom and Gomorrah, Gideon says to God, "Do not let your anger burn against me, let me speak one more time" (v. 39; cf. Gen 18:32). Gideon requests that the opposite be done with respect to the dew and the fleece: This time the dew should appear on the ground but *not* on the fleece. Remarkably and patiently, God complies with this second request for a sign that will be more extraordinary than the first (vv. 39-40). Only then is Gideon ready to go off to battle.

7:1-23. God had chosen a weak and unlikely leader in Gideon (6:15). Similarly, God also desires a small and weak army to fight the Midianites. A small number of warriors in Israel's army would compel Israel to acknowledge that it was God alone who had won the victory, and not human strength. Israel could not boast, "My own hand has delivered me" (v. 2). Gideon begins with thirty-two thousand soldiers, which would have been an emormous army in this ancient period. The Hebrew word for "thousand" (אלף *'elep*) can also mean tribal "unit." Thus an earlier version of the story may have been about 32 "units" (not "thousands") of soldiers with perhaps ten soldiers in each unit, for a total of 320 soldiers. Even 320 would be a large army in this time period.

Whatever the earlier version, the text's present form presumes the huge army of 32,000 men. (We will later learn that the Midianite army numbers 120,000 soldiers!) God seeks to reduce the number of Gideon's army through two tests. The first test is drawn from the laws of the books of Deuteronomy. The law specifies that if any warrior is "afraid or disheartened," he should return home from battle lest he discourage the other troops (Deut 20:8). When Gideon instructs the fearful to return home, 22,000 men leave, and only 10,000 remain. Given Gideon's past fearfulness, we may wonder whether he was tempted to join those who went back home. Gideon does stay, perhaps a signal that he himself is beginning to change. Still not satisfied, God devises a second test to reduce the number of soldiers even more. All the fighters who kneel down at a watering hole and drink by putting their hands to their mouths are excluded. The tiny minority of 300 who lapped the water with their tongues like dogs are chosen as Gideon's little army (vv. 4-7). This small band of doglike soldiers will take on the hordes of Midianites, who are as "thick as locusts" so that they cannot be counted (v. 12; cf. 6:5).

God commands Gideon to attack, "for I have given it into your hand" (v. 9). Such divine assurance ought to have been sufficient grounds for Gideon's ready obedience. But God knows this fearful Gideon and offers him another sign of reassurance. Gideon and his servant sneak down to the enemy camp and overhear words spoken by the Midianites about their fear of Gideon and his army. Gideon is encouraged, worships God, and calls his soldiers to attack (vv. 9-15). Their unorthodox military strategy involves a nighttime raid as Gideon's men surround the enemy camp. Each of the 300 soldiers will blow a trumphet and then smash a clay jar that conceals a torch inside. The Midianites' still dark night will be pierced by the simultaneous sound of 300 trumpets coming from every direction and the explosion of light as 300 torches suddenly light up the night sky. The enemy soldiers will be so terrified and confused they will fight and kill one another. As Gideon's army performs this strategy to instill terror in the enemy, Gideon tells them to shout, "For the LORD and for Gideon!" (vv. 18, 20). The praise of Gideon along with the Lord may suggest a subtle shift in Gideon's perception of himself. Gideon had earlier felt that he was nothing (6:15) and the Lord was everything (7:15). But now in this shout Gideon claims a piece of the spotlight along with God.

This subtle shift is also apparent when we compare Gideon's attack in Judges 7 with Joshua's attack on the city of Jericho in Joshua 2. The tactics of Israel's army surrounding the enemy, blowing trumpets, and shouting all find a parallel in Joshua's conquest of Jericho. However, Joshua's command to shout did not give glory to Joshua himself but only to the Lord: "For the LORD has given you the city" (Josh 2:16). In contrast, Gideon desires to claim credit along with God in his shout: "For the LORD *and* for Gideon." Gideon is taking over some of God's prerogatives.

7:24–8:3. Gideon initially gathered his army from some of the middle and northern tribes of Israel in Canaan (Manasseh, Asher, Zebulun, and Naphtali; 6:35; 7:23). Gideon had not at first invited the important northern tribe of Ephraim to join in the battle. However, he does call them to help in the very last phase of the battle against the Midianites. They succeed in capturing the two "captains" of the Midianite army, Oreb ("Raven") and Zeeb ("Wolf"). The psalmist lists these two names as enemy leaders of Midian whom Israel had conquered during the time of the judges (Ps 83:11).

The warriors from the tribe of Ephraim bring the heads of Oreb and Zeeb to Gideon, but they also bring a complaint to him. They are angry that Gideon did not call them at the beginning of the conflict with Midian, and "they upbraided him violently" (8:1). The possibility of internal conflict or even civil war within Israel arises for the first time in the book of Judges. As the judges era continues, this internal conflict or social disintegration will emerge as a major theme as the judges become less and less effective as unifiers of the Israelite people. The book of Judges will end with an all-out civil war as Israelite tribes attack and nearly exterminate their brother tribe of Benjamin (Judges 20–21). This time the conflict between Gideon and the tribe of Ephraim does not end with civil war but with negotiated resolution. Gideon demonstrates diplomatic skill as he flatters the Ephraimites for achieving what Gideon could not do in capturing the two Midianite generals: "What have I been able to do in comparison to you?" Gideon has learned well from God's skill in responding to Gideon's own objections and laments. Gideon follows God's example and patiently offers a gracious response to the Ephraimites' complaint. Gideon soothes their anger and averts a crisis (8:2-3).

REFLECTIONS

1. Before going into battle, Gideon sets up a test for God involving the fleece of sheep's wool and the morning dew. Other biblical figures used conditions and tests to determine whether God was present and active in a given situation. Sometimes the conditions involved natural or ordinary needs. For example, Jacob agreed to accept the Lord as his God if the Lord would "give me bread to eat and clothing to wear" and return him "to my father's house in peace" (Gen 28:18-22 NRSV). At other times, miraculous or extraordinary signs of God's power were requested. Moses requested a sign that he could bring to the Israelites to convince them that God was the power behind his leadership. God gave him two miraculous signs: the healing of his leprous hand and the staff that turned into a serpent (Exod 4:1-9). Jesus also used both ordinary and miraculous signs of God's power in his ministry. In the story of the paralyzed man who was lowered through a hole in the roof, Jesus first spoke ordinary words, "Friend, your sins are forgiven you" (Luke 5:20 NRSV). But some onlookers grumbled that Jesus' words were blasphemy, since forgiving sins was something only God could do. Thus Jesus gave an extraordinary sign of God's power by healing the paralyzed man "so that you may know that the Son of Man has authority on earth to forgive sins" (Luke 5:24 NRSV).

Like Gideon, we yearn for signs, both ordinary and extraordinary, that God is alive and at work in our lives. The disciple Thomas wanted such tangible signs of Jesus' presence after the resurrection. Thomas was not satisfied with ordinary words and reports; he demanded to see the miracle of Jesus risen from the dead for himself. Jesus granted him that direct evidence of his presence. But Jesus also reminded him, "Blessed are those who have not seen and yet have come to believe" (John 20:29 NRSV). The story of Gideon reminds us of God's graciousness in giving us those occasional signs and glimpses of God's presence and power at work in our lives. Sometimes those signs are natural and ordinary glimpses of God's quiet blessings that are always there but often go unnoticed or unappreciated. At other times and more rarely, God may give us a more dramatic or extraordinary sign. Others may brush off such experiences as coincidence or blind chance, but the eyes of faith may perceive them as the hand of God. At still other times, God's people may yearn for a sign from God that never comes. At such times, we join the psalmist's lament and cry, "How long, O LORD? Will you forget me forever?/ How long will you hide your face from me?" (Ps 13:1 NRSV)?

2. One of the major thematic tensions in this section involves the balance between divine agency and human participation in accomplishing God's work in the world. On one hand, God reduces Gideon's huge army from 32,000 to 300 in order to demonstrate that the victory will rely primarily on God's power alone, and not on human strength. God is concerned that Israel will wrongly "take credit away from me, saying, 'My own hand has delivered me' " (7:2). On the other hand, Gideon inserts his own name in the shout of praise and glory associated with the victory to come: "For the LORD and for Gideon" (7:18-20).

This tension reflects a larger, ongoing dialogue within Scripture about the balance between divine agency and human responsibility. On the one hand, Moses emphasizes the primacy of God's action and the passivity of humans in the conflict with Pharaoh and Israel's exodus out of Egypt. Moses advises the Israelites, "The LORD will fight for you, and you have only to keep still" (Exod 14:14 NRSV). The apostle Paul speaks of the death of his human self and its replacement with Christ: "I have been crucified with Christ; and it is no longer I who live but it is Christ who lives in me" (Gal 2:19-20 NRSV). On the other hand, the Bible contains many laws and proverbs that presume that humans have the ability, freedom, and responsibility to work with God to do God's will. Scripture also includes stories of human action that caused God to adjust or alter divine plans. Moses' prayer changed God's mind when Israel worshiped the golden calf (Exod 32:11-14). The pleas of the Syrophoenecian woman caused Jesus to reverse his decision and heal her daughter (Mark 7:24-30). God clearly takes into account human actions, words, and freedom as God works in the world. Indeed, even within the book of Judges itself God used the freedom and actions of many human actors to achieve God's purposes. Ehud's devious trick with his hidden sword (3:12-30) or Jael's feigned hospitality to the Canaanite general Sisera (4:17-24) were human actions that God did not seem to plan but that did contribute to God's defeat of Israel's enemies. The Song of Deborah and Barak in Judges 5 praises God for the defeat of the Canaanites (5:2-5, 31), but it also praises humans like Deborah, "the mother of Israel" (5:7), the commanders "who offered themselves willingly" (5:9), and Jael as "the most blessed of women" (5:24). As few in number as they were, even the 300 soldiers of Gideon played some role in God's defeat of the Midianites.

Thus we may affirm Gideon's insistence that recognition be given to him along with the Lord in defeating Midian. We generally applaud those with feelings of worthlessness, like Gideon, who discover over time a sense of self-worth and value. But God's concern about Israel's taking all the credit for itself instead of attributing it to God flashes a warning light at the same time. Surely humans contribute to the divine cause, but God knows that humans have a tendency to cross the line, forget God, and take all the credit for themselves. Maintaining a balance between primary reliance on God and an affirmation of human talents and creativity in achieving God's will in the world is difficult, but necessary. In the case of Gideon, we will see that he will begin to cross the line and lose that balance when he crosses the Jordan River in the next section, beginning with Judg 8:4. Gideon's worthwhile self-affirmation will eventually begin to evolve into self-absorption.

Judges 8:4-35, A Complex Gideon: Kingship and Idolatry

NIV

⁴Gideon and his three hundred men, exhausted yet keeping up the pursuit, came to the Jordan and crossed it. ⁵He said to the men of Succoth, "Give my troops some bread; they are worn out, and I am still pursuing Zebah and Zalmunna, the kings of Midian."

⁶But the officials of Succoth said, "Do you already have the hands of Zebah and Zalmunna in your possession? Why should we give bread to your troops?"

⁷Then Gideon replied, "Just for that, when the LORD has given Zebah and Zalmunna into my hand, I will tear your flesh with desert thorns and briers."

⁸From there he went up to Peniel[a] and made the same request of them, but they answered as the men of Succoth had. ⁹So he said to the men of Peniel, "When I return in triumph, I will tear down this tower."

¹⁰Now Zebah and Zalmunna were in Karkor with a force of about fifteen thousand men, all that were left of the armies of the eastern peoples; a hundred and twenty thousand swordsmen had fallen. ¹¹Gideon went up by the route of the nomads east of Nobah and Jogbehah and fell upon the unsuspecting army. ¹²Zebah and Zalmunna, the two kings of Midian, fled, but he pursued them and captured them, routing their entire army.

NRSV

4Then Gideon came to the Jordan and crossed over, he and the three hundred who were with him, exhausted and famished.[a] 5So he said to the people of Succoth, "Please give some loaves of bread to my followers, for they are exhausted, and I am pursuing Zebah and Zalmunna, the kings of Midian." 6But the officials of Succoth said, "Do you already have in your possession the hands of Zebah and Zalmunna, that we should give bread to your army?" 7Gideon replied, "Well then, when the LORD has given Zebah and Zalmunna into my hand, I will trample your flesh on the thorns of the wilderness and on briers." 8From there he went up to Penuel, and made the same request of them; and the people of Penuel answered him as the people of Succoth had answered. 9So he said to the people of Penuel, "When I come back victorious, I will break down this tower."

10Now Zebah and Zalmunna were in Karkor with their army, about fifteen thousand men, all who were left of all the army of the people of the east; for one hundred twenty thousand men bearing arms had fallen. 11So Gideon went up by the caravan route east of Nobah and Jogbehah, and attacked the army; for the army was off its guard. 12Zebah and Zalmunna fled; and he pursued them and took the two kings of Midian, Zebah and Zalmunna, and threw all the army into a panic.

a8 Hebrew Penuel, a variant of Peniel; also in verses 9 and 17

a Gk: Heb pursuing

¹³Gideon son of Joash then returned from the battle by the Pass of Heres. ¹⁴He caught a young man of Succoth and questioned him, and the young man wrote down for him the names of the seventy-seven officials of Succoth, the elders of the town. ¹⁵Then Gideon came and said to the men of Succoth, "Here are Zebah and Zalmunna, about whom you taunted me by saying, 'Do you already have the hands of Zebah and Zalmunna in your possession? Why should we give bread to your exhausted men?'" ¹⁶He took the elders of the town and taught the men of Succoth a lesson by punishing them with desert thorns and briers. ¹⁷He also pulled down the tower of Peniel and killed the men of the town.

¹⁸Then he asked Zebah and Zalmunna, "What kind of men did you kill at Tabor?"

"Men like you," they answered, "each one with the bearing of a prince."

¹⁹Gideon replied, "Those were my brothers, the sons of my own mother. As surely as the Lord lives, if you had spared their lives, I would not kill you." ²⁰Turning to Jether, his oldest son, he said, "Kill them!" But Jether did not draw his sword, because he was only a boy and was afraid.

²¹Zebah and Zalmunna said, "Come, do it yourself. 'As is the man, so is his strength.'" So Gideon stepped forward and killed them, and took the ornaments off their camels' necks.

²²The Israelites said to Gideon, "Rule over us—you, your son and your grandson—because you have saved us out of the hand of Midian."

²³But Gideon told them, "I will not rule over you, nor will my son rule over you. The Lord will rule over you." ²⁴And he said, "I do have one request, that each of you give me an earring from your share of the plunder." (It was the custom of the Ishmaelites to wear gold earrings.)

²⁵They answered, "We'll be glad to give them." So they spread out a garment, and each man threw a ring from his plunder onto it. ²⁶The weight of the gold rings he asked for came to seventeen hundred shekels,^a not counting the ornaments, the pendants and the purple garments worn by the kings of Midian or the chains that were on their camels' necks. ²⁷Gideon made the gold into an ephod, which he placed in Ophrah,

^a26 That is, about 43 pounds (about 19.5 kilograms)

13When Gideon son of Joash returned from the battle by the ascent of Heres, ¹⁴he caught a young man, one of the people of Succoth, and questioned him; and he listed for him the officials and elders of Succoth, seventy-seven people. ¹⁵Then he came to the people of Succoth, and said, "Here are Zebah and Zalmunna, about whom you taunted me, saying, 'Do you already have in your possession the hands of Zebah and Zalmunna, that we should give bread to your troops who are exhausted?'" ¹⁶So he took the elders of the city and he took thorns of the wilderness and briers and with them he trampled^a the people of Succoth. ¹⁷He also broke down the tower of Penuel, and killed the men of the city.

18Then he said to Zebah and Zalmunna, "What about the men whom you killed at Tabor?" They answered, "As you are, so were they, every one of them; they resembled the sons of a king." ¹⁹And he replied, "They were my brothers, the sons of my mother; as the Lord lives, if you had saved them alive, I would not kill you." ²⁰So he said to Jether his firstborn, "Go kill them!" But the boy did not draw his sword, for he was afraid, because he was still a boy. ²¹Then Zebah and Zalmunna said, "You come and kill us; for as the man is, so is his strength." So Gideon proceeded to kill Zebah and Zalmunna; and he took the crescents that were on the necks of their camels.

22Then the Israelites said to Gideon, "Rule over us, you and your son and your grandson also; for you have delivered us out of the hand of Midian." ²³Gideon said to them, "I will not rule over you, and my son will not rule over you; the Lord will rule over you." ²⁴Then Gideon said to them, "Let me make a request of you; each of you give me an earring he has taken as booty." (For the enemy^b had golden earrings, because they were Ishmaelites.) ²⁵"We will willingly give them," they answered. So they spread a garment, and each threw into it an earring he had taken as booty. ²⁶The weight of the golden earrings that he requested was one thousand seven hundred shekels of gold (apart from the crescents and the pendants and the purple garments worn by the kings of Midian, and the collars that were on the necks of their camels). ²⁷Gideon made an ephod

^a With verse 7, Compare Gk: Heb *he taught*   ^b Heb *they*

NIV

his town. All Israel prostituted themselves by worshiping it there, and it became a snare to Gideon and his family.

²⁸Thus Midian was subdued before the Israelites and did not raise its head again. During Gideon's lifetime, the land enjoyed peace forty years.

²⁹Jerub-Baal son of Joash went back home to live. ³⁰He had seventy sons of his own, for he had many wives. ³¹His concubine, who lived in Shechem, also bore him a son, whom he named Abimelech. ³²Gideon son of Joash died at a good old age and was buried in the tomb of his father Joash in Ophrah of the Abiezrites.

³³No sooner had Gideon died than the Israelites again prostituted themselves to the Baals. They set up Baal-Berith as their god and ³⁴did not remember the LORD their God, who had rescued them from the hands of all their enemies on every side. ³⁵They also failed to show kindness to the family of Jerub-Baal (that is, Gideon) for all the good things he had done for them.

NRSV

of it and put it in his town, in Ophrah; and all Israel prostituted themselves to it there, and it became a snare to Gideon and to his family. ²⁸So Midian was subdued before the Israelites, and they lifted up their heads no more. So the land had rest forty years in the days of Gideon.

²⁹Jerubbaal son of Joash went to live in his own house. ³⁰Now Gideon had seventy sons, his own offspring, for he had many wives. ³¹His concubine who was in Shechem also bore him a son, and he named him Abimelech. ³²Then Gideon son of Joash died at a good old age, and was buried in the tomb of his father Joash at Ophrah of the Abiezrites.

³³As soon as Gideon died, the Israelites relapsed and prostituted themselves with the Baals, making Baal-berith their god. ³⁴The Israelites did not remember the LORD their God, who had rescued them from the hand of all their enemies on every side; ³⁵and they did not exhibit loyalty to the house of Jerubbaal (that is, Gideon) in return for all the good that he had done to Israel.

COMMENTARY

The typical model of the judges cycle would conclude the story of Gideon at this point with a statement about the victory over the enemy Midian and the number of years of rest that followed. But the Gideon narrative does not end here. Rather, the story begins a new scene in 8:4 as Gideon crosses the Jordan River out of Canaan in hot pursuit of two Midianite kings named Zebah and Zalmunna. The psalmist mentions their names as Midianite princes who coveted Israel's land (Ps 83:11). Gideon's 300 soldiers are "exhausted and famished" from all their fighting (v. 4). The Lord plays no role in the action of these last episodes. One gets the sense that it is Gideon alone, not his soldiers or the Lord, who is pushing the action and calling the shots.

8:4-21. Gideon and his army come to the towns of Succoth and then Penuel, east of the Jordan. They ask for some bread, but the residents of these cities refuse to offer them hospitality. The story does not explicitly say who the residents of Succoth and Penuel are. Are they Canaanites? Are

they fellow Israelites from the east Jordanian tribe of Gad? The town of Succoth was settled by the tribe of Gad, according to Josh 13:24-28. Penuel is a town associated with the ancestor Jacob and his wrestling match with God (Gen 32:30-32). These associations suggest that the townspeople are Israelites refusing to help fellow Israelites. In response to their inhospitality, Gideon promises revenge upon them after he returns from capturing the two Midianite kings (vv. 7, 9). Later Gideon will do what he threatened. He will trample the inhabitants of Succoth with wilderness thorns and briars, and he will topple the tower of Penuel and kill its people (vv. 16-17).

The violence and severity of the revenge Gideon takes on his fellow Israelites for their admittedly inhospitable attitude seems out of proportion. The taunting of Gideon by Succoth and Penuel (vv. 6, 15) was hardly just cause to kill everyone in the towns. Gideon has seemingly lost his diplomatic skill and graciousness, displayed in the dispute with the Ephraimites (vv. 1-3). He has crossed a line as well as the Jordan River (v. 4). He displays the overweening arrogance of the primeval and brutish Lamech, who boasted to his wives, "I have killed a man for wounding me, a young man for striking me. If Cain is avenged sevenfold, truly Lamech seventy-sevenfold" (Gen 4:23-24 NRSV). These themes of Israel's own inhospitality toward other Israelites and the severe revenge and civil war that ensue will grow larger as we move through Judges. The final episode of chaps. 19–21 describes a full-blown version of these themes, which will mark the total collapse of Israel's unity and the end of the judges era.

Personal revenge or retribution plays a role not only with Succoth and Penuel but also with Gideon's motivation in pursuing the two kings of Midian, Zebah and Zalmunna. When Gideon finally captures them, he asks them about the Israelites they killed at Tabor. The kings' answer to Gideon is interesting: "As you are, so were they, every one of them; they resembled the sons of a king" (v. 18). The implication is clear: Gideon has the appearance of a "son of a king." More-over, Gideon is about to kill two kings. Does that mean that Gideon will himself step into their role of king in their stead? In this context, Gideon issues his own law of vengeance much as a king might do. He justifies his execution of the kings as revenge for their having killed his brothers. He thus instructs his oldest son to kill the kings. However, his son refuses out of fear and timidity (v. 20). Gideon's son is a reflection of the earlier and more timid Gideon who had refused God's command to kill the enemy early in his career (6:15). But Gideon has changed. He has become bolder, more self-assured, and more willing to take matters into his own hands without the help of the Lord. Thus Gideon kills the kings himself. He also takes the royal emblems, the crescents hanging from the necks of the kings' camels, as booty and keeps them for himself (v. 21). Has Gideon begun to step over the line from a temporary judge to a king? And if so, is that a good thing or a bad thing? The next episodes will explore those questions.

8:22-28. The Israelites are impressed with Gideon's newly discovered boldness, independence, and assertiveness as a leader. They say to Gideon, "Rule [מָשַׁל *māšal*] over us, you and your son and your grandson also." They do not use the word "king" (מֶלֶךְ *melek*), but they do suggest a dynasty

of Gideon's line to rule into the future. The reason the people offer to Gideon is that "you have delivered us out of the hand of Midian." The Lord had earlier been concerned that Israel might take credit away from the Lord and say, "My own hand has delivered me" (7:2). These words to Gideon that *he* was the one who delivered Israel with no mention of the Lord suggest that what God feared has come to pass. Israel has forgotten all that God had done, just as the prophet had warned earlier in the Gideon story (6:7-10).

Gideon seems to turn down the people's request that he and his son and grandson become rulers over Israel. Sounding quite pious, Gideon replies, "I will not rule over you, and my son will not rule over you; the LORD will rule over you" (8:23). Gideon appears to wash his hands of any role in guiding Israel into the future and instead leaves it up to God alone. Gideon's statement is taken by some scholars as a positive reflection of the view of the writers of this story. The intended meaning of the story, they argue, is a critique of all human kingship or dynastic rule in favor of a theocratic ideal in which God alone is King and Ruler over Israel. This implies an affirmation of total human equality that plays down the need for human hierarchy or leadership. However, the message of the Gideon story in this regard seems more nuanced than a simple rejection of all human kingship or leadership. The narrator of the story has placed Gideon's claim—that God alone rules Israel with no room for human leadership—in a literary context that suggests something is wrong with this statement. First of all, Gideon has been acting more and more like an independent and improper king. He had no need of the Lord when he took the law into his own hands and went on his spree of personal revenge in this chapter. Moreover, he accumulates gold (vv. 24-26), a sign of a bad king, according to the law of the king in Deut 17:17. Second, Gideon crafts a cult object, called an ephod, which becomes an idol: "All Israel prostituted themselves to it, and it became a snare to Gideon and to his family" (v. 27). This, too, is a sign of a bad king, according to the law in Deut 17:20.[39]

How does this religious ephod relate to the

---

39. David Jobling, "Deuteronomic Political Theory in Judges and 1 Samuel 1–12," in *The Sense of Biblical Narrative: Structural Analyses in the Hebrew Bible*, JSOTSup 39 (Sheffield: JSOT, 1988) 1:66-67.

issue of human politics and kingship? An ephod is associated with ceremonial garments of priests (Exodus 28; 39). It was probably used as a device for receiving oracles and guidance from a deity. Since Gideon had renounced any overt claim to rule for himself, he makes an ephod as an instrument of divination to provide a way to maintain contact between God and Israel. However, his manufacture and sole control of the ephod and the connection to God suggest that Gideon may in fact be hiding his power and rule behind the cloak of religious trappings and pious claims that "the LORD will rule over you." In this sense, the ephod becomes an idol, a graven image of God that Gideon controls. Israel worships a humanly constructed image instead of the true God, who is beyond human control and who judges all human beings and their institutions of power. The God of Israel surely can work in and through human beings and their structures of community and national life. But this God of Israel cannot be captured or uncritically identified with any one human form, image, or institution.

We can also read this connection of Gideon's refusal to rule Israel and the making of an ephod in a more straightforward way. Gideon may simply want no part in trying to rule Israel, with all its difficulties and conflicts. He constructs the ephod as a mechanical device for divine oracles so that he will not need to take responsibility for guiding the affairs of the nation. The ephod becomes a substitute for human leadership of the community. However, the ephod can never take the place of the dynamic and complex interactions of God, human leaders, and the people of Israel. In this reading, Gideon has acted wrongly, but not because he veils his human power behind an idolatrous image of God. Rather, Gideon abandons his responsibility to lead Israel as a servant and partner with God. His refusal leaves a power vacuum that is only inadequately filled by a mechanical and idolatrous oracular device. The narrative may be intentionally ambiguous and suggestive of both readings. Either reading of Gideon's actions—that he is a covert king or that he has abandoned all responsibility for leadership—indicates that something has gone terribly wrong with the system of the judges.

The full extent of Gideon's offense in making the idol emerges when one considers the episode in Israel's history that it most resembles. In effect, Gideon replays the sin of Aaron and the Israelites when they made and worshiped the golden calf at Mt. Sinai (Exodus 32). When God conquered Pharaoh and his army, Israel received booty of gold and silver jewelry from the Egyptians (Exod 3:21-22; 12:35-36). Later at Mt. Sinai, Aaron the priest collected all the gold earrings the Israelites had received from the Egyptians and melted them down to make a golden calf. They worshiped the golden calf, proclaiming it to be the god "who brought you out of the land of Egypt" (Exod 32:8 NRSV). Gideon does what Aaron did. He asks the Israelites to give up their golden earrings plundered from the enemy, makes an ephod from the gold, and sets the ephod up at his home in Ophrah, and Israel worships it as an idol. Just as their ancestors had claimed that the golden calf had delivered them out of Egypt, so also the Israelites now claim that Gideon and not the Lord was the one "who delivered us out of the hand of Midian" (8:22). More than any other OT story, the golden calf story represents the defining paradigm of Israel's rebellion against the Lord. The association of Gideon's ephod with that story suggests that the road of the judges era has taken a decidedly negative turn.

The ominous character of Gideon's idolatry is further signaled by the fact that Gideon's ephod is a literary echo of a later story in the book of Judges. The story of Micah and his idolatrous "ephod" marks the culminating endpoint of Israel's downward spiral into religious disintegration (17:5; 18:14-20). The Gideon story begins the transition into that downward slide. At the start of his career, Gideon had broken down pagan altars and idols in his hometown of Ophrah (6:24-27). At the end of his life, Gideon constructs an idol, which leads Israel astray in his hometown of Ophrah (8:27). The final portrait of Gideon is mixed. He failed as a religious leader, but he remained successful as a military leader. He subdued Midian, and Israel had rest for forty years (8:28; see 3:11; 5:31).

8:29-35. These verses conclude the Gideon cycle and show again the complexity and ambiguity of Gideon's character. Both names for Gideon reappear together: Jerubbabel (v. 29) and Gideon (v. 30). On one hand, Jerubbaal, or Gideon, seems to retire from any role in leading the people of Israel; he "went to live in his own house" (v. 29). On the other hand, Gideon has "many wives" and seventy sons (v. 30). Both details provide a hint that Gideon has become more than just a simple wheat farmer from Ophrah (6:11). Larger numbers of wives and offspring often accompany kingship. The law of the king in Deuteronomy explicitly prohibits Israel's king from acquiring "many wives for himself, or else his heart will turn away" (Deut 17:17); King Solomon violated the prohibition of having many wives (1 Kgs 11:3). The mention of Gideon's seventy sons reflects the large number of offspring kings typically have. In particular, the wicked King Ahab of Samaria had "seventy sons" (2 Kgs 10:1). Moreover, Gideon takes a female slave from the city of Shechem as a wife or concubine. Sexual entanglements with Shechem had led to disastrous results before in Israel's history (Genesis 34). This time the relationship between Israel and the concubine in Shechem leads to the birth of a son, whom Gideon names "Abimelech," meaning "My Father Is King" (v. 31). Through his son's name, Gideon may be covertly proclaiming himself king. He was a successful ruler in terms of military victories (v. 28), but Gideon was a poor leader in religious affairs involving the idolatrous ephod (vv. 24-27). Gideon is an ambiguous figure, refusing to accept the office of ruler or kingship (vv. 22-23), and yet he is acting in some ways as a covert king. In the next generation, Gideon's son Abimelech will openly declare himself king in spite of Gideon's claim that "my sons will not rule over you" (v. 23). Abimelech's attempt at monarchy will be short and violent, and it will end in tragedy (chap. 9).

For now, however, Gideon's life ends peacefully "at a good old age." Gideon achieved much that was good in his life, but his reign as judge also showed the cracks of a deteriorating system of leadership. While Gideon was alive, Israel worshiped his ephod as an idol, a graven image of the Lord. When Gideon dies, Israel goes even further in violating the first of the Ten Commandments: Israel "relapsed and prostituted themselves with the Baals." Their religious situation returns to what it was at the beginning of the Gideon story, before Gideon pulled down his father's Baal altar (6:25-27). They forgot the Lord, but they also committed another major sin: "they did not exhibit loyalty to the house of Jerubbaal (that is, Gideon) in return for all the good that he had done in Israel" (v. 35). The details of this offense against Gideon's house, or family, will be the subject of the next chapter in the judges era, Abimelech's disastrous attempt to become king in Israel.

REFLECTIONS

1. Gideon is a character who changes radically over the course of his reign as a judge. He begins as an overly passive and fearful leader, constantly in need of reassurance. At the midpoint of his career, he finds a balance of both self-affirmation and the affirmation of God's role as deliverer: "For the LORD and for Gideon" (8:18, 20). By the end of his battles with Midian, Gideon begins asserting himself to the exclusion of God in unwarranted acts of personal revenge, even against his fellow Israelites. The final blow comes when Gideon makes the ephod, which replaces the Lord as an object of worship.

Remarkably, God works through Gideon all through his life. When Gideon was hesitant and fainthearted, God patiently gave him the signs he needed to bolster his courage. When Gideon later became focused on his own glory more than the praise of God, God still gave forty years of peace to Israel by defeating the Midianites. As one surveys the Scriptures, it becomes clear that God repeatedly works through flawed and imperfect people. Abraham sometimes doubted and endangered God's promises to him, but God continued to use him and his descendants as a blessing to "all the families of the earth" (Gen 12:3 NRSV). Jacob was hardly an exemplary person, deceiving his father and stealing his brother's birthright. Yet God chose him as the carrier of the promise. King David committed adultery and murdered his loyal soldier Uriah to cover up his affair. Yet God chose him and his dynasty forever. The disciple Peter denied Jesus three times, and the other disciples all deserted Jesus during his trial, which led to Jesus' execution on the cross. Yet God used Peter and the other disciples as the first preachers of the gospel (Acts 2). Whether we feel wholly inadequate for what God calls us to do or whether we sometimes think too highly of ourselves and forget God, the lesson of Gideon teaches us that God can still accomplish God's will through us and sometimes in spite of us.

2. The story of Gideon raises the issue of the relationship of religion and politics. In the end, did Gideon hide his drive for power and self-glorification with the word and power of God? Or did he run away from his responsibility and the responsibility of his family to lead Israel on a more permanent and stable basis, since the system of temporary leadership by judges was starting to unravel? Either option seems to be rejected by the writer or narrator of the Gideon story. The book of Judges does not promote a theocratic ideal in which God alone is King and no human leader exists. When Gideon expressed such an ideal, his words were set in a negative context that implicitly condemned his claim. In the end, Judges affirms the need for a king, a human ruler, who guides Israel to faith and allegiance to the Lord. This pro-king perspective of Judges is demonstrated by the important refrain that encloses the last section of the book, describing Israel's basic problem as Israel spins out of control into political and religious chaos: "In those days there was no king in Israel; all the people did what was right in their own eyes" (17:6; 21:25). Israel comes to need a more stable form of human leadership.

On the other hand, the Gideon story makes clear that this king must be of a special type, conforming to certain criteria. The king must take seriously the responsibility to rule. Those in authority must be open and accountable in the exercise of power. They stand under divine scrutiny and judgment. The mediation of the Lord's will should not be too closely identified with the ruler's will as it was with Gideon's ephod. God's word must remain free, independent, and able to critique the governing power. A prophet like the one who appeared earlier in the Gideon story (6:7-10) typically fulfilled this role in Israel's monarchy. Examples include the prophets Samuel (1 Samuel 15), Nathan (2 Samuel 12), and Elijah (1 Kings 18). Each spoke God's critical words of judgment to Israel's kings. Governments and leaders in communities of all kinds continue to need independent voices who are willing to speak the truth boldly and to criticize constructively. The quality of Gideon's rule fell short in a number of these criteria of good leadership and good kings. The kingship of Gideon's son Abimelech will move even further away from the ideal kingship to which Judges looks forward.

Judges 9:1-57, Abimelech: A Troubled Foray into Kingship

9 Abimelech son of Jerub-Baal went to his mother's brothers in Shechem and said to them and to all his mother's clan, ²"Ask all the citizens of Shechem, 'Which is better for you: to have all seventy of Jerub-Baal's sons rule over you, or just one man?' Remember, I am your flesh and blood."

³When the brothers repeated all this to the citizens of Shechem, they were inclined to follow Abimelech, for they said, "He is our brother." ⁴They gave him seventy shekels*ᵃ* of silver from the temple of Baal-Berith, and Abimelech used it to hire reckless adventurers, who became his follow-

a4 That is, about 1 3/4 pounds (about 0.8 kilogram)

9 Now Abimelech son of Jerubbaal went to Shechem to his mother's kinsfolk and said to them and to the whole clan of his mother's family, ²"Say in the hearing of all the lords of Shechem, 'Which is better for you, that all seventy of the sons of Jerubbaal rule over you, or that one rule over you?' Remember also that I am your bone and your flesh." ³So his mother's kinsfolk spoke all these words on his behalf in the hearing of all the lords of Shechem; and their hearts inclined to follow Abimelech, for they said, "He is our brother." ⁴They gave him seventy pieces of silver out of the temple of Baal-berith with which Abimelech hired worthless and reckless fellows,

ers. [5]He went to his father's home in Ophrah and on one stone murdered his seventy brothers, the sons of Jerub-Baal. But Jotham, the youngest son of Jerub-Baal, escaped by hiding. [6]Then all the citizens of Shechem and Beth Millo gathered beside the great tree at the pillar in Shechem to crown Abimelech king.

[7]When Jotham was told about this, he climbed up on the top of Mount Gerizim and shouted to them, "Listen to me, citizens of Shechem, so that God may listen to you. [8]One day the trees went out to anoint a king for themselves. They said to the olive tree, 'Be our king.'

[9]"But the olive tree answered, 'Should I give up my oil, by which both gods and men are honored, to hold sway over the trees?'

[10]"Next, the trees said to the fig tree, 'Come and be our king.'

[11]"But the fig tree replied, 'Should I give up my fruit, so good and sweet, to hold sway over the trees?'

[12]"Then the trees said to the vine, 'Come and be our king.'

[13]"But the vine answered, 'Should I give up my wine, which cheers both gods and men, to hold sway over the trees?'

[14]"Finally all the trees said to the thornbush, 'Come and be our king.'

[15]"The thornbush said to the trees, 'If you really want to anoint me king over you, come and take refuge in my shade; but if not, then let fire come out of the thornbush and consume the cedars of Lebanon!'

[16]"Now if you have acted honorably and in good faith when you made Abimelech king, and if you have been fair to Jerub-Baal and his family, and if you have treated him as he deserves— [17]and to think that my father fought for you, risked his life to rescue you from the hand of Midian [18](but today you have revolted against my father's family, murdered his seventy sons on a single stone, and made Abimelech, the son of his slave girl, king over the citizens of Shechem because he is your brother)— [19]if then you have acted honorably and in good faith toward Jerub-Baal and his family today, may Abimelech be your joy, and may you be his, too! [20]But if you have not, let fire come out from Abimelech and con-

who followed him. [5]He went to his father's house at Ophrah, and killed his brothers the sons of Jerubbaal, seventy men, on one stone; but Jotham, the youngest son of Jerubbaal, survived, for he hid himself. [6]Then all the lords of Shechem and all Beth-millo came together, and they went and made Abimelech king, by the oak of the pillar[a] at Shechem.

[7]When it was told to Jotham, he went and stood on the top of Mount Gerizim, and cried aloud and said to them, "Listen to me, you lords of Shechem, so that God may listen to you.

[8] The trees once went out
    to anoint a king over themselves.
So they said to the olive tree,
    'Reign over us.'
[9] The olive tree answered them,
    'Shall I stop producing my rich oil
      by which gods and mortals are
        honored,
    and go to sway over the trees?'
[10] Then the trees said to the fig tree,
    'You come and reign over us.'
[11] But the fig tree answered them,
    'Shall I stop producing my sweetness
      and my delicious fruit,
    and go to sway over the trees?'
[12] Then the trees said to the vine,
    'You come and reign over us.'
[13] But the vine said to them,
    'Shall I stop producing my wine
      that cheers gods and mortals,
    and go to sway over the trees?'
[14] So all the trees said to the bramble,
    'You come and reign over us.'
[15] And the bramble said to the trees,
    'If in good faith you are anointing me
      king over you,
    then come and take refuge in my
      shade;
    but if not, let fire come out of the
      bramble
    and devour the cedars of Lebanon.'
[16]"Now therefore, if you acted in good faith and honor when you made Abimelech king, and if you have dealt well with Jerubbaal and his house, and have done to him as his actions

[a] Cn: Meaning of Heb uncertain

NIV

sume you, citizens of Shechem and Beth Millo, and let fire come out from you, citizens of Shechem and Beth Millo, and consume Abimelech!"

²¹Then Jotham fled, escaping to Beer, and he lived there because he was afraid of his brother Abimelech.

²²After Abimelech had governed Israel three years, ²³God sent an evil spirit between Abimelech and the citizens of Shechem, who acted treacherously against Abimelech. ²⁴God did this in order that the crime against Jerub-Baal's seventy sons, the shedding of their blood, might be avenged on their brother Abimelech and on the citizens of Shechem, who had helped him murder his brothers. ²⁵In opposition to him these citizens of Shechem set men on the hilltops to ambush and rob everyone who passed by, and this was reported to Abimelech.

²⁶Now Gaal son of Ebed moved with his brothers into Shechem, and its citizens put their confidence in him. ²⁷After they had gone out into the fields and gathered the grapes and trodden them, they held a festival in the temple of their god. While they were eating and drinking, they cursed Abimelech. ²⁸Then Gaal son of Ebed said, "Who is Abimelech, and who is Shechem, that we should be subject to him? Isn't he Jerub-Baal's son, and isn't Zebul his deputy? Serve the men of Hamor, Shechem's father! Why should we serve Abimelech? ²⁹If only this people were under my command! Then I would get rid of him. I would say to Abimelech, 'Call out your whole army!'"ᵃ

³⁰When Zebul the governor of the city heard what Gaal son of Ebed said, he was very angry. ³¹Under cover he sent messengers to Abimelech, saying, "Gaal son of Ebed and his brothers have come to Shechem and are stirring up the city against you. ³²Now then, during the night you and your men should come and lie in wait in the fields. ³³In the morning at sunrise, advance against the city. When Gaal and his men come out against you, do whatever your hand finds to do."

³⁴So Abimelech and all his troops set out by night and took up concealed positions near

ᵃ29 Septuagint; Hebrew him." Then he said to Abimelech, "Call out your whole army!"

NRSV

deserved— ¹⁷for my father fought for you, and risked his life, and rescued you from the hand of Midian; ¹⁸but you have risen up against my father's house this day, and have killed his sons, seventy men on one stone, and have made Abimelech, the son of his slave woman, king over the lords of Shechem, because he is your kinsman— ¹⁹if, I say, you have acted in good faith and honor with Jerubbaal and with his house this day, then rejoice in Abimelech, and let him also rejoice in you; ²⁰but if not, let fire come out from Abimelech, and devour the lords of Shechem, and Beth-millo; and let fire come out from the lords of Shechem, and from Beth-millo, and devour Abimelech." ²¹Then Jotham ran away and fled, going to Beer, where he remained for fear of his brother Abimelech.

²²Abimelech ruled over Israel three years. ²³But God sent an evil spirit between Abimelech and the lords of Shechem; and the lords of Shechem dealt treacherously with Abimelech. ²⁴This happened so that the violence done to the seventy sons of Jerubbaal might be avengedᵃ and their blood be laid on their brother Abimelech, who killed them, and on the lords of Shechem, who strengthened his hands to kill his brothers. ²⁵So, out of hostility to him, the lords of Shechem set ambushes on the mountain tops. They robbed all who passed by them along that way; and it was reported to Abimelech.

²⁶When Gaal son of Ebed moved into Shechem with his kinsfolk, the lords of Shechem put confidence in him. ²⁷They went out into the field and gathered the grapes from their vineyards, trod them, and celebrated. Then they went into the temple of their god, ate and drank, and ridiculed Abimelech. ²⁸Gaal son of Ebed said, "Who is Abimelech, and who are we of Shechem, that we should serve him? Did not the son of Jerubbaal and Zebul his officer serve the men of Hamor father of Shechem? Why then should we serve him? ²⁹If only this people were under my command! Then I would remove Abimelech; I would sayᵇ to him, 'Increase your army, and come out.'"

³⁰When Zebul the ruler of the city heard the words of Gaal son of Ebed, his anger was kindled.

ᵃ Heb might come ᵇ Gk: Heb and he said

NIV

Shechem in four companies. ³⁵Now Gaal son of Ebed had gone out and was standing at the entrance to the city gate just as Abimelech and his soldiers came out from their hiding place.

³⁶When Gaal saw them, he said to Zebul, "Look, people are coming down from the tops of the mountains!"

Zebul replied, "You mistake the shadows of the mountains for men."

³⁷But Gaal spoke up again: "Look, people are coming down from the center of the land, and a company is coming from the direction of the soothsayers' tree."

³⁸Then Zebul said to him, "Where is your big talk now, you who said, 'Who is Abimelech that we should be subject to him?' Aren't these the men you ridiculed? Go out and fight them!"

³⁹So Gaal led out*a* the citizens of Shechem and fought Abimelech. ⁴⁰Abimelech chased him, and many fell wounded in the flight—all the way to the entrance to the gate. ⁴¹Abimelech stayed in Arumah, and Zebul drove Gaal and his brothers out of Shechem.

⁴²The next day the people of Shechem went out to the fields, and this was reported to Abimelech. ⁴³So he took his men, divided them into three companies and set an ambush in the fields. When he saw the people coming out of the city, he rose to attack them. ⁴⁴Abimelech and the companies with him rushed forward to a position at the entrance to the city gate. Then two companies rushed upon those in the fields and struck them down. ⁴⁵All that day Abimelech pressed his attack against the city until he had captured it and killed its people. Then he destroyed the city and scattered salt over it.

⁴⁶On hearing this, the citizens in the tower of Shechem went into the stronghold of the temple of El-Berith. ⁴⁷When Abimelech heard that they had assembled there, ⁴⁸he and all his men went up Mount Zalmon. He took an ax and cut off some branches, which he lifted to his shoulders. He ordered the men with him, "Quick! Do what you have seen me do!" ⁴⁹So all the men cut branches and followed Abimelech. They piled them against the stronghold and set it on fire over the people inside. So all the people in the tower

a39 Or Gaal went out in the sight of

NRSV

³¹He sent messengers to Abimelech at Arumah,*a* saying, "Look, Gaal son of Ebed and his kinsfolk have come to Shechem, and they are stirring up*b* the city against you. ³²Now therefore, go by night, you and the troops that are with you, and lie in wait in the fields. ³³Then early in the morning, as soon as the sun rises, get up and rush on the city; and when he and the troops that are with him come out against you, you may deal with them as best you can."

34So Abimelech and all the troops with him got up by night and lay in wait against Shechem in four companies. ³⁵When Gaal son of Ebed went out and stood in the entrance of the gate of the city, Abimelech and the troops with him rose from the ambush. ³⁶And when Gaal saw them, he said to Zebul, "Look, people are coming down from the mountain tops!" And Zebul said to him, "The shadows on the mountains look like people to you." ³⁷Gaal spoke again and said, "Look, people are coming down from Tabbur-erez, and one company is coming from the direction of Elon-meonenim."*c* ³⁸Then Zebul said to him, "Where is your boast*d* now, you who said, 'Who is Abimelech, that we should serve him?' Are not these the troops you made light of? Go out now and fight with them." ³⁹So Gaal went out at the head of the lords of Shechem, and fought with Abimelech. ⁴⁰Abimelech chased him, and he fled before him. Many fell wounded, up to the entrance of the gate. ⁴¹So Abimelech resided at Arumah; and Zebul drove out Gaal and his kinsfolk, so that they could not live on at Shechem.

42On the following day the people went out into the fields. When Abimelech was told, ⁴³he took his troops and divided them into three companies, and lay in wait in the fields. When he looked and saw the people coming out of the city, he rose against them and killed them. ⁴⁴Abimelech and the company that was*e* with him rushed forward and stood at the entrance of the gate of the city, while the two companies rushed on all who were in the fields and killed them. ⁴⁵Abimelech fought against the city all that day; he took the city, and killed the people that were in it; and he razed the city and sowed it with salt.

a Cn See 9.41. Heb Tormah   *b* Cn: Heb are besieging   *c* That is Diviners' Oak   *d* Heb mouth   *e* Vg and some Gk Mss: Heb companies that were

NIV

of Shechem, about a thousand men and women, also died.

⁵⁰Next Abimelech went to Thebez and besieged it and captured it. ⁵¹Inside the city, however, was a strong tower, to which all the men and women—all the people of the city—fled. They locked themselves in and climbed up on the tower roof. ⁵²Abimelech went to the tower and stormed it. But as he approached the entrance to the tower to set it on fire, ⁵³a woman dropped an upper millstone on his head and cracked his skull.

⁵⁴Hurriedly he called to his armor-bearer, "Draw your sword and kill me, so that they can't say, 'A woman killed him.'" So his servant ran him through, and he died. ⁵⁵When the Israelites saw that Abimelech was dead, they went home.

⁵⁶Thus God repaid the wickedness that Abimelech had done to his father by murdering his seventy brothers. ⁵⁷God also made the men of Shechem pay for all their wickedness. The curse of Jotham son of Jerub-Baal came on them.

NRSV

46When all the lords of the Tower of Shechem heard of it, they entered the stronghold of the temple of El-berith. ⁴⁷Abimelech was told that all the lords of the Tower of Shechem were gathered together. ⁴⁸So Abimelech went up to Mount Zalmon, he and all the troops that were with him. Abimelech took an ax in his hand, cut down a bundle of brushwood, and took it up and laid it on his shoulder. Then he said to the troops with him, "What you have seen me do, do quickly, as I have done." ⁴⁹So every one of the troops cut down a bundle and following Abimelech put it against the stronghold, and they set the stronghold on fire over them, so that all the people of the Tower of Shechem also died, about a thousand men and women.

50Then Abimelech went to Thebez, and encamped against Thebez, and took it. ⁵¹But there was a strong tower within the city, and all the men and women and all the lords of the city fled to it and shut themselves in; and they went to the roof of the tower. ⁵²Abimelech came to the tower, and fought against it, and came near to the entrance of the tower to burn it with fire. ⁵³But a certain woman threw an upper millstone on Abimelech's head, and crushed his skull. ⁵⁴Immediately he called to the young man who carried his armor and said to him, "Draw your sword and kill me, so people will not say about me, 'A woman killed him.'" So the young man thrust him through, and he died. ⁵⁵When the Israelites saw that Abimelech was dead, they all went home. ⁵⁶Thus God repaid Abimelech for the crime he committed against his father in killing his seventy brothers; ⁵⁷and God also made all the wickedness of the people of Shechem fall back on their heads, and on them came the curse of Jotham son of Jerubbaal.

COMMENTARY

Two observations begin the exploration of Judges 9: Abimelech is the first person in the Bible overtly to assert for himself the title of "king," and Abimelech's violent and vengeful brand of kingship is the antithesis of the kind of ruler the book of Judges advocates. This judgment appears most clearly in Jotham's fable, which Martin Buber has called "the strongest anti-monarchical poem of world literature."[40] Abimelech's experi-

40. Martin Buber, "Books of Judges and Book of Judges," in *Kingship of God* (New York: Harper & Row, 1967) 75.

ment in kingship ultimately comes to an ignoble and abrupt end. After Abimelech, Israel's mode of governance will revert to the system of temporary judges in Jephthah and Samson (chaps. 10–16). Ultimately, however, the experiment in judgeship itself will suffer the same fate as Abimelech's violent brand of kingship and come to a similar disastrous end (chaps. 17–21).

9:1-21. Abimelech's father was a son of Gideon. His mother was a concubine or woman slave from the city of Shechem. As the son of a slave woman, Abimelech had less status than the seventy other sons of Gideon, whose mothers were not concubines. Abimelech desires to overcome his low status by first establishing a power base with the inhabitants of Shechem, his mother's hometown. He argues that his single leadership would be less taxing and preferable to being ruled by all the seventy sons of Gideon. He also appeals to his kinship with the Shechemites: "I am your bone and your flesh." The leaders of Shechem agree to support him because "he is our brother" (v. 3). They give him money to hire an army of "worthless and reckless fellows" (v. 4). His first act is to go and kill "his brothers," the seventy sons of Gideon, "on one stone." Two ironies flow from this brutal mass murder. The first irony is that Abimelech's macho savagery against his seventy Israelite brothers "on one stone" will be answered at the end of his life by a woman's "millstone" thrown upon his head (vv. 5, 53, 56).[41] The second irony is that the Shechemites, who felt secure in their support of Abimelech because "he is our brother," should have learned from this massacre how Abimelech treats his "brothers." Indeed, Abimelech will eventually attack and kill all his Shechemite "brothers" just as he had killed his brothers who were the sons of Gideon (vv. 3, 34-49, 57).

After Abimelech kills Gideon's seventy sons, the leaders of Shechem and Beth-millo make him "king" in a covenant ceremony at "the oak of the pillar at Shechem." The mention of the oak and the pillar is likely a reference to a Canaanite worship site (see Gen 35:4). Shechem as a city had both positive and negative memories for Israel. Israel remembered a brutal confrontation

with the Canaanites of Shechem headed by a man named Hamor (Genesis 34). After Joshua's conquest of Canaan, Shechem became a famous Israelite site for covenant ceremonies of blessing and curse (Joshua 24). The bones of the revered ancestor Jacob were also buried at Shechem (Josh 24:32). Later in Israel's history, Shechem gained more negative associations after King Solomon's death when the united kingdom of Israel was split into two kingdoms, northern Israel and southern Judah. Solomon's son Rehoboam, who ruled the southern kingdom of Judah, was initially crowned king at Shechem (1 Kgs 12:1). Rehoboam's rival, King Jeroboam of the northern kingdom of Israel, then built his own royal palace at Shechem as a rival of the southern capital of Jerusalem (1 Kgs 12:25). Thus Shechem conjured up associations with covenants of curse and blessing as well as troubled and divisive kingships in Israel's memory.

Once Abimelech is declared king at Shechem, Jotham steps onto the stage. Jotham is the one remaining son of Gideon who had escaped the slaughter of Gideon's family. He stands on top of Mt. Gerizim, a place tradition had associated with covenants and proclaiming a blessing (Deut 27:12; Josh 8:33). However, Jotham proclaims not a blessing but a curse on Abimelech and the residents of Shechem in the form of a fable about trees and a bramble bush (vv. 8-15). In the fable, the trees symbolize the people of Shechem who are looking for someone to anoint as king over them. They ask various fruit trees and vines, who all say no to kingship (vv. 8-13). Finally, they ask a worthless bramble bush, who invites them to "come and take refuge in my shade" (v. 15). "Shade" (צל *ṣēl*) as protection was a frequent image associated with kings in the ancient Near East. However, the scrawny bramble bush offers little actual shade; its only real value is as kindling for fire. The bramble bush represents Abimelech, who becomes the king of the "trees" of Shechem. They join forces in a covenant with a meager blessing—the thin shade of a bramble bush—and a much more dangerous curse—a forest fire started with the kindling of the bramble (v. 15).

In the fable itself, curse and blessing are dependent on whether the "trees" of Shechem act "in good faith" in anointing Abimelech as king (v. 15). Jotham's explanation of the fable expands this key condition for curse or blessing. The central

---

41. T. A. Boogart, "Stone for Stone: Retribution in the Story of Abimelech and Shechem," *JSOT* 32 (1985) 45-56; J. Gerald Janzen, "A Certain Woman in the Rhetoric of Judges 9," *JSOT* 38 (1987) 33-37.

question is this: Did the people of Shechem act "in good faith and honor *with Jerubbaal and with his house*" when they crowned Abimelech king (vv. 16, 19-20)? Gideon, or Jerubbaal, had risked his life to save Shechem from the Midian invaders. Is Shechem showing proper gratitude and honor toward Gideon by crowning the murderer of his sons as king? If the answer is yes, then Shechem will rejoice. On the other hand, if crowning Abimelech, who massacred the seventy sons of Gideon (or Jerubbaal), dishonored the house of Gideon, then "let fire come from Abimelech" to destroy the towns of Shechem and Beth-millo, and let fire from Shechem and Beth-millo also destroy Abimelech (v. 20). Of course, Jotham's conditions already contain their answer. Abimelech, and by association the Shechemites, has grievously dishonored Gideon's house, and thus the curse will indeed come into effect. The rest of the story of Abimelech recounts the working out of this curse.

9:22-57. Abimelech rules for only three years (v. 22). Other rulers of Israel in the judges period typically ruled for forty years or longer. The brevity of Abimelech's reign is the eventual result of God's sending "an evil spirit between Abimelech and the lords of Shechem" (v. 23). God's Spirit had inspired the model judge Othniel to victory (3:10). God's Spirit had also come upon Gideon with somewhat less dramatic effect, but he was at least successful in uniting some of the Israelite tribes (see the Commentary on 6:34). In Abimelech's case, the divine Spirit actually causes division and conflict between people rather than uniting them. God sends the evil and divisive spirit as just retribution for the murder of Gideon's seventy sons. The conflict starts as the Shechemites begin to ambush and rob travelers "out of hostility" to Abimelech (v. 25). The conflict intensifies when a Canaanite named "Gaal" (related to the Hebrew verb נעל [*gāʿal*, "to loathe," "to abhor"]) moves into Shechem and wins the loyalty of the lords of Shechem away from Abimelech. Just as Abimelech had appealed to his mother's kinship with the Shechemites, so also Gaal appeals to the Shechemites' kinship bond to their earlier Canaanite ancestor "Hamor father of Shechem" (v. 28; see Genesis 34).

Zebul is Abimelech's one remaining supporter in Shechem. He gets wind of Gaal's plot to win the allegiance of Shechem away from Abimelech and

promptly informs him. Abimelech then launches a surprise attack on the city of Shechem that moves in three phases. First, Abimelech's army defeats Gaal and his forces (vv. 34-41). It would have been reasonable for Abimelech to have ended his attack at that point, satisfied with eliminating Gaal and his supporters. However, he takes revenge to an extreme in a manner similar to his father, Gideon. Gideon had earlier destroyed the towns of Succoth and Penuel, including the tower of Penuel, in retaliation for their taunts against him (8:4-17). Abimelech likewise takes vengeance to an extreme. In the second phase of his attack on the next day, he kills all the common people of Shechem who came out in the morning to work in the fields outside the city. Abimelech's disagreement was with Gaal and the lords of Shechem, not with these commoners of Shechem. Yet he kills them all. Then Abimelech enters the city itself, burns it to the ground, and sows it with salt so that nothing will ever grow there again (vv. 42-45). The third phase of Abimelech's attack is aimed at the inner circle of Shechem's leaders, the "lords of the Tower of Shechem." These lords shut themselves up in the tower, which functioned as a temple of the Canaanite god El-berith (meaning "god of the covenant"). The god's name recalls the covenant that Abimelech made with Shechem, which Jotham interpreted in his fable as a covenant of curse. The fable's curse about Abimelech as the fiery bramble bush (v. 20) literally comes true as Abimelech and his army frantically gather bundles of brush and set fire to them at the base of the tower to burn it, killing about a thousand men and women in the process (vv. 46-49).

Abimelech's frenzied attacks of unwarranted and extreme revenge show a portrait of a madman out of control. The final episode in this violent despot's life is his seemingly random attack on the town of Thebez, which was not involved in the Shechem affair. One senses that Abimelech is randomly slaughtering people for no apparent reason. Attacks on towers characterize the vengeful rampages of both Gideon and Abimelech. Gideon had attacked the tower at Penuel (8:17); Abimelech had earlier attacked the tower of Shechem (9:46-49). Abimelech assaults still another tower, the tower of Thebez (9:50-52). It is at this tower that Abimelech meets his end when "a certain woman" at the top of the tower throws a "mill-stone," which hits Abimelech and crushes his skull (v. 53). Before he dies, Abimelech commands his armorbearer to drive his sword into him lest people say of Abimelech, "A woman killed him." For this macho, violent madman, that would be the ultimate shame. The irony is, of course, that this story has been remembered throughout the ages. Abimelech is repaid with death and shame for his savagery against Gideon's sons every time the story is retold. Abimelech joins the ranks of the Canaanite general Sisera, who also died at the hand of a woman. The major

difference is that Sisera had been an enemy, a Canaanite. Abimelech was the son of one of Israel's judges who killed and fought against his own people. The enemy is no longer only foreign generals. The enemy has become one of Israel's own rulers. The social fabric of Israel has experienced a major tear. The question will be whether Abimelech's tenure was a momentary lapse from which Israel will shortly recover. Or has Israel begun an irreversible downhill slide into social and religious chaos? The stories of the next major judges, Jephthah and Samson, will lead us further into answers to those questions.

REFLECTIONS

1. It may trouble us to read that God may at times send an evil spirit within communities or groups to stir up conflict, divisiveness, and disunity. God usually seems on the side of harmony, unity, and reconciliation within communities. The apostle Paul urges the Christian community to live harmoniously together as the body of Christ, whose members "though many, are one body" and who live "in the one Spirit" (1 Cor 12:12-13 NRSV). Psalm 133 declares, "How very good and pleasant it is when kindred live together in unity. . . . For there the LORD ordained his blessing, life forevermore" (Ps 133:1, 3 NRSV). Yet there are circumstances when God does disrupt unified communities when they have become too powerful and their actions stand too strongly in opposition to the will and purpose of God. The classic example is the story of the tower of Babel (Gen 11:1-9), another tower story in the Bible, which echoes the attack on the tower of Shechem. Humanity had unified itself for the purpose of building a tower to reach to the heavens in order to "make a name for ourselves" (Gen 11:4 NRSV). God discerned that this world-unifying project had self-centeredness and rebellion written all over it. Thus God confused the tower builders' language and scattered them across the earth. The humans' rebellious power was thereby dispersed and limited. The violent alliance of Abimelech and the Shechemites was similarly self-centered and rebellious in its intentions. Thus God's spirit stirred up divisions among them so that their power would be diffused and their treachery finally ended.

The rise and fall of modern-day empires, hate groups, dictators, and oppressive systems invite consideration of how God may be working today in our own world and time in analogous ways. Even communities of God's people who are severely conflicted with hateful feelings of vengeance must ask themselves hard questions. Is the community's extreme ill will in part God's judgment on the community for past purposes and actions that have run counter to the purposes God may have envisioned for that community? Of course, some conflict and disagreement within a community are normal and even desirable for a vital and creative group. However, a given community can reach a point when conflict becomes so hurtful and deep that it paralyzes rather than energizes the community or groups within the community. Then it is time for soul searching and serious evaluation of the community's mission and its relationships to God and to other communities with whom it relates.

2. The story of Abimelech is sometimes interpreted as a general indictment of any form of kingship or centralized form of government within Israel. However, Judges 9 and its fable indict a specific form of kingship characterized by gaining power through brute force and violence. The major issue with Abimelech and Shechem is that they did not "exhibit loyalty to the house of" Jerubbabel/Gideon when they participated in the massacre of Gideon's seventy sons (8:35; 9:16-20, 56-57). Gideon had risked his life for them, and they returned evil for good. In the final analysis, the book of Judges will support certain forms of kingship and centralized authority. The positive attributes of such a model of kingship for the book of Judges would include the following elements: (1) a dynasty or family line of rulers whom God would choose; (2) a king who would unite all Israel, not by force or violence, but by persuasion and an earned loyalty; and (3) a king who would be faithful and subject to God's guidance and who would lead the people in devotion to the one true God of Israel. Abimelech fell short in every category. The politics of Abimelech—ruthless violence, hunger for power, back-stabbing vengeance, irrational assault, the worship of other gods—are roundly condemned in the strongest terms in Judges 9. Such violence in political life repeated itself often in Israel's history of kingship (1 Kgs 15:29; 2 Kgs 9:1–10:17), and violence has continued to mar the political struggles of human communities across the globe and throughout history up to the present day. Judges 9 provides a realistic portrait of the potential evil of human politics, power, and violence.

3. The disloyalty and ingratitude that Abimelech and the Shechemites displayed to their deliverer Gideon is a mirror of the disloyalty and lack of gratitude that Israel as a people showed toward the Lord. Religion and politics are intertwined in the stories. Israel's disloyalty to God begins and ends the Gideon cycle (6:7-10; 8:33-35). That religious disloyalty seeps into the political life of Israel. Israelites forgot how to show gratefulness and fidelity both to their God, who saved them from Egypt, and to their human leader Gideon, who delivered them from Midian. The quality of our theology shapes and influences the quality of both our political and our personal relationships. Good theology ought to have practical effects on how humans relate to each other.

Judges 10:1-5, Tola and Jair: Two Minor Judges

NIV	NRSV
10 After the time of Abimelech a man of Issachar, Tola son of Puah, the son of Dodo, rose to save Israel. He lived in Shamir, in the hill country of Ephraim. [a]He led Israel twenty-three years; then he died, and was buried in Shamir. [3]He was followed by Jair of Gilead, who led Israel twenty-two years. [4]He had thirty sons, who rode thirty donkeys. They controlled thirty towns in Gilead, which to this day are called Havvoth Jair.[b] [5]When Jair died, he was buried in Kamon.	**10** After Abimelech, Tola son of Puah son of Dodo, a man of Issachar, who lived at Shamir in the hill country of Ephraim, rose to deliver Israel. [2]He judged Israel twenty-three years. Then he died, and was buried at Shamir. [3]After him came Jair the Gileadite, who judged Israel twenty-two years. [4]He had thirty sons who rode on thirty donkeys; and they had thirty towns, which are in the land of Gilead, and are called Havvoth-jair to this day. [5]Jair died, and was buried in Kamon.
[a]2 Traditionally *judged*; also in verse 3 [b]4 Or *called the settlements of Jair*	

COMMENTARY

A second interlude of the so-called minor judges appears at the end of this middle phase of the judges period (6:1–10:5). Three separate notices of minor judges appear in the book of Judges, one for each of the three phases of the judges era:

(1) Shamgar, at the middle of the first victorious and faithful phase in 3:31; (2) Tola and Jair at the end of the transitional phase in 10:1-5; and (3) Ibzan, Elon, and Abdon at the middle of the third tragic phase of the judges in 12:8-15. The first

minor judge, Shamgar, mirrored the positive success of the major judges of the first phase (Ehud, Deborah/Barak) as he was victorious over Israel's enemy and "delivered Israel" (3:31). The two minor judges in 10:1-5, Tola and Jair, reflect the ambiguous and transitional character of the two judges or rulers in this middle phase of the judges, Gideon and Abimelech. On one hand, Gideon successfully defeated the Midianites and gave Israel rest from its enemies for forty years (8:28). On the other hand, Gideon led Israel into idolatry (8:27), Abimelech violently seized power as king (9:5-6), and both of them used excessive violence in acts of personal revenge (8:4-17; 9:22-57).

Similarly, the first minor judge in this period, Tola, successfully "rose to deliver Israel" and ruled for twenty-three years. Tola's success mirrors the success of Gideon. However, the second minor judge, Jair, never is said to have delivered Israel or defeated an enemy. Jair's judgeship of twenty-two years seems selfishly preoccupied with internal consolidation of the family's power and wealth: thirty sons who ride on thirty donkeys and possess thirty towns. Jair seems less oriented to helping Israel or serving God and more oriented to helping himself and his own family. Thus the transition from Tola's successful deliverance of Israel to Jair's preoccupation with himself and his family's welfare is a microcosm of the turn from Gideon's deliverance to Abimelech's self-absorbed grab for power.

REFLECTIONS

1. The interludes of the minor judges have the literary effect of providing pauses of relative calm and stability within the increasingly chaotic and unstable era of the judges. God's work through these minor judges suggests not so much God's dramatic intervention as God's quiet and often hidden sustaining work within the ordinary life of families, communities, and nations. Such momentary respites of order and stability in the lives of individuals and communities allow time for renewal before we face the next round of challenges and difficulties. The minor judge episodes function as "narrative sabbaths," brief moments of relative quiet and refreshment. The minor judge interlude allows some brief narrative time for readers to ponder their reactions and their role in the events that have transpired before we are thrown again into the dilemmas, struggles, and tragedies of major judges like Jephthah and Samson.

2. The two minor judges, Tola and Jair, represent a transition in the era of the judges, as do the major judges Gideon and Abimelech. As implied readers of Judges who have read only this far in the book, however, we may not be able to discern whether these judges in the middle section of Judges represent a major turning point downward in Israel's national life or only a momentary relapse from which it will recover with the subsequent judgeships of Jephthah and Samson. Of course, when we survey the whole book with the chaos and the tragedy of the final chapters, Judges 17–21, we then can know the answer. The events of 6:1–10:5 do indeed mark a major turning point and a defining moment of decline and transition.

This experience of readers who may have some unclarity about the significance of events when we are still in the midst of them and cannot see the long view or the final outcome is analogous to our experience in the life of faith. When in the midst of a time of despair or other difficulty, we may not be able to know what our future holds. Are we at the beginning of a downward slide into a long and arduous experience of suffering with no foreseeable end? Or is this only a momentary setback, a brief time of struggle from which we will soon recover? In such times, we remember God's faithfulness to God's people over the long haul in the past. Remembrances of God's past loyalty and love provide a long view, reaching backward, that may help to put moments of difficult transition in perspective. We also have God's promises for the future of divine presence, strength, and ultimate victory over all things—even death—to sustain us with a long perspective that reaches forward (Rom 8:37-39). Even as Israel turns toward social and religious disintegration at this point in the book, Israel can be sustained by God's past love and future promises that somehow God will continue to preserve and shape Israel toward a hopeful future. Out of Israel's struggle and transition into decline will eventually come Israel's new life, new promises, and new hope. However, it may be difficult to see any of that clearly now. Israel, as God's people in every time and place, must live by faith and not by sight.

JUDGES 10:6–12:15, JEPHTHAH, IBZAN, ELON, AND ABDON

OVERVIEW

The narrative of Jephthah begins the third and final phase of the individual judge stories. The first phase (3:7–5:31) had featured consistently faithful and victorious judges (Othniel, Ehud, Deborah/Barak). The second transitional phase (6:1–10:5) included the judge Gideon and his son Abimelech, who represented the beginning of the downfall of the judges. Gideon was successful in defeating Israel's enemies and giving Israel rest for forty years. However, the leadership of Gideon and Abimelech began to degenerate into religious idolatry and selfish acts of violence aimed not only at external enemies but also at other Israelites. The third phase of the judge stories (10:6–16:31) portrays two major judges, Jephthah and Samson. These judges continue the descent into a widening distance from God and a growing inability to unite and defend Israel against its enemies for a sustained period of time. Both Jephthah and Samson experience a deeply tragic turnabout in their lives. A foolish vow compels Jephthah to sacrifice the life of his only daughter, and a reckless revelation to Delilah leads Samson into disgrace and death. Their individual stories of tragedy become precursors of Israel's collective tragedy and disintegration in the final section of the book, chaps. 17–21.

A key theme in the Jephthah narrative is the entrapment of human language that leads to death. Jephthah's vow forces him to kill or sacrifice his one child, his daughter, who represents his only link to future life. The name "Jephthah" means in Hebrew "he opens" (יפתח *yiptāḥ*), and the climax of his story is when Jephthah opens his mouth to speak the terrible vow he cannot take back: "For I have opened my mouth to the LORD, and I cannot take back my vow" (11:35-36). In the final scene, fellow Israelites from the tribe of Ephraim are forced to say a single word with a different dialect ("sibboleth" instead of "shibboleth"). Because they pronounce this one word differently, 42,000 of the Ephraimites die at the hands of Jephthah and his army. Human words and dialogue are important throughout Jephthah's story; five scenes form the structural backbone, and a dialogue stands at the center of each scene. The scenes include (1) Israel and the Lord (10:6-16), (2) the elders of Gilead and Jephthah (10:17–11:11), (3) Jephthah and the Ammonite king (11:12-28), (4) Jephthah and his daughter (11:29-38), and (5) Jephthah and the Ephraimites (12:1-7).[42]

These five scenes and their central dialogues reveal Israel's deepening failure to remain faithful to God and united to one another. This growing failure emerges when we compare the Jephthah narrative with the preceding judge stories and the plot that is repeated in each story. The early judge stories spoke of Israel's sin in brief and general terms, but the Jephthah story concentrates more extensively on Israel's sin as the worship of other gods (10:6; cf. 3:12; 4:1). The enemy's oppression is briefly noted in the earlier stories but occupies much more space in the Jephthah cycle (10:6-16; cf. 3:13; 4:2). Israel's cry of distress led to immediate divine deliverance in the earlier stories (3:15; 4:3-7). But Israel's cry and repentance in the Jephthah tale lead to God's harsh rebuke of Israel's sin and God's initial refusal to deliver

42. Barry Webb, *The Book of the Judges: An Integrated Reading* (Sheffield: JSOT, 1987) 41-78.

Israel (10:10-14). Previous judges had united several Israelite tribes (including Ephraim) in the battle against their enemies (3:27; 5:14). Jephthah is unable to unite even one entire tribe but only the district or clan of Gilead, located east of the Jordan. Moreover, he ends up killing 42,000 Ephraimites who were part of the Israelite people. Disunity rather than unity in Israel characterizes Jephthah's tenure as judge. Gideon had also had a dispute with the Ephraimites, but he had resolved the quarrel peacefully (8:1-3). In contrast, Jephthah's dispute with Ephraim ends with a slaughter (12:1-6). The early judge stories kept the spotlight on

God and the military deliverance, but Jephthah's story focuses much more on the human judge and less attention on God. The early judges gain forty or more years of "rest" from Israel's enemies (3:30; 5:31; 8:28). However, Jephthah reigns for only six years and does not gain "rest" from Israel's enemies (12:7). At every point of comparison, Jephthah indicates a degradation from previous judge stories.[43]

43. Lawson Stone, "From Tribal Confederation to Monarchic State: The Editorial Perspective of the Book of Judges" (Ph.D. diss., Yale University; Ann Arbor: University Microfilms, 1987) 260-391, provides an extended argument for the redactional shaping of the individual judge stories into three phases of gradual decline.

Judges 10:6–11:11, Israel, the Lord, and Jephthah

NIV

[6]Again the Israelites did evil in the eyes of the LORD. They served the Baals and the Ashtoreths, and the gods of Aram, the gods of Sidon, the gods of Moab, the gods of the Ammonites and the gods of the Philistines. And because the Israelites forsook the LORD and no longer served him, [7]he became angry with them. He sold them into the hands of the Philistines and the Ammonites, [8]who that year shattered and crushed them. For eighteen years they oppressed all the Israelites on the east side of the Jordan in Gilead, the land of the Amorites. [9]The Ammonites also crossed the Jordan to fight against Judah, Benjamin and the house of Ephraim; and Israel was in great distress. [10]Then the Israelites cried out to the LORD, "We have sinned against you, forsaking our God and serving the Baals."

[11]The LORD replied, "When the Egyptians, the Amorites, the Ammonites, the Philistines, [12]the Sidonians, the Amalekites and the Maonites[a] oppressed you and you cried to me for help, did I not save you from their hands? [13]But you have forsaken me and served other gods, so I will no longer save you. [14]Go and cry out to the gods you have chosen. Let them save you when you are in trouble!"

[15]But the Israelites said to the LORD, "We have sinned. Do with us whatever you think best, but please rescue us now." [16]Then they got rid of the foreign gods among them and served the LORD. And he could bear Israel's misery no longer.

[a]12 Hebrew; some Septuagint manuscripts Midianites

NRSV

6The Israelites again did what was evil in the sight of the LORD, worshiping the Baals and the Astartes, the gods of Aram, the gods of Sidon, the gods of Moab, the gods of the Ammonites, and the gods of the Philistines. Thus they abandoned the LORD, and did not worship him. [7]So the anger of the LORD was kindled against Israel, and he sold them into the hand of the Philistines and into the hand of the Ammonites, [8]and they crushed and oppressed the Israelites that year. For eighteen years they oppressed all the Israelites that were beyond the Jordan in the land of the Amorites, which is in Gilead. [9]The Ammonites also crossed the Jordan to fight against Judah and against Benjamin and against the house of Ephraim; so that Israel was greatly distressed.

10So the Israelites cried to the LORD, saying, "We have sinned against you, because we have abandoned our God and have worshiped the Baals." [11]And the LORD said to the Israelites, "Did I not deliver you[a] from the Egyptians and from the Amorites, from the Ammonites and from the Philistines? [12]The Sidonians also, and the Amalekites, and the Maonites, oppressed you; and you cried to me, and I delivered you out of their hand. [13]Yet you have abandoned me and worshiped other gods; therefore I will deliver you no more. [14]Go and cry to the gods whom you have chosen; let them deliver you in the time of your

[a] Heb lacks Did I not deliver you

NIV

17When the Ammonites were called to arms and camped in Gilead, the Israelites assembled and camped at Mizpah. 18The leaders of the people of Gilead said to each other, "Whoever will launch the attack against the Ammonites will be the head of all those living in Gilead."

11 Jephthah the Gileadite was a mighty warrior. His father was Gilead; his mother was a prostitute. 2Gilead's wife also bore him sons, and when they were grown up, they drove Jephthah away. "You are not going to get any inheritance in our family," they said, "because you are the son of another woman." 3So Jephthah fled from his brothers and settled in the land of Tob, where a group of adventurers gathered around him and followed him.

4Some time later, when the Ammonites made war on Israel, 5the elders of Gilead went to get Jephthah from the land of Tob. 6"Come," they said, "be our commander, so we can fight the Ammonites."

7Jephthah said to them, "Didn't you hate me and drive me from my father's house? Why do you come to me now, when you're in trouble?"

8The elders of Gilead said to him, "Nevertheless, we are turning to you now; come with us to fight the Ammonites, and you will be our head over all who live in Gilead."

9Jephthah answered, "Suppose you take me back to fight the Ammonites and the LORD gives them to me—will I really be your head?"

10The elders of Gilead replied, "The LORD is our witness; we will certainly do as you say." 11So Jephthah went with the elders of Gilead, and the people made him head and commander over them. And he repeated all his words before the LORD in Mizpah.

NRSV

distress." 15And the Israelites said to the LORD, "We have sinned; do to us whatever seems good to you; but deliver us this day!" 16So they put away the foreign gods from among them and worshiped the LORD; and he could no longer bear to see Israel suffer.

17Then the Ammonites were called to arms, and they encamped in Gilead; and the Israelites came together, and they encamped at Mizpah. 18The commanders of the people of Gilead said to one another, "Who will begin the fight against the Ammonites? He shall be head over all the inhabitants of Gilead."

11 Now Jephthah the Gileadite, the son of a prostitute, was a mighty warrior. Gilead was the father of Jephthah. 2Gilead's wife also bore him sons; and when his wife's sons grew up, they drove Jephthah away, saying to him, "You shall not inherit anything in our father's house; for you are the son of another woman." 3Then Jephthah fled from his brothers and lived in the land of Tob. Outlaws collected around Jephthah and went raiding with him.

4After a time the Ammonites made war against Israel. 5And when the Ammonites made war against Israel, the elders of Gilead went to bring Jephthah from the land of Tob. 6They said to Jephthah, "Come and be our commander, so that we may fight with the Ammonites." 7But Jephthah said to the elders of Gilead, "Are you not the very ones who rejected me and drove me out of my father's house? So why do you come to me now when you are in trouble?" 8The elders of Gilead said to Jephthah, "Nevertheless, we have now turned back to you, so that you may go with us and fight with the Ammonites, and become head over us, over all the inhabitants of Gilead." 9Jephthah said to the elders of Gilead, "If you bring me home again to fight with the Ammonites, and the LORD gives them over to me, I will be your head." 10And the elders of Gilead said to Jephthah, "The LORD will be witness between us; we will surely do as you say." 11So Jephthah went with the elders of Gilead, and the people made him head and commander over them; and Jephthah spoke all his words before the LORD at Mizpah.

COMMENTARY

The two scenes that begin the Jephthah narrative function as mirror images. In the first scene (10:6-16), *the Lord* rebuffs Israel for asking for help after the Israelites had earlier rejected the Lord: "You have abandoned me and worshiped other gods" (10:13). In the second scene (10:17–11:11), *Jephthah* rebukes the elders of Gilead for asking for his help after the elders had earlier rejected him. His words closely resemble the words used by the Lord: "Are you not the very ones who rejected me?" In spite of the initial rebuke, however, both scenes end with the Lord and Jephthah responding favorably to the pleas for help. Although similar, these paired scenes also illustrate a crucial distinction. The Lord responds graciously to Israel's cry of distress with no appreciable benefit to the Lord. In fact, Israel increasingly rejects the Lord in favor of other gods in spite of the Lord's favor. On the other hand, Jephthah's response to the cries of distress leads to his elevation from the status of a rejected son of a prostitute to "the head and commander" of the people of Gilead. God acts out of unrequited love, while Jephthah acts out of self-interest.

10:6-16. The Jephthah cycle opens with the usual introductory description of Israel again doing "what was evil in the sight of the LORD." However, the nature of the evil involving the worship of other gods has worsened. In the previous era of Gideon, Israel had worshiped only Canaanite or Amorite gods (6:10, 25; 8:33). In the era of Jephthah, the Israelites extend their religious devotion to a virtual supermarket of foreign gods from Canaan, Aram, Sidon, Moab, Ammon, and Philistia (v. 6). As punishment for their increasing disloyalty, the Lord allows the foreign nations of Philistia and Ammon to oppress Israel for eighteen years. As in the other judge episodes, the Israelites "cried to the LORD" for help (v. 10; see 3:9, 15; 4:3; 6:7).

But this time the Israelites add something to their typical cry for aid. They speak words of repentance and remorse for their sinful ways: "We have sinned against you" (v. 10). Israel has never confessed its sin in this way before in the judges stories. Unfortunately, the condition of the people has deteriorated to such a state that the Lord receives these words of repentance as a shallow ploy to manipulate God. The words do not convince the Lord in the light of the repeated backsliding of Israel in the past. God had saved the Israelites from seven different oppressors in the past. Yet, each time the Israelites had rejected the Lord and returned to worshiping the gods of those same oppressing nations (cf. v. 6 and vv. 11-12). Thus the Lord comes to a startling and terrifying conclusion: "therefore I will deliver you no more" (v. 13). The divine pronouncement is Israel's death sentence. Without God's presence and deliverance, Israel is doomed. The Lord urges Israel to "go and cry" for help from these other foreign gods that Israel had repeatedly worshiped. "Let them deliver you" (v. 14).

The Israelites are persistent, however, and beg God with a second word of repentance (v. 15). Moreover, the Israelites bolster their words with action: They "put away" their alien gods and worship the Lord. The next line is crucial, but its meaning is debated. The Lord "could no longer bear to see Israel suffer" (v. 16). Many commentators assume that Israel's actions and words have convinced the Lord of Israel's genuine and deep remorse. This profound repentance, they argue, is what causes the Lord to alter the earlier pronouncement of never again delivering Israel. Another biblical example of this divine change of heart in response to human repentance to which these commentators point is that of the city of Nineveh in the book of Jonah. The inhabitants of Nineveh repented after hearing Jonah's words of doom, and their repentance caused God to spare the city from destruction (Jonah 3:10; see Jer 18:7-8). Many commentators conclude that the same dynamic is at work here.[44]

However, the Lord's reaction in v. 16 is more ambiguous and indeterminate than such an interpretation allows. The verb translated "to bear" (קצר *qāṣar*) often carries connotations of frustration, loss of patience, anger, and exasperation (Num 21:4-5; Zech 11:8-9). It is the verb used when Samson becomes so exasperated with Delilah's constant nag-

---

44. See Robert G. Boling, *Judges*, AB 6A (Garden City, N.Y.: Doubleday, 1975) 193; J. Alberto Soggin, *Judges*, OTL (Philadelphia: Westminster, 1981) 203.

ging that he reveals the secret of his strength (16:16). Thus one might well read the Lord's response in v. 16 not as God's joyful agreement to deliver Israel because of its genuine and sustained repentance. Rather, the Lord knows that this repentance will again be temporary and shallow, but the Lord in total exasperation and anger "cannot bear to see Israel suffer." It is Israel's *suffering,* not Israel's deep repentance, that motivates any potential change in the Lord's plans.[45] We assume that God will somehow reluctantly intervene. However, the text does not say that the Lord immediately raises up a deliverer as in the earlier judge stories. The reader is left to wonder how God is involved in the next series of events and whether those events will lead to Israel's deliverance from its enemies. As we shall see, this ambiguity about God's role in the judgeship of Jephthah is the first of a number of indeterminate moments in the story of Jephthah the judge.

10:17–11:11. The next scene opens with the Ammonite army getting ready to fight Israel. Meanwhile, the Israelites in the Transjordan region of Gilead are frantically scrambling to find a military leader who is willing to fight the Ammonites. They offer a reward to the one who will step forward: "He shall be head over all the inhabitants of Gilead" (10:18). The narrator interrupts the flow of the story to introduce a "mighty warrior" named Jephthah. Jephthah is an Israelite from Gilead, but he has some deficits according to Israel's social code: He is "the son of a prostitute," an outcast from his family, and a leader of outlaws who raid villages in the foreign "land of Tob" for a living (10:1-3). Jephthah's character reminds us

of the ill-fated Abimelech, who was the despised son of a concubine (8:31), in conflict with his other brothers (9:5), and the leader of outlaws (9:4). These associations with the negative figure of Abimelech do not bode well for Jephthah's future, but in the end (unlike Abimelech) he will be called one who "judged Israel six years" (12:7).

In 11:4, the narrator returns to the story about the Ammonites' making war on the Israelite people of Gilead. Although the Gileadites had earlier rejected Jephthah as one of their own, the elders of Gilead beg Jephthah in their distress to return home and save his people from the Ammonite oppressors. Just as Israel had earlier rejected God and then returned to call on God for help, so also the people of Gilead return to call on Jephthah for help. Jephthah asks a legitimate question: "Are you not the very ones who rejected me?" But the Gileadites insist and offer Jephthah the position of leader "over all the inhabitants of Gilead" if he conquers the Ammonites. Jephthah then accepts the offer to fight the Ammonites with a condition that links his mission with the Lord's plan: if "the LORD gives them over to me" (11:9). This is Jephthah's first vow involving the Lord; his second vow will be more problematic (11:29-40). The elders of Gilead then pledge, "The LORD will be witness between us," and the deal is struck "before the LORD at Mizpah" (11:9-11). This sudden cluster of references to "the LORD" suggests to the reader that Jephthah may indeed be the Lord's chosen agent to deliver Israel in spite of his questionable character. Our interest is piqued and focused on this ambiguous character, who is both "mighty warrior" and "son of a prostitute," both pious adherent to the Lord and shrewd negotiator for his own interests.

---

45. Robert Polzin, *Moses and the Deuteronomist: A Literary Study of the Deuteronomic History* (New York: Seabury, 1980) 177; Webb, *The Book of the Judges,* 45-48.

REFLECTIONS

1. Israel's words of repentance and God's refusal to accept the repentance as sufficient or genuine invite reflection on the role of human repentance in motivating God's forgiveness and acts of compassion. God often does accept repentance and a change of heart as sufficient grounds to grant a person or group mercy and compassion. The psalmist reminds us that "the sacrifice acceptable to God is a broken spirit;/ a broken and contrite heart,/ O God, you will not despise" (Ps 51:17 NRSV). God speaks through the prophet Jeremiah in a similar vein: "At one moment I may declare concerning a nation or a kingdom, that I will pluck up and break down and destroy it, but if that nation, concerning which I have spoken, turns from its evil, I will change my mind about the disaster that I intended to bring on it" (Jer 18:7-8 NRSV).

Yet even in cases of true repentance and God's change of mind concerning judgment, the repentant people sometimes must still suffer negative consequences from their misdeeds. For example, God forgave the Israelites for their worship of the golden calf at Mt. Sinai (Exod 32:10, 14). However, some of the Israelites still suffered death and a plague for their sin (Exod 35:25-28, 34-35). Later in the wilderness, Moses' appeal to God's merciful nature caused God to forgive Israel's sin of refusing to enter the promised land of Canaan (Num 14:10-20). But again severe consequences accompanied the forgiveness: The old generation of Israelites would have to die in the wilderness, and God would allow only a new generation of Israelites born in the wilderness to enter the land of Canaan (Num 14:21-35).

At other times in the Bible, words and even actions that display human repentance have no effect on God. At times, the people have become so corrupt and disloyal at their core that no hope for true and sustained repentance seems possible. An important example is God's indictment of Israel's shallow repentance in Hos 5:8–6:6. Israel utters words of repentance, but God knows these words are manipulative, hollow, and not heartfelt. God seems genuinely at a loss on how to turn Israel around:

What shall I do with you, O Ephraim?
  What shall I do with you, O Judah?
Your love is like a morning cloud,
  like the dew that goes away early. (Hos 6:4 NRSV)

A classic example of Israel's shallow repentance is recorded in Jeremiah 34. The prophet Jeremiah proclaimed doom on the city of Jerusalem and its king, Zedekiah. As a result, the king issued a decree setting all Israelite slaves free in accordance with a widely ignored biblical law that commanded the periodic release of all Israelite slaves. The king hoped the freeing of Israelite slaves would demonstrate to God that Zedekiah and his people were truly repentant. This in turn would motivate God to deliver Israel from the Babylonian army, which had surrounded the city. However, when the Babylonian army got up and left for a time to attend to another crisis elsewhere, the Israelites immediately rescinded the decree and took back all their slaves once again. God angrily denounced Israel's shallow repentance and promised that the Babylonian army would return to destroy Jerusalem (Jer 34:12-32). Israel had become so rebellious at its very core that it was no longer capable of sincere and sustained repentance. That is the situation in which we find Israel in Judg 10:10-16. At this point, Israel has rejected the Lord so many times after the Lord's repeated interventions to save Israel that Israel can no longer be trusted.

The Bible is well acquainted with the full range of human responses to God's compassionate and loving nature. Sometimes God's love causes a person to see the error of his or her ways and to begin a whole new life of faithfulness and obedience (Luke 19:1-10). More often, God's promise and love may begin a process of slow growth and change, with ups and downs that offer glimpses of genuine repentance that may not be fully realized on this side of the grave. Major biblical figures like Abraham, Jacob, and King David, for whom we have more biographical detail, offer realistic examples of lives of faith that sometimes falter. At other times, an individual or community may reach a point of such degradation or entrapment in misguided rebellion or sinfulness that they may be incapable of true and lasting repentance. Like an addict who will say anything to get another fix or an abuser who will deny everything to avoid exposing an awful secret, people can become almost hopelessly entangled in their self-delusions and manipulative ploys. The only resort to genuine transformation in such cases is to "hit bottom" so that the lie is exposed, the truth is set free, and the old pattern reaches an end. In such extreme cases, only then does new life have a chance to emerge as a genuine possibility. This is where the book of Judges is heading. Israel will hit bottom in chapters 17–21 as the social fabric of Israel will disintegrate and its sense of faith and morality will descend into chaos. People of faith need much wisdom and much humility when they try to discern at what point they and those with whom they minister stand on the continuum of human repentance. Is it genuine, partial, or a shallow manipulative ploy? In some cases, we may need to leave judgments concerning the genuineness of human repentance to God's wisdom when our own insights in such matters reach their limits.

2. One of the most remarkable features of the Lord's response to Israel's shallow repentance is that the Lord does not simply abandon Israel entirely. Instead, the story reports that God "could no longer bear to see Israel suffer" (10:16). This is a word of grace in the midst of human failure. Even though Israel deserves to be oppressed by the very nations and foreign gods whom they had worshiped, the Lord is moved to save them from the punishment the Lord had imposed. The manner of God's salvation in this particular case is not immediately apparent. Such bewilderment and unclarity are often what we experience when we stand in the midst of a time of trial and suffering. Where is God in this? How will God act to save? In the midst of our wonderment, we can be supported by the knowledge that God cannot bear too long to see God's people suffer, no matter how deserved the suffering may be. We can hope and expect that God will not allow us to undergo more difficulty or trial than we can endure with God's help (1 Cor 10:13).

3. God has used many unlikely people to accomplish God's purposes throughout the book of Judges. God's agents have included a left-handed assassin named Ehud, a woman judge and prophet named Deborah, a non-Israelite woman named Jael, and a timid Gideon, who was the weakest of the weak. Yet Jephthah appears to be the most unlikely person of God among them all. He is the son of a prostitute, an outcast from his own family, and the leader of a band of outlaws. He is also a sly negotiator as he gains for himself the position of leader of all Gilead in return for his willingness to fight Ammon. At the same time, he acknowledges the Lord's role in giving him victory over Ammon (11:9) and brings his political covenant with the elders of Gilead into the realm of religious faith (11:11). We are left wondering at this point whether Jephthah, at his core, is a genuinely good and faithful person who has simply made the best of the unfortunate circumstances of his life, which were beyond his control. Or is Jephthah a cynical politician who is looking out only for his own interests, using religion to mask his quest for political power and position? Even by the end of the story of Jephthah, we will not be able to answer these questions definitively. Jephthah will remain an ambiguous character. Yet God will use him to judge Israel for six years (12:7), and Jephthah will be listed in the New Testament Letter to the Hebrews as one of Israel's heroes of faith (Heb 11:32). God does not use plastic saints but flesh-and-blood sinners to work God's will in the world. That may be a comforting word of reassurance for those who yearn to be useful to the purposes of God and yet who know all too well their own failures and inadequacies.

Judges 11:12-40, Jephthah, His Daughter, and the Ammonites

NIV	NRSV
12Then Jephthah sent messengers to the Ammonite king with the question: "What do you have against us that you have attacked our country?"	12Then Jephthah sent messengers to the king of the Ammonites and said, "What is there between you and me, that you have come to me to fight against my land?" 13The king of the Ammonites answered the messengers of Jephthah, "Because Israel, on coming from Egypt, took away my land from the Arnon to the Jabbok and to the
13The king of the Ammonites answered Jephthah's messengers, "When Israel came up out of Egypt, they took away my land from the Arnon	

NIV

to the Jabbok, all the way to the Jordan. Now give it back peaceably."

¹⁴Jephthah sent back messengers to the Ammonite king, ¹⁵saying:

"This is what Jephthah says: Israel did not take the land of Moab or the land of the Ammonites. ¹⁶But when they came up out of Egypt, Israel went through the desert to the Red Sea*ᵃ* and on to Kadesh. ¹⁷Then Israel sent messengers to the king of Edom, saying, 'Give us permission to go through your country,' but the king of Edom would not listen. They sent also to the king of Moab, and he refused. So Israel stayed at Kadesh.

¹⁸"Next they traveled through the desert, skirted the lands of Edom and Moab, passed along the eastern side of the country of Moab, and camped on the other side of the Arnon. They did not enter the territory of Moab, for the Arnon was its border.

¹⁹"Then Israel sent messengers to Sihon king of the Amorites, who ruled in Heshbon, and said to him, 'Let us pass through your country to our own place.' ²⁰Sihon, however, did not trust Israel*ᵇ* to pass through his territory. He mustered all his men and encamped at Jahaz and fought with Israel.

²¹"Then the LORD, the God of Israel, gave Sihon and all his men into Israel's hands, and they defeated them. Israel took over all the land of the Amorites who lived in that country, ²²capturing all of it from the Arnon to the Jabbok and from the desert to the Jordan.

²³"Now since the LORD, the God of Israel, has driven the Amorites out before his people Israel, what right have you to take it over? ²⁴Will you not take what your god Chemosh gives you? Likewise, whatever the LORD our God has given us, we will possess. ²⁵Are you better than Balak son of Zippor, king of Moab? Did he ever quarrel with Israel or fight with them? ²⁶For three hundred years Israel occupied Heshbon, Aroer, the surrounding settlements and all the towns along the Arnon. Why didn't you retake them during that time? ²⁷I have not wronged you, but you are doing

ᵃ16 Hebrew Yam Suph; that is, Sea of Reeds   ᵇ20 Or however, would not make an agreement for Israel

NRSV

Jordan; now therefore restore it peaceably." ¹⁴Once again Jephthah sent messengers to the king of the Ammonites ¹⁵and said to him: "Thus says Jephthah: Israel did not take away the land of Moab or the land of the Ammonites, ¹⁶but when they came up from Egypt, Israel went through the wilderness to the Red Sea*ᵃ* and came to Kadesh. ¹⁷Israel then sent messengers to the king of Edom, saying, 'Let us pass through your land'; but the king of Edom would not listen. They also sent to the king of Moab, but he would not consent. So Israel remained at Kadesh. ¹⁸Then they journeyed through the wilderness, went around the land of Edom and the land of Moab, arrived on the east side of the land of Moab, and camped on the other side of the Arnon. They did not enter the territory of Moab, for the Arnon was the boundary of Moab. ¹⁹Israel then sent messengers to King Sihon of the Amorites, king of Heshbon; and Israel said to him, 'Let us pass through your land to our country.' ²⁰But Sihon did not trust Israel to pass through his territory; so Sihon gathered all his people together, and encamped at Jahaz, and fought with Israel. ²¹Then the LORD, the God of Israel, gave Sihon and all his people into the hand of Israel, and they defeated them; so Israel occupied all the land of the Amorites, who inhabited that country. ²²They occupied all the territory of the Amorites from the Arnon to the Jabbok and from the wilderness to the Jordan. ²³So now the LORD, the God of Israel, has conquered the Amorites for the benefit of his people Israel. Do you intend to take their place? ²⁴Should you not possess what your god Chemosh gives you to possess? And should we not be the ones to possess everything that the LORD our God has conquered for our benefit? ²⁵Now are you any better than King Balak son of Zippor of Moab? Did he ever enter into conflict with Israel, or did he ever go to war with them? ²⁶While Israel lived in Heshbon and its villages, and in Aroer and its villages, and in all the towns that are along the Arnon, three hundred years, why did you not recover them within that time? ²⁷It is not I who have sinned against you, but you are the one who does me wrong by making war on me. Let the LORD, who is judge, decide today for the Israelites or for the

ᵃ Or Sea of Reeds

NIV

me wrong by waging war against me. Let the LORD, the Judge,[a] decide the dispute this day between the Israelites and the Ammonites."

²⁸The king of Ammon, however, paid no attention to the message Jephthah sent him.

²⁹Then the Spirit of the LORD came upon Jephthah. He crossed Gilead and Manasseh, passed through Mizpah of Gilead, and from there he advanced against the Ammonites. ³⁰And Jephthah made a vow to the LORD: "If you give the Ammonites into my hands, ³¹whatever comes out of the door of my house to meet me when I return in triumph from the Ammonites will be the LORD's, and I will sacrifice it as a burnt offering."

³²Then Jephthah went over to fight the Ammonites, and the LORD gave them into his hands. ³³He devastated twenty towns from Aroer to the vicinity of Minnith, as far as Abel Keramim. Thus Israel subdued Ammon.

³⁴When Jephthah returned to his home in Mizpah, who should come out to meet him but his daughter, dancing to the sound of tambourines! She was an only child. Except for her he had neither son nor daughter. ³⁵When he saw her, he tore his clothes and cried, "Oh! My daughter! You have made me miserable and wretched, because I have made a vow to the LORD that I cannot break."

³⁶"My father," she replied, "you have given your word to the LORD. Do to me just as you promised, now that the LORD has avenged you of your enemies, the Ammonites. ³⁷But grant me this one request," she said. "Give me two months to roam the hills and weep with my friends, because I will never marry."

³⁸"You may go," he said. And he let her go for two months. She and the girls went into the hills and wept because she would never marry. ³⁹After the two months, she returned to her father and he did to her as he had vowed. And she was a virgin.

From this comes the Israelite custom ⁴⁰that each year the young women of Israel go out for four days to commemorate the daughter of Jephthah the Gileadite.

a27 Or Ruler

NRSV

Ammonites." ²⁸But the king of the Ammonites did not heed the message that Jephthah sent him.

²⁹Then the spirit of the LORD came upon Jephthah, and he passed through Gilead and Manasseh. He passed on to Mizpah of Gilead, and from Mizpah of Gilead he passed on to the Ammonites. ³⁰And Jephthah made a vow to the LORD, and said, "If you will give the Ammonites into my hand, ³¹then whoever comes out of the doors of my house to meet me, when I return victorious from the Ammonites, shall be the LORD's, to be offered up by me as a burnt offering." ³²So Jephthah crossed over to the Ammonites to fight against them; and the LORD gave them into his hand. ³³He inflicted a massive defeat on them from Aroer to the neighborhood of Minnith, twenty towns, and as far as Abel-keramim. So the Ammonites were subdued before the people of Israel.

³⁴Then Jephthah came to his home at Mizpah; and there was his daughter coming out to meet him with timbrels and with dancing. She was his only child; he had no son or daughter except her. ³⁵When he saw her, he tore his clothes, and said, "Alas, my daughter! You have brought me very low; you have become the cause of great trouble to me. For I have opened my mouth to the LORD, and I cannot take back my vow." ³⁶She said to him, "My father, if you have opened your mouth to the LORD, do to me according to what has gone out of your mouth, now that the LORD has given you vengeance against your enemies, the Ammonites." ³⁷And she said to her father, "Let this thing be done for me: Grant me two months, so that I may go and wander[a] on the mountains, and bewail my virginity, my companions and I." ³⁸"Go," he said and sent her away for two months. So she departed, she and her companions, and bewailed her virginity on the mountains. ³⁹At the end of two months, she returned to her father, who did with her according to the vow he had made. She had never slept with a man. So there arose an Israelite custom that ⁴⁰for four days every year the daughters of Israel would go out to lament the daughter of Jephthah the Gileadite.

a Cn: Heb go down

COMMENTARY

The dramatic point of tension and resolution in previous judge stories involved the defeat of the enemy and its leader. Othniel defeated the king of Aram (3:10). Ehud assassinated the fat King Eglon (3:21-23). Deborah foretold and Jael actually committed the assassination of the Canaanite general Sisera (4:9, 21). Gideon annihilated the Midianites in a surprise attack at night (7:19-23). We would expect that the climax of the Jephthah story would be his military defeat of the Ammonites, who were oppressing Israel. Jephthah does defeat them, but the battle is narrated in only two short verses (vv. 32-33). What replaces the military victory as the center of the story's tension and climax is the vow Jephthah makes to the Lord before the battle (vv. 30-31) and its fulfillment after the battle (vv. 34-40). Jephthah vows to offer to the Lord as a burnt offering whoever or whatever comes out of the door of his house when he comes home from battle (v. 31). The one to be sacrificed ends up being Jephthah's only child, his daughter. As we shall see, a number of uncertainties and ambiguities surround this climactic episode. The history of interpretation of this text runs the gamut from extolling the virtue of Jephthah and his daughter in their willing sacrifice to vilifying Jephthah as an evil father and perpetrator of patriarchal violence. However, before we examine the ambiguities of Jephthah's vow, the scene opens with an extended set of negotiations between Jephthah and the king of the Ammonites in vv. 12-28.

11:12-28. Jephthah has been elevated by the elders of Gilead from a rogue leader of bandits to the more honored role of a military commander of Gilead's army. Before leading the army into battle, however, Jephthah steps into another role as statesman and diplomat in an attempt to broker a peaceful resolution to the conflict with Ammon. Jephthah demonstrates his verbal abilities in presenting persuasive arguments about conflicting claims to the land of Gilead. Unfortunately, the Ammonite king in the end remains unpersuaded, and military conflict becomes the only option.

Jephthah begins the negotiations by sending a messenger to the Ammonites to ask why Ammon is attacking the Israelite region of Gilead. The Ammonite king sends a messenger in reply who argues that Israel wrongly stole this land of the Ammorites in the Transjordan area when Israel first came from Egypt on its way to the promised land (v. 13). In a lengthy rejoinder, Jephthah rehearses the story of Numbers 21, which recounts Israel's experience in this region. As the Israelites tried to reach Canaan, which was the land the Lord had given them, the Israelites had to cross one of three nations that lay on the eastern boundary of Canaan. Those nations included Moab, Edom, and the land of the Amorites. Israel did not seek to take away "the land of Moab or the land of the Ammonites" or any other land besides Canaan (v. 15). However, Edom and Moab refused to allow Israel to cross their territories to get to Canaan (vv. 16-18). The only option left to Israel was to go through the land of the Amorites, whose leader was King Sihon. The Amorites also refused to honor Israel's reasonable request to pass through the land. In addition to refusing Israel's request, the Amorites also viciously attacked Israel in an act of aggression. But "the LORD" saved Israel and defeated the aggressive Amorites. As a result, the Lord gave the Amorites' land to Israel as their rightful possession in the area east of the Jordan River (v. 21-23).

Jephthah then asks the Ammonites two key questions in his argument: "Should you not possess what your god Chemosh gives you to possess? And should we not be the ones to possess everything that the LORD our God has conquered for our benefit?" (v. 24). The questions imply that each nation has its legitimate god with a certain territory alloted to it, no more and no less. This view is in line with that of Deut 32:8-9:

When the Most High apportioned the nations,
  when he divided humankind,
he fixed the boundaries of the peoples
  according to the number of the gods;
the LORD's own portion was his people,
  Jacob his alloted share. (NRSV)

One difficulty in the Judges text is that the god Chemosh is usually portrayed as the chief god of the nation of Moab and not of Ammon. Ammon's chief god is Milcom, or Molech (Num 21:29; 2 Kgs 23:13). However, Jephthah apparently assumes an almost interchangeable identification of the nations of Ammon and Moab. This close association of Moab and Ammon appears elsewhere in Judges (3:13) and in the OT (Gen 19:36-38; Deut 2:17-19). The association with Moab and the god Chemosh may also recall the remarkable narrative of the Moabite king who offered up his only son as a burnt offering in a conflict with Israel, causing Moab to be spared (2 Kgs 3:26-27). The upcoming scene with Jephthah's sacrifice of his only child as part of a vow before a military battle may be an echo of this Moabite act, an act that was at once effective and also abominable.

Jephthah continues his argument as he moves from history and theology to practicality. If the east Jordan region of the Amorites belonged to Ammon, why did Ammon allow the Israelites to dwell in the region for three hundred years (v. 26)? It makes little sense for Ammon suddenly to raise objections when Ammon has been silent for such a long time. In the end, however, Jephthah correctly senses that none of these arguments will likely sway the Ammonite king. Thus Jephthah throws down the gauntlet by inviting the Lord to be the judge of this dispute and "decide today for the Israelites or the Ammonites" (v. 27). Jephthah takes on the role of a prosecuting attorney in a lawsuit with Ammon with the Lord sitting as judge in the divine court. The statement is in effect a declaration of war as the Lord's decision will be determined by whomever wins the military battle between the two opponents. Jephthah's extended arguments indeed have no effect in persuading the Ammonites to back down, and so the stage is set for the conflict to begin (v. 28).

The literary effects of this extended negotiation are several. First, the negotiations retard the building tension and push back the climax to a point further into the story. Second, Jephthah's diplomacy establishes him as an able (if not always successful) negotiator. Knowing of his ability to negotiate will later cause the reader to wonder why the skillful Jephthah does not negotiate with God when his foolish vow forces him to sacrifice his daughter. Third, the references to Moab and the god Chemosh suggest a negative association of Jephthah with the Moabite king who offered his child as a burnt offering as a means of inducing his god to give him a victory (2 Kgs 3:26-27).

Fourth, Jephthah's arguments also suggest positive aspects of his character. He seems to know the faith traditions of Israel's past, and he presents himself as a rational statesman who desires peace rather than war. He is not an aggressor, and yet he is also not a coward. He refuses to back down in fear before the Ammonite threat. He ultimately entrusts his future and his fate into the hands of the Lord. Jephthah emerges as a complex character with both negative and positive dimensions that will continue throughout the next climactic scenes involving his vow and his daughter.

11:29-40. When the negotiations with the Ammonite king conclude, "the spirit of the LORD came upon Jephthah" (v. 29). This is the first explicit indication in the story that the Lord has indeed chosen Jephthah to deliver Israel from the Ammonites. Everything up to this point has involved human initiative: the elders of Gilead negotiating with Jephthah to be their leader, and Jephthah negotiating on his own initiative with the Ammonite king. The Lord's name has been invoked along the way at several points, but no overt statement has indicated the Lord's actual involvement with Jephthah. But now the Spirit of the Lord has come upon Jephthah just as the Spirit had come upon previous judges. The divine Spirit was a positive element in Othniel's defeat of the enemy king of Aram (3:10). The Spirit of the Lord had relatively little positive effect on Gideon, however, who remained timid and fearful even after receiving the Spirit (6:34). In the case of Abimelech, God sent an evil spirit that did not cause unity and strength but conflict and discord among the Israelites. Thus, when we read that Jephthah received the Spirit of the Lord, we are poised to wonder whether this will have a positive or a negative effect. Part of the effect of the Spirit is an ability to unite and call forth volunteers from among the tribes of Israel. Jephthah accomplishes this rallying of troops with some success as he passes "through Gilead and Manasseh." This is not a large call of many Israelite tribes but involves only a small localized area in the territory outside of Canaan and east of the Jordan River. The judges seem less and less able to muster substantial coalitions of tribes as we move through the individual judge stories from Othniel to Ehud to Deborah/Barak and Gideon. Indeed, the next and final judge after Jephthah, Samson, will lead no Israelites in battle. Samson will fight all his battles against the Philistines alone. This increasing inability to unify Israel's tribes is part of the social disintegration of the nation as the era of the judges waned.

Once we have been assured that the Spirit of the Lord has come upon Jephthah, we are prepared by the previous judge stories to assume that battle and victory for Israel will follow immediately. However, that assumption is disrupted by a startling and somewhat ambiguous pledge or vow made by Jephthah to the Lord. If the Lord gives Jephthah victory over the Ammonites, then Jephthah promises to offer as a burnt offering either "whoever" (NRSV) or "whatever" (NIV) first "comes out of the doors of my house to meet me" when he returns home from the battle. The Hebrew text (אשׁר 'ăšer) is ambiguous as to whether Jephthah intended his vow to involve the offering of a human being ("whoever") or an animal ("whatever"). Some scholars argue that Jephthah's words must intend a human sacrifice. G. F. Moore offers his own strong opinion, "That a human victim is intended is, in fact, as plain as words can make it; the language is inapplicable to an animal, and a vow to offer the first sheep or goat that he comes across—not to mention the possibility of an unclean animal—is trivial to absurdity."[46]

Other scholars argue just as adamantly that Jephthah's vow would assume an animal sacrifice in the light of the structure of Iron Age houses unearthed in this area. Domesticated animals apparently lived along with humans inside the typical house of this period.[47] In my judgment, Jephthah's language is left intentionally ambivalent by the narrator so that the reader cannot know for sure what Jephthah's real intention was.

Another issue arises in trying to understand the significance of Jephthah's vow. What is the relationship of Jephthah's vow and the coming of the Spirit of the Lord upon him? Phyllis Trible argues that Jephthah's vow is an act of unfaithfulness. She assumes Jephthah is aware that he has just received the Lord's Spirit. Knowing this, the Spirit-filled Jephthah should trust that God's Spirit is all he needs to guarantee victory over the Ammonites. However, his additional vow after receiving the Spirit means that he does not yet trust God sufficiently. His vow

is a calculated ploy to manipulate God as a way to ensure victory.[48] In contrast to Trible, who separates the good spirit from Jephthah's bad vow, Cheryl Exum maintains that the vow is not made in opposition to the divine Spirit. Rather, the vow is made under the influence of the Lord's Spirit. The problem is not the vow as such, argues Exum. Faithful Israelites frequently made vows to God. The revered ancestor Jacob vowed to worship the Lord if the Lord would take care of his needs (Gen 28:20-22). The pious Hannah vowed to dedicate her son to the Lord's service if the Lord would grant her the ability to have children (1 Sam 1:9-11). The problem with Jephthah's vow was not making the vow itself but its careless wording and content. Jephthah recklessly vowed to offer "whoever" or "whatever" came out of his house as a burnt offering. If he had promised to erect an altar or worship the Lord when he returned in victory, the vow would have been much less problematic.[49]

I would argue that the act of taking the vow in itself *in this specific context* is indeed problematic, but not for the reason Trible cites. We are not told whether Jephthah is aware of having received the divine Spirit. Therefore, we cannot join Trible in condemning him for failing to trust in a divine Spirit that he may not have been aware he had been given. Yet there is another basis on which we can condemn Jephthah. While vows may be properly offered to God in some contexts, Jephthah wrongly uses the vow *in this particular context* as a bribe or leverage to influence the divine judge in the context of a court case. Jephthah has himself set up the conflict with the Ammonites as a court battle with the Lord as judge (11:27). According to Deuteronomy's laws, any bribes or gifts to judges are strictly prohibited lest they unduly influence the judges' decisions (Deut 16:19). This prohibition is grounded in Israel's understanding of God, who "is not partial and takes no bribe" (Deut 10:17 NRSV).[50] Thus Jephthah's vow in itself violates a deeply held Israelite norm in regard to the prohibition of gifts or bribes to judges. Exum is surely correct that the wording and content of the vow are also reckless

---

46. G. F. Moore, *Judges*, ICC (New York: Scribners, 1901) 299.

47. Robert G. Boling, *Judges*, AB 6A (Garden City, N.Y.: Doubleday, 1975) 208.

48. Phyllis Trible, "The Daughter of Jephthah: An Inhuman Sacrifice," in *Texts of Terror, Literary-Feminist Readings of Biblical Narratives* (Philadelphia: Fortress, 1984) 93-116.

49. J. Cheryl Exum, "The Tragic Vision and Biblical Narrative: The Case of Jephthah," in *Signs and Wonders: Biblical Texts in Literary Focus*, ed. J. Cheryl Exum (n.p.: SBL, 1989) 66-67.

50. Michael Goldberg, "The Story of the Moral: Gifts or Bribes in Deuteronomy?" *Int.* 38 (1984) 15-25.

and problematic in that it opens the door to all kinds of inappropriate sacrifices, including unclean animals or humans. But any vow, no matter its content, in this particular setting of a court case with God as judge is illicit and inappropriate.

Jephthah has received "the spirit of the LORD" as a gift of strength, and he has made the vow as a bribe to influence God's decision as judge in order to guarantee himself the victory. What will God's response be? We learn immediately that the Lord gave the Ammonites into Jephthah's hand, and Jephthah "inflicted a massive defeat on them" (vv. 32-33). Ordinarily such a victory would be the climax of an individual judge story, but in this case the attention of the narrator rests elsewhere. Jephthah returns home from his victory. Remembering his open-ended vow, the reader wonders who or what will first come out of his house. The narrator reports the tragic scene: "there was his daughter coming out to meet him with timbrels and dancing." Jephthah's daughter was doing what Israelite women often did: welcoming victorious soldiers home with music and dance. Women led by Miriam celebrated Israel's victory over Egypt at the Red Sea (Exod 15:19-21), and women later celebrated King David's military victories in a similar manner (1 Sam 8:6-7).

But this moment of great triumph for Jephthah turns into bitter tragedy and pain. His thoughtless vow meant that he would have to sacrifice his daughter as a burnt offering to the Lord. The sacrifice is all the more poignant because she is his only link to future generations: "she was his only child; he had no son or daughter except her" (v. 34). Jephthah's first words are somewhat troubling, for they paint him as the victim and offer no consolation to his daughter. Jephthah accuses his daughter of bringing trouble on him, as if she is somehow responsible for his reckless vow (v. 35). He appears capable of seeing the world only through his own eyes. His self-centered character is heightened by the contrast with his daughter. She dutifully accepts her fate for the sake of her father and Israel's security: "do to me according to what has gone out of your mouth" (v. 36). She makes only one request: that she and her companions be allowed to "wander on the mountains" and "bewail my virginity" for a period of two months (v. 37). She does so, and then she returns to her father, "who did with her according to the vow he had made." No description of

the actual killing of the daughter is given beyond this. An additional note emphasizes her virginity: "she had never slept with a man" (v. 39). The scene concludes with an ongoing custom in which the daughters of Israel would go out for four days each year either "to lament" (NRSV) the death of Jephthah's daughter or to "commemorate" (NIV) her willing sacrifice (v. 40).

In a thorough and helpful study of this text, David Marcus summarizes the fascinating history of interpretation of this tragic and troubling text, which divides into two major groups.[51] On one hand, Jewish and Christian interpreters up to the Middle Ages consistently assumed that Jephthah did indeed kill his daughter and offer her up as a burnt offering to God. For example, the Aramaic Targum acknowledged that while Jephthah did sacrifice his daughter, the practice was henceforth prohibited in Israel. The Church Father Origen believed the sacrifice of Jephthah's daughter to prefigure the willing sacrifice and death of the Christian martyrs. Jewish exegetes like Rashi and Nachmanides appealed to the "plain sense" of the text's meaning that Jephthah did indeed kill his daughter as a sacrificial offering.

On the other hand, a second major group of interpreters have argued that Jephthah did *not* actually kill his daughter, but rather dedicated her to a life of virginity or celibacy. The earliest example of this line of interpretation is the medieval Jewish commentator David Kimchi, who wrote:

It is quite clear that he did not kill her because the text [in verse 37] does not say "I will mourn for my life," [but only "will mourn for my virginity"]. This indicates that he did not kill her but rather that she did not know a man [remained a virgin], because the text says [verse 39] "she did not know a man."[52]

Many subsequent Jewish and Christian interpreters adopted this line of interpretation, assuming that Jephthah's daughter remained alive but celibate. Indeed, Christian scholars associated the medieval practice of nuns vowing their lives to celibate service to God with the model of Jephthah's daughter. In support of their position, these interpreters point to v. 39, which does not actually state that Jephthah killed his daughter but simply that he "did with her according to the vow he had made." This line of interpretation found

---

51. David Marcus, *Jephthah and His Vow* (Lubbock, Tex.: Texas Tech Press, 1986) 8-9.
52. Quoted in ibid., 8.

its way into George Frederic Handel's oratorio entitled *Jephtha* first performed in 1752. In Handel's retelling of the biblical story, an angel intervenes just when Jephthah is about to kill his daughter and sings these words:

Rise, Jephtha. And ye reverend priests, withhold the slaughterous hand. No vow can disannul the law of God, nor such was its intent, when rightly scanned, yet still shall be fulfilled. Thy daughter, Jephtha, thou must dedicate to God, in pure and virgin state for ever.

This angelic interruption of the sacrifice mirrors a similar motif in Abraham's near sacrifice of his son in Genesis 22.

Despite these alternative renderings, the dominant interpretation remains that Jephthah did indeed kill his daughter and offer her as a burnt offering. Martin Luther's comment on the text is typical: "Some affirm he did not sacrifice her, but the text is clear enough."[53] However, I find more convincing the conclusion of the careful study by David Marcus that the Jephthah story contains "ambiguities consciously devised by the narrator" to be "open to a number of interpretations" so that "the text, as it stands now, admits the possibility of either conclusion."[54] The effect of the ambivalence is to heighten suspense, to draw the reader into wrestling with the moral dilemmas and ambiguities of the story, and to increase the sense of horror at a possibility so repulsive that it is not described but left only as an imagined potentiality. This central ambiguity of the entire story—whether Jephthah killed his daughter or not—reflects the overall ambiguity of Jephthah's character. In the end, whether Jephthah's daughter was sacrificed or lived a life of celibacy, Jephthah's vow remains foolish, wrong, and unnecessary. Yet at the same time, Jephthah received "the spirit of the LORD" and successfully delivered Israel from the Ammonite oppression. The scale of evaluation, however, will be tipped more toward the negative and against Jephthah in the concluding episode as he deals treacherously with his fellow Israelites from the tribe of Ephraim (12:1-6).

---

53. Martin Luther, *Die Deutsche Bibel* (Weimar: Hermann Böhlaus Nachfolger, 1939) 131.

54. Marcus, *Jephthah and His Vow,* 52.

REFLECTIONS

1. Part of the ambiguity of this story is that it touches upon the opposition of two strong convictions or values promoted in biblical literature. On one hand, the offering up of children as burnt offerings to the gods was viewed as an abhorrent pagan abomination that profaned the name of the Lord (Lev 18:21; 20:2-5; 2 Kgs 23:10; Jer 32:35). Indeed, this repugnant practice was most closely associated with the god Molech, the god of the Ammonites, the very people against whom Jephthah was fighting. On the other hand, the Old Testament expresses the conviction that every firstborn child belonged to the Lord and was theoretically to be offered up as a sacrifice to the Lord (Exod 13:2; 22:29). This conviction lay in the background of the account of the Lord's killing of the firstborn of the Egyptians in the tenth plague of the exodus story (Exod 4:22-23). God commanded certain provisions by which the firstborn children of the Israelites could be "redeemed" and thus spared from death. Parents could substitute certain animals as burnt offerings (Exod 13:13; 34:20). They could also substitute for their children individual members of the special tribe of Levites who were dedicated to lifelong service in the Lord's sanctuary (Num 3:12-13; 8:15-18). The Lord's legitimate claim on all firstborn children likely underlies in part the story of God's command to Abraham to offer his son Isaac as a burnt offering to the Lord in Genesis 22. The same theme of the sacrifice of the firstborn child lies behind Paul's understanding of the death of Jesus as God's offering up his only Son as a sacrifice: "He who did not withhold his own Son, but gave him up for all of us, will he not with him also give us everything else?" (Rom 8:32 NRSV). Jon Levenson has argued that this theme of the death and sacrifice of the firstborn or beloved child is deeply rooted and common in both Jewish and Christian theological traditions.[55]

---

55. Jon Levenson, *The Death and Resurrection of the Beloved Son: The Transformation of Child Sacrifice in Judaism and Christianity* (New Haven: Yale University Press, 1993).

The willingness to give up what is most precious in service to God remains an enduring biblical value. At the same time, the protection of children against violence and abuse, even if religiously motivated, is demonstrated by the many ways in which the firstborn children could be "redeemed." Abraham's willingness to sacrifice Isaac is never held up as a model to be emulated; it was a one-time and unique demonstration of faith from which all subsequent sacrifices in ancient Israel of animals, grain, or acts of justice and contrition drew merit. In the same way, God's willingness to allow Jesus to die on the cross was a one-time, unrepeatable sacrifice and not a literal example for human parents to follow in regard to their children.

As for Jephthah's willingness to sacrifice his daughter, we must remember its place within the larger structure of thematic development within the book of Judges. Jephthah's judgeship represents the third and most negative phase of the individual judges. We have moved from good and faithful judges in 3:7–5:31 to a transitional phase of somewhat effective but religiously unfaithful judges in 6:1–10:5 to the third phase of tragic and ultimately failed judges in 10:6–16:31. Jephthah falls within the last and most negative period of the era. His willingness to kill or sacrifice his daughter in an unnecessary and illicit vow must be evaluated as a symptom of a deteriorating system of leadership under the judges.

2. Feminist scholars have rightly condemned Jephthah's callous and unjust treatment of his daughter. Her meek and submissive acquiescence to her father's foolish vow cannot excuse Jephthah, nor can it be taken as an enduring model for women or daughters in their relationship to men or fathers. As is often the case in many communities and societies, the woman here is anonymous, powerless, and the victim of deathly forces over which she has little control or involvement. Her negative experience differs markedly from the first woman and daughter we encountered at the beginning of Judges. There the daughter had a name, Achsah. She took bold initiatives for the sake of her own well-being as she asked her father for life-giving springs of water as part of her inheritance (1:11-15). In contrast, Jephthah's daughter can ask her father only for two months reprieve from her death sentence or (in some interpretations) two months of mourning for her life of celibacy.

What emerges as one surveys all the women in the book of Judges is that the welfare and status of women become signs of the religious and political health of the society. In the initial stages of the judges era, when Israel was united and faithful to God, the women in the stories held positions of some power and exercised independent initiative. The women who appear early in the judges period—Achsah (1:11-15), Deborah, and Jael (chaps. 4–5)—are among some of the strongest women characters in the Bible. By the time we have reached the third phase of the era in the judgeship of Jephthah, the fate of women has deteriorated along with Israel's social and religious life, as the fate of Jephthah's daughter illustrates. That deterioration in the role of the women will continue with the fate of several women in the Samson story (chaps. 13–16). This social and religious regression will reach a horrifying low point with the rape and murder of the Levite's concubine in chapter 19 and the forcible kidnapping of hundreds of young women by the men of the tribe of Benjamin in chapter 21. The book of Judges suggests that the well-being and treatment of women and children (especially daughters) in a community or nation can serve as a measuring stick for the overall health and faithfulness of the community's religious and political life. In a similar way, the Old Testament prophets saw the mistreatment of widows and orphans and other marginalized groups as a symptom of a deeper social and religious deterioration at the core of the nation (Isa 10:2). This measuring stick remains an enduring and relevant index for the health of contemporary communities and societies as well.[56]

---

56. For a survey of women characters in the book of Judges, see Michael O'Connor, "The Women in the Book of Judges," *HAR* 10 (1986) 227-93; and J. Cheryl Exum, "Feminist Criticism: Whose Interests Are Being Served?" in Gale A. Yee, ed., *Judges and Method: New Approaches in Biblical Studies* (Minneapolis: Fortress, 1995) 65-90.

3. Certain tensions emerge in attempting to understand the nature of God's involvement in the events of Jephthah's story. The Lord vows never again to deliver Israel because of its repeated disloyalty, and yet the Lord cannot bear to see Israel suffer (10:13, 16). Jephthah negotiates his own rise to the position of judge over Israel. In every other case, God has been the prime mover in calling the judges to their role. The Lord does give the victory to Jephthah (11:32), but it is not entirely clear whether the victory comes solely as a result of the Lord's giving Jephthah the divine Spirit (11:29). Did Jephthah's vow to the Lord help in any way to convince God to secure the victory over the Ammonites (11:30-31)? The story does not give a clear answer. One senses that God is somehow more distant and not as directly in control of events as in the previous judge stories. Although God remains involved, God seems at the same time to be growing increasingly frustrated with Israel and more willing to allow Israel to go on its misguided course and suffer the consequences. The elders of Gilead choose the son of a prostitute as their judge, and the Lord allows it. Jephthah vows to sacrifice what first comes out of his house. When it is his daughter, God does not intervene to nullify the tragic consequences as God had done in Genesis 22 with Abraham and Isaac. There may be times in our lives when God remains present, but may also allow us to suffer the tragic consequences of our own rebellious actions and sin. God does not save us from every mistake. God often allows us the freedom to fail. Such failures and acts of rebellion may become opportunities to reconsider our priorities, to mature in our decision making, and to grow in faith. At other times, such failures may drive us to despair. Whether we take advantage of those opportunities for growth in the midst of failure remains an open question and an ongoing challenge that we are likely to encounter more than once in our lifetime.

Judges 12:1-7, Jephthah and the Ephraimites

NIV

12 The men of Ephraim called out their forces, crossed over to Zaphon and said to Jephthah, "Why did you go to fight the Ammonites without calling us to go with you? We're going to burn down your house over your head."

²Jephthah answered, "I and my people were engaged in a great struggle with the Ammonites, and although I called, you didn't save me out of their hands. ³When I saw that you wouldn't help, I took my life in my hands and crossed over to fight the Ammonites, and the LORD gave me the victory over them. Now why have you come up today to fight me?"

⁴Jephthah then called together the men of Gilead and fought against Ephraim. The Gileadites struck them down because the Ephraimites had said, "You Gileadites are renegades from Ephraim and Manasseh." ⁵The Gileadites captured the fords of the Jordan leading to Ephraim, and whenever a survivor of Ephraim said, "Let me cross over," the men of Gilead asked him, "Are you an Ephraimite?" If he replied, "No," ⁶they said, "All

NRSV

12 The men of Ephraim were called to arms, and they crossed to Zaphon and said to Jephthah, "Why did you cross over to fight against the Ammonites, and did not call us to go with you? We will burn your house down over you!" ²Jephthah said to them, "My people and I were engaged in conflict with the Ammonites who oppressed us[a] severely. But when I called you, you did not deliver me from their hand. ³When I saw that you would not deliver me, I took my life in my hand, and crossed over against the Ammonites, and the LORD gave them into my hand. Why then have you come up to me this day, to fight against me?" ⁴Then Jephthah gathered all the men of Gilead and fought with Ephraim; and the men of Gilead defeated Ephraim, because they said, "You are fugitives from Ephraim, you Gileadites—in the heart of Ephraim and Manasseh."[b] ⁵Then the Gileadites took the fords of the Jordan against the Ephraimites. Whenever one of the fugitives of Ephraim said,

a Gk OL, Syr H: Heb lacks *who oppressed us* *b* Meaning of Heb uncertain: Gk omits *because . . . Manasseh*

NIV

right, say 'Shibboleth.' " If he said, "Sibboleth," because he could not pronounce the word correctly, they seized him and killed him at the fords of the Jordan. Forty-two thousand Ephraimites were killed at that time.

7Jephthah led[a] Israel six years. Then Jephthah the Gileadite died, and was buried in a town in Gilead.

a7 Traditionally *judged*; also in verses 8-14

NRSV

"Let me go over," the men of Gilead would say to him, "Are you an Ephraimite?" When he said, "No," 6they said to him, "Then say Shibboleth," and he said, "Sibboleth," for he could not pronounce it right. Then they seized him and killed him at the fords of the Jordan. Forty-two thousand of the Ephraimites fell at that time.

7Jephthah judged Israel six years. Then Jephthah the Gileadite died, and was buried in his town in Gilead.[a]

a Gk: Heb *in the towns of Gilead*

COMMENTARY

The final episode in the Jephthah cycle involves his conflict, not with an external enemy but with a fellow Israelite tribe, the tribe of Ephraim. Ephraim is a northern tribe located on the western side of the Jordan River in the hill country of Canaan. Ephraim was a dominant and important northern tribe throughout much of ancient Israel's history. The book of Judges uses this tribe as a barometer of Israel's cohesion and social unity as a people. In the earliest and most positive phase of the judges era, the individual judges called on the tribe of Ephraim to join in the conflict against the enemy, and they immediately responded (3:27; 4:5; 5:14). In the second transitional phase under the judge Gideon, the tribe of Ephraim is called into the conflict against Midian at a late stage. The Ephraimites complain bitterly to Gideon about not being invited earlier to join in the battle. Gideon soothes their hurt feelings and peacefully resolves the internal dispute with Ephraim (7:24-25; 8:1-3). In this third and most negative phase of the judges era, beginning with Jephthah, the Ephraimites are bitterly disappointed that they were not invited to join Jephthah's fight against the Ammonites. Although a skillful negotiator in the past, Jephthah does not deal with their complaint diplomatically. Instead, he fights against the Ephraimites and kills 42,000 of them. This civil war with Ephraim uncovers a growing rift within Israel itself. This intra-Israelite conflict is a sign of the dissolution of the nation of Israel, which will only worsen when a full-scale

civil war erupts in Judges 19–21 with devastating results.

12:1-3. Verse 1 opens the scene with the Ephraimites preparing for battle and confronting Jephthah with a question. Why did he not call on the Ephraimites to join in his fight against the Ammonites? The question is a close parallel to the Ephraimites' question to Gideon in 8:1. However, their hostility is much more intense now than at the time of Gideon. The Ephraimites vow to burn Jephthah's "house" down over him. The threat is somewhat hollow in that the death or lifelong virginity of Jephthah's only daughter guarantees that he has no "house" in the sense of future progeny. Jephthah responds that he had, indeed, called on the Ephraimites to help in fighting the Ammonites, but they "did not deliver me from their hand" (v. 2). Jephthah's claim to have invited Ephraim to join the fight is not attested anywhere in the preceding story (see 11:29). The reader is led to conclude that this is a bald-faced lie. We begin to wonder whether any of Jephthah's many words, including his confessions of faith in God, were genuine and true. The Ephraimites are not satisfied with his answer to their complaint, and so the battle between Jephthah and his fellow Israelites from Ephraim begins.

12:4. One of the other causes of the fight is the Ephraimites' taunt or accusation that the Transjordanian people of Gilead are only פליטים (*pĕlîṭîm*), "fugitives" (NRSV) or perhaps better "renegades" (NIV), from Ephraim who have abandoned their true home tribe (v. 4). Such taunts and desires for personal vengeance had earlier led Gideon to attack his fellow Israelites (8:4-9, 13-17). Once again, matters involving the judge's personal pride and tribal jealousies override the need for unity and cohesion as the people of God. Jephthah's leadership fails to offer any substantive or positive vision for uniting Israel once the Ammonite enemy has been defeated. Instead, Jephthah engages in ruthless power politics to defeat and kill what he perceives to be the internal enemy of Ephraim.

12:5-6. One of the methods Jephthah employs to identify and isolate his internal enemies is the boundary of language and of dialect. Jephthah knows well the power of words to entrap and bring death. Jephthah's army of Gileadites secures the fords, or crossing points, on the Jordan River, the geographical boundary between his parochial region of Gilead east of the Jordan and the rest of Israel in the land of Canaan, which lies to the west of the Jordan River. Jephthah's defeat of the invading Ephraimite army causes the Ephraimite soldiers who escaped from the battle to become the "fugitives of Ephraim," the same derisive label the Ephraimites had used for the men of Gilead (v. 5; see v. 4). When these Ephraimite fugitives try to cross the Jordan to leave Gideon and return home to Ephraim on the western side, the Gilead soldiers first make them say the word "Shibboleth" (שִׁבֹּלֶת *šibbōlet*), which means either "ear of corn" or "stream." People of Gilead east of the Jordan pronounced this word with an initial "sh" sound in their dialect. People of Ephraim from west of the Jordan pronounced the same word with an initial "s," and not "sh," sound. Thus Jephthah's soldiers are able to detect the Ephraimites by their dialect, and they kill them as they try to cross the river. The narrator reports that an enormous number, 42,000 Ephraimites, were killed at that time (v. 6). This scene at the fords of the Jordan River recalls an earlier judge, Ehud, who also seized the fords of the Jordan River and killed thousands there. However, Ehud fought against Israel's enemies, the Moabites, and not against fellow Israelites (3:28-29). In contrast, Jephthah has slaughtered his countrymen, the Ephraimites, at the fords of the Jordan. Jephthah's massacre of his own people suggests a disintegration of Israel's unity from the inside, a growing threat more ominous than any outside enemy.

12:7. This gradual decline in Israel's well-being as a nation is also suggested by the fact that Jephthah's reign as a judge is the shortest of any of the judges thus far. Previous judges had won periods of forty to eighty years of peace and "rest" for Israel (3:30; 5:31; 8:28). Jephthah judged Israel for only six years. In contrast to the previous judges, the narrator does not report that Israel obtained any period of "rest" or peace in his time. Jephthah dies a parochial "Gileadite" more than a unifying and heroic judge who left a lasting legacy for all Israel (v. 12).

REFLECTIONS

Up to this point, Jephthah's character has appeared to be quite ambivalent. At times he seems a faithful follower of the Lord and an able leader of the army who defeats the Ammonites. At other times, Jephthah appears manipulative, unwilling to trust the Lord, and tragically entrapped by his own words. In this last scene of his life, the scales of judgment tip decidedly against him in comparison to previous judges and their treatment of the tribe of Ephraim. Earlier judges had successfully rallied the Ephraimites to their side. But Jephthah succeeds only in antagonizing the Ephraimites and then slaughtering them. Just as Jephthah had killed his own daughter and family member, so also now he kills his own Israelite brothers and members of the broader Israelite family.

When a common external enemy is defeated or disappears, a power vacuum often occurs within a group or community. This is true of large groups and nations, and it is true of small groups, religious communities, and families. The sudden disappearance of a common enemy or purpose often allows old tribal jealousies and conflicts over power within the group to erupt. What is required is something Jephthah did not offer. Such groups or communities need strong leadership to help them discover and unite behind a positive and compelling vision for their identity and mission. Good leaders help individuals and groups within their community to form and rally around positive goals and purposes. Such goals transcend parochial interests and center the community's attention on the larger good of the group and its mission within the larger context in which it lives and works.

Judges 12:8-15, Ibzan, Elon, and Abdon: Three Minor Judges

NIV	NRSV
8After him, Ibzan of Bethlehem led Israel. 9He had thirty sons and thirty daughters. He gave his daughters away in marriage to those outside his clan, and for his sons he brought in thirty young women as wives from outside his clan. Ibzan led Israel seven years. 10Then Ibzan died, and was buried in Bethlehem.	8After him Ibzan of Bethlehem judged Israel. 9He had thirty sons. He gave his thirty daughters in marriage outside his clan and brought in thirty young women from outside for his sons. He judged Israel seven years. 10Then Ibzan died, and was buried at Bethlehem.
11After him, Elon the Zebulunite led Israel ten years. 12Then Elon died, and was buried in Aijalon in the land of Zebulun.	11After him Elon the Zebulunite judged Israel; and he judged Israel ten years. 12Then Elon the Zebulunite died, and was buried at Aijalon in the land of Zebulun.
13After him, Abdon son of Hillel, from Pirathon, led Israel. 14He had forty sons and thirty grandsons, who rode on seventy donkeys. He led Israel eight years. 15Then Abdon son of Hillel died, and was buried at Pirathon in Ephraim, in the hill country of the Amalekites.	13After him Abdon son of Hillel the Pirathonite judged Israel. 14He had forty sons and thirty grandsons, who rode on seventy donkeys; he judged Israel eight years. 15Then Abdon son of Hillel the Pirathonite died, and was buried at Pirathon in the land of Ephraim, in the hill country of the Amalekites.

COMMENTARY

The three so-called minor judges in 12:8-15 appear in the midst of the major judgeships of Jephthah (chaps. 10–12) and Samson (chaps. 13–16). These three judges—Ibzan, Elon, and Abdon—reflect the same progressive decline in effectiveness that has been noted among the major judges Jephthah and Samson, who comprise this third and most negative phase of the judges era. This third cluster of minor judges emerges as ineffectual leaders in comparison to the two previous groups of minor judges, associated with phase one and phase two of the judges period. The first minor judge in the positive phase was Shamgar (3:31), who defeated the Philistines and "delivered Israel." The second group of minor judges included Tola and Jair (10:1-5) during the second transitional phase of the judges era. Tola successfully "delivered Israel" and reigned for

twenty-three years. The description of Jair's tenure as judge is less positive in that he did not "deliver Israel." His reign focused less on Israel as a whole and more on the welfare of his own family and their possession of donkeys and towns. His reign, however, lasted for a fairly long period of twenty-two years.

The third group of minor judges here does not compare favorably with the previous minor judges. No minor judge in this third group is said to "deliver" Israel. Their rule brings benefit only to themselves and not to the nation of Israel as a whole. The details about these judges involve only their own families and their deaths and burials. The lengths of their reigns (seven years, ten years, eight years) are relatively short in comparison to the previous minor judges (10:1-5, 23 years, 22 years). These minor judges (Ibzan, Elon,

Abdon) combine with Jephthah and Samson to embody the disintegration of Israel in the third and most negative phase of the individual judge stories.

This uneventful interlude of three minor judges has a literary effect similar to treading water and going nowhere. It is almost as if God needs this time to consider the options of what to do next with this people Israel who seem repeatedly inclined toward rebellion and self-destruction. God had earlier said there would be no more deliver-

ance for Israel (10:13). Would God return to that position after the misguided judgeship of Jephthah? Or would God dramatically intervene in some new way when the next cycle began with Israel's evil and the resulting oppression by an enemy? The brief respite of the minor judges provides some time for God and the reader to interrupt the cycle of major judgeships, to contemplate the implications of the disturbing events of the past, and to consider the range of options for Israel's future.

REFLECTIONS

The temporary intermission provided by the minor judges at this unsettled point in the era of the judges may provoke some reflections on those times in our own lives when we need such moments of respite. Significant or traumatic events and transitions in our lives often require that we interrupt our normal routine and pattern to make some space for contemplation and assessment. We need to carve out space and time for thoughtful reflection, prayer, decision making, discussion, and rest. Such moments are especially important in times of chaos, transition, uncertainty, or conflict. Israel was going through such unsettled times, and the minor judges provide a moment of calm in the midst of a turbulent and uncertain future.

JUDGES 13:1–16:31, SAMSON, THE LAST JUDGE

OVERVIEW

The seventeenth-century poet John Milton retold the biblical story of Samson in an epic poem entitled *Samson Agonistes*. Milton himself had tragically become blind, and he put this searching question into Samson's mouth:

Why was my breeding ordered and prescribed
As of a person separate to God,
Designed for great exploits; if I must die
Betrayed, captive, and both my eyes put out . . . ?
(Line 30)

Milton's question captures the essential riddle of great expectations and tragic humiliation that is the story of Samson. More than any previous judge, Samson is wondrously chosen by God from birth. He is a special judge, a Nazarite called to deliver Israel from the oppressive Philistines. Tragically, all our expectations about what a judge should be fall apart in Samson. He leads no

Israelites into battle. He marries a Philistine woman. He attends drinking parties with the enemy. He spends the night with a foreign prostitute. He engages only in personal vendettas with little sense of working in service to God or for the well-being of all Israel. He succumbs to Delilah's pleas to know the secret of his strength, which leads to imprisonment, torture, and blindness. In the end, Samson prays to God to let him die and destroy the Philistines and the temple of the god Dagon in the process. Samson is no ordinary judge. He plays an important and even climactic role as the last of the judges of Israel in the book of Judges.

The importance of the Samson cycle for the book of Judges is demonstrated by the extensive number of motifs the writers or editors have borrowed from earlier judge narratives and incorporated into the Samson saga. The following is a list of sixteen important allusions to other parts of Judges, both allusive parallels and contrasts.[57]

(1) In the first chapter of Judges, the role of the tribe of Judah was positive, bold, and courageous in leading the fight against Israel's enemy (1:1-15). In the Samson story, the people of Judah simply acquiesce to the Philistines' oppressive rule over them. They show no courage or ability to resist the enemy (15:9-11). Instead, they betray their own judge Samson, bind him with ropes, and hand him over to the Philistines (15:12-13).

(2) Judges 3:6 condemned the Israelites for intermarrying with other nations, since marriage with foreigners led to worshiping foreign gods. Samson loved and married a foreign woman (14:1-4). His marriage violated God's prohibition to the Israelites in 2:2: "For your part, do not make a covenant with the inhabitants of this land" (2:2). Moreover, Samson also slept with a foreign prostitute (זנה *zōnâ*, 16:1-3). The same Hebrew root (זנה *znh*) is used to describe Israel's "prostituting" and "lusting" after foreign gods elsewhere in Judges (2:17; 8:33).

(3) The last rogue judge, Samson, is the reverse image of the first model judge, Othniel (1:11-15; 3:7-11). Othniel's exemplary marriage to the Israelite Achsah contrasts with Samson's troubled marriage and relationships with foreign women. Othniel leads Israelite soldiers in a successful holy war. Samson is a loner who has no desire to lead Israel in any way. Othniel "delivered" Israel from its enemy and gave Israel "rest," or peace, for forty years (3:9, 11). Samson will only "begin to deliver Israel" from the Philistines, and no period of rest will result from his judgeship (13:5; 16:31).

(4) In all the previous judge stories, it is always *Israel* who cries in distress and causes God to intervene (3:15; 4:3; 6:7; 10:10). In the Samson story, *Samson* replaces Israel as the one who cries out to God, once when he is dying of thirst (15:18-19) and once at the end of his life, when he desires revenge on the Philistines (16:28-30). In both cases, God responds to Samson's cry just as God had responded to the Israelites' cry of distress in the previous stories.

(5) The early judge Ehud approached the fat king Eglon with a sword hidden at his side, and he said, "I have a secret message for you, O king" (3:19). Similarly, secrets figure prominently throughout the Samson story: the angel's secret identity (13:17-18), the secret that Samson's marriage to a Philistine woman is from the Lord (14:4), the riddle and its secret solution (12:18), the secret of Samson's strength in his uncut hair (16:4-17), the secret that the Lord had left Samson when his head was shaved (16:20), and the secret of Samson's hair growing back, which allowed him one last opportunity to bring revenge on the Philistines (16:22-30).

(6) One of the early minor judges, Shamgar, killed six hundred Philistines with an oxgoad (3:31). Samson killed one thousand Philistines with the jawbone of an ass (15:14-17).

(7) Jael the Kenite killed the Canaanite general Sisera by putting him to sleep in her tent and then secretly "driving" a tent peg into his head (4:21). Similarly, Delilah tries to capture Samson by putting him to sleep and "driving" (תקע *tāqaʿ*; the same verbs as in 4:21) a tent peg or pin into the long braid of hair on his head (16:14). In the end, Jael succeeds in killing Israel's enemy, Sisera, and Delilah succeeds in the plot to kill Israel's judge, Samson (16:18-31).

(8) The judge Gideon began his career by pulling down the altar of the Canaanite god Baal (6:25-27). Samson ends his career by pushing down the pillars of the temple of the Philistine god Dagon (16:23-31).

(9) Gideon's main mission to fight the Midianites was momentarily diverted by a personal vendetta against the inhabitants of the towns of Succoth and Penuel who had taunted him (8:4-9, 13-17). Similarly, Jephthah's primary fight with the Ammonites was interrupted when as an act of personal revenge he killed thousands of Ephraimites who had taunted him (12:1-6). Samson's career as a judge was devoted entirely to personal vendettas and individual acts of revenge against the Philistines (14:19; 15:7, 14-17; 16:28-30). What was occasional with Gideon and Jephthah became Samson's whole mission: a self-centered desire for personal revenge with no awareness of serving God or leading all Israel.

(10) Several elements in God's call of Gideon to be a judge in 6:11-24 reappear in the story of Samson's birth and call to be a deliverer of Israel

---

57. The list of allusions to other sections of Judges and their significance has been drawn primarily from the discussion of Edward Greenstein, "The Riddle of Samson," *Prooftexts* 1 (1981) 237-60; and Barry Webb, *The Book of the Judges: An Integrated Reading* (Sheffield: JSOT, 1987) 162-74; in addition to my own independent work.

in 13:1-25. Shared motifs include the dramatic appearance of an angel of the Lord (6:11-12; 13:3); the request for confirmation and repetition of signs (6:17-18; 13:8); the fear of death due to seeing the Lord (6:22; 13:22); the reassurance that the people involved will not die (6:23; 13:23); the offering of a kid and a grain offering to the Lord on a rock (6:19-20; 13:19); a divine fire that springs up from the altar, accompanied by the disappearance of the angel (6:21; 13:20-21); and the divine commissioning of Gideon and Samson to deliver Israel (6:14; 13:5).

(11) Gideon employed three hundred men with torches in the attack against the Midianites (7:16, 20-23). Samson employed three hundred foxes with torches tied between their tails in the attack against the Philistines (15:1-8).

(12) It is only with Samson that the Philistine threat, first mentioned in the Jephthah story, is addressed (13:5; 16:30).

(13) A centerpiece of the Jephthah story is that he keeps his vow to sacrifice his daughter, despite the tragic consequences (11:29-40). One of the central elements of the Samson story is that he does *not* keep his vows. He breaks all three nazirite vows by eating unclean food, drinking alcohol, and cutting his hair (13:4-5; see Num 6:1-8). He ate unclean food in the form of honey from a lion's corpse (14:8-9). He drank alcohol or wine at a seven-day drinking festival in honor of his wedding to the Philistine woman (14:10-12). He allowed his hair to be cut after Delilah's incessant pleas (16:17-20).

(14) Jephthah's victory against the Ammonites led unintentionally to the death and burning of the daughter whom he loved (11:30-31, 34-40). Samson's victory against the Philistines led unintentionally to the death and burning of the wife whom he loved (15:1-6).

(15) In 14:3 and 7, Samson desired the woman from Timnah as a wife because "she pleased Samson." The phrase in Hebrew literally reads, "she was right in the eyes of Samson." The phrase is unusual when applied to humans as an object, but it appears to be an intentional echo of a key phrase that frames the last section of Judges (chaps. 17–21). The same phrase is used for all Israelites in 17:6 and 21:25: "All the people did what was right in their own eyes." Samson's roving eyes, illicit sexual liaisons, and vengeful

murder of Philistines resemble the Israelites' doing whatever was right in their own eyes in Judges 17–21. They worshiped idols (17:1-6). They committed sexual immorality and murder (19:22-30). And Israelites killed each other, nearly exterminating the tribe of Benjamin (20:35-48).

(16) Samson's shaved head portends his imminent capture and death at the hands of the Philistines (16:17-21; see 13:3-5). However, a note of hope emerges when "the hair of his head began to grow again" (16:22). Similarly, the Israelites' attack and near extinction of their own fellow tribe of Benjamin portends the end of Israel's twelve-tribe union (19:22–20:46). However, a note of hope emerges when six hundred Benjaminite soldiers manage to escape the battle and live on to repopulate the tribe (20:47).

How are we to interpret these many allusions to other parts of the book of Judges in the Samson story? These literary echoes suggest that the present form of the story was shaped and edited at a late stage of the book's composition, when much of the other material in Judges had already been written and set in place. Also, Samson is an embodiment of all that was wrong with the judges who preceded him. On one hand, Samson is the opposite of what the good judges were in the early part of the judges era. He is the reverse image of the first model judge, Othniel. Samson also embodies the worst of the negative characteristics that began to appear in the last two phases of the judges era with Gideon and Jephthah: personal vendettas, selfish rage, reluctance to lead, inability to rally the tribes of Israel into a united community, covenants with foreigners, and breaking of covenant vows. In short, Samson represents the implosion of the whole judge system. The judges have gradually deteriorated in effectiveness as religious and military leaders over the course of three distinct phases in the book of Judges. Samson is the end of the line in that deterioration. He is the judge who no longer leads Israel or obeys God. Moreover, he only begins to deliver Israel from the Philistines (13:5), and he does not gain any years of rest for his people.

Samson is the embodiment not only of the judges but also of the whole nation of Israel.[58] He breaks all of his covenant vows as a Nazirite in

58. Greenstein, "The Riddle of Samson," 247-55.

the same way that Israel repeatedly broke its covenant obligations in worshiping idols. Samson's entanglements with foreign women are a metaphor for Israel's "lusting" after foreign gods. Samson spurned all the obligations of the nazirite covenant to which his parents had been faithful (13:1-24). In the same manner, the new generation of Israelites after the death of Joshua spurned the covenant of their faithful parents (2:6-23). Just as God responded repeatedly to Israel's cry of distress in spite of its disobedience, so also God responded each time to Samson's cry of distress (15:18-19; 16:28-30).

Just as Samson embodies the judges and Israel, so also he embodies one other important feature of the book of Judges: the kind of divine love that simply cannot let go. Samson loves even when the loved one repeatedly betrays that love and loyalty. Samson's wife betrayed the answer to his riddle (14:17), and yet he continued to love her (15:1). One scholar has argued that the answer to the riddle in 14:18 ("What is sweeter than honey? What is stronger than a lion?") implies an additional and unspoken answer—namely, love.[59] Delilah betrayed

Samson four different times, and yet he continued to return to her and love her (16:1-21). Samson was betrayed not only by the women he loved but even by his fellow Israelites. The tribe of Judah betrayed their own judge, Samson, to the Philistines, and yet he did not take revenge on Judah (15:9-17). The special intensity of Samson's connection with God—the special birth involving the angelic visitor and the frequent infusion of the divine Spirit (13:25; 14:6, 19; 15:14)—suggests that Samson's character may reveal something deeper and more direct about God's character than did previous judges. Samson's tenacious and often irrational love provides a metaphor for God's unfailing love in spite of Israel's repeated betrayals. Samson was a pushover whenever his beloved cried, begged, and pleaded with him. If we shake our heads in puzzlement over Samson's relentless love for those who betrayed him, then we must do the same for God's amazingly patient and relentless love for Israel throughout the book of Judges. Ironically, the most disobedient and ineffective of all Israel's judges becomes the best window into the heart and character of Israel's God. With Samson, we come to the core of the meaning of the book of Judges for our understanding of the judges, of Israel, and of God.

59. Philip Nel, "The Riddle of Samson (Judge 14, 14.18)," *Biblica* 66 (1985) 534-45.

Judges 13:1-25, The Birth of Samson

13 Again the Israelites did evil in the eyes of the LORD, so the LORD delivered them into the hands of the Philistines for forty years.

[2]A certain man of Zorah, named Manoah, from the clan of the Danites, had a wife who was sterile and remained childless. [3]The angel of the LORD appeared to her and said, "You are sterile and childless, but you are going to conceive and have a son. [4]Now see to it that you drink no wine or other fermented drink and that you do not eat anything unclean, [5]because you will conceive and give birth to a son. No razor may be used on his head, because the boy is to be a Nazirite, set apart to God from birth, and he will begin the deliverance of Israel from the hands of the Philistines."

[6]Then the woman went to her husband and told him, "A man of God came to me. He looked like an angel of God, very awesome. I didn't ask

13 The Israelites again did what was evil in the sight of the LORD, and the LORD gave them into the hand of the Philistines forty years.

2There was a certain man of Zorah, of the tribe of the Danites, whose name was Manoah. His wife was barren, having borne no children. [3]And the angel of the LORD appeared to the woman and said to her, "Although you are barren, having borne no children, you shall conceive and bear a son. [4]Now be careful not to drink wine or strong drink, or to eat anything unclean, [5]for you shall conceive and bear a son. No razor is to come on his head, for the boy shall be a nazirite[a] to God from birth. It is he who shall begin to deliver Israel from the hand of the Philistines." [6]Then the woman came and told her husband, "A man of God came to me, and his appearance was like

[a] That is *one separated* or *one consecrated*

NIV

him where he came from, and he didn't tell me his name. ⁷But he said to me, 'You will conceive and give birth to a son. Now then, drink no wine or other fermented drink and do not eat anything unclean, because the boy will be a Nazirite of God from birth until the day of his death.'"

⁸Then Manoah prayed to the LORD: "O Lord, I beg you, let the man of God you sent to us come again to teach us how to bring up the boy who is to be born."

⁹God heard Manoah, and the angel of God came again to the woman while she was out in the field; but her husband Manoah was not with her. ¹⁰The woman hurried to tell her husband, "He's here! The man who appeared to me the other day!"

¹¹Manoah got up and followed his wife. When he came to the man, he said, "Are you the one who talked to my wife?"

"I am," he said.

¹²So Manoah asked him, "When your words are fulfilled, what is to be the rule for the boy's life and work?"

¹³The angel of the LORD answered, "Your wife must do all that I have told her. ¹⁴She must not eat anything that comes from the grapevine, nor drink any wine or other fermented drink nor eat anything unclean. She must do everything I have commanded her."

¹⁵Manoah said to the angel of the LORD, "We would like you to stay until we prepare a young goat for you."

¹⁶The angel of the LORD replied, "Even though you detain me, I will not eat any of your food. But if you prepare a burnt offering, offer it to the LORD." (Manoah did not realize that it was the angel of the LORD.)

¹⁷Then Manoah inquired of the angel of the LORD, "What is your name, so that we may honor you when your word comes true?"

¹⁸He replied, "Why do you ask my name? It is beyond understanding.ᵃ" ¹⁹Then Manoah took a young goat, together with the grain offering, and sacrificed it on a rock to the LORD. And the LORD did an amazing thing while Manoah and his wife watched: ²⁰As the flame blazed up from the altar toward heaven, the angel of the LORD ascended

ᵃ18 Or is wonderful

NRSV

that of an angelᵃ of God, most awe-inspiring; I did not ask him where he came from, and he did not tell me his name; ⁷but he said to me, 'You shall conceive and bear a son. So then drink no wine or strong drink, and eat nothing unclean, for the boy shall be a naziriteᵇ to God from birth to the day of his death.'"

8Then Manoah entreated the LORD, and said, "O LORD, I pray, let the man of God whom you sent come to us again and teach us what we are to do concerning the boy who will be born." ⁹God listened to Manoah, and the angel of God came again to the woman as she sat in the field; but her husband Manoah was not with her. ¹⁰So the woman ran quickly and told her husband, "The man who came to me the other day has appeared to me." ¹¹Manoah got up and followed his wife, and came to the man and said to him, "Are you the man who spoke to this woman?" And he said, "I am." ¹²Then Manoah said, "Now when your words come true, what is to be the boy's rule of life; what is he to do?" ¹³The angel of the LORD said to Manoah, "Let the woman give heed to all that I said to her. ¹⁴She may not eat of anything that comes from the vine. She is not to drink wine or strong drink, or eat any unclean thing. She is to observe everything that I commanded her."

15Manoah said to the angel of the LORD, "Allow us to detain you, and prepare a kid for you." ¹⁶The angel of the LORD said to Manoah, "If you detain me, I will not eat your food; but if you want to prepare a burnt offering, then offer it to the LORD." (For Manoah did not know that he was the angel of the LORD.) ¹⁷Then Manoah said to the angel of the LORD, "What is your name, so that we may honor you when your words come true?" ¹⁸But the angel of the LORD said to him, "Why do you ask my name? It is too wonderful."

19So Manoah took the kid with the grain offering, and offered it on the rock to the LORD, to him who worksᶜ wonders.ᵈ ²⁰When the flame went up toward heaven from the altar, the angel of the LORD ascended in the flame of the altar while Manoah and his wife looked on; and they fell on their faces to the ground. ²¹The angel of

ᵃ Or the angel   ᵇ That is one separated or one consecrated
ᶜ Gk Vg: Heb and working   ᵈ Heb wonders, while Manoah and his wife looked on

NIV

in the flame. Seeing this, Manoah and his wife fell with their faces to the ground. ²¹When the angel of the LORD did not show himself again to Manoah and his wife, Manoah realized that it was the angel of the LORD.

²²"We are doomed to die!" he said to his wife. "We have seen God!"

²³But his wife answered, "If the LORD had meant to kill us, he would not have accepted a burnt offering and grain offering from our hands, nor shown us all these things or now told us this."

²⁴The woman gave birth to a boy and named him Samson. He grew and the LORD blessed him, ²⁵and the Spirit of the LORD began to stir him while he was in Mahaneh Dan, between Zorah and Eshtaol.

NRSV

the LORD did not appear again to Manoah and his wife. Then Manoah realized that it was the angel of the LORD. ²²And Manoah said to his wife, "We shall surely die, for we have seen God." ²³But his wife said to him, "If the LORD had meant to kill us, he would not have accepted a burnt offering and a grain offering at our hands, or shown us all these things, or now announced to us such things as these."

24The woman bore a son, and named him Samson. The boy grew, and the LORD blessed him. ²⁵The spirit of the LORD began to stir him in Mahaneh-dan, between Zorah and Eshtaol.

COMMENTARY

The Samson narrative opens with the usual introductory formula, announcing that Israel again has done evil and the Lord has allowed the Philistines to oppress them for forty years. If this were the typical judges cycle, we would expect the Israelites to cry in distress, prompting God to send a deliverer. In this case, the Israelites do not know enough even to cry out. Instead, God must take the initiative in sending an angel to announce the birth of a son "who shall begin to deliver Israel from the hand of the Philistines" (v. 5). The deliverance will be partial, suggesting that the judge paradigm is increasingly losing effectiveness. The Philistines will return as Israel's oppressors later in 1 Samuel under the kingships of Saul and David (see 1 Sam 4:1-11).

The birth of this deliverer is announced to the barren, or childless, wife of a man named Manoah from the tribe of Dan. The angel instructs the mother-to-be not to drink wine or alcohol and not to eat unclean food. These same prohibitions presumably apply to the son about to be born, along with one additional prohibition: "no razor is to come on his head" (vv. 4-5). The reason for the prohibitions is that this son will be a "Nazirite" to God from birth. The word "nazirite" (נזיר *nāzîr*) means "separated one" or "consecrated one," signifying someone specially dedicated for

service to God. The law for the Nazirite is found in Num 6:1-21 and specifies three obligations: no wine, no cutting of hair, and no touching of a corpse. The laws in Numbers 6 assume that the nazirite vow is taken on voluntarily by an adult for a limited period rather than given at birth for a lifetime. However, the special dedication of a Nazirite from the womb suggests an extraordinary act of consecration by God. The special character of this son who is about to be born is underscored by the fact that the mother is barren. The motif of the barren wife to whom God gives a child is associated with several famous female ancestors of Israel's history: Sarah and her son, Isaac (Gen 11:30; 21:1-7); Rebekah and her sons, Jacob and Esau (Gen 25:21-26); Rachel and her sons, Joseph and Benjamin (Gen 29:31; 30:22-24; 35:16-20); and Hannah and her son Samuel (1 Sam 1:1-28). The nazirite vow and the barren woman who gives birth raise enormous expectations in the reader to look for something extraordinary from this son who is about to be born.

The wife of Manoah reports the encounter to her husband. She tells him that "a man of God" whose appearance was like that of "an angel of God" came to her with the news of the imminent birth of a son. She simply accepts his words as true, not pressing to know from where he came or what his name is (vv. 6-7). Manoah's wife explains that the boy will be a Nazirite to God from birth, as the man of God had said. Then she adds her own ominous words: His nazirite mission will extend from birth "to the day of his death" (v. 7). Her words allude in a tragic way to the final scene of the Samson story (16:23-31).

The husband, Manoah, is not satisfied with this secondhand report from his wife. He prays to God to send the man of God again to confirm the news and to teach them what they are to do with the boy who will be born. God grants Manoah's request. The man of God comes to Manoah's wife in the field, and she runs and brings her husband to meet him. After the man of God, who is indeed an angel of God, repeats the nazirite instructions, Manoah invites him to stay and eat. Manoah wants to prepare a kid or young goat as a meal. The hospitality is reminiscent of Abraham's invitation to the three men of God in Gen 18:1-15. The angel of God demurs, saying he will not eat the food, but Manoah can offer the kid as a burnt offering to the Lord. Still unaware that this is an angel, Manoah asks, "What is your name?" The angel replies, "Why do you ask my name? It is too wonderful" (vv. 17-18). This exchange is a direct allusion to the famous wrestling match between the ancestor Jacob and the angel of God (Gen 32:29).

After Manoah offers up a burnt offering, the angel ascends in the flame up to heaven. Now Manoah knows this was an angel of the Lord. He is fearful that he and his wife will die because "we have seen God" (v. 22). This concern reflects a common OT notion that any human who sees God face to face will die (Exod 33:20). But Manoah's wife assures him that they will not die. God has come, not to destroy them, but to give them life in the form of a son soon to be born (v. 23). In due time, Manoah's wife gives birth to a son, whom she names Samson. The Lord blesses the boy as he grows, and "the spirit of the LORD began to stir him" (v. 24).

This opening episode of the Samson story is saturated with allusions to the wider biblical tradition. The famous barren mothers, the nazirite vow, the angels' visit to Abraham and Sarah, the wrestling match with Jacob, and seeing God face to face all point to the birth of this son as an extraordinarily momentous event. These allusions all suggest that God has pulled out all the stops and is investing enormous divine power and hope in this one son about to be born. After the debacle of the Jephthah story and the brief respite of the minor judges in 12:8-15, God is now intervening in a dramatic and unprecedented way to save Israel. Even so, God realizes that even this child will only "begin to deliver Israel from the hand of the Philistines" (v. 5).

REFLECTIONS

1. When it comes to believing and trusting in what God promises, the Bible affirms that a variety of responses is available and legitimate. The first scene of the story presents us with two quite different approaches in the wife of Manoah and Manoah himself. The wife of Manoah simply trusts what the man of God tells her. She does not require or ask for his source of authority or his name (13:6). In spite of the obstacle of her barrenness, she is willing to trust that God will somehow find a way to make the promise come true. Her strong faith finds a New Testament counterpart in the angel's promise to Mary that she would be the mother of Jesus. Mary accepted the angel's words, saying, "Let it be with me according to your word" (Luke 1:38 NRSV). Likewise, the women at Jesus' tomb on Easter morning believed without question the angels' words that Jesus had risen from the dead (Luke 24:1-9).

However, not all of God's people find it easy to trust God's promises without some sort of sign or confirmation. In Judges 13, the husband, Manoah, needs some assurance that his wife's report is truly a word from God. His request echoes the experience of Abraham and his struggle to believe God's promise of a son and of a land in Genesis 15. On one hand, Abraham trusted God's promise of a son (Gen 15:6). On the other hand, a part of Abraham needed an additional sign and confirmation of God's promise of the land (Gen 15:8-19). In the New Testament retelling of the first Easter story, the women came from Jesus' tomb and relayed to the disciples what the angel had said about Jesus' resurrection. But the text reports that "these words seemed to them an idle tale" (Luke 24:11 NRSV). The confirmation came in Jesus' resurrection appearances to the disciples. Examples include the scene on the road to Emmaus (Luke 24:13-35) and the confrontation of the risen Jesus with doubting Thomas, the disciple who wanted proof that Jesus was alive (John 20:19-29). In each of these cases, God took seriously and accepted those who expressed their doubts and struggles to believe. To those who doubt, God often offers signs and assurances that are visible to the eyes of faith.

2. The parents of Samson emerge as faithful and obedient models of faith who desire that God "teach us what we are to do concerning the boy" (13:8). We have seen this motif of a faithful generation of parents once before in the book of Judges. In chapter 2, the previous generation of Israelites under the leadership of Joshua had "worshiped the LORD all the days of Joshua" (2:7). However, after the death of that generation, "another generation grew up after them, who did not know the LORD" (2:10). The parents of Samson display a strong faith similar to that of the generation of Joshua. As readers at this early point in the Samson story, we wonder whether the son Samson and the generation of Israelites he represents will continue to be faithful. Or will Samson and his generation fail to maintain their covenant loyalty to the Lord? By the end of the Samson saga, we will see that the paradigm of an old faithful generation of parents, followed by a disobedient and rebellious generation will, indeed, be repeated in the story of Manoah and his wife and their son, Samson. The paradigm raises the ever-present challenges of an older generation's passing on its faith tradition to a new generation.

3. The many allusions to important biblical traditions of consecration and special service in Judges 13 demonstrate that the divine investment in this son named Samson as a deliverer of Israel is enormous. At the same time, the continuing decline in the effectiveness of the whole judges system of leadership and the degradation of Israel's social and religious life pose massive obstacles to God's will to deliver Israel yet again. This combination of intense divine energy and a resistant people and system of leadership will result only in Israel's partial deliverance: Samson "shall begin to deliver Israel from the hand of the Philistines" (v. 5). This observation may lead us to reflect on the role of humans and human systems and institutions both to advance and to thwart the efficiency and effectiveness of God's will's being done in a given situation. Ultimately, God's final will and loving purpose for the people of God and for the whole creation will be done. As the apostle Paul affirms, nothing "in all creation will be able to separate us from the love of God in Christ Jesus our Lord" (Rom 8:39 NRSV). However, God's specific will in particular circumstances may be helped or hindered by what humans and other forces in the world may do.

Judges 14:1-20, Samson the Riddler

NIV	NRSV
14 Samson went down to Timnah and saw there a young Philistine woman. ²When he returned, he said to his father and mother, "I have seen a Philistine woman in Timnah; now get her for me as my wife."	**14** Once Samson went down to Timnah, and at Timnah he saw a Philistine woman. ²Then he came up, and told his father and mother, "I saw a Philistine woman at Timnah; now get her for me as my wife." ³But his father and
³His father and mother replied, "Isn't there an acceptable woman among your relatives or among all our people? Must you go to the uncircumcised Philistines to get a wife?"	mother said to him, "Is there not a woman among your kin, or among all our*a* people, that you must go to take a wife from the uncircumcised Philis-
But Samson said to his father, "Get her for me.	*a* Cn: Heb *my*

NIV

She's the right one for me." [4](His parents did not know that this was from the LORD, who was seeking an occasion to confront the Philistines; for at that time they were ruling over Israel.) [5]Samson went down to Timnah together with his father and mother. As they approached the vineyards of Timnah, suddenly a young lion came roaring toward him. [6]The Spirit of the LORD came upon him in power so that he tore the lion apart with his bare hands as he might have torn a young goat. But he told neither his father nor his mother what he had done. [7]Then he went down and talked with the woman, and he liked her.

[8]Some time later, when he went back to marry her, he turned aside to look at the lion's carcass. In it was a swarm of bees and some honey, [9]which he scooped out with his hands and ate as he went along. When he rejoined his parents, he gave them some, and they too ate it. But he did not tell them that he had taken the honey from the lion's carcass.

[10]Now his father went down to see the woman. And Samson made a feast there, as was customary for bridegrooms. [11]When he appeared, he was given thirty companions.

[12]"Let me tell you a riddle," Samson said to them. "If you can give me the answer within the seven days of the feast, I will give you thirty linen garments and thirty sets of clothes. [13]If you can't tell me the answer, you must give me thirty linen garments and thirty sets of clothes."

"Tell us your riddle," they said. "Let's hear it." [14]He replied,

"Out of the eater, something to eat;
    out of the strong, something sweet."

For three days they could not give the answer.

[15]On the fourth[a] day, they said to Samson's wife, "Coax your husband into explaining the riddle for us, or we will burn you and your father's household to death. Did you invite us here to rob us?"

[16]Then Samson's wife threw herself on him, sobbing, "You hate me! You don't really love me. You've given my people a riddle, but you haven't told me the answer."

"I haven't even explained it to my father or mother," he replied, "so why should I explain it

a15 Some Septuagint manuscripts and Syriac; Hebrew seventh

NRSV

tines?" But Samson said to his father, "Get her for me, because she pleases me." [4]His father and mother did not know that this was from the LORD; for he was seeking a pretext to act against the Philistines. At that time the Philistines had dominion over Israel.

[5]Then Samson went down with his father and mother to Timnah. When he came to the vineyards of Timnah, suddenly a young lion roared at him. [6]The spirit of the LORD rushed on him, and he tore the lion apart barehanded as one might tear apart a kid. But he did not tell his father or his mother what he had done. [7]Then he went down and talked with the woman, and she pleased Samson. [8]After a while he returned to marry her, and he turned aside to see the carcass of the lion, and there was a swarm of bees in the body of the lion, and honey. [9]He scraped it out into his hands, and went on, eating as he went. When he came to his father and mother, he gave some to them, and they ate it. But he did not tell them that he had taken the honey from the carcass of the lion.

[10]His father went down to the woman, and Samson made a feast there as the young men were accustomed to do. [11]When the people saw him, they brought thirty companions to be with him. [12]Samson said to them, "Let me now put a riddle to you. If you can explain it to me within the seven days of the feast, and find it out, then I will give you thirty linen garments and thirty festal garments. [13]But if you cannot explain it to me, then you shall give me thirty linen garments and thirty festal garments." So they said to him, "Ask your riddle; let us hear it." [14]He said to them,

"Out of the eater came something to eat.
Out of the strong came something sweet."

But for three days they could not explain the riddle.

[15]On the fourth[a] day they said to Samson's wife, "Coax your husband to explain the riddle to us, or we will burn you and your father's house with fire. Have you invited us here to impoverish us?" [16]So Samson's wife wept before him, saying, "You hate me; you do not really love me. You have asked a riddle of my people, but you have not explained it to me." He said to her, "Look, I

a Gk Syr: Heb seventh

to you?" ¹⁷She cried the whole seven days of the feast. So on the seventh day he finally told her, because she continued to press him. She in turn explained the riddle to her people.

¹⁸Before sunset on the seventh day the men of the town said to him,

"What is sweeter than honey?
  What is stronger than a lion?"

Samson said to them,

"If you had not plowed with my heifer,
  you would not have solved my riddle."

¹⁹Then the Spirit of the LORD came upon him in power. He went down to Ashkelon, struck down thirty of their men, stripped them of their belongings and gave their clothes to those who had explained the riddle. Burning with anger, he went up to his father's house. ²⁰And Samson's wife was given to the friend who had attended him at his wedding.

have not told my father or my mother. Why should I tell you?" ¹⁷She wept before him the seven days that their feast lasted; and because she nagged him, on the seventh day he told her. Then she explained the riddle to her people. ¹⁸The men of the town said to him on the seventh day before the sun went down,

"What is sweeter than honey?
  What is stronger than a lion?"

And he said to them,

"If you had not plowed with my heifer,
  you would not have found out my riddle."

¹⁹Then the spirit of the LORD rushed on him, and he went down to Ashkelon. He killed thirty men of the town, took their spoil, and gave the festal garments to those who had explained the riddle. In hot anger he went back to his father's house. ²⁰And Samson's wife was given to his companion, who had been his best man.

COMMENTARY

Judges 13 had prepared the reader to have great expectations for Samson as a deliverer of Israel. However, his first recorded action as an adult seems quickly to dash those expectations. He falls in love with a Philistine woman and orders his mother and father, "Get her for me as my wife" (v. 2). Samson's parents know that their covenant with God condemns intermarriage with foreigners (3:6) and making covenants with non-Israelites (2:2). Thus they try to dissuade Samson from marrying the Philistine woman, but he will not take no for an answer. He insists that "she pleases me" (היא ישרה בעיני *hî' yāšěrâ bě'ênāy*; lit., "she is right in my eyes"). The phrase is an echo of the important refrain that characterizes all Israel in the final and most tragic section of Judges: "all the people did what was right in their own eyes" (17:6; 21:25).

14:4. Just when we are ready to condemn Samson for his roving eye, however, the narrator interrupts with a word to the reader. Samson's parents did not know that "this was from the LORD"! The Lord wanted Samson to marry the Philistine woman in order to create "a pretext to act against the Philistines." Remarkably, God

steers Samson to disobey God's own covenant prohibitions against intermarriage in order to help Israel and act against the Philistine oppressors. This is one of many ironies and inverted expectations that we will encounter in the chaotic and unsettled situation in which Samson lives and through which God works at the end of the judges era. The parents' lack of knowledge about the unexpected ways in which God was working in Samson will also be a recurring theme in the narrative.

14:5-9. Samson convinces his parents to join him in "going down" to the town of Timnah to marry the Philistine woman. Their journey into Philistine territory will lead to Samson's breaking two of his three nazirite vows: drinking wine or anything produced from the grapevine (13:4; Num 6:4) and eating anything that is unclean, especially anything associated with the corpse of an animal or a human (13:4; Num 6:6-8). They come to the "vineyards of Timnah." The mention of a vineyard immediately raises warning flags, since the Nazirite is to avoid anything produced from grapes. Suddenly a young lion roars at Samson, the Spirit of the Lord rushes upon him, and he tears apart the lion barehanded. The nazirite instructions in chap. 13 had said nothing about a prohibition against Samson's touching a corpse; that prohibition is mentioned only in the general nazirite law in Numbers 6. Thus the reader may wonder whether Samson's touching the corpse of a lion (itself an unclean animal, Lev 11:27) may technically not be a violation of his nazirite covenant. Samson's parents again do not know about the incident with the lion. In any case, Samson and his parents visit the Philistine woman and then return home. Sometime later, Samson is on his way to the wedding and travels the same road as before. He sees the carcass of the lion he had killed with a swarm of bees and their honey in the carcass. He eats the honey, which is ritually contaminated by the unclean corpse of an unclean animal. The reader now knows that Samson has broken his first nazirite vow, but again his parents are unaware (vv. 8-9).

14:10-11. Samson's father goes down to arrange for the marriage, and Samson "made a feast" as was the custom for weddings (v. 10). The word for "feast" here (משתה *mišteh*) suggests a drinking feast, and so Samson seems to have broken now the second of his nazirite vows: "be careful not to drink wine or strong drink" (13:4; Num 6:3-4). However, the reader may wonder still whether these are serious infractions, since the angel had applied these two prohibitions to the parents but not explicitly (perhaps implicitly?) to Samson. At least Samson's hair remains uncut, and it will be that third and last vow of his nazirite covenant that will remain fulfilled until the last episode with Delilah.

14:12-18a. As part of the seven-day feast, Samson proposes a riddle to his wedding guests and places a wager of sixty garments that the guests cannot solve it. The riddle is this: "Out of the eater came something to eat. Out of the strong came something sweet." The answer to the riddle, on the surface, is Samson's dead lion with its sweet honey, about which the guests know nothing. After three days of guessing, the guests demand that Samson's new wife beg him for the answer to the riddle "or we will burn you and your father's house with fire" (v. 15). She begs Samson for the answer until the seventh day of the feast. He finally relents and tells her the answer to the riddle, and then she passes it on to the Philistine guests: "What is sweeter than honey? What is stronger than a lion?" (v. 18). There may be more than this surface-level meaning to the riddle, however, in the context of the larger Samson story. The solution is given in the form of two questions. The interrogatives invite further searching on the reader's part to consider another level of meaning as to what might be stronger than a lion and sweeter than honey. One scholar has argued that a more subtle answer to the two questions and an implied solution to the larger riddle of the Samson story itself is the answer "love." Love is both incredibly strong and incredibly sweet for both Samson and his women, but more significantly for God and the people of Israel. God's powerful and sweet love cannot let Israel go, no matter how disobedient they are.

14:18b-20. Samson gives a sexually crude and angry response to the wedding guests: "If you had not plowed with my heifer, you would not have found out my riddle" (v. 18). The Spirit of God rushes on Samson yet again. He then angrily goes to the neighboring Philistine city of Ashkelon, kills thirty men, steals their garments, and gives the stolen clothing to the wedding guests in payment for the wager they had made and Samson had lost. Hot-headed Samson heads back home, leaving his wife with the Philistines. In Samson's absence, his wife is married off again to the best man at Samson's wedding (vv. 19-20).

REFLECTIONS

In the topsy-turvy world of a disintegrating Israelite society, the Lord works in mysterious and seemingly contradictory ways. The Lord is behind Samson's desire for a Philistine wife, a desire that contradicts earlier covenant prohibitions for intermarriage in Judg 2:2 and 3:6. The Spirit of the Lord rushed on Samson two times in this episode, and each time Samson disobeyed clear prohibitions of the covenant. The divine Spirit gave Samson the strength to kill the young lion (14:6). Yet that eventually led to his breaking the nazirite prohibition of touching a corpse or eating anything unclean. The Spirit of the Lord also rushed upon Samson when he murdered the thirty men of Ashkelon, stole their clothing, and then used his ill-gotten gains to pay off his wager. Samson kills and steals out of personal revenge and hot-headed anger, violations of the commandments against killing and stealing without community sanction (Deut 5:17, 19).

God seems constrained to work through such devious and sinful means in the disordered context of a splintered and rebellious Israelite nation. God is free to contravene the very laws God has given to Israel for the sake of God's mercy and love for the people and for the sake of the punishment of the oppressive Philistines. Although laws and ordered structures are important and helpful, the priority remains on God's will and God's compassion, which may at times override institutional policy, governmental regulation, and even divine law.

Judges 15:1-20, Samson the Avenger

NIV

15 Later on, at the time of wheat harvest, Samson took a young goat and went to visit his wife. He said, "I'm going to my wife's room." But her father would not let him go in.

²"I was so sure you thoroughly hated her," he said, "that I gave her to your friend. Isn't her younger sister more attractive? Take her instead."

³Samson said to them, "This time I have a right to get even with the Philistines; I will really harm them." ⁴So he went out and caught three hundred foxes and tied them tail to tail in pairs. He then fastened a torch to every pair of tails, ⁵lit the torches and let the foxes loose in the standing grain of the Philistines. He burned up the shocks and standing grain, together with the vineyards and olive groves.

⁶When the Philistines asked, "Who did this?" they were told, "Samson, the Timnite's son-in-law, because his wife was given to his friend."

So the Philistines went up and burned her and her father to death. ⁷Samson said to them, "Since you've acted like this, I won't stop until I get my revenge on you." ⁸He attacked them viciously and slaughtered many of them. Then he went down and stayed in a cave in the rock of Etam.

⁹The Philistines went up and camped in Judah, spreading out near Lehi. ¹⁰The men of Judah asked, "Why have you come to fight us?"

"We have come to take Samson prisoner," they answered, "to do to him as he did to us."

¹¹Then three thousand men from Judah went down to the cave in the rock of Etam and said to Samson, "Don't you realize that the Philistines are rulers over us? What have you done to us?"

NRSV

15 After a while, at the time of the wheat harvest, Samson went to visit his wife, bringing along a kid. He said, "I want to go into my wife's room." But her father would not allow him to go in. ²Her father said, "I was sure that you had rejected her; so I gave her to your companion. Is not her younger sister prettier than she? Why not take her instead?" ³Samson said to them, "This time, when I do mischief to the Philistines, I will be without blame." ⁴So Samson went and caught three hundred foxes, and took some torches; and he turned the foxes*ᵃ* tail to tail, and put a torch between each pair of tails. ⁵When he had set fire to the torches, he let the foxes go into the standing grain of the Philistines, and burned up the shocks and the standing grain, as well as the vineyards and*ᵇ* olive groves. ⁶Then the Philistines asked, "Who has done this?" And they said, "Samson, the son-in-law of the Timnite, because he has taken Samson's wife and given her to his companion." So the Philistines came up, and burned her and her father. ⁷Samson said to them, "If this is what you do, I swear I will not stop until I have taken revenge on you." ⁸He struck them down hip and thigh with great slaughter; and he went down and stayed in the cleft of the rock of Etam.

9Then the Philistines came up and encamped in Judah, and made a raid on Lehi. ¹⁰The men of Judah said, "Why have you come up against us?" They said, "We have come up to bind Samson, to do to him as he did to us." ¹¹Then three thousand men of Judah went down to the cleft

ᵃ Heb *them*   ᵇ Gk Tg Vg: Heb lacks *and*

NIV

He answered, "I merely did to them what they did to me."

[12]They said to him, "We've come to tie you up and hand you over to the Philistines."

Samson said, "Swear to me that you won't kill me yourselves."

[13]"Agreed," they answered. "We will only tie you up and hand you over to them. We will not kill you." So they bound him with two new ropes and led him up from the rock. [14]As he approached Lehi, the Philistines came toward him shouting. The Spirit of the LORD came upon him in power. The ropes on his arms became like charred flax, and the bindings dropped from his hands. [15]Finding a fresh jawbone of a donkey, he grabbed it and struck down a thousand men.

[16]Then Samson said,

"With a donkey's jawbone
  I have made donkeys of them.[a]
With a donkey's jawbone
  I have killed a thousand men."

[17]When he finished speaking, he threw away the jawbone; and the place was called Ramath Lehi.[b]

[18]Because he was very thirsty, he cried out to the LORD, "You have given your servant this great victory. Must I now die of thirst and fall into the hands of the uncircumcised?" [19]Then God opened up the hollow place in Lehi, and water came out of it. When Samson drank, his strength returned and he revived. So the spring was called En Hakkore,[c] and it is still there in Lehi.

[20]Samson led[d] Israel for twenty years in the days of the Philistines.

a16 Or made a heap or two; the Hebrew for donkey sounds like the Hebrew for heap.   b17 Ramath Lehi means jawbone hill.   c19 En Hakkore means caller's spring.   d20 Traditionally judged

NRSV

of the rock of Etam, and they said to Samson, "Do you not know that the Philistines are rulers over us? What then have you done to us?" He replied, "As they did to me, so I have done to them." [12]They said to him, "We have come down to bind you, so that we may give you into the hands of the Philistines." Samson answered them, "Swear to me that you yourselves will not attack me." [13]They said to him, "No, we will only bind you and give you into their hands; we will not kill you." So they bound him with two new ropes, and brought him up from the rock.

14When he came to Lehi, the Philistines came shouting to meet him; and the spirit of the LORD rushed on him, and the ropes that were on his arms became like flax that has caught fire, and his bonds melted off his hands. [15]Then he found a fresh jawbone of a donkey, reached down and took it, and with it he killed a thousand men. [16]And Samson said,

"With the jawbone of a donkey,
  heaps upon heaps,
with the jawbone of a donkey
  I have slain a thousand men."

[17]When he had finished speaking, he threw away the jawbone; and that place was called Ramath-lehi.[a]

18By then he was very thirsty, and he called on the LORD, saying, "You have granted this great victory by the hand of your servant. Am I now to die of thirst, and fall into the hands of the uncircumcised?" [19]So God split open the hollow place that is at Lehi, and water came from it. When he drank, his spirit returned, and he revived. Therefore it was named En-hakkore,[b] which is at Lehi to this day. [20]And he judged Israel in the days of the Philistines twenty years.

a That is The Hill of the Jawbone   b That is The Spring of the One who Called

COMMENTARY

15:1-8. Samson's hot-headed exploits of personal revenge against the Philistines continue. Samson discovers that his Philistine wife has been given to another man and vows to "do mischief to the Philistines" in retaliation. He implies that

his earlier killing and stealing (14:19) had been reckless and sinful when he says that this time his revenge "will be without blame" (v. 4). Samson's "mischief" involves attaching torches to the tails of three hundred foxes and letting them loose to burn up the grain fields, vineyards, and olive groves of the Philistines. When the Philistines learn that Samson was behind the "mischief," they up the ante in a spiral of retaliatory violence by burning Samson's Philistine wife and her father (v. 6; see 14:15). Samson then vows revenge, and "he struck them down hip and thigh with great slaughter" (v. 8).

15:9-13. The spiral of revenge keeps growing as the Philistines in turn attack the tribe of Judah in the hope of capturing Samson. The tribe of Judah had been an exemplary leader among the Israelites in chap. 1. They had been the first and most successful tribe to lead an attack against the Canaanites (1:1-15). However, in this period of the disintegration of Israel under the judges, even the tribe of Judah cannot or will not resist Israel's oppressors. Instead, they betray God's designated deliverer, Samson, by binding him and surrendering him to the Philistines (vv. 12-13).

15:14-17. The Spirit of the Lord once again rushes upon Samson, and he breaks the ropes that bind him. He finds a jawbone of a donkey. As with the lion carcass (14:5-9), Samson again touches a part of an animal corpse, which defiles him and breaks his nazirite vow (Num 6:6). Samson uses the jawbone to kill a thousand Philistines and then utters a proud boast about the "heaps upon heaps" he has killed (v. 16). The boast is reminiscent of the primeval figure Lamech, who boasted of the revenge he took upon those who hurt him (Gen 4:23-24). Samson's exploits also find a parallel in the earlier minor judge Shamgar, who killed six hundred Philistines with an oxgoad (3:31). The hill on which Samson threw away the donkey's jawbone is remembered by its name, "Ramath-lehi," "The Hill of the Jawbone" (v. 17).

15:18-20. The next scene introduces the first of two times when Samson calls upon God for help. Although God's Spirit has repeatedly rushed upon Samson, it is not clear whether Samson is aware that God has been working through him. Samson seems, in his own mind, to be driven by the desire for personal revenge and nothing else. However, now he acknowledges that it is the Lord who has "granted this great victory by the hand of your servant" (v. 18). In spite of Samson's disobedience and breach of his nazirite covenant, Samson stays connected to God. He prays to God, asking, "Am I now to die of thirst?" In previous judge stories, it was always Israel who cried out in distress, and not the judges. Samson, who is both judge and a metaphor for Israel itself, cries out to the Lord. And as in previous judge stories, the Lord responds to Samson's cry. God splits open a rock, and water flows from it. The place was named "En-hakkore," "The Spring of the One Who Called" (vv. 18-19). This scene of thirst and the provision of water recalls Israel's experience in the wilderness as the people traveled from Egypt to the promised land and God miraculously provided water from a rock (Exod 17:1-7). The parallel with Israel's experience further cements the identification of Samson not only as a judge but also as a metaphor for all Israel.

REFLECTIONS

The central theme of this section of the Samson story is best summarized by Samson himself, "As they did to me, so I have done to them" (15:11). Samson's relationship to the Philistines dances between two poles, either legalistic vengeance as expressed in Samson's statement or a passionate and reckless love as expressed for his Philistine wife (14:3) and later for Delilah (16:4). Samson loves his women, even though he is repeatedly betrayed by them. This dance between vengeful legalism and unrelenting and generous love first appeared in the book of Judges in the juxtaposition of the story of the Canaanite king Adoni-bezek (1:5-7) and the story of Achsah, daughter of the Israelite Othniel (1:11-15). After his capture and punishment, the Canaanite king conceded, "As I have done, so God has paid me back" (1:7). He sees the world through the lens of legalistic retribution. On the other hand, Achsah received from her father an inheritance of land as a gift. Then she boldly asked for an additional area that contains springs of water, and her father graciously and generously gave her two such areas with springs of life-giving water (1:14-15). Achsah saw the world through the lens of a parent's unconditional and generous love. Both of these themes have been weaving in and out of the stories of the judges throughout the book. Israel has done evil, and God has sent an enemy in punishment. Israel has cried out in distress, and God has sent a deliverer to save them. As Israel's sin and disloyalty have increased over the course of the judges era, however, God's love and generosity have been strained to a near breaking point. God's work in and through Samson is one more attempt by God to embody in a leader both responsible accountability and retribution and an unconditional divine love that cannot let Israel go.

God strains to reconcile these two poles in the relationship with Israel throughout Judges. On one hand, God proclaims to Israel, "I will never break my covenant with you" (2:1). On the other hand, God threatens to end the relationship and let Israel receive its just punishment: "You have abandoned me and worshiped other gods; therefore I will deliver you no more" (10:13). Samson embodies these two poles—vengeful retribution and unrelenting love—in his life and relationships. Ultimately, like the two pillars of Dagon's temple (16:30-31), these two opposing poles of vengeance and love will crush Samson and lead to his death. The reader may wonder how God is faring under the strain of holding this rebellious Israel accountable for its actions even as God loves Israel with an unfailing love.

Judges 16:1-3, Samson and the Prostitute

NIV

16 One day Samson went to Gaza, where he saw a prostitute. He went in to spend the night with her. ²The people of Gaza were told, "Samson is here!" So they surrounded the place and lay in wait for him all night at the city gate. They made no move during the night, saying, "At dawn we'll kill him."

³But Samson lay there only until the middle of the night. Then he got up and took hold of the doors of the city gate, together with the two posts, and tore them loose, bar and all. He lifted them to his shoulders and carried them to the top of the hill that faces Hebron.

NRSV

16 Once Samson went to Gaza, where he saw a prostitute and went in to her. ²The Gazites were told,ᵃ "Samson has come here." So they circled around and lay in wait for him all night at the city gate. They kept quiet all night, thinking, "Let us wait until the light of the morning; then we will kill him." ³But Samson lay only until midnight. Then at midnight he rose up, took hold of the doors of the city gate and the two posts, pulled them up, bar and all, put them on his shoulders, and carried them to the top of the hill that is in front of Hebron.

ᵃ Gk: Heb lacks *were told*

COMMENTARY

Samson's love life continues with a brief nocturnal liaison with a Philistine prostitute in Gaza (v. 1). If Samson can point, however imperfectly, to the vastness of God's love, Samson can also symbolize the fickle love and loyalty of Israel. His night with the "prostitute" (זונה *zōnâ*) recalls God's charge against the Israelites for "prostituting" (זנה *zānâ*) themselves with all manner of foreign gods (2:17; 8:33).

The Philistines in Gaza discover that Samson is in town. Seeking further revenge, they decide to wait until dawn to capture Samson as he leaves the prostitute and departs through the city gate. But Samson leaves at midnight and eludes capture. With his enormous strength, Samson also picks up the city gate and its two posts and carries them for miles to the Israelite town of Hebron, where he sets them up on a hill as an act of humiliation and defiance aimed at Israel's Philistine oppressors (vv. 2-3).

REFLECTIONS

Samson's illicit sexual relationship with the Philistine prostitute reminds the reader in some ways of the two Israelite spies who visited Rahab, the Canaanite prostitute, in the city of Jericho (Josh 2:1-24). One key difference between the two stories is that Samson is there for his own personal gratification. The two Israelite spies were in Jericho not for their own pleasure but on a spy mission on behalf of all Israel. Samson's liaison with the prostitute signifies Israel's lusting after other gods for the sake of personal gratification and self-centered desires. The Jericho spies were doing the opposite. They risked their lives and well-being for the sake of the larger community.

However, there are also significant similarities between the two stories. Both stories proclaim the ultimate power and authority of Israel's God over all other gods and powers. Jericho's walls came tumbling down. Samson's theft of Gaza's city gates makes a similar statement about God's authority even over the Philistines. The city gate is the place of political decision making and the rendering of justice. Samson's feat of pulling up the city gate and planting it on a hill in Israel portends the eventual political and military defeat of the Philistines by the Israelites. It also prefigures Samson's final act of defiance when he will push down another entrance and two pillars in the Philistine temple of Dagon. That final act in the Samson saga will entail not only Israel's partial triumph over the Philistine oppressors but also the Lord's ultimate victory over the Philistine god Dagon (16:23-31).

Samson's act of political defiance stands in a long series of biblical people of God who have defied the powers of human authority and government when they have acted oppressively and contrary to God's will. Moses defied Pharaoh and the Egyptian empire, saying, "Let my people go" (Exodus 5–15). Amos boldly condemned King Jeroboam for the nation's ill treatment of the poor (Amos 7:10-17). Daniel remained faithful in the face of persecution for his faith because he knew God's authority supersedes all worldly authorities (Daniel 1–12). When the authorities tried to prevent Peter and the other apostles from proclaiming the gospel of Jesus Christ, they replied, "We must obey God rather than any human authority" (Acts 5:29 NRSV). Samson's placing the Gaza gates on the hill outside Hebron is one more affirmation that "thine is the kingdom and the power and the glory forever and ever. Amen."

Judges 16:4-31, Delilah and the Death of Samson

NIV

⁴Some time later, he fell in love with a woman in the Valley of Sorek whose name was Delilah. ⁵The rulers of the Philistines went to her and said, "See if you can lure him into showing you the secret of his great strength and how we can overpower him so we may tie him up and subdue him. Each one of us will give you eleven hundred shekels*a* of silver."

⁶So Delilah said to Samson, "Tell me the secret of your great strength and how you can be tied up and subdued."

⁷Samson answered her, "If anyone ties me with seven fresh thongs*b* that have not been dried, I'll become as weak as any other man."

a5 That is, about 28 pounds (about 13 kilograms)   *b7 Or bowstrings; also in verses 8 and 9*

NRSV

4After this he fell in love with a woman in the valley of Sorek, whose name was Delilah. ⁵The lords of the Philistines came to her and said to her, "Coax him, and find out what makes his strength so great, and how we may overpower him, so that we may bind him in order to subdue him; and we will each give you eleven hundred pieces of silver." ⁶So Delilah said to Samson, "Please tell me what makes your strength so great, and how you could be bound, so that one could subdue you." ⁷Samson said to her, "If they bind me with seven fresh bowstrings that are not dried out, then I shall become weak, and be like anyone else." ⁸Then the lords of the Philistines brought her seven fresh bowstrings that had not dried out, and she bound him with them. ⁹While men were

[8]Then the rulers of the Philistines brought her seven fresh thongs that had not been dried, and she tied him with them. [9]With men hidden in the room, she called to him, "Samson, the Philistines are upon you!" But he snapped the thongs as easily as a piece of string snaps when it comes close to a flame. So the secret of his strength was not discovered.

[10]Then Delilah said to Samson, "You have made a fool of me; you lied to me. Come now, tell me how you can be tied."

[11]He said, "If anyone ties me securely with new ropes that have never been used, I'll become as weak as any other man."

[12]So Delilah took new ropes and tied him with them. Then, with men hidden in the room, she called to him, "Samson, the Philistines are upon you!" But he snapped the ropes off his arms as if they were threads.

[13]Delilah then said to Samson, "Until now, you have been making a fool of me and lying to me. Tell me how you can be tied."

He replied, "If you weave the seven braids of my head into the fabric ⌊on the loom⌋ and tighten it with the pin, I'll become as weak as any other man." So while he was sleeping, Delilah took the seven braids of his head, wove them into the fabric [14]and[a] tightened it with the pin.

Again she called to him, "Samson, the Philistines are upon you!" He awoke from his sleep and pulled up the pin and the loom, with the fabric.

[15]Then she said to him, "How can you say, 'I love you,' when you won't confide in me? This is the third time you have made a fool of me and haven't told me the secret of your great strength." [16]With such nagging she prodded him day after day until he was tired to death.

[17]So he told her everything. "No razor has ever been used on my head," he said, "because I have been a Nazirite set apart to God since birth. If my head were shaved, my strength would leave me, and I would become as weak as any other man."

[18]When Delilah saw that he had told her everything, she sent word to the rulers of the Philistines, "Come back once more; he has told me everything." So the rulers of the Philistines re-

[a] 13,14 Some Septuagint manuscripts; Hebrew "⌊I can⌋, if you weave the seven braids of my head into the fabric ⌊on the loom⌋." [14]So she

lying in wait in an inner chamber, she said to him, "The Philistines are upon you, Samson!" But he snapped the bowstrings, as a strand of fiber snaps when it touches the fire. So the secret of his strength was not known.

[10]Then Delilah said to Samson, "You have mocked me and told me lies; please tell me how you could be bound." [11]He said to her, "If they bind me with new ropes that have not been used, then I shall become weak, and be like anyone else." [12]So Delilah took new ropes and bound him with them, and said to him, "The Philistines are upon you, Samson!" (The men lying in wait were in an inner chamber.) But he snapped the ropes off his arms like a thread.

[13]Then Delilah said to Samson, "Until now you have mocked me and told me lies; tell me how you could be bound." He said to her, "If you weave the seven locks of my head with the web and make it tight with the pin, then I shall become weak, and be like anyone else." [14]So while he slept, Delilah took the seven locks of his head and wove them into the web,[a] and made them tight with the pin. Then she said to him, "The Philistines are upon you, Samson!" But he awoke from his sleep, and pulled away the pin, the loom, and the web.

[15]Then she said to him, "How can you say, 'I love you,' when your heart is not with me? You have mocked me three times now and have not told me what makes your strength so great." [16]Finally, after she had nagged him with her words day after day, and pestered him, he was tired to death. [17]So he told her his whole secret, and said to her, "A razor has never come upon my head; for I have been a nazirite[b] to God from my mother's womb. If my head were shaved, then my strength would leave me; I would become weak, and be like anyone else."

[18]When Delilah realized that he had told her his whole secret, she sent and called the lords of the Philistines, saying, "This time come up, for he has told his whole secret to me." Then the lords of the Philistines came up to her, and brought the money in their hands. [19]She let him fall asleep on her lap; and she called a man, and

[a] Compare Gk: in verses 13-14, Heb lacks and make it tight . . . into the web   [b] That is one separated or one consecrated

NIV

turned with the silver in their hands. ¹⁹Having put him to sleep on her lap, she called a man to shave off the seven braids of his hair, and so began to subdue him.ᵃ And his strength left him.

²⁰Then she called, "Samson, the Philistines are upon you!"

He awoke from his sleep and thought, "I'll go out as before and shake myself free." But he did not know that the LORD had left him.

²¹Then the Philistines seized him, gouged out his eyes and took him down to Gaza. Binding him with bronze shackles, they set him to grinding in the prison. ²²But the hair on his head began to grow again after it had been shaved.

²³Now the rulers of the Philistines assembled to offer a great sacrifice to Dagon their god and to celebrate, saying, "Our god has delivered Samson, our enemy, into our hands."

²⁴When the people saw him, they praised their god, saying,

"Our god has delivered our enemy
    into our hands,
the one who laid waste our land
    and multiplied our slain."

²⁵While they were in high spirits, they shouted, "Bring out Samson to entertain us." So they called Samson out of the prison, and he performed for them.

When they stood him among the pillars, ²⁶Samson said to the servant who held his hand, "Put me where I can feel the pillars that support the temple, so that I may lean against them." ²⁷Now the temple was crowded with men and women; all the rulers of the Philistines were there, and on the roof were about three thousand men and women watching Samson perform. ²⁸Then Samson prayed to the LORD, "O Sovereign LORD, remember me. O God, please strengthen me just once more, and let me with one blow get revenge on the Philistines for my two eyes." ²⁹Then Samson reached toward the two central pillars on which the temple stood. Bracing himself against them, his right hand on the one and his left hand on the other, ³⁰Samson said, "Let me die with the Philistines!" Then he pushed with all his might, and down came the temple on the rulers and all the people in it. Thus he killed many more when he died than while he lived.

ᵃ 19 Hebrew; some Septuagint manuscripts *and he began to weaken*

NRSV

had him shave off the seven locks of his head. He began to weaken,ᵃ and his strength left him. ²⁰Then she said, "The Philistines are upon you, Samson!" When he awoke from his sleep, he thought, "I will go out as at other times, and shake myself free." But he did not know that the LORD had left him. ²¹So the Philistines seized him and gouged out his eyes. They brought him down to Gaza and bound him with bronze shackles; and he ground at the mill in the prison. ²²But the hair of his head began to grow again after it had been shaved.

23Now the lords of the Philistines gathered to offer a great sacrifice to their god Dagon, and to rejoice; for they said, "Our god has given Samson our enemy into our hand." ²⁴When the people saw him, they praised their god; for they said, "Our god has given our enemy into our hand, the ravager of our country, who has killed many of us." ²⁵And when their hearts were merry, they said, "Call Samson, and let him entertain us." So they called Samson out of the prison, and he performed for them. They made him stand between the pillars; ²⁶and Samson said to the attendant who held him by the hand, "Let me feel the pillars on which the house rests, so that I may lean against them." ²⁷Now the house was full of men and women; all the lords of the Philistines were there, and on the roof there were about three thousand men and women, who looked on while Samson performed.

28Then Samson called to the LORD and said, "Lord GOD, remember me and strengthen me only this once, O God, so that with this one act of revenge I may pay back the Philistines for my two eyes."ᵇ ²⁹And Samson grasped the two middle pillars on which the house rested, and he leaned his weight against them, his right hand on the one and his left hand on the other. ³⁰Then Samson said, "Let me die with the Philistines." He strained with all his might; and the house fell on the lords and all the people who were in it. So those he killed at his death were more than those he had killed during his life. ³¹Then his brothers and all his family came down and took him and brought him up and buried him between Zorah and Eshtaol in the tomb of his father Manoah. He had judged Israel twenty years.

ᵃ Gk: Heb *She began to torment him*   ᵇ Or *so that I may be avenged upon the Philistines for one of my two eyes*

NIV

³¹Then his brothers and his father's whole family went down to get him. They brought him back and buried him between Zorah and Eshtaol in the tomb of Manoah his father. He had led[a] Israel twenty years.

a 31 Traditionally *judged*

COMMENTARY

16:4-5. After the one-night liaison in Gaza, Samson "falls in love" with a woman named Delilah (v. 4). She is from the valley of Sorek, which lies within the Israelite land of Canaan, not far from Jerusalem. Scholars disagree about whether Delilah is an Israelite, a Canaanite, or a Philistine. The text remains intentionally ambivalent about her ethnicity so that the reader may wonder whether Samson has at last "come home" to Israel in obedience to his parents' wishes to find a woman to love from among "our people" (14:3). The name "Delilah" (דלילה *dĕlîlâ*) means "flirtatious," which fits her role in the story. The Philistines had earlier coaxed Samson's wife to betray him in the matter of the riddle (14:15-20). Similarly, the Philistines coax Delilah to find out the secret to the riddle of Samson's superhuman strength. Whereas earlier the Philistines had threatened Samson's wife with death (14:15), this time they offer Delilah an enormous bribe of "eleven hundred pieces of silver" (v. 5).

16:6-14. Delilah then tries to coax the secret of Samson's strength from him. On three different occasions he lies to Delilah about the secret of his power. First, Samson tells her that his strength will vanish if he is bound by seven fresh bowstrings. Then he suggests that he will lose his power if he is bound by new ropes. Finally, he tells Delilah that he will become a normal man if his hair is plaited into seven braids, which are then woven into a web and made tight with a pin. All of these are lies. It is this third false reason that begins to build suspense. Samson's admission that his strength has something to do with his hair is getting dangerously close to the truth about the one nazirite vow he has not yet broken (13:5). Moreover, the scene with Samson sleeping and Delilah weaving the hair of his head and "making

it tight with the pin" (lit., "she thrust the pin/tent peg") reminds the reader of an earlier story in Judges 4. Jael, the Kenite woman, like Delilah, was not clearly allied with either Israel or Israel's enemy Sisera. As he slept, she "thrust" (תקע *tāqaʿ*; the same verb as in 16:14) a tent peg into his temple and killed him (4:17-21). The parallel is a foreboding sign that Samson is moving closer to his own downfall and death.

16:15-22. Delilah pleads one more time with Samson to reveal his secret, appealing to his love for her. After days of nagging, Samson is "tired to death" (v. 16), a figurative image that will soon become a literal fact. Samson gives in and tells her the secret of his nazirite vow and that his hair cannot be cut: "If my head were shaved . . . I would become weak, and be like anyone else" (v. 17). Delilah senses that this time Samson is telling the truth. She again lets him fall asleep in her lap and then has a man cut Samson's hair. Samson's strength begins to leave him, but he appears unaware of his loss: "he did not know that the LORD had left him" (v. 20). Samson's figurative blindness to his real condition of weakness and divine abandonment is made literal and physical as the Philistines capture him and "gouged out his eyes" (v. 21).

Samson is bound and forced to do what is traditionally the work of women and slaves: "he ground at the mill in the prison" (v. 21; see Exod 11:5; Job 31:10). Samson has been totally transformed and humiliated. He was once a paragon of male bravado, a man of extraordinary physical strength and the knower of deep secrets unknown to others. Now Samson takes the role of a blind female servant, a captive of war, an exile in a foreign land. Indeed, his fate is a mirror image of the later experience of Israel in exile. Lamentations 5:13 laments that in exile "young men are compelled to grind." Samson's shaved head is not only a violation of his nazirite vow but also the mark of a person who is taken into exile. Isaiah 7:20 predicts the exile of the northern kingdom of Israel by the Assyrians with this image: "On that day the Lord will shave with a razor hired beyond the River—with the king of Assyria—the head and the hair of the feet, and it will take off the beard as well." Deuteronomy 21:12 speaks of the treatment of female captives of war: "suppose you see among the captives a beautiful woman whom you desire and want to marry . . . she shall shave her head." Samson is a feminized captive and exile, a paradigm of Israel in exile, seemingly abandoned by God.

However, the scene does not end in total despair but with what James Crenshaw has described as "one of those pregnant sentences that is the mark of genius."[60] Verse 22 concludes, "But the hair of his head began to grow again after it had been shaved." The new growth of Samson's hair may yet provide hope for some kind of vindication and purpose in the midst of Samson's captivity and exile among the Philistines.

16:23-27. The setting for the final scene of the Samson story is the grand temple of the Philistine god Dagon, which is filled with "the lords of the Philistines." The Philistines are celebrating a grand festival of sacrifice and thanksgiving to their god, who "has given Samson our enemy into our hand" (v. 23). Samson had entertained the Philistines once before at the wedding feast of his Philistine wife. Then he had offered a secret riddle to which they found a solution. The Philistines again command Samson to entertain them; he performs to a full house with standing room only for an additional 3,000 Philistines who are on the roof of the temple (v. 27).

16:28-30. Once before Samson had called upon God in prayer when he was weakened by thirst (15:18). One more time he calls on God in prayer. "Strengthen me," he prays, "so that with this one act of revenge I may pay back the

---

60. James Crenshaw, "The Samson Saga: Filial Devotion or Erotic Attachment?" *ZAW* 86 (1974) 501.

Philistines for my eyes" (v. 28). Samson continues to define his actions in terms of personal vendetta and revenge. He remains blind, however, to the larger significance of his mission as an agent of God's deliverance for the sake of the future of the whole people of Israel. Nevertheless, God will use Samson for one last defeat of the Philistines.

In a story filled with secrets and riddles, Samson accomplishes his final act of defeating the Philistines through one final secret. Samson pretends that he is so weak that he must lean on the "pillars on which the house rests" (v. 26). Then, calling on the Lord, Samson leans his full weight aganst the middle pillars of the temple. Dramatically, he prays, "Let me die with the Philistines" (v. 30). Samson strains "with all his might," which has returned along with his growing hair. The pillars buckle, the roof collapses, and the victory party for Dagon becomes a Philistine disaster of death and destruction. Samson dies along with thousands of Philistines. Ironically, Samson has killed more Philistines in his death than all those he killed during his life (v. 30). In the midst of this final triumph, Samson remains a tragic figure, forever blind to the larger purposes for which God had used him. Samson saw only personal revenge in this event; the Lord sees deliverance for God's people and the Lord's victory in the cosmic battle against Dagon, the god of the Philistines.

16:31. Samson's family takes his body and buries him in the tomb of his father, a sign of a life that has ended and come full circle. In the end, Samson "judged Israel twenty years," as compared to the much longer forty years of Philistine oppression (13:1). God had invested enormous divine energy in this last of the judges. Even so, Samson was only able to "begin to deliver Israel" from the Philistines (13:5). The Philistines would return as a major threat to Israel, beginning with the events in 1 Samuel 4. In Samson, the line of Israel's military deliverers called judges comes to an end within the book of Judges. The system of leadership under the judges has finally self-destructed and collapsed under its own weight along with the Philistine temple of Dagon.

REFLECTIONS

1. Samson's many relationships with women invite critical reflection on the role and portraits of women in the Samson saga. His mother is a positive model of faithfulness and trust. However, the other women in his life are not so positively portrayed. They are objects of desire, nagging and tempting Samson into economic ruin, sexual immorality, and ultimately death. Moreover, each of these women is in some way caught in the web of the pressures, economics, and powers of a male-dominated society. Samson's wife is threatened and forced to betray him. She is ultimately killed and burned along with her father (14:14; 15:16). Samson uses the prostitute at Gaza for a night of self-gratification (16:1-3). Delilah is pressured by an enormous bribe from the Philistines to betray her lover. Both the prostitute and Delilah are used by men in exchange for money.[61]

It was noted in the reflections on Jephthah's daughter in Judges 11 that the decline in the well-being of women as we move through the book of Judges parallels the gradual disintegration and decline of Israel as a society and a religious community. The women in the Samson story continue to reflect this downward trend in social and religious degradation. Their portraits will find parallels in our own time and communities.

2. One of the most dramatic points in Judges 16 is Samson's request for God to let him "die with the Philistines" (v. 30). This expression to God of a death wish is not unique to Samson. Other great figures of the Bible reached such points of despair that they also asked God to let them die. Moses was overcome with the burdens of leading the rebellious Israelites through the wilderness and requested that God put him to death (Num 11:10-15). The prophet Elijah sat under a tree in despair because he alone had been faithful to God and yet had been no more effective than his predecessors in leading Israel to faith in God. So he asked God, "take away my life" (1 Kgs 19:4). Jeremiah was so severely persecuted for prophesying God's word that he wished he had been killed in his mother's womb (Jer 20:17). The prophet Jonah sulked under a bush because God had shown mercy to the Assyrian city of Nineveh. Jonah was so upset by God's generosity to this pagan city that he asked God to "please take my life from me" (Jonah 4:3). In each of these cases, however, God always refused the request to put the person to death and instead sent the person on to continue his mission. Samson's request for God to let him die is the only time such a request is granted in the Old Testament.

Samson's uniqueness in this regard may stem from two reasons. One reason is that Samson represents the end of the line of the judges. He is more than just another judge. He embodies the office of the judge, which comes to an end with him. Thus, God's allowing Samson to die is God's allowing the office or system of judge as a means of leading and saving Israel to die. Another reason for Samson's uniqueness is that he embodies Israel as a nation. The shaved head, the forced grinding at the mill, and the binding and captivity of Samson are all images of exile and captivity. They prefigure the exile Israel will later experience under kingship. The northern kingdom of Israel will be conquered by the Assyrians and be sent into exile (2 Kings 17). Later, the southern kingdom of Judah will succumb to the power of the Babylonian empires, and its population will be exiled (2 Kings 24–25). The exile will be a kind of death for Israel. The Temple in Jerusalem will be destroyed as was the Philistine temple of Dagon. The system of kingship will end, just as the era of the judges also came to an end. Israel and Judah will lose their strength as Samson had done. The prophets will castigate Israel for its blindness to its sin before the exile (Isa 6:9-13) and its blindness to the deliverance God is working out for the sake of the exiles (Isa 43:19). The prophet Ezekiel spoke of Israel's exile as the death of a nation in his image of Israel as a valley filled with dry bones (Ezek 37:1-14).

61. See J. Cheryl Exum, "Samson's Women," in *Fragmented Women: Feminist (Sub)versions of Biblical Narratives* (Valley Forge, Pa.: Trinity, 1993) 61-93.

Thus Samson's request to die and God's acquiescence to that request reflect Samson's larger role as a symbol of the system of judges as an institution and a metaphor for Israel as a nation and its eventual fate of exile.

3. The Samson story holds on to a thread (or hair) of hope as it notes that Samson's hair begins to grow back after it has been shaved (16:22). If his shaved head represents exile and captivity, then the new growth of hair represents hope in the midst of exile. The Deuteronomistic History of Joshua–2 Kings ends with Israel in exile. But it also ends with a brief note of hope that parallels Samson's growing hair. In 2 Kgs 25:27-30, the king of Judah, who is in exile, is released from prison and allowed to dine with the king of Babylon. This hint of hope and opening to some kind of possible future functions in a way similar to the growing hair of Samson. As we emerge from the tragedies and downfalls that beset us, we may yet discover such glimpses of hope, such openings to the future, such hints that God is working in hidden ways to redeem and save and heal, of which we may not be fully aware.

4. One of the overriding themes of the Samson story is Israel's learning that its future depends entirely on God's guidance and strength, not its own. Samson represents the prideful and boastful Israel who goes it alone, thinking for the most part that he does not need anyone else to help him. Yet there are glimpses of Samson's recognition of his limits, once when he was dying of thirst and a final time when he was dying at the hand of the Philistines. It is only when Samson reaches the end of his rope and slams up against his dependence on God that he comes to some realization of his need for God.[62] This was God's experience with Israel as well. That experience is definitively summarized in the Song of Moses in Deuteronomy 32:

> Indeed the LORD will vindicate his people,
> > have compassion on his servants,
> when he sees that their power is gone. (Deut 32:36 NRSV)

Israel will then begin to come to the realization that its future and hope lie not in a particular institution of leadership (whether judges or kings) or in its own strength or virtue. The future of God's people lies in trusting and worshiping the one God who is worthy of such trust:

> See now that I, even I, am he:
> > there is no god besides me.
> I kill and I make alive:
> > I wound and I heal;
> > and no one can deliver from my hand. (Deut 32:39 NRSV)

5. In the history of Christian biblical interpretation, one of the dominant ways in which Samson has been interpreted is as a prefigurement, or type, of Christ. In spite of his dubious moral character, Samson has functioned over the centuries in sermons, art, and interpretation as a precursor to Jesus' life and death. The parallels are many. Samson's special birth and the angel's announcement to his mother in Judges 13 functioned as a model for the writer of Jesus' birth story and announcement in Luke 1–2. The title of "Nazorean" is applied to Jesus, a possible allusion to the special status of a "Nazirite," similar to Samson, in Matt 2:23. The Spirit of the Lord came upon Samson just as it came upon Jesus as he did battle with Satan in the wilderness (Luke 3:21-22; 4:1-13). However, the most important parallels involve Samson's suffering and death as a type of Jesus' suffering and death on the cross. Samson was betrayed by his own people, by Judah and by the women he loved. He was beaten and tortured. Samson's outstretched arms on the two pillars of the Philistine temple were read by Christian interpreters as a prefigurement of Jesus' outstretched arms on the cross. In his death, Samson destroyed the enemy and its god. Similarly, interpreters saw Jesus' death as destroying

---

62. J. Cheryl Exum, "The Theological Dimension of the Samson Saga," *VT* 33 (1983), 30-45.

sin and death and defeating the powers and principalities of this world who resisted God's will for creation.

Perhaps at a deeper level, the Samson story affirms God's willingness to enter into the full sinfulness and rebellion of humankind in order to accomplish the purposes of God in the world. At some level, the figure of Samson embodies not only the institution of judgeship or the nation of Israel, but also God's amazing and relentless love. God keeps coming back to God's sinful people, responding to their cries of distress and promising to stay with them in and through their failures, their captivities, their exiles, and even their deaths. Whether it is the human nation of Israel or the individual person of Jesus, God is present and at work in an incarnational way in the blood and mess and chaos of human life. In that promise is a word of hope even when we come to the end and death of the era of the judges in the man Samson.

JUDGES 17:1–21:25

CONCLUSION: ISRAEL'S DISINTEGRATION

OVERVIEW

The stories of chaps. 17–21 conclude the book of Judges with a portrait of Israel in religious and social chaos. The gradual decline in the individual judge stories from the ideal of Othniel in chap. 3 to the tragic judgeships of Jephthah and Samson in chaps. 10–16 ends in chaps. 17–21 with Israel's near disintegration as a covenant community of God. In these chapters, the era of the judges has ended. Idols are worshiped. Priests are hired for personal gain. Defenseless foreigners are mercilessly attacked. Strangers are mistreated. An Israelite woman is brutally raped and murdered by Israelites. The entire Israelite tribe of Benjamin is nearly exterminated by fellow Israelites. Additional Israelite men, women, and children are killed. Other women are kidnapped and forced to become wives of Benjaminite men. Israel seems oblivious to the extent of its disobedience and disloyalty to the covenant with God. Yet God remains to work in and through the perverse actions of Israel in order to preserve its life and prepare for a whole new way of leading and guiding Israel through the institution of the king (1–2 Samuel).

The narratives in chaps. 17–21 no longer follow the cyclical pattern of the individual judge stories of chaps. 3–16, in which Israel does evil, God sends an enemy, Israel cries to God, God sends a judge to deliver Israel, and Israel again does evil (see 2:11-19). Instead, Judges 17–21 is a collection of originally disparate stories that contain no foreign aggressor or enemy and no judge or deliverer to lead Israel. These varied and originally separate stories have been brought together and artfully shaped to form a dramatic conclusion to the book. The stories divide into two major sections: Chapters 17–18 focus on the religious dimensions of Israel's decline (idols,

priests, abuse of holy war), and chaps. 19–21 deal more with the social dimensions of Israel's disintegration (inhospitality, rape, murder, deception, civil war, the near extinction of an Israelite tribe). This two-part conclusion corresponds with the book's two-part introduction, which likewise focuses on the social fragmentation (1:1–2:5) and religious deterioration (2:6–3:6) of Israel in the land of Canaan.

Although different in focus, the two sections of chaps. 17–18 (religious chaos) and chaps. 19–21 (social upheaval) contain several overlapping details and themes. Both sections feature an individual "Levite," a member of the special priestly tribe of Israel (cf. Josh 18:7; 21:1-42). In the first section, a Levite man travels from the southern town of Bethlehem in Judah to the hill country of Ephraim (17:7-8). In the second section, another Levite man travels from the hill country of Ephraim to Bethlehem of Judah and then back to northern Ephraim (19:1, 18). One Levite is originally from southern Judah, and the other Levite is originally from northern Ephraim. The actions of the two Levite men, representing the major tribes of northern and southern Israel, are implicitly condemned. Both sections begin with an event involving the individual Levite and personal or family matters (chaps. 17; 19), which then spirals into a larger tribal conflict involving either foreigners (chap. 18) or fellow Israelites (chap. 20). The conclusion of each section involves the preservation of an Israelite tribe through abhorrent but seemingly necessary means. After having lost its original land allotment in Canaan, the tribe of Dan migrates to the foreign town of Laish. Dan destroys the small and defenseless village on the northern margins of Canaan and takes it over as its own city and territory, so that the tribe can have a place to live (18:27-31). Likewise, after having been nearly exterminated as a tribe in a civil war with the rest of Israel, the six hundred surviving men of the tribe of Benjamin secure their tenuous future by kidnapping young girls who will become their wives (21:8-24). In each case, innocent victims suffer with no mechanism for accountability or redress because of the absence of political leadership.[63]

An important refrain brackets the concluding section of chaps. 17–21, at both its beginning (17:6) and its end (21:25): "In those days there was no king in Israel; all the people did what was right in their own eyes." Part of the refrain, "In those days there was no king in Israel," also appears in 18:1 and 19:1. Scholars generally agree that this refrain provides a key insight into the perspective of the later writers and editors who shaped the book of Judges. However, scholars disagree about the meaning of the refrain. Some argue that it was added at a late date in Israel's history, sometime after the exile of Israel by the Assyrians (2 Kings 17) and the exile of Judah by the Babylonians (2 Kings 24–25). They point to the key reference to the period of Israel's exile in the phrase "the time the land went into captivity," in 18:30. These scholars view the meaning of the refrain in a positive light, arguing that it is a declaration of moral freedom and spiritual renewal for the Israelites in exile under either the Assyrians (722 BCE) or the Babylonians (586 BCE). According to this perspective, the refrain signals an opportunity to start over in hope and promotes creative experiments for community life after the demise of kingship in Israel.[64] Other scholars view the refrain as an entirely negative evaluation of Israel in the period of the judges. They tend to date the final form of the book and its refrain to the time either before the Assyrian exile or before the Babylonian exile, when the Israelite monarchy was still in place. The refrain, they argue, points to the need for a king as the only viable solution

to protect Israel from its own self-induced social and religious dissolution. Some scholars argue that the concluding chapters of Judges and the refrain were intended negatively, either as a polemic against the northern kingdom's worship centers in Dan and Bethel (see 2 Kgs 12:25-33), as an attack against the erratic leadership of Saul in comparison to the stable kingship of David, or as a general apology for dynastic kingship, as opposed to the occasional and flawed leadership of the judges.[65]

As the analysis of the individual chapters will show, the refrain and the concluding section of Judges as a whole should be understood as both a negative portrayal of Israel in this period at the end of the judges era and as an affirmation of the hope of God's continuing presence with the community in spite of its unfaithfulness. The flip side of the refrain about the absence of a king and everybody's doing what is right in his or her own eyes is the phrase repeated frequently throughout Judges: "the Israelites did what was evil in the eyes of the LORD" (2:11; 3:7, 12; 4:1; 6:1; 10:6; 13:1). In the present form of Judges, the Israelites' doing "evil in the eyes of the LORD" is functionally equivalent to doing "what is right in their own eyes." This negative interpretation of the refrain in 17:6 and 21:25 is further supported by the use of the same phrase for Samson's errant and misguided yearning for a Philistine wife: "she is right in my eyes" (NRSV, "she pleases me"; 14:3, 7). Elsewhere in the OT, humans' "doing what is right in their own eyes" typically connotes presumption, arrogance, and failure to act according to the will of God. In Deut 12:8, Moses commands Israel, "You shall not act as we are acting here today, everyone doing what is right in their own eyes" (literal translation of the Hebrew; NRSV, "all of us according to our own desires"; NIV, "everyone as he sees fit").

Moreover, the narratives in Judges 17–21 portray the systematic breaking of nearly all of the Ten Commandments (see Exod 20:1-17; Deut 5:6-21). Israelites worship other gods and idols

63. F. Crüsemann, *Der Widerstand gegen das Königtum* (Neukirchen-Vluyn: Neukirchener Verlag, 1978) 157-58.

64. Examples of positive readings of the refrain include Robert Boling, "In Those Days There Was No King in Israel," in *A Light Unto My Path: Old Testament Studies in Honor of Jacob M. Myers,* ed. H. Bream et al. (Philadelphia: Temple, 1974) 33-48; and William Dumbrell, " 'In Those Days There Was No King in Israel; Every Man Did What Was Right in His Own Eyes': The Purpose of the Book of Judges Reconsidered," *JSOT* 25 (1983) 23-33.

65. Martin Noth, "The Background of Judges 17–18," in *Israel's Prophetic Heritage,* ed. B. W. Anderson and W. Harrelson (London: SCM, 1962) 68-85; Yairah Amit, "Literature in the Service of Political Studies in Judges 19–21," in *Politics and Theopolitics in the Bible and Postbiblical Literature,* ed. H. G. Reventlow et al. (Sheffield, JSOT, 1994) 28-40; and Lawson Stone, "From Tribal Confederation to Monarchic State: The Editorial Perspective of the Book of Judges" (Ph.D. diss., Yale University; Ann Arbor: University Microfilms, 1987) 458, 471-77.

(17:3-5), take the Lord's name in vain (17:13), dishonor parents (17:1-2), brutally kill innocent victims (18:27; 19:26-29; 21:10), commit adultery and rape (19:22-25), steal other's property (17:2; 18:21-27), bear false witness (20:1-7), and covet what belongs to their neighbor (18:27-31; 21:8-24). This failure to obey the central commandments outlined in Deuteronomy 5 suggests that "doing what was right in their own eyes" was something less than a positive experience of spiritual renewal (see 2:17; 3:4).

Was the absence of a monarch ("there was no king") the basic cause of this moral and religious failure in Israel? And would the rise of kingship in Israel rectify the chaos at the end of the judges period by creating a permanent state of obedience and faithfulness in Israel? As noted above, this concluding section of Judges and the entire book itself had a long history of composition and editing. Early stories of individual judges were collected and edited over many generations, probably extending from a time early in the Israelite monarchy to the exilic or post-exilic period. At an earlier stage, the book of Judges likely functioned as an apologetic piece to support kingship in Israel, particularly the southern Judean dynasty of King David and his successors. The geographical progression of both the introduction in 1:1–2:5 and the individual judge stories in 3:7–16:31 suggest a preference for the southern tribe of Judah as success and faithfulness among the southern tribes gradually decline into failure and disobedience as one moves further north among the tribes of Israel. The introduction concludes with the expulsion of what will be the northernmost tribe, Dan, from its land (1:34-36), and the individual judge stories conclude with the tragic death of the judge Samson, who is also from the northern tribe of Dan (13:2; 16:23-31). This pro-Judean and pro-kingship perspective may well have been the product of the editors who worked on the books of the Deuteronomistic History (Deuteronomy–2 Kings) during the reigns of Hezekiah (2 Kings 18–20) and Josiah (2 Kings 22–23) or at other times during the monarchy.

However, the narratives of the exile of the northern kingdom (2 Kings 17), and especially the exile of the southern kingdom of Judah (2 Kings 24–25), suggest that the final form of Judges came to be read within the broader perspective of the whole Deuteronomistic History, which extends from Deuteronomy to 2 Kings. That history encompasses Israel's narrated experience through a number of different political contexts: the unique office of Moses as covenant mediator, Joshua's leadership of the conquest and the temporary judges who followed him, Israel's kings in both northern Israel and southern Judah, and the time of the exile and the end of kingship. Looking back from the perspective of the exile, Israel came to know that each of these human political contexts and institutions was initially moderately successful but in the end ultimately flawed. Each period of leadership (Moses, Joshua–Judges, Kings) evidenced a similar pattern of initial success followed by deterioration and the ultimate dissolution of the old system. Moses successfully led Israel out of Egypt, but Israel in its trek through the wilderness grew increasingly rebellious against God (Deut 31:27-29). The old wilderness generation of Israelites, including Moses himself, was condemned to die in the desert without entering the promised land. An entirely new generation would inherit the land of Canaan (Deut 1:22-45; see Numbers 13–14). During the period of Joshua and the judges, Israel experienced initial success in its conquest. However, the book of Judges traces the gradual decline of the judges era from moderate success into gradual decline, culminating in social and religious chaos and disintegration (Judges 17–21). During the period of the kings in Israel, the initial success of David and Solomon in the united monarchy gradually deteriorated into the divided kingdoms of north and south (1 Kings 11–12), the exile of the northern kingdom (2 Kings 17), and finally the exile of the southern kingdom of Judah and the apparent end of the Davidic kingship in its traditional form (2 Kings 24–25).

Thus Judges, within the final form of the Deuteronomistic History, functions as a sober and realistic example of what eventually happens to any form of human governance or polity among the people of God. Every form of human leadership or power, whether a Mosaic covenant mediator or a judge or a king, may be moderately appropriate and helpful for a given time and context. But no human institution or structure is immune from the larger and deeper problem that infects humanity itself: namely, human sinfulness, rebellion against God, and self-absorbed quests for power, vengeance, and resources through strategies of violence, delusion, and theft. The book of Judges is not simply an apology for kingship, as if the presence of kings would be the one, ideal guarantee of Israel's long-term adherence to the covenant with God. Rather, the institution of Israelite judges was a paradigm of the way in which God must work in an imperfect world through necessary but inevitably flawed human structures, ideologies, and institutions. Such human structures and arrangements of power and resources may work for a time in given contexts and periods, but they will eventually deteriorate. God allows such institutions and structures to run their course and die in order that new arrangements and structures may be born. God allowed the structure of leadership through temporary judges to "hit bottom" in the social and religious chaos of Judges 17–21. Israel would struggle to

find a new way of governance through the new institution of kingship (1–2 Samuel, 1–2 Kings). Like the judges, the institution of kingship would function effectively for a time, but eventually disintegrate in the exile. Israel would then need again to struggle to find an appropriate polity and structure to reconstitute itself as the people of God, whether it remained in diaspora or returned to the land. Aspects of kingship remained alive in Judaism in the form of a hope for the Messiah, but leadership in the community took other forms in the meantime. Thus the book of Judges is a sober and mature portrait of the necessity for human structures of leadership and power, the inevitability of their corruption and eventual decline, and the gracious willingness of God to work in and through such flawed human structures and communities in order to accomplish God's purposes in the world.

JUDGES 17:1–18:31, IDOLS, HIRED PRIESTS, AND UNHOLY CONQUESTS

NIV	NRSV
17Now a man named Micah from the hill country of Ephraim [2]said to his mother, "The eleven hundred shekels[a] of silver that were taken from you and about which I heard you utter a curse—I have that silver with me; I took it."	**17**There was a man in the hill country of Ephraim whose name was Micah. [2]He said to his mother, "The eleven hundred pieces of silver that were taken from you, about which you uttered a curse, and even spoke it in my hearing,—that
Then his mother said, "The LORD bless you, my son!"	silver is in my possession; I took it; but now I will return it to you."[a] And his mother said, "May my son be blessed by the LORD!" [3]Then he returned the
[3]When he returned the eleven hundred shekels of silver to his mother, she said, "I solemnly consecrate my silver to the LORD for my son to make a carved image and a cast idol. I will give it back to you."	eleven hundred pieces of silver to his mother; and his mother said, "I consecrate the silver to the LORD from my hand for my son, to make an idol of cast metal." [4]So when he returned the money to his
[4]So he returned the silver to his mother, and she took two hundred shekels[b] of silver and gave them to a silversmith, who made them into the image and the idol. And they were put in Micah's house.	mother, his mother took two hundred pieces of silver, and gave it to the silversmith, who made it into an idol of cast metal; and it was in the house of Micah. [5]This man Micah had a shrine, and he
[5]Now this man Micah had a shrine, and he made an ephod and some idols and installed one of his sons as his priest. [6]In those days Israel had no king; everyone did as he saw fit.	made an ephod and teraphim, and installed one of his sons, who became his priest. [6]In those days there was no king in Israel; all the people did what was right in their own eyes.

_a2 That is, about 28 pounds (about 13 kilograms)   _b4 That is, about 5 pounds (about 2.3 kilograms)

_a The words _but now I will return it to you_ are transposed from the end of verse 3 in Heb

NIV

[7] A young Levite from Bethlehem in Judah, who had been living within the clan of Judah, [8] left that town in search of some other place to stay. On his way[a] he came to Micah's house in the hill country of Ephraim.

[9] Micah asked him, "Where are you from?"

"I'm a Levite from Bethlehem in Judah," he said, "and I'm looking for a place to stay."

[10] Then Micah said to him, "Live with me and be my father and priest, and I'll give you ten shekels[b] of silver a year, your clothes and your food." [11] So the Levite agreed to live with him, and the young man was to him like one of his sons. [12] Then Micah installed the Levite, and the young man became his priest and lived in his house. [13] And Micah said, "Now I know that the LORD will be good to me, since this Levite has become my priest."

18 In those days Israel had no king.

And in those days the tribe of the Danites was seeking a place of their own where they might settle, because they had not yet come into an inheritance among the tribes of Israel. [2] So the Danites sent five warriors from Zorah and Eshtaol to spy out the land and explore it. These men represented all their clans. They told them, "Go, explore the land."

The men entered the hill country of Ephraim and came to the house of Micah, where they spent the night. [3] When they were near Micah's house, they recognized the voice of the young Levite; so they turned in there and asked him, "Who brought you here? What are you doing in this place? Why are you here?"

[4] He told them what Micah had done for him, and said, "He has hired me and I am his priest."

[5] Then they said to him, "Please inquire of God to learn whether our journey will be successful."

[6] The priest answered them, "Go in peace. Your journey has the LORD's approval."

[7] So the five men left and came to Laish, where they saw that the people were living in safety, like the Sidonians, unsuspecting and secure. And since their land lacked nothing, they were prosperous.[c] Also, they lived a long way from the Sidonians and had no relationship with anyone else.[d]

a8 Or To carry on his profession   b10 That is, about 4 ounces (about 110 grams)   c7 The meaning of the Hebrew for this clause is uncertain.   d7 Hebrew; some Septuagint manuscripts with the Arameans

NRSV

[7] Now there was a young man of Bethlehem in Judah, of the clan of Judah. He was a Levite residing there. [8] This man left the town of Bethlehem in Judah, to live wherever he could find a place. He came to the house of Micah in the hill country of Ephraim to carry on his work.[a] [9] Micah said to him, "From where do you come?" He replied, "I am a Levite of Bethlehem in Judah, and I am going to live wherever I can find a place." [10] Then Micah said to him, "Stay with me, and be to me a father and a priest, and I will give you ten pieces of silver a year, a set of clothes, and your living."[b] [11] The Levite agreed to stay with the man; and the young man became to him like one of his sons. [12] So Micah installed the Levite, and the young man became his priest, and was in the house of Micah. [13] Then Micah said, "Now I know that the LORD will prosper me, because the Levite has become my priest."

18 In those days there was no king in Israel. And in those days the tribe of the Danites was seeking for itself a territory to live in; for until then no territory among the tribes of Israel had been allotted to them. [2] So the Danites sent five valiant men from the whole number of their clan, from Zorah and from Eshtaol, to spy out the land and to explore it; and they said to them, "Go, explore the land." When they came to the hill country of Ephraim, to the house of Micah, they stayed there. [3] While they were at Micah's house, they recognized the voice of the young Levite; so they went over and asked him, "Who brought you here? What are you doing in this place? What is your business here?" [4] He said to them, "Micah did such and such for me, and he hired me, and I have become his priest." [5] Then they said to him, "Inquire of God that we may know whether the mission we are undertaking will succeed." [6] The priest replied, "Go in peace. The mission you are on is under the eye of the LORD."

[7] The five men went on, and when they came to Laish, they observed the people who were there living securely, after the manner of the Sidonians, quiet and unsuspecting, lacking[c] nothing on earth, and possessing wealth.[d] Furthermore, they were far from the Sidonians and had no dealings with Aram.[e] [8] When they came to their

a Or Ephraim, continuing his journey   b Heb living, and the Levite went   c Cn Compare 18.10: Meaning of Heb uncertain   d Meaning of Heb uncertain   e Symmachus: Heb with anyone

NIV

[8]When they returned to Zorah and Eshtaol, their brothers asked them, "How did you find things?"

[9]They answered, "Come on, let's attack them! We have seen that the land is very good. Aren't you going to do something? Don't hesitate to go there and take it over. [10]When you get there, you will find an unsuspecting people and a spacious land that God has put into your hands, a land that lacks nothing whatever."

[11]Then six hundred men from the clan of the Danites, armed for battle, set out from Zorah and Eshtaol. [12]On their way they set up camp near Kiriath Jearim in Judah. This is why the place west of Kiriath Jearim is called Mahaneh Dan[a] to this day. [13]From there they went on to the hill country of Ephraim and came to Micah's house.

[14]Then the five men who had spied out the land of Laish said to their brothers, "Do you know that one of these houses has an ephod, other household gods, a carved image and a cast idol? Now you know what to do." [15]So they turned in there and went to the house of the young Levite at Micah's place and greeted him. [16]The six hundred Danites, armed for battle, stood at the entrance to the gate. [17]The five men who had spied out the land went inside and took the carved image, the ephod, the other household gods and the cast idol while the priest and the six hundred armed men stood at the entrance to the gate.

[18]When these men went into Micah's house and took the carved image, the ephod, the other household gods and the cast idol, the priest said to them, "What are you doing?"

[19]They answered him, "Be quiet! Don't say a word. Come with us, and be our father and priest. Isn't it better that you serve a tribe and clan in Israel as priest rather than just one man's household?" [20]Then the priest was glad. He took the ephod, the other household gods and the carved image and went along with the people. [21]Putting their little children, their livestock and their possessions in front of them, they turned away and left.

[22]When they had gone some distance from Micah's house, the men who lived near Micah were called together and overtook the Danites.

[a]12 Mahaneh Dan means Dan's camp.

NRSV

kinsfolk at Zorah and Eshtaol, they said to them, "What do you report?" [9]They said, "Come, let us go up against them; for we have seen the land, and it is very good. Will you do nothing? Do not be slow to go, but enter in and possess the land. [10]When you go, you will come to an unsuspecting people. The land is broad—God has indeed given it into your hands—a place where there is no lack of anything on earth."

[11]Six hundred men of the Danite clan, armed with weapons of war, set out from Zorah and Eshtaol, [12]and went up and encamped at Kiriath-jearim in Judah. On this account that place is called Mahaneh-dan[a] to this day; it is west of Kiriath-jearim. [13]From there they passed on to the hill country of Ephraim, and came to the house of Micah.

[14]Then the five men who had gone to spy out the land (that is, Laish) said to their comrades, "Do you know that in these buildings there are an ephod, teraphim, and an idol of cast metal? Now therefore consider what you will do." [15]So they turned in that direction and came to the house of the young Levite, at the home of Micah, and greeted him. [16]While the six hundred men of the Danites, armed with their weapons of war, stood by the entrance of the gate, [17]the five men who had gone to spy out the land proceeded to enter and take the idol of cast metal, the ephod, and the teraphim.[b] The priest was standing by the entrance of the gate with the six hundred men armed with weapons of war. [18]When the men went into Micah's house and took the idol of cast metal, the ephod, and the teraphim, the priest said to them, "What are you doing?" [19]They said to him, "Keep quiet! Put your hand over your mouth, and come with us, and be to us a father and a priest. Is it better for you to be priest to the house of one person, or to be priest to a tribe and clan in Israel?" [20]Then the priest accepted the offer. He took the ephod, the teraphim, and the idol, and went along with the people.

[21]So they resumed their journey, putting the little ones, the livestock, and the goods in front of them. [22]When they were some distance from the home of Micah, the men who were in the

[a]That is Camp of Dan   [b]Compare 17.4, 5; 18.14: Heb teraphim and the cast metal

23As they shouted after them, the Danites turned and said to Micah, "What's the matter with you that you called out your men to fight?"

24He replied, "You took the gods I made, and my priest, and went away. What else do I have? How can you ask, 'What's the matter with you?'"

25The Danites answered, "Don't argue with us, or some hot-tempered men will attack you, and you and your family will lose your lives." 26So the Danites went their way, and Micah, seeing that they were too strong for him, turned around and went back home.

27Then they took what Micah had made, and his priest, and went on to Laish, against a peaceful and unsuspecting people. They attacked them with the sword and burned down their city. 28There was no one to rescue them because they lived a long way from Sidon and had no relationship with anyone else. The city was in a valley near Beth Rehob.

The Danites rebuilt the city and settled there. 29They named it Dan after their forefather Dan, who was born to Israel—though the city used to be called Laish. 30There the Danites set up for themselves the idols, and Jonathan son of Gershom, the son of Moses,a and his sons were priests for the tribe of Dan until the time of the captivity of the land. 31They continued to use the idols Micah had made, all the time the house of God was in Shiloh.

a30 An ancient Hebrew scribal tradition, some Septuagint manuscripts and Vulgate; Masoretic Text *Manasseh*

houses near Micah's house were called out, and they overtook the Danites. 23They shouted to the Danites, who turned around and said to Micah, "What is the matter that you come with such a company?" 24He replied, "You take my gods that I made, and the priest, and go away, and what have I left? How then can you ask me, 'What is the matter?'" 25And the Danites said to him, "You had better not let your voice be heard among us or else hot-tempered fellows will attack you, and you will lose your life and the lives of your household." 26Then the Danites went their way. When Micah saw that they were too strong for him, he turned and went back to his home.

27The Danites, having taken what Micah had made, and the priest who belonged to him, came to Laish, to a people quiet and unsuspecting, put them to the sword, and burned down the city. 28There was no deliverer, because it was far from Sidon and they had no dealings with Aram.a It was in the valley that belongs to Beth-rehob. They rebuilt the city, and lived in it. 29They named the city Dan, after their ancestor Dan, who was born to Israel; but the name of the city was formerly Laish. 30Then the Danites set up the idol for themselves. Jonathan son of Gershom, son of Moses,b and his sons were priests to the tribe of the Danites until the time the land went into captivity. 31So they maintained as their own Micah's idol that he had made, as long as the house of God was at Shiloh.

a Cn Compare verse 7: Heb *with anyone*   b Another reading is *son of Manasseh*

COMMENTARY

17:1-13. The narrative of Israel's degeneration into religious chaos begins with a man named Micah (v. 1). In Hebrew (מיכה *mîkâ*), this name means "Who is like the Lord?" The name implies that no god, idol, or other representation can ever compare with or substitute for the Lord. The Lord resists being tamed or captured by any humanly created image, structure, or institution. Ironically, this man named Micah will in the end seek to do what his name denies is possible: He will try to capture God in an idol and manipulate God for

his own personal gain (vv. 4-5, 12-13). The reader senses immediately the topsy-turvy nature of this family's religious life. The son, Micah, stole from his own mother eleven hundred pieces of silver, an enormous sum equal to what Delilah received for betraying her lover Samson (16:4). He had knowingly taken the money, even though he had heard his mother utter a curse against anyone who would steal it. Micah's actions as an individual reflect the actions of the nation of Israel. Israel was repeatedly warned about the consequences and curses for violating God's covenant (2:1-5, 20-23; 6:7-10; 10:10-16), and yet the nation repeatedly and openly disobeyed God. The son, Micah, returns the silver to his mother. She does not offer any word of reproof at all but asks for the Lord's blessing on him. One senses the total absence of accountability and responsibility in this family. The mother then consecrates the silver to the Lord "to make an idol of cast metal" (v. 3). She offers only two hundred of the eleven hundred pieces of silver to a silversmith to make the idol for her son (v. 4). Religion is here twisted and distorted. Curses become blessings. Consecration to the Lord becomes idolatry. Vows of offerings are only partially fulfilled. The scene ends with a tidy personal shrine for the son, Micah, with the silver idol, devices for getting oracles from God ("an ephod and teraphim"), and Micah's own son as a priest. The refrain about no king and everybody's doing "what was right in their own eyes" (v. 6) reflects the religious chaos exemplified in this opening scene of chap. 17 and functions as an overarching commentary on the entire period described in chaps. 17–21. The same refrain is repeated at 21:25 and thus brackets this entire concluding section of Judges.

The scene shifts from Micah and his personal shrine to another young man, a Levite from the town of Bethlehem in Judah. The Levites in Judah were descendants of the priestly line of Aaron (Josh 21:4). The Levite leaves his home in Judah "to live wherever he could find a place" (v. 8). The sense of the Levite's aimless wandering without any guide again reflects Israel's loss of leadership in this period when "there was no king" (v. 6). Eventually, the Levite comes to Micah's house in Ephraim, and he hires the Levite as his own priest for ten pieces of silver (vv. 8-12). The levitical priest simply sells his clerical services to anyone with sufficient money. Micah's theology of divine manipulation becomes clear in his comment that he now knows God will prosper him "because the Levite has become my priest" (v. 13). Micah believes that just as God can be captured in a humanly crafted idol, so also God's favor can be guaranteed by buying the right priest. Religion has been reduced to a privatized manipulation of God for personal gain.

18:1-31. The narrative action shifts from the private shrine of Micah to "the tribe of the Dan-

ites," who are in search of a new territorial home. The narrator reminds the reader once again of Israel's lack of leadership: "in those days there was no king in Israel" (v. 1; see 17:6; 19:1; 21:25). Like the aimless and wandering Levite in 17:8, the Danites are wandering aimlessly in search of land. The tribe of Dan had originally settled in their inheritance of land in the western border of Canaan, but they had been driven out by the native Amorites (1:34-36; Josh 19:40-47). Dan was among several Israelite tribes in Judges 1 that allowed foreigners and their gods to remain in Canaan in violation of the holy war laws, but the tribe of Dan was the only Israelite tribe that was so weak that it was actually chased off its inherited land.

Having lost their initial land inheritance, the Danites engage in a new conquest for land. An earlier story in Josh 19:47 recounts Dan's conquest of a city called Leshem. Judges 18 provides an alternate version of the same conquest, but the name of the city is changed from "Leshem" to "Laish." The actions of the tribe of Dan follow roughly the narrative pattern of previous Israelite conquests, especially the spy story in Numbers 13–14 and the conquest of the city of Jericho in Judges 2 and 6. Elements of this holy war pattern in Judges 18 include sending spies (v. 2), receiving a divine command to conquer the land (vv. 3-6), gaining inside information about the inhabitants (v. 7), the spies' report and the people's reaction (vv. 8-10), and the march and the actual conquest of the city or land (vv. 11-13, 27-28).[66] The story of the Danite conquest of the city of Laish, however, distorts three crucial elements of the conquest pattern. One element is the oracle from God. Previous conquest stories included a clear oracle and command from the Lord to conquer the land or city, mediated through a reliable messenger, either Moses or Joshua. In the case of Dan's conquest, the hired levitical priest in Micah's idolatrous shrine is unreliable as a messenger for the Lord. The Levite seems more than willing to sell his soul as well as his oracles to the highest bidder (vv. 18-20). Moreover, the Levite provides an ambiguous oracle that in Hebrew (לכו לשלום נכח יהוה דרככם *lĕkû lĕšālôm nōkaḥ YHWH darkĕkem*) literally reads: "Go in peace. Your way is *in front of the Lord*" (v.

---

66. Abraham Malamat, "The Danite Migration and the Pan-Israelite Exodus-Conquest: A Biblical Narrative Pattern," *Bib* 22 (1992) 1-17.

6). The NIV translates the second sentence of the oracle as indicating "the LORD's approval" of the Danites' plan to conquer Laish. The NRSV provides an equally plausible translation, indicating that the Danites' plan is subject to God's critical judgment: "The mission you are on is under the eye of the LORD." The ambiguity of the oracle invites readers to question the legitimacy of the Danites' plan to conquer Laish.

A second element of the holy war conquest pattern that is distorted in comparison to previous conquest accounts is the strength and aggression of the enemy relative to Israel. The model of holy war conquest emphasizes Israel's weakness, the enemy's strength and aggressiveness, and the Lord's ability to overcome the odds and give Israel the victory (Num 13:27-33; Josh 6:1, 16, 20; 10:1-11; 11:1-5). The Danites' conquest of Laish turns this model of holy war on its head. The Danites are the military aggressors. The inhabitants of Laish are "living securely" without the need for military defenses, walls, or strong allies nearby. They are "quiet and unsuspecting" (vv. 7, 27-28). The Danites' attack on the weak and peaceful people of Laish seems less like a legitimate holy war conquest and more like Amalek's wicked aggression against the "faint and weary" Israelites in the wilderness (Deut 25:17-19). The Lord remains largely uninvolved in carrying out the actual conquest, another sign of the illegitimacy of the Danites' attack on Laish.

A third element of the holy war pattern is a prohibition on anyone's ever living again in the city once it has been destroyed (Josh 6:26) and the devotion of all the city's wealth to the Lord

(Josh 6:17-19; 7:1-26). In violation of the holy war laws, the Danites "rebuild the city and lived in it" (v. 28), changing the name of the city from "Laish" to "Dan." Moreover, the Danites covet the wealth of Laish (vv. 7, 10), and there is no report that they dedicate any of the wealth to the Lord. Instead, they steal the Levite and the idols from the personal shrine of Micah and forcibly transfer them to their rebuilt city of Dan (vv. 14-26, 30-31). The Danites worship at this illegitimate site of idolatry even though the true "house of God was at Shiloh," where the ark of God was maintained (v. 31; see 1 Samuel 1–3). The Danite sanctuary remained, along with a levitical priest in the line of Moses, "until the time the land went into captivity" (v. 30), a reference to the exile of the northern kingdom of Israel in 721 BCE (2 Kings 17). The sanctuary at Dan eventually became associated with the idolatrous golden calves set up by the Israelite king Jeroboam in Dan and Bethel (1 Kgs 12:25-31). Therefore, although the Danite conquest of Laish seems to have the general outline of a holy war conquest, the distortions of three crucial elements condemn the Danites in their aggressive military takeover of Laish. The ambiguous divine oracle is given through a suspect mediator (a hired Levite and idolator). Dan is the powerful aggressor against the weak and defenseless city of Laish. Finally, Dan fails to devote the city and its wealth to the Lord, taking it over for themselves and setting up an idolatrous worship site. The portrait of the tribe of Dan that emerges from this chapter is that of a greedy bully who picks on the weak and serves idols of wealth and power rather than God.

REFLECTIONS

On the surface of these stories, a tone of religious devotion swirls in the air. There is talk of God, dedication to worship, the hiring of priests, the seeking of divine oracles, the building of worship sites, and many of the elements of a holy war conquest. However, scratch a little deeper, and these surface features of religiosity and piety reveal a profound ailment that reaches to the core of Israel's heart. Israel has lost touch with God and God's covenant traditions and commandments. Israel is devoted to other gods, idols, wealth, and power as substitutes for knowing and loving the Lord alone (Deut 6:4-5). Manipulation of God for private gain replaces sacrifices and service to the purpose and mission of God in the world. Individuals try to shrink God to a private household shrine rather than bow down in worshipful humility before the God who is the maker and judge of all creation. Micah and the Danites are examples of Israel's attempt to make God small and manageable. But attempts to confine or domesticate God will lead to judgment and disaster. Israel will suffer a near-death experience in the final chapters that follow. What will be even more amazing is that the Lord will not give up on Israel. God will find a way to remain faithful to the promises God made to this recalcitrant people, preserving them and bringing creative new forms of community life out of the chaos of religious and social degradation.

The stories of Judges 17–18 invite us to reflect critically on the practices of individual congregations, institutions, denominations, and religions. To what extent do our surface rhetoric and actions reflect and promote a true and deep knowledge and love of the God of Jesus Christ? Do our lives and practices embody a lively and devoted commitment to God and familiarity with Scripture? Or are our religious words and actions simply a smoke screen to veil real devotion to the interests of self, the power politics of the world, the worship of greed, and the resistance to responsibility and accountability for the well-being of others? Scripture reminds us that not everything that is "spiritual," "religious," and "godly" is necessarily true, good, or of the Lord. The devil delights to dress in religious garb. Thus 1 John 4:1 counsels the faithful to "test the spirits to see whether they are from God; for many false prophets have gone out into the world" (NRSV). Jesus reminds his followers, "Not everyone who says to me, 'Lord, Lord,' will enter the kingdom of heaven" (Matt 7:21 NRSV). Jesus asked, "Why do you call me 'Lord, Lord,' and do not do what I tell you?" He followed this question with a parable about a man who dug deeply and built his house on a solid rock foundation that resisted the devastating floods that inevitably come. Another person built a house on shallow ground without any foundation, and "great was the ruin of that house" (Luke 6:46-49). Judges 17–18 reflects the ruin of Israel as it built its house on the shallow ground of idolatry, greed, and power. The catastrophic flood of social disintegration will soon follow in chapters 19–21, the horrific consequence of everybody's doing "what was right in their own eyes."

JUDGES 19:1–21:25, THE LEVITE'S CONCUBINE AND WAR WITHIN ISRAEL

OVERVIEW

It has been noted throughout the book of Judges that the changing power relationships, independence, and treatment of the many women characters in the book function as benchmarks for the health and faithfulness of God's people. Early on in the judges era, women like Achsah (1:11-15), Deborah (4:4-10), and Jael (4:17-22) displayed glimpses of boldness, leadership, and power as subjects of their destinies in the midst of a largely patriarchal context. Israel seemed to function more effectively as a religious and social community. As the period of the judges began its long decline, women became objects of men's foolish vows (Jephthah's daughter, 11:29-40), the objects of men's desire (14:1-3; 16:1), and the purchased instruments for schemes of male vengeance (16:5). This general decline from woman as the subject of independent action to woman as

the object of men's actions and desires in the book of Judges coincides with the gradual decline in the health of Israel's social and religious life during the judges era. That decline culminates with the atrocity of rape and murder committed against the Levite's concubine in Judges 19, certainly one of the most brutal and violent scenes in all of Scripture.

The interplay of an individual Israelite (Samson, Micah) or a particular tribe (Dan) functioning as a symbol or metaphor for all Israel is a narrative device that continues into Judges 19–21. Certainly the horror of the rape and murder of the Levite's concubine must be taken seriously in its own right as a matter of patriarchal violence against women. However, its juxtaposition with the fractious civil war in chaps. 20–21 invites the reader to consider the fate of this woman, who has been raped, murdered, and cut into twelve pieces, as a gruesome metaphor for the social body of the twelve-tribe union of Israel. Increasingly in the book of Judges, Israel has been dishonored, attacked, killed, and split into pieces by other Israelites. Hints of these internal tribal divisions and conflicts began already in the Song of Deborah and Barak in 5:15-17 and in Gideon's conflict with the Ephraimites and the people of Penuel and Succoth (8:1-9, 13-17). The internal violence and social dissolution within Israel gradually escalated with Abimelech's murder of his seventy half-brothers (9:5), Jephthah's killing of 42,000 Ephraimites (12:1-6), Judah's betrayal of Samson to the Philistines (15:9-13), and Samson's unwillingness to lead any Israelite tribes in a coalition against the Philistines. The fabric of Israel's tribal union gradually unraveled into a disheveled heap of threads.

Judges 19:1-30, The Atrocity at Gibeah

NIV

19 In those days Israel had no king.

Now a Levite who lived in a remote area in the hill country of Ephraim took a concubine from Bethlehem in Judah. [2]But she was unfaithful to him. She left him and went back to her father's house in Bethlehem, Judah. After she had been there four months, [3]her husband went to her to persuade her to return. He had with him his servant and two donkeys. She took him into her father's house, and when her father saw him, he gladly welcomed him. [4]His father-in-law, the girl's father, prevailed upon him to stay; so he remained with him three days, eating and drinking, and sleeping there.

[5]On the fourth day they got up early and he prepared to leave, but the girl's father said to his son-in-law, "Refresh yourself with something to eat; then you can go." [6]So the two of them sat down to eat and drink together. Afterward the girl's father said, "Please stay tonight and enjoy yourself." [7]And when the man got up to go, his father-in-law persuaded him, so he stayed there that night. [8]On the morning of the fifth day, when he rose to go, the girl's father said, "Refresh yourself. Wait till afternoon!" So the two of them ate together.

[9]Then when the man, with his concubine and his servant, got up to leave, his father-in-law, the girl's father, said, "Now look, it's almost evening. Spend the night here; the day is nearly over. Stay and enjoy yourself. Early tomorrow morning you can get up and be on your way home." [10]But, unwilling to stay another night, the man left and

NRSV

19 In those days, when there was no king in Israel, a certain Levite, residing in the remote parts of the hill country of Ephraim, took to himself a concubine from Bethlehem in Judah. [2]But his concubine became angry with[a] him, and she went away from him to her father's house at Bethlehem in Judah, and was there some four months. [3]Then her husband set out after her, to speak tenderly to her and bring her back. He had with him his servant and a couple of donkeys. When he reached[b] her father's house, the girl's father saw him and came with joy to meet him. [4]His father-in-law, the girl's father, made him stay, and he remained with him three days; so they ate and drank, and he[c] stayed there. [5]On the fourth day they got up early in the morning, and he prepared to go; but the girl's father said to his son-in-law, "Fortify yourself with a bit of food, and after that you may go." [6]So the two men sat and ate and drank together; and the girl's father said to the man, "Why not spend the night and enjoy yourself?" [7]When the man got up to go, his father-in-law kept urging him until he spent the night there again. [8]On the fifth day he got up early in the morning to leave; and the girl's father said, "Fortify yourself." So they lingered[d] until the day declined, and the two of them ate and drank.[e] [9]When the man with his concubine and his servant got up to leave, his father-in-law, the girl's father, said to him, "Look, the day has worn on until it is almost evening. Spend the night. See, the day has drawn to a close. Spend the night

[a] Gk OL: Heb *prostituted herself against*   [b] Gk: Heb *she brought him*   [c] Compare verse 7 and Gk: Heb *they*   [d] Cn: Heb *Linger*   [e] Gk: Heb lacks *and drank*

went toward Jebus (that is, Jerusalem), with his two saddled donkeys and his concubine.

[11]When they were near Jebus and the day was almost gone, the servant said to his master, "Come, let's stop at this city of the Jebusites and spend the night."

[12]His master replied, "No. We won't go into an alien city, whose people are not Israelites. We will go on to Gibeah." [13]He added, "Come, let's try to reach Gibeah or Ramah and spend the night in one of those places." [14]So they went on, and the sun set as they neared Gibeah in Benjamin. [15]There they stopped to spend the night. They went and sat in the city square, but no one took them into his home for the night.

[16]That evening an old man from the hill country of Ephraim, who was living in Gibeah (the men of the place were Benjamites), came in from his work in the fields. [17]When he looked and saw the traveler in the city square, the old man asked, "Where are you going? Where did you come from?"

[18]He answered, "We are on our way from Bethlehem in Judah to a remote area in the hill country of Ephraim where I live. I have been to Bethlehem in Judah and now I am going to the house of the LORD. No one has taken me into his house. [19]We have both straw and fodder for our donkeys and bread and wine for ourselves your servants—me, your maidservant, and the young man with us. We don't need anything."

[20]"You are welcome at my house," the old man said. "Let me supply whatever you need. Only don't spend the night in the square." [21]So he took him into his house and fed his donkeys. After they had washed their feet, they had something to eat and drink.

[22]While they were enjoying themselves, some of the wicked men of the city surrounded the house. Pounding on the door, they shouted to the old man who owned the house, "Bring out the man who came to your house so we can have sex with him."

[23]The owner of the house went outside and said to them, "No, my friends, don't be so vile. Since this man is my guest, don't do this disgraceful thing. [24]Look, here is my virgin daughter, and his concubine. I will bring them out to you now, and you can use them and do to them whatever

here and enjoy yourself. Tomorrow you can get up early in the morning for your journey, and go home."

[10]But the man would not spend the night; he got up and departed, and arrived opposite Jebus (that is, Jerusalem). He had with him a couple of saddled donkeys, and his concubine was with him. [11]When they were near Jebus, the day was far spent, and the servant said to his master, "Come now, let us turn aside to this city of the Jebusites, and spend the night in it." [12]But his master said to him, "We will not turn aside into a city of foreigners, who do not belong to the people of Israel; but we will continue on to Gibeah." [13]Then he said to his servant, "Come, let us try to reach one of these places, and spend the night at Gibeah or at Ramah." [14]So they passed on and went their way; and the sun went down on them near Gibeah, which belongs to Benjamin. [15]They turned aside there, to go in and spend the night at Gibeah. He went in and sat down in the open square of the city, but no one took them in to spend the night.

[16]Then at evening there was an old man coming from his work in the field. The man was from the hill country of Ephraim, and he was residing in Gibeah. (The people of the place were Benjaminites.) [17]When the old man looked up and saw the wayfarer in the open square of the city, he said, "Where are you going and where do you come from?" [18]He answered him, "We are passing from Bethlehem in Judah to the remote parts of the hill country of Ephraim, from which I come. I went to Bethlehem in Judah; and I am going to my home.[a] Nobody has offered to take me in. [19]We your servants have straw and fodder for our donkeys, with bread and wine for me and the woman and the young man along with us. We need nothing more." [20]The old man said, "Peace be to you. I will care for all your wants; only do not spend the night in the square." [21]So he brought him into his house, and fed the donkeys; they washed their feet, and ate and drank.

[22]While they were enjoying themselves, the men of the city, a perverse lot, surrounded the house, and started pounding on the door. They said to the old man, the master of the house,

[a] Gk Compare 19.29. Heb *to the house of the LORD*

NIV

you wish. But to this man, don't do such a disgraceful thing."

²⁵But the men would not listen to him. So the man took his concubine and sent her outside to them, and they raped her and abused her throughout the night, and at dawn they let her go. ²⁶At daybreak the woman went back to the house where her master was staying, fell down at the door and lay there until daylight.

²⁷When her master got up in the morning and opened the door of the house and stepped out to continue on his way, there lay his concubine, fallen in the doorway of the house, with her hands on the threshold. ²⁸He said to her, "Get up; let's go." But there was no answer. Then the man put her on his donkey and set out for home.

²⁹When he reached home, he took a knife and cut up his concubine, limb by limb, into twelve parts and sent them into all the areas of Israel. ³⁰Everyone who saw it said, "Such a thing has never been seen or done, not since the day the Israelites came up out of Egypt. Think about it! Consider it! Tell us what to do!"

NRSV

"Bring out the man who came into your house, so that we may have intercourse with him." ²³And the man, the master of the house, went out to them and said to them, "No, my brothers, do not act so wickedly. Since this man is my guest, do not do this vile thing. ²⁴Here are my virgin daughter and his concubine; let me bring them out now. Ravish them and do whatever you want to them; but against this man do not do such a vile thing." ²⁵But the men would not listen to him. So the man seized his concubine, and put her out to them. They wantonly raped her, and abused her all through the night until the morning. And as the dawn began to break, they let her go. ²⁶As morning appeared, the woman came and fell down at the door of the man's house where her master was, until it was light.

27In the morning her master got up, opened the doors of the house, and when he went out to go on his way, there was his concubine lying at the door of the house, with her hands on the threshold. ²⁸"Get up," he said to her, "we are going." But there was no answer. Then he put her on the donkey; and the man set out for his home. ²⁹When he had entered his house, he took a knife, and grasping his concubine he cut her into twelve pieces, limb by limb, and sent her throughout all the territory of Israel. ³⁰Then he commanded the men whom he sent, saying, "Thus shall you say to all the Israelites, 'Has such a thing ever happened*ª since the day that the Israelites came up from the land of Egypt until this day? Consider it, take counsel, and speak out.'"

ª Compare Gk: Heb ³⁰And all who saw it said, "Such a thing has not happened or been seen

COMMENTARY

19:1-3. Judges 19 begins by describing again the absence of leadership and accountability in this period of Israel's life: "In those days, when there was no king in Israel . . ." (v. 1; see 17:6; 18:1; 21:25). The refrain builds an expectation that chaos, disorder, and disobedience will characterize the stories that follow. The earlier narrative in chap. 17 had featured a Levite from Bethlehem in southern Judah who traveled north

to Ephraim. This narrative in chap. 19 features a Levite from northern Ephraim who travels south to Bethlehem in Judah. His "concubine" or wife of secondary rank had left the Levite, her husband, four months earlier and returned home to live with her father. The reason for her leaving is open to two different interpretations. The NRSV translates the Hebrew verb זנה (*zānâ;* lit., "to commit adultery," "prostitute oneself") in v. 2 as "she became angry with him," implying that the Levite had done something wrong to cause her to leave. Since a woman could not initiate a divorce in ancient Israel, the very act of a woman's leaving her husband would be construed as committing adultery. But leaving her husband in such a way suggests the husband probably had been abusive or done something else wrong, causing her to be angry and to leave. The NIV translates the same verb as "she was unfaithful to him," indicating that the concubine was the one responsible for causing the separation through her adulterous action with another man. However, the subsequent actions of the Levite, who goes to the father's house "to speak tenderly to her and bring her back," seem to imply that he had been in the wrong. The similar phrase, "to speak tenderly to her" (לדבר על-לבה lĕdabbēr 'al-libbāh), was used to describe the man Shechem as he sought to persuade the Israelite woman Dinah to marry him after he had already raped her (Gen 34:3). This association with Shechem plants a seed of suspicion in the reader's mind about the dubious character of this Levite. While the concubine's father appears delighted to see his daughter's husband come for her (v. 3), the reader does not know the feelings of the concubine herself. She remains an object passed from father to husband with no apparent opportunity for her to approve or disapprove of their decision concerning her fate.

The concubine's father practices an exaggerated hospitality, repeatedly insisting that the Levite remain to eat and drink and enjoy himself in a feast of male bonding over the course of five days. The Levite appears weak and unable to say no to his father-in-law until finally, late into the fifth day, the Levite and his concubine take off to return to northern Ephraim (vv. 9-10). The Levite's unwise decision to leave so late in the day forces him and his party (the concubine, a servant, and two donkeys) to seek shelter overnight in a stranger's house. The Levite avoids seeking shelter in the city of Jerusalem because non-Israelites, Jebusites, lived there: "we will not turn aside into a city of foreigners" (vv. 10-12). The Levite wrongly assumes he will receive more hospitality in the Israelite town of Gibeah, which is located in the tribal territory of Benjamin. As things turn out, the Levite and his party would probably have fared better with foreigners than with their fellow Israelites.

19:14-15. The Levite enters the Israelite town of Gibeah and sits waiting in the open square for an invitation from some hospitable resident to spend the night at his or her house. Extending hospitality to strangers was an important and deeply held custom in the ancient Near East, and particularly so in Israel. The covenant code in Exodus (Exod 22:21; 23:9), the priestly laws of Leviticus (Lev 19:33-34), and the deuteronomic law code (Deut 16:14; 26:12) all command Israel to extend generous hospitality to the stranger or sojourner. God "loves the stranger," and God instructs Israel, "You shall also love the stranger, for you were strangers in the land of Egypt" (Deut 10:18-19). The deuteronomic law also instructs Israelites to be generous in hospitality to Levites, since they have no land of their own and their lives are to be dedicated in service to the Lord (Deut 16:14; 26:12). Therefore, if the Israelites in the town of Gibeah had known their religious traditions and values well, they would have fallen all over each other to offer hospitality to this man who is both a sojourner and a Levite. "But no one," says the text, "took them to spend the night" (v. 15). This is a time when there is no king, no teacher of the law, and no knowledge or fear of the Lord in the land. Ironically, it is the Levites as a tribe who were charged by Moses to teach the Israelites "to observe diligently all the words of this law" (Deut 31:12). If Gibeah is any sign of what is typical in Israel, the Levites have failed miserably as teachers of the law in regard to hospitality.[67]

19:16-26. Finally, late into the evening an old man who was originally from Ephraim but is living as a resident alien in the Benjaminite town of Gibeah offers them a place to sleep in his house (vv. 16-21). It is questionable whether such a resident alien even had the legal right to extend hospitality to strangers. At any rate, his generosity puts the native residents of Gibeah in an extremely bad light. The Levite assures the old man that they have plenty of provisions; all they need is a roof over their heads. While they eat and drink and enjoy the old man's generous hospitality, "the men of the city, a perverse lot" surround

---

67. Victor Matthews, "Hospitality and Hostility in Genesis 19 and Judges 19," *BTB* 22 (1992) 3-11.

the house and pound on the door. They demand that the strange man, the Levite, be brought out "so that we might have intercourse with him" (v. 22; lit., "so that we might know him"). In an act of twisted male hospitality, the old Ephraimite man refuses to cave in to this threat of homosexual rape against the Levite, offering instead his virgin daughter and the Levite's concubine. The Levite suddenly intervenes, "seized his concubine, and put her out to them" (v. 25). In the Levite's hands, his concubine becomes a dispensable victim and a substitute sacrifice who undergoes the horror and abuse that he would have experienced. "They wantonly raped her, and abused her all through the night until the morning" (v. 25). The concubine manages to crawl to the door of the old man's house and then collapses, either unconscious or dead (v. 26).[68]

The scene is a clear echo of the Genesis story of Sodom and Gomorrah, in which the two angels of the Lord were traveling and received hospitality from Lot (Gen 19:1-29). The wicked men of Sodom similarly surrounded the house and pounded at Lot's door. They demanded that the two strangers come out "so that we may know them" (Gen 19:5). Lot offered his two daughters in their stead. However, before this could be done, the two angels of the Lord struck blind the residents of Sodom. On the next day, God destroyed the two wicked cities of Sodom and Gomorrah in a hail of fire and brimstone. The two cities became legendary in Israel's tradition for their wickedness, their inhospitality to strangers, and God's total annihilation of them (Deut 29:23; Jer 49:18; Amos 4:11). The atrocity at Gibeah in Judges 19 offers no divine intervention to protect the woman. Thus Gibeah's evil men go over the edge and transgress in ways even worse than the residents of Sodom.[69]

19:27-28. Although subtly construed, the

most sinister character in the narrative may be the Levite himself. He had earlier "spoken tenderly" to his concubine in an effort to persuade her to return with him from her father's house (v. 3). But the reader even then may have wondered what the Levite had done to cause her to leave him in the first place. The events following the concubine's rape may provide some reasons. After having handed over his concubine to the mob outside the house, the Levite might be expected to be tortured all night by guilt, shame, and remorse for his action. Instead, he apparently goes to bed and sleeps (v. 27). He does not rush out of the house in the morning in search of his concubine. Instead, he makes preparations to leave and opens the door only when he is ready to continue his journey. The Levite is totally self-absorbed, unremorseful, and unfeeling.

When the Levite finally opens the door, "there was his concubine lying at the door of the house, with her hands on the threshold" (v. 27). The image of this tortured and raped woman on the doorstep should have brought to tears any human with an ounce of compassion. Now would be a moment for him to "speak tenderly" to her, gently lifting her battered body and carrying her to a bed in the house where she could be nursed and allowed time to begin to heal her broken body and spirit—if she was not already dead. What we get instead are the callous and gruff words of the Levite to the concubine, "Get up, we are going." She does not answer. Her inability to respond suggests either unconsciousness or death, and the reader is left wondering. The Levite picks up her limp body, puts it on the donkey, and "sets out for his home" (v. 28). The scene is a reversal of the first woman we encounter in the book of Judges, Achsah, daughter of Caleb. In 1:11-15, a bold and buoyant Achsah had dismounted from her donkey to ask her loving father for the gift of life-giving springs of water. Her father, Caleb, generously gave his daughter not one but two springs of water. The love, generosity, and promotion of life and well-being that characterized the relationship between women and men at the beginning of Judges are tragically absent here at the end of Judges.

19:29-30. When the Levite arrives at his home, he takes a knife and grasps his concubine (v. 29). The verb "to grasp" (חזק ḥāzaq) is the

---

68. Insightful analyses of this story are offered from a feminist-literary perspective by Phyllis Trible, "An Unnamed Woman, The Extravagance of Violence," in *Texts of Terror: Literary-Feminist Readings of Biblical Narratives* (Philadelphia: Fortress, 1984) 65-91; and from a womanist perspective by Koala Jones-Warsaw, "Toward a Womanist Hermeneutic: A Reading of Judges 19–21," in *A Feminist Companion to Judges,* ed. Athalya Brenner (Sheffield: JSOT, 1993) 172-86.

69. For various perspectives on the literary, historical, and thematic relationship between Genesis 19 and Judges 19–21, see Stuart Lasine, "Guest and Host in Judges 19: Lot's Hospitality in an Inverted World," *JSOT* 29 (1984) 37-59; Susan Niditch, "The 'Sodomite' Theme in Judges 19–20: Family, Community, and Social Disintegration," *CBQ* 44 (1982) 365-78; and Matthews, "Hospitality and Hostility in Genesis 19 and Judges 19," 3-11.

same Hebrew verb used in v. 25 when the Levite "seized" his concubine to put her out and expose her to the mob of wicked men. The verb suggests a rough and abusive handling of her body. The Levite then "cut her into twelve pieces, limb by limb" and sends each piece of her dismembered body to one of the twelve tribes of Israel as a grisly call to arms. His act is a morbid and twisted adaptation of a customary means of calling up an emergency military force in the ancient Near East. King Saul, for example, summoned the twelve tribes of Israel to join in a battle by cutting up and sending out twelve parts of an ox (1 Sam 11:7). But when did the Levite's concubine actually die? When she lay at the doorstep after the night of abuse? During the journey home on the donkey? Or at the hands of the Levite as he cut her into pieces? The reader is never actually told. Mieke Bal suggests that "as her death began at her exposure and ends with her dismemberment, we cannot know when exactly she dies, and we must not know it. . . . She dies several times, or rather, she never stops dy-

ing."[70] In any case, the Levite is as culpable in her death as anyone in the story from his first "seizing" of her in v. 25 to the last "grasping" of her in v. 29. As the Levite sends her body parts out to Israel, he accompanies them with a message, "Has such a thing ever happened since the day that the Israelites came up from the land of Egypt until this day?" (v. 30). But what exactly is the outrageous "thing"? Is it the brutal rape of this woman? The inhospitality shown toward the Levite? Or, at least in the reader's mind, is it the truly outrageous and brutal dismemberment, desecretion, and perhaps even murder of the woman by the cold and calculating Levite? Has the concubine become simply an instrument for the Levite to use to drum up support for his desire for personal revenge for the inhospitality shown to him? We will learn more in the next scene.

70. Mieke Bal, "A Body of Writing: Judges 19," in *A Feminist Companion to Judges,* ed. Athalya Brenner (Sheffield: JSOT, 1993) 222. See also Bal, *Death and Dissymmetry: The Politics of Coherence in the Book of Judges* (Chicago: University of Chicago Press, 1988) 83-93.

REFLECTIONS

1. The dismembered body of a woman who has been raped constitutes an outrageous horror in the midst of Israel. The portrait of this woman is a tragedy that has been repeated time and again throughout history from the ancient period until today. Violence, sexual abuse, neglect, and suffering have been the experience of far too many women in countries and cultures across the globe. The unnamed concubine in Judges 19 is a metaphor for all the nameless women who endure public or private abuse and suffering in our societies. This story of the Levite's concubine calls the reader to "consider it, take counsel, and speak out" (19:30).

2. The pattern of exaggerated hospitality followed by violent inhospitality occurred in an earlier narrative in Judges when the Kenite woman Jael invited the Canaanite general Sisera into her tent for protection, food, drink, and rest. She then proceeded to pound a tent peg into the temple of his sleeping head (4:17-22). This breach of the ancient hospitality code had occurred among foreigners, but Jael's act contributed to the victory Israel won against the Canaanites. It was part of the strange means by which "God subdued King Jabin of Canaan before the Israelites" (4:23). The story of Judges 19 likewise portrays an exaggerated hospitality followed by violent inhospitality. Unlike Judges 4, this act of inhospitality occurs "in the family" of Israel. The attack against the Levite's concubine involves Israel's attack, not against a foreign enemy, but against its own body politic. To paraphrase Pogo, Israel has met the enemy, "and the enemy is us!"

Israel's worst internal enemy emerges as the Levite, the holy man who is supposed to be dedicated to the service of the Lord. The shocking implications for the critique of religious leaders parallel the effect of Jesus' story of the good Samaritan (Luke 10:25-37). The two holy men, the priest and the Levite, passed by the man who had been robbed and beaten, much as the Levite gruffly stepped over the body of his concubine with the words, "Get up, we are going." It was only the outsider or foreigner, the Samaritan, who stopped and offered help, hospitality, and generosity to the man. We wonder how much better it would have been for the Levite and his concubine had they agreed to stay overnight with the non-Israelites in Jerusalem, the Jebusites (vv. 10-12). Even the great ancestor Abraham looked less than virtuous next to the fear of God displayed by the Canaanite king Abimelech in Gen 20:1-18. These stories suggest that outsiders and foreigners often display values and virtues closer to the biblical tradition than do God's own people, who claim to follow the will of God.

3. Israel's actions in Judges 19 contradict the instructions concerning the treatment of strangers and outsiders found elsewhere in Scripture. According to the larger biblical tradition, extending hospitality to strangers may be an opportunity to encounter God in the form of a human being in need. Abraham and Sarah offered hospitality to three men who visited them with a promise, and the strangers turned out to be the Lord visiting them (Genesis 18). The New Testament Letter to the Hebrews alludes to Abraham and Sarah's experience: "Let mutual love continue. Do not neglect to show hospitality to strangers, for by doing that some have entertained angels without knowing it" (Heb 13:1-2). In the last judgment scene in Matthew 25, when the good sheep are separated from the wicked goats, the good sheep are those who have fed the hungry, clothed the naked, visited the prisoners, and welcomed the stranger. Without realizing it, those who practice such hospitality to others do it to Jesus as well: "Truly, I tell you, just as you did it to one of the least of these who are members of my family, you did it to me" (Matt 25:40). Offering hospitality to strangers is an opportunity to encounter God. The abuse or neglect of strangers is an affront to God.

Judges 20:1–21:25, An Unholy Civil War

NIV

20 Then all the Israelites from Dan to Beer-sheba and from the land of Gilead came out as one man and assembled before the LORD in Mizpah. ²The leaders of all the people of the tribes of Israel took their places in the assembly of the people of God, four hundred thousand soldiers armed with swords. ³(The Benjamites heard that the Israelites had gone up to Mizpah.) Then the Israelites said, "Tell us how this awful thing happened."

⁴So the Levite, the husband of the murdered woman, said, "I and my concubine came to Gibeah in Benjamin to spend the night. ⁵During the night the men of Gibeah came after me and surrounded the house, intending to kill me. They raped my concubine, and she died. ⁶I took my concubine, cut her into pieces and sent one piece to each region of Israel's inheritance, because they committed this lewd and disgraceful act in Israel. ⁷Now, all you Israelites, speak up and give your verdict."

⁸All the people rose as one man, saying, "None of us will go home. No, not one of us will return to his house. ⁹But now this is what we'll do to

NRSV

20 Then all the Israelites came out, from Dan to Beer-sheba, including the land of Gilead, and the congregation assembled in one body before the LORD at Mizpah. ²The chiefs of all the people, of all the tribes of Israel, presented themselves in the assembly of the people of God, four hundred thousand foot-soldiers bearing arms. ³(Now the Benjaminites heard that the people of Israel had gone up to Mizpah.) And the Israelites said, "Tell us, how did this criminal act come about?" ⁴The Levite, the husband of the woman who was murdered, answered, "I came to Gibeah that belongs to Benjamin, I and my concubine, to spend the night. ⁵The lords of Gibeah rose up against me, and surrounded the house at night. They intended to kill me, and they raped my concubine until she died. ⁶Then I took my concubine and cut her into pieces, and sent her throughout the whole extent of Israel's territory; for they have committed a vile outrage in Israel. ⁷So now, you Israelites, all of you, give your advice and counsel here."

⁸All the people got up as one, saying, "We will not any of us go to our tents, nor will any of us

Gibeah: We'll go up against it as the lot directs. [10]We'll take ten men out of every hundred from all the tribes of Israel, and a hundred from a thousand, and a thousand from ten thousand, to get provisions for the army. Then, when the army arrives at Gibeah[a] in Benjamin, it can give them what they deserve for all this vileness done in Israel." [11]So all the men of Israel got together and united as one man against the city.

[12]The tribes of Israel sent men throughout the tribe of Benjamin, saying, "What about this awful crime that was committed among you? [13]Now surrender those wicked men of Gibeah so that we may put them to death and purge the evil from Israel."

But the Benjamites would not listen to their fellow Israelites. [14]From their towns they came together at Gibeah to fight against the Israelites. [15]At once the Benjamites mobilized twenty-six thousand swordsmen from their towns, in addition to seven hundred chosen men from those living in Gibeah. [16]Among all these soldiers there were seven hundred chosen men who were left-handed, each of whom could sling a stone at a hair and not miss.

[17]Israel, apart from Benjamin, mustered four hundred thousand swordsmen, all of them fighting men.

[18]The Israelites went up to Bethel[b] and inquired of God. They said, "Who of us shall go first to fight against the Benjamites?"

The LORD replied, "Judah shall go first."

[19]The next morning the Israelites got up and pitched camp near Gibeah. [20]The men of Israel went out to fight the Benjamites and took up battle positions against them at Gibeah. [21]The Benjamites came out of Gibeah and cut down twenty-two thousand Israelites on the battlefield that day. [22]But the men of Israel encouraged one another and again took up their positions where they had stationed themselves the first day. [23]The Israelites went up and wept before the LORD until evening, and they inquired of the LORD. They said, "Shall we go up again to battle against the Benjamites, our brothers?"

The LORD answered, "Go up against them."

return to our houses. [9]But now this is what we will do to Gibeah: we will go up[a] against it by lot. [10]We will take ten men of a hundred throughout all the tribes of Israel, and a hundred of a thousand, and a thousand of ten thousand, to bring provisions for the troops, who are going to repay[b] Gibeah of Benjamin for all the disgrace that they have done in Israel." [11]So all the men of Israel gathered against the city, united as one.

[12]The tribes of Israel sent men through all the tribe of Benjamin, saying, "What crime is this that has been committed among you? [13]Now then, hand over those scoundrels in Gibeah, so that we may put them to death, and purge the evil from Israel." But the Benjaminites would not listen to their kinsfolk, the Israelites. [14]The Benjaminites came together out of the towns to Gibeah, to go out to battle against the Israelites. [15]On that day the Benjaminites mustered twenty-six thousand armed men from their towns, besides the inhabitants of Gibeah. [16]Of all this force, there were seven hundred picked men who were left-handed; every one could sling a stone at a hair, and not miss. [17]And the Israelites, apart from Benjamin, mustered four hundred thousand armed men, all of them warriors.

[18]The Israelites proceeded to go up to Bethel, where they inquired of God, "Which of us shall go up first to battle against the Benjaminites?" And the LORD answered, "Judah shall go up first."

[19]Then the Israelites got up in the morning, and encamped against Gibeah. [20]The Israelites went out to battle against Benjamin; and the Israelites drew up the battle line against them at Gibeah. [21]The Benjaminites came out of Gibeah, and struck down on that day twenty-two thousand of the Israelites. [23c] The Israelites went up and wept before the LORD until the evening; and they inquired of the LORD, "Shall we again draw near to battle against our kinsfolk the Benjaminites?" And the LORD said, "Go up against them." [22]The Israelites took courage, and again formed the battle line in the same place where they had formed it on the first day.

[24]So the Israelites advanced against the Benjaminites the second day. [25]Benjamin moved out

---

NIV

²⁴Then the Israelites drew near to Benjamin the second day. ²⁵This time, when the Benjamites came out from Gibeah to oppose them, they cut down another eighteen thousand Israelites, all of them armed with swords.

²⁶Then the Israelites, all the people, went up to Bethel, and there they sat weeping before the LORD. They fasted that day until evening and presented burnt offerings and fellowship offerings*a* to the LORD. ²⁷And the Israelites inquired of the LORD. (In those days the ark of the covenant of God was there, ²⁸with Phinehas son of Eleazar, the son of Aaron, ministering before it.) They asked, "Shall we go up again to battle with Benjamin our brother, or not?"

The LORD responded, "Go, for tomorrow I will give them into your hands."

²⁹Then Israel set an ambush around Gibeah. ³⁰They went up against the Benjamites on the third day and took up positions against Gibeah as they had done before. ³¹The Benjamites came out to meet them and were drawn away from the city. They began to inflict casualties on the Israelites as before, so that about thirty men fell in the open field and on the roads—the one leading to Bethel and the other to Gibeah.

³²While the Benjamites were saying, "We are defeating them as before," the Israelites were saying, "Let's retreat and draw them away from the city to the roads."

³³All the men of Israel moved from their places and took up positions at Baal Tamar, and the Israelite ambush charged out of its place on the west*b* of Gibeah.*c* ³⁴Then ten thousand of Israel's finest men made a frontal attack on Gibeah. The fighting was so heavy that the Benjamites did not realize how near disaster was. ³⁵The LORD defeated Benjamin before Israel, and on that day the Israelites struck down 25,100 Benjamites, all armed with swords. ³⁶Then the Benjamites saw that they were beaten.

Now the men of Israel had given way before Benjamin, because they relied on the ambush they had set near Gibeah. ³⁷The men who had been in ambush made a sudden dash into Gibeah, spread out and put the whole city to the sword.

a26 Traditionally peace offerings   *b33 Some Septuagint manuscripts and Vulgate; the meaning of the Hebrew for this word is uncertain.*
c33 Hebrew Geba, a variant of Gibeah

NRSV

against them from Gibeah the second day, and struck down eighteen thousand of the Israelites, all of them armed men. ²⁶Then all the Israelites, the whole army, went back to Bethel and wept, sitting there before the LORD; they fasted that day until evening. Then they offered burnt offerings and sacrifices of well-being before the LORD. ²⁷And the Israelites inquired of the LORD (for the ark of the covenant of God was there in those days, ²⁸and Phinehas son of Eleazar, son of Aaron, ministered before it in those days), saying, "Shall we go out once more to battle against our kinsfolk the Benjaminites, or shall we desist?" The LORD answered, "Go up, for tomorrow I will give them into your hand."

29So Israel stationed men in ambush around Gibeah. ³⁰Then the Israelites went up against the Benjaminites on the third day, and set themselves in array against Gibeah, as before. ³¹When the Benjaminites went out against the army, they were drawn away from the city. As before they began to inflict casualties on the troops, along the main roads, one of which goes up to Bethel and the other to Gibeah, as well as in the open country, killing about thirty men of Israel. ³²The Benjaminites thought, "They are being routed before us, as previously." But the Israelites said, "Let us retreat and draw them away from the city toward the roads." ³³The main body of the Israelites drew back its battle line to Baal-tamar, while those Israelites who were in ambush rushed out of their place west*a* of Geba. ³⁴There came against Gibeah ten thousand picked men out of all Israel, and the battle was fierce. But the Benjaminites did not realize that disaster was close upon them.

35The LORD defeated Benjamin before Israel; and the Israelites destroyed twenty-five thousand one hundred men of Benjamin that day, all of them armed.

36Then the Benjaminites saw that they were defeated.*b*

The Israelites gave ground to Benjamin, because they trusted to the troops in ambush that they had stationed against Gibeah. ³⁷The troops in ambush rushed quickly upon Gibeah. Then they put the whole city to the sword. ³⁸Now the agreement between the main body of Israel and

a Gk Vg: Heb in the plain   *b This sentence is continued by verse 45.*

NIV

38The men of Israel had arranged with the ambush that they should send up a great cloud of smoke from the city, 39and then the men of Israel would turn in the battle.

The Benjamites had begun to inflict casualties on the men of Israel (about thirty), and they said, "We are defeating them as in the first battle." 40But when the column of smoke began to rise from the city, the Benjamites turned and saw the smoke of the whole city going up into the sky. 41Then the men of Israel turned on them, and the men of Benjamin were terrified, because they realized that disaster had come upon them. 42So they fled before the Israelites in the direction of the desert, but they could not escape the battle. And the men of Israel who came out of the towns cut them down there. 43They surrounded the Benjamites, chased them and easilya overran them in the vicinity of Gibeah on the east. 44Eighteen thousand Benjamites fell, all of them valiant fighters. 45As they turned and fled toward the desert to the rock of Rimmon, the Israelites cut down five thousand men along the roads. They kept pressing after the Benjamites as far as Gidom and struck down two thousand more.

46On that day twenty-five thousand Benjamite swordsmen fell, all of them valiant fighters. 47But six hundred men turned and fled into the desert to the rock of Rimmon, where they stayed four months. 48The men of Israel went back to Benjamin and put all the towns to the sword, including the animals and everything else they found. All the towns they came across they set on fire.

21 The men of Israel had taken an oath at Mizpah: "Not one of us will give his daughter in marriage to a Benjamite."

2The people went to Bethel,b where they sat before God until evening, raising their voices and weeping bitterly. 3"O LORD, the God of Israel," they cried, "why has this happened to Israel? Why should one tribe be missing from Israel today?"

4Early the next day the people built an altar and presented burnt offerings and fellowship offerings.c

5Then the Israelites asked, "Who from all the tribes of Israel has failed to assemble before the

a43 The meaning of the Hebrew for this word is uncertain.   b2 Or
to the house of God   c4 Traditionally peace offerings

NRSV

the men in ambush was that when they sent up a cloud of smoke out of the city 39the main body of Israel should turn in battle. But Benjamin had begun to inflict casualties on the Israelites, killing about thirty of them; so they thought, "Surely they are defeated before us, as in the first battle." 40But when the cloud, a column of smoke, began to rise out of the city, the Benjaminites looked behind them—and there was the whole city going up in smoke toward the sky! 41Then the main body of Israel turned, and the Benjaminites were dismayed, for they saw that disaster was close upon them. 42Therefore they turned away from the Israelites in the direction of the wilderness; but the battle overtook them, and those who came out of the citya were slaughtering them in between.b 43Cutting downc the Benjaminites, they pursued them from Nohahd and trod them down as far as a place east of Gibeah. 44Eighteen thousand Benjaminites fell, all of them courageous fighters. 45When they turned and fled toward the wilderness to the rock of Rimmon, five thousand of them were cut down on the main roads, and they were pursued as far as Gidom, and two thousand of them were slain. 46So all who fell that day of Benjamin were twenty-five thousand arms-bearing men, all of them courageous fighters. 47But six hundred turned and fled toward the wilderness to the rock of Rimmon, and remained at the rock of Rimmon for four months. 48Meanwhile, the Israelites turned back against the Benjaminites, and put them to the sword—the city, the people, the animals, and all that remained. Also the remaining towns they set on fire.

21 Now the Israelites had sworn at Mizpah, "No one of us shall give his daughter in marriage to Benjamin." 2And the people came to Bethel, and sat there until evening before God, and they lifted up their voices and wept bitterly. 3They said, "O LORD, the God of Israel, why has it come to pass that today there should be one tribe lacking in Israel?" 4On the next day, the people got up early, and built an altar there, and offered burnt offerings and sacrifices of well-being. 5Then the Israelites said, "Which of all the tribes of Israel did not come up in the assembly to the

a Compare Vg and some Gk Mss: Heb cities   b Compare Syr:
Meaning of Heb uncertain   c Gk: Heb Surrounding   d Gk: Heb
pursued them at their resting place

NIV

LORD?" For they had taken a solemn oath that anyone who failed to assemble before the LORD at Mizpah should certainly be put to death.

⁶Now the Israelites grieved for their brothers, the Benjamites. "Today one tribe is cut off from Israel," they said. ⁷"How can we provide wives for those who are left, since we have taken an oath by the LORD not to give them any of our daughters in marriage?" ⁸Then they asked, "Which one of the tribes of Israel failed to assemble before the LORD at Mizpah?" They discovered that no one from Jabesh Gilead had come to the camp for the assembly. ⁹For when they counted the people, they found that none of the people of Jabesh Gilead were there.

¹⁰So the assembly sent twelve thousand fighting men with instructions to go to Jabesh Gilead and put to the sword those living there, including the women and children. ¹¹"This is what you are to do," they said. "Kill every male and every woman who is not a virgin." ¹²They found among the people living in Jabesh Gilead four hundred young women who had never slept with a man, and they took them to the camp at Shiloh in Canaan.

¹³Then the whole assembly sent an offer of peace to the Benjamites at the rock of Rimmon. ¹⁴So the Benjamites returned at that time and were given the women of Jabesh Gilead who had been spared. But there were not enough for all of them.

¹⁵The people grieved for Benjamin, because the LORD had made a gap in the tribes of Israel. ¹⁶And the elders of the assembly said, "With the women of Benjamin destroyed, how shall we provide wives for the men who are left? ¹⁷The Benjamite survivors must have heirs," they said, "so that a tribe of Israel will not be wiped out. ¹⁸We can't give them our daughters as wives, since we Israelites have taken this oath: 'Cursed be anyone who gives a wife to a Benjamite.' ¹⁹But look, there is the annual festival of the LORD in Shiloh, to the north of Bethel, and east of the road that goes from Bethel to Shechem, and to the south of Lebonah."

²⁰So they instructed the Benjamites, saying, "Go and hide in the vineyards ²¹and watch. When the girls of Shiloh come out to join in the dancing, then rush from the vineyards and each of you

NRSV

LORD?" For a solemn oath had been taken concerning whoever did not come up to the LORD to Mizpah, saying, "That one shall be put to death." ⁶But the Israelites had compassion for Benjamin their kin, and said, "One tribe is cut off from Israel this day. ⁷What shall we do for wives for those who are left, since we have sworn by the LORD that we will not give them any of our daughters as wives?"

8Then they said, "Is there anyone from the tribes of Israel who did not come up to the LORD to Mizpah?" It turned out that no one from Jabesh-gilead had come to the camp, to the assembly. ⁹For when the roll was called among the people, not one of the inhabitants of Jabesh-gilead was there. ¹⁰So the congregation sent twelve thousand soldiers there and commanded them, "Go, put the inhabitants of Jabesh-gilead to the sword, including the women and the little ones. ¹¹This is what you shall do; every male and every woman that has lain with a male you shall devote to destruction." ¹²And they found among the inhabitants of Jabesh-gilead four hundred young virgins who had never slept with a man and brought them to the camp at Shiloh, which is in the land of Canaan.

13Then the whole congregation sent word to the Benjaminites who were at the rock of Rimmon, and proclaimed peace to them. ¹⁴Benjamin returned at that time; and they gave them the women whom they had saved alive of the women of Jabesh-gilead; but they did not suffice for them.

15The people had compassion on Benjamin because the LORD had made a breach in the tribes of Israel. ¹⁶So the elders of the congregation said, "What shall we do for wives for those who are left, since there are no women left in Benjamin?" ¹⁷And they said, "There must be heirs for the survivors of Benjamin, in order that a tribe may not be blotted out from Israel. ¹⁸Yet we cannot give any of our daughters to them as wives." For the Israelites had sworn, "Cursed be anyone who gives a wife to Benjamin." ¹⁹So they said, "Look, the yearly festival of the LORD is taking place at Shiloh, which is north of Bethel, on the east of the highway that goes up from Bethel to Shechem, and south of Lebonah." ²⁰And they instructed the Benjaminites, saying, "Go and lie in wait in the vineyards, ²¹and watch; when the

NIV

seize a wife from the girls of Shiloh and go to the land of Benjamin. ²²When their fathers or brothers complain to us, we will say to them, 'Do us a kindness by helping them, because we did not get wives for them during the war, and you are innocent, since you did not give your daughters to them.'"

²³So that is what the Benjamites did. While the girls were dancing, each man caught one and carried her off to be his wife. Then they returned to their inheritance and rebuilt the towns and settled in them.

²⁴At that time the Israelites left that place and went home to their tribes and clans, each to his own inheritance.

²⁵In those days Israel had no king; everyone did as he saw fit.

NRSV

young women of Shiloh come out to dance in the dances, then come out of the vineyards and each of you carry off a wife for himself from the young women of Shiloh, and go to the land of Benjamin. ²²Then if their fathers or their brothers come to complain to us, we will say to them, 'Be generous and allow us to have them; because we did not capture in battle a wife for each man. But neither did you incur guilt by giving your daughters to them.'" ²³The Benjaminites did so; they took wives for each of them from the dancers whom they abducted. Then they went and returned to their territory, and rebuilt the towns, and lived in them. ²⁴So the Israelites departed from there at that time by tribes and families, and they went out from there to their own territories.

²⁵In those days there was no king in Israel; all the people did what was right in their own eyes.

COMMENTARY

20:1-48. The Israelites respond en masse to the Levite's urgent call to arms precipitated by the rape of his concubine and the distribution of her body parts to all twelve tribes. In ironic contrast to the concubine's dismembered body, "all the Israelites" assemble "in one body" at Mizpah (v. 1). The mention of Mizpah recalls the story of Jephthah and his daughter. Jephthah was selected as a judge at Mizpah, and it was there that he made his tragic and reckless vow, which led to the death and sacrifice of his daughter (11:29-40). The association with Jephthah does not bode well for what is about to take place. Previous attempts to unite Israel's twelve tribes against foreign enemies gradually deteriorated over the course of the judges era, culminating in the later judges who attacked fellow Israelites (Gideon, Jephthah) and in the individualistic Samson, who did not lead or unite any Israelites but carried out his personal acts of revenge by himself. However, in this period of chaos and distintegration, the Israelites come together for the purpose of taking revenge on one of their own tribes, the tribe of Benjamin. They gather to consider taking revenge on Benjamin because its territory includes

the town of Gibeah, the site of the atrocity against the Levite's concubine (19:12-15).

The Israelites ask the Levite to explain what happened at Gibeah in Benjamin. The Levite responds with a distorted and edited version of events. His report of the outrage at Gibeah differs markedly at certain crucial points from the actual narrated events in 19:22-30. The Levite's distortions begin with his claim that it was "the lords of Gibeah" who rose up against him (v. 5) rather than the less significant group of "perverse men of the city" (19:22). The Levite claims that the men "intended to kill me" (v. 5), while the actual intent was to "have intercourse with him" (19:22). The Levite fails to mention that he was the one who "seized his concubine" and threw her out to the mob. Moreover, he claims that "they raped my concubine until she died" (v. 5). The actual narrative never makes it clear that the men of Gibeah killed her; the reader knows that the Levite himself probably had a role in killing her either through neglect, forcing her to ride the long journey on the donkey, or cutting her body into pieces. The Levite's version of the story is designed to exaggerate the guilt of the people of Gibeah and to avoid any guilt or responsibility on his own part for having exposed his concubine to rape and murder. The Levite engages in the age-old game of creating an enemy in order to avoid his own responsibility or role in perpetuating an evil situation or action.

The Israelites respond to the Levite's accusation against the city of Gibeah by sending troops to attack the city and "repay Gibeah of Benjamin for all the disgrace that they have done in Israel" (v. 10). The text emphasizes again that "all the men of Israel" are "united as one" in their attack against Gibeah (v. 11). A matter of personal revenge involving a Levite has now expanded to become a national and tribal affair. A total of 26,000 troops from the tribe of Benjamin (including some specially skilled left-handed warriors) come out to support the city of Gibeah against the attack of the huge army of 400,000 warriors from the other Israelite tribes (vv. 14-17).

Like the tribe of Dan, who had misused a holy war model in its conquest of the city of Laish (18:27-31), the Israelites use aspects of the holy war in this ill-conceived civil war against one of their own tribes. They go up to the holy site of Bethel and inquire of God, "Which of us shall go up first to battle against the Benjaminites?" The Lord answers, "Judah shall go up first" (v. 18). The question and the oracle's response echo the opening scene in the book of Judges, when the Israelites had asked the Lord who should be first to go up to fight against "the Canaanites." God had also answered then, "Judah shall go up" (1:1-2). The oracle in Judges 1 had shown the favored status of Judah, and God gave Judah victory in its battle with Canaan (1:4-10). But in Judges 20, the choice of Judah to lead the assault against Benjamin implicates Judah along with the other tribes in their ill-conceived attempt to destroy a part of Israel. Insofar as "all Israelites" are involved in this civil war, all Israelites are implicitly condemned by these actions, including Judah.

The judgment against all Israel, including Judah, is further demonstrated by the results of the three separate battles against the Benjaminites in Judges 20. In the first battle, the Benjaminites are victorious and kill 22,000 Israelites. Israel weeps before the Lord, crying out for help as they had done when the Lord sent enemy oppressors to attack them for their disobedience (vv. 19-23; see 2:1-5; 3:9, 15; 4:3; 6:6; 10:10). As earlier in

the book of Judges, Israel's weeping and crying are reactions to the oppression of enemies that God used to punish Israel for its evil ways. In previous episodes of the judges, God used foreign nations, such as the Canaanites or the Ammonites or the Philistines, as instruments of judgment. In chap. 20, God uses one of Israel's own tribes, the tribe of Benjamin, as an instrument of judgment against the rest of Israel.

The Israelites again seek an oracle from the Lord, asking, "Shall we again draw near to battle against our kinsfolk the Benjaminites?" God says yes, but the oracle again does not promise victory (v. 23; note the transposition of vv. 22 and 23 in the NRSV). The Israelites dutifully attack Benjamin a second time, but they suffer another defeat and the deaths of an additional 18,000 men (vv. 24-25). The Israelites weep again and seek a third oracle from God, and this time God promises Israel's victory and Benjamin's defeat (vv. 26-28). In their third battle with Benjamin, the Israelites employ a military strategy of ambush and deception similar to the strategy used in the successful holy war campaign against the city of Ai (Josh 8:29-42). The successful strategy is a sign that this battle is God's just punishment on the tribe of Benjamin for its disobedience, just as the two previous battles had been God's judgment on the other tribes of Israel.

The battle scene concludes with a body count of Benjaminites killed in battle. The Benjaminites had started out with about 26,000 warriors (v. 15). In various phases of the third and last battle, the Israelites killed a group of 18,000 Benjaminite soldiers (v. 24), then a group of 5,000 Benjaminites (v. 45), and finally a group of 2,000 Benjaminite warriors (v. 45). Only 600 Benjaminite men remain of the whole tribe; these 600 had escaped the battle and "fled toward the wilderness" (v. 47). The Israelites then proceed to kill all the remaining Benjaminite population of elders, women, children, and animals. The tribe of Benjamin was nearly exterminated from the face of the earth, except for the slender thread of 600 escaped survivors. Would a part of Israel be forever destroyed by fellow Israelites? That is the question that hangs over the narrative as we move into the next scene.

21:1-25. The question of the survival of the tribe of Benjamin is heightened by a foolish vow the Israelites had made in the course of their deliberations at Mizpah. They had promised that none of them would give their daughters in marriage to any Benjaminite man (v. 1). Mizpah was the same location where Jephthah had made his reckless vow to offer as a burnt offering whatever or whoever first came out of his house when he returned victorious from battle. What came first out of his house happened to be his one and only child, his daughter. Jephthah was thus forced to sacrifice her, effectively wiping out his family line (11:29-40). The Israelites' vow at Mizpah threatens to create a similar result for the tribe of Benjamin, effectively wiping out any hope for the tribe's future life. The remnant of the tribe of Benjamin consists of only 600 men and no women to bear children for a new generation (20:46-48). The Israelites cry for a third time to God, but their cry reveals their ignorance about their own responsibility and guilt in nearly exterminating the tribe of Benjamin. They ask God, "Why has it come to pass that today there should be one tribe lacking in Israel" (v. 3)? They need only look in the mirror for the answer. The sinfulness of all Israel, including Benjamin, is responsible for this crisis (20:11). Israel seems unable to acknowledge its own guilt in the matter, much as the Levite in the rape and murder of his concubine.

The Israelites suddenly wake up and realize that they cannot allow Benjamin as a tribe to be annihilated in spite of their foolish vow. They remember a second vow they had made at Mizpah: that any group who did not come to Mizpah and join the coalition against Benjamin would "be put to death" (v. 5). They also recall that one group of Israelites from Jabesh-gilead had not been present at Mizpah (vv. 8-9). Thus, in a bizarre move, they decide to attack the residents of Jabesh-gilead out of "compassion for Benjamin their kin" (v. 6). Where is their compassion for their kin of Jabesh-gilead? The Israelites kill everyone in Jabesh-gilead except "four hundred young virgins who had never slept with a man" (v. 12). They offer the 400 virgin women of Jabesh-Gilead to the 600 Benjaminite men who had escaped the battle and proclaim peace to them (v. 13-14). However, 200 of the 600 Benjaminite men still

have no wives. Thus the Israelites come up with another bizarre scheme. They instruct the Benjaminites to lie in wait at the yearly festival at Shiloh and kidnap the young virgins as they dance during the festival. In this way, the Benjaminites will get wives for themselves. But since these women were not given voluntarily by the fathers or brothers at Shiloh, the Israelites will not technically have violated the Mizpah vow, which involved willingly giving daughters to the Benjaminite men (vv. 15-22). The Israelites seem unaware that kidnapping and rape violate basic covenant obligations more severely than any single vow. The Israelites are simply multiplying the crime that was first committed against the Levite's concubine. The Benjaminites do indeed kidnap the virgin women at Shiloh and return to their tribal territory to raise families and build up their tribal population once again (vv. 23-24).

The book of Judges comes to a close with the refrain that began this section in 17:6: "In those days there was no king in Israel; all the people did what was right in their own eyes" (v. 25), reminding the reader again of the chaos and disintegration that have occurred between the two refrains. Religious idolatry, unholy wars of conquest against a peaceful and defenseless people, abuse of strangers, rape, murder, personal revenge, deception, civil war, and more rape, murder, and kidnapping of young women all combine to portray an Israel in turmoil and near death. What is most remarkable is that God has been at work in and through this chaos, even as God's Spirit moved over the primeval chaos of creation to form the heavens and the earth (Gen 1:1-5). God has been true to the divine promise to preserve Israel's survival in the land in spite of its constant and escalating rebellion and disobedience. And just as surely as God created the cosmos out of chaos, so too God will create a new Israel out of the chaos at the end of the judges period. The stories that follow in 1–2 Samuel and 1–2 Kings chronicle a bold new experiment with kingship in Israel, a new venture with its own set of glorious heights, culminating in King David, and tragic lows, ending in the exile of the nation to a foreign land.

REFLECTIONS

1. The Levite dodged his role and responsibility for the concubine's rape and death by misrepresenting the complex moral texture of the events leading up to the crimes that were committed. He simplified the calculus of guilt by laying all the blame on the residents of Gibeah. Similarly, the tribes of Israel seem totally unaware of the ways in which their evil actions have led to the near extinction of one of their own tribes, the tribe of Benjamin. "O Lord," they ask, "why has it come to pass that today there should be one tribe lacking in Israel?" The desire to pass the buck and not acknowledge our own sin and failure goes back as far as the story of Adam and Eve in the garden of Eden (Gen 3:8-13) or to the story of Aaron and the golden calf at the foot of Mt. Sinai (Exod 32:3-4, 22-24). Humans regularly resist taking responsibility for their own misdeeds. We seek to place blame on anyone but ourselves. Some find it difficult to offer a true and heartfelt confession of failure to God and to people whom they have hurt. But such confession and acknowledgment of wrongdoing are a necessary first step in restoring broken relationships with God and with other human beings. Confession is good for our souls, but it is often hard for our lips to speak the words with integrity and truthfulness.

2. Scholars have often understood the final section of Judges (chaps. 17–21) as propaganda by one group aimed against other groups within Israel. Some argue that these stories condemn the northern kingdom of Israel and favor the southern kingdom of Judah. Others suggest that the stories imply a condemnation of the kingship of Saul (who was from Gibeah of the tribe of Benjamin, 1 Sam 10:26) and support for the kingship of David, based in Jerusalem. Still others see an implied critique of one levitical group of priests versus another group of Levites. Some of these intra-Israelite rivalries may have played a role in earlier stages in the writing and shaping of these stories. But in their present form, these narratives intentionally include all tribes and groups as taking part in and being responsible for the social and religious collapse of Israel at the end of the judges period. One idolatrous Levite or priest is from the south and the tribe of Judah, and the other callous and self-absorbed Levite is from the north and the tribe of Ephraim. "All Israel" is involved in the misguided civil war and the killing and kidnapping of women that follow. All the tribes of Israel experience defeat in the battle, a sign of God's judgment against them. Benjamin (the tribe of King Saul) is defeated and judged, but so is the tribe of Judah (the tribe of King David). This blanket condemnation of all Israel echoes the angel's words of judgment against all the Israelites at the beginning of the book (Judg 2:4). All have sinned and fallen short of the glory of God (Rom 3:23).

3. The Israelite tribes acted in bizarre and reprehensible ways to avoid the technicalities of violating the reckless vow that prohibited them from offering their daughters to the remnant of Benjaminite men. On one hand, their actions display a rigid legalism in trying to keep the vow at any cost. On the other hand, their actions show a total disregard for the basic covenantal obligations of love and preserving the life and well-being of their neighbor. When the Israelite tribes totally annihilated Jabesh-Gilead and sanctioned the kidnapping of the women of Shiloh in order to protect themselves from breaking their vow, they give evidence of having lost their moral and covenantal bearings. Preoccupation with legalistic and technical obedience to certain rules or laws without an accompanying sense of the principles of faithfulness and love that undergird such laws and temper their rigid application is a recipe for disaster.

4. The singular tragedy of the rape and murder of the Levite's concubine is compounded and multiplied many times over by the events that follow the Levite's manipulation of the facts. His distorted report leads to a spiraling cycle of violence and revenge, which only multiplies the crime. Thousands more people are killed. Hundreds more women are forcibly taken. Such is the demonic power of group evil, mob violence, and the human desire for ever more vengeance and retribution. The Bible recommends a good and more perfect way in which vengeance belongs to God alone, evil is answered with good, and enemies are loved rather than hated (Lev 19:18; Matt 5:38-48; Rom 12:14-21). Such ideals are often difficult to translate into reality, but even the so-called *lex talionis*—"an eye for an eye, a tooth for a tooth, a life for a life"—at least puts a limit on retribution and revenge. We may, perhaps, begin there and then work, however imperfectly, toward the more difficult but preferred ideal.

5. Lingering theological questions remain at the end of the book of Judges about the place and role of God in the midst of this unholy mess of human violence, idolatry, blind disobedience, war, and atrocities. God remains involved in these tragic events to judge and punish the Israelites through their own ill-conceived plans and strategies (20:18, 23, 27-28, 35). God remains ominously silent in response to the Israelites' question of "why has it come to pass. . . ?" (21:3). But the reader knows well that the Israelites have brought this crisis upon themselves through their own disobedience. There is no king in Israel, no leader, no teacher, no guide who can unite Israel in renewed commitment to God and to the covenant God made with Israel. For the moment, everyone is doing what is right in his or her own eyes. As we come to the end of Judges, God has allowed Israel to experience the violent harvest of its long history of disobedience.

But God is not finished with Israel yet. Just as Samson's hair began to grow and offered a glimpse of hope, so also the tribe of Benjamin is pulled back just in time from the brink of extinction. Israel's twelve tribes are preserved. God remains committed to this people, because God has promised to do so: "I will never break my covenant with you" (2:1). God's patient love has been stretched nearly to the breaking point during the era of Gideon, Jephthah, Samson, and the Levite's concubine. But the Spirit of God is stirring again in new ways in Israel in the chaos at the end of Judges. God will raise up a new order of kings and prophets in Israel who will lead God's people effectively for a time. But the time of kings and prophets, like the era of the judges, will also come to an end. The kings of Israel, like the judges of old, will give way to new means of leadership, new structures of community, and new avenues for the Spirit of God to work in the world.

The book of Judges invites us to assess our own times and communities and modes of leadership. Are they effective and faithful instruments for promoting the will and purposes of God in the world? Are we sufficiently open to the new futures and possibilities God is creating out of the chaos and churning of our own time? In the words of God speaking through a prophet in a time of exile and chaos, "I am about to do a new thing;/ now it springs forth; do you not perceive it?" (Isa 43:19 NRSV).

THE BOOK OF RUTH

INTRODUCTION, COMMENTARY, AND REFLECTIONS
BY
KATHLEEN A. ROBERTSON FARMER

THE BOOK OF
RUTH

INTRODUCTION

T he book of Ruth contains an artistically constructed, kaleidoscopic narrative that is more like an extended parable than a historical report. The story is told with extreme narrative economy (a style that includes deliberate gaps or silences that leave many details unexplained) and with a characteristic disregard for historical or political details. The narrator uses symbolic names (such as the names of Naomi's sons, signifying in advance that they are not long for this world), word play (such as puns and double entendres), and the purposeful repetition of words and phrases to highlight themes and underline ambiguities. The "sophisticated literary artistry of the author" is marked by "the conscious intentional employment of multiple levels of meaning in the narrative."[1]

THE INTERPRETIVE CHALLENGE

In form and function, the book of Ruth closely resembles both the book of Jonah and the story Nathan tells to David in 2 Sam 12:1-7, without Nathan's accusatory line ("You are the man!") at the end. Like Nathan's story, and like Jonah, Ruth has the power of revealing us to ourselves *as we are* rather than as we think we ought to be. But unlike Nathan's story, Ruth and Jonah are *not* presented to us by a prophet who is willing and able to tell us who we are within the dynamics of the story.

Thus the interpretive challenge in both stories lies in the area of identification. We can rather easily argue that Jonah was a personification of the Jewish audience to whom the

1. Moshe J. Bernstein, "Two Multivalent Readings in the Ruth Narrative," *JSOT* 50 (1991) 15-16.

book itself was addressed. "Israel itself is symbolized in Jonah's person, a stubborn and self-isolating Israel that is always occupied with itself, evading the actual will of God, and unaware that God loves other peoples just as much as Israel itself."[2] But which of the characters in the book of Ruth can be said to mirror the people of God?

Generations of interpreters have held up the character of Ruth as a model of morality. Like the "good Samaritan" in Luke 10:30-37, Ruth is an admirable character from an ethnic group that was despised and rejected by those who considered themselves to be the "people of God." Ruth's admirability tempts interpreters to tell themselves and their audiences, "We *ought* to be or act like this." But an interpreter's advice to "go and do likewise" (as wise as it may be) never comes to an audience with the force of revelation. Nathan's exclamation in 2 Sam 12:7 has revelatory power because it uses the mirror of the story to reveal David to himself. But seeing themselves mirrored in the character for whom the book of Ruth is named will not lead an audience either to repentance or to hope for their own redemption.

REDEMPTION AND IDENTIFICATION

The purposeful repetition of key terms in the book of Ruth encourages us to consider Naomi as the character who most closely mirrors the attitudes and experiences of the people of God, including both Israel and the church. Repetition indicates that "redemption" is a key concern in the story of Ruth. The book is only eighty-five verses long, but the word "redeem" (גאל *gāʾal*) and its derivatives ("redeemer," "redemption") are used some twenty-three times. Asking who or what is redeemed leads to the discovery that Naomi is the ultimate recipient of redemption in the story.

On a superficial level, we might say that the story of Ruth is about redemption defined in a secular manner, as the restoration of property to its original owners or as the healing of a break in a branch of a family tree. The final scene in the story (4:13-17), however, hints at a deeper level of meaning. In 4:14 the audience discovers that Naomi is to be "redeemed" through the child whose conception was said to have been given by the LORD (4:13). The women of Bethlehem, who know how bitter Naomi has been about the emptiness of her life, tell us that this "redeemer" will "restore" or "reverse" Naomi's "life" (using the word נפש [*nepeš*], which is often translated "soul").

Reversal is the essence of redemption. Within the story world Naomi is the primary object of redemption. It is Naomi whose life is turned around, whose feelings of bitterness, emptiness, and hopelessness are reversed. Ruth's faithfulness is only the *instrument* God uses to accomplish Naomi's redemption.

If the story told in the book of Ruth is to be redemptive for the people of God, then the people of God must identify themselves with the one who *is* redeemed. The story of Ruth becomes a story of redemption for Israel only if Israel can be persuaded to believe that the

2. Gerhard Lohfink, *The Bible: Now I Get It! A Form-Criticism Handbook,* trans. Daniel Coogan (Garden City, N.Y.: Doubleday, 1979) 83.

redemptive efforts made by God on Naomi's behalf will be made by God on Israel's behalf as well.

Ruth, the outsider, the representative of a group that Deut 23:3 refuses to admit to "the assembly of the LORD," is the agent or tool God uses to bring about the redemption of Israel/Naomi. The parable-like form of the narrative encourages us to see not just that we *ought* to be like Ruth but that we *are* like Naomi. And when we see ourselves reflected in the story as we really are (rather than as we think we ought to be), the good news comes to us as revelation rather than application.

Thus a redemptive reading of Ruth will assume that the story is primarily concerned with the faithfulness of God rather than with the faithfulness of the people of God. In Ruth, redemption is based on grace, not merit. Redemption is not a reward given to Naomi because of her exemplary behavior. God chooses to redeem those who seem to have done little to deserve redemption. And God chooses to use those who seem unqualified according to human standards of judgment to accomplish God's purposes in the world. The admirability of the "other" in the story (be they Samaritan or Moabite) should serve primarily to convict us of our own repeated failures to recognize the despised "other" as an agent of God's redemptive activity in the world.

CANONICAL LOCATIONS AND THEIR IMPLICATIONS

Different Bibles place the book of Ruth in different locations. In Christian Bibles (following the Septuagint), Ruth is found in the "Former Prophets," the traditional name for the narrative sequence from Joshua to 2 Kings. But the Hebrew Bible puts Ruth among the Writings, the division of the canon that includes wisdom literature and Psalms. In the Hebrew text, Ruth is one of the *Megilloth* ("The Five Scrolls") set apart for liturgical use in the major religious festivals of Judaism. Ruth is read aloud in the synagogue as a part of the two-day celebration of *Shavuot*, the Feast of Weeks (which is also called Pentecost because it falls fifty days—seven weeks plus one day—after the beginning of Passover). The Feast of Weeks celebrates both the end of the grain harvest season and the giving of the Torah, marking the covenant between Yahweh and the people of Israel.[3] The connection between the festival and the book is both seasonal (the action in Ruth takes place during the grain harvest) and symbolic (God's love for Israel culminates in a marriage/covenant oriented toward redemption).

The canonizers responsible for the order of the books in Christian Bibles may not have intended to convey any particular theological meaning by their placement of Ruth between Judges and 1 Samuel. They may have intended merely to put as many books as possible in chronological order. However, once it was done (for whatever reason) it must be acknowledged that "the narrative that includes [Ruth] differs from the narrative that excludes it."[4] When Ruth is read in between Judges and Samuel, it functions both as a

---

3. See Abraham P. Bloch, *The Biblical and Historical Background of the Jewish Holy Days* (New York: KTAV, 1978) 179-89.

4. David Jobling, "Ruth Finds a Home: Canon, Politics, Method," in *The New Literary Criticism and the Hebrew Bible,* ed. J. Cheryl Exum and David J. A. Clines (Valley Forge: Trinity Press International, 1993) 126.

spacer and as a bridge between the end of the period when "there was no king in Israel" (Judg 21:25) and the beginning of the united monarchy. On the one hand, the opening of Ruth ("In the days when the Judges ruled") implies that the period of the judges is an era now gone by, making the book of Judges seem quite distant and separate from the action in 1 Samuel. On the other hand, the way Ruth begins with a reference to the judges and ends with a reference to David informs the reader in advance that the episodes in Samuel dealing with Saul are little more than a detour on the road to the dynasty that really matters, the Davidic line of kings.[5]

Taken together, Judges 19–21 and Ruth seem to condemn the origins of Saul and commend the origins of David for ethical rather than ethnic reasons.[6] God's rejection of Saul can be anticipated by the reader who notes that Saul comes from Gibeah (the source of the appalling behavior described in Judges 19–21). Saul has an ethnically "pure" family tree, but he seems to have inherited his ancestors' tendency to disregard God's sovereignty. In contrast, David's family tree is rooted in the remarkably loyal behavior of a foreigner who has voluntarily chosen to join herself and her future to the Lord. Thus if Ruth is read in between Judges and 1 Samuel, it seems to function as a "witness to the moral legitimacy of the Davidic monarchy."[7] When Judges, Ruth, and Samuel are read together as a single story, it seems that David, with his "outsider" blood, is more of an insider with God than is Saul, whose bloodlines are not tainted by intermarriage but whose ancestors *acted* in a tainted way.

In the Hebrew Bible, Ruth is surrounded by post-exilic, poetic and wisdom-oriented texts. The reader who encounters Ruth among the Writings is more inclined to see the story as a parable than as an apology, or as an example story rather than royal propaganda. Many of the psalms are assigned to David, and a large section of 1 Chronicles (chaps. 10–29) is devoted to the kingship of David. In this literary context, the book of Ruth seems to assume the greatness rather than defend the legitimacy of the Davidic line of kings. Thus readers of Ruth in the Hebrew Bible are more likely to conclude that it teaches a lesson that could function equally well in any historical setting. An early rabbinic interpreter says Ruth was written "to teach how great is the reward of those who do deeds of kindness,"[8] and a modern literary critic says that the moral of the story is, "Common people achieve uncommon ends when they act unselfishly toward each other."[9]

Since many of the Writings are obviously post-exilic in origin, Ruth's placement in the Hebrew Bible tends to support those who think the story of Ruth was developed in the fifth century BCE as a way of casting doubt on the wisdom of Ezra and Nehemiah's attempt to cast all foreign wives out of the restoration community of Israel.[10]

5. Ibid., 130-31.

6. See Warren Austin Gage, "Ruth Upon the Threshing Floor and the Sin of Gibeah: A Biblical-Theological Study," *Westminster Theological Journal* 51 (1989) 369-75.

7. Ibid., 370.

8. *Ruth Rabbah* II.14, L. Rabinowitz, trans. (London: Socino Press, 1939).

9. Jack M. Sasson, "Ruth," in *The Literary Guide to the Bible,* ed. Robert Alter and Frank Kermode (Cambridge, Mass.: Harvard University Press, 1987) 321.

10. Although this idea has circulated since the early 1800s, it has been given its best modern presentation by André LaCocque, "Ruth," in *The Feminine Unconventional: Four Subversive Figures in Israel's Tradition* (Minneapolis: Fortress, 1990) 84-116.

THE AMBIGUITY OF DATING

We cannot date the composition of the book of Ruth with any degree of certainty. The linguistic evidence is so ambiguous that equally valid arguments can be formulated to support either an early or a late date.[11]

Some readers jump from the observation of Ruth's function in its literary context in Christian Bibles to the conclusion that Ruth was *written* in David's time as an attempt to establish David's right to the throne. However, an apology for the righteous origins of the Davidic dynasty might have served the purposes of later writers as well. The exilic editors of the Deuteronomic History (the narrative sequence from Joshua to Kings) were interested in reflecting on faithful and unfaithful forms of leadership in Israel and Judah, and the post-exilic work of the chronicler was dedicated to exalting the successful kingship of David over against the failures of Saul.

In his own lifetime, David would have been known as a successful and powerful king who had overcome the military opponents of Israel and expanded the borders of the kingdom, while creating a sense of national identity among various tribal and ethnic groups. But David's greatest fame in Israel came in retrospect, as people in later times looked back on the beginnings of the Davidic dynasty, which had become remarkable for its stability and longevity. Long after David's own time, as the gap between the theological ideals projected onto human kingship and the historical realities perpetrated by human kings continued to widen, the faithful in Israel began to look for a future king descended from David (a "messiah" [מָשִׁיחַ *māšîaḥ*], meaning "an anointed one") whose reign would bring about true security, justice, and well-being. Thus David's significance did not diminish with time but grew even greater in the years just before and just after the Babylonian Exile (587–539 BCE).

READING RUTH IN VARIOUS LIFE SETTINGS

Reading history through the lens of Ruth is more like looking through a kaleidoscope than a microscope. While the dominant themes of redemption and insider/outsider dynamics remain constant within the story, every rotation of the proposed background against which the story is read causes these themes to fall into a different pattern. Every attempt to fill in the silences in the story produces a new shade of meaning.

If we imagine an audience of people in David's own time concerned with the purity of David's bloodline, we can see how reading Ruth might have persuaded them that the Moabite "taint" in David's ancestry was "redeemed" when the Moabite in question was shown to be an admirable convert to Judaism.[12] If we imagine an audience at a later date concerned with what it was that qualified one line of kings to rule "forever," we can see how reading Ruth may have convinced them that lovingkindness (not ethnic purity) gave birth to the messianic line of kings. If Ruth is read by people who are gravely concerned

---

11. Edward L. Greenstein, *Essays on Biblical Method and Translation,* BJS 92 (Atlanta, 1989) 14-15.
12. Murray D. Gow, *The Book of Ruth: Its Structure, Theme, and Purpose* (Leicester: Apollos, 1992) 182.

over the fragmentation of Israel, it may seem that "in the reunion of Ruth and Naomi, whom even death will not separate, the old sad break between the families of Lot and Abraham is repaired, and from that reforging of patriarchal bonds, there will be a new birth of salvation."[13] And if the book is read and studied by people who are being forced to choose between those who want to cast all foreign influences out of their community of faith (Neh 13:1-3) and those who insist that the "house of the LORD" should be a "house of prayer for all peoples" (Isa 56:1-8), such an audience must have heard the story of Ruth as supporting the fruitfulness of the inclusive position.

In fact, the parabolic nature of the narrative makes tenuous every attempt to pin its origins down to one particular setting in the life of Israel. The enduring appeal of Ruth depends precisely upon this non-specificity, which allows the story to function effectively as revelation in our own as well as in Israel's eyes. When the kaleidoscope of history spins into our own time, we must consider how people in a country that is in the process of tightening its immigration laws in order to protect its cultural identity will see or hear themselves reflected in the dynamics of the text. Every new reader is challenged afresh to recognize his or her own present reality mirrored in a narrative that both convicts us of our lack of merit and assures us of God's redemptive inclinations.

13. Harold Fisch, "Ruth and the Structure of Covenant History," *VT* 32 (1982) 435.

BIBLIOGRAPHY

Verse-by-verse analyses plus theological reflections that will be helpful in preaching, teaching, and personal study can be found in:

Bush, Frederic. *Ruth/Esther*. WBC 9. Dallas: Word, 1996. Extensive bibliographies and detailed analyses of the Hebrew text make this volume an outstanding resource for further study.

Campbell, Edward F., Jr. *Ruth*. AB 7. Garden City, N.Y.: Doubleday, 1975. Although slightly dated, this is still the most accessible, well-balanced, and theologically sound commentary available in English.

Hubbard, Robert L., Jr. *The Book of Ruth*. NICOT. Grand Rapids: Eerdmans, 1988. Contains very helpful surveys of the range of opinions and the arguments used to support scholarly theories of the origins, purposes, themes, and theological perspectives of Ruth.

The following give readers helpful or provocative insights into the different ways Ruth can be understood, depending on the assumptions one brings to the reading of the text:

Bos, Johanna W. H. *Ruth, Esther, Jonah*. Knox Preaching Guides. Edited by John H. Hayes. Atlanta: John Knox, 1986.

Fewell, Danna Nolan, and David Miller Gunn. *Compromising Redemption: Relating Characters in the Book of Ruth*. Literary Currents in Biblical Interpretation. Louisville: Westminster/John Knox, 1990. Uses both interpretive storytelling and formal literary analyses to question traditional assumptions about the exemplary nature of the characters in Ruth.

Kates, Judith A., and Gail Twersky Reimer, eds. *Reading Ruth: Contemporary Women Reclaim a Sacred Story*. New York: Ballantine, 1994. Allows women's experiences in the modern world to illuminate and be illuminated by the book of Ruth.

LaCocque, André. "Ruth." In *The Feminine Unconventional: Four Subversive Figures in Israel's Tradition.* OBT. Minneapolis: Fortress, 1990. Pictures Ruth as a post-exilic parable that subverts the xenophobic policies of Ezra and Nehemiah.

Sasson, Jack M. *Ruth: A New Translation with a Philological Commentary and a Formalist-Folklorist Interpretation.* Baltimore: John Hopkins University Press, 1979. Casts a great deal of light on the way traditional literary forms affect our readings of the biblical text.

Trible, Phyllis. "A Human Comedy." In *God and the Rhetoric of Sexuality.* OBT. Philadelphia: Fortress, 1978. Presents Ruth and Naomi as admirable examples of how brave and bold women can survive in a man's world and become both the recipients and the agents of God's blessings.

OUTLINE OF RUTH

I. Ruth 1:1-22, Turn, Turn, Turn

A. 1:1-5, Turning Away

B. 1:6-22, Turning Back
   1:6-14, "Return to Your Mother's House"
   1:15-18, "Don't Tell Me to Turn My Back on You!"
   1:19-22, Turning Bitter

II. Ruth 2:1-23, Known and Unknown

A. 2:1-16, Portrait of a "Worthy" Man
   2:1-7, "Happening" to Find the Right Field
   2:8-16, Boaz "Notices" Ruth

B. 2:17-23, "Kindness" Has Not Forsaken the Living or the Dead

III. Ruth 3:1-18, Uncovering and Recovering

A. 3:1-7, The Plan: Uncovering

B. 3:8-13, Recovering: Midnight on the Threshing Floor

C. 3:14-18, The Beginning of an End to Emptiness

IV. Ruth 4:1-22, The Roots of Israel's Redemption

A. Ruth 4:1-11*a*, Boaz Settles the Matter
   4:1-4, The Trap Is Baited and Set
   4:5-6, The Trap Is Sprung
   4:7-11*a*, Legal Formalities

B. 4:11*b*-17, Naming the Mothers of the Messiah
   4:11*b*-12, Blessing the Union
   4:13-17, Redemption Incarnate

C. 4:18-22, David's Family Tree

RUTH 1:1-22

TURN, TURN, TURN

OVERVIEW

The action in the opening chapter of the book of Ruth revolves around Naomi. She provides the thread of narrative continuity in the chapter. We follow her from Bethlehem to Moab and back. She turns away from the promised land in a time of need and turns back in a time of plenty. Naomi is the object of Ruth's pledge of loyalty. And, when Naomi and Ruth arrive in Bethlehem, Naomi is the center of the whole town's attention (1:19).[14]

The word שוב (*šûb*), variously translated as "turn," "return," "go back," "turn back," and "brought back," occurs fifteen times in the book of Ruth, twelve times in the first chapter (1:6, 7, 8, 10, 11, 12, 15*a*, 15*b*, 16, 21, 22*a*, 22*b*). In the HB, *šûb* ("turn"/"return") is frequently used in a figurative sense to describe mental, emotional, or spiritual reversals. The word can refer to apostasy (turning away from God, as in Judg 2:19) as well as to repentance (turning back to God, as in 1 Kgs 8:33). Thus even when "turn"/"return" or "turn back" is used in a seemingly neutral (geographical) sense, it retains some of these moral overtones. Ruth and Naomi can both be said to be "returnees" ("who came back from the country of Moab," 1:22, 2:6; 4:3) in more than one sense of the word.

The frequent repetition of "turn" may also be used to alert the audience to the role that reversals play in this part of the story (as well as in the book as a whole). The chapter begins in the midst of a famine and ends in the midst of a barley harvest. The ones who look for more abundant life in Moab find death there instead. Naomi's life turns from "full" in the midst of famine to "empty" in the midst of plenty, and Naomi herself turns from "sweet" to "bitter" (1:20-21). In chap-

ter 4, the word *šûb* will be used again to describe the final reversal in the story: The child born to Ruth and Boaz will be "a restorer of life" (משיב *mēšîb*; lit., "will cause life to turn around") for Naomi.

The fact that this story is said to take place "in the days when the judges 'judged' " may carry more meaning than merely a historical identification. Several indicators suggest that the narrator wants us to connect the beginning of Ruth with the end of Judges. The twofold repetition of "Bethlehem in Judah" in Ruth 1:1-2 prods us to make a mental connection between this unidentified man and the escalating spiral of sin and violence portrayed in the final chapters of Judges (which in the LXX and in the Christian canon immediately precede Ruth).

The story in Judges 17–18, about the opportunistic levite who tended the idolatrous shrine that was eventually appropriated by the Danites, begins with nearly identical language: "Now there was a young man of Bethlehem in Judah" (Judg 17:7). Similarly, the story of gang rape, murder, dismemberment, civil war, and genocide told in Judges 19–21 begins with "a certain Levite" who took for himself a "concubine from Bethlehem in Judah" (Judg 19:1).

Furthermore, when the character called "a certain man" in Ruth 1:1 is given a name in 1:2, it is a name that is guaranteed to remind the reader of the recurring theme of Judges 17–21. The name "Elimelech" can be taken as an affirmation meaning "My God is King." But the final chapters in Judges illustrate in a stark and graphic manner that in those days no one (not even God) was king in Israel (Judg 17:6; 18:1; 19:1; 21:25). Thus the story of Ruth begins in a way that reminds us of the evil that can happen when the LORD does *not* reign supreme in Israel. The book of Judges illustrates the ways in which lack of loyalty

---

14. Vincent L. Tollers, "Narrative Control in the Book of Ruth," in *Mappings of the Biblical Terrain: The Bible as Text,* ed. Vincent L. Tollers and John Maier (Lewisburg: Bucknell University Press, 1989) 255.

and kindness among the children of Israel leads to division and death. In contrast, Ruth demonstrates what can happen when even a foreigner whose origins are despised in Israel chooses loyalty and kindness as a way of life.

RUTH 1:1-5, TURNING AWAY

<table>
<tr><td>

NIV

1 In the days when the judges ruled,[a] there was a famine in the land, and a man from Bethlehem in Judah, together with his wife and two sons, went to live for a while in the country of Moab. [2]The man's name was Elimelech, his wife's name Naomi, and the names of his two sons were Mahlon and Kilion. They were Ephrathites from Bethlehem, Judah. And they went to Moab and lived there.

[3]Now Elimelech, Naomi's husband, died, and she was left with her two sons. [4]They married Moabite women, one named Orpah and the other Ruth. After they had lived there about ten years, [5]both Mahlon and Kilion also died, and Naomi was left without her two sons and her husband.

[a]1 Traditionally judged

</td><td>

NRSV

1 In the days when the judges ruled, there was a famine in the land, and a certain man of Bethlehem in Judah went to live in the country of Moab, he and his wife and two sons. [2]The name of the man was Elimelech and the name of his wife Naomi, and the names of his two sons were Mahlon and Chilion; they were Ephrathites from Bethlehem in Judah. They went into the country of Moab and remained there. [3]But Elimelech, the husband of Naomi, died, and she was left with her two sons. [4]These took Moabite wives; the name of the one was Orpah and the name of the other Ruth. When they had lived there about ten years, [5]both Mahlon and Chilion also died, so that the woman was left without her two sons and her husband.

</td></tr>
</table>

COMMENTARY

1:1. Biblical authors sometimes speak of famines as a consequence of or punishment for the sins of the people of God (see Amos 4:6; Hos 4:1-3). But the phrase "there was a famine in the land" may also be used as the conventional beginning of an example story (as in Gen 12:10; 26:1).

1:2. The sojourners are said to be "Ephrathites," which in this context seems to be the name of a clan or sub-tribal grouping. The source of 1 Chr 2:19-20, 50 suggests that Bethlehem was founded by the descendants of a woman named Ephrath, the wife of Caleb. It is particularly appropriate for a story that centers around a woman to identify her family by the name of the clan's matriarch. The narrator in Gen 35:19 considers "Ephrathah" simply another name for Bethlehem, which would also be congruent with the usage of "Ephrathah" in Ruth 4:11. The only

other time the whole term "Ephrathite from Bethlehem in Judah" is used in the OT is in 1 Sam 17:12, when David is identified as the son of "an Ephrathite of Bethlehem in Judah." However, the speaker in Judg 12:5 uses "Ephrathites" to refer to people from Ephraim. This latter usage suggests still another connection between the beginning of Ruth and the end of Judges, since both of the stories in Judges 17–21 begin "in the hill country of Ephraim." The word "Ephrathites" may also have ironic overtones as it is used here, since it apparently comes from a root (פרה *pārâ*) meaning "fruitful," "fertile," or "productive." These travelers, who come from either a clan or an area known for its "fruitfulness," find only barrenness and death in Moab.

The term translated "country of Moab" is spelled in two slightly different ways in Ruth. "Country" is spelled שׂדי (*śĕdê*, construct form) in

1:1-2 and in one of the two occurrences in 1:6 (as well as in 1:22; 2:6) but שׂדה (*śĕdēh*, construct form) in the second occurrence in 1:6 (and also in Ruth 4:3). The latter spelling is the more common in texts other than Ruth (see Gen 36:35; Num 21:20; 1 Chr 1:46; 8:8). This variation in spelling may be more significant than it seems at first glance. In the unpointed (unvocalized) Hebrew text, "country" (*śĕdê*) is identical to Shaddai (שׁדי *śadday*), the name Naomi uses for God in 1:20-21. Thus the place where Naomi's troubles begin and the name of the God she blames for bringing these troubles upon her would have looked as well as sounded alike in the earliest forms of the text. (See Commentary on 1:20-21.)

In modern English usage, the word "country" is an ambiguous term that can refer either to a political state or to a rural (as opposed to an urban) area. There is some question as to how the terms *śĕdê* and *śĕdēh* should be translated here. Since the singular form of the same word (שׂדה *śādeh*) is used later in Ruth to refer to the "field" in which Ruth gleans (2:2-3, 8, 22) and to the parcel of land that Naomi is selling (4:3), we might reasonably infer that the narrator uses *śĕdê mô'āb/śĕdēh mô'āb* to refer in a nonspecific way to rural areas under cultivation, where there is some hope of escaping the famine that prevails in Bethlehem.

In any case, the symbolic force that the name "Moab" would have had in the minds of Israelite audiences matters here more than does the travelers' geographical destination. In the ears of an Israelite audience, almost any reference to Moab would have carried negative moral and emotional connotations. Genesis 19 reflects Israelite feelings of contempt for Moabites, claiming that Moab (and Ammon) had incestuous beginnings. When the Israelites were traveling in the wilderness after their escape from bondage in Egypt, their encounters with Moabites were either hostile (Numbers 22) or shameful (Numbers 25). After the Israelite tribes began to settle in Canaan, their enmity with Moab continued (Judges 3); and hostilities flourished through the periods of the united and divided monarchies (2 Samuel 8; Isaiah 15–16; Jer 48:38; Ezek 25:8-11; Amos 2:1-3; Zeph 2:9). Deuteronomy 23:3 bans Moabites and their descendants down to the tenth generation from entering "the assembly of the LORD."

1:3-5. The narrative begins (as an ancient audience would have expected a story to begin) by naming the man, the head of the family, first. In the first two verses, Naomi is merely a member of Elimelech's family. She is *"his"* wife, and Mahlon and Chilion are *"his"* two sons. But in v. 3 the storyteller shifts the focus of attention to Naomi: Elimelech becomes "the husband of Naomi," and Naomi is left with *"her"* two sons. When the sons also die, we are told that "the woman was left without *her* two sons and *her* husband" (1:5). Naomi will be the center of narrative attention throughout the rest of the chapter.

The names given to Naomi's sons are symbolic of the short-lived role they will play in the story. "Mahlon" sounds like the disease that hit the Egyptians before the exodus (Exod 15:26), and "Chilion" seems to come from the root כלה (*kālâ*), meaning "to perish." The narrator tells us that Mahlon and Chilion "married" Moabite women (NIV) or "took" (NRSV) Moabite wives, using the root נשׂא (*nś'*) instead of the more usual word for "take" (לקח *lqḥ*). The term used in Ruth 1:4 (נשׂא *nś'*) is used only nine times in the OT to refer to marriage: in Judg 21:23 (reminding us once again of the links between the beginning of Ruth and the end of Judges); in Ezra 9:2, 12; 10:44 and Neh 13:25 (where the taking of foreign wives is condemned); and in 2 Chr 11:21; 13:21; 24:3 (in reference to the taking of multiple wives).

REFLECTIONS

The book of Ruth begins with a series of small ironies. Famine covers the area known as the "House of Bread" (Bethlehem). Members of a clan named "Fruitfulness" move to Moab in order to live, but end up dying one after another, leaving no "fruit" (children) behind them. Even audiences who were not already predisposed to seeing Moab as a symbol of evil would be able to infer that Moab in this story is a place of death and destruction, swallowing up those who turn to it for sustenance.

The parabolic nature of the introduction to Ruth encourages us to see ourselves and our own lives reflected in the circumstances of the story. But the revelatory power of a parable depends on its audience's understanding of the *implications* of the facts of the story. When Jesus told the parable of the good Samaritan to his Judean audience, he knew the implications involved in making the hero of the story a Samaritan. The parable would not have made its point if most of the people in the audience had not considered themselves morally superior to Samaritans. In order to hear the same point in our own time, modern audiences need to recognize (but not share or condone) the ancient audience's cultural prejudices. Before we can decide what corresponds to Moab in our lives today, we have to ask, "What are the things we think we despise until we are forced to turn to them in times of crisis?" Or "What do we seek out in desperate times that ends up killing us or making our lives unfruitful?"

A deuteronomistic historian may have seen the use of נשא (*nāśāʾ*) in 1:4 (they "took" wives) as a way of highlighting the relationship between the end of Judges and the beginning of Ruth. But an audience in the post-exilic period must have heard in the use of this term for "marriage" an echo of the language Ezra and Nehemiah were using as they tried to persuade the Jews to abandon the foreign wives they had "taken." It has been suggested that Ruth is a subversive parable that was written specifically to undermine the authority of the priests who were trying to "purify" Israel by ostracizing foreign women.[15] Like parables in general, Ruth begins in a way that encourages people to identify themselves with the characters and their attitudes. An audience that had begun to be persuaded by Ezra and Nehemiah's language might have felt that the use of *nāśāʾ* gave an appropriately negative connotation to the joining of Israelite men with Moabite women. But, again like parables in general, the story of Ruth will eventually subvert, or cause the audience to question their initial assumptions. Whether the story of Ruth was originally written for this purpose, it certainly must have functioned this way in Second Temple Judaism (i.e., after 520–515 BCE).

When conflicts of opinion arise in our own communities of faith concerning who is acceptable and who is not, we can encourage people to notice that more than one opinion is expressed by the faith communities reflected in the biblical text. Part of the good news to be preached on the basis of the book of Ruth is that the attitudes toward outsiders expressed in Ezra 9–10 and Neh 13:23-27 were not shared by all biblical authorities. The xenophobia reflected in Ezra–Nehemiah is contradicted explicitly in Isaiah 56 and implicitly in the book of Ruth.

15. André LaCocque, "Ruth," in *The Feminine Unconventional: Four Subversive Figures in Israel's Tradition,* OBT (Minneapolis: Fortress, 1990) 84-116.

RUTH 1:6-22, TURNING BACK

Ruth 1:6-14, "Return to Your Mother's House"

NIV	NRSV
⁶When she heard in Moab that the Lord had come to the aid of his people by providing food for them, Naomi and her daughters-in-law prepared to return home from there. ⁷With her two daughters-in-law she left the place where she had been living and set out on the road that would take them back to the land of Judah.	6Then she started to return with her daughters-in-law from the country of Moab, for she had heard in the country of Moab that the Lord had considered his people and given them food. 7So she set out from the place where she had been living, she and her two daughters-in-law, and they went on their way to go back to the land of Judah.

NIV

[8]Then Naomi said to her two daughters-in-law, "Go back, each of you, to your mother's home. May the LORD show kindness to you, as you have shown to your dead and to me. [9]May the LORD grant that each of you will find rest in the home of another husband."

Then she kissed them and they wept aloud [10]and said to her, "We will go back with you to your people."

[11]But Naomi said, "Return home, my daughters. Why would you come with me? Am I going to have any more sons, who could become your husbands? [12]Return home, my daughters; I am too old to have another husband. Even if I thought there was still hope for me—even if I had a husband tonight and then gave birth to sons— [13]would you wait until they grew up? Would you remain unmarried for them? No, my daughters. It is more bitter for me than for you, because the LORD's hand has gone out against me!"

[14]At this they wept again. Then Orpah kissed her mother-in-law good-by, but Ruth clung to her.

NRSV

[8]But Naomi said to her two daughters-in-law, "Go back each of you to your mother's house. May the LORD deal kindly with you, as you have dealt with the dead and with me. [9]The LORD grant that you may find security, each of you in the house of your husband." Then she kissed them, and they wept aloud. [10]They said to her, "No, we will return with you to your people." [11]But Naomi said, "Turn back, my daughters, why will you go with me? Do I still have sons in my womb that they may become your husbands? [12]Turn back, my daughters, go your way, for I am too old to have a husband. Even if I thought there was hope for me, even if I should have a husband tonight and bear sons, [13]would you then wait until they were grown? Would you then refrain from marrying? No, my daughters, it has been far more bitter for me than for you, because the hand of the LORD has turned against me." [14]Then they wept aloud again. Orpah kissed her mother-in-law, but Ruth clung to her.

COMMENTARY

1:6-7. Clearly Naomi is the focus of the narrator's attention. *She* started to return with *her* daughters-in-law, because *"she* had heard. . . . " (v. 6), and *"she* set out from the place where *she* had been living" (v. 7). The phrase "back to the land of Judah" in v. 7 must also refer to Naomi alone, since Ruth and Orpah had not come from there originally.

In v. 6, the word translated "food" is לחם (*leḥem*), which can mean either "bread" or "food." The narrator uses an implied pun to make a point: Naomi decided to return home after the deaths of her husband and sons, because she had heard that "bread" (*leḥem*) had returned to "The House of Bread" (בית-לחם *bêt-leḥem*).

The word that is translated "daughter-in-law" (כלה *kallâ*) in 1:6-8, and 22 is used in most other passages to mean "bride" (as in Isa 49:18; 61:10; 62:5). Ruth and Orpah are Naomi's sons' "brides." The narrator may use this particular term to add a further touch of pathos to the story and to make the two women seem younger and more eligible for second mar-

riages. Naomi herself is said to address the younger women as "my daughters" in 1:11-13.

1:8-9. Naomi wants her sons' brides to remarry. Commentators have sometimes been puzzled by the use of the phrase "mother's house" in v. 8. Elsewhere in the HB widowed women are expected or advised to return to their fathers' houses (Gen 38:11; Lev 22:13). The term "mother's house" (בית אמה *bêt 'immāh*) occurs only four times in Scripture: once here in Ruth 1:8, once in Gen 24:8 (the Rebekah story), and twice in the Song of Songs (3:4; 8:2). In each case this phrase appears in a story about or by a woman, and in each case the context is related to marriage arrangements. Naomi's statement in v. 9 makes it clear that urging each of them to go back to her "mother's house" is equivalent to encouraging them to look for new husbands. Going back to the mother's house is a first step in the process that will allow them to find "rest" or "security" (מנוחה *měnûḥâ*) in another husband's house.

In the written form of the Hebrew text, v. 9 is a declarative sentence: "The LORD *will* deal kindly with you." The early scribes amended it to read as a wish. Read as a declarative statement, Naomi's words might seem like an affirmation of faith. However, if we take what Naomi says as an affirmation, rather than a wish, then Naomi would seem to be implying that her own miserable situation has come about because she has not dealt kindly with the dead! (See further discussion at Commentary on 1:21.)

The terms "kindly" (NRSV) and "kindness" (NIV) in v. 8 are feeble attempts to translate the Hebrew word חסד (*ḥesed*). In the HB, *ḥesed* has far more theological significance than "kindness" has in common English usage. *Ḥesed* is considered an essential part of the nature of God and is frequently used to describe God's acts of unmerited grace and mercy. But (as v. 8 implies), human beings are also able to do or to show *ḥesed* to one another. To do or to show *ḥesed* means to demonstrate lovingkindness and loyalty that extends far beyond what the law requires, beyond anything the recipient expects or deserves to receive.[16]

Naomi's wish in v. 8 implies that both of her sons' brides have been kind and loyal to their husbands and to her beyond the call of duty. Naomi hopes that the LORD will follow *their* example! Furthermore, Naomi clearly thinks that the LORD's *ḥesed* toward Orpah and Ruth should provide them with "security" or "rest" (*měnûḥâ*) in the form of new husbands.

1:10-13. When the younger women say they would rather return with Naomi to her home than return to their own homes (v. 10), Naomi comes up with a series of arguments meant to persuade them that they will be better off going back to their own mothers' houses. Naomi's logic seems to be based on a customary practice known in modern times as the "levirate marriage" (after the Latin word *levir,* meaning "brother-in-law"). If an Israelite man died before he produced any offspring, his brother was expected to marry the widow and to allow the firstborn son of their

union to carry on the dead man's "name" (Deut 25:5-10). Similar practices were customary in Hittite, Assyrian, and Ugaritic societies, and texts from these neighboring cultures indicate that such marriages allowed the deceased man's family to keep his property under their control.[17] It is unclear whether this was the rationale behind Deut 25:5-10. In any case, Naomi seems to assume that if she had other living sons, they might have married their brothers' widows and thus provided them with the "security" they needed.

Naomi's statements that she "has no more sons in her" and is too old now to have another husband are followed by two rhetorical questions in v. 13 that assume the answer no. Naomi knows she is not able to provide Orpah and Ruth with the husbands she thinks they need in order to have "security" or "rest." The word used twice in v. 15 to mean "sister-in-law" reminds the listener of the levirate code in Deuteronomy. The only biblical uses of the root יבם (*ybm*) are found here in Ruth (in the feminine, translated "sister-in-law") and in the "law of the levirate" in Deut 25:5-10 (in the masculine, translated "brother-in-law").

The questions Naomi asks in v. 13 are also meant to remind us of the story of Tamar and Judah (Genesis 38), which illustrates how levirate marriage customs functioned (or failed to function) on at least one occasion in Israel's memory. After Tamar's first two husbands (both sons of Judah) had died, Judah said to his daughter-in-law, "Remain a widow in your father's house until my son Shelah grows up," all the while intending to ignore any further claims she might make upon his family (Gen 38:11). Naomi's argument implies that Ruth's and Orpah's situation is even more hopeless than Tamar's was. Naomi thinks there is not even the remotest possibility that levirate customs could provide a satisfactory solution to their mutual dilemma. Later in the story, Naomi's next of kin will be called a "redeemer," but never a "brother-in-law."

Naomi's final argument has to do with her own apparently hopeless situation. The future may seem uncertain for Orpah and Ruth, but Naomi thinks her own situation is even more bitter than theirs. They might still remarry and have children,

16. Katherine Doob Sakenfeld, *Faithfulness in Action: Loyalty in Biblical Perspective,* OBT (Philadelphia: Fortress, 1985); H. J. Zobel, *Theological Dictionary of the Old Testament,* vol. 5 (Grand Rapids: Eerdmans, 1986) 44-64; Edward F. Campbell, "Naomi, Boaz, and Ruth: *Hesed* and Change," in *God's Steadfast Love: Essays in Honor of Prescott Harrison Williams, Jr.,* Austin Seminary Bulletin (1990) 64-74.

17. Raymond Westbrook, *Property and Family in Biblical Law,* JSOT-Sup 113 (Sheffield: Sheffield Academic, 1991) 69-89.

but the older woman seems to have "no hope" (v. 12). In v. 9, Naomi expressed the wish that the LORD would deal even more kindly with Orpah and Ruth than they deserved. But v. 13 indicates that Naomi does not think the LORD has dealt kindly with her at all. Unlike the land of the Ephrathites, which is able to recover from famine, Naomi expects never to become fruitful again.

Naomi is "bitter" (מר *mar*, v. 13), as she will say again in vv. 19-20, and she blames the LORD for bringing about the situation in which she finds herself: "the hand of the LORD has turned against me." She argues that it does not make logical sense for Orpah and Ruth to align themselves with someone who seems to have the hand of the LORD turned against her.

The narrator uses the same root word for "turn"/"return" (שוב *šûb*) in all of the turning points in this scene: When Naomi decides to *return* home, she tells her daughters-in-law to *return* to their homes because the LORD's hand has *turned* against her. "Turn"/"return" occurs both in the narration and in the dialogue, serving to integrate both components of the text,[18] and it "carries the whole movement and tension of the episode."[19]

18. Basil Rebera, "Lexical Cohesion in Ruth: A Sample," in *Perspectives on Language and Text,* ed. Edgar W. Conrad and Edward G. Newing (Winona Lake, In.: Eisenbrauns, 1987) 131-38.
19. Edward F. Campbell, Jr., *Ruth,* AB 7 (New York: Doubleday, 1975) 79.

1:14. In vv. 6-13 the daughters-in-law are addressed as a unit and respond as a unit: "they wept" (v. 9), and "they said" (v. 10). Here they again weep in unison, and then they become individuals, acting separately for the first time in the story. Orpah's leave-taking is recorded in the briefest possible manner. Having been persuaded by Naomi's arguments in vv. 11-13, Orpah kisses Naomi good-bye and then simply vanishes from the narrator's point of view. Orpah functions as a foil for Ruth, who acts in an exactly opposite way. Unlike Orpah, Ruth is not persuaded. She "clings" to her mother-in-law (note the verb דבק [*dābaq*], which can also be used to refer to a marriage relationship, as in Gen 2:24; 1 Kgs 11:2, or to Israel's ideal relationship with God, as in Josh 22:5). And unlike Orpah, who is never given a speaking voice in the story, Ruth makes a lengthy, forceful, and impassioned speech that dismisses all of Naomi's arguments as irrelevant.

The word for "mother-in-law" (חמות *ḥāmôt*) occurs here for the first time. The narrator uses this term, meaning "husband's mother" here and in 2:11, 18, 19, 23; 3:1, 6, 16. But Ruth herself never uses this word to address Naomi. Ruth uses the term only when she tells Naomi that *Boaz* has said, "Do not return to your mother-in-law empty-handed." Outside the book of Ruth, "mother-in-law" is found only in Mic 7:6.

REFLECTIONS

The formal, written record of a society seldom reflects a true picture of day-to-day life within that society. Historians, reporters, journalists, filmmakers, and storytellers may neglect the mundane details of everyday relationships, but these are the "facts" of life that affect the majority of people in the most significant ways. Naomi's reference to the "mother's house" gives us an oblique glimpse into one of the (most unreported) roles played by Israelite women in daily affairs.[20] The narrator who reports that Ishmael's mother "got a wife for him" does not seem to think this was exceptional behavior on Hagar's part (Gen 21:21), and Naomi does not see marriage from "the mother's house" as a foreign institution. Although the official, formal records speak only of a father's power over his daughter's choices, "Israelite women apparently had a role equal to if not greater than their husbands in arranging the marriages of their children."[21]

Orpah (whose name seems to mean "back of the neck") does everything society, custom, and the authority figures in her life expect her to do. She obeys her mother-in-law's instructions and returns to her own mother's house, weeping as she goes. While rabbinic legends say that the

20. Carol Meyers, "Returning Home: Ruth 1:8 and the Gendering of the Book of Ruth," in *A Feminist Companion to Ruth,* ed. Athalya Brenner (Sheffield: Sheffield Academic, 1993) 113.
21. Ibid., 112.

four giant warriors mentioned in 2 Sam 21:22 were Orpah's sons, the official biblical records ignore her. Orpah seems to have been a model of obedient womanhood, and the LORD may have eventually dealt kindly with her, as she had dealt with Naomi and her family (1:8); but no one elected to tell her story. In a similar way, many modern women who have chosen traditional life-styles, living lives of obedience to the expectations of society or of the authority figures in their lives, may feel that no one is interested in telling their stories. "Orpah's journey home helps us to reconsider the silent and silenced among us, the women who stand both on the threshold of the women's movement and on the threshold of traditional beliefs and practices."[22]

We should stress that the biblical narrator does not condemn Orpah. Nor should we. The Orpahs as well as the Ruths among us deserve to be remembered and celebrated. But considering Orpah's choice to return to her mother's house encourages us to ask, "What in one's past does one reclaim? To what does one return? How does one return to the 'mother's house' without losing the redefinition of self and society discovered in the wilderness?"[23]

It is very important for the interpreter of Ruth to note that the relationship between Ruth and Naomi is *described* by the narrator, not *prescribed* as a rule for anyone else's behavior. If Ruth's actions are taken to be prescriptive (if the interpreter moves from the observation that this is the way Ruth acted to the conclusion that this is the way *all* daughters-in-law should act), then the book of Ruth becomes an oppressive instrument. Katherine Doob Sakenfeld describes a gathering of Japanese women who "expressed strong distaste for the story [of Ruth], explaining that it was much used by male church leaders as biblical warrant for completely self-sacrificing devotion of daughter-in-law to mother-in-law, a cultural tradition they sought to challenge."[24] While the relationship between mother-in-law and daughter-in-law translates differently in different cultural settings and among different persons, there is nothing in the biblical text of Ruth to justify our using it to impose or to reinforce standards of behavior in our own times.

22. Bonnie Miller-McLemore, "Returning to the 'Mother's House': A Feminist Look at Orpah," *The Christian Century* (April 17, 1991) 430.
23. Ibid.
24. Katherine Doob Sakenfeld, " 'Feminist' Theology and Biblical Interpretation," in *Biblical Theology: Problems and Perspectives,* ed. Steven J. Kraftchick, Charles D. Meyers, Jr., and Ben C. Ollenburger (Nashville: Abingdon, 1995) 257.

Ruth 1:15-18, "Don't Tell Me to Turn My Back on You!"

NIV

15"Look," said Naomi, "your sister-in-law is going back to her people and her gods. Go back with her."

16But Ruth replied, "Don't urge me to leave you or to turn back from you. Where you go I will go, and where you stay I will stay. Your people will be my people and your God my God. 17Where you die I will die, and there I will be buried. May the LORD deal with me, be it ever so severely, if anything but death separates you and me." 18When Naomi realized that Ruth was determined to go with her, she stopped urging her.

NRSV

15So she said, "See, your sister-in-law has gone back to her people and to her gods; return after your sister-in-law." 16But Ruth said,
"Do not press me to leave you
    or to turn back from following you!
Where you go, I will go;
    where you lodge, I will lodge;
your people shall be my people,
    and your God my God.
17 Where you die, I will die—
    there will I be buried.
May the LORD do thus and so to me,
    and more as well,
    if even death parts me from you!"
18When Naomi saw that she was determined to go with her, she said no more to her.

COMMENTARY

1:15. Both the NRSV and the NIV refer to Orpah's "gods" with a lowercase letter *g*, which seems to indicate to the English reader that Orpah and her fellow Moabites worshiped a variety of gods. But when the same Hebrew word אלהים (*'ĕlōhîm*) occurs again in v. 16, both translations use an uppercase *G* to indicate that Ruth intends to worship Naomi's one and only God. However, an impartial observer must note that the words used in vv. 15-16 are identical in Hebrew. The difference occurs in English only because the translators have come to their readings of the text with some previous assumptions concerning Moabite worship practices. It might be argued that OT references to Moabite religion seem to know of only one Moabite deity: Chemosh (see Num 21:29; Judg 11:24; 1 Kgs 11:7, 33; 2 Kgs 23:13; Jer 48:7, 13, 46; except for Baal-peor in Num 25:1-3, which seems to mean "The Lord of Peor" and also probably refers to Chemosh). So when *'ĕlōhîm* is used in the context of Orpah's return to her mother's house, it may be that "the most natural assumption is that Chemosh is intended."[25]

1:16. When Ruth finally speaks up, her words have overtones of indignation that the usual English translations fail to capture. The word עזב (*'āzab*), translated "leave" in this verse, frequently connotes "changing primary allegiance" (as in Gen 2:24, which uses both דבק [*dābaq*, to "cling to"] and עזב [*'āzab*, to "leave"]).[26] *'Āzab* is the word used when Israel is said to "abandon" or "forsake" the LORD (as in Judg 10:10) or the LORD's commandments (as in Deut 29:24). Ruth is indignant because Naomi is urging her to abandon her present loyalties and to turn her back on her previous commitments.

Ruth uses verbs that state her intentions for the future: "I will go"; "I will lodge"; "I will die"; and "I will be buried." But the clauses translated here as "your God *will be* my God" and "your people *will be* my people" actually contain no verbs at all. In Hebrew, this simple juxtapositioning of nouns ("your God, my God; your people, my people") most frequently represents a statement of present rather than future reality. It is possible that Ruth means for these clauses to stand as an explanation for the rest of her declaration. Ruth has *already* committed herself to the LORD by whom she swears in v. 17. She has already committed herself to the family into which she married.[27] These firm and present loyalties explain Ruth's determination to "cling" to Naomi and her indignation at being asked to return to her family of origin. In effect, Ruth says: "Your God *is* my God, and your people *are* my people; *therefore*, where you go I will go, and where you lodge I will lodge. And it makes me angry when you urge me to abandon these commitments!"

1:17. The oath formula used here is found elsewhere in the OT (e.g., 1 Kgs 19:2), but only in 1 Sam 20:13 and in this verse from Ruth does it use Yahweh (יהוה *YHWH*, "LORD") rather than Elohim (אלהים *'ĕlōhîm*, "God"). The oath assumes that the LORD is one who reads the intentions of the heart and punishes lies. If Ruth's husband had been alive, or if she had been living in her father's house, such an oath might not have been considered binding. But according to Num 30:9, "every vow of a widow or of a divorced woman, by which she has bound herself, shall be binding upon her."

1:18. The Hebrew can be understood in at least two ways. Either Naomi stopped urging Ruth to go back (as the NIV assumes), or Naomi stopped speaking to Ruth altogether. The NRSV translation ("she said no more to her") leaves room for either understanding.

---

25. Alastair Hunter, "How Many Gods Had Ruth?" *Scottish Journal of Theology* 34 (1981) 433.

26. Ilona Rashkow, "Ruth: The Discourse of Power and the Power of Discourse," in *A Feminist Companion to Ruth,* ed. Athalya Brenner (Sheffield: Sheffield Academic, 1993) 31.

27. Ibid., 32.

REFLECTIONS

Ruth was neither legally required nor customarily expected to remain with her mother-in-law. Thus her speech in vv. 16-17 must be understood as an act of *ḥesed,* showing love and loyalty over and beyond what is considered normal or expected. Ruth's actions seem to reflect her name, an apparent pun recalling the sounds of the words for "woman friend" (רעות *rĕ'ût,* as in Exod 11:2) and "satiation" or "full-to-overflowing" (רויה *rĕwāyâ,* as in Ps 23:5). Naomi takes a commonsense approach to the future as she tries to reason with Ruth. She sees no way that Ruth could benefit personally from continued association with her. Reason alone could not justify Ruth's decision to "cling" to her mother-in-law. Her words and actions are governed by loyalty and love, rather than by logic.

In Jewish tradition, the interchange between Naomi and Ruth is used as a pattern for testing the sincerity of converts to Judaism. Noting that Naomi says "go back" (שבנה *šōbnâ*) three times (v. 8, 11, 12) to both Orpah and Ruth, the rabbis concluded that "a would-be proselyte should be repulsed three times." And, as Naomi tried to convince Ruth that accompanying her would have its disadvantages, the rabbis concluded that the would-be convert must be told about the possible hardships involved in becoming a Jew.[28] Naomi says "go back" once more to Ruth alone (v. 15), but after Ruth's firm response, "she stopped urging her," leading the rabbis to think that "a proselyte is not to be overburdened or cross-examined too closely."[29]

How do we read Naomi's character? The narrative does not assign an emotion or an attitude to the statement in v. 18 that says, literally, "When she realized she was determined to go with her she ceased speaking to her." The narrator does not tell us how to interpret Naomi's silence. Is Naomi overwhelmed with gratitude and thus silenced, or does she refuse to speak as a sign of anger?

Some readers suggest that Naomi may have preferred to go back home without the burden of a Moabite daughter-in-law. After all, Naomi's people had despised the Moabites for generations before and after the time in which this story is set. If we assume that she shared the "conventional prejudices" of her society against Moabites, then "Naomi's silence at Ruth's unshakable commitment to accompany her emerges as resentment, irritation, frustration, unease."[30] This reading of Naomi's reaction to Ruth's clinging is supported by the way she appears to ignore Ruth in the next scene, when they arrive back in Bethlehem (vv. 19-21). At the very least we might say that Naomi did not want to go home to Bethlehem accompanied by a Moabite reminder of all she had lost.

However, those who prefer to interpret Naomi's silence as appreciation or gratitude argue that "Naomi is the only one who could have told the Bethlehemites about Ruth's kindness, later mentioned by Boaz (2:11)."[31] Or they claim that "it could only have been because of Naomi's conduct that both her daughters-in-law cleaved to her, were prepared to surrender their past" on her behalf.[32]

28. *Ruth Rab.* II 16; *Yebam,* 47a; *Rashi* i 16. See D. R. G. Beattie, *Jewish Exegesis of the Book of Ruth,* JSOTSup 2 (1977) 104, 205-6.

29. *Rashi* i 18; Beattie, *Jewish Exegesis of the Book of Ruth,* 104.

30. Danna Nolan Fewell and David M. Gunn, " 'A Son Is Born to Naomi!': Literary Allusions and Interpretation in the Book of Ruth," *JSOT* 40 (1988) 104.

31. Vincent L. Tollers, "Narrative Control in the Book of Ruth," in *Mappings of the Biblical Terrain: The Bible as Text,* ed. Vincent L. Tollers and John Maier (Lewisburg: Bucknell University Press, 1989) 254.

32. Frieda Clark Hyman, "Ruth—A Pure Dove of Israel," *Judaism* 38 (1989) 61.

Ruth 1:19-22, Turning Bitter

<table>
<tr>
<td valign="top">

NIV

¹⁹So the two women went on until they came to Bethlehem. When they arrived in Bethlehem, the whole town was stirred because of them, and the women exclaimed, "Can this be Naomi?"

²⁰"Don't call me Naomi,ᵃ " she told them. "Call me Mara,ᵇ because the Almightyᶜ has made my life very bitter. ²¹I went away full, but the LORD has brought me back empty. Why call me Naomi? The LORD has afflictedᵈ me; the Almighty has brought misfortune upon me."

²²So Naomi returned from Moab accompanied by Ruth the Moabitess, her daughter-in-law, arriving in Bethlehem as the barley harvest was beginning.

ᵃ *20 Naomi* means *pleasant*; also in verse 21.   ᵇ*20 Mara* means *bitter.*   ᶜ*20* Hebrew *Shaddai*; also in verse 21   ᵈ*21* Or *has testified against*

</td>
<td valign="top">

NRSV

19So the two of them went on until they came to Bethlehem. When they came to Bethlehem, the whole town was stirred because of them; and the women said, "Is this Naomi?" ²⁰She said to them,

"Call me no longer Naomi,ᵃ
    call me Mara,ᵇ
      for the Almightyᶜ has dealt bitterly with
      me.
²¹ I went away full,
    but the LORD has brought me back empty;
why call me Naomi
    when the LORD has dealt harshly withᵈ
    me,
    and the Almightyᶜ has brought calamity
      upon me?"

22So Naomi returned together with Ruth the Moabite, her daughter-in-law, who came back with her from the country of Moab. They came to Bethlehem at the beginning of the barley harvest.

ᵃ That is *Pleasant*   ᵇ That is *Bitter*   ᶜ Traditional rendering of Heb *Shaddai*   ᵈ Or *has testified against*

</td>
</tr>
</table>

COMMENTARY

1:19. The "whole town" was stirred, but only the women speak to Naomi. Their communal question may simply express surprise at her sudden appearance, after an absence of more than ten years, or it may imply that Naomi's appearance has changed considerably during her absence.

1:20-21. Naomi's circumstances have certainly turned for the worse, as she makes clear with a bitter pun based on the root meanings of two Hebrew names. Naomi says that her given name, which sounds like the Hebrew words for "pleasant" (נעם *nōʿam*) or "sweet" (נעים *nāʿîm*), does not fit her current circumstances. It would be more accurate now for her friends to call her Mara (which sounds like מרה [*mārâ*], the feminine form of the Hebrew word for "bitter").

Two sets of opposites are rhymed (in antithetical parallelism) in order to explain Naomi's bit-

tersweet pun. In meaning, bitter is as far from sweet as empty is from full. "Sweet" may have been an appropriate name for Naomi when she was "full." But "bitter" better fits her "empty" state. The polarity between *full* and *empty* will come up again in 3:17, when Ruth brings an apron full of grain back from the threshing floor and tells Naomi that Boaz had told her not to go back to Naomi "empty."

Once again (in v. 20 as in v. 13) Naomi's bitterness is connected with her assumption that the LORD's hand has been turned against her. Early rabbis saw three possible ways of reading the consonants of the word מרה (*mrh*), translated "dealt harshly with me" (NRSV) or "has afflicted me" (NIV). The word might mean "to testify," "to afflict," or "to be concerned with." Early Greek and Latin translations opted for the meaning "afflict." The Masoretic Hebrew text chose the form meaning "testify against."[33] If Naomi is using the legal term "testified against me" (as in 1 Sam 12:3; 2 Sam 1:16), then her statement would seem to imply that she feels she has done something wrong and is being punished by God. The reader's sense that Naomi feels guilty is strengthened if a declarative sense of the verb is kept in v. 9 (the LORD will deal kindly with you, as you have dealt kindly with the dead and with me).

Naomi uses two different names for God in vv. 20-21. The poetic parallelism equates *Shaddai* (translated "Almighty" in most English versions) with *Yahweh* (traditionally translated LORD). This is not a particularly new idea: Exodus 6:2 also implies that the LORD (Yahweh) was known to the patriarchs as El Shaddai (traditionally translated "God Almighty" or "Almighty God"). But Naomi's use of "Shaddai" in this context of fertility (fullness) reversed to barrenness (emptiness) is particularly striking.

As mentioned in the Commentary on 1:2, the word "Shaddai" (שׁדי *šadday*) is similar in sound and identical in spelling (in the consonantal text) to the word שׁדי (*šĕdê*), which is used in Ruth for the "country of" or the "fields of" Moab. At the very least, a Hebrew-speaking audience must have noticed the echoing of sounds between the use of "Shaddai" in vv. 20-21 and *šĕdê* in v. 22. The narrator has already demonstrated a penchant for wordplay. Thus we should seriously consider the possibility that this phonological echo was a deliberate attempt to call attention to the ironic possibilities inherent in the similar sounds of Hebrew words.

The original meaning or actual derivation of the divine name "Shaddai" is open to debate. Based on similarities between *shaddai* and other words in Hebrew, as well as in related Semitic languages, suggestions have been made ranging from "mountain" to "fields," from "breasts" to "demons" or "destroyers." Greek and Latin translators decided that "Shaddai" must refer to "the omnipotent one," and English versions followed suit with the traditional rendering "Almighty."[34]

Whatever the origins of the name may be, there is no doubt that Shaddai sounds very much like the Hebrew words שׂדה (*śādeh*, "field"/"fertile country"), שׁדי (*šĕdê*, "breasts of"), and שׁד (*šōd*, "destruction"). Hebrew storytellers have never been known to limit their puns to linguistically derived etymologies. The narrator in Ruth may have been aware of nothing more than the polar possibilities of meaning inherent in the sound of the traditional name "Shaddai." But such an awareness on the part of the speaker and the audience would give an ironic twist to Naomi's complaint. Both her former fullness and her present emptiness originate with the God whose name reminds people of both fertility and destruction. The narrator may also have expected listeners to connect Naomi's God language with her experiences in the "fields" (fertile country) of Moab. A few texts suggest that the name "Shaddai" may once have had Moabite connections.[35] In the third and fourth oracles of Balaam (the prophet who was called by the king of Moab to curse the Israelites as they camped in Moabite territory), Balaam describes himself as one who "sees the vision of Shaddai" (Num 24:4, 16).

1:22. The final verse of the first chapter looks both backward and forward. It summarizes the essential happenings of the first chapter and sets the stage for the action in the second chapter, which takes place in the period between "the beginning of the barley harvest" and "the end of the barley and the wheat harvests" (2:23).

The thematic term "turn"/"return" is used twice in the final verse of the first chapter. The first usage in v. 22 (ותשׁב *wattāšob*) is identical in form to the very first usage in the book (1:6). This repetition creates an envelope structure around the first part of Naomi's story. The second usage in this verse takes the form השׁבה (*haššābâ*, "the returnee"), which will appear again in 4:3.

In the homecoming scene (vv. 19-21), Naomi seemed to be so involved in her own bitterness that she ignored the presence of Ruth. But now the narrator reminds us that Ruth is still very much in the picture. She is called by name and described according to both her family of origin (Moabitess) and her family of choice (daughter-in-law).

33. Edward F. Campbell, Jr., *Ruth,* AB 7 (Garden City, N.Y.: Doubleday, 1975) 77.

34. For an excellent overview of scholarly suggestions and arguments, see David Biale, "The God with Breasts: El Shaddai in the Bible," *History of Religions* 21 (1982) 240-56.

35. Jo Ann Hackett, *The Balaam Text from Deir 'Alla,* HSM 31 (Chico, Calif.: Scholars Press, 1984) 85-89.

This is the first time in the story that Ruth is called "the Moabite/Moabitess." This designation may be used by the narrator to reflect the way the people of Bethlehem think of Ruth—as an outsider. In the coming chapters there will be a repeated emphasis on Ruth's ethnic background, even when it does not seem natural or needed in the narrative (note 2:2, 6, 21; 4:5, 10). The fact that the story belabors this aspect of Ruth's identity may indicate something of the author's intentions.[36]

36. André LaCocque, "Ruth," in *The Feminine Unconventional: Four Subversive Figures in Israel's Tradition,* OBT (Minneapolis: Fortress, 1990) 85.

REFLECTIONS

No matter how central her role in the story may be, Naomi comes across in this first chapter as a rather unattractive character. She knows that her name means "sweet" or "sweetness," but she does not feel sweet. Life has not been sweet for Naomi. Furthermore, Naomi does not act in the way we expect the faithful to act. She blames the LORD for the emptiness she now feels. She neither asks nor expects the LORD to come to her aid as God had come "to the aid of his people by providing food for them."[37] In modern times we might say that Naomi is in one of the stages of the grieving process. Like many of us who have suffered losses that leave us feeling empty, Naomi fears that her loss of husband and sons is the result of divine judgment. She may even feel that she is somehow to blame for their deaths.

Also like others who are caught up in the throes of their own grief, Naomi seems to lack gratitude for the support she has received from Ruth. When the two travelers arrive in Bethlehem, Naomi complains that she went away full—with a husband, two sons, and a promising future—and that she is coming back empty, because of the LORD. She speaks to the women of the town as if Ruth were neither present nor important to her. In this stage of her grief, Naomi's emptiness has not been affected by Ruth's pledge of undying loyalty.

From the beginning of the story it has been clear that Naomi is the character who is most in need of redemption. Her situation cries out for a reversal or a recovery. If members of a modern audience feel no need to be redeemed, they may be reluctant to identify themselves and their own situations with Naomi's situation. Thus, if you are inclined to preach or to teach Ruth as a parable of God's grace, you will need to lead your listeners to recognize that they, like Naomi, have pockets of emptiness in their lives that cannot be filled through their own efforts.

The narrative we call the story of Ruth will eventually tell us how Naomi is persuaded to let go of her bitterness, how her emptiness is filled with new life, how her redemption becomes the first step in the redemption of the people of God. Nevertheless, the memory of Naomi is a bittersweet one. We know more about the bitter side of Naomi than of the sweet. Might we not say the same about most of the people of God? Are not most of us really more like Naomi than we are like Ruth? At best most of us might say we have lived bittersweet lives of faith. Most of us can probably say that (like Naomi) we have more often been the recipients than the givers of loving kindness/faithfulness. Yet it can be said

> that this bitter, grieving Naomi has succeeded in achieving what many missionaries hope for: someone has chosen to follow her God, and she (Naomi) has become an instrument for this choice not by putting on a "happy face" but by being her true self. For Ruth, Naomi's truthful expression of her grief and bitterness does not obscure what Ruth has seen as a member of her family for the last ten years nor what she knows about Naomi's faith.[38]

Thus it seems that Naomi's story would serve as an appropriate basis for a sermon on All Saints Day. Just as Memorial Day is a secular holiday meant to honor those who have died

37. D. F. Rauber, "Literary Values in the Bible: The Book of Ruth," *JBL* 89 (1970) 27-37.
38. Nancy V. Lee, "Choices in the Book of Ruth," *The Japan Christian Quarterly* 54 (1988) 236.

in the country's service and to remember those we continue to love, even though they are no longer a physical part of our lives, so also All Saints Day is a time set aside in the church year for the remembrance of those who have died in the faith. This "memorial day" of the church is celebrated either on the first day of November (the day after Halloween) or on the first Sunday in November.

In older English versions of the Bible, we find references to the "saints" in the Old Testament as well as in the New Testament. One of the words that gets translated as "saints" in the Old Testament is a form of the Hebrew word for lovingkindness or faithfulness above and beyond the ordinary. According to that definition, we might easily say that Ruth should be included among the "saints" whom we remember on All Saints Day. It is easy to see how Ruth's actions toward Naomi might be described as faithfulness above and beyond the call of duty. Ruth probably comes as close to conforming to our traditional expectations of what a saint is like as any Old Testament character ever does. However, in the Christian tradition the people who are called saints have not all demonstrated an extraordinary degree of faithfulness, patience, or piety. In fact, the apostle Paul uses the term "saints" to refer to all who are a part of the body of Christ. Under this definition, all Christians, past, present, and future, can be considered a part of the communion of saints. And in Matt 27:52 the saints are even said to include the pre-Christian faithful.

It is easy to see how we might include Ruth among the communion of saints. Ruth plays an important, even an essential role in the carrying out of God's will in the world. Ruth is the change-agent whose loving faithfulness reflects God's faithfulness to Naomi. But in the last analysis, we need to acknowledge that this festival of All Saints is not about the faithfulness of the saints at all. It is, rather, a celebration of the faithfulness of God.[39] Because Naomi does not come across as a model of sainthood or faithfulness as we usually understand it, because Naomi does not act as we expect the faithful to act, it is easier for us to see that her story is about the faithfulness of God, and not about the faithfulness of humankind. Thus there is a message of good news for those who can see themselves mirrored in the character of Naomi: God can use us, as weak and as faulty as we may be, just as God used Naomi, even in the midst of her bitterness and grief, to accomplish some small part in the work of God in the world. Like Naomi, we can be called "saints," not because we have been extraordinarily faithful to God but because God has been extraordinarily faithful to us.

39. Marion Soards, Thomas Dozeman, and Kendall McCabe, *Preaching the Common Lectionary Year B: After Pentecost 2* (Nashville: Abingdon, 1993) 132-33.

RUTH 2:1-23

KNOWN AND UNKNOWN

OVERVIEW

The center section of Ruth is organized around the polarities of knowing and not knowing, leaving and cleaving. Various forms of ידע (*yāda'*, "to know") are used in chaps. 2–3, along with other words having similar meanings (such as "recognize," "eyes"/"sight," etc.). Boaz is "known" as a member of Elimelech's clan. Ruth is a foreigner (one who is unknown) who comes to a people that she "did not know before" (2:11 NRSV). Boaz, who is "known" to Naomi, "notices" the one who is unknown (2:10) and acknowledges her right to his protection. In keeping with the narrator's interest in knowing and not knowing, we find a pattern of repetition of the word for "eyes" (עינים *ênayim*) in this section of the book. Ruth uses the phrase "to find favor in the eyes of" in 2:2 (to Naomi, about her intentions), in 2:10 (to Boaz), and again in 2:13, at the end of her conversation with Boaz. Boaz also tells Ruth to keep her "eyes" on the field that is being reaped (2:9).

Chapter 3 will exploit the sexual as well as the cognitive connotations of "knowing," but chap. 2 merely hints at potential relationships that might develop between members of the clan and the stranger in their midst by exploring the thematic contrast between the polarities of leaving and cleaving (forsaking and clinging), which were first introduced in the preceding chapter. In chap. 1 Ruth was said to "cling"/"cleave"/"stay close" (דבק *dābaq*) to her mother-in-law, whom she stubbornly refused to "leave"/"forsake"/"abandon" (עזב '*āzab*). In this chapter, Boaz tells Ruth to "cling"/"cleave"/"stay close" (*dābaq*) to his workers (v. 8) and praises her for having "abandoned" or "left" ('*āzab*) her father, her mother, and her native land in order to accompany Naomi back to Bethlehem (2:11). Boaz uses the word '*āzab* again when he orders his workers to "leave" some extra stalks of grain for Ruth to glean (2:16); Naomi uses '*āzab* in 2:20, as she praises the one "whose kindness has not *forsaken* the living or the dead;" and both Ruth and Naomi use *dābaq* ("stay close") again in 2:21, 23.

Chapter 2 should raise questions in the audience's mind with regard to insider/outsider dynamics in Israel as well as in our own communities. Who is "family," and who is not? Who is "foreign," and who is not? How does an outsider become an insider? What are the rights, the privileges, and the obligations shared by those who belong to the "insider" group?

Once again, an interpretive ambiguity arises with regard to the discernment of Boaz's character. How do we explain his motives? Why does Boaz do and say what he does? Does his piety go any deeper than the words he speaks in 2:4, 12? Does this portrayal of Boaz picture him as a totally admirable man or not? Is he magnanimous in his treatment of Ruth, or does Ruth have to nudge him into a sense of his responsibilities?

RUTH 2:1-16, PORTRAIT OF A "WORTHY" MAN

Ruth 2:1-7, "Happening" to Find the Right Field

NIV

2 Now Naomi had a relative on her husband's side, from the clan of Elimelech, a man of standing, whose name was Boaz.

²And Ruth the Moabitess said to Naomi, "Let me go to the fields and pick up the leftover grain behind anyone in whose eyes I find favor."

Naomi said to her, "Go ahead, my daughter." ³So she went out and began to glean in the fields behind the harvesters. As it turned out, she found herself working in a field belonging to Boaz, who was from the clan of Elimelech.

⁴Just then Boaz arrived from Bethlehem and greeted the harvesters, "The LORD be with you!"

"The LORD bless you!" they called back.

⁵Boaz asked the foreman of his harvesters, "Whose young woman is that?"

⁶The foreman replied, "She is the Moabitess who came back from Moab with Naomi. ⁷She said, 'Please let me glean and gather among the sheaves behind the harvesters.' She went into the field and has worked steadily from morning till now, except for a short rest in the shelter."

NRSV

2 Now Naomi had a kinsman on her husband's side, a prominent rich man, of the family of Elimelech, whose name was Boaz. ²And Ruth the Moabite said to Naomi, "Let me go to the field and glean among the ears of grain, behind someone in whose sight I may find favor." She said to her, "Go, my daughter." ³So she went. She came and gleaned in the field behind the reapers. As it happened, she came to the part of the field belonging to Boaz, who was of the family of Elimelech. ⁴Just then Boaz came from Bethlehem. He said to the reapers, "The LORD be with you." They answered, "The LORD bless you." ⁵Then Boaz said to his servant who was in charge of the reapers, "To whom does this young woman belong?" ⁶The servant who was in charge of the reapers answered, "She is the Moabite who came back with Naomi from the country of Moab. ⁷She said, 'Please, let me glean and gather among the sheaves behind the reapers.' So she came, and she has been on her feet from early this morning until now, without resting even for a moment."[a]

[a] Compare Gk Vg: Meaning of Heb uncertain

COMMENTARY

2:1. The narrator's introduction of Boaz begins (v. 1) and ends (v. 3) with a reference to the family/clan of Elimelech. He and Boaz are said to be members of the same sub-tribal grouping, but the specific relationship between them is left vague. The narrator says that Boaz is Elimelech's מידע (*měyuddā*ʿ), spelled in a way that usually means "acquaintance," "close friend" or "companion" (as in Ps 55:14). Scribal notations in the Masoretic text suggest that it should be read as מדע (*mōdāʿ*), which seems to mean "kinsman" or "relative" in its only other biblical occurrence (in Prov 7:4). Both *měyuddāʿ* and *mōdāʿ* are derivatives of the root meaning "to know."

Since Boaz is from the same clan as Elimelech,

the two men clearly must be related in some way. However, given the ways in which the narrator plays with the various permutations of the root "to know" in this center section of the book, it seems more than likely that the original spelling (connoting an acquaintance rather than a close relative) represented the narrator's deliberate intentions. Boaz may be a relative, but the narrator does not want to raise our hopes prematurely concerning his degree of closeness to Elimelech. Rather, the storyteller allows the tension in the story to build. It is not at all clear at first just how Boaz's relationship to Elimelech is going to be of help to Naomi. Only after Ruth reports on her successful encounter with Boaz does Naomi tell us he is a "near one" (קרוב *qārôb*) and a גאל (*gōʾēl*), a relationship that involves certain obligations. (See the discussion of *gōʾēl* in the Commentary on 2:20.)

Whether we read the word as *mĕyuddāʿ* or as *mōdāʿ*, it is very likely that the relational term used in v. 1 is neutral with regard to Boaz's family obligations. The narrator introduces Boaz without implying that he has any legal or moral obligation to support Naomi.[40] In contrast, the terms that will be used in v. 20 suggest that Boaz either can or should do something to alleviate the widow's "emptiness."

In v. 1, this man Boaz (who is related in some way to Naomi's husband) is also called a גבור חיל (*gibbôr ḥayil*). Both *gibbôr* and *ḥayil* have root meanings associated with the concepts of strength and power. The phrase is used as a statement of approbation in a variety of situations and seems to have different connotations, depending on the context in which it is used. In Josh 1:14; 6:2; 8:3; and Judg 11:1, *gibbôr ḥayil* clearly refers to "warriors," to "soldiers" (NRSV), and to "fighting men" (NIV). But translators have decided that in 1 Sam 9:1 its usage best describes Kish as "a man of wealth" (NRSV) or "a man of standing" (NIV); that David was "a man of valor" (NRSV) or "a brave man" (NIV) in 1 Sam 16:18; that Jeroboam was "very able" (NRSV) or "a man of standing" (NIV) in 1 Kgs 11:28; and that Naaman was "a valiant soldier" (NIV) or "a mighty warrior" (NRSV) in 2 Kgs 5:1. In a few contexts, *ḥayil* seems to mean "procreative power" or "the ability to produce offspring" (as in Job 21:7; Joel 2:22); thus it might be translated as "virility."[41]

Most interpreters think the context in Ruth implies that Boaz is "a man of substance"[42] or "a property holder."[43] The most creatively appropriate suggestion comes from Danna Nolan Fewell and David M. Gunn, who think *gibbôr ḥayil* should be translated "a pillar of society."[44] Fewell and Gunn explain that this

English idiom . . . plays well on both the notion of strength (*ḥayil*) and the fact that "Boaz" is also the name of one of the pillars of the temple (1 Kgs 7.15-22, 41-42). Furthermore, we understand the phrase to suggest that Boaz is an important man in the community, a man of reputation, a man of worth, a man of social and economic standing.[45]

The NIV combines both words into a single meaning that emphasizes Boaz's reputation in the community ("a man of standing"), while the NRSV says that Boaz is both "prominent" (*gibbôr*) and "rich" (*ḥayil*). However, when Boaz uses *ḥayil* to describe Ruth (3:11), the NRSV translates the word as "worthy." Consistency as well as context would be better served by using "worthy" to describe both Boaz and Ruth (in 2:1 and 3:11). In both contexts, *ḥayil* refers to the way Boaz and Ruth are perceived in the community. The use of *ḥayil* in both verses seems to suggest that they are a well-matched pair.

2:2. The narrator once again calls Ruth "the Moabite/Moabitess," even though the designation seems superfluous and redundant in the context. The narrator clearly wants us to keep Ruth's ethnic identity in mind. However, referring to Moab here also creates a phonological echo between this verse and 1:22. Ruth uses שדה (*śādeh*) to mean "field." Thus the same two words (*śādeh* and Moab) are used in this verse as were used in 1:22 (where they meant the "country of Moab"). Ruth says she wants to "glean," which the NIV accurately translates as "pick up the leftover grain." The laws in Lev 19:9-10 and 23:22 forbade Israelite landowners to strip their fields completely clean as they harvested their crops. Harvesters were supposed to leave both the standing grain at the edges of every field and the grains that were accidentally missed during the regular harvesting process for the use of the "poor" and the "resident alien," who had no land of their own to cultivate. Deuteronomy 24:19 states a slightly different version of the law: "When you reap your harvest in your field and forget a sheaf in the field, you shall not go back to get it; it shall be left for the alien, the orphan, and the widow" (NRSV).

2:3. "As it happened" (NRSV) or "as it turned out" (NIV) is literally "her happening happened." This phrase appears to mean "as luck would have it" or "by chance she happened onto." When the

40. Cf. Campbell, *Ruth,* 88-90, who notes the use of the verb ידע *ydʿ* in treaty-covenant terminology and translates מידע (*mĕyuddāʿ*) as "covenant-brother."

41. C. J. Labuschagne, "The Crux in Ruth 4:11," *ZAW* 79 (1967) 365.

42. Campbell, *Ruth,* 90.

43. Jack M. Sasson, *Ruth: A New Translation with a Philological Commentary and a Formalist-Folklorist Interpretation* (Baltimore: Johns Hopkins University Press, 1979) 39.

44. Danna Nolan Fewell and David M. Gunn, "Boaz, Pillar of Society: Measures of Worth in the Book of Ruth," *JSOT* 45 (1989) 45-59.

45. Ibid., 54.

word is used elsewhere in the Hebrew Bible (e.g., Gen 24:12; 27:20), it is God who is said to cause something to happen. But here the narrator carefully avoids any specific reference to God's agency.

2:4. The first interchange between Boaz and his workers may reflect a standardized greeting formula. We have heard Boaz described in the third person as a "pillar" of the community. Now we are allowed to hear for ourselves the manner in which such a "pillar" speaks. Both Boaz and Naomi seem to use a slightly archaic form of Hebrew, indicating (perhaps) that they belong to an older generation.

2:5-7. Boaz addresses "the servant who was in charge of the reapers" (NRSV), called "the foreman of the reapers" in the NIV. In the NRSV, the masculine form of the word נער (na'ar) is translated "servant" in vv. 5-6, but the feminine form of the same word (נערה na'ărâ) is translated "young woman" in v. 5. The basic sense of both terms has to do with youth rather than with servanthood. But both words are used in a secondary sense to connote a person with subservient status. Thus when Boaz asks the na'ar who is in charge of the reapers, "To whom does this na'ărâ belong?" he might mean "To whom does this 'servant woman' belong?" (in the sense of ownership) or "To which clan or family does this 'young woman' belong?"

In v. 6 the young man/servant in charge of the harvesters clarifies Ruth's status by describing her first of all as "the Moabite woman" and then as the one "who came back with Naomi from the country of Moab." In v. 7 he tells Boaz that Ruth asked both to "glean" and to "gather" (אסף 'āsap) "among the sheaves."

The meaning of the last part of the foreman's speech is unclear in Hebrew. All translations emend the text in some way in an attempt to make sense of what the foreman says about Ruth. With emendations, the text can be taken to mean either that Ruth has been working in the field since morning or that she has been standing there waiting for Boaz to arrive.[46] Many critics think that Ruth (either out of ignorance or out of boldness) has asked the foreman for permission to do something out of the ordinary.[47] The word "gather" (used in addition to "glean") may imply a departure from the usual way in which gleaning was done, or Ruth's request to glean "among the sheaves" may go beyond the usual practice.[48] It is not even clear whether the custom of the land guaranteed Ruth the right to glean. The laws in Lev 19:9-10; 23:22; and Deut 24:19 give gleaning rights to the "sojourner" or to the resident alien (using the Hebrew word גר gēr). But in v. 10 Ruth calls herself a נכריה (nokriyyâ, a female foreigner), which may mean that she is not entitled to glean and needs to get permission first.[49]

The NIV follows those emendations that picture Ruth as already working in the field before the arrival of Boaz. The NRSV preserves some of the ambiguity of the Hebrew text by using the phrase "on her feet," which could imply either that she was standing and waiting or that she was working. (See Reflections at 2:8-16 and 2:17-23.)

46. Campbell, *Ruth,* 94-96; Sasson, *Ruth,* 47; Robert L. Hubbard, *The Book of Ruth,* NICOT (Grand Rapids: Eerdmans, 1988) 149, 152.
47. See Frederic Bush, *Ruth/Esther,* WBC 9 (Dallas: Word, 1996) 114.
48. Hubbard, *The Book of Ruth,* 148, 176.
49. Deut 15:3 and 23:20 seem to indicate that Israel's laws did not protect the "foreigner" (m. s. נכרי nokrî) as they protected the "sojourner" (גר gēr) from exploitation.

Ruth 2:8-16, Boaz "Notices" Ruth

NIV

8So Boaz said to Ruth, "My daughter, listen to me. Don't go and glean in another field and don't go away from here. Stay here with my servant girls. 9Watch the field where the men are harvesting, and follow along after the girls. I have told the men not to touch you. And whenever you are thirsty, go and get a drink from the water jars the men have filled."

NRSV

8Then Boaz said to Ruth, "Now listen, my daughter, do not go to glean in another field or leave this one, but keep close to my young women. 9Keep your eyes on the field that is being reaped, and follow behind them. I have ordered the young men not to bother you. If you get thirsty, go to the vessels and drink from what the young men have drawn." 10Then she fell pros-

NIV

[10]At this, she bowed down with her face to the ground. She exclaimed, "Why have I found such favor in your eyes that you notice me—a foreigner?"

[11]Boaz replied, "I've been told all about what you have done for your mother-in-law since the death of your husband—how you left your father and mother and your homeland and came to live with a people you did not know before. [12]May the LORD repay you for what you have done. May you be richly rewarded by the LORD, the God of Israel, under whose wings you have come to take refuge."

[13]"May I continue to find favor in your eyes, my lord," she said. "You have given me comfort and have spoken kindly to your servant—though I do not have the standing of one of your servant girls."

[14]At mealtime Boaz said to her, "Come over here. Have some bread and dip it in the wine vinegar."

When she sat down with the harvesters, he offered her some roasted grain. She ate all she wanted and had some left over. [15]As she got up to glean, Boaz gave orders to his men, "Even if she gathers among the sheaves, don't embarrass her. [16]Rather, pull out some stalks for her from the bundles and leave them for her to pick up, and don't rebuke her."

NRSV

trate, with her face to the ground, and said to him, "Why have I found favor in your sight, that you should take notice of me, when I am a foreigner?" [11]But Boaz answered her, "All that you have done for your mother-in-law since the death of your husband has been fully told me, and how you left your father and mother and your native land and came to a people that you did not know before. [12]May the LORD reward you for your deeds, and may you have a full reward from the LORD, the God of Israel, under whose wings you have come for refuge!" [13]Then she said, "May I continue to find favor in your sight, my lord, for you have comforted me and spoken kindly to your servant, even though I am not one of your servants."

14At mealtime Boaz said to her, "Come here, and eat some of this bread, and dip your morsel in the sour wine." So she sat beside the reapers, and he heaped up for her some parched grain. She ate until she was satisfied, and she had some left over. [15]When she got up to glean, Boaz instructed his young men, "Let her glean even among the standing sheaves, and do not reproach her. [16]You must also pull out some handfuls for her from the bundles, and leave them for her to glean, and do not rebuke her."

COMMENTARY

2:8-11. The way in which one emends v. 7 makes a difference in how one understands Boaz and his actions. If Ruth is standing at the edge of the field when Boaz arrives, it is easy to see why Boaz notices her immediately. If she is already working in the field with a number of others, his noticing her seems more remarkable. If Ruth has been waiting for the landowner's permission to begin working, then vv. 8-9 can be seen to mean little more than the granting of that permission. But if Ruth is thought to have been working in the field already, then what Boaz does in vv. 8-9 appears to be an unsolicited act of kindness, above and beyond the expectations of custom or duty. This latter reading is the traditional interpretation,

bolstered by the observation that Ruth's response to Boaz's first speech seems to indicate that his actions go beyond the strict performance of the laws on gleaning (v. 10).

In v. 8 Boaz addresses Ruth as "my daughter," which could be understood as either a traditional form of address from an older person to a woman who is considerably younger (cf. 1:11-13) or as a form of address that emphasizes the superior status of the speaker. When Boaz tells Ruth to stick close to his "young women" (NRSV) or " servant girls" (NIV), he uses רבק (dābaq), the same word for "cling" or "keep close," which the narrator used in 1:14 to describe the way Ruth "clung" to Naomi.

Ruth's question in v. 10 involves a pun based on two different forms of the same word.[50] The word translated "foreigner" (נכריה *nokriyyâ*) comes from the same root (נכר *nkr*) as the word translated "take notice." In effect, Ruth says, "Why do you 'recognize' me [notice me], when I am 'one who is not recognized' [a foreigner]?" Boaz's answer in v. 11 picks up the two central themes in the chapter. He knows (has been told) that Ruth had to forsake the people and places she knew so well in order to come to live with a people she did not know.

2:12-13. Like Naomi in 1:8-9, Boaz makes a pious wish for Ruth's future, based on her commendable behavior in the past. The word כנף (*kānāp*) is translated in its usual sense of "wing" in v. 12, but in 3:9 the same word will be translated "cloak" (NRSV) or the "corner of a garment" (NIV). Boaz's metaphor implies that the God of Israel is like a mother hen (or some other type of bird) that protects its young by sheltering them under its wing (as in Deut 32:11; Ps 91:4). Since the "wings" represent a place of refuge, the metaphor refers essentially to the LORD's protection.

Boaz apparently assumes that Ruth's future is in the hands of the LORD. Ruth's reply in the first part of v. 13 subtly suggests that the LORD may be waiting for Boaz to act! In modern colloquial terms, we might say that Ruth challenges Boaz to "put his money where his mouth is."

In the last half of v. 13, Ruth says that Boaz has treated her as kindly as he would treat one of his own "servants" (using the word שפחה [*šiphâ*], which is traditionally translated "maid" or "maidservant"), even though she is not in fact one of his servants.

We know very little about the functioning of social hierarchies in Israel. Translators have assumed that the meaning of *šiphâ* varies according to the context in which it is used. In Exod 11:5, the "maidservant" is associated with menial labor and seems to be at the opposite end of the social spectrum from the ruling classes. In some OT texts, the *šiphâ* seems to be a maid who is eligible to bear the children of her mistress' husband (such as Hagar, Bilhah, or Zilpah). In some texts, *šiphâ* is translated "female slave" (as in Gen 12:16; 24:35). However, *šiphâ* is also closely related to the Hebrew word for "clan" or "extended family"

(משפחה *mišpāhâ*). These overtones of kinship connected with servitude might be better communicated in English by translating *šiphâ* as "family servant." It is possible that a family servant was considered a member of his or her owner's clan, and thus could expect better treatment from family members than could the נכריה (*nokriyyâ*), "foreign woman," Ruth knows herself to be. (See the laws in Lev 25:35-46 regarding the treatment of fellow Israelites who have been forced by poverty into positions of servitude.)

When Ruth uses the phrase "speak to the heart of" in v. 13, she is using language that could be construed in one of two ways. The phrase can mean simply to speak kindly (as in Gen 50:21) or to "encourage" someone (as in 2 Sam 19:7). But in several other texts the idiom is used in the context of courtship or persuasion in a sexual sense (as in Gen 34:3; Judg 19:3; Hos 2:14).[51] Ruth (or the narrator) may be hinting that Boaz's speech sounds like "sweettalking."

2:14-16. In the ancient world, traveling away from home, leaving the protection of one's friends and relatives behind, was a risky business. Travelers had to depend on hospitality customs, which changed a stranger into a temporary member of the host's family, in order to survive. When hospitality was offered and accepted, it was generally understood that the protection of the host's clan was extended to the guest. Hospitality codes were a matter of custom rather than law, but several Old Testament narratives give us a glimpse of these customs at work in biblical times. When unknown travelers are invited into people's homes in Genesis 18–19; 24 and Judges 19, the sharing of food is always mentioned. Thus it seems that the sharing of food is a hospitality ritual associated with the offering of protection to the unprotected. When Boaz gives Ruth food and drink, he may be offering her (or acknowledging that she has) a kind of honorary membership in his clan.[52]

In v. 7 the young man in charge of the reapers said that Ruth had asked to glean "among the sheaves." This is what Boaz now tells his men to let her do (v. 15), suggesting that this was not the usual way gleaning was done. Furthermore,

50. Campbell, *Ruth,* 98.

51. Ibid., 100-101.
52. Jack M. Sasson, "Ruth," *The Literary Guide to the Bible,* ed. Robert Alter and Frank Kermode (Cambridge, Mass.: Harvard University Press, 1987) 324-25.

Boaz tells them deliberately to "abandon" (עזב 'āzab) an extra amount of the standing grain for Ruth's benefit.

In v. 9 Boaz said he had told his men not to "touch" Ruth. Now he orders them neither to "humiliate" her (v. 15) nor to "restrain" her from gathering as much as she can (v. 16).

REFLECTIONS

The story of Ruth lives within the sociocultural assumptions of its narrator. The modern interpreter of Ruth needs to recognize (but need not approve of) the world pictured by the narrator. However, if Ruth is to function as a revelatory text in the modern world, modern audiences will need to see how the situations of the characters in the story correspond to modern situations. The preacher or teacher needs to ask, What types of people in our society face the same kinds of problems as Naomi and Ruth faced in the world they inhabited? The narrator assumes that Ruth and Naomi live in a rural, agrarian society in which women have to depend on men in order to survive. This is a world in which women are valued primarily for their ability to produce sons to carry on the patrilineal system;[53] a world in which women without fathers, husbands, or sons are denied access to the legal and financial structures of the community. The narrator (and the original audience) assumes that women like Naomi and Ruth have no socially acceptable means of supporting themselves except begging and gleaning.

Thus, in order to decide who corresponds to Ruth and Naomi in our own society, we have to ask, Who is forced by circumstances beyond their control to glean what they can from the bounty of others? Who in our world has no choice but to live on what is left over after those in control of the basic resources for life have taken everything they want or need? The modern interpreter thus concludes that a "widow" is not merely a woman who has lost her husband but anyone in our society (male or female) who has to rely on the charitable whims of others for food and shelter.

Furthermore, Naomi comes from and Ruth immigrates to a community in which foreigners (particularly foreign women) traditionally were viewed with suspicion, as a potential source of temptation to sin (as in, e.g., 1 Kgs 11:1-8; Prov 5:1-20). Many biblical references indicate that Ruth's ancestry and culture were held in contempt by the people of her new homeland. If Israel had an official "immigration policy" in the time of the judges, undoubtedly Moabites would have been listed as "undesirable elements." Moabites were banned from the assembly of the LORD because of their ancestors' sins. In order to decide who corresponds to a "Moabite" in our society, we need to consider not just those who are strangers in our midst, but those whom we have banned from the fellowship of worshiping Christians.

In modern times, ongoing debates over immigration laws indicate that many people feel burdened by the presence of foreigners in their midst—even if these outsiders profess undying allegiance to us and to our God, as Ruth did to Naomi. The people in our congregations may find it hard to believe that refugees, immigrants, or people requesting political asylum might someday become the instruments of our redemption. But there is no doubt that the biblical narrator pictures Ruth as an immigrant, entering the "promised land" from the same direction and for many of the same reasons as Naomi's ancestors had done in previous generations. Thus interpreters of Ruth will need to lead their audiences to consider some of the characteristics Ruth has in common with "outsiders" who are seeking entrance into our own country or into our communities today. For instance, it might be argued that Ruth came into Israel seeking (and finding) greater economic security than she had in her native land. (Elimelech

---

53. See Esther Fuchs, "The Literary Characterization of Mothers and Sexual Politics in the Hebrew Bible," in *Feminist Perspectives on Biblical Scholarship,* ed. Adela Yarbro Collins (Chico, Calif.: Scholars Press, 1985) 117-36, who argues that the narrator makes Ruth behave in ways that reflect and promote male desires and prerogatives.

and his family had gone to Moab for the same reason.) Impoverished Israelites may have complained that Ruth took work or resources away from the native poor of Bethlehem.

Some readers might be tempted to see Ruth as a model immigrant, one who is acceptable because she is perfectly assimilated into the society and religion she has adopted as her own. But this "melting pot" perspective has a shadow side. Some groups of immigrants have discovered that promises of assimilation into the dominant culture raise false hopes. United Methodist Bishop Roy Sano has said, "If there is any biblical account that describes the story behind Asian Americans' dreams in America, it appears in the book of Ruth. . . . The greater part of our people came with a determination to live the same story in its secular or religious versions. However, an analysis of our actual situation suggests that another story would be more honest and humanizing."[54]

In fact, many immigrants' experiences have not matched the "dream" that an assimilated Ruth represents. We might ask which is flawed—the dream or the reality? Perhaps the "parable" of Ruth should be addressed only to the dominant majority in each community of faith. The dominant (insider) group needs constantly to be reminded that they can neither survive nor accomplish the mission to which they are called without the active assistance of "foreigners" in their midst.

54. Roy Sano, "Ethnic Liberation Theology: Neo-Orthodoxy Reshaped or Replaced?" *Christianity and Crisis* 11:10 (1975) 258-59.

RUTH 2:17-23, "KINDNESS" HAS NOT FORSAKEN THE LIVING OR THE DEAD

NIV

[17]So Ruth gleaned in the field until evening. Then she threshed the barley she had gathered, and it amounted to about an ephah.[a] [18]She carried it back to town, and her mother-in-law saw how much she had gathered. Ruth also brought out and gave her what she had left over after she had eaten enough.

[19]Her mother-in-law asked her, "Where did you glean today? Where did you work? Blessed be the man who took notice of you!"

Then Ruth told her mother-in-law about the one at whose place she had been working. "The name of the man I worked with today is Boaz," she said.

[20]"The LORD bless him!" Naomi said to her daughter-in-law. "He has not stopped showing his kindness to the living and the dead." She added, "That man is our close relative; he is one of our kinsman-redeemers."

[21]Then Ruth the Moabitess said, "He even said to me, 'Stay with my workers until they finish harvesting all my grain.'"

a17 That is, probably about 3/5 bushel (about 22 liters)

NRSV

17So she gleaned in the field until evening. Then she beat out what she had gleaned, and it was about an ephah of barley. [18]She picked it up and came into the town, and her mother-in-law saw how much she had gleaned. Then she took out and gave her what was left over after she herself had been satisfied. [19]Her mother-in-law said to her, "Where did you glean today? And where have you worked? Blessed be the man who took notice of you." So she told her mother-in-law with whom she had worked, and said, "The name of the man with whom I worked today is Boaz." [20]Then Naomi said to her daughter-in-law, "Blessed be he by the LORD, whose kindness has not forsaken the living or the dead!" Naomi also said to her, "The man is a relative of ours, one of our nearest kin."[a] [21]Then Ruth the Moabite said, "He even said to me, 'Stay close by my servants, until they have finished all my harvest.'" [22]Naomi said to Ruth, her daughter-in-law, "It is better, my daughter, that you go out with his young women, otherwise you might be bothered

a Or one with the right to redeem

²²Naomi said to Ruth her daughter-in-law, "It will be good for you, my daughter, to go with his girls, because in someone else's field you might be harmed."

²³So Ruth stayed close to the servant girls of Boaz to glean until the barley and wheat harvests were finished. And she lived with her mother-in-law.

in another field." ²³So she stayed close to the young women of Boaz, gleaning until the end of the barley and wheat harvests; and she lived with her mother-in-law.

COMMENTARY

2:17-20. Thanks to Boaz's largess, Ruth is able to bring a large amount of barley (about half a bushel) home to Naomi, plus whatever she has left over from the "parched grain" Boaz had given her to eat (v. 14). When Naomi finds out that it is Boaz who has taken such "notice" of Ruth (using the same word used in v. 10), she calls down a blessing upon him. The antecedent of the expression "whose kindness has not forsaken the living or the dead" (v. 20) is unclear. Naomi's words may mean that Boaz's recognition of Ruth proves that *Boaz* has not "forsaken" either them or their deceased husbands. Or the words may mean that Boaz's actions indicate that the LORD has not "forsaken" them. The NIV takes the decision away from the reader by inserting the word "LORD" as the subject and making the relative clause into a declarative sentence. The NIV clearly wants the reader to conclude that Naomi sees the LORD's hand at work in Boaz's actions.

Now, for the first time, Naomi tells Ruth that Boaz is a "close relative" (קרוב *qārôb*, from the root meaning "near"). In fact, Naomi says, he is a גאל (*gōʾēl*), "one of our nearest kin" (NRSV) or "one of our kinsman-redeemers" (NIV). The word *gōʾēl* comes from the root גאל (*gāʾal*, "to redeem" or "to recover"). In Israelite law codes, a *gōʾēl* is a designated male family member (brother, uncle, or cousin) who is expected to recover (rescue, ransom, buy back, redeem) that which has been (or is in danger of being) removed from family control by poverty, war, death, etc. The literature of ancient Israel refers to customs and duties related to the recovery (or redemption) of people (Lev 25:47-55), of property (Lev 25:25-34; Jer 32:6-15), and of prestige (through the

taking of revenge, Num 35:19-27; 2 Sam 14:4-11). But the circumstances in Ruth (at least as far as they have been explained by the narrator) do not seem to conform to any of the legal codes preserved in Scripture. At this point in the story, it is not at all clear to the modern reader what Boaz might be expected to "redeem."

In 1:12-13 it seemed that Naomi had given up hope that traditional levirate marriage practices would ever be of benefit to her. Now, however, Naomi seems to think that "the living and the dead" will be able to benefit in some way from the attraction between her *gōʾēl* and her daughter-in-law. It would seem that the dead could benefit only if their names were kept alive in Israel, as levirate marriages were meant to do. But the legal codes contained in the Bible do not speak of a connection between levirate marriage practices and the redemption or recovery of property. The story of Ruth seems to excerpt elements associated with both customs and to combine them in a unique way. It would be reasonable for us to assume that ancient audiences were familiar with a much larger body of customary law than the codes preserved in Scripture. Naomi's excitement in v. 20 seems to indicate that she sees possibilities that we do not. It also seems that Naomi's attitude toward Ruth is changing. Naomi includes Ruth in the kinship circle when she says that Boaz is "one of *our* closest relatives."

2:21-23. In v. 21, Ruth quotes Boaz as having said "cling to my young men," whereas, in fact, he said (in v. 8) "cling to my young women." Like Boaz, Naomi tells Ruth to stick close to the *women* workers (v. 22). Naomi is afraid that Ruth might be importuned (פגע *pāgaʿ*), using the same word that was translated "urge" (NIV) or "press" (NRSV) in 1:16, if she tries to better herself by going to some other landowner's field.

Taken at face value, Naomi's advice to Ruth sounds very motherly: Stick close to the *women* workers in Boaz's fields. However, it is also possible that Naomi's concern is prompted by self-interest. Now that it appears that Boaz has taken more than a passing interest in Ruth, Naomi may be beginning to see how a marriage between her *gō'ēl* and her daughter-in-law could result in a solution to her own problems.

As in the previous chapter, the final verse both summarizes the essential points made in this chapter and sets the stage for the action in the following chapter. Verse 23 tells us that about seven weeks have passed since Ruth and Naomi had arrived in Bethlehem (the usual period of time between the beginning of the barley harvest in 1:22 and the end of the wheat harvest in 2:23). However, Ruth and Naomi are still widows, still living on the leftovers of the harvest in Bethlehem. Naomi's expectations that "the living and the dead" would benefit from Boaz's attraction to Ruth have not been met. Thus we are persuaded that their situation is dire enough to justify the drastic measures that will be taken in the following chapter.

REFLECTIONS

Providence, like beauty, is in the eye of the beholder. While the narrator does not specifically say that Ruth's "happening" to find Boaz's field was a part of God's plan, members of the audience may conclude that such happenings only seem accidental to human eyes. "For Ruth and Boaz it was an accident, but not for God."[55] Naomi's exclamation in 2:20 can also be taken as the perception of God's providence at work, as the NIV translation dictates.

This chapter in Ruth raises the question of the relationship between divine plans and human agency. To what extent does the working out of God's plans depend on the willingness of humans to be God's "hands" (or in this case "wings") in the world? After Boaz piously wishes that the LORD will repay Ruth for her loyalty to Naomi, Ruth reminds Boaz that he can (and should) act as God's agent in ameliorating her present circumstances. Ruth's reply, "May I continue to find favor in *your* sight" (2:13 NRSV, italics added), reminds Boaz that she and her mother-in-law also need earthly, physical help, which he is in a position to supply. Ruth even has to hint to Boaz that he might help make his pious wish come true by accepting her as a member of his extended family.[56]

In an oral performance, a narrator can use intonations and gestures to communicate attitudes such as sarcasm and irony, boldness, and feigned or genuine deference on the part of the speakers. But the written text lacks intonation patterns, and the narrator gives us very few clues with which to judge the motives or the emotions of the characters in the story. The narrator in Ruth (in line with the practice of most biblical storytellers) usually reports only *what* the characters say and do, not why or how. These gaps or silences in the text lure members of the audience into drawing their own conclusions about the sincerity (or the sarcasm) of any statement.

When Boaz was first described as a "worthy" man in the story, the original storyteller may have used an intonation pattern that turned the phrase "a worthy man" into a tongue-in-cheek evaluation of Boaz's character. The sound of the original speaker's voice may have made the listener wonder whether Boaz's "worthiness" was only skin deep. Is Boaz a man who speaks in a pious manner but has to be nudged into giving his close relatives' widows a helping hand? It is equally possible that the original speaker's tone of voice assured the audience that Boaz truly was an admirable man.

55. Ronald M. Hals, *The Theology of the Book of Ruth* (Philadelphia: Fortress, 1969) 12.
56. Jack M. Sasson, *Ruth: A New Translation with a Philological Commentary and a Formalist-Folklorist Interpretation* (Baltimore: Johns Hopkins University Press, 1979) 49-52.

It is up to the reader of the text to decide whether Ruth's speeches in 2:10, 13 are genuinely humble, submissive, and grateful or whether she speaks with a tinge of impatience or irony in her voice. How would you feel if you were Ruth, waiting for this pillar of the community to give you permission to glean enough for you and your mother-in-law to live on, and all he said was "may the LORD reward you"? Would you feel more sarcastic than humble as you reminded this "worthy" man that he himself has a part to play in God's plans for you (2:13)?

When the narrator has Ruth use the term *nokriyyâ* to describe herself in 2:10, a post-exilic audience must have heard echoes of the contempt Ezra and Nehemiah had for the נכריות (*nokriyyôt*, "foreign women") who had married Israelite men. Although the early rabbis thought that a convert like Ruth should be accepted as an equal in Israel,[57] a close examination of Ruth's first attempts to act like a normal member of the Bethlehem community raises a few doubts concerning the community's initial willingness to accept her as one of their own. Why, for instance, was it necessary for Boaz to tell his men (on three separate occasions) not to bother this stranger in their midst? Although the translations sound neutral with regard to where Ruth sat when Boaz invited her to share the harvesters' lunch, the Hebrew hints that she sat to the side of the other workers, not among them. The narrator continues to call Ruth "the Moabite/Moabitess" from the beginning of the chapter (2:2, 6) to the end (2:22).

Boaz may have been worried that the other community members would think less of him if he gave special favors to a Moabite. What would the people of Bethlehem say if he, a pillar of the community, allowed an outsider—someone from a despised ethnic group, someone who has never before worked or paid taxes in their community—access to the fields they have cultivated all year? What would happen to the work ethic if she were given more grain than the law strictly allowed? Would other poor people flock to his fields expecting the same? Would his current field hands demand special privileges as well?

This chapter in Ruth also raises the question of how the faithful should deal with the "widows" (the dispossessed and the powerless) in their communities. Israelite laws regarding the care of the poor assumed that most people lived in rural, agriculturally based communities (see Exod 22:21-24; 23:6-11; Lev 19:9-10; Deut 10:17-19; 14:28-29; 15:7-11; 24:17-22; 26:12-13). The change to a largely urban, industrialized society in our time makes it difficult to decide how we should translate into modern practices these ancient instructions for the care of the people. Interpreters of the biblical text need to consider whether (and how) the laws of gleaning and tithing and protecting the powerless apply for us today.

Again, it may be necessary for the interpreter of Ruth to examine the role of the reader's identification within the dynamics of the story. Unlike an accusatory prophetic text, which prompts people to react defensively, a parable like Ruth allows people to make discoveries about themselves that have the force of revelation. But the content of that revelation will vary according to the location of the reader's identification. As teachers and preachers of the parable of Ruth, our task is to retell the story in such a way that our listeners recognize their own present realities mirrored in the dynamics of the narrative. Who shall we say seems to play a Boaz-like part in the modern world? Do we resemble Boaz and the reapers in the field in our dealings with the dispossessed and the powerless in our society? Do we give them pious words in response to their pleas instead of material relief for their needs? Do we allow those without resources of their own to "glean" only after we have taken everything we want from our "fields"? Do we give them the leftovers that we, the pillars of the community, do not want or do not want to bother with? Are we reluctant to set aside perfectly good resources for their use, telling ourselves that they have not helped to "grow" or to "tend" them? Are food pantries the modern equivalent of gleaning? What would be the modern equivalent of offering hospitality to an unknown traveler?

---

57. *Ruth Rab.* III.5.

RUTH 3:1-18

Uncovering and Recovering

Overview

The third chapter of Ruth consists of three distinct scenes. The word גלה (gālâ, "uncover") dominates the first scene (vv. 1-7), and the similar-sounding גאל (gāʾal, "recover," "redeem," "act as next-of-kin") prevails in the second (vv. 8-13). The deliberate use of word play, ambiguity, and *double entendre* in these first two scenes creates a dramatic tension that the final scene (vv. 14-18) serves to prolong rather than resolve. The words שכב (šākab, "lie down") and ידע (yādaʿ, "know") occur in all three scenes and weave a thread of continuity between them.

In this chapter, the narrator's penchant for puns develops into a mischievous use of words and phrases that may be understood to have either innocent or sexually suggestive meanings. In other Old Testament texts, "to know" and "to lie down" are each used as euphemisms for sexual intercourse. When Ruth asks Boaz to take her "under his wing" in v. 9, she uses the same phrase that is used in Ezek 16:8 as a metaphor for marriage. The word מרגלות (margĕlôt, "feet") comes from a root commonly used in euphemisms for the genitals (see Isa 7:20); "uncover" is frequently found in texts prohibiting sexual relationships between close relatives (Lev 18:6-19); and "threshing floors" were traditionally associated with sex for hire (Hos 9:1).

The clustering together of so many terms that have both innocent denotations (face-value meanings) and sexually suggestive connotations must be considered a deliberate narrative ploy.[58] Misplaced prudery may tempt modern readers to cover up the sexually suggestive nature of the text, but doing so robs the story of an essential element of its meaning.

The suggestive language used here encourages us to compare this situation with other, similar situations recorded in Scripture. Naomi's plan is not without biblical precedent. Both Ruth and Naomi could trace their ancestry back to women who had decided to take similarly drastic actions in order to accomplish similar ends (Genesis 19 and 38).[59]

Again in this chapter narrative gaps or silences force each reader to evaluate and to come to some conclusions about what motivates the words and actions of the characters. The reader must decide whether Ruth appears to be "a willing marionette in the hands of a crafty, strong-willed mother-in-law"[60] or whether she demonstrates initiative, pluck, and *chutzpah* as she manipulates Boaz into giving her what she wants and needs.[61]

Does Ruth merely encourage a shy or hesitant Boaz to follow his own inclinations, as traditional piety often assumes? Or does the plan formulated by Naomi and carried out by Ruth constitute entrapment, as some other readers suggest?[62] In order to evaluate Boaz's character, we must first decide whether Boaz had a moral or legal obligation to do something about Naomi and Ruth's precarious economic situation. If we decide that he did, then we must ask, Why had he not done so before? Did Boaz have to be shamed into doing his duty, or had he truly not seen a way to help

---

58. Barbara Green, "The Plot of the Biblical Story of Ruth," *JSOT* 23 (1982) 61; Edward F. Campbell, Jr., *Ruth,* AB 7 (Garden City, N.Y.: Doubleday, 1975) 131; Calum Carmichael, "Treading in the Book of Ruth," *ZAW* 92 (1980) 248-66.

59. The notable similarities between these stories have been highlighted and analyzed persuasively by H. Fisch, "Ruth and the Structure of Covenant History," *VT* (1982) 425-37; and Anthony Phillips, "The Book of Ruth—Deception and Shame," *Journal of Jewish Studies* 37 (1986) 1-17.

60. Vincent L. Tollers, "Narrative Control in the Book of Ruth," in *Mappings of the Biblical Terrain: The Bible as Text,* ed. Vincent L. Tollers and John Maier (Lewisburg: Bucknell University Press, 1989) 254.

61. Sasson, *Ruth,* 230.

62. See Athalya Brenner, *The Israelite Woman: Social Role and Literary Type in Biblical Narrative* (Sheffield: JSOT, 1985) 107; Anthony Phillips, "The Book of Ruth—Deception and Shame," *JJS* 37 (1986) 14-16.

until Ruth pointed it out to him? Did Ruth have to prick his conscience, or did she simply help him to see a way in which he could do חסד (*ḥesed*), "kindness" beyond the call of obligation or duty?

Some interpreters suggest that Boaz finds it difficult to justify his attraction to a Moabite woman and needs some way to make his inclinations seem like a virtuous concern for the interests of the living and the dead.[63] Others think that Boaz had to be shamed into doing what he ought to have done all along.[64] As you read chapter 3, keep an open mind to the multiple interpretive possibilities inherent in the text.

63. Danna Nolan Fewell and David M. Gunn, "Boaz, Pillar of Society: Measures of Worth in the Book of Ruth," *JSOT* 45 (1989) 49.
64. E.g., Phillips, "The Book of Ruth—Deception and Shame."

RUTH 3:1-7, THE PLAN: UNCOVERING

NIV

3 One day Naomi her mother-in-law said to her, "My daughter, should I not try to find a home[a] for you, where you will be well provided for? [2]Is not Boaz, with whose servant girls you have been, a kinsman of ours? Tonight he will be winnowing barley on the threshing floor. [3]Wash and perfume yourself, and put on your best clothes. Then go down to the threshing floor, but don't let him know you are there until he has finished eating and drinking. [4]When he lies down, note the place where he is lying. Then go and uncover his feet and lie down. He will tell you what to do."

[5]"I will do whatever you say," Ruth answered. [6]So she went down to the threshing floor and did everything her mother-in-law told her to do.

[7]When Boaz had finished eating and drinking and was in good spirits, he went over to lie down at the far end of the grain pile. Ruth approached quietly, uncovered his feet and lay down.

a1 Hebrew find rest *(see Ruth 1:9)*

NRSV

3 Naomi her mother-in-law said to her, "My daughter, I need to seek some security for you, so that it may be well with you. [2]Now here is our kinsman Boaz, with whose young women you have been working. See, he is winnowing barley tonight at the threshing floor. [3]Now wash and anoint yourself, and put on your best clothes and go down to the threshing floor; but do not make yourself known to the man until he has finished eating and drinking. [4]When he lies down, observe the place where he lies; then, go and uncover his feet and lie down; and he will tell you what to do." [5]She said to her, "All that you tell me I will do."

[6]So she went down to the threshing floor and did just as her mother-in-law had instructed her. [7]When Boaz had eaten and drunk, and he was in a contented mood, he went to lie down at the end of the heap of grain. Then she came stealthily and uncovered his feet, and lay down.

COMMENTARY

3:1-2. In the first chapter, Naomi urged Ruth to return to her mother's house, praying that the LORD would grant her מנוחה (*mĕnûḥâ*), "security" (NRSV) or "rest" (NIV), by giving her a second husband (1:9). In 3:1 the term מנוח (*mānôaḥ*, which the NRSV translates as "security" and the NIV as "home") is spelled slightly differently and seems to refer to a "resting place," or a place to

settle down (see Gen 8:9) rather than to rest itself. As a widow and a foreigner, without property or protector, Ruth has no home of her own. As the last few words in the preceding chapter remind us, "she lived with her mother-in-law." Gleaning would have provided Ruth and Naomi with little more than hand-to-mouth subsistence. So Naomi sees the need to plan for her daughter-in-law's (and her own?) future. Naomi's hopes had been raised by the attention Boaz paid to Ruth at their first encounter. But as the harvest season draws to an end without any further action from Boaz, Naomi sees that she and Ruth will need to "work out their own destinies."[65]

It was clear that Naomi had marriage in mind when she used the term "rest" in 1:9, and the same seems to be true here. Naomi mentions Ruth's need for security in one breath (v. 1) and Boaz in the next (v. 2).

The word Naomi uses in v. 2 to describe Boaz as their "kinsman" differs from the relational terms she used in 2:20. In 2:20, Naomi called Boaz a גאל (gō'ēl, a "kinsman-redeemer"). But in 3:2, as in 2:1, she uses a kinship designation derived from the root meaning "to know" (ידע yd'). Other forms of knowing appear in vv. 3, 11, and 18, providing a framework for the rest of the narrator's "carefully contrived ambiguity."[66]

3:3. Washing, anointing (or perfuming oneself), and donning one's best clothes may symbolize either the end of a period of mourning (cf. 2 Sam 12:20) or the preparation of a bride for a wedding (cf. Ezek 16:9).[67] Audience members who were fully aware of the euphemistic uses of "know" (see, e.g., Gen 4:1, 17, 25) must have been amused at the double meaning inherent in Naomi's advice, "Do not make yourself *known* to the man until he has finished eating and drinking."

3:4-7. The storyteller uses "uncover," "feet," and "lie down" both in Naomi's instructions and in the description of Ruth's actions (vv. 4, 7). In Hebrew, each of these words carries suggestive associations that are not obvious in English translations. Before the reader tries to decide what Naomi wants to happen on the threshing floor, some attention must be given to the secondary freight these words must have carried in the minds of a Hebrew-speaking audience.

Like the English word "sleep," the word שכב (šākab, "lie down") can be used in an innocent manner. But the word is also frequently used to imply sexual intercourse (e.g., Gen 19:33-35;

30:15-16; 38:26). Similarly, the word translated "uncover" (גלה gālâ) assumes sexual overtones when it is used in combination with words such as "nakedness" (ערוה 'erwâ), as in laws governing sexual relationships (Lev 18:6-19). "Nakedness" in such contexts seems to be a euphemism for genitalia (see Isa 47:3). However, in other combinations, the same root meaning of "uncover" is carried over into the realm of religious experience, where it becomes a technical term for "revelation" (as in Deut 29:29; Isa 40:5; 53:1).

In Deut 27:20, gālâ means "removed" (the man who "lies down" [šākab] with his father's wife is cursed, because he has "removed" [gālâ] his father's "wing" or garment [כנף kānāp]). But in other contexts, gālâ becomes a political or historical term when it refers to a person who is "removed" from the land (taken into captivity or exile), as in 2 Kgs 25:21 and Jer 52:27. And in the account of Ezra's post-exilic campaign to eliminate all marriages between Israelite men and foreign women, this same root is used a collective noun (גולה gôlâ), designating those who had returned from exile (see Ezra 9:4).

By juxtaposing the similar-sounding words gālâ ("uncover," "reveal," "remove") and גאל (gā'al, "recover," "redeem," "restore"), the narrator encourages the audience to consider ways in which "uncovering" (with all its possible innuendoes) can lead to "recovering"—to the redemption of what was lost.

Naomi tells Ruth to uncover Boaz's "feet" (or the place where his feet are), rather than his "nakedness," but the word translated "feet" is also commonly used as a euphemism meaning "private parts." It would be more accurate, then, to translate the word as "lower body" than "feet." Modern translations sometimes substitute modern euphemisms, so that the reader of an English version is seldom aware of the way the word "feet" functions in the Hebrew text. Thus, for instance, both the NIV and the NRSV use "relieving himself," where the Hebrew idiom says, literally, "uncovering his feet" (see, e.g., Judg 3:24; 1 Sam 24:3), the NRSV of Ezek 16:25 says, "offering *yourself* [lit.. your feet] to every passerby," and Deut 28:25 says "the afterbirth that comes out from between her *thighs* [lit., her feet]."

---

65. Phyllis Trible, "A Human Comedy," in *God and the Rhetoric of Sexuality*, OBT (Philadelphia: Fortress, 1978) 195.

66. Campbell, *Ruth*, 131.

67. Barbara Green, "The Plot of the Biblical Story of Ruth," *JSOT* 23 (1982) 61.

RUTH 3:8-13, RECOVERING: MIDNIGHT ON THE THRESHING FLOOR

NIV

[8] In the middle of the night something startled the man, and he turned and discovered a woman lying at his feet.

[9] "Who are you?" he asked.

"I am your servant Ruth," she said. "Spread the corner of your garment over me, since you are a kinsman-redeemer."

[10] "The LORD bless you, my daughter," he replied. "This kindness is greater than that which you showed earlier: You have not run after the younger men, whether rich or poor. [11] And now, my daughter, don't be afraid. I will do for you all you ask. All my fellow townsmen know that you are a woman of noble character. [12] Although it is true that I am near of kin, there is a kinsman-redeemer nearer than I. [13] Stay here for the night, and in the morning if he wants to redeem, good; let him redeem. But if he is not willing, as surely as the LORD lives I will do it. Lie here until morning."

NRSV

[8] At midnight the man was startled, and turned over, and there, lying at his feet, was a woman! [9] He said, "Who are you?" And she answered, "I am Ruth, your servant; spread your cloak over your servant, for you are next-of-kin."[a] [10] He said, "May you be blessed by the LORD, my daughter; this last instance of your loyalty is better than the first; you have not gone after young men, whether poor or rich. [11] And now, my daughter, do not be afraid, I will do for you all that you ask, for all the assembly of my people know that you are a worthy woman. [12] But now, though it is true that I am a near kinsman, there is another kinsman more closely related than I. [13] Remain this night, and in the morning, if he will act as next-of-kin[a] for you, good; let him do it. If he is not willing to act as next-of-kin[a] for you, then, as the LORD lives, I will act as next-of-kin[a] for you. Lie down until the morning."

[a] Or one with the right to redeem

COMMENTARY

The stories preserved in Genesis 19 and 38 (both of which involve tricks played by women without husbands or children on men who are related to them in some way) must lurk in the background of our minds as we listen to Naomi's plan and watch Ruth carry the scheme out with a variation or two of her own. "No one could have heard the story of 'Ruth the Moabitess' without thinking of Lot's daughter (Ruth's ancestress) and the incestuous beginning of the Moabite nation."[68] A reader who remembers how Lot's daughters managed to impregnate themselves without their father's knowledge might suspect that Naomi's plan "depends on Boaz being merry with wine and consequently having no clear memory of what happened."[69] It is quite possible that

when he is startled awake and finds himself lying half naked next to a Moabite woman, "Boaz imagines that Ruth has done what her ancestress, Lot's daughter, did before her."[70]

The root word גאל (g'l) is used six times in vv. 9-13 (once in v. 9, twice in v. 12, three times in v. 13) and thus comes to dominate this midnight scenario. As a verb, gā'al is translated "redeem" in the NIV and "act as next-of-kin" in the NRSV. The noun form, gō'ēl, is translated "next-of-kin" in the NRSV and "kinsman-redeemer" in the NIV. The term is difficult to translate because the same root is used to describe (1) the action of recovering that which was lost (or about to be lost) to a given family and (2) the family member who was expected to perform that action.

3:8-9. Verse 8 begins with ויהי (wayĕhî), sometimes translated "and it came to pass." This phrase

68. Warren Austin Gage, "Ruth Upon the Threshing Floor and the Sin of Gibeah: A Biblical-Theological Study," *Westminster Theological Journal* 51 (1989) 370.

69. Phillips, "The Book of Ruth—Deception and Shame," 14.

70. Ibid.

usually indicates the start of a new scene. In the previous scene, Naomi had said "he will tell you what to do" (v. 4), and Ruth had promised to do everything Naomi told her to do. But Ruth does not wait until Boaz tells her what to do. Rather, *she* tells *him* what he should do, using words that were not supplied by Naomi.[71]

In her earlier conversational exchanges with Boaz, Ruth had referred to herself as a נכריה (*nokriyyâ*), a foreigner (2:10), who had been treated more like a שפחה (*šipḥâ*), a family servant (2:13). Now in v. 9 she tells Boaz that she is his אמה (*'āmâ*), again translated "servant" in both the NRSV and the NIV. Although in most biblical contexts the words *šipḥâ* and *'āmâ* seem to be interchangeable, many scholars think that an *'āmâ* has higher social status than a *šipḥâ*.[72] Sasson[73] and Campbell[74] think that there is some reason to believe that an *'āmâ* was eligible for marriage with her master, and Ilona Rashkow suggests that Ruth has used "three progressively more familiar terms . . . to describe herself to Boaz."[75]

First Ruth identifies herself as his *'āmâ*, then she asks Boaz to "spread" his כנף (*kānāp*; NRSV, "cloak"; NIV, "corner of garment") over his *'āmâ*. The NIV takes this second use of *'āmâ* as "over me." Boaz had used the plural of the word *kānāp* ("wing") in 2:12 to refer to the protection of the LORD. Now Ruth repeats Boaz's words back to him in a context that gives a new shade of meaning to his original utterance. In Ruth's request (v. 9), the word *kānāp* ("wing"/"cloak") retains the connotation of protection it had in 2:12. But when a woman asks a man to take her "under his wing," the metaphor assumes sexual overtones (as in Deut 27:20; Ezek 16:8). Again in 3:9, as in 2:13, Ruth challenges Boaz to take action to make his pious wishes come true.

Interpreters are divided over two issues related to Ruth's speech in v. 9: (1) Should the words "spread your wing" ("spread the corner of your garment/your cloak over your servant") be understood as a marriage proposal or merely a request for sexual relations? (2) Is Ruth making one request or two? Should we understand her words to mean that she equates the function of redemption with marriage (or sexual relations) with Boaz? Is she saying, "Since you are a *gō'ēl* [next-of-kin/kinsman-redeemer], you should marry me?" Or should Ruth's mention of "redemption" be considered a separate issue from marriage?

While many readers assume that Ruth is asking Boaz to fulfill the levirate marriage customs, in fact the biblical laws concerning "redemption" say nothing about marriage, let alone levirate marriage. However, it is quite possible that the laws preserved in Scripture represent only a fraction of the customary laws that existed in any given period or locality. The narrator may assume a body of customary law in which marriage and redemption are equated or closely linked. If so, these laws have not been preserved for our edification.

There is no doubt that the institutions of redemption and levirate marriage (as they are described in the biblical texts) had similar purposes. While the levirate laws state that they are concerned with keeping a "name" alive, a large body of evidence indicates that one's name is more closely connected to inheritance than to bloodline or memory. The complaint that the daughters of Zelophehad brought to Moses (Num 27:1-11) "presupposes that the 'name' of a man . . . could be preserved only in association with the inheritance of land by his descendants."[76] A levirate marriage was meant "to provide the deceased with an heir to his estate,"[77] so that his family would not lose title to his land. Redemption was similarly concerned with keeping family property under family control.

3:10-13. It can be argued that Boaz's words in these verses provide adequate clues for deciding between the interpretive possibilities presented to us in vv. 9-10.[78] Since Boaz says, "I will do for you all that you ask" (v. 11), and then proceeds to arrange his marriage with Ruth, we should be able to assume that he understood Ruth's

71. Johanna W. H. Bos, "Out of the Shadows: Genesis 38; Judges 4:17-22; Ruth 3," *Semeia* 42 (1988) 62.

72. E. M. MacDonald, *The Position of Women as Reflected in Semitic Codes of Law* (Toronto: University of Toronto Press, 1931) 62; Paul Joüon, *Ruth: Commentaire philologique et exétique*, Subsidia Biblica 9 (Rome: Pontifical Biblical Institute, 1986) 57; Adele Berlin, *Poetics and Interpretation of Biblical Narrative*, Bible and Literature 9 (Sheffield: Almond, 1983) 88-89.

73. Jack M. Sasson, *Ruth: A New Translation with a Philological Commentary and a Formalist-Folklorist Interpretation* (Baltimore: Johns Hopkins University Press, 1979) 53.

74. Edward F. Campbell, Jr., *Ruth*, AB 7 (Garden City, N.Y.: Doubleday, 1975) 101.

75. Ilona Rashkow, "Ruth: The Discourse of Power," in *A Feminist Companion to Ruth*, ed. Athalya Brenner (Sheffield: Sheffield Academic, 1993) 39.

76. Martin Noth, *Numbers*, OTL (Philadelphia: Westminster, 1968) 211.

77. Raymond Westbrook, *Property and Family in Biblical Law*, JSOTSup 113 (Sheffield: Sheffield Academic, 1991) 74.

78. Barbara Green, "The Plot of the Biblical Story of Ruth," *JSOT* 23 (1982) 63.

request as a proposal of marriage, rather than a request for sexual relations per se. This assumption is further supported by the observation that in Ezek 16:8 the image of "spreading a wing over" is closely connected with "pledging" oneself and entering into a covenant with the one over whom the wing or cloak is spread.

The fact that the storyteller has Boaz give two different answers in vv. 11-12 (each beginning with ועתה [wĕ ʿattâ], indicating that they are separate conclusions to separate requests)[79] suggests that Ruth's request for the protection of marriage is separable from (not automatically tied to) her request for "redemption." In v. 11 Boaz responds to Ruth's request for marriage, and in v. 12 he responds to her reminder that he is a גאל (gō ʾēl). "The first he can promise to do; the second depends on one factor outside his control."[80]

Boaz says that someone has a prior claim, or a closer kinship, to Naomi (or to Naomi's husband) than he does. Leviticus 25:48-49 lists brothers, uncles, or uncles' sons (first cousins) as responsible for the redemption of family members who are forced to sell themselves into bondage. However, the story never tells us precisely how Boaz was related to Elimelech (see Commentary on 4:3).

Assuming that Ruth's request for marriage is not automatically tied to Boaz's status as a potential "redeemer" allows us to address another debated point in the interpretation of this text. In v. 10 Boaz says that this current act of "loyalty" or "kindness" (חסד ḥesed) on Ruth's part is greater than her former ḥesed. But the narrator leaves it up to the listener (or reader) to decide what Boaz means either by Ruth's former act of ḥesed or by this act of ḥesed.

The word ḥesed has been used two times before in this story, both times by Naomi. In 1:8, Naomi prayed that the LORD would show ḥesed to her daughters-in-law as they had shown it to her and to "the dead." In 2:20, Naomi takes Boaz's tokens of favor to Ruth as a sign that the LORD had not stopped showing ḥesed "to the living and the dead." It seems reasonable to assume that, in Boaz's mind, Ruth's former ḥesed was directed to her now-deceased husband, brother-in-law, and father-in-law and to her still-living mother-in-law.

It is somewhat more difficult to determine what

Boaz means by this latter act of ḥesed on Ruth's part, which he takes to be even greater than the first one (3:10). Does Boaz think that he is the beneficiary in this latter act of ḥesed? Does he think that Ruth has done him a kindness by choosing him (an old man, with no heir of his own) as a marriage partner in preference to a younger man? Or does Boaz see that both the living (Naomi) and the dead (Elimelech, Mahlon, and Kilion) will benefit from Ruth's action here, just as they benefited from Ruth's ḥesed in the past?

Separating Ruth's request for marriage from her request for redemption allows us to distinguish between the beneficiaries of these separate requests. Boaz's remarks in v. 10 indicate that Ruth could have remedied her own situation by getting any one of the younger men to marry her (which may explain her initial interest in the men who worked in Boaz's fields). But only marriage to one of Elimelech's closest relatives (a kinsman-redeemer) could address both the needs of Ruth's family of choice (living and dead) and Ruth's needs for the security of a home of her own. If we assume that Ruth makes two separate suggestions, one for her own benefit ("Take me under your wing") and one for the benefit of the living and the dead ("Act as the redeemer you are qualified to be"), then it seems that the action Boaz calls "this last instance of your loyalty" refers to Ruth's concern for Naomi and her "emptiness" (i.e., her dead family).

In v. 11 Boaz agrees to marry Ruth, assuring her that the townspeople think she is "a worthy woman," and in v. 13 he swears that one way or another he will see to the recovery (redemption) of what was lost after the deaths of Elimelech, Mahlon, and Kilion. Up to this point in the story, we have not been told precisely what Boaz is being asked to redeem or recover. We can only deduce, from what has been said so far, that "Boaz as a redeemer will provide Naomi, as well as Ruth, with [economic] security."[81]

The term אשת חיל (ʾēšet ḥayil; NRSV, "a worthy woman"; NIV, "a woman of noble character") is the feminine equivalent of what Boaz was called in 2:1 (גבור חיל gibbôr ḥayil). Boaz might be saying that Ruth's first marriage (to Mahlon) "had conferred upon her credentials proper enough for her to (re)marry a gibbôr ḥayil."[82] But it seems just

79. Sasson, Ruth, 86.
80. Green, "The Plot of the Biblical Story of Ruth," 63.

81. Johanna W. H.Bos, "Out of the Shadows: Genesis 38; Judges 4:17-22; Ruth 3," Semeia 42 (1988) 63.
82. Ibid.

as likely that Boaz uses this term because Ruth has already earned a reputation for good works (as 2:11 indicates). Since this chapter is so heavily packed with double entendre, we ought also to remember that *ḥayil* can have overtones meaning "procreative power," the ability to have a large family (see the Commentary on 2:1 and 4:11). (See Reflections at 3:14-18.)

RUTH 3:14-18, THE BEGINNING OF AN END TO EMPTINESS

NIV

¹⁴So she lay at his feet until morning, but got up before anyone could be recognized; and he said, "Don't let it be known that a woman came to the threshing floor."

¹⁵He also said, "Bring me the shawl you are wearing and hold it out." When she did so, he poured into it six measures of barley and put it on her. Then he[a] went back to town.

¹⁶When Ruth came to her mother-in-law, Naomi asked, "How did it go, my daughter?"

Then she told her everything Boaz had done for her ¹⁷and added, "He gave me these six measures of barley, saying, 'Don't go back to your mother-in-law empty-handed.'"

¹⁸Then Naomi said, "Wait, my daughter, until you find out what happens. For the man will not rest until the matter is settled today."

[a]15 Most Hebrew manuscripts; many Hebrew manuscripts, Vulgate and Syriac *she*

NRSV

14So she lay at his feet until morning, but got up before one person could recognize another; for he said, "It must not be known that the woman came to the threshing floor." ¹⁵Then he said, "Bring the cloak you are wearing and hold it out." So she held it, and he measured out six measures of barley, and put it on her back; then he went into the city. ¹⁶She came to her mother-in-law, who said, "How did things go with you,[a] my daughter?" Then she told her all that the man had done for her, ¹⁷saying, "He gave me these six measures of barley, for he said, 'Do not go back to your mother-in-law empty-handed.'" ¹⁸She replied, "Wait, my daughter, until you learn how the matter turns out, for the man will not rest, but will settle the matter today."

[a]Or "Who are you,

COMMENTARY

3:14. The final scene takes place at first light. Given the common association between threshing floors and prostitution, we might interpret Boaz's wish for Ruth to leave the threshing floor "before anyone could be recognized" as an attempt to protect either her reputation as a "worthy woman" or his own reputation in order not to jeopardize the plan he will carry out in the next chapter.

3:15. Various attempts have been made to explain the significance of the barley Boaz gives to Ruth. The text says that Boaz gave her six "barleys," usually interpreted as six "measures" of one size or another. This amount of grain might represent a bride-price or a marriage settlement.[83] It might be the price for the option to buy the parcel of land that we learn about in the next chapter. It could be interpreted as a token of apology to Naomi, because her scheme did not work out precisely as she had hoped,[84] or it might be understood as Ruth's payment for services rendered during the night.[85] Some think the phrase "six barleys" should be understood as six grains, symbolizing the restoration

83. Sasson, *Ruth*, 98. See also Étan Levine, *The Aramaic Version of Ruth*, AnBib 58 (Rome: Pontifical Biblical Institute, 1973) 95-96.

84. See Pierre Crapon de Caprona, *Ruth la Moabite* (Geneva: Labor et Fides, 1982) 88-89.

85. G. May, "Ruth's Visit to the High Place at Bethlehem," *Journal of the Royal Asiatic Society of Great Britain and Ireland* (1939) 77.

of "seed" to Elimelech's line.[86] Early Jewish interpreters thought the six grains (seeds) represented six male descendants, each of whom would be blessed with six blessings.[87] Phillips concludes that having been tricked into thinking he has been compromised, "Boaz seeks to save his own reputation and keep Naomi quiet at the same time by signaling by the gift of grain that he will now do what he ought all along to have put in motion."[88]

3:16. Naomi's question is literally, "Who are you, my daughter?" Boaz used the same words in v. 9. But Naomi is not really asking for identification. The phrase may simply be an idiom suggesting that Ruth has arrived home before it is light enough for Naomi to see for sure who it is (in which case, it should be translated, "It is you, my daughter?"). But the words might also be understood as Naomi's way of asking whether Ruth's status has changed overnight. Both the NIV and the NRSV translations imply that Naomi is asking Ruth whether her plan has succeeded. This interpretation is justified by the observation that Ruth replies to Naomi's question by telling her "all that the man had done for her."[89]

3:17-18. Back in v. 15, the narrator did not tell us whether Boaz said anything at all when he gave the grain to Ruth, so it is unclear whether we should take Ruth's words in v. 17 as a factual report of events. However, it is clear that the word רֵיקָם (*rêqām*; NIV and NRSV, "empty-handed") is identical to the term used by Naomi to describe her "emptiness" in 1:21. Whether Boaz in fact said, "Do not go back to your mother-in-law *empty*," it seems likely that the barley given to Ruth was meant to send a message of some kind to Naomi. Naomi's words in v. 18 indicate that she understands the barley as a sign from Boaz that "he will settle the matter today."

Ruth has asked for marriage and redemption. Boaz has pledged to see both done. If Naomi is the intended recipient of the redemption (as 4:14 seems to indicate), then the suspense generated in this chapter has to do with how Boaz will accomplish this task. The levirate marriage laws, at least in the form in which we know them, do not expect Boaz to offer marriage to Ruth. If Boaz had been one of Elimelech's brothers, he might have felt obliged to marry *Naomi*. But such a marriage would not have solved Ruth's problems. Nor would a marriage between Naomi and Boaz keep the "name" of the dead alive in Israel, since Naomi was past the age of childbearing (1:11). Thus the narrator cleverly builds suspense by leading the audience to wonder how both women's problems can be solved by a marriage between Boaz and Ruth.

---

86. Bos, "Out of the Shadows," 56.
87. *Ruth Rab.* VII.2; Levine, *The Aramaic Version of Ruth,* 96.
88. Anthony Phillips, "The Book of Ruth—Deception and Shame," *JJS* 37 (1986) 14.
89. See Murray D. Gow, *The Book of Ruth: Its Structure, Theme and Purpose* (Leicester: Apollos, 1992) 72.

REFLECTIONS

1. Again, the eyes of faith may see God working behind the scenes in chap. 3, but the narrator carefully avoids saying anything about divine agency. The evidence could just as easily lead one to conclude that "God only helps those who help themselves,"[90] or that "God's plan is unconsciously carried out by the Naomis of this world who think they are only working out their own destiny."[91]

In this chapter as in the preceding one, the narrator uses echoing phrases to raise the question of correspondences between human actions and divine actions. On the threshing floor at midnight, Ruth repeats Boaz's words back to him, as she did in the gleaning scene. This time she hints to Boaz that shelter under the LORD's "wings" (1:12) might very well take the shape of shelter under Boaz's "wing" (3:9). In other words, Ruth "challenges Boaz to be the occasion of divine blessing in her life."[92] Preachers and teachers may conclude that, like Boaz, we need more than one reminder that we have a role to play in making our pious wishes for others come true. And, like Boaz, those of us who are the "pillars" of our own religious communities may need to be taught how to do *ḥesed* by the "foreigners" in our midst.

---

90. Phillips, "The Book of Ruth—Deception and Shame," 16.
91. Vincent L. Tollers, "Narrative Control in the Book of Ruth," in *Mappings of the Biblical Terrain: The Bible as Text,* ed. Vincent L. Tollers and John Maier (Lewisburg: Bucknell University Press, 1989) 252.
92. Phyllis Trible, "A Human Comedy," in *God and the Rhetoric of Sexuality,* OBT (Philadelphia: Fortress, 1978) 184.

2. The most heated debates concerning the interpretation of the book of Ruth revolve around the action on the threshing floor. What really happened there? Are we supposed to know? Should we be shocked by Naomi's plan and Ruth's behavior? Or should we admire the way these women have taken steps to guarantee both their own futures and the continuity of their family tree?

The similarity between chapter 3 of Ruth and the story of Tamar in Genesis 38 reminds us that Tamar's father-in-law, Judah, acknowledged that Tamar's behavior (which might have been condemned as incestuous by normal standards) was more justifiable than his. He had avoided doing what was right: providing Tamar with a child to carry on the "name" of the dead. Judah's failure to do what was right forced Tamar to take drastic measures to see justice done. In a similar way, Boaz acknowledges that Ruth's behavior is actually an act of *ḥesed*. This does not mean that Ruth's behavior (if known to the people of Bethlehem) would have been condoned. Even if nothing more happened between Ruth and Boaz than the conversation reported in 3:8-13, Ruth's actions (coming to the threshing floor, lying next to a sleeping man who was not her husband) would undoubtedly have been judged scandalous according to the standards of the society in which she lived. The question is whether the end result in this case justifies the means.

The reluctance of modern readers to see any scandalous overtones in this scene may stem from a need to reinforce deep-seated beliefs that the virtuous are rewarded. Since Ruth's actions seem to have had positive results, what she did must have been something good. This wishful thinking is aided and abetted by translators who fail (or refuse) to communicate the undertones as well as the overtones of the original language to the non-Hebrew-speaking audience. If we acknowledge that what Ruth did is both scandalous (in the eyes of the world) and an act of loving-kindness, then we can prompt modern audiences to consider which canons of socially acceptable behavior they might be willing to defy in order to "do" *ḥesed*—loving-kindness above and beyond the call of duty.

3. The debate that rages over the admirability (or lack thereof) of the actions portrayed in Ruth 3:1-13 is not trivial. There are serious theological implications. If Ruth is read with a "merit theology," then the happy ending that comes in the final chapter will seem to be the result of the courage, initiative, loyalty, and altruism of the human characters involved in the scene at the threshing floor. There are ample warrants for reading the story in this way. While the biblical texts frequently remind us that it is not our faithfulness that causes God to love us, it is clear that human faithfulness is highly valued by God. The book of Ruth can be said to suggest that the effective communication of God's love in the world depends on faithful human behavior, that God uses faithful human behavior to communicate God's love.

A number of appealing sermon topics can be derived from a merit-based reading of Ruth. We can truthfully say that the story of Ruth demonstrates that loving-kindness (*ḥesed*) can transform emptiness into occasions for hope, that *ḥesed* alone (and not the purity of one's ancestral line) qualifies us to become servants of the LORD. We might conclude that the book of Ruth and Gal 3:26-29 agree that it is not our physical ancestry but our faithfulness to God that identifies us as descendants of Abraham and heirs to the promise. Ruth might be pictured as the model foreigner Isaiah of Babylon had in mind when he said that the LORD will give a monument and a name better than sons and daughters to foreigners who choose to join themselves to the LORD (Isa 56:3-7). We could say that Ruth's willingness to commit herself and her future to the LORD allows God to work through her to transform Naomi's emptiness into fullness. Ruth acts as an agent of God's *ḥesed* when she herself shows *ḥesed* to Naomi.

Reading Ruth with a theology of grace (unmerited love) allows us to consider that none of the human characters acted in totally admirable or altruistic ways. The deliberate ambiguity of the narrator allows us to choose. Is redemption (which plays such a large part in the story) given as a *reward* for the behavior portrayed in this chapter or in spite of it?

RUTH 4:1-22

THE ROOTS OF ISRAEL'S REDEMPTION ·

OVERVIEW

In the preceding chapter, Ruth *uncovered* Boaz and asked him to *recover* ("redeem") that which was lost. In this chapter, Boaz *uncovers* the ear of the "nearer redeemer" and challenges him to *recover* (redeem) the land that had belonged to Elimelech. Used in a technical sense in legal texts, "redemption" seems to refer to the process by which people, property, and prestige are restored to a family who has lost them through poverty, violence, or some other cause. But the word "redeem" is also used figuratively to mean to "rescue," "save," or "liberate" people from danger, distress, or oppression.[93] When Ruth tells Boaz, "You are a redeemer" (see 3:9), it is not completely clear what she is asking Boaz to do. In 4:3 we hear for the first time in the story that there is property that needs to be redeemed.

The difficulty in trying to understand what is going on in chap. 4 stems from two facts: (1) The customs or laws assumed by the story world are no longer known to us; they have been lost in the mists of time. (2) In the process of transmitting the text, some changes have been made, so that none of the solutions suggested by interpreters can make complete sense of the text as it now stands.

It becomes apparent in 4:14-17 that the loss that mattered most to Naomi is one that can be redeemed by the birth of a child. This may be related to the "parcel of land" mentioned in 4:3 by assuming that a male child is needed to carry on the title to the property that had belonged to Elimelech. In order for the property to remain in Elimelech's family, there needs to be a male heir

to inherit it. But we can only speculate as to whether the purchase (or redemption) of the field triggers the levirate obligation to raise up an heir for the dead,[94] or whether the redemption of property and the raising up an heir for that property are considered separate and unconnected actions until Boaz makes the connection voluntarily, as a surprise move.

In v. 4, the word "redeem" (גאל *gāʾal*) is equated with "acquire," "make one's own" (קנה *qānâ*). The encounter between Boaz and the nearer redeemer is structured around the word *qnh* (translated "buy" or "acquire"), which occurs six times in vv. 4-10 (once in vv. 4, 8, 9, 10, and twice in v. 5).

The word שֵׁם (*šēm*, "name") occurs seven times in this chapter (once in vv. 5, 11, 14; twice in vv. 10 and 17), but only the final use of the term seems to be part of an actual naming formula. In vv. 5 and 10, "name" takes on the connotation of "title to the land," while in vv. 11 and 14 it seems to refer to reputation or fame.

The genealogy with which the book of Ruth ends looks forward to the birth of David and backward to Perez, the child of a Canaanite widow who tricked the father of her deceased husband into having intercourse with her. Thus we are told that neither of Obed's parents has an impeccable line of descent. Ruth's ancestry can be traced to an incestuous union between Lot and one of his daughters (Genesis 19), and Boaz is descended from an illicit union between Judah and his daughter-in-law (Genesis 38)!

93. See Ringgren, *TDOT* 2:353-54.

94. Raymond Westbrook, *Property and Family in Biblical Law,* JSOT-Sup 113 (Sheffield: Sheffield Academic, 1991) 67.

RUTH 4:1-11*a*, BOAZ SETTLES THE MATTER

Ruth 4:1-4, The Trap Is Baited and Set

NIV

4 Meanwhile Boaz went up to the town gate and sat there. When the kinsman-redeemer he had mentioned came along, Boaz said, "Come over here, my friend, and sit down." So he went over and sat down.

²Boaz took ten of the elders of the town and said, "Sit here," and they did so. ³Then he said to the kinsman-redeemer, "Naomi, who has come back from Moab, is selling the piece of land that belonged to our brother Elimelech. ⁴I thought I should bring the matter to your attention and suggest that you buy it in the presence of these seated here and in the presence of the elders of my people. If you will redeem it, do so. But if you*a* will not, tell me, so I will know. For no one has the right to do it except you, and I am next in line."

"I will redeem it," he said.

a4 Many Hebrew manuscripts, Septuagint, Vulgate and Syriac; most Hebrew manuscripts he

NRSV

4 No sooner had Boaz gone up to the gate and sat down there than the next-of-kin,*a* of whom Boaz had spoken, came passing by. So Boaz said, "Come over, friend; sit down here." And he went over and sat down. ²Then Boaz took ten men of the elders of the city, and said, "Sit down here"; so they sat down. ³He then said to the next-of-kin,*a* "Naomi, who has come back from the country of Moab, is selling the parcel of land that belonged to our kinsman Elimelech. ⁴So I thought I would tell you of it, and say: Buy it in the presence of those sitting here, and in the presence of the elders of my people. If you will redeem it, redeem it; but if you will not, tell me, so that I may know; for there is no one prior to you to redeem it, and I come after you." So he said, "I will redeem it."

a Or one with the right to redeem

COMMENTARY

4:1-2. Archaeological digs have revealed that the gate area of most Israelite towns included a courtyard lined with benches. Biblical texts indicate that many business transactions, including the settling of disputes, were conducted in this area, with townspeople acting as witnesses or as the jury. When Boaz gets the next-of-kin and ten elders to sit down with him in the gate, he is in effect convening a court of law.

As soon as the stage is set, the closer kinsman arrives on the scene. Both the NRSV and the NIV have Boaz call the next of kin "friend," but in fact Boaz uses פלני אלמני (*pĕlōnî ʾalmōnî*), a Hebrew idiom that suggests that the man's name is not important to the story. When the same phrase is used to describe a place rather than a person in 2 Kgs 6:8, both the NIV and the NRSV have "such and such a place." Thus it seems that the English idiom "so and so" might better com-

municate the storyteller's intentions. The medieval Rabbi Rashi seems to have been the first to suggest that *pĕlōnî ʾalmōnî* should be translated "So-and-So," explaining that "his name is not written because he was not willing to redeem."[95]

4:3. There are a number of interpretive ambiguities in this verse. For the first time in the story a piece of land or a field belonging to Elimelech has been explicitly mentioned. Is this simply a literary device to preserve the surprise of the story? Or should we have known from Naomi's and Ruth's references to a redeemer that a parcel of land was implied? Is Boaz saying that Naomi *is about to sell* or that she *has already sold* this piece of property? Should the phrase "our brother Elimelech" be understood literally or figuratively?

95. D. R. G. Beattie, *Jewish Exegesis of the Book of Ruth,* JSOTSup 2 (1977) 109.

The verb that Boaz uses (מכר *mākar*, "sold") is in the perfect tense, which ordinarily indicates a completed action. Thus we could understand Boaz to mean that Naomi (or Elimelech) had already sold the field in question, perhaps during the famine that motivated the family's move to Moab. So what is needed is a redeemer to buy the property back, and thus restore it to the control of the clan or extended family. But if this were the case, Boaz's words in vv. 5 and 9 would not make sense. Thus both the NIV and the NRSV opt for a present-tense translation: Naomi "*is* selling."

Women could own, buy, sell, and inherit property in Israel (see Num 27:1-8; 36:1-12; Job 42:15; Prov 31:16). Most of the cultures of the ancient Near East allowed men to make their wives or daughters their heirs.[96] Texts from the Jewish community on the island of Elephantine in the sixth century BCE indicate that a childless widow in that community could inherit property from her husband, and the apocryphal book of Judith is about a widow who both inherited from her husband (Jdt 8:7) and had the right to bequeath her property as she wished (Jdt 16:21-24). The biblical laws "specify those who have a right to the property insofar as there are no contrary provisions made. They do not say the wife cannot inherit if the husband, before he dies, chooses to make her his heir."[97] Thus Naomi may have inherited from her deceased husband the parcel of land to which Boaz refers. One way of reading v. 5 even suggests that both Naomi and Ruth could claim ownership of the land in question. Since the story says that Naomi and Ruth have been living on gleanings from the grain harvest, however, we can assume that mere ownership of the field was not enough to support the two women.

It is highly unlikely that a piece of arable land would have been left unclaimed and unused during the ten or more years that Elimelech and his family stayed in Moab. So it is conceivable that the task of buying or redeeming the land would include regaining control of it from someone who had held it in Naomi's absence. This seems to have been the problem faced by the woman whose son was revived by Elisha. When she returned home after having lived elsewhere during seven years of famine in her own land, she had to "appeal to the king for her house and her land" (2 Kgs 8:1-6). It may even have been So-and-So who had claimed and used the land in the intervening years, since he knew that he was the next-of-kin. If that is the case, then Boaz would be suggesting in v. 4 that So-and-So should pay Naomi for the land he has been using since Naomi and her family left for Moab.

In speaking to So-and-So, Boaz calls Elimelech "our brother" (אחינו *'aḥînû*). Interpreters who are inclined to take this term literally conclude that Boaz, So-and-So, and Elimelech shared at least one parent. Other interpreters note that the common Hebrew usage of "brother" is seldom precise. The word "brother" can also be used to describe relationships between cousins (brothers' sons) and between uncles and nephews.

4:4. When Boaz reminds So-and-So that it is his duty to buy (or to pay for) the field that legally belongs to Elimelech's heirs, he uses an idiom that in Hebrew means "I thought I would *uncover* your ear." The insipid English translations (NRSV, "I thought I would tell you of it"; NIV, "I thought I would bring it to your attention") obscure the way in which the narrator links the uncovering done by Ruth on the threshing floor with the uncovering done by Boaz at the city gate. In chap. 4, as in chap. 3, uncovering is closely related to recovering. The NIV inserts the word "right" ("to redeem") into Boaz's sentence. But it is really not clear whether redemption in this case involves a right of first refusal or an obligation to buy.

Boaz has chosen to call So-and-So to account for his actions in a very public forum. Having been openly challenged in the presence of ten elders (and assorted other townspeople), So-and-So states his willingness to make amends. He says, "I will buy." (See Reflections at 4:13-17.)

96. Eryl W. Davie, "Inheritance Rights and the Hebrew Levirate Marriage: Part I," *VT* 31, 2 (1981) 138.

97. Thomas Thompson and Dorothy Thompson, "Some Legal Problems in the Book of Ruth," *VT* (1968) 98.

Ruth 4:5-6, The Trap Is Sprung

⁵Then Boaz said, "On the day you buy the land from Naomi and from Ruth the Moabitess, you acquire[a] the dead man's widow, in order to maintain the name of the dead with his property."

⁶At this, the kinsman-redeemer said, "Then I cannot redeem it because I might endanger my own estate. You redeem it yourself. I cannot do it."

[a]5 Hebrew; Vulgate and Syriac *Naomi, you acquire Ruth the Moabitess,*

⁵Then Boaz said, "The day you acquire the field from the hand of Naomi, you are also acquiring Ruth[a] the Moabite, the widow of the dead man, to maintain the dead man's name on his inheritance." ⁶At this, the next-of-kin[b] said, "I cannot redeem it for myself without damaging my own inheritance. Take my right of redemption yourself, for I cannot redeem it."

[a]OL Vg: Heb *from the hand of Naomi and from Ruth* [b]Or *one with the right to redeem*

COMMENTARY

Interpretations of the interchange between Boaz and So-and-So can vary widely, because a word that was written one way in the consonantal text was vocalized by the Masoretes to read another way.[98] The original consonants in the text of v. 5 (קניתי *qnyty*) imply that Boaz says, "The day you acquire the land . . . *I* acquire the dead man's widow." But both the NIV and the NRSV accept the scribal emendation that changes the written form of the verb ("I acquire") to קניתה (*qānîtâ*), "*you* acquire" or "you are acquiring."

The amended form ("you acquire") implies (1) that a levirate-type of obligation is connected to the ownership of the land and (2) that So-and-So either does not know, has forgotten, or wants to ignore this connection. Beattie thinks this emendation originated because of a misunderstanding: "Since, when he buys the land, Boaz also takes Ruth as his wife (vv. 9, 10), it was assumed that the two things belonged together and that the redeemer of the land should take Ruth in marriage as a condition of his redemption, and so קניתי *qānîtî* was taken to be second person."[99] If we assume that the levirate customarily applied to more than brothers-in-law, and if we read the text as it was pointed by the Masoretes ("The day you acquire the field . . . *you* acquire the widow, to maintain the dead man's name on his inheritance"), then it seems that Boaz is saying that "if

the nearest relative is willing to perform one legal custom which was to his advantage, he should in logic be willing to perform the other which was not. . . . He could not decently choose one and reject the other."[100] This reading assumes that Boaz has shamed the nearer redeemer by publicly exposing his willingness to perform only the profitable parts of his redemptive duties. However, if we keep the original consonantal spelling, so that Boaz says, "*I* have acquired" or "*I* am acquiring," then it seems that marrying Ruth in order to produce a child who will keep Elimelech's line alive is not necessarily connected with the redemption of the land.

The words used in v. 5 (NIV, "to maintain the name of the dead with his property"; NRSV, "to maintain the dead man's name on his inheritance") echo the levirate language used in Deut 25:6-7. But neither Boaz nor So-and-So fits the category of persons to whom the law in Deuteronomy 25 is addressed (i.e., they are not "brothers living together" with Elimelech). Commentators have proposed a number of theories to explain the differences between what the Ruth account seems to assume and what the law in Deuteronomy commands. It has been suggested that the "rules" assumed in Ruth (1) represent a local, geographical variant; (2) that they testify to customs that preceded the codification of the law; or (3) that they reflect later stages of development

98. See D. R. G. Beattie, "Kethibh and Qere in Ruth 4:5," *VT* 21 (1971) 490-94.

99. Ibid., 494.

100. Phillips, "The Book of Ruth—Deception and Shame," 9.

in the application of the spirit of the laws to concrete situations.[101]

So-and-So's reaction to Boaz's announcement indicates that more is at stake here than literally keeping the name of the dead alive. Since neither Ruth nor Tamar (whose story in Genesis 38 more closely fits the levirate laws) actually called her children by the name of the deceased husband, we may deduce that "name" (שֵׁם *šēm*) was not meant to be taken literally in this context. Furthermore, Boaz says he intends to "maintain the dead man's name *on his inheritance.*" Thus it seems that this use of "name" might have the sense of "title" or "claim of ownership" of the land. In other words, Boaz firmly intends to let his and Ruth's first child be known as Elimelech's heir. In effect, Boaz says, "I feel it is only fair to tell you, before you redeem [or acquire] this piece of property, that I plan to marry Ruth in order to raise up a future claimant to the title of that land."

The laws concerning the redemption of land say that land that was sold to a redeemer "shall remain with the purchaser until the year of jubilee; in the jubilee it shall be released, and the property shall be returned" (Lev 25:28). However, the command to return the property assumes that someone with a legitimate claim to its title would still be alive to accept its return. In this case, it must have seemed quite likely that Elimelech's line would die out. So-and-So was willing to buy or redeem the land as long as it seemed that he would never have to give the land back. Once So-and-So had paid for the land in question, it would remain a part of his own inheritance. But if Boaz provided Elimelech and Mahlon with an heir, So-and-So (and his heirs) would eventually lose both the purchase price and the land itself.

It seems best to assume that neither Boaz nor So-and-So was legally obliged to "maintain the dead man's name on his inheritance." It makes better logical and narrative sense to assume that Boaz's announcement comes as a surprise to both So-and-So and the audience.[102] If we keep the original form of the text (*I* am acquiring), then it seems that the surprise Boaz springs on So-and-So is the announcement that Boaz *voluntarily* is going to take on the duties of a levirate marriage. So-and-So had not foreseen the possibility that Boaz would marry Ruth or that Boaz would pledge "to raise up the name of the deceased over his inheritance." The suspense engendered by events in the preceding chapter is thus resolved in a satisfying manner. The audience is supposed to think, "Aha! What a clever (and unexpected) solution to both widows' problems!" (See Reflections at 4:13-17.)

101. Westbrook, *Property and Family in Biblical Law,* 63.

102. Barbara Green, "The Plot of the Biblical Story of Ruth," *JSOT* 23 (1982) 59.

Ruth 4:7-11*a*, Legal Formalities

[7](Now in earlier times in Israel, for the redemption and transfer of property to become final, one party took off his sandal and gave it to the other. This was the method of legalizing transactions in Israel.)

[8]So the kinsman-redeemer said to Boaz, "Buy it yourself." And he removed his sandal.

[9]Then Boaz announced to the elders and all the people, "Today you are witnesses that I have bought from Naomi all the property of Elimelech, Kilion and Mahlon. [10]I have also acquired Ruth the Moabitess, Mahlon's widow, as my wife, in order to maintain the name of the dead with his property, so that his name will not disappear from

[7]Now this was the custom in former times in Israel concerning redeeming and exchanging: to confirm a transaction, the one took off a sandal and gave it to the other; this was the manner of attesting in Israel. [8]So when the next-of-kin[a] said to Boaz, "Acquire it for yourself," he took off his sandal. [9]Then Boaz said to the elders and all the people, "Today you are witnesses that I have acquired from the hand of Naomi all that belonged to Elimelech and all that belonged to Chilion and Mahlon. [10]I have also acquired Ruth the Moabite, the wife of Mahlon, to be my wife, to maintain

a Or *one with the right to redeem*

NIV	NRSV
among his family or from the town records. Today you are witnesses!" ¹¹Then the elders and all those at the gate said, "We are witnesses. May the LORD make the woman who is coming into your home like Rachel and Leah, who together built up the house of Israel.	the dead man's name on his inheritance, in order that the name of the dead may not be cut off from his kindred and from the gate of his native place; today you are witnesses." ¹¹Then all the people who were at the gate, along with the elders, said, "We are witnesses. May the LORD make the woman who is coming into your house like Rachel and Leah, who together built up the house of Israel.

COMMENTARY

4:7-8. A shoe, or a sandal, functions as a symbol for the right to buy or redeem the land that had belonged to Elimelech.[103] Giving up the sandal signals So-and-So's willingness to give up his right to claim or redeem the property Elimelech had left behind when he went to Moab. The narrator's statement that "this was the custom in former days" indicates that the story is being told to people who live in a much later time than the time in which Boaz and So-and-So lived. The narrator's audience no longer exchanged sandals in order to confirm or legalize a transaction, so this detail in the story needed to be explained to them.

Deuteronomy 25:7-10 says that a widow whose husband's brother refuses to perform the levirate duties has the right to pull the sandal off his foot and spit in his face in the presence of elders. Ruth 4:7 indicates that taking off a sandal in front of witnesses represents a legal transaction. However, the verbs "to pull off" (שלף *šālap*) and "to take off" (חלץ *ḥālaṣ*) come from completely different Hebrew roots. Apparently the law of the levirate allowed the widow to perform an action that publicly declared that the brother-in-law had given up all claims to the land that had belonged to his deceased brother. If he was not willing to marry the widow and raise up sons for the deceased

man, then he had to forfeit his right to claim or to redeem the land. Some critics think that Boaz (in 4:5) was making the same point to the nearer redeemer.[104] However, So-and-So is never called "brother-in-law."

4:9-11a. Once the sandal is in his possession, Boaz turns to the elders and to all the townspeople who happen to be in the area at that time, publicly declaring that he has acquired both the land and Ruth (vv. 9-10). The legal nature of his declaration is underscored by the fact that his speech begins and ends with the formula "today you are witnesses" (vv. 9-10). Since Boaz uses the same word to describe what he has done both to the land and to Ruth, some readers have wondered whether Ruth is being bought and sold like a piece of property. However, the word קנה (*qānâ*), translated here as "acquire" or "buy," has a spectrum of meanings ranging from "purchase" to "create" to "possess." In Ps 74:2 and Exod 15:13-16, *qānâ* is used as a synonym for "redemption." Thus we should probably understand *qānâ* here to mean "make one's own."[105] In front of witnesses, as if in a court of law, Boaz declares that he has made both the land and Ruth his own. The people reply, "We are witnesses," and the legalities are concluded. (See Reflections at 4:13-17.)

---

103. Robert Gordis, "Love, Marriage, and Business in the Book of Ruth," in *A Light Unto My Path: Old Testament Studies in Honor of Jacob M. Myers,* ed. H. N. bream et al. (Philadelphia: Temple University Press, 1977) 247.

104. Phillips, "The Book of Ruth—Deception and Shame," 9.
105. Edward F. Campbell, Jr., *Ruth,* AB 7 (Garden City, N.Y.: Doubleday, 1975) 159.

RUTH 4:11b-17, NAMING THE MOTHERS OF THE MESSIAH

Ruth 4:11b-12, Blessing the Union

NIV	NRSV
May you have standing in Ephrathah and be famous in Bethlehem. [12]Through the offspring the LORD gives you by this young woman, may your family be like that of Perez, whom Tamar bore to Judah."	May you produce children in Ephrathah and bestow a name in Bethlehem; [12]and, through the children that the LORD will give you by this young woman, may your house be like the house of Perez, whom Tamar bore to Judah."

COMMENTARY

After they have performed their legal function as witnesses, the same collective voice of the elders and the people assembled at the gate pronounces a blessing on the upcoming marriage. The blessing contains three wishes: The first concerns Boaz's bride; the second concerns Boaz himself; and the third concerns his "house." The first and third parts of the blessing refer to the "house" of Israel and the "house" of Perez. Jacob-Israel was the father of Judah through Leah, and Judah was the father of Perez through Tamar. Boaz is a descendant of both houses.

"House" (בית bêt) is clearly a figure of speech meaning "lineage" or "descendants." In the first part of the blessing, it is clear that the wish is for Ruth to produce as many offspring as did Rachel and Leah (the wives of Jacob-Israel). The last part of the blessing is a wish that the descendants of Ruth and Boaz will rival those of Judah and Tamar. But the middle part of the blessing is more difficult to understand. Literally, the Hebrew says, "May you make/do חיל [ḥayil]" in Ephrathah and "call a name" in Bethlehem. As we saw earlier,

the word ḥayil can mean "strength" or "worth" derived from physical, moral, or financial power. But ḥayil also occurs in the special sense of "potency" or "the ability to produce offspring." Thus it seems that all three parts of the blessing are concerned with the fruitfulness of the marriage. The NRSV understands ḥayil in this way when it translates the middle wish, "May you produce children in Ephrathah and bestow a name in Bethlehem." While Ephrathah is the name of the clan to which Boaz belongs, mentioning it again at this point makes particularly good sense because of the name's association with fertility.[106]

While the blessing is addressed to a man, each of its parts reminds us of the women who have had essential roles in maintaining the continuity of the family in the past: Leah, the mother of Judah; Ephrat, the mother of the clan named after her; and Tamar, the mother of Perez. (See Reflections at 4:13-17.)

106. C. J. Labuschagne, "The Crux in Ruth 4:11," ZAW 79 (1967) 365-66.

Ruth 4:13-17, Redemption Incarnate

NIV	NRSV
[13]So Boaz took Ruth and she became his wife. Then he went to her, and the LORD enabled her to conceive, and she gave birth to a son. [14]The women said to Naomi: "Praise be to the LORD,	13So Boaz took Ruth and she became his wife. When they came together, the LORD made her conceive, and she bore a son. [14]Then the women said to Naomi, "Blessed be the LORD, who has not

NIV

who this day has not left you without a kinsman-redeemer. May he become famous throughout Israel! ¹⁵He will renew your life and sustain you in your old age. For your daughter-in-law, who loves you and who is better to you than seven sons, has given him birth."

¹⁶Then Naomi took the child, laid him in her lap and cared for him. ¹⁷The women living there said, "Naomi has a son." And they named him Obed. He was the father of Jesse, the father of David.

NRSV

left you this day without next-of-kin;ᵃ and may his name be renowned in Israel! ¹⁵He shall be to you a restorer of life and a nourisher of your old age; for your daughter-in-law who loves you, who is more to you than seven sons, has borne him." ¹⁶Then Naomi took the child and laid him in her bosom, and became his nurse. ¹⁷The women of the neighborhood gave him a name, saying, "A son has been born to Naomi." They named him Obed; he became the father of Jesse, the father of David.

ᵃOr one with the right to redeem

COMMENTARY

4:13. In 1:4 we were told that Mahlon and Chilion "took" Moabite wives (using the verb נשא *nāśāʾ*). In 4:10, Boaz declared that he had "acquired" Ruth (using the verb קנה *qānâ*). But when the narrator reports on the actual marriage between Ruth and Boaz, two more traditional terms are used: לקח (*lāqaḥ,* also meaning "took") and ותהי-לו לאשה (*watĕhî-lô lĕʾiššâ,* "she became his wife"). Then the narrator tells us (with a euphemism) that "Boaz went into her" (NRSV, "they came together"; the NIV leaves out this bit of information). The consummation of the marriage is clearly a human activity. However, in the narrator's eyes, the conception of a child is a gift from God ("the LORD made her conceive"). Like Rachel and Leah—indeed, like all the mothers of the promised line—Ruth conceives only by the grace of God (Gen 21:1-2; 25:21; 29:31-32; 30:22-23).

4:14-17. When the women say that the child is Naomi's "redeemer" (גאל *gōʾēl*) in v. 14, the legally minded may see this as a reference to the property that had once belonged to Elimelech. If Naomi had had another son of her own, presumably that son would have inherited everything from his dead father and brothers. As Naomi's "son," Obed is the heir who will "maintain the name of the dead with his property." But the women of the town define the child's role in a different way. In their opinion, the child's significance is formulated completely in terms of his meaning for Naomi.[107]

The phrase קרא שם (*qārāʾ šēm,* "to call a name") occurs twice in vv. 17, creating the impression that the women of Bethlehem give the baby more than one name. The NIV changes the first use of *qārāʾ šēm* to "say," but the NRSV represents the Hebrew accurately. Naming speeches usually consist of a pun linking the baby's name with an explanation of its meaning. If the way Rachel and Leah named their children is used as a pattern (see Gen 29:32-35; 30:6, 8, 11, 13, 18-19, 24), then we would expect the first part of v. 17 to say that the child's name resembled sounds in the phrase "a son is born to Naomi." But there seems to be no relationship between this phrase and the name "Obed." Since the phrase "to call a name" is also used in vv. 11 and 14 in the sense of becoming famous, its first use in v. 17 might be taken to mean "significance" or "importance." If so, then the verse should be translated as "A son has been born to Naomi."[108]

Ruth's son is Naomi's "redeemer," but redemption for Naomi takes the form of a reversal of the emptiness that has embittered her. It is poetically fitting for the narrator to use the same women

107. Fokkelien Van Dijk-Hemmes, "Traces of Women's Texts in the Hebrew Bible," in *On Gendering Texts: Female and Male Voices in the Hebrew Bible,* ed. Athalya Brenner and Fokkelien Van Dijk-Hemmes (Leiden: E. J. Brill, 1993) 106.
108. Robert L. Hubbard, *The Book of Ruth,* NICOT (Grand Rapids: Eerdmans, 1988) 15.

who absorbed Naomi's bitterness in 1:20-21 to assure her that the LORD has not abandoned her; the child whose conception was given by the LORD will turn Naomi's life around. This fifteenth use of the word שׁוב (šûb; NRSV, "restore"; NIV, "renew") marks the final reversal in Naomi's story. The word נפשׁ (nepeš; NIV and NRSV, "life") refers to the whole person or to the innermost self. When Ps 23:3 uses the same two words, most translations render them as "restore" and "soul." Naomi's "life" has gone from fullness to emptiness and back to fullness again. Because

Ruth the Moabite loves her, Naomi will be "sustained" (NIV) or "nourished" (NRSV) rather than empty in her "old age." Clearly the women think there is more to redemption than the retention of property within the family.

Obed, the ancestor of the Davidic kings, personifies Naomi's redemption. After political kingship disappears altogether from Israel and Judah, the faithful will still look for a descendant of Obed (a "messiah") to become redemption incarnate for the people of God.

REFLECTIONS

1. In the story world, the townspeople's blessing is presented as a traditional wish, something they might have said to any bride and groom. Presumably, the people sitting at the gate were unaware of Ruth's clandestine visit to the threshing floor. But for the narrator's audience, the blessing must seem ironically appropriate. For the audience who knows both the traditions of Israel and the story of Ruth, the blessing is more than a generic wish for fruitfulness in a marriage. The audience is aware that the three women who are named in the blessing have well-known stories attached to them in Israel's tradition. Not only did these women play a part in building up the house of Israel, but they did so in particularly deceptive ways. Tamar, Rachel, and Leah are all remembered as tricksters whose deceptions had reproductive consequences (Gen 29:21–30:19; 38:1-30). A further touch of irony results from the recollection that Rachel and Leah once complained to Israel that their own father (Laban) treated them like *nokriyyōt*, foreign women (Gen 31:15)!

Although Rachel, the younger of Jacob's wives, is listed first in the blessing, Leah is the mother of Judah. The people of Bethlehem traced their ancestry to Judah through Perez, one of the twins born after Tamar tricked Judah into having intercourse with her. But this reference to Tamar and Judah must remind the audience of more than just the Bethlehemites' ancestry. An audience familiar with Tamar's story must have seen resemblances between her situation and Ruth's situation, between Tamar's actions and Ruth's actions. Both women are childless widows. Both widows have male relatives who might be expected to ameliorate their situations, but who choose not to do so. Each woman takes her reproductive future into her own hands. Each "uncovers" a man who can give her a child qualified to keep the "name" of the dead alive in Israel. The genealogy in Ruth 4:18-22 will trace the family tree through the fathers, but the blessing in 4:11-12 reminds us that it is the mothers of the messianic line who made sure that the continuity of the family line remained unbroken. To modern eyes, these women may seem to have sold out to "the patriarchal institution of the levirate, which ensures the patrilineage of a deceased husband."[109] But it might also be argued that they have undermined the male Israelites' belief that God favors submissive, non-aggressive behavior on the part of women.

2. The references to Rachel and Tamar might also have had political significance. Rachel was the mother of Joseph and thus was the ancestress of the northern kingdom's dominant tribes (Ephraim and Manasseh). Leah was the mother of Judah, the dominant tribe of the

---

109. Esther Fuchs, "The Literary Characterization of Mothers and Sexual Politics in the Hebrew Bible," in *Feminist Perspectives on Biblical Scholarship,* ed. Adela Yarbro Collins (Chico, Calif.: Scholars Press, 1985) 130.

southern kingdom. Tamar appears to have been a Canaanite woman. Ezra 4:1-3 tells us how the returned exiles (the remnants of Judah/Leah's descendants) spurned the remnants of Rachel's descendants, and Ezra 10 tells us how they rejected the foreign wives of men descended from Judah. But the first part of the blessing in Ruth 4:11*b* names Rachel (the northern ancestress) first and emphatically declares that both Rachel and Leah together built up the house of Israel. And in the final part of the blessing, "Boaz is blessed by the prayer that his house may be like that 'of Perez whom Tamar [a Canaanite!] bore' to the patriarch Judah as the result of an irregular connection (so the Judeans were in no position to throw stones at their northern neighbors)."[110]

3. Boaz and his well-wishers in 4:11-12 think of Ruth's value in terms of her ability to "build up" her husband's "house." In the world of the story, women seem to acquire value in men's eyes primarily by giving birth to sons who will carry their fathers' "names" (both gene pools and property claims) into the future. But the women of Bethlehem refuse to be limited by this patriarchal evaluation. They tell Naomi that "the son is to be valued because of his *mother*! This child will be a blessing, they say, 'for your daughter-in-law, who loves you, has borne him, and she means more than seven sons!' "[111]

The story thus ends, as it began, with Naomi. After all is said and done, Naomi is the recipient of redemption. Ruth is neither seen nor heard to speak in the conclusion of the book bearing her name. Nevertheless, Ruth (not Naomi) will be remembered as one of the mothers of the Messiah.

4. Whether or not the book of Ruth was *written* in post-exilic times, when it was *heard* in that era it must have made a difference in people's attitudes toward the foreigners in their midst. Clearly Naomi is the character who best reflects the experiences of the *gôlâ*, the remnant who returned home after the exile: "Naomi is a figure for the Jewish people in a phase from which God has hidden his face."[112] Naomi herself was a remnant; she was the one who was "left" (1:3, 5). If the people of Israel in the post-exilic period could identify with Naomi's bitterness, if they felt as empty as Naomi felt returning to Judah after a long sojourn away from home, then they might also have understood from the story of Ruth that redemption (recovery from the emptiness and the bitter losses of the exile) could come from the very foreigners Ezra and Nehemiah wanted to cast out of the covenant community. If, on the other hand, the listeners identified with the "worthy" Boaz, they might have noticed that this pillar of Israelite society had to be called to responsibility by a foreign woman.[113] Identification within the dynamics of the Ruth story might very well have helped to persuade people in the time of Nehemiah-Ezra that "foreigners who joined themselves to the LORD" (Isa 56:6) were an essential part of the LORD's plan for Israel's redemption.

110. See M. Smith, *Palestinian Parties and Politics That Shaped the Old Testament* (New York: Columbia University Press, 1971) 161-62.
111. Nancy V. Lee, "Choices in the Book of Ruth," *The Japan Christian Quarterly* 54 (1988) 242.
112. Haim Chertok, "The Book of Ruth—Complexities Within Simplicity," *Judaism* 35 (1986) 295.
113. Phyllis Trible, "A Human Comedy," in *God and the Rhetoric of Sexuality,* OBT (Philadelphia: Fortress, 1978) 184.

RUTH 4:18-22, DAVID'S FAMILY TREE

NIV	NRSV
[18]This, then, is the family line of Perez: Perez was the father of Hezron, [19]Hezron the father of Ram, Ram the father of Amminadab,	18Now these are the descendants of Perez: Perez became the father of Hezron, [19]Hezron of Ram, Ram of Amminadab, [20]Amminadab of Nahshon, Nahshon of Salmon, [21]Salmon of Boaz, Boaz of Obed, [22]Obed of Jesse, and Jesse of David.

NIV

²⁰Amminadab the father of Nahshon,
  Nahshon the father of Salmon,^a
²¹Salmon the father of Boaz,
  Boaz the father of Obed,
²²Obed the father of Jesse,
  and Jesse the father of David.

^a20 A few Hebrew manuscripts, some Septuagint manuscripts and Vulgate (see also verse 21 and Septuagint of 1 Chron. 2:11); most Hebrew manuscripts *Salma*

COMMENTARY

When the Anchor Bible commentary on Ruth was published in 1975, it could accurately be said that "there is all but universal agreement that verses 18-22 form a genealogical appendix to the Ruth story and are not an original part of it."[114] But more recent scholarship is inclined to argue that the genealogy functions "as an integral part of the text as it has been received."[115] Since there is no genealogy of David in the books of Samuel, this list of ancestors in Ruth serves an essential purpose: "to situate the characters of this story among the body of known personalities in the tradition."[116] Thus it seems that the attachment of the genealogy to the story of Ruth must be at least as old as the inclusion of the book in the narrative sequence from Genesis to Kings.

The genealogy begins with Perez, which makes Boaz the seventh "son" named in the list of David's ancestors. David himself was said to be a seventh son in 1 Chr 2:15, although 1 Sam 17:12-15 calls him the youngest of Jesse's eight sons.

Since the narrative puts so much emphasis on maintaining the name of the dead on his inheritance, the failure to mention either Elimelech or Mahlon in the genealogy is striking. Boaz is counted as the father of Obed, and Obed "builds up the house" of Boaz, not the house of Mahlon. Whatever legal fiction was maintained in order to make Obed the heir to Elimelech's property, the narrator clearly thinks that the line leading to the birth of David runs through Boaz.

In most Hebrew manuscripts, the name of Boaz's father is spelled "Salma" (here and in 1 Chr 2:11). Some manuscripts of the Septuagint spell the name "Salmon," as does Matt 1:5. Matthew's list of ancestors from Abraham to Jesus names Rahab as the wife of Salmon and the mother of Boaz (a detail that is not found in the Hebrew Bible). Most commentators assume that Matthew is referring to the Rahab whose story is told in Josh 2:1-21; 6:22-23. Like Ruth, Rahab was a non-Israelite woman who chose to align herself with Israel and with Israel's God. If Rahab, the Canaanite prostitute from Jericho, was the mother of Boaz, then Obed, the "root" of David's family tree, had both a Moabite mother and a Canaanite grandmother. On one side, the line leading to Obed runs from the unnamed mother of Moab to Ruth. On the other side, the line leads from Leah, the mother of Judah, to Tamar, the mother of Perez, and to Rahab, the mother of Boaz.

114. Campbell, *Ruth,* 172.
115. Ernst R. Wendland, "Structural Symmetry and Its Significance in the Book of Ruth," in *Issues in Bible Translation,* ed. Philip C. Stine, UBS Monograph Series 3 (New York: United Bible Societies, 1988) 36. See also Adele Berlin, *Poetics and Interpretation of Biblical Narrative* (Winona Lake, Ind.: Eisenbrauns, 1994) 109-10; Johannes C. de Moor, "The Poetry of the Book of Ruth, Part II," *Orientalia,* N.S. 55 (1986) 42-43.
116. Berlin, *Poetics and Interpretation of Biblical Narrative,* 110.

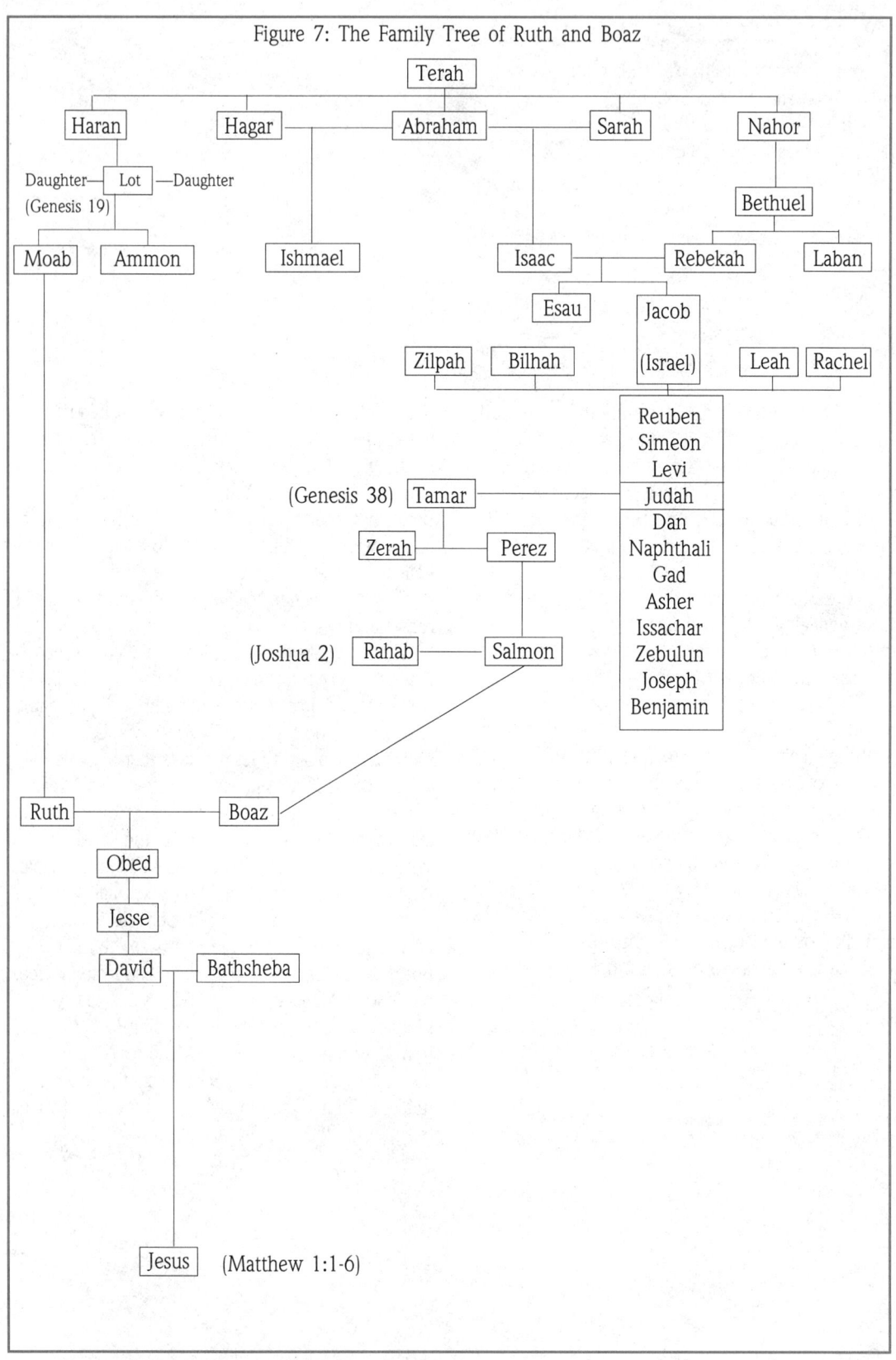

Figure 7: The Family Tree of Ruth and Boaz

REFLECTIONS

In 4:13 the narrator tells us that the LORD made Ruth conceive. This assertion stands out as the only place in the book in which the narrator makes a statement about God's actions. All of the other references to God in the story are found in the mouths of the characters, who express a variety of beliefs about the nature and purposes of God.

Naomi's picture of God reflects (or perhaps is distorted by) her grief. When Naomi speaks to Orpah and Ruth in 1:13 and to the women of Bethlehem in 1:20-21, she blames the LORD for her bereavement. It is not clear whether she thinks she has done something wrong (perhaps fleeing to Moab in the midst of a famine) for which she is being punished, or whether she thinks the LORD's hand has been arbitrarily raised against her.

As her grief begins to heal, Naomi invokes the LORD's blessing on Boaz when Ruth brings back a load of grain from gleaning in Boaz's field (2:20). While it is not clear whether the phrase "whose kindness has not forsaken the living or the dead" refers to Boaz or to the LORD, it is clear that Naomi is now thinking of the LORD as a potential source of blessing.

In a similar way, we can see that what Boaz says and thinks about God is shaped (or perhaps distorted) by the fact that Boaz is wealthy and secure in his position in the community. Feeling blessed by God, he repeatedly calls upon the LORD to bless or to reward those with whom Boaz is pleased (2:12; 3:10).

Ruth, the non-Israelite convert to the mother-in-law's faith, has the least to say about the LORD. After she tells Naomi that "your God will be my God," she swears an oath by the God of Israel, which means something like, "May the LORD strike me dead if I don't keep my pledge" (1:17). Ruth is confident that she has put her future into the hands of a God who has power over life and death.

The women of Bethlehem also see the LORD as a source of life. They praise God with a collective voice in 4:14, because it is clear to them that God has provided Naomi with a "redeemer." However, it might also be said that human beings personify and communicate the loving-kindness of God to each other in this story. Everything the LORD gives, including the conception of the child, comes through human interaction. We might conclude that God's love embodied in humankind gives birth to the messianic line.

Interpretations of the book of Ruth in the life of the church can be divided into essentially two groups, depending on how the following questions are answered: Is the line of the redeemer "chosen" *because* of the faithfulness of its human components or *in spite of* their all-too human behavior? Are Tamar, Rahab, and Ruth included in Matthew's genealogy because of or in spite of who they were? Do we credit their ḥesed or God's ḥesed for the birth of the messianic line?

On the one hand, it is quite possible to argue that "the genealogy . . . underscores the great reward granted Ruth for her loyalty; she is the honored ancestress of a great Israelite leader."[117] Ruth's faithfulness seems to be an essential element in the carrying out of God's plans for the world through the lineage of David. "It is the faith of Rahab and Ruth, not their pedigree, that commends them to be the mothers of kings."[118]

On the other hand, it is equally possible to argue that the story of Ruth is more about the faithfulness of God than about the faithfulness of humankind. If we consider the role the book of Ruth plays as a part of the Deuteronomistic History, we might conclude either that the ancestry of the Davidic line of kings is better than the line of Saul, or that *both* lines leading to human kingship in Israel are flawed. The marriage between Ruth (the descendant of Moab)

---

117. Hubbard, *The Book of Ruth*, 22.
118. Warren Austin Gage, "Ruth Upon the Threshing Floor and the Sin of Gibeah: A Biblical-Theological Study," *Westminster Theological Journal* 51 (1989) 375.

and Boaz (the descendant of Tamar) can be seen either as a redemption of their ancestors' stories or as one more echo in Israel's sustained confession of sin as recorded in Joshua through 2 Kings.

Within the context of the whole canon, the book of Ruth can be considered a parable of the nature of God's love. The parable says that Ruth persisted in offering Naomi love and support, even in the face of Naomi's rejection, just as God persists in loving us, even in the face of our rejection. But the specific stories associated with the line of the Messiah read more like a confession of sin than a catalog of virtues. The stories told about the ancestors of Ruth and Boaz make it clear that the messianic king comes from a well-established line of tricksters who have mixed and not always admirable motives for what they do. Whatever determined David's eligibility to father the messianic line of kings, we can be sure that it was neither the ethnic nor the moral purity of his ancestral line! The collective point these stories make is *not* that the mothers and fathers of the Messiah were exceptionally worthy people, but that God can use even the least likely agents to bring about redemption. When the Gospel of Matthew adds Rahab to the list of David's ancestors and Jesus to the list of those whose ancestry is nothing to brag about, the theological point remains the same: It is God's grace and not our own merit that brings forth the redeemer of the world.

We who consider ourselves the people of God are frequently tempted to think that redemption comes as a reward to those who are faithful. We need to be reminded on a regular basis that God's faithfulness, not our own, brings about redemption. All of the characters in the story of Ruth have mixed motives. They have both self-serving and altruistic agendas. "They are all human, yet out of the tangle of human interactions God's redemption occurs."[119]

Because Ruth is the human catalyst for the redemptive transformations in Naomi's life, and because Ruth's acts of loving-kindness communicate the persistence of God's love to Naomi, we are tempted to hold Ruth up as a model for our own morality. But, in fact, most of us should see ourselves mirrored in the character of Naomi. Naomi reflects the reality of who we are: We are the recipients of unmerited love, and our redemption is due to someone else's ḥesed, not our own.

At the same time, however, it must be said that readers who recognize that there are ways in which they *are* like Ruth may also hear a redemptive message in the story. Renita Weems notes that an African American woman might at various times see her life experiences reflected in "Ruth the woman, Ruth the foreigner, Ruth the unelected woman, Ruth the displaced widow, or, perhaps, Ruth the ancestress of the king of Israel, King David, to name a few."[120] Seeing one's own reality mirrored in the character of Ruth may assure those who feel like Moabites in their own modern contexts that God does not choose agents of redemption according to human standards or according to the expectations of society, that God can and may be working through them and through their relationships with others to transform emptiness into fullness. But for someone else (teachers, preachers, or writers of commentaries) to insist that a reader *ought* to be like Ruth must be considered repressive rather than redemptive.

We who think we have been chosen by God are often tempted to exclude those we perceive to be "the other." Thus we need to be reminded on a regular basis that God often chooses "the other" to help carry out God's purposes in the world. Rather than encouraging people to be like Ruth, we need to challenge them to *see* Ruth reflected in the "other," however the "other" is currently defined. In preaching or teaching from the book of Ruth, we need to ask, Who is the "Moabite" in the eyes of *our* community of faith? Who do we despise on the basis of their origins (Gen 19:30-37) or blame for the decline in our own morals (Num 25:1-2)? To whom do we deny admittance into "the assembly of the LORD" (Deut 23:3-6)? Might God use such a one to bring about *our* redemption?

---

119. Alice Ogden Bellis, *Helpmates, Harlots, Heroes: Women's Stories in the Hebrew Bible* (Louisville: Westminster/John Knox, 1994) 211.

120. Renita J. Weems, "African American Women and the Bible," in *Stony the Road We Trod,* ed. Cain Hope Felder (Minneapolis: Fortress, 1991) 67-68.

THE FIRST AND SECOND
BOOKS OF SAMUEL

INTRODUCTION, COMMENTARY, AND REFLECTIONS
BY
BRUCE C. BIRCH

THE FIRST AND SECOND BOOKS OF
SAMUEL

INTRODUCTION

The books of 1 and 2 Samuel witness to one of the most crucial periods of transition and change in the story of ancient Israel. At the opening of 1 Samuel, Israel is a loose federation of tribes, experiencing both external threat from the militarily superior Philistines and internal crisis because of the corruption of the priestly house of Eli at Shiloh, where the ark was maintained and covenant traditions were preserved (see Overview for chaps. 1–7). At the conclusion of 2 Samuel, an emerging monarchy is firmly in place under David. He has weathered various threats to the integrity of the kingdom, and is preparing to establish a hereditary dynasty in Israel. The momentous changes necessitated by this transition to kingship provide some of the most dramatic stories in the Old Testament. These stories not only narrate dramatic events but also introduce us to some of the most striking characters in the biblical story. Samuel, Saul, and David, whose stories overlap, dominate the pages of the books of Samuel. Moreover, even the supporting cast is remarkable for the variety of sharply drawn characters that flesh out the pages of these stories—Hannah, Eli, Jonathan, Michal, Joab, Abigail, Abishai, Abner, Bathsheba, Nathan, Amnon, Tamar, Absalom, Mephibosheth, to name only a few. Yet, beyond these personalities and events, the books of Samuel make clear that the Lord is at work in these turbulent times. On the surface, these stories may seem preoccupied with political power, but we will discover that these narratives testify to the true power of the Lord, acting in and through personalities and events to bring Israel to a new future in keeping with God's purposes.

TITLE AND DIVISION OF THE BOOKS OF SAMUEL

The books of 1 and 2 Samuel were originally one book. The oldest Hebrew manuscript from Qumran (4QSam[a]) includes both 1 and 2 Samuel on a single scroll. Moreover, the Talmud references allude to a single book of Samuel. The division into two books was probably introduced by the Greek translators (the Septuagint), perhaps to create scrolls of a more manageable size. In Septuagint manuscripts, the books of Samuel and Kings are divided into four books called 1–4 Kingdoms. This division and its designations were adopted by Jerome in his Latin translation (the Vulgate) and became the common designation in Roman Catholic Bibles until the mid-twentieth century. The manuscripts of the Masoretic text (Hebrew) assume a one-book arrangement. The division into 1 and 2 Samuel did not appear until the fifteenth century and became common with the first printed editions of the Hebrew Bible in the sixteenth century.[1]

The decision about the place at which to divide the books was undoubtedly influenced by the custom of concluding books with the death of a major figure (e.g., Joseph/Genesis; Moses/Deuteronomy; Joshua/Joshua). Thus the division of the books of Samuel was placed after the death of Saul. It is curious, however, that the two versions of Saul's death are separated by this division (1 Samuel 31; 2 Samuel 1). The retention of the name "Samuel" for the divided arrangement also creates the anomaly of a 2 Samuel named for the prophet Samuel, who does not appear at all in the book.

TEXT OF THE BOOKS OF SAMUEL

The Hebrew text of 1 and 2 Samuel (the Masoretic text) on which English translations have been routinely based is in extremely poor condition.[2] Its text for these books is much shorter than the text of the ancient Greek translation of the Hebrew Bible, the Septuagint (LXX), and other ancient versions of the text of 1 and 2 Samuel. Until recently, many scholars assumed that the Greek translators had simply added traditions known to them and thus expanded the text. However, other scholars offered a different explanation—namely, that the Hebrew text had suffered numerous omissions and copying errors. This latter assumption was confirmed by the discovery, beginning in 1952, of three fragmentary Samuel manuscripts in the library of the ancient community of Qumran, beside the shores of the Dead Sea.[3] The most important of these, 4QSam[a], was written in the first century BCE and contains large portions of 1 and 2 Samuel in a well-preserved condition. The second, 4QSam[b], dates from the mid-third century but contains only poorly preserved fragments of a small portion of 1 Samuel. And the third, 4QSam[c], also from the first century, contains only fragments of 1 Samuel 25 and 2 Samuel 14–15.

The failure to publish many of the Qumran texts promptly has delayed the impact of

---

1. See P. Kyle McCarter, *I Samuel,* AB 8 (Garden City, N.Y.: Doubleday, 1984) 3-4.
2. McCarter (ibid., 5-11) has the fullest description of the textual witnesses for the books of Samuel, and the textual sections of his chapter-by-chapter commentary represent the most detailed treatment of textual problems in these books.
3. See E. C. Ulrich, Jr., *The Qumran Text of Samuel and Josephus,* HSM 19 (Missoula, Mont.: Scholars Press, 1978).

this material on English translations of the books of Samuel. However, the work of Ulrich and McCarter (both cited above) has given wide circulation to the longer LXX/Qumran readings for 1 and 2 Samuel. Frank Cross used the Qumran material in translating the books of Samuel for the NAB (1970). More recent translations (including the NRSV and the NIV, used in this commentary) have been able to use this textual material, and as a consequence have often adopted many of the longer readings reflected in the LXX and Qumran texts.

LITERARY COMPOSITION OF THE BOOKS OF SAMUEL

It is generally agreed that analysis of the process by which the books of Samuel were composed comprises one of the most complex subjects in twentieth-century biblical study. Current views on the literary composition of 1 and 2 Samuel offer no clear-cut consensus. I can only summarize briefly some of the major positions and approaches concerning the formation of the books of Samuel. Later, some of the critical assumptions that serve as the basis for this commentary will be made clear.

Earlier Approaches. Repetitions, doublets, contradictions, and contrasting viewpoints in the stories and traditions of 1 and 2 Samuel led scholars in the late nineteenth and early twentieth centuries to look for multiple literary strands or sources that could be traced throughout the books of Samuel.[4] Some identified literary sources in the books of Samuel that they thought were continuations of those present in the Pentateuch, but this view was largely abandoned in the early twentieth century. A more prominent theory involved the view that the books of Samuel were made up of an early and a late source. Although details differed, many scholars until the mid-twentieth century defended some variation on this hypothesis. The early source was thought to offer a more positive assessment of the development of monarchy in Israel and also to be more historically reliable. The late source was responsible for additions to the text that created inconsistencies and redundancies. This late source was negative toward kingship and considered to provide a less reliable historical source for the period. This theory of an early and a late source has been largely abandoned. Both supportive and antagonistic attitudes toward kingship in Israel are likely to have arisen from Saul's time onward and not simply to be the product of late experience with kings. Furthermore, the negative views associated with the kingship of Saul disappear in positive approval of David when he enters the story. In sum, theories of composition for the books of Samuel have become more complex. Moreover, few scholars think that the traditions now included in the books of Samuel offer a neutral historical reconstruction of that period.

In 1926, Leonhard Rost published his influential study of 2 Samuel 9–20 and 1 Kings 1–2,[5] which he identified as an independent narrative written by a single author who lived

---

4. For a detailed discussion of representative scholars and viewpoints in early and recent research on the books of Samuel, see James W. Flanagan, "Samuel, Book of 1–2: Text, Composition and Content," in *The Anchor Bible Dictionary*, 6 vols., ed. David Noel Freedman (New York: Doubleday, 1992) 5:958-61.

5. Leonhard Rost, *Die Überlieferung von der Thronnachfolge Davids,* BWANT 3/6 (Stuttgart: Kohlhammer, 1926); English trans.: *The Succession to the Throne of David,* trans. Michael D. Rutter and David M. Gunn (Sheffield: Almond, 1982).

close to the time of the events themselves. Rost believed that the focus for this narrative was in answering the question, Who will succeed David on the throne? Building on Rost's hypothesis, Gerhard von Rad argued that the succession narrative was an early example of history writing, albeit a history that assumes divine providence acted through persons and events in the narrative.[6] Rost's work has been the starting point for an unusual degree of interest in these chapters of 2 Samuel, and many of Rost's conclusions have been modified, including the contention that succession is the central interest of these chapters (see Overview for 2 Samuel 9:1–20:26). Nevertheless, his view of a coherent pre-existing narrative used as a source by the author of 1 and 2 Samuel is still widely accepted.

This claim for the existence of a succession narrative as a source document for the compiler of 1 and 2 Samuel has influenced a flurry of claims for other independent pre-existing sources that were incorporated into the books of Samuel—not as intertwined sources but as stories in a sequence. Other proposed sources included an ark narrative (1 Samuel 4–6; 2 Samuel 6), a history of David's rise (1 Samuel 16–2 Samuel 5:10), and a birth story of Samuel (1 Samuel 1–3).

In 1943, Martin Noth proposed that the whole of the Former Prophets (Joshua–2 Kings, excluding Ruth in the English Bible) constituted a single great history work influenced by deuteronomic theological perspectives and written during the time of the Babylonian exile.[7] His basic argument for a deuteronomistic historian (Dtr) is still widely accepted, although some now argue persuasively that this Deuteronomistic History was written before the destruction of Jerusalem and was then supplemented to take account of those events. Noth did identify the deuteronomic historian with most of the material and viewpoint attributed to the so-called Late Source of earlier scholarship—that is, negative to kingship and historically unreliable. This broad identification is no longer accepted. Most now regard the final shape of 1 and 2 Samuel to be the work of the deuteronomistic historian, but the extent of that role is debated, with some claiming that the deuteronomist did little more than mechanical redaction with occasional theological comment and others claiming single, unified authorship of the whole of 1 and 2 Samuel by the deuteronomist.[8]

Recent Emphases. Scholarship on the books of Samuel since 1960 has been prolific and varied, but one may highlight several prominent areas in the discussion. Many scholars

6. Gerhard von Rad, "Der Anfang der Geschichtsschreibung im alten Israel," *Archiv fur Kulturgeschichte* 32 (1944) 1-42; English translation: "The Beginning of History Writing in Ancient Israel," in *The Problem of the Hexateuch and Other Essays,* trans. E. W. Trueman Dicken (New York: McGraw-Hill, 1966) 166-204.

7. Martin Noth, *Überlieferungsgeschichtliche Studien. Die sammeln und bearbeitenden Geschichtswerke im Alten Testament* (Tubingen: Niemeyer, 1943); English translation: *The Deuteronomistic History,* trans. J. Doull, JSOTSup 15 (Sheffield: JSOT, 1981).

8. The most careful and nuanced treatment of the deuteronomistic influences and traditions in the books of Samuel is that of T. Veijola, *Das Konigtum in der Beurteilung der deuteronomistischen Historiographie. Eine redaktions-geschichtliche Untersuchung,* Annales Academiae Scientiarum Fennicae B, 193 (Helsinki: Suomalainen Tiedeakatemia, 1977). Robert Polzin has recently argued in a series of volumes that the text from Joshua through 2 Kings is the work of a single deuteronomistic author. His volumes on the books of Samuel are *Samuel and the Deuteronomist: A Literary Study of the Deuteronomic History,* Part Two: *1 Samuel* (San Francisco: Harper & Row, 1989) and *David and the Deuteronomist: A Literary Study of the Deuteronomic History,* Part Three: *2 Samuel* (Bloomington: Indiana University Press, 1993).

continued to work with the traditional tools and approaches of historical-critical scholarship but with much greater attention to the complexity of the Samuel material. In addition, they have tended to examine longer segments of the Samuel narratives and with greater attention to the final form of the text in these segments as well as in the books of Samuel as a whole. Significant studies, based on historical-critical methods, have focused on the ark narrative, the rise of kingship in Israel, the history of David's rise, David's consolidation of his kingdom, the court history of David (the succession narrative), and the so-called appendixes to the books of Samuel. (See the Overview sections on each of these narrative segments for more detailed discussion and bibliography.)

Some scholars still discern evidence of pre-deuteronomistic editions of Samuel traditions incorporating, and in some cases helping to form, the larger narrative segments just mentioned above. Perhaps the most thoroughgoing example of such a viewpoint appears in McCarter's Anchor Bible commentary. Building on the work of Weiser and Birch, McCarter argues that

> the First Book of Samuel derives its basic shape from a prophetic history of the origin of the monarchy that was intended to present the advent of kingship in Israel as a concession to a wanton demand of the people . . . the history was written to set forth according to a prophetic perspective the essential elements of the new system by which Israel would be governed. The prophet, whom the example of Samuel showed to be capable of ruling alone, would continue to be the people's intercessor with Yahweh. The king . . . would be subject not only to the instruction and admonition of the prophet acting in his capacity as Yahweh's spokesman but even to prophetic election and rejection.[9]

This prophetic history, dating to the late eighth century, is especially evident in segments of narrative on the birth of Samuel (1 Samuel 1–3), the role of Samuel as judge and deliverer (1 Samuel 7), the rise of kingship and the role of the prophet in those events (1 Samuel 8–12), the rejection of Saul (1 Samuel 13 and 15), the anointing of David (1 Samuel 16), Saul's consultation with the ghost of Samuel (1 Samuel 28), elements of the dynastic oracle (2 Samuel 7), the sin of David and his confrontation by Nathan (2 Samuel 11–12), and David's census and God's judgment (2 Samuel 24).

Recent decades have seen the impact of social-scientific methods and comparative social-world models on study of the books of Samuel and the transition period these traditions represent in the history of Israel. The publication of Gottwald's groundbreaking study on tribal Israel in the period of Joshua and Judges[10] had a catalytic effect on Samuel studies. Interest focused on describing the centralization process that moved Israel from

---

9. McCarter, *I Samuel*, 21. McCarter builds on work by Artur Weiser, *The Old Testament: Its Formation and Development*, trans. B. M. Barton (New York: Association Press, 1961; German original 1948); and Bruce C. Birch, *The Rise of the Israelite Monarchy: The Growth and Development of 1 Samuel 7–15*, SBLDS 27 (Missoula, Mont.: Scholars Press, 1976).

10. Norman K. Gottwald, *The Tribes of Yahweh: A Sociology of the Religion of Liberated Israel, 1250–1050 B.C.* (Maryknoll, N.Y.: Orbis, 1979).

its tribal existence to a monarchic nation-state. Most social-world critics think a complex pattern of social and economic pressures led toward centralization, but also produced resistance to that centralization. Many believe the political reality of the Philistines' pressure and the economic reality of limited resources led not to a full-fledged kingship under Saul and David, but to something more like a paramount tribal chieftaincy, which was not free politically or economically to embrace fully the model of a royal state.[11] That remains for Solomon to accomplish. The narratives of Samuel represent not history per se but a telling of Israel's story that seeks to unify diverse perspectives in the service of a social unity centered in Jerusalem and based on Yahwistic religion.

> Differences and contradictions in the stories have ecological, political, social, economic, and religious bases. By their existence, the texts signal continuing hope for social unity grounded in belief. The unifying force of Yahwist religion is central to the stories. Tensions among factions and perspectives that can be felt, for the most part, follow from contemporary differences rather than successive revisions of the texts. Hence, 1–2 Samuel, although formed from separate traditions, cycles, and stories, is a unified account that captures the urgency of the compilers' time.[12]

Recent scholarship has also seen the application of literary-critical methodologies to 1 and 2 Samuel. These studies have focused on the final form of the text with little interest in traditional questions of sources or processes of composition. Literary critics assume that the narrative as it stands possesses artistic integrity and must be analyzed as such. These approaches have been largely uninterested in historical questions and are largely skeptical that genuine correlations are possible between these stories and the actual course of Israel's history. The study by David Gunn, devoted to the succession narrative, represented a break with many of the assumptions of traditional historical criticism and treated the succession narrative as a part of a larger integrated whole in the books of Samuel.[13] More recently, works by Polzin and Fokkelman involve a close literary reading of the texts of 1 and 2 Samuel that has moved in an entirely different direction from traditional historical-critical scholarship on the books of Samuel.[14] Their treatments postulate and seek to demonstrate a literary integrity in the books of Samuel that neither admits to previous sources or editions in these narratives nor shows any interest or confidence in these texts as sources for Israel's history in the time of Saul and David. The narrative is understood to be largely the product of the literary efforts and theological concerns of a later single author (for Polzin, it is the deuteronomist).

Finally, there has been a resurgence of interest in the theological interpretation of the

---

11. See James W. Flanagan, "Chiefs in Israel," *JSOT* 20 (1981) 47-73; Frank S. Frick, *The Formation of the State in Ancient Israel: A Survey of Methods and Theories*, SWBA 4 (Sheffield: JSOT, 1985).

12. Flanagan, "Samuel, Books of 1–2," *ABD* 5:961.

13. David M. Gunn, *The Story of King David: Genre and Interpretation*, JSOTSup 6 (Sheffield: JSOT, 1978).

14. See Polzin, *Samuel and the Deuteronomist* and *David and the Deuteronomist;* J. P. Fokkelman, *Narrative Art and Poetry in the Books of Samuel,* 2 vols. (Assen: Van Gorcum, 1981; 1986).

books of Samuel. In the search for sources and in the effort to identify various historical elements in the text, the theological importance of the books of Samuel as a whole had been neglected. However, this situation has changed dramatically since 1970. There is increasing recognition that the books of Samuel represent Israel's theological struggle to adapt its faith to radically changed social realities and that many of the issues concerning the relationship of God's providence to human power are of continuing concern to the Jewish and Christian communities. The work of Walter Brueggemann has been of critical importance in the renewal of theological interest in the books of Samuel. In countless articles, monographs, and books he has pioneered the reshaping of traditional assumptions that these books are only of "historical" interest. His commentary on the books of Samuel represents the culminating statement of his work on this literature.[15]

Recent Samuel scholarship has been rich and eclectic. There is no clear consensus on many of the critical issues in interpreting the book, but a general agreement seems to be emerging that scholarship on the books of Samuel in the future is likely to draw on a variety of approaches and methodologies (historical-critical, social-world, literary, theological). Perhaps such multifaceted approaches are the best hope of doing justice to the complexity and richness of these books.

CRITICAL ASSUMPTIONS

The Commentary and Reflections on the books of Samuel make a number of critical assumptions that need to be made explicit.

1. The emphasis of this work will be on the *final form* of 1 and 2 Samuel as a literary witness whose integrity and meaning do not depend on analysis and recovery of the earlier sources and editions that have brought the narrative to its present final form. This final form is probably the product of the deuteronomistic historian, who allowed earlier sources and editions to remain visible. These earlier elements may contribute distinctive emphases to the narrative. The concern, however, will not be to separate and recover these earlier sources and editions from the final form of the text, but to examine how they contribute to the books of Samuel in their present form. The long process by which these traditions have been shaped is not recoverable. My analysis will begin with the whole rather than the parts. Where earlier sources and editions have been left visible, I will comment on the emphases of these elements as they contribute to an enriched understanding of the books of Samuel in their present final form.

For the purpose of this commentary, the most important of the earlier sources and editions are listed here:

Independent literary units that existed prior to the work of the narrator and are responsible for the final shape of the books of Samuel. These include an ark narrative (1

---

15. Walter Brueggemann, *First and Second Samuel,* Interpretation (Louisville: John Knox, 1990). His many other articles and books related to the books of Samuel are too numerous to mention here, but they are cited throughout this commentary.

Samuel 4–6); a history of the rise of David (1 Sam 16:1–2 Sam 5:10); and a court history (so-called succession narrative; 2 Samuel 9–20). Other narrative segments of 1 and 2 Samuel seem intentionally shaped as literary units, but it is less clear that they predate the work of the artistic hand responsible for the whole of these books.

A prophetic edition of these narratives may have joined and interpreted early traditions and sources prior to the work of the deuteronomist. The conclusions of McCarter, mentioned earlier, seem to have merit, though I am not as confident as McCarter that the work of this prophetic editor can be as precisely identified as he believes. It is not possible to isolate a prophetic edition in the present form of the books of Samuel. Rather, one may identify a prophetic theology of kingship and an emphasis on the peculiar role of the prophets in relation to kings within certain narratives. These prophetic interests and emphases will be noted as they appear in the final form of the text. This emphasis is apparent especially in 1 Samuel 1–3; 7–15; 16; 28; and 2 Samuel 7; 11–12; 24 (see Commentary on these sections and chapters).

Even if the deuteronomistic historian is responsible for the whole of 1 and 2 Samuel, there are certain *narrative segments that reflect deuteronomistic language and theological interests.* Compared to other portions of the Deuteronomistic History, there are fewer of these distinctively deuteronomistic passages, which suggests that a large part of the narrative of 1 and 2 Samuel already existed in a form that the deuteronomistic historian found congenial. Many of the distinctly deuteronomistic passages incorporate the Samuel narratives into the form and structure adopted elsewhere for the Deuteronomistic History—e.g., elements of the farewell speech of Samuel (1 Samuel 12) or the archival notices on Saul's kingship (1 Sam 13:1-2; 14:47-51). In general, I will not try to identify every verse that might be argued as distinctively deuteronomistic;[16] instead, I will simply note those places where a deuteronomistic perspective or use of language influences the analysis of the larger narrative. I do not regard the deuteronomist as simply an annotator. By what has been included, excluded, and added to earlier sources, the deuteronomist has worked as the literary artist and theological commentator responsible for the books of Samuel as we now have them.

2. There is an identifiable and significant *socio-historical context* to which the narratives of 1 and 2 Samuel give witness, even if that witness is now interpretively shaped by the perspectives and contexts of later Israelite generations. These stories are rooted in a time of considerable social and political transformation in the life of Israel, and these realities challenged the theological categories by which Israel understood its life in relation to God. This transformative period was so crucial to Israel's understanding of itself that its events and personalities were still being assessed politically and theologically at the time of the exile, when the work of the deuteronomistic historian fixed these narratives in their present form.

16. A helpful and thoughtful delineation of the deuteronomistic portions of 1 and 2 Samuel may be found in McCarter, *I Samuel,* 14-17, and *II Samuel,* 4-8, although McCarter is generally more confident than I in arguing the presence of a deuteronomistic hand in very small additions to some chapters.

The books of Samuel open with a loose federation of tribal groups gripped by a crisis, both external and internal, that threatens the very existence of Israel, and they end on the eve of an emergent hereditary monarchy that will preside over an established nation-state. This transformation represents a considerable achievement. The narratives in 1 and 2 Samuel are not historical in the sense of our modern positivistic understandings of history. Rather, they blend historical realism with artistic and theological imagination. Attention to the imaginative elements of these narratives has led some to miss the historically realistic style by which these narratives depict the nature of this historical crisis and social transformation. Likewise, the historically realistic style has led others mistakenly to treat the books of Samuel as history writing and to overlook the artistic and imaginative freedom with which many elements of the story have been shaped.

The socio-historical context at the beginning of 1 Samuel includes the external threat of incorporation into a Philistine empire that sought to expand into Israelite territory c. 1000 BCE (1 Samuel 4). The internal crisis in this same period is reflected in the loose tribal association that proves incapable of meeting such a crisis (1 Samuel 4) and the corruption of the institutions of Yahwism, which gave tribal Israel whatever unity it possessed (1 Samuel 2–3). The end of the book of Judges describes a state of political chaos and moral decadence that results in idolatry and barbarous behavior (Judges 17–21), a time when "there was no king in Israel; every man did what was right in his own eyes" (Judg 17:6; 18:1; 19:1; 21:25). There is little reason to think that Israel could survive these internal and external crises.

Yet, by the end of 2 Samuel, Israel has been transformed socially and politically. Although details may be debated, it is clear that this transformation included political centralization and the emergence of governantal structures (first to chieftaincy then to monarchy) capable of uniting tribal Israel and coping with the crises it faced. This transformation included movement economically from marginal tribal, agrarian existence to a period of prosperity that included extended trade and the emergence of wealth. This development also required new structures of social management and practice. Many of the narratives of 1 and 2 Samuel are concerned to make legitimate, politically and theologically, these newly emerging political and economic structures. Saul, David, Jerusalem, the Temple—all in turn are the subject of narrative apologists in the books of Samuel (e.g., Saul, 1 Sam 9:1–10:16; David, 1 Sam 16:1–2 Sam 5:10; Jerusalem, 2 Sam 5:6-10; 6:1-19; Temple, 2 Sam 24:18-25). But the narratives also reflect the resistance to new centralized political and economic structures: Kingship is opposed (1 Samuel 8); David cannot build the Temple (2 Samuel 7); David's census brings judgment (2 Sam 24:1-17). These narratives reflect the challenge, tensions, and promise of a transformative moment in Israel's life. Elements of historical realism in the narratives allow us a view of the socio-historical context for this moment in Israel's story, but the narratives exercise artistic imagination in presenting the personalities, the events, and the divine will that mediated Israel's transformation.

3. *The role of personality* in Israel's story of this period is central. Samuel, Saul, and

David loom over the story in overlapping domination of the narrative landscape (Samuel, 1 Samuel 1–28; Saul, 1 Samuel 9–2 Samuel 1; David, 1 Samuel 16–2 Samuel 24). First, Samuel, then Saul, and finally David are presented as crucial to Israel's future, but where any two are present in the story, tension and conflict arise, as if there is room for only one of these dominant personalities in the spotlight. In the end, it is David, "the man after God's own heart," who fascinates Israel's storytellers.

Yet, for all the intense interest in David, these narratives do not neglect the role of others in the story. No segment of the Old Testament is filled with a richer cast of characters, and their portraits are vividly drawn. Even characters that occupy a single episode (e.g., Abigail, 1 Samuel 25) are often drawn as full and intriguing figures who play crucial roles in the drama that will find its climax in David. More than in earlier narratives in the canon (the Pentateuch, Joshua, Judges) the personalities of 1 and 2 Samuel are described in terms of inner motives and struggles as well as actions.

The telling of these stories depicts the personalities in artistic as well as historical terms. A historically realistic style is blended with artistic imagination. The narrator is not concerned with just the "truth" of fact but with the "truth" of meaning for Israel, especially where David is concerned. It does not matter who really killed Goliath (David, 1 Samuel 17, or Elhanan, 2 Sam 21:19). The combination of piety and courage in the dramatic, but fanciful, story of a youthful David's triumph captures the imagination of Israel and allows one to be confident that Israel's new future is assured. The story of Israel's transformation from tribe to kingdom is grounded in a historical experience, but the story of this time is peopled by characters that are, at times, portrayed in painstakingly realistic terms and, at other times, seem to stride off the page larger than life. Both the imaginative and the realistic elements are important in conveying Israel's memory of this crucial time.

4. To paint David and other crucial characters solely in human historical terms might suggest that Israel's transformation in that period was simply the product of human activity. But the authors of 1 and 2 Samuel understand that Israel's new future results from the working of *the providence of God.* It is the Lord (Yahweh) who shapes the events and personalities of this time. Sociopolitical realities and leadership are bent to the divine purpose.

In a world of human politics preoccupied with the issues of power, the issue for the narratives of Samuel is, Where does true power lie? These narrators understand that, in the juxtaposition of human power and divine will, God possesses the final authority. The poetry of Hannah's song (1 Sam 2:1-10) and of David's song (2 Sam 22:2-51) frames the entirety of 1 and 2 Samuel by announcing a divine purpose at work in the world that overturns and reverses the usual patterns of power. Consistent with this literary frame, a barren woman can give birth to the prophet of God's future for Israel (1 Samuel 1), a devastating Philistine victory can be turned into Philistine defeat without human help (1 Samuel 4–6), the king demanded by the people can nevertheless become God's anointed one (1 Samuel 8–10), even anointed kings can be rejected for unfaithfulness (1 Samuel

13; 15), an eighth son of an obscure family can become the future of Israel and the man after God's own heart (1 Samuel 16), a fugitive with a renegade band of followers sought by the king can receive the divine promise of eternal dynasty (2 Samuel 7), and even Israel's greatest and most beloved king can be judged by God (2 Samuel 12) and bring tragedy upon his own family (2 Samuel 13–18). In human terms, many of these events seem unlikely, but the narratives of Samuel understand all of these (and more) as a part of God's providence at work to bring Israel's future into being.

In 1 and 2 Samuel, the divine shaping of events is assumed, and even stated by the main characters in the narrative. This working of divine power does not usually occur by direct intervention in events, although the ark narratives (1 Samuel 4–6) suggest that God's purposes might not require human agency. Nevertheless, God's will is usually brought to pass through human events and personalities. The narratives make clear that divine power lies behind the human drama. For example, the lengthy narration of David's rise (1 Samuel 16–2 Sam 5:10) has as its central theological motif the conviction that "God was with him" (1 Sam 16:18; 18:14, 28), and it concludes after David is fully enthroned over Israel and Judah, "David became greater and greater, for the LORD, the God of hosts, was with him" (2 Sam 5:10 NRSV).

NARRATIVE UNITS AND EMPHASES IN THE BOOKS OF SAMUEL

Completely apart from judgments about earlier independent sources still visible in 1 and 2 Samuel, there is a developing scholarly consensus about the major segments into which the narrative falls. A brief description of these units gives a sense of the flow of the narrative and its major emphases. For a fuller description of these units and their themes, as well as references to the relevant scholarly literature, see the Overview sections for each of the segments.

1 Sam 1:1–4:1a. As the books of Samuel open, Israel is faced with a grave crisis, both internal and external, but we are not introduced to that crisis directly. Instead, we hear the story of Hannah, a barren woman who prays to the Lord and makes a vow (1:11). She asks the Lord to remember her, which the story tells us the Lord does (1:19). The story of Hannah's barrenness opens to the story of Israel's barren future. She bears a son, Samuel, the prophet who leads Israel through its time of crisis and through whom God will establish a kingship in Israel. Hannah's song (2:1-10) speaks of a God who brings the future in dramatic reversals and foreshadows the remarkable emergence of David as the climax of this story, an eighth son who becomes king. Childs has identified this song as "an interpretive key for this history which is, above all, to be understood from a theocentric perspective."[17] He has also shown that it has a counterpart at the end of 2 Samuel (chap. 22), a song that celebrates the Lord as the power behind David's successes. Thus a story that will be rich in human characters and events is framed as the work of the Lord.

17. Brevard S. Childs, *Introduction to the Old Testament as Scripture* (Philadelphia: Fortress, 1979) 273.

This opening segment of 1 Samuel goes on to depict the tragic corruption of the priestly house of Eli at Shiloh (2:11-36). But against this background of covenant disobedience at the heart of Israel, chaps. 1–3 provide a story of the birth, growth, legitimization, and establishment of Samuel as the prophetic leader who will bring Israel through crisis to a new day. By the end of chap. 3, Samuel is established as God's prophetic voice, and judgment has been pronounced on the house of Eli.

1 Sam 4:1b–7:1. This section of narrative identifies the external crisis of Israel. It tells a dramatic story of Philistine threat, defeat of Israel, and capture of the ark (chap. 4). Nevertheless, the Philistines do not turn out to have the upper hand. The ark of the covenant itself mediates the powerful presence of the Lord, defeating the Philistine god Dagon and bringing plagues upon the Philistine people. In humiliation, the Philistines finally send the ark on a cart back into Israelite territory (chaps. 5–6). I agree with those who have argued that this so-called ark history did not originally continue in 2 Samuel 6 (see the Overview on this section for a detailed discussion). That story does, of course, include the ark, but it focuses on David in a way quite unlike the style in 1 Samuel 4–6, where human characters play a small role.

These stories about the ark are remarkable, because Samuel, who was so carefully introduced in the preceding chapters, is absent. The only connection to chaps. 1–3 is the report of the death of Eli's sons when the ark is captured and of Eli's death when he hears the tragic news (4:12-22). Human leadership plays no role in these events; the divine power mediated by the ark is equal to the challenge of the Philistine crisis. As a result, the ensuing human demand for a king seems unnecessary. The Lord is sovereign and governs Israel's history, even in the face of threat from Philistine armies and gods. Whatever is to unfold in Israel's story in 1 and 2 Samuel will be because God allows or wills it.

1 Sam 7:2-17. Suddenly Samuel reappears in the story. In this unusual narrative, Samuel faces a Philistine threat and leads Israel to victory, but not through his own military leadership. Through prayer and mediation of divine power against the enemy, Samuel meets the threat (7:2-14). This victory is followed by the notice of a circuit that Samuel travels, "administering justice" in Israel (7:15-17). The portrait in this chapter is of Samuel single-handedly carrying on the covenant tradition and giving the leadership necessary for Israel's welfare. Once again, the narrative's effect is to render the coming request for a king unnecessary. Israel has the power of God and the leadership of Samuel. What more is needed? If kingship is nevertheless to come, then it is because God wills it, not because the situation of Israel demanded it.

1 Sam 8:1–15:35. These chapters focus on the establishment of kingship in Israel and the installation of Saul as the first holder of this office. There can be little doubt that these narratives have gone through a complex literary process that cannot be entirely recovered (see earlier discussion in this Introduction and also the Overview for these chapters). There is also an emerging consensus that the socio-historical realities behind these narratives were more complex than response to the Philistine crisis. Economic developments leading to accumulation of wealth and to the centralized forms of govern-ment needed to safeguard that wealth undoubtedly played a role in the development of Israelite monarchy, but these processes lie in the background of the narrative.

As the narratives now stand, the internal and external crises of Israel have driven some to demand a king. These chapters preserve a divided opinion on this matter. Some narratives clearly view kingship as sinful, allowed by an indulgent God (chaps. 8 and 12), while other narratives see the choice of Saul and his kingship as an act of God's providential grace (9:1–10:16; 11:1-15). This divided opinion is now widely understood as being rooted in genuine division within Israel at an early time. These traditions undoubtedly reflect Israel's struggle over the appropriate relationship of human power to divine power as expressed in the institutions of governance in Israel. Economic and political pressures were demand-ing new patterns of institutional leadership, but how was covenant obedience and divine authority preserved when human power grew more centralized and prominent in Israel?

The prophet plays a crucial role in representing the initiative of God (anointing, 10:1), in voicing the covenant demands of God on king and people (Samuel's farewell address, chap. 12), and in holding kings accountable to God (Saul's rejection, 13:8-15; 15:1-35). This prophetic role also occurs in David's story. The roles of the prophet in these narratives have led some scholars to suggest a prophetic editing of significant portions of the narratives in 1 and 2 Samuel, including the diverse material on the establishment of kingship (see the fuller discussion in the Overview on this section).

The political and theological interests reflected in 1 Samuel 8–15 are played out around the person of Saul. Many interpreters have noted the tragic character of his story (see the Overview on this section). The narratives reflect an awareness that David is the true climax of the story and of God's purposes in the story. Saul, in spite of his gifts, beyond what seems deserved by his faults, appears destined for failure and tragedy. Saul's story is not his own; it is a preparation for David. Saul's shortcomings are exposed in these stories (esp. chaps. 13–15). He does not appear to have the gifts required to usher in Israel's new future. Yet, the narrator is aware that Saul pays the personal price for Israel's future as one destined to fail so that another might succeed. It is fitting that much later in the narrative, after David has become the focus of attention, there is a pause for compassion and tribute to Saul and his son Jonathan on the occasion of their tragic deaths (2 Samuel 1).

1 Sam 16:1–2 Sam 5:10. The focus shifts to David. Story after story celebrates the courage, leadership, resourcefulness, piety, and political skill of David. Saul appears as a foil to David—driven, impulsive, cruel, fickle, and ineffective. Many scholars believe these narratives existed as an earlier collection, often called the "History of David's Rise" (see the Overview on this section).

With the appearance of David, the divisions and struggles evident in 1 Samuel 8–15 begin to recede into the background. The theme of Hannah's song reappears forcefully in these stories; God is at work in great historical reversals—to bring low and to exalt. In 1 Samuel 16, we are introduced to an eighth son of an obscure family who tends sheep. By

2 Sam 5:3, he has become the king of Judah and Israel. The activity of God through these events is made explicit at the conclusion of the whole narrative segment, "David became greater and greater, for the LORD, the God of hosts, was with him" (2 Sam 5:10 NRSV). God's presence with David is a central theme of this narrative section (see 1 Sam 16:18; 17:37; 18:12, 14, 28; 20:13). David is portrayed as a man of piety and prayer alongside his prowess as warrior and leader (e.g., 1 Sam 17:45-47; 23:1-5).

The narrator is concerned to legitimize the kingship of David and to overcome objections that might be raised against his claim on the throne. Thus various episodes in this section seek to counter charges that might be made against David. McCarter has listed the following charges that these narratives seek to refute and explain:[18]

1. David sought to advance himself at Saul's expense.
2. David was a deserter.
3. David was an outlaw.
4. David was a Philistine mercenary.
5. David was implicated in Saul's death.
6. David was implicated in Abner's death.
7. David was implicated in Ishbaal's death.

Alongside these apologetic efforts is a growing procession of witnesses who acknowledge David's right and destiny to Israel's throne: Jonathan, Michal, the servants of Achish, Ahimelech, Abigail, and finally Saul himself (1 Sam 24:20). After Saul's death (1 Samuel 31; 2 Samuel 1), David first becomes king over Judah (2 Sam 2:1-4), and after a series of complicated events, which includes the deaths of Abner and Ishbaal, David becomes king over Israel as well (2 Sam 5:3). In the final event of this drama of David's rise, David takes Jerusalem as his capital city (2 Sam 5:6-9). In David and Jerusalem, God has established a new future for Israel.

2 Sam 5:11–8:18. David remains the focus of the narrative, but in this segment the tone is not as celebrative as it was for David's rise. Enthusiasm gives way to official records and affairs of state. David sits on the throne; bureaucracy and ideology seem to close around him. Flanagan has observed a symmetry of arrangement that suggests a shift from tribal, covenant realities to state, royal ideology.[19] Family genealogy (2 Sam 5:13-16) gives way to officers of the court (2 Sam 8:15-18). War to bring deliverance from the Philistine threat (2 Sam 5:17-25) gives way to wars of national expansion and empire building (2 Sam 8:1-14). The central symbol of tribal covenant relationship to God, the ark, is brought to Jerusalem (2 Sam 6:1-20) and made secondary by God's announcement through the prophet Nathan of an eternal covenant with David (2 Sam 7:1-29). The center of Israel's life has shifted. God's covenant promises for Israel's future are now identified with the future of the Davidic dynasty. Conflict in Israel over kingship has now disappeared or been overridden by the claim that David is the destiny for Israel toward which God has been moving.

18. P. Kyle McCarter, "The Apology of David," *JBL* 99 (1980) 499-502.
19. James W. Flanagan, "Social Transformation and Ritual in 2 Samuel 6," in *The Word of the Lord Shall Go Forth*, ed. Carol L. Meyers and M. O'Connor (Winona Lake, Ind.: Eisenbrauns, 1983) 361-72.

2 Sam 9:1–20:26. This is the segment of 2 Samuel usually designated as the succession narrative or the court history of David. Most scholars agree that this narrative segment existed independently prior to the time it was incorporated into the larger narrative of the books of Samuel. However, recent arguments have been advanced against considering 1 Kings 1–2 to be the continuation or conclusion of this narrative (see the Overview on 2 Sam 9:1–20:26 for a detailed discussion of critical issues).

There is a general consensus that, with these chapters, the narrative makes a sudden and dramatic shift in its portrayal of David. The key to this shift is 2 Samuel 11–12, which recount David's adultery with Bathsheba, his murder of Uriah, his marriage to Bathsheba, and his confrontation by the prophet Nathan. David's repentance spares his own life, but Nathan announces God's judgment of violence unleashed in David's own family. The remaining narratives provide detailed accounts of the tragic consequences of David's own sin: Amnon's rape of Tamar (13:1-22), Absalom's killing of Amnon and his banishment (13:23-39), Absalom's rebellion and David's humiliating retreat from Jerusalem (chaps. 14–17), the defeat and death of Absalom; David's overwhelming grief (chaps. 18–19), and continued rebellion in the kingdom (chap. 20).

As many have noted, literary style and emphasis change markedly in this segment of David's story. Gone is the assurance of state ideology that marked the previous narrative on David as king and the exuberance of the narrative on David's rise. These are stories in which the humanity, pathos, and vulnerability of David come to the fore. We are allowed to see David in decline and suffering. The literary style is unusually subtle and sensitive (see the Overview on this section for further details on style and perspective in this narrative). It focuses on human agency in these stories of tragedy in David's family; yet, it makes clear, in understated ways, that God's providence nevertheless encompasses even these painful human moments (cf. 2 Sam 11:27*b;* 17:14*b*). The result of this intensely human portrait of David is that readers approach the end of the books of Samuel in a chastened mood. The achievement of human political power is not without its dangers. The temptation to think of human power as autonomous is considerable. To wield that power in the service of self-interest and in disregard of God's ultimate authority and rule is to incur judgment. Even David takes such a course of action at considerable cost.

2 Sam 21:1–24:25. These chapters, commonly called appendixes to the books of Samuel, have been most often treated as a miscellaneous collection of David traditions inserted by a rough hand prior to David's deathbed scene in 1 Kings 1–2. However, there is a symmetrical arrangement to these materials that suggests a significant intention. There are two narratives, one focused on expiation of Saul's guilt (2 Sam 21:1-14) and the other on expiation of David's guilt (2 Sam 24:1-25). There are two lists of heroes and their deeds (2 Sam 21:15-22; 23:8-39). Finally, at the heart of this section are two songs: a thanksgiving by David for the Lord's deliverance (2 Sam 22:1-51, parallel to Psalm 18) and a song that celebrates God's promise to David (2 Sam 23:1-7). This pattern reminds us of the pattern in 2 Sam 5:11–8:18 and has led some to suggest that the earlier movement from tribal to royal realities is being reversed in these appendixes—to reassert tribal, covenantal perspectives at the end of David's story (see the Overview on 2 Sam 21:1–24:25 for fuller discussion of scholarly proposals on these chapters).

In many ways the ideology of royal absolutism has been deconstructed by the judgment on David's sin with Bathsheba and Uriah, and the tragic events in David's family that ensued. Yet, at the end of chap. 20, David's power is reestablished, and he asserts that power to quell a rebellion. Without the so-called appendixes, the story would continue in 1 Kings 1–2 with deathbed vendettas by David and bloodbaths by Solomon. This material (chaps. 21–24) stays or moderates the reconstruction of royal absolutist power. The narratives in these chapters provide a reminder that, even when David feels most powerful, he is accountable to forces and authority beyond his own (the execution of Saul's son, chap. 21; the census, chap. 24). The lists of heroes make clear that it was never David alone through whom God was working to bring Israel's future. David was the leader of a heroic community. The two great songs at the heart of this section place into the mouth of David acknowledgment and celebration of the power of God working through him. In spite of earlier sin and judgment, these final appendixes return to the David anticipated by the song of Hannah at the start of the books of Samuel. It is the Lord who "brings low and exalts" and who "exalts the power of his anointed" (1 Sam 2:7*b*, 10*b*). Just as the Lord had heeded the prayer of Hannah (1 Sam 1:19) to open the story of kingship in Israel, so also that story concludes with the Lord heeding the prayer of David (2 Sam 24:25).

BIBLIOGRAPHY

Commentaries:

Anderson, A. A. *2 Samuel.* WBC 11. Waco: Word, 1989. A comprehensive critical commentary with valuable surveys of previous scholarly work.

Brueggemann, Walter. *First and Second Samuel.* Interpretation. Louisville: John Knox, 1990. An expository commentary with valuable theological insights.

Gordon, R. P. *1 and 2 Samuel.* Old Testament Guides. Sheffield: JSOT, 1984. A brief but reliable guide to the main interpretive issues.

Hertzberg, Hans Wilhelm. *I and II Samuel.* OTL. Philadelphia: Westminster, 1964. A classic historical-critical treatment of the books of Samuel.

Klein, Ralph W. *1 Samuel.* WBC 10. Waco: Word, 1983. A comprehensive critical commentary with valuable surveys of previous scholarly work.

McCarter, P. Kyle. *I Samuel.* AB 8. Garden City, N.Y.: Doubleday, 1980.

———. *II Samuel.* AB 9. Garden City, N.Y.: Doubleday, 1984. The best available treatment of text-critical issues in the books of Samuel, valuable for its careful critical analysis of literary and traditio-historical issues.

Other Helpful Studies:

Alter, Robert. *The Art of Biblical Narrative.* New York: Basic Books, 1981. A foundational study of the features of Hebrew narrative texts.

Birch, Bruce C. *The Rise of the Israelite Monarchy: The Growth and Development of I Samuel 7–15.* SBLDS

27. Missoula, Mont.: Scholars Press, 1976. A dissertation that advanced the thesis of prophetic interests evident in a pre-Dtr editing of materials in the books of Samuel.

Brueggemann, Walter. *David's Truth in Israel's Imagination and Memory.* Philadelphia: Fortress, 1985. Theological essays on focal themes for different segments of the narratives that give Israel's testimony concerning David.

————. *Power, Providence, and Personality: Biblical Insight into Life and Ministry.* Louisville: Westminster/John Knox, 1990. Insightful studies of selected texts and theological themes in the books of Samuel.

Carlson, R. A. *David, the Chosen King: A Traditio-Historical Approach to the Second Book of Samuel.* Stockholm: Almqvist och Wiksell, 1964. A helpful discussion of 2 Samuel organized around the themes of David under blessing and under curse.

Childs, Brevard S. *Introduction to the Old Testament as Scripture.* Philadelphia: Fortress, 1979. Discussion of the canonical shape and context for the books of Samuel.

Fokkelmann, J. P. *Narrative Art and Poetry in the Books of Samuel.* 2 vols. Assen: Van Gorcum, 1981 and 1986. Detailed analysis of the literary structures and functions of the texts in the books of Samuel.

Gunn, David M. *The Fate of King Saul.* JSOTSup 14. Sheffield: JSOT, 1980.

————. *The Story of King David.* JSOTSup 6. Sheffield: JSOT, 1978. Analysis of the literary features of these key narratives and the central characters around which they are constructed.

Miller, Patrick D., Jr., and J. J. M. Roberts. *The Hand of the Lord: A Reassessment of the "Ark Narrative" of 1 Samuel.* Johns Hopkins Near Eastern Studies. Baltimore: Johns Hopkins University Press, 1977. The most thorough treatment of the "ark narrative" in 1 Samuel 4–6 and of the scholarly theses related to these narratives; distinguished by its use of comparative Near Eastern materials and its cogent argument against inclusion of 2 Samuel 6 as a part of the "ark narrative."

Polzin, Robert. *David and the Deuteronomist: A Literary Study of the Deuteronomic History.* Part Three: *2 Samuel.* Bloomington: Indiana University Press, 1993.

————. *Samuel and the Deuteronomist: A Literary Study of the Deuteronomic History.* Part Two: *1 Samuel.* San Francisco: Harper & Row, 1989. Detailed literary analysis of the books of Samuel that argues the case for a single author of the Deuteronomistic History of which these books are a part.

Rad, Gerhard von. "Der Anfang der Geschichtsschreibung im alten Israel." *Archiv für Kulturgeschichte* 32 (1944) 1-42. English translation: "The Beginning of History Writing in Ancient Israel." In *The Problem of the Hexateuch and Other Essays.* Translated by E. W. Trueman Dicken. New York: McGraw-Hill, 1966. A classic essay that still marks the starting point for all modern discussion of the theological perspective of the "succession narrative" in 2 Samuel.

Rost, Leonhard. *Die Überlieferung von der Thronnachfolge Davids.* BWANT 3/6. Stuttgart: Kohlhammer, 1926. English translation: *The Succession to the Throne of David.* Translated by Michael D. Rutter and David M. Gunn. Sheffield: Almond, 1982. The classic study that popularized the hypothesis that 2 Samuel 9–20 and 1 Kings 1–2 are a connected literary product of a single author focused on the theme of succession to the throne of David.

Other important studies on particular narrative sections of the books of Samuel are cited in the notes to the Overview sections spread throughout the commentary.

OUTLINE OF FIRST AND SECOND SAMUEL

I. 1 Samuel 1:1–31:13

    A. 1 Samuel 1:1–7:17, Samuel and the Crisis of Israel
        1:1–4:1*a*, Samuel and the Word of the Lord
            1:1-28, The Birth of Samuel
            2:1-10, The Song of Hannah
            2:11-36, Corruption of the House of Eli
            3:1–4:1*a*, The Call of Samuel
        4:1*b*–7:1, The Philistine Crisis and the Capture of the Ark
            4:1*b*-22, The Philistines, the Ark, and the House of Eli
            5:1-12, The Ark with the Philistines
            6:1–7:1, The Return of the Ark
        7:2-17, Samuel as Judge of Israel

    B. 1 Samuel 8:1–15:35, The Kingship of Saul
        8:1-22, Demand and Warning
        9:1–11:15, Saul Becomes King
            9:1–10:16, The Anointing of Saul
            10:17-27*a*, Saul Among the Baggage
            10:27*b*–11:15, Saul Delivers Jabesh-gilead
        12:1-25, Samuel's Address to Israel
        13:1–15:35, The Exploits and Rejection of Saul
            13:1-23, Saul Rejected from Dynasty
            14:1-52, Jonathan and Saul Against the Philistines
            15:1-35, Saul Rejected from Kingship

    C. 1 Samuel 16:1–31:13, The Rise of David and the Decline of Saul
        16:1-13, The Anointing of David
        16:14-23, David Is Introduced to Saul's Court
        17:1-58, David Defeats Goliath
        18:1–20:42, David and the Household of Saul
            18:1-30, Saul's Jealousy at David's Success
            19:1-24, Saul's Threat to David's Life
            20:1-42, The Friendship of Jonathan and David
        21:1–26:25, David as Fugitive
            21:1-9, David and Ahimelech at Nob
            21:10-15, David Plays the Madman
            22:1-5, The Entourage of David
            22:6-23, Saul Massacres the Priests at Nob
            23:1-29, Narrow Escapes from Saul
            24:1-22, David Spares Saul's Life
            25:1-44, Abigail Saves David from Bloodguilt

1 SAMUEL 1:1–7:17, SAMUEL AND
THE CRISIS OF ISRAEL

OVERVIEW

These chapters introduce the books of 1 and 2 Samuel as the story of a reshaping moment in Israel's history. As 1 Samuel opens, a transformation is about to take place in Israel's life. By the end of 2 Samuel, that transformation, for good or for ill, has been completed. The time of the judges has ended, and the reign of Israelite kings has begun. The threatened conquest of tribal Israel by external enemies, such as the Philistines (the threat at the end of Judges and at the opening of 1 Samuel), is over and the kingdom of David is established with secure borders. The violence and lack of moral direction signaled by the closing chapters of Judges (Judges 17–21)[20] is replaced by the mediators of God's Word: the prophets and God's anointed ones, the kings. No longer will it be said, "In those days there was no king in Israel; all the people did what was right in their own eyes" (Judg 21:25).

First Samuel 1–7 sets the stage for these transformations in Israel. The reader is drawn into an Israelite world in crisis. On the one hand, the crisis is internal. The sons of Eli, the priest at Shiloh where the ark of the covenant is kept, have corrupted the religious practices of Israel for their own gain (2:11-17). Eli seems powerless to change or control their behavior (2:22-25). Since God will not tolerate such faithlessness (2:25b, 27-36), there is no future for the house of Eli (4:12-22). On the other hand, the crisis of Israel is external. The Philistines wage a war of conquest on Israel and even capture the ark of the covenant as the spoils of victory (4:1b-11), but God will not tolerate the victory of Israel's enemies or the

humiliation of the ark (5:1–7:1). There is no future for Philistine conquest of Israel (7:3-14).

Chapters 1–7 introduce not only Israel's crisis, but also the key figure through whom God will work to resolve the crisis, Samuel. We are told of his birth as the gracious act of God (1:1-28), his childhood and vocational shaping at Shiloh (2:11, 18, 26; 3:1-18), his establishment as the prophet of God's Word (3:19–4:1a), and his leadership in the face of the Philistine threat (7:3-17). Samuel plays the central role in these chapters as the instrument of God's will in the midst of Israel. Samuel is the first of three great men whose overlapping stories dominate this time of transition in Israel and who take up the whole of the books of Samuel: Samuel, Saul, and David. One may see Samuel as the representative of older, tribal Israel and its traditions. Yet, Samuel will also be the instrument through whom God will act to bring about a new, royal Israel with its perils and possibilities.

It has long been recognized that 1 Samuel 1–7 contains at least three distinct literary segments: (1) Chapters 1–3 tell of Samuel's birth and childhood and the corruption of the house of Eli; (2) chaps. 4–6 narrate the Philistine threat and the capture of the ark; and (3) chap. 7 establishes the leadership of Samuel. The sudden and total absence of Samuel in chaps. 4–6 especially suggests that the deuteronomistic historian (see Introduction) has used separate sources in compiling the books of Samuel. These segments may have originated separately, but in their present place in the Deuteronomistic History they are closely interconnected. Scholars such as Willis and Polzin[21] have

---

20. In the Deuteronomistic History, which stretches from Joshua to 2 Kings, the book of 1 Samuel follows immediately after Judges. Early English Bibles changed the order of books in the canon and placed the book of Ruth between Judges and 1 Samuel.

21. See John T. Willis, "An Anti-Elide Narrative Tradition from a Prophetic Circle at the Ramah Sanctuary," *JBL* 90 (1971) 288-308; "Samuel Versus Eli: I Sam. 1-7," *TZ* 35 (1979) 201-12; Robert Polzin, *Samuel and the Deuteronomist* (San Francisco: Harper & Row, 1989) 18-79.

made a strong case for a reading that focuses on the literary continuity of these segments in the story of Israel as it is now told by the deuteronomistic historian. Although this commentary will break the text into segments at logical points for convenience of discussion, the chief focus nevertheless will be on the final form in which these chapters (and, indeed, the whole of 1 Samuel) tell and interpret the story of Israel in this time of transformation.

1 Samuel 1:1–4:1a, Samuel and the Word of the Lord

OVERVIEW

These chapters provide a crucial introduction to the books of Samuel. In the story of a single family and an elderly priest at Shiloh, we are made aware of important events that will transform Israel's future and of a past way of life in Israel that will be no more. These chapters look back to the book of Judges and to the historical and moral limitations that have brought Israel to a moment of crisis. At the same time, they look forward to a future that God's transforming initiatives will make possible for Israel in the midst of crisis.

There are several distinct segments in these chapters. We hear the story of Samuel's birth (1:1-28), an account of the corruption of the priestly house of Eli at Shiloh (2:11-36), and a narrative that establishes the authority of Samuel in Israel as an alternative to the house of Eli (3:1–4:1a). But the song of Hannah (2:1-10) stands at the center of this section. It not only celebrates the grace-given birth of a child, but also it looks beyond that moment to celebrate the birth of a new Israel with a king as a grace-given possibility for Israel's future. The song of Hannah tells us that we are hearing more than the local stories of Elkanah's family and Eli's family. The events that link the fate of these two families will determine the future of Israel.

Of course, these chapters introduce us to Samuel as the key figure who will give leadership for the beginning of this period of crisis and transformation. This section begins with his birth as a gift of grace in response to Hannah's plea and vow (1:1-28), and it ends with Samuel fully established in Israel as a prophet of God's Word (3:19–4:1a). Yet, as important as Samuel is, these chapters even more importantly establish God as the One who will determine Israel's future. Samuel is an agent of God's sovereignty and initiative. Every segment of this opening section to the books of Samuel stresses God's role as the One whose will and word will shape Israel's new life. Samuel will play a key role, but it will be as the instrument of what God is doing in Israel.

The initial chapters of the books of Samuel focus on God's raising up of new leadership in Israel to meet the moral crisis created by the corruption of Eli's sons (2:11-36). It is significant that moral crisis takes priority over political crisis in the opening of the books of Samuel. We do not hear of the Philistines and the grave threat they represent to Israel's political future until chapter 4. Instead, the concern is initially for the lack of faithful and decisive leadership in Israel. The reader of the Deuteronomistic History cannot help connecting this lack of leadership to the violence and moral lack of direction that characterized Israel at the end of the book of Judges (e.g., the rape and murder of the Levite's concubine, Judges 19; the near genocidal war that follows, Judges 20–21; and the summary comment, Judg 21:25). God must raise up faithful leadership, first Samuel and ultimately David, before the political crisis of Israel can be resolved.

God begins Israel's transformation in this time of crisis not with great men and events, but with the distress of a barren woman. Such a beginning reminds us of the unlikely paths God's grace often takes, and it signals to us that the coming kingdom itself is to be understood as the gift of divine grace.

1 Samuel 1:1-28, The Birth of Samuel

NIV

1 There was a certain man from Ramathaim, a Zuphite[a] from the hill country of Ephraim, whose name was Elkanah son of Jeroham, the son of Elihu, the son of Tohu, the son of Zuph, an Ephraimite. ²He had two wives; one was called Hannah and the other Peninnah. Peninnah had children, but Hannah had none.

³Year after year this man went up from his town to worship and sacrifice to the LORD Almighty at Shiloh, where Hophni and Phinehas, the two sons of Eli, were priests of the LORD. ⁴Whenever the day came for Elkanah to sacrifice, he would give portions of the meat to his wife Peninnah and to all her sons and daughters. ⁵But to Hannah he gave a double portion because he loved her, and the LORD had closed her womb. ⁶And because the LORD had closed her womb, her rival kept provoking her in order to irritate her. ⁷This went on year after year. Whenever Hannah went up to the house of the LORD, her rival provoked her till she wept and would not eat. ⁸Elkanah her husband would say to her, "Hannah, why are you weeping? Why don't you eat? Why are you downhearted? Don't I mean more to you than ten sons?"

⁹Once when they had finished eating and drinking in Shiloh, Hannah stood up. Now Eli the priest was sitting on a chair by the doorpost of the LORD's temple.[b] ¹⁰In bitterness of soul Hannah wept much and prayed to the LORD. ¹¹And she made a vow, saying, "O LORD Almighty, if you will only look upon your servant's misery and remember me, and not forget your servant but give her a son, then I will give him to the LORD for all the days of his life, and no razor will ever be used on his head."

¹²As she kept on praying to the LORD, Eli observed her mouth. ¹³Hannah was praying in her heart, and her lips were moving but her voice was not heard. Eli thought she was drunk ¹⁴and said to her, "How long will you keep on getting drunk? Get rid of your wine."

¹⁵"Not so, my lord," Hannah replied, "I am a woman who is deeply troubled. I have not been drinking wine or beer; I was pouring out my soul

a1 Or from Ramathaim Zuphim   _b9 That is, tabernacle_

NRSV

1 There was a certain man of Ramathaim, a Zuphite[a] from the hill country of Ephraim, whose name was Elkanah son of Jeroham son of Elihu son of Tohu son of Zuph, an Ephraimite. ²He had two wives; the name of the one was Hannah, and the name of the other Peninnah. Peninnah had children, but Hannah had no children.

3Now this man used to go up year by year from his town to worship and to sacrifice to the LORD of hosts at Shiloh, where the two sons of Eli, Hophni and Phinehas, were priests of the LORD. ⁴On the day when Elkanah sacrificed, he would give portions to his wife Peninnah and to all her sons and daughters; ⁵but to Hannah he gave a double portion,[b] because he loved her, though the LORD had closed her womb. ⁶Her rival used to provoke her severely, to irritate her, because the LORD had closed her womb. ⁷So it went on year by year; as often as she went up to the house of the LORD, she used to provoke her. Therefore Hannah wept and would not eat. ⁸Her husband Elkanah said to her, "Hannah, why do you weep? Why do you not eat? Why is your heart sad? Am I not more to you than ten sons?"

9After they had eaten and drunk at Shiloh, Hannah rose and presented herself before the LORD.[c] Now Eli the priest was sitting on the seat beside the doorpost of the temple of the LORD. ¹⁰She was deeply distressed and prayed to the LORD, and wept bitterly. ¹¹She made this vow: "O LORD of hosts, if only you will look on the misery of your servant, and remember me, and not forget your servant, but will give to your servant a male child, then I will set him before you as a nazirite[d] until the day of his death. He shall drink neither wine nor intoxicants,[e] and no razor shall touch his head."

12As she continued praying before the LORD, Eli observed her mouth. ¹³Hannah was praying silently; only her lips moved, but her voice was not heard; therefore Eli thought she was drunk. ¹⁴So Eli said to her, "How long will you make a drunken spectacle of yourself? Put away your wine."

a Compare Gk and 1 Chr 6.35-36: Heb Ramathaim-zophim   _b Syr: Meaning of Heb uncertain_   _c Gk: Heb lacks and presented herself before the LORD_   _d That is one separated or one consecrated_   _e Cn Compare Gk Q Ms 1.22: MT then I will give him to the LORD all the days of his life_

NIV

to the Lord. ¹⁶Do not take your servant for a wicked woman; I have been praying here out of my great anguish and grief."

¹⁷Eli answered, "Go in peace, and may the God of Israel grant you what you have asked of him."

¹⁸She said, "May your servant find favor in your eyes." Then she went her way and ate something, and her face was no longer downcast.

¹⁹Early the next morning they arose and worshiped before the Lord and then went back to their home at Ramah. Elkanah lay with Hannah his wife, and the Lord remembered her. ²⁰So in the course of time Hannah conceived and gave birth to a son. She named him Samuel,ᵃ saying, "Because I asked the Lord for him."

²¹When the man Elkanah went up with all his family to offer the annual sacrifice to the Lord and to fulfill his vow, ²²Hannah did not go. She said to her husband, "After the boy is weaned, I will take him and present him before the Lord, and he will live there always."

²³"Do what seems best to you," Elkanah her husband told her. "Stay here until you have weaned him; only may the Lord make good hisᵇ word." So the woman stayed at home and nursed her son until she had weaned him.

²⁴After he was weaned, she took the boy with her, young as he was, along with a three-year-old bull,ᶜ an ephahᵈ of flour and a skin of wine, and brought him to the house of the Lord at Shiloh. ²⁵When they had slaughtered the bull, they brought the boy to Eli, ²⁶and she said to him, "As surely as you live, my lord, I am the woman who stood here beside you praying to the Lord. ²⁷I prayed for this child, and the Lord has granted me what I asked of him. ²⁸So now I give him to the Lord. For his whole life he will be given over to the Lord." And he worshiped the Lord there.

ᵃ20 *Samuel* sounds like the Hebrew for *heard of God.*   ᵇ23 Masoretic Text; Dead Sea Scrolls, Septuagint and Syriac *your*   ᶜ24 Dead Sea Scrolls, Septuagint and Syriac; Masoretic Text *with three bulls*   ᵈ24 That is, probably about 3/5 bushel (about 22 liters)

NRSV

¹⁵But Hannah answered, "No, my lord, I am a woman deeply troubled; I have drunk neither wine nor strong drink, but I have been pouring out my soul before the Lord. ¹⁶Do not regard your servant as a worthless woman, for I have been speaking out of my great anxiety and vexation all this time." ¹⁷Then Eli answered, "Go in peace; the God of Israel grant the petition you have made to him." ¹⁸And she said, "Let your servant find favor in your sight." Then the woman went to her quarters,ᵃ ate and drank with her husband,ᵇ and her countenance was sad no longer.ᶜ

19They rose early in the morning and worshiped before the Lord; then they went back to their house at Ramah. Elkanah knew his wife Hannah, and the Lord remembered her. ²⁰In due time Hannah conceived and bore a son. She named him Samuel, for she said, "I have asked him of the Lord."

21The man Elkanah and all his household went up to offer to the Lord the yearly sacrifice, and to pay his vow. ²²But Hannah did not go up, for she said to her husband, "As soon as the child is weaned, I will bring him, that he may appear in the presence of the Lord, and remain there forever; I will offer him as a naziriteᵈ for all time."ᵉ ²³Her husband Elkanah said to her, "Do what seems best to you, wait until you have weaned him; only—may the Lord establish his word."ᶠ So the woman remained and nursed her son, until she weaned him. ²⁴When she had weaned him, she took him up with her, along with a three-year-old bull,ᵍ an ephah of flour, and a skin of wine. She brought him to the house of the Lord at Shiloh; and the child was young. ²⁵Then they slaughtered the bull, and they brought the child to Eli. ²⁶And she said, "Oh, my lord! As you live, my lord, I am the woman who was standing here in your presence, praying to the Lord. ²⁷For this child I prayed; and the Lord has granted me the petition that I made to him. ²⁸Therefore I have lent him to the Lord; as long as he lives, he is given to the Lord."

She left him there forʰ the Lord.

ᵃ Gk: Heb *went her way*   ᵇ Gk: Heb lacks *and drank with her husband*   ᶜ Gk: Meaning of Heb uncertain   ᵈ That is *one separated* or *one consecrated*   ᵉ Cn Compare Q Ms: MT lacks *I will offer him as a nazirite for all time*   ᶠ MT: Q Ms Gk Compare Syr *that which goes out of your mouth*   ᵍ Q Ms Gk Syr: MT *three bulls*   ʰ Gk (Compare Q Ms) and Gk at 2.11: MT *And he* (that is, Elkanah) *worshiped there before*

COMMENTARY

The book of 1 Samuel opens with a localized story of dynamics in a single family, but this story is more than it seems on first glance. The story ends with the birth of Samuel and his dedication at Shiloh. Samuel is to play a central role in the transformation from a tribal Israel to an Israelite kingdom. Further, this family story introduces not only a main character in the story ahead but also many of the themes and issues that will mark the telling of that story.

On one level, 1 Sam 1:1-28 is a family drama. We meet the family of Elkanah and his two wives, Hannah and Peninnah. The tension in this family comes from the barrenness of Hannah. Although Elkanah loves Hannah and treats her with kindness, Peninnah taunts and provokes Hannah for her childlessness. With this situation as background, the focus shifts to Hannah. On a visit to the sanctuary at Shiloh, she prays fervently to the Lord for the gift of a child and vows to dedicate any such child to the Lord. The priest of Shiloh, Eli, observes her at prayer and, after initially mistaking her behavior as drunkenness, blesses the vow she has made. Subsequently, Hannah does bear a son to Elkanah and names him Samuel. After the child is weaned, she brings Samuel to Shiloh and leaves him there in service dedicated to the Lord. Throughout this family drama, God is the determining power. It is God who has "closed her womb" (vv. 5-6); it is God to whom Hannah prays and makes her vow (vv. 10-11); it is God whom Eli invokes to grant Hannah's petition (v. 17); it is God who "remembers" Hannah and grants her request (v. 19); and it is God to whom the child, Samuel, is given in service (vv. 27-28). God works providentially in the events of this story.

On another level, this story does more than simply get Samuel onstage. There are many ties between the telling of this family story and the wider story of Israel's journey to kingship and kingdom, which is the central focus of 1 and 2 Samuel. Robert Polzin has suggested that the situation in Elkanah's family is intended as a parable of Israel's situation at this moment in its history.[22] Hannah's anxiety

over having no children, even though Elkanah loves her, parallels Israel's anxiety over having no king in spite of the care and love of God. The taunting of Peninnah, described as a rival (see Commentary on 1:6), suggests the taunts of Israel's neighboring "rival" nations, who have kings. The granting of a son to Hannah and the future granting of a king to Israel do not occur without conditions. The son (the king?) is to be dedicated to the Lord. Elkanah, who loved Hannah even without a child, voices the central condition that comes with all gifts of God's grace, whether child or king: "May the LORD establish his word" (v. 23). When Israel's first king, Saul, is later rejected from kingship, God tells Samuel it is because Saul has not "established my word" (1 Sam 15:11; NRSV, "carried out my commands"; NIV, "carried out my instructions").

The narrative of 1:1-28 contains several distinct elements. Verses 1-2 introduce us to Elkanah, Hannah, and Peninnah and state the central issue of Hannah's childlessness. Verses 3-8 serve as exposition, giving the reader information on the rivalry with Peninnah, the love of Elkanah, and the bitterness of Hannah that are necessary background to the story of Hannah's vow at Shiloh and her encounter with the priest Eli, which follows in vv. 9-18. This vow and the narration of its fulfillment (vv. 19-20) constitute the central focus of the chapter. What precedes is background exposition, and what follows in the final section—with the weaning, presentation, and dedication of Samuel (vv. 21-28)—suggests future implications for Israel flowing from Hannah's vow and its fulfillment.

1:1-2. Elkanah is introduced as an Ephraimite from Ramathaim. A later tradition in 1 Chr 6:27, 34 (MT 6:12, 19) makes Elkanah a Levite, but this may be a late attempt to give Samuel a proper priestly ancestry. Ramathaim is mentioned only here; Elkanah's hometown appears in v. 19 and in 2:11 simply as Ramah. In subsequent chapters, Samuel is associated with a town named Ramah in the tribal territory of Benjamin. These two places are probably not the same, but it is impossible to sort out the confusion with certainty. Elkanah's ancestor Zuph seems to give his name to both a clan (Elkanah is a Zuphite, v. 1a) and a geographic region (Saul's search for lost asses

---

22. Robert Polzin, *Samuel and the Deuteronomist: A Literary Study of the Deuteronomic History,* Part Two: *1 Samuel* (San Francisco: Harper & Row, 1989) 18-30.

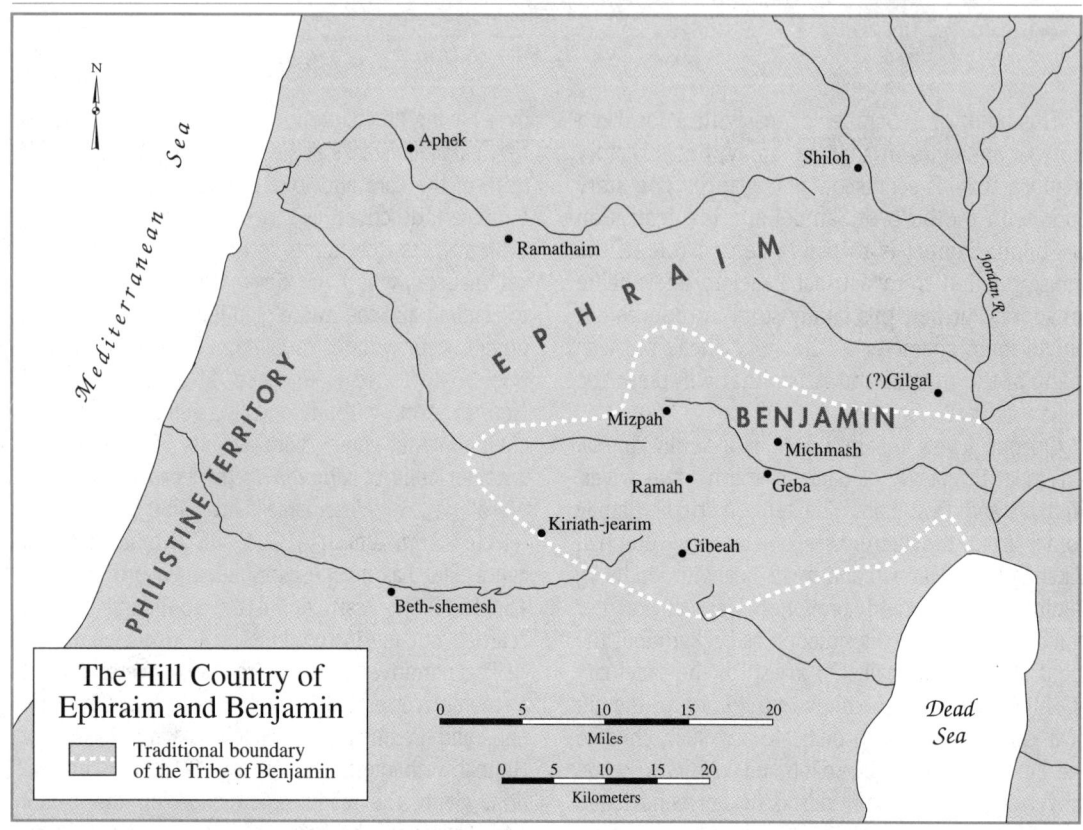

The Hill Country of
Ephraim and Benjamin

Traditional boundary
of the Tribe of Benjamin

takes him to a land called Zuph, where he encounters Samuel, 9:5).

Elkanah has two wives. Monogamy was not yet established as the only acceptable practice, and many biblical figures had multiple wives (e.g., Abraham, Jacob, David). Hannah was the first wife, and Peninnah was the second (MT, "second"; NRSV and NIV, "other"). The main issue creating the drama in this story is stated simply and clearly at the end of v. 2: "Peninnah had children, but Hannah had no children." This note may imply that the reason why Elkanah took a second wife was to give him children and heirs, since Hannah remained childless. The names of the wives may connote something of their role in the story: "Hannah" (חנה *ḥannâ*) means "charming," "attractive," indicating her role as the wife Elkanah loves (v. 5); "Peninnah" (פננה *pĕninnâ*) means "fertile" or "prolific," indicating her identity as childbearer.

1:3-8. This section gives us background on the tensions among Hannah, Peninnah, and Elkanah that arose year after year on the occasion of a special pilgrimage to the sanctuary at Shiloh. It appears to have been an act of special devotion on the part of Elkanah, and not a pilgrimage as a part of a stipulated observance (1:3, 21). It was a time for family worship and sacrifice.

Shiloh, at this time, was a major sanctuary of the Israelite tribes and was the resting place for the "ark of God" (3:3). As such it is a place especially associated with the presence of the God of Israel, whom Elkanah worships here as the "LORD of hosts" or "Yahweh of the armies" (v. 3). This is a longer form of the proper name for Israel's God, which some have suggested may mean "one who creates [heavenly] armies."[23] This name may especially be connected with God as the warrior who fights for Israel against its enemies, as in the hero/heroine stories of the book of Judges or in the victory of Samuel through God's aid (1 Samuel 7). The passing reference to Eli and his two sons, Hophni and Phinehas (v. 3*b*), foreshadows the significant role they play in the story a short time later (cf. 1 Sam 2:12-17).

This annual visit to Shiloh was a time when Hannah's childlessness became a particular burden.

23. See P. Kyle McCarter, *I Samuel,* AB 8 (Garden City, N.Y.: Doubleday, 1980) 59.

The distribution of meat from the sacrifice underlined her solitary state. While Peninnah and her sons and daughters would receive a large portion of the sacrifice, Hannah would be entitled only to her one portion. Elkanah would give Hannah a double portion out of his love for her (v. 5), but this surely only emphasized her isolation in a society where wives were valued when they bore children.

This situation was made worse by the taunting of Peninnah, whose provocation and irritation of Hannah, year after year, reduced her to tears and refusal to eat (vv. 6-7). Peninnah is described as a "rival" (צרה *sārâ*), a term seldom used in describing family relationships and often translated as "enemy" or "adversary" in describing relationships between peoples or nations. The choice of language here suggests that the relationship of Israel without a king taunted by its neighboring kingdoms may be reflected in the family tension between Hannah and Peninnah. The themes of barrenness and the rivalry between wives is known from the earlier biblical stories of Sarah and Hagar (Genesis 16), and Rachel and Leah (Gen 29:31–30:24), where these mothers and their sons also represent the relationships between tribes and peoples.

Elkanah appears in the midst of this conflict as a kind and well-intentioned man. He loves Hannah and tries to treat her with care (v. 5), but he cannot quite understand the depth of her despair. In v. 8, he pleads with her to eat and not be sad. He rather plaintively asks if his love is not worth more to her than ten sons. As we shall see, Hannah's answer to this question is no. She still desires a son, much as Israel will still desire a king in spite of God's love and care (1 Samuel 8). Elkanah may mean well, but he places himself, and not the plight of Hannah, in the central focus. He significantly does not tell Hannah that *she* is worth more to *him* than ten sons.[24]

Twice in this section the reader is told that "the LORD had closed her [Hannah's] womb" (vv. 5-6). On the one hand, this statement reminds us of God's ultimate power to determine all futures, whether Hannah's or Israel's. But, on the other hand, both of these statements describe Hannah's state by someone else. Others may see Hannah's barrenness as a sign of God's rejection. Elkanah loves

her, though God has closed her womb; Peninnah taunts her, because God has closed her womb. Both lover and provoker treat Hannah as God-forsaken. It is eventually God's response to Hannah that will prove this to be a premature judgment.

1:9-18. Here we come to the heart of the story. The narrative moves from what happened year after year to the events of a particular year when Hannah left the sacrificial meal and "presented herself before the LORD" (v. 9). Such action probably occurred near the entrance to the sanctuary where the ark was housed, because Eli, the head of the priestly family that served the sanctuary at Shiloh, was seated there. In her distress and bitterness, Hannah has nevertheless taken the initiative to bring her case to God. She prays and makes a vow (vv. 10-11).

Hannah's vow (v. 11) appeals to the same "LORD of hosts" to whom Elkanah brings his annual sacrifice. She asks that God "remember" her, and her appeal is brought as one in misery, with only the lowly state of a servant before God. She assumes that the God of Israel might care for those hurting and without status, an assumption beautifully elaborated in Hannah's song in 2:1-10. The "God of armies" might also remember a distressed, childless woman like Hannah.

Her request is straightforward: She asks for a male child. But if she were to receive this gift of God's grace, she vows to give back to God the gift she receives. She promises to dedicate her son as a Nazirite. Nazirites marked their commitment by abstaining from wine or other strong drink and by never cutting their hair (v. 11*b*). Such vows of dedication did not usually last for a lifetime, as the regulations in Num 6:1-21 suggest. They did set aside individuals for unusual service to God, sometimes in military service. Samson is the chief biblical example of a Nazirite. Perhaps Hannah knew his story because Samson's unnamed mother, too, was childless when God promised her a son and laid down the conditions of his dedication as a Nazirite (Judg 13:1-24). Samson's dedication was also to be lifelong, although as we know it did not turn out that way.

At this point, we discover that Hannah has been praying silently while moving her lips, and that Eli, who observed her, mistook this for drunken behavior and rebuked her (vv. 12-14), which initiated dialogue between them. Hannah responds with a

---

24. See Yairah Amit, " 'Am I Not More Devoted to You Than Ten Sons?' (1 Samuel 1.8): Male and Female Interpretations," in *A Feminist Companion to Samuel and Kings,* ed. A. Brenner (Sheffield: Sheffield Academic, 1994) 68-76.

passionate defense of her actions. It is not wine or strong drink, but her soul that she has been "pouring out" before God (v. 15). She admits to being a "deeply troubled" woman, a phrase (קשת-רוח *qĕšat-rûaḥ*) that Ahlstrom has proposed is better translated as "hard, obstinate or stubborn of spirit."[25] Hannah persists in her request for a child from God, an act that effectively foreshadows the persistence of Israel in its request for a king. Hannah further admits to "great anxiety and vexation" but begs of Eli that she not be counted as a "worthless woman" (v. 16). The word "worthless" (בליעל *bĕliyyaʿal*) appears later in 1 Sam 2:12 to describe the sons of Eli and in 10:27 to describe troublesome opponents of the kingship of Saul. It also describes the violent wrongdoers of Gibeah in Judg 19:22 and the power of chaos in Ps 18:5. What Hannah has requested out of her great anxiety will indeed have great effect on the future of Israel. Hannah's petition and vow have been laid in the hands of God.

Eli responds without ever learning the content of Hannah's vow. Perhaps he responds to the passion of her trust in God's grace. He simply announces a blessing on her request and sends her forth in peace (v. 17). His comment is as much an expression of confidence that God *will* respond to such a fervent and trusting petition as it is a hope that God will do so. Little does he realize what the child who results from this vow will mean to his own priestly family. Eli's language in this speech introduces the first two of seven uses of the verb "to ask" (שאל *šāʾal*) in this chapter. Instead of "the petition you have made," this expression might be rendered "the asking you have asked." This verb appears in the name of Samuel and his connection to Saul. It will be commented on further in relation to vv. 20 and 28.

1:19-20. Hannah responds with a modest request to be viewed favorably by this priest who has mistaken her for a drunken woman, and then she returns to her husband. No longer sad, she has rested her future in God's hands. That trust is well placed. When Hannah returns home and has sexual relations with Elkanah, "the Lord remembered her" (v. 19). It is the precise fulfillment of the request Hannah had made in v. 11. She gives birth to a son and names him Samuel (v. 20). She explains this name by linking it to the verb "to ask" (*šāʾal*), which we have already noted in Eli's speech

(v. 17). But Samuel's name (שמואל *šĕmûʾēl*) does not seem derived from this verb. It is Saul (שאול *šāʾûl*) whose name is drawn from the verb "to ask." This has led many previous commentators to suggest that this was originally a birth story for Saul and that at a later time Samuel displaced him in the story.[26] Such a view does not seem likely. There is little in this story that fits Saul's story in any way (i.e., different parents and home, no evidence of Saul's being dedicated to service at Shiloh). Perhaps the play on words here is instead intended to link the future of Samuel to that of Saul (see Commentary on 1:28).

1:21-28. Elkanah and his family returned to Shiloh for their yearly sacrifice, but Samuel is not immediately dedicated to God's service, as Hannah had vowed. Hannah does not go to Shiloh but asks that she might wait until the boy, Samuel, is weaned and reaffirms her intention to dedicate the boy as a Nazirite at that time (vv. 21-22).

Elkanah readily agrees but makes a statement that sounds an important theme for the opening of 1 Samuel: "Only—may the Lord establish his word" (v. 23). Elkanah alludes to the larger purpose for which the boy Samuel is to be dedicated. The issue of Nazirite vows is no longer in view. Samuel is to become a prophet, a mediator of God's Word to all of Israel (3:19–4:1*a*). In this role, Samuel is later to reject Saul as one who did not establish God's word (15:11). We become aware in Elkanah's statement that we are not simply beginning the story of Samuel, but the story of God's Word working through Samuel in Israel. The actual dedication of Samuel may occur after his weaning, but God's Word will not ultimately be stayed.

In due course, Hannah takes Samuel to Shiloh along with appropriate offerings and sacrifices (v. 24) and presents the boy to Eli. She identifies herself as the distraught woman with whom Eli had spoken (v. 25). She then uses the very words Eli had used in v. 17: "The Lord has granted me the petition that I made to him" (v. 27). The child Samuel is "the asking that I asked," once again returning to the verb *šāʾal*, "to ask." Further, she continues (v. 28) to link Samuel even more directly to this verb. The verb *šāʾal* can also have the meaning "to lend"

25. G. W. Ahlstrom, "1 Samuel 1:15," *Biblica* 60 (1979) 254.

26. See, e.g., McCarter, *I Samuel*, 62-63. For a discussion of the problems with this view and alternatives along the lines I have taken here, see John T. Willis, "Cultic Elements in the Story of Samuel's Birth and Dedication," *ST* 26 (1972) 54; and Polzin, *Samuel and the Deuteronomist*, 24-25.

in the sense of "requested" or "designated for a purpose." Hannah says, "I have *lent* him to the LORD," and further, "as long as he lives, he *is given* to the LORD." The form of this final verb is identical to the name of Saul (שָׁאוּל *šā'ûl*). For as long as Samuel lives, "he is *Saul* to the LORD." This statement comes as a climactic conclusion to the chapter. Samuel is both requested from and loaned back to the Lord. But his future, as one dedicated to God, is inextricably linked with Saul, as we shall later see. It is not Samuel who has invaded a birth story of Saul; it is Saul whom the narrative has caused to invade Samuel's story, linking their futures together in God's purposes for Israel. Samuel, "as long as he lives," has no future that does not include Saul. Hannah has spoken her son's future, and with that, she leaves him in Shiloh "for the LORD" (v. 28*b*).

REFLECTIONS

The books of Samuel begin with a salvation story. New life comes out of barrenness. Hope rises from hopelessness. Despair is transformed into thanksgiving and praise.

In 1 Samuel 1, the focus is on Hannah, a woman distraught over the limits faced by childless women in her world and taunted by a rival who has no compassion. By trusting her plight to God, Hannah claimed the new future God can make possible to those in barren, hopeless circumstances. Her story has roots in Israel's past. God had remembered Rachel, and she had been given a child (Gen 30:22). God had remembered the Hebrews in bondage in Egypt (Exod 2:24) and delivered them into new life as a people. Hannah opens her misery and need to God and asks for God to remember her.

Hannah's story also points to Israel's future. It is significant that a story that is to climax in the royal greatness of David begins in the bereft circumstances of Hannah. The future of Israel is to be a gift of God's grace as surely as Israel's past had been. Over and over again in the books of Samuel, God will find possibilities for new life and hopeful futures in persons and circumstances that seem impossible by human standards. Threatened by external enemies and internal corruption, Israel's future at the time of Hannah's story is bleak, but the birth of Samuel to a barren woman who boldly asks for God's grace gives hope that God can transform Israel's future even as Hannah's future is transformed—and Hannah's son, Samuel, is to play a central role in God's plan. God remembered Hannah; God will once again remember Israel.

If this is a story of God's grace for Hannah and for Israel, it can also be the story of God's grace for us. As persons of faith and as the church, we can learn from Hannah something of the dynamics of grace that might transform our futures and address the forms of hopelessness and pain that we face.

1. We can learn from Hannah the importance of expressing our need before God. Sometimes we are more intent on presenting a portrait of the vigor of our faith than in confessing our struggles, our anxieties, and our pains. This is true of individuals, congregations, and denominations. In our religious life, we admire positive thinking, goal setting, problem solving, and program planning. We often seem to believe that the right spiritual discipline, the proper church-growth program, or the most thoroughgoing strategic planning process will meet our needs. Hannah simply and straightforwardly expressed her need to God. In doing so, she recognized that wholeness in her life lay beyond those things she could control and rested in God as the larger reality of her life. Sometimes facing our needs as persons and as churches can open new possibilities, not of our making but of God's.

2. We can learn from Hannah the trustful persistence required to claim God's grace. Hannah boldly asked that God remember her. She prayed passionately, as a woman of "stubborn spirit" (see Commentary on 1:15), and she trusted that God's grace was available to her. There is an audacity to this persistent trustfulness that does not always fit well with the gentility of Sunday morning religion in the modern church. Some years ago, a well-known government official stopped attending a Washington, D.C., church that included a time for sharing of concerns before intercessory prayers. He claimed he did not come to church to hear people "let their guts hang out." There is a certain audacity to the insistence that God's grace is ours. Those who passionately express their hopeful claim on that grace may be judged unacceptable in their behavior, even as Hannah was judged by Eli to be drunk. The bold and passionate claim that God's justice is a promise for all people regardless of race issued in behavior by early civil rights advocates that many judged inappropriate and thus condemned.

God responded to the stubborn insistence of Hannah. Elkanah's love was not enough. She asked of God yet further expressions of grace, and God gave it. We will learn soon in 1 Samuel that the grace of God in the leaders of Israel's past was not enough. Israel insisted on a king, and God complied. In reading these stories, some might judge Hannah and Israel as audaciously ungrateful. Yet, Jesus spoke in praise of the persistent widow in Luke 18:1-8, and he urged his followers to persist in making their needs known to God in prayer. God has constantly created new possibilities of grace out of our stubborn insistence that God remember us yet again.

3. We can learn from Hannah that the proper response to the gift of God's grace is to give it back. If we attempt to keep it as a possession, we will lose it. Hannah knew this from the beginning and vowed to give back of the grace God might grant. When the time comes, Hannah's response teaches us something of proper response to the gifts of God. When the infant Samuel is weaned, Hannah returns to the sanctuary with offerings and sacrifices, and she dedicates the child to God.

When grace brings new life, we, too, must give back of the grace we have received. This will include worship, which is the giving back of grace as praise. It will further include dedicating the grace we have received to the service of God. In every generation there has been a need for some in the church to move beyond receiving grace to returning grace. The curious possibilities in the word שׁאל (šāʾal) model the needed response. What was *asked* must become what is *lent back*. People and communities of faith must become less concerned over who and how many have received God's grace and more concerned with the ways in which God's grace is given back into God's service.

1 Samuel 2:1-10, The Song of Hannah

NIV	NRSV
2 Then Hannah prayed and said:	2 Hannah prayed and said,
"My heart rejoices in the LORD; in the LORD my horn*a* is lifted high. My mouth boasts over my enemies, for I delight in your deliverance.	"My heart exults in the LORD; my strength is exalted in my God.*a* My mouth derides my enemies, because I rejoice in my*b* victory.
2"There is no one holy*b* like the LORD; there is no one besides you; there is no Rock like our God.	2 "There is no Holy One like the LORD, no one besides you; there is no Rock like our God.
3"Do not keep talking so proudly or let your mouth speak such arrogance, for the LORD is a God who knows, and by him deeds are weighed.	3 Talk no more so very proudly, let not arrogance come from your mouth; for the LORD is a God of knowledge, and by him actions are weighed. 4 The bows of the mighty are broken, but the feeble gird on strength.
a1 Horn here symbolizes strength; also in verse 10. *b2 Or no Holy One*	*a* Gk: Heb *the LORD* *b* Q Ms: MT *your*

NIV

[4]"The bows of the warriors are broken,
  but those who stumbled are armed with
    strength.
[5]Those who were full hire themselves out for
    food,
  but those who were hungry hunger no more.
She who was barren has borne seven children,
  but she who has had many sons pines away.

[6]"The Lord brings death and makes alive;
  he brings down to the grave[a] and raises up.
[7]The Lord sends poverty and wealth;
  he humbles and he exalts.
[8]He raises the poor from the dust
  and lifts the needy from the ash heap;
he seats them with princes
  and has them inherit a throne of honor.

"For the foundations of the earth are the Lord's;
  upon them he has set the world.
[9]He will guard the feet of his saints,
  but the wicked will be silenced in darkness.

"It is not by strength that one prevails;
[10] those who oppose the Lord will be
    shattered.
He will thunder against them from heaven;
  the Lord will judge the ends of the earth.

"He will give strength to his king
  and exalt the horn of his anointed."

[a]6 Hebrew *Sheol*

NRSV

[5] Those who were full have hired themselves
    out for bread,
  but those who were hungry are fat with
    spoil.
The barren has borne seven,
  but she who has many children is forlorn.
[6] The Lord kills and brings to life;
  he brings down to Sheol and raises up.
[7] The Lord makes poor and makes rich;
  he brings low, he also exalts.
[8] He raises up the poor from the dust;
  he lifts the needy from the ash heap,
to make them sit with princes
  and inherit a seat of honor.[a]
For the pillars of the earth are the Lord's,
  and on them he has set the world.

[9] "He will guard the feet of his faithful ones,
  but the wicked shall be cut off in
    darkness;
  for not by might does one prevail.
[10] The Lord! His adversaries shall be shattered;
  the Most High[b] will thunder in heaven.
The Lord will judge the ends of the earth;
  he will give strength to his king,
  and exalt the power of his anointed."

[a] Gk (Compare Q Ms) adds *He grants the vow of the one who vows,
and blesses the years of the just*   [b] Cn Heb *against him he*

COMMENTARY

1 Samuel 2 begins by telling us that Hannah prayed, but what follows is not just a prayer but a hymn. Hannah sings! Her song is offered to us as the only appropriate response to her experience of God's wondrous grace. Hannah's song (2:1-10) is only loosely connected to the narratives that precede and follow it; nevertheless, on several different levels it serves an important role in these opening chapters of 1 Samuel.

First, these verses are a song of praise and thanksgiving by a barren woman whose womb has been opened. There is much in this hymn appropriate as a response by Hannah to the miracle that has issued in the birth of Samuel (chap. 1). The language of v. 1 is the language of

personal praise to God, and Hannah gives praise for "my victory" (NRSV, reading with Qumran MSS; the NIV reads "your" with the MT). The "enemies" of v. 1*b* and the references to arrogant and proud speech in v. 3 can be read as references to Peninnah and her taunting of Hannah. Verse 5*b* speaks of God's reversal of fortunes to give the barren one seven children while one with many children is left forlorn. Although Hannah is later recorded as bearing only five more children (v. 21), her hope for seven (a common number representing completion and fulfillment) is appropriate at this point in the story. She has certainly experienced the reversal wrought by God's power, of which this verse speaks.

It has long been recognized, however, that the reference of this hymn is broader than the story of Hannah's barrenness and the birth of Samuel. Many have noted the similarities of language and style to Psalm 113 and other hymns of praise in the psalter. It may well be that Hannah's praise has been drawn from a pool of hymnic praise known to Israel in its worship traditions. This possibility has led many to treat Hannah's song as a late and secondary intrusion into the text. Even though Hannah's song may draw on wider doxological traditions in Israel, however, it functions here as a key text to introduce the whole of the books of Samuel by relating Hannah's new future to a new future opening up for Israel.

Thus a second level of meaning for the song of Hannah becomes available when we recognize that she sings not just as the mother of Samuel but as a mother of Israel. It is a song that moves from lifting high the horn of Hannah (v. 1*a*, NIV; NRSV, "strength is exalted") to lifting high the horn of God's anointed (the king, 10*b*, NIV; NRSV, "power of his anointed"). The song suggests hope for the movement of struggling, perishing Israel to established nation, which is the story of the books of Samuel. Hannah's singing further reinforces what we have seen foreshadowed in chap. 1: Samuel's birth is tied to the birth of kingship in Israel. Israel's fortunes, like Hannah's, can be reversed. Thus the song of Hannah is intended to broaden our horizons beyond that of Hannah's personal story. Her song speaks of a whole catalog of reversals that are possible through the power of God: weakness made strength, the lowly made exalted, the hungry filled, the poor made rich, the barren given children (vv. 4-8*a*). At the end of Hannah's song, God's anointed one, the king, is to be understood as the gift of God as surely as was the child whose birth is celebrated at the opening of the song.

Although many have commented on similarities between Hannah's song and Psalm 113, only a few have noted the remarkable similarity of language and theme with 2 Samuel 22 (which appears in almost identical form in Psalm 18).[27] The

superscription to Psalm 18 says that David addressed this song of thanksgiving to God "on the day when the LORD delivered him from the hand of all his enemies and from the hand of Saul" (Ps 18:1). The whole saga of the books of Samuel is bracketed by the singing of Hannah and David. Hannah's victory, given by God, points forward to God's anointed one. David, God's anointed king, celebrates God's victory on his behalf, reflecting on the many obstacles he has overcome. Both songs stress the power of God to reverse apparently fixed human fortunes. Both Hannah's son, Samuel, and David must face conflict with Saul as God's failed king and their enemy. Again Hannah's song anticipates God's power to overcome such conflict, while David's song recalls such conflict already overcome. Seen in tandem with 2 Samuel 22, Hannah's song in 1 Sam 2:1-10 cannot be regarded as a mere intrusion into the flow of the narrative. Rather, it states doxologically the theological motifs that will dominate the whole of the story about to unfold in the books of Samuel. We shall expect to find these motifs echoed at various points throughout the story.

Finally, the song of Hannah should be understood as a witness to the central role of God's providence. Her song is a clear and unequivocal offering of praise to God, who is the power behind all of the events about to unfold, as surely as God was the power that opened the womb of Hannah. In the story of Hannah in chap. 1, and in all the episodes that will unfold in the chapters ahead, we will encounter the influence of remarkable men and women on the fate of Israel in the midst of extraordinary historical circumstances. Yet, central to the witness of 1 and 2 Samuel is the conviction that it is the presence of God with these characters and in the midst of this history that makes the crucial difference for Israel's future. Hannah's song celebrates and gives witness to this power of divine providence to create possibilities for the future that seem impossible through human and historical resources alone. Who would have thought there was a new future for Hannah? Who would think that Israel, as its plight unfolds in 2:11–7:2, has any future? It is

---

27. See R. A. Carlson, *David, the Chosen King* (Stockholm: Almqvist & Wiksell, 1964) 45-46; Brevard S. Childs, *Introduction to the Old Testament as Scripture* (Philadelphia: Fortress, 1979) 274; Walter Brueggemann, "I Samuel 1: A Sense of a Beginning," *ZAW* 102 (1990) 33-48; and Polzin, *Samuel and the Deuteronomist*, 31-34. Polzin includes a detailed chart of linguistic and thematic similarities. Randall C. Bailey, "The Redemption of

YHWH: A Literary Critical Function of the Songs of Hannah and David," *Biblical Interpretation* 3 (1995) 213-31, sees these bracketing hymns focused for exiles on a more hopeful aspect of God's character than the character of God displayed in the rest of the books of Samuel.

the Lord (Yahweh) who is incomparable (v. 2), who knows and weighs (v. 3b), who reverses the fortunes of the strong and the weak (vv. 4-8a), who is the creator of the earth itself (v. 8b), who guards the faithful (v. 9a), who judges the earth (v. 10c), and who upholds the king (v. 10de). Behind the human drama and the historical circumstances of these stories in the books of Samuel lies the certainty of God's providential working. Hannah's song passionately affirms God's providential presence in human history.

2:1-3. The song begins in an intensely personal style more characteristic of songs of thanksgiving than the more generalized praise of hymns. This is appropriate to the setting as Hannah's passionate offering of praise for God's deliverance. She sings in v. 1 of "my heart," "my strength," "my God," and "my enemies," and speaks of the victory in which she rejoices.[28] Such praise is immediately followed by three statements about the incomparability of God (v. 2). There is no one like the Lord, the Holy One, the Rock. Hannah's personal joy depends on divine power, a power manifested in holiness and strength, a power worthy of worship but offering safety in times of trouble. Hannah's singing gives praise to God as the source of her deliverance.

In the second phrase of the song, she uses a Hebrew idiom רמה קרני (rāmâ qarnî), literally, "my horn is raised" (v. 1a). This is a common metaphor in Hebrew poetry, used to evoke the image of a horned beast. The horn itself is a sign of strength; to "raise a horn" is to affirm power and dignity; hence, the NRSV abandons the metaphor and simply translates the image as "strength." The image of the horn appears in Hebrew literature as a sign of victory or success (e.g., Pss 89:17; 92:10), and it is sometimes used with specific reference to God's giving of children (see esp. 1 Chr 25:5, "All these were the children of Heman . . . in accordance with God's promise to raise up his horn," author's trans.). Such usage makes the image of the horn particularly appropriate for expressing Hannah's joy. The special significance of this image in Hannah's song is that what begins in v. 1 as the raising of Hannah's horn concludes in v. 10 with the raising of the

king's horn. The power of God, which can make the barren woman rejoice in a child, can also transform threatened tribal Israel into a kingdom.

Verse 3 provides a warning. If Hannah rejoices, those who are inclined to pride or arrogance must beware. God both knows (presumably of such prideful and arrogant attitudes) and weighs actions (if such prideful arrogance is acted upon). In the light of Hannah's story, Peninnah's taunting and ridicule of Hannah come immediately to mind (1:6). But this hymn does not identify Peninnah, leaving the text open for us to consider all who might arrogantly oppose God's will or pridefully think they can control their own destiny apart from God.

2:4-8. In these verses, Hannah's song becomes a catalog of surprising reversals that are wrought by God's power. The recital is divided into two groups with dramatic effect. Verses 4-5 speak in passive voice of groups whose fortunes are reversed, but God is not named as the agent of these transformations. The text focuses on the strong who are made weak (the mighty, v. 4; the full, v. 5a) and the weak who are made strong (the feeble, v. 4; the hungry, v. 5a). Verse 5b reverses the order, beginning with the weak. This time the subject is the barren woman who is given seven children, while the woman with many children is forlorn. The poem confirms Hannah's experience, given emphasis in this recital of God's power to transform the customary human realities. The number seven is probably an ideal number here and does not need to be reconciled with the five additional children Hannah later bears (v. 21). We might also observe that this first group of reversals begins with the "mighty" whose bows are broken (v. 4a). Perhaps this allusion foreshadows the reversal of fortunes that will bring David to the throne when Saul and Jonathan are killed in battle against the Philistines, with David mourning, "How the mighty have fallen" (2 Sam 1:19, 25, 27).

In vv. 6-8d, Hannah's song names the Lord as the power behind these reversals. The focus shifts from the hope of those in need of God's transforming power to a doxology in praise of the transforming One. An astonishing series of active verbs emphasizes God's power behind both negative and positive human experience. It is the Lord who "kills," who "brings down to Sheol," who "makes poor," who "brings low." The Lord also "brings to life," "raises up," "makes rich," "exalts," "raises up," "lifts," and "makes them sit and

---

28. The NRSV also includes "my victory" by adopting the reading from Qumran MSS. The NIV stays with the MT and reads "your victory," thus creating a contrast. It is Hannah's celebration, but it is God's victory.

inherit." The positive list is longer, naming the "poor" and the "needy" as recipients (v. 8). Further v. 8cd describes the fate of these poor and needy people as sitting with princes and inheriting a throne. The poet points the reader ahead both to lowly Israel's taking a place among the kingdoms and to David as a shepherd and eighth son who nevertheless will be king.[29]

The identity of this God who can accomplish such reversals is revealed in v. 8ef. God is the Creator. The hope of Hannah and the hope of Israel are rooted in the same power that holds the cosmos aloft over the seas of chaos. God has placed the world on its foundations, and God is the Rock (v. 2b) on which those in need and without power can rely. Hannah has experienced the power of the Creator in her time of need, and she sings about it as the reality to which all in need may turn.

2:9-10. Moral implications flow from this recital. The God of these reversals is a God who distinguishes between the faithful and the wicked (v. 9ab). Indeed, "the LORD will judge the ends of the earth" (v. 10c). The faithful are those who trust God's power to transform their lives and the social realities in which they live. The wicked are those who trust in their own might, power, and wealth. The list of groups whose fortunes are reversed in vv. 4-8d is here equated with the faithful and the wicked in the eyes of God. God will care for the faithful, but the wicked, God will "cut off in darkness" (v. 9b).

The last phrase of v. 9 serves not just as a conclusion to the verse, but also as a key to all of Hannah's song. It states a crucial principle for the story of Israel that unfolds in the books of Samuel: "For not by might does one prevail" (v. 9c). Human efforts to secure one's own destiny will not prevail apart from trust in what God is doing. In Hannah's song, all of the ways of human power can be reversed through the power of God: military might, wealth, family. It is God's power that endures.

At this point (v. 10a), the song bursts forth in an ecstatic cry of God's name—the Lord (Yahweh)![30] A series of phrases (v. 10a-c) celebrates the power of God, who shatters adversaries, thunders on high, and judges the earth. Who can doubt that it is the power of such a God that prevails and not human might?

Finally, and rather surprisingly, the power of God so passionately celebrated is linked to the king. Hannah's song concludes in v. 10de by announcing that God will give strength to the king and raise the "horn" (NRSV, "exalt the power") of the anointed (מָשִׁיחַ māšîaḥ). God's investment in this king is underlined by the use of the possessive. It is God's king and God's anointed one. The song, which began by celebrating God's gift of a child to Hannah, anticipates the gift of God's king to Israel; and it is Hannah's son, the prophet Samuel, who will anoint Israel's kings, Saul (10:1) and David (16:13). As we shall see, the advent of kingship in Israel was controversial. But Hannah's song at the beginning of this story makes clear that God is at work in these events; there will be no king but that he is God's king.

---

29. At this point, the LXX adds "He grants the vow of the one who vows," which would seem to give a more explicit reference to Hannah's story; but the LXX also omits much of the preceding verse. The NRSV takes note of this alternative in a footnote.

30. The NRSV is to be preferred over the NIV, which has omitted the conjunction "for" or "because" that links the final phrase of v. 9 causally to the first two phrases. In v. 10a, it is unlikely that "LORD" can be read as an object the way the NIV has it. There are longer additions to v. 10 in the LXX and in 4QSam. The LXX addition is similar to Jer 9:23-24, and the Qumran addition is different but fragmentary. See P. Kyle McCarter, *I Samuel,* AB 8 (Garden City, N.Y.: Doubleday, 1984) 69-70, for a full discussion of these textual problems.

REFLECTIONS

1. The song of Hannah is one of the Bible's most eloquent voices, testifying to God as the true source of transforming power. Its key line, "For not by might does one prevail" (1 Sam 2:9c NRSV), is a needed word in every generation, for it speaks to one of the most perennial of human temptations: the temptation to believe that we can control our own destiny and, perhaps, the course of history as well.

We live in a world that constantly evidences a belief in human might. Militarism, in its modern technological guise, has made the twentieth century the bloodiest century of human history; yet it is easier to raise budgets for weapons than for diplomacy. Consumer-driven market realities control our cultural preferences and appetites, and elections are influenced more by financial resources than by political ideas. Even at the personal level we live within a culture that worships self-fulfillment and the many programs to achieve it. Even in the church, energy seems too often directed to issues of membership growth, institutional maintenance, and popularity of programs than to discernment of what God is doing in the world.

The experience out of which Hannah sings offers hope to Israel and to us that a different reality is at work in the world from what we customarily acknowledge. Hannah's hope becomes hope for Israel and for us that power is not irrevocably tilted in favor of those the world defines as powerful—definitions that leave many powerless and without hope. Hannah sings of a God whose transforming power can reverse those patterns. She sings of a God who does not accept the world's power arrangements. She sings of a God whose might is not wielded in a disinterested fashion. God is heavily invested in the welfare of the weak, the powerless, the poor, the hungry, the dispossessed, the barren.

It is not accidental that Israel's hope for a king is voiced through the experience and the song of a barren woman whose petition has been heard. If God's transforming power for Israel takes the shape of a king, then Israel's king cannot be disinterested. Israel's king must be God's king, God's anointed one (1 Sam 2:10). The leadership of such a king must reflect the priorities of a God invested in those without power and might by the world's standards—those the world believes cannot possibly prevail. God's anointed one must serve the reversals of power about which Hannah sings (see Ps 72:1-4, 12-14).

This connection of anointed king to barren woman suggests that leadership in God's community in every generation cannot be either disinterested or self-serving. Leadership of God's people must reflect God's investment in the transformation of social realities that are biased against the weak, the poor, and the powerless. The church must identify with those who wait for God's reversals of grace. It is the surprising shape of God's power to which Paul points in 1 Cor 1:27-29:

> God chose what is foolish in the world to shame the wise; God chose what is weak in the world to shame the strong; God chose what is low and despised in the world, things that are not, to reduce to nothing things that are, so that no one might boast in the presence of God. (NRSV)

The raised horn of those who have been anointed to leadership in the church must be rooted in the raised horn of those who once were barren but are given new life in God's grace and power.

2. For Christians, the melody of Hannah's song is echoed in the song of Mary, known as the Magnificat (Luke 1:46-55). The strong similarities of language and theme have led many scholars to suggest that the song of Hannah was known to the Gospel writer. Both songs celebrate a wondrous birth, enabled by God's grace. Both songs preface and look to the coming of an anointed one (Messiah), although only Hannah's song uses this actual word. Both songs see the power of God as transforming power in behalf of the powerless.

Thus Mary, the mother of Jesus, is part of a long tradition. The mother of the Messiah (the "anointed one") for the church has an ancestry that includes the mothers of Israel, like Hannah. Many of these mothers, like Hannah and Mary, were singers. Miriam sang of God's deliverance in Exodus 15. Deborah sang of God's victory in Judges 5. These mothers were singers of new possibilities. They were singers of new communities and new power arrangements. The songs of mothers remind us that our story as the church is a part of what God has been doing since creation itself (1 Sam 2:8b), since the first giving of God's promise to raise up a people (Luke 1:55). The history of God's salvation does not originate with Jesus or with the church. The church is a part of the larger activity of God from creation onward. To be the community of Jesus as the Messiah is to be related to a God whose story is always larger than the church's story. It is to be related to a God whose transforming power on behalf of the powerless does not originate in Jesus Christ but was already known to Hannah and simply finds new expression in the song Mary sings for the church.

1 Samuel 2:11-36, Corruption of the House of Eli

NIV

[11]Then Elkanah went home to Ramah, but the boy ministered before the LORD under Eli the priest.

[12]Eli's sons were wicked men; they had no regard for the LORD. [13]Now it was the practice of the priests with the people that whenever anyone offered a sacrifice and while the meat was being boiled, the servant of the priest would come with a three-pronged fork in his hand. [14]He would plunge it into the pan or kettle or caldron or pot, and the priest would take for himself whatever the fork brought up. This is how they treated all the Israelites who came to Shiloh. [15]But even before the fat was burned, the servant of the priest would come and say to the man who was sacrificing, "Give the priest some meat to roast; he won't accept boiled meat from you, but only raw."

[16]If the man said to him, "Let the fat be burned up first, and then take whatever you want," the servant would then answer, "No, hand it over now; if you don't, I'll take it by force."

[17]This sin of the young men was very great in the LORD's sight, for they[a] were treating the LORD's offering with contempt.

[18]But Samuel was ministering before the LORD—a boy wearing a linen ephod. [19]Each year his mother made him a little robe and took it to him when she went up with her husband to offer the annual sacrifice. [20]Eli would bless Elkanah and his wife, saying, "May the LORD give you children by this woman to take the place of the one she prayed for and gave to the LORD." Then they would go home. [21]And the LORD was gracious to Hannah; she conceived and gave birth to three sons and two daughters. Meanwhile, the boy Samuel grew up in the presence of the LORD.

[22]Now Eli, who was very old, heard about everything his sons were doing to all Israel and how they slept with the women who served at the entrance to the Tent of Meeting. [23]So he said to them, "Why do you do such things? I hear from all the people about these wicked deeds of yours. [24]No, my sons; it is not a good report that I hear spreading among the LORD's people. [25]If a

a17 Or men

NRSV

[11]Then Elkanah went home to Ramah, while the boy remained to minister to the LORD, in the presence of the priest Eli.

[12]Now the sons of Eli were scoundrels; they had no regard for the LORD [13]or for the duties of the priests to the people. When anyone offered sacrifice, the priest's servant would come, while the meat was boiling, with a three-pronged fork in his hand, [14]and he would thrust it into the pan, or kettle, or caldron, or pot; all that the fork brought up the priest would take for himself.[a] This is what they did at Shiloh to all the Israelites who came there. [15]Moreover, before the fat was burned, the priest's servant would come and say to the one who was sacrificing, "Give meat for the priest to roast; for he will not accept boiled meat from you, but only raw." [16]And if the man said to him, "Let them burn the fat first, and then take whatever you wish," he would say, "No, you must give it now; if not, I will take it by force." [17]Thus the sin of the young men was very great in the sight of the LORD; for they treated the offerings of the LORD with contempt.

[18]Samuel was ministering before the LORD, a boy wearing a linen ephod. [19]His mother used to make for him a little robe and take it to him each year, when she went up with her husband to offer the yearly sacrifice. [20]Then Eli would bless Elkanah and his wife, and say, "May the LORD repay[b] you with children by this woman for the gift that she made to[c] the LORD"; and then they would return to their home.

[21]And[d] the LORD took note of Hannah; she conceived and bore three sons and two daughters. And the boy Samuel grew up in the presence of the LORD.

[22]Now Eli was very old. He heard all that his sons were doing to all Israel, and how they lay with the women who served at the entrance to the tent of meeting. [23]He said to them, "Why do you do such things? For I hear of your evil dealings from all these people. [24]No, my sons; it is not a good report that I hear the people of the LORD spreading abroad. [25]If one person sins against

a Gk Syr Vg: Heb with it   b Q Ms Gk: MT give   c Q Ms Gk: MT for the petition that she asked of   d Q Ms Gk: MT When

man sins against another man, God[b] may mediate for him; but if a man sins against the LORD, who will intercede for him?" His sons, however, did not listen to their father's rebuke, for it was the LORD's will to put them to death.

[26]And the boy Samuel continued to grow in stature and in favor with the LORD and with men.

[27]Now a man of God came to Eli and said to him, "This is what the LORD says: 'Did I not clearly reveal myself to your father's house when they were in Egypt under Pharaoh? [28]I chose your father out of all the tribes of Israel to be my priest, to go up to my altar, to burn incense, and to wear an ephod in my presence. I also gave your father's house all the offerings made with fire by the Israelites. [29]Why do you[c] scorn my sacrifice and offering that I prescribed for my dwelling? Why do you honor your sons more than me by fattening yourselves on the choice parts of every offering made by my people Israel?'

[30]"Therefore the LORD, the God of Israel, declares: 'I promised that your house and your father's house would minister before me forever.' But now the LORD declares: 'Far be it from me! Those who honor me I will honor, but those who despise me will be disdained. [31]The time is coming when I will cut short your strength and the strength of your father's house, so that there will not be an old man in your family line [32]and you will see distress in my dwelling. Although good will be done to Israel, in your family line there will never be an old man. [33]Every one of you that I do not cut off from my altar will be spared only to blind your eyes with tears and to grieve your heart, and all your descendants will die in the prime of life.

[34]"'And what happens to your two sons, Hophni and Phinehas, will be a sign to you—they will both die on the same day. [35]I will raise up for myself a faithful priest, who will do according to what is in my heart and mind. I will firmly establish his house, and he will minister before my anointed one always. [36]Then everyone left in your family line will come and bow down before him for a piece of silver and a crust of bread and plead, "Appoint me to some priestly office so I can have food to eat."'"

[a]25 Or the judges   [b]29 The Hebrew is plural.

another, someone can intercede for the sinner with the LORD;[a] but if someone sins against the LORD, who can make intercession?" But they would not listen to the voice of their father; for it was the will of the LORD to kill them.

26Now the boy Samuel continued to grow both in stature and in favor with the LORD and with the people.

27A man of God came to Eli and said to him, "Thus the LORD has said, 'I revealed[b] myself to the family of your ancestor in Egypt when they were slaves[c] to the house of Pharaoh. [28]I chose him out of all the tribes of Israel to be my priest, to go up to my altar, to offer incense, to wear an ephod before me; and I gave to the family of your ancestor all my offerings by fire from the people of Israel. [29]Why then look with greedy eye[d] at my sacrifices and my offerings that I commanded, and honor your sons more than me by fattening yourselves on the choicest parts of every offering of my people Israel?' [30]Therefore the LORD the God of Israel declares: 'I promised that your family and the family of your ancestor should go in and out before me forever'; but now the LORD declares: 'Far be it from me; for those who honor me I will honor, and those who despise me shall be treated with contempt. [31]See, a time is coming when I will cut off your strength and the strength of your ancestor's family, so that no one in your family will live to old age. [32]Then in distress you will look with greedy eye[e] on all the prosperity that shall be bestowed upon Israel; and no one in your family shall ever live to old age. [33]The only one of you whom I shall not cut off from my altar shall be spared to weep out his[f] eyes and grieve his[g] heart; all the members of your household shall die by the sword.[h] [34]The fate of your two sons, Hophni and Phinehas, shall be the sign to you— both of them shall die on the same day. [35]I will raise up for myself a faithful priest, who shall do according to what is in my heart and in my mind. I will build him a sure house, and he shall go in and out before my anointed one forever. [36]Everyone who is left in your family shall come to implore him for a piece of silver or a loaf of bread,

[a] Gk Compare Q Ms: MT another, God will mediate for him   [b] Gk Tg Syr: Heb Did I reveal   [c] Q Ms Gk: MT lacks slaves   [d] Q Ms Gk: MT then kick   [e] Q Ms Gk: MT will kick   [f] Q Ms Gk: MT your   [g] Q Ms Gk: Heb your   [h] Q Ms See Gk: MT die like mortals

and shall say, Please put me in one of the priest's places, that I may eat a morsel of bread.'"

COMMENTARY

After Hannah's song, the narrative resumes to begin the story of disaster facing the priestly house of Eli. The author identifies the corruption of Eli's sons and the abuse of the priestly office as the precipitating cause for the coming judgment of God against the house of Eli. The counterpoint to this story of impending disaster is a constant thread of attention to the rise of Samuel. In this story of corruption and doom, there is, nevertheless, a developing sense of anticipation for the new things in store for Israel, which God will do through Samuel.

The literary structure of this section seems very carefully crafted so as to contrast the wickedness of Eli's sons, Hophni and Phinehas, with the goodness of Hannah's son, Samuel.[31] The most fully developed portions of the story focus on the corruption of Eli's sons and the consequences that flow from their behavior. Verses 12-17 identify the past patterns of consistent and habitual abuse of the priestly office by Eli's sons. Verses 22-25 tell of an ineffectual attempt by Eli to curb their behavior. The sons ignore him, a response that characterizes the present lamentable state of affairs in the story. Finally, vv. 27-36 shift to the future disastrous consequences of this behavior for the house of Eli by means of an oracle of judgment brought to Eli by a "man of God."

A brief episode in the middle of the sorry story of Eli's sons concludes the prior story of Hannah (vv. 19-21). It brings closure to Hannah's story in ironic fashion, since Eli pronounces a blessing for her faithfulness even as his household is falling under a curse for its lack of faithfulness.

Threaded throughout this largely negative story are six short notices on Samuel's rise and growth in favor with God and people. They provide an understated counterpoint to the story of Eli's sons

in this last portion of chap. 2 (vv. 11, 18, 21b, 26), but they extend into chap. 3, where they bracket a more fully developed story of Samuel as the vehicle of God's word (3:1, 19). Each of these notices of Samuel's positive development is immediately prefaced or followed by a comment about the sin and corruption of Eli's sons. The contrast is especially heightened by use of the Hebrew verb גדל (gādal), meaning to "become great" or "grow." Verse 17 notes that it was the sins of Eli's sons that "became great," while three of the five following references to Samuel note that he "grew up in the presence of the LORD" (v. 21b), "in stature and in favor with the LORD and with the people" (v. 26), and as a man for whom God "let none of his words fall to the ground" (3:19 NRSV).

2:11-17. The narrative resumes with the notice that Elkanah returns home (Hannah is not mentioned), while Samuel, identified only as "the boy" (נער na'ar), stayed to serve the Lord under the tutelage of Eli (v. 11). The section ends by referring to Eli's sons also as "boys" (נערים nĕ'ārîm), but they are contemptuous of the Lord and have become great sinners in the Lord's eyes (v. 17). The term na'ar is here used as an indicator of subordinate status and not simply chronological age. Samuel must have been quite young, just beginning his service in Shiloh, whereas Eli's sons clearly were old enough to be given some priestly responsibilities. This section describes their failure in those responsibilities.

The account gives a harsh and unequivocating judgment. Eli's sons are not named (except to announce their death, v. 34), but their sinful behavior is carefully noted. They are identified as "scoundrels" (בליעל bĕliyya'al, v. 12; NIV, "wicked men"), a title Hannah disavows when she pleads with Eli not to think her a "worthless woman" (1:16). Eli's sons have achieved this dubious status by showing disregard for the Lord (v. 12b) and for the duties of priests (v. 13a).

Verses 13b-14 describe the customary practice

---

31. This view is opposed to those that see the Samuel material in this chapter as separate and redactional. See John T. Willis, "Samuel Versus Eli: I Sam. 1-7," *TZ* 35 (1979) 201-12, for a detailed defense of the unity of this chapter and, indeed, the whole of 1 Samuel 1-7.

of providing the priests' portion at Shiloh, while vv. 15-16 detail the abuse of this practice (this is made clearer in the NIV translation). Ordinarily, while the meat was boiling, a fork would be thrust in and whatever it brought out would go to the priests. Eli's sons, however, would send a servant to insist on a choice cut from all of the meat, including the fatty portions, which were specially reserved for dedication to the Lord. Further, they insisted that their choice be made before it was boiled so that the priests could roast the choicest portions for themselves. If Israelites objected to this arrogant behavior, hoping at least to burn the fatty portions before the Lord, they were threatened with violence (v. 16). The narrative affirms that such practices are contemptuous and constitute great sin in the eyes of God (v. 17).

2:18-21. The failure of Eli's sons in their priestly duties is followed by a notice concerning Samuel's education as a priest. The "linen ephod" he wore is not to be confused with a more elaborate outer garment also called an ephod and worn by priests (see v. 28). The white linen fabric here is elsewhere associated with priests and angels. David wears a "linen ephod" when he dances before the ark (2 Sam 6:14).

This notice about Samuel's clothing bridges to a brief account of the small robe Hannah would make and bring to Samuel each year. Verses 19-21 bring closure to Hannah's story. Eli blesses her; she then has five additional children. Soon the story will announce the death of Eli's children (v. 34). The verb שָׁאַל (šāʾal) is used again to describe Samuel as the "gift" or "asking" that Hannah has now "lent" to the Lord, a play on words that, we have seen, ties the fate of Hannah's son Samuel to Saul, Israel's first king (see Commentary on 1:20, 27-28). A final notice of Samuel's growth in the presence of God (v. 21b) signals a return to the story of Eli's sons and their growth in sin.

2:22-26. A poignant encounter unfolds. Eli has heard of his sons' despicable behavior. Indeed, he has additionally heard that they are having sexual relations with women serving in the sanctuary (v. 22). He attempts to confront them. Using strong words, he calls their actions "evil dealings/wicked deeds" (v. 23), informing them that their actions are widely known (v. 24) and making clear that such acts constitute sin against God (v. 25). But he speaks to no

avail. They will not listen (v. 25b). Eli, who is very old (v. 22a; 4:15 reports him to be ninety-eight), cannot exercise authority over these wanton sons. Perhaps this confrontation between father and sons has come too late.

The final phrase of v. 25 is difficult to understand: "for it was the will of the LORD to kill them." The text assumes that the coming deaths of Hophni and Phinehas are encompassed in the will of God for Israel at this time in its life. As surely as God is bringing something to birth for Israel through Hannah and Samuel, God is the power that will bring Eli's sons to the death their sin has made necessary. The description of the sins of Eli's sons makes clear that they have chosen this particular path. The path of corruption represented by Eli's sons must end so that something new can begin for the life of Israel.

Verse 26 makes it clear where that new life is emerging. Even as we learn from Eli's words to his sons that their evil reputation has spread among the people (v. 24), we hear that Samuel is growing in favor not only with God but also with the people. This notice of Hannah's son is particularly reminiscent of a later comment—about Mary's son in Luke 2:52.

2:27-36. A "man of God" appears before Eli and pronounces a prophetic oracle of God's judgment on the house of Eli. Many have suggested that this speech came from the hand of the deuteronomistic historian (Dtr). Particularly toward the end of this speech, the perspective shifts from the immediate events that will involve Samuel and Eli's household to concerns for the priestly office in Solomon's Temple. Such a perspective would be consistent with Dtr's wider view in telling the whole story of Israel. Dtr elsewhere uses programmatic speeches at crucial points to clarify the direction and perspective of his theological view of history (see esp. the speech by a "man of God" to Jeroboam in 1 Kgs 13:1-3). Certain phrases are characteristic of deuteronomistic vocabulary—e.g., "do according to what is in my heart and in my mind" (v. 35).

This speech may indeed reflect the broader interests of Dtr, but it also plays an important and carefully crafted role in the flow of the surrounding narrative. The deaths of Hophni and Phinehas are announced. The beginning of the end is at hand for the priestly house of Eli and for Shiloh.

Samuel will be the immediate successor to Eli's authority in Israel, even if Dtr gives us a glimpse over a longer term.

This speech is a classic example of a prophetic judgment speech. It opens with the use of the messenger formula ("Thus says the LORD . . . "), making clear that the "man of God" is speaking for God. The first half of the speech provides an accusation in which the sin of Eli's house is made clear (vv. 27-29). Signaled by "therefore," the oracle moves to an announcement of judgment against Eli's house (vv. 30-36). There is no narrative conclusion to the chapter. It ends abruptly with the conclusion of the speech.

As is customary in prophetic speech, God speaks in the first person through the "man of God" to Eli. God reminds Eli that his priestly service may be traced back to the time of bondage in Egypt, when Eli's ancestor was chosen to be priest (vv. 27-28). Three priestly duties given to that ancestor and his descendants are named: "to go up to my altar, to offer incense, to wear an ephod," and in return certain offerings were given to the priests (v. 28). Many think the ancestor intended here is Moses and that Eli is a part of a Mushite line of priestly authority that could trace its genealogy to the time of the Israelite bondage in Egypt; "Hophni" and "Phinehas" are Egyptian names.[32] Eli is simply reminded that he holds office and authority by God's designation, handed down through generations of Eli's ancestors. Moreover, that designation assumes the faithful discharge of the lineage's priestly duties.

In the context of these expectations as God's priest, Eli is charged with abuse of his priestly office in relation to sacrifices and offerings and with honoring his sons more than God (v. 29). Perhaps Eli's sons were the prime offenders, but God's judgment charges Eli with complicity in their apostasy. Did Eli also eat the choice parts pirated from worshipers? Could he have done more to stop such behavior? However, it is now too late; the speech moves to the pronouncement of judgment for the contempt shown to God.

God acknowledges the making of a promise to Eli's ancestor that his line should serve God as priests forever (v. 30a). However, God also declares that only those who honor God can be honored by God. Those who despise God can only be treated with contempt (v. 30b). God's promise does not offer an unconditional guarantee of privilege. God promises to return honor for honor and contempt for contempt. The consequences are dire. No one in the entire priestly family of Eli will live to old age (vv. 31-32). This priestly house is to end.

There is one exception, and here is where the horizon of Dtr broadens beyond the immediate story of Eli and Samuel and the coming kingship. One will be spared, but even he shall eventually die weeping and grieving (v. 33). The other members of Eli's house will die violent deaths. It is widely agreed that this verse alludes to Abiathar and his survival from Saul's massacre of the priests at Nob (22:6-23). Abiathar becomes high priest, along with Zadok, under David; but in the purge after Solomon takes the throne, Abiathar is deposed and banished (1 Kgs 2:27). The sign to Eli that these events shall come to pass will be the deaths of his sons, Hophni and Phinehas, on the same day (v. 34). This brings us back to Eli's family, and the fulfillment of this sign is recorded in 4:11.

Again, in vv. 35-36, the longer view of Dtr asserts itself. God promises to raise up a "faithful priest" to do what is in God's heart and mind and to serve "before my anointed one forever." God promises to build a "sure house" for this priest (a phrase reminiscent of the sure house God promises to establish for David in 2 Sam 7:16). Most scholars believe this statement is a reference to Zadok and Solomon's designation of Zadok and his house as the permanent priesthood of the Temple in Jerusalem. Priestly house and royal house become closely linked. The Zadokite priesthood is generally thought to trace its ancestry to Aaron rather than to Moses. Dtr may be commenting on later post-exilic priestly conflicts. Verse 36 is puzzling, but it may indicate later descendants of Eli's house (through Abiathar?) who were forced to beg for bread from the Temple. Scholars have suggested that this may reflect the later menial and subservient status of Levites at the Temple (see Deut 18:6-8; 2 Kgs 23:9).

32. The history of priestly office in Israel is a complex subject, and some of these genealogical claims may be attempts to justify authority among later priestly groups. See the discussion in Richard D. Nelson, *Raising Up a Faithful Priest: Community and Priesthood in Biblical Theology* (Louisville: Westminster/John Knox, 1993) 1-16. The view of a Mushite connection to Eli still rests largely on the work of Frank M. Cross, "The Priestly Houses of Early Israel," in *Canaanite Myth and Hebrew Epic* (Cambridge, Mass.: Harvard University Press, 1973) 195-215.

REFLECTIONS

Any preaching or teaching from 1 Sam 2:11-36 will bring the reader face to face with the issue of God's judgment. This is a story of sin and its consequences. Many North American Christians are not very comfortable with these themes. Optimism, positive thinking, joyful possibility—these sound so much more promising for an attractive, upbeat faith. Stories like this one come as a shock.

How do we make sense of the notion that God's promises can be abrogated or rejected? God made a promise forever to Eli's ancestor (2:30), but God cancels the promise because Israel has treated God with contempt. There are consequences to the contempt of God, and in this story the consequence is death. We in the church like to think of ourselves as recipients of God's promise. Could our sin lead to the cancellation of that promise?

We are shocked by the statement at the end of 2:25, "It was the will of the LORD to kill them" (NRSV). This does not mean that God desired their deaths. But God must exact the consequences of sin. In general, the Bible does not deal with this difficult theme in a rigid or mechanistic way. God does not determine the actions of Eli's sons. God does not choose the moral course that leads to death, but the death Hophni and Phinehas bring upon themselves is from God because God will not rescue them from the consequences of their own sin. Nor can we expect guarantees for life if we make death-dealing moral choices. The promise inherent in life itself can be broken if we render it meaningless. An old spiritual sings, "God gave Noah the rainbow sign; no more water, the fire next time." God's promises are not given with immunity from God's judgment. We can refuse the grace inherent in God's promise, and the consequence may be death.

The God angrily confronting Eli is no warm, fuzzy God. We cannot speak of the grace of God, seen growing in Samuel, without acknowledging the wrath and judgment of God, exacting consequences for the sins of Eli's sons. To preach this text is to acknowledge that moral choices as leaders in God's community do have something to do with life and death. Relationship to God is demanding and dangerous. Those who would serve God place themselves under both God's grace and God's judgment—not just under God's grace. This would certainly alter concepts of ordained ministry in an age where too many see the role of pastor or priest as only a job or a profession. Perhaps this episode concerning Eli's sons can help us to reflect on the risky business of leadership in God's community. To treat leadership roles in self-serving ways is to treat God with contempt, and there might be more at stake than a job.

1 Samuel 3:1–4:1a, The Call of Samuel

NIV

3 The boy Samuel ministered before the LORD under Eli. In those days the word of the LORD was rare; there were not many visions.

²One night Eli, whose eyes were becoming so weak that he could barely see, was lying down in his usual place. ³The lamp of God had not yet gone out, and Samuel was lying down in the temple[a] of the LORD, where the ark of God was. ⁴Then the LORD called Samuel.

Samuel answered, "Here I am." ⁵And he ran to Eli and said, "Here I am; you called me."

a3 That is, tabernacle

NRSV

3 Now the boy Samuel was ministering to the LORD under Eli. The word of the LORD was rare in those days; visions were not widespread.

2At that time Eli, whose eyesight had begun to grow dim so that he could not see, was lying down in his room; ³the lamp of God had not yet gone out, and Samuel was lying down in the temple of the LORD, where the ark of God was. ⁴Then the LORD called, "Samuel! Samuel!"[a] and he said, "Here I am!" ⁵and ran to Eli, and said,

a Q Ms Gk See 3.10: MT the LORD called Samuel

NIV

But Eli said, "I did not call; go back and lie down." So he went and lay down.

⁶Again the LORD called, "Samuel!" And Samuel got up and went to Eli and said, "Here I am; you called me."

"My son," Eli said, "I did not call; go back and lie down."

⁷Now Samuel did not yet know the LORD: The word of the LORD had not yet been revealed to him.

⁸The LORD called Samuel a third time, and Samuel got up and went to Eli and said, "Here I am; you called me."

Then Eli realized that the LORD was calling the boy. ⁹So Eli told Samuel, "Go and lie down, and if he calls you, say, 'Speak, LORD, for your servant is listening.'" So Samuel went and lay down in his place.

¹⁰The LORD came and stood there, calling as at the other times, "Samuel! Samuel!"

Then Samuel said, "Speak, for your servant is listening."

¹¹And the LORD said to Samuel: "See, I am about to do something in Israel that will make the ears of everyone who hears of it tingle. ¹²At that time I will carry out against Eli everything I spoke against his family—from beginning to end. ¹³For I told him that I would judge his family forever because of the sin he knew about; his sons made themselves contemptible,*a* and he failed to restrain them. ¹⁴Therefore, I swore to the house of Eli, 'The guilt of Eli's house will never be atoned for by sacrifice or offering.'"

¹⁵Samuel lay down until morning and then opened the doors of the house of the LORD. He was afraid to tell Eli the vision, ¹⁶but Eli called him and said, "Samuel, my son."

Samuel answered, "Here I am."

¹⁷"What was it he said to you?" Eli asked. "Do not hide it from me. May God deal with you, be it ever so severely, if you hide from me anything he told you." ¹⁸So Samuel told him everything, hiding nothing from him. Then Eli said, "He is the LORD; let him do what is good in his eyes."

¹⁹The LORD was with Samuel as he grew up, and he let none of his words fall to the ground. ²⁰And all Israel from Dan to Beersheba recognized

a13 Masoretic Text; an ancient Hebrew scribal tradition and Septuagint *sons blasphemed God*

NRSV

"Here I am, for you called me." But he said, "I did not call; lie down again." So he went and lay down. ⁶The LORD called again, "Samuel!" Samuel got up and went to Eli, and said, "Here I am, for you called me." But he said, "I did not call, my son; lie down again." ⁷Now Samuel did not yet know the LORD, and the word of the LORD had not yet been revealed to him. ⁸The LORD called Samuel again, a third time. And he got up and went to Eli, and said, "Here I am, for you called me." Then Eli perceived that the LORD was calling the boy. ⁹Therefore Eli said to Samuel, "Go, lie down; and if he calls you, you shall say, 'Speak, LORD, for your servant is listening.'" So Samuel went and lay down in his place.

¹⁰Now the LORD came and stood there, calling as before, "Samuel! Samuel!" And Samuel said, "Speak, for your servant is listening." ¹¹Then the LORD said to Samuel, "See, I am about to do something in Israel that will make both ears of anyone who hears of it tingle. ¹²On that day I will fulfill against Eli all that I have spoken concerning his house, from beginning to end. ¹³For I have told him that I am about to punish his house forever, for the iniquity that he knew, because his sons were blaspheming God,*a* and he did not restrain them. ¹⁴Therefore I swear to the house of Eli that the iniquity of Eli's house shall not be expiated by sacrifice or offering forever."

¹⁵Samuel lay there until morning; then he opened the doors of the house of the LORD. Samuel was afraid to tell the vision to Eli. ¹⁶But Eli called Samuel and said, "Samuel, my son." He said, "Here I am." ¹⁷Eli said, "What was it that he told you? Do not hide it from me. May God do so to you and more also, if you hide anything from me of all that he told you." ¹⁸So Samuel told him everything and hid nothing from him. Then he said, "It is the LORD; let him do what seems good to him."

¹⁹As Samuel grew up, the LORD was with him and let none of his words fall to the ground. ²⁰And all Israel from Dan to Beer-sheba knew that Samuel was a trustworthy prophet of the LORD. ²¹The LORD continued to appear at Shiloh, for the LORD revealed himself to Samuel at Shiloh by the word

a Another reading is *for themselves*

NIV

that Samuel was attested as a prophet of the LORD. [21]The LORD continued to appear at Shiloh, and there he revealed himself to Samuel through his word.

4 And Samuel's word came to all Israel.

NRSV

4 of the LORD. [1]And the word of Samuel came to all Israel.

COMMENTARY

This chapter, traditionally labeled "The Call of Samuel," does more than that title suggests. It authorizes and legitimizes Samuel as the only source of God's Word during the oncoming period of radical dislocation and transformation in Israel. Simultaneously it provides the final word of judgment on and removal from authority of the priestly house of Eli (although we have had previous word of this in 2:27-36). The chapter begins with Samuel as a boy, learning from Eli, and it ends with Samuel as God's prophet (3:20), replacing Eli as the authority at Shiloh (3:21).

3:1. This verse reintroduces us to the cast of characters, Samuel and Eli, and suggests that the main focus of the reader's concern should be on the rarity of God's word. No longer a child, Samuel has become a young man in the service of the Lord under Eli at Shiloh. The text has carefully noted the progress of Samuel's growth and service (1 Sam 2:11, 18, 21, 26). He has learned from Eli, gained favor with the people, and, most important, matured in the presence and favor of the Lord. All this prepares him for his transformation to a new role of leadership.

Eli has just received an extended pronouncement of judgment on his priestly house from an unknown prophet (1 Sam 2:27-36). We must read chap. 3 under the shadow of this judgment, waiting to see how the Lord will provide for leadership in Israel when the priestly leadership at Shiloh has failed so utterly. Nevertheless, as the chapter opens Samuel is still serving "under Eli."

The central issue of this chapter is introduced in v. 1*b:* The "word of the LORD" is rare, and "visions" have become uncommon in Israel. Consequently, what is about to happen to Samuel is unusual and prepares us for his unique role. Verse 7 explains that, during the night, Samuel was experiencing the "word of the LORD," but he did not know it. In v. 11, Samuel does receive the Lord's word, and in v. 15 the experience is described as a "vision." In the person of Samuel, the situation of v. 1*b* is about to be reversed. The chapter closes with an extended notice of Samuel's new role as the channel of the Lord's word in Israel (3:19–4:1*a*). This special concern for the word of the Lord and the authorization of Samuel as its medium is consistent with the theological concerns of the prophetic editor whom many scholars believe had a crucial role in the shaping of 1 Samuel (see the Introduction).

3:2-18. This narrative gives an account of Samuel's revelatory experience at Shiloh. Although these verses are usually described as the call of Samuel, they do not show the typical pattern of a prophetic call narrative. There is neither a formal commissioning of Samuel to be a prophet nor the typical expression of a prophet's unworthiness for the call (cf., e.g., Isa 6:1-13). This passage is better understood as a theophany, a report about God's appearance in the human world. This account would seem to have much in common with Egyptian and Mesopotamian theophanic narratives of religious functionaries who sleep in a shrine in order to receive a dream or visionary message from the deity.[33]

33. Some continue to defend this chapter as a modified call narrative, following the position of Murray Newman, "The Prophetic Call of Samuel," in *Israel's Prophetic Heritage,* ed. B. W. Anderson and W. Harrelson (New York: Harper & Row, 1962) 86-97. More convincing seem the treatments of those who see the chapter as a theophanic narrative: e.g., Ralph W. Klein, *1 Samuel,* WBC 10 (Waco: Word, 1983) 31; Michael Fishbane, "I Samuel 3: Historical Narrative and Narrative Poetics," in *Literary Interpretations of Biblical Narratives,* vol. 2, ed. K. R. Gros Louis and J. S. Ackerman (Nashville: Abingdon, 1982) 192.

First Samuel 3 serves less to call Samuel as a prophet than to inaugurate him as a prophet, mediating the word of the Lord.

The story of Samuel's theophanic experience falls into three distinct parts: vv. 2-9 describe the initial setting and experience in which Samuel does not recognize the approach of the Lord; vv. 10-14 report the Lord's message to Samuel; vv. 15-18 tell of Samuel's reluctant reporting of the message to Eli. Although Samuel is the central figure in the story, Eli plays an important role in each segment as well.

The story takes place during the night in the temple (tent sanctuary) at Shiloh. Samuel is sleeping near the ark of the Lord (v. 3), while Eli is lying down in his usual place, presumably somewhere outside the inner temple precincts (v. 2).

We are told that the "lamp of God had not yet gone out" (v. 3). At its most literal level, this expression may indicate the time prior to dawn. Priestly protocol called for the burning of lamps in the sanctuary from evening to morning (Exod 27:20-21). But this phrase may convey multiple levels of meaning. As Polzin has noted, this story opens with the vocabulary of sight and insight.[34] *Visions* are infrequent. Eli's *eyesight* is growing dim; he cannot *see.* The *lamp* has not yet gone out. This visual vocabulary prepares us for an ironic contrast. The boy Samuel sleeps near the ark, which is a source of divine presence and illumination, but he cannot perceive what is really happening, whereas the priest Eli, nearly blind and sleeping apart from the divine presence of the ark, finally perceives that the Lord is speaking to Samuel. In this context, the expression "the lamp of God had not yet gone out" may refer both to the near extinguishing of divine vision in Israel (v. 1*b*) and to the waning of Eli's literal vision as well as his role as a priestly source of spiritual vision (v. 2).

Three times God calls Samuel, and each time he runs to Eli, presuming the old priest has summoned him (vv. 4-8). We need not think, as some commentators have suggested, that Samuel is unusually naive or dense. He is still a youth and living in a time when the word and vision of the Lord are rare. In fact, the text goes to unusual lengths to suggest that Samuel has no basis on which to recognize the

34. Robert Polzin, *Samuel and the Deuteronomist: A Literary Study of the Deuteronomic History,* Part Two: *1 Samuel* (San Francisco: Harper & Row, 1989) 49-54.

Lord's summons. Verse 7 tells us that Samuel did not yet *know* the Lord, nor had the word of the Lord been *revealed* to him. Since Samuel has been ministering under the instruction of Eli at the Lord's sanctuary in Shiloh, we may presume that Samuel knew something about the Lord, but that he had not yet had revelatory experience of the Lord. Therefore, it is not reasonable to expect Samuel to recognize what is taking place.

When Samuel comes to Eli a third time, the old priest *perceives* "that the LORD was calling the boy" (v. 8*b*). The blind priest *sees* what is taking place, whereupon Eli gives Samuel a proper response to make (v. 9).

Verses 10-14 record the full content of the divine revelation to Samuel. The climactic moment follows the three futile calls. Together they form an emphatic number sequence (cf. Num 22:22-33; Amos 1:3, 6, 9, 11, 13). Samuel makes the response suggested to him by Eli, but he omits the explicit use of the divine name (v. 10), perhaps reinforcing the notice of v. 7 that Samuel does not yet *know* the Lord.

At this point, the Lord "came and stood" before Samuel, indicating a visionary as well as an auditory experience. The message of the Lord begins with the announcement that the Lord is "about to do something in Israel that will make the ears of everyone who hears of it tingle" (v. 11; see the same expression in 2 Kgs 21:12; Jer 19:3). The divine word to be pronounced bears immediate significance for the house of Eli. Simultaneously, it announces a divine action that will be recognized by all who hear of it as a turning point in God's relationship with Israel.

God pronounces a word of judgment on the priestly house of Eli. The wording of v. 12 recognizes that judgment has already been pronounced on Eli's family in 2:27-36. This new word confirms and makes irrevocable that judgment. Once again it is clear that Eli himself is not corrupt or unfaithful. His sons have engaged in despicable and corrupt activities, and Eli has not been able to "restrain" (כהה *kāhâ*) them (v. 13). Standard Hebrew lexicons give the meaning of this word as "rebuke," and some translations (e.g., NEB) have followed this meaning. However, this meaning surely cannot be correct, since Eli did "rebuke" his sons (2:22-25). The NRSV and the NIV both follow the suggestion that this word is related to a root meaning "to be weak," thus in this text meaning "to restrain" or "to weaken." Eli rebuked his sons, but he could not control them. The judgment is harsh: Eli and his entire priestly lineage, once promised authority forever (2:30), are now to be "punished" (NRSV; NIV, "judged") forever (v. 13). This judgment cannot be ritually averted either by sacrifice or by offering (v. 14).

Unlike the previous announcement of God's judgment against the house of Eli, there is no mention of survivors (2:33) or successor priestly houses (2:35). The emphasis here is less on this divine word of judgment as news to Eli than on the inauguration of Samuel as the prophetic recipient and proclaimer of the divine word.

In the final section of this story (vv. 15-18), Samuel must communicate the Lord's harsh word of judgment to Eli. He delays until morning, afraid to face Eli with this difficult judgment (v. 15). The statement that Samuel "opened the doors of the house of the LORD," which may have been his usual duty, takes on new meaning, since Samuel is opening a new means of access to God's word in Israel.

Eli takes the initiative by calling to Samuel, and he softens a difficult moment for Samuel by gently addressing him as "my son." Ironically, Samuel makes the same response ("Here I am") that he made in the night when he mistakenly thought Eli was calling him (v. 16). Eli instructs Samuel to report his experience, leaving out nothing. When Samuel does so, Eli wins our admiration by the integrity of his forthright response (v. 18). The aging priest again identifies the source of this revelatory word: "It is the LORD." He then gracefully accepts the divine verdict. Although he knows that the consequences of his sons' sins have fallen upon him personally and on his whole house, he can nevertheless respond in terms of acceptance rather than self-interest. God knows what is good even though this means relinquishment and loss for Eli and his family. It is remarkable that, in spite of Eli's inability to control his sons, he is never described in these chapters as personally culpable or lacking in integrity and faithful intent. God's way into the future for Israel will not include Eli, but Eli acknowledges the priority of divine will over his own. The roles of Eli and Samuel have now been reversed. It is Eli who looks to Samuel for instruction in the word of the Lord. Eli's authority has ended, but Samuel's has just begun.

3:19–4:1a. The real climax of this passage comes in the final notice that identifies Samuel as the Lord's fully authorized prophet. The first half of 4:1 functions as the concluding word to this unit rather than as the opening word to the ark narrative that follows. (The LXX has a much longer reading for this verse, which includes mention of the continued wickedness of Eli's sons.) The situation described in 3:1 has changed. The word of the Lord is no longer rare, but reliably present in the midst of Israel through Samuel.

Verse 19 implies that Samuel has grown to adulthood, but in sharp contrast to 3:7, the Lord is now present with him and lets "none of his words fall to the ground." Samuel's words prove reliable and trustworthy. Indeed, we are told that this reputation stretched the length of the land, "from Dan to Beer-sheba" (3:20). But this reputation is now identified with a definite role. All of Israel knows Samuel to be "attested as a prophet of the LORD" (3:20; the NRSV inexplicably changes the verb into an adjective, "was a trustworthy prophet . . ."). Samuel is a נביא (*nābî'*), the Hebrew term for "prophet." The narrator in 2:27 was reluctant to use this formal term for the "man of God" who gave the oracle of judgment to Eli. In 1 Samuel, this term is reserved for Samuel, the Lord's prophet.

With great irony, 3:21 reports that the Lord continued to appear at *Shiloh.* Although the place remains the same, the reader is aware that a great change has been made. What had been the ritual center under the leadership of Eli has now become the center for the prophetic word under the leadership of Samuel.

An interesting pattern appears in the concluding lines of this account. The Lord continues to give Samuel revelatory experience "by the word of the LORD" (3:21*b;* the NIV reduces the divine name to a pronoun, "through his word."). The following clause states that "the word of *Samuel* came to all Israel" (4:1*a*). This progression is a telling comment on the way in which a prophet mediates the divine word. The prophet may be the channel through whom God speaks, but one should not confuse the divine word with the prophet's words. God's word comes to the prophet, but the prophet must pass that word on in his own words. The prophet speaks *for* God, not *as* God.

REFLECTIONS

1. In the church's use of this text the focus has almost always been on 3:2-10 as a simple story of God's call and the way in which we often fail to recognize it. In such traditional use, the passage becomes a generalized story of God's calling and the need for discernment so that we do not mistake God's voice for the human voices of authority that surround us.

Although this reading depends on a legitimate element of the story, it ignores the fact that God's call did not come to Samuel—nor does it come to us—in general circumstances. This is not a narrative of Samuel's general religious awakening. It is not simply another experience on the road to religious maturity. Samuel is called by God in a time of spiritual desolation, religious corruption, political danger, and social upheaval. The word of the Lord is rare; the sons of Eli are corrupt; the Philistines are about to threaten Israel's survival; the pressures to move toward kingship will soon grow to overwhelming.

If the context for Samuel's experience is harsh, so too is the message he is told to bring. We sometimes celebrate so-called mountaintop religious experiences as ends in themselves, without considering what the God we encounter in religious experience demands of us. Samuel is called to deliver a harsh message of judgment that is necessary if there is to be a hopeful new beginning for Israel in this trying time. There is no time to dwell on childlike faith experiences. The call is to a prophetic task. The text will not allow us to dwell on the theophanic experience as an end in itself. This text reminds us of the spiritual challenges and social transformations that God's call brings. We are urged not only to discern God's voice but to listen to what it asks of us as well. We are called to become the channel for God's prophetic word to our own time.

2. First Samuel 3:1–4:1*a* reminds us of God's constant presence in the endings and the beginnings of human history. This is a story of endings. The people despair at the corruption of Eli's sons and the failure of leadership in a crucial time. But the message of this story is that corrupt institutions and oppressive practices need not endure. God opposes them. In the harsh word of judgment given to Samuel for Eli is the hopeful proclamation that God will not acquiesce to evil. This has already been anticipated in doxological terms by Hannah's song in 2:1-10. It now finds concrete historical reality in God's announced end to the house of Eli.

Eli's calm and faithful acceptance of this harsh word is itself a model of faith in difficult circumstances. He is not the central cause of corruption in the order God will sweep away, but he is invested in that order. He, too, will pay a price in God's judgment on his sons. Historically the church, too, has found itself invested in corrupt orders it did not entirely create. Accepting God's judgment in times of social transformation and spiritual challenge involves us in the pain of Eli's complicity and calls us to reflect his trustful willingness to let God "do what is good."

But this is also a story of new beginnings. To dwell on the judgment of Eli's house is to fail to rejoice in God's initiative to raise up new prophetic leadership. We cannot mourn so deeply what seems to be passing that we miss the signs of what God is bringing to birth: "There is a chance for newness, and that chance is rooted in Hannah's piety, in Israel's daring doxology, in Eli's yielding, in Samuel's availability, in God's resolve to do a new thing."[35]

God's new beginning is not just the stirring of a boy's religious sensitivities. The chapter opens with the absence of God's word and ends with the proclamation of God's word through Samuel. The story opens with corrupt and discredited religious leadership in place and closes with new and vigorous leadership, recognized by all Israel. We are being prepared to recognize that, in the difficult days of social upheaval ahead for Israel, there is already a new beginning: God's initiative for new possibilities in spite of the failure and the passing away of old patterns. The movement of Samuel is from messenger of God's word of judgment for Eli to ongoing prophet of God's word

---

35. Walter Brueggemann, *First and Second Samuel,* Interpretation (Louisville: John Knox, 1990) 27.

for all Israel. Those who read this text need to see the link between the proclamation of endings and the provision for ongoing leadership that enables God's new beginnings. It will not be enough to proclaim judgment without taking responsibility for what lies beyond judgment.

3. This story reminds us that the divine word is often mediated through human words. In our efforts to discern God's will, we recognize in this story the need for community. First Samuel, then Eli, and finally all Israel requires the mediation of others to hear and understand God's word for their lives.

With humility, we realize that, like Samuel, we may not ourselves recognize the call of God. It may be others, like Eli, who discern the divine presence first and name the divine name so that we may be enabled to respond. This text calls for openness to seeking the advice and wisdom of others who might aid us in discerning God's call.

In fear and trembling, we understand with Eli that the harsh words others may speak in criticism of our practices may be the word of God's judgment. The person through whom such words of judgment are mediated may be as unlikely as an apprentice sleeping in the sanctuary, but the word delivered is nonetheless the word of God. The response demanded of us may be as difficult as Eli's relinquishment of vested interest to trust in God's will. We are challenged by this text to recognize that God's word for us sometimes comes harshly, and asks of us difficult choices.

In gratitude, we recognize with all Israel the continuing presence of God's word in our midst, and we give thanks for God's prophets who bring us hope as well as judgment. God's word requires prophets, but this text reminds us that the two cannot be confused. God's word comes to Samuel, but Samuel's words come to all Israel. This is a foundation stone in understanding the preaching task in the life of the church. Our words rest on faithful discernment of God's word, but they will never be identical to God's word. Humility is an appropriate posture as we respond to the call to mediate God's word. Further on in the story, we may have occasion to wonder whether Samuel has remembered this. Nevertheless, we are reminded in this text of the necessary mediation to the community by those who audaciously receive the gift of God's word and attempt to communicate it in their own words.

1 Samuel 4:1*b*–7:1, The Philistine Crisis and the Capture of the Ark

OVERVIEW

First Samuel 4:1*b*–7:1 provides an abrupt change of scene and focus. Chapter 4 tells the story of a Philistine military campaign against Israel. Not only is Israel defeated initially, but when the ark of the covenant, a sacred symbol of the presence of Yahweh, is brought onto the field to ensure victory, it is captured, and Israel suffers an even greater defeat. The sons of Eli are killed, and Eli himself dies in shock at the news of the ark's capture. In chap. 5 we have an account of what happens while the ark is with the Philistines, and chap. 6 tells how the Philistines finally sent the ark back to Israelite territory. The entire story stresses the ultimate sovereignty of the Lord (Yahweh) over the Philistines and

their gods despite appearances to the contrary in the initial defeat of Israel.

Since the work of Leonhard Rost, most scholars have viewed 1 Samuel 4–6 as a separate story, usually referred to as the "Ark Narrative."[36] In this view, the main character of chaps. 4–6 is the ark of the covenant itself. This ark narrative concludes in 2 Samuel 6 with the story of David's finding and

---

36. Leonhard Rost, *The Succession to the Throne of David*, trans. M. D. Rutter and D. M. Gunn (Sheffield: Almond, 1982; original German publication, 1926). Anthony F. Campbell, *The Ark Narrative (1 Sam 4–6; 2 Sam 6): A Form-Critical and Traditio-Historical Study*, SBLDS 16 (Missoula, Mont.: Scholars Press, 1975), represents a development of Rost's classic view and contains an excellent history of research on these chapters.

installing the ark in Jerusalem. This narrative was written in the late Davidic or early Solomonic period to legitimize the Davidic dynasty by associating it with the ark, which was a sacred symbol of God's presence during the time of the tribal league. Then the ark narrative was incorporated into the later Deuteronomistic History. Most scholars think its presence there is somewhat intrusive.

Recent studies have raised some serious alternatives to this view. Patrick D. Miller and J. J. M. Roberts[37] have argued forcefully that an original ark narrative included the portions of 1 Samuel 2 that deal with the corruption of the house of Eli. They argue that this original narrative did not include 2 Samuel 6 and that it dates prior to David's defeat of the Philistines. The account stresses the hand of Yahweh as an expression of divine power and encourages trust in God's control of events even in a time of apparent defeat. Robert Polzin[38] is representative of recent literary studies of the books of Samuel that are little concerned with the early history of the text. He stresses the interconnections between chaps. 4–6 and the surrounding material in 1 Samuel 1–7 and discusses the role these chapters might play in the larger Deuteronomistic History addressed to exiles in Babylon. He finds these interconnections so numerous and so skillfully made that he sees little value in speculating on the prior existence of an independent ark narrative.

It seems likely that these chapters did have a separate history. Even the casual reader has the sense of an abrupt change with chap. 4. Samuel, whose birth and future leadership have dominated chaps. 1–3, drops entirely out of the story. With no introduction, the Philistines are threatening the future of Israel. Events rather than characters occupy the attention of the story. Although the deaths of Hophni and Phinehas serve in the present arrangement of 1 Samuel to fulfill the words of the man of God to Eli in 2:34, chap. 4 itself makes nothing of this. In fact, chap. 4 does not reflect any anti-Elide sentiment or suggest that the death of Eli's sons (or of Eli himself) had anything to do with their sin. Chapter 2, with its careful

counterpoint between Samuel and the sons of Eli, seems too much a literary unity to support the suggestion that the ark narrative originally included the anti-Elide portions of the chapter (contra Miller and Roberts).

Although 1 Samuel 4–6 may have had a separate literary pre-history, these chapters have been artfully incorporated into the context of 1 Samuel 1–7 and into the larger purposes of the Deuteronomistic History. To perceive these interconnections as skillfully created does not necessitate the suggestion of a single author (contra Polzin), but can be seen as a tribute to the skill of a historian who utilized a variety of materials to produce a telling of Israel's story for the sake of a generation in exile. The story of Israel's early loss of the ark would have been of obvious interest to exiles who had lost the ark in the destruction of Jerusalem (with Polzin). Although we may see evidence of earlier source materials used by the historian and make observations about them, our primary emphasis must be on the story of Israel in this transformative period as it is now told in the full text before us.

We can now make some observations about the nature of the narrative material in 1 Samuel 4–6 and about the way in which this narrative segment now functions in its present position in the books of Samuel. Miller and Roberts have made an especially important contribution to the study of these chapters by their investigation of numerous texts from the ancient Near East that chronicle the capture of a nation's gods in battle and their subsequent return.[39] Taking images of gods as spoils of war was common, as was displaying them in the victorious nation's temple. Frequently these images were returned. Miller and Roberts cite texts that interpret such events not only from the point of view of the victor but also those that speak from the perspective of the defeated. For the victor, such events demonstrated the superiority of their gods. Told from the perspective of the defeated, it was important to reaffirm the sovereignty of their god and to assert that even the defeat was an act of their god's will, perhaps out of anger with the people. The eventual return of the image was understood as having

---

37. Patrick D. Miller and J. J. M. Roberts, *The Hand of the Lord: A Reassessment of the "Ark Narrative" of 1 Samuel* (Baltimore: Johns Hopkins, 1977).

38. Polzin, *Samuel and the Deuteronomist*, 2-8, 55-79. See also John T. Willis, "Samuel Versus Eli: I Sam. 1-7," *TZ* 35 (1979).

39. Miller and Roberts, *The Hand of the Lord*.

been compelled by the god's desire to return and not by the magnanimity of the enemy.

Miller and Roberts make a convincing case for understanding the ark narrative in 1 Samuel 4–6 as an account of a disastrous defeat and the capture of the ark from the point of view of an Israel trying to understand how this could have happened. The account seeks to interpret events theologically by seeing the "hand of Yahweh" in the entire course of events. God has allowed the defeat and the ark's capture (chap. 4); in captivity, the ark serves as the vehicle for Yahweh to humiliate the Philistines and their god Dagon (chap. 5); and God's power ultimately brings the ark home to Israel (chap. 6). Although events appear to suggest otherwise, the ark narrative makes clear that the Lord (Yahweh) was always the determinative power behind the course of events. Within 1 Samuel 4–6 it is not made clear what motivated Israel's God to allow such a defeat. However, the placement of the ark narrative in 1 Samuel 1–7 suggests an answer to this question: It was the corruption of the priestly leadership of Israel in the house of Eli at Shiloh.[40] The deuteronomistic historian has artfully used the ark narrative to play an important function not only in the immediate context of 1 Samuel and the story of the rise of kingship in Israel but also in the larger context of the Deuteronomistic History as a narration of Israel's story addressed to exiles.

In 1 Samuel 1–7 everything points toward the emergence of kingship in Israel. First Samuel 1–3 introduced the reader to the internal factors that contributed to the need for kingship. The priestly house of Eli at Shiloh had become corrupt. Yet, God was at work. Samuel was born as the gift of God to Hannah, and he was raised to be given authority as God's prophet, replacing Eli at Shiloh as the trustworthy representative of God in Israel (3:19–4:1*a*). Chapters 4–6 now introduce the reader to the external factors leading to kingship in Israel. The Philistines have defeated Israel and have captured the ark. There is a danger that political autonomy and identity for Israel may be swallowed up permanently by this enemy. But the message of the ark narrative is that here, too, God is at work. God is still in control of these events,

allowing the capture of the ark (chap. 4), humiliating the Philistines and their god Dagon (chap. 5), and motivating the return of the ark to Israelite territory (chap. 6). In their present arrangement, these two segments are tied together by the deaths of Eli and his sons in 4:12-18. These deaths now function as the fulfillment of God's judgment on the corruption of the house of Eli, announced by both the unnamed man of God (2:27-36) and Samuel (3:11-18). As we shall see, chap. 7 brings together these internal and external forces that move Israel toward kingship. Samuel meets the Philistines, and the Philistines are defeated. Once again, God is at work, using the prophet Samuel, who replaced Eli, to meet the external threat of the enemy. The perspective of this story seems to be that kingship was coming, but that it was not really needed. God was at work dealing with the internal and the external crises.

In the larger framework of the Deuteronomistic History the ark narrative may have a special significance for the community of exiles to whom that history was addressed. The exiles had also suffered defeat and lost the ark. They could not fail to identify with the plight of Israel when the ark was captured by the Philistines. This connection to the experience of exile seems explicit in the naming of Phinehas' son by his dying wife in 4:21-22, "The glory has *gone into exile* from Israel" (author's trans. גלה [*gālâ*]; the NRSV and the NIV use the less descriptive "departed"). The "glory" (כבוד *kābôd*) refers to God's own being and is strikingly similar to the image in Ezek 10:18 for the departure of God's glory from the Temple in the exile experience. Chapters 5–6 of the ark narrative, which emphasize the continued sovereignty of God, the humiliation of the enemy, and return to the land, would be especially hopeful for exiles who read this history, trusting that God was also continuing to be active on their behalf. For exiles who read 1 Samuel 4–6, the message is that God continues to be at work even in apparent defeat. For exiles, kingship has ended, but God's sovereignty has not. In this larger deuteronomistic context, kingship has come and gone. First Samuel 4–6 may suggest that kingship had not really been needed. God's sovereignty is sufficiently reliable.

In the commentary below we will look more closely at each of the distinct episodes in the drama of the Philistines and the ark.

---

40. It is not necessary to include portions of chap. 2 in an original ark narrative (as do Miller and Roberts) in order to observe this connection in the present arrangement of 1 Samuel 1–7. An original ark narrative may have included some other motivation for Yahweh's action or none at all. See Willis, "Samuel Versus Eli," 204-7.

1 Samuel 4:1*b*-22, The Philistines, the Ark, and the House of Eli

NIV

Now the Israelites went out to fight against the Philistines. The Israelites camped at Ebenezer, and the Philistines at Aphek. ²The Philistines deployed their forces to meet Israel, and as the battle spread, Israel was defeated by the Philistines, who killed about four thousand of them on the battlefield. ³When the soldiers returned to camp, the elders of Israel asked, "Why did the LORD bring defeat upon us today before the Philistines? Let us bring the ark of the LORD's covenant from Shiloh, so that it*ª* may go with us and save us from the hand of our enemies."

⁴So the people sent men to Shiloh, and they brought back the ark of the covenant of the LORD Almighty, who is enthroned between the cherubim. And Eli's two sons, Hophni and Phinehas, were there with the ark of the covenant of God.

⁵When the ark of the LORD's covenant came into the camp, all Israel raised such a great shout that the ground shook. ⁶Hearing the uproar, the Philistines asked, "What's all this shouting in the Hebrew camp?"

When they learned that the ark of the LORD had come into the camp, ⁷the Philistines were afraid. "A god has come into the camp," they said. "We're in trouble! Nothing like this has happened before. ⁸Woe to us! Who will deliver us from the hand of these mighty gods? They are the gods who struck the Egyptians with all kinds of plagues in the desert. ⁹Be strong, Philistines! Be men, or you will be subject to the Hebrews, as they have been to you. Be men, and fight!"

¹⁰So the Philistines fought, and the Israelites were defeated and every man fled to his tent. The slaughter was very great; Israel lost thirty thousand foot soldiers. ¹¹The ark of God was captured, and Eli's two sons, Hophni and Phinehas, died.

¹²That same day a Benjamite ran from the battle line and went to Shiloh, his clothes torn and dust on his head. ¹³When he arrived, there was Eli sitting on his chair by the side of the road, watching, because his heart feared for the ark of

ª3 Or he

NRSV

In those days the Philistines mustered for war against Israel,*ª* and Israel went out to battle against them;*ᵇ* they encamped at Ebenezer, and the Philistines encamped at Aphek. ²The Philistines drew up in line against Israel, and when the battle was joined,*ᶜ* Israel was defeated by the Philistines, who killed about four thousand men on the field of battle. ³When the troops came to the camp, the elders of Israel said, "Why has the LORD put us to rout today before the Philistines? Let us bring the ark of the covenant of the LORD here from Shiloh, so that he may come among us and save us from the power of our enemies." ⁴So the people sent to Shiloh, and brought from there the ark of the covenant of the LORD of hosts, who is enthroned on the cherubim. The two sons of Eli, Hophni and Phinehas, were there with the ark of the covenant of God.

5When the ark of the covenant of the LORD came into the camp, all Israel gave a mighty shout, so that the earth resounded. ⁶When the Philistines heard the noise of the shouting, they said, "What does this great shouting in the camp of the Hebrews mean?" When they learned that the ark of the LORD had come to the camp, ⁷the Philistines were afraid; for they said, "Gods have*ᵈ* come into the camp." They also said, "Woe to us! For nothing like this has happened before. ⁸Woe to us! Who can deliver us from the power of these mighty gods? These are the gods who struck the Egyptians with every sort of plague in the wilderness. ⁹Take courage, and be men, O Philistines, in order not to become slaves to the Hebrews as they have been to you; be men and fight."

10So the Philistines fought; Israel was defeated, and they fled, everyone to his home. There was a very great slaughter, for there fell of Israel thirty thousand foot soldiers. ¹¹The ark of God was captured; and the two sons of Eli, Hophni and Phinehas, died.

12A man of Benjamin ran from the battle line,

ª Gk: Heb lacks In those days the Philistines mustered for war against Israel   ᵇ Gk: Heb against the Philistines   ᶜ Meaning of Heb uncertain   ᵈ Or A god has

NIV

God. When the man entered the town and told what had happened, the whole town sent up a cry.

[14]Eli heard the outcry and asked, "What is the meaning of this uproar?"

The man hurried over to Eli, [15]who was ninety-eight years old and whose eyes were set so that he could not see. [16]He told Eli, "I have just come from the battle line; I fled from it this very day."

Eli asked, "What happened, my son?"

[17]The man who brought the news replied, "Israel fled before the Philistines, and the army has suffered heavy losses. Also your two sons, Hophni and Phinehas, are dead, and the ark of God has been captured."

[18]When he mentioned the ark of God, Eli fell backward off his chair by the side of the gate. His neck was broken and he died, for he was an old man and heavy. He had led[a] Israel forty years.

[19]His daughter-in-law, the wife of Phinehas, was pregnant and near the time of delivery. When she heard the news that the ark of God had been captured and that her father-in-law and her husband were dead, she went into labor and gave birth, but was overcome by her labor pains. [20]As she was dying, the women attending her said, "Don't despair; you have given birth to a son." But she did not respond or pay any attention.

[21]She named the boy Ichabod,[b] saying, "The glory has departed from Israel"—because of the capture of the ark of God and the deaths of her father-in-law and her husband. [22]She said, "The glory has departed from Israel, for the ark of God has been captured."

a18 Traditionally judged   b21 Ichabod means no glory.

NRSV

and came to Shiloh the same day, with his clothes torn and with earth upon his head. [13]When he arrived, Eli was sitting upon his seat by the road watching, for his heart trembled for the ark of God. When the man came into the city and told the news, all the city cried out. [14]When Eli heard the sound of the outcry, he said, "What is this uproar?" Then the man came quickly and told Eli. [15]Now Eli was ninety-eight years old and his eyes were set, so that he could not see. [16]The man said to Eli, "I have just come from the battle; I fled from the battle today." He said, "How did it go, my son?" [17]The messenger replied, "Israel has fled before the Philistines, and there has also been a great slaughter among the troops; your two sons also, Hophni and Phinehas, are dead, and the ark of God has been captured." [18]When he mentioned the ark of God, Eli[a] fell over backward from his seat by the side of the gate; and his neck was broken and he died, for he was an old man, and heavy. He had judged Israel forty years.

[19]Now his daughter-in-law, the wife of Phinehas, was pregnant, about to give birth. When she heard the news that the ark of God was captured, and that her father-in-law and her husband were dead, she bowed and gave birth; for her labor pains overwhelmed her. [20]As she was about to die, the women attending her said to her, "Do not be afraid, for you have borne a son." But she did not answer or give heed. [21]She named the child Ichabod, meaning, "The glory has departed from Israel," because the ark of God had been captured and because of her father-in-law and her husband. [22]She said, "The glory has departed from Israel, for the ark of God has been captured."

a Heb he

COMMENTARY

This chapter is divided into two distinct segments. The first segment (vv. 1*b*-11) tells the story of a Philistine attack on Israel. After an initial defeat, the elders of Israel decide to bring the ark of the covenant onto the field of battle. Although fearful, the Philistines do battle again. The defeat of Israel is catastrophic, and the ark itself is captured. The remainder of the chapter (vv. 12-22) offers a detailed response to the disastrous news of the defeat and capture of the ark. The priest of Shiloh, Eli, dies in shock upon hearing that his sons are dead and the ark has been taken, and his daughter-in-law dies in childbirth.

4:1b-11. Abruptly the Philistines enter the story. Nothing in chaps. 1–3 has prepared us for this external threat to Israel. The Philistines gather

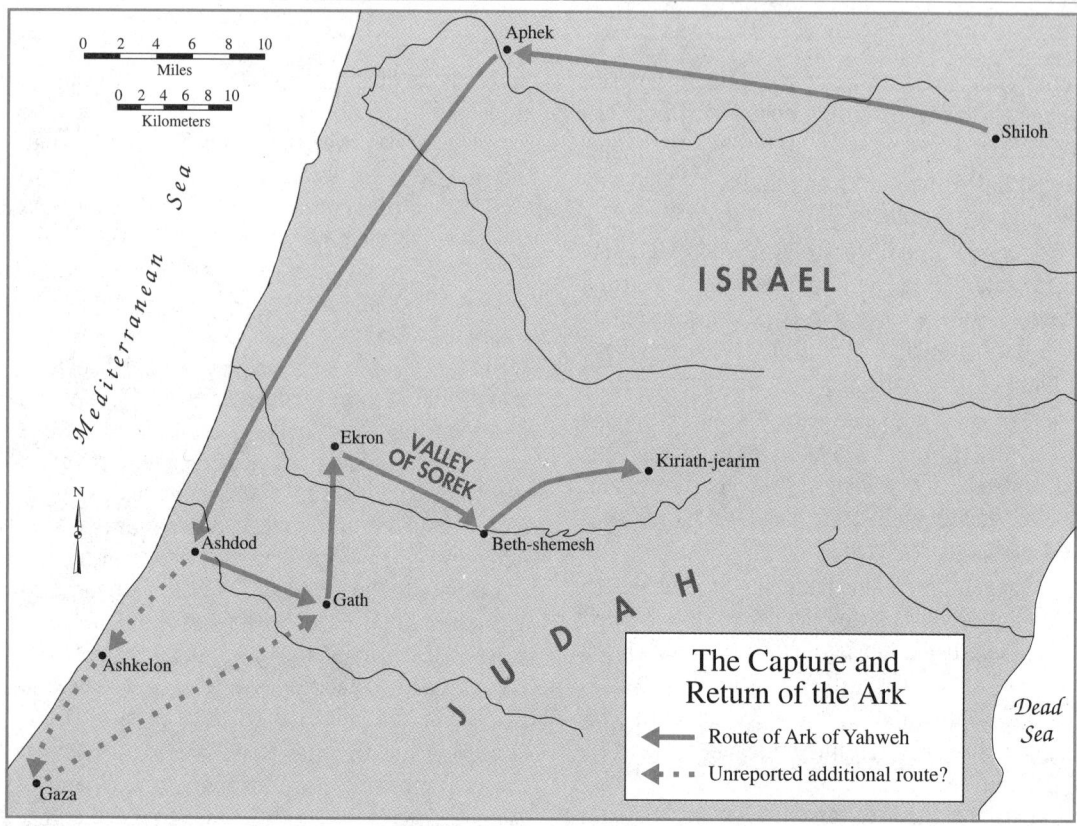

Map showing locations including Aphek, Shiloh, ISRAEL, Ekron, VALLEY OF SOREK, Kiriath-jearim, Ashdod, Beth-shemesh, Gath, JUDAH, Ashkelon, Gaza, Mediterranean Sea, and Dead Sea.

The Capture and Return of the Ark

⟵ Route of Ark of Yahweh

⟵ ⋯ Unreported additional route?

for war at Aphek, a site east of modern-day Tel-Aviv, while the Israelites gather to meet them at Ebenezer (probably a different site from the Ebenezer of 7:12). No motivation is given for the battle. This account is not interested in political history. We know of animosity between Israelites and Philistines from the stories of Samson in Judges 13–16. Moreover, throughout the books of Samuel the Philistines are among the chief adversaries of Israel until David's decisive victories over them (2 Sam 5:17-25). In the ark narrative, the Philistines are treated as a general threat to Israel's security and well-being.

The Philistines were a people who established themselves on the coastal plain to the southwest of Israelite territory as a part of an invasion of sea peoples in the late thirteenth century BCE. They became the ruling class of the Canaanite population, already settled in the coastal plain, and were largely associated with the five great cities mentioned in 6:17. Some of the accounts of conflict with Israel found in 1 and 2 Samuel suggest that the Philistines had ambitions to expand their territory at the expense of the Israelite tribes (e.g.,

the suggestion in 1 Samuel 13–14 of Philistine garrisons in Israelite territory).

The first section of chap. 4 has a symmetrical (chiastic) structure.

vv. 1*b*-2	first defeat by the Philistines
vv. 3	speech of the elders of Israel
vv. 4-5	bringing of the ark to battle
vv. 6-9	speech of the Philistines
v. 10	second defeat by the Philistines; capture of the ark

The ark stands at the center of this account, and its fate will be the main concern of chaps. 5–6. The speeches on either side of the appearance of the ark concern Israelite and Philistine perceptions of what the ark symbolizes about Israel's God.

In the initial skirmish, Israel is defeated with a loss of four "thousands" of men. It is widely agreed that the Hebrew term for "thousand" (אֶלֶף *'elep*) designates a tribal or a military unit of an indeterminate size.[41] The loss is probably fewer

41. See P. Kyle McCarter, *I Samuel,* AB 8 (Garden City, N.Y.: Doubleday, 1980) 107, for a fuller discussion.

than fifty men. This first defeat is a humiliation but not yet a disaster for Israel.

When the elders of Israel hear the report of this battle they immediately have a diagnosis of the situation (v. 3): The Lord has caused their defeat. The situation can be remedied by bringing the "ark of the covenant of the LORD" from Shiloh. Then, God will "come among us and save us from the power of our enemies." The problem for the elders is no more than the need to have God present at the scene of battle. The reader, however, has information not apparent to the elders. When we hear in v. 4 that Hophni and Phinehas are to carry the ark into battle, we suspect that the defeat might have more to do with God's judgment than with God's absence, and this judgment is not yet complete.

In v. 4, the people send to Shiloh and bring "the ark of the covenant of the LORD of hosts, who is enthroned on the cherubim." This lengthy epithet for the ark implies that it functioned in several ways in Israelite tradition. The ark was a box or chest that served as a repository for the tablets of the law given to Moses on Mt. Sinai (Exod 25:21; Deut 10:3-5); thus it was called the "ark of the covenant" (e.g., Josh 3:6) or the "ark of the testimony" (e.g., Exod 25:22). Further, the ark was the sign of the enthroned presence of Yahweh. It was regarded as a throne pedestal above which Yahweh was invisibly enthroned. Thus the ark could be referred to as God's footstool (1 Chr 28:2; Pss 99:5; 132:7; Lam 2:1). God's invisible throne was flanked by winged cherubim, part animal and part human figures known to us from Canaanite iconography, in which the god El is depicted on a throne supported by cherubim. Usually kept in the sanctuary (during this period at Shiloh), the ark symbolized the royal presence of Yahweh in the midst of Israel. But the ark was also fitted with rings and poles to make it movable (Exod 25:12-13), and it played a special role in Israel's holy wars. It was carried into battle to ensure that Yahweh would be present and fight on behalf of Israel (see Joshua 6 and the ark's crucial role at Jericho). In v. 3, the elders clearly understand the presence of the ark as the key to deliverance from their enemies, the Philistines. The title "LORD of hosts" (יהוה צבאות *YHWH ṣĕbā'ôt*, v. 4) is a reference to this military role of the ark and might be rendered "LORD of the armies."

When the ark arrives in the Israelite battle camp,

the army raises the prolonged ritual shout associated with holy war (תרועה *tĕrû'â*), whereupon, the earth itself trembles (v. 5). This noise has the desired effect: When the Philistines hear the roar, they respond anxiously over this turn of events.

The Philistine speech initially demonstrates the dread that falls upon them. They are startled by the ritual outcry coming from the camp of Israel (whom they refer to as "Hebrews," probably a somewhat pejorative designation, v. 6). Informed of the arrival of the ark, they interpret this as the arrival of "gods" in Israel's camp. "Woe to us! For nothing like this has happened before," they cry (v. 7). They despair at their chances before the "power of these mighty gods" (v. 8). The Philistines may be intentionally portrayed as ignorant of Israelite belief, since the use of the plural "gods" suggests that Israelites were polytheists. This statement makes their next utterance even more remarkable. It is the Philistines who draw a parallel with the great moment of Israelite deliverance in the exodus. It is the Philistines who confess exodus faith (v. 8*b*). They know of the plagues with which Yahweh struck Egypt, although they suggest that this happened in the wilderness and, again, was done by "gods." They are informed but not entirely accurate in their information. Nevertheless, it is the Philistines who alert the reader to exodus parallels and possibilities (a theme to which the Philistines return in 6:6).

The tide seems to be turning toward Israel. The ark is present; the shouting is invoking terror in the enemy; the God of exodus is at work. But the Philistines do not respond as expected. They do not retreat in panic. They admonish themselves with calls to have courage, to "be men and fight" (v. 9). They will not be slaves to Israel, suggesting that this was what Israel had been to them. This may indicate an oppressive history between Philistines and Israelites behind the story, but it is not of central concern in the telling of this story.

The outcome of a second battle is reported with devastating economy (v. 10). The verbs dominate: "fought," "defeated," "fled," "fell," "captured," "died." Both armies fight, but Israel is defeated. It is Israel's army that flees, not just retreating but dispersing and going home. Thirty "thousands" of Israelites have fallen (see Commentary on 4:2). The ark is captured; Hophni and Phinehas die.

This last notice prepares us for the shift of scene to Shiloh in v. 12.

The account simply reports the outcome of the battle, but the dilemma left in the wake of battle is theological, and not just political. The ark had been present. The elders assumed that God would be present as well. Yet, the outcome was again defeat. This could mean that Israel's God was powerless, but subsequent events (chap. 5) will demonstrate that this is not the case. The theological crisis of these events arises out of the recognition that defeat must have been the will of God.

4:12-22. The scene shifts to Shiloh, opening with a messenger's arrival from the battlefield. We are immediately made aware of Eli, the priest at Shiloh, as the focus of this account. He sits anxiously beside the gate, waiting for news, and his anxiety is not for his sons but for the ark (v. 13). The messenger has torn his clothes and placed dirt upon his head, traditional signs of grief; but Eli is ninety-eight years old and blind, so he cannot see these visible signs of bad news (v. 15). When he first enters the city, the messenger gives the news, and the city cries out (v. 13). Eli hears this outcry and asks about its meaning.

The messenger's report to Eli is remarkably similar to the report given to David of Saul's death in 2 Sam 1:1-4, also by a messenger who arrives with torn clothes and dirt on his head (cf. esp. 1 Sam 4:16-17 with 2 Sam 1:3-4). In each case, the messenger refers to his recent escape from the battle, is asked about the situation, reports a defeat and scattering of the army, and brings news of the death of two persons in the battle. Verse 17 also reports the capture of the ark. In chap. 4 the defeat of Israel foreshadows a later time when the future of Israel will be in jeopardy. The enemy is the same, but the consequences quite different. The one signals the end of the house of Eli, but the other marks the rise of the house of David. Israel may be defeated, but God's purposes for judgment or grace will go forward.

To our surprise, Eli does not respond to the news of his sons' deaths. It is at the news of the capture of the ark that he falls from his seat, breaks his neck, and dies (v. 18). The ark narrative itself makes no connection to the statement by the man of God to Eli that the deaths of Hophni and Phinehas would be the sign of God's

eventual judgment against the whole of the house of Eli (2:34). We as readers are left to make that connection. We are positioned to understand the events of chap. 4 as a part of God's judgment, although chap. 4 itself displays no interest or awareness of this theme.

The final phrase of v. 18 reports that Eli "judged Israel forty years." We would not have thought to number Eli among the judges of Israel. He appears in 1 Samuel 1–4 solely as a priest at Shiloh. This note is probably an effort of the deuteronomistic historian to incorporate Eli into the chronological scheme of his history. To Dtr, all of the leaders in Israel before the start of kingship were understood as judges and their years were reported, usually in round numbers of forty or twenty (see the book of Judges).

The final episode of this chapter (vv. 19-22) gives us a brief and poignant human vignette, used to make a theological comment on the meaning of these events. An unnamed woman, identified only as Eli's daughter-in-law and the wife of Phinehas, is pregnant. The tragic news of the capture of the ark and the deaths of Eli and Phinehas brings on labor (v. 19). It does not go well, and she is near to death, but she gives birth to a son (v. 20). We presume that she dies, but not before naming her son "Ichabod." Although the precise derivation of the name is uncertain, the mother interprets the name to mean "the glory has departed from Israel" (v. 21), which refers specifically to the capture of the ark (v. 22). The verb used here means "to go into exile" (גלה *gālâ*), and "glory" (כבוד *kābôd*) refers not to the ark itself but to the presence of God enthroned over the ark. God has gone into exile. It is an image reminiscent of Ezekiel's vision of God's glory departing from the Temple over the mountains (Ezek 10:18). It seems like the end of the story for Israel. The Philistines had invoked exodus imagery, but this seems like a reverse exodus: God departs, leaving Israel in bondage. It is well to remember that this material, although speaking of events near the end of the twelfth century BCE, is part of a larger history work addressed to Babylonian exiles. We can imagine a particularly sharp identification of exiles with this moment in the story, which would also make subsequent developments in chaps. 5–6 of special interest to those readers.

REFLECTIONS

The end of chapter 4 focuses the central question raised here for Israel and for every generation: How do we maintain faith when "the glory has departed"? What becomes of our trust in God when God appears to be absent or impotent? It is a perennial question of human experience. For Christians, it is the question of Good Friday, the moment when human hope seems lost forever in the suffering of the cross, and Jesus himself cries out with the words of Ps 22:1, "My God, my God, why have you forsaken me?"

The story of 1 Samuel 4 suggests for our initial reflection on this unfolding drama (we must remember that this is only the first episode in a longer ark narrative) both a false and a hopeful response to this question of the absence of God. Clues to these responses are found in the contrasting speeches of the elders of Israel (4:3-4) and of the Philistines (4:6-9).

1. In the response of the elders of Israel to the news of the first defeat by the Philistines we see the danger of equating the presence of God with the material trappings of religion. It is easy to mistake our symbols for the God to whom they point. The elders of Israel assumed that the presence of the ark would ensure God's presence, and that that presence would take the form of a victory. Perhaps exiles reading this tale through the work of the deuteronomistic historian would have thought of a similar attitude toward the Temple as a guarantee of God's presence and Israel's security (see the temple sermon in Jeremiah 7). Modern readers of this story would do well to ponder the ways in which we tend to equate the presence of God with impressive buildings or furnishings, with burgeoning memberships, or with popular programs. In response to perceived "enemies" of the church, we are likely to wheel out these evidences of success as testimony to God with us.

The witness of this opening episode in the ark narrative is that trust in symbols alone is misplaced trust. It is a form of idolatry. A pastor recently confided to me that a catastrophic fire that had destroyed a large and imposing church building may have been the best thing to happen to that congregation in some time. "We discovered that the building may have been distracting us from some of the things God had in mind for us."

The tragedy for Israel, and perhaps for us, is that idols must sometimes fail for us to see what we have done. The failure of the ark was a national tragedy with painful consequences. Likewise, confrontation with our misplaced trust is often painful. Cherished programs and beloved buildings must sometimes be lost in order for us to see that the presence of God is not defined by such things.

2. It is, perhaps, an intentional irony that it is the Philistines who give us the clue to a more faithful and hopeful response in times of the apparent absence of God. In their somewhat panicked, not quite accurate way, they nevertheless point us to the exodus tradition. While the elders of Israel trust in the ark, the Philistines remind us to remember how the presence of God has been made known in the past. In the face of defeat, it is the enemy who voices the memory of exodus and God's deliverance from bondage in Egypt. The Philistines voice what they do not fully understand, but they remind us of the importance of reclaiming our own exodus memory.

It is from exodus memory that Israel and the church have discerned a pattern of exodus faith, claimed and reclaimed by countless generations. In situations of distress we, like Israel at the sea, despair of hope for any way into the future. Death seems about to have the final word; we can see no possibilities for life. It is the faith growing out of the experience of those who walked through the midst of the sea to new life, that through God unexpected deliverance is made available. In God there is always a way into the future and a further word of life to be spoken over against the apparent finality of death.[42]

42. Bruce C. Birch, *Let Justice Roll Down: The Old Testament, Ethics, and Christian Life* (Louisville: Westminster/John Knox, 1991) 131-32.

In 1 Samuel 4, death seems to have spoken a final word—the four "thousands," the thirty "thousands," Hophni and Phinehas, Eli, the unnamed wife of Phinehas, the hopes of Israel—all dead! Exodus faith believes this is not the final word, and the Philistines remind us to remember. Perhaps it is significant that the chapter ends with a birth. It is a shadowed birth in ominous circumstances, but it is new life in the midst of death nevertheless. Exodus faith urges us to trust that in God death is never the final word, but life has a further word to speak. In 1 Samuel 4, it is not yet clear what that word of new life might be for Israel, so the chapter ends with the necessity of trustful waiting—trust that God is not finished yet with Israel. It is a word to us as well. In times when God seems absent, we are called to trustful waiting because we know of the exodus God. With the prophet of the exile we can affirm that "those who wait for the Lord shall renew their strength, they shall mount up with wings like eagles, they shall run and not be weary, they shall walk and not faint" (Isa 40:31).

1 Samuel 5:1-12, The Ark with the Philistines

NIV

5 After the Philistines had captured the ark of God, they took it from Ebenezer to Ashdod. ²Then they carried the ark into Dagon's temple and set it beside Dagon. ³When the people of Ashdod rose early the next day, there was Dagon, fallen on his face on the ground before the ark of the Lord! They took Dagon and put him back in his place. ⁴But the following morning when they rose, there was Dagon, fallen on his face on the ground before the ark of the Lord! His head and hands had been broken off and were lying on the threshold; only his body remained. ⁵That is why to this day neither the priests of Dagon nor any others who enter Dagon's temple at Ashdod step on the threshold.

⁶The Lord's hand was heavy upon the people of Ashdod and its vicinity; he brought devastation upon them and afflicted them with tumors.ᵃ ⁷When the men of Ashdod saw what was happening, they said, "The ark of the god of Israel must not stay here with us, because his hand is heavy upon us and upon Dagon our god." ⁸So they called together all the rulers of the Philistines and asked them, "What shall we do with the ark of the god of Israel?"

They answered, "Have the ark of the god of Israel moved to Gath." So they moved the ark of the God of Israel.

⁹But after they had moved it, the Lord's hand was against that city, throwing it into a great

ᵃ6 Hebrew; Septuagint and Vulgate *tumors. And rats appeared in their land, and death and destruction were throughout the city*

NRSV

5 When the Philistines captured the ark of God, they brought it from Ebenezer to Ashdod; ²then the Philistines took the ark of God and brought it into the house of Dagon and placed it beside Dagon. ³When the people of Ashdod rose early the next day, there was Dagon, fallen on his face to the ground before the ark of the Lord. So they took Dagon and put him back in his place. ⁴But when they rose early on the next morning, Dagon had fallen on his face to the ground before the ark of the Lord, and the head of Dagon and both his hands were lying cut off upon the threshold; only the trunk ofᵃ Dagon was left to him. ⁵This is why the priests of Dagon and all who enter the house of Dagon do not step on the threshold of Dagon in Ashdod to this day.

6The hand of the Lord was heavy upon the people of Ashdod, and he terrified and struck them with tumors, both in Ashdod and in its territory. ⁷And when the inhabitants of Ashdod saw how things were, they said, "The ark of the God of Israel must not remain with us; for his hand is heavy on us and on our god Dagon." ⁸So they sent and gathered together all the lords of the Philistines, and said, "What shall we do with the ark of the God of Israel?" The inhabitants of Gath replied, "Let the ark of God be moved on to us."ᵇ So they moved the ark of the God of Israel to Gath.ᶜ ⁹But after they had brought it to Gath,ᵈ the hand of the Lord was against the city,

ᵃ Heb lacks *the trunk of*   ᵇ Gk Compare Q Ms: MT *They answered, "Let the ark of the God of Israel be brought around to Gath."*   ᶜ Gk: Heb lacks *to Gath*   ᵈ Q Ms: MT lacks *to Gath*

NIV

panic. He afflicted the people of the city, both young and old, with an outbreak of tumors.[a] [10]So they sent the ark of God to Ekron.

As the ark of God was entering Ekron, the people of Ekron cried out, "They have brought the ark of the god of Israel around to us to kill us and our people." [11]So they called together all the rulers of the Philistines and said, "Send the ark of the god of Israel away; let it go back to its own place, or it[b] will kill us and our people." For death had filled the city with panic; God's hand was very heavy upon it. [12]Those who did not die were afflicted with tumors, and the outcry of the city went up to heaven.

[a]9 Or *with tumors in the groin* (see Septuagint)　　[b]11 Or *he*

NRSV

causing a very great panic; he struck the inhabitants of the city, both young and old, so that tumors broke out on them. [10]So they sent the ark of the God of Israel[a] to Ekron. But when the ark of God came to Ekron, the people of Ekron cried out, "Why[b] have they brought around to us[c] the ark of the God of Israel to kill us[c] and our[d] people?" [11]They sent therefore and gathered together all the lords of the Philistines, and said, "Send away the ark of the God of Israel, and let it return to its own place, that it may not kill us and our people." For there was a deathly panic[e] throughout the whole city. The hand of God was very heavy there; [12]those who did not die were stricken with tumors, and the cry of the city went up to heaven.

[a]Q Ms Gk: MT lacks *of Israel*　　[b]Q Ms Gk: MT lacks *Why*
[c]Heb *me*　　[d]Heb *my*　　[e]Q Ms reads *a panic from the* LORD

COMMENTARY

Although Israel has been defeated by the Philistines, the message of this chapter is that the Lord (Yahweh) has not. The theme of chap. 5 is the power of the Lord. This theme is emphasized by the repeated use of the phrase "the hand of the Lord/God" (vv. 6, 7, 9, 11). In all four instances, the "hand of the Lord/God" is exercised against the Philistines as a demonstration of the power of Israel's God, Yahweh. Use of "hand" (יד *yād*) in this way indicates strength, might, or power. By contrast, the Philistine god Dagon loses his hands in this episode (v. 4). Further, three times the author states that the "hand of the LORD" is "heavy" (vv. 6, 7, 11). The word "heavy" in vv. 6 and 11 is from the same root as the word "glory" (כבד *kbd*; v. 7 uses another root [קשה *qšh*], also meaning "to be heavy"). In 4:21-22, the "glory" had departed from Israel, but now this same *kābôd* ("glory," "heavy") is evident in the Lord's power against the Philistines. The account of chap. 5 makes clear that God has not been vanquished or lost power. Rather, the course of events serves God's purposes.

This episode of God's power unfolds in two stages. First, there is a drama in which the Lord (Yahweh) defeats the Philistine god Dagon (vv. 1-5). Then there is an account of the affliction of

the Philistines with a plague of tumors, which progresses from one Philistine city to another and leaves the Philistines urging that the ark be relinquished (vv. 6-12).

5:1-5. The Philistines carry the ark of the covenant triumphantly to Ashdod (v. 1), one of the five principal cities of Philistia, located roughly in the center of Philistine territory, close to the sea. They install the ark in a temple for the god Dagon and place it next to Dagon's image (v. 2). This portion of the ark story seems to regard Dagon as the primary god of the Philistines (see also Judg 16:23; 1 Chr 10:10), but his background is Semitic. The Philistines probably adopted his worship along with other practices of the essentially Canaanite population they ruled. Dagon was present in the pantheon of a number of ancient cities (e.g., Ebla, Mari, Ugarit), and in the Ugaritic texts he appears as the father of Baal. The name "Dagon" is related to Semitic words for "rain clouds" and "grain," fitting connections for a fertility god. The temple of Dagon in Ashdod was later destroyed by the Hasmonean ruler Jonathan in 147 BCE (1 Macc 10:83-84; 11:4).

It was a common practice in the ancient world to carry off the image of the god of a vanquished enemy.[43] Although the ark was not an image of Yahweh, the Philistines' reaction in 4:5-9 shows their awareness that the ark symbolized the presence of the Israelite deity. To place the ark next to the image of Dagon in his temple would certainly indicate the submission and perhaps defeat of Yahweh by Dagon; it may also have reflected the incorporation of Yahweh's power as a subordinate deity into Dagon's sovereignty. The superiority of Dagon over Yahweh was made visible in the ritual sphere, even as Philistia had defeated Israel in the political sphere. These Philistine expectations were not, however, to be fulfilled.

On the first morning after the installation of the ark in the Philistine temple, the people of Ashdod found the image of Dagon lying face down before the ark (v. 3). It must have been a shock to find the great Dagon in a posture of obeisance and submission before the "ark of the covenant of the LORD of hosts" (4:4 NRSV). They put Dagon back in his place. When they rise early on the next morning and come to Dagon's temple, they again find his image face down before the ark, but this time his head and his hands are broken off and are lying on the threshold of the temple (v. 4). Dagon is "reduced to a stump, without a head for thinking or hands for acting."[44] The text provides a dramatic portrait of a vanquished Dagon. He is rendered helpless before Yahweh. Perhaps Dagon's hands on the threshold even suggest that he made a futile attempt to escape, or perhaps that the demons and spirits sometimes said to guard thresholds (in this instance to a sacred place) could not help him. Almost as an aside, the story includes an etiological note (v. 5), citing this event as the reason why priests and others do not step on the threshold of the temple of Dagon in Ashdod. In any event, a great reversal has taken place. The one apparently without power has proved powerful; the one thought to have been defeated has emerged victorious. The reader is reminded of Hannah's song in 2:1-10 and its celebration of God's power to make such reversals. Lest there be any doubt, the story

moves from Dagon rendered powerless without hands to an account of the heavy hand of the Lord against the Philistines.

5:6-12. The biblical author mentions the hand of the Lord four times in this section (vv. 6, 7, 9, 11). This image of the power of God is now directed against the Philistines, who had dared to challenge that power. Dagon, their god, has been exposed as helpless and ineffectual. The consequences fall upon the Philistines, who now are without protection.

A plague of tumors breaks out among the people of Ashdod (v. 6). The Septuagint and the Vulgate include a longer version of v. 6, which most recent commentators and a number of recent translations have adopted as the preferred reading (the NIV includes it in a footnote). The addition to v. 6 might be translated: "Mice [or rats] swarmed up from their ships, and the mice [or rats] went into their land. Then there was a deathly panic in the city."[45] This reference to mice or rats in the longer text makes sense of the symbolic golden offerings of tumors and mice sent back with the ark in 6:4-5, 11. They are offerings intended to ward off a plague in the cities associated with mice (or rats) swarming out of Philistine ports into the cities.

The Hebrew word translated here as "tumors" (עפלים 'ŏpālîm) means "hill," "mound," or "swelling." Since Martin Luther, most commentators have associated these tumors with the bubonic plague. This dreaded disease takes its name from its most visible symptom, the growth of inflamed tumerous boils called "buboes." It is also well known that bubonic plague was associated with the fleas that infested rodents as carriers of the disease and often spread through rodents on ships in port cities.[46]

For the ark story, however, the ultimate cause of this plague is the hand of the Lord. Plague is one of the ways in which God's power and judgment on enemies are expressed in the Hebrew tradition (see 2 Samuel 24; Hab 3:5). The Philistine references to the exodus tradition in 4:8 and 6:6 would certainly prompt the reader to remember the role of plague in the exodus drama

43. See Patrick D. Miller, Jr., and J. J. M. Roberts, *The Hand of the Lord: A Reassessment of the "Ark Narrative" of 1 Samuel,* Johns Hopkins Near Eastern Studies (Baltimore: Johns Hopkins University Press, 1977), for discussions of ancient Near Eastern parallels to the practices reflected in this chapter.

44. Ralph W. Klein, *1 Samuel,* WBC 10 (Waco: Word, 1983) 50. Miller and Roberts, *The Hand of the Lord,* 46, also note a reference in the Ugaritic texts to the goddess Anat wearing a girdle of hands from vanquished enemies and with their heads hanging down her back.

45. See McCarter, *1 Samuel,* 119-20, for a full discussion of the textual problems here.

46. Apparently the term used in the Septuagint can indicate not only the swelling of a hill or a tumerous growth but also the buttocks. This led the Jewish historian Josephus (*Antiquities of the Jews* 6.3) to associate the plague here with dysentery. The MT repoints the Hebrew word to give a meaning associated with dysentery.

as well (see esp. Exod 9:15-16). In the ancient world, widespread disease was usually considered to be of divine origin. With Dagon defeated and a plague upon them, it is not surprising that the Philistines quickly turned to appease Israel's God by returning the ark to Israel.

An assembly of the lords of the Philistines is hastily convened (v. 8). Each of the five Philistine cities was ruled by a lord, and in times of crisis they acted in concert. The people of Ashdod say that the ark cannot remain among them, because they blame its presence for the fate of Dagon and the plague (v. 7). Almost arrogantly the people of Gath say they will take it (v. 8b); but when the ark arrives in Gath the hand of the Lord turns against them, and the plague breaks out in Gath (v. 9). Without consultation or request, the ark is sent on to Ekron, where it is received with despair (v. 10). The hand of the Lord and the plague also take a toll of the Ekronites (vv. 11b-12). The lords of the Philistines are again called, and the people demand that the ark be returned to its place in Israel (v. 11a). The ark and the accompanying hand of the Lord have been on a procession of death through the Philistine cities. In each of these cities, the language of plague is accompanied by the language of holy war. We are told in vv. 6 (LXX), 9, and 11 that a "panic" (מהומה mĕhûmâ) swept the cities, a word used to describe the holy panic that sweeps the enemy when God fights for Israel (14:15, 20, 22; Deut 7:23). This is what Israel had hoped for when they brought the ark to the field of battle against the Philistines. The holy panic had been withheld on that occasion, but now it breaks forth against all three of the Philistine cities that hold the ark captive. God had allowed the defeat of Israel for other purposes, but God is not powerless before Philistine enemies. Panic and plague sweep their cities. Verse 12 ends this segment of the ark story with the outcry of a Philistine city to match the outcry of Shiloh (4:13).

The power of the Lord associated with the ark has now been experienced by Israelite and Philistine alike. Israel experienced that power in the withholding of God's hand; the Philistines experienced it in the striking of God's hand. In terms of the larger story, it is now clear that the Philistines are a threat to Israel, but not to the Lord (Yahweh). The Philistines need not be feared by those who trust and honor the Lord.

REFLECTIONS

"God has no hands but our hands," states an aphorism popular in many contemporary church circles. This episode of the ark story (chap. 5) is a dramatic rebuttal of that notion. The aphorism suggests that God has no power to act in the world apart from human agency. Yet, in this episode the "hand of the LORD" is constantly at work without the mediation of any human agent, and the enemies of God are rendered handless (Dagon) and helpless (the Philistines). It is remarkable for the books of Samuel to include this story in which human characters play no role at all in the course of events, for most of the stories in Samuel are dominated by powerful and often charismatic personalities. The absence of human characters in the drama of the ark story may serve as a reminder of the ultimate reality of divine power when royal power gets under way.

It can serve as a reminder to us as well. Not everything is of our making in matters of faith and ultimate purpose in history. We live in a society frequently tempted to worship human power. Human capacities have been extended. We can affect our own future from the manipulation of the psyche to the destruction of the planet. These are heady powers. Yet, in this century of the greatest human power we have witnessed the results of those powers used only for human self-interest: holocaust, ethnic cleansing, racism, apartheid, terrorism, war, environmental destruction.

This attitude carries over to the church as well. We often imagine that God's grace is dependent on our efforts. We are sometimes so busy doing things for God that we fail to notice what God is doing. We need the reminder of this ark story that the hand of God is constantly at work exposing the idols in our midst as impotent and directing us to real power in the divine purposes at work in the world. When our programs and missions become efforts to manage and control God's grace for the sake of institutional success, we run the risk of finding our efforts reduced to powerless torsos without hands. Our idolatrous efforts cannot really make a difference, and we run the risk of finding ourselves numbered among God's enemies.

Walter Brueggemann calls our attention to important Gospel parallels here:

> The phrase "They rose early on the next morning" (v. 4) calls to mind the Easter formula of the Gospels (Matt. 28:1; Mark 16:2; Luke 24:1). Like those women in the Gospel narrative, the Philistines came to the temple "early the next morning" expecting to find a triumphant Dagon and a defeated Yahweh. In the Gospel they came expecting to find the power of death regnant and the defeat of Jesus. In neither case did the morning visitors find what they expected.
>
> The expectation of both the Philistines and the women in the Gospel failed to recognize that the power for life belongs to Yahweh.[47]

For resurrection people, the word is the same as this word to Israel in the ark story: The hand that makes the difference between life and death in the world belongs to God. What our hands do must be decided in the light of that truth.

47. Walter Brueggemann, *First and Second Samuel,* Interpretation (Louisville: John Knox, 1990) 36.

1 Samuel 6:1–7:1, The Return of the Ark

NIV

6 When the ark of the LORD had been in Philistine territory seven months, [2]the Philistines called for the priests and the diviners and said, "What shall we do with the ark of the LORD? Tell us how we should send it back to its place."

[3]They answered, "If you return the ark of the god of Israel, do not send it away empty, but by all means send a guilt offering to him. Then you will be healed, and you will know why his hand has not been lifted from you."

[4]The Philistines asked, "What guilt offering should we send to him?"

They replied, "Five gold tumors and five gold rats, according to the number of the Philistine rulers, because the same plague has struck both you and your rulers. [5]Make models of the tumors and of the rats that are destroying the country, and pay honor to Israel's god. Perhaps he will lift his hand from you and your gods and your land. [6]Why do you harden your hearts as the Egyptians and Pharaoh did? When he[a] treated them harshly, did they not send the Israelites out so they could go on their way?

[7]"Now then, get a new cart ready, with two cows that have calved and have never been yoked. Hitch the cows to the cart, but take their

[a]6 That is, God

NRSV

6 The ark of the LORD was in the country of the Philistines seven months. [2]Then the Philistines called for the priests and the diviners and said, "What shall we do with the ark of the LORD? Tell us what we should send with it to its place." [3]They said, "If you send away the ark of the God of Israel, do not send it empty, but by all means return him a guilt offering. Then you will be healed and will be ransomed;[a] will not his hand then turn from you?" [4]And they said, "What is the guilt offering that we shall return to him?" They answered, "Five gold tumors and five gold mice, according to the number of the lords of the Philistines; for the same plague was upon all of you and upon your lords. [5]So you must make images of your tumors and images of your mice that ravage the land, and give glory to the God of Israel; perhaps he will lighten his hand on you and your gods and your land. [6]Why should you harden your hearts as the Egyptians and Pharaoh hardened their hearts? After he had made fools of them, did they not let the people go, and they departed? [7]Now then, get ready a new cart and two milch cows that have never borne a yoke, and yoke the cows to the cart, but take their calves home, away from them. [8]Take the ark of

[a]Q Ms Gk: MT *and it will be known to you*

NIV

calves away and pen them up. [8]Take the ark of the LORD and put it on the cart, and in a chest beside it put the gold objects you are sending back to him as a guilt offering. Send it on its way, [9]but keep watching it. If it goes up to its own territory, toward Beth Shemesh, then the LORD has brought this great disaster on us. But if it does not, then we will know that it was not his hand that struck us and that it happened to us by chance."

[10]So they did this. They took two such cows and hitched them to the cart and penned up their calves. [11]They placed the ark of the LORD on the cart and along with it the chest containing the gold rats and the models of the tumors. [12]Then the cows went straight up toward Beth Shemesh, keeping on the road and lowing all the way; they did not turn to the right or to the left. The rulers of the Philistines followed them as far as the border of Beth Shemesh.

[13]Now the people of Beth Shemesh were harvesting their wheat in the valley, and when they looked up and saw the ark, they rejoiced at the sight. [14]The cart came to the field of Joshua of Beth Shemesh, and there it stopped beside a large rock. The people chopped up the wood of the cart and sacrificed the cows as a burnt offering to the LORD. [15]The Levites took down the ark of the LORD, together with the chest containing the gold objects, and placed them on the large rock. On that day the people of Beth Shemesh offered burnt offerings and made sacrifices to the LORD. [16]The five rulers of the Philistines saw all this and then returned that same day to Ekron.

[17]These are the gold tumors the Philistines sent as a guilt offering to the LORD—one each for Ashdod, Gaza, Ashkelon, Gath and Ekron. [18]And the number of the gold rats was according to the number of Philistine towns belonging to the five rulers—the fortified towns with their country villages. The large rock, on which[a] they set the ark of the LORD, is a witness to this day in the field of Joshua of Beth Shemesh.

[19]But God struck down some of the men of Beth Shemesh, putting seventy[b] of them to death because they had looked into the ark of the LORD. The people mourned because of the heavy blow

a18 A few Hebrew manuscripts (see also Septuagint); most Hebrew manuscripts *villages as far as Greater Abel, where* b19 A few Hebrew manuscripts; most Hebrew manuscripts and Septuagint *50,070*

NRSV

the LORD and place it on the cart, and put in a box at its side the figures of gold, which you are returning to him as a guilt offering. Then send it off, and let it go its way. [9]And watch; if it goes up on the way to its own land, to Beth-shemesh, then it is he who has done us this great harm; but if not, then we shall know that it is not his hand that struck us; it happened to us by chance."

[10]The men did so; they took two milch cows and yoked them to the cart, and shut up their calves at home. [11]They put the ark of the LORD on the cart, and the box with the gold mice and the images of their tumors. [12]The cows went straight in the direction of Beth-shemesh along one highway, lowing as they went; they turned neither to the right nor to the left, and the lords of the Philistines went after them as far as the border of Beth-shemesh.

[13]Now the people of Beth-shemesh were reaping their wheat harvest in the valley. When they looked up and saw the ark, they went with rejoicing to meet it.[a] [14]The cart came into the field of Joshua of Beth-shemesh, and stopped there. A large stone was there; so they split up the wood of the cart and offered the cows as a burnt offering to the LORD. [15]The Levites took down the ark of the LORD and the box that was beside it, in which were the gold objects, and set them upon the large stone. Then the people of Beth-shemesh offered burnt offerings and presented sacrifices on that day to the LORD. [16]When the five lords of the Philistines saw it, they returned that day to Ekron.

[17]These are the gold tumors, which the Philistines returned as a guilt offering to the LORD: one for Ashdod, one for Gaza, one for Ashkelon, one for Gath, one for Ekron; [18]also the gold mice, according to the number of all the cities of the Philistines belonging to the five lords, both fortified cities and unwalled villages. The great stone, beside which they set down the ark of the LORD, is a witness to this day in the field of Joshua of Beth-shemesh.

[19]The descendants of Jeconiah did not rejoice with the people of Beth-shemesh when they greeted[b] the ark of the LORD; and he killed seventy men of them.[c] The people mourned because the

a Gk: Heb *rejoiced to see it* b Gk: Heb *And he killed some of the people of Beth-shemesh, because they looked into* c Heb *killed seventy men, fifty thousand men*

NIV

the LORD had dealt them, [20]and the men of Beth Shemesh asked, "Who can stand in the presence of the LORD, this holy God? To whom will the ark go up from here?"

[21]Then they sent messengers to the people of Kiriath Jearim, saying, "The Philistines have returned the ark of the LORD. Come down and take it up to your place."

7 [1]So the men of Kiriath Jearim came and took up the ark of the LORD. They took it to Abinadab's house on the hill and consecrated Eleazar his son to guard the ark of the LORD.

NRSV

LORD had made a great slaughter among the people. [20]Then the people of Beth-shemesh said, "Who is able to stand before the LORD, this holy God? To whom shall he go so that we may be rid of him?" [21]So they sent messengers to the inhabitants of Kiriath-jearim, saying, "The Philistines have returned the ark of the LORD. Come down and take it up to you."

7 [1]And the people of Kiriath-jearim came and took up the ark of the LORD, and brought it to the house of Abinadab on the hill. They consecrated his son, Eleazar, to have charge of the ark of the LORD.

COMMENTARY

This section constitutes the final act in the drama of the ark of the Lord. The Philistines, hoping for an end to the afflictions that have plagued them, devise a plan for returning the ark (6:1-9). The plan is carried out, and the ark is welcomed with rejoicing and sacrifice by the people of Beth-shemesh (6:10-16). Following a short summary of the reparation offerings sent with the ark (6:17-18), there is a final episode concerning an outbreak of divine power against the people of Beth-shemesh and their subsequent decision to lodge the ark at Kiriath-jearim (6:19–7:1).

As in chap. 5, the story does not emphasize the ark itself, but the power of the Lord, who acts in freedom and sovereignty. This power is acknowledged by the Philistines in their references to God's "hand" against them (vv. 3, 5, 9), and this episode ends with God's power mysteriously breaking out against the Israelites of Beth-shemesh after the ark arrives there (v. 19). The power of God is not controlled by any party, but shows itself in ways that emphasize the sovereign freedom of God.

In the larger framework of 1 Samuel, the ark story of chaps. 4–6 is now complete. The Philistines, who constituted the external threat to Israel's future, have proved ineffectual before the superior power of the Lord (Yahweh). Their apparent victory was but a passing moment, and the hand of the Lord exposed the Philistines and their god Dagon as weak and powerless. The Philistine threat is not yet removed, however. That development will occur in

chap. 7. In the course of dealing with the external Philistine threat, God has also brought to an end the corrupt house of Eli at Shiloh (4:12-18). This development ties the ark story to the previous story of Hannah, Eli, and Samuel in chaps. 1–3 and prepares the reader for the return of Samuel to the story in chap. 7. This passage concludes with the designation of a priest, Eleazar (7:1), to care for the ark. Yet, the question of political leadership for Israel's future remains unresolved.

6:1-9. The ark remained in Philistine territory for seven months (v. 1); we may presume these were months of continued afflictions of tumors and mice (see Commentary on 5:6). In the light of the prominent exodus language and imagery in this chapter, we are reminded of the seven days of the first plague against Egypt in Exod 7:25. The Philistines summon priests and diviners (not lords as in 5:8, 11) and ask them both what to do with the ark and what they should send with the ark when returning it to its place (v. 2). The tone seems exasperated, and the questions seem to assume that the ark must be returned; but the question is over the proper method for doing so.

What unfolds in vv. 3-9 is an elaborate plan focused on two elements: the sending of a reparation offering with the ark (vv. 3-5) and a plan for the physical return of the ark that allows for a final testing of the power of Israel's God (vv. 7-9). In v. 6, the Philistines, as they did at the beginning of the ark story (4:8), make a remarkably direct reference to the exodus experience. It is Israel's enemies, the Philistines, who give us the key: The ark story is an exodus story. We have already seen exodus language and themes in chaps. 4–5. Chapter 6 is heavily influenced by exodus images and parallels as well.[48]

The priests and diviners urge that the ark not be sent from Philistine territory empty. This calls to mind God's promise to Moses that Israel would not go from Egypt "empty-handed" (Exod 3:21). In Exod 11:2 and 12:35-36, this promise is fulfilled with objects of gold and silver (כלי [kĕlî], "objects," is used in 1 Sam 6:8, 15 and Exod 12:35). Deuteronomy 15:13 also urges that slaves not be freed and sent out "empty-handed," because Israelites were once slaves in Egypt. In 1 Samuel, the priests and diviners counsel the payment of a "guilt-offering" (vv. 3-4, 8, 17). The Hebrew word used here (אשם 'āšām) is most often a substitutionary offering to remove impurity, but in this instance it is to be understood as the payment of reparations to appease Israel's God and to obtain relief from the afflictions the people have suffered. The priests and diviners hope that such an offering would provide for healing and ransom and that it would turn aside the "hand" of Israel's God (v. 3b). In effect, the Philistines now acknowledge the power of the Lord (Yahweh). In chap. 5, the narrator spoke of events as the "hand of the LORD"; in chap. 6 the Philistines speak of events as the "hand of the God of Israel" (vv. 3, 5, 9).

The "guilt offering" is to take the form of "five gold tumors and five gold mice" (v. 4; NIV, "rats"). These were to be placed in a container and transported with the ark out of Philistine territory. The number, shape, and material of these objects all give meaning to this symbolic act. The number five corresponds to the five lords of the Philistine cities (v. 4). All are said to have been afflicted, even though chap. 5 mentioned only three of the five. In v. 17, the five cities are named in connection with the five gold tumors, but v. 18 suggests that there were many more gold mice. The number of mice is said to represent every Philistine habitation, "both fortified cities and unwalled villages." These objects are made of gold, making them very valuable and,

therefore, suitable for the payment of reparations to appease the anger of Israel's God. The shape of these objects clearly represents the afflictions that have come upon the Philistines. By sending away these representations of the tumors and the rodents that have plagued their people and cities, the Philistines hope to rid themselves of God's judgmental hand (v. 5). The extent to which this "hand" has been felt is reflected in the hope that God's hand will be lightened from upon "you, your gods and your land" (v. 5b).

Verses 5b-6 justify the Philistine plan by means of a remarkable appeal to the exodus tradition. The strategy is described as intended to "give glory to the God of Israel." This development is a reversal of the departure of "glory" from Israel after the capture of the ark in 4:21-22. We are also reminded of Exod 14:4, 17, where God describes the exodus deliverance as "gaining glory" over Pharaoh and Egypt. In both instances, God's glory is contrasted to the "hardening" of the pharaoh's heart. This tradition is known to the Philistines in the ark story, and in v. 6 the priests and diviners argue against a "hardening" of Philistine hearts lest they meet the same fate as Pharaoh and Egypt. God had "made fools" (התעלל hit'allēl, hithpael) of the Egyptians (the same word is used in Exod 10:2), and they still had to let the Israelites go. The argument seems to be that delay in letting the ark go could only result in further harm and humiliation. The return of the ark may be understood as a new exodus event—a release from bondage and a return to the land of Israel. Perhaps in the light of the exile language in 4:21, exiles were also meant to take hope in this story told to them through the Deuteronomistic History. Release and return are possible through the power of the Lord.

The Hebrew root כבד (kbd) continues to play a key role here, as it did in chaps. 4–5. This root is behind both the words for "glory" and for "heavy." In v. 6, it is also the root translated "harden," which we might read as "to make heavy." The root "lighten" (קלל qll) is the semantic opposite of this root. Thus vv. 5b-6 urge the Philistines to "give glory" (kbd) to God; maybe God will "lighten his hand"; but do not "make heavy/harden" (kbd) your heart.

In vv. 7-9, the focus shifts to plans for the physical return of the ark to Israelite territory. The

---

48. See David Daube, *The Exodus Pattern in the Bible* (London: Faber & Faber, 1963).

use of a new cart and cows that have not yet known a yoke (v. 7) is consistent with other biblical and ancient references to the care for the purity of objects and animals used in rituals or associated with holy objects like the ark. The cows are eventually sacrificed by the people of Beth-shemesh (v. 14), which may have been the Philistines' intent as well. The selection of milk cows and their separation from their calves seems to be a peculiar Philistine wrinkle designed to make a final test of Yahweh's power. The cows, unused to the yoke and separated from their calves, are to be set loose to pull the cart with the ark and the golden offerings. If they go toward Beth-shemesh into Israelite territory, then it was indeed God's hand that had afflicted them; but if they should instead return to their calves or wander aimlessly, then the affliction might be mere chance (v. 9). The Philistines hold out one final hope that they might discredit Israel's God and salvage some relief from their humiliation. It proves to be a false hope.

6:10-16. The test begins. The cows do not waver. They go straight toward Beth-shemesh, "turning neither to the right nor to the left" (v. 12). Trailing in their wake are the lords of the Philistines, who watch as the ark arrives in the fields of Beth-shemesh. Fourteen miles west of Jerusalem, not far from the Philistine city of Ekron, Beth-shemesh may have been territory disputed by Israel and Philistia (see 2 Chr 28:18).

The people of Beth-shemesh greet the ark with great rejoicing (v. 13). The outcries of Shiloh when the ark was captured (4:13) are now replaced by the cries of celebration in Beth-shemesh at its return. The cart provides the wood and the cows become the sacrifice as the people of Beth-shemesh use a large stone in the field of Joshua as an altar upon which to offer ritual thanks to God for what must have seemed a miraculous turn of events. The Philistine lords watch this celebration and return to Ekron (v. 16).

Verse 15 is often considered a secondary addition to the story. Levites are rarely mentioned in the books of Samuel (only in 2 Sam 15:24), and their removal of the ark and offering of sacrifices repeats what has already taken place in v. 14. It may be that later editors thought the ark should only properly be handled by priests.

6:17-18. These verses summarize the guilt of-

ferings and their significance. The five gold tumors symbolize the five central cities of the Philistines, which are named here. Verse 18 suggests that the golden mice (or rats) represent all Philistine towns and villages and must number many more than five. This notice may indicate that all Philistia participated in the payment of reparations. Verse 18 adds an etiological note that the stone in Joshua's field remains as a witness "to this day."

6:19–7:1. Just when the story seems to be over, we encounter a disturbing episode. The ark story began with the Israelites' presumption that the ark gave them some control over the use of God's power. They were mistaken, as the capture of the ark and their defeat made clear (chap. 4). As the ark story comes to a close and the ark returns to the Israelites, this episode seems like a warning that the presence of God is still a dangerous matter and cannot be presumed upon. Israel, in the time of David, learns this lesson again when Uzzah is struck down for touching the ark as it is transferred to Jerusalem (2 Sam 6:6-7).

The Masoretic Text and the Septuagint differ on what took place. Some Israelites, the sons of Jeconiah, either looked into the ark (MT) or refused to join in the celebration (LXX; the NRSV follows the LXX; the NIV follows the MT). Because of this violation of the ark's holiness, or because of a refusal to honor the ark, God strikes down seventy men (v. 19).[49] The mood of welcome disappears. The people of Beth-shemesh mourn and ask whether anyone can stand before this holy God. They want to get rid of the ark (v. 20). They send to the town of Kireath-jearim, a Gibeonite city, which may have included a ritual center. The references to the "house of Abinadab" and the "consecration" of his son Eleazar to care for the ark may refer to a priestly household, which would seem to be an appropriate place for a holy object like the ark. Josephus, the Jewish historian, suggests that the reason for God's smiting of men at Beth-shemesh was that none of them were priests (his text does not appear to contain the reference to Levites in v. 15).[50] If this was the issue, then the move to Kireath-jearim placed the ark in the proper priestly care it deserved.

---

49. The Hebrew text adds 50,000 men, but the additional number is inserted in ungrammatical fashion, is absent in the LXX, and is rejected by most translators and commentators. See P. Kyle McCarter, *I Samuel*, AB 8 (Garden City, N.Y.: Doubleday, 1980) 131, for a full discussion of the textual problems in 6:19.

50. Josephus *Antiquities of the Jews* 6:16.

Eleazar is not an Israelite, and he plays no wider role in Israel's story. The ark now has a proper custodian, but Israel still has no real political or ritual leadership to replace the house of Eli. God's power is not defeated or diminished, but it is not yet clear what God has in store for Israel's future.

REFLECTIONS

Chapter 6 completes the story traditionally called "the ark narrative." The ark of the covenant does, indeed, play a central role in the story, but is the ark really the focus? Both Israelites and Philistines thought so, but each learned, with some difficulty, that the ark symbolized the presence and power of the Lord (Yahweh), but that the ark did not guarantee control of that power. Israel expected victory by the ark's presence on the battlefield (4:1-11). They were defeated. The Philistines expected triumph when they installed the ark as a trophy in the temple of Dagon (5:1-12). They were humiliated and afflicted. The Israelites of Beth-shemesh expected restored well-being to accompany the return of the ark (6:19–7:1). They were assaulted. In each episode, Israelite or Philistine failed to see that true power lies not in the ark but in the holy God to whom the ark pointed, and that God will not be managed or controlled.

This is not the portrait of a warm, fuzzy, friendly deity. The God of the ark story in 1 Samuel 4–6 is mysterious, dangerous, and, above all, possessed of sovereign freedom. This is not the portrait of God favored by positive-thinking, make-God-appealing, church-growth strategies. "God is so good" a well-known praise song croons repeatedly. Well, yes! God is good. But God is also holy, mysterious, and powerful. This story reminds us that there is a side of the reality of God that cannot be reduced to a tool for providing positive life experiences. Relationship to God can be demanding and even risky. Manipulation and management of holy symbols for our own ends can be downright dangerous.

We live in a time when politicians almost routinely invoke religious language and symbolism in their political campaigns and public image making. How different is this from bringing out the ark in the hope that our enemies will flee in panic? Is there a true sense of God's holy power as the reality behind the symbols and images? A recent American president was well known for his use of religious language to gain support for policy initiatives, but it was equally well known that he was a member of no church and did not participate in public worship except for official occasions. Such seemingly cynical use of religious symbols reflects a disregard for the divine reality to which those symbols point. The disturbing message of the incident at Beth-shemesh is that the judging hand of God can be felt by those who claim to be divine allies but fail to honor God, as easily as it is felt by those who openly declare opposition to God's purposes in the world.

It is, perhaps, in the nature of institutionalized religion to want to control or manage divine power and to limit divine freedom. But the God of the ark story is similar to the God who spoke through Moses on Mt. Sinai, saying, "I will be gracious to whom I will be gracious, and will show mercy to whom I will show mercy" (Exod 33:19; see Paul's quote of this text in Rom 9:15). To modern sensibilities, this may seem like divine arbitrariness, but it is instead divine freedom. In every generation there are those in the church who imagine that they can make lists of those who are deserving of God's mercy (or, as in the ark story, deserving of God's judging hand). In Jesus' time, some of his opponents among the scribes and Pharisees objected to his association with those they had defined as being outside of God's mercy. In our own time, voices claiming to speak for God have put forward lists of those deserving of God's judgment and unworthy of God's mercy. Such lists have included persons with AIDS, feminists, immigrants who do not speak English, gays or lesbians, non-middle-class African Americans, those who would allow abortions, and the poor in general. Even in localized and personal relationships there is a distressing tendency to treat those with whom we disagree as apostates and ourselves as being backed by divine power. The ark story suggests that the freedom of God will not allow God's power to be wielded on behalf of self-serving interests or in disregard of the need to honor God's purposes above our own. No cause, regardless of how righteous it seems, can claim God's grace as a possession or God's judgment as a weapon. Both God's grace and God's judgment come as a divine gift, and that gift is given out of sovereign freedom.

The Israelites of Shiloh and Beth-shemesh were clear about who deserved the judging hand of God against them: the Philistines. When the Philistines won the battle, they were clear about who had been deserted by the hand of God: the Israelites. Both were wrong. God's purposes went forward according to God's plan. Those who fail to discern what God is doing and insist on trying to control God's power for their own plan court disaster. Lives of faith lived in respect for God's freedom are lives of discernment. We seek to discern what God is doing in the world and align our efforts to God's. The tendency of the church is to think it is incumbent on God to follow our carefully laid plans. We must scan the horizon, seeking to discern God at work in people, movements, events, and programs that make for wholeness, justice, and love. To our surprise we may sometimes find testimony to God at work in the mouths of those we thought were Philistines.

Perhaps, in the end, the Philistines ironically modeled the proper response. They sought to understand God's activity in their own time by remembering what God had done before. It was the Philistines who called to mind the exodus-shaped activity of God. They gave God gifts that suggested honor and respect for God's holiness and power. They acknowledged the freedom of God by allowing the ark to make its own way toward its own future—and they followed. Maybe their only real mistake at this point was that they eventually turned back.

1 Samuel 7:2-17, Samuel as Judge of Israel

NIV	NRSV
[2]It was a long time, twenty years in all, that the ark remained at Kiriath Jearim, and all the people of Israel mourned and sought after the LORD. [3]And Samuel said to the whole house of Israel, "If you are returning to the LORD with all your hearts, then rid yourselves of the foreign gods and the Ashtoreths and commit yourselves to the LORD and serve him only, and he will deliver you out of the hand of the Philistines." [4]So the Israelites put away their Baals and Ashtoreths, and served the LORD only.	2From the day that the ark was lodged at Kiriath-jearim, a long time passed, some twenty years, and all the house of Israel lamented[a] after the LORD.
	3Then Samuel said to all the house of Israel, "If you are returning to the LORD with all your heart, then put away the foreign gods and the Astartes from among you. Direct your heart to the LORD, and serve him only, and he will deliver you out of the hand of the Philistines." 4So Israel put away the Baals and the Astartes, and they served the LORD only.
[5]Then Samuel said, "Assemble all Israel at Mizpah and I will intercede with the LORD for you." [6]When they had assembled at Mizpah, they drew water and poured it out before the LORD. On that day they fasted and there they confessed, "We have sinned against the LORD." And Samuel was leader[a] of Israel at Mizpah.	5Then Samuel said, "Gather all Israel at Mizpah, and I will pray to the LORD for you." 6So they gathered at Mizpah, and drew water and poured it out before the LORD. They fasted that day, and said, "We have sinned against the LORD." And Samuel judged the people of Israel at Mizpah.
[7]When the Philistines heard that Israel had assembled at Mizpah, the rulers of the Philistines came up to attack them. And when the Israelites	7When the Philistines heard that the people of Israel had gathered at Mizpah, the lords of the Philistines went up against Israel. And when the
[a]6 Traditionally *judge*	[a] Meaning of Heb uncertain

NIV

heard of it, they were afraid because of the Philistines. [8]They said to Samuel, "Do not stop crying out to the LORD our God for us, that he may rescue us from the hand of the Philistines." [9]Then Samuel took a suckling lamb and offered it up as a whole burnt offering to the LORD. He cried out to the LORD on Israel's behalf, and the LORD answered him.

[10]While Samuel was sacrificing the burnt offering, the Philistines drew near to engage Israel in battle. But that day the LORD thundered with loud thunder against the Philistines and threw them into such a panic that they were routed before the Israelites. [11]The men of Israel rushed out of Mizpah and pursued the Philistines, slaughtering them along the way to a point below Beth Car.

[12]Then Samuel took a stone and set it up between Mizpah and Shen. He named it Ebenezer,[a] saying, "Thus far has the LORD helped us." [13]So the Philistines were subdued and did not invade Israelite territory again.

Throughout Samuel's lifetime, the hand of the LORD was against the Philistines. [14]The towns from Ekron to Gath that the Philistines had captured from Israel were restored to her, and Israel delivered the neighboring territory from the power of the Philistines. And there was peace between Israel and the Amorites.

[15]Samuel continued as judge over Israel all the days of his life. [16]From year to year he went on a circuit from Bethel to Gilgal to Mizpah, judging Israel in all those places. [17]But he always went back to Ramah, where his home was, and there he also judged Israel. And he built an altar there to the LORD.

[a]12 *Ebenezer* means *stone of help.*

NRSV

people of Israel heard of it they were afraid of the Philistines. [8]The people of Israel said to Samuel, "Do not cease to cry out to the LORD our God for us, and pray that he may save us from the hand of the Philistines." [9]So Samuel took a sucking lamb and offered it as a whole burnt offering to the LORD; Samuel cried out to the LORD for Israel, and the LORD answered him. [10]As Samuel was offering up the burnt offering, the Philistines drew near to attack Israel; but the LORD thundered with a mighty voice that day against the Philistines and threw them into confusion; and they were routed before Israel. [11]And the men of Israel went out of Mizpah and pursued the Philistines, and struck them down as far as beyond Beth-car.

[12]Then Samuel took a stone and set it up between Mizpah and Jeshanah,[a] and named it Ebenezer;[b] for he said, "Thus far the LORD has helped us." [13]So the Philistines were subdued and did not again enter the territory of Israel; the hand of the LORD was against the Philistines all the days of Samuel. [14]The towns that the Philistines had taken from Israel were restored to Israel, from Ekron to Gath; and Israel recovered their territory from the hand of the Philistines. There was peace also between Israel and the Amorites.

[15]Samuel judged Israel all the days of his life. [16]He went on a circuit year by year to Bethel, Gilgal, and Mizpah; and he judged Israel in all these places. [17]Then he would come back to Ramah, for his home was there; he administered justice there to Israel, and built there an altar to the LORD.

[a] Gk Syr: Heb *Shen* [b] That is *Stone of Help*

COMMENTARY

With chapter 7 we come to an important crossroad in the story of 1 Samuel. In chaps. 1–3, we were introduced to the internal crisis in Israel. Eli's sons had become corrupt, and the entire priestly house of Eli at Shiloh was judged and condemned. In chaps. 4–6, the external crisis in Israel was introduced. The Philistines defeated Israel in battle and captured the ark of the covenant. In each of these crises, God was at work creating unexpected,

new possibilities. To meet the internal need for faithful and authentic leadership, God raised up Samuel to be God's prophet. To meet the external need to demonstrate where true power lies, God humiliated the Philistine god Dagon and afflicted the Philistine cities with tumors and mice, forcing the return of the ark. At the end of chaps. 1–3, *God's word,* mediated through the prophet Samuel, has replaced the authority of Eli and his corrupt sons

(3:19–4:1). At the end of chaps. 4–6, *God's hand* has been felt by Philistine and Israelite, making clear that God's sovereign freedom and power are unrivaled in the world.

Now these two strands of Israel's story come together in chap. 7. Samuel, absent from chaps. 4–6, appears again in a central role, exercising authentic and legitimate leadership over Israel. The Philistines appear again as a military threat, and this time, through the mediation of Samuel, a great victory is won and Israel enjoys a time of release from Philistine threat.

In bare outline, chap. 7 includes a ceremony in which Samuel leads Israel in putting aside foreign gods (vv. 3-4); an assembly at Mizpah, interrupted by a Philistine attack and a subsequent victory over the Philistines through the intercession of Samuel (vv. 5-12); a summary of the extent of Philistine subjugation during the time of Samuel (vv. 13-14); and a notice of the circuit Samuel regularly made as judge of Israel (vv. 15-17).

The role of Samuel is central in each segment of chap. 7. Indeed, it is Samuel's role in chap. 7 that brings together and resolves for the moment the issues of crisis for Israel raised in chaps. 1–6. We have already seen Samuel as a "trustworthy prophet of the LORD" (4:20). We may also presume that by being reared and mentored by Eli at Shiloh, Samuel had some training in priestly duties. In chap. 7, we see both a continuation and an expansion of these prophetic and priestly roles for Samuel as well as the addition of a judicial role.

Samuel appears in the role of intercessor for the people before God (v. 5). The verb used here (פלל *pālal*; NIV, "intercede"; the NRSV unsatisfactorily translates as "pray") is the same verb used in Eli's question to his corrupt sons in 2:25: "If someone sins against the Lord, who can make intercession?" Samuel himself now seems to be the answer to that question. In 12:19, the people implore Samuel to continue in the role of intercessor (*pālal*), and Samuel responds in 12:23, "Far be it from me that I should sin against the Lord by ceasing to intercede [*pālal*] for you" (NIV; the NRSV again simply translates "pray"). In 7:5, Samuel intercedes for the people in a ceremony of repentance, but the role of intercessor is also consistent with the people's appeal for him to call on God for aid against the Philistine threat in 7:8.

Representing the people's needs before God is a role frequently taken up by later prophets (e.g., Amos, Jeremiah, Joel), and it reminds us of the role of Moses as intercessor. Indeed, Samuel is twice mentioned alongside Moses in the role of intercessor for the people (Ps 99:6; Jer 15:1).

Samuel appears in vv. 7-12 as the prophetic performer of holy war rites prior to the victory of the Lord.[51] Samuel is not himself a charismatic deliverer but a prophetic agent helping to mediate God's deliverance. The connection of prophets to such holy warfare is seen in 1 Kgs 20:13-14; 22:5-12; and 2 Kgs 3:11-19. We are also reminded of Deborah, who was called a prophetess and was not herself a military deliverer (Judges 4). The roles of both intercessor and mediator of the holy war elaborate Samuel's leadership as a prophet and are primarily connected with the account of victory over the Philistines in vv. 5-12. This heightening of Samuel's role as a prophet would be consistent with the existence of a prophetic version of Israel's story for this period (see Introduction).

Another role for Samuel, not necessarily related to his identity as a prophet, is reflected in the four references to him as "judging" Israel (vv. 6, 15, 16, 17). The root שפט (*špṭ*, "to judge") implies the administration of justice and probably involves the interpreting of covenant law and tradition related to the Mosaic covenant. Samuel's role as judge is connected in vv. 15-17 with a small circuit in central Israelite territory (mainly Benjaminite land), in which Samuel apparently traveled to interpret and administer covenant justice. He is often viewed here as keeping older covenant traditions alive in a time when the ark is lost, Shiloh may be destroyed, the leadership of the house of Eli is ended, and, in spite of the optimistic notice of v. 13, the Philistine threat is not yet ended. The reference in v. 6 seems to be an effort to identify the judge of vv. 15-17 with the prophet of vv. 5-12; they are both Samuel. This title of "judge" also makes Samuel the clear successor to Eli (who was said to have judged Israel for 40 years [4:18]) and to earlier "judges" of Israel in the book of Judges. These earlier "judges"

51. The nature of holy war traditions will be further discussed in connection with a closer look at 7:5-12. For additional detail on the prophet's role in holy war, see Bruce C. Birch, *The Rise of the Israelite Monarchy: The Growth and Development of I Samuel 7–15,* SBLDS 27 (Missoula, Mont.: Scholars Press, 1976) 17-19; Patrick D. Miller, "The Divine Council and the Prophetic Call to War," *VT* 18 (1968) 100-107.

included military deliverers and those who played some judicial function as covenant interpreters. Samuel's activity in vv. 15-17 seems more like the latter. The final statement in v. 17 tells us that Samuel built an altar at Ramah. In this chapter, he also conducts a water ritual related to penance (v. 6) and offers a burnt offering (v. 9). These suggest priestly activities, even if Samuel does not appear fully in the role of priest.

These testimonies to the breadth and efficacy of Samuel's leadership suggest that God has raised up the leadership necessary to meet Israel's crises and that a king is not really necessary (the people's request comes in the next chapter). Prophetic leadership would have been enough. McCarter thinks that Samuel's role and accomplishments reflect David's later success and are intended to diminish the unique role of David.[52]

First Samuel 7 shows some evidence of the process through which the traditions developed. The episode of victory over the Philistines and the heightened role of Samuel in that episode (vv. 5-12) are consistent with an earlier prophetic version of Israel's story for this period (see the Introduction). The special language and interests of the deuteronomistic historian (Dtr) are reflected in vv. 3-4, the last phrase of v. 6, and vv. 13-15 (some of the evidence for this judgment will be commented upon in the detailed examination of this chapter). Whatever the earlier history of these materials, however, they have now all been assembled into the present form of the text by the creative work of the deuteronomistic historian, and it is this final telling of Israel's story that should occupy primary attention. After a closer look at the various segments of this chapter, we will return to comments on the role of chap. 7 as a whole in its wider contexts.

7:2-4. Verse 2 forms a transition from the ark story in chaps. 4–6 to the narrative of chap. 7. It assumes that we know something of the story that led to the ark's lodging at Kireath-jearim and speaks of the passage of twenty years. The expression that Israel "lamented [NRSV; NIV, "mourned"] after the LORD" suggests that this was an unsettled and difficult time for Israel. The

attack of the Philistines in v. 10 indicates that the threat from these perennial enemies had continued in spite of the experience with the ark.

In vv. 3-4, Samuel challenges all of Israel to give up idolatrous practices as a condition for deliverance from the Philistines. These verses have been widely recognized as deuteronomistic in both language and theme.[53] The concern for purity of worship and the theme of return to the Lord are central to the theology of Deuteronomy and Dtr.[54] Verses 3-4 seem very similar to Josh 24:23-24 and Judg 10:6-16, both thought to show Dtr influence. Each of these texts calls for Israel to put away foreign gods and identifies those gods with the Baals and Astartes of Canaanite worship. They further call on Israel to "direct your heart to the LORD" and "serve" the Lord. Baal was the Canaanite storm god and chief god related to the fertility of the land; Astarte was a Canaanite goddess of fertility and war and closely associated with Baal. Their names almost became clichéd expressions for any idolatrous deities (see 12:10; Judg 2:13; 3:7; 10:6, 10).

Verses 2-4 seem to be a deuteronomistic passage creating a transition from the ark story of chaps. 4–6 to the story of Samuel and the Philistine victory in 7:5-12. This transition has two important effects. First, these verses now imply that the disaster when the ark was captured was due to Israel's idolatry and not to the corruption of the house of Eli. The crisis with the Philistines did not end with the return of the ark. The people now need to repent of their apostasy if they are to be delivered out of the hand of the Philistines. Second, these verses now tie this episode into the pattern of sin (usually idolatry), distress as punishment, appeal to God, repentance, deliverance, and a period of peace that organizes the stories of the book of Judges; this pattern is described in Judg 2:11–3:6. Israel's story in 1 Samuel 1–7 is to be read as a continuation of the story of tribal Israel. Israel has sinned, and that sin is now interpreted as idolatry. They have suffered oppres-

52. P. Kyle McCarter, *I Samuel*, AB 8 (Garden City, N.Y.: Doubleday, 1980) 150. See also Robert Polzin, *Samuel and the Deuteronomist: A Literary Study of the Deuteronomic History*, Part Two: *1 Samuel* (San Francisco: Harper & Row, 1989) 76-77.

53. See Birch, *Rise of the Israelite Monarchy*, 16-17; Ralph W Klein, *1 Samuel*, WBC 10 (Waco: Word, 1983) 64-66; McCarter, *I Samuel*, 142-43. The expression "with all your heart" is common in Deut and Dtr (Deut 4:29; 6:5; 10:12; 11:13; 13:4; 26:16; 30:2, 6, 10; Josh 22:5; 23:14; 1 Sam 12:20, 24; 1 Kgs 8:23; 14:8; 2 Kgs 10:31). The fuller phrase "to return to the LORD with all the heart" is found in Deut 30:10; 1 Kgs 8:48; 2 Kgs 23:25.

54. See Hans Walter Wolff, "The Kerygma of the Deuteronomic Historical Work," in *The Vitality of Old Testament Traditions* (Atlanta: John Knox, 1975) 83-100.

sion and distress at the hands of the Philistines (twenty- or forty-year periods are typical in Judges). They have appealed to the Lord (v. 2, "lamented after the LORD"). They respond to Samuel's appeal and put away the foreign gods. The stage is now set for deliverance, for Samuel portrayed as judge, and for the ensuing period of peace (see Commentary on 7:13-14 and 7:15).

7:5-12. Samuel calls an assembly of the people at Mizpah for the purpose of interceding for the people's sin (v. 5). This seems to repeat the assembly Samuel addressed in vv. 3-4, and the people's fasting and confession in v. 6 seem unnecessary in light of their action of putting away the Baals and Astartes in v. 4. The water pouring ritual in v. 6 is unknown elsewhere, but is clearly a part of a ritual of penitence here.

Mizpah is an important cultic center in the tribal territory of Benjamin, north of Jerusalem. It plays an important role in 1 Samuel as part of Samuel's judicial circuit (7:16) and the site where Saul was selected as king by lot (10:17). The notice that Samuel "judged" the people there (v. 6) is unexpected, since no judicial activity is involved. In this verse, Dtr is probably reminding us to read the coming story of deliverance from the Philistines in the light of the pattern of the book of Judges. The notice here identifies the intercessor/holy war agent/prophet Samuel with the Samuel who judges Israel in vv. 15-17.

The Philistines hear of this assembly, and the lords of the Philistines bring a force up against Israel (v. 7) and attack them (v. 10). Perhaps the Philistines considered the assembly a prelude to rebellion or simply an opportune moment to gain advantage; their motives are not made clear.

The Israelites turn in fear to Samuel and insist that the prophet who interceded for their sins also act as intercessor to seek God's salvation from the Philistines. They asked Samuel to *cry out* and *pray* so that God might *save* (v. 8). Samuel offers a lamb as a whole burnt offering; then he *cries out,* and God *answers* (v. 9). The verbs in these verses expose an important dynamic in Israel's faith. It is the cry of human distress that mobilizes God's response and salvation (see, e.g., 12:8, 10; Exod 2:23; 3:7). The people do not cry directly to God, but Samuel is asked to cry out on their behalf. This action emphasizes his role as prophetic mediator. Prayer now stands as the middle term

between the outcry on behalf of the people's need and the advent of God's salvation. The burnt offering, a sacrifice devoted entirely to God, represents utter reliance on God's deliverance; and when Samuel takes up the people's petition and cries out, God's answer follows (v. 9*b*).

The events of v. 10*b* (v. 10*a* simply notes the Philistine attack) make clear that trust in God is all that was necessary.

The tradition of miraculous delivery from the Philistines . . . seems clearly to be a holy war tradition. The encounter is prefaced by sacrifice (vs. 9); it is Yahweh himself who fights, calling into service the forces of nature (vs. 10) and throwing the enemy into confusion (vs. 10). These are among the primary motifs of holy war. The language itself is the language of holy war. The verb המם [*hmm* "to throw into confusion or panic"] appears five times and always in a holy war context [Josh 10:10; Judg 4:15; 1 Sam 7:10; 2 Sam 22:15//Ps 18:14]. In all but Judg 4 Yahweh's victory is accompanied by meteorological phenomena such as thunder, lightning or hail.[55]

The victory belongs entirely to the Lord, and the enemy is routed before Israel (v. 10*b*), with Israelites engaging in the pursuit after the outcome is decided (v. 11). This victory reverses the rout of the Israelites by the Philistines attested in 4:3.

Samuel erects a stone and names it Ebenezer, "stone of help," to commemorate the Lord's help against the Philistines (v. 12). This act recalls the place where Israel assembled to do battle with the Philistines on the disastrous occasion when the ark was captured (4:1). It seems unlikely that this Ebenezer near Mizpah and the earlier Ebenezer near Aphek could be the same place, but geography is not the crucial matter here. What matters is that, by God's power and through the mediation of God's prophet, the defeat of Israel at Ebenezer (chap. 4) has been reversed by a victory of Ebenezer (chap. 7). The Philistines have been routed and defeated. Most significantly, God has not been defeated, as the capture of the ark might have implied. When Israel was in need, God helped, and that help sufficed.

7:13-14. These verses show Dtr completing the framework begun in vv. 2-4. Such a framework is common in the book of Judges. Now that

55. Birch, *Rise of the Israelite Monarchy,* 17-18. On features of holy war, see R. de Vaux, *Ancient Israel: Its Life and Institutions* (London: Darton, Longman and Todd, 1961) 258-60, and F. M. Cross, "The Divine Warrior in Israel's Early Cult," in *Biblical Motifs,* ed. A. Altmann (Cambridge, Mass.: Harvard University Press, 1966) 11-39.

God has brought deliverance, the land enjoys a time of peace for the lifetime of the judge ("all the days of Samuel"). In form and vocabulary, these verses are similar to the notes that conclude the deliverance accounts in the book of Judges.[56]

The far-reaching effects claimed by vv. 13-14 for the victory over the Philistines cannot be regarded as accurate. The claim here is that the Philistines were not only subdued but also did not even enter the land of Israel during Samuel's lifetime (v. 13), that the territory was returned to Israel, and that there was peace with the Amorites (v. 14). Many episodes in the subsequent story of 1 Samuel show the Philistines occupying Israelite territory and engaging in military actions against the Israelites (e.g., chaps. 13–14; 17–18) during the life of Samuel. Eventually, Saul loses his life in a great battle against the Philistines (1 Samuel 31; 2 Samuel 1); it is David who finally removes the Philistine threat (2 Sam 5:17-25).

The importance of these verses is not historical but theological. The "hand of the LORD" has proved victorious against the Philistines (v. 13). Israel, under the leadership of Samuel, has nothing to fear from the "hand of the Philistines" (vv. 3, 8, 14). This theme of the power of God's hand also ties the victory of chap. 7 to the humiliation and affliction of the Philistines, brought by the "hand of the LORD" in the ark story (chaps. 5–6). The claim here is that Israel can trust this demonstrated power of the Lord and the leadership of Samuel. There is no need for the king whom the people will request in chap. 8. That the idealized picture of vv. 13-14 does not become historical reality may be understood as the product of the people's failure to trust in the Lord's power and the Lord's prophet by insisting on a king.

7:15-17. In the present form of this chapter, the notice of Samuel as judge of Israel for his lifetime (v. 15) makes Samuel the successor to Eli, who was said to have judged Israel in 4:18, and places Samuel in the long succession of judges over Israel recorded in the book of Judges. Verses 16-17 give us a glimpse of the activity of Samuel

that might lie as reality behind such a title. Samuel traveled a small circuit of towns to administer justice. In a time when the Shiloh priesthood is scattered and discredited and Shiloh itself may be destroyed or left non-functional by the Philistines, Samuel appears here as one laboring to keep the tradition of the covenant law alive. Since we are told he built an altar at Ramah, perhaps we can imagine him performing ritual as well as judicial functions. Ramah was the hometown of Samuel, and the other places were towns with important cultic backgrounds (Bethel, Gilgal, and Mizpah). All are close together, so we should imagine that Samuel is maintaining a foothold for the endangered covenant tradition, not making grand rounds throughout Israel.

Having looked more closely at the segments of the chapter, it is now possible to comment on the role of 1 Samuel 7 in its wider contexts. This chapter seems to play a pivotal role both in the opening section of 1 Samuel (chaps. 1–7) and in the wider Deuteronomistic History.

Chapter 7 concludes the epoch of Israel's history that began with the book of Judges. Samuel becomes the last of the judges. He is made the successor both of those judges who were connected with Israel's deliverance from an enemy[57] and of those judges who are connected with the administration of justice and the oversight of covenant traditions (the so-called minor judges). The picture of 1 Samuel 7 is intended to convince us that this pattern of leadership and of trust in the Lord was adequate to Israel's needs. Chapter 8 will begin the story of kingship, and the era of judges will be gone forever.

Chapter 7 serves as the resolution of Israel's internal and external crises that have been described in 1 Samuel 1–6. The infant Samuel, a gift of God's grace to Hannah, has grown to adulthood as a prophet, a gift of God's grace to Israel. As God's prophet, Samuel is the successor to the corrupt house of Eli, which has been discredited and removed from influence. As God's prophet, Samuel is the mediator of the power of the Lord's hand, which can give deliverance from enemies. The power that humiliated the Philistines through the ark is now mediated through God's prophet. This could be the

---

56. The verb (כנע *kāna'*, "subdue") appears in the niphal primarily in the Dtr framework of Judges (Judg 3:30; 8:28; 11:33; in hiphil Judg 4:23). The expression "the hand of the LORD was against . . ." appears in Deut 2:15; Judg 2:15; 1 Sam 12:15, which are deuteronomistic, and also in 1 Sam 5:9, which connects this episode back to the ark narrative. The term "Amorite" (v. 14) is also the term used by Deuteronomy (and the Elohist) for the non-Israelite peoples of the area.

57. Samuel is not himself a military deliverer but is the agent through which God's deliverance is mediated. His role is most analogous to that of Deborah, one of the earlier judges.

happy ending to the story, but the people in chap. 8 will insist on a king instead.

Chapter 7 plays an important role as a reference point in the ongoing story of Israel as told by the deuteronomist. Most immediately it is the counterpoint against which we must read the story of the people's request for a king in 1 Samuel 8. Samuel led the people to put away foreign gods and serve the Lord *only* (7:3-4). In 8:7-8, God interprets the request for a king as equivalent to Israel's rebellions in idolatry. Serving a king is equated to serving other gods. The result of such folly is also made clear in relation to chap. 7.

Whereas Samuel cried to the Lord and the Lord answered (7:9), the people, with the king they have chosen, will cry to the Lord, and the Lord will not answer (8:18). In the broader perspective of the deuteronomist, this chapter (and its negative counterpoint in chap. 8) may present a word to the generation of exiles to which this history is addressed. They have trusted kings, and the result was exile. Chapter 7 suggests to such exilic readers that they can still cry out, and God will answer if their trust is truly in the Lord (and the Lord's prophets?), and not in their own institutions.

REFLECTIONS

The second verse of the well-known hymn "Come, Thou Fount of Every Blessing" begins:

Here I raise mine Ebenezer;
Hither by thy help I'm come;
And I hope, by thy good pleasure,
Safely to arrive at home.

Countless Christians have sung these lines, affirming their need for help and safe arrival home without having any idea what it means to "raise mine Ebenezer." It is 1 Sam 7:12 from which we learn that an Ebenezer ("a stone of help") is a reminder of the only sure source of help and safety. God helps! This chapter is a witness to the dangers of false security and the source of true security.

1. False security is ultimately a matter of idolatry. It is not just a deuteronomistic conceit that this chapter begins with a call to put aside foreign gods (7:3-4). Loyalty and trust in the Lord are the basic issue here. The appeal of the Baals and the Astartes must be understood in broad terms as the failure to "direct your heart to the LORD" (7:3 NRSV). They represent the many other things that can claim the loyalty of Israel and of us. In 1 Samuel 7, we read this call to "put away foreign gods" and "serve the LORD only" in the light of the ark, on one side (chaps. 4–6), and the king, on the other (chap. 8). Neither is worthy of ultimate trust. The ark is an object, and the king is a man; neither can save of its own accord. The attempt to manipulate the ark for the sake of security led to disaster. To trust in a king ultimately leads to exile. Both ark and king have value only as representatives of the true power that lies with the hand of the Lord.

It is the Philistines who represent the fears of Israel over their own security. The Philistines are, in 1 Samuel, the representatives of worldly, political, and technical power. They are organized, efficient, technologically superior in military might. Israel had been defeated by them twice, and they had captured the ark. Israel feared that the Philistines were the wave of the future, and they were afraid (7:7). But Philistine power had already been exposed as idolatrous. Their god Dagon had no true power. Philistine might, however, could not protect their cities and people from the hand of the Lord. The Philistines proved as fearful and vulnerable as the Israelites. They may have taken the ark, but they could not hold it. In 1 Samuel 7 the Philistines are defeated, not by superior technical and political power, but by the thunder of God.

We live in a world that cannot imagine this turn of events. We admire, even worship, political power and technical expertise. We consider this realistic and not idolatrous. We sometimes see the dangers in such loyalties, but then we want symbols (arks) or leadership (kings) that yoke our trust in God to political and technical power. It is seldom that we dare serve God *only*. Even our frequent preoccupation with efficient, successful, technically up-to-date congregations and denominational structures seems more like an emulation of the Philistines than a trust in God's power to bring new possibilities in unexpected ways.

We are so allied with public power and technical expertise in our culture that it is hard for us to grant reality to this story of God's victory. Brueggemann notes, "Insofar as this text concerns war and national public power, it is, in our day, the marginal peoples who rely on strategies of thunder in the face of superior technology."[58] It is the oppressed and the dispossessed who know they stand no chance if their hope rests in power defined by the world's terms. It is also in personal experiences of powerlessness, grief, and loss that we know reality is not defined ultimately by worldly, technical, and political power. The history of the faith communities who have gone before us gives frequent testimony to the unlikely reversals, societal and personal, that have been made possible by God's hand, much to the bewilderment of the world's power arrangements. Even in our recent history, we have seen the dismantlement of the Soviet Union, the destruction of the Berlin wall, the fall of dictatorship in the Philippines, the end of apartheid in South Africa, and an agreement between Palestinians and Israelis. These are the reversals of which Hannah sang and seemed unlikely judged solely by human capabilities and stratagems. They are the reversals hoped for by those who can only trust that the thunder of God can rout the Philistines.

2. The verbs of 7:8-9 tell us something of Israel's covenantal alternative to idolatrous loyalties. In the face of Philistine threat, the people ask Samuel to *cry out* and *pray* on their behalf, so that the Lord might *save* them. In response to their request, Samuel does *cry out,* and the Lord does *answer.* Further, this chapter is bracketed by *fasting* and *confession* in 7:6 and the *administration of justice* in 7:15-17. All of these verbs speak of a reliance on covenantal relationship to God's power, and not of reliance on human power and capability. Such a pattern of trust in the Lord contrasts with the apparent superiority of Philistine power, which strikes fear in Israelite hearts. We know from chaps. 4–6 that Philistine power rests on idolatrous loyalties that cannot save.

God's salvation is mobilized by the outcry of human need and distress, but it is focused by prayer, repentance, and the administration of justice. The outcry alone brings divine response (7:9). From Exodus onward (e.g., Exod 2:23; 3:7), Israel's God has been known as a God who responds to the cry of human distress. God's salvation is seen in the new possibilities for life and hope that arise in the midst of and in spite of that distress. In reading again in this story of God's willingness to answer the outcry, we can take renewed hope that God is at work even in the most oppressive and hopeless circumstances. This is true completely apart from any human activity. But prayer, repentance, and the administration of justice are ways in which the covenantal faith community aligns with and joins in the saving activity of God.

The people ask Samuel to cry out and to pray for them. The outcry is the voicing of pain, but prayer is the conscious sharing of our experience with God and openness to God's experience shared with us. Does the victory of 1 Samuel 7 suggest that prayer can save? No, it is God who saves. But is God responsive to prayer? Yes, but in God's own time and way. We dare to pray for our needs, even to pray for the defeat of enemies, but we must then trust that the future and its possibilities will be opened in God's own way. God is not manipulated by our prayers.

Likewise, repentance and the administration of justice are the ways in which the covenant community seeks to renew its own life and the life of its society through alignment with the purposes of God. In repentance, we examine our own lives and institutions for patterns that

58. Walter Brueggemann, *First and Second Samuel,* Interpretation (Louisville: John Knox, 1990) 53.

serve our self-interests rather than God's. We recognize in repentance that we, too, can align ourselves with the enemies of God. In the administration of justice, the covenant community seeks to create structures that make for the wholeness (*shalom*) that is the goal of covenant life to which God has called us. Like Samuel, we are often called upon to preserve a witness to such wholeness in the midst of and in spite of considerable brokenness. We dare to say in a broken world that there is another reality, and justice points to that reality by seeking to value and bring to wholeness every human life and the whole of creation.

These activities also do not themselves "save" us, although the frenetic activities of some congregations suggest a belief that salvation can be programmed. God's salvation always comes as freely and unexpectedly as the thunder of the Lord. Repentance and justice are part of covenant community lived in trust that the God who thunders is the locus of true security, and the loyalties that we seek to manage through human means are idolatrous. They are not worthy of ultimate trust. The ark story, followed by this story of Samuel and the victory of God, teaches us that God's ways of saving will sometimes surprise our expectations. If God responds to our outcries, it will not be in mechanical or managed ways. We will be surprised by grace, but we can trust its reality. The world will still urge us to loyalties and trust that are idolatrous, but covenant faith insists that only the hand of the Lord can save us.

1 SAMUEL 8:1–15:35, THE KINGSHIP OF SAUL

OVERVIEW

With these chapters we come to the main subject of the books of Samuel: the beginnings of kingship in Israel. Chapters 1–7 provide a prologue to this main story. The establishment of kingship represented a major transformation for Israel. It was not only a change in institutional structures but also a major shift in categories for understanding the nature of Israel's life as a community and its relationship to God. Such transformations could not take place without stresses and conflicts. The books of Samuel in general, and chaps. 8–15 in particular, reflect the tensions and ambiguities of these transitional times. These tensions are evident in distinct but interrelated dimensions of the story that unfold in 1 Samuel 8–15.

Israel's transformation was *theological.* The old traditions of covenant community resisted and came into conflict with the emerging ideology of royal community. Covenant community had been rooted in an understanding of the sovereignty of God. Israel was the people of a divine king. When Gideon was asked by some of the people to become king following his victory over Midian he refused, saying, "I will not rule over you, and my son will not rule over you; the Lord will rule over you" (Judg 8:23).

Earthly kingship was seen by some as a rejection of divine kingship. Covenant community was understood as a tradition of special relationship to God, who had been made known to Israel through the exodus experience and the covenant making at Mt. Sinai. Israel's understanding of this covenant God and the community that lived in relationship to this God set them apart from other communities in the world. The desire to have a king arises in 1 Samuel 8 as the impulse to be "like other nations" (vv. 5, 20). For Israel, the available models for kingship were to be found in the small kingdoms that were Israel's neighbors. How could the uniqueness of Israel's faith and relationship to God be maintained if Israel's life became patterned more like the surrounding nations? How could Israel have an earthly king without undermining the sovereignty of God?

Israel's transformation was *sociopolitical.* The emergence of kingship in Israel did not result from an abstract theological debate. Real crises, both internal and external, exposed the weaknesses of Israel's tribal life and created the pressure to adopt kingship as an alternative. When Samuel became old, his sons proved to be corrupt and unworthy successors to judge Israel (8:1-3). The house of Eli before Samuel had fallen under God's judgment for its corruption. It is in this context that the elders of Israel come to request a king (8:4-5). Even after a king is chosen, tensions over spheres of authority remain and can be seen in the conflicts between Samuel and Saul (13:1-15; 15:1-35).

External sociopolitical pressures came in the form of the Philistine military threat. The deuteronomistic historian does not want to present the Philistines as a legitimate reason for kingship. Samuel is presented as ending the Philistine threat in 7:13-14, and the Philistine crisis does not figure at all in the elders' request for a king in chap. 8 (although it may be hinted at in v. 20). Nevertheless, other texts in this section make clear that the threat of permanent Philistine conquest was a factor in the establishment of kingship. Saul is anointed in 10:1 with the explicit charge to deliver Israel from the Philistines. Chapters 13–14 show Saul addressing all of his initial efforts at relief from the Philistine threat. Kingship implies centralized leadership, standing armies, and unified authority. These are needed to defeat an enemy like the Philistines, but these are all new patterns for the life of Israel and stand in tension with older patterns. The conflicts with Samuel in chaps. 13–15 are not only theological in character, but also represent conflicts over authority and conduct in military matters. Samuel represents older holy war traditions, and Saul represents emerging patterns common to the ways in which kings conduct military campaigns.

Recent work on the sociological background to this period of transformation to monarchy has made clear that emerging population pressure and economic surplus were a part of the pressure to move from localized tribal patterns to centralized royal systems of social organization.[59] New patterns of land consolidation and political power necessitated a strong centralized system to protect these emerging vested interests. Kingship was the logical development to meet these needs. A military crisis, like the Philistine threat, may have provided the opportunity for transition to kingship, but vested economic and political power interests stood to gain more than simply relief from Philistine pressure. It must be stressed that these social and demographic factors are never explicitly stated in the text of the books of Samuel as a justification for kingship. They are the factors we can discern behind and through the story.

These social factors also create theological tensions. Covenant faith arose in response to oppression and marginalization and was never at home with vested-interest power arrangements. The theological unease of the covenant tradition with some of the emerging sociopolitical power arrangements that accompany kingship will be a source of tension visible at various points in the books of Samuel (e.g., "the ways of the king," 1 Sam 8:11-18).

Israel's transformation was *character driven.* The testimony of the books of Samuel is that this crucial transition period in Israel's life was dominated by the leadership and personalities of Samuel, Saul, and David. The character and activity of Israel's God, Yahweh, also play a pivotal role in the story of this period and in the lives of these three leaders. In 1 Samuel 8–15, David has not yet entered the story, although his crucial place in the story is sometimes foreshadowed (e.g., 13:14; 15:28). In these chapters, the characters of Samuel, Saul, and the Lord (Yahweh) all reflect the tensions and ambiguities of this transition time.

Samuel appears as God's prophet. As such he is commanded by God to give the people a king (8:7, 9, 22), and he is God's agent in designating and anointing Saul (9:27–10:8, 17-27). But Samuel also represents the older tribal traditions, and he sometimes appears as intransigent and subversive of kingship in general and of Saul in particular (8:6, 10-17; 10:17-19; 13:1-15; 15:1-35).

Saul, as Israel's first king, is portrayed as an attractive, effective leader (esp. chap. 11), and the reader sympathizes with him when he seems undermined by Samuel (13:1-15; 15:1-35). Yet, he also at times seems vacillating and indecisive, prone to impulsive decisions, and unable to see the consequences of his actions (e.g., 14:36-46; Saul's character problems come out more strongly in chaps. 16–31). He represents, at times, Israel's bright future, but at other times, Israel's miscalculation. He does not appear effective at bridging from the old order to the new.

59. See, e.g., L. Marvin Chaney, "Ancient Palestinian Peasant Movements and the Formation of Premonarchic Israel," in *Palestine in Transition,* ed. D. N. Freedman and D. F. Graf (Sheffield: Almond, 1983) 39-90; James W. Flanagan, "Chiefs in Israel," *JSOT* 20 (1981) 47-73; Frank S. Frick, *The Formation of the State in Ancient Israel* (Sheffield: JSOT, 1988); Norman K. Gottwald, "Early Israel and the Canaanite Socioeconomic System," in Freedman and Graf, *Palestine in Transition,* 25-37.

God clearly authorizes the establishment of kingship in Israel (8:7, 9, 22) and designates Saul as the first king (9:15-18). Yet, God clearly regards this development as sinful and as a rejection of God's own rule (8:7-9). It is God's prophet who claims that God has rejected Saul (15:26), but then it is God who chooses David as the "man after God's own heart" (13:14). God clearly directs the course of events, but God's motives and goals are not always clear. Some of this ambiguity may reside in traditions that differ on whether kingship can be reconciled with the covenant tradition.

These tensions of a transition time in Israel's life are reflected in the complexity of the literature in 1 Samuel 8–15. These chapters have proved notoriously difficult for both the scholar and the church reader. Kingship seems condemned at one point and welcomed at another. Saul seems to become king three times. He is rejected by Samuel twice. Later in 1 Samuel, David is introduced to Saul twice, David spares Saul's life twice, and Saul commits suicide twice. The times were complex. So, too, the literature of 1 Samuel (esp. chaps. 8–15) probably went through a complex history of development. Here are some observations that may help in reading this section of 1 Samuel.

(1) In these chapters, we are not dealing with history writing as such but with literary and theological interpretations of history. The storytellers make no effort to be objective. They have perspectives on the stories they want to share, and those perspectives often reflect the situations of later Israel, to whom they are telling the story (e.g., exiles in Babylon).

(2) The episodes that form the present shape of 1 Samuel probably went through a complex process of development. Older views of 1 Samuel divided the book into an early source that was positive to kingship and a late source that was negative to kingship. This approach has largely proved unsuccessful and has been abandoned, although many Bible reference books still reflect this theory. Most scholars now recognize that support and opposition to kingship were a part of the experience of Israel at the time of the transition to kingship.

There is wide agreement that a deuteronomistic historian is responsible for the final shape of these chapters as a part of his larger work from Joshua through 2 Kings. He was more than just an editor, but a creative storyteller in his own right, telling the story of Israel's life for the sake of a generation in exile in Babylon. At times he contributed material of his own (e.g., chap. 12), while at other times he shaped an already extant story through additions and transitions (e.g., chap. 8). We will see his special interests showing through more clearly at some points than at others.

There was also an earlier prophetic edition of these stories (see the Introduction for fuller details), and his interest in the role of prophets and in a prophetic view of kingship can be seen clearly at various points. It is not possible or even desirable to divide the traditions of 1 Samuel into "sources" or to become preoccupied with the pre-canonical development of the text. It is helpful to see the way the tradition picks up the witness of previous generations and incorporates that witness into a new telling of the story. Although the text of the canon is now relatively fixed, this process continues as church and synagogue read and tell the story of Israel in ways that speak to a new generation.

(3) It is the final shape of the story as it now appears in the canonical text of 1 and 2 Samuel that we must seek to understand and appropriate. In the commentary that follows on chaps. 8–15, we will reflect on the story as a theological and literary witness in its present form. This form is not the product of haphazard editing but is a final creative telling of the story. Although occasionally evidences of the process through which the traditions passed will be observed, the overriding concern will always be to understand and to find meaning in the story of Israel's establishment of kingship as it is now presented to us in the book of 1 Samuel and in the larger frame of the story of Israel from Joshua to 2 Kings.

In general terms, 1 Samuel 8–15 divides into two large segments. Chapters 8–12 tell us how Saul became king; chaps. 13–15 tell us how Saul lost kingship. Each of these segments begins and ends in an encounter with the prophet Samuel, who is obviously a key figure for this segment of 1 Samuel.

1 Samuel 8:1-22, Demand and Warning

NIV

8 When Samuel grew old, he appointed his sons as judges for Israel. ²The name of his firstborn was Joel and the name of his second was Abijah, and they served at Beersheba. ³But his sons did not walk in his ways. They turned aside after dishonest gain and accepted bribes and perverted justice.

⁴So all the elders of Israel gathered together and came to Samuel at Ramah. ⁵They said to him, "You are old, and your sons do not walk in your ways; now appoint a king to lead[a] us, such as all the other nations have."

⁶But when they said, "Give us a king to lead us," this displeased Samuel; so he prayed to the LORD. ⁷And the LORD told him: "Listen to all that the people are saying to you; it is not you they have rejected, but they have rejected me as their king. ⁸As they have done from the day I brought them up out of Egypt until this day, forsaking me and serving other gods, so they are doing to you. ⁹Now listen to them; but warn them solemnly and let them know what the king who will reign over them will do."

¹⁰Samuel told all the words of the LORD to the people who were asking him for a king. ¹¹He said, "This is what the king who will reign over you will do: He will take your sons and make them serve with his chariots and horses, and they will run in front of his chariots. ¹²Some he will assign to be commanders of thousands and commanders of fifties, and others to plow his ground and reap his harvest, and still others to make weapons of war and equipment for his chariots. ¹³He will take your daughters to be perfumers and cooks and bakers. ¹⁴He will take the best of your fields and vineyards and olive groves and give them to his attendants. ¹⁵He will take a tenth of your grain and of your vintage and give it to his officials and attendants. ¹⁶Your menservants and maidservants and the best of your cattle[b] and donkeys he will take for his own use. ¹⁷He will take a tenth of your flocks, and you yourselves will become his slaves. ¹⁸When that day comes, you will cry out for relief from the king you have chosen, and the LORD will not answer you in that day."

a5 Traditionally *judge*; also in verses 6 and 20   b16 Septuagint; Hebrew *young men*

NRSV

8 When Samuel became old, he made his sons judges over Israel. ²The name of his firstborn son was Joel, and the name of his second, Abijah; they were judges in Beer-sheba. ³Yet his sons did not follow in his ways, but turned aside after gain; they took bribes and perverted justice.

4Then all the elders of Israel gathered together and came to Samuel at Ramah, ⁵and said to him, "You are old and your sons do not follow in your ways; appoint for us, then, a king to govern us, like other nations." ⁶But the thing displeased Samuel when they said, "Give us a king to govern us." Samuel prayed to the LORD, ⁷and the LORD said to Samuel, "Listen to the voice of the people in all that they say to you; for they have not rejected you, but they have rejected me from being king over them. ⁸Just as they have done to me,[a] from the day I brought them up out of Egypt to this day, forsaking me and serving other gods, so also they are doing to you. ⁹Now then, listen to their voice; only—you shall solemnly warn them, and show them the ways of the king who shall reign over them."

10So Samuel reported all the words of the LORD to the people who were asking him for a king. ¹¹He said, "These will be the ways of the king who will reign over you: he will take your sons and appoint them to his chariots and to be his horsemen, and to run before his chariots; ¹²and he will appoint for himself commanders of thousands and commanders of fifties, and some to plow his ground and to reap his harvest, and to make his implements of war and the equipment of his chariots. ¹³He will take your daughters to be perfumers and cooks and bakers. ¹⁴He will take the best of your fields and vineyards and olive orchards and give them to his courtiers. ¹⁵He will take one-tenth of your grain and of your vineyards and give it to his officers and his courtiers. ¹⁶He will take your male and female slaves, and the best of your cattle[b] and donkeys, and put them to his work. ¹⁷He will take one-tenth of your flocks, and you shall be his slaves. ¹⁸And in that day you will cry out because of your king, whom

a Gk: Heb lacks *to me*   b Gk: Heb *young men*

NIV

¹⁹But the people refused to listen to Samuel. "No!" they said. "We want a king over us. ²⁰Then we will be like all the other nations, with a king to lead us and to go out before us and fight our battles."

²¹When Samuel heard all that the people said, he repeated it before the LORD. ²²The LORD answered, "Listen to them and give them a king."

Then Samuel said to the men of Israel, "Everyone go back to his town."

NRSV

you have chosen for yourselves; but the LORD will not answer you in that day."

19But the people refused to listen to the voice of Samuel; they said, "No! but we are determined to have a king over us, ²⁰so that we also may be like other nations, and that our king may govern us and go out before us and fight our battles." ²¹When Samuel had heard all the words of the people, he repeated them in the ears of the LORD. ²²The LORD said to Samuel, "Listen to their voice and set a king over them." Samuel then said to the people of Israel, "Each of you return home."

COMMENTARY

In this chapter, the elders of Israel come to Samuel and demand a king. The kingship, which was hinted at in various ways in chaps. 1–7, now becomes the explicit focus of the story. This is the issue we have been prepared for in the opening chapters of 1 Samuel. We have seen kingship coming, but in 1 Samuel 7 we are told, in effect, that it is not needed. The leadership of God's prophet Samuel was enough. His faithful judging of Israel had replaced the corruption of the house of Eli, and his mediation of God's power had resulted in the defeat of the Philistines. We are prepared and meant to be unsympathetic to the elders' request in 8:4-5.

After a brief report on the corruption of Samuel's sons, the main episode unfolds as a series of conversations between three participants: the elders of Israel, Samuel, and God. The long recitation by Samuel on the "ways of the king" in vv. 10-18 forms the centerpiece for the chapter.

Most scholars have found evidence of the special themes and vocabulary of the deuteronomistic historian in this chapter. This will be particularly noted in the discussion of vv. 8 and 18 and in the theme of apostasy raised in God's speech in vv. 7-9. The mediating role of Samuel between God and people makes this material consistent with the emphasis on his role as a prophet in an earlier prophetic edition of this tradition.[60] The

emphasis in this commentary will be on chap. 8 as it now functions in its present form.

8:1-3. Samuel has grown old (vv. 1, 5). We presume he has judged Israel faithfully and well. When he addresses Israel a final time and proclaims his innocence, none can raise complaint against him (12:3-5). But all is not well.

Ironically, it is Samuel's sons who have grown corrupt. Samuel himself had replaced Eli, not because of the sin of the old priest himself, but because of the perverse practices of Eli's sons, Hophni and Phinehas (2:12-17). This notice of the sin of Samuel's sons prepares us for the elders of Israel to request a new arrangement in vv. 4-5.

Samuel had appointed his two sons, Joel and Abijah, to be judges in Beersheba. It is surprising to have two individuals exercising this function in the same location, and to imagine that Samuel's influence stretched as far south as Beersheba. The Jewish historian Josephus knew a tradition that assigned one of the sons to Bethel.[61] These sons, however, were no Samuels. In a series of blunt phrases, the problem is stated in v. 3. They have not followed in their father's ways; they seek profit for themselves; they accept bribes; they "perverted justice." These include explicit violations of covenant law on profits (Exod 18:21), bribes (Exod 23:8), and the administration of justice (Exod 23:2, 6, 8). They were practices later harshly condemned by the prophets (see Isa 1:23;

60. See Bruce C. Birch, *The Rise of the Israelite Monarchy: The Growth and Development of I Samuel 7–15*, SBLDS 27 (Missoula, Mont.: Scholars Press, 1976) 22-29; and P. Kyle McCarter, *I Samuel*, AB 8 (Garden City, N.Y.: Doubleday, 1980) 156-59.

61. Josephus *Antiquities of the Jews* 6.32.

5:23; Amos 5:7, 12). These actions struck at the heart of the covenant relationship that judges in Israel were intended to protect and uphold.

Justice is the fundamental issue at stake in this episode of the story. The Hebrew verb שׁפט (šāpaṭ, "to judge") and the noun משׁפט (mišpāṭ, "justice") play an important role here. Chapter 7 concluded with a notice that Samuel "judged" Israel and "administered justice" (7:15-17). Chapter 8 opens with a notice that his sons "judged" Israel and "perverted justice" (vv. 1-3). The request of the elders (vv. 5, 20) is for a king "to judge us" (šāpaṭ; NRSV, "to govern"; NIV, "to lead"). When God later tells Samuel to warn the people, it is to tell them the "mišpāṭ of the king" (NRSV, "ways of the king"; NIV, "what the king . . . will do").[62] A central question posed by this chapter is, Where is justice to come from with Samuel growing old? It does not appear that his sons are the answer. Samuel is displeased (v. 6) by the request for a "king to judge us," and his speech later (vv. 10-17) does not hold out the hope that justice can come from a king. Perhaps only God's prophet, like Samuel, can be trusted to guard justice in Israel. When Israel does have kings, it is the prophets Samuel (1 Samuel 13; 15) and Nathan (2 Samuel 12) who will have the authority to confront Saul and David with violations of justice and covenant obedience.

8:4-9. The elders of Israel approach Samuel in his hometown of Ramah (v. 4). It is not clear what segment of Israel this represents. Verse 10 refers to them as "the people who were asking him for a king," which seems to imply that this is not a representative, all-Israel delegation. The fact that they are not worried by Samuel's suggestion of the burdens of kingship in vv. 10-17 has led some to speculate that this gathering represents the more influential and wealthy in Israel, who were most likely to gain from the move to kingship.

The complaint of the elders (v. 5a) repeats the language of the notice in vv. 1-3: Samuel is old, and his sons do not follow in his ways. There is no suggestion in the text that this was an illegitimate concern. But the remedy proposed by the elders takes a bold turn (v. 5b). They ask for a king! They want this king to govern them. Since the verb here is šāpaṭ, "to judge," it seems clear that they envision this king as a successor to Samuel, who had been "judging" them (7:15-17). They want Samuel to "appoint" this king, but most surprising in their request (demand?) is that they want to be "like other nations." This phrase is repeated in the people's insistence on a king in v. 20. The law of the king in Deut 17:14 uses a similar phrase to describe the people's desire for a king, and then surrounds this desire with laws that guard and restrict the role of the king. To become "like other nations" represented a significant shift for Israel—a shift away from distinctive community to conformity with the patterns of other peoples. What was at stake was Israel's identity and particularity.

Samuel does not pick up on this issue. He is displeased, but his displeasure seems personally focused on his replacement as judge by a king (v. 6). When Samuel prays to God, we have the sense that the people are being reported to a higher authority by someone who has been personally affronted. God certainly saw Samuel's response as one of personal rejection and thus soothed him (v. 7).

God's response is surprising. God commands Samuel to "listen to the voice of the people" (v. 7). God repeats this command twice (vv. 9, 22), each time in slightly stronger terms. The imperative of שׁמע (šāmaʿ, "to listen" or "to hear") often carries the implication of "obey." God immediately acquiesces to the demand of the people and proceeds to sooth Samuel. Only then does God voice the divine concerns raised by the people's request. To seek an earthly king was a rejection of God's rule as divine king. It was a challenge to divine sovereignty, and at root it was idolatrous. God equated the desire for a king with Israel's forsaking of the Lord in favor of serving other gods. Israel had been doing this since God brought them out of Egypt (an adroit reminder of exodus as the origin of Israel in God's deliverance, v. 8). The elders' request is a rejection of God, not of Samuel. The issue is idolatry (like other nations) and apostasy (only God is king), not personal affront. What Samuel is now experiencing is the same idolatrous behavior God had seen before ("so also they are doing to you," v. 8b), not something uniquely directed at Samuel.

The Hebrew term מאס (māʾas, "to reject") is a

---

62. The "mišpāṭ of the king" will be discussed further below. It can be noted here, however, that the NIV translation is woefully inadequate. It obscures the connection of this term to "justice" and the fact that the text may be referring to a formal document or code of royal responsibilities (see 10:25; Deut 17:18-19).

key term. The people's action is described here and later in Samuel's speech at Mizpah (10:19) as a "rejection" of God as king. The term next appears as a description of God's action toward Saul, "Because you have rejected the word of the LORD, he has also rejected you from being king" (15:23; cf. 15:26; 16:1). As Gunn has observed, "The use of the motif of rejection . . . formally links Saul's fate with Yahweh's understanding of his own treatment at the hands of the people."[63] This rejection of God casts a shadow over Saul's kingship from the beginning.

Nevertheless, God instructs Samuel again to "listen to their voice" (v. 9*a*). God does not approve, but God permits. The tone is indulgent and tolerant, almost resigned. But Samuel is also told to "solemnly warn them" (v. 9*b*, the verb is given emphasis by the addition of an infinitive). The verb עוד (*'ûd*) means to "give witness" and in this emphatic form can mean to "give warning." In effect, Samuel as God's prophet becomes witness to the dangers of the path the people have chosen. The content of Samuel's witness is to be the משפט המלך (*mišpaṭ hammelek*, vv. 9, 11). The phrase seems to indicate some formal standard for the behavior of kings. Both 1 Sam 10:25 (using a similar phrase) and Deut 17:18-19 imply a written document to which kings were accountable. Both of these passages, however, imply that the document was some sort of restraint on the abuse of kingship, whereas Samuel's speech in vv. 10-18 provides a catalog of abuse. Some have seen the phrase as connoting the rights of the king, while others have seen it merely as descriptive of the conduct of the king. Clearly there is an ironic contrast between the concern of the elders for "justice" and the use of the term "justice" (*mišpaṭ*) for this recitation of oppressive royal behavior. Veijola, noting the common use of the term "witness" or "warn" in connection with treaties or agreements, suggests that Samuel is instructed by God to lay out before the people, with proper warnings, the terms of an ironic royal treaty.[64] In effect, God tells Samuel to let them know what they're in for. "They wanted justice? Tell them the kind of justice they can expect from a king." Still, God granted the people's request.

Samuel was to warn them, but he was also to do what they asked.

8:10-18. Samuel's speech is a catalog of the royal abuse of power. Many have observed that it seems to reflect Israel's later experience with its own kings, especially Solomon. Thus the deuteronomistic historian may be suggesting that the request for a king was the beginning of the path to exile. Mendelsohn, however, has shown that this picture could also fit Canaanite royal practices as early as the thirteenth century BCE (Ugarit and Alalakh).[65] If so, Samuel's speech may describe the excesses of pagan kingship rather than being a description of Israel's own royal experience. The practices reflected in vv. 11-17 fit well with the foreign practices forbidden to Israel's kings in the law of the king (Deut 17:14-20). Perhaps these views are not mutually exclusive. An old document detailing the abusive practices of foreign kings may well have suited the deuteronomistic historian's needs in critiquing Israel's royal abuses.

Whatever the origin of this portrait of kingship, it is clear that Samuel is using it in an attempt to dissuade the Israelite elders from their request for a king. Although v. 10 says that Samuel reported the words of the Lord, there is no suggestion that he revealed to the elders the Lord's instruction to grant their request. In fact, after God instructs Samuel a third time to "listen to their voice," Samuel still does not tell the people of God's acquiescence in their request and sends them home (v. 22). For Polzin, this is evidence that Samuel is dragging his feet in spite of God's willingness to grant a king. He believes the *mišpaṭ hammelek* must have included duties of the king toward the people as well as the privileges Samuel details; thus Samuel is intentionally giving only half the picture.[66]

Whatever Samuel's motives, he clearly paints a negative portrait of kingship, and it is clearly intended to convince the people to withdraw their request. The royal practices Samuel highlighted were those of conscripting young men for military service, farming royal holdings, and manufacture

63. David M. Gunn, *The Fate of King Saul: An Introduction of a Biblical Story* (Sheffield: JSOT, 1980) 60.

64. T. Veijola, *Das Königtum in der Beurteilung der Deuteronomistischen Historiographie,* Annales Academiae Scientiarum Fennicae Series B 198 (Helsinki: Suomalainen Tiedeaktemia, 1977) 60.

65. Isaac Mendelsohn, "Samuel's Denunciation of Kingship in the Light of Akkadian Documents from Ugarit," *BASOR* 143 (1956) 17-22.

66. Robert Polzin, *Samuel and the Deuteronomist: A Literary Study of the Deuteronomic History,* Part Two: *1 Samuel* (San Francisco: Harper & Row, 1989) 85-88. Polzin also holds the opinion that the practices Samuel details are typical and expected of kings and do not constitute abuse of power. Samuel merely gives these normal royal practices a negative spin.

of implements (vv. 11-12) and young women for perfumers, cooks, and bakers (v. 13). The king would also take the best of the productive land and redistribute it to his own retainers (v. 14). He would require a tenth of all forms of wealth—grain, vineyards, flocks, cattle, donkeys, and slaves (vv. 15-17). All these are practices attested for Israelite and non-Israelite kings.[67]

Samuel's speech portrays royal privilege as grasping and debilitating. Four times he uses the verb "to take" (לקח *lāqaḥ*) and twice the verb "to confiscate one tenth" (עשׂר *'āśar*) as the main action of his description (vv. 11, 13, 14, 15, 16, 17). What is the "justice" of a king? A king will take, take, take, take, take, take! Even more dramatically, Samuel describes the end result of this grasping: "you shall be his slaves" (v. 17*b*). To serve a king is to return to bondage, to reverse what God had done in the exodus deliverance (v. 8). The fate Samuel described would undercut the very identity of Israel as God's delivered people. For the security of a king, the people would surrender their freedom. "The monarchy substitutes human power for the availability of Yahweh."[68]

Samuel concludes by saying the day will come when the people will "cry out because of your king . . . but the LORD will not answer" (v. 18). The cry and answer that brought deliverance under Samuel (7:9) are reversed. The pattern of outcry and divine answer, which had been Israel's hope and security from the exodus onward, is now broken (Exod 2:23-25; 3:7-8). This sequence had particularly marked the period of the judges, but under a king the time of divine answer is ended. The phrase "in that day" may indicate the historian's word to his audience that in exile "that day" had already come, and "in that day" God could not save them from the fate they had chosen. Significantly, v. 18 describes this choice as the king "you have chosen for yourselves." Even in the law of the king in Deut 17:15, which allows a king in Israel, it is to be one "whom the Lord your God will choose." The people's request is seen in v. 18 as an attempt at self-willed choice by the people. God will allow a king, but the ongoing story in 1 Samuel suggests that God will

choose him. Chapter 9 is a story of Saul's designation by God, not by the people.

8:19-22. In counterpoint to God's instruction that Samuel "listen to the voice of the people" (vv. 7, 9, 22), the people "refused to listen to the voice of Samuel" (v. 19). Samuel's warning has no effect. The response is a resounding "No!" Some have suggested that the people's disregard of Samuel's speech shows that these were the Israelites who would benefit from a royal system. The story seems to suggest their stubbornness in the face of Samuel's warning more than their sense that it would not apply to them. In any case, Samuel offered no real alternative, so it is not surprising that the people insisted on having a king.

The reasons for having a king are expanded. The people still desire to be "like other nations" and to have a king "to govern" them, but in addition they want the king to "go out before us and fight our battles" (v. 20). This is the first hint of a military justification for kingship. Perhaps the Philistine threat is behind this vague remark.

When Samuel reports the people's determination to the Lord, he is instructed a third time to "listen" and to "set a king over them." Instead of immediately doing so, Samuel sends the people home (v. 22). This could be read as intentional recalcitrance on Samuel's part, but it may simply be an ending of this episode in order to move the story on to the various traditions on how Saul became the first king (chaps. 9–11).

When we look back at the entire episode in 1 Samuel 8, it is clear that the people have a legitimate complaint. The system is breaking down, and Samuel seems unwilling or unable to offer a remedy. It would seem that both Samuel and the elders, with their request, appear in the story as false options. Samuel is defensive and foot-dragging. He sees the request as a personal affront and is not immediately responsive to the people's needs or God's command. The elders, on the other hand, seem to want more than the corrective to a legitimate problem. They are motivated by the desire to emulate their neighbors and to give up the difficult vocation of covenant community, which makes them different. Self-interest and status seem to occupy them, and they make a more emotional than thoughtful response to the issues raised by Samuel's warning.

It is God who seems willing to risk a new

---

67. See Ralph W. Klein, *1 Samuel*, WBC 10 (Waco: Word, 1983) 77-78, for particulars on these practices.

68. Walter Brueggemann, *First and Second Samuel*, Interpretation (Louisville: John Knox, 1990) 65.

choice, even against the divine self-interest. God's acquiescence does seem more indulgent than gracious, but there is a sense that God knows more and is willing to risk more than Samuel or the elders. Or perhaps God is willing to let his covenant partners take their own risks, even when God believes their choice to be unwise. God knows that kingship in these terms is idolatrous and sinful. Still, kingship is authorized and perhaps not unredeemable (as Samuel later suggests in 12:14), but the risk is great. Saul will fall victim to that risk. Perhaps God is already looking ahead to David and his special role in the story of Israel's kings. It may take the failure of Saul to allow the possibilities of David.

REFLECTIONS

1. It was not easy for Israel to live as covenant community in partnership with God. It was clear from Exodus onward that the covenant model was an alternative to the models of community that prevailed in the world of Israel's neighbors.[69] That alternative model included a recognition of God's sovereignty, which did not require hierarchical forms of leadership in the human community. But the lure of conformity is seductive, and the pressures toward cultural accommodation are great. "Appoint for us a king . . . like other nations" (8:5). The people said to Samuel, in effect, "We don't want to be different anymore. We want to be like everyone else. The pressures of alternative living are too great." One of the issues raised by this episode for the community of faith in every generation is the lure and the danger of cultural accommodation.

Like Israel, the church is called to be in the world, but not of the world. The pattern of the church's life is defined by relationship with God in continuity with the covenant model of Israel and with the community of new covenant in Jesus Christ, shaped by the early church. The qualities of such faith communities include love, justice, peace, compassion, and worship. This is not an easy calling. The pressures toward cultural conformity are great, and we live in a culture that often elevates a different set of qualities from those of the covenant model. They include self-interest and self-fulfillment, political and military power, acquisition and consumption. It is understandably tempting to want to be like everyone else, both as persons and as institutions.

The special warning for us in 1 Samuel 8 is the way in which authentic crisis may support the desire to be "like other nations." The crisis of leadership created by Samuel's age and the corruption of his sons was real, but in the response to this crisis Israel's authentic identity as a covenant people was compromised. Likewise, the church's greatest temptations to accommodation often come in struggles to deal with authentic challenges or to respond to genuine crises in the church or the society.

A man whose father was a pastor in California at the start of World War II confided that his father had been guilt stricken for his entire life because he had failed to say a word of protest when a close personal friend and neighbor of Japanese descent was taken to an internment camp and had his home and business seized. As a pastor in the community, he thought he might have made a difference, but he remained silent. The crisis of the war with Japan was real, but he compromised his deepest faith commitments because of the pressure of public sentiment and the fear of seeming different. It is a pressure to be "like other nations" that we all have known. At its simplest, it is a personal unwillingness to be identified as a person of faith in our communities and workplaces. At its most demonic, it is a church that accommodates itself to evil in the name of patriotism and produces a Nazi Germany or an ethnic cleansing.

The church as an institution is vulnerable to this danger of responding to crisis by becoming "like other nations." Many denominations and congregations have become concerned over membership decline. Outreach and evangelism are always legitimate concerns for the church, but

---

69. For fuller discussions of covenant community as an alternative model, see Walter Brueggemann, *Prophetic Imagination* (Philadelphia: Fortress, 1978) chap. 2, and Bruce C. Birch, *Let Justice Roll Down,* 172-84.

not at the cost of the church's basic faith identity. In contemporary America the emphasis on individual independence and self-reliance is enormous, and the notion of relating to others in community is not always popular. In our eagerness to reach the world, the temptation is to compromise the basic identity of God's covenant people. But it is simply not possible to be a person of covenant faith without being a part of the covenant community. The church could become "like other nations," but it would cease to be the church. In its desire to be relevant, the church must also guard against sacrificing its authentic calling and identity for the sake of the latest fad, success scheme, or ideology that comes along. The desire to be "like other nations" is never a legitimate motivation for change or unwillingness to change.

2. Reflection on 1 Samuel 8 raises questions on the difficult relationship of faith community to political institutions. Israel did not have the sharp separation of sacred and secular institutions that American society assumes, but the basic issues remain the same. When does trust in human power become a rejection of divine power? How does our recognition of divine authority relate to our recognition of human authority? How do citizenship and discipleship interact? Chapter 8 does not so much offer answers to these questions as it puts them on our agenda. These questions provide a lens and a focus for reading the stories of Saul and David, which lie ahead. These questions also provide a framework for reflection on the uneasy relationship between divine power and human power in our own settings and institutions as citizens of a modern nation and members of contemporary churches. This chapter reminds us that communities of faith are not isolated from the arenas of public power. Our decisions about relationship to God affect the way we live in the sociopolitical world.

In this story, the elders and Samuel both suggest dangers that still face us in the modern church. The elders have a legitimate concern for justice, but are willing to erode the authority of God for the sake of stronger centers of human power. Samuel is protective of the integrity of God, but represents a vested interest in the way things have always been done. Chapter 8 offers no simple right-and-wrong way to adjudicate the claims of citizenship and faith. It merely demands an awareness of the interrelated character of these claims.

The elders' initial approach asks us to consider where the church's support of traditional ways of doing things has allowed or perpetuated injustice. Have we raised up leaders who close their eyes to patterns of abuse in the name of protecting the status quo? The elders' request for a king raises questions about our willingness to grasp for security when the need is for justice. To what degree does the church support public policies that provide instant gratification at the expense of long-term problem solving? We want forceful, even authoritarian, leaders to deal with issues of crime, drug trafficking, deteriorating cities, welfare abuse, and the collapse of family structures. But there is often little support for long-term systemic efforts to address the underlying issues of poverty, consumerism, racism, and societal values that create the dysfunctions in our communities and families. Samuel's catalog of oppressive royal practices ought to give us pause as citizens and as people of faith. Like other nations before us, we may be too willing to sacrifice freedom and justice for the sake of security.

The ultimate issue raised by 1 Samuel 8 is, To what degree have we let our trust in human authority overshadow our trust in God? This is the issue placed before us for the reading of the remainder of 1 and 2 Samuel. It is also placed before us as people of faith who must grapple with issues of public power and authority. Where does faith draw its boundaries? At what point do our loyalties to human institutions have to give way to the higher loyalty we owe to God? There is no set answer, but there are many examples of those who were forced to make such a decision. Martin Luther opposed the ecclesiastical power of a pope. Martin Luther King, Jr., opposed the civil power of a state. In 1 Samuel 8, God gives Israel the freedom to choose a king, but God does not give up the claim of divine sovereignty. We, too, have the freedom to participate boldly in making the decisions of public life, but if we read this chapter carefully we should do so with some degree of humility (and repentance?) in recognition that human power is only subordinate to divine power.

1 Samuel 9:1–11:15, Saul Becomes King

OVERVIEW

The spotlight shifts from the question of whether to have a king to the question of who will be king. These chapters contain three separate stories relating how Saul was designated as the first king of Israel. In 9:1–10:16, Saul is anointed and commissioned by the prophet Samuel. In 10:17-27, Saul is chosen by lot and found hiding among the baggage before being acclaimed by the people. In 11:1-15, Saul delivers Jabesh-gilead from the Ammonites in a style reminiscent of the judges, and the people make Saul king.

Yet kingship arrives uneasily in Israel. Samuel's speech in 10:18-19 reminds the people that their desire for a king is a rejection of God's rule. Even after Saul is chosen by lot and legitimated by the people, there are those who complain and withhold their allegiance (10:27). After Saul's deliverance of Jabesh-gilead, some desire to put such complainers to death (11:12-13). Samuel's farewell speech in chap. 12 renews and extends Samuel's objections to kingship and his warnings about its dangers. In 13:1-15 and 15:1-35, Saul has no sooner become king than he is rejected from kingship by Samuel. In chaps. 9–11, Saul has his brief moment in the story, but it is clear that the older Israelite tradition represented by Samuel is still ambiguous about kingship. Saul is not able to win over the Israelite tradition. It remains for David to do that.

These chapters may have gone through a complex literary history. Traditionally these stories were each assigned to an early pro-monarchical source and a late anti-monarchical source. This approach has been largely abandoned. Nevertheless, each episode does seem to have a different perspective on kingship in general and Saul in particular. It is likely that these episodes had separate literary origins, but they are now connected and interrelated by a creative hand that presented these traditions as part of a single witness to this important period of transformation in Israel. It is my belief that this artful, interconnected story was first the product of prophetically influenced circles with a distinctive theology of kingship in mind. I will note places where this prophetic theology comes into view. This prophetically influenced telling of the story was incorporated into the Deuteronomistic History work, and the Dtr historian made his own creative literary contributions. Nevertheless, the emphasis will not be on the literary prehistory of these chapters, but on their witness in the present final form of the text. The full text as we now have it is the telling of the story of kingship that Israel itself finally fixed and passed on as its accepted version of these important events. Listening to the voice of this full witness is our chief task.

1 Samuel 9:1–10:16, The Anointing of Saul

NIV

9 There was a Benjamite, a man of standing, whose name was Kish son of Abiel, the son of Zeror, the son of Becorath, the son of Aphiah of Benjamin. [2]He had a son named Saul, an impressive young man without equal among the Israelites—a head taller than any of the others.

[3]Now the donkeys belonging to Saul's father Kish were lost, and Kish said to his son Saul, "Take one of the servants with you and go and look for the donkeys." [4]So he passed through the

NRSV

9 There was a man of Benjamin whose name was Kish son of Abiel son of Zeror son of Becorath son of Aphiah, a Benjaminite, a man of wealth. [2]He had a son whose name was Saul, a handsome young man. There was not a man among the people of Israel more handsome than he; he stood head and shoulders above everyone else.

3Now the donkeys of Kish, Saul's father, had strayed. So Kish said to his son Saul, "Take one of the boys with you; go and look for the don-hill country of Ephraim and through the area around Shalisha, but they did not find them. They went on into the district of Shaalim, but the donkeys were not there. Then he passed through the territory of Benjamin, but they did not find them.

5When they reached the district of Zuph, Saul said to the servant who was with him, "Come, let's go back, or my father will stop thinking about the donkeys and start worrying about us."

6But the servant replied, "Look, in this town there is a man of God; he is highly respected, and everything he says comes true. Let's go there now. Perhaps he will tell us what way to take."

7Saul said to his servant, "If we go, what can we give the man? The food in our sacks is gone. We have no gift to take to the man of God. What do we have?"

8The servant answered him again. "Look," he said, "I have a quarter of a shekel*a* of silver. I will give it to the man of God so that he will tell us what way to take." 9(Formerly in Israel, if a man went to inquire of God, he would say, "Come, let us go to the seer," because the prophet of today used to be called a seer.)

10"Good," Saul said to his servant. "Come, let's go." So they set out for the town where the man of God was.

11As they were going up the hill to the town, they met some girls coming out to draw water, and they asked them, "Is the seer here?"

12"He is," they answered. "He's ahead of you. Hurry now; he has just come to our town today, for the people have a sacrifice at the high place. 13As soon as you enter the town, you will find him before he goes up to the high place to eat. The people will not begin eating until he comes, because he must bless the sacrifice; afterward, those who are invited will eat. Go up now; you should find him about this time."

14They went up to the town, and as they were entering it, there was Samuel, coming toward them on his way up to the high place.

15Now the day before Saul came, the Lord had revealed this to Samuel: 16"About this time tomorrow I will send you a man from the land of Benjamin. Anoint him leader over my people Israel; he will deliver my people from the hand

a8 That is, about 1/10 ounce (about 3 grams)

keys." 4He passed through the hill country of Ephraim and passed through the land of Shalishah, but they did not find them. And they passed through the land of Shaalim, but they were not there. Then he passed through the land of Benjamin, but they did not find them.

5When they came to the land of Zuph, Saul said to the boy who was with him, "Let us turn back, or my father will stop worrying about the donkeys and worry about us." 6But he said to him, "There is a man of God in this town; he is a man held in honor. Whatever he says always comes true. Let us go there now; perhaps he will tell us about the journey on which we have set out." 7Then Saul replied to the boy, "But if we go, what can we bring the man? For the bread in our sacks is gone, and there is no present to bring to the man of God. What have we?" 8The boy answered Saul again, "Here, I have with me a quarter shekel of silver; I will give it to the man of God, to tell us our way." 9(Formerly in Israel, anyone who went to inquire of God would say, "Come, let us go to the seer"; for the one who is now called a prophet was formerly called a seer.) 10Saul said to the boy, "Good; come, let us go." So they went to the town where the man of God was.

11As they went up the hill to the town, they met some girls coming out to draw water, and said to them, "Is the seer here?" 12They answered, "Yes, there he is just ahead of you. Hurry; he has come just now to the town, because the people have a sacrifice today at the shrine. 13As soon as you enter the town, you will find him, before he goes up to the shrine to eat. For the people will not eat until he comes, since he must bless the sacrifice; afterward those eat who are invited. Now go up, for you will meet him immediately." 14So they went up to the town. As they were entering the town, they saw Samuel coming out toward them on his way up to the shrine.

15Now the day before Saul came, the Lord had revealed to Samuel: 16"Tomorrow about this time I will send to you a man from the land of Benjamin, and you shall anoint him to be ruler over my people Israel. He shall save my people from the hand of the Philistines; for I have seen the suffering of*a* my people, because their outcry

a Gk: Heb lacks the suffering of

NIV

of the Philistines. I have looked upon my people, for their cry has reached me."

[17]When Samuel caught sight of Saul, the LORD said to him, "This is the man I spoke to you about; he will govern my people."

[18]Saul approached Samuel in the gateway and asked, "Would you please tell me where the seer's house is?"

[19]"I am the seer," Samuel replied. "Go up ahead of me to the high place, for today you are to eat with me, and in the morning I will let you go and will tell you all that is in your heart. [20]As for the donkeys you lost three days ago, do not worry about them; they have been found. And to whom is all the desire of Israel turned, if not to you and all your father's family?"

[21]Saul answered, "But am I not a Benjamite, from the smallest tribe of Israel, and is not my clan the least of all the clans of the tribe of Benjamin? Why do you say such a thing to me?"

[22]Then Samuel brought Saul and his servant into the hall and seated them at the head of those who were invited—about thirty in number. [23]Samuel said to the cook, "Bring the piece of meat I gave you, the one I told you to lay aside."

[24]So the cook took up the leg with what was on it and set it in front of Saul. Samuel said, "Here is what has been kept for you. Eat, because it was set aside for you for this occasion, from the time I said, 'I have invited guests.'" And Saul dined with Samuel that day.

[25]After they came down from the high place to the town, Samuel talked with Saul on the roof of his house. [26]They rose about daybreak and Samuel called to Saul on the roof, "Get ready, and I will send you on your way." When Saul got ready, he and Samuel went outside together. [27]As they were going down to the edge of the town, Samuel said to Saul, "Tell the servant to go on ahead of us"—and the servant did so—"but you stay here awhile, so that I may give you a message from God."

10 Then Samuel took a flask of oil and poured it on Saul's head and kissed him, saying, "Has not the LORD anointed you leader over his inheritance?[a] [2]When you leave me today, you will

NRSV

has come to me." [17]When Samuel saw Saul, the LORD told him, "Here is the man of whom I spoke to you. He it is who shall rule over my people." [18]Then Saul approached Samuel inside the gate, and said, "Tell me, please, where is the house of the seer?" [19]Samuel answered Saul, "I am the seer; go up before me to the shrine, for today you shall eat with me, and in the morning I will let you go and will tell you all that is on your mind. [20]As for your donkeys that were lost three days ago, give no further thought to them, for they have been found. And on whom is all Israel's desire fixed, if not on you and on all your ancestral house?" [21]Saul answered, "I am only a Benjaminite, from the least of the tribes of Israel, and my family is the humblest of all the families of the tribe of Benjamin. Why then have you spoken to me in this way?"

[22]Then Samuel took Saul and his servant-boy and brought them into the hall, and gave them a place at the head of those who had been invited, of whom there were about thirty. [23]And Samuel said to the cook, "Bring the portion I gave you, the one I asked you to put aside." [24]The cook took up the thigh and what went with it[a] and set them before Saul. Samuel said, "See, what was kept is set before you. Eat; for it is set[b] before you at the appointed time, so that you might eat with the guests."[c]

So Saul ate with Samuel that day. [25]When they came down from the shrine into the town, a bed was spread for Saul[d] on the roof, and he lay down to sleep.[e] [26]Then at the break of dawn[f] Samuel called to Saul upon the roof, "Get up, so that I may send you on your way." Saul got up, and both he and Samuel went out into the street.

[27]As they were going down to the outskirts of the town, Samuel said to Saul, "Tell the boy to go on before us, and when he has passed on, stop here yourself for a while, that I may make known to you the word of God."

10 [1]Samuel took a vial of oil and poured it on his head, and kissed him; he said, "The LORD has anointed you ruler over his people Israel. You shall reign over the people of the LORD and

NIV

meet two men near Rachel's tomb, at Zelzah on the border of Benjamin. They will say to you, 'The donkeys you set out to look for have been found. And now your father has stopped thinking about them and is worried about you. He is asking, "What shall I do about my son?" '

³"Then you will go on from there until you reach the great tree of Tabor. Three men going up to God at Bethel will meet you there. One will be carrying three young goats, another three loaves of bread, and another a skin of wine. ⁴They will greet you and offer you two loaves of bread, which you will accept from them.

⁵"After that you will go to Gibeah of God, where there is a Philistine outpost. As you approach the town, you will meet a procession of prophets coming down from the high place with lyres, tambourines, flutes and harps being played before them, and they will be prophesying. ⁶The Spirit of the LORD will come upon you in power, and you will prophesy with them; and you will be changed into a different person. ⁷Once these signs are fulfilled, do whatever your hand finds to do, for God is with you.

⁸"Go down ahead of me to Gilgal. I will surely come down to you to sacrifice burnt offerings and fellowship offerings,ᵃ but you must wait seven days until I come to you and tell you what you are to do."

⁹As Saul turned to leave Samuel, God changed Saul's heart, and all these signs were fulfilled that day. ¹⁰When they arrived at Gibeah, a procession of prophets met him; the Spirit of God came upon him in power, and he joined in their prophesying. ¹¹When all those who had formerly known him saw him prophesying with the prophets, they asked each other, "What is this that has happened to the son of Kish? Is Saul also among the prophets?"

¹²A man who lived there answered, "And who is their father?" So it became a saying: "Is Saul also among the prophets?" ¹³After Saul stopped prophesying, he went to the high place.

¹⁴Now Saul's uncle asked him and his servant, "Where have you been?"

"Looking for the donkeys," he said. "But when

ᵃ8 Traditionally *peace offerings*

NRSV

you will save them from the hand of their enemies all around. Now this shall be the sign to you that the LORD has anointed you rulerᵃ over his heritage: ²When you depart from me today you will meet two men by Rachel's tomb in the territory of Benjamin at Zelzah; they will say to you, 'The donkeys that you went to seek are found, and now your father has stopped worrying about them and is worrying about you, saying: What shall I do about my son?' ³Then you shall go on from there further and come to the oak of Tabor; three men going up to God at Bethel will meet you there, one carrying three kids, another carrying three loaves of bread, and another carrying a skin of wine. ⁴They will greet you and give you two loaves of bread, which you shall accept from them. ⁵After that you shall come to Gibeath-elohim,ᵇ at the place where the Philistine garrison is; there, as you come to the town, you will meet a band of prophets coming down from the shrine with harp, tambourine, flute, and lyre playing in front of them; they will be in a prophetic frenzy. ⁶Then the spirit of the LORD will possess you, and you will be in a prophetic frenzy along with them and be turned into a different person. ⁷Now when these signs meet you, do whatever you see fit to do, for God is with you. ⁸And you shall go down to Gilgal ahead of me; then I will come down to you to present burnt offerings and offer sacrifices of well-being. Seven days you shall wait, until I come to you and show you what you shall do."

9As he turned away to leave Samuel, God gave him another heart; and all these signs were fulfilled that day. ¹⁰When they were going from thereᶜ to Gibeah,ᵈ a band of prophets met him; and the spirit of God possessed him, and he fell into a prophetic frenzy along with them. ¹¹When all who knew him before saw how he prophesied with the prophets, the people said to one another, "What has come over the son of Kish? Is Saul also among the prophets?" ¹²A man of the place answered, "And who is their father?" Therefore it became a proverb, "Is Saul also among the prophets?" ¹³When his prophetic frenzy had ended, he went home.ᵉ

14Saul's uncle said to him and to the boy,

ᵃ Gk: Heb lacks *over his people Israel. You shall . . . anointed you ruler*   ᵇ Or *the Hill of God*   ᶜ Gk: Heb *they came there*   ᵈ Or *the hill*   ᵉ Cn: Heb *he came to the shrine*

NIV	NRSV
we saw they were not to be found, we went to Samuel." ¹⁵Saul's uncle said, "Tell me what Samuel said to you." ¹⁶Saul replied, "He assured us that the donkeys had been found." But he did not tell his uncle what Samuel had said about the kingship.	"Where did you go?" And he replied, "To seek the donkeys; and when we saw they were not to be found, we went to Samuel." ¹⁵Saul's uncle said, "Tell me what Samuel said to you." ¹⁶Saul said to his uncle, "He told us that the donkeys had been found." But about the matter of the kingship, of which Samuel had spoken, he did not tell him anything.

COMMENTARY

With the opening of chap. 9 there is a sudden shift in scene and subject matter. Chapter 8 ended in ambiguity. There would be a king in Israel. God had ordered Samuel to listen to the people's request. But the matter of kingship is still problematic. God would grant the request, but understood it as a rejection of God's own rule; and Samuel had warned of the oppressive policies of such a king. In chap. 9, these ambiguities are left behind for the moment. The attention of the narrative shifts to the questions of who and how. In three separate episodes, of which this is the first, the answer to who is always Saul. The answer to how is a bit more complex.

In this story, Saul is anointed for his role by the prophet Samuel. Saul is designated by God and brought to Samuel through the circumstances of a search for lost donkeys. In the anointing by God's prophet, Saul is legitimized for his role as ruler (נגיד *nāgîd,* "ruler," leader," not מלך *melek,* "king"; see Commentary below) to deliver Israel from the Philistines (9:16; 10:1), and he receives God's Spirit (10:10). Saul's commissioning is declared by Samuel to be the "word of God" (9:27*b*).

There is no hint of ambiguity about kingship or Saul in this account. There is no reluctance evidenced by Samuel or by God to this authorization of Saul to his role. The motive for this designation of Saul is God's salvation. God has chosen Saul to bring deliverance from the Philistines (a motive absent in chap. 8). There is no indication in this account that God is acting in response to the people's desires. Saul and kingship have their moment in the story without qualification.

The anointing of Saul by the prophet Samuel is bracketed by the story of a young man's search

for his father's lost donkeys. After a brief introduction of Saul's background in vv. 1-2, a tale unfolds of lost donkeys, young men, journeys, and a seer who might help them (vv. 3-13). This story seems totally unrelated to any of the matters that have occupied the attention of 1 Samuel 1–8. Since the work of Gressman, most scholars have agreed that this material is marked by folkloristic elements: indefinite time, an unnamed city, the motif of journeying and searching, and an ideal youth as hero.[70] Saul and his young servant companion search for the lost animals. Their search is futile, and they resolve to consult a man of God at a nearby city. They have run out of bread and discuss how they will pay for his advice. They meet maidens coming to draw water who tell them in some detail of the arrival of a man of God to offer a sacrifice. These verses (vv. 3-13) are rich in detail, leisurely in pace, and seemingly unrelated to matters of significance in the wider story of 1 Samuel.

At v. 14 there is a dramatic shift. The unknown man of God/seer is revealed to be Samuel. The reader knows him, although Saul does not. The pace and mood of the story shift. In a flashback we are told that God had told Samuel of Saul's coming (vv. 15-17). We learn that Saul is God's choice for king, and, in a series of events, Saul is anointed, receives the Spirit of God, and prophesies with a band of prophets. This segment of the story (9:14–10:13) has been shaped by the pattern typical of prophetic call narratives (see Excursus, "The Call Narrative Form in 1 Samuel 9:1–

---

70. For a fuller discussion, see Bruce C. Birch, "The Development of the Tradition of the Anointing of Saul, 1 Sam 9:1–10:16," *JBL* 90 (1971) 57-58.

10:16," 1040-42). Samuel disposes of the matter of the lost donkeys (v. 20). This is no longer the focus. God's purposes, Israel's deliverance, rulers, prophets, God's Spirit—these are the central focus of the story, and they are related to the larger themes of 1 Samuel 1–7. In 10:14-16, Saul returns home, and the focus again becomes the lost donkeys. Saul keeps the "matter of the kingship" a secret (v. 16*b*).

It is possible that the story of the lost donkeys and the story of the anointing by Samuel originated separately, but if so, they have now been artfully combined and interrelated. The episode as it now stands may well have originated from prophetic circles that emphasized the importance of the prophetic role in authorizing Israel's kings. To be legitimate, kings must be anointed by God's prophet and receive God's Spirit. This prophetic perspective on kingship may be behind the arrangement of the ongoing story. In 10:17-27, Saul, God's anointed one, is given public recognition; and in 11:1-15, Saul demonstrates the power of God's Spirit by delivering the people of Jabesh-gilead. We will see a similar pattern in the beginning of David's story in 1 Samuel 16–17.

In 1 Sam 9:1–10:16, each segment of the story is constructed around dialogues with two brief narrative intervals and a stylized introduction.

9:1-4	Introduction of Saul and the search for the donkeys
9:5-10	Saul and his servant companion
9:11-14	Young men and the maidens
9:15-17	God and Samuel
9:18-21	Samuel and Saul—first day
9:22-25	(Narrative of the banquet)
9:26–10:8	Samuel and Saul—second day
10:9-13	(Narrative of Saul's prophesying)
10:14-16	Saul and his uncle

These first two conversations and the final one focus on the lost donkeys. The three conversations in the central portion of the story give us the theological center and the narrative climax of the story. In 9:15-17, we learn that it is God's initiative that is theologically central to these events. In 9:26–10:8, God's initiative is fulfilled and the story reaches its climax in the anointing of Saul as ruler to deliver Israel. Samuel the prophet is the connecting link between God and Saul.

9:1-2. Saul is introduced into the story for the first time by the use of an introductory formula, giving us his genealogy and some basic information about him. The pattern is a bit unusual, since it begins not with Saul but with his father, Kish (see 17:12; Judg 3:15; 1 Kgs 11:26). Saul is from an influential family in the tribe of Benjamin. The phrase "man of wealth" (גבור חיל *gibbôr ḥayil*) can also mean "mighty warrior," and we might take it to mean that Saul's father is a powerful and influential man. Further, we are told that Saul is both more handsome and physically taller than most men. This notice is reminiscent of other specially destined characters in the biblical story (Joseph, Gen 39:6; David, 1 Sam 16:12, 18; 17:42; Absalom, 2 Sam 14:25). This is not a story of humble beginnings or of the ugly duckling. Saul is introduced to us as a young man with good prospects.

9:3-10. Saul is sent by his father to find some strayed donkeys, and he takes a young man (probably a servant) with him. The pace of the story is unhurried, and it lingers over many details, such as the route of the search through territories of uncertain identity (v. 4). After a futile search, Saul wants to turn back out of concern that his father might become more worried about him than about the donkeys (v. 5); but his companion has heard of a man of God in a nearby town and suggests that they ask him about the donkeys (v. 6). Saul worries about what to give for payment, since they are out of bread (v. 7). But the young man finds a quarter shekel of silver (v. 8), and so they go to find the man of God (v. 10). Elements of their conversation will come back to mind later in the story when Samuel tells Saul of signs that he will receive. The first sign would be a man bringing news that the donkeys have been found and that Saul's father is worried about him (10:2), and the second would be a man who will give them bread (10:3-4).

In our first encounter with Saul, he seems young and inexperienced. The servant-companion seems more resourceful than Saul. There is little to make us think that Saul is a man of destiny. Perhaps this is in itself significant. Saul does nothing to appear ambitious or in any way seeking kingship. We are introduced to Saul completely apart from the usual political maneuverings that lead to leadership or high office. At this point, Saul is a passive participant in the story of his own destiny. He is to be chosen, not to choose.

There is a brief parenthetical comment in v. 9. The author of this story felt the need to explain to readers that a man who used to be called a "seer" was the same as what was now known to the readers of the story as a "prophet." Both terms designated one to whom inquiries could be made about matters of concern seeking insight into the future or advice on a course of action. This is a bit confusing, since the term "seer" is not used until v. 11. There the "man of God" is referred to as a "seer." It would seem that all three terms are being used somewhat interchangeably in this chapter. The nameless "man of God" will suddenly be revealed as Samuel in v. 14. The author apparently thought readers would be confused when the prophet Samuel is addressed as "seer" instead of as "prophet."

9:11-14. As Saul and his companion approach the city, they meet young girls coming down from the hill to draw water. They ask the maidens, "Is the seer here?" (v. 11). They receive an effusive answer, detailing the arrival of the seer, his custom to offer sacrifice at the shrine there, and his practice of hosting a banquet for invited guests after the sacrifice (vv. 12-13). After they leave the girls and enter the city, the two young men meet the seer on his way to the shrine, and it is none other than Samuel (v. 14). Saul clearly does not know Samuel (cf. vv. 18-19), but the reader now suspects that something more significant than lost donkeys is afoot.

9:15-17. A flashback informs the reader that behind Saul's seemingly innocent search is a divine initiative. What is taking place is a part of God's plan. A day earlier God had spoken to the prophet Samuel that on the next day God would send to him a man from the tribe of Benjamin. There is no rationale for God's choice. Saul, as we know from our glimpse of him earlier in the chapter, has not sought leadership of the kingdom. God has not picked him out because he has already distinguished himself in leadership in any

way. The choice of Saul is to be an act of sovereign freedom on the part of God. It surely is not what the elders had in mind in their request for a king. Perhaps Samuel thought he would have a voice in the choosing. When Saul comes into view the next day, God speaks again to Samuel, saying, "This is the man" (v. 17). God alone has chosen, bypassing Samuel and the elders and offering no explanation for the choice.

God's intended course of action, however, is made very clear. There is a role for Samuel and for Saul in what God is doing. The verbs and their subjects are straight to the point: "I will send . . . you shall anoint . . . he shall save" (v. 15). God's own motive for this plan of action is also clear, "I have seen." What God had seen was the suffering of Israel at the hand of the Philistines. The outcry of the people had come to the Lord. Three times in the brief speech to Samuel (v. 16) God speaks of Israel as "my people." The language of God's concern is the language of the exodus God, who sees suffering, hears the outcry, and acts to deliver (Exod 2:23-25; 3:7-8). Ironically, in 1 Samuel 1–8 it has been primarily the Philistines who have reminded us of the exodus God (4:8; 6:6; but see also God's reminder in 8:8). Once again this exodus God acts to bring salvation to Israel.

Samuel is to "anoint" Saul to be "ruler" (v. 16 NRSV; NIV, "leader") over Israel. It is significant that the term "king" (מלך *melek*) is not used. Instead, both here and in 10:1, we find the term נגיד (*nāgîd*). The precise meaning of this term has been widely debated. Some have argued that Saul was not initially authorized as king but as some sort of military commander in the face of the Philistine threat. His role only developed toward full kingship as he continued in office, acquired court officers, and hoped to begin a dynastic succession with his son Jonathan. However, both David (25:30; 2 Sam 5:2; 6:21; 7:8) and Solomon (1 Kgs 1:20, 35) are referred to as *nāgîd* in contexts that are related to kingship. Even though the term "king" is not used in the story of Saul's anointing, the final line declares that Saul kept the "matter of the kingship" to himself (10:16). Clearly, the story as it now stands understands Saul's role as royal and not just military. Mettinger has made a convincing case for understanding *nāgîd* as a term for king-designate.[71] This meaning would fit well here, since Saul has been designated as king but has not yet taken office in Israel. The intention in God's command is to start Saul on a path to a royal destiny.

Whatever *nāgîd* came to designate as an office in Israel, we should not overlook an important significance to the title within the literary framework of the story itself. The noun *nāgîd* seems to be derived from the verb נגד (*nāgad*, "to make known"), which appears mainly in its hiphil form הגיד (*higgîd*). This verb appears six times in the story (9:6, 8, 18, 19; 10:15, 16). Literally, *nāgîd* means "the made known one" or "the designated one." The use of the noun and the verb stresses that Saul does not on his own become king. He is "designated" by God. This role for Saul is "made known" by God to Samuel and through Samuel to Saul.

The act of anointing legitimates Saul in this office.[72] There are many references to the anointing of kings in Israel; some are by the people (2 Sam 2:4; 5:3; 2 Kgs 11:12; 23:30) and others by God's prophet (9:16; 10:1; 15:1, 17; 16:12-13; 2 Sam 12:7; 2 Kgs 9:3, 6, 12; 2 Chr 22:7). Both types may well reflect God as the ultimate source of authorization, with people or prophet acting as God's signifying agent in the ritual of anointing. Certainly prophetic circles would stress the necessity of God's prophet in this role for the legitimization of kings. The account of Saul's anointing seems to be from such circles, since it highlights the role of Samuel. As we will see in the discussion of 10:1, an important consequence of anointing in this prophetic tradition may be the receiving of God's Spirit. In any case, kings in Israel came to be known as Yahweh's "anointed one" (משיח *māšîaḥ*). When the hope for God's "anointed one" was projected into the future as an eschatological hope, it became the expectation of God's coming Messiah. In a sense, Saul is Israel's first "messiah"; thus important themes in Israel's story find a beginning.

In v. 17 (see also 10:1), Samuel is told that Saul will "rule" over Israel. This term (עצר *'āṣar*) means literally "to keep in bounds." It may be taken in the sense of "govern" or "administer" and is an activity not limited to kings. It indicates more than a military role for Saul.[73]

It is important to note that for 9:1–10:16, the motivating factor for the establishment of kingship in Israel is the Philistine crisis. There is no hint of a request from the elders or of the situation with Samuel's sons. Kingship and Saul as the king-designate appear in this story as a part of God's saving response to Israel's cry of distress. None of the ambiguity that was noted in connection with kingship in chap. 8 is present in this account.

9:18-21. Saul obviously does not know or recognize Samuel, and he inquires about the seer. After a curt acknowledgment that he is the seer, Samuel gives a more elaborate response that must have amazed Saul (v. 19). In quick order, Saul is ordered up to the shrine, invited to dinner with Samuel, and told he is staying the night. Samuel further says that he will tell Saul everything on his "mind" (לב *lēb*, "heart," often translated "mind," since ancient Israelites understood the heart to be the seat of thought and understanding). Saul undoubtedly thought that the lost donkeys were uppermost in his "mind." Samuel dismisses this concern by informing Saul that the donkeys have been found. Saul is to give no further "thought" (*lēb*) to them (v. 20a). Something new and more significant is about to be placed on the "mind/heart" of Saul. In the end, he will be transformed; God will give him "another heart" (*lēb*, 10:9).

Samuel ends his speech to Saul with an enigmatic question (v. 20b): "On whom is Israel's desire fixed, if not on you and on all your ancestral house?" In this NRSV translation (and the similar one in the NIV), the emphasis seems to be on Saul and his family as the fulfillment of Israel's desires—namely, a leader, a king. It may also be translated, "To whom belong all desirable things in Israel . . . ?" This rendering highlights the wealth and benefits that might flow to Saul

---

71. T. N. D. Mettinger, *King and Messiah: The Civil and Sacral Legitimation of the Israelite Kings,* CB Old Testament Series 8 (Lund: C. W. K. Gleerup, 1976). Mettinger builds on an earlier suggestion by A. Alt, "The Formation of the Israelite State in Palestine," in *Essays on Old Testament History and Religion* (Oxford: Basil Blackwell, 1966) 195.

72. On anointing and its significance, see E. Kutsch, *Salbung als Rechtsakt im Alten Testament und in alten Orient,* BZAW 88 (Berlin: Alfred Topelmann, 1963). For the importance of anointing to the prophetic ideology of kingship, see Rolf Knierim, "The Messianic Concept in the First Book of Samuel," in *Jesus and the Historian,* ed. T. Trotter (Philadelphia: Westminster, 1968) 31.

73. Robert Polzin, *Samuel and the Deuteronomist: A Literary Study of the Deuteronomic History,* Part Two: *1 Samuel* (San Francisco: Harper & Row, 1989) 94, takes this verb to mean "constrain," "hinder," "imprison" and sees it as a divine prediction of the dire consequences of kingship. Given the positive outlook on Saul throughout this account, such negative meanings seem unlikely.

and his family when he rules Israel. In either case, lost donkeys are of little consequence when Saul has these prospects ahead of him.

In v. 21, Saul finally senses that something extraordinary is taking place. He may not fully understand what Samuel is alluding to, but he objects that he is not the right person. He claims that he is from an insignificant tribe and a humble family. In a somewhat bewildered tone he asks why Samuel has spoken to him in this way. Saul's objections sound much like those raised by earlier figures in the biblical story, particularly Moses and Gideon. Such objections are a standard feature of call stories, in which God calls and commissions persons to a task in the divine plan. The standardized pattern of such call narratives has influenced the shape of this story about Saul. Since this pattern stretches over several sections of this episode it is appropriate to briefly consider the call narrative pattern as a whole and its influence on this story.

❖   ❖   ❖   ❖

EXCURSUS: THE CALL NARRATIVE FORM IN 1 SAMUEL 9:1–10:16

Norman Habel has provided the most definitive description of a basic literary structure in prophetic call narratives.[74] He based his work on examination of the calls of Moses, Gideon, and the classical prophets for whom we have a call story. All of the elements Habel discerned in such call narratives are present in the Saul story (1 Sam 9:1–10:16). They occur in a somewhat altered order, modified to account for the presence of the prophet Samuel as a third-party mediator of God's call to Saul. This role of Samuel is one of the special interests and emphases of this story and is consistent with the view that the story was shaped in prophetic circles.

The elements of this formal structure in the Samuel/Saul account are: (1) divine confrontation, (2) introductory word, (3) objection, (4) commission, (5) sign, and (6) reassurance.

THE DIVINE CONFRONTATION, 9:15

It is God who takes the initiative. In most call stories, God confronts directly the one to be commissioned, but here God contacts Samuel, God's prophet. The situation is similar to that of the prophet Elijah (1 Kgs 19:15-16), when the prophet is commanded to anoint Elisha as his successor (interestingly, also to anoint Jehu as king of Israel). The direct nature of the divine encounter is emphasized by the Hebrew idiom for direct revelation, "the Lord had uncovered Samuel's ear" (9:15 NRSV; NIV, "revealed").

THE INTRODUCTORY WORD, 9:16-17

This element in the structure spells out the basis for the commission to come later. God is still speaking to Samuel, and the purpose of the call is simple and clear: It is to raise up a deliverer for Israel against the Philistines. The urgency is underlined by the statement that God has seen the affliction and heard the outcry of "my people." The language is reminiscent of the call of Moses (Exod 3:7-9), and the need for a deliverer against an enemy is like the situation in Gideon's call (Judg 6:11-24).

This revelatory word to Samuel anticipates the actual commissioning of Saul, which comes later.

74. Norman Habel, "The Form and Significance of the Call Narratives," *ZAW* 77 (1965) 297-323. Wolfgang Richter, *Die sogenannten vorprophetischen Berufungsberichte. Eine literaturwissenschaftliche Studie zu 1 Sam 9:1-10, 16; Ex 3f.; und Ri 6:11b-17,* FRLANT 101 (Göttingen: Vandenhoeck und Ruprecht, 1970), sees the calls of Moses, Gideon, and Saul following a different format from that described by Habel. In my opinion, what Richter describes are variants of Habel's pattern adapted to different stories and settings, and not a separate formal type. See my fuller, more technical discussion of the call pattern for Saul in Bruce C. Birch, "The Development of the Tradition of the Anointing of Saul, 1 Sam 9:1–10:16," *JBL* 90 (1971) 60-68.

The language of 9:16-17 is substantially repeated in 10:1. In God's eyes, Saul has already been commissioned, even though Samuel has yet to communicate this fact to Saul. The Hebrew word שלח (šālaḥ, "send") is a key word in most prophetic call narratives, but in this Samuel/Saul story it appears in the word to Samuel (9:16) and not in the actual commissioning (10:1). In a sense, Saul is already "sent" by God before he ever encounters Samuel and is told of this "sending."

THE OBJECTION, 9:21

The recipient of God's call now objects that he is unworthy or inadequate of such a calling. Ordinarily this element would come after the commissioning. Here Saul receives only a foreshadowing of the commission in Samuel's statement that he and his family have been singled out for a distinctive role in Israel (v. 20b). Of course, the reader knows the full commission, since it was revealed to Samuel the day before. The content of Saul's objection is much like Gideon's. However, since it comes before the full statement of the task before him, Saul's objection, unlike Gideon's, is not that he is unequal to the task (Judg 6:15), but that he is unworthy of the choice itself.

THE COMMISSION, 10:1

The commissioning itself is prefaced by Samuel's statement that this is the "word of God" (9:27; cf. NIV, weakly, "message from God"), emphasizing the role of the prophet as a mediator of God's call in this story. The commission is virtually identical to God's words given to Samuel on the day before, except that the Philistines are not specifically named. Saul is to be a deliverer for Israel from all its "enemies." The commission is similar to that of Gideon (Judg 6:14), beginning with a rhetorical question (see NIV; the NRSV makes it a statement) that emphasizes divine initiative and ends in a commission to be a deliverer from military threat. Unlike Gideon, Saul's commission is accompanied by an act—Samuel's anointing of Saul. This is a new element, not typically present in call narratives, because this story deals with a king. Saul is to be God's anointed one, as נגיד (nāgîd), "leader," or as מלך (melek), "king." The Lord is the one who anoints Saul, a claim made twice in this verse (reading the longer version of the Greek).

THE SIGN, 10:1b, 5-7a, 9-10

In most call narratives, the sign comes after the reassurance. It confirms the presence of God with the one called. Here Samuel promises a "sign" already at the end of Samuel's commissioning and anointing (10:1b) and speaks of "signs" just prior to the words of reassurance given to Saul in v. 7. Although Samuel predicts these "signs" before the reassurance, they are fulfilled in vv. 9-10.

There has been considerable debate over the nature of this sign. Verse 1b speaks of a "sign" in the singular, but vv. 7 and 9 refer to "signs." Samuel's speech to Saul in vv. 2-6 speaks of three events that will befall Saul, but vv. 10-11 narrate the fulfillment of only one of these events. These discrepancies cannot be resolved easily. As it now stands, the story seems to regard the episode of Saul's encounter with a band of prophets and his receiving of God's Spirit with them as the most important confirming event—the sign of God's presence with Saul. The other two events predicted by Samuel have to do with the lost donkeys portion of the story, and this element of the story has given way to the more important call of Saul to be God's deliverer. Their fulfillment is not the focus of the story's interest.

THE REASSURANCE, 10:7*b*

The reassurance formula "for God will be with you" is an important part of call stories. Usually it occurs in the first person as God speaks directly to the one called, but here it is in the third person as God's call is mediated to Saul through the prophet Samuel.

All of the elements of Habel's description of the typical call narrative are here, although somewhat altered by the mediating presence of Samuel as God's prophet. The call narrative and the role of Samuel emphasize the importance of the prophets as God's agents in authorizing and legitimizing kings in Israel.

❖   ❖   ❖   ❖

9:22-25. Saul and his servant companion are brought to a banquet hall, where a sumptuous meal has been prepared, and Saul is treated as the honored guest. There are thirty guests, and Saul is given a special portion of the meat. Some have wished to see symbolic significance in these particulars. Others have seen the banquet itself as foreshadowing a coronation feast. However, such suggestions are speculative. We can say with certainty only that Saul, as an inexperienced young man just arrived in the city, dined as an honored guest with the great prophet Samuel on that day (v. 24*b*). Saul is then taken to spend the night, presumably at Samuel's house, to end a remarkable day. But even more remarkable events are to come on the next day.

9:26–10:13. The next morning Samuel takes Saul to the edge of the town and sends his servant on ahead. Then Samuel, announcing this moment as an occasion to "make known" the "word of God" (9:27*b*), anoints Saul and commissions him as *nāgîd* to deliver Israel from its enemies (10:1; most of this verse is missing in the Hebrew text, but the longer version is present in the Septuagint and the Vulgate; the NRSV and most recent translations have adopted this longer reading. The NIV includes it in a footnote). The nature of anointing and the role of *nāgîd* have already been discussed in connection with 9:15-17. The anointing and the commissioning of Saul (10:1) repeat the language of God's instructions to Samuel earlier, except that specific mention of the Philistines is replaced by a more general reference to "enemies" of Israel. This is the climactic moment of the story. Saul, a young man in search of lost donkeys, has instead been designated to rule a kingdom. The reader is left to marvel at the boldness of God's initiative. This is not likely the candidate

the elders would have chosen. Even Samuel is bluntly told, "Here is the man!" (9:17). Whatever happens in subsequent episodes to win approval for Saul's kingship among the people, we are clear that in the beginning Saul was God's man.

Samuel promises a sign (10:1*b*), and then speaks of three events that will take place after Saul leaves him. First, two men will meet him to say that the donkeys have been found and that his father is worried about him. Saul had earlier suggested that his father would be worried (9:5), and Samuel had told him the donkeys were found (9:20). This report to Saul would seem only to confirm what he already knows and resolve the lost donkeys theme in the story. Second, Saul will encounter three men who will give him bread. This seems to resolve the lament of Saul in 9:7 that they were out of bread.

The third event is most important in the story. Saul will meet a band of prophets coming down from a shrine, playing instruments. They will be caught up in a prophetic ecstasy, and Saul will be seized by the "spirit of the Lord" and join them in their charismatic prophesying. This is the only one of the three predicted events for which the fulfillment is narrated. According to 10:10, Saul does meet this band of prophets, becomes possessed of God's Spirit, and prophesies with them.

There is an important connection between anointing and the receiving of God's Spirit in 1 Samuel.[75] David also receives God's Spirit after being anointed by the prophet Samuel (16:13). Later, when the Spirit of God empowers Saul to deliver the people of Jabesh-gilead, it is a public demonstration of the power of the Spirit Saul has

---

75. See Rolf Knierim, "The Messianic Concept in the First Book of Samuel," in *Jesus and the Historian*, ed. T. Trotter (Philadelphia: Westminster, 1968).

already received in his anointing. God's anointed kings are the recipients of God's Spirit, and for Saul both the anointing and the Spirit are mediated to him by the prophets.

Through the events of anointing and possession of God's Spirit, Saul is transformed. Twice in this segment of the story there are indications of the radical nature of this transformation. In v. 6*b*, Samuel says that when the Spirit comes upon him Saul will "be turned into a different person," and in v. 9*a* the text tells us that as Saul left Samuel "God gave him another heart." There is a tension of timing here. Was Saul a changed man before or after meeting the prophets and receiving the Spirit? It matters little. Through these events Saul is changed from the naive young man we saw at the beginning of the story. Then his "heart/mind" (לב *lēb*) was only on donkeys (see Commentary on 9:19-20), but now Saul has a new "heart" (*lēb*, 10:9). Saul's story begins with another witness to a common biblical theme: the power of God to choose and use persons who seem unlikely agents of God's purposes when measured in human terms (Jacob, Moses, Gideon, Ruth, David, Amos, a peasant woman from Nazareth named Mary). God sees with a different eye. Through God's Spirit, Saul becomes a "different man."

Just how "different" Saul is may be in part measured by the response of witnesses to Saul's prophesying (10:11-13). People who know him as the son of Kish are amazed, and this amazement gives rise to a popular saying, "Is Saul also among the prophets?" Another story of how this saying arose appears in 19:18-24. Gunn has pointed out that the saying appears to have an affirming context in 1 Samuel 10 but a disapproving context in chap. 19. In the first passage, Saul is recognized to have the status of a prophet, while in the second it seems to confirm him as a raving madman.[76] Of course, one comes before Saul's rejection and the other after. In the context of 1 Samuel 10, the people's amazement becomes a confirmation that Saul is indeed a different person. He is Spirit-filled, therefore, God empowered. In the wake of chap. 8, we have to wonder if this is what the elders had in mind. This is not a king who will come to the throne through the usual processes of politics and power. If there is to be

76. David M. Gunn, *The Fate of King Saul*, JSOTSup 14 (Sheffield: JSOT, 1980) 63.

a king in Israel, this story seems to suggest that he will be chosen on God's terms. The reign of such a king, then, will also be judged on God's terms. This idea has ramifications for the fate of Saul as the story continues.

In 10:7 Saul is authorized to "do whatever you see fit to do." This would seem to be the permission to get about the business for which he has been commissioned: to bring deliverance. Many would see this actualized in chap. 11 when Saul, through the power of God's Spirit, delivers the people of Jabesh-gilead. But immediately in 10:8 Samuel commands Saul to go to Gilgal and wait for him to come and offer sacrifices. The wait is to last seven days, and Samuel will "show you what you shall do." It is as if Saul is authorized in 10:7, and in 10:8 Samuel asserts that he is still in charge. This verse clearly is the background to the first conflict between Samuel and Saul (13:1-15), which leads to Saul's rejection by Samuel. It reminds us that however positive the picture of Saul and kingship is in 9:1–10:16, there is a deep ambiguity in the wider tradition about kingship in general and Saul in particular. Israel was not of one mind as it faced these transforming changes from old order to new.

10:14-16. At the end of 10:13 we are told simply that Saul went home. Suddenly we are back in the lost donkey story. Saul's uncle questions him and learns that the two men went to Samuel for help in finding the donkeys (v. 14). Perhaps finding this encounter with the eminent Samuel surprising, the uncle asks what Samuel said (v. 15). All Saul reports is that Samuel told him that the donkeys had been found. The episode concludes with the notice that Saul intentionally kept the "matter of the kingship" a secret (v. 16). This gives the reader a way of understanding why subsequent episodes on Saul's accession to the kingship do not seem to know of this anointing by Samuel. But this final notice makes clear that, as the text now stands, Saul's anointing was a "matter of the kingship," and *nāgîd* as used here (9:16; 10:1) is not understood in some narrow meaning of military leadership alone. This story is intended as the first step by Saul to the throne. The kingdom remains a secret for the moment, but the reader knows that God has acted. In spite of ambiguous beginnings (chap. 8), if there will be a king in Israel, it will be God's king.

REFLECTIONS

1. The most obvious point to be drawn from 1 Sam 9:1–10:16 is that God uses unexpected persons and works through surprising circumstances. This is, of course, a common biblical theme (Joseph, Moses, Gideon, Ruth, Esther, Mary, Paul); and it is seen again in 1 Samuel when David is chosen as the man after God's own heart, even though he is the eighth son and but a boy (1 Sam 16:1-13). That this theme is so common in the Bible should not lead us to the conclusion that it is trite, but that it is centrally important. Over and again the biblical story tells us that men and women who become crucial to God's purposes would have been overlooked if measured only by the usual human standards. God looked beyond these standards and saw new possibilities. God saw in Saul the "different person" (10:6) and the "other heart" (10:9) that lay within this inexperienced young man. It would seem that Saul's story (and the many other stories of unlikely persons called by God) might urge the church to reconsider the standards of discernment that usually prevail in identifying and nurturing leadership in the church. It is often easier to tick off lists of qualifications than to discern the capacity to be transformed by God's Spirit and to become one of those who manifest the heart received from God.

Saul is not just a surprising choice, but the circumstances of his anointing are unlikely as well. It is commonplace to refer to this story as one in which Saul went looking for lost donkeys but found a kingdom. There is a word here both for those who experience God's call (like Saul) and for those who might be God's agents in mediating God's call (like Samuel). The person God needs and the occasion for claiming that person to God's purposes may present themselves in the most ordinary and unexpected circumstances. The church is prone to develop "leadership training events" or "Christian vocation conferences" and the like in its formal efforts to develop and nurture leaders for the faith community. These have their place, but Saul's story suggests that a part of our energies must be devoted to listening for God's voice to say, "Here is the one." This will not always come through our formal programs.

We must be careful not to romanticize this theme. Saul was not a person of no real gifts miraculously transformed into a king. We cannot expect a sense of God's calling and authorization to give us gifts and talents we never had before. We can, however, expect that through the power of God's Spirit we can become persons that we never were before, and the gifts we possess can be put to new purpose and given new focus by God's giving of "another heart" (10:9): " 'Another heart' (10:9) suggests a total revisioning of the world in a way that shatters old perceptions, invites new commitments, and requires new actions."[77] Saul has been given new possibilities for his life, and the text suggests such new possibilities for Israel as well. To read this text in the church is to expect transformation and change if we are open to God's calling. We cannot settle for business as usual. We cannot settle for more efficient leadership. We cannot settle for success defined as safety and stability. What those who saw Saul seized by the Spirit observed was unsettling and disturbing to them. "There is a new creation: everything old has passed away; see, everything has become new!" (2 Cor 5:17 NRSV).

2. The real point of this story of Saul's calling (and of our own) focuses on the one who calls. This is a story of *God's initiative* and *God's Spirit* as the source of newness. The newness of God for Saul and for Israel does not come from calculating reason or careful political maneuvering. This was surely what the elders wanted and expected (chap. 8). They wanted a general, an administrator, and a royal symbol of stability and safety. Instead they got Saul, seized by the power of the Spirit in ways that amazed, perhaps embarrassed, those who knew him (10:11-12). He did not look like a leader who could be managed in the people's interests. The Spirit often appears unmanageable in the world's terms. When the Spirit powerfully filled

---

77. Walter Brueggemann, *First and Second Samuel,* Interpretation (Louisville: John Knox, 1990) 77.

those present at Pentecost, onlookers sneered that they were drunk (Acts 2:13), even as Hannah had been accused of drunkenness by Eli when she was merely occupied with God (1:14).

For the people of God, whether Israel or the church, genuine newness comes first from *God's initiative.* The people may demand, as did the elders of Israel (chap. 8), but God will choose, as made evident in Saul ("Here is the man," 9:17). In the church, most denominations or traditions have elaborate structures and mechanisms for making choices of leadership or program. It is important that we constantly and prayerfully examine these to ensure that they are accountable to the choosing of God. The church's processes should always be, in part, a discernment of what God has chosen as the path to newness in the church's life and mission.

For the people of God, genuine newness is not only initiated by God but also empowered and made possible by *God's Spirit.* In God's Spirit, Saul was made new, and it took surprising, amazing form as he prophesied with the prophets. Openness to God's Spirit in the community of faith will lead us down unexpected paths. In its institutional forms, the church is like other human institutions. It tends to prefer patterns that can be managed and controlled. If kept oriented to faithful purposes, this can even be good stewardship. But the power of God's Spirit, constantly working to transform the church and the world, means that a central element of our life will be unmanageable and uncontrollable. God's Spirit seizes, surprises, upsets, transforms, and reorients. Without openness to this empowerment of the Spirit, the church cannot be made new.

The pattern of God's choosing and the Spirit of God empowering is one with considerable resonance in the biblical tradition. In 1 Sam 9:1–10:16, Saul is chosen by God, is anointed by the prophet Samuel on God's command, and receives God's Spirit. The result is to give Israel its first king. In 1 Sam 16:1-13, David is singled out as God's choice, is anointed by Samuel, and receives God's Spirit. The result is not only a king for Israel, but also a dynasty (the house of David) descended from the man "after God's own heart." In Luke 3:21-22//Matt 3:13-17//Mark 1:9-11, Jesus is baptized (anointed) by John, the Spirit descends upon Jesus, and God's voice claims him as "beloved Son" (the language of God's affirmation is taken from Ps 2:7, a royal psalm, and Isa 42:1). The result is the beginning of the career of Jesus as Messiah, the anointed one. In Acts 2 the apostles and those assembled with them are anointed by tongues of flame, and the Spirit descends upon them. The result is the Pentecost birth of the church. This places us as the church today in the line of the pattern that began with Saul. Are we still the God-chosen, Spirit-filled church? Saul is eventually rejected and loses the Spirit. Could the church suffer the same fate? Do we continue to live out the promise of newness that the Spirit brings, or have we like Saul gotten diverted by our own self-interest? We may continue on in Saul's story with more than a little interest in his fate.

1 Samuel 10:17-27a, Saul Among the Baggage

NIV	NRSV
[17]Samuel summoned the people of Israel to the LORD at Mizpah [18]and said to them, "This is what the LORD, the God of Israel, says: 'I brought Israel up out of Egypt, and I delivered you from the power of Egypt and all the kingdoms that oppressed you.' [19]But you have now rejected your God, who saves you out of all your calamities and distresses. And you have said, 'No, set a king over us.' So now present yourselves before the LORD by your tribes and clans."	17Samuel summoned the people to the LORD at Mizpah [18]and said to them,[a] "Thus says the LORD, the God of Israel, 'I brought up Israel out of Egypt, and I rescued you from the hand of the Egyptians and from the hand of all the kingdoms that were oppressing you.' [19]But today you have rejected your God, who saves you from all your calamities and your distresses; and you have said, 'No! but set a king over us.' Now therefore
	[a] Heb *to the people of Israel*

NIV

²⁰When Samuel brought all the tribes of Israel near, the tribe of Benjamin was chosen. ²¹Then he brought forward the tribe of Benjamin, clan by clan, and Matri's clan was chosen. Finally Saul son of Kish was chosen. But when they looked for him, he was not to be found. ²²So they inquired further of the LORD, "Has the man come here yet?"

And the LORD said, "Yes, he has hidden himself among the baggage."

²³They ran and brought him out, and as he stood among the people he was a head taller than any of the others. ²⁴Samuel said to all the people, "Do you see the man the LORD has chosen? There is no one like him among all the people."

Then the people shouted, "Long live the king!"

²⁵Samuel explained to the people the regulations of the kingship. He wrote them down on a scroll and deposited it before the LORD. Then Samuel dismissed the people, each to his own home.

²⁶Saul also went to his home in Gibeah, accompanied by valiant men whose hearts God had touched. ²⁷But some troublemakers said, "How can this fellow save us?"

NRSV

present yourselves before the LORD by your tribes and by your clans."

20Then Samuel brought all the tribes of Israel near, and the tribe of Benjamin was taken by lot. ²¹He brought the tribe of Benjamin near by its families, and the family of the Matrites was taken by lot. Finally he brought the family of the Matrites near man by man,ᵃ and Saul the son of Kish was taken by lot. But when they sought him, he could not be found. ²²So they inquired again of the LORD, "Did the man come here?"ᵇ and the LORD said, "See, he has hidden himself among the baggage." ²³Then they ran and brought him from there. When he took his stand among the people, he was head and shoulders taller than any of them. ²⁴Samuel said to all the people, "Do you see the one whom the LORD has chosen? There is no one like him among all the people." And all the people shouted, "Long live the king!"

25Samuel told the people the rights and duties of the kingship; and he wrote them in a book and laid it up before the LORD. Then Samuel sent all the people back to their homes. ²⁶Saul also went to his home at Gibeah, and with him went warriors whose hearts God had touched. ²⁷But some worthless fellows said, "How can this man save us?"

ᵃ Gk: Heb lacks *Finally . . . man by man*   ᵇ Gk: Heb *Is there yet a man to come here?*

COMMENTARY

The scene shifts to an assembly of Israel, called by Samuel, at Mizpah. The transition is not smooth. No passage of time is noted, but the Saul who is chosen by lot and acclaimed king is not the boy we just left in the previous episode. Samuel, who had anointed Saul in 10:1, does not seem to know him now. This may well have been an independent story of how Saul became king. In its present position, following the story of Saul's anointing by Samuel, this episode now functions as the public acclamation of Saul's designation as king, which was kept secret until this moment (v. 16*b*). Here the people become involved in acknowledging God's choice for king (v. 24).

Samuel's speech at the beginning of the Mizpah assembly (vv. 18-19) recalls the negative evalu-

ation given of kingship in chap. 8. Some have claimed this speech to be the work of the deuteronomistic historian, but the text includes no special Dtr vocabulary; it is more appropriately understood as a prophetic judgment speech (see Commentary on 10:18-19). The later portion of this episode at Mizpah involves God in directly selecting Saul and proclaims Saul as God's chosen one. Thus the Mizpah story seems to reflect the deep ambiguity in Israel over kingship. In fact, the story ends with references to supporters and detractors of Saul (vv. 26-27*a*). The public beginnings of kingship in Israel were unsettled and disturbing. How can the people's rejection of God still result in Saul as God's chosen one?

10:17-19. We have already encountered

Mizpah as the scene of the penitential ceremony Samuel was conducting when the Philistines attacked (7:7-11). On that occasion, through the mediation of Samuel, a great victory was won. Chapter 7 seemed to show that kingship was unnecessary to deal with the Philistine threat. To assemble Israel at Mizpah for kingmaking may have been intended to recall that victory and to suggest that this activity was unneeded.

Certainly Samuel's opening speech to this assembly set a negative tone for the proceedings. The pattern of this speech is typical of prophetic judgment speeches against the nation,[78] and it underlines Samuel's prophetic role. His speech opens with a long form of the prophetic *messenger formula* ("Thus says the LORD, the God of Israel," v. 18a). The words that follow are in the first person, as if God were speaking directly through Samuel as God's prophetic messenger. God's speech to Israel begins with a *recitation of saving acts.* God recalls the exodus deliverance out of bondage in Egypt and also mentions deliverance from "all the kingdoms that were oppressing you" (v. 18b). This phrase may refer to those who opposed Israel's settlement in the land or to threats from enemies during the time of the judges. What is significant is that these enemies are described as "kingdoms." It was Israel's enemies who had kings, and they were overcome by God's power acting through and for Israel without benefit of a king! This opening to God's speech through Samuel reminds Israel that they have been the recipients of God's salvation.

By contrast, the *accusation* in v. 19a charges that Israel had "rejected your God who saves you from all your calamities and your distresses." Israel had done this by asking for a king. This charge is emphasized by characterizing Israel's response to the Lord as an emphatic "No!" This accusation recalls the assembly at Ramah in chap. 8 and the people's demand to Samuel for a king. Israel's sin is its rejection of God. The verb "reject" (מאס *mā'as*) is common in prophetic judgment speeches. This is the same charge against Israel as in 8:7, but there God added the accusation that Israel worshiped foreign gods (8:8). This

motif is more typical of the deuteronomistic historian but is missing in 10:18-19.[79]

The *announcement of judgment,* often introduced by the words "Now, therefore . . ." (as in v. 19b), usually follows the accusation in a prophetic judgment speech. What we expect is God's judgment as a response to the people's rejection of the God who saved them. What we find instead is a bland summons for the people to present themselves by tribes and clans. That this is "before the LORD" indicates some cultic ceremony. What follows in vv. 20-24 is the account of God's choosing of Saul as king. As we will see, God is active in this process, and Samuel proclaims Saul as "the one whom the LORD has chosen" (v. 24). The divine will asserts itself, not in judgment, but in claiming Israel's king as the Lord's king. The story suggests that time will tell whether Saul in particular or kingship in general is a judgment. But it will not be because God has withdrawn from Israel in this kingmaking moment.

10:20-24. The actual drama of Saul's selection is played out in two acts. First, there is a lot-casting ceremony (vv. 20-21). Then there is the search for Saul among the baggage and his acclamation by Samuel and the people (vv. 22-24).

Assembled before the Lord, Israel is "brought near" by tribe, and the tribe of Benjamin is "taken." The families of Benjamin are "brought near," and the family of Matri is "taken." The men of Matri are "brought near" man by man, and Saul, the son of Kish, is "taken." The process is very similar to the lot-casting described in Josh 7:14-18, where lots were cast to identify Achan as the violator of the holy ban. Lots were also cast to indicate Jonathan as the vow breaker in 14:40-42, although the process there probably involved the Urim and Thummim and the choice between two options until a final decision is made. Both of these parallels are stories for the designation of an offender against God and Israel, which may suggest that the use of lots was an intentional continuation of the negative tone toward kingship in v. 19; still, positive statements

78. Claus Westermann, *Basic Forms of Prophetic Speech* (Philadelphia: Westminster, 1967) 98-101, 182-83.

79. Those who argue that 10:17-27a is deuteronomistic often compare 10:18-19 to Judg 6:7-10 and 1 Sam 8:7-8, but the Dtr influence in those passages is clearest in the theme of the worship of foreign gods, which is absent in 10:17-27a. For fuller discussion see Bruce C. Birch, *The Rise of the Israelite Monarchy: The Growth and Development of I Samuel 7–15,* SBLDS 27 (Missoula, Mont.: Scholars Press, 1976) 47-50; and P. Kyle McCarter, *I Samuel,* AB 8 (Garden City, N.Y.: Doubleday, 1980) 195.

on Saul as God's chosen one in v. 24 make this claim doubtful.

The final phrase of v. 21 says that when Saul was sought, he could not be found. This is problematic, since the method described for casting lots requires the physical presence of tribes, families, and individuals. They are "brought near," and one is then "taken" (i.e., designated). In v. 21, the people inquire of God (the Hebrew word is שָׁאַל [šā'al], from which the name "Saul" is derived; thus they "sauled" for Saul). According to the Hebrew text, the people question God: "Is there a man yet to come here?" (v. 22). This query seems to imply that the lot-casting was unsuccessful and that the people turn to the Lord for further help. Both the NRSV and the NIV adopt a Septuagint reading that merely indicates that Saul cannot be found. This leaves the mystery of how he could have been designated while hidden. Some scholars believe that two accounts, one of lot casting and one of Saul's being pointed out directly by God among the baggage, have been combined. As it stands, we have to imagine Saul designated by lot and then somehow running to hide before he is really noticed.

In any case, God becomes very active in designating Saul from v. 22 onward. The people "inquire" of the Lord; the Lord points Saul out, hiding in the baggage (v. 22); and Saul is proclaimed by Samuel as the one "chosen by the LORD" (v. 24a). There is a sense of excitement and affirmation regarding Saul in this portion of the story. When Saul stood, he was "head and shoulders taller than any of them" (v. 23; cf. 9:2), a physical sign that Saul was, indeed, the divine choice. Samuel, normally dour, seems to be enthusiastic when he says, "There is no one like him among all the people." The people shout, "Long live the king!" (v. 24b; a cry associated elsewhere with accession to the throne, 2 Sam 16:16; 1 Kgs 1:25; 2 Kgs 11:12).

Apart from Samuel's opening speech in vv. 18-19, this account is very positive, even joyous, over the selection of Saul. Saul is God's chosen and is now acclaimed by Samuel and the people. The people had rejected God (v. 19), but God has chosen Saul (v. 24). The people may have sinned, but God refuses to withdraw from their future.

10:25-27. Samuel next recites to the people the מִשְׁפַּט הַמְּלֻכָה (mišpaṭ hammĕlukâ), some set of regu-

lations to govern the rule of the king (NRSV, "rights and duties of the kingship"; NIV, "regulations of the kingship"). Samuel records them in a book and deposits it before the Lord—i.e., in a sanctuary (v. 25). This immediately brings to mind the law of the king in Deut 17:14-20, which defines the obligations of the king and requires him to make a copy of "this law" (perhaps meaning all of Deuteronomy). In any case, v. 25 seems to indicate some written, legal document to hold the king accountable before God.

Is this *mišpaṭ hammĕlukâ* to be identified with the מִשְׁפַּט הַמֶּלֶךְ (mišpaṭ hammelek), which Samuel makes known to the people in 8:9? Translated as "ways of the king" (NRSV), 8:9 introduces Samuel's negative speech about the oppressive practices of kings as a warning to the people. The two references (8:9; 10:25) are most often taken as unrelated. Yet, the similarity in terminology is striking. In Samuel's speech (chap. 8), he could well have drawn from a document on the practices of kings but for his purposes highlighted only the negative burdens that royal privilege would impose on the people. The NRSV rendering of 10:25 as "rights and duties of the kingship" emphasizes the usual expectation that the Hebrew word מִשְׁפָּט (mišpāṭ, "justice") would include responsibilities as well as privileges attached to kingship.

According to the final phrase of v. 25, Samuel sends everyone home, including Saul, who goes back to Gibeah (v. 26a). This seems odd. It would seem that Saul should now begin the business of being king. It may be that his return home is necessary to prepare for chap. 11, where Saul is summoned from his fields to rescue Jabesh-gilead and is again proclaimed king. The historian is combining and harmonizing several stories detailing Saul's accession to kingship.

Verses 26b-27 include an especially interesting note indicating Israel's divided mind over kingship. Even after the acclamation at Mizpah, there were both supporters and opponents of Saul's kingship. Saul was accompanied to his home by supporters described as "warriors" (NRSV) or "valiant men" (NIV). The word so translated is חַיִל (ḥayil), which can indicate strength or prowess in battle, but can also signify wealth and influence. Since economic wealth and political influence were often accompanied and protected by military power in Israel's world, it is easy to see how this word includes all these nuances. We may have here an indication that the support for kingship in general and Saul in particular came from those with influence and wealth in Israel. The elders who approached Samuel asking for a king in chap. 8 would also seem to possess power and privilege. According to v. 26, God had touched the hearts of these men. Saul's support from the influential and powerful was surely essential if he was to have a chance at success, and God's hand is involved even in this garnering of support.

Yet kingship comes to Saul and to Israel as an ambiguous thing. There are detractors, described in v. 27a as בליעל (bĕliyyaʿal; NRSV, "worthless fellows"; NIV, "troublemakers"). These renegades and malcontents sneer, "How can this man save us?" They despise Saul and give him no gifts (which may have symbolized fealty to the new king). But Saul holds his peace. This notice is surely related to 11:12-13. Following Saul's victory at Jabesh-gilead, his supporters want to put his detractors to death. Saul had been the source of "saving" in Israel, and he refuses to allow such bloodshed. (This incident will be discussed further in the Commentary on chap. 11.)

The word bĕliyyaʿal was used in 2:12 to describe the unscrupulous sons of Eli. It is clear that this word usually indicated the most undesirable people in Israel. Yet we should remember that Eli mistook Hannah for bĕliyyaʿal in 1:14-16. Later,

when David gathers men around him in the wilderness, his support comes from the discontented and outcasts of Israel (22:1-3). In the story of 1 Samuel, true power comes from God, and its form in the life of Israel does not always follow the usual patterns of human power and privilege. The elders may demand a king, but God will choose an inexperienced boy. The men of power may collect around the newly acclaimed Saul, but the "worthless ones" may have the final word as they later gather around a fugitive David.

Indeed, the worthless ones may voice the crucial question at this point in the story: Can Saul save? In the unfolding drama of 1 Samuel, there are both immediate and long-term answers to this question. In the very next episode of the story (chap. 11), Saul does save the city and the people of Jabesh-gilead. But in the longer term, God rejects Saul, who commits terrifying and unbalanced deeds. Can Saul save? Perhaps God working through Saul could save. The deliverance of Jabesh-gilead was made possible by the possession of God's mighty Spirit (11:6). His rejection will come when he ignores the command of God through God's prophet (chaps. 13 and 15), and his demented behavior will come after God's Spirit leaves him (16:14). The story of 1 Samuel may be a story of the source of true saving. Saul alone cannot save. The worthless ones raised a more important question than they knew.

REFLECTIONS

First Samuel 10:17-27a has been a neglected episode among the stories of the rise of kingship in Israel. At best it is considered curious that the chosen king should be hiding among the baggage. Yet, themes are touched on in this brief episode that are among the most central aspects of the biblical message.

1. This passage begins with God's word through Samuel that in spite of God's past deliverance Israel has rejected "your God who saves you" by desiring a king (10:18-19). Yet, a short time later it is God who reveals Saul hiding among the baggage (10:22), and Samuel declares him "the one whom the LORD has chosen" (10:24). This has struck many commentators as inconsistent or at least odd. How could a passage that begins with God's rejection of the people because of their desire for a king end in the designation of Saul as God's chosen king? Many have resorted to theories of divergent accounts unskillfully wed in 10:17-27a, one negative to kingship, another positive.

It would seem that those who find this pattern strange have forgotten how frequently in the biblical story God responds to human sin with grace. Sin is judged and called to account, but it is not God's final word. In this passage, Samuel's speech is a prophetic judgment of the people in direct and unvarnished terms. But God's final action is to redeem even the kingship through the grace of divine election. The king will be *God's* chosen one, not the people's. One is reminded of God's speech in Hosea's well-known oracle:

When Israel was a child, I loved him,
   and out of Egypt I call my son.
The more I called them,
   the more they went from me . . .
   My heart recoils within me;
   my compassion grows warm and tender.
I will not execute my fierce anger . . .
I will return them to their homes, says the LORD.
(Hos 11:1-2*a,* 8*b*-9*a,* 11*b* NRSV)

Time and again in the biblical story, God's saving occurs in spite of human sin. God turns potential disasters as a result of human sin into opportunities for divine grace. Joseph says to his reconciled brothers, "Even though you intended to do harm to me, God intended it for good" (Gen 50:20 NRSV). From the flood story to Jonah's message of doom to the Ninevites, God's grace has a way of having the last word. It is the very same dynamic that stands at the heart of the Christian gospel, "But God proves his love for us in that while we still were sinners Christ died for us" (Rom 5:8 NRSV). In the story of Israel's kingship, the people may have turned away from God in desiring a king; but it is clear that God will not turn away from them, even in the matter of a king. Saul will have his chance as God's chosen one.

2. A second important theme in this episode focuses on the unlikely moments of Saul's hiding in the baggage (10:22-23) and on the complaining of "worthless fellows" that Saul cannot save them (10:27*a*). This question recurs in many forms throughout 1 and 2 Samuel: "Who can save?" The question has individual and social dimensions.

On an individual level, Saul is apparently reluctant to be chosen. Like Moses and Gideon before him, he does not think he is the one to save Israel. God must seek him out and insist that he is the chosen one. It is not up to Saul alone to save. It is God with Saul (10:7) who can save. Over and over again those called in the biblical story must be reassured that it is God with them who saves: "I have chosen you and not cast you off; do not fear, for I am with you, do not be afraid, for I am your God; I will strengthen you, I will help you, I will uphold you with my victorious right hand" (Isa 41:9*b*-10 NRSV).

Most of us today are inclined to hide in the baggage. We are reluctant to think that we might be the very one through whom God's salvation might work. Our fear frequently arises because we only gauge our own human resources and fail to trust in what God might work through us and our limited gifts. The life of the church is full of baggage-searching efforts, insisting that with God's grace this one or that one might really give the leadership needed. The trick is to be certain that we are prayerfully attuned to God's choices and not our own. God's choosing may lead, as with Saul, to some less obvious nominees through whom God's saving grace might work.

The question of who can save is also a social question. All Israel is divided by this question. It is the worthless ones who dare to voice it (10:26-27*a*). The question is directed to our corporate institutions and those who hold office in them. For Israel, it was kingship in general and Saul in particular. For us it may be denominational structures and leaders (bishops, elders, presbytery executives, moderators, officers, and staff members) or it may be secular institutions of governance and the officeholders or civil servants who work in them. Israel's story once again suggests that the structures and the persons alone cannot save. The worthless ones are properly skeptical if Saul's supporters think that kingship or Saul of their own accord can save Israel. The story of 1 Samuel has already made this point. The piety and integrity of Eli could not save his sons or his household;

the ark could not save Israel. It is God's power that saves, and that power can work through persons and institutions. Through Samuel, God saves Israel from the Philistines in chap. 7. In the power of God's Spirit, Saul will save Jabesh-gilead in chap. 11. But when Saul tries to save on his own terms and in disregard for God as the source of saving power, he is rejected as God's chosen one and his story takes a tragic turn (chap. 15).

It has always been tempting for the church and its leaders to trust institutional structures and officeholders as the source of salvation rather than the God who might work through those institutions and leaders. As with the kingship, God can redeem even our sometimes sinful churches—but only if we recognize the choices God is making in our midst, rather than insisting on our own customs or preferences.

The same observation can be made about secular societal institutions and leaders. They, too, can become idols, and there are many who believe, in the name of patriotism, that some pattern of government or legislation or leadership can save us. Alone these things cannot save us. Only when self-interest and vested interest are given up to God's interests can salvation be fully present in our societal structures.

It is significant that the skeptical question of who can save is raised by those whom Israel labeled "worthless ones." Often, from biblical times to the present, it is through those whom society labels worthless that the patterns of God's grace in our midst are revealed. In the end the skepticism toward Saul is, unfortunately, well founded. Jesus associated with outcasts and sinners. The early church broke down barriers between Jew and Greek, male and female, slave and free (Gal 3:28). Saint Francis reclaimed the gospel as good news for the poor. John Wesley left comfortable pews to preach to miners in open fields. African Americans and black South Africans declared that racist institutions could save no one and acted accordingly. It would do well for Christians and citizens today to listen to the voices of those dismissed as worthless ones. Perhaps their voices can be a reminder that even the most cherished customs, economic systems, political platforms, or religious systems cannot save. It is only through constant discernment of what God is doing in our midst, and attention to the surprising patterns of God's grace, that any institution or leader can become a part of God's saving work in the world.

1 Samuel 10:27b–11:15, Saul Delivers Jabesh-gilead

NIV

They despised him and brought him no gifts. But Saul kept silent.

11 Nahash the Ammonite went up and besieged Jabesh Gilead. And all the men of Jabesh said to him, "Make a treaty with us, and we will be subject to you."

²But Nahash the Ammonite replied, "I will make a treaty with you only on the condition that I gouge out the right eye of every one of you and so bring disgrace on all Israel."

³The elders of Jabesh said to him, "Give us seven days so we can send messengers throughout Israel; if no one comes to rescue us, we will surrender to you."

⁴When the messengers came to Gibeah of Saul and reported these terms to the people, they all

NRSV

They despised him and brought him no present. But he held his peace.

No one was left of the Israelites across the Jordan whose right eye Nahash, king of the Ammonites, had not gouged out. But there were seven thousand men who had escaped from the Ammonites and had entered Jabesh-gilead.ᵃ

11 About a month later,ᵇ Nahash the Ammonite went up and besieged Jabesh-gilead; and all the men of Jabesh said to Nahash, "Make a treaty with us, and we will serve you." ²But Nahash the Ammonite said to them, "On this condition I will make a treaty with you, namely that I gouge out everyone's right eye, and thus

ᵃ Q Ms Compare Josephus, *Antiquities* VI.v.1 (68-71): MT lacks *Now Nahash . . . entered Jabesh-gilead.* ᵇ Q Ms Gk: MT lacks *About a month later*

NIV

wept aloud. ⁵Just then Saul was returning from the fields, behind his oxen, and he asked, "What is wrong with the people? Why are they weeping?" Then they repeated to him what the men of Jabesh had said.

⁶When Saul heard their words, the Spirit of God came upon him in power, and he burned with anger. ⁷He took a pair of oxen, cut them into pieces, and sent the pieces by messengers throughout Israel, proclaiming, "This is what will be done to the oxen of anyone who does not follow Saul and Samuel." Then the terror of the LORD fell on the people, and they turned out as one man. ⁸When Saul mustered them at Bezek, the men of Israel numbered three hundred thousand and the men of Judah thirty thousand.

⁹They told the messengers who had come, "Say to the men of Jabesh Gilead, 'By the time the sun is hot tomorrow, you will be delivered.'" When the messengers went and reported this to the men of Jabesh, they were elated. ¹⁰They said to the Ammonites, "Tomorrow we will surrender to you, and you can do to us whatever seems good to you."

¹¹The next day Saul separated his men into three divisions; during the last watch of the night they broke into the camp of the Ammonites and slaughtered them until the heat of the day. Those who survived were scattered, so that no two of them were left together.

¹²The people then said to Samuel, "Who was it that asked, 'Shall Saul reign over us?' Bring these men to us and we will put them to death."

¹³But Saul said, "No one shall be put to death today, for this day the LORD has rescued Israel."

¹⁴Then Samuel said to the people, "Come, let us go to Gilgal and there reaffirm the kingship." ¹⁵So all the people went to Gilgal and confirmed Saul as king in the presence of the LORD. There they sacrificed fellowship offerings*ᵃ* before the LORD, and Saul and all the Israelites held a great celebration.

ᵃ15 Traditionally *peace offerings*

NRSV

put disgrace upon all Israel." ³The elders of Jabesh said to him, "Give us seven days' respite that we may send messengers through all the territory of Israel. Then, if there is no one to save us, we will give ourselves up to you." ⁴When the messengers came to Gibeah of Saul, they reported the matter in the hearing of the people; and all the people wept aloud.

5Now Saul was coming from the field behind the oxen; and Saul said, "What is the matter with the people, that they are weeping?" So they told him the message from the inhabitants of Jabesh. ⁶And the spirit of God came upon Saul in power when he heard these words, and his anger was greatly kindled. ⁷He took a yoke of oxen, and cut them in pieces and sent them throughout all the territory of Israel by messengers, saying, "Whoever does not come out after Saul and Samuel, so shall it be done to his oxen!" Then the dread of the LORD fell upon the people, and they came out as one. ⁸When he mustered them at Bezek, those from Israel were three hundred thousand, and those from Judah seventy*ᵃ* thousand. ⁹They said to the messengers who had come, "Thus shall you say to the inhabitants of Jabesh-gilead: 'Tomorrow, by the time the sun is hot, you shall have deliverance.'" When the messengers came and told the inhabitants of Jabesh, they rejoiced. ¹⁰So the inhabitants of Jabesh said, "Tomorrow we will give ourselves up to you, and you may do to us whatever seems good to you." ¹¹The next day Saul put the people in three companies. At the morning watch they came into the camp and cut down the Ammonites until the heat of the day; and those who survived were scattered, so that no two of them were left together.

12The people said to Samuel, "Who is it that said, 'Shall Saul reign over us?' Give them to us so that we may put them to death." ¹³But Saul said, "No one shall be put to death this day, for today the LORD has brought deliverance to Israel."

14Samuel said to the people, "Come, let us go to Gilgal and there renew the kingship." ¹⁵So all the people went to Gilgal, and there they made Saul king before the LORD in Gilgal. There they sacrificed offerings of well-being before the LORD, and there Saul and all the Israelites rejoiced greatly.

ᵃ Q Ms Gk: MT *thirty*

COMMENTARY

If we had not already been introduced to Saul as Israel's first king in previous chapters, this episode would look like a story from the book of Judges. Saul seems like one of the charismatic deliverers of Israel, empowered by God's Spirit in times of crisis. The crisis here is caused by the cruelty and oppression of Nahash, the king of Ammon, who has laid siege to Jabesh-gilead (vv. 1-4). When the inhabitants of Jabesh send a desperate appeal for help, it is Saul who hears the news while plowing his field, whereupon he is filled with the Spirit of God. He summons the tribal militia and mounts a campaign that successfully delivers the people of Jabesh-gilead (vv. 5-11). Following this victory, some want to put to death those who opposed Saul, but Saul intervenes (vv. 12-13), and he is then made king in Gilgal (vv. 14-15). Until the kingmaking at the end of the chapter, this story shows no knowledge of Saul in connection with kingship. There is no indication of any previous anointing (10:1) or public acclamation (10:24) of Saul as king over Israel. The account is very positive toward Saul, picturing him as a hero and deliverer of Israel. It would appear that this story is an independent tradition indicating that Saul became king as a spontaneous acclamation following his demonstrated leadership in delivering Jabesh-gilead. As we will see later, some attempt has been made to harmonize this account with other stories on Saul's rise to kingship by having Samuel suggest in v. 14 that the people are going to Gilgal to "renew" the kingship. Verse 15, however, says straightforwardly that the people "made Saul king before the Lord in Gilgal."

Chapter 11 may have originated as an independent tradition on Saul's rise to kingship, but in its present context it confirms a kingship already revealed to Saul and to Israel. Saul had already received the Spirit of God as a result of his anointing by Samuel (10:5-6, 10), and he had been presented and acclaimed before the people at Mizpah (10:17-24). Still, Saul had not begun active rule over Israel. Samuel had sent him and the people home from Mizpah (10:25b). The coming of God's Spirit on Saul in this episode (11:6) empowers him not to prophesy but to lead

Israel to deliverance from an enemy, the Ammonites. Saul publicly demonstrates the power of God's Spirit in leadership of Israel. The "renewal" of the kingship in Gilgal (11:14) now marks the beginning of Saul's active rule of Israel as a proven leader possessed of God's Spirit.

Chapter 11 is also tied to its wider context by the key concept of salvation. Chapter 10 had ended with the crucial question of the "worthless ones": "How can this man *save* us?" (10:27a). The Hebrew root יָשַׁע (*yš'*) plays a key role in this chapter. As a verb, it is translated "save" or "deliver," and as a noun, "salvation" or "deliverance." Brueggemann has seen that this theme is central to each part of the dramatic story of chap. 11.[80]

The problem:	If there is no one to *save* us (v. 3)
The intervention:	You shall have *deliverance* (v. 9)
The resolution:	The Lord has wrought *deliverance* in Israel (v. 13)

Saul can save, but only as an agent of God's deliverance, which he himself confesses in v. 13. Those whom the supporters of Saul want to put to death in v. 12 are likely the "worthless ones/troublemakers," who cast doubt on Saul's ability to save in 10:27a. Saul refuses to allow their death, and in doing so begins to function as an authority for sacral justice in Israel (see discussion below). This ironically casts a shadow forward, since it will be Saul's later violations in matters of sacral justice that lead Samuel to reject Saul as king (chaps. 13 and 15).

10:27b–11:4. The story opens with a description of the cruel siege of Jabesh-gilead by Nahash the Ammonite. The NRSV includes a long addition to the text that now appears at the end of chap. 10 (the addition is actually unnumbered but will be treated here as 10:27b). This material is from a manuscript found at Qumran (Dead Sea Scroll 4QSam[a]) and was also known by the Jewish historian Josephus.[81] The NIV has chosen not to include it. The addition provides helpful back-

80. Walter Brueggemann, *First and Second Samuel,* Interpretation (Louisville: John Knox, 1990) 83.

81. Josephus *Antiquities of the Jews* 6.68-71. See McCarter, *I Samuel,* 199, for a discussion and reconstruction of the Qumran text.

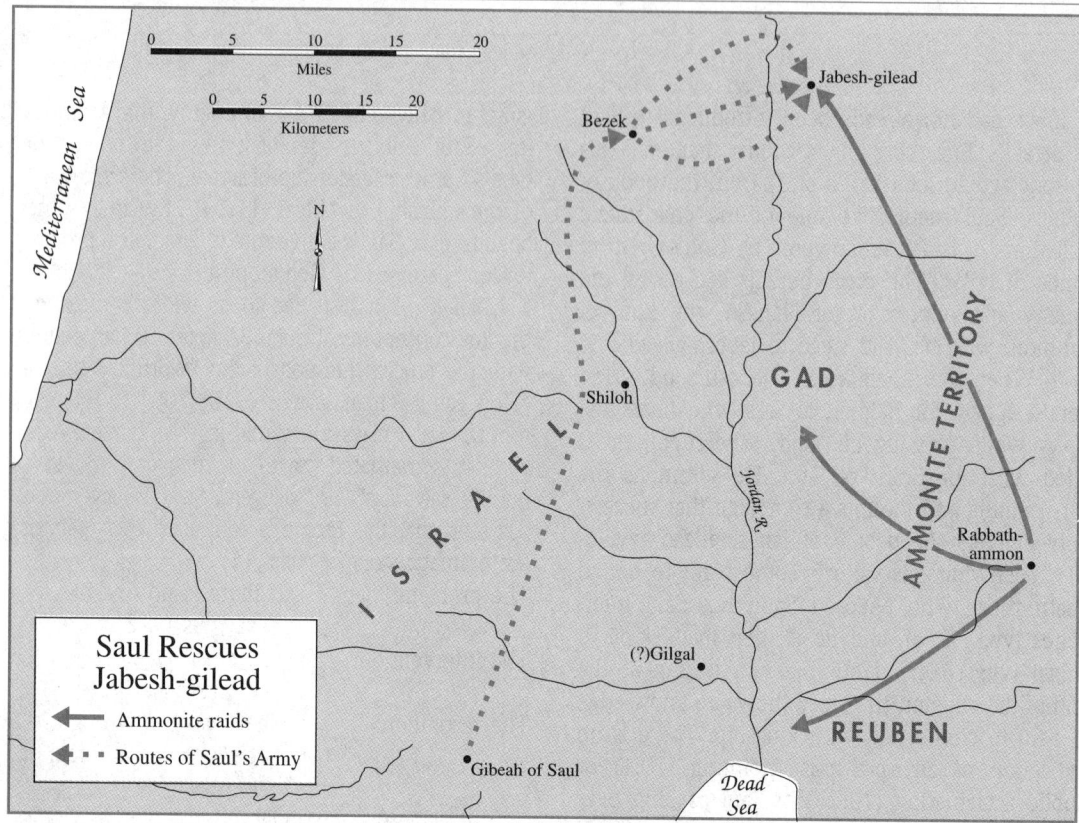

Saul Rescues
Jabesh-gilead

← Ammonite raids

◄ ··· Routes of Saul's Army

ground on the siege. Nahash, the ruler of Ammon, is described as a cruel oppressor. The name "Nahash" is related to the Hebrew for "snake" (נחש *nāḥāš*). Nahash had systematically gouged out the right eyes of the men of Gad and Reuben, and seven thousand men from these tribes had taken refuge in Jabesh-gilead. Gad and Reuben were Israelite tribes located to the east of the Jordan in territory perennially under dispute with the Ammonites, one of several Transjordanian kingdoms. Jabesh-gilead is usually located in the Transjordanian portion of the tribe of Manasseh and has always seemed too far north to have been an object of Ammonite conquest. The longer text from Qumran makes clear that Nahash is pursuing refugees from his oppressive campaign against Gad and Reuben. His intent in gouging out eyes was to deprive the Israelites of a *deliverer* (a theme that returns in 11:3). Presumably, one-eyed men are not very effective warriors. This cruel policy of Nahash, outlined in the Qumran addition, provides the background to Nahash's terms of surrender to the besieged inhabitants of Jabesh-gilead in 11:2. They had offered to surrender and make a treaty

of service to Nahash (11:1), but Nahash had accepted only on condition that their right eyes be gouged out, thus disgracing Israel.

The elders of Jabesh-gilead asked for seven days to send out word through Israel. Their intent was to find someone to *save* them. If no one was found, they would surrender (v. 3). Surprisingly, Nahash does not respond. Perhaps he was simply confident that nothing could save Jabesh-gilead in so short a time.

In v. 4, messengers from Jabesh-gilead reach Gibeah (identified here with Saul), and the inhabitants weep at the news of the desperate situation. The book of Judges reports a special relationship between these two cities that grew out of an earlier crisis. The tribes of Israel went to war against the tribe of Benjamin for atrocities committed by the men of Gibeah against the concubine of a Levite from Ephraim (Judges 19–21). Jabesh-gilead had refused to send men to participate in the punishment of Gibeah, and for this they were attacked and four hundred virgin daughters of Jabesh-gilead were given to the survivors of Benjamin to rebuild the population of the tribe (Judg 21:1-14). Thus many families of

Gibeah included ties of kinship to Jabesh-gilead. It is now in Gibeah that a deliverer for Jabesh is found in the person of Saul. Later in the books of Samuel, the men of Jabesh-gilead repay the deliverance of Saul by retrieving his body at great risk from the Philistines to give it a proper burial (1 Sam 31:11-13; 2 Sam 2:4*b*-7).

11:5-11. This section of the story focuses entirely on Saul and his response to the plight of Jabesh-gilead. It is his response that makes a difference and brings deliverance. When the news of the siege comes, Saul is simply working in the fields with oxen like any ordinary citizen (v. 5). This account knows nothing of royal designation for Saul. When Saul asks why people are weeping and is told the news, the response is immediate. Simultaneously the Spirit of God comes upon him with power, and he becomes very angry (v. 6). The language is strikingly similar to that used of Samson in Judg 14:6, 19; 15:14, and many of the heroes of Judges were said to have received God's Spirit as the source of their power (Othniel, Gideon, Jephthah). For Saul, human anger at oppression and divine empowerment to effect a change through God's Spirit come together. It is out of this combination of righteous anger and divine power that the action of salvation comes in this story. Although Saul is clearly the hero of this story, there is a clear stress on God as the ultimate source of deliverance. It is the Spirit of God that empowers Saul; it is the dread of the Lord (v. 8) that fell upon Israel and brought response to Saul's summons; and it is the Lord to whom Saul finally gives credit for deliverance (v. 13).

Saul summons the tribal levy. This is the only example of this calling out of tribal military resources outside of the book of Judges. He does this by cutting his oxen into pieces and sending them throughout Israel with the threat that whoever does not respond to the call might face a similar fate (v. 7). This is reminiscent of the Levite's sending pieces of his concubine's body to summon Israel to punish those responsible for her death (Judg 19:29-30). The reference to Samuel in this verse is widely regarded as a secondary addition. Samuel plays no role in this story until the kingmaking at the end of the chapter.

The "dread of the LORD" falls upon Israel, and the people respond (v. 7*b*). This phrase and the motif of God's Spirit suggest that we are dealing with the influence of holy war traditions. It is God who fights for Israel in such righteous causes.

When the people are mustered by Saul at Bezek, they number three hundred thousand. The word for "thousand" in Hebrew (אלף *'elep*) may also be translated as "contingent," which may be a more realistic rendering.

Word is sent to Jabesh-gilead that before midday on the next day they would have *deliverance* (v. 9), and the people of Jabesh-gilead rejoice. The inhabitants then give Nahash an ambiguous message. The Hebrew word יצא (*yāṣā'*) means literally "come out." It can be used in the sense of "surrender" or "give ourselves up" as in v. 3, but it can also mean "come out to do battle." The people of Jabesh-gilead give a cleverly ambiguous reply to Nahash: "Tomorrow, we will come out to you, and you may do to us whatever seems good to you" (v. 10). Nahash is lulled into believing capitulation is at hand, when the people of Jabesh-gilead plan to join in Saul's attack on the Ammonites. Both the NIV and the NRSV obscure this play on words.

The actual battle and Saul's victory are recorded briefly in v. 11. Saul divides his company into three forces. They attack the Ammonites in the morning and complete the victory during the heat of the day. Presumably the Ammonites are taken off guard, thinking that surrender is near. The victory is complete, and no further interest is shown in Nahash or the Ammonites. Interest focuses on Saul.

11:12-15. In the aftermath of victory, people approach Samuel demanding that those who questioned the reign of Saul be put to death (v. 12). This group may be the "worthless men/troublemakers" of 10:27*a* who wondered aloud whether Saul could save them. Now Saul has saved Israel, and those who doubted are in jeopardy. This incident is widely interpreted as a desire for petty vengeance and Saul's response as evidence of his magnanimity. However, Knierim has emphasized that the matter is one of sacral justice and not simple vengeance and mercy.

The request of the people for the punishment of Saul's slanderers is not at all an act of "petty vengeance." It is a necessity of sacral justice. . . . After Saul's victory, it was proven by divine judgment that the despisers had not merely slandered Saul but also Yahweh's messiah, and with that Yahweh himself. . . . The desire of the people . . . is a legitimate and necessary demand to execute judgment against the convicted slanderers of Yahweh.[82]

82. Rolf Knierim, "The Messianic Concept in the First Book of Samuel," in *Jesus and the Historian,* ed. T. Trotter (Philadelphia: Westminster, 1968) 33.

In 10:27*a* these opponents of Saul are already called בני בליעל (*běnê běliyya'al*, "worthless ones"). In the Old Testament, a "worthless man" is one who slanders God or breaks sacral law (1:16; 2:12; Deut 13:14; Judg 19:22; 20:13; Nah 1:11), destroys justice (1 Kgs 21:10; Prov 19:28), destroys life (Prov 16:27), or rebels against the king (2 Sam 16:7; 20:1; 23:7; Job 34:18)—and all of these acts call for the judgment of death. The text itself is quite clear that Saul did not pardon these opponents because he was feeling generous. He states in apodictic form:

No man shall be put to death on this day . . . because God has delivered Israel. A legal pronouncement is made on the basis of God's act of salvation and not because of Saul's magnanimity. What is significant about this is the apparent transfer to Saul of the right to make judgments in the sacral/legal realm. . . . In v. 12 the people approach Samuel with the matter, but in v. 13 it is Saul who deals with the question. It is natural that Samuel as the judge of Israel and authority in such matters should be approached, but it is clear that the outcome shows Saul in the position to act authoritatively [instead of Samuel].[83]

Saul's exercise of authority properly recognizes God as the ultimate authority both for this judgment and for the victory that preceded it. Ironically

83. Birch, *The Rise of the Israelite Monarchy*, 61-62.

it will be a disregard for sacral law and God's authority that Samuel will use as the basis for Saul's later rejection.

In v. 14, Samuel summons the people to Gilgal with the curious purpose of "renewing" the kingship, but in v. 15 it is the people who make Saul king before the Lord. This text may reflect a tradition of the people involved in kingmaking without the involvement of God's prophet. Verse 14 would then represent the prophetic tradition introducing Samuel into this story and harmonizing it with the earlier kingmaking role of Samuel by speaking of the Gilgal ceremony as a "renewal" of kingship. The effect of the text as it now stands is to make Saul's victory and the ceremony at Gilgal a confirmation of Saul's earlier designation as Israel's king.

This narrative provides an overwhelmingly positive portrait of Saul and the basis for his kingship. It is appropriate that the story ends with the rejoicing of Saul and all Israel at Gilgal (v. 15*b*). However, the biblical tradition associated with Gilgal does not remain entirely positive. In the time of Hosea, when Israel had suffered from the abuses of royal power, the prophet proclaimed, "They made kings, but not through me. . . . Every evil of theirs began at Gilgal; there I came to hate them" (Hos 8:4*a*; 9:15*a* NRSV).

REFLECTIONS

There can be no doubt that Saul is the narrative center of this story. It is his heroic moment, and the tone of the story is one of unstinting approval for Saul. But if Saul is the narrative center, the theological center of this story is focused on the theme of salvation. This is a story of salvation, both in the immediate sense of the crisis in Jabesh-gilead and in a larger sense within the book of 1 Samuel.

The immediate context for this focus on salvation begins in 10:19. Including that verse, there are five uses (10:19, 27; 11:3, 9, 13) of the root ישע (*yš'*) as either a verb ("to save," "to deliver") or a noun ("salvation," "deliverance"). Samuel claims that Israel has rejected their God, who *saves* them (10:19). Some have doubts that Saul can *save* them (10:27). The people of Jabesh-gilead fear that no one can *save* them (11:3). Word is sent that Saul will *save* them (11:9). Saul affirms that it was God who *saved* them. At the center stands the perennial fear in times of crisis that no salvation is possible. On one side stand the rejection of God and the doubts about leadership. Can they possibly save us (see the Reflections in previous chapter)? On the other side stands the affirmation that our leaders can bring salvation, but only if it is understood that the salvation they bring originates in God. This salvation drama in the story of Israel and Saul can teach us much about our own continuing quest for salvation.

1. Salvation is ultimately from God. It is God who truly saves. Samuel feared that in demanding a king the people were rejecting the God who saves (10:19). At least at this moment in the story Saul's response in 11:13 suggests that even a king can recognize God as the true source of all deliverance. For us, who live in a time that values individual self-sufficiency and puts increasing trust in technological solutions to problems, it is sometimes difficult to recognize our need for the salvation that comes from God. Israel was in a time of transition when it must have been tempted to leave God behind as part of the old order. But even in a story of new leadership and heroism there must be recognition that God is the source of all genuine salvation in every age, old and new.

2. God's salvation does not operate in isolation from human agency. The biblical story is filled with examples of the men and women God has involved in the work of salvation in the world. In this story, the agent of God's salvation is Saul. God's Spirit is at work to bring deliverance, but it is Saul who is seized by God's Spirit and empowered by it (11:6). What is kindled in Saul is anger, and that anger is directed at the cruel oppression that Nahash has inflicted on the people of Jabesh-gilead. The order here is significant. Saul does not become angry and then become Spirit-filled; it is the reverse. The anger is, of course, Saul's, but the implication is that it also grows out of the Spirit of God, which has grasped him. The suggestion is that the anger is also God's. Perhaps this story is teaching us what can happen when divine Spirit and human anger are focused together on oppression. The story of Saul as an instrument of God's deliverance here will help us to recognize that through God's Spirit, power beyond our rational and pragmatic expectations is available to us. But it will also require human involvement in the pain and struggle of those whose plight should rouse us to anger and action.

3. Salvation is sociopolitical as well as spiritual. Stories such as this one are important reminders that God's salvation has to do with the divine desire for human wholeness in all aspects of broken human existence. There are many voices in our time that use the concept of salvation only in reference to religious or spiritual matters. They imagine that God desires only to "save" us by establishing or restoring faith relationship in communion with God. The biblical concept of God's salvation is much broader than this; God's salvation includes not only a concern to establish faith but also to foster justice and to seek peace. In our time, the liberation theologies have seen the sociopolitical dimensions of God's salvation most clearly. Indeed, the Hebrew words for "save" and "salvation" can also be translated as "liberate" and "liberation." God's salvation is at work not only in the holy moment of covenant making on Mt. Sinai but also in the liberating spirit that rouses Saul to righteous anger on behalf of justice for Jabesh-gilead. In our own time, perhaps, God's salvation is best seen in those whose lives have exemplified deep biblical and spiritual roots combined with the active work of compassion and justice—the love of God joined with and reflected in the love of neighbor—Dietrich Bonhoeffer, Dorothy Day, Martin Luther King, Jr., Thomas Merton, Mother Teresa.

4. Salvation cannot remain passive in the face of suffering. It must act. God's Spirit is roused to action by human suffering, and those who would live in relation to the divine Spirit will likewise be stirred. Jesus inaugurated his ministry by reading from Isa 61:1-2:

> The Spirit of the Lord is upon me,
>> because he has anointed me to bring good news to the poor.
> He has sent me to proclaim release to the captives
>> and recovery of sight to the blind,
>> to let the oppressed go free,
> to proclaim the year of the Lord's favor. (Luke 4:18-19 NRSV)

In the power of God's Spirit upon him, Saul is "proclaiming release to the captives" in 1 Samuel 11. The Spirit empowers us to action in the face of oppression and suffering, but it is not without cost. Some are troubled that "saving action" in this story involves war as an instrument of divine and human justice. The salvation wrought by the Spirit does not operate as a *deus ex machina,* magically righting wrong with no human cost. It is not war that is affirmed in stories such as this. What is affirmed is the value of those who live and suffer on the underside of history. What is affirmed is that God has not forgotten them. What is affirmed is that violence is already being done in situations of oppression, and not to respond would be violence itself. God cannot will that nothing be done in the face of such brutality—whether in Jabesh-gilead or in countless modern experiences of oppression and suffering. The fall of oppressors is often costly and violent because of the violence that oppression introduces into human experience, not because violence is what God desires. In biblical times or our own, to do nothing in the face of brutality and injustice is sometimes the greater violence.

1 Samuel 12:1-25, Samuel's Address to Israel

NIV

12 Samuel said to all Israel, "I have listened to everything you said to me and have set a king over you. ²Now you have a king as your leader. As for me, I am old and gray, and my sons are here with you. I have been your leader from my youth until this day. ³Here I stand. Testify against me in the presence of the LORD and his anointed. Whose ox have I taken? Whose donkey have I taken? Whom have I cheated? Whom have I oppressed? From whose hand have I accepted a bribe to make me shut my eyes? If I have done any of these, I will make it right."

⁴"You have not cheated or oppressed us," they replied. "You have not taken anything from anyone's hand."

⁵Samuel said to them, "The LORD is witness against you, and also his anointed is witness this day, that you have not found anything in my hand."

"He is witness," they said.

⁶Then Samuel said to the people, "It is the LORD who appointed Moses and Aaron and brought your forefathers up out of Egypt. ⁷Now then, stand here, because I am going to confront you with evidence before the LORD as to all the righteous acts performed by the LORD for you and your fathers.

⁸"After Jacob entered Egypt, they cried to the LORD for help, and the LORD sent Moses and Aaron, who brought your forefathers out of Egypt and settled them in this place.

⁹"But they forgot the LORD their God; so he sold them into the hand of Sisera, the commander of the army of Hazor, and into the hands of the Philistines and the king of Moab, who fought against them. ¹⁰They cried out to the LORD and said, 'We have sinned; we have forsaken the LORD

NRSV

12 Samuel said to all Israel, "I have listened to you in all that you have said to me, and have set a king over you. ²See, it is the king who leads you now; I am old and gray, but my sons are with you. I have led you from my youth until this day. ³Here I am; testify against me before the LORD and before his anointed. Whose ox have I taken? Or whose donkey have I taken? Or whom have I defrauded? Whom have I oppressed? Or from whose hand have I taken a bribe to blind my eyes with it? Testify against me*ᵃ* and I will restore it to you." ⁴They said, "You have not defrauded us or oppressed us or taken anything from the hand of anyone." ⁵He said to them, "The LORD is witness against you, and his anointed is witness this day, that you have not found anything in my hand." And they said, "He is witness."

⁶Samuel said to the people, "The LORD is witness, whoᵇ appointed Moses and Aaron and brought your ancestors up out of the land of Egypt. ⁷Now therefore take your stand, so that I may enter into judgment with you before the LORD, and I will declare to youᶜ all the saving deeds of the LORD that he performed for you and for your ancestors. ⁸When Jacob went into Egypt and the Egyptians oppressed them,ᵈ then your ancestors cried to the LORD and the LORD sent Moses and Aaron, who brought forth your ancestors out of Egypt, and settled them in this place. ⁹But they forgot the LORD their God; and he sold them into the hand of Sisera, commander of the army of King Jabin ofᵉ Hazor, and into the hand

ᵃ Gk: Heb lacks *Testify against me*   ᵇ Gk: Heb lacks *is witness, who* ᶜ Gk: Heb lacks *and I will declare to you*   ᵈ Gk: Heb lacks *and the Egyptians oppressed them*   ᵉ Gk: Heb lacks *King Jabin of*

NIV

and served the Baals and the Ashtoreths. But now deliver us from the hands of our enemies, and we will serve you.' [11]Then the LORD sent Jerub-Baal,[a] Barak,[b] Jephthah and Samuel,[c] and he delivered you from the hands of your enemies on every side, so that you lived securely.

[12]"But when you saw that Nahash king of the Ammonites was moving against you, you said to me, 'No, we want a king to rule over us'—even though the LORD your God was your king. [13]Now here is the king you have chosen, the one you asked for; see, the LORD has set a king over you. [14]If you fear the LORD and serve and obey him and do not rebel against his commands, and if both you and the king who reigns over you follow the LORD your God—good! [15]But if you do not obey the LORD, and if you rebel against his commands, his hand will be against you, as it was against your fathers.

[16]"Now then, stand still and see this great thing the LORD is about to do before your eyes! [17]Is it not wheat harvest now? I will call upon the LORD to send thunder and rain. And you will realize what an evil thing you did in the eyes of the LORD when you asked for a king."

[18]Then Samuel called upon the LORD, and that same day the LORD sent thunder and rain. So all the people stood in awe of the LORD and of Samuel.

[19]The people all said to Samuel, "Pray to the LORD your God for your servants so that we will not die, for we have added to all our other sins the evil of asking for a king."

[20]"Do not be afraid," Samuel replied. "You have done all this evil; yet do not turn away from the LORD, but serve the LORD with all your heart. [21]Do not turn away after useless idols. They can do you no good, nor can they rescue you, because they are useless. [22]For the sake of his great name the LORD will not reject his people, because the LORD was pleased to make you his own. [23]As for me, far be it from me that I should sin against the LORD by failing to pray for you. And I will teach you the way that is good and right. [24]But be sure to fear the LORD and serve him faithfully with all your heart; consider what great things he has done for you. [25]Yet if you persist in doing evil, both you and your king will be swept away."

[a]11 Also called *Gideon*; Syriac; Hebrew *Bedan* and Syriac *Samson*   [b]11 Some Septuagint manuscripts and Syriac; Hebrew *Bedan*   [c]11 Hebrew; some Septuagint manuscripts

NRSV

of the Philistines, and into the hand of the king of Moab; and they fought against them. [10]Then they cried to the LORD, and said, 'We have sinned, because we have forsaken the LORD, and have served the Baals and the Astartes; but now rescue us out of the hand of our enemies, and we will serve you.' [11]And the LORD sent Jerubbaal and Barak,[a] and Jephthah, and Samson,[b] and rescued you out of the hand of your enemies on every side; and you lived in safety. [12]But when you saw that King Nahash of the Ammonites came against you, you said to me, 'No, but a king shall reign over us,' though the LORD your God was your king. [13]See, here is the king whom you have chosen, for whom you have asked; see, the LORD has set a king over you. [14]If you will fear the LORD and serve him and heed his voice and not rebel against the commandment of the LORD, and if both you and the king who reigns over you will follow the LORD your God, it will be well; [15]but if you will not heed the voice of the LORD, but rebel against the commandment of the LORD, then the hand of the LORD will be against you and your king.[c] [16]Now therefore take your stand and see this great thing that the LORD will do before your eyes. [17]Is it not the wheat harvest today? I will call upon the LORD, that he may send thunder and rain; and you shall know and see that the wickedness that you have done in the sight of the LORD is great in demanding a king for yourselves." [18]So Samuel called upon the LORD, and the LORD sent thunder and rain that day; and all the people greatly feared the LORD and Samuel.

19All the people said to Samuel, "Pray to the LORD your God for your servants, so that we may not die; for we have added to all our sins the evil of demanding a king for ourselves." [20]And Samuel said to the people, "Do not be afraid; you have done all this evil, yet do not turn aside from following the LORD, but serve the LORD with all your heart; [21]and do not turn aside after useless things that cannot profit or save, for they are useless. [22]For the LORD will not cast away his people, for his great name's sake, because it has pleased the LORD to make you a people for himself. [23]Moreover as for me, far be it from me that I

[a] Gk Syr: Heb *Bedan*   [b] Gk: Heb *Samuel*   [c] Gk: Heb *and your ancestors*

NRSV

should sin against the LORD by ceasing to pray for you; and I will instruct you in the good and the right way. 24Only fear the LORD, and serve him faithfully with all your heart; for consider what great things he has done for you. 25But if you still do wickedly, you shall be swept away, both you and your king."

COMMENTARY

Chapter 12 consists entirely of a speech by Samuel to Israel, with occasional responses by the people. There is a curious lack of narrative framework for this address. No time or place is given. The voice of the narrator merely tells us when Samuel or the people begin to speak and narrates the fulfillment of a sign in v. 18.

This chapter is frequently called the "farewell address" of Samuel because of the prophet's reference to his advanced age in v. 2 and the clear implication that some transitions of leadership are taking place with the advent of kingship. But it is not really accurate to treat this as Samuel's retirement. Toward the end of this chapter, Samuel emphasizes that he will continue to pray for Israel and to "instruct you in the good and the right way" (v. 23). He is still active in the course of events hereafter, as his two rejections of Saul in chaps. 13 and 15 make clear. Further, it will be Samuel who anoints David as Saul's successor (16:1-13) and who gives David refuge when he flees from Saul (19:18-24). In this last episode, Samuel remains active as the leader of a community of prophets. It is well to take Samuel's speech as a marker of transition in his role, but not as his farewell.

Since the work of Martin Noth[84] most scholars have recognized 1 Samuel 12 as one of the key passages, often in the form of speeches by main characters, that stand at turning points in the Deuteronomistic History (Dtr) and serve to integrate its various sections (e.g., Josh 1:11-15; 23–24; 2 Samuel 7; 1 Kgs 8:14-61). There is much evidence of deuteronomistic language and themes,

but these occur primarily in vv. 6-15 and 20-25, leading some scholars to suggest that vv. 1-5, 16-19 may reflect an earlier tradition that the deuteronomistic historian has used as the context for his programmatic speech by Samuel.[85] The earlier verses focus on a vindication and demonstration of authority for Samuel as God's prophet. The Dtr additions in vv. 6-15 and 20-25 focus on the vindication of God and the faithlessness of the people as a basis for renewed covenant possibilities even in the age of kings. The vindication of God's prophet in vv. 1-5 gives added authority to Samuel's affirmation of God and judgment of the people in the remainder of the chapter.

The chapter falls into distinct segments: vv. 1-5, the exoneration of Samuel; vv. 6-15, covenant-influenced address contrasting faithfulness of God and sin of the people; vv. 16-18, the giving of a sign; v. 19, the people's confession of sin and request for intercession; vv. 20-25, closing homiletical admonitions.

12:1-5. Since the place is not named, we must assume that the scene is still Gilgal, where chap. 11 ended. Samuel's speech to the people uses both legal ("testify," "witness") and cultic ("before the LORD and before his anointed") language, so the matter of Samuel's innocence seems to be set in terms of sacral justice. The fact that testimony takes place "before God's anointed" and that "God's anointed" is affirmed as a witness (vv. 3a, 5a) suggests that the king played a role in sacral justice. We have seen this role developing (perhaps at the expense of Samuel) in 11:12-13.

84. Martin Noth, *Uberlieferungsgeschichtliche Studien,* 2nd ed. (Tübingen: Max Niemeyer, 1957) 5; Eng. trans.: *The Deuteronomistic History* (Sheffield: University of Sheffield Press, 1981).

85. See P. Kyle McCarter, *I Samuel,* AB 8 (Garden City, N.Y.: Doubleday, 1980) 212-21, which includes an excellent listing of the deuteronomistic influences in the chapter. See also Bruce C. Birch, *The Rise of the Israelite Monarchy: The Growth and Development of I Samuel 7–15,* SBLDS 27 (Missoula, Mont.: Scholars Press, 1976) 64-68.

The thematic focus of this first speech is on Samuel's vindication of himself before the people. There are several important particulars. First, he declares that he has fulfilled his role as kingmaker (v. 1). He has set a king over Israel in response to what the people requested. This action obviously calls to mind the demand of the elders in chap. 8, but there is no hint in 12:1-5 that this was a sinful request (as it was in chap. 8). Indeed, the king is twice called "God's anointed" (משיח *māšîaḥ*) in these verses (3*a*, 5*a*), a designation that relates to the very positive tradition of the anointing of Saul in 9:1–10:16. The idea of the request for a king as something sinful is introduced only in the second part (vv. 6-15, the Dtr portion) of Samuel's speech in chap. 12, and then in connection with the defeat of Nahash, the Ammonite. Clearly, the relationship of chap. 12 to the preceding chapters is a complex one. It may well be that vv. 1-5 stem from an earlier prophetic edition of this literature (see the Introduction) that stresses Samuel's prophetic role but treats kings positively as the Lord's anointed. In any case, Samuel here cites his role in kingmaking as a proper carrying out of his responsibilities.

Samuel acknowledges the presence of the new king and draws a contrast to his own advanced age (v. 2). He also refers to his sons as part of the people. There is no hint of the problematic behavior of these sons that led to the demand for a king (8:1-4). Samuel calls attention to the long years of leadership he has given, reminding the people that he began as a youth and has led them until he is now old and gray. Clearly Samuel is alluding to a change of leadership even if he is not signaling his complete retirement. If one may judge from subsequent developments in 1 Samuel, the king will now give leadership in governance and military matters. Samuel, as prophet, intends to retain some authority and leadership in covenantal matters. This notion fits well with his intention, declared later in this chapter, to pray and provide moral teaching (v. 23) to the people. That these matters have not been so neatly separated in Israel will lead to trouble between Saul and Samuel.

Finally, Samuel declares that he is innocent of any charge that he has used his leadership role for personal gain. Samuel asks five questions in which he declares his innocence of corrupt practices: taking an ox, taking a donkey, defrauding, oppressing, and

taking a bribe (v. 3). He calls for testimony by anyone who might challenge him and say that he has done these things. The assumption is that if no one comes forward, Samuel's protestation of innocence stands (cf. Num 16:15; Deut 26:13-14; Job 31). Significantly, three of the five potential violations of office use the term "take" (לקח *lāqaḥ*). This is the same verb used frequently in Samuel's warning speech about the practices of a king (8:11-18). Kings "take," but Samuel has not "taken." It is not just the person of Samuel that is vindicated here, but the type of leadership represented by the authority of prophets rather than the authority of kings. It is the community of covenant contrasted with the unknown shape that monarchy may take in Israel.[86]

The people respond to Samuel's demand for exoneration with a ringing endorsement of his innocence (v. 4). They declare that Samuel has not used his office for gain. Samuel then formalizes this as a matter of sacral justice by declaring the Lord and the Lord's anointed as solemn witnesses to his innocence, with the people acknowledging this witness (v. 5).

12:6-15. There is almost universal agreement that this portion of chap. 12 is from the hand of Dtr and stands as one of the programmatic speeches that the historian uses to mark the transition from one period of Israel's story to the next. This speech marks the transition from the era of the judges to the era of the kings in Israel's life. There is also broad agreement that the speech reflects the influence of the covenant form also attested in Joshua 24 and the book of Deuteronomy. The role of Samuel here is that of covenant mediator, as was also the case with Moses and Joshua. Formal elements of a covenant pattern influenced by the patterns of ancient treaties have frequently been pointed out in this speech.[87] This pattern includes an introduction or summons to hear, historical prologue, stipulations or require-

---

86. So Walter Brueggemann, *First and Second Samuel*, Interpretation (Louisville: John Knox, 1990) 90; McCarter, *I Samuel*, 218-19. McCarter argues that the original account had a threefold shape reflecting prophetic interests and editing. Verses 1-5 contrast the prophet favorably to the king; vv. 16-19 demonstrate the power of the prophet; v. 23 foretells the future shape of the office of prophet. The Dtr historian has added to this account the admonitions and evaluations of kingship found in vv. 6-15 and portions of vv. 20-25.

87. This discussion of covenant form in 1 Samuel 12 is especially indebted to Dennis J. McCarthy, *Treaty and Covenant: A Study in Form in the Ancient Oriental Documents and in the Old Testament* (Rome: Pontifical Biblical Institute, 1963) 141-44, and James Muilenburg, "The Form and Structure of the Covenantal Formulations," *VT* 9 (1959) 347-65.

ments, blessings and curses, and divine witnesses. The pattern, perhaps influenced by ancient treaty forms (often involving investiture of kings in office), has been adapted to the particular viewpoint of Dtr that the request for a king was a sin of the people. The emphasis throughout is on the fidelity of the people rather than on the king.

Verse 6 opens with an invocation of the Lord as witness (NRSV, which reads with LXX). McCarthy has noted that in ancient treaty forms divine witnesses were often listed at the opening of the treaties.[88] The God called upon to witness this solemn recitation is identified as the God of the exodus tradition, and in particular the God who appoints leaders like Moses and Aaron. With God as witness, Israel is called upon to "take your stand . . . before the LORD" (cf. Josh 24:1). The express purpose here is Samuel's intention to "enter into judgment with you" (v. 7*a*). The ceremony is not for covenant making but is occasioned by covenant breaking, and perhaps intended for covenant renewing.

Samuel announces a recitation of the Lord's saving deeds toward Israel (v. 7*b*; cf. Josh 24:2-13). The emphasis of this recitation is on God's faithfulness to Israel in times of crisis, with particular attention given to the way in which God has provided leadership for these crises. By contrast, Samuel emphasizes the people's recurring sin, usually in the form of forgetting the Lord (v. 9) and worshiping idols (v. 10). The pattern in this historical recital is the pattern present in the book of Judges: the people sin, a crisis (usually an enemy) arises, the people cry to the Lord, and the Lord sends a deliverer. Samuel begins with the exodus story (v. 8), which opens not with Israel's sin, but with Jacob's simple entry into Egypt, where the Egyptians oppressed them (Israel), and then God's sending of Moses and Aaron, who delivered Israel out of Egypt.

Samuel then moves to the period of the judges (vv. 9-11). Here the cycle begins with the people's sin and proceeds through the pattern typical of the book of Judges (crisis, cry, deliverer). Samuel names three enemies who brought crisis to Israel (v. 9): Sisera/King Jabin, the Philistines, and the king of Moab. These cases do not reflect the order of events in the book of Judges. Sisera was de-

88. McCarthy, *Treaty and Covenant,* 141.

feated by Deborah and her general Barak (Judges 4–5). The Philistines appear as a threat in connection with the deliverance of Shamgar (Judg 3:31), the exploits of Samson (Judges 13–16), and the holy war of Samuel (1 Samuel 7). We do not know to which of these moments Samuel was referring. King Eglon of Moab oppressed Israel and was killed by Ehud (Judg 3:12-30). In v. 10, Samuel recalls the outcry of the people in these crises, confessing their sin and renewed loyalty to the Lord. The language of this verse is strongly deuteronomistic in tone—e.g., the reference to serving the "Baals and Astartes" (cf. 7:3-4). In v. 11, Samuel moves on to name deliverers raised up by God in response to the people's cry of need and repentance: Jerubbaal (another name for Gideon), Bedan, Jephthah, and Samuel. Except for Samuel, those named do not correspond to any of the enemies listed in v. 9. Bedan is not known to us except for an obscure reference in 1 Chr 7:17; the LXX reads "Barak" instead of "Bedan," a reading adopted by both the NRSV and the NIV. The LXX also reads "Samson" instead of "Samuel" (adopted by the NRSV, but mentioned in a footnote in the NIV). Despite these ambiguities, Samuel's point is clear: God provided the leadership necessary to meet crises and give Israel security and peace (v. 11*b*).

Samuel moves on to the most recent crisis with Nahash of Ammon (v. 12). The prophet charges that Israel has changed the pattern out of a failure to trust in God's deliverance. When this crisis arose, Israel did not cry out to God and confidently await God's response. Instead, they demanded a king, and in doing so rejected the kingship of God. This is a different version of events from what we have seen in 1 Samuel 11, where Saul was pictured as a deliverer empowered by God's Spirit in the mold of the judges. The elevation to kingship in that story came after the victory, and in earlier chapters the people's demand for a king came long before the crisis with Ammon (1 Samuel 8). Again, although the ambiguities cannot be resolved, we understand Samuel's claim. Israel in the present moment is accused of a failure to trust in God's deliverance. Instead of crying to God for help, Israel has demanded a king.

Verse 13 shifts from recitation of the past to presentation in the present. Samuel presents the king; he acknowledges kingship as an accomplished fact. Surprisingly, the king is presented both as chosen by the people and as established in authority over Israel by God. The people have demanded, but the king they receive is still from God.

Then vv. 14-15 present the conditions under which people and king can still live within the framework of covenant relationship to God. Even though the kingship originated out of sinful request, there is a future for king and people in relation to God—though with conditions. The listings in vv. 14-15 correspond to the listing of stipulations or requirements in other covenant texts and in ancient treaties (Deuteronomy 12–26; Josh 24:14). The consequences, good and bad, that flow from obedience or disobedience to these requirements reflect the blessings and curses associated with this covenant/treaty form (Deuteronomy 28; Josh 24:20). There are five conditions from which blessing flows, and all reflect the loyalty to the Lord required of Israel and its king. These are followed by two conditions, which will result in judgment:

Obedience to the Lord (v. 14)		Disobedience to the Lord (v. 15)
If you will:	fear	If you will not:
	serve	
	heed his voice	heed his voice
	not rebel	If you do: rebel
	follow	
Then:	it will be well	Then: the hand of the LORD will be against you and your king

The judgment stated in v. 15 is especially interesting, since the hand of the Lord was prominent in judgment against both Philistines and Israelites in the ark story of 1 Samuel 4–6. It is also worth commenting that Samuel includes people and king together in presenting covenant possibilities and covenant dangers. Israel may have a king, and the king may be established by God as a concession to Israel, but the king must obey the covenant.

12:16-19. Samuel has ended his covenant speech. Now he demonstrates his prophetic power: his ability to call and have the Lord answer. It was the time of the wheat harvest when rain was rare, but Samuel called upon the Lord to send a thunderstorm as a sign of the people's sin in asking for a king, and the Lord sent a thunderstorm. This act is reminiscent of events in Samuel's victory over the Philistines in 7:8-10 (see also Elijah's calling forth a drought from the Lord, 1 Kgs 17:1). Thunderstorms are also connected with the appearance of God (theophany). The fear of the people that they may die (v. 19) suggests that they feared the holy presence of God in this storm. They ask for Samuel to intercede for them, and they confess that their demand for a king was evil. The effect of this development is not only to reassert divine authority but to establish Samuel's prophetic authority as God's representative as well. "All the people greatly feared the LORD and Samuel" (v. 18*b*; cf. Exod 14:31*b* for a similar statement on the Lord and Moses). Samuel had vindicated himself (vv. 1-5) and God (vv. 6-15) before the people, and the authority of God and the prophet are now demonstrated to powerful effect. This is hardly a retirement ceremony for Samuel. Kingship may be an accomplished reality in Israel, but God's prophet still claims considerable authority. He has not asked for the undoing of kingship. Indeed, Samuel has helped to establish the king, but the future of king and people still lies within the framework of covenant obedience, and Samuel remains the covenant mediator.

12:20-25. This section is less formal and more homiletical in tone. It even has a pastoral quality as Samuel responds to the people's fearful confession with the classic formula of reassurance, "Do not be afraid" (v. 20*a*). This section again shows marks of the deuteronomic historian—e.g., the phrase "serve the LORD with all your heart" (v. 20). When we remember that Dtr probably wrote and compiled his history in the context of Babylonian exile, we might wonder whether this last section is particularly directed at reassuring and admonishing the exiles. The "fear not" formula is perhaps best known from the great prophet of the exile we know as Second Isaiah (e.g., Isa 41:10, 14; 43:1, 5). There are reassurances that the people can turn back to the Lord and serve the Lord in spite of sin (v. 20*b*), and reaffirmations of God's election of Israel and the tie of God's name to Israel as a people (v. 22). The people are admonished not to turn aside after "useless things." The Hebrew word תֹהוּ (tōhû) is used in Gen 1:2 to indicate chaos and by Second Isaiah in reference to idols (Isa 41:29; 44:9). Samuel ends his homily with a more concise statement of conditions for blessing and curse (vv. 24-25; cf. vv. 14-15). Israel is called to fear and serve the Lord, but if they do wickedness then Israel and its king will be "swept away." Again, in the context of exile, the possibility of being permanently "swept away," both king and people, is a very real fear. Samuel offers some hope, but the consequences of failure are harsh. For exiles reading this historian's story of early Israel—Samuel,

Saul, and eventually David—the story is often a parable of their own struggles.

In the midst of Samuel's final speech (v. 23), the prophet speaks about his own future role (perhaps reflecting the role of prophets in Israel's later history, including the exile experience). For all of his judgment pronounced on Israel's sin, Samuel vows never to sin against the Lord by ceasing to pray for the people and to instruct them in the "good and right way." The people can count on the prophet's continual intercession and moral instruction. It is an interesting and instructive view of the prophet's role beyond the announcement of God's word.

REFLECTIONS

First Samuel 12 is the ideal preaching and teaching text. Its form is already a teaching sermon. Of course, Samuel's words to Israel may need some translation to the situation of the modern church, but not as much as we might think. The issues with which Samuel and Israel were struggling are perennial issues in the life of the church in every generation, including our own.

1. On one level, Samuel's concern and the focus of this chapter are on the way in which old and cherished values can relate to new realities. Situations of change for the faith community and the social contexts in which faith is lived can bring both threat and possibility. Samuel spoke to Israel at a time when many saw the king as a hopeful new reality in their midst. The patterns of covenant community and Samuel's lifelong investment in the leadership of Israel seemed threatened and were probably regarded by many as outmoded. Samuel saw this as an issue of trust in God. The danger was that the God of covenant might seem as outmoded as the older patterns of community and leadership.

Samuel's speech is a word against moral compromise in the name of realistic politics. Changing situations may demand new institutions and new social structures, but Samuel asserts that fundamental moral reality has not changed. That moral reality is rooted in the God who covenants with the community and is faithful to that covenant. Samuel's recital of God's faithfulness in times of crisis can be continued down to the present. New kings or new elected officials or new political parties or new patterns of regulations and governance may become necessary, but these things do not ultimately endure and cannot be the locus of our trust. When we lose sight of God's reign, we risk idolatry in the worship of structures we have made for ourselves. We place ourselves in danger of being "swept away" because these things do not endure.

> Chapter 12 asserts without reservation that there is another governance that merits and must have more of our attention. There is a leadership that does not "take," that does not seek its own. There is a community that could "serve faithfully." This chapter intends to renew in ancient Israel a moral vision of the historical process when that moral vision was skewed by fear, calculation, and vested interest. The renewed moral vision of the historical process is as urgent now as then—lest we all be "swept away."[89]

There is also in this text another insight into times of transition. The speech of Samuel also asserts that the affirmation of old values (covenant) can embrace new forms and realities (kingship). Samuel judges the request for kingship sinful, but this new reality can be

89. Brueggemann, *First and Second Samuel,* 96-97.

encompassed within the covenant framework. Samuel does not ask the people to depose the king, but challenges king and people to renewed covenant obedience. Moral steadfastness need not be reactionary and backward looking. Faithful response need not go back to the future, but can go on to the future—even in changed circumstances we might not have chosen—in confidence that all futures are God's future. In the book of 1 Samuel, there is much that looks back to what God has done and seeks to preserve the covenant relationship forged in that history. But at the same time, much in 1 Samuel looks ahead, beyond the struggles within and without, to David, the man after God's own heart. And in the larger perspective of the canon, it looks beyond David to the Messiah, God with us. Those in our own time who are troubled by changes that threaten valued faith perspectives are right to call for care, lest we reject the reign of God for the sake of our own constructions of reality. But equal care must be exercised that we do not fail to discern what God is doing new in our midst and mindlessly hold to the old and familiar. Times of change, even crisis, bring not only threat but also new possibility. Samuel's speech in the context of a history for exiles may have been intended both to renew covenant loyalties and to affirm that God is still at work in the radically changed realities of their lives: "I am about to do a new thing; now it springs forth, do you not perceive it?" (Isa 43:19*a* NRSV). Samuel's speech is a word to the increasingly polarized political climate of our times. God both preserves and makes new. The challenge is to discernment, not to the choosing of sides.

2. This chapter is also an important text for reflection on the meaning of leadership in the faith community or in the society. Both Samuel and the new king (unnamed here) are assumed in this text to be accountable to the same covenant demands for obedience that are laid upon the people. Samuel opens his conduct as a leader to the people's judgment and witness (12:1-5). In Samuel's challenge to covenant obedience and warning of dangers to disobedience (12:14-15, 24-25), no distinction is drawn between king and people. This text is a fundamental rejection of the notion that leadership brings privileged position. Not even prophets or kings could claim this. This has been a perennial issue in political and religious institutions. Recent decades have seen a constant stream of revelations exposing violations of trust by those who hold offices of leadership in society or church. Often these corrupt practices grow less out of pure malevolence than out of the misguided notion that offices of leadership confer privileged position on their holders—that to hold such offices is to escape the standards expected of the people. The flagrant cases make news headlines. The list includes presidents and Wall Street managers, Republicans and Democrats, men and women. In the church, leadership has suffered the same abuses and illusions of privileged position. The list here includes bishops, denominational treasurers, pastors of local churches, and lay officeholders. These are the offenders, but Samuel's speech suggests that their offenses may grow out of a flawed notion of office and leadership. Can we affirm with Samuel that office should confer no privilege or personal gain? Can we agree that the future of a leader is intimately tied to the future of the people? Do we accept or even promote patterns of deference and privilege between office holder and citizen, or between clergy and laity, that create the climate for abuse?

Along with his warning about kingship in chap. 8, the text of Samuel's speech in chap. 12 has a rich history in the English tradition. English politicians and writers have cited Samuel as support for making the monarchy accountable to the people in the signing of the Magna Charta and for constitutional monarchy in the seventeenth century. Early American patriots, such as Thomas Paine, used Samuel to support democratic forms of leadership that are fully accountable to the people.

Samuel has sometimes been pictured as defensive and crotchety. This may reflect our unhappiness with him in his treatment of Saul later in the story (chaps. 13; 15). It is possible, however, to view him in chap. 12 as a model of admirable traits of leadership. He is unswerving in his determination not to use his office for personal gain. He recognizes that God, and not he, is the true shaping force of history. Although with warnings, he makes a place for the new reality of kingship in Israel. And perhaps his new role, outlined in 12:23, is an especially important word about leadership. When the time of Samuel's formal leadership at the head of the people came to an end, he did not simply abandon his tie to the people but promised to be unceasing in prayer and instruction in the good and right way. One wonders whether the activities of prayer and instruction might sometimes be more enduring than the activities of office and power. Recent American presidents have often left office simply to lead lives of personal pleasure and relaxation. Jimmy Carter, however, a man of prayer and religious conviction, has devoted himself since his presidency to mediation of international conflicts, Habitat for Humanity, and his center in Atlanta dedicated to issues of peace and justice in the world. One wonders whether this is not more in the spirit of Samuel, who did not leave office to go home to his own interests, but continued in prayer for and instruction of the people he had once led in power.

1 Samuel 13:1–15:35, The Exploits and Rejection of Saul

OVERVIEW

Now that Saul is firmly established as king, and Samuel's speech in chap. 12 has given us a pause for theological reflection on covenant, king, and people, the narrative resumes with the career of Saul. It is to be brief and unhappy. The two central episodes are rejection stories (13:8-15; 15:1-35). Again, Samuel plays a central role as God's prophet. He confronts Saul with violations of covenant obedience and sacral law, and then announces God's judgment. The section ends with the mournful note that "the LORD was sorry that he had made Saul king over Israel." Saul will remain in the story for the rest of 1 Samuel, but the focus will shift to David beginning with chap. 16.

Surrounding these two rejection stories are traditions that narrate Saul's efforts against the Philistines. These sections provide a good deal of data about the historical circumstances of the time. Israel exists in a desperate position. Saul's efforts seem admirable and sometimes effective, but even here Saul seems overshadowed by his own son Jonathan. The episode in chap. 14 that almost leads to the death of Jonathan already begins to cast a shadow over Saul's leadership and judgment. In this entire section we have the feeling that we are not really hearing about Saul's reign but are being prepared for the appearance of David.

1 Samuel 13:1-23, Saul Rejected from Dynasty

13 Saul was ⌞thirty,⌟[a] years old when he became king, and he reigned over Israel ⌞forty-⌟[b] two years.

[2]Saul[c] chose three thousand men from Israel; two thousand were with him at Micmash and in the hill country of Bethel, and a thousand were with Jonathan at Gibeah in Benjamin. The rest of the men he sent back to their homes.

[3]Jonathan attacked the Philistine outpost at Geba, and the Philistines heard about it. Then

[a1] A few late manuscripts of the Septuagint; Hebrew does not have *thirty*. [b1] See the round number in Acts 13:21; Hebrew does not have *forty*. [c1,2] Or *and when he had reigned over Israel two years,* [2]he

13 Saul was . . .[a] years old when he began to reign; and he reigned . . . and two[b] years over Israel.

2Saul chose three thousand out of Israel; two thousand were with Saul in Michmash and the hill country of Bethel, and a thousand were with Jonathan in Gibeah of Benjamin; the rest of the people he sent home to their tents. [3]Jonathan defeated the garrison of the Philistines that was at Geba; and the Philistines heard of it. And Saul blew the trumpet throughout all the land, saying,

[a] The number is lacking in the Heb text (the verse is lacking in the Septuagint). [b] *Two* is not the entire number; something has dropped out.

Saul had the trumpet blown throughout the land and said, "Let the Hebrews hear!" [4]So all Israel heard the news: "Saul has attacked the Philistine outpost, and now Israel has become a stench to the Philistines." And the people were summoned to join Saul at Gilgal.

[5]The Philistines assembled to fight Israel, with three thousand[a] chariots, six thousand charioteers, and soldiers as numerous as the sand on the seashore. They went up and camped at Micmash, east of Beth Aven. [6]When the men of Israel saw that their situation was critical and that their army was hard pressed, they hid in caves and thickets, among the rocks, and in pits and cisterns. [7]Some Hebrews even crossed the Jordan to the land of Gad and Gilead.

Saul remained at Gilgal, and all the troops with him were quaking with fear. [8]He waited seven days, the time set by Samuel; but Samuel did not come to Gilgal, and Saul's men began to scatter. [9]So he said, "Bring me the burnt offering and the fellowship offerings.[b]" And Saul offered up the burnt offering. [10]Just as he finished making the offering, Samuel arrived, and Saul went out to greet him.

[11]"What have you done?" asked Samuel.

Saul replied, "When I saw that the men were scattering, and that you did not come at the set time, and that the Philistines were assembling at Micmash, [12]I thought, 'Now the Philistines will come down against me at Gilgal, and I have not sought the LORD's favor.' So I felt compelled to offer the burnt offering."

[13]"You acted foolishly," Samuel said. "You have not kept the command the LORD your God gave you; if you had, he would have established your kingdom over Israel for all time. [14]But now your kingdom will not endure; the LORD has sought out a man after his own heart and appointed him leader of his people, because you have not kept the LORD's command."

[15]Then Samuel left Gilgal[c] and went up to Gibeah in Benjamin, and Saul counted the men who were with him. They numbered about six hundred.

[16]Saul and his son Jonathan and the men with

"Let the Hebrews hear!" [4]When all Israel heard that Saul had defeated the garrison of the Philistines, and also that Israel had become odious to the Philistines, the people were called out to join Saul at Gilgal.

5The Philistines mustered to fight with Israel, thirty thousand chariots, and six thousand horsemen, and troops like the sand on the seashore in multitude; they came up and encamped at Michmash, to the east of Beth-aven. [6]When the Israelites saw that they were in distress (for the troops were hard pressed), the people hid themselves in caves and in holes and in rocks and in tombs and in cisterns. [7]Some Hebrews crossed the Jordan to the land of Gad and Gilead. Saul was still at Gilgal, and all the people followed him trembling.

8He waited seven days, the time appointed by Samuel; but Samuel did not come to Gilgal, and the people began to slip away from Saul.[a] [9]So Saul said, "Bring the burnt offering here to me, and the offerings of well-being." And he offered the burnt offering. [10]As soon as he had finished offering the burnt offering, Samuel arrived; and Saul went out to meet him and salute him. [11]Samuel said, "What have you done?" Saul replied, "When I saw that the people were slipping away from me, and that you did not come within the days appointed, and that the Philistines were mustering at Michmash, [12]I said, 'Now the Philistines will come down upon me at Gilgal, and I have not entreated the favor of the LORD'; so I forced myself, and offered the burnt offering." [13]Samuel said to Saul, "You have done foolishly; you have not kept the commandment of the LORD your God, which he commanded you. The LORD would have established your kingdom over Israel forever, [14]but now your kingdom will not continue; the LORD has sought out a man after his own heart; and the LORD has appointed him to be ruler over his people, because you have not kept what the LORD commanded you." [15]And Samuel left and went on his way from Gilgal.[b] The rest of the people followed Saul to join the army; they went up from Gilgal toward Gibeah of Benjamin.[c]

Saul counted the people who were present with him, about six hundred men. [16]Saul, his son

NIV

them were staying in Gibeah[a] in Benjamin, while the Philistines camped at Micmash. [17]Raiding parties went out from the Philistine camp in three detachments. One turned toward Ophrah in the vicinity of Shual, [18]another toward Beth Horon, and the third toward the borderland overlooking the Valley of Zeboim facing the desert.

[19]Not a blacksmith could be found in the whole land of Israel, because the Philistines had said, "Otherwise the Hebrews will make swords or spears!" [20]So all Israel went down to the Philistines to have their plowshares, mattocks, axes and sickles[b] sharpened. [21]The price was two thirds of a shekel[c] for sharpening plowshares and mattocks, and a third of a shekel[d] for sharpening forks and axes and for repointing goads.

[22]So on the day of the battle not a soldier with Saul and Jonathan had a sword or spear in his hand; only Saul and his son Jonathan had them.

[23]Now a detachment of Philistines had gone out to the pass at Micmash.

[a]16 Two Hebrew manuscripts; most Hebrew manuscripts *Geba,* a variant of *Gibeah* [b]20 Septuagint; Hebrew *plowshares* [c]21 Hebrew *pim*; that is, about 1/4 ounce (about 8 grams) [d]21 That is, about 1/8 ounce (about 4 grams)

NRSV

Jonathan, and the people who were present with them stayed in Geba of Benjamin; but the Philistines encamped at Michmash. [17]And raiders came out of the camp of the Philistines in three companies; one company turned toward Ophrah, to the land of Shual, [18]another company turned toward Beth-horon, and another company turned toward the mountain[a] that looks down upon the valley of Zeboim toward the wilderness.

[19]Now there was no smith to be found throughout all the land of Israel; for the Philistines said, "The Hebrews must not make swords or spears for themselves"; [20]so all the Israelites went down to the Philistines to sharpen their plowshares, mattocks, axes, or sickles;[b] [21]The charge was two-thirds of a shekel[c] for the plowshares and for the mattocks, and one-third of a shekel for sharpening the axes and for setting the goads.[d] [22]So on the day of the battle neither sword nor spear was to be found in the possession of any of the people with Saul and Jonathan; but Saul and his son Jonathan had them.

[23]Now a garrison of the Philistines had gone out to the pass of Michmash.

[a] Cn Compare Gk: Heb *toward the border* [b] Gk: Heb *plowshare* [c] Heb *was a pim* [d] Cn: Meaning of Heb uncertain

COMMENTARY

The use of a special formula (although incomplete) announces the formal beginning of Saul's reign in v. 1. Saul is now king, but the story of his rise to the throne almost immediately becomes the story of his fall from kingship. In Saul's story there is no honeymoon for the new monarch. Chapter 13 is a narrative of Saul's external conflict with the Philistines and internal conflict with Samuel. Saul does not succeed in overcoming either of these conflicts, and they eventually bring him to a tragic end.

The immediate challenge for Saul's reign is the war against Philistine domination. Verses 2-7a begin a detailed account of military encounters with the Philistines and the particular exploits of Saul and his son Jonathan (introduced here for the first time). The story of these military campaigns and their eventual limited success in parts of the tribal territory of Benjamin continues in vv. 15b-23 and on into chap. 14.

In the midst of this account of military tactics and maneuvers we find an episode of conflict between Saul and the prophet Samuel (vv. 7b-15a). Saul, faced with a deteriorating military situation, had offered the sacrifices necessary to begin battle. Samuel had told him to wait for his arrival. One presumes that the prophet would have offered these sacrifices. When Samuel arrives to find that Saul had proceeded without him, he angrily denounces Saul and announces that God will seek another "man after his own heart" to whom the kingdom will be given.

There are numerous problems in this chapter: (1) Samuel's instruction of Saul to wait at Gilgal for seven days (v. 8) seems related to the command of Samuel in 10:8, but in chap. 10 Saul

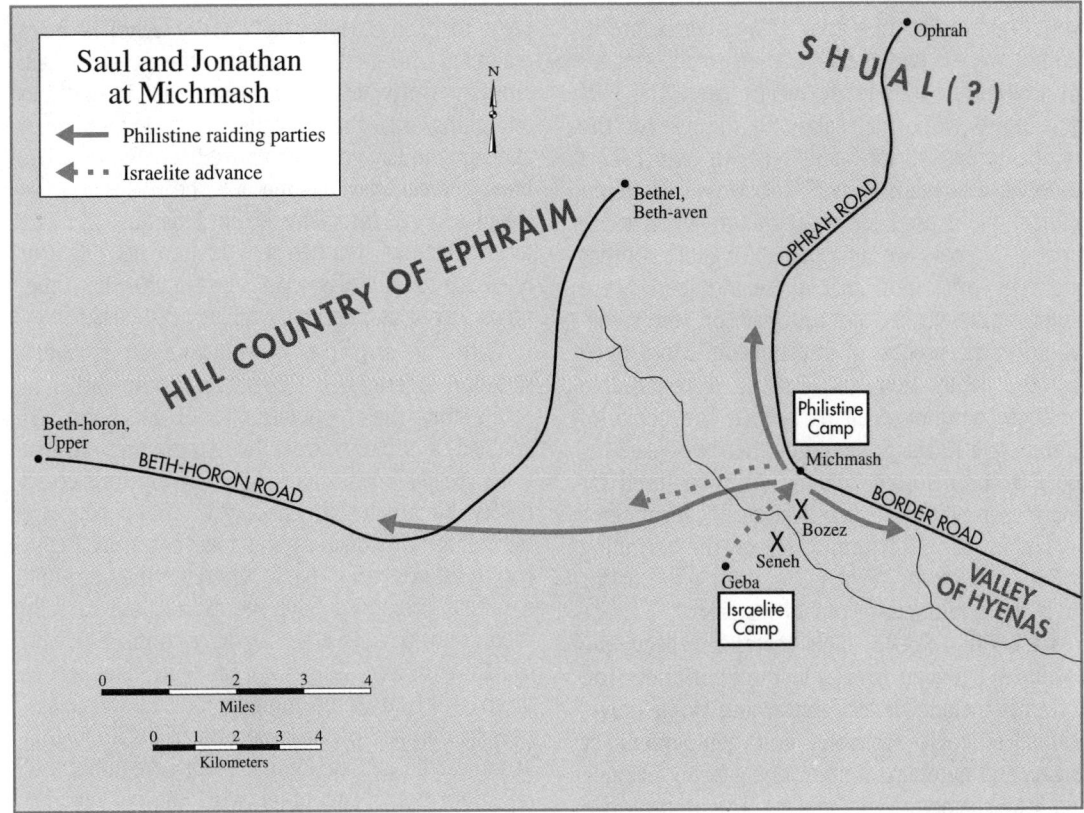

Saul and Jonathan at Michmash

← Philistine raiding parties

◄ · · · Israelite advance

was a boy and not yet king. In chap. 13, Saul is a warrior king with a grown warrior son. (2) The narrative seems to speak of the military exploits of Saul and Jonathan in a confused and overlapping way (cf. v. 3 with v. 4). This situation has led some scholars to suggest that an account of a successful campaign by Saul has been interwoven with an account of Jonathan's deeds.[90] (3) Almost all commentators have recognized a confusion in biblical references to Gibeah (גבעה gib'â) and Geba (גבע geba'). Although these two places have traditionally been seen as separate locations only three miles apart in Benjaminite territory, the two often appear interchangeably in different manuscript traditions and within narrative episodes (e.g., cf. v. 15 with v. 16). Miller has made a plausible case that references to Geba, to Geba of Benjamin, to Gibeah, to Gibeath, to Gibeah of Benjamin, to Gibeah of Saul, and to Gibeath-elohim all refer to the same general geographic location.[91] Some of these matters are commented

on further below, but in general the difficulties of this chapter cannot be fully resolved. Chapter 13 does not seem an entirely smooth literary piece, but the significance for Saul's story of conflicts with the Philistines and with Samuel seems clear, and that will be our focus.

13:1. This is the formula typically used to introduce the reign of a king in the books of Kings (e.g., 1 Kgs 14:21; 22:42). It is also used later for Ishbaal (2 Sam 2:10) and David (2 Sam 5:4). The formula usually states the age of the king at accession and the number of years of his reign, but in Saul's case the formula appears to be incomplete. The MT literally reads that Saul was one year old when he began his reign. A number may have dropped out, as the NRSV rendering suggests by leaving a blank space. Three LXX manuscripts read the number 30, which the NIV has adopted, but most LXX texts omit the entire verse. The age of thirty seems young for Saul to have a warrior son like Jonathan a verse later, however.

The last part of the formula is also incomplete. The Hebrew text reads two years for Saul's reign, but in an unusual form of the number 2 that

90. See Ralph W Klein, *1 Samuel,* WBC 10 (Waco: Word, 1983) 123-28, for a more detailed discussion of various proposals.

91. J. M. Miller, "Geba/Gibeah of Benjamin," *VT* 25 (1975) 145-66.

would seem to require another number before it. Many have felt two years too short to account for the events of Saul's reign, in any case. The NIV reads forty-two by appealing to the use of the round number 40 for Saul's reign in Acts 13:21. Josephus also reads forty,[92] but forty is a round number often used for a generation when more precise numbers are unknown. We must content ourselves by saying that these numbers were either unknown to the historian or lost somewhere in the process of transmission. Most agree that the deuteronomistic historian is responsible for these chronological markers in the books of Samuel and Kings. Some argue that two years fits the Dtr chronological scheme, and was used for that reason whether it was historically accurate or not. In any case, the formula signals the beginning of Saul's kingship. What follows, for good or for ill, is the tradition's record of his reign.

13:2-7a, 15b-23. This material reflects the hostilities between Israel and the Philistines. The accounts include details concerning troop movements, strategic locations and deployment of forces, and numbers of men. There is no dialogue and little character development. The literary style is straightforward and almost bare of stylistic devices (vv. 5-6 show a brief descriptive flourish). The impression is of annalistic material or official records of these military encounters.

This military material in chap. 13 sets the stage for the more developed narrative of events in chap. 14. Saul is presented as a capable military leader who has assembled a significant force (v. 2). He is encamped at Michmash and Jonathan at Gibeah/Geba. Jonathan takes bold action (foreshadowing his role in chap. 14?) and wins a victory over the garrison of Philistines at Gibeah/Geba (v. 3). This act gains the attention of the Philistines and causes Saul to blow the trumpet and summon the Israelite levy (v. 4). A major Philistine army encamps at Michmash to put down this rebellion (v. 5).

In Saul's summons (v. 3b), he says, "Let the Hebrews hear!" This expression is problematic, because Israelites never referred to themselves as Hebrews. Elsewhere the term is pejorative and is applied to them by others. Later, in v. 7, the scattering of Israelite troops includes a further refer-

ence to "some Hebrews." Many scholars have emended the text to remove these references. Norman Gottwald has proposed that in addition to calling out the Israelite tribal levy Saul is appealing to Israelites who have become *apiru*/Hebrew mercenaries fighting for the Philistines, as David and his men later do in 1 Samuel 27. The term "Hebrew" is often said to have its origin in reference to an outlaw class called *apiru* who sometimes served as mercenary military retainers.[93]

With the arrival of a Philistine army, Saul's situation deteriorates. Only a brief time earlier in Saul's story, the empowerment of God's Spirit had enabled a victory over the Ammonites against even greater odds (chap. 11). The contrast could hardly be greater in chap. 13. The people are trembling with distress and take cowardly flight, hiding themselves in panic wherever they can find a refuge (vv. 6-7). Saul seems helpless to rally them, and in v. 15b he can only count 600 who remain with him. This is not the Spirit-filled leader of chap. 11. It is the moment of Saul's helplessness in the face of the desertion of his army that becomes the setting for the story of conflict and rejection in the encounter with Samuel (vv. 7b-15a). Saul's loss of God's Spirit is not noted until 16:14, but the power of God's Spirit seems already dormant in Saul.

The last portion of the chapter gives further reports on military movements and deployments. The Philistines are encamped at Michmash and send out smaller forces in three directions (vv. 17-18). Saul and Jonathan remain at Gibeah/Geba with their depleted force (vv. 15b-16), but the chapter ends by calling attention to the Philistine force deployed to the pass at Michmash. The stage is set for the bold raid of Jonathan, which begins chap. 14.

As an aside from the main story, vv. 19-22 report that the Philistines had a monopoly on ironworking in the region. The Israelites (called Hebrews by the Philistines, v. 19) were not allowed to have smiths. Even farm implements had to be obtained from the Philistine smiths, and at considerable cost as well (vv. 20-21). Thus Israelite armies under Saul did not have iron fighting weapons. Only Saul and Jonathan possessed sword or spear of iron (v. 22). The impact of this note is to heighten the readers' sense of the

92. Josephus *Antiquities of the Jews* 6.14.9.

93. Norman K. Gottwald, *The Tribes of Yahweh: A Sociology of the Religion of Liberated Israel, 1250–1050 B.C.E.* (Maryknoll: Orbis, 1979) 423-24.

overwhelming odds faced by Saul, Jonathan, and the Israelite warriors.

13:7b-15a. This is the first of two episodes telling of Saul's rejection by Samuel (cf. also chap. 15). In the present form of the text, this story is tied to the instruction of Samuel to the young Saul in 10:8. The prophet commands Saul to go to Gilgal and wait seven days for Samuel's arrival to offer sacrifices. Verse 8 sets the stage for following events by reporting that Saul waits the seven days appointed by Samuel, but the prophet does not come to Gilgal. We have already briefly noted the problems with this chronology. The events of 10:17–12:25 could hardly have taken place in seven days. Further, the young Saul of 10:8 is now a man with a grown son in 13:8. Nevertheless, there is no other possible reference for the command to wait at Gilgal. The historian has apparently chosen to ignore the chronological problems in favor of focusing on Saul's obedience to the command of the prophet Samuel. The story even seems artificially to move Saul to Gilgal (v. 7b) and back again to Gibeah/Geba (v. 15) to make this possible.

Saul is occupied with the strategic military situation. His troops are scattering in panic after having seen the superior strength of the Philistines. A battle seems imminent, but in the holy war traditions of Israel sacrifices must be offered before a battle in order to seek the Lord's favor. It is not only a matter of required ritual but also for Saul a matter of his troops' morale. How can he hold his men if they do not have confidence that the Lord will aid their cause against the oppressor Philistines?

Saul fails to see that this is a theological as well as a strategic situation. Samuel had commanded him to wait, and the prophet had specified that he would arrive to make the sacrifices. The burnt offering and the offering of well-being (peace or fellowship offering, NIV) are the very sacrifices Samuel mentioned in 10:8 and reserved to himself. We have already seen Samuel offering sacrifices before battle (7:9-10) in a victorious encounter with the Philistines. Hence, the ritual may be a prophetic prerogative, and thus not to be usurped by kings. Kings, after all, were new to Israel and had no claim on traditional rituals.

No sooner does Saul proceed with the sacrifices than Samuel appears. It is hard to avoid some suspicion at the timing of his entrance. Samuel's encounter with Saul occurs in the form of a prophetic accusation and announcement of judgment. Samuel responds to Saul's greeting with an accusing question, "What have you done?" (v. 11a). "The prophetic accusation to an individual person was often a matter of the prophet's establishing the facts of the case through questions exactly as it occurs in the regular judicial process. . . . [It is] similar to a hearing in which the prophet is one who hears and the king is the one heard."[94] Saul's response is defensive, shifting responsibility to Samuel, "The people were slipping away from me, and . . . *you* [the pronoun here is emphatic] did not come" (v. 11b). Saul goes on to state his desire to have the favor of the Lord in battle and claims that he "forced himself" to make the sacrifices (v. 12). He offered them reluctantly, he claims.

Saul seems sympathetic here. To most readers his rationale sounds reasonable and his actions understandable. We are unprepared for the harshness of Samuel's response. He brands Saul's actions foolish and charges Saul with failing to keep the commandment of the Lord (v. 13a). Prophetic accusation is then followed by announcement of punishment, and again Samuel's response seems exceptionally harsh. Samuel announces that the Lord would have established Saul's kingdom forever (v. 13b). This is a new motif in 1 Samuel, and it foreshadows the dynastic promise later given to David by the prophet Nathan (2 Samuel 7). Samuel continues by saying that now Saul's kingdom will not continue (v. 14a). Saul is denied the hope of dynasty for his house. The reader has just been introduced to Jonathan; both here and in the following chapter he appears as an attractive and capable leader. However, Samuel makes clear that Jonathan will not succeed his father as king. Further, Samuel declares that the Lord has already selected Saul's successor, "a man after his own heart," and has appointed him נגיד (*nāgîd*, "ruler," "prince," "designate to the throne," v. 14b). This is clearly a reference ahead to David, who will be anointed by Samuel in 16:13 as Saul's successor. David's shadow is cast over Saul from the very beginning of his reign. The phrase "a man after his own heart" is often taken as a reference to David's character, as if it refers to some special quality that singled David out. McCarter has shown clearly, however, that this

94. Claus Westermann, *Basic Forms of Prophetic Speech* (Philadelphia: Westminster, 1967) 144.

phrase refers not to David's character but to God's freedom.[95] The kingdom is given to "a man of God's own choosing" (cf. the use of this phrase in 14:7; 2 Sam 7:21; Ps 20:4; Jer 3:15). This phrase looks ahead to David because this is the direction God wills. This emphasis on God's free choice of the anointed one as designated through prophets is consistent with the prophetic theology of kingship, visible in 9:1–10:16, the episode to which this story is tied through the command of Samuel the prophet.

Again Samuel asserts with finality that Saul has not kept the Lord's commandment (v. 14*b*). What was this commandment? What does Samuel see as the offense? Is the failure to follow Samuel's instructions the equivalent of violating the commandment of the Lord? Is the punishment announced by Samuel out of proportion to the offense? The text does not answer all of our questions. We are inclined to respond to the personalities at play here. Saul seems well meaning and concerned for his people. Samuel seems angry, temperamental, and reactionary. The modern reader is inclined to feel that he is overreacting. We should probably not underestimate the depth of the issues involved in the transitions taking

95. P. Kyle McCarter, *I Samuel,* AB 8 (Garden City, N.Y.: Doubleday, 1980) 229.

place with the establishment of kingship for the first time in Israel. How much power are kings to have? Should their authority extend to religious matters? Should the office of king usurp the office of the prophet/covenant mediator? Should kingship in Israel include the concept of dynasty? Samuel is not an attractive personality in these stories, but the issues are more than a clash of personalities. They are issues that will prove to be life-and-death matters in Israel, and from the perspective of the historians who later shaped this narrative (perhaps both prophetic and deuteronomistic) the deathly possibilities inherent in royal power seem more obvious than they may to the contemporary reader. Perhaps these historians knew of later times in Israel's story when hundreds of prophets were co-opted by royal power in the time of Ahab (1 Kgs 22:6).

Saul is not to be Israel's future, and in chap. 15 he is even rejected as the legitimate king of Israel's present in the story of 1 Samuel. Perhaps the tradition does not itself fully know why Saul deserved this fate, but it does know that David was God's choice for Israel's future and that Saul's brief reign was not finally characterized by the presence of God's Spirit.

REFLECTIONS

This first story of Saul's rejection before he even has a chance to establish his reign is a tale with sober lessons to teach. These reflections grow out of the beginning of a tragedy that will not, perhaps cannot, be averted.

1. This tale of conflict between Samuel and Saul is set in a context that calls for the exercise of power on several different levels. Military power must be exercised in the face of the Philistine threat. The power of leadership is called for to maintain readiness and morale among Saul's own fighting men. The power of religious authority is crucial in Israel, where all wars are to be fought as holy wars in obedience to God's purpose and will. In each of these interrelated arenas there were decisions to be made and actions to be taken, and these were a matter of life and death.

But these issues of power could not be decided in the abstract. They came entangled in the personalities of Samuel and Saul. Samuel is a reluctant participant in the enterprise of kingship. He is fearful that kingship will erode the covenant tradition he has upheld faithfully. He will be supplanted to some degree by any shape of developing royal leadership. In his prophetic role, he designated Saul, and he feels bound to hold Saul accountable to the Lord whom Samuel serves as prophet. Saul is a young man in a role with no precedent in Israel. His inexperience as king is matched by Israel's inexperience at having kings. He is faced with an overwhelming military challenge and a deteriorating capability for meeting that challenge. He seems naive in his understanding of relationship to the religious authority of Samuel.

What begins in the conflict here, continues in the total rejection of chap. 15, and finally ends when Saul takes his own life in 1 Samuel 31 is a tragedy borne of the peculiar mix of personality and power issues that mark the lives of Samuel and Saul. What we must understand is that this mixing of personality and power is always the case. We wish it were not so. We long for purity in moral decision making, hoping for some rational, objective method of knowing the will of God and determining the ethical course of action. Or we long for ideal personalities with no human flaws to make these decisions for us. If only we had the ideal president or the ideal pastor. But this difficult story of Samuel and Saul reminds us that moral decisions are made in the context of complex, often ambiguous, power dilemmas, and they are made by real people, with their personal flaws and vested interests.

In the ongoing story of 1 Samuel it is clear that alongside the messy issues of personality and power, God is at work opening new possibilities for Israel. Beyond the arenas of human power is a working of divine power. The ark stories in chaps. 4–6 make the reality of this power visible. The hand of Yahweh is at work in these events. This episode already looks ahead to God's choosing of David (v. 14). This seems a quick and harsh verdict on Saul, but the stakes for Israel are high. It is not too early to suggest that the constant prayer and inquiry after God's will that mark so many David stories are in distinct contrast to the well-meaning, but self-possessed blundering forward of Saul. Saul always seems to act on his own authority rather than in communication with God. It is a warning to our own well-intentioned efforts that are, nevertheless, centered only in our own power and authority.

2. The conflict between Samuel and Saul is a matter not only of personalities but also of role or office. Samuel is a prophet, but in the circumstances of his time he also serves in judicial and priestly roles that maintain the older covenant traditions of Israel. Saul is Israel's new king, an office not known before in Israel and considered by some antagonistic to the covenant tradition. The conflict here is a reflection of the need to determine the relationship that should exist between the authority of kings and the authority of prophets.

While modern readers often sympathize with Saul in this and subsequent episodes (Samuel comes off as a considerably unlikable grouch!), it would be well for American readers in particular to remember their own history. The founders of the United States thought there were good reasons to separate religious and governance roles. They did not wish kings to control religious rituals and practices, and they had in some cases come to the American colonies to escape the abuse of such royal authority used to restrict religious practice. Eventually in Israel kings began to co-opt many of the prophets or persecute those whom they could not co-opt. We may sympathize with Saul as a person, but we should not be so quick to dismiss his actions as trivial. It is often by seemingly innocent and trivial acts that authority is undermined or liberties eroded, in our own time as surely as in ancient Israel. Samuel may be a harsh character in this story, but we would do well to consider him a warning to our complacency when religious symbols are appropriated for civil or political purposes or for partisan ideological commitments in our own time. This is surely one of the issues to be considered in the heated debate over prayer in public schools. Even if the intention is noble, do we want to set the precedent of allowing civil authority to authorize or, as some would have it, administer religious observance? Those who answer this question in the negative may seem as harsh and unreasoning as would Samuel to some.

1 Samuel 14:1-52, Jonathan and Saul Against the Philistines

NIV

14 ¹One day Jonathan son of Saul said to the young man bearing his armor, "Come, let's go over to the Philistine outpost on the other side." But he did not tell his father.

²Saul was staying on the outskirts of Gibeah under a pomegranate tree in Migron. With him were about six hundred men, ³among whom was Ahijah, who was wearing an ephod. He was a son of Ichabod's brother Ahitub son of Phinehas, the son of Eli, the LORD's priest in Shiloh. No one was aware that Jonathan had left.

⁴On each side of the pass that Jonathan intended to cross to reach the Philistine outpost was a cliff; one was called Bozez, and the other Seneh. ⁵One cliff stood to the north toward Micmash, the other to the south toward Geba.

⁶Jonathan said to his young armor-bearer, "Come, let's go over to the outpost of those uncircumcised fellows. Perhaps the LORD will act in our behalf. Nothing can hinder the LORD from saving, whether by many or by few."

⁷"Do all that you have in mind," his armor-bearer said. "Go ahead; I am with you heart and soul."

⁸Jonathan said, "Come, then; we will cross over toward the men and let them see us. ⁹If they say to us, 'Wait there until we come to you,' we will stay where we are and not go up to them. ¹⁰But if they say, 'Come up to us,' we will climb up, because that will be our sign that the LORD has given them into our hands."

¹¹So both of them showed themselves to the Philistine outpost. "Look!" said the Philistines. "The Hebrews are crawling out of the holes they were hiding in." ¹²The men of the outpost shouted to Jonathan and his armor-bearer, "Come up to us and we'll teach you a lesson."

So Jonathan said to his armor-bearer, "Climb up after me; the LORD has given them into the hand of Israel."

¹³Jonathan climbed up, using his hands and feet, with his armor-bearer right behind him. The Philistines fell before Jonathan, and his armor-bearer followed and killed behind him. ¹⁴In that

NRSV

14 ¹One day Jonathan son of Saul said to the young man who carried his armor, "Come, let us go over to the Philistine garrison on the other side." But he did not tell his father. ²Saul was staying in the outskirts of Gibeah under the pomegranate tree that is at Migron; the troops that were with him were about six hundred men, ³along with Ahijah son of Ahitub, Ichabod's brother, son of Phinehas son of Eli, the priest of the LORD in Shiloh, carrying an ephod. Now the people did not know that Jonathan had gone. ⁴In the pass,ᵃ by which Jonathan tried to go over to the Philistine garrison, there was a rocky crag on one side and a rocky crag on the other; the name of the one was Bozez, and the name of the other Seneh. ⁵One crag rose on the north in front of Michmash, and the other on the south in front of Geba.

⁶Jonathan said to the young man who carried his armor, "Come, let us go over to the garrison of these uncircumcised; it may be that the LORD will act for us; for nothing can hinder the LORD from saving by many or by few." ⁷His armor-bearer said to him, "Do all that your mind inclines to.ᵇ I am with you; as your mind is, so is mine."ᶜ ⁸Then Jonathan said, "Now we will cross over to those men and will show ourselves to them. ⁹If they say to us, 'Wait until we come to you,' then we will stand still in our place, and we will not go up to them. ¹⁰But if they say, 'Come up to us,' then we will go up; for the LORD has given them into our hand. That will be the sign for us." ¹¹So both of them showed themselves to the garrison of the Philistines; and the Philistines said, "Look, Hebrews are coming out of the holes where they have hidden themselves." ¹²The men of the garrison hailed Jonathan and his armor-bearer, saying, "Come up to us, and we will show you something." Jonathan said to his armor-bearer, "Come up after me; for the LORD has given them into the hand of Israel." ¹³Then Jonathan climbed up on his hands and feet, with his armor-bearer following after him. The Philistinesᵈ fell before Jonathan,

ᵃ Heb *Between the passes*   ᵇ Gk: Heb *Do all that is in your mind. Turn*   ᶜ Gk: Heb lacks *so is mine*   ᵈ Heb *They*

NIV

first attack Jonathan and his armor-bearer killed some twenty men in an area of about half an acre.[a]

[15]Then panic struck the whole army—those in the camp and field, and those in the outposts and raiding parties—and the ground shook. It was a panic sent by God.[b]

[16]Saul's lookouts at Gibeah in Benjamin saw the army melting away in all directions. [17]Then Saul said to the men who were with him, "Muster the forces and see who has left us." When they did, it was Jonathan and his armor-bearer who were not there.

[18]Saul said to Ahijah, "Bring the ark of God." (At that time it was with the Israelites.)[c] [19]While Saul was talking to the priest, the tumult in the Philistine camp increased more and more. So Saul said to the priest, "Withdraw your hand."

[20]Then Saul and all his men assembled and went to the battle. They found the Philistines in total confusion, striking each other with their swords. [21]Those Hebrews who had previously been with the Philistines and had gone up with them to their camp went over to the Israelites who were with Saul and Jonathan. [22]When all the Israelites who had hidden in the hill country of Ephraim heard that the Philistines were on the run, they joined the battle in hot pursuit. [23]So the LORD rescued Israel that day, and the battle moved on beyond Beth Aven.

[24]Now the men of Israel were in distress that day, because Saul had bound the people under an oath, saying, "Cursed be any man who eats food before evening comes, before I have avenged myself on my enemies!" So none of the troops tasted food.

[25]The entire army[d] entered the woods, and there was honey on the ground. [26]When they went into the woods, they saw the honey oozing out, yet no one put his hand to his mouth, because they feared the oath. [27]But Jonathan had not heard that his father had bound the people with the oath, so he reached out the end of the staff that was in his hand and dipped it into the honeycomb. He raised his hand to his mouth, and his eyes brightened.[e] [28]Then one of the soldiers told him, "Your father bound the army under a strict oath, saying, 'Cursed be any man who eats food today!' That is why the men are faint."

a14 Hebrew half a yoke; a "yoke" was the land plowed by a yoke of oxen in one day.   b15 Or a terrible panic   c18 Hebrew; Septuagint "Bring the ephod." (At that time he wore the ephod before the Israelites.)   d25 Or Now all the people of the land   e27 Or his strength was renewed

NRSV

and his armor-bearer, coming after him, killed them. [14]In that first slaughter Jonathan and his armor-bearer killed about twenty men within an area about half a furrow long in an acre[a] of land. [15]There was a panic in the camp, in the field, and among all the people; the garrison and even the raiders trembled; the earth quaked; and it became a very great panic.

16Saul's lookouts in Gibeah of Benjamin were watching as the multitude was surging back and forth.[b] [17]Then Saul said to the troops that were with him, "Call the roll and see who has gone from us." When they had called the roll, Jonathan and his armor-bearer were not there. [18]Saul said to Ahijah, "Bring the ark[c] of God here." For at that time the ark[c] of God went with the Israelites. [19]While Saul was talking to the priest, the tumult in the camp of the Philistines increased more and more; and Saul said to the priest, "Withdraw your hand." [20]Then Saul and all the people who were with him rallied and went into the battle; and every sword was against the other, so that there was very great confusion. [21]Now the Hebrews who previously had been with the Philistines and had gone up with them into the camp turned and joined the Israelites who were with Saul and Jonathan. [22]Likewise, when all the Israelites who had gone into hiding in the hill country of Ephraim heard that the Philistines were fleeing, they too followed closely after them in the battle. [23]So the LORD gave Israel the victory that day.

The battle passed beyond Beth-aven, and the troops with Saul numbered altogether about ten thousand men. The battle spread out over the hill country of Ephraim.

24Now Saul committed a very rash act on that day.[d] He had laid an oath on the troops, saying, "Cursed be anyone who eats food before it is evening and I have been avenged on my enemies." So none of the troops tasted food. [25]All the troops[e] came upon a honeycomb; and there was honey on the ground. [26]When the troops came upon the honeycomb, the honey was dripping out; but they did not put their hands to their mouths, for they feared the oath. [27]But Jonathan had not heard his father charge the troops with

a Heb yoke   b Gk: Heb they went and there   c Gk the ephod   d Gk: Heb The Israelites were distressed that day   e Heb land

NIV

²⁹Jonathan said, "My father has made trouble for the country. See how my eyes brightened[a] when I tasted a little of this honey. ³⁰How much better it would have been if the men had eaten today some of the plunder they took from their enemies. Would not the slaughter of the Philistines have been even greater?"

³¹That day, after the Israelites had struck down the Philistines from Micmash to Aijalon, they were exhausted. ³²They pounced on the plunder and, taking sheep, cattle and calves, they butchered them on the ground and ate them, together with the blood. ³³Then someone said to Saul, "Look, the men are sinning against the Lord by eating meat that has blood in it."

"You have broken faith," he said. "Roll a large stone over here at once." ³⁴Then he said, "Go out among the men and tell them, 'Each of you bring me your cattle and sheep, and slaughter them here and eat them. Do not sin against the Lord by eating meat with blood still in it.'"

So everyone brought his ox that night and slaughtered it there. ³⁵Then Saul built an altar to the Lord; it was the first time he had done this.

³⁶Saul said, "Let us go down after the Philistines by night and plunder them till dawn, and let us not leave one of them alive."

"Do whatever seems best to you," they replied.

But the priest said, "Let us inquire of God here."

³⁷So Saul asked God, "Shall I go down after the Philistines? Will you give them into Israel's hand?" But God did not answer him that day.

³⁸Saul therefore said, "Come here, all you who are leaders of the army, and let us find out what sin has been committed today. ³⁹As surely as the Lord who rescues Israel lives, even if it lies with my son Jonathan, he must die." But not one of the men said a word.

⁴⁰Saul then said to all the Israelites, "You stand over there; I and Jonathan my son will stand over here."

"Do what seems best to you," the men replied.

⁴¹Then Saul prayed to the Lord, the God of Israel, "Give me the right answer."[b] And Jonathan and Saul were taken by lot, and the men were

---

a29 Or my strength was renewed   b41 Hebrew; Septuagint "Why have you not answered your servant today? If the fault is in me or my son Jonathan, respond with Urim, but if the men of Israel are at fault, respond with Thummim."

NRSV

the oath; so he extended the staff that was in his hand, and dipped the tip of it in the honeycomb, and put his hand to his mouth; and his eyes brightened. ²⁸Then one of the soldiers said, "Your father strictly charged the troops with an oath, saying, 'Cursed be anyone who eats food this day.' And so the troops are faint." ²⁹Then Jonathan said, "My father has troubled the land; see how my eyes have brightened because I tasted a little of this honey. ³⁰How much better if today the troops had eaten freely of the spoil taken from their enemies; for now the slaughter among the Philistines has not been great."

31After they had struck down the Philistines that day from Michmash to Aijalon, the troops were very faint; ³²so the troops flew upon the spoil, and took sheep and oxen and calves, and slaughtered them on the ground; and the troops ate them with the blood. ³³Then it was reported to Saul, "Look, the troops are sinning against the Lord by eating with the blood." And he said, "You have dealt treacherously; roll a large stone before me here."[a] ³⁴Saul said, "Disperse yourselves among the troops, and say to them, 'Let all bring their oxen or their sheep, and slaughter them here, and eat; and do not sin against the Lord by eating with the blood.'" So all of the troops brought their oxen with them that night, and slaughtered them there. ³⁵And Saul built an altar to the Lord; it was the first altar that he built to the Lord.

36Then Saul said, "Let us go down after the Philistines by night and despoil them until the morning light; let us not leave one of them." They said, "Do whatever seems good to you." But the priest said, "Let us draw near to God here." ³⁷So Saul inquired of God, "Shall I go down after the Philistines? Will you give them into the hand of Israel?" But he did not answer him that day. ³⁸Saul said, "Come here, all you leaders of the people; and let us find out how this sin has arisen today. ³⁹For as the Lord lives who saves Israel, even if it is in my son Jonathan, he shall surely die!" But there was no one among all the people who answered him. ⁴⁰He said to all Israel, "You shall be on one side, and I and my son Jonathan will be on the other side." The people said to

---

a Gk: Heb me this day

NIV

cleared. ⁴²Saul said, "Cast the lot between me and Jonathan my son." And Jonathan was taken.

⁴³Then Saul said to Jonathan, "Tell me what you have done."

So Jonathan told him, "I merely tasted a little honey with the end of my staff. And now must I die?"

⁴⁴Saul said, "May God deal with me, be it ever so severely, if you do not die, Jonathan."

⁴⁵But the men said to Saul, "Should Jonathan die—he who has brought about this great deliverance in Israel? Never! As surely as the LORD lives, not a hair of his head will fall to the ground, for he did this today with God's help." So the men rescued Jonathan, and he was not put to death.

⁴⁶Then Saul stopped pursuing the Philistines, and they withdrew to their own land.

⁴⁷After Saul had assumed rule over Israel, he fought against their enemies on every side: Moab, the Ammonites, Edom, the kingsᵃ of Zobah, and the Philistines. Wherever he turned, he inflicted punishment on them.ᵇ ⁴⁸He fought valiantly and defeated the Amalekites, delivering Israel from the hands of those who had plundered them.

⁴⁹Saul's sons were Jonathan, Ishvi and Malki-Shua. The name of his older daughter was Merab, and that of the younger was Michal. ⁵⁰His wife's name was Ahinoam daughter of Ahimaaz. The name of the commander of Saul's army was Abner son of Ner, and Ner was Saul's uncle. ⁵¹Saul's father Kish and Abner's father Ner were sons of Abiel.

⁵²All the days of Saul there was bitter war with the Philistines, and whenever Saul saw a mighty or brave man, he took him into his service.

ᵃ47 Masoretic Text; Dead Sea Scrolls and Septuagint *king*   ᵇ47 Hebrew; Septuagint *he was victorious*

NRSV

Saul, "Do what seems good to you." ⁴¹Then Saul said, "O LORD God of Israel, why have you not answered your servant today? If this guilt is in me or in my son Jonathan, O LORD God of Israel, give Urim; but if this guilt is in your people Israel,ᵃ give Thummim." And Jonathan and Saul were indicated by the lot, but the people were cleared. ⁴²Then Saul said, "Cast the lot between me and my son Jonathan." And Jonathan was taken.

43Then Saul said to Jonathan, "Tell me what you have done." Jonathan told him, "I tasted a little honey with the tip of the staff that was in my hand; here I am, I will die." ⁴⁴Saul said, "God do so to me and more also; you shall surely die, Jonathan!" ⁴⁵Then the people said to Saul, "Shall Jonathan die, who has accomplished this great victory in Israel? Far from it! As the LORD lives, not one hair of his head shall fall to the ground; for he has worked with God today." So the people ransomed Jonathan, and he did not die. ⁴⁶Then Saul withdrew from pursuing the Philistines; and the Philistines went to their own place.

47When Saul had taken the kingship over Israel, he fought against all his enemies on every side—against Moab, against the Ammonites, against Edom, against the kings of Zobah, and against the Philistines; wherever he turned he routed them. ⁴⁸He did valiantly, and struck down the Amalekites, and rescued Israel out of the hands of those who plundered them.

49Now the sons of Saul were Jonathan, Ishvi, and Malchishua; and the names of his two daughters were these: the name of the firstborn was Merab, and the name of the younger, Michal. ⁵⁰The name of Saul's wife was Ahinoam daughter of Ahimaaz. And the name of the commander of his army was Abner son of Ner, Saul's uncle; ⁵¹Kish was the father of Saul, and Ner the father of Abner was the son of Abiel.

52There was hard fighting against the Philistines all the days of Saul; and when Saul saw any strong or valiant warrior, he took him into his service.

ᵃ Vg Compare Gk: Heb ⁴¹ *Saul said to the LORD, the God of Israel*

COMMENTARY

This is Jonathan's story. He boldly initiates action against the Philistines and leads the Israelites in a decisive victory against their enemy. Saul also plays a major role in the story, but in contrast to his son Jonathan, Saul appears cautious, given to pious ritual, and ultimately foolish in his decisions. Saul's actions prevent the victory from being as great as it might have been and jeopardize Jonathan's life.

Chapter 14 presupposes the background on the Philistine war that was reported in 13:1-7a, 15b-23, but stylistically this episode is very different. Unlike the sparse, annalistic quality of chap. 13, the account in chap. 14 is a masterpiece of narrative storytelling. It uses dialogue extensively, includes plot and subplot, and develops two characters (Jonathan and Saul). Numerous studies have demonstrated that this chapter is one of the finest examples of narrative prose in the Hebrew Bible.[96]

There is also a constant influence in this chapter from the holy war theology and its understanding that it is Yahweh who fights for Israel and can alone give victory. This influence pervades the entire chapter.[97]

v. 6	In the very making of his proposal to attack the Philistine garrison, Jonathan affirms that it is the Lord who must in reality win the victory. God's power bears no relationship to numbers of men.
vv. 10, 12	Entry into the fray depends on a sign that the Lord has "given them into our hand." This phrase is one of the most typical formulae in holy war texts (Josh 6:2, 12; 8:1, 7; 10:8, 12, 19; Judg 11:30, 32; 12:3). It is used (vv. 36-37) in an oracular inquiry directed to the Lord.
v. 15	The enemy is stricken with God's panic (Gen 35:5; Exod 23:27;

Isa 2:10, 19), and there is an earthquake (1 Sam 4:5; Amos 8:8; Joel 2:10).

v. 20	The enemy is thrown into confusion (Judg 7:22, and in verbal form 1 Sam 7:10; Exod 14:24; Josh 10:10; 2 Sam 22:15).
v. 23	Victory is ascribed to the Lord by a salvation formula ("The LORD saved Israel on that day," 1 Sam 4:3; 7:8).
v. 31	The totality of victory is expressed in a common formula used in holy war texts ("The LORD struck down the Philistines that day from Michmash to Aijalon," 1 Sam 15:5-7; Num 21:30; Judg 11:33; Josh 10:10).
v. 45	Even in the attempt to ransom Jonathan's life, the people ascribe the victory to divine aid.

The victory is Yahweh's victory. It is Jonathan who trusts in and defers to God's providence even as he takes bold action. As he proposes the attack to his weaponbearer, Jonathan says, "*Perhaps* [NIV; NRSV, "It may be"] the LORD will act in our behalf. Nothing can hinder the LORD from saving, whether by many or by few" (v. 6). Jonathan does not presume on God's freedom, but he is certain that if victory is possible it will come from the Lord. He then acts in confidence that God will save when God wills it.

Saul, in contrast, relies excessively on ritual. He tends to remain passive and unresponsive until he can ensure the Lord's favor by oracular means or by the taking of oaths (vv. 2-3, 18-19, 24, 36-37, 46). Perhaps this puts his rejection in chap. 13 in a new light as a part of Saul's need to hide behind ritual assurance even at the expense of infringing on Samuel's prerogatives. He might have fared better to go boldly into battle without the sacrifices. We will return to these issues at a later point.

In any case, chap. 14 introduces us to Jonathan as a hero, but exposes Saul as a man whose cautious piety and foolish actions nearly lead to the tragic cost of Jonathan's life. The people must redeem Jonathan from Saul's own folly. Perhaps the larger tragedy of Saul's story in 1 Samuel is

---

96. For detailed discussion of the literary features of 1 Samuel 14, see J. Blenkinsopp, "Jonathan's Sacrilege, 1 Sam 14:1-46: A Study in Literary History," *CBQ* 26 (1964) 423-49; David Jobling, "Saul's Fall and Jonathan's Rise: Tradition and Redaction in 1 Sam 14:1-46," *JBL* 95 (1976) 367-76.

97. The following list is an adaptation from Bruce C. Birch, *The Rise of the Israelite Monarchy: The Growth and Development of I Samuel 7-15*, SBLDS 27 (Missoula, Mont.: Scholars Press, 1976) 89-90.

that no one can eventually redeem Saul from the tragic cost of his own folly. In the end, Saul's piety is revealed as self-serving, not God-fearing. It is Jonathan who truly trusts in divine freedom and divine saving. Ultimately, Saul stands in contrast not only to Jonathan but also to David.

14:1-5. This story begins dramatically with Jonathan's proposal to attack the Philistine garrison accompanied only by his armorbearer (v. 1). Only then does the storyteller set the scene. The Philistines are at Michmash, while Saul and only six hundred men are at Gibeah (vv. 2, 16; Geba in v. 5). Saul is sitting under a tree, accompanied by Ahijah, a priest in the line of Eli, who carries an ephod (vv. 2-3). The text opens with Jonathan as a man of action and Saul passively waiting for something to develop. The priest and the ephod are significant in the light of the role that ritual plays for Saul in this story. Here the ephod seems to be a ceremonial garment that contains in a pocket or pouch the sacred oracles, Urim and Thummim, which are used later in the story.

No one in Saul's camp knows that Jonathan and his armorbearer have gone. They must climb down through a rocky gorge that separates Philistines and Israelites and come back up the other side (vv. 5-6).

14:6-23. With the scene set, action resumes with Jonathan again stating his intention (v. 6), but he adds a derogatory reference to the Philistines as the uncircumcised. More important, he sets his action in the context of God's providence: "Perhaps the LORD will act for us." He does not infringe on divine freedom or presume somehow to control God's action. He expresses a hope in what he trusts is possible through the Lord, "for nothing can hinder the LORD from saving by many or by few" (v. 6).

The armorbearer, in his only speech, expresses solidarity with Jonathan (v. 7). Such men were more than servants; they were also close martial companions to leaders like Jonathan. David later becomes Saul's armorbearer and distinguishes himself in battle. In this story, Jonathan's armorbearer is a full participant in the crucial battle that Jonathan precipitates with the Philistines.

Jonathan proposes a method for determining whether his proposed attack is the will of the Lord (vv. 8-10). The sign will be that the Philistines who first see them urge them to come up (taunt-

ing them to come up and fight?). Jonathan and his companion show themselves, and the Philistines taunt them, calling them "Hebrews" (a derogatory term) who have come up out of their holes from hiding (v. 11). The Philistines dare them to come up, whereupon they will show them a thing or two (v. 12). A battle ensues in which Jonathan and his companion wreak havoc on the Philistine ranks (vv. 13-14). It is clear that the Lord is, indeed, with them, as is evident in the onset of panic and an earthquake, which characterize the Lord's fighting for Israel (v. 15).

Saul's camp at Gibeah notices the fighting in the Philistine camp (v. 16). Instead of joining the fray immediately, Saul takes the roll of his troops and discovers that Jonathan and his armorbearer are missing (v. 17). He calls for the priest Ahijah, presumably to consult after God's will in this situation. The Masoretic Text (Hebrew) reads that Ahijah brought the ark out to Saul (v. 18). This does not seem likely, given the fate of the ark in 1 Samuel 6 and the need for David to find it later in 2 Samuel 6. The LXX (Greek) text reads "ephod" here. This seems a more appropriate reading, particularly in the light of v. 3, where the ephod is mentioned. This reference also makes sense of v. 19, where the tumult grows so great among the Philistines that Saul finally decides he can wait no longer. He commands Ahijah to "withdraw your hand." Presumably Ahijah was interrupted in the process of consulting the Urim and Thummim (mentioned later in v. 41). They may have been carried in a pouch on the ephod (see Exod 28:30; Lev 8:8), from which they would be withdrawn to give their judgment on Saul's military prospects. Eight times in 1 Samuel the ephod is mentioned as a priestly garment from which a divine oracle is often sought (2:28; 14:3, 18; 21:9; 22:18; 23:6, 9; 30:7).

Saul and his men join the conflict (v. 20), whereupon they are joined by Hebrew mercenaries who had been fighting for the Philistines (v. 21) and Israelites who had hidden in panic earlier (v. 22; see 13:6-7). The text makes clear that it is the Lord who gives Israel victory on that day (v. 23*a*). The battle extends far beyond the area around Gibeah and Michmash into the hill country of Ephraim, with Saul's army swelling to ten thousand men (v. 23*b*).

14:24-30. Against the backdrop of this improbable victory another deadly drama begins to unfold as a result of an oath Saul lays upon his troops (v. 24). The narrator labels this action from the beginning as "very rash" (the NRSV and most commentators read with the LXX here; the Greek text specifies an act regarded as a blunder). Saul's oath lays a curse on any of his troops who eat food before nightfall and the completion of Saul's vengeance on his enemies. The purpose of such an oath is to help ensure victory by making a sacrificial commitment. However, this was a foolish move, for two reasons. First, Saul's army eventually becomes faint for lack of food (vv. 28, 31), and they cannot physically pursue the victory to its fullest extent. More important for this story, not everyone—including Saul's son, Jonathan (v. 27)—is present to hear of this oath.

In the course of battle, Jonathan, seeing a honeycomb, dips his staff into the honey and eats from it (v. 27). The food energizes him ("his eyes brightened"). Then others tell him of his father's oath. Remarkably, Jonathan immediately criticizes his father openly: "My father has troubled the land. . . . How much better if today the troops had eaten freely . . . for now the slaughter among the Philistines has not been great" (vv. 29-30). Father and son are now set ominously against each other. It will not be the last time, for Jonathan eventually becomes the friend of David and his supporter for the throne (1 Samuel 20). For now, Jonathan's innocent act of nourishment places him inadvertently under the curse of Saul's oath.

14:31-35. For a brief moment the story's attention shifts from Jonathan to the wider consequences of Saul's foolish oath. Famished after long fighting without food, Saul's troops begin to slaughter sheep and cattle and eat the meat without the ritual draining of the blood required by Israelite law (vv. 31-32). Saul's oath has led to massive sacral sin by his army. Saul orders that a large stone be placed in front of him, which becomes an altar for ritual slaughter and draining of the blood (vv. 33-34). It is said to be the first altar Saul built to the Lord, implying that others had been made as well (v. 35).

14:36-46. In the flush of victory by day, Saul proposes to pursue the Philistines through the night, but Saul, heeding the urging of his priest, pauses to consult the Lord (v. 36). Presumably this meant the seeking of some oracular assurance

through the priest (Urim and Thummim?) before taking action. However, on this occasion there is no answer (v. 37). Saul does not then make his own decision. He presumes that he cannot get assurance because of someone's sin (v. 38), and he, again rashly, proclaims that even if this sin is in his own son Jonathan, he will surely die (v. 39). There follows an elaborate process of lot-casting with the Urim and the Thummim. The names of these two objects, cast or withdrawn in the process, seem to mean "cursed" and "counted whole," hence each inquiry could give a positive or a negative verdict. This process could be used by posing questions (as in v. 37) or by choosing between groups of potentially guilty persons (as in vv. 40-42). Saul's first question forces a choice between the people on one side and Jonathan/Saul on the other. When father and son are taken, Saul poses a choice between himself and Jonathan. (The LXX includes additional material claiming that the people tried to dissuade Saul from continuing at this point.) Jonathan is taken; he confesses to having eaten honey and expresses a willingness to die (v. 43). The irony at this point in the story is significant. Jonathan ate food in utter ignorance of his father's oath. If there was sin here, it was in the making of such a misguided oath (one recalls the oath of Jephthah and the willing death of his innocent daughter, Judges 11) or the widespread, knowing violation by the people in eating meat with the blood still in it, which violates sacral law. But it is Jonathan, the undisputed hero of the day, who is taken by lot and who offers himself to die. Distressingly, Saul states his willingness to carry out this death penalty (v. 44), but the people will not hear of it. Claiming that Jonathan worked with God in bringing them victory, they counter Saul's oath with one of their own, "As the LORD lives, not one hair of his head shall fall to the ground" (v. 45). Sadly the story ends with a report that the moment for a wider Israelite victory had passed. The pursuit ends, and the Philistines return to their own strongholds (v. 46).

14:47-52. The final section of this chapter includes three small notices. The first (vv. 47-48) is a summary of Saul's military campaigns. It assesses positively Saul's leadership in matters of warfare. Some have thought the list too extensive and suggest that a later list of David's victories has been placed here. However, such an explanation is not really necessary. Independent traditions confirm Saul's campaigns against Ammonites, Philistines, and Amalekites. It is not unreasonable that he had conflicts with others among Israel's traditional enemies. What remains important is that a portion of the tradition remembers Saul as successful and valiant. In answer to the earlier question of the skeptics, "Can Saul save?" (10:27), this notice says, "Yes, Saul did save Israel for a time." It is significant that this positive notice is placed before the final story of Saul's rejection from kingship in chap. 15.

A second notice tells us of Saul's family (vv. 49-51). His son Ishvi is mentioned only here, unless this is a variant name for Ishbaal (2 Samuel 2–4). Jonathan, Malchishua, and Abinadab (not named here) are reported to have died with Saul at Mt. Gilboa in 31:2 (see 1 Chr 9:49). Saul's two daughters, Merab and Michal, play a later role in connection with marriage to David (18:17-27), with Michal becoming David's wife. This is the only time Saul's wife, Ahinoam, is named. Abner, the commander of Saul's army, plays a key role in the later story, and he appears here as Saul's uncle, although confusion over the relationship of Kish and Ner may mean that Saul and Abner were cousins (see 9:1; 1 Chr 8:33; 9:36, 39).

In the final notice (v. 52), we see Saul's method for gathering fighting men to his service. It reflects the beginning of a standing army in Israel and constitutes the very manner by which David later enters Saul's service (16:18) and becomes Saul's armorbearer (16:21).

REFLECTIONS

On the surface, this story is about warfare, heroic deeds, and strange rituals. At a deeper level, this story concerns the relationship between piety and moral responsibility, particularly the moral responsibility that comes with leadership.

The commentary has pointed to the great contrast between Jonathan and Saul. It is ironic that Jonathan seems the more kingly of the two, but we know from chap. 13 that he will not be king after his father. On initial glance, Jonathan seems pragmatic, a man of action and bold initiative. Yet, it is Jonathan who trusts in God's purposes to work through "many or by few," who gives God credit for victory, and who knows that human desires and divine purpose may not always coincide. "Perhaps," he says, "the LORD will act for us." Saul seems the more pious, surrounding himself with priest and ephod, resorting to ritual assurance before taking action, pledging solemn oaths as a sign of commitment. Yet, it is Saul who seems unable to act in trust that God's purposes will go forward one way or another. He wants assurance of outcomes before he begins. He wants his piety to be recognized and perhaps obligate God to his purposes. From the drama played out between this father and son, we learn important things about the nature and limitations of true piety when faced with the moral decisions of public policy (in this instance, warfare against oppressors).

1. Piety is not a substitute for human wisdom and responsible action. Jonathan acted boldly to take an initiative he thought promising. In his "Perhaps . . ." of v. 6, he holds open the possibility that the course of events could show that his action was not the direction of God's purposes, and he would then have broken off his attack or changed strategies. By contrast, Saul let his acts of piety (rituals and oaths) substitute for his own wisdom and his own action. His nervous consultations at strategic moments and his foolish oath did not impress or obligate God. They sapped the war effort, almost took the life of his own son, and left the end result short of what it might have been.

It is endlessly tempting, from Saul's generation to our own, to let piety become an end in itself, as if acting religious were the chief thing required of those who would serve the God who can save. We refrain from our own saving activity in favor of energy spent on rituals and institutional patterns that divert our attention from moral challenges rather than focusing us on them. Such self-serving religious ritual and practice are ultimately a failure of trust in God and a failure to understand that the world is the arena of God's activity. We, like Jonathan, are called to discern what actions might best serve God's salvation and to move forward. Such discernment and action may have to be modified in the light of further understandings of God's will, but inaction coupled with fearful hiding behind religious rituals and practices will never serve God's saving purposes.

2. Piety, especially ritual observance, cannot protect us from moral risk taking. Even the most faithful among us are given no path to certitude that guarantees the outcome of our actions. Saul wanted to resolve the "perhaps" of Jonathan's initiative before he took action. In an apt phrase, Robert Polzin accuses Saul of engaging in "ritual concealment."[98] Saul is so obsessed with rituals and oaths that might determine or even influence the course of divine action that he borders on sorcery and divination. He wants a formula for success before he risks his resources. Needless to say, this is not an attitude limited to the time of Saul. Too many leaders in church and society are reluctant to take positions until it is clear which way the wind is blowing. In politics, this is expediency; but in the church it is a lack of faith.

3. Piety must ultimately honor the freedom of God. We cannot by our pious practices and observances coerce or obligate divine grace. Nothing can hinder the salvation of the Lord, and we will never cease to be surprised by grace. The "Perhaps . . ." of Jonathan was a more authentic expression of faith than the fearful ritual seeking of certitude by Saul, because it grew out of trust in God's saving purposes and a willingness to live and act within the mysteries of God's saving grace. Some of the opponents of Jesus in the Gospels thought they knew the paths of observance that would guarantee divine favor and grace. There is no lack of such attitudes in some quarters in the church today.

The freedom of God does not depend on popular support or large numbers. Jonathan knew that God can save through the many or the few. Saul thought he could do nothing with his six hundred, and Jonathan acted with two. Trustful action in the hope that "perhaps the Lord will act for us" happens too seldom in the modern church. We wait for full funding, additional staffing, rising memberships, fully resourced programs, and denominational authorization. We could find ourselves under the tree with Saul, consulting priest and ephod, or taking oaths in the form of resolutions when God chooses to act for justice and salvation. God's action may be served by the few who can choose to move boldly in trust that the path of God's grace will be revealed as we move forward.

98. Robert Polzin, *Samuel and the Deuteronomist: A Literary Study of the Deuteronomic History,* Part Two: *1 Samuel* (San Francisco: Harper & Row, 1989) 138.

1 Samuel 15:1-35, Saul Rejected from Kingship

NIV

15 Samuel said to Saul, "I am the one the Lord sent to anoint you king over his people Israel; so listen now to the message from the Lord. [2]This is what the Lord Almighty says: 'I will punish the Amalekites for what they did to Israel when they waylaid them as they came up from Egypt. [3]Now go, attack the Amalekites and totally destroy[a] everything that belongs to them. Do not spare them; put to death men and

[a]3 The Hebrew term refers to the irrevocable giving over of things or persons to the Lord, often by totally destroying them; also in verses 8, 9, 15, 18, 20 and 21.

NRSV

15 Samuel said to Saul, "The Lord sent me to anoint you king over his people Israel; now therefore listen to the words of the Lord. [2]Thus says the Lord of hosts, 'I will punish the Amalekites for what they did in opposing the Israelites when they came up out of Egypt. [3]Now go and attack Amalek, and utterly destroy all that they have; do not spare them, but kill both man and woman, child and infant, ox and sheep, camel and donkey.'"

[4]So Saul summoned the people, and numbered

NIV

women, children and infants, cattle and sheep, camels and donkeys.'"

⁴So Saul summoned the men and mustered them at Telaim—two hundred thousand foot soldiers and ten thousand men from Judah. ⁵Saul went to the city of Amalek and set an ambush in the ravine. ⁶Then he said to the Kenites, "Go away, leave the Amalekites so that I do not destroy you along with them; for you showed kindness to all the Israelites when they came up out of Egypt." So the Kenites moved away from the Amalekites.

⁷Then Saul attacked the Amalekites all the way from Havilah to Shur, to the east of Egypt. ⁸He took Agag king of the Amalekites alive, and all his people he totally destroyed with the sword. ⁹But Saul and the army spared Agag and the best of the sheep and cattle, the fat calves*ᵃ* and lambs—everything that was good. These they were unwilling to destroy completely, but everything that was despised and weak they totally destroyed.

¹⁰Then the word of the Lᴏʀᴅ came to Samuel: ¹¹"I am grieved that I have made Saul king, ⌐ᵃuse he has turned away from me and has not carried out my instructions." Samuel was troubled, and he cried out to the Lᴏʀᴅ all that night.

¹²Early in the morning Samuel got up and went to meet Saul, but he was told, "Saul has gone to Carmel. There he has set up a monument in his own honor and has turned and gone on down to Gilgal."

¹³When Samuel reached him, Saul said, "The Lᴏʀᴅ bless you! I have carried out the Lᴏʀᴅ's instructions."

¹⁴But Samuel said, "What then is this bleating of sheep in my ears? What is this lowing of cattle that I hear?"

¹⁵Saul answered, "The soldiers brought them from the Amalekites; they spared the best of the sheep and cattle to sacrifice to the Lᴏʀᴅ your God, but we totally destroyed the rest."

¹⁶"Stop!" Samuel said to Saul. "Let me tell you what the Lᴏʀᴅ said to me last night."

"Tell me," Saul replied.

¹⁷Samuel said, "Although you were once small

ᵃ9 Or the grown bulls; the meaning of the Hebrew for this phrase is uncertain.

NRSV

them in Telaim, two hundred thousand foot soldiers, and ten thousand soldiers of Judah. ⁵Saul came to the city of the Amalekites and lay in wait in the valley. ⁶Saul said to the Kenites, "Go! Leave! Withdraw from among the Amalekites, or I will destroy you with them; for you showed kindness to all the people of Israel when they came up out of Egypt." So the Kenites withdrew from the Amalekites. ⁷Saul defeated the Amalekites, from Havilah as far as Shur, which is east of Egypt. ⁸He took King Agag of the Amalekites alive, but utterly destroyed all the people with the edge of the sword. ⁹Saul and the people spared Agag, and the best of the sheep and of the cattle and of the fatlings, and the lambs, and all that was valuable, and would not utterly destroy them; all that was despised and worthless they utterly destroyed.

10The word of the Lᴏʀᴅ came to Samuel: ¹¹"I regret that I made Saul king, for he has turned back from following me, and has not carried out my commands." Samuel was angry; and he cried out to the Lᴏʀᴅ all night. ¹²Samuel rose early in the morning to meet Saul, and Samuel was told, "Saul went to Carmel, where he set up a monument for himself, and on returning he passed on down to Gilgal." ¹³When Samuel came to Saul, Saul said to him, "May you be blessed by the Lᴏʀᴅ; I have carried out the command of the Lᴏʀᴅ." ¹⁴But Samuel said, "What then is this bleating of sheep in my ears, and the lowing of cattle that I hear?" ¹⁵Saul said, "They have brought them from the Amalekites; for the people spared the best of the sheep and the cattle, to sacrifice to the Lᴏʀᴅ your God; but the rest we have utterly destroyed." ¹⁶Then Samuel said to Saul, "Stop! I will tell you what the Lᴏʀᴅ said to me last night." He replied, "Speak."

17Samuel said, "Though you are little in your own eyes, are you not the head of the tribes of Israel? The Lᴏʀᴅ anointed you king over Israel. ¹⁸And the Lᴏʀᴅ sent you on a mission, and said, 'Go, utterly destroy the sinners, the Amalekites, and fight against them until they are consumed.' ¹⁹Why then did you not obey the voice of the Lᴏʀᴅ? Why did you swoop down on the spoil, and do what was evil in the sight of the Lᴏʀᴅ?" ²⁰Saul said to Samuel, "I have obeyed the voice of the Lᴏʀᴅ, I have gone on the mission on which

NIV

in your own eyes, did you not become the head of the tribes of Israel? The LORD anointed you king over Israel. [18]And he sent you on a mission, saying, 'Go and completely destroy those wicked people, the Amalekites; make war on them until you have wiped them out.' [19]Why did you not obey the LORD? Why did you pounce on the plunder and do evil in the eyes of the LORD?"

[20]"But I did obey the LORD," Saul said. "I went on the mission the LORD assigned me. I completely destroyed the Amalekites and brought back Agag their king. [21]The soldiers took sheep and cattle from the plunder, the best of what was devoted to God, in order to sacrifice them to the LORD your God at Gilgal."

[22]But Samuel replied:

"Does the LORD delight in burnt offerings and
    sacrifices
  as much as in obeying the voice of the
    LORD?
To obey is better than sacrifice,
  and to heed is better than the fat of rams.
[23]For rebellion is like the sin of divination,
  and arrogance like the evil of idolatry.
Because you have rejected the word of the
    LORD,
  he has rejected you as king."

[24]Then Saul said to Samuel, "I have sinned. I violated the LORD's command and your instructions. I was afraid of the people and so I gave in to them. [25]Now I beg you, forgive my sin and come back with me, so that I may worship the LORD."

[26]But Samuel said to him, "I will not go back with you. You have rejected the word of the LORD, and the LORD has rejected you as king over Israel!"

[27]As Samuel turned to leave, Saul caught hold of the hem of his robe, and it tore. [28]Samuel said to him, "The LORD has torn the kingdom of Israel from you today and has given it to one of your neighbors—to one better than you. [29]He who is the Glory of Israel does not lie or change his mind; for he is not a man, that he should change his mind."

[30]Saul replied, "I have sinned. But please honor me before the elders of my people and before Israel; come back with me, so that I may worship

NRSV

the LORD sent me, I have brought Agag the king of Amalek, and I have utterly destroyed the Amalekites. [21]But from the spoil the people took sheep and cattle, the best of the things devoted to destruction, to sacrifice to the LORD your God in Gilgal." [22]And Samuel said,

"Has the LORD as great delight in burnt
    offerings and sacrifices,
  as in obedience to the voice of the LORD?
Surely, to obey is better than sacrifice,
  and to heed than the fat of rams.
[23] For rebellion is no less a sin than divination,
  and stubbornness is like iniquity and
    idolatry.
Because you have rejected the word of the
    LORD,
  he has also rejected you from being king."

[24]Saul said to Samuel, "I have sinned; for I have transgressed the commandment of the LORD and your words, because I feared the people and obeyed their voice. [25]Now therefore, I pray, pardon my sin, and return with me, so that I may worship the LORD." [26]Samuel said to Saul, "I will not return with you; for you have rejected the word of the LORD, and the LORD has rejected you from being king over Israel." [27]As Samuel turned to go away, Saul caught hold of the hem of his robe, and it tore. [28]And Samuel said to him, "The LORD has torn the kingdom of Israel from you this very day, and has given it to a neighbor of yours, who is better than you. [29]Moreover the Glory of Israel will not recant[a] or change his mind; for he is not a mortal, that he should change his mind." [30]Then Saul[b] said, "I have sinned; yet honor me now before the elders of my people and before Israel, and return with me, so that I may worship the LORD your God." [31]So Samuel turned back after Saul; and Saul worshiped the LORD.

[32]Then Samuel said, "Bring Agag king of the Amalekites here to me." And Agag came to him haltingly.[c] Agag said, "Surely this is the bitterness of death."[d] [33]But Samuel said,

"As your sword has made women childless,
  so your mother shall be childless among
    women."

---

[a] Q Ms Gk: MT *deceive*   [b] Heb *he*   [c] Cn Compare Gk: Meaning of Heb uncertain   [d] Q Ms Gk: MT *Surely the bitterness of death is past*

NIV

the LORD your God." ³¹So Samuel went back with Saul, and Saul worshiped the LORD.

³²Then Samuel said, "Bring me Agag king of the Amalekites."

Agag came to him confidently,ᵃ thinking, "Surely the bitterness of death is past."

³³But Samuel said,

"As your sword has made women childless,
    so will your mother be childless among
        women."

And Samuel put Agag to death before the LORD at Gilgal.

³⁴Then Samuel left for Ramah, but Saul went up to his home in Gibeah of Saul. ³⁵Until the day Samuel died, he did not go to see Saul again, though Samuel mourned for him. And the LORD was grieved that he had made Saul king over Israel.

ᵃ32 Or *him trembling, yet*

NRSV

And Samuel hewed Agag in pieces before the LORD in Gilgal.

34Then Samuel went to Ramah; and Saul went up to his house in Gibeah of Saul. ³⁵Samuel did not see Saul again until the day of his death, but Samuel grieved over Saul. And the LORD was sorry that he had made Saul king over Israel.

COMMENTARY

In this chapter Saul is rejected as legitimate king over Israel. As in chap. 13, he has violated the instructions of Samuel, the prophet of the Lord. Twice we are told that the Lord "regretted" having made Saul king over Israel (vv. 11, 35) because "he has turned back from following me, and has not carried out my commands" (v. 11). In the confrontation with Saul, Samuel claims that God has already "torn" the kingdom from Saul and "given it to a neighbor of yours, who is better than you" (v. 28). The text is already looking ahead to David, who waits just offstage (chap. 16) and will occupy the central attention of the tradition for the remainder of the books of Samuel. Saul's career as God's anointed king over Israel ends almost as soon as it starts.

The setting for this episode is a war with the Amalekites, an ancient enemy of Israel. Samuel, speaking as the Lord's prophet, commands Saul to exterminate the Amalekites in order to avenge wrongs committed against Israel when they came out of Egypt (vv. 1-3). The Amalekite background and the holy war practice of חרם (ḥērem) will be discussed further below. It is important to note here that both Amalekites and ḥērem are secondary

interests in this episode. Instead, the primary issue is obedience to the direct command of the Lord. No question is raised by the text (though it is by some commentators) about the appropriateness of a campaign against the Amalekites or the morality of the utter extermination of enemies (ḥērem). These questions often arise out of sympathy for the hapless Saul and in reaction to the harshness of Samuel. For this story, the issue is Saul's obedience to God's commands; no suggestion is made that these commands were illegitimate. If we raise those issues, we must recognize that they are our concerns and not those of 1 Samuel.

As we will see, this chapter includes prophetic patterns and concerns. Samuel is a prophet of the Lord. He announces the word of the Lord with the use of the full messenger formula (v. 2), receives the word of the Lord expressing divine regret, and pronounces an oracle of judgment against Saul for his failure to obey the word of the Lord (see esp. vv. 22-23). As many have observed, the key word around which the entire episode hinges is שׁמע (šāmaʿ, "to hear"), which, particularly in conjunction with the term "voice" or "command of the LORD," often means "to obey."

This verb appears in vv. 1, 14, 19, 20, 22 (2x), and 24. Saul's failure to "hear/obey" is the reason for his rejection as king. This theme would have been theologically important to the prophetic circles that shaped the Saul story, and it was also an important concern to the deuteronomistic historian (cf. 12:14-15), who incorporated this material into his larger history work (see Introduction).

Chapter 15 has important thematic ties to its larger context. There is a reference in v. 1 to the anointing of Saul in 10:1 (another episode with strong prophetic emphases). The theme of obedience to God's voice and commandment is the condition laid down by Samuel for the well-being of king and people in 12:14-15. Chapter 15 must also be read with chaps. 13 and 14 as the final episode in a section on Saul's career as king that seems primarily concerned with explaining the reasons for Saul's failure. There are similarities to 13:7*b*-15*a*, which have led some to see chap. 15 as a variant account of that earlier rejection story. But both seem to have been shaped by prophetic circles so as to present a growing pattern of crisis, leading first to the loss of dynasty and then to the loss of Saul's own kingship. Chapter 16 begins with the grief of Samuel, mentioned at the end of this episode (v. 35), and Saul's encounter with Samuel's ghost in chap. 28 clearly knows and uses the rejection story in chap. 15.

Just as Saul's obedience is at issue, so also is the people's obedience. Saul's references to the people's role in the violation of the *ḥērem* (vv. 15, 21, 24) are often treated simply as efforts by Saul to avoid full blame. But it is the narrator, and not Saul, who reports (v. 9) that "Saul *and the people* spared. . . ." Saul was the people's king. God acquiesced, but commanded Samuel in 8:22, "Make for *them* a king." In Samuel's speech to Israel (chap. 12), Saul is "the king whom *you* have chosen, for whom *you* have asked" (v. 13), and the people confess that they have sinned by "demanding a king for *ourselves*" (v. 19). Both king and people are held accountable: "If both you and the king . . . will follow the LORD your God, it will be well. . . . But if you do wickedly, you shall be swept away, both you and your king" (vv. 14, 25). In the present story, chap. 15 involves the people in the charge of disobedience along with Saul. His rejection is the rejection of

the people's king. Chapter 16 then opens significantly with God's announcement that "I have provided for *myself* a king among his [Jesse's] sons" (v. 1*b*).

Since this chapter signals an end to Saul's legitimized rule, it is a natural point at which to raise questions of meaning concerning this abortive experience with kingship. One may also assess the character of Saul and his confronter, Samuel, as well as the role of God in this failed enterprise. Was Saul guilty? Was his offense so great? Was God fair? Had God doomed Saul from the start? Was Samuel too harsh? Was he representing God or his own reactionary interests? Earlier responses to these questions paint a harsh portrait of Saul as surely deserving of what he received. "What wonder was it then, that the Lord rejected him, whose best service was an act of vile dissimulation? . . . He continued, to the last, proud, and cruel, and profane."[99] Scholars have more recently tended to see Saul as a tragic figure and, hence, treat both Samuel and God rather harshly in assessment of this episode. "Samuel's passion for covenant requirements reaches ideological proportions, because he is unwilling (or unable) to relate his demands to the political realities with which Saul must struggle. . . . Samuel's absolutist claims here are subtle and multidimensioned. Most broadly, Samuel's one issue is uncompromising loyalty to Yahweh. At another level, his claim is uncompromising loyalty to Samuel, who is the only valid voice of Yahweh."[100] Opinion on this chapter and on the assessment of Saul, Samuel, and God at this point is more varied than for any other issues in the books of Samuel. We will return to discuss these matters further after a closer look at the text of chapter 15.

15:1-3. The episode opens with Samuel's report to Saul of a divine command. He begins by reminding Saul about the source of his authority. It was Samuel whom God sent to anoint Saul in the first place (v. 1*a*). It is the prophet who speaks

99. Thomas Robinson, "The Character of Saul," in *Scripture Characters or a Practical Improvement of the Principal Histories from the Time of the Judges to the End of the Old Testament* (London, 1790) 49, quoted in David M. Gunn, *The Fate of King Saul,* JSOTSup 14 (Sheffield: JSOT, 1980) 42-43.

100. Walter Brueggemann, *First and Second Samuel,* Interpretation (Louisville: John Knox, 1990) 109-10. See also Gunn, *The Fate of King Saul;* W. Lee Humphreys, "The Tragedy of King Saul: A Study of the Structure of 1 Sam 9-31," *JSOT* 6 (1978) 18-27; and J. Cheryl Exum and William J. Whedbee, "Isaac, Samson, and Saul: Reflections on the Comic and Tragic Visions," *Semeia* 32 (1984) 5-40.

and who now voices what is to be the crucial issue of this chapter, "Now therefore listen to the words of the LORD" (v. 1*b*). The Hebrew verb שׁמע (*šāmaʿ*) means "listen" or "hear," but in covenantal contexts (especially deuteronomistic) it often means "obey." To obey is not only to hear but also to do. Saul is called to hear and to do "the words of the LORD." Saul may be king, but he is still subject to the word of the Lord as mediated by the prophet Samuel.

Samuel begins his speech with the full messenger formula, which underlines his claim to speak God's word, "Thus says the LORD of hosts" (v. 2*a*). The term "hosts" (צבאות *ṣĕbāʾôt*) means "armies" and emphasizes the God who fights as a warrior for Israel—an appropriate way of referring to God on this occasion. Samuel orders a campaign against the Amalekites as punishment for the opposition of the Amalekites against Israel at the time of the exodus from Egypt (v. 2). Saul is to attack and "utterly destroy" the Amalekites—every person and every animal (v. 3).

The Amalekites were a nomadic people living primarily in the Negeb and the Sinai, south of Israelite territory. On the journey through the wilderness from Egypt, Israel had been attacked by the Amalekites and won a victory over them at Rephidim (Exod 17:8-16), after which God promised to "blot out the remembrance of Amalek from under heaven" (17:14). Samuel's announcement that the time of Amalek's punishment had come is similar to the command in Deut 25:17-19 that Amalek should be destroyed for its past crimes. Brueggemann has suggested that Samuel's command is a "dangerous political irrelevancy" because there is no evidence that the Amalekites posed any real threat to Israel's life, but instead is an ideological test.[101] We should remember, however, that David was later forced into military encounter with the Amalekites on three occasions (27:8; 30:1-31; 2 Sam 8:12). In the positive summary of Saul's military achievements in 14:48, the victory of the Amalekites is listed as a rescue from the hands of those who plundered Israel. Conflict with Amalekites seemed to be a frequent factor in the life of Judah especially, and one could see Saul undertaking a campaign against them as a way of extending his influence into this important southern tribe (exactly what

David did later). Hence, it does not seem necessary to see the Amalekite campaign as an occasion manufactured by Samuel for a test of Saul's obedience.

Saul is to "utterly/totally destroy" every man, woman, child, and beast belonging to the Amalekites. The Hebrew verb חרם (*ḥāram*, also translated "to exterminate," "to place under the ban") is used in connection with warfare for the practice of dedicating to God all of a conquered enemy and their possessions by killing and burning. The practice is associated with holy war, in which the battle has sacral purpose and God is often said to fight as a warrior for Israel (Josh 6:17; 10–11). Deuteronomic law (Deut 13:12-18; 20:1-20) provides prescripts for such practices. Even though the practice is primarily attested for the period before kingship in Israel, the *ḥērem* seems to be an ideal kept alive among the prophets. Ahab is confronted by the prophets for not carrying out the ban (1 Kgs 20:42), and later oracles of judgment may reflect the concept applied to those who become the enemies of God's purposes in the world (e.g., Joel 2). Although associated with the concept of holy war, the practice seems infrequently applied, and recent scholarship has stressed that the notion and institutions of holy war itself do not seem standardized or uniformly applied at different times and places in Israel's story.[102] What seems to be at stake in 1 Samuel 15 is not Saul's violation of a norm for holy war. It is, instead, his failure to carry out the explicit command of the Lord as mediated by the prophet Samuel on this occasion. The text does not reflect at all upon whether the command of *ḥērem* is legitimate or morally worthy of obedience (an area often explored by those seeking to justify Saul's actions). The text treats the content of the command matter-of-factly and focuses entirely on the issue of obedience or disobedience to God's words/commands.

15:4-9. These verses describe Saul's campaign against the Amalekites. The numbers for Saul's men seem inflated; the word אלף (*ʾelep*) may not mean "thousand" but instead "group," "battalion," or "unit" (v. 4). Significantly, a force for Judah is listed separately, which suggests that Saul may be undertaking this campaign as a way of

---

101. Brueggemann, *First and Second Samuel*, 110.

102. See the excellent survey in Norman K. Gottwald, "War, Holy," in *IDBSup* (Nashville: Abingdon, 1976) 942-44; and the comprehensive study by Susan Niditch, *War in the Hebrew Bible: A Study in the Ethics of Violence* (New York: Oxford University Press, 1993).

building alliances with this large southern tribe. A "city of the Amalekites" (v. 5) has not been identified with any certainty and stands in tension with the nomadic life usually associated with the Amalekites. The Kenites, another southern desert people who lived among the Amalekites, are offered amnesty before the battle begins out of respect for past cooperative relations between Kenites and Israelites (v. 6; cf. Exodus 18; Judg 4:11-22, and David's similar treatment of the Kenites in 1 Sam 27:10; 30:29). Amalek is defeated over a wide territory (v. 7).

The report on the carrying out of the command to "utterly destroy" (*ḥāram*) is crucial for this episode. Verse 8 states that Agag, king of Amalek, was spared but that the rest of the Amalekites were destroyed. The reference must be to a particular group of Amalekites, since Amalekites continue to give trouble later to David (chap. 30). The next verse (v. 9) significantly states that "Saul and the people" not only kept Agag alive, but they also kept the best of the sheep, cattle, fatlings, and lambs. What was valuable was saved, and only what was "despised and worthless" was destroyed. Offering God only what is despised and worthless would seem a thoughtless act at best and contemptuous at worst. In any case, commanded by God to "utterly destroy," Saul and the people have "spared."

15:10-23. The word of the Lord comes again to Samuel (v. 10), and its content is surprising. God "regrets" having made Saul king (v. 11). The confrontation with Saul is bracketed with divine regret, for the chapter ends by saying again that the Lord was "sorry" to have made Saul king (v. 35*b;* the Hebrew word here is the same [נחם *nāḥam*]; this verb also appears as the expression of divine regret over the creation of humankind prior to the flood in Gen 6:6-7). The experiment with Saul is over. God has already rendered a judgment, and it remains for Samuel to confront Saul and deliver that judgment. The basis of God's judgment is clear: "He has turned back from following me, and has not carried out my commands" (v. 11*a*).

The report of Samuel's anger and nightlong crying out to the Lord has been variously interpreted. Some see it simply as an expression of Samuel's outrage at Saul expressed in a venting of that anger in communion with God. Others

have seen the verse as an expression of prophetic intercession to God, perhaps hoping to avert such a final judgment against Saul. The text does not resolve this ambiguity.

Samuel then journeys to meet Saul, ironically finding him at Gilgal (v. 12), the place of Saul's confirmation in kingship (11:14-15) and his first confrontation with Samuel (13:7*b*-15*a*). Samuel had heard that Saul was erecting a monument for himself at Carmel (v. 12), probable evidence of self-aggrandizement on Saul's part.

The meeting of Samuel with Saul is shaped by the influence of prophetic speeches of indictment (accusation) and judgment (as also in 13:7*b*-15), with the accusation becoming clear through a series of questions posed by Samuel to Saul in a process resembling a judicial hearing (vv. 13-21). When the indictment against Saul is clear, Samuel announces judgment in the form of a poetic oracle that is remarkably similar to passages in the classical prophets (vv. 22-23; cf. Hos 6:6).[103]

Saul greets Samuel warmly and explicitly claims that he has fulfilled the Lord's command (v. 13). But countering Saul's implicit claim to have "listened," Samuel listens and hears the sound of sheep and cattle (v. 14). Saul admits this livestock is from the Amalekite raid, but he claims "the *people* spared the best" of the livestock for sacrifice. The rest, he claims, "*we* have utterly destroyed" (v. 15). Saul excludes himself from the sparing, but includes himself in utterly destroying. It is a pattern to which Saul returns in vv. 20*b*-21*a*, where he claims, "*I* have utterly destroyed the Amalekites. But from the spoil the *people* took sheep and cattle" for sacrifice.

In the ensuing exchange between Samuel and Saul, the issue of listening/obedience is central. Samuel interrupts Saul's justification for sparing the livestock to announce God's word (v. 16). Although v. 17 is difficult to interpret, Samuel seems to claim that Saul, as king of Israel, is responsible for the people's actions. He cannot separate their actions from his own. After reminding Saul of the task to which he has been commanded (v. 18), Samuel challenges, "Why did you not obey [שמע *šāmaʿ*] the word of the Lord?" The taking of spoil

---

103. See Bruce C. Birch, *The Rise of the Israelite Monarchy: The Growth and Development of I Samuel 7–15,* SBLDS 27 (Missoula, Mont.: Scholars Press, 1976) 98-103, for a fuller treatment of these prophetic speech forms.

is labeled as "evil in the sight of the LORD" (v. 19). Yet, Saul insists that he has "obeyed the voice of the LORD," but in the same breath comes the revelation that he has brought the Amalekite king Agag as a captive (v. 20). We are given no clue in the chapter to the purpose of this hostage taking. Could it have been for the prestige of parading the captive king? Could it have been to force some agreement or cessation of hostilities with other Amalekite groups? We do not know, but Agag as a captive violates the commanded ban.

Samuel then announces judgment on Saul. Samuel rejects the notion that bringing sheep and cattle for sacrifice provides an acceptable substitute for obedience to the command of the Lord. The Lord does not delight in such rituals when they become a substitute for obedience (v. 22; the verb שמע [šāmaʿ] is used twice in this verse, and a synonym, הקשב [hiqšîb, hiphil, "to heed"], is used as well). This elevation of obedience over sacrifice is a central theme in the prophets (Isa 1:10-13; Amos 5:21-24; Hos 6:6; Mic 6:6-8). Saul's disobedience is called "rebellion" and "stubbornness" and is equated with the sins of divination, iniquity, and idolatry (v. 23a). It is a harsh judgment, one that often seems disproportionate to Saul's deeds, but this is because most modern readers do not accept the command of ḥērem as legitimate. It is clear from Samuel's judgment speech that the issue was not the specific "sparing" of livestock and king but the matter of obedience to the word of the Lord. Verse 23b contains the devastating consequence: Because Saul "rejected" the Lord's word, the Lord has "rejected" him as king. The verb here is the same as that used in 8:7 for God's statement that the people had "rejected" (מאס māʾas) the Lord as king over them. The rejection of Saul is also a rejection of the people's king. Rejection has come full circle. King and people stand convicted in this account.

How guilty was Saul? Did he really believe he had carried out the command of God? Did he really bring all of those sheep and cattle (the best) for sacrifice? David Gunn is representative of a number of scholars who want to defend Saul as a tragic victim here.

If Samuel's bitter contrast between obedience and sacrifice only makes sense when it is assumed that he saw a significant incompatibility between "devotion" (ḥrm)

and "sacrifice" (zbḥ) of the booty, so Saul's (and the people's) actions and subsequent protestations that the command had been fulfilled only make sense when it is assumed that they, for their part, saw no significant incompatibility. . . . Saul's crime is either that he was ignorant of some technical implications of two sacral concepts (ḥrm and zbḥ) or, if he were aware of them, that he wrongly evaluated them as unimportant.[104]

Gunn and others with similar viewpoints are correct in their assumption that the story intends to generate some sympathy for Saul and that the harshness of the penalty for Saul seems disproportionate. The account is too rich and nuanced for simplistic readings that simply make Saul a villain (likewise Samuel or God). We must remember that the account is trying to make sense of historical events that resulted in Saul's tragic demise and David's eventual triumph. History often does not seem fair, but historians and storytellers seek to understand these events (in this case theologically as well as historically). In this account, Saul is treated sympathetically; but his attempt to pass responsibility to the people, his later confession that he "listened" to the people and not to God (v. 24), and his sparing of King Agag, for which no purpose is given, are enough for the tradition to judge him guilty of disobedience, even if his intention to sacrifice the livestock at Gilgal were an honorable delay of "utterly destroying" rather than a hasty justification of taking plunder. Disobedience ("not listening") is unacceptable in God's anointed king. Saul is not just any man, and he is not rejected as a man, but as the holder of the office of anointed one (v. 17 recalls this status).

15:24-31. Saul responds to Samuel's announcement of judgment with a confession. Again the issue is expressed, not in terms of the specifics of ḥērem but as violation (sin, transgression) of the commandment of the Lord and the words of the Lord's prophet. Saul explains that he "feared the *people* and *listened* to their voice" (v. 24). He pleads for forgiveness and asks that Samuel return with him to worship the Lord (v. 25); but Samuel will not do that, and he repeats the devastating judgment (v. 26; cf. v. 23b).

The author has painted a desperate picture. Samuel turns to go; Saul grasps for him in pleading. Samuel's robe is caught and torn (v. 27). The moment gives Samuel one last opportunity, and

104. David M. Gunn, *The Fate of King Saul*, JSOTSup 14 (Sheffield: JSOT, 1980) 50, 53-54.

he seems harsh indeed. He uses the ripped garment as a symbolic action to reinforce God's word, in a manner characteristic of later prophets. One thinks especially of the prophet Ahijah of Shiloh, who meets Jeroboam on the road and tears a cloak and symbolically gives him the pieces, which represent the tribes torn from the rule of Solomon's son Rehoboam (1 Kgs 11:29-32). Samuel declares that God has torn the kingdom from Saul "this day." But he adds one very significant piece of information: God has already given the kingdom to "a neighbor of yours, who is better than you" (v. 28), referring, of course, to David. Saul's kingship has effectively ended, although he continues in the trappings of royalty for some time. David waits in the wings to make his entrance in the next chapter.

Verse 29 has long been recognized as problematic. Samuel claims that the "Glory of Israel" (i.e., God) does not "lie" (the NRSV's "recant" is an odd choice for the word here) or "change his mind; for he is not a mortal that he should change his mind." The word translated here as "change his mind" is נחם (niham, niphal), the same word used in vv. 1 and 35 to say that God "regretted" (i.e., "changed his mind," also sometimes translated "repented") the choice of Saul. Most interpreters have read v. 29 as a general statement of divine character reinforcing the irrevocability of Saul's rejection. Still, this verse seems a puzzling contradiction of the "regret" of God seen in vv. 1 and 35. Fretheim has argued convincingly that v. 29 refers not to Saul's rejection but to God's commitment made to David (without David's name) in v. 28b.[105] God may have "regretted/repented" of the choice of Saul, but v. 29 now announces an unshakable commitment to David. The text foreshadows the divine covenant with David. The intention is not to say that God never repents of anything but that this particular commitment is unshakable. The two places where niham is used to speak of God as "not repenting" both refer to God's commitment to David. Verse 29 is a near duplicate of a passage in Balaam's speeches in Num 23:19, where the concern is also a foreshadowing of divine commitment to David. The

same verb used to speak of God's not repenting appears in a Davidic covenant setting in Ps 110:4. Although the verb is different, the theme is equivalent in Ps 132:11: "The Lord swore to David a sure oath, from which he will *not turn back*" (NRSV). The theme of God's character being revealed in regretting/repenting and not regretting/repenting will be discussed at a later point.

Saul again confesses his sin, but he asks Samuel at least to honor him before the people by returning with him to worship the Lord (v. 30). Samuel agrees, an act that shows some compassion in allowing Saul to save face before Israel (v. 31).

15:32-35. Samuel is not finished. He commands that Agag, the Amalekite king, be brought before him. Agag seems to foresee his doom (v. 32). After a brief oracle of judgment (v. 33*a*), Samuel himself completes the *ḥērem* against the Amalekites by cutting Agag to pieces (v. 33*b*), presumably with a sword, even as Agag had killed many people with the sword.

Samuel leaves for Ramah and Saul for Gibeah (v. 34), but it is the prophet's permanent exit from Saul's story. We are told that Samuel does not see Saul again until the day of Samuel's death (v. 35). This notice foreshadows Saul's later encounter with Samuel's ghost (chap. 28) before the battle that ends with his own death. The brief encounter in 19:18-24 stands in tension with this statement.

Samuel grieves over Saul (v. 35), a motif that continues into the beginning of David's story (16:1). The author does not hint that this grief is false or only over the failure of Samuel's plans. The narrative portrays Samuel as a complex character of harsh words and actions, but also with his own indications of humanity.

The chapter ends with the statement again that the Lord "regretted" the choice of Saul (v. 35*b*). God's purposes are central to 1 Samuel, and God has determined that a new course must be set. The kingship of Saul can no longer serve God's intentions for Israel.

What do we make of this story and its role in 1 Samuel? The answer to this question revolves around both the actions and the character of the three central figures: Saul, Samuel, and God.

Did Saul sin? Yes. The charge of "not listening" to the command/word of the Lord is a serious one in many OT texts. Did he sin knowingly, and was his punishment proportionate to his mis-

---

105. Terence E. Fretheim, "Divine Foreknowledge, Divine Constancy, and the Rejection of Saul's Kingship," *CBQ* 47 (1985) 595-602. This provocative and insightful article has informed my discussion of many of the issues in this chapter.

deeds? These questions are not so easy to answer. The witnesses to Saul's story clearly have some sympathy with him. He is treated not as a villain, but as a tragic man who meant well for Israel. To this degree, the treatments of Gunn, Humphreys, Exum/Whedbee, and others have provided important correctives to excessive vilification of Saul in many earlier studies. But in 1 Samuel, God focuses on Israel's future, not Saul's. Saul is not devoid of admirable human traits, but he has weaknesses as well. Chapters 13–15 are designed to show that the course of his kingship is not going well. Israel's future is at stake, and the theme of God's regret in 15:1, 35 expresses the divine decision that Saul is not the direction. God will chart a new course with David, and Saul will not be Israel's future.

Gunn and others have suggested that chap. 15 (and its wider context in 1 Samuel) reveals the "dark side" of God. Saul is fated to fail, and God is ruthlessly manipulative and less than honorable.[106] There are certainly questions of fairness to be raised concerning the actions of God, if our perspective were only from the personal fate of Saul. There is a "dark side" to the portrait of God here because God's larger purposes for Israel and for kingship are judged incapable of fulfillment through Saul and through kingship as defined in the story of Saul. Saul was not fated to fail. God had intended that Saul would deliver Israel (9:16; 10:1) and empowered him with the divine Spirit for such tasks (chap. 11). Saul's failures were his own, and were not forced on him by God. It is clear by chap. 15 that the tradition, although sympathetic to Saul, sees in David God's new enterprise for the sake of Israel. Saul could not have gotten them there. In fact, kingship as defined by Saul was not working to benefit Israel. Kingship itself had to be put on a new basis.

Saul was the people's king (8:22), whereas David will be the king God makes for "myself" (16:1). Saul and the people were a conditional experiment that depended on obedience (12:14-15, 25), but Davidic kingship would rest on God's unconditional commitment. God's choice of David would ultimately lead to a new basis for the role of the anointed one. That role rested not on the people and the king's obedience, but on God's

faithfulness. Does this mean the divine relationship to the king changed from Saul to David? Perhaps so. The tradition recognizes a difference.

I will establish the throne of his kingdom forever . . . when he commits iniquity I will punish him . . . but I will not take my steadfast love from him, as I took it from Saul, whom I put away from before you. (2 Sam 7:13-15 NRSV)

Fretheim addresses these issues in a similar fashion:

While the kingship of Saul was explicitly conditioned by the obedience of both king and people (12:14-15, 25), the kingship of David was not. God placed the kingship on an entirely new footing compared to that of Saul. Why? Because God learned something from the experience (and experiment) with Saul. . . . Given what has happened to the conditionally established kingship of Saul, God determines that only a new tack will have a chance of succeeding, viz., an unconditional commitment to the Davidic king. . . . It is of great importance to recognize that God's primary concern in all of this is for the future of *Israel* (cf. 9:16; 10:1; 12:22). Saul's disobedience and other unkingly behavior may not seem to our minds to be sufficient justification for the divine rejection. But chaps. 13–15 (cf. 1 Sam 28:18) would seem to be concerned to chart a trend or direction in the nature of Saul's kingship. . . . It is possible that the whole people would be swept away (12:14-15, 25) if this pattern in the kingship were allowed to continue.[107]

Measured in individual terms, this seems unfair to Saul, but the portrait of the books of Samuel is of a God responding to human history, not unrolling a predetermined script. The theme of divine regret/repentance especially suggests a God who responds and alters course in the pursuit of divine purposes. I mentioned earlier that the theme of divine regret (נחם *niham*, niphal) also appears in the story of the flood in Gen 6:6; the analogy with 1 Samuel 15 is an apt one. God's regret results both in judgment and in a new beginning based on God's covenant commitment, even in spite of human sin (see Gen 8:21-22). According to the story of 1 Samuel, kingship will find a new basis in David, which is guaranteed by God's commitment in spite of the conduct of people and the king. The tradition recognizes that it was different for Saul (2 Sam 7:13-15), and in that sense he was a tragic figure. David, too, will sin, and he will suffer consequences for his sin

---

106. See Gunn, *The Fate of King Saul,* 123-24, and also the others cited in n. 78.

107. Fretheim, "Divine Foreknowledge, Divine Constancy, and the Rejection of Saul's Kingship," 599-601.

(see 2 Sam 11-20); but God's faithfulness will allow the lineage of God's anointed one to endure as the source of hope in Israel even when earthly kingdoms seem to have perished through disobedience and when only the eschatological hope of a coming anointed one ("messiah") remains.

What of Samuel? Is he unduly harsh? Is he a single issue ideologue?[108] Prophets would not win personality awards. Samuel, indeed, is representative of an older, threatened political and religious order, and we know he was resistant to the idea of kingship (chap. 8). But the tradition portrays him in chap. 15 as one whose central focus is the word of the Lord. The text matter-of-factly reports Samuel's command to Saul as coming from the Lord. When Samuel's vested interests got in the way of God's purposes, the tradition forthrightly showed God dealing with Samuel as an obstruction (chaps. 8; 16). There is no suggestion of that in chap. 15. Samuel does represent the old order, which is passing away in

Israel, and we may fairly judge that he does not possess the full vision of God's future. In chap. 16, as we will see, he is still looking for the wrong things and must be directed by God (16:7). But Samuel not only rejects Saul—he anoints David, an even more radical departure from the old order. Samuel has limits and shortcomings, and he is harsh and often unlikable, but the tradition seems to believe that in chap. 15 he was doing the will of God in rejecting Saul so that the project with David could begin. If he is unbending in chap. 15, it is because the tradition reflected in that chapter regards listening/obedience as non-negotiable. The ongoing Jewish tradition remembered Samuel as faithful prophet, not as an ideological obstructionist (Sir 46:13-20).

In the end it is fitting, perhaps, that Samuel's grief marks the end of Saul's time as king (v. 35). There is no reason to regard this as self-serving or inauthentic sorrow. Samuel began his career announcing rejection to a man he probably cared for deeply (Eli, chap. 3). There is a certain symmetry in his career (even beyond the grave, chap. 28) that it ended in the same fashion.

108. See Walter Brueggemann, *First and Second Samuel,* Interpretation (Louisville: John Knox, 1990) 110, for a vigorous argument on behalf of this view.

REFLECTIONS

Chapter 15 is an important turning point in the story of 1 Samuel, but it has also proved a difficult episode for modern readers in response to the story. It is important to separate several issues that necessarily arise for the reader.

1. In reading and appropriating this story, we must forthrightly acknowledge that holy war, as its practice is reflected in this story, cannot be a morally defensible practice for us. In devoting both plunder and people of a vanquished enemy to the Lord, the practice of holy war treats people as mere property and shows no regard for the sanctity of life. Once defined as an enemy, Amalekite lives were given no worth. Such practices are not, of course, limited to ancient times. Holocaust and Hiroshima stand as symbols of modern policies of extermination in dealing with enemies. But such policies, even in war, no longer have broad moral support, and readers of 1 Samuel 15 are often shocked that God and Samuel would order such an action.

It is important to note that the text of 1 Samuel 15 treats the command of holy war against the Amalekites as a legitimate command of the Lord. We may disagree that such a policy could ever be God's will, but this is not questioned by Saul or by the storyteller. Thus Saul's action in sparing King Agag cannot be seized upon as the act of a moral reformer demonstrating compassion over against the hard-heartedness of Samuel. The motive for bringing back a captive king is glory, not compassion. In preaching this text, we can (perhaps must) reject the content of ancient standards of morality in the matter of holy war while at the same time taking seriously the confrontation over obedience to the divine word in this story.

2. The episode in chap. 15 provides occasion to reflect on how often we know what the word of the Lord demands, but alter it to suit our own needs. If we set aside the difficult issue of holy war for a moment, the issue for us in this text is, as it was for Saul, obedience. What happens when we know the will of God but fail to do it—worse, when we only do it in part—the parts that are convenient? Paul lamented, "For I do not do the good I want, but the evil I do not want is what I do" (Rom 7:19). We can fill in our own issues and experience, but almost all of us, if we are honest, know how easy it is to make our own adjustments to what we know God is demanding of us. We want to honor God in our own way, not in God's way. We want to make our own adjustments ("Just a small difference really!"). When the rich young ruler came to Jesus, he was certain he was ready for full obedience. But when Jesus told him to sell all he had, it was not the shape of obedience he had in mind (Matt 19:16-30; Mark 10:17-31; Luke 18:18-30). I'm certain the price of discipleship seemed harsh to the young ruler. When we read of the rejection of Saul for his failure to do what he knew was demanded of him as God's command, we can sympathize with him and the high price he paid for a few alterations in carrying out the command. But if we choose to follow his path and make our own alterations in what we know God is asking of us in obedience, then we had better look over our shoulders occasionally for the approach of a Samuel.

3. Much of the focus of modern readers' discomfort and assessment of Saul as a tragic figure centers on the issue of proportionality. Was the judgment of God announced by Samuel against Saul harsher than his infraction deserved? He had hardly begun his reign before he was rejected as king. Saul may have used poor judgment, but he does not seem a man of ill will.

We live in a society that gives fairness a high value. We make bestsellers out of books such as *When Bad Things Happen to Good People.*[109] Although Saul, unlike Job, is not a completely innocent man, many still feel that 1 Samuel 15 raises a theodicy issue. Did Saul's actions completely justify rejection by God? As modern readers, all too aware of our own flaws, we identify with Saul and doubt that we could meet such rigorous divine standards.

Yet, the story of Saul and of our lives does not operate solely in a retributive-justice framework. Saul is not rejected because he passed some dividing line of behavior that is marked "deserving" on one side and "undeserving" on the other. It has simply become clear in the story that Saul cannot be God's future for Israel. Disobedience to God's Word, Saul's need for the assurance of ritual and oath, his indecision and inability to assess situations clearly (all demonstrated in the episodes of chaps. 13–15) have made this evident. Israel's future is at stake, and God acts to move toward a new future in David.

In our society, both secular and religious institutions struggle over the standards that should apply and the judgments that should be made concerning leadership. Too often matters of seniority, goodwill, old-boy networks, or simple avoidance of conflict stand in the way of judgments over what will move us forward in obedience to God's will and in concern for the welfare of our communities and churches. We allow general qualities of goodness to substitute for the gifts of leadership. A "Peanuts" cartoon shows Charlie Brown saying to Linus that when he grows up he would like to be a prophet. Linus replies that this is an admirable goal, but "most turn out to be false prophets." Charlie Brown responds, "Well, at least I'll be a sincere false prophet." There are those who at times must make decisions that remove persons from leadership or deny them access to leadership roles (e.g., judicatory bodies that assess candidates for ministry). These persons will often be worthy and admirable in other ways. If our unwillingness to make difficult decisions causes us to allow persons to continue in leadership when they do not have the gifts for that role, then we will have failed the future of the

109. Harold S. Kushner, *When Bad Things Happen to Good People* (New York: Schocken, 1981).

institutions we serve. Those who make such difficult decisions will often seem as harsh as does Samuel in this account.

4. Samuel has sometimes been accused of rejecting Saul out of vested interests in maintaining the ideology of an old order. This is always a danger for those who must make judgments concerning leadership. But this story suggests that Samuel acted out of obedience to God's command and that he was personally filled with grief for Saul. We, like Samuel, cannot come to decisions concerning leadership without vested interests. But we can submit our decisions to prayerful discernment of God's will for the future rather than our own, and we cannot make such decisions in isolation from the personal pathos all such decisions involve. We do well to remember that if Samuel rejected Saul with any thought of returning to the safety of an old, familiar order of things, God did not let this happen. God summoned Samuel out of his grief and sent him to anoint David (16:1), an even more radical departure from the old patterns and ideologies of the tribal league. If we are tempted to reject leaders in the name of God, hoping for the comfort of the "way we've always done things," we can be certain that God will find yet more challenging ways of raising up leaders to move us toward the future of God's kingdom.

1 SAMUEL 16:1–31:13, THE RISE OF DAVID AND THE DECLINE OF SAUL

OVERVIEW

David comes onstage at this point in the story and does not relinquish center stage for the remainder of the books of Samuel. Other major characters recede into the background or play only supporting roles. Samuel, the prophet whose forceful presence has dominated the early chapters of 1 Samuel, anoints David as king and then disappears from the story. Saul, Israel's first king, still occupies the throne, but Israel has no future with Saul; he seems, in the remaining chapters of 1 Samuel, to be primarily a foil for the rising star of David. His death, at the end of 1 Samuel, provides a tragic counterpoint to the final accession of David to the throne. David is the climactic point to which the story of 1 Samuel has been building, and we now hear his story in astonishing detail. The tradition clearly understands that God's intentions for Israel's future are bound up in this man David.

Since the work of Leonhard Rost, most scholars have accepted the identification of a unified literary composition, commonly called the history of David's rise, that tells the story of David until his accession to the kingship of Judah and Israel.[110] The precise beginning and ending of this history Rise remain in dispute.[111] I agree with those who see the beginning of this composition in 16:14-23 with the introduction of David to Saul's court as a musician and armorbearer. The conclusion may be found in the formula that declares God's presence with David in 2 Sam 5:10. The story of David's anointing (6:1-13) is an important introduction to the history of David's rise, added by a prophetic historian who incorporated the history

110. The original work of Leonhard Rost was published in 1926, but is now available in English translation as *The Succession to the Throne of David,* trans. David M. Gunn (Sheffield: Almond, 1982). Rost's brief suggestion of a history of the rise of David has received considerable attention in recent years. See the treatment of this scholarship in P. Kyle McCarter, "The Apology of David," *JBL* 99 (1980) 489-504. For a minority view that understands all of 1 Samuel as a unified literary composition rather than a product of several sources or editions, see Robert Polzin, *Samuel and the Deuteronomist: A Literary Study of the Deuteronomic History,* Part Two: *1 Samuel* (San Francisco: Harper & Row, 1989).

111. Some would see the beginning of the history of David's rise at 16:1, and others would even include chap. 15. A few would see the conclusion extending beyond 5:10 in 2 Samuel. See the discussion of these critical issues in P. Kyle McCarter, "The Apology of David," *JBL* 99 (1980) 499-502, as well as his summary of the role of the history of the Rise of David in the larger composition of 1 Samuel in P. Kyle McCarter, *I Samuel,* AB 8 (Garden City, N.Y.: Doubleday, 1980) 27-30.

into his larger work, covering most of 1 Samuel (see the Introduction). This prophetic historian used the story of David's anointing to create a bridge between the rejection of Saul (chap. 15) and the beginning of David's story (16:14-23) and is also responsible for the episode with the ghost of Samuel in chap. 28.

This history of the rise of David does not focus on David as an established royal figure. Rather, it conveys a David who begins as an eighth son and a shepherd, yet becomes king of all Israel through an unlikely series of trials and successes. David is the outsider who makes good, the underdog who triumphs, the outcast who returns in power. Brueggemann reminds us that such stories are told and celebrated by the marginal, who find hope in the early David stories for their own rise from marginalization.[112] David is a marginal figure himself, a nobody whose successes are resented by the established power (Saul) and who is forced to become something of an outlaw.[113] These stories celebrate David as the raw yet charismatic hero of those denied the gentility of established power. The David we will encounter in these stories is not idealized. He is both pious and pragmatic, idealistic and self-serving, fearless and calculating.

A compelling argument has been made that a central purpose for the writing of the history of the rise of David was to legitimate his claim to the throne and to provide an apology to counter claims that might have been made against David's right to the kingship. McCarter offers the following list of potential charges against David that this narrative seeks to counter:

1. David sought to advance himself at court at Saul's expense.
2. David was a deserter.
3. David was an outlaw.
4. David was a Philistine mercenary.
5. David was implicated in Saul's death.
6. David was implicated in Abner's death.
7. David was implicated in Ishbaal's death.[114]

In each of these instances the storyteller takes pains to show that David was guiltless and that his rise to power was lawful and legitimate. Each of these charges is argued as untrue or understandable in the circumstances. We will see this more clearly in discussing individual chapters.

If David occupies the stage in these stories, God is nevertheless the director of the drama. The clear and constant theological theme of these chapters is that the Lord was with David. This claim occurs first in the mouth of a servant speaking to Saul of David (16:18), and it recurs explicitly in 17:37; 18:12, 14, 28; 20:13; and 2 Sam 5:10. This final reference provides a theological summary of the history of David's rise: "And David became greater and greater, for the LORD, the God of hosts, was with him." Throughout these stories, even where the formula of divine presence does not explicitly appear, it is clear that David represents what God is doing to secure Israel's future and well-being. As we will see in 16:1-13, God initiated the David story in Israel by choosing David "for myself" (16:1). What follows in the remaining chapters of 1 Samuel is a unique combination of theological confidence in God's presence with David and honesty about the raw events of this political process and the men and women who lived through it.

---

112. Walter Brueggemann, *David's Truth in Israel's Imagination and Memory* (Philadelphia: Fortress, 1985) 19-23.

113. Both Niels Peter Lemche, "David's Rise," *JSOT* 10 (1978) 23, and George Mendenhall, *The Tenth Generation: The Origins of the Biblical Tradition* (Baltimore: Johns Hopkins University Press, 1973) 135-36, treat David as a Habiru (a kind of outlaw class of the socially marginal in the ancient world). John L. McKenzie, *The Old Testament Without Illusion* (Chicago: Thomas More, 1979) 236, calls David a "bloodthirsty, oversexed bandit."

114. McCarter, "The Apology of David," 499-502. McCarter is building on the earlier work of Artur Weiser, "Die Legitimation des Königs David: zur Eigenart und Entstehung der sogen. Geschichte von Davids Aufstieg," *VT* 16 (1966) 325-54.

1 Samuel 16:1-13, The Anointing of David

NIV

16The LORD said to Samuel, "How long will you mourn for Saul, since I have rejected him as king over Israel? Fill your horn with oil and be on your way; I am sending you to Jesse of Bethlehem. I have chosen one of his sons to be king."

²But Samuel said, "How can I go? Saul will hear about it and kill me."

The LORD said, "Take a heifer with you and say, 'I have come to sacrifice to the LORD.' ³Invite Jesse to the sacrifice, and I will show you what to do. You are to anoint for me the one I indicate."

⁴Samuel did what the LORD said. When he arrived at Bethlehem, the elders of the town trembled when they met him. They asked, "Do you come in peace?"

⁵Samuel replied, "Yes, in peace; I have come to sacrifice to the LORD. Consecrate yourselves and come to the sacrifice with me." Then he consecrated Jesse and his sons and invited them to the sacrifice.

⁶When they arrived, Samuel saw Eliab and thought, "Surely the LORD's anointed stands here before the LORD."

⁷But the LORD said to Samuel, "Do not consider his appearance or his height, for I have rejected him. The LORD does not look at the things man looks at. Man looks at the outward appearance, but the LORD looks at the heart."

⁸Then Jesse called Abinadab and had him pass in front of Samuel. But Samuel said, "The LORD has not chosen this one either." ⁹Jesse then had Shammah pass by, but Samuel said, "Nor has the LORD chosen this one." ¹⁰Jesse had seven of his sons pass before Samuel, but Samuel said to him, "The LORD has not chosen these." ¹¹So he asked Jesse, "Are these all the sons you have?"

"There is still the youngest," Jesse answered, "but he is tending the sheep."

Samuel said, "Send for him; we will not sit down[a] until he arrives."

¹²So he sent and had him brought in. He was ruddy, with a fine appearance and handsome features.

---

[a]11 Some Septuagint manuscripts; Hebrew *not gather around*

NRSV

16The LORD said to Samuel, "How long will you grieve over Saul? I have rejected him from being king over Israel. Fill your horn with oil and set out; I will send you to Jesse the Bethlehemite, for I have provided for myself a king among his sons." ²Samuel said, "How can I go? If Saul hears of it, he will kill me." And the LORD said, "Take a heifer with you, and say, 'I have come to sacrifice to the LORD.' ³Invite Jesse to the sacrifice, and I will show you what you shall do; and you shall anoint for me the one whom I name to you." ⁴Samuel did what the LORD commanded, and came to Bethlehem. The elders of the city came to meet him trembling, and said, "Do you come peaceably?" ⁵He said, "Peaceably; I have come to sacrifice to the LORD; sanctify yourselves and come with me to the sacrifice." And he sanctified Jesse and his sons and invited them to the sacrifice.

⁶When they came, he looked on Eliab and thought, "Surely the LORD's anointed is now before the LORD."[a] ⁷But the LORD said to Samuel, "Do not look on his appearance or on the height of his stature, because I have rejected him; for the LORD does not see as mortals see; they look on the outward appearance, but the LORD looks on the heart." ⁸Then Jesse called Abinadab, and made him pass before Samuel. He said, "Neither has the LORD chosen this one." ⁹Then Jesse made Shammah pass by. And he said, "Neither has the LORD chosen this one." ¹⁰Jesse made seven of his sons pass before Samuel, and Samuel said to Jesse, "The LORD has not chosen any of these." ¹¹Samuel said to Jesse, "Are all your sons here?" And he said, "There remains yet the youngest, but he is keeping the sheep." And Samuel said to Jesse, "Send and bring him; for we will not sit down until he comes here." ¹²He sent and brought him in. Now he was ruddy, and had beautiful eyes, and was handsome. The LORD said, "Rise and anoint him; for this is the one." ¹³Then Samuel took the horn of oil, and anointed him in the presence of his brothers; and the spirit of the LORD came mightily upon David from that day forward. Samuel then set out and went to Ramah.

---

[a] Heb *him*

Then the LORD said, "Rise and anoint him; he is the one."

¹³So Samuel took the horn of oil and anointed him in the presence of his brothers, and from that day on the Spirit of the LORD came upon David in power. Samuel then went to Ramah.

COMMENTARY

Chapter 16 contains two episodes that introduce David. The first (vv. 1-13) designates David as God's choice; the second (vv. 14-23) identifies David as Saul's choice. The narrator wanted to emphasize the priority of God's initiative. The human actions that occur in the coming chapters constitute the acting out of a divine plan for Israel's future. The stories about David are the stories of God's anointed one. God's designation of David takes place in secret, and the reader thus possesses knowledge that only Samuel and David's family possess in the story. The episode of David's introduction to Saul's court (vv. 14-23) is thus a public presentation of David, and the reader knows more of the significance of this debut than does Saul. In v. 1, God chooses David "for myself" as a king, while in vv. 14-23 Saul thinks he is only choosing a musician and armorbearer.

The account of David's anointing by the prophet Samuel was probably placed as an introduction to the history of David's rise, which begins with v. 14. No mention is made of Samuel's anointing of David outside of 16:1-13. The theme of the Spirit that comes upon David (v. 13) and leaves Saul (v. 14) links the two episodes that introduce us to David. Likewise, the theme of Samuel's grief in v. 1 links this episode backward to the story of Saul's rejection, where Samuel's grief is mentioned (15:35).

The key word in vv. 1-13 is ראה (rā'â, "to see," vv. 1, 6, 7, 12). It is also used in vv. 17-18, where it provides a thematic link between the episodes of the chapter. Chapter 15 described the rejection of Saul as a function of not "listening." The election of David is now presented as an exercise in right "seeing." Twice in this chapter the verb rā'â is used with the specialized meaning of "provide"—seeing in the sense of discerning or

choosing. In v. 1, God says, "I have provided [seen] for myself a king," and in v. 17, Saul says, "Provide [see] for me someone who can play." God sees more than Saul can see in David. In the anointing episode, God sees more than Samuel. In vv. 6-7, Samuel (the seer! 9:19) sees only outward appearance, but God sees the heart. The story has now gone full circle. At the beginning of Samuel's story it was Eli who could not see, visions were rare, and the lamp of God was dim (3:1-2). Now it is Samuel who does not see clearly, and God must directly indicate the proper choice. At the center of this episode is a drama of right seeing. In it, the author underlines the theme of appearance and reality, which is central to this text. The reality of God's future for Israel does not always appear clear to human eyes, even to those of a prophet.

The anointing of David also follows a pattern we have seen before in the story of Saul. The career of God's anointed one (משיח māšîaḥ) involves anointing by a prophet, after which both Saul and David experience the possession of God's Spirit (10:1, 9-10; 11:6 for Saul; 16:13 for David). David's reception of the Spirit seems more immediate and is said to be effective "from that day forward" (v. 13). Both men then make a public debut (10:17-27; 16:14-23) and subsequently perform a mighty deed of valor that validates them as individuals possessed of God's Spirit (chaps. 11 and 17). But Saul's actions led to rejection, whereas David's story will culminate in confirmation and covenant.

Central to this theology of God's anointed one is the role of the prophet, who is God's agent to anoint, reject, or confirm (Nathan, 2 Samuel 7). In chap. 16, the prophetic interests are still clear, but the portrait of Samuel as an individual performing the prophetic role is less than flattering. He must be roused out of immobilizing grief (v. 1), he is fearful of the task laid out for him (v. 2), and he is rebuked for rushing to judgment (vv. 6-7). He seems old and passive, unable to see as God wishes him to see. Throughout the chapter, there is a constant dialogue between God and Samuel, as if he must be instructed at each step. Nevertheless, he is the prophet through whom God chooses to work. One has the impression that the prophetic role is being honored by the tradition even when the individual is not totally effective.

16:1-5. The story of David begins with divine initiative. God's speech in v. 1 begins with a note of reproof to Samuel. The season of grief is over (cf. 15:35). God has rejected Saul, and Samuel is dwelling on what might have been. God is already looking to the future. Indeed, the choice has already been made: "I have provided [seen] for *myself* a king." This new chosen one is among the sons of Jesse in Bethlehem. Samuel is told to fill his horn with oil (for an obvious anointing) and go there. Samuel had been commissioned to "make for *them* [the people] a king" (8:22). This act will provide a new dimension of God's initiative for Israel's future, with its twin crises of leadership and Philistine threat. David will be God's own king.

Samuel responds in fear: "If Saul hears of it, he will kill me" (v. 2a). To anoint a new king while Saul still physically occupies the throne would be treason. God tells Samuel to take a heifer along so that he can claim to be journeying to Bethlehem for a sacrifice (v. 2b), but once there the purpose is clear. Samuel is to invite Jesse and his sons to the sacrifice and anoint the one God names. God almost seems indulgent with Samuel in saying, "I will tell you what to do." The suggestion that God has participated in a lie (the God who claimed not to lie in 15:29) is a false issue. As in 9:19-24, the anointing would almost certainly have been accompanied by sacrifice and ritual eating together. God appears to be simply instructing Samuel on practicalities that he seems unable to decide for himself in his fearful state. In effect, he is told by God, "You don't have to confess treason, Samuel. Tell them something acceptable." If in chap. 8 God was willing to step back a little to let the people chart the course they demanded, that time has now ended. God

is firmly in authority over the course of events this time. Kingship will have a new basis in God's initiative, not that of the people.

The elders of Bethlehem are afraid and ask Samuel if he comes peaceably (v. 4). It seems less that they fear danger from Samuel directly than the controversy with Saul that he might bring into their midst. They do not know that he has come to anoint a successor to Saul, but they know that he is in conflict with Saul. Samuel soothes them by declaring peaceable intent. He merely announces a sacrifice and invites Jesse and his sons to join him (v. 5).

16:6-11. In this drama, Jesse and his sons seem to be the only persons present with Samuel. The sons of Jesse are brought before Samuel one at a time. When Eliab (the eldest, 17:13) comes forward, Samuel is ready to choose him. But the issue is proper "seeing." The text says that Samuel "looked on [ראה *rāʾâ*] Eliab" and thought that Eliab surely must be the Lord's anointed. God immediately replies with a rebuke. Samuel, God warns, must not "look" at appearance or stature. The verb here is נבט (*nābaṭ*) rather than *rāʾâ*, "to see." The implication may be that Samuel was "looking" but not really "seeing." Saul had been handsome and tall (9:2; 10:23). Such matters of appearance did not justify a decision. God pronounces Eliab to be "rejected" (מאס *māʾas*), the same term used of Saul in 15:23, 26 when he was "rejected" as king. It is also the same word used in 8:7 to describe the people's "rejection" of God as king. Eliab cannot move Israel beyond the stalemates of "rejection." Mettinger has suggested that "Eliab is something of a 'new Saul,' so that in his rejection Saul is denounced in effigy." He further suggests that the process here is something like the choosing of Saul by lots. As each son is brought forward, Samuel in some manner determines a divine judgment of yes or no. As with Saul, Samuel almost took Eliab's stature as the sign of his chosenness. But when God finally makes a choice, the chosen one is absent and must be brought onstage.[115]

God declares further that the Lord "sees" differently from mortals, who settle for outward appearance. The Lord "sees" the heart (v. 7), the

---

115. T. N. D. Mettinger, *King and Messiah: The Civil and Sacral Legitimation of the Israelite Kings,* ConBOT 8 (Lund: CWK Gleerup, 1976) 175-79.

inner person, and not the outward appearance. "Heart" has to do with the will and character of a person. David is the man after God's own heart (13:14), the man whom God has chosen. Human appearance will not determine reality for Israel this time.

The other sons of Jesse are paraded forward (vv. 8-10). Two are named, Abinadab and Shammah, but the other four are lumped together and left nameless. All are designated as "not chosen." Samuel asks Jesse if all his sons are present, and Jesse reports that there is one other who is tending the sheep (v. 11). Samuel sends for him. Virtually all scholars agree that David's identity as a shepherd (a theme mentioned in each of the three introductory stories for David, 16:19; 17:15, 34-36) foreshadows his role as king. "Shepherd" was a common title for kings both in Israel and in the ancient Near East. It is also significant that David is the eighth son. This means that he is far down in the line of succession. God, as with Jacob and Joseph, once again reaches out to take a younger son, an unlikely prospect for success, and finds in him the hope of Israel's future. From this moment and throughout the stories of the rise of David there is an element of cheering on the underdog and the outsider.[116] God "sees" possibilities even when others do not: "God chose what is low and despised in the world, things that are not, to reduce to nothing things that are" (1 Cor 1:28).

16:12-13. At last David makes his appearance.

116. This is a theme particularly stressed by Brueggemann's treatment of the stories of the rise of David, Walter Brueggemann, *David's Truth in Israel's Imagination and Memory* (Philadelphia: Fortress, 1985) 19-40.

He is passive, the object of our regard. It is not yet time for him to take action. Remarkably, when he enters, the text tells us, he is "ruddy, had beautiful eyes, and was handsome" (v. 12*a*). Appearance may not be what counts for God's choice, but the text almost seems to delight in saying that he could be handsome anyway. "This is the one!" God declares (v. 12*b*). This handsome one must also be the one with the heart to be God's anointed. So Samuel is commanded to anoint him, and he does so before all the sons of Jesse (v. 13*a*). Then "the spirit of the LORD came mightily upon David from that day forward" (v. 13*b*). God's anointed one is marked, as was Saul, by the receiving of the Spirit. But unlike Saul, the Spirit comes upon David as soon as he is anointed and stays with him from that day forward. Saul's experience with the prophets (10:9-13) and in delivering Ammon (11:6) suggests a different understanding of the way in which the Spirit might be present for Saul, although the departure of the Spirit from Saul (v. 14) might indicate the Spirit was with him until that moment. In any case, David is now fully God's anointed king, with oil and with Spirit.

It should be noted that although David's name has been used throughout this discussion he is not named in the text until this final verse of the anointing story. The naming of this anointed one as David comes as a dramatic and climactic introduction to one whose story will become the very center of Israel's life and who will grasp Israel's imagination for generations to come. Samuel, by contrast, quietly leaves the stage and returns to Ramah (v. 13*b*). His time is over.

REFLECTIONS

1. Once again we have a story that reminds us of the unlikely vessels of God's grace. God's choice is David, a shepherd, an eighth son, from the village of Bethlehem, from a family that has no obvious pedigree. The theme of David as an unlikely instrument for Israel's hope continues throughout the story of his early years. We are always in wonder that this man David is the one for whom God has prepared us, of whom Hannah sang in hope. Can this boy defeat the Philistine champion? Can this upstart warrior escape the wrath of Saul? Can this fugitive and outlaw become a king? Can a man who hires himself out to the Philistines win Israel's heart?

One of the most basic themes of the entire biblical message is that God finds possibilities for grace in the most unexpected places and through the most unlikely persons. To choose the youngest son, who labors as a shepherd, to be Israel's future king is to ignore the usual arrangements for power and influence in the ancient world. Unlike Saul's father, Kish, David's father, Jesse, is not described as "a man of wealth" (9:1, the word can also mean "power").

The family tree of David is not distinguished. Jesse's grandmother was Ruth, an immigrant Moabite woman (Ruth 4:17). His grandfather was Boaz, whose ancestors included a Canaanite woman who was almost executed for adultery (Tamar, Genesis 38) and a Canaanite prostitute from Jericho (Rahab, Joshua 2). In the world's usual power arrangements, this would not be the stuff of royal lineage, but in God's plans sometimes "the last shall be first" (Matt 19:30; 20:16; Mark 10:31; Luke 13:30), even an absent eighth son tending the sheep. Of course, the unlikely journey of God's grace through the line of David leads to Jesus, born in a stable, a Galilean, a carpenter's son, and finally a crucified criminal. But Jesus is the true anointed One (Messiah) in whom God meets us for the most unlikely of all moments of grace. And the genealogy of Jesus in Matthew 1 includes younger sons like Jacob, David, and Solomon as well as naming those unlikely mothers Tamar, Rahab, and Ruth.

This story of the choosing of David can serve as a reminder that we still live in communities for which the patterns of power seek to become permanently entrenched. Too often we fail to look for possibilities of grace and hope beyond the traditional channels of power, influence, and success. We ignore the possibilities in those who are customarily absent from the gatherings of power (the inner cities, the elderly, immigrants who speak languages other than English, those of a different race from ours). We do not believe that God can find hope for a new future among the marginalized and the dispossessed. In our own personal moments of estrangement and self-doubt, we do not believe that God can find possibilities for grace in us.

2. Related to this theme of God's unexpected choices is our tendency, like Samuel, to confuse appearance for reality. It is almost trite to note that we live in a culture oriented to image and appearance. Products are sold by the appearance of youth and sexuality, which have nothing to do with the product itself. Tobacco brings cancerous death, but sells by appeal to chic and macho appearances. Children are ostracized at school for not wearing the proper brand names, and sometimes robbed of coveted items when they do wear them. Political campaigners seek to polish a successful media image rather than to convince voters by their positions on issues.

God's word to Samuel (16:7) is hopeful in such a time. When so many are fooled by appearances, it is comforting and encouraging to hear that God looks on the heart, that God can see past the preoccupation with image and appearance that characterizes our time. If the church is both to discern and to mediate God's grace in the world, then it, too, must seek to look on the heart—to see as God sees. It must look beyond appearances in order to grapple with the concerns and address the needs of the human heart. Nothing less will be acceptable for the life of God's people, no matter how successful our institutional appearance might be. If we succumb to the temptation to choose for appearance alone, then God's rebuke to Samuel will be our own.

The irony of this text is that when David appears, he, too, is handsome. This text does not argue against our efforts to make ourselves, our communities, our programs attractive. It is a question of priorities. Appearance alone is no substitute for matters of the heart, but if we tend faithfully to matters of the heart, the grace of God within will often show an attractive face to the world.

1 Samuel 16:14-23, David Is Introduced to Saul's Court

NIV

¹⁴Now the Spirit of the LORD had departed from Saul, and an evil[a] spirit from the LORD tormented him.

¹⁵Saul's attendants said to him, "See, an evil

[a]14 Or *injurious*; also in verses 15, 16 and 23

NRSV

14Now the spirit of the LORD departed from Saul, and an evil spirit from the LORD tormented him. ¹⁵And Saul's servants said to him, "See now, an evil spirit from God is tormenting you. ¹⁶Let our lord now command the servants who attend

NIV

spirit from God is tormenting you. ¹⁶Let our lord command his servants here to search for someone who can play the harp. He will play when the evil spirit from God comes upon you, and you will feel better."

¹⁷So Saul said to his attendants, "Find someone who plays well and bring him to me."

¹⁸One of the servants answered, "I have seen a son of Jesse of Bethlehem who knows how to play the harp. He is a brave man and a warrior. He speaks well and is a fine-looking man. And the LORD is with him."

¹⁹Then Saul sent messengers to Jesse and said, "Send me your son David, who is with the sheep." ²⁰So Jesse took a donkey loaded with bread, a skin of wine and a young goat and sent them with his son David to Saul.

²¹David came to Saul and entered his service. Saul liked him very much, and David became one of his armor-bearers. ²²Then Saul sent word to Jesse, saying, "Allow David to remain in my service, for I am pleased with him."

²³Whenever the spirit from God came upon Saul, David would take his harp and play. Then relief would come to Saul; he would feel better, and the evil spirit would leave him.

NRSV

you to look for someone who is skillful in playing the lyre; and when the evil spirit from God is upon you, he will play it, and you will feel better." ¹⁷So Saul said to his servants, "Provide for me someone who can play well, and bring him to me." ¹⁸One of the young men answered, "I have seen a son of Jesse the Bethlehemite who is skillful in playing, a man of valor, a warrior, prudent in speech, and a man of good presence; and the LORD is with him." ¹⁹So Saul sent messengers to Jesse, and said, "Send me your son David who is with the sheep." ²⁰Jesse took a donkey loaded with bread, a skin of wine, and a kid, and sent them by his son David to Saul. ²¹And David came to Saul, and entered his service. Saul loved him greatly, and he became his armor-bearer. ²²Saul sent to Jesse, saying, "Let David remain in my service, for he has found favor in my sight." ²³And whenever the evil spirit from God came upon Saul, David took the lyre and played it with his hand, and Saul would be relieved and feel better, and the evil spirit would depart from him.

COMMENTARY

This is the second of three episodes that introduce David into the story. No one of the three shows knowledge of the others, but together they introduce David from complementary perspectives. What was a secret, subversive choosing of David by God (vv. 1-13) becomes a public, visible choosing of David by Saul (vv. 14-23). On the surface, Saul seems to be the subject of this episode, with his needs for relief from an "evil spirit" occupying central attention. A young musician named David is brought in to aid him. But the reader, because of the anointing story in vv. 1-13, knows that David is more than just a musician in this story. Saul has brought the future king into his own court. Fokkelman has highlighted the irony of this moment, "While Saul and his court think they are welcoming a musician,

we realize that the Saulide monarchy is dragging in a Trojan Horse."[117]

The key word that sets the theme for this episode is רוח (*rûaḥ*), "spirit." It provides a link back to the anointing story, where "the spirit of the LORD came mightily upon David from that day forward" (v. 13). Now v. 14 reports that "the spirit of the LORD departed from Saul" (v. 14*a*) and "an evil spirit from the LORD tormented him" (v. 14*b*). Both Saul and David may have been anointed, but it seems that only one of them may possess the Lord's Spirit at a time and thus be the legitimate anointed one in the eyes of God and on the throne of Israel. The evil spirit that plagues Saul seems to be some sort of affliction that comes

117. J. P. Fokkelman, *Narrative Art and Poetry in the Books of Samuel,* vol. 2: *The Crossing Fates (I Sam 13–31 and II Sam 1)* (Assen: Van Gorcum, 1986) 135.

and goes, since David's playing can make it depart (v. 23). The various references to "spirit" will be commented on further in the discussion of the verses below. The notion of an evil spirit "from the LORD" is disturbing to us. Does this simply make Saul a victim of God's anger? We must remember that seldom does the biblical story recognize secondary causation. All things ultimately come from God. This does not absolve Saul from responsibility for his own behavior. We must also avoid rationalizing this text too quickly. The evil spirit here is more than just some ancient code for what we might call sickness or mental illness. Saul is a troubled man, and as the people's king he reflects a troubled Israel (as we have seen in previous chaps., esp. 8 and 15). Both Saul and Israel are alienated from God. David is God's solution for both. This episode in 16:14-23 brings David immediately into the household of Saul, and with healing results. In the longer term, the episode introduces David into the household of Israel with hope for its future well-being. Although the immediate context is Saul's malady, God's ultimate plan for Israel in David is recognized and given voice through Saul's servant, "the LORD is with him" (v. 18).

16:14-19. We have noted that the Lord's Spirit departs from Saul and that an evil spirit arrives to plague him (v. 1). Although God's Spirit came more than once to Saul (10:10; 11:6), its departure here seems permanent. Possession of God's Spirit was a sign of Saul's status as God's anointed one, and it is now David who possesses God's Spirit (16:13). By contrast, the evil spirit can come and go repeatedly as the troubled mind and spirit of Saul are given healing attention, in the case of this account, by David's music (v. 23). This is apparently some affliction that is not without precedent, for Saul's servants suggest that a musician skilled with the lyre can soothe and bring relief to him (vv. 15-16). There is a possible known remedy for such troubling of the spirit. It is not fruitful to attempt some precise medical or psychological diagnosis of Saul as some have done. We know that Saul, at later points in the story, evidences brooding and melancholy states, fits of anger and rage that issue in violence, and irrational actions that divert him from the needs of his kingdom and finally lead to his own suicide. That this evil spirit is attributed to God indicates that, for the author, Saul's condition has a spiritual dimension. He is alienated from God and from the power of God's Spirit for well-being. All things come from God, but the preceding chapters help us to understand that Saul's actions have cut him off from the well-being that would be available to him in relationship to God.

Music is often associated, in both ancient and modern literature, with healing powers. Saul's servants are certain that music will help to soothe his troubled state, and they suggest a search for a musician skilled on the lyre. Saul accepts the suggestion and commands that his servants "provide for me someone who can play well" (v. 17). The verb here is the same focused use of *ra'ah,* "to see," "to search out," that was used by God in 16:1, "I have provided for myself. . . ." David was first provided by God, and now provided to Saul. A young servant immediately responds to Saul's command with "I have seen [*ra'â*] a son of Jesse the Bethlehemite" and reports that this son of Jesse is "skillful in playing." Here is the first testimony in the biblical tradition to David as a musician. David's skills as a musician, singer, and composer of songs become a standard part of the tradition about him. He is called the "beloved singer of Israel" in 2 Sam 23:1 (NIV; the NRSV abandons this reading; see Commentary on 2 Sam 23:1-7). He is cited as a composer of psalms and patron of music in 2 Sam 6:5; 1 Chr 6:31; and 16:7-42 and in the superscriptions of more than eighty psalms. Klein cites a reference in the Qumran materials that David wrote 3,600 psalms and 450 songs.[118]

The testimony of the servant continues on to cite a number of other qualities of this son of Jesse. He is a "man of valor, a warrior, prudent in speech, and a man of good presence" (v. 18). This recital goes beyond the needs of this episode, where only a musician is sought. These qualities anticipate the actions and qualities of the David we will see in the chapters immediately ahead (chaps. 17–20). Most important, the servant testifies that "the LORD is with him" (v. 18*b*), a major theological theme in the stories of David's rise, culminating in the great summation of 2 Sam 5:10 (see also 1 Sam 17:37; 18:12, 14, 28; 20:13). We are placed on notice that what begins here is part

---

118. Ralph W Klein, *1 Samuel,* WBC 10 (Waco: Word, 1983) 165. See also James L. Mays, "The David of the Psalms," *Int.* 40 (1986) 143-55.

of a larger divine plan and not just a strategy to relieve Saul's illness.

The man described here is not the untried boy of vv. 11-13. He is also not the boy, untested in battle, who fells Goliath in chap. 17, a tension we will deal with in later discussion. Apparently this able man is still doing some sheeptending, as Saul's request of Jesse in v. 19 suggests. Saul's request (command?) names David publicly for the first time. It is ironic that the first utterance of David's name in the Bible is on the lips of Saul, the man he will replace as Israel's king.

16:20-23. David makes his appearance and enters Saul's service. His role is still largely passive. He is the subject of only two verbs here, "David took the lyre and played it" (v. 23). We await chap. 17 for the introduction of David as a man of bold action, although the qualities cited by the servant in v. 18 anticipate such bold leadership.

Jesse sends gifts to Saul (v. 20), whereupon Saul receives David into his service (v. 21). We are reminded of Saul's recruiting of able warriors into his service (14:52*b*). It does not appear that Saul received David only for his abilities as a musician. In fact, v. 21 says that David became Saul's personal armorbearer, which, as we have seen in the story of Jonathan's exploits (chap. 14), signifies someone like a companion at arms. Most significant, v. 21 notes that "Saul loved him greatly." Alongside the public story of emerging kingship in Israel there begins here a personal story of relationships between David and the household of Saul. The tragedy of Saul's insane jealousy toward David at a later point in the story is compounded by this simple statement of Saul's great love for David. It is not only Saul's kingdom that is torn (chap. 15) but his heart as well.

Saul requests of Jesse that David remain permanently in his service (v. 22), which highlights Saul's special regard for David. Verse 23 returns to the theme of Saul's illness/evil spirit. When it plagues him, then it is indeed David who can lift this oppressive spirit. David is the source of well-being, the possessor of the Lord's Spirit who can drive back evil spirits. The word translated as "relieved" (רוח *rāwaḥ*) is a verbal form from the same root as "spirit." David not only removes the troubling spirit but also is the source of life and well-being through the Spirit. David provides momentary relief to Saul; he is the long-term hope for Israel.

REFLECTIONS

There is a famous painting of Saul and David by the Dutch master Rembrandt van Rijn. Saul is in the foreground dressed in the turban and finery of an oriental potentate. His expression is sad and melancholy. We know that this is a man in despair. He grips a spear, and something about his grasp on that weapon and the set of his jaw tells us that there is not only sadness here, but danger as well. There is a potential for evil in this troubled man. In the background, almost hidden in the shadows, is David, with harp in hand. We know the story. We know that his task is to soothe this troubled man. There is something hopeful about his presence. We know there is another reality than this powerful, troubled, and potentially evil man in the foreground. David is present as the future, but we know it is an endangered future. We hope he will be good at dodging spears.

Our tendency is often to define power as dangerous and potentially evil. As we move into the twenty-first century, distrust of those in authority is very high. We have seen the madness come forward and brandish the spear—in holocausts, gulags, ethnic cleansings, tribal wars of genocide. Our text does not absolve God of these evil spirits, and we, too, wonder why God's world should allow for such possibilities. Even short of horrors and atrocities, we often view those who have the power of governance or leadership as troubled and self-serving. The episode of David's introduction to Saul's court and Rembrandt's painting remind us that troubled and corrupt power is not the only possibility.

God has allowed for such evil in the world, but both spear and harp can represent power used faithfully for God's purposes. If our world is plagued, like Saul, by evil spirits that are also ultimately from God, then God has not left us defenseless against such evil.

In this episode it is the harp we find first in David's hand. David will, in future episodes, also be a warrior, and the spear can be wielded for good (David) or ill (Saul). But against the evil spirits that trouble the holders of power, David comes first as a singer of hope. It may well be that the church, like David, will be called to sing in the face of power edging into madness—to sing of hope, alternative possibilities, new futures. Such singing is not a substitute for faithful action in the arenas of power and influence, but perhaps faithful singing must precede faithful action as acknowledgment that the Spirit that drives out evil comes from God with us and not from our power alone.

In the painting Saul holds the spear. He has not used it yet, but he will later use it in an attempt to kill David, the singer (chap. 18). But the spear or the sword (used in these stories as symbols of military power) will be used in David's hand to kill Goliath and eventually drive oppressors from the land. There may be a part of us that wishes God's purposes worked only through the harp or that the providence of God included only benevolent spirits and not evil spirits. But God has become active in human history with all of its complexities and ambiguities. In order to move toward David, God must move away from Saul, and this leaves Saul plagued and troubled. This, too, is God's doing. The hope of harp and song simply reminds us that God has not left us defenseless in the face of troubled power and that the spear will not always be in Saul's hand.

1 Samuel 17:1-58, David Defeats Goliath

NIV

17 Now the Philistines gathered their forces for war and assembled at Socoh in Judah. They pitched camp at Ephes Dammim, between Socoh and Azekah. ²Saul and the Israelites assembled and camped in the Valley of Elah and drew up their battle line to meet the Philistines. ³The Philistines occupied one hill and the Israelites another, with the valley between them.

⁴A champion named Goliath, who was from Gath, came out of the Philistine camp. He was over nine feet[a] tall. ⁵He had a bronze helmet on his head and wore a coat of scale armor of bronze weighing five thousand shekels[b]; ⁶on his legs he wore bronze greaves, and a bronze javelin was slung on his back. ⁷His spear shaft was like a weaver's rod, and its iron point weighed six hundred shekels.[c] His shield bearer went ahead of him.

⁸Goliath stood and shouted to the ranks of Israel, "Why do you come out and line up for battle? Am I not a Philistine, and are you not the servants of Saul? Choose a man and have him come down to me. ⁹If he is able to fight and kill me, we will become your subjects; but if I overcome him and kill him, you will become our

a4 Hebrew was six cubits and a span (about 3 meters)   b5 That is, about 125 pounds (about 57 kilograms)   c7 That is, about 15 pounds (about 7 kilograms)

NRSV

17 Now the Philistines gathered their armies for battle; they were gathered at Socoh, which belongs to Judah, and encamped between Socoh and Azekah, in Ephes-dammim. ²Saul and the Israelites gathered and encamped in the valley of Elah, and formed ranks against the Philistines. ³The Philistines stood on the mountain on the one side, and Israel stood on the mountain on the other side, with a valley between them. ⁴And there came out from the camp of the Philistines a champion named Goliath, of Gath, whose height was six[a] cubits and a span. ⁵He had a helmet of bronze on his head, and he was armed with a coat of mail; the weight of the coat was five thousand shekels of bronze. ⁶He had greaves of bronze on his legs and a javelin of bronze slung between his shoulders. ⁷The shaft of his spear was like a weaver's beam, and his spear's head weighed six hundred shekels of iron; and his shield-bearer went before him. ⁸He stood and shouted to the ranks of Israel, "Why have you come out to draw up for battle? Am I not a Philistine, and are you not servants of Saul? Choose a man for yourselves, and let him come down to me. ⁹If he is able to fight with me and kill me, then we will be your servants; but if I

a MT: Q Ms Gk four

subjects and serve us." [10]Then the Philistine said, "This day I defy the ranks of Israel! Give me a man and let us fight each other." [11]On hearing the Philistine's words, Saul and all the Israelites were dismayed and terrified.

[12]Now David was the son of an Ephrathite named Jesse, who was from Bethlehem in Judah. Jesse had eight sons, and in Saul's time he was old and well advanced in years. [13]Jesse's three oldest sons had followed Saul to the war: The firstborn was Eliab; the second, Abinadab; and the third, Shammah. [14]David was the youngest. The three oldest followed Saul, [15]but David went back and forth from Saul to tend his father's sheep at Bethlehem.

[16]For forty days the Philistine came forward every morning and evening and took his stand.

[17]Now Jesse said to his son David, "Take this ephah[a] of roasted grain and these ten loaves of bread for your brothers and hurry to their camp. [18]Take along these ten cheeses to the commander of their unit.[b] See how your brothers are and bring back some assurance[c] from them. [19]They are with Saul and all the men of Israel in the Valley of Elah, fighting against the Philistines."

[20]Early in the morning David left the flock with a shepherd, loaded up and set out, as Jesse had directed. He reached the camp as the army was going out to its battle positions, shouting the war cry. [21]Israel and the Philistines were drawing up their lines facing each other. [22]David left his things with the keeper of supplies, ran to the battle lines and greeted his brothers. [23]As he was talking with them, Goliath, the Philistine champion from Gath, stepped out from his lines and shouted his usual defiance, and David heard it. [24]When the Israelites saw the man, they all ran from him in great fear.

[25]Now the Israelites had been saying, "Do you see how this man keeps coming out? He comes out to defy Israel. The king will give great wealth to the man who kills him. He will also give him his daughter in marriage and will exempt his father's family from taxes in Israel."

[26]David asked the men standing near him, "What will be done for the man who kills this Philistine and removes this disgrace from Israel?

a[17] That is, probably about 3/5 bushel (about 22 liters)   b[18] Hebrew thousand   c[18] Or some token; or some pledge of spoils

prevail against him and kill him, then you shall be our servants and serve us." [10]And the Philistine said, "Today I defy the ranks of Israel! Give me a man, that we may fight together." [11]When Saul and all Israel heard these words of the Philistine, they were dismayed and greatly afraid.

[12]Now David was the son of an Ephrathite of Bethlehem in Judah, named Jesse, who had eight sons. In the days of Saul the man was already old and advanced in years.[a] [13]The three eldest sons of Jesse had followed Saul to the battle; the names of his three sons who went to the battle were Eliab the firstborn, and next to him Abinadab, and the third Shammah. [14]David was the youngest; the three eldest followed Saul, [15]but David went back and forth from Saul to feed his father's sheep at Bethlehem. [16]For forty days the Philistine came forward and took his stand, morning and evening.

[17]Jesse said to his son David, "Take for your brothers an ephah of this parched grain and these ten loaves, and carry them quickly to the camp to your brothers; [18]also take these ten cheeses to the commander of their thousand. See how your brothers fare, and bring some token from them."

[19]Now Saul, and they, and all the men of Israel, were in the valley of Elah, fighting with the Philistines. [20]David rose early in the morning, left the sheep with a keeper, took the provisions, and went as Jesse had commanded him. He came to the encampment as the army was going forth to the battle line, shouting the war cry. [21]Israel and the Philistines drew up for battle, army against army. [22]David left the things in charge of the keeper of the baggage, ran to the ranks, and went and greeted his brothers. [23]As he talked with them, the champion, the Philistine of Gath, Goliath by name, came up out of the ranks of the Philistines, and spoke the same words as before. And David heard him.

[24]All the Israelites, when they saw the man, fled from him and were very much afraid. [25]The Israelites said, "Have you seen this man who has come up? Surely he has come up to defy Israel. The king will greatly enrich the man who kills him, and will give him his daughter and make his family free in Israel." [26]David said to the men who stood by him, "What shall be done for the man

a Gk Syr: Heb among men

NIV

Who is this uncircumcised Philistine that he should defy the armies of the living God?"

27They repeated to him what they had been saying and told him, "This is what will be done for the man who kills him."

28When Eliab, David's oldest brother, heard him speaking with the men, he burned with anger at him and asked, "Why have you come down here? And with whom did you leave those few sheep in the desert? I know how conceited you are and how wicked your heart is; you came down only to watch the battle."

29"Now what have I done?" said David. "Can't I even speak?" 30He then turned away to someone else and brought up the same matter, and the men answered him as before. 31What David said was overheard and reported to Saul, and Saul sent for him.

32David said to Saul, "Let no one lose heart on account of this Philistine; your servant will go and fight him."

33Saul replied, "You are not able to go out against this Philistine and fight him; you are only a boy, and he has been a fighting man from his youth."

34But David said to Saul, "Your servant has been keeping his father's sheep. When a lion or a bear came and carried off a sheep from the flock, 35I went after it, struck it and rescued the sheep from its mouth. When it turned on me, I seized it by its hair, struck it and killed it. 36Your servant has killed both the lion and the bear; this uncircumcised Philistine will be like one of them, because he has defied the armies of the living God. 37The LORD who delivered me from the paw of the lion and the paw of the bear will deliver me from the hand of this Philistine."

Saul said to David, "Go, and the LORD be with you."

38Then Saul dressed David in his own tunic. He put a coat of armor on him and a bronze helmet on his head. 39David fastened on his sword over the tunic and tried walking around, because he was not used to them.

"I cannot go in these," he said to Saul, "because I am not used to them." So he took them off. 40Then he took his staff in his hand, chose five smooth stones from the stream, put them in

NRSV

who kills this Philistine, and takes away the reproach from Israel? For who is this uncircumcised Philistine that he should defy the armies of the living God?" 27The people answered him in the same way, "So shall it be done for the man who kills him."

28His eldest brother Eliab heard him talking to the men; and Eliab's anger was kindled against David. He said, "Why have you come down? With whom have you left those few sheep in the wilderness? I know your presumption and the evil of your heart; for you have come down just to see the battle." 29David said, "What have I done now? It was only a question." 30He turned away from him toward another and spoke in the same way; and the people answered him again as before.

31When the words that David spoke were heard, they repeated them before Saul; and he sent for him. 32David said to Saul, "Let no one's heart fail because of him; your servant will go and fight with this Philistine." 33Saul said to David, "You are not able to go against this Philistine to fight with him; for you are just a boy, and he has been a warrior from his youth." 34But David said to Saul, "Your servant used to keep sheep for his father; and whenever a lion or a bear came, and took a lamb from the flock, 35I went after it and struck it down, rescuing the lamb from its mouth; and if it turned against me, I would catch it by the jaw, strike it down, and kill it. 36Your servant has killed both lions and bears; and this uncircumcised Philistine shall be like one of them, since he has defied the armies of the living God." 37David said, "The LORD, who saved me from the paw of the lion and from the paw of the bear, will save me from the hand of this Philistine." So Saul said to David, "Go, and may the LORD be with you!"

38Saul clothed David with his armor; he put a bronze helmet on his head and clothed him with a coat of mail. 39David strapped Saul's sword over the armor, and he tried in vain to walk, for he was not used to them. Then David said to Saul, "I cannot walk with these; for I am not used to them." So David removed them. 40Then he took his staff in his hand, and chose five smooth stones from the wadi, and put them in his shepherd's

NIV

the pouch of his shepherd's bag and, with his sling in his hand, approached the Philistine.

⁴¹Meanwhile, the Philistine, with his shield bearer in front of him, kept coming closer to David. ⁴²He looked David over and saw that he was only a boy, ruddy and handsome, and he despised him. ⁴³He said to David, "Am I a dog, that you come at me with sticks?" And the Philistine cursed David by his gods. ⁴⁴"Come here," he said, "and I'll give your flesh to the birds of the air and the beasts of the field!"

⁴⁵David said to the Philistine, "You come against me with sword and spear and javelin, but I come against you in the name of the Lord Almighty, the God of the armies of Israel, whom you have defied. ⁴⁶This day the Lord will hand you over to me, and I'll strike you down and cut off your head. Today I will give the carcasses of the Philistine army to the birds of the air and the beasts of the earth, and the whole world will know that there is a God in Israel. ⁴⁷All those gathered here will know that it is not by sword or spear that the Lord saves; for the battle is the Lord's, and he will give all of you into our hands."

⁴⁸As the Philistine moved closer to attack him, David ran quickly toward the battle line to meet him. ⁴⁹Reaching into his bag and taking out a stone, he slung it and struck the Philistine on the forehead. The stone sank into his forehead, and he fell facedown on the ground.

⁵⁰So David triumphed over the Philistine with a sling and a stone; without a sword in his hand he struck down the Philistine and killed him.

⁵¹David ran and stood over him. He took hold of the Philistine's sword and drew it from the scabbard. After he killed him, he cut off his head with the sword.

When the Philistines saw that their hero was dead, they turned and ran. ⁵²Then the men of Israel and Judah surged forward with a shout and pursued the Philistines to the entrance of Gath ͣ and to the gates of Ekron. Their dead were strewn along the Shaaraim road to Gath and Ekron. ⁵³When the Israelites returned from chasing the Philistines, they plundered their camp. ⁵⁴David took the Philistine's head and brought it to Jerusalem, and he put the Philistine's weapons in his own tent.

ͣ52 Some Septuagint manuscripts; Hebrew a valley

NRSV

bag, in the pouch; his sling was in his hand, and he drew near to the Philistine.

41The Philistine came on and drew near to David, with his shield-bearer in front of him. ⁴²When the Philistine looked and saw David, he disdained him, for he was only a youth, ruddy and handsome in appearance. ⁴³The Philistine said to David, "Am I a dog, that you come to me with sticks?" And the Philistine cursed David by his gods. ⁴⁴The Philistine said to David, "Come to me, and I will give your flesh to the birds of the air and to the wild animals of the field." ⁴⁵But David said to the Philistine, "You come to me with sword and spear and javelin; but I come to you in the name of the Lord of hosts, the God of the armies of Israel, whom you have defied. ⁴⁶This very day the Lord will deliver you into my hand, and I will strike you down and cut off your head; and I will give the dead bodies of the Philistine army this very day to the birds of the air and to the wild animals of the earth, so that all the earth may know that there is a God in Israel, ⁴⁷and that all this assembly may know that the Lord does not save by sword and spear; for the battle is the Lord's and he will give you into our hand."

48When the Philistine drew nearer to meet David, David ran quickly toward the battle line to meet the Philistine. ⁴⁹David put his hand in his bag, took out a stone, slung it, and struck the Philistine on his forehead; the stone sank into his forehead, and he fell face down on the ground.

50So David prevailed over the Philistine with a sling and a stone, striking down the Philistine and killing him; there was no sword in David's hand. ⁵¹Then David ran and stood over the Philistine; he grasped his sword, drew it out of its sheath, and killed him; then he cut off his head with it.

When the Philistines saw that their champion was dead, they fled. ⁵²The troops of Israel and Judah rose up with a shout and pursued the Philistines as far as Gath ͣ and the gates of Ekron, so that the wounded Philistines fell on the way from Shaaraim as far as Gath and Ekron. ⁵³The Israelites came back from chasing the Philistines, and they plundered their camp. ⁵⁴David took the

ͣ Gk Syr: Heb Gai

⁵⁵As Saul watched David going out to meet the Philistine, he said to Abner, commander of the army, "Abner, whose son is that young man?"

Abner replied, "As surely as you live, O king, I don't know."

⁵⁶The king said, "Find out whose son this young man is."

⁵⁷As soon as David returned from killing the Philistine, Abner took him and brought him before Saul, with David still holding the Philistine's head.

⁵⁸"Whose son are you, young man?" Saul asked him.

David said, "I am the son of your servant Jesse of Bethlehem."

head of the Philistine and brought it to Jerusalem; but he put his armor in his tent.

⁵⁵When Saul saw David go out against the Philistine, he said to Abner, the commander of the army, "Abner, whose son is this young man?" Abner said, "As your soul lives, O king, I do not know." ⁵⁶The king said, "Inquire whose son the stripling is." ⁵⁷On David's return from killing the Philistine, Abner took him and brought him before Saul, with the head of the Philistine in his hand. ⁵⁸Saul said to him, "Whose son are you, young man?" And David answered, "I am the son of your servant Jesse the Bethlehemite."

COMMENTARY

This is certainly the best known of all the stories of David. People who have no religious background or biblical knowledge recognize and know the broad outlines of the story of David and Goliath. Moreover, within 1 Samuel this story seems to occupy a special position. It is the most detailed in the telling of all the stories of David. Robert Alter says that this chapter represents as close as one can come in the Hebrew Bible to an epic style of storytelling—rich and explicit detail, extensive use of vivid dialogue, strong characterization and interaction of characters.[119] At the center of this epic drama, David emerges as the central actor whose bold action and unwavering faith capture our imagination. He is unquestionably the man for Israel's future, and the popularity of the story suggests that he becomes here a man for future generations as well.

Many scholars think that David did not kill Goliath. In 2 Sam 21:19 (cf. also 23:24), a biblical author reports that Elhanan of Bethlehem killed Goliath the Gittite. In 1 Samuel 17, Goliath is named only twice (vv. 4, 23), and David's opponent is usually referred to simply as "the Philistine." The Goliath killed by Elhanan was said to possess a spear with a shaft "like a weaver's beam," a detail also used in describing the armor of David's opponent in 17:7. The name "Goliath"

may have been transferred from Elhanan's deed to the account of David's victory over a Philistine champion. The chronicler attempts to harmonize these stories by having Elhanan kill Lahmi, a cousin of Goliath (1 Chr 20:5). Whatever the historical truth, the name "Goliath" became firmly fixed in the tradition as the giant warrior vanquished by the courageous boy David. In fact, it became one of the defining stories of the tradition about David in early Judaism and on through generations in church and synagogue. The writer of Sirach, singing the praises of famous men in Israel's past, wrote of David:

In his youth did he not kill a giant,
    and take away the people's disgrace,
when he whirled the stone in the sling
    and struck down the boasting Goliath?
For he called on the Lord, the Most High,
    and he gave strength to his right arm
to strike down a mighty warrior,
    and to exalt the power of his people.
(Sir 47:4-5 NRSV)

In its present form, this chapter serves as the reader's third introduction to David. As we shall see, this introduction shows no awareness of the previous episodes of David's anointing or introduction to Saul's court as a musician (chap. 16). This creates certain tensions in the flow of the larger story that cannot be resolved or harmonized. The dramatic story of 1 Samuel 17 does

119. Robert Alter, *The Art of Biblical Narrative* (New York: Basic Books, 1981) 150-51.

provide an important complement to the episodes of chap. 16. There David was first "provided" by God in the story of his anointing (16:1-13) and then "provided" to Saul to banish his evil spirits (16:14-23), but in both of these stories David is essentially passive. He never speaks; his only action is to play the lyre (16:23). Now, in chap. 17, David reveals a talent for speech and action. He is not just the object of others' descriptions. His two rhetorically powerful speeches to Saul (vv. 34-37) and to Goliath (vv. 45-47) form the theological heart of this story. His actions are reported throughout the chapter, but especially in the climactic moment of the battle with the Philistine champion, David becomes a man of bold and effective action. In vv. 48-51, David is the subject of fifteen verbs, placing him at the center of a bold action drama. He ran—put his hand—took out—slung—struck—prevailed—striking down—killing—ran—stood over—grasped—drew—killed—cut off. David is now introduced to us not only as God's man and Saul's man, but also as his own man. Speaking of the contrast and complementarity of chaps. 16 and 17, Alter wrote:

The joining of the two accounts leaves us swaying in the dynamic interplay between two theologies, two conceptions of kingship and history, two views of David the man. In one, the king is imagined as God's instrument, elected through God's own initiative, manifesting his authority by commanding the realm of spirits good and evil, a figure who brings healing and inspires love. In the other account, the king's election is, one might say, ratified rather than initiated by God; instead of the spirit descending, we have a young man ascending through his own resourcefulness, cool courage, and quick reflexes, and also through his rhetorical skill. . . . Without both these versions of David's beginnings and his claim to legitimacy as monarch, the Hebrew writer would have conveyed less than what he conceived to be the full truth about his subject.[120]

Unfortunately, 1 Samuel 17 poses difficult textual problems.[121] The Old Greek text (LXX[B] and other related MSS) is considerably shorter than the Hebrew text (MT) on which our translations of chap. 17 are based. Missing from LXX[B] are vv. 12-31, 41, 48*b*, 50, and 55-58 (also 18:1-5). These verses are present in other manuscript families of the LXX, but the majority of scholars

at present argue that the shorter text is the more original and that the MT and other LXX manuscripts represent an expansion of the story. A few would even see this expansion as the combination of two completely independent accounts, but the verses missing from LXX[B] do not really make a very complete or coherent account on their own. In short, the textual history of this chapter is complex. In this commentary, I will interpret the text in its present form as it now stands in the Hebrew text of 1 Samuel, though occasionally noting problems posed by variant readings.

17:1-11. Verses 1-3 set the scene. The Philistines are back. This relentless enemy still poses a serious threat to Israel's future. Saul was anointed and commissioned to face this threat (9:16; 10:1), and in this tale he is attempting to do so—although, as we shall see, his efforts seem to have bogged down. The Philistine and Israelite armies are encamped on opposite ridges with a valley in between. This confrontation occurred in the southwest of Judah near the Philistine border and the cities of Ekron and Gath.

Into the valley, a man named Goliath of Gath comes to challenge Israel (v. 4). The name is thought by many to be an authentic Philistine name similar to names from other regions settled by the sea peoples. He is called a "champion" (אִשׁ-הַבֵּנַיִם '*iš-habbēnayim*; lit., "a man between the two"). Roland de Vaux has collected a number of references, from the Bible and from the ancient Near East, that indicate that a tradition of single, representative combat was not unusual in the ancient world (see, e.g., 2 Sam 21:15-22; 23:20; Paris/Menelaus and Hector/Achilles in the *Iliad*).[122] Goliath has come forth to challenge an Israelite representative to such combat (v. 8). The fight will be to the death. Moreover, the Philistine asserts that the army of the losing combatant would become the servants of the opposing army (v. 9). In fact, as de Vaux's study shows, such combats seldom resolved the issue so completely, and battles usually ensued, as at the end of this story; but the winning of such a combat could give great psychological advantage to the victorious side.

The text does not rush quickly to describe the

120. Ibid., 152-53.
121. See P. Kyle McCarter, *I Samuel*, AB 8 (Garden City, N.Y.: Doubleday, 1980) 286-309; and Ralph W. Klein, *I Samuel*, WBC 10 (Waco: Word, 1983) 168-75, for detailed discussions of the textual issues.

122. Roland de Vaux, "Single Combat in the Old Testament," in *The Bible and the Ancient Near East*, trans. D. McHugh (Garden City, N.Y.: Doubleday, 1971) 122-35.

combat. Instead, it lingers in detail on the intimidating appearance of the challenger. The MT gives his height as six cubits and a span (all LXX texts read four cubits and a span). The greater of these would make Goliath 9 feet 9 inches tall, while the lesser would make him 6 feet 9 inches. By ancient standards, even this lower figure would be an impressive height. The larger figure would be taller than any known human remains. In any case, this imposing stature is the source of the notion popular from ancient times to the present that David's victory was over a giant.

The text is more impressed with Goliath's armor than with his height. Three verses (vv. 5-7) are devoted to detailed descriptions of his armaments. The portrait is of an invulnerable warrior. His entire body is covered with state-of-the-art armor. We are intended to envision him as impregnable—an impression David will prove wrong! Not only is he armored, but also he is armed. He has a javelin slung on his back (some think this is a scimitar); he carries a huge spear with a massive iron head; and we know from the end of the story (v. 51) that he has a sword.

This intimidating champion of the Philistines issues his challenge and then taunts Israel, "Today I defy the ranks of Israel! Give me a man, that we may fight together" (v. 10). Challenge becomes humiliating taunt. The Philistine's demand for a "man" foreshadows his later judgment (and Saul's) that Israel instead sends a "boy" (vv. 33, 42). David will prove this judgment wrong, but for the time being the intimidating tactics of the Philistine are effective. Saul and all Israel are "dismayed and greatly afraid." The king who was to be Israel's deliverer and all his army are immobilized by fear.

17:12-30. This entire section is missing in the shorter LXX[B] text, which goes immediately to v. 31 and David's appearance before Saul as a potential champion for Israel. In the present shape of the story, this lengthy section introduces David in a way that sharpens the contrast with the bombastic bully Goliath.

At an almost leisurely pace, David is introduced as the eighth son of Jesse from Bethlehem in Judah (v. 12). As in chap. 16, David is a shepherd (v. 15), but, significantly, his three oldest brothers have joined the service of Saul and are with Saul's army (v. 13). In the larger narrative of the rise of David, this is an important portrait of Jesse's family as loyal servants to Saul. David has the menial task of shuttling back and forth from flock to father's house to battlefront, carrying supplies and messages while still having responsibilities for tending sheep (vv. 15, 17-18). After the Philistine's challenge has gone unanswered for forty days (v. 16), David is serendipitously sent to the battlecamp with grain and bread for his brothers, along with cheese as a gift for their commander (vv. 17-18). He is to return with news and tokens from his brothers for Jesse. The introduction of David in this story is as ordinary and unremarkable as the introduction of Goliath is dramatic and intimidating.

As chance would have it, David arrives at Saul's camp just as the armies are taking their positions on opposite sides of the valley, with war cries splitting the air (v. 20). He seems typical of what we would expect of a young man come to the scene of the action. He quickly dumps his baggage with the quartermaster to find his brothers and see what is happening on the front lines (v. 22; Would Saul have been hiding in the baggage? 10:22). He finds his brothers just as Goliath (named here for the second time, v. 23) steps forth to issue his challenge. The response around him is fear and retreat (v. 24). The men of Saul's army speak of him in awe ("Get a load of that guy!") and have no doubt that Goliath's arrogant challenge is meant to defy Israel (v. 25*a*); but they can report the rewards offered by the king to face him only in wistful tones. There is no hint that, even in return for such rewards, anyone will go out against the Philistine. The king has offered wealth, marriage into the royal family, and "to make his family free in Israel" for the man who kills Goliath (v. 25*b*). It is not clear what this final phrase means. Most believe it represents some remission of obligations (taxation, military service) to the family of a victorious volunteer. As if he has not heard correctly, David asks the man to repeat this recital of rewards, but in doing so he adds comments of his own that are revealing (v. 26). He characterizes one who would win such rewards as "taking away the reproach from Israel." David understands the lack of Israelite response as shameful. Israel lies discredited as long as none dare take up the challenge. Further, the reproach is not merely to Israel or to Saul. It is to Israel's God, for David understands that these are "the armies of the living God" that Goliath has defied. David becomes the first to describe this confrontation in theological terms. It is not Saul, the king anointed to bring God's deliverance, who invokes the power of God. It is this newly arrived shepherd boy. He sees clearly what Saul and the rest of Israel apparently do not: that to respond only in terms of the Philistine trust in force of arms leaves them in the clutches of fear and death, but to understand the Philistine offense as being against a living God is to open up powerful and unexpected resources for life. It is David, and not Saul, who will embody this.

In what almost seems a distraction from the main story, Eliab, the oldest son of Jesse, overhears his young brother quizzing soldiers about the royal rewards, and his reaction seems typical of older brothers to kid brothers (v. 28). He is angry; he overreacts; he accuses David of abandoning his responsibilities with the sheep; he labels David as presumptuous and evil-hearted; he accuses David of boyish voyeurism, just showing up to gawk at the battle. David does what all little brothers do. He says, in effect, "Who asked you?" (v. 29), and goes right on with what he was doing (v. 30). This encounter only serves to heighten the coming drama. The reader knows that David has not abandoned his sheep (v. 20), that he is there at his father's bidding, and that, far from being "evil-hearted," David is the man after God's own heart (13:14) and the one whom God has chosen by looking on the heart (16:7). We suspect what Eliab does not, that in this seemingly ordinary, curious boy there is a surprising possibility for God's response to the "reproach of Israel." In the camp of the faint-hearted, this boy accused of an evil heart will prove to have the most courageous heart.

17:31-40. Saul hears about David's inquiries and sends for him (v. 31). There is no indication that Saul is already acquainted with David or knows anything about him. Just as the reader was introduced to David again in v. 12, so also Saul must now be introduced to him.

David is certainly not in awe of the king's presence. He speaks first and does so to console the king by urging him not to lose heart because of the arrogant Philistine (v. 32a). Referring to himself as Saul's servant, David then volunteers to go out against the Philistine (v. 32b). Saul is dismayed and responds that David is only a boy in contrast to the seasoned Philistine warrior (v. 33). The contrast between boy and man is made throughout the account until David proves he is more than man enough in the end. Saul's judgment is next echoed by Goliath himself (v. 42).

David makes the first of two great speeches in this chapter, which reveal both his rhetorical skill and the foundation of faith on which his actions rest. Saul has assumed that the power necessary for deliverance must lie in the realm of military might. Of armies and arms, David has no experience. David's speech is designed to demonstrate to Saul that power and courage can have other sources than military experience, and these sources for David are both practical and spiritual.

David speaks first of his life as a shepherd, an ordinary occupation but one with its own dangers and challenges (vv. 34-35). David already has experience with deliverance. When lions and bears would seize a lamb, David would not hesitate to confront these beasts, even if they turned on him. He would pursue, rescue, seize, strike down, and kill these animals. The verbs are similar to those used in the action climax of David's battle with the Philistine champion. Indeed, after speaking of his experience with marauding beasts, David vows to do the same to one who had "defied the armies of the living God" (v. 36). We might note that those armies stand paralyzed while a boy proposes to defend the honor of the living God. The armies do not act as if they believe in such a God.

David has spoken boldly of his own courage and strength, but in v. 37 he gives the credit for this to God. It was "the LORD" who "saved" from lion and bear; it is "the LORD" who "will save" from the hand of the Philistine. David is the first in this account to offer the name of Israel's God, Yahweh (trans. "LORD"). It is Yahweh who saves and who is the true source of any power David may have—to save from beasts of animal or human variety. Saul, the would-be deliverer from the hand of the Philistines, is reduced to echoing the faith of this boy. He is convinced and bids him go and then pronounces the name Yahweh himself, not as the source of his strength but as the One who goes with David (v. 37). First, Saul's servant had pronounced this theme to the stories of the rise of David (16:18); now Saul himself recognizes this truth, "The LORD is/will be with him."

Saul may have uttered the divine name, but he cannot give up his own reliance on human military power. He attempts to clothe David in his own armor (vv. 38-39).

Saul does not understand anything. He has uttered Yahweh's name. But he wants to outdo Goliath on Goliath's terms. . . . So he offers armor, helmet, coat of mail, sword—David "tried in vain to go" with such encumbrance. David's contrast is with both Saul and Goliath. Unlike them, he goes unencumbered ("I am not used to them"). Both of them—the one a braggart, the other a coward—trust in arms.[123]

David is the model of another way, of those without the benefit of superior arms and armies who nevertheless trust that God can make deliverance possible against the odds, that there is hope even when faced with apparently hopeless situations. David refuses the armor, and he takes only his staff, his sling, and five smooth stones—the equipment of a shepherd (v. 40)—to meet the Philistine.

17:41-47. The Philistine champion can hardly believe his eyes. As he approaches, shieldbearer in front of him, he sees David is only a boy, "ruddy and handsome" (vv. 41-42), and he responds with contempt, "Am I a dog that you come to me with sticks?" (v. 43a). The reader, of course, remembers that this Philistine has been ominously compared with animals (v. 36). Goliath curses David by his gods, but they are left nameless and by implication are judged insignificant and ineffectual (v. 43b). He taunts David, threatening to leave his flesh to the birds and the beasts (v. 44). The portrait is of a warrior who is arrogant, boastful, self-assured.

By contrast, David seems calmly confident. To Goliath he directs a second remarkable speech. As he did to Saul earlier, David gives voice to the source of his confidence in the Lord's power to deliver. He begins with the contrast that is obvious to all who view them on the field of battle. Goliath comes with the confidence of armed might (sword, spear, and javelin), but David comes only in the name of the Lord—here given full title "the LORD of hosts, the God of the armies of Israel" (v. 45). It is that Lord who delivers, David declares, and will give the Philistine into his hand. David will strike him down,

cut off his head, and leave the bodies of the entire Philistine army as carrion for the birds and beasts (v. 46). David can give it back to the Philistine in the rhetorical battle as well as the coming physical one.

Verses 46b-47 attest to the true purpose of this contest. It must happen so that "all the earth may know there is a God in Israel, and that all this assembly may know that the Lord does not save by sword and spear; for the battle is the Lord's and he will give you into our hand." Deliverance does not come through trust in human might. God delivers in spite of "spear and sword" for the sake of the world's knowledge of the source of true power and the special relationship of that power to Israel. This theme was also central in the exodus story of God's deliverance (see, e.g., Exod 7:5; 14:4, 18), and it was central to the exiles when the power of their God among the nations was in doubt (see, e.g., Ezek 6:7, 10, 13-14; 7:4, 9, 27). In this story, those who need to "know" include both the Philistines and the Israelites of Saul's army. Both parties must know that the Lord saves! The array of swords and spears on either hillside represents power that cannot ultimately save. David "calls Israel away from its imitation of the nations and calls the nations away from their foolish defiance of Yahweh."[124] David comes with courage and hope, not because of superior weapons or training, but because his trust is in the surprising possibilities of God's deliverance.

17:48-51. When the combat comes, the narrative moves swiftly. Action verbs tumble over one another. After all the buildup, the climax is almost over as quickly as it starts (vv. 48-49). David runs, puts his hand in the bag, takes a stone, slings it, and strikes the Philistine. The stone finds a vulnerable, unarmored spot on the forehead. The stone sinks; the Philistine falls.

Verse 50 almost seems like an aside, observing what we have already seen, but perhaps emphasizing the odds against it by noting that David did not even carry a sword. David finishes the matter by drawing the Philistine's own sword, killing him, and cutting off his head (v. 51). David has carried out his intentions declared to the Philistine challenger (v. 46). The reaction of the Philistine

---

123. Walter Brueggemann, *David's Truth in Israel's Imagination and Memory* (Philadelphia: Fortress, 1985) 33.

124. Walter Brueggemann, *First and Second Samuel,* Interpretation (Louisville: John Knox, 1990) 132.

army is immediate: They flee. They had no intention of passively becoming the servants of Israel, as Goliath's challenge had proposed.

17:52-58. There remains only the aftermath of this sudden and surprising victory. Israel's army pursues the Philistines back into their own cities and territories (v. 52) and returns to plunder their camp (v. 53). In a problematic note, v. 54 says that David takes the head of the Philistine to Jerusalem and puts Goliath's armor in his own tent. Jerusalem is not an Israelite city until David himself captures it in 2 Sam 5:6-9. As for the armor, David later retrieves the sword of Goliath from the sanctuary at Nob (21:8-9). It may be that Goliath's head ended up at Jerusalem later as a relic of David's victory. No widely accepted resolution of these tensions has been suggested.

The episode of David's victory ends with a strange incident. After Saul has watched this improbable victory, he asks his commander, "Abner, whose son is this young man?" Abner does not know (v. 55). Saul instructs Abner to make inquiries and find out whose son he is (v. 56). Finally, Abner simply brings David before Saul (dragging the severed head! v. 57), and Saul asks David, "Whose son are you?" to which David replies, "I am the son of your servant Jesse the Bethlehemite" (v. 58). David noticeably does not give his name. What is going on here? How could Saul not know the boy he tried to outfit with his armor and talked with before the battle? Certainly this story shows no knowledge of David as a member of Saul's inner court circle (16:14-23).

Polzin has ingeniously proposed that Saul's question of David was really a demand to acquire David's allegiance as a "son" of Saul—i.e., one committed in loyalty to Saul. "Saul thereby asks David formally to renounce Jesse's paternity in favor of his own."[125] David shrewdly avoids this commitment by citing only his biological sonship and noting Jesse as the king's servant, but refusing to pledge such loyalty in his own name. Polzin thus affirms that Saul knew David as his armorbearer all along and was now seeking to secure David's pledge of loyalty. The withheld pledge marks the beginning of tensions between the two. Polzin's thesis of continuous, single authorship for virtually the whole of 1 Samuel (including chaps. 16–17) forces him to play down the problems with this view of v. 58. It makes less sense to see Saul's question of Abner (v. 55) and his command to inquire about David (v. 56) as matters of David's allegiance to Saul. It also remains problematic to see David as Saul's musician and armorbearer, who entered permanent service with Saul in 16:21-22, as the same David who is commuting from the sheepfold to bring food to his brothers at Saul's camp. Further, would Saul's armorbearer be so unfamiliar with arms and armor as in 17:38-39, or would Saul show no signs of recognition or familiarity? It is far more likely that the episodes of 16:1-13, 14-23 and 17:1-58 are three separate introductions to David with differing conceptions of how David became known to Saul. They have come together in a collection of David traditions without any extensive effort to resolve the tensions between them. I believe Polzin is correct, however, to see David's reply in v. 58*b* as a wary one, not even revealing his name. The exchange seems tense and foreshadows further tension to come.

125. Robert Polzin, *Samuel and the Deuteronomist: A Literary Study of the Deuteronomic History,* Part Two: *1 Samuel* (San Francisco: Harper & Row, 1989) 175, see the full discussion, 171-76.

REFLECTIONS

The story of David and Goliath has become one of the best known of all biblical stories and something of a cultural icon. Its imagery and influence can be seen in an amazing variety of ways from biblical times to the present. Painters, sculptors, musicians, and poets have made the story their subject. For example, David was the patron saint of Florence during the Renaissance, and that city's remarkable cadre of painters and sculptors almost all used David as a subject, the favorite view being of David with the head of Goliath. In a single month recently, I heard a recording of a song on David and Goliath by the jazz group Take 6, had a student share with me delight at discovering Joseph Heller's comic rendering of this story in his novel *God Knows,*[126] rediscovered Emily Dickinson's David/Goliath poem "I Took My

126. Joseph Heller, *God Knows* (New York: Knopf, 1984).

Power in My Hand," and viewed the magnificent Flemish tapestries of the David and Goliath story hanging in the Washington National Cathedral.

The use of the David/Goliath story as a metaphor for the hopes of the underdog has become a cultural cliché. In the 1996 United States presidential elections, Bob Dole compared his election hopes against Bill Clinton to David versus Goliath. Cereal ads used the imagery of this story to suggest that cereal can make Davids out of young boys. The victory of the U.S. Women's Gymnastics team at the 1996 Atlanta Olympics was praised as a David over Goliath victory, even though the gender of the participants was different.

Some of these uses of the story are, of course, superficial. Some simply illustrate the natural appeal of stories in all cultures that feature resourceful children winning over evil forces against the odds. But even these witness to a deeper level of meaning that has made the David and Goliath story such a perennial favorite. The story is not simply a matter of rooting for the underdog. It embodies the hopes of all persons when they are faced with overwhelming and evil power that there is a way to overcome that power and win the future. This story has been told and retold especially by the weak, the oppressed, the marginal, and the powerless—those who do not simply hope for a David but see themselves as David, faced with the giants of oppression, and who know that their only hope lies with a living God. Their own courage and resourcefulness will not be enough, and the human power even of their friends will lie paralyzed and ineffectual like the armies of Saul. It is the oppressed and the marginalized who know better than most of us that the Philistines of the world cannot be bested on their own terms. Whole systems of power, technology, and violence cannot be beaten by creating countersystems of power, technology, and violence. Arms races may create stalemates between opponents bristling with arms, but cannot bring peace. This is the reason why the violence of crime is not overcome by counterviolence in brutal prisons and capital punishment. The David and Goliath story is the story of those who know the truth of David's words, "The Lord does not save by sword or spear."

David is not just the courageous underdog. He is the one who knows that there are resources beyond the technology of kingdoms. His is an alternative to the way of swords and empires. To be sure, his way in this story is not a pacifist option. The enemy is struck down, and David must stand bravely in opposition to oppressive power. But his way, if not pacifist in the face of oppressive power, is subversive of that power. Ultimately his trust is not in the technology of force but in the subversive power of truth. And the truth in this story is that God is ultimately in opposition to arrogant and self-serving power and its violence. Trust in God nurtures hope that there is a way into the future where there seems no way, that there may be a chink in the impregnable armor, that a well-placed stone of opposition can bring down seemingly impregnable systems of oppression that loom as armored giants. We must relearn this lesson of God-trusting opposition to oppression in every generation. I confess that I did not believe that I would see in my lifetime the collapse of the Berlin Wall (and all that it symbolized) or the end of the system of apartheid in South Africa. I had forgotten this story of God-trusting persistence in the face of the giants.

This story also reminds us that speech is as important as action. David's two speeches to Saul and to Goliath give meaning to the action he takes. The affirmation of a "living God" enables one to go forth against the technologies of death. The affirmation that our purpose is that "all may know there is a God" saves our opposition to evil from becoming self-serving and arrogant. The acknowledgment that "the Lord does not save by sword or spear" makes us imaginative and resourceful in seeking alternatives to the intimidation of the powerful.

The contrast in this story is not just between David's God and the nameless (and ultimately powerless) gods of the Philistines. It is also between David's faith and the lack of faith of Saul and Israel. They can think of nothing more to do than to imitate poorly the very forces of oppressive power they oppose. Well-meaning movements and efforts for justice in the church and society sometimes clank around in the armor of Saul, attempting to imitate and best oppression on its own terms. When the church imagines that its mission can go forward only with massive numbers, large budgets, corporate styles of planning, and hierarchical structures of authority, then maybe we should read this story again. It is God who saves, not Goliath. God saves, not without human agents, but in ways that astonish us in our usual ways of measuring influence and power.

The David and Goliath story is the truth needed by those who are "the least of these" and face the overwhelming power of violent and death-dealing systems. This story teaches and hopefully engenders trust that the resources of a living God can still best the "principalities and powers" of this world. This is not a passive, inactive posture. It requires faithful and truthful speech, courageous confrontation, and the trust that by God's grace a well-placed stone might prove superior to the armor of a Goliath or a Saul.

1 Samuel 18:1–20:42, David and the Household of Saul

OVERVIEW

Now that David has been introduced—as shepherd anointed by Samuel, as musician brought into the service of Saul, and as unlikely hero against Goliath—there follows a series of chapters that trace David's relationships—with Saul, with Saul's family, and with the wider public in Israel. These chapters establish key themes for the remainder of the stories about Saul and David. These themes will make clear why the end must come in the triumph of David and the tragedy of Saul. In chap. 18, David is both the object of love—from Jonathan, Michal, and all Israel—and the object of growing hostility from Saul. The danger from Saul's jealous anger appears in chap. 18 but escalates in chap. 19 into a direct threat that forces David to become a fugitive from the royal household. Chapter 20 is a moving story of the love and friendship between David and Jonathan, which nevertheless cannot bring David back into favor. Their pledges foreshadow the transfer of the kingdom from Saul to David and not to Jonathan. From this point forward, David is a fugitive, on the run from Saul's anger.

A number of scholars understand 18:1-5 as the conclusion of the David and Goliath story in chap. 17.[127] I disagree and take these verses as the first episode of a chapter focusing on David's relationships in the royal household and the implications of this situation for the future of king and kingdom in Israel. It may well be that the first phrase of 18:1 is intended to create a bridge to chap. 17 ("After David had finished talking to Saul . . ."), but Jonathan, the focus of 18:1-5, does not appear and plays no role in the Goliath story. However, his love for David (stated twice, vv. 1, 3) provides one of the major themes of chap. 18: the growing love for David both in the royal household and in all Israel (vv. 16, 20, 22, 28). This love for David, especially in Saul's own family, is the counterpoint for Saul's anger and growing hostility toward David. Saul is losing the throne to David. These issues were not yet on the table in chap. 17, but 18:1-5 introduces them in a way tied crucially to the remainder of chap. 18 and the two chapters that follow (19–20).

127. See Klein, *1 Samuel,* 168-83; McCarter, *I Samuel,* 299-309; H. W. Hertzberg, *I and II Samuel: Introduction and Commentary,* OTL (Philadelphia: Westminster, 1964) 142-55.

1 Samuel 18:1-30, Saul's Jealousy at David's Success

NIV

18 After David had finished talking with Saul, Jonathan became one in spirit with David, and he loved him as himself. ²From that day Saul kept David with him and did not let him return to his father's house. ³And Jonathan made a covenant with David because he loved him as himself. ⁴Jonathan took off the robe he was wearing and gave it to David, along with his tunic, and even his sword, his bow and his belt.

⁵Whatever Saul sent him to do, David did it so successfully*a* that Saul gave him a high rank in the army. This pleased all the people, and Saul's officers as well.

⁶When the men were returning home after David had killed the Philistine, the women came out from all the towns of Israel to meet King Saul with singing and dancing, with joyful songs and with tambourines and lutes. ⁷As they danced, they sang:

"Saul has slain his thousands,
and David his tens of thousands."

⁸Saul was very angry; this refrain galled him. "They have credited David with tens of thousands," he thought, "but me with only thousands. What more can he get but the kingdom?" ⁹And from that time on Saul kept a jealous eye on David.

¹⁰The next day an evil*b* spirit from God came forcefully upon Saul. He was prophesying in his house, while David was playing the harp, as he usually did. Saul had a spear in his hand ¹¹and he hurled it, saying to himself, "I'll pin David to the wall." But David eluded him twice.

¹²Saul was afraid of David, because the Lᴏʀᴅ was with David but had left Saul. ¹³So he sent David away from him and gave him command over a thousand men, and David led the troops in their campaigns. ¹⁴In everything he did he had great success,*c* because the Lᴏʀᴅ was with him. ¹⁵When Saul saw how successful*d* he was, he was afraid of him. ¹⁶But all Israel and Judah loved David, because he led them in their campaigns.

¹⁷Saul said to David, "Here is my older daughter Merab. I will give her to you in marriage; only

a5 Or wisely   b10 Or injurious   c14 Or he was very wise   d15 Or wise

NRSV

18 When David*a* had finished speaking to Saul, the soul of Jonathan was bound to the soul of David, and Jonathan loved him as his own soul. ²Saul took him that day and would not let him return to his father's house. ³Then Jonathan made a covenant with David, because he loved him as his own soul. ⁴Jonathan stripped himself of the robe that he was wearing, and gave it to David, and his armor, and even his sword and his bow and his belt. ⁵David went out and was successful wherever Saul sent him; as a result, Saul set him over the army. And all the people, even the servants of Saul, approved.

6As they were coming home, when David returned from killing the Philistine, the women came out of all the towns of Israel, singing and dancing, to meet King Saul, with tambourines, with songs of joy, and with musical instruments.*b* ⁷And the women sang to one another as they made merry,

"Saul has killed his thousands,
and David his ten thousands."

⁸Saul was very angry, for this saying displeased him. He said, "They have ascribed to David ten thousands, and to me they have ascribed thousands; what more can he have but the kingdom?" ⁹So Saul eyed David from that day on.

10The next day an evil spirit from God rushed upon Saul, and he raved within his house, while David was playing the lyre, as he did day by day. Saul had his spear in his hand; ¹¹and Saul threw the spear, for he thought, "I will pin David to the wall." But David eluded him twice.

12Saul was afraid of David, because the Lᴏʀᴅ was with him but had departed from Saul. ¹³So Saul removed him from his presence, and made him a commander of a thousand; and David marched out and came in, leading the army. ¹⁴David had success in all his undertakings; for the Lᴏʀᴅ was with him. ¹⁵When Saul saw that he had great success, he stood in awe of him. ¹⁶But all Israel and Judah loved David; for it was he who marched out and came in leading them.

17Then Saul said to David, "Here is my elder daughter Merab; I will give her to you as a wife;

a Heb he   b Or triangles, or three-stringed instruments

serve me bravely and fight the battles of the LORD." For Saul said to himself, "I will not raise a hand against him. Let the Philistines do that!"

18But David said to Saul, "Who am I, and what is my family or my father's clan in Israel, that I should become the king's son-in-law?" 19So*a* when the time came for Merab, Saul's daughter, to be given to David, she was given in marriage to Adriel of Meholah.

20Now Saul's daughter Michal was in love with David, and when they told Saul about it, he was pleased. 21"I will give her to him," he thought, "so that she may be a snare to him and so that the hand of the Philistines may be against him." So Saul said to David, "Now you have a second opportunity to become my son-in-law."

22Then Saul ordered his attendants: "Speak to David privately and say, 'Look, the king is pleased with you, and his attendants all like you; now become his son-in-law.'"

23They repeated these words to David. But David said, "Do you think it is a small matter to become the king's son-in-law? I'm only a poor man and little known."

24When Saul's servants told him what David had said, 25Saul replied, "Say to David, 'The king wants no other price for the bride than a hundred Philistine foreskins, to take revenge on his enemies.'" Saul's plan was to have David fall by the hands of the Philistines.

26When the attendants told David these things, he was pleased to become the king's son-in-law. So before the allotted time elapsed, 27David and his men went out and killed two hundred Philistines. He brought their foreskins and presented the full number to the king so that he might become the king's son-in-law. Then Saul gave him his daughter Michal in marriage.

28When Saul realized that the LORD was with David and that his daughter Michal loved David, 29Saul became still more afraid of him, and he remained his enemy the rest of his days.

30The Philistine commanders continued to go out to battle, and as often as they did, David met with more success*b* than the rest of Saul's officers, and his name became well known.

a19 Or *However,*   *b30* Or *David acted more wisely*

only be valiant for me and fight the LORD's battles." For Saul thought, "I will not raise a hand against him; let the Philistines deal with him." 18David said to Saul, "Who am I and who are my kinsfolk, my father's family in Israel, that I should be son-in-law to the king?" 19But at the time when Saul's daughter Merab should have been given to David, she was given to Adriel the Meholathite as a wife.

20Now Saul's daughter Michal loved David. Saul was told, and the thing pleased him. 21Saul thought, "Let me give her to him that she may be a snare for him and that the hand of the Philistines may be against him." Therefore Saul said to David a second time,*a* "You shall now be my son-in-law." 22Saul commanded his servants, "Speak to David in private and say, 'See, the king is delighted with you, and all his servants love you; now then, become the king's son-in-law.'" 23So Saul's servants reported these words to David in private. And David said, "Does it seem to you a little thing to become the king's son-in-law, seeing that I am a poor man and of no repute?" 24The servants of Saul told him, "This is what David said." 25Then Saul said, "Thus shall you say to David, 'The king desires no marriage present except a hundred foreskins of the Philistines, that he may be avenged on the king's enemies.'" Now Saul planned to make David fall by the hand of the Philistines. 26When his servants told David these words, David was well pleased to be the king's son-in-law. Before the time had expired, 27David rose and went, along with his men, and killed one hundred*b* of the Philistines; and David brought their foreskins, which were given in full number to the king, that he might become the king's son-in-law. Saul gave him his daughter Michal as a wife. 28But when Saul realized that the LORD was with David, and that Saul's daughter Michal loved him, 29Saul was still more afraid of David. So Saul was David's enemy from that time forward.

30Then the commanders of the Philistines came out to battle; and as often as they came out, David had more success than all the servants of Saul, so that his fame became very great.

a Heb *by two*   *b* Gk Compare 2 Sam 3.14: Heb *two hundred*

COMMENTARY

This chapter consists of four distinct narrative episodes and a concluding comment. The narratives each feature a member of the royal household in some kind of relationship to David: vv. 1-5, Jonathan's love for David; vv. 6-16, Saul's growing hostility toward David; vv. 17-19, the proposed marriage of David to Merab; vv. 20-29, Michal's love for David and their marriage; v. 30, concluding comment.

Saul's relationship to David is the focus of vv. 6-16, but Saul and his actions are a part of the three episodes involving his children as well. The context for the events narrated in this chapter is twofold. Much of the action occurs within the royal household of Saul, to which David clearly has access in the beginning of the chapter and to which David gains membership as the king's son-in-law by the end of the chapter. At the same time there is regular attention throughout the chapter to David's growing public following. His larger reputation and the deeds that build public acclaim are a constant element in the development of events and the actions of characters in this chapter.

The episodes of this chapter are linked by interwoven themes of David's rise, on the one hand, and Saul's decline, on the other hand. There are three linking elements to the positive portrait of David's inexorable movement toward the kingship.

(1) David is surrounded and gifted with *love*. Six times in this chapter we are told that David is loved. Two of Saul's children loved David, and that love is mentioned twice for each: Jonathan in vv. 1, 3, and Michal in vv. 22, 28. All of Israel and Judah loved David (v. 16). Even Saul's servants loved David, a fact Saul cynically uses in setting up what he hopes will be David's death (v. 22; see also v. 5). In this chapter David does little to promote or reciprocate this love (but see chap. 20). Love seems to come to him as gift and destiny.[128] We catch only distant glimpses of his public leadership in military campaigns as any offered explanation of what inspired such love. Ironically, Saul was first said to love David (16:21), but as his family, household, and all Israel come to love David, Saul cannot. This may be an important clue to the character of Saul.

128. See D. M. Gunn, "David and the Gift of the Kingdom," *Semeia* 3 (1975) 14-45.

(2) The love David receives is coupled with the *success* he achieves. Four times in the chapter we are told that David is successful: as a warrior (v. 5), in all his undertakings (v. 14), in the eyes of Saul (v. 15), and especially against the Philistines, which leads to his fame (v. 30). David's success comes primarily in accomplishing what Saul was anointed and commissioned to do: to bring deliverance from the Philistines. To observe that Saul saw this success (v. 15) is to note his bitter recognition of David's effectiveness and, by implication, his own failure. At least this seems to be how Saul takes it, for he seems unable to enjoy David's successes as a part of the leadership he has raised up and encouraged. For Saul, David's success is not reason for celebration but for his removal. Part of the building drama of the chapter is that the obstacles Saul throws up to David's success become the foundations for David's greater successes—his dispatch to the battlefront (v. 13); his offer of Michal in exchange for Philistine foreskins as the bridal price (vv. 24-27).

(3) The picture of the love and success that come to David is built up through the events and personalities reported in narratives of public and court life. However, this narrative detail leads to a theological conclusion. Not only is David loved and successful, but also *the Lord is with him.* Twice the narrator gives us this theological comment as an explanation for the unfolding events (vv. 12, 14). It is the sounding again of a key theme already introduced in 16:18, and that will continue as a theme throughout the narratives of the rise of David (see the concluding affirmation in 2 Sam 5:10). The theme appears a third time in this chapter, significantly to record Saul's own realization that "the LORD was with David" (v. 28). Saul, along with the reader, is forced to recognize that within the human events narrated here a divine intention is at work. David is God's future for Israel, and he will not be denied.

Over against this celebration of David unfolds a dark counterdrama for Saul. When the love and success surrounding David find expression in the song of the women, praising David more extravagantly than they praise Saul (v. 7), Saul's response is *anger* (v. 8) and an "eyeing" of David (v. 9), which must be interpreted as "suspicion" and/or "jealousy." Most of Saul's actions throughout the chapter can be understood as expressions of this anger and jealousy. Saul once loved David (16:21), but at the end of this chapter the final verdict is that "Saul was David's enemy from that day forward" (v. 29).

Coupled with the acting out of Saul's anger is Saul's growing *fear*. Anger and fear, as modern psychology knows, often go hand in hand. Saul has been rejected by Samuel as king; now his actual grip on the kingdom is slipping. Saul becomes the first to voice that the future of the kingdom is David (v. 8), although the reader has known this since Samuel's anointing of David (16:1-13). So beneath Saul's angry and hostile response to David is an escalation of fear and anxiety. "Saul was *afraid* of David" (v. 12). Then Saul "stood in *awe* of him" (ירא *yārēʾ*, a term that indicates anxiety, apprehension, v. 15). Finally, after David has turned every obstacle from Saul into success, and Saul has acknowledged that "the LORD was with David," we read that "Saul was *still more afraid* of David" (v. 29).

In the midst of this human drama, the narrator discerns a divine intention. For Saul, this finds expression in "an evil spirit from God" that seizes him and sends him into a rage against David (v. 10). Saul's own anger and fear exemplify a deeper alienation from God and God's purposes for Israel. Saul cannot be Israel's future. His own actions demonstrate why this must be so, but the giving and withholding of God's Spirit for good or for evil will make certain that it is so.

Is Saul fated to fail and David destined to succeed? Some recent treatments of this narrative have seen Saul as only, or primarily, a victim and have understood his story as one of tragic fate.[129] David, of course, in such a view is destined to greatness. Both men are little more than pawns in the plot of a story predetermined by the storyteller's conception of divine intention. Such a view does not, however, do justice to the complexity of these stories. Chapter 18 offers a good example of this complexity. Before the "evil spirit from God" comes upon Saul (v. 10), he has already responded to the success of his own

commander with anger and jealousy, seeing only danger to his throne and not benefits to his kingdom (vv. 8-9). The evil spirit that comes upon Saul intermittently does not appear responsible for Saul's actions, fating him to failure, but in this instance its presence almost seems brought on by Saul's turn to self-serving and eventually evil responses to David's success.[130] Paul Ricoeur has suggested that in this narrative we should understand Saul as both victim and perpetrator.[131] Saul is not compelled to evil action by the "evil spirit from God." Indeed, chap. 18 goes to unusual lengths to expose the inner thoughts and motives of a man, Saul, bent on sinful protection of his own interests (see esp. vv. 17, 21, 25). The narrator tells us of both the actions or motives of the human characters and of the divine purposes that can be discerned acting through and in spite of these human agents. God's purpose in these narratives is fated to have its way, but Saul and David may, nevertheless, choose their courses of action within those divine purposes. It is part of the artistic complexity and brilliance of these stories that both human action and divine intent are made credible.[132] Such excellence helps to account for the appeal of these stories to those confessing communities who today affirm both human freedom and divine providence.

As in chap. 17, the text of LXX[B] is considerably shorter than the Hebrew text reflected in most translations. Most scholars believe the shorter Greek text may have been original and that the Hebrew text represents later expansion. These additions are scattered throughout chap. 18 and seem to emphasize the hostility of Saul for David, making clear that David was innocent of any provocation for this hostility. For example, the entire Merab incident is missing in LXX[B]. The addition shows David as humbly professing himself unworthy and Saul as underhanded and double-dealing. I will make occasional observations on

129. See David M. Gunn, *The Fate of King Saul*, JSOTSup 14 (Sheffield: JSOT, 1980); W. Lee Humphreys, *The Tragic Vision and the Hebrew Tradition*, OBT (Philadelphia: Fortress, 1985) esp. 38-41.

130. Robert Polzin, *Samuel and the Deuteronomist: A Literary Study of the Deuteronomic History*, Part Two: *1 Samuel* (San Francisco: Harper & Row, 1989) 180, discusses the evil spirit that plagues Saul as potentially both cause and effect of Saul's deranged and evil actions.

131. Paul Ricoeur, *The Symbolism of Evil* (Boston: Beacon, 1969) 232-60. This work came to my attention through the use of Ricoeur's categories by Walter Brueggemann, "Narrative Coherence and Theological Intentionality in 1 Samuel 18," *CBQ* 55 (1993) 229, 241-42.

132. For a helpful discussion of 1 Samuel 18 as an "imaginative construal" of human and political events as divine providence see Walter Brueggemann, *Power, Providence, and Personality* (Louisville: Westminster/John Knox, 1990) 24-48, esp. 40.

important textual variants, but, in general, will interpret the Hebrew text on which most translations are based.[133]

18:1-5. Abruptly Jonathan enters the story. The opening phrase of v. 1 tries to bridge back to the close of chap. 17, but the themes of vv. 1-5 all point forward to the remainder of chap. 18 and beyond. Jonathan experiences an immediate bonding with David—his soul was bound to David's soul (v. 1). No motivation is given for this bonding, but it is obviously deeply personal. The word translated here as "soul" is נפשׁ (*nepeš*), a word that indicates the essential life of a person or animal. It encompasses the whole being of a person (hence, the NIV translation using the word "spirit" is misleading and potentially confusing, since the Hebrew word for "spirit" [רוח *rûaḥ*] does play a role in this chapter at a later point [v. 10]). Further, Jonathan "loved" David; such love transcended Jonathan's own self-interest. His love for David was indistinguishable from that of his own life. Saul's action in not allowing David to return home (v. 2) almost constitutes an adoption of David into the royal household, a status further authorized by David's marriage to Saul's daughter Michal at the end of this chapter (v. 27).

Recent studies of the term "love" (אהב *'āhab*) have emphasized that in addition to the implications of personal and emotional commitment the term often carries dimensions of social and political loyalty.[134] In v. 3, Jonathan's love is stated again, using the same language as in v. 1, but this time it is connected with the making of a covenant with David. One is tempted to see these two expressions of Jonathan's love as indications of personal (v. 1) and political commitment (v. 3) to David. Jonathan has, for good or for ill, cast his future with David. He has bound himself to David not only in terms of personal loyalty (see the expansion of this to the concept of חסד *ḥesed* in chap. 20), but also, more formally, in a covenant.

We are not explicitly told the content of the covenant between David and Jonathan, but Jonathan's actions in v. 4 may give an indication. Jonathan strips off his robe, his armor, his sword, and his belt and gives them all to David. This,

though undoubtedly a generous personal gesture, is surely more than that. The robe, in particular, symbolizes the kingdom. Hence, Jonathan's action authorizes David for the throne.[135] The tearing of a robe represented the tearing of the kingdom from Saul in 15:28, where Samuel also promised that it would be given into the hand of "a neighbor of yours, who is better than you." Jonathan is the potential heir to Saul's throne, but now he gives his robe and other royal accoutrements to David at the start of a chapter clearly designed to show David as better than Saul—prospering in success as Saul descends into fearful and jealous actions. The implication seems to be that Jonathan already sees David as Israel's future. The covenant between them might well be a formal recognition of loyalty to that end. (This reading gains support as the continuing relationship of David and Jonathan unfolds in chaps. 19–20.)

We hear nothing of David's response to Jonathan's remarkable expressions of love for him. At this point we receive only a first report of David's success (v. 5). The verb the NRSV translates here as "went out" (יצא *yāṣā'*; the NIV has a remarkably free translation of this verse) often indicates a military mission against an enemy, and David's success leads to Saul's appointment of him as commander of the army. David's initial success is as a warrior in Saul's service. In this role he receives the approval of "all the people" and significantly of "the servants of Saul." Almost before we know it is an issue, the affections of Saul's family, household, and subjects have been captured by David.

18:6-16. This long central section narrates the transformation of Saul. By the end of v. 16, it is clear that Saul has become unworthy of the throne. He has given in to petty and self-serving hostility toward David.

The turning point is the song of the women who are welcoming Saul and David home from "killing the Philistine" (v. 6). It is unlikely that we are intended to see this as the return from the victory over Goliath. Verse 5 makes clear that

---

133. For a fuller discussion of textual matters see P. Kyle McCarter, *I Samuel*, AB 8 (Garden City, N.Y.: Doubleday, 1980) 301-21; Ralph W. Klein, *1 Samuel*, WBC 10 (Waco: Word, 1983) 185-87.

134. See J. A. Thompson, "The Significance of the Verb *Love* in the David-Jonathan Narratives in 1 Samuel," *VT* 24 (1974) 334-38.

135. See David Jobling, *The Sense of Biblical Narrative: Structural Analyses in the Hebrew Bible I,* JSOTSup 7 (Sheffield: JSOT, 1986) 19-20. Gunn, *The Fate of King Saul,* 80, points out that David will receive equipment from Jonathan that he would not accept from Saul in 17:38-39, but Brueggemann rightly notes that Saul is trying to equip David for battle (which he does not need), but Jonathan is legitimating him for the throne (which he does need), Brueggemann, "Narrative Coherence and Theological Intentionality in 1 Samuel 18," 233.

David has been given a command and was sent out in the service of Saul, and the women's welcome home implies some passage of time for David to establish his reputation in battle. To the accompaniment of instruments, the women from the towns of Israel come dancing and singing, "Saul has killed his thousands, and David his ten thousands" (v. 7). This couplet of Hebrew poetry is in a familiar pattern of intensifying parallelism, in which the second element expands and intensifies the meaning of the first element.[136] In fact, the word in the second element does not have the precise meaning "ten thousand" but can be translated "many" or "multitude"; nevertheless, the pattern requires it to mean more than the thousand attributed to Saul. Usually the subject in such parallelisms does not change, but here the subject of the first is Saul and of the second David. The implication seems to be that the women did not simply unintentionally offend Saul, but really elevated David's deeds over those of the king.

Saul clearly understands the song as belittling to him, and his response is to be angry and displeased (v. 8), which is the seed from which violence and madness will grow. Ironically Saul first gives voice to the ultimate issue at stake. He correctly perceives that the issue is legitimate claim to the kingdom, and he correctly senses that his own grip on that legitimate claim is slipping: "What more can he have but the kingdom?" (v. 8b). The note that he "eyed" David thereafter alludes to suspicion and jealousy (v. 9). Saul is unable to see David's success and growing reputation as anything but threatening.

It is significant that Saul's hostile and self-protective response is followed by a notice of his possession by "an evil spirit from God" (v. 10). Saul seems to suffer intermittent seizures by this "evil spirit," which does not seem the cause of his other problematic behaviors so much as additional evidence of his unbalanced state. We are told that Saul "raved"; the word here is the verb often translated as "prophesy" (נבא *nābā'*). In 10:10 Saul was seized by God's Spirit and he "prophesied" as a positive sign of his anointing. Now his seizure by "an evil spirit from God" results in the ravings of a madman.

These "ravings" come upon Saul while David is playing music to soothe him (cf. 16:23). Saul is holding a spear, and as David plays, Saul throws the spear at him, forcing David to elude him twice (vv. 10b-11). For the first of several times in this chapter, the narrator gives us access to Saul's thoughts and, thus, his motives. In this case, outward action and inner thought coincide, for Saul thought to pin David to the wall and then threw his spear to do so. Later, Saul seems to become more duplicitous, saying one thing outwardly while the narrator lets us hear entirely different motives inwardly. Saul is now caught in a vicious cycle with David. David's music soothes him at the onset of his seizures by this "evil spirit," but the presence of David kindles Saul's anger and jealousy toward the growing popularity of his servant. Saul is a troubled and torn man.

Verses 10-11 are a near duplicate of 19:9-10. They are missing from LXX[B], and many scholars think they have become displaced and inserted here from chap. 19. In any case, the incident shows well the increasing instability and hostility of Saul at this point in the story.

Although David's life was in danger (v. 11), Saul was the one "afraid" (v. 12). The narrator is clear about the reason for such fear. Saul is afraid because God was with David but had parted from Saul. These human events are a part of what God is doing in and through these events. For Saul, fear leads to increasingly self-serving actions. He sends David out to battle (v. 13). This commission has the effect of removing him from court and placing him in a position of threat. Some see a demotion in David's placement as commander of a thousand (a military unit), when v. 5 reported that Saul set him over the army. Whatever Saul's intent, David is neither killed nor relegated to obscurity. He is "successful" in everything he does (v. 14), and the whole land comes to "love" him (v. 16). As before, the narrator makes sure we know that such success happens because "the LORD was with him" (v. 14). Saul's fear escalates to "awe" of David (the NIV translates "afraid of" for both of the different words in vv. 12 and 14, but the word in v. 14 indicates something more like "anxiety" or "trembling").

18:17-19. Saul's fear and awe lead to murderous plots against David. Saul offers his daughter Merab to David, saying he desires only David's

---

136. See Robert Alter, *The Art of Biblical Poetry* (New York, Basic Books, 1985); Adele Berlin, "Parallelism," in *Anchor Bible Dictionary* (New York: Doubleday, 1992) 5:155-62.

bravery and skill as a warrior in return (v. 17a). But immediately after Saul's speech the narrator opens Saul's inner dialogue to us. Saul intends that when David attempts to prove himself worthy of this status, he will be killed by the Philistines (v. 17b). Saul's offer of marriage may be related to the reward promised to the one who killed Goliath (17:25), but the biblical author does not make this connection explicit. Saul seems to be growing increasingly duplicitous. When the time comes for Merab to marry, he gives her to another (v. 19). Royal daughters are given and royal wives are acquired throughout the books of Samuel largely as an outgrowth of political purposes on the part of the kings themselves and those seeking to influence them.

David simply responds with a statement of humility concerning his unworthiness for the position of son-in-law to the king (v. 18). In this segment and the next, we are given information about the thoughts and feelings of both Saul and Michal, but we gain no access to David's inner thoughts and motives. We do not know whether he saw through Saul's plots, how he felt about this betrayal, whether he reciprocated Michal's love (v. 20), or whether he saw the plots as opportunities to further ambition. While we gain remarkable insight into the character of Saul and Michal, the character of David remains opaque.[137]

18:20-30. This section opens with a remarkable and revealing statement that "Michal loved David" (v. 20).[138] It is the only time in Hebrew Scripture where a woman is said to love a man, and where a woman's feelings precipitate a marriage. In this case, the fact of Michal's love pleases Saul because of his own devious purposes. His interior thoughts are again revealed by the narrator as being focused on a plot to have David killed

by the Philistines (v. 21). But it is bold for Michal to both love and to make that love known (reported twice, vv. 20, 28) in a time of politically arranged marriages. We are told nothing of what motivated this love, and we are never told that David reciprocated it. In fact, when the offer of marriage to Michal is made known to David, his response is distinctly pragmatic and impersonal, "David was well pleased to be the king's son-in-law" (v. 26). It was the position, and not the woman, that attracted David.

Most of this section is taken up with the plotting of Saul, a portrait of distinctly inappropriate royal behavior. The offer to become the king's son-in-law is made a second time (v. 21b), but through the mediation of Saul's servants. They are commanded to flatter David with a strange mixture of truth and falsehood (v. 22): the king delights in you (lie); his servants "love" you (probably true, cf. v. 5). They are further instructed on what to say when David makes another self-effacing statement about his unworthiness (as with Merab). Are these statements genuine? Does David see through the plot? Is he playing along because he sees an opportunity? These matters are left unclear. The servants are to say that Saul expects no bride-price except one hundred Philistine foreskins (v. 25). Just so the reader will not fail to get the point, the narrator interrupts to say explicitly that Saul was sending David out to be killed (v. 25b). Ironically, David adopts a similar strategy of removing a man by sending him into battle when he sends Uriah to his death in 2 Samuel 11.

David goes immediately to gain the bridal price, and he returns with *two hundred* Philistine foreskins. The Greek text (LXX) and 2 Sam 3:14 both have "one hundred"; the NRSV adopts this reading, but the NIV stays with the MT's "two hundred." Perhaps David is so enthusiastic to become the son-in-law Saul does not want that he actually doubles the number of foreskins. The marriage is made; the brevity of the report about it may suggest Saul's reluctant compliance.

The text makes explicit Saul's recognition of the realities facing him (v. 28). The Lord is with David, and Michal loves him. Saul has been betrayed by his God and his family. Little wonder that v. 29a reports Saul as "still more afraid of David." Since Saul seems unable to join in the celebration of David, whom he also once loved

137. Alter, *The Art of Biblical Narrative,* 114-20, uses chaps. 18–19 as the primary focus for his discussion of "Characterization and the Art of Reticence" in Hebrew narrative. His detailed discussion of the various techniques for revealing character, as well as keeping character hidden, is extremely helpful. All of these techniques are used in Samuel 18: inference from actions, outward speech, interior dialogue, and the narrator's explicit statements.

138. For this and all subsequent discussions of texts involving Michal, I am indebted to a remarkable collection of scholarly and artistic treatments of Michal's story, *Telling Queen Michal's Story: An Experiment in Comparative Interpretation,* ed. David J. A. Clines and Tamara C. Eskenazi, JSOTSup 119 (Sheffield: JSOT, 1991). Included in this collection is a previously published article that has especially influenced my own views of these texts: J. Cheryl Exum, "Murder They Wrote: Ideology and the Manipulation of Female Presence in Biblical Narrative," in *The Pleasure of Her Text: Feminist Readings of Biblical and Historical Texts,* ed. A. Bach (Philadelphia: Trinity Press International, 1990) 45-68.

(16:21), he now sadly becomes "David's enemy from that time forward" (v. 29*b*). Saul has cast his lot with enmity against David, and tragically this act places him in opposition to what God is doing in behalf of Israel's future.

In a final verse (v. 30) we hear a report of David's "success" against the Philistines and his growing fame. David is fulfilling the task originally given to Saul.

REFLECTIONS

1. Walter Brueggemann has made an imaginative use of 1 Samuel 18 in reflecting on pastoral care in the practice of ministry.[139] He suggests that because our own lives have the quality of narrated story, our attentiveness to narratives such as this chapter can have transforming effect. The key lies in imaginatively attending to our stories alongside the biblical story. Pastoral care in the context of biblical faith is an act of imaginative attending to texts such as this one and to the narratives of our lives. The imaginative juxtaposition of biblical story with personal story creates new possibilities both for understanding the claims of faith and for living transformed lives in the light of those claims.

In 1 Samuel 18 the text models for us ways in which the data of "love" and "success" can be described. The biblical story shows a complexity of human interactions and motives, yet reveals within those human stories an insistent divine story ("Yahweh was with him"). Pastoral care attends to the human stories of our lives while challenging us to imaginatively perceive the insistence of another story that changes us beyond the ability of psychology or sociology to describe. Stories like those in 1 Samuel 18 provide opportunity for transforming pastoral care, because in the retelling these texts are experienced as both our story and not our story. Such texts provide a ground for redescribing and reconstructing our own lives.

> It takes no great imagination, while considering Saul or David, to find our life peopled with Jonathan and Merab and Michal and singing women and ruthless spears and applauding crowds. We draw very close to the narrative and we participate. When we do draw close, criticism is overcome and the text narrates for us another world, a world in which love is possible and hatred goes crazy, in which success is rampant and the king fails, in which Yahweh is present in transformative ways. David's world is rich with people. In our *retelling* of David's story and David's world, "our story" is *repeopled*. . . . When these stories are absent from our experience, everything is likely to be "explained." But then noticing is not possible: thrones are never risked, songs are never sung, swords are never thrown, foreskins are never acquired, names are never precious. When everything is "explained" life is denied and no new life is imaginable.[140]

2. By the end of chap. 18, Saul is engaged in a devious plot to end David's life, and his own life is gripped by fear and enmity. But the chapter did not begin that way. All of this grew from the seed of anger, envy, and jealousy at the success of another. The escalation from this small beginning to Saul's eventual tragic collapse was not necessary. All of us experience occasions of unwarranted and self-serving anger, jealousy that the successes of another were not our own. What the episodes of this chapter make clear is that evil and tragedy grow first from the small seeds of ordinary acts born of our own worst impulses. We cannot blame God for these acts, nor could Saul, but God's judgment will not be absent when we act to injure others out of our own anger and envy. We may not plot murder, but there are many ways to do hostile injury, from malicious gossip to political campaigns of character assassination. Saul is a sad reminder that jealous anger is a common human experience, but it makes all the difference whether we resolve it in repentance and reconciliation or take the escalating road to evil and madness.

---

139. Walter Brueggemann, *Power, Providence, and Personality* (Louisville: Westminster/John Knox, 1990) 41-48.
140. Ibid., 47-48.

By the same token "love" and "success" are not guaranteed by God's grace apart from the acts of responsibility and commitment taken in the dailiness of our lives. Jonathan and Michal heard the same praise given for David that Saul heard. Jonathan in particular could have acted as Saul did in jealous protection of his own interests. What makes for the love and success of David's story here, in contrast to the fear and evil that overshadow Saul's story, are the simple acts of David's attention to the tasks given him, the courage of Jonathan and Michal to love without regard to self-interest, and the willingness of the women to sing in honest celebration of things that deserve celebrating. This narrative insists that God is at work in our lives, but not apart from ordinary acts of human courage and faithfulness or human sin and madness. If God is with us, or if we have become alienated from God, it is not simply preordained. It is the daily conduct of our own lives that will allow others to make those judgments about us.

1 Samuel 19:1-24, Saul's Threat to David's Life

NIV

19Saul told his son Jonathan and all the attendants to kill David. But Jonathan was very fond of David ²and warned him, "My father Saul is looking for a chance to kill you. Be on your guard tomorrow morning; go into hiding and stay there. ³I will go out and stand with my father in the field where you are. I'll speak to him about you and will tell you what I find out."

⁴Jonathan spoke well of David to Saul his father and said to him, "Let not the king do wrong to his servant David; he has not wronged you, and what he has done has benefited you greatly. ⁵He took his life in his hands when he killed the Philistine. The LORD won a great victory for all Israel, and you saw it and were glad. Why then would you do wrong to an innocent man like David by killing him for no reason?"

⁶Saul listened to Jonathan and took this oath: "As surely as the LORD lives, David will not be put to death."

⁷So Jonathan called David and told him the whole conversation. He brought him to Saul, and David was with Saul as before.

⁸Once more war broke out, and David went out and fought the Philistines. He struck them with such force that they fled before him.

⁹But an evil*ᵃ* spirit from the LORD came upon Saul as he was sitting in his house with his spear in his hand. While David was playing the harp, ¹⁰Saul tried to pin him to the wall with his spear, but David eluded him as Saul drove the spear into the wall. That night David made good his escape.

ᵃ9 Or injurious

NRSV

19Saul spoke with his son Jonathan and with all his servants about killing David. But Saul's son Jonathan took great delight in David. ²Jonathan told David, "My father Saul is trying to kill you; therefore be on guard tomorrow morning; stay in a secret place and hide yourself. ³I will go out and stand beside my father in the field where you are, and I will speak to my father about you; if I learn anything I will tell you." ⁴Jonathan spoke well of David to his father Saul, saying to him, "The king should not sin against his servant David, because he has not sinned against you, and because his deeds have been of good service to you; ⁵for he took his life in his hand when he attacked the Philistine, and the LORD brought about a great victory for all Israel. You saw it, and rejoiced; why then will you sin against an innocent person by killing David without cause?" ⁶Saul heeded the voice of Jonathan; Saul swore, "As the LORD lives, he shall not be put to death." ⁷So Jonathan called David and related all these things to him. Jonathan then brought David to Saul, and he was in his presence as before.

8Again there was war, and David went out to fight the Philistines. He launched a heavy attack on them, so that they fled before him. ⁹Then an evil spirit from the LORD came upon Saul, as he sat in his house with his spear in his hand, while David was playing music. ¹⁰Saul sought to pin David to the wall with the spear; but he eluded Saul, so that he struck the spear into the wall. David fled and escaped that night.

11Saul sent messengers to David's house to

NIV

¹¹Saul sent men to David's house to watch it and to kill him in the morning. But Michal, David's wife, warned him, "If you don't run for your life tonight, tomorrow you'll be killed." ¹²So Michal let David down through a window, and he fled and escaped. ¹³Then Michal took an idol[b] and laid it on the bed, covering it with a garment and putting some goats' hair at the head.

¹⁴When Saul sent the men to capture David, Michal said, "He is ill."

¹⁵Then Saul sent the men back to see David and told them, "Bring him up to me in his bed so that I may kill him." ¹⁶But when the men entered, there was the idol in the bed, and at the head was some goats' hair.

¹⁷Saul said to Michal, "Why did you deceive me like this and send my enemy away so that he escaped?"

Michal told him, "He said to me, 'Let me get away. Why should I kill you?'"

¹⁸When David had fled and made his escape, he went to Samuel at Ramah and told him all that Saul had done to him. Then he and Samuel went to Naioth and stayed there. ¹⁹Word came to Saul: "David is in Naioth at Ramah"; ²⁰so he sent men to capture him. But when they saw a group of prophets prophesying, with Samuel standing there as their leader, the Spirit of God came upon Saul's men and they also prophesied. ²¹Saul was told about it, and he sent more men, and they prophesied too. Saul sent men a third time, and they also prophesied. ²²Finally, he himself left for Ramah and went to the great cistern at Secu. And he asked, "Where are Samuel and David?"

"Over in Naioth at Ramah," they said.

²³So Saul went to Naioth at Ramah. But the Spirit of God came even upon him, and he walked along prophesying until he came to Naioth. ²⁴He stripped off his robes and also prophesied in Samuel's presence. He lay that way all that day and night. This is why people say, "Is Saul also among the prophets?"

[a]13 Hebrew teraphim; also in verse 16

NRSV

keep watch over him, planning to kill him in the morning. David's wife Michal told him, "If you do not save your life tonight, tomorrow you will be killed." ¹²So Michal let David down through the window; he fled away and escaped. ¹³Michal took an idol[a] and laid it on the bed; she put a net[b] of goats' hair on its head, and covered it with the clothes. ¹⁴When Saul sent messengers to take David, she said, "He is sick." ¹⁵Then Saul sent the messengers to see David for themselves. He said, "Bring him up to me in the bed, that I may kill him." ¹⁶When the messengers came in, the idol[c] was in the bed, with the covering[b] of goats' hair on its head. ¹⁷Saul said to Michal, "Why have you deceived me like this, and let my enemy go, so that he has escaped?" Michal answered Saul, "He said to me, 'Let me go; why should I kill you?'"

18Now David fled and escaped; he came to Samuel at Ramah, and told him all that Saul had done to him. He and Samuel went and settled at Naioth. ¹⁹Saul was told, "David is at Naioth in Ramah." ²⁰Then Saul sent messengers to take David. When they saw the company of the prophets in a frenzy, with Samuel standing in charge of[b] them, the spirit of God came upon the messengers of Saul, and they also fell into a prophetic frenzy. ²¹When Saul was told, he sent other messengers, and they also fell into a frenzy. Saul sent messengers again the third time, and they also fell into a frenzy. ²²Then he himself went to Ramah. He came to the great well that is in Secu;[d] he asked, "Where are Samuel and David?" And someone said, "They are at Naioth in Ramah." ²³He went there, toward Naioth in Ramah; and the spirit of God came upon him. As he was going, he fell into a prophetic frenzy, until he came to Naioth in Ramah. ²⁴He too stripped off his clothes, and he too fell into a frenzy before Samuel. He lay naked all that day and all that night. Therefore it is said, "Is Saul also among the prophets?"

[a] Heb took the teraphim   [b] Meaning of Heb uncertain   [c] Heb the teraphim   [d] Gk reads to the well of the threshing floor on the bare height

COMMENTARY

This chapter tells the tale of four escapes (vv. 1-7; 8-10; 11-17; 18-24). Although it is David whose life is in danger, the chapter focuses on Saul. His descent into degenerate violence and madness becomes complete.

The entire narrative presents an escalation of Saul's murderous intent toward David. Saul no longer disguises his efforts to have his rival killed. In each of the four episodes, Saul takes direct action against David in full public view.

In this chapter, the extent of opposition to Saul is exposed, as is the breadth of David's support. Saul's efforts to kill David are thwarted by his own children, Jonathan (vv. 1-7) and Michal (vv. 11-17), by David's own agility (vv. 8-10), and by the prophet Samuel with the aid of God's Spirit (vv. 18-24).

By the end of the final episode we have witnessed the final and total delegitimation of Saul as he lies prostrate before Samuel, naked and raving (v. 24). He has moved from anger, fear, and devious plotting in chap. 18 to obsessive murderous action and madness in chap. 19. There may be some episodes yet to be played out, but there is no doubt that Saul is no longer God's anointed king. In fact, God may have rejected Saul as king (chap. 15), but Saul's own actions have made himself a despicable and pitiable human being.

19:1-7. Saul's murderous intentions are now in the open. He speaks to his son Jonathan and his servants about killing David (v. 1). His plots to get the Philistines to do his dirty work had failed (chap. 18), so Saul intends to take matters directly into his own hands. The irony is that he makes this known to those whom we know love David (18:1, 3, 22). Saul does not seem in touch with reality. In v. 1*b* we are told that Jonathan "took great delight" in David. The verb here (חפץ *ḥāpēṣ*) is the same as the one Saul used in lying to David that the "king is delighted with you," while in reality Saul was plotting his death (18:22). Jonathan's delight in David is the truth, and he warns David of Saul's intention to kill him (v. 2), helps him devise a hiding place, and offers to be David's advocate with Saul (v. 3). David seems to hide in the very field where Jonathan speaks with his father, suggesting to some scholars that David was intended to overhear the conversation (v. 3).

Jonathan's speech is both passionate and eloquent. He seems to have a flair for rhetoric, which reminds us of the eloquent speeches of David to Saul and Goliath in chap. 17. Perhaps this was a common trait that drew these friends together. Jonathan's attempt to sway his father begins by contrasting the sin Saul intends against David with David's innocence of any sin against Saul (v. 4). Further, David has rendered "good service" to Saul (v. 4). Most would see in this phrase affirmation of David's loyalty to a formal commitment of service required of those who serve the king. In v. 5*a*, Jonathan argues that David has even gone beyond the simple doing of his duty and courageously risked his life in vanquishing the Philistine (Goliath). This led to a great victory for Israel, and Jonathan reminds Saul that the king had seen and rejoiced in this mighty deed and that the Lord had been behind this victory. Jonathan then concludes by returning to the theme of David's innocence (v. 5*b*). By emphasizing that Saul would be killing David without cause, Jonathan may be raising the threat of bloodguilt on the house of Saul for the taking of innocent life (cf. Abigail's effort to keep David from bloodguilt in 25:31).

Saul is persuaded; he even swears an oath in the name of the Lord (Yahweh) that David shall not be put to death (v. 6). Jonathan completes his mediation on David's behalf by personally bringing him the news and escorting him back to the court to resume his duties (v. 7). It is to be a brief restoration.

19:8-10. In v. 8, further conflict with the Philistines is reported. David goes out to meet them in battle (we hear no report of Saul's involvement), and, as before, he is successful. The Philistines flee before his attack. As in chap. 18, David does nothing more throughout these episodes of Saul's growing hostility than carry out his duties as a warrior (and musician) in the service of Saul.

The battle notice is immediately followed by a repeat of the incident reported in 18:10-11 (many scholars think 19:9-10 is the original location and that the incident has been duplicated by addition to chap. 18). The evil spirit from God once again comes over Saul (v. 9), and he is caught up in a moment of madness. As with 18:10-11, the notion of an evil spirit may be a way of describing a psychological or emotional disorder. Such illness was for Israel from God and encompassed in God's purposes. Especially in these stories of the rejected Saul, his illness or madness was evidence of his alienation from God.

As David is playing music, to soothe Saul in such times, Saul attempts to kill David with a spear, but David is too agile. The spear is embedded harmlessly in the wall (v. 10). Now Saul has directly attempted to kill David, and David is forced to escape. We are forced to some disturbing conclusions about Saul. The juxtaposition of the battle notice and the attempt on David's life forces us to see a relationship between the two. In the light of chap. 18 (esp. v. 8), we must assume that Saul is motivated by jealousy at David's success in the very task Saul himself was commissioned to perform—deliverance from the Philistines. Saul's deadly actions against David have nothing to do with an offense by David, but grow from Saul's sense of his own inadequacy.

Saul has also now become an oath breaker. The oath he swore in the Lord's name (v. 6) has been quickly and very personally broken. It apparently meant nothing. Brueggemann notes how lightly Saul has broken this oath to preserve a life when he tenaciously held on to an oath for death that almost took Jonathan's life in 14:24, 44.[141]

19:11-17. First it was Jonathan who intervened to save David from Saul, now it is Michal who saves him, for like Jonathan she "loved" David (18:20, 28). Saul has placed men at David's house, intending to kill him the next morning (v. 11a). Michal apparently has some knowledge of her father's intent, and she warns David that he must escape that night (v. 11b). This initiative on her part is like that taken by Jonathan in v. 2.

Michal's efforts on behalf of David are, however, quite different from Jonathan's. Jonathan became David's rhetorical advocate with Saul, but Michal takes direct action in David's behalf. Perhaps Saul was beyond rhetoric. Michal lowers David out of a window to enable his escape (v. 12). She then creates a cover story to buy him time. She takes a teraphim (some kind of household idol; cf. Gen. 31:19-35; Judg 17:5; 18:14,

17-18, 20) and places it as a dummy in David's bed, using goat hair for the head, and covers it with clothes (v. 13). When Saul's men come to take David and kill him, she tells her first lie by reporting that he is sick (v. 14). Saul sends his men back, telling them to bring David in his sick bed and that he will kill him anyway (v. 15). Saul has even lost any sense of honor in his obsession with ridding himself of David. Michal's deception is then discovered (v. 16), and Saul confronts his daughter, demanding to know why she has aided his enemy (v. 17a). Michal then tells a second lie on David's behalf, but also to mollify her father and, perhaps, to protect herself. She says that David threatened her (v. 17b). In reality, she has been the initiator at every point. Adele Berlin has pointed out that in terms of usual biblical expectations, Jonathan has acted the more feminine role and Michal the more masculine.[142] It is Jonathan who uses words and Michal who takes aggressive and physical action. She boldly made her love for David known in the beginning (not the usual woman's prerogative in those times), and she took greater risks in protecting David by actively deceiving and lying to Saul.

As for Saul, he is now exposed as both murderous and obsessed. He has been abandoned and betrayed by his own family. He is isolated without support in his efforts and bereft even of his own honor.

19:18-24. The chapter concludes with a strange episode. David escapes from Saul's capital in Gibeah and goes north to Ramah, the hometown of the prophet Samuel (v. 18). It seems unlikely that he would have gone north, since his own tribal territory is Judah, and all of his subsequent adventures as a fugitive occur in this southern territory. This episode, which will later include an encounter between Samuel and Saul, also stands in tension with the notice (15:35) that Samuel did not see Saul again until the day of his death. It may be that these tensions are less important to the storyteller than the need to use a story that affirms public support for David from

---

141. Walter Brueggemann, *First and Second Samuel,* Interpretation (Louisville: John Knox, 1990) 142.

142. Adele Berlin, "Characterization in Biblical Narrative: David's Wives," *JSOT* 23 (1982) 70-72. Berlin also points out that this same reversal can be seen in David's response to Jonathan and Michal: "The feelings of love and tenderness that David might have been expected to have for Michal are all reserved for Jonathan." See 1 Sam 20:41; 2 Sam 1:26.

the prophet Samuel and that underscores Saul's isolation and madness.

David reports to Samuel all that has transpired (v. 18*b*). We cannot imagine him being too surprised. They settle at Naioth in Ramah. Naioth is probably not a place name, as the NRSV and the NIV suggest. It may best be translated as "camps" or "huts" and seems to be a location at Ramah, perhaps the kind of settlement that housed communities of prophets.[143] Saul hears of David's presence there and sends men to capture him (vv. 19-20*a*).

When Saul's men arrive, they see Samuel standing at the head of the assembly of prophets who are caught up in the ecstatic state of prophesying. Then the "spirit of God" falls upon these messengers of Saul, and they, too, fall into a prophetic frenzy (v. 20). We saw this ecstatic behavior associated with the prophets and the possession of God's Spirit in 10:9-10 when Saul was seized by God's Spirit as a sign of his special status as God's anointed one. At that time, Saul was given another heart, indicating some transformation to enable him in his commission as the anointed one (10:9). Here Saul's messengers seem immobilized by the Spirit's frenzy and unable to carry out their mission. When Saul hears of this situation, he sends a second group of men who have the same experience. Saul sends a third group, with like results (v. 21).

Finally, Saul must go himself (v. 22); no one

can do his dirty work for him. Before he even reaches the place where David and Samuel are, he is also seized by the Spirit of God (v. 23). He falls into the same ecstatic frenzy as the others while apparently continuing to Naioth in Ramah. When there, he strips off his clothes and falls on the ground before Samuel and lies naked for an entire day and night. It is a scene of Saul's final and total humiliation and his complete loss of authority as God's anointed king. Before God's prophet, the Spirit of God, which once authorized him (10:9-10), now leaves Saul naked, prostrate, humiliated, and powerless. David then makes good his escape (20:1*a*).

The final phrase of v. 24 relates this experience once more to the saying "Is Saul also among the prophets?" In 10:11-12, this proverb seems to imply an answer of yes and to confirm Saul as God's anointed one. He is given "another heart" to pursue his commission to deliver Israel. Saul is once again "among the prophets," but this time it is only as an object of humiliation and pity. The Spirit of God can both authorize and judge. Saul is no longer worthy. Instead of receiving another heart, Saul is immobilized, and David, the man after God's own heart, escapes. It is even possible, as Wilson suggests, that the implied answer to the saying "Is Saul also among the prophets?" has now become "No, Saul is no prophet; he is insane!"[144]

---

143. See the discussion in P. Kyle McCarter, *I Samuel*, AB 8 (Garden City, N.Y.: Doubleday, 1980) 328.

144. Robert R. Wilson, *Prophecy and Society in Ancient Israel* (Philadelphia: Fortress, 1980) 183.

REFLECTIONS

The theme of this chapter is sad but obvious. It is a chronicle of the total undoing of Saul. David himself and even Yahweh recede for a moment into the background. This is the final unfolding of the cautionary moral tale of Saul that began in chap. 18 with anger and jealousy at the success of another. It is often our failure to address the roots of evil in the ordinary that allows evil to flourish and corrode our lives. Saul was not an inherently evil man who rose to high places only to have his sinful nature finally catch up with him. He had his flaws and failures, but until 18:8 he seemed basically a good man who intended well. Those who do terrible and violent deeds do not usually begin by intending such actions. To ignore or justify our own petty thoughts and deeds is to risk the path of Saul. Saul was rejected by God as king; he could not bring Israel into the future God intended. But he was the sponsor and mentor of that future for Israel in David. He was not rejected as a man, and he, like his son Jonathan, could have allowed the throne to pass to David, a man he once loved (16:21).

Again we encounter a notice of the "evil spirit from the LORD" that came upon Saul and led to his attempt on David's life with the spear, which seems so constantly present with Saul. This theme reminds us of Saul's alienation from God and God's rejection of Saul as a part of the divine plan for Israel. God has, indeed, caused the anguish that grips Saul and sends him periodically into a rage, but the text takes care to comment on Saul's own human motives of anger, jealousy, and self-interest. These are not the Lord's doing. The "evil spirit from the LORD" may indicate intermittent losses of control and judgment, but Saul's descent into murderous obsession and madness is largely accomplished in chaps. 18–19 in those moments of complete self-possession rather than spirit possession. He became ruled by anger, jealousy, rage, obsession, and fear. He allowed these emotions to overwhelm his beginning with David, when he loved David (16:21). Saul's end as a king may have been rooted in his rejection by God through Samuel, but his end as a good and faithful man began in ordinary moments where jealous anger was allowed to obscure love.

But if David is in the background here, Jonathan and Michal are not. Their courageous speech and deeds form a counterpart to Saul's descent into madness and murder. Their disregard for self-interest is a total contrast to Saul's obsession with his own standing. These profiles of faithfulness and courage motivated by love are worth noting for their modeling of alternative paths to the self-destructive path taken by Saul.

1 Samuel 20:1-42, The Friendship of Jonathan and David

NIV

20 Then David fled from Naioth at Ramah and went to Jonathan and asked, "What have I done? What is my crime? How have I wronged your father, that he is trying to take my life?"

²"Never!" Jonathan replied. "You are not going to die! Look, my father doesn't do anything, great or small, without confiding in me. Why would he hide this from me? It's not so!"

³But David took an oath and said, "Your father knows very well that I have found favor in your eyes, and he has said to himself, 'Jonathan must not know this or he will be grieved.' Yet as surely as the LORD lives and as you live, there is only a step between me and death."

⁴Jonathan said to David, "Whatever you want me to do, I'll do for you."

⁵So David said, "Look, tomorrow is the New Moon festival, and I am supposed to dine with the king; but let me go and hide in the field until the evening of the day after tomorrow. ⁶If your father misses me at all, tell him, 'David earnestly asked my permission to hurry to Bethlehem, his hometown, because an annual sacrifice is being made there for his whole clan.' ⁷If he says, 'Very well,' then your servant is safe. But if he loses his temper, you can be sure that he is determined to harm me. ⁸As for you, show kindness to your

NRSV

20 David fled from Naioth in Ramah. He came before Jonathan and said, "What have I done? What is my guilt? And what is my sin against your father that he is trying to take my life?" ²He said to him, "Far from it! You shall not die. My father does nothing either great or small without disclosing it to me; and why should my father hide this from me? Never!" ³But David also swore, "Your father knows well that you like me; and he thinks, 'Do not let Jonathan know this, or he will be grieved.' But truly, as the LORD lives and as you yourself live, there is but a step between me and death." ⁴Then Jonathan said to David, "Whatever you say, I will do for you." ⁵David said to Jonathan, "Tomorrow is the new moon, and I should not fail to sit with the king at the meal; but let me go, so that I may hide in the field until the third evening. ⁶If your father misses me at all, then say, 'David earnestly asked leave of me to run to Bethlehem his city; for there is a yearly sacrifice there for all the family.' ⁷If he says, 'Good!' it will be well with your servant; but if he is angry, then know that evil has been determined by him. ⁸Therefore deal kindly with your servant, for you have brought your servant into a sacred covenant[a] with you. But if there is

a Heb *a covenant of the LORD*

servant, for you have brought him into a covenant with you before the LORD. If I am guilty, then kill me yourself! Why hand me over to your father?"

⁹"Never!" Jonathan said. "If I had the least inkling that my father was determined to harm you, wouldn't I tell you?"

¹⁰David asked, "Who will tell me if your father answers you harshly?"

¹¹"Come," Jonathan said, "let's go out into the field." So they went there together.

¹²Then Jonathan said to David: "By the LORD, the God of Israel, I will surely sound out my father by this time the day after tomorrow! If he is favorably disposed toward you, will I not send you word and let you know? ¹³But if my father is inclined to harm you, may the LORD deal with me, be it ever so severely, if I do not let you know and send you away safely. May the LORD be with you as he has been with my father. ¹⁴But show me unfailing kindness like that of the LORD as long as I live, so that I may not be killed, ¹⁵and do not ever cut off your kindness from my family—not even when the LORD has cut off every one of David's enemies from the face of the earth."

¹⁶So Jonathan made a covenant with the house of David, saying, "May the LORD call David's enemies to account." ¹⁷And Jonathan had David reaffirm his oath out of love for him, because he loved him as he loved himself.

¹⁸Then Jonathan said to David: "Tomorrow is the New Moon festival. You will be missed, because your seat will be empty. ¹⁹The day after tomorrow, toward evening, go to the place where you hid when this trouble began, and wait by the stone Ezel. ²⁰I will shoot three arrows to the side of it, as though I were shooting at a target. ²¹Then I will send a boy and say, 'Go, find the arrows.' If I say to him, 'Look, the arrows are on this side of you; bring them here,' then come, because, as surely as the LORD lives, you are safe; there is no danger. ²²But if I say to the boy, 'Look, the arrows are beyond you,' then you must go, because the LORD has sent you away. ²³And about the matter you and I discussed—remember, the LORD is witness between you and me forever."

²⁴So David hid in the field, and when the New Moon festival came, the king sat down to eat.

guilt in me, kill me yourself; why should you bring me to your father?" ⁹Jonathan said, "Far be it from you! If I knew that it was decided by my father that evil should come upon you, would I not tell you?" ¹⁰Then David said to Jonathan, "Who will tell me if your father answers you harshly?" ¹¹Jonathan replied to David, "Come, let us go out into the field." So they both went out into the field.

¹²Jonathan said to David, "By the LORD, the God of Israel! When I have sounded out my father, about this time tomorrow, or on the third day, if he is well disposed toward David, shall I not then send and disclose it to you? ¹³But if my father intends to do you harm, the LORD do so to Jonathan, and more also, if I do not disclose it to you, and send you away, so that you may go in safety. May the LORD be with you, as he has been with my father. ¹⁴If I am still alive, show me the faithful love of the LORD; but if I die,ᵃ ¹⁵never cut off your faithful love from my house, even if the LORD were to cut off every one of the enemies of David from the face of the earth." ¹⁶Thus Jonathan made a covenant with the house of David, saying, "May the LORD seek out the enemies of David." ¹⁷Jonathan made David swear again by his love for him; for he loved him as he loved his own life.

¹⁸Jonathan said to him, "Tomorrow is the new moon; you will be missed, because your place will be empty. ¹⁹On the day after tomorrow, you shall go a long way down; go to the place where you hid yourself earlier, and remain beside the stone there.ᵃ ²⁰I will shoot three arrows to the side of it, as though I shot at a mark. ²¹Then I will send the boy, saying, 'Go, find the arrows.' If I say to the boy, 'Look, the arrows are on this side of you, collect them,' then you are to come, for, as the LORD lives, it is safe for you and there is no danger. ²²But if I say to the young man, 'Look, the arrows are beyond you,' then go; for the LORD has sent you away. ²³As for the matter about which you and I have spoken, the LORD is witnessᵇ between you and me forever."

²⁴So David hid himself in the field. When the new moon came, the king sat at the feast to eat. ²⁵The king sat upon his seat, as at other times,

ᵃ Meaning of Heb uncertain ᵇ Gk: Heb lacks witness

²⁵He sat in his customary place by the wall, opposite Jonathan,ᵃ and Abner sat next to Saul, but David's place was empty. ²⁶Saul said nothing that day, for he thought, "Something must have happened to David to make him ceremonially unclean—surely he is unclean." ²⁷But the next day, the second day of the month, David's place was empty again. Then Saul said to his son Jonathan, "Why hasn't the son of Jesse come to the meal, either yesterday or today?"

²⁸Jonathan answered, "David earnestly asked me for permission to go to Bethlehem. ²⁹He said, 'Let me go, because our family is observing a sacrifice in the town and my brother has ordered me to be there. If I have found favor in your eyes, let me get away to see my brothers.' That is why he has not come to the king's table."

³⁰Saul's anger flared up at Jonathan and he said to him, "You son of a perverse and rebellious woman! Don't I know that you have sided with the son of Jesse to your own shame and to the shame of the mother who bore you? ³¹As long as the son of Jesse lives on this earth, neither you nor your kingdom will be established. Now send and bring him to me, for he must die!"

³²"Why should he be put to death? What has he done?" Jonathan asked his father. ³³But Saul hurled his spear at him to kill him. Then Jonathan knew that his father intended to kill David.

³⁴Jonathan got up from the table in fierce anger; on that second day of the month he did not eat, because he was grieved at his father's shameful treatment of David.

³⁵In the morning Jonathan went out to the field for his meeting with David. He had a small boy with him, ³⁶and he said to the boy, "Run and find the arrows I shoot." As the boy ran, he shot an arrow beyond him. ³⁷When the boy came to the place where Jonathan's arrow had fallen, Jonathan called out after him, "Isn't the arrow beyond you?" ³⁸Then he shouted, "Hurry! Go quickly! Don't stop!" The boy picked up the arrow and returned to his master. ³⁹(The boy knew nothing of all this; only Jonathan and David knew.) ⁴⁰Then Jonathan gave his weapons to the boy and said, "Go, carry them back to town."

⁴¹After the boy had gone, David got up from

ᵃ25 Septuagint; Hebrew *wall. Jonathan arose*

upon the seat by the wall. Jonathan stood, while Abner sat by Saul's side; but David's place was empty.

26Saul did not say anything that day; for he thought, "Something has befallen him; he is not clean, surely he is not clean." ²⁷But on the second day, the day after the new moon, David's place was empty. And Saul said to his son Jonathan, "Why has the son of Jesse not come to the feast, either yesterday or today?" ²⁸Jonathan answered Saul, "David earnestly asked leave of me to go to Bethlehem; ²⁹he said, 'Let me go; for our family is holding a sacrifice in the city, and my brother has commanded me to be there. So now, if I have found favor in your sight, let me get away, and see my brothers.' For this reason he has not come to the king's table."

30Then Saul's anger was kindled against Jonathan. He said to him, "You son of a perverse, rebellious woman! Do I not know that you have chosen the son of Jesse to your own shame, and to the shame of your mother's nakedness? ³¹For as long as the son of Jesse lives upon the earth, neither you nor your kingdom shall be established. Now send and bring him to me, for he shall surely die." ³²Then Jonathan answered his father Saul, "Why should he be put to death? What has he done?" ³³But Saul threw his spear at him to strike him; so Jonathan knew that it was the decision of his father to put David to death. ³⁴Jonathan rose from the table in fierce anger and ate no food on the second day of the month, for he was grieved for David, and because his father had disgraced him.

35In the morning Jonathan went out into the field to the appointment with David, and with him was a little boy. ³⁶He said to the boy, "Run and find the arrows that I shoot." As the boy ran, he shot an arrow beyond him. ³⁷When the boy came to the place where Jonathan's arrow had fallen, Jonathan called after the boy and said, "Is the arrow not beyond you?" ³⁸Jonathan called after the boy, "Hurry, be quick, do not linger." So Jonathan's boy gathered up the arrows and came to his master. ³⁹But the boy knew nothing; only Jonathan and David knew the arrangement. ⁴⁰Jonathan gave his weapons to the boy and said to him, "Go and carry them to the city." ⁴¹As

NIV

the south side ⌊of the stone⌋ and bowed down before Jonathan three times, with his face to the ground. Then they kissed each other and wept together—but David wept the most.

⁴²Jonathan said to David, "Go in peace, for we have sworn friendship with each other in the name of the LORD, saying, 'The LORD is witness between you and me, and between your descendants and my descendants forever.'" Then David left, and Jonathan went back to the town.

NRSV

soon as the boy had gone, David rose from beside the stone heap[a] and prostrated himself with his face to the ground. He bowed three times, and they kissed each other, and wept with each other; David wept the more.[b] ⁴²Then Jonathan said to David, "Go in peace, since both of us have sworn in the name of the LORD, saying, 'The LORD shall be between me and you, and between my descendants and your descendants, forever.'" He got up and left; and Jonathan went into the city.[c]

[a] Gk: Heb *from beside the south*   [b] Vg: Meaning of Heb uncertain
[c] This sentence is 21.1 in Heb

COMMENTARY

David's time in the court of Saul is over. He dare not return, because Saul will kill him. He will be a fugitive for the immediate future. But there is a final scene yet to play. The deep and committed friendship of Jonathan with David is the focus of this chapter. Although the external issue revolves around determining whether David must permanently absent himself from Saul's court, the real issue is focused on the ability of the friendship of Jonathan and David to survive this crisis and on the meaning of that commitment for Israel's future and the future of their descendants. Jonathan must struggle with conflicting loyalties to family responsibility and covenanted commitment to his friend. David must balance his instinct for survival with his loyalty to Jonathan and his need to honor Jonathan's obligation to Saul, even though Saul is now David's enemy. The exchanges between them are moving, honest, and, in the end, heartbreaking, for these friends will be forced to part. There are no portraits in the Bible of love and loyalty between friends to match this one. It is a friendship, with personal and political dimensions, that shapes Israel's future as surely as it shapes the futures of Jonathan and David themselves.

The first half of the chapter is taken up by an extended conversation between David and Jonathan. Initially, David petitions Jonathan for help in determining his status in Saul's court and the seriousness of Saul's threats on his life (vv.

1-11). They devise a plan involving David's absence from an important banquet. In a second segment of the conversation (vv. 12-17), the roles are reversed, and Jonathan petitions David to remember him and his descendants when he comes into the power of his kingdom. Many scholars believe this section is a secondary addition to the text because it anticipates the kind treatment David gives to Jonathan's son, Mephibosheth, in 2 Samuel 9.[145] They note that David's question in v. 10 is answered in vv. 18-23 and suggest that the addition of vv. 12-17 was a later attempt to bridge between the history of David's rise and the succession narrative. In any case, the present form of the text makes the friendship and loyalty between David and Jonathan the context for commenting on David's relationship to the house of Saul on two horizons. On the near horizon, David's innocence of wrongdoing against Saul is acknowledged and affirmed by Saul's own son. David did not come to power through any injustice against the house of Saul. Innocence is a major concern of the history of David's rise. On the distant horizon, David's loyalty to the house of Saul through Jonathan, even after he becomes king, is promised and anticipated. This loyalty is a concern for the succession narrative in 2 Samuel. The extended conversation between David and Jonathan ends with a plan for communicating what Jonathan has discovered (vv. 18-23).

145. See McCarter, *I Samuel,* 342-45; Ralph W. Klein, *1 Samuel,* WBC 10 (Waco: Word, 1983) 205.

The second half of the chapter carries out the two friends' plan. David is absent from the banquet, and Jonathan offers an explanation (vv. 24-29). Saul lashes out angrily at Jonathan, and his murderous intentions toward David become clear (vv. 30-34). Jonathan gets news to David, and the chapter ends with a tearful and moving parting of the friends (vv. 35-42).

A key theological term in this episode is חֶסֶד (ḥesed), which is difficult to translate adequately. It appears often in connection with Israel's covenant with God where it is frequently used to describe God's covenant love and loyalty. It has often been translated as "steadfast love," "lovingkindness," or "mercy." In this passage, both David and Jonathan appeal to this concept (vv. 8, 14-15). The NRSV translates as "deal kindly" (v. 8) and "faithful love" (vv. 14-15); the NIV uses "kindness" for all three occurrences. Sakenfeld, in the most thorough and useful study of ḥesed, suggests that the term really indicates both the attitude and the action of loyalty in relationships. Her analysis is particularly helpful in reflecting on the role of loyalty in this relationship between David and Jonathan.[146]

This is a story of conflicting claims of loyalty. The conflict is between the familial and the covenantal. Jonathan has responsibility as a son to his father; for that matter, David has obligations as a son-in-law to Saul. But Saul's intention to kill David places family loyalty in conflict with a covenant made between Jonathan and David (vv. 8, 16; 18:3). In 1 Samuel 20, ḥesed is used only in reference to this covenant commitment between the two friends. The conflict of loyalties also occurs between the personal and the political. The "love" (v. 17; 18:1, 3) and "loyalty" (vv. 8, 14-15) between David and Jonathan are not limited to the personal and intimate relationship between them. Both terms also reflect sociopolitical loyalties and commitments. Jonathan and David both understand that it is not just their personal future at stake but the political future of Israel. Saul angrily insists that Jonathan's political interests as heir to the throne require that he set aside the shameful choice of personal commitment to David (vv. 30-31). Jonathan knows that loyalty to David is not simply to a friend but to

one who will be king instead of him, and he asks of David loyalty as a king and not just as a friend (vv. 13-16).

Some have seen Jonathan in this chapter choosing exclusively for David and against Saul.[147] This is true, in a sense. Jonathan not only supports and protects David against the wrath of his father, but he also seems to see the most clearly of anyone in the story that David represents God's future for Israel. Jonathan alone gives voice to a sense of the Lord's working through David in these events (vv. 12, 14, 16, 22, 23, 42). In a way, Jonathan chooses for the Lord and not just for David. But this choice is not allowed to be absolute and unambiguous. Jonathan must, for the sake of loyalty to David, oppose his father and risk his father's violence (v. 33); but he refuses to abandon his father or the demands of familial loyalty. He knows his father, Saul, is doomed; he knows David is Israel's future. He can protect that future, but he cannot go with it. In this chapter, the term "father" (אָב ʾāb) is used fourteen times, emphasizing the painful relationship that Jonathan cannot escape. Saul is his father. He loves David, but he does not go with him. He stays with Saul at some personal risk and with the knowledge that he is on a sinking ship. In the end, he dies fighting with his father in a battle that cannot be won (31:2). It is little wonder that David, who better than anyone knows of Jonathan's loyalty, can sing on hearing of the death of father and son, "Saul and Jonathan, beloved and lovely! In life and in death they were not divided" (2 Sam 1:23a).

20:1-11. David is on the run. After leaving Ramah, he meets with Jonathan to plead his innocence (v. 1). Jonathan refuses to believe that his father wishes to kill David and appeals to his close relationship with Saul to argue that Saul would have told him (v. 2). This does not fit well with the notice of 19:1 that Saul spoke with Jonathan in particular about killing David. Either separate accounts of events have been combined without regard to such tensions or episodes are not necessarily in chronological order. David hypothesizes that Saul wouldn't tell Jonathan because he knew such a plot would grieve his son (v. 3). This statement foreshadows reality; when Jonathan learns beyond doubt that his father in-

146. Katharine Doob Sakenfeld, *Faithfulness in Action: Loyalty in Biblical Perspective,* OBT (Philadelphia: Fortress, 1985) 1-15.

147. Brueggemann, *First and Second Samuel,* 153.

tends to kill David, he does indeed grieve (v. 34). The depth of relationship between Jonathan and David is shown by Jonathan's ready willingness to do what David asks without knowing yet what it is (v. 4).

Although the events of chap. 19 would seem to leave no doubt about Saul's intent, David enlists Jonathan's help in determining his standing with Saul and the extent of his danger. David plans to absent himself from an important feast he would have been expected to attend. When his absence is noted by Saul, Jonathan is to say that David has gone to Bethlehem for a yearly sacrifice with his family (vv. 5-6). If the king accepts the excuse, all is well; but if the king is angry, then it will indicate that Saul means to do evil toward David (v. 7).

David concludes his petition by asking that Jonathan show *ḥesed* "loyalty" toward him because of the "covenant" between them (v. 8*a*; see 18:3). Further, David declares that if he is guilty he would just as soon Jonathan would kill him (v. 8*b*). In this verse, the depth of loyalty and commitment that supports this friendship is exposed. The relationship is not just a casual attraction between youthful comrades in arms. Their friendship is a covenanted relationship originating in love (v. 17; 18:1, 3) and maintained in a loyalty prepared to accept the personal and the political implications of the commitment between them. In the larger framework of 1 Samuel, this account once again affirms David's innocence of offense against the house of Saul and shows Saul's son supporting David in this claim.

David asks how Jonathan will bring news to him if the news is bad (v. 10). The presumption is that if Saul does wish to kill David, it will be risky to be seen with him. The two friends walk out into a field (v. 11). The narrative appears to continue in v. 18, where the plan devised involves David's hiding in the field. In the present form of the text, however, Jonathan opens a new conversation in which roles are reversed. Jonathan now petitions David.

20:12-17. This section begins with Jonathan's vow not only to tell David if his father means him harm, but also to help him escape to safety. He swears in the name of "the LORD, the God of Israel" and invokes the name of the Lord repeatedly throughout this speech (vv. 12-16). He even

places himself at risk if he fails to honor this vow (v. 13*a*). Jonathan sees that they are players in more than a human drama. It is God's future for Israel that is at stake, and not simply his personal friend David.

Jonathan's focus shifts to that future in blessing and petition. In blessing, Jonathan invokes the Lord's presence with David "as he has been with my father" (v. 13*b*). The theme of "God is with him [David]," a major motif of the history of David's rise, is now invoked by Saul's own son. But Jonathan also seems to be recognizing a transfer of divine presence from his father to David. Implicit in his language is acknowledgment that the Lord is no longer with Saul, but Jonathan willingly invokes the Lord's presence for David as Israel's future. Saul already belongs to Israel's past.

Blessing for the future gives way to petition for the future in vv. 14-15. The roles of Jonathan and David are reversed. David, who was in danger at the present, had asked Jonathan for help. Jonathan now foresees a danger to his descendants and requests David for help in the future. Both of these friends appeal to *ḥesed* "loyalty/faithful love/kindness" and the covenant between them as the basis for aid. Jonathan first appeals to *ḥesed* for himself if he is still alive (v. 14), and then to *ḥesed* for his descendants (v. 15). Jonathan sees a future when David will become king and the Lord will destroy his enemies and the enemies of Israel (v. 15); indeed, he covenants with David that it may be so (v. 16). In effect, Jonathan acknowledges the coming kingship of David, but he also knows that the house of Saul has become the enemy of this future king. He knows that the enemies of the Lord's anointed will be "cut off" (כרת *kārat*, a verb used twice in v. 15) and appeals to David that he and his house not be numbered among those enemies. (The LXX of v. 16 reads, "may the name of Jonathan not be 'cut off' from the house of David.") Jonathan separates himself from the opposition of the house of Saul to David and asks David to make a place for his name and his household in the coming future kingdom. He makes David swear an oath out of love (v. 17). The text notes "for he loved him as he loved his own life"; it is unclear whether the subject is Jonathan or David. It would seem that David is swearing on the basis of his love for Jonathan (v. 17*a*). This would make the swearing of David's love a complement to Jonathan's love of David "as his own soul" in 18:1, 3.

What Jonathan fears and the help he requests both come to pass at a later point in the story. In 2 Samuel 9, when David's enemies have been vanquished, including most of the house of Saul, David seeks out the surviving son of Jonathan, Mephibosheth, to show him *ḥesed* (2 Sam 9:1, 3, 7) for the sake of Jonathan. David restores land to him and gives him a place at the royal table.

20:18-23. The two friends devise a plan that will enable Jonathan to communicate to David what he finds out about Saul's intent. Jonathan will shoot arrows in the field near where David is hiding. Then, when Jonathan instructs his servant where to find the arrows, he will, by his instructions, reveal to David what he knows about Saul's plan (vv. 19-22). Jonathan's sense of the Lord's providence is evident. If David must flee for his own safety, Jonathan is confident that the "LORD has sent you away" (v. 22b). As the friends part, Jonathan invokes the Lord as witness to what has passed between them (v. 23). It is no light thing; it is "forever."

20:24-34. The scene shifts to the feast of the new moon at Saul's court, where David's chair is empty (vv. 24-25). His absence elicits no response for the first night of the feast because Saul assumes that David has become unclean for some reason and cannot attend (v. 26). There were a variety of ways this could occur (e.g., contact with a dead body, an emission of bodily fluids, etc.). But when David is absent a second night, Saul asks for an explanation from Jonathan. Jonathan uses the prepared excuse that David has been summoned to be with his family in Bethlehem (vv. 27-29). Interestingly, Jonathan reports that David came to him, and he gave permission for his absence, which seems a bit presumptuous on Jonathan's part.

The mood suddenly and violently shifts. Saul, perhaps with the clarity of his own paranoid obsession with David, has seen straight through Jonathan, and he turns his anger on his own son (v. 30). He launches into a merciless tirade, slandering even Jonathan's mother in the process. But in his anger he sees clearly: Jonathan has "chosen" David, and Saul believes it is to Jonathan's shame. The reference to the shame of Jonathan's mother's nakedness or genitals is perhaps a suggestion that

Jonathan was a shame from the moment of his birth. Saul cannot even bring himself to pronounce the name of David (also v. 27). Throughout this tirade, he calls David only the "son of Jesse," as if this were an epithet. Perhaps it is a derogatory comment aimed at David's humble family.

Saul, in his anger, knows the future. He simply does not accept it. He angrily declares to Jonathan what Jonathan already knows: As long as the "son of Jesse" lives, there will be no kingdom for Jonathan (v. 31a). Lest Jonathan have any doubt, Saul demands that he bring the "son of Jesse" to him, for he is a "son of death" (v. 31b; the NRSV and the NIV lose the graphic imagery here by rendering "he will surely die/he must die"). Jonathan makes one last desperate attempt to plead David's innocence (v. 32). It is more than Saul can take. Rejected by God, he now seems rejected by his own son. The violence directed heretofore at David explodes toward Jonathan, and Saul hurls his spear at his son (v. 33a). Jonathan knows that David was right; only violence and death can await David in Saul's court (v. 33b). He leaves the table and the court in anger and grieves (as David had known he would, v. 3), over his friend's fate and his own disgrace (v. 34).

20:35-42. The scene shifts to the field where Jonathan and David had arranged their rendezvous. The narrative lingers over the details of Jonathan's shooting of arrows and his instructions to the boy with him (vv. 35-40). It is almost as if the narrative is reluctant to end, for at its end these two friends will part forever. The signal is given in the coded responses to the servant boy: David is not safe in the court of Saul. Jonathan's speech offers a double meaning when he urges his servant, "Hurry, be quick, do not linger!" (v. 38). It is an instruction David, too, must heed.

Jonathan dismisses his servant, and the friends meet for a final time face to face. It is a scene of considerable pathos, and for once David, often the passive objective of passions around him, becomes the proactive partner. He prostrates himself before Jonathan three times; the two men kiss and weep, but the text says, "David wept the more" (v. 41). There is no embarrassment at the deep affection that passes between these two warriors and friends. The author of this political drama of the kingdom pauses to note the passion and the grief of this moment.

Jonathan has the last word, and, as previously, it is Jonathan who sees with the eyes of faith and trusts that the Lord is at work even in these painful events. He sends David forth in peace (a contrast to the violence manifested by Saul), and he recalls the mutual oaths sworn in the name of the Lord. His words invoke the presence of that same Lord as the guarantor of the ties between Jonathan and David and between Jonathan's house and David's house "forever" (v. 42). They physically part from each other, but they are forever bound in covenant loyalty.

REFLECTIONS

This chapter is centrally important to any biblical reflection on a theology of friendship. The Bible is filled with many stories that illustrate the importance of relationships, but on closer examination most of these have to do with relationships of family (husbands, wives, parents, children, extended family) or of roles in society (governance, economics, religious leadership, military crises). There are not many texts that deal with relationship of friends, adults who need not have established relationships of commitment to each other, but have done so nevertheless. Jonathan and David could have related to each other at greater personal distance through the positions and roles each held: crown prince to military commander; son of Saul to son-in-law of Saul. But from the beginning the relationship of these two went beyond that of family and social role. Jonathan loved David "as his own soul" (18:1, 3), and David loved Jonathan "as his own life" (20:17). Modeled here is friendship that chooses for a depth of intimacy and commitment that was not a given responsibility of family or social position. It was grounded in covenant between the two and was practiced through the loyalty each gave to and claimed from the other.

The danger here, of course, is that we may give in to a romantic sentimentality about friendship and wax eloquent about all of the positive virtues of love, commitment, and loyalty as if they operated in detachment from the historical, social, and even theological contexts where friendship must be lived. It is perhaps significant and thought-provoking that our most eloquent story of human friendship in the Bible does not end happily ever after. Perhaps this helps us to guard against rendering the important truths of this story of friendship in the pastels of a Madison Avenue commercial.

As Sakenfeld has reminded us, "loyalty" (*ḥesed*) is the key to understanding the human commitments modeled here in the friendship of Jonathan and David.[148] But it is good to remind ourselves of the breadth and depth of this key theme.

1. This story tells us of the ambiguity and pain of loyalty. The commitment between friends modeled here is not without cost. The choices made are not always simple and clear-cut. The friendship of these two men requires risk and self-sacrifice. Commitments of loyalty are not made in a vacuum.

Jonathan is not free to choose for David in isolation from responsibilities to his father, Saul. He must make painful choices that honor his commitments as loyal friend while not giving up responsibilities as a son. While Jonathan helps David to safety, he also chooses to remain with his father, even to death. In D. H. Lawrence's play *David,* much of the drama is centered on the tension between Jonathan's ties to his friend as future king and his father as rejected king. Jonathan realizes that his soul belongs to David, but that his life belongs to Saul. When the friends finally part, Jonathan says to David, "I would not see thy new day, David. For thy wisdom is the wisdom of the subtle and behind thy passion lies prudence. Thy virtue is in thy wit and thy shrewdness. But in Saul have I known the magnanimity of a man."[149]

148. Sakenfeld, *Faithfulness in Action.*
149. D. H. Lawrence, *David,* reprinted in *Religious Drama I: Five Plays,* ed. M. Halverson (New York: Meridian, 1957) 265-66.

The story of friendship between David and Jonathan suggests that love and loyalty are always experienced in the midst of ambiguous claims and responsibilities. The experience of friendship can lead to painful as well as fulfilling decisions. We live in a societal context prone to cheap relationships. Many live under the illusion that their own self-fulfillment and self-gratification are the primary goals of relationship. But pursuit of such shallow relationships can never result in the experience of loyal friendship given and received. Loyalty requires honoring of commitments, concern for the other as fully as for self, parting as well as being with, giving rather than grasping, pain along with joy.

2. This is also a story of the politics of loyalty. In the commentary it is noted that key terms such as "love" and "loyalty" are not limited in their meaning to the personal and intimate dimensions of human relationship. The love and loyalty in the friendship of Jonathan and David surely had such personal dimensions, as the moving scene of their parting demonstrates. But at every point in the story it is clear that these two friends knew that their commitment had implications for the kingdom. Jonathan's choice for David was a matter of shifted political loyalty as well as personal loyalty.

Friendships always have social contexts and social consequences. This is clear, for example, in our society in the matter of interracial friendships and relationships. To bind oneself in loyal friendship to a person of another race is to move against the grain of a society still blighted by significant elements of racism and to model an alternative to that racism, often at considerable risk and pain. Jonathan saw a different future for Israel in David and chose that future as well as that person in his friendship for David. In our friendships, we make not only personal choices but also choices for the future of the communities of which we are a part. To choose friendships with those most like ourselves will limit the future open to our communities. Jonathan chose against what tradition dictated as his self-interest. The challenge to find loyalty in relationships today across traditional lines of race, class, sexual orientation, and national self-interest will determine the future. The church in such a time would do well to read Jonathan's story carefully.

3. Finally, this story points to God as guarantor of loyalty. Over and again, largely in the voice and witness of Jonathan, we are reminded that loyalty in human relationships finds its full meaning as commitment made in the name of the Lord. It is trust that the future is God's future that makes pain and ambiguity endurable. It is the hope that God's future will come that allows us to risk challenging the vested interests and human cowardice that, in the name of stability and convention, undermine loyalty and love. Jonathan could choose against his own self-interest and his father's restricted vision of the future because his horizon was God's future. His vision encompassed more than the present realities of homicidal father, fugitive friend, risky intercession, and tearful parting. Beyond these events, Jonathan could see God's future for Israel, and David could respond in loyal commitment even to Jonathan's descendants in trust that God's future would come. In the complexities of our own relationships, our horizons are often too limited to the human possibilities that seem available in the present moment. One of the functions of this text and of the church that reads it is to offer the horizon of God's future as hopeful possibility to those who struggle to see past the pain and ambiguity of present circumstance to suggest that there is a larger vision that our relationships can serve. Those who would offer loyal friendship in the midst of life's struggles give up self-interest and risk painful struggle not only for the sake of the friend but also for the future of God's kingdom that such loyalty makes possible.

1 Samuel 21:1–26:25, David as Fugitive

OVERVIEW

These chapters contain stories from the period of time when David was a fugitive trying to stay one step ahead of Saul. The character of David becomes more active in these stories in contrast to his largely passive role in the stories of his time in Saul's court. During this period, David gathers a personal military force around himself (22:1-5) and lives the life of an outlaw. These episodes, as a part of the history of David's rise, explain David's actions in ways that avoid public disapproval and maintain his innocence of wrongdoing.[150] David has been forced into fugitive life by the unjust pursuit of Saul. Although Saul commits violent atrocities (22:6-23), David spares Saul's life and seeks reconciliation with him (24:1-22; 26:1-

25). David receives the support of important figures, and their support shows his innocence of wrongdoing and the growing recognition of his coming kingship. Ahimelech willingly shares holy bread with him (21:1-9). The king of Moab gives him refuge (22:3-4). The prophet Gad supports him (22:5). Abiathar seeks refuge with David as a survivor of Saul's massacre at Nob, and David is in no way responsible for that act of madness (22:6-23). Abigail's resourcefulness keeps David from bloodguilt in the death of Nabal (25:1-44). Although David is a fugitive, he is not a lawless man who acts in ways inappropriate for one who would be king. Eventually, in a rare lucid moment, even Saul recognizes David's innocence and blesses him (26:21-25).

150. P. Kyle McCarter, "The Apology of David," *JBL* 99 (1980) 500.

1 Samuel 21:1-9, David and Ahimelech at Nob

NIV	NRSV
21 David went to Nob, to Ahimelech the priest. Ahimelech trembled when he met him, and asked, "Why are you alone? Why is no one with you?"	**21**[a] David came to Nob to the priest Ahimelech. Ahimelech came trembling to meet David, and said to him, "Why are you alone, and no one with you?" [2]David said to the priest Ahimelech, "The king has charged me with a matter, and said to me, 'No one must know anything of the matter about which I send you, and with which I have charged you.' I have made an appointment[b] with the young men for such and such a place. [3]Now then, what have you at hand? Give me five loaves of bread, or whatever is here." [4]The priest answered David, "I have no ordinary bread at hand, only holy bread—provided that the young men have kept themselves from women." [5]David answered the priest, "Indeed women have been kept from us as always when I go on an expedition; the vessels of the young men are holy even when it is a common journey; how much more today will their vessels be holy?" [6]So the priest gave him the holy bread; for there was no bread there except the bread of
[2]David answered Ahimelech the priest, "The king charged me with a certain matter and said to me, 'No one is to know anything about your mission and your instructions.' As for my men, I have told them to meet me at a certain place. [3]Now then, what do you have on hand? Give me five loaves of bread, or whatever you can find."	
[4]But the priest answered David, "I don't have any ordinary bread on hand; however, there is some consecrated bread here—provided the men have kept themselves from women."	
[5]David replied, "Indeed women have been kept from us, as usual whenever[a] I set out. The men's things[b] are holy even on missions that are not holy. How much more so today!" [6]So the priest gave him the consecrated bread, since there was no bread there except the bread of the Presence that had been removed from before the LORD and	

a5 Or from us in the past few days since   *b5 Or bodies*

a Ch 21.2 in Heb   *b Q Ms Vg Compare Gk: Meaning of MT uncertain*

NIV

replaced by hot bread on the day it was taken away.

⁷Now one of Saul's servants was there that day, detained before the LORD; he was Doeg the Edomite, Saul's head shepherd.

⁸David asked Ahimelech, "Don't you have a spear or a sword here? I haven't brought my sword or any other weapon, because the king's business was urgent."

⁹The priest replied, "The sword of Goliath the Philistine, whom you killed in the Valley of Elah, is here; it is wrapped in a cloth behind the ephod. If you want it, take it; there is no sword here but that one."

David said, "There is none like it; give it to me."

NRSV

the Presence, which is removed from before the LORD, to be replaced by hot bread on the day it is taken away.

7Now a certain man of the servants of Saul was there that day, detained before the LORD; his name was Doeg the Edomite, the chief of Saul's shepherds.

8David said to Ahimelech, "Is there no spear or sword here with you? I did not bring my sword or my weapons with me, because the king's business required haste." ⁹The priest said, "The sword of Goliath the Philistine, whom you killed in the valley of Elah, is here wrapped in a cloth behind the ephod; if you will take that, take it, for there is none here except that one." David said, "There is none like it; give it to me."

COMMENTARY

When David is on the run, his first encounter is with the priest Ahimelech at Nob. This is only the first portion of a dramatic story that has its tragic resolution in 22:6-23, when Saul has the entire priestly community at Nob massacred for helping David. Here we read the story of Ahimelech's assistance to David, which leads to that tragedy. In this first story of David as fugitive, we see two elements emerge that are characteristic of this entire section on David's adventures as a fugitive from Saul. First, David becomes much more proactive than he has appeared in chaps. 18–20. He is not content to react to the actions of others, but he asserts himself, often in unconventional ways. Second, Ahimelech is the first of what will be a growing list of those who recognize David as future king. This recognition is not always explicit, but David's influence is seen as broadening and his support growing. The king's own son and daughter had already helped David escape from Saul. This episode adds the aid of Ahimelech, the head of the surviving Elide priesthood that once served the ark in Shiloh.

21:1-6. David's flight brings him to Nob, where remnants of the priestly line of Eli settled after the destruction of Shiloh and the loss of the ark. Ahimelech, the leader of this priestly community, was the son of Ahitub, Eli's grandson

(22:9), and a brother of Ahijah, who carried the ephod for Saul in his earlier campaign against the Philistines (14:3, 18).

Ahimelech comes trembling with fear to meet David (v. 1). He asks David why he has come alone. It would presumably be unusual for a commander of Saul's army to be about by himself (also unarmed, as it turns out); so it is understandable that Ahimelech would fear that something was amiss. David boldly lies, claiming that Saul has sent him on a secret mission (v. 2). Ahimelech does not seem to question this statement. Word of David's fugitive status may not have been widely known at this point.

David further reveals that he has a force of men with him somewhere nearby. He needs food for himself and his men. He asks for five loaves but also expresses willingness to accept anything that is at hand (v. 3). Ahimelech answers that he has no "ordinary" bread, but only "holy" bread (v. 4). The two terms here make an important contrast that David will also use in his reply (v. 5). The word חל (ḥōl) means "ordinary," "profane," "secular" and is the opposite of קדש (qōdeš) "holy," "sacred." Ahimelech was referring to the holy bread of the presence (see v. 6), twelve loaves baked from pure wheat flour and placed before Yahweh on each sabbath. According to

Exod 25:30; 35:13; and Lev 24:5-9, such bread was to be eaten by Aaron and his sons—i.e., the priests. Ahimelech is willing to give this bread to David, but only if he has met the conditions of ritual holiness. In this case, Ahimelech inquires after only one such condition. David and his men must not have engaged recently in sexual intercourse (v. 4*b*). The laws of purity required that those in contact with holy things must observe sexual abstinence. David replies that he and his men always observe sexual abstinence when on a military mission (v. 5*a*). He is probably referring to practices associated with holy war, when those fighting a righteous cause were expected to observe certain rules of purity (see Deut 23:9-14; Josh 3:5). (Ironically, it is later Uriah's dedication in keeping himself pure for battle that prevents him from sleeping with his wife, Bathsheba, to David's annoyance and his own doom [2 Sam 11:11-12].) David tells Ahimelech that even though the mission might be "secular" (*ḥōl*) his men keep their "vessels" (bodies, sexual members?) "holy" (*qōdeš*). He implies that this is especially the case on this occasion (v. 5*b*). Ahimelech is apparently convinced by David's word on this matter. As a result, he gives David the bread of the presence as food for his men.

The text has provided an interesting play on the words for the "holy," "sacred" and the "profane," "ordinary." Ahimelech has only "holy" bread, but gives it up to those in need of "ordinary" bread. David is on an "ordinary," "common" mission, but claims to observe the rules of "holiness" and receives "holy" bread for provision. The ordinary boundaries between the sacred and the profane have been collapsed in the face of David's need and God's kingdom, which is coming in David.

Did David tell the truth? We do not really know. Jesus refers to this incident as a violation of ritual law (Matt 12:3-4; Mark 2:25-26; Luke 6:3-4), but this may not indicate that David was

impure, only that by Jesus' time ritual law reserved such holy bread only for priests, and it would not have mattered whether David and his men were ritually holy. The importance of this story does not lie so much in the truth of David's statements but in the availability of holy things for what God is doing through David. David obtains the help of the most influential priestly authority in the land. He certainly exercises a bold freedom in ritual matters, in marked contrast to Saul's behavior (see esp. chap. 14). Were Samuel to rebuke him for this incident, one cannot imagine David agonized and undone by it.

21:7-9. The episode closes with two brief notes. This exchange between David and Ahimelech is observed by Doeg, an Edomite and a servant of Saul (v. 7). Nothing is made of this now, but in 22:6-23 it is Doeg who becomes the informer to Saul of this exchange, and Doeg eventually is ordered to do Saul's dirty work of slaughtering the priests. Edomites are traditional enemies of Israel throughout the Bible, so Doeg's identity as an Edomite is probably intended to mark him for the reader as a potential villain.

David had apparently fled Saul's court in such haste that he took no weapons, and he asks Ahimelech if any can be supplied to him (v. 8). In response to this second request, Ahimelech reports that what is available is the sword of Goliath, which has been carefully kept, wrapped in fine cloth and stored behind the ephod. He offers it, and David gladly takes it (v. 9). We do not know how it came to be at Nob. This does not accord with the note in 17:54, although the LXX there reads that it was placed in the "temple of the LORD," which might indicate a sanctuary like Nob. Of greatest importance here is the way in which possession of the sword makes visible and explicit the memory of David's greatest public triumph. Power, prestige, and recognition are flowing David's way throughout these stories in spite of the sense of danger and urgency in his flight.

REFLECTIONS

In this story of David and the holy bread it is clear that David represents the future God is bringing for the sake of Israel. The laws of holiness are intended to show honor and respect for the holiness of God, but never as an end in themselves. When such rituals and traditions themselves stand in the way of God's larger purposes, they must give way to the needs of

God's kingdom. One has a sense in reading this story that Ahimelech is properly discharging his duty as keeper of holy things, but he does not question David too closely or draw the lines of ritual purity too closely (e.g., limiting the eating of the bread to priests only). He asks of David a respect for those holy traditions, but willingly gives holy things for God's purposes in a world that is itself profane and ordinary. What good are holy things if they cannot make a difference in a world where some seek to kill others and prevent the advent of God's kingdom?

For his part, David has boldly asserted that he has honored the requirements of holiness but insists on the importance of his needs in the struggles for God's kingdom taking place in the profane world. In a well-known article, Walter Brueggemann has suggested that David is put forward in the tradition as God's trusted creature. This story is one of the texts to which he points to show David modeling the freedom God has given to humankind—a freedom to seize boldly the possibilities of every moment. In David we see a man who understands that God has trusted him with his moment in history and can risk new understandings and new possibilities. In this story, David

> breaks the notion of "holy" away from the shrine and moves it out into the normal affairs of men. . . . David is not bound by the normal notion of what is *qōdeš*. He subordinates that conventional notion to the problem at hand, namely his safe get-away. . . . If *qōdeš* still functions as a meaningful term, it now means the well-being of his party on the way to royal power. Against the narrower notions of holy which had been held he risks a new understanding . . . . Both David and Jesus overturn conventional notions of what is sacred.[151]

Notions of the holy are still often held within the sanctuary and the traditions of institutional religious practice. David's story asserts that holiness received in the sanctuary can make holy the struggles of the ordinary, and it is in that wider, profane world that God is bringing the kingdom. But make no mistake—it is risky business to discern and choose for what God is doing in the world and to offer the sanctuary's holy resources for the sake of God's work in the world. We will see this in its starkest terms when the story of Nob continues to its tragic end in chap. 22. Then we must return to reflect on the cost of leaving the enclave of the sanctuary to become involved in the coming of the kingdom.

In the Gospels, Jesus uses this story of David in one of his earliest confrontations with the Pharisees (Mark 2:23-28; Luke 6:1-5; Matthew puts it later in Jesus' ministry, Matt 12:1-8). He was confronted by the religious leaders for plucking grain on the sabbath. Jesus appealed to the example of David, who, in need of food, ate the bread of the presence, "which it was not lawful for any but the priests to eat," and gave it to his companions. In the Gospel of Mark, Jesus then states that "the sabbath was made for humankind, not humankind for the sabbath" (Mark 2:27). For Jesus in Mark's Gospel, human need takes priority over ritual observance, and he implies, in approval of David, that laws of ritual holiness are subordinate not only to human need but also to the larger purposes and priorities demanded by God's kingdom. In all three of the Gospel accounts, Jesus proclaims that "the Son of Man is Lord of the sabbath." David's bold redefinition of holiness stands as a precedent for a christological claim that Jesus, the son of David, has likewise redefined holiness in keeping with the needs of God's kingdom rather than the requirements for ritual holiness or sacred institution. To oppose the powers that defend such ritual holiness is, however, serious business. For Jesus, this leads to the cross; for David, this act leads to a later massacre of all of the priests at Nob (22:6-23).

151. Walter Brueggemann, "The Trusted Creature," *CBQ* 31 (1969) 488-89.

1 Samuel 21:10-15, David Plays the Madman

NIV

¹⁰That day David fled from Saul and went to Achish king of Gath. ¹¹But the servants of Achish said to him, "Isn't this David, the king of the land? Isn't he the one they sing about in their dances:

" 'Saul has slain his thousands,
  and David his tens of thousands'?"

¹²David took these words to heart and was very much afraid of Achish king of Gath. ¹³So he pretended to be insane in their presence; and while he was in their hands he acted like a madman, making marks on the doors of the gate and letting saliva run down his beard.

¹⁴Achish said to his servants, "Look at the man! He is insane! Why bring him to me? ¹⁵Am I so short of madmen that you have to bring this fellow here to carry on like this in front of me? Must this man come into my house?"

NRSV

10David rose and fled that day from Saul; he went to King Achish of Gath. ¹¹The servants of Achish said to him, "Is this not David the king of the land? Did they not sing to one another of him in dances,

'Saul has killed his thousands,
  and David his ten thousands'?"

¹²David took these words to heart and was very much afraid of King Achish of Gath. ¹³So he changed his behavior before them; he pretended to be mad when in their presence.ᵃ He scratched marks on the doors of the gate, and let his spittle run down his beard. ¹⁴Achish said to his servants, "Look, you see the man is mad; why then have you brought him to me? ¹⁵Do I lack madmen, that you have brought this fellow to play the madman in my presence? Shall this fellow come into my house?"

ᵃ Heb *in their hands*

COMMENTARY

This brief and strange episode adds Achish, the Philistine king of Gath, to the growing list of those who recognize David as king. The use of the term "king" (מלך *melek*) for David by the servants of Achish (v. 11) is sometimes taken as a textual mistake (an editorial slip, a redactional inconsistency). More likely it is but one more addition to the growing list of those who clearly see David as Israel's future and know Saul is king in name only.

Why did David go to Gath? We are not told. Perhaps he sought anonymity and safety from Saul by hiring himself out as mercenary to Achish, the king of Gath. He does this at a later point, but with full knowledge of his identity by Achish. Achish accepted his service and placed David in charge of Ziklag (27:1–28:2). In this story, one of the points seems to be the growing reputation and recognition of David. He cannot hide—even in a non-Israelite setting. The servants of Achish (Philistines no less) not only recognize him, but pronounce him the king of the land (as opposed to Saul, who thinks he is). They even know the

songs sung in celebration of David's killing of their fellow Philistines (v. 11)!

David makes a quick assessment of this situation and decides he has miscalculated in thinking Gath was a place he could hide. He is afraid, as well he should have been (v. 12). Thinking quickly (our more active David in this section), he bangs/marks/spits on the gateposts (translators read this difficult text differently) and lets spit dribble down his beard. In short, he acts insane. He acts like a fool while they try to restrain him (v. 13). The strategy works. Achish, thinking David mad, announces that he has enough madmen without bringing one more into the house. Apparently they release him, since 22:1 has him escaping from there to another place. No doubt this story was told with the intent to ridicule the Philistines as well—"Don't we all know those Philistines have more than their share of madmen?"

This brief story serves to introduce Achish, who plays a larger role later in the story. It shows David as resourceful when in danger. That the

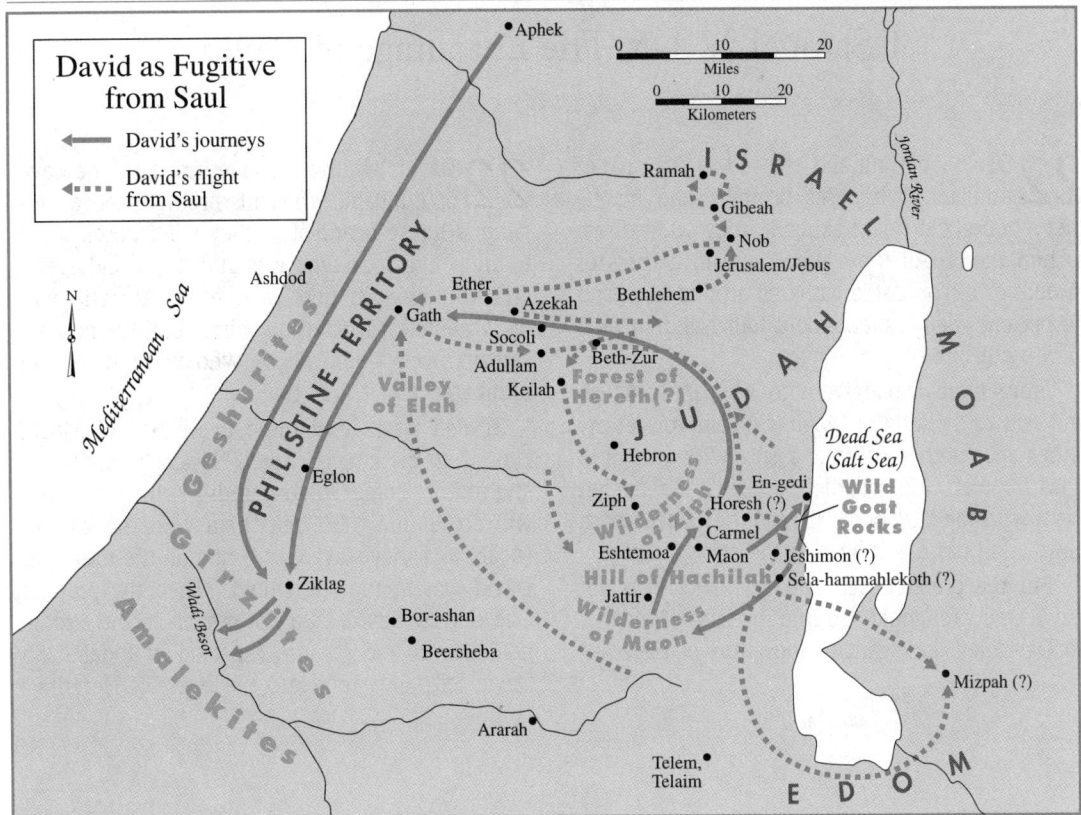

Map: David as Fugitive from Saul. Legend — David's journeys; David's flight from Saul. Labeled locations include Aphek, Ramah, Gibeah, Nob, Jerusalem/Jebus, Bethlehem, Ashdod, Ether, Azekah, Gath, Socoli, Beth-Zur, Adullam, Keilah, Forest of Hereth(?), Eglon, Hebron, Ziph, Horesh(?), En-gedi, Wild Goat Rocks, Dead Sea (Salt Sea), Ziklag, Eshtemoa, Carmel, Maon, Jeshimon(?), Sela-hammahlekoth(?), Jattir, Bor-ashan, Beersheba, Hill of Hachilah, Wilderness of Maon, Wilderness of Ziph, Telem, Telaim, Ararah, Mizpah(?), and regions Israel, Judah, Moab, Edom, Philistine Territory, Geshurites, Girzites, Amalekites, Mediterranean Sea, Jordan River, Wadi Besor, Valley of Elah.

story, though brief, was enjoyed by Israel is reflected by two references to it in the superscriptions of Psalms 34 and 56. But the greatest significance of this odd encounter lies in the growing accumulation of witnesses to David's coming kingship. David is God's anointed one. Samuel knows it. Jonathan and Michal know it. Many in Israel seem to sense it, even if they do not fully recognize it. Ahimelech seems to know it. Now even the nations begin to acknowledge God's anointed one. What the Philistines see in David is not a fugitive but the king of the land (v. 11), and a moment later "a madman." This strategy bespeaks cleverness on David's part, but in the larger biblical drama the nations often see the ways of God's anointed and the coming of God's kingdom as madness.

REFLECTIONS

This strange episode comes immediately after David's bold redefinition of holiness in the taking of the bread of presence for food (see Reflections at 21:1-9). David's masquerade as a madman reminds us of the odd form holiness can sometimes take. The Philistines discern the truth of David as Israel's future king, but they dismiss its significance because his madness does not fit their definition of a threat to their interests. Likewise, we may often see God's holy purpose at work in the world, but ignore its significance because it does not fit our expectations for the activities of grace. Many great figures in the history of the church have been considered "mad" for their actions, only to have history judge them to have been instruments of God's holy purposes. This is an odd tale, but it is the first recognition of David's kingship by the nations. To the nations, God's anointed one seems a harmless madman. To proclaim a crucified criminal as God's anointed one (Messiah) must have seemed equally mad to the nations in Jesus' time.

1 Samuel 22:1-5, The Entourage of David

NIV

22 David left Gath and escaped to the cave of Adullam. When his brothers and his father's household heard about it, they went down to him there. ²All those who were in distress or in debt or discontented gathered around him, and he became their leader. About four hundred men were with him.

³From there David went to Mizpah in Moab and said to the king of Moab, "Would you let my father and mother come and stay with you until I learn what God will do for me?" ⁴So he left them with the king of Moab, and they stayed with him as long as David was in the stronghold.

⁵But the prophet Gad said to David, "Do not stay in the stronghold. Go into the land of Judah." So David left and went to the forest of Hereth.

NRSV

22 David left there and escaped to the cave of Adullam; when his brothers and all his father's house heard of it, they went down there to him. ²Everyone who was in distress, and everyone who was in debt, and everyone who was discontented gathered to him; and he became captain over them. Those who were with him numbered about four hundred.

3David went from there to Mizpeh of Moab. He said to the king of Moab, "Please let my father and mother come[a] to you, until I know what God will do for me." ⁴He left them with the king of Moab, and they stayed with him all the time that David was in the stronghold. ⁵Then the prophet Gad said to David, "Do not remain in the stronghold; leave, and go into the land of Judah." So David left, and went into the forest of Hereth.

ᵃ Syr Vg: Heb *come out*

COMMENTARY

This brief portion of the story consists of two short notes. The first tells of the growing entourage that begins to form around David (vv. 1-2). The second reports on David's brief trip to Moab, apparently to take his parents out of harm's way (vv. 3-5). These notes continue the accumulation of witnesses and support that David is gathering.

22:1-2. David takes refuge in the cave of Adullam. Although the precise location is uncertain, it was definitely in the tribal territory of Judah, probably somewhere between Hebron and Gath. From this location David could get word to his family. Hence, we are not surprised to learn that he is joined by his brothers and all of his father's household (v. 1). They could well have been in danger from Saul's anger at David. This seems confirmed when David moves his own parents to Moab for a while (v. 3). David seems to have had the unqualified support of his family throughout his career. Even the quarrel with Eliab in 17:28-30 is not a serious division, but only the natural squabbling of older and younger brothers.

Of greater interest is the notice (v. 2) that David is joined in his fugitive enclave by the distressed, the indebted, and the discontent. David becomes their leader, and their number grows to four hundred (later to six hundred, 23:13; 25:13; 27:2; 30:9-10). In short, David's personal force is made up of those who are marginal or outcast in society. This group is the beginning of a personal military force that David maintained as loyal to him and that stood apart from the kingdom's own military even after he became king. The origins of this group suggest that there may have been a socioeconomic basis to the conflict between David and Saul in addition to personal jealousy and animosity. David, as an eighth son of a rather undistinguished family, may be seen as the hero and champion of socially and economically marginal groups over against wealthier landholders. Certainly Saul continues to avoid David's name and call him a "son of Jesse," as if this were derogatory (see 22:7), which may indicate a contempt for David's humble birth and lack of social position. The rise of David may threaten social realignment in Israel. Mendenhall has taken this text and others as evidence that David is a "Hebrew," a term used in a derogatory way about groups that live as outlaws without social status or power.[152] There may also be a northern Israel/southern Judah split reflected here as David begins building a southern, Judean, power base for himself; Saul was from the northern tribe of Benjamin.

22:3-5. David apparently enjoys friendly relations with Moab. He makes a trip to Mizpeh, where he asks the king of Moab to keep his father and mother safe until he is clear about his future (v. 1). Of course, the book of Ruth preserves a tradition that David's own great-grandmother was a Moabite woman (Ruth 4:18-22). It is noteworthy that in asking for this favor David again casually expresses confidence that his future is in God's hands: "until I know what God will do for me" (v. 1*b*). He does not view the kingdom as

something he seizes by his own efforts, but constantly sees the possibilities of his future as expressions of God's will. David does leave his parents in Moab for a time, although it is uncertain what is meant by the phrase "all the time that David was in the stronghold" (v. 4). Now the king of Moab has been added to the list of those who seem to support David as the future of Israel. David's influence and political base are broadening.

Suddenly a prophet named Gad appears and orders David back to Judah (v. 5). We know nothing about Gad; later he functions as a court prophet during the reign of David (2 Sam 24:11-19). This small note is significant in two ways. First, it indicates prophetic support for David, along with his anointing by Samuel and the incident at Ramah (19:18-24). Second, it moves David back into Judah, where the remaining drama of David's rise to kingship will be played out and where David will build his own base of support.

152. George M. Mendenhall, "The 'Vengeance' of Yahweh," in *The Tenth Generation: The Origins of the Biblical Tradition* (Baltimore: Johns Hopkins University Press, 1973) 135-38.

REFLECTIONS

We cannot read this notice in 1 Sam 22:2 about David's attracting to himself the outcasts of the land without remembering that Jesus, the son of David, also attracted the outcasts of his time. There is a word about the nature of God's kingdom as opposed to human kingdoms here. God's kingdom does not find its membership in the usual patterns of power and influence. It is often "the least of these" who become significant, and the "last will become first." David is clear in the midst of the mundane concerns of these verses that his kingdom will be a result of what "God will do for me." It will not be of his own making.

This is an important reminder about the nature of God's people and God's kingdom for a time like ours, when strategies of church growth urge homogeneity and upward mobility as growth principles. I am certain that those gathering to David did not look in his time like a formula designed for success. Certainly, the representatives of institutional religion in Jesus' time did not think he was making wise choices about those who became associated with him. But if David and Jesus drew the troubled and the outcast to themselves because they offered hope and new life to all, can the church in our time do less and still serve the kingdom of God? "Come to me, all you that are weary and are carrying heavy burdens, and I will give you rest" (Matt 11:28 NRSV).

1 Samuel 22:6-23, Saul Massacres the Priests at Nob

NIV	NRSV
⁶Now Saul heard that David and his men had been discovered. And Saul, spear in hand, was seated under the tamarisk tree on the hill at	6Saul heard that David and those who were with him had been located. Saul was sitting at Gibeah, under the tamarisk tree on the height,

Gibeah, with all his officials standing around him. [7]Saul said to them, "Listen, men of Benjamin! Will the son of Jesse give all of you fields and vineyards? Will he make all of you commanders of thousands and commanders of hundreds? [8]Is that why you have all conspired against me? No one tells me when my son makes a covenant with the son of Jesse. None of you is concerned about me or tells me that my son has incited my servant to lie in wait for me, as he does today."

[9]But Doeg the Edomite, who was standing with Saul's officials, said, "I saw the son of Jesse come to Ahimelech son of Ahitub at Nob. [10]Ahimelech inquired of the LORD for him; he also gave him provisions and the sword of Goliath the Philistine."

[11]Then the king sent for the priest Ahimelech son of Ahitub and his father's whole family, who were the priests at Nob, and they all came to the king. [12]Saul said, "Listen now, son of Ahitub."

"Yes, my lord," he answered.

[13]Saul said to him, "Why have you conspired against me, you and the son of Jesse, giving him bread and a sword and inquiring of God for him, so that he has rebelled against me and lies in wait for me, as he does today?"

[14]Ahimelech answered the king, "Who of all your servants is as loyal as David, the king's son-in-law, captain of your bodyguard and highly respected in your household? [15]Was that day the first time I inquired of God for him? Of course not! Let not the king accuse your servant or any of his father's family, for your servant knows nothing at all about this whole affair."

[16]But the king said, "You will surely die, Ahimelech, you and your father's whole family."

[17]Then the king ordered the guards at his side: "Turn and kill the priests of the LORD, because they too have sided with David. They knew he was fleeing, yet they did not tell me."

But the king's officials were not willing to raise a hand to strike the priests of the LORD.

[18]The king then ordered Doeg, "You turn and strike down the priests." So Doeg the Edomite turned and struck them down. That day he killed eighty-five men who wore the linen ephod. [19]He also put to the sword Nob, the town of the priests,

with his spear in his hand, and all his servants were standing around him. [7]Saul said to his servants who stood around him, "Hear now, you Benjaminites; will the son of Jesse give every one of you fields and vineyards, will he make you all commanders of thousands and commanders of hundreds? [8]Is that why all of you have conspired against me? No one discloses to me when my son makes a league with the son of Jesse, none of you is sorry for me or discloses to me that my son has stirred up my servant against me, to lie in wait, as he is doing today." [9]Doeg the Edomite, who was in charge of Saul's servants, answered, "I saw the son of Jesse coming to Nob, to Ahimelech son of Ahitub; [10]he inquired of the LORD for him, gave him provisions, and gave him the sword of Goliath the Philistine."

11The king sent for the priest Ahimelech son of Ahitub and for all his father's house, the priests who were at Nob; and all of them came to the king. [12]Saul said, "Listen now, son of Ahitub." He answered, "Here I am, my lord." [13]Saul said to him, "Why have you conspired against me, you and the son of Jesse, by giving him bread and a sword, and by inquiring of God for him, so that he has risen against me, to lie in wait, as he is doing today?"

14Then Ahimelech answered the king, "Who among all your servants is so faithful as David? He is the king's son-in-law, and is quick[a] to do your bidding, and is honored in your house. [15]Is today the first time that I have inquired of God for him? By no means! Do not let the king impute anything to his servant or to any member of my father's house; for your servant has known nothing of all this, much or little." [16]The king said, "You shall surely die, Ahimelech, you and all your father's house." [17]The king said to the guard who stood around him, "Turn and kill the priests of the LORD, because their hand also is with David; they knew that he fled, and did not disclose it to me." But the servants of the king would not raise their hand to attack the priests of the LORD. [18]Then the king said to Doeg, "You, Doeg, turn and attack the priests." Doeg the Edomite turned and attacked the priests; on that day he killed eighty-five who wore the linen ephod. [19]Nob, the city of the

a Heb *and turns aside*

with its men and women, its children and infants, and its cattle, donkeys and sheep.

²⁰But Abiathar, a son of Ahimelech son of Ahitub, escaped and fled to join David. ²¹He told David that Saul had killed the priests of the LORD. ²²Then David said to Abiathar: "That day, when Doeg the Edomite was there, I knew he would be sure to tell Saul. I am responsible for the death of your father's whole family. ²³Stay with me; don't be afraid; the man who is seeking your life is seeking mine also. You will be safe with me."

priests, he put to the sword; men and women, children and infants, oxen, donkeys, and sheep, he put to the sword.

20But one of the sons of Ahimelech son of Ahitub, named Abiathar, escaped and fled after David. ²¹Abiathar told David that Saul had killed the priests of the LORD. ²²David said to Abiathar, "I knew on that day, when Doeg the Edomite was there, that he would surely tell Saul. I am responsible*a* for the lives of all your father's house. ²³Stay with me, and do not be afraid; for the one who seeks my life seeks your life; you will be safe with me."

a Gk Vg: Meaning of Heb uncertain

COMMENTARY

This episode resumes the story line begun in 21:1-9. Doeg the Edomite, who saw David with Ahimelech (21:7), reports this meeting to Saul. The consequences are tragic. In this story, Saul hits bottom in his madness. He is possessed by his violent obsession with David and is out of control. We suspected something ominous might come from the note about Doeg in 21:7, but as readers we are shocked at the massacre that results. In the larger context, David has been gaining support from key figures and broadening his base among the people. Here we see Saul alienating and turning against his own support.

22:6-10. Saul is at Gibeah, his hometown and capital. As is frequently the case, Saul holds a spear (18:10; 19:9, 10; 26:7-8, 11-12, 16; 2 Sam 1:6). He has already hurled it at David and Jonathan on separate occasions. He is sitting beneath a tamarisk tree, and his servants are around him (v. 6). Saul addresses them as "Benjaminites," suggesting that this group is made up only of those closest to Saul, his own tribesmen and kinfolk (v. 7). Saul seems to be brooding. The immediate tone of his address to these close servants is accusatory. He asks a rhetorical question (Will David reward you?), followed by an amazing accusation: "Is that why all of you have conspired against me?" (v. 8*a*). He apparently believes that all of these kinsmen in his service would conspire against him for gain. The suggestion must have

been a shock. It was customary to reward service with land and promotion to military command. Surely Saul had already done so for some of these. Perhaps he is calling to their attention that David, a fugitive, can hardly offer such reward.

Saul's bill of particulars for the charge of conspiracy includes the accusation that none of them have disclosed the covenant (NRSV, "league") made between his son Jonathan and David (whom Saul only refers to disparagingly as "son of Jesse"), or that Jonathan has stirred David up "to lie in wait" (v. 8). This means that Saul believes his own son is plotting with his enemy for his death, an accusation we, as readers, know is untrue. This reference may be preparing us for the two stories in which David does, indeed, have the life of Saul in his hand, but refuses to take the life of God's anointed one (chaps. 24 and 26). There is a pathetic quality to Saul's speech. At one point (v. 8*b*) he pleads, "None of you is sorry for me." Saul seems to know about the commitment of Jonathan in loyalty to David. They had already confronted each other over this matter (20:30-34). Saul's madness seems to have taken a paranoid turn. He imagines that Jonathan's commitment to David is a plot to ambush him, and he accuses his own men of knowing about this. This must have seemed outrageous and unwarranted to Saul's men. In the text, they remain speechless.

It is Doeg, a non-Israelite, an Edomite, who

finds his tongue. In v. 9 he reports having seen David with Ahimelech at Nob, and he levels three charges. He claims that Ahimelech "inquired of the LORD" for David, gave him provisions, and gave him the sword of Goliath (v. 10). We know the last two of these to be true based on the account in 21:1-9. It is the first we have heard of the first charge, although Ahimelech later seems to admit that it is true (v. 15). "To inquire of the LORD" means to seek an oracle of guidance, in this case for David. This is a function associated with priests or prophets, and persons presumably would seek them out to make such inquiries. As we have seen before in 1 Samuel, there is an ironic play on words here, since the verb שָׁאַל (*šā'al*, "to ask," "to inquire") is the root of Saul's own name. While Saul was seeking David, David was seeking a *šā'al* from Ahimelech.

22:11-19. Saul demands the appearance not only of Ahimelech but also of the entire company of priests who live at Nob (v. 11). These priests are the remnants of the house of Eli. According to 14:3, Ahimelech's brother Ahijah has accompanied Saul on his Philistine campaigns and used the ephod to help give him guidance. There is little to suggest that this entire Elide priesthood had been anything other than completely loyal to Saul. Yet, when Saul greets Ahimelech, it is with a contemptuous command to "Listen!" and a refusal to use his name. Ahimelech respectfully makes himself available and refers to Saul as "my lord" (v. 12), but Saul without preamble accuses him of conspiracy and repeats the three charges made by Doeg. Saul adds to this his own paranoid notion that this enables David to "lie in wait" to ambush Saul.

Ahimelech's response and defense are extraordinary and masterful. He defends himself by defending David's innocence (v. 14). Why should he not receive and aid David? David is known as the most faithful of Saul's servants; he is the king's son-in-law; he is the commander of Saul's bodyguard (NIV, reading with the LXX; the NRSV adopts a strange translation here that has no textual support). He is honored in the royal household. Ahimelech could well imagine that he would be in trouble should he not aid one such as this. It should be noted that throughout his speech, Ahimelech, in contrast to Saul, always uses David's name.

Ahimelech continues his defense by appealing to precedent (v. 15a). He admits inquiring of the Lord for David, but argues that he has done it many times before. Further, he claims that he and his whole priestly house knew nothing of the enmity between Saul and David (v. 15b). He had no reason to think things had changed from his previous dealings with David. Throughout this last plea, Ahimelech refers to himself as Saul's "servant."

Saul does not hesitate for a moment. There is no discussion, no debate. The sentence is death, presumably for treason against the king, and it is death not just for Ahimelech but for the entire company of priests (v. 16). The hesitation comes not from Saul, but from the king's own royal bodyguard. Saul orders them to carry out the death sentence, and they refuse (v. 17). It is a telling moment in Saul's story. He is now isolated in his madness from his own men. They will not attack priests of the Lord. Their respect for God's priests is greater than Saul's. Saul is alone in his obsession. Almost pathetically Saul turns in his isolation to Doeg the Edomite (v. 18). He has no stake in priests of the Lord, so he does Saul's bidding and slaughters eighty-five priests that day (v. 19). Tradition amplifies the horror of this moment; the LXX reads 305 priests, and Josephus reads 385 priests. The massacre is carried to the city of Nob itself, which Saul puts to the sword, killing men, women, children, and livestock (v. 20). Saul, who disobeyed the command to put the Amalekites to the ban (חרם *ḥērem;* see chap. 15), now totally exterminates the remaining members of the priestly family, who served before the ark of the covenant, as if they were the enemies of the Lord. Saul's mad act brings to sad fulfillment the judgment pronounced on the house of Eli in 2:31-32.

22:20-23. The judgment against the house of Eli speaks of one who would escape to weep and grieve (1 Sam 2:33). This prediction is fulfilled when Abiathar, the son of Ahimelech, escapes the massacre and flees to David (v. 20) and reports the news of this tragedy to David (v. 21). In contrast to Saul's irresponsible actions, David immediately takes the responsibility (v. 22). He remembers seeing Doeg, and he says flatly, "I am responsible for the lives of all your father's house." It is Saul who has acted like a criminal, and it is

David who acts like a king. David receives Abiathar into his entourage with reassurance, along with the warning that Abiathar is now marked by Saul even as David is marked (v. 23).

REFLECTIONS

What can be said about the violent madness seen in a story such as this? We want to cry out in protest. Truthfully we want God to do something about it—to intervene. After all, we have seen constant evidences of God's hand moving David toward Israel's future. We have seen God rejecting Saul, and an evil spirit from God coming to plague him. Is not God in control here? But in the books of Samuel, God is at work largely through and in spite of human agency. God does not remove either David or Saul from responsibility for his own actions. Even the evil spirit that plagues Saul is an indication of his alienation from divine power and the guidance of God's Spirit, but it is not in evidence as a coercive power making Saul's decisions for him.

The hard truth of this terrible story is that Saul has become an evil man. He was not inherently so or destined to be so. He is not devoid of qualities even now that arouse our sympathy. But he has become evil in the obsessive desire to maintain his hold on power. At its worst, evil cannot distinguish between friend and foe, and now Saul has turned on his allies and imagines conspiracy from his friends. The outcome is terrible to behold.

The hard truth of human freedom is that God does not stay the hand of one bent on evil. God does not intervene to save the priests of Nob, whose lives are devoted to the service of the Lord. In our own century, we wish that God had stayed the hand of evil—in the holocaust deaths of millions in the death camps, in the genocidal wars and ethnic cleansings of resurgent tribalism and nationalism, in Vietnamese villages destroyed in misbegotten efforts to save them—but God has not intervened. In our time, as in Saul's, human freedom may be used for evil. The desire to gain or maintain power over others still leads to acts of mindless violence.

God does not intervene to prevent the possibilities of evil in the service of power. In 1 Samuel, God is at work making clear that Israel's future of promise lies with David and that Saul cannot be that future. But God, in these stories, works through human agency. If God is with David, it is not to supernaturally predetermine his successes. They are the product of David's gifts used in the service of God. Unfortunately, this story is centered on a man alienated from God, and God does not limit what Saul can do in the grip of evil and madness. The trust that God gives in human freedom, which is apparent in the books of Samuel, means that such freedom can be used for good or for evil. We know this is also true in our own time, for acts of terrible violence are a part of our daily news. If God is present at such times, it is not to make decisions or to determine actions for us. It is to support and enable the response of good in the face of evil. It is to provide alternatives for our future that move away from evil.

In this story, David models what is required in the face of evil. David takes responsibility for what has come to pass and moves on toward God's future. The violence was Saul's, but it is David who says, "I am responsible." The priests of Nob are tragically gone, but Abiathar can be sheltered, and a different kingdom from Saul's can be brought into being. The realities of evil are evident in every generation. The names Auschwitz, My Lai, Soweto, Hiroshima, Belfast, Sarajevo, Rwanda, Mogadishu, and Selma are a partial roll call of evil in our own time. Those who would participate in the bringing of God's future cannot be those who say, "We had nothing to do with those things." God's future lies with those who, like David, say, "We are responsible." It is a choosing of responsibility when the perpetrators of evil have chosen irresponsibility. As David then offered to Abiathar, we must also then offer the vision of a future free from fear, allied with life, and safe for all (1 Sam 22:23).

1 Samuel 23:1-29, Narrow Escapes from Saul

NIV

23 When David was told, "Look, the Philistines are fighting against Keilah and are looting the threshing floors," ²he inquired of the LORD, saying, "Shall I go and attack these Philistines?"

The LORD answered him, "Go, attack the Philistines and save Keilah."

³But David's men said to him, "Here in Judah we are afraid. How much more, then, if we go to Keilah against the Philistine forces!"

⁴Once again David inquired of the LORD, and the LORD answered him, "Go down to Keilah, for I am going to give the Philistines into your hand." ⁵So David and his men went to Keilah, fought the Philistines and carried off their livestock. He inflicted heavy losses on the Philistines and saved the people of Keilah. ⁶(Now Abiathar son of Ahimelech had brought the ephod down with him when he fled to David at Keilah.)

⁷Saul was told that David had gone to Keilah, and he said, "God has handed him over to me, for David has imprisoned himself by entering a town with gates and bars." ⁸And Saul called up all his forces for battle, to go down to Keilah to besiege David and his men.

⁹When David learned that Saul was plotting against him, he said to Abiathar the priest, "Bring the ephod." ¹⁰David said, "O LORD, God of Israel, your servant has heard definitely that Saul plans to come to Keilah and destroy the town on account of me. ¹¹Will the citizens of Keilah surrender me to him? Will Saul come down, as your servant has heard? O LORD, God of Israel, tell your servant."

And the LORD said, "He will."

¹²Again David asked, "Will the citizens of Keilah surrender me and my men to Saul?"

And the LORD said, "They will."

¹³So David and his men, about six hundred in number, left Keilah and kept moving from place to place. When Saul was told that David had escaped from Keilah, he did not go there.

¹⁴David stayed in the desert strongholds and in the hills of the Desert of Ziph. Day after day Saul searched for him, but God did not give David into his hands.

NRSV

23 Now they told David, "The Philistines are fighting against Keilah, and are robbing the threshing floors." ²David inquired of the LORD, "Shall I go and attack these Philistines?" The LORD said to David, "Go and attack the Philistines and save Keilah." ³But David's men said to him, "Look, we are afraid here in Judah; how much more then if we go to Keilah against the armies of the Philistines?" ⁴Then David inquired of the LORD again. The LORD answered him, "Yes, go down to Keilah; for I will give the Philistines into your hand." ⁵So David and his men went to Keilah, fought with the Philistines, brought away their livestock, and dealt them a heavy defeat. Thus David rescued the inhabitants of Keilah.

6When Abiathar son of Ahimelech fled to David at Keilah, he came down with an ephod in his hand. ⁷Now it was told Saul that David had come to Keilah. And Saul said, "God has given[a] him into my hand; for he has shut himself in by entering a town that has gates and bars." ⁸Saul summoned all the people to war, to go down to Keilah, to besiege David and his men. ⁹When David learned that Saul was plotting evil against him, he said to the priest Abiathar, "Bring the ephod here." ¹⁰David said, "O LORD, the God of Israel, your servant has heard that Saul seeks to come to Keilah, to destroy the city on my account. ¹¹And now, will[b] Saul come down as your servant has heard? O LORD, the God of Israel, I beseech you, tell your servant." The LORD said, "He will come down." ¹²Then David said, "Will the men of Keilah surrender me and my men into the hand of Saul?" The LORD said, "They will surrender you." ¹³Then David and his men, who were about six hundred, set out and left Keilah; they wandered wherever they could go. When Saul was told that David had escaped from Keilah, he gave up the expedition. ¹⁴David remained in the strongholds in the wilderness, in the hill country of the Wilderness of Ziph. Saul sought him every day, but the LORD[c] did not give him into his hand.

15David was in the Wilderness of Ziph at Horesh

a Gk Tg: Heb *made a stranger of*   *b* Q Ms Compare Gk: MT *Will the men of Keilah surrender me into his hand? Will*   *c* Q Ms Gk: MT *God*

¹⁵While David was at Horesh in the Desert of Ziph, he learned that Saul had come out to take his life. ¹⁶And Saul's son Jonathan went to David at Horesh and helped him find strength in God. ¹⁷"Don't be afraid," he said. "My father Saul will not lay a hand on you. You will be king over Israel, and I will be second to you. Even my father Saul knows this." ¹⁸The two of them made a covenant before the LORD. Then Jonathan went home, but David remained at Horesh.

¹⁹The Ziphites went up to Saul at Gibeah and said, "Is not David hiding among us in the strongholds at Horesh, on the hill of Hakilah, south of Jeshimon? ²⁰Now, O king, come down whenever it pleases you to do so, and we will be responsible for handing him over to the king."

²¹Saul replied, "The LORD bless you for your concern for me. ²²Go and make further preparation. Find out where David usually goes and who has seen him there. They tell me he is very crafty. ²³Find out about all the hiding places he uses and come back to me with definite information.^a Then I will go with you; if he is in the area, I will track him down among all the clans of Judah."

²⁴So they set out and went to Ziph ahead of Saul. Now David and his men were in the Desert of Maon, in the Arabah south of Jeshimon. ²⁵Saul and his men began the search, and when David was told about it, he went down to the rock and stayed in the Desert of Maon. When Saul heard this, he went into the Desert of Maon in pursuit of David.

²⁶Saul was going along one side of the mountain, and David and his men were on the other side, hurrying to get away from Saul. As Saul and his forces were closing in on David and his men to capture them, ²⁷a messenger came to Saul, saying, "Come quickly! The Philistines are raiding the land." ²⁸Then Saul broke off his pursuit of David and went to meet the Philistines. That is why they call this place Sela Hammahlekoth.^b ²⁹And David went up from there and lived in the strongholds of En Gedi.

^a23 Or *me at Nacon*   ^b28 *Sela Hammahlekoth* means *rock of parting.*

when he learned that^a Saul had come out to seek his life. ¹⁶Saul's son Jonathan set out and came to David at Horesh; there he strengthened his hand through the LORD.^b ¹⁷He said to him, "Do not be afraid; for the hand of my father Saul shall not find you; you shall be king over Israel, and I shall be second to you; my father Saul also knows that this is so." ¹⁸Then the two of them made a covenant before the LORD; David remained at Horesh, and Jonathan went home.

¹⁹Then some Ziphites went up to Saul at Gibeah and said, "David is hiding among us in the strongholds of Horesh, on the hill of Hachilah, which is south of Jeshimon. ²⁰Now, O king, whenever you wish to come down, do so; and our part will be to surrender him into the king's hand." ²¹Saul said, "May you be blessed by the LORD for showing me compassion! ²²Go and make sure once more; find out exactly where he is, and who has seen him there; for I am told that he is very cunning. ²³Look around and learn all the hiding places where he lurks, and come back to me with sure information. Then I will go with you; and if he is in the land, I will search him out among all the thousands of Judah." ²⁴So they set out and went to Ziph ahead of Saul.

David and his men were in the wilderness of Maon, in the Arabah to the south of Jeshimon. ²⁵Saul and his men went to search for him. When David was told, he went down to the rock and stayed in the wilderness of Maon. When Saul heard that, he pursued David into the wilderness of Maon. ²⁶Saul went on one side of the mountain, and David and his men on the other side of the mountain. David was hurrying to get away from Saul, while Saul and his men were closing in on David and his men to capture them. ²⁷Then a messenger came to Saul, saying, "Hurry and come; for the Philistines have made a raid on the land." ²⁸So Saul stopped pursuing David, and went against the Philistines; therefore that place was called the Rock of Escape.^c ^{29d}David then went up from there, and lived in the strongholds of En-gedi.

^aOr *saw that*   ^bCompare Q Ms Gk: MT *God*   ^cOr *Rock of Division;* Meaning of Heb uncertain   ^dCh 24.1 in Heb

COMMENTARY

On first glance this chapter has nothing new to tell us. Saul—still obsessive and dangerous—is pursuing David. David stays just out of Saul's reach by virtue of his own wits and astute judgment. At first this seems to be just another chase and escape episode. But on second reading, some important additions to the portrayal of David's character appear. In his rescue of the inhabitants of Keilah (vv. 1-5), David risks his own best interests for the sake of others in need. There seems to be little to gain politically, and Keilah does not prove grateful or reliable (v. 12). David, however, shows himself capable of more than pragmatic, political self-interest. In addition, the entire episode with Keilah shows David engaged in an ongoing exchange with God that seems both natural and comfortable. He inquires of God as a matter of course in important matters. We have seen David gaining support throughout the preceding chapters. Although he is a fugitive, it is clear that David is Israel's future and Saul is in decline. Now v. 14*b* makes clear why Saul cannot succeed in his efforts to destroy David, "Saul sought him every day but the LORD did not give him into his hand." What we witness here is not constant divine, supernatural intervention. It is the simple truth that David, as a man who inquires naturally and regularly of God, has the strength of faith at his disposal. Along with his own courage and resourcefulness David has the resources of his own trustful relationship with God, and for the narrator of these chapters that makes all the difference between David and Saul. God is committed to David as Israel's future and is present in these events to bring that future to pass, but David must trust and act in accord with that divine commitment. It is not enough to trust in his own considerable gifts. Saul, however, has given in entirely to his own self-interested need for power and to violence in support of maintaining that power.

23:1-5. A report reaches David that the Judean city Keilah is under attack by the Philistines, who were apparently taking grain from the threshing floors (v. 1). Keilah was in the region of Judah, close to Philistine territory and vulnerable to attack. Faced with a situation calling for action, David prays. He asks God if he should go to Keilah's aid. God's answer is, "Yes! Go! Save them!" (v. 2). We are not told the means of inquiry. It may have been by use of the ephod in the possession of Abiathar and mentioned in v. 6 (see chap. 14 on use of the ephod to inquire of God). It is significant that David is immediately responsive to Keilah's predicament. No special tie to this town is mentioned; there is no obvious political advantage to David. Rather, the risk is great to David, not only from the Philistines, but also, as events develop, from exposing himself to the pursuit of Saul. Apart from building general goodwill in Judah, David's primary motivation seems to be compassion for Keilah's plight.

David's men are afraid (v. 3). It is understandable that fighting the Philistines almost on the borders of Philistia might be a daunting prospect. To allay their fears, David prays again (v. 4). This time the Lord's response is even more specific, "I will give them into your hand." So David fights for Keilah and is victorious (v. 5). He captures the Philistine livestock and delivers the city. The narrative focuses on David, both as a man of prayer and as a man of action. It is a combination seldom seen for Saul. Even in chap. 14, where he consults God through his priest, Saul seems unwilling to act in trust of the guidance he has sought.

23:6-14. Verse 6 notes the presence of Abiathar and the ephod he carries as a part of David's retinue. The resources of the religious establishment of Israel (what is left of it) are now with David.

The scene then shifts to Saul and his obsession with David. Saul believes David has made a mistake by entering a closed city where he can be trapped (v. 7), hence Saul gathers his army for a siege of Keilah (v. 8). The situation is reminiscent of those who thought they had Samson trapped inside a city (Judg 16:1-3). It is interesting that Saul here voices the belief that God has given David into his hand—an unbelievable delusion on the part of Saul, who has just slaughtered all of God's priests. Either he is deluded and unaware of his true situation, or he refuses to acknowledge it. The truth is made clear to the reader at the end of this episode: "The LORD did not give him into his hand" (v. 14*b*).

We are not told how, but word of Saul's mobilization reaches David, whereupon he summons Abiathar (v. 9). Now David explicitly uses the ephod to inquire of the Lord. He asks if Saul really will come against Keilah, and God responds that Saul will (vv. 10-11). Twice in this inquiry David refers to himself as God's servant. He is also clear that Keilah is endangered because of him. David inquires further. Will the men of Keilah surrender David to save themselves? The Lord answers that they will (v. 12). David cannot stay. With his six hundred men, he leaves Keilah before Saul can arrive (v. 13). Having no destination, they "wandered wherever they could go." Saul gives up the siege of Keilah, but not the pursuit. Verse 14 says that he seeks David every day. David stays in the hill country, finally moving to the wilderness of Ziph, an area closer to Hebron.

23:15-18. Verse 15 actually begins in the MT with "David saw," but the unpointed consonants of the verb are identical to the verb "to be afraid." It does not make sense that David is just now "learning/saw" that Saul had come out to kill him (as the NRSV and the NIV have it). In the light of Jonathan's reassurance in v. 17, it would seem that this episode begins in v. 15 by noting David's fear, his vulnerability: "David was afraid, for Saul had come out to seek his life; David was in the wilderness of Ziph, at Horesh."

It is in the time of David's fear that his friend Jonathan comes to him (v. 16). We hear nothing of the communication or the logistics that made this possible. In the moment of need, Jonathan is there to strengthen him, but he does so "through the LORD." This is a friendship shared in the context of faith. Jonathan seems to understand that they participate in the larger purposes of God's future for Israel. Jonathan's initial words are words of reassurance that we associate with divine messengers, "Fear not!" Jonathan speaks further in the confident tones of pronouncement. David need not fear, because Saul will not find him—because David will be king—because Jonathan gives up his first position in inheritance of the throne to become second to David—because even Saul knows that this is true (v. 17). This is a remarkable series of assertions. Perhaps

the confident tone is because Jonathan spoke "through the LORD." The mood is almost one of prophetic pronouncement. Most amazing is Jonathan's final assertion that Saul also knows David will be king. We do not question that what Jonathan says is true. We have suspected that Saul's compulsive pursuit of David is rooted in what Saul dares not admit to himself. Now his son has said aloud what Saul cannot himself yet voice. That final confession of David as Israel's future king is yet to come from Saul himself (24:20). All know the truth of David's coming kingship. Saul will be the last to know, or at least to acknowledge publicly that he knows. Again the friends covenant together (as in 18:3; 20:16-17), and they go their separate ways. It is their last face-to-face meeting.

23:19-29. This chapter contains yet one more tale of escape. Perhaps the author intends that we not forget that David still has enemies and the danger is real. We have seen support coming to him so often in the previous stories that we may forget how perilous David's situation really is.

While David is hiding in the region of Ziph, some men of that region go to Saul at Gibeah. They reveal David's hiding place and offer to hand him over to the king (vv. 19-20). Saul's response is ironic. He invokes God's blessing on these Ziphites for showing him "compassion" (חמל *ḥāmal*, v. 21). It is the very word used when Saul spared King Agag's life in 15:3, 9, 15. Now he would connect compassion with the taking of David's life. He sends the men of Ziph back for a precise reconnaissance and promises to join them for the final hunt when David is located (vv. 22-23). Saul recognizes that David is "very cunning" (v. 22) and knows that capture of David is no sure thing until it is accomplished.

The time for speeches is over. Verses 24-29 are all action—a kind of cat and mouse game. Saul is now on the chase, and David is on the run (v. 25). In the wilderness of Maon, Saul gets close to his objective. David is on one side of a mountain and Saul on the other, but Saul seems to be circling in on his prey (v. 26). Just then messengers come with word of a Philistine attack (v. 27). We are not told precisely where or in what strength, but it is a situation serious enough to cause Saul to break off the effort to capture David and to turn his attention to the Philistines (v. 28).

Even Saul cannot ignore the threat Philistines posed to Israel's survival. How ironic that the Philistines whom David attacked at the beginning of the chapter should save him now. They name the place "Rock of Division or Parting" or "Rock of Escape" to commemorate this incident. David makes good his escape and moves to En-gedi, beside the Dead Sea (v. 29).

REFLECTIONS

Once again this chapter invites us to ponder the interrelationship between divine will and human circumstances. In these escape stories, God does not dramatically intervene to save David. Everything is explainable in human terms. David takes courageous action; he makes wise decisions; he reacts swiftly to circumstances. Yet the narrative is confident that divine providence is at work. The workings of divine grace are not radically separated in character from the workings of David's considerable human skills.

Especially significant is David's confidence that divine providence plays a role even as he marshals and uses his own skills effectively. He not only acts, but he also prays. He has resources of faith as well as a capable mind, a fleet foot, and a strong arm. His prayers do not seem perfunctory or merely habitual. David prays and acts in crisis situations as if both efforts make a difference. This suggests that for the narrator of these stories divine providence is understood to require both the trust and the agency of David. God is at work, but God also counts on David to be at work. It is together that God and David will bring Israel's future.

For people of faith in the modern church the temptation is often to separate the workings of divine providence from our own human agency. Even further, many choose to emphasize only one or the other. Some imagine they can pray for God's will and do nothing. Others seem to think they can build the kingdom of God by their own efforts alone. Prayer groups and social action committees in congregations frequently have no overlapping membership. David models a different response. His constant combination of prayer and action suggests that we, too, must stand in the tension between trust in what God is doing and response as we ourselves do what we can do. It is, perhaps, trustful prayer that enables wise discernment of what we must do. In discussion of David's story, I have heard some remark that they wish God were with them as God was with David. Perhaps it takes bold prayer, like David's, to claim the truth that God *is* with us in our own faithful actions to move toward God's future.

1 Samuel 24:1-22, David Spares Saul's Life

NIV

24 After Saul returned from pursuing the Philistines, he was told, "David is in the Desert of En Gedi." [2]So Saul took three thousand chosen men from all Israel and set out to look for David and his men near the Crags of the Wild Goats.

[3]He came to the sheep pens along the way; a cave was there, and Saul went in to relieve himself. David and his men were far back in the cave. [4]The men said, "This is the day the LORD spoke of when he said[a] to you, 'I will give your enemy into your hands for you to deal with as you wish.'" Then David crept up unnoticed and cut off a corner of Saul's robe.

a4 Or "Today the LORD is saying

NRSV

24 When Saul returned from following the Philistines, he was told, "David is in the wilderness of En-gedi." [2]Then Saul took three thousand chosen men out of all Israel, and went to look for David and his men in the direction of the Rocks of the Wild Goats. [3]He came to the sheepfolds beside the road, where there was a cave; and Saul went in to relieve himself.[a] Now David and his men were sitting in the innermost parts of the cave. [4]The men of David said to him, "Here is the day of which the LORD said to you, 'I will give your enemy into your hand, and you

a Heb to cover his feet

NIV

5Afterward, David was conscience-stricken for having cut off a corner of his robe. 6He said to his men, "The LORD forbid that I should do such a thing to my master, the LORD's anointed, or lift my hand against him; for he is the anointed of the LORD." 7With these words David rebuked his men and did not allow them to attack Saul. And Saul left the cave and went his way.

8Then David went out of the cave and called out to Saul, "My lord the king!" When Saul looked behind him, David bowed down and prostrated himself with his face to the ground. 9He said to Saul, "Why do you listen when men say, 'David is bent on harming you'? 10This day you have seen with your own eyes how the LORD delivered you into my hands in the cave. Some urged me to kill you, but I spared you; I said, 'I will not lift my hand against my master, because he is the LORD's anointed.' 11See, my father, look at this piece of your robe in my hand! I cut off the corner of your robe but did not kill you. Now understand and recognize that I am not guilty of wrongdoing or rebellion. I have not wronged you, but you are hunting me down to take my life. 12May the LORD judge between you and me. And may the LORD avenge the wrongs you have done to me, but my hand will not touch you. 13As the old saying goes, 'From evildoers come evil deeds,' so my hand will not touch you.

14"Against whom has the king of Israel come out? Whom are you pursuing? A dead dog? A flea? 15May the LORD be our judge and decide between us. May he consider my cause and uphold it; may he vindicate me by delivering me from your hand."

16When David finished saying this, Saul asked, "Is that your voice, David my son?" And he wept aloud. 17"You are more righteous than I," he said. "You have treated me well, but I have treated you badly. 18You have just now told me of the good you did to me; the LORD delivered me into your hands, but you did not kill me. 19When a man finds his enemy, does he let him get away unharmed? May the LORD reward you well for the way you treated me today. 20I know that you will surely be king and that the kingdom of Israel will be established in your hands. 21Now swear to me by the LORD that you will not cut off my descen-

NRSV

shall do to him as it seems good to you.'" Then David went and stealthily cut off a corner of Saul's cloak. 5Afterward David was stricken to the heart because he had cut off a corner of Saul's cloak. 6He said to his men, "The LORD forbid that I should do this thing to my lord, the LORD's anointed, to raise my hand against him; for he is the LORD's anointed." 7So David scolded his men severely and did not permit them to attack Saul. Then Saul got up and left the cave, and went on his way.

8Afterwards David also rose up and went out of the cave and called after Saul, "My lord the king!" When Saul looked behind him, David bowed with his face to the ground, and did obeisance. 9David said to Saul, "Why do you listen to the words of those who say, 'David seeks to do you harm'? 10This very day your eyes have seen how the LORD gave you into my hand in the cave; and some urged me to kill you, but I spared[a] you. I said, 'I will not raise my hand against my lord; for he is the LORD's anointed.' 11See, my father, see the corner of your cloak in my hand; for by the fact that I cut off the corner of your cloak, and did not kill you, you may know for certain that there is no wrong or treason in my hands. I have not sinned against you, though you are hunting me to take my life. 12May the LORD judge between me and you! May the LORD avenge me on you; but my hand shall not be against you. 13As the ancient proverb says, 'Out of the wicked comes forth wickedness'; but my hand shall not be against you. 14Against whom has the king of Israel come out? Whom do you pursue? A dead dog? A single flea? 15May the LORD therefore be judge, and give sentence between me and you. May he see to it, and plead my cause, and vindicate me against you."

16When David had finished speaking these words to Saul, Saul said, "Is this your voice, my son David?" Saul lifted up his voice and wept. 17He said to David, "You are more righteous than I; for you have repaid me good, whereas I have repaid you evil. 18Today you have explained how you have dealt well with me, in that you did not kill me when the LORD put me into your hands. 19For who has ever found an enemy, and sent the

a Gk Syr Tg Vg: Heb *it* (my eye) *spared*

NIV

dants or wipe out my name from my father's family."

²²So David gave his oath to Saul. Then Saul returned home, but David and his men went up to the stronghold.

NRSV

enemy safely away? So may the LORD reward you with good for what you have done to me this day. ²⁰Now I know that you shall surely be king, and that the kingdom of Israel shall be established in your hand. ²¹Swear to me therefore by the LORD that you will not cut off my descendants after me, and that you will not wipe out my name from my father's house." ²²So David swore this to Saul. Then Saul went home; but David and his men went up to the stronghold.

COMMENTARY

One of the dangers of power is its seduction to violence.[153] The temptation is to resort to violence as a way of gaining, maintaining, or holding on to power. Saul has fallen victim to this temptation. Although he did not gain his throne by violence, but by the gift of God, he has resorted to increasing violence as he felt power shifting from himself toward David. Thus far, the balance of power has been on Saul's side. He is the king; he has the power. As the popularity of David grew, Saul first became violent toward David himself. David was forced to become a fugitive from Saul's murderous intentions. But violence tends to breed violence. Saul's paranoid grasping after his own power led to violent turns toward those who supported David, and eventually toward those he only imagined to support David. His violence lashed out at his own son Jonathan, his own servants, and in deadliest fashion to the whole community of the priests of Nob.

In chaps. 18–23, as Saul's bent to violence increased, his hold on power ironically decreased. We have seen in these chapters a shifting of power away from Saul and toward David, as one after another the witnesses to David's future kingship step forward. At the beginning of these chapters, Saul was powerful and David was vulnerable; but in 1 Samuel 24 the situation is reversed. In this episode, it will be Saul who is vulnerable and David who holds power over his life. In the final speech of this chapter, Saul himself will finally confess this knowledge that David will be king (24:20). The shift of power to David is finally complete; even Saul must acknowledge it. It is a great reversal like those Hannah's song foresees (1 Sam 2:1-10). The eighth son from a family of little influence or wealth, forced to live as an outlaw and fugitive, nevertheless will be Israel's future king because he is the man after God's own heart (13:14).

In this great reversal of power, David now faces the temptation to violence that power brings. This is the first of three chapters (chaps. 24–26) that focus on whether David will use violence in order to gain or hold power. Like Saul, power has come to him as a gift. Will he, like Saul, resort to the violence that power makes so readily available?

Chapter 24 relates an incident in which Saul's life is unexpectedly placed in David's hands, but out of respect for God's anointed one David cannot kill him, as his men urge him to do. Instead he cuts off a piece of Saul's robe and uses it to confront Saul. David speaks of his own innocence and compassion, and he presents the evidence of his sparing of Saul. Saul, shocked out of his madness into lucidity, confesses his own repayment of David's goodness by evil and acknowledges that the future of Israel's kingship lies with David. The chapter is organized with a succinct narrative account of the incident (vv. 1-7), followed by the two lengthy and eloquent

153. Walter Brueggemann, *Power, Providence, and Personality* (Louisville: Westminster/John Knox, 1990) 49-89, has used the stories of David's rise to kingship as the focus for reflection on the interrelationship of power and violence. He has given special attention to 1 Samuel 24–26 as crucial for understanding David's relationship to these issues. My own discussion is indebted at many points to the stimulus of his treatment of these chapters.

speeches, the first by David (vv. 8-15) and the second by Saul (vv. 16-21).

This episode is closely paralleled by the story in 1 Samuel 26. Most scholars believe that these stories are variant witnesses to the same incident. Although some details differ, there are extensive similarities of language, detail, and theme in the two accounts.[154] There is no agreement on which account is earlier or more authentic. In the present arrangement, the two similar episodes are used to build a sequence (with the story of David/Nabal/Abigail in 1 Samuel 25 between them) on David's facing of issues of power, violence, bloodguilt, and innocence.

The viewpoint of the narrator and editor of these stories as they now stand is that David refused to gain or hold power by violence. David spares Saul's life (v. 24); he is persuaded by Abigail to spare Nabal (v. 25); he spares Saul again (v. 26).[155] In this first episode of the sequence in chaps. 24–26, David has the opportunity to kill Saul, who has become his enemy and seeks his life, but David refuses. The claim of the story is that David is free of bloodguilt toward the house of Saul. He did not gain power by raising his own hand against God's anointed one. He has received the kingdom as the gift of God's grace and not by the grasp of his own hand.[156] The story suggests that David models an alternative to the usual power arrangements and breaks the connection of power with violence, although he must live close to its temptations. Subsequent chapters continue to raise these issues. Can such an alternative to the interconnections of power and violence be maintained?

24:1-7. Surely this story was told with amazement and humor. Saul again receives a report on

David's whereabouts (v. 1). He sets out with three thousand men into the wilderness around En-gedi (v. 2). Saul comes to a convenient cave and, feeling the urge of nature, he goes inside to defecate (v. 3a). The expression "to cover his feet" is a euphemism for this bodily function. Saul's circumstances are surely intended to emphasize both the fact that he had reason to enter the cave alone and that he was in an extremely vulnerable position. Remarkably, David and his men are hiding in the back of this very cave (v. 3b). It is an astonishing turn of events. The hunter has now become the potential prey.

David's men are immediately certain that this opportunity has been given to them by the Lord, and they urge David to take advantage of it. They quote a promise of the Lord, unknown to us elsewhere, that predicts a day when the Lord will give the enemy into David's hand and he should "do to him as it seems good to you" (v. 4a). They clearly have in mind the ending of Saul's pursuit by the ending of Saul's life. Perhaps David is tempted by this; the text does not say. But clearly he will lose face or leadership if he does nothing with such an opportunity. The possibility of violence could easily be justified in such circumstances. Saul has amply made clear his violent intent toward David. With Saul gone, would not David's way be clear to the throne? We imagine many such possibilities churning within David, but what he does amazes us (and surely his men as well). He creeps forward and cuts off a piece of Saul's robe (v. 4b).

How could this happen? The text is short on details. Perhaps it was very dark, and they were very close. Perhaps Saul had laid his robe aside while relieving himself. Perhaps he fell asleep afterward. The focus is not on the details, but the act itself is full of meaning. We know that the royal robe itself is a powerful symbol of authority. Jonathan symbolizes his willingness to pass royal authority on to David by clothing him in his own robe in 18:4. The torn robe of Samuel in 15:28 was used by the prophet to symbolize the tearing of the kingdom from Saul and giving it to his neighbor, "who is better than you." Now David holds in his hand the torn piece of Saul's robe, and Saul's very life is effectively in David's power. The verb "cut off" (כרת *kārat*) is used four times in this chapter (vv. 4, 5, 12, 22). Jonathan uses this verb to plead with David that his family not

---

154. Ralph W. Klein, *1 Samuel,* WBC 10 (Waco: Word, 1983) 236-37, gives a detailed chart of the extensive parallels between 1 Samuel 24 and 26.

155. Traditional historical-critical treatments of these chapters have been preoccupied with similarities between chaps. 24 and 26 and have focused on questions concerning historicity and the history of composition. More recent commentators have observed that the sequence of chaps. 24–26 as it now stands serves to shift from David as one whose life is endangered to David as one who spares life. Each of these chapters is connected to important earlier themes in the narrative of David's rise. Robert Polzin, *Samuel and the Deuteronomist: A Literary Study of the Deuteronomic History,* Part Two: *1 Samuel* (San Francisco: Harper & Row, 1989) 203-15, provides an excellent and representative discussion of these matters.

156. David M. Gunn, "David and the Gift of the Kingdom (2 Sam 2–4, 9–20; 1 Kgs 1–2)," *Semeia* 3 (1975) 14-45, has helpfully developed the categories of gift and grasp for understanding the successes and failures of David. When David receives the kingdom as a gift of God and acts accordingly, all is well; but when David attempts to grasp the power of the kingdom for his own purposes, all goes awry.

be "cut off" when David comes to the throne (20:14-16), and at the end of this encounter Saul will similarly ask David to swear that he will not "cut off" Saul's family or name in Israel (v. 21). David Gunn makes a plausible case that the literal phrase here, "to cut off the skirt," is a euphemism for cutting off the penis, thus leaving Saul without manhood or future. David does not actually do this, but the phrase suggests to the audience of this story the possibility of this drastic act and the extent of Saul's vulnerability.[157] This act of cutting off potentially represents David's power over Saul's life, over his royal authority, over his manhood, over his descendants, and over his future.

David has acted magnanimously and spared Saul's life, but he is still immediately filled with remorse. He is "stricken to the heart" (v. 5) at what he has done, but one has the impression that he is most devastated by what he might have done. He refers to Saul twice in v. 6 as "the LORD's anointed" and calls him "my lord." David's fear is that he might have "raised my hand against him." David has acted with compassion, but he has stared into the abyss of violence. He knows how close he was to raising his hand against the Lord's anointed one. Power has been shifting from Saul to David, and now Saul is completely in David's power. David knows the ease by which vulnerability can be violently exploited and how thin is the line between knowing this and acting on it. He is overwhelmed by what he has discovered within himself. On this occasion he holds back the violence and resists it successfully. At a later point in David's story, at the height of his royal power, he gives in. He takes Bathsheba, and he kills Uriah (2 Samuel 11). Even now, in a cave in the Judean wilderness, David knows and recoils from this capacity within himself.

David's stress on Saul as "the LORD's anointed" (twice in v. 5) also shows a knowledge on David's part that to strike Saul is to strike the office itself. He comes back to his respect for the office of "the LORD's anointed" when he speaks to Saul (v. 10). After all, David is himself "the LORD's anointed." The respect for one designated by the Lord may be genuine, but it cannot be without some degree of self-interest. David surely does not want to set a precedent that violence can be legitimately authorized against one God has chosen.[158] David restrains his men, perhaps with some difficulty, since he is forced to "scold them severely," and allows Saul to exit the cave (v. 7).

24:8-15. David follows Saul from the cave and places himself in the vulnerable position. He addresses Saul respectfully by his office as "My lord, the king" and bows to the ground in homage (v. 8). We do not immediately have Saul's reaction, for David begins a lengthy speech.

David first declares himself innocent of the charge that he ever desired to harm Saul (v. 9). We must remember that while David is speaking to Saul within the story, the larger narrative is defending David of such a charge. David offers as dramatic evidence of his innocence the piece of Saul's robe and rehearses the circumstances of Saul's vulnerability in the cave (vv. 10-11). David is explicit about what might have happened, "I could have killed you; others urged me to do it." David even uses the language of divine providence, "The LORD gave you into my hand" (v. 10). This is the language used most often in holy war for the disposal of God's enemies. David implies that Saul has become God's enemy, and David could have been the instrument of God's judgment on Saul. But David "spared" him.

At the moment David shows Saul the piece of robe, the evidence of his compassion, he shifts to more intimate language and calls Saul "my father" (v. 11*a*). David contrasts his action with Saul's, "I have not sinned . . . you are hunting me" (v. 11*b*).

Finally, David shifts to juridical language in his appeal to Saul (v. 12). David is willing to let the Lord judge between them. David has not taken vengeance but will leave such vengeance to God: "My hand shall not be against you." He reinforces this affirmation with a saying, "Out of the wicked comes forth wickedness" (v. 13). David is not among the wicked, so his hand will not do violence to Saul. By contrast, Saul, the king of Israel, seeks to do violence—and against whom? David self-deprecatingly describes himself as "a dead dog" or "a flea" (v. 14) compared to Saul's royal power. David's refusal to raise a hand against Saul seems more than a refusal for the moment; it seems almost to be a vow. David will not seize the throne by violence against the person of Saul.

---

157. David M. Gunn, *The Fate of King Saul,* JSOTSup 14 (Sheffield: JSOT, 1980) 92-95.

158. This element of David's self-interest is discussed very helpfully in Keith Whitelam, "The Defense of David," *JSOT* 29 (1984) 73.

It is for the Lord to judge such things, not David, and David is certain that in the Lord's judgment he will be vindicated (v. 15).

David's speech is a remarkable and impassioned refusal of the usual patterns of power and violence. He chooses not to take vengeance and seize power over Saul, who has become his enemy. Although the word is not used, David in effect forgives Saul and offers to end the enmity between them. By a bold act of compassion, David breaks the cycle of violence that Saul has initiated.

24:16-22. Saul now speaks. We have been in suspense, wondering what his response might be. It is not what we would expect: "Is this your voice, my son David?" (v. 16). Saul returns the intimate address of David, who spoke to him as a father (v. 11). We remember that once Saul loved David (16:21). Brueggemann has pointed out that Saul's plaintive question echoes the question of the aged Isaac, uncertain of the identity of his son (Gen 27:18, 32).[159] The effect is to stress Saul's vulnerability and fearfulness. Like the blessing stolen from Isaac by Jacob, the kingdom is about to be transferred from a once, but no longer, powerful Saul to the bold youth of David.

Before speaking further, Saul weeps (v. 16*b*). It is a moment filled with pathos. One imagines all the failed possibilities for Saul's life caught up in this weeping. David has made Saul face what he has become. Perhaps he weeps for what he might have been or what he once was.

The Saul who speaks after the weeping seems a different man from the one we have seen in recent chapters of the story. He can lucidly face and speak the truth of his life, although it is a harsh truth. He begins with the juridical language that concluded David's speech, and he pronounces a verdict (v. 17): David is the righteous one in this conflict. Saul has repaid good with evil. Saul equates his actions with evil. Out of Saul's own mouth, David is acquitted and declared righteous. The telling of this story will vindicate David from charges of conspiring against Saul. It is an unexpected reversal: The fugitive is righteous and good; the king is evil. One is reminded of the same verdict ("she is more righ-

teous than I") by Judah concerning Tamar when she was about to be executed (Gen 38:26).

Saul continues in a remarkable series of candid acknowledgments. It is as if he is suddenly empowered to recognize and speak the truth, even though it convicts him of evil.

He acknowledges David's magnanimity in sparing his life (v. 18*a*).

He acknowledges that it was the Lord who gave him into David's hand (v. 18*b*).

He acknowledges that he cannot be David's enemy, for who would send an enemy away safely (v. 19*a*)?

He acknowledges that David deserves good as a reward for what he has done (v. 19*b*).

Finally, in one of the climactic moments of the history of David's rise, Saul utters the words "I know." His confession is what others in the story and the reader have known for some time: "I know that you shall surely be king, and that the kingdom of Israel is in your hand" (v. 20). The verb מלך (*mālak*) is formulated in a particularly emphatic way, "you shall *surely* be king." Saul is the last to know. Jonathan told David that Saul knew (23:17), but we must hear it from the mouth of Saul himself. Now the transition is complete. Saul has conceded the kingdom and acknowledged David as the future—a future Saul had failed to forestall.

Saul has one final plea. He asks David to swear an oath that he will not "cut off" his descendants after him or wipe out his name (v. 21). The verb "cut off" is the same as the word used for the action of "cutting off" Saul's robe; thus David holds Saul's future in his hands. But David had already made a covenant with Jonathan not to "cut off" his descendants (20:14-17). Even in this matter, David has acted ahead of Saul in "steadfast love" (*ḥesed*) toward Jonathan. David swears this also to Saul, but with no comment (v. 22).

The two depart, but Saul to Gibeah and David to his wilderness stronghold. Saul may have acknowledged David's coming kingship, but David will not put himself into Saul's hand again. The transfer of power is complete, but the final days of Saul must still be completed; David must wait.

---

159. Walter Brueggemann, *First and Second Samuel,* Interpretation (Louisville: John Knox, 1990) 171.

REFLECTIONS

Even Saul has now confessed David as Israel's future. It is an important moment in the plot of this story, but the context in which this confession comes is equally important because this moment has not been reached by the usual power arrangements. Power has been transferring to David throughout these stories, but David has not used it to seize the kingdom. In this dramatic episode, Saul, who has become David's enemy, is in David's power. David could have killed him, but he did not. He spared Saul. David was even remorseful over his temptation to do violence against Saul. He refused to exploit Saul's vulnerability and returned good for evil. He refused to act in vengeance. These are not the usual ways in which power is exercised in David's world—or, for that matter, in our own. It reminds us of Hannah's song, which already signaled that the coming of God's kingdom would be marked by reversals from the usual patterns of power: "The LORD makes poor and makes rich; he brings low, he also exalts" (2:7).

In David's action in this story, we see one whose final moment in receiving power is enabled by forgiveness and compassion. He breaks the cycle of violence and vengeance, and new possibilities are opened. Even Saul is freed for a lucid moment of knowing and speaking the truth—about David, about himself, about the future of Israel. All who come to hold power must face the issues of violence. There is no alternative in the human world. Power always lives close to the possibilities of violence by some means. In this story, it is David who must face that reality. He must look squarely at the possibility of violence within himself. He quails at what he sees, for violence is closer to the surface than most are forced to recognize or admit. But he does not give in to the violence within him.

To hold power does not mean that we will surrender to our violent impulses. David models an alternative to such surrender. Compassion, remorse, forgiveness, and responsibility can allow power to turn from violence. Such qualities of grace can break the tenacious connection between power and violence and allow new options.

To forgive and to act with compassion does not mean to ignore the realities of violence and evil that confront us. David's appeal to Saul asked for an end to pursuit and a declaration of innocence. But to follow David's alternative way is to refuse to return violence with violence. Recent studies in the patterns of abuse within families document the sad truth that many victims become victimizers themselves. They are caught in a vicious and continuous cycle of abuse and violence. The cycle is broken not by acceptance of the evil done, but by forgiveness that frees the victim from the need for vengeance and enables a new future. David and Saul do not go home together as if nothing had ever happened between them, but David's bold refusal of violence and his compassion on his own enemy broke the cycle and enabled them to go their separate ways into a new future.

It would seem that this alternative of forgiveness and compassion holds the hope for breaking some of the societal patterns of violence in which we are enmeshed as well. One wonders if widespread and strident support for capital punishment and the right to carry concealed weapons is not the desire for vengeance that returns violence for the violent assaults of crime, drug trafficking, and loss of respect for authority that afflict our communities. The desire to return violence for violence is a part of longstanding conflicts such as the Israeli/Palestinian hostilities. When Soviet-sponsored oppression was lifted from the Balkan states, freedom did not lead to peace but to vengeful ethnic cleansings, inflicting violence on supposed enemies in return for years of violence suffered under oppression. Such cycles of violence can go on endlessly unless someone courageously breaks the cycle.

What might happen if persons in power chose to practice a politics of compassion and forgiveness in place of the politics of coercion, manipulation, and violence? What would happen if the alternative practiced by David replaced the usual patterns of power? The kingdom gained by compassion and not by violence was the dream of prophets who hoped for a time when swords would be beaten into plowshares (Isa 2:4; Mic 4:3). For Christians, such an alternative is modeled in Jesus of Nazareth, who announced a kingdom that did not conform to the usual power arrangements—that called for the forgiveness of enemies (Matt 5:24; Luke 6:27, 35), the love of the neighbor (Matt 22:39; Mark 12:31; Luke 10:25-37), the giving of one's life for the sake of the kingdom (Matt 10:39; Mark 8:35; Luke 17:33). In 1 Samuel 24 and David's refusal to gain the kingdom by violence, we can, perhaps, see why the early church also proclaimed Jesus of Nazareth to be the son of David.

1 Samuel 25:1-44, Abigail Saves David from Bloodguilt

NIV

25 Now Samuel died, and all Israel assembled and mourned for him; and they buried him at his home in Ramah.

Then David moved down into the Desert of Maon.[a] [2]A certain man in Maon, who had property there at Carmel, was very wealthy. He had a thousand goats and three thousand sheep, which he was shearing in Carmel. [3]His name was Nabal and his wife's name was Abigail. She was an intelligent and beautiful woman, but her husband, a Calebite, was surly and mean in his dealings.

[4]While David was in the desert, he heard that Nabal was shearing sheep. [5]So he sent ten young men and said to them, "Go up to Nabal at Carmel and greet him in my name. [6]Say to him: 'Long life to you! Good health to you and your household! And good health to all that is yours!

[7]" 'Now I hear that it is sheep-shearing time. When your shepherds were with us, we did not mistreat them, and the whole time they were at Carmel nothing of theirs was missing. [8]Ask your own servants and they will tell you. Therefore be favorable toward my young men, since we come at a festive time. Please give your servants and your son David whatever you can find for them.' "

[9]When David's men arrived, they gave Nabal this message in David's name. Then they waited.

[10]Nabal answered David's servants, "Who is this David? Who is this son of Jesse? Many servants are breaking away from their masters these days. [11]Why should I take my bread and water, and the meat I have slaughtered for my shearers, and give it to men coming from who knows where?"

[12]David's men turned around and went back.

[a]*1 Some Septuagint manuscripts; Hebrew* Paran

NRSV

25 Now Samuel died; and all Israel assembled and mourned for him. They buried him at his home in Ramah.

Then David got up and went down to the wilderness of Paran.

[2]There was a man in Maon, whose property was in Carmel. The man was very rich; he had three thousand sheep and a thousand goats. He was shearing his sheep in Carmel. [3]Now the name of the man was Nabal, and the name of his wife Abigail. The woman was clever and beautiful, but the man was surly and mean; he was a Calebite. [4]David heard in the wilderness that Nabal was shearing his sheep. [5]So David sent ten young men; and David said to the young men, "Go up to Carmel, and go to Nabal, and greet him in my name. [6]Thus you shall salute him: 'Peace be to you, and peace be to your house, and peace be to all that you have. [7]I hear that you have shearers; now your shepherds have been with us, and we did them no harm, and they missed nothing, all the time they were in Carmel. [8]Ask your young men, and they will tell you. Therefore let my young men find favor in your sight; for we have come on a feast day. Please give whatever you have at hand to your servants and to your son David.' "

[9]When David's young men came, they said all this to Nabal in the name of David; and then they waited. [10]But Nabal answered David's servants, "Who is David? Who is the son of Jesse? There are many servants today who are breaking away from their masters. [11]Shall I take my bread and my water and the meat that I have butchered for my shearers, and give it to men who come from I do not know where?" [12]So David's young men

NIV

When they arrived, they reported every word. [13]David said to his men, "Put on your swords!" So they put on their swords, and David put on his. About four hundred men went up with David, while two hundred stayed with the supplies.

[14]One of the servants told Nabal's wife Abigail: "David sent messengers from the desert to give our master his greetings, but he hurled insults at them. [15]Yet these men were very good to us. They did not mistreat us, and the whole time we were out in the fields near them nothing was missing. [16]Night and day they were a wall around us all the time we were herding our sheep near them. [17]Now think it over and see what you can do, because disaster is hanging over our master and his whole household. He is such a wicked man that no one can talk to him."

[18]Abigail lost no time. She took two hundred loaves of bread, two skins of wine, five dressed sheep, five seahs[a] of roasted grain, a hundred cakes of raisins and two hundred cakes of pressed figs, and loaded them on donkeys. [19]Then she told her servants, "Go on ahead; I'll follow you." But she did not tell her husband Nabal.

[20]As she came riding her donkey into a mountain ravine, there were David and his men descending toward her, and she met them. [21]David had just said, "It's been useless—all my watching over this fellow's property in the desert so that nothing of his was missing. He has paid me back evil for good. [22]May God deal with David,[b] be it ever so severely, if by morning I leave alive one male of all who belong to him!"

[23]When Abigail saw David, she quickly got off her donkey and bowed down before David with her face to the ground. [24]She fell at his feet and said: "My lord, let the blame be on me alone. Please let your servant speak to you; hear what your servant has to say. [25]May my lord pay no attention to that wicked man Nabal. He is just like his name—his name is Fool, and folly goes with him. But as for me, your servant, I did not see the men my master sent.

[26]"Now since the LORD has kept you, my master, from bloodshed and from avenging yourself with your own hands, as surely as the LORD lives

[a]18 That is, probably about a bushel (about 37 liters) [b]22 Some Septuagint manuscripts; Hebrew *with David's enemies*

NRSV

turned away, and came back and told him all this. [13]David said to his men, "Every man strap on his sword!" And every one of them strapped on his sword; David also strapped on his sword; and about four hundred men went up after David, while two hundred remained with the baggage.

[14]But one of the young men told Abigail, Nabal's wife, "David sent messengers out of the wilderness to salute our master; and he shouted insults at them. [15]Yet the men were very good to us, and we suffered no harm, and we never missed anything when we were in the fields, as long as we were with them; [16]they were a wall to us both by night and by day, all the while we were with them keeping the sheep. [17]Now therefore know this and consider what you should do; for evil has been decided against our master and against all his house; he is so ill-natured that no one can speak to him."

[18]Then Abigail hurried and took two hundred loaves, two skins of wine, five sheep ready dressed, five measures of parched grain, one hundred clusters of raisins, and two hundred cakes of figs. She loaded them on donkeys [19]and said to her young men, "Go on ahead of me; I am coming after you." But she did not tell her husband Nabal. [20]As she rode on the donkey and came down under cover of the mountain, David and his men came down toward her; and she met them. [21]Now David had said, "Surely it was in vain that I protected all that this fellow has in the wilderness, so that nothing was missed of all that belonged to him; but he has returned me evil for good. [22]God do so to David[a] and more also, if by morning I leave so much as one male of all who belong to him."

[23]When Abigail saw David, she hurried and alighted from the donkey, and fell before David on her face, bowing to the ground. [24]She fell at his feet and said, "Upon me alone, my lord, be the guilt; please let your servant speak in your ears, and hear the words of your servant. [25]My lord, do not take seriously this ill-natured fellow, Nabal; for as his name is, so is he; Nabal[b] is his name, and folly is with him; but I, your servant, did not see the young men of my lord, whom you sent.

[26]"Now then, my lord, as the LORD lives, and as you yourself live, since the LORD has restrained

[a] Gk Compare Syr: Heb *the enemies of David*   [b] That is *Fool*

NIV

and as you live, may your enemies and all who intend to harm my master be like Nabal. 27And let this gift, which your servant has brought to my master, be given to the men who follow you. 28Please forgive your servant's offense, for the LORD will certainly make a lasting dynasty for my master, because he fights the LORD's battles. Let no wrongdoing be found in you as long as you live. 29Even though someone is pursuing you to take your life, the life of my master will be bound securely in the bundle of the living by the LORD your God. But the lives of your enemies he will hurl away as from the pocket of a sling. 30When the LORD has done for my master every good thing he promised concerning him and has appointed him leader over Israel, 31my master will not have on his conscience the staggering burden of needless bloodshed or of having avenged himself. And when the LORD has brought my master success, remember your servant."

32David said to Abigail, "Praise be to the LORD, the God of Israel, who has sent you today to meet me. 33May you be blessed for your good judgment and for keeping me from bloodshed this day and from avenging myself with my own hands. 34Otherwise, as surely as the LORD, the God of Israel, lives, who has kept me from harming you, if you had not come quickly to meet me, not one male belonging to Nabal would have been left alive by daybreak."

35Then David accepted from her hand what she had brought him and said, "Go home in peace. I have heard your words and granted your request."

36When Abigail went to Nabal, he was in the house holding a banquet like that of a king. He was in high spirits and very drunk. So she told him nothing until daybreak. 37Then in the morning, when Nabal was sober, his wife told him all these things, and his heart failed him and he became like a stone. 38About ten days later, the LORD struck Nabal and he died.

39When David heard that Nabal was dead, he said, "Praise be to the LORD, who has upheld my cause against Nabal for treating me with contempt. He has kept his servant from doing wrong and has brought Nabal's wrongdoing down on his own head."

Then David sent word to Abigail, asking her to

NRSV

you from bloodguilt and from taking vengeance with your own hand, now let your enemies and those who seek to do evil to my lord be like Nabal. 27And now let this present that your servant has brought to my lord be given to the young men who follow my lord. 28Please forgive the trespass of your servant; for the LORD will certainly make my lord a sure house, because my lord is fighting the battles of the LORD; and evil shall not be found in you so long as you live. 29If anyone should rise up to pursue you and to seek your life, the life of my lord shall be bound in the bundle of the living under the care of the LORD your God; but the lives of your enemies he shall sling out as from the hollow of a sling. 30When the LORD has done to my lord according to all the good that he has spoken concerning you, and has appointed you prince over Israel, 31my lord shall have no cause of grief, or pangs of conscience, for having shed blood without cause or for having saved himself. And when the LORD has dealt well with my lord, then remember your servant."

32David said to Abigail, "Blessed be the LORD, the God of Israel, who sent you to meet me today! 33Blessed be your good sense, and blessed be you, who have kept me today from bloodguilt and from avenging myself by my own hand! 34For as surely as the LORD the God of Israel lives, who has restrained me from hurting you, unless you had hurried and come to meet me, truly by morning there would not have been left to Nabal so much as one male." 35Then David received from her hand what she had brought him; he said to her, "Go up to your house in peace; see, I have heeded your voice, and I have granted your petition."

36Abigail came to Nabal; he was holding a feast in his house, like the feast of a king. Nabal's heart was merry within him, for he was very drunk; so she told him nothing at all until the morning light. 37In the morning, when the wine had gone out of Nabal, his wife told him these things, and his heart died within him; he became like a stone. 38About ten days later the LORD struck Nabal, and he died.

39When David heard that Nabal was dead, he said, "Blessed be the LORD who has judged the case of Nabal's insult to me, and has kept back his servant from evil; the LORD has returned the

NIV

become his wife. ⁴⁰His servants went to Carmel and said to Abigail, "David has sent us to you to take you to become his wife."

⁴¹She bowed down with her face to the ground and said, "Here is your maidservant, ready to serve you and wash the feet of my master's servants." ⁴²Abigail quickly got on a donkey and, attended by her five maids, went with David's messengers and became his wife. ⁴³David had also married Ahinoam of Jezreel, and they both were his wives. ⁴⁴But Saul had given his daughter Michal, David's wife, to Paltiel⁴ son of Laish, who was from Gallim.

⁴44 Hebrew *Palti*, a variant of *Paltiel*

NRSV

evildoing of Nabal upon his own head." Then David sent and wooed Abigail, to make her his wife. ⁴⁰When David's servants came to Abigail at Carmel, they said to her, "David has sent us to you to take you to him as his wife." ⁴¹She rose and bowed down, with her face to the ground, and said, "Your servant is a slave to wash the feet of the servants of my lord." ⁴²Abigail got up hurriedly and rode away on a donkey; her five maids attended her. She went after the messengers of David and became his wife.

43David also married Ahinoam of Jezreel; both of them became his wives. 44Saul had given his daughter Michal, David's wife, to Palti son of Laish, who was from Gallim.

COMMENTARY

This is the second account in a sequence of three chapters dealing with the temptation to violence that comes with power. In each account, David's innocence of such violence is demonstrated, and his coming kingship is cleared from suspicion of bloodguilt. In chap. 24 and in the similar episode yet to come (chap. 26), David restrains his impulse to do violence against Saul and refuses to take the king's life. In chap. 25, David must be restrained by the intervention of Abigail to keep from incurring bloodguilt by taking revenge on her husband, Nabal.

Numerous scholars have commented on a sense of stereotyped character and formal, unrealistic plot to chap. 25. Berlin writes, "The plot, as well as the characters, is unrealistic. It could be reduced to: 'fair maiden' Abigail is freed from the 'wicked ogre' and marries 'prince charming.' This suggests that this is not just another episode in the biography of David, but an exemplum."[160] These observations in no way diminish the important role of chap. 25, particularly the role it plays in the sequence on David's refusal to use violence in chaps. 24–26. All three of these chapters, with long rhetorical speeches placed in the mouths of the key characters, seem somewhat artificial. This itself, how-

ever, may give us a clue that the author is using this sequence of chapters to make some major points of his own.[161]

Chapter 25 is constructed in such a way that character and plot point beyond the narrative boundaries of the chapter. We can sketch the broad outline of some of these interconnections and will discuss details in the verse-by-verse commentary.

The character of Nabal in this story seems to represent Saul in many details.[162] In the immediate context of chaps. 24–26, Nabal, like Saul, is spared from the vengeful hand of David, although chap. 25 requires the intervention of Abigail. Nabal is also one who returns evil for good, a characteristic Saul admits about himself (24:17). Nabal's name and actions are the marks of a fool (25:25) and reflect the confession Saul makes in 26:21, "I have been a fool." Nabal's response to David's request is to treat him as a servant breaking away from a master (25:10), which reflects David's treatment by Saul since chap. 19. Most important, Nabal's death, not by the hand of David but by the hand of the Lord, prefigures

160. Adele Berlin, "Characterization in Biblical Narrative: David's Wives," *JSOT* 23 (1982) 77.

161. See Polzin, *Samuel and the Deuteronomist*, 268n. 10, for a response to critics who use the artifice of chaps. 24–26 as an excuse to dismiss their significance in the larger history.

162. Numerous scholars have noticed the Saul-Nabal connection. Polzin (ibid., 211-12) gives one of the more detailed discussions of the issue.

Saul's death. Abigail's speeches twice look ahead to Saul's death while also speaking of her hus-band. In 25:26, Abigail swears by the Lord, "Let your enemies and those who seek to do evil to my lord be like Nabal." The only one "seeking" to do evil to David outside this story is Saul. When Abigail later says, "If anyone should rise up to pursue you and to seek your life" (v. 29*a*), it is impossible not to think of Saul's pursuit, which has dominated the story in recent chapters. She continues, "The lives of your enemies he [God] shall sling out as from the hollow of a sling" (v. 29*b*). Immediately we think of Goliath, vanquished by a stone from David's sling. But when Nabal is later struck dead by the Lord, the act is accompanied by the notice that "he became like a stone" (v. 37). David's enemies, whether Goliath, Nabal, or Saul, are slung out like a stone to their own death. Both Nabal and Saul die because they opposed David, and in doing so opposed God's future for Israel.

David is saved from incurring bloodguilt by Abigail, but in the process we are exposed to a darker side of David's character than we have seen thus far. Although he is restrained by Abigail's timely intervention, David is willing to kill, and to do so on a major scale in wiping out all the males in Nabal's household (v. 22). Some have characterized David's activity in this episode as a protection rack-eteer. This assessment will require discussion, but could add to the darker Davidic portrait drawn in this chapter. This side of David's character foreshad-ows a later time when his willingness to kill is not restrained, and he sends Uriah to his death in order to take Bathsheba for himself (2 Samuel 11). The consequences of this surrender to his own violent side are monumental for David and his family (2 Samuel 12–20). In both incidents, David seeks to kill a man and then marries his wife. Due to Abigail, who acts as an instrument of the Lord, David does not kill Nabal, and the later marriage is not tainted by bloodguilt. With Uriah and Bathsheba, David does kill, and the marriage is shadowed by blood.

Abigail is the central character in this episode, even though David's coming kingship remains the larger context. She appears as the agent through whose gifts the Lord is at work to restrain David from violence.[163] In contrast to Nabal and his foolishness, Abigail recognizes in David the future king of Israel and understands the danger that bloodguilt would constitute to that kingship. It is through her remarkable human gifts that the word and will of God are made clear to David and he is able to step back from the danger. Her gifts include intelligence, beauty, excellence in speech, resourcefulness, and a willingness to take action. Levenson sees her as the model of the wise woman (contrasted to the fool) and relates her to the "ideal woman" of Prov 31:10-31.[164] Bach objects that she can hardly be the "ideal woman," since she "refers to her husband as a fool (v. 25), sides with his enemy, and does not even mourn his death." Bach sees her as a figure with pro-phetic connections, speaking God's word to David and pronouncing the first prophecy of a "sure house" for David (v. 28).[165] This phrase certainly looks ahead to Nathan's dynastic oracle in 2 Samuel 7. It may be significant that Abigail's story comes after the death of Samuel (v. 1) and before Nathan has entered the story. Abigail is the bridge between these prophets for God's Word, whether she holds an overt office as prophet or not. An additional element of Abigail's character has been recognized by Berlin, who sees her as a mirror image of Bathsheba.[166] Uriah is a good man, but Bathsheba can do nothing to save him. Nabal is a worthless man, but Abigail goes to great lengths to save him. David is drawn to Bathsheba in an encounter of illicit sex, but Abigail, though she marries David, is not involved sexually with him at all, and the marriage is completely legitimate. For Bathsheba, David kills; for Abigail, David refrains from killing.

Through the characters and the roles they play in this story, chap. 25 serves as the central piece in the defense of David (chaps. 24–26) against the charge of using violence to gain the throne. At the same time, this chapter brings to fruition the themes of divine destiny in David's rise and foreshadows the themes of dynasty and downfall in David's future.

25:1. With the briefest of notices, we learn that Samuel has died. It is the end of an important

163. See Walter Brueggemann, *Power, Providence, and Personality* (Louisville: Westminster/John Knox, 1990) 62.

164. Jon D. Levenson, "1 Samuel 25 as Literature and History," *CBQ* 40 (1978) 11-28. This excellent article has influenced much of my understanding of this chapter.

165. Alice Bach, "The Pleasure of Her Text," in *The Pleasure of Her Text: Feminist Readings of Biblical and Historical Texts,* ed. Alice Bach (Philadelphia: Trinity Press International, 1990) 29, 34.

166. Berlin, "Characterization in Biblical Narrative," 76.

time of transition in Israel. For good or for ill, Israel now stands fully in the era of kings. Samuel had anointed Saul and presided over his rejection. He had anointed David and saw the beginnings of his rise to kingship. Perhaps the narrator has waited until this moment to report Samuel's death so that we can first hear the confession of David's kingship from the mouth of Saul himself (24:20). David's kingship and Israel's future are secure. The notice that David went down to the wilderness of Paran is changed by almost all commentators to read with the LXX, "the wilderness of Maon."

25:2-8. The story opens with the introduction of two characters we have not previously met. The first is Nabal, but we are introduced to his property and wealth before we ever learn his name (v. 2).[167] We are told that he is a "very great man" (NRSV; NIV, "rich"; the phrase probably indicates influence as well as wealth). He has "three thousand sheep and a thousand goats," and we are told that it is shearing time, a time of celebration and profit-making from the flocks. Finally (v. 3) we are told his name. This must have raised the eyebrows of Hebrew readers, for his name means "fool" or "churl." The word נבל (*nābāl*) appears frequently in wisdom contexts as the opposite of the wise man, one who is a glutton (Prov 30:22), a miser (Jer 17:11), who does not believe in God (Pss 14:1; 53:1), and is a general embarrassment (Prov 17:21). A *nābāl* is stupid, but in a vicious and mean-spirited manner, not in the harmless way of the simpleton. In v. 3*b*, Nabal is characterized as "surly and mean." Especially interesting is the long description of a *nābāl* in Isa 32:5-8, which includes the refusal of the *nābāl* to give food and drink to those in need of them (Isa 32:6), the precise violation of hospitality that Nabal commits against David in this story. Verse 3*b* also tells us that Nabal was a Calebite, one of the most influential clans of Judah, with its chief city in Hebron.

In the midst of v. 3 we are also briefly introduced to Abigail, who provides a contrast to Nabal. We are given her name first and then told that she is "clever/intelligent" (NRSV/NIV) and "beautiful." The word used here is שׂכל (*śekel*, "understanding," "intellect"), and Abigail is said to have "good understanding." She is a striking contrast to her husband, who is "surly and mean," but we cannot help thinking that she matches better with David, who is described as "handsome" in 16:12, using the same term as used here for Abigail's beauty. Both have inner qualities of "heart" (David) and "understanding/intelligence" (Abigail) that distinguish them beyond their good looks.

The action of the story begins with a delegation of ten men sent from David, who had heard it was shearing time (vv. 4-5). This time was one of revelry and feasting, and David believes this is the opportune moment to make a request of Nabal in Carmel. The emissaries are given careful instructions in courtesy and respect. They are to greet Nabal with a threefold greeting of "Peace" (שלום *šālôm*), a wish for well-being and wholeness to Nabal, to his house, and to all he has (v. 6). David's request is then to be conveyed to Nabal. His men have been with Nabal's shepherds, and David avows that no harm has come to them and nothing has been missing during that time (v. 7). On the basis of this protection, he asks for consideration at this feast time and is willing to take whatever Nabal might have at hand to give them by way of provisions (v. 8). David closes his message by referring to himself and his men as Nabal's servants, and to himself as "your son David," an intimate term of address used by Saul in chaps. 24 and 26 to address David.

Is this request legitimate or is it a veiled threat? Some commentators have seen David's greeting of peace and his statement affirming that the shepherds have not been harmed as veiled language for the lack of peace and the harm that will come to the shepherds if his request is not granted. In this view, David is a racketeer engaged in a protection scam.[168] This view seems more influenced by old gangster movies than by the biblical narrative. The shepherds themselves elaborate enthusiastically about David to Abigail and describe David's men as "a wall to us both night and day" (v. 16). In the protection rackets of gangster imagery, no real protection is ever given from any danger except from the collectors themselves. In the wilderness areas of Judah, the dangers to flocks from predators and thieves were quite real, but with David's men there, no sheep had been lost (even to David's men). Nabal's

---

167. Levenson, "1 Samuel 25 as Literature and History," 13-17, includes this observation in a detailed and helpful characterization of Nabal.

168. See, e.g., Walter Brueggemann, *First and Second Samuel*, Interpretation (Louisville: John Knox, 1990) 176, 179.

shepherds seem to believe that the presence and protection of David's men is an asset. David himself seems to believe that a genuine service had been rendered (v. 21). Certainly David's request seems respectful rather than demanding, although one would think that the simple rules of hospitality and common sense would warn Nabal against offending a man with an armed band of six hundred men. It would seem well for us to avoid seeing David's request as racketeering without further information on the customs of the time in such matters.

25:9-13. After Nabal has heard the request from David's men (v. 9), his response is as contemptuous as their tone had been respectful. He asks mockingly, "Who is David? Who is the son of Jesse?" (v. 10*a*). The implication is that David is a nobody. Even worse, Nabal suggests that David is no more than a runaway servant or slave, escaping from a master (v. 10*b*). The reference may be intended for us to think of Saul's pursuit of his "servant" David. There is considerable irony here, since a few verses later Nabal's own servants turn against him, describing him as "so ill-natured that no one can speak to him" (v. 17). Nabal ends his contemptuous response by claiming that his food and drink are for his own shearers and not for men without standing, like David and his entourage (v. 11). Not only has Nabal refused the request, but also he has demeaned those who brought it.

David's response is swift and harsh. Upon hearing the report (v. 12), David orders his men to strap on their swords and arms himself as well. He leaves two hundred men to guard the baggage and sets out with four hundred armed men (v. 13). David clearly intends to revenge the insult to his men and their request with violence, and unlike his opportunities to strike Saul (chaps. 24 and 26), he does not hesitate to choose this violent course of action.

25:14-17. Remarkably one of Nabal's servants comes to Abigail in distress about the situation (v. 14). He appears to be one of the shepherds in the field, for he seems to know of David and his men and to represent those who enjoyed their protection while in the field. He speaks of this experience with David in the first-person plural, and, as we have noted, he speaks to Abigail very positively about David and the servants' relationship to him (vv. 15-16). Somehow he has learned of

Nabal's insults to David's messengers and reports to Abigail of her husband's behavior (v. 14*b*). He also seems to know that this response will bring disaster ("evil") upon Nabal's whole household (v. 17). Whether he has a report of David's armed approach or simply knows from experience how David will respond we do not know. It is clear that he expects Abigail to be able to do something about the situation. He calls Nabal a בן-בליעל (*ben-bĕliyyaʿal*), "a worthless man, a good-for-nothing" (NRSV, "ill-natured"; NIV, "wicked man"). This is the same term used of those who were contemptuous of Saul in 10:26-27; Nabal has, like them, spurned the future king. The same term was also used of Eli's worthless sons (2:12) and of Eli's mistaken judgment about Hannah (1:16). Nabal is now labeled by his own servant as a worthless fool. But the servant clearly hopes for more from Abigail.

25:18-31. Abigail takes over the story at this point. If David was quick to take action for violence, Abigail matches his decisiveness in the effort to avoid violence. She takes action by gathering elaborate provisions for David's men. The narrative lingers over the precise details of the food and drink as they are loaded on donkeys, perhaps marveling at Abigail's ability to assemble so much on such short notice (v. 18). She sends the provisions on ahead with servants, promising that she herself will follow (v. 19). One is reminded of the gifts sent ahead by Jacob to soothe a potentially murderous Esau (Genesis 32). The narrative makes a point of noting that she does not tell her husband, Nabal (v. 19*b*).

Abigail follows after the provisions on her donkey, whereupon she meets David and his men on the way (v. 20). It is noteworthy that she is not willing to sit home and hope the provisions will appease David. Her own personal involvement carries considerable risk, given the hostile intentions of David. The meeting of Abigail with David gives the narrator the opportunity to reemphasize that hostile intent. We are given access to David's vow of vengeance (vv. 21-22). David recalls his protection of Nabal's men and flocks and characterizes what Nabal has done as having "returned me evil for good." This clearly links Nabal with Saul in 24:17 and suggests that the narrator does not see David as being engaged in some morally questionable scam. But David is on the brink of violence for the sake of vengeance, having vowed to kill all the males of Nabal's household (v. 22). The Hebrew text here translates literally "all who piss upon the wall," a euphemism for male gender by reference to their means of urination (cf. v. 34).

The account returns to Abigail, who dismounts and falls on the ground in obeisance before David (v. 23). At this point the focus shifts from the actions of Abigail to the speech of Abigail. She is as eloquent as she is decisive, but she is also strategic. Constantly throughout her speeches she addresses David as "my lord" and speaks of herself as "your servant," literally "your maidservant." Her initial words are disarming in the light of David's vow. She boldly claims all the guilt as hers alone (v. 24). What is David to do? He has vowed the death of all males in Nabal's household, and a woman is now taking all the blame. At the very least it blunts David's resolve and allows her a hearing. Although she has accepted blame, she does not hesitate to indicate where actual blame belongs, nor is she reluctant to describe her husband with candor (v. 25a). She pleads that David not take seriously an איש הבליעל (’îš habbĕliyya‘al), a "worthless man." She boldly claims that his name, "Nabal," describes him. "Fool [nābāl] is his name, and folly [נבלה nĕbālâ] is with him." (Isa 32:5 also makes this connection, "For the fool utters foolishness [nĕbālâ].") She subtly contrasts herself to her husband. If David had dealt with her, none of this would have happened, but she did not see the young men David sent (v. 25b).

Abigail counters David's vow with a vow of her own, taken in the name of the Lord and of David's own life (v. 26a). Abigail's language in this section of her speech makes constant reference to the Lord (Yahweh) and to what the Lord is doing in these events. Abigail gives voice to the word and will of God here in a manner very reminiscent of the prophets. She claims that the Lord has restrained David from bloodguilt and the taking of vengeance with his own hand (v. 26b). Since the intervention has been entirely through the agency of Abigail, we must conclude that her actions of intervention were God's actions. God, through Abigail, has kept David from actions that would argue against his worthiness for kingship. In chaps. 24 and 26, David makes clear that God's anointed one is not to be killed; in this chapter, he must learn that neither is God's anointed one to engage in unnecessary killing. To take violent vengeance on Nabal would constitute serious moral

and practical impediments to David's future kingship. One could hardly imagine the later crowning of David at Hebron (2 Sam 2:1-4) if he had wiped out the entire household of a prominent Calebite.

Abigail goes on to express the hope that David's "enemies and those who seek to do evil to my lord be like Nabal" (v. 26b). According to Abigail's speech, Nabal is as good as dead, but not by David's hand. It is Saul who "seeks" David for evil. Saul's death, not by David's hand, is foreshadowed here as well (as chaps. 24 and 26 make clear).

The provisions are offered as a blessing (NRSV, "present"; NIV, "gift") for David's men (v. 27), and Abigail, having already accepted guilt, asks for forgiveness (v. 28a). What Abigail offers in return is a word about David's future. Her words are prophetic in tone and explicitly anticipate the dynastic oracle of the prophet Nathan (2 Samuel 7). Abigail proclaims that the Lord will make for David a "sure house" in Israel (v. 28b). It is the first direct reference to the Davidic dynasty and is the same phrase used for dynastic promise in 2 Sam 7:11, 17, 26-27; 1 Kgs 2:24; 11:38. This affirmation of David for Israel's future goes beyond even Saul's confession in 24:20. Abigail implies that such a promise is deserved because David is fighting the battles of the Lord. It is less clear what she means by claiming that evil will not be found in David for his entire lifetime, since this is not the case as his story unfolds. Some believe she is speaking primarily of his innocence at this point in the story.

Abigail again turns to speak of those who pursue David as enemies who seek his life (v. 29). Saul is the only one who comes to mind. In a colorful metaphor, she announces God's protection for David. He will be "bound in the bundle of the living under the care of the LORD your God." Enemies like Saul receive their own metaphor, apparently drawn from David's victory over Goliath. They will be "slung out as from the hollow of a sling." Nabal, as David's enemy in this story, is eventually struck by the Lord and becomes "like a stone" (v. 37).

Abigail understands that David will be instrumental for Israel's future, and she knows this from the Lord. She boldly sums up what she has done for David and proclaims his future at the same time. When the Lord has done all the good spoken about David (Abigail seems privy to this divine information) and has appointed him "prince over Israel" (נגיד *nāgîd*, the term used in 9:16 for king-designate, referring to Saul), then David will be free of guilt over spilling innocent blood. His kingship can be claimed without taint. The implication is that David has been saved from this fate. Abigail subtly takes credit by asking that when the Lord has dealt well with David, he "remember" her (v. 31). This request eventually results in David's marriage to Abigail.

25:32-35. David's response is simple and direct, and in most ways it defers to Abigail as the chief actor in this drama. He speaks in doxology by pronouncing a threefold blessing. In these blessings are both praise and recognition. He recognizes that it is the Lord who has met him in Abigail (v. 32). He recognizes Abigail's "good sense/good judgment" (v. 33*a*), a quality that again marks her as a wise woman (see Prov 11:22). He recognizes that her action has kept him from bloodguilt and vengeance by his own hand (v. 33*b*). It is this last recognition that gives David pause for further reflection. Without Abigail, David's impulse to do violence against the men of Nabal's house would have been unrestrained (v. 34), and David's claim to the kingdom would have been clouded by bloodguilt against a prominent Calebite family in Judah. David has stared into the abyss of his own violence yet again. As he reflects on what might have been, we learn that Abigail herself had been in danger, for David credits the Lord God of Israel with restraining him from hurting Abigail (v. 34*a*). David is sober and chastened after having faced this woman of courage, resourcefulness, and persuasive speech. David receives the provisions she has brought and sends her home with the blessing of peace that he had tried to give to her husband, Nabal (v. 35). David acknowledges her persuasive voice and grants her petition (lit., "I have lifted up your face," v. 35*b*).

25:36-38. When Abigail returns home, Nabal is feasting and drunk, a state consistent with the gluttonous behavior associated elsewhere with a "fool." She tells him nothing until the next morning (v. 36). His feast is described as "like a king," but ironically he has left an actual king outside the feast and without provision except for the intervention of Abigail. The next morning, when the wine has drained out of Nabal (perhaps a wordplay, since *nābāl* can also mean "wineskin"), Abigail tells him what she has done (v. 37*a*). His

reaction is immediate and harsh: "His heart died within him; he became like a stone" (v. 37*b*). Nabal's "merry heart" (v. 36*b*) is now stilled and hardened. Ten days later, the Lord strikes Nabal so that he dies (26:10 suggests this could also become the fate of Saul). It is the Lord who takes vengeance, and not David. "The fool has said in his heart there is no God" (Pss 14:1; 53:1), but here God has struck the heart of the fool. Nabal has offended God in treating God's anointed one with contempt. In chaps. 24 and 26 David refrains from acting against God's anointed one, knowing that one cannot injure God's anointed with impunity. Nabal, the fool, demonstrates the wisdom of David in this matter. Abigail has saved David from interfering with this divine justice.

25:39-44. David responds to the news of Nabal's death with another doxology (cf. vv. 32-33). His offer of praise to the Lord clearly acknowledges the right of God to judge him and the evil that he had almost committed (v. 39). In praising the Lord for keeping him from such evildoing, he tacitly equates the action of Abigail with the action of God. In these events, Abigail was the embodiment of God's activity on behalf of David.

David woos Abigail; he sends a delegation to "take you to him as his wife" (v. 40). This "taking" does not seem like the royal actions in the warning of Samuel (8:11-18) or the illicit seizure of Uriah's wife, Bathsheba (2 Sam 11:4). Abigail is a free woman and responds willingly (although some feel her response in v. 41 is excessively subservient). As she had done before, she rides out to meet David. The accompanying five maids signify her wealth and importance. She becomes David's wife (v. 42).

Verses 43-44 are not a part of the story itself. They offer further notices about David's marriages, undoubtedly placed here because of his marriage to Abigail. We are told that David also married Ahinoam of Jezreel (v. 43). Most believe this is the Jezreel mentioned as a city in Judah, near Maon and Carmel (Josh 15:56), and not the northern and better-known Jezreel. Levenson and Halpern have made clear the probable importance of these marriages in solidifying Judahite support for David and explaining the quick action to crown David king in Hebron after the death of Saul (2 Sam 2:1-4).[169] In Abigail's case, David

___

169. Jon D. Levenson and Baruch Halpern, "The Political Import of David's Marriages," *JBL* 99 (1980) 507-18.

became the head of a wealthy Calebite household, and the marriage to Ahinoam at least made him part of another important clan of Judah. Levenson's suggestion that Ahinoam was the same one who was the only named wife of Saul (14:50) has little support.[170] It seems unlikely that such an audacious act, with its claim on the throne of Saul, would stand without comment in the biblical narrative. Ahinoam later gives birth to David's

first son, Amnon, whose rape of Tamar sets off a series of violent episodes in David's family (2 Samuel 13). Abigail also bears a son, named either Chileab (2 Sam 3:3) or Daniel (1 Chr 3:1).

While David is concluding influential marriages in Judah, Saul acts to deprive him of his own daughter Michal by giving her to another man, Palti (v. 44). This act would appear to be an effort to deprive David of any legitimate claim on the Saulide line.

170. Jon D. Levenson, "1 Samuel 25 as Literature and History," *CBQ* 40 (1978) 27.

REFLECTIONS

1. "Beloved, never avenge yourselves, but leave room for the wrath of God; for it is written, 'Vengeance is mine, I will repay, says the Lord' " (Rom 12:19 NRSV; cf. Heb 10:30). The story of Abigail's saving David from bloodguilt could almost use this line from the apostle Paul as an Aesop-like moral at the end of the story. First Samuel 25 could serve as a parable on the truth and importance of this statement by Paul. Yet, Paul himself is actually quoting the Torah in Deut 32:35, and the principle of vengeance reserved to God and not to be taken into one's own hands is an important Hebrew moral principle (see also Prov 20:22; 24:29).

This notion that vengeance belongs to God is widely misunderstood. Many modern Christians would read Paul's statement as a remnant of some harsh, judgmental Old Testament God. But Mendenhall has shown that God's vengeance is not an arbitrary or capricious divine wrath, but an expression of divine governance related to justice and righteousness as operative and maintained by God in the world.[171] Even more important, the reservation of vengeance to God removes justification for human vengeance. If "vengeance is mine, says the Lord," then it cannot be yours or mine. Both Abigail and David state the most important outcome of Abigail's intervention—namely, that David did not take vengeance into his own hands (vv. 26, 33).

The forestalling of vengeance by one's own hand opens the possibilities for creative moral action and discernment of God's providence. Paul's reflection on vengeance as the Lord's is followed by this statement: "No, 'if your enemies are hungry, feed them; if they are thirsty, give them something to drink' " (Rom 12:20 NRSV). Paul is quoting Jesus' teachings (Matt 5:44; 25:35; Luke 6:27), but it is Abigail who has already acted this out. In her actions to forestall vengeance, new possibilities are made available. Lives are saved, of course, but the future kingdom God is making for Israel through David is saved as well. God does act against Nabal, but David is not tainted with Nabal's blood. In their marriage, both David and Abigail claim a future that could not have been possible in the aftermath of a vengeful raid. In the surrounding chapters 24 and 26, David's restraint from violence leads to Saul's concession of the kingdom, a legitimization David could never have had by killing Saul.

2. "Blessed are the peacemakers, for they will be called the children of God" (Matt 5:9 NRSV). Peacemaking and acting as a partner in God's family are allied in this saying of Jesus. Abigail models it. David is reminded of it by Abigail on the verge of violating the peace, and he sees God's action in Abigail (1 Sam 25:32, 39). To do good rather than evil is to align our actions with what God is doing. To be peacemakers is to seek the unity of human moral agency with divine agency; Abigail models this. Her husband Nabal models its opposite. Evil appears as foolishness and removal from God.

171. George M. Mendenhall, "The 'Vengeance' of Yahweh," in *The Tenth Generation: The Origins of the Biblical Tradition* (Baltimore: Johns Hopkins University Press, 1973) 69-104.

Peace in the Hebrew sense of *šālôm* means wholeness and well-being. David announces such a hope for peace through his men (v. 6), but the actions of Nabal prevent it. To act the fool is to create brokenness. Evil appears here as moral disregard and self-preoccupation. This also characterizes Saul, who has become evil in the sense of playing the fool (which he admits in 26:21). He was not inherently evil and did not begin his kingship by intending the evil use of power. He became one who returned evil for good (24:17) through his own foolishness. In our own time, it is often easier to confront great forces of obvious evil (Hitlers and Stalins, KKK and Bull Connors, apartheid and ethnic cleansing) than to confront our own mean-spirited foolishness and the evil that results. It is easy to desire peacemaking and turning from vengeance as the work of diplomats and Nobel prize winners. It is more difficult to rush, like Abigail, into the breaches of daily life where foolishness provokes violence and standing between the two is risky business.

3. This is an unusual story in the Hebrew Bible because a woman, Abigail, appears as the chief protagonist. Hebrew biblical narrative in general is the product of a highly patriarchal culture, and women usually appear as secondary characters in men's stories, with some notable exceptions.[172] Even in Abigail's case, the story is in the context of the larger story of David's rise to kingship. But this distinct episode belongs to Abigail. She is the only character in contact with all the other characters in the story. After the initial description of the crisis, she is the clear decision maker and action taker. Except for his initial resolve to violence, which is seen as a rash and unconsidered action, even David primarily responds to her initiatives. Abigail is pictured with bold qualities of character: intelligence, direct and persuasive speech, decisiveness, good sense, and vision. Most unusual is that Abigail is seen as the surrogate for Yahweh (the Lord). Her actions are the agency for God's actions and are recognized as such by David (and, therefore, by the narrator of this history). Abigail both acts for God and speaks for God, and this acting and speaking are the salvation of the future king. She saves him from bloodguilt and the terrible burden this would place on his kingship.

Some have reacted negatively to Abigail because of her deferential speech and her initiation and acceptance of marriage to David. We should not be too harsh on her for acting within the framework of her own time. It was a patriarchal culture, and there was little place in it for unmarried women. Unusual to her time was her bold initiative to secure a marriage of her own choosing. That she secures a safe place for her own future we should not begrudge her.

Abigail is an important biblical model of moral courage and peacemaking. She dealt with both the evil of Nabal and the danger of David in a forthright and resourceful way, and at considerable risk to herself. She could well have experienced violence from Nabal or from David. It is significant that, as a woman of wealth and privilege, she was approached in trustful confidence by the servants of the household seeking help. She models peacemaking in her ability to see issues at stake beyond the immediate situation and in enabling others (here most notably David) to see the long-term consequences of immediate acts of passion and self-gratification.

In her own initiatives, Abigail never loses sight of the larger movement of divine initiative, but she boldly claims a part in that providential movement. She persuasively relates present moral action to the larger vision of God's future and dares to place herself in a position to mediate the present in the light of that vision.

We live in a world constantly needing restraint from violence, and we could always do with more Abigails. She stands as a model in her own context for actions that avoid vengeance and make for peace. Our context is radically different from that of Abigail, but the tasks are no less urgent. Abigail acted boldly within the framework available to her, and in doing so she shaped the future of God's kingdom. Men and women may find in her example the encouragement to act for God's kingdom in opposition to the violence of our own time.

---

172. See Alice Ogden Bellis, *Helpmates, Harlots, Heroes: Women's Stories in the Hebrew Bible* (Louisville: Westminster/John Knox, 1994), for a helpful survey of women's stories and the considerable scholarly literature now available on them.

1 Samuel 26:1-25, David Spares Saul's Life Again

NIV

26 The Ziphites went to Saul at Gibeah and said, "Is not David hiding on the hill of Hakilah, which faces Jeshimon?"

²So Saul went down to the Desert of Ziph, with his three thousand chosen men of Israel, to search there for David. ³Saul made his camp beside the road on the hill of Hakilah facing Jeshimon, but David stayed in the desert. When he saw that Saul had followed him there, ⁴he sent out scouts and learned that Saul had definitely arrived.ᵃ

⁵Then David set out and went to the place where Saul had camped. He saw where Saul and Abner son of Ner, the commander of the army, had lain down. Saul was lying inside the camp, with the army encamped around him.

⁶David then asked Ahimelech the Hittite and Abishai son of Zeruiah, Joab's brother, "Who will go down into the camp with me to Saul?"

"I'll go with you," said Abishai.

⁷So David and Abishai went to the army by night, and there was Saul, lying asleep inside the camp with his spear stuck in the ground near his head. Abner and the soldiers were lying around him.

⁸Abishai said to David, "Today God has delivered your enemy into your hands. Now let me pin him to the ground with one thrust of my spear; I won't strike him twice."

⁹But David said to Abishai, "Don't destroy him! Who can lay a hand on the Lord's anointed and be guiltless? ¹⁰As surely as the Lord lives," he said, "the Lord himself will strike him; either his time will come and he will die, or he will go into battle and perish. ¹¹But the Lord forbid that I should lay a hand on the Lord's anointed. Now get the spear and water jug that are near his head, and let's go."

¹²So David took the spear and water jug near Saul's head, and they left. No one saw or knew about it, nor did anyone wake up. They were all sleeping, because the Lord had put them into a deep sleep.

¹³Then David crossed over to the other side and stood on top of the hill some distance away;

NRSV

26 Then the Ziphites came to Saul at Gibeah, saying, "David is in hiding on the hill of Hachilah, which is opposite Jeshimon."ᵃ ²So Saul rose and went down to the Wilderness of Ziph, with three thousand chosen men of Israel, to seek David in the Wilderness of Ziph. ³Saul encamped on the hill of Hachilah, which is opposite Jeshimonᵃ beside the road. But David remained in the wilderness. When he learned that Saul had come after him into the wilderness, ⁴David sent out spies, and learned that Saul had indeed arrived. ⁵Then David set out and came to the place where Saul had encamped; and David saw the place where Saul lay, with Abner son of Ner, the commander of his army. Saul was lying within the encampment, while the army was encamped around him.

6Then David said to Ahimelech the Hittite, and to Joab's brother Abishai son of Zeruiah, "Who will go down with me into the camp to Saul?" Abishai said, "I will go down with you." ⁷So David and Abishai went to the army by night; there Saul lay sleeping within the encampment, with his spear stuck in the ground at his head; and Abner and the army lay around him. ⁸Abishai said to David, "God has given your enemy into your hand today; now therefore let me pin him to the ground with one stroke of the spear; I will not strike him twice." ⁹But David said to Abishai, "Do not destroy him; for who can raise his hand against the Lord's anointed, and be guiltless?" ¹⁰David said, "As the Lord lives, the Lord will strike him down; or his day will come to die; or he will go down into battle and perish. ¹¹The Lord forbid that I should raise my hand against the Lord's anointed; but now take the spear that is at his head, and the water jar, and let us go." ¹²So David took the spear that was at Saul's head and the water jar, and they went away. No one saw it, or knew it, nor did anyone awake; for they were all asleep, because a deep sleep from the Lord had fallen upon them.

13Then David went over to the other side, and stood on top of a hill far away, with a great distance between them. ¹⁴David called to the army

ᵃ4 Or *had come to Nacon*

ᵃ Or *opposite the wasteland*

NIV

there was a wide space between them. ¹⁴He called out to the army and to Abner son of Ner, "Aren't you going to answer me, Abner?"

Abner replied, "Who are you who calls to the king?"

¹⁵David said, "You're a man, aren't you? And who is like you in Israel? Why didn't you guard your lord the king? Someone came to destroy your lord the king. ¹⁶What you have done is not good. As surely as the LORD lives, you and your men deserve to die, because you did not guard your master, the LORD's anointed. Look around you. Where are the king's spear and water jug that were near his head?"

¹⁷Saul recognized David's voice and said, "Is that your voice, David my son?"

David replied, "Yes it is, my lord the king." ¹⁸And he added, "Why is my lord pursuing his servant? What have I done, and what wrong am I guilty of? ¹⁹Now let my lord the king listen to his servant's words. If the LORD has incited you against me, then may he accept an offering. If, however, men have done it, may they be cursed before the LORD! They have now driven me from my share in the LORD's inheritance and have said, 'Go, serve other gods.' ²⁰Now do not let my blood fall to the ground far from the presence of the LORD. The king of Israel has come out to look for a flea—as one hunts a partridge in the mountains."

²¹Then Saul said, "I have sinned. Come back, David my son. Because you considered my life precious today, I will not try to harm you again. Surely I have acted like a fool and have erred greatly."

²²"Here is the king's spear," David answered. "Let one of your young men come over and get it. ²³The LORD rewards every man for his righteousness and faithfulness. The LORD delivered you into my hands today, but I would not lay a hand on the LORD's anointed. ²⁴As surely as I valued your life today, so may the LORD value my life and deliver me from all trouble."

²⁵Then Saul said to David, "May you be blessed, my son David; you will do great things and surely triumph."

So David went on his way, and Saul returned home.

NRSV

and to Abner son of Ner, saying, "Abner! Will you not answer?" Then Abner replied, "Who are you that calls to the king?" ¹⁵David said to Abner, "Are you not a man? Who is like you in Israel? Why then have you not kept watch over your lord the king? For one of the people came in to destroy your lord the king. ¹⁶This thing that you have done is not good. As the LORD lives, you deserve to die, because you have not kept watch over your lord, the LORD's anointed. See now, where is the king's spear, or the water jar that was at his head?"

¹⁷Saul recognized David's voice, and said, "Is this your voice, my son David?" David said, "It is my voice, my lord, O king." ¹⁸And he added, "Why does my lord pursue his servant? For what have I done? What guilt is on my hands? ¹⁹Now therefore let my lord the king hear the words of his servant. If it is the LORD who has stirred you up against me, may he accept an offering; but if it is mortals, may they be cursed before the LORD, for they have driven me out today from my share in the heritage of the LORD, saying, 'Go, serve other gods.' ²⁰Now therefore, do not let my blood fall to the ground, away from the presence of the LORD; for the king of Israel has come out to seek a single flea, like one who hunts a partridge in the mountains."

²¹Then Saul said, "I have done wrong; come back, my son David, for I will never harm you again, because my life was precious in your sight today; I have been a fool, and have made a great mistake." ²²David replied, "Here is the spear, O king! Let one of the young men come over and get it. ²³The LORD rewards everyone for his righteousness and his faithfulness; for the LORD gave you into my hand today, but I would not raise my hand against the LORD's anointed. ²⁴As your life was precious today in my sight, so may my life be precious in the sight of the LORD, and may he rescue me from all tribulation." ²⁵Then Saul said to David, "Blessed be you, my son David! You will do many things and will succeed in them." So David went his way, and Saul returned to his place.

COMMENTARY

This episode is a close parallel to chap. 24. Both have the same basic plot, though with differing details and some new emphases appearing in chap. 26. This is also the final chapter in a sequence of three episodes dealing with the temptation to violence that comes with power and David's avoidance of such violence. In chaps. 24 and 26, David has the opportunity to kill Saul, but he chooses against violence. In chap. 25, he is saved from violence against the house of Nabal by the intervention of Abigail. In all three chapters, the narrator understands violence to have been avoided because God was working providentially to bring David's kingdom to fruition. Violence would have created an impediment to his kingship over all Israel.

These three chapters also represent Saul's last hurrah. What remains after these stories are only the details surrounding his death (chaps. 28 and 31). In chaps. 24–26, we see Saul's relinquishment of the kingdom. Saul himself acknowledges David's coming kingdom in chap. 24. In chap. 25, Saul's death is foreshadowed in the fate of Nabal, and in chap. 26, Saul's death is even more explicitly foretold.

Many of the basic elements in the story of chap. 26 have already been treated in the discussion of chap. 24. The commentary on chap. 26 will stress those elements that differ from chap. 24. Some of these new and distinctive elements are:

❖ the role of Abishai as David's companion in the venture;
❖ the heightened sense of divine providence;
❖ the foreshadowing of Saul's death;
❖ the taking of Saul's spear and water jar;
❖ the taunting of Abner;
❖ David's suggestion of motivation for Saul's pursuit;
❖ Saul's final benediction to David.

26:1-5. Ziphites again report to Saul about David's whereabouts (v. 1; cf. 23:19). As before, Saul gathers a sizable force (3,000 men) to pursue his obsession (v. 2). Saul makes a base camp, and David, hearing that Saul has come into the area, sends out spies to locate him (vv. 3-4). With this information, David himself goes to find Saul asleep for the night, with Abner his commander at his side, and the army encircling him (v. 5). Unlike chap. 24, Saul has not come serendipitously into David's power. David has sought him out, and he will next take the initiative to go into Saul's camp. It is a more active David, seeking advantage over Saul, than we saw in chap. 24.

26:6-12. David speaks to Ahimelech the Hittite and to Abishai, Joab's brother, to see if they are daring enough go with him into Saul's camp. Abishai takes up the challenge eagerly (v. 6). We presume that Ahimelech declined. Abishai is one of the sons of Zeruiah, David's sister (1 Chr 2:16). Abishai and his two brothers, Joab and Asahel, are prominent members of David's warrior band. Joab becomes David's chief military commander, and Asahel is killed in an incident that starts a blood feud with difficult consequences for David (2 Samuel 2). Abishai was a member of David's elite "Thirty" and had been involved in numerous exploits that required a ready sword (2 Sam 2:18-24; 3:30; 10:9-14; 16:5-11; 18:2-14; 20:6-10; 21:16-17). David complains at one point, "These men, the sons of Zeruiah, are too violent for me" (2 Sam 3:39). Given this reputation, it is not surprising that Abishai volunteered for David's daring mission.

They find Saul sleeping with his spear stuck in the ground beside him, while Abner and the army surrounding him also sleep (v. 7). Abishai is ready to kill Saul. He claims that "God has given your enemy into your hand," but then wishes to be the extension of David's hand and pin Saul to the ground with one thrust of Saul's own spear (v. 8). David restrains him by claiming that no one can strike God's anointed and remain guiltless (v. 9). David's restraint no doubt reflects a mixture of compassion and respect for the office of king as God's anointed one. After all, David is himself God's anointed (see discussion of 24:1-22).

Abishai must have been difficult to hold back. David argues that the life of Saul must be in God's hands, not theirs. He details three ways in which Saul might meet his fate (v. 10): He will be struck down by God (as was Nabal, 25:38); he will die of natural causes ("his day will come to die"); or he will die in battle. It is this last possibility that is to be Saul's fate, although the fatal blow is not to be from the enemy's hand (chap. 31). David's urgent argument to Abishai is that Saul's death is coming, and it should not come at their hands.

David proposes that they take the spear and a water jug nearby and leave (v. 11). These will prove that they had the opportunity to harm Saul. They take these things and make their way out of the camp with no one knowing of their presence (v. 12a). But the note in v. 12b suggests that this act of human daring was assisted by divine providence: "Because a deep sleep from the LORD had fallen upon them." More than in chap. 24, the narrator has emphasized the activity of God through and beside the actions of the human participants in the story. The events leading to Israel's future in David are subject to divine governance. David seems to sense this. His refusal to burden his coming kingship with the blood of Saul grows out of trust that God's way with Saul will take its own course. Five times in his speech to Abishai (vv. 9-11) David mentions the name of the Lord. The narrator, by telling us of the deep sleep from the Lord (v. 12), lets us know that God is also enabling the course of David's future.

26:13-16. Standing on a hill at a distance, David calls to the sleeping army and singles out Abner in particular (vv. 13-14). Abner, the commander of Saul's army (14:50-51), plays a crucial role in future events. He does not seem initially to recognize David (v. 14b). David addresses him with contempt, as a soldier who has failed in his duty. He taunts Abner for having a reputation as a warrior but failing to keep adequate watch over "your lord, the king" (v. 15). David boldly claims that Abner deserves to die for having failed to protect the Lord's anointed, and he calls attention to the missing spear and water jug—proof that the king's life had been in jeopardy even while Saul slept in the midst of his army (v. 16). It may be that David's death sentence against Abner is intended to foreshadow and justify Joab's later killing of Abner, even though the immediate cause at the time was a matter of family vengeance for Joab (2 Sam 3:27). The protection of the life of God's anointed one is no small matter in these stories. David succeeds in ridiculing Abner for disregard of Saul, while David places himself in the position of honoring Saul by sparing his life when the king was in his power. It is the fugitive and outlaw who has best guarded the king's life.

26:17-25. Instead of two formal monologues by David and Saul, as in chap. 24, there is here an exchange of speeches between the two. It is Saul who recognizes David, and his initial response is unexpectedly intimate, "Is this your voice, my son David?" (v. 17). In all three of Saul's speeches he addresses David as "my son" (vv. 17, 21, 25). Even more remarkable, in each of these places he also uses David's name. We have become accustomed in previous chapters to Saul's contemptuous and dismissive reference to David as "the son of Jesse." Unlike 24:11, however, David does not address Saul as "my father." He addresses Saul formally but respectfully as "my lord, O king" and refers to himself deferentially as Saul's "servant" (vv. 17b-18).

As in chap. 24, David declares his innocence of wrongdoing toward the king (v. 18), but his speech in v. 19 probes further the motivation of Saul's pursuit of David. He raises the possibility that the Lord has roused Saul to pursue him; but it does not appear that David believes this, and he suggests that an offering would be enough to put the relationship right. David then ventures that other men have stirred Saul against him. Here he seems more passionate, suggesting this is where he believes blame belongs. "May they be cursed before the LORD," David exclaims. Such opponents, he claims, are driving him out of the land of Israel, the heritage of the Lord. David surprisingly suggests that they are driving him to the service of other gods (v. 19b). David's claim here may be a preparation for his move in chap. 27 into the service of Achish, the Philistine king of Gath. This must have been a controversial element in David's career, and his speech (v. 19) suggests that others have driven him to seek refuge outside the land of Israel. It would not have been David's choice. In fact, David pleads with Saul to relent from his pursuit so that David might not die away from the land of the Lord (v. 20a). Saul has mounted a big-game hunt for a mere flea (v. 20b).

Saul responds in a confession (v. 21). It is briefer than Saul's speech in 24:16-21, but it is more striking because Saul admits to wrongdoing. Bluntly Saul states, "I have done wrong." He calls himself a fool (recalling Nabal in chap. 25) and admits he has made a mistake. In the midst of this self-critique, Saul also invites David to return, although it is not clear whether this means to the service of Saul or back to the royal household. He vows no harm will come to David and recognizes that David has already had opportunity to harm him but has not done so. As it turns out, this is the last story in which Saul pursues David, but 27:4 suggests that this is only because David left Israelite territory.

David dramatically shows the spear (perhaps the same one previously thrown at him) and offers to return it (v. 22). Although he continues to speak to Saul, David's focus shifts to his own vindication before the Lord. He seeks nothing from Saul. Perhaps he realizes that he already has the kingdom from Saul and can ask for nothing more. Instead, David gives voice to his hope and trust that the Lord rewards righteousness and faithfulness, that David's own life will be precious in the sight of the Lord, and that the Lord will deliver him from all trouble (vv. 23*a*, 24). He recognizes that the Lord was present in the events that gave Saul into his hand (v. 23*b*). David gave back Saul's life, but it is to the Lord that David looks for his life (v. 24*a*). In the parallel accounts of chaps. 24 and 26, the trustful faith of David is more evident in chap. 26. David has refrained from the temptation to violence as a means to power, but it was trust in the Lord's ability to bring David's future in God's own way that enabled David to refuse violence as a means to his own future. This is David's last speech to Saul, and in it he has moved away from concern with Saul. David now focuses on the Lord as the source of Israel's future and his own.

Saul's final response is a less explicit concession than his conceding of the kingdom to David in 24:20, but it is more sweeping. He pronounces a blessing on David and acknowledges that David's success is assured. Saul's final sentence uses two intensive grammatical constructions (infinitives absolute) to express the strength of his final knowledge of David's future: "You will *indeed* do many things and will *surely* succeed in them" (v. 25). David and Saul part for the last time.

REFLECTIONS

Saul and David are finished with each other. Kingship has been conceded to David. David has refused violence as a means to achieve power. Chapters 24–26 have had moments of intense human drama with life and death hanging in the balance (see Reflections on chaps. 24 and 25). Yet, through it all it is clear that the Lord is at work in these human events. For the most part, there is no effort in the telling of the story to demarcate human and divine action. God's actions are often seen in and through the action of human events (the exception is the deep sleep of 26:12). It is together that divine providence and human agency have modeled a way to power that is not based on violence. The restraint of David and the intervention of Abigail are significant as human moral acts in the face of violent potential. But their actions are not without resources rooted in trust that the Lord is at work, and both Abigail and David give credit for God's presence in their own actions.

In our own modern experience, the tendency is to separate human and divine agency in dealing with the issues of violence and power. There are those, on the one hand, who expect God to make moral decisions for them or to take the crucial moral actions. They pray for righteousness, peace, and justice but do nothing to enable it. They treat the Bible as a prescriptive rule book through which they hope God will direct them. On the other hand, there are those who imagine that human resources alone are adequate to build the future. They trust only those possibilities that emerge out of empirical data or rational analysis. They do not trust that God is also at work. They miss opportunities that come as surprises of graceful possibility and are overlooked by inventories of human resources alone. Particularly in the arenas of power politics there often seems to be little room for qualities of compassion, restraint, patience, and mediation. Such qualities are often considered soft—not realistic politics in the world's terms.

Chapter 26 suggests that there are alternatives in dealing with the issues of power and violence. David models a willingness to receive the kingdom on God's terms by refusing violence as a means to power and trusting that God will open other options for dealing with

Saul. The alternative to David in this story is Abishai, who knows no way but violence on his own terms. The boundary between the two is small. David knows how close he is to Abishai's way, and the story of Abigail's intervention in chap. 25 tells us that David is capable of choosing that way. But Abishai's way would have polarized David's kingdom. To seize by force the objects or goals we desire is often to destroy the very thing we hoped to gain. Whether we look at hardened lines of conflict in international disputes or in family dynamics, one often suspects that Abishai's way has prevailed. We try to force the future we desire through various degrees of physical, political, and emotional violence. Like David, we all live too close for comfort to the temptation to force our will, to retaliate, and to justify our attempts to control.

In this story, David does restrain Abishai, even as he was himself restrained by Abigail. It suggests that there is a moral alternative to the violent practices of power that are evident in our marriages and families, our power politics and military might, and our economic and racial divisions. But this alternative requires imaginative discernment of God at work in the midst of our own actions. Qualities of compassion, righteousness, faithfulness, and trust are evident in these stories. But reading these stories teaches us that such qualities will appear only when we give up our own attempts to force the future and instead choose partnership with God, who constantly gives us our future as a gift and bids us receive it rather than grasp it.[173]

173. See D. M. Gunn, "David and the Gift of the Kingdom," *Semeia* 3 (1975) 14-45.

1 Samuel 27:1–28:2, David in the Service of the Philistines

NIV

27 But David thought to himself, "One of these days I will be destroyed by the hand of Saul. The best thing I can do is to escape to the land of the Philistines. Then Saul will give up searching for me anywhere in Israel, and I will slip out of his hand."

²So David and the six hundred men with him left and went over to Achish son of Maoch king of Gath. ³David and his men settled in Gath with Achish. Each man had his family with him, and David had his two wives: Ahinoam of Jezreel and Abigail of Carmel, the widow of Nabal. ⁴When Saul was told that David had fled to Gath, he no longer searched for him.

⁵Then David said to Achish, "If I have found favor in your eyes, let a place be assigned to me in one of the country towns, that I may live there. Why should your servant live in the royal city with you?"

⁶So on that day Achish gave him Ziklag, and it has belonged to the kings of Judah ever since. ⁷David lived in Philistine territory a year and four months.

⁸Now David and his men went up and raided the Geshurites, the Girzites and the Amalekites. (From ancient times these peoples had lived in

NRSV

27 David said in his heart, "I shall now perish one day by the hand of Saul; there is nothing better for me than to escape to the land of the Philistines; then Saul will despair of seeking me any longer within the borders of Israel, and I shall escape out of his hand." ²So David set out and went over, he and the six hundred men who were with him, to King Achish son of Maoch of Gath. ³David stayed with Achish at Gath, he and his troops, every man with his household, and David with his two wives, Ahinoam of Jezreel, and Abigail of Carmel, Nabal's widow. ⁴When Saul was told that David had fled to Gath, he no longer sought for him.

5Then David said to Achish, "If I have found favor in your sight, let a place be given me in one of the country towns, so that I may live there; for why should your servant live in the royal city with you?" ⁶So that day Achish gave him Ziklag; therefore Ziklag has belonged to the kings of Judah to this day. ⁷The length of time that David lived in the country of the Philistines was one year and four months.

8Now David and his men went up and made raids on the Geshurites, the Girzites, and the Amalekites; for these were the landed settlements

NIV

the land extending to Shur and Egypt.) ⁹Whenever David attacked an area, he did not leave a man or woman alive, but took sheep and cattle, donkeys and camels, and clothes. Then he returned to Achish.

¹⁰When Achish asked, "Where did you go raiding today?" David would say, "Against the Negev of Judah" or "Against the Negev of Jerahmeel" or "Against the Negev of the Kenites." ¹¹He did not leave a man or woman alive to be brought to Gath, for he thought, "They might inform on us and say, 'This is what David did.'" And such was his practice as long as he lived in Philistine territory. ¹²Achish trusted David and said to himself, "He has become so odious to his people, the Israelites, that he will be my servant forever."

28 In those days the Philistines gathered their forces to fight against Israel. Achish said to David, "You must understand that you and your men will accompany me in the army."

²David said, "Then you will see for yourself what your servant can do."

Achish replied, "Very well, I will make you my bodyguard for life."

NRSV

from Telam*a* on the way to Shur and on to the land of Egypt. ⁹David struck the land, leaving neither man nor woman alive, but took away the sheep, the oxen, the donkeys, the camels, and the clothing, and came back to Achish. ¹⁰When Achish asked, "Against whom*b* have you made a raid today?" David would say, "Against the Negeb of Judah," or "Against the Negeb of the Jerahmeelites," or, "Against the Negeb of the Kenites." ¹¹David left neither man nor woman alive to be brought back to Gath, thinking, "They might tell about us, and say, 'David has done so and so.'" Such was his practice all the time he lived in the country of the Philistines. ¹²Achish trusted David, thinking, "He has made himself utterly abhorrent to his people Israel; therefore he shall always be my servant."

28 In those days the Philistines gathered their forces for war, to fight against Israel. Achish said to David, "You know, of course, that you and your men are to go out with me in the army." ²David said to Achish, "Very well, then you shall know what your servant can do." Achish said to David, "Very well, I will make you my bodyguard for life."

a Compare Gk 15.4: Heb *from of old* *b* Q Ms Gk Vg: MT lacks *whom*

COMMENTARY

In spite of chaps. 24 and 26, the enmity between David and Saul has not ended, or at least David is not willing to trust that it has ended. David believes that he can only find safety by leaving the area of Saul's authority. He feels compelled to take refuge in Philistine territory and to support his company by doing service to Achish, the king of Gath. In the history of David's rise, this episode justifies the Philistine interlude in David's career by claiming that it was forced by Saul. The story goes on to claim further that David was not really disloyal. Rather, he turned the occasion of his service to the advantage of Judah and duped the Philistines in the process.

This chapter, and its continuation in chap. 29, includes no explicit theological interests. God remains hidden in this portion of the story. As for

David, we have seen much to admire in him thus far. Much of what we have seen bears out the judgment of the servant who first brought him to Saul's attention in 16:18: He is "skillful in playing, a man of valor, a warrior, prudent in speech, and a man of good presence; and the LORD is with him." In this chapter, we are reminded that David can also be tough, opportunistic, and cunning. He is capable of ruthless behavior. We have seen some of this side of David as well from time to time (most notably in the rage from which Abigail restrains him, chap. 25). David is presented here as a warrior, looking out for himself and his entourage as best he can. He could be ruthlessly effective in pursuit of his own needs for security and political gain.

27:1-4. David does not think he is safe from

Saul's murderous intentions. David has six hundred men with him, along with their entire households, including women and children; he himself now has two wives (vv. 2-3). With such a large party, he cannot indefinitely elude Saul. He can think of no better alternative than to leave Saul's territory, and that means moving into Philistine territory as the one place Saul certainly will not pursue him (v. 1). It is a calculated risk. For one who aspired to the throne of Israel, such consort with Israel's enemy would be hard to explain. Perhaps only David would have dared it. He seems to have considered this strategy earlier (21:11-16), but he was recognized and forced to abandon the attempt. Perhaps this was too close in time to some of his own exploits against the Philistines. It may be that David is now perceived as the enemy of the king of Israel, Saul. In any case, David and his company, including Abigail and Ahinoam, are received into residence in Gath. When Saul hears that David is in Gath, he does abandon his pursuit (v. 4). It is the permanent end of the threat from Saul, for he is soon caught up in the events that end his life.

27:5-7. David approaches Achish, the king of Gath, with a proposal. He asks that he be assigned a town where he can be of service to Achish rather than living in Gath itself (v. 5). We presume that David would have to render service to the Philistine king in some way in order to be allowed to live in Gath or any other place in his kingdom. David's move is a shrewd one, since it places the execution of his service to Achish at a remove from close scrutiny by the king. Achish accepts the proposal and assigns David the town of Ziklag as the location for David's service (v. 6a), perhaps as a kind of feudal territory. The text notes that Ziklag continued to be regarded as a personal holding of the Davidic kings in Judah down to the time of the writing of the account (v. 6b). Verse 7 inserts a chronological note that David was in Philistine service for one year and four months.

27:8-12. Presumably David's assignment was to pacify the enemies of Philistine Gath in the region of Ziklag, which lay on the boundary between the territory of Gath and a region that included the settlements of the Israelite tribe of Judah as well as a number of other settled and semi-nomadic peoples of the southern region

known as the Negeb. David's actions while at Ziklag were calculated to build his own power base in Judah while fooling Achish into believing that he was giving exemplary service.

Using Ziklag as a base, David made raids on the Geshurites, the Girzites, and the Amalekites (v. 8). These were traditional enemies of the Israelites, particularly the tribe of Judah. These peoples lived in the wilderness areas south of Judah into the Sinai peninsula, but often raided Judahite villages. David's own people are victimized at Ziklag by an Amalekite raid (chap. 30), although this act may be in retaliation for what David had done. David's forays against these traditional enemies surely enhanced his reputation in Judah, and in the process extended David's political base in Judah. In these raids, David leaves no one alive—man, woman, or child—but takes considerable spoils in the form of livestock or garments, which he brings back to Achish (v. 9). This activity seems ironic, since Saul was rejected for taking such spoil after a war with the Amalekites (chap. 15). But David is under no prophetically mediated divine command of *ḥērem* here. Indeed, his killing of all the people in these raids turns out to have a ruthless but practical purpose for David and does not involve holy war strictures. Warfare against enemies is also outside the framework of concern for bloodguilt, which occupied our attention in chaps. 24–26.

Achish, who is no doubt pleased with the additions to his wealth and the subduing of troublesome enemies, asks David for a report on his raids. David shrewdly but falsely reports that he has been raiding "the Negeb of Judah," "the Negeb of the Jerahmeelites," or "the Negeb of the Kenites" (v. 10). The Jerahmeelites and the Kenites are both southern peoples allied with Judah and perhaps considered their kindred. David casually lies to Achish that his raids have been in the general southern region (Negeb) against Israelite villages of the tribe of Judah and their allies. It is to cover this lie that David must leave no witnesses alive to tell the truth of his raids (v. 11). The subterfuge seems to work, for Achish believes that David must have made himself utterly odious to his own people (after all, David is himself from the tribe of Judah), and as a result Achish considers David to have proved himself an entirely trustworthy servant (v. 12).

28:1-2. David's strategy may have worked too well. The worst possible situation develops: war against Israel by the gathered forces of the Philistines (v. 1*a*). Achish is so confident of the loyalty of David and his men that he calls them out as part of the military force from Gath to take part in the campaign against Israel (v. 1*b*). David is in an extremely difficult political dilemma. If he is forced to fight against Israel, he will be unable to justify any claim on the Israelite throne; but if he refuses loyal service to Achish, his own life and those of his company will be in immediate danger. David chooses to bluff for the moment. He almost casually responds to Achish that he is ready to serve him (v. 2*a*). Matters go from bad to worse

when Achish, perhaps pleased with David's ready response, makes David and his men the personal bodyguard of the Philistine king (v. 2*b*). Now David cannot even hope to seek refuge on the obscure outskirts of the battle. A king's bodyguard must surround the king and fight for his protection. Such a position in battle is visible and prominent. Achish considers this an honor to David, but David is in a terrible position.

Suddenly, the account breaks off. We are left suspended. The outcome of David's dilemma will not be told until this story resumes in 29:1. Instead, the scene shifts to give us a last pathos-filled glimpse of Saul on the eve of this coming battle with the Philistines (28:3-25).

REFLECTIONS

This is a report that revels in David's shrewd manipulation of enemies and justifies what might otherwise be a questionable time of service with the Philistines. There is no need to import artificial theological comment into the chapter. David is God's future for Israel, but he is no saint. The narrative does not flinch from this reality. We know God's hand is with David, but in this moment it is hidden. We are left with a story that reflects the brutal realities of the time, and a David who seeks to survive within the framework of those realities. In this story, David cannot wait for more favorable options but must choose boldly for his own survival and the lives of his company. We are asked simply to attend to the story of these events in confidence that the reality of God's purposes behind the story has not changed.

In similar fashion, people of faith in every generation are asked to attend to the story of their own lives in trust that God is the reality that moves history—even when the hand of God seems hidden and the brutal realities that are a part of human experience seem remote from God's purposes. It is in facing harsh circumstances that are so often a part of human experience that we avoid a naive, romantic view of God's purposes in the world, and how we effectively serve those purposes. We, like David, may also be asked to act boldly in circumstances that do not give us ideal options or absolute moral clarity.

1 Samuel 28:3-25, Saul and the Ghost of Samuel

NIV

³Now Samuel was dead, and all Israel had mourned for him and buried him in his own town of Ramah. Saul had expelled the mediums and spiritists from the land.

⁴The Philistines assembled and came and set up camp at Shunem, while Saul gathered all the Israelites and set up camp at Gilboa. ⁵When Saul saw the Philistine army, he was afraid; terror filled his heart. ⁶He inquired of the LORD, but the LORD did not answer him by dreams or Urim or proph-

NRSV

3Now Samuel had died, and all Israel had mourned for him and buried him in Ramah, his own city. Saul had expelled the mediums and the wizards from the land. ⁴The Philistines assembled, and came and encamped at Shunem. Saul gathered all Israel, and they encamped at Gilboa. ⁵When Saul saw the army of the Philistines, he was afraid, and his heart trembled greatly. ⁶When Saul inquired of the LORD, the LORD did not answer him, not by dreams, or by Urim, or by prophets.

ets. ⁷Saul then said to his attendants, "Find me a woman who is a medium, so I may go and inquire of her."

"There is one in Endor," they said.

⁸So Saul disguised himself, putting on other clothes, and at night he and two men went to the woman. "Consult a spirit for me," he said, "and bring up for me the one I name."

⁹But the woman said to him, "Surely you know what Saul has done. He has cut off the mediums and spiritists from the land. Why have you set a trap for my life to bring about my death?"

¹⁰Saul swore to her by the LORD, "As surely as the LORD lives, you will not be punished for this."

¹¹Then the woman asked, "Whom shall I bring up for you?"

"Bring up Samuel," he said.

¹²When the woman saw Samuel, she cried out at the top of her voice and said to Saul, "Why have you deceived me? You are Saul!"

¹³The king said to her, "Don't be afraid. What do you see?"

The woman said, "I see a spirit*ᵃ* coming up out of the ground."

¹⁴"What does he look like?" he asked.

"An old man wearing a robe is coming up," she said.

Then Saul knew it was Samuel, and he bowed down and prostrated himself with his face to the ground.

¹⁵Samuel said to Saul, "Why have you disturbed me by bringing me up?"

"I am in great distress," Saul said. "The Philistines are fighting against me, and God has turned away from me. He no longer answers me, either by prophets or by dreams. So I have called on you to tell me what to do."

¹⁶Samuel said, "Why do you consult me, now that the LORD has turned away from you and become your enemy? ¹⁷The LORD has done what he predicted through me. The LORD has torn the kingdom out of your hands and given it to one of your neighbors—to David. ¹⁸Because you did not obey the LORD or carry out his fierce wrath against the Amalekites, the LORD has done this to you today. ¹⁹The LORD will hand over both Israel and you to the Philistines, and tomorrow you and

ᵃ13 Or see spirits; or see gods

⁷Then Saul said to his servants, "Seek out for me a woman who is a medium, so that I may go to her and inquire of her." His servants said to him, "There is a medium at Endor."

8So Saul disguised himself and put on other clothes and went there, he and two men with him. They came to the woman by night. And he said, "Consult a spirit for me, and bring up for me the one whom I name to you." ⁹The woman said to him, "Surely you know what Saul has done, how he has cut off the mediums and the wizards from the land. Why then are you laying a snare for my life to bring about my death?" ¹⁰But Saul swore to her by the LORD, "As the LORD lives, no punishment shall come upon you for this thing." ¹¹Then the woman said, "Whom shall I bring up for you?" He answered, "Bring up Samuel for me." ¹²When the woman saw Samuel, she cried out with a loud voice; and the woman said to Saul, "Why have you deceived me? You are Saul!" ¹³The king said to her, "Have no fear; what do you see?" The woman said to Saul, "I see a divine being*ᵃ* coming up out of the ground." ¹⁴He said to her, "What is his appearance?" She said, "An old man is coming up; he is wrapped in a robe." So Saul knew that it was Samuel, and he bowed with his face to the ground, and did obeisance.

15Then Samuel said to Saul, "Why have you disturbed me by bringing me up?" Saul answered, "I am in great distress, for the Philistines are warring against me, and God has turned away from me and answers me no more, either by prophets or by dreams; so I have summoned you to tell me what I should do." ¹⁶Samuel said, "Why then do you ask me, since the LORD has turned from you and become your enemy? ¹⁷The LORD has done to you just as he spoke by me; for the LORD has torn the kingdom out of your hand, and given it to your neighbor, David. ¹⁸Because you did not obey the voice of the LORD, and did not carry out his fierce wrath against Amalek, therefore the LORD has done this thing to you today. ¹⁹Moreover the LORD will give Israel along with you into the hands of the Philistines; and tomorrow you and your sons shall be with me; the LORD will also give the army of Israel into the hands of the Philistines."

ᵃ Or a god; or gods

NIV

your sons will be with me. The LORD will also hand over the army of Israel to the Philistines."

²⁰Immediately Saul fell full length on the ground, filled with fear because of Samuel's words. His strength was gone, for he had eaten nothing all that day and night.

²¹When the woman came to Saul and saw that he was greatly shaken, she said, "Look, your maidservant has obeyed you. I took my life in my hands and did what you told me to do. ²²Now please listen to your servant and let me give you some food so you may eat and have the strength to go on your way."

²³He refused and said, "I will not eat."

But his men joined the woman in urging him, and he listened to them. He got up from the ground and sat on the couch.

²⁴The woman had a fattened calf at the house, which she butchered at once. She took some flour, kneaded it and baked bread without yeast. ²⁵Then she set it before Saul and his men, and they ate. That same night they got up and left.

NRSV

20Immediately Saul fell full length on the ground, filled with fear because of the words of Samuel; and there was no strength in him, for he had eaten nothing all day and all night. ²¹The woman came to Saul, and when she saw that he was terrified, she said to him, "Your servant has listened to you; I have taken my life in my hand, and have listened to what you have said to me. ²²Now therefore, you also listen to your servant; let me set a morsel of bread before you. Eat, that you may have strength when you go on your way." ²³He refused, and said, "I will not eat." But his servants, together with the woman, urged him; and he listened to their words. So he got up from the ground and sat on the bed. ²⁴Now the woman had a fatted calf in the house. She quickly slaughtered it, and she took flour, kneaded it, and baked unleavened cakes. ²⁵She put them before Saul and his servants, and they ate. Then they rose and went away that night.

COMMENTARY

This episode records the final desperate hours of Saul before his death. On the eve of battle with the Philistines, Saul violates his own proscription of necromancy in Israel by seeking out a medium to bring up the ghost of the prophet Samuel. Instead of the reassurance or release he seeks, Saul is reminded by a hostile Samuel of his rejection and is told of his impending death in battle along with his sons. Even from the grave, Samuel remains Saul's nemesis.

Saul has reached absolute bottom. He is fearful and anxious and seeks to inquire of the Lord, but no mode of inquiry brings results (v. 6). He comes to the full realization that God is not with him. We have known it, and perhaps Saul has suspected it, since he was forced to acknowledge David as future king (24:20). But on the eve of battle with the Philistines, the full realization of his isolation from God drives Saul to despair. He understands rightly that Samuel had been the key to God's presence with him earlier. Indeed, the fates of Samuel and Saul have been intertwined from the beginning. Even Samuel's birth story

(chap. 1) was filled with allusions to Saul's name. It seems only fitting that the two should appear together at the end.

In a sense this is the end of Samuel's era as well as of Saul's. Saul has failed as the people's king, but God's alternative to Saul is not a return to the rigid orthodoxy and old traditionalism of Samuel. Samuel began in a time when there was no word of the Lord in the land (3:1). Now chap. 28 returns to a situation where there is no word of the Lord (v. 6), and even the ghost of Samuel can only speak harshly of endings, not of beginnings. Another avenue for the presence of God in Israel has become available with David. Samuel anointed him, but he has operated quite independently of the old ways represented by Samuel. A central theme of the stories of David's rise has been, "God was with him" (e.g., 16:18; 2 Sam 5:10). Unlike Saul, David has no problem inquiring of God and receiving a response (22:10, 13, 15; 23:2, 4; 30:8; 2 Sam 2:1; 5:19, 23). Through David, God has opened a new path for God's future with Israel. Saul and Samuel are both about to be left behind. A new boldness and directness in relating to God have appeared in David that reject both the anxious ritualism of Saul and the inflexible orthodoxy of Samuel. Saul and Samuel together in this story point only to deathly realities for Israel. By contrast, David bears God's possibilities of life for Israel.

An introductory word must be said about the woman in this story. She is a necromancer, whose practices were consistently forbidden in Israel as inconsistent with the worship of Yahweh. Translators have often labeled her a "witch" (see discussion of the Hebrew terms below). It is a term that carries dark and sinister connotations, and is not at all specific to the actual meanings of the terms used in the story. Older commentary on this text often vilified her and even suggested that she was somehow responsible for leading Saul astray in his final hours. Yet, in the context of a careful reading of the story, this unnamed woman is a person of courage and compassion. Her vocation may not be compatible with the worship of Yahweh, but she is intended in her strength and caring to be a contrast to the weak, pathetic, and unfaithful Saul. The story intentionally compares this so-called king to this forbidden woman and finds Saul the loser in the comparison.

Scholars have frequently pointed out difficulties in the placement and composition of this chapter.[174] According to v. 4, the Philistines are already encamped at Shunem, near the site of the final battle, but in 29:1 they are still gathering much farther south at Aphek. The chapter would fit better chronologically after chap. 30. Such a re-organization would, of course, remove the chapter from its disruptive position in the story of David's dilemma in the service of the Philistines. Still, we should also reckon with the possibility that it was just such a pause in David's story that was intended by those who placed chap. 28 here. Saul's tragic fate is then contrasted with David's near miraculous good fortune in chap. 29. The close ties of this chapter to chap. 15 (cf. 28:16-18 and 15:16-28) and the heightened role of Samuel suggest that this chapter received some reworking as part of a prophetic edition of these stories (see Introduction).

174. See P. Kyle McCarter, *I Samuel*, AB 8 (Garden City, N.Y.: Doubleday, 1980) 422-23; Ralph W Klein, *I Samuel*, WBC 10 (Waco: Word, 1983) 268-74.

28:3-7. The episode opens bluntly. It quickly gives us three pieces of information:

(1) Samuel is dead (v. 3*a*). This restates the notice of 25:1 and serves to reintroduce Samuel into the story.

(2) Saul had expelled "mediums" and "wizards" (NRSV)/"spiritists" (NIV) from the land. This is consistent with what seems to be a constant opposition of Yahwism to such practices (see Lev 19:31; 20:6, 27; Deut 18:11). This notice introduces unauthorized means of seeking guidance alongside notice of Samuel, who was a prophet, an authorized means of seeking guidance. Saul will soon be in the awkward position of seeking to consult a prophet (authorized) through a medium (unauthorized), which he had forbidden in Israel.

(3) The Philistines are gathering for a major military campaign against Israel. Forces are already arrayed opposite one another in the valley of Jezreel (v. 4), the Philistines at Shunem on the north and the Israelites at Gilboa on the south.

With this background, the scene shifts to Saul, who remains the central focus throughout. Saul is terrified at the sight of the army the Philistines have assembled (v. 5). His impulse is not to devise a plan of action (even a strategic retreat), but to find some instruction about what to do. He tries to inquire of the Lord. There is a play on words here, for the verb "to ask," "to inquire" is שָׁאַל (*šāʾal*), the word from which Saul's own name is derived. Saul "sauled" the Lord. He uses three traditional means of inquiry: dreams, the casting of sacred lots (here only Urim mentioned; usually Urim and Thummim), and prophets. The scene is reminiscent of chap. 14, where Jonathan took bold action, voicing trust in the Lord, while Saul sought ritual reassurance before doing anything until it was almost too late. On the eve of his battle with the Philistines, Saul is seeking ritual certainty rather than drawing up battle plans. He is ruled by fear and not by trust. The Lord does not answer. It is ironic that another means of seeking guidance from the Lord—namely, through priest and ephod—has been lost to Saul by his own deadly violence against the priestly community at Nob (22:6-23). Abiathar and the ephod are now with David, and in 30:7-8 David will use them confidently and successfully to receive a word from the Lord.

In his anxiety and fear, Saul goes beyond the bounds of faithful covenant practices to seek out a medium, violating his own prohibition. He sends servants to find a medium so he can "saul" (inquire of) her. They find one at Endor (v. 7), which is behind the Philistine lines.

The word translated "medium" in vv. 3, 7, 9 and as "spirit" in v. 8 is אוב (*'ôb*), a word referring to ancestral spirits or images representing them. Lust, who has written the most detailed analysis on wizardry and necromancy in ancient Israel, connects the word with the Hebrew for "father" (אב *'āb*), referring to the spirits of "fathers" who have died.[175] It often appears in the plural, as in vv. 3 and 9, and connotes those who summon such spirits or ancestors, a "medium." Verse 7 is more explicit and speaks twice of "a woman of [i.e., dealing with] ancestral spirits." Verse 8 speaks in the singular of the "spirit" Saul wishes the woman to conjure up. Other texts suggest that such necromancers may either summon and "inquire of" spirits (Deut 18:11) or be possessed by spirits and speak for them (Lev 20:27). The term translated "wizard" or "spiritist" (vv. 3, 9) is ידעני (*yiddě'ōnî*), a word related to the verb "to know" (ידע *yāda'*), which Lust understands as ghosts knowledgeable of the future. Saul's prohibition in vv. 3 and 9 implies a banning of those who traffic in such ghosts, hence a "wizard."

28:8-14. Saul goes to the woman at Endor, in disguise and at night, accompanied by two of his men (v. 8*a*). He must furtively sneak behind enemy lines to seek this forbidden reassurance. It is not a picture to inspire confidence in Saul's leadership. He requests the woman to call up a specific ancestral spirit (*'ôb*), whom he will name (v. 8*b*). She is cautious. She cites Saul's prohibition of mediums and wizards and wonders aloud if they are trying to entrap her (v. 9). To violate royal decree is to risk death. She does not seem to be in the business of regularly flaunting this royal prohibition. Ironically, to reassure her that she will come to no harm, Saul swears by the Lord (Yahweh), even as he violates the commandments of covenant with the Lord (v. 10).

The woman still seems cautious as she asks, "Who do you want brought up?" Saul answers, "Samuel" (v. 11). The narrative shows no interest

in rituals or details of the conjuring process. Suddenly, Samuel is there. Some commentators have suggested that he appeared before the woman could do anything to summon him. When she sees Samuel, the woman suddenly also recognizes Saul. She cries out at the deception and names what Saul has sought to hide, "You are Saul!" (v. 12). Saul reassures her but rushes on to the matter he came for, "What do you see?" (v. 13*a*). At first she reports that she sees "a divine being" or "a god" (v. 13*b;* the NIV reads "spirit," but the word is אלהים [*'ĕlōhîm*], "god" or "gods") coming up from the ground. Saul anxiously asks for her to describe its appearance, and she reports seeing an old man wrapped in a robe (v. 14*a*). It is enough; Saul knows him, and he bows to the ground before Samuel (v. 14*b*). The word for "robe" (מעיל *mě'îl*) is associated both with Samuel and with royalty. It is the word for the robe that Samuel tore at the time of Saul's rejection in 15:27. It is the word for the robe Hannah brought to the boy Samuel each year at Shiloh (2:19). It is the word for the robe passed to David by Jonathan (18:4) and the robe that David cut a piece from when Saul was in his power (24:5). The ghost of Samuel comes cloaked in the robe associated with prophecy and kingship, and Saul cannot help knowing him. But it is the cloak of authority that Saul cannot possess or keep. It appears now on the dead Samuel like a shroud, and when Samuel is finished it represents the shroud of Saul as well. Saul greets the ghost of Samuel on the ground, which is where Samuel last saw him in humiliating circumstances (19:24).

28:15-19. Death has not mellowed Samuel. He is as harsh and unyielding as we remember him. He is angry at being disturbed from the sleep of death (v. 15*a*). We wonder what Saul could possibly have had in mind to summon this crotchety nemesis in his time of need. Yet, Saul pours out his troubles in a rush of words: the Philistines—war—God—turned away—no answer (v. 15*b*). Finally, Saul truthfully speaks the heart of his problem: "I have summoned you to tell me what I should do." We cannot imagine this line from David. David constantly inquires of God, but he is never at a loss for what to do in crisis. At the risk of using a cliché, there is something of the old piece of folk wisdom that "God helps those who help themselves" in the contrast be-

175. J. Lust, "On Wizards and Prophets," in *Studies in Prophecy,* VTSup 26 (Leiden: E. J. Brill, 1974) 133-42. See Ralph W. Klein, *1 Samuel,* WBC 10 (Waco: Word, 1983) 270, for other etymological suggestions.

tween Saul and David. David may inquire of God over a course of action (as in 30:7-8), but Saul seems to want God or God's prophet to tell him what to do.

Samuel replies scornfully, "Why then do you ask [שָׁאַל *šā'al*] me?" He voices what Saul now knows: God has abandoned him and is his enemy (v. 16). The ghost of Samuel has seized the floor, and his harsh rhetoric pours over the hapless Saul. Saul is reminded that what has happened is just what Samuel said would happen: The kingdom has been torn from him and given to his neighbor (v. 17). The language is identical to 15:28, except that Samuel now names the neighbor: David! Saul is reminded of his sin in not exterminating the Amalekites; the emphasis is not on the deed itself, however, but on Saul's failure to "obey the voice of the LORD" (v. 18). David will take spoils from Amalek without criticism (chap. 30). But the day of Samuel and holy war commandments of tribal covenant practice is over.

The final word of Samuel's ghost addresses neither the past nor its fulfillment in Saul's present crisis. It concerns the future and Saul's final fate. Samuel reveals that the Lord will give Israel into the hand of the Philistines, and Saul, along with his sons, will die in the battle on the next day (v. 19). As if to signal the abruptness and the finality of Saul's end, the séance with Samuel is ended. There is no word of departure, no appeal, no discussion, no further conversation. It is over—the séance, the coming battle, the experiment with the people's king, the life of Saul!

28:20-25. Saul once again is on the ground, a powerless man, at the departure of Samuel (v. 20; cf. 19:24). These last verses are anticlimactic. Saul is devastated emotionally and weak physically. He has eaten nothing all day and night, perhaps fasting in preparation for battle (v. 20*b*). The woman takes charge in caring response to Saul's terror-stricken state (v. 21*a*). She demands that Saul listen to her because she has listened to him and risked her life (vv. 21*b*-22*a*). She offers Saul food to strengthen him, and he refuses; but his servants join the woman in urging him until he finally rises from the ground to sit on the bed (vv. 22*b*-23). Quickly and generously, the woman slaughters a calf, bakes cakes, and prepares them for Saul (v. 24). In the house of this forbidden woman, behind enemy lines, and in the dead of night, Saul eats a final royal meal and departs (v. 25).

REFLECTIONS

Saul is faced here with a genuine crisis and deserves our sympathy. But the portrait of Saul in this episode is not one of courage in the face of crisis. The Saul of this story is sad and pathetic—a despairing, beaten man. His energy is not spent facing crisis and giving leadership in what must have been a terrifying moment for all of Israel. Instead of facing his destiny, he is still seeking ways to know and control his destiny. In desperation, he turns to idolatrous practices. In fear of the future, he returns to a past that cannot save him.

The episode of chapter 28 is strange. This story of mediums and ghosts is easy to dismiss as odd or interesting, but in no way our story. Yet, in many ways we live in a very Saul-like era. We are deeply anxious and fearful of the future. The hostile forces that face us are different from Saul's Philistines, but no less deadly. We are assaulted by media-driven consumer values that erode our sense of self-worth, reduce our sexuality to a marketing commodity, and create a deadly acceptance of violent behavior in streets, schools, and homes, as well as between nations.

People of faith should be able to respond with resources of life in the face of such death-dealing crises. But too often we, like Saul, have lost touch with the future as God's future. The trustful living and bold facing of the future modeled by David in these stories is replaced by anxious Saul-like efforts to know and control our destiny, efforts that seem cut off from trustful confidence that God is with us.

1. The failure of a trustful faith leads us to embrace idolatrous practices in the effort to know and control our destiny. We live in an age of the popularity of the soothsayer and the quick fix on the future. Horoscopes may be mere entertainment for some people, but are taken very seriously by others as daily guides for living. Bestseller lists regularly carry titles that promise to make ancient secret knowledge available to modern readers. Psychic hotlines peddle their wares regularly on late-night television. Radio and TV evangelists urge us to purchase their explanations of biblical prophecies that will supposedly make clear the course of future events. Even something as benign as the Meyers-Briggs test indicators is sometimes misconstrued as dictating what is possible and what is not, what will happen and what will not. There seems to be an unending stream of new corporate management systems, and the church is often tempted to adopt the latest as the means to congregational growth and success.

Some of these examples may be empty hoaxes, while others misapply useful tools. All risk becoming idolatrous substitutes for openness to the future God is bringing. These and many other modern systems and devices tempt us to seek knowledge and control of our future as a substitute for trustful receiving and responding to the future. Like Saul, we often want certainty in advance.

2. The failure of trustful faith also leads us to refuse God's future by desperately calling up the past. In politics this often leads to a kind of nostalgia for the past as a time free of the crises that beset us. But the past is to be remembered and not reborn; the past is to be learned from and built upon, not resurrected. Restoration of our past, like the ghost of Samuel, often turns out crankier than we remembered. A recent presidential candidate remembered and extolled the community spirit he knew and valued in the late 1940s and early 1950s. He claimed that we could recover it, but African Americans from the South and women who lived in that time do not share his nostalgia.

In religious life we also call up the past as a way of refusing the future. "We've always done it that way" is an old familiar cry in the church. We invoke tradition, hoping, like Saul, that it will tell us what to do. But the ghosts of our past, if we dare to listen to them, may tell a word about the death of one way into the future so that another can be born. Like the tragic, coming death of Saul and his sons, such deaths of failed faithfulness are genuinely painful. The prophetic spirit of our own past as people of faith will always point us forward to God, who will not be confined to the past. We must sometimes face our own death so that God's future can be born. Sometimes "those who would gain their life must lose it" (Matt 10:39; Mark 8:35; Luke 17:33; John 12:25).

1 Samuel 29:1-11, David Dismissed from the Battle with Saul

NIV	NRSV
29 The Philistines gathered all their forces at Aphek, and Israel camped by the spring in Jezreel. ²As the Philistine rulers marched with their units of hundreds and thousands, David and his men were marching at the rear with Achish. ³The commanders of the Philistines asked, "What about these Hebrews?"	**29** Now the Philistines gathered all their forces at Aphek, while the Israelites were encamped by the fountain that is in Jezreel. ²As the lords of the Philistines were passing on by hundreds and by thousands, and David and his men were passing on in the rear with Achish, ³the commanders of the Philistines said, "What are these Hebrews doing here?" Achish said to the commanders of the Philistines, "Is this not David, the servant of King Saul of Israel, who has been with me now for days and years? Since he deserted to me I have found no fault in him to this day." ⁴But the commanders of the Philistines were angry with him; and the commanders of the
Achish replied, "Is this not David, who was an officer of Saul king of Israel? He has already been with me for over a year, and from the day he left Saul until now, I have found no fault in him."	
⁴But the Philistine commanders were angry with him and said, "Send the man back, that he may return to the place you assigned him. He	

NIV

must not go with us into battle, or he will turn against us during the fighting. How better could he regain his master's favor than by taking the heads of our own men? [5]Isn't this the David they sang about in their dances:

" 'Saul has slain his thousands,
    and David his tens of thousands'?"

[6]So Achish called David and said to him, "As surely as the LORD lives, you have been reliable, and I would be pleased to have you serve with me in the army. From the day you came to me until now, I have found no fault in you, but the rulers don't approve of you. [7]Turn back and go in peace; do nothing to displease the Philistine rulers."

[8]"But what have I done?" asked David. "What have you found against your servant from the day I came to you until now? Why can't I go and fight against the enemies of my lord the king?"

[9]Achish answered, "I know that you have been as pleasing in my eyes as an angel of God; nevertheless, the Philistine commanders have said, 'He must not go up with us into battle.' [10]Now get up early, along with your master's servants who have come with you, and leave in the morning as soon as it is light."

[11]So David and his men got up early in the morning to go back to the land of the Philistines, and the Philistines went up to Jezreel.

NRSV

Philistines said to him, "Send the man back, so that he may return to the place that you have assigned to him; he shall not go down with us to battle, or else he may become an adversary to us in the battle. For how could this fellow reconcile himself to his lord? Would it not be with the heads of the men here? [5]Is this not David, of whom they sing to one another in dances,

    'Saul has killed his thousands,
        and David his ten thousands'?"

6Then Achish called David and said to him, "As the LORD lives, you have been honest, and to me it seems right that you should march out and in with me in the campaign; for I have found nothing wrong in you from the day of your coming to me until today. Nevertheless the lords do not approve of you. [7]So go back now; and go peaceably; do nothing to displease the lords of the Philistines." [8]David said to Achish, "But what have I done? What have you found in your servant from the day I entered your service until now, that I should not go and fight against the enemies of my lord the king?" [9]Achish replied to David, "I know that you are as blameless in my sight as an angel of God; nevertheless, the commanders of the Philistines have said, 'He shall not go up with us to the battle.' [10]Now then rise early in the morning, you and the servants of your lord who came with you, and go to the place that I appointed for you. As for the evil report, do not take it to heart, for you have done well before me.[a] Start early in the morning, and leave as soon as you have light." [11]So David set out with his men early in the morning, to return to the land of the Philistines. But the Philistines went up to Jezreel.

[a] Gk: Heb lacks *and go to the place . . . done well before me*

COMMENTARY

This chapter is a continuation of 27:1–28:2. David had offered himself and his men in service to Achish the king of Gath and had been given Ziklag as an outpost for keeping the enemies of Gath pacified and enriching the coffers of Achish. Although David had launched campaigns against the traditional enemies of Judah, he had fooled Achish into thinking he was raiding his own people. In 28:1-2, David was placed in an awkward position by being called out to join Philistine forces in a campaign against Israel. We were left in suspense while the scene shifted to Saul's meeting with Samuel's ghost in 28:3-25. This episode tells us how David was saved from the politically disastrous position of doing battle against Israel. Saul's total desolation (28:3-25) stands in contrast to this story of David's astonishing resilience and good fortune.

29:1-5. The Philistines have gathered at Aphek, the same site where the disastrous capture of the ark had occurred earlier (4:1). The Israelites are already in Jezreel below Mt. Gilboa, where the final battle with Saul will take place (v. 1). The troops mustered by the lords of the five Philistine cities are passing in review before the commanders (presumably those designated for command of the combined military forces) when David and his men ride past near the rear of the column as a part of Achish's troops (v. 2). The commanders seem astonished, "What are these Hebrews doing here?" (v. 3*a*). They use the derogatory term "Hebrew" (עברי *'ibrî*), signifying a marginal, socially outcast class of people. It is a term found elsewhere on Philistine lips concerning Israelites (4:6, 9; 13:3, 19; 14:11, 21). Again the account reminds us of David's ties to the marginal and oppressed groups within Israel.

Achish makes the first of three vigorous defenses of David's acceptability in this chapter (v. 3*b*). He identifies David by name and by calling him the servant of King Saul of Israel. This does not seem to help, whereupon Achish goes on quickly to say that David has been in his service for some time. He identifies David as a deserter, which perhaps explains his initial linking of David with Saul. He avows to have found no fault in David. As readers, of course, we know differently. David has been duping Achish while ingratiating himself to the people of Judah (27:8-12).

The commanders are not easily persuaded. They are angry with Achish and demand that he send David back to Ziklag. They regard him as a liability in battle, one who could turn on the Philistines during the heat of battle (v. 4). They raise the possibility that David would buy his way back into favor with his lord (Saul) by offering the heads of Philistine soldiers. Further, now that Achish has named him, the commanders know his reputation. He is the same David celebrated in song and dance, along with Saul, for having killed Philistines (v. 5): "Saul has killed his thousands, and David his ten thousands." It is easy to understand the commander's unease about David's presence. It may be fortunate that they let David leave unimpeded.

29:6-11. Achish must break the news to David. Oddly, he does so by swearing an oath in the name of the Lord (Yahweh). Perhaps this was an honor to David's God, or perhaps it is just an anachronism. For the second time Achish vigorously defends David (v. 6). Ironically, he begins by citing David's honesty; we know David does not deserve this accolade. Achish argues that David should be included in the campaign; he has found nothing wrong with David. Now Achish says the lords of the Philistines do not approve, presumably backing up their commanders' objections. Achish sends David home in peace, but warns him to do nothing to offend the Philistine lords (v. 7). Perhaps this indicates that David's safety is somewhat in question; he had better not call any more attention to himself.

In what must surely be a tongue-in-cheek response, David protests his loyalty and expresses disappointment at not being included in the Philistine military effort (v. 8). He must surely have been inwardly relieved. Many have suggested that David's final phrases have an intended double meaning. When he expresses the desire to "fight against the enemies of my lord the king," he does not name the king. Achish assumes it is a reference to himself, but David may have been referring to Saul. Perhaps in battle David thought he would seize the opportunity to turn the tide for Israel.

A third time Achish declares David innocent of wrongdoing. Here he seems to get carried away rhetorically: "You are as blameless in my sight as an angel of God" (v. 9). Surely there was some humor in the telling of a story in which a Philistine king sees David as an angel of God! Still David must return home; he cannot do battle. He will have to be content with the good regard of Achish and not take the commanders' disapproval ("evil report") to heart (v. 10; the longer NRSV text in this verse reflects a reading with the LXX, which the NIV does not adopt). David leaves for Ziklag as the Philistines move north to meet the Israelites at Jezreel (v. 11).

REFLECTIONS

There are no explicit theological statements in this chapter, but in the larger history of David's rise we have heard many times that "God was with him." Even without an explicit statement, that seems obvious once again in this chapter.

Everything seems to come up roses for David. The future of Israel in David simply will not be denied or shadowed. What looks compromising of that future always seems to take a turn for the best. This story, as with most of the stories of David's rise, seems to be told from the perspective of the marginal who revel in the adventures and triumphs of one of their own. Even Philistine kings (Achish) declare David guiltless, but they do not know the half of it. He is really guiltless from Israel's perspective, because he has used his service to Achish to dupe the hated Philistines and to serve Judah. For marginal and embattled Israelites of future generations, this becomes literature of hope in times when there is little to hope for and even less to celebrate.

Yet in David, and the telling of his stories, it can be affirmed that God's future is coming. Those in power are not quite as in control as they think. This is why David's remarkable stories have been read and reread with wonder and hope, generation after generation. Even today, those who read these stories in the church of the marginal and the oppressed will recognize their hope in David and be heartened and astonished by his narrow escapes, bold actions, and faithful trust. Those who read these stories in the church of the powerful must suspect that they may not know the full story of what God is doing (like Achish) unless they can strive to read outside their own privileged context. They must seek to read stories such as this one in solidarity with those who know that grace usually comes as subversive power—like David.

1 Samuel 30:1-31, David and the Amalekite Raid on Ziklag

NIV

30 David and his men reached Ziklag on the third day. Now the Amalekites had raided the Negev and Ziklag. They had attacked Ziklag and burned it, [2]and had taken captive the women and all who were in it, both young and old. They killed none of them, but carried them off as they went on their way.

[3]When David and his men came to Ziklag, they found it destroyed by fire and their wives and sons and daughters taken captive. [4]So David and his men wept aloud until they had no strength left to weep. [5]David's two wives had been captured—Ahinoam of Jezreel and Abigail, the widow of Nabal of Carmel. [6]David was greatly distressed because the men were talking of stoning him; each one was bitter in spirit because of his sons and daughters. But David found strength in the LORD his God.

[7]Then David said to Abiathar the priest, the son of Ahimelech, "Bring me the ephod." Abiathar

NRSV

30 Now when David and his men came to Ziklag on the third day, the Amalekites had made a raid on the Negeb and on Ziklag. They had attacked Ziklag, burned it down, [2]and taken captive the women and all[a] who were in it, both small and great; they killed none of them, but carried them off, and went their way. [3]When David and his men came to the city, they found it burned down, and their wives and sons and daughters taken captive. [4]Then David and the people who were with him raised their voices and wept, until they had no more strength to weep. [5]David's two wives also had been taken captive, Ahinoam of Jezreel, and Abigail the widow of Nabal of Carmel. [6]David was in great danger; for the people spoke of stoning him, because all the people were bitter in spirit for their sons and daughters. But David strengthened himself in the LORD his God.

[a] Gk: Heb lacks *and all*

brought it to him, [8]and David inquired of the LORD, "Shall I pursue this raiding party? Will I overtake them?"

"Pursue them," he answered. "You will certainly overtake them and succeed in the rescue."

[9]David and the six hundred men with him came to the Besor Ravine, where some stayed behind, [10]for two hundred men were too exhausted to cross the ravine. But David and four hundred men continued the pursuit.

[11]They found an Egyptian in a field and brought him to David. They gave him water to drink and food to eat— [12]part of a cake of pressed figs and two cakes of raisins. He ate and was revived, for he had not eaten any food or drunk any water for three days and three nights.

[13]David asked him, "To whom do you belong, and where do you come from?"

He said, "I am an Egyptian, the slave of an Amalekite. My master abandoned me when I became ill three days ago. [14]We raided the Negev of the Kerethites and the territory belonging to Judah and the Negev of Caleb. And we burned Ziklag."

[15]David asked him, "Can you lead me down to this raiding party?"

He answered, "Swear to me before God that you will not kill me or hand me over to my master, and I will take you down to them."

[16]He led David down, and there they were, scattered over the countryside, eating, drinking and reveling because of the great amount of plunder they had taken from the land of the Philistines and from Judah. [17]David fought them from dusk until the evening of the next day, and none of them got away, except four hundred young men who rode off on camels and fled. [18]David recovered everything the Amalekites had taken, including his two wives. [19]Nothing was missing: young or old, boy or girl, plunder or anything else they had taken. David brought everything back. [20]He took all the flocks and herds, and his men drove them ahead of the other livestock, saying, "This is David's plunder."

[21]Then David came to the two hundred men who had been too exhausted to follow him and who were left behind at the Besor Ravine. They came out to meet David and the people with him.

[7]David said to the priest Abiathar son of Ahimelech, "Bring me the ephod." So Abiathar brought the ephod to David. [8]David inquired of the LORD, "Shall I pursue this band? Shall I overtake them?" He answered him, "Pursue; for you shall surely overtake and shall surely rescue." [9]So David set out, he and the six hundred men who were with him. They came to the Wadi Besor, where those stayed who were left behind. [10]But David went on with the pursuit, he and four hundred men; two hundred stayed behind, too exhausted to cross the Wadi Besor.

[11]In the open country they found an Egyptian, and brought him to David. They gave him bread and he ate; they gave him water to drink; [12]they also gave him a piece of fig cake and two clusters of raisins. When he had eaten, his spirit revived; for he had not eaten bread or drunk water for three days and three nights. [13]Then David said to him, "To whom do you belong? Where are you from?" He said, "I am a young man of Egypt, servant to an Amalekite. My master left me behind because I fell sick three days ago. [14]We had made a raid on the Negeb of the Cherethites and on that which belongs to Judah and on the Negeb of Caleb; and we burned Ziklag down." [15]David said to him, "Will you take me down to this raiding party?" He said, "Swear to me by God that you will not kill me, or hand me over to my master, and I will take you down to them."

[16]When he had taken him down, they were spread out all over the ground, eating and drinking and dancing, because of the great amount of spoil they had taken from the land of the Philistines and from the land of Judah. [17]David attacked them from twilight until the evening of the next day. Not one of them escaped, except four hundred young men, who mounted camels and fled. [18]David recovered all that the Amalekites had taken; and David rescued his two wives. [19]Nothing was missing, whether small or great, sons or daughters, spoil or anything that had been taken; David brought back everything. [20]David also captured all the flocks and herds, which were driven ahead of the other cattle; people said, "This is David's spoil."

[21]Then David came to the two hundred men who had been too exhausted to follow David, and

NIV

As David and his men approached, he greeted them. ²²But all the evil men and troublemakers among David's followers said, "Because they did not go out with us, we will not share with them the plunder we recovered. However, each man may take his wife and children and go."

²³David replied, "No, my brothers, you must not do that with what the LORD has given us. He has protected us and handed over to us the forces that came against us. ²⁴Who will listen to what you say? The share of the man who stayed with the supplies is to be the same as that of him who went down to the battle. All will share alike." ²⁵David made this a statute and ordinance for Israel from that day to this.

²⁶When David arrived in Ziklag, he sent some of the plunder to the elders of Judah, who were his friends, saying, "Here is a present for you from the plunder of the LORD's enemies."

²⁷He sent it to those who were in Bethel, Ramoth Negev and Jattir; ²⁸to those in Aroer, Siphmoth, Eshtemoa ²⁹and Racal; to those in the towns of the Jerahmeelites and the Kenites; ³⁰to those in Hormah, Bor Ashan, Athach ³¹and Hebron; and to those in all the other places where David and his men had roamed.

NRSV

who had been left at the Wadi Besor. They went out to meet David and to meet the people who were with him. When David drew near to the people he saluted them. ²²Then all the corrupt and worthless fellows among the men who had gone with David said, "Because they did not go with us, we will not give them any of the spoil that we have recovered, except that each man may take his wife and children, and leave." ²³But David said, "You shall not do so, my brothers, with what the LORD has given us; he has preserved us and handed over to us the raiding party that attacked us. ²⁴Who would listen to you in this matter? For the share of the one who goes down into the battle shall be the same as the share of the one who stays by the baggage; they shall share alike." ²⁵From that day forward he made it a statute and an ordinance for Israel; it continues to the present day.

²⁶When David came to Ziklag, he sent part of the spoil to his friends, the elders of Judah, saying, "Here is a present for you from the spoil of the enemies of the LORD"; ²⁷it was for those in Bethel, in Ramoth of the Negeb, in Jattir, ²⁸in Aroer, in Siphmoth, in Eshtemoa, ²⁹in Racal, in the towns of the Jerahmeelites, in the towns of the Kenites, ³⁰in Hormah, in Bor-ashan, in Athach, ³¹in Hebron, all the places where David and his men had roamed.

COMMENTARY

David returns to Ziklag to find it burned and looted by Amalekite raiders. All the women and children, including David's two wives, have been taken captive. David immediately pursues the Amalekites, defeats them, and recovers the captives, along with considerable spoils. This victory for David, of course, provides a simple and immediate contrast to the defeat Saul and the Israelite army suffer in chap. 31. Yet, the real interest of the story does not seem to be in David's victory over the Amalekites itself, but in David's character—the way he conducts himself—throughout the episode. Here, too, David stands in contrast to Saul, but it is the inept and despairing Saul of chap. 28 in view rather than the Saul dying in battle of chap. 31. Key elements in this contrast include:

(1) Both Saul and David are described as being

in "great distress" (28:15; 30:6). Both men are in leadership crises. Saul is on the eve of a great battle with the Philistines and does not know what to do. His response to "great distress" is to consult in desperation a medium, forbidden to worshipers of the covenant Lord, and to ask the ghost of Samuel what he is to do. David is in "great distress" because he has returned to the destruction of Ziklag and the capture of its women and children, and his men are so angry that they threaten to stone him (v. 6). The NRSV translates this verb (צרר ṣārar) as to be in "great danger," but this is inadequate. The reference is not to external threat but to David's inner turmoil. The key phrase comes at the end of v. 6, "But David strengthened himself in the LORD his God." David knows where his greatest strength lies. His confident faith here is the very antithesis to the desperate and fearful Saul creeping by night to the medium at Endor.

(2) When Saul inquired of the Lord (28:6) he received no answer from any of the acceptable forms of inquiry. In contrast, David calls on Abiathar to bring out the ephod, and he inquires of the Lord whether he should pursue the Amalekites (30:7-8). David receives strong reassurance from the Lord, "Pursue, for you shall surely overtake and shall surely rescue" (two emphatic infinitive constructions). We could interpret this contrast simply as the difference between divine disfavor and divine favor. The story is deeply biased in favor of David as God's future for Israel. But it would be a mistake to see this contrast simply as a victimization of Saul and to understand his distance from God as solely of divine making. Saul was rejected as the king God desired for Israel, but apart from a desire for ritual certainty before crucial battles (see chaps. 13; 14; 28) Saul is never portrayed as a man who "strengthened himself in the LORD." He does not pray to the Lord. He does not express trust in the Lord. The ephod is with David because Saul massacred the priestly community where it resided. Saul has been driven by his own jealousy, anger, and violence without reference to what he perceived the Lord to be doing. If the Lord does not answer Saul (28:6), he should hardly be surprised, since he has lived in separation from the Lord. By contrast, David has prayed to, consulted with, and given credit to the Lord throughout the course of these stories. There is a trustful confidence that marks David's interaction with the Lord. David is in communication with the Lord because he has never broken off the lines of communication.

(3) In the sad episode at Endor, Saul is a king who can hardly be recognized as such. His behavior is the antithesis of royal behavior. He violates his own royal decrees. He seeks ghosts who might tell him what to do. He is fearful and without authority. In the end, even the medium must command him to act in his own best interest (28:21-22). In chap. 30, David, who is not yet king, gives royal leadership that prefigures his coming kingdom. After consulting with God, he takes command with a bold plan of action. But he seems even more the king after the victory is won when he makes the decision to share the spoils with those who stayed to guard the baggage

(vv. 21-25). It is a judicial decision that reorders the social hierarchy that has previously prevailed. The decision treats all who participate, in whatever role, with equity and moves against the creation of haves and have-nots. It no doubt reflects David's own experience of being an eighth son, a fugitive, and one whose own entourage was gathered from the dispossessed (22:2). But it also reflects the authority to make such decisions that goes with kingship. In equally generous spirit, but with calculated political gain, David also distributes spoils to the chief cities of Judah, building and broadening his political base (vv. 26-31). Again such generous, diplomatic, and pragmatic action bespeaks royal authority. Saul is the king who acts as no king; David is the not-yet king who acts with royal authority.

30:1-6. The Amalekites seem to be constantly entangled in Israel's story. When David and his men return to find Ziklag in ashes and their women and children taken captive (vv. 1-3), it seems natural to assume that this was Amalekite retaliation for the raids David had conducted against them while in the service of Achish (27:8). David's absence had provided them with an opportunity. The Amalekites had taken captive everyone left in Ziklag (v. 2), whereas David had systematically left no survivors in his Amalekite raids (27:9). This contrast does not arise out of some more compassionate inclination on the part of the Amalekites but on the difference in strategic situation. David could not allow word to reach Achish of the true character of his raids. The Amalekites' taking of prisoners was probably more common, since women and children could be considered plunder and were profitable. Their capture alive was a matter of economics, and not mercy.

The immediate response to this catastrophe is grief (v. 4). The people weep, and David weeps with them for his wives, Ahinoam and Abigail, who were both taken (v. 5). But weeping is followed by bitterness and anger, and it focuses on David (v. 6). After all, he was their leader. Perhaps he should have foreseen the vulnerability of Ziklag when all the fighting men were taken to join the Philistine force. Their anger is so great that the people speak of stoning David. This causes David "great distress," but "David strengthened himself in the LORD his God." It is a marvelous view of a man in crisis who knows he possesses faith resources as well as his own human resources. There is a quiet, confident trust that characterizes David's faith here. Piety alone will not suffice. David goes on in this story to take action, utilizing his own considerable skills as leader and warrior. But David models the man of faith who knows that something beyond his own human skills is available to those who trust in the God of whom Hannah sang (2:1-10)—the God who reverses the fortunes of the powerful on behalf of the powerless.

30:7-10. David calls for Abiathar to bring the ephod (v. 7). Abiathar had brought the ephod with him as the lone survivor of Saul's massacre of the priests of Nob (23:6). David inquires of God through priest and ephod, "Shall I pursue? Shall I overtake?" God's answer comes without elaboration, "Pursue! You shall surely overtake. You shall surely deliver" (v. 8). The answer is immediate and emphatic. We have already noted the stark contrast to the silence of God and the isolation of Saul (28:6). It is still up to David to give leadership in a concrete plan of pursuit and deliverance. He takes six hundred men who have already traveled three days from Aphek and pursues the Amalekites to the Wadi Besor, presumably south into the Negeb. Here David leaves two hundred men who are too exhausted to go farther (vv. 9-10). It seems clear that these two hundred also served to guard the supply baggage so that the pursuit could make all necessary speed (v. 24). We hear no more of anger toward David. Leadership has channeled grief and frustration into action.

30:11-15. David and his men get a helpful break when they encounter an Egyptian abandoned in the desert for three days without food or water. David immediately gives him hospitality, and the food and water revive him (vv. 11-12). He had been a slave of the Amalekites and had been abandoned in the desert when he became ill (v. 13). He confirms that this was the very band of Amalekites who had burned Ziklag (v. 14), and David recruits his help to take them to these Amalekites. The young Egyptian agrees, on the condition that his life be spared and that he not be returned to his master (v. 15). This Egyptian is the first of several parties in this account to receive the generosity of David. In each instance, David seems compassionate and responsive to those without power, but in each he also acts in ways that enhance his reputation and claim

for kingship. In short, David is acting as a wise king might act.

30:16-20. With the help of the Egyptian, the Amalekites are overtaken. They are eating, drinking, and dancing in celebration of their victory and enjoyment of their plunder (v. 16). The picture is of raiders who think they are beyond the reach of any possible pursuit. David attacks, and the battle extends through the following day. Only four hundred Amalekites on camels escape, too swift for David to overtake (v. 17). The success is complete. David's wives and all the other captives are recovered (vv. 18-19). All of the plunder of the Amalekites is taken, along with extensive herds of livestock. All of the material goods are given over to David's authority as if he were a triumphant king, "This is David's spoil" (v. 20).

One cannot help remembering that Saul was condemned for having taken Amalekite spoil (chap. 15). Now, David is celebrated for the taking of Amalekite spoil. Clearly things have changed in Israel. It should be remembered that although the occasion is the taking of Amalekite spoil and the preserving of King Agag's life, the explicit sin of Saul was in failing to obey the explicit command of the Lord through the prophet Samuel. Samuel had declared the Amalekite campaign a holy war and commanded the total destruction of all people and goods. What has changed in Israel is not simply that David can do what Saul could not, although the story is certainly biased toward David. What has changed is that Samuel and the old traditions of the tribal league, such as holy war, have passed from the scene. David's military campaign stands under no divine command. There is no Samuel to disobey. The taking of Amalekite spoil is set in a new and different context. Indeed, David himself sought authorization for his Amalekite campaign; he did not need a prophet to order it or a holy war tradition to structure it. The issue was never Amalekite spoil but a new freedom exercised by David in relationship to the Lord that was not possible for Saul. The strictures of tribal Yahwism no longer hold, and there is no longer a Samuel to maintain them.

30:21-25. When David and his men return to where the two hundred had been left with the baggage, an issue arises. Those who had done battle do not wish to share the spoil with those who remained behind (vv. 21-22). Some among David's men, labeled "corrupt and worthless men," wish to allow those with the baggage only the recovery of their wives and children. This surely was the traditional economic arrangement; those who fought got the plunder. David intervenes and demonstrates both generosity and a willingness to make a decision about the distribution of these goods that is kingly in character. David determines that all should share equally in the economic goods gained in the Amalekite victory whether they fought in the battle or guarded the supplies (v. 24). David declares a theological basis for his policy: It is the Lord who gives the victory, so any gain comes as a gift of grace, even to those who did battle; thus all are to share in these gifts (v. 23). Further, David makes this "a statute and an ordinance," and it will hold until the time of the narrator who tells this tale (v. 25). The declaration of new laws for the basis of distributing economic goods is an action we would expect of a king. David boldly decides the issue and claims an authority that anticipates his kingship. This authority is exercised on behalf of generosity and equity by one who himself has

been deprived in the context of traditional economic arrangements—an eighth son, one left to run errands for his brothers who did battle, a fugitive, a leader of marginal men in Israel.

30:26-31. David's generosity is not ended. He distributes the goods captured from the Amalekites even beyond the circle of his own men. He sends spoil to his "friends, the elders of Judah" (v. 26a). His message to them is an invitation to share in the "spoil of the enemies of the LORD" (v. 26b). The implication is interesting. One is either a "friend of David" or an "enemy of the LORD." David is established as the mediator of relationship to the Lord. To be for David is to join in God's purposes for Israel. David's largess to the elders of Judah is not without important political implications. David is building the base in Judah from which his kingship will first be declared. The names of the cities of Judah are listed like the roll call of a political convention (vv. 27-31); the list ends with Hebron, where David will first be declared and crowned king (2 Sam 2:1-4).

REFLECTIONS

The kingdom of Saul is finished. He is not yet crowned, but in this chapter it is David who acts like a king. David is already demonstrating qualities of the kingdom God is bringing to Israel.

1. It is a kingdom that finds its pragmatic power in giving, and not taking. With the abandoned Egyptian, the two hundred men left exhausted with the baggage, and in the distribution of spoil to the cities of Judah, David acts out of generosity, and not possession. Samuel had warned of a king who would take and take and take (8:11-18), but David is not to be that king. One of the important dimensions observed here about David's generosity is that it is not separated from his exercise of pragmatic power and authority. We so often treat acts of generosity as acts apart from normal reality. We step back to do an altruistic deed or to give a generous gift, assuming that we will then resume the patterns of realistic economics and politics. David's generosity is genuine, but it also serves him well in his own political goals. From the Egyptian, he receives the intelligence he needs to overtake the Amalekites. Among his own men, he establishes a cohesive solidarity that was not possible in the usual arrangements of haves and have-nots. With the cities of Judah, he builds a broad base for future rule based on a confidence that David will seek the welfare of all and not simply the enrichment of the royal house. Simply put, this chapter suggests that the politics of giving not only makes good theological and ethical sense, but it also makes better political sense than the politics of taking.

This is difficult for many to understand or accept in our consumer society, based on profitability. The study of American values entitled *Habits of the Heart* suggests that as a society we are abandoning communitarian values in favor of individualistic values, and one of the casualties is a traditional spirit of generosity in American life.[176] In one of the lowest taxed

---

176. Robert Bellah et al., *Habits of the Heart: Individualism and Commitment in American Life* (Berkeley: University of California Press, 1985).

of all developed nations, there is a growing resentment at having to give up any of our economic resources to the common good of the community. In churches we are now told that the baby boomer generations do not appreciate the concept of stewardship. They resent the notion of giving and are more comfortable with patterns of funding that move to a payment-for-services mode. One recent stewardship expert suggested posted fees in churches for weddings, funerals, Sunday school registration for children, and the like. David's story suggests that community based on taking, holding, and possessing cannot be the community of God's kingdom.

2. It is a kingdom that is willing to rearrange the customary patterns of economic distribution. David boldly declared a new equity in economic resources between those who fought the battles and those who maintained the supplies and guarded the base camp. After all, if some had stayed to guard Ziklag, the Amalekites could not have raided them, but all the fighting men probably wanted in on the glory and profit of the Philistine campaign. Although the matter immediately at hand dealt with the sharing of goods from a military campaign, David showed a willingness to examine and change traditional arrangements of economic power for the sake of equity and justice.

Walter Brueggemann reminds us of the similarity between David's decision and Jesus' parable of the workers in Matt 20:1-16. Those who began work early in the day were paid the same wages as those who came late. When some complain, the householder says, "I choose to give to this last as I give to you. . . . Do you begrudge my generosity? So the last will be first, and the first last" (Matt 20:15-16). Brueggemann remarks, "This Matthean text is a parable of the kingdom. Our narrator has some sense that with David a new kingdom is at hand. Israel is at the threshold of the last becoming first. The new king orders a new social possibility."[177]

3. It is a kingdom that knows its resources for crisis are spiritual as well as sociopolitical, economic, or psychological. Nowhere is the character of the kingdom God is bringing in David made clearer than in v. 6. In the midst of grief over his own loss and a leadership crisis that could become life-threatening, "David strengthened himself in the LORD his God." David was possessed of considerable resources of his own: courage, leadership, prowess as a warrior, resourcefulness. Yet, David always seemed to be aware that these alone were not sufficient apart from a faith that placed his human skills in partnership with what God was doing in Israel and in his own life. For David, faith was not a separate reality to be honored apart from the other arenas of his life. It was in and through his faith in the Lord that David approached all else and utilized his considerable human gifts.

We live in a society prone to isolate and compartmentalize religious experience. After honoring the spiritual dimensions of our life on Sunday, we return to work and personal relationships, where we often try to operate entirely by rational and empirical modes of knowing and doing that are in our own control. Without a nurturing of spiritual resources, we suffer a loss of identity and our doing becomes indistinguishable from all of the other interests that seek to influence public policy and societal conduct. David, without strengthening himself in the Lord, would have been just one more minor ancient Near Eastern potentate. Instead, he was the man after God's own heart.

177. Walter Brueggemann, *First and Second Samuel,* Interpretation (Louisville: John Knox, 1990) 205.

1 Samuel 31:1-13, The Battle of Gilboa and the Death of Saul

NIV

31 Now the Philistines fought against Israel; the Israelites fled before them, and many fell slain on Mount Gilboa. ²The Philistines pressed hard after Saul and his sons, and they killed his sons Jonathan, Abinadab and Malki-Shua. ³The fighting grew fierce around Saul, and when the archers overtook him, they wounded him critically.

⁴Saul said to his armor-bearer, "Draw your sword and run me through, or these uncircumcised fellows will come and run me through and abuse me."

But his armor-bearer was terrified and would not do it; so Saul took his own sword and fell on it. ⁵When the armor-bearer saw that Saul was dead, he too fell on his sword and died with him. ⁶So Saul and his three sons and his armor-bearer and all his men died together that same day.

⁷When the Israelites along the valley and those across the Jordan saw that the Israelite army had fled and that Saul and his sons had died, they abandoned their towns and fled. And the Philistines came and occupied them.

⁸The next day, when the Philistines came to strip the dead, they found Saul and his three sons fallen on Mount Gilboa. ⁹They cut off his head and stripped off his armor, and they sent messengers throughout the land of the Philistines to proclaim the news in the temple of their idols and among their people. ¹⁰They put his armor in the temple of the Ashtoreths and fastened his body to the wall of Beth Shan.

¹¹When the people of Jabesh Gilead heard of what the Philistines had done to Saul, ¹²all their valiant men journeyed through the night to Beth Shan. They took down the bodies of Saul and his sons from the wall of Beth Shan and went to Jabesh, where they burned them. ¹³Then they took their bones and buried them under a tamarisk tree at Jabesh, and they fasted seven days.

NRSV

31 Now the Philistines fought against Israel; and the men of Israel fled before the Philistines, and many fell[a] on Mount Gilboa. ²The Philistines overtook Saul and his sons; and the Philistines killed Jonathan and Abinadab and Malchishua, the sons of Saul. ³The battle pressed hard upon Saul; the archers found him, and he was badly wounded by them. ⁴Then Saul said to his armor-bearer, "Draw your sword and thrust me through with it, so that these uncircumcised may not come and thrust me through, and make sport of me." But his armor-bearer was unwilling; for he was terrified. So Saul took his own sword and fell upon it. ⁵When his armor-bearer saw that Saul was dead, he also fell upon his sword and died with him. ⁶So Saul and his three sons and his armor-bearer and all his men died together on the same day. ⁷When the men of Israel who were on the other side of the valley and those beyond the Jordan saw that the men of Israel had fled and that Saul and his sons were dead, they forsook their towns and fled; and the Philistines came and occupied them.

8The next day, when the Philistines came to strip the dead, they found Saul and his three sons fallen on Mount Gilboa. ⁹They cut off his head, stripped off his armor, and sent messengers throughout the land of the Philistines to carry the good news to the houses of their idols and to the people. ¹⁰They put his armor in the temple of Astarte;[b] and they fastened his body to the wall of Beth-shan. ¹¹But when the inhabitants of Jabesh-gilead heard what the Philistines had done to Saul, ¹²all the valiant men set out, traveled all night long, and took the body of Saul and the bodies of his sons from the wall of Beth-shan. They came to Jabesh and burned them there. ¹³Then they took their bones and buried them under the tamarisk tree in Jabesh, and fasted seven days.

a Heb *and they fell slain*   *b* Heb plural

COMMENTARY

It is ended. The kingdom of Saul is no more. There will be no deliverance. Saul and his sons lie dead on Mt. Gilboa at the hand of the Philistines. It is for David to have the final word about Saul and Jonathan in 2 Sam 1:19-27. In 1 Samuel 31, the account of Saul's death is told in simple, straightforward terms. The narrator gives us no additional comment. Except for David's eulogy, all has been spoken of Saul.

There is a second, variant account of Saul's death in 2 Sam 1:1-16, where an Amalekite comes to David claiming to have ended Saul's life at the king's own request. This account will be evaluated in discussion of that chapter. It is unclear whether it should be taken as a differing account or simply as a boastful claim by an Amalekite.

31:1-7. With the briefest of reports, it is clear that the battle with the Philistines has gone disastrously for Israel. The Israelite troops have been slaughtered in their flight on the slopes of Mt. Gilboa (v. 1). The reader has an uncanny feeling of returning to the beginning of this story of 1 Samuel. Nothing seems to have changed from the time of the Israelite defeat and the capture of the ark in 1 Samuel 4. Saul had made no real difference in the Philistine crisis. Kingship, as Saul had exercised it, was no more effective than the tribal levy that was defeated in that earlier disaster.

Saul has lost his army, and in short order he loses his sons in battle as well—three of them: Jonathan, Abinadab, and Malchishua (v. 2). A fourth son survives to play a role in later events (2 Sam 2:8-11). Saul had been left alone by God and Samuel, and he is now alone on the battlefield. The archers are turning attention to his position, and Saul has been wounded (v. 3).

Saul had been unable to make decisions on the eve of this battle (chap. 28), but in his final moment he is decisive. He asks his armorbearer to draw his sword and kill him, lest the Philistines capture and humiliate him (v. 4*a*). He retains enough fight to scornfully call them the "uncircumcised." He will not give his enemies the pleasure of taking him alive and shaming Israel. The armorbearer is afraid and will not do it. Perhaps he is too devoted to Saul, or he is afraid to strike down God's anointed one. Without hesitation or word, Saul falls upon his own sword in a final heroic gesture (v. 4*b*). Seeing this, the armorbearer falls upon his sword and dies with his king (v. 5). King, sons, servants, and army all lie dead upon Mt. Gilboa (v. 6). The Isra-

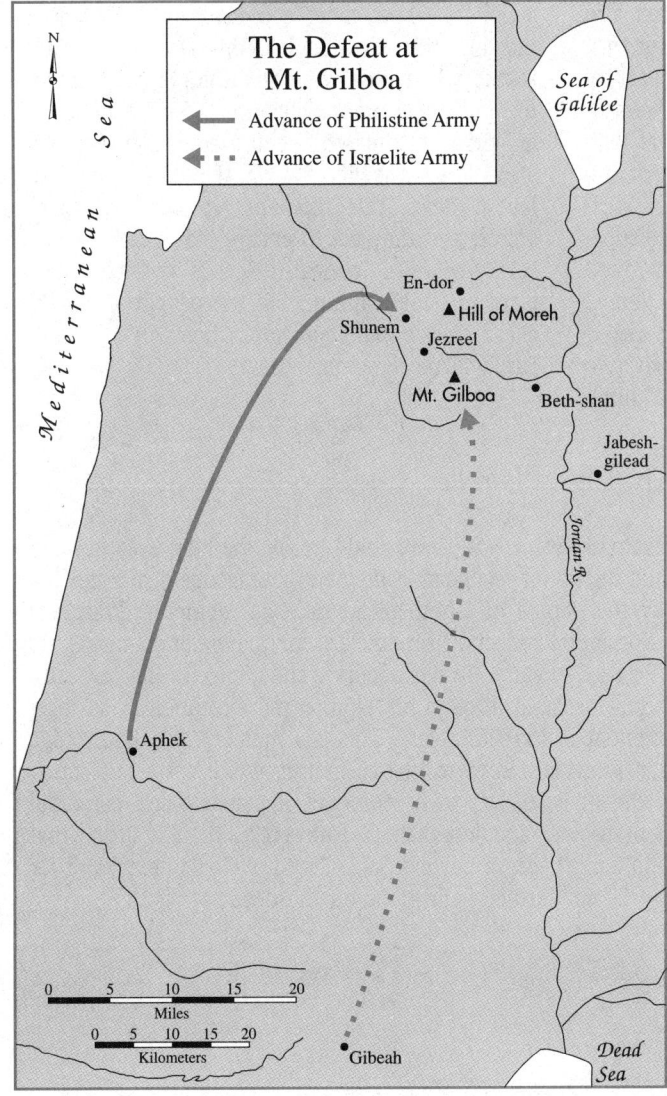

The Defeat at Mt. Gilboa

← Advance of Philistine Army

←--- Advance of Israelite Army

elites of the region, even beyond the Jordan, hear of this massive defeat and flee from their cities. The Philistines occupy the entire territory (v. 7). It is the end of Saul; the defeat is of such proportions that we wonder whether it is the end of Israel.

31:8-13. The Philistines find the bodies of Saul and his sons (v. 8). They do not seem to be looking for him or to know that Saul is dead. It was the ordinary practice to strip the battlefield dead for items of value. No doubt Saul and his sons would be recognizable by their armor and weapons. Saul's bold act has robbed them of the possibility of humiliating his person. All they can do is mutilate his body. They cut off his head, strip his armor, and send news of the extent of their victory to their people (v. 9; the text also notes their idols, probably a scornful comment). Beheading was probably intended as an act of triumphant scorn. We remember David's beheading of Goliath after his victory (17:51). The Philistines place Saul's armor in the temple of Astarte, a goddess associated with Canaanite religion. Such a display is no doubt intended to show the superiority of Philistine deities over the God of Israel. We remember the display of the ark in the temple of Dagon (5:2) and the deposit of Goliath's sword in a holy place (17:54; 21:9-10). Saul's body (we do not know if this included his head) is hung on the walls of Beth-shan, a northern city under Philistine control (v. 10). This was probably intended as an act of public humiliation, although Saul's self-inflicted death robbed the Philistines of a more effective public ridicule. The Philistines did not capture him; they did not even kill him.

The final word of this chapter is not, however, of death and humiliation but of honor. When word of Saul's fate reaches the people of Jabesh-gilead (v. 11), they do not hesitate. All of the fighting men of the city march through the night to retrieve the bodies of Saul and his sons from where the Philistines have hung them. They return with the bodies and burn them (v. 12). They then bury the bones under a tamarisk tree in Jabesh-gilead and fast in Saul's honor (v. 13). The people of Jabesh-gilead could not forget or ignore the debt they owe Saul for his swift and valiant rescue when they were at the mercy of Nahash, the king of Ammon (chap. 11). Saul had begun his time as king with courageous and effective leadership as befits a king. For the people of Jabesh-gilead, this moment remains worthy of honor, and they act to ensure that this honor be bestowed even in death. Saul is not to have a place in Israel's future, but the people of Jabesh-gilead ensure that Saul's royal moments in Israel's past will be remembered.

REFLECTIONS

This is not the moment to celebrate or evaluate Saul. He could not be the king Israel needed or God desired, but he deserves the dignity of recognizing his own courageous death and the notice of the honor given him by the people of Jabesh-gilead as royal moments. Preachers should resist coming to this text for moral reflection on suicide, for the tradition makes no moral comment about the means of Saul's death. He did not have the choice of life or death, only the choice of further humiliation for Israel through his capture and execution or a kingly act that brought an end to this moment of Israelite defeat. This is a moment to acknowledge the need for communal silence and grieving and to resist explanatory words for a brief time. Such restraint is often needed in the midst of our own moments of personal and corporate grief. It remains for David to celebrate Saul and Jonathan (2 Sam 1:17-27). It is fitting that David should have the last word on Saul, because beyond Saul, David is God's next word for Israel. (See 2 Sam 1:1-10 and 1:11-27 for further Reflections on the death of Saul.)

OVERVIEW

The division between the books of Samuel is artificial. In the Hebrew manuscripts they were one continuous book, but the division was introduced in the Greek and Latin versions. It must have seemed convenient to divide this lengthy book into two, and the death of Saul seemed a natural point of division. After all, several other biblical books end with the death of important figures (Moses, Joshua). This, however, creates the impression that 1 Samuel is Saul's story and 2 Samuel is David's. Any careful reader of 1 Samuel to this point will know that this is not the case. David has been the primary focus since he was introduced in 1 Samuel 16. He is even anticipated in several passages before that (e.g., 1 Sam 13:14; 15:28).

2 SAMUEL 1:1–5:10, DAVID BECOMES KING

OVERVIEW

Second Samuel 1:1–5:10 is the conclusion of the history of the rise of David, which began with 1 Sam 16:1. Most scholars believe this was an independent narrative, now incorporated into the larger Deuteronomistic History (see Introduction and the Overview on 1 Sam 16:1–31:13). This narrative of David's rise to the throne concludes with the formula in 2 Sam 5:10, "And David became greater and greater, for the LORD, the God of hosts was with him." The purpose of this narrative on David's rise was not simply to report events, but to make clear in the telling that David achieved the throne by legitimate means. He was both worthy of the throne and intended by God for Israel's throne.

The narrative task of bringing David to the throne and legitimizing him on it is not finished with the death of Saul (1 Samuel 31). It was clearly not self-evident to all in that time that David should become king. He becomes king immediately only over Judah (2 Sam 2:1-4). The rest of Israel, although in disarray following the Philistine defeat, follows Saul's son Ishbosheth/Ishbaal, who was supported on the throne by Abner, Saul's commander (2 Sam 2:8). Complex events that eventually bring David to the throne of Israel as well as Judah include the assassinations of Abner and Ishbosheth/Ishbaal (3:6-39; 4:1-12). The narrative of these events clearly has as a central purpose the exoneration of David from any blame in these deaths. It is not enough that David become king but that he is legitimated in doing so. He is not tainted by bloodguilt, nor has he conspired against the house of Saul. These chapters have as their central purpose the legitimization of David's claim on the throne. What better way to begin than by reporting David's genuine anger and grief over the deaths of Saul and Jonathan?

2 Samuel 1:1-16, A Report of Saul's Death

NIV	NRSV
1 After the death of Saul, David returned from defeating the Amalekites and stayed in Ziklag two days. ²On the third day a man	**1** After the death of Saul, when David had returned from defeating the Amalekites, David remained two days in Ziklag. ²On the third

NIV

arrived from Saul's camp, with his clothes torn and with dust on his head. When he came to David, he fell to the ground to pay him honor.

[3]"Where have you come from?" David asked him.

He answered, "I have escaped from the Israelite camp."

[4]"What happened?" David asked. "Tell me."

He said, "The men fled from the battle. Many of them fell and died. And Saul and his son Jonathan are dead."

[5]Then David said to the young man who brought him the report, "How do you know that Saul and his son Jonathan are dead?"

[6]"I happened to be on Mount Gilboa," the young man said, "and there was Saul, leaning on his spear, with the chariots and riders almost upon him. [7]When he turned around and saw me, he called out to me, and I said, 'What can I do?'

[8]"He asked me, 'Who are you?'

"'An Amalekite,' I answered.

[9]"Then he said to me, 'Stand over me and kill me! I am in the throes of death, but I'm still alive.'

[10]"So I stood over him and killed him, because I knew that after he had fallen he could not survive. And I took the crown that was on his head and the band on his arm and have brought them here to my lord."

[11]Then David and all the men with him took hold of their clothes and tore them. [12]They mourned and wept and fasted till evening for Saul and his son Jonathan, and for the army of the LORD and the house of Israel, because they had fallen by the sword.

[13]David said to the young man who brought him the report, "Where are you from?"

"I am the son of an alien, an Amalekite," he answered.

[14]David asked him, "Why were you not afraid to lift your hand to destroy the LORD's anointed?"

[15]Then David called one of his men and said, "Go, strike him down!" So he struck him down, and he died. [16]For David had said to him, "Your blood be on your own head. Your own mouth testified against you when you said, 'I killed the LORD's anointed.'"

NRSV

day, a man came from Saul's camp, with his clothes torn and dirt on his head. When he came to David, he fell to the ground and did obeisance. [3]David said to him, "Where have you come from?" He said to him, "I have escaped from the camp of Israel." [4]David said to him, "How did things go? Tell me!" He answered, "The army fled from the battle, but also many of the army fell and died; and Saul and his son Jonathan also died." [5]Then David asked the young man who was reporting to him, "How do you know that Saul and his son Jonathan died?" [6]The young man reporting to him said, "I happened to be on Mount Gilboa; and there was Saul leaning on his spear, while the chariots and the horsemen drew close to him. [7]When he looked behind him, he saw me, and called to me. I answered, 'Here sir.' [8]And he said to me, 'Who are you?' I answered him, 'I am an Amalekite.' [9]He said to me, 'Come, stand over me and kill me; for convulsions have seized me, and yet my life still lingers.' [10]So I stood over him, and killed him, for I knew that he could not live after he had fallen. I took the crown that was on his head and the armlet that was on his arm, and I have brought them here to my lord."

[11]Then David took hold of his clothes and tore them; and all the men who were with him did the same. [12]They mourned and wept, and fasted until evening for Saul and for his son Jonathan, and for the army of the LORD and for the house of Israel, because they had fallen by the sword. [13]David said to the young man who had reported to him, "Where do you come from?" He answered, "I am the son of a resident alien, an Amalekite." [14]David said to him, "Were you not afraid to lift your hand to destroy the LORD's anointed?" [15]Then David called one of the young men and said, "Come here and strike him down." So he struck him down and he died. [16]David said to him, "Your blood be on your head; for your own mouth has testified against you, saying, 'I have killed the LORD's anointed.'"

COMMENTARY

The book of 2 Samuel opens with another report of Saul's death. The narrator has given us a report of Saul's final moments on Mt. Gilboa in 1 Samuel 31, but, in the context of the story, David does not yet know of Saul's fate. This episode reports Saul's death as it comes to David.

Such a reporting to David would simply reinforce what we already know, except that when the report is given it provides a somewhat different accounting of Saul's death. The messenger is an Amalekite. Saul seems to be fatally entangled with Amalekites (see 1 Samuel 15). This Amalekite brings word that he chanced upon the wounded Saul, who asked him to take his life. The Amalekite did so and has brought David the insignia of royal office—crown and armlet. He no doubt expected reward and favor for this. This accounting is quite different from that of 1 Samuel 31, where Saul takes his own life rather than be captured and humiliated by the Philistines. The existence of these two accounts has raised questions. Which is the story of what really happened? Have two sources with different versions been combined here? The two accounts, however, need not raise such questions. The Amalekite could be a mere opportunist who chanced upon Saul's body and enhanced his tale in order to seek David's favor. Since the narrator has given us another story of Saul's death already (1 Samuel 31), we may regard the Amalekite report with suspicion. We will probably never know what really happened. What is important in this version (2 Samuel 1) is that David has no other information than this Amalekite's report, and David's response is based on that information.

To focus on questions of historicity or sources would be to miss the genuinely new element in this account—namely, David's response to the news of Saul's death. It is spontaneous grief, not joy and celebration. It is not what the Amalekite expected. David himself speaks of it later, "When the one who told me, 'See, Saul is dead,' thought he was bringing good news, I seized him and killed him" (4:10). David's grief and execution of the Amalekite constitute the most important focus of this episode. David is cleared of complicity in Saul's death. (How did he get those royal insignia?) He is innocent even of unseemly celebration. (Look how spontaneous was his grief!) He has given honor and protection to the Lord's anointed one. (He is himself the Lord's anointed.)

1:1-10. The phrase "after the death of Saul" signals the basis on which 1 and 2 Samuel are divided. The era of Saul has ended. Although David's story had already begun, he is now left alone at center stage.

David has been back at Ziklag for two days (v. 1), following the Amalekite campaign (1 Samuel 30). This notice subtly reminds the reader that David was occupied with the Amalekites far to the south at the time of the battle on Mt. Gilboa, thereby suggesting that he could not have been involved in Saul's death. On the third day, a messenger arrives from Saul's camp. It is clear that the news is not good, for his clothes are torn and he has dirt on his head, in keeping with traditional signs of mourning (v. 2). After he falls in homage before David, there follows a battle report in the form of an interrogation. David asks three questions and receives answers that convey what has happened (vv. 3-10). The reader of the books of Samuel has a strange sense of having seen this scene before. The messenger, the signs of mourning, the questions and answers resemble closely the account of the messenger who brought news to Eli of the defeat of Israel, the death of his sons, and the capture of the ark (1 Sam 4:12-18). Once again the news is of catastrophic defeat, the end of a family's leadership in Israel, and the emergence of an overriding question of what has happened to God's presence in Israel's midst. This time the answer to the question of God's presence will be David!

Still, it is not yet time for David. This episode involves a report of endings, not new beginnings. In answer to David's rapid-fire questioning, the messenger reveals that he has come from Israel's camp (v. 3) and brings news that the Israelite army has fled. Many have fallen in battle, including Saul and Jonathan (v. 4). One can almost sense David's suspicions that all is not simple and straightforward when he asks the messenger how he knows of the deaths of Saul and Jonathan (v. 5). The answer requires a tale.

The messenger reports that he was on Mt. Gilboa. It is not at all clear what his role was. He does not seem to have been a part of the army of Saul or of the Philistines. It would seem that he is a scavenger of the battlefield, a pilferer among the fallen. He reports that he encountered Saul, leaning upon his spear, with Philistine chariots and horsemen closing in on his position (v. 6). How appropriate—even ironic—that Saul should lean in his final moments on the spear that seemed always with him—to throw at David or at Jonathan or to be stolen from his side at night by David. The messenger relates that Saul called to him and asked his identity (v. 7). The messenger answered him, "I am an Amalekite" (v. 8). An Amalekite! As we listen in on this report, we are astonished. Is Saul fated to encounter Amalekites at all his moments of loss—of kingdom (1 Samuel 15) and of life? The Amalekite reports that Saul beseeched him to kill him (v. 9a). Saul seems to be already badly wounded in this accounting. He tells the Amalekite that he is seized by "convulsions" (NRSV; NIV, "throes of death"), yet his life lingers (v. 9b). So the Amalekite reports that he killed Saul; he believed Saul could not have lived anyway (v. 10a). The tone is matter-of-fact, almost casual. The Amalekite presents David with Saul's crown and armlet, emphasizing that he has brought them to "my lord" (v. 10b). Such royal insignia were signs of office and authority. It is now clear that the Amalekite knew of David's potential claim on Israel's throne. We will learn that one of Saul's sons, and Saul's general Abner, survived the battle and sought to continue the house of Saul; but the Amalekite did not seek to return Saul's royal insignia to his own house. He brought them to David, seeking to win favor. He no doubt believed that David would celebrate the death of Saul as his enemy, and that he, having brought not only the good news but also the symbols of kingship and its authority, would be celebrated too. He must have expected a reward. It shows, however, how little this outsider, this Amalekite, really understood of Israel's kings as God's anointed ones or of David's complex relationship to Saul.

1:11-16. David's response was immediate and must have been surprising to the Amalekite messenger. David responds in unreserved grief—tearing his clothes, weeping, fasting until the evening—and he is joined by all the men with him (vv. 11-12). There is no suggestion of pretense or artificiality in David's grief. The Amalekite had come with news he no doubt judged worthy of celebration. He did not understand the importance of Saul or of the office of king as God's anointed to Israel. He did not understand the depth of loss when Saul, Jonathan, and the army of Israel had all been swept away.

At evening David returns to question the young man who had come as messenger. He asks, "Where do you come from?" And he hears in answer, "I am the son of a resident alien, an Amalekite" (v. 13). An Amalekite, living as a sojourner in Israel—it is as if the identity of the messenger had not registered with David earlier. No doubt David's recent loss to the Amalekite raid and his subsequent pursuit and victory were fresh in his mind (1 Samuel 30). Now, he has suffered loss at the hands of an Amalekite again. One can feel the growing menace in David's voice as he asks a question that is in effect an accusation, "Were you not afraid to lift your hand to destroy the LORD's anointed?" (v. 14). David had been afraid to do so. On two occasions, Saul had been in his power, and David had refused to strike him out of respect for Saul as the Lord's anointed one (1 Samuel 24 and 26). Now Saul has been struck down by an Amalekite—a people with a long history of animosity toward Israel and a nemesis to both Saul and David. David cannot allow the inviolability of God's anointed to be broken. He cannot allow the precedent of letting violence to God's anointed go unpunished. He cannot allow his own loyalty to Saul as God's anointed one to be questioned. The Amalekite has unknowingly violated sacred territory, expecting a reward. His ignorance cannot save him; he receives a death sentence instead. David quickly and summarily orders the Amalekite struck down (v. 15). His own confession has condemned him, and David announces the bloodguilt that lies upon the Amalekite for his deed (v. 16). By implication, David declares his own innocence of bloodguilt in Saul's death. He has avenged Saul's death, not taken advantage of it. The opportunism of the Amalekite led to death, and not favor. As an outsider, he never fully understood what was at stake.

REFLECTIONS

Much of the attention to this text has focused on issues of historicity in relation to the account of Saul's death in 1 Samuel 31. What really happened? Which account is accurate? This is not, however, an important issue to the narrator of the history of David's rise or to the larger Deuteronomistic History of which it is a part—and it should not be the focus of our reading. It does not matter whether the Amalekite was lying or telling the truth. Either way, David acted on the basis of what he knew of how Saul died, and the focus is on his loyalty and grief overriding his ambition and self-interest. This theme is further heightened by the song of lament for Saul and Jonathan that follows in 1:17-27. David responded as much for the community as for himself. Whatever Saul had done to David, the striking of God's anointed one (whether an Amalekite deed or an Amalekite lie) struck at the heart of Israel, and such an act could not be allowed to stand unavenged.

Readers often find this account oddly troubling. If Saul were really mortally wounded, they feel that the Amalekite really did nothing very wrong. Even if he just happened along and took the crown and armlet to David with a tale, hoping for reward, they do not feel that he deserved to die. In this country, we are raised to admire opportunism. We often have little loyalty to anything beyond the opportunistic advance of our own interests. The lovable con man is a staple of our novels and movies. The important study of American values *Habits of the Heart*[178] documents the diminishment of communitarian values in favor of a purely individualistic value structure. In American religious life, there has always been a strong segment of believers who elevate personal salvation above considerations of commitment to church or human community. Such perspectives often seem little more than pious opportunism.

The character of David certainly has an opportunistic streak. He knows how to protect and advance his own self-interests, and even in this episode it is in his political interest not to seem in any way complicit in Saul's death. But David also has genuine loyalties that transcend and restrict his opportunism. He has loyalty to Israel and is genuinely grieved at the Philistine defeat of Israel's armies. He has loyalty to the commitments he makes. He had joined in covenant to Jonathan and will honor that commitment, even to Jonathan's descendants (chap. 9). He has loyalty to the Lord. Saul was God's anointed one, and even though Saul treated him as an enemy David refused to harm Saul (1 Samuel 24 and 26). At many points in David's story his relationship to God affects the course of his own personal actions. Even following the grieving of Saul's death, David inquires of God before taking political action (2:1-4). The Amalekite, who believed that he was bringing good news that cleared the throne for an opportunistic David, found that his news was not immediately good news. He did not reckon with loyalties that transcended personal ambitions. Our own reading of this story often fails to credit David with motives or loyalties that transcend his own self-interest. Perhaps this is a reflection of our own predilections rather than a careful reading of David's own story.

A story such as this one calls us to examine our own loyalties and behavior. In a society that often admires and rewards self-interested behavior, we are summoned in this story to witness David's righteous anger on behalf of the community's loss and in loyalty to God's anointed one—even when this loss might bring him personal advantage. Do we still have the capacity to become as righteously angry over violations of community as over violations of our personal ambitions? Are we prepared to grieve over the loss of the community's authority and integrity as well as over our own? Our answers to such questions will determine where we find our place in this story—with the Amalekite or with David.

---

178. Robert Bellah et al., *Habits of the Heart: Individualism and Commitment in American Life* (Berkeley: University of California Press, 1985).

2 Samuel 1:17-27, David's Lament for Saul and Jonathan

[17]David took up this lament concerning Saul and his son Jonathan, [18]and ordered that the men of Judah be taught this lament of the bow (it is written in the Book of Jashar):

[19]"Your glory, O Israel, lies slain on your
　　heights.
　　How the mighty have fallen!

[20]"Tell it not in Gath,
　　proclaim it not in the streets of Ashkelon,
　lest the daughters of the Philistines be glad,
　　lest the daughters of the uncircumcised
　　　rejoice.

[21]"O mountains of Gilboa,
　　may you have neither dew nor rain,
　　nor fields that yield offerings ⌞of grain⌟.
　For there the shield of the mighty was defiled,
　　the shield of Saul—no longer rubbed with
　　　oil.

[22]From the blood of the slain,
　　from the flesh of the mighty,
　the bow of Jonathan did not turn back,
　　the sword of Saul did not return unsatisfied.

[23]"Saul and Jonathan—
　　in life they were loved and gracious,
　　and in death they were not parted.
　They were swifter than eagles,
　　they were stronger than lions.

[24]"O daughters of Israel,
　　weep for Saul,
　who clothed you in scarlet and finery,
　　who adorned your garments with
　　　ornaments of gold.

[25]"How the mighty have fallen in battle!
　　Jonathan lies slain on your heights.
[26]I grieve for you, Jonathan my brother;
　　you were very dear to me.
　Your love for me was wonderful,
　　more wonderful than that of women.

[27]"How the mighty have fallen!
　　The weapons of war have perished!"

[17]David intoned this lamentation over Saul and his son Jonathan. [18](He ordered that The Song of the Bow[a] be taught to the people of Judah; it is written in the Book of Jashar.) He said:

[19] Your glory, O Israel, lies slain upon your
　　high places!
　　How the mighty have fallen!
[20] Tell it not in Gath,
　　proclaim it not in the streets of Ashkelon;
　or the daughters of the Philistines will rejoice,
　　the daughters of the uncircumcised will exult.

[21] You mountains of Gilboa,
　　let there be no dew or rain upon you,
　　nor bounteous fields![b]
　For there the shield of the mighty was defiled,
　　the shield of Saul, anointed with oil no
　　　more.

[22] From the blood of the slain,
　　from the fat of the mighty,
　the bow of Jonathan did not turn back,
　　nor the sword of Saul return empty.

[23] Saul and Jonathan, beloved and lovely!
　　In life and in death they were not divided;
　they were swifter than eagles,
　　they were stronger than lions.

[24] O daughters of Israel, weep over Saul,
　　who clothed you with crimson, in luxury,
　　who put ornaments of gold on your apparel.

[25] How the mighty have fallen
　　in the midst of the battle!

　Jonathan lies slain upon your high places.
[26] 　I am distressed for you, my brother
　　　Jonathan;
　greatly beloved were you to me;
　　your love to me was wonderful,
　　passing the love of women.

[27] How the mighty have fallen,
　　and the weapons of war perished!

a Heb *that The Bow*　　b Meaning of Heb uncertain

COMMENTARY

David's grief finds moving expression in a lament for Saul and Jonathan. The poetry is passionate, unreserved, and genuine in its communication of loss. This song of lament is widely regarded as the composition of David himself. It is a fitting memorial to Saul and Jonathan and their accomplishments on behalf of Israel, and it is especially appropriate that this memorial should be from David. His song reminds us of the depth of loss that the death of Saul and Jonathan meant for Israel. The focus of 1 Samuel 16–31 on the rise of David and the conflict between David and Saul causes us to lose sight of the full meaning of Saul's kingship for Israel. We have seen Saul's obsession and jealousy, and we have watched his descent into desperation and fear. Nevertheless, in a time of Philistine conquest and domination, Saul led Israel back to some sense of identity and renewed freedom. His small kingdom and his successes against the Philistines kept alive the hope that Israel's story had not ended. The courage and leadership of his son Jonathan was well-known and widely admired. Now Saul is gone; the crown prince Jonathan is gone; Israel has been defeated and dispersed by yet another Philistine army. As readers we have hope that in David Israel's kingdom and its story may yet find a new future. But David and the remnants of Israel have no assurance of this. The depth of loss and defeat is so great that it must be acknowledged and mourned before one may dare to hope for any future. David's personal story is set aside for public grief. His time may come, but in this moment of loss it is the time of Saul and Jonathan that must be honored. Without Saul and Jonathan, David's story would not be possible.

David's song is in the form of a dirge or lament for the dead, known in Hebrew as a קינה (*qînâ*). It is a type of song in honor of the dead that looks backward on the accomplishments of those being remembered and honored. It often addresses the dead in the second person. There is a frequent contrasting of "then" and "now" or "past" and "present" in such dirges. The song honors the dead, and, hence, no ill is spoken of them. There is no mention or address to God in a *qînâ*. As in David's lament here, even theological concerns are set aside in the experience of a deeply human moment. There is a distinctive poetic rhythm to the *qînâ*, although variations in it are possible, as is the case in this text. This type of funerary lament is distinguished from the lament of distress found in the psalms. Such distress laments are cries for help addressed to God, which realistically express the distress of the moment but look forward in anticipation of deliverance. There is no *qînâ* in the psalter.[179]

The poetic lament occurs in vv. 19-27. Verses 17-18 form an introduction to the song. The refrain "How the mighty have fallen" is used three times (vv. 19, 25, 27). It appears at the beginning and end of the piece, and its presence in v. 25 seems to divide the lament into two unequal segments. The first part focuses on the exploits of Saul and Jonathan and the mourning of their deaths (vv. 19-24), whereas the second focuses more on David's personal grief over the loss of Jonathan (vv. 25-26).

1:17-18. These verses introduce the poetic piece, which starts in v. 19. David's song is announced in v. 17 as a *qînâ* in honor of Saul and Jonathan. Even the verb in this verse is derived from the same root as the noun *qînâ*.

Verse 18 has been subject to a variety of translations and interpretations.[180] There are three distinct elements to the verse. The first is the phrase "to teach the sons of Judah." The second is the single Hebrew word for "bow" (קשת *qešet*), the same weapon of war used by Jonathan in v. 22. The third element is the expression "[Behold], it is written in the Book of Jashar." There is general agreement that this final expression indicates a collection of poems or songs from which this lament of David was taken by the editor, who placed it appropriately after the narrative accounts of Saul's death. The Book of Jashar is also mentioned in Josh 10:12-13 as the source of the poem celebrating the standing still of the sun at Gibeon. This may have been an anthology of poems (now lost to us) celebrating the heroic deeds of various Israelites. The word "Jashar" is

---

179. Claus Westermann, "Struktur und Geschichte der Klage im Alten Testament," *ZAW* 66 (1954) 46, gives a detailed sketch of the differences between these two types of lament.

180. For a full discussion of the various proposals, see A. A. Anderson, *2 Samuel*, WBC 11 (Dallas: Word, 1989) 15; P. Kyle McCarter, *II Samuel*, AB 9 (Garden City, N.Y.: Doubleday, 1984) 67-68.

sometimes translated as "the Upright" or "the Just" (הישׁר *hayyāšār*).

The first two elements of the verse may be understood in two different ways. These may constitute a superscription to David's song in the fashion of the superscriptions that preface many of the psalms. According to this model, the first phrase would be an admonition that the song should be taught to the sons of Judah. It is to be preserved as an important memory in Israel. The word "bow" would then be the title of the poem. Such a title could be taken as a key word from the mention of Jonathan's favorite weapon in v. 22, or it could be an epithet for Jonathan and/or Saul themselves, much as "the chariots of Israel and its horsemen" is used to designate Elijah and Elisha (2 Kgs 2:12; 13:14). Another view would combine these first two elements and read them as a single phrase, "to teach the sons of Judah the bow." In this view, the phrase would announce the intention to use this lament to encourage the sons of Judah to learn military skills following the example of Saul and Jonathan. There are difficulties of grammatical construction that make the second option less likely, and the phrases are likely a superscription and a title to the poem.

1:19-20. In grand and poetic language David addresses Israel to mourn its "glory," which has been slain (v. 19*a*). This is not the common Hebrew word for "glory." The word here is צבי (*ṣĕbî*), which means "beauty," "honor," or "splendor." It can also mean "gazelle." In either usage the term is commonly regarded as an epithet for Saul (or for both Saul and Jonathan). Kings are frequently described in idealistic and heroic terms as handsome and magnificent. Animal images are often used for heroes in ancient literature as well. Either as the "Splendor of Israel" or as the "Gazelle of Israel," this invitation to grief would seem to have Saul, the king, as its object.

The phrase "slain upon your high places" uses a term (במה *bāmâ*) that is later associated with the wooded heights of idolatrous worship and sacrifice. Accordingly some have wanted to see here a comment on Saul's death as idolatrous sacrifice—perhaps a deuteronomistic comment on Saul's kingship and eventually all kingship as idolatrous.[181] If, however, as most suppose, this is

early poetry authored by David himself, the term *bāmâ* need not indicate a place of idolatrous worship. Indeed, the basic meaning of the word seems to indicate any rounded swelling of landscape or even of body parts—e.g., buttocks. Given Saul's well-attested death on Mt. Gilboa and the reference to this location in v. 21, we should take the term here to mean only a "height."

The first use of the refrain is in v. 19*b*. The term "mighty" (i.e., mighty men, warriors) does not mean Israelite warriors in general but Saul and Jonathan in particular. Israel's heroes have perished. The refrain becomes a punctuation of grief for this song of loss.

The opening exclamation of grief is followed in v. 20 by a fervent wish that is nevertheless contrary to reality. David's wish, and surely that of all Israel, is that news of this loss could be kept from the Philistine home cities, for there the news will be greeted with rejoicing and exultation. In reality the Philistines sent news of victory to their home cities immediately, perhaps with Saul's armor as a trophy (1 Sam 31:9). Ashkelon and Gath are two of the five Philistine city states, and, of course, Gath is where David served the Philistine king Achish for a time. He knows the Philistines well. It is particularly galling to think of Philistine joy at the expense of Israelite loss. A measure of David's contempt for this Philistine foe can be seen in the use of the term "uncircumcised" as a derogatory description (see also 1 Sam 17:26, where David uses the term in contempt of Goliath). The description of the daughters of the Philistines in arrogant rejoicing is balanced later in the poem by a summons to the daughters of Israel that they may weep over Saul, a more fitting response to such a great loss (v. 24).

1:21. David turns to the mountains of Gilboa, where Saul was killed, and calls for them to be without dew or rain and to have no fields of bounteous harvest (v. 21*a*).[182] In effect, David has uttered a curse upon Gilboa. Such desolation on its slopes is the only fitting memorial to such a loss. Cut off from its life-giving water both above

---

181. See Robert Polzin, *David and the Deuteronomist: A Literary Study of the Deuteronomic History*, Part Three: *2 Samuel* (Bloomington: Indiana University Press, 1993) 15-16.

182. The words translated "bounteous fields" (NRSV) and "fields that yield offerings of grain" (NIV; שׂדי תרומת *śĕdê tĕrûmōt*) are notoriously difficult to translate, and numerous emendations of the text have been suggested, none of which have received a wide following. See Anderson, *2 Samuel*, 21; and McCarter, *II Samuel*, 69-71, 75-76, for fuller discussion of the proposals.

and below, Gilboa would only be a place of death because there the shield of the "mighty" was defiled (v. 21b). The poetic parallel makes clear that Saul is the warrior meant here. It is his shield that will no longer be oiled in preparation for battle. The use of the phrase "anointed with oil" also reminds us that Saul himself was God's anointed one, but that he, too, no longer exists.

1:22-24. We have already mentioned the contrast between "then" and "now" as a characteristic of the *qînâ*, or funerary lament. In this segment, the present reality of loss and defeat is contrasted with the memory of Saul and Jonathan as magnificent and valiant warriors for Israel. The tone of this section is more intimate and personal, more passionate.

In v. 22 we are suddenly in the heat of battle, but it is not the final battle of defeat. The imagery attests to the prowess of Saul and Jonathan as warriors. Jonathan with bow and Saul with sword did not hesitate to draw the blood or pierce the flesh (fat) of the enemy. Blood and fat are often associated with sacrifice, and this language may suggest that the victories of Saul and Jonathan were like sacrifices offered up to the Lord. The weapons of Saul and Jonathan found their mark and were victorious even over the "mighty" (גבורים *gibbôrîm*; the same word used of Saul and Jonathan in vv. 19, 21, 25, 27) who fought for the enemy.

David's song looks beyond the exploits of battle to remember Saul and Jonathan as beloved in Israel and as gracious or charming (v. 23a). The NRSV's use of "lovely" suggests appearance, but the word here (נעים *nā'îm*, "gracious," "charming"; it can also mean "pleasant," which may be how it is used in v. 26b) is more indicative of manner or character. Further, David sings that in life and in death this father and son were not parted. The NRSV translation is to be preferred. Life and death form a poetic merism, with two opposites indicating a totality—i.e., Saul and Jonathan were never divided. In the final images of the verse (v. 23b), these two mighty men of Israel are compared in swiftness to eagles and in strength to lions. In this verse, we may be dealing with the natural hyperbole that is characteristic of eulogies. Because so much of our encounter with Saul has involved his obsessive and violent pursuit of David, we do not think of him as gracious and beloved, although our portrait of Jonathan might

fit these terms. We certainly do not think of the relationship between Saul and Jonathan as one of constant unity. They quarreled violently, and because of David (1 Sam 20:30-34; 22:8). No doubt the portrait here is due in part to the graciousness of David, placing Israel's departed king in the best light. Nevertheless, we should also remember that Israel's experience with Saul was not seen primarily through the lens of the struggle with David. David's memory of a loved and gracious Saul may be his own memories of a time before their conflict, when Saul loved David (1 Sam 16:21); but it may also speak for Israel, who saw in Saul and his son Jonathan those who gave them hope in the face of Philistine threat and pride in identity as Israelites. If Jonathan and Saul had conflicts, we should remember that Jonathan loyally stayed by his father's side rather than go with David. Jonathan chose against his love for David to honor and support Saul in spite of their differences. They were not divided, even by their dispute over David, and they died together on the field of battle. David sings of a truth in Israel's experience of Saul and Jonathan that transcends the flaws and struggles of their lives to celebrate their gifts and mourn their loss.

In contrast to the arrogant rejoicing of the daughters of the Philistines (v. 20), David summons the daughters of Israel to weep for Saul (v. 24). It is tears that are appropriate, not laughter. They are to mourn for his loss, remembering the honor and glory with which he had clothed them. The imagery of crimson garments and gold ornaments represents the well-being that Saul returned to Israel. Crimson and gold are the trappings of royalty. In a time of Philistine defeat and occupation, Saul brought a royal presence into the midst of Israel and dared in such a time to dream of kingdom. If he failed to establish an enduring kingdom, he nevertheless gave birth to that possibility for Israel. Again the language is poetic hyperbole. It should not be taken to mean that David is addressing only the daughters of the wealthy.[183]

1:25-27. The use of the refrain in v. 25a marks the transition to a new section of the lament. It is the most personal segment in its use of language, almost as if we have moved from leadership in public grief to David's own private

183. Contra Walter Brueggemann, *First and Second Samuel*, Interpretation (Louisville: John Knox, 1990) 216.

sorrow. It is the only segment of the lament cast in the first person. The focus of this section is on Jonathan and the deep personal loss his death meant for David. The king is put aside for the moment in this intimate mourning of the loss of a friend. It is no longer the "splendor" or "glory" of Israel that lies slain upon the high places. It is simply and tragically Jonathan who lies slain there (v. 25*b*).

The poetry of grief in v. 26 reflects the deep and personal relationship of David and Jonathan and the covenant bonds between them, portrayed in 1 Sam 18:1-4; 20:1-42; 23:15-18. David speaks of his own deep distress and speaks of Jonathan as "brother" (v. 26*a*). This term of familial relationship and closeness may refer both to David's relationship to Jonathan as the husband of his sister Michal and to their commitment in a covenant based on *ḥesed* ("faithfulness," "steadfast love"). Covenant partners are often referred to as "brothers."

David speaks of the depth of personal relationship between them. The two verbs used are the same two used in v. 23*a* to speak of Saul and Jonathan, but the application is more personal. The NRSV confusingly translates נעם (*nā'ēm*) as "beloved," which makes it seem as if the verb "to love" (אהב *'āhab*) appears three times in v. 26*b* and points to the wrong corresponding verb in v. 23*a*. David speaks here of the great pleasure and graciousness he found in Jonathan. The NIV translates it more felicitously, "you were very dear to me." David calls to memory Jonathan's love (18:1, 3; 20:17). It was wonderful, and it surpassed the love of women (v. 26*b*). David unreservedly gives public expression to the love on which his friendship with Jonathan was based. As observed in the Commentary on 18:1-4, such love was not only personal but political in character as well. Jonathan's love for David found expression in the surrender of his claim to the throne (18:4), and the verb "to love" appears often in connection with covenant partners to indicate commitment. It was, indeed, wondrous that Jonathan could give up so much for the love of his friend.

Some have felt that the statement of this love, which for David surpassed the love of women, is indicative of a homosexual relationship between David and Jonathan.[184] There is nothing in the language of this verse that explicitly suggests this or rules it out. Of course, David's many liaisons with women are well known and in some cases notorious (2 Samuel 11). We should be alert to the possibility that this phrase says less about David's sexual orientation than it says about the status of women in ancient Israel. In an era of arranged marriages, love was not considered the basis of most relationships between men and women. Liaisons with women existed either in the context of marriage, where the purpose was child-bearing, or in illicit contexts, where the purpose was to satisfy lust. Love of women in such limited contexts might indeed pale in comparison to the deep and personal commitment represented by the love of David and Jonathan for each other.

The final use of the refrain in v. 27 signals the end of David's song of lament. The "weapons of war" that have perished here are Saul and Jonathan themselves. David has been the instrument of the unreserved and public expression of grief. He has dared to speak both personally of his own loss and corporately of Israel's loss. Set aside for this moment are both political prospects and divine intentions for Israel's future. It is a deeply human moment that belongs to Saul and Jonathan.

184. See Tom Horner, *Jonathan Loved David: Homosexuality in Biblical Times* (Philadelphia: Westminster, 1978).

REFLECTIONS

David's singing of Israel's grief and his own invites us to consider our own capacity for public grief and the healing that can flow from such expression.

In 1963 I was a seminary student in Dallas, Texas, when President John F. Kennedy was assassinated. I remember vividly the days of public and national grief. My mind still fills with the images of the caisson and the riderless horse and the endless lines of mourners who filed past the bier while millions filed with them via the television screen. There were poetic words of tribute and loss to accompany the rituals. And there was a strange unity and community in grief, as if in acknowledging our loss we were bound together in a human experience that

2 SAMUEL 1:17-27 REFLECTIONS

transcended partisan politics and vested interests. As it was for David, the customary politics of the kingdom were set aside for the moment. The humanness at the heart of the political process was exposed and cared for. In this spirit, bipartisan efforts passed the Civil Rights Act of 1963 in the days following the death of JFK. It was by no means politics as usual.

Only a few short years later, the assassination of Martin Luther King, Jr., in 1968 also brought the country to a standstill. Grief this time was also expressed as rage, and many cities experienced violent outbursts of anger and loss. The hope and promise of a man who symbolized unity beyond the deep racial divisions in our country had been cut down by an assassin's bullet. In the wrenching aftermath of this tragedy, it was again an occasion for public grief that captured a nation's attention, refocused the dream for which King had died, and turned a nation's loss toward new resolve in the struggles against racism. King's nationally televised funeral service brought the nation to a standstill and focused the public attention on King's legacy, which lives beyond the loss felt so deeply by so many.

Unfortunately these signal events in American life may be exceptions and not the rule. Only a short distance from the Lincoln Memorial in Washington, D.C., is the Vietnam War Memorial. It does not announce its presence in monumental fashion. It is a silent, dark granite gash in the green earth inscribed with the mute names of every American military person lost in the Vietnam war. Endless lines pass by its surfaces and stop to find and read names that represent their losses in the midst of a nation's loss. It is the most visited monument in the nation's capital and obviously speaks eloquently to the need of many to acknowledge public grief. But this monument speaks in silent testimony to those who make their way to its site while the nation as a whole has yet to speak much publicly about this chapter of defeat and loss. Vietnam veterans returned to a nation that did not want to hear about their war. They are often called a lost generation of veterans whose sacrifices have been largely unacknowledged because to do so would be to face our moment of national loss and pain in that war. Triumphal politics silence the Davidic voices who would grieve the slain and mourn the defeats. In similar fashion, we are only now learning that voices of triumph obscured the cost and loss suffered in the Persian Gulf War.

David has introduced into this ongoing story of politics and kingdoms the truth taught by all of Israel's laments. It is as important to sing publicly of our hurts as it is to sing of our triumphs. It is only by acknowledging the depths of loss that we can open to God's new thing in our midst. David sings Israel to an acknowledgment of loss that will allow them to surrender Saul as a future that can no longer be. Such singing enables the turning to God's new future. We must remember that David's story not only has roots in the experience of his own time but is being retold by the deuteronomistic historian, who is telling the story to exiles in Babylon who have also lost a king and a kingdom. Imagine the meaning of David's song of lament heard anew beside the rivers of Babylon by those who despaired of singing the Lord's song (Ps 137:4). David summons those non-singers to sing their loss, and his singers invite us to join in the singing. It is the singing of our hurts that truly orders our priorities. Even the kingdom can wait. Politics and consuming as usual can wait when we allow our grief and pain to teach us what is genuinely valued and needed in our lives. We know the truth of this in moments like the JFK and the King funerals, when much that seemed important was put on hold for a while.

David's singing may model a role for the church. The church should be the place where death can be faced for the painful reality that it is and where our human loss and grief can be voiced. It should be a place where we dare to speak of kingdoms we hoped for that have suffered defeat and have left us despairing of justice or peace or hope. This is the point of the cross as a central symbol of the Christian faith. The brokenness of our lives and our world must be acknowledged and voiced. David teaches us that we cannot move to joy, renewal, and praise too soon. We must make a place for our pain. Our wounds cannot heal if they are not exposed. It is only after encounter with the cross and the loss it represents that resurrection can speak a meaningful word of life. The poetry of pain and grief allows the lost kingdom of Saul to give way to the renewed kingdom of David. The church can sing with David and become a place where pain and loss are acknowledged publicly and their power over us is broken. This can enable a turning toward God's new future for ourselves, for our nation, for our world.

2 Samuel 2:1-11, David Becomes King at Hebron

NIV

2 In the course of time, David inquired of the LORD. "Shall I go up to one of the towns of Judah?" he asked.

The LORD said, "Go up."

David asked, "Where shall I go?"

"To Hebron," the LORD answered.

[2]So David went up there with his two wives, Ahinoam of Jezreel and Abigail, the widow of Nabal of Carmel. [3]David also took the men who were with him, each with his family, and they settled in Hebron and its towns. [4]Then the men of Judah came to Hebron and there they anointed David king over the house of Judah.

When David was told that it was the men of Jabesh Gilead who had buried Saul, [5]he sent messengers to the men of Jabesh Gilead to say to them, "The LORD bless you for showing this kindness to Saul your master by burying him. [6]May the LORD now show you kindness and faithfulness, and I too will show you the same favor because you have done this. [7]Now then, be strong and brave, for Saul your master is dead, and the house of Judah has anointed me king over them."

[8]Meanwhile, Abner son of Ner, the commander of Saul's army, had taken Ish-Bosheth son of Saul and brought him over to Mahanaim. [9]He made him king over Gilead, Ashuri[a] and Jezreel, and also over Ephraim, Benjamin and all Israel.

[10]Ish-Bosheth son of Saul was forty years old when he became king over Israel, and he reigned two years. The house of Judah, however, followed David. [11]The length of time David was king in Hebron over the house of Judah was seven years and six months.

[a] 9 Or Asher

NRSV

2 After this David inquired of the LORD, "Shall I go up into any of the cities of Judah?" The LORD said to him, "Go up." David said, "To which shall I go up?" He said, "To Hebron." [2]So David went up there, along with his two wives, Ahinoam of Jezreel, and Abigail the widow of Nabal of Carmel. [3]David brought up the men who were with him, every one with his household; and they settled in the towns of Hebron. [4]Then the people of Judah came, and there they anointed David king over the house of Judah.

When they told David, "It was the people of Jabesh-gilead who buried Saul," [5]David sent messengers to the people of Jabesh-gilead, and said to them, "May you be blessed by the LORD, because you showed this loyalty to Saul your lord, and buried him! [6]Now may the LORD show steadfast love and faithfulness to you! And I too will reward you because you have done this thing. [7]Therefore let your hands be strong, and be valiant; for Saul your lord is dead, and the house of Judah has anointed me king over them."

[8]But Abner son of Ner, commander of Saul's army, had taken Ishbaal[a] son of Saul, and brought him over to Mahanaim. [9]He made him king over Gilead, the Ashurites, Jezreel, Ephraim, Benjamin, and over all Israel. [10]Ishbaal,[a] Saul's son, was forty years old when he began to reign over Israel, and he reigned two years. But the house of Judah followed David. [11]The time that David was king in Hebron over the house of Judah was seven years and six months.

[a] Gk Compare 1 Chr 8.33; 9.39: Heb *Ish-bosheth*, "man of shame"

COMMENTARY

Abruptly the time of mourning is ended. Political realities will not wait. Saul is dead, and the Israelites have scattered. The Philistines occupy the country. If David is to be a part of Israel's future, he must act. The first part of this chapter consists of three brief reports, each suggesting elements in the complex politics of the kingdom. Saul's death has left a vacuum of leadership, and various forces rush to fill the space he has left: vv. 1-4a, after inquiring of God, David moves to Hebron, where he is anointed king by the men of Judah; vv. 4b-7, David responds to the loyalty of Jabesh-gilead in rescuing the body of Saul. His first act as king in Judah is to offer favor to a key group of Israelites; vv. 8-11, Abner makes Ishbosheth king over Israel in Mahanaim.

There is no simple way forward after Saul's death. This portion of the story marks the beginning of a period of conflicting loyalties and ambitions. It is a story of politics and violence, but at the same time a story of God's future for Israel that finally comes to fruition in David.

2:1-4a. David is still at Ziklag. Saul is dead. Israel's future is at stake. David does not hesitate to act and move toward power, but characteristically his first act is to inquire of the Lord. He has a specific course of action in mind, and the posing of the question in this form suggests that he is using the sacred lots (see 1 Sam 23:9; 30:7). But the narrative has no interest in ritual processes. Only the question and its answer are important: "Should I go up to one of the cities of Judah?" "Yes!" says the Lord. "To which one?" David asks. "Hebron!" (v. 1). David's natural impulse is to consult with the Lord before taking action. This may be an intentional contrast to the way in which Abner makes Ishbosheth king in Mahanaim (vv. 8-9). David's strength ultimately rests in divine power, not in human power.

Hebron was one of the towns to which David distributed the spoil of his Amalekite victory (1 Sam 30:31). It has a long history of connection with Israel's ancestors (Gen 13:18; 23:19; 35:27; 37:14), but in the tribal period of Israel it was a Calebite town (Josh 15:13-14; Judg 1:20) and may not have been considered a city of Judah until after David unified the territory. It is significant that David's two wives are named in the notice that he went up to Hebron. Abigail had been the wife of Nabal, a prominent Calebite landholder, and Ahinoam was from Jezreel, which was a town near Carmel, the city of Nabal. The account emphasizes that David is already related by marriage to two important clans in the area of Hebron

and may already have claims on important land-holdings by virtue of those marriages.

In v. 3, David, all of his men (presumably six hundred; cf. 1 Sam 27:2), and their households settled in the "towns of Hebron." This would imply at least 2,000 people, and even if the "towns of Hebron" implies the surrounding region rather than just the city of Hebron, this is a sizable population transfer. Many scholars have suggested that this sounds more like a takeover of Hebron than a simple move, although it may have been an acceptable takeover to the inhabitants of Hebron. The verb עלה (ʾālâ, "to go up") is used elsewhere with a military connotation (e.g., 5:17, 19), and David does "go up" with a seasoned fighting force of six hundred men. Hebron would hardly be in a position to refuse David hospitality. Some have suggested that David may have done this with Philistine approval.[185] There is not yet any notice in the story that he has left Philistine service or positioned himself as a Philistine enemy. His break with the Philistines does not seem to come until he is made king of Israel (5:17).

Only after David has, in effect, occupied Hebron do the "men of Judah" come to Hebron and "anoint" David king over the house of Judah (v. 4a). These may be the same individuals as the "elders of Judah" who received David's gifts in 1 Sam 30:26. Whatever the earlier relationship between Judah and Hebron, they are now joined in David's kingship over a "house of Judah," with its capital in Hebron.

It is significant that the people "anoint" David. He had already been secretly anointed by the prophet Samuel (1 Sam 16:13). This earlier anointing led to David's receiving God's Spirit and being designated as the "anointed of the LORD." Here we seem to be dealing with an anointing ritual that does not confer sacral status but represents the people's authorization of the ruler. In 19:10, the people anoint Absalom as a sign of their authorization, but it does not make him the Lord's anointed. The significance here is that David is legitimated by both God and people. His rule is established with the broadest possible basis. The immediate contrast to this will be the imposition of a king on the throne of Israel by Abner in vv. 8-9.

Judah has for the moment separated from Is-

185. A. A. Anderson, *2 Samuel*, WBC 11 (Waco: Word, 1989) 22-23.

rael. Judah has chosen one of its own as king. The fate of Israel, scattered and defeated, is not immediately clear, whereas the people of Judah have acted to secure their own future. Such Judahite action may be seen as a rebellion against Israel as a Saulide kingdom. This would help to explain the hostilities that break out into war between Israel and Judah in 2:12-32.

2:4b-7. David is given a report on the people of Jabesh-gilead (v. 4*b*), who rescued Saul's body from the walls of Beth-shan and gave it a proper burial (1 Sam 31:11-13). Their kindness to Saul was in gratitude for his rescue of Jabesh-gilead from the siege of Nahash, the king of Ammon (1 Samuel 11).

David's first act after becoming king of Judah is to send a gracious message to a northern Israelite group (vv. 5-7). Jabesh-gilead was an important town in the Transjordan and was not far from Mahanaim, where a Saulide capital would be established under the reign of Saul's son Ishbosheth (vv. 8-9). David offers commendation and friendship to an Israelite community in the heart of the remaining Saulide kingdom.

David begins by blessing them in the name of the Lord because of the loyalty they had shown to Saul in his burial (v. 5). The term for "loyalty" here is חסד (*hesed*), a word associated with covenants and commitments (also translated as "kindness," "faithfulness," or "steadfast love"). It was a term favored by David and Jonathan in describing the depth of their friendship and commitment to each other (1 Sam 20:8, 14-15). It is a principle respected and employed by David in honoring his personal and royal commitments (9:1, with Jonathan's son, Mephibosheth; 10:2, in a treaty with the Ammonites).

In return, David invokes the "steadfast love/kindness" (*hesed*) and "faithfulness" of the Lord on behalf of the Jabesh-gileadites (v. 6*a*). Further, David himself promises "favor" toward them. The term used here is טובה (*tôbâ*; lit., "goodness"). The NRSV's translation "reward" suggests material benefits, but David is simply offering friendship and goodwill. He offers relationship and not "reward." It is significant that David invokes God's beneficence before offering his own goodwill. It conveys a sense that David understands his own authority as being derived from that of the Lord. It also serves to make his own goodwill an extension of God's favor, a

connection that he no doubt hopes the people of Jabesh-gilead will find attractive. His final word is not quite so subtle. Although he encourages them to be brave and strong, he bluntly reminds them that Saul is dead, but Judah has just anointed David king (v. 7). The message to Jabesh-gilead is that they can hang on to those things that are gone, or they can look to new beginnings with David. At this point, David cannot realistically expect an explicit political alliance with Jabesh-gilead. They are too far north, and both Philistines and the remnants of a Saulide kingdom lie between. He is, however, building influence and goodwill in the north, and this effort seems to bear fruit in the future (5:1-3).

2:8-11. The first two verses of this section narrate the establishment of a continuing Saulide kingdom (vv. 8-9). The narrative does not dwell on this continuation of Israel, but strikes a contrast with the beginnings of David's kingdom, described earlier in the chapter.

David's kingship in Judah begins with his inquiring of the Lord (v. 1). David seeks divine authorization. By contrast, vv. 8-9 report that Abner *took* Ishbosheth, and *brought* him to Mahanaim, and *made* him king. The harsh verbs of these verses portray an Israelite kingship authorized by the political and military power of Abner.

Abner was the commander of Saul's army (1 Sam 17:55; 20:25; 26:5) and a cousin (or uncle) of Saul (1 Sam 14:50). It seems clear that, after the death of Saul, Abner was the effective power in Israel, but he does not have a clear claim to the throne and must install the remaining son of Saul on the throne as a figurehead. This assessment of Abner's power seems confirmed by later events when his defection to David and subsequent death leave Ishbosheth vulnerable to assassination (3:6–4:12).

Ishbosheth appears to be the remaining son of Saul. His name, as it appears in 2 Samuel, has always been considered a scribal comment. His name is reported in 1 Chr 8:33; 9:39 as "Eshbaal," which means "Baal exists." Some would, with a slight emendation, read "Ishbaal," "Man of Baal." Most scholars consider the name reported in 1 Chronicles as historically original,[186] and many translations have adopted this name in

---

186. See P. Kyle McCarter, *II Samuel*, AB 9 (Garden City, N.Y.: Doubleday, 1984) 85-87, for a detailed discussion of the linguistic and textual proposals related to this name.

place of Ishbosheth in 2 Samuel (including the NRSV). However, the actual text for 2 Samuel reads the name as "Ishbosheth," which means "Man of shame." The widely accepted hypothesis is that later editors or scribes (perhaps the deuteronomistic historian), reflecting the struggle with Baalism in later periods, replaced the offending Baal element of the name with the Hebrew word for "shame" (בשׁת *bōšet*). Such a linguistic substitution as a theological comment is known elsewhere in the biblical tradition (e.g., Jer 11:13). In Saul's time, the term בעל (*baʿal*), which means "lord," was not yet connected with Canaanite idolatry as a threat to the worship of Yahweh. The noun may even have been used as a term of honor and respect for God. Jonathan also had a son with a name that included the element *baʿal*, and the text of 2 Samuel also shows his name altered by the use of the term *bōšet* (see Commentary on 2 Sam 9:1-13). We do not know much about Ishbosheth/Ishbaal. He was not with Saul and his other sons at Mt. Gilboa, and most assume that this means he was too young to join the fighting men.

Mahanaim is an important town in the Transjordan. It seems clear that any continuation of Israelite rule would have been forced to locate its center outside of Philistine-dominated territory. There is no evidence that Philistine hegemony extended beyond the Jordan River, so Mahanaim was a safe place for Abner to attempt a rebuilding of the Israelite kingdom. The list of geographic territories for Ishbosheth's rule in v. 9 is a claim to most, if not all, of Saul's previous kingdom, but it is a hope rather than a reality.

The chronological notes of vv. 10-11 are characteristic of the deuteronomistic historian and are probably from his hand. The actual figures used present some problems. It is highly unlikely that Ishbosheth was forty years old at the start of his reign. This would make him older than Jonathan and heir to the throne ahead of Jonathan. David was only thirty years old when his reign began (5:4), and he was of similar age to Jonathan. There are many indications that Ishbosheth was a boy. He did not fight at Gilboa. He was dominated and controlled by Abner as if Abner were regent to the throne. In the later dispute over Rizpah, Saul's concubine, it is Abner who has sexual relations with her, and not Ishbosheth. The taking of the king's harem was a frequent sign of accession to the throne in ancient times (see Absalom later, 16:21-22). Ishbosheth may have been too young to have exercised this sign of authority himself (see Commentary on 3:6-11).

The note of two years for Ishbosheth's reign may well be accurate (v. 10), but it is difficult to explain why David's reign at Hebron is listed as having been so much longer (seven and a half years, v. 11). The usual assumption has been that when Ishbosheth was killed and the elders of Israel made David king as well, he soon thereafter moved his capital to Jerusalem. This note, if accurate, would suggest that David reigned from Hebron for five and a half years after becoming king over Judah *and* Israel.

REFLECTIONS

It would be understandable if readers took a cynical view of these notices in 2:1-11. Saul has received his moment of honor and respect. Now it is politics as usual. Yet, even the honored past must give way to the future, and the realities of power must be acknowledged.

The short notices of this passage do, however, offer a contrast in dealing with the realities of power. Abner *takes, brings,* and *makes* a king. He imposes authority and forces a political ideology on the land. David inquires of God, acts decisively himself, and submits to the anointing of the people. He is not without his own authority or the influence of his own considerable will. But he is willing to submit his own authority to a partnership with God, on the one hand, and with the community, on the other hand.

What an instructive metaphor this is for any calling to leadership in the secular world or in the church. Whether in our churches or in our governments, we want leaders with authority who can take decisive action. But too often our leadership is exposed as exercising such authority with no loyalty beyond their own self-interest. Hardly a month goes by without the news of some major scandal of failed public or ecclesiastical trust—presidential advisers, bishops, senators, denominational treasurers. It is significant that in the notice that stands between the models of David and Abner for kingship, David commends the men of Jabesh-gilead for their loyalty to the interests of a king who cannot repay their deed. It is an act of integrity utterly without self-interest. Leadership appropriate to God's kingdom is always shared leadership, accountable to God and community. Whether we speak of pastors or of presidents, David's model has much to commend it.

2 Samuel 2:12-32, A Battle and a Blood Feud

NIV

12Abner son of Ner, together with the men of Ish-Bosheth son of Saul, left Mahanaim and went to Gibeon. 13Joab son of Zeruiah and David's men went out and met them at the pool of Gibeon. One group sat down on one side of the pool and one group on the other side.

14Then Abner said to Joab, "Let's have some of the young men get up and fight hand to hand in front of us."

"All right, let them do it," Joab said.

15So they stood up and were counted off—twelve men for Benjamin and Ish-Bosheth son of Saul, and twelve for David. 16Then each man grabbed his opponent by the head and thrust his dagger into his opponent's side, and they fell down together. So that place in Gibeon was called Helkath Hazzurim.*a*

17The battle that day was very fierce, and Abner and the men of Israel were defeated by David's men.

18The three sons of Zeruiah were there: Joab, Abishai and Asahel. Now Asahel was as fleet-footed as a wild gazelle. 19He chased Abner, turning neither to the right nor to the left as he pursued him. 20Abner looked behind him and asked, "Is that you, Asahel?"

"It is," he answered.

21Then Abner said to him, "Turn aside to the right or to the left; take on one of the young men and strip him of his weapons." But Asahel would not stop chasing him.

22Again Abner warned Asahel, "Stop chasing me! Why should I strike you down? How could I look your brother Joab in the face?"

23But Asahel refused to give up the pursuit; so Abner thrust the butt of his spear into Asahel's stomach, and the spear came out through his

a16 Helkath Hazzurim means field of daggers or field of hostilities.

NRSV

12Abner son of Ner, and the servants of Ish-baal*a* son of Saul, went out from Mahanaim to Gibeon. 13Joab son of Zeruiah, and the servants of David, went out and met them at the pool of Gibeon. One group sat on one side of the pool, while the other sat on the other side of the pool. 14Abner said to Joab, "Let the young men come forward and have a contest before us." Joab said, "Let them come forward." 15So they came forward and were counted as they passed by, twelve for Benjamin and Ishbaal*a* son of Saul, and twelve of the servants of David. 16Each grasped his opponent by the head, and thrust his sword in his opponent's side; so they fell down together. Therefore that place was called Helkath-hazzurim,*c* which is at Gibeon. 17The battle was very fierce that day; and Abner and the men of Israel were beaten by the servants of David.

18The three sons of Zeruiah were there, Joab, Abishai, and Asahel. Now Asahel was as swift of foot as a wild gazelle. 19Asahel pursued Abner, turning neither to the right nor to the left as he followed him. 20Then Abner looked back and said, "Is it you, Asahel?" He answered, "Yes, it is." 21Abner said to him, "Turn to your right or to your left, and seize one of the young men, and take his spoil." But Asahel would not turn away from following him. 22Abner said again to Asahel, "Turn away from following me; why should I strike you to the ground? How then could I show my face to your brother Joab?" 23But he refused to turn away. So Abner struck him in the stomach with the butt of his spear, so that the spear came out at his back. He fell there, and died where he lay. And all those who came to the place where Asahel had fallen and died, stood still.

a Gk Compare 1 Chr 8.33; 9.39: Heb Ish-bosheth, "man of shame"
b That is Field of Sword-edges

NIV

back. He fell there and died on the spot. And every man stopped when he came to the place where Asahel had fallen and died.

²⁴But Joab and Abishai pursued Abner, and as the sun was setting, they came to the hill of Ammah, near Giah on the way to the wasteland of Gibeon. ²⁵Then the men of Benjamin rallied behind Abner. They formed themselves into a group and took their stand on top of a hill.

²⁶Abner called out to Joab, "Must the sword devour forever? Don't you realize that this will end in bitterness? How long before you order your men to stop pursuing their brothers?"

²⁷Joab answered, "As surely as God lives, if you had not spoken, the men would have continued the pursuit of their brothers until morning.ᵃ"

²⁸So Joab blew the trumpet, and all the men came to a halt; they no longer pursued Israel, nor did they fight anymore.

²⁹All that night Abner and his men marched through the Arabah. They crossed the Jordan, continued through the whole Bithronᵇ and came to Mahanaim.

³⁰Then Joab returned from pursuing Abner and assembled all his men. Besides Asahel, nineteen of David's men were found missing. ³¹But David's men had killed three hundred and sixty Benjamites who were with Abner. ³²They took Asahel and buried him in his father's tomb at Bethlehem. Then Joab and his men marched all night and arrived at Hebron by daybreak.

ᵃ27 Or *spoken this morning, the men would not have taken up the pursuit of their brothers*; or *spoken, the men would have given up the pursuit of their brothers by morning*   ᵇ29 Or *morning*; or *ravine*; the meaning of the Hebrew for this word is uncertain.

NRSV

24But Joab and Abishai pursued Abner. As the sun was going down they came to the hill of Ammah, which lies before Giah on the way to the wilderness of Gibeon. 25The Benjaminites rallied around Abner and formed a single band; they took their stand on the top of a hill. 26Then Abner called to Joab, "Is the sword to keep devouring forever? Do you not know that the end will be bitter? How long will it be before you order your people to turn from the pursuit of their kinsmen?" 27Joab said, "As God lives, if you had not spoken, the people would have continued to pursue their kinsmen, not stopping until morning." 28Joab sounded the trumpet and all the people stopped; they no longer pursued Israel or engaged in battle any further.

29Abner and his men traveled all that night through the Arabah; they crossed the Jordan, and, marching the whole forenoon,ᵃ they came to Mahanaim. 30Joab returned from the pursuit of Abner; and when he had gathered all the people together, there were missing of David's servants nineteen men besides Asahel. 31But the servants of David had killed of Benjamin three hundred sixty of Abner's men. 32They took up Asahel and buried him in the tomb of his father, which was at Bethlehem. Joab and his men marched all night, and the day broke upon them at Hebron.

ᵃ Meaning of Heb uncertain

COMMENTARY

The background to this episode is war between the house of Saul and the house of David (cf. 3:1, 6). This is probably not the story of the outbreak of that war, although it would seem to be the account of a major confrontation at an early point in this period of hostility. When the forces of Abner and the forces of Joab confront each other across the pool at Gibeon, the assumption is that there will be a battle of some sort (vv. 12-14). The narrative of 2 Samuel is not interested in telling us why the house of Saul and the house of David are at war. Does Israel regard David's kingship over Judah as a rebellion and a seizing of territory belonging to Israel? Has David made overt claims on the throne of Israel? We do not know of any such claims. It may well be that David, even as king in Hebron, is still working as a vassal of the Philistines. We do not have any record of a break with the Philistines at this point. Only after he becomes king of Israel (5:1-3) does

David seem to become an enemy of the Philistines. If Abner and his men are at Gibeon trying to reassert Israelite control of the central hill country, Saul's home area in Benjamin, then an encounter with Joab could well be an encounter with forces in service to the Philistines.

The narrator of this episode is less concerned with the larger geopolitics of the region than with this encounter as the setting for the killing of Asahel by Abner (v. 23). This act sets in motion a complex series of events that do constitute a threat to David's kingship over all of Israel. These events will continue to unfold beyond this episode through chaps. 3–4. God's kingdom under David does not come in a vacuum but in the midst of difficult political realities and personal tragedies.

2:12-17. Abner, who was commander of the army under Saul and is now the power behind the rule of Ishbosheth, leads a military party back into the central hill country from which Israel had been driven by the Philistines (v. 12). The verb יצא (*yāṣā*, "to go out") used in this context has military connotations. They have come from Mahanaim, the Transjordanian town from which Ishbosheth now perpetuates the rule of the house of Saul, to Gibeon, a non-Israelite city aligned with Israel since the days of Joshua (Joshua 9). Gibeon is in the middle of Benjaminite tribal territory and close to Saul's capital at Gibeah. Several times in this account the Israelites with Abner are referred to as Benjaminites (vv. 15, 25, 31). This may well be a mission sent to test the extent of Philistine control over Benjaminite home territory.

At the same time, Joab, commanding some of the men of David, went out (*yāṣā*) to meet them at the pool of Gibeon (v. 13). Joab is David's nephew, the son of his sister Zeruiah (1 Chr 2:16). This is our first meeting with him, but he will figure prominently in the story of David from this point onward. Joab and his men seem already to be in Gibeon, and they meet with Abner's force at a place called the pool of Gibeon. The two groups face each other across the pool (v. 13*b*). We have already mentioned the possibility that David's men are still serving as vassals of the Philistines. They may be patrolling this territory for the Philistines.

Perhaps in an attempt to avoid full-scale conflict Abner proposes a representative combat between twelve of his men (called Benjaminites) and twelve of Joab's men; Joab agrees to this (vv. 14-15). Older commentary on this text describes this encounter as a game or a contest that got out of hand and turned deadly. More recent scholarship has made clear the widespread use of representative combat in the ancient Near East and has advanced evidence that the verb שׂחק (*śāḥaq*), often translated as "to play," can also mean "to contest in hand to hand combat."[187]

The fight is quickly over (v. 16). This verse may represent only the final stage of the combat. It would appear that each pair of opponents became locked in struggle with daggers so that all twenty-four opponents fell wounded if not dead. The narrator reports that this event gave rise to the naming of the place as "Field of Daggers or Hostilities" (v. 16*b*). Suddenly, without explanation, a wider battle is reported, and it is one that Abner and the Israelite men lose (v. 17). Did some not honor the terms of the representative combat? Of course, such a battle broke out after David killed Goliath as well (1 Samuel 17). This battle following the combat of the young men seems to be the context in which the events of vv. 18-32 are narrated. It was those events, and not the wider battle, that was of interest to the narrator.

2:18-32. The three sons of David's sister Zeruiah are the macho men of the books of Samuel. They are fierce and formidable warriors, but also are rash and intemperate. We already met Abishai, who, as the companion of David, had to be restrained from killing Saul in his sleep (1 Sam 26:6-12). Joab eventually becomes the commander of David's armies, but he will also be involved in numerous events that require a quick sword and a willingness to use it. In this story, the focus is on the third brother, Asahel, who is said to be as fast of foot as a gazelle (v. 18).

In the heat of battle, perhaps as the Israelites are trying to retreat, Asahel pursues Abner with dogged persistence (v. 19). The impression is that Abner is not as fast as Asahel, but he is a more seasoned warrior. Abner clearly knows Asahel and makes certain of his identity (v. 20). Twice he tries to persuade Asahel to break off the pursuit. He urges him to seize one of the other men and take spoil for himself (v. 21). When Asahel persists

---

187. Roland de Vaux, "Single Combat in the Old Testament," in *The Bible and the Ancient Near East*, trans. D. McHugh (Garden City, N.Y.: Doubleday, 1971) 122-35.

in pursuit, Abner pleads that he does not wish to hurt him. He worries about facing Joab if he should strike down Asahel (v. 22). As it turns out, this worry was warranted (see chap. 3). Asahel refuses to break off the pursuit. The end comes quickly with the practiced efficiency of the experienced warrior. When Abner sees that there is no alternative but to kill or be killed, he strikes Asahel with the butt of his spear so that the end passes through his body (v. 23a). It may have been an unexpected stroke with the back of the spear. The account seems to be at great pains to show that Abner was forced into combat against his will in killing Asahel. Others come to the place where Asahel lies and stand silent and still, perhaps in shock at the loss of one of these seemingly invincible brothers (v. 23b).

The remaining brothers, Joab and Abishai, take up the pursuit of Abner, but they do not seem as fleet of foot (v. 24). At nightfall Abner and his remaining Israelites/Benjaminites take a stand on a hilltop with Joab, Abishai, and their men apparently at a distance, perhaps on an opposite hill (v. 25). Abner calls out a proposal to end the fighting. He speaks of his men and the men of David as kinsmen and suggests that their battle can only become more bitter (v. 26). Joab takes the opening. Perhaps it allows him to disengage with honor. He, too, refers to the two opposing forces as kinsmen and admits that without Abner's initiative the battle would have continued until morning (v. 27). Joab sounds the trumpet, and the battle ends (v. 28). There is irony in Abner's proposal to cease hostilities. He asks the question, "Is the sword to keep devouring forever?" (v. 26a). The imagery of the "sword devouring" appears only one additional time in 2 Samuel. Instead of a plea for peace, it is a casual justification for the murder of Uriah, which David orders Joab to carry out, saying, "The sword devours one and then the other" (11:25).

There remains of this account only the sad aftermath of war: the return home of those who survived (vv. 29, 32b); the listing of the body count for those who cannot return home (nineteen of David's men, but three hundred and sixty of Abner's men, vv. 30-31); and the burial of Asahel in his father's tomb in Bethlehem (v. 32a). It has been a great loss for the men of Israel, but the death of Asahel clearly leaves Joab without any feeling of victory. The full repercussions of this event have yet to play themselves out.

REFLECTIONS

It is in the Advent season that churches sing of the angelic proclamation of "Peace on earth! Goodwill to all people!" It is a most satisfying way to think of the advent of God's kingdom and the coming of God's anointed one. But this text is far from that imagery. David is God's anointed one, and the kingdom God will establish through him is being born. Yet, the events of this narrative are of war, not of peace—of violence, and not of goodwill.

It is natural for readers to ask why David's lament over the cost of war in the lives of Saul and Jonathan (1:19-27) and David's praise for the "loyalty/steadfast love" of Jabesh-gilead (2:4b-7) must be followed by a story of such senseless violence and death. We want God's kingdom to be announced and fully present. We want to think about God's kingdom as abstracted from the realities of war and blood feuds, politics and ideologies. This text reminds us that God's kingdom cannot take shape in human history without recognition of these realities. David cannot establish God's kingdom for Israel, and God's purposes cannot go forward apart from facing and dealing with such realities. David will have to deal with the Abners and the Joabs, the civil wars and the Philistine wars, his own faithfulness and the seductions of his own power.

In our own time, we may sing with the angelic choirs at Christmastide, but the gospel story and the church calendar will eventually take us to Herod's court, to Pilate's judgment, and to Golgotha. It is good to sing of our hope for "peace on earth," but the church in our time will have to listen to the stories of atrocities in Rwanda, renewed ethnic killing in Bosnia, and widespread abuse and rape of women in our own society that fill our newspapers. It is these stories, like the war story of 2 Sam 2:12-32, that remind us why God's kingdom is needed in our midst. We need God's kingdom to come precisely because the world is often violent, unjust, and cruel. Blood is shed, and death is real in our world just as in David's.

The story of this war episode offers no glib answers or moral aphorisms. It tells us what the world, where David must establish his kingdom, is like. His first act as king of Judah was to praise the *ḥesed* of Jabesh-gilead. He must now deal with the political realities that drive the violence of Abner and Joab and their men. In the chapters just ahead (chaps. 3–4), events actually get more complex politically, and more people die. David must face these realities and nevertheless find a way to establish the kingdom. If we in our turn are to be agents for the bringing of God's kingdom, it will not be enough to sing of peace and settle for a fuzzy hope that it will come. We, like David, will have to find realistic strategies that deal with the ambiguous political realities standing as barriers to the coming of the kingdom. To do that, we will have to face the realities of wars and rumors of wars. We will have to hear and tell the stories of violence that make clear the tragic cycle of injury and revenge that threatens God's kingdom in our time as surely as it threatened God's kingdom through David. Only by recognizing such patterns of violence and naming the blind self-interest that motivates such patterns can we hope to break the hold of violent patterns and move toward the fullness of God's kingdom.

2 Samuel 3:1-5, David's Sons

NIV

3 The war between the house of Saul and the house of David lasted a long time. David grew stronger and stronger, while the house of Saul grew weaker and weaker.

²Sons were born to David in Hebron:

His firstborn was Amnon the son of Ahinoam of Jezreel;

³his second, Kileab the son of Abigail the widow of Nabal of Carmel;

the third, Absalom the son of Maacah daughter of Talmai king of Geshur;

⁴the fourth, Adonijah the son of Haggith;

the fifth, Shephatiah the son of Abital;

⁵and the sixth, Ithream the son of David's wife Eglah.

These were born to David in Hebron.

NRSV

3 There was a long war between the house of Saul and the house of David; David grew stronger and stronger, while the house of Saul became weaker and weaker.

²Sons were born to David at Hebron: his first-born was Amnon, of Ahinoam of Jezreel; ³his second, Chileab, of Abigail the widow of Nabal of Carmel; the third, Absalom son of Maacah, daughter of King Talmai of Geshur; ⁴the fourth, Adonijah son of Haggith; the fifth, Shephatiah son of Abital; ⁵and the sixth, Ithream, of David's wife Eglah. These were born to David in Hebron.

COMMENTARY

This short section includes a summarizing note (v. 1) and a list of the sons born to David at Hebron (vv. 2-5). It seems intrusive here, since v. 6 resumes the story of the enmity between Abner and Joab, which began with the death of Asahel in 2:18-32.

Verse 1 is an important programmatic statement reminding us that David's kingship over a unified Israel did not come immediately or with-

out cost. There was a "long war." Interestingly, this war is characterized not by geography (north and south) but by the two houses claiming the throne. It was a war between the house of Saul and the house of David. The ghost of past conflict between David and Saul is not easily exorcised. Yet, the path to the future is clear. David grew constantly stronger while the house of Saul grew progressively weaker. Perhaps the conflict went on so long precisely because David would not seize a unified kingdom by frontal assault. As we shall see, he is careful not to be seen as having plotted the deaths of Israel's leaders. It is important that Israel come to him with the gift of kingdom. We should imagine the war, then, as one of border hostilities and skirmishing rather than as a campaign by David to impose his rule on Israel.

The list of David's sons is information that is not directly pertinent at this point in the story, but it is the first hint of the issue of succession, which will loom so large at a later point in the story. We know almost nothing about three of these sons beyond their names in this list (cf. 1 Chr 3:1-9, where it is combined with the list in 5:13-16): Chileab (whose mother, Abigail, is known to us from 1 Samuel 25), Shephatiah, and Ithream. The remaining three will become well known to us in later struggles over succession to the throne. Amnon, Absalom, and Adonijah all play significant roles in the difficult and tragic events of David's later life (see 2 Samuel 13–20; 1 Kings 1–2).

2 Samuel 3:6-39, The Death of Abner

NIV

6During the war between the house of Saul and the house of David, Abner had been strengthening his own position in the house of Saul. 7Now Saul had had a concubine named Rizpah daughter of Aiah. And Ish-Bosheth said to Abner, "Why did you sleep with my father's concubine?"

8Abner was very angry because of what Ish-Bosheth said and he answered, "Am I a dog's head—on Judah's side? This very day I am loyal to the house of your father Saul and to his family and friends. I haven't handed you over to David. Yet now you accuse me of an offense involving this woman! 9May God deal with Abner, be it ever so severely, if I do not do for David what the LORD promised him on oath 10and transfer the kingdom from the house of Saul and establish David's throne over Israel and Judah from Dan to Beersheba." 11Ish-Bosheth did not dare to say another word to Abner, because he was afraid of him.

12Then Abner sent messengers on his behalf to say to David, "Whose land is it? Make an agreement with me, and I will help you bring all Israel over to you."

13"Good," said David. "I will make an agreement with you. But I demand one thing of you: Do not come into my presence unless you bring Michal daughter of Saul when you come to see me." 14Then David sent messengers to Ish-Bosheth son of Saul, demanding, "Give me my wife Michal, whom I betrothed to myself for the price of a hundred Philistine foreskins."

15So Ish-Bosheth gave orders and had her taken away from her husband Paltiel son of Laish. 16Her

NRSV

6While there was war between the house of Saul and the house of David, Abner was making himself strong in the house of Saul. 7Now Saul had a concubine whose name was Rizpah daughter of Aiah. And Ishbaal[a] said to Abner, "Why have you gone in to my father's concubine?" 8The words of Ishbaal[b] made Abner very angry; he said, "Am I a dog's head for Judah? Today I keep showing loyalty to the house of your father Saul, to his brothers, and to his friends, and have not given you into the hand of David; and yet you charge me now with a crime concerning this woman. 9So may God do to Abner and so may he add to it! For just what the LORD has sworn to David, that will I accomplish for him, 10to transfer the kingdom from the house of Saul, and set up the throne of David over Israel and over Judah, from Dan to Beer-sheba." 11And Ishbaal[a] could not answer Abner another word, because he feared him.

12Abner sent messengers to David at Hebron,[c] saying, "To whom does the land belong? Make your covenant with me, and I will give you my support to bring all Israel over to you." 13He said, "Good; I will make a covenant with you. But one thing I require of you: you shall never appear in my presence unless you bring Saul's daughter Michal when you come to see me." 14Then David sent messengers to Saul's son Ishbaal,[d] saying, "Give me my wife Michal, to whom I became engaged at the price of one hundred foreskins of the Philistines." 15Ishbaal[d] sent and took her from

a Heb And he   b Gk Compare 1 Chr 8.33; 9.39: Heb Ish-bosheth,
"man of shame"   c Gk: Heb where he was   d Heb Ish-bosheth

NIV

husband, however, went with her, weeping behind her all the way to Bahurim. Then Abner said to him, "Go back home!" So he went back.

[17]Abner conferred with the elders of Israel and said, "For some time you have wanted to make David your king. [18]Now do it! For the LORD promised David, 'By my servant David I will rescue my people Israel from the hand of the Philistines and from the hand of all their enemies.'"

[19]Abner also spoke to the Benjamites in person. Then he went to Hebron to tell David everything that Israel and the whole house of Benjamin wanted to do. [20]When Abner, who had twenty men with him, came to David at Hebron, David prepared a feast for him and his men. [21]Then Abner said to David, "Let me go at once and assemble all Israel for my lord the king, so that they may make a compact with you, and that you may rule over all that your heart desires." So David sent Abner away, and he went in peace.

[22]Just then David's men and Joab returned from a raid and brought with them a great deal of plunder. But Abner was no longer with David in Hebron, because David had sent him away, and he had gone in peace. [23]When Joab and all the soldiers with him arrived, he was told that Abner son of Ner had come to the king and that the king had sent him away and that he had gone in peace.

[24]So Joab went to the king and said, "What have you done? Look, Abner came to you. Why did you let him go? Now he is gone! [25]You know Abner son of Ner; he came to deceive you and observe your movements and find out everything you are doing."

[26]Joab then left David and sent messengers after Abner, and they brought him back from the well of Sirah. But David did not know it. [27]Now when Abner returned to Hebron, Joab took him aside into the gateway, as though to speak with him privately. And there, to avenge the blood of his brother Asahel, Joab stabbed him in the stomach, and he died.

[28]Later, when David heard about this, he said, "I and my kingdom are forever innocent before the LORD concerning the blood of Abner son of Ner. [29]May his blood fall upon the head of Joab and upon all his father's house! May Joab's house

NRSV

her husband Paltiel the son of Laish. [16]But her husband went with her, weeping as he walked behind her all the way to Bahurim. Then Abner said to him, "Go back home!" So he went back.

17Abner sent word to the elders of Israel, saying, "For some time past you have been seeking David as king over you. [18]Now then bring it about; for the LORD has promised David: Through my servant David I will save my people Israel from the hand of the Philistines, and from all their enemies." [19]Abner also spoke directly to the Benjaminites; then Abner went to tell David at Hebron all that Israel and the whole house of Benjamin were ready to do.

20When Abner came with twenty men to David at Hebron, David made a feast for Abner and the men who were with him. [21]Abner said to David, "Let me go and rally all Israel to my lord the king, in order that they may make a covenant with you, and that you may reign over all that your heart desires." So David dismissed Abner, and he went away in peace.

22Just then the servants of David arrived with Joab from a raid, bringing much spoil with them. But Abner was not with David at Hebron, for David[a] had dismissed him, and he had gone away in peace. [23]When Joab and all the army that was with him came, it was told Joab, "Abner son of Ner came to the king, and he has dismissed him, and he has gone away in peace." [24]Then Joab went to the king and said, "What have you done? Abner came to you; why did you dismiss him, so that he got away? [25]You know that Abner son of Ner came to deceive you, and to learn your comings and goings and to learn all that you are doing."

26When Joab came out from David's presence, he sent messengers after Abner, and they brought him back from the cistern of Sirah; but David did not know about it. [27]When Abner returned to Hebron, Joab took him aside in the gateway to speak with him privately, and there he stabbed him in the stomach. So he died for shedding[b] the blood of Asahel, Joab's[c] brother. [28]Afterward, when David heard of it, he said, "I and my kingdom are forever guiltless before the LORD for the blood of Abner son of Ner. [29]May the guilt[d]

a Heb *he* b Heb lacks *shedding* c Heb *his* d Heb *May it*

NIV

never be without someone who has a running sore or leprosy*a* or who leans on a crutch or who falls by the sword or who lacks food."

³⁰(Joab and his brother Abishai murdered Abner because he had killed their brother Asahel in the battle at Gibeon.)

³¹Then David said to Joab and all the people with him, "Tear your clothes and put on sackcloth and walk in mourning in front of Abner." King David himself walked behind the bier. ³²They buried Abner in Hebron, and the king wept aloud at Abner's tomb. All the people wept also.

³³The king sang this lament for Abner:

"Should Abner have died as the lawless die?
³⁴   Your hands were not bound,
     your feet were not fettered.
You fell as one falls before wicked men."

And all the people wept over him again.

³⁵Then they all came and urged David to eat something while it was still day; but David took an oath, saying, "May God deal with me, be it ever so severely, if I taste bread or anything else before the sun sets!"

³⁶All the people took note and were pleased; indeed, everything the king did pleased them. ³⁷So on that day all the people and all Israel knew that the king had no part in the murder of Abner son of Ner.

³⁸Then the king said to his men, "Do you not realize that a prince and a great man has fallen in Israel this day? ³⁹And today, though I am the anointed king, I am weak, and these sons of Zeruiah are too strong for me. May the LORD repay the evildoer according to his evil deeds!"

a29 The Hebrew word was used for various diseases affecting the skin—not necessarily leprosy.

NRSV

fall on the head of Joab, and on all his father's house; and may the house of Joab never be without one who has a discharge, or who is leprous,*a* or who holds a spindle, or who falls by the sword, or who lacks food!" ³⁰So Joab and his brother Abishai murdered Abner because he had killed their brother Asahel in the battle at Gibeon.

31Then David said to Joab and to all the people who were with him, "Tear your clothes, and put on sackcloth, and mourn over Abner." And King David followed the bier. ³²They buried Abner at Hebron. The king lifted up his voice and wept at the grave of Abner, and all the people wept. ³³The king lamented for Abner, saying,

"Should Abner die as a fool dies?
³⁴ Your hands were not bound,
     your feet were not fettered;
   as one falls before the wicked
     you have fallen."

And all the people wept over him again. ³⁵Then all the people came to persuade David to eat something while it was still day; but David swore, saying, "So may God do to me, and more, if I taste bread or anything else before the sun goes down!" ³⁶All the people took notice of it, and it pleased them; just as everything the king did pleased all the people. ³⁷So all the people and all Israel understood that day that the king had no part in the killing of Abner son of Ner. ³⁸And the king said to his servants, "Do you not know that a prince and a great man has fallen this day in Israel? ³⁹Today I am powerless, even though anointed king; these men, the sons of Zeruiah, are too violent for me. The LORD pay back the one who does wickedly in accordance with his wickedness!"

a A term for several skin diseases; precise meaning uncertain

COMMENTARY

This episode constitutes an unfolding drama with Abner at its center, but the innocence of David as its objective. This drama falls into several distinct acts within the narrative of the chapter: vv. 6-11 tell of Abner's conflict with Ishbosheth; vv. 12-21 detail Abner's negotiations with David and the planned covenant with Israel; vv. 22-27 narrate the circumstances of Abner's death at the hands of Joab; vv. 28-39 describe David's cursing of Joab and his elaborate lamentation and honoring of Abner. The purpose of the episode within the larger history of the rise of David is made clear by v. 37: "So all the people and all Israel understood that day that the king had no part in the killing of Abner, son of Ner." David is innocent of the violence that took the life of Abner, commander of the northern armies. The bloodguilt falls on Joab (v. 29), and not on David. It is conceivable that David benefited from Abner's death, if Abner is seen as a potential rival of David, but a similar case could be made that this untimely death was problematic for David's relationship to northern Israel and robbed him of an important strategic ally in terms of other goals (e.g., ridding Israel of Philistine domination).

The account of Abner's death possesses a viewpoint of its own for this complex series of events. No doubt the telling of this story would be different from other viewpoints. The present account is *biased positively toward Abner*. Abner appears as a strong and forceful leader of Israel. By contrast, Ishbosheth is weak and vacillating. After Abner's death even David voices the opinion that "a prince and a great man has fallen this day in Israel" (v. 38). Abner is not viewed as a threat to David. In fact, it is Abner who gives voice on two occasions to the conviction that David is the man the Lord has chosen to lead all Israel and to bring deliverance from the Philistines (vv. 9, 18). The present account is equally clear about the *guilt of Joab*. Joab's cause against Abner is not presented as a just cause, but as a petty personal feud that has placed the interests of David and Israel in jeopardy. David curses Joab and lays the bloodguilt for Abner's death upon Joab and his family (vv. 28-29). Joab's act of killing is a murder (v. 30), and this bloodguilt may eventually be what allows Solomon to take Joab's life at a later point when it suits Solomon's interests (1 Kgs 2:31-34). The present account, by contrast, is concerned to demonstrate *David's innocence.* David is not involved in plotting Abner's death and does not incur bloodguilt (v. 37). He curses Joab and gives Abner the honor of a state funeral with elaborate lamentation. Of course, it is also notable that Joab, unlike the Amalekite who took Saul's life (1:1-16) or the two who will bring Ishbosheth's head to David in the next episode (4:1-12), is not killed. David curses him, but seems still to need him. Perhaps David could not move to take Joab's life because he was related to David by family or was simply too influential and powerful. What seems to begin here is a dark and complex relationship between Joab and David. David will often rely on Joab for both honorable and sinister purposes (cf. 10:7-19 and

11:14-25). He seems to need Joab, but seems also to recognize in him a violence that is dangerous and compromises the kingdom (v. 39).

These events might have been told from other perspectives and have taken quite a different shape. The story would have a different spin were it told from the perspective of Joab's clan or the perspective of those in Israel still suspicious of David's motives or the perspective of the surviving members of the house of Saul (e.g., Ishbosheth and Michal). The invective of Shimei (16:7-8) when David is retreating from Jerusalem suggests that some thought David had incurred bloodguilt in the events that led to his kingship and the collapse of the house of Saul.

The present narrative is biased in favor of David's innocence, but it is the only telling of these events that we have. One can only speculate about the relation of this telling to the historical course of events or David's so-called true motives behind his public actions. Some, desiring to paint a more cynical portrait of David, have ventured so far as to suggest that David desired and plotted the death of Abner. His public shock and lamentation, then, were a sham.[188] In the absence of other tellings of this story, such alternative reconstructions are mere speculation and should be treated with caution.

3:6-11. Verse 6 seems to be a further comment on v. 1 and resumes the main story line after the insertion of the notice on David's sons in vv. 2-5. War continues between the houses of Saul and David, but the focus now shifts to Abner, who has made his position stronger within the house of Saul (v. 6*b*). Since Abner was already acknowledged as the power behind the throne of Ishbosheth (2:8-9), this development is not a surprise.

A tale of conflict between Abner and Ishbosheth unfolds in vv. 7-11. (The NRSV, following 1 Chr 8:33; 9:39, reads "Ishbaal" instead of "Ishbosheth" for the name of Saul's son. See Commentary on 2 Sam 2:8-11 for a discussion of this matter.) Ishbosheth confronts Abner over having had sexual relations with Rizpah, a concubine of his father, Saul. In this story, Rizpah does not emerge as a character in her own right, but is a symbolic pawn in power struggles related to the throne. In a later story (21:8-14), she appears in a tragic episode involving the death of her sons. Her courage and perseverance eventually command the attention and response of David himself. Here, however, she is simply named as the concubine of Saul.

The status of such concubines is a matter of some debate. Some regard Rizpah as a slave attached to the household of Saul who attained significance by bearing him two sons.[189] Others believe that such concubines were legitimate wives of a second rank, perhaps drawn from lower economic classes.[190] The naming of her father would tend to confirm that she was not a slave. In any case, it is clear that her two sons fathered by Saul were considered a legitimate part of the house of Saul and certainly gave Rizpah additional status in the royal household.

It has long been noted that sexual relations with a king's wives or concubines is an act used by claimants to the throne to establish their right to succession. Such action can establish legitimacy to a claim on the throne or serve to usurp the claim of the present occupant of the throne. In this instance, Ishbosheth may have taken Abner's relations with Rizpah to be an implicit threat to his own kingship and a potential claim on the throne by Abner himself. Similar events occur in two other instances with David's sons. Absalom asserts his claim on David's throne by sleeping with David's ten concubines (2 Samuel 20–22). Later, Adonijah asks for Abishag, the concubine of David's old age, as a wife. This is treated as an act of sedition by Solomon and is used as a pretext to kill his half brother and rival for the throne (1 Kgs 2:17-25). Such symbolic sexual acts with royal wives and concubines by claimants to the throne are known elsewhere in the ancient world as well, and many believe the action of Abner must be seen as a challenge to Ishbosheth's royal authority.[191] Why did Ishbosheth not take Rizpah as a wife himself? Then Abner could have sexual relations with her only by committing the crime of adultery. It may be that Ishbosheth was too young and was still only a boy (see Commentary on 2:10-11).

189. See P. Kyle McCarter, *II Samuel,* AB 9 (Garden City, N.Y.: Doubleday, 1984) 112-13, for this view.

190. See A. A. Anderson, *2 Samuel,* WBC 11 (Waco: Word, 1989) 55-56, and the more technical studies he cites for this view.

191. See M. Tsevat, "Marriage and Monarchical Legitimacy in Ugarit and Israel," *JSS* 3 (1958) 237-43.

Abner's angry response leaves unclear whether Ishbosheth's charge was just or not. Abner is indignant, but his indignation could be construed as anger over Ishbosheth's accusation as false or over the accusation as dealing with a trivial matter compared to the loyalty Abner had shown to the house of Saul. He begins his angry response by claiming that Ishbosheth's accusation has insulted him as a "dog's head of Judah," presumably an epithet of worthlessness (v. 8a). Abner feels publicly demeaned. He contrasts this with his loyalty (*ḥesed*) shown to the house of Saul and specifically states that he has not given Ishbosheth over to David (v. 8b). Perhaps this remark is intended as a veiled threat. To Abner, the matter of Rizpah is of small consequence compared to his service, and Ishbosheth has demeaned that service.

Abruptly, Abner seems to resolve to do the very thing he had threatened. In vv. 8-9, he vows by his own well-being before God to shift his support to David and establish his kingdom from Dan to Beersheba. Surprisingly he cites the promise of the Lord to David for such a kingdom and places his own support in the service of that promise. Abner vows to become the agent of God's promise to David. We do not have any record of so specific a divine promise made to David, although his anointing by Samuel and the many references to David as God's choice for king would carry the implicit promise of such an established kingdom. Certainly there is no story of a divine oath sworn to David, but this may simply indicate the widespread recognition of divine favor attached to David and his future reign. We should note that Abner refers to David's reign over Israel and Judah, indicating the dual nature of David's kingship from the beginning.

Our final picture of Ishbosheth is of a pitiful, fearful man. He is powerless to do anything to stop the defection of Abner. The real power clearly rests with Abner, not Ishbosheth, and Ishbosheth is afraid (v. 11).

3:12-21. In v. 12, Abner makes good his threat and enters into negotiations with David. He sends messengers to propose a covenant with David. It is clear that Abner approaches David not as a refugee but as a chieftain with considerable power and influence. He offers as his part of a covenant with David to deliver not only his own support but also the allegiance of the northern tribes of Israel. We have no reason to doubt that he can deliver on the promise. However, the rhetorical question that begins Abner's negotiations with David is not entirely clear. It may be that the question, "To whom does the land belong?" is a reference to Abner's acknowledgment of the Lord's oath to give all of the land into David's rule (vv. 9-10). The answer to the rhetorical question is, then, "To David, of course!"

David readily agrees to a covenant with Abner, but not without his own condition. If Abner is to meet with David to negotiate an alliance, then he is to bring Saul's daughter Michal with him (v. 13). The language is forceful. Abner may not even appear before David without bringing Michal. Saul had been forced to marry his daughter Michal to David when he produced the brideprice of Philistine foreskins (1 Sam 18:20-27). David now alludes to this brideprice (v. 14) as his legal claim that the marriage to Michal is still in effect. When David had been forced to flee from Saul's court, with the aid of Michal and Jonathan, Saul had married her to a man named Palti (1 Sam 25:44). Saul hoped to remove any claim by David on kinship to the house of Saul that might strengthen Davidic claims on the throne. Now that second marriage is declared void by the reassertion of David's claim, and Michal is forcibly taken from Paltiel (v. 15, a longer form of the name), who follows her, weeping, until Abner threateningly tells him to return home (v. 16). Although Michal's arrival at David's capital is not recounted, we may assume that she was delivered to him, since she makes a later appearance as part of David's household (6:16, 20-23). By reclaiming his marriage to Michal, David solidifies both a legal and a popular tie to the house of Saul. This no doubt increases his acceptability to a broad segment of the northern Israelite populace. In all of this Michal has no say. She once loved David (1 Sam 18:20), but she has now become a pawn in a larger complex of political maneuvering.

It is odd that David's formal request for the return of Michal goes to Ishbosheth, who then has her taken from Paltiel (vv. 14-15). In v. 16, however, it is clearly Abner who is delivering her to David. It is likely that Ishbosheth was not aware of Abner's actual negotiations with David or of David's condition. David's legal claim on Michal is asserted through the official channel of the Saulide king Ishbosheth, because the negotiations with Abner are still secret. Abner is still the true power behind

Ishbosheth, so it is not surprising that Ishbosheth complies, although he must certainly have known it would strengthen Davidic claims.

After negotiations with David, Abner turns to deal with the elders of Israel (v. 17a). This should not be understood as a formal body, but simply a meeting of representative leaders from the northern tribes. Abner's speech to them implies that there has already been considerable support in the north for David as king (v. 17b). Abner announces to them that the time has come to make it happen, and he supports that claim by making an appeal to David as the one promised by the Lord to bring deliverance from the Philistines (v. 18). This must have been a powerful incentive to those who had only recently suffered a brutal defeat at the hands of the Philistines, and Abner's appeal is also a reminder of the failure of the house of Saul to bring relief from Philistine oppression. Abner makes a special effort to speak directly to the Benjaminites, the tribesmen of Saul's house (v. 19a). It is not clear if this was in a separate meeting, but it does imply that negotiations with Saul's own tribe required additional attention and delicacy. Nevertheless, the word brought to David at Hebron by Abner is pointed in its statement that Israel and the "whole house of Benjamin" are ready to act in David's favor (v. 19b).

With a company of only twenty men, Abner meets with David at Hebron, where he is welcomed with a feast (v. 20). Final negotiations are completed for a covenant-making ceremony with Israel that will establish David's rule over "all that your heart desires" (v. 21). Abner addresses David as "my lord, the king," and the mood is festive. When Abner departs to rally Israel for the covenant ceremony, the text tells us for the first of three times that Abner departed in "peace" (שׁלום šālôm, vv. 21b, 22b, 23b). The narrator wants to be clear that all was well between David and Abner. Perhaps of equal importance, the narrative is clear that alliance with Israel was not made through coercion but through negotiations and covenant.

3:22-30. Joab enters the story, and events take a dark turn. He had just returned from leading one of David's raiding parties, presumably of the sort that David conducted in the name of the Philistines from Ziklag (v. 22a). In the light of subsequent events, one wonders if Joab's absence from Hebron at the time of Abner's visit was intentional on David's part. Joab comes with the spoils of war, and the text reminds us again that Abner had departed in peace (v. 22b). Immediately Joab receives a report that Abner has been in Hebron and again that Abner left David in peace (v. 23). Joab's response is immediate and bitter. He confronts David and suggests that David has allowed an enemy to escape (v. 24). He argues that Abner could only have deception and spying as his purposes in coming to David (v. 25). No response of David is recorded, but Joab clearly received no encouragement, since he subsequently took matters into his own hands. Joab must be seen as a figure with two interests that work against the acceptability of an alliance with Abner. The first is his hatred and distrust of Abner, stemming from Abner's killing of Joab's brother Asahel in the battle described in 2:12-32. Joab sees himself as the legitimate bearer of a claim for vengeance against Abner, although ordinarily bloodguilt would not be recognized for a death suffered in war—i.e., it was not considered murder. The second of Joab's interests in this matter has to do with influence on David. Joab eventually becomes commander of David's armies (8:16), but it is reasonable to think that Abner might have assumed this role if he had lived. In any case, Abner would have been a powerful and influential military adviser and leader within David's kingdom, and this would make him Joab's natural rival for David's favor.

Joab does not hesitate to take ruthless action in his own interests. He sends messengers to intercept Abner and seek his return to Hebron (v. 26). Again, the cautious narrative makes clear that David knew nothing of this (v. 26b). When Abner returns, Joab pulls him into a chamber of the gate as if to confer with him, but instead Joab stabs him in the stomach, and Abner dies (v. 27). Twice the narrative attributes this death to vengeance for Asahel's death (vv. 27b, 30; Joab's brother Abishai is included in v. 30, although he seems to have played no direct role). However, the verdict of the narrative on this deed is clear. The death of Abner is called a murder, while the death of Asahel in battle is named a killing (v. 30).

It is murder that carries bloodguilt, and this is David's immediate concern in response to news of Abner's death. David declares himself and his kingdom innocent of this wrongfully shed blood (v. 28), and he lays the guilt upon Joab and the

house of Joab's father (v. 29a). David goes farther and pronounces a curse upon the house of Joab (v. 29b) that includes disease, violence, and hunger. The reference to one "who holds a spindle" may imply men who are not fit for battle and must do women's work. The curse is vigorous and unflinching in its terms, but why did David not act more directly against Joab as he did in avenging the bloodguilt incurred by the Amalekite in killing Saul (1:1-16), or as he will later do in avenging the death of Ishbosheth (4:1-12)? In effect, David leaves this particular matter to the Lord (explicit in v. 39b), while David himself continues to make extensive use of the services of Joab (e.g., 8:16; 20:23). It may be that Joab and his family are too influential and centrally important in David's military forces to act against him or dispense with him. Certainly, v. 39 indicates some frustration on David's part for his lack of political options in dealing with the violence of the sons of Zeruiah. It is clear that even kings have political limitations on their choices—at least if they are to continue as king. Eventually Joab's bloodguilt for the death of Abner is cited by David from his deathbed as reason for Solomon to kill him (1 Kgs 2:5-6). It may be that the story here is shaped to help justify the death of Joab as part of an initial Solomonic court purge.

3:31-39. David may be innocent, as the narrative claims, but it is also possible that no one will believe him. The need to establish public credibility for David's claim to non-involvement is clearly a factor in the elaborate public mourning and state funeral given for Abner. David is sending a message to the northern tribes that this killing was not his desired outcome. Indeed, Abner's death seems more a problem to David than an asset.

David orders the people, including Joab (a public humiliation?), into mourning for Abner with the tearing of clothes and the wearing of sackcloth (v. 31). David himself follows the bier and leads in weeping at Abner's burial in Hebron (v. 32). He sings a lament for Abner (vv. 33-34), recalling his similar but much more elaborate lament for Saul and Jonathan (1:17-27). The first line is addressed to Israel as a rhetorical question, suggesting that Abner did not deserve such an ignoble death (that of a fool or an outlaw, v. 33b). The remaining lines are addressed in the second person to the deceased, a feature common to funerary laments (although this one is not composed in the קִינָה *qînâ* pattern as in 1:17-27). Although Abner was not bound and fettered like a criminal, he died like one (v. 34*a*). David labels those who killed Abner as the wicked before whom Abner fell by treachery (v. 34*b*). David fasts the entire day, in spite of the people's urging him to eat (v. 35). David is the chief of the mourners for Abner, and although his sentiments may be genuine, it is clear that his mourning bears political significance.

From the perspective of this narrative, David's efforts are efficacious. The people noticed and were pleased by David's response, although the narrator admits that the people seemed to be pleased with almost everything David did (v. 36). We have already noted the declaration of David's innocence and the people's recognition of his innocence in v. 37 as the key verse to this chapter. David is not complicit in the death of Abner. The people know it; the narrative wants the reader to know it. Indeed, David's final words in this matter are a magnanimous tribute to Abner as "a prince and a great man" (v. 38) and a final statement of impotence in the face of the violence of Joab's family (v. 39). David's vow in v. 39*b* entrusts vengeance in this matter to the Lord.

Was David innocent of the death of Abner? Those who take a more cynical view of David believe not and argue that David plotted Abner's death.[192] It is hard, however, to maintain the case that Abner's death was an advantage to David rather than a setback. David was on the verge of achieving kingship over all Israel when Joab impulsively acted. What is important to observe is that this narrative is not in doubt about David's innocence. Historical possibilities beyond this telling of the story are possible, but completely speculative, and this way of telling the story is what Israelite tradition has preserved as its belief. Others, ancient and modern, will no doubt continue to believe David somehow guilty in these matters. Conspiracy theories were probably as popular in ancient Israel as in modern America. Shimei's outburst against David is probably a good example (16:7-8). There remains one more death to be narrated (Ishbosheth, 4:1-12) before we can reflect fully on these complex interrelationships of power and violence, innocence and guilt.

Although the larger concern is David's innocence, this episode is unusual because David is not its center. It is Abner who dominates this story—even in his death. David's words of honor and respect in v. 38 do not ring hollow. David, as a "prince and a great man" himself, can recognize and pay tribute to another, even though David had once taunted Abner over his failure to protect the king (1 Sam 26:14-16).

Abner does not have the aura of divine destiny about him as does David. No narrator claims that "God was with him." Perhaps he is a secular counterpart to David—warrior, leader, diplomat—but he is not God's anointed. Abner does recognize the Lord at work in the events bringing David to the throne, and he is able to align himself willingly with those divine purposes (3:9, 18).

No doubt Abner acted with all the self-interest that we might expect a warrior and a man of influence to possess. In 2:8-9, he acts with decisive power to establish Ishbosheth on the throne and himself as the power behind the throne. Yet, it was a time of crisis when Israel was scattered and defeated. Without Abner, it is clear that no Israelite kingdom would have continued in the north. In spite of self-interest there is a kind of integrity to Abner. He did not seize the throne himself. Even the incident with Rizpah does not seem like a move toward the throne for himself, since the result was a move toward David. His claim of loyalty to the house of Saul is believable (3:8). Even in moving his allegiance to David there is no hint that he would do violence to Ishbosheth, although Ishbosheth's accusation wounded and angered him (3:7-8). His address to the elders of Israel suggests that the move to David was motivated by the best interests of Israel against their most deadly enemy, the Philistines (3:17-18).

Abner must have possessed a great deal of power, but in this episode and the preceding story of Asahel's death he does not act with raw power. He tried twice to dissuade Asahel from pursuit before he was forced to kill him (2:18-23). He negotiated terms with David. He negotiated terms with the elders of Israel. He moved to base Israel's future on covenant agreements and not simply on his personal influence (3:12, 21).

Abner is no saint, but he seems very different as a warrior and as a man from Joab. Ironically, it is Joab and not David who gains the most from

192. See VanderKam, "Davidic Complicity in the Deaths of Abner and Eshbaal," 533, who writes, "David both desired and planned the death of Abner." See also N. P. Lemche, "David's Rise," *JSOT* 10 (1978) 17-18.

Abner's death. Although cursed in the moment he rises to ever greater power and influence under David, Joab is at his most visible in the stories of David's decline and his troubled family. What would the mature years of David's reign have been like with Abner as a right-hand man rather than Joab? Joab is such an ambiguous figure that David from his deathbed feels compelled to advise Solomon to kill him in final payment for the bloodguilt incurred with the death of Abner (1 Kgs 2:5-6, 28-34). Of course, Joab had opposed Solomon for the throne and would have been dangerous to leave alive.

REFLECTIONS

1. We live in an age enamored of superstars. We want to focus on the Davids who rise to the top. We often fail to look beyond to those who make a difference in the second, third, or fourth ranks of leadership. It may make a difference whether those places are filled by Abners or Joabs. It may be worth caring whether people of integrity are neutralized by violence, although the weapon for our time is as likely to be the violence of ideology as that of the knife. We tend to expend great energy on processes to elect presidents, to choose bishops, to select school superintendents, or to hire chiefs of police. But we need to devote far more energy to opposing those persons and processes that drive good people from the lesser offices of public or church service, from day-to-day ministry, from classroom teaching, or from routine police work. Those who might serve the Davids of our time with integrity are too often victims of the self-interested, calculated violence of the Joabs among us. The weapons of violence include more than physical assault. Persons of integrity are often driven from leadership in church and community by character assassination, intolerable pay and working conditions, polarized ideological rhetoric, and lack of support. We can hope for leaders of integrity in our highest levels of political or church leadership, but they will fail if we do not find ways to support them with scores of Abners rather than Joabs.

2. The issues of violence are never far from the arenas of public or ecclesiastical power. We cannot naively hope for unblemished Davids who will save us. In this story, David may be innocent; but thanks to Joab, David's kingdom can never be innocent again, and Abner is dead. We must read the story of yet another death, Ishbosheth (4:1-12), and then we can reflect more fully on the complex interrelationship between power and violence and the future of God's kingdom in the midst of these realities. (See Reflections at 4:1-12.)

2 Samuel 4:1-12, The Death of Ishbosheth

NIV

4 When Ish-Bosheth son of Saul heard that Abner had died in Hebron, he lost courage, and all Israel became alarmed. ²Now Saul's son had two men who were leaders of raiding bands. One was named Baanah and the other Recab; they were sons of Rimmon the Beerothite from the tribe of Benjamin—Beeroth is considered part of Benjamin, ³because the people of Beeroth fled to Gittaim and have lived there as aliens to this day.

⁴(Jonathan son of Saul had a son who was lame in both feet. He was five years old when the news

NRSV

4 When Saul's son Ishbaal*a* heard that Abner had died at Hebron, his courage failed, and all Israel was dismayed. ²Saul's son had two captains of raiding bands; the name of the one was Baanah, and the name of the other Rechab. They were sons of Rimmon a Benjaminite from Beeroth—for Beeroth is considered to belong to Benjamin—³(Now the people of Beeroth had fled to Gittaim and are there as resident aliens to this day).

a Heb lacks *Ishbaal*

NIV

about Saul and Jonathan came from Jezreel. His nurse picked him up and fled, but as she hurried to leave, he fell and became crippled. His name was Mephibosheth.)

⁵Now Recab and Baanah, the sons of Rimmon the Beerothite, set out for the house of Ish-Bosheth, and they arrived there in the heat of the day while he was taking his noonday rest. ⁶They went into the inner part of the house as if to get some wheat, and they stabbed him in the stomach. Then Recab and his brother Baanah slipped away.

⁷They had gone into the house while he was lying on the bed in his bedroom. After they stabbed and killed him, they cut off his head. Taking it with them, they traveled all night by way of the Arabah. ⁸They brought the head of Ish-Bosheth to David at Hebron and said to the king, "Here is the head of Ish-Bosheth son of Saul, your enemy, who tried to take your life. This day the LORD has avenged my lord the king against Saul and his offspring."

⁹David answered Recab and his brother Baanah, the sons of Rimmon the Beerothite, "As surely as the LORD lives, who has delivered me out of all trouble, ¹⁰when a man told me, 'Saul is dead,' and thought he was bringing good news, I seized him and put him to death in Ziklag. That was the reward I gave him for his news! ¹¹How much more—when wicked men have killed an innocent man in his own house and on his own bed—should I not now demand his blood from your hand and rid the earth of you!"

¹²So David gave an order to his men, and they killed them. They cut off their hands and feet and hung the bodies by the pool in Hebron. But they took the head of Ish-Bosheth and buried it in Abner's tomb at Hebron.

NRSV

4Saul's son Jonathan had a son who was crippled in his feet. He was five years old when the news about Saul and Jonathan came from Jezreel. His nurse picked him up and fled; and, in her haste to flee, it happened that he fell and became lame. His name was Mephibosheth.ᵃ

5Now the sons of Rimmon the Beerothite, Rechab and Baanah, set out, and about the heat of the day they came to the house of Ishbaal,ᵇ while he was taking his noonday rest. ⁶They came inside the house as though to take wheat, and they struck him in the stomach; then Rechab and his brother Baanah escaped.ᶜ ⁷Now they had come into the house while he was lying on his couch in his bedchamber; they attacked him, killed him, and beheaded him. Then they took his head and traveled by way of the Arabah all night long. ⁸They brought the head of Ishbaalᵇ to David at Hebron and said to the king, "Here is the head of Ishbaal,ᵇ son of Saul, your enemy, who sought your life; the LORD has avenged my lord the king this day on Saul and on his offspring."

9David answered Rechab and his brother Baanah, the sons of Rimmon the Beerothite, "As the LORD lives, who has redeemed my life out of every adversity, ¹⁰when the one who told me, 'See, Saul is dead,' thought he was bringing good news, I seized him and killed him at Ziklag—this was the reward I gave him for his news. ¹¹How much more then, when wicked men have killed a righteous man on his bed in his own house! And now shall I not require his blood at your hand, and destroy you from the earth?" ¹²So David commanded the young men, and they killed them; they cut off their hands and feet, and hung their bodies beside the pool at Hebron. But the head of Ishbaalᵇ they took and buried in the tomb of Abner at Hebron.

ᵃ In 1 Chr 8.34 and 9.40, *Merib-baal*   ᵇ Heb *Ish-bosheth*   ᶜ Meaning of Heb of verse 6 uncertain

COMMENTARY

This episode recounts the third death to which David must respond during his ascent to the throne of Judah and Israel. The death of Ishbosheth now leaves the throne of Israel unoccupied. The story of Ishbosheth's death and David's response is remarkably similar to that of the death of Saul at the hand of the Amalekite (1:1-16). In each story someone kills a king and brings the news to David, expecting to find favor with him. Instead, they pay with their own lives for the bloodguilt they have incurred. The narrative of Abner's death is longer and more complex but raises the same issue of bloodguilt in relation to David's kingdom (3:6-39).

The issue of bloodguilt has been a central concern in the history of the rise of David. The episode on the death of Ishbosheth is the end of a long sequence of narrative episodes seeking to establish David's innocence of bloodguilt. In 1 Samuel 24–26, David avoided bloodguilt. Twice he resisted the opportunity to take the life of Saul and incur bloodguilt for the killing of the Lord's anointed (1 Samuel 24 and 26). In 1 Samuel 25, the intervention of Abigail saved David from angrily killing Nabal and incurring bloodguilt. Now, David cannot avoid association with killings that incur bloodguilt, but the narratives seek to demonstrate that the bloodguilt does not belong to David. He is innocent of involvement and instead acts to avenge the slain and exact the consequences of bloodguilt. He orders the deaths of the Amalekite who took the life of Saul (1:1-16) and the sons of Rimmon, who bring to David the head of Ishbosheth (4:1-12). Following the death of Abner, David cursed his own military commander, Joab, and elaborately mourned the fallen Abner (3:6-39). Violence and death have come close to the kingdom, but David has not taken innocent blood to advance his kingdom, argues the narrative.

Undoubtedly there were those in Israel who did not regard David as innocent of bloodguilt in these deaths. When David retreats from Jerusalem at the time of Absalom's rebellion, a man named Shimei comes out to curse the seemingly defeated David:

"Out! Out! Murderer! Scoundrel! The LORD has avenged on all of you the blood of the house of Saul, in whose place you have reigned; and the LORD has given the kingdom into the hand of your son Absalom. See, disaster has overtaken you; for you are a man of blood." (16:7-8)

Recently a number of interpreters have argued in favor of David's complicity in these deaths. They view the present story as political propaganda used to whitewash a politically calculating and opportunistic David. For example, in the death of Ishbosheth, Lemche writes of the two murderers, "No sooner had they murdered their master than they hastened to Hebron to receive their reward, and of course David perforce had to execute his hired assassins if he was to maintain his innocence."[193] Such a reading reflects a more cynical view of David and political power in general, but there is little explicit support in the text for this view of David's role. To be sure, we must recognize the apologetic character of the entire history of David's rise. Moreover, David may well have benefited from deaths that he did not himself arrange. Still, there is no clear evidence for his complicity in these deaths.

The accounts of Davidic innocence in these matters are not naive political idealizations, at least not as they are now incorporated into the larger framework of the books of Samuel and the Deuteronomistic History. David may be innocent, but these narratives clearly imply that violence is, nevertheless, a reality in the kingdom. David's faithful rule must be established in the face of brutal and violent realities, and David must deal with these realities in spite of his innocence in creating them. We begin to understand that power in the kingdom can never be totally innocent so long as the kingdom itself is brutal and violent. In the longer view of David's story, we are being prepared for the day when David gives in to the temptations of power and commits violent acts for reasons of pure self-interest (adultery with Bathsheba and the murder of Uriah, 2 Samuel 11). Using the helpful vocabulary of David Gunn, we must first hear the story of how the kingdom came to David as a *gift* before we can fully comprehend the dangers of seeking to gain or maintain the kingdom by *grasp*.[194] The narrator understands that David has received the kingdom as the Lord's gift, not as the result of his grasping manipulation of events and propaganda. The story does not idealize David, but makes even clearer the dangers of believing that the kingdom can be grasped through one's own power. The story of David's grasping of power and its consequences lies yet ahead of us.

4:1-3. The scene shifts to the north for reaction to the death of Abner. Ishbosheth's (in accordance with the chronicler, the NRSV reads "Ishbaal" rather than "Ishbosheth"; see the Com-

193. Lemche, "David's Rise," 17.
194. David M. Gunn, "David and the Gift of the Kingdom (2 Sam 2–4, 9–20; 1 Kgs 1–2)," *Semeia* 3 (1975) 14-45.

mentary on 2:8-9 for a discussion of the alternatives for the name of Saul's son) courage fails, and all Israel is distressed (v. 1). Of course, Ishbosheth was afraid of the threat Abner posed when he was alive (3:11); now that Abner is dead, Ishbosheth is still afraid. It is hard to know what Ishbosheth or Israel knew about Abner's negotiations with David. Since Abner had conferred with the elders of Israel, their dismay must reflect not simply the loss of Abner but the loss of the alliance he was negotiating with David. It is clear that without Abner the prospects of the north and their bargaining power with David are diminished. As for Ishbosheth, he was properly fearful. With or without Abner, he seems to have no future.

Verse 2 introduces Baanah and Rechab, who were captains of raiding bands in Ishbosheth's army. The account is at some pains to establish that they were Benjaminites, even though they were from Beeroth, which was a traditional Gibeonite city. This makes Ishbosheth's assassins his own kinsmen. Although details are not supplied, it is clear that Beeroth was annexed by the tribe of Benjamin, forcing the Gibeonite inhabitants to relocate in Gittaim (v. 3). These events may lie behind the blood feud that led the Gibeonites to exact vengeance upon the house of Saul in 2 Sam 21:1-9.

4:4. This verse is a parenthesis, which does not advance the story of this episode, but prepares us for a later story in chap. 9. It tells us that Saul's son Jonathan had a son named Mephibosheth. He had been injured and permanently crippled by a fall suffered in the hasty escape from Jezreel at the time of Israel's defeat on Mt. Gilboa and the deaths of Saul and Jonathan. The name "Mephibosheth" is reported in 1 Chr 8:34; 9:40 as "Meribbaal." Most scholars believe that this is another instance where later editors were offended by the element "baal" as part of a royal family name. They substituted בשׁת (*bōšet*), the Hebrew word for "shame," in place of the supposed idolatrous element of the name (see the discussion of Ishbosheth in the Commentary on 2:8-9).

The insertion of this note is odd. It may be that the narrator wishes us to know that with the death of Ishbosheth the line of Saul will not end. Further, it anticipates the loyalty (חסד *ḥesed*) that David will yet show to the house of Saul in keeping with the covenant he made with Jonathan

(1 Samuel 20). In the midst of a story of violence and treachery against the house of Saul, loyalty and commitment are also anticipated.

4:5-8. The account of the murderous deed itself starts at an oddly leisurely pace as Baanah and Rechab come to Ishbosheth's house during his noontime rest (v. 5). The literary style implies careful deliberation, not impulsive action. The next two verses almost seem like variant versions of the killing of Ishbosheth. Each could stand alone. In v. 6, the men come inside on the pretext of obtaining wheat (a communal storehouse?), strike Ishbosheth in the stomach, and escape. In v. 7, they enter the house and find Ishbosheth lying on his couch. The fatal action is narrated in a brutal series of verbs: "They attacked him, killed him, and beheaded him." Then they take his head and travel through the night to Hebron. It may be that v. 7 simply added detail to the spare account in v. 6.

Arriving at Hebron, they present Ishbosheth's head to David, clearly expecting praise and honor for their deed (v. 8). They present their grisly trophy as vengeance for David on Saul, an enemy who had sought David's life. They clearly do not understand David or the situation they have created. Reward or favor will not be their lot.

4:9-12. David answers Baanah and Rechab with an oath taken in the name of the Lord, whom David recognizes as the source of his deliverance from adversity (v. 9). He ominously recalls for them the fate of the Amalekite who had brought news that he had killed Saul, thinking it good news. His fate was death (v. 10). Saul had been wounded and asked for his own death to avoid being captured by the Philistines. Now, David reminds his would-be benefactors, a righteous man has been murdered in his own bed. Ishbosheth is not, like his father, God's anointed king, but he is righteous (i.e., innocent). That makes Baanah and Rechab evildoers, and their blood is required to recompense the bloodguilt they have incurred (v. 11). In verbs as harsh and quick as the reporting of their own deed, David commands the fate of these two assassins: "They killed them; they cut off their hands and feet, and hung their bodies beside the pool at Hebron." While his assassins are humiliated in their death, Ishbosheth is honored in his death. It is ironic, however, that his burial is in the same tomb as Abner.

REFLECTIONS

As has been noted, this episode on the death of Ishbosheth is the last in a sequence of stories dealing with the juxtaposition of power and violence, guilt and innocence, in the history of David's rise.[195] In our reading of these stories and in reflection on their intersection with our own experience, two dangerously distorted interpretive readings must be avoided.

The first is a reading that makes the mistake of thinking that the claims for David's innocence mean that the kingdom is innocent or that the seductive temptation to violence for the sake of power can be ignored. David's innocence cannot be read as an end in itself. This is the danger of *pious naïveté*. David's claim to innocence was not bought at the price of non-involvement in the brutal realities of a violent world. He was forced to recognize the temptation to violence in himself (1 Samuel 24–26) and to respond justly and faithfully to the violence of others (2 Samuel 1–4). In our own world, the temptation to think that innocent faith can provide an escape from the realities of a broken world is a delusion and an abdication of responsibility. As in David's story, God's kingdom is come in the midst of the world and its sinful realities, not apart from them. People of faith cannot use their own supposed innocence to hide from or ignore a world enamored of violence. To do so is to work against the coming of God's kingdom.

The second reading that must be avoided is one that believes that no innocence can be preserved in the midst of violence and cannot see the possibilities of God's kingdom in the midst of a brutal world. This is the danger of *secularized cynicism*. In our cynical age, there are many who believe that faithfulness and integrity are not possible in the precincts of power. They believe that religious faith is either irrelevant to political power or a mere tool of political power. Reading David's story from this perspective sees only propaganda for Davidic power and is certain that David was manipulating events behind the scenes. Such readings see manipulation, self-interest, survival, and compromise with violence as the only possibilities for dealing with power in our own world.

Over against these dangerous and distorted readings, the church must read David's story in these episodes with the conviction that there is an alternative to our naïveté and our cynicism. The church's attentive reading of these stories of David's encounters with violence on the way to power in God's new kingdom can teach us about the realities of violence, power, and God's kingdom in our own time.

1. These stories teach us that there is no completely innocent power. Power is never far from violence or the temptation to violence. As an individual, David may be innocent of bloodguilt in these stories. But as a king he must rule in a kingdom saturated with violence. To have power is to have responsibility for recognizing and responding to violence, in David's world or in our own. The Christian faith radicalizes this understanding in its central salvation story. Jesus—the Messiah, the anointed One, the son of David—must face the violence of the world in his own crucifixion in order to bring God's kingdom. The innocent one, nevertheless, takes on the bloodguilt of a violent world.

2. These stories also teach us that there can be faithful leadership in the face of violence. Brutality, violence, manipulation, and self-interest do not have the final word in these stories. One can responsibly exercise power without giving in to the violence that is always near at hand. David's innocence in these stories is not merely political propaganda but is serious moral witness on the part of the community that preserved and told these stories. (The portion of David's story that unfolds from the adultery with Bathsheba and the killing of Uriah in 2 Samuel 11 deals with the consequences that result when power does give in to the temptations of violence.)

---

195. Walter Brueggemann also reads these stories in terms of the issues of violence and power in *Power, Providence, and Personality* (Louisville: Westminster/John Knox, 1990) 49-85. Our readings are congenial, but with different emphases.

Faithful leadership for the sake of God's kingdom requires action in opposition to violence. Like David, we must oppose and hold accountable those who promote and condone violence in the expectation of profit, fame, or pleasure. A recent news article told of the recasting of two films with additional scenes of sex and violence to avoid a PG rating and gain a more profitable R rating. "On any given day in America, 480 women and children will be forcibly raped, 5,670 women will be assaulted by a male intimate partner and four women and three children will be murdered by a family member."[196] Every season of political campaigning is now marred by "attack ads" and character assassination in the hopes of gaining electoral favor. The church must be in the forefront of those willing to join decisive action against these predilections to violence in our midst.

Faithful leadership for the sake of God's kingdom requires grief at the losses we have suffered. David could not bring a new kingdom apart from his ability to lead his people in grief over their losses of Saul, Jonathan, Abner, and Ishbosheth. The church, too, will not be credible in its leadership for alternatives to dangerous streets, troubled homes, and desensitized public appetites for violence if it is not seen as grieving over the losses we have experienced. A church perceived as merely tending to its own institutional health will have no credibility in leadership for alternatives to violence in our time. It was the prophet Amos who indicted those who, even though not guilty of direct violence, "lie on beds of ivory . . . sing idle songs to the sound of the harp . . . but are not grieved over the ruin of Joseph" (Amos 6:4-6 NRSV). It is our grief that sharpens our awareness of the price we have paid for violence and enables us to look beyond to the new possibilities of God's kingdom. Resurrection does not immediately follow crucifixion in the gospel story. The grief of the disciples while Jesus lay three days in the tomb is a necessary prelude to the new hope of resurrection.

3. These stories, finally, teach us that it is ultimately God who redeems the kingdom. Throughout the stories of the rise of David there have been constant reminders that as David moved toward his own power, he recognized that the ultimate power for newness in Israel comes from the Lord. God makes faithful leadership possible in the midst of and in spite of violence. It is God's kingdom that stands as the alternative to human kingdoms ruled by violence and self-interest. To give faithful leadership in God's kingdom does not require perfection (David is far from that), but it implies an integrity rooted in an alternative vision of the source of true power. David is cunning, resourceful, formidable in battle, and shrewd in his political dealings. He can compete on the fields of human power. But what sets him apart in these stories is his constant possession of a vision that transcends human power and is rooted in the power of God as the hope for newness in Israel. He refuses to accept the kingdom from those who would give it on violent terms. In the Christian gospel story, human kingdoms flex muscles in crucifixion, but resurrection has the final word of newness in spite of such violence. For David and for us, it is God's kingdom that brings newness and will not be denied. Between the blindness of naïveté and the paralysis of cynicism, enabled by our own action and grief, lies the possibility of God's faithful kingdom in a world of violence.

196. Mary Pipher, *Reviving Ophelia: Saving the Selves of Adolescent Girls* (New York: Ballantine, 1994) 219.

2 Samuel 5:1-5, David Made King by Israel

NIV

5 All the tribes of Israel came to David at Hebron and said, "We are your own flesh and blood. ²In the past, while Saul was king over

NRSV

5 Then all the tribes of Israel came to David at Hebron, and said, "Look, we are your bone and flesh. ²For some time, while Saul was

NIV

us, you were the one who led Israel on their military campaigns. And the LORD said to you, 'You will shepherd my people Israel, and you will become their ruler.'"

³When all the elders of Israel had come to King David at Hebron, the king made a compact with them at Hebron before the LORD, and they anointed David king over Israel.

⁴David was thirty years old when he became king, and he reigned forty years. ⁵In Hebron he reigned over Judah seven years and six months, and in Jerusalem he reigned over all Israel and Judah thirty-three years.

NRSV

king over us, it was you who led out Israel and brought it in. The LORD said to you: It is you who shall be shepherd of my people Israel, you who shall be ruler over Israel." ³So all the elders of Israel came to the king at Hebron; and King David made a covenant with them at Hebron before the LORD, and they anointed David king over Israel. ⁴David was thirty years old when he began to reign, and he reigned forty years. ⁵At Hebron he reigned over Judah seven years and six months; and at Jerusalem he reigned over all Israel and Judah thirty-three years.

COMMENTARY

This brief report brings us to the climactic moment of the history of David's rise. He had earlier been anointed king over Judah (2:4a). Now the northern tribes of Israel, the remnants of the kingdom of Saul, come to anoint David as their king. David becomes king of all Israel.

As the elders of Israel affirm David, they recall a promise of the Lord that David would be "shepherd of my people Israel" (v. 2). Hearing this phrase, we realize with a start that we have completed an incredible journey, starting with David as shepherd of his father's flocks to David as "shepherd of my people Israel." He has moved from boy to king—from eighth son to the throne. The narrative recounting this climactic moment is surprisingly brief and matter-of-fact. The narrative has confidently foreseen this moment all along. It now simply states in the voice of the people that the Lord's promises have been fulfilled in David.

5:1-3. The tribes of Israel come to David at Hebron (v. 1a). The text no doubt implies that tribal representatives were sent; v. 3, in fact, refers to this delegation as the "elders of Israel." They appeal to David to become their king. They have nowhere else to go. Ishbosheth is dead, and there is no likely successor. They have no bargaining power. Their military leader, Abner, is dead, and his position of strength for negotiations with David is now lost. They come now to David almost as petitioners, beseeching him to accept them and rule over them.

This very compact narrative of only three verses articulates a basis for this completion of David's rise to kingship over all Israel in the words and actions of the elders of Israel. They appeal to kinship (v. 1a), to their previous experience with David (v. 2a), and to the promise of the Lord (v. 2b). Then they enter into covenant with David (v. 3a) and anoint him as king (v. 3b).

The elders open their petition to David by claiming, "We are your bone and flesh." This expression usually denotes blood kinship (cf. Gen 29:14; Judg 9:2). At a later point in the story, David uses a similar phrase to note his kinship to Judah in contrast to all of Israel (19:13), but this would not rule out Israel's use of the phrase to appeal to kinship as the basis for agreement with David. David has now reclaimed Saul's daughter Michal as his legal wife (3:13-16). Although tribal ties represent the closest kinship (e.g., David with Judah and Saul with Benjamin) the notion of a broader kinship among the tribal groups of Israel emerged fairly early. By the time of the Deuteronomistic History, the notion of the kinship of all Israel was a fixed dogma. For that reason, some have suggested a deuteronomistic influence in these verses.[197] It does not seem likely that this phrase is being used as a covenantal formula rather than a plea based on kinship.[198]

---

197. See P. Kyle McCarter, *II Samuel,* AB 9 (Garden City, N.Y.: Doubleday, 1984) 131-32.
198. Contra Walter Brueggemann, "Of the Same Flesh and Bone (Gen 2,23a)," *CBQ* 32 (1970) 535.

In v. 2a, the Israelites appeal to their past experience with David. They do so in a way that explicitly renounces their loyalty to Saul. They recall that even in the days of Saul "it was you who led out Israel and brought it in." This phrase specifically refers to David's military leadership in command of Israelite troops (1 Sam 18:13, 16). Perhaps these were some of the people who cheered that "Saul has slain his thousands, but David his ten thousands." It was not Saul who gave them hope, they now claim—it was *you*! As readers, we have known from 1 Samuel 16 on that the future of Israel belongs to David and not to Saul. This scene is the final moment of recognition.

The elders of Israel are also clear that the Lord has been at work in bringing them to this moment (v. 2b). They know of a promise by the Lord that David should be "shepherd over my people Israel" and "ruler over Israel." We do not know of such a promise verbalized in the narrative by the Lord in these terms. But we have known David as the man to whom God promised kingship over Israel, and the roles of shepherd and ruler are consistent with the destiny toward which God has constantly moved David's journey. The term "shepherd" (רעה *rō'eh*) is a common designation for kings and political leaders, both in Israel and in the wider ancient Near East.[199] The title is a reminder of responsibility to care for and protect the people as a shepherd would do for the flock. One suspects, however, that in this context we are intended to recall David's own beginnings as a shepherd boy (1 Sam 16:11; 17:15). Now he has become a shepherd king. Israel also uses the term נגיד (*nāgîd*), "prince," "king-designate" (see the discussion of this term in Commentary on 9:16; 10:1). Some have suggested that Israel was cautiously avoiding the term "king." However, David does not become king until the covenant making and anointing in v. 3, where the term "king"

is used twice. The use of *nāgîd* in v. 2 may simply be as "king-designate."

Of special significance is the use of "shepherd" and *nāgîd* together in reference to David in Nathan's oracle of dynastic promise: "I took you from the pasture, from following the sheep to be prince over my people Israel" (7:8). The promise of the Lord here articulated by the elders of Israel seems to anticipate and prepare us for Nathan's oracle. This connection may be further support for those who see deuteronomistic influence in 5:1-2, since such influence is generally recognized in the final shaping of 2 Samuel 7.

In v. 3, the elders of Israel come to Hebron (did they come twice?) for covenant making. It is King David (note the full title) who is the subject of the verb here. The basis of Davidic rule over Israel will not be raw power, but willingness on his part to enter covenant. His kingship is established on the basis of a covenant involving mutual recognition of needs and responsibilities. The people then anoint him as king over Israel. This anointing is the counterpart of the anointing by Judah in 2:4a. But both of these anointings by the people only serve to ratify the anointing of David by the Lord through the prophet Samuel (1 Sam 16:13). David's journey to the throne as the Lord's anointed one is now complete.

5:4-5. These are chronological notes, probably from the deuteronomistic historian. David is surprisingly young by our standards—only thirty—when he begins to reign. He rules surprisingly long by ancient standards—forty years, making him a ripe age of seventy when he dies. The number forty may be a rounded number, as it often is in the Old Testament, but it fits rather closely into other chronological data on David. Verse 5 seems more specific, giving us years and months at Hebron along with years and months at Jerusalem. This, of course, is premature on the part of the historian, since Jerusalem is not yet in David's hands.

199. See A. A. Anderson, *2 Samuel*, WBC 11 (Waco: Word, 1989) 76.

REFLECTIONS

God keeps promises. David is now king in Israel, and the kingdom is established with God's king and not the people's. Already this kingdom promises newness. The shape of power in this kingdom will be governed by shepherding and covenant making. The imagery is of care and mutuality. Israel's future hope has for the moment become its present hope.

Although the shape of human governance, political and religious, has seldom maintained the ideal of shepherding and covenant making, these have remained significant images in the vision of Israel and the church through generations to the present. From the Twenty-third Psalm to Jesus' declaration of his own death, "I am the good shepherd who lays down his life for the sheep" (see John 10:11), the image of the shepherd has been a central expression of the church's vision of leadership in the service of God's kingdom. Covenant has likewise been central to the understanding of Israel and the church that leadership never functions apart from a mutual community of recognized needs and responsibilities. This brief passage only lifts these images briefly into view, but it is a beginning in David that points us to rich new understandings of God's kingdom for Israel's future and for our own.

2 Samuel 5:6-10, David Captures Jerusalem

NIV

⁶The king and his men marched to Jerusalem to attack the Jebusites, who lived there. The Jebusites said to David, "You will not get in here; even the blind and the lame can ward you off." They thought, "David cannot get in here." ⁷Nevertheless, David captured the fortress of Zion, the City of David.

⁸On that day, David said, "Anyone who conquers the Jebusites will have to use the water shaft[a] to reach those 'lame and blind' who are David's enemies.[b]" That is why they say, "The 'blind and lame' will not enter the palace."

⁹David then took up residence in the fortress and called it the City of David. He built up the area around it, from the supporting terraces[c] inward. ¹⁰And he became more and more powerful, because the LORD God Almighty was with him.

a8 Or use scaling hooks   b8 Or are hated by David   c9 Or the Millo

NRSV

6The king and his men marched to Jerusalem against the Jebusites, the inhabitants of the land, who said to David, "You will not come in here, even the blind and the lame will turn you back"—thinking, "David cannot come in here." 7Nevertheless David took the stronghold of Zion, which is now the city of David. 8David had said on that day, "Whoever would strike down the Jebusites, let him get up the water shaft to attack the lame and the blind, those whom David hates."[a] Therefore it is said, "The blind and the lame shall not come into the house." 9David occupied the stronghold, and named it the city of David. David built the city all around from the Millo inward. 10And David became greater and greater, for the LORD, the God of hosts, was with him.

a Another reading is those who hate David

COMMENTARY

David is now king over all Israel, north and south, but oddly the final episode in the history of David's rise does not focus on the royal office but on the royal capital. The final note involves the politics of geography, not the politics of leadership. In a brief, almost cryptic, passage we are told that David captured the Jebusite city of Jerusalem and made it the "city of David" (vv. 7, 9). It is a text fraught with many problems of translation and interpretation, as the verse-to-verse commentary will make clear. Verse 10 pronounces a theological verdict on the entire history of David's rise: "David became greater and greater, for the LORD, the God of hosts,

was with him." God's presence with David throughout the trials of his rise to the throne of Israel has been a major theological theme since it was first sounded in 1 Sam 16:18 (see the Overview for 1 Sam 16:1–31:13). It now stands almost as a benediction on all that has transpired in the story of David to this point. Beyond this point, we encounter traditions on the manner in which David consolidated and conducted his rule of Israel.

As for Jerusalem, it is fitting that this city make its appearance alongside David as he takes up the kingship of all Israel. This brief episode is only a beginning, but as a royal theology develops from the reign of David onward, it will rest on two great pillars of belief and trust. The first is that God has chosen David and his dynasty forever. David is clearly chosen for the throne of Israel by God, and in the dynastic oracle from the prophet Nathan in 2 Samuel 7, this election extends to the Davidic dynasty forever. The second conviction of royal theology is that God has chosen Mt. Zion in Jerusalem as the holy habitation of God. This belief obviously received its great boost from Solomon's building of the Temple on Mt. Zion. Jerusalem becomes not just David's city, but a holy city. Nevertheless, this Jerusalem element of royal theology begins in this brief story of David's capture of Jerusalem to be his capital. It will be further developed by the story of David's transfer of the ark of the covenant to Jerusalem in the next chapter. Psalm 132, which commemorates David's search for the ark, ends in praise for each of these elements of Davidic royal theology: the promise to David and the choice of Mt. Zion in Jerusalem. This understated story of David's capture of Jerusalem provides the beginning of that city's important role in Israel's faith and its continued existence today as a city considered holy by three great religions: Judaism, Christianity, and Islam.

This story of David's capture of Jerusalem gives no rationale for the undertaking. Why did David want or need Jerusalem? It has long been commonplace in analyzing David's action to suppose that he was looking for a way to locate his capital on neutral ground, unrelated to either Judah or Israel. Jerusalem is almost on the boundary between the tribal territories of Judah and the northern tribes who finally came to David in 5:1-3. Since Jerusalem was a Jebusite city, neither Judah nor Israel could claim David's capital city as its own. David captured it with "his men" (v. 6), and it became the "city of David" (vv. 7, 9). Jerusalem was also a well-known city from ancient times. It is mentioned in the Ebla archives (c. 2500 BCE), Egyptian execration texts (19th cent. BCE), and the Amarna letters (14th cent. BCE). It is usually identified with the city of Salem, where Abraham encountered the priest-king Melchizedek (Gen 14:17-20). Jerusalem is described as one of the Canaanite centers that Israel could not capture or assimilate (Josh 15:63; Judg 1:21); a successful raid or skirmish with the Jebusites of

Jerusalem may be indicated in Judg 1:8. A deity named Shalem is mentioned in the Ugaritic texts, and thus the name of Jerusalem may mean "establishment of (the god) Shalem." In later Israelite times the name is associated with the Hebrew word שלום ($\check{s}\bar{a}l\hat{o}m$), meaning "peace/wholeness." To possess Jerusalem as his capital undoubtedly added a measure of credibility and prestige to David's infant kingdom.

5:6-9. Without any explanation or hint of motivation, David and his men march against the Jebusite city of Jerusalem (v. 6*a*). There can be little doubt that the phrase "his men" refers to the mercenary force loyal to David that has been with him through much of his time in the wilderness and his service to the Philistines. David's capture of Jerusalem will owe nothing to the militias of Judah or Israel. This means that there is a literal sense to David's naming of the city as "the city of David" (v. 9*a*; see also v. 7). It could be regarded as a personal, royal possession.

We know little about the Jebusites. Opinion is divided among scholars on whether they are a Canaanite clan or a small, autonomous ethnic group apart from the Canaanites. Either is possible. In spite of the exchange of some hostile words and taunts in this brief episode, it seems clear that David took the city without great loss of life and, as Gottwald argues persuasively, "retained the Jebusites in their former home, even though this put them in the administrative heart of his new Israelite kingdom."[200] Mendenhall believes this gave David the administrators, managers, scribes, and merchants who enabled him to successfully launch a nation-state. The tribal cultures of Israel and Judah would not have required or possessed many of these skills.[201]

In v. 6*b*, the Jebusites appear to taunt David, believing their city to be impregnable. Their taunt is the first of three puzzling references in this passage to the "blind and the lame" (see also v. 8). Most believe that this first reference expresses the Jebusite belief that Jerusalem is so strong and secure that even "the blind and the lame" could defend it. The narrator even shares the Jebusites' thoughts that David could be disregarded as a

---

200. Norman K. Gottwald, *The Tribes of Yahweh: A Sociology of the Religion of Liberated Israel, 1250–1050 B.C.E.* (Maryknoll, N.Y.: Orbis, 1979) 571.

201. George E. Mendenhall, "The Monarchy," *Int.* 29 (1975) 160.

threat: "David cannot come in here." One presumes that David, with his force of men, is outside the wall, threatening siege.

The narrative is so eager that it gives outcome before any details. Verse 7 simply announces, as if in response to the Jebusite taunt, that David did capture the "stronghold of Zion" and that further he audaciously renamed it after himself, "the city of David." This is the first reference to Zion, and this is usually taken as a designation of the hill on the southeast of the city that may have been a citadel at this time. It becomes better known, of course, as the designation of the hill on which Solomon builds the Temple, Mt. Zion.

An extremely brief account suggests the manner of David's capture of Jerusalem in v. 8. The text is so cryptic in its details that it has been often suggested that the text has become corrupted or shortened. It seems clear that David took the city by stealth rather than by force. David issues a challenge to those who would join him in attacking the Jebusites. Both the NRSV and the NIV follow the majority opinion and depict David and his men using a water shaft to enter the city, perhaps taking it by surprise. The difficult word here is צנור (ṣinnôr), a rare word appearing elsewhere only in Ps 42:7, where it is generally taken to mean "waterfall." Various other proposals have been made for this word, including "grappling hooks," "weapon," and even the "male sexual organ" in an oath-taking ceremony. McCarter believes the term means "windpipe" and that David is instructing his men to strike a lethal blow, thereby not leaving any lame or blind.[202] The classic suggestion that David used the city's access to its own water supply as a vulnerable point from which to take the city seems most likely. The verb may imply the cutting off of the water supply rather than scrambling up a shaft. The shaft discovered in 1867 connecting the spring of Gihon with the old stronghold of Jerusalem is probably not the Jebusite ṣinnôr.[203]

In 1 Chr 11:4-9, the account of the capture of Jerusalem is elaborated by an offer from David that the first to attack the Jebusites would be made commander in chief of his army. In this account, Joab meets this challenge and is the first to attack. Accordingly, he is put in a position of command by David. This may be an authentic detail that has been omitted by the writer of 2 Samuel, since this book often demeans Joab.

The references to the "lame and blind" in v. 6 are puzzling. The first reference may simply be a turning back of the Jebusite taunt. David refers to the defenders of Jerusalem as the "lame and blind" and declares his hatred of them. This may be simply the rhetoric of battle taunts. The final sentence of v. 8 takes this matter of the blind and the lame as the etiology of a custom or prohibition denying the lame and the blind access to the Temple ("house"). We do not know of such a regulation, although disabled persons could not become priests (Lev 21:18). Since the Temple did not even exist in David's time, the verse seems artificial and contrived. It does not help to consider "house" to mean "palace," as some have suggested, since we know of no such regulation for the palace either. No proposal has gained a consensus.

The final outcome of this encounter is stated clearly in v. 9a. David not only captured Jerusalem but also occupied it and renamed it as his own city, "the city of David." In v. 9b, we are told that David did some building. The meaning of "Millo" is uncertain. The NRSV leaves the term untranslated to indicate a region of the city. Recent archaeological work suggests that the term may refer to a system of terraces supported by retaining walls, and the NIV translation reflects this understanding. Solomon is also said to have done construction work on the Millo (1 Kgs 9:15, 24; 11:27), which suggests that he extended or improved terracing already begun by David.

5:10. We have already noted this verse as a final theological comment for the history of the rise of David. The longer, formal name of God is used: "the Lord, the God of hosts." At the beginning of the books of Samuel, this name was associated with the ark of the covenant and the hope of Israel, expressed in the prayer of Hannah (1 Sam 1:11; 4:4). Now the ark is lost, but God has raised up David. Just as the ark represented God's presence in Israel, so also God is with David. Significantly, in the next chapter David brings back the ark to Jerusalem, but it will no longer be the chief sign of God's presence. God's presence in Israel is now seen in David, who

202. See the discussion in A. A. Anderson, *2 Samuel*, WBC 11 (Waco: Word, 1989) 84, and the alternative proposed by P. Kyle McCarter, *II Samuel*, AB 9 (Garden City, N.Y.: Doubleday, 1984) 139-40.
203. See J. Shiloh, "The City of David: Archaeological Project: Third Season—1980," *Biblical Archaeologist* 44 (1981) 170.

grows stronger and stronger. There is an implicit contrast here. The house of Saul has grown weaker and weaker and has all but disappeared. The threat of the Philistines will be immediately addressed in the remainder of chapter 5. David's strength has now grown until he can meet this deadly enemy of Israel, and they will then grow weaker and weaker. We have followed David's story as the hope for Israel's future. That future has now arrived.

REFLECTIONS

We have come to the concluding moment in a remarkable tale of God's newness for Israel. That newness has taken the shape of David, but it now also introduces Jerusalem. God's future for Israel is tied up not only with a man but also with a place. Jerusalem (Zion) becomes a holy place. This has not yet fully taken place. Here Jerusalem becomes David's city. With the later building of the Temple by Solomon, it will become God's holy habitation. Here we stand only at the introduction of this city that is to figure so remarkably in Israel's story. Just as Moses is forever connected to Sinai, so also David will be forever connected to Zion. Gese has spoken of this as a reshaping of Israel's memory from Sinai-Torah to Zion-Torah.[204] That reshaping process has begun in this moment when Jerusalem becomes David's city.

This beginning of the Jerusalem tradition seems unpromising. It speaks of conquest and of exclusion of the disabled. Jerusalem was a Jebusite city, perhaps named after a Jebusite god. One can hardly see here the beginning of an expansive and hopeful vision for Jerusalem as God's holy habitation. Yet, we should remember that David began as the unpromising eighth son who tended sheep for his undistinguished family. It is God who makes something of the boy and of the place.

From this unpromising beginning unfolds an expansive vision of God's city to complement God's king. Jerusalem becomes the focus of a new vision of God's presence in our midst. This finds expression, of course, in the building of Solomon's Temple (1 Kings 6). God's dwelling on Mt. Zion becomes the sign of God's involvement in the midst of God's people and human history: "For the LORD has chosen Zion; he has desired it for his habitation: 'This is my resting place forever; here I will reside, for I have desired it' " (Ps 132:13-14 NRSV). When Jerusalem and the Temple are destroyed, this expansive vision survives as hope for more than an earthly city. The vision of God's new Jerusalem becomes ultimate hope for the triumph of God's rule and measure for all earthly cities where human rulers hold power. From Ezekiel's elaborate vision of the new Jerusalem (Ezekiel 40–48) to the apocalyptic vision of God's new Jerusalem descending from the heavens (Rev 21:1-4), the vision that arises from Jerusalem both encompasses and transcends the possibilities for earthly cities and those who govern there. If David's city begins with exclusion of the lame and the blind, this is not where it ends. The vision of Jerusalem expands to become inclusive of all human hopes and possibilities: "I saw the holy city, the New Jerusalem, coming down out of heaven from God. . . . 'See, the home of God is among mortals. He will dwell with them as their God; they will be his peoples, and God himself will be with them; he will wipe every tear from their eyes. Death will be no more; mourning and crying and pain will be no more, for the first things have passed away' " (Rev. 21:2-4).

The text of 2 Sam 5:6-10 should be preached as the humble beginnings from which this expansive vision grows. Jerusalem occupies a special and passionate place in the Israelite tradition that survives even into the present day, when Jerusalem is a unique and holy place to three of the world's great religions: "If I forget you, O Jerusalem, let my right hand wither! Let my tongue cling to the roof of my mouth, if I do not remember you, if I do not set Jerusalem above my highest joy" (Ps 137:5-6 NRSV). If these passions give rise to tensions, they also give rise to a hopeful vision that transcends the tensions: "Pray for the peace of

204. Hartmut Gese, "The Davidic Covenant and the Zion Tradition," in *Essays on Biblical Theology* (Minneapolis: Augsburg, 1981) 60-92.

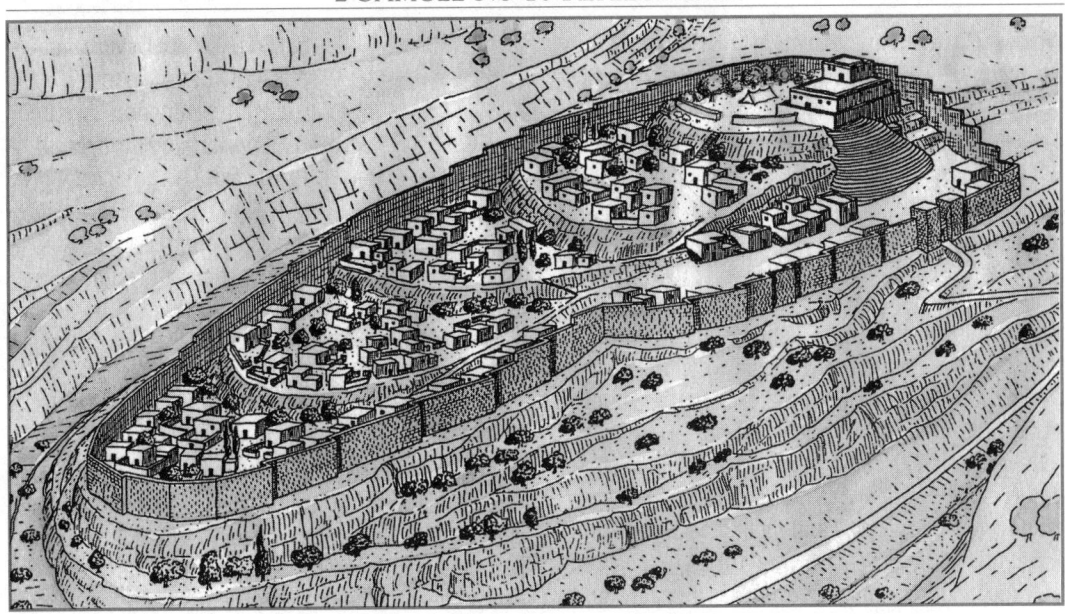

Figure 8: Jerusalem at the Time of David

Jerusalem: May they prosper who love you. Peace be within your walls, and security within your towers. . . . For the sake of the house of the LORD our God, I will seek your good" (Ps 122:6-7, 9 NRSV).

This text encourages us to reflect on the importance of holy place in religious experience. In our mobile society, we lose sight of the possibilities for place as a bearer of tradition and a repository for the sense of God's presence. In reading the story of David, we are not only reading of kings and kingdoms, but of the dwelling of God in their midst. Jerusalem becomes a reminder of this, lest the course of human events become an end in itself. It is good in our own time to consider the way in which our sanctuaries and the historic places of our various denominations can be for us holy places that serve as repositories of memory and tradition—that remind us of God's story in the midst of our own. It is also good to rekindle in our preaching, our teaching, our hymnody, and our liturgies the expansive vision of God's new Jerusalem. This vision, grown from the modest beginnings of David's city, reminds us of the larger vision that our modest places must always serve and be judged by. When the places of our religious life begin to become "our" places rather than God's place—when we only exclude and have failed to open to God's more inclusive vision—then we need to hear again the story of Jerusalem with its beginnings in conquest and its completion as the crown of God's coming kingdom. Like Jerusalem, our places can be transformed by the vision of God's presence.

2 SAMUEL 5:11–8:18, DAVID CONSOLIDATES HIS KINGDOM

OVERVIEW

It is almost anticlimactic for the story to continue. We began with a hope and an expectation of newness in Israel with the birth of Hannah's child Samuel, and the singing of Hannah's song of God's reversals of customary power in 1 Sam 1:1–2:10. The focus of 1 Samuel 1–7 was on Israel's crises and the hopeful expectation, symbolized by the prophet Samuel, that God would bring newness into the midst of crisis. That expectation for God's new future has been identified with the hope for a king in Israel since 1 Samuel 8. Expectation for God's new future has focused on David since 1 Samuel 16. It became clear that David was God's future for Israel and God's king for a new Israelite kingdom. We have been moving with growing anticipation toward David's ascent to Israel's throne, and now it has come to pass.

Nevertheless, Israel's story and David's story continue. This section (2 Sam 5:11–8:18) is concerned with the consolidation and legitimization of David's kingdom. It is one thing to become king and another thing to establish a secure and enduring kingdom. David the tribal hero and chieftain must become David the ruler of a nation.

From a literary standpoint, this section does not possess the thematic coherence and unity that have long been noted for the great artistic literary pieces that stand on either side. The history of David's rise (1 Sam 16:1–2 Sam 5:10) provides the passion and excitement of David as hero of the tribes, opposed by Saul but destined for greatness by the enduring presence of God. The succession narrative, which follows (2 Samuel 9–20; 1 Kings 1–2), chronicles the decline of David and his family into excesses of power and intrigue, with God's judgment articulated by Nathan's oracle (2 Sam 12:1-15) as the background. This section on David's consolidation of the kingdom presents neither the passion nor the pathos of these other narrative segments of David's story. The narrative segments within the chapters seem to be a collection of independent narratives ranging from battle report to prophetic oracle of promise and reflect no common author or narrative style.

The collection of these independent traditions is not, however, haphazard. James Flanagan has persuasively argued that this section has six segments that have been artistically arranged to suggest a movement in David's story from settlement with the old order to the emergence of genuinely new patterns for Israel's life.[205] The units are arranged chiastically:

205. James W. Flanagan, "Social Transformation and Ritual in 2 Samuel 6," in *The Word of the Lord Shall Go Forth: Festschrift for D. N. Freedman*, ed. C. L. Meyers and M. O'Connor (Winona Lake, Ind.: Eisenbrauns, 1983) 361-72.

A	5:13-16, list of David's family
B	5:17-25, defeat of the Philistines; kingdom secured
C	6:1-23, the ark brought to Jerusalem
C′	7:1-29, Nathan's oracle of dynastic promise
B′	8:1-14, defeat of Israel's neighbors; kingdom expanded
A′	8:15-18, list of David's officials

The first three units represent the foundation of David's kingship in concerns appropriate to the earlier tribal existence of Israel as God's covenant people. David's marriages and his children (5:13-16) witness to the importance of kinship networks in earlier tribal life. His victory over the Philistines (5:17-25) ends the threat of a perennial enemy of tribal Israel. The bringing of the ark to Jerusalem (6:1-23) makes the royal capital also the covenant shrine, as was Shiloh, and the ancient symbol of God's presence and power is honored in the new kingdom. In these notices and actions, David is presented as one who makes alliances with the old order of covenantal Israel in order to secure the kingdom and to settle or make peace with old issues that brought Saul to grief.

In the last three units of the section, David's story moves to new horizons. New bases of security are established for Israel's future. Kinship gives way to royal bureaucracy as the basis of power (5:13-16; 8:15-18). Security from a threatening enemy gives way to royal conquest and expansion of borders and the security of territorial domination (5:17-25; 8:1-14). At the center of the section, the theology of God's presence symbolized by the ark gives way to a theology of God's promise that makes Davidic dynasty itself a theological symbol of God's care for Israel (6:1-23; 7:1-29). Kingdom is theologically wedded to God's continuing guidance of Israel's future.

The reader is gripped by a tension between two responses that seem naturally invoked by these stories and reports. On the one hand, we acknowledge the passing of the old order even as David makes his peace with that older reality in Israel. On the other hand, we celebrate the arrival of full nationhood and the emergence of new and unexpected patterns of God's grace in David and his dynasty. Both are authentic responses to God's truth revealed in passing order and emerging order. The emergence of Israel as a nation is not without cost. As we shall see, the new bases of royal power bring new threats of royal ideology and abuse of power. But to remain in the tribal

patterns of covenantal Israel had already proved costly, as seen in the crises that opened the books of Samuel (see Overview for 1 Sam 1:1–7:17). The key to this section is the great oracle of God's promise to David in 2 Samuel 7. If the kingdom is to be more than ideology or power, it will be because God redeems it and works through it.

2 Samuel 5:11-25, Economic and Political Security

NIV

[11]Now Hiram king of Tyre sent messengers to David, along with cedar logs and carpenters and stonemasons, and they built a palace for David. [12]And David knew that the LORD had established him as king over Israel and had exalted his kingdom for the sake of his people Israel.

[13]After he left Hebron, David took more concubines and wives in Jerusalem, and more sons and daughters were born to him. [14]These are the names of the children born to him there: Shammua, Shobab, Nathan, Solomon, [15]Ibhar, Elishua, Nepheg, Japhia, [16]Elishama, Eliada and Eliphelet.

[17]When the Philistines heard that David had been anointed king over Israel, they went up in full force to search for him, but David heard about it and went down to the stronghold. [18]Now the Philistines had come and spread out in the Valley of Rephaim; [19]so David inquired of the LORD, "Shall I go and attack the Philistines? Will you hand them over to me?"

The LORD answered him, "Go, for I will surely hand the Philistines over to you."

[20]So David went to Baal Perazim, and there he defeated them. He said, "As waters break out, the LORD has broken out against my enemies before me." So that place was called Baal Perazim.[a] [21]The Philistines abandoned their idols there, and David and his men carried them off.

[22]Once more the Philistines came up and spread out in the Valley of Rephaim; [23]so David inquired of the LORD, and he answered, "Do not go straight up, but circle around behind them and attack them in front of the balsam trees. [24]As soon as you hear the sound of marching in the tops of the balsam trees, move quickly, because that will

[a]20 Baal Perazim means *the lord who breaks out.*

NRSV

11King Hiram of Tyre sent messengers to David, along with cedar trees, and carpenters and masons who built David a house. [12]David then perceived that the LORD had established him king over Israel, and that he had exalted his kingdom for the sake of his people Israel.

13In Jerusalem, after he came from Hebron, David took more concubines and wives; and more sons and daughters were born to David. [14]These are the names of those who were born to him in Jerusalem: Shammua, Shobab, Nathan, Solomon, [15]Ibhar, Elishua, Nepheg, Japhia, [16]Elishama, Eliada, and Eliphelet.

17When the Philistines heard that David had been anointed king over Israel, all the Philistines went up in search of David; but David heard about it and went down to the stronghold. [18]Now the Philistines had come and spread out in the valley of Rephaim. [19]David inquired of the LORD, "Shall I go up against the Philistines? Will you give them into my hand?" The LORD said to David, "Go up; for I will certainly give the Philistines into your hand." [20]So David came to Baal-perazim, and David defeated them there. He said, "The LORD has burst forth against[a] my enemies before me, like a bursting flood." Therefore that place is called Baal-perazim.[b] [21]The Philistines abandoned their idols there, and David and his men carried them away.

22Once again the Philistines came up, and were spread out in the valley of Rephaim. [23]When David inquired of the LORD, he said, "You shall not go up; go around to their rear, and come upon them opposite the balsam trees. [24]When you hear the sound of marching in the tops of the balsam

[a] Heb *paraz*   [b] That is *Lord of Bursting Forth*

NIV

mean the LORD has gone out in front of you to strike the Philistine army." ²⁵So David did as the LORD commanded him, and he struck down the Philistines all the way from Gibeon*a* to Gezer.

a25 Septuagint (see also 1 Chron. 14:16); Hebrew Geba

NRSV

trees, then be on the alert; for then the LORD has gone out before you to strike down the army of the Philistines." ²⁵David did just as the LORD had commanded him; and he struck down the Philistines from Geba all the way to Gezer.

COMMENTARY

The remainder of chap. 5 contains several short notices that deal primarily with the economic and political security of David's new kingdom. There is a brief mention of trade and diplomatic relations established with Hiram king of Tyre (vv. 11-12); a listing of the children born to David in Jerusalem (vv. 13-16); and two accounts of decisive victories over the Philistines (vv. 17-21, 22-25). The cumulative effect of these notices shows David as being effective in making his fledgling kingdom secure and viable. David ends the ongoing threat from the Philistines, which Saul had failed to meet. The building of a palace with cedar obtained from Hiram of Tyre reflects the beginning of new economic patterns with Jerusalem as the new center of the emerging Davidic kingdom.

5:11-12. Suddenly the scope of David's story expands. We no longer read of local realities, which were the focus of the narratives of David's rise to the throne. The scope has become international, and David receives ambassadors from a neighboring king, Hiram of Tyre (v. 11*a*). Further, along with the ambassadors come cedar and the skilled carpenters and masons who will build a palace for David. This, no doubt, suggests the establishment of trade relations between David's fledgling kingdom and the Phoenician trading center of Tyre. Hiram would have not supplied such goods and services without getting something in return. We do not have the details, but it is clear that new economic arrangements have been made. Kingdoms require economic bases to survive and grow beyond the simpler needs of tribal life. It is significant that this notice of economic arrangements with Tyre is the first action reported for David as king of all Israel.

We have moved from tribal reality to royal reality. Cedar is the symbol of wealth, but its opulence is also the source of the temptation to imagine that wealth makes a king self-sufficient and aloof from covenant demands for justice. Jeremiah speaks of kings who build houses of cedar and imagine themselves great while ignoring the concerns of justice and righteousness that demonstrate knowledge of the Lord (Jer 22:13-18). New possibilities for kingdom bring new dangers, but for the moment David is certain that these new realities are further evidence of the favor of God on his kingdom (v. 12). The costs and dangers of such kingdoms are to be faced in the future.

5:13-16. These verses list the children born to David while in Jerusalem. It corresponds to the list of his children born at Hebron in 3:2-5. Unlike that list, only the names of the sons are mentioned here. Their mothers remain anonymous, except for the mother of Solomon, whom we know from 2 Sam 12:24 was Bathsheba. This is the first reference to Solomon and points us toward a significant development in the story of David and the kingship.

The other, nameless mothers of David's Jerusalem children are lumped together in the notice that David "took" more concubines and wives (v. 13*a*). The verb "took" (לקח *lāqaḥ*) recalls the warning of Samuel in 1 Sam 8:11-18 about the "ways of the king" and anticipates David's "taking" of Bathsheba in 2 Sam 11:4 (the NRSV and NIV translate it weakly as "get"). This is also the first mention of concubines (v. 13*a*). The acquisition of a harem of wives and concubines was a symbol of power and influence among ancient kings (see Solomon's later practice in 1 Kings 11). David is indeed beginning to give Israel a king "like the other nations" (1 Sam 8:5, 20). Verse 13*b* also mentions the birth of daughters, but like the mothers they are left nameless. Women do not figure in the usual patriarchal patterns of royal reality. Except for Solomon, none of the sons mentioned here will play any further role in Israel's story.

5:17-25. In two brief accounts, David seems to end the Philistine threat that had clouded Israel's future for over a generation. David succeeds in the task for which Saul was anointed as Israel's first king, but that ended for Saul in failure and death. It is likely that David's ending of the Philistine menace involved more than two battles (2 Sam 8:1 may reflect this). These may have been decisive victories and may have been intended to balance the two great defeats suffered by Israel in the earlier stories of the books of Samuel (1 Samuel 4 and 31). These accounts symbolize David's success at giving Israel military security; they do not seem to occur in the chronological order of David's actions in the early days of his kingship. For example, many commentators have suggested that at least one of these victories must have come before the capture of Jerusalem. Certainly the chapter should not be regarded as giving a reliable historical sequence of events.[206]

As it now stands, the encounters with the Philistines are initiated by the news of David's acceptance of kingship over Israel (i.e., the northern, previously Saulide, tribes who had been the constant enemies of Philistia). We must consider the possibility that, until this point, the Philistines had still regarded David as a vassal of the king of Gath. The narrator has not reported that David had broken this relationship. Hence, his kingship over Judah may have been considered a development in David's control over a southern territory that he was supposed to be managing for the king of Gath. In any case, the break with the Philistines is made inevitable by his kingship over all Israel, which would have made clear his intention to throw off Philistine domination. David is now clearly the enemy, and the Philistines must act against his perceived rebellion (vv. 1-2).

Initially David is forced to seek refuge in his stronghold (perhaps Adullum, 1 Sam 22:1, 4; 24:22). In v. 19 we still see the David known to us before he became king. He inquires of the Lord whether he should engage the Philistines. The means of inquiry is not clear but could have been by ephod or lots. The Lord answers that David should engage them, for the Lord will give the Philistines into David's hand. The theme of God's presence with David and David's recognition of his reliance on God's guidance has carried over from the narratives of David's rise. He has not yet become the self-sufficient monarch. When David defeats the Philistines (v. 20*a*), he gives the credit to the Lord, using the metaphor of a flood bursting upon the enemy; from that image is derived the name for remembrance of the place, Baal-perazim (v. 20*b*).[207] In the abandonment, capture, and removal of Philistine idols (v. 21), the reader cannot help recalling the Philistine capture of the ark and its subsequent sojourn in Philistine territory (1 Samuel 4–6). Through David, God has reversed Israel's fortunes.

The second battle occurs in the same general region (v. 22). It is not clear what the relationship of the two encounters might have been. Perhaps this is a force sent out in response to the first defeat, but it could also be a separate incident at another time, suggesting a period of hostilities between David and the Philistines. Once again David inquires of the Lord, and the Lord's response this time involves a particular strategy (vv. 23-24). David is not to engage them directly, but he must flank the Philistine force and come against them from the rear through a stand of balsam trees. When David hears "the sound of marching in the tops of the balsam trees" he is to strike, for he will know that the Lord has already gone ahead to strike the Philistines. This imagery is probably intended to refer to a rush of wind in the treetops. Wind is often an image of divine power in battle accounts that reflect the holy war imagery where God fights for Israel (see the storm imagery in 1 Sam 7:10; 12:18). David follows the Lord's instruction and wins a great victory, driving the Philistines back into their home territory (v. 25). Except for a brief reference in 8:1, this is the last we hear of the Philistines as a threat to Israel. David accomplishes what Saul could not and ends the time of Philistine domination.

---

206. See the discussion of these matters in Anderson, *2 Samuel,* 92-94, and in N. L. Tidwell, "The Philistine Incursions into the Valley of Rephaim," VTSup 30 (1979) 190-212.

207. C. L. Seow, *Myth, Drama, and the Politics of David's Dance,* HSM 44 (Atlanta: Scholars Press, 1989) 80-90, argues that Yahweh should be seen here as the divine warrior of holy war tradition "bursting forth" against the waters as in primordial battle. This "bursting forth" is paralleled in the Lord's "bursting forth" against Uzzah in 2 Sam 6:8. Certainly Seow is correct that both of the battle accounts in 5:17-25 reflect the holy war tradition associated with the ark. McCarter, *II Samuel,* 183, in a similar vein argues that these battle accounts, with their holy war language, are intended as a necessary introduction to the procession of the ark, symbolizing the God of holy war tradition, which follows in chap. 6.

At the end of this chapter, David has brought his new kingdom fully into the arena of nations. His united kingdom of Israel and Judah has a capital in Jerusalem, the beginning of international trade, and military security against its most feared enemy. David is now fully a king and has established a kingdom in more than name only. It is the Lord who is still recognized by David and by the narrator as the power at work through David, but the ominous seduction of cedar, with its implications of wealth and power, is now also a part of the story.

REFLECTIONS

No one would deny the importance of achieving economic and political security for a nation. In these stories, David does so and appears to maintain his sense of the kingdom as ultimately relying for true security on the Lord. This unit, with its brief episodes, is significant for its record of David's achievements and for its hint of the dangers that come with the power to make such achievements. A palace of cedar is little to ask as a reward (v. 11), and even in its building David is quick to acknowledge the Lord as the source of all he has achieved. But cedar and victory are dangerous commodities and require careful handling. These dangers remain for later episodes in David's story to explore.

Economic wealth and political victory are still seductive and dangerous commodities, and recent decades have given us a procession of political and ecclesiastical leaders who have fallen victim to these seductive dangers. Our text suggests no remedy but constant recognition of our true security in the Lord and our awareness of the dangers that come with the necessary exercise of power.

2 Samuel 6:1-23, David Brings the Ark to Jerusalem

NIV

6 David again brought together out of Israel chosen men, thirty thousand in all. ²He and all his men set out from Baalah of Judah*a* to bring up from there the ark of God, which is called by the Name,*b* the name of the LORD Almighty, who is enthroned between the cherubim that are on the ark. ³They set the ark of God on a new cart and brought it from the house of Abinadab, which was on the hill. Uzzah and Ahio, sons of Abinadab, were guiding the new cart ⁴with the ark of God on it,*c* and Ahio was walking in front of it. ⁵David and the whole house of Israel were celebrating with all their might before the LORD, with songs*d* and with harps, lyres, tambourines, sistrums and cymbals.

⁶When they came to the threshing floor of Nacon, Uzzah reached out and took hold of the ark of God, because the oxen stumbled. ⁷The LORD's

a2 That is, Kiriath Jearim; Hebrew Baale Judah, a variant of Baalah of Judah   b2 Hebrew; Septuagint and Vulgate do not have the Name. c3,4 Dead Sea Scrolls and some Septuagint manuscripts; Masoretic Text cart 4and they brought it with the ark of God from the house of Abinadab, which was on the hill   d5 See Dead Sea Scrolls, Septuagint and 1 Chronicles 13:8; Masoretic Text celebrating before the LORD with all kinds of instruments made of pine.

NRSV

6 David again gathered all the chosen men of Israel, thirty thousand. ²David and all the people with him set out and went from Baale-judah, to bring up from there the ark of God, which is called by the name of the LORD of hosts who is enthroned on the cherubim. ³They carried the ark of God on a new cart, and brought it out of the house of Abinadab, which was on the hill. Uzzah and Ahio,*a* the sons of Abinadab, were driving the new cart ⁴with the ark of God;*b* and Ahio*a* went in front of the ark. ⁵David and all the house of Israel were dancing before the LORD with all their might, with songs*c* and lyres and harps and tambourines and castanets and cymbals.

⁶When they came to the threshing floor of Nacon, Uzzah reached out his hand to the ark of God and took hold of it, for the oxen shook it. ⁷The anger of the LORD was kindled against Uzzah; and God struck him there because he reached out his hand to the ark;*d* and he died there beside the ark of God. ⁸David was angry because the LORD

a Or and his brother   b Compare Gk: Heb and brought it out of the house of Abinadab, which was on the hill with the ark of God   c Q Ms Gk 1 Chr 13.8: Heb fir trees   d 1 Chr 13.10 Compare Q Ms: Meaning of Heb uncertain

anger burned against Uzzah because of his irreverent act; therefore God struck him down and he died there beside the ark of God.

⁸Then David was angry because the LORD's wrath had broken out against Uzzah, and to this day that place is called Perez Uzzah.ᵃ

⁹David was afraid of the LORD that day and said, "How can the ark of the LORD ever come to me?" ¹⁰He was not willing to take the ark of the LORD to be with him in the City of David. Instead, he took it aside to the house of Obed-Edom the Gittite. ¹¹The ark of the LORD remained in the house of Obed-Edom the Gittite for three months, and the LORD blessed him and his entire household.

¹²Now King David was told, "The LORD has blessed the household of Obed-Edom and everything he has, because of the ark of God." So David went down and brought up the ark of God from the house of Obed-Edom to the City of David with rejoicing. ¹³When those who were carrying the ark of the LORD had taken six steps, he sacrificed a bull and a fattened calf. ¹⁴David, wearing a linen ephod, danced before the LORD with all his might, ¹⁵while he and the entire house of Israel brought up the ark of the LORD with shouts and the sound of trumpets.

¹⁶As the ark of the LORD was entering the City of David, Michal daughter of Saul watched from a window. And when she saw King David leaping and dancing before the LORD, she despised him in her heart.

¹⁷They brought the ark of the LORD and set it in its place inside the tent that David had pitched for it, and David sacrificed burnt offerings and fellowship offeringsᵇ before the LORD. ¹⁸After he had finished sacrificing the burnt offerings and fellowship offerings, he blessed the people in the name of the LORD Almighty. ¹⁹Then he gave a loaf of bread, a cake of dates and a cake of raisins to each person in the whole crowd of Israelites, both men and women. And all the people went to their homes.

²⁰When David returned home to bless his house-

ᵃ8 *Perez Uzzah* means *outbreak against Uzzah.*   ᵇ17 Traditionally *peace offerings;* also in verse 18

had burst forth with an outburst upon Uzzah; so that place is called Perez-uzzah,ᶠ to this day. ⁹David was afraid of the LORD that day; he said, "How can the ark of the LORD come into my care?" ¹⁰So David was unwilling to take the ark of the LORD into his care in the city of David; instead David took it to the house of Obed-edom the Gittite. ¹¹The ark of the LORD remained in the house of Obed-edom the Gittite three months; and the LORD blessed Obed-edom and all his household.

12It was told King David, "The LORD has blessed the household of Obed-edom and all that belongs to him, because of the ark of God." So David went and brought up the ark of God from the house of Obed-edom to the city of David with rejoicing; ¹³and when those who bore the ark of the LORD had gone six paces, he sacrificed an ox and a fatling. ¹⁴David danced before the LORD with all his might; David was girded with a linen ephod. ¹⁵So David and all the house of Israel brought up the ark of the LORD with shouting, and with the sound of the trumpet.

16As the ark of the LORD came into the city of David, Michal daughter of Saul looked out of the window, and saw King David leaping and dancing before the LORD; and she despised him in her heart.

17They brought in the ark of the LORD, and set it in its place, inside the tent that David had pitched for it; and David offered burnt offerings and offerings of well-being before the LORD. ¹⁸When David had finished offering the burnt offerings and the offerings of well-being, he blessed the people in the name of the LORD of hosts, ¹⁹and distributed food among all the people, the whole multitude of Israel, both men and women, to each a cake of bread, a portion of meat,ᵍ and a cake of raisins. Then all the people went back to their homes.

20David returned to bless his household. But Michal the daughter of Saul came out to meet David, and said, "How the king of Israel honored himself today, uncovering himself today before the eyes of his servants' maids, as any vulgar fellow might shamelessly uncover himself!" ²¹David said

ᵃ That is *Bursting Out Against Uzzah*   ᵇ Vg: Meaning of Heb uncertain

NIV

hold, Michal daughter of Saul came out to meet him and said, "How the king of Israel has distinguished himself today, disrobing in the sight of the slave girls of his servants as any vulgar fellow would!"

[21]David said to Michal, "It was before the LORD, who chose me rather than your father or anyone from his house when he appointed me ruler over the LORD's people Israel—I will celebrate before the LORD. [22]I will become even more undignified than this, and I will be humiliated in my own eyes. But by these slave girls you spoke of, I will be held in honor."

[23]And Michal daughter of Saul had no children to the day of her death.

NRSV

to Michal, "It was before the LORD, who chose me in place of your father and all his household, to appoint me as prince over Israel, the people of the LORD, that I have danced before the LORD. [22]I will make myself yet more contemptible than this, and I will be abased in my own eyes; but by the maids of whom you have spoken, by them I shall be held in honor." [23]And Michal the daughter of Saul had no child to the day of her death.

COMMENTARY

Scholars generally agree that David's installation of the ark of God in Jerusalem was of pivotal significance to the establishment and legitimization of his kingdom. Yet, interpretation of 2 Samuel 6 has been extremely varied.

Leonhard Rost first proposed that this chapter was part of an independent ark narrative that began with 1 Samuel 4–6 and concluded with the bringing of the ark to Jerusalem in 2 Samuel 6.[208] Following Rost, the ark narrative was understood until recently as one of the sources incorporated into a larger history work by the deuteronomistic historian. More recent scholarship has raised questions about the inclusion of 2 Samuel 6 in such an ark narrative.[209] This chapter seems to be part of David's story, and, unlike 1 Samuel 4–6, the ark itself does not seem to be the major character of the story. The transition between 1 Samuel 4–6 and 2 Samuel 6 is not a smooth one and has led many to propose that something must have dropped out if these chapters existed as an independent document. Nevertheless, it seems clear

that the author responsible for writing and placing 2 Samuel 6 knew of the ark narratives in 1 Samuel 4–6 and intentionally built on that earlier episode concerning the ark of God. Certain patterns seem to be an intentional relating of the two ark-related narratives. In 1 Samuel 4, there are two Philistine victories that lead to the loss of the ark, whereas two victories of Israel over the Philistines (2 Sam 5:17-25) and the loss of the Philistine idols (5:21) preface the recovery of the ark in 2 Samuel 6. The loss of the ark signaled the end of the house of Eli (1 Sam 4:12-18); now the recovery of the ark occasions a confrontation with Michal that signals with finality the end of the house of Saul (2 Sam 6:20-23). The religious and political futures of Israel now focus on David. Even the ark seems to need his patronage as it is restored to a central place in Israelite life. The ark (and the Lord it represented) seemed to take care of itself in 1 Samuel 5–6.

Psalm 132 has long been recognized as a liturgical remembrance of David's transfer of the ark. It opens by describing a search for and a procession of the ark (Ps 132:1-9) and concludes with affirmations of God's promises concerning David and Zion (Ps 132:10-18). This is similar to the progression in 2 Samuel—from procession of the ark (chap. 6) to the oracle of dynastic promise to David (chap. 7). Psalm 132 may well be an older remembrance of the ark procession and the

208. Leonhard Rost, *The Succession to the Throne of David,* trans. M. D. Rutter and D. M. Gunn, JSOTSup (Sheffield: Almond, 1982; original German edition, 1926).

209. Patrick D. Miller and J. J. M. Roberts, *The Hand of the Lord: A Reassessment of the "Ark Narrative" of 1 Samuel* (Baltimore: Johns Hopkins University Press, 1977), make a convincing argument that 2 Samuel 6 was not a part of an independent ark narrative. For an opposing view, see Anthony F. Campbell, *The Ark Narrative (1 Sam 4–6; 2 Sam 6): A Form-Critical and Traditio-Historical Study,* SBLDS 16 (Missoula, Mont.: Scholars Press, 1975).

Davidic promise than the present narrative forms of 2 Samuel 6–7. Influential Scandinavian scholars have stressed the ritual and mythological background of the ark procession, arguing that 2 Samuel 6 was a story composed to justify later liturgical practices of processing the ark and was without historical basis in the reign of David.[210] More recent scholarship has reasserted the importance of 2 Samuel 6 as the record of a pivotal historical moment in David's kingship, although the telling of the story has been shaped to help legitimate Davidic rule.[211] Liturgy, as reflected in Psalm 132, celebrates this event but does not create it.

The procession of the ark to Jerusalem, initiated by David, was significant on many levels. Flanagan has suggested that this complexity of meanings marks the ark procession as a rite of passage that allows and encourages transformations from old order to new order that would not have been possible in a less liminal moment.[212] Although they are interrelated, different levels of meaning can be discerned in the ark procession story.

(1) The transfer of the ark served to legitimate Davidic rule. The ark of God was the most sacred symbol of tribal, covenantal Israel. It represented the holy war traditions of Yahweh as the divine warrior who fought for Israel, and the traditions of Yahweh as divine king whose enthroned presence was represented by the ark (see Commentary on 1 Sam 4:4). David's transfer of the ark to Jerusalem links the kingship of God to Davidic rule. Likewise, God's protection of Israel was now channeled through the protection of God's anointed king.

(2) The removal of the ark from the house of Abinadab and the death of Uzzah, Abinadab's son, sever previous arrangements for custody of the ark. Custody is transferred to the house of David.

In effect, David becomes the patron of the ark—a priestly role—and the older covenantal religious traditions it represents. By honoring the ark and restoring it to a position of respect, David avoids the conflict that brought grief to Saul. He positions himself as the preserver rather than the threat to the older religious traditions.

(3) The procession of the ark serves as a public ritual to inaugurate Jerusalem, not only as royal capital but also as the religious center of Israel's life.[213] This makes Jerusalem the successor to Shiloh and ties religious center and political center together in David's city and David's rule. The kingdom of David and the city of Jerusalem possess both theological and political implications, leading to the emergence of a David-Zion theology.

(4) The narrative of the ark procession reveals David's personal character, especially his unique ability to blend piety and politics. On the one hand, the honoring of the ark is a pious act, acknowledging the centrality of the Lord's rule in David's kingdom. On the other hand, the procession of the ark is a shrewd and calculated move by David to appease forces that might otherwise oppose him. It is a part of David's uniqueness in Israel's story that both of these aspects seem authentic to David. Brueggemann captures the ambiguity of Davidic character in such moments:

Insofar as the narrative looks back, the advent of the ark bespeaks genuine religious seriousness on David's part. Insofar as the event looks forward, there is a hint of political calculation and manipulation in David's act. Both factors are present. The wonder is that David is able to hold them together in a kind of personal authenticity that resists choosing one factor or the other.[214]

(5) The procession of the ark helps to establish a ritual, liturgical base for the development of a theology of kingship in Israel. Certainly the evidence from Psalm 132, as well as other references in the psalms, makes clear that the transfer of the ark to Jerusalem was the subject of ongoing liturgical celebration in Israel's worship life. C. L. Seow, in an important study of this chapter, suggests persuasively that David may have shaped this procession as a ritual drama drawn from an

210. Norwegian Sigmund Mowinckel first advanced his arguments for an ark procession as part of an annual Israelite New Year's festival in the 1920s. His most definitive work was translated into English as *The Psalms in Israel's Worship,* 2 vols., trans. D. R. Ap-Thomas (Nashville: Abingdon, 1962). A. Bentzen had earlier argued that 2 Samuel 6 reflects ancient combat myths and is a narrativizing of liturgical motifs. See "The Cultic Use of the Story of the Ark in Samuel," *JBL* 67 (1948) 37-53.

211. See Terence E. Fretheim, "The Cultic Use of the Ark of the Covenant in the Monarchical Period" (Th.D. diss., Princeton Theological Seminary, 1967); and P. Kyle McCarter, "The Ritual Dedication of the City of David in 2 Samuel 6," in *The Word of the Lord Shall Go Forth: Festschrift for D. N. Freedman,* ed. C. L. Meyers and M. O'Connor (Winona Lake, Ind.: Eisenbrauns, 1983) 273-78.

212. James W. Flanagan, "Social Transformation and Ritual in 2 Samuel 6," in *The Word of the Lord Shall Go Forth: Festschrift for D. N. Freedman,* ed. C. L. Meyers and M. O'Connor (Winona Lake, Ind.: Eisenbrauns, 1983) 361-72.

213. McCarter, "The Ritual Dedication of the City of David in 2 Samuel 6," 273-78, particularly stresses this narrative as involving the inauguration of Jerusalem for its important role in Israel's life.

214. Walter Brueggemann, *First and Second Samuel,* Interpretation (Louisville: John Knox, 1990) 249.

ancient mythic pattern chronicling the victory of the divine warrior and his subsequent victorious procession to ascend the royal throne.[215] Such a pattern seems to shape the narrative of 2 Samuel 6. The ritual pattern associated with the divine warrior in the ancient Near East is now claimed for Israel's God, Yahweh. The various elements of this ritual drama include:

❖ victory over enemies (5:17-25) as the necessary prelude to the victory procession of chap. 6;

❖ a ceremonial procession of the victorious divine warrior in joyous celebration;

❖ demonstrations of divine power, such as the smiting of Uzzah (Seow suggests that this might have been a ritual battle at the threshing floor [v. 6] to reenact the death of the Lord's enemies, but this must be regarded as somewhat speculative);

❖ the role of dancing as reflective of the dance of all creation in celebration of the divine warrior's victory;

❖ the ascent and installation of the ark (vv. 17-18) as an enthronement of the divine warrior in kingship;

❖ a ritual banquet and distribution of food, displaying the divine king's graciousness (v. 19).

In effect, this ritual drama enacts the procession of the victorious divine warrior to his rightful place as divine king. In the narrative of 2 Samuel 6, this ritual drama is appropriated in a manner that makes David and his kingship the representative of the Lord as divine warrior king.

In vv. 16 and 20-23, an intense drama is played out within the larger narrative between David and Saul's daughter Michal. This episode seems intrusive within the story of the transfer of the ark, and opinion is divided on whether the encounter with Michal is an original part of the narrative. Much has been written recently on the character of Michal.[216] She has been depicted both as a vindictive nag and as a rightfully incensed victim of political manipulation by David. The episode

will be examined more carefully below, but the encounter in its present form has less to do with the personalities of Michal and David than with the delegitimizing of Saulide claims. The episode serves to announce the end of any possibility of an heir to the throne through Michal.

6:1-5. We have just read about two great victories over the Philistines (5:17-25). When v. 1 tells us that David "again" musters "thirty thousand men," we expect a further account of military engagements. Instead David and his entire entourage go to Baalah of Judah (NIV; NRSV, "Baale-judah") to bring the ark of God to Jerusalem. Instead of a new military engagement, this is to be the triumphal procession of the God responsible for those victories against the Philistines (5:20*b*, 24*b*).

Unlike the apparent implication of Ps 132:6, no search for the ark is necessary. The ark of God is not lost, but it has been neglected. According to 1 Sam 6:21–7:1, the ark had rested in the house of Abinadab in Kireath-jearim, a Gibeonite town in the territory of Judah. According to 2 Sam 6:3-4, the ark is removed from the house of Abinadab, placed on a new cart, and sent on its way accompanied by the two sons of Abinadab, Uzzah and Ahio. The discrepancy in place names for the ark's resting place may be explained by alternative names for the same location. Kiriath-jearim is identified with Kiriath-baal in Josh 15:60; 18:14, and with Baalah in Josh 15:9. Baalah of Judah could be a variant of these alternative names for Kiriath-jearim.

The full formal designation for the ark is used in v. 2: "the ark of God which is called by the name of the Lord of hosts who is enthroned on the cherubim." This same full name of the ark is also used in 1 Sam 4:4 at the beginning of the ark narrative (see Commentary on 1 Sam 4:1*b*-11). The use of this full designation connects David to the range of traditions connected to the ark. For tribal Israel, the ark of God was the chief symbol of the Lord's presence in the midst of Israel. It was a gilded box made of acacia wood (Exod 25:10-22; 37:1-9) surmounted by winged cherubim, which served as a pedestal for the invisibly enthroned Yahweh (the Lord). The title for Israel's God as "Lord of hosts" is rooted in the holy war tradition of Israel's God as a divine warrior who fights for them and is the true leader of the armies ("hosts"). By the use of the ark's

215. C. L. Seow, *Myth, Drama, and the Politics of David's Dance,* HSM 44 (Atlanta: Scholars Press, 1989).

216. An outstanding collection of writings on Michal is found in David J. A. Clines and Tamara C. Eskenazi, eds., *Telling Queen Michal's Story,* JSOTSup 119 (Sheffield: JSOT, 1991). Particularly helpful is J. Cheryl Exum, "Murder They Wrote: Ideology and the Manipulation of Female Presence in Biblical Narrative," in *The Pleasure of Her Text: Feminist Readings of Biblical and Historical Texts,* ed. Alice Bach (Philadelphia: Trinity Press International, 1990) 45-68.

full title, the reader is reminded that when David brings the ark to Jerusalem he is associating his own kingdom with the presence, the military power, and the kingship of Israel's covenant God, Yahweh. David is, in effect, proclaiming a powerful divine alliance for himself in this public ritual.

The procession moves toward Jerusalem. The use of the cart and oxen is reminiscent of the Philistines' ridding themselves of the ark in 1 Samuel 6. Once again the ark moves to a new resting place, but this time it is not accompanied at a distance by watchful and anxious Philistines (1 Sam 6:12). David himself and the whole house of Israel dance and play instruments "before the LORD with all their might" (v. 5). The mood is one of joy and celebration appropriate to the triumphal procession of the Lord, who had been victorious over the Philistines.

6:6-11. The procession of the ark to Jerusalem is interrupted. As the ark approaches the threshing floor of Nacon, the oxen stumble and the ark teeters. Uzzah reaches out his hand to steady the ark (v. 6). The anger of the Lord flares, and God strikes Uzzah dead (v. 7). We are shocked. What has Uzzah done to deserve this? The Hebrew text uses an obscure word of uncertain meaning. The NIV has translated the phrase as "because of his irreverent act." The NRSV follows the reading in 1 Chr 13:10, which is supported by a fragmentary Qumran manuscript, "because he reached out his hand to the ark." What is clear is that the ark possesses great holiness and power. It may not be treated casually. The death of Uzzah is reminiscent of the fate that befell the inhabitants of Beth-shemesh when they looked inside the ark (1 Sam 6:19). Uzzah may have desired to help, but his casual touching of the holy ark carries a terrible price. David clearly does not find this price acceptable. With unusual candor, v. 8 records David's anger toward God. The note about David's anger uses the same verb, translated as "burst forth" (פרץ *pāras*), that was used for the "bursting forth" of God's power against the Philistines in the holy war account of 5:20.[217] Uzzah

has been treated like the enemy of God and of Israel, and David does not find this acceptable. He fears bringing such a dangerous holy object into his own city (vv. 9-10a). Accordingly, the procession is halted, and the ark is lodged in the house of Obed-edom, a Gittite who presumably lives nearby (v. 10b). There the ark remains for three months, which v. 11 tells us were months of blessing for Obed-edom and his household. Ironically, just as David had sojourned among the Gittites before receiving his kingdom and claiming Jerusalem as his capital, so, too, the ark of God rests with a Gittite before proceeding to Jerusalem and the triumphant installation of Israel's divine warrior-king, Yahweh.

6:12-19. The death of Uzzah ends any authority that the house of Abinadab might have had over the ark of God. In v. 12, David receives word that the house of Obed-edom has been blessed, so he resumes the procession of the ark into Jerusalem. There is no further word of Abinadab or his sons as custodians of the ark. David seems more directly involved than before. It is David who "brought up" the ark (v. 12); it is David who "sacrificed" an ox and a fatling after processing only six paces (v. 13); it is David who "danced before the LORD with all his might" clad only in a linen ephod (v. 14). It is David's house that now serves as custodian of the ark.

With great ceremony, the ark is installed in Jerusalem. The ark, and the God whose presence it represents, is given an honored place and is housed in a special tent sanctuary where burnt offerings and offerings of well-being are made (v. 17). Blessings are pronounced on the people in the name of the Lord of hosts (v. 18). The divine warrior has now become a source of blessing in the midst of the people. Food is distributed among the people—bread, meat, and raisins—as a ceremonial meal befitting the conclusion of the triumphant processional of Israel's victorious God (v. 19). Banquets and public distribution of food were common in ancient Near Eastern coronation rights, which would support the notion that Israel's God is being installed as a divine king. God's enthroned presence, represented by the ark, now resides in the midst of David's city.

In the midst of this public ritual and celebration, v. 16 pulls us aside as observers of one who has not participated in the joy of the day. Michal, identified every time she is mentioned in this

217. Because of the similarity of the verbs, Seow, *Myth, Drama, and the Politics of David's Dance,* 97-104, speculates that the procession of the divine warrior represented by the ark may have included a mock battle, reenacting the victory over the Philistines. But he admits that the present text treats Uzzah's death entirely as a historical occurrence and not as a mock death of Philistine enemies.

chapter as the "daughter of Saul," is inside looking on from a window. This position alone marks her as a non-participant. She focuses on David's dancing, described here as exuberant in his leaping before the Lord. We are told only that as she sees David dancing, she "despised him in her heart." For now we know nothing of the motivations for such despising. The notice anticipates the later confrontation between David and Michal after the celebrations are over (vv. 20-23).

6:20-23. The account of the ark's transfer to Jerusalem does not end on a high note of celebration and joy. The final verses of the chapter are taken up in a bitter family dispute between David and Michal.[218] She is always identified in this chapter as the daughter of Saul, underlining her role as the representative of the Saulide line. Saul had reluctantly given her as wife to David after his payment of a brideprice of two hundred Philistine foreskins (1 Sam 18:20-29), but she was given to Palti as wife when David became a fugitive from Saul (1 Sam 25:44). David required Abner to restore Michal to him as a condition for accepting Abner's support, and Michal was forcibly taken from a weeping Palti and brought to David (2 Sam 3:15-16). At one time, the story reported that "Michal loved David" (1 Sam 18:20), but nothing of that love remains.

David seems to know nothing of the impending confrontation and returns to bless his own household following the public ceremonies with the ark (v. 20a). He is met by Michal, who immediately confronts David with criticism of his public behavior (v. 20). She begins with sarcasm, "How the king of Israel honored himself today." It is clear from what follows that she believes he has dishonored himself.

Much has been written about Michal's displeasure.[219] There are three elements in her angry tirade (v. 20b). The first is that David has uncovered himself. In his dancing, presumably he exposed his genitals. This may well have been unusual behavior for a king. A second motive for her anger is that this took place before "the

slave girls of his servants" (NIV; NRSV, "his servants' maids")—in other words, before women of the lowest socioeconomic class. It seems to matter to Michal that David has behaved this way before lower-class women, but we are not told why. Finally, Michal calls David a "vulgar fellow" who has "shamelessly" uncovered himself. She seems to feel that his behavior was inappropriate for a king. He has lowered himself to the basest of men. Perhaps as a royal herself she has her own conception of protocol, and this son of a shepherd does not meet the standard. Michal's feelings have been made clear, but we are left to speculate on all that lies behind them.

David's response to Michal clearly makes the issue one of legitimacy for his kingship and as a corollary the end of Saulide hopes for a royal future (vv. 21-22). David immediately contrasts his status as God's chosen king with God's rejection of Saul ("your father") and all of his household (v. 21a). David reminds her that he is "prince over Israel" by the Lord's choice, and it was for the Lord that he danced (v. 21b). David seems to agree that his behavior was shameless, undignified, and humiliating even in his own eyes (v. 22a), but it was for the Lord. As for the servants' maids, David accepts their honor even when Michal believes he has only earned dishonor (v. 22b). Michal is put in her place as the daughter of a dishonored and rejected king. David is the chosen of God and is honored by even the lowest classes of his people. The political implications are clear: The house of Saul has no say in matters of the kingdom. David draws his authority and legitimation from the Lord and from the people.

The final verse of the chapter (v. 23) ends all Saulide hopes. Michal will remain childless to her death. There will be no son to unite the Davidic and Saulide houses. Again the text leaves details unclear. Many have speculated that David put her aside as a wife; others have suggested that Michal would have nothing to do with David. Some have interpreted this verse as implying God's judgment on Michal. None of these things are said. All are left as possibilities for our speculation.

In this brief episode, we are told about the substance of the confrontation, but most of the motives behind it are left unstated. Robert Alter suggests that this invitation to "multiple interpretations" may be precisely the point:

With a fine sense of the tactics of exposition, the narrator tells us exactly what Michal is feeling but not

---

218. Two articles by David J. A. Clines have been particularly helpful on this segment of Michal's story: "Michal Observed: An Introduction to Reading her Story," and "The Story of Michal, Wife of David, in Its Sequential Unfolding," both in Clines and Eskenazi, *Telling Queen Michal's Story,* 24-63, 129-40.

219. See Clines's survey of the many suggestions and positions taken relative to Michal in this story, "Michal Observed: An Introduction to Reading her Story," in ibid., 52-61.

why. . . . The scorn for David welling up in Michal's heart is thus plausibly attributable in some degree to all of the following: the undignified public spectacle which David just now is making of himself; Michal's jealousy over the moment of glory David is enjoying while she sits alone, a neglected co-wife, back at the provisional palace; Michal's resentment over David's indifference to her all these years, over the other wives he has taken, over being torn away from the devoted Palti; David's dynastic ambitions—now clearly revealed in his establishing the Ark in the "City of David"—which will irrevocably displace the house of Saul. The distance between the spouses is nicely indicated here by the epithets chosen for each: she is the "daughter of Saul," and she sees him as the king.

Michal's subsequent words to David seize on the immediate occasion, the leaping and cavorting, as the particular reason for her anger, but the biblical writer knows as well as any psychologically minded modern that one's emotional reaction to an immediate stimulus can have a complicated prehistory; and by suppressing any causal explanation in his initial statement of Michal's scorn, he beautifully suggests the "overdetermined" nature of her contemptuous ire, how it bears the weight of everything that has not been said but obliquely intimated about the relation between Michal and David.[220]

220. Robert Alter, *The Art of Biblical Narrative* (New York: Basic Books, 1981) 123.

REFLECTIONS

1. There have been many occasions when 2 Samuel 6 has been used as a justification for dance and bodily movement as a part of Christian worship. It is no doubt true that dance was a more natural part of Israelite worship than our own, but such a use of this text misses its main point. Dance is not here simply a neutral method for the praise of God. David's dancing before the ark as it is transferred to Jerusalem, the city of David, points to a pivotal transfer of political power and a transforming possibility for new theological understandings of God's power in relation to public power. David's intense personal involvement is either a genuine recognition and honoring of true power in the Lord (represented by the ark) or a manipulation of religious symbols for the sake of his own enhanced power. This account invites us to reflect on how thin the line is between these two possibilities.

I am writing these words on the very day of the inauguration of a president of the United States. The ceremony will be filled with religious symbols and personalities. These religious trappings embody both possibilities and dangers. They symbolize ties to older traditions in honor and respect for the values of religious customs that we wish to preserve and draw upon in public life. They represent the danger of cynically manipulating religious symbols for the advancement of ideologies or personal power. There is no easy mediation between these two alternatives, and unless religious values are to be totally absent from the public arena we must run the risk of these dangers for the sake of the possibilities. To separate religious symbolism and public power is to risk giving up the notion of moral accountability in public life altogether.

Worship, in our experience, is seldom this risky. Unlike David, we mostly observe rather than participate. Unlike those who saw Uzzah fall, we seldom recognize the power of God's holy presence. Unlike Michal, we fail to voice the political threat that arises from the juncture of religious symbol and political power.

This text and these reflections can offer no glib antidotes to the safe and comfortable rituals of our sanctuaries or the taken-for-granted use of religious symbols in public ceremonies. It would seem that 2 Samuel 6 simply reminds us that divine power and human political power must be intentionally brought together as David is trying to do. It is a risky business, as Uzzah's death reminds us and Nathan the prophet will later point out to David (2 Samuel 12). The alternative is to live with the illusion that our own structures of political power are the ultimate reality, to live with the illusion that religious symbols can be hoarded away from public responsibility or cynically manipulated for the sake of human power arrangements. It is out of such illusions that kingdoms have fallen and nations have perished.

2. While it is clear that the confrontation between Michal and David is intended to address matters of Davidic and Saulide claims on the kingdom, the story is also revealing of gender politics in ancient Israel. Michal had boldly dared to love David and to make that love known (1 Sam 18:20). Yet, David is never said to have loved her, although marriage to her was politically advantageous to him. Three times Michal is given to a man as wife for political reasons (David, 1 Sam 18:27; Paltiel, to spite David, 1 Sam 25:44; David again, as the price for alliance with Abner, 2 Sam 3:14-16). In all of this we lose sight of her love, for love was not allowed a role in such political matters. By 2 Sam 6:20-23, this love appears long dead. When her resentment pours out upon David, the text treats the issue as one of the legitimation of claims on the kingdom. Michal is always called the daughter of Saul, for she is used here as the representative of Saulide claims.

But that is just the point: Michal is always getting used for claims other than her own. Her claim of love was given no power in her world. Her sad and bitter story may be used by the writer to further the men's story of kingdom and power, but it reminds us that the books of Samuel know another reality that David ignores at his peril. The books of Samuel began in the Lord's regard for another childless woman, Hannah. Hannah's song testified to the Lord's commitment to reverse the fortunes of the oppressed and the exploited. David has known this reversal of grace himself in his rise as God's chosen one, from shepherd to king. As his kingdom interests bring Michal's story to a bitter end, David is in the dangerous position of claiming to honor the Lord while completing the final humiliation of one who had once offered him love. Michal's story anticipates the day when David will learn that even God's chosen king must face God's judgment for having been preoccupied with his own power and self-interest (the Bathsheba story, 2 Samuel 11–12). In reading Michal's story, we do well to examine our own refusals of love for the sake of power, our own disregard of women's interests as irrelevant to the public interest, our own efforts to honor the Lord while not fully honoring the priorities to which the Lord has called us.

3. It is the death of Uzzah that most often disturbs readers of this chapter. Why should he be struck dead for what seems a helpful act? It is unlikely that any response we may give will make us comfortable with this God who brings death rather than life. But the point of this strange and disturbing episode may well be that encounter with God is a risky business—not to be taken causally or lightly, as is frequently our custom.

We know nothing about Uzzah. We do know that the ark was, by law, to be carried on poles by Levites, but it has instead been loaded on an oxcart (reminiscent of the Philistines in 1 Samuel 6). Was Uzzah responsible for this? Is his haste to prevent the toppling of the ark but his own attempt to avoid the consequences of poor judgment in transporting the holy presence? As a priest, did he not know that touching the ark is forbidden? Such questions cannot be answered, but the death of Uzzah can stand as a reminder of the danger of trying to manage God's holiness. What should be reverence and awe before God gives way to the notion that we can put our hands on God. That way lies death—perhaps not as dramatic as Uzzah's but just as fatal. Jesus called those who thought they could control God's holiness by their own efforts "whitewashed tombs . . . full of dead men's bones" (Matt 23:27 NRSV).

2 Samuel 7:1-17, Nathan's Dynastic Oracle

NIV	NRSV
7 After the king was settled in his palace and the LORD had given him rest from all his enemies around him, ²he said to Nathan the prophet, "Here I am, living in a palace of cedar, while the ark of God remains in a tent."	**7** Now when the king was settled in his house, and the LORD had given him rest from all his enemies around him, ²the king said to the prophet Nathan, "See now, I am living in a house of cedar, but the ark of God stays in a

NIV

³Nathan replied to the king, "Whatever you have in mind, go ahead and do it, for the LORD is with you."

⁴That night the word of the LORD came to Nathan, saying:

⁵"Go and tell my servant David, 'This is what the LORD says: Are you the one to build me a house to dwell in? ⁶I have not dwelt in a house from the day I brought the Israelites up out of Egypt to this day. I have been moving from place to place with a tent as my dwelling. ⁷Wherever I have moved with all the Israelites, did I ever say to any of their rulers whom I commanded to shepherd my people Israel, "Why have you not built me a house of cedar?"'

⁸"Now then, tell my servant David, 'This is what the LORD Almighty says: I took you from the pasture and from following the flock to be ruler over my people Israel. ⁹I have been with you wherever you have gone, and I have cut off all your enemies from before you. Now I will make your name great, like the names of the greatest men of the earth. ¹⁰And I will provide a place for my people Israel and will plant them so that they can have a home of their own and no longer be disturbed. Wicked people will not oppress them anymore, as they did at the beginning ¹¹and have done ever since the time I appointed leaders*a* over my people Israel. I will also give you rest from all your enemies.

"'The LORD declares to you that the LORD himself will establish a house for you: ¹²When your days are over and you rest with your fathers, I will raise up your offspring to succeed you, who will come from your own body, and I will establish his kingdom. ¹³He is the one who will build a house for my Name, and I will establish the throne of his kingdom forever. ¹⁴I will be his father, and he will be my son. When he does wrong, I will punish him with the rod of men, with floggings inflicted by men. ¹⁵But my love will never be taken away from him, as I took it away from Saul, whom I removed from before you. ¹⁶Your house and your kingdom will

a11 Traditionally judges

NRSV

tent." ³Nathan said to the king, "Go, do all that you have in mind; for the LORD is with you."

4But that same night the word of the LORD came to Nathan: ⁵Go and tell my servant David: Thus says the LORD: Are you the one to build me a house to live in? ⁶I have not lived in a house since the day I brought up the people of Israel from Egypt to this day, but I have been moving about in a tent and a tabernacle. ⁷Wherever I have moved about among all the people of Israel, did I ever speak a word with any of the tribal leaders*a* of Israel, whom I commanded to shepherd my people Israel, saying, "Why have you not built me a house of cedar?" ⁸Now therefore thus you shall say to my servant David: Thus says the LORD of hosts: I took you from the pasture, from following the sheep to be prince over my people Israel; ⁹and I have been with you wherever you went, and have cut off all your enemies from before you; and I will make for you a great name, like the name of the great ones of the earth. ¹⁰And I will appoint a place for my people Israel and will plant them, so that they may live in their own place, and be disturbed no more; and evildoers shall afflict them no more, as formerly, ¹¹from the time that I appointed judges over my people Israel; and I will give you rest from all your enemies. Moreover the LORD declares to you that the LORD will make you a house. ¹²When your days are fulfilled and you lie down with your ancestors, I will raise up your offspring after you, who shall come forth from your body, and I will establish his kingdom. ¹³He shall build a house for my name, and I will establish the throne of his kingdom forever. ¹⁴I will be a father to him, and he shall be a son to me. When he commits iniquity, I will punish him with a rod such as mortals use, with blows inflicted by human beings. ¹⁵But I will not take*b* my steadfast love from him, as I took it from Saul, whom I put away from before you. ¹⁶Your house and your kingdom shall be made sure forever before me;*c* your throne shall be established forever. ¹⁷In accordance with all these words and with all this vision, Nathan spoke to David.

*a Or any of the tribes   b Gk Syr Vg 1 Chr 17.13: Heb shall not depart
c Gk Heb Mss: MT before you; Compare 2 Sam 7.26, 29*

NIV

endure forever before me[a]; your throne will be established forever.'"

[17]Nathan reported to David all the words of this entire revelation.

[a]16 Some Hebrew manuscripts and Septuagint; most Hebrew manuscripts *you*

COMMENTARY

This chapter is the most important theological text in the books of Samuel and perhaps in the entire Deuteronomistic History. With the kingdom secure and his own house (palace) built, David expresses the desire to build a house (temple) for the Lord. Initially, the prophet Nathan approves of this task (vv. 1-3). God's word comes to Nathan in the night with an oracle in response to David's desire (vv. 4-16): The Lord does not need or desire a house (vv. 4-7). The Lord has chosen and cared for David (vv. 8-11*a*), and, instead, the Lord will establish a house (dynasty) for David (v. 11*b*). A son will come after David and be established on the throne; he will build a house (temple) for the Lord (vv. 12-13). This throne will be established forever; the Lord will relate to these descendants of David as father to son; they may be chastised for their sin, but, unlike with Saul, God's steadfast love will be with them forever (vv. 14-16). Nathan conveys this oracle to David (v. 17).

It is readily apparent that this chapter relies on a word play, involving the variant meanings of a single word, to convey its central theme. The common Hebrew noun בית (*bayit*) can, depending on context, mean "house," "dwelling," "palace," "temple," or "dynasty." All of these meanings may play a role in 2 Sam 7:1-17, but the crucial theological focus is on the relationship between temple and dynasty.

This passage is foundational for the appearance and development of a Davidic theology in Israel alongside the covenant theology of tribal Israel. The text of this chapter did not appear full blown in David's time. Most scholars agree that the text of 2 Sam 7:1-17 has undergone a complex history, and, as it now stands, it reflects the development and appropriation of many generations in Israel. There is no scholarly consensus, however, on the

details of the literary history of this text.[221] Almost all would see the final form of 2 Sam 7:1-17 as having been shaped by the deuteronomistic historian (in the verse-by-verse commentary, evidence of deuteronomistic language and themes will be noted). McCarthy proposed that 2 Samuel 7 should be regarded as one of the programmatic speeches that appear at crucial junctures in the Deuteronomistic History (e.g., Joshua 23; 1 Samuel 12; 1 Kgs 8:14-66).[222] These speeches look back on the past and ahead to the future and offer theological evaluations of Israel's history and prospects. His proposal has proved widely persuasive. A substantial majority of scholars would also see some elements of 2 Sam 7:1-17 as having originated with David, but proposals for the development of the chapter between the time of David and the Deuteronomistic History vary significantly. McCarter has offered a proposal for the development of 2 Sam 7:1-17 in three stages, each reflecting differing interests and emphases, which seems helpful and persuasive: "The earliest form of Nathan's oracle was a promise of dynasty to David made in connection with his declared intention to build a temple for Yahweh. This ancient document was expanded by a writer with a less favorable view towards the temple and towards David himself. The final form of the passage was the work of a Deuteronomistic editor who further

221. See the extremely helpful survey and evaluation of the vast literature interpreting 2 Samuel 7 in P. Kyle McCarter, *II Samuel*, AB 9 (Garden City, N.Y.: Doubleday, 1984) 209-31. His treatment is an invaluable guide to the many proposals made concerning the development of this key chapter. A few recent voices argue for the literary unity of 2 Samuel 7 and deny any history of development reflected in the text. John Van Seters, *In Search of History: Historiography in the Ancient World and the Origins of Biblical History* (New Haven: Yale University Press, 1983) 273, argues "from the point of view of form criticism there is no reason why the whole chapter cannot be considered the work of one author."

222. Dennis J. McCarthy, "II Samuel 7 and the Structure of the Deuteronomic History," *JBL* 84 (1965) 131-38.

amended it to express his own point of view."[223] McCarter identifies the second stage in this process with circles reflecting a "prophetic theology of kingship coming to terms with the historical reality of the Davidic dynasty."[224] He characterizes the progression of theological perspectives through these stages as follows:

(1) "You have promised to build a house for me. Therefore I shall build a house for you."[225] Dynastic promise was initially understood as divine response to David's intention to build God a temple. This earliest level is found in vv. 1*a*, 2-3, 11*b*-12, 13*b*-15*a*.

(2) "You will not build me a house. I shall build you a house."[226] A prophetic editing of the text, found in vv. 4-9*a*, 15*b*, argues that a temple was not needed and that the gift of dynastic promise was not a response to David's plan to build a temple but a free act of divine grace.

(3) "You will not build me a house. Your son will build me a house."[227] The final version of the deuteronomistic historian, present in vv. 1*b*, 9*b*-11*a*, 13*a*, 16, softens the negative attitude of the prophetic version toward the Temple. It makes God's refusal to David only temporary and allows for a positive attitude toward Solomon's building of the Temple.

One could argue with the attribution of particular verses or phrases, but in general the process of development McCarter suggests makes sense against the backdrop of Israel's changing history and the place of temple and dynasty in that history. Psalms 89:19-37; 132:11-18; and 1 Chr 17:1-15 represent other important texts in which the themes of dynastic promise to David and God's dwelling on Mt. Zion (Temple) are seen as pillars of the royal theology that develops in Israel from David onward.

In its present form, 2 Sam 7:1-17 serves multiple purposes in the ongoing story of 1–2 Samuel as well as in the larger biblical story. It serves to explain why David did not build a Temple but why his son Solomon later is able to do so. It seeks to legitimize the principle of dynastic succession, which was new to Israel, by making it the will and promise of the Lord. It made clear

that God's graceful presence was not dependent on a temple, even though Solomon would later be allowed to build one. It makes clear that God's promise to David would endure, even though times of chastising judgment would arise. (This emphasis might have been especially important to the exilic audience of the Deuteronomistic History.) Finally, it became an important text to articulate Jewish messianic expectations in a time when there was no Davidic monarch on the throne. This development, of course, led to the appropriation of this text by the early Christian church, who understood Jesus as the continuation of this promise to the line of David.

The oracle of Nathan in 2 Sam 7:4-16 locates God's grace toward Israel in an unconditional and everlasting promise to the line of David. This was a new theological understanding in Israel and stood in tension with the conditional "if" of the Mosaic covenant at Mt. Sinai.[228] Yet, the Davidic promise did not displace the Sinai covenant. God's promise to David was understood to stand in continuity with God's previous acts of salvation on behalf of Israel. The conditional "if" of covenant is now encompassed by the "nevertheless" of unconditional promise. Obedience to covenant requirements is still demanded. Judgment, even of Davidic kings, is still the consequence of covenant disobedience (7:14*b*), but the commitment of God to steadfast love toward David's line and the Davidic kingdom is everlasting and cannot be broken (7:15-16). As will be discussed further below, this notion advances a theme of unconditional divine grace that makes this text centrally important to later Protestant understandings of justification by grace rather than works.

The theology of 2 Sam 7:1-17 is not politically disinterested, and this text has not always been seen or used in accordance with high-minded purposes. Especially in its present position in David's story, this text legitimizes dynastic power and the interests of the Davidic state in maintain-

---

223. McCarter, *II Samuel*, 223.
224. Ibid., 229.
225. Ibid., 224.
226. Ibid., 225.
227. Ibid., 230.

228. Ps 132:12 contains a conditional form of the dynastic promise: "If your sons keep my covenant and my decrees that I shall teach them, their sons also, forevermore, shall sit on your throne" (NRSV). The covenantal "if" is preserved here, and this may be an earlier form of the dynastic promise than 2 Sam 7:4-16. The unconditional character of the promise develops as the line of David does, in fact, consolidate its power and establish its continuity. A theology to justify this in spite of the inevitable better and worse occupants of the throne has developed that understands God's promise as unconditional, although allowing for chastisement, and this is now reflected in 2 Sam 7:4-16.

ing power. As Flanagan's understanding of the structure of these chapters reminds us (see the Overview to 2 Sam 5:11–8:18), 2 Samuel 7 represents the turning point from continuity with older tribal realities and traditions (symbolized by the ark, chap. 6) to new understandings of God's presence in the Davidic kingdom.[229] The struggle for survival against the Philistines is over (5:17-25), and the expansion to empire is about to begin (8:1-14). Brueggemann calls the perspective of this chapter "the sure truth of the state" to emphasize the ideological orientation and interests of this text.

In the move from tribe to state, we are moving into ideology, into a justification of present forms of power and social organization and into propaganda, in which truth is what is advantageous. Note, I do not argue that this is dishonest or lightly perverted. I argue rather that the shift of perception caused by a monopoly of wealth and power invites such distortion, which then becomes systematic distortion. . . . I do not believe there is a predistorted text of these things. That is, there never was a "Nathan oracle" which was not ideologically intentional. Moreover, I shall say that this "sure truth," distorted as it is, is foundationally the vehicle for important faith resources.[230]

Israel's theology is now invested in the Davidic kingdom and its particular shape of political power. Chapter 7 is a recital by those who see new possibilities given by God in commitment to David. Nathan's oracle becomes the source of trust in the certainty of God's promise. But 2 Samuel 7 is also a recital by those likely to benefit from the power arrangements of kingdom. The oracle, then, becomes the source of temptation to manipulate the language of God's promise for the sake of vested interests. This text is at one and the same time a locus for both hope and danger.

7:1-3. David is now settled in his newly built "house of cedar" (see 5:11), and the kingdom is at peace (v. 1). The concept of "rest from enemies" given by the Lord (see also v. 11*a*) is a frequent theme in deuteronomistic texts (Deut 12:9-10; 25:19; Josh 21:44; 22:4; 23:1; 1 Kgs 5:4; 8:56). David is disturbed by the contrast between the luxury of his own house and the "tent" that houses the ark of God (v. 2). The clear implication is that David would like to build a temple for the Lord. Temple building was an activity often undertaken by ancient Near Eastern kings to legitimize their rule and to ensure favor from their gods.[231] A temple in Jerusalem would relate the Lord's presence, symbolized by the ark, to a permanent structure in David's city.

David expresses his concern to Nathan, the prophet (v. 2*a*). This is the first mention of Nathan, and we receive no information about him except that he is a "prophet" (נביא *nābî'*). He appears to have been an influential member of David's court in Jerusalem, with access to the king. He later confronts David over his sin with Bathsheba (2 Samuel 12) and plays a role in the accession of Solomon (1 Kings 1). Nathan's initial response to David's desire to build a temple for the Lord is one of approval. Nathan tells David to carry out his intentions and blesses him with the formula "the LORD is with you" (v. 3). We have seen this formula as a central theme in the history of David's rise (see Commentary on 5:10). David came to power through bold action in confidence that the Lord was with him. In v. 3, it appears that this pattern will continue with a bold Davidic plan to build the Lord a temple.

7:4-7. Nathan spoke too quickly. The Lord has a word to communicate on this matter, and it comes to Nathan in the night (v. 4). The word that Nathan is to take to David (vv. 5-16) is introduced with the messenger formula characteristic of prophetic oracles: "Thus says the LORD. . . ."

The initial element of God's word to David focuses on divine rejection of David's proposal to build a temple for the Lord (vv. 5-7). The tone is not angry but firm. David is God's servant and is addressed as such (vv. 5, 8), but David is not the one to build such a house for the Lord (v. 5*b*). God has not desired or needed a house (i.e., a permanent, fixed dwelling). God recalls that the divine dwelling has been a tent since the days of the deliverance out of Egypt (v. 6) and that at no time has a divine request been made of Israel's leaders to build a "house of cedar" for the Lord (v. 7). The issue here is one of divine freedom, represented by the movable tent-sanctuary, which is threatened by the notion of a permanent, localized temple and the implication that divine pres-

229. James W. Flanagan, "Social Transformation and Ritual in 2 Samuel 6," in *The Word of the Lord Shall Go Forth: Festschrift for D. N. Freedman,* ed. C. L. Meyers and M. O'Connor (Winona Lake, Ind.: Eisenbrauns, 1983).

230. Walter Brueggemann, *David's Truth in Israel's Imagination and Memory* (Philadelphia: Fortress, 1985) 72.

231. G. W. Ahlstrom, *Royal Administration and National Religion in Ancient Palestine* (Leiden: E. J. Brill, 1982) 3-8.

ence can be confined or captured. God, who is accustomed to "moving about among all the people of Israel," treats the desire to build a temple as an attempt to domesticate and control the presence of God. It is an abridgment of sovereign freedom. This clearly stated attitude against the building of a temple makes v. 13 problematic, since it seems to approve the later building of a temple by David's son Solomon.

7:8-11a. The use of the words "Now, therefore . . ." and a repeated messenger formula signal a new focus in God's word to David through the prophet. What follows is a review of God's favorable history with David and an extension of that favor through David to Israel's future. God's refusal to permit David to build a temple is not to be seen as a sign of divine disfavor. God has been with David, and through David God will bless Israel's future. This section is powered by verbs of decisive divine action. The first three point to God's gracious history with David:

I took you from the pasture (v. 8*b*)
I have been with you (v. 9*a*)
I have cut off all your enemies (v. 9*a*)

The second three point to a future of God's graciousness with David and Israel:

I will make you a great name (v. 9*b*)
I will appoint a place for my people Israel (v. 10*a*)
I will give you rest from all your enemies (v. 11)

Many have suggested that the three phrases that point to the future show deuteronomistic influence and the desire to reassure a generation in exile that God's promise still holds. The theme of rest from enemies is a common deuteronomistic theme (see Commentary on 7:1-3), and v. 10, in particular, appears to address a generation that has lost a kingdom, rather than David, who has just gained one.

7:11b-17. Verse 11*b* begins a new section of God's promise, as indicated by the connecting word *moreover*. But it also signals the theological and literary center of this oracle. The expression "The LORD declares to you that the LORD himself will establish a house for you" (v. 11*b*) alone is cast in third-person rather than first-person address. This shift calls attention to the climactic character of the verse and has led some to argue that it was originally the continuation of v. 3 and

represents the oldest literary layer of the text (see the discussion of McCarter's proposal above).

Startlingly, God reverses David's proposal. David cannot build a house for the Lord; the Lord will build a house for David. Using the potential for multiple meanings in the word ביח (*bayit*, "house"), God rejects "temple" but promises "dynasty." The grace shown to David in the past will now extend into the future. This promise is not simply for David, but for the line of David that will come after him.

The immediate consequence of this promise is to be a son who will succeed David on the throne (v. 12). This, of course, will be Solomon (1 Kings 1). It is this son who will be allowed to build "a house for my name" (v. 13*a*). This verse is thought by many to be from the deuteronomist. It seems to be a later legitimization of the Solomonic Temple in spite of God's rejection of such temples in vv. 5-7. The effect is to make God's refusal of a temple only temporary, but the remaining tension between vv. 5-7 and v. 13*a* is still evident. Verse 13*a* uses the typical deuteronomistic idea that it is God's name and not God's own self that dwells in the Temple (see Deut 12:11; 14:23; 16:2; 26:2).

The promise of a "house" for David extends beyond Solomon. The throne of the kingdom is to be established and made secure "forever" (repeated three times in vv. 13, 16). Abigail had already foretold a "sure house" for David (1 Sam 25:28), and God has now promised everlasting dynasty extending from David to secure a future of promise for Israel.

This promise will establish intimate relationship. The relationship between God and the king will be as that of a father to a son (v. 14; cf. the language of Pss 2:7; 89:26-27). It was not uncommon in the ancient world to conceptualize the king as the adopted son of the national god. Further, this promise is unconditional. God may chastise the king for disobeying God's covenant demands ("iniquity"), and there will be appropriate consequences (v. 14*b*). But even this will not cause God to cease in "steadfast love" toward David's line, as had happened to Saul (v. 15). The tragedy of Saul cannot be repeated. God is permanently and unconditionally committed to David and what flows from David for Israel's future. God's commitment takes the form of "steadfast love" (חסד *ḥesed*), a term connected with the loyalty required of covenant relationships. Verse 17 reports that Nathan conveyed to David all that the Lord had spoken.

REFLECTIONS

1. Nathan's oracle speaks to us of the necessary risk of deep faith held close to political ideology. It speaks to us out of the recognition that God has taken the risk of historical concreteness. Chapter 7 is the witness of those who have discerned God's unconditional grace in relation to David and to David's kingdom. It is a bold and audacious claim, and such a claim is not without its dangers. There are clear ideological interests in this text. It runs dangerously close to political propaganda. Indeed, later kings of Judah seem to use Davidic royal theology to simply undergird their own privileged position of power without regard to the God whose promise they exploit (e.g., see the indictment of a king by Jeremiah, Jer 2:3-19).

In spite of the danger, this text is a summons to stand boldly in the tension created by faith commitment and political engagement—to stand between God's interests and the world's interests. The pressure is to resolve the tension. Indeed, readings of 2 Sam 7:1-17 tend to read the oracle either as a bold statement of grace or as crass political propaganda.[232] Likewise, the church resists reading this text as a challenge to stand in the tension of faith and ideology. We are prone either to withdraw from the world's interests into unengaged piety or to ignore God's interests and slip into ideologically co-opted or culturally accommodated religiosity.

God has taken the risk of engaging with the political interests of kingdom. This text summons the church to risk such engagement as well. To respond to this summons will be to get ecclesiastical hands dirty: debating public policy on important issues; upholding value commitments and integrity in public institutions; standing in opposition to power structures when God's justice demands it; supporting power structures when mutually affirmed goals allow it. We may, like David, have occasions to repent when the interests of power tempt us over the line and we act in our own interests (personal or institutional) rather than in God's interests. Second Samuel 7 reminds us that the alternative to this risky tension of faith and political ideology cannot be disinterested, unengaged religion. That is not what God has modeled for us. In David, God risks the dangers of ideological manipulation of faith for the sake of bringing the grace of divine promise into close engagement with public and political realities. The church can do no less.

2. Nathan's oracle introduces a new theological language of unconditional grace into Israel's story. "This ideological utterance is the root of evangelical faith in the Bible: that is, faith that relies on the free promise of the gospel. Heretofore, God's commitments to Israel are regularly and characteristically conditional."[233] The promise to David does not remove the "if" of moral demand that we associate with God's covenant given to Israel at Sinai. Even kings may be chastised and made to suffer the consequences of their sin. This promise, however, does encompass the "if" in a divine commitment that endures in spite of sin. God's grace provides a bedrock of hope even in the midst of sin's consequences.

This unconditional promise may be one of the very reasons why Israel's tradition endures. Exile to Babylon came as a particular challenge to Israel's faith. Seemingly, nation, king, Temple, and national identity had been swept away. The retelling of David's story by the deuteronomistic historian in exilic times offered the chance to reclaim this promise and reaffirm that God is never finished with this commitment to David and to David's line. The promise holds and offers a constant basis of hope to God's people.

232. McCarter, *II Samuel,* 210, cites the views of R. H. Pfeiffer, *Introduction to the Old Testament,* rev. ed. (New York: Harper and Bros., 1948), who regarded 2 Samuel 7 as "a mire of unintelligible verbiage" (p. 372), characterized by confusion and illiteracy and a "complete misunderstanding of the religion in the period of . . . David" (p. 373). The author, whose style is "consistently wretched," is at once "prolix" and "banal" (p. 372); he "repeats himself *ad nauseam*" (p. 373).

233. Walter Brueggemann, *First and Second Samuel,* Interpretation (Louisville: John Knox, 1990) 257.

This theme of unconditional grace in the promise to David is consistent with the articulation of "justification by grace" in the letters of Paul (cf. Rom 3:28; Gal 2:16-21). For that reason, 2 Samuel 7 has been an important text in Protestant traditions in which it is frequently cited and preached upon in connection with the theme of God's grace.

3. The promise of an enduring line for David is one of the foundations for the rise of messianic hopes in Judaism. When the prospects of the present kingdom seemed bleak, the prophets turned to this statement of enduring promise through David for the hope that God is always bringing a new David in every circumstance. God has promised an anointed one who will again bear God's Spirit and establish God's intended kingdom.

> A shoot shall come out from the stump of Jesse,
>   and a branch shall grow out of his roots.
> The spirit of the LORD shall rest on him,
>   the spirit of wisdom and understanding,
>   the spirit of counsel and might,
>   the spirit of knowledge and the fear of the LORD.
> (Isa 11:1-2 NRSV)

In the circumstances surrounding exile and its aftermath, Judaism relied on the promise of God to David for the hope that God had not abandoned the historical enterprise. Even when there was no political kingdom, there was a David coming and a hope that God's anointed one would set things right. Exile contributed to an understanding that God's kingdom might not be tied to any one political kingdom, but the promise is nevertheless trustworthy within the historical process. The people of Israel could remain hopeful even under successive dominations by the empires.

The early Christian church saw Jesus in the light of this promise. The claim that Jesus was born in the line of David and thus inherits God's promise to David is not casually made. Jesus was seen as the Messiah, God's anointed one, announcing a kingdom of God with transforming power in this world. In the church today, 2 Sam 7:1-11, 16 appears in the *Revised Common Lectionary* as the lection for the fourth Sunday in Advent, Cycle B, the season when we anticipate Jesus' coming as the promised one. It is coupled with the Gospel reading of the annunciation to Mary (Luke 1:26-38) to indicate the church's recognition of continuity between Mary, the mother of Messiah, and David, the father of the messianic line. The angel Gabriel's announcement is, in part, a reaffirmation of the everlasting promise to David:

> And now, you will conceive in your womb and bear a son, and you will name him Jesus. He will be great, and will be called the Son of the Most High [cf. 2 Sam 7:14], and the Lord God will give to him the throne of his ancestor David. He will reign over the house of Jacob forever, and of his kingdom there will be no end. (Luke 1:31-33 NRSV)

Incarnation is connected to Davidic promise. Each brings divine presence close to human political realities. Each suggests that we cannot know God's promises apart from engagement with the risks and possibilities of the human historical process. In the lections of Advent we wait again each year for the coming of the son of David and the Son of God, confident that God's promise still holds in the historical moment of every generation.

Mary's response to the news of her son was to sing the beautiful song that we call the Magnificat (Luke 1:46-55; it appears as an alternative reading for the psalm in the lections for the fourth Sunday of Advent, Cycle B). Mary's song is a celebration of the transforming reversals of hope that the Messiah (her son, God's Son) will bring in the political and economic orders of human history. As we listen to her song in anticipation of Jesus, we remember that it is based on Hannah's song (1 Sam 2:1-10). Hannah's song also anticipated such reversals of hope in the coming of God's anointed king and the transforming grace he would bring. God's anticipated king in Hannah's song was David.

To read God's enduring promise to David in this text today is to be reminded of the roots and the challenge of our own messianic hope. To trust in God's promise to David and to claim Jesus as having been born into the line of that promise is to understand God's work as being endlessly engaged with the issues of justice and power that must be faced to establish God's kingdom in every age. In the light of this biblical promise, the church must understand its own faith as being endlessly engaged with these same realities.

2 Samuel 7:18-29, The Prayer of David

NIV

[18]Then King David went in and sat before the LORD, and he said:

"Who am I, O Sovereign LORD, and what is my family, that you have brought me this far? [19]And as if this were not enough in your sight, O Sovereign LORD, you have also spoken about the future of the house of your servant. Is this your usual way of dealing with man, O Sovereign LORD?

[20]"What more can David say to you? For you know your servant, O Sovereign LORD. [21]For the sake of your word and according to your will, you have done this great thing and made it known to your servant.

[22]"How great you are, O Sovereign LORD! There is no one like you, and there is no God but you, as we have heard with our own ears. [23]And who is like your people Israel—the one nation on earth that God went out to redeem as a people for himself, and to make a name for himself, and to perform great and awesome wonders by driving out nations and their gods from before your people, whom you redeemed from Egypt?[a] [24]You have established your people Israel as your very own forever, and you, O LORD, have become their God.

[25]"And now, LORD God, keep forever the promise you have made concerning your servant and his house. Do as you promised, [26]so that your name will be great forever. Then men will say, 'The LORD Almighty is God over Israel!' And the house of your servant David will be established before you.

a23 See Septuagint and 1 Chron. 17:21; Hebrew wonders for your land and before your people, whom you redeemed from Egypt, from the nations and their gods.

NRSV

[18]Then King David went in and sat before the LORD, and said, "Who am I, O Lord GOD, and what is my house, that you have brought me thus far? [19]And yet this was a small thing in your eyes, O Lord GOD; you have spoken also of your servant's house for a great while to come. May this be instruction for the people,[a] O Lord GOD! [20]And what more can David say to you? For you know your servant, O Lord GOD! [21]Because of your promise, and according to your own heart, you have wrought all this greatness, so that your servant may know it. [22]Therefore you are great, O LORD God; for there is no one like you, and there is no God besides you, according to all that we have heard with our ears. [23]Who is like your people, like Israel? Is there another[b] nation on earth whose God went to redeem it as a people, and to make a name for himself, doing great and awesome things for them,[c] by driving out[d] before his people nations and their gods?[e] [24]And you established your people Israel for yourself to be your people forever; and you, O LORD, became their God. [25]And now, O LORD God, as for the word that you have spoken concerning your servant and concerning his house, confirm it forever; do as you have promised. [26]Thus your name will be magnified forever in the saying, 'The LORD of hosts is God over Israel'; and the house of your servant David will be established before you. [27]For you, O LORD of hosts, the God of Israel, have made this revelation to your servant, saying, 'I will build you a house'; therefore your servant has found courage to pray this prayer to you. [28]And now, O Lord GOD, you are God, and your words

a Meaning of Heb uncertain b Gk: Heb one c Heb you d Gk 1 Chr 17.21: Heb for your land e Cn: Heb before your people, whom you redeemed for yourself from Egypt, nations and its gods

NIV	NRSV
²⁷"O LORD Almighty, God of Israel, you have revealed this to your servant, saying, 'I will build a house for you.' So your servant has found courage to offer you this prayer. ²⁸O Sovereign LORD, you are God! Your words are trustworthy, and you have promised these good things to your servant. ²⁹Now be pleased to bless the house of your servant, that it may continue forever in your sight; for you, O Sovereign LORD, have spoken, and with your blessing the house of your servant will be blessed forever."	are true, and you have promised this good thing to your servant; ²⁹now therefore may it please you to bless the house of your servant, so that it may continue forever before you; for you, O Lord GOD, have spoken, and with your blessing shall the house of your servant be blessed forever."

COMMENTARY

David responds to the oracle of dynastic promise with a prayer. It is a remarkable prayer and quite unlike the spontaneous, almost conversational, communication with God that has marked David's story to this point. In style, this prayer is formal, and in mood it seems calculating. It manages to be both deferential and audacious, qualities revealed in key repetitions in the prayer. David refers to himself ten times as "your servant." He addresses God with the exceedingly formal title "Lord GOD" (אדני יהוה ʾădōnāy YHWH; cf. NIV, "Sovereign Lord") seven times and as "LORD of hosts" twice. The divine appellation "Lord GOD" is used nowhere else in the books of Samuel. These repeated designations suggest an acknowledgment of divine power by a deferential David. Such deference is matched, however, by an audacious David who forcefully reminds God of the dynastic promise, perhaps even demanding fidelity to this promise. The use of the word "house" to mean "dynasty" appears seven times (see Commentary on 7:1-17), and the term "forever" (עולם ʿôlām) is used five times. These repetitions are largely in the last six verses of the passage.

In structure, the prayer begins with David's expressions of deference (vv. 18-21), moves to praise of God's incomparability and benevolence toward Israel (vv. 22-24), and concludes with David's insistent restatement of the dynastic promise (vv. 25-29). Brueggemann felicitously refers to this threefold structure of David's prayer as "def-

erence, doxology, and demand."²³⁴ The final section of this prayer actually contains two petitions, both bold claims on God's fidelity to the promise of the dynastic oracle. David asks that God "do as you promised" (v. 25) and that God "bless the house of your servant" (v. 29).²³⁵

There has been considerable debate about the literary history of this text. Most scholars agree that there is evidence of the deuteronomistic historian in the passage, especially in vv. 22-26.²³⁶ There may have been a version of David's prayer that accompanied earlier versions of Nathan's oracle. It is hard to separate out such an earlier version with any certainty. The urgency with which David appeals for the fulfillment of God's promise to the line of David suggests that the present text reflects a time when historic circumstances have called that promise into question. This would, of course, fit well with the deuteronomistic historian's setting in exile. The urgent need of exiles to hear this promise anew and to hear David insisting on its fulfillment may be the shaping influence of David's prayer as we now

234. Ibid., 259. See also the discussion in Walter Brueggemann, *David's Truth in Israel's Imagination and Memory* (Philadelphia: Fortress, 1985) 77-81.

235. See the analysis of this prayer in Patrick D. Miller, *They Cried to the Lord: The Form and Theology of Biblical Prayer* (Minneapolis: Fortress, 1994) 345-46.

236. A few scholars have seen the entire prayer as a deuteronomistic composition, e.g., Frank M. Cross, *Canaanite Myth and Hebrew Epic* (Cambridge, Mass.: Harvard University Press, 1973) 254. Most have seen the Dtr influence only in 7:22-26, e.g., T. N. D. Mettinger, *King and Messiah: The Civil and Sacral Legitimation of the Israelite Kings,* ConBOT 8 (Lund: CWK Gleerup, 1976) 51.

read it. A supporting piece of evidence might be found in the unusual use of the divine designation "Lord GOD," which is never used elsewhere in the books of Samuel but is characteristically used by the exilic prophet Ezekiel (217 times).

7:18-21. David begins with a formula typically used for polite deference to a superior, "Who am I . . . ?" and continues in this deferential tone (v. 18). He refers to himself as servant (vv. 19-21) and addresses God four times as "Lord GOD" (vv. 18-20). David speaks of himself and the matter of his house (dynasty) as being "small" in God's eyes (v. 19; cf. also this usage in Solomon's prayer, 1 Kgs 3:7). All that has happened to bring David this far (v. 18) and to bestow whatever "greatness" (v. 21) David possesses is credited to the "word" and to the "will" of God (NIV; the NRSV uses "promise" and "heart" of God).

In its language, the opening to David's prayer bespeaks humility before God. Yet, the formal tone is quite different from the previous occasions when David "inquired" of the Lord. Gone is the sense of intimate piety, and it seems replaced by more florid, court language. Has this public prayer been shaped by reasons of state rather than by habits of faith? It is hard to say, but the prayer of David the king seems different from the prayer of David the shepherd/warrior/fugitive.

7:22-24. This section is given over entirely to praise of God. The stress is on the incomparability of God (v. 22), as evidenced in graciousness toward Israel (v. 23). This makes Israel unique among the nations (v. 23a). The entire salvation history of Israel is suggested in the phrases of v. 23. It is here that most scholars find language that evidences the deuteronomistic style (e.g., the stress on the Lord's "name," v. 23).

Verse 24 links God to Israel in a version of the well-known covenant formula, "I will be their God and they will be my people" (Exod 6:7; Lev 26:12; Ezek 11:20; 37:27; Hos 2:23). Interestingly, the status of God's people will last "forever" (v. 24b). The conditional covenant of Sinai relating God and people is now altered by the unconditional language of the Davidic dynastic promise (v. 16). Praise of God has been inescapably linked to the future of the Davidic regime as implied in the commitment to the people "forever." This tie to Davidic promise is made explicit in the final section of the prayer.

7:25-29. The climactic section of David's prayer is signaled by the use of the Hebrew word ועתה (wĕ ʿattâ), "and now." This adverb is used, especially in covenantal formulations, to move from past remembrance to present action and is usually used by a stronger party to demand an action from a lesser party.[237] David uses this adverb three times in this section (vv. 25, 28, 29), giving his prayer an exceptionally audacious tone. David is now demanding fidelity from God.

Verse 25 moves directly to audacious petition. After reminding God of the word already spoken (i.e., Nathan's oracle), David petitions God to "confirm it forever; do as you have promised." The term "forever" (עולם ʿôlām), applied to the people in covenant with God (v. 24), is now applied to dynastic promise to David. David's prayer then immediately links this to the glorification of God's name, which will be "forever" (v. 26a), but not in its own right. The magnification of God's name is tied to Israel and the house of David (v. 26b). David demands God's fidelity to an everlasting link of God's name, Israel, and the house of David. Brueggemann writes:

David has gone very far in . . . taking the initiative for the relation with God. That is exactly what we expect from state truth, with reference to God. Its program is to make God a responsive patron. In 7:26 we have a shrewd piece of dynastic self-service. It is promised that Yahweh's name will be magnified . . . but he has now linked it to the dynastic claim. He has fixed it so that Yahweh cannot be magnified unless David is magnified as well. Thus David is linked to Yahweh. And along the way, Israel is identified with David.[238]

In v. 27, David recalls and restates the central promise of the dynastic oracle, "I will build you a house [dynasty]" (cf. v. 11b, where the verb is "make"). He claims that it is the remembrance of that promise that has given him the courage to pray so boldly. With two additional phrases introduced by wĕ ʿattâ, David continues in this bold vein. In v. 28, David acknowledges that "God is God" and that God's words are true, but he then links God's divine truth to the promise of this "good thing" to David. David audaciously suggests that the veracity of God's word is at stake. In v.

237. See James Muilenburg, "The Form and Structure of the Covenantal Formulations," *VT* 9 (1959) 347-65, for a discussion of this adverb in covenantal texts.
238. Brueggemann, *David's Truth in Israel's Imagination and Memory*, 80.

29, David further petitions for a blessing. One would think that the promise of dynasty was enough, but the point here seems to be the continuity of the promise. The word "forever" is used twice, and the blessing asked for—demanded—is but a further way of stating the "good thing" that has been done for David in the promise of dynasty. This verse is a not-too-subtle reminder to God that this promise was to be everlasting. Significantly, the prayer ends on the word "forever." The prayer that began in deference ends with unmitigated demand.

Throughout his story, David has prayed. Perhaps it is to be expected that his prayers as shepherd and as warrior would be different from his prayers as king. He must now lead a nation's prayers and represent a people's interests. The language is now formal, public language. The interests are in a dynastic future and not a personal future. But the object to which prayer is directed is still an acknowledged sovereign God. David boldly claims the promise; he will later also experience the accountability that comes with that promise (cf. 7:14; 12:1-14).

REFLECTIONS

It is doubtful that David's prayer would ever be used as an Old Testament reading alongside the Lord's prayer. It is not the model we desire in answer to the disciples' request, "Lord, teach us to pray" (Luke 11:1). Although David's prayer acknowledges divine sovereignty, it also boldly makes claims on the sovereign God. Its tone is not that of disinterested praise or acknowledgment of need before God. The interests of state ideology are not far beneath the surface.

Yet, there is a quality to David's prayer, and to Hebrew prayer in general, that has much to teach us. Our tendency in prayer is to seek both language and tone that we imagine acceptable before God. By contrast, Hebrew prayer brings before God the entire gamut of human experience and the moods appropriate to them. The laments of the psalter are often cited in this regard. Anger, resentment, desire for vengeance, frustration with God's seeming inattention—a whole range of human feeling and experience seldom expressed in our prayer (esp. public prayer) finds expression in Hebrew prayer. God does not require a sanitized version of our most passionate struggles.

The boldness of David's prayer is in keeping with this quality of Hebrew prayer. David unabashedly expresses his claim on God's fidelity to the promise given to his dynasty. If this is tainted by ideological state interests, God must also know that these political interests are of concern to David. They are often of concern to us, but they seldom are offered to God in prayer. David, while boldly making his claims, constantly acknowledges divine sovereignty and freedom. To lay our claims before God is not to imagine that we actually control God.

To pray on behalf of our political self-interest is, of course, dangerous prayer. We run the risk of thinking we can domesticate God in our own interests. We may forget to lay such prayer alongside acknowledgment of divine sovereignty and thereby render prayer a mere instrument of public propaganda. This sometimes happens in the cynical uses of religious language and symbols that political candidates imagine will win votes.

But to pray on behalf of our political self-interest, while dangerous, is also necessary lest we submit only a portion of our humanity to the sovereignty of God's will in the conscious act of prayer. There is a need to pray about our political arrangements lest we think final authority lies in such arrangements. The act of prayer itself is a recognition of God's interests, which extend beyond our own self-interest. God is capable of judging the heart by which such prayers are offered and of responding to the humility or cynicism found there. It may ultimately be more dangerous to pray only the "safe" prayers on what we imagine are the "acceptable" topics in the "appropriate" moods. Such prayers are ultimately a failure of trust in the comprehensive freedom and sovereignty of God.

2 Samuel 8:1-14, David's Victories

NIV

8 In the course of time, David defeated the Philistines and subdued them, and he took Metheg Ammah from the control of the Philistines.

²David also defeated the Moabites. He made them lie down on the ground and measured them off with a length of cord. Every two lengths of them were put to death, and the third length was allowed to live. So the Moabites became subject to David and brought tribute.

³Moreover, David fought Hadadezer son of Rehob, king of Zobah, when he went to restore his control along the Euphrates River. ⁴David captured a thousand of his chariots, seven thousand charioteers[a] and twenty thousand foot soldiers. He hamstrung all but a hundred of the chariot horses.

⁵When the Arameans of Damascus came to help Hadadezer king of Zobah, David struck down twenty-two thousand of them. ⁶He put garrisons in the Aramean kingdom of Damascus, and the Arameans became subject to him and brought tribute. The LORD gave David victory wherever he went.

⁷David took the gold shields that belonged to the officers of Hadadezer and brought them to Jerusalem. ⁸From Tebah[b] and Berothai, towns that belonged to Hadadezer, King David took a great quantity of bronze.

⁹When Tou[c] king of Hamath heard that David had defeated the entire army of Hadadezer, ¹⁰he sent his son Joram[d] to King David to greet him and congratulate him on his victory in battle over Hadadezer, who had been at war with Tou. Joram brought with him articles of silver and gold and bronze.

¹¹King David dedicated these articles to the LORD, as he had done with the silver and gold from all the nations he had subdued: ¹²Edom[e] and Moab, the Ammonites and the Philistines, and Amalek. He also dedicated the plunder taken from Hadadezer son of Rehob, king of Zobah.

¹³And David became famous after he returned

---

a4 Septuagint (see also Dead Sea Scrolls and 1 Chron. 18:4); Masoretic Text *captured seventeen hundred of his charioteers*   b8 See some Septuagint manuscripts (see also 1 Chron. 18:8); Hebrew *Betah.*   c9 Hebrew *Toi,* a variant of *Tou;* also in verse 10   d10 A variant of *Hadoram*   e12 Some Hebrew manuscripts, Septuagint and Syriac (see also 1 Chron. 18:11); most Hebrew manuscripts *Aram*

NRSV

8 Some time afterward, David attacked the Philistines and subdued them; David took Metheg-ammah out of the hand of the Philistines.

2He also defeated the Moabites and, making them lie down on the ground, measured them off with a cord; he measured two lengths of cord for those who were to be put to death, and one length[a] for those who were to be spared. And the Moabites became servants to David and brought tribute.

3David also struck down King Hadadezer son of Rehob of Zobah, as he went to restore his monument[b] at the river Euphrates. 4David took from him one thousand seven hundred horsemen, and twenty thousand foot soldiers. David hamstrung all the chariot horses, but left enough for a hundred chariots. 5When the Arameans of Damascus came to help King Hadadezer of Zobah, David killed twenty-two thousand men of the Arameans. 6Then David put garrisons among the Arameans of Damascus; and the Arameans became servants to David and brought tribute. The LORD gave victory to David wherever he went. 7David took the gold shields that were carried by the servants of Hadadezer, and brought them to Jerusalem. 8From Betah and from Berothai, towns of Hadadezer, King David took a great amount of bronze.

9When King Toi of Hamath heard that David had defeated the whole army of Hadadezer, 10Toi sent his son Joram to King David, to greet him and to congratulate him because he had fought against Hadadezer and defeated him. Now Hadadezer had often been at war with Toi. Joram brought with him articles of silver, gold, and bronze; 11these also King David dedicated to the LORD, together with the silver and gold that he dedicated from all the nations he subdued, 12from Edom, Moab, the Ammonites, the Philistines, Amalek, and from the spoil of King Hadadezer son of Rehob of Zobah.

13David won a name for himself. When he returned, he killed eighteen thousand Edomites[c] in the Valley of Salt. 14He put garrisons in Edom;

---

a Heb *one full length*   b Compare 1 Sam 15.12 and 2 Sam 18.18
c Gk: Heb *returned from striking down eighteen thousand Arameans*

NIV	NRSV
from striking down eighteen thousand Edomites[a] in the Valley of Salt.	throughout all Edom he put garrisons, and all the Edomites became David's servants. And the LORD gave victory to David wherever he went.
14He put garrisons throughout Edom, and all the Edomites became subject to David. The LORD gave David victory wherever he went.	

a13 A few Hebrew manuscripts, Septuagint and Syriac (see also 1 Chron. 18:12); most Hebrew manuscripts *Aram* (that is, Arameans)

COMMENTARY

This section records the military triumphs of David and the territorial expansion of his kingdom. The style is annalistic rather than that of storytelling. The chapter seems to be a collection of archival notices. Each segment records a people conquered or brought into the sphere of Davidic influence. This chapter records the movement from small kingdom to small empire.

The order of reporting in the chapter should not be taken as a chronological history. The record presents victories and annexations of territory stretching over many years during David's reign. This section parallels the section on David's victories over the Philistines in 2 Sam 5:17-25. The purpose of David's military exploits has shifted from defense to empire building. This is in keeping with the symmetrical structure Flanagan has detected for 5:11–8:18 as David's story moves from older, tribal connections to emerging patterns of kingdom and empire[239] (see the Overview to 5:11–8:18). Because David's victories over the Philistines occupy an earlier position in this structure, there is only a very brief mention of Philistine victory here (v. 1).

The key theological theme in this chapter is sounded in vv. 6b and 14b, where it is noted that "the LORD gave victory to David wherever he went." There is little doubt that the intention of the historian[240] is to picture the growth of a small Israelite empire by the subjugation of neighboring

territories as evidence of divine favor toward David. By itself this would be a theme in continuity with the "God was with him" theme of the history of David's rise. However, the theological statement of vv. 6b and 14b stands in some tension with the tendency of empires to trust in human power. Verse 13a begins by stating that "David won a name for *himself*," and almost every segment of the chapter records David's prowess, and often his cruelty, as a conqueror. The reader arrives at the end of the chapter with an overall impression of reliance on human power in empire building in spite of the attributions of David's victories to the Lord in vv. 6b, 14b. This tension between divine power and human power arrangements will frequently occupy our attention in the episodes that lie ahead in David's story.

8:1-2. The chapter begins with brief notices of victories over the Philistines and the Moabites. David's victory over the Philistines has already been recorded in 5:17-25, and for that reason probably receives little attention here. This may be an additional victory not specifically mentioned earlier. We have little idea of the proper chronology for the several Philistine battles mentioned here and in chap. 5. This particular battle may be mentioned because it involves annexation of territory. The NRSV and the NIV treat "Metheg-ammah" as a place name, but such a place is unknown to us otherwise. The parallel text in 1 Chr 18:1 reads, "Gath and its surrounding villages."

Verse 2 records a victory over Moab, although no reason is given for hostilities with this neighboring kingdom. Indeed, the king of Moab had given refuge to David's family while he was a fugitive from Saul (1 Sam 22:3-4), and later tradition claims that David's great-grandmother was

239. James W. Flanagan, "Social Transformation and Ritual in 2 Samuel 6," in *The Word of the Lord Shall Go Forth: Festschrift for D. N. Freedman,* ed. C. L. Meyers and M. O'Connor (Winona Lake, Ind.: Eisenbrauns, 1983).

240. P. Kyle McCarter, *II Samuel,* AB 9 (Garden City, N.Y.: Doubleday, 1984) 251, believes the deuteronomistic historian is responsible for compiling this section from available archival material. There is little by way of language that indicates deuteronomistic composition, so this conclusion is possible but unlikely.

the Moabite woman Ruth (Ruth 4:21-22). This makes David's harsh treatment of Moabite captives even more surprising. The method of measuring with a cord to determine those to be singled out for mass execution is particularly gruesome and is not attested elsewhere. The writer of 1 Chr 18:2 omits the matter altogether, and the Greek text changes the ratio to half and half for survivors and those executed. The crucial matter for the interests of this chapter is that Moab becomes a vassal state in a growing Davidic empire.

8:3-8. These verses give a more detailed report of a campaign against Aramean contingents in Syria. David's primary adversary is King Hadadezer of Rehob of Zobah (v. 3). Zobah is an Aramean territory east of the Anti-Lebanon mountain range and north of Damascus. We know of a Beth-rehob near the southern slopes of Mt. Hermon, and this may have been Hadadezer's home. David seems to have attacked Hadadezer's territory when he was away to the north near the Euphrates River (v. 3*b*). The battle probably widened into a general Aramean conflict, since the Arameans of Damascus come to the aid of Hadadezer (v. 5) and since David's final victory is over this entire Aramean territory (v. 6). Damascus, a vassal or ally state of Zobah at this point, will rise to become the dominant Aramean capital by late in Solomon's reign (1 Kgs 11:23-25).

It is uncertain what the relationship is between this report and the account of campaigns against the Arameans in 10:6-19. Since these accounts also involve Hadadezer and end in Aramean defeat and subjugation, most interpreters would regard the two passages as reports drawn from the same Davidic campaign against the Arameans. Whether these reflect different battles and events in such a campaign or are variant accounts of the same battles is not clear (see Commentary on 10:1-19).

David's victory is decisive, and significant attention is given to the plunder. We are told of large numbers of horses and men captured by David (v. 4). He keeps only 100 chariots and hamstrings the remaining 1,600 horses. He apparently could not incorporate more into his own forces

and refused to leave them usable by his enemy. Verse 5*b* records that 22,000 Aramean fighting men have been killed by David's forces. Gold shields belonging to Hadadezer are carried triumphally to Jerusalem (v. 7), and great quantities of bronze are taken (v. 8), perhaps as part of the tribute exacted in v. 6. The chronicler claims that this bronze was used by Solomon to fashion ritual objects for the Temple on Mt. Zion (1 Chr 18:8).

The tone of this account is harsh. Again no explicit motive for war with the Arameans is mentioned. The motivation seems to be territorial expansion of David's realm (v. 6). The note attributing David's victories to the Lord's hand (v. 6*b*) seems incongruous when it appears in the midst of this account of territorial conquest and plunder.

8:9-12. Hamath was a neo-Hittite city-state to the north of Zobah, and King Toi of this city was delighted with David's victory over Hadadezer, with whom he had often been at war (vv. 9-10). King Toi sends his son Joram with congratulations and tribute of gold, silver, and bronze to David (v. 10). David dedicates this tribute to the Lord, along with the booty he took in his other campaigns (v. 11). Verse 12 goes on to list David's conquests from which the dedicated plunder has come. In addition to the campaigns mentioned in this chapter, this summary mentions Edom, the Ammonites, and Amalek. The verb used for David's action toward these people is "subdue" (כבשׁ *kābaš*), indicating conquest and subjugation. None of the campaigns reported in this chapter seem to have been a response to provocation.

8:13-14. These verses contain two concluding formulae that stand in tension with each other and a brief note on the subjugation of Edom. The latter appears as an added note, almost an afterthought to the previous notices. It records a great slaughter of Edomites (18,000, v. 13) and the incorporation of Edom into David's growing empire as a vassal state (v. 14).

The two formulae attribute David's success on the one hand to the Lord (v. 14*b*, a repeat of v. 6*b*), and on the other hand to David's own considerable powers (v. 13*a*, "David won a name for *himself*"). Empire as a testimony to human power stands in tension with kingdom as the gift of God.

REFLECTIONS

The theological issue of this chapter lies in the very tension with which it ends. Is David's success as an empire builder a testimony to his own achievement or to the grace of God? For the moment, these attributions stand side by side, but it is clear that the successes of power raise the temptation to imagine such power to be autonomous. The David who inquired of the Lord at almost every turn in the stories of his rise to kingship does not ask for divine guidance in these conquests. He simply "defeats," "takes," "kills," "strikes down," and "subdues." These are the verbs of autonomous power. When it is reported that the Lord gave him victory, it almost seems to be a divine indulgence of David's imagined autonomy. A dangerous tension has been established nonetheless. That tension is resolved in divine judgment on David in 2 Samuel 12, when the illusion of autonomous power leads to injustice and violence.

We should be disturbed by the unjustified exercise of power for ideological political purposes here. There are no suggested motives for David's campaigns beyond expansion of his own political power and influence. And the means for achieving this expansion of power are violent. The word for "victory" in 8:6b, 14b is more frequently translated as "salvation," "deliverance," or "liberation." It is a sobering reminder that it is all too easy to justify our own ideological interests as divinely sanctioned. God's salvation becomes our victory. The text here walks a thin line. God may, indeed, be at work in these matters of the kingdom, but the tendency of human power to act as if it were autonomous stands side by side with the claim of divine activity.

In our own successes, we are much more prone to take credit for ourselves, our congregation, or our nation than to recognize the enabling activity of God. When we fail to give this recognition, the methods by which we pursue success are even more likely to do violence in some way to others as the price of our accomplishments. Power brings with it the dangerous illusion of autonomy. The temptation is then to invoke the name of God only after the fact as a blessing on what we have done for our own purposes. Nevertheless, persons and communities of faith cannot avoid the exercise of power in the public arena, for to do so would be a failure of trust that God is at work in those arenas. The alternative is the constant prayerful discernment of the divine will in the very processes of making decisions in the exercise of power. Early in his career, David modeled such a constancy of prayer and seeking of the divine will. Here, David at the height of his career is in danger of forgetting this process. To preach this chapter is to be warned of the danger that results when God is acknowledged only as an afterthought. The next step is to forget God altogether and risk the violent consequences of our own unchecked temptations to autonomous power.

2 Samuel 8:15-18, The Officers of David's Court

NIV

[15]David reigned over all Israel, doing what was just and right for all his people. [16]Joab son of Zeruiah was over the army; Jehoshaphat son of Ahilud was recorder; [17]Zadok son of Ahitub and Ahimelech son of Abiathar were priests; Seraiah was secretary; [18]Benaiah son of Jehoiada was over the Kerethites and Pelethites; and David's sons were royal advisers.[a]

[a]18 Or were priests

NRSV

[15]So David reigned over all Israel; and David administered justice and equity to all his people. [16]Joab son of Ahilud was over the army; Jehoshaphat son of Ahilud was recorder; [17]Zadok son of Ahitub and Ahimelech son of Abiathar were priests; Seraiah was secretary; [18]Benaiah son of Jehoiada was over[a] the Cherethites and the Pelethites; and David's sons were priests.

[a] Syr Tg Vg 20.23; 1 Chr 18.17: Heb lacks was over

COMMENTARY

This small section is generally regarded as a conclusion to the material on the consolidation of David's kingdom before the start of the succession narrative in chap. 9 (see Introduction). It offers a summarizing statement of David's rule (v. 15) and a listing of his most important officials (vv. 16-18). The section on David as king began with a listing of David's family (5:13-16), in keeping with tribal concern for kinship. But with the kingdom secure, a dynastic promise given, and an empire begun, the stress shifts from family to officers of the court. Loyalties to family and tribe must give way to loyalties to king and kingdom.

8:15. As David's reign over all Israel is affirmed (v. 15*a*) there is a significant acknowledgment of "justice and equity" at the heart of David's rule, and this is for the sake of "all his people." Things have changed in Israel. Many tribal patterns have been replaced by the emerging power arrangements of the kingdom. Yet, this text suggests that centrally important covenant commitments have not been left behind, but have been transferred to new royal structures. David, as king, takes up the mantle of administrator of covenant justice. David has now reached the pinnacle of his power, and yet he is presented as remaining aware of covenant obligation and the welfare of all Israel. This perspective is in keeping with portraits elsewhere of the ideal king (Ps 89:14; Isa 9:7; Jer 22:3; 23:5). It will remain to be seen whether David will keep these commitments in view as he settles into a position of power and influence heretofore unknown in Israel.

8:16-18. Here we get a closer look at the organization of the royal bureaucracy. Under David, Israel is taking on the shape of kingdoms known elsewhere in the region. David is consolidating and organizing royal power in ways that will run the risk of the very dangers against which Samuel warned (1 Sam 8:11-18). He places pairs of officials in control of military, economic, and religious life. A similar list appears in 2 Sam 20:23-26 with the addition of Ira, the Jairite, a priest, and Adoniram as supervisor of the labor details.

Joab is to command the army, and Benaiah is in charge of mercenary forces (Cherethites and Pelethites, v. 18*b*). Both of these commands represent something new in Israel: a standing professional army and the use of mercenary forces. Reliance on tribal levies for defense is a thing of the past, and military power now centers its loyalty on the king, and not on the tribe. The identity of the two mercenary groups cannot be determined with certainty. The Cherethites have often been identified as Cretans and the Pelethites as a sub-group of the Philistines. They may be groups who, like the Philistines, came to the area as part of the Sea People's invasion, and they seem to have been recruited into the force David assembled around himself while at Ziklag (see the reference to "the Negeb of the Cherethites" in 1 Sam 30:14).[241]

Jehoshaphat, who is listed as "recorder," should be considered the chief civil servant in charge of state records and documents (v. 16*b*). Among the functions of such records would be provision of the basis for taxation and conscription. Seraiah (v. 17*b*), listed as "secretary," was more than just a scribe but should probably be seen as a "secretary of state" (the rendering used in the NEB) and an adviser to David.[242]

In the listing of priests under David, the names of Ahimelech and Abiathar have probably become reversed (v. 17*a*). The parallel list in 20:25 lists Abiathar (not Ahimelech) as David's priest, and 1 Sam 22:20; 23:6; 30:7 identify Abiathar's father as Ahimelech.[243] Zadok and Abiathar share the office of high priest under David until Abiathar is banished by Solomon after David's death (1 Kgs 2:35). Abiathar was the only survivor of Saul's massacre of the priests of Nob and joined David's entourage at that time (1 Sam 22:6-23). The final reference to David's sons as priests is curious (v. 18*b*). This may mean that the priesthood was not yet hereditary or was limited to those of Levite descent. The chronicler, concerned with levitical matters, seems to have changed the designation to make David's sons only "high officials" (1 Chr 18:17). David's sons do not seem to be designated as priests in the larger public role given to Zadok and Abiathar. They may have functioned as priests in the royal household—i.e., chaplains within the royal family.

241. See the fuller discussion of these groupings in P. Kyle McCarter, *II Samuel*, AB 9 (Garden City, N.Y.: Doubleday, 1984) 256.

242. See T. N. D. Mettinger, *Solomonic State Officials*, ConBOT 5 (Lund: CWK Gleerup, 1971) 52-62, for a full discussion of officials during the time of David.

243. See McCarter's discussion of the textual problems and their solution, *II Samuel*, 253-55.

REFLECTIONS

The ideals of covenant loyalty stand side by side with the organization of state bureaucracy. Therein lies both the challenge and the danger for David and for all who would seek to relate faith to public power. David may actualize the dangers against which Samuel warned (1 Sam 8:11-18); the mechanisms for royal "taking" are all in place. Or David may remain committed to the covenant God, who has been "with him" to this point. These are the perennial choices of people who would not compartmentalize religious faith away from the public arena. One of the lessons to be learned from the books of Samuel is that God is not removed from the arenas of public political power. God cannot be served in a privatized fashion. But the juxtaposition of covenant values and bureaucratic power arrangements implies a genuine risk. David will fall victim to the temptations of autonomous power in his taking of Bathsheba and his murder of Uriah (2 Samuel 11). So, too, has our own history known such abuses of power, from the taking of Native American land to the violent defense of racial segregation to the arrogance of Watergate. But while the nearness of covenant to power may tempt David and us to the sins of power, the nearness of power to covenant allows for the judgment and redemption of power. Such judgment and redemption will also be a part of David's story, because commitment to covenant loyalty allows access to the voice of the prophet Nathan (2 Samuel 12). Such judgment and redemption will be possible for us only to the degree that our bureaucratic arrangements allow access to covenantal voices within the arrangements of power.

2 SAMUEL 9:1–20:26, DAVID'S FAMILY AND DAVID'S THRONE

OVERVIEW

Since the work of Leonhard Rost, most scholars have assumed that 2 Sam 9:1–20:26 and 1 Kgs 1:1–2:46 are a unified narrative incorporated into the Deuteronomistic History.[244] Rost, and most scholars since him, called this piece the "succession narrative," because, he claimed, the central concern of these texts was to answer the question of 1 Kgs 1:20, 27: "Who should sit on the throne of my lord the king after him?" This question of succession to the throne of David is resolved by the accession of Solomon and the purging of his opponents (1 Kings 1–2). Earlier portions of the story remove Amnon (2 Samuel 13) and Absalom (2 Samuel 14–19) as potential heirs to the throne and make clear that there will be no descendants

of Saul to claim the throne (2 Samuel 9). The calamitous family events that surround this drama of succession are given theological justification by the story of David's sin and judgment in the matter of Bathsheba and Uriah (2 Samuel 11–12).

Following Rost, great stress has been placed on the unusual artistic quality of the succession narrative. Its rich use of narrative detail and its full development of character, especially the intimate portraits of personal emotions and motivations, have been widely praised. Von Rad has persuasively argued that the succession narrative represents the advent of a new form of history writing in ancient Israel that elevates and celebrates human reality by demonstrating "an emancipated spirituality, modernized and freed from cultus."[245]

244. The English translation of Leonhard Rost's 1926 work is available as *The Succession to the Throne of David,* trans. M. D. Rutter and D. M. Gunn, JSOTSup (Sheffield: Almond, 1982). See A. A. Anderson, *2 Samuel,* WBC 11 (Waco: Word, 1989) xxvi-xxviii, for a discussion of earlier work on which Rost's influential hypothesis was based.

245. Gerhard von Rad, "The Beginnings of Historical Writing in Ancient Israel," in *The Problem of the Hexateuch and Other Essays,* trans. E. W. Trueman Dicken (New York: McGraw-Hill, 1966; orig. German edition, 1944) 204.

Although there has been general agreement on the conclusion of the succession narrative with 1 Kgs 2:46*b,* "So the kingdom was established in the hand of Solomon," there has been less agreement about its beginning.[246] Rost suggested that it commenced in 2 Samuel 9, but he recognized earlier elements that might be a part of the succession theme (e.g., 2 Sam 6:23). Other suggestions have been made, but without an emerging consensus. The proposed beginning in 2 Samuel 9 does seem abrupt. The story of Gibeonite revenge on the house of Saul, which now appears as an appendix in 2 Samuel 21, may belong with the story of David's hospitality to the remaining Saulide survivor (2 Samuel 9). Still, although the beginning is difficult to determine, most scholars continue to view the so-called succession narrative as one of three already existing compositions incorporated by the deuteronomist into his larger history work: ark narrative (1 Samuel 4–6 [some include 2 Samuel 6]); history of David's rise (1 Sam 16:1–2 Sam 5:10); succession narrative (2 Samuel 9–20; 1 Kings 1–2).

Although Rost's hypothesis has proven very influential, recent challenges have been raised to fundamental aspects of his view. First, the question has been raised as to whether succession to the throne is really the central theme of this entire block of narrative. Gunn suggests that the focus of this narrative is not on legitimizing Solomon for the throne. Rather, the focus is on "David's fortunes through accession, rebellion and succession."[247] McCarter would agree with Gunn that succession is a central concern only for the final portion of the narrative (1 Kings 1–2).[248] He argues that the so-called succession narrative is really a series of independent thematic pieces (e.g., David's treatment of the surviving sons of Saul; David's sin with Bathsheba; Amnon's rape of Tamar; Absalom's rebellion) that are organized as a more personal history of David's family and fortunes in the later years of his reign and are related to succession only by the addition of 1 Kings 1–2.

Gunn and McCarter are only representative of numerous recent challenges to Rost's hypothesis.

Questions have also been raised about the narrative in 2 Samuel 9–20 and 1 Kings 1–2 as the product of a superior artistic hand separate from the rest of 1 and 2 Samuel. Robert Alter has asserted that "the evidence for a unified imaginative conception of the whole David story seems to me to be persuasive."[249] Robert Polzin has subjected the entire David story to close analysis as part of his argument that David's story, as well as the whole of the Deuteronomistic History, stems from a single author.[250] Both represent a growing number of voices arguing that changes in style or emphasis in this portion of David's story constitute an intentional artistic strategy rather than evidence of a separate narrative source. Most scholars, however, continue to discern some stylistic differences between the history of David's rise and the succession narrative and find the episodes devoted to David's actions as king (2 Sam 5:11–8:18) even more distinct. They would see the present shape of 2 Samuel as the product of a gifted editor using multiple sources rather than the product of a single authorial hand.[251]

A number of recent interpretations of David's story have focused on the character of David rather than on the literary history of the text. Seen from this perspective, there seems to be a sharp division in David's story, with the dividing point coming in the Bathsheba/Uriah episode (2 Samuel 11–12). R. A. Carlson has argued that stories prior to this account of David's sin show David as the recipient of blessing. From that point onward, however, we read the story of David under a curse. The David we see under blessing is confident, bold, decisive, and energetic. David under curse appears tentative, anxious, inactive, and anguished.[252] Alter and Brueggemann have observed a similar shift in the narrative portrait of David, but they have characterized this as a shift from focus on David's public life to his private

246. See Anderson, *2 Samuel,* xxv-xxxvi, for a survey of critical views on the character and limits of the succession narrative.

247. D. M. Gunn, *The Story of King David: Genre and Interpretation,* JSOTSup 6 (Sheffield: JSOT, 1978) 14.

248. McCarter, *II Samuel,* 9-16. See also Peter Ackroyd, "The Succession Narrative (So-called)," *Int.* 35 (1981) 383-96.

249. Robert Alter, *The Art of Biblical Narrative* (New York: Basic Books, 1981) 119.

250. Robert Polzin, *David and the Deuteronomist: A Literary Study of the Deuteronomic History,* Part Three: *2 Samuel* (Bloomington: Indiana University Press, 1993) esp. 221n. 1.

251. See McCarter, *II Samuel,* 4-16, for a discussion of major hypotheses on the literary structure and history of this material.

252. R. A. Carlson, *David, the Chosen King: A Traditio-Historical Approach to the Second Book of Samuel* (Uppsala: Almqvist and Wiksell, 1964).

life. The former is a story of unparalleled success, but the latter is filled with considerable ambiguity and anguish.

One of the most striking aspects of the entire David story is that until his career reaches its crucial breaking point with his murder-by-proxy of Uriah after his adultery with Bathsheba, almost all his speeches are in public situations and can be read as politically motivated. It is only after the death of the child born of his union with Bathsheba that the personal voice of a shaken David begins to emerge.[253]

[In] the "Rise of David," the narrative focuses exclusively and with severe discipline only upon the *public* David, screening out any probe of David's person, attitude, or motive.... The incredible miscalculation (sin?) with Uriah and Bathsheba opens David, according to the narrator, to the awareness of ambiguity of a moral kind.... And from that shattering moment, the narrator, the community around the story, and perhaps David, are permitted to enter a new world of personal interiority with all its problematic of anguish, ambiguity, ambition, and ambivalence. The public David continues to function, but the public David is no longer able or permitted to override, censor, and ignore the personal David. Now the two are placed in a deep and unresolvable tension.[254]

In 2 Samuel 9–20 and 1 Kings 1–2, the focus is on David the man, not on David the king. As readers of this segment of David's story, we will be forced to ponder the meaning of our humanity in the face of power. These narratives are not devoid of ideological interests, but reflection on political power must stand side by side with reflection on human vulnerability. Such stories of humanness in the midst of power have implications for our understandings of kingdom and of our own humanity.[255]

If a shift in the presentation of David takes place in 2 Samuel 9–20 and 1 Kings 1–2, this is also true for the depiction of God's role in this

story. Gerhard von Rad, in a classic treatment of this narrative, has argued that God is more hidden in these stories than in previous narratives.[256] This feature allows a greater role for and emphasis on human freedom,[257] but this less overtly visible God has not surrendered the historical process to human autonomy. Although David models freedom in all its possibilities and temptations, the narrative makes clear that God has not let go of David and is still acting to shape the course of Israel's future through David. Von Rad has noted three crucial texts in which God's continued engagement with David's story becomes visible: 2 Sam 11:27; 12:24-25; and 17:14. These texts will receive special attention in the subsequent commentary.[258] In addition to these references to explicit divine involvement, Brueggemann has called attention to two texts in which David expresses faith and trust in God's continued engagement with his life and Israel's future: 2 Sam 15:24-29 and 16:12.[259] These, likewise, will receive special attention.

Beginning with chapter 9 and ending with chapter 20, each episode is part of a continuous narrative. The logical conclusion of this narrative comes in 1 Kings 1–2 with the death of David and the accession of Solomon, but these chapters obviously lie beyond the scope of our commentary on the books of Samuel. Chapters 21–24 are a diverse collection of materials that do not stand in narrative sequence with chaps. 9–20. They are usually referred to as appendixes to the books of Samuel. Questions pertaining to the arrangement, placement, and purpose of these chapters will be taken up in the Overview to 2 Sam 21:1–24:25.

---

253. Alter, *The Art of Biblical Narrative,* 119.
254. Walter Brueggemann, *David's Truth in Israel's Imagination and Memory* (Philadelphia: Fortress, 1985) 42-43.
255. Indeed, Brueggemann has suggested that these stories of David's human vulnerability provide the clues for understanding the generalized reflections on created humanity found in the Yahwist narratives of Genesis 2–11. See Walter Brueggemann, "David and His Theologian," *CBQ* 30 (1968) 156-81.

256. Von Rad, "The Beginnings of Historical Writing in Ancient Israel."
257. See Walter Brueggemann, "The Trusted Creature," *CBQ* 31 (1969) 484-98, and "On Trust and Freedom: A Study of Faith in the Succession Narrative," *Int.* 26 (1972) 3-19.
258. Von Rad, "The Beginnings of Historical Writing in Ancient Israel," 198.
259. Brueggemann, *David's Truth in Israel's Imagination and Memory,* 53. Brueggemann also adds 1 Kings 2:2-4 to the three texts identified by von Rad as texts witnessing to God's continued involvement.

2 Samuel 9:1-13, David's Hospitality to Mephibosheth

NIV	NRSV
9 David asked, "Is there anyone still left of the house of Saul to whom I can show kindness for Jonathan's sake?"	**9** David asked, "Is there still anyone left of the house of Saul to whom I may show kindness for Jonathan's sake?" [2]Now there was a

NIV

²Now there was a servant of Saul's household named Ziba. They called him to appear before David, and the king said to him, "Are you Ziba?"

"Your servant," he replied.

³The king asked, "Is there no one still left of the house of Saul to whom I can show God's kindness?"

Ziba answered the king, "There is still a son of Jonathan; he is crippled in both feet."

⁴"Where is he?" the king asked.

Ziba answered, "He is at the house of Makir son of Ammiel in Lo Debar."

⁵So King David had him brought from Lo Debar, from the house of Makir son of Ammiel.

⁶When Mephibosheth son of Jonathan, the son of Saul, came to David, he bowed down to pay him honor.

David said, "Mephibosheth!"

"Your servant," he replied.

⁷"Don't be afraid," David said to him, "for I will surely show you kindness for the sake of your father Jonathan. I will restore to you all the land that belonged to your grandfather Saul, and you will always eat at my table."

⁸Mephibosheth bowed down and said, "What is your servant, that you should notice a dead dog like me?"

⁹Then the king summoned Ziba, Saul's servant, and said to him, "I have given your master's grandson everything that belonged to Saul and his family. ¹⁰You and your sons and your servants are to farm the land for him and bring in the crops, so that your master's grandson may be provided for. And Mephibosheth, grandson of your master, will always eat at my table." (Now Ziba had fifteen sons and twenty servants.)

¹¹Then Ziba said to the king, "Your servant will do whatever my lord the king commands his servant to do." So Mephibosheth ate at David's*ᵃ* table like one of the king's sons.

¹²Mephibosheth had a young son named Mica, and all the members of Ziba's household were servants of Mephibosheth. ¹³And Mephibosheth lived in Jerusalem, because he always ate at the king's table, and he was crippled in both feet.

ᵃ11 Septuagint; Hebrew my

NRSV

servant of the house of Saul whose name was Ziba, and he was summoned to David. The king said to him, "Are you Ziba?" And he said, "At your service!" ³The king said, "Is there anyone remaining of the house of Saul to whom I may show the kindness of God?" Ziba said to the king, "There remains a son of Jonathan; he is crippled in his feet." ⁴The king said to him, "Where is he?" Ziba said to the king, "He is in the house of Machir son of Ammiel, at Lo-debar." ⁵Then King David sent and brought him from the house of Machir son of Ammiel, at Lo-debar. ⁶Mephibosheth*ᵃ* son of Jonathan son of Saul came to David, and fell on his face and did obeisance. David said, "Mephibosheth!"*ᵃ* He answered, "I am your servant." ⁷David said to him, "Do not be afraid, for I will show you kindness for the sake of your father Jonathan; I will restore to you all the land of your grandfather Saul, and you yourself shall eat at my table always." ⁸He did obeisance and said, "What is your servant, that you should look upon a dead dog such as I?"

⁹Then the king summoned Saul's servant Ziba, and said to him, "All that belonged to Saul and to all his house I have given to your master's grandson. ¹⁰You and your sons and your servants shall till the land for him, and shall bring in the produce, so that your master's grandson may have food to eat; but your master's grandson Mephibosheth*ᵃ* shall always eat at my table." Now Ziba had fifteen sons and twenty servants. ¹¹Then Ziba said to the king, "According to all that my lord the king commands his servant, so your servant will do." Mephibosheth*ᵃ* ate at David's*ᵇ* table, like one of the king's sons. ¹²Mephibosheth*ᵃ* had a young son whose name was Mica. And all who lived in Ziba's house became Mephibosheth's*ᶜ* servants. ¹³Mephibosheth*ᵃ* lived in Jerusalem, for he always ate at the king's table. Now he was lame in both his feet.

ᵃ Or Merib-baal: See 4.4 note *ᵇ Gk: Heb my* *ᶜ Or Merib-baal's: See 4.4 note*

COMMENTARY

With his kingdom secure, David abruptly becomes concerned about his covenant with Jonathan, which required David to show loyalty to Jonathan's descendants (cf. 1 Sam 20:14-17, 42; 23:18; 24:21-22). David's fulfillment of this covenant obligation provides the theme for this chapter. Together with 2 Samuel 10, this passage portrays David as a man of loyalty and good faith in his personal and royal dealings. The term חסד (ḥesed) appears as David's intention in 9:1, 3, 7 and in 10:2.

David's dealings with Jonathan's surviving son, Mephibosheth, is foreshadowed by the brief account of the accident that left Mephibosheth lame (2 Sam 4:4). This episode is also related to later material—when Mephibosheth and the servant Ziba play important roles in the encounters that mark David's retreat from Jerusalem at the time of Absalom's rebellion (cf. 16:1-4; 19:24-31).

Many scholars believe that 2 Samuel 21 originally preceded 2 Samuel 9.[260] In the necessary chronological sequence of events the execution of the sons of Saul to revenge Saul's wrongdoing against the Gibeonites, which is the subject of chap. 21, must come prior to David's searching out of Mephibosheth as the sole survivor of the house of Saul. Although it is possible that chap. 21 has been displaced from its original literary context prior to chap. 9, there is no clear evidence for this point as its original placement. As we shall see, chap. 21 plays an important role in the structure of the appendixes to 2 Samuel 21–24.

Chapter 9 opens with David's question and then proceeds by means of three dialogues: David/Ziba (vv. 2-4); David/Mephibosheth (vv. 5-8); David/Ziba again (vv. 9-11a). Concluding comments in vv. 11b-13 make clear that David's intentions to provide hospitality to Jonathan's son were carried out.

9:1-4. David's question (v. 1) introduces the theme of the chapter: David's covenant with Jonathan. With his kingdom secure, David turns his attention to the fulfillment of the covenant he swore to Jonathan (1 Sam 20:14-17, 42). He intends to show ḥesed (the loyalty often associated with covenants; see the Commentary on 1

Samuel 20) to any who are still left from the house of Saul. The use of the word "still" implies that events have preceded this account that leave in doubt the question of survivors in the line of Saul. This doubt has led to the suggestion, mentioned above, that the account of the killing of seven sons of Saul to satisfy Gibeonite demands for vengeance (2 Sam 21:1-14) originally preceded 2 Samuel 9. Indeed, the sparing of Mephibosheth from these acts of revenge is mentioned explicitly there (21:7). But, even without the grim tale of 2 Samuel 21, there would be some doubt about the survival of Saul's line. Following Saul's own death (1 Samuel 31; 2 Samuel 1) David's kingship is established through events that include the killing of Saul's general, Abner, and the assassination of Saul's son Ishbosheth (2 Samuel 2–4).[261] These events, which mark the fall of any vestige of Saulide rule, no doubt signaled the confiscation of Saulide land holdings and the dispersal of the remaining family of Saul. When David announces his desire to show "loyalty" or "kindness" (חסד ḥesed) to the house of Saul in keeping with his commitment to Jonathan, one has reason to wonder about the sincerity of such a declaration.

Ziba is introduced as a servant of the house of Saul who is summoned by David and then offers David his service (v. 2). David has clearly sought Ziba out in his quest for surviving descendants of Saul, and he asks Ziba the same question he voiced earlier (v. 3). Ziba knows of a son of Jonathan and identifies him as being "crippled in his feet" (see 2 Sam 4:4); he is living in the household of Machir in Lo-debar, which is in the Transjordan (v. 4). This site is close to Mahanaim, where Ishbosheth located his capital, and to Jabesh-gilead, a city with special ties to the house of Saul (see 1 Sam 11:1-13; 31:11-13; 2 Sam 2:4b-7).

9:5-8. David sends for this son of Jonathan (v. 5), and only when he appears before David is he finally named, both by the narrator and by David (v. 6). The chronicler records his name as

---

260. See McCarter, *II Samuel*, 263.

261. David M. Gunn, *The Story of King David*, JSOTSup 6 (Sheffield: JSOT, 1978) 68, makes a strong case for the relationship of 2 Samuel 9 to the events narrated in 2 Samuel 2–4. This raises doubts about chap. 9 as the beginning of a new narrative and suggests a closer connection between the history of the rise of David and the succession narrative than usually argued.

Meribaal (1 Chr 8:34; 9:40), probably another instance where the deuteronomistic historian has replaced the element בעל (ba'al, "lord" or "master") in the name with the word בשת (bōšet, "shame") because of the association of the title ba'al with the name of the Canaanite deity Baal.[262]

There is a strong emphasis in this account on the difference in power between David and Mephibosheth (also with Ziba earlier). Mephibosheth falls on his face, does obeisance (the Hebrew word here is often translated as "worship" [שחה šāḥâ]), and refers to himself as David's servant (v. 6). Following David's gracious act toward him, Mephibosheth again does obeisance ("worships") and refers to himself not only as servant but self-deprecatingly as a "dead dog" as well (v. 8). The implication is that he is worthless compared to David. The result of this subservience by Mephibosheth is to highlight David's power and privilege and to make David's act of kindness toward Mephibosheth seem remarkably gracious. David addresses Mephibosheth with the classic formula of reassurance associated with salvation oracles, "Fear not!" (v. 7a). He then cites his covenant obligation to Jonathan, Mephibosheth's father, and restores the land of Saul to this grandson of Israel's first king. David further vows that Mephibosheth will henceforth eat at the king's table (v. 7). To sit at table with the king is a privilege that accords Mephibosheth status akin to the sons of the king (v. 11). Some have said that there is a political purpose to David's invitation to the royal table—namely, that he is placing the remaining heir of Saul where an eye can be kept on him.[263] This may be true, but such a motive is not made explicit in the text, and the narrator of the story clearly considers this an honor, and not house arrest (v. 11). The restoration of Saulide land to Mephibosheth implies that it had been confiscated, perhaps after the death

of Ishbaal, and was in David's possession as royal property until this time.

9:9-11a. Abruptly David again summons Ziba (v. 9a). Mephibosheth's departure is not mentioned. David reports his action in returning land to Mephibosheth (v. 9b) and commissions Ziba, his sons, and his servants to work and manage the land on behalf of this new master (v. 10a). Ziba's household is substantial: fifteen sons and twenty servants (v. 10b). It seems possible that Ziba, a former servant of Saul, was already managing this land as royal property for David and that he is here simply informed that he and the land have a new master in Mephibosheth. Ziba's management of the land is to provide Mephibosheth with food, even though the narrator reports again that he will eat at the king's table (v. 10b). Perhaps Mephibosheth, now as a royal landowner, must provide his share for the provisioning of the royal court. Ziba, deferentially referring to himself again as David's servant, accepts this commission and vows to carry it out (v. 11a).

9:11b-13. These verses conclude the account by reporting on the outcome of the matters revealed in the dialogues between David, Ziba, and Mephibosheth. The text refers twice again to Mephibosheth's eating at the king's table (vv. 11b, 13a). One of these references (v. 11b) adds the note equating this role to the status of one of the king's own sons. Mephibosheth has a son named Mica (v. 12a), who is included in the list of four sons born to Mephibosheth according to the chronicler's account (1 Chr 8:34-35; 9:40-41). Thus the line of Saul, through Jonathan, continues. The covenant vow made by David to Jonathan is kept, and David appears as a man of loyalty (ḥesed) to his commitments.

The final verse of the chapter mentions again that Mephibosheth was "lame in both his feet" (v. 13b; see v. 3; 4:4). This description reminds readers that this malady makes him an unlikely candidate for the throne; hence, he is not a threat to David.

Four times it is stressed in this chapter that Mephibosheth was to eat at the king's table the rest of his days (vv. 7b, 10b, 11b, 13a). As mentioned above, some have seen this as a form of house arrest—David shrewdly keeping an eye on a potential rival for the throne. In such a reading, this becomes a story of ideological politics masquerading as compassion. We are led to ques-

---

262. See McCarter, *II Samuel*, 124-25, 128, for a detailed discussion of the textual evidence and the various proposals made in relation to the name "Mephibosheth." A similar emendation was also made for the name "Ishbaal," which appears in 2 Samuel as "Ishbosheth." See the Commentary on 2 Sam 4:1 and the discussion of "Mephibosheth" in the Commentary on 2 Sam 4:4. It should also be noted that Rizpah, the concubine of Saul, also had a son named Mephibosheth (21:8). Most scholars agree that these are two individuals with the same or similar names.

263. See, e.g., H. W. Hertzberg, *I and II Samuel: A Commentary,* trans. J. S. Bowden, OTL (Philadelphia: Westminster, 1964; German ed. 1960) 299.

David's Empire

Tebah

Cun

ZOBAH

Berothai

Mt. Lebanon

BETH-REHOB

N

Mt. Hermon

Damascus

Tyre

MAACAH

Mediterranean Sea

Sea of
Chinnereth

GESHUR

TOB

Yarmuk R.

Jabbok R.

ISRAEL

AMMON

Jordan R.

Rabbah

Jerusalem

PHILISTIA

JUDAH

Dead
Sea

Arnon R.

MOAB

0   10   20
Miles

0   10   20
Kilometers

tion whether power can act with genuine compassion rather than solely in its own self-interest.

But this reading does not seem supported by the text itself. The stress on covenant relationship with Jonathan, the reference to making Mephibosheth like one of the king's sons, and the restoration of land to Mephibosheth are all elements that seem genuinely in the interests of Mephibosheth's welfare. It is true that the acts of a king were never neutral and without political significance, but in this case David's interests seem well served by his appearing magnanimous rather than coercive toward the remnant of the house of Saul.

The question remains as to why unusual stress is given to Mephibosheth's eating at the king's table. Robert Polzin has made the intriguing suggestion that this theme in 2 Samuel 9 must be read in connection with the reference in 2 Kgs 25:29 that Jehoiachin, the Davidic king carried into exile from Jerusalem to Babylon, "every day of his life dined regularly in the king's presence."[264] Although English translations vary

---

264. Polzin, *David and the Deuteronomist,* 103-4. Polzin also connects this theme in 2 Samuel 9 with the reference in 1 Sam 2:36 to the survivor of Eli's priestly house requesting "one of the priest's places that I may eat a morsel of bread." The parallel suggested does not contain the phrase "eat continually," refers to priestly remnants rather than to royal remnants, and does not draw on the image of being invited to the royal table. In short, the connection seems less compelling here than that suggested with 2 Kgs 25:29.

slightly, the Hebrew phrase, appearing only in 2 Sam 9:7, 10, 13 and 2 Kgs 25:29, is אכל תמיד ('ākal tāmîd), "to eat continually." Mephibosheth, the remnant of Saul's house, "eating continually" at the king's table foreshadows Jehoiachin, the remnant of David's house in exile, "eating continually" at the king's table. Through this connection within the Deuteronomistic History, 2 Samuel 9 suggests that the last word for the house of Saul, for the house of David, and for Israel's future is that of *ḥesed*, "covenant loyalty."

The foundational character of that *ḥesed* may appear in v. 3 of this chapter, when David refers to the *ḥesed* he intends to demonstrate as the "*ḥesed* of God" ("the kindness of God"). David acts not just out of friendship to Jonathan but out of covenant commitment between the two that finds its grounding in God's covenant commitment. "Show me the faithful love [*ḥesed*] of the LORD," Jonathan implores David (1 Sam 20:14). If David's treatment of Mephibosheth foreshadows Israel's story in exile and the fate of his own royal line, then this account suggests to the exilic readers of the Deuteronomistic History that they, too, can count on God's *ḥesed*, and the land that belonged to them might also be restored.

REFLECTIONS

1. Seen in the light of the hopeful meaning this episode may have held for exiles, a seemingly odd episode of David's loyalty and kindness becomes a testimony to divine loyalty and kindness. We read as those who constantly find ourselves cut off from our full future—existing as remnants with little hope for fullness of life except for the *ḥesed* of God, a divine sovereign who restores us to wholeness and invites us to sit at table.

Medieval and Renaissance Christian artists sometimes pictured David and Mephibosheth in the paintings, stained-glass windows, and sculptures they produced. Often when they did, the food they depicted on the king's table was the bread and the cup of the eucharistic meal. David's kindness was understood as God's kindness (v. 3), and the king's table to which we are all invited is ultimately God's table.

2. This episode, however, can also be read within its own framework in David's story as a witness to the capacity for compassion to co-exist with political expediency. David's actions need not be read as simply one or the other. In our own experience, we often react cynically to expressions of compassion or altruism by public officeholders. We suspect their motivation is solely for public image and political advantage.

We are correct to examine such expressions for evidence of genuine regard and, perhaps more important, to remember and hold officials accountable for actions that are consistent with their statements of compassionate concern. Nevertheless, people of faith should welcome the notion that commitments born of compassion and regard for the well-being of others should be considered politically advantageous. If such values were consistently rewarded, it would encourage more persons committed to those values to seek public office. Unfortunately, we too often say we want our leaders to demonstrate qualities such as compassionate regard for others, but we reward political actions that are advantageous only to the special interests from which we profit.

David had no interest in encouraging the house of Saul to make claims on the throne, but he honored the covenant of friendship that he had made with Jonathan and acted with *ḥesed*. We need not apologize for pursuing or supporting others in appropriate political goals. But the measure of our actions in pursuit of political ends must be in terms of values such as those honored by David in this story: loyalty, respect, steadfast love, and the well-being of others.

2 Samuel 10:1-19, War with the Ammonites and the Arameans

NIV

10 In the course of time, the king of the Ammonites died, and his son Hanun succeeded him as king. ²David thought, "I will show kindness to Hanun son of Nahash, just as his father showed kindness to me." So David sent a delegation to express his sympathy to Hanun concerning his father.

When David's men came to the land of the Ammonites, ³the Ammonite nobles said to Hanun their lord, "Do you think David is honoring your father by sending men to you to express sympathy? Hasn't David sent them to you to explore the city and spy it out and overthrow it?" ⁴So Hanun seized David's men, shaved off half of each man's beard, cut off their garments in the middle at the buttocks, and sent them away.

⁵When David was told about this, he sent messengers to meet the men, for they were greatly humiliated. The king said, "Stay at Jericho till your beards have grown, and then come back."

⁶When the Ammonites realized that they had become a stench in David's nostrils, they hired twenty thousand Aramean foot soldiers from Beth Rehob and Zobah, as well as the king of Maacah with a thousand men, and also twelve thousand men from Tob.

⁷On hearing this, David sent Joab out with the entire army of fighting men. ⁸The Ammonites came out and drew up in battle formation at the entrance to their city gate, while the Arameans of Zobah and Rehob and the men of Tob and Maacah were by themselves in the open country.

NRSV

10 Some time afterward, the king of the Ammonites died, and his son Hanun succeeded him. ²David said, "I will deal loyally with Hanun son of Nahash, just as his father dealt loyally with me." So David sent envoys to console him concerning his father. When David's envoys came into the land of the Ammonites, ³the princes of the Ammonites said to their lord Hanun, "Do you really think that David is honoring your father just because he has sent messengers with condolences to you? Has not David sent his envoys to you to search the city, to spy it out, and to overthrow it?" ⁴So Hanun seized David's envoys, shaved off half the beard of each, cut off their garments in the middle at their hips, and sent them away. ⁵When David was told, he sent to meet them, for the men were greatly ashamed. The king said, "Remain at Jericho until your beards have grown, and then return."

6When the Ammonites saw that they had become odious to David, the Ammonites sent and hired the Arameans of Beth-rehob and the Arameans of Zobah, twenty thousand foot soldiers, as well as the king of Maacah, one thousand men, and the men of Tob, twelve thousand men. ⁷When David heard of it, he sent Joab and all the army with the warriors. ⁸The Ammonites came out and drew up in battle array at the entrance of the gate; but the Arameans of Zobah and of Rehob, and the men of Tob and Maacah, were by themselves in the open country. 9When Joab saw that the battle was set against

⁹Joab saw that there were battle lines in front of him and behind him; so he selected some of the best troops in Israel and deployed them against the Arameans. ¹⁰He put the rest of the men under the command of Abishai his brother and deployed them against the Ammonites. ¹¹Joab said, "If the Arameans are too strong for me, then you are to come to my rescue; but if the Ammonites are too strong for you, then I will come to rescue you. ¹²Be strong and let us fight bravely for our people and the cities of our God. The Lord will do what is good in his sight."

¹³Then Joab and the troops with him advanced to fight the Arameans, and they fled before him. ¹⁴When the Ammonites saw that the Arameans were fleeing, they fled before Abishai and went inside the city. So Joab returned from fighting the Ammonites and came to Jerusalem.

¹⁵After the Arameans saw that they had been routed by Israel, they regrouped. ¹⁶Hadadezer had Arameans brought from beyond the River[a]; they went to Helam, with Shobach the commander of Hadadezer's army leading them.

¹⁷When David was told of this, he gathered all Israel, crossed the Jordan and went to Helam. The Arameans formed their battle lines to meet David and fought against him. ¹⁸But they fled before Israel, and David killed seven hundred of their charioteers and forty thousand of their foot soldiers.[b] He also struck down Shobach the commander of their army, and he died there. ¹⁹When all the kings who were vassals of Hadadezer saw that they had been defeated by Israel, they made peace with the Israelites and became subject to them.

So the Arameans were afraid to help the Ammonites anymore.

a16 That is, the Euphrates   b18 Some Septuagint manuscripts (see also 1 Chron. 19:18); Hebrew *horsemen*

him both in front and in the rear, he chose some of the picked men of Israel, and arrayed them against the Arameans; ¹⁰the rest of his men he put in the charge of his brother Abishai, and he arrayed them against the Ammonites. ¹¹He said, "If the Arameans are too strong for me, then you shall help me; but if the Ammonites are too strong for you, then I will come and help you. ¹²Be strong, and let us be courageous for the sake of our people, and for the cities of our God; and may the Lord do what seems good to him." ¹³So Joab and the people who were with him moved forward into battle against the Arameans; and they fled before him. ¹⁴When the Ammonites saw that the Arameans fled, they likewise fled before Abishai, and entered the city. Then Joab returned from fighting against the Ammonites, and came to Jerusalem.

15But when the Arameans saw that they had been defeated by Israel, they gathered themselves together. ¹⁶Hadadezer sent and brought out the Arameans who were beyond the Euphrates; and they came to Helam, with Shobach the commander of the army of Hadadezer at their head. ¹⁷When it was told David, he gathered all Israel together, and crossed the Jordan, and came to Helam. The Arameans arrayed themselves against David and fought with him. ¹⁸The Arameans fled before Israel; and David killed of the Arameans seven hundred chariot teams, and forty thousand horsemen,[a] and wounded Shobach the commander of their army, so that he died there. ¹⁹When all the kings who were servants of Hadadezer saw that they had been defeated by Israel, they made peace with Israel, and became subject to them. So the Arameans were afraid to help the Ammonites any more.

a 1 Chr 19.18 and some Gk Mss read *foot soldiers*

COMMENTARY

This chapter contains the first two of three reports on conflicts in a war between David's Israelite kingdom and a coalition of Ammonite and Aramean kingdoms. The first report tells of the Ammonite insult to David's envoys, the assembling of an Ammonite-Aramean coalition to op-

pose David's army under Joab, and an initial victory for Israel (vv. 1-14). David seems to follow this victory with separate campaigns against the Arameans and the Ammonites. A second report tells of David's victory over a widened coalition of Aramean kingdoms (10:15-19). A final report will narrate the siege and eventual capture of Rabbah, the capital of Ammon (11:1; 12:26-31).

These military accounts allude to the theme of David's חסד (hesed, "loyalty") in chapter 9. There David showed hesed toward Mephibosheth in loyalty to the covenant of friendship between David and Mephibosheth's father, Jonathan. In chap. 10, David seeks to show hesed in his public political dealings by sending envoys to reaffirm his loyalty to Ammon on the occasion of the death of their king, Nahash (v. 2). The portrait of chaps. 9 and 10 is of David as a man who honors commitments and acts with integrity to uphold those commitments in his personal and public dealings.

The military campaign against Ammonites and Arameans also defines the context for the story of David's adultery with Bathsheba and the arranged killing of her husband, Uriah, during the siege of Rabbah (11:2-25). There is a sad and ironic contrast between David's willingness to go to war to defend an insult to his hesed (chap. 10) and his subsequent willingness to abandon hesed to his subjects by committing adultery and murder.

10:1-5. Nahash, the king of the Ammonites, has died and has been succeeded by his son Hanun (v. 1). David sends envoys to express his condolences to Hanun, an action that David understands as an expression of loyalty (hesed) to Hanun in return for loyal treatment (hesed) David had received from Hanun's father, Nahash (v. 2). This language toward Ammonite kings may surprise the reader. Nahash had been a brutal enemy of Israel during the days of Saul and had been defeated by Saul when Nahash laid siege to the city of Jabesh-gilead (see 1 Samuel 11). However, the language in the opening verses of this chapter reflects the relationship of allies. Some have speculated that friendly relations developed between David and Ammon when David was fleeing from Saul. Nahash and David became allies against a common enemy in Saul.[265] Others speculate that the alliance was not between equals and that Ammon had been forced by Saul's victory into a relationship of subservience to Israel, which now

carries over to David's kingdom.[266] This background would help to explain the hostile treatment of David's envoys by Hanun, but it assumes a vassal relationship of Ammon to Israel that seems unlikely during the tenuous kingship of Saul.

Whatever the earlier relationship, David is now king of a secure and increasingly powerful Israelite kingdom. Hanun's advisers among the Ammonite princes see David's envoys as potential spies for an eventual Israelite overthrow of Ammon (v. 3b). They discount any honorable intention in the sending of envoys with condolences (v. 3a), and they humiliate David's representatives by shaving half of their beards and cutting off the lower portion of their garments, exposing their manhood (v. 4). Such acts explicitly reject the loyalty (hesed) that David had sought to demonstrate.

When the envoys return to Israelite territory, David, hearing of their treatment and their shame, goes compassionately to meet them at Jericho. He urges them to remain there until their beards grow back, erasing the external signs of their shameful treatment. David's personal attention to their plight is characteristic of his regard for his subjects, especially those in his service. Small acts of compassion like this make David's treatment of Uriah in the following chapter even more shocking.

10:6-14. The intentional humiliation of David's official envoys functions as an act of war. The Ammonite king has insulted David himself. David's honor and the integrity of his hesed toward Hanun's father have been called into question. The Ammonites clearly understood that war would result, and they proceeded immediately to recruit allies among the Aramean kingdoms of the region. The Arameans of Beth-rehob and Zobah may be the same coalition of kingdoms located south and east of Mt. Hermon that were mentioned in David's campaigns in 8:3-8, particularly since the Arameans are led by a king named Hadadezer, who is also mentioned later in this account (10:16). Most scholars believe that 8:3-8 represents the final victory in the war described in chap. 10.[267] Chapter 8 is a summary of David's conquests and was not intended to imply that all these victories took place at that early point in

265. So A. A. Anderson, *2 Samuel*, WBC 11 (Waco: Word, 1989) 146; and P. Kyle McCarter, *II Samuel*, AB 9 (Garden City, N.Y.: Doubleday, 1984) 270. McCarter, however, thinks the act of loyalty from Nahash to David was when David was received at Mahanaim by a son of Nahash, named Shobi, while retreating from Absalom (2 Sam 17:27). He believes the account of the war in chap. 10 has been misplaced chronologically in the present arrangement.

266. So Walter Brueggemann, *First and Second Samuel*, Interpretation (Louisville: John Knox, 1990) 269-70.

267. See Anderson, *2 Samuel*, 146.

David's kingship. Maacah and Tob are also small Aramean kingdoms located in the region east of the Sea of Galilee and probably under the influence of Hadadezer and the larger Aramean kingdom of Zobah (10:16). The numbers of men may not be as large as most translations suggest, since the Hebrew word usually translated "thousand" (אֶלֶף 'elep) can also mean a "military unit" of variable size. The account in 1 Chr 19:6-7 suggests that the Ammonites hired the Arameans as mercenaries.

David does not himself go to battle. He sends his general Joab (v. 7), a trusted commander who had been with David from the days of his conflict with Saul. Joab brings his army up to face the Ammonites outside the gate of their city (presumably their capital, Rabbah), and finds himself with two battle-fronts, since the Aramean forces draw up in the open country behind him (v. 8). It is not clear whether Joab was surprised by this tactic or anticipated it, but he responds quickly by taking a picked force under his own command to face the Arameans while leaving the rest of his army under the command of his brother Abishai to face the Ammonites (vv. 9-10). If possible, they are to assist one another should either front prove too difficult (v. 11). Joab's final admonition before battle is notable. He urges courage, both for the sake of "our people and for the cities of our God" (v. 12*a*). This may refer to the cities of David's kingdom in general or to the Israelite cities of the Transjordan, which would be in more immediate danger if the battle were lost. Finally, Joab offers a statement of reliance on the will of the Lord: "May the LORD do what seems good to him" (v. 12*b*). We are accustomed to hearing this kind of trustful expression of faith from the mouth of David, but not from Joab, who usually displays a more pragmatic inclination.

Joab's two-front attack is successful. The Arameans are routed, and the Ammonites retreat back into their walled city (vv. 13-14). Apparently, Joab and his army are not prepared either to lay siege to the city or to pursue the Arameans back into their own territory. The Israelites return to Jerusalem (v. 14*b*), but the war is far from over. This was only the opening skirmish.

10:15-19. The Arameans correctly understand that David is not through with them, and they decide to take the initiative against him. Under the leadership of Hadadezer (cf. 2 Sam 8:3-8), the Aramean city-states from beyond the Euphrates River (NIV, "the River") gather to oppose David. Hadadezer places the army under the command of his own general, Shobach (vv. 15-16). This time, David himself leads an Israelite force to meet the Arameans, a measure of the seriousness with which he takes this threat (v. 17). By contrast, in the following chapter David will remain at home for the siege of Rabbah. Such a siege may have required a longer campaign, and the king's protracted absence was not desirable; nevertheless, there seems to be an intended contrast between the active David of chap. 10 and the idle David of chap. 11.

The place or region where these armies engage one another is Helam, probably located in the northern Transjordan (v. 17). The outcome never seems in doubt: David and his army rout the Arameans, with a great loss of Aramean lives and the death of Shobach, their general (v. 18). The coalition of Aramean kings under Hadadezer recognize their defeat and sue for peace, but peace in this instance is clearly acceptance of subjection to Israel and the end of Aramean assistance to the Ammonites (v. 19). The borders of David's kingdom are expanded, and the enemy who started this war is now isolated. The campaign against the Ammonites will follow in short order (11:1).

REFLECTIONS

This chapter reminds us that David, as God's anointed king, is forced to deal with the same matters of state that all political leaders must face. We are reminded that David is a man of war as well as a man of faith. Israel, even as a kingdom ruled by God's chosen king, must live among the nations and deal with the conflicts that arise between nations. Covenant faith and covenant community cannot function in a vacuum apart from the world. Indeed, in the books of Samuel, piety is always held close to politics, and chap. 10 reminds us that God's people are not protected from the messiness of the world. This chapter does not reflect deeply on these matters, but there do seem to be two small clues worthy of notice.

1. It is clearly important to the narrator of this text that David sought to act with the integrity of *ḥesed* in dealing with the politics of nations and did not limit such "loyalty" to personal relationships (as in chap. 9). The same commitment to loyalty that marks the covenant relationship between Israel and God is to mark our personal and public dealings with one another. We are not to hold separate sets of values and commitments in our personal and public lives. Both are to be governed by the *ḥesed* that God, in covenant relationship, demonstrates toward us.

2. Joab voices a willingness to place trust ultimately in God while doing his human best to cope with a situation of grave conflict (v. 12). In the stories of David, Joab often represents the pragmatic warrior. He is certainly not a figure of piety and faith. Yet, in David's kingdom power is to be wielded in the presence and promise of God. David most often models this trust, but it is here also a hallmark of those who serve him. Even in the messy conflicts of power that erupt in war there is the need to recognize the power of God that holds any exercise of power accountable. In the recognition of God's power to do what "seems good to him" is the safeguard against the service of our own self-interests. When power is used in the service of self-interest and in the illusion of human autonomy, divine presence can be experienced as judgment. David is about to learn this.

2 Samuel 11:1-27, David's Adultery with Bathsheba

NIV

11 In the spring, at the time when kings go off to war, David sent Joab out with the king's men and the whole Israelite army. They destroyed the Ammonites and besieged Rabbah. But David remained in Jerusalem.

²One evening David got up from his bed and walked around on the roof of the palace. From the roof he saw a woman bathing. The woman was very beautiful, ³and David sent someone to find out about her. The man said, "Isn't this Bathsheba, the daughter of Eliam and the wife of Uriah the Hittite?" ⁴Then David sent messengers to get her. She came to him, and he slept with her. (She had purified herself from her uncleanness.) Then*ᵃ* she went back home. ⁵The woman conceived and sent word to David, saying, "I am pregnant."

⁶So David sent this word to Joab: "Send me Uriah the Hittite." And Joab sent him to David. ⁷When Uriah came to him, David asked him how Joab was, how the soldiers were and how the war was going. ⁸Then David said to Uriah, "Go down to your house and wash your feet." So Uriah left the palace, and a gift from the king was sent after him. ⁹But Uriah slept at the entrance to the palace with all his master's servants and did not go down to his house.

ᵃ4 Or with her. When she purified herself from her uncleanness,

NRSV

11 In the spring of the year, the time when kings go out to battle, David sent Joab with his officers and all Israel with him; they ravaged the Ammonites, and besieged Rabbah. But David remained at Jerusalem.

2It happened, late one afternoon, when David rose from his couch and was walking about on the roof of the king's house, that he saw from the roof a woman bathing; the woman was very beautiful. ³David sent someone to inquire about the woman. It was reported, "This is Bathsheba daughter of Eliam, the wife of Uriah the Hittite." ⁴So David sent messengers to get her, and she came to him, and he lay with her. (Now she was purifying herself after her period.) Then she returned to her house. ⁵The woman conceived; and she sent and told David, "I am pregnant."

6So David sent word to Joab, "Send me Uriah the Hittite." And Joab sent Uriah to David. ⁷When Uriah came to him, David asked how Joab and the people fared, and how the war was going. ⁸Then David said to Uriah, "Go down to your house, and wash your feet." Uriah went out of the king's house, and there followed him a present from the king. ⁹But Uriah slept at the entrance of the king's house with all the servants of his lord, and did not go down to his house.

NIV

¹⁰When David was told, "Uriah did not go home," he asked him, "Haven't you just come from a distance? Why didn't you go home?"

¹¹Uriah said to David, "The ark and Israel and Judah are staying in tents, and my master Joab and my lord's men are camped in the open fields. How could I go to my house to eat and drink and lie with my wife? As surely as you live, I will not do such a thing!"

¹²Then David said to him, "Stay here one more day, and tomorrow I will send you back." So Uriah remained in Jerusalem that day and the next. ¹³At David's invitation, he ate and drank with him, and David made him drunk. But in the evening Uriah went out to sleep on his mat among his master's servants; he did not go home.

¹⁴In the morning David wrote a letter to Joab and sent it with Uriah. ¹⁵In it he wrote, "Put Uriah in the front line where the fighting is fiercest. Then withdraw from him so he will be struck down and die."

¹⁶So while Joab had the city under siege, he put Uriah at a place where he knew the strongest defenders were. ¹⁷When the men of the city came out and fought against Joab, some of the men in David's army fell; moreover, Uriah the Hittite died.

¹⁸Joab sent David a full account of the battle. ¹⁹He instructed the messenger: "When you have finished giving the king this account of the battle, ²⁰the king's anger may flare up, and he may ask you, 'Why did you get so close to the city to fight? Didn't you know they would shoot arrows from the wall? ²¹Who killed Abimelech son of Jerub-Besheth*? Didn't a woman throw an upper millstone on him from the wall, so that he died in Thebez? Why did you get so close to the wall?' If he asks you this, then say to him, 'Also, your servant Uriah the Hittite is dead.'"

²²The messenger set out, and when he arrived he told David everything Joab had sent him to say. ²³The messenger said to David, "The men overpowered us and came out against us in the open, but we drove them back to the entrance to the city gate. ²⁴Then the archers shot arrows at your servants from the wall, and some of the king's men died. Moreover, your servant Uriah the Hittite is dead."

*21 Also known as *Jerub-Baal* (that is, Gideon)

NRSV

¹⁰When they told David, "Uriah did not go down to his house," David said to Uriah, "You have just come from a journey. Why did you not go down to your house?" ¹¹Uriah said to David, "The ark and Israel and Judah remain in booths;ᵃ and my lord Joab and the servants of my lord are camping in the open field; shall I then go to my house, to eat and to drink, and to lie with my wife? As you live, and as your soul lives, I will not do such a thing." ¹²Then David said to Uriah, "Remain here today also, and tomorrow I will send you back." So Uriah remained in Jerusalem that day. On the next day, ¹³David invited him to eat and drink in his presence and made him drunk; and in the evening he went out to lie on his couch with the servants of his lord, but he did not go down to his house.

14In the morning David wrote a letter to Joab, and sent it by the hand of Uriah. ¹⁵In the letter he wrote, "Set Uriah in the forefront of the hardest fighting, and then draw back from him, so that he may be struck down and die." ¹⁶As Joab was besieging the city, he assigned Uriah to the place where he knew there were valiant warriors. ¹⁷The men of the city came out and fought with Joab; and some of the servants of David among the people fell. Uriah the Hittite was killed as well. ¹⁸Then Joab sent and told David all the news about the fighting; ¹⁹and he instructed the messenger, "When you have finished telling the king all the news about the fighting, ²⁰then, if the king's anger rises, and if he says to you, 'Why did you go so near the city to fight? Did you not know that they would shoot from the wall? ²¹Who killed Abimelech son of Jerubbaal?ᵇ Did not a woman throw an upper millstone on him from the wall, so that he died at Thebez? Why did you go so near the wall?' then you shall say, 'Your servant Uriah the Hittite is dead too.'"

22So the messenger went, and came and told David all that Joab had sent him to tell. ²³The messenger said to David, "The men gained an advantage over us, and came out against us in the field; but we drove them back to the entrance of the gate. ²⁴Then the archers shot at your servants from the wall; some of the king's servants are dead; and your servant Uriah the Hittite is dead

ᵃ Or *at Succoth*   ᵇ Gk Syr Judg 7.1: Heb *Jerubbesheth*

NIV

²⁵David told the messenger, "Say this to Joab: 'Don't let this upset you; the sword devours one as well as another. Press the attack against the city and destroy it.' Say this to encourage Joab."

²⁶When Uriah's wife heard that her husband was dead, she mourned for him. ²⁷After the time of mourning was over, David had her brought to his house, and she became his wife and bore him a son. But the thing David had done displeased the LORD.

NRSV

also." ²⁵David said to the messenger, "Thus you shall say to Joab, 'Do not let this matter trouble you, for the sword devours now one and now another; press your attack on the city, and overthrow it.' And encourage him."

26When the wife of Uriah heard that her husband was dead, she made lamentation for him. ²⁷When the mourning was over, David sent and brought her to his house, and she became his wife, and bore him a son.

COMMENTARY

In this chapter, the reader senses a major shift in David's story. The shift may be described in a variety of ways: from the public to the personal, from power to vulnerability, from blessing to curse,[268] from gift to grasp.[269] In the course of this subtly crafted narrative, David's world is transformed. Things will no longer be the same. David uses royal power abusively to satisfy his own personal desires. Moreover, the violence he had earlier avoided (1 Samuel 24–26) spirals out of control in his own personal life. Adultery and deceit lead to murder, and the violence that stains David's hands will spread to his own family (chaps. 12–19).

The story may be seen as a tale of royal power told in four episodes, each with a complication that further enmeshes David in sin: (1) v. 1, an introductory verse that places David at home while his army lays siege to Rabbah; (2) vv. 2-5, the adultery. David sees a beautiful woman (Bathsheba) bathing and exercises royal privilege to "take" her. Complication: Bathsheba becomes pregnant; (3) vv. 6-13, the cover-up; David brings Uriah, Bathsheba's husband, home from the front to sleep with his wife and remove suspicion over the child's paternity—complication: Uriah is too dedicated as a soldier and will not "go down" to his house while comrades are still in the field; and (4) vv. 14-25, the murder. David arranges with Joab for Uriah to die in battle. Complication:

Other innocent lives are lost in an ill-advised military tactic; and (5) vv. 26-27, the aftermath. David and Bathsheba marry to preserve public honor, and they have a son. Complication: What David had done was "evil in the eyes of the LORD."

The final sentence of chap. 11 points beyond the boundaries of the story. In the books of Samuel, the story is not just about the rise of royal power in Israel. It is also the story of God's power as the true force shaping Israel's future. For chap. 11 as a story of David, a king, the marriage and birth would have been the end of the matter. But as a story of David, God's anointed king, the matter is not ended. The story continues in chap. 12 when Nathan the prophet confronts David by announcing divine judgment for what he had done in taking Bathsheba and killing Uriah.

The narrative of David and Bathsheba is also set more widely in the context of public events. The war with Ammon and the siege of Rabbah provide the framework and the backdrop for the story. The siege begins in 11:1 and concludes in 12:26-31. In 1 Sam 8:20, the elders of Israel had demanded a king who would "go out before us and fight our battles." The prophet Samuel had warned them of the dangers from kings who "take" from the people for their own interests (1 Sam 8:11-18). Now David no longer leads his troops into battle. He remains idle in Jerusalem while his men are fighting at Rabbah (v. 1), and he "takes" what he sees and desires for himself (v. 4).

The repercussions go beyond the framework of the war with Ammon. David's use of power for personal desire is like a virus unleashed in his

268. R. A. Carlson, *David, The Chosen King: A Traditio-Historical Approach to the Second Book of Samuel* (Stockholm: Almqvist och Wiksell, 1964).
269. David M. Gunn, *The Story of King David*, JSOTSup 6 (Sheffield: JSOT, 1978).

own family (see Nathan's oracle of judgment on David, 12:10-12). Episodes of rape, murder, and rebellion mark the unfolding tragedy of David's family history (chaps. 13–19).[270] David in chap. 11 charts a tragic path of abused power for his own sons to follow.

11:1-5. The background for the story is the siege of Rabbah. This campaign against the capital city of Ammon is the final chapter of the wars narrated in chap. 10. David sends Joab to lay siege to Rabbah, while David remains in Jerusalem. The taking of Rabbah is not narrated until 12:26-31. We see the events of this story against the backdrop of the public realities of a nation at war with a neighbor. The embedding of this story of sexual violence within a story of the violence of war may be intentional. David, left behind in Jerusalem, "takes" the woman he desires (v. 4) and eventually is summoned to Rabbah to personally "take" the city (12:28-29).[271]

The reason why David remains in Jerusalem is not explained. It seems to be a part of the narrative art of the author to leave ambiguities that allow us to imagine differing possibilities.[272] Has David lost interest in military leadership? Is he now too valuable as king to go on such campaigns (see 21:17)? Is the siege a tedious matter, and can David give time only to the final "taking" of the city? In any case, the picture is that of an idle king, pacing about on the roof of his palace when he spies a beautiful woman at her bath (v. 2). Further, a contrast is established between the stay-at-home David and the wronged husband, Uriah, who is away fighting the king's battles.

The story unfolds with a remarkable economy of narration. The author emphasizes the action with little mention of motivations, emotions, or feelings. About the woman we are told only that she was bathing and beautiful. From this slender

evidence some have been certain that Bathsheba had conspired to be seen by the king. Hertzberg accuses Bathsheba of "feminine flirtation": "We must, however, ask whether Bathsheba did not count on this possibility [of being seen]."[273] Nicol suggests that "even if it was not deliberate, Bathsheba's bathing in a place so clearly open to the king's palace can hardly indicate less than a contributory negligence on her part."[274] Others are equally clear that Bathsheba is simply the victim, both of David and of the narrator by objectifying her in the story.[275] The matter of Bathsheba's complicity is left unaddressed and, therefore, ambiguous. It must be observed, however, that the account shows no interest in Bathsheba's guilt in this matter and does not suggest that Bathsheba's bathing was an act of seduction. The narrator lays the moral responsibility entirely on David. It is what "David had done" that "was evil in the eyes of the LORD" (v. 27*b*), and it is against David that Nathan announces God's judgment (12:7).

David inquires after the identity of the woman he has seen (v. 3). He asks, "Is this not Bathsheba, daughter of Eliam, the wife of Uriah the Hittite?"[276] David receives no confirmation of this identification. The purpose of the question is to identify her for the reader. She is identified primarily by her ties to father and husband. In fact, she is not again called by her own name, Bathsheba, until after the death of the child she conceives with David (12:24). She is called only "the wife of Uriah" or "the woman." Even in the genealogy of Jesus in Matt 1:6 she is called the "wife of Uriah." The emphasis here is on the adultery of David and his guilt, but it is a point made at the expense of robbing Bathsheba of any developed character or identity in the story. Adele Berlin observes that Bathsheba is "a complete non-person. She is not even a minor character,

---

270. McCarter, *II Samuel*, 290-91, sees 2 Samuel 11–12 as a preface added by a prophetic author to a story on the events surrounding Absalom's rebellion (2 Samuel 13–19), although the prophetic author's direct contribution may be limited to 11:27*b*-12:15*a*. This may well be the case, since chaps. 13–19 do not refer explicitly to the events of chaps. 11–12. These chapters seem more like a lens through which to view David's sin and judgment in subsequent chapters.

271. For discussion of the significant combination of war, sex, and violence in this chapter, see Mieke Bal, *Lethal Love: Feminist Literary Readings of Biblical Love Stories* (Bloomington: Indiana University Press, 1987) 10-36; J. P. Fokkelman, *Narrative Art and Poetry in the Books of Samuel*, vol. 1: *King David* (Assen: van Gorcum, 1981) 41-70.

272. The crucial role of ambiguity in the narrative art of this chapter has been convincingly discussed in Gale A. Yee, " 'Fraught with Background': Literary Ambiguity in II Samuel 11," *Int.* 42 (1988) 240-53.

273. Hans Wilhelm Hertzberg, *I and II Samuel,* OTL (Philadelphia: Westminster, 1964) 309.

274. George G. Nicol, "Bathsheba, a Clever Woman?" *Expository Times* 99 (1988) 360.

275. J. Cheryl Exum, *Fragmented Women: Feminist (Sub)versions of Biblical Narratives* (Valley Forge: Trinity Press International, 1993) 170-201.

276. The verbs in this sentence give no other subject than David. Both the NRSV and the NIV imply a third party reporting back to David, but the question is David's seeking of confirmation. See Randall C. Bailey, *David in Love and War: The Pursuit of Power in 2 Samuel 10–12,* JSOTSup 75 (Sheffield: JSOT, 1990) 85. David's inquiry after the woman's identity need not imply others voyeuristically gazing with David at the bathing Bathsheba, contra Exum, *Fragmented Women,* 174-75.

but simply part of the plot. This is why she is not considered guilty of adultery. She is not an equal party to the adultery, but only the means whereby it was achieved."[277]

The actual act of adultery is narrated with surprising economy in v. 4. The narrative is powered by verbs in short phrases. David "sent," "took," and "lay." Bathsheba "came," "returned," and "conceived." Is this the record of a rape? According to Exum, "the text seems ambivalent on the matter. 'Sent' and 'took' indicate aggression on David's part; on the other hand, the two verbs of which Bathsheba is the subject, 'came' and 'returned,' are not what one would expect if resistance were involved. The king sends for a subject and she obeys. His position of power gives him an advantage: he 'takes.' "[278] This is coercive, self-indulgent use of power to satisfy sexual lust on David's part. He intentionally violates a marriage and breaks the law of the Lord. If Bathsheba "came" to him, it implies passivity more than consent. It is a verb that follows the statement that the king "sent messengers and he took her." Both the NRSV and the NIV soften the text here and inaccurately imply consent by translating "David sent messengers to get her." In these translations, there is no "taking," as Samuel warned that kings would do (1 Sam 8:11-18), and the messengers, rather than David, are made the implied subject of the verb. "Taking" is reduced to "fetching," and Bathsheba's "coming" is made the response to a summons rather than acquiescence in a seizure.[279] In the ongoing story of David's family, this scene of coercive sex foreshadows Amnon's rape of Tamar (chap. 13) and Absalom's rape of the ten wives of David (on the very same palace roof, 16:21-22). In this narrative, David is clearly treated as the offender and Bathsheba as a used woman. David did not take her with a desire for ongoing relationship or marriage. It is only the pregnancy that keeps the episode from being a one-night stand, and even then David hopes to deceive Uriah into thinking the child is his rather than David's. It is only the lack

of attention to Bathsheba's point of view altogether that allows issues of seduction, honor, or consent on her part to be raised at all.[280]

The parenthetical statement (v. 4) that Bathsheba was "purifying herself after her period" is not an explanation of the bathing in v. 1. It is a note that makes clear the paternity of the child conceived by Bathsheba. Since she had just had a period and since her husband is on the battlefront, the child must be David's.

A tawdry but straightforward story of royal lust is suddenly complicated. Bathsheba, who has not spoken at all, now makes a transforming speech. She conceives and reports to the king, "I am pregnant" (v. 5). David is now threatened with exposure of his lustful taking of Bathsheba, his violation of another man's marriage, and his breaking of the law of the Lord (see Deut 22:22). David thought his power gave him control, but he could not control Bathsheba's body and the conception that took place within her. Her words now propel the story into a new and tragic dimension.

11:6-13. In response to Bathsheba's words, David launches a cover-up. He sends a message to Joab, summoning Uriah home from the battlefront (v. 6). Joab always seems somewhere nearby when questionable actions are afoot. David intends to get Uriah to sleep with his wife so that he might appear to be the child's father.[281]

Uriah was a member of David's elite thirty (23:39). He is consistently identified as "the Hittite." This may mean that he was a mercenary serving as an officer in David's military, but some think the Jerusalem nobility may have had Hittite associations and were incorporated into Israel with David's capture of Jerusalem.[282] "Uriah" is a Yahwistic name meaning "Yahweh is my light,"

---

277. Adele Berlin, "Characterization in Biblical Narrative: David's Wives," *JSOT* 23 (1982) 73.

278. Exum, *Fragmented Women*, 172.

279. Hertzberg, *I and II Samuel*, 310, writes that "her consciousness of the danger into which adultery was leading her . . . must have been outweighed by her realization of the honour of having attracted the king." It is troubling that coercive use of power for the sake of royal lust is so easily transmuted into an honor.

280. Exum refers to this objectivization of Bathsheba by the narrator as being "raped by the pen." This is the title of her chapter on Bathsheba in *Fragmented Women*, 170-201. I would stop short of accusing scholars who note the ambiguities left by the narrator as complicit in the crime of "narrative rape." Those who resolve those ambiguities by scapegoating Bathsheba and softening David's guilt may deserve the accolade. For a response to the issues Exum raises, see George G. Nicol, "The Alleged Rape of Bathsheba: Some Observations on Ambiguity in Biblical Narrative," *JSOT* 73 (1997) 43-54.

281. It is David's persistent attempts to pass paternity of the child onto Uriah that undercut Randall Bailey's thesis (*David in Love and War*, 88) that this story is concerned with "political marriage" rather than "sexual lust." David is clearly trying to avoid marriage. The notion that David required the wife of another man to produce a legitimate heir when he had so many other wives and sons stretches credulity and forces Bailey to locate this episode unconvincingly after the death of Absalom.

282. See Anderson, *2 Samuel*, 153.

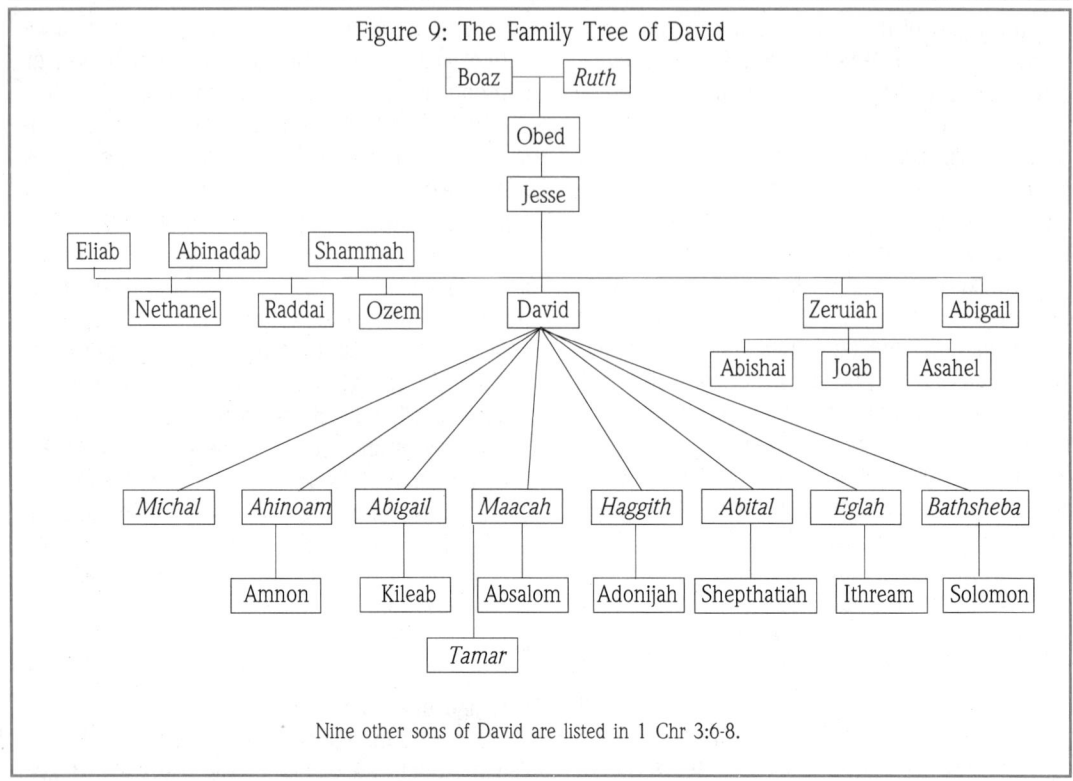

Figure 9: The Family Tree of David

Nine other sons of David are listed in 1 Chr 3:6-8.

which would indicate identification with Israel's God.

As with Bathsheba, David "sends" and Uriah "comes," but there is no "taking." This time David must persuade and manipulate. When Uriah appears, David inquires after the progress of the siege, as if this report were the purpose of the summons (v. 7). He asks after the welfare (שלום *šālôm*, "peace," "well-being") of Joab, the army, and the war (the NRSV and the NIV obscure this threefold asking about *šālôm*). These queries are ironic, since David's actions will later cause death—the absence of *šālôm*—to dominate the story (vv. 15, 17, 21, 24-26).

David urges Uriah to "go down to your house and wash your feet" and sends a present with him (v. 8). The phrase "wash your feet" is a euphemism for having sexual intercourse, which v. 11 shows Uriah clearly understood. But Uriah does not "go down." He sleeps with the king's servants at the gate (v. 9). David is told that Uriah did not "go down," and he summons Uriah to ask why he did not (v. 10). The constant concern to get Uriah to "go down" to his house gives an

urgent, almost frantic tone to the story. David is desperate that the cover-up succeed.

In contrast to David's desperation, Uriah seems calm and principled. He tells David that he cannot enjoy his house—eating, drinking, and taking sexual pleasure with his wife—while the ark, Joab, and the armies of Israel and Judah remain encamped in the field, enduring the hardships of the siege at Rabbah (v. 11). The reference to booths (Sukkot) here may refer to temporary camp structures or be taken as a place name for the encampment, Succoth. This statement seems a genuine expression of loyalty and commitment on the part of one of David's elite military men. There is no suggestion in the text that Uriah knew of his wife's pregnancy and suspected David's true purposes.[283]

The mention of the ark reminds us that David was once ill at ease until there should be a house for the ark (2 Sam 7:2; Ps 132:1-5). Now he is at ease in Jerusalem while the ark is still in the field with the army.

283. Contra Hertzberg, *I and II Samuel,* 310; Meir Sternberg, *The Poetics of Biblical Narrative* (Bloomington: University of Indiana Press, 1985) 201-13.

David makes one more attempt to get Uriah to his house. He gets Uriah drunk, but when evening comes Uriah still sleeps with the king's servants and does not "go down" to his house (v. 13). Unwittingly, Uriah has sealed his own doom, but the picture left with the reader is one of contrast between the principled obedience of Uriah and the increasingly desperate actions of David. David has once again encountered the limits of royal power. He cannot control Uriah's principles.

11:14-25. It is chilling how easily cover-up plan shifts to murder plot. As before, it begins with a message from David to Joab, but this time Uriah must carry the cruel order for his own death (v. 14). The letter orders Joab to place Uriah in the midst of heavy fighting and withdraw support (v. 15). Thus Uriah is to be given a hero's death in battle. He is to be honored in death for the sake of preserving David's honor in life. This section of the story is dominated by forms of the verb "to die" (מות *mût*, vv. 15, 17, 21, 24, 26). God's anointed king has become an agent of death. Self-interested use of power has led David into a deadly chain of events from seizure to deception to death.

Joab quickly carries out David's order, and Uriah is killed (vv. 16-17), but not without further cost. The effort to expose Uriah leads to the death of others from among "the servants of David" (v. 17). This leads to an elaborate reporting of events to David. Joab sends a messenger to David (v. 18) but anticipates that David will become angry at the loss of troops that resulted from a foray so close to the city walls (vv. 19-20) and that he will recall the death of Abimelech when a woman threw a millstone on him from the wall (v. 21; cf. Judg 9:50-55).[284] If David responds in this angry manner, the messenger is to add the news, "Your servant Uriah the Hittite is dead too" (v. 21*b*).

In v. 22, the messenger makes his report to David, and the Hebrew text does not report an angry response on his part. Nevertheless, vv. 23-24 report a speech by the messenger justifying the tactic that took them close to the wall and

cost lives among the servants of David. He ends with the news that Uriah was also dead. The Greek text of these verses does include the angry response of David in virtually identical language to the anticipation of his anger by Joab. This fuller text makes more sense out of the messenger's defensive response and the mollifying news of Uriah's death.

David sends a callous and cynical response back to Joab (v. 25): "Do not let this thing be evil in your eyes, for the sword devours now one, now another." The NRSV and the NIV soften the opening phrase and in the process lose a precise parallel with the closing comment of the chapter (v. 27*b*). David presumes to say that what has happened is not an evil thing. It is just the unfortunate cost of war. Get on with the siege. David engages in a moral cover-up to match the cover-up of his actual deeds. Perhaps he is trying to convince himself as much as Joab that this was an act of war and not an act of murder. He is not so calmly accepting of the costs of war when the reported death is that of his own son Absalom (18:33). David speaks as if the matter is finished. He imagines his sinful deeds can be masked by the inevitable loss of life that takes place in war.

11:26-27. These verses report the developments David had hoped for in arranging the death of Uriah and one further development beyond his control. In quick succession, Uriah's death is reported to Bathsheba; she observes the proper rituals of mourning for her husband; David "sends" and "brings" her to the palace; David and Bathsheba marry; and a son is born. This is the course of events for which David had hoped and plotted. The king's honor has been publicly preserved. David surely imagines that all is well and the matter is finished.

At this point, the moral perspective of the Lord enters the picture. David had urged Joab not to let this matter be "evil in your eyes" (v. 25*a*), setting aside any human moral qualms. But the text now tells us that "the thing that David has done was evil in the eyes of the LORD" (v. 27*b*, author's trans.). Again both the NRSV and the NIV soften the moral judgment made in the text and obscure the parallel with v. 25*a*. From God's perspective this matter is not finished. David's power cannot control the judgment of God. David believes the story has ended, but this final notice

---

284. The reference to Abimelech seems awkward and ill placed. Some have suggested that it is a reference intended to function metaphorically as a comment on aspects of the wider story in chap. 11. See Mieke Bal, *Lethal Love: Feminist Literary Readings of Biblical Love Stories* (Bloomington: Indiana University Press, 1987) 10-36, for extensive discussion of the options here and the connection of this text with the emergence of a biblical theme of the "lethal woman."

of God's viewpoint alerts the reader that there is a further act to this drama, and chap. 12 will make this clear to David as well when he is confronted with his sin by the prophet Nathan.

REFLECTIONS

1. This is a classic story of the arrogant misuse of power for personal whim. It is remarkable that a story so negative to David was preserved and passed on in the tradition. Indeed, the idealized Davidic portrait by the chronicler omits this episode. We should be grateful that the tradition had the courage to present Israel's greatest king with a portrait that includes his weaknesses and vulnerability as well as his accomplishments and power. This sordid and disillusioning episode in David's story serves as a cautionary tale on the nearness of violence to those who live with power. It reminds us that even those most admired and most accomplished are not immune to the temptation of power.

Those possessed of power and surrounded by admirers and supporters often succumb to the illusion that they are in control of their own destiny and can define the terms of the morality that governs their actions. David experienced the limits of his power and control. He could not control Bathsheba's pregnancy, Uriah's principles, or God's moral judgment. One can hardly consider this a word limited in application to an ancient king when our own news has been filled in recent years with stories of politicians, clergy, military officers, and teachers guilty of sexual misconduct and manipulation of others for the sake of self-interest. In many of these instances, abuses were committed under the illusion that the authority of their office, rank, or influence would protect them. The tragedy of lives undone and accomplishments overshadowed by acts committed under such an illusion of power is an almost weekly story in our communities and nation.

The story of David's adultery and murder reminds us of the deadly spiral of violence that can escalate from a single sinful act. For David, an initial act born of lust led to an elaborate and deceitful attempt at cover-up and finally to murder. Perhaps the dramas of our lives are not always on this grand scale, but we should not imagine that because we have stopped short of murder that this is not our story. We all know that we have at times acted to exploit others for our own self-interest, and we know too well how easily a lie to cover our tracks can involve us in complex deceits and additional acts that compound and deepen our original complicity.

2. Evidence that this story strikes close to home can be seen in the many efforts to soften the impact of the story. This is apparent in the endless fascination with the tale of David and Bathsheba through the generations and the many efforts to find some justification or mitigating circumstances that avoid the simple conclusion that David, the hero of our story, has become an adulterer and a murderer. These efforts are seen not only in scholarly treatments, from the ancient rabbis to modern academics, but also in numerous treatments of the David and Bathsheba story in art, poetry, literature, and film.[285]

As modern readers, teachers, and preachers, we must face the harsh realities of the story and avoid the temptation to soften them. To do so will mean countering many distorted readings of this story already present in past interpretation and popular cultural. These distorted readings take several forms:

Scapegoating. Perhaps the most common distortion of this story through the ages is the effort to portray Bathsheba as a seductress or co-conspirator, thereby transforming David to some degree from perpetrator to victim. The story gives us nothing explicit to substantiate such views and, in fact, shows little interest in Bathsheba as a subject at all. Yet, the following excerpt from a turn-of-the-century treatment of this story has been typical of many treatments

---

285. See J. Cheryl Exum, "Bathsheba Plotted, Shot, and Painted," in *Plotted, Shot, and Painted: Cultural Representations of Biblical Women,* JSOTSup 215 (Sheffield: Sheffield Academic, 1996) 19-53.

of the episode down to the present: "No one of good moral character could have acted as she did in her seduction and conquest of David. She doubtless exposed herself that the king might be tempted; she willingly came to the palace when she was sent for; and conspired with David for the murder of her husband."[286] This scapegoating of Bathsheba as the temptress who led David astray was present in some ancient rabbinic efforts to soften David's guilt, and it is still present in some church education curriculum treatments. Recent movie and television treatments of the story uniformly show Bathsheba engaging in seductive behavior and usually portray her as the initiator of the relationship by means of such behavior.[287] Joseph Heller's novel on David has Bathsheba say, "I made up my mind to meet you. A king and all that too—who could resist? So I began bathing on my roof every evening to attract you."[288] These efforts to make Bathsheba the initiator are unfortunately consistent with a common defense in cases of the rape and abuse of women: "She asked for it." Even the NRSV's and the NIV's softening of the verb "take" to make David's messengers merely "getting" Bathsheba (v. 4a) shows our unwillingness to face the coercion in David's action. This would suggest that it might be difficult to face similarly coercive behaviors between the sexes in our own experience.

Rationalizing. Another common effort to soften the harsh realities of this story is the search for mitigating circumstances that help to explain, if not justify, David's actions. In a 1985 film, *King David,*[289] Bathsheba reveals to a shocked David that Uriah is an abusive husband, thus giving David a noble motive for the act of murder and the rescue of an abused woman. The ancient rabbis sought to lessen David's guilt in a variety of ways. Some claimed the chain of events was due to the marriage of a Hittite man to an Israelite wife and that the marriage to David rectified that unacceptable state. Others claimed that Satan appeared as a bird and when David shot an arrow at it, the screen shielding Bathsheba at her bath was toppled, and the chain of events was begun.[290] Another form of rationalizing David's great sin has been to claim that his repentance was correspondingly great, as evidenced by Psalm 51. Such a traditional argument usually seems to mean that we can ignore the sordid story of 1 Samuel 11.

Romanticizing. Some readers prefer to describe Bathsheba as the beautiful woman with whom "David fell in love when he saw her bathing." What better way to soften the harshness of this story than to make it a love story? Indeed, David and Bathsheba often make the list of the world's great lovers, alongside Romeo and Juliet, Anthony and Cleopatra, and others. Hollywood could not resist this temptation, and many people's view of this story is colored by the sweeping romance of Gregory Peck and Susan Hayward in Darryl F. Zanuck's 1951 film *David and Bathsheba.*[291] This film presents Uriah as a soldier with no interest in his wife, David as lonely in his royal office, and Bathsheba as a neglected wife who finds her true love in David. But the biblical text does not give us a romance. David has no interest in an ongoing relationship or marriage until Bathsheba becomes pregnant, and even then he prefers the solution of making Uriah the father. Romances do not begin with "taking" and end with murder, and we romanticize this tale at our own peril. There is too much in present popular culture that romanticizes violence and the abuse of women.

When we preach and teach this story, we must be clear: It is a story of a fallen hero. One cannot help recalling David's own lament over Saul and Jonathan, "How the mighty have fallen" (2 Sam 1:19). This time it is David who has fallen, and the fall is not in battle but in moral character. The difficulty we have in facing the harsh reality of this story is a testimony to the ease with which we excuse our own sin. But if we can face David's sin for what it is,

286. Morton Bryan Wharton, *Famous Men of the Old Testament* (New York: E. B. Treat, 1903) 213.
287. See Exum, "Bathsheba Plotted, Shot, and Painted," 19-53.
288. Joseph Heller, *God Knows* (New York: Dell, 1984) 312.
289. *King David,* Paramount Pictures, directed by Bruce Beresford, produced by Martin Elfand, starring Richard Gere.
290. Reported in Michael E. Williams, ed. *The Storyteller's Companion to the Bible,* vol. 3: *Judges–Kings* (Nashville: Abingdon, 1992) 122-23.
291. *David and Bathsheba,* Twentieth Century Fox, directed by Henry King, produced by Darryl F. Zanuck.

we may better face our own. This theme will continue in the confrontation with Nathan in chap. 12.

To preach this story will require an honest facing of our own complicity with David. To face the sin of our greatest biblical heroes can allow us to face our own impulses to use others for the fulfillment of our own desires and to face the tragic ease with which we can become entangled in growing webs of sinful acts as we try to cover up and avoid accountability for our own manipulation of others. This story is especially directed to those whose positions of power, leadership, and influence provide constant opportunity for manipulating or exploiting those in more vulnerable positions. Our newspapers today are filled with stories of those—from presidents to pastors—who have abused the power of their offices for the fulfillment of their own self-interested desires or gains. Perhaps we need to preach this bleak side of David's story more often, not simply to point fingers at the sins of the mighty but to acknowledge how often we excuse and emulate them.

2 Samuel 12:1-15a, Nathan's Confrontation of David

NIV

12 The LORD sent Nathan to David. When he came to him, he said, "There were two men in a certain town, one rich and the other poor. ²The rich man had a very large number of sheep and cattle, ³but the poor man had nothing except one little ewe lamb he had bought. He raised it, and it grew up with him and his children. It shared his food, drank from his cup and even slept in his arms. It was like a daughter to him.

⁴"Now a traveler came to the rich man, but the rich man refrained from taking one of his own sheep or cattle to prepare a meal for the traveler who had come to him. Instead, he took the ewe lamb that belonged to the poor man and prepared it for the one who had come to him."

⁵David burned with anger against the man and said to Nathan, "As surely as the LORD lives, the man who did this deserves to die! ⁶He must pay for that lamb four times over, because he did such a thing and had no pity."

⁷Then Nathan said to David, "You are the man! This is what the LORD, the God of Israel, says: 'I anointed you king over Israel, and I delivered you from the hand of Saul. ⁸I gave your master's house to you, and your master's wives into your arms. I gave you the house of Israel and Judah. And if all this had been too little, I would have given you even more. ⁹Why did you despise the word of the LORD by doing what is evil in his eyes? You struck down Uriah the Hittite with the sword and took his wife to be your own. You killed him with

NRSV

But the thing that David had done displeased the LORD,

12 ¹and the LORD sent Nathan to David. He came to him, and said to him, "There were two men in a certain city, the one rich and the other poor. ²The rich man had very many flocks and herds; ³but the poor man had nothing but one little ewe lamb, which he had bought. He brought it up, and it grew up with him and with his children; it used to eat of his meager fare, and drink from his cup, and lie in his bosom, and it was like a daughter to him. ⁴Now there came a traveler to the rich man, and he was loath to take one of his own flock or herd to prepare for the wayfarer who had come to him, but he took the poor man's lamb, and prepared that for the guest who had come to him." ⁵Then David's anger was greatly kindled against the man. He said to Nathan, "As the LORD lives, the man who has done this deserves to die; ⁶he shall restore the lamb fourfold, because he did this thing, and because he had no pity."

7Nathan said to David, "You are the man! Thus says the LORD, the God of Israel: I anointed you king over Israel, and I rescued you from the hand of Saul; ⁸I gave you your master's house, and your master's wives into your bosom, and gave you the house of Israel and of Judah; and if that had been too little, I would have added as much more. ⁹Why have you despised the word of the LORD, to do what is evil in his sight? You have struck down Uriah the Hittite with the sword, and have

NIV

the sword of the Ammonites. ¹⁰Now, therefore, the sword will never depart from your house, because you despised me and took the wife of Uriah the Hittite to be your own.'

¹¹"This is what the LORD says: 'Out of your own household I am going to bring calamity upon you. Before your very eyes I will take your wives and give them to one who is close to you, and he will lie with your wives in broad daylight. ¹²You did it in secret, but I will do this thing in broad daylight before all Israel.'"

¹³Then David said to Nathan, "I have sinned against the LORD."

Nathan replied, "The LORD has taken away your sin. You are not going to die. ¹⁴But because by doing this you have made the enemies of the LORD show utter contempt,[a] the son born to you will die."

¹⁵After Nathan had gone home,

[a]14 Masoretic Text; an ancient Hebrew scribal tradition *this you have shown utter contempt for the LORD*

NRSV

taken his wife to be your wife, and have killed him with the sword of the Ammonites. ¹⁰Now therefore the sword shall never depart from your house, for you have despised me, and have taken the wife of Uriah the Hittite to be your wife. ¹¹Thus says the LORD: I will raise up trouble against you from within your own house; and I will take your wives before your eyes, and give them to your neighbor, and he shall lie with your wives in the sight of this very sun. ¹²For you did it secretly; but I will do this thing before all Israel, and before the sun." ¹³David said to Nathan, "I have sinned against the LORD." Nathan said to David, "Now the LORD has put away your sin; you shall not die. ¹⁴Nevertheless, because by this deed you have utterly scorned the LORD,[a] the child that is born to you shall die." ¹⁵Then Nathan went to his house.

[a] Ancient scribal tradition: Compare 1 Sam 25.22 note: Heb *scorned the enemies of the LORD*

COMMENTARY

In the previous chapter David "sent" in order to "take" (11:4). Now it is the Lord who "sends," and it is in order to speak. God sends Nathan, a prophet, to David. Nathan is to confront David and speak of God's judgment of him, because the "thing that David had done was evil in the eyes of the LORD" (11:27b, author's trans.).

It has often been noted that Nathan's confrontation with David in 12:1-15a stands out as different in style and content from the storytelling style of the succession narrative (2 Samuel 9–20; 1 Kings 1–2).[292] For most of the succession narrative, God's perspective and God's shaping of events are conveyed in minimal comments that remind the reader of a larger reality at work. The verse quoted above (11:27b) is such a comment, and the story would flow smoothly from that notice of God's displeasure to the consequence stated in 12:15b, "The LORD struck the child that Uriah's wife bore to David, and it became very

ill." So it is unusual to have a prophet arrive and offer a detailed spelling out of God's judgment on David's sin. McCarter has argued compellingly that chaps. 10–12 have been affixed by a prophetic editor "as a kind of theological preface" to the subsequent story of Absalom's rebellion and the havoc in David's family that preceded and followed that rebellion.[293] McCarter admits, however, that only 12:1-15a may actually stem from the hand of this prophetic editor.[294] In my opinion, the story of David's sin and the tragic events that culminated in Absalom's rebellion were already joined in the succession narrative. The knowledge of David's adultery and the death of Uriah could not be ignored by that historian. The prophetic addition of the confrontation and judgment from the Lord through Nathan additionally makes the case that David has already been judged, has repented, and has suffered the consequences of his sin in the tragedies that afflict his

292. See the discussion of the interpretive history of this chapter in George W. Coats, "Parable, Fable, and Anecdote: Storytelling in the Succession Narrative," *Int.* 35 (1981) 368-82.

293. P. Kyle McCarter, *II Samuel*, AB 9 (Garden City, N.Y.: Doubleday, 1984) 276.

294. Ibid., 304-9.

family, so the dynasty (Solomon in particular) could continue free of taint from these events.

The account of this prophetic encounter has three parts: vv. 1-7*a*, the parable and David's response to it; vv. 7*b*-12, a prophetic oracle announcing judgment; vv. 13-15*a*, David's repentance.

12:1-7a. David had thought the matter of Bathsheba and Uriah to be finished, but the Lord has not finished with it. The Lord sends Nathan to him. The introduction of the prophet into the story is abrupt and unexpected. We met Nathan previously in chap. 7, where he announced the oracle of God's promise to David. He is present now for a quite different purpose. Readers often assume that Nathan had access to David and could speak to him openly. Nevertheless, even a prophet must frame his speech carefully in the presence of power; so Nathan does not approach the matter of concern directly. Instead, he tells David a story involving a case of injustice.

Nathan's story is usually understood as a parable.[295] Parables operate out of a tension between the expected and the actual events. Actual events usually reverse the expectations of the hearer and in doing so make the point intended by the recital of the parable. Some have called this text a "juridical parable," which intentionally disguises a real-life situation in order to draw a guilty party into passing judgment on himself.[296] Other examples of juridical parables are 2 Sam 14:1-20; 1 Kgs 20:35-43; and Isa 5:1-7.

Nathan's parable presents David with a tale of contrasts. There is a rich man and a poor man. There are the large flocks and herds of the rich man, and the single ewe lamb that is the prized possession of the poor man (vv. 2-3). Nathan's story expands at this point to describe the closeness of the poor man to his lamb. It was like his child; it ate, drank, and slept with him (v. 3*b*). When a guest came to the rich man's house, he was reluctant to take a lamb from his own flocks to feed his guest. It is at this point that the parable takes its unexpected turn. Without explanation, the rich man simply takes the poor man's beloved

lamb and feeds it to his guest (v. 4). We are shocked at such a heartless act, particularly since it is disguised to the rich man's guest as hospitality—crass injustice masquerading as graciousness.

Before speaking of David's reaction, we should note that this scene does not seem like a customary session of royal judicial practice. Kings did have a role in administering justice, but this instance is not presented as a real-life case for David to decide. No names, places, witnesses, or other petitioners are in evidence. Instead, we find an encounter between prophet and king in which Nathan has chosen the rhetorical device of a parable of injustice for his purpose in confronting David.

David's reaction is like our own. He is shocked and angry by the arbitrary action of the rich man (v. 5*a*). Yet, he does not yet recognize his own "taking" (11:4) in the "taking" of the rich man (v. 4). David does not yet realize that he has become the king against whose "taking" Samuel warned the people (1 Sam 8:11-19). David swears by the life of the Lord that any man who would do such a thing is a בֶן־מָוֶת (*ben-māwet*), literally, a "son of death" (v. 5*b*). This is usually interpreted to mean "one who deserves to die" (cf. 1 Sam 20:31-32, where Saul refers to David as a *ben-māwet* and Jonathan responds, "Why should he be put to death?"). This comment, however, expresses David's feeling toward such a man and does not constitute a formal sentence of death. In v. 6, David's sense of legal remedy for such a situation is expressed in terms of fourfold restitution (see Exod 22:1). His sense of the offense is made clear in v. 6*b*, "because he had no pity." The Hebrew word for "pity" (חָמַל *ḥāmāl*) here may be thought of in terms of "compassion," especially the "compassion" that saves from death.[297] Lacking compassion, the rich man sent the poor man's lamb to slaughter; likewise, David sent Uriah to his death.

The dramatic climax of Nathan's strategy and the moment of recognition for David come in v. 7*a*: "You are the man!" David is the one who had much and took the possession of one who had little; David is the exploiter, the perpetrator of injustice. Some have argued that Nathan's parable does not correspond exactly to David's

---

295. See W. M. W. Roth, "You Are the Man! Structural Interaction in 2 Samuel 10–12," *Semeia* 8 (1977) 1-13. See also Coats, "Parable, Fable, and Anecdote," although Coats unconvincingly wants to argue that Nathan's story is more like a fable than a parable.

296. Uriel Simon, "The Poor Man's Ewe-Lamb: An Example of a Juridical Parable," *Biblica* 48 (1967) 207-42.

297. George Coats, "II Samuel 12:1-7a," *Int.* 40 (1986) 171-72, finds this same Hebrew root used for the "compassion" that Pharaoh's daughter showed in saving the infant Moses from death and that later Moses showed in intervening to save Israel from death at the hands of God's judgment for the golden calf at Sinai.

crimes. The lamb seems to represent Bathsheba, the one wife of Uriah, whereas David had many wives. Yet, it is the lamb that is killed, not its owner, who loved it. But the parable is not intended as an allegory in which each detail corresponds to the exact crimes of David. David's use of his position of power and wealth to "take" what belonged to another is *like* the deed of the rich man. The exact detailing of David's crimes remains for the direct and explicit speech of the judgment oracle that follows (7*b*-12). The parable creates the moment of recognition after David has himself rendered a judgment on the injustice of such privileged "taking."

12:7b-12. Nathan leaves the indirection of parable and risks the directness of confrontational speech that takes the form of a prophetic announcement of God's judgment. It opens with the messenger formula, "Thus says the LORD . . ." (repeated again at the start of v. 11), which emphasizes the prophet's role in speaking God's word and signals that the prophet will speak in the first person, as if the Lord were speaking directly. God recites to David the benevolent deeds done on his behalf (vv. 7*b*-8). This is followed by the accusation detailing David's offenses (v. 9). The formulaic element "Now, therefore . . ." signals the announcement of punishment that will come as judgment for David's sin (vv. 10-12).

God reviews the history of divine graciousness toward David; it is a history dominated by "giving," in contrast to David's "taking" (vv. 7-8). The anointing probably refers to David's anointing by the prophet Samuel (1 Sam 16:13). God saved David from Saul and gave all that was Saul's to David, eventually including the kingdoms of Israel and Judah. It is uncertain what is meant by the reference to "your master's wives," since there is no tradition that David ever took the wives of Saul for himself. Surprisingly, God states a willingness to have given David even more (v. 8*b*), but David has now moved from gift to grasp.[298]

What was veiled and implied in Nathan's parable becomes bold and explicit in the indictment of v. 9. What David has done is given theological meaning in the opening of this indictment. He has "despised the word of the LORD" and done "what is evil in his sight" (v. 9*a*). This is dangerous language, for Saul was rejected as king be-

cause he had "rejected the word of the LORD" (1 Sam 15:26). Again David's deeds are named as "evil" in God's eyes, echoing the language of 11:27*b* and contradicting David's false reassurance to Joab that their murderous deeds were not "evil" but the mere by-product of war (see Commentary on 11:25). David's deeds are not just offenses against Bathsheba and Uriah; they are offenses against God's Word. Even in the later announcement of punishment, God makes clear that in taking Bathsheba for his own wife, "you have despised me" (v. 10*b*).

Again the indictment names David's sin as "taking" Uriah's wife for his own and brackets that accusation of adultery with a twofold statement of David's murder of Uriah (v. 9*b*). David was not present when Uriah was killed in battle ("struck down by the sword"; "killed him with the sword of the Ammonites"), but God's indictment is explicit: *"You . . . struck down . . . killed."*

"Now, therefore . . ." signals God's pronouncement of punishment for David's sin. The "sword will never depart from your house" (v. 10*a*). "I will raise up trouble against you from within your own house" (v. 11*a*). The violence David has done against Uriah and Bathsheba will be visited on David's own family. The story of David, as it unfolds from this point forward, is indeed violent and tragic. It includes the death of a child, an incestuous rape, a murder of revenge, a son's armed rebellion, and that son's subsequent death. God's statement of having given David's wives to a "neighbor" who will lie with them in public, doing before all Israel what David did in secret (vv. 11*b*-12), foreshadows Absalom's public taking of David's wives and concubines in a tent on the palace roof (16:21-22). It was an act of defiance, a taking of David's royal prerogatives to symbolize Absalom's seizure of David's throne. That shameful moment is here given a theological interpretation as being retribution for David's own adultery.

12:13-15a. The shock of Nathan's dramatic accusation "You are the man!" is almost equaled by David's immediate response to God's judgment, "I have sinned against the LORD" (v. 13*a*). David has not lost the capacity to choose for the Lord, and the only avenue back to relationship is the one he has taken, confession and repentance. Power defers to piety. David did not turn on Nathan or reject Nathan's harsh words. He did

---

298. See David M. Gunn, "David and the Gift of the Kingdom (2 Sam 2–4, 9–20; 1 Kgs 1–2)," *Semeia* 3 (1975) 14-45.

not assert his authority or attempt to justify or deny. His confession is as simple and direct as was the moment of recognition that followed the parable. David is the man; David is the sinner. David has dealt violence and death, and violence and death are to return as his judgment. But in his confession, life continues to assert itself. Nathan announces that David's sin has been put aside, and he will not die (v. 13*b*). God's forgiveness can be as simple and direct as David's repentance. But the continuing claim of life made possible by David's response does not remove all consequence of sin. What David has done cannot be undone. Life can be reclaimed and continue in the midst of the consequences of sin, but the tragic reverberations from David's sin will continue to be felt in his family. David has "utterly scorned the LORD," and he may live, but the child conceived by Bathsheba from her union with David will die (v. 14). Nathan has spoken God's word, and he departs the scene as quickly as he appeared (v. 15*a*).

REFLECTIONS

1. This story concerns the speaking of judgment to power. Power is always tempted to live in the illusion that it is autonomous and self-sufficient. Powerful people in powerful positions often imagine that they can define reality in their own terms. David had succumbed to the illusion of royal reality as ultimate authority. Nathan has come to speak to him the truth of the matter, that there is a divine reality before which royal reality is judged. In our own time, the prophetic task is still to speak the truth of divine reality in a world that is obsessed with the self-defining realities of political and economic power. If the church would speak prophetically as a part of its ministry, then it must be willing to speak the truth in the presence of power. There is a divine governance of history that transcends human institutions. There is a divine power at work in history that judges human uses of power. In the eyes of God, the powerless are as valued as the powerful, and the exploitation of these powerless ones is evil. The achievements of power will mean nothing if they are bought at the price of exploiting the weak and the vulnerable. This is the reality of the world the prophet (and the prophetic community) speaks as truth in the presence of power.

But such speech is dangerous. Those who would be prophetic must risk speaking directly to those who hold power. It is not enough to speak about the misuse of power at a distance from power. If the church would make a difference with its prophetic speaking, it must find ways to be heard by those who hold power. This may necessitate finding ways of commanding attention, as Nathan did in his use of parable. "One cannot address royal power directly, especially royal power so deeply in guilt. It is permissible to talk about speaking truth to power, but if truth is to have a chance with power, it must be done with some subtlety."[299] But even for Nathan, there came a moment when royal power was attentive and the unvarnished truth of evil in the service of power had to be named and faced. The risk of this moment is real, and the church cannot imagine that the speaking of truth to power will not be costly at times. It will not always be a David who stands before us. At other times in the biblical story, the response to prophetic confrontation of the king was not repentance. Ahab and Jezebel sought Elijah's life; Manasseh slaughtered the prophets; Jehoiakim held Jeremiah's words in contempt.

2. An important and overlooked aspect of this story is that both Nathan and David stand within and represent the community of faith. As the church, we cannot afford to read this story as a call simply to become Nathans, pointing fingers at and naming the sins of others. Both Nathan and David are part of God's covenant community, and each plays a role in God's plan for Israel.

This story is not concerned with the opposition of the wholly righteous to the unredeemably wicked. Its lesson is that righteousness and sin exist side by side even within the covenant

---

299. Walter Brueggemann, *David's Truth in Israel's Imagination and Memory* (Philadelphia: Fortress, 1985) 63.

community. Thus, the church is never in the position of selecting only one of these roles. It is called to *proclaim God's judgment* on all that opposes God's desire for justice and fullness of life, but it is also required to *receive and acknowledge judgment* for its own participation in the conditions that create brokenness.[300]

3. This story focuses primarily on the speaking of judgment, but it also speaks of the possibilities of confession and repentance in the face of judgment. David's immediate and direct confession of sin (v. 13*a*) is almost as surprising as Nathan's climactic, "You are the man!" (v. 7*a*). David has committed crimes, and from this brokenness will come consequences. They will unfold in the death of the child and the tragedies that will infect David's family. David has unleashed death, but in his confession he reclaims the possibilities of life in the midst of death. He moves from his own self-pronounced verdict that he is a "son of death" (12:5*b*) to Nathan's quiet word, "You will not die" (12:13*b*).

If, as the church, we attend only to Nathan's judgment and fail to note David's repentance, then we run the risk of settling for guilt as the goal of our prophetic speech. Dramatic confrontation and naming of sin in sermons, resolutions, and public forums can often be quite successful in stirring guilt for complicity in the brokenness that is present in our world. But guilt is ultimately static and backward-looking in regret for things done that cannot be undone. David's confession models a first step toward repentance. In the Hebrew concept, repentance is related to the word meaning "to turn." To repent is to turn and go in a new direction. Repentance is dynamic and forward-looking in hope for a new direction away from patterns of brokenness. The good news of this text is that we are not left in guilt but are called to repentance. This does not mean that we are free from the consequences of sin. David has enacted self-centered abuses of power that will return to haunt him through his own children. It does, however, mean that judgment is not the final word; repentance makes a further word of life possible in the face of judgment. If the church speaks the truth to power, it should never be with a self-satisfied assumption that judgment is the final word. We should always speak judgment in the hope that confession and repentance might make life possible in spite of the deathly powers unleashed by sin.

In many medieval synagogue manuscripts of 2 Samuel 12, a gap was left by the copyist in the text following David's confession of sin in v. 13*a*. This was to give the opportunity for the reading of Psalm 51, the great penitential psalm that carries this superscription: "A Psalm of David, when the prophet Nathan came to him, after he had gone in to Bathsheba." This psalm expresses the attitude of repentance, rather than guilt, which the church seeks when it speaks in judgment:

> Have mercy on me, O God,
> according to your steadfast love;
> according to your abundant mercy
> blot out my transgressions.
> Wash me thoroughly from my iniquity,
> and cleanse me from my sin
>
> . . .
>
> Create in me a clean heart, O God,
> and put a new and right spirit within me.
> Do not cast me away from your presence,
> and do not take your holy spirit from me.
> (Ps 51:1-2, 10-11 NRSV)

---

300. Bruce C. Birch and Larry L. Rasmussen, *The Predicament of the Prosperous* (Philadelphia: Westminster, 1978) 128.

2 Samuel 12:15b-25, The Death of the Child of David and Bathsheba

NIV

the LORD struck the child that Uriah's wife had borne to David, and he became ill. ¹⁶David pleaded with God for the child. He fasted and went into his house and spent the nights lying on the ground. ¹⁷The elders of his household stood beside him to get him up from the ground, but he refused, and he would not eat any food with them.

¹⁸On the seventh day the child died. David's servants were afraid to tell him that the child was dead, for they thought, "While the child was still living, we spoke to David but he would not listen to us. How can we tell him the child is dead? He may do something desperate."

¹⁹David noticed that his servants were whispering among themselves and he realized the child was dead. "Is the child dead?" he asked.

"Yes," they replied, "he is dead."

²⁰Then David got up from the ground. After he had washed, put on lotions and changed his clothes, he went into the house of the LORD and worshiped. Then he went to his own house, and at his request they served him food, and he ate.

²¹His servants asked him, "Why are you acting this way? While the child was alive, you fasted and wept, but now that the child is dead, you get up and eat!"

²²He answered, "While the child was still alive, I fasted and wept. I thought, 'Who knows? The LORD may be gracious to me and let the child live.' ²³But now that he is dead, why should I fast? Can I bring him back again? I will go to him, but he will not return to me."

²⁴Then David comforted his wife Bathsheba, and he went to her and lay with her. She gave birth to a son, and they named him Solomon. The LORD loved him; ²⁵and because the LORD loved him, he sent word through Nathan the prophet to name him Jedidiah.ᵃ

ᵃ25 Jedidiah means loved by the LORD.

NRSV

The LORD struck the child that Uriah's wife bore to David, and it became very ill. ¹⁶David therefore pleaded with God for the child; David fasted, and went in and lay all night on the ground. ¹⁷The elders of his house stood beside him, urging him to rise from the ground; but he would not, nor did he eat food with them. ¹⁸On the seventh day the child died. And the servants of David were afraid to tell him that the child was dead; for they said, "While the child was still alive, we spoke to him, and he did not listen to us; how then can we tell him the child is dead? He may do himself some harm." ¹⁹But when David saw that his servants were whispering together, he perceived that the child was dead; and David said to his servants, "Is the child dead?" They said, "He is dead."

20Then David rose from the ground, washed, anointed himself, and changed his clothes. He went into the house of the LORD, and worshiped; he then went to his own house; and when he asked, they set food before him and he ate. ²¹Then his servants said to him, "What is this thing that you have done? You fasted and wept for the child while it was alive; but when the child died, you rose and ate food." ²²He said, "While the child was still alive, I fasted and wept; for I said, 'Who knows? The LORD may be gracious to me, and the child may live.' ²³But now he is dead; why should I fast? Can I bring him back again? I shall go to him, but he will not return to me."

24Then David consoled his wife Bathsheba, and went to her, and lay with her; and she bore a son, and he named him Solomon. The LORD loved him, ²⁵and sent a message by the prophet Nathan; so he named him Jedidiah,ᵃ because of the LORD.

ᵃ That is Beloved of the LORD

COMMENTARY

This segment of the text leaves the didactic style of Nathan's prophetic oracle and returns to a storytelling mode. This section may be the original continuation of 11:27b, before the prophetic addition of Nathan's confrontation with David. The death of David and Bathsheba's child becomes only the first of a series of tragic experiences of death and/or violence in David's family. Moreover, we now understand these experiences in the light of Nathan's pronouncement of God's judgment on David. David's confession reclaims his own life, but such reclaiming is costly. David's own life continues in the midst of the deadly realities he has himself introduced into his own personal story. The first costly experience of this deathly presence in the royal household comes in the death of the son conceived in David's adulterous liaison with Bathsheba. Nathan had already said that the child would die (v. 14). Verses 15b-23 narrate the events surrounding the child's death. Verses 24-25 anticipate a new future and new life with the birth of Solomon, whom the Lord loves and who will become the first king in an ongoing dynasty from David.

12:15b-23. The opening of this bitter story leaves no room for doubt: "The LORD struck the child that Uriah's wife bore to David, and it became very ill" (v. 15b). The death that David brought to another family now enters his own. In the view of this narrator, there was a cost to be paid, and the Lord is the agent exacting the moral cost of David's deathly crimes. Since the price is the life of a child, we may find this view of God difficult to understand and accept, but the text does not address this issue.

The narrative focuses on David. By now we should not be surprised at this. David is clearly attached to the child and pleads with God for the child's life (v. 16a). The conception of this child altered the life of king and kingdom. To have lost so much and then lose the child as well seems unbearable. David refuses food, keeping vigil through the night, and his servants become distressed, urging him to eat (vv. 16b-17). After seven days, the child dies, and the servants are afraid to tell David. They fear that his grief will deepen and that he may even do himself harm

(v. 18). David perceives the reality of the moment without being told. He asks his whispering servants if the child is dead, and they confirm that it is so (v. 19).

It is at this point in the story that David's actions confound his servants (and readers). Custom dictates that mourning should begin, with its attendant lamentation and ceremonies of grief. Instead of these expected practices, David begins a series of purposeful activities not usually associated with a time of mourning (v. 20). The verbs dominate the story: David rose, washed, anointed himself, changed clothes, entered the house of the Lord, worshiped, went to his own house, requested food, and ate. In short, David resumed his life and the practices of his customary routines.

His servants, who were disturbed over David's unrestrained distress during the child's illness, are equally dismayed at his behavior after the child's death. David has reversed the usual custom. His servants cannot restrain themselves. "What are you doing?" they ask (v. 21). David's response shows a remarkable ability to face the realities of life and death and his own complicity in those things that make for life and death. He fasted and wept while the child was ill in petition for the graciousness of God and in hope that God's mercy would grant the child life (v. 22). But when this was not to be, David accepted the reality of death and rejected fasting and weeping in favor of relinquishment and resumption of life (v. 23). He refuses to bow to the power of death and accepts his inability to restore his son. "I shall go to him, but he will not return to me" (v. 23b).

Walter Brueggemann has seen in this story one evidence of a new portrait of humanity that emerges in the story of David. David is the model of God's "trusted creature" who acts with boldness and freedom to claim the gifts of life with which humanity is trusted.

David's reaction to the death of his child and thus to the reality of all death is not to be viewed as stoic resignation.... David has a fresh view of the meaning of life and death, where his proper hopes and proper fears are to be located. This is more than a violation of common practice. It is an act of profound faith in the face of the most precious tabus of his people. David had discerned, for whatever reasons, that the issues of his life are not to be found in cringing fear before the powers of death, but rather in his ability to embrace and abandon, to love and to leave, to take life as it comes not with indifference but with freedom, not with callousness but with buoyancy.... For him there is none of the conventional paralysis in death. He knew death belonged legitimately to history, and he had no illusions about entering some kind of faith which did not know death.[301]

12:24-25. David's affirmation of life in the face of death is followed by a report of new life. In rapid succession, David comforts Bathsheba, goes to her, lies with her, and she then bears a second son (v. 24*a*). This is the first time since Bathsheba was introduced (11:3) that she is named in her own right and not referred to as "the wife of Uriah." In the birth of this second child, she becomes more than the occasion for David's sin. In fact, Bathsheba is later to play a very active role in helping this son succeed to the throne of David (1 Kgs 1:11-31).

This son is named Solomon (v. 24*b*), a name usually associated with the word שלום (*šālôm*, "peace," "wholeness"). This is an ironic name in

the light of the events that preceded his birth, but perhaps it should be seen as the "peace/wholeness" hoped for in the new beginning of his birth. That this is a genuine new beginning with hope of a new future is affirmed by the notice that "the LORD loved him" (v. 24*b*). Further, God sends the prophet Nathan, this time as a bearer of hope rather than judgment. Nathan names the child "Jedidiah," a name that means "beloved of the LORD [Yahweh]" (v. 25). This name is not used elsewhere about Solomon and may be considered a private name, while "Solomon" was to be the child's throne name as Israel's third king.

The consequences of death and violence unleashed by David's sin are not yet played out. Tragic events lie ahead, but this notice already foreshadows that the promise of dynasty to David will remain firm and that Solomon need not carry into his own reign the judgment given to his father. Indeed, this may be part of the purpose of this entire narrative: to show that the sins of David have been judged and paid for. Solomon and the Davidic dynasty are free from guilt.

301. Walter Brueggemann, "The Trusted Creature," *CBQ* 31 (1969) 490.

REFLECTIONS

1. This is a difficult story for modern readers in the church. We do not wish to think that the lives of innocent children are exacted by God as punishment for a parent's sin. But this text assumes that all things ultimately come from God, including the illness of this child. From this point of view, all deaths are a part of the mystery of God's providence. God can and does use the circumstances of our lives to further the purposes of divine grace and judgment. This story does not, however, make a generalized claim about the deaths of all children.

The emphasis in this story is on David, who thought he could be the controller of life and death for his own ends, but must now discover that he is not autonomous and cannot control life and death, even though he is the king. Life and death exist in human history as a part of the mystery of God's providence, and not as a matter to be taken into human hands.

What also offends modern readers is the total focus on David. It is David who is the subject of this narrative—his loss, his grief, and finally his response in the face of the tragic cost. The child and Bathsheba are only elements of the plot in this episode of David's story, and they are not even named. This storytelling is simply endlessly fascinated with David and his meaning for Israel. This is less an intentional belittling of other characters in the story than a mark of the enormous importance David came to hold for Israel. That attention still focuses on David even in these episodes of sin, judgment, loss, and pain is a remarkable testimony to the ability of Israel's storytellers to face the realities of David's weakness and vulnerability while yet affirming his vitality and importance in Israel's story. This suggests that the tradition about David has something to teach us in observing his vulnerable moments and not simply in celebrating his triumphs.

2. This story reminds us that in the community of faith, life always has a further word to speak. There is something about the death of a child that heightens the offense of death. Life is unexpectedly cut short. Such a death seems unnatural, unfair. It is surely this same sense of offense that leads David to his severe pain and grief when faced with the potential loss of his son. David's grief and our own when faced with the reality of such untimely death is an appropriate acknowledgment of the reality and power of death in our human existence. It is an expression of our vulnerability and a recognition that we are not autonomous and in control. Even a life of piety and faith does not give us safe conduct around the necessity of facing death's power. The death of a child brings us more unexpectedly and harshly into the presence of that power. In our own grief, in our care of others in their grief, we must allow for the acknowledgment and voicing of the pain that comes with death's power. We must refuse to deny the reality of death's power.

But David's response to the death of the child is an important word to us about the power of life, which does not take away the offense of death. It simply refuses to let death have the final word. Death invades and inflicts its pain, but life goes on. In grieving the death of a child, it is all too easy to let that child's death become the most important thing about him or her. But even in a foreshortened life, the gift of that child's life among us is more important than his or her death. If, like David, we dwell not on death but on life, then we align ourselves with the importance that the gift of a life be remembered and affirmed. That life need not be eclipsed by letting death have the final word. To go on with life is not heartless or stoic and does not require us to deny the pain of loss. It is to affirm that the power of life is stronger than the power of death, and if we live that as true for our own lives we can affirm it as true for our children who die before us.[302]

For Christians, this understanding is at the heart of resurrection faith. Christ's resurrection does not remove or nullify the offense of the cross. Resurrection is simply God's refusal to let death have the final word. There is a further word of life that God speaks in the face of death and against the power of death (see Romans 6). David claimed the power of life at the very moment that death seemed to prevail. To read his story is to understand that we can do the same.

302. See Bruce C. Birch, "Biblical Faith and the Loss of Children," *The Christian Century* 100 (1983) 965-67.

2 Samuel 12:26-31, The Capture of Rabbah

NIV

26Meanwhile Joab fought against Rabbah of the Ammonites and captured the royal citadel. 27Joab then sent messengers to David, saying, "I have fought against Rabbah and taken its water supply. 28Now muster the rest of the troops and besiege the city and capture it. Otherwise I will take the city, and it will be named after me."

29So David mustered the entire army and went to Rabbah, and attacked and captured it. 30He took the crown from the head of their king[a]—its weight was a talent[b] of gold, and it was set with precious stones—and it was placed on David's head. He took a great quantity of plunder from the city 31and brought out the people who were

a30 Or *of Milcom* (that is, Molech)   b30 That is, about 75 pounds (about 34 kilograms)

NRSV

26Now Joab fought against Rabbah of the Ammonites, and took the royal city. 27Joab sent messengers to David, and said, "I have fought against Rabbah; moreover, I have taken the water city. 28Now, then, gather the rest of the people together, and encamp against the city, and take it; or I myself will take the city, and it will be called by my name." 29So David gathered all the people together and went to Rabbah, and fought against it and took it. 30He took the crown of Milcom[a] from his head; the weight of it was a talent of gold, and in it was a precious stone; and it was placed on David's head. He also brought forth the spoil of the city, a very great amount. 31He brought out the people who were in it, and set them to

a Gk See 1 Kings 11.5, 33: Heb *their kings*

NIV

there, consigning them to labor with saws and with iron picks and axes, and he made them work at brickmaking.[a] He did this to all the Ammonite towns. Then David and his entire army returned to Jerusalem.

[a]*31 The meaning of the Hebrew for this clause is uncertain.*

NRSV

work with saws and iron picks and iron axes, or sent them to the brickworks. Thus he did to all the cities of the Ammonites. Then David and all the people returned to Jerusalem.

COMMENTARY

The story moves from private matters back to the public arena and resumes the account of the Ammonite campaign, left off at 11:1. This military confrontation with a neighboring kingdom had begun in the humiliation of David's ambassadors in 10:1-5 and now concludes with the capture and pillage of the Ammonite capital city, Rabbah.

Developments in this final stage of the siege of Rabbah take an ironic turn. David had remained in Jerusalem while Joab conducted the siege (11:1). This simple fact provides the context for the account of David's adultery with Bathsheba and subsequent murder of her husband Uriah. Further, Nathan had confronted David with his crimes and pronounced God's judgment on him. Now, with all the personal damage done, Joab summons David to participate in the final defeat of Rabbah (v. 27). Joab has brought the city to submission by attacking its water supply (v. 27b). But out of loyalty to David, he sends word that he believes it more appropriate that David's name be associated with the fall of the city rather than his own (v. 28). It is a worthy and perhaps prudent gesture on the part of a loyal commander.

David responds to this summons and goes to Rabbah. The account is dominated by the verb "to take" (לכד *lākad,* vv. 28 [2x], 29). How much more appropriate it is for David to be engaged in "taking" the city of Israel's enemies than for him to be idle in Jerusalem "taking" the wife of his loyal commander Uriah (11:4). David "takes" not only the city but also spoils from the city (v. 30b), including a massive gold and jewel-encrusted crown taken from the idol of Ammon's god, Milcom, which is placed on David's head (v. 30a). He subjects the people of Ammon to forced labor to dismantle the defenses of their own cities (v. 31). Ammon was almost certainly incorporated territorially into the Davidic empire. The tradition allows David to capture, take plunder, use slave labor, and return to Jerusalem without moral comment. There is no memory of the story of Saul, who had been judged for such actions. There is no prophet Samuel to declare such campaigns as governed by the laws of holy war and חרם (*ḥērem;* see the Commentary on 1 Sam 15:1-35). The prophet Nathan is silent about such older tribal institutions. We have left tribal reality behind, and the Israelite tradition now stands fully in the reality of kingship. Royal concerns for territory, enemies made subject people, and economic gain now govern the story. In this military report, these concerns are assumed as appropriate to the reality of kings without further comment. (These few verses simply complete the narrative of David's Ammonite-Aramaean wars, begun in chap. 10. See Reflections at 10:1-19.)

2 Samuel 13:1-22, Amnon Rapes Tamar

NIV

13 In the course of time, Amnon son of David fell in love with Tamar, the beautiful sister of Absalom son of David.

NRSV

13 Some time passed. David's son Absalom had a beautiful sister whose name was Tamar; and David's son Amnon fell in love with

NIV

²Amnon became frustrated to the point of illness on account of his sister Tamar, for she was a virgin, and it seemed impossible for him to do anything to her.

³Now Amnon had a friend named Jonadab son of Shimeah, David's brother. Jonadab was a very shrewd man. ⁴He asked Amnon, "Why do you, the king's son, look so haggard morning after morning? Won't you tell me?"

Amnon said to him, "I'm in love with Tamar, my brother Absalom's sister."

⁵"Go to bed and pretend to be ill," Jonadab said. "When your father comes to see you, say to him, 'I would like my sister Tamar to come and give me something to eat. Let her prepare the food in my sight so I may watch her and then eat it from her hand.'"

⁶So Amnon lay down and pretended to be ill. When the king came to see him, Amnon said to him, "I would like my sister Tamar to come and make some special bread in my sight, so I may eat from her hand."

⁷David sent word to Tamar at the palace: "Go to the house of your brother Amnon and prepare some food for him." ⁸So Tamar went to the house of her brother Amnon, who was lying down. She took some dough, kneaded it, made the bread in his sight and baked it. ⁹Then she took the pan and served him the bread, but he refused to eat.

"Send everyone out of here," Amnon said. So everyone left him. ¹⁰Then Amnon said to Tamar, "Bring the food here into my bedroom so I may eat from your hand." And Tamar took the bread she had prepared and brought it to her brother Amnon in his bedroom. ¹¹But when she took it to him to eat, he grabbed her and said, "Come to bed with me, my sister."

¹²"Don't, my brother!" she said to him. "Don't force me. Such a thing should not be done in Israel! Don't do this wicked thing. ¹³What about me? Where could I get rid of my disgrace? And what about you? You would be like one of the wicked fools in Israel. Please speak to the king; he will not keep me from being married to you." ¹⁴But he refused to listen to her, and since he was stronger than she, he raped her.

¹⁵Then Amnon hated her with intense hatred.

NRSV

her. ²Amnon was so tormented that he made himself ill because of his sister Tamar, for she was a virgin and it seemed impossible to Amnon to do anything to her. ³But Amnon had a friend whose name was Jonadab, the son of David's brother Shimeah; and Jonadab was a very crafty man. ⁴He said to him, "O son of the king, why are you so haggard morning after morning? Will you not tell me?" Amnon said to him, "I love Tamar, my brother Absalom's sister." ⁵Jonadab said to him, "Lie down on your bed, and pretend to be ill; and when your father comes to see you, say to him, 'Let my sister Tamar come and give me something to eat, and prepare the food in my sight, so that I may see it and eat it from her hand.'" ⁶So Amnon lay down, and pretended to be ill; and when the king came to see him, Amnon said to the king, "Please let my sister Tamar come and make a couple of cakes in my sight, so that I may eat from her hand."

7Then David sent home to Tamar, saying, "Go to your brother Amnon's house, and prepare food for him." ⁸So Tamar went to her brother Amnon's house, where he was lying down. She took dough, kneaded it, made cakes in his sight, and baked the cakes. ⁹Then she took the pan and set them[a] out before him, but he refused to eat. Amnon said, "Send out everyone from me." So everyone went out from him. ¹⁰Then Amnon said to Tamar, "Bring the food into the chamber, so that I may eat from your hand." So Tamar took the cakes she had made, and brought them into the chamber to Amnon her brother. ¹¹But when she brought them near him to eat, he took hold of her, and said to her, "Come, lie with me, my sister." ¹²She answered him, "No, my brother, do not force me; for such a thing is not done in Israel; do not do anything so vile! ¹³As for me, where could I carry my shame? And as for you, you would be as one of the scoundrels in Israel. Now therefore, I beg you, speak to the king; for he will not withhold me from you." ¹⁴But he would not listen to her; and being stronger than she, he forced her and lay with her.

15Then Amnon was seized with a very great loathing for her; indeed, his loathing was even greater than the lust he had felt for her. Amnon

ᵃ Heb and poured

NIV

In fact, he hated her more than he had loved her. Amnon said to her, "Get up and get out!"

[16]"No!" she said to him. "Sending me away would be a greater wrong than what you have already done to me."

But he refused to listen to her. [17]He called his personal servant and said, "Get this woman out of here and bolt the door after her." [18]So his servant put her out and bolted the door after her. She was wearing a richly ornamented[a] robe, for this was the kind of garment the virgin daughters of the king wore. [19]Tamar put ashes on her head and tore the ornamented[b] robe she was wearing. She put her hand on her head and went away, weeping aloud as she went.

[20]Her brother Absalom said to her, "Has that Amnon, your brother, been with you? Be quiet now, my sister; he is your brother. Don't take this thing to heart." And Tamar lived in her brother Absalom's house, a desolate woman.

[21]When King David heard all this, he was furious. [22]Absalom never said a word to Amnon, either good or bad; he hated Amnon because he had disgraced his sister Tamar.

a18 The meaning of the Hebrew for this phrase is uncertain.   *b19* The meaning of the Hebrew for this word is uncertain.

NRSV

said to her, "Get out!" [16]But she said to him, "No, my brother;[a] for this wrong in sending me away is greater than the other that you did to me." But he would not listen to her. [17]He called the young man who served him and said, "Put this woman out of my presence, and bolt the door after her." [18](Now she was wearing a long robe with sleeves; for this is how the virgin daughters of the king were clothed in earlier times.[b]) So his servant put her out, and bolted the door after her. [19]But Tamar put ashes on her head, and tore the long robe that she was wearing; she put her hand on her head, and went away, crying aloud as she went.

[20]Her brother Absalom said to her, "Has Amnon your brother been with you? Be quiet for now, my sister; he is your brother; do not take this to heart." So Tamar remained, a desolate woman, in her brother Absalom's house. [21]When King David heard of all these things, he became very angry, but he would not punish his son Amnon, because he loved him, for he was his firstborn.[c] [22]But Absalom spoke to Amnon neither good nor bad; for Absalom hated Amnon, because he had raped his sister Tamar.

a Cn Compare Gk Vg: Meaning of Heb uncertain   *b* Cn: Heb *were clothed in robes*   *c* QMs Gk: MT lacks *but he would not punish . . . firstborn*

COMMENTARY

This shocking episode narrates a brutal and incestuous rape. Tamar is the object of lustful desire by her half brother Amnon. The story reports in graphic detail Amnon's plot to get Tamar alone, his violent rape of her, and his callous discarding of her afterward. Her brother, Absalom, urges her silence and broods on his own plans for vengeance and ambitions. Their father, David, is angry but takes no action against Amnon. The story is truly what Phyllis Trible has labeled "a text of terror."[303]

Unlike Bathsheba (chap. 11), Tamar has voice and action in this story, and she speaks and acts with wisdom and courage. Nevertheless, in sig-

303. Phyllis Trible, "Tamar: The Royal Rape of Wisdom," in *Texts of Terror: Literary-Feminist Readings of Biblical Narratives* (Philadelphia: Fortress, 1984) 37-64.

nificant ways this remains a story of men set in the man's world of power and politics. Tamar is introduced not in her own right but as the sister of Absalom and the object of Amnon's desire (v. 1). Absalom and Amnon are sons of David and rivals to succeed him on the throne. For the narrator of this story, the rape of Tamar is not of interest as a personal tragedy for Tamar but as an offense to the family of Absalom, which leads to Absalom's vengeful killing of Amnon and his subsequent banishment by David. Tamar's rape sets in motion a course of events that eventually eliminates the two leading contenders for the Davidic throne. Tamar is an event rather than a person in this story. When the event is over, she disappears, while Absalom and Amnon play out the effects of the event that are of greatest interest to the narrator.

In the larger context, this story is a part of an unfolding chronicle of the violence David has unleashed in his own family.[304] He has himself modeled the wanton behavior that "takes" by power whatever is desired (Bathsheba, chap. 11) and is willing to kill for his own self-interest (Uriah, chap. 11). Now his sons follow in his footsteps, to the grief of Tamar. In this larger context, these violent events are also a part of the "trouble against you from within your own house" (12:11a), which Nathan the prophet announced as God's judgment for David's sin. Tamar is a victim not only of Amnon's lust but also of David's sin and God's judgment.

We have little choice but to attend to the drama of tragedy in David's house and power politics in David's kingdom, for David is the fascination and focus of the books of Samuel. Nevertheless, we can also choose to see the tragedy and pain of Tamar the person in spite of the narrator's emphasis on her rape as the excuse for Absalom's revenge. We need not victimize Tamar again by failing to note her courage and resourcefulness in the face of danger or by refusing to acknowledge the full reality of the suffering and humiliation inflicted upon her, not only by Amnon, who raped her, but also by David and Absalom, who see her tragedy primarily as a complication in kingdom politics.[305]

13:1-7. The story begins with the naming of David's son Absalom, for it is in his fate that the narrator is interested. Tamar is named only after her identity as Absalom's beautiful sister is stated (v. 1a). Indeed, she is bracketed by two princes, for Amnon, the half brother of Absalom, is said to love her (v. 1b). Amnon is David's oldest son (3:2-5) and, therefore, David's likely successor. Absalom was probably next in line for the throne, since Chileab (3:3) does not appear in any stories and is believed to have died. This story is not told

for its own sake but for its effect on the succession to the throne.[306]

It becomes increasingly apparent that Amnon's so-called love is really lust. He is described as being obsessed with Tamar to the point of illness (v. 2a). Tamar is not available to him. She is his sister, a fact reinforced by constant use of brother/sister language in this chapter. She is a virgin, undoubtedly sequestered and protected in women's quarters with other marriageable women of the court. The narrative is straightforward; Amnon's so-called love is frustration that he cannot do with Tamar what he pleases (v. 2b).

Jonadab is introduced as a friend of Amnon, the nephew of David, and a "crafty" man (v. 3). Amnon reveals the problem of his "love" for Tamar (again identified as Absalom's sister, v. 4). The tone of the text is misleading. Amnon's intentions are later exposed as the violence of incest and rape, but the text treats his plotting with Jonadab as if the issue were merely the plight of a lovesick young man. We are well warned by this story of the innocent guises that can mask violence. Jonadab devises a plan, with the sole intent of isolating Amnon alone with Tamar. Amnon is to feign illness, and when he is visited by his father, David, he is to ask that Tamar be sent to make cakes and feed him in his illness (v. 5). Amnon follows this plan to the letter (v. 6). David once again becomes complicit (this time probably unwittingly) in sending someone to a violent fate—first Uriah, now Tamar (v. 7).

13:8-14. Tamar comes innocently to Amnon's house, and what the reader knows to be a charade is played out. Her actions are efficient and caring. She performs all the necessary operations for the baking of cakes (v. 8), but Amnon refuses to eat and instead sends everyone from the room (v. 9). Amnon implores her to come into his chamber and feed him (presumably a separate bedchamber where he is lying in bed feigning illness, v. 10). It is at this point that all pretense vanishes on Amnon's part (v. 11). There is no illness; there is no love. There is "grasping/seizing" (חזק ḥāzaq, a verb that emphasizes strength) and desire,

304. Burke O. Long, "Wounded Beginnings: David and Two Sons," in *Images of Man and God: Old Testament Short Stories in Literary Focus*, ed. by Burke O. Long (Sheffield: Almond, 1981) 26-34, treats this episode as a short story in its own right that is incorporated into the plot of the larger compositions of the succession narrative and the Deuteronomistic History.

305. A notable example of telling and interpreting this story from Tamar's point of view can be found in Pamela Cooper-White, *The Cry of Tamar: Violence Against Women and the Church's Response* (Minneapolis: Fortress, 1995) 1-14. My discussion has also been informed by an unpublished seminar paper on this chapter by Mary Petrina Boyd.

306. A. A. Anderson, *2 Samuel*, WBC 11 (Waco: Word, 1989) 172, suggests that "Amnon's love for Tamar was, largely, part of his plan to put Absalom and his family in their place! . . . Although Amnon was attracted by Tamar's beauty he hoped, even more so, both to gratify his sexual desires and to humiliate Absalom through Tamar, at the same time." Although this is possible, there is little explicit evidence of this in the text.

"Come, lie with me, my sister." It is uncertain whether laws against incest were in force at this time (Lev 18:9, 11; 20:17; Deut 27:22) or whether they applied to the royal family. Tamar later suggests that marriage would have been possible (v. 13*b*). It may be that the frequent use of "brother/sister" language points to disregard of filial loyalties rather than to a charge of incest.

The intent to rape, however, is clear. Amnon has not made an invitation; he has voiced a demand and will not be denied. Tamar names the intent, "No, my brother, do not force me" (v. 12*a*). The meaning of the verb ענה (*'ānâ*, "force") is connected with concepts of humiliation and oppression. Tamar sees clearly that rape is Amnon's intention (the same verb is used in v. 14, when Amnon carries out that intention).

Unlike Bathsheba in 11:4, Tamar resists the lustful grasp of royal power—in speech and in action. Trible has emphasized Tamar's courageous voicing of wise counsel in the face of dire threat.[307] She quickly marshals arguments against Amnon's intended violence, in his own interests as well as hers. She first argues that such a thing is simply not done in Israel, and she names this act with the term נבלה (*nĕbālâ*, v. 12*b*). A widely used traditional translation of this term is "folly" or "foolishness" (KJV, RSV), but recent scholarship and translators have recognized the inadequacy of this rendering. Phillips notes that this term is "a general expression for serious disorderly and un- ruly action resulting in the breakup of an existing relationship. . . . It indicates the end of an existing order consequent upon breach of rules which maintained that order."[308] The renderings in the NRSV ("vile [thing]") and the NIV ("wicked thing") are more appropriate. Tamar argues that Amnon's deed would violate deeply held princi- ples that guard the Israelite social order.

Taking a second, more practical tack, Tamar laments that she would have to live in shame, but more pointedly Amnon's reputation would be ru- ined. He would be regarded as "one of the נבלים *nĕbālîm*] in Israel"—i.e., "a fool," "a scoundrel" (v. 13*a*). We are reminded of Nabal, in 1 Samuel 25, whose name and actions were from this same root word.

307. Trible, *Texts of Terror*, 36-64.
308. A. Phillips, "NEBALAH—a Term for Serious Disorderly and Unruly Conduct," *VT* 25 (1975) 241.

Finally, Tamar begs Amnon to speak with David and arrange a marriage. She believes David would not refuse the relationship (v. 13*b*). It is not clear whether such marriages of half siblings in the royal family were acceptable, but Tamar is probably right that David would agree to it rather than face the scandal that is about to erupt. After all, David has defied convention for the sake of lust himself. This plea on Tamar's part is a sad testimony to her recognition of the powerless role that women occupied in ancient Israel. She knows that if Amnon is determined, he can have her, but she urges him to do this in a way that accords her some honor and respect.

Tamar's speech is remarkable for its wise counsel under such desperate circumstances. Her arguments are compelling, and she is able to appeal to Amnon's interests as well as her own. Yet, Amnon refuses to listen to her. He rejects wise speech in favor of physical power and violence. The rape is reported in direct and brutal terms (v. 14). Amnon was stronger than Tamar, so he forced her (the verb is *'ānâ* again; cf. v. 12). The final verb שכב (*šākab*, "to lay") appears in the Hebrew text without its customary preposition "with," used to indicate con- sensual sexual intercourse. The result is a construc- tion that accords with the brutal crudity of our modern expression, making the final phrase of this verse, "and he laid her." The NIV combines the effect of the verbs "force" and "lay" to tersely translate, "he raped her." The notice that Amnon was stronger than Tamar implies physical resistance on her part. To wise speech, Tamar adds courageous action, but she is overpowered.

13:15-19. Just as this account began with Amnon's feelings, so also now that rape has been committed, Amnon's feelings continue to occupy the narrative. He is filled with intense hatred (v. 15; NRSV, "loathing"). His so-called love (v. 1) is exposed as lust and the power to do violence. The reversal from desire to repulsion is immediate and revealing. He had no regard for Tamar beyond the gratification of his own desires. Now he can- not face what he has done. He orders Tamar, "Get up and get out!" (v. 15*b*). Amnon has used Tamar, and he is now through with her.

Again Tamar boldly protests. Although bruised, bleeding, and humiliated, Tamar understands the repercussions of what is happening. She is not paralyzed by Amnon's violence and hatred, but sees her interests clearly. She argues that to send her away now would be an even greater wrong than he has already committed (v. 16). According to Israelite law, Amnon is now guilty of the rape of an unbetrothed virgin, and the law demanded that he make the bridal payment and marry her (Exod 22:16-17; see also Deut 22:28-29). Although she has been brutalized, to be sent away would subject Tamar to the cultural horror of a life of permanent shame, unmarriageability, and childlessness. She would be deprived even of the limited opportunities available to women for life as a full part of the community. The marriage required by law in such a situation would at least give her some rights and some sense of public honor.

For the second time, Amnon will not listen to Tamar (v. 16b; cf. v. 14a). He calls his servant and has Tamar forcibly removed from his presence and the door bolted (vv. 17, 18b). It is the last recorded contact he has with her; he is through with her. No shred of regard for her fate is revealed.

Perhaps Amnon thought that was the end of the matter and that Tamar would slink away in silence and shame. But Tamar will not participate in a conspiracy of silence. She boldly makes public what Amnon has done and forces the world of power and kingdom to face the reality of this violence and her humiliation. Apparently princesses wore a special garment that signified their virginity and marriageability (v. 18a). Tamar now tears this garment and goes forth in grief and public lamentation, with ashes on her head, with her hand raised upon her head, and with loud weeping (v. 19). Tamar's public outcry ensures that the chain of consequences will now flow unbroken from Amnon's act (and originally from David's acts of adultery and murder). Violence will beget violence.

13:20-22. Tamar's speaking and acting are finished in the story. The narrator's interest shifts to the repercussions of these events in the world of royal power. It is Absalom who will now be the central figure. He meets his sister in her grief and humiliation and seems to know that it is Amnon who has done this thing (v. 20a). Absalom urges Tamar to "be quiet for now, my sister; he is your brother; do not take this to heart" (v. 20b). Absalom's response minimizes Tamar's pain and humiliation and suggests to Tamar that not much

can be done, since it is a family matter. She is urged to silence and the stifling of feelings. Some suggest that in the light of Absalom's later revenge against Amnon, he is not minimizing Tamar's experience but merely biding his time.[309] Absalom was certainly deeply offended by Amnon's assault on his sister. Nevertheless, he does not share with Tamar his anger toward Amnon or even his sympathy with her plight.[310] Absalom's revenge seems to be more a matter of restoring family honor and securing his own place in the succession than a matter of solidarity with Tamar. He does take her into his house, where she remains a "desolate" woman, a term that indicates her status as a woman without hope of marriage or family who must live with permanent public humiliation (v. 20b).

On hearing of this atrocity, King David responds by becoming "very angry" (v. 21a). But his anger is of little consequence. We are told that he will not punish Amnon because he loves him as his firstborn (v. 21b).[311] David does nothing. We have known David as a man of decisive action, but in this and subsequent episodes narrating the drama of his own family, David is curiously passive and indecisive. Perhaps David is himself so morally compromised by his own flagrant crimes (chap. 11) that he cannot confront the excesses of his sons. David may be angry, but he joins the conspiracy of silence around the rape of Tamar, and in doing so he unwittingly allows Absalom's murderous revenge to run its course. It is to this further violence that v. 22 points. Absalom speaks neither "good nor bad" to Amnon, which may mean he avoided him altogether. Instead Absalom nurtures hatred for his brother because Amnon had raped (the word is 'ānâ again) his sister, Tamar.

309. C. C. Conroy, *Absalom, Absalom! Narrative and Language in 2 Sam 13–20*, AnBib 81 (Rome: Pontifical Biblical Institute, 1978) 35, finds in Absalom's spare response a "tone of tenderness." Trible, *Texts of Terror*, 51, suggests that Absalom is not minimizing but using euphemisms that underscore the unspeakable horror of the rape. See Cooper-White's response to Trible and discussion of this issue in *The Cry of Tamar*, 8-9, 265.

310. Walter Brueggemann, *First and Second Samuel*, Interpretation (Louisville: John Knox, 1990) 288-89, writes that "Absalom assures his sister he will carry her wrong in his heart." Although subsequent events may show that he did so, the text does not depict Absalom as assuring Tamar that her burden is shared. In fact, though he may take the matter to heart, he tells Tamar not to do so (v. 20).

311. The Septuagint, with some support from the Qumran texts, is the basis for the fuller text of the NRSV. Most commentators have adopted this reading, but the NIV follows the briefer Hebrew text.

REFLECTIONS

1. Although this is a story of princes and princesses in an ancient kingdom, the violence it narrates is shockingly timeless. Pamela Cooper-White has found in the text of this ancient story a witness to issues of violence against women that are still with us.

Tamar's story, sadly, is still modern
❖ Tamar was sexually assaulted, not by a stranger, but by someone she knew.
❖ The violation took place not in a dark alley or in a desolate park, but by a member of her own family in his home.
❖ Tamar was exploited through one of her most vulnerable traits—her kindness and her upbringing to take care of the other.
❖ Tamar said no; her no was not respected.
❖ When Tamar sought help, she was told to keep quiet.
❖ The process for achieving justice and restitution was taken out of her hands entirely and carried forward by her brother—it became men's business.
❖ In the end, it was her perpetrator for whom her father mourned, not for her.
❖ The end of Tamar's story happens without her.[312]

The pattern of Tamar's story is repeated in the story of many modern women who are the victims of rape or incest, yet whose experience has been denied or hidden.

This text is not read publicly in the church, and it is seldom preached. Persons experienced at Bible study in the church are often shocked to have this story called to their attention. They had no idea such a story was a part of the biblical tradition. It is as if the silence counseled by Absalom (v. 20) has extended through the centuries to the present. It is easy to understand why the story has been ignored. We do not like to be faced with the brutal realities of which this story speaks. Even less do we like to think such stories are a part of our Scripture. What does it mean that David's line, from which the Messiah is to come, has been determined by the course of such violent events?

While it is easy to understand why many would prefer not to read this story, there are important reasons why it should be read. In reading this story, we are forced to recognize our own experience in this ancient tale. There is an empowerment that comes from recognizing that this story names present realities as well as those long past. If such stories are read as part of our biblical tradition, similar stories can be faced in our own lives, in the lives of our family and friends, and in the life of our communities. To read of the courage and wisdom of Tamar may encourage those who have been victimized in our own time to give voice to their own experience, so that conspiracies of silence do not allow continued violence to be denied or ignored. To read of Tamar's pain can enable others to voice their own pain so that it is not borne alone. If the church can be the place of such reading and such voicing, then there is hope that the church might provide a community prepared to take action against continued patterns of violence against women in our culture and to stand in caring support of those who have already been victimized.

2. This story is also a reminder of the way in which resorting to violence and exploitation gives rise to continuing chains of tragedy and suffering. Acts of violence are seldom isolated events. David's own actions in the "taking" of Bathsheba and the murder of Uriah provided the model for Amnon's violent use of power to fulfill his own desires. Amnon's brutal rape of Tamar kindles a hatred in Absalom that will lead to further violence (13:23-36). Absalom's violent revenge will result in alienation, which leads to rebellion, war, and further death (chaps. 15–19). It is no different in our own time. Those who brutalize others have often been witnesses to or victims of such violence themselves.

---

312. Pamela Cooper-White, *The Cry of Tamar: Violence Against Women and the Church's Response* (Minneapolis: Fortress, 1995) 4-5.

In this story, it is David who might have broken the chain of violence he himself had begun. But, though angered, he does nothing, and his refusal to act continues the chain. In reading this story, we are encouraged to recognize the ways in which we grow angry at the violence of our society, but choose not to act. We live in a society in which gun ownership continues to rise and schools have been forced to develop policies to deal with weapons brought to school. Drive-by shootings are a reality in every urban area of the country. Bombings of the federal building in Oklahoma City and at the Atlanta Olympics in 1996 raise the specter of domestic terrorism. Dozens of African American churches have been burned in senseless acts of destruction. We live in a violent world in which genocidal war masquerades as "ethnic cleansing" in Bosnia, where tourists are slaughtered in Luxor for the sake of a political statement, and where the potential for peace in the Middle East is undermined by violent Arab and Israeli extremists. These are dramatic evidences of violence, but they are fueled by a tolerance of violence in smaller ways, such as an unwillingness to face the acceptance of violence as commonplace in our entertainment media (where women are often the victims of graphic and sexually charged acts of violence), and a growing lack of civility in personal and political relationships. David's example should teach us that anger is not enough. Tolerance and inaction in the face of violence fosters further violence. Because David did nothing, this story ends with a hatred that will continue the chain of violence. Our tolerance and inaction in the face of violence will likewise ensure the continuity of violence in our midst.

2 Samuel 13:23-39, Absalom Kills Amnon

NIV

²³Two years later, when Absalom's sheepshearers were at Baal Hazor near the border of Ephraim, he invited all the king's sons to come there. ²⁴Absalom went to the king and said, "Your servant has had shearers come. Will the king and his officials please join me?"

²⁵"No, my son," the king replied. "All of us should not go; we would only be a burden to you." Although Absalom urged him, he still refused to go, but gave him his blessing.

²⁶Then Absalom said, "If not, please let my brother Amnon come with us."

The king asked him, "Why should he go with you?" ²⁷But Absalom urged him, so he sent with him Amnon and the rest of the king's sons.

²⁸Absalom ordered his men, "Listen! When Amnon is in high spirits from drinking wine and I say to you, 'Strike Amnon down,' then kill him. Don't be afraid. Have not I given you this order? Be strong and brave." ²⁹So Absalom's men did to Amnon what Absalom had ordered. Then all the king's sons got up, mounted their mules and fled.

³⁰While they were on their way, the report came to David: "Absalom has struck down all the king's sons; not one of them is left." ³¹The king

NRSV

²³After two full years Absalom had sheepshearers at Baal-hazor, which is near Ephraim, and Absalom invited all the king's sons. ²⁴Absalom came to the king, and said, "Your servant has sheepshearers; will the king and his servants please go with your servant?" ²⁵But the king said to Absalom, "No, my son, let us not all go, or else we will be burdensome to you." He pressed him, but he would not go but gave him his blessing. ²⁶Then Absalom said, "If not, please let my brother Amnon go with us." The king said to him, "Why should he go with you?" ²⁷But Absalom pressed him until he let Amnon and all the king's sons go with him. Absalom made a feast like a king's feast.ᵃ ²⁸Then Absalom commanded his servants, "Watch when Amnon's heart is merry with wine, and when I say to you, 'Strike Amnon,' then kill him. Do not be afraid; have I not myself commanded you? Be courageous and valiant." ²⁹So the servants of Absalom did to Amnon as Absalom had commanded. Then all the king's sons rose, and each mounted his mule and fled.

30While they were on the way, the report

ᵃ Gk Compare Q Ms: MT lacks *Absalom made a feast like a king's feast*

NIV

stood up, tore his clothes and lay down on the ground; and all his servants stood by with their clothes torn.

³²But Jonadab son of Shimeah, David's brother, said, "My lord should not think that they killed all the princes; only Amnon is dead. This has been Absalom's expressed intention ever since the day Amnon raped his sister Tamar. ³³My lord the king should not be concerned about the report that all the king's sons are dead. Only Amnon is dead."

³⁴Meanwhile, Absalom had fled.

Now the man standing watch looked up and saw many people on the road west of him, coming down the side of the hill. The watchman went and told the king, "I see men in the direction of Horonaim, on the side of the hill."ᵃ

³⁵Jonadab said to the king, "See, the king's sons are here; it has happened just as your servant said."

³⁶As he finished speaking, the king's sons came in, wailing loudly. The king, too, and all his servants wept very bitterly.

³⁷Absalom fled and went to Talmai son of Ammihud, the king of Geshur. But King David mourned for his son every day.

³⁸After Absalom fled and went to Geshur, he stayed there three years. ³⁹And the spirit of the kingᵇ longed to go to Absalom, for he was consoled concerning Amnon's death.

ᵃ34 Septuagint; Hebrew does not have this sentence. ᵇ39 Dead Sea Scrolls and some Septuagint manuscripts; Masoretic Text But ˌthe spirit of, David the king

NRSV

came to David that Absalom had killed all the king's sons, and not one of them was left. ³¹The king rose, tore his garments, and lay on the ground; and all his servants who were standing by tore their garments. ³²But Jonadab, the son of David's brother Shimeah, said, "Let not my lord suppose that they have killed all the young men the king's sons; Amnon alone is dead. This has been determined by Absalom from the day Amnonᵃ raped his sister Tamar. ³³Now therefore, do not let my lord the king take it to heart, as if all the king's sons were dead; for Amnon alone is dead."

³⁴But Absalom fled. When the young man who kept watch looked up, he saw many people coming from the Horonaim roadᵇ by the side of the mountain. ³⁵Jonadab said to the king, "See, the king's sons have come; as your servant said, so it has come about." ³⁶As soon as he had finished speaking, the king's sons arrived, and raised their voices and wept; and the king and all his servants also wept very bitterly.

³⁷But Absalom fled, and went to Talmai son of Ammihud, king of Geshur. David mourned for his son day after day. ³⁸Absalom, having fled to Geshur, stayed there three years. ³⁹And the heart ofᶜ the king went out, yearning for Absalom; for he was now consoled over the death of Amnon.

ᵃ Heb he   ᵇ Cn Compare Gk: Heb the road behind him   ᶜ Q Ms Gk: MT And David

---

COMMENTARY

The unfolding story of tragic events in David's family continues. After biding his time for two years, Absalom takes revenge for the rape of Tamar by killing his half-brother Amnon. Although this act has the immediate effect of forcing Absalom into exile from Jerusalem, nevertheless, it places him next in the line of succession to David's throne. In this ongoing story, family events are never far separated from the machinations of power in the affairs of the kingdom, and it is the eventual outcome of these power struggles that most interests the narrator. Although this episode records Amnon's death, Absalom is the main focus of the narrative. These

events are part of the prelude to Absalom's rebellion (chaps. 15–19).

13:23-29. Absalom invites the royal household to a sheepshearing at his properties some miles to the north of Jerusalem (v. 1). This was undoubtedly not an invitation to the special work of shearing but to the celebration and feasting that follow the work (see 1 Sam 25:2-8). Although the initial invitation is to the "king's sons," presumably accompanied by their usual entourages, Absalom makes a special invitation to David, the king, himself (v. 2). This may have been an expected custom and courtesy. David graciously declines the invitation, on grounds that the king's presence with all of the necessary attending servants would be a burden on Absalom's hospitality. Although Absalom presses, the king maintains his refusal, but gives a royal blessing on the occasion (v. 3).

There is no way to know whether Absalom had already planned this event as the setting for his revenge or if the absence of David gave him an opportune moment, which he seized. Perhaps David was suspicious when Absalom singled out Amnon as one whose presence he especially desired. David questions the need of Amnon's attendance (v. 4), but when Absalom insists, David finally allows Amnon and all the other princes to travel to Absalom's feast (v. 5). Whether planned or serendipitous, Absalom finally has what his vengeance requires: the presence of Amnon away from the watchful eye of David and a location away from Jerusalem that will allow for his own escape.

Absalom orders his servants to murder Amnon. He instructs them to wait until Amnon is drunk with wine and to kill him at Absalom's command (v. 28a). Lest his servants waver in their loyalty, Absalom assures them that he will take full responsibility for the command and urges their courage and valor (v. 28b). Like his father, Absalom does not kill directly but orders murder through the hands of loyal servants (cf. David's order to Joab, 11:14-15). Absalom's trust in his servants' loyalty is well placed. With the command, "Strike Amnon!" the deed is done; no details of the actual murder are recorded. We hear only that the servants did as commanded and that the rest of the king's sons flee on mules. They undoubtedly feared a wholesale massacre of royal heirs. Absalom's purpose at the moment seems limited to revenge. He does not yet plan a rebellion and seizing of power. If so, he might have waited until an occasion when David was present and struck him as well.

13:30-39. The narrative lingers dramatically over a false report that came to David claiming that Absalom had killed all of the king's sons (v.

30). David tears his garments and lies prostrate in grief over the prospect of such a terrible loss (v. 31). His grief proves misplaced, but it foreshadows a later moment of terrible grief when it is Absalom who lies dead (18:33[19:1]). Strangely, Jonadab, the friend who had plotted with Amnon in his rape of Tamar, advises the king that it is surely only Amnon who is dead (vv. 32-33). He has no explicit report to this effect, but he cites the rape of Tamar as the source of Absalom's animosity. Jonadab expected something like this, perhaps because he himself feared retaliation for his part in the matter.

Jonadab's confident assertion is borne out a short time later when the watchman sees many people coming on the road to Jerusalem (v. 34). They are the king's sons, who arrive weeping bitterly over the assassination of their brother, and no doubt out of fear for their own lives (v. 36). Jonadab takes credit for his accurate prediction (v. 35).

In the midst of this narration of David's anxious waiting, we are told for the first of three times that "Absalom fled" (vv. 34a, 37, 38). Absalom takes refuge with his maternal grandfather, Talmai, the king of Geshur (v. 37; cf. 3:3). He remains there for three years (v. 38). We are told that David mourned daily for his son (v. 37b), but the text is ambiguous at first about which son he mourned—Amnon, who was dead, or Absalom, who was a fugitive in exile from his own land. Verse 39 resolves this ambiguity. It is Absalom for whom David's heart longs. The text tells us that he is consoled over Amnon's death; now he misses the son who yet lives. David's ability to face death and go on with life reminds us of the story of the death of his first son with Bathsheba (12:15b-23). We wonder why David did not simply bring Absalom home. Yet, there are limits to what even a king can do. Absalom is guilty of the murder of the crown prince. Even David might find it difficult to excuse such a crime publicly, in spite of his personal longings. It takes a complicated negotiation, engineered by Joab, to bring him home (chap. 14).

REFLECTIONS

This tragic story of revenge and murder is yet another link in the chain of violence that began with David's adultery with Bathsheba and murder of Uriah. Now David's two oldest sons have repeated his actions: One has taken for himself the object of his sexual desire, and the other has killed for the sake of his own personal and political interests. Tragically, the result of following their father's path is that one son is dead and the other in exile. The overriding message of this text is once again that violence leads to yet more violence (see Reflections at 13:1-22).

The difference here is that Absalom believed his violence against Amnon was just recompense for Amnon's rape of Tamar (although we cannot rule out Absalom's political interests in the succession as a factor). But this does not end the matter. Absalom has continued the chain of violence, and the chain has not yet played out its consequences. It is in reading this story in our time that we must learn that righteous violence continues the chain of violence, as surely as violence done out of baser motives. Absalom's solution of taking justice violently into his own hands is as unacceptable as David's refusal to take action at all (v. 21). Neither denial nor violent retaliation ends the chain of violence.

Recently, the FBI made arrests of a group planning to bomb the homes of anti-abortion leaders. The actions of this group were intended to be righteous retaliation for the bombing of several abortion clinics in which one person had been killed. What a strange turn of events. In the name of preserving life and protecting freedom of choice, opposing groups are willing to take life and permanently end choice. The cycle of violence will continue unless someone steps forward willing to break that cycle.

One wonders whether the rising tide of public opinion in support of capital punishment is not motivated more by a righteous desire for revenge than by any real desire to break the patterns that lead to violent crimes. Such a willingness simply to justify the return of violence for violence will not break patterns of violent crime in our communities. The way of Absalom runs the risk of deepening the alienation in our own communities rather than resolving it. As with Absalom, so with us, the consequences could be great.

2 Samuel 14:1-33, The Restoration of Absalom

<table>
<tr><th>NIV</th><th>NRSV</th></tr>
<tr><td>

14 Joab son of Zeruiah knew that the king's heart longed for Absalom. [2]So Joab sent someone to Tekoa and had a wise woman brought from there. He said to her, "Pretend you are in mourning. Dress in mourning clothes, and don't use any cosmetic lotions. Act like a woman who has spent many days grieving for the dead. [3]Then go to the king and speak these words to him." And Joab put the words in her mouth.

[4]When the woman from Tekoa went[a] to the king, she fell with her face to the ground to pay him honor, and she said, "Help me, O king!"

[5]The king asked her, "What is troubling you?"

She said, "I am indeed a widow; my husband is dead. [6]I your servant had two sons. They got into a fight with each other in the field, and no one was there to separate them. One struck the other and killed him. [7]Now the whole clan has risen up against your servant; they say, 'Hand over

</td><td>

14 Now Joab son of Zeruiah perceived that the king's mind was on Absalom. [2]Joab sent to Tekoa and brought from there a wise woman. He said to her, "Pretend to be a mourner; put on mourning garments, do not anoint yourself with oil, but behave like a woman who has been mourning many days for the dead. [3]Go to the king and speak to him as follows." And Joab put the words into her mouth.

[4]When the woman of Tekoa came to the king, she fell on her face to the ground and did obeisance, and said, "Help, O king!" [5]The king asked her, "What is your trouble?" She answered, "Alas, I am a widow; my husband is dead. [6]Your servant had two sons, and they fought with one another in the field; there was no one to part them, and one struck the other and killed him. [7]Now the whole family has risen against your servant. They say, 'Give up the man who struck his brother, so that we may kill him for the life of his brother whom he murdered, even if we destroy the heir

</td></tr>
</table>

[a]4 Many Hebrew manuscripts, Septuagint, Vulgate and Syriac; most Hebrew manuscripts *spoke*

NIV

the one who struck his brother down, so that we may put him to death for the life of his brother whom he killed; then we will get rid of the heir as well.' They would put out the only burning coal I have left, leaving my husband neither name nor descendant on the face of the earth."

[8]The king said to the woman, "Go home, and I will issue an order in your behalf."

[9]But the woman from Tekoa said to him, "My lord the king, let the blame rest on me and on my father's family, and let the king and his throne be without guilt."

[10]The king replied, "If anyone says anything to you, bring him to me, and he will not bother you again."

[11]She said, "Then let the king invoke the LORD his God to prevent the avenger of blood from adding to the destruction, so that my son will not be destroyed."

"As surely as the LORD lives," he said, "not one hair of your son's head will fall to the ground."

[12]Then the woman said, "Let your servant speak a word to my lord the king."

"Speak," he replied.

[13]The woman said, "Why then have you devised a thing like this against the people of God? When the king says this, does he not convict himself, for the king has not brought back his banished son? [14]Like water spilled on the ground, which cannot be recovered, so we must die. But God does not take away life; instead, he devises ways so that a banished person may not remain estranged from him.

[15]"And now I have come to say this to my lord the king because the people have made me afraid. Your servant thought, 'I will speak to the king; perhaps he will do what his servant asks. [16]Perhaps the king will agree to deliver his servant from the hand of the man who is trying to cut off both me and my son from the inheritance God gave us.'

[17]"And now your servant says, 'May the word of my lord the king bring me rest, for my lord the king is like an angel of God in discerning good and evil. May the LORD your God be with you.'"

[18]Then the king said to the woman, "Do not keep from me the answer to what I am going to ask you."

"Let my lord the king speak," the woman said.

NRSV

as well.' Thus they would quench my one remaining ember, and leave to my husband neither name nor remnant on the face of the earth."

[8]Then the king said to the woman, "Go to your house, and I will give orders concerning you." [9]The woman of Tekoa said to the king, "On me be the guilt, my lord the king, and on my father's house; let the king and his throne be guiltless." [10]The king said, "If anyone says anything to you, bring him to me, and he shall never touch you again." [11]Then she said, "Please, may the king keep the LORD your God in mind, so that the avenger of blood may kill no more, and my son not be destroyed." He said, "As the LORD lives, not one hair of your son shall fall to the ground."

[12]Then the woman said, "Please let your servant speak a word to my lord the king." He said, "Speak." [13]The woman said, "Why then have you planned such a thing against the people of God? For in giving this decision the king convicts himself, inasmuch as the king does not bring his banished one home again. [14]We must all die; we are like water spilled on the ground, which cannot be gathered up. But God will not take away a life; he will devise plans so as not to keep an outcast banished forever from his presence.[a] [15]Now I have come to say this to my lord the king because the people have made me afraid; your servant thought, 'I will speak to the king; it may be that the king will perform the request of his servant. [16]For the king will hear, and deliver his servant from the hand of the man who would cut both me and my son off from the heritage of God.' [17]Your servant thought, 'The word of my lord the king will set me at rest'; for my lord the king is like the angel of God, discerning good and evil. The LORD your God be with you!"

[18]Then the king answered the woman, "Do not withhold from me anything I ask you." The woman said, "Let my lord the king speak." [19]The king said, "Is the hand of Joab with you in all this?" The woman answered and said, "As surely as you live, my lord the king, one cannot turn right or left from anything that my lord the king has said. For it was your servant Joab who commanded me; it was he who put all these words into the mouth of your servant. [20]In order to

a Meaning of Heb uncertain

NIV

[19]The king asked, "Isn't the hand of Joab with you in all this?"

The woman answered, "As surely as you live, my lord the king, no one can turn to the right or to the left from anything my lord the king says. Yes, it was your servant Joab who instructed me to do this and who put all these words into the mouth of your servant. [20]Your servant Joab did this to change the present situation. My lord has wisdom like that of an angel of God—he knows everything that happens in the land."

[21]The king said to Joab, "Very well, I will do it. Go, bring back the young man Absalom."

[22]Joab fell with his face to the ground to pay him honor, and he blessed the king. Joab said, "Today your servant knows that he has found favor in your eyes, my lord the king, because the king has granted his servant's request."

[23]Then Joab went to Geshur and brought Absalom back to Jerusalem. [24]But the king said, "He must go to his own house; he must not see my face." So Absalom went to his own house and did not see the face of the king.

[25]In all Israel there was not a man so highly praised for his handsome appearance as Absalom. From the top of his head to the sole of his foot there was no blemish in him. [26]Whenever he cut the hair of his head—he used to cut his hair from time to time when it became too heavy for him—he would weigh it, and its weight was two hundred shekels[a] by the royal standard.

[27]Three sons and a daughter were born to Absalom. The daughter's name was Tamar, and she became a beautiful woman.

[28]Absalom lived two years in Jerusalem without seeing the king's face. [29]Then Absalom sent for Joab in order to send him to the king, but Joab refused to come to him. So he sent a second time, but he refused to come. [30]Then he said to his servants, "Look, Joab's field is next to mine, and he has barley there. Go and set it on fire." So Absalom's servants set the field on fire.

[31]Then Joab did go to Absalom's house and he said to him, "Why have your servants set my field on fire?"

[32]Absalom said to Joab, "Look, I sent word to you and said, 'Come here so I can send you to

[a]26 That is, about 5 pounds (about 2.3 kilograms)

NRSV

change the course of affairs your servant Joab did this. But my lord has wisdom like the wisdom of the angel of God to know all things that are on the earth."

21Then the king said to Joab, "Very well, I grant this; go, bring back the young man Absalom." 22Joab prostrated himself with his face to the ground and did obeisance, and blessed the king; and Joab said, "Today your servant knows that I have found favor in your sight, my lord the king, in that the king has granted the request of his servant." 23So Joab set off, went to Geshur, and brought Absalom to Jerusalem. 24The king said, "Let him go to his own house; he is not to come into my presence." So Absalom went to his own house, and did not come into the king's presence.

25Now in all Israel there was no one to be praised so much for his beauty as Absalom; from the sole of his foot to the crown of his head there was no blemish in him. 26When he cut the hair of his head (for at the end of every year he used to cut it; when it was heavy on him, he cut it), he weighed the hair of his head, two hundred shekels by the king's weight. 27There were born to Absalom three sons, and one daughter whose name was Tamar; she was a beautiful woman.

28So Absalom lived two full years in Jerusalem, without coming into the king's presence. 29Then Absalom sent for Joab to send him to the king; but Joab would not come to him. He sent a second time, but Joab would not come. 30Then he said to his servants, "Look, Joab's field is next to mine, and he has barley there; go and set it on fire." So Absalom's servants set the field on fire. 31Then Joab rose and went to Absalom at his house, and said to him, "Why have your servants set my field on fire?" 32Absalom answered Joab, "Look, I sent word to you: Come here, that I may send you to the king with the question, 'Why have I come from Geshur? It would be better for me to be there still.' Now let me go into the king's presence; if there is guilt in me, let him kill me!" 33Then Joab went to the king and told him; and he summoned Absalom. So he came to the king and prostrated himself with his face to the ground before the king; and the king kissed Absalom.

NIV

the king to ask, "Why have I come from Geshur? It would be better for me if I were still there!"' Now then, I want to see the king's face, and if I am guilty of anything, let him put me to death."

³³So Joab went to the king and told him this. Then the king summoned Absalom, and he came in and bowed down with his face to the ground before the king. And the king kissed Absalom.

COMMENTARY

This chapter continues the narration of events in the aftermath of Amnon's rape of Tamar (13:1-22) and Absalom's vengeance killing of Amnon (13:23-39). Absalom has passed three years in exile from Jerusalem, fearing retribution (13:38). This chapter tells first of Absalom's return to Jerusalem, through the timely intervention of David's right-hand man, Joab, and a wise woman from Tekoa, whom Joab recruits for his scheme (vv. 1-24). David is involved in rendering a hypothetical judgment that is used in a manner similar to Nathan's parable (12:1-7) to enable David to see his own action and allow Absalom's return to Jerusalem, but not into the king's presence. Verses 25-27 give the reader a fuller description of Absalom's attractiveness. Finally, the story tells of Absalom's use of Joab again, after two years, to bring about a personal restoration of relationship to his father, David (vv. 28-33). The relationship may be genuine, but it is fragile. Five years of bitter separation between father and son cannot be easily bridged or forgotten. The kiss of reconciliation comes too late (v. 33), and almost immediately Absalom begins his plans for rebellion (chap. 15).

Many scholars believe vv. 15-17 have become displaced and that they properly follow v. 7.[313] These verses return to the hypothetical case of the woman's surviving son after David has already rendered judgment in this matter and the woman has given up her role as the aggrieved widow (vv. 8-11). The argument in favor of this reordering is persuasive, and the discussion will follow that reordered pattern.

14:1-7, 15-17. Joab takes the initiative to restore Absalom because of his regard for David (v. 1). As subsequent events reveal, Joab has no personal concern for Absalom (cf. 14:29-33; 18:14). Perhaps Joab believes that he can take David's mind off of Absalom and restore his mind to matters of the kingdom (cf. 19:1-8).

Without preamble, Joab launches a stratagem by bringing a wise woman from Tekoa, approximately ten miles south of Jerusalem. He instructs her to take on the role of a widow woman in mourning and to go before the king (v. 2). Joab gives her the words to say. There has been some debate about the character and role of the woman from Tekoa.[314] The use of the adjective "wise" (חכמה ḥăkāmâ, v. 2a) probably does not indicate a formal office (e.g., sage or teacher). It may indicate that she was "clever" or "shrewd." Joab may have given her the "words" that define the hypothetical case she brings to David, but her interaction with David and the skill with which she manipulates his response draw the reader's admiration. She flatters David, saying that he has "wisdom like the wisdom of the angel of God" (v. 20). Since she clearly enables David to see things he cannot see for himself, we are left with the judgment that she is certainly as wise as the

313. See P. Kyle McCarter, *II Samuel*, AB 9 (Garden City, N.Y.: Doubleday, 1984) 345-46; Anderson, *2 Samuel*, 185-86.

314. The poles of opinion are defined by Claudia V. Camp, "The Wise Women of 2 Samuel: A Role Model for Women in Early Israel," *CBQ* 43 (1981) 14-29, who argues that this woman must have had considerable standing and authority in her own community, and by Alice Ogden Bellis, *Helpmates, Harlots, and Heroes: Women's Stories in the Hebrew Bible* (Louisville: Westminster/John Knox, 1994) 154, who writes, "The woman is merely playing a role that has been scripted for her by a man. Although she is called wise, there is a problem. Either her own work is attributed to a man, a real enough possibility, or she is not really wise." The first of the positions probably argues for more than can be said on the basis of this text, and the second underestimates the skill and latitude the woman exercises in the role assigned her by Joab.

king and, therefore, deserving of the adjective that describes her in v. 2.[315]

In vv. 4-7, the woman comes before David as a petitioner seeking the king's aid. She plays the hypothetical role of a widow whose two sons have fought, and tragically one has killed the other. Now, her family demands that the surviving son be given up and executed as a murderer, thus leaving her with no sons and with no one to carry on her dead husband's name and lineage. Verses 15-17 seem to continue this telling of the woman's story and express the motivation that caused her to bring her case before the king. She seeks deliverance by the king from the strict demands that justice would impose upon her, cutting her and her son off from the "heritage of God" (v. 16). She ends with the appropriate flattery of the king's ability to discern "good and evil" and invokes the name of the Lord (v. 17).

Like Nathan's parable (12:1-4), the woman's story seems to be a juridical parable designed to elicit a judgment from David on his own situation and then point out to him the parallels in his own life.[316] Unlike Nathan, the woman's case is directed toward eliciting an action of reconciliation on David's part rather than evoking a judgment against the king. The outcome is not as sharp and dramatic as in the case of Nathan's parable,[317] but it succeeds in forcing David out of the strict dictates of the law, which he must uphold as king, and into the thinking of unthinkable alternatives. He is forced to consider the possibilities of mercy, new future, and an end to violence and vengeance.

14:8-11. The king is moved to mercy and promises to issue orders on the woman's behalf (v. 8). The woman constantly interrupts the king in the process of his ruling. She declares that she will bear the guilt (v. 9a), presumably the guilt that might be incurred from going against the letter of the law. She further declares that the king and his throne will be guiltless (v. 9b). Even if David does not yet see his own situation in the woman's story, the reader certainly catches the irony of such a declaration. David and his throne are not guiltless. The reader is forced to remember the chain of violence that stretches from David to Amnon and to Absalom. David's throne and the pretenders to it are awash in guilt. David reassures the woman that his own authority will reach out against any who speak against her (v. 10).

The woman persists and wants explicit reassurance in the name of the Lord that the "avenger of blood" will not take her son's life (v. 11a). Some regard this "avenger of blood" as an officer in the community for seeing that justice is done in cases such as the murder the woman reports. Others see this role as one assumed by a member of the family with the responsibility to seek blood vengeance in such cases. Indeed, the woman does refer to her family as having "risen against" her (v. 7).[318] In any case, David gives her the reassurance she desires and pronounces an oath: "As the LORD lives, not one hair of your son shall fall to the ground" (v. 11b). It is the same guarantee of safety that the people used to protect Jonathan against Saul's unwise execution of the letter of the law (1 Sam 14:45). It also binds David by an oath, after which the woman abandons her role and reveals the true matter that David has pronounced upon. Whether such an oath is binding when the hypothetical case is unmasked may be debatable, but the real force here is moral, and not legal suasion.

14:12-14, 18-20. David has been led by the woman's skillfully played role to compromise the law of blood vengeance. As Brueggemann has aptly stated it, "When the 'killer' is acknowledged to be a beloved son, vengeance can be overcome."[319] The woman can now drop her ruse and reveal the true nature of the concern for which Joab sent her. It is a moment of risk and courage. One does not meddle lightly in the king's family matters. Her tone becomes deferential as she asks and receives permission to speak a word to the king (v. 12).

315. Walter Brueggemann, *First and Second Samuel,* Interpretation (Louisville: John Knox, 1990) 292, writes, "Perhaps 'wise' means one who is able to discern, articulate, and practice life outside the categories of bureaucratic perception, the capacity to see connections and hidden forces that are not visible in conventional modes of administrative thought."

316. On juridical parables, see Uriel Simon, "The Poor Man's Ewe-Lamb: An Example of a Juridical Parable," *Biblica* 48 (1967) 207-42.

317. Willey makes the interesting argument that the woman's story is a "clever parody" of the Nathan parable: "By setting up a tale similar to the Nathan tale, the narrator raises our expectations for a similarly luminous outcome, but then fails splendidly to deliver. This importunate woman reads not as a second Nathan, come again to set things straight, but as a parody of his methods, fit for a king doomed to moral confusion." See Patricia K. Willey, "The Importunate Woman of Tekoa and How She Got Her Way," in *Reading Between Texts: Intertextuality and the Hebrew Bible,* ed. Danna Nolan Fewell, Literary Currents in Biblical Interpretation (Louisville: Westminster/John Knox, 1992) 115-31, esp. 128.

318. See the discussion in A. A. Anderson, *2 Samuel,* WBC 11 (Waco: Word, 1989) 188.

319. Brueggemann, *First and Second Samuel,* 293.

The intent of the woman's speech is clear, although some elements are problematic and uncertain. She tells David straightforwardly that in rendering judgment on her hypothetical case he has convicted himself, inasmuch as he has allowed himself to lose a beloved son by banishment (v. 13*b*). In effect, David has played the role of the blood avenger toward Absalom. She suggests that this is an offense against the people of God, perhaps indicating Absalom's popularity with the people (v. 13*a*). Verse 14*a* seems to be speaking of Amnon's death as something that cannot be undone, much as water spilled on the ground cannot be retrieved. She argues that God would find a way to restore an outcast (v. 14*b*). This section of the woman's speech is awkward and oblique in its application to David. Perhaps the indirection is a mark of deference before the king. Nevertheless, the intent of the speech is clear: If David can restore the son to the woman in her hypothetical case, then he can find a way to restore Absalom to his own family and kingdom.

David not only sees the woman's point, but he sees behind it. He insists on her candor (v. 18) and asks if the hand of Joab is in this charade (v. 19*a*). The woman admits that it was Joab's doing, but not without considerable flattery of the king and his wise ability to see and know all things (vv. 19*b*-20). With the stratagem uncovered, the woman no doubt fears how the king will react. So she praises David extravagantly as having "wisdom like the wisdom of the angel of God."

14:21-24. Now that he sees, David acts. He sees that the case brought to him is really a petition about Absalom, and he grants the petition and orders that Absalom be brought home (v. 21). He deals directly with Joab, who seems to be present, and the woman is suddenly gone from the story. Joab knows he has pushed the boundaries of his friendship and loyalty to David, and he acknowledges David's decision with deference, flattery, and blessing. But he also clearly takes credit for the idea (v. 22).

But the matter is not settled. David has been pressed to act as a father, but he cannot give up the role of king. Joab brings Absalom to Jerusalem (v. 23), but David will not allow Absalom into his presence (v. 24). The father has brought him home, but the king will not receive him. This situation will continue for two full years (v. 28).

A reconciling moment has come near, but it has passed without actualization.

14:25-27. The narrative pauses for a personal note about Absalom. We are told of his handsome appearance (v. 25), and we remember the striking appearance of Saul (1 Sam 9:2) and his tragic fate. We also recall the Lord's reminder to the prophet Samuel that God looks not on appearance but on the heart (1 Sam 16:7); nevertheless the storyteller cannot resist noting the handsome appearance of David when he enters the story (1 Sam 16:12). Absalom is admired for his physical perfection and a magnificent head of hair (vv. 25*b*-26). This particular description foreshadows Absalom's fate, when he will be caught fast by his hair in a tree while attempting to escape the defeat of his military force. This is usually interpreted as the entanglement of his hair; his vanity becomes his undoing. A final and poignant personal note is added when the narrator reports that Absalom has three sons and one daughter, but only the daughter is named (v. 27). Her name is Tamar, a testimony to the feelings Absalom carried for his violated sister. Even if he took Amnon's life in part for his own political purposes, there is little reason to doubt that Absalom was deeply troubled by the defiling of his sister, Tamar.

14:28-33. Two years have passed without Absalom's return to the court. It is almost as if he is under house arrest (v. 28). Absalom takes the initiative to change this situation, and, like his father, he knows that Joab is the man to make things happen. Absalom sends for Joab, but twice Joab ignores the prince's summons (v. 29). Joab is loyal to the father, not the son. Absalom resorts to extreme measures. He orders his servants to set Joab's field on fire (v. 30), and this brings Joab to ask what in the world Absalom is doing (v. 31). Absalom then makes clear his desire to be brought before the king and suggests he would rather be in exile or even executed if he is still considered guilty (v. 32). It is a risky and bold move. David must make good his full rehabilitation at court or complete the demands of blood guilt, now delayed five years.

Again Joab is the go-between, and when David hears the message he does send for Absalom. With appropriate deference, Absalom prostrates himself before the king, and "the king kissed Absalom" (v. 33). This is often treated as a reconciliation between father and son. The NRSV subtitles this section "David Forgives Absalom." Perhaps David's kiss could have signaled a restored relationship, but we have the impression that the kiss came at least two years too late. At no point does David take the initiative to restore Absalom to relationship. When the kiss finally comes, it is because Absalom forces the moment. David has not seen Absalom for five years. Even when official forgiveness allows Absalom's return to Jerusalem, David makes clear that personal forgiveness is not offered. David's mind was on Absalom (14:1), but he seems unable to allow the father in him to take precedence over the king. The text is clear: It is the king who kisses Absalom, not the father. David's kiss seems grudging and formal, and we are given no indication that David's heart, which may long for Absalom (14:1), is allowed to take precedence over royal policy. We are not surprised when chap. 15 begins the story of Absalom's overt rebellion and attempt to seize David's throne.

REFLECTIONS

This episode in the drama of David's family and kingdom speaks to us of the opportunity for new beginnings and of how easily those opportunities can be missed.

1. The first part of the story is a hopeful testimony that it is possible to move beyond vengeance to a new beginning. The cycle of violence and the dislocations it creates can be broken. This is genuine good news for those of us who read this story in a time when violence has reached such deadly and far-reaching proportions in our society. That the cycle of violence can be broken is also good news for those who know the deadly patterns of violence and vengeance in their own families. Patterns of abuse, exploitation, and alienation have divided our own families as surely as the family of David, and the results are often a paralysis that imagines no new beginnings are possible and the continuation of patterns of abuse from one generation to the next.

In this narrative on the possibility of a new beginning, Joab, of all people, first envisions an alternative future—a future not dictated by custom, traditional patterns, or juridical realities. Why was it not possible for Absalom to come home and make a new beginning? But the real power for new beginnings comes through courageous and imaginative speech that allows David to perceive an alternative future. A wise and resourceful woman tells a story that imagines vengeance could be foregone in favor of compassion. In that story, David sees new possibilities for his own story and breaks the demands of custom and law to allow the return of an outcast and the dropping of demands for further blood.

In our society, our churches, and our own lives we are often so busy analyzing the reality of our situations that we fail to imagine more hopeful scenarios and tell stories that make them possible. Pastoral care in our churches has borrowed the insights of the psychotherapy movement and understood how helpful it can be to retell the story of our past and claim the past without being controlled by it. This story suggests that we should also be telling stories of our future in ways that open new possibilities and release us from the tyranny of our own present. We have identified the form of the woman's story as "parable," a type of story that speaks of the familiar but surprises the listener with new realities about his or her own life. Christians, of course, think of Jesus' parables and the way in which they opened new possibilities for the listener. For this story, we cannot help recalling the parable of the prodigal son (Luke 15:11-32), a story of a son whose choices alienated and exiled him from the love of a father. Like the woman's story to David, Jesus' parable suggests that separation need not be the accepted reality. There can be return, forgiveness, and new beginnings.

The church is also in the business of telling stories through which persons can come to see themselves and their possibilities in new ways. The biblical story itself can serve in this way. In our preaching and teaching, in our study and devotion, we should seek ways to allow the biblical story to intersect our own stories and encourage openness to the new possibilities that come out of those intersections. Likewise, the sharing of our own faith stories and the witness of ways in which we have experienced the overcoming of fear and alienation can allow others to envision those same possibilities in their lives. The woman's story was one in which she refused to let the law have the last word about her son. The community of faith, like the woman, should constantly tell stories that affirm the ultimate worth of all persons regardless of the circumstances that make them outcasts and separate them from one another. This enables the church, like David, to act in ways that redeem the outcast and move beyond alienation.

2. Tragically, this episode in David's story is not just about new beginnings made possible, but also about opportunities lost. Because of the woman's courageous and imaginative speech, David saw an alternative future in relationship to his son, but when Absalom returned to Jerusalem, David failed to actualize that new future. He does not see his son or receive him. Two years of silent proximity pass, and Absalom forces an encounter. David kisses Absalom, but the kiss comes too late.

In the parable of the prodigal son, the father also kisses the son (Luke 15:20), but there the kiss marks the graceful seizing of the moment when a new future can be realized. The father's kiss comes immediately, spontaneously, unconditionally. David could not act in grace and forgiveness when the moment for it came, and the moment passed. The kiss comes too late, and a resentful Absalom begins to plot rebellion (15:1-12).

The courageous and imaginative telling of our biblical and faith stories can create possibilities for new beginnings. But the moment for those new beginnings must be acted upon. Whether it is the moment of hopeful new alternatives for our lives, for our churches, or for our communities, it requires a giving up of past realities defined by habit, custom, tradition, or fear for the risk of grace. We cannot embrace the future and nurse the wounds of the past. David wanted his son nearby, but he could not embrace him. David wanted a new beginning as a father, but he could not abandon the juridical judgment of the king.

In Israel's story, God has the experience of a parent with an exiled child in the time of Israel's Babylonian exile. God's response, through the prophet of the exile, is to say: "I, I am He who blots out your transgressions for my own sake, and I will not remember your sins" (Isa 43:25 NRSV). God risks the speaking of forgiveness and understands such forgiving as being for God's "own sake." For his own sake, David needed to forgive and claim the new future opened by the wise woman's imaginative speech. For our own sake, as persons of faith and as the church, we need to model God's forgiveness in the world. We must speak imaginatively of new beginnings in lives and communities, leave alienated pasts behind in forgiveness, and embrace the new futures made possible in God's grace.

2 Samuel 15:1–20:22, Absalom's Rebellion

OVERVIEW

The story of Absalom's rebellion stands as the centerpiece of the so-called succession narrative. The stories of Amnon's rape of Absalom's sister, Tamar, and Absalom's subsequent murder of Amnon (chaps. 13–14) are primarily narrated to explain how it came to be that David's son Absalom was so alienated from David that he tried to seize the throne. This entire course of events is the grim fulfillment of the judgment pronounced by the prophet Nathan on David for his sin in the adultery with Bathsheba and the murder of Uriah (chap. 12).

The narration of Absalom's rebellion unfolds primarily in a series of conversations between characters in the story. There is a noticeable lack of interest in historical detail while the focus remains on the unfolding personal drama between David and his rebellious son. Other characters enter the story as they support or oppose David in this time of revolt. While Absalom's rebellion is an event dealing with the future course of political power in Israel, it is in the end a personal tragedy that ends in David's grief over yet another son (18:33).

2 Samuel 15:1-12, The Seeds of Revolt

NIV

15 In the course of time, Absalom provided himself with a chariot and horses and with fifty men to run ahead of him. ²He would get up early and stand by the side of the road leading to the city gate. Whenever anyone came with a complaint to be placed before the king for a decision, Absalom would call out to him, "What town are you from?" He would answer, "Your servant is from one of the tribes of Israel." ³Then Absalom would say to him, "Look, your claims are valid and proper, but there is no representative of the king to hear you." ⁴And Absalom would add, "If only I were appointed judge in the land! Then everyone who has a complaint or case could come to me and I would see that he gets justice."

⁵Also, whenever anyone approached him to bow down before him, Absalom would reach out his hand, take hold of him and kiss him. ⁶Absalom behaved in this way toward all the Israelites who came to the king asking for justice, and so he stole the hearts of the men of Israel.

⁷At the end of four*ᵃ* years, Absalom said to the king, "Let me go to Hebron and fulfill a vow I made to the LORD. ⁸While your servant was living at Geshur in Aram, I made this vow: 'If the LORD takes me back to Jerusalem, I will worship the LORD in Hebron.*ᵇ*'"

⁹The king said to him, "Go in peace." So he went to Hebron.

¹⁰Then Absalom sent secret messengers throughout the tribes of Israel to say, "As soon as you hear the sound of the trumpets, then say, 'Absalom is king in Hebron.'" ¹¹Two hundred men from Jerusalem had accompanied Absalom. They had been invited as guests and went quite innocently, knowing nothing about the matter. ¹²While Absalom was offering sacrifices, he also sent for Ahithophel the Gilonite, David's counselor, to come from Giloh, his hometown. And so the conspiracy gained strength, and Absalom's following kept on increasing.

ᵃ7 Some Septuagint manuscripts, Syriac and Josephus; Hebrew forty
ᵇ8 Some Septuagint manuscripts; Hebrew does not have in Hebron.

NRSV

15 After this Absalom got himself a chariot and horses, and fifty men to run ahead of him. ²Absalom used to rise early and stand beside the road into the gate; and when anyone brought a suit before the king for judgment, Absalom would call out and say, "From what city are you?" When the person said, "Your servant is of such and such a tribe in Israel," ³Absalom would say, "See, your claims are good and right; but there is no one deputed by the king to hear you." ⁴Absalom said moreover, "If only I were judge in the land! Then all who had a suit or cause might come to me, and I would give them justice." ⁵Whenever people came near to do obeisance to him, he would put out his hand and take hold of them, and kiss them. ⁶Thus Absalom did to every Israelite who came to the king for judgment; so Absalom stole the hearts of the people of Israel.

⁷At the end of four*ᵃ* years Absalom said to the king, "Please let me go to Hebron and pay the vow that I have made to the LORD. ⁸For your servant made a vow while I lived at Geshur in Aram: If the LORD will indeed bring me back to Jerusalem, then I will worship the LORD in Hebron."*ᵇ* ⁹The king said to him, "Go in peace." So he got up, and went to Hebron. ¹⁰But Absalom sent secret messengers throughout all the tribes of Israel, saying, "As soon as you hear the sound of the trumpet, then shout: Absalom has become king at Hebron!" ¹¹Two hundred men from Jerusalem went with Absalom; they were invited guests, and they went in their innocence, knowing nothing of the matter. ¹²While Absalom was offering the sacrifices, he sent for*ᶜ* Ahithophel the Gilonite, David's counselor, from his city Giloh. The conspiracy grew in strength, and the people with Absalom kept increasing.

ᵃ Gk Syr: Heb forty   *ᵇ Gk Mss: Heb lacks in Hebron*   *ᶜ Or he sent*

COMMENTARY

This episode divides into two scenes. The first (vv. 1-6) describes the activity of Absalom as he ingratiates himself to the people of Israel and gathers popular support at the expense of David's reputation. The second scene (vv. 7-12) tells of Absalom's overt declaration of rebellion against David from the ancient capital city of Judah in Hebron.

15:1-6. Apparently only a short time after Absalom's reunion with David (14:33), Absalom surrounds himself with the trappings of a royal prince and heir apparent. The chariot, horses, and fifty men (presumably soldiers) that accompany him on his movements in and around Jerusalem (v. 1) must have given Absalom considerable public visibility. We do not know whether he was officially considered the heir to the throne; at a later point when David's son Adonijah declares his claim to the throne, he, too, surrounds himself with chariots, horses, and fifty men (1 Kgs 1:5). This may well be an entourage that indicates potential royal status.

Absalom embarks on a strategy of ingratiating himself with those who are discontent with David's system of administering justice. Absalom would position himself in the gate to encounter those who brought a suit before the king (v. 2). He would express sympathy with their case as well as decry the lack of anyone available to hear the case (v. 3). Absalom then avowed that if he were judge in the land all who had a cause could come before him and receive justice (v. 4). Clearly Absalom is exploiting a weakness in David's system of justice in order to build public support, but it is difficult to tell just what the nature of the discontent was toward David's justice. The king in Israel had a judicial function and was required to render judgments on difficult cases that could not be clearly ruled upon in other judicial arenas (cf. Ps 72:1-4, 12-14; Isa 11:3-5). Twice we have seen this role of the king exploited to bring personal matters before David (by Nathan, 12:1-15; by the wise woman of Tekoa, 14:1-24). It may have been that in this time it had become too difficult to gain access to David in order to bring a case before him. Or perhaps there was a feeling that David should appoint an official to hear cases on his behalf. Some believe that Absalom's offer to act in this role is an effort

to appear as an innovator proposing solutions on the people's behalf.[320] David may have been unwilling to delegate royal authority in this manner, a reluctance Absalom now exploits.

Whatever the particulars, discontent with David's justice must have been widespread, as evidenced by Absalom's success at garnering support for his rebellion. Absalom, whom we know was handsome (14:25-26), clearly also possesses personal charm. He embraces and kisses those who bow before him (vv. 5-6*a*) and in this way "stole the hearts of the people of Israel" (v. 6*b*). The people are made to feel that they have a friend in the royal court. No doubt, Absalom's appeal to those who felt they were denied adequate attention from the king's justice were supplemented by those who had other reasons to want David's rule overturned. When David retreats from Jerusalem, for instance, he encounters those who still hold a grudge against him for having displaced the house of Saul (cf. 16:3, 5-8).

15:7-12. Absalom has built his popular base of support, and now the moment for overt rebellion has come. Most take the reference to four years in v. 7 as the time since his reunion with David (14:33). Only then would Absalom have had the freedom to engage in the activities of vv. 1-6. That Absalom felt the need to seize the throne while David was yet alive may be the best evidence that he was not clearly designated as the successor to the throne. His rehabilitation may not have included restoration of his succession rights.

Once again Absalom asks permission of David to make a journey with an entourage from the court (cf. 13:23-29). One would think David might think twice about this request. This time Absalom claims the need to go to Hebron to offer sacrifices in fulfillment of a vow he made while exiled in Geshur (vv. 7-8). The king gives permission and ironically wishes him peace (v. 9).

Absalom's true intent becomes clear in v. 10. He sends secret messengers throughout Israel. With the blowing of the ram's horn (a traditional part of enthronement rituals; see 1 Kgs 1:34; 2

---

320. See K. W. Whitelam, *The Just King: Monarchical Judicial Authority in Ancient Israel,* JSOTSup 12 (Sheffield: University of Sheffield Press, 1979) 140-41.

Kgs 9:13), Absalom is to be pronounced king at Hebron. Hebron was a symbolically appropriate place for this announced coup. It was an ancient Yahwistic shrine and the capital of the tribe of Judah. Absalom himself was born there (3:2-3), but more important David was anointed king in Hebron over both Judah (2:4) and Israel (5:1). It may well be that the people of Hebron were disgruntled over the movement of David's capital from Hebron to Jerusalem and welcomed Absalom's attention to its status. In any case, Absalom's launch of revolt from the capital of Judah makes clear that his rebellion had the support of both the northern and southern tribes of Israel. He was not simply exploiting discontent from die-hard Saulides.

Absalom had shrewdly brought two hundred men as his guests from Jerusalem. The text tells us they were innocent and did not know what was about to happen (v. 11). This was a clever move on Absalom's part. No doubt the two hundred were primarily those whom Absalom considered friends and supporters. By being with him in Hebron, they are already implicated in his declared usurpation of the throne. They are hardly in a position to disavow loyalty to Absalom, as some might have done in the greater safety of Jerusalem. From David's side, it appears that many influential men have cast their lot with Absalom. The story particularly calls our attention to the defection of one of David's "counselors" (advisers) to give assistance to Absalom (v. 12). His name is Ahithophel, and the effort to thwart his shrewd advice becomes a chief interest later in the story (16:15–17:29).

Absalom's attack on Jerusalem must have come quickly but not immediately. Verse 12*b* suggests that some time was spent in Hebron to allow for support to gather strength. Interestingly, the narrator calls Absalom's rebellion a "conspiracy" (קֶשֶׁר *qāšar*), the same word used much earlier by Saul in accusing his own supporters of having collaborated with David against him (1 Sam 22:8, 13). The decisive moment has passed. Israel faces a civil war, and shockingly Absalom has seized the initiative and appears to have growing strength and numbers (v. 12*b*). We thought David's fugitive days were over, but he must flee for his life once again. (See Reflections at 15:13–16:14.)

2 Samuel 15:13–16:14, The Retreat from Jerusalem

NIV

¹³A messenger came and told David, "The hearts of the men of Israel are with Absalom."

¹⁴Then David said to all his officials who were with him in Jerusalem, "Come! We must flee, or none of us will escape from Absalom. We must leave immediately, or he will move quickly to overtake us and bring ruin upon us and put the city to the sword."

¹⁵The king's officials answered him, "Your servants are ready to do whatever our lord the king chooses."

¹⁶The king set out, with his entire household following him; but he left ten concubines to take care of the palace. ¹⁷So the king set out, with all the people following him, and they halted at a place some distance away. ¹⁸All his men marched past him, along with all the Kerethites and Pelethites; and all the six hundred Gittites who had

NRSV

13A messenger came to David, saying, "The hearts of the Israelites have gone after Absalom." ¹⁴Then David said to all his officials who were with him at Jerusalem, "Get up! Let us flee, or there will be no escape for us from Absalom. Hurry, or he will soon overtake us, and bring disaster down upon us, and attack the city with the edge of the sword." ¹⁵The king's officials said to the king, "Your servants are ready to do whatever our lord the king decides." ¹⁶So the king left, followed by all his household, except ten concubines whom he left behind to look after the house. ¹⁷The king left, followed by all the people; and they stopped at the last house. ¹⁸All his officials passed by him; and all the Cherethites, and all the Pelethites, and all the six hundred Gittites who had followed him from Gath, passed on before the king.

19Then the king said to Ittai the Gittite, "Why

NIV

accompanied him from Gath marched before the king.

¹⁹The king said to Ittai the Gittite, "Why should you come along with us? Go back and stay with King Absalom. You are a foreigner, an exile from your homeland. ²⁰You came only yesterday. And today shall I make you wander about with us, when I do not know where I am going? Go back, and take your countrymen. May kindness and faithfulness be with you."

²¹But Ittai replied to the king, "As surely as the LORD lives, and as my lord the king lives, wherever my lord the king may be, whether it means life or death, there will your servant be."

²²David said to Ittai, "Go ahead, march on." So Ittai the Gittite marched on with all his men and the families that were with him.

²³The whole countryside wept aloud as all the people passed by. The king also crossed the Kidron Valley, and all the people moved on toward the desert.

²⁴Zadok was there, too, and all the Levites who were with him were carrying the ark of the covenant of God. They set down the ark of God, and Abiathar offered sacrifices*ᵃ* until all the people had finished leaving the city.

²⁵Then the king said to Zadok, "Take the ark of God back into the city. If I find favor in the LORD's eyes, he will bring me back and let me see it and his dwelling place again. ²⁶But if he says, 'I am not pleased with you,' then I am ready; let him do to me whatever seems good to him."

²⁷The king also said to Zadok the priest, "Aren't you a seer? Go back to the city in peace, with your son Ahimaaz and Jonathan son of Abiathar. You and Abiathar take your two sons with you. ²⁸I will wait at the fords in the desert until word comes from you to inform me." ²⁹So Zadok and Abiathar took the ark of God back to Jerusalem and stayed there.

³⁰But David continued up the Mount of Olives, weeping as he went; his head was covered and he was barefoot. All the people with him covered their heads too and were weeping as they went up. ³¹Now David had been told, "Ahithophel is among the conspirators with Absalom." So David prayed, "O LORD, turn Ahithophel's counsel into foolishness."

ᵃ24 Or Abiathar went up

NRSV

are you also coming with us? Go back, and stay with the king; for you are a foreigner, and also an exile from your home. ²⁰You came only yesterday, and shall I today make you wander about with us, while I go wherever I can? Go back, and take your kinsfolk with you; and may the LORD show*ᵃ* steadfast love and faithfulness to you." ²¹But Ittai answered the king, "As the LORD lives, and as my lord the king lives, wherever my lord the king may be, whether for death or for life, there also your servant will be." ²²David said to Ittai, "Go then, march on." So Ittai the Gittite marched on, with all his men and all the little ones who were with him. ²³The whole country wept aloud as all the people passed by; the king crossed the Wadi Kidron, and all the people moved on toward the wilderness.

24Abiathar came up, and Zadok also, with all the Levites, carrying the ark of the covenant of God. They set down the ark of God, until the people had all passed out of the city. ²⁵Then the king said to Zadok, "Carry the ark of God back into the city. If I find favor in the eyes of the LORD, he will bring me back and let me see both it and the place where it stays. ²⁶But if he says, 'I take no pleasure in you,' here I am, let him do to me what seems good to him." ²⁷The king also said to the priest Zadok, "Look,*ᵇ* go back to the city in peace, you and Abiathar,*ᶜ* with your two sons, Ahimaaz your son, and Jonathan son of Abiathar. ²⁸See, I will wait at the fords of the wilderness until word comes from you to inform me." ²⁹So Zadok and Abiathar carried the ark of God back to Jerusalem, and they remained there.

30But David went up the ascent of the Mount of Olives, weeping as he went, with his head covered and walking barefoot; and all the people who were with him covered their heads and went up, weeping as they went. ³¹David was told that Ahithophel was among the conspirators with Absalom. And David said, "O LORD, I pray you, turn the counsel of Ahithophel into foolishness."

32When David came to the summit, where God was worshiped, Hushai the Archite came to meet him with his coat torn and earth on his head. ³³David said to him, "If you go on with me,

ᵃ Gk Compare 2.6: Heb lacks may the LORD show   ᵇ Gk: Heb Are you a seer or Do you see?   ᶜ Cn: Heb lacks and Abiathar

³²When David arrived at the summit, where people used to worship God, Hushai the Arkite was there to meet him, his robe torn and dust on his head. ³³David said to him, "If you go with me, you will be a burden to me. ³⁴But if you return to the city and say to Absalom, 'I will be your servant, O king; I was your father's servant in the past, but now I will be your servant,' then you can help me by frustrating Ahithophel's advice. ³⁵Won't the priests Zadok and Abiathar be there with you? Tell them anything you hear in the king's palace. ³⁶Their two sons, Ahimaaz son of Zadok and Jonathan son of Abiathar, are there with them. Send them to me with anything you hear."

³⁷So David's friend Hushai arrived at Jerusalem as Absalom was entering the city.

16 When David had gone a short distance beyond the summit, there was Ziba, the steward of Mephibosheth, waiting to meet him. He had a string of donkeys saddled and loaded with two hundred loaves of bread, a hundred cakes of raisins, a hundred cakes of figs and a skin of wine.

²The king asked Ziba, "Why have you brought these?"

Ziba answered, "The donkeys are for the king's household to ride on, the bread and fruit are for the men to eat, and the wine is to refresh those who become exhausted in the desert."

³The king then asked, "Where is your master's grandson?"

Ziba said to him, "He is staying in Jerusalem, because he thinks, 'Today the house of Israel will give me back my grandfather's kingdom.'"

⁴Then the king said to Ziba, "All that belonged to Mephibosheth is now yours."

"I humbly bow," Ziba said. "May I find favor in your eyes, my lord the king."

⁵As King David approached Bahurim, a man from the same clan as Saul's family came out from there. His name was Shimei son of Gera, and he cursed as he came out. ⁶He pelted David and all the king's officials with stones, though all the troops and the special guard were on David's right and left. ⁷As he cursed, Shimei said, "Get out, get out, you man of blood, you scoundrel! ⁸The LORD has repaid you for all the blood you shed in the

you will be a burden to me. ³⁴But if you return to the city and say to Absalom, 'I will be your servant, O king; as I have been your father's servant in time past, so now I will be your servant,' then you will defeat for me the counsel of Ahithophel. ³⁵The priests Zadok and Abiathar will be with you there. So whatever you hear from the king's house, tell it to the priests Zadok and Abiathar. ³⁶Their two sons are with them there, Zadok's son Ahimaaz and Abiathar's son Jonathan; and by them you shall report to me everything you hear." ³⁷So Hushai, David's friend, came into the city, just as Absalom was entering Jerusalem.

16 When David had passed a little beyond the summit, Ziba the servant of Mephibosheth^a met him, with a couple of donkeys saddled, carrying two hundred loaves of bread, one hundred bunches of raisins, one hundred of summer fruits, and one skin of wine. ²The king said to Ziba, "Why have you brought these?" Ziba answered, "The donkeys are for the king's household to ride, the bread and summer fruit for the young men to eat, and the wine is for those to drink who faint in the wilderness." ³The king said, "And where is your master's son?" Ziba said to the king, "He remains in Jerusalem; for he said, 'Today the house of Israel will give me back my grandfather's kingdom.'" ⁴Then the king said to Ziba, "All that belonged to Mephibosheth^a is now yours." Ziba said, "I do obeisance; let me find favor in your sight, my lord the king."

⁵When King David came to Bahurim, a man of the family of the house of Saul came out whose name was Shimei son of Gera; he came out cursing. ⁶He threw stones at David and at all the servants of King David; now all the people and all the warriors were on his right and on his left. ⁷Shimei shouted while he cursed, "Out! Out! Murderer! Scoundrel! ⁸The LORD has avenged on all of you the blood of the house of Saul, in whose place you have reigned; and the LORD has given the kingdom into the hand of your son Absalom. See, disaster has overtaken you; for you are a man of blood."

⁹Then Abishai son of Zeruiah said to the king, "Why should this dead dog curse my lord the king? Let me go over and take off his head." ¹⁰But

^a Or *Merib-baal:* See 4.4 note

NIV

household of Saul, in whose place you have reigned. The LORD has handed the kingdom over to your son Absalom. You have come to ruin because you are a man of blood!"

⁹Then Abishai son of Zeruiah said to the king, "Why should this dead dog curse my lord the king? Let me go over and cut off his head."

¹⁰But the king said, "What do you and I have in common, you sons of Zeruiah? If he is cursing because the LORD said to him, 'Curse David,' who can ask, 'Why do you do this?'"

¹¹David then said to Abishai and all his officials, "My son, who is of my own flesh, is trying to take my life. How much more, then, this Benjamite! Leave him alone; let him curse, for the LORD has told him to. ¹²It may be that the LORD will see my distress and repay me with good for the cursing I am receiving today."

¹³So David and his men continued along the road while Shimei was going along the hillside opposite him, cursing as he went and throwing stones at him and showering him with dirt. ¹⁴The king and all the people with him arrived at their destination exhausted. And there he refreshed himself.

NRSV

the king said, "What have I to do with you, you sons of Zeruiah? If he is cursing because the LORD has said to him, 'Curse David,' who then shall say, 'Why have you done so?'" ¹¹David said to Abishai and to all his servants, "My own son seeks my life; how much more now may this Benjaminite! Let him alone, and let him curse; for the LORD has bidden him. ¹²It may be that the LORD will look on my distress,ᵃ and the LORD will repay me with good for this cursing of me today." ¹³So David and his men went on the road, while Shimei went along on the hillside opposite him and cursed as he went, throwing stones and flinging dust at him. ¹⁴The king and all the people who were with him arrived weary at the Jordan;ᵇ and there he refreshed himself.

ᵃ Gk Vg: Heb *iniquity*   ᵇ Gk: Heb lacks *at the Jordan*

COMMENTARY

The central portion of the narrative of Absalom's rebellion has a symmetrical structure.[321]

A	15:13–16:14, David's retreat from Jerusalem
B	16:15–17:23, the conflict of advisers
B′	17:24–19:8, the conflict of armies
A′	19:9-43, David's return to Jerusalem

This account of David's retreat from Jerusalem in the face of Absalom's advance on the capital city provides the opportunity for narration of five encounters that reveal to us something of David's support and opposition as well as evidence of his still considerable strength of character in the face of adversity. Information on the panicked beginning and the progress of David's retreat is found in 15:13-18, 23, 30-31; 16:5, 14. The encounters along the way include those with Ittai the Gittite (16:19-22), Abiathar and Zadok (16:24-29), Hushai the Archite (15:32-36), Ziba (16:1-4), and Shimei (16:5-13). This account conveys an atmosphere of near panic, and decisions are made quickly in the heat of the moment with no opportunity for careful planning or strategy on David's part. The advantage seems to rest with Absalom, although he is himself offstage, and we hear only of his arrival to Jerusalem in v. 37.

15:13-18. A messenger brings David the ominous news that the "hearts of the Israelites have gone after Absalom" (v. 13). By contrast, David's constituency seems to be the bureaucracy of Je-

321. For a more detailed analysis of literary structures in these chapters, see C. C. Conroy, *Absalom, Absalom! Narrative and Language in 2 Sam 13–20,* AnBib 81 (Rome: Pontifical Biblical Institute, 1978) 89. See also A. A. Anderson, *2 Samuel,* WBC 11 (Waco: Word, 1989) 202.

rusalem, whom he now summons to escape (v. 14). These verses speak of David's household, his officials, his servants, and the mercenary troops that are in his personal service. The implication is clear: The people are with Absalom. The odds do not look good for David.

The message brought to David must have indicated that Absalom was on the move toward Jerusalem. David's pleas are urgent, yet David takes command, and the order of the day is haste. He clearly does not regard Jerusalem as the ground on which he wishes to meet Absalom. Perhaps he fears encirclement or harm to the city. What David orders is a strategic retreat so that he may choose a more suitable time and place to meet Absalom's threat. All who are loyal to David in Jerusalem are evacuated except for ten concubines left to care for the royal household (v. 16). This reference clearly prepares for Absalom's action reported in 16:22.

David stops at the outskirts of the city to take stock of his entourage (v. 17). Those who pass in review (v. 18) are intended to give us some idea of David's remaining military resources. These consist primarily of non-Israelite mercenaries whose loyalty is to David and not to Israel as a nation. The manuscript evidence for this verse is very uncertain,[322] and many commentators believe the reference to the "six hundred" is an indication of David's personal army, retained from the days of his wilderness skirmishes with Saul and his service of the Philistines at Ziklag (cf. 1 Sam 23:13; 27:2; 30:9). Cherethites, Pelethites, and Gittites are mercenary groups of non-Israelites in David's service.

15:19-23. The first of five encounters for David during his retreat from Jerusalem is with Ittai, the commander of the Gittite troops in David's service. This may well be a contingent of fighting men from Gath whose loyalty David had won while serving as the Philistine commander of Ziklag under the king of Gath. David suggests in his comments to Ittai that he joined David only "yesterday" (v. 20a), which may indicate that the Gittite troops were not a part of David's longstanding personal army, but had joined him more recently.

David's speech to Ittai is gracious and generous. He speaks of Ittai's foreign status and suggests that this need not be Ittai's battle. He releases Ittai and his men from obligation, along with their families and households, and blesses them with steadfast love (חסד *hesed*) and faithfulness from the Lord (v. 20). Ittai's response is equally gracious and generous. He pledges loyalty to David in the name of David's God, Yahweh (the Lord), and by David's own life. Ittai declares that his lot is with David in life or in death (v. 21). David accepts this pledge, and Ittai, his men, and their families all march into exile with David (v. 22). Sakenfeld has called attention to the parallel of this encounter with Naomi's effort to bid farewell to Ruth and her subsequent pledge of loyalty in Ruth 1:8, 16-17.[323] Like Ruth, Ittai is a foreigner who chooses loyalty to an Israelite and to Israel's God over alternatives that might have led to greater safety and less risk. In this context, we may be intended to see a contrast between Absalom, the disloyal son, and Ittai, the foreigner who is more loyal than the son. In the final battle against Absalom, Ittai is made one of the three top commanders (18:2, 5).

The route of David's retreat is through the Kidron Valley, which lies between Jerusalem and the Mount of Olives. The procession is one of weeping and sorrow. The wilderness, into which the procession heads, seems symbolic (v. 23).

15:24-30. David next encounters the priests Abiathar and Zadok, who come bearing the ark of the covenant (v. 24). It would seem logical to bring the ark with David's entourage as a sign of God's presence in their midst, but David rejects this alternative in a characteristic mixture of piety and pragmatism. He sends the ark and the priests back into Jerusalem. He realizes that possession even of this sacred object offers no guarantee of God's favor (cf. Israel's experience in 1 Samuel 4). It is not for David to command the presence of God. If David finds favor in God's eyes, then God will bring him back into the presence of the ark and Jerusalem, where it resides (v. 25). But if David finds no favor in God's eyes, the ark will not save him. God will do what seems right in the divine will (v. 26). David places his trust in the providence of God, not in the ark as a sacred object he can possess. This speech by David is reminiscent of the pious trust he relied on in the period when he was a fugitive from Saul in the wilderness. It is appropriate as he heads into

322. P. Kyle McCarter, *II Samuel*, AB 9 (Garden City, N.Y.: Doubleday, 1984) 363-64, discusses the textual issues in detail.

323. Katherine D. Sakenfeld, *The Meaning of Hesed in the Hebrew Bible: A New Inquiry*, HSM 17 (Missoula, Mont.: Scholars Press, 1978) 1-8.

the wilderness again as a fugitive that his faith should once again become the basis of his trust. His future is entrusted to the hand of God.

Yet, David's trustful faith does not rule out his own pragmatic action. This mixture of piety and pragmatism has often marked David's bold actions in the past. If Zadok and Abiathar must return to Jerusalem with their two sons (v. 27), they can at least be David's eyes and ears in Absalom's city. David lays the foundation for an intelligence network and informs the priests where he will be waiting so that word can be brought to him (v. 28). The two priests return with the ark to Jerusalem to carry out this mandate.

David and his people proceed on their way over the Mount of Olives (v. 30). David weeps; his head is covered; he walks on bare feet. This is not the portrait of a political or military retreat. It is a penitential procession. David has cast his fate in the hands of God, and he moves forward in penance and in supplication for God's mercy. His people join him in these acts of ritual penance.

15:31-37. Even on his penitential journey David is active, receiving intelligence, meeting friends and foes, and making decisions. He receives word that one of his trusted advisers, Ahithophel, has joined Absalom's rebellion against him (cf. v. 12). His first response is to place this matter in God's hands—he prays. He asks God to turn the counsel of Ahithophel to foolishness (v. 31). We are reminded of David's frequent resort to prayer in time of trial before he became king. As he arrives at the summit of the Mount of Olives, where there was a place of worship, Hushai appears to meet him (v. 32), almost as if he were the answer to David's prayer. Indeed, Hushai will become the means for defeating the counsel of Ahithophel.

Hushai arrives in torn garments and with dirt on his head, clearly prepared to join the grieving procession into exile (v. 32). But David has other plans for this loyal friend. We are seeing David at his best. He has no master strategy, but seizes opportunities as they are presented and makes them work in his favor. David reminds us in the encounters during his retreat of the opportunistic, yet piously trustful David we saw in his early career. Ittai, the military man, is most useful in the wilderness with David. But his priests and now his friend will be of greater use in Jerusalem. David sends Hushai, like Abiathar and Zadok, back to the city to infiltrate Absalom's followers. Hushai is to pretend to defect to Absalom. David hopes that Hushai might find ways to counter the defection of Ahithophel (v. 34). It would seem that David thinks of Hushai primarily as a spy, working with Abiathar and Zadok to send information to David by means of their two sons (vv. 35-36). What David cannot foresee is that Hushai will actually be called upon to advise Absalom, thus directly countering Ahithophel's advice (cf. 16:15–17:14). Hushai, referred to as David's friend, does return to the city just as Absalom is entering it (v. 37).

16:1-4. David's next encounter, as he passes beyond the Mount of Olives, is with a figure we have met before. Ziba, a servant of Saul who had been assigned by David to care for properties of Jonathan's remaining son, Mephibosheth (chap. 9), meets David bearing gifts (16:1). Ziba's appearance is something of a surprise. As an old Saulide loyalist, he might have welcomed the overthrow of David and thus support Absalom. But Ziba is shrewd; he may know enough not to count the father out in this struggle. He may see this moment as his opportunity to become more than a servant to those with land and authority. He brings substantial provisions to David and his company, surely a welcome gift for this hasty departure, and the king is pleasantly surprised at such largess (16:1-2). Such a gift makes clear that Ziba sides with David. But David shrewdly asks where Mephibosheth stands (v. 3a), and Ziba replies that Mephibosheth has remained in Jerusalem hoping that Absalom's rebellion will see the return to him of Saul's kingdom (v. 3b). We do not know the truth of this matter, and Mephibosheth will later dispute this report (19:24-30). It does not seem reasonable that Absalom's seizure of the throne should raise hopes for the return of the throne to the house of Saul. Is Ziba simply opportunistic at Mephibosheth's expense? For the moment we are left to wonder, but David acts on what he hears and declares that all of Mephibosheth's holdings are now Ziba's property (v. 4a), a decision for which Ziba is appropriately grateful and deferential toward David (v. 4b).

16:5-10a. David has received the loyalty of an old Saulide supporter, but his next encounter is with the unleashed anger and venom of a Saulide supporter who has not reconciled himself to the reign of David in Saul's place. When David reaches Bahurim, moving toward the Jordan River, a man named Shimei, whose family belongs to the house of Saul, comes to meet David—not with gifts, but with cursing (v. 5). He throws stones at David and his party and hurls accusations as well (vv. 6-8). His voice must represent many yet remaining in Israel who hold David responsible for the deaths of Saul, Ishbosheth, and Abner. Shimei calls David a murderer and a man of blood. It may well be that the handing over of Saul's sons to Gibeonite vengeance (recorded in 21:1-9) had also taken place prior to this time in David's story. Shimei calls for blood vengeance against David for the blood of the house of Saul, and he sees Absalom's revolt as the instrument of the Lord's judgment against David. Saulide hopes and animosities are alive and well in Israel. Shimei thinks the moment for Saulide vengeance has come, and he boldly announces as much to David, even in the presence of David's loyal fighting men.

Naturally, it is Abishai, brother of Joab and one of the hotheaded sons of Zeruiah, who wants to respond by calling Shimei a "dead dog" and cutting off his head (v. 9). David has had to deal with the hot-tempered and violent responses of Abishai and his brother Joab before (1 Sam 26:8-9; 2 Sam 3:30, 39), and he quickly heads off Abishai's retaliatory response (v. 10a). David's response reveals his trustful faith in the face of grave challenge.

16:10b-12. David cannot afford petty retaliation at this moment, but his response is more than pragmatism. David takes this moment of cursing to reflect on his position before God and his trust that it is God's grace and not Abishai's sword that can counter Shimei's cursing. David reflects that Shimei's cursing may be a part of what God has done in this moment (v. 10b), and he chooses to endure the curses as a part of what God's providence has brought to him. After all, David muses, his own son Absalom is in open revolt against him (v. 11). What are curses and stones compared to the threat from which they are in retreat? David recognizes that it is not the goodwill of Shimei that he needs, but the grace and mercy of God in his time of distress (v. 12a). He expresses a hope, almost a prayer, that Shimei's curses may be countered and replaced by God's goodness (v. 12b). In this moment we again see David as we have seen him before at his best. He trusts God and recognizes his reliance on God's providence, while moving forward himself with the most effective action he can take on his own behalf. It is a juxtaposition of political realism and trusting faith that is part of what so fascinates us about David and has made him such an influential figure in Jewish and Christian tradition.

16:13-14. So the procession continues on down to the Jordan, with Shimei unmolested in his cursing and stone throwing. One senses that David is out of immediate danger once he reaches the Jordan River. The scene now shifts to Absalom's court and the strategic counsel he receives.

REFLECTIONS

This segment of the narrative gives us a portrait of David marked by considerable pathos. He is a man under judgment whose own son has turned against him. He has experienced tragedy and death; now he faces the shame of flight from his own capital city. We can hardly help recalling the words of David's own lament over Saul and Jonathan, "How the mighty have fallen" (1:19b).

Yet there emerges in this account of retreat a remarkable testimony to the resilience of David's faith and the strength of his character. The David we see is not without the flaws that have brought tragedy to him, but he is, nevertheless, a David who models for us the power of faith to overcome the power of sin and death. In the midst of what is almost a Davidic passion narrative, we begin to see the power of God to bring new life.

1. David begins this journey as a sinner who has paid a high price as the consequence of his sin. But he is not undone by this realization of his own guilt. David teaches us that in the face of sin and its death-dealing consequences, we must ultimately rely on the power of God's grace. David will return if he "finds favor in the eyes of the Lord" (15:25) and if the "Lord will look on my distress" and "repay me with good" (16:12). This is not the "good" he deserves but the "good" that comes only as God's grace. He trusts that in spite of sin there is a future to be received in God's providence. In contrast, many who come to the realization of their own sin and are faced with its consequences in their lives find themselves mired in guilt, unable to move on from a past that has crumbled and move toward the possibilities of God's new future. Sometimes when our own sinful choices have resulted in broken relationships and ruined lives, we seem to believe that broken reality is all we deserve. David models the bold faith that believes the good news—new life is available to us through the "goodness" of God, even when we do not deserve it. In the midst of the apparent loss of his kingdom, a consequence of his own sin, David trusts that in God there is a future for him. Although he does not know that this future will mean his kingdom regained, he trusts boldly in God's providence to give him a future: "Let him do to me what seems good to him" (15:26).

David also teaches us in this story that piety is not passive in its waiting for God's goodness to bring new life and new future. On this journey in retreat from Jerusalem, David is meeting and dealing with friends and enemies in a way that reflects his considerable skill at shaping his own future while trusting that its shape ultimately rests with God. He plans, deploys, gathers information, and makes careful decisions. Piety does not ask for the abandonment of political realism or shrewd decision making in our own interests. Some persons of faith seem to assume that piety necessitates a kind of political naïveté and passivity in the face of life's personal and societal challenges. God may provide openings to new life, but we surely must be willing to open doors and find ways to move forward through them. Faith does not ask us to resign ourselves to the future God has in store, but to boldly claim that future and participate with God in its emergence.

2. A special notice must be given to David's unwillingness to use the ark to his advantage. He refused to manipulate the authentic religious symbol of covenant faith for his own self-interest. In a day that sees frequent appeal to religious symbols for the promotion of narrow ideological claims, it is refreshing to read of David's refusal. We, also, should be wary of too easily claiming the symbols of our faith to lend authority to causes that cannot stand on their own merits. This is not an appeal for the absence of religious language in public life. It is an appeal that we not use such language or symbols as a cynical Madison Avenue technique to lend respectability to our causes. David refused to use the ark, but he did not hesitate to speak the language of faith in his dealings with those he met and in the strategic decisions he made on his journey. It is the substance of our faith and its values that must be present in the public arena, not simply its symbols for the sake of appearances and public image.

2 Samuel 16:15–17:29, The Strategies of Ahithophel and Hushai

NIV

¹⁵Meanwhile, Absalom and all the men of Israel came to Jerusalem, and Ahithophel was with him. ¹⁶Then Hushai the Arkite, David's friend, went to Absalom and said to him, "Long live the king! Long live the king!"

¹⁷Absalom asked Hushai, "Is this the love you show your friend? Why didn't you go with your friend?"

NRSV

15Now Absalom and all the Israelites[a] came to Jerusalem; Ahithophel was with him. ¹⁶When Hushai the Archite, David's friend, came to Absalom, Hushai said to Absalom, "Long live the king! Long live the king!" ¹⁷Absalom said to Hushai, "Is this your loyalty to your friend? Why did you not go with your friend?" ¹⁸Hushai said

a Gk: Heb all the people, the men of Israel

NIV

¹⁸Hushai said to Absalom, "No, the one chosen by the LORD, by these people, and by all the men of Israel—his I will be, and I will remain with him. ¹⁹Furthermore, whom should I serve? Should I not serve the son? Just as I served your father, so I will serve you."

²⁰Absalom said to Ahithophel, "Give us your advice. What should we do?"

²¹Ahithophel answered, "Lie with your father's concubines whom he left to take care of the palace. Then all Israel will hear that you have made yourself a stench in your father's nostrils, and the hands of everyone with you will be strengthened." ²²So they pitched a tent for Absalom on the roof, and he lay with his father's concubines in the sight of all Israel.

²³Now in those days the advice Ahithophel gave was like that of one who inquires of God. That was how both David and Absalom regarded all of Ahithophel's advice.

17 Ahithophel said to Absalom, "I would*ᵃ* choose twelve thousand men and set out tonight in pursuit of David. ²I would*ᵇ* attack him while he is weary and weak. I would*ᵇ* strike him with terror, and then all the people with him will flee. I would*ᵇ* strike down only the king ³and bring all the people back to you. The death of the man you seek will mean the return of all; all the people will be unharmed." ⁴This plan seemed good to Absalom and to all the elders of Israel.

⁵But Absalom said, "Summon also Hushai the Arkite, so we can hear what he has to say." ⁶When Hushai came to him, Absalom said, "Ahithophel has given this advice. Should we do what he says? If not, give us your opinion."

⁷Hushai replied to Absalom, "The advice Ahithophel has given is not good this time. ⁸You know your father and his men; they are fighters, and as fierce as a wild bear robbed of her cubs. Besides, your father is an experienced fighter; he will not spend the night with the troops. ⁹Even now, he is hidden in a cave or some other place. If he should attack your troops first,*ᶜ* whoever hears about it will say, 'There has been a slaughter among the troops who follow Absalom.' ¹⁰Then even the bravest soldier, whose heart is like the

a1 Or *Let me*   *b2* Or *will*   *c9* Or *When some of the men fall at the first attack*

NRSV

to Absalom, "No; but the one whom the LORD and this people and all the Israelites have chosen, his I will be, and with him I will remain. ¹⁹Moreover, whom should I serve? Should it not be his son? Just as I have served your father, so I will serve you."

²⁰Then Absalom said to Ahithophel, "Give us your counsel; what shall we do?" ²¹Ahithophel said to Absalom, "Go in to your father's concubines, the ones he has left to look after the house; and all Israel will hear that you have made yourself odious to your father, and the hands of all who are with you will be strengthened." ²²So they pitched a tent for Absalom upon the roof; and Absalom went in to his father's concubines in the sight of all Israel. ²³Now in those days the counsel that Ahithophel gave was as if one consulted the oracle*ᵃ* of God; so all the counsel of Ahithophel was esteemed, both by David and by Absalom.

17 Moreover Ahithophel said to Absalom, "Let me choose twelve thousand men, and I will set out and pursue David tonight. ²I will come upon him while he is weary and discouraged, and throw him into a panic; and all the people who are with him will flee. I will strike down only the king, ³and I will bring all the people back to you as a bride comes home to her husband. You seek the life of only one man,*ᵇ* and all the people will be at peace." ⁴The advice pleased Absalom and all the elders of Israel.

⁵Then Absalom said, "Call Hushai the Archite also, and let us hear too what he has to say." ⁶When Hushai came to Absalom, Absalom said to him, "This is what Ahithophel has said; shall we do as he advises? If not, you tell us." ⁷Then Hushai said to Absalom, "This time the counsel that Ahithophel has given is not good." ⁸Hushai continued, "You know that your father and his men are warriors, and that they are enraged, like a bear robbed of her cubs in the field. Besides, your father is expert in war; he will not spend the night with the troops. ⁹Even now he has hidden himself in one of the pits, or in some other place. And when some of our troops*ᶜ* fall at the first attack, whoever hears it will say, 'There has

a Heb *word*   *b* Gk: Heb *like the return of the whole (is) the man whom you seek*   *c* Gk Mss: Heb *some of them*

heart of a lion, will melt with fear, for all Israel knows that your father is a fighter and that those with him are brave.

[11]"So I advise you: Let all Israel, from Dan to Beersheba—as numerous as the sand on the seashore—be gathered to you, with you yourself leading them into battle. [12]Then we will attack him wherever he may be found, and we will fall on him as dew settles on the ground. Neither he nor any of his men will be left alive. [13]If he withdraws into a city, then all Israel will bring ropes to that city, and we will drag it down to the valley until not even a piece of it can be found."

[14]Absalom and all the men of Israel said, "The advice of Hushai the Arkite is better than that of Ahithophel." For the LORD had determined to frustrate the good advice of Ahithophel in order to bring disaster on Absalom.

[15]Hushai told Zadok and Abiathar, the priests, "Ahithophel has advised Absalom and the elders of Israel to do such and such, but I have advised them to do so and so. [16]Now send a message immediately and tell David, 'Do not spend the night at the fords in the desert; cross over without fail, or the king and all the people with him will be swallowed up.'"

[17]Jonathan and Ahimaaz were staying at En Rogel. A servant girl was to go and inform them, and they were to go and tell King David, for they could not risk being seen entering the city. [18]But a young man saw them and told Absalom. So the two of them left quickly and went to the house of a man in Bahurim. He had a well in his courtyard, and they climbed down into it. [19]His wife took a covering and spread it out over the opening of the well and scattered grain over it. No one knew anything about it.

[20]When Absalom's men came to the woman at the house, they asked, "Where are Ahimaaz and Jonathan?"

The woman answered them, "They crossed over the brook."[a] The men searched but found no one, so they returned to Jerusalem.

[21]After the men had gone, the two climbed out of the well and went to inform King David. They said to him, "Set out and cross the river at once;

[a]20 Or "They passed by the sheep pen toward the water."

been a slaughter among the troops who follow Absalom.' [10]Then even the valiant warrior, whose heart is like the heart of a lion, will utterly melt with fear; for all Israel knows that your father is a warrior, and that those who are with him are valiant warriors. [11]But my counsel is that all Israel be gathered to you, from Dan to Beer-sheba, like the sand by the sea for multitude, and that you go to battle in person. [12]So we shall come upon him in whatever place he may be found, and we shall light on him as the dew falls on the ground; and he will not survive, nor will any of those with him. [13]If he withdraws into a city, then all Israel will bring ropes to that city, and we shall drag it into the valley, until not even a pebble is to be found there." [14]Absalom and all the men of Israel said, "The counsel of Hushai the Archite is better than the counsel of Ahithophel." For the LORD had ordained to defeat the good counsel of Ahithophel, so that the LORD might bring ruin on Absalom.

[15]Then Hushai said to the priests Zadok and Abiathar, "Thus and so did Ahithophel counsel Absalom and the elders of Israel; and thus and so I have counseled. [16]Therefore send quickly and tell David, 'Do not lodge tonight at the fords of the wilderness, but by all means cross over; otherwise the king and all the people who are with him will be swallowed up.'" [17]Jonathan and Ahimaaz were waiting at En-rogel; a servant-girl used to go and tell them, and they would go and tell King David; for they could not risk being seen entering the city. [18]But a boy saw them, and told Absalom; so both of them went away quickly, and came to the house of a man at Bahurim, who had a well in his courtyard; and they went down into it. [19]The man's wife took a covering, stretched it over the well's mouth, and spread out grain on it; and nothing was known of it. [20]When Absalom's servants came to the woman at the house, they said, "Where are Ahimaaz and Jonathan?" The woman said to them, "They have crossed over the brook[a] of water." And when they had searched and could not find them, they returned to Jerusalem.

[21]After they had gone, the men came up out of the well, and went and told King David. They

[a] Meaning of Heb uncertain

NIV

Ahithophel has advised such and such against you." [22]So David and all the people with him set out and crossed the Jordan. By daybreak, no one was left who had not crossed the Jordan.

[23]When Ahithophel saw that his advice had not been followed, he saddled his donkey and set out for his house in his hometown. He put his house in order and then hanged himself. So he died and was buried in his father's tomb.

[24]David went to Mahanaim, and Absalom crossed the Jordan with all the men of Israel. [25]Absalom had appointed Amasa over the army in place of Joab. Amasa was the son of a man named Jether,[a] an Israelite[b] who had married Abigail,[c] the daughter of Nahash and sister of Zeruiah the mother of Joab. [26]The Israelites and Absalom camped in the land of Gilead.

[27]When David came to Mahanaim, Shobi son of Nahash from Rabbah of the Ammonites, and Makir son of Ammiel from Lo Debar, and Barzillai the Gileadite from Rogelim [28]brought bedding and bowls and articles of pottery. They also brought wheat and barley, flour and roasted grain, beans and lentils,[d] [29]honey and curds, sheep, and cheese from cows' milk for David and his people to eat. For they said, "The people have become hungry and tired and thirsty in the desert."

[a]25 Hebrew *Ithra,* a variant of *Jether* [b]25 Hebrew and some Septuagint manuscripts; other Septuagint manuscripts (see also 1 Chron. 2:17) *Ishmaelite* or *Jezreelite* [c]25 Hebrew *Abigal,* a variant of *Abigail* [d]28 Most Septuagint manuscripts and Syriac; Hebrew *lentils, and roasted grain*

NRSV

said to David, "Go and cross the water quickly; for thus and so has Ahithophel counseled against you." [22]So David and all the people who were with him set out and crossed the Jordan; by daybreak not one was left who had not crossed the Jordan.

[23]When Ahithophel saw that his counsel was not followed, he saddled his donkey and went off home to his own city. He set his house in order, and hanged himself; he died and was buried in the tomb of his father.

[24]Then David came to Mahanaim, while Absalom crossed the Jordan with all the men of Israel. [25]Now Absalom had set Amasa over the army in the place of Joab. Amasa was the son of a man named Ithra the Ishmaelite,[a] who had married Abigal daughter of Nahash, sister of Zeruiah, Joab's mother. [26]The Israelites and Absalom encamped in the land of Gilead.

[27]When David came to Mahanaim, Shobi son of Nahash from Rabbah of the Ammonites, and Machir son of Ammiel from Lo-debar, and Barzillai the Gileadite from Rogelim, [28]brought beds, basins, and earthen vessels, wheat, barley, meal, parched grain, beans and lentils,[b] [29]honey and curds, sheep, and cheese from the herd, for David and the people with him to eat; for they said, "The troops are hungry and weary and thirsty in the wilderness."

[a]1 Chr 2.17: Heb *Israelite* [b]Heb *and lentils and parched grain*

COMMENTARY

It is Absalom's time onstage. The scene shifts from the pathos of David's retreat from Jerusalem to the self-confident air of Absalom's triumphant procession into Jerusalem. The narrator emphasizes the strategic moves by which Absalom will consolidate his grip on David's kingdom. The developments within Absalom's camp unfold in several scenes: 16:15-19 Hushai, David's friend, insinuates himself into the counsel of Absalom; 16:20-23, on Ahithophel's advice Absalom publicly takes possession of David's concubines; 17:1-4, Ahithophel gives his advice on the strategy Absalom should follow in defeating David; 17:5-

14, Hushai offers competing advice; 17:15-22, David is warned and makes good his escape; 17:23, Ahithophel commits suicide; 17:24-29, David and Absalom maneuver their forces and prepare for battle.

Some questions have been raised about the literary unity of this section.[324] Absalom's taking of David's concubines (16:20-23) seems a strange diversion when he appears otherwise to be in hot pursuit of David. Further, Hushai's advice is declared the better (17:14), and Ahithophel appar-

324. See A. A. Anderson, *2 Samuel,* WBC 11 (Waco: Word, 1989) 212-13, for a discussion of various proposals.

ently commits suicide in disgrace (17:23); but in the end, it is Ahithophel's advice that is taken (17:24), and Hushai warns David in time to escape (17:15-16). However, the narrator is less interested in these idiosyncrasies than in the theological issues that shape the account. For example, Ahithophel's advice is confounded by the misleading advice of Hushai in answer to David's prayer in 15:31, "O Lord, I pray you, turn the counsel of Ahithophel into foolishness." Further, David may have been warned in a timely way by Hushai and may have taken appropriate action (17:15-16, 22), but the crucial power at work behind these events and on David's behalf is the Lord: "For the LORD had ordained to defeat the good counsel of Ahithophel, so that the Lord might bring ruin on Absalom" (17:14b). The incident involving the concubines reminds us of Nathan's prophecy against David that "I will take your wives before your eyes, and give them to your neighbor, and he shall lie with your wives in the sight of this very sun. For you did it secretly; but I will do this thing before all Israel and before the sun" (12:11-12). The narrative emphasizes that David has been judged. This violence from the hand of his own son is a part of that judgment. But the Lord has not taken the kingdom from David. He has been chastised, but the promise to David's dynasty is a firm promise, stated in 7:14-16 in Nathan's oracle.

16:15-19. When Absalom enters Jerusalem, Ahithophel is with him, and their first encounter is with David's friend Hushai (v. 15). Hushai's task, following David's instruction (15:32-37), is to make believable his own defection to Absalom's camp and to attempt to counter Ahithophel's advice. His words to Absalom display a marvelous facility with rhetorical duplicity. He greets Absalom with "Long live the king!" carefully avoiding mention of the name of the king whose long life he desires (v. 16). When Absalom questions the "loyalty" (חסד *ḥesed*) of one who would desert a friend (v. 17), Hushai coyly claims loyalty only to the one chosen by God and the people (v. 18). The reader, of course, knows that Hushai believes this to be David, while Absalom's ego, no doubt, allows him to believe it is he. Finally, however, even clever phrases must give way to the bold lie that allows Hushai access to the inner councils of Absalom: "I will serve you," he lies (v. 19).

16:20–17:14. Absalom turns first to Ahitho-

phel for counsel (16:20). Ahithophel's advice is so highly regarded that it is treated as if it were an oracle from God (v. 23). Ahithophel's reputation is a force to be reckoned with, and the danger to David from his advice is serious. His advice comes in two parts.

First, Ahithophel advises Absalom to humiliate David publicly by openly engaging in sexual intercourse with the ten concubines David had left at the palace (v. 21; cf. 15:16). Ahithophel suggests that this action will make Absalom "odious" to David in the hearing of all Israel and will strengthen Absalom's supporters (16:21b). Absalom pitches a tent on the roof and publicly takes his father's concubines (16:22). Such action fulfills Nathan's judgment against David (12:11-12) that his wives will be taken publicly, whereas he had taken Uriah's wife in secret. Perhaps Absalom's tent is pitched on the palace roof from which David first viewed Bathsheba. It does not seem likely, as some have suggested, that Absalom's action established any legal claim on the throne.[325] His action seems symbolic; it is an act of defiance and a seizing of David's prerogatives as king. Such defiant public gestures often do win public support from those who gravitate to the apparent winning side in political conflicts. Ironically, Absalom's dramatic act is for the reader a fulfillment of Yahweh's judgment and thus serves notice that Absalom, even in this moment of apparent humiliation of his father, is not really in control of events.

Ahithophel's second piece of advice is strategic. He offers Absalom a plan to end his campaign swiftly and surgically (17:1-3). Ahithophel himself proposes to lead a force of twelve thousand (the word for "thousand" [אלף *'elep*] can also mean a "contingent" or "battalion") in a quick strike on David that very night while he is "weary and discouraged." In the ensuing panic and flight, Ahithophel will strike down David alone, minimizing the loss of life among the others with David. Ahithophel assumes that with David gone, the others can be pacified and returned to their homes without need of a protracted war. He uses the imagery of a bride returning to her husband to describe this strategy. It is a bold and brilliant plan, one that pleases Absalom and the elders of

---

325. See the discussion of these matters in ibid., 214. See also the Commentary on 2 Sam 3:7-10, where Abner's taking of Saul's concubine raises similar issues.

Israel (17:4). This plan might have worked, except for the intervention of Hushai. David's hasty retreat from the fords of the Jordan after hearing of this plan suggests that he knew he would be in danger from such a strategy (17:22).

Absalom decides to consult Hushai for advice as well, and reports to him what Ahithophel has already counseled (17:5-6). Wasting no time, Hushai declares that Ahithophel's plan is not good (17:7). Whereas Ahithophel's advice was offered directly and succinctly, Hushai's speech is eloquent and complex. He marshals all of his considerable rhetorical resources to sway opinion away from Ahithophel's plan (17:8-10). Hushai does not move directly to an alternative plan. He recalls David's considerable reputation as a warrior and notes the field experience of the seasoned warriors who are with him. Such a cunning warrior would not allow himself to be found dispirited and unprepared in the midst of his troops; he would be hidden (17:8b-9a). David and his troops are enraged like a bear robbed of cubs (17:8a); therefore, they are more dangerous at present. Hushai suggests that when Absalom's less experienced troops meet David's seasoned warriors, it is Absalom's troops who are likely to panic at the first losses to David and his warriors (17:9b-10). While pretending to give Absalom advice, Hushai actually pays tribute to David and builds up the image of David's invincibility among Absalom's supporters.

Hushai offers an alternative plan that involves the raising of an army from all Israel (17:11a, Dan to Beersheba suggests that Absalom's support is not regionalized). He may be appealing to Absalom's ego by suggesting that he should lead this mighty army personally (17:11b). In Hushai's plan, this mighty army would sweep over David's force wherever they encountered him, and if he took refuge in a city they would drag it into the valley to capture him (vv. 12-13). Hushai is in wonderful form as a rhetorical orator at this point. The reader knows that Hushai's plan is intended to buy time for David to organize his resistance, but its grandiose design and the lure of a heroic battle and its accompanying victory win the day with Absalom and his advisers. They declare Hushai's plan better than Ahithophel's (17:14a). However, the narrator lets the reader in on the reality truly at work here: "The Lord had ordained to defeat the good counsel of Ahithophel" (17:14b). David had prayed while Absalom marched, and David's prayer (15:31) has been answered. Kings and pretenders struggle for the throne, but the Lord controls the ultimate course of Israel's history and David's dynasty.

17:15-23. Hushai seems to have prevailed, but the events that follow presume that Ahithophel's strategy is followed. Hushai sends a warning to David, carried by the sons of Zadok and Abiathar, David's priests who have stayed in Jerusalem to spy on Absalom's activity. Although Hushai reports on the counsel given by Ahithophel and himself, he urges David to move quickly so that Ahithophel's plan would not have a chance of success (vv. 15-16). The narrator includes a dramatic episode concerning the narrow escape of the messengers, Jonathan and Ahimaaz, who are hidden in a well by supporters (vv. 17-20). When they report to David, they emphasize the danger imposed by Ahithophel's strategy (v. 21). David quickly crosses the Jordan and moves out of reach of Ahithophel's proposed quick-strike force. The account exhibits no trust that Hushai's apparent triumph as an adviser will hold. Indeed, the military movements that follow in the story show little relation to either strategy. The narrative about dueling advisers may be intended primarily to emphasize the conviction that God will ultimately determine the outcome of events.

Ahithophel responds to the defeat of his plan (perhaps also to intelligence that David's quick action had rendered it unfeasible) by setting his house in order and hanging himself (v. 23). Many have noted the similarity to the report of Judas's death in the Gospels (cf. Matt 27:5). Both men betrayed God's anointed one.

17:24-29. The final verses of this chapter report troop movements and preparations in advance of the final military encounter, in which the success or failure of Absalom's rebellion will be determined.

David moves to Mahanaim in the Transjordan, while Absalom crosses the Jordan, too late to catch David at the fords there (v. 24), and Absalom goes on to camp in Gilead (v. 26). Absalom appoints Joab's nephew Amasa to lead his troops (v. 25). Perhaps by this move he hopes to claim for himself some of the charisma of Joab's warrior family.

Verses 27-29 report that David is given extensive provisions at Mahanaim by three prominent families of supporters, one Ammonite and two Israelite. The reader learns that not all have deserted him for Absalom. David still has support and resources to draw upon. Hushai's rhetoric and warning have bought him time, and he is now rested and provisioned. The stage is set for the final confrontation of father and son.

REFLECTIONS

Sixteenth- and seventeenth-century English writers were fascinated with this confrontation between Ahithophel and Hushai.[326] From Chaucer to Shakespeare to Dryden, Ahithophel has been seen as synonymous with treachery, disloyalty, and political machination for one's own gain. Ahithophel has been compared with Judas, and their suicides are considered appropriate for their disloyalty. A verb was even coined in seventeenth-century England for the act of disloyal treachery: "to Ahithophel." Hushai, quite the opposite, has been widely admired for his loyalty and willingness to risk his own welfare for the sake of that loyalty. John Dryden, in *Absalom and Achitophel,* may have seen his own satire as the wisdom of Hushai. In that work, he sought to confound the treachery of Absalom-like politicians and the deception of Ahithophel-like advisers, which he saw leading England astray in his time.

The story and the metaphors it affords are no longer so familiar, but the moral types represented by Ahithophel and Hushai are as prominent in the modern imagination as ever. The clever but treacherous turncoat and the undercover loyalist are staples of modern fiction and caricatures that often appear in analysis of public affairs. Loyalty and betrayal remain topics of modern fascination.

We are not as prone as our seventeenth-century counterparts to read biblical stories as straightforward allegories of our own times, events, and personalities. Yet, the story of these two advisers raises probing questions for us in a time when loyalties are perhaps too easily shifted and we are often reluctant to take risks even for the loyalties we have chosen. How often are our loyalties shifted in order to be on a "winning side," as with Ahithophel? Are we, like Hushai, willing to risk rejection, ridicule, even danger for the sake of the commitments we have made? The retreating, humiliated, and betrayed David of these stories does not look like a good investment for the loyalty of Hushai. The tendency of modern predilections is to be with the majority, the popular, the apparent locus of power. But God's future often does not accord with expectations measured in terms of human power and success. David was the eighth son of a little-known family, but he was the man after God's own heart. For Christians, commitment to a "crucified One" seems a poor investment of loyalty if measured by the standards of modern realpolitik.

Ultimately, the proper reading of this story requires that we acknowledge the working of God's will as the measure of all loyalties. God is at work preserving a future for David and confounding the rebellion of Absalom. Trust in this providential working of God in the course of human history is not a reason for resigned and passive waiting. Like Hushai, we work on behalf of those loyalties that seem most worthy and in line with what we understand God may be doing. In these efforts, we make ourselves available as the channels through which God's providence may operate. Like Hushai, we may become the means whereby God confounds treachery, self-serving ambitions, and murderous intent in the cynical politics of our own Ahithophels.

326. For specific references on the wealth of 16th- and 17th-century references to Ahithophel and Hushai, see Larry Carver, "Ahithophel," in *A Dictionary of Biblical Tradition in English Literature,* ed. David Lyle Jeffrey (Grand Rapids: Eerdmans, 1992) 27-28.

2 Samuel 18:1-18, The Defeat and Death of Absalom

18 David mustered the men who were with him and appointed over them commanders of thousands and commanders of hundreds. ²David sent the troops out—a third under the command of Joab, a third under Joab's brother Abishai son of Zeruiah, and a third under Ittai the Gittite. The king told the troops, "I myself will surely march out with you."

³But the men said, "You must not go out; if we are forced to flee, they won't care about us. Even if half of us die, they won't care; but you are worth ten thousand of us.ª It would be better now for you to give us support from the city."

⁴The king answered, "I will do whatever seems best to you."

So the king stood beside the gate while all the men marched out in units of hundreds and of thousands. ⁵The king commanded Joab, Abishai and Ittai, "Be gentle with the young man Absalom for my sake." And all the troops heard the king giving orders concerning Absalom to each of the commanders.

⁶The army marched into the field to fight Israel, and the battle took place in the forest of Ephraim. ⁷There the army of Israel was defeated by David's men, and the casualties that day were great—twenty thousand men. ⁸The battle spread out over the whole countryside, and the forest claimed more lives that day than the sword.

⁹Now Absalom happened to meet David's men. He was riding his mule, and as the mule went under the thick branches of a large oak, Absalom's head got caught in the tree. He was left hanging in midair, while the mule he was riding kept on going.

¹⁰When one of the men saw this, he told Joab, "I just saw Absalom hanging in an oak tree."

¹¹Joab said to the man who had told him this, "What! You saw him? Why didn't you strike him to the ground right there? Then I would have had to give you ten shekelsᵇ of silver and a warrior's belt."

¹²But the man replied, "Even if a thousand shekelsᶜ were weighed out into my hands, I would

ª3 Two Hebrew manuscripts, some Septuagint manuscripts and Vulgate; most Hebrew manuscripts *care; for now there are ten thousand like us* ᵇ11 That is, about 4 ounces (about 115 grams) ᶜ12 That is, about 25 pounds (about 11 kilograms)

18 Then David mustered the men who were with him, and set over them commanders of thousands and commanders of hundreds. ²And David divided the army into three groups:ª one third under the command of Joab, one third under the command of Abishai son of Zeruiah, Joab's brother, and one third under the command of Ittai the Gittite. The king said to the men, "I myself will also go out with you." ³But the men said, "You shall not go out. For if we flee, they will not care about us. If half of us die, they will not care about us. But you are worth ten thousand of us;ᵇ therefore it is better that you send us help from the city." ⁴The king said to them, "Whatever seems best to you I will do." So the king stood at the side of the gate, while all the army marched out by hundreds and by thousands. ⁵The king ordered Joab and Abishai and Ittai, saying, "Deal gently for my sake with the young man Absalom." And all the people heard when the king gave orders to all the commanders concerning Absalom.

6So the army went out into the field against Israel; and the battle was fought in the forest of Ephraim. ⁷The men of Israel were defeated there by the servants of David, and the slaughter there was great on that day, twenty thousand men. ⁸The battle spread over the face of all the country; and the forest claimed more victims that day than the sword.

9Absalom happened to meet the servants of David. Absalom was riding on his mule, and the mule went under the thick branches of a great oak. His head caught fast in the oak, and he was left hangingᶜ between heaven and earth, while the mule that was under him went on. ¹⁰A man saw it, and told Joab, "I saw Absalom hanging in an oak." ¹¹Joab said to the man who told him, "What, you saw him! Why then did you not strike him there to the ground? I would have been glad to give you ten pieces of silver and a belt." ¹²But the man said to Joab, "Even if I felt in my hand the weight of a thousand pieces of silver, I would not raise my hand against the king's son; for in

ª Gk: Heb *sent forth the army* ᵇ Gk Vg Symmachus: Heb *for now there are ten thousand such as we* ᶜ Gk Syr Tg: Heb *was put*

NIV

not lift my hand against the king's son. In our hearing the king commanded you and Abishai and Ittai, 'Protect the young man Absalom for my sake.*' [a] 13And if I had put my life in jeopardy[b]—and nothing is hidden from the king—you would have kept your distance from me."

14Joab said, "I'm not going to wait like this for you." So he took three javelins in his hand and plunged them into Absalom's heart while Absalom was still alive in the oak tree. 15And ten of Joab's armor-bearers surrounded Absalom, struck him and killed him.

16Then Joab sounded the trumpet, and the troops stopped pursuing Israel, for Joab halted them. 17They took Absalom, threw him into a big pit in the forest and piled up a large heap of rocks over him. Meanwhile, all the Israelites fled to their homes.

18During his lifetime Absalom had taken a pillar and erected it in the King's Valley as a monument to himself, for he thought, "I have no son to carry on the memory of my name." He named the pillar after himself, and it is called Absalom's Monument to this day.

*12 A few Hebrew manuscripts, Septuagint, Vulgate and Syriac; most Hebrew manuscripts may be translated *Absalom, whoever you may be.*
*13 Or *Otherwise, if I had acted treacherously toward him*

NRSV

our hearing the king commanded you and Abishai and Ittai, saying: For my sake protect the young man Absalom! 13On the other hand, if I had dealt treacherously against his life[a] (and there is nothing hidden from the king), then you yourself would have stood aloof." 14Joab said, "I will not waste time like this with you." He took three spears in his hand, and thrust them into the heart of Absalom, while he was still alive in the oak. 15And ten young men, Joab's armor-bearers, surrounded Absalom and struck him, and killed him.

16Then Joab sounded the trumpet, and the troops came back from pursuing Israel, for Joab restrained the troops. 17They took Absalom, threw him into a great pit in the forest, and raised over him a very great heap of stones. Meanwhile all the Israelites fled to their homes. 18Now Absalom in his lifetime had taken and set up for himself a pillar that is in the King's Valley, for he said, "I have no son to keep my name in remembrance"; he called the pillar by his own name. It is called Absalom's Monument to this day.

a Another reading is *at the risk of my life*

COMMENTARY

The story of Absalom's rebellion now moves quickly to its tragic climax. The description of the final battle and David's victory is reported briefly and matter-of-factly (vv. 6-8). What clearly concerns the narrator more is making clear that David was in no way involved in the death of Absalom. This may have been a necessary apologetic for reestablishing David's rule in an Israel where Absalom had received widespread support. In this telling of the story of Absalom's defeat and death, the narrator is at great pains to explain that David was not even allowed to participate personally in the battle (vv. 2b-4) and that David went to great lengths in attempting to ensure the personal safety of Absalom (vv. 5, 12). Joab is given total responsibility for Absalom's death. His role in David's story seems to be that of the heavy who does the dirty work while

David remains apart with reputation intact (cf. the deaths of Abner, 3:27; Uriah, 11:16-17).

18:1-5. David organizes his troops for the battle with Absalom using the traditional military units of "thousands" and "hundreds" (v. 1; these terms do not indicate precise numbers). He divides his force into three contingents (v. 2), two commanded by his longtime companions, the warrior brothers Joab and Abishai, and the third by the mercenary Ittai the Gittite, whose loyalty was noted in the report of David's retreat from Jerusalem (15:19-22).

The account lingers over the details of two claims that are clearly of great importance in this story. The first is that David does not actually participate in the battle that leads to the defeat and death of Absalom. He wished to accompany his troops (v. 2*b*), but they would not allow it. The king is considered too valuable ("worth ten thousand of us," v. 3), and he is urged to remain in the city (Mahanaim?), providing support. David acquiesces to their judgment (v. 4).

Second, David gives explicit instructions to Joab, Abishai, and Ittai, which "all the people heard," that Absalom is not to be personally harmed (v. 5). It is David, the concerned father, who dominates the moments before the final battle, not David the aggrieved king. "Deal gently," David pleads and urges this for his own sake, not for the sake of Absalom. The author pictures David as being personally invested in the welfare of his son, a portrait that may have been designed by the narrator to assuage Absalom's followers after his death and to aid in reestablishing David's rule.

18:6-8. The battle is joined; its description is terse and pointed. The fighting takes place in the "forest of Ephraim," probably a forested area in the Transjordan (v. 6). The "men of Israel" are massively defeated by "the servants of David" (v. 7). These phrases may suggest that Absalom's largely conscripted army was no match for the seasoned professional warriors of David. Hushai's advice and warning bought David the time to organize and choose the field of battle, and in these conditions Absalom's people's army was no match for the experienced warriors of David. The loss of twenty thousand may be intended to indicate losses of twenty units designated as "thousands" rather than indicating actual numbers.[327] As the battle widens, the report indicates that the forest claims more than the sword (v. 8), a tribute to David's wise choice of terrain for what may have been a battle more like guerrilla warfare than the open meeting of armies in the field.

18:9-18. The scene shifts to Absalom. It is not clear whether he is leading troops in battle or attempting to flee the battlefield. What happens, however, is not the result of a military encounter. Absalom's mule takes him beneath an oak tree, and his head becomes caught in its branches, leaving him suspended "between heaven and

earth" (v. 9). Since the time of Josephus,[328] interpreters have related this event to the notice of Absalom's magnificent head of hair (14:26) and assumed that his hair became entangled in the overhanging boughs of the tree. Brueggemann suggests that Absalom's suspension reflects the tensions in which the narrative itself now stands suspended. "Absalom is suspended between life and death, between the sentence of a rebel and the value of a son, between the severity of the king and the yearning of the father."[329] Over against the harshness of the battle and its terrible losses stand the last words of David, "Deal gently."

The desire of the father does not dominate events in this moment. Rather, the harsh pragmatism of Joab assumes control of events, perhaps intended by the author to shift any blame that might attach to David for Absalom's death. A soldier reports Absalom's predicament to Joab (v. 10), and Joab admonishes him for not having killed Absalom on the spot. The exchange between Joab and the soldier emphasizes for the reader the clarity of David's desire and command concerning the safety of Absalom. The soldier would not risk raising his hand against the king's son for any amount of reward, because he had clearly heard the king's command (v. 12). Furthermore, he does not believe Joab would have backed him up if he had killed Absalom (v. 13). Absalom's death cannot be blamed on overzealous troops. Joab must personally take matters into his own hands. He takes three spears and thrusts them into Absalom; only then do his personal armorbearers also join in ensuring the death of the rebellious son (vv. 14-15). Absalom's blood is on Joab's hands alone. Only with Absalom's death are the battle and the pursuit ended (v. 16).

Absalom is buried in the forest, his grave marked by a heap of stones (v. 17). This is an honorable burial; he is not left dishonored as carrion for the animals (cf. the fate of Saul's sons in 21:1-14). Nevertheless, Absalom is not buried with the royal family. He is left on the field of battle where his rebellion ended in failure. The note in v. 18 seems to be an added parenthesis by an editor who wanted to take note of a pillar that Absalom himself had erected in the Valley of

327. P. Kyle McCarter, *II Samuel,* AB 9 (Garden City, N.Y.: Doubleday, 1984) 405, suggests the losses may have been as few as between 100 and 280, but most would estimate the numerical strength of a "thousand" as more than five to fourteen soldiers. This may be more the strength of a "hundred" (cf. v. 1). In any case, we should think of the loss to Absalom's army in this battle as twenty "units." See G. E. Mendenhall, "The Census Lists of Numbers 1 and 26," *JBL* 77 (1958) 52-66, for a comprehensive discussion of the term אלף (*'elep*), "thousand."

328. Josephus *Antiquities of the Jews* 7.239.

329. Walter Brueggemann, *First and Second Samuel,* Interpretation (Louisville: John Knox, 1990) 319.

the Kings (perhaps the Kidron Valley in Jerusalem), which still stood in his own time and was known by Absalom's name. The notice that Absalom had no sons may mean that the three sons mentioned as having been born to Absalom in 14:27 had not survived into adulthood. The monument mentioned here no doubt led to the naming of a later Roman period tomb in the Kidron Valley as the "Tomb of Absalom," a popular designation that this Hellenistic tomb retains today. (See Reflections at 18:19–19:8a.)

2 Samuel 18:19–19:8a, David's Grief Over Absalom's Death

NIV

¹⁹Now Ahimaaz son of Zadok said, "Let me run and take the news to the king that the LORD has delivered him from the hand of his enemies."

²⁰"You are not the one to take the news today," Joab told him. "You may take the news another time, but you must not do so today, because the king's son is dead."

²¹Then Joab said to a Cushite, "Go, tell the king what you have seen." The Cushite bowed down before Joab and ran off.

²²Ahimaaz son of Zadok again said to Joab, "Come what may, please let me run behind the Cushite."

But Joab replied, "My son, why do you want to go? You don't have any news that will bring you a reward."

²³He said, "Come what may, I want to run."

So Joab said, "Run!" Then Ahimaaz ran by way of the plain[a] and outran the Cushite.

²⁴While David was sitting between the inner and outer gates, the watchman went up to the roof of the gateway by the wall. As he looked out, he saw a man running alone. ²⁵The watchman called out to the king and reported it.

The king said, "If he is alone, he must have good news." And the man came closer and closer.

²⁶Then the watchman saw another man running, and he called down to the gatekeeper, "Look, another man running alone!"

The king said, "He must be bringing good news, too."

²⁷The watchman said, "It seems to me that the first one runs like Ahimaaz son of Zadok."

"He's a good man," the king said. "He comes with good news."

²⁸Then Ahimaaz called out to the king, "All is well!" He bowed down before the king with his

NRSV

19Then Ahimaaz son of Zadok said, "Let me run, and carry tidings to the king that the LORD has delivered him from the power of his enemies." ²⁰Joab said to him, "You are not to carry tidings today; you may carry tidings another day, but today you shall not do so, because the king's son is dead." ²¹Then Joab said to a Cushite, "Go, tell the king what you have seen." The Cushite bowed before Joab, and ran. ²²Then Ahimaaz son of Zadok said again to Joab, "Come what may, let me also run after the Cushite." And Joab said, "Why will you run, my son, seeing that you have no reward[a] for the tidings?" ²³"Come what may," he said, "I will run." So he said to him, "Run." Then Ahimaaz ran by the way of the Plain, and outran the Cushite.

24Now David was sitting between the two gates. The sentinel went up to the roof of the gate by the wall, and when he looked up, he saw a man running alone. ²⁵The sentinel shouted and told the king. The king said, "If he is alone, there are tidings in his mouth." He kept coming, and drew near. ²⁶Then the sentinel saw another man running; and the sentinel called to the gatekeeper and said, "See, another man running alone!" The king said, "He also is bringing tidings." ²⁷The sentinel said, "I think the running of the first one is like the running of Ahimaaz son of Zadok." The king said, "He is a good man, and comes with good tidings."

28Then Ahimaaz cried out to the king, "All is well!" He prostrated himself before the king with his face to the ground, and said, "Blessed be the LORD your God, who has delivered up the men who raised their hand against my lord the king." ²⁹The king said, "Is it well with the young man Absalom?" Ahimaaz answered, "When Joab sent your servant,[b] I saw a great tumult, but I do not

a23 That is, the plain of the Jordan

a Meaning of Heb uncertain   b Heb the king's servant, your servant

NIV

face to the ground and said, "Praise be to the LORD your God! He has delivered up the men who lifted their hands against my lord the king."

²⁹The king asked, "Is the young man Absalom safe?"

Ahimaaz answered, "I saw great confusion just as Joab was about to send the king's servant and me, your servant, but I don't know what it was."

³⁰The king said, "Stand aside and wait here." So he stepped aside and stood there.

³¹Then the Cushite arrived and said, "My lord the king, hear the good news! The LORD has delivered you today from all who rose up against you."

³²The king asked the Cushite, "Is the young man Absalom safe?"

The Cushite replied, "May the enemies of my lord the king and all who rise up to harm you be like that young man."

³³The king was shaken. He went up to the room over the gateway and wept. As he went, he said: "O my son Absalom! My son, my son Absalom! If only I had died instead of you—O Absalom, my son, my son!"

19 Joab was told, "The king is weeping and mourning for Absalom." ²And for the whole army the victory that day was turned into mourning, because on that day the troops heard it said, "The king is grieving for his son." ³The men stole into the city that day as men steal in who are ashamed when they flee from battle. ⁴The king covered his face and cried aloud, "O my son Absalom! O Absalom, my son, my son!"

⁵Then Joab went into the house to the king and said, "Today you have humiliated all your men, who have just saved your life and the lives of your sons and daughters and the lives of your wives and concubines. ⁶You love those who hate you and hate those who love you. You have made it clear today that the commanders and their men mean nothing to you. I see that you would be pleased if Absalom were alive today and all of us were dead. ⁷Now go out and encourage your men. I swear by the LORD that if you don't go out, not a man will be left with you by nightfall. This will be worse for you than all the calamities that have come upon you from your youth till now."

⁸So the king got up and took his seat in the gateway.

NRSV

know what it was." ³⁰The king said, "Turn aside, and stand here." So he turned aside, and stood still.

31 Then the Cushite came; and the Cushite said, "Good tidings for my lord the king! For the LORD has vindicated you this day, delivering you from the power of all who rose up against you." ³²The king said to the Cushite, "Is it well with the young man Absalom?" The Cushite answered, "May the enemies of my lord the king, and all who rise up to do you harm, be like that young man."

33*a*The king was deeply moved, and went up to the chamber over the gate, and wept; and as he went, he said, "O my son Absalom, my son, my son Absalom! Would I had died instead of you, O Absalom, my son, my son!"

19 It was told Joab, "The king is weeping and mourning for Absalom." ²So the victory that day was turned into mourning for all the troops; for the troops heard that day, "The king is grieving for his son." ³The troops stole into the city that day as soldiers steal in who are ashamed when they flee in battle. ⁴The king covered his face, and the king cried with a loud voice, "O my son Absalom, O Absalom, my son, my son!" ⁵Then Joab came into the house to the king, and said, "Today you have covered with shame the faces of all your officers who have saved your life today, and the lives of your sons and your daughters, and the lives of your wives and your concubines, ⁶for love of those who hate you and for hatred of those who love you. You have made it clear today that commanders and officers are nothing to you; for I perceive that if Absalom were alive and all of us were dead today, then you would be pleased. ⁷So go out at once and speak kindly to your servants; for I swear by the LORD, if you do not go, not a man will stay with you this night; and this will be worse for you than any disaster that has come upon you from your youth until now." ⁸Then the king got up and took his seat in the gate. The troops were all told, "See, the king is sitting in the gate"; and all the troops came before the king.

a Ch 19.1 in Heb

COMMENTARY

The narrative continues with a report of the aftermath of Absalom's death. The tragic news of the son's death is brought to the waiting father, and his all-consuming grief threatens to overwhelm the effect of the victory. The pathos of David's grief is portrayed in a graphic manner that has touched the hearts of generations who have read this story and made it a virtual icon of parental anguish.

The story builds dramatically to the moment when David receives the tragic news of Absalom's death. Fourteen verses (18:19-32) stretch the tension as rival runners bring word to an anxious father who pleads for news of the welfare of his son. David receives word of the victory, but almost dismisses it, seeking news of Absalom. When David learns of Absalom's death, the victory is entirely hidden from view by the magnitude of his grief (18:33). David's role as father, protecting even a rebellious son, is allowed to prevail over any portrait of him as ruthless king putting down a rebellion against his rule. It remains for Joab to see the demoralizing effect of David's grief on his supporters and the belittling of their service on behalf of David and his throne. Joab, in his usual direct way, confronts David and coaxes him to resume the role of king in spite of the pain of the father (19:1-8).

18:19-32. This detailed narration of the messengers sent to bring word to David heightens the drama of the waiting father and the terrible news that he must hear. Ahimaaz, the son of Zadok, wishes to bring the report to David. He is bubbling with youthful excitement about the great victory, which he understands as the Lord's deliverance of David (v. 19). Joab knows that since Absalom is dead, David will not receive this as good news. He tells Ahimaaz that he cannot go "because the king's son is dead" (v. 20). It would not do to send the son of a high royal official, the priest Zadok, with such news. David has killed the bearer of bad tidings before (cf. 1:15-16). Joab knows that the news of this death will not be welcomed as was the news of Uriah's death (11:21). David will not dismiss this death as the unfortunate consequence of war (11:25). Better to send a Cushite, a foreigner, an outsider, with such news (v. 21). But even after the Cushite

departs, Ahimaaz pleads to run to David as well. He seems aware of the risk, but asks to be allowed to run "come what may!" (vv. 22-23). Joab reminds him that this news will carry no reward (v. 22), but he gives in, and Ahimaaz, taking an alternative route, outruns the Cushite (v. 23).

The focus of the narrative shifts to David's perspective, waiting at the gates of the city with a sentinel, straining for first sight of the messengers who might bring news of the battle (v. 24). First one runner is sighted, then another. The first is recognized as Ahimaaz, and David leaps to grasp a straw of hope. Ahimaaz is a good man; he must bring good news (vv. 25-27). Perhaps David assumes that Joab would not risk the life of the son of Zadok with bad news and David's anger.

Ahimaaz blurts out an "All is well" as he falls prostrate before David. His formal report is in the form of a thanksgiving to the Lord,[330] and he speaks only of the victory (v. 28). This is not what interests David; he presses for information on "the young man" Absalom (v. 29a). Ahimaaz suffers a failure of nerve. Joab told him that Absalom was dead, but he cannot bring himself to tell David (compassion for David? fear for his own safety?). He reports only a commotion but no knowledge of its meaning (v. 29b). He does not have news of what David most wants to know. The victory is of little interest to the anxious father. He tells Ahimaaz to stand aside (v. 30).

It remains for the Cushite unwittingly to bring the tragic news to David. He, too, reports the news of victory as the welcome deliverance of the Lord (v. 31), and when David asks of Absalom, the Cushite reports his death as the welcome death of one who rose up to harm the king (v. 32). There is no sense that this would not come as good news to a threatened king. But it is not the king who receives the news; it is the father.

18:33. There is no more poignant portrayal of human grief and desolation in all of Scripture than in this single verse. David, who had received the news of his infant son's death with stoic resignation (12:19-23) is undone by news of Absalom's

---

330. See C. C. Conroy, *Absalom, Absalom! Narrative and Language in 2 Sam 13–20*, AnBib 81 (Rome: Pontifical Biblical Institute, 1978) 72, esp. n. 116.

death. The battle, the rebellion, the throne—all of this is irrelevant in this moment. David is wracked with unrestrained grief and cries out in anguish. No longer is Absalom the "young man" (18:5, 29, 32). He is "my son" (five times in this verse), and Absalom (three times in this verse). David has grieved with poetic eloquence over Saul and Jonathan (1:17-27), and with stoic resignation over his infant son (12:19-23). But this time there is no capacity for eloquence, and the king is not resigned to this ending of a father's hopes. This is the most elemental and deeply human moment in all of David's story. David has now borne the full cost of his own descent into violence, and the judgment pronounced by Nathan has now played itself out in the violent consequences to his own family. It may be David's knowledge of his own role in bringing this moment of lost hopes and shattered relationship that makes his grief so inconsolable.

19:1-8a. As usual, Joab notices that there is a kingdom to run here. It is to Joab that the grief of the king and the effect of his mourning on the people are reported (vv. 1-2). Reports of the king's reaction cause troops that should have returned in celebration of victory to creep back into the city as if they had done something wrong and should be ashamed (v. 3). David does not even notice this behavior. The cries of "my son, Absalom," which seemed moving and understandable in 18:33, begin to seem self-indulgent in 19:4.

Joab boldly enters the royal residence and confronts the king. Perhaps only Joab could have spoken as directly and candidly as he now speaks to David. He tells David that he has shamed those who supported him, fought for him, and saved his life and the lives of his family (v. 5). Joab accuses David of having twisted values, loving those who hate him and hating those who love him (v. 6a). Joab shares his impression that David would gladly have heard news of the death of every member of his company if Absalom, a rebel and a murderer, were yet alive (v. 6b). It is a remarkable speech for anyone to make to a king, but Joab is not finished. He ends with a threat: David must appear in public to speak a word of kindness to his supporters or, Joab swears by the Lord, not a single man will stay the night with him, and David will be finished (v. 7). This almost sounds like a threat by Joab to lead a rebellion or desertion of David himself.

To his credit, David gathers himself and takes a seat in the gate, presumably as a sign of support and welcome to his returning and victorious warriors (v. 8). Word of this royal presence passes among the troops, and they gather around the king for whom they have fought. We cannot imagine that the grief we have glimpsed is assuaged, but in the necessities of the moment, the king takes the place of the father.

REFLECTIONS

The heart-rending scene of David's grief over Absalom's death is a scene of such universal human pathos that it has attracted unusual attention, from ancient times to our own era. The tragic moment addresses the reader on multiple levels.

1. First and foremost, David depicts the depths of a father's grief at the loss of a son. Whatever the circumstances, whatever the strains on the relationship, every parent can identify with the pain of having one's own child die first. Many know and recognize the cry of David's loss without understanding any of the complexities of the relationship between David and Absalom. David's poignant statement that he would willingly have died in Absalom's place has become particularly emblematic of parental willingness to sacrifice one's own welfare to preserve the life of one's child. Those who know something of Absalom's rebellion find this story particularly relevant to parents of children who take self-destructive paths from which parental love, though willing to sacrifice, cannot save them. The power of this portrait of parental grief gives this moment in David's story a familiarity and emotional identification that function apart from the complexities of the story in 2 Samuel.

2. The preaching of this text, however, should point beyond emotional identification with parental loss to some of the deeper issues encompassed in this climactic moment of David's grief. David is caught in a tension between his roles as father and as king. Absalom is a rebel and a traitor against the king, but he is nevertheless loved by the father. Earlier David, alienated from Absalom, had called him only "the young man Absalom" (18:5), but now Absalom is "my son," and David utters this phrase repeatedly (five times) in anguish and grief.

David is caught in a tragic conflict between public and private roles. As king, he must regard Absalom as a criminal whose fate is deserved, but as father he cannot accept such an end for his son. As king, he has vast power to influence events, but as a grief-stricken father he has no power to bring his son back to life. Frederick Buechner reminds us that when David wished he had died instead of Absalom, "he meant it, of course. If he could have done the boy's dying for him, he would have done it. If he could have paid the price for the boy's betrayal of him, he would have paid it. If he could have given his own life to make the boy alive again, he would have given it. But even a king can't do things like that. As later history was to prove, it takes a God."[331]

This poignant moment in David's story is a reminder to us of the difficulty of balancing public responsibility and familial loyalty. Like David, we often learn to love when it is too late. When David's love would have made a difference, he was only the king—allowing Absalom's return, but not allowing access to the father's love. In our own society, the lesson of David's grief is not simply a matter of personal relationships but of societal ones as well. We grieve the violence that breaks out all too often in the rebellion of sons and daughters, but we have not reached out in ways that would have forestalled violence and rebellion. Issues of poverty, education, familial dysfunction, substance abuse, and consumerist values distort the future of many of our sons and daughters who then attempt to seize their birthright in violent ways—increased gun violence, the growth of paramilitary cults, increased intolerance in public discourse, and growing lack of respect for all forms of authority. We may mourn, like David, when inattention to such alienation produces an Oklahoma City federal building bombing or a Unabomber, but the time for addressing alienation with compassion, forgiveness, and attention to genuine needs comes, as with David, before the point of tragic consequences. David's weeping must move us in response to those of our sons and daughters who are alienated and in rebellion before we, too, must weep the tragic consequences. The challenge is to break the cycle before we come to these tragic moments of grief, personal or societal. David's human emotions became visible when it was too late. In his story, one wonders what might have been avoided if David's heart had overflowed with love and forgiveness at an earlier moment rather than with grief in this tragic demonstration after Absalom is gone (see Reflections at 14:1-33).

3. But David's weeping may in part be for himself as well as for Absalom. David's suffering and loss are not innocent. It is David's own modeling of grasping, arrogant power that Absalom has emulated. It is judgment on David's sin that is playing itself out in the tragedies of his family. This drama of sin and judgment, passing tragically from fathers to sons, is a theme that has attracted the attention of Christian writers from Augustine to the present. They have found in this final scene of the drama of Absalom's rebellion a tragic and sobering outcome to the conflict between the exercise of self-interested human free will and the irresistible workings of divine providence. This they believed was a perennial tension in human existence lived within the framework of divine will. Absalom's loss was not just a human tragedy but a result of divine justice. Augustine writes in *On Christian Doctrine*: "He mourned over his son's death, not because of his own loss, but because he knew to what punishment so impious an adulterer and parricide had been hurried."[332] It may well be that this scene continues to have a tragic attraction for modern readers for this same reason. David's grief speaks to us not simply of parental loss but of his recognition that his own sins, Absalom's sins, and God's

331. Frederick Buechner, *Peculiar Treasures: A Biblical Who's Who* (San Francisco: Harper & Row, 1979) 6.
332. Augustine, *On Christian Doctrine*, 3.21.30, cited in Frans De Bruyn, "Absalom," in *A Dictionary of Biblical Tradition in English Literature*, ed. David Lyle Jeffrey (Grand Rapids: Eerdmans, 1992) 12.

justice have all helped to bring this tragic moment to pass. We recognize in David's grief our own grief over many losses we have experienced not simply as victims but as perpetrators. How much greater the grief when we know that we have helped to bring its cause. It is the despair of our soul coupled with the grief of our heart.

With the advent of the novel in the eighteenth century, writers were drawn to the universal elements of this story of a divided father and son ending in the father's grief. Thomas Hardy called this chapter the "finest example of [prose narrative] that I know, showing beyond its power and pathos the highest artistic cunning."[333] The two most celebrated uses of this story of a son's rebellion and a father's grief are in William Faulkner's *Absalom, Absalom!* and Alan Paton's *Cry, the Beloved Country.* Both find in the racially divided societies of the early twentieth-century American South and mid-century South African apartheid parallels to the story of Absalom and David. In both novels and the modern settings they chronicle, sons are brought to grief by the injustices their fathers first put in place and the sons inevitably imitate. Too late the fathers must recognize the price their sons have paid for their father's sins as well as their own, and the emptiness of the grief with which the fathers are left.

Absalom went to war against his father in an effort to seize for himself a place he had lost by imitating the violence his own father had used to get what he desired. This vicious cycle is not unknown to the parents and children of every generation. We know that we have modeled behavior and values that subsequent generations will imitate—to our sorrow. If we identify with the grief of David over his son, it is because we too often experience it as our own, or that of others close to us.

This scene of David's desolation will forever touch the human heart with its portrait of a father's pain. One can hope that it will also remind us that time can run out. There are stories in which the prodigal son does not come home and the waiting father's embrace is empty.

333. Cited in ibid., 14.

2 Samuel 19:8*b*-43, David Returns to Jerusalem

NIV

"The king is sitting in the gateway," they all came before him.

Meanwhile, the Israelites had fled to their homes. [9]Throughout the tribes of Israel, the people were all arguing with each other, saying, "The king delivered us from the hand of our enemies; he is the one who rescued us from the hand of the Philistines. But now he has fled the country because of Absalom; [10]and Absalom, whom we anointed to rule over us, has died in battle. So why do you say nothing about bringing the king back?"

[11]King David sent this message to Zadok and Abiathar, the priests: "Ask the elders of Judah, 'Why should you be the last to bring the king back to his palace, since what is being said throughout Israel has reached the king at his quarters? [12]You are my brothers, my own flesh and blood. So why should you be the last to bring

NRSV

Meanwhile, all the Israelites had fled to their homes. [9]All the people were disputing throughout all the tribes of Israel, saying, "The king delivered us from the hand of our enemies, and saved us from the hand of the Philistines; and now he has fled out of the land because of Absalom. [10]But Absalom, whom we anointed over us, is dead in battle. Now therefore why do you say nothing about bringing the king back?"

[11]King David sent this message to the priests Zadok and Abiathar, "Say to the elders of Judah, 'Why should you be the last to bring the king back to his house? The talk of all Israel has come to the king.*a* [12]You are my kin, you are my bone and my flesh; why then should you be the last to bring back the king?' [13]And say to Amasa, 'Are you not my bone and my flesh? So may God do

a Gk: Heb *to the king, to his house*

NIV

back the king?' [13]And say to Amasa, 'Are you not my own flesh and blood? May God deal with me, be it ever so severely, if from now on you are not the commander of my army in place of Joab.'"

[14]He won over the hearts of all the men of Judah as though they were one man. They sent word to the king, "Return, you and all your men." [15]Then the king returned and went as far as the Jordan.

Now the men of Judah had come to Gilgal to go out and meet the king and bring him across the Jordan. [16]Shimei son of Gera, the Benjamite from Bahurim, hurried down with the men of Judah to meet King David. [17]With him were a thousand Benjamites, along with Ziba, the steward of Saul's household, and his fifteen sons and twenty servants. They rushed to the Jordan, where the king was. [18]They crossed at the ford to take the king's household over and to do whatever he wished.

When Shimei son of Gera crossed the Jordan, he fell prostrate before the king [19]and said to him, "May my lord not hold me guilty. Do not remember how your servant did wrong on the day my lord the king left Jerusalem. May the king put it out of his mind. [20]For I your servant know that I have sinned, but today I have come here as the first of the whole house of Joseph to come down and meet my lord the king."

[21]Then Abishai son of Zeruiah said, "Shouldn't Shimei be put to death for this? He cursed the LORD's anointed."

[22]David replied, "What do you and I have in common, you sons of Zeruiah? This day you have become my adversaries! Should anyone be put to death in Israel today? Do I not know that today I am king over Israel?" [23]So the king said to Shimei, "You shall not die." And the king promised him on oath.

[24]Mephibosheth, Saul's grandson, also went down to meet the king. He had not taken care of his feet or trimmed his mustache or washed his clothes from the day the king left until the day he returned safely. [25]When he came from Jerusalem to meet the king, the king asked him, "Why didn't you go with me, Mephibosheth?"

[26]He said, "My lord the king, since I your servant am lame, I said, 'I will have my donkey saddled and will ride on it, so I can go with the

NRSV

to me, and more, if you are not the commander of my army from now on, in place of Joab.'" [14]Amasa[a] swayed the hearts of all the people of Judah as one, and they sent word to the king, "Return, both you and all your servants." [15]So the king came back to the Jordan; and Judah came to Gilgal to meet the king and to bring him over the Jordan.

[16]Shimei son of Gera, the Benjaminite, from Bahurim, hurried to come down with the people of Judah to meet King David; [17]with him were a thousand people from Benjamin. And Ziba, the servant of the house of Saul, with his fifteen sons and his twenty servants, rushed down to the Jordan ahead of the king, [18]while the crossing was taking place,[b] to bring over the king's household, and to do his pleasure.

Shimei son of Gera fell down before the king, as he was about to cross the Jordan, [19]and said to the king, "May my lord not hold me guilty or remember how your servant did wrong on the day my lord the king left Jerusalem; may the king not bear it in mind. [20]For your servant knows that I have sinned; therefore, see, I have come this day, the first of all the house of Joseph to come down to meet my lord the king." [21]Abishai son of Zeruiah answered, "Shall not Shimei be put to death for this, because he cursed the LORD's anointed?" [22]But David said, "What have I to do with you, you sons of Zeruiah, that you should today become an adversary to me? Shall anyone be put to death in Israel this day? For do I not know that I am this day king over Israel?" [23]The king said to Shimei, "You shall not die." And the king gave him his oath.

[24]Mephibosheth[c] grandson of Saul came down to meet the king; he had not taken care of his feet, or trimmed his beard, or washed his clothes, from the day the king left until the day he came back in safety. [25]When he came from Jerusalem to meet the king, the king said to him, "Why did you not go with me, Mephibosheth?"[c] [26]He answered, "My lord, O king, my servant deceived me; for your servant said to him, 'Saddle a donkey for me,[d] so that I may ride on it and go with the king.' For your servant is lame. [27]He has slandered

a Heb He   b Cn: Heb the ford crossed   c Or Merib-baal: See 4.4 note   d Gk Syr Vg: Heb said, 'I will saddle a donkey for myself

NIV

king.' But Ziba my servant betrayed me. ²⁷And he has slandered your servant to my lord the king. My lord the king is like an angel of God; so do whatever pleases you. ²⁸All my grandfather's descendants deserved nothing but death from my lord the king, but you gave your servant a place among those who eat at your table. So what right do I have to make any more appeals to the king?"

²⁹The king said to him, "Why say more? I order you and Ziba to divide the fields."

³⁰Mephibosheth said to the king, "Let him take everything, now that my lord the king has arrived home safely."

³¹Barzillai the Gileadite also came down from Rogelim to cross the Jordan with the king and to send him on his way from there. ³²Now Barzillai was a very old man, eighty years of age. He had provided for the king during his stay in Mahanaim, for he was a very wealthy man. ³³The king said to Barzillai, "Cross over with me and stay with me in Jerusalem, and I will provide for you."

³⁴But Barzillai answered the king, "How many more years will I live, that I should go up to Jerusalem with the king? ³⁵I am now eighty years old. Can I tell the difference between what is good and what is not? Can your servant taste what he eats and drinks? Can I still hear the voices of men and women singers? Why should your servant be an added burden to my lord the king? ³⁶Your servant will cross over the Jordan with the king for a short distance, but why should the king reward me in this way? ³⁷Let your servant return, that I may die in my own town near the tomb of my father and mother. But here is your servant Kimham. Let him cross over with my lord the king. Do for him whatever pleases you."

³⁸The king said, "Kimham shall cross over with me, and I will do for him whatever pleases you. And anything you desire from me I will do for you."

³⁹So all the people crossed the Jordan, and then the king crossed over. The king kissed Barzillai and gave him his blessing, and Barzillai returned to his home.

⁴⁰When the king crossed over to Gilgal, Kimham crossed with him. All the troops of Judah and half the troops of Israel had taken the king over.

⁴¹Soon all the men of Israel were coming to the king and saying to him, "Why did our brothers,

NRSV

your servant to my lord the king. But my lord the king is like the angel of God; do therefore what seems good to you. ²⁸For all my father's house were doomed to death before my lord the king; but you set your servant among those who eat at your table. What further right have I, then, to appeal to the king?" ²⁹The king said to him, "Why speak any more of your affairs? I have decided: you and Ziba shall divide the land." ³⁰Mephibosheth*ᵃ* said to the king, "Let him take it all, since my lord the king has arrived home safely."

31Now Barzillai the Gileadite had come down from Rogelim; he went on with the king to the Jordan, to escort him over the Jordan. ³²Barzillai was a very aged man, eighty years old. He had provided the king with food while he stayed at Mahanaim, for he was a very wealthy man. ³³The king said to Barzillai, "Come over with me, and I will provide for you in Jerusalem at my side." ³⁴But Barzillai said to the king, "How many years have I still to live, that I should go up with the king to Jerusalem? ³⁵Today I am eighty years old; can I discern what is pleasant and what is not? Can your servant taste what he eats or what he drinks? Can I still listen to the voice of singing men and singing women? Why then should your servant be an added burden to my lord the king? ³⁶Your servant will go a little way over the Jordan with the king. Why should the king recompense me with such a reward? ³⁷Please let your servant return, so that I may die in my own town, near the graves of my father and my mother. But here is your servant Chimham; let him go over with my lord the king; and do for him whatever seems good to you." ³⁸The king answered, "Chimham shall go over with me, and I will do for him whatever seems good to you; and all that you desire of me I will do for you." ³⁹Then all the people crossed over the Jordan, and the king crossed over; the king kissed Barzillai and blessed him, and he returned to his own home. ⁴⁰The king went on to Gilgal, and Chimham went on with him; all the people of Judah, and also half the people of Israel, brought the king on his way.

41Then all the people of Israel came to the king, and said to him, "Why have our kindred the people of Judah stolen you away, and brought

ᵃ Or *Merib-baal*: See 4.4 note

NIV

the men of Judah, steal the king away and bring him and his household across the Jordan, together with all his men?"

⁴²All the men of Judah answered the men of Israel, "We did this because the king is closely related to us. Why are you angry about it? Have we eaten any of the king's provisions? Have we taken anything for ourselves?"

⁴³Then the men of Israel answered the men of Judah, "We have ten shares in the king; and besides, we have a greater claim on David than you have. So why do you treat us with contempt? Were we not the first to speak of bringing back our king?"

But the men of Judah responded even more harshly than the men of Israel.

NRSV

the king and his household over the Jordan, and all David's men with him?" ⁴²All the people of Judah answered the people of Israel, "Because the king is near of kin to us. Why then are you angry over this matter? Have we eaten at all at the king's expense? Or has he given us any gift?" ⁴³But the people of Israel answered the people of Judah, "We have ten shares in the king, and in David also we have more than you. Why then did you despise us? Were we not the first to speak of bringing back our king?" But the words of the people of Judah were fiercer than the words of the people of Israel.

COMMENTARY

Absalom's rebellion and the civil war it brought are over, but the aftermath of these events leaves a troubled political reality in the kingdom as David retakes his throne. The grieving father must give way to the judicious king if David's reign is to be effectively reestablished. Not even David's return to Jerusalem is without troublesome political details, and the first portion of this section details the negotiations that make David's return possible (vv. 8b-18a). As David crosses the Jordan to begin the final leg of his return journey, he encounters three persons. They remind us of the encounters that marked his retreat from Jerusalem (15:13–16:14). In fact, two of these are direct counterparts of those earlier encounters: with Shimei (vv. 18b-23) and with Mephibosheth (vv. 24-30). The third is with a powerful supporter of David, Barzillai, with whom David negotiates a continuing alliance (vv. 31-40; cf. 17:27-29). The chapter closes with a confrontation between the northern tribes of Israel and Judah over David's crossing of the Jordan and his escort back to Jerusalem (vv. 41-43). This dispute apparently sets the stage for a further rebellion against David, led by a man named Sheba (chap. 20).

David's retreat from Jerusalem in the face of Absalom's advance was discussed earlier as being narrated in the manner of a procession of penance. Now that Absalom is dead and David's

forces have been victorious, we might expect a triumphant and celebratory return to Jerusalem. Yet, the tone of this narrative is not triumphal. The wise, if world-weary, David we saw in the retreat from Jerusalem (15:13–16:14) is the David we still see in this report of return. He makes judicious and compassionate decisions. He takes decisive action when needed. There is no overt expression of theological themes in this account, but one wonders if this telling is not still governed by David's expression in his retreat from Jerusalem: "If I find favor in the eyes of the LORD, he will bring me back and let me see both it and the place where [the ark] stays" (15:25). David is returning, not in triumph, but in humility. He is a sinner, but he still finds favor in the eyes of the Lord.

19:8b-18a. Although the victory over Absalom is won, these verses make clear that it is no simple matter for David to resume the throne. There are political complexities to be addressed and political loyalties to be won. The reference to the anointing of Absalom (v. 10), about which we had not heard before, suggests that David may have been officially deposed by the people. He may have won the victory, but the people must invite him to resume the throne, perhaps even by being anointed again. This is what some scholars believe took place at Gilgal, an ancient site connected with kingship from Saul's time (1 Sam 11:15), where David meets the representatives of Israel and Judah (vv. 15, 40).[334]

The notice that the Israelites had fled to their homes (v. 8*b*) indicates the dispersal of the army raised by Absalom, but the political division among the people is not ended. Some remember the deliverance from enemies that David had won for them in the past and urge that he be brought back now that Absalom is defeated (v. 9). Not all agree, as the use of dispute to describe the advancing of this argument suggests. David takes political action in the face of this uncertainty. He uses his loyal priests, Zadok and Abiathar, to make a political overture to the elders of Judah. David urges Judah to take the initiative in restoring him to the throne, and he bases his appeal on his kinship with Judah (vv. 11-12). He was a Judean himself, and Judah had been the first to make him king (2:4). Ironically the appeal to "my bone and my flesh" echoes the claim of kinship that northern Israel made in asking David to be king (5:1). Now David is playing Judah off against northern Israel.

David is willing to make concessions to win back Judah's political loyalty. In an astonishing bid for the loyalty of those in Judah who supported Absalom, David offers to make Amasa commander of his army, replacing Joab (v. 13). Amasa was a distant kinsman of David and Joab, and he was chosen by Absalom to lead the rebel army (17:25). This move would be as if President Lincoln had invited Robert E. Lee to replace Ulysses S. Grant at the conclusion of the American Civil War. Such a dramatic concession must speak to the uncertainty of David's political situation that he should feel such a gesture was needed. Further, he is directly displacing Joab, a reality that Joab could not accept. David may harbor animosity toward Joab for having killed Absalom, although we are never explicitly told that David knew this. The young man refusing Joab's urging to kill Absalom may have been right when he said, "There is nothing hidden from the king" (18:13).

David's political strategy seems to work, since Amasa sways Judah and they send an invitation for David to return (v. 14). Representatives of Judah meet at Gilgal to welcome David as he crosses the Jordan on his return to Jerusalem (v. 15). This apparently effective political overture to Judah will, however, create new problems in David's relationship to the northern tribes of Israel (vv. 41-43).

Among those who hurry to Gilgal to meet David are Shimei, the pro-Saulide Benjaminite who had cursed David on his retreat (v. 16; cf. 16:5-8), and Ziba, the servant of Saul to whom David had given the land allotted to Mephibosheth, also on the retreat from Jerusalem (v. 17; cf. 16:1-4). Now on his return journey David must deal again with these men and issues.

19:18*b*-23. Although it was primarily Judah who came to escort David back to Jerusalem, Shimei had arrived with a thousand Benjaminites (v. 17*a*). Shimei had good reason to be worried. When David seemed near to defeat and was barely escaping Jerusalem ahead of Absalom, Shimei had cursed David and attributed David's fate to the blood of Saul's house on his hands. David had restrained Abishai from killing Shimei (16:5-13). Now Absalom is defeated, and David has the upper hand. Shimei takes the initiative by falling before David, confessing the wrong he has done to him, and asking for mercy (v. 19). He claims that he is the first from the "house of Joseph" to meet David (v. 20), which means the first from the northern tribes to support David.

Again it is Abishai who wants to kill him, but we should not take this simply as a violent impulse. Abishai cites Shimei's offense as cursing the Lord's anointed, which is indeed a serious crime (v. 21). But as before, David intervenes on behalf of Shimei. David mildly rebukes Abishai (and his brother Joab), suggesting that he is distancing himself from the violence of these "sons of Zeruiah" and does not wish them as adversaries (v. 22*a*).[335] David had voiced reservations before about the "sons of Zeruiah" at the time of Abner's death (3:39).

David relates the mercy he shows on "this day" as appropriate to the day he is "king over Israel." We are reminded of the time Saul's supporters wanted to put some of his opponents to death, and Saul declared that "no one shall be put to death this day" (1 Sam 11:13). Immediately after

---

334. See T. N. D. Mettinger, *King and Messiah: The Civil and Sacral Legitimation of the Israelite Kings,* ConBOT 8 (Lund: CWK Gleerup, 1976) 118-23.

335. The noun שׂטן (*śāṭān*) may not mean "adversary" in the sense of an opponent of David, but "accuser" in the sense of the legal accuser of Shimei (cf. Zech 3:1). David would be rejecting Abishai's attempt to play that accusatory role.

this Saul was anointed at Gilgal (1 Sam 11:14-15). Such a sequence has led some to believe that David is being anointed again at Gilgal and that amnesty for opponents such as Shimei has become a part of the tradition surrounding the anointing and accession of Israel's kings.[336] Of course, David has ample political motives for showing such mercy to Shimei, since his support among the northern tribes is not yet assured. Conciliation toward Shimei seems wise on David's part as an effort to renegotiate his own kingship and its necessary base of support.[337]

David pronounces his verdict, "You shall not die," and gives it force by taking an oath (v. 23). But political memories are long. Shimei's curse against the Lord's anointed one has still not been avenged. On his deathbed, David will charge Solomon to deal with Shimei in accordance with his offense (1 Kgs 2:8-9). David's oath and his need for northern support prevented him from doing so, but Solomon is not restrained by this oath. On a pretext, Solomon will have Shimei put to death (1 Kgs 2:36-46).

19:24-30. David is next met by Mephibosheth, the son of Jonathan and the grandson of Saul (see chap. 9). He is unkempt and dirty, since he has not washed or otherwise taken care of himself since the day David left Jerusalem (v. 24). The implication is that Mephibosheth's actions were acts of mourning and solidarity with David in his plight. David meets him with a challenge, "Why did you not go with me, Mephibosheth?" (v. 25). Mephibosheth was not one of those whom David met on his desperate retreat from Jerusalem. It was Ziba, the servant of Saul who had been charged with the care of the Saulide lands David had given to Mephibosheth, who met David on the road. Ziba had brought provisions for David and charges against Mephibosheth that he had remained in Jerusalem in hopes of regaining the kingdom of Saul (16:1-4). David had rewarded Ziba by declaring that all that had belonged to Mephibosheth henceforth belonged to Ziba.

Even now, as David crosses the Jordan, Ziba has come with fifteen sons and twenty servants to help transport David's household and be at his

service (v. 17*b*). But Mephibosheth is now here to speak for himself, and he tells quite a different story. In answer to David's challenge, Mephibosheth claims that Ziba had deceived David. Mephibosheth had charged Ziba to saddle a donkey so he could join David. Being lame, he must ride to do so. But Ziba, he claims, had taken the donkey for himself, left Mephibosheth helpless behind, and slandered his good name before David (vv. 26-27*a*). Mephibosheth throws himself on David's mercy and whatever David might decide (v. 27*b*). He claims that he has already received David's generosity and has no right to ask more (v. 28). He is eloquent and convincing in his claim that he would not violate David's goodwill. Who is telling the truth? David is faced with utterly contradictory stories, and the narrator offers no hints about where the truth might lie.

David does not hesitate; he makes a royal decision. The land, and presumably the household that accompanies the land, is to be divided between Ziba and Mephibosheth (v. 29). There is no time to adjudicate this dispute. David chooses to believe that Mephibosheth could be speaking the truth, and he acts to ensure his continued generosity to the house of Saul. Mephibosheth might well have protested that all of the land should be his and that Ziba should be punished, but he does not. He responds in loyalty and gratitude and with the surprising statement that Ziba could take all the land, since David had returned in safety (v. 30). This statement alone seems to confirm that Mephibosheth speaks out of loyalty and not expedience.

19:31-40. Barzillai is a Gileadite who had helped to provision David's army in the Transjordan when he was preparing for the battle with Absalom (v. 32; cf. 17:27-29). He, too, now meets David at the crossing of the Jordan (v. 31). He appears in the role of David's host, bidding farewell to his royal guest, and David attempts to repay the kindness by urging Barzillai to come and live at David's court (v. 33). No doubt David is anxious to continue the alliance with this powerful and influential supporter, but one need not see his offer as an effort to co-opt or control Barzillai. Indeed, Barzillai is probably more valuable to David in the Transjordan, which is where Barzillai desires to remain. Barzillai cites his age of eighty years, and with an appealing sense of

---

336. Mettinger, *King and Messiah,* 119.

337. K. W. Whitelam, *The Just King: Monarchical Judicial Authority in Ancient Israel,* JSOTSup 12 (Sheffield: University of Sheffield Press, 1979) 145, gives a detailed accounting of the negotiating process that may have been necessary for David's return to the throne.

mild self-mockery claims that he is well beyond the ability to enjoy courtly pleasures (v. 35). He will only accompany David a short way and then return to live out his years in his own family home (vv. 36-37*a*).

Barzillai does ask that Chimham, who must be his son, be taken into David's court to serve at David's pleasure (v. 37*b*). David gladly accepts this offer (v. 38); indeed, on his deathbed he urges Solomon to offer continued generosity toward the sons of Barzillai (1 Kgs 2:7). When David and those accompanying him have crossed the Jordan, he kisses Barzillai, who then departs for his home (v. 39). The procession continues on to Gilgal, but, significantly, those accompanying David now include "half the people of Israel" as well as the people of Judah (v. 40).

19:41-43. It is the people of Israel, the representatives of the northern tribes, who now speak up in resentment of the initiative taken by Judah to bring David back to Jerusalem (v. 41). Tribal and regional animosities boil to the surface in an angry exchange of claims about who has priority in David's kingdom. Judah claims kinship to David and innocence of any intention to gain from their initiative (v. 42). But Israel claims to have a larger stake in the kingdom by virtue of having ten tribes, and they were the first to speak of bringing David back (v. 43). These jealous claims are not resolved. The text states that Judah's words were fiercer than Israel's, giving the impression that Judah simply outshouted or even threatened their northern counterparts. Absalom may be defeated, but the tribal divisions that he exploited are still present in the kingdom. As old animosities resurface, one final episode of rebellion against David's kingship occurs: the rebellion of Sheba (chap. 20). (See Reflections at 20:1-22.)

2 Samuel 20:1-22, Sheba's Rebellion

NIV

20 Now a troublemaker named Sheba son of Bicri, a Benjamite, happened to be there. He sounded the trumpet and shouted,

"We have no share in David,
　no part in Jesse's son!
Every man to his tent, O Israel!"

²So all the men of Israel deserted David to follow Sheba son of Bicri. But the men of Judah stayed by their king all the way from the Jordan to Jerusalem.

³When David returned to his palace in Jerusalem, he took the ten concubines he had left to take care of the palace and put them in a house under guard. He provided for them, but did not lie with them. They were kept in confinement till the day of their death, living as widows.

⁴Then the king said to Amasa, "Summon the men of Judah to come to me within three days, and be here yourself." ⁵But when Amasa went to summon Judah, he took longer than the time the king had set for him.

⁶David said to Abishai, "Now Sheba son of Bicri will do us more harm than Absalom did. Take your master's men and pursue him, or he will find fortified cities and escape from us." ⁷So Joab's

NRSV

20 Now a scoundrel named Sheba son of Bichri, a Benjaminite, happened to be there. He sounded the trumpet and cried out,

"We have no portion in David,
　no share in the son of Jesse!
Everyone to your tents, O Israel!"

²So all the people of Israel withdrew from David and followed Sheba son of Bichri; but the people of Judah followed their king steadfastly from the Jordan to Jerusalem.

3David came to his house at Jerusalem; and the king took the ten concubines whom he had left to look after the house, and put them in a house under guard, and provided for them, but did not go in to them. So they were shut up until the day of their death, living as if in widowhood.

4Then the king said to Amasa, "Call the men of Judah together to me within three days, and be here yourself." ⁵So Amasa went to summon Judah; but he delayed beyond the set time that had been appointed him. ⁶David said to Abishai, "Now Sheba son of Bichri will do us more harm than Absalom; take your lord's servants and pursue him, or he will find fortified cities for himself, and escape from us." ⁷Joab's men went out after

NIV

men and the Kerethites and Pelethites and all the mighty warriors went out under the command of Abishai. They marched out from Jerusalem to pursue Sheba son of Bicri.

⁸While they were at the great rock in Gibeon, Amasa came to meet them. Joab was wearing his military tunic, and strapped over it at his waist was a belt with a dagger in its sheath. As he stepped forward, it dropped out of its sheath.

⁹Joab said to Amasa, "How are you, my brother?" Then Joab took Amasa by the beard with his right hand to kiss him. ¹⁰Amasa was not on his guard against the dagger in Joab's hand, and Joab plunged it into his belly, and his intestines spilled out on the ground. Without being stabbed again, Amasa died. Then Joab and his brother Abishai pursued Sheba son of Bicri.

¹¹One of Joab's men stood beside Amasa and said, "Whoever favors Joab, and whoever is for David, let him follow Joab!" ¹²Amasa lay wallowing in his blood in the middle of the road, and the man saw that all the troops came to a halt there. When he realized that everyone who came up to Amasa stopped, he dragged him from the road into a field and threw a garment over him. ¹³After Amasa had been removed from the road, all the men went on with Joab to pursue Sheba son of Bicri.

¹⁴Sheba passed through all the tribes of Israel to Abel Beth Maacahᵃ and through the entire region of the Berites, who gathered together and followed him. ¹⁵All the troops with Joab came and besieged Sheba in Abel Beth Maacah. They built a siege ramp up to the city, and it stood against the outer fortifications. While they were battering the wall to bring it down, ¹⁶a wise woman called from the city, "Listen! Listen! Tell Joab to come here so I can speak to him." ¹⁷He went toward her, and she asked, "Are you Joab?"

"I am," he answered.

She said, "Listen to what your servant has to say."

"I'm listening," he said.

¹⁸She continued, "Long ago they used to say, 'Get your answer at Abel,' and that settled it. ¹⁹We are the peaceful and faithful in Israel. You are trying to destroy a city that is a mother in

ᵃ14 Or Abel, even Beth Maacah; also in verse 15

NRSV

him, along with the Cherethites, the Pelethites, and all the warriors; they went out from Jerusalem to pursue Sheba son of Bichri. ⁸When they were at the large stone that is in Gibeon, Amasa came to meet them. Now Joab was wearing a soldier's garment and over it was a belt with a sword in its sheath fastened at his waist; as he went forward it fell out. ⁹Joab said to Amasa, "Is it well with you, my brother?" And Joab took Amasa by the beard with his right hand to kiss him. ¹⁰But Amasa did not notice the sword in Joab's hand; Joab struck him in the belly so that his entrails poured out on the ground, and he died. He did not strike a second blow.

Then Joab and his brother Abishai pursued Sheba son of Bichri. ¹¹And one of Joab's men took his stand by Amasa, and said, "Whoever favors Joab, and whoever is for David, let him follow Joab." ¹²Amasa lay wallowing in his blood on the highway, and the man saw that all the people were stopping. Since he saw that all who came by him were stopping, he carried Amasa from the highway into a field, and threw a garment over him. ¹³Once he was removed from the highway, all the people went on after Joab to pursue Sheba son of Bichri.

14Shebaᵃ passed through all the tribes of Israel to Abel of Beth-maacah;ᵇ and all the Bichritesᶜ assembled, and followed him inside. ¹⁵Joab's forcesᵈ came and besieged him in Abel of Beth-maacah; they threw up a siege ramp against the city, and it stood against the rampart. Joab's forces were battering the wall to break it down. ¹⁶Then a wise woman called from the city, "Listen! Listen! Tell Joab, 'Come here, I want to speak to you.'" ¹⁷He came near her; and the woman said, "Are you Joab?" He answered, "I am." Then she said to him, "Listen to the words of your servant." He answered, "I am listening." ¹⁸Then she said, "They used to say in the old days, 'Let them inquire at Abel'; and so they would settle a matter. ¹⁹I am one of those who are peaceable and faithful in Israel; you seek to destroy a city that is a mother in Israel; why will you swallow up the heritage of the Lord?" ²⁰Joab answered, "Far be it from me, far be it, that I should swallow up or destroy! ²¹That is not the case! But a man

ᵃ Heb He   ᵇ Compare 20.15: Heb and Beth-maacah   ᶜ Compare Gk Vg: Heb Berites   ᵈ Heb They

NIV

Israel. Why do you want to swallow up the LORD's inheritance?"

²⁰"Far be it from me!" Joab replied, "Far be it from me to swallow up or destroy! ²¹That is not the case. A man named Sheba son of Bicri, from the hill country of Ephraim, has lifted up his hand against the king, against David. Hand over this one man, and I'll withdraw from the city."

The woman said to Joab, "His head will be thrown to you from the wall."

²²Then the woman went to all the people with her wise advice, and they cut off the head of Sheba son of Bicri and threw it to Joab. So he sounded the trumpet, and his men dispersed from the city, each returning to his home. And Joab went back to the king in Jerusalem.

NRSV

of the hill country of Ephraim, called Sheba son of Bichri, has lifted up his hand against King David; give him up alone, and I will withdraw from the city." The woman said to Joab, "His head shall be thrown over the wall to you." ²²Then the woman went to all the people with her wise plan. And they cut off the head of Sheba son of Bichri, and threw it out to Joab. So he blew the trumpet, and they dispersed from the city, and all went to their homes, while Joab returned to Jerusalem to the king.

COMMENTARY

The intertribal rivalries and political tensions that threatened David's kingship during Absalom's rebellion have one more convulsive episode to be played out. A man named Sheba, from the Saulide tribe of Benjamin, declares a secession from Davidic rule and apparently receives significant northern Israelite support. This separatist movement seems to have been provoked by the dispute between representatives of Judah and Israel at the end of chap. 19 over priority in support of the restoration of David's rule. It is doubtful, especially in the light of the outcome, that Sheba's revolt enjoyed the support of most northern Israelites. His separatist movement more likely reflects the political rivalries and fragmentation that Absalom exploited. David's victory over Absalom did not immediately end those tensions. To reestablish his reign, David must deal with rebellious leaders like Sheba if he is to reunify his kingdom. Even though Sheba is finally betrayed and his threat ended, the episode makes clear that the final years of David's reign were not years of halcyon contentment. The divisions that finally permanently rupture the kingdom after Solomon's death are already present in David's kingdom. In fact, the rallying cry for secessionist northern dissenters is the same later in Jeroboam's time (1 Kgs 12:16) as in Sheba's (v. 1).

Sheba's revolt also functions as the backdrop for narrating a further dark episode in Joab's story.

This time he is responsible for the murder of Amasa (vv. 4-13), whom David had appointed to command the army in his place (19:13). As with his killing of Abner (3:27), Uriah (11:16-17), and Absalom (18:14), Joab does not hesitate to kill when he judges it to be in his own interest or his own assessment of the king's interests. The narrative simply reports the murder of Amasa without comment, but on his deathbed David charges Solomon to hold Joab accountable for the blood of Abner and Amasa (1 Kgs 2:5-6). Political memories can be long in Israel.

The completion of chap. 20 seems to represent a break in the narrative of David's later years. Most have judged chaps. 21–24 to be appendixes to the book. These chapters do not continue the chronological narration of events toward the end of David's kingship. Some have believed that 1 Kings 1–2 are the continuation of the main narrative and conclude the so-called succession narrative with the account of Solomon's accession to the throne (see the Overview for chaps. 9–20). In their present form, those chapters certainly conclude David's story by narrating his death and the events immediately surrounding it, but they were probably not originally connected to 2 Samuel 20. With chap. 20 we come to the conclusion, not of David's life, but of an apologetic account of the events that led to and resolved Absalom's rebellion against his own father. The slant is pro-David, narrating tragic events but making clear that they were not of David's making (including the murder of Amasa). David may have suffered struggles and setbacks, but he is still worthy of God's promise, and so is his dynasty.[338]

20:1-3. Sheba, identified as a scoundrel or troublemaker, was one of the Israelites present at the angry confrontation between Israelites and Judahites in 19:41-43. His response to the apparently successful claims of Judah for priority with David is to declare that Israel has nothing to do with David (v. 1). His outcry is a call to secession and separatism for the northern tribes of Israel, and it may have been a traditional separatist slogan. In any case, it is used again in a remarkably similar situation of failed negotiations between north and south when Jeroboam leads the north into the breakaway that permanently divides the Israelite kingdom (1 Kgs 12:16). Sheba is a Benjaminite, perhaps even a distant relative of Saul, if Bichri is related to Becorath (9:1). Perhaps Sheba is part of the one thousand Benjaminites who accompanied Shimei to meet David (19:16).

Sheba's cry receives support, but it is unclear what is meant by the expression "all the people of Israel followed Sheba" (v. 2). It surely does not mean that the whole of the northern tribes joined Sheba's rebellion, for no battles with northern forces seem to ensue. The phrase could indicate that the Israelites present at the crossing of the Jordan left with Sheba in an act of defiance. The second half of the verse narrows the reference to those who met David at the Jordan to accompany him back to Jerusalem. Since those present on that occasion were primarily Benjaminites, like Sheba himself, it may have been that Sheba's tangible support came primarily from his own tribe. That he does not gain widespread support in Israel seems clear by his ignoble end (vv. 14-22).

David's first act in Jerusalem is to set aside the ten concubines he had left in Jerusalem (15:16). These are the women of his household whom Absalom had violated sexually in a public display of contempt for David and assertion of his own authority as king (16:20-23). Although David provides for

their care, they are condemned to a future without husbands or children, as if they were widows (v. 3). David's act here does not have any clearly discernible connection to Sheba's revolt. It seems unlikely that this is an act to appease northern sensibilities, and even less likely that David is giving up the keeping of concubines (his son Solomon takes the practice to new heights).[339] More likely, David acts to preserve his own honor by refusing to restore to his household the women Absalom has defiled. The narrator is concerned not only with Sheba's rebellion but also with other matters that took place in this same period.

20:4-13. The murder of Amasa by Joab is another drama that plays itself out against the backdrop of Sheba's rebellion. Amasa was the Judahite commander of Absalom's army whom David appointed over his own army in a conciliatory gesture to win back support of the tribe of Judah and others who had followed Absalom (19:13). This appointment displaced Joab, who was out of favor with David for killing Absalom. Joab had, earlier in David's career, reacted to the defection of Abner, Saul's general and a potential rival, by killing him (3:27).

In the wake of Sheba's defiance, David summons Amasa with his first assignment as commander of David's army. He is to gather the militia of Judah and come ready before David in three days. He does not do so in the time allotted (v. 4). Scholars offer various interpretations of this failure.[340] Was it an act of deliberate refusal to obey on Amasa's part? Was the time simply too short to accomplish the task? Was the short time limit a deliberate trap to ensure Amasa's failure? We do not have enough information to determine which of these was the case.

David turns to one of his old warrior companions, Abishai (one of the sons of Zeruiah and the brother of Joab), to take the mercenary forces, which were under separate command from the tribal militia, and pursue Sheba quickly (vv. 6-7). David is presented as being genuinely worried about the threat from Sheba—one potentially greater than that posed by Absalom. Absalom fomented a rebellion against David, but Sheba represents a potential threat to the unity of the kingdom itself.

338. See P. Kyle McCarter, *II Samuel*, AB 9 (Garden City, N.Y.: Doubleday, 1984) 9-16, for a detailed discussion of this view and its alternatives.

339. Contra Walter Brueggemann, *First and Second Samuel*, Interpretation (Louisville: John Knox, 1990) 330.

340. Cf. ibid., 330-31; A. A. Anderson, *2 Samuel*, WBC 11 (Waco: Word, 1989) 240; McCarter, *II Samuel*, 432.

David will, in this successful campaign against Sheba, keep this unity intact by force; but Sheba's separatist movement foreshadows the eventual division of the kingdom under Jeroboam (1 Kings 12).

Belatedly, Amasa comes to meet Joab and the army at Gibeon (v. 8a). The troops of Judah may have been with him. Joab goes out to meet him and, in an apparent ruse, intentionally drops his sword, only to retrieve it and plunge it into Amasa's belly as he grasps Amasa's beard to kiss him in greeting (vv. 8b-10). It is a scene narrated with grisly details: Amasa's entrails fall onto the ground; Joab strikes only one blow and leaves Amasa to die wallowing in his own blood on the road (v. 12). An ultimatum is issued: Whoever favors Joab and David should follow Joab (v. 11). The order of loyalties expressed here is significant. The ultimatum does not work immediately. With Amasa's agonized body in the road, people (presumably Amasa's troops) simply stop in the road (v. 12). Finally, Joab's man drags Amasa's body aside and covers it; only then do all the troops join in the pursuit of Sheba (v. 13).

This episode is probably narrated in such detail to make clear that Amasa's murder was not David's doing. Amasa was, no doubt, an influential man in Judah, and his murder presented a serious political complication for David. This account is apologetic in character. "This was the work of Joab, acting on his own initiative and motivated by his usual sense of ruthless expediency, probably augmented in this case by envy and injured pride."[341]

20:14-22. Sheba does not seem able to generate an effective army. He is described primarily as being on the run with David's force in pursuit. David's haste in ordering this pursuit was probably an effort to keep Sheba from having time to gather a force and organize a campaign. Ironically, David's strategy is consistent with the advice of Ahithophel to Absalom and might well have been effective against David if Hushai had not intervened (16:15–17:14).

341. McCarter, *II Samuel*, 432.

David's initial fear that Sheba would hole up in a fortified city (v. 6) comes to pass. Sheba takes refuge in Abel of Beth-maacah, a city in the north of Israel near Dan (v. 14); it may be associated with the Aramaean kingdom of Maacah (10:6). He seems to have only a force from his own clan, the Bichrites, with him. Joab lays siege to the city, a matter in which he has some expertise (11:1; 12:26-31). The siege proceeds methodically and would no doubt have been effective (v. 15), but Joab is halted by the words of a "wise woman" from the walls of the city (v. 16).

The woman describes herself as a representative of peace and faithfulness in Israel and speaks of the "heritage of the LORD." She presents alternatives to the destruction of her city, known for its wisdom and as a "mother in Israel" (vv. 18-19). The contrast with Joab could hardly be greater. He represents ruthless power and the will to violence in settling issues. He considers his actions in the light of pragmatic self-interest, not out of concern for the "heritage of the LORD." He would not hesitate to destroy even the most important city if it stood in his way. The wise woman of Abel reminds us of other women in the books of Samuel who offered peaceful and conciliatory alternatives to violence and confrontation: Abigail (1 Samuel 25) and the wise woman of Tekoa (2 Sam 14:1-24).

But Joab is willing to deal if he can get what he is after. He is nothing if not pragmatic. Joab declares that his real objective is not to destroy the city, but to capture and deal with Sheba, a rebel against David's rule. If he alone were given up, the city and all in it would be left alone; Joab would withdraw (v. 21a). The wise woman promises the head of Sheba (v. 21b). It is a peaceful alternative for the city, but not for Sheba. After proper consultation with the people, Sheba's head is thrown over the wall, and the siege is lifted (v. 22). The unity of the kingdom is restored—but by force, not by persuasion.

REFLECTIONS

1. The events that follow Absalom's death show David and his kingdom enmeshed in a complex series of political and military dealings. God is not explicitly visible in these chapters, and the kingdom reflects abiding tensions that foreshadow a troubled future. In his retreat from Jerusalem, David had trusted his troubled future to the goodness of God and the faithfulness of God's promises (16:12). As the narrative of David's story through this troubled period comes to an end, we are forced to understand that if God's promise is trustworthy it will be in the midst of the troubled realities of power and politics, not as a way around those realities.

Many in our own day turn to faith in the hope that the promises of God can give them a means to bypass the harsh realities of the world. That hope is an illusion. Like David, we will be forced to trust in those promises through days that are filled with conflict, difficult decisions, shifting human loyalties, and the seeming lack of God's presence. In the midst of harsh realities in politics and relationships, we will also encounter loyal relationships (like Barzillai) and wise words (like the woman of Abel), and we must receive and be guided by them. But beyond these human moments of hope must be a trust that God's promises are sure even in a troubled world and in the troubles of our lives.

Trust is a quality that is often in short supply in our materialistic world. Trust requires an ability to look beyond the immediacy of our struggles and brokenness. Trust requires remembering and living out of God's promises even in days when God seems distant or absent. God is not overtly visible in the account of troubling political events in this chapter, and David has been through tragic events that were a consequence of his own sin. But God's promise has not been revoked, and in the midst of his troubles, David chose to trust in that promise (16:12). It may be that trust, rooted in the memory of God's promise, gives us eyes to see God's goodness in the midst of trouble—in the loyalty of a friend, in wise words from an unexpected source, in the faithful support of a community, or in the opening of unforeseen possibilities.

2. Chapters 19–20 are not resurrection moments in David's story. They are testimony to the realities of brokenness and violence that surround the exercise of human political power. But the promise has been voiced and is still certain. David is God's anointed king. He has been to the depths of personal despair in the death of Absalom and to the desperation of political failure in the loss of his kingdom, and he has trusted in the goodness of God's promise (16:12). We, like David, can trust God's promise; but we, like him, must do so in continued engagement with the complexities of our personal and political lives. We could do far worse than to face those complexities with compassion for those who have wronged us (Shimei), acceptance of ambiguities we cannot resolve (Ziba and Mephibosheth), appreciation for the loyalties of friends and family (Barzillai), decisiveness when difficult action must be taken to avoid further division (Sheba), and willingness to entertain wise alternatives (the wise woman of Abel).

These stories of the struggles and brokenness of David's later years do not contain dramatic religious experiences to reassure David of God's presence. In our own troubled world and the troubled moments of our own lives, we, too, seldom receive dramatic religious experiences to reassure us. Like David, we are required to remember God's promises as they have been made known to us and to trust that God is in the midst of our decisions and relationships, enabling our most faithful responses to the events of our lives.

2 Samuel 20:23-26, David's Officers

NIV	NRSV
[23]Joab was over Israel's entire army; Benaiah son of Jehoiada was over the Kerethites and Pelethites; [24]Adoniram[a] was in charge of forced labor; Jehoshaphat son of Ahilud was recorder; [25]Sheva was secretary; Zadok and Abiathar were priests; [26]and Ira the Jairite was David's priest.	[23]Now Joab was in command of all the army of Israel;[a] Benaiah son of Jehoiada was in command of the Cherethites and the Pelethites; [24]Adoram was in charge of the forced labor; Jehoshaphat son of Ahilud was the recorder; [25]Sheva was secretary; Zadok and Abiathar were priests; [26]and Ira the Jairite was also David's priest.
[a]24 Some Septuagint manuscripts (see also 1 Kings 4:6 and 5:14); Hebrew *Adoram*	[a] Cn: Heb *Joab to all the army, Israel*

COMMENTARY

The final segment before the "appendixes" to the books of Samuel (chaps. 21–24) is a list of David's officers. It is a parallel to the list in 8:15-18. Most scholars believe the list in chap. 8 reflects an earlier period of David's reign and that the list here reflects David's later kingdom.[342] The presence of this bureaucratic list as the conclusion to this section (chaps. 9–20) suggests that, for the moment, stability has been restored and the administrative apparatus of the kingdom is in place.

Most of the officers of the court are listed in pairs: two military, two administrative, two priestly offices. This arrangement may reflect an interest in preventing too great a concentration of power in any one of the persons in these areas.

There are some additions to and variations on the list of 8:15-18. Sheva is now secretary rather than Seraiah. There is a new office: "Adoram was

in charge of the forced labor" (v. 24a). The practice of using forced labor, a policy continued and expanded by Solomon (1 Kgs 5:13; 9:15-22), came to be much hated. This practice may have begun as a use of slaves or non-Israelite laborers, but eventually Israelites were also conscripted for the building of Solomon's royal buildings and the Temple. Such conscription of labor sounds like the dangers of which the prophet Samuel warned (1 Sam 8:10-18), and such an office in this list seems to move farther from the ideals of covenant community into royal bureaucracy. We know nothing about Ira the Jairite or what it means to say that he was David's priest (v. 26). His position in the list displaces the listing of David's sons as priests in 8:18. Ira does not seem to have the cultic status of Zadok and Abiathar, who are elsewhere connected with the ark and the corporate cultus of Jerusalem. Perhaps Ira was a royal chaplain to David.

---

342. T. N. D. Mettinger, *Solomonic State Officials: A Study of the Civil Government Officials of the Israelite Monarchy,* ConBOT 5 (Lund: Gleerup, 1971) 7.

2 SAMUEL 21:1–24:25, A FINALE OF DAVID TRADITIONS

OVERVIEW

These final chapters represent an interruption in the chronological narration of David's story. Those who have defended the hypothesis of a succession narrative see the account of Solomon's accession to the throne (1 Kings 1–2) as the natural continuation of 2 Samuel 20. The narratives of 21:1-14 and 24:1-25 are not set in the later years of David's life and have nothing to do with royal succession. The poems of 22:1-51 and 23:1-7 possess no narrative setting, and the lists of 21:15-22 and 23:8-39 are drawn from the period of David's exploits against the Philistines. Most scholars have treated these chapters as intrusive appendixes, a miscellany of David-related material that was appended to the story in a complex and frag-

mented redactional process at a point prior to his deathbed scene.[343] Interpreters have also recognized the symmetrical or ring-like arrangement of these chapters:[344]

A	21:1-14, a narrative on the expiation of Saul's guilt
B	21:15-22, a list of heroes and their deeds
C	22:1-51, a song of thanksgiving for the Lord's deliverance

---

343. See Anderson, *2 Samuel,* 247-48; McCarter, *II Samuel,* 18-19.
344. This symmetrical arrangement was first given detailed description by Karl Budde, *Die Bucher Samuel erklart,* KHCAT 8 (Tubingen: Mohr, 1902) 304, and his description has been adopted by many since.

C′	23:1-7, a song in celebration of God's promise to David
B′	23:8-39, a list of heroes and their deeds
A′	24:1-25, a narrative on the expiation of David's guilt

Despite this literary structure, these chapters have been treated primarily as a miscellany without intentional or substantive connection to the preceding books of Samuel. Only recently have voices begun to suggest that these chapters conclude the book of 2 Samuel with a distinctive ideological and theological voice. Scholars have suggested that these chapters taken together make a concluding comment on the story of kingship in Israel and the story of David in particular as that has been narrated in the books of Samuel.[345]

My own position on these chapters is similar to that taken by Walter Brueggemann in his recent studies of these chapters.[346] He notes the symmetrical arrangement of narratives in 2 Samuel 5–8, chapters that move David's story from tribal ideology to royal ideology (see the Overview for 2 Samuel 5–8), and suggests that these final chapters of 2 Samuel move in the other direction, from a high royal theology back to tribal, covenantal understandings of David's story. He notes that "the story ends with a king beset by self-serving political arrogance and autonomy" and argues that "chapters 21–24 are a gathering of materials to form a counterpart to the aggrandizement of absolute David, and perhaps intend to reverse the *rite of passage* in chapters 5–8 in order to provide David 'passage' back into the pre-absolute world of tribal fidelity . . . [these chapters are] a dismantling or deconstruction of an extravagantly royal David who has become unacceptable to the old tribal theory."[347]

I would suggest a slightly different relationship of these chapters to their preceding context. Chapter 20 does not leave us with a reality of royal

absolutism that needs deconstruction. Royal absolutism in David's story was at its height in 2 Samuel 10 (conquest of nations) and 2 Samuel 11 (the personal behavior of "taking"). David's acting out of royal absolutism is reflected in the behavior of his sons Amnon (in the rape of Tamar, chap. 13) and Absalom (in his seizing of the throne, chaps. 15–18). But such absolutism as acceptable royal behavior for God's king has already been deconstructed in the narrative by the judgment of the Lord pronounced by Nathan (chap. 12), and in the tragic events that unfold in David's own family, bringing him to grief as a king and as a man (chaps. 13–20). In these tragic episodes, we see a newly vulnerable and fallible David, but we also glimpse some of the qualities that made David God's king earlier in his story. These qualities are especially evident in his expression of trust to God's mercy and will in 15:25-26 and in David's wise and compassionate dealings with enemies and friends both as he retreated from Jerusalem (15:13–16:14) and as he returned (19:8*b*-40). The ideology of royal absolutism has been exposed and found wanting; glimpses of David as the Lord's anointed, covenantal king are visible in spite of David's vulnerability.

At the end of chap. 20, however, David has been reestablished as king. Moreover, Joab's actions suggest the possibility of a return to rule by absolute royal power. Without the intervening testimony of chaps. 21–24, David's story would proceed to the cynical politics of deathbed vendettas by David and political bloodbaths by Solomon (1 Kings 1–2). What intervenes in chaps. 21–24 is not a deconstruction of royal absolutism but the effort to stay or to moderate its reconstruction. David is still vulnerable and capable of self-serving political acts (e.g., the execution of Saul's sons, chap. 21; the census, chap. 24), but he is capable of recognizing an authority beyond his own, that of the Lord. The lists show David not as the sole hero of a royal public relations effort, but as the leader of a heroic community. The two great songs celebrate David only in relation to the Lord, who chose him and acts through him, and in spite of David's sin and God's judgment. When the story moves on to Solomon and the ideology of empire, it does so only after including the testimony of these so-called appen-

345. Most notably, Brevard S. Childs, *Introduction to the Old Testament as Scripture* (Philadelphia: Fortress, 1979) 273-75; Walter Brueggemann, "2 Samuel 21-24: An Appendix of Deconstruction?" *CBQ* 50 (1988) 383-97; Robert Polzin, *David and the Deuteronomist: A Literary Study of the Deuteronomic History*, Part Three: *2 Samuel* (Bloomington: Indiana University Press, 1993) 202-14.

346. See Brueggemann's recent treatments of these chapters in *First and Second Samuel*, 336-57, and Walter Brueggemann, *Power, Providence, and Personality* (Louisville: Westminster/John Knox, 1990) 86-115.

347. Brueggemann, *Power, Providence and Personality*, 88, 90.

dixes. But these chapters bracket David's story by ending on the same note that was struck by Hannah's song in the beginning of the story of Israel's kingship. It is the Lord who "brings low and exalts," and it is the Lord who "exalts the power of his anointed" (1 Sam 2:7b, 10b).

2 Samuel 21:1-14, Gibeonite Vengeance

NIV

21 During the reign of David, there was a famine for three successive years; so David sought the face of the LORD. The LORD said, "It is on account of Saul and his blood-stained house; it is because he put the Gibeonites to death."

²The king summoned the Gibeonites and spoke to them. (Now the Gibeonites were not a part of Israel but were survivors of the Amorites; the Israelites had sworn to ˻spare˼ them, but Saul in his zeal for Israel and Judah had tried to annihilate them.) ³David asked the Gibeonites, "What shall I do for you? How shall I make amends so that you will bless the LORD's inheritance?"

⁴The Gibeonites answered him, "We have no right to demand silver or gold from Saul or his family, nor do we have the right to put anyone in Israel to death."

"What do you want me to do for you?" David asked.

⁵They answered the king, "As for the man who destroyed us and plotted against us so that we have been decimated and have no place anywhere in Israel, ⁶let seven of his male descendants be given to us to be killed and exposed before the LORD at Gibeah of Saul—the LORD's chosen one."

So the king said, "I will give them to you."

⁷The king spared Mephibosheth son of Jonathan, the son of Saul, because of the oath before the LORD between David and Jonathan son of Saul. ⁸But the king took Armoni and Mephibosheth, the two sons of Aiah's daughter Rizpah, whom she had borne to Saul, together with the five sons of Saul's daughter Merab,ᵃ whom she had borne to Adriel son of Barzillai the Meholathite. ⁹He handed them over to the Gibeonites, who killed and exposed them on a hill before the LORD. All seven of them fell together; they were put to death during the first days of the harvest, just as the barley harvest was beginning.

NRSV

21 Now there was a famine in the days of David for three years, year after year; and David inquired of the LORD. The LORD said, "There is bloodguilt on Saul and on his house, because he put the Gibeonites to death." ²So the king called the Gibeonites and spoke to them. (Now the Gibeonites were not of the people of Israel, but of the remnant of the Amorites; although the people of Israel had sworn to spare them, Saul had tried to wipe them out in his zeal for the people of Israel and Judah.) ³David said to the Gibeonites, "What shall I do for you? How shall I make expiation, that you may bless the heritage of the LORD?" ⁴The Gibeonites said to him, "It is not a matter of silver or gold between us and Saul or his house; neither is it for us to put anyone to death in Israel." He said, "What do you say that I should do for you?" ⁵They said to the king, "The man who consumed us and planned to destroy us, so that we should have no place in all the territory of Israel— ⁶let seven of his sons be handed over to us, and we will impale them before the LORD at Gibeon on the mountain of the LORD."ᵃ The king said, "I will hand them over."

⁷But the king spared Mephibosheth,ᵇ the son of Saul's son Jonathan, because of the oath of the LORD that was between them, between David and Jonathan son of Saul. ⁸The king took the two sons of Rizpah daughter of Aiah, whom she bore to Saul, Armoni and Mephibosheth;ᵇ and the five sons of Merabᶜ daughter of Saul, whom she bore to Adriel son of Barzillai the Meholathite; ⁹he gave them into the hands of the Gibeonites, and they impaled them on the mountain before the LORD. The seven of them perished together. They were put to death in the first days of harvest, at the beginning of barley harvest.

10Then Rizpah the daughter of Aiah took sackcloth, and spread it on a rock for herself, from

ᵃ8 Two Hebrew manuscripts, some Septuagint manuscripts and Syriac (see also 1 Samuel 18:19); most Hebrew and Septuagint manuscripts *Michal*

ᵃ Cn Compare Gk and 21.9: Heb *at Gibeah of Saul, the chosen of the LORD*   ᵇ Or *Merib-baal:* See 4.4 note   ᶜ Two Heb Mss Syr Compare Gk: MT *Michal*

NIV

¹⁰Rizpah daughter of Aiah took sackcloth and spread it out for herself on a rock. From the beginning of the harvest till the rain poured down from the heavens on the bodies, she did not let the birds of the air touch them by day or the wild animals by night. ¹¹When David was told what Aiah's daughter Rizpah, Saul's concubine, had done, ¹²he went and took the bones of Saul and his son Jonathan from the citizens of Jabesh Gilead. (They had taken them secretly from the public square at Beth Shan, where the Philistines had hung them after they struck Saul down on Gilboa.) ¹³David brought the bones of Saul and his son Jonathan from there, and the bones of those who had been killed and exposed were gathered up.

¹⁴They buried the bones of Saul and his son Jonathan in the tomb of Saul's father Kish, at Zela in Benjamin, and did everything the king commanded. After that, God answered prayer in behalf of the land.

NRSV

the beginning of harvest until rain fell on them from the heavens; she did not allow the birds of the air to come on the bodiesᵃ by day, or the wild animals by night. ¹¹When David was told what Rizpah daughter of Aiah, the concubine of Saul, had done, ¹²David went and took the bones of Saul and the bones of his son Jonathan from the people of Jabesh-gilead, who had stolen them from the public square of Beth-shan, where the Philistines had hung them up, on the day the Philistines killed Saul on Gilboa. ¹³He brought up from there the bones of Saul and the bones of his son Jonathan; and they gathered the bones of those who had been impaled. ¹⁴They buried the bones of Saul and of his son Jonathan in the land of Benjamin in Zela, in the tomb of his father Kish; they did all that the king commanded. After that, God heeded supplications for the land.

ᵃ Heb *them*

COMMENTARY

This narrative describes how a claim of bloodguilt on the house of Saul, for a wrong committed against the Gibeonites, led to the execution of seven of Saul's remaining sons. The cursing of Shimei as David retreats from Jerusalem accuses David of having the blood of Saul's house on his hands (16:8). This accusation may have as its background the events narrated in 21:1-14. The events narrated here do not follow chronologically on the rebellion of Sheba in chap. 20. This story comes from an earlier time in David's reign, although we find no mention of these events elsewhere in the books of Samuel or Chronicles. The narrator knows of David's kindness to Mephibosheth because of his oath to Jonathan (v. 7). Moreover, 1 Samuel 9, which tells the story of David and Mephibosheth, seems to presuppose that he is the only one left of the house of Saul (9:1). This reference has caused some to propose that chap. 21 has been displaced from an original position prior to chap. 9, but there is no evidence to support this hypothesis.

Although the story is grim and tragic, the narrative may be intended to absolve David of any direct responsibility for the elimination of Saul's heirs. Taken in this straightforward fashion, an unspecified offense of Saul against the Gibeonites has caused a famine because that offense has not been expiated. David is only the one to whom God reveals the cause of the famine (v. 1). Further, David has no direct responsibility for the death of the remaining sons of the house of Saul; it is the Gibeonites who carry out vengeance on Saul's heirs (vv. 4-6). David even spares one of Saul's sons (v. 7) and later gives these seven, along with the bones of Saul and Jonathan, honored burial (vv. 12-14).

But the account is capable of a more cynical reading. We have no knowledge of the offense against the Gibeonites that issued in this charge of bloodguilt against the house of Saul. This is unusual in a pro-David narrative that lost no opportunity to discredit Saul. In this story, the bloodguilt of Saul is made known only to David, although the Gibeonites seem to feel the accusation is warranted. It is David, however, who initiates negotiations with the Gibeonites over this matter. Brueggemann has suggested that the charge against Saul could simply be a piece of "Davidic fabrication" that serves as a pretext for

David to eliminate any future Saulide claim on his throne, and does so in the name of religious expiation of guilt.[348] But even if the offense against the Gibeonites is not fabricated, we can judge David to be capable of political opportunism in using an old charge of bloodguilt to eliminate potential rivals. At the point in David's story where a vulnerable and chastened David has regained power and used it to consolidate his reign (chap. 20), this narrative begins a series of appendixes that step outside the chronology of David's story and remind the reader that royal reality is not identical with the royal ideal of efficient, bureaucratized, religiously sanctioned power. Instead of high royal ideology, we see either a local chieftain who must expiate bloodguilt and bow to powers beyond his control or a ruthless politician who takes advantage of a suspicious charge against an old enemy to eliminate his heirs as potential rivals. In either case, this narrative works against any idealized high theology of kingship focused on David.

21:1-6. A three-year famine grips the land. In this crisis, David inquires of the Lord, only to be told that the land suffers under bloodguilt incurred by Saul for an offense against the Gibeonites. But there are gaps in this information. Why does the land now suffer punishment during the time of David for an offense committed by Saul, who has already been rejected and met a tragic death for his failures before God? What did Saul do to the Gibeonites? By what means did David inquire of God? How is it that he alone comes to know of Saul's bloodguilt? These questions are never answered and leave the account ambiguous. Is this an innocent story of the expiation of guilt or a convenient pretext for political opportunism by David?

We have no record elsewhere of an action by Saul against the Gibeonites. Verse 2 says that Saul tried to exterminate them and attributes this to excessive nationalistic sentiment for Israel and Judah, which caused him to violate the special covenant made between Israel and the Gibeonites in Joshua's time (Josh 9:3-27). Although the Gibeonites were a non-Israelite people (here called Amorites), they had enjoyed a special relationship to Israel. However, their city and territory were very near Saul's capital and home at Gibeah. Saul may have tried to annex or somehow control this territory and met resistance that led to Gibeonite deaths.

The Gibeonites are pictured as reticent in this entire matter. They do not call for vengeance, but are approached by David (v. 2a), who alone seems to have received divine word that the famine is connected with Saul's bloodguilt. David seeks a renewed blessing from the Gibeonites and asks them to name the means of expiation (v. 3). The Gibeonites cautiously advise the king that it is not within their authority to exact monetary reparations or to exact the death penalty (v. 4a). Again David takes the initiative by assuming the authority for any penalty exacted in expiation of Saul's bloodguilt (v. 4b). It is by royal authority that things will be put right.

When the Gibeonites finally speak their mind, it is to seek the penalty against Saul's house that he supposedly sought against the Gibeonites—extermination. Saul's offense is described as genocidal in character (v. 5), though details are still vague and unspecified. The proposed penalty for Saul's act is the execution of seven of Saul's sons at the hands of the Gibeonites (v. 6). The meaning of the verb יקע (*yāqaʿ*) is uncertain here, and translators have argued on behalf of an astonishing range of options ("impaling," "dismemberment," "crucifixion in the sun," "hanging," "hurling down").[349] Since this is to be done "before the LORD," it should be envisioned as a ritual execution. David agrees to hand over these seven sons. The act may be intended as more symbolic than actually effective in ending the house of Saul. Perhaps the number seven represents completion. As we shall see, David spares Jonathan's son, Mephibosheth (v. 7; chap. 9), and the seven sons of Saul who were executed surely included some old enough to have sons of their own to carry on the Saulide line. For David's political purposes, it does eliminate all possible immediate Saulide rivals to the throne.

21:7-9. The executions are carried out, with the notable exception of David's protection of Mephibosheth (v. 7), Jonathan's son, because of the covenant sworn between David and Jonathan (1 Sam 18:3; 20:17, 42; 23:18). Chapter 9 tells the story of David and Mephibosheth in some detail, and the opening of that chapter seems to imply that Mephibosheth is the only remaining

---

348. Walter Brueggemann, *First and Second Samuel,* Interpretation (Louisville: John Knox, 1990) 336-38.

349. See R. Polzin, "HWQYʿ and Covenantal Institutions in Early Israel," *HTR* 62 (1969) 236.

direct descendant of Saul. For this reason, some have suggested that chap. 21 once preceded chap. 9.

The seven executed sons are named in v. 8. They include two sons of Saul by Rizpah, who was Saul's concubine and, after Saul's death, was the object of tension between Abner and Ish-bosheth (3:7-11). One of Rizpah's sons is also named Mephibosheth, but he is in no way to be identified with Jonathan's son. The remaining five were grandsons of Saul, born to his daughter Merab,[350] who was married to a son of Barzillai. If this is the same Barzillai associated with the support of David during Absalom's revolt (17:27-29; 19:31-40), it is surprising that his grandsons would be killed with David's tacit approval. Some have argued that these two men are not the same person.[351]

David hands these Saulide sons into the hand of the Gibeonites, who carry out the executions at the beginning of the barley harvest (v. 9). This timing may have been significant—as an expectation that expiation of Saul's bloodguilt would bring an end to the famine.

21:10-14. Suddenly and surprisingly the narrative focus shifts away from David to Rizpah, the concubine of Saul and mother of two sons executed by the Gibeonites. Dressed for mourning, she keeps vigil by the bodies of her sons and the others who have been executed (v. 10). The bodies have apparently been left exposed to birds and wild animals as a further act of humiliation and dishonor, but Rizpah refuses to accept this fate for her sons and fends off the scavengers day and night.

When Rizpah's lonely vigil is reported to David (v. 11), he is apparently moved to action. We are not told of David's inner motivation, but he acts to honor the dead. He begins by retrieving the bones of Saul and Jonathan from the people of Jabesh-gilead, who had stolen the bodies of their heroes from their humiliating display on the walls of the Philistine city of Beth-shan (v. 12; cf. 1 Sam 31:11-13). He gives their bones and the bodies of those now executed an honorable burial (vv. 13-14a). Saul and Jonathan are laid to rest in the tomb of Saul's father, Kish (v. 14a). Only after their burial does God heed prayers on behalf of the famine-parched land (v. 14b). Some scholars think this story stands in conflict with 1 Sam 31:12, where it is reported that the bodies of Saul and Jonathan had been burned, but v. 13 clearly states that after the burning their bones were buried under a tamarisk tree in Jabesh-gilead. The burning of the bodies was not so intense or protracted as to destroy the bones.

---

350. The Hebrew text reads "Michal," but Michal was never married to a son of Barzillai and is explicitly said to have borne no children (6:23). The Greek text reads "Merab," and most translations have followed this reading.

351. See Hans Wilhelm Hertzberg, *I and II Samuel,* OTL (Philadelphia: Westminster, 1964) 384.

REFLECTIONS

1. This story is told in a manner that does not allow certainty on whether to read it as an innocent but somewhat primitive story of the expiation of guilt or as a cynical exercise in royal political opportunism (see Commentary). This ambiguity may well point to a reality worth noting for our time as well as for David's: the ease with which political expediency can masquerade as religious duty. It is often as difficult to distinguish innocent religiosity from self-serving hypocrisy in our modern public forums as it is in this story. Since the stakes, as in this tale, are often serious life-and-death issues, it behooves us to examine carefully religious calls to action. The clothing of religious duty cannot provide a safe conduct around careful public scrutiny of proposed policies or programs. This is not a call to "keep religion out of politics," but to recognize that religious values and claims in the political arena must be subject to the same critical scrutiny as secular claims. If religious motivations prove sincere and recommended policies prove sound, the outcome will be stronger for undergoing careful scrutiny. But if closer examination reveals hypocrisy and cynical self-serving uses of religious language, then all will be well served by the exposure of such tactics. Determination of David's motives lies beyond our further examination, but the ambiguous telling of this story serves to make us more vigilant in writing our own story.

2. The brief moment in the spotlight occupied by Rizpah in this story is worthy of our notice. David, the king, holds all the power, but Rizpah, with quiet moral persistence, forces the king to act on the side of honor and humanity. Too often we give in to the claims of human political power to be all-powerful, but Rizpah reminds us that this is not the full truth about reality. There is a moral power that can affect even kings, if we choose to wield it. In our own time, women in Argentina and El Salvador have stood up publicly and persistently as the "mothers of the disappeared," insisting that disregard for the common humanity of countless sons and husbands could not go unremarked. Like Rizpah, they kept a vigil that brought the notice of powers that could eventually make changes. Oppressive regimes were forced to change and give way in the face of a witness devoid of apparent political power, but possessed of moral power that proved capable of making a political difference. Rizpah's moment in this story is small, but her moral persistence makes her witness great.

2 Samuel 21:15-22, David's Warriors

[15]Once again there was a battle between the Philistines and Israel. David went down with his men to fight against the Philistines, and he became exhausted. [16]And Ishbi-Benob, one of the descendants of Rapha, whose bronze spearhead weighed three hundred shekels[a] and who was armed with a new ⌞sword⌟, said he would kill David. [17]But Abishai son of Zeruiah came to David's rescue; he struck the Philistine down and killed him. Then David's men swore to him, saying, "Never again will you go out with us to battle, so that the lamp of Israel will not be extinguished."

[18]In the course of time, there was another battle with the Philistines, at Gob. At that time Sibbecai the Hushathite killed Saph, one of the descendants of Rapha.

[19]In another battle with the Philistines at Gob, Elhanan son of Jaare-Oregim[b] the Bethlehemite killed Goliath[c] the Gittite, who had a spear with a shaft like a weaver's rod.

[20]In still another battle, which took place at Gath, there was a huge man with six fingers on each hand and six toes on each foot—twenty-four in all. He also was descended from Rapha. [21]When he taunted Israel, Jonathan son of Shimeah, David's brother, killed him.

[22]These four were descendants of Rapha in Gath, and they fell at the hands of David and his men.

a16 That is, about 7 1/2 pounds (about 3.5 kilograms)   b19 Or son of Jair the weaver   c19 Hebrew and Septuagint; 1 Chron. 20:5 son of Jair killed Lahmi the brother of Goliath

15The Philistines went to war again with Israel, and David went down together with his servants. They fought against the Philistines, and David grew weary. [16]Ishbi-benob, one of the descendants of the giants, whose spear weighed three hundred shekels of bronze, and who was fitted out with new weapons,[a] said he would kill David. [17]But Abishai son of Zeruiah came to his aid, and attacked the Philistine and killed him. Then David's men swore to him, "You shall not go out with us to battle any longer, so that you do not quench the lamp of Israel."

18After this a battle took place with the Philistines, at Gob; then Sibbecai the Hushathite killed Saph, who was one of the descendants of the giants. [19]Then there was another battle with the Philistines at Gob; and Elhanan son of Jaare-oregim, the Bethlehemite, killed Goliath the Gittite, the shaft of whose spear was like a weaver's beam. [20]There was again war at Gath, where there was a man of great size, who had six fingers on each hand, and six toes on each foot, twenty-four in number; he too was descended from the giants. [21]When he taunted Israel, Jonathan son of David's brother Shimei, killed him. [22]These four were descended from the giants in Gath; they fell by the hands of David and his servants.

a Heb was belted anew

COMMENTARY

The second element in the appendixes is a list of the exploits of David's warriors during the war with the Philistines. The list is composed of four items, each with some narrative detail, describing the triumph of one of David's men over a giant warrior of the Philistines. Each item begins with a report about a battle with the Philistines (vv. 15, 18-20), and v. 22 summarizes the entire list, "These four were descended from the giants in Gath; they fell by the hands of David and his servants."

Although David is valued as the "lamp of Israel" (v. 17), such a judgment occurs in a context of his weariness and removal from battle. David may be the king whose very being is important to Israel, but he no longer leads heroically in battle. In all four segments of the list, David's men do the heroic deeds. David's elevation to the high role of "lamp of Israel" seems hollow when placed alongside the diminishment of his actual deeds in leading Israel. The attribution of his triumph over Goliath to another hero (v. 19) may be a part of this intentional diminishment of David. The author may be suggesting that the claims of importance for the "lamp of Israel" may be exaggerated and that Israel does not really need David.

21:15-17. David plays a role only in the first part of the list (vv. 15-17), a portrait with some tension in its portrayal of David. He grows weary in battle and is about to be overcome by one of the giants who fought for the Philistines (vv. 15-16). This Philistine warrior and the subsequent three are all described as "descendants of הרפה" (*hārāpâ*, vv. 16, 18, 20, 22), which is taken by some as a reference to the "Rephaim," who were legendary giants in Canaan before the coming of the Israelites (Gen 15:20; Deut 2:11; 3:11; Josh 17:15), hence, to be translated here as "giants" (NRSV). But others have taken this term for a family name and have translated it as "descendants of Rapha" (NIV).

David is rescued by Abishai from the threat occasioned by his weariness (v. 17*a*). Again he is forced to rely on the sons of Zeruiah (Abishai's brother is Joab). Following this narrow escape, David's men swore that he should no longer go into battle. As king, he is too valuable to risk in battle (cf. 18:3). They fear that his death would "quench the lamp of Israel" (v. 17*b*). This phrase represents a high theology of kingship that values the king as light and life in the midst of Israel, but ironically it works against the exercise of genuine leadership or the direct action on the part of David. Brueggemann has suggested that the juxtaposition of David's weariness and his removal from the arena of mighty deeds in these verses makes the affirmation that David is the "lamp of Israel" ironic and ambiguous.[352] The high theology of kingship is called into question. Is such a symbolically valued king needed if he no longer leads? In the following list of mighty deeds against the Philistines, David is conspicuous by his absence.

21:18-22. David no longer appears in this list of heroic exploits. The heroic victories of three of his men are celebrated. It is the second of these three that has provoked greatest comment. In v. 19, Elhanan, a Bethlehemite, is given credit for having killed Goliath. In the far better known story of 1 Samuel 17, it is, of course, David who is the Bethlehemite who kills Goliath, whose spear, in both stories, is described as being like a "weaver's beam" (1 Sam 17:7). Scholars have offered numerous suggestions to explain this discrepancy.[353] They range from suggesting that Elhanan is another name for David himself to the view that this is an intentional debunking of the David mystique by attributing his greatest victory to another warrior. The chronicler reports (1 Chr 20:5) that Elhanan killed Lahmi, a brother of Goliath, which is widely taken as an attempt by the historian to harmonize these two traditions. We cannot resolve this discrepancy with certainty, but the effect of the notice here is to diminish David's role in the Philistine wars. The final notice of v. 22 makes the mention of David alongside his men seem irrelevant. David does nothing in this listing of mighty deeds except to retire in weariness from the field of battle.

---

352. Brueggemann, *Power, Providence, and Personality,* 92-93.
353. See the discussion of various proposals in A. A. Anderson, *2 Samuel,* WBC 11 (Waco: Word, 1989) 255.

2 Samuel 22:1-51, A Psalm of Thanksgiving from David

NIV

22 David sang to the Lord the words of this song when the Lord delivered him from the hand of all his enemies and from the hand of Saul. ²He said:

"The Lord is my rock, my fortress and my
  deliverer;
³ my God is my rock, in whom I take refuge,
  my shield and the horn*ᵃ* of my salvation.
He is my stronghold, my refuge and my
    savior—
  from violent men you save me.
⁴I call to the Lord, who is worthy of praise,
  and I am saved from my enemies.

⁵"The waves of death swirled about me;
  the torrents of destruction overwhelmed
    me.
⁶The cords of the grave*ᵇ* coiled around me;
  the snares of death confronted me.
⁷In my distress I called to the Lord;
  I called out to my God.
From his temple he heard my voice;
  my cry came to his ears.

⁸"The earth trembled and quaked,
  the foundations of the heavens*ᶜ* shook;
  they trembled because he was angry.
⁹Smoke rose from his nostrils;
  consuming fire came from his mouth,
  burning coals blazed out of it.
¹⁰He parted the heavens and came down;
  dark clouds were under his feet.
¹¹He mounted the cherubim and flew;
  he soared*ᵈ* on the wings of the wind.
¹²He made darkness his canopy around him—
  the dark*ᵉ* rain clouds of the sky.
¹³Out of the brightness of his presence
  bolts of lightning blazed forth.
¹⁴The Lord thundered from heaven;
  the voice of the Most High resounded.
¹⁵He shot arrows and scattered ⌊the enemies⌋,
  bolts of lightning and routed them.
¹⁶The valleys of the sea were exposed

ᵃ3 Horn here symbolizes strength. *ᵇ6* Hebrew *Sheol*   *ᶜ8* Hebrew;
Vulgate and Syriac (see also Psalm 18:7) *mountains*   *ᵈ11* Many
Hebrew manuscripts (see also Psalm 18:10); most Hebrew manuscripts
appeared   *ᵉ12* Septuagint and Vulgate (see also Psalm 18:11);
Hebrew *massed*

NRSV

22 David spoke to the Lord the words of this song on the day when the Lord delivered him from the hand of all his enemies, and from the hand of Saul. ²He said:

The Lord is my rock, my fortress, and my
  deliverer,
³ my God, my rock, in whom I take refuge,
  my shield and the horn of my salvation,
  my stronghold and my refuge,
  my savior; you save me from violence.
⁴ I call upon the Lord, who is worthy to be
    praised,
  and I am saved from my enemies.

⁵ For the waves of death encompassed me,
  the torrents of perdition assailed me;
⁶ the cords of Sheol entangled me,
  the snares of death confronted me.

⁷ In my distress I called upon the Lord;
  to my God I called.
From his temple he heard my voice,
  and my cry came to his ears.

⁸ Then the earth reeled and rocked;
  the foundations of the heavens trembled
  and quaked, because he was angry.
⁹ Smoke went up from his nostrils,
  and devouring fire from his mouth;
  glowing coals flamed forth from him.
¹⁰ He bowed the heavens, and came down;
  thick darkness was under his feet.
¹¹ He rode on a cherub, and flew;
  he was seen upon the wings of the wind.
¹² He made darkness around him a canopy,
  thick clouds, a gathering of water.
¹³ Out of the brightness before him
  coals of fire flamed forth.
¹⁴ The Lord thundered from heaven;
  the Most High uttered his voice.
¹⁵ He sent out arrows, and scattered them
  —lightning, and routed them.
¹⁶ Then the channels of the sea were seen,
  the foundations of the world were laid
    bare
  at the rebuke of the Lord,

NIV

and the foundations of the earth laid bare
at the rebuke of the LORD,
    at the blast of breath from his nostrils.

17"He reached down from on high and took
        hold of me;
    he drew me out of deep waters.
18He rescued me from my powerful enemy,
    from my foes, who were too strong for me.
19They confronted me in the day of my disaster,
    but the LORD was my support.
20He brought me out into a spacious place;
    he rescued me because he delighted in me.

21"The LORD has dealt with me according to my
        righteousness;
    according to the cleanness of my hands he
        has rewarded me.
22For I have kept the ways of the LORD;
    I have not done evil by turning from my
        God.
23All his laws are before me;
    I have not turned away from his decrees.
24I have been blameless before him
    and have kept myself from sin.
25The LORD has rewarded me according to my
        righteousness,
    according to my cleanness*a* in his sight.

26"To the faithful you show yourself faithful,
    to the blameless you show yourself
        blameless,
27to the pure you show yourself pure,
    but to the crooked you show yourself
        shrewd.
28You save the humble,
    but your eyes are on the haughty to bring
        them low.
29You are my lamp, O LORD;
    the LORD turns my darkness into light.
30With your help I can advance against a troop*b*;
    with my God I can scale a wall.

31"As for God, his way is perfect;
    the word of the LORD is flawless.
He is a shield
    for all who take refuge in him.
32For who is God besides the LORD?
    And who is the Rock except our God?

*a25 Hebrew; Septuagint and Vulgate (see also Psalm 18:24) to the
cleanness of my hands   b30 Or can run through a barricade*

NRSV

at the blast of the breath of his nostrils.

17 He reached from on high, he took me,
    he drew me out of mighty waters.
18 He delivered me from my strong enemy,
    from those who hated me;
    for they were too mighty for me.
19 They came upon me in the day of my calamity,
    but the LORD was my stay.
20 He brought me out into a broad place;
    he delivered me, because he delighted in
        me.

21 The LORD rewarded me according to my
        righteousness;
    according to the cleanness of my hands
        he recompensed me.
22 For I have kept the ways of the LORD,
    and have not wickedly departed from my
        God.
23 For all his ordinances were before me,
    and from his statutes I did not turn aside.
24 I was blameless before him,
    and I kept myself from guilt.
25 Therefore the LORD has recompensed me
        according to my righteousness,
    according to my cleanness in his sight.

26 With the loyal you show yourself loyal;
    with the blameless you show yourself
        blameless;
27 with the pure you show yourself pure,
    and with the crooked you show yourself
        perverse.
28 You deliver a humble people,
    but your eyes are upon the haughty to
        bring them down.
29 Indeed, you are my lamp, O LORD,
    the LORD lightens my darkness.
30 By you I can crush a troop,
    and by my God I can leap over a wall.
31 This God—his way is perfect;
    the promise of the LORD proves true;
    he is a shield for all who take refuge in him.

32 For who is God, but the LORD?
    And who is a rock, except our God?
33 The God who has girded me with strength*a*

a Q Ms Gk Syr Vg Compare Ps 18.32: MT God is my strong refuge

NIV

³³It is God who arms me with strength^a
and makes my way perfect.
³⁴He makes my feet like the feet of a deer;
he enables me to stand on the heights.
³⁵He trains my hands for battle;
my arms can bend a bow of bronze.
³⁶You give me your shield of victory;
you stoop down to make me great.
³⁷You broaden the path beneath me,
so that my ankles do not turn.

³⁸"I pursued my enemies and crushed them;
I did not turn back till they were destroyed.
³⁹I crushed them completely, and they could
not rise;
they fell beneath my feet.
⁴⁰You armed me with strength for battle;
you made my adversaries bow at my feet.
⁴¹You made my enemies turn their backs in
flight,
and I destroyed my foes.
⁴²They cried for help, but there was no one to
save them—
to the LORD, but he did not answer.
⁴³I beat them as fine as the dust of the earth;
I pounded and trampled them like mud in
the streets.

⁴⁴"You have delivered me from the attacks of
my people;
you have preserved me as the head of nations.
People I did not know are subject to me,
⁴⁵   and foreigners come cringing to me;
as soon as they hear me, they obey me.
⁴⁶They all lose heart;
they come trembling^b from their strongholds.

⁴⁷"The LORD lives! Praise be to my Rock!
Exalted be God, the Rock, my Savior!
⁴⁸He is the God who avenges me,
who puts the nations under me,
⁴⁹   who sets me free from my enemies.
You exalted me above my foes;
from violent men you rescued me.
⁵⁰Therefore I will praise you, O LORD, among
the nations;
I will sing praises to your name.

^a33 Dead Sea Scrolls, some Septuagint manuscripts, Vulgate and Syriac (see also Psalm 18:32); Masoretic Text *who is my strong refuge*   ^b46 Some Septuagint manuscripts and Vulgate (see also Psalm 18:45); Masoretic Text *they arm themselves.*

NRSV

has opened wide my path.^a
³⁴ He made my^b feet like the feet of deer,
and set me secure on the heights.
³⁵ He trains my hands for war,
so that my arms can bend a bow of
bronze.
³⁶ You have given me the shield of your
salvation,
and your help^c has made me great.
³⁷ You have made me stride freely,
and my feet do not slip;
³⁸ I pursued my enemies and destroyed them,
and did not turn back until they were
consumed.
³⁹ I consumed them; I struck them down, so
that they did not rise;
they fell under my feet.
⁴⁰ For you girded me with strength for the
battle;
you made my assailants sink under me.
⁴¹ You made my enemies turn their backs to me,
those who hated me, and I destroyed
them.
⁴² They looked, but there was no one to save
them;
they cried to the LORD, but he did not
answer them.
⁴³ I beat them fine like the dust of the earth,
I crushed them and stamped them down
like the mire of the streets.

⁴⁴ You delivered me from strife with the
peoples;^d
you kept me as the head of the nations;
people whom I had not known served
me.
⁴⁵ Foreigners came cringing to me;
as soon as they heard of me, they obeyed
me.
⁴⁶ Foreigners lost heart,
and came trembling out of their
strongholds.

⁴⁷ The LORD lives! Blessed be my rock,
and exalted be my God, the rock of my
salvation,
⁴⁸ the God who gave me vengeance

^a Meaning of Heb uncertain   ^b Another reading is *his*   ^c Q Ms: MT *your answering*   ^d Gk: Heb *from strife with my people*

NIV

⁵¹He gives his king great victories;
    he shows unfailing kindness to his anointed,
    to David and his descendants forever."

NRSV

and brought down peoples under me,
⁴⁹ who brought me out from my enemies;
    you exalted me above my adversaries,
    you delivered me from the violent.

⁵⁰ For this I will extol you, O Lᴏʀᴅ, among
        the nations,
    and sing praises to your name.
⁵¹ He is a tower of salvation for his king,
    and shows steadfast love to his anointed,
    to David and his descendants forever.

COMMENTARY

This is the first of two songs that stand at the heart of the appendixes to the books of Samuel. It is a royal psalm of thanksgiving, attributed to David "when the Lᴏʀᴅ delivered him from the hand of all his enemies, and from the hand of Saul" (v. 1), and is a duplicate of Psalm 18. McCann has made a strong case that this psalm of thanksgiving had an eschatological orientation in Israel and in the psalter. It functioned to proclaim "the reign of God amid circumstances that suggest God does *not* reign."[354] Even in its setting in 2 Samuel, this psalm refers less to a celebration of the end of troubles for David himself and more to a confidence that God will bring deliverance for the house of David into the future (v. 51*c*).

This song, probably shaped in Israel's liturgical history, is now placed at the end of the books of Samuel as David's reflection on his entire career and as a theological comment on the books of Samuel. It complements the song of Hannah (1 Sam 2:1-10), celebrating in retrospect the same ultimate reality of the Lord's sovereignty that Hannah's song anticipated.[355] As we shall see, many themes appear in both these poetic pieces, which bracket the narratives of 1 and 2 Samuel.

The song falls into three distinct pieces. The separate emphases of these segments are crucial to understanding the role this song now plays

when it is placed in the mouth of David at the conclusion of his career (i.e., when the kingdom is secure from enemies).

The first section (vv. 1-20) is a thanksgiving for deliverance. It emphasizes the celebration of God's power to deliver from the threat of chaos. The king appears only as a supplicant. Verse 7 is the thematic key of this section, "I called . . . he heard. . . ." The poet focuses exclusively on the grace-filled activity of God's salvation.

The second section (vv. 21-28) extols human moral virtue and the power of righteousness to gain the Lord's favor. Both wisdom and deuteronomic influence have been attributed to this section, because it seems to accept a doctrine of strict retribution that is characteristic of these two traditions. The thematic key to this section comes in v. 24, "I was blameless before him." Here the emphasis is on human ability to claim God's grace by virtue of one's own righteousness.

The final section (vv. 29-51) offers yet another perspective. In the king's voice, God's ultimate power is acknowledged as central (e.g., v. 29, "Indeed, you are my lamp, O Lᴏʀᴅ"), but side by side with this acknowledgment is an affirmation of the king's own abilities and deeds (e.g., v. 30, "By you I can crush a troop"). This section is filled with the affirmation of heroic acts and mighty gifts, all celebrated in action verbs whose subject is "I." But constantly alongside the deeds of the royal "I," the poet acknowledges the divine, empowering "Thou." The king achieves great things through admirable abilities, but all that he does

354. J. Clinton McCann, Jr., *Psalms,* in *The New Interpreter's Bible,* vol. 4 (Nashville: Abingdon, 1996) 747.
355. See Brevard S. Childs, *Introduction to the Old Testament as Scripture* (Philadelphia: Fortress, 1979) 273-74; Brueggemann, *First and Second Samuel,* 339.

is enabled by the grace-filled activity of God, who deserves to be praised (v. 50). But God's salvation and steadfast love are given through God's king and God's anointed one: "David and his descendants forever" (v. 51). As a theological comment on David's story—indeed, the whole story of God's movement in Israel toward and through David—the final section of this psalm serves as a corrective to the first two segments.

God's salvation (emphasized in vv. 1-20) is crucial to Israel's future, but the stories of the books of Samuel stress the unique combination of divine providence with human personality, through which God has chosen to work. These stories do not fit the dictum of the exodus experience, "The LORD will fight for you, and you have only to keep still" (Exod 14:14). God's grace in deliverance is worthy of celebration, but if 1 and 2 Samuel celebrate divine power they also celebrate the man after God's own heart: David. Even when David grew weary (21:15), there were mighty men and mighty deeds through which God's deliverance was made visible.

In section two of this psalm (vv. 22-28), the emphasis on the king's righteousness and obedience as the source of God's blessing also does not ring completely true. At this point, near the end of David's story, we know that he did not remain blameless and without guilt. The king's moral virtue alone, even when the king is David, cannot assure God's salvation. A developing ideology of kingship may wish to assert royal control over the destiny of Israel, but the story of David makes clear that such an ideology stands on shaky ground. We can only read the assertions of vv. 21-28 ironically in the light of David's career, marred by his own guilt in "the matter of Uriah the Hittite" (1 Kgs 15:4).

It is only in section three of this song (vv. 29-51) that we come to the combination of royal gifts with the ultimate empowering (and forgiving) grace of God, which makes the future possible for God's people. "The outcome of such a three part juxtaposition is that the king who might wish to claim virtue and achievement for himself is like every other Israelite. He is only an empty-handed suppliant before Yahweh, totally dependent on Yahweh's willingness to listen and to answer and

intervene."[356] The king is nothing without the grace of God; nevertheless, God has chosen to work through David and the subsequent kings of his line. God has chosen to work messianically—that is, through God's anointed one. It is this combination of divine providence and human action that uniquely summarizes the books of Samuel and the story of David in particular.

22:1-20. Verse 1 serves as a superscription to this psalm, identifying the first-person royal voice in the psalm as David and identifying the occasion as the day when David was delivered from all his enemies and from Saul. The psalm itself does not derive from a specific time of deliverance, but instead to God's deliverance of God's king in all times of distress.

These initial verses are a thanksgiving for deliverance from distress. They open with a doxology in praise of the Lord that utilizes a rush of terms and titles signifying God's role as rescuer and protector (vv. 2-4). All of these terms are personalized by "the royal narrator" with the use of the possessive pronoun "my": rock, fortress, deliverer, refuge, shield, horn of salvation, stronghold, savior.

Doxology gives way to descriptions of distress in vv. 5-6. Such language is associated elsewhere with descriptions of chaos and Sheol (cf. Ps 116:3; Jonah 2:5-6a), and the stress is on the powerlessness of the royal suppliant before such chaotic forces: waves of death, torrents of perdition, cords of Sheol, and snares of death.

Verse 7 is the dramatic turning point in this part of the psalm. The king cries out, and God hears. It is classic exodus language, reflecting the covenantal traditions of Israel (Exod 2:23). What follows in vv. 8-20 is a richly embroidered poetic portrait of God's salvation—eminently capable of meeting the challenge of the chaotic powers described in vv. 5-6 and resulting in the salvation of the royal suppliant. The king's only role in this first segment of chap. 22 is that of one in need who cries out to God. God is the deliverer, described in theophanic terms arriving in power to work deliverance in a time of distress. Elements

---

356. Brueggemann, *Power, Providence, and Personality,* 97. Unlike Brueggemann I do not see the third section as a return to single-minded emphasis on God's grace alone, as in section one. God's willingness to act as "Thou" to the king's "I" is unique. The psalm ultimately affirms God's intention to act in and through God's "anointed" one in spite of human sin and guilt, which makes it so appropriate as a theological summation to the books of Samuel, and for Christians a prelude to God's "messianic" future.

of earthquake, smoke, and fire accompany God's appearance (vv. 8-9). God commands the clouds, rides on cherubs and the wind, thunders with his voice, hurls the lightning, and lays bare the sea and the earth's foundations with a blast from the divine nostrils (vv. 10-16). God's theophany delivers the suppliant. Matching the torrent of doxology in vv. 2-4 is a rush of verbs signifying deliverance in vv. 17-20: God "reached . . . took . . . drew me out . . . delivered . . . was my stay . . . brought me out . . . delighted in me." We reach the end of this first segment of the psalm surfeited in the language of divine salvation and grace. The poem focuses exclusively on God as the bringer of salvation.

22:21-28. Some have found the shift in language so startling with these verses that they discern a different author. In my view, this dramatic shift is an intentional literary device that serves well the purpose of this psalm. These verses shift the emphasis from divine saving initiatives to human righteousness and obedience and human moral ability to deserve God's blessing.

In tones reminiscent of Deuteronomy or Proverbs, this portion of the psalm asserts the importance of righteousness and obedience to God's covenant as moral qualities that God takes seriously. The psalmist parades terms indicative of the moral life for our attention: "righteousness," "cleanness of hands," "his ordinances before me," "his statutes I did not turn aside," "blameless," "kept from guilt," "loyal," "pure," "humble." We are torn between two sentiments as we read this section. We are properly impressed with the demands of the moral life lived in covenant obedience. Surely the Lord does regard such qualities, and we are reassured that such values matter in the eyes of God. But we also remember that these words are placed in the mouth of David, and when this Davidic voice claims, "I was blameless before him, and I kept myself from guilt" (v. 24a), we know that this has not always been the case. The words of such lofty ideals placed in the mouth of the man who took Bathsheba and killed Uriah become ironic and self-indicting. The words of this section are no less true as statements of what God desires, but David does not stand guiltless. This segment of the psalm stands as a testimony to the moral demands placed upon one who would be God's person, but in the light of David's story, we are grateful that we have already heard testi-

mony in vv. 2-20 to God's grace given without merit. Taken alone, these verses might well become the basis of a high royal theology that imagines the king can control his own fate or is blameless because he stands above blame. But because we know David's story, we know that this can never be true. Even David stands guilty before God. Fortunately, this segment of the psalm does not stand alone and must be read in the context of the full psalm.

22:29-51. The final segment of this psalm is a song of victory. It celebrates both the success of human action and the enabling power of God that makes such actions effective. In the first two verses of this section, we hear praise for God as "my lamp" who "lightens my darkness" (v. 29), followed by the affirmations that "I can crush a troop" or "leap over a wall" (v. 30). Even these human feats of prowess, however, are accomplished only "by you" and "by my God." It is significant that David here celebrates God as "lamp" when in 21:17b David's men feared to risk his life lest it quench the "lamp of Israel." David's light depends on God's light.

Throughout the remainder of this psalm, the royal voice celebrates the feats he has accomplished against enemies. Such language is sometimes placed in an exultant first-person voice: "I pursued . . . destroyed . . . did not turn back . . . consumed . . . struck down . . . they fell" (vv. 38-39). But the affirmations of the royal "I" are constantly balanced by acknowledgment of a divine "Thou" who enables victory against enemies and prowess as warrior. The voice speaking here admits that "your help has made me great" (v. 36b). Celebration of victory is punctuated with praise for the Lord who gives the victory (vv. 32, 47, 50).

It is with the final verse (v. 51) that the full contrast of this final section with the first two sections of the song becomes clear. God is the true source of deliverance (vv. 2-20), and human righteousness does count (vv. 21-28). But in David and his descendants, God has chosen to work salvation through the Davidic king and to show steadfast love by means of the anointed one. The king alone cannot secure the future in righteousness—even David is a sinner—and God has chosen not to act alone but through David, God's anointed king. In the end, this psalm celebrates this partnership for the sake of Israel's salvation.

REFLECTIONS

Many important elements of this psalm are given reflection in the section on Psalm 18 in volume IV of *The New Interpreter's Bible*. I limit reflections here to aspects that seem especially significant to the setting of this psalm at the conclusion of David's story.

1. Some of the imagery of this psalm will seem strange to our modern ears, especially the dramatic theophanic images of 22:8-20. Yet, the threat of chaos is a reality with which most can identify. Brueggemann writes, "Indeed, chaos (and not guilt) is the besetting issue in our common experience. The threat of chaos is known most intimately in broken interpersonal relationships. The same threat is known most massively and publicly in relation to the looming danger of nuclear holocaust."[357]

2. In some ways we have retained a sense of the invading reality of chaos and its threat to our attempts at ordered meaning to our lives, but we have lost the corresponding language of deliverance that speaks in the same elemental way against the threat of chaos. We live in a time enamored of our own human capacities. When these capacities fail to deliver us from the crises (the times of chaos) in our life, we often discover that we have lost touch with a sense of divine power capable of driving back the darkness and restoring order in the midst of chaos.

Recovery of a sense of a power beyond our own human capacities requires a boldness of speech about God's power beyond our power, as this psalm models. Such speech does not allow denial of our need for deliverance, as if we could save ourselves. Such speech does not sink into despair that chaos cannot be overcome, for it boldly speaks of a power capable of overcoming chaos.

In terms of this psalm, our generation (and especially the church) has been drawn to the ordered, moral universe suggested by the second section of this psalm (22:21-28). The cool, rational, didactic approach of obeying commandments and seeking righteousness tempts us into thinking that our own efforts can control chaos. In the face of difficult and divisive moral issues (such as sexual orientation, abortion, the changing shape of the family, economic materialism, and nuclear war), the church is more prone to establish study commissions, to pass carefully worded resolutions, or sometimes to seek settlement of the issue by legislation that defines righteousness. One of the teachings of this psalm may be that such didactic approaches to vexing moral questions only have their place in the context of a more elemental confidence and celebration of God's power to overcome chaos and to establish the kingdom. Such a confidence in God's ultimate reign over creation and history may let us regard our own efforts as less ultimate. Such a confidence may allow acceptance of differences in the confidence that God will ultimately vanquish the genuine enemies of God's kingdom. Such a confidence will require a boldness of speech about God's salvation that recognizes that our own moral efforts remain important, but cannot alone save us.

3. In the end this psalm teaches us something about God's willingness to act with, through, and even in spite of our humanness—both in David's story and our own. This psalm declares that God has chosen to make Israel's salvation (and ours) a divine-human enterprise. In this psalm, it is the confession of the human "I" that what enables wholeness and success in our own efforts is the power of the divine "Thou." In the Christian faith, the word for this confessional reality is *incarnation*. We know God's steadfast love through God's "anointed" (v. 51), through "messiah" (the Hebrew term for "anointed one"). For Christians, the claim that Jesus Christ was born in the line of David is precisely made in order to claim as a part

---

357. Walter Brueggemann, *First and Second Samuel,* Interpretation (Louisville: John Knox, 1990) 342.

of the meaning of Christ the story of God acting in, through, and in spite of David. In incarnation, Christians claim the tradition summarized by this psalm and its ultimate celebration of a divine-human partnership through which salvation comes. Hannah's song (1 Sam 2:1-10) began the story of God's salvation through David, and Mary's song (Luke 1:46-55) echoed it to begin the story of God's salvation through Jesus. Now this psalm of deliverance, obedience, and partnership between God and God's anointed one ends David's story and is echoed in the New Testament claim that Jesus, divine and human, is the son of David.

2 Samuel 23:1-7, David's Last Words

NIV

23 These are the last words of David:

"The oracle of David son of Jesse,
    the oracle of the man exalted by the Most
        High,
the man anointed by the God of Jacob,
    Israel's singer of songs[a]:

2"The Spirit of the LORD spoke through me;
    his word was on my tongue.
3The God of Israel spoke,
    the Rock of Israel said to me:
'When one rules over men in righteousness,
    when he rules in the fear of God,
4he is like the light of morning at sunrise
    on a cloudless morning,
like the brightness after rain
    that brings the grass from the earth.'

5"Is not my house right with God?
    Has he not made with me an everlasting
        covenant,
    arranged and secured in every part?
Will he not bring to fruition my salvation
    and grant me my every desire?
6But evil men are all to be cast aside like
        thorns,
    which are not gathered with the hand.
7Whoever touches thorns
    uses a tool of iron or the shaft of a spear;
    they are burned up where they lie."

a1 Or *Israel's beloved singer*

NRSV

23 Now these are the last words of David:
The oracle of David, son of Jesse,
    the oracle of the man whom God
        exalted,[a]
the anointed of the God of Jacob,
    the favorite of the Strong One of Israel:

2 The spirit of the LORD speaks through me,
    his word is upon my tongue.
3 The God of Israel has spoken,
    the Rock of Israel has said to me:
One who rules over people justly,
    ruling in the fear of God,
4 is like the light of morning,
    like the sun rising on a cloudless morning,
    gleaming from the rain on the grassy land.

5 Is not my house like this with God?
    For he has made with me an everlasting
        covenant,
    ordered in all things and secure.
Will he not cause to prosper
    all my help and my desire?
6 But the godless are[b] all like thorns that are
        thrown away;
    for they cannot be picked up with the
        hand;
7 to touch them one uses an iron bar
    or the shaft of a spear.
    And they are entirely consumed in fire
        on the spot.[c]

a Q Ms: MT *who was raised on high*   b Heb *But worthlessness*
c Heb *in sitting*

COMMENTARY

This is the second of the two songs that stand together at the heart of the so-called appendixes (2 Samuel 21–24). Although it is considerably shorter, this poetic piece, like 22:1-51, is a statement of idealized royal theology. Together these two songs at the end of David's career serve as a counterpart to the song of Hannah in 1 Sam 2:1-10. Hannah sang in anticipation of God's anointed one and the power of God through this royal agent to reverse the injustices of the world. The songs set in the mouth of David in 22:1-51 and 23:1-7 make clear that God has not abandoned the divine resolve to work through God's anointed king. These "last words of David" in 23:1-7 emphasize that God's covenant promise is everlasting (v. 5). Moreover, the well-being of God's people requires that the king rule "justly" and in the "fear of God" (vv. 3-4). After the stories of David's abuse of power and the tragic re-enactment of those abuses by his sons and others in his kingdom (2 Samuel 11–20), these last words of David come as a reminder of the royal ideal to which God will hold the anointed one in spite of the temptations presented by royal power. This poem articulates the continuing hope that God's king can be an agent of God's Word and Spirit (v. 2), in spite of the shortcomings of David. It speaks of the hope for just rule through kingship understood as divine gift, not simply as the result of human power. It is against such hope, centered in what God is doing in Israel's midst, that not only David but all future kings in the line of David can be held accountable, and God's commitment to "everlasting covenant" can be understood. The politics of royal power must be measured against the demands of divine justice and the certainty of divine commitment.

Interestingly, these "last words of David" are presented as an "oracle" of David (v. 1a). The word נְאֻם (nĕʾum), here translated "oracle," usually refers to a "prophetic utterance." Since David speaks of God's word on his tongue and the Spirit of the Lord speaking through him (v. 2), we conclude that David is portrayed here as a prophetic figure, receiving and proclaiming the word of the Lord as well as functioning as God's anointed king (v. 1b). Perhaps this picture of

David as prophet originated with some of the other prophetic influences that we have noticed earlier in the books of Samuel (see Introduction).

In keeping with a common pattern for such oracles (see Balaam's oracle, Num 24:3, 15), there is an introduction of the oracle giver and an acknowledgment of God as the source of this word in vv. 1-2, followed by the direct reporting of God's word in vv. 3-4. David interrupts this word from the Lord (v. 5), affirming that his rule has embodied this word and that, as a consequence, he has received God's covenant and blessing (v. 5). Verses 6-7 resume and conclude God's word. It has often been noticed that the word of the Lord in vv. 4, 6-7 bears similarities to wisdom literature in its contrast of the righteous and the wicked, its use of metaphors drawn from nature, and its appeal to the fear of God.

23:1-2. Following a superscription that labels this song as the "last words of David" (v. 1a), David announces that he speaks an "oracle," which comes through him as God's "word" enabled by the "Spirit of the Lord" (vv. 1-2). The vocabulary is that of prophetic utterance, and the opening formula is virtually identical to that used by Balaam in beginning his oracle in Num 24:3. As readers of 2 Samuel, we have seen the temptation to understand royal power through taking and grasping (as the prophet Samuel had warned, 1 Sam 8:10-18), but now in the poetic oracle of a prophetic David, we hear him acknowledge that it is God who exalts a man to kingship (v. 1b);[358] it is not a human accomplishment. The king is the anointed of God (v. 1b) and not of the people. It is from the "Strong One of Israel" that favor comes (v. 1b),[359] and not from the wielding of political power. The testimony of this song does not come as a summing up of David's wisdom and experience. It comes through the "Spirit of

---

358. We read אֵל (ʾēl, "God"; see NRSV) with the Dead Sea Scroll fragment 4QSamᵃ in place of עַל (ʿal, "on high" or "Most High"; see NIV) in the MT. See P. Kyle McCarter, *II Samuel*, AB 9 (Garden City, N.Y.: Doubleday, 1984) 477, for a detailed discussion of alternatives.

359. The traditional rendering of this phrase as "the sweet singer [or psalmist] of Israel" (NIV, "Israel's singer of songs") is possible, but most recent commentators and translations have read the terms זְמִרוֹת יִשְׂרָאֵל (zĕmirôt yiśrāʾēl) as an epithet for God parallel to the phrase "God of Jacob" in the preceding line. It is variously translated as "protector of Israel," "Strong One of Israel" (NRSV), or "Stronghold of Israel." See ibid., 480.

the LORD" as God's "word" on David's tongue (v. 2). At the end of David's story, we are reminded in this song that God has been the initiator and shaper of a new future for Israel.

23:3-4. David announces and speaks the word of God; the text of this word begins in v. 3*b* (the NIV indicates this with quotation marks). The king is to rule justly and in the fear of God (v. 3*b*). When justice and piety are joined in the rule of the kingdom, then the result will be like the benefits of light from the sun and rain on the land in a well-ordered creation (v. 4). The imagery from nature and the admonition to the fear of God are reminiscent of wisdom literature. But wise rule here clearly arises from attending to matters of justice that temper the exercise of self-interested power. And wise rule requires that the king recognize God as the source from which royal power is derived, if it is to give life as sun and rain give life to the earth.

David's story has not always reflected this commitment to justice. As a result, death rather than life became actualized in his family and kingdom. But the ideal of kingship as God's anointed requires justice at the heart of any exercise of power, lest it be used to exploit, manipulate, or oppress. Those responsible for these final chapters of 2 Samuel have not allowed the tragic stories of grasping, self-interested power that marked the later years of David and his family to have the final word. Israel's poets can imagine a vision of the just and faithful king that outlives the realities of David's failures. This song leaves as David's legacy a royal ideal that is more enduring than royal reality, which always falls short of God's intentions (see Psalm 72 for a fuller poetic articulation of this ideal). The king can be a source of life and renewal to God's people, but only by attending to the justice and faithfulness that are the conditions of life-giving rule.

23:5. This verse seems like a comment by David instead of God's word. Read in this way, there is an exuberant quality to David's break into

the moment with his own word: "Is not my house like this with God?" Our first reaction might be incredulous. David's house has been far from justice and faithfulness in previous episodes, and yet the humility of David in retreat from Jerusalem and the grief of David as bereft father have shown us a David defined by more than self-serving power.

The key to David's outburst may be found in his answer to his own question (v. 5*b*). The capacity for David's house to be just and faithful lies not in what David or those who come after him can achieve, but in God's commitment in "everlasting covenant" with David and his line (reflecting 2 Sam 7:14-16). If justice and faithfulness were left to human capacities alone, all would be doomed to fail. David can sin, but he can reclaim the vision of just and faithful rule because God's commitment never wavers. God is the true source of order, security, prosperity, and help (v. 5*b*). These do not exist as human achievements but as God-given possibilities, given again and again in everlasting covenant. David's house cannot be "like this" alone, but only "with God" (v. 5*a*). God's fidelity makes justice and faithfulness possible in spite of our sinful grasping after power.

23:6-7. These verses resume the divine oracle David is declaring. They provide an antithesis to vv. 3*b*-4. If the just and faithful king brings the renewal of life, then the "godless" (NRSV) or "evil" (NIV) bring death. The poet uses imagery, not of renewed and productive nature, but of thorns that choke life and cause pain (v. 6). Their fate is to perish (v. 7). The Hebrew word here is בְלִיַּעַל (*bĕliyyaʿal*), a word often translated as "worthless ones" but is also associated with injustice and impiety—i.e., the opposite of God's king as envisioned in v. 3*b*. It is interesting to note that, following Hannah's song (1 Sam 2:1-10), with its anticipation of God's justice through God's anointed one, we immediately see the contrast to God's anointed in the injustices committed by Eli's sons, who are also called *bĕliyyaʿal* (1 Sam 2:12).

REFLECTIONS

Those responsible for the appendixes in chaps. 21–24 knew the realistic story of David's misuse of power and its consequences. As readers of 2 Samuel, we, too, have seen David misuse his power to take and kill, and we have seen the consequences in his own family. We know the unfortunate reality alongside the hoped-for ideal of God's anointed king. But the segments of the appendixes, and this poetic song in particular, seek to reimagine the future from the perspective of what God is doing in David (and in kingship), and not through what David has done. This is the key. Israel's future and our own future are not dependent on what human power has realistically done or can do. For those who dare to imagine it, and give poetic voice to it, the future is God's future and, therefore, is always open to the possibilities of justice, faithfulness, and life no matter how realistic might be our assessment of the powers of oppression, sin, and death. Surrounded by a troubled and broken world and the crises of our own lives, we lose sight of God's power at work beyond and in spite of our own human limitations and sin. In the name of realism, we define ourselves, our goals, our communities by our failures and not by our visions. We settle for problems to solve rather than ideals to embody.

We live in a world where even the best of our leaders, in church and nation, seem to acquiesce in the so-called realities of violence, marketplace, self-sufficiency, and arrogant certitude. Even in facing these realities as problematic we allow them to define the terms of our life. There is a dearth of those who would reimagine the future in different terms. In particular, the church should give leadership in such reimagining because we know the reality of God beyond the realities of the world. We should dare to dream dreams and see visions, because we trust that God is at work to bring possibilities for life, hope, love, and justice that go beyond the sum total of our human capacities. To read David's final song should not lead us to sneer at its unrealistic idealism. We should instead hear in its images the call to declare anew for our time that God's justice and faithfulness define the vision that leads to life. This is the truth of the world's reality, no matter how often we fall short of fully actualizing that vision. David's song calls us to reimagine our future as God's future. If we are so busy in the church realistically analyzing our institutional and societal issues that we fail to dream dreams or see visions, then we will perish like the "worthless ones" of 23:6-7. If, however, we claim with David the everlasting covenant of God's promise (23:5), then the hope of our future will be based in a reality that transcends the powers of this world. Our hope can never settle for the realistic assessment of human possibilities. Just and faithful human rule is always rooted in the trustworthiness of God's promises.

2 Samuel 23:8-39, Exploits of David's Warriors

NIV

[8]These are the names of David's mighty men:

Josheb-Basshebeth,[a] a Tahkemonite,[b] was chief of the Three; he raised his spear against eight hundred men, whom he killed[c] in one encounter.

[9]Next to him was Eleazar son of Dodai the Ahohite. As one of the three mighty men, he was with David when they taunted the Philistines gathered ⌊at Pas Dammim,⌋[d] for battle. Then the men of Israel retreated, [10]but he stood his ground and struck down the Philistines till his hand grew

a8 Hebrew; some Septuagint manuscripts suggest *Ish-Bosheth,* that is, *Esh-Baal* (see also 1 Chron. 11:11 *Jashobeam*).   b8 Probably a variant of *Hacmonite* (see 1 Chron. 11:11)   c8 Some Septuagint manuscripts (see also 1 Chron. 11:11); Hebrew and other Septuagint manuscripts *Three; it was Adino the Eznite who killed eight hundred men*   d9 See 1 Chron. 11:13; Hebrew *gathered there.*

NRSV

[8]These are the names of the warriors whom David had: Josheb-basshebeth a Tahchemonite; he was chief of the Three;[a] he wielded his spear[b] against eight hundred whom he killed at one time.

[9]Next to him among the three warriors was Eleazar son of Dodo son of Ahohi. He was with David when they defied the Philistines who were gathered there for battle. The Israelites withdrew, [10]but he stood his ground. He struck down the Philistines until his arm grew weary, though his hand clung to the sword. The LORD brought about a great victory that day. Then the people came back to him—but only to strip the dead.

a Gk Vg Compare 1 P5 11.11: Meaning of Heb uncertain   b 1 Chr 11.11: Meaning of Heb uncertain

tired and froze to the sword. The LORD brought about a great victory that day. The troops returned to Eleazar, but only to strip the dead.

[11] Next to him was Shammah son of Agee the Hararite. When the Philistines banded together at a place where there was a field full of lentils, Israel's troops fled from them. [12] But Shammah took his stand in the middle of the field. He defended it and struck the Philistines down, and the LORD brought about a great victory.

[13] During harvest time, three of the thirty chief men came down to David at the cave of Adullam, while a band of Philistines was encamped in the Valley of Rephaim. [14] At that time David was in the stronghold, and the Philistine garrison was at Bethlehem. [15] David longed for water and said, "Oh, that someone would get me a drink of water from the well near the gate of Bethlehem!" [16] So the three mighty men broke through the Philistine lines, drew water from the well near the gate of Bethlehem and carried it back to David. But he refused to drink it; instead, he poured it out before the LORD. [17] "Far be it from me, O LORD, to do this!" he said. "Is it not the blood of men who went at the risk of their lives?" And David would not drink it.

Such were the exploits of the three mighty men.

[18] Abishai the brother of Joab son of Zeruiah was chief of the Three.[e] He raised his spear against three hundred men, whom he killed, and so he became as famous as the Three. [19] Was he not held in greater honor than the Three? He became their commander, even though he was not included among them.

[20] Benaiah son of Jehoiada was a valiant fighter from Kabzeel, who performed great exploits. He struck down two of Moab's best men. He also went down into a pit on a snowy day and killed a lion. [21] And he struck down a huge Egyptian. Although the Egyptian had a spear in his hand, Benaiah went against him with a club. He snatched the spear from the Egyptian's hand and killed him with his own spear. [22] Such were the exploits of Benaiah son of Jehoiada; he too was as famous as the three mighty men. [23] He was held

[11] Next to him was Shammah son of Agee, the Hararite. The Philistines gathered together at Lehi, where there was a plot of ground full of lentils; and the army fled from the Philistines. [12] But he took his stand in the middle of the plot, defended it, and killed the Philistines; and the LORD brought about a great victory.

[13] Towards the beginning of harvest three of the thirty[c] chiefs went down to join David at the cave of Adullam, while a band of Philistines was encamped in the valley of Rephaim. [14] David was then in the stronghold; and the garrison of the Philistines was then at Bethlehem. [15] David said longingly, "O that someone would give me water to drink from the well of Bethlehem that is by the gate!" [16] Then the three warriors broke through the camp of the Philistines, drew water from the well of Bethlehem that was by the gate, and brought it to David. But he would not drink of it; he poured it out to the LORD, [17] for he said, "The LORD forbid that I should do this. Can I drink the blood of the men who went at the risk of their lives?" Therefore he would not drink it. The three warriors did these things.

[18] Now Abishai son of Zeruiah, the brother of Joab, was chief of the Thirty.[d] With his spear he fought against three hundred men and killed them, and won a name beside the Three. [19] He was the most renowned of the Thirty,[e] and became their commander; but he did not attain to the Three.

[20] Benaiah son of Jehoiada was a valiant warrior[f] from Kabzeel, a doer of great deeds; he struck down two sons of Ariel[g] of Moab. He also went down and killed a lion in a pit on a day when snow had fallen. [21] And he killed an Egyptian, a handsome man. The Egyptian had a spear in his hand; but Benaiah went against him with a staff, snatched the spear out of the Egyptian's hand, and killed him with his own spear. [22] Such were the things Benaiah son of Jehoiada did, and won a name beside the three warriors. [23] He was renowned among the Thirty, but he did not attain to the Three. And David put him in charge of his bodyguard.

[24] Among the Thirty were Asahel brother of

NIV

in greater honor than any of the Thirty, but he was not included among the Three. And David put him in charge of his bodyguard.

24Among the Thirty were:

Asahel the brother of Joab,
Elhanan son of Dodo from Bethlehem,
25Shammah the Harodite,
Elika the Harodite,
26Helez the Paltite,
Ira son of Ikkesh from Tekoa,
27Abiezer from Anathoth,
Mebunnai*a* the Hushathite,
28Zalmon the Ahohite,
Maharai the Netophathite,
29Heled*b* son of Baanah the Netophathite,
Ithai son of Ribai from Gibeah in Benjamin,
30Benaiah the Pirathonite,
Hiddai*c* from the ravines of Gaash,
31Abi-Albon the Arbathite,
Azmaveth the Barhumite,
32Eliahba the Shaalbonite,
the sons of Jashen,
Jonathan 33son of*d* Shammah the Hararite,
Ahiam son of Sharar*e* the Hararite,
34Eliphelet son of Ahasbai the Maacathite,
Eliam son of Ahithophel the Gilonite,
35Hezro the Carmelite,
Paarai the Arbite,
36Igal son of Nathan from Zobah,
the son of Hagri,*f*
37Zelek the Ammonite,
Naharai the Beerothite, the armor-bearer of
    Joab son of Zeruiah,
38Ira the Ithrite,
Gareb the Ithrite
39and Uriah the Hittite.
There were thirty-seven in all.

a27 Hebrew; some Septuagint manuscripts (see also 1 Chron. 11:29) *Sibbecai*   *b29* Some Hebrew manuscripts and Vulgate (see also 1 Chron. 11:30); most Hebrew manuscripts *Heleb*   *c30* Hebrew; some Septuagint manuscripts (see also 1 Chron. 11:32) *Hurai*   *d33* Some Septuagint manuscripts (see also 1 Chron. 11:34); Hebrew does not have *son of*.   *e33* Hebrew; some Septuagint manuscripts (see also 1 Chron. 11:35) *Sacar*   *f36* Some Septuagint manuscripts (see also 1 Chron. 11:38); Hebrew *Haggadi*

NRSV

Joab; Elhanan son of Dodo of Bethlehem; 25Shammah of Harod; Elika of Harod; 26Helez the Paltite; Ira son of Ikkesh of Tekoa; 27Abiezer of Anathoth; Mebunnai the Hushathite; 28Zalmon the Ahohite; Maharai of Netophah; 29Heleb son of Baanah of Netophah; Ittai son of Ribai of Gibeah of the Benjaminites; 30Benaiah of Pirathon; Hiddai of the torrents of Gaash; 31Abi-albon the Arbathite; Azmaveth of Bahurim; 32Eliahba of Shaalbon; the sons of Jashen: Jonathan 33son of*a* Shammah the Hararite; Ahiam son of Sharar the Hararite; 34Eliphelet son of Ahasbai of Maacah; Eliam son of Ahithophel the Gilonite; 35Hezro*b* of Carmel; Paarai the Arbite; 36Igal son of Nathan of Zobah; Bani the Gadite; 37Zelek the Ammonite; Naharai of Beeroth, the armor-bearer of Joab son of Zeruiah; 38Ira the Ithrite; Gareb the Ithrite; 39Uriah the Hittite—thirty-seven in all.

a Gk: Heb lacks *son of*   *b* Another reading is *Hezrai*

COMMENTARY

In the symmetrical arrangement of the appendixes to 2 Samuel, this list of David's warriors and their exploits corresponds to the list in 21:15-21. This section, however, is actually composed of two lists separated by a brief narrative about David and his men: vv. 8-12, a list of the Three and their exploits; this list identifies David's most prominent warriors and documents their prowess in single-handed combat against the Philistines; vv. 13-17, a narrative account of an incident involving David and three unnamed warriors (the editor may have assumed they were the Three); the account stresses the solidarity between David and his men.; vv. 18-39, a list of the Thirty, apparently a military unit made up of David's most effective fighting men; the list details exploits of two who rose to military command positions and simply names others; the list concludes with Uriah the Hittite (see 2 Samuel 11).

This section is in keeping with the tendency of the appendixes to offer alternatives to the bureaucracy and ideology of kingship that characterize the narratives of David at the height of his power. The lists here are remarkable for the absence of any reference to David. Israel had other heroes than David. The kingdom and its successes, particularly against the Philistines, were not totally dependent on David. However, the mention of victory as the gift of the Lord (vv. 10, 12) makes clear that the kingdom's future has been in God's hands. Brueggemann sees theonomous and democratic tendencies working together here in an alternative reading of the David tradition:

> It is likely that the *theonomous* inclination of the narrative, which credits Yahweh, and the *democratic* tendency, which names other heroes, are related to each other. State absolutism will attempt to silence theonomy and to nullify democracy. The list thus makes an important statement about social power. The list specifies and celebrates theonomous, democratic power as the proper way of David's rule; and it warns against absolutism which would credit neither Yahweh nor other human heroes.[360]

When David does appear in this section, it is in a narrative (vv. 13-17) that stresses his solidar-

ity with his men, the common humanity he shares with them, and his wise refusal to elevate himself above them. It cannot be accidental that the list of the Thirty ends this section with the naming of Uriah the Hittite (v. 39). The mention of his name speaks eloquently without explicit moralizing. He is among those heroes on whose exploits the kingdom and David's successes depended. He was among those with whom David once acknowledged a deep solidarity. Our knowledge of the reason for his untimely departure from the ranks of the Thirty (2 Samuel 11) speaks volumes about the dangers of a royal ideology and practice that loses touch with its foundations in the work of the Lord and the support of the community.

23:8-12. Three great warriors are named and praised for their effectiveness in single-handed combat against the Philistines, often in situations where the Israelite army had fled in panic. Their names are Josheb-basshebeth,[361] Eleazar, and Shammah. We know nothing of their deeds outside of these notices. They do not appear as companions of David elsewhere in the stories of David, although the editor who arranged the material of this chapter may have assumed they were the unnamed three of vv. 13-17. Josheb-basshebeth was the chief or commander of the Three. The "Three" seems to be a designation for a formal elite unit or rank in Israel's militia under David, at least in the early period of the Philistine wars (note vv. 8, 19, 23).

Twice in recounting the exploits of the Three, the narrator gives credit for their victory to the Lord (vv. 10, 12). This recognition of the power of God working through human exploits characterizes the traditions about the early David and his successes (see the concluding summary of the rise of David, 2 Sam 5:10), but is notably absent in the accounts of David's wars as king (2 Samuel 8 and 10). The narrator responsible for arranging these appendixes may have intended to reaffirm

---

360. Brueggemann, *First and Second Samuel,* 348.

361. Some Greek MSS read this name as "Eshbaal" or "Ishbaal," which may have been deliberately altered to remove the element "baal" from the name (see Commentary on 2:8). 1 Chr 11:11 has the name as "Jashobeam." The chronicler also has variant names for many in the list of the Thirty as well as some additional names. See P. Kyle McCarter, *II Samuel,* AB 9 (Garden City, N.Y.: Doubleday, 1984) 489-99, for a detailed discussion of the many textual variants in the names listed here and in 1 Chronicles.

this theonomous principle as a corrective to the tendency of royal ideology to self-sufficiency.

23:13-17. This brief narrative tells of a time when a Philistine garrison occupied David's home in Bethlehem (v. 14). David, who is at his stronghold in the cave of Adullam (v. 13), tells three of his warriors that he wants a drink from the well in Bethlehem (v. 15). In this very human and intimate portrait, David is unfettered by royal pretensions and office. He shares his basic, human desires with his men.

But this story is also about the loyalty of David's men to him. At considerable risk, they break through the Philistine defenses at Bethlehem, draw water from the well there, and bring it back to David (v. 16*a*). It is an act of foolishly touching bravery and solidarity with their leader.

David's response is truly remarkable for its instinctive grasp of what is at stake here. David perceives that water brought at such risk and such commitment cannot be treated as the ordinary drink that might be brought by a subordinate to one in authority. In the mere bringing of such a costly gift there was a solidarity between David and his men that could not be broken by the exercise of his own satisfaction. David pours the water on the ground, but he does so as an act of offering to the Lord (v. 16*b*). The water is treated, not as worthless, but as so valuable that it can be offered only to God. David stands in solidarity with his men, refusing to be the one worthy of such a gift. He treats the water as a sacrament, saying that it represents the very blood of the men who risked their lives for it (v. 17).

This is not the David of kingly office and royal authority who is "worth ten thousand of us" (18:3). David's leadership is recognized here as rooted in solidarity with his men, not his elevation above them. It is a fitting reminder near the end of David's story of the qualities that brought him to leadership and eventually to the throne, lest the temptations of royal power isolate him from the possibilities of solidarity with his people.

23:18-39. The chapter closes with a list of the Thirty. This group, like the Three, seems to be an elite corps of warriors on whom David relied, particularly early in his career. The author gives two of them special treatment by reporting some of their heroic exploits. One of these is Abishai, the brother of Joab, and a frequent, if hotheaded, companion of David in his early exploits (see, e.g., 1 Sam 26:6-8; 2 Sam 16:9-12). Abishai is credited here with becoming commander of the Thirty (vv. 18-19). Benaiah is also accorded this extended treatment (vv. 20-23), and his mighty deeds are recounted. He, too, rises to a position of command. He was placed in charge of David's bodyguard (v. 23), which probably meant the mercenaries who formed David's own personal militia. Benaiah later plays a role in the palace intrigues around the succession to the throne when David is on his deathbed (1 Kings 1–2).

The remainder of the Thirty are simply listed by name, with some reference to family or place (vv. 24-39). The concluding formula states that there were thirty-seven men in all (v. 39), but it is impossible to find this many names even with the inclusion of Abishai, Benaiah, and the Three. The most striking feature of the list is the absence of one name, Joab. Joab is David's most frequent military companion, and, aside from David, the most prominent military leader in Israel. He is listed twice as the commander of David's army (8:16; 20:23). He was the brother of Abishai, commander of the Thirty, and of Asahel, also listed in the Thirty (v. 24), who was killed by Abner in an incident while David was king of Judah (2:18-23). Perhaps, as commander of the army Joab was considered to be above and outside the Three and the Thirty. Ending this list of heroes with the name of Uriah the Hittite makes a final comment on a less than heroic side of David's tradition.

REFLECTIONS

1. Effective and charismatic leaders always face the danger of creating a cult of personality among their followers, thus losing touch with the very people who admire them and helped to make for their success. History is replete with examples. The two lists (23:8-12, 18-39) and the intervening narrative (23:13-17) of this section seem intended to warn of this danger with respect to David. David was not the only man helping to forge Israel's future by brave and sacrificial deeds, and what made him most effective as a leader was his solidarity with his men, not his authority over them.

This intended corrective to the David tradition can serve as a warning to us as well. It is all too easy for those in positions of leadership to become isolated and to forget the many contributions made by persons who contribute without getting as much recognition—elected officials forget voters, clergy ignore laity, teachers patronize students, parents demean or overprotect children. The configurations of power that seem most admired in our society and in our churches tend to be hierarchical, self-sufficient, and self-promoting. This section suggests that this is a false perception. Real leadership and true power arise out of recognition of solidarity with community and with God. Such solidarity is offered here as a corrective to the ideology of royal power that led David into tragedy and loss. We may read this section as a corrective to our own tendencies to follow David's example (2 Samuel 11–20) into false ideologies of autonomous and isolated power.

2. There is a helpful insight for the church in the story of David's thirst and the water his men procured at great risk, only to have David pour it out before the Lord. The story suggests that the church might think more carefully about the role of liturgical acts in acknowledging and calling us to solidarity with one another. Liturgical acts, when properly focused on God and engaged in as the work of the community, have the power to subvert the imagination in favor of possibilities that undermine accepted notions of power and authority in the world. When we come together as a community before God, liturgical acts call us away from autonomy into solidarity, away from grasping into giving, and away from self-congratulation to acknowledgment of interdependence and mutual need. If the church is to participate in the emergence of new power arrangements for a new community, then it will first have to risk acts of liturgical imagination that, like David's pouring out of the water, create a sense of solidarity with one another before God. We refuse to allow personal satisfaction or fulfillment (drinking the water) as an appropriate goal for our liturgical life together. Worship is directed to God rather than to our own needs. Worship is the work that makes community, not our own self-fulfillment.

2 Samuel 24:1-25, David's Census and the Threshing Floor of Araunah

NIV

24 Again the anger of the LORD burned against Israel, and he incited David against them, saying, "Go and take a census of Israel and Judah."

²So the king said to Joab and the army commanders[a] with him, "Go throughout the tribes of Israel from Dan to Beersheba and enroll the fighting men, so that I may know how many there are."

³But Joab replied to the king, "May the LORD your God multiply the troops a hundred times over, and may the eyes of my lord the king see it. But why does my lord the king want to do such a thing?"

[a]2 Septuagint (see also verse 4 and 1 Chron. 21:2); Hebrew *Joab the army commander*

NRSV

24 Again the anger of the LORD was kindled against Israel, and he incited David against them, saying, "Go, count the people of Israel and Judah." ²So the king said to Joab and the commanders of the army,[a] who were with him, "Go through all the tribes of Israel, from Dan to Beer-sheba, and take a census of the people, so that I may know how many there are." ³But Joab said to the king, "May the LORD your God increase the number of the people a hundredfold, while the eyes of my lord the king can still see it! But why does my lord the king want to do this?" ⁴But the king's word prevailed against Joab and the commanders of the army. So Joab and the com-

[a]1 Chr 21.2 Gk: Heb *to Joab the commander of the army*

NIV

[4]The king's word, however, overruled Joab and the army commanders; so they left the presence of the king to enroll the fighting men of Israel.

[5]After crossing the Jordan, they camped near Aroer, south of the town in the gorge, and then went through Gad and on to Jazer. [6]They went to Gilead and the region of Tahtim Hodshi, and on to Dan Jaan and around toward Sidon. [7]Then they went toward the fortress of Tyre and all the towns of the Hivites and Canaanites. Finally, they went on to Beersheba in the Negev of Judah.

[8]After they had gone through the entire land, they came back to Jerusalem at the end of nine months and twenty days.

[9]Joab reported the number of the fighting men to the king: In Israel there were eight hundred thousand able-bodied men who could handle a sword, and in Judah five hundred thousand.

[10]David was conscience-stricken after he had counted the fighting men, and he said to the LORD, "I have sinned greatly in what I have done. Now, O LORD, I beg you, take away the guilt of your servant. I have done a very foolish thing."

[11]Before David got up the next morning, the word of the LORD had come to Gad the prophet, David's seer: [12]"Go and tell David, 'This is what the LORD says: I am giving you three options. Choose one of them for me to carry out against you.'"

[13]So Gad went to David and said to him, "Shall there come upon you three[a] years of famine in your land? Or three months of fleeing from your enemies while they pursue you? Or three days of plague in your land? Now then, think it over and decide how I should answer the one who sent me."

[14]David said to Gad, "I am in deep distress. Let us fall into the hands of the LORD, for his mercy is great; but do not let me fall into the hands of men."

[15]So the LORD sent a plague on Israel from that morning until the end of the time designated, and seventy thousand of the people from Dan to Beersheba died. [16]When the angel stretched out his hand to destroy Jerusalem, the LORD was grieved because of the calamity and said to the angel who was afflicting the people, "Enough!

[a]13 Septuagint (see also 1 Chron. 21:12); Hebrew seven

NRSV

manders of the army went out from the presence of the king to take a census of the people of Israel. [5]They crossed the Jordan, and began from[a] Aroer and from the city that is in the middle of the valley, toward Gad and on to Jazer. [6]Then they came to Gilead, and to Kadesh in the land of the Hittites;[b] and they came to Dan, and from Dan[d] they went around to Sidon, [7]and came to the fortress of Tyre and to all the cities of the Hivites and Canaanites; and they went out to the Negeb of Judah at Beer-sheba. [8]So when they had gone through all the land, they came back to Jerusalem at the end of nine months and twenty days. [9]Joab reported to the king the number of those who had been recorded: in Israel there were eight hundred thousand soldiers able to draw the sword, and those of Judah were five hundred thousand.

[10]But afterward, David was stricken to the heart because he had numbered the people. David said to the LORD, "I have sinned greatly in what I have done. But now, O LORD, I pray you, take away the guilt of your servant; for I have done very foolishly." [11]When David rose in the morning, the word of the LORD came to the prophet Gad, David's seer, saying, [12]"Go and say to David: Thus says the LORD: Three things I offer[d] you; choose one of them, and I will do it to you." [13]So Gad came to David and told him; he asked him, "Shall three[e] years of famine come to you on your land? Or will you flee three months before your foes while they pursue you? Or shall there be three days' pestilence in your land? Now consider, and decide what answer I shall return to the one who sent me." [14]Then David said to Gad, "I am in great distress; let us fall into the hand of the LORD, for his mercy is great; but let me not fall into human hands."

[15]So the LORD sent a pestilence on Israel from that morning until the appointed time; and seventy thousand of the people died, from Dan to Beer-sheba. [16]But when the angel stretched out his hand toward Jerusalem to destroy it, the LORD relented concerning the evil, and said to the angel who was bringing destruction among the people, "It is enough; now stay your hand." The angel of

[a] Gk Mss: Heb encamped in Aroer south of [b] Gk: Heb to the land of Tahtim-hodshi [c] Cn Compare Gk: Heb they came to Dan-jaan and [d] Or hold over [e] 1 Chr 21.12 Gk: Heb seven

Withdraw your hand." The angel of the LORD was then at the threshing floor of Araunah the Jebusite.

¹⁷When David saw the angel who was striking down the people, he said to the LORD, "I am the one who has sinned and done wrong. These are but sheep. What have they done? Let your hand fall upon me and my family."

¹⁸On that day Gad went to David and said to him, "Go up and build an altar to the LORD on the threshing floor of Araunah the Jebusite." ¹⁹So David went up, as the LORD had commanded through Gad. ²⁰When Araunah looked and saw the king and his men coming toward him, he went out and bowed down before the king with his face to the ground.

²¹Araunah said, "Why has my lord the king come to his servant?"

"To buy your threshing floor," David answered, "so I can build an altar to the LORD, that the plague on the people may be stopped."

²²Araunah said to David, "Let my lord the king take whatever pleases him and offer it up. Here are oxen for the burnt offering, and here are threshing sledges and ox yokes for the wood. ²³O king, Araunah gives all this to the king." Araunah also said to him, "May the LORD your God accept you."

²⁴But the king replied to Araunah, "No, I insist on paying you for it. I will not sacrifice to the LORD my God burnt offerings that cost me nothing."

So David bought the threshing floor and the oxen and paid fifty shekels*ᵃ* of silver for them. ²⁵David built an altar to the LORD there and sacrificed burnt offerings and fellowship offerings.*ᵇ* Then the LORD answered prayer in behalf of the land, and the plague on Israel was stopped.

ᵃ24 That is, about 1 1/4 pounds (about 0.6 kilogram)   ᵇ25 Traditionally peace offerings

the LORD was then by the threshing floor of Araunah the Jebusite. ¹⁷When David saw the angel who was destroying the people, he said to the LORD, "I alone have sinned, and I alone have done wickedly; but these sheep, what have they done? Let your hand, I pray, be against me and against my father's house."

18That day Gad came to David and said to him, "Go up and erect an altar to the LORD on the threshing floor of Araunah the Jebusite." ¹⁹Following Gad's instructions, David went up, as the LORD had commanded. ²⁰When Araunah looked down, he saw the king and his servants coming toward him; and Araunah went out and prostrated himself before the king with his face to the ground. ²¹Araunah said, "Why has my lord the king come to his servant?" David said, "To buy the threshing floor from you in order to build an altar to the LORD, so that the plague may be averted from the people." ²²Then Araunah said to David, "Let my lord the king take and offer up what seems good to him; here are the oxen for the burnt offering, and the threshing sledges and the yokes of the oxen for the wood. ²³All this, O king, Araunah gives to the king." And Araunah said to the king, "May the LORD your God respond favorably to you."

24But the king said to Araunah, "No, but I will buy them from you for a price; I will not offer burnt offerings to the LORD my God that cost me nothing." So David bought the threshing floor and the oxen for fifty shekels of silver. ²⁵David built there an altar to the LORD, and offered burnt offerings and offerings of well-being. So the LORD answered his supplication for the land, and the plague was averted from Israel.

COMMENTARY

This unusual narrative forms the counterpart to the narrative that opened the appendixes to the books of Samuel (21:1-14). The word "again," which begins v. 1, suggests a formal link between the two stories as episodes that begin with the Lord's anger. Some have suggested that these two stories originally belonged together and were located earlier in the collection of David's stories.

Yet others have found several different and independent traditions brought together in chap. 24. These efforts to reconstruct an earlier, complex literary history for this chapter have neither been convincing nor generated a consensus.[362] It seems more likely that, whatever the earlier literary history of this narrative, it was placed here in its present form as a part of the symmetrically arranged appendixes to the books of Samuel (see Overview for 21:1–24:25) to play a role in the conclusion of the David tradition.

The story is organized into three distinct but related episodes: vv. 1-9, the census—incited by God, ordered by David, carried out by Joab; vv. 10-17, the judgment—David's repentance, Gad's announcement, the plague, God's mercy, David's confession; vv. 18-25, the altar—Gad's announcement, the purchase of the threshing floor, the building of an altar, the end of the threat. The story leaves many questions unaddressed. Why was God angry with Israel? Why is a census such a threat to the people? How does David come to realize that he has sinned? Why does God show mercy in the judgment by pestilence? The narrator does not seem interested in reporting motives behind events but instead to allow the character of David to be revealed in the course of events. Such an interest makes chap. 24 an appropriate final comment on David for the books of Samuel.

24:1-9. The story opens with the unexplained anger of God toward Israel. Further, God "incited David" to commit an act that later in the story is clearly regarded as sinful (v. 1). We are uncomfortable with questions these assertions raise about the justice of God, but the narrator gives no attention to this concern and passes quickly on to the course of events with the focus on David. The portrait of God as the instigator of sinful actions must have made subsequent generations uncomfortable, since the retelling of this story by the chronicler attributes the instigation to the "adversary" (שָׂטָן *śāṭān*) instead of to the Lord (1 Chr 21:1). The issues raised are similar to those raised by the prologue to the book of Job, in which both the Lord and the "adversary" (*śāṭān*) play a role in trying to instigate Job to sin.

David is to "count the people"—i.e., take a

census (v. 1*b*). It is never clear that David realizes that this administrative impulse has been instigated by the Lord. David, as so often before, entrusts this task to his chief of staff, Joab, and presents it as his own royal command. David says nothing about divine initiative, nor does he say anything about royal purpose in wanting to know "how many there are" (v. 2).

We begin to sense that there is more to this issue than meets the eye when Joab, with great deference but unmistakable firmness, questions David's wisdom in undertaking this census (v. 3). Joab's opposition is even more persistent in the parallel account in 1 Chr 21:2-6, where he even refuses to carry out the order fully. We notice that this task is to be carried out by Joab with the commanders of the army (i.e., it may require military force) and that they disapprove as well, which is made clear when David must override the objections of Joab and the commanders by royal fiat (v. 4*a*). In the face of full royal authority, Joab and the commanders obey the king (v. 4*b*). Verses 5-8 report the carrying out of the census. The locations mentioned refer to the extremities of the Davidic kingdom, implying that all who fell within these boundaries were counted. The phrase "from Dan to Beersheba" commonly designates the whole of Israel (v. 2). The process took nine months and twenty days (v. 8).

What was so threatening about a census, and why did it require the participation of the army? We begin to sense an answer to this question with Joab's report back to David (v. 9). The census enumerated the number of fighting men in the kingdom—800,000 in Israel and 500,000 in Judah. Only the able-bodied men have been counted. Such a census is the prelude to a military draft. Later, under Solomon, it is clear that such a census also provides the basis for conscripting forced labor and for taxation (1 Kgs 4:7-19, 27-28; 5:13-14). No wonder such a census might be resisted by the people and require the army to carry it out. David has taken a major step away from tribal military behavior and toward centralized royal control of such matters. His census constitutes a step toward the fulfillment of the prophet Samuel's dire warning against kings who "take" from the people (1 Sam 8:10-18). Such a royal census is not a neutral act, but a testimony to state power and intent to use that power. David

---

362. See A. A. Anderson, *2 Samuel*, WBC 11 (Waco: Word, 1989) 282-84, for a discussion of the many proposals made for the literary formation of this chapter.

(even though "incited" by God) has given in to the temptation to order his kingdom in the manner of state politics in the other kingdoms of the ancient world. David's Israel is becoming "like the other nations" (1 Sam 8:4, 20).

24:10-17. This section is bracketed by David's realization and confession of the sin he has committed (vv. 10, 17). We are not told how David came to this realization, but what is significant (perhaps the more so for seeming so spontaneous) is that David is not wholly captured by the ideology of state power and its bureaucratic practices. He retains a capacity for governance that considers the perspective of the people and a willingness to acknowledge and respond to his own weaknesses. Even in his two confessions of sin in this section, he progresses from petitioning God for his own forgiveness (v. 10) to petitioning God to spare the people of Israel and to let judgment fall entirely on David and his house (v. 17).

A new character enters David's story at this point, but it is not a new role. A prophet brings the word of God's judgment and its consequences, but the prophet is not Nathan (chaps. 7 and 12); it is a prophet named Gad (v. 11). The word Gad brings is odd. David may choose the consequences of the sin he has committed—but what a choice it is! Gad offers the terrible triad of famine, war, and pestilence, known in later prophetic preaching on God's judgment (Jer 14:12; 15:2; 21:7, 9; 24:10; 27:8; Ezek 5:12; 6:12). The time sequences occur in descending order: three years of famine (reading with the Greek text and 1 Chr 21:12; the Hebrew text reads "seven"), three months of military pursuit by enemies, or three days of pestilence (v. 13).

David's response to this terrible dilemma of choice is in keeping with the portrait of his faithful side presented in these final chapters. He places his trust in the God who is now judging him, and, in the face of the judgment, he expresses hope in God's mercy (v. 14). In the hands of God, one might hope for mercy—not so from human hands. This choice eliminates one of the possible consequences—namely, pursuit by an enemy— but it leaves famine and pestilence as possibilities. David chooses no further, and it is the Lord who apparently makes the final choice and sends a pestilence (v. 15).

It is unclear how long the pestilence runs unchecked, but "until the appointed time" is not the full three days threatened because God's mercy does intervene. David's trust is justified. The damage is still great; seventy thousand die from disease (v. 15*b*). Without explanation, an angel of the Lord appears in the story as the agent of God's judgment by pestilence. As the angel approaches Jerusalem, God stays its destroying hand with the declaration: "It is enough" (v. 16).[363] The spot where the pestilence stops is the threshing floor of a Jebusite named Araunah, which is significant for the final episode of this chapter. Verse 17 records David's second confession of sin prior to God's relenting mercy, since it treats his words as a response to the destruction wrought by the angel of pestilence. Just as God responds in mercy, so also David responds by offering himself in place of the people. But God's mercy is not the result of David's confession; it is the unexplained grace of God in which David trusted (v. 14). If God can judge, God can also show mercy (cf. Hos 11:8-9). The Lord repents of anger, and David repents of sin. In this divine and human responsiveness lie the hope of Israel's future and the possibility of renewed relationship between God and God's king.

24:18-25. The prophet Gad instructs David to build an altar at the threshing floor where the plague had stopped (v. 17). David's response is one of obedience, and the subsequent course of events completes David's faithful response to God's judgment and mercy in an act of ritual piety. Verses 18-24 narrate the negotiations for the purchase of the threshing floor by David from Arauna. Arauna is initially awed by the king's presence and the gravity of the occasion, so he offers to give the threshing floor as well as oxen and wood for sacrifice (in 1 Chr 21:20-23, this generosity is also motivated by the presence of the angel with a drawn sword). David refuses this offer by saying that he cannot offer to the Lord what cost him nothing, and he insists on paying full price (v. 24).

Only when the altar is built and the sacrifice has been made does the account end by saying that the Lord answered David's supplications and

---

363. The angel has a more extended and dramatic role in the chronicler's account, where he stands with sword drawn over Jerusalem while David's repentance and the episode with the altar and sacrifice at the threshing floor of Arauna (Chronicles, Ornan) are played out. Only after the sacrifice is the sword sheathed (1 Chr 21:15-27).

ended the plague (v. 25; in 1 Chr 21:27, the angel sheaths his sword). The impression is that God initiated mercy, but that David's response in acknowledging God and confessing his own sin with appropriate acts of ritual piety were necessary to end the threat of judgment completely. The confession is enacted in worship wherein the gift of God's mercy is acknowledged and received. Anything less than authentic worship would not restore relationship broken by sin.

This final episode may have been preserved because of a tradition that linked this altar on Arauna's threshing floor with the eventual site of the Jerusalem Temple. In 1 Chr 22:1, David declares this Jebusite threshing floor to be the site of a future temple and actually begins making preparations for its construction by stockpiling building materials (1 Chr 22:2-16).

With chap. 24 we come to the end of the books of Samuel and to the end of David's story. (1 Kings 1–2 focus on the accession of Solomon; David is dying.) It is significant that the books of Samuel end with the prayerful petition of David in a time of need and with God's merciful response to that need. The books of Samuel began in a similar way, with the prayerful petition of Hannah and God's merciful response (1 Samuel 1). At beginning and end, this story turns on trust in the mercy of God. Early in 1 Samuel we are told that Israel's old system of leadership was corrupt (Eli's sons), and in the end David himself has been corrupted. However, God's mercy endures. Moreover, the true source from which Israel's future always comes is acknowledged in acts of worship (Hannah's and David's) that frame the books of Samuel. Brueggemann speaks of these framing stories in this way:

> The Samuel corpus is thus framed at beginning and end with powerful affirmations about God's fidelity and Israel's (Hannah's and David's) capacity to trust, submit, and pray. The decisive affirmation at beginning and end of the narrative concerns the overriding sovereignty of God.[364]

Chapter 24 (and the appendixes of chaps. 21–24) redirects our attention from the flawed David, seduced by the availability of royal power and co-opted by the patterns of state ideology. The David we finally see in the appendixes is the David who, in spite of his human vulnerability, has a capacity for faith, for prayer, for worship that points beyond himself to the Lord as David's true source of power, as Israel's genuine hope for a future, as every generation's sure promise of mercy.

364. Walter Brueggemann, *First and Second Samuel*, Interpretation (Louisville: John Knox, 1990) 256.

REFLECTIONS

1. At first glance, many readers feel that the events that develop in this chapter seem out of proportion to the taking of a census, which precipitates the crisis. But much depends on where we locate ourselves as readers. To those who have power, or feel they have access to those in power, bureaucratic processes most often seem benign, necessary, or neutral. But to those who live their lives outside the circles of power and on the margins of the social order, such processes are threatening and dangerous—even a census. For the 1990 United States Census, the percentage of those who remained uncounted in the inner cities of the largest metropolitan areas has been estimated as high as 25 percent. Among the poor and the immigrant residents of our cities, many felt that to be found and counted was to be put at risk. The bureaucracies of state power were not to be trusted; better to be anonymous and uncounted. To give information to such bureaucracies was to be uncertain of how that information would be used. Would such information be shared with taxation authorities, with immigration officials, with police departments?

To read this final story of David is to realize how casually those who hold authority and power exercise it without considering how the bureaucracies of power are experienced by those at the margins of society. Even programs designed to help those in need are sometimes burdened with such bureaucratic complexity that many conclude that the help offered is intended to be unobtainable. Too often the practices of institutional power structures have as their primary interest their own self-perpetuation. It is too easy for political or ecclesiastical institutions to lose sight of the communities they are to serve. This odd story of a census stands as a reminder that we must look at our programs and policies through the eyes of those at the margins if we are to be certain that our efforts contribute to the wholeness of all whom our actions touch.

2. What makes this story remarkable, however, is that David, in the midst of his own exercise of self-serving bureaucratic power, recognized his actions for what they were—sinful—and he confessed. What opened from that confession were new possibilities for facing the consequences of his action, for rekindling his care for the community, and for restoring relationship to God.

The dangers of self-interested power do not go wholly unrecognized in our own time, but the response is often reform rather than repentance, renewed practice rather than renewed prayer. David's example here might encourage us, in the face of the dangers brought by uncaring power, not to rush so quickly into new blueprints for more responsive institutions or better-flowing organizational charts. Confession and prayer, whether in secular or religious settings, offer possibilities for the future that grow out of restored relationships, rather than new solutions offered out of the same old institutional assumptions. Confession and prayer offer foundations for facing unpleasant consequences that spring from our self-interested exercise of power, rather than attempting to cover those consequences (or postpone them) with a flurry of new activity.

In our own time, we have watched the remarkable proceedings of South Africa's Truth and Reconciliation Commission, chaired by Bishop Desmond Tutu, as it has engaged in the public practice of confession in an effort to heal a deeply divided nation. It is not insignificant that this commission is led by a bishop of the Anglican Church, for if the church reads its own Scripture, including stories like this one, then it knows something of the power of confession to create new possibilities.

The practice of confession and prayer is the foundation for recognizing where God's mercy is at work in the midst of the brokenness our human actions inevitably bring. Prayer does not so much mobilize God's mercy as articulate our own trust in God's mercy. God's mercy is already at work, but our own trustful prayer makes the possibilities that grow from divine mercy more visible. Prayer changes the horizon of our vision to include discernment of what God is doing alongside our analysis of the human possibilities. Prayer that encompasses our own self-examination and confession—that reaches in hope for restored and renewed possibilities—is the first act on the path to actualizing God's new future in our lives and in our communities.

3. It is appropriate that the books of Samuel end with worship and the responsiveness of God in mercy (v. 25). In a story filled with remarkable personalities and complex political events, we might be tempted to think that the stories of Samuel, Saul, and David are stories of human power. But from the story of Hannah to this final story of census, plague, and altar, we have been reminded that God's providence is at work in the characters and the events of this decisive period in Israel. Worship as the final act of this story is the appropriate recognition of divine reality working in and through human history. To read this story is to know that this is true for our history as well as for Israel's. In the consequences that flow from our own acts of bureaucratic disregard and institutional power, we experience God's judgment and contribute to our own brokenness. If in confession and prayer we recognize our failings and trust in God's mercy, new possibilities for restored relationship are opened to us. Community and communion, with others and with God, can be imagined in ways that transform our future and provide new paths of response. Like David at the end of these books of Samuel, our only appropriate response to this gift of new future in God's mercy is worship—the acknowledgment of God as the true source of all futures and our only hope for a foretaste of God's kingdom in the midst of our human kingdoms.

TRANSLITERATION SCHEMA

HEBREW AND ARAMAIC TRANSLITERATION

Consonants:

א	=	ʾ	ט	=	ṭ	פ or ף	=	p		
ב	=	b	י	=	y	צ or ץ	=	ṣ		
ג	=	g	כ or ך	=	k	ק	=	q		
ד	=	d	ל	=	l	ר	=	r		
ה	=	h	מ or ם	=	m	שׂ	=	ś		
ו	=	w	נ or ן	=	n	שׁ	=	š		
ז	=	z	ס	=	s	ת	=	t		
ח	=	ḥ	ע	=	ʿ					

Masoretic Pointing:

Pure-long			Tone-long			Short			Composite *shewa*		
הָ	=	â	ָ	=	ā	ַ	=	a	ֲ	=	ă
ִי or ֵי	=	ê	ֵ	=	ē	ֶ	=	e	ֱ or ֵ	=	ĕ
ִי or ִ	=	î				ִ	=	i			
וֹ or ֹ	=	ô	ֹ	=	ō	ָ	=	o	ֳ	=	ŏ
וּ or ֻ	=	û				ֻ	=	u			

GREEK TRANSLITERATION

α	=	a	ι	=	i	ρ	=	r
β	=	b	κ	=	k	σ or ς	=	s
γ	=	g	λ	=	l	τ	=	t
δ	=	d	μ	=	m	υ	=	y
ε	=	e	ν	=	n	φ	=	ph
ζ	=	z	ξ	=	x	χ	=	ch
η	=	ē	ο	=	o	ψ	=	ps
θ	=	th	π	=	p	ω	=	ō

Index of Excursuses, Maps, Charts, and Illustrations

ABBREVIATIONS

BCE	Before the Common Era
CE	Common Era
c.	circa
cf.	compare or contrast
chap(s).	chapter(s)
esp.	especially
fem.	feminine
lit.	literally
LXX	Septuagint
masc.	masculiine
MS(S)	manuscript(s)
MT	Masoretic Text
n.(n.)	note(s)
NT	New Testament
OL	Old Latin
OT	Old Testament
v(v).	verse(s)
Vg	Vulgate

Names of Biblical Books

Gen	Nah	1–4 Kgdms	John
Exod	Hab	Add Esth	Acts
Lev	Zeph	Bar	Rom
Num	Hag	Bel	1–2 Cor
Deut	Zech	1–2 Esdr	Gal
Josh	Mal	4 Ezra	Eph
Judg	Ps (Pss)	Jdt	Phil
1–2 Sam	Job	Ep Jer	Col
1–2 Kgs	Prov	1–4 Macc	1–2 Thess
Isa	Ruth	Pr Azar	1–2 Tim
Jer	Cant	Pr Man	Titus
Ezek	Eccl	Sir	Phlm
Hos	Lam	Sus	Heb
Joel	Esth	Tob	Jas
Amos	Dan	Wis	1–2 Pet
Obad	Ezra	Matt	1–3 John
Jonah	Neh	Mark	Jude
Mic	1–2 Chr	Luke	Rev

Names of Dead Sea Scrolls and Related Texts

1Q, 2Q, 3Q, etc.   Numbered caves of Qumran, followed by abbreviation of biblical or apocryphal book

Orders and Tractates in Mishnaic and Related Literature

'Abot	'Abot
Menah.	Menahot
Rab.	Rabbah (following abbreviation for biblical book)
Yoma	Yoma (= Kippurim)

ABBREVIATIONS

Commonly Used Periodicals, Reference Works, and Serials

AAR	American Academy of Religion
AB	Anchor Bible
ABD	*Anchor Bible Dictionary*
AnBib	Analecta biblica
AASOR	Annual of the American Schools of Oriental Research
ANEP	J.B. Pritchard (ed.), Ancient Near East in Pictures
ANET	J.B. Pritchard (ed.), *Ancient Near Eastern Texts*
ATANT	Abhandlungen zur Theologie des Alten und Neuen Testaments
BAR	*Biblical Archaeologist Reader*
BASOR	*Bulletin of the American Schools of Oriental Research*
BBB	Bonner biblische Beitrage
BETL	Bibliotheca ephemeridum theologicarum lovaniensium
Bib	*Biblica*
BDB	F. Brown, S.R. Driver, and C. A. Briggs, *Hebrew and English* Lexicon of the Old Testament
BJS	Brown Judaic Studies
BN	*Biblische Notizen*
BTB	Biblical Theology Bulletin
BWANT	Beitrage zur Wissenschaft vom Alten und Neuen Testament
BZ	*Biblische Zeitschrift*
BZAW	Beihefte zur *ZAW*
ConBOT	Coniectanea biblica, Old Testament
CBQ	*Catholic Biblical Quarterly*
FRLANT	Forschungen zur Religion und Literatur des Alten und Neuen Testaments
HAT	Handbuch zum Alten Testament
HSM	Harvard Semitic Monographs
ICC	International Critical Commentary
IDB	*Interpreter's Dictionary of the Bible*
IDBSup.	*Interpreter's Dictionary of the Bible, Supplementary Volume*
Int.	*Interpretation*
ITC	International Theological Commentary
JAAR	*Journal of the American Academy of Religion*
JBL	*Journal of Biblical Literature*
JETS	*Journal of the Evangelical Theological Society*
JJS	
JPS	Jewish Publication Society
JSOT	*Journal for the Study of the Old Testament*
JSOTSup	Journal for the Study of the Old Testament—Supplement Series
JSS	*Journal of Jewish Studies*
KB	L. Koehler and W. Baumgartner, *Lexicon in Veteris Testamenti libros*
LCL	Loeb Classical Library
KJV	King James, or Authorized, Version
NCB	New Century Bible
NEB	New English Bible
NIB	*New Interpreter's Bible*
NICOT	New International Commentary on the Old Testament
NIGTC	The New International Greek Testament Commentary
NIV	New International Version
NRSV	New Revised Standard Verion
OBT	Overtures to Biblical Theology
OTL	Old Testament Library
PEFQS	Palestine Exploration Fund, Quarterly Statement
PEQ	Palestine Exploration Quarterly
REB	Revised English Bible
RSV	Revised Standard Version
SAB	Stuttgarter biblische Aufsatzbände
SBLDS	SBL Dissertation Series
SBLMS	SBL Monograph Series
SBT	Studies in Biblical Theology
SJLA	Studies in Judaism in Late Antiquity
SOTSMS	Society for Old Testament Study Monograph Series
ST	Studia theologica
SVTP	Studia in Veteris Testamenti pseudepigrapha
SWBA	Social World of Biblical Antiquity
TDOT	G. Kittel and G. Friedrich (eds.), *Theological Dictionary of the New Testament*
TynBul	*Tyndale Bulletin*

TZ	Theologische Zeitschrift
UBS	United Bible Societies
UF	Ugarit-Forschungen
VT	Vetus Testamentum
VTSup	Vetus Testamentum, Supplements
WBC	Word Biblical Commentary
WMANT	Wissenschaftliche Monographienzum Alten und Neuen Testament
WTJ	Westminster Theological Journal
ZAW	Zeitschrift für die alttestamentliche Wissenschaft
ZTK	Zeitschrift fur Theologie und Kirche